The Broadview Anthology of

VICTORIAN
POETRY

AND POETIC THEORY

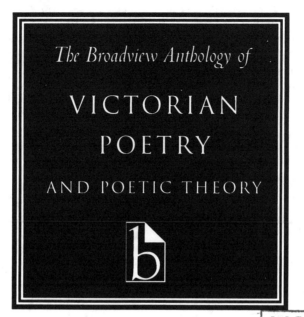

The Broadview Anthology of

VICTORIAN POETRY

AND POETIC THEORY

EDITED BY

THOMAS J. COLLINS

& VIVIENNE J. RUNDLE

ASSISTANT EDITORS: WAI YING LEE & KIRSTEN MUNRO

BROADVIEW ANTHOLOGIES OF ENGLISH LITERATURE

broadview press

NATIONAL LIBRARY OF CANADA CATALOGUING IN PUBLICATION

The Broadview Anthology of Victorian poetry and poetic theory

(Broadview anthologies of English literature)
Includes bibliographical reference and index.
ISBN 1-55111-100-4

1. English poetry— 19th Century. I. Collins, Thomas J., 1936–. II.
Rundle, Vivienne Jill. III. Series.

PR1223.B68   1999   821'.808   C99-931886-1

Broadview Press, Ltd. is an independent, international publishing house, incorporated in 1985. Broadview believes in shared ownership, both with its employees and with the general public; since the year 2000 Broadview shares have traded publicly on the Toronto Venture Exchange under the symbol BDP.

We welcome comments and suggestions regarding any aspect of our publications—please feel free to contact us at the addresses below or at broadview@broadviewpress.com.

North America
PO Box 1243,
Peterborough, Ontario
Canada K9J 7H5
PO Box 1015,
3576 California Road,
Orchard Park, NY, USA 14127
Tel: (705) 743-8990;
Fax: (705) 743-8353
email: customerservice@broadviewpress.com

UK, Ireland, and continental Europe
NBN Plymbridge
Estover Road
Plymouth
UK PL6 7PY
Tel: +44 (0) 1752 202301;
Fax: +44 (0) 1752 202331;
Fax Order Line: +44 (0) 1752 202333;
Cust Ser: cservs@nbnplymbridge.com
Orders: orders@nbnplymbridge.com

Australia and New Zealand
UNIREPS,
University of New South Wales
Sydney, NSW, 2052
Australia
Tel: 61 2 9664 0999;
Fax: 61 2 9664 5420
email: info.press@unsw.edu.au

www. broadviewpress.com

Broadview Press gratefully acknowledges the financial support of the Government of Canada through the Book Publishing Industry Development Program for our publishing activities.

Cover design by George Kirkpatrick

PRINTED IN CANADA

Editorial Preface

Our initial but vastly overambitious intention for this anthology was to publish a single volume which would include a representative selection of Victorian poetry, poetic theory, and non-fiction prose. But as we progressed in reading (much of it for the first time for us) the work of non-canonical poets, both female and male, and as we surveyed the wide-ranging nature of Victorian theoretical discourse, we concluded that a single large volume could accommodate only poetry and poetic theory. This volume represents the result of that decision.

In preparing *The Broadview Anthology of Victorian Poetry and Poetic Theory*, we were guided by four criteria: the desire to include as full a representation of lesser-known poets as possible; the desire also to provide the widest possible range of selections from poets long established in the canon of Victorian English literature; the desire to recognize the ways in which the perceived canon has changed over time and is continuing to change; and, finally, the desire to include a more exhaustive selection of theoretical commentary than has hitherto been available in a single volume. Given these criteria, the size and extensive scope of this anthology is the inevitable result.

We were, however, forced to make difficult choices in selecting material in order to keep this anthology within manageable (and bindable) limits. At the outset we decided that we would avoid, insofar as possible, using brief excerpts from longer works. The long poem is such a central part of Victorian poetry that we were determined to give such works an appropriate amount of space. Readers will, therefore, find the whole of Alfred Tennyson's *In Memoriam,* four complete books from Robert Browning's *The Ring and the Book,* and two complete books from Elizabeth Barrett Browning's *Aurora Leigh.* In order to accommodate these longer works, and others, as well as a generous selection of theoretical prose, the publisher has adopted a two-column format, thereby allowing the inclusion of considerably more material than would have otherwise been possible.

The selection process was influenced by several factors. We determined that our interpretation of the term "Victorian" would not be restrictive. To define one's selective limits as Queen Victoria's reign (1837–1901) imposes arbitrary historical limitations on choice, and the notion of historical periodicity is, at best, questionable. Readers will, therefore, find poetry which is pre-1837 (Felicia Hemans, John Clare, the early Tennyson, for example), and post-1901 (Charlotte Mew, Alice Meynell, and Elizabeth Robins, for example). The selection process was also significantly shaped by the editors' perception of the aesthetic quality of particular poems, the topical nature of some poems, and the contemporary importance and influence of theoretical essays. We endeavoured to take into account, and to have the anthology reflect, the extensive amount of critical work undertaken over the past generation. In addition, we have included some poems widely read and/or influential in their times (Coventry Patmore's *Angel in the House* is a good example), even though they might not be held in such high esteem today.

Another influential factor in our decisions about what to print was the response of scholars from various parts of the world to our request for reactions to the initial, very tentative, table of contents that we published on the Victoria Research Web almost five years ago. The table of contents in this volume differs markedly from the original one, and we want to thank all those colleagues (too many to name individually) who responded so generously to our call for assistance and suggestions. Many of the good things about this anthology (but none of the faults) are a result of that Internet interchange.

Gender issues have been the subject of some of the most interesting and controversial discussions in the study of Victorian poetry for the past decade or more. It will be evident to readers that the selection process was informed significantly by these discussions. Perhaps even more so than in other areas of English literature, recent anthologizing in Victorian literature has focused on providing—at last—a fuller representation of the work of women poets beyond the standard choices from Elizabeth Barrett Browning and Christina Rossetti. The publication of large anthologies devoted entirely to Victorian women poets has been of enormous value to students, to the profession, and particularly to us.

The Broadview Anthology of Victorian Poetry and Poetic Theory attempts to achieve a balance which includes the voices of both men and women poets and theorists. This should not be taken to imply any criticism of those efforts by other scholars to collect and to discuss solely the work of women poets. Indeed, as suggested above, compiling an anthology such as this would have been much more difficult had it not been for the work of recovery and reassessment carried out by such scholars as Isobel Armstrong, in *Victorian Poetry: Poetry, poetics, and politics* (Routledge, 1993), Angela Leighton, in *Victorian Women Poets: Writing Against the Heart* (Harvester Wheatsheaf, 1992), and Angela Leighton and Margaret Reynolds, editors of *Victorian Women Poets: An Anthology* (Blackwell, 1995) to name but a few. In her excellent introduction to *Victorian Women Poets,* Margaret Reynolds makes an interesting observation about the Victorian "conversation," particularly among women poets: "There are numerous poems addressed by one poet to another as if carrying on a conversation with one another" (xxx). She cites, among others, Letitia Elizabeth Landon's stanzas on Hemans and Dora Greenwell's poems on Barrett Browning. Men were also, obviously, engaged in this direct conversation: Sydney Dobell and James Thomson, for instance, also wrote poems on Barrett Browning. This idea of conversation can, we believe, be profitably expanded to include the somewhat more wide-ranging notion of direct and indirect dialogue among poets, theorists, and the Victorian (and modern) communities of writers and readers.

Some critics have suggested in recent years that prose fiction was the prevailing Victorian genre. Its importance is unarguable. But as we worked on this anthology we were struck more acutely than ever before (even after decades of teaching), by the sheer volume of poetry published in annuals, periodicals, and collections by both men and women, a good deal of which, for both sexes, has only recently been recovered. In that poetry, and related theory, we perceived an intense dialogue of writers interacting with one another, and their predecessors, directly and indirectly, on all manner of topics important in their time, and still important in ours. "Intertextuality" was not in the vocabulary of the Victorians, but it was certainly in their practice. For a discussion of this subject, framed in slightly different terms, see, for example, Isobel Armstrong's incisive analysis of the poetic and intellectual currents and countercurrents involving Arthur Henry Hallam, Tennyson, William J. Fox, Browning, male and female feminists, and John Stuart Mill in Chapter 1, "Two Systems of Concentric Circles" of her *Victorian Poetry.* We hope that this work will provide readers with a more comprehensive sense than hitherto possible, drawing from material available in a single anthology, of the extent of this interactive dialogue in poetry, in theory, and between poetry and theory.

EDITORIAL NOTE

Readers will find moderate annotation, for our desire has been to remain as unobtrusive as possible. Annotation is restricted, almost without exception, to the explanatory, and our guiding principle has been brevity and clarity.

In the Poetry section, we have used the normal practice of ordering chronologically by the birth dates of the poets; poems are arranged chronologically for each poet by publication date, with a few exceptions (for example, Matthew Arnold and Thomas Hardy). Dates of first publication are given when known, and dates of composition, if known, are given in brackets—both at the end of poems. In the Theory section, we have arranged the essays by date of publication, primarily because many of the essays interact with one another and with their contemporary intellectual and cultural circumstances.

Finally, we would like to thank all those individuals who have so helpfully responded to our seemingly endless series of questions about matters of content and form. In addition to our Internet advisors, they are: David Bentley, George Bornstein, Chris Brown, Wolfram Burghardt, Nigel Crowther, Doug Gerber, Jim Good, Don Hair, Jim Hatch, Bruce Howe, Adrienne Kertzer, Margot Louis, Lorne Macdonald, Brenda MacEachern, Anne McWhir, Ninian Mellamphy, Elizabeth Murray, Victor Neufeldt, David Oakleaf, Tilottama Rajan, Marjorie Ratcliffe, R.J. Shroyer, Patricia Srebrnik, Lisa Surridge, Jane Toswell, and Mary Louise Young. We received great help from our graduate student assistants: Susan Birkwood at the beginning of the project and Natalie Sliscovic in its final stages. Wai Ying Lee and Kirsten Munro, also graduate students, have contributed so much to this anthology, in quality and quantity, that the least we could do is give them title-page recognition as Assistant Editors. And, as always and in everything, the members of the English Department office staff at the University of Western Ontario (Pat Dibsdale, Teresa MacDonald, Anne McFarland, and Beth McIntosh) have been immensely helpful. At Broadview Press, Don LePan has been forbearing and kind, Eileen Eckert has nobly endured the exhausting job of proofreading, and Kathryn Brownsey (the actual "maker" of this book) has exhibited estimable skill, saintly patience, and the endurance of an Ironman triathlete.

TJC
VJR
JULY 15, 1999

————————

Contents

POETRY

POETIC THEORY

INDEXES

POETRY
ॐॐ

Anonymous

ↄ⃝ↄↄↄ

A New Song on the
Birth of the Prince of Wales

Who was born on Tuesday, November 9, 1841

There's a pretty fuss and bother both in country
    and in town,
Since we have got a present, and an heir unto the
    Crown,
A little Prince of Wales so charming and so sly,
And the ladies shout with wonder, What a pretty
    little boy!

5 He must have a little musket, a trumpet and a kite,
A little penny rattle, and silver sword so bright,
A little cap and feather with scarlet coat so smart,
And a pretty little hobby horse to ride about the
    park.

Price Albert he will often take the young Prince on
    his lap,
10 And fondle him so lovingly, while he stirs about
    the pap,[1]
He will pin on his flannel before he takes his nap,
Then dress him out so stylish with his little clouts[2]
    and cap.

He must have a dandy suit to strut about the town,
John Bull[3] must rake together six or seven
    thousand pound,

15 You'd laugh to see his daddy, at night he
    homeward runs,
With some peppermint or lollipops, sweet cakes
    and sugar plums.

He will want a little fiddle, and a little German
    flute,
A little pair of stockings and a pretty pair of boots,
With a handsome pair of spurs, and a golden
    headed cane,
20 And a stick of barley sugar, as long as Drury Lane.[4]

An old maid ran through the palace, which did the
    nobs[5] surprize,
Bawling out, he's got his daddy's mouth, his
    mammy's nose and eyes,
He will be as like his daddy as a frigate to a ship,
If he'd only got mustachios upon his upper lip.

25 Now to get these little niceties the taxes must be
    rose,
For the little Prince of Wales wants so many suits
    of clothes,
So they must tax the frying pan, the windows and
    the doors,
The bedsteads and the tables, kitchen pokers, and
    the floors.
—1841?, 1871 (1841)

---

[1] the female breast; also, soft food given to babies.

[2] archaic term for cloth or leather for patching. Here possibly meaning boots.

[3] the typical Englishman.

[4] a well-known London street, location of the famous Drury Lane Theatre, founded 1663.

[5] members of the upper classes.

Thomas Ashe
1836 – 1889

Thomas Ashe, born in Dublin, was a novelist, poet, and miscellaneous writer.

⊱⊰

Corpse-Bearing

I remember, they sent
    Some one to me, who said,
"You were his friend while he lived:
    Be so now he is dead."

5   So I went next day to the house;
    And a woman nodded to me,
As I sat alone in thought:—
    Said, "Sir, would you like to see

The poor dead body upstairs,
10   Before we rivet the lid?"
But I said, "I would rather not:
    For the look would never be hid

"From my sight, day after day,
    From my soul, year after year.
15 Enough to look on the pall:
    Enough to follow the bier."

So the mourners gather'd at last;
    And the poor dead body was put
In a hearse with mournful plumes,
20   And the door of the hearse was shut.

And when the mourners were all
    In the coaches, ready to start,
The sorrowing parent came
    To me, and whisper'd apart.

25 He smiled as well as he could;
    And the import of what he said
Was, that I should bear at the feet,
    And his son would bear at the head.

He was ever my friend;
30   And I was happy to be
Of ever so small use still
    To one who had so loved me.

But, what a weight, O God!
    Was that one coffin to bear!
35 Like a coffin of lead!
    And I carry it everywhere

About, wherever I go!
    If I lift the slightest thing,
That requires an effort to lift,
40   The effort at once will bring

The whole weight into my hands,
    And I carry the corpse at the feet;
And feel as if it would drop,
    And slip out of its winding-sheet.

45 I have made a vow in my heart,
    Whatever the friends may say,
Never to carry a corpse
    Again, to my dying day.
  —1871 (1859-60)

To Two Bereaved

You must be sad; for though it is to Heaven,
  'Tis hard to yield a little girl of seven.
Alas, for me, 'tis hard my grief to rule,
Who only met her as she went to school;
5 Who never heard the little lips so sweet
Say even "Good morning," though our eyes would
  meet
As whose would fain be friends! How must you
  sigh,
Sick for your loss, when even so sad am I,
Who never clasp'd the small hands any day!
10 Fair flowers thrive round the little grave, I pray.
—1876 (1874)

Walter Savage Landor
1775 – 1864

Walter Savage Landor wrote prolifically in prose and verse in English, Latin, and Italian. From 1814 to 1835, and again from 1858 until his death, he lived in Italy, fleeing England because of debt and litigation. His *Imaginary Conversations*, 152 prose dialogues between historical and legendary characters, were highly regarded by his contemporaries, and his verse collections—*Hellenics* (1846, 1847), *Italics* (1848), *Last Fruit Off an Old Tree* (1853), and *Heroic Idylls* (1863)—exhibit classical control and stylistic economy.

For An Epitaph At Fiesole

Lo! where the four mimosas blend their shade,
In calm repose at last is Landor laid;
For ere he slept he saw them planted here
  By her his soul had ever held most dear,
And he had lived enough when he had dried her tear.
—1831

Ianthe Leaves

Ianthe! you are call'd to cross the sea!
  A path forbidden *me*!
Remember, while the Sun his blessing sheds
  Upon the mountain-heads,
5 How often we have watch'd him laying down
  His brow, and dropt our own
Against each other's, and how faint and short
  And sliding the support!
What will succeed it now? Mine is unblest,
10 Ianthe! nor will rest
But on the very thought that swells with pain.
  O bid me hope again!
O give me back what Earth, what (without you)
  Not Heaven itself can do—
15 One of the golden days that we have past;
  And let it be my last!
Or else the gift would be, however sweet,
  Fragile and incomplete.
—1831

Dying Speech of an Old Philosopher

I strove with none, for none was worth my strife:
  Nature I loved, and, next to Nature, Art:
I warm'd both hands before the fire of Life;
  It sinks; and I am ready to depart.
—1849

Death's Language

Death stands above me, whispering low
  I know not what into my ear:
Of his strange language all I know
  Is, there is not a word of fear.
—1853

Her Name

Well I remember how you smiled
  To see me write your name upon
The soft sea-sand... *"O, what a child!*
  You think you're writing upon stone!"

5 I have since written what no tide
  Shall ever wash away; what men
Unborn shall read o'er ocean wide
  And find Ianthe's name again.
—1853

A Foreign Ruler

He says, *My reign is peace*, so slays
A thousand in the dead of night.
Are you all happy now? he says,
And those he leaves behind cry *quite*.

5 He swears he will have no contention,
And sets all nations by the ears;
He shouts aloud, *No intervention!*
Invades, and drowns them all in tears.
—1863

John Clare
1793 – 1864

John Clare, the Northamptonshire peasant-poet, was interested in the sights and sounds of the natural world. After an obscure youth as a ploughboy, he first won acclaim for his *Poems Descriptive of Rural Life* (1820). He subsequently published *The Village Minstrel* (1821) and *The Rural Muse* (1834). Clare's mental (and physical) health was extremely fragile, and in July 1837, he was committed to an asylum.

☙☙☙

"I Am"

1

I am—yet what I am, none cares or knows;
  My friends forsake me like a memory lost:—
I am the self-consumer of my woes;—
  They rise and vanish in oblivion's host,
5 Like shadows in love's frenzied stifled throes:—
And yet I am, and live—like vapours tost

2

Into the nothingness of scorn and noise,—
  Into the living sea of waking dreams,
Where there is neither sense of life or joys,
10   But the vast shipwreck of my lifes esteems;
Even the dearest, that I love the best
Are strange—nay, rather stranger than the rest.

3

I long for scenes, where man hath never trod
  A place where woman never smiled or wept
15 There to abide with my Creator, God;
  And sleep as I in childhood, sweetly slept,
Untroubling, and untroubled where I lie,
The grass below—above the vaulted sky.
    —1848 (1846)

An Invite to Eternity

1

Wilt thou go with me sweet maid
  Say maiden wilt thou go with me
Through the valley depths of shade
Of night and dark obscurity
5 Where the path hath lost its way
Where the sun forgets the day
Where there's nor life nor light to see
Sweet maiden wilt thou go with me

2

Where stones will turn to flooding streams
10 Where plains will rise like ocean waves
Where life will fade like visioned dreams
And mountains darken into caves
Say maiden wilt thou go with me
Through this sad non-identity
15 Where parents live and are forgot
And sisters live and know us not

3

Say maiden wilt thou go with me
In this strange death of life to be
To live in death and be the same
20 Without this life, or home, or name
At once to be, & not to be
That was, and is not—yet to see
Things pass like shadows—and the sky
Above, below, around us lie

4

25 The land of shadows wilt thou trace
And look—nor know each others face
The present mixed with reasons gone
And past, and present all as one
Say maiden can thy life be led
30 To join the living with the dead
Then trace thy footsteps on with me
We're wed to one eternity
—1848 (1847–48)

The Old Year

1

The Old Year's gone away
To nothingness and night
We cannot find him all the day
Nor hear him in the night
5 He left no footstep mark or place
In either shade or sun
Tho' last year he'd a neighbours face
In this he's known by none

2

All nothing every where
10 Mists we on mornings see
They have more substance when they're here
And more of form than he
He was a friend by every fire
In every cot and hall
15 A guest to every hearts desire
And now he's nought at all

3

Old papers thrown away
Or garments cast aside
E'en the talk of yesterday
20 Are things identified
But time once torn away

No voices can recall
The eve of new years day
Left the old one lost to all
—1873 (1845)

The Yellowhammer [1]

When shall I see the white thorn leaves agen
And Yellowhammers gath'ring the dry bents[2]
By the Dyke side on stilly moor or fen
Feathered wi love and natures good intents
5 Rude is the nest this Architect invents
Rural the place wi cart ruts by dyke side
Dead grass, horse hair and downy headed bents
Tied to dead thistles she doth well provide
Close to a hill o' ants where cowslips bloom
10 And shed o'er meadows far their sweet perfume
In early Spring when winds blow chilly cold
The yellow hammer trailing grass will come
To fix a place and choose an early home
With yellow breast and head of solid gold
—1920 (1842–64)

Sonnet: "I Am"

I feel I am;—I only know I am,
And plod upon the earth, as dull and void:
Earth's prison chilled my body with its dram
Of dullness, and my soaring thoughts destroyed,
5 I fled to solitudes from passions dream,
But strife persued—I only know, I am,
I was a being created in the race
Of men disdaining bounds of place and time:—
A spirit that could travel o'er the space
10 Of earth and heaven,—like a thought sublime,
Tracing creation, like my maker, free,—
A soul unshackled—like eternity,

---

[1] a kind of small bird.

[2] stiff-stemmed grasses.

Spurning earth's vain and soul debasing thrall
But now I only know I am,—that's all.
—1935 (1842–64)

Stanzas
"The passing of a dream"

1

The passing of a dream
 Are the thoughts I have to day
Cloud shadows they all seem
 And pass as soon away
5 Their meaning and their shade
 I cannot well define
The little left unsaid
 Seems others, and not mine

2

Here's a place so dainty dress't
10 That o'er my vision swim
Like a land in the far west
 But alas my vision's dim
The trees are not the trees
 Under which I used to play
15 And the flowers they cannot please
 For I am sad to day

3

Here's the shumac all on fire
 Like hot coals amid the green
It might please my heart's desire
20 If elsewhere the place had been
Here dreams their troubles make
 To a body without pain
When shall my mind awake
 In its own loved scenes again
—1935 (1842–64)

"There is a charm in Solitude that cheers"

There is a charm in Solitude that cheers
 A feeling that the world knows nothing of
A green delight the wounded mind endears
After the hustling world is broken off
5 Whose whole delight was crime at good to scoff
Green solitude his prison pleasure yields
The bitch fox heeds him not—birds seem to laugh
He lives the Crusoe of his lonely fields
Which dark green oaks his noontide leisure shields
—1949 (1842–64)

Stanzas
"Black absence hides upon the past"

1

Black absence hides upon the past
 I quite forget thy face
And memory like the angry blast
 Will love's last smile erace
5 I try to think of what has been
 But all is blank to me
And other faces pass between
 My early love and thee

2

I try to trace thy memory now
10 And only find thy name
Those inky lashes on thy brow
 Black hair, and eyes the same
Thy round pale face of snowy dyes
 There's nothing paints thee there
15 A darkness comes before my eyes
 For nothing seems so fair

3

I knew thy name so sweet and young
 'Twas music to my ears
A silent word upon my tongue

20   A hidden thought for years
Dark hair and lashes swarthy too
    Arched on thy forehead pale
All else is vanished from my view
    Like voices on the gale
—1949 (1844?)

The Winter's Spring

1

The winter comes I walk alone
    I want no birds to sing
To those who keep their hearts their own
    The winter is the Spring
5 No flowers to please—no bees to hum
    The coming Springs already come

2

I never want the christmas rose
    To come before its time
The seasons each as God bestows
10 Are simple and sublime
I love to see the snow storm hing
    'Tis but the winter garb of Spring

3

I never want the grass to bloom
    The snow-storm's best in white
15 I love to see the tempest come
    And love its piercing light
The dazzled eyes that love to cling
O'er snow white meadows sees the Spring

4

I love the snow the crimpling snow
20 That hangs on every thing
It covers every thing below
    Like white doves brooding wing
A landscape to the aching sight
A vast expance of dazzling light

5

25 It is the foliage of the woods
That winter's bring—The dress
White easter of the year in bud
That makes the winter Spring
The frost and snow his poseys bring
30 Natures white spirits of the Spring
—1949 (1847)

An Anecdote of Love

When April & dew brings primroses here
    I think love of you at the Spring o' the year
Did I harbour bad words when your garter fell off
I to stoop was deterred but I stood not to scoff
5 A bitt of brown list of small value must be
But as it lay there 'twas a diamond to me

Ere back you turned to pick it up
    I noticed well the place
For children there for violets stoop
10 With many a rosey face
I fain would stoop myself you see
    But dare not well presume
The Blackbird sung out let it be
    The maid was in her bloom

15 How beautiful that ancle was
    From which that garter fell
And lusty was the bonny lass
    Whose name I dare not tell
I know the colour of her gown
20 Her bonnet Ribbon too
The fairest maiden in the town
    Is she that wears the blue

Though years have gone but when I see
    The green spot where it fell
25 The stitchwort flower delighteth me
    There blooming in the dell

And years may come no winter seers
The green haunts of the Dove
Those wild flowers stand the bl[i]ght of years
30 Sweet anecdotes of love—
—1964 (1842–64)

To Miss B.

1

Odd rot it[1] what a shame it is
That love should puzzles grow
That we the one we seek should miss
    And change from top to toe
5   The Gilafers a Gilafer
And nature owns the plan
And strange a thing it is to me
A man cant be a man

2

I traced the woods and mountains brow
10 And felt as feels a man
Love pleased me then that puzzles now
    E'en do the best I can
Nature her same green mantle spread
    And boundless is her span
15 The same bright sun is o'er my head
    But I can't be a man

3

The turf is green and fair the sky
And nature still divine
And summot lovely fills my eye
20 Just like this love of mine
And though I love—it may not be
For do the best I can

Mong such disordered company
I cannot be a man

4

25 Th[r]ough married ties—affections ties
And all the ties of love
I struggled to be just and wise
But just I cannot prove
The Bible says that God is love
30 I like so wise a plan
But was it ordered from above
That love was [not] wi' man

5

This contradiction puzzles me
And it may puzzle all
35 Was Adam thus fore doomed to be
Our misery by his fall
Eves fall has been a fall to me
And do the best I can
Woman—I neither love nor see
40 And cannot be a man
—1964 (1842–64)

"The thunder mutters louder..."

The thunder mutters louder & more loud
    With quicker motion hay folks ply the rake
Ready to burst slow sails the pitch black cloud
& all the gang a bigger haycock make
5 To sit beneath—the woodland winds awake
The drops so large wet all thro' in an hour
A tiney flood runs down the leaning rake
In the sweet hay yet dry the hay folks cower
& some beneath the waggon shun the shower
—1984 (1845)

---

[1] an oath. "Odd" is a corruption of "God," so the expression means
"God rot it." A related variation is "Drat."

Felicia Hemans
1793 – 1835

Felicia Hemans, although by dates a late-Romantic poet, is also regarded as the initiator of a tradition of Victorian women's poetry. She was one of six children born to George Browne and Felicity Wagner. The family was deserted by her father when she was fourteen, about the time she published her first volume of verse. In 1812 Felicia married Captain Alfred Hemans, who left his family in 1818 after fathering five children; it is little wonder that her poetry concerns women's domestic responsibilities in relation to the unreliable behaviour of men. The fourteen volumes of verse published between 1818 and her death in 1835 reflect these themes, as well as those of heroic suicide, the conflict between public and private spheres of activity, and the relationship between love and creativity.

೧೨೧

The Suliote Mother

[[It] is related, in a French life of Ali Pasha,[1] that several of the Suliote women, on the advance of the Turkish troops into the mountain fastnesses, assembled on a lofty summit, and, after chanting a wild song, precipitated themselves with their children, into the chasm below, to avoid becoming the slaves of the enemy.]

She stood upon the loftiest peak,
    Amidst the clear blue sky;
A bitter smile was on her cheek,
    And a dark flash in her eye.

5 "Dost thou see them, boy?—through the dusky
    pines
Dost thou see where the foeman's armor shines?
Hast thou caught the gleam of the conqueror's
    crest?
My babe, that I cradled on my breast!
Wouldst thou spring from thy mother's arms with
    joy?
10 —That sight hath cost thee a father, boy!"

    For in the rocky strait beneath,
        Lay Suliote sire and son:

    They had heaped high the piles of death
        Before the pass was won.

15 "They have crossed the torrent, and on they come:
Woe for the mountain hearth and home!
There, where the hunter laid by his spear,
There, where the lyre hath been sweet to hear,
There, where I sang thee, fair babe! to sleep,
20 Naught but the blood-stain our trace shall keep!

    And now the horn's loud blast was heard,
        And now the cymbal's clang,
    Till even the upper air was stirred,
        As cliff and hollow rang.

25 "Hark! they bring music, my joyous child!
What saith the trumpet to Suli's wild?
Doth it light thine eye with so quick a fire,
As if at a glance of thine armèd sire?
Still!—be thou still!—there are brave men low:
30 Thou wouldst not smile couldst thou see him
    now!"

    But nearer came the clash of steel,
        And louder swelled the horn,
    And farther yet the tambour's peal
        Through the dark pass was borne.

---

[1] Turkish pasha of Janina (1741–1822).

35 "Hear'st thou the sound of their savage mirth?
Boy! thou wert free when I gave thee birth,—
Free, and how cherished, my warrior's son!
He too hath blessed thee, as I have done!
Ay, and unchained must his loved ones be—
40 Freedom, young Suliote! for thee and me!"

    And from the arrowy peak she sprung,
      And fast the fair child bore:—
    A veil upon the wind was flung,
      A cry—and all was o'er!
—1825

The Lady of The Castle

From the "Portrait Gallery," an unfinished poem.

"If there be but one spot on thy name,
One eye thou fearest to meet, one human voice
Whose tones thou shrinkest from—Woman! veil
    thy face,
And bow thy head—and die!"

5 Thou seest her pictured with her shining hair,
    (Famed were those tresses in Provençal song,)
Half braided, half o'er cheek and bosom fair
    Let loose, and pouring sunny waves along
Her gorgeous vest. A child's light hand is roving
10 Midst the rich curls; and, oh! how meekly loving
Its earnest looks are lifted to the face
Which bends to meet its lip in laughing grace!
Yet that bright lady's eye, methinks, hath less
Of deep, and still, and pensive tenderness,
15 Than might beseem a mother's; on her brow
    Something too much there sits of native scorn,
And her smile kindles with a conscious glow,
    As from the thought of sovereign beauty born.
These may be dreams—but how shall woman tell
20 Of woman's shame, and not with tears? She fell!
That mother left that child!—went hurrying by

Its cradle—haply not without a sigh,
Haply one moment o'er its rest serene
She hung. But no! it could not thus have been,
25 For *she went on*!—forsook her home, her hearth,
All pure affection, all sweet household mirth,
To live a gaudy and dishonored thing,
Sharing in guilt the splendors of a king.

Her lord, in very weariness of life,
30 Girt on his sword for scenes of distant strife.
He recked no more of glory: grief and shame
Crushed out his fiery nature, and his name
Died silently. A shadow o'er his halls
Crept year by year: the minstrel passed their walls;
35 The warder's horn hung mute. Meantime the child
On whose first flowering thoughts no parent
    smiled,
A gentle girl, and yet deep-hearted, grew
Into sad youth; for well, too well, she knew
Her mother's tale! Its memory made the sky
40 Seem all too joyous for her shrinking eye;
Checked on her lip the flow of song, which fain
Would there have lingered; flushed her cheek to
    pain,
If met by sudden glance; and gave a tone
Of sorrow, as for something lovely gone,
45 E'en to the spring's glad voice. Her own was low
And plaintive. Oh! there lie such depths of woe
In a *young* blighted spirit! Manhood rears
A haughty brow, and age has done with tears;
But youth bows down to misery, in amaze
50 At the dark cloud o'ermantling its fresh days;—
And thus it was with her. A mournful sight
    In one so fair—for she indeed was fair;
Not with her mother's dazzling eyes of light—
    Hers were more shadowy, full of thought and
      prayer,
55 And with long lashes o'er a white-rose cheek
Drooping in gloom, yet tender still and meek,
Still that fond child's—and oh! the brow above

So pale and pure! so formed for holy love
To gaze upon in silence!—But she felt
60 That love was not for her, though hearts would melt
Where'er she moved, and reverence mutely given
Went with her; and low prayers, that called on
      heaven
To bless the young Isaure.

                              One sunny morn
With alms before her castle gate she stood,
65 Midst peasant groups: when, breathless and
      o'erworn,
      And shrouded in long weeds of widowhood,
A stranger through them broke. The orphan maid,
With her sweet voice and proffered hand of aid,
Turned to give welcome; but a wild sad look
70 Met hers—a gaze that all her spirit shook;
And that pale woman, suddenly subdued
By some strong passion, in its gushing mood,
Knelt at her feet, and bathed them with such tears
As rain the hoarded agonies of years
75 From the heart's urn; and with her white lips
      pressed
The ground they trod; then, burying in her vest
Her brow's deep flush, sobbed out—"Oh
      undefiled!
I am thy mother—spurn me not, my child!"

Isaure had prayed for that lost mother; wept
80 O'er her stained memory, while the happy slept
In the hushed midnight; stood with mournful gaze
Before yon picture's smile of other days,
But never breathed in human ear the name
Which weighed her being to the earth with shame.
85 What marvel if the anguish, the surprise,
The dark remembrances, the altered guise,
Awhile o'erpowered her? From the weeper's touch
She shrank—'twas but a moment—yet too much
For that all-humbled one; its mortal stroke
90 Came down like lightning, and her full heart broke
At once in silence. Heavily and prone

She sank, while o'er her castle's threshold stone,
Those long fair tresses—*they* still brightly wore
Their early pride, though bound with pearls no
      more—
95 Bursting their fillet,[1] in sad beauty rolled,
And swept the dust with coils of wavy gold.

Her child bent o'er her—called her: 'twas too late
Dead lay the wanderer at her own proud gate!
The joy of courts, the star of knight and bard—
100 How didst thou fall, O bright-haired Ermengarde!
—1826

To Wordsworth

Thine is a strain to read among the hills,
      The old and full of voices,—by the source
Of some free stream, whose gladdening presence
      fills
      The solitude with sound; for in its course
5 Even such is thy deep song, that seems a part
Of those high scenes, a fountain from their heart.

Or its calm spirit fitly may be taken
      To the still breast in sunny garden bowers,
Where vernal winds each tree's low tones awaken,
10   And bud and bell with changes mark the hours.
There let thy thoughts be with me, while the day
Sinks with a golden and serene decay.

Or by some hearth where happy faces meet,
      When night hath hushed the woods, with all
      their birds,
15 There, from some gentle voice, that lay were sweet
      As antique music, linked with household words;
While in pleased murmurs woman's lip might
      move,
And the raised eye of childhood shine in love.

_____
[1] ribbon.

Or where the shadows of dark solemn yews
20   Brood silently o'er some lone burial-ground,
Thy verse hath power that brightly might diffuse
        A breath, a kindling, as of spring, around;
From its own glow of hope and courage high,
And steadfast faith's victorious constancy.

25 True bards and holy!—thou art e'en as one
        Who, by some secret gift of soul or eye,
In every spot beneath the smiling sun,
        Sees where the springs of living waters lie:
Unseen awhile they sleep—till, touched by thee,
30 Bright healthful waves flow forth, to each glad
        wanderer free.
        —1826

Casabianca [1]

The boy stood on the burning deck
        Whence all but he had fled;
The flame that lit the battle's wreck,
        Shone round him o'er the dead.

5   Yet beautiful and bright he stood,
        As born to rule the storm;
A creature of heroic blood,
        A proud, though child-like form.

The flames roll'd on—he would not go
10   Without his Father's word;
That Father, faint in death below,
        His voice no longer heard.

He call'd aloud:—"Say, Father, say
        If yet my task is done?"

15 He knew not that the chieftain lay
        Unconscious of his son.

"Speak, Father!" once again he cried,
        "If I may yet be gone!"
And but the booming shots replied,
20   And fast the flames roll'd on.

Upon his brow he felt their breath,
        And in his waving hair,
And look'd from that lone post of death,
        In still, yet brave despair.

25 And shouted but once more aloud,
        "My Father! must I stay?"
While o'er him fast, through sail and shroud,
        The wreathing fires made way.

They wrapt the ship in splendour wild,
30   They caught the flag on high,
And stream'd above the gallant child,
        Like banners in the sky.

There came a burst of thunder sound—
        The boy—oh! where was he?
35 Ask of the winds that far around
        With fragments strew'd the sea!—

With mast, and helm, and pennon fair,
        That well had borne their part—
But the noblest thing which perish'd there
40   Was that young faithful heart!
        —1826

---

[1] "Young Casabianca, a boy about thirteen years old, son to the Admiral
of Orient, remained at his post (in the Battle of the Nile) after the ship
had taken fire, and all the guns has been abandoned; and perished in the
explosion of the vessel, when the flames had reached the powder."
(Hemans's note.)

Properzia Rossi

[*Properzia Rossi, a celebrated female sculptor of Bologna, possessed also of talents for poetry and music, died in consequence of an unrequited attachment. A painting, by Ducis, represents her showing her last work, a basso-relievo of Ariadne,[1] to a Roman knight, the object of her affection, who regards it with indifference.*]

"Tell me no more, no more
Of my soul's lofty gifts! Are they not vain
To quench its haunting thirst for happiness?
Have I not loved, and striven, and failed to bind
5   One true heart unto me, whereon my own
Might find a resting-place, a home for all
Its burden of affections? I depart,
Unknown, though Fame goes with me; I must leave
The earth unknown. Yet it may be that death
10   Shall give my name a power to win such tears
As would have made life precious."

I

One dream of passion and of beauty more!
And in its bright fulfilment let me pour
My soul away! Let earth retain a trace
15   Of that which lit my being, though its race
Might have been loftier far. Yet one more dream!
From my deep spirit one victorious gleam
Ere I depart! For thee alone, for thee!
May this last work, this farewell triumph be—
20   Thou, loved so vainly! I would have enshrined
Something immortal of my heart and mind,
That yet may speak to thee when I am gone,
Shaking thine inmost bosom with a tone
Of lost affection,—something that may prove
25   What she hath been, whose melancholy love
On thee was lavished; silent pang and tear,

And fervent song that gushed when none were near,
And dream by night, and weary thought by day,
Stealing the brightness from her life away—
30   While thou—Awake! not yet within me die!
Under the burden and the agony
Of this vain tenderness—my spirit, wake!
Even for thy sorrowful affection's sake,
Live! in thy work breathe out!—that he may yet,
35   Feeling sad mastery there, perchance regret
Thine unrequited gift.

II

It comes! the power
Within me born flows back—my fruitless dower
That could not win me love. Yet once again
I greet it proudly, with its rushing train
40   Of glorious images: they throng—they press—
A sudden joy lights up my loneliness—
I shall not perish all!

The bright work grows
Beneath my hand, unfolded as a rose,
Leaf after leaf, to beauty; line by line,
45   I fix my thought, heart, soul, to burn, to shine,
Through the pale marble's veins. It grows!—and now
I give my own life's history to thy brow,
Forsaken Ariadne!—thou shalt wear
My forms, my lineaments; but oh! more fair,
50   Touched into lovelier being by the glow
Which in me dwells, as by the summer light
All things are glorified. From thee my woe
Shall yet look beautiful to meet his sight,
When I am passed away. Thou art the mould,
55   Wherein I pour the fervent thoughts, the untold,
The self-consuming! Speak to him of me,
Thou, the deserted by the lonely sea,
With the soft sadness of thine earnest eye—
Speak to him, lorn one! deeply, mournfully,
60   Of all my love and grief! Oh! could I throw
Into thy frame a voice—a sweet, and low,
And thrilling voice of song! when he came nigh,
To send the passion of its melody

---

[1]   in Greek myth, King Minos's daughter, who gave Theseus the thread by which he found his way out of the Minotaur's Labyrinth. Theseus initially swore to love Ariadne, but eventually abandoned her on the isle of Naxos.

Through his pierced bosom—on its tones to bear
65 My life's deep feeling as the southern air
Wafts the faint myrtle's breath—to rise, to swell,
To sink away in accents of farewell,
Winning but one, *one* gush of tears, whose flow
Surely my parted spirit yet might know,
70 If love be strong as death!

III

Now fair thou art,
Thou form, whose life is of my burning heart!·
Yet all the vision that within me wrought,
    I cannot make thee. Oh! I might have given
Birth to creations of far nobler thought;
75   I might have kindled, with the fire of heaven,
Things not of such as die! But I have been
Too much alone! A heart whereon to lean,
With all these deep affections that o'erflow
My aching soul, and find no shore below;
80 An eye to be my star; a voice to bring
Hope o'er my path like sounds that breathe of spring.
These are denied me—dreamt of still in vain.
Therefore my brief aspirings from the chain
Are ever but as some wild fitful song,
85 Rising triumphantly, to die ere long
In dirge-like echoes.

IV

Yet the world will see
Little of this, my parting work! in thee.
    Thou shalt have fame! Oh, mockery! give the reed
From storms a shelter—give the drooping vine
90 Something round which its tendrils may entwine—
    Give the parched flower a rain-drop, and the meed
Of love's kind words to woman! Worthless fame!
That in *his* bosom wins not for my name
The abiding place it asked! Yet how my heart,
95 In its own fairy world of song and art
Once beat for praise! Are those high longings o'er?
That which I have been can I be no more?
Never! oh, never more! though still thy sky
Be blue as then, my glorious Italy!

100 And though the music, whose rich breathings fill
Thin air with soul, be wandering past me still;
And though the mantle of thy sunlight streams
Unchanged on forms, instinct with poet-dreams.
Never! oh, never more! Where'er I move,
105 The shadow of this broken-hearted love
Is on me and around! Too well *they* know
    Whose life is all within, too soon and well,
When there the blight hath settled! But I go
    Under the silent wings of peace to dwell;
110 From the slow wasting, from the lonely pain,
The inward burning of those words—*"in vain,"*
    Seared on the heart—I go. 'Twill soon be past!
Sunshine and song, and bright Italian heaven,
    And thou, oh! thou, on whom my spirit cast
115 Unvalued wealth—who knowest not what was given
In that devotedness—the sad, and deep,
And unrepaid—farewell! If I could weep
Once, only once, beloved one! on thy breast,
Pouring my heart forth ere I sink to rest!
120 But that were happiness!—and unto me
Earth's gift is *fame.* Yet I was formed to be
So richly blessed! With thee to watch the sky,
Speaking not, feeling but that thou wert nigh;
With thee to listen, while the tones of song
125 Swept even as part of our sweet air along—
To listen silently; with thee to gaze
On forms, the deified of olden days—
This had been joy enough; and hour by hour,
From its glad well-springs drinking life and power,
130 How had my spirit soared, and made its fame
    A glory for thy brow! Dreams, dreams!—the fire
Burns faint within me. Yet I leave my name—
    As a deep thrill may linger on the lyre
When its full chords are hushed—awhile to live,
135 And one day haply in thy heart revive
Sad thoughts of me. I leave it, with a sound,
A spell o'er memory, mournfully profound;
I leave it on my country's air to dwell—
Say proudly yet—*"'Twas hers who loved me well!"*
—1828

The Memorial Pillar

[*On the road-side, between Penrith and Appleby, stands a small pillar with this inscription:*—"*This pillar was erected, in the year 1656, by Ann, Countess-Dowager of Pembroke, for a memorial of her last parting, in this place, with her good and pious mother, Margaret, Countess-Dowager of Cumberland, on the 2d April, 1616.*"]

"Hast thou through Eden's wild-wood vales, pursued
Each mountain scene magnificently rude,
Nor with attention's lifted eye revered
That modest stone, by pious Pembroke reared,
Which still records, beyond the pencil's power,
The silent sorrows of a parting hour?"—ROGERS.

Mother and child! whose blending tears
    Have sanctified the place,
Where, to the love of many years
    Was given one last embrace—
5   Oh! ye have shrined a spell of power,
Deep in your record of that hour.

A spell to waken solemn thought—
    A still, small under tone,
That calls back days of childhood fraught
10   With many a treasure gone;
And smites, perchance, the hidden source,
Though long untroubled—of remorse.

For who, that gazes on the stone
    Which marks your parting spot,
15 Who but a mother's love hath known—
    The *one* love changing not?
Alas! and haply learned its worth
First with the sound of "Earth to earth!"

But thou, high-hearted daughter! thou,
20   O'er whose bright honored head
Blessings and tears of holiest flow
    E'en here were fondly shed—

Thou from the passion of the grief,
In its full burst, couldst draw relief.

25 For, oh! though painful be the excess,
    The might wherewith it swells,
In nature's fount no bitterness
    Of nature's mingling dwells;
And thou hadst not, by wrong or pride,
30 Poisoned the free and healthful tide.

But didst thou meet the face no more
    Which thy young heart first knew?
And all—was all in this world o'er
    With ties thus close and true?
35 It was! On earth no other eye
Could give thee back thine infancy.

No other voice could pierce the maze
    Where, deep within thy breast,
The sounds and dreams of other days
40   With memory lay at rest;
No other smile to thee could bring
A gladdening, like the breath of spring.

Yet, while thy place of weeping still
    Its lone memorial keeps,
45 While on thy name, midst wood and hill,
    The quiet sunshine sleeps,
And touches, in each graven line,
Of reverential thought a sign;

Can I, while yet these tokens wear
50   The impress of the dead,
Think of the love embodied there
    As of a vision fled?
A perished thing, the joy and flower
And glory of one earthly hour?

55 Not so!—I will not bow me so
    To thoughts that breathe despair!
A loftier faith we need below,

Life's farewell words to bear.
Mother and child!—your tears are past—
60 Surely your hearts have met at last.

—1828

The Grave of a Poetess [1]

"Ne me plaignez pas—si vous saviez
Combien de peines ce tombeau m'a épargnées!" [2]

I stood beside thy lowly grave;
    Spring odors breathed around,
And music, in the river wave,
    Passed with a lulling sound.

5 All happy things that love the sun
    In the bright air glanced by,
And a glad murmur seemed to run
    Through the soft azure sky.

Fresh leaves were on the ivy bough
10   That fringed the ruins near;
Young voices were abroad—but thou
    Their sweetness couldst not hear.

And mournful grew my heart for thee!
    Thou in whose woman's mind
15 The ray that brightens earth and sea,
    The light of song, was shrined.

Mournful, that thou wert slumbering low,
    With a dread curtain drawn

Between thee and the golden glow
20   Of this world's vernal[3] dawn.

Parted from all the song and bloom
    Thou wouldst have loved so well,
To thee the sunshine round thy tomb
    Was but a broken spell.

25 The bird, the insect on the wing,
    In their bright reckless play,
Might feel the flush and life of spring—
    And thou wert passed away.

But then, e'en then, a nobler thought
30   O'er my vain sadness came;
The immortal spirit woke, and wrought
    Within my thrilling frame.

Surely on lovelier things, I said,
    Thou must have looked ere now,
35 Than all that round our pathway shed
    Odors and hues below.

The shadows of the tomb are here,
    Yet beautiful is earth!
What see'st thou, then, where no dim fear,
40   No haunting dream hath birth?

Here a vain love to passing flowers
    Thou gavest; but where thou art,
The sway is not with changeful hours—
    There love and death must part.

45 Thou hast left sorrow in thy song,
    A voice not loud but deep
The glorious bowers of earth among,
    How often didst thou weep?

---

[1] "Extrinsic interest has lately attached to the fine scenery of Woodstock, near Kilkenny, on account of its having been the last residence of the author of *Psyche.* Her grave is one of many in the churchyard of the village. The river runs smoothly by. The ruins of an ancient abbey, that have been partially converted into a church, reverently throw their mantle of tender shadow over it.—*Tales by the O'Hara Family.*" (Hemans's note.)

[2] "Do not grieve—if you knew how much pain this grave has spared me!"

---

[3] spring.

Where couldst thou fix on mortal ground
50 Thy tender thoughts and high?—
Now peace the woman's heart hath found,
    And joy the poet's eye.
—1828

The Image In Lava [1]

Thou thing of years departed!
    What ages have gone by
Since here the mournful seal was set
    By love and agony.

5 Temple and tower have mouldered,
    Empires from earth have passed,
And woman's heart hath left a trace
    Those glories to outlast!

And childhood's fragile image,
10   Thus fearfully enshrined,
Survives the proud memorials reared
    By conquerors of mankind.

Babe! wert thou brightly slumbering
    Upon thy mother's breast
15 When suddenly the fiery tomb
    Shut round each gentle guest?

A strange, dark fate o'ertook you,
    Fair babe and loving heart!
One moment of a thousand pangs—
20   Yet better than to part!

Haply of that fond bosom
    On ashes here impressed,
Thou wert the only treasure, child!
    Whereon a hope might rest.

25 Perchance all vainly lavished
    Its other love had been,
And where it trusted, naught remained
    But thorns on which to lean.

Far better, then, to perish,
30   Thy form within its clasp,
Than live and lose thee, precious one
    From that impassioned grasp.

Oh! I could pass all relics
    Left by the pomps of old,
35 To gaze on this rude monument
    Cast in affection's mould.

Love! human love! what art thou?
    Thy print upon the dust
Outlives the cities of renown
40   Wherein the mighty trust!

Immortal, oh! immortal
    Thou art, whose earthly glow
Hath given these ashes holiness—
    It must, it *must* be so!
—1828

The Indian With His Dead Child [2]

In the silence of the midnight
    I journey with my dead;
In the darkness of the forest-boughs
    A lonely path I tread.

---

[1] "The impression of a woman's form, with an infant clasped to the bosom, found at the uncovering of Herculaneum." (Hemans's note.)

[2] "An Indian, who had established himself in a township of Maine, feeling indignantly the want of sympathy evinced towards him by the white inhabitants, particularly on the death of his only child, gave up his farm soon afterwards, dug up the body of his child, and carried it with him two hundred miles through the forests to join the Canadian Indians.—See Tudor's *Letters on the Eastern States of America.*" (Hemans's note.)

But my heart is high and fearless,
    As by mighty wings upborne;
The mountain eagle hath not plumes
    So strong as love and scorn.

I have raised thee from the grave-sod,
    By the white man's path defiled;
On to the ancestral wilderness
    I bear thy dust, my child!

I have asked the ancient deserts
    To give my dead a place,
Where the stately footsteps of the free
    Alone should leave a trace.

And the tossing pines made answer—
    "Go, bring us back thine own!"
And the streams from all the hunters' hills
    Rushed with an echoing tone.

Thou shalt rest by sounding waters
    That yet untamed may roll;
The voices of that chainless host
    With joy shall fill thy soul.

In the silence of the midnight
    I journey with the dead,
Where the arrows of my father's bow
    Their falcon flight have sped.

I have left the spoilers' dwellings
    For evermore behind;
Unmingled with their household sounds,
    For me shall sweep the wind.

Alone, amidst their hearth-fires,
    I watched my child's decay;
Uncheered, I saw the spirit-light
    From his young eyes fade away.

When his head sank on my bosom,
    When the death-sleep o'er him fell,
Was there one to say, "A friend is near?"
    There was none!—pale race, fare-well!

To the forests, to the cedars,
    To the warrior and his bow,
Back, back!—I bore thee laughing thence,
    I bear thee slumbering now!

I bear thee unto burial
    With the mighty hunters gone;
I shall hear thee in the forest-breeze,
    Thou wilt speak of joy, my son!

In the silence of the midnight
    I journey with the dead;
But my heart is strong, my step is fleet,
    My father's path I tread.
—1830

The Rock of Cader Idris

[*It is an old tradition of the Welsh bards, that on the summit of the mountain Cader Idris is an excavation resembling a couch; and that whoever should pass a night in that hollow, would be found in the morning either dead, in a frenzy, or endowed with the highest poetical inspiration.*]

I lay on that rock where the storms have their
    dwelling,
    The birthplace of phantoms, the home of the
      cloud;
Around it forever deep music is swelling,
    The voice of the mountain-wind, solemn and
      loud.
'Twas a midnight of shadows all fitfully streaming,
    Of wild waves and breezes, that mingled their
      moan;
Of dim shrouded stars, as from gulfs faintly
      gleaming;

And I met the dread gloom of its grandeur
     alone.

I lay there in silence—a spirit came o'er me;
10   Man's tongue hath no language to speak what I
          saw;
Things glorious, unearthly, passed floating before
          me,
     And my heart almost fainted with rapture and
          awe.
I viewed the dread beings around us that hover,
     Though veiled by the mists of mortality's
          breath;
15 And I called upon darkness the vision to cover,
     For a strife was within me of madness and
          death.

I saw them—the powers of the wind and the ocean,
     The rush of whose pinions bears onward the
          storms;
Like the sweep of the white rolling wave was their
          motion—
20 I *felt* their dim presence, but knew not their
          forms!

I saw them—the mighty of ages departed—
     The dead were around me that night on the hill:
From their eyes, as they passed, a cold radiance
          they darted,—
     There was light on my soul, but my heart's
          blood was chill.

25 I saw what man looks on, and dies—but my spirit
     Was strong, and triumphantly lived through
          that hour;
And, as from the grave, I awoke to inherit
     A flame all immortal, a voice, and a power!
Day burst on that rock with the purple cloud
          crested,
30 And high Cader Idris rejoiced in the sun;—
But oh! what new glory all nature invested,
     When the sense which gives soul to her beauty
          was won!

—1834

James Henry
1798 – 1876

James Henry, educated in classics and then medicine at Trinity College, Dublin, had a large and successful medical practice despite his controversial opinions. From 1841 he devoted his life to the study of Virgil, whom he had admired from boyhood. With his wife and later his daughter, Henry travelled through Europe on foot, visiting libraries and hunting for manuscripts and rare editions of Virgil. In addition to scholarly commentaries, Henry wrote travelogues, a considerable amount of poetry, and numerous pamphlets.

❦

"Two hundred men and eighteen killed..."

Two hundred men and eighteen killed[1]
    For want of a second door!
Ay, for with two doors, each ton coal
    Had cost one penny more.

5 And what is it else makes England great,
    At home, by land, by sea,
But her cheap coal, and eye's tail turned
    Toward strict economy?

But if a slate falls off the roof
10   And kills a passer-by,
Or if a doctor's dose too strong
    Makes some half-dead man die,

We have coroners and deodands
    And inquests, to no end,
15 And every honest Englishman's
    The hapless sufferer's friend,

And householder's or doctor's foe,
    For he has nought to lose,
And fain will, if he can, keep out
20   Of that poor dead man's shoes.

But if of twice a hundred men,
    And eighteen more, the breath
Is stopped at once in a coal pit,
    It's quite a natural death;

25 For, God be praised! the chance is small
    That either you or I
Should come, for want of a second door,
    In a coal pit to die.

Besides, 'twould cost a thousand times
30   As much, or something more,
To make to every pit of coal
    A second, or safety door,

As all the shrouds and coffins cost
    For those who perish now
35 For want of a second door, and that's
    No trifle, you'll allow;

---

[1] "At ten o'clock on the morning of Thursday, January 16, 1862, the great iron beam of the steam-engine which worked the pumps of the Hester coal pit near Hartley in Northumberland, snapped across, and a portion of the beam, 40 tons in weigh, fell into the shaft in such a manner as not only to cut off all communication between the interior of the pit and the outer world, but entirely to obstruct all passage of pure air into, and foul air out of, the pit. All the persons who were at work below at the time, two hundred and eighteen in number, were of course suffocated, nor was it until the seventh day after the accident that access could be had to the interior of the pit, or anything, beyond the mere fact of their entombment, ascertained concerning the helpless and unfortunate victims of that 'auri sacra fames' which so generally, so heartlessly, so pertinaciously refuses the poor workers in the coal mines of England, even the sad resource of a second staple or air shaft. See the *Illustrated London News* of January 25, and February 1, 1862." (Henry's note.)

And trade must live, though now and then
    A man or two may die;
So merry sing "God bless the Queen,"
40   And long live you and I;

And, Jenny, let each widow have
    A cup of congo[1] strong,
And every orphan half a cup,
    And so I end my song,

45 With prayer to God to keep coal cheap,
    Both cheap and plenty too,
And if the pit's a whole mile deep,
    What is it to me or you?

For though we're mortal too, no doubt,
50   And Death for us his sithe
Has ready still, the chance is small
    We ever die of stithe.

And if we do, our gracious Queen
    Will, sure, a telegram send,
55 To say how sore she grieves for us
    And our untimely end;

And out of her own privy purse
    A sovereign down will pay,
To have us decently interred
60   And put out of the way;

And the burial service shall for us
    In the churchyard be read,
And more bells rung and more hymns sung
    Than if we had died in bed:

65 For such an accident as this
    May never occur again,
And till it does, one door's enough
    For pumps, air, coal, and men;

And should it occur—which God forbid!—
70   And stifle every soul,
Remember well, good Christians all,
    Not one whit worse the coal.
    —1866 (1862)

---

[1] a kind of black Chinese tea.

Thomas Hood
1799 – 1845

Thomas Hood, the poet, novelist, and essayist, was a man of letters whose career spanned both the Romantic and Victorian eras. Perpetually beset by ill-health and financial woes, Hood joined the *London Magazine* in 1821 where he encountered De Quincey, Hazlitt, Lamb, and Wordsworth. Hood produced a succession of varied works—*Odes and Addresses to Great People* (1825), *Whims and Oddities* (1826 and 1827), *National Tales* (1827), and *The Plea of the Midsummer Fairies* (1827). Noted for his mastery of the pun, his metrical skill, and his comic verse, Hood is equally celebrated for such humanitarian poems as "The Song of the Shirt" (1843), and "The Bridge of Sighs" (1844).

∽∾∽∾

The Song of the Shirt

With fingers weary and worn,
    With eyelids heavy and red,
A woman sat, in unwomanly rags,
    Plying her needle and thread—
5   Stitch! stitch! stitch!
In poverty, hunger, and dirt,
    And still with a voice of dolorous pitch
She sang the "Song of the Shirt."

"Work! work! work!
10 While the cock is crowing aloof!
    And work—work—work,
Till the stars shine through the roof!
It's Oh! to be a slave
    Along with the barbarous Turk,[1]
15 Where woman has never a soul to save,
    If this is Christian work!

"Work—work—work
Till the brain begins to swim;
    Work—work—work
20 Till the eyes are heavy and dim!
Seam, and gusset, and band,
    Band, and gusset, and seam,
Till over the buttons I fall asleep,
    And sew them on in a dream!

25 "Oh, Men, with Sisters dear!
    Oh, men, with Mothers and Wives!
It is not linen you're wearing out,
    But human creatures' lives!
        Stitch—stitch—stitch,
30 In poverty, hunger, and dirt,
Sewing at once, with a double thread,
    A Shroud as well as a Shirt.

"But why do I talk of Death?
    That Phantom of grisly bone,
35 I hardly fear its terrible shape,
    It seems so like my own—
    It seems so like my own,
        Because of the fasts I keep;
Oh, God! that bread should be so dear,
40 And flesh and blood so cheap!

"Work—work—work!
    My labour never flags;
And what are its wages? A bed of straw,
    A crust of bread—and rags.
45 That shatter'd roof—and this naked floor—
    A table—a broken chair—

---

[1] The English—and most Europeans—historically considered the Old Ottoman Empire a barbaric and savage civilization; hence, "Turk" became a derogatory epithet.

And a wall so blank, my shadow I thank
   For sometimes falling there!

"Work—work—work!
50 From weary chime to chime,
   Work—work—work—
As prisoners work for crime!
   Band, and gusset, and seam,
   Seam, and gusset, and band,
55 Till the heart is sick, and the brain benumb'd,
   As well as the weary hand.

"Work—work—work,
In the dull December light,
   And work—work—work,
60 When the weather is warm and bright—
While underneath the eaves
   The brooding swallows cling
As if to show me their sunny backs
   And twit me with the spring.

65 "Oh! but to breathe the breath
Of the cowslip and primrose sweet—
   With the sky above my head,
And the grass beneath my feet,

For only one short hour
70   To feel as I used to feel,
Before I knew the woes of want,
   And the walk that costs a meal!

"Oh! but for one short hour!
   A respite however brief!
75 No blessed leisure for Love or Hope,
   But only time for Grief!
A little weeping would ease my heart,
   But in their briny bed
My tears must stop, for every drop
80   Hinders needle and thread!"

With fingers weary and worn,
   With eyelids heavy and red,
A woman sat in unwomanly rags,
   Plying her needle and thread—
85   Stitch! stitch! stitch!
   In poverty, hunger, and dirt,
And still with a voice of dolorous pitch,—
Would that its tone could reach the Rich!—
She sang this "Song of the Shirt!"
—1843

William Barnes
1801 – 1886

William Barnes was a clergyman, poet, and local antiquary. He was the author of three series of *Poems of Rural Life in the Dorset Dialect* (1854, 1859, 1862), and in a modest way may be thought of as a regionalist predecessor of Thomas Hardy.

❧

Uncle an' Aunt

How happy uncle us'd to be
O' zummer time, when aunt an' he
O' Zunday evenens, eärm in eärm,
Did walk about their tiny farm,
5   While birds did zing an' gnats did zwarm,
Drough grass a'most above their knees,
An' roun' by hedges an' by trees
    Wi' leafy boughs a-swaÿen.

His hat wer broad, his cwoat wer brown,
10   Wi' two long flaps a-hangen down;
An' vrom his knee went down a blue
Knit stocken to his buckled shoe;
An' aunt did pull her gown-taïl drough
Her pocket-hold, to keep en neat,
15   As she mid walk, or teäke a seat
    By leafy boughs a-swaÿen.

An' vu'st they'd goo to zee their lots
O' pot-eärbs in the geärden plots;
An' he, i'-may-be, by the hatch,
20   Would zee aunt's vowls upon a patch
O' zeeds, an' vow if he could catch
Em wi' his gun, they shoudden vlee
Noo mwore into their roosten tree,
    Wi' leafy boughs a-swaÿen.

25   An' then vrom geärden they did pass
Drough orcha'd out to zee the grass,
An' if the apple-blooth, so white,

Mid be at all a-touch'd wi' blight;
An' uncle, happy at the zight,
30   Did guess what cider there mid be
In all the orcha'd, tree wi' tree,
    Wi' tutties[1] all a-swaÿen.

An' then they stump'd along vrom there
A-vield, to zee the cows an' meäre;
35   An' she, when uncle come in zight,
Look'd up, an' prick'd her ears upright,
An' whicker'd out wi' all her might;
An' he, a-chucklen, went to zee
The cows below the sheädy tree,
40   Wi' leafy boughs a-swaÿen.

An' last ov all, they went to know
How vast the grass in meäd did grow;
An' then aunt zaid 'twer time to goo
In hwome,—a-holden up her shoe,
45   To show how wet he were wi' dew.
An' zoo they toddled hwome to rest,
Lik' doves a-vlee-en to their nest,
    In leafy boughs a-swaÿen.
—1840

Polly Be-En Upzides Wi' Tom

Ah! yesterday, d'ye know, I voun'
Tom Dumpy's cwoat an' smock-frock, down
Below the pollard out in groun';

---

[1] small bunches of flowers.

An' zoo I slyly stole
5 An' took the smock-frock up, an' tack'd
The sleeves an' collar up, an' pack'd
Zome nice sharp stwones, all fresh a-crack'd,
'Ithin each pocket-hole.

An' in the evenen, when he shut
10 Off work, an' come an' donn'd his cwoat,
Their edges gi'ed en sich a cut,
How we did stan' an' laugh!
An' when the smock-frock I'd a-zow'd
Kept back his head an' hands, he drow'd
15 Hizzelf about, an' teäv'd,[1] an' blow'd,
Lik' any up-tied calf.

Then in a veag[2] away he flung
His frock, an' after me he sprung,
An' mutter'd out sich dreats, an' wrung
20 His vist up sich a size!
But I, a-runnen, turn'd an' drow'd
Some doust, a-pick'd up vrom the road,
Back at en wi' the wind, that blow'd
It right into his eyes.

25 An' he did blink, an' vow he'd catch
Me zomehow yet, an' be my match.
But I wer nearly down to hatch
Avore he got vur on;
An' up in chammer, nearly dead
30 Wi' runnen, lik' a cat I vled,
An' out o' window put my head
To zee if he wer gone.

An' there he wer, a-prowlen roun'
Upon the green; an' I look'd down
35 An' told en that I hoped he voun'
He mussen think to peck
Upon a body zoo, nor whip

_____

[1] to throw oneself about energetically.

[2] a violent fit of anger.

The meäre to drow me off, nor tip
Me out o' cart ageän, nor slip
40 Cut hoss-heäir down my neck.
—1841

The Vaïces that Be Gone

When evenen sheädes o' trees do hide
A body by the hedge's zide,
An' twitt'ren birds, wi' plaÿsome flight,
Do vlee to roost at comen night,
5 Then I do saunter out o' zight
In orcha'd, where the pleäce woonce rung
Wi' laughs a-laugh'd an' zongs a-zung
By vaïces that be gone.

There's still the tree that bore our swing,
10 An' others where the birds did zing;
But long-leav'd docks do overgrow
The groun' we trampled beäre below,
Wi' merry skippens to an' fro
Bezide the banks, where Jim did zit
15 A-plaÿen o' the clarinit
To vaïces that be gone.

How mother, when we us'd to stun
Her head wi' all our naïsy fun,
Did wish us all a-gone vrom home:
20 An' now that zome be dead, an' zome
A-gone, an' all the pleäce is dum',
How she do wish, wi' useless tears,
To have ageän about her ears
The vaïces that be gone.

25 Vor all the maïdens an' the bwoys
But I, be marri'd off all woys,
Or dead an' gone; but I do bide
At hwome, alwone, at mother's zide,
An' often, at the evenen-tide,
30 I still do saunter out, wi' tears,

Down drough the orcha'd, where my ears
   Do miss the vaïces gone.
—1841

Childhood

Aye, at that time our days wer but vew,
  An' our lim's wer but small, an' a-growen;
An' then the feäïr worold wer new,
  An' life wer all hopevul an' gaÿ;
5   An' the times o' the sprouten o' leaves,
  An' the cheäk-burnen seasons o' mowen,
An' binden o' red-headed sheaves,
  Wer all welcome seasons o' jaÿ.

Then the housen seem'd high, that be low,
10 An' the brook did seem wide that is narrow,
An' time, that do vlee, did goo slow,
  An' veelens now feeble wer strong,
An' our worold did end wi' the neämes
  Ov the Sha'sbury Hill or Bulbarrow;
15 An' life did seem only the geämes
  That we plaÿ'd as the days rolled along.

Then the rivers, an' high-timber'd lands,
  An' the zilvery hills, 'ithout buyen,
Did seem to come into our hands
20 Vrom others that own'd em avore;
An' all zickness, an' sorrow, an' need,
  Seem'd to die wi' the wold vo'k a-dyen,
An' leäve us vor ever a-freed
  Vrom evils our vorefathers bore.

25 But happy be childern the while
  They have elders a-liven to love em,
An' teäke all the wearisome tweil
  That zome hands or others mus' do;
Like the low-headed shrubs that be warm,
30 In the lewth[1] o' the trees up above em,

---
[1] shelter.

A-screen'd vrom the cwold blowen storm
That the timber avore em must rue.
—1858

The Turnstile

Ah! sad wer we as we did peäce
  The wold church road, wi' downcast feäce,
The while the bells, that mwoan'd so deep
Above our child a-left asleep,
5 Wer now a-zingen all alive
Wi' tother bells to meäke the vive.
Bur up at woone pleäce we come by,
'Twer hard to keep woone's two eyes dry:
On Steän-cliff road, 'ithin the drong,[2]
10 Up where, as vo'k do pass along,
The turnen stile, a-païnted white,
Do sheen by day an' show by night.
Vor always there, as we did goo
To church, thik stile did let us drough,
15 Wi' spreaden eärms that wheel'd to guide
Us each in turn to tother zide.
An' vu'st ov all the traïn he took
My wife, wi' winsome gaït an' look;
An' then zent on my little maïd,
20 A-skippen onward, overjaÿ'd
To reach ageän the pleäce o' pride,
Her comely mother's left han' zide.
An' then, a-wheelen roun', he took
On me, 'ithin his third white nook.
25 An' in the fourth, a-sheäkèn wild,
He zent us on our giddy child.
But eesterday he guided slow
My downcast Jenny, vull o' woe,
An' then my little maïd in black,
30 A-walken softly on her track;
An' after he'd a-turn'd ageän,
To let me goo along the leäne,

---
[2] narrow path.

He had noo little bwoy to vill
His last white eärms, an' they stood still.
—1859

Jaÿ A-Pass'd

When leaves, in evenen winds, do vlee,
Where mornen aïr did strip the tree,
The mind can waït vor boughs in spring
To cool the elem-sheäded ring.
5   Where orcha'd blooth's[1] white sceäles do vall
Mid come the apple's blushen ball.
Our hopes be new, as time do goo,
A-measur'd by the zun on high,
Avore our jaÿs do pass us by.

10   When ice did melt below the zun,
An' weäves along the stream did run,
I hoped in Maÿ's bright froth to roll,
Lik' jess'my[2] in a lily's bowl.
Or, if I lost my loose-bow'd swing,
15   My wrigglen kite mid pull my string,
An' when noo ball did rise an' vall,

Zome other geäme wud still be nigh,
Avore my jaÿs all pass'd me by.

I look'd, as childhood pass'd along,
20   To walk, in leäter years, man-strong,
An' look'd ageän, in manhood's pride,
To manhood's sweetest chaïce, a bride:
An' then to childern, that mid come
To meäke my house a dearer hwome.
25   But now my mind do look behind
Vor jaÿs; an' wonder, wi' a sigh,
When 'twer my jaÿs all pass'd me by.

Wer it when, woonce, I miss'd a call
To rise, an' seem'd to have a vall?
30   Or when my Jeäne to my hands left
Her vew bright keys, a dolevul heft?[3]
Or when avore the door I stood,
To watch a child a-gone vor good?
Or where zome crowd did laugh aloud;
35   Or when the leaves did spring, or die?
When did my jaÿ all pass me by?
—1864

---

[1] blossom.

[2] jasmine.

[3] a sorrowful weight.

Letitia E. Landon
L.E.L.
1802 – 1838

Letitia Elizabeth Landon, the poet and novelist well known in her own time as L.E.L., was born in Chelsea. She wrote to support her family, producing, tirelessly, five volumes of poetry in seven years: *The Fate of Adelaide* (1821), *The Improvisatrice* (1824), *The Troubadour* (1825), *The Golden Violet* (1827), and *The Venetian Bracelet, the Lost Pleiad, A History of the Lyre, and Other Poems* (1828). Landon embraces the Romantic aesthetic of spontaneity, yet tends to elaborate typically Victorian topics (indulging at times in excesses of Victorian sentimentality). As well as poetry, she published four novels between 1831 and 1838. She married George Maclean, the colonial governor of Cape Coast Castle in Ghana, and accompanied him back to the Gold Coast despite rumours that Maclean was a bigamist. Four months later, L.E.L. was found dead in her room with a bottle of prussic acid in her hand.

ഏഩൕ

from *The Improvisatrice*

Advertisement

Poetry needs no Preface: if it do not speak for itself, no comment can render it explicit. I have only, therefore, to state that *The Improvisatrice* is an attempt to illustrate that species of inspiration common in Italy, where the mind is warmed from earliest childhood by all that is beautiful in nature and glorious in art. The character depicted is entirely Italian,—a young female with all the loveliness, vivid feeling, and genius of her own impassioned land. She is supposed to relate her own history; with which are intermixed the tales and episodes which various circumstances call forth.

L.E.L.

I am a daughter of that land,
Where the poet's lip and the painter's hand
Are most divine,—where the earth and sky,
Are picture both and poetry—
5   I am of Florence. 'Mid the chill
Of hope and feeling, oh! I still
Am proud to think to where I owe
My birth, though but the dawn of woe!

My childhood passed 'mid radiant things,
10 Glorious as Hope's imaginings;
Statues but known from shapes of the earth,
By being too lovely for mortal birth;
Paintings whose colours of life were caught
From the fairy tints in the rainbow wrought;
15 Music whose sighs had a spell like those
That float on the sea at the evening's close;
Language so silvery, that every word
Was like the lute's awakening chord;
Skies half sunshine, and half starlight;
20 Flowers whose lives were a breath of delight;
Leaves whose green pomp knew no withering;
Fountains bright as the skies of our spring;
And songs whose wild and passionate line
Suited a soul of romance like mine.

25   My power was but a woman's power;
Yet, in that great and glorious dower
Which Genius gives, I had my part:
I poured my full and burning heart
In song, and on the canvass made
30   My dreams of beauty visible;
I knew not which I loved the most—
    Pencil or lute,—both loved so well.

Oh, yet my pulse throbs to recall,
When first upon the gallery's wall
35 Picture of mine was placed, to share
Wonder and praise from each one there!
Sad were my shades; methinks they had
Almost a tone of prophecy—
I ever had, from earliest youth,
40 A feeling what my fate would be.

My first was of a gorgeous hall,
Lighted up for festival;
Braided tresses, and cheeks of bloom,
Diamond agraff,[1] and foam-white plume;
45 Censers of roses, vases of light,
Like what the moon sheds on a summer night.
Youths and maidens with linked hands,
Joined in the graceful sarabands,[2]
Smiled on the canvass; but apart
50 Was one who leant in silent mood
As revelry to sick heart
Were worse than veriest solitude.
Pale, dark-eyed, beautiful, and young,
Such as he had shone o'er my slumbers,
55 When I had only slept to dream
Over again his magic numbers.

Divinest Petrarch! he whose lyre,
Like morning light, half dew, half fire,
To Laura and to love was vowed—
60 He looked on one, who with the crowd
Mingled, but mixed not; on whose cheek
There was a blush, as if she knew
Whose look was fixed on hers. Her eye,
Of a spring-sky's delicious blue,
65 Had not the language of that bloom,
But mingling tears, and light, and gloom,
Was raised abstractedly to Heaven:—
No sign was to her lover given.
I painted her with golden tresses,

70 Such as float on the wind's caresses,
When the laburnums wildly fling
Their sunny blossoms to the spring,
A cheek which had the crimson hue
Upon the sun touched nectarine;
75 A lip of perfume and of dew;
A brow like twilight's darkened line.
I strove to catch each charm that long
Has lived,—thanks to her lover's song!
Each grace he numbered one by one,
80 That shone in her of Avignon.[3]

I ever thought that poet's fate
Utterly lone and desolate.
It is the spirit's bitterest pain
To love, to be beloved again;
85 And yet between a gulf which ever
The hearts that burn to meet must sever.
And he was vowed to one sweet star,
Bright yet to him, but bright afar.

O'er some, Love's shadow may but pass
90 As passes the breath-stain o'er glass;
And pleasures, cares, and pride combined,
Fill up the blank Love leaves behind.
But there are some whose love is high,
Entire, and sole idolatry;
95 Who, turning from a heartless world,
Ask some dear thing, which may renew
Affection's severed links, and be
As true as they themselves are true.
But Love's bright fount is never pure;
100 And all his pilgrims must endure
All passion's mighty suffering
Ere they may reach the blessed spring.
And some who waste their lives to find
A prize which they may never win:
105 Like those who search for Irem's[4] groves,
Which found, they may not enter in.

---

[1] a kind of hook used as a clasp.

[2] a slow, elegant Spanish dance in triple time.

[3] a southern French city which served as the papal seat in 1309–77.

[4] a paradise named in the Koran.

Where is the sorrow but appears
In Love's long catalogue of tears?
And some there are who leave the path
110   In agony and fierce disdain;
But bear upon each cankered breast
     The scar that never heals again.

     My next was of a minstrel too,
Who proved that woman's hand might do,
115 When, true to the heart pulse, it woke
     The harp. Her head was bending down,
As if in weariness, and near,
     But unworn, was a laurel crown.
She was not beautiful, if bloom
120 And smiles form beauty; for, like death,
Her brow was ghastly; and her lip
Was parched, as fever were its breath.
There was a shade upon her dark,
Large, floating eyes, as if each spark
125 Of minstrel ecstasy was fled,
Yet leaving them no tears to shed;
Fixed in their hopelessness of care,
And reckless in their great despair.
She sat beneath a cypress tree,
130   A little fountain ran beside,
And, in the distance, one dark rock
     Threw its long shadow o'er the tide;
And to the west, where the nightfall
Was darkening day's gemm'd coronal,[1]
135 Its white shafts crimsoning in the sky,
Arose the sun-god's sanctuary.
I deemed, that of lyre, life, and love
     She was a long, last farewell taking;—
That, from her pale and parched lips,
140   Her latest, wildest song was breaking.

SAPPHO'S SONG [2]

Farewell, my lute!—and would that I
     Had never waked thy burning chords!
Poison has been upon thy sigh,
     And fever has breathed in thy words.

5 Yet wherefore, wherefore should I blame
     Thy power, thy spell, my gentlest lute?
I should have been the wretch I am,
     Had every chord of thine been mute.

It was my evil star above,
10   Not my sweet lute, that wrought me wrong:
It was not song that taught me love,
     But it was love that taught me song.

If song be past, and hope undone,
     And pulse, and head, and heart, are flame;
15 It is thy work, thou faithless one!
     But, no!—I will not name thy name!

Sun-god! lute, wreath are vowed to thee!
     Long be their light upon my grave—
My glorious grave—yon deep blue sea:
20   I shall sleep calm beneath its wave!

FLORENCE! with what idolatry
     I've lingered in thy radiant halls,
Worshipping, till my dizzy eye
     Grew dim with gazing on those walls,
25 Where Time had spared each glorious gift
By Genius unto Memory left!
And when seen by the pale moonlight,
More pure, more perfect, though less bright,
What dreams of song flashed on my brain,
30 Till each shade seemed to live again;
And then the beautiful, the grand,

---

[1] a crown or coronet.

[2] Sappho was a Greek lyric poet, born on the island of Lesbos (?–650 BC).

The glorious of my native land,
In every flower that threw its veil
Aside, when wooed by the spring gale;
35   In every vineyard, where the sun,
His task of summer ripening done,
Shone on their clusters, and a song
Came lightly from the peasant throng;—
In the dim loveliness of night,
40   In fountains with their diamond light,
In aged temple, ruined shrine,
And its green wreath of ivy twine;—
In every change of earth and sky,
Breathed the deep soul of poesy.

45   As yet I loved not;—but each wild,
High thought I nourished raised a pyre
For love to light; and lighted once
By love, it would be like the fire
The burning lava floods that dwell
50   In Etna's[1] cave unquenchable.

        .   .   .   .   .

—1824

Erinna [2]

Was she of spirit race, or was she one
Of earth's least earthly daughters, one to whom
A gift of loveliness and soul is given,
Only to make them wretched?

There is an antique gem, on which her brow
Retains its graven beauty even now.
Her hair is braided, but one curl behind
Floats as enamour'd of the summer wind;
The rest is simple. Is she not too fair
Even to think of maiden's sweetest care?
The mouth and brow are contrasts. One so fraught
With pride, the melancholy pride of thought
Conscious of power, and yet forced to know
How little way such power as that can go;
Regretting, while too proud of the fine mind,
Which raises but to part it from its kind:
But the sweet mouth had nothing of all this;
It was a mouth the rose had lean'd to kiss
For her young sister, telling, now though mute,
How soft an echo it was to the lute.
The one spoke genius, in its high revealing;
The other smiled a woman's gentle feeling.
It was a lovely face: the Greek outline
Flowing, yet delicate and feminine;
The glorious lightning of the kindled eye,
Raised, as it communed with its native sky.
A lovely face, the spirit's fitting shrine;
The one almost, the other quite divine.

———————————

My hand is on the lyre, which never more
With its sweet commerce, like a bosom friend,
Will share the deeper thoughts which I could trust
Only to music and to solitude.
5   It is the very grove, the olive grove,
Where first I laid my laurel crown aside,
And bathed my fever'd brow in the cold stream;
As if that I could wash away the fire
Which from that moment kindled in my heart.
10   I well remember how I flung myself,
Like a young goddess, on a purple cloud
Of light and odour—the rich violets
Were so ethereal in bloom and breath:
And I,—I felt immortal, for my brain

———————————

[1] volcanic mountain in eastern Sicily.

[2] "Introductory Notice: Among the obligations I owe to 'The Brides of Florence,' and to the information contained in its interesting notes, I must refer particularly for the origin of the present poem. In one of those notes is the first, indeed the only account I ever met with of Erinna. The following short quotation is sufficient for my present purpose:—'Erinna was a poetess from her cradle, and she only lived to the completion of her eighteenth year.—Of Erinna very little is known; there is in the Grecian Anthology a sepulchral epigram by Antipater on this young poetess.' A poem of the present kind had long floated on my imagination; and this gave it a local habitation and a name. There seemed to me just enough known of Erinna to interest; and I have not attempted to write a classical fiction; feelings are what I wish to narrate, not incidents; my aim has been to draw the portrait and trace the

changes of a highly poetical mind, too sensitive perhaps of the chill and bitterness belonging even to success. The feelings which constitute poetry are the same in all ages, they are acted upon by similar causes. Erinna is an ideal not a historical picture, and as such I submit it less to the judgment than to the kindness of my friends." (Landon's note.)

15 Was drunk and mad with its first draught of fame.
'Tis strange there was one only cypress tree,
And then, as now, I lay beneath its shade.
The night had seen me pace my lonely room,
Clasping the lyre I had no heart to wake,
20 Impatient for the day: yet its first dawn
Came cold as death; for every pulse sank down,
Until the very presence of my hope
Became to me a fear. The sun rose up;
I stood alone mid thousands; but I felt
25 Mine inspiration; and, as the last sweep
Of my song died away amid the hills,
My heart reverberated the shout which bore
To the blue mountains and the distant heaven
ERINNA's name, and on my bended knee,
30 Olympus,[1] I received thy laurel crown.

And twice new birth of violets have sprung,
Since they were first my pillow, since I sought
In the deep silence of the olive grove
The dreamy happiness which solitude
35 Brings to the soul o'erfill'd with its delight:
For I was like some young and sudden heir
Of a rich palace heap'd with gems and gold,
Whose pleasure doubles as he sums his wealth
And forms a thousand plans of festival;
40 Such were my myriad visions of delight.
The lute, which hitherto in Delphian[2] shades
Had been my twilight's solitary joy,
Would henceforth be a sweet and breathing bond
Between me and my kind. Orphan unloved,
45 I had been lonely from my childhood's hour,
Childhood whose very happiness is love:
But that was over now; my lyre would be
My own heart's true interpreter, and those
To whom my song was dear, would they not bless
50 The hand that waken'd it? I should be loved

_____

[1] the mountain home of the gods in Greek mythology.

[2] of Delphi, or the oracle of Apollo which was located there.

For the so gentle sake of those soft chords
Which mingled others' feelings with mine own.

Vow'd I that song to meek and gentle thoughts.
To tales that told of sorrow and of love,
55 To all our nature's finest touches, all
That wakens sympathy: and I should be
Alone no longer; every wind that bore,
And every lip that breathed one strain of mine,
Henceforth partake in all my joy and grief.
60 Oh! glorious is the gifted poet's lot,
And touching more than glorious: 't is to be
Companion of the heart's least earthly hour;
The voice of love and sadness, calling forth
Tears from their silent fountain: 't is to have
65 Share in all nature's loveliness; giving flowers
A life as sweet, more lasting than their own;
And catching from green wood and lofty pine
Language mysterious as musical;
Making the thoughts, which else had only been
70 Like colours on the morning's earliest hour,
Immortal, and worth immortality;
Yielding the hero that eternal name
For which he fought; making the patriot's deed
A stirring record for long after time;
75 Cherishing tender thoughts, which else had pass'd
Away like tears; and saving the loved dead
From death's worst part—its deep forgetfulness.

From the first moment when a falling leaf,
Or opening bud, or streak of rose-touch'd sky,
80 Waken'd in me the flush and flow of song,
I gave my soul entire unto the gift
I deem'd mine own, direct from heaven; it was
The hope, the bliss, the energy of life;
I had no hope that dwelt not with my lyre,
85 No bliss whose being grew not from my lyre,
No energy undevoted to my lyre.
It was my other self, that had a power;
Mine, but o'er which I had not a control.
At times it was not with me, and I felt

90 A wonder how it ever had been mine:
And then a word, a look of loveliness,
A tone of music, call'd it into life;
And song came gushing, like the natural tears,
To check whose current does not rest with us.

95   Had I lived ever in the savage woods,
Or in some distant island, which the sea
With wind and wave guards in deep loneliness;
Had my eye never on the beauty dwelt
Of human face, and my ear never drank
100 The music of a human voice; I feel
My spirit would have pour'd itself in song,
Have learn'd a language from the rustling leaves
The singing of the birds, and of the tide.
Perchance, then, happy had I never known
105 Another thought could be attach'd to song
Than of its own delight. Oh! let me pause
Over this earlier period, when my heart
Mingled its being with its pleasures, fill'd
With rich enthusiasm, which once flung
110 Its purple colouring o'er all things of earth,
And without which our utmost power of thought
But sharpens arrows that will drink our blood.
Like woman's soothing influence o'er man,
Enthusiasm is upon the mind;
115 Softening and beautifying that which is
Too harsh and sullen in itself. How much
I loved the painter's glorious art, which forms
A world like, but more beautiful than this;
Just catching nature in her happiest mood!
120 How drank I in fine poetry, which makes
The hearing passionate, fill'd with memories
Which steal from out the past like rays from clouds!
And then the sweet songs of my native vale,
Whose sweetness and whose softness call'd to mind
125 The perfume of the flowers, the purity
Of the blue sky; Oh, how they stirr'd my soul!
Amid the many golden gifts which heaven
Has left, like portions of its light, on earth,
None hath such influence as music hath.

130 The painter's hues stand visible before us
In power and beauty; we can trace the thoughts
Which are the workings of the poet's mind:
But music is a mystery, and viewless
Even when present, and is less man's act,
135 And less within his order; for the hand
That can call forth the tones, yet cannot tell
Whither they go, or if they live or die,
When floated once beyond his feeble ear;
And then, as if it were an unreal thing,
140 The wind will sweep from the neglected strings
As rich a swell as ever minstrel drew.

    A poet's word, a painter's touch, will reach
The innermost recesses of the heart,
Making the pulses throb in unison
145 With joy or grief, which we can analyze;
There is the cause for pleasure and for pain:
But music moves us, and we know not why;
We feel the tears, but cannot trace their source.
Is it the language of some other state,
150 Born of its memory? For what can wake
The soul's strong instinct of another world,
Like music? Well with sadness doth it suit,
To hear the melancholy sounds decay,
And think (for thoughts are life's great human links,
155 And mingle with our feelings,) even so
Will the heart's wildest pulses sink to rest.

    How have I loved, when the red evening fill'd
Our temple with its glory, first, to gaze
On the strange contrast of the crimson air,
160 Lighted as if with passion, and flung back,
From silver vase and tripod rich with gems,
To the pale statues round, where human life
Was not, but beauty was, which seemed to have
Apart existence from humanity:
165 Then, to go forth where the tall waving pines
Seem'd as behind them roll'd a golden sea,
Immortal and eternal; and the boughs,
That darkly swept between me and its light,

Were fitting emblems of the worldly cares
170 That are the boundary between us and heaven;
Meanwhile, the wind, a wilful messenger
Lingering amid the flowers on his way,
At intervals swept past in melody,
The lutes and voices of the choral hymn
175 Contending with the rose-breath on his wing!
Perhaps it is these pleasures' chiefest charm,
They are so indefinable, so vague.
From earliest childhood all too well aware
Of the uncertain nature of our joys,
180 It is delicious to enjoy, yet know
No after consequence will be to weep.
Pride misers with enjoyment, when we have
Delight in things that are but of the mind:
But half humility when we partake
185 Pleasures that are half wants, the spirit pines
And struggles in its fetters, and disdains
The low base clay to which it is allied.
But here our rapture raises us: we feel
What glorious power is given to man, and find
190 Our nature's nobleness and attributes,
Whose heaven is intellect; and we are proud
To think how we can love those things of earth
Which are least earthly; and the soul grows pure
In this high communing, and more divine.
195 This time of dreaming happiness pass'd by,
Another spirit was within my heart;
I drank the maddening cup of praise, which grew
Henceforth the fountain of my life; I lived
Only in others' breath; a word, a look,
200 Were of all influence on my destiny:
If praise they spoke, 'twas sunlight to my soul;
Or censure, it was like the scorpion's sting.

And a yet darker lesson was to learn—
The hollowness of each; that praise, which is
205 But base exchange of flattery; that blame,
Given by cautious coldness, which still deems
'Tis safest to depress; that mockery,
Flinging shafts but to show its own keen aim;

That carelessness, whose very censure's chance;
210 And, worst of all, the earthly judgment pass'd
By minds whose native clay is unredeem'd
By aught of heaven, whose every thought falls foul
Plague spot on beauty which they cannot feel,
Tainting all that it touches with itself.
215 O dream of fame, what hast thou been to me
But the destroyer of life's calm content!
I feel so more than ever, that thy sway
Is weaken'd over me. Once I could find
A deeper and dangerous delight in thee;
220 But that is gone. I am too much awake.
Light has burst o'er me, but not morning's light;
'Tis such light as will burst upon the tomb,
When all but judgment's over. Can it be,
That these fine impulses, these lofty thoughts,
225 Burning with their own beauty, are but given
To make me the low slave of vanity,
Heartless and humbled? O my own sweet power,
Surely thy songs were made for more than this!
What a worst waste of feeling and of life
230 Have been the imprints on my roll of time,
Too much, too long! To what use have I turn'd
The golden gifts in which I pride myself?
They are profaned; with their pure ore I made
A temple resting only on the breath
235 Of heedless worshippers. Alas! that ever
Praise should have been what it has been to me
The opiate of my heart. Yet I have dream'd
Of things which cannot be; the bright, the pure,
That all of which the heart may only dream;
240 And I have mused upon my gift of song,
And deeply felt its beauty, and disdain'd
The pettiness of praise to which at times
My soul has bow'd; and I have scorn'd myself
For that my cheek could burn, my pulses beat
245 At idle words. And yet, it is in vain
For the full heart to press back every throb
Wholly upon itself. Ay, fair as are
The visions of a poet's solitude,
There must be something more for happiness;

250 They seek communion. It had seem'd to me
A miser's selfishness, had I not sought
To share with others those impassion'd thoughts,
Like light, or hope, or love, in their effects.
When I have watch'd the stars write on the sky
255 In characters of light, have seen the moon
Come like a veil'd priestess from the east,
While, like a hymn, the wind swell'd on mine ear,
Telling soft tidings of eve's thousand flowers,
Has it not been the transport of my lute
260 To find its best delight in sympathy?
Alas! the idols which our hopes set up,
They are Chaldean[1] ones, half gold, half clay;
We trust, we are deceived, we hope, we fear,
Alike without foundation; day by day
265 Some new illusion is destroyed, and life
Gets cold and colder on towards its close.
Just like the years which make it, some are check'd
By sudden blights in spring; some are dried up
By fiery summers; others waste away
270 In calm monotony of quiet skies,
And peradventure these may be the best:
They know no hurricanes, no floods that sweep
As a God's vengeance were upon each wave;
But then they have no ruby fruits, no flowers
275 Shining in purple, and no lighted mines
Of gold and diamond. Which is the best,—
Beauty and glory, in a southern clime,
Mingled with thunder, tempest; or the calm
Of skies that scarcely change, which, at the least,
280 If much of shine they have not, have no storms?
I know not: but I know fair earth or sky
Are self-consuming in their loveliness,
And the too radiant sun and fertile soil
In their luxuriance run themselves to waste,
285 And the green valley and the silver stream
Become a sandy desert. Oh! the mind,
Too vivid in its lighted energies,

May read its fate in sunny Araby.[2]
How lives its beauty in each Eastern tale,
290 Its growth of spices, and its groves of balm!
They are exhausted; and what is it now?
A wild and burning wilderness. Alas!
For such similitude. Too much this is
The fate of this world's loveliest and best.

295   Is there not a far people, who possess
Mysterious oracles of olden time,
Who say that this earth labours with a curse,
That it is fallen from its first estate,
And is now but the shade of what it was?
300 I do believe the tale. I feel its truth
In my vain aspirations, in the dreams
That are revealings of another world,
More pure, more perfect than our weary one,
Where day is darkness to the starry soul.

305   O heart of mine! my once sweet paradise
Of love and hope! how changed thou art to me!
I cannot count thy changes: thou hast lost
Interest in the once idols of thy being;
They have departed, even as if wings
310 Had borne away their morning; they have left
Weariness, turning pleasure into pain,
And too sure knowledge of their hollowness.

   And that too is gone from me; that which was
My solitude's delight! I can no more
315 Make real existence of a shadowy world.
Time was, the poet's song, the ancient tale
Were to me fountains of deep happiness,
For they grew visible in my lonely hours,
As things in which I had a deed and part;
320 Their actual presence had not been more true:
But these are bubbling sparkles, that are found
But at the spring's first source. Ah! years may bring
The mind to its perfection, but no more

---

[1] Magic and astrology flourished in Chaldea/Babylonia.

[2] Arabia.

Will those young visions live in their own light;
325 Life's troubles stir life's waters all too much,
Passions chase fancies, and, though still we dream,
The colouring is from reality.

Farewell, my lyre! thou hast not been to me
All I once hoped. What is the gift of mind,
330 But as a barrier to so much that makes
Our life endurable,—companionship,
Mingling affection, calm and gentle peace,
Till the vex'd spirit seals with discontent
A league of sorrow and of vanity,
335 Built on a future which will never be!

And yet I would resign the praise that now
Makes my cheek crimson, and my pulses beat,
Could I but deem that when my hand is cold,
And my lip passionless, my songs would be
340 Number'd 'mid the young poet's first delights;
Read by the dark-eyed maiden in an hour
Of moonlight, till her cheek shone with its tears;
And murmur'd by the lover when his suit
Calls upon poetry to breathe of love.
345 I do not hope a sunshine burst of fame,
My lyre asks but a wreath of fragile flowers.
I have told passionate tales of breaking hearts,
Of young cheeks fading even before the rose;
My songs have been the mournful history
350 Of woman's tenderness and woman's tears;
I have touch'd but the spirit's gentlest chords,—
Surely the fittest for my maiden hand;—
And in their truth my immortality.

Thou lovely and lone star, whose silver light,
355 Like music o'er the waters, steals along
The soften'd atmosphere; pale star, to thee
I dedicate the lyre, whose influence
I would have sink upon the heart like thine.

In such an hour as this, the bosom turns
360 Back to its early feelings; man forgets

His stern ambition and his worldly cares,
And woman loathes the petty vanities
That mar her nature's beauty; like the dew,
Shedding its sweetness o'er the sleeping flowers
365 Till all their morning freshness is revived,
Kindly affections, sad, but yet sweet thoughts
Melt the cold eyes, long, long unused to weep.
O lute of mine, that I shall wake no more!
Such tearful music linger on thy strings,
370 Consecrate unto sorrow and to love;
Thy truth, thy tenderness, be all thy fame!
—1826

"Preface" to The Venetian Bracelet, The Lost Pleiad, A History of the Lyre, and Other Poems

Diffidence of their own abilities, and fear, which heightens the anxiety for public favour, are pleas usually urged by the youthful writer: may I, while venturing for the first time to speak of myself, be permitted to say they far more truly belong to one who has had experience of both praise and censure. The feelings which attended the publication of the "Improvisatrice," are very different from those that accompany the present volume. I believe I *then* felt little beyond hope, vague as the timidity which subdued it, and that excitement which every author must know: *now* mine is a "farther looking hope;" and the timidity which apprehended the verdict of others, is now deepened by distrust of my own powers. Or, to claim my poetical privilege, and express my meaning by a simile, I should say, I am no longer one who springs forward in the mere energy of exercise and enjoyment; but rather like the Olympian racer, who strains his utmost vigour, with the distant goal and crown in view. I have devoted my whole life to one object: in society I have but sought the material for solitude. I can imagine but one interest in existence,—that which has filled my past, and haunts my future,—the perhaps vain desire, when I am nothing, of leaving one of those memories at once a good and a glory. Believing, as I do, in the great and excellent influence of poetry, may I hazard the expression of what I have myself sometimes trusted to do? A highly cultivated state of society must ever have for concomitant evils, that selfishness, the result of indolent indulgence; and that heartlessness attendant on refinement, which too often hardens while it polishes. Aware that to elevate I must first soften, and that if I wished to purify I must first touch, I have ever endeavoured to bring forward grief, disappointment, the fallen leaf, the faded flower, the broken heart, and the early grave. Surely we must be less worldly, less interested, from this sympathy with the sorrow in which our unselfish feelings alone can take part. And now a few words on a subject, where the variety of the opinions offered have left me somewhat in the situation of the prince in the fairy tale, who, when in the vicinity of the magic fountain, found himself so distracted by the multitude of voices that directed his way, as to be quite incapable of deciding which was the right path. I allude to the blame and eulogy which have been equally bestowed on my frequent choice of love as my source of song. I can only say, that for a woman, whose influence and whose sphere must be in the affections, what subject can be more fitting than one which it is her peculiar province to refine, spiritualize, and exalt? I have always sought to paint it self-denying, devoted, and making an almost religion of its truth; and I must add, that such as I would wish to draw her, woman actuated by an attachment as intense as it is true, as pure as it is deep, is not only more admirable as a heroine, but also in actual life, than one whose idea of love is that of light amusement, or at worst of vain mortification. With regard to the frequent application of my works to myself, considering that I sometimes pourtrayed love unrequited, then betrayed, and again destroyed by death—may I hint the conclusions are not quite logically drawn, as assuredly the same mind cannot have suffered such varied modes of misery. However, if I must have an unhappy passion, I can only console myself with my own perfect unconsciousness of so great a misfortune. I now leave the following poems to their fate: they must speak for themselves. I could but express my anxiety, an anxiety only increased by a popularity beyond my most sanguine dreams.

With regard to those whose former praise encouraged, their best recompense is the happiness they bestowed. And to those whose differing opinion expressed itself in censure, I own, after the first chagrin was past, I never laid down a criticism by which I did not benefit, or trust to benefit. I will conclude by apostrophizing the hopes and fears they excited, in the words of the Mexican king—"Ye have been the feathers of my wings."

—1829

The Nameless Grave

A nameless grave,—there is no stone
  To sanctify the dead:
O'er it the willow droops alone,
  With only wild flowers spread.

5 "Oh, there is nought to interest here,
  No record of a name,
A trumpet call upon the ear,
  High on the roll of fame.

"I will not pause beside a tomb
10 Where nothing calls to mind
Aught that can brighten mortal gloom,
  Or elevate mankind;—

"No glorious memory to efface
  The stay of meaner clay;
15 No intellect whose heavenly trace
  Redeem'd our earth:—away!"

Ah, these are thoughts that well may rise
  On youth's ambitious pride;
But I will sit and moralize
20 This lowly stone beside.

Here thousands might have slept, whose name
  Had been to thee a spell,
To light thy flashing eyes with flame,—
  To bid thy young heart swell.

25 Here might have been a warrior's rest,
  Some chief who bravely bled,
With waving banner, sculptured crest,
  And laurel on his head.

That laurel must have had its blood,
30 That blood have caused its tear,—
Look on the lovely solitude—
  What! wish for warfare here!

A poet might have slept,—what! he
  Whose restless heart first wakes
35 Its lifepulse into melody,
  Then o'er it pines and breaks?—

He who hath sung of passionate love,
  His life a feverish tale:—
Oh! not the nightingale, the dove
40 Would suit its quiet vale.

See, I have named your favourite two,—
  Each had been glad to crave
Rest 'neath this turf's unbroken dew,
  And such a nameless grave!
—1829

The Factory

'Tis an accursed thing!

There rests a shade above yon town,
  A dark funeral shroud:
'Tis not the tempest hurrying down,
  'Tis not a summer cloud.

5 The smoke that rises on the air
  Is as a type and sign;
A shadow flung by the despair
  Within those streets of thine.

That smoke shuts out the cheerful day
10 The sunset's purple hues,
The moonlight's pure and tranquil ray,
  The morning's pearly dews.

Such is the moral atmosphere
  Around thy daily life;
15 Heavy with care, and pale with fear,
  With future tumult rife.

There rises on the morning wind
  A low appealing cry,
A thousand children are resign'd
20 To sicken and to die!

We read of Moloch's[1] sacrifice,
  We sicken at the name,
And seem to hear the infant cries—
  And yet we do the same;—

25 And worse—'twas but a moment's pain
  The heathen altar gave,
But we give years,—our idol, Gain,
  Demands a living grave!

---

[1] the god of the ancient Phoenicians and Ammonites to whom children were sacrificed by burning.

How precious is the little one,
    Before his mother's sight,
With bright hair dancing in the sun,
    And eyes of azure light!

He sleeps as rosy as the south,
    For summer days are long;
A prayer upon the little mouth,
    Lull'd by his nurse's song.

Love is around him, and his hours
    Are innocent and free;
His mind essays its early powers
    Beside his mother's knee.

When afteryears of trouble come,
    Such as await man's prime,
How will he think of that dear home,
    And childhood's lovely time!

And such should childhood ever be,
    The fairy well; to bring
To life's worn, weary memory
    The freshness of its spring.

But here the order is reversed,
    And infancy, like age,
Knows of existence but its worst,
    One dull and darken'd page;—

Written with tears and stamp'd with toil,
    Crush'd from the earliest hour,
Weeds darkening on the bitter soil
    That never knew a flower.

Look on yon child, it droops the head,
    Its knees are bow'd with pain;
It mutters from its wretched bed,
    "O, let me sleep again!"

Alas! 'tis time, the mother's eyes
    Turn mournfully away;
Alas! 'tis time, the child must rise,
    And yet it is not day.

The lantern's lit—she hurries forth,
    The spare cloak's scanty fold
Scarce screens her from the snowy north,
    The child is pale and cold.

And wearily the little hands
    Their task accustom'd ply;
While daily, some 'mid those pale bands,
    Droop, sicken, pine, and die.

Good God! to think upon a child
    That has no childish days,
No careless play, no frolics wild,
    No words of prayer and praise!

Man from the cradle—'tis too soon
    To earn their daily bread,
And heap the heat and toil of noon
    Upon an infant's head.

To labour ere their strength be come,
    Or starve,—is such the doom
That makes of many an English home
    One long and living tomb?

Is there no pity from above,—
    No mercy in those skies;
Hath then the heart of man no love,
    To spare such sacrifice?

O, England! though thy tribute waves
    Proclaim thee great and free,
While those small children pine like slaves,
    There is a curse on thee!
    —1835

Carthage [1]

"Early on the morning following, I walked to the site of the great Carthage,—of that town, at the sound of whose name mighty Rome herself had so often trembled,—of Carthage, the mistress of powerful and brave armies, of numerous fleets, and of the world's commerce, and to whom Africa, Spain, Sardinia, Corsica, Sicily, and Italy herself bowed in submission as to their sovereign—in short,—*'Carthago, dives opum, studiisque asperrima belli:'* [2] I was prepared to see but few vestiges of its former grandeur, it had so often suffered from the devastating effects of war, that I knew many could not exist; but my heart sunk within me when ascending one of its hills, (from whose summit the eye embraces a view of the whole surrounding country to the edge of the sea,) I beheld nothing more than a few scattered and shapeless masses of masonry. The scene that once was animated by the presence of nearly a million of warlike inhabitants is now buried in the silence of the grave; no living soul appearing, if we occasionally except a soldier going or returning from the fort, or the solitary and motionless figure of an Arab, watching his flocks from the summit of the fragment of some former palace or temple."—Sir G. Temple's *Excursions in the Mediterranean.*

Low it lieth—earth to earth—
All to which that earth gave birth—
Palace, market-street, and fane; [3]
Dust that never asks in vain,
5 Hath reclaim'd its own again.
     Dust, the wide world's king.
Where are now the glorious hours

Of a nation's gather'd powers?
Like the setting of a star,
10 In the fathomless afar;
     Time's eternal wing
Hath around those ruins cast
The dark presence of the past.

Mind, what art thou? dost thou not
15 Hold the vast earth for thy lot?
In thy toil, how glorious.
What dost thou achieve for us,
Over all victorious!
     Godlike thou dost seem.
20 But the perishing still lurks
In thy most immortal works;
Thou dost build thy home on sand,
And the palace-girdled strand
     Fadeth like a dream.
25 Thy great victories only show
All is nothingness below.
—1837

Felicia Hemans

No more, no more—oh, never more returning,
  Will thy beloved presence gladden earth;
No more wilt thou with sad, yet anxious, yearning
  Cling to those hopes which have no mortal birth.
5 Thou art gone from us, and with thee departed,
  How many lovely things have vanished too:
Deep thoughts that at thy will to being started,
  And feelings, teaching us our own were true.
Thou hast been round us, like a viewless spirit,
10 Known only by the music on the air;
The leaf or flowers which thou hast named inherit
A beauty known but from thy breathing there:
For thou didst on them fling thy strong emotion.
  The likeness from itself the fond heart gave;
15 As planets from afar look down on ocean,
  And give their own sweet image to the wave.

---

[1] an ancient city and state in northern Africa, founded by the Phoenicians near present-day Tunis, and destroyed by the Romans in 146 BC.

[2] "Carthage, rich in resources, most fierce in the arts of war."

[3] temple or church.

And thou didst bring from foreign lands their
    treasures,
    As floats thy various melody along;
We know the softness of Italian measures,
20   And the grave cadence of Castilian song.
A general bond of union is the poet,
    By its immortal verse is language known,
And for the sake of song do others know it—
    One glorious poet makes the world his own.
25 And thou—how far thy gentle sway extended!
    The heart's sweet empire over land and sea;
Many a stranger and far flower was blended
    In the soft wreath that glory bound for thee.
The echoes of the Susquehanna's[1] waters
30   Paused in the pine-woods words of thine to hear;
And to the wide Atlantic's younger daughters
    Thy name was lovely, and thy song was dear.

Was not this purchased all too dearly?—never
    Can fame atone for all that fame hath cost.
35 We see the goal, but know not the endeavour
    Nor what fond hopes have on the way been lost.
What do we know of the unquiet pillow,
    By the worn check and tearful eyelid prest,
When thoughts chase thoughts, like the tumultuous
    billow,
40   Whose very light and foam reveals unrest?
We say, the song is sorrowful, but know not
    What may have left that sorrow on the song:
However mournful words may be, they show not
    The whole extent of wretchedness and wrong.
45 They cannot paint the long sad hours, passed only
    In vain regrets o'er what we feel we are.
Alas! The kingdom of the lute is lonely—
    Cold is the worship coming from afar.

Yet what is mind in woman but revealing
50   In sweet clear light the hidden world below,

By quicker fancies and a keener feeling
    Than those around, the cold and careless, know?
What is to feed such feeling, but to culture
    A soil whence pain will never more depart?
55 The fable of Prometheus and the vulture,[2]
    Reveals the poet's and the woman's heart.
Unkindly are they judged—unkindly treated—
    By careless tongues and by ungenerous words;
While cruel sneer, and hard reproach, repeated,
60   Jar the fine music of the spirit's chords.
Wert thou not weary—thou whose soothing
    numbers
    Gave other lips the joy thine own had not.
Didst thou not welcome thankfully the slumbers
    Which closed around thy mourning human lot?

65 What on this earth could answer thy requiring,
    For earnest faith—for love, the deep and true,
The beautiful, which was thy soul's desiring,
    But only from thyself its being drew.
How is the warm and loving heart requited
70   In this harsh world, where it awhile must dwell.
Its best affections wronged, betrayed, and slighted—
    Such is the doom of those who love too well.
Better the weary dove should close its pinion,
    Fold up its golden wings and be at peace,
75 Enter, O ladye, that serene dominion,
    Where earthy cares and earthy sorrows cease.
Fame's troubled hour has cleared, and now replying,
    A thousand hearts their music ask of thine.
Sleep with a light the lovely and undying
80   Around thy grave—a grave which is a shrine.
—1838

---

[1] river flowing through New York, Pennsylvania, and Maryland into Chesapeake Bay.

[2] Prometheus stole fire from heaven and bestowed it upon humanity, subsequently earning the wrath of Zeus. Prometheus's punishment was to be chained to a rock where a vulture arrived each day to devour his liver, which always grew back after the encounter.

Rydal Water and Grasmere Lake

The Residence of Wordsworth

Not for the glory on their heads
  Those stately hill-tops wear,
Although the summer sunset sheds
  Its constant crimson there.
5 Not for the gleaming lights that break
  The purple of the twilight lake,
Half dusky and half fair,
  Does that sweet valley seem to be
A sacred place on earth to me.

10 The influence of a moral spell
  Is found around the scene,
Giving new shadows to the dell,
  New verdure to the green.
With every mountain-top is wrought
15 The presence of associate thought,
A music that has been;
  Calling that loveliness to life
With which the inward world is rife.

His home—our English poet's home—
20 Amid these hills is made;
Here, with the morning, hath he come,
  There, with the night delay'd.
On all things is his memory cast,
  For every place wherein he past
25 Is with his mind array'd,
  That, wandering in a summer hour,
Ask'd wisdom of the leaf and flower.

Great poet, if I dare to throw
  My homage at thy feet,
30 'Tis thankfulness for hours which thou
  Hast made serene and sweet;
As wayfarers have incense thrown
  Upon some mighty altar-stone,
Unworthy, and yet meet,

35 The human spirit longs to prove
  The truth of its uplooking love.

Until thy hand unlock'd its store,
  What glorious music slept!
Music that can be hush'd no more
40 Was from our knowledge kept.
But the great Mother gave to thee
  The poet's universal key,
And forth the fountains swept—
  A gushing melody forever,
45 The witness of thy high endeavours.

Rough is the road which we are sent,
  Rough with long toils and pain;
And when upon the steep ascent,
  A little way we gain,
50 Vex'd with our own perpetual care,
  Little we heed what sweet things are
Around our pathway blent;
  With anxious steps we hurry on,
The very sense of pleasure gone.

55 But thou dost in this feverish dream
  Awake a better mood,
With voices from the mountain stream,
  With voices from the wood.
And with their music dost impart
60 Their freshness to the world-worn heart,
Whose fever is subdued
  By memories sweet with other years,
By gentle hopes, and soothing tears.

A solemn creed is thine, and high,
65 Yet simple as a child,
Who looketh hopeful to yon sky
  With eyes yet undefiled.
By all the glitter and the glare
  This life's deceit and follies wear,
70 Exalted, and yet mild,
  Conscious of those diviner powers
Brought from a better world than ours.

Thou hast not chosen to rehearse
    The old heroic themes;
75 Thou hast not given to thy verse
    The heart's impassion'd dreams.
Forth flows thy song as waters flow
    So bright above—so clam below,
Wherein the heaven seems
    Eternal as the golden shade
80 Its sunshine on the stream hath laid.

The glory which thy spirit hath,
    Is round life's common things,
And flingeth round our common path,
85   As from an angel's wings,
A light that is not of our sphere,
    Yet lovelier for being here,
Beneath whose presence springs
    A beauty never mark'd before,
90 Yet once known, vanishing no more.

How often with the present sad,
    And weary with the past,
A sunny respite have we had,
    By but a chance look cast
95 Upon some word of thine that made
    The sullenness forsake the shade,
Till shade itself was past:
    For Hope divine, serene, and strong,
Perpetual lives within thy song.

100 Eternal as the hills thy name,
    Eternal as thy strain;
So long as ministers of Fame
    Shall Love and Hope remain.
The crowded city in its streets,
105   The valley, in its green retreats,
Alike thy words retain.
    What need hast thou of sculptured stone?—
Thy temple, is thy name alone.
—1838

Infanticide in Madagascar [1]

A luxury of summer green
    Is on the southern plain,
And water-flags, with dewy screen,
    Protect the ripening grain.
5 Upon the sky is not a cloud
    To mar the golden glow,
Only the palm-tree is allow'd
    To fling its shade below.

And silvery, 'mid its fertile brakes,
10   The winding river glides,
And every ray in heaven makes
    Its mirror of its tides.
And yet it is a place of death—
    A place of sacrifice;
15 Heavy with childhood's parting breath
    Weary with childhood's cries.

The mother takes her little child—
    Its face is like her own;
The cradle of her choice is wild—
20   Why is it left alone?
The trampling of the buffalo
    Is heard among the reeds,
And sweeps around the carrion crow
    That amid carnage feeds.

25 O! outrage upon mother Earth
    To yonder azure sky;
A destined victim from its birth,
    The child is left to die.
We shudder that such crimes disgrace
30   E'en yonder savage strand;
Alas! and hath such crime no trace
    Within our English land?

---

[1] island off the southeastern coast of Africa, colonized by the French.

Pause, ere we blame the savage code
    That such strange horror keeps;
35 Perhaps within her sad abode
    The mother sits and weeps,
And thinks how oft those eyelids smiled,
    Whose close she may not see,
And says, "O, would to God, my child,
40   I might have died for thee!"

Such law of bloodshed to annul
    Should be the Christian's toil;
May not such law be merciful,
    To that upon our soil?
45 Better the infant eyes should close
    Upon the first sweet breath,
That weary for their last repose,
    A living life in death!

Look on the children of our poor
50   On many an English child:
Better that it had died secure
    By yonder river wild.
Flung careless on the waves of life,
    From childhood's earliest time,
55 They struggle, one perpetual strife,
    With hunger and with crime.

Look on the crowded prison-gate—
    Instructive love and care
In early life had saved the fate
60   That waits on many there.
Cold, selfish, shunning care and cost,
    The poor are left unknown;
I say, for every soul thus lost,
    We answer with our own.
  —1838

R.E. Egerton Warburton
1804 – 1891

Rowland E. Egerton Warburton, educated at Eton and Oxford, was a man of property, an ardent foxhunter, and a minor poet whose main poetic interest was in hunt-ing songs. His *Poems, Epigrams, and Sonnets* was published in 1877.

❧❧❧

Past and Present

On four-horse coach, whose luggage pierced the
  sky,
  Perch'd on back seat, like clerk on office-stool,
  While wintry winds my dangling heels kept cool,
  In Whitney white envelop'd and blue tie,
5 Unpillow'd slumber from my half-closed eye
    Scared by the shrill tin horn; when welcome
    Yule
Brought holiday season, it was thus from school
  I homeward came some forty years gone by.
Thus two long days and one long night I rode,
10 Stage after stage, till the last change of team
  Stopp'd, splash'd and panting, at my sire's
    abode.
How nowaday from school comes home my son?
  Through duct and tunnel by a puff of steam,
  Shot like a pellet from his own pop-gun.

—1877

Elizabeth Barrett Browning
1806 — 1861

Long before she met and married Robert Browning, Elizabeth Barrett Browning's popularity and reputation as a major Victorian poet was well established. The eldest of eleven children, Barrett was a confined invalid by twenty-two, dominated by her patriarchal father, Edward. Her literary activity, however, could not be contained so easily: after teaching herself Latin and Greek, Elizabeth Barrett anonymously published *The Battle of Marathon* (1820), at the age of fourteen, *An Essay on Mind, with Other Poems* (1826), when she was twenty, and a translation of *Prometheus Bound* in 1838. Her reputation was established with *The Seraphim and Other Poems* (1838), which was her first signed volume, and *Poems* (1844), which features the famous plea to the social consciences of

Victorian middle classes, "The Cry of the Children." Elizabeth Barrett and Robert Browning began corresponding in January, 1845, but he did not visit her until 21 May. They secretly married in 1846 and settled in Italy, where their son, Robert (Pen) Weidemann, was born. Barrett Browning published the well-known sequence, *Sonnets from the Portuguese*, in the 1850 volume, *Poems*, and her productivity continued with *Casa Guidi Windows* (1851), and *Poems Before Congress* (1860). Her most important and impressive work, however, is the verse novel, *Aurora Leigh* (1857), which considers and discusses, against a melodramatic Victorian backdrop, the role of poetry, the female as both writer and heroine, and the circumscribed role of women.

∽∾∽

The Romaunt of the Page [1]

I

A knight of gallant deeds
  And a young page at his side,
From the holy war in Palestine [2]
  Did slow and thoughtful ride,
5 As each were a palmer [3] and told for beads
  The dews of the eventide.

IV

"O young page," said the knight,
  "A noble page art thou!
Thou fearest not to steep in blood
10   The curls upon thy brow;

And once in the tent, and twice in the fight,
  Didst ward me a mortal blow."

III

"O brave knight," said the page,
  "Or ere we hither came,
15 We talked in tent, we talked in field,
  Of the bloody battle-game;
But here, below this greenwood bough,
  I cannot speak the same.

IV

"Our troop is far behind,
20   The woodland calm is new;
Our steeds, with slow grass-muffled hoofs
  Tread deep the shadows through;
And, in my mind, some blessing kind
  Is dropping with the dew.

V

25 "The woodland calm is pure—
  I cannot choose but have

---

[1] a romance; romantic poem or study.

[2] otherwise known as the Crusades (between 1095 and 1270); usually at the request of the pope, Western European Christians led military expeditions to recover Jerusalem and the other Palestinian places of pilgrimage known as the Holy Land from Muslim control.

[3] a pilgrim carrying a palm leaf to represent his pilgrimage to the Holy Land.

A thought from these, o' the beechen-trees,
    Which in our England wave,
And of the little finches fine
30 Which sang there while in Palestine
    The warrior-hilt we drave.

VI

"Methinks, a moment gone,
    I heard my mother pray!
I heard, sir knight, the prayer for me
35   Wherein she passed away;
And I know the heavens are leaning down
    To hear what I shall say."

VII

The page spake calm and high,
    As of no mean degree;
40 Perhaps he felt in nature's broad
    Full heart, his own was free:
And the knight looked up to his lifted eye,
    Then answered smilingly—

VIII

"Sir page, I pray your grace!
45   Certes, I meant not so
To cross your pastoral mood, sir page,
    With the crook of the battle-bow;
But a knight may speak of a lady's face,
I ween, in any mood or place,
50   If the grasses die or grow.

IX

"And this I meant to say—
    My lady's face shall shine
As ladies' faces use, to greet
    My page from Palestine;
55 Or, speak she fair or prank she gay,
    She is no lady of mine.

X

"And this I meant to fear—
    Her bower may suit thee ill;
For, sooth, in that same field and tent,
60   Thy *talk* was somewhat still:
And fitter thy hand for my knightly spear
    Than thy tongue for my lady's will!"

XI

Slowly and thankfully
    The young page bowed his head;
65 His large eyes seemed to muse a smile,
    Until he blushed instead,
And no lady in her bower, pardiè,[1]
    Could blush more sudden red:
"Sir Knight,—thy lady's bower to me
70   Is suited well," he said.

XII

Beati, beati, mortui!
    From the convent on the sea,
    One mile off, or scarce so nigh,
    Swells the dirge as clear and high
75   As if that, over break and lea,
    Bodily the wind did carry
    The great altar of Saint Mary,
    And the fifty tapers burning o'er it,
    And the Lady Abbess dead before it,
80   And the chanting nuns whom yester-week
    Her voice did charge and bless,—
    Chanting steady, chanting meek,
    Chanting with a solemn breath,
    Because that they are thinking less
85   Upon the dead than upon death.
Beati, beati, mortui!
    Now the vision in the sound
    Wheeleth on the wind around;
    Now it sweepeth back, away—
90   The uplands will not let it stay

---

[1] by god; indeed.

To dark the western sun:
Mortui!—away at last,—
Or ere the page's blush is past!
And the knight heard all, and the page heard none.

XIII

95 "A boon, thou noble knight,
    If ever I servèd thee!
Though thou art a knight and I am a page,
    Now grant a boon to me;
And tell me sooth, if dark or bright,
100 If little loved or loved aright
    Be the face of thy ladye."

XIV

Gloomily looked the knight—
    "As a son thou hast servèd me,
And would to none I had granted boon
105   Except to only thee!
For haply then I should love aright,
For then I should know if dark or bright
    Were the face of my ladye.

XV

"Yet it ill suits my knightly tongue
110   To grudge that granted boon,
That heavy price from heart and life
    I paid in silence down;
The hand that claimed it, cleared in fine
My father's fame: I swear by mine,
115   That price was nobly won!

XVI

"Earl Walter was a brave old earl,
    He was my father's friend;
And while I rode the lists at court
    And little guessed the end,
120 My noble father in his shroud
Against a slanderer lying loud,
    He rose up to defend.

XVII

"Oh, calm below the marble grey
    My father's dust was strown!
125 Oh, meek above the marble grey
    His image prayed alone!
The slanderer lied: the wretch was brave—
For, looking up the minster-nave,[1]
He saw my father's knightly glaive[2]
130   Was changed from steel to stone.

XVIII

"Earl Walter's glaive was steel,
    With a brave old hand to wear it,
And dashed the lie back in the mouth
Which lied against the godly truth
135   And against the knightly merit:
The slanderer, 'neath the avenger's heel,
Struck up the dagger in appeal
From stealthy lie to brutal force—
And out upon the traitor's corse
140   Was yielded the true spirit.

XIX

"I would mine hand had fought that fight
    And justified my father!
I would mine heart had caught that wound
    And slept beside him rather!
145 I think it were a better thing
Than murdered friend and marriage-ring
    Forced on my life together.

XX

"Wail shook Earl Walter's house;
    His true wife shed no tear;
150 She lay upon her bed as mute
    As the earl did on his bier:
Till—'Ride, ride fast,' she said at last,
'And bring the avengèd's son anear!

---

[1] the central part of the monastery church.

[2] a broadsword.

Ride fast, ride free, as a dart can flee,
155 For white of blee with waiting for me
Is the corse in the next chambère.'

XXI

"I came, I knelt beside her bed;
Her calm was worse than strife:
'My husband, for thy father dear,
160 Gave freely when thou wast not here
His own and eke my life.
A boon! Of that sweet child we make
An orphan for thy father's sake,
Make thou, for ours, a wife.'

XXII

165 "I said, 'My steed neighs in the court,
My bark[1] rocks on the brine,
And the warrior's vow I am under now
To free the pilgrim's shrine;
But fetch the ring and fetch the priest
170 And call that daughter of thine,
And rule she wide from my castle on Nyde
While I am in Palestine.'

XXIII

"In the dark chambère, if the bride was fair,
Ye wis, I could not see,
175 But the steed thrice neighed, and the priest fast
prayed,
And wedded fast were we.
Her mother smiled upon her bed
As at its side we knelt to wed,
And the bride rose from her knee
180 And kissed the smile of her mother dead,
Or ever she kissed me.

XXIV

"My page, my page, what grieves thee so,
That the tears run down thy face?"—

_____
[1] small sail boat.

"Alas, alas! mine own sistèr
185 Was in thy lady's case:
But _she_ laid down the silks she wore
And followed him she wed before,
Disguised as his true servitor,
To the very battle-place."

XXV

190 And wept the page, but laughed the knight,
A careless laugh laughed he:
"Well done it were for thy sistèr,
But not for my ladye!
My love, so please you, shall requite
195 No woman, whether dark or bright,
Unwomaned if she be."

XXVI

The page stopped weeping and smiled cold—
"Your wisdom may declare
That womanhood is proved the best
200 By golden brooch and glossy vest
The mincing ladies wear;
Yet is it proved, and was of old,
Anear as well, I dare to hold,
By truth, or by despair."

XXVII

205 He smiled no more, he wept no more,
But passionate he spake—
"Oh, womanly she prayed in tent,
When none beside did wake!
Oh, womanly she paled in fight,
210 For one belovèd's sake!—
And her little hand, defiled with blood,
Her tender tears of womanhood
Most woman-pure did make!"

.

XXVIII

—"Well done it were for thy sistèr,
215 Thou tellest well her tale!
But for my lady, she shall pray

I' the kirk[1] of Nydesdale.
Not dread for me but love for me
    Shall make my lady pale;
220 No casque shall hide her woman's tear—
It shall have room to trickle clear
    Behind her woman's veil."

XXIX

—"But what if she mistook thy mind
    And followed thee to strife,
225 Then kneeling did entreat thy love
    As Paynims[2] ask for life?"
—"I would forgive, and evermore
Would love her as my servitor,
    But little as my wife.

XXX

230 "Look up—there is a small bright cloud
    Alone amid the skies!
So high, so pure, and so apart,
    A woman's honour lies."
The page looked up—the cloud was sheen—
235 A sadder cloud did rush, I ween,
    Betwixt it and his eyes.

XXXI

Them dimly dropped his eyes away
    From welkin unto hill—
Ha! who rides there?—the page is 'ware,
240   Though the cry at his heart is still:
And the page seeth all and the knight seeth none,
Though banner and spear do fleck the sun,
    And the Saracens[3] ride at will.

XXXII

He speaketh calm, he speaketh low,—
245   "Ride fast, my master, ride,

---

[1] church.

[2] non-Christians.

[3] referring to Moslems in the time of the Crusades.

Or ere within the broadening dark
    The narrow shadows hide."
"Yea, fast, my page, I will do so,
    And keep thou at my side."

XXXIII

250 "Now nay, now nay, ride on thy way,
    Thy faithful page precede.
For I must loose on saddle-bow
My battle-casque[4] that galls, I trow,
    The shoulder of my steed;
255 And I must pray, as I did vow.
    For one in bitter need.

XXXIV

"Ere night I shall be near to thee,—
    Now ride, my master, ride!
Ere night, as parted spirits cleave
260 To mortals too beloved to leave,
    I shall be at thy side."
The knight smiled free at the fantasy,
    And adown the dell did ride.

XXXV

Had the knight looked up to the page's face,
265   No smile the word had won;
Had the knight looked up to the page's face,
    I ween he had never gone:
Had the knight looked back to the page's geste,[5]
    I ween he had turned anon,
270 For dread was the woe in the face so young,
And wild was the silent geste that flung
Casque, sword to earth, as the boy downsprung
    And stood—alone, alone.

XXXVI

He clenched his hands as if to hold
275   His soul's great agony—

---

[4] helmet.

[5] demeanour; gesture.

"Have I renounced my womanhood,
　　For wifehood unto *thee*,
And is this the last, last look of thine
　　That ever I shall see?

XXXVII

280 "Yet God thee save, and mayst thou have
　　A lady to thy mind,
More woman-proud and half as true
　　As one thou leav'st behind!
And God me take with HIM to dwell—
285 For HIM I cannot love too well,
　　As I have loved my kind."

XXXVIII

SHE looketh up, in earth's despair,
　　The hopeful heavens to seek;
That little cloud still floateth there,
290 　　Whereof her loved did speak:
How bright the little cloud appears!
Her eyelids fall upon the tears,
　　And the tears down either cheek.

XXXIX

The tramp of hoof, the flash of steel—
95 　　The Paynims round her coming!
The sound and sight have made her calm,—
　　False page, but truthful woman;
She stands amid them all unmoved:
A heart once broken by the loved
300 　　Is strong to meet the foeman.

XL

"Ho, Christian page! art keeping sheep,
　　From pouring wine-cups resting?"—
"I keep my master's noble name,
　　For warring, not for feasting;
05 And if that here Sir Hubert were,
My master brave, my master dear,
　　Ye would not stay the questing."

XLI

"Where is thy master, scornful page,
　　That we may slay or bind him?"—
310 "Now search the lea and search the wood,
　　And see if ye can find him!
Nathless, as hath been often tried,
Your Paynim heroes faster ride
　　Before him than behind him."

XLII

315 "Give smoother answers, lying page,
　　Or perish in the lying!"—
"I trow that if the warrior brand
Beside my foot, were in my hand,
　　'Twere better at replying!"
320 They cursed her deep, they smote her low,
They cleft her golden ringlets through;
　　The Loving is the Dying.

XLIII

She felt the scimitar gleam down,
　　And met it from beneath
325 With smile more bright in victory
　　Than any sword from sheath,—
Which flashed across her lip serene,
Most like the spirit-light between
　　The darks of life and death.

XLIV

330 *Ingemisco, ingemisco!*
From the convent on the sea,
Now it sweepeth solemnly,
As over wood and over lea
Bodily the wind did carry
335 The great altar of St. Mary,
And the fifty tapers paling o'er it,
And the Lady Abbess stark before it.
And the weary nuns with hearts that faintly
Beat along their voices saintly
340 *Ingemisco, ingemisco!*
Dirge for abbess laid in shroud

Sweepeth o'er the shroudless dead,
Page or lady, as we said,
With the dews upon her head,
345 All as sad if not as loud.
    Ingemisco, ingemisco!
Is ever a lament begun
By any mourner under sun,
Which, ere it endeth, suits but *one*?
—1844

Lady Geraldine's Courtship:

A Romance of the Age.

*A Poet writes to his Friend. Place—A Room in
Wycombe Hall. Time—Late in the evening.*

I

Dear my friend and fellow-student, I would lean
    my spirit o'er you!
Down the purple of this chamber tears should
    scarcely run at will.
I am humbled who was humble. Friend, I bow my
    head before you:
You should lead me to my peasants, but their faces
    are too still.

II

5 There's a lady, an earl's daughter,—she is proud
    and she is noble,
And she treads the crimson carpet and she breathes
    the perfumed air,
And a kingly blood sends glances up, her princely
    eye to trouble,
And the shadow of a monarch's crown is softened
    in her hair.

III

She has halls among the woodlands, she has castles
    by the breakers,

10 She has farms and she has manors, she can threaten
    and command:
And the palpitating engines snort in steam across
    her acres,
As they mark upon the blasted heaven the measure
    of the land.

IV

There are none of England's daughters who can
    show a prouder presence;
Upon princely suitors' praying she has looked in
    her disdain.
15 She was sprung of English nobles, I was born of
    English peasants;
What was *I* that I should love her, save for
    competence to pain?

V

I was only a poor poet, made for singing at her
    casement,
As the finches or the thrushes, while she thought of
    other things
Oh, she walked so high above me, she appeared to
    my abasement,
20 In her lovely silken murmur, like an angel clad in
    wings!

VI

Many vassals bow before her as her carriage sweeps
    their doorways;
She has blest their little children, as a priest or
    queen were she:
Far too tender, or too cruel far, her smile upon the
    poor was,
For I thought it was the same smile which she used
    to smile on *me*.

VII

25 She has voters in the Commons, she has lovers in
    the palace,

And, of all the fair court-ladies, few have jewels half
    as fine;
Oft the Prince has named her beauty 'twixt the red
    wine and the chalice:
Oh, and what was *I* to love her? my beloved, my
    Geraldine!

VIII

Yet I could not choose but love her: I was born to
    poet-uses,
30 To love all things set above me, all of good and all
    of fair.
Nymphs of mountain, not of valley, we are wont to
    call the Muses;[1]
And in nympholeptic[2] climbing, poets pass from
    mount to star.

IX

And because I was a poet, and because the public
    praised me,
With a critical deduction for the modern writer's
    fault,
35 I could sit at rich men's tables,—though the
    courtesies that raised me,
Still suggested clear between us the pale spectrum
    of the salt.

X

And they praised me in her presence—"Will your
    book appear this summer?"
Then returning to each other—"Yes, our plans are
    for the moors."
Then with whisper dropped behind me—"There
    he is! the latest comer.
40 Oh, she only likes his verses! what is over, she
    endures.

---

[1] in Greek and Roman mythology, the nine goddesses, daughters of
Zeus and Mnemosyne, who presided over the arts and sciences.

[2] the passion or frenzy caused by desire for an unattainable ideal; often
the emotion is aroused in the male by a beautiful young girl.

XI

"Quite low-born, self educated! somewhat gifted
    though by nature,
And we make a point of asking him,—of being
    very kind.
You may speak, he does not hear you! and, besides,
    he writes no satire,—
All these serpents kept by charmers leave the
    natural sting behind."

XII

45 I grew scornfuller, grew colder, as I stood up there
    among them,
Till as frost intense will burn you, the cold
    scorning scorched my brow;
When a sudden silver speaking, gravely cadenced,
    over-rung them,
And a sudden silken stirring touched my inner
    nature through.

XIII

I looked upward and beheld her: with a calm and
    regnant spirit,
50 Slowly round she swept her eyelids, and said clear
    before them all—
"Have you such superfluous honour, sir, that able
    to confer it
You will come down, Mister Bertram, as my guest
    to Wycombe Hall?"

XIV

Here she paused; she had been paler at the first
    word of her speaking,
But, because a silence followed it, blushed
    somewhat, as for shame:
55 Then, as scorning her own feeling, resumed
    calmly—"I am seeking
More distinction than these gentlemen think
    worthy of my claim.

XV

"Ne'ertheless, you see, I seek it—not because I am
a woman,"
(Here her smile sprang like a fountain and, so,
overflowed her mouth)
"But because my woods in Sussex[1] have some
purple shades at gloaming
60 Which are worthy of a king in state, or poet in his
youth.

XVI

"I invite you, Mister Bertram, to no scene for
worldly speeches—
Sir, I scarce should dare—but only where God
asked the thrushes first:
And if *you* will sing beside them, in the covert of
my beeches,
I will thank you for the woodlands,—for the
human world, at worst."

XVII

65 Then she smiled around right childly, then she
gazed around right queenly,
And I bowed—I could not answer; alternated light
and gloom—
While as one who quells the lions, with a steady eye
serenely,
She, with level fronting eyelids, passed out stately
from the room.

XVIII

Oh, the blessèd woods of Sussex, I can hear them
still around me,
70 With their leafy tide of greenery still rippling up
the wind!
Oh, the cursèd woods of Sussex! where the hunter's
arrow found me,
When a fair face and a tender voice had made me
mad and blind!

XIX

In that ancient hall of Wycombe thronged the
numerous guests invited,
And the lovely London ladies trod the floors with
gliding feet;
75 And their voices low with fashion, not with feeling,
softly freighted
All the air about the windows with elastic laughters
sweet.

XX

For at eve the open windows flung their light out
on the terrace
Which the floating orbs of curtains did with
gradual shadow sweep,
While the swans upon the river, fed at morning by
the heiress,
80 Trembled downward through their snowy wings at
music in their sleep.

XXI

And there evermore was music, both of instrument
and singing,
Till the finches of the shrubberies grew restless in
the dark;
But the cedars stood up motionless, each in a
moonlight's ringing,
And the deer, half in the glimmer, strewed the
hollows of the park.

XXII

85 And though sometimes she would bind me with
her silver-corded speeches
To commix my words and laughter with the
converse and the jest,
Oft I sat apart and, gazing on the river through the
beeches,
Heard, as pure the swans swam down it, her pure
voice o'erfloat the rest.

---

[1] a county of southern England.

XXIII

In the morning, horn of huntsman, hoof of steed
and laugh of rider,
90 Spread out cheery from the courtyard till we lost
them in the hills,
While herself and other ladies, and her suitors left
beside her,
Went a-wandering up the gardens through the
laurels and abeles.

XXIV

Thus, her foot upon the new-mown grass,
bareheaded, with the flowing
Of the virginal white vesture gathered closely to her
throat,
95 And the golden ringlets in her neck just quickened
by her going,
And appearing to breathe sun for air, and doubting
if to float,—

XXV

With a bunch of dewy maple, which her right hand
held above her,
And which trembled a green shadow in betwixt her
and the skies,
As she turned her face in going, thus, she drew me
on to love her,
00 And to worship the divineness of the smile hid in
her eyes.

XXVI

For her eyes alone smile constantly; her lips have
serious sweetness,
And her front is calm, the dimple rarely ripples on
the cheek;
But her deep blue eyes smile constantly, as if they
in discreetness
Kept the secret of a happy dream she did not care
to speak.

XXVII

105 Thus she drew me the first morning, out across
into the garden,
And I walked among her noble friends and could
not keep behind.
Spake she unto all and unto me—"Behold, I am
the warden
Of the song-birds in these lindens, which are cages
to their mind.

XXVIII

"But within this swarded circle into which the
lime-walk brings us,
110 Whence the beeches, rounded greenly, stand away
in reverent fear,
I will let no music enter, saving what the fountain
sings us
Which the lilies round the basin may seem pure
enough to hear.

XXIX

"The live air that waves the lilies waves the slender
jet of water
Like a holy thought sent feebly up from soul of
fasting saint:
115 Whereby lies a marble Silence, sleeping (Lough the
sculptor wrought her),
So asleep she is forgetting to say Hush!—a fancy
quaint.

XXX

"Mark how heavy white her eyelids! not a dream
between them lingers;
And the left hand's index droppeth from the lips
upon the cheek:
While the right hand,—with the symbol-rose held
slack within the fingers,—
120 Has fallen backward in the basin—yet this Silence
will not speak!

XXXI

"That the essential meaning growing may exceed
  the special symbol,
Is the thought as I conceive it: it applies more high
  and low.
Our true noblemen will often through right
  nobleness grew humble,
And assert an inward honour by denying outward
  show."

XXXII

125 "Nay, your Silence," said I, "truly, holds her
  symbol-rose but slackly,
Yet *she holds it*, or would scarcely be a Silence to
  our ken:
And your nobles wear their ermine on the outside,
  or walk blackly
In the presence of the social law as mere ignoble
  men.

XXXIII

"Let the poets dream such dreaming! madam, in
  these British islands
130 'Tis the substance that wanes ever, 'tis the symbol
  that exceeds.
Soon we shall have nought but symbol: and, for
  statues like this Silence,
Shall accept the rose's image—in another case, the
  weed's."

XXXIV

"Not so quickly," she retorted,—"I confess,
  where'er you go, you
Find for things, names—shows for actions, and
  pure gold for honour clear:
135 But when all is run to symbol in the Social, I will
  throw you
The world's book which now reads dryly, and sit
  down with Silence here."

XXXV

Half in playfulness she spoke, I thought, and half
  in indignation;
Friends, who listened, laughed her words off, while
  her lovers deemed her fair:
A fair woman, flushed with feeling, in her noble-
  lighted station
140 Near the statue's white reposing—and both bathed
  in sunny air!

XXXVI

With the trees round, not so distant but you heard
  their vernal murmur,
And beheld in light and shadow the leaves in and
  outward move,
And the little fountain leaping toward the sun-
  heart to be warmer,
Then recoiling in a tremble from the too much
  light above.

XXXVII

145 'Tis a picture for remembrance. And thus, morning
  after morning.
Did I follow as she drew me by the spirit to her
  feet.
Why, her greyhound followed also! dogs—we both
  were dogs for scorning—
To be sent back when she pleased it and her path
  lay through the wheat.

XXXVIII

And thus, morning after morning, spite of vows
  and spite of sorrow,
150 Did I follow at her drawing, while the week-days
  passed along,—
Just to feed the swans this noontide, or to see the
  fawns to-morrow,
Or to teach the hill-side echo some sweet Tuscan in
  a song.

XXXIX

Ay, for sometimes on the hill-side, while we sate
    down in the gowans,[1]
With the forest green behind us and its shadow cast
    before,
155 And the river running under, and across it from the
    rowans
A brown partridge whirring near us till we felt the
    air it bore,—

XL

There, obedient to her praying, did I read aloud
    the poems
Made to Tuscan flutes, or instruments more
    various of our own;
Read the pastoral parts of Spenser, or the subtle
    interflowings
160 Found in Petrarch's[2] sonnets—here's the book, the
    leaf is folded down!

XLI

Or at times a modern volume, Wordsworth's
    solemn-thoughted idyl,
Howitt's ballad-verse, or Tennyson's enchanted
    reverie,—
Or from Browning some "Pomegranate," which, if
    cut deep down the middle,
Shows a heart within blood-tinctured, of a veined
    humanity.

XLII

165 Or at times I read there, hoarsely, some new poem
    of my making:
Poets ever fail in reading their own verses to their
    worth,
For the echo in you breaks upon the words which
    you are speaking,

And the chariot wheels jar in the gate through
    which you drive them forth.

XLIII

After, when we were grown tired of books, the
    silence round us flinging
170 A slow arm of sweet compression, felt with beatings
    at the breast,
She would break out on a sudden in a gush of
    woodland singing,
Like a child's emotion in a god—a naiad tired of
    rest.

XLIV

Oh, to see or hear her singing! scarce I know which
    is divinest,
For her looks sing too—she modulates her gestures
    on the tune,
175 And her mouth stirs with the song, like song; and
    when the notes are finest,
'Tis the eyes that shoot out vocal light and seem to
    swell them on.

XLV

Then we talked—oh, how we talked! her voice, so
    cadenced in the talking,
Made another singing—of the soul! a music
    without bars:
While the leafy sounds of woodlands, humming
    round where we were walking,
180 Brought interposition worthy-sweet,—as skies
    about the stars.

XLVI

And she spake such good thoughts natural, as if she
    always thought them;
She had sympathies so rapid, open, free as bird on
    branch,
Just as ready to fly east as west, whichever way
    besought them,

[1] a yellow or white wild-flower, especially a daisy.

[2] Francesco Petrarca (1304–74), Italian poet.

In the birchen-wood a chirrup, or a cock-crow in
    the grange.

XLVII

185 In her utmost lightness there is truth—and often
    she speaks lightly,
Has a grace in being gay which even mournful
    souls approve,
For the root of some grave earnest thought is
    under-struck so rightly
As to justify the foliage and the waving flowers
    above.

XLVIII

And she talked on—*we* talked, rather! upon all
    things, substance, shadow,
190 Of the sheep that browsed the grasses, of the
    reapers in the corn,
Of the little children from the schools, seen
    winding through the meadow,
Of the poor rich world beyond them, still kept
    poorer by its scorn.

XLIX

So, of men, and so, of letters—books are men of
    higher stature,
And the only men that speak aloud for future times
    to hear;
195 So, of mankind in the abstract, which grows slowly
    into nature,
Yet will lift the cry of "progress," as it trod from
    sphere to sphere.

L

And her custom was to praise me when I said,—
    "The Age culls simples,
With a broad clown's back turned broadly to the
    glory of the stars.
We are gods by our own reck'ning, and may well shut
    up the temples,

200 And wield on, amid the incense-steam, the thunder
    of our cars.

LI

"For we throw our acclamations of self-thanking,
    self-admiring,
With, at every mile run faster,—'O the wondrous
    wondrous age!'
Little thinking if we work our SOULS as nobly as
    our iron,
Or if angels will commend us at the goal of
    pilgrimage.

LII

205 "Why, what *is* this patient entrance into nature's
    deep resources
But the child's most gradual learning to walk
    upright without bane!
When we drive out, from the cloud of steam,
    majestical white horses,
Are we greater than the first men who led black
    ones by the mane?

LIII

"If we trod the deeps of ocean, if we struck the stars
    in rising,
210 If we wrapped the globe intensely with one hot
    electric breath,
'Twere but power within our tether, no new spirit-
    power comprising,
And in life we were not greater men, nor bolder
    men in death."

LIV

She was patient with my talking; and I loved her,
    loved her certes
As I loved all heavenly objects, with uplifted eyes
    and hands;
215 As I loved pure inspirations, loved the graces, loved
    the virtues,

In a Love content with writing his own name on
    desert sands.

LV

Or at least I thought so, purely; thought no idiot
    Hope was raising
Any crown to crown Love's silence, silent Love that
    sate alone:
Out, alas! the stag is like me, he that tries to go on
    grazing
220 With the great deep gun-wound in his neck, then
    reels with sudden moan.

LVI

It was thus I reeled. I told you that her hand had
    many suitors;
But she smiles them down imperially as Venus did
    the waves,
And with such a gracious coldness that they cannot
    press their futures
On the present of her courtesy, which yieldingly
    enslaves.

LVII

225 And this morning as I sat alone within the inner
    chamber
With the great saloon beyond it, lost in pleasant
    thought serene,
For I had been reading Camoëns,[1] that poem you
    remember,
Which his lady's eyes are praised in as the sweetest
    ever seen.

LVIII

And the book lay open, and my thought flew from
    it, taking from it
230 A vibration and impulsion to an end beyond its
    own,

As the branch of a green osier,[2] when a child would
    overcome it,
Springs up freely from his claspings and goes
    swinging in the sun.

LIX

As I mused I heard a murmur; it grew deep as it
    grew longer,
Speakers using earnest language—"Lady Geraldine,
    you *would!*"
235 And I heard a voice that pleaded, ever on in accents
    stronger,
As a sense of reason gave it power to make its
    rhetoric good.

LX

Well I knew that voice; it was an earl's, of soul that
    matched his station,
Soul completed into lordship, might and right read
    on his brow;
Very finely courteous; far too proud to doubt his
    domination
240 Of the common people, he atones for grandeur by
    a bow.

LXI

High straight forehead, nose of eagle, cold blue
    eyes of less expression
Then resistance, coldly casting off the looks of
    other men,
As steel, arrows; unelastic lips which seem to taste
    possession
And be cautious lest the common air should injure
    or distrain.

LXII

245 For the rest, accomplished, upright,—ay, and
    standing by his order

---

[1] Luis de Camoëns (1524–80), Portuguese poet.

[2] willow tree.

With a bearing not ungraceful; fond of art and
    letters too;
Just a good man made a proud man,—as the sandy
    rocks that border
A wild coast, by circumstances, in a regnant ebb
    and flow.

LXIII

Thus, I knew that voice, I heard it, and I could not
    help the hearkening:
250 In the room I stood up blindly, and my burning
    heart within
Seemed to seethe and fuse my senses till they ran
    on all sides darkening,
And scorched, weighed like melted metal round my
    feet that stood therein.

LXIV

And that voice, I heard it pleading, for love's sake,
    for wealth, position,
For the sake of liberal uses and great actions to be
    done:
255 And she interrupted gently, "Nay, my lord, the old
    tradition
Of your Normans, by some worthier hand than
    mine is, should be won."

LXV

"Ah, that white hand!" he said quickly,—and in his
    he either drew it
Or attempted—for with gravity and instance she
    replied,
"Nay, indeed, my lord, this talk is vain, and we had
    best eschew it
260 And pass on, like friends, to other points less easy
    to decide."

LXVI

What he said again, I know not: it is likely that his
    trouble

Worked his pride up to the surface, for she
    answered in slow scorn,
"And your lordship judges rightly. Whom I marry
    shall be noble,
Ay, and wealthy. I shall never blush to think how
    he was born."

LXVII

265 There, I maddened! her words stung me. Life swept
    through me into fever,
And my soul sprang up astonished, sprang full-
    statured in an hour.
Know you what it is when anguish, with
    apocalyptic NEVER,
To a Pythian[1] height dilates you, and despair
    sublimes to power?

LXVIII

From my brain the soul-wings budded, waved a
    flame about my body,
270 Whence conventions coiled to ashes. I felt self-
    drawn out, as man,
From amalgamate false natures, and I saw the skies
    grow ruddy
With the deepening feet of angels, and I knew what
    spirits can.

LXIX

I was mad, inspired—say either (anguish worketh
    inspiration)
Was a man or beast—perhaps so, for the tiger roars
    when speared;
275 And I walked on, step by step along the level of my
    passion—
Oh my soul! and passed the doorway to her face,
    and never feared.

---

[1] an allusion to the "Pythian shriek" of the priestess of Apollo at Delphi
while under divine influence.

LXX

He had left her, peradventure, when my footstep
    proved my coming,
But for *her*—she half arose, then sate, grew scarlet
    and grew pale.
Oh, she trembled! 'tis so always with a worldly man
    or woman
80 In the presence of true spirits; what else *can* they do
    but quail?

LXXI

Oh, she fluttered like a tame bird, in among its
    forest brothers
Far too strong for it; then drooping, bowed her
    face upon her hands;
And I spake out wildly, fiercely, brutal truths of her
    and others:
I, she planted in the desert, swathed her, windlike,
    with my sands.

LXXII

85 I plucked up her social fictions, bloody-rooted
    though leaf-verdant,
Trod them down with words of shaming,—all the
    purple and the gold,
All the "landed stakes" and lordships, all that spirits
    pure and ardent
Are cast out of love and honour because chancing
    not to hold.

LXXIII

"For myself I do not argue," said I, "though I love
    you, madam.
90 But for better souls that nearer to the height of
    yours have trod:
And this age shows, to my thinking, still more
    infidels to Adam
Than directly, by profession, simple infidels to
    God.

LXXIV

"Yet, O God," I said, "O grave," I said, "O
    mother's heart and bosom,
With whom first and last are equal, saint and
    corpse and little child!
295 We are fools to your deductions, in these figments
    of heart-closing;
We are traitors to your causes, in these sympathies
    defiled.

LXXV

"Learn more reverence, madam, not for rank or
    wealth—*that* needs no learning:
That comes quickly, quick as sin does, ay, and
    culminates to sin;
But for Adam's seed, MAN! Trust me, 'tis a clay
    above your scorning,
300 With God's image stamped upon it, and God's
    kindling breath within.

LXXVI

"What right have you, madam, gazing in your
    palace mirror daily,
Getting so by heart your beauty which all others
    must adore,
While you draw the golden ringlets down your
    fingers, to vow gaily
You will wed no man that's only good to God, and
    nothing more?

LXXVII

305 "Why, what right have you, made fair by that same
    God, the sweetest woman
Of all women He has fashioned, with your lovely
    spirit face
Which would seem so near to vanish if its smile
    were not so human,
And your voice of holy sweetness, turning common
    words to grace,—

LXXVIII

"What right *can* you have, God's other works to
    scorn, despise, revile them
310 In the gross, as mere men, broadly—not as *noble*
    men, forsooth,—
As mere Pariahs of the outer world, forbidden to
    assoil them
In the hope of living, dying, near that sweetness of
    your mouth?

LXXIX

"Have you any answer, madam? If my spirit were
    less earthly,
If its instrument were gifted with a better silver
    string,
315 I would kneel down where I stand, and say—
    Behold me! I am worthy
Of thy loving, for I love thee. I am worthy as a
    king.

LXXX

"As it is—your ermined pride, I swear, shall feel
    this stain upon her,
That *I*, poor, weak, tost with passion, scorned by
    me and you again,
Love you, madam, dare to love you, to my grief
    and your dishonour,
320 To my endless desolation, and your impotent
    disdain!"

LXXXI

More mad words like these—mere madness! friend,
    I need not write them fuller,
For I hear my hot soul dropping on the lines in
    showers of tears.
Oh, a woman! friend, a woman! why, a beast had
    scarce been duller
Than roar bestial loud complaints against the
    shining of the spheres.

LXXXII

325 But at last there came a pause. I stood all vibrating
    with thunder
Which my soul had used. The silence drew her face
    up like a call.
Could you guess what word she uttered? She
    looked up, as if in wonder,
With tears beaded on her lashes, and said—
    "Bertram!"—it was all.

LXXXIII

If she had cursed me, and she might have, or if
    even, with queenly bearing
330 Which at need is used by women, she had risen up
    and said,
"Sir, you are my guest, and therefore I have given
    you a full hearing:
Now, beseech you, choose a name exacting
    somewhat less, instead!"—

LXXXIV

I had borne it: but that "Bertram"—why, it lies
    there on the paper
A mere word, without her accent, and you cannot
    judge the weight
335 Of the calm which crushed my passion: I seemed
    drowning in a vapour;
And her gentleness destroyed me whom her scorn
    made desolate.

LXXXV

So, struck backward and exhausted by that inward
    flow of passion
Which had rushed on, sparing nothing, into forms
    of abstract truth,
By a logic agonising through unseemly
    demonstration,
340 And by youth's own anguish turning grimly grey
    the hairs of youth,—

LXXXVI

By the sense accursed and instant, that if even I
    spake wisely
I spake basely—using truth, if what I spake indeed
    was true,
To avenge wrong on a woman—*her*, who sate there
    weighing nicely
A poor manhood's worth, found guilty of such
    deeds as I could do!—

LXXXVII

345 By such wrong and woe exhausted—what I
    suffered and occasioned,—
As a wild horse through a city runs with lightning
    in his eyes,
And then dashing at a church's cold and passive
    wall, impassioned,
Strikes the death into his burning brain, and
    blindly drops and dies—

LXXXVIII

So I fell, struck down before her—do you blame
    me, friend, for weakness?
350 'Twas my strength of passion slew me!—fell before
    her like a stone;
Fast the dreadful world rolled from me on its
    roaring wheels of blackness:
When the light came I was lying in this chamber
    and alone.

LXXXIX

Oh, of course she charged her lacqueys to bear out
    the sickly burden,
And to cast it from her scornful sight, but not
    beyond the gate;
355 She is too kind to be cruel, and too haughty not to
    pardon
Such as man as I; 'twere something to be level to
    her hate.

XC

But for me—you now are conscious why, my
    friend, I write this letter,
Now my life is read all backward, and the charm of
    life undone.
I shall leave her house at dawn; I would to-night, if
    I were better—
360 And I charge my soul to hold my body
    strengthened for the sun.

XCI

When the sun has dyed the oriel, I depart, with no
    last gazes,
No weak moanings (one word only, left in writing
    for her hands),
Out of reach of all derision, and some unavailing
    praises,
To make front against this anguish in the far and
    foreign lands.

XCII

365 Blame me not. I would not squander life in
    grief—I am abstemious.
I but nurse my spirit's falcon that its wing may soar
    again.
There's no room for tears of weakness in the blind
    eyes of a Phemius:
Into work the poet kneads them, and he does not
    die *till then*.

CONCLUSION

I

Bertram finished the last pages, while along the
    silence ever
370 Still in hot and heavy splashes fell the tears on every
    leaf.
Having ended, he leans backward in his chair, with
    lips that quiver
From the deep unspoken, ay, and deep unwritten
    thoughts of grief.

II

Soh! how still the lady standeth! 'Tis a dream—a
  dream of mercies!
'Twixt the purple lattice-curtains how she standeth
  still and pale!
375 'Tis a vision, sure, of mercies, sent to soften his
  self-curses,
Sent to sweep a patient quiet o'er the tossing of his
  wail.

III

"Eyes," he said, "now throbbing though me! are ye
  eyes that did undo me?
Shining eyes, like antique jewels set in Parian
  statue-stone![1]
Underneath that calm white forehead are ye ever
  burning torrid
380 O'er the desolate sand-desert of my heart and life
  undone?"

IV

With a murmurous stir uncertain, in the air the
  purple curtain
Swelleth in and swelleth out around her motionless
  pale brows,
While the gliding of the river sends a rippling noise
  for ever
Through the open casement whitened by the
  moonlight's slant repose.

V

385 Said he—"Vision of a lady! stand there silent, stand
  there steady!
Now I see it plainly, plainly now I cannot hope or
  doubt—
There, the brows of mild repression—there, the
  lips of silent passion,

---

[1] fine, white marble from the Greek island, Paros.

Curvèd like an archer's bow to send the bitter
  arrows out."

VI

Ever, evermore the while in a slow silence she kept
  smiling,
390 And approached him slowly, slowly, in a gliding
  measured pace;
With her two white hands extended as if praying
  one offended,
And a look of supplication gazing earnest in his
  face.

VII

Said he—"Wake me by no gesture,—sound of
  breath, or stir of vesture!
Let the blessèd apparition melt not yet to its divine!
395 No approaching—hush, no breathing! or my heart
  must swoon to death in
The too utter life thou bringest, O thou dream of
  Geraldine!"

VIII

Ever, evermore the while in a slow silence she kept
  smiling,
But the tears ran over lightly from her eyes and
  tenderly:—
"Dost thou, Bertram, truly love me? Is no woman
  far above me
400 Found more worthy of thy poet-heart than such a
  one as *I*?"

IX

Said he—"I would dream so ever, like the flowing
  of that river,
Flowing ever in a shadow greenly onward to the sea!
So, thou vision of all sweetness, princely to a full
  completeness
Would my heart and life flow onward, deathward,
  through this dream of THEE!"

X

405 Ever, evermore the while in a slow silence she kept
    smiling,
While the silver tears ran faster down the blushing
    of her cheeks;
Then with both her hands enfolding both of his,
    she softly told him,
"Bertram, if I say I love thee,…'tis the vision only
    speaks."

XI

Softened, quickened to adore her, on his knee he
    fell before her,
410 And she whispered low in triumph, "It shall be as I
    have sworn.
Very rich he is in virtues, very noble—noble, certes;
And I shall not blush in knowing that men call him
    lowly born."
—1844

The Dead Pan [1]

Excited by Schiller's "Götter Griechenlands," and
partly founded on a well-known tradition mentioned in a
treatise of Plutarch ("De Oraculorum Defectu"), accord-
ing to which, at the hour of the Saviour's agony, a cry of
"Great Pan is dead!" swept across the waves in the hearing
of certain mariners,—and the oracles ceased.

It is in all veneration to the memory of the deathless
Schiller that I oppose a doctrine still more dishonouring
to poetry than to Christianity.

As Mr. Kenyon's graceful and harmonious paraphrase
of the German poem was the first occasion of the turning
of my thoughts in this direction, I take advantage of the
pretence to indulge my feelings (which overflow on other
grounds) by inscribing my lyric to that dear friend and
relative, with the earnestness of appreciating esteem as well
as of affectionate gratitude.—1844.

I

Gods of Hellas, gods of Hellas,[2]
  Can ye listen in your silence?
Can your mystic voices tell us
Where ye hide? In floating islands,
5 With a wind that evermore
Keeps you out of sight of shore?
        Pan, Pan is dead.

II

In what revels are ye sunken
In old Æthiopia?
10 Have the Pygmies made you drunken,
Bathing in mandragora[3]
Your divine pale lips that shiver
Like the lotus in the river?
        Pan, Pan is dead.

III

15 Do ye sit there still in slumber,
In gigantic Alpine rows?
The black poppies out of number
Nodding, dripping from your brows
To the red lees of your wine,
20 And so kept alive and fine?
        Pan, Pan is dead.

IV

Or lie crushed your stagnant corses
Where the silver spheres roll on,
Stung to life by centric forces
25 Thrown like rays out from the sun?—
While the smoke of your old altars
Is the shroud that round you welters?
        Great Pan is dead.

---

[1] the Greek god of flocks and herds who invented the pan-pipe and lost
in a contest with Apollo; Pan is typically represented with the horns,
ears, and legs of a goat on a man's body.

[2] ancient Greek name of Greece.

[3] the mandrake, a Mediterranean plant of the nightshade family, having
a forked fleshy root which supposedly resembles the human form;
mandragora is the use of the root as a narcotic.

V

"Gods of Hellas, gods of Hellas"
30 Said the old Hellenic tongue,—
Said the hero-oaths, as well as
Poets' songs the sweetest sung:
Have ye grown deaf in a day?
Can ye speak not yea or nay,
35   Since Pan is dead?

VI

Do ye leave your rivers flowing
All alone, O Naiades,
While your drénchèd locks dry slow in
This cold feeble sun and breeze?
40 Not a word the Naiads say,
Though the rivers run for aye;
        For Pan is dead.

VII

From the gloaming of the oak-wood,
O ye Dryads, could ye flee?
45 At the rushing thunderstroke, would
No sob tremble through the tree?
Not a word the Dryads say,
Though the forests wave for aye;
        For Pan is dead.

VIII

50 left the mountain places,
Oreads wild, for other tryst?
Shall we see no sudden faces
Strike a glory though the mist?
Not a sound the silence thrills
55 Of the everlasting hills:
        Pan, Pan is dead.

IX

O twelve gods of Plato's vision,
Crowned to starry wanderings,
With your chariots in procession
60 And your silver clash of wings!

Very pale ye seem to rise,
Ghosts of Grecian deities,
        Now Pan is dead!

X

Jove,[1] that right hand is unloaded
65 Whence the thunder did prevail,
While in idiocy of godhead
Thou art staring the stars pale!
And thine eagle, blind and old,
Roughs his feathers in the cold.
70   Pan, Pan is dead.

XI

Where, O Juno,[2] is the glory
Of thy regal look and tread?
Will they lay, for evermore, thee
On thy dim, strait, golden bed?
75 Will thy queendom all lie hid
Meekly under either lid?
        Pan, Pan is dead.

XII

Ha, Apollo![3] floats his golden
Hair all mist-like where he stands,
80 While the Muses hang enfolding
Knee and foot with faint wild hands?
'Neath the clanging of thy bow,
Niobe[4] looked lost as thou!
        Pan, Pan is dead.

---

[1] another name for Jupiter, the Roman god of thunder and lightning; his Greek equivalent is Zeus.

[2] the wife of Jupiter, the most important goddess of the Roman state.

[3] the Greek and Roman god of reason, intelligence, music, prophecy, medicine, and the sun.

[4] the daughter of Tantalus; Apollo and Artemis, angered by Niobe's boast of being superior to their mother, Leto, slew her seven sons and daughters and turned her into stone.

XIII

85 Shall the casque with its brown iron
Pallas'[1] broad blue eyes eclipse,
And no hero take inspiring
From the god-Greek of her lips?
'Neath her olive dost thou sit,
90 Mars[2] the mighty, cursing it?
  Pan, Pan is dead.

XIV

Bacchus, Bacchus![3] on the panther
He swoons, bound with his own vines;
And his Mænads slowly saunter,
95 Head aside, among the pines,
While they murmur dreamingly
"Evohe!—ah—evohe!—
  Ah, Pan is dead!"

XV

Neptune[4] lies beside the trident,
100 Dull and senseless as a stone;
And old Pluto[5] deaf and silent
Is cast out into the sun:
Ceres[6] smileth stern thereat,
"We *all* now are desolate—
105   Now Pan is dead."

XVI

Aphrodite![7] dead and driven
As thy native foam thou art;
With the cestus long done heaving
On the white calm of thine heart!
110 *Ai Adonis!*[8] at that shriek
Not a tear runs down her cheek—
  Pan, Pan is dead.

XVII

And the Loves, we used to know from
One another, huddled lie,
115 Frore as taken in a snow-storm,
Close beside her tenderly;
As if each had weakly tried
Once to kiss her as he died.
  Pan, Pan is dead.

XVIII

120 What, and Hermes?[9] Time enthralleth
All thy cunning, Hermes, thus,
And the ivy blindly crawleth
Round thy brave caduceus?
Hast thou no new message for us,
125 Full of thunder and Jove-glories?
  Nay, Pan is dead.

XIX

Crownèd Cybele's[10] great turret
Rocks and crumbles on her head;
Roar the lions of her chariot
130 Toward the wilderness, unfed:
Scornful children are not mute,—

---

[1] one of the names of Athena, Greek goddess of wisdom, war, and weaving, born from Zeus's head.

[2] the Roman god of war; his Greek equivalent is Ares.

[3] another name for Dionysus, Greek god of wine who loosens inhibitions and inspires creativity in music and poetry. Maenads were female followers of Bacchus, traditionally associated with divine possession and frenzied rites.

[4] the Roman god of the sea; his Greek counterpart is Poseidon.

[5] the Roman god of the Underworld; his Greek equivalent is Hades.

[6] the Roman goddess of corn; her Greek counterpart is Demeter.

---

[7] Greek goddess of love and beauty; her Roman counterpart is Venus.

[8] In Greek mythology, Adonis was a beautiful youth loved by Aphrodite, fatally wounded by a boar's tusk. He was also a resurrection god, from whose blood springs the anemone.

[9] the Greek god of messages, thieves, and tricksters; his Roman counterpart is Mercury.

[10] a mother goddess first worshipped in Phrygia and later in Greece.

"Mother, mother, walk afoot,
     Since Pan is dead!"

XX

In the fiery-hearted centre
135 Of the solemn universe,
Ancient Vesta,[1]—who could enter
To consume thee with this curse?
Drop thy grey chin on thy knee,
O thou palsied Mystery!
140   For Pan is dead.

XXI

Gods, we vainly do adjure you,—
Ye return nor voice nor sign!
Not a votary could secure you
Even a grave for your Divine:
145 Not a grace, to show thereby
Here these grey old gods do lie.
        Pan, Pan is dead.

XXII

Even that Greece who took your wages
Calls the obolus[2] outworn;
150 And the hoarse, deep-throated ages
Laugh your godships unto scorn:
And the poets do disclaim you,
Or grow colder if they name you—
        And Pan is dead.

XXIII

155 Gods bereavèd, gods belated,
With your purples rent asunder.
Gods discrowned and desecrated,
Disinherited of thunder!
Now, the goats may climb and crop

160 The soft grass on Ida's[3] top—
        Now Pan is dead.

XXIV

Calm, of old, the bark went onward,
When a cry more loud than wind
Rose up, deepened, and swept sunward
165 From the pilèd Dark behind;
And the sun shrank and grew pale,
Breathed against by the great wail—
        "Pan, Pan is dead."

XV

And the rowers from the benches
170 Fell, each shuddering on his face,
While departing Influences
Struck a cold back through the place;
And the shadow of the ship
Reeled along the passive deep—
175   "Pan, Pan is dead."

XXVI

And that dismal cry rose slowly
And sank slowly through the air,
Full of spirit's melancholy
And eternity's despair!
180 And they heard the words it said—
PAN IS DEAD—GREAT PAN IS DEAD—
        PAN, PAN IS DEAD.

XXVII

'Twas the hour when One in Sion[4]
Hung for love's sake on a cross;
185 When His brow was chill with dying
And His soul was faint with loss;
When His priestly blood dropped downward
And His kingly eyes looked throneward—
        Then, Pan was dead.

---

[1] Roman goddess of the hearth; equated with Greek goddess Hestia.

[2] ancient Greek coin.

[3] mountain near Troy.

[4] the hill of Jerusalem on which the city of David was built.

XXVIII

190 By the love, He stood alone in,
His sole Godhead rose complete,
And the false gods fell down moaning
Each from off his golden seat;
All the false gods with a cry
195 Rendered up their deity—
        Pan, Pan was dead.

XXIX

Wailing wide across the islands,
They rent, vest-like, their Divine;
And a darkness and a silence
200 Quenched the light of every shrine;
And Dodona's[1] oak swang lonely
Henceforth, to the tempest only:
        Pan, Pan was dead.

XXX

Pythia[2] staggered, feeling o'er her
205 Her lost god's forsaking look;
Straight her eyeballs filmed with horror
And her crispy fillets shook
And her lips gasped, through their foam,
For a word that did not come.
210   Pan, Pan was dead.

XXXI

O ye vain false gods of Hellas,
Ye are silent evermore!
And I dash down this old chalice
Whence libations ran of yore.
215 See, the wine crawls in the dust
Wormlike—as your glories must,
        Since Pan is dead.

XXXII

Get to dust, as common mortals,
By a common doom and track!
220 Let no Schiller from the portals
Of that Hades call you back,
Or instruct us to weep all
At your antique funeral.
        Pan, Pan is dead.

XXXIII

225 By your beauty, which confesses
Some chief Beauty conquering you,—
By our grand heroic guesses
Through your falsehood at the True,—
We will weep *not!* earth shall roll
230 Heir to each god's aureole—
        And Pan is dead.

XXXIV

Earth outgrows the mythic fancies
Sung beside her in her youth,
And those debonair romances
235 Sound but dull beside the truth.
Phœbus'[3] chariot-course is run:
Look up, poets, to the sun!
        Pan, Pan is dead.

XXXV

Christ hath sent us down the angels;
240 And the whole earth and the skies
Are illumed by altar-candles
Lit for blessèd mysteries;
And a priest's hand through creation
Waveth calm and consecration:
245   And Pan is dead.

XXXVI

Truth is fair: should we forgo it?
Can we sigh right for a wrong?

---

[1] sanctuary and oracle of Zeus in northern Greece.

[2] the prophetess (sibyl) of Apollo at Delphi.

---

[3] "bright": epithet of the sun-god Apollo.

God Himself is the best Poet,
And the Real is His song.
250 Sing His truth out fair and full,
And secure His beautiful!
        Let Pan be dead!

XXXVII

Truth is large: our aspiration
Scarce embraces half we be.
255 Shame, to stand in His creation
And doubt truth's sufficiency!—
To think God's song unexcelling
The poor tales of our own telling—
        When Pan is dead!

XXXVIII

260 What is true and just and honest,
What is lovely, what is pure,
All of praise that hath admonisht,
All of virtue,—shall endure;
These are themes for poets' uses,
265 Stirring nobler than the Muses,
        Ere Pan was dead.

XXXIX

O brave poets, keep back nothing,
Nor mix falsehood with the whole!
Look up Godward; speak the truth in
270 Worthy song from earnest soul:
Hold, in high poetic duty,
Truest Truth the fairest Beauty!
        Pan, Pan is dead.

—1844

The Cry of the Children

"Φεῦ, φεῦ, τί προσδέρκεσθέ μ' ὄμμασιν, τέκνα;" [1]
—Medea.

I

Do ye hear the children weeping, O my
    brothers,
    Ere the sorrow comes with years?
They are leaning their young heads against their
    mothers,
    And *that* cannot stop their tears.
5 The young lambs are bleating in the meadows,
    The young birds are chirping in the nest,
The young fawns are playing with the shadows,
    The young flowers are blowing toward the
        west—
But the young, young children, O my brothers,
10   They are weeping bitterly!
They are weeping in the playtime of the others,
    In the country of the free.

II

Do you question the young children in the sorrow
    Why their tears are falling so?
15 The old man may weep for his to-morrow
    Which is lost in Long Ago;
The old tree is leafless in the forest,
    The old year is ending in the frost,
The old wound, if stricken, is the sorest,
20   The old hope is hardest to be lost:
But the young, young children, O my brothers,
    Do you ask them why they stand
Weeping sore before the bosoms of their mothers,
    In our happy Fatherland?

III

25 They look up with their pale and sunken faces,
    And their looks are sad to see,

---

[1] Euripedes, *Medea*, l. 1040: "Oh! What is the meaning of your glance at me, children."

For the man's hoary anguish draws and presses
    Down the cheeks of infancy;
"Your old earth," they say, "is very dreary,
30   Our young feet," they say, "are very weak;
Few paces have we taken, yet are weary—
    Our grave-rest is very far to seek:
Ask the aged why they weep, and not the children,
    For the outside earth is cold,
35 And we young ones stand without, in our
      bewildering,
    And the graves are for the old.

IV

"True," say the children, "it may happen
    That we die before our time:
Little Alice died last year, her grave is shapen
40   Like a snowball, in the rime.
We looked into the pit prepared to take her:
    Was no room for any work in the close clay!
From the sleep wherein she lieth none will wake her,
    Crying, 'Get up, little Alice! it is day.'
45 If you listen by that grave, in sun and shower,
    With your ear down, little Alice never cries;
Could we see her face, be sure we should not know
    her,
    For the smile has time for growing in her eyes:
And merry go her moments, lulled and stilled in
50   The shroud by the kirk-chime.
It is good when it happens," say the children,
    "That we die before our time."

V

Alas, alas, the children! they are seeking
    Death in life, as best to have:
55 They are binding up their hearts away from
      breaking,
    With a cerement from the grave.
Go out, children, from the mine and from the city,
    Sing out, children, as the little thrushes do;
Pluck your handfuls of the meadow-cowslips pretty,
60   Laugh aloud, to feel your fingers let them
      through!

But they answer, "Are your cowslips of the meadows
    Like our weeds anear the mine?
Leave us quiet in the dark of the coal-shadows,
    From your pleasures fair and fine!

VI

65 "For oh," say the children, "we are weary,
    And we cannot run or leap;
If we cared for any meadows, it were merely
    To drop down in them and sleep.
Our knees tremble sorely in the stooping,
70   We fall upon our faces, trying to go;
And, underneath our heavy eyelids drooping
    The reddest flower would look as pale as snow.
For, all day, we drag our burden tiring
    Through the coal-dark, underground;
75 Or, all day, we drive the wheels of iron
    In the factories, round and round.

VII

"For all day the wheels are droning, turning;
    Their wind comes in our faces,
Till our hearts turn, our heads with pulses burning,
80   And the walls turn in their places:
Turns the sky in the high window, blank and reeling,
    Turns the long light that drops adown the wall,
Turn the black flies that crawl along the ceiling:
    All are turning, all the day, and we with all.
85 And all day the iron wheels are droning,
    And sometimes we could pray,
'O ye wheels' (breaking out in a mad moaning),
    'Stop! be silent for to-day!'"

VIII

Ay, be silent! Let them hear each other breathing
90   For a moment, mouth to mouth!
Let them touch each other's hands, in a fresh
      wreathing
    Of their tender human youth!
Let them feel that this cold metallic motion
    Is not all the life God fashions or reveals:
95 Let them prove their living souls against the notion

That they live in you, or under you, O wheels!
Still, all day, the iron wheels go onward,
    Grinding life down from its mark;
And the children's souls which God is calling
    sunward,
100   Spin on blindly in the dark.

IX

Now tell the poor young children, O my brothers,
    To look up to Him and pray;
So the blessed One who blesseth all the others,
    Will bless them another day.
105 They answer, "Who is God that He should hear us,
    While the rushing of the iron wheels is stirred?
When we sob aloud, the human creatures near us
    Pass by, hearing not, or answer not a word.
And *we* hear not (for the wheels in their resounding)
110   Strangers speaking at the door:
Is it likely God, with angels singing round Him,
    Hears our weeping any more?

X

"Two words, indeed, of praying we remember,
    And at midnight's hour of harm,
115 'Our Father,' looking upward in the chamber,
    We say softly for a charm.
We know no other words except 'Our Father,'
    And we think that, in some pause of angels'
    song,
God may pluck them with the silence sweet to
    gather,
120   And hold both within His right hand which is
    strong.
'Our Father!' If He heard us, He would surely
    (For they call Him good and mild)
Answer, smiling down the steep world very purely,
    'Come and rest with me, my child.'"

XI

125 "But, no!" say the children, weeping faster,
    "He is speechless as a stone:
And they tell us, of His image is the master

Who commands us to work on.
Go to!" say the children,—"up in Heaven,
130   Dark, wheel-like, turning clouds are all we find.
Do not mock us; grief has made us unbelieving:
    We look up for God, but tears have made us
    blind."
Do you hear the children weeping and disproving,
    O my brothers, what ye preach?
135 For God's possible is taught by His world's loving,
    And the children doubt of each.

XII

And well may the children weep before you!
    They are weary ere they run;
They have never seen the sunshine, nor the glory
140   Which is brighter than the sun.
They know the grief of man, without its wisdom;
    They sink in man's despair, without its calm;
Are slaves, without the liberty in Christdom,
    Are martyrs, by the pang without the palm;
145 Are worn as if with age, yet unretrievingly
    The harvest of its memories cannot reap,—
Are orphans of the earthly love and heavenly.
    Let them weep! let them weep!

XIII

They look up with their pale and sunken faces,
150   And their look is dread to see,
For they mind you of their angels in high places,
    With eyes turned on Deity.
"How long," they say, "how long, O cruel nation,
    Will you stand, to move the world, on a
    child's heart,—
155 Stifle down with a mailed heel its palpitation,
    And tread onward to your throne amid the
    mart?
Our blood splashes upward, O gold-heaper,
    And your purple shows your path!
But the child's sob in the silence curses deeper
160   Than the strong man in his wrath."
    —1844

A Man's Requirements

I

Love me, Sweet, with all thou art,
　　Feeling, thinking, seeing;
Love me in the lightest part,
　　Love me in full being.

II

5　Love me with thine open youth
　　In its frank surrender;
With the vowing of thy mouth
　　With its silence tender.

III

Love me with thine azure eyes,
10　　Made for earnest granting;
Taking colour from the skies,
　　Can Heaven's truth be wanting?

IV

Love me with their lids, that fall
　　Snow-like at first meeting;
15　Love me with thine heart, that all
　　Neighbours then see beating.

V

Love me with thine hand stretched out
　　Freely—open-minded:
Love me with thy loitering foot,—
20　　Hearing one behind it.

VI

Love me with thy voice, that turns
　　Sudden faint above me;
Love me with thy blush that burns
　　When I murmur *Love me!*

VII

25　Love me with thy thinking soul,
　　Break it to love-sighing;

Love me with thy thoughts that roll
　　On through living—dying.

VIII

Love me in thy gorgeous airs,
30　　When the world has crowned thee;
Love me, kneeling at thy prayers,
　　With the angels round thee.

IX

Love me pure, as musers do,
　　Up the woodlands shady:
35　Love me gaily, fast and true,
　　As a winsome lady.

X

Through all hopes that keep us brave,
　　Farther off or nigher,
Love me for the house and grave,
40　　And for something higher.

XI

Thus, if thou wilt prove me, Dear,
　　Woman's love no fable,
I will love *thee*—half a year—
　　As a man is able.
—1850

Sonnets From the Portuguese [1]

III

Unlike are we, unlike, O princely Heart!
　　Unlike our uses and our destinies.
Our ministering two angels look surprise
On one another, as they strike athwart
5　Their wings in passing. Thou, bethink thee, art
A guest for queens to social pageantries,

---

[1] Presented as translations from the Portuguese language, the sequence consists of forty-four sonnets.

With gages[1] from a hundred brighter eyes
Than tears even can make mine, to play thy part
Of chief musician. What hast *thou* to do
10   With looking from the lattice-lights at me,
A poor, tired, wandering singer, singing through
The dark, and leaning up a cypress tree?
The chrism[2] is on thine head,—on mine, the
        dew,—
And Death must dig the level where these agree.

XXII

When our two souls stand up erect and strong,
Face to face, silent, drawing nigh and nigher,
Until the lengthening wings break into fire
At either curvèd point,—what bitter wrong
5   Can the earth do to us, that we should not long
Be here contented? Think. In mounting higher,
The angels would press on us and aspire
To drop some golden orb of perfect song
Into our deep, dear silence. Let us stay
10   Rather on earth, Belovèd,—where the unfit
Contrarious moods of men recoil away
And isolate pure spirits, and permit
A place to stand and love in for a day,
With darkness and the death-hour rounding it.

XXIX

I think of thee!—my thoughts do twine and bud
About thee, as wild vines, about a tree,
Put out broad leaves, and soon there's nought to see
Except the straggling green which hides the wood.
5   Yet, O my palm-tree, be it understood
I will not have my thoughts instead of thee
Who art dearer, better! Rather, instantly
Renew thy presence; as a strong tree should,
Rustle thy boughs and set thy trunk all bare,
10   And let these bands of greenery which insphere thee

---

[1]   pledges.

[2]   consecrated oil.

Drop heavily down,—burst, shattered, everywhere!
Because, in this deep joy to see and hear thee
And breathe within thy shadow a new air,
I do not think of thee—I am too near thee.

XLIII

How do I love thee? Let me count the ways.
I love thee to the depth and breadth and height
My soul can reach, when feeling out of sight
For the ends of Being and ideal Grace.
5   I love thee to the level of everyday's
Most quiet need, by sun and candle-light.
I love thee freely, as men strive for Right;
I love thee purely, as they turn from Praise.
I love thee with the passion put to use
10   In my old griefs, and with my childhood's faith.
I love thee with a love I seemed to lose
With my lost saints—I love thee with the breath,
Smiles, tears, of all my life!—and, if God choose,
I shall but love thee better after death.
—1850 (1845–47)

The Runaway Slave at Pilgrim's Point

I

I stand on the mark beside the shore
    Of the first white pilgrim's bended knee,
Where exile turned to ancestor,
    And God was thanked for liberty.
5   I have run through the night, my skin is as dark,
I bend my knee down on this mark:
    I look on the sky and the sea.

II

O pilgrim-souls, I speak to you!
    I see you come proud and slow
10   From the land of the spirits pale as dew
    And round me and round me ye go.
O pilgrims, I have gasped and run
All night long from the whips of one
    Who in your names works sin and woe!

78

III

15 And thus I thought that I would come
    And kneel here where ye knelt before,
And feel your souls around me hum
    In undertone to the ocean's roar;
And lift my black face, my black hand,
20 Here, in your names, to curse this land
    Ye blessed in freedom's, evermore.

IV

I am black, I am black,
    And yet God made me, they say:
But if He did so, smiling back
25   He must have cast His work away
Under the feet of His white creatures,
With a look of scorn, that the dusky features
    Might be trodden again to clay.

V

And yet He has made dark things
30   To be glad and merry as light:
There's a little dark bird sits and sings,
    There's a dark stream ripples out of sight,
And the dark frogs chant in the safe morass,
And the sweetest stars are made to pass
35   O'er the face of the darkest night.

VI

But *we* who are dark, we are dark!
    Ah God, we have no stars!
About our souls in care and cark
    Our blackness shuts like prison-bars:
40 The poor souls crouch so far behind
That never a comfort can they find
    By reaching through the prison-bars.

VII

Indeed we live beneath the sky,
    That great smooth Hand of God stretched out
45 On all His children fatherly,
    To save them from the dread and doubt

Which would be if, from this low place,
All opened straight up to His face
    Into the grand eternity.

VIII

50 And still God's sunshine and His frost,
    They make us hot, they make us cold,
As if we were not black and lost;
    And the beasts and birds, in wood and fold,
Do fear and take us for very men:
55 Could the whip-poor-will or the cat of the glen
    Look into my eyes and be bold?

IX

I am black, I am black!
    But, once, I laughed in girlish glee,
For one of my colour stood in the track
60   Where the drivers drove, and looked at me,
And tender and full was the look he gave—
Could a slave look *so* at another slave?—
    I look at the sky and sea.

X

And from that hour our spirits grew
65   As free as if unsold, unbought:
Oh, strong enough, since we were two,
    To conquer the world, we thought.
The drivers drove us day by day;
We did not mind, we went one way,
70   And no better a freedom sought.

XI

In the sunny ground between the canes,
    He said "I love you" as he passed;
When the shingle-roof rang sharp with the rains,
    I heard how he vowed it fast:
75 While others shook he smiled in the hut,
As he carved me a bowl of the cocoa-nut
    Through the roar of the hurricanes.

XII

I sang his name instead of a song,
    Over and over I sang his name,
80 Upward and downward I drew it along
    My various notes,—the same, the same!
I sang it low, that the slave-girls near
Might never guess, from aught they could hear,
    It was only a name—a name.

XIII

85 I look on the sky and the sea.
    We were two to love, and two to pray:
Yes, two, O God, who cried to Thee,
    Though nothing didst Thou say!
Coldly Thou sat'st behind the sun:
90 And now I cry who am but one,
    Thou wilt not speak to-day.

XIV

We were black, we were black,
    We had no claim to love and bliss,
What marvel if each went to wrack?
95   They wrung my cold hands out of his
They dragged him—where? I crawled to touch
His blood's mark in the dust…not much,
    Ye pilgrim-souls, though plain as *this!*

XV

Wrong, followed by a deeper wrong!
100   Mere grief's too good for such as I:
So the white men brought the shame ere long
    To strangle the sob of my agony.
They would not leave me for my dull
Wet eyes!—it was too merciful
105   To let me weep pure tears and die.

XVI

I am black, I am black!
    I wore a child upon my breast,
An amulet that hung too slack,
    And, in my unrest, could not rest:

110 Thus we went moaning, child and mother,
    One to another, one to another,
        Until all ended for the best.

XVII

For hark! I will tell you low, low,
    I am black, you see,—
115 And the babe who lay on my bosom so,
    Was far too white, too white for me;
As white as the ladies who scorned to pray
Beside me at church but yesterday,
    Though my tears had washed a place for my
        knee.

XVIII

120 My own, own child! I could not bear
    To look in his face, it was so white;
I covered him up with a kerchief there,
    I covered his face in close and tight:
And he moaned and struggled, as well might be,
125 For the white child wanted his liberty—
    Ha, ha! he wanted the master-right.

XIX

He moaned and beat with his head and feet,
    His little feet that never grew;
He struck them out, as it was meet,
130   Against my heart to break it through:
I might have sung and made him mild,
But I dared not sing to the white-faced child
    The only song I knew.

XX

I pulled the kerchief very close:
135   He could not see the sun, I swear,
More, then, alive, than now he does
    From between the roots of the mango…where?
I know where. Close! A child and mother
Do wrong to look at one another
140   When one is black and one is fair.

XXI

Why, in that single glance I had
    Of my child's face,…I tell you all,
I saw a look that made me mad!
    The *master's* look, that used to fall
145 On my soul like his lash…or worse!
And so, to save it from my curse,
    I twisted it round in my shawl.

XXII

And he moaned and trembled from foot to head,
    He shivered from head to foot;
150 Till after a time, he lay instead
    Too suddenly still and mute.
I felt, beside, a stiffening cold:
I dared to lift up just a fold,
    As in lifting a leaf of the mango-fruit.

XXIII

155 But *my* fruit…ha, ha!—there, had been
    (I laugh to think on't at this hour!)
Your fine white angels (who have seen
    Nearest the secret of God's power)
And plucked my fruit to make them wine,
160 And sucked the soul of that child of mine
    As the humming-bird sucks the soul of the
       flower.

XXIV

Ha, ha, the trick of the angels white!
    They freed the white child's spirit so.
I said not a word, but day and night
165   I carried the body to and fro,
And it lay on my heart like a stone, as chill.
—The sun may shine out as much as he will:
    I am cold, though it happened a month ago.

XXV

From the white man's house, and the black man's
       hut,
170   I carried the little body on;

The forest's arms did round us shut,
    And silence through the trees did run:
They asked no question as I went,
They stood too high for astonishment,
175   They could see God sit on His throne.

XXVI

My little body, kerchiefed fast,
    I bore it on through the forest, on;
And when I felt it was tired at last,
    I scooped a hole beneath the moon:
180 Through the forest-tops the angels far,
With a white sharp finger from every star,
    Did point and mock at what was done.

XXVII

Yet when it was all done aright,—
    Earth, 'twixt me and my baby, strewed,—
185 All, changed to black earth,—nothing white,—
    A dark child in the dark!—ensued
Some comfort, and my heart grew young;
I sate down smiling there and sung
    The song I learnt in my maidenhood.

XXVIII

190 And thus we two were reconciled,
    The white child and black mother, thus;
For as I sang it soft and wild,
    The same song, more melodious,
Rose from the grave whereon I sate:
195 It was the dead child singing that,
    To join the souls of both of us.

XXIX

I look on the sea and the sky.
    Where the pilgrims' ships first anchored lay
The free sun rideth gloriously,
200   But the pilgrim-ghosts have slid away
Through the earliest streaks of the morn:
My face is black, but it glares with a scorn
    Which they dare not meet by day.

XXX

Ha!—in their stead, their hunter sons!
205   Ha, ha! they are on me—they hunt in a ring!
Keep off! I brave you all at once,
    I throw off your eyes like snakes that sting!
You have killed the black eagle at nest, I think:
Did you ever stand still in your triumph, and shrink
210   From the stroke of her wounded wing?

XXXI

(Man, drop that stone you dared to lift!—)
    I wish you who stand there five abreast,
Each, for his own wife's joy and gift,
    A little corpse as safely at rest
215 As mine in the mangoes! Yes, but *she*
May keep live babies on her knee,
    And sing the song she likes the best.

XXXII

I am not mad: I am black.
    I see you staring in my face—
220 I know you staring, shrinking back,
    Ye are born of the Washington-race,
And this land is the free America,
And this mark on my wrist—(I prove what I say)
    Ropes tied me up here to the flogging-place.

XXXIII

225 You think I shrieked then? Not a sound!
    I hung, as a gourd hangs in the sun;
I only cursed them all around
    As softly as I might have done
My very own child: from these sands
230 Up to the mountains, lift your hands,
    O slaves, and end what I begun!

XXXIV

Whips, curses; these must answer those!
    For in this UNION you have set
Two kinds of men in adverse rows,

235   Each loathing each; and all forget
The seven wounds in Christ's body fair,
    While HE sees gaping everywhere
    Our countless wounds that pay no debt.

XXXV

Our wounds are different. Your white men
240   Are, after all, not gods indeed,
Nor able to make Christs again
    Do good with bleeding. *We* who bleed
(Stand off!) we help not in our loss!
We are too heavy for our cross,
245   And fall and crush you and your seed.

XXXVI

I fall, I swoon! I look at the sky.
    The clouds are breaking on my brain;
I am floated along, as if I should die
    Of liberty's exquisite pain.
250 In the name of the white child waiting for me
In the death-dark where we may kiss and agree,
White men, I leave you all curse-free
    In my broken heart's disdain!
—1850

Aurora Leigh

FIRST BOOK

Of writing many books there is no end;[1]
     And I who have written much in prose and
         verse
For others' uses, will write now for mine,—
Will write my story for my better self,[2]
5 As when you paint your portrait for a friend,
Who keeps it in a drawer and looks at it
Long after he has ceased to love you, just

---

[1] See Ecclesiastes 12:12.

[2] Aurora, age 26 or 27, is writing her life story retrospectively.

To hold together what he was and is.
I, writing thus, am still what men call young;
10 I have not so far left the coasts of life
To travel inward, that I cannot hear
That murmur of the outer Infinite[1]
Which unweaned babies smile at in their sleep
When wondered at for smiling; not so far,
15 But still I catch my mother at her post
Beside the nursery door, with finger up,
"Hush, hush—here's too much noise!" while her
    sweet eyes
Leap forward, taking part against her word
In the child's riot. Still I sit and feel
20 My father's slow hand, when she had left us both,
Stroke out my childish curls across his knee,
And hear Assunta's[2] daily jest (she knew
He liked it better than a better jest)
Inquire how many golden scudi[3] went
25 To make such ringlets. O my father's hand,
Stroke heavily, heavily the poor hair down,
Draw, press the child's head closer to thy knee!
I'm still too young, too young, to sit alone.

I write. My mother was a Florentine,
30 Whose rare blue eyes were shut from seeing me
When scarcely I was four years old, my life
A poor spark snatched up from a failing lamp
Which went out therefore. She was weak and frail;
She could not bear the joy of giving life,
35 The mother's rapture slew her. If her kiss
Had left a longer weight upon my lips
It might have steadied the uneasy breath,
And reconciled and fraternised my soul
With the new order. As it was, indeed,
40 I felt a mother-want about the world,

And still went seeking, like a bleating lamb
Left out at night in shutting up the fold,—
As restless as a nest-deserted bird
Grown chill through something being away,
    though what
45 It knows not. I, Aurora Leigh, was born
To make my father sadder, and myself
Not overjoyous, truly. Women know
The way to rear up children (to be just),
They know a simple, merry, tender knack
50 Of tying sashes, fitting baby-shoes,
And stringing pretty words that make no sense,
And kissing full sense into empty words,
Which things are corals[4] to cut life upon,
Although such trifles: children learn by such,
55 Love's holy earnest in a pretty play
And get not over-early solemnised,
But seeing, as in a rose-bush, Love's Divine
Which burns and hurts not,[5]—not a single
    bloom,—
Become aware and unafraid of Love.
60 Such good do mothers. Fathers love as well
—Mine did, I know,—but still with heavier brains,
And wills more consciously responsible,
And not as wisely, since less foolishly;
So mothers have God's license to be missed.

65 My father was an austere Englishman,
Who, after a dry lifetime spent at home
In college-learning, law, and parish talk,
Was flooded with a passion unaware,
His whole provisioned and complacent past
70 Drowned out from him that moment. As he stood
In Florence, where he had come to spend a month
And note the secret of Da Vinci's[6] drains,
He musing somewhat absently perhaps

---

[1] Cf. William Wordsworth's "Ode: Intimations of Immortality from Recollections of Early Childhood" (1807).

[2] common nineteenth-century Italian name meaning "Our Lady, received into Heaven."

[3] a former coin of Italy and Sicily.

---

[4] a toy made of polished coral, given to infants to assist teething (*OED*).

[5] See Exodus 3:2.

[6] Leonardo da Vinci (1452–1519), Florentine artist, celebrated as a painter, sculptor, architect, engineer, and scientist.

Some English question...whether men should pay
75 The unpopular but necessary tax
With left or right hand—in the alien sun
In that great square of the Santissima[1]
There drifted past him (scarcely marked enough
To move his comfortable island scorn)
80 A train of priestly banners, cross and psalm,
The white-veiled rose-crowned maidens holding up
Tall tapers, weighty for such wrists, aslant
To the blue luminous tremor of the air,
And letting drop the white wax as they went
85 To eat the bishop's wafer at the church;
From which long trail of chanting priests and girls,
A face flashed like a cymbal on his face
And shook with silent clangour brain and heart,
Transfiguring him to music. Thus, even thus,
90 He too received his sacramental gift
With eucharistic meanings; for he loved.

And thus beloved, she died. I've heard it said
That but to see him in the first surprise
Of widower and father, nursing me,
95 Unmothered little child of four years old,
His large man's hands afraid to touch my curls,
As if the gold would tarnish,—his grave lips
Contriving such a miserable smile
As if he knew needs must, or I should die,
100 And yet 'twas hard,—would almost make the stones
Cry out for pity.[2] There's a verse he set
In Santa Croce[3] to her memory,—
"Weep for an infant too young to weep much
When death removed this mother"—stops the mirth
105 To-day on women's faces when they walk
With rosy children hanging on their gowns,
Under the cloister to escape the sun
That scorches in the piazza. After which
He left our Florence and made haste to hide

110 Himself, his prattling child, and silent grief,
Among the mountains above Pelago;
Because unmothered babes, he thought, had need
Of mother nature more than others use,
And Pan's[4] white goats, with udders warm and full
115 Of mystic contemplations, come to feed
Poor milkless lips of orphans like his own—
Such scholar-scraps he talked, I've heard from
    friends,
For even prosaic men who wear grief long
Will get to wear it as a hat aside
120 With a flower stuck in't. Father, then, and child,
We lived among the mountains many years,
God's silence on the outside of the house,
And we who did not speak too loud within,
And old Assunta to make up the fire,
125 Crossing herself whene'er a sudden flame
Which lightened from the firewood, made alive
That picture of my mother on the wall.

The painter drew it after she was dead,
And when the face was finished, throat and hands,
130 Her cameriera[5] carried him, in hate
Of the English-fashioned shroud, the last brocade
She dressed in at the Pitti;[6] "he should paint
No sadder thing than that," she swore, "to wrong
Her poor signora."[7] Therefore very strange
135 The effect was. I, a little child, would crouch
For hours upon the floor with knees drawn up,
And gaze across them, half in terror, half
In adoration, at the picture there,—
That swan-like supernatural white life
140 Just sailing upward from the red stiff silk
Which seemed to have no part in it nor power

---

[1] the church of the Santissima Annunziata in Florence.

[2] See Luke 19:40.

[3] a church in Florence.

[4] the god of woods, fields, and flocks, having a human body with goat's legs, horns, and ears.

[5] Italian waiting woman.

[6] The Pitti Palace was the official residence of the grand dukes of Tuscany in the nineteenth century.

[7] lady.

To keep it from quite breaking out of bounds.
For hours I sat and stared. Assunta's awe
And my poor father's melancholy eyes
145 Still pointed that way. That way went my thoughts
When wandering beyond sight. And as I grew
In years, I mixed, confused, unconsciously,
Whatever I last read or heard or dreamed,
Abhorrent, admirable, beautiful,
150 Pathetical, or ghastly, or grotesque,
With still that face…which did not therefore change,
But kept the mystic level of all forms,
Hates, fears, and admirations, was by turns
Ghost, fiend, and angel, fairy, witch, and sprite,
155 A dauntless Muse[1] who eyes a dreadful Fate,[2]
A loving Psyche who loses sight of Love,[3]
A still Medusa[4] with mild milky brows
All curdled and all clothed upon with snakes
Whose slime falls fast as sweat will; or anon
160 Our Lady of the Passion, stabbed with swords
Where the Babe sucked;[5] or Lamia[6] in her first
Moonlighted pallor, ere she shrunk and blinked
And shuddering wriggled down to the unclean;
Or my own mother, leaving her last smile
165 In her last kiss upon the baby-mouth
My father pushed down on the bed for that,—
Or my dead mother, without smile or kiss,

Buried at Florence. All which images,
Concentred on the picture, glassed themselves
170 Before my meditative childhood, as
The incoherencies of change and death
Are represented fully, mixed and merged,
In the smooth fair mystery of perpetual Life.
And while I stared away my childish wits
175 Upon my mother's picture (ah, poor child!),
My father, who through love had suddenly
Thrown off the old conventions, broken loose
From chin-bands[7] of the soul, like Lazarus,[8]
Yet had no time to learn to talk and walk
180 Or grow anew familiar with the sun,—
Who had reached to freedom, not to action, lived,
But lived as one entranced, with thoughts, not
        aims,—
Whom love had unmade from a common man
But not completed to an uncommon man,—
185 My father taught me what he had learnt the best
Before he died and left me,—grief and love.
And, seeing we had books among the hills,
Strong words of counselling souls confederate
With vocal pines and waters,—out of books
190 He taught me all the ignorance of men,
And how God laughs in heaven when any man
Says "Here I'm learned; this, I understand;
In that, I am never caught at fault or doubt."
He sent the schools to school, demonstrating
195 A fool will pass for such through one mistake,
While a philosopher will pass for such,
Through said mistakes being ventured in the gross
And heaped up to a system.
                                        I am like,
They tell me, my dear father. Broader brows
200 Howbeit, upon a slenderer undergrowth
Of delicate features,—paler, near as grave;
But then my mother's smile breaks up the whole,
And makes it better sometimes than itself.

---

[1] In Greek mythology, the nine Muses, the offspring of Zeus and Mnemosyne, presided over the arts; the nine are Calliope, Clio, Thalia, Melpomene, Euterpe, Terpsichore, Erato, Polyhymnia, and Urania.

[2] The three Fates, daughters of Erebus and Night, were Clotho ("the spinner"), Lachesis ("the measurer"), and Atropos ("she who cannot be avoided").

[3] The marriage of Eros, or Cupid, with Psyche was ruined when she disobeyed his orders and attempted to view him unawares.

[4] the Gorgon, loved by Poseidon and mother of Chrysaor and Pegasus. Medusa was transformed by Athene into a snake-haired monster whose glance turned men into stone; she was eventually beheaded by Perseus.

[5] See Luke 2:35.

[6] In Greek mythology, Lamia's children were killed by Hera, jealous of the mortal's relationship with Zeus. Thereafter, Lamia sought out and killed the children of others in revenge; see also Keats's "Lamia."

[7] a shroud; winding-cloth.

[8] See John 11:1–53.

So, nine full years, our days were hid with God
205 Among his mountains: I was just thirteen,
Still growing like the plants from unseen roots
In tongue-tied Springs,—and suddenly awoke
To full life and life's needs and agonies
With an intense, strong, struggling heart beside
210 A stone-dead father. Life, struck sharp on death,
Makes awful lightning. His last word was "Love—"
"Love, my child, love, love!"—(then he had done
     with grief)
"Love, my child." Ere I answered he was gone,
And none was left to love in all the world.

215 There, ended childhood. What succeeded next
I recollect as, after fevers, men
Thread back the passage of delirium,
Missing the turn still, baffled by the door;
Smooth endless days, notched here and there with
     knives,
220 A weary, wormy darkness, spurred i' the flank
With flame, that it should eat and end itself
Like some tormented scorpion. Then at last
I do remember clearly how there came
A stranger with authority, not right
225 (I thought not), who commanded, caught me up
From old Assunta's neck; how, with a shriek,
She let me go,—while I, with ears too full
Of my father's silence to shriek back a word,
In all a child's astonishment at grief
230 Stared at the wharf-edge where she stood and
     moaned,
My poor Assunta, where she stood and moaned!
The white walls, the blue hills, my Italy,
Drawn backward from the shuddering steamer-deck,
Like one in anger drawing back her skirts
235 Which suppliants catch at. Then the bitter sea
Inexorably pushed between us both
And, sweeping up the ship with my despair,
Threw us out as a pasture to the stars.

Ten nights and days we voyaged on the deep;
240 Ten nights and days without the common face
Of any day or night; the moon and sun
Cut off from the green reconciling earth,
To starve into a blind ferocity
And glare unnatural; the very sky
245 (Dropping its bell-net down upon the sea,
As if no human heart should 'scape alive)
Bedraggled with the desolating salt,
Until it seemed no more that holy heaven
To which my father went. All new and strange;
250 The universe turned stranger, for a child.

Then, land!—then, England! oh, the frosty cliffs
Looked cold upon me. Could I find a home
Among those mean red houses through the fog?
And when I heard my father's language first
255 From alien lips which had no kiss for mine
I wept aloud, then laughed, then wept, then wept,
And some one near me said the child was mad
Through much sea-sickness. The train swept us on:
Was this my father's England? the great isle?
260 The ground seemed cut up from the fellowship
Of verdure, field from field, as man from man;
The skies themselves looked low and positive,
As almost you could touch them with a hand,
And dared to do it they were so far off
265 From God's celestial crystals; all things blurred
And dull and vague. Did Shakespeare and his mates
Absorb the light here?—not a hill or stone
With heart to strike a radiant colour up
Or active outline on the indifferent air.

270 I think I see my father's sister stand
Upon the hall-step of her country-house
To give me welcome. She stood straight and calm,
Her somewhat narrow forehead braided tight
As if for taming accidental thoughts
275 From possible pulses; brown hair pricked with gray
By frigid use of life (she was not old,
Although my father's elder by a year),

A nose drawn sharply, yet in delicate lines;
A close mild mouth, a little soured about
280 The ends, through speaking unrequited loves
Or peradventure niggardly half-truths;
Eyes of no colour,—once they might have smiled,
But never, never have forgot themselves
In smiling; cheeks, in which was yet a rose
285 Of perished summers, like a rose in a book,
Kept more for ruth than pleasure,—if past bloom,
Past fading also.
                              She had lived, we'll say,
A harmless life, she called a virtuous life,
A quiet life, which was not life at all
290 (But that, she had not lived enough to know),
Between the vicar and the county squires,
The lord-lieutenant[1] looking down sometimes
From the empyrean[2] to assure their souls
Against chance vulgarisms, and, in the abyss,
295 The apothecary, looked on once a year
To prove their soundness of humility.
The poor-club[3] exercised her Christian gifts
Of knitting stockings, stitching petticoats,
Because we are of one flesh, after all,
300 And need one flannel (with a proper sense
Of difference in the quality)—and still
The book-club, guarded from your modern trick
Of shaking dangerous questions from the crease,
Preserved her intellectual. She had lived
305 A sort of cage-bird life, born in a cage,
Accounting that to leap from perch to perch
Was act and joy enough for any bird.
Dear heaven, how silly are the things that live
In thickets, and eat berries!
                              I, alas,
310 A wild bird scarcely fledged, was brought to her
   cage,

***

[1] the official, though mostly ceremonial, governor of a county.

[2] i.e., heaven.

[3] a charitable club collecting clothes or funds for the poor.

And she was there to meet me. Very kind.
Bring the clean water, give out the fresh seed.

She stood upon the steps to welcome me,
Calm, in black garb. I clung about her neck,—
315 Young babes, who catch at every shred of wool
To draw the new light closer, catch and cling
Less blindly. In my ears my father's word
Hummed ignorantly, as the sea in shells,
"Love, love, my child." She, black there with my
   grief,
320 Might feel my love—she was his sister once—
I clung to her. A moment she seemed moved,
Kissed me with cold lips, suffered me to cling,
And drew me feebly through the hall into
The room she sat in.
                              There, with some strange spasm
325 Of pain and passion, she wrung loose my hands
Imperiously, and held me at arm's length,
And with two grey-steel naked-bladed eyes
Searched through my face,—ay, stabbed it through
   and through,
Through brows and cheeks and chin, as if to find
330 A wicked murderer in my innocent face,
If not here, there perhaps. Then, drawing breath,
She struggled for her ordinary calm—
And missed it rather,—told me not to shrink,
As if she had told me not to lie or swear,—
335 "She loved my father and would love me too
As long as I deserved it." Very kind.

I understood her meaning afterward;
She thought to find my mother in my face,
And questioned it for that. For she, my aunt,
340 Had loved my father truly, as she could,
And hated, with the gall of gentle souls,
My Tuscan mother who had fooled away
A wise man from wise courses, a good man
From obvious duties, and, depriving her,
345 His sister, of the household precedence,
Had wronged his tenants, robbed his native land,

And made him mad, alike by life and death,
In love and sorrow. She had pored for years
What sort of woman could be suitable
350 To her sort of hate, to entertain it with,
And so, her very curiosity
Became hate too, and all the idealism
She ever used in life was used for hate,
Till hate, so nourished, did exceed at last
355 The love from which it grew, in strength and heat,
And wrinkled her smooth conscience with a sense
Of disputable virtue (say not, sin)
When Christian doctrine was enforced at church.

And thus my father's sister was to me
360 My mother's hater. From that day she did
Her duty to me (I appreciate it
In her own word as spoken to herself),
Her duty, in large measure, well pressed out[1]
But measured always. She was generous, bland,
365 More courteous than was tender, gave me still
The first place,—as if fearful that God's saints
Would look down suddenly and say "Herein
You missed a point, I think, through lack of love."
Alas, a mother never is afraid
370 Of speaking angerly[2] to any child,
Since love, she knows, is justified of love.

And I, I was a good child on the whole,
A meek and manageable child. Why not?
I did not live, to have the faults of life:
375 There seemed more true life in my father's grave
Than in all England. Since *that* threw me off
Who fain would cleave (his latest will, they say,
Consigned me to his land), I only thought
Of lying quiet there where I was thrown
380 Like sea-weed on the rocks, and suffering her
To prick me to a pattern with her pin,
Fibre from fibre, delicate leaf from leaf,

And dry out from my drowned anatomy
The last sea-salt left in me.
                                    So it was.
385 I broke the copious curls upon my head
In braids, because she liked smooth-ordered hair.
I left off saying my sweet Tuscan words
Which still at any stirring of the heart
Came up to float across the English phrase
390 As lilies (*Bene* or *Che che*),[3] because
She liked my father's child to speak his tongue.
I learnt the collects and the catechism,[4]
The creeds, from Athanasius[5] back to Nice,
The Articles, the Tracts *against* the times[6]
395 (By no means Buonaventure's "Prick of Love"),[7]
And various popular synopses of
Inhuman doctrines never taught by John,
Because she liked instructed piety.
I learnt my complement of classic French
400 (Kept pure of Balzac and neologism)
And German also, since she liked a range
Of liberal education,—tongues, not books.
I learnt a little algebra, a little
Of the mathematics,—brushed with extreme flounce
405 The circle of the sciences, because
She misliked women who are frivolous.
I learnt the royal genealogies
Of Oviedo, the internal laws
Of the Burmese empire,—by how many feet
410 Mount Chimborazo outsoars Teneriffe.
What navigable river joins itself

---

[1] See Luke 6:38.

[2] i.e., angrily.

[3] "good" or "well, well."

[4] the manual of Christian doctrine arranged in the form of question and answer, intended for instructing those to be confirmed.

[5] The Athanasian creed forms part of the basic tenets of faith in the liturgy of the Church of England.

[6] In 1833 and 1841, *Tracts for the Times* was published by the Oxford High Church warning against the secularization of the church, and calling for a strengthened reliance on Catholic principles.

[7] *Stimulus Divini Amoris* (The Prick, or Goad, of Love), incorrectly attributed to St. Buonaventure, is a devotional work which emphasizes an emotional, rather than logical, approach to the mysteries.

To Lara, and what census of the year five
Was taken at Klagenfurt,—because she liked
A general insight into useful facts.
415 I learnt much music,—such as would have been
As quite impossible in Johnson's day
As still it might be wished—fine sleights of hand
And unimagined fingering, shuffling off
The hearer's soul through hurricanes of notes
420 To a noisy Tophet; and I drew…costumes
From French engravings, nereids neatly draped
(With smirks of simmering godship): I washed in
Landscapes from nature (rather say, washed out).
I danced the polka and Cellarius,
425 Spun glass, stuffed birds, and modelled flowers in
        wax,
Because she liked accomplishments in girls.
I read a score of books on womanhood
To prove, if women do not think at all,
They may teach thinking (to a maiden aunt
430 Or else the author),—books that boldly assert
Their right of comprehending husband's talk
When not too deep, and even of answering
With pretty "may it please you," or "so it is,"—
Their rapid insight and fine aptitude,
435 Particular worth and general missionariness,
As long as they keep quiet by the fire
And never say "no" when the world says "ay,"
For that is fatal,—their angelic reach
Of virtue, chiefly used to sit and darn,
440 And fatten household sinners,—their, in brief,
Potential faculty in everything
Of abdicating power in it: she owned
She liked a woman to be womanly,
And English women, she thanked God and sighed
445 (Some people always sigh in thanking God)
Were models to the universe. And last
I learnt cross-stitch, because she did not like
To see me wear the night with empty hands
A-doing nothing. So, my shepherdess
450 Was something after all (the pastoral saints
Be praised for't), leaning lovelorn with pink eyes

To match her shoes, when I mistook the silks;
Her head uncrushed by that round weight of hat
So strangely similar to the tortoise-shell
455 Which slew the tragic poet.
                              By the way,
The works of women are symbolical.
We sew, sew, prick our fingers, dull our sight,
Producing what? A pair of slippers, sir,
To put on when you're weary—or a stool
460 To stumble over and vex you…"curse that stool!"
Or else at best, a cushion, where you lean
And sleep, and dream of something we are not
But would be for your sake. Alas, alas!
This hurts most, this—that, after all, we are paid
465 The worth of our work, perhaps.
                              In looking down
Those years of education (to return)
I wonder if Brinvilliers suffered more
In the water-torture…flood succeeding flood
To drench the incapable throat and split the veins…
470 Than I did. Certain of your feebler souls
Go out in such a process; many pine
To a sick, inodorous light; my own endured:
I had relations in the Unseen, and drew
The elemental nutriment and heat
475 From nature, as earth feels the sun at nights,
Or as a babe sucks surely in the dark.
I kept the life thrust on me, on the outside
Of the inner life with all its ample room
For heart and lungs, for will and intellect,
480 Inviolable by conventions. God,
I thank thee for that grace of thine!
                              At first
I felt no life which was not patience,—did
The thing she bade me, without heed to a thing
Beyond it, sat in just the chair she placed,
485 With back against the window, to exclude
The sight of the great lime-tree on the lawn,
Which seemed to have come on purpose from the
        woods
To bring the house a message,—ay, and walked

Demurely in her carpeted low rooms,
490 As if I should not, hearkening my own steps,
Misdoubt I was alive. I read her books,
Was civil to her cousin, Romney Leigh,
Gave ear to her vicar, tea to her visitors,
And heard them whisper, when I changed a cup
495 (I blushed for joy at that),—"The Italian child,
For all her blue eyes and her quiet ways,
Thrives ill in England: she is paler yet
Than when we came the last time; she will die."

"Will die." My cousin, Romney Leigh, blushed too,
500 With sudden anger, and approaching me
Said low between his teeth, "You're wicked now?
You wish to die and leave the world a-dusk
For others, with your naughty light blown out?"
I looked into his face defyingly;
505 He might have known that, being what I was,
'Twas natural to like to get away
As far as dead folk can: and then indeed
Some people make no trouble when they die.
He turned and went abruptly, slammed the door,
510 And shut his dog out.
                         Romney, Romney Leigh.
I have not named my cousin hitherto,
And yet I used him as a sort of friend;
My elder by few years, but cold and shy
And absent...tender, when he thought of it,
515 Which scarcely was imperative, grave betimes,
As well as early master of Leigh Hall,
Whereof the nightmare sat upon his youth,
Repressing all its seasonable delights,
And agonising with a ghastly sense
520 Of universal hideous want and wrong
To incriminate possession. When he came
From college to the country, very oft
He crossed the hill on visits to my aunt,
With gifts of blue grapes from the hothouses,
525 A book in one hand,—mere statistics (if
I chanced to lift the cover), count of all

The goats whose beards grow sprouting down
      toward hell
Against God's separative judgment-hour.
And she, she almost loved him,—even allowed
530 That sometimes he should seem to sigh my way;
It made him easier to be pitiful,
And sighing was his gift. So, undisturbed,
At whiles she let him shut my music up
And push my needles down, and lead me out
535 To see in that south angle of the house
The figs grow black as if by a Tuscan rock,
On some light pretext. She would turn her head
At other moments, go to fetch a thing,
And leave me breath enough to speak with him,
540 For his sake; it was simple.
                            Sometimes too
He would have saved me utterly, it seemed,
He stood and looked so.
                         Once, he stood so near,
He dropped a sudden hand upon my hand
Bent down on woman's work, as soft as rain—
545 But then I rose and shook it off as fire,
The stranger's touch that took my father's place
Yet dared seem soft.
                       I used him for a friend
Before I ever knew him for a friend.
'Twas better, 'twas worse also, afterward:
550 We came so close, we saw our differences
Too intimately. Always Romney Leigh
Was looking for the worms, I for the gods.
A godlike nature his; the gods look down,
Incurious of themselves; and certainly
555 'Tis well I should remember, how, those days,
I was a worm too, and he looked on me.

A little by his act perhaps, yet more
By something in me, surely not my will,
I did not die. But slowly, as one in swoon,
560 To whom life creeps back in the form of death,
With a sense of separation, a blind pain
Of blank obstruction, and a roar i' the ears

Of visionary chariots which retreat
As earth grows clearer…slowly, by degrees;
565 I woke, rose up…where was I? in the world;
For uses therefore I must count worth while.

I had a little chamber in the house,
As green as any privet-hedge a bird
Might choose to build in, though the nest itself
570 Could show but dead-brown sticks and straws; the
walls
Were green, the carpet was pure green, the straight
Small bed was curtained greenly, and the folds
Hung green about the window which let in
The out-door world with all its greenery.
575 You could not push your head out and escape
A dash of dawn-dew from the honeysuckle,
But so you were baptized into the grace
And privilege of seeing…
First, the lime
(I had enough there, of the lime, be sure,—
580 My morning-dream was often hummed away
By the bees in it); past the lime, the lawn,
Which, after sweeping broadly round the house,
Went trickling through the shrubberies in a stream
Of tender turf, and wore and lost itself
585 Among the acacias, over which you saw
The irregular line of elms by the deep lane
Which stopped the grounds and dammed the
overflow
Of arbutus and laurel. Out of sight
The lane was; sunk so deep, no foreign tramp
590 Nor drover of wild ponies out of Wales
Could guess if lady's hall or tenant's lodge
Dispensed such odours,—though his stick well-
crooked
Might reach the lowest trail of blossoming briar
Which dipped upon the wall. Behind the elms,
595 And through their tops, you saw the folded hills
Striped up and down with hedges (burly oaks
Projecting from the line to show themselves),

Through which my cousin Romney's chimneys
smoked
As still as when a silent mouth in frost
600 Breathes, showing where the woodlands hid Leigh
Hall;
While, far above, a jut of table-land,
A promontory without water, stretched,—
You could not catch it if the days were thick,
Or took it for a cloud; but, otherwise,
605 The vigorous sun would catch it up at eve
And use it for an anvil till he had filled
The shelves of heaven with burning thunder-bolts,
Protesting against night and darkness:—then,
When all his setting trouble was resolved
610 To a trance of passive glory, you might see
In apparition on the golden sky
(Alas, my Giotto's background!) the sheep run
Along the fine clear outline, small as mice
That run along a witch's scarlet thread.

615 Not a grand nature. Not my chestnut-woods
Of Vallombrosa, cleaving by the spurs
To the precipices. Not my headlong leaps
Of waters, that cry out for joy or fear
In leaping through the palpitating pines,
620 Like a white soul tossed out to eternity
With thrills of time upon it. Not indeed
My multitudinous mountains, sitting in
The magic circle, with the mutual touch
Electric, panting from their full deep hearts
625 Beneath the influent heavens, and waiting for
Communion and commission. Italy
Is one thing, England one.
On English ground
You understand the letter,—ere the fall
How Adam lived in a garden. All the fields
630 Are tied up fast with hedges, nosegay-like;
The hills are crumpled plains, the plains parterres,
The trees, round, woolly, ready to be clipped,
And if you seek for any wilderness
You find, at best, a park. A nature tamed

635 And grown domestic like a barn-door fowl,
Which does not awe you with its claws and beak,
Nor tempt you to an eyrie too high up,
But which, in cackling, sets you thinking of
Your eggs to-morrow at breakfast, in the pause
640 Of finer meditation.
           Rather say,
A sweet familiar nature, stealing in
As a dog might, or child, to touch your hand
Or pluck your gown, and humbly mind you so
Of presence and affection, excellent
645 For inner uses, from the things without.

I could not be unthankful, I who was
Entreated thus and holpen. In the room
I speak of, ere the house was well awake,
And also after it was well asleep,
650 I sat alone, and drew the blessing in
Of all that nature. With a gradual step,
A stir among the leaves, a breath, a ray,
It came in softly, while the angels made
A place for it beside me. The moon came,
655 And swept my chamber clean of foolish thoughts.
The sun came, saying, "Shall I lift this light
Against the lime-tree, and you will not look?
I make the birds sing—listen! but, for you,
God never hears your voice, excepting when
660 You lie upon the bed at nights and weep."

Then, something moved me. Then, I wakened up
More slowly than I verily write now,
But wholly, at last, I wakened, opened wide
The window and my soul, and let the airs
665 And out-door sights sweep gradual gospels in,
Regenerating what I was. O, Life,
How oft we throw it off and think,—"Enough,
Enough of life in so much!—here's a cause
For rupture;—herein we must break with Life,
670 Or be ourselves unworthy; here we are wronged,
Maimed, spoiled for aspiration: farewell, Life!"
And so, as froward babes, we hide our eyes
And think all ended.—Then, Life calls to us
In some transformed, apocalyptic voice,
675 Above us, or below us, or around:
Perhaps we name it Nature's voice, or Love's,
Tricking ourselves, because we are more ashamed
To own our compensations than our griefs:
Still, Life's voice!—still, we make our peace with
    Life.

680 And I, so young then, was not sullen. Soon
I used to get up early, just to sit
And watch the morning quicken in the gray,
And hear the silence open like a flower
Leaf after leaf,—and stroke with listless hand
685 The woodbine through the window, till at last
I came to do it with a sort of love,
At foolish unaware: whereat I smiled,—
A melancholy smile, to catch myself
Smiling for joy.
           Capacity for joy
690 Admits temptation. It seemed, next, worth while
To dodge the sharp sword set against my life;
To slip down stairs through all the sleepy house,
As mute as any dream there, and escape
As a soul from the body, out of doors,
695 Glide through the shrubberies, drop into the lane,
And wander on the hills an hour or two,
Then back again before the house should stir.

Or else I sat on in my chamber green,
And lived my life, and thought my thoughts, and
    prayed
700 My prayers without the vicar; read my books
Without considering whether they were fit
To do me good. Mark, there. We get no good
By being ungenerous, even to a book,
And calculating profits,—so much help
705 By so much reading. It is rather when
We gloriously forget ourselves and plunge
Soul-forward, headlong, into a book's profound,

Impassioned for its beauty and salt of truth—
'Tis then we get the right good from a book.

10 I read much. What my father taught before
From many a volume, Love re-emphasised
Upon the self-same pages: Theophrast
Grew tender with the memory of his eyes,
And Ælian made mine wet. The trick of Greek
15 And Latin he had taught me, as he would
Have taught me wrestling or the game of fives
If such he had known,—most like a shipwrecked
    man
Who heaps his single platter with goats' cheese
And scarlet berries; or like any man
20 Who loves but one, and so gives all at once,
Because he has it, rather than because
He counts it worthy. Thus, my father gave;
And thus, as did the women formerly
By young Achilles, when they pinned a veil
25 Across the boy's audacious front, and swept
With tuneful laughs the silver-fretted rocks,
He wrapt his little daughter in his large
Man's doublet, careless did it fit or no.

But, after I had read for memory,
30 I read for hope. The path my father's foot
Had trod me out (which suddenly broke off
What time he dropped the wallet of the flesh
And passed), alone I carried on, and set
My child-heart 'gainst the thorny underwood,
35 To reach the grassy shelter of the trees.
Ah babe i' the wood, without a brother-babe!
My own self-pity, like the red-breast bird,
Flies back to cover all that past with leaves.

Sublimest danger, over which none weeps,
40 When any young wayfaring soul goes forth
Alone, unconscious of the perilous road,
The day-sun dazzling in his limpid eyes,
To thrust his own way, he an alien, through
The world of books! Ah, you!—you think it fine,

745 You clap hands—"A fair day!"—you cheer him on,
As if the worst, could happen, were to rest
Too long beside a fountain. Yet, behold,
Behold!—the world of books is still the world,
And wordlings in it are less merciful
750 And more puissant. For the wicked there
Are winged like angels; every knife that strikes
Is edged from elemental fire to assail
A spiritual life; the beautiful seems right
By force of beauty, and the feeble wrong
755 Because of weakness; power is justified
Though armed against Saint Michael; many a crown
Covers bald foreheads. In the book-world, true,
There's no lack, neither, of God's saints and kings,
That shake the ashes of the grave aside
760 From their calm locks and undiscomfited
Look steadfast truths against Time's changing mask.
True, many a prophet teaches in the roads;
True, many a seer pulls down the flaming heavens
Upon his own head in strong martyrdom
765 In order to light men a moment's space.
But stay!—who judges?—who distinguishes
'Twixt Saul and Nahash justly, at first sight,
And leaves king Saul precisely at the sin,
To serve king David? who discerns at once
770 The sound of the trumpets, when the trumpets blow
For Alaric as well as Charlemagne?
Who judges wizards, and can tell true seers
From conjurers? the child, there? Would you leave
That child to wander in a battle-field
775 And push his innocent smile against the guns;
Or even in a catacomb,—his torch
Grown ragged in the fluttering air, and all
The dark a-mutter round him? not a child.

I read books bad and good—some bad and good
780 At once (good aims not always make good books:
Well-tempered spades turn up ill-smelling soils
In digging vineyards even); books that prove
God's being so definitely, that man's doubt
Grows self-defined the other side the line,

785 Made atheist by suggestion; moral books,
Exasperating to license; genial books,
Discounting from the human dignity;
And merry books, which set you weeping when
The sun shines,—ay, and melancholy books,
790 Which make you laugh that any one should weep
In this disjointed life for one wrong more.

The world of books is still the world, I write,
And both worlds have God's providence, thank God,
To keep and hearten: with some struggle, indeed,
795 Among the breakers, some hard swimming through
The deeps—I lost breath in my soul sometimes
And cried "God save me if there's any God,"
But, even so, God saved me; and, being dashed
From error on to error, every turn
800 Still brought me nearer to the central truth.

I thought so. All this anguish in the thick
Of men's opinions…press and counter-press,
Now up, now down, now underfoot, and now
Emergent…all the best of it, perhaps,
805 But throws you back upon a noble trust
And use of your own instinct,—merely proves
Pure reason stronger than bare inference
At strongest. Try it,—fix against heaven's wall
The scaling-ladders of school logic—mount
810 Step by step!—sight goes faster; that still ray
Which strikes out from you, how, you cannot tell,
And why, you know not (did you eliminate,
That such as you indeed should analyse?)
Goes straight and fast as light, and high as God.

815 The cygnet finds the water, but the man
Is born in ignorance of his element
And feels out blind at first, disorganised
By sin i' the blood,—his spirit-insight dulled
And crossed by his sensations. Presently
820 He feels it quicken in the dark sometimes,
When, mark, be reverent, be obedient,
For such dumb motions of imperfect life

Are oracles of vital Deity
Attesting the Hereafter. Let who says
825 "The soul's a clean white paper," rather say,
A palimpsest, a prophet's holograph
Defiled, erased and covered by a monk's,—
The apocalypse, by a Longus! poring on
Which obscene text, we may discern perhaps
830 Some fair, fine trace of what was written once,
Some upstroke of an alpha and omega
Expressing the old scripture.
                              Books, books, books!
I had found the secret of a garret-room
Piled high with cases in my father's name,
835 Piled high, packed large,—where, creeping in and
     out
Against the giant fossils of my past,
Like some small nimble mouse between the ribs
Of a mastodon, I nibbled here and there
At this or that box, pulling through the gap,
840 In heats of terror, haste, victorious joy,
The first book first. And how I felt it beat
Under my pillow, in the morning's dark,
An hour before the sun would let me read!
My books! At last because the time was ripe,
845 I chanced upon the poets.
                              As the earth
Plunges in fury, when the internal fires
Have reached and pricked her heart, and, throwing
     flat
The marts and temples, the triumphal gates
And towers of observation, clears herself
850 To elemental freedom—thus, my soul,
At poetry's divine first finger-touch,
Let go conventions and sprang up surprised,
Convicted of the great eternities
Before two worlds.
                              What's this, Aurora Leigh,
855 You write so of the poets, and not laugh?
Those virtuous liars, dreamers after dark,
Exaggerators of the sun and moon,
And soothsayers in a tea-cup?

                        I write so
Of the only truth-tellers now left to God,
860 The only speakers of essential truth,
Opposed to relative, comparative,
And temporal truths; the only holders by
His sun-skirts, through conventional gray glooms;
The only teachers who instruct mankind
865 From just a shadow on a charnel-wall
To find man's veritable stature out
Erect, sublime,—the measure of a man,
And that's the measure of an angel, says
The apostle. Ay, and while your common men
870 Lay telegraphs, gauge railroads, reign, reap, dine,
And dust the flaunty carpets of the world
For kings to walk on, or our president,
The poet suddenly will catch them up
With his voice like a thunder,—"This is soul,
875 This is life, this word is being said in heaven,
Here's God down on us! what are you about?"
How all those workers start amid their work,
Look round, look up, and feel, a moment's space,
That carpet-dusting, though a pretty trade,
880 Is not the imperative labour after all.

My own best poets, am I one with you,
That thus I love you,—or but one through love?
Does all this smell of thyme about my feet
Conclude my visit to your holy hill
885 In personal presence, or but testify
The rustling of your vesture through my dreams
With influent odours? When my joy and pain,
My thought and aspiration like the stops
Of pipe or flute, are absolutely dumb
890 Unless melodious, do you play on me
My pipers,—and if, sooth, you did not blow,
Would no sound come? or is the music mine,
As a man's voice or breath is called his own,
Inbreathed by the Life-breather? There's a doubt
895 For cloudy seasons!
                        But the sun was high
When first I felt my pulses set themselves

For concord; when the rhythmic turbulence
Of blood and brain swept outward upon words,
As wind upon the alders, blanching them
900 By turning up their under-natures till
They trembled in dilation. O delight
And triumphs of the poet, who would say
A man's mere "yes," a woman's common "no,"
A little human hope of that or this,
905 And says the word so that it burns you through
With a special revelation, shakes the heart
Of all the men and women in the world,
As if one came back from the dead and spoke,
With eyes too happy, a familiar thing
910 Become divine i' the utterance! while for him
The poet, speaker, he expands with joy;
The palpitating angel in his flesh
Thrills inly with consenting fellowship
To those innumerous spirits who sun themselves
915 Outside of time.
                        O life, O poetry,
—Which means life in life! cognisant of life
Beyond this blood-beat, passionate for truth
Beyond these senses!—poetry, my life,
My eagle, with both grappling feet still hot
920 From Zeus's thunder, who hast ravished me
Away from all the shepherds, sheep, and dogs,
And set me in the Olympian roar and round
Of luminous faces for a cup-bearer,
To keep the mouths of all the godheads moist
925 For everlasting laughters,—I myself
Half drunk across the beaker with their eyes!
How those gods look!
                        Enough so, Ganymede,
We shall not bear above a round or two.
We drop the golden cup at Heré's foot
930 And swoon back to the earth,—and find ourselves
Face-down among the pine-cones, cold with dew,
While the dogs bark, and many a shepherd scoffs,
"What's come now to the youth?" Such ups and
        downs
Have poets.

Am I such indeed? The name
935 Is royal, and to sign it like a queen
Is what I dare not,—though some royal blood
Would seem to tingle in me now and then,
With sense of power and ache,—with imposthumes
And manias usual to the race. Howbeit
940 I dare not: 'tis too easy to go mad
And ape a Bourbon in a crown of straws;
The thing's too common.
                                    Many fervent souls
Strike rhyme on rhyme, who would strike steel on
        steel
If steel had offered, in a restless heat
945 Of doing something. Many tender souls
Have strung their losses on a rhyming thread,
As children cowslips: the more pains they take,
The work more withers. Young men, ay, and maids,
Too often sow their wild oats in tame verse,
950 Before they sit down under their own vine
And live for use. Alas, near all the birds
Will sing at dawn,—and yet we do not take
The chaffering swallow for the holy lark.
In those days, though, I never analysed,
955 Not even myself. Analysis comes late.
You catch a sight of Nature, earliest,
In full front sun-face, and your eyelids wink
And drop before the wonder of't; you miss
The form, through seeing the light. I lived, those
        days,
960 And wrote because I lived—unlicensed else;
My heart beat in my brain. Life's violent flood
Abolished bounds,—and, which my neighbour's
        field,
Which mine, what mattered? it is thus in youth!
We play at leap-frog over the god Term;
965 The love within us and the love without
Are mixed, confounded; if we are loved or love,
We scarce distinguish: thus, with other power;
Being acted on and acting seem the same:
In that first onrush of life's chariot-wheels,
970 We know not if the forests move or we.

And so, like most young poets, in a flush
Of individual life I poured myself
Along the veins of others, and achieved
Mere lifeless imitations of live verse,
975 And made the living answer for the dead,
Profaning nature. "Touch not, do not taste,
Nor handle,"—we're too legal, who write young:
We beat the phorminx till we hurt our thumbs,
As if still ignorant of counterpoint;
980 We call the Muse,—"O Muse, benignant Muse,"—
As if we had seen her purple-braided head,
With the eyes in it, start between the boughs
As often as a stag's. What make-believe,
With so much earnest! what effete results
985 From virile efforts! what cold wire-drawn odes
From such white heats!—bucolics, where the cows
Would scare the writer if they splashed the mud
In lashing off the flies,—didactics, driven
Against the heels of what the master said;
990 And counterfeiting epics, shrill with trumps
A babe might blow between two straining cheeks
Of bubbled rose, to make his mother laugh;
And elegiac griefs, and songs of love,
Like cast-off nosegays picked up on the road,
995 The worse for being warm: all these things, writ
On happy mornings, with a morning heart,
That leaps for love, is active for resolve,
Weak for art only. Oft, the ancient forms
Will thrill, indeed, in carrying the young blood.
1000 The wine-skins, now and then, a little warped,
Will crack even, as the new wine gurgles in.
Spare the old bottles!—spill not the new wine.

By Keats's soul, the man who never stepped
In gradual progress like another man,
1005 But, turning grandly on his central self,
Ensphered himself in twenty perfect years
And died, not young (the life of a long life
Distilled to a mere drop, falling like a tear
Upon the world's cold cheek to make it burn
1010 For ever); by that strong excepted soul,

I count it strange and hard to understand
That nearly all young poets should write old,
That Pope was sexagenary at sixteen,
And beardless Byron academical,
015 And so with others. It may be perhaps
Such have not settled long and deep enough
In trance, to attain to clairvoyance,—and still
The memory mixes with the vision, spoils,
And works it turbid.
          Or perhaps, again,
020 In order to discover the Muse-Sphinx,
The melancholy desert must sweep round,
Behind you as before.—
             For me, I wrote
False poems, like the rest, and thought them true
Because myself was true in writing them.
025 I peradventure have writ true ones since
With less complacence.
           But I could not hide
My quickening inner life from those at watch.
They saw a light at a window, now and then,
They had not set there: who had set it there?
030 My father's sister started when she caught
My soul agaze in my eyes. She could not say
I had no business with a sort of soul,
But plainly she objected,—and demurred
That souls were dangerous things to carry straight
035 Through all the spilt saltpetre of the world.
She said sometimes "Aurora, have you done
Your task this morning? have you read that book?
And are you ready for the crochet here?"—
As if she said "I know there's something wrong;
040 I know I have not ground you down enough
To flatten and bake you to a wholesome crust
For household uses and proprieties,
Before the rain has got into my barn
And set the grains a-sprouting. What, you're green
045 With out-door impudence? you almost grow?"
To which I answered, "Would she hear my task,
And verify my abstract of the book?
Or should I sit down to the crochet work?

Was such her pleasure?" Then I sat and teased
1050 The patient needle till it split the thread,
Which oozed off from it in meandering lace
From hour to hour. I was not, therefore, sad;
My soul was singing at a work apart
Behind the wall of sense, as safe from harm
1055 As sings the lark when sucked up out of sight
In vortices of glory and blue air.

And so, through forced work and spontaneous work,
The inner life informed the outer life,
Reduced the irregular blood to a settled rhythm,
1060 Made cool the forehead with fresh-sprinkling
    dreams,
And, rounding to the spheric soul the thin,
Pined body, struck a colour up the cheeks
Though somewhat faint. I clenched my brows
    across
My blue eyes greatening in the looking-glass,
1065 And said "We'll live, Aurora! we'll be strong.
The dogs are on us—but we will not die."

Whoever lives true life will love true love.
I learnt to love that England. Very oft,
Before the day was born, or otherwise
1070 Through secret windings of the afternoons,
I threw my hunters off and plunged myself
Among the deep hills, as a hunted stag
Will take the waters, shivering with the fear
And passion of the course. And when at last
1075 Escaped, so many a green slope built on slope
Betwixt me and the enemy's house behind,
I dared to rest, or wander, in a rest
Made sweeter for the step upon the grass,
And view the ground's most gentle dimplement
1080 (As if God's finger touched but did not press
In making England), such an up and down
Of verdure,—nothing too much up or down,
A ripple of land; such little hills, the sky
Can stoop to tenderly and the wheatfields climb;
1085 Such nooks of valleys lined with orchises,

Fed full of noises by invisible streams;
And open pastures where you scarcely tell
White daisies from white dew,—at intervals
The mythic oaks and elm-trees standing out
1090 Self-poised upon their prodigy of shade,—
I thought my father's land was worthy too
Of being my Shakespeare's.

              Very oft alone,
Unlicensed; not unfrequently with leave
To walk the third with Romney and his friend
1095 The rising painter, Vincent Carrington,
Whom men judge hardly as bee-bonneted,
Because he holds that, paint a body well,
You paint a soul by implication, like
The grand first Master. Pleasant walks! for if
1100 He said "When I was last in Italy,"
It sounded as an instrument that's played
Too far off for the tune—and yet it's fine
To listen.

        Often we walked only two
If cousin Romney pleased to walk with me.
1105 We read, or talked, or quarrelled, as it chanced.
We were not lovers, nor even friends well-matched:
Say rather, scholars upon different tracks,
And thinkers disagreed: he, overfull
Of what is, and I, haply, overbold
1110 For what might be.

           But then the thrushes sang,
And shook my pulses and the elms' new leaves:
At which I turned, and held my finger up,
And bade him mark that, howsoe'er the world
Went ill, as he related, certainly
1115 The thrushes still sang in it. At the word
His brow would soften,—and he bore with me
In melancholy patience, not unkind,
While breaking into voluble ecstasy
I flattered all the beauteous country round,
1120 As poets use, the skies, the clouds, the fields,
The happy violets hiding from the roads
The primroses run down to, carrying gold;
The tangled hedgerows, where the cows push out

Impatient horns and tolerant churning mouths
1125 'Twixt dripping ash-boughs,—hedgerows all alive
With birds and gnats and large white butterflies
While look as if the May-flower had caught life
And palpitated forth upon the wind;
Hills, vales, woods, netted in a silver mist,
1130 Farms, granges, doubled up among the hills;
And cattle grazing in the watered vales,
And cottage-chimneys smoking from the woods,
And cottage-gardens smelling everywhere,
Confused with smell of orchards. "See," I said,
1135 "And see! is God not with us on the earth?
And shall we put Him down by aught we do?
Who says there's nothing for the poor and vile
Save poverty and wickedness? behold!"
And ankle-deep in English grass I leaped
1140 And clapped my hands, and called all very fair.

In the beginning when God called all good,
Even then was evil near us, it is writ;
But we indeed who call things good and fair,
The evil is upon us while we speak;
1145 Deliver us from evil, let us pray.

SECOND BOOK

Times followed one another. Came a morn
I stood upon the brink of twenty years,
And looked before and after, as I stood
Woman and artist,—either incomplete,
5 Both credulous of completion. There I held
The whole creation in my little cup,
And smiled with thirsty lips before I drank
"Good health to you and me, sweet neighbour mine,
And all these peoples."

           I was glad, that day;
10 The June was in me, with its multitudes
Of nightingales all singing in the dark,
And rosebuds reddening where the calyx split.
I felt so young, so strong, so sure of God!

So glad, I could not choose be very wise!
15 And, old at twenty, was inclined to pull
My childhood backward in a childish jest
To see the face of't once more, and farewell!
In which fantastic mood I bounded forth
At early morning,—would not wait so long
20 As even to snatch my bonnet by the strings,
But, brushing a green trail across the lawn
With my gown in the dew, took will and away
Among the acacias of the shrubberies,
To fly my fancies in the open air
25 And keep my birthday, till my aunt awoke
To stop good dreams. Meanwhile I murmured on
As honeyed bees keep humming to themselves,
"The worthiest poets have remained uncrowned
Till death has bleached their foreheads to the bone;
30 And so with me it must be unless I prove
Unworthy of the grand adversity,
And certainly I would not fail so much.
What, therefore, if I crown myself to-day
In sport, not pride, to learn the feel of it,
35 Before my brows be numbed as Dante's own
To all the tender pricking of such leaves?
Such leaves! what leaves?"
                                    I pulled the branches down
To choose from.
                    "Not the bay! I choose no bay
(The fates deny us if we are overbold),
40 Nor myrtle—which means chiefly love; and love
Is something awful which one dares not touch
So early o' mornings. This verbena strains
The point of passionate fragrance; and hard by,
This guelder-rose, at far too slight a beck
45 Of the wind, will toss about her flower-apples.
Ah—there's my choice,—that ivy on the wall,
That headlong ivy! not a leaf will grow
But thinking of a wreath. Large leaves, smooth
    leaves,
Serrated like my vines, and half as green.
50 I like such ivy, bold to leap a height
'Twas strong to climb; as good to grow on graves

As twist about a thyrsus; pretty too
(And that's not ill) when twisted round a comb."
Thus speaking to myself, half singing it,
55 Because some thoughts are fashioned like a bell
To ring with once being touched, I drew a wreath
Drenched, blinding me with dew, across my brow,
And fastening it behind so, turning faced
…My public!—cousin Romney—with a mouth
60 Twice graver than his eyes.
                                        I stood there fixed,—
My arms up, like the caryatid, sole
Of some abolished temple, helplessly
Persistent in a gesture which derides
A former purpose. Yet my blush was flame,
65 As if from flax, not stone.
                                "Aurora Leigh,
The earliest of Auroras!"
                                        Hand stretched out
I clasped, as shipwrecked men will clasp a hand,
Indifferent to the sort of palm. The tide
Had caught me at my pastime, writing down
70 My foolish name too near upon the sea
Which drowned me with a blush as foolish. "You,
My cousin!"
                    The smile died out in his eyes
And dropped upon his lips, a cold dead weight,
For just a moment, "Here's a book I found!
75 No name writ on it—poems, by the form;
Some Greek upon the margin,—lady's Greek
Without the accents. Read it? Not a word.
I saw at once the thing had witchcraft in't,
Whereof the reading calls up dangerous spirits:
80 I rather bring it to the witch."
                                        "My book.
You found it"…
                        "In the hollow by the stream
That beech leans down into—of which you said
The Oread in it has a Naiad's heart
And pines for waters."
                            "Thank you."
                                            "Thanks to *you*

85 My cousin! that I have seen you not too much
Witch, scholar, poet, dreamer, and the rest,
To be a woman also."
                          With a glance
The smile rose in his eyes again and touched
The ivy on my forehead, light as air.
90 I answered gravely "Poets needs must be
Or men or women—more's the pity."
                                    "Ah,
But men, and still less women, happily,
Scarce need be poets. Keep to the green wreath,
Since even dreaming of the stone and bronze
95 Brings headaches, pretty cousin, and defiles
The clean white morning dresses."
                                  "So you judge!
Because I love the beautiful I must
Love pleasure chiefly, and be overcharged
For ease and whiteness! well, you know the world,
100 And only miss your cousin, 'tis not much.
But learn this; I would rather take my part
With God's Dead, who afford to walk in white
Yet spread His glory, than keep quiet here
And gather up my feet from even a step
105 For fear to soil my gown in so much dust.
I choose to walk at all risks.—Here, if heads
That hold a rhythmic thought, much ache perforce,
For my part I choose headaches,—and to-day's
My birthday."
              "Dear Aurora, choose instead
110 To cure them. You have balsams."
                                   "I perceive.
The headache is too noble for my sex.
You think the heartache would sound decenter,
Since that's the woman's special, proper ache,
And altogether tolerable, except
115 To a woman."
              Saying which, I loosed my wreath,
And swinging it beside me as I walked,
Half-petulant, half-playful, as we walked,
I sent a sidelong look to find his thought,—
As falcon set on falconer's finger may,

120 With sidelong head, and startled, braving eye,
Which means, "You'll see—you'll see! I'll soon take
     flight,
You shall not hinder." He, as shaking out
His hand and answering "Fly then," did not speak,
Except by such a gesture. Silently
125 We paced, until, just coming into sight
Of the house-windows, he abruptly caught
At one end of the swinging wreath, and said
"Aurora!" There I stopped short, breath and all.

"Aurora, let's be serious, and throw by
130 This game of head and heart. Life means, be sure,
Both heart and head,—both active, both complete,
And both in earnest. Men and women make
The world, as head and heart make human life.
Work man, work woman, since there's work to do
135 In this beleaguered earth, for head and heart,
And thought can never do the work of love:
But work for ends, I mean for uses, not
For such sleek fringes (do you call them ends,
Still less God's glory?) as we sew ourselves
140 Upon the velvet of those baldaquins[1]
Held 'twixt us and the sun. That book of yours,
I have not read a page of; but I toss
A rose up—it falls calyx down, you see!
The chances are that, being a woman, young
145 And pure, with such a pair of large, calm eyes,
You write as well…and ill…upon the whole,
As other women. If as well, what then?
If even a little better,…still, what then?
We want the Best in art now, or no art.
150 The time is done for facile settings up
Of minnow gods, nymphs here and tritons there;
The polytheists have gone out in God,
That unity of Bests. No best, no God!
And so with art, we say. Give art's divine,
155 Direct, indubitable, real as grief,
Or leave us to the grief we grow ourselves
Divine by overcoming with mere hope

---

[1] a ceremonial canopy for a doorway, altar, or throne.

And most prosaic patience. You, you are young
As Eve with nature's daybreak on her face,
160 But this same world you are come to, dearest coz,
Has done with keeping birthdays, saves her wreaths
To hang upon her ruins,—and forgets
To rhyme the cry with which she still beats back
Those savage, hungry dogs that hunt her down
165 To the empty grave of Christ. The world's hard pressed;
The sweat of labour in the early curse
Has (turning acrid in six thousand years)
Become the sweat of torture. Who has time,
An hour's time…think!—to sit upon a bank
170 And hear the cymbal tinkle in white hands?
When Egypt's slain, I say, let Miriam sing!—
Before—where's Moses?"

                "Ah, exactly that.
Where's Moses?—is a Moses to be found?
You'll seek him vainly in the bulrushes,
175 While I in vain touch cymbals. Yet concede,
Such sounding brass has done some actual good
(The application in a woman's hand,
If that were credible, being scarcely spoilt,)
In colonising beehives."

                "There it is!—
180 You play beside a death-bed like a child,
Yet measure to yourself a prophet's place
To teach the living. None of all these things
Can women understand. You generalise
Oh, nothing,—not even grief! Your quick-breathed
    hearts,
185 So sympathetic to the personal pang,
Close on each separate knife-stroke, yielding up
A whole life at each wound, incapable
Of deepening, widening a large lap of life
To hold the world-full woe. The human race
190 To you means, such a child, or such a man,
You saw one morning waiting in the cold,
Beside that gate, perhaps. You gather up
A few such cases, and when strong sometimes
Will write of factories and of slaves, as if
195 Your father were a negro, and your son

A spinner in the mills. All's yours and you,
All, coloured with your blood, or otherwise
Just nothing to you. Why, I call you hard
To general suffering. Here's the world half-blind
200 With intellectual light, half-brutalised
With civilisation, having caught the plague
In silks from Tarsus, shrieking east and west
Along a thousand railroads, mad with pain
And sin too!…does one woman of you all
205 (You who weep easily) grow pale to see
This tiger shake his cage?—does one of you
Stand still from dancing, stop from stringing pearls,
And pine and die because of the great sum
Of universal anguish?—Show me a tear
210 Wet as Cordelia's, in eyes bright as yours,
Because the world is mad. You cannot count,
That you should weep for this account, not you!
You weep for what you know. A red-haired child
Sick in a fever, if you touch him once,
215 Though but so little as with a finger-tip,
Will set you weeping; but a million sick…
You could as soon weep for the rule of three
Or compound fractions. Therefore, this same world,
Uncomprehended by you, must remain
220 Uninfluenced by you.—Women as you are,
Mere women, personal and passionate,
You give us doating mothers, and perfect wives,
Sublime Madonnas, and enduring saints!
We get no Christ from you,—and verily
225 We shall not get a poet, in my mind."

"With which conclusion you conclude!"…
                           "But this,
That you, Aurora, with the large live brow
And steady eyelids, cannot condescend
To play at art, as children play at swords,
230 To show a pretty spirit, chiefly admired
Because true action is impossible.
You never can be satisfied with praise
Which men give women when they judge a book
Not as mere work but as mere woman's work,

235 Expressing the comparative respect
Which means the absolute scorn. 'Oh, excellent,
What grace, what facile turns, what fluent sweeps,
What delicate discernment…almost thought!
The book does honour to the sex, we hold.
240 Among our female authors we make room
For this fair writer, and congratulate
The country that produces in these times
Such women, competent to…spell.'"
                              "Stop there,"
I answered, burning through his thread of talk
245 With a quick flame of emotion,—"You have read
My soul, if not my book, and argue well
I would not condescend…we will not say
To such a kind of praise (a worthless end
Is praise of all kinds), but to such a use
250 Of holy art and golden life. I am young,
And peradventure weak—you tell me so—
Through being a woman. And, for all the rest,
Take thanks for justice. I would rather dance
At fairs on tight-rope, till the babies dropped
255 Their gingerbread for joy,—than shift the types
For tolerable verse, intolerable
To men who act and suffer. Better far
Pursue a frivolous trade by serious means,
Than a sublime art frivolously."
                              "You,
260 Choose nobler work than either, O moist eyes
And hurrying lips and heaving heart! We are young,
Aurora, you and I. The world,—look round,—
The world, we're come to late, is swollen hard
With perished generations and their sins:
265 The civiliser's spade grinds horribly
On dead men's bones, and cannot turn up soil
That's otherwise than fetid. All success
Proves partial failure; all advance implies
What's left behind; all triumph, something crushed
270 At the chariot-wheels; all government, some wrong
And rich men make the poor, who curse the rich,
Who agonise together, rich and poor,
Under and over, in the social spasm

And crisis of the ages. Here's an age
275 That makes its own vocation! here we have stepped
Across the bounds of time! here's nought to see,
But just the rich man and just Lazarus,
And both in torments, with a mediate gulf,
Though not a hint of Abraham's bosom. Who
280 Being man, Aurora, can stand calmly by
And view these things, and never tease his soul
For some great cure? No physic for this grief,
In all the earth and heavens too?"
                              "You believe
In God, for your part?—ay? that He who makes
285 Can make good things from ill things, best from
        worst,
As men plant tulips upon dunghills when
They wish them finest?"
                              "True. A death-heat is
The same as life-heat, to be accurate,
And in all nature is no death at all,
290 As men account of death, so long as God
Stands witnessing for life perpetually,
By being just God. That's abstract truth, I know,
Philosophy, or sympathy with God:
But I, I sympathise with man, not God
295 (I think I was a man for chiefly this),
And when I stand beside a dying bed,
'Tis death to me. Observe,—it had not much
Consoled the race of mastodons to know,
Before they went to fossil, that anon
300 Their place would quicken with the elephant.
They were not elephants but mastodons;
And I, a man, as men are now and not
As men may be hereafter, feel with men
In the agonising present."
                              "Is it so,"
305 I said, "my cousin? is the world so bad,
While I hear nothing of it through the trees?
The world was always evil,—but so bad?"

"So bad, Aurora. Dear, my soul is grey
With poring over the long sum of ill;

310 So much for vice, so much for discontent,
So much for the necessities of power,
So much for the connivances of fear,
Coherent in statistical despairs
With such a total of distracted life,…

315 To see it down in figures on a page,
Plain, silent, clear, as God sees through the earth
The sense of all the graves,—that's terrible
For one who is not God, and cannot right
The wrong he looks on. May I choose indeed,

320 But vow away my years, my means, my aims,
Among the helpers, if there's any help
In such a social strait? The common blood
That swings along my veins is strong enough
To draw me to this duty."
                              Then I spoke.

325 "I have not stood long on the strand of life,
And these salt waters have had scarcely time
To creep so high up as to wet my feet:
I cannot judge these tides—I shall, perhaps.
A woman's always younger than a man

330 At equal years, because she is disallowed
Maturing by the outdoor sun and air,
And kept in long-clothes past the age to walk.
Ah well, I know you men judge otherwise!
You think a woman ripens, as a peach,

335 In the cheeks chiefly. Pass it to me now;
I'm young in age, and younger still, I think,
As a woman. But a child may say amen
To a bishop's prayer and feel the way it goes,
And I, incapable to loose the knot

340 Of social questions, can approve, applaud
August compassion, Christian thoughts that shoot
Beyond the vulgar white of personal aims.
Accept my reverence."
                          There he glowed on me
With all his face and eyes. "No other help?"

345 Said he—"no more than so?"
                              "What help?" I asked.
"You'd scorn my help,—as Nature's self, you say,
Has scorned to put her music in my mouth

Because a woman's. Do you now turn round
And ask for what a woman cannot give?"

350 "For what she only can, I turn and ask,"
He answered, catching up my hands in his,
And dropping on me from his high-eaved brow
The full weight of his soul,—"I ask for love,
And that, she can; for life in fellowship

355 Through bitter duties—that, I know she can;
For wifehood—will she?"
                          "Now," I said, "may God
Be witness 'twixt us two!" and with the word,
Meseemed I floated into a sudden light
Above his stature,—"am I proved too weak

360 To stand alone, yet strong enough to bear
Such leaners on my shoulder? poor to think,
Yet rich enough to sympathise with thought?
Incompetent to sing, as blackbirds can,
Yet competent to love, like HIM?"
                                      I paused;

365 Perhaps I darkened, as the lighthouse will
That turns upon the sea. "It's always so.
Anything does for a wife."
                              "Aurora, dear,
And dearly honoured,"—he pressed in at once
With eager utterance,—"you translate me ill.

370 I do not contradict my thought of you
Which is most reverent, with another thought
Found less so. If your sex is weak for art
(And I, who said so, did but honour you
By using truth in courtship), it is strong

375 For life and duty. Place your fecund heart
In mine, and let us blossom for the world
That wants love's colour in the grey of time.
My talk, meanwhile, is arid to you, ay,
Since all my talk can only set you where

380 You look down coldly on the arena-heaps
Of headless bodies, shapeless, indistinct!
The Judgment-Angel scarce would find his way
Through such a heap of generalised distress
To the individual man with lips and eyes,

385 Much less Aurora. Ah, my sweet, come down,
And hand in hand we'll go where yours shall touch
These victims, one by one! till, one by one,
The formless, nameless trunk of every man
Shall seem to wear a head with hair you know,
390 And every woman catch your mother's face
To melt you into passion."
                                        "I am a girl,"
I answered slowly; "you do well to name
My mother's face. Though far too early, alas,
God's hand did interpose 'twixt it and me,
395 I know so much of love as used to shine
In that face and another. Just so much;
No more indeed at all. I have not seen
So much love since, I pray you pardon me,
As answers even to make a marriage with
400 In this cold land of England. What you love
Is not a woman, Romney, but a cause:
You want a helpmate, not a mistress, sir,
A wife to help your ends,—in her no end.
Your cause is noble, your ends excellent,
405 But I, being most unworthy of these and that,
Do otherwise conceive of love. Farewell."

"Farewell, Aurora? you reject me thus?"
He said.
              "Sir, you were married long ago.
You have a wife already whom you love,
410 Your social theory. Bless you both, I say.
For my part, I am scarcely meek enough
To be the handmaid of a lawful spouse.
Do I look a Hagar,[1] think you?"
                                        "So you jest."

"Nay, so, I speak in earnest," I replied.
415 "You treat of marriage too much like, at least,
A chief apostle: you would bear with you
A wife...a sister...shall we speak it out?
A sister of charity."
                            "Then, must it be

---
[1] the mother of Ishmael by Abraham.

Indeed farewell? And was I so far wrong
420 In hope and in illusion, when I took
The woman to be nobler than the man,
Yourself the noblest woman, in the use
And comprehension of what love is,—love,
That generates the likeness of itself
425 Through all heroic duties? so far wrong,
In saying bluntly, venturing truth on love,
'Come, human creature, love and work with me,'—
Instead of 'Lady, thou art wondrous fair,
And, where the Graces walk before, the Muse
430 Will follow at the lightning of their eyes,
And where the Muse walks, lovers need to creep:
Turn round and love me, or I die of love.'"

With quiet indignation I broke in.
"You misconceive the question like a man,
435 Who sees a woman as the complement
Of his sex merely. You forget too much
That every creature, female as the male,
Stands single in responsible act and thought
As also in birth and death. Whoever says
440 To a loyal woman, 'Love and work with me,'
Will get fair answers if the work and love,
Being good themselves, are good for her—the best
She was born for. Women of a softer mood,
Surprised by men when scarcely awake to life,
445 Will sometimes only hear the first word, love,
And catch up with it any kind of work,
Indifferent, so that dear love go with it.
I do not blame such women, though, for love,
They pick much oakum; earth's fanatics make
450 Too frequently heaven's saints. But *me* your work
Is not the best for,—nor your love the best,
Nor able to commend the kind of work
For love's sake merely. Ah, you force me, sir,
To be overbold in speaking of myself:
455 I too have my vocation,—work to do,
The heavens and earth have set me since I changed
My father's face for theirs, and, though your world
Were twice as wretched as you represent,

Most serious work, most necessary work
60 As any of the economists.' Reform,
Make trade a Christian possibility,
And individual right no general wrong;
Wipe out earth's furrows of the Thine and Mine,
And leave one green for men to play at bowls,
65 With innings for them all!…What then, indeed,
If mortals are not greater by the head
Than any of their prosperities? what then,
Unless the artist keep up open roads
Betwixt the seen and unseen,—bursting through
70 The best of your conventions with his best,
The speakable, imaginable best
God bids him speak, to prove what lies beyond
Both speech and imagination? A starved man
Exceeds a fat beast: we'll not barter, sir,
75 The beautiful for barley.—And, even so,
I hold you will not compass your poor ends
Of barley-feeding and material ease,
Without a poet's individualism
To work your universal. It takes a soul,
80 To move a body: it takes a high-souled man,
To move the masses, even to a cleaner stye:
It takes the ideal, to blow a hair's-breadth off
The dust of the actual.—Ah, your Fouriers[1] failed,
Because not poets enough to understand
85 That life develops from within.—For me,
Perhaps I am not worthy, as you say,
Of work like this: perhaps a woman's soul
Aspires, and not creates: yet we aspire,
And yet I'll try out your perhapses, sir,
90 And if I fail…why, burn me up my straw
Like other false works—I'll not ask for grace;
Your scorn is better, cousin Romney. I
Who love my art, would never wish it lower
To suit my stature. I may love my art.
95 You'll grant that even a woman may love art,
Seeing that to waste true love on anything
Is womanly, past question."
                                    I retain

_____
[1] Charles Fourier (1772–1837), French social theorist.

The very last word which I said that day,
As you the creaking of the door, years past,
500 Which let upon you such disabling news
You ever after have been graver. He,
His eyes, the motions in his silent mouth,
Were fiery points on which my words were caught,
Transfixed for ever in my memory
505 For his sake, not their own. And yet I know
I did not love him…nor he me…that's sure…
And what I said is unrepented of,
As truth is always. Yet…a princely man!—
If hard to me, heroic for himself!
510 He bears down on me through the slanting years,
The stronger for the distance. If he had loved,
Ay, loved me, with that retributive face,…
I might have been a common woman now
And happier, less known and less left alone,
515 Perhaps a better woman after all,
With chubby children hanging on my neck
To keep me low and wise. Ah me, the vines
That bear such fruit are proud to stoop with it.
The palm stands upright in a realm of sand.

520 And I, who spoke the truth then, stand upright,
Still worthy of having spoken out the truth,
By being content I spoke it though it set
Him there, me here.—O woman's vile remorse,
To hanker after a mere name, a show,
525 A supposition, a potential love!
Does every man who names love in our lives
Become a power for that? is love's true thing
So much best to us, that what personates love
Is next best? A potential love, forsooth!
530 I'm not so vile. No, no—he cleaves, I think,
This man, this image,—chiefly for the wrong
And shock he gave my life, in finding me
Precisely where the devil of my youth
Had set me, on those mountain-peaks of hope
535 All glittering with the dawn-dew, all erect
And famished for the noon,—exclaiming, while
I looked for empire and much tribute, "Come,

I have some worthy work for thee below.
Come, sweep my barns and keep my hospitals,
540 And I will pay thee with a current coin
Which men give women."
                                As we spoke, the grass
Was trod in haste beside us, and my aunt,
With smile distorted by the sun,—face, voice
As much at issue with the summer-day
545 As if you brought a candle out of doors,
Broke in with "Romney, here!—My child, entreat
Your cousin to the house, and have your talk,
If girls must talk upon their birthdays. Come."

He answered for me calmly, with pale lips
550 That seemed to motion for a smile in vain,
"The talk is ended, madam, where we stand.
Your brother's daughter has dismissed me here;
And all my answer can be better said
Beneath the trees, than wrong by such a word
555 Your house's hospitalities. Farewell."

With that he vanished. I could hear his heel
Ring bluntly in the lane, as down he leapt
The short way from us.—Then a measured speech
Withdrew me. "What means this, Aurora Leigh?
560 My brother's daughter has dismissed my guests?"

The lion in me felt the keeper's voice
Through all its quivering dewlaps; I was quelled
Before her,—meekened to the child she knew:
I prayed her pardon, said "I had little thought
565 To give dismissal to a guest of hers,
In letting go a friend of mine who came
To take me into service as a wife,—
No more than that, indeed."
                                "No more, no more?
Pray Heaven," she answered, "that I was not mad.
570 I could not mean to tell her to her face
That Romney Leigh had asked me for a wife,
And I refused him?"
                                "Did he ask?" I said;

"I think he rather stooped to take me up
For certain uses which he found to do
575 For something called a wife. He never asked."

"What stuff!" she answered; "are they queens, these
      girls?
They must have mantles, stitched with twenty silks,
Spread out upon the ground, before they'll step
One footstep for the noblest lover born."

580 "But I am born," I said with firmness, "I,
To walk another way than his, dear aunt."

"You walk, you walk! A babe at thirteen months
Will walk as well as you," she cried in haste,
"Without a steadying finger. Why, you child,
585 God help you, you are groping in the dark,
For all this sunlight. You suppose, perhaps,
That you, sole offspring of an opulent man,
Are rich and free to choose a way to walk?
You think, and it's a reasonable thought,
590 That I, beside, being well to do in life,
Will leave my handful in my niece's hand
When death shall paralyse these fingers? Pray,
Pray, child, albeit I know you love me not,
As if you loved me, that I may not die!
595 For when I die and leave you, out you go
(Unless I make room for you in my grave),
Unhoused, unfed, my dear poor brother's lamb
(Ah heaven!—that pains!)—without a right to crop
A single blade of grass beneath these trees,
600 Or cast a lamb's small shadow on the lawn,
Unfed, unfolded! Ah, my brother, here's
The fruit you planted in your foreign loves!—
Ay, there's the fruit he planted! never look
Astonished at me with your mother's eyes,
605 For it was they who set you where you are,
An undowered orphan. Child, your father's choice
Of that said mother disinherited
His daughter, his and hers. Men do not think
Of sons and daughters, when they fall in love,

610 So much more than of sisters; otherwise
   He would have paused to ponder what he did,
   And shrunk before the clause in the entail
   Excluding offspring by a foreign wife
   (The clause set up a hundred years ago
615 By a Leigh who wedded a French dancing-girl
   And had his heart danced over in return);
   But this man shrank at nothing, never thought
   Of you, Aurora, any more than me—
   Your mother must have been a pretty thing,
620 For all the coarse Italian blacks and browns,
   To make a good man, which my brother was,
   Unchary of the duties to his house;
   But so it fell indeed. Our cousin Vane,
   Vane Leigh, the father of this Romney, wrote
625 Directly on your birth, to Italy,
   'I ask your baby daughter for my son,
   In whom the entail now merges by the law.
   Betroth her to us out of love, instead
   Of colder reasons, and she shall not lose
630 By love or law from henceforth'—so he wrote;
   A generous cousin was my cousin Vane.
   Remember how he drew you to his knee
   The year you came here, just before he died,
   And hollowed out his hands to hold your cheeks,
635 And wished them redder,—you remember Vane.
   And now his son, who represents our house,
   And holds the fiefs and manors in his place,
   To whom reverts my pittance when I die
   (Except a few books and a pair of shawls),
640 The boy is generous like him, and prepared
   To carry out his kindest word and thought
   To you, Aurora. Yes, a fine young man
   Is Romney Leigh; although the sun of youth
   Has shone too straight upon his brain, I know,
645 And fevered him with dreams of doing good
   To good-for-nothing people. But a wife
   Will put all right, and stroke his temples cool
   With healthy touches."…
                           I broke in at that.
   I could not lift my heavy heart to breathe

650 Till then, but then I raised it, and it fell
   In broken words like these—"No need to wait:
   The dream of doing good to…me, at least,
   Is ended, without waiting for a wife
   To cool the fever for him. We've escaped
655 That danger,—thank Heaven for it."
                                    "You," she cried,
   "Have got a fever. What, I talk and talk
   An hour long to you,—I instruct you how
   You cannot eat or drink or stand or sit
   Or even die, like any decent wretch
660 In all this unroofed and unfurnished world,
   Without your cousin,—and you still maintain
   There's room 'twixt him and you for flirting fans
   And running knots in eyebrows? You must have
   A pattern lover sighing on his knee?
665 You do not count enough, a noble heart
   (Above book-patterns) which this very morn
   Unclosed itself in two dear fathers' names
   To embrace your orphaned life? Fie, fie! But stay,
   I write a word, and counteract this sin."

670 She would have turned to leave me, but I clung.
   "O sweet my father's sister, hear my word
   Before you write yours. Cousin Vane did well,
   And cousin Romney well,—and I well too,
   In casting back with all my strength and will
675 The good they meant me. O my God, my God!
   God meant me good, too, when He hindered me
   From saying 'yes' this morning. If you write
   A word, it shall be 'no.' I say no, no!
   I tie up 'no' upon His altar-horns,
680 Quite out of reach of perjury! At least
   My soul is not a pauper; I can live
   At least my soul's life, without alms from men;
   And if it must be in heaven instead of earth,
   Let heaven look to it,—I am not afraid."

685 She seized my hands with both hers, strained them
        fast,
   And drew her probing and unscrupulous eyes

Right through me, body and heart. "Yet, foolish
   Sweet,
You love this man. I've watched you when he came,
And when he went, and when we've talked of him:
690   I am not old for nothing; I can tell
The weather-signs of love: you love this man."

Girls blush sometimes because they are alive,
Half wishing they were dead to save the shame.
The sudden blush devours them, neck and brow;
695   They have drawn too near the fire of life, like gnats,
And flare up bodily, wings and all. What then?
Who's sorry for a gnat...or girl?
                              I blushed.
I feel the brand upon my forehead now
Strike hot, sear deep, as guiltless men may feel
700   The felon's iron, say, and scorn the mark
Of what they are not. Most illogical
Irrational nature of our womanhood,
That blushes one way, feels another way,
And prays, perhaps another! After all,
705   We cannot be the equal of the male
Who rules his blood a little.
                              For although
I blushed indeed, as if I loved the man,
And her incisive smile, accrediting
That treason of false witness in my blush,
710   Did bow me downward like a swathe of grass
Below its level that struck me,—I attest
The conscious skies and all their daily suns,
I think I loved him not,—nor then, nor since,
Nor ever. Do we love the schoolmaster,
715   Being busy in the woods? much less, being poor,
The overseer of the parish? Do we keep
Our love to pay our debts with?
                              White and cold
I grew next moment. As my blood recoiled
From that imputed ignominy, I made
720   My heart great with it. Then, at last, I spoke,
Spoke veritable words but passionate,
Too passionate perhaps...ground up with sobs

To shapeless endings. She let fall my hands
And took her smile off, in sedate disgust,
725   As peradventure she had touched a snake,—
A dead snake, mind!—and, turning round, replied,
"We'll leave Italian manners, if you please.
I think you had an English father, child,
And ought to find it possible to speak
730   A quiet 'yes' or 'no,' like English girls,
Without convulsions. In another month
We'll take another answer—no, or yes."
With that, she left me in the garden-walk.

I had a father! yes, but long ago—
735   How long it seemed that moment. Oh, how far,
How far and safe, God, dost thou keep thy saints
When once gone from us! We may call against
The lighted windows of thy fair June-heaven
Where all the souls are happy,—and not one,
740   Not even my father, look from work or play
To ask, "Who is it that cries after us,
Below there, in the dusk?" Yet formerly
He turned his face upon me quick enough,
If I said "Father." Now I might cry loud;
745   The little lark reached higher with his song
Than I with crying. Oh, alone, alone,—
Not troubling any in heaven, nor any on earth,
I stood there in the garden, and looked up
The deaf blue sky that brings the roses out
750   On such June mornings.
                              You who keep account
Of crisis and transition in this life,
Set down the first time Nature says plain "no"
To some "yes" in you, and walks over you
In gorgeous sweeps of scorn. We all begin
755   By singing with the birds, and running fast
With June-days, hand in hand: but once, for all,
The birds must sing against us, and the sun
Strike down upon us like a friend's sword caught
By an enemy to slay us, while we read
760   The dear name on the blade which bites at us!—
That's bitter and convincing: after that,

We seldom doubt that something in the large
Smooth order of creation, though no more
Than haply a man's footstep, has gone wrong.
765 Some tears fell down my cheeks, and then I smiled,
As those smile who have no face in the world
To smile back to them. I had lost a friend
In Romney Leigh; the thing was sure—a friend,
Who had looked at me most gently now and then,
770 And spoken of my favourite books, "our books,"
With such a voice! Well, voice and look were now
More utterly shut out from me I felt,
Than even my father's. Romney now was turned
To a benefactor, to a generous man,
775 Who had tied himself to marry…me, instead
Of such a woman, with low timorous lids
He lifted with a sudden word one day,
And left, perhaps, for my sake.—Ah, self-tied
By a contract, male Iphigenia[1] bound
780 At a fatal Aulis for the winds to change
(But loose him, they'll not change), he well might seem
A little cold and dominant in love!
He had a right to be dogmatical,
This poor, good Romney. Love, to him, was made
785 A simple law-clause. If I married him,
I should not dare to call my soul my own
Which so he had bought and paid for: every thought
And every heart-beat down there in the bill;
Not one found honestly deductible
790 From any use that pleased him! He might cut
My body into coins to give away
Among his other paupers; change my sons,
While I stood dumb as Griseld,[2] for black babes
Or piteous foundlings; might unquestioned set
795 My right hand teaching in the Ragged Schools,
My left hand washing in the Public Baths,

What time my angel of the Ideal stretched
Both his to me in vain. I could not claim
The poor right of a mouse in a trap, to squeal,
800 And take so much as pity from myself.

Farewell, good Romney! if I loved you even
I could but ill afford to let you be
So generous to me. Farewell, friend, since friend
Betwixt us two, forsooth, must be a word
805 So heavily overladen. And, since help
Must come to me from those who love me not,
Farewell, all helpers—I must help myself,
And am alone from henceforth.—Then I stooped
And lifted the soiled garland from the earth,
810 And set it on my head as bitterly
As when the Spanish monarch crowned the bones
Of his dead love. So be it. I preserve
That crown still,—in the drawer there! twas the first.
The rest are like it;—those Olympian crowns,
815 We run for, till we lose sight of the sun
In the dust of the racing chariots!
                              After that,
Before the evening fell, I had a note,
Which ran,—"Aurora, sweet Chaldean, you read
My meaning backward like your eastern books,
820 While I am from the west, dear. Read me now
A little plainer. Did you hate me quite
But yesterday? I loved you for my part;
I love you. If I spoke untenderly
This morning, my beloved, pardon it;
825 And comprehend me that I loved you so
I set you on the level of my soul,
And overwashed you with the bitter brine
Of some habitual thoughts. Henceforth, my flower,
Be planted out of reach of any such,
830 And lean the side you please, with all your leaves!
Write woman's verses and dream woman's dreams;
But let me feel your perfume in my home
To make my sabbath after working-days.
Bloom out your youth beside me,—be my wife."

---

[1] the daughter of Agamemnon who was sacrificed at Aulis when the Greek fleet was stranded during its voyage to Troy.

[2] the patient wife who survives the trials and tortures by her husband as he tests the limits of her devotion and obedience; a popular literary figure, there are different versions provided by Boccaccio, Petrarch, and Chaucer.

835 I wrote in answer—"We Chaldeans discern
Still farther than we read. I know your heart,
And shut it like the holy book it is,
Reserved for mild-eyed saints to pore upon
Betwixt their prayers at vespers. Well, you're right,
840 I did not surely hate you yesterday;
And yet I do not love you enough to-day
To wed you, cousin Romney. Take this word,
And let it stop you as a generous man
From speaking farther. You may tease, indeed,
845 And blow about my feelings or my leaves,
And here's my aunt will help you with east winds
And break a stalk, perhaps, tormenting me;
But certain flowers grow near as deep as trees,
And, cousin, you'll not move my root, not you,
850 With all your confluent storms. Then let me grow
Within my wayside hedge, and pass your way!
This flower has never as much to say to you
As the antique tomb which said to travellers, 'Pause,
Siste, viator.'" Ending thus, I sighed.

855 The next week passed in silence, so the next,
And several after: Romney did not come
Nor my aunt chide me. I lived on and on,
As if my heart were kept beneath a glass,
And everybody stood, all eyes and ears,
860 To see and hear it tick. I could not sit,
Nor walk, nor take a book, nor lay it down,
Nor sew on steadily, nor drop a stitch,
And a sigh with it, but I felt her looks
Still cleaving to me, like the sucking asp
865 To Cleopatra's breast, persistently
Through the intermittent pantings. Being observed,
When observation is not sympathy,
Is just being tortured. If she said a word,
A "thank you," or an "if it please you, dear,"
870 She meant a commination,[1] or, at best,
An exorcism against the devildom
Which plainly held me. So with all the house.

---

[1] a threat of divine vengeance.

Susannah could not stand and twist my hair
Without such glancing at the looking-glass
875 To see my face there, that she missed the plait.
And John,—I never sent my plate for soup,
Or did not send it, but the foolish John
Resolved the problem, 'twixt his napkined thumbs,
Of what was signified by taking soup
880 Or choosing mackerel. Neighbours who dropped in
On morning visits, feeling a joint wrong,
Smiled admonition, sat uneasily,
And talked, with measured, emphasised reserve,
Of parish news, like doctors to the sick,
885 When not called in,—as if, with leave to speak,
They might say something. Nay, the very dog
Would watch me from his sun-patch on the floor,
In alternation with the large black fly
Not yet in reach of snapping. So I lived.

890 A Roman died so; smeared with honey, teased
By insects, stared to torture by the moon:
And many patients souls 'neath English roofs
Have died like Romans. I, in looking back,
Wish only, now, I had borne the plague of all
895 With meeker spirits than were rife at Rome.

For, on the sixth week, the dead sea broke up,
Dashed suddenly through beneath the heel of Him
Who stands upon the sea and earth and swears
Time shall be nevermore. The clock struck nine
900 That morning too,—no lark was out of tune,
The hidden farms among the hills breathed straight
Their smoke toward heaven, the lime-tree scarcely
      stirred
Beneath the blue weight of the cloudless sky,
Though still the July air came floating through
905 The woodbine at my window, in and out,
With touches of the out-door country news
For a bending forehead. There I sat, and wished
That morning-truce of God would last till eve,
Or longer. "Sleep," I thought, "late sleepers,—sleep,
910 And spare me yet the burden of your eyes."

Then, suddenly, a single ghastly shriek
Tore upward from the bottom of the house.
Like one who wakens in a grave and shrieks,
The still house seemed to shriek itself alive,
915 And shudder through its passages and stairs
With slam of doors and clash of bells.—I sprang,
I stood up in the middle of the room,
And there confronted at my chamber-door
A white face,—shivering, ineffectual lips.

920 "Come, come," they tried to utter, and I went:
As if a ghost had drawn me at the point
Of a fiery finger through the uneven dark,
I went with reeling footsteps down the stair,
Nor asked a question.
                              There she sat, my aunt,—
925 Bolt upright in the chair beside her bed,
Whose pillow had no dint! she had used no bed
For that night's sleeping, yet slept well. My God,
The dumb derision of that grey, peaked face
Concluded something grave against the sun,
930 Which filled the chamber with its July burst
When Susan drew the curtains ignorant
Of who sat open-eyed behind her. There
She sat…it sat…we said "she" yesterday…
And held a letter with unbroken seal
935 As Susan gave it to her hand last night:
All night she had held it. If its news referred
To duchies or to dunghills, not an inch
She'd budge, 'twas obvious, for such worthless odds:
Nor, though the stars were suns and overburned
940 Their spheric limitations, swallowing up
Like wax the azure spaces, could they force
Those open eyes to wink once. What last sight
Had left them blank and flat so,—drawing out
The faculty of vision from the roots,
945 As nothing more, worth seeing, remained behind?

Were those the eyes that watched me, worried me?
That dogged me up and down the hours and days,
A beaten, breathless, miserable soul?

And did I pray, a half-hour back, but so,
950 To escape the burden of those eyes…those eyes?
"Sleep late" I said?—
                              Why, now, indeed, they sleep.
God answers sharp and sudden on some prayers,
And thrusts the thing we have prayed for in our face,
A gauntlet with a gift in't. Every wish
955 Is like a prayer, with God.
                              I had my wish
To read and meditate the thing I would,
To fashion all my life upon my thought,
And marry or not marry. Henceforth none
Could disapprove me, vex me, hamper me.
960 Full ground-room, in this desert newly made,
For Babylon or Baalbec,—when the breath,
Now choked with sand, returns for building towns.

The heir came over on the funeral day,
And we two cousins met before the dead,
965 With two pale faces. Was it death or life
That moved us? When the will was read and done,
The official guests and witnesses withdrawn,
We rose up in a silence almost hard,
And looked at one another. Then I said,
970 "Farewell, my cousin."
                              But he touched, just touched
My hatstrings, tied for going (at the door
The carriage stood to take me), and said low,
His sister a little unsteady through his smile,
"Siste, viator."
                              "Is there time," I asked,
975 "In these last days of railroads, to stop short
Like Cæsar's chariot (weighing half a ton)
On the Appian road, for morals?"
                              "There is time,"
He answered grave, "for necessary words,
Inclusive, trust me, of no epitaph
980 On man or act, my cousin. We have read
A will, which gives you all the personal goods
And funded moneys of your aunt."
                              "I thank

Her memory for it. With three hundred pounds
We buy, in England even, clear standing-room
985 To stand and work in. Only two hours since,
I fancied I was poor."
                    "And, cousin, still
You're richer than you fancy. The will says,
Three hundred pounds, and any other sum
Of which the said testatrix dies possessed.
990 I say she died possessed of other sums."

"Dear Romney, need we chronicle the pence?
I'm richer than I thought—that's evident.
Enough so."
                "Listen rather. You've to do
With business and a cousin," he resumed,
995 "And both, I fear, need patience. Here's the fact.
The other sum (there *is* another sum,
Unspecified in any will which dates
After possession, yet bequeathed as much
And clearly as those said three hundred pounds)
1000 Is thirty thousand. You will have it paid
When?…where? My duty troubles you with words."

He struck the iron when the bar was hot;
No wonder if my eyes sent out some sparks.
"Pause there! I thank you. You are delicate
1005 In glosing gifts;—but I, who share your blood,
Am rather made for giving, like yourself,
Than taking, like your pensioners. Farewell."

He stopped me with a gesture of calm pride.
"A Leigh," he said, "gives largesse and gives love,
1010 But gloses never: if a Leigh could glose,
He would not do it, moreover, to a Leigh,
With blood trained up along nine centuries
To hound and hate a lie from eyes like yours.
And now we'll make the rest as clear: Your aunt
1015 Possessed these moneys."
                        "You will make it clear,
My cousin, as the honour of us both,
Or one of us speaks vainly! that's not I.

My aunt possessed this sum,—inherited
From whom, and when? bring documents, prove
    dates."
1020 "Why now indeed you throw your bonnet off
As if you had time left for a logarithm!
The faith's the want. Dear cousin, give me faith,
And you shall walk this road with silken shoes,
As clean as any lady of our house
1025 Supposed the proudest. Oh, I comprehend
The whole position from your point of sight.
I oust you from your father's halls and lands
And make you poor by getting rich—that's law;
Considering which, in common circumstance,
1030 You would not scruple to accept from me
Some compensation, some sufficiency
Of income—that were justice; but, alas,
I love you,—that's mere nature; you reject
My love,—that's nature also; and at once,
1035 You cannot, from a suitor disallowed,
A hand thrown back as mine is, into yours
Receive a doit, a farthing,—not for the world!
That's woman's etiquette, and obviously
Exceeds the claim of nature, law, and right,
1040 Unanswerable to all. I grant, you see,
The case as you conceive it,—leave you room
To sweep your ample skirts of womanhood,
While, standing humbly squeezed against the wall,
I own myself excluded from being just,
1045 Restrained from paying indubitable debts,
Because denied from giving you my soul.
That's my misfortune!—I submit to it
As if, in some more reasonable age,
'Twould not be less inevitable. Enough.
1050 You'll trust me, cousin, as a gentleman,
To keep your honour, as you count it, pure,
Your scruples (just as if I thought them wise)
Safe and inviolate from gifts of mine."
I answered mild but earnest. "I believe
1055 In no one's honour which another keeps,
Nor man's nor woman's. As I keep, myself,

My truth and my religion, I depute
No father, though I had one this side death,
Nor brother, though I had twenty, much less you,
1060 Though twice my cousin, and once Romney Leigh,
To keep my honour pure. You face, to-day,
A man who wants instruction, mark me, not
A woman who wants protection. As to a man,
Show manhood, speak out plainly, be precise
1065 With facts and dates. My aunt inherited
This sum, you say—"
                          "I said she died possessed
Of this, dear cousin."
                          "Not by heritage.
Thank you: we're getting to the facts at last.
Perhaps she played at commerce with a ship
1070 Which came in heavy with Australian gold?
Or touched a lottery with her finger-end,
Which tumbled on a sudden into her lap
Some old Rhine tower or principality?
Perhaps she had to do with a marine
1075 Sub-transatlantic railroad, which pre-pays
As well as pre-supposes? or perhaps
Some stale ancestral debt was after-paid
By a hundred years, and took her by surprise?—
You shake your head, my cousin; I guess ill."

1080 "You need not guess, Aurora, nor deride;
The truth is not afraid of hurting you.
You'll find no cause, in all your scruples, why
Your aunt should cavil at a deed of gift
'Twixt her and me."
                          "I thought so—ah! a gift."

1085 "You naturally thought so," he resumed.
"A very natural gift."
                          "A gift, a gift!
Her individual life being stranded high
Above all want, approaching opulence,
Too haughty was she to accept a gift
1090 Without some ultimate aim: ah, ah, I see,—
A gift intended plainly for her heirs,

And so accepted…if accepted…ah,
Indeed that might be; I am snared perhaps
Just so. But, cousin, shall I pardon you,
1095 If thus you have caught me with a cruel springe?"

He answered gently, "Need you tremble and pant
Like a netted lioness? is't my fault, mine,
That you're a grand wild creature of the woods
And hate the stall built for you? Any way,
1100 Though triply netted, need you glare at me?
I do not hold the cords of such a net;
You're free from me, Aurora!"
                          "Now may God
Deliver me from this strait! This gift of yours
Was tendered…when? accepted…when?" I asked.
1105 "A month…a fortnight since? Six weeks ago
It was not tendered; by a word she dropped
I know it was not tendered nor received.
When was it? bring your dates."
                          "What matters when?
A half-hour ere she died, or a half-year,
1110 Secured the gift, maintains the heritage
Inviolable with law. As easy pluck
The golden stars from heaven's embroidered stole
To pin them on the grey side of this earth,
As make you poor again, thank God."
                          "Not poor
1115 Nor clean again from henceforth, you thank God?
Well, sir—I ask you—I insist at need,—
Vouchsafe the special date, the special date."

"The day before her death-day," he replied,
"The gift was in her hands. We'll find that deed,
1120 And certify that date to you."
                          As one
Who has climbed a mountain-height and carried up
His own heart climbing, panting in his throat
With the toil of the ascent, takes breath at last,
Looks back in triumph—so I stood and looked.
1125 "Dear cousin Romney, we have reached the top
Of this steep question, and may rest, I think.

But first,—I pray you pardon, that the shock
And surge of natural feeling and event
Has made me oblivious of acquainting you
1130 That this, this letter (unread, mark, still sealed),
Was found enfolded in the poor dead hand:
That spirit of hers had gone beyond the address,
Which could not find her though you wrote it
    clear,—
I know your writing, Romney,—recognise
1135 The open-hearted *A*, the liberal sweep
Of the *G*. Now listen,—let us understand:
You will not find that famous deed of gift,
Unless you find it in the letter here,
Which, not being mine, I give you back.—Refuse
1140 To take the letter? well then—you and I,
As writer and as heiress, open it
Together, by your leave.—Exactly so:
The words in which the noble offering's made
Are nobler still, my cousin; and, I own,
1145 The proudest and most delicate heart alive,
Distracted from the measure of the gift
By such a grace in giving, might accept
Your largesse without thinking any more
Of the burthen of it, than King Solomon
1150 Considered, when he wore his holy ring
Charactered over with the ineffable spell,
How many carats of fine gold made up
Its money-value: so, Leigh gives to Leigh!
Or rather, might have given, observe,—for that's
1155 The point we come to. Here's a proof of gift,
But here's no proof, sir, of acceptancy,
But, rather, disproof. Death's black dust, being
    blown,
Infiltrated through every secret fold
Of this sealed letter by a puff of fate,
1160 Dried up for ever the fresh-written ink,
Annulled the gift, disutilized the grace,
And left these fragments."
                As I spoke, I tore
The paper up and down, and down and up
And crosswise, till it fluttered from my hands,

1165 As forest-leaves, stripped suddenly and rapt
By a whirlwind on Valdarno, drop again,
Drop slow, and strew the melancholy ground
Before the amazèd hills…why, so, indeed,
I'm writing like a poet, somewhat large
1170 In the type of the image, and exaggerate
A small thing with a great thing, topping it:—
But then I'm thinking how his eyes looked, his,
With what despondent and surprised reproach!
I think the tears were in them as he looked;
1175 I think the manly mouth just trembled. Then
He broke the silence.
              "I may ask, perhaps,
Although no stranger…only Romney Leigh,
Which means still less…than Vincent Carrington,
Your plans in going hence, and where you go.
1180 This cannot be a secret."
                 "All my life
Is open to you, cousin. I go hence
To London, to the gathering-place of souls,
To live mine straight out, vocally, in books;
Harmoniously for others, if indeed
1185 A woman's soul, like man's, be wide enough
To carry the whole octave (that's to prove),
Or, if I fail, still purely for myself.
Pray God be with me, Romney."
                 "Ah, poor child,
Who fight against the mother's 'tiring hand,
1190 And choose the headsman's! May God change His
    world
For your sake, sweet, and make it mild as heaven,
And juster than I have found you."
                 But I paused.
"And you, my cousin?"—
              "I," he said,—"you ask?
You care to ask? Well, girls have curious minds
1195 And fain would know the end of everything,
Of cousins therefore with the rest. For me,
Aurora, I've my work; you know my work;
And, having missed this year some personal hope,
I must beware the rather that I miss

200 No reasonable duty. While you sing
Your happy pastorals of the meads and trees,
Bethink you that I go to impress and prove
On stifled brains and deafened ears, stunned deaf,
Crushed dull with grief, that nature sings itself,
205 And needs no mediate poet, lute or voice,
To make it vocal. While you ask of men
Your audience, I may get their leave perhaps
For hungry orphans to say audibly
'We're hungry, see,'—for beaten and bullied wives
210 To hold their unweaned babies up in sight,
Whom orphanage would better, and for all
To speak and claim their portion…by no means
Of the soil,…but of the sweat in tilling it;
Since this is nowadays turned privilege,
215 To have only God's curse on us, and not man's.
Such work I have for doing, elbow-deep
In social problems,—as you tie your rhymes,
To draw my uses to cohere with needs
And bring the uneven world back to its round,
220 Or, failing so much, fill up, bridge at least
To smoother issues some abysmal cracks
And feuds of earth, intestine heats have made
To keep men separate,—using sorry shifts
Of hospitals, almshouses, infant schools,
225 And other practical stuff of partial good
You lovers of the beautiful and whole
Despise by system."
                    "*I* despise? The scorn
Is yours, my cousin. Poets become such
Through scorning nothing. You decry them for
230 The good of beauty sung and taught by them,
While they respect your practical partial good
As being a part of beauty's self. Adieu!
When God helps all the workers for His world,
The singers shall have help of Him, not last."

235 He smiled as men smile when they will not speak
Because of something bitter in the thought;
And still I feel his melancholy eyes
Look judgment on me. It is seven years since:

I know not if 'twas pity or 'twas scorn
1240 Has made them so far-reaching: judge it ye
Who have had to do with pity more than love
And scorn than hatred. I am used, since then,
To other ways, from equal men. But so,
Even so, we let go hands, my cousin and I,
1245 And in between us rushed the torrent-world
To blanch our faces like divided rocks,
And bar for ever mutual sight and touch
Except through swirl of spray and all that roar.

FIFTH BOOK

Aurora Leigh, be humble. Shall I hope
To speak my poems in mysterious tune
With man and nature?—with the lava-lymph
That trickles from successive galaxies
5 Still drop by drop adown the finger of God
In still new worlds?—with summer-days in this
That scarce dare breathe they are so beautiful?
With spring's delicious trouble in the ground,
Tormented by the quickened blood of roots,
10 And softly pricked by golden crocus-sheaves
In token of the harvest-time of flowers?
With winters and with autumns,—and beyond
With the human heart's large seasons, when it
        hopes
And fears, joys, grieves, and loves?—with all that
        strain
15 Of sexual passion, which devours the flesh
In a sacrament of souls? with mother's breasts
Which, round the new-made creatures hanging
        there,
Throb luminous and harmonious like pure
        spheres?—
With multitudinous life, and finally
20 With the great escapings of ecstatic souls,
Who, in a rush of too long prisoned flame,
Their radiant faces upward, burn away
This dark of the body, issuing on a world
Beyond our mortal?—can I speak my verse

25 So plainly in tune to these things and the rest
That men shall feel it catch them on the quick
As having the same warrant over them
To hold and move them if they will or no,
Alike imperious as the primal rhythm
30 Of that theurgic[1] nature?—I must fail,
Who fail at the beginning to hold and move
One man,—and he my cousin, and he my friend,
And he born tender, made intelligent,
Inclined to ponder the precipitous sides
35 Of difficult questions; yet, obtuse to *me*,
Of *me*, incurious! likes me very well,
And wishes me a paradise of good,
Good looks, good means, and good digestion,—ay,
But otherwise evades me, puts me off
40 With kindness, with a tolerant gentleness,—
Too light a book for a grave man's reading! Go,
Aurora Leigh: be humble.

　　　　　　　　There it is,
We women are too apt to look to one,
Which proves a certain impotence in art.
45 We strain our natures at doing something great,
Far less because it's something great to do,
Than haply that we, so, commend ourselves
As being not small, and more appreciable
To some one friend. We must have mediators
50 Betwixt our highest conscience and the judge;
Some sweet saint's blood must quicken in our palms,
Or all the like in heaven seems slow and cold:
Good only being perceived as the end of good,
And God alone pleased,—that's too poor, we think,
55 And not enough for us by any means.
Ay—Romney, I remember, told me once
We miss the abstract when we comprehend.
We miss it most when we aspire,—and fail.

Yet, so, I will not.—This vile woman's way
60 Of trailing garments shall not trip me up:
I'll have no traffic with the personal thought
In Art's pure temple. Must I work in vain,

Without the approbation of a man?
It cannot be; it shall not. Fame itself,
65 That approbation of the general race,
Presents a poor end (though the arrow speed
Shot straight with vigorous finger to the white),
And the highest fame was never reached except
By what was aimed above it. Art for art,
70 And good for God Himself, the essential Good!
We'll keep our aims sublime, our eyes erect,
Although our woman-hands should shake and fail;
And if we fail…But must we?—

　　　　　　　　Shall I fail?
The Greeks said grandly in their tragic phrase,
75 "Let no one be called happy till his death."
To which I add,—Let no one till his death
Be called unhappy. Measure not the work
Until the day's out and the labour done,
Then bring your gauges. If the day's work's scant,
80 Why, call it scant; affect no compromise;
And, in that we have nobly striven at least,
Deal with us nobly, women though we be,
And honour us with truth if not with praise.

　　　·　　　·　　　·　　　·　　　·　　　·

The critics say that epics have died out
140 With Agamemnon and the goat-nursed gods;
I'll not believe it. I could never deem,
As Payne Knight did (the mythic mountaineer
Who travelled higher than he was born to live,
And showed sometimes the goitre in his throat
145 Discoursing of an image seen through fog),
That Homer's heroes measured twelve feet high.
They were but men:—his Helen's hair turned grey
Like any plain Miss Smith's who wears a front;
And Hector's infant whimpered at a plume
150 As yours last Friday at a turkey-cock.
All actual heroes are essential men,
And all men possible heroes: every age,
Heroic in proportions, double-faced,
Looks backward and before, expects a morn
155 And claims an epos.

---
[1] supernatural or divine force.

                    Ay, but every age
Appears to souls who live in't (ask Carlyle)
Most unheroic. Ours, for instance, ours:
The thinkers scout it, and the poets abound
Who scorn to touch it with a finger-tip:
160 A pewter age,—mixed metal, silver-washed;
An age of scum, spooned off the richer past,
An age of patches for old gaberdines,
An age of mere transition, meaning nought
Except that what succeeds must shame it quite
165 If God please. That's wrong thinking, to my mind,
And wrong thoughts make poor poems.
                              Every age,
Through being beheld too close, is ill-discerned
By those who have not lived past it. We'll suppose
Mount Athos carved, as Alexander schemed,
170 To some colossal statue of a man.
The peasants, gathering brushwood in his ear,
Had guessed as little as the browsing goats
Of form or feature of humanity
Up there,—in fact, had travelled five miles off
175 Or ere the giant image broke on them,
Full human profile, nose and chin distinct,
Mouth, muttering rhythms of silence up the sky
And fed at evening with the blood of suns;
Grand torso,—hand, that flung perpetually
180 The largesse of a silver river down
To all the country pastures. 'Tis even thus
With times we live in,—evermore too great
To be apprehended near.
                    But poets should
Exert a double vision; should have eyes
185 To see near things as comprehensively
As if afar they took their point of sight,
And distant things as intimately deep
As if they touched them. Let us strive for this.
I do distrust the poet who discerns
190 No character or glory in his times,
And trundles back his soul five hundred years,
Past moat and drawbridge, into a castle-court,
To sing,—oh, not of lizard or of toad

Alive i' the ditch there,—'twere excusable,
195 But of some black chief, half knight, half sheep-lifter,
Some beauteous dame, half chattel and half queen,
As dead as must be, for the greater part,
The poems made on their chivalric bones;
And that's no wonder: death inherits death.

200 Nay, if there's room for poets in this world
A little overgrown (I think there is),
Their sole work is to represent the age,
Their age, not Charlemagne's,—this live,
        throbbing age,
That brawls, cheats, maddens, calculates, aspires,
205 And spends more passion, more heroic heat,
Betwixt the mirrors of its drawing-rooms,
Than Roland with his knights at Roncesvalles.
To flinch from Modern varnish, coat or flounce,
Cry out for togas and the picturesque,
210 Is fatal,—foolish too. King Arthur's self
Was commonplace to Lady Guenever;
And Camelot to minstrels seemed as flat
As Fleet Street to our poets.
                        Never flinch,
But still, unscrupulously epic, catch
215 Upon the burning lava of a song
The full-veined, heaving, double-breasted Age:
That, when the next shall come, the men of that
May touch the impress with reverent hand, and say
"Behold,—behold the paps we have all sucked!
220 This bosom seems to beat still, or at least
It sets ours beating: this is living art,
Which thus presents and thus records true life."

What form is best for poems? Let me think
Of forms less, and the external. Trust the spirit,
225 As sovran nature does, to make the form;
For otherwise we only imprison spirit
And not embody. Inward evermore
To outward,—so in life, and so in art
Which still is life.
                    Five acts to make a play.

230 And why not fifteen? why not ten? or seven?
What matter for the number of the leaves,
Supposing the tree lives and grows? exact
The literal unities of time and place,
When 'tis the essence of passion to ignore
235 Both time and place? Absurd. Keep up the fire,
And leave the generous flames to shape themselves.

'Tis true the stage requires obsequiousness
To this or that convention; "exit" here
And "enter" there; the points for clapping, fixed,
240 Like Jacob's white-peeled rods before the rams,
And all the close-curled imagery clipped
In manner of their fleece at shearing-time.
Forget to prick the galleries to the heart
Precisely at the fourth act,—culminate
245 Our five pyramidal acts with one act more,
We're lost so: Shakespeare's ghost could scarcely
        plead
Against our just damnation. Stand aside;
We'll muse for comfort that, last century,
On this same tragic stage on which we have failed,
250 A wigless Hamlet would have failed the same.

And whosoever writes good poetry,
Looks just to art. He does not write for you
Or me,—for London or for Edinburgh;
He will not suffer the best critic known
255 To step into his sunshine of free thought
And self-absorbed conception and exact
An inch-long swerving of the holy lines.
If virtue done for popularity
Defiles like vice, can art, for praise or hire,
260 Still keep its splendour and remain pure art?
Eshew such serfdom. What the poet writes,
He writes: mankind accepts it if it suits,
And that's success: if not, the poem's passed
From hand to hand, and yet from hand to hand,
265 Until the unborn snatch it, crying out
In pity on their fathers' being so dull,
And that's success too.

                I will write no plays;
Because the drama, less sublime in this,
Makes lower appeals, submits more menially,
270 Adopts the standard of the public taste
To chalk its height on, wears a dog-chain round
Its regal neck, and learns to carry and fetch
The fashions of the day to please the day,
Fawns close on pit and boxes, who clap hands
275 Commending chiefly its docility
And humour in stage-tricks,—or else indeed
Gets hissed at, howled at, stamped at like a dog,
Or worse, we'll say. For dogs, unjustly kicked,
Yell, bite at need; but if your dramatist
280 (Being wronged by some five hundred nobodies
Because their grosser brains most naturally
Misjudge the fineness of his subtle wit)
Shows teeth an almond's breadth, protests the
        length
Of a modest phrase,—"My gentle countrymen,
285 "There's something in it haply of your fault,"—
Why then, besides five hundred nobodies,
He'll have five thousand and five thousand more
Against him,—the whole public,—and all the hoofs
Of King Saul's father's asses, in full drove,
290 And obviously deserve it. He appealed
To these,—and why say more if they condemn,
Than if they praise him?—Weep, my Æschylus,
But low and far, upon Sicilian shores!
For since 'twas Athens (so I read the myth)
295 Who gave commission to that fatal weight
The tortoise, cold and hard, to drop on thee
And crush thee,—better cover thy bald head;
She'll hear the softest hum of Hyblan bee
Before thy loudest protestation!
                            Then
300 The risk's still worse upon the modern stage.
I could not, for so little, accept success,
Nor would I risk so much, in ease and calm,
For manifester gains: let those who prize,
Pursue them: I stand off. And yet, forbid,
305 That any irreverent fancy or conceit

Should litter in the Drama's throne-room where
The rulers of our art, in whose full veins
Dynastic glories mingle, sit in strength
And do their kingly work,—conceive, command,
310 And, from the imagination's crucial heat,
Catch up their men and women all a-flame
For action, all alive and forced to prove
Their life by living out heart, brain, and nerve,
Until mankind makes witness, "These be men
315 As we are," and vouchsafes the greeting due
To Imogen and Juliet—sweetest kind
On art's side.
                          'Tis that, honouring to its worth
The drama, I would fear to keep it down
To the level of the footlights. Dies no more
320 The sacrificial goat, for Bacchus slain,
His filmed eyes fluttered by the whirling white
Of choral vestures,—troubled in his blood,
While tragic voices that clanged keen as swords,
Leapt high together with the altar-flame
325 And made the blue air wink. The waxen mask,
Which set the grand still front of Themis' son
Upon the puckered visage of a player,—
The buskin, which he rose upon and moved,
As some tall ship first conscious of the wind
330 Sweeps slowly past the piers,—the mouthpiece, where
The mere man's voice with all its breaths and breaks
Went sheathed in brass, and clashed on even heights
Its phrasèd thunders,—these things are no more,
Which once were. And concluding, which is clear,
335 The growing drama has outgrown such toys
Of simulated stature, face, and speech,
It also peradventure may outgrow
The simulation of the painted scene,
Boards, actors, prompters, gaslight, and costume,
340 And take for a worthier stage the soul itself,
Its shifting fancies and celestial lights,

With all its grand orchestral silences
To keep the pauses of its rhythmic sounds.

Alas, I still see something to be done,
345 And what I do falls short of what I see,
Though I waste myself on doing. Long green days,
Worn bare of grass and sunshine,—long calm nights,
From which the silken sleeps were fretted out,
Be witness for me, with no amateur's
350 Irreverent haste and busy idleness
I set myself to art! What then? what's done?
What's done, at last?
                          Behold, at last, a book.
If life-blood's necessary, which it is,—
(By that blue vein athrob on Mahomet's brow,
355 Each prophet-poet's book must show man's blood!)
If life-blood's fertilising, I wrung mine
On every leaf of this,—unless the drops
Slid heavily on one side and left it dry.
That chances often: many a fervid man
360 Writes books as cold and flat as graveyard stones
From which the lichen's scraped; and if Saint Preux
Had written his own letters, as he might,
We had never wept to think of the little mole
'Neath Julie's[1] drooping eyelid. Passion is
365 But something suffered, after all.
                          While Art
Sets action on the top of suffering:
The artist's part is both to be and do,
Transfixing with a special, central power
The flat experience of the common man,
370 And turning outward, with a sudden wrench,
Half agony, half ecstasy, the thing
He feels the inmost,—never felt the less
Because he sings it. Does a torch less burn
For burning next reflectors of blue steel,
375 That *he* should be the colder for his place

---

[1] characters from Rousseau's *La Nouvelle Héloïse* (1761), an adaptation
of the tale of Abelard and Eloisa.

'Twixt two incessant fires,—his personal life's,
And that intense refraction which burns back
Perpetually against him from the round
Of crystal conscience he was born into
380 If artist-born? O sorrowful great gift
Conferred on poets, of a twofold life,
When one life has been found enough for pain!
We, staggering 'neath our burden as mere men,
Being called to stand up straight as demi-gods,
385 Support the intolerable strain and stress
Of the universal, and send clearly up
With voices broken by the human sob,
Our poems to find rhymes among the stars!

But soft,—a "poet" is a word soon said,
390 A book's a thing soon written. Nay, indeed,
The more the poet shall be questionable,
The more unquestionably comes his book.
And this of mine—well, granting to myself
Some passion in it,—furrowing up the flats,
395 Mere passion will not prove a volume worth
Its gall and rags even. Bubbles round a keel
Mean nought, excepting that the vessel moves.
There's more than passion goes to make a man
Or book, which is a man too.
                              I am sad.
400 I wonder if Pygmalion had these doubts
And, feeling the hard marble first relent,
Grow supple to the straining of his arms,
And tingle through its cold to his burning lip,
Supposed his senses mocked, supposed the toil
405 Of stretching past the known and seen to reach
The archetypal Beauty out of sight,
Had made his heart beat fast enough for two,
And with his own life dazed and blinded him!
Not so; Pygmalion loved,—and whoso loves
410 Believes the impossible.
                        But I am sad:
I cannot thoroughly love a work of mine,
Since none seems worthy of my thought and hope
More highly mated. He has shot them down,

My Phœbus Apollo, soul within my soul,
415 Who judges, by the attempted, what's attained,
And with the silver arrow from his height
Has struck down all my works before my face
While I said nothing. Is there aught to say?
I called the artist but a greatened man.
420 He may be childless also, like a man.

I laboured on alone. The wind and dust
And sun of the world beat blistering in my face;
And hope, now for me, now against me, dragged
My spirits onward, as some fallen balloon,
425 Which, whether caught by blossoming tree or bare,
Is torn alike. I sometimes touched my aim,
Or seemed,—and generous souls cried out "Be
    strong,
Take courage; now you're on our level,—now!
The next step saves you!" I was flushed with praise,
430 But, pausing just a moment to draw breath,
I could not choose but murmur to myself
"Is this all? all that's done? and all that's gained?
If this then be success, 'tis dismaller
Than any failure."
              O my God, my God,
435 O supreme Artist, who as sole return
For all the cosmic wonder of Thy work,
Demandest of us just a word...a name,
"My Father!" thou hast knowledge, only thou,
How dreary 'tis for women to sit still,
440 On winter nights by solitary fires,
And hear the nations praising them far off,
Too far! ay, praising our quick sense of love,
Our very heart of passionate womanhood,
Which could not beat so in the verse without
445 Being present also in the unkissed lips
And eyes undried because there's none to ask
The reason they grew moist.
                        To sit alone
And think for comfort how, that very night,
Affianced lovers, leaning face to face
450 With sweet half-listenings for each other's breath,

Are reading haply from a page of ours,
To pause from a thrill (as if their cheeks had
    touched)
When such a stanza, level to their mood,
Seems floating their own thought out—"So I feel
455 For thee,"—"And I, for thee: this poet knows
What everlasting love is!"—how, that night,
Some father, issuing from the misty roads
Upon the luminous round of lamp and hearth
And happy children, having caught up first
460 The youngest there until it shrink and shriek
To feel the cold chin prick its dimples through
With winter from the hills, may throw i' the lap
Of the eldest (who has learnt to drop her lids
To hide some sweetness newer than last year's)
465 Our book and cry,…"Ah you, you care for rhymes;
So here be rhymes to pore on under trees,
When April comes to let you! I've been told
They are not idle as so many are,
But set hearts beating pure as well as fast.
470 'Tis yours, the book; I'll write your name in it,
That so you may not lose, however lost
In poet's lore and charming reverie,
The thought of how your father thought of *you*
In riding from the town."
                To have our books
475 Appraised by love, associated with love,
While *we* sit loveless! is it hard, you think?
At least 'tis mournful. Fame, indeed, 'twas said,
Means simply love. It was a man said that:
And then, there's love and love: the love of all
480 (To risk in turn a woman's paradox)
Is but a small thing to the love of one.
You bid a hungry child be satisfied
With a heritage of many corn-fields: nay,
He says he's hungry,—he would rather have
485 That little barley-cake you keep from him
While reckoning up his harvests. So with us
(Here, Romney, too, we fail to generalise):
We're hungry.
           Hungry! but it's pitiful

To wail like unweaned babes and suck our thumbs
490 Because we're hungry. Who, in all this world
(Wherein we are haply set to pray and fast
And learn what good is by its opposite),
Has never hungered? Woe to him who has found
The meal enough! if Ugolino's[1] full,
495 His teeth have crunched some foul unnatural thing,
For here satiety proves penury
More utterly irremediable. And since
We needs must hunger,—better, for man's love,
Than God's truth! better, for companions sweet,
500 Than great convictions! let us bear our weights,
Preferring dreary hearths to desert souls.
Well, well! they say we're envious, we who rhyme;
But I, because I am a woman perhaps
And so rhyme ill, am ill at envying.
505 I never envied Graham his breadth of style,
Which gives you, with a random smutch or two,
(Near sighted critics analyse to smutch)
Such delicate perspectives of full life:
Nor Belmore, for the unity of aim
510 To which he cuts his cedarn poems, fine
As sketchers do their pencils: nor Mark Gage,
For that caressing colour and trancing tone
Whereby you're swept away and melted in
The sensual element, which with a back wave
515 Restores you to the level of pure souls
And leaves you with Plotinus.[2] None of these,
For native gifts or popular applause,
I've envied; but for this,—that when by chance
Says some one,—"There goes Belmore, a great man!
520 He leaves clean work behind him, and requires
No sweeper up of the chips,"…a girl I know,
Who answers nothing, save with her brown eyes,
Smiles unaware as if a guardian saint
Smiled in her:—for this, too,—that Gage comes
    home

---

[1] Count Ugolino Della Gherardesca (d. 1289), despot ruler of Pisa
(1284–88).

[2] Neoplatonist philosopher (c. 205–70).

525 And lays his last book's prodigal review
Upon his mother's knee, where, years ago,
He laid his childish spelling-book and learned
To chirp and peck the letters from her mouth,
As young birds must. "Well done," she murmured then;
530 She will not say it now more wonderingly:
And yet the last "Well done" will touch him more,
As catching up to-day and yesterday
In a perfect chord of love: and so, Mark Gage,
I envy you your mother!—and you, Graham,
535 Because you have a wife who loves you so,
She half forgets, at moments, to be proud
Of being Graham's wife, until a friend observes,
"The boy here, has his father's massive brow,
Done small in wax…if we push back the curls."
540 Who loves me? Dearest father,—mother sweet,—
I speak the names out sometimes by myself,
And make the silence shiver. They sound strange,
As Hindostanee to an Ind-born man
Accustomed many years to English speech;
545 Or lovely poet-words grown obsolete,
Which will not leave off singing. Up in heaven
I have my father,—with my mother's face
Beside him in a blotch of heavenly light;
No more for earth's familiar, household use,
550 No more. The best verse written by this hand,
Can never reach them where they sit, to seem
Well-done to *them*. Death quite unfellows us,
Sets dreadful odds betwixt the live and dead,
And makes us part as those at Babel did
555 Through sudden ignorance of a common tongue.
A living Cæsar would not dare to play
At bowls with such as my dead father is.

And yet this may be less so than appears,
This change and separation. Sparrows five
560 For just two farthings, and God cares for each.
If God is not too great for little cares,
Is any creature, because gone to God?
I've seen some men, veracious, nowise mad,
Who have thought or dreamed, declared and testified,
565 They heard the Dead a-ticking like a clock
Which strikes the hours of the eternities,
Beside them, with their natural ears,—and known
That human spirits feel the human way
And hate the unreasoning awe which waves them off
570 From possible communion. It may be.
At least, earth separates as well as heaven.
For instance, I have not seen Romney Leigh
Full eighteen months…add six, you get two years.
They say he's very busy with good works,—
575 Has parted Leigh Hall into almshouses.
He made one day an almshouse of his heart,
Which ever since is loose upon the latch
For those who pull the string.—I never did.

It always makes me sad to go abroad,
580 And now I'm sadder that I went to-night,
Among the lights and talkers at Lord Howe's.
His wife is gracious, with her glossy braids,
And even voice, and gorgeous eyeballs, calm
As her other jewels. If she's somewhat cold,
585 Who wonders, when her blood has stood so long
In the ducal reservoir she calls her line
By no means arrogantly? she's not proud;
Not prouder than the swan is of the lake
He has always swum in;—'tis her element;
590 And so she takes it with a natural grace,
Ignoring tadpoles. She just knows perhaps
There *are* who travel without outriders,
Which isn't her fault. Ah, to watch her face,
When good Lord Howe expounds his theories
595 Of social justice and equality!
'Tis curious, what a tender, tolerant bend
Her neck takes: for she loves him, likes his talk,
"Such clever talk—that dear, odd Algernon!"
She listens on, exactly as if he talked
600 Some Scandinavian myth of Lemures,
Too pretty to dispute, and too absurd.

She's gracious to me as her husband's friend,
And would be gracious, were I not a Leigh,
Being used to smile just so, without her eyes,
605 On Joseph Strangways the Leeds mesmerist,
And Delia Dobbs the lecturer from "the States"
Upon the "Woman's question." Then, for him,
I like him; he's my friend. And all the rooms
Were full of crinkling silks that swept about
510 The fine dust of most subtle courtesies.
What then?—why then, we come home to be sad.

How lovely, One I love not looked to-night!
She's very pretty, Lady Waldemar.
Her maid must use both hands to twist that coil
515 Of tresses, then be careful lest the rich
Bronze rounds should slip:—she missed, though, a
        grey hair,
A single one,—I saw it; otherwise
The woman looked immortal. How they told,
Those alabaster shoulders and bare breasts,
520 On which the pearls, drowned out of sight in milk,
Were lost, excepting for the ruby-clasp!
They split the amaranth velvet-bodice down
To the waist or nearly, with the audacious press
Of full-breathed beauty. If the heart within
525 Were half as white!—but, if it were, perhaps
The breast were closer covered and the sight
Less aspectable, by half, too.
                            I heard
The young man with the German student's look—
A sharp face, like a knife in a cleft stick,
530 Which shot up straight against the parting line
So equally dividing the long hair,—
Say softly to his neighbour, (thirty-five
And mediæval) "Look that way, Sir Blaise.
She's Lady Waldemar—to the left—in red—
535 Whom Romney Leigh, our ablest man just now,
Is soon about to marry."
                        Then replied
Sir Blaise Delorme, with quiet, priestlike voice,
Too used to syllable damnations round

To make a natural emphasis worth while:
640 "Is Leigh your ablest man? the same, I think,
Once jilted by a recreant pretty maid
Adopted from the people? Now, in change,
He seems to have plucked a flower from the other
        side
Of the social hedge."
                        "A flower, a flower," exclaimed
645 My German student,—his own eyes full-blown
Bent on her. He was twenty, certainly.

Sir Blaise resumed with gentle arrogance,
As if he had dropped his alms into a hat
And gained the right to counsel,—"My young
        friend,
650 I doubt your ablest man's ability
To get the least good or help meet for him,
For pagan phalanstery[1] or Christian home,
From such a flowery creature."
                                "Beautiful!"
My student murmured rapt,—"Mark how she stirs!
655 Just waves her head, as if a flower indeed,
Touched far off by the vain breath of our talk."

At which that bilious Grimwald (he who writes
For the Renovator), who had seemed absorbed
Upon the table-book of autographs
660 (I dare say mentally he crunched the bones
Of all those writers, wishing them alive
To feel his tooth in earnest), turned short round
With low carnivorous laugh,—"A flower, of course!
She neither sews nor spins,—and takes no thought
665 Of her garments...falling off."
                                The student flinched;
Sir Blaise, the same; then both, drawing back their
        chairs
As if they spied black-beetles on the floor,
Pursued their talk, without a word being thrown

---

[1] a community of people living together, free of external regulation and
holding property in common. The term was used by Fourier in his
socialist scheme for the reorganization of society.

To the critic.
                    Good Sir Blaise's brow is high
670 And noticeably narrow: a strong wind,
You fancy, might unroof him suddenly,
And blow that great top attic off his head
So piled with feudal relics. You admire
His nose in profile, though you miss his chin;
675 But, though you miss his chin, you seldom miss
His ebon cross worn innermostly (carved
For penance by a saintly Styrian monk
Whose flesh was too much with him), slipping
       through
Some unaware unbuttoned casualty
680 Of the under-waistcoat. With an absent air
Sir Blaise sat fingering it and speaking low,
While I, upon the sofa, heard it all.

"My dear young friend, if we could bear our eyes,
Like blessedest Saint Lucy, on a plate,
685 They would not trick us into choosing wives,
As doublets, by the colour. Otherwise
Our fathers chose,—and therefore, when they had
       hung
Their household keys about a lady's waist,
The sense of duty gave her dignity;
690 She kept her bosom holy to her babes,
And, if a moralist reproved her dress,
'Twas, 'Too much starch!'—and not, 'Too little
       lawn!'"

"Now, pshaw!" returned the other in a heat,
A little fretted by being called "young friend,"
695 Or so I took it,—"for Saint Lucy's sake,
If she's the saint to swear by, let us leave
Our fathers,—plagued enough about our sons!"
(He stroked his beardless chin) "yes, plagued, sir,
       plagued:
The future generations lie on us
700 As heavy as the nightmare of a seer;
Our meat and drink grow painful prophecy:
I ask you,—have we leisure, if we liked,

To hollow out our weary hands to keep
Your intermittent rushlight of the past
705 From draughts in lobbies? Prejudice of sex
And marriage-law…the socket drops them through
While we two speak,—however may protest
Some over-delicate nostrils like your own,
'Gainst odours thence arising."
                              "You are young,"
710 Sir Blaise objected.
                    "If I am," he said
With fire,—"though somewhat less so than I seem,
The young run on before, and see the thing
That's coming. Reverence for the young, I cry.
In that new church for which the world's near ripe,
715 You'll have the younger in the Elder's chair,
Presiding with his ivory front of hope
O'er foreheads clawed by cruel carrion-birds
Of life's experience."
                    "Pray your blessing, sir,"
Sir Blaise replied good-humouredly,—"I plucked
720 A silver hair this morning from my beard,
Which left me your inferior. Would I were
Eighteen and worthy to admonish you!
If young men of your order run before
To see such sights as sexual prejudice
725 And marriage-law dissolved,—in plainer words,
A general concubinage expressed
In a universal pruriency,—the thing
Is scarce worth running fast for, and you'd gain
By loitering with your elders."
                              "Ah," he said,
730 "Who, getting to the top of Pisgah-hill,[1]
Can talk with one at bottom of the view,
To make it comprehensible? Why, Leigh
Himself, although our ablest man, I said,
Is scarce advanced to see as far as this,
735 Which some are: he takes up imperfectly
The social question—by one handle—leaves

---

[1] the summit from which Moses saw the promised land: Deuteronomy 3:27 and 34:1–4.

The rest to trail. A Christian socialist
Is Romney Leigh, you understand."
                                "Not I.
I disbelieve in Christian-pagans, much
740 As you in women-fishes. If we mix
Two colours, we lose both, and make a third
Distinct from either. Mark you! to mistake
A colour is the sign of a sick brain,
And mine, I thank the saints, is clear and cool:
745 A neutral tint is here impossible.
The church—and by the church, I mean, of course
The catholic, apostolic, mother-church,—
Draws lines as plain and straight as her own walls;
Inside of which are Christians obviously
750 And outside...dogs."[1]
                 "We thank you. Well I know
The ancient mother-church would fain still bite,
For all her toothless gums,—as Leigh himself
Would fain be a Christian still, for all his wit.
Pass that; you two may settle it, for me.
755 You're slow in England. In a month I learnt
At Göttingen[2] enough philosophy
To stock your English schools for fifty years;
Pass that, too. Here alone, I stop you short,
— Supposing a true man like Leigh could stand
760 Unequal in the stature of his life
To the height of his opinions. Choose a wife
Because of a smooth skin?—not he, not he!
He'd rail at Venus' self for creaking shoes,
Unless she walked his way of righteousness:
765 And if he takes a Venus Meretrix[3]
(No imputation on the lady there),
Be sure that, by some sleight of Christian art,
He has metamorphosed and converted her
To a Blessed Virgin."
                "Soft!" Sir Blaise drew breath
770 As if it hurt him—"Soft! no blasphemy,

I pray you!"
            "The first Christians did the thing:
Why not the last?" asked he of Göttingen,
With just that shade of sneering on the lip,
Compensates for the lagging of the beard,—
775 "And so the case is. If that fairest fair
Is talked of as the future wife of Leigh,
She's talked of too, at least as certainly,
As Leigh's disciple. You may find her name
On all his missions and commissions, schools,
780 Asylums, hospitals,—he had her down,
With other ladies whom her starry lead
Persuaded from their spheres, to his country-place
In Shropshire, to the famed phalanstery
At Leigh Hall, christianised from Fourier's[4] own
785 (In which he has planted out his sapling stocks
Of knowledge into social nurseries),
And there, they say, she has tarried half a week,
And milked the cows, and churned, and pressed the
      curd,
And said 'my sister' to the lowest drab
790 Of all the assembled castaways; such girls!
Ay, sided with them at the washing-tub—
Conceive, Sir Blaise, those naked perfect arms,
Round glittering arms, plunged elbow-deep in suds,
Like wild swans hid in lilies all a-shake."

795 Lord Howe came up. "What, talking poetry
So near the image of the unfavouring Muse?
That's you, Miss Leigh: I've watched you half an
      hour,
Precisely as I watched the statue called
A Pallas in the Vatican;[5]—you mind
800 The face, Sir Blaise?—intensely calm and sad,
As wisdom cut it off from fellowship,—
But *that* spoke louder. Not a word from *you*!

---

[1] Revelation 22:14.

[2] German university founded in 1734.

[3] a prostitute.

---

[4] Charles Fourier (d. 1837), French socialist.

[5] The statue is also called Minerva Medica and La Dea Salus, standing in the "Braccio Nuovo" of the Vatican Museum.

And these two gentlemen were bold, I marked,
And unabashed by even your silence."
                                        "Ah,"
805 Said I, "my dear Lord Howe, you shall not speak
To a printing woman who has lost her place
(The sweet safe corner of the household fire
Behind the heads of children), compliments,
As if she were a woman. We who have clipt
810 The curls before our eyes may see at least
As plain as men do. Speak out, man to man;
No compliments, beseech you."
                                "Friend to friend,
Let that be. We are sad to-night, I saw,
(—Good night, Sir Blaise! ah, Smith—he has
    slipped away),
815 I saw you across the room, and stayed, Miss Leigh,
To keep a crowd of lion-hunters off,
With faces toward your jungle. There were three;
A spacious lady, five feet ten and fat,
Who has the devil in her (and there's room)
820 For walking to and fro upon the earth,
From Chipewa to China; she requires
Your autograph upon a tinted leaf
'Twixt Queen Pomare's and Emperor
    Soulouque's.[1]
Pray give it; she has energies, though fat:
825 For me, I'd rather see a rick on fire
Than such a woman angry. Then a youth
Fresh from the backwoods, green as the underboughs,
Asks modestly, Miss Leigh, to kiss your shoe,
And adds, he has an epic in twelve parts,
830 Which when you've read, you'll do it for his boot:
All which I saved you, and absorb next week
Both manuscript and man,—because a lord
Is still more potent than a poetess
With any extreme republican. Ah, ah,
835 You smile, at last, then."
                                "Thank you."

---

[1] Queen Pomare IV of Tahiti (1813–77); Faustin-Elie Soulouque
(c. 1782–1867), president of Haiti in 1847 who declared himself
Emperor Faustin I of Haiti in 1849.

                                        "Leave the smile,
I'll lose the thanks for't,—ay, and throw you in
My transatlantic girl, with golden eyes,
That draw you to her splendid whiteness as
The pistil of a water-lily draws,
840 Adust with gold. Those girls across the sea
Are tyrannously pretty,—and I swore
(She seemed to me an innocent, frank girl)
To bring her to you for a woman's kiss,
Not now, but on some other day or week:
845 —We'll call it perjury; I give her up."

"No, bring her."
                    "Now," said he, "you make it hard
To touch such goodness with a grimy palm.
I thought to tease you well, and fret you cross,
And steel myself, when rightly vexed with you,
850 For telling you a thing to tease you more."

"Of Romney?"
                "No, no; nothing worse," he cried,
"Of Romney Leigh than what is buzzed about,—
That *he* is taken in an eye-trap too,
Like many half as wise. The thing I mean
855 Refers to you, not him."
                            "Refers to me."
He echoed,—"Me! You sound it like a stone
Dropped down a dry well very listlessly
By one who never thinks about the toad
Alive at the bottom. Presently perhaps
860 You'll sound your 'me' more proudly—till I
    shrink."

"Lord Howe's the toad, then, in this question?"
                                                "Brief,
We'll take it graver. Give me sofa-room,
And quiet hearing. You know Eglinton,
John Eglinton, of Eglinton in Kent?"

865 "Is *he* the toad?—he's rather like the snail,
Known chiefly for the house upon his back:

Divide the man and house—you kill the man;
That's Eglinton of Eglinton, Lord Howe."

He answered grave. "A reputable man,
870 An excellent landlord of the olden stamp,
If somewhat slack in new philanthropies,
Who keeps his birthdays with a tenants' dance,
Is hard upon them when they miss the church
Or hold their children back from catechism,
875 But not ungentle when the agèd poor
Pick sticks at hedge-sides: nay, I've heard him say,
'The old dame has a twinge because she stoops;
'That's punishment enough for felony.'"

"O tender-hearted landlord! may I take
880 My long lease with him, when the time arrives
For gathering winter-faggots!"
                              "He likes art,
Buys books and pictures…of a certain kind;
Neglects no patent duty; a good son"…

"To a most obedient mother. Born to wear
885 His father's shoes, he wears her husband's too:
Indeed I've heard it's touching. Dear Lord Howe,
You shall not praise *me* so against your heart,
When I'm at worst for praise and faggots."
                                        "Be
Less bitter with me, for…in short," he said,
890 "I have a letter, which he urged me so
To bring you…I could scarcely choose but yield;
Insisting that a new love, passing through
The hand of an old friendship, caught from it
Some reconciling odour."
                         "Love, you say?
895 My lord, I cannot love: I only find
The rhyme for love,—and that's not love, my lord.
Take back your letter."
                       "Pause: you'll read it first?"

"I will not read it: it is stereotyped;[1]
The same he wrote to,—anybody's name,
900 Anne Blythe the actress, when she died so true
A duchess fainted in a private box:
Pauline the dancer, after the great *pas*[2]
In which her little feet winked overhead
Like other fire-flies, and amazed the pit:
905 Or Baldinacci, when her F in alt[3]
Had touched the silver tops of heaven itself
With such a pungent spirit-dart, the Queen
Laid softly, each to each, her white-gloved palms,
And sighed for joy: or else (I thank your friend)
910 Aurora Leigh,—when some indifferent rhymes,
Like those the boys sang round the holy ox
On Memphis-highway, chance perhaps to set
Our Apis-public lowing. Oh, he wants,
Instead of any worthy wife at home,
915 A star upon his stage of Eglinton?
Advise him that he is not overshrewd
In being so little modest: a dropped star
Makes bitter waters, says a Book I've read,[4]—
And there's his unread letter."
                               "My dear friend,"
920 Lord Howe began…
                    In haste I tore the phrase.
"You mean your friend of Eglinton, or me?"

"I mean you, you," he answered with some fire.
"A happy life means prudent compromise;
The tare runs through the farmer's garnered sheaves,
925 And though the gleaner's apron holds pure wheat
We count her poorer. Tare with wheat, we cry,
And good with drawbacks. You, you love your art,

---

[1] a printing process where a relief printing plate is cast in a mould made from composed type or an original plate; a widely held but fixed and oversimplified image or idea.

[2] the virtuoso set piece of a ballet; more commonly, the phrase is used to describe the *pas de deux* of two dancers.

[3] a high note in the upper register in music.

[4] Revelation 8:10–11.

And, certain of vocation, set your soul
On utterance. Only, in this world we have made
930 (They say God made it first, but if He did
'Twas so long since, and, since, we have spoiled it
      so,
He scarce would know it, if He looked this way,
From hells we preach of, with the flames blown
      out),
—In this bad, twisted, topsy-turvy world
935 Where all the heaviest wrongs get uppermost,—
In this uneven, unfostering England here,
Where ledger-strokes and sword-strokes count
      indeed,
But soul-strokes merely tell upon the flesh
They strike from,—it is hard to stand for art,
940 Unless some golden tripod from the sea
Be fished up, by Apollo's divine chance,
To throne such feet as yours, my prophetess,
At Delphi.[1] Think,—the god comes down as fierce
As twenty bloodhounds, shakes you, strangles you,
945 Until the oracular shriek shall ooze in froth!
At best 'tis not all ease,—at worst too hard:
A place to stand on is a 'vantage gained,
And here's your tripod. To be plain, dear friend,
You're poor, except in what you richly give;
950 You labour for your own bread painfully
Or ere you pour our wine. For art's sake, pause."

I answered slow,—as some wayfaring man,
Who feels himself at night too far from home,
Makes steadfast face against the bitter wind.
955 "Is art so less a thing than virtue is,
That artists first must cater for their ease
Or ever they make issue past themselves
To generous use? Alas, and is it so,
That we, who would be somewhat clean, must
      sweep

960 Our ways as well as walk them, and no friend
Confirm us nobly,—'Leave results to God,
But you, be clean?' What! 'prudent compromise
Makes acceptable life,' you say instead,
You, you, Lord Howe?—in things indifferent, well.
965 For instance, compromise the wheaten bread
For rye, the meat for lentils, silk for serge,
And sleep on down, if needs, for sleep on straw;
But there, end compromise. I will not bate
One artist-dream on straw or down, my lord,
970 Nor pinch my liberal soul, though I be poor,
Nor cease to love high, though I live thus low."

So speaking, with less anger in my voice
Than sorrow, I rose quickly to depart;
While he, thrown back upon the noble shame
975 Of such high-stumbling natures, murmured words,
The right words after wrong ones. Ah, the man
Is worthy, but so given to entertain
Impossible plans of superhuman life,—
He sets his virtues on so raised a shelf,
980 To keep them at the grand millennial height,
He has to mount a stool to get at them;
And, meantime, lives on quite the common way,
With everybody's morals.
                              As we passed,
Lord Howe insisting that his friendly arm
985 Should oar me across the sparkling brawling stream
Which swept from room to room,—we fell at once
On Lady Waldemar. "Miss Leigh," she said,
And gave me such a smile, so cold and bright,
As if she tried it in a 'tiring glass[2]
990 And liked it; "all to-night I've strained at you
As babes at baubles held up out of reach
By spiteful nurses ('Never snatch,' they say),
And there you sat, most perfectly shut in
By good Sir Blaise and clever Mister Smith
995 And then our dear Lord Howe! at last indeed
I almost snatched. I have a world to speak

---

[1] a religious sanctuary of ancient Greece, dedicated to Apollo and situated on Mount Parnassus; thought of as the navel of the earth, it was the seat of the Pythia, the priestess of Apollo, who delivered her riddling responses there. The tripod is the bronze altar on which the priestess sits.

[2] a mirror.

About your cousin's place in Shropshire, where
I've been to see his work…our work,—you heard
I went?…and of a letter yesterday,
In which if I should read a page or two
You might feel interest, though you're locked of
    course
In literary toil.—You'll like to hear
Your last book lies at the phalanstery,
As judged innocuous for the elder girls
And younger women who care for books.
We all must read, you see, before we live,
Till slowly the ineffable light comes up
And, as it deepens, drowns the written word,—
So said your cousin, while we stood and felt
A sunset from his favourite beech-tree seat.
He might have been a poet if he would,
But then he saw the higher thing at once
And climbed to it. I think he looks well now,
Has quite got over that unfortunate…
Ah, ah…I know it moved you. Tender-heart!
You took a liking to the wretched girl.
Perhaps you thought the marriage suitable,
Who knows? a poet hankers for romance,
And so on. As for Romney Leigh, 'tis sure
He never loved her,—never. By the way,
You have not heard of *her*…? quite out of sight,
And out of saving? lost in every sense?"

She might have gone on talking half an hour
And I stood still, and cold, and pale, I think,
As a garden-statue a child pelts with snow
For pretty-pastime. Every now and then
I put in "yes" or "no," I scarce knew why;
The blind man walks wherever the dog pulls,
And so I answered. Till Lord Howe broke in:
"What penance takes the wretch who interrupts
The talk of charming women? I, at last,
Must brave it. Pardon, Lady Waldemar!
The lady on my arm is tired, unwell,
And loyally I've promised she shall say

No harder word this evening, than…good-night;
The rest her face speaks for her."—Then we went.

And I breathe large at home. I drop my cloak
Unclasp my girdle, loose the band that ties
My hair…now could I but unloose my soul!
We are sepulchred alive in this close world,
And want more room.
                The charming woman there—
This reckoning up and writing down her talk
Affects me singularly. How she talked
To pain me! woman's spite.—You wear steel-mail:
A woman takes a housewife[1] from her breast
And plucks the delicatest needle out
As 'twere a rose, and pricks you carefully
'Neath nails, 'neath eyelids, in your nostrils,—say,
A beast would roar so tortured,—but a man,
A human creature, must not, shall not flinch,
No, not for shame.
              What vexes, after all,
Is just that such as she, with such as I,
Knows how to vex. Sweet heaven, she takes me up
As if she had fingered me and dog-eared me
And spelled me by the fireside half a life!
She knows my turns, my feeble points.—What
    then?
The knowledge of a thing implies the thing;
Of course, she found *that* in me, she saw *that*,
Her pencil underscored *this* for a fault,
And I, still ignorant. Shut the book up,—close!
And crush that beetle in the leaves.
                  O heart,
At last we shall grow hard too, like the rest,
And call it self-defence because we are soft.

And after all, now…why should I be pained
That Romney Leigh, my cousin, should espouse
This Lady Waldemar? And, say, she held
Her newly-blossomed gladness in my face,…

----

[1] a small case for needles, etc. (*OED*).

'Twas natural surely, if not generous,
Considering how, when winter held her fast,
1070 I helped the frost with mine, and pained her more
Than she pains me. Pains me!—but wherefore
    pained?
'Tis clear my cousin Romney wants a wife,—
So, good!—The man's need of the woman, here,
Is greater than the woman's of the man,
1075 And easier served; for where the man discerns
A sex (ah, ah, the man can generalise,
Said he), we see but one, ideally
And really: where we yearn to lose ourselves
And melt like white pearls in another's wine,
1080 He seeks to double himself by what he loves,
And make his drink more costly by our pearls.
At board, at bed, at work and holiday,
It is not good for man to be alone,
And that's his way of thinking, first and last,
1085 And thus my cousin Romney wants a wife.
But then my cousin sets his dignity
On personal virtue. If he understands
By love, like others, self-aggrandisement,
It is that he may verily be great
1090 By doing rightly and kindly. Once he thought,
For charitable ends set duly forth
In Heaven's white judgment-book, to marry…ah,
We'll call her name Aurora Leigh, although
She's changed since then!—and once, for social
    ends,
1095 Poor Marian Erle, my sister Marian Erle,
My woodland sister, sweet maid Marian,
Whose memory moans on in me like the wind
Through ill-shut casements, making me more sad
Than ever I find reasons for. Alas,
1100 Poor pretty plaintive face, embodied ghost!
He finds it easy then, to clap thee off
From pulling at his sleeve and book and pen,—
He locks thee out at night into the cold
Away from butting with thy horny eyes
1105 Against his crystal dreams, that now he's strong
To love anew? that Lady Waldemar

Succeeds my Marian?
              After all, why not?
He loved not Marian, more than once he loved
Aurora. If loves at last that Third,
1110 Albeit she prove as slippery as spilt oil
On marble floors, I will not augur him
Ill-luck for that. Good love, howe'er ill-placed,
Is better for a man's soul in the end,
Than if he loved ill what deserves love well.
1115 A pagan, kissing for a step of Pan
The wild-goat's hoof-print on the loamy down,
Exceeds our modern thinker who turns back
The strata…granite, limestone, coal, and clay,
Concluding coldly with, "Here's law! where's
    God?"

1120 And then at worst,—if Romney loves her not,—
At worst,—if he's incapable of love,
Which may be—then indeed, for such a man
Incapable of love, she's good enough;
For she, at worst too, is a woman still
1125 And loves him…as the sort of woman can.

My loose long hair began to burn and creep,
Alive to the very ends, about my knees:
I swept it backward as the wind sweeps flame,
With the passion of my hands. Ah, Romney laughed
1130 One day…(how full the memories come up!)
"—Your Florence fire-flies live on in your hair,"
He said, "it gleams so." Well, I wrung them out,
My fire-flies; made a knot as hard as life
Of those loose, soft, impracticable curls.
1135 And then sat down and thought…"She shall not
    think
Her thought of me,"—and drew my desk and
    wrote.

"Dear Lady Waldemar, I could not speak
With people round me, nor can sleep to-night
And not speak, after the great news I heard
1140 Of you and of my cousin. May you be

Most happy; and the good he meant the world,
Replenish his own life. Say what I say,
And let my word be sweeter for your mouth,
As you are *you*…I only Aurora Leigh."
45 That's quiet, guarded: though she hold it up
Against the light, she'll not see through it more
Than lies there to be seen. So much for pride;
And now for peace, a little. Let me stop
All writing back…"Sweet thanks, my sweetest friend,
50 You've made more joyful my great joy itself."
—No, that's too simple! she would twist it thus,
"My joy would still be as sweet as thyme in drawers,
"However shut up in the dark and dry;
"But violets, aired and dewed by love like yours,
55 "Out-smell all thyme: we keep that in our clothes,
"But drop the other down our bosoms till
"They smell like"…ah, I see her writing back
Just so. She'll make a nosegay of her words,
And tie it with blue ribbons at the end
60 To suit a poet;—pshaw!
                        And then we'll have
The call to church, the broken, sad, bad dream
Dreamed out at last, the marriage-vow complete
With the marriage-breakfast; praying in white
    gloves,
Drawn off in haste for drinking pagan toasts
65 In somewhat stronger wine than any sipped
By gods since Bacchus had his way with grapes.

A postscript stops all that and rescues me.
"You need not write. I have been overworked,
And think of leaving London, England even,
70 And hastening to get nearer the sun
Where men sleep better. So, adieu."—I fold
And seal,—and now I'm out of all the coil;
I breathe now, I spring upward like a branch
The ten-years school-boy with a crooked stick
75 May pull down to his level in search of nuts,
But cannot hold a moment. How we twang
Back on the blue sky, and assert our height,
While he stares after! Now, the wonder seems

That I could wrong myself by such a doubt.
1180 We poets always have uneasy hearts,
    Because our hearts, large-rounded as the globe,
    Can turn but one side to the sun at once.
    We are used to dip our artist-hands in gall
    And potash, trying potentialities
1185 Of alternated colour, till at last
    We get confused, and wonder for our skin
    How nature tinged it first. Well—here's the true
    Good flesh-colour; I recognise my hand,—
    Which Romney Leigh may clasp as just a friend's,
1190 And keep his clean.
                        And now, my Italy.
    Alas, if we could ride with naked souls
    And make no noise and pay no price at all,
    I would have seen thee sooner, Italy,
    For still I have heard thee crying through my life,
1195 Thou piercing silence of ecstatic graves,
    Men call that name!
                        But even a witch to-day
    Must melt down golden pieces in the nard
    Wherewith to anoint her broomstick ere she rides;
    And poets evermore are scant of gold,
1200 And if they find a piece behind the door
    It turns by sunset to a withered leaf.
    The Devil himself scarce trusts his patented
    Gold-making art to any who make rhymes,
    But culls his Faustus from philosophers [1]
1205 And not from poets. "Leave my Job," said God; [2]
    And so the Devil leaves him without pence,
    And poverty proves plainly special grace.
    In these new, just, administrative times
    Men clamour for an order of merit: why?
1210 Here's black bread on the table and no wine!

---

[1] See Marlowe's *The Tragical History of Doctor Faustus* (1604), and Goethe's drama, *Faust* (1808 and 1832). Faust is a philosopher and alchemist who sells his soul to the devil in return for the secret of alchemy, wealth, and power.

[2] Cf. Job 42:10.

At least I am a poet in being poor,
Thank God. I wonder if the manuscript
Of my long poem, if 'twere sold outright,
Would fetch enough to buy me shoes to go
1215 A-foot (thrown in, the necessary patch
For the other side the Alps)? It cannot be.
I fear that I must sell this residue
Of my father's books, although the Elzevirs[1]
Have fly-leaves over-written by his hand
1220 In faded notes as thick and fine and brown
As cobwebs on a tawny monument
Of the old Greeks—*conferenda hæc cum his—*
Corruptè citat—lege potiùs,[2]
And so on, in the scholar's regal way
1225 Of giving judgment on the parts of speech,
As if he sat on all twelve thrones up-piled,
Arraigning Israel.[3] Ay, but books and notes
Must go together. And this Proclus too,
In these dear quaint contracted Grecian types,
1230 Fantastically crumpled like his thoughts
Which would not seem too plain; you go round
    twice
For one step forward, then you take it back
Because you're somewhat giddy; there's the rule
For Proclus.[4] Ah, I stained this middle leaf
1235 With pressing in't my Florence iris-bell,
Long stalk and all: my father chided me
For that stain of blue blood,—I recollect
The peevish turn his voice took,—"Silly girls,
Who plant their flowers in our philosophy
1240 To make it fine, and only spoil the book!
No more of it, Aurora." Yes—no more!
Ah, blame of love, that's sweeter than all praise
Of those who love not! 'tis so lost to me,

I cannot, in such beggared life, afford
1245 To lose my Proclus,—not for Florence even.

The kissing Judas, Wolff,[5] shall go instead,
Who builds us such a royal book as this
To honour a chief-poet, folio-built,
And writes above, "The house of Nobody!"
1250 Who floats in cream, as rich as any sucked
From Juno's breasts,[6] the broad Homeric lines,
And, while with their spondaic prodigious mouths
They lap the lucent margins as babe-gods,
Proclaims them bastards. Wolff's an atheist:
1255 And if the Iliad fell out, as he says,
By mere fortuitous concourse of old songs,
Conclude as much too for the universe.

That Wolff, those Platos: sweep the upper shelves
As clean as this, and so I am almost rich,
1260 Which means, not forced to think of being poor
In sight of ends. To-morrow: no delay.
I'll wait in Paris till good Carrington
Dispose of such and, having chaffered for[7]
My book's price with the publisher, direct
1265 All proceeds to me. Just a line to ask
His help.
            And now I come, my Italy,
My own hills! Are you 'ware of me, my hills,
How I burn toward you? do you feel to-night
The urgency and yearning of my soul,
1270 As sleeping mothers feel the sucking babe
And smile?—Nay, not so much as when in heat
Vain lightnings catch at your inviolate tops
And tremble while ye are steadfast. Still ye go
Your own determined, calm, indifferent way

---

[1] a family of printers, working in Amsterdam, Leyden, and the Hague (1592–1680); the printers were famous for their editions of the classics.

[2] "Compare this with that. Corruptly or incorrectly cited."

[3] Cf. Matthew 19:28.

[4] Proclus of Byzantium (c. 411–85); the last major writer of the Neo-platonic school.

[5] Friedrich Augustus Wolf—EBB's spelling is incorrect—(1759–1824); his *Prolegomena to Homer* (1795) argues that the *Iliad* and *Odyssey* are not works by a single, identifiable poet, but works composed by a number of authors.

[6] The Milky Way was said to originate from Juno's flowing milk—from Hyginus's *Poetica Astronomica* 2:43.

[7] haggled over.

75 Toward sunrise, shade by shade, and light by light,
Of all the grand progression nought left out,
As if God verily made you for yourselves
And would not interrupt your life with ours.
—1857

A Curse for a Nation

PROLOGUE

I heard an angel speak last night,
    And he said "Write!
Write a Nation's curse for me,
And send it over the Western Sea."

5 I faltered, taking up the word:
    "Not so, my lord!
If curses must be, choose another
To send thy curse against my brother.

"For I am bound by gratitude,
10   By love and blood,
To brothers of mine across the sea,
Who stretch out kindly hands to me."

"Therefore," the voice said, "shalt thou write
    My curse to-night.
15 From the summits of love a curse is driven,
As lightning is from the tops of heaven."

"Not so," I answered. "Evermore
    My heart is sore
For my own land's sins: for little feet
20 Of children bleeding along the street:

"For parked-up honours that gainsay
    The right of way:
For almsgiving through a door that is
Not open enough for two friends to kiss:

25 "For love of freedom which abates
    Beyond the Straits:
For patriot virtue starved to vice on
Self-praise, self-interest, and suspicion:

"For an oligarchic parliament,
30   And bribes well-meant.
What curse to another land assign,
When heavy-souled for the sins of mine?"

"Therefore," the voice said, "shalt thou write
    My curse to-night.
35 Because thou hast strength to see and hate
A foul thing done *within* thy gate."

"Not so," I answered once again.
    "To curse, choose men.
For I, a woman, have only known
40 How the heart melts and the tears run down."

"Therefore," the voice said, "shalt thou write
    My curse to-night.
Some women weep and curse, I say
(And no one marvels), night and day.

45 "And thou shalt take their part to-night,
    Weep and write.
A curse from the depths of womanhood
Is very salt, and bitter, and good."

So thus I wrote, and mourned indeed,
50   What all may read.
And thus, as was enjoined on me,
I send it over the Western Sea.
—1860

A Musical Instrument

I

What was he doing, the great god Pan,[1]
   Down in the reeds by the river?
Spreading ruin and scattering ban,[2]
Splashing and paddling with hoofs of a goat,
5   And breaking the golden lilies afloat
      With the dragon-fly on the river.

II

He tore out a reed, the great god Pan,
   From the deep cool bed of the river:
The limpid water turbidly ran,
10   And the broken lilies a-dying lay,
And the dragon-fly had fled away,
      Ere he brought it out of the river.

III

High on the shore sat the great god Pan
   While turbidly flowed the river;
15   And hacked and hewed as a great god can,
With his hard bleak steel at the patient reed,
Till there was not a sign of the leaf indeed
      To prove it fresh from the river.

IV

He cut it short, did the great god Pan,
20   (How tall it stood in the river!)

Then drew the pith,[3] like the heart of a man,
Steadily from the outside ring,
And notched the poor dry empty thing
   In holes, as he sat by the river.

V

25 "This is the way," laughed the great god Pan
      (Laughed while he sat by the river),
"The only way, since gods began
To make sweet music, they could succeed."
Then, dropping his mouth to a hole in the reed,
30   He blew in power by the river.

VI

Sweet, sweet, sweet, O Pan!
   Piercing sweet by the river!
Blinding sweet, O great god Pan!
The sun on the hill forgot to die,
35 And the lilies revived, and the dragon-fly
      Came back to dream on the river.

VII

Yet half a beast is the great god Pan,
   To laugh as he sits by the river,
Making a poet out of a man:
40 The true gods sigh for the cost and pain,—
For the reed which grows nevermore again
      As a reed with the reeds in the river.
                              —1862

---

[1] the god of woods, fields, and flocks, having a human body with goat's legs, horns, and ears. According to Greek myth, the nymph Syrinx, in attempting to escape Pan's pursuit of her, was metamorphosed into a reed in a stream. Pan turned the reed into a shepherd's pipe.

[2] curses; condemnation.

[3] the central tissue.

Frederick Tennyson
1807 – 1898

As the brother of the more famous Alfred, Frederick, with Charles Tennyson (1808–97), contributed to Alfred's first major publication, *Poems By Two Brothers*

(1826). Somewhat more than half the volume was by Alfred; Frederick wrote only three or four of the poems, and the rest were by Charles.

⁂

Old Age

As when into the garden paths by night
One bears a lamp, and with its sickly glare
Scatters the burnished flowers a-dreaming there,
Palely they show like spectres in his sight,
Lovely no more, disfurnished of delight,
Some folded up and drooping o'er the way,
Their odours spent, their colour changed to gray,
Some that stood queen-like in the morning light
Fallen discrowned: so the low-burning loves
That tremble in the hearts of aged men
Cast their own light upon the world that moves
Around them, and receive it back again.
Old joys seem dead, old faces without joys;
Laughter is dead. There is no mirth in boys.
—1913

Caroline Norton
1808 – 1877

Caroline Norton was the daughter of the Scottish novelist Henrietta Callander, granddaughter of the dramatist and politician Richard Brinsley Sheridan, and great-granddaughter of the novelist Frances Sheridan. Caroline married George Norton in 1827 and soon discovered, as her first American editor delicately wrote, that he was "a man of a lower range of feelings" than she. The marriage was an unhappy one emotionally, intellectually, and even politically (Norton was a Whig and her husband was a Tory MP). After her husband's death in 1875,

Norton married a long-time friend, but died shortly thereafter. Norton was ardently engaged in contemporary debates on married women's rights and on child labour, which she vigorously opposed and which forms the subject of "A Voice from the Factories" (1836). From the publication of her first collection, *The Sorrows of Rosalie* (1829), her poetry was well-received by her peers, and Hartley Coleridge, famously remarking that she was "the Byron of modern poetesses," identified her in 1840 as the foremost woman poet writing in England.

⌘

From *Voice From the Factories*

I

When fallen man from Paradise was driven
    Forth to a world of labour, death, and
        care;
Still, of his native Eden, bounteous Heaven
    Resolved one brief memorial to spare,
5   And gave his offspring an imperfect share
    Of that lost happiness, amid decay;
    Making their first *approach* to life seem fair,
    And giving, for the Eden past away,
CHILDHOOD, the weary life's long happy holyday.

IX

Ever a toiling *child* doth make us sad:
    'T is an unnatural and mournful sight,
75   Because we feel their smiles should be so glad,
    Because we know their eyes should be so bright.
    What is it, then, when, tasked beyond their
        might,
    They labour all day long for others' gain,—
    Nay, trespass on the still and pleasant night,
80   While uncompleted hours of toil remain?
Poor little FACTORY SLAVES—for YOU these lines
    complain!

X

Beyond all sorrow which the wanderer knows,
    Is that these little pent-up wretches feel;
    Where the air thick and close and stagnant
        grows,
85   And the low whirring of the incessant wheel
    Dizzies the head, and makes the senses reel:
    There, shut for ever from the gladdening sky,
    Vice premature and Care's corroding seal
    Stamp on each sallow cheek their hateful die,
90 Line the smooth open brow, and sink the
    saddened eye.

XI

For them the fervid summer only brings
    A double curse of stifling withering heat;
For them no flowers spring up, no wild bird
        sings,
No moss-grown walks refresh their weary
        feet;—
95   No river's murmuring sound;—no wood-walk,
        sweet
With many a flower the learned slight and
        pass;—
Nor meadow, with pale cowslips thickly set

Amid the soft leaves of its tufted grass,—
Lure *them* a childish stock of treasures to amass.

XIV

Mark the result. Unnaturally debarred
All nature's fresh and innocent delights,
20 While yet each germing energy strives hard,
And pristine good with pristine evil fights;
When every passing dream the heart excites,
And makes even *guarded* virtue insecure;
Untaught, unchecked, they yield as vice invites:
25 With all around them cramped, confined,
    impure,
Fast spreads the moral plague which nothing new
    shall cure.

XV

Yes, this reproach is added; (infamous
In realms which own a Christian monarch's
    sway!)
Not suffering *only* is their portion, thus
30 Compelled to toil their youthful lives away:
Excessive labour works the SOUL's decay—
Quenches the intellectual light within—
Crushes with iron weight the mind's free play—
Steals from us LEISURE purer thoughts to
    win—
35 And leaves us sunk and lost in dull and native sin.

XVI

Yet in the British Senate men rise up,
(The freeborn and the fathers of our land!)
And while these drink the dregs of Sorrow's cup,
Deny the sufferings of the pining band.
40 With nice-drawn calculations at command,
They prove—rebut—explain—and reason long;
Proud of each shallow argument they stand,
And prostitute their utmost powers of tongue
Feebly to justify this great and glaring wrong.

XVII

145 So rose, with such a plausible defence
Of the unalienable RIGHT OF GAIN,
Those who against Truth's brightest eloquence
Upheld the cause of torture and of pain:
And fear of Property's Decrease made vain,
150 For years, the hope of Christian Charity
To lift the curse from SLAVERY's dark domain,
And send across the wide Atlantic sea
The watchword of brave men—the thrilling
    shout, "BE FREE!"

XVIII

What is to be a slave? Is 't not to spend
155 A life bowed down beneath a grinding ill?—
To labour on to serve another's end,—
To give up leisure, health, and strength, and
    skill—
And give up each of these *against your will?*
Hark to the angry answer:—"Theirs is not
160 A life of slavery; if they labour,—still
We *pay* their toil. Free service is their lot;
And what their labour yields, by us is fairly got."

XIX

Oh, Men! blaspheme not Freedom! Are they
    free
Who toil until the body's strength gives way?
165 Who may not set a term for Liberty,
Who have no time for food, or rest, or play,
But struggle through the long unwelcome day
Without the leisure to be good or glad?
Such is their service—call it what you may.
170 Poor little creatures, overtasked and sad,
Your Slavery hath no name,—yet is its Curse
    as bad!

XX

Again an answer. "'Tis their parents' choice.
By *some* employ the poor man's child must earn
Its daily bread; and infants have no voice

175　In what the allotted task shall be: they learn
　　What answers best, or suits the parents' turn."
　　Mournful reply! Do not your hearts inquire
　　Who tempts the parents' penury? They yearn
　　Toward their offspring with a strong desire,
180　But those who starve *will* sell, even what they
　　most require.

XXI

　　We grant their class must labour—young and
　　old;
　　We grant the child the needy parents' tool:
　　But still our hearts a better plan behold;
　　No bright Utopia of some dreaming fool,
185　But rationally just, and good by rule.
　　Not against TOIL, but TOIL's EXCESS we pray,
　　(Else were we nursed in Folly's simplest school);
　　That so our country's hardy children may
　　Learn not to loathe, but bless, the well apportioned
　　day.

XXII

190　One more reply! The *last* reply—the great
　　Answer to all that sense or feeling shows,
　　To which all others are subordinate:—
　　"The Masters of the Factories must lose
　　By the abridgment of these infant woes.
195　Show us the remedy which shall combine
　　Our equal gain with their increased repose—
　　Which shall not make our trading class repine,
　　But to the proffered boon its strong effects
　　confine."

XXIII

　　Oh! shall it then be said that TYRANT acts
200　Are those which cause our country's looms to
　　thrive?
　　That Merchant England's prosperous trade
　　exacts
　　This bitter sacrifice, e'er she derive
　　That profit due, for which the feeble strive?

　　Is her commercial avarice so keen,
205　That in her busy multitudinous hive
　　Hundreds must die like insects, scarcely seen,
　　While the thick-thronged survivors work where
　　they have been?

XXIV

　　Forbid it, Spirit of the glorious Past
　　Which gained our Isle the surname of 'The
　　Free,'
210　And made our shores a refuge at the last
　　To all who would not bend the servile knee,
　　The vainly-vanquished sons of Liberty!
　　Here ever came the injured, the opprest,
　　Compelled from the Oppressor's face to flee—
215　And found a home of shelter and of rest
　　In the warm generous heart that beat in England's
　　breast.

XLIV

　　Examine and decide. Watch through his day
　　One of these little ones. The sun hath shone
390　An hour, and by the ruddy morning's ray,
　　The last and least, he saunters on alone.
　　See where, still pausing on the threshold stone,
　　He stands, as loth to lose the bracing wind;
　　With wistful wandering glances backward
　　thrown
395　On all the light and glory left behind,
　　And sighs to think that HE must darkly be
　　confined!

XLV

　　Enter with him. The stranger who surveys
　　The little natives of that dreary place
　　(Where squalid suffering meets his shrinking
　　gaze),
400　Used to the glory of a young child's face,
　　Its changeful light, its coloured sparkling grace,
　　(Gleams of Heaven's sunshine on our shadowed
　　earth!)

Starts at each visage wan, and bold, and base,
Whose smiles have neither innocence nor
mirth,—
And comprehends the Sin original from birth.

XLVI

There the pale Orphan, whose unequal strength
Loathes the incessant toil it *must* pursue,
Pines for the cool sweet evening's twilight
length,
The sunny play-hour, and the morning's dew:
Worn with its cheerless life's monotonous hue,
Bowed down, and faint, and stupified it stands;
Each half-seen object reeling in its view—
While its hot, trembling, languid little hands
Mechanically heed the Task-master's commands.

XLVII

There, sounds of wailing grief and painful
blows
Offend the ear, and startle it from rest;
(While the lungs gasp what air the place
bestows;)
Or misery's joyless vice, the ribald jest,
Breaks the sick silence: staring at the guest
Who comes to view their labour, they beguile
The unwatched moment; whispers half supprest
And mutterings low, their faded lips defile,—
While gleams from face to face a strange and sullen
smile.

XLVIII

These then are his Companions: he, too young
To share their base and saddening merriment,
Sits by: his little head in silence hung;
His limbs cramped up; his body weakly bent;
Toiling obedient, till long hours so spent
Produce Exhaustion's slumber, dull and deep.
The Watcher's stroke,—bold—sudden—
violent,—
Urges him from that lethargy of sleep,

And bids him wake to Life,—to labour and to
weep!

XLIX

But the day hath its End. Forth then he hies
With jaded, faltering step, and brow of pain;
Creeps to that shed,—his HOME,—where
happy lies
The sleeping babe that cannot toil for Gain;
Where his remorseful Mother tempts in vain
With the best portion of their frugal fare:
Too sick to eat—too weary to complain—
He turns him idly from the untasted share,
Slumbering sinks down unfed, and mocks her
useless care.

L

Weeping she lifts, and lays his heavy head
(With all a woman's grieving tenderness)
On the hard surface of his narrow bed;
Bends down to give a sad unfelt caress,
And turns away;—willing her God to bless,
That, weary as he is, he need not fight
Against that long-enduring bitterness,
The VOLUNTARY LABOUR of the Night,
But sweetly slumber on till day's returning light.

LI

Vain hope! Alas! unable to forget
The anxious task's long, heavy agonies,
In broken sleep the victim labours yet!
Waiting the boding stroke that bids him rise,
He marks in restless fear each hour that flies—
Anticipates the unwelcome morning prime—
And murmuring feebly, with unwakened eyes,
"Mother! Oh Mother! is it yet THE TIME?"—
Starts at the moon's pale ray—or clock's far
distant chime.

LII

460 Such is *his* day and night! Now then return
Where your OWN slumber in protected ease;
They whom no blast may pierce, no sun may
  burn;
The lovely, on whose cheeks the wandering
  breeze
Hath left the rose's hue. Ah! not like these
465 Does the pale infant-labourer ask to be:
He craves no tempting food—no toys to
  please—
Not Idleness,—but less of agony;
Not Wealth,—but comfort, rest, CONTENTED
POVERTY.

LIII

There is, among all men, in every clime,
470 A difference instinctive and unschooled:
God made the MIND unequal. From all time
By fierceness conquered, or by cunning fooled,
The World hath had its Rulers and its Ruled:—
Yea—uncompelled—men abdicate free choice,
475 Fear their own rashness, and, by thinking cooled,
Follow the counsel of some trusted voice;—
A self-elected sway, wherein their souls rejoice.

LIV

Thus, for the most part, willing to obey,
Men rarely set Authority at naught:
480 Albeit a weaker or a worse than they
May hold the rule with such importance fraught:
And thus the peasant, from his cradle taught
That some must *own*, while some must *till* the
  land,
Rebels not—murmurs not—even in his thought.
485 Born to his lot, he bows to high command,
And guides the furrowing plough with a contented
hand.

LV

But, if the weight which habit renders light
Is made to gall the Serf who bends below—
The dog that watched and fawned, prepares to
  bite!
490 Too rashly strained, the cord snaps from the
  bow—
Too tightly curbed, the steeds their riders
  throw—
And so, (at first contented his fair state
Of customary servitude to know,)
Too harshly ruled, the poor man learns to hate
495 And curse the oppressive law that bids him serve
the Great.

LVI

THEN first he asks his gloomy soul the CAUSE
Of his discomfort; suddenly compares—
Reflects—and with an angry Spirit draws
The envious line between his lot and theirs,
500 Questioning the JUSTICE of the unequal shares.
And from the gathering of this discontent,
Where there is strength, REVOLT his standard
  rears;
Where there is weakness, evermore finds vent
The sharp annoying cry of sorrowful complaint.

LVII

505 Therefore should Mercy, gently and serene,
Sit by the Ruler's side, and share his Throne:—
Watch with unerring eye the passing scene,
And bend her ear to mark the feeblest groan;
Lest due Authority be overthrown,
510 And they that ruled perceive (too late confest!)
Permitted Power might still have been their own,
Had they but watched that none should be
  opprest—
No just complaint despised—no WRONG left
  unredrest.
—1836

The Creole Girl

Elle etait de ce monde, ou les plus belles choses
  Ont le pire destin;
Et Rose, elle a vecu ce que vivent les Roses,
  L'espace d'un matin! [1]

She came to England from the island clime
  Which lies beyond the far Atlantic wave;
She died in early youth—before her time—
  "Peace to her broken heart, and virgin grave!"

5   She was the child of Passion, and of Shame,
  English her father, and of noble birth;
Though too obscure for good or evil fame,
  Her unknown mother faded from the earth.

And what that fair West Indian did betide,
10   None knew but he, who least of all might tell,—
But that she lived, and loved, and lonely died,
  And sent this orphan child with him to dwell.

Oh! that a fair, an innocent young face
  Should have a poison in its looks alone,
15 To raise up thoughts of sorrow and disgrace
  And shame most bitter, although not his own:

Cruel were they who flung that heavy shade
  Across the life whose days did but begin;
Cruel were they who crush'd her heart, and made
20   *Her* youth pay penance for *his* youth's wild sin:

Yet so it was;—among her father's friends
  A cold compassion made contempt seem light,
But in "the world," no justice e'er defends
  The victims of their tortuous wrong and
    right:—

25 And "moral England," striking down the weak,
  And smiling at the vices of the strong,
On her, poor child! her parent's guilt would wreak,
  And that which was her grievance, made her
    wrong.

The world she understood not; nor did they
30   Who made that world,—her, either, understand;
The very glory of her features' play
  Seem'd like the language of a foreign land;

The shadowy feelings, rich and wild and warm,
  That glow'd and mantled in her lovely face,—
35 The slight full beauty of her youthful form,
  Its gentle majesty, its pliant grace,—

The languid lustre of her speaking eye,
  The indolent smile of that bewitching mouth,
(Which more than all betray'd her natal sky,
40   And left us dreaming of the sunny South,)—

The passionate variation of her blood,
  Which rose and sank, as rise and sink the waves,
With every change of her most changeful mood,
  Shock'd sickly Fashion's pale and guarded slaves.

45 And so in this fair world she stood alone,
  An alien 'mid the ever-moving crowd,
A wandering stranger, nameless and unknown
  Her claim to human kindness disallow'd.

But oft would Passion's bold and burning gaze,
50   And Curiosity's set frozen stare,
Fix on her beauty in those early days,
  And coarsely thus her loveliness declare!

Which she would shrink from, as the gentle plant,
  Fern-leaved Mimosa [2] folds itself away;

---

[1] "She was of this world where the most beautiful things have the worst fate. She lived like the rose in the space of a morning."

[2] plant with yellow flowers and sensitive leaflets which droop when touched.

55 Suffering and sad;—for easy 'twas to daunt
     One who on earth had no protecting stay.

And often to her eye's transparent lid
     The unshed tears would rise with sudden start,
And sink again, as though by Reason chid,
60   Back to their gentle home, her wounded heart,

Even as some gushing fountain idly wells
     Up to the prison of its marble side,
Whose power the mounting wave forever quells,—
     So rose her tears—so stemm'd by virgin pride.

65 And so more lonely each succeeding day,
     As she her lot did better understand,
She lived a life which had in it decay,
     A flower transplanted to too cold a land,—

Which for a while gives out a hope of bloom,
70   Then fades and pines, because it may not feel
The freedom and the warmth which gave it room
     The beauty of its nature to reveal.

For vainly would the heart accept its lot,
     And rouse its strength to bear avow'd contempt,
75 Scorn *will* be felt as scorn—deserved or not—
     And from its bitter spell none stand exempt

There is a basilisk[1] power in human eyes
     When they would look a fellow-creature down,
Neath which the faint soul fascinated lies,
80   Struck by the cold sneer and the with'ring
          frown.

But one there was among the cruel crowd,
     Whose nature *half* rebell'd against the chain,
Which fashion flung around him; though too proud
     To own that slavery's weariness and pain.

85 Too proud; perhaps too weak; for Custom still
     Curbs with an iron bit the souls born free;
They start and chafe, yet bend them to the will
     Of this most nameless ruler,—so did he.

And even unto *him* the worldly brand
90   Which rested on her, half her charm effaced;
Vainly all pure and radiant did she stand,—
     Even unto *him* she was a thing disgraced.

Had she been early doom'd a cloister'd nun,
     To Heaven devoted by an holy vow—
95 His union with that poor deserted one
     Had seem'd not *more* impossible than now.

He *could* have loved her—fervently and well;
     But still the cold world with its false allure,
Bound his free liking in an icy spell,
100   And made its whole foundation insecure.

But not like meaner souls, would he, to prove
     A vulgar admiration, her pursue;
For though his glance after her would rove,
     As something beautiful, and strange, and new.

105 They were withdrawn if but her eye met his,
     Or, for an instant if their light remain'd,
They soften'd into gentlest tenderness,
     As asking pardon that his look had pain'd.

And she was nothing unto him,—nor he
110   Aught unto her; but each of each did dream
In the still hours of thought, when we are free
     To quit the real world for things which seem.

When in his heart Love's folded wings would stir,
     And bid his youth choose out a fitting mate,
115 *Against his will* his thoughts roam'd back to her,
     And all around seem'd blank and desolate.

---

[1] a fatal glance; derived from the legend of a mythical lizard-like creature
with a lethal look and glance.

When, in his worldly haunts, a smother'd sigh
   Told he had won some lady of the land,
The dreaming glances of *his* earnest eye
   Beheld far off the Creole orphan stand;

20

And to the beauty by his side he froze,
   As though she were not fair, nor he so young,
And turn'd on her such looks of cold repose
   As check'd the trembling accents of her tongue,

25 And bid her heart's dim passion seek to hide
   Its gathering strength, although the task be
     pain,
Lest she become that mock to woman's pride—
   A wretch that loves unwoo'd, and loves in vain.

So in his heart she dwelt,—as one may dwell
30   Upon the verge of a forbidden ground;
And oft he struggled hard to break the spell
   And banish her, but vain the effort found;

For still along the winding way which led
   Into his inmost soul, unbidden came
35 Her haunting form,—and he was visited
   By echoes soft of her unspoken name,

Through the long night, when those we love *seem*
   near,
   However cold, however far away,
Borne on the wings of floating dreams, which cheer
40   And give us strength to meet the struggling day.

And when in twilight hours *she* roved apart,
   Feeding her love-sick soul with visions fair,
The shadow of *his* eyes was on her heart,
   And the smooth masses of his shining hair

45 Rose in the glory of the evening light,
   And, where she wander'd glided, evermore,

A star which beam'd upon her world's lone night
   Where nothing glad had ever shone before.

But vague and girlish was that love,—no hope,
150   Even of familiar greeting, ever cross'd
Its innocent, but, oh! most boundless scope;
   She loved him,—and she knew her love was
     lost.

She gazed on him, as one from out a bark,
   Bound onward to a cold and distant strand,
155 Some lovely bay, some haven fair may mark,
   Stretching far inward to a sunnier land;

Who, knowing he must still sail on turns back
   To watch with dreaming and most mournful
     eyes
The ruffling foam which follows in his track,
160   Or the deep starlight of the shoreless skies.

Oh! many a hopeless love like this may be,—
   For love will live that never looks to win
Gems rashly lost in Passion's stormy sea,
   Not to be lifted forth when once cast in!

PART II

So time roll'd on, till suddenly that child
   Of southron clime and feelings, droop'd and
     pined;
Her cheek wax'd paler, and her eye grew wild,
   And from her youthful form all strength
     declined.

5 Twas then I knew her; late and vainly call'd
   To "minister unto a mind diseased,"—
When on her heart's faint sickness all things pall'd
   And the deep inward pain was never eased:

Her step was always gentle, but at last
10   It fell as lightly as a wither'd leaf
In autumn hours; and wheresoe'er she pass'd
    Smiles died away, she look'd so full of grief.

And more than ever from that world, where still
    Her father hoped to place her, she would shrink;
15 Loving to be alone, her thirst to fill
    From the sweet fountain where the dreamers
      drink.

One eve, beneath the acacia's waving bough,
    Wrapt in these lonely thoughts she sate and
      read;
Her dark hair parted from her sunny brow,
20   Her graceful arm beneath her languid head;

And droopingly and sad she hung above
    The open page, whereon her eyes were bent,
With looks of fond regret and pining love;
    Nor heard my step, so deep was she intent.

25 And when she me perceived, she did not start,
    But lifted up those soft dark eyes to mine,
And smiled, (that mournful smile which breaks the
      heart!)
    Then glanced again upon the printed line.

"What readest thou?" I ask'd. With fervent gaze,
30   As though she would have scann'd my inmost
      soul,
She turn'd to me, and, as a child obeys
    The accustom'd question of revered control,

She pointed to the title of that book,
    (Which, bending down, I saw was "Coralie,"
35 Then gave me one imploring piteous look,
    And tears, too long restrain'd, gush'd fast and
      free.

It was a tale of one, whose fate had been
    Too like her own to make that weeping strange;
Like her, transplanted from a sunnier scene;
40   Like her, all dull'd and blighted by the change.

No further word was breathed between us two;—
    No confidence was made to keep or break;—
But since that day, which pierced my soul quite
      thro',
    My hand the dying girl would faintly take,

45 And murmur, as its grasp (ah! piteous end!)
    Return'd the feeble pressure of her own,
"Be with me to the last,—for thou, dear friend,
    Hast all my struggles, all my sorrow known!"

She died!—The pulse of that untrammell'd heart
50   Fainted to stillness. Those most glorious eyes
Closed on the world where she had dwelt apart
    And her cold bosom heaved no further sighs.

She died!—and no one mourn'd except her sire,
    Who for a while look'd out with eyes more dim;
55 Lone was her place beside his household fire,
    Vanish'd the face that ever smiled on him.

And no one said to him—"Why mournest thou?"
    Because she was the unknown child of shame;
(Albeit her mother better kept the vow
60   Of faithful love, than some who keep their
      fame.)

Poor mother, and poor child!—unvalued lives!
    Wan leaves that perish'd in obscurest shade!
While round me still the proud world stirs and
      strives,
    Say, Shall I weep that ye are lowly laid?

65 Shall *I* mourn for ye? No!—and least for thee,
    Young dreamer, whose pure heart gave way
      before

Thy bark was launch'd upon Love's stormy sea,
    Or treachery wreck'd it on the farther shore.

Least, least of all for thee! Thou art gone hence?
70   Thee never more shall scornful looks oppress,
Thee the world wrings not with some vain pretence,
    Nor chills thy tears, nor mocks at thy distress.

From man's unjustice, from the cold award
    Of the unfeeling thou hast pass'd away;
75 Thou 'rt at the gates of light where angels guard
    Thy path to realms of bright eternal day.

There shall thy soul its chains of slavery burst,
    There, meekly standing before God's high
        throne,
Thou'lt find the judgments of our earth reversed,
80   And answer for no errors but thine own.
    —1840

The Poet's Choice

'Twas in youth, that hour of dreaming;
  Round me, visions fair were beaming,
Golden fancies, brightly gleaming,
        Such as start to birth
5 When the wandering restless mind,
Drunk with beauty, thinks to find
Creatures of a fairy kind
        Realized on Earth!

Then, for me, in every dell
10 Hamadryads[1] seem'd to dwell
(They who die, as Poet's tell,
        Each with her own tree);
And sweet mermaids, low reclining,
Dim light through their grottos shining,

15 Green weeds round their soft limbs twining,
        Peopled the deep Sea.

Then, when moon and stars were fair,
Nymph-like visions fill'd the air,
With blue wings and golden hair
20   Bending from the skies;
And each cave by echo haunted
In its depth of shadow granted,
Brightly, the Egeria[2] wanted,
        To my eager eyes.

25 But those glories pass'd away;
Earth seem'd left to dull decay,
And my heart in sadness lay,
        Desolate, uncheer'd;
Like one wrapt in painful sleeping,
30 Pining, thirsting, waking, weeping,
Watch thro' Life's dark midnight keeping,
        Till THY form appear'd!

THEN my soul, whose erring measure
Knew not where to find true pleasure,
35 Woke and seized the golden treasure
        Of thy human love;
And looking on thy radiant brow,
My lips in gladness breathed the vow
Which angels, not more fair than thou,
40   Have register'd above.

And now I take my quiet rest,
With my head upon thy breast,
I will make no further quest
        In Fancy's realms of light;
45 Fay, nor nymph, nor winged spirit,
Shall my store of love inherit;
More thy mortal charm doth merit
        Than dream, however bright.

---

[1] a wood nymph whose life was intertwined with that of the tree she lived in.

[2] a nymph who advised and dictated laws to Numa, the second king of Rome.

And my soul, like some sweet bird
50 Whose song at summer eve is heard,
When the breeze, so lightly stirr'd,
      Leaves the branch unbent,—
Sits and all triumphant sings,
Folding up her brooding wings,
55 And gazing out on earthly things
      With a calm content.
—1840

Sonnet IV

Be frank with me, and I accept my lot;
  But deal not with me as a grieving child,
Who for the loss of that which he hath not
  Is by a show of kindness thus beguiled.
5 Raise not for me, from its enshrouded tomb,
  The ghostly likeness of a hope deceased;
Nor think to cheat the darkness of my doom
  By wavering doubts how far thou art released:
This dressing Pity in the garb of Love,—
10   This effort of the heart to *seem* the same,—
These sighs and lingerings, (which nothing prove
  But that thou leav'st me with a kind of
    shame,)—
Remind me more, by their most vain deceit,
Of the dear loss of all which thou dost counterfeit.
—1840

Sonnet VIII

To My Books

Silent companions of the lonely hour,
  Friends, who can never alter or forsake,
Who for inconstant roving have no power,
  And all neglect, perforce, must calmly take,—

5 Let me return to YOU; this turmoil ending
  Which worldly cares have in my spirit wrought,
And, o'er your old familiar pages bending,
  Refresh my mind with many a tranquil thought,
Till, haply meeting there, from time to time,
10   Fancies, the audible echo of my own,
'Twill be like hearing in a foreign clime
  My native language spoke in friendly tone,
And with a sort of welcome I shall dwell
On these, my unripe musings, told so well.
—1840

Sonnet XI

The Weaver

Little they think, the giddy and the vain,
  Wandering at pleasure 'neath the shady trees,
While the light glossy silk or rustling train
  Shines in the sun or flutters in the breeze,
5 How the sick weaver plies the incessant loom,
  Crossing in silence the perplexing thread,
Pent in the confines of one narrow room,
  Where droops complainingly his cheerless
    head:—
Little they think with what dull anxious eyes,
10   Nor by what nerveless, thin, and trembling
    hands,
The devious mingling of those various dyes
  Where wrought to answer Luxury's commands.
But the day cometh when the tired shall rest,—
Where weary Lazarus leans his head on Abraham's
    breast![1]
—1840

---

[1] at rest with one's ancestors. Abraham was the first patriarch and ancestor of the Hebrews: Genesis 12:25.

Edward FitzGerald
1809 – 1883

Edward FitzGerald, poet and translator, graduated from Trinity College, Cambridge, in 1830. He is best known for his adaptation and translation of the *Rubáiyát* of *Omar Khayyám* (1859), which initiated Robert Browning's reply in "Rabbi Ben Ezra" (1864).

❧

Rubáiyát of Omar Khayyám [1]

1

Wake! For the Sun, who scattered into flight
   The Stars before him from the Field of Night,
Drives Night along with them from Heav'n
      and strikes
The Sultán's Turret with a Shaft of Light.

2

5 Before the phantom of False morning[2] died,
Methought a Voice within the Tavern cried,
   "When all the Temple is prepared within,
Why nod the drowsy Worshiper outside?"

3

And, as the Cock crew, those who stood before
10 The Tavern shouted—"Open, then, the Door!
   You know how little while we have to stay,
And, once departed, may return no more."

4

Now the New Year[3] reviving old Desires,
The thoughtful Soul to Solitude retires,

15 Where the WHITE HAND OF MOSES on the
         Bough[4]
Puts out, and Jesus from the Ground suspires.[5]

5

Iram[6] indeed is gone with all his Rose,
And Jamshyd's[7] Sevn'-ringed Cup where no one
         knows;
   But still a Ruby kindles in the Vine,
20 And many a Garden by the Water blows.

6

And David's lips are locked; but in divine
High-piping Pehlevi,[8] with "Wine! Wine! Wine!
   Red Wine!"—the Nightingale cries to the Rose
That sallow cheek of hers to incarnadine.

7

25 Come, fill the Cup, and in the fire of Spring
Your Winter-garment of Repentance fling;
   The Bird of Time has but a little way
To flutter—and the Bird is on the Wing.

---

[1] Omar Khayyám, or Omar the Tent-maker, was a Persian poet and astronomer of the eleventh century. *Rubáiyát* is the plural form of *rubai*, or quatrain.

[2] "A transient light on the Horizon about an hour before the…True Dawn; a well-known phenomenon in the East." (FitzGerald's note.)

[3] The Persian New Year begins with the vernal equinox.

---

[4] See Exodus 4:6.

[5] The Persians believed that the healing power of Jesus resided in his breath.

[6] "A royal Garden now sunk somewhere in the Sands of Arabia." (FitzGerald's note.)

[7] a legendary king of Persia; his seven-ringed cup symbolized the seven heavens, the seven planets, the seven seas, etc.

[8] David the holy singer; Pehlevi is the ancient literary language of Persia.

8

Whether at Naishápur[1] or Babylon,
30 Whether the Cup with sweet or bitter run,
    The Wine of Life keeps oozing drop by drop,
The Leaves of Life keep falling one by one.

9

Each Morn a thousand Roses brings, you say;
Yes, but where leaves the Rose of Yesterday?
35   And this first Summer month that brings the
            Rose
Shall take Jamshyd and Kaikobad[2] away.

10

Well, let it take them! What have we to do
With Kaikobád the Great, or Kaikhosru?[3]
    Let Zál and Rustum[4] bluster as they will,
40 Or Hátim[5] call to Supper—heed not you.

11

With me along the strip of Herbage strown
That just divides the desert from the sown,
    Where name of Slave and Sultán is forgot—
And Peace to Mahmúd[6] on his golden Throne!

12

45 A Book of Verses underneath the Bough,
A Jug of Wine, a Loaf of Bread—and Thou
    Beside me singing in the Wilderness—
Oh, Wilderness were Paradise enow!

13

Some for the glories of This World; and some
50 Sigh for the Prophet's[7] Paradise to come;
    Ah, take the Cash, and let the Credit go,
Nor heed the rumble of a distant Drum![8]

14

Look to the blowing Rose about us—"Lo,
Laughing," she says, "into the world I blow,
55   At once the silken tassel of my Purse
Tear, and its Treasure[9] on the Garden throw."

15

And those who husbanded the Golden Grain,
And those who flung it to the winds like Rain,
    Alike to no such aureate Earth are turned
60 As, buried once, Men want dug up again.

16

The Worldly Hope men set their Hearts upon
Turns Ashes—or it prospers; and anon,
    Like Snow upon the Desert's dusty Face,
Lighting a little hour or two—is gone.

17

65 Think, in this battered Caravanserai[10]
Whose Portals are alternate Night and Day,
    How Sultán after Sultán with his Pomp
Abode his destined Hour, and went his way.

18

They say the Lion and the Lizard keep
70 The Courts where Jamshyd gloried and drank
            deep;

---

[1] the village in Persia where Omar was born.

[2] the founder of a celebrated dynasty.

[3] King.

[4] son and father who were warriors.

[5] according to FitzGerald, "a type of oriental generosity."

[6] a sultan who conquered India.

---

[7] Muhammad's.

[8] "A Drum—beaten outside a Palace." (FitzGerald's note.)

[9] "The Rose's Golden Centre." (FitzGerald's note.)

[10] an Oriental inn.

And Bahrám,[1] that great Hunter—the Wild
    Ass
Stamps o'er his Head, but cannot break his Sleep.

19

I sometimes think that never blows so red
The Rose as where some buried Caesar[2] bled;
    That every Hyacinth[3] the Garden wears
Dropped in her Lap from some once lovely Head.

20

And this reviving Herb whose tender Green
Fledges the River-Lip on which we lean—
    Ah, lean upon it lightly! for who knows
From what once lovely Lip it springs unseen!

21

Ah my Belovèd, fill the Cup that clears
TODAY of past Regrets and future Fears:
    Tomorrow!—Why, Tomorrow I may be
Myself with Yesterday's Sev'n thousand Years.

22

For some we loved, the loveliest and the best
That from his Vintage rolling Time hath pressed,
    Have drunk their Cup a Round or two before,
And one by one crept silently to rest.

23

And we, that now make merry in the Room
They left, and Summer dresses in new bloom,
    Ourselves must we beneath the Couch of Earth
Descend—ourselves to make a Couch—for whom?

24

Ah, make the most of what we yet may spend,
Before we too into the Dust descend;
    Dust into Dust, and under Dust to lie,
Sans Wine, sans Song, sans Singer, and—sans End!

25

Alike for those who for TODAY prepare,
And those that after some TOMORROW stare,
    A Muezzín[4] from the Tower of Darkness cries,
"Fools, your Reward is neither Here nor There."

26

Why, all the Saints and Sages who discussed
Of the Two Worlds so wisely—they are thrust
    Like foolish Prophets forth; their Words to Scorn
Are scattered, and their Mouths are stopped with
    Dust.[5]

27

Myself when young did eagerly frequent
Doctor and Saint, and heard great argument
    About it and about; but evermore
Came out by the same door where in I went.

28

With them the seed of Wisdom did I sow,
And with mine own hand wrought to make it
    grow;
    And this was all the Harvest that I reaped—
"I came like Water, and like Wind I go."

29

Into this Universe, and *Why* not knowing
Nor *Whence*, like Water willy-nilly flowing;
    And out of it, as Wind along the Waste,
I know not *Whither*, willy-nilly blowing.

---

[1] a Persian ruler who died in a swamp while pursuing a wild ass.

[2] Roman general and dictator (102?–44 BC).

[3] Hyacinthus, in Greek mythology, was a youth accidentally killed by his friend Apollo; the hyacinth flower sprang up where Hyacinthus's blood had flowed.

---

[4] the officer who calls the faithful to prayer from a tower of the Mosque.

[5] The Muslims threw dust into the air to confound enemies of the faith.

30

What, without asking, hither hurried *Whence?*
And, without asking, *Whither* hurried hence!
     Oh, many a Cup of this forbidden Wine[1]
120 Must drown the memory of that insolence!

31

Up from the Earth's Center through the Seventh
     Gate
I rose, and on the Throne of Saturn[2] sate,
     And many a Knot unraveled by the Road;
But not the Master-knot of Human Fate.

32

125 There was the Door to which I found no Key;
There was the Veil through which I might not see;
     Some little talk awhile of ME and THEE[3]
There was—and then no more of THEE and ME.

33

Earth could not answer; nor the Seas that mourn
130 In flowring Purple, of their Lord forlorn;
     Nor rolling Heaven, with all his Signs[4] revealed
And hidden by the sleeve of Night and Morn.

34

Then of the THEE IN ME who works behind
The Veil, I lifted up my hands to find
     A lamp amid the Darkness; and I heard,
135 As from Without—"THE ME WITHIN THEE
     BLIND!"

35

Then to the Lip of this poor earthen Urn
I leaned, the Secret of my Life to learn;

---

[1] Alcohol is forbidden to faithful Moslems.

[2] the seat of knowledge. According to the ancients, Saturn was lord of the seventh of the concentric spheres or heavens surrounding the earth.

[3] "Some dividual [sic] Existence or Personality distinct from the whole." (FitzGerald's note.)

[4] of the zodiac.

And Lip to Lip it murmured—"While you live,
140 Drink!—for, once dead, you never shall return."

36

I think the Vessel, that with fugitive
Articulation answered, once did live,
     And drink; and Ah! the passive Lip I kissed,
And many Kisses might it take—and give!

37

145 For I remember stopping by the way
To watch a Potter thumping his wet Clay;[5]
     And with its all-obliterated Tongue
It murmured—"Gently, Brother, gently, pray!"

38

And has not such a Story from of Old
150 Down Man's successive generations rolled
     Of such a clod of saturated Earth
Cast by the Maker into Human mold?

39

And not a drop that from our Cups we throw
For Earth to drink of,[6] but may steal below
155   To quench the fire of Anguish in some Eye
There hidden—far beneath, and long ago.

40

As then the Tulip, for her morning sup
Of Heav'nly Vintage, from the soil looks up,
     Do you devoutly do the like, till Heav'n
160 To Earth invert you—like an empty Cup.

41

Perplexed no more with Human or Divine,
Tomorrow's tangle to the winds resign,

---

[5] Compare Robert Browning's "Rabbi ben Ezra," ll. 26–27.

[6] the custom of pouring some wine on the ground before drinking. "The precious Liquor is not lost, but sinks into the ground to refresh the dust of some poor Wine-worshipper foregone." (FitzGerald's note.)

And lose your fingers in the tresses of
The Cypress-slender Minister of Wine.[1]

42

65 And if the Wine you drink, the Lip you press,
End in what All begins and ends in—Yes;
　　Think then you are TODAY what YESTERDAY
You were—TOMORROW you shall not be less.

43

So when that Angel of the darker Drink
70 At last shall find you by the river brink,
　　And offering his Cup, invite your Soul
Forth to your Lips to quaff—you shall not shrink.

44

Why, if the Soul can fling the Dust aside,
And naked on the Air of Heaven ride,
75 　　Were 't not a Shame—were 't not a Shame for
　　　　him
In this clay carcass crippled to abide?

45

'Tis but a Tent where takes his one day's rest
A Sultán to the realm of Death addressed;
　　The Sultán rises, and the dark Ferrásh[2]
80 Strikes, and prepares it for another Guest.

46

And fear not lest Existence closing your
Account, and mine, should know the like no more;
　　The Eternal Sáki from that Bowl has poured
Millions of Bubbles like us, and will pour.

47

85 When You and I behind the Veil are past,
Oh, but the long, long while the World shall last,

Which of our Coming and Departure heeds
As the Sea's self should heed a pebble-cast.

48

A Moment's Halt—a momentary taste
190 Of BEING from the Well amid the Waste—
　　And Lo!—the phantom Caravan has reached
The NOTHING it set out from—Oh, make haste!

49

Would you that spangle of Existence spend
About THE SECRET—quick about it, Friend!
195 　　A Hair perhaps divides the False and True—
And upon what, prithee, may life depend?

50

A Hair perhaps divides the False and True—
Yes; and a single Alif[3] were the clue—
　　Could you but find it—to the Treasure-house,
200 And peradventure to THE MASTER too;

51

Whose secret Presence, through Creation's veins
Running Quicksilver-like, eludes your pains;
　　Taking all shapes from Máh to Máhi,[4] and
They change and perish all—but He remains;

52

205 A moment guessed—then back behind the Fold
Immersed of Darkness round the Drama rolled
　　Which, for the Pastime of Eternity,
He doth Himself contrive, enact, behold.

53

But if in vain, down on the stubborn floor
210 Of Earth, and up to Heav'n's unopening Door,

---

[1] woman servant who passes the wine.

[2] servant who takes down the tent.

---

[3] a simple vertical line, the first letter of the Arabic alphabet.

[4] "From Fish to Moon." (FitzGerald's note.)

You gaze TODAY, while You are You—how then
TOMORROW, You when shall be You no more?

54

Waste not your Hour, nor in the vain pursuit
Of This and That endeavor and dispute;
    Better be jocund with the fruitful Grape
215 Than sadden after none, or bitter, Fruit.

55

You know, my Friends, with what a brave Carouse
I made a Second Marriage in my house;
    Divorced old barren Reason from my Bed,
220 And took the Daughter of the Vine to Spouse.

56

For "IS" and "IS-NOT" though with Rule and Line,
And "UP-AND-DOWN" by Logic, I define,
    Of all that one should care to fathom, I
Was never deep in anything but—Wine.

57

225 Ah, but my Computations, People say
Reduced the Year to better reckoning?[1]—Nay,
    'Twas only striking from the Calendar
Unborn Tomorrow, and dead Yesterday.

58

And lately, by the Tavern Door agape,
230 Came shining through the Dusk an Angel Shape
    Bearing a Vessel on his Shoulder; and
He bid me taste of it; and 'twas—the Grape!

59

The Grape that can with Logic absolute
The Two-and-Seventy jarring Sects,[2] confute;

---

235 The sovereign Alchemist that in a trice
Life's leaden metal into Gold transmute;

60

The mighty Mahmúd, Allah-breathing Lord,
That all the misbelieving and black Horde[3]
    Of Fears and Sorrows that infest the Soul
240 Scatters before him with his whirlwind Sword.

61

Why, be this Juice the growth of God, who dare
Blaspheme the twisted tendril as a Snare?
    A Blessing, we should use it, should we not?
And if a Curse—why, then, Who set it there?

62

245 I must abjure the Balm of Life, I must,
Scared by some After-reckoning ta'en on trust
    Or lured with Hope of some Diviner Drink,
To fill the Cup—when crumbled into Dust!

63

Oh threats of Hell and Hopes of Paradise!
250 One thing at least is certain—*This* Life flies;
    One thing is certain and the rest is Lies—
The Flower that once has blown forever dies.

64

Strange, is it not? that of the myriads who
Before us passed the door of Darkness through,
255   Not one returns to tell us of the Road,
Which to discover we must travel too.

65

The Revelations of Devout and Learn'd
Who rose before us, and as Prophets burned,[4]
    Are all but Stories, which, awoke from Sleep,
260 They told their comrades, and to Sleep returned.

66

I sent my Soul through the Invisible,
Some letter of that After-life to spell;
    And by and by my Soul returned to me,
And answered, "I Myself am Heav'n and Hell"—

67

265 Heaven but the Vision of fulfilled Desire,
And Hell the Shadow from a Soul on fire
    Cast on the Darkness into which Ourselves,
So late emerged from, shall so soon expire.

68

We are no other than a moving row
270 Of Magic Shadow-shapes that come and go
    Round with the Sun-illumined Lantern held
In Midnight by the Master of the Show;

69

But helpless Pieces of the Game He plays
Upon this Checkerboard of Nights and Days;
275   Hither and thither moves, and checks, and slays,
And one by one back in the Closet lays.

70

The Ball no question makes of Ayes and Noes,
But Here or There as strikes the Player[1] goes;
    And He that tossed you down into the Field,
280 *He* knows about it all—HE knows—HE knows!

71

The Moving Finger writes, and, having writ,
Moves on; nor all your Piety nor Wit
    Shall lure it back to cancel half a Line,
Nor all your Tears wash out a Word of it.

72

285 And that inverted Bowl they call the Sky,
Whereunder crawling cooped we live and die,

    Lift not your hands to *It* for help—for It
As impotently moves as you or I.

73

With Earth's first Clay They did the Last Man
    knead,
290 And there of the Last Harvest sowed the Seed;
    And the first Morning of Creation wrote
What the Last Dawn of Reckoning shall read.

74

YESTERDAY *This* Day's Madness did prepare;
TOMORROW'S Silence, Triumph, or Despair.
295   Drink! for you know not whence you came, nor
        why;
Drink, for you know not why you go, nor where.

75

I tell you this—When, started from the Goal,
Over the flaming shoulders of the Foal
    Of Heav'n Parwín and Mustarí they flung,
300 In my predestined Plot of Dust and Soul.[2]

76

The Vine had struck a fiber; which about
If clings my Being—let the Dervish[3] flout;
    Of my Base metal may be filed a Key.
That shall unlock the Door he howls without.

77

305 And this I know: whether the one True Light
Kindle to Love, or Wrath—consume me quite.
    One Flash of It within the Tavern caught
Better than in the Temple lost outright.

---

[1] polo player.

[2] The speaker's fate was predestined, and related to the relationship of the stars and planets, the Pleiades (Parwin) and Jupiter (Mushtari), which were "flung" by the Gods.

[3] an ascetic who would despise alcohol as a means of perceiving truth.

78

What! out of senseless Nothing to provoke
310 A conscious Something to resent the yoke
　　Of unpermitted Pleasure, under pain
Of Everlasting Penalties, if broke!

79

What! from his helpless Creature be repaid
Pure Gold for what he lent him dross-allayed—
315 　　Sue for a Debt he never did contract,
And cannot answer—Oh, the sorry trade!

80

O Thou, who didst with pitfall and with gin[1]
Beset the Road I was to wander in,
　　Thou wilt not with Predestined Evil round
320 Enmesh, and then impute my Fall to Sin!

81

O Thou, who Man of Baser Earth didst make.
And ev'n with Paradise devise the Snake,
　　For all the Sin wherewith the Face of Man
Is blackened—Man's forgiveness give—and take!

———————

82

325 As under cover of departing Day
Slunk hunger-stricken Ramazán[2] away,
　　Once more within the Potter's house alone
I stood, surrounded by the Shapes of Clay—

83

Shapes of all Sorts and Sizes, great and small
330 That stood along the floor and by the wall;
　　And some loquacious Vessels were; and some
Listened perhaps, but never talked at all.

84

Said one among them—"Surely not in vain
My substance of the common Earth was ta'en
335 　　And to this Figure molded, to be broke,
Or trampled back to shapeless Earth again."

85

Then said a Second—"Ne'er a peevish Boy
Would break the Bowl from which he drank in joy;
　　And He that with his hand the Vessel made
340 Will surely not in after Wrath destroy."

86

After a momentary silence spake
Some Vessel of a more ungainly Make:
　　"They sneer at me for leaning all awry;
What! did the Hand, then, of the Potter shake?"

87

345 Whereat someone of the loquacious Lot—
I think a Súfi[3] pipkin—waxing hot—
　　"All this of Pot and Potter—Tell me then,
Who is the Potter, pray, and who the Pot?"

88

"Why," said another, "Some there are who tell
350 Of one who threatens he will toss to Hell
　　The luckless Pots he marred in making—Pish!
He's a Good Fellow, and 'twill all be well."

89

"Well," murmured one, "Let whoso make or buy,
My Clay with long Oblivion is gone dry;
355 　　But fill me with the old familiar Juice,
Methinks I might recover by and by."

[1] trap.

[2] the month of fasting between sunrise and sunset.

[3] Persian mystic.

90

So while the Vessels one by one were speaking
The little Moon looked in that all were seeking;[1]
    And then they jogged each other, "Brother!
        Brother!
Now for the Porter's shoulder-knot[2] a-creaking!"

———————

91

Ah, with the Grape my fading Life provide,
And wash the Body whence the Life has died,
    And lay me, shrouded in the living Leaf,
By some not unfrequented Garden-side—

92

That ev'n my buried Ashes such a snare
Of Vintage shall fling up into the Air
    As not a True-believer passing by
But shall be overtaken unaware.

93

Indeed the Idols I have loved so long
Have done my credit in this World much wrong,
    Have drowned my Glory in a shallow Cup,
And sold my Reputation for a Song.

94

Indeed, indeed, Repentance oft before
I swore—but was I sober when I swore?
    And then and then came Spring, and Rose-in-
        hand
My threadbare Penitence apieces tore.

95

And much as Wine has played the Infidel,
And robbed me of my Robe of Honor—Well,

I wonder often what the Vintners buy
One-half so precious as the stuff they sell.

96

Yet Ah, that Spring should vanish with the Rose!
That Youth's sweet-scented manuscript should close!
    The Nightingale that in the branches sang,
Ah whence, and whither flown again, who knows!

97

Would but the Desert of the Fountain yield
One glimpse—if dimly, yet indeed, revealed,
    To which the fainting Traveler might spring,
As springs the trampled herbage of the field.

98

Would but some wingèd Angel ere too late
Arrest the yet unfolded Roll of Fate,
    And make the stern Recorder otherwise
Enregister, or quite obliterate!

99

Ah, Love! could you and I with Him conspire
To grasp this sorry Scheme of Things entire,
    Would not we shatter it to bits—and then
Remold it nearer to the Heart's Desire!

———————

100

Yon rising Moon that looks for us again—
How oft hereafter will she wax and wane;
    How oft hereafter rising look for us
Through this same Garden—and for *one* in vain!

101

And when like her, O Sákí, you shall pass
Among the Guests Star-scattered on the Grass,
    And in your joyous errand reach the spot
Where I made One—turn down an empty Glass!

TAMÁM[3]

—1859, 1889 (1857)

———————

[1] "At the close of the Fasting Month, Ramazán…the first Glimpse of the new Moon…is looked for with the utmost Anxiety and hailed with all Acclamation." (FitzGerald's note.)

[2] straps on which the wine jars were carried by the porter.

[3] "It is ended."

Alfred Tennyson
1809–1892

Alfred Tennyson was the most popular and prolific of Victorian poets. While Robert Browning was struggling to find his poetic voice, and an audience, as late as 1850, Tennyson in that year became Poet Laureate. Born into a large family marked by poverty and madness, Tennyson survived a difficult childhood and entered Trinity College, Cambridge, in 1827. There he met and befriended Arthur Henry Hallam, whose death in 1833 occasioned Tennyson's most important poem, *In Memoriam A.H.H.* (1850). With Hallam, Tennyson was a member of the informal debating and discussion group, the Cambridge Apostles. There is no doubt that discussions in this group influenced *Poems, Chiefly Lyrical* (1830), and *Poems* (1832). Stung by hostile critical reaction, and suffering from Hallam's loss, Tennyson spent the years from 1833 to 1850 writing *In Memoriam*, revising his early poetry and writing a number of new poems, all for inclusion in the two volumes published as *Poems* in 1842. His poetic productivity, including *Idylls of the King* (1859–74), continued until his death.

ഗൢഗ

Mariana [1]

With blackest moss the flower-plots
    Were thickly crusted, one and all:
The rusted nails fell from the knots
    That held the pear to the gable-wall.
5 The broken sheds looked sad and strange:
    Unlifted was the clinking latch;
    Weeded and worn the ancient thatch
Upon the lonely moated grange.
        She only said, "My life is dreary,
10   He cometh not," she said;
        She said, "I am aweary, aweary,
           I would that I were dead!"

Her tears fell with the dews at even;
    Her tears fell ere the dews were dried;
15 She could not look on the sweet heaven,
    Either at morn or eventide.
After the flitting of the bats,
    When thickest dark did trance [2] the sky,
    She drew her casement-curtain by,

20 And glanced athwart the glooming flats.
        She only said, "The night is dreary,
         He cometh not," she said;
        She said, "I am aweary, aweary,
           I would that I were dead!"

25 Upon the middle of the night,
    Waking she heard the night-fowl crow:
The cock sung out an hour ere light:
    From the dark fen the oxen's low
Came to her: without hope of change,
30   In sleep she seemed to walk forlorn,
    Till cold winds woke the gray-eyed morn
About the lonely moated grange.
        She only said, "The day is dreary,
         He cometh not," she said;
35   She said, "I am aweary, aweary,
           I would that I were dead!"

About a stone-cast from the wall
    A sluice with blackened waters slept,
And o'er it many, round and small,
40   The clustered marish-mosses crept.
Hard by a poplar shook alway,
    All silver-green with gnarlèd bark:
    For leagues no other tree did mark
The level waste, the rounding gray.

---

[1] For a detailed presentation of materials related to Tennyson's poems, sources, annotations, textural variants, etc., see *The Poems of Tennyson*, ed. Christopher Ricks, 2nd ed., 3 vols. (Berkeley: University of California Press, 1987).

[2] to throw into a trance.

45   She only said, "My life is dreary,
         He cometh not," she said;
      She said, "I am aweary, aweary,
         I would that I were dead!"

And ever when the moon was low;
50   And the shrill winds were up and away,
In the white curtain, to and fro,
    She saw the gusty shadow sway.
But when the moon was very low,
    And wild winds bound within their cell,
55   The shadow of the poplar fell
Upon her bed, across her brow.
      She only said, "The night is dreary,
         He cometh not," she said;
      She said, "I am aweary, aweary.
60   I would that I were dead!"

All day within the dreamy house,
    The doors upon their hinges creaked;
The blue fly sung in the pane; the mouse
    Behind the mouldering wainscot shrieked,
65   Or from the crevice peered about.
      Old faces glimmered through the doors,
      Old footsteps trod the upper floors,
    Old voices called her from without.
      She only said, "My life is dreary,
70   He cometh not," she said;
      She said, "I am aweary, aweary,
         I would that I were dead!"

The sparrow's chirrup on the roof,
    The slow clock ticking, and the sound
75 Which to the wooing wind aloof
    The poplar made, did all confound
Her sense; but most she loathed the hour
    When the thick-moted sunbeam lay
    Athwart the chambers, and the day
80 Was sloping toward his western bower.
      Then, said she, "I am very dreary,
         He will not come," she said;

      She wept, "I am aweary, aweary,
         Oh God, that I were dead!"
—1830

Supposed Confessions of a Second-Rate Sensitive Mind [1]

O God! my God! have mercy now.
  I faint, I fall. Men say that Thou
Didst die for me, for such as *me*,
Patient of ill, and death, and scorn,
5 And that my sin was as a thorn
Among the thorns that girt Thy brow,
Wounding Thy soul.—That even now,
In this extremest misery
Of ignorance, I should require
10 A sign! and if a bolt of fire
Would rive the slumbrous summer noon
While I do pray to Thee alone,
Think my belief would stronger grow!
Is not my human pride brought low?
15 The boastings of my spirit still?
The joy I had in my freewill
All cold, and dead, and corpse-like grown?
And what is left to me, but Thou,
And faith in Thee? Men pass me by;
20 Christians with happy countenances—
And children all seem full of Thee!
And women smile with saint-like glances
Like Thine own mother's when she bowed
Above Thee, on that happy morn
25 When angels spake to men aloud,
And Thou and peace to earth were born.
Goodwill to me as well as all—
I one of them: my brothers they:
Brothers in Christ—a world of peace
30 And confidence, day after day;

---

[1] published in 1830 with the longer title "…Mind Not In Unity With Itself"; not reprinted until restored in 1884.

And trust and hope till things should cease,
And then one Heaven receive us all.

How sweet to have a common faith!
To hold a common scorn of death!
35 And at a burial to hear
The creaking cords which wound and eat
Into my human heart, whene'er
Earth goes to earth, with grief, not fear,
With hopeful grief, were passing sweet!

40 Thrice happy state again to be
The trustful infant on the knee!
Who lets his rosy fingers play
About his mother's neck, and knows
Nothing beyond his mother's eyes.
45 They comfort him by night and day;
They light his little life alway;
He hath no thought of coming woes;
He hath no care of life or death;
Scarce outward signs of joy arise,
50 Because the Spirit of happiness
And perfect rest so inward is;
And loveth so his innocent heart,
Her temple and her place of birth,
Where she would ever wish to dwell,
55 Life of the fountain there, beneath
Its salient springs, and far apart,
Hating to wander out on earth,
Or breathe into the hollow air,
Whose chillness would make visible
60 Her subtil, warm, and golden breath,
Which mixing with the infant's blood,
Fulfils him with beatitude.
Oh! sure it is a special care
Of God, to fortify from doubt,
65 To arm in proof,[1] and guard about
With triple-mailèd trust, and clear
Delight, the infant's dawning year.

Would that my gloomèd fancy were
As thine, my mother, when with brows
70 Propt on thy knees, my hands upheld
In thine, I listened to thy vows,
For me outpoured in holiest prayer—
For me unworthy!—and beheld
Thy mild deep eyes upraised, that knew
75 The beauty and repose of faith,
And the clear spirit shining through.
Oh! wherefore do we grow awry
From roots which strike so deep? why dare
Paths in the desert? Could not I
80 Bow myself down, where thou hast knelt,
To the earth—until the ice would melt
Here, and I feel as thou hast felt?
What Devil had the heart to scathe
Flowers thou hadst reared—to brush the dew
85 From thine own lily, when thy grave
Was deep, my mother, in the clay?
Myself? Is it thus? Myself? Had I
So little love for thee? But why
Prevailed not thy pure prayers? Why pray
90 To one who heeds not, who can save
But will not? Great in faith, and strong
Against the grief of circumstance
Wert thou, and yet unheard. What if
Thou pleadest still, and seest me drive
95 Through utter dark a full-sailed skiff,
Unpiloted i' the echoing dance
Of reboant[2] whirlwinds, stooping low
Unto the death, not sunk! I know
At matins and at evensong,
100 That thou, if thou wert yet alive,
In deep and daily prayers wouldst strive
To reconcile me with thy God.
Albeit, my hope is gray, and cold
At heart, thou wouldest murmur still—
105 "Bring this lamb back into Thy fold,
My Lord, if so it be Thy will."

---

[1] armour.

---

[2] re-bellowing.

Wouldst tell me I must brook the rod
And chastisement of human pride;
That pride, the sin of devils, stood
10 Betwixt me and the light of God!
That hitherto I had defied
And had rejected God—that grace
Would drop from his o'er-brimming love,
As manna on my wilderness,
15 If I would pray—that God would move
And strike the hard, hard rock,[1] and thence,
Sweet in their utmost bitterness,
Would issue tears of penitence
Which would keep green hope's life. Alas!
20 I think that pride hath now no place
Nor sojourn in me. I am void,
Dark, formless, utterly destroyed.
Why not believe then? Why not yet
Anchor thy frailty there, where man
25 Hath moored and rested? Ask the sea
At midnight, when the crisp slope[2] waves
After a tempest, rib and fret
The broad-imbasèd beach, why he
Slumbers not like a mountain tarn?
30 Wherefore his ridges are not curls
And ripples of an inland mere?
Wherefore he moaneth thus, nor can
Draw down into his vexèd pools
All that blue heaven which hues and paves
35 The other? I am too forlorn,
Too shaken: my own weakness fools
My judgment, and my spirit whirls,
Moved from beneath with doubt and fear.

"Yet," said I, in my morn of youth,
40 The unsunned freshness of my strength,
When I went forth in quest of truth,
"It is man's privilege to doubt,
If so be that from doubt at length,

Truth may stand forth unmoved of change,
145 An image with profulgent brows,
And perfect limbs, as from the storm
Of running fires and fluid range
Of lawless airs, at last stood out
This excellence and solid form
150 Of constant beauty. For the Ox
Feeds in the herb, and sleeps, or fills
The horned valleys all about,
And hollows of the fringed hills
In summer heats, with placid lows
155 Unfearing, till his own blood flows
About his hoof. And in the flocks
The lamb rejoiceth in the year,
And raceth freely with his fere,[3]
And answers to his mother's calls
160 From the flowered furrow. In a time,
Of which he wots not, run short pains
Through his warm heart; and then, from whence
He knows not, on his light there falls
A shadow; and his native slope,
165 Where he was wont to leap and climb,
Floats from his sick and filmed eyes,
And something in the darkness draws
His forehead earthward, and he dies.
Shall man live thus, in joy and hope
170 As a young lamb, who cannot dream,
Living, but that he shall live on?
Shall we not look into the laws
Of life and death, and things that seem,
And things that be, and analyse
175 Our double nature, and compare
All creeds till we have found the one,
If one there be?" Ay me! I fear
All may not doubt, but everywhere
Some must clasp Idols. Yet, my God,
180 Whom call I Idol? Let Thy dove
Shadow me over,[4] and my sins

---

[1] Numbers 20:2.

[2] sloping.

[3] companion.

[4] to protect with wings.

Be unremembered, and Thy love
Enlighten me. Oh teach me yet
Somewhat before the heavy clod
185   Weighs on me, and the busy fret
Of that sharp-headed worm begins
In the gross blackness underneath.

O weary life! O weary death!
O spirit and heart made desolate!
190   O damned vacillating state!
—1830

The Poet

The poet in a golden clime was born,
    With golden stars above;
Dowered with the hate of hate, the scorn of scorn,
    The love of love.

5   He saw through life and death, through good and
        ill,
    He saw through his own soul.
The marvel of the everlasting will,
    An open scroll,

Before him lay: with echoing feet he threaded
10   The secretest walks of fame:
The viewless arrows of his thoughts were headed
    And winged with flame,

Like Indian reeds blown[1] from his silver tongue,
    And of so fierce a flight,
15   From Calpè unto Caucasus[2] they sung,
    Filling with light

And vagrant melodies the winds which bore
    Them earthward till they lit;

Then, like the arrow-seeds of the field flower,[3]
20   The fruitful wit

Cleaving, took root, and springing forth anew
    Where'er they fell, behold,
Like to the mother plant in semblance, grew
    A flower all gold,

25   And bravely furnished all abroad to fling
    The wingèd shafts of truth,
To throng with stately blooms the breathing spring
    Of Hope and Youth.

So many minds did gird their orbs with beams,
30   Though one did fling the fire.
Heaven flowed upon the soul in many dreams
    Of high desire.

Thus truth was multiplied on truth, the world
    Like one great garden showed,
35   And through the wreaths of floating dark upcurled,
    Rare sunrise flowed.

And Freedom reared in that august sunrise
    Her beautiful bold brow,
When rites and forms[4] before his burning eyes
40   Melted like snow.

There was no blood upon her maiden robes
    Sunned by those orient skies;
But round about the circles of the globes
    Of her keen eyes

45   And in her raiment's hem was traced in flame
    WISDOM, a name to shake
All evil dreams of power—a sacred name.
    And when she spake,

---

[1] arrows shot from blowpipes.

[2] from Gibraltar, Europe's western limit, to the Caucasus Mountains in the east.

[3] the dandelion.

[4] traditional forms of church and state.

Her words did gather thunder as they ran,
50   And as the lightning to the thunder
Which follows it, riving the spirit of man,
   Making earth wonder,

So was their meaning to her words. No sword
   Of wrath her right arm whirled,
55 But one poor poet's scroll, and with *his* word
   She shook the world.

—1830

The Poet's Mind

I

Vex not thou the poet's mind
   With thy shallow wit:
Vex not thou the poet's mind;
   For thou canst not fathom it.
5 Clear and bright it should be ever,
Flowing like a crystal river;
Bright as light, and clear as wind.

II

Dark-browed sophist, come not anear;
   All the place is holy ground;
10   Hollow smile and frozen sneer
      Come not here.
Holy water will I pour[1]
Into every spicy flower
Of the laurel-shrubs that hedge it around.
15 The flowers would faint at your cruel cheer.
   In your eye there is death,
   There is frost in your breath
Which would blight the plants.
      Where you stand you cannot hear
20   From the groves within
      The wild-bird's din.
In the heart of the garden the merry bird chants.
It would fall to the ground if you came in.

---

[1] exorcism.

In the middle leaps a fountain
25   Like sheet lightning,
   Ever brightening
With a low melodious thunder;
All day and all night it is ever drawn
   From the brain of the purple mountain
30   Which stands in the distance yonder:
It springs on a level of bowery lawn,
And the mountain draws it from Heaven above,
And it sings a song of undying love;
And yet, though its voice be so clear and full,
35 You never would hear it; your ears are so dull;
So keep where you are: you are foul with sin;
It would shrink to the earth if you came in.
—1830

The Mystic [2]

Angels have talked with him, and showed him
   thrones:
Ye knew him not: he was not one of ye,
Ye scorned him with an undiscerning scorn:
Ye could not read the marvel in his eye,
5 The still serene abstraction: he hath felt
The vanities of after and before;
Albeit, his spirit and his secret heart
The stern experiences of converse lives,
The linkèd woes of many a fiery change
10 Had purified, and chastened, and made free.
Always there stood before him, night and day,
Of wayward varycolored circumstance
The imperishable presences serene
Colossal, without form, or sense, or sound,
15 Dim shadows but unwaning presences
Fourfacèd to four corners of the sky:
And yet again, three shadows, fronting one,
One forward, one respectant,[3] three but one;

---

[2] Published in 1830, the only blank verse poem in the volume, *Poems, Chiefly Lyrical*, it was not reprinted in subsequent editions.

[3] looking backward.

And yet again, again and evermore,
20   For the two first were not, but only seemed,
One shadow in the midst of a great light,
One reflex from eternity on time,
One mighty countenance of perfect calm,
Awful with most invariable eyes.
25   For him the silent congregated hours,
Daughters of time, divinely tall, beneath
Severe and youthful brows, with shining eyes
Smiling a godlike smile (the innocent light
Of earliest youth pierced through and through with
    all
30   Keen knowledges of low-embowèd eld)
Upheld, and ever hold aloft the cloud
Which droops lowhung on either gate of life,
Both birth and death: he in the centre fixt,
Saw far on each side through the grated gates
35   Most pale and clear and lovely distances.
He often lying broad awake, and yet
Remaining from the body, and apart
In intellect and power and will, hath heard
Time flowing in the middle of the night,
40   And all things creeping to a day of doom.
How could ye know him? Ye were yet within
The narrower circle; he had wellnigh reached
The last, which with a region of white flame,
Pure without heat, into a larger air
45   Upburning, and an ether of black blue,
Investeth and ingirds all other lives.
    —1830

The Kraken [1]

Below the thunders of the upper deep,
  Far, far beneath in the abysmal sea,
His ancient, dreamless, uninvaded sleep
The Kraken sleepeth: faintest sunlights flee
5   About his shadowy sides: above him swell
Huge sponges of millennial growth and height;

And far away into the sickly light,
From many a wondrous grot and secret cell
Unnumbered and enormous polypi
10   Winnow with giant arms the slumbering green.
There hath he lain for ages and will lie
Battening upon huge seaworms in his sleep,
Until the latter fire shall heat the deep;
Then once by man and angels to be seen,
15   In roaring he shall rise and on the surface die.
    —1830

The Lady of Shalott

PART I

On either side the river lie
  Long fields of barley and of rye,
That clothe the wold and meet the sky;
And through the field the road runs by
5   To many-towered Camelot;[2]
And up and down the people go,
Gazing where the lilies blow
Round an island there below,
    The island of Shalott.

10   Willows whiten, aspens quiver,
Little breezes dusk and shiver
Through the wave that runs for ever
By the island in the river
    Flowing down to Camelot.
15   Four gray walls, and four gray towers,
Overlook a space of flowers,
And the silent isle imbowers
    The Lady of Shalott.

By the margin, willow-veiled,
20   Slide the heavy barges trailed
By slow horses; and unhailed
The shallop flitteth silken-sailed

---

[1] although published in 1830, not reprinted until 1872.

[2] seat of King Arthur's Court.

Skimming down to Camelot:
But who hath seen her wave her hand?
25 Or at the casement seen her stand?
Or is she known in all the land,
    The Lady of Shalott?

Only reapers, reaping early
In among the bearded barley,
30 Hear a song that echoes cheerly
From the river winding clearly,
    Down to towered Camelot:
And by the moon the reaper weary,
Piling sheaves in uplands airy,
35 Listening, whispers "'Tis the fairy
    Lady of Shalott."

PART II

There she weaves by night and day
A magic web with colours gay.
She has heard a whisper say,
40 A curse is on her if she stay
    To look down to Camelot.
She knows not what the curse may be,
And so she weaveth steadily,
And little other care hath she,
45   The Lady of Shalott.

And moving through a mirror clear
That hangs before her all the year,
Shadows of the world appear.
There she sees the highway near
50   Winding down to Camelot:
There the river eddy whirls,
And there the surly village-churls,
And the red cloaks of market girls,
    Pass onward from Shalott.

55 Sometimes a troop of damsels glad,
An abbot on an ambling pad,
Sometimes a curly shepherd-lad,
Or long-haired page in crimson clad,

Goes by to towered Camelot;
60 And sometimes through the mirror blue
The knights come riding two and two:
She hath no loyal knight and true,
    The Lady of Shalott.

But in her web she still delights
65 To weave the mirror's magic sights,
For often through the silent nights
A funeral, with plumes and lights
    And music, went to Camelot:
Or when the moon was overhead,
70 Came two young lovers lately wed;
"I am half sick of shadows," said
    The Lady of Shalott.

PART III

A bow-shot from her bower-eaves,
He rode between the barley-sheaves,
75 The sun came dazzling through the leaves,
And flamed upon the brazen greaves
    Of bold Sir Lancelot.
A red-cross knight for ever kneeled
To a lady in his shield,
80 That sparkled on the yellow field,
    Beside remote Shalott.

The gemmy bridle glittered free,
Like to some branch of stars we see
Hung in the golden Galaxy.
85 The bridle bells rang merrily
    As he rode down to Camelot:
And from his blazoned baldric slung
A mighty silver bugle hung,
And as he rode his armour rung,
90   Beside remote Shalott.

All in the blue unclouded weather
Thick-jewelled shone the saddle-leather,
The helmet and the helmet-feather
Burned like one burning flame together,

95 As he rode down to Camelot.
As often through the purple night,
Below the starry clusters bright,
Some bearded meteor, trailing light,
    Moves over still Shalott.

100 His broad clear brow in sunlight glowed;
On burnished hooves his war-horse trode;
From underneath his helmet flowed
His coal-black curls as on he rode,
    As he rode down to Camelot.
105 From the bank and from the river
He flashed into the crystal mirror,
"Tirra lirra," by the river
    Sang Sir Lancelot.

She left the web, she left the loom,
110 She made three paces through the room,
She saw the water-lily bloom,
She saw the helmet and the plume,
    She looked down to Camelot.
Out flew the web and floated wide;
115 The mirror cracked from side to side;
"The curse is come upon me," cried
    The Lady of Shalott.

PART IV

In the stormy east-wind straining,
The pale yellow woods were waning,
120 The broad stream in his banks complaining,
Heavily the low sky raining
    Over towered Camelot;
Down she came and found a boat
Beneath a willow left afloat,
125 And round about the prow she wrote
    The Lady of Shalott.

And down the river's dim expanse
Like some bold seër in a trance,
Seeing all his own mischance—
130 With a glassy countenance

Did she look to Camelot.
And at the closing of the day
She loosed the chain, and down she lay;
The broad stream bore her far away,
135   The Lady of Shalott.

Lying, robed in snowy white
That loosely flew to left and right—
The leaves upon her falling light—
Through the noises of the night
140   She floated down to Camelot:
And as the boat-head wound along
The willowy hills and fields among,
They heard her singing her last song,
    The Lady of Shalott.

145 Heard a carol, mournful, holy,
Chanted loudly, chanted lowly,
Till her blood was frozen slowly,
And her eyes were darkened wholly,
    Turned to towered Camelot.
150 For ere she reached upon the tide
The first house by the water-side,
Singing in her song she died,
    The Lady of Shalott.

Under tower and balcony,
155 By garden-wall and gallery,
A gleaming shape she floated by,
Dead-pale between the houses high,
    Silent into Camelot.
Out upon the wharfs they came,
160 Knight and burgher, lord and dame,
And round the prow they read her name,
    The Lady of Shalott.

Who is this? and what is here?
And in the lighted palace near
165 Died the sound of royal cheer;
And they crossed themselves for fear,
    All the knights at Camelot:

But Lancelot mused a little space;
He said, "She has a lovely face;
170 God in his mercy lend her grace,
    The Lady of Shalott."
—1832

To —.[1] With the Following Poem
[The Palace of Art]

I send you here a sort of allegory,
    (For you will understand it) of a soul,
A sinful soul possessed of many gifts,
    A spacious garden full of flowering weeds,
5 A glorious Devil, large in heart and brain,
    That did love Beauty only, (Beauty seen
In all varieties of mould and mind)
And Knowledge for its beauty; or if Good,
Good only for its beauty, seeing not
10 That Beauty, Good, and Knowledge, are three sisters
That doat upon each other, friends to man,
Living together under the same roof,
And never can be sundered without tears.
And he that shuts Love out, in turn shall be
15 Shut out from Love, and on her threshold lie
Howling in outer darkness. Not for this
Was common clay ta'en from the common earth
Moulded by God, and tempered with the tears
Of angels to the perfect shape of man.
—1832

The Palace of Art

I built my soul a lordly pleasure-house,
    Wherein at ease for aye to dwell.
I said, "O Soul, make merry and carouse,
    Dear soul, for all is well."

5 A huge crag-platform, smooth as burnished brass
    I chose. The rangèd ramparts bright
From level meadow-bases of deep grass
    Suddenly scaled the light.

Thereon I built it firm. Of ledge or shelf
10   The rock rose clear, or winding stair.
My soul would live alone unto herself
    In her high palace there.

And "while the world runs round and round," I
    said,
    "Reign thou apart, a quiet king,
15 Still as, while Saturn whirls, his stedfast shade
    Sleeps on his luminous ring."[2]

To which my soul made answer readily:
    "Trust me, in bliss I shall abide
In this great mansion, that is built for me,
20   So royal-rich and wide."

        *   *   *   *

Four courts I made, East, West and South and
    North,
    In each a squarèd lawn, wherefrom
The golden gorge of dragons spouted forth
    A flood of fountain-foam.

25 And round the cool green courts there ran a row
    Of cloisters, branched like mighty woods,
Echoing all night to that sonorous flow
    Of spouted fountain-floods.

And round the roofs a gilded gallery
30   That lent broad verge to distant lands,
Far as the wild swan wings, to where the sky
    Dipt down to sea and sands.

---

[1] probably addressed to R.C. Trench, a member of the Cambridge Apostles. Tennyson remarked that Trench "said, when we were at Trinity together, 'Tennyson, we cannot live in Art.' This poem is the embodiment of my own belief that the Godlike life is with man and for man."

---

[2] the shadow of the whirling Saturn.

From those four jets four currents in one swell
    Across the mountain streamed below
35 In misty folds, that floating as they fell
    Lit up a torrent-bow.

And high on every peak a statue seemed
    To hang on tiptoe, tossing up
A cloud of incense of all odour steamed
40   From out a golden cup.

So that she thought, "And who shall gaze upon
    My palace with unblinded eyes,
While this great bow will waver in the sun,
    And that sweet incense rise?"

45 For that sweet incense rose and never failed,
    And, while day sank or mounted higher,
The light aërial gallery, golden-railed,
    Burnt like a fringe of fire.

Likewise the deep-set windows, stained and traced,
50   Would seem slow-flaming crimson fires
From shadowed grots of arches interlaced,
    And tipt with frost-like spires.

    *   *   *   *

Full of long-sounding corridors it was,
    That over-vaulted grateful gloom,
55 Through which the livelong day my soul did pass,
    Well-pleased, from room to room.

Full of great rooms and small the palace stood,
    All various, each a perfect whole
From living Nature, fit for every mood
60   And change of my still soul.

For some were hung with arras green and blue,
    Showing a gaudy summer-morn,
Where with puffed cheek the belted hunter blew
    His wreathèd bugle-horn.

65 One seemed all dark and red—a tract of sand,
    And some one pacing there alone,
Who paced for ever in a glimmering land,
    Lit with a low large moon.

One showed an iron coast and angry waves.
70   You seemed to hear them climb and fall
And roar rock-thwarted under bellowing caves,
    Beneath the windy wall.

And one, a full-fed river winding slow
    By herds upon an endless plain,
75 The ragged rims of thunder brooding low,
    With shadow-streaks of rain.

And one, the reapers at their sultry toil.
    In front they bound the sheaves. Behind
Were realms of upland, prodigal in oil,
80   And hoary to the wind.[1]

And one a foreground black with stones and slags,
    Beyond, a line of heights, and higher
All barred with long white cloud the scornful crags,
    And highest, snow and fire.

85 And one, an English home—gray twilight poured
    On dewy pastures, dewy trees,
Softer than sleep—all things in order stored,
    A haunt of ancient Peace.

Nor these alone, but every landscape fair,
90   As fit for every mood of mind,
Or gay, or grave, or sweet, or stern, was there
    Not less than truth designed.

    *   *   *   *

Or the maid-mother by a crucifix,
    In tracts of pasture sunny-warm,

---

[1] the white underside of the olive leaf.

95   Beneath branch-work of costly sardonyx
        Sat smiling, babe in arm.

    Or in a clear-walled city on the sea,
        Near gilded organ-pipes, her hair
    Wound with white roses, slept St Cecily;[1]
100   An angel looked at her.

    Or thronging all one porch of Paradise
        A group of Houris bowed to see
    The dying Islamite, with hands and eyes
        That said, We wait for thee.

105   Or mythic Uther's deeply-wounded son[2]
        In some fair space of sloping greens
    Lay, dozing in the vale of Avalon,
        And watched by weeping queens.[3]

    Or hollowing one hand against his ear,
110   To list a foot-fall, ere he saw
    The wood-nymph, stayed the Ausonian king to hear
        Of wisdom and of law.

    Or over hills with peaky tops engrailed,[4]
        And many a tract of palm and rice
115   The throne of Indian Cama[5] slowly sailed
        A summer fanned with spice.

    Or sweet Europa's mantle blew unclasped,
        From off her shoulder backward borne:
    From one hand drooped a crocus: one hand
        grasped
120   The mild bull's golden horn.

Or else flushed Ganymede,[6] his rosy thigh
    Half-buried in the Eagle's down,
Sole as a flying star shot through the sky
    Above the pillared town.

125 Nor these alone: but every legend fair
    Which the supreme Caucasian[7] mind
Carved out of Nature for itself, was there,
    Not less than life, designed.

       *   *   *   *

Then in the towers I placed great bells that swung,
130   Moved of themselves, with silver sound;
And with choice paintings of wise men I hung
    The royal dais round.

For there was Milton like a seraph strong,
    Beside him Shakespeare bland and mild;
135 And there the world-worn Dante grasped his song,
    And somewhat grimly smiled.

And there the Ionian father of the rest;[8]
    A million wrinkles carved his skin;
A hundred winters snowed upon his breast,
140   From cheek and throat and chin.

Above, the fair hall-ceiling stately-set
    Many an arch high up did lift,
And angels rising and descending met
    With interchange of gift.

145 Below was all mosaic choicely planned
    With cycles of the human tale
Of this wide world, the times of every land
    So wrought, they will not fail.

---

1 the patron saint of music.

2 King Arthur.

3 Avalon, the Celtic isle to which the dead Arthur was borne by the weeping queens.

4 serrated.

5 the Hindu God of young love.

6 Trojan boy carried off to Olympus by Zeus in the form of a bird.

7 Indo-European.

8 Homer.

The people here, a beast of burden slow,
150   Toiled onward, pricked with goads and stings;
Here played, a tiger, rolling to and fro
         The heads and crowns of kings;

Here rose, an athlete, strong to break or bind
         All force in bonds that might endure,
155 And here once more like some sick man declined,
         And trusted any cure.

But over these she trod: and those great bells
         Began to chime. She took her throne:
She sat betwixt the shining Oriels,
160   To sing her songs alone.

And through the topmost Oriels' coloured flame
         Two godlike faces gazed below;
Plato the wise, and large-browed Verulam,[1]
         The first of those who know.

165 And all those names, that in their motion were
         Full-welling fountain-heads of change,
Betwixt the slender shafts were blazoned fair
         In diverse raiment strange:

Through which the lights, rose, amber, emerald,
         blue,
170   Flushed in her temples and her eyes,
And from her lips, as morn from Memnon,[2] drew
         Rivers of melodies.

No nightingale delighteth to prolong
         Her low preamble all alone,
175 More than my soul to hear her echoed song
         Throb through the ribbèd stone;

Singing and murmuring in her feastful mirth,
         Joying to feel herself alive,

---

[1] Francis Bacon (Lord Verulam).

[2] a statue near Thebes that made music when touched by the sun.

Lord over Nature, Lord of the visible earth,
180   Lord of the senses five;

Communing with herself: "All these are mine,
         And let the world have peace or wars,
'Tis one to me." She—when young night divine
         Crowned dying day with stars,

185 Making sweet close of his delicious toils—
         Lit light in wreaths and anadems,[3]
And pure quintessences of precious oils
         In hollowed moons of gems,

To mimic heaven; and clapt her hands and cried,
190   "I marvel if my still delight
In this great house so royal-rich, and wide,
         Be flattered to the height.

"O all things fair to sate my various eyes!
         O shapes and hues that please me well!
195 O silent faces of the Great and Wise,
         My Gods, with whom I dwell!

"O God-like isolation which art mine,
         I can but count thee perfect gain,
What time I watch the darkening droves of swine
200   That range on yonder plain.

"In filthy sloughs they roll a prurient skin,
         They graze and wallow, breed and sleep;
And oft some brainless devil enters in,
         And drives them to the deep."

205 Then of the moral instinct would she prate
         And of the rising from the dead,
As hers by right of full-accomplished Fate;
         And at the last she said:

---

[3] crowns.

"I take possession of man's mind and deed.
210   I care not what the sects may brawl.
I sit as God holding no form of creed,
      But contemplating all."

*   *   *   *

Full oft the riddle of the painful earth
      Flashed through her as she sat alone,
215 Yet not the less held she her solemn mirth,
      And intellectual throne.

And so she throve and prospered: so three years
      She prospered: on the fourth she fell,
Like Herod, when the shout was in his ears,
220   Struck through with pangs of hell.

Lest she should fail and perish utterly,
      God, before whom ever lie bare
The abysmal deeps of Personality,
      Plagued her with sore despair.

225 When she would think, where'er she turned her
      sight
      The airy hand confusion wrought,
Wrote, "Mene, mene,"[1] and divided quite
      The kingdom of her thought.

Deep dread and loathing of her solitude
230   Fell on her, from which mood was born
Scorn of herself; again, from out that mood
      Laughter at her self-scorn.

"What! is not this my place of strength," she said,
      "My spacious mansion built for me,
235 Whereof the strong foundation-stones were laid
      Since my first memory?"

But in dark corners of her palace stood
      Uncertain shapes; and unawares

On white-eyed phantasms weeping tears of blood,
240   And horrible nightmares,

And hollow shades enclosing hearts of flame,
      And, with dim fretted[2] foreheads all,
On corpses three-months-old at noon she came,
      That stood against the wall.

245 A spot of dull stagnation, without light
      Or power of movement, seemed my soul,
'Mid onward-sloping motions infinite
      Making for one sure goal.

A still salt pool, locked in with bars of sand,
250   Left on the shore; that hears all night
The plunging seas draw backward from the land
      Their moon-led waters white.

A star that with the choral starry dance
      Joined not, but stood, and standing saw
255 The hollow orb of moving Circumstance[3]
      Rolled round by one fixed law.

Back on herself her serpent pride had curled.
      "No voice," she shrieked in that lone hall,
"No voice breaks through the stillness of this world:
260   One deep, deep silence all!"

She, mouldering with the dull earth's mouldering
      sod,
      Inwrapt tenfold in slothful shame,
Lay there exilèd from eternal God,
      Lost to her place and name;

265 And death and life she hated equally,
      And nothing saw, for her despair,

---

[1] from Daniel 5:23–27: "MENE; God hath numbered thy kingdom, and finished it."

[2] worm-fretted.

[3] Tennyson's comment: "Some old writer calls the Heavens 'The Circumstance.'"

But dreadful time, dreadful eternity,
   No comfort anywhere;

Remaining utterly confused with fears,
270   And ever worse with growing time,
And ever unrelieved by dismal tears,
   And all alone in crime:

Shut up as in a crumbling tomb, girt round
   With blackness as a solid wall,
275 Far off she seemed to hear the dully sound
   Of human footsteps fall.

As in strange lands a traveller walking slow,
   In doubt and great perplexity,
A little before moon-rise hears the low
280   Moan of an unknown sea;

And knows not if it be thunder, or a sound
   Of rocks thrown down, or one deep cry
Of great wild beasts; then thinketh, "I have found
   A new land, but I die."

285 She howled aloud, "I am on fire within.
   There comes no murmur of reply.
What is it that will take away my sin,
   And save me lest I die?"

So when four years were wholly finished,
290   She threw her royal robes away.
"Make me a cottage in the vale," she said,
   "Where I may mourn and pray.

"Yet pull not down my palace towers, that are
   So lightly, beautifully built:
295 Perchance I may return with others there
   When I have purged my guilt."
   —1832

The Hesperides [1]

The Northwind fallen, in the newstarrèd night
Zidonian Hanno, voyaging beyond
The hoary promontory of Soloë
Past Thymiaterion, in calmèd bays,
5 Between the southern and the western Horn,
Heard neither warbling of the nightingale,
Nor melody o' the Libyan lotusflute
Blown seaward from the shore; but from a slope
That ran bloombright into the Atlantic blue,
10 Beneath a highland leaning down a weight
Of cliffs, and zoned below with cedarshade,
Came voices, like the voices in a dream,
Continuous, till he reached the outer sea.

SONG
I

The golden apple, the golden apple, the
   hallowed fruit,
15 Guard it well, guard it warily,
Singing airily,
Standing about the charmèd root.
Round about all is mute,
As the snowfield on the mountain-peaks,
20 As the sandfield at the mountain-foot.
Crocodiles in briny creeks
Sleep and stir not: all is mute.
If ye sing not, if ye make false measure,
We shall lose eternal pleasure,
25 Worth eternal want of rest.
Laugh not loudly: watch the treasure
Of the wisdom of the west.
In a corner wisdom whispers. Five and three
(Let it not be preached abroad) make an awful
   mystery.
30 For the blossom unto threefold music bloweth;

---

[1] The daughters of Hesperus, who lived in the west where the sun sets, guarded the golden apples given by Earth to Hera; Hercules slew the guardian dragon and stole the apples.

Evermore it is born anew;
And the sap to threefold music floweth,
From the root
Drawn in the dark,
35 Up to the fruit,
Creeping under the fragrant bark,
Liquid gold, honeysweet, through and through.
Keen-eyed Sisters, singing airily,
Looking warily
40 Every way,
Guard the apple night and day,
Lest one from the East come and take it away.

II

Father Hesper,[1] Father Hesper, watch, watch, ever
  and aye,
Looking under silver hair with a silver eye.
45 Father, twinkle not thy stedfast sight;
Kingdoms lapse, and climates change, and races die;
Honour comes with mystery;
Hoarded wisdom brings delight.
Number, tell them over and number
50 How many the mystic fruittree holds,
Lest the redcombed dragon slumber
Rolled together in purple folds.
Look to him, father, lest he wink, and the golden
  apple be stolen away,
For his ancient heart is drunk with overwatchings
  night and day,
55 Round about the hallowed fruittree curled—
Sing away, sing aloud evermore in the wind,
  without stop,
Lest his scalèd eyelid drop,
For he is older than the world.
If he waken, we waken,
60 Rapidly levelling eager eyes.
If he sleep, we sleep,
Dropping the eyelid over the eyes.
If the golden apple be taken

The world will be overwise.
65 Five links, a golden chain, are we,
Hesper, the dragon, and sisters three,
Bound about the golden tree.

III

Father Hesper, Father Hesper, watch, watch, night
  and day,
Lest the old wound of the world be healèd,
70 The glory unsealèd,
The golden apple stolen away,
And the ancient secret revealèd.
Look from west to east along:
Father, old Himala[2] weakens, Caucasus[3] is bold
  and strong.
75 Wandering waters unto wandering waters call;
Let them clash together, foam and fall.
Out of watchings, out of wiles,
Comes the bliss of secret smiles.
All things are not told to all.
80 Half-round the mantling night is drawn,
Purplefringèd with even and dawn.
Hesper hateth Phosphor,[4] evening hateth morn.
Every flower and every fruit the redolent breath
Of this warm seawind ripeneth,
85 Arching the billow in his sleep;
But the landwind wandereth,
Broken by the highland-steep,
Two streams upon the violet deep:
For the western sun and the western star,
90 And the low west wind, breathing afar,
The end of day and beginning of night
Make the apple holy and bright;
Holy and bright, round and full, bright and blest,
Mellowed in a land of rest;
95 Watch it warily day and night;
All good things are in the west.

---

[1] Hesperus as the evening star.

[2] the Himalayas in India.

[3] the Caucasus mountains in the east.

[4] the morning star.

Till midnoon the cool east light
Is shut out by the round of the tall hillbrow;
But when the fullfaced sunset yellowly
100 Stays on the flowering arch of the bough,
The luscious fruitage clustereth mellowly,
Goldenkernelled, goldencored,
Sunset-ripened above on the tree.
The world is wasted with fire and sword,
105 But the apple of gold hangs over the sea.
Five links, a golden chain, are we,
Hesper, the dragon, and sisters three,
Daughters three,
Bound about
110 All round about
The gnarlèd bole of the charmèd tree.
The golden apple, the golden apple, the hallowed
    fruit,
Guard it well, guard it warily,
Watch it warily,
115 Singing airily,
Standing about the charmèd root.
—1832

The Lotos-Eaters

"Courage!" he said,[1] and pointed toward
    the land,
"This mounting wave will roll us shoreward soon."
In the afternoon they came unto a land
In which it seemèd always afternoon.
5 All round the coast the languid air did swoon,
Breathing like one that hath a weary dream.
Full-faced above the valley stood the moon;
And like a downward smoke, the slender stream
Along the cliff to fall and pause and fall did seem.

10 A land of streams! some, like a downward smoke,
Slow-dropping veils of thinnest lawn, did go;
And some through wavering lights and shadows
    broke,
Rolling a slumbrous sheet of foam below.
They saw the gleaming river seaward flow
15 From the inner land: far off, three mountain-tops,
Three silent pinnacles of agèd snow,
Stood sunset-flushed: and, dewed with showery
    drops,
Up-clomb the shadowy pine above the woven
    copse.

The charmèd sunset lingered low adown
20 In the red West: through mountain clefts the dale
Was seen far inland, and the yellow down
Bordered with palm, and many a winding vale
And meadow, set with slender galingale;[2]
A land where all things always seemed the same!
25 And round about the keel with faces pale,
Dark faces pale against that rosy flame,
The mild-eyed melancholy Lotos-eaters came.

Branches they bore of that enchanted stem,
Laden with flower and fruit, whereof they gave
30 To each, but whoso did receive of them,
And taste, to him the gushing of the wave
Far far away did seem to mourn and rave
On alien shores; and if his fellow spake,
His voice was thin, as voices from the grave;
35 And deep-asleep he seemed, yet all awake,
And music in his ears his beating heart did make.

They sat them down upon the yellow sand,
Between the sun and moon upon the shore;
And sweet it was to dream of Fatherland,
40 Of child, and wife, and slave; but evermore
Most weary seemed the sea, weary the oar,
Weary the wandering fields of barren foam.
Then some one said, "We will return no more;"

---

[1] Odysseus urging his men to continue their journey homeward.

[2] aromatic herb.

And all at once they sang, "Our island home
45 Is far beyond the wave; we will no longer roam."

CHORIC SONG

I

There is sweet music here that softer falls
Than petals from blown roses on the grass,
Or night-dews on still waters between walls
Of shadowy granite, in a gleaming pass;
50 Music that gentlier on the spirit lies,
Than tired eyelids upon tired eyes;
Music that brings sweet sleep down from the
    blissful skies.
Here are cool mosses deep,
And through the moss the ivies creep,
55 And in the stream the long-leaved flowers weep,
And from the craggy ledge the poppy hangs in sleep.

II

Why are we weighed upon with heaviness,
And utterly consumed with sharp distress,
While all things else have rest from weariness?
60 All things have rest: why should we toil alone,
We only toil, who are the first of things,
And make perpetual moan,
Still from one sorrow to another thrown:
Nor ever fold our wings,
65 And cease from wanderings,
Nor steep our brows in slumber's holy balm;
Nor harken what the inner spirit sings,
"There is no joy but calm!"
Why should we only toil, the roof and crown of
    things?

III

70 Lo! in the middle of the wood,
The folded leaf is wooed from out the bud
With winds upon the branch, and there
Grows green and broad, and takes no care,
Sun-steeped at noon, and in the moon
75 Nightly dew-fed; and turning yellow

Falls, and floats adown the air.
Lo! sweetened with the summer light,
The full-juiced apple, waxing over-mellow,
Drops in a silent autumn night.
80 All its allotted length of days,
The flower ripens in its place,
Ripens and fades, and falls, and hath no toil,
Fast-rooted in the fruitful soil.

IV

Hateful is the dark-blue sky,
85 Vaulted o'er the dark-blue sea.
Death is the end of life; ah, why
Should life all labour be?
Let us alone. Time driveth onward fast,
And in a little while our lips are dumb.
90 Let us alone. What is it that will last?
All things are taken from us, and become
Portions and parcels of the dreadful Past.
Let us alone. What pleasure can we have
To war with evil? Is there any peace
95 In ever climbing up the climbing wave?
All things have rest, and ripen toward the grave
In silence; ripen, fall and cease:
Give us long rest or death, dark death, or dreamful ease.

V

How sweet it were, hearing the downward stream,
100 With half-shut eyes ever to seem
Falling asleep in a half-dream!
To dream and dream, like yonder amber light,
Which will not leave the myrrh-bush on the height;
To hear each other's whispered speech;
105 Eating the Lotos day by day,
To watch the crisping ripples on the beach,
And tender curving lines of creamy spray;
To lend our hearts and spirits wholly
To the influence of mild-minded melancholy;
110 To muse and brood and live again in memory,
With those old faces of our infancy
Heaped over with a mound of grass,

Two handfuls of white dust, shut in an urn of
    brass!

VI

Dear is the memory of our wedded lives,
115 And dear the last embraces of our wives
And their warm tears: but all hath suffered change:
For surely now our household hearths are cold:
Our sons inherit us: our looks are strange:
And we should come like ghosts to trouble joy.
120 Or else the island princes over-bold
Have eat our substance, and the minstrel sings
Before them of the ten years' war in Troy,
And our great deeds, as half-forgotten things.
Is there confusion in the little isle?
125 Let what is broken so remain.
The Gods are hard to reconcile:
'Tis hard to settle order once again.
There *is* confusion worse than death,
Trouble on trouble, pain on pain,
130 Long labour unto agèd breath,
Sore task to hearts worn out by many wars
And eyes grown dim with gazing on the pilot-stars.

VII

But, propt on beds of amaranth[1] and moly,[2]
How sweet (while warm airs lull us, blowing lowly)
135 With half-dropt eyelid still,
Beneath a heaven dark and holy,
To watch the long bright river drawing slowly
His waters from the purple hill—
To hear the dewy echoes calling
140 From cave to cave through the thick-twinèd vine—
To watch the emerald-coloured water falling
Through many a woven acanthus[3]-wreath divine!
Only to hear and see the far-off sparkling brine,

---

[1] an immortal flower.

[2] an herb with magical powers.

[3] a sacred plant.

Only to hear were sweet, stretched out beneath the
    pine.

VIII

145 The Lotos blooms below the barren peak:
The Lotos blows by every winding creek:
All day the wind breathes low with mellower tone:
Through every hollow cave and alley lone
Round and round the spicy downs the yellow
    Lotos-dust is blown.
150 We have had enough of action, and of motion we,
Rolled to starboard, rolled to larboard, when the
    surge was seething free,
Where the wallowing monster spouted his foam-
    fountains in the sea.
Let us swear an oath, and keep it with an equal
    mind,
In the hollow Lotos-land to live and lie reclined
155 On the hills like Gods together, careless of mankind.
For they lie beside their nectar, and the bolts are
    hurled
Far below them in the valleys, and the clouds are
    lightly curled
Round their golden houses, girdled with the
    gleaming world:
Where they smile in secret, looking over wasted
    lands,
160 Blight and famine, plague and earthquake, roaring
    deeps and fiery sands,
Clanging fights, and flaming towns, and sinking
    ships, and praying hands.
But they smile, they find a music centred in a
    doleful song
Steaming up, a lamentation and an ancient tale of
    wrong,
Like a tale of little meaning though the words are
    strong;
165 Chanted from an ill-used race of men that cleave
    the soil,
Sow the seed, and reap the harvest with enduring
    toil,

Storing yearly little dues of wheat, and wine and oil;
Till they perish and they suffer—some, 'tis
    whispered—down in hell
Suffer endless anguish, others in Elysian valleys
    dwell,
70 Resting weary limbs at last on beds of asphodel.
Surely, surely, slumber is more sweet than toil, the
    shore
Than labour in the deep mid-ocean, wind and
    wave and oar;
Oh rest ye, brother mariners, we will not wander
    more.
—1832

The Two Voices [1]

A still small voice spake unto me,
  "Thou art so full of misery,
Were it not better not to be?"

Then to the still small voice I said;
5 "Let me not cast in endless shade
What is so wonderfully made." [2]

To which the voice did urge reply;
  "Today I saw the dragon-fly
Come from the wells where he did lie.

10 "An inner impulse rent the veil
Of his old husk: from head to tail
Came out clear plates of sapphire mail.

"He dried his wings: like gauze they grew;
Through crofts and pastures wet with dew
15 A living flash of light he flew."

I said, "When first the world began,
Young Nature through five cycles ran,
And in the sixth she moulded man.

"She gave him mind, the lordliest
20 Proportion, and, above the rest,
Dominion in the head and breast." [3]

Thereto the silent voice replied;
"Self-blinded are you by your pride:
Look up through night: the world is wide.

25 "This truth within thy mind rehearse,
That in a boundless universe
Is boundless better, boundless worse.

"Think you this mould of hopes and fears
Could find no statelier than his peers
30 In yonder hundred million spheres?"

It spake, moreover, in my mind:
"Though thou wert scattered to the wind,
Yet is there plenty of the kind."

Then did my response clearer fall:
35 "No compound of this earthly ball
Is like another, all in all."

To which he answered scoffingly;
"Good soul! suppose I grant it thee,
Who'll weep for thy deficiency?

40 "Or will one beam be less intense,
When thy peculiar difference
Is cancelled in the world of sense?"

I would have said, "Thou canst not know,"
But my full heart, that worked below,
45 Rained through my sight its overflow.

---

[1] published in 1842, but dated "1833." Tennyson's son, Hallam, describes it as "begun under the cloud of his overwhelming sorrow after the death of Arthur Hallam," which Tennyson learned about on 1 October 1833. But correspondence shows that a version of the poem was in existence as early as June of that year.

[2] Psalm 139:11–14.

[3] Psalm 8:6.

Again the voice spake unto me:
"Thou art so steeped in misery,
Surely 'twere better not to be.

"Thine anguish will not let thee sleep,
50 Nor any train of reason keep:
Thou canst not think, but thou wilt weep."

I said, "The years with change advance:
If I make dark my countenance,[1]
I shut my life from happier chance.

55 "Some turn this sickness yet might take,
Even yet." But he: "What drug can make
A withered palsy cease to shake?"

I wept, "Though I should die, I know
That all about the thorn will blow
60 In tufts of rosy-tinted snow;

"And men, through novel spheres of thought
Still moving after truth long sought,
Will learn new things when I am not."

"Yet," said the secret voice, "some time,
65 Sooner or later, will gray prime
Make thy grass hoar with early rime.

"Not less swift souls that yearn for light,
Rapt after heaven's starry flight,
Would sweep the tracts of day and night.

70 "Not less the bee would range her cells,
The furzy prickle fire the dells,
The foxglove cluster dappled bells."

I said that "all the years invent;
Each month is various to present
75 The world with some development.

"Were this not well, to bide mine hour,
Though watching from a ruined tower
How grows the day of human power?"

"The highest-mounted mind," he said,
80 "Still sees the sacred morning spread
The silent summit overhead.

"Will thirty seasons render plain
Those lonely lights that still remain,
Just breaking over land and main?

85 "Or make that morn, from his cold crown
And crystal silence creeping down,
Flood with full daylight glebe and town?

"Forerun thy peers, thy time, and let
Thy feet, millenniums hence, be set
90 In midst of knowledge, dreamed not yet.

"Thou hast not gained a real height,
Nor art thou nearer to the light,
Because the scale is infinite.

"'Twere better not to breathe or speak,
95 Than cry for strength, remaining weak,
And seem to find, but still to seek.

"Moreover, but to seem to find
Asks what thou lackest, thought resigned,
A healthy frame, a quiet mind."

100 I said, "When I am gone away,
'He dared not tarry,' men will say,
Doing dishonour to my clay."

"This is more vile," he made reply,
"To breathe and loathe, to live and sigh,
105 Than once from dread of pain to die.

---

[1] Job 14:20.

"Sick art thou—a divided will
Still heaping on the fear of ill
The fear of men, a coward still.

"Do men love thee? Art thou so bound
10 To men, that how thy name may sound
Will vex thee lying underground?

"The memory of the withered leaf
In endless time is scarce more brief
Than of the garnered Autumn-sheaf.

15 "Go, vexèd Spirit, sleep in trust;
The right ear, that is filled with dust,
Hears little of the false or just."

"Hard task, to pluck resolve," I cried,
"From emptiness and the waste wide
20 Of that abyss, or scornful pride!¹

"Nay—rather yet that I could raise
One hope that warmed me in the days
While still I yearned for human praise.

"When, wide in soul and bold of tongue,
25 Among the tents I paused and sung,
The distant battle flashed and rung.

"I sung the joyful Pæan clear,
And, sitting, burnished without fear
The brand, the buckler, and the spear—

30 "Waiting to strive a happy strife,
To war with falsehood to the knife,
And not to lose the good of life—

"Some hidden principle to move,
To put together, part and prove,
35 And mete the bounds of hate and love—

"As far as might be, to carve out
Free space for every human doubt,
That the whole mind might orb about—

"To search through all I felt or saw,
140 The springs of life, the depths of awe,
And reach the law within the law:

"At least, not rotting like a weed,
But, having sown some generous seed,
Fruitful of further thought and deed,

145 "To pass, when Life her light withdraws,
Not void of righteous self-applause,
Nor in a merely selfish cause—

"In some good cause, not in mine own,
To perish, wept for, honoured, known,
150 And like a warrior overthrown;

"Whose eyes are dim with glorious tears,
When, soiled with noble dust, he hears
His country's war-song thrill his ears:

"Then dying of a mortal stroke,
155 What time the foeman's line is broke,
And all the war is rolled in smoke."

"Yea!" said the voice, "thy dream was good,
While thou abodest in the bud.
It was the stirring of the blood.

160 "If Nature put not forth her power
About the opening of the flower,
Who is it that could live an hour?

"Then comes the check, the change, the fall,
Pain rises up, old pleasures pall.
165 There is one remedy for all.

---

¹ *Paradise Lost* 10.282–83.

"Yet hadst thou, through enduring pain,
Linked month to month with such a chain
Of knitted purport, all were vain.

"Thou hadst not between death and birth
170 Dissolved the riddle of the earth.
So were thy labour little-worth.

"That men with knowledge merely played,
I told thee—hardly nigher made,
Though scaling slow from grade to grade;

175 "Much less this dreamer, deaf and blind,
Named man, may hope some truth to find,
That bears relation to the mind.

"For every worm beneath the moon
Draws different threads, and late and soon
180 Spins, toiling out his own cocoon.

"Cry, faint not: either Truth is born
Beyond the polar gleam forlorn,
Or in the gateways of the morn.

"Cry, faint not, climb: the summits slope
185 Beyond the furthest flights of hope,
Wrapt in dense cloud from base to cope.

"Sometimes a little corner shines,
As over rainy mist inclines
A gleaming crag with belts of pines.

190 "I will go forward, sayest thou,
I shall not fail to find her now.
Look up, the fold[1] is on her brow.

"If straight thy track, or if oblique,
Thou know'st not. Shadows thou dost strike,
195 Embracing cloud, Ixion-like;[2]

"And owning but a little more
Than beasts, abidest lame and poor,
Calling thyself a little lower

"Than angels. Cease to wail and brawl![3]
200 Why inch by inch to darkness crawl?
There is one remedy for all."

"O dull, one-sided voice," said I,
"Wilt thou make everything a lie,
To flatter me that I may die?

205 "I know that age to age succeeds,
Blowing a noise of tongues and deeds,
A dust of systems and of creeds.

"I cannot hide that some have striven,
Achieving calm, to whom was given
210 The joy that mixes man with Heaven:

"Who, rowing hard against the stream,
Saw distant gates of Eden gleam,
And did not dream it was a dream;

"But heard, by secret transport led,
215 Even in the charnels of the dead,
The murmur of the fountain-head—

"Which did accomplish their desire,
Bore and forbore, and did not tire,
Like Stephen, an unquenchèd fire.

220 "He heeded not reviling tones,
Nor sold his heart to idle moans,
Though cursed and scorned, and bruised with
     stones:

"But looking upward, full of grace,
He prayed, and from a happy place
225 God's glory smote him on the face."[4]

---

[1] "cloud." (Tennyson's note.)

[2] "Ixion embraced a cloud, hoping to embrace a goddess." (Tennyson's note.)

---

[3] ll. 196–99: Ecclesiastes 3:19 and Psalm 8:4–5.

[4] ll. 222–25: Acts 7:55.

The sullen answer slid betwixt:
"Not that the grounds of hope were fixed,
The elements were kindlier mixed."

I said, "I toil beneath the curse,
30 But, knowing not the universe,
I fear to slide from bad to worse.

"And that, in seeking to undo
One riddle, and to find the true,
I knit a hundred others new:

35 "Or that this anguish fleeting hence,
Unmanacled from bonds of sense,
Be fixed and frozen to permanence:

"For I go, weak from suffering here:
Naked I go, and void of cheer:[1]
40 What is it that I may not fear?"

"Consider well," the voice replied,
"His face, that two hours since hath died;
Wilt thou find passion, pain or pride?

"Will he obey when one commands?
45 Or answer should one press his hands?
He answers not, nor understands.

"His palms are folded on his breast:
There is no other thing expressed
But long disquiet merged in rest.

50 "His lips are very mild and meek:
Though one should smite him on the cheek,
And on the mouth, he will not speak.

"His little daughter, whose sweet face
He kissed, taking his last embrace,
55 Becomes dishonour to her race—

"His sons grow up that bear his name,
Some grow to honour, some to shame,—[2]
But he is chill to praise or blame.

"He will not hear the north-wind rave,
260 Nor, moaning, household shelter crave
From winter rains that beat his grave.

"High up the vapours fold and swim:
About him broods the twilight dim:
The place he knew forgetteth him."[3]

265 "If all be dark, vague voice," I said,
"These things are wrapt in doubt and dread,
Nor canst thou show the dead are dead.

"The sap dries up: the plant declines.
A deeper tale my heart divines.
270 Know I not Death? the outward signs?

"I found him when my years were few;
A shadow on the graves I knew,
And darkness in the village yew.

"From grave to grave the shadow crept:
275 In her still place the morning wept:
Touched by his feet the daisy slept.

"The simple senses crowned his head:
'Omega! thou art Lord,' they said,
'We find no motion in the dead.'

280 "Why, if man rot in dreamless ease,[4]
Should that plain fact, as taught by these,
Not make him sure that he shall cease?

---

1 Ecclesiastes 5:15.

2 Job 14:21.

3 Psalm 103:16, Job 7:10.

4 *Hamlet* 1.5.32–33.

"Who forged that other influence,
That heat of inward evidence,
285 By which he doubts against the sense?

"He owns the fatal gift of eyes,
That read his spirit blindly wise,
Not simple as a thing that dies.

"Here sits he shaping wings to fly:
290 His heart forebodes a mystery:
He names the name Eternity.

"That type of Perfect in his mind
In Nature can he nowhere find.
He sows himself on every wind.

295 "He seems to hear a Heavenly Friend,
And through thick veils to apprehend
A labour working to an end.

"The end and the beginning vex
His reason: many things perplex,
300 With motions, checks, and counterchecks.

"He knows a baseness in his blood
At such strange war with something good,
He may not do the thing he would.[1]

"Heaven opens inward, chasms yawn,
305 Vast images in glimmering dawn,
Half shown, are broken and withdrawn.

"Ah! sure within him and without,
Could his dark wisdom find it out,
There must be answer to his doubt,

310 "But thou canst answer not again.
With thine own weapon art thou slain,
Or thou wilt answer but in vain.

"The doubt would rest, I dare not solve.
In the same circle we revolve.
315 Assurance only breeds resolve."

As when a billow, blown against,
Falls back, the voice with which I fenced
A little ceased, but recommenced.

"Where wert thou when thy father played
320 In his free field, and pastime made,
A merry boy in sun and shade?

"A merry boy they called him then,
He sat upon the knees of men
In days that never come again.

325 "Before the little ducts began
To feed thy bones with lime, and ran
Their course, till thou wert also man:

"Who took a wife, who reared his race,
Whose wrinkles gathered on his face,
330 Whose troubles number with his days:

"A life of nothings, nothing-worth,
From that first nothing ere his birth
To that last nothing under earth!"

"These words," I said, "are like the rest:
335 No certain clearness, but at best
A vague suspicion of the breast:

"But if I grant, thou mightst defend
The thesis which thy words intend—
That to begin implies to end;

340 "Yet how should I for certain hold,
Because my memory is so cold,
That I first was in human mould?

---

[1] ll. 301–03: Romans 7:18–19 and Galatians 5:17.

"I cannot make this matter plain,
But I would shoot, howe'er in vain,
45 A random arrow from the brain.

"It may be that no life is found,
Which only to one engine bound
Falls off, but cycles always round.

"As old mythologies relate,[1]
50 Some draught of Lethe might await
The slipping through from state to state.

"As here we find in trances, men
Forget the dream that happens then,
Until they fall in trance again.

55 "So might we, if our state were such
As one before, remember much,
For those two likes might meet and touch.

"But, if I lapsed from nobler place,
Some legend of a fallen race
60 Alone might hint of my disgrace;

"Some vague emotion of delight
In gazing up an Alpine height,
Some yearning toward the lamps of night;

"Or if through lower lives I came—
65 Though all experience past became
Consolidate in mind and frame—

"I might forget my weaker lot;
For is not our first year forgot?
The haunts of memory echo not.

70 "And men, whose reason long was blind,
From cells of madness unconfined,
Oft lose whole years of darker mind.

"Much more, if first I floated free,
As naked essence, must I be
375 Incompetent of memory:

"For memory dealing but with time,
And he with matter, could she climb
Beyond her own material prime?

"Moreover, something is or seems,
380 That touches me with mystic gleams,
Like glimpses of forgotten dreams—

"Of something felt, like something here;
Of something done, I know not where;
Such as no language may declare."

385 The still voice laughed. "I talk," said he,
"Not with thy dreams. Suffice it thee
Thy pain is a reality."

"But thou," said I, "hast missed thy mark,
Who sought'st to wreck my mortal ark,
390 By making all the horizon dark.

"Why not set forth, if I should do
This rashness, that which might ensue
With this old soul in organs new?

"Whatever crazy sorrow saith,
395 No life that breathes with human breath
Has ever truly longed for death.[2]

"'Tis life, whereof our nerves are scant,
Oh life, not death, for which we pant;
More life, and fuller, that I want."[3]

---

[1] Pythagoras's metempsychosis, and Plato's myth of Er: *Republic* 10.

[2] Job 3:20–21.

[3] John 10:10.

400 I ceased, and sat as one forlorn.
Then said the voice, in quiet scorn,
"Behold, it is the Sabbath morn."

And I arose, and I released
The casement, and the light increased
405 With freshness in the dawning east.

Like softened airs that blowing steal,
When meres begin to uncongeal,
The sweet church bells began to peal.

On to God's house the people prest:
410 Passing the place where each must rest,
Each entered like a welcome guest.

One walked between his wife and child,
With measured footfall firm and mild,
And now and then he gravely smiled.

415 The prudent partner of his blood
Leaned on him, faithful, gentle, good,
Wearing the rose of womanhood.

And in their double love secure,
The little maiden walked demure,
420 Pacing with downward eyelids pure.

These three made unity so sweet,
My frozen heart began to beat,
Remembering its ancient heat.

I blest them, and they wandered on:
425 I spoke, but answer came there none:
The dull and bitter voice was gone.

A second voice was at mine ear,
A little whisper silver-clear,
A murmur, "Be of better cheer."

430 As from some blissful neighbourhood,
A notice faintly understood,
"I see the end, and know the good."

A little hint to solace woe,
A hint, a whisper breathing low,
435 "I may not speak of what I know."

Like an Æolian harp that wakes
No certain air, but overtakes
Far thought with music that it makes:

Such seemed the whisper at my side:
440 "What is it thou knowest, sweet voice?" I cried.
"A hidden hope," the voice replied:

So heavenly-toned, that in that hour
From out my sullen heart a power
Broke, like the rainbow from the shower,

445 To feel, although no tongue can prove,
That every cloud, that spreads above
And veileth love, itself is love.

And forth into the fields I went,
And Nature's living motion lent
450 The pulse of hope to discontent.

I wondered at the bounteous hours,
The slow result of winter showers:
You scarce could see the grass for flowers.

I wondered, while I paced along:
455 The woods were filled so full with song,
There seemed no room for sense of wrong;

And all so variously wrought,
I marvelled how the mind was brought
To anchor by one gloomy thought;

460 And wherefore rather I made choice
To commune with that barren voice,
Than him that said, "Rejoice! Rejoice!"
—1842

St Simeon Stylites [1]

Although I be the basest of mankind,
From scalp to sole one slough and crust of sin,
Unfit for earth, unfit for heaven, scarce meet
For troops of devils, mad with blasphemy,
5   I will not cease to grasp the hope I hold
Of saintdom, and to clamour, mourn and sob,
Battering the gates of heaven with storms of prayer,
Have mercy, Lord, and take away my sin.

Let this avail, just, dreadful, mighty God,
10 This not be all in vain, that thrice ten years,
Thrice multiplied by superhuman pangs,
In hungers and in thirsts, fevers and cold,
In coughs, aches, stitches, ulcerous throes and
    cramps,
A sign betwixt the meadow and the cloud,
15 Patient on this tall pillar I have borne
Rain, wind, frost, heat, hail, damp, and sleet, and
    snow;
And I had hoped that ere this period closed
Thou wouldst have caught me up into thy rest,
Denying not these weather-beaten limbs
20 The meed of saints, the white robe and the palm.[2]

O take the meaning, Lord: I do not breathe,
Not whisper, any murmur of complaint.
Pain heaped ten-hundred-fold to this, were still
Less burthen, by ten-hundred-fold, to bear,
25 Than were those lead-like tons of sin that crushed
My spirit flat before thee.
                    O Lord, Lord,

Thou knowest I bore this better at the first,
For I was strong and hale of body then;
And though my teeth, which now are dropt away,
30 Would chatter with the cold, and all my beard
Was tagged with icy fringes in the moon,
I drowned the whoopings of the owl with sound
Of pious hymns and psalms, and sometimes saw
An angel stand and watch me, as I sang.
35 Now am I feeble grown; my end draws nigh;
I hope my end draws nigh: half deaf I am,
So that I scarce can hear the people hum
About the column's base, and almost blind,
And scarce can recognise the fields I know;
40 And both my thighs are rotted with the dew;
Yet cease I not to clamour and to cry,
While my stiff spine can hold my weary head,
Till all my limbs drop piecemeal from the stone,
Have mercy, mercy: take away my sin.

45   O Jesus, if thou wilt not save my soul,
Who may be saved? who is it may be saved?[3]
Who may be made a saint, if I fail here?
Show me the man hath suffered more than I.
For did not all thy martyrs die one death?
50 For either they were stoned, or crucified,
Or burned in fire, or boiled in oil, or sawn
In twain beneath the ribs; but I die here
Today, and whole years long, a life of death.
Bear witness, if I could have found a way
55 (And heedfully I sifted all my thought)
More slowly-painful to subdue this home
Of sin, my flesh, which I despise and hate,
I had not stinted practice, O my God.

For not alone this pillar-punishment,
60 Not this alone I bore: but while I lived
In the white convent down the valley there,
For many weeks about my loins I wore
The rope that haled the buckets from the well,

---

[1] although published in 1842, written in 1833.

[2] Revelation 7:9.

[3] Matthew 19:25.

Twisted as tight as I could knot the noose;
65 And spake not of it to a single soul,
Until the ulcer, eating through my skin,
Betrayed my secret penance, so that all
My brethren marvelled greatly. More than this
I bore, whereof, O God, thou knowest all.

70 Three winters, that my soul might grow to thee,
I lived up there on yonder mountain side.
My right leg chained into the crag, I lay
Pent in a roofless close of ragged stones;
Inswathed sometimes in wandering mist, and twice
75 Blacked with thy branding thunder, and sometimes
Sucking the damps for drink, and eating not,
Except the spare chance-gift of those that came
To touch my body and be healed, and live:
And they say then that I worked miracles,
80 Whereof my fame is loud amongst mankind,
Cured lameness, palsies, cancers.[1] Thou, O God,
Knowest alone whether this was or no.
Have mercy, mercy! cover all my sin.[2]

Then, that I might be more alone with thee,
85 Three years I lived upon a pillar, high
Six cubits, and three years on one of twelve;
And twice three years I crouched on one that rose
Twenty by measure; last of all, I grew
Twice ten long weary weary years to this,
90 That numbers forty cubits from the soil.

I think that I have borne as much as this—
Or else I dream—and for so long a time,
If I may measure time by yon slow light,
And this high dial, which my sorrow crowns—
95 So much—even so.
                    And yet I know not well,
For that the evil ones come here, and say,
"Fall down, O Simeon: thou hast suffered long

For ages and for ages!" then they prate
Of penances I cannot have gone through,
100 Perplexing me with lies; and oft I fall,
Maybe for months, in such blind lethargies
That Heaven, and Earth, and Time are choked.
                                        But yet
Bethink thee, Lord, while thou and all the saints
Enjoy themselves in heaven, and men on earth
105 House in the shade of comfortable roofs,
Sit with their wives by fires, eat wholesome food,
And wear warm clothes, and even beasts have stalls,
I, 'tween the spring and downfall of the light,
Bow down one thousand and two hundred times,
110 To Christ, the Virgin Mother, and the saints;
Or in the night, after a little sleep,
I wake: the chill stars sparkle; I am wet
With drenching dews, or stiff with crackling frost.
I wear an undressed goatskin on my back;
115 A grazing iron collar grinds my neck;
And in my weak, lean arms I lift the cross,
And strive and wrestle with thee till I die:
O mercy, mercy! wash away my sin.

O Lord, thou knowest what a man I am;
120 A sinful man, conceived and born in sin:[3]
'Tis their own doing; this is none of mine;
Lay it not to me. Am I to blame for this,
That here come those that worship me? Ha! ha!
They think that I am somewhat. What am I?
125 The silly people take me for a saint,
And bring me offerings of fruit and flowers:
And I, in truth (thou wilt bear witness here)
Have all in all endured as much, and more
Than many just and holy men, whose names
130 Are registered and calendared for saints.

Good people, you do ill to kneel to me.
What is it I can have done to merit this?
I am a sinner viler than you all.

---

[1] Acts 8:7.

[2] Psalm 85:2.

[3] Psalm 51: 5.

It may be I have wrought some miracles,
35 And cured some halt and maimed; but what of that?
It may be, no one, even among the saints,
May match his pains with mine; but what of that?
Yet do not rise; for you may look on me,
And in your looking you may kneel to God.
40 Speak! is there any of you halt or maimed?
I think you know I have some power with Heaven
From my long penance: let him speak his wish.

    Yes, I can heal him. Power goes forth from me.
They say that they are healed. Ah, hark! they shout
45 "St Simeon Stylites." Why, if so,
God reaps a harvest in me. O my soul,
God reaps a harvest in thee. If this be,
Can I work miracles and not be saved?
This is not told of any. They were saints.
50 It cannot be but that I shall be saved;
Yea, crowned a saint. They shout, "Behold a saint!"
And lower voices saint me from above.
Courage, St Simeon! This dull chrysalis
Cracks into shining wings, and hope ere death
55 Spreads more and more and more, that God hath
    now
Sponged and made blank of crimeful record all
My mortal archives.
        O my sons, my sons,
I, Simeon of the pillar, by surname
Stylites, among men; I, Simeon,
60 The watcher on the column till the end;
I, Simeon, whose brain the sunshine bakes;
I, whose bald brows in silent hours become
Unnaturally hoar with rime, do now
From my high nest of penance here proclaim
65 That Pontius and Iscariot by my side
Showed like fair seraphs. On the coals I lay,
A vessel full of sin: all hell beneath
Made me boil over. Devils plucked my sleeve,
Abaddon and Asmodeus caught at me.
70 I smote them with the cross; they swarmed again.
In bed like monstrous apes they crushed my chest:

They flapped my light out as I read: I saw
Their faces grow between me and my book;
With colt-like whinny and with hoggish whine[1]
175 They burst my prayer. Yet this way was left,
And by this way I 'scaped them. Mortify
Your flesh, like me, with scourges and with thorns;
Smite, shrink not, spare not. If it may be, fast
Whole Lents, and pray. I hardly, with slow steps,
180 With slow, faint steps, and much exceeding pain,
Have scrambled past those pits of fire, that still
Sing in mine ears. But yield not me the praise:
God only through his bounty hath thought fit,
Among the powers and princes of this world,
185 To make me an example to mankind,
Which few can reach to. Yet I do not say
But that a time may come—yea, even now,
Now, now, his footsteps smite the threshold stairs
Of life—I say, that time is at the doors
190 When you may worship me without reproach;
For I will leave my relics in your land,
And you may carve a shrine about my dust,
And burn a fragrant lamp before my bones,
When I am gathered to the glorious saints.

195   While I spake then, a sting of shrewdest pain
Ran shrivelling through me, and a cloudlike change,
In passing, with a grosser film made thick
These heavy, horny eyes. The end! the end!
Surely the end! What's here? a shape, a shade,
200 A flash of light. Is that the angel there
That holds a crown? Come, blessèd brother, come.
I know thy glittering face. I waited long;
My brows are ready. What! deny it now?
Nay, draw, draw, draw nigh. So I clutch it. Christ!
205 'Tis gone: 'tis here again; the crown! the crown![2]
So now 'tis fitted on and grows to me,
And from it melt the dews of Paradise,
Sweet! sweet! spikenard, and balm, and frankincense.

---

1 Cf. *The Tempest* 2.2.8–10.

2 Revelation 1:7–10.

Ah! let me not be fooled, sweet saints: I trust
210 That I am whole, and clean, and meet for Heaven.

Speak, if there be a priest, a man of God,
Among you there, and let him presently
Approach, and lean a ladder on the shaft,
And climbing up into my airy home,
215 Deliver me the blessèd sacrament;
For by the warning of the Holy Ghost,
I prophesy that I shall die tonight,
A quarter before twelve.
                                   But thou, O Lord,
Aid all this foolish people;[1] let them take
220 Example, pattern: lead them to thy light.
—1842

Ulysses[2]

It little profits that an idle king,[3]
By this still hearth, among these barren crags,
Matched with an agèd wife, I mete and dole
Unequal laws unto a savage race,
5 That hoard, and sleep, and feed, and know not me.

I cannot rest from travel: I will drink
Life to the lees: all times I have enjoyed
Greatly, have suffered greatly, both with those
That loved me, and alone; on shore, and when
10 Through scudding drifts the rainy Hyades[4]
Vext the dim sea: I am become a name;
For always roaming with a hungry heart
Much have I seen and known; cities of men

And manners, climates, councils, governments,
15 Myself not least, but honoured of them all;
And drunk delight of battle with my peers,
Far on the ringing plains of windy Troy.
I am a part of all that I have met;
Yet all experience is an arch wherethrough
20 Gleams that untravelled world, whose margin fades
For ever and for ever when I move.
How dull it is to pause, to make an end,
To rust unburnished, not to shine in use!
As though to breathe were life. Life piled on life
25 Were all too little, and of one to me
Little remains: but every hour is saved
From that eternal silence, something more,
A bringer of new things; and vile it were
For some three suns to store and hoard myself,
30 And this gray spirit yearning in desire
To follow knowledge like a sinking star,
Beyond the utmost bound of human thought.

This is my son, mine own Telemachus,
To whom I leave the sceptre and the isle—
35 Well-loved of me, discerning to fulfil
This labour, by slow prudence to make mild
A rugged people, and through soft degrees
Subdue them to the useful and the good.
Most blameless is he, centred in the sphere
40 Of common duties, decent not to fail
In offices of tenderness, and pay
Meet adoration to my household gods,
When I am gone. He works his work, I mine.

There lies the port; the vessel puffs her sail:
45 There gloom the dark broad seas. My mariners
Souls that have toiled, and wrought, and thought
      with me—
That ever with a frolic welcome took
The thunder and the sunshine, and opposed
Free hearts, free foreheads—you and I are old;
50 Old age hath yet his honour and his toil;
Death closes all: but something ere the end,

---

[1] Psalm 74:18.

[2] Tennyson's comment on the poem: "The poem was written soon after Arthur Hallam's death, and it gives the feeling about the need of going forward and braving the struggle of life perhaps more simply than anything in *In Memoriam*."

[3] Ulysses, King of Ithaca, has returned to his island from Troy, after ten years of wandering. He now prepares to set sail for his legendary final voyage: *Odyssey* 11.

[4] clouds believed to bring storms.

Some work of noble note, may yet be done,
Not unbecoming men that strove with Gods.
The lights begin to twinkle from the rocks:
55 The long day wanes: the slow moon climbs: the deep
Moans round with many voices. Come, my friends,
'Tis not too late to seek a newer world.
Push off, and sitting well in order smite
The sounding furrows; for my purpose holds
60 To sail beyond the sunset, and the baths
Of all the western stars, until I die.
It may be that the gulfs will wash us down:
It may be we shall touch the Happy Isles,[1]
And see the great Achilles, whom we knew.
65 Though much is taken, much abides; and though
We are not now that strength which in old days
Moved earth and heaven; that which we are, we are;
One equal temper of heroic hearts,
Made weak by time and fate, but strong in will
70 To strive, to seek, to find, and not to yield.
—1842

Tiresias [2]

I wish I were as in the years of old,
While yet the blessèd daylight made itself
Ruddy through both the roofs of sight, and woke
These eyes, now dull, but then so keen to seek
5 The meanings ambushed under all they saw,
The flight of birds, the flame of sacrifice,
What omens may foreshadow fate to man
And woman, and the secret of the Gods.
My son, the Gods, despite of human prayer,
10 Are slower to forgive than human kings.
The great God, Arês, burns in anger still
Against the guiltless heirs of him from Tyre,
Our Cadmus, out of whom thou art, who found
Beside the springs of Dircê, smote, and stilled

---

[1] the Isles of the Blest.

[2] Although the poem was published in 1885, Hallam Tennyson notes
that it was "partly written at the same time" as "Ulysses" (1833).

15 Through all its folds the multitudinous beast,
The dragon, which our trembling fathers called
The God's own son.
                  A tale, that told to me,
When but thine age, by age as winter-white
As mine is now, amazed, but made me yearn
20 For larger glimpses of that more than man
Which rolls the heavens, and lifts, and lays the deep,
Yet loves and hates with mortal hates and loves,
And moves unseen among the ways of men.
Then, in my wanderings all the lands that lie
25 Subjected to the Heliconian ridge
Have heard this footstep fall, although my wont
Was more to scale the highest of the heights
With some strange hope to see the nearer God.
One naked peak—the sister of the sun
30 Would climb from out the dark, and linger there
To silver all the valleys with her shafts—
There once, but long ago, five-fold thy term
Of years, I lay; the winds were dead for heat;
The noonday crag made the hand burn; and sick
35 For shadow—not one bush was near—I rose
Following a torrent till its myriad falls
Found silence in the hollows underneath.
There in a secret olive-glade I saw
Pallas Athene climbing from the bath
40 In anger; yet one glittering foot disturbed
The lucid well; one snowy knee was prest
Against the margin flowers; a dreadful light
Came from her golden hair, her golden helm
And all her golden armour on the grass,
45 And from her virgin breast, and virgin eyes
Remaining fixt on mine, till mine grew dark
For ever, and I heard a voice that said
"Henceforth be blind, for thou hast seen too much,
And speak the truth that no man may believe."
50 Son, in the hidden world of sight, that lives
Behind this darkness, I behold her still,
Beyond all work of those who carve the stone,
Beyond all dreams of Godlike womanhood,
Ineffable beauty, out of whom, at a glance,

55 And as it were, perforce, upon me flashed
The power of prophesying—but to me
No power—so chained and coupled with the curse
Of blindness and their unbelief, who heard
And heard not, when I spake of famine, plague,
60 Shrine-shattering earthquake, fire, flood,
       thunderbolt,
And angers of the Gods for evil done
And expiation lacked—no power on Fate,
Theirs, or mine own! for when the crowd would roar
For blood, for war, whose issue was their doom,
65 To cast wise words among the multitude
Was flinging fruit to lions; nor, in hours
Of civil outbreak, when I knew the twain
Would each waste each, and bring on both the yoke
Of stronger states, was mine the voice to curb
70 The madness of our cities and their kings.
       Who ever turned upon his heel to hear
My warning that the tyranny of one
Was prelude to the tyranny of all?
My counsel that the tyranny of all
75 Led backward to the tyranny of one?
       This power hath worked no good to aught that
              lives,
And these blind hands were useless in their wars.
O therefore that the unfulfilled desire,
The grief for ever born from griefs to be,
80 The boundless yearning of the Prophet's heart—
Could *that* stand forth, and like a statue, reared
To some great citizen, win all praise from all
Who past it, saying, "That was he!"
                            In vain!
Virtue must shape itself in deed, and those
85 Whom weakness or necessity have cramped
Within themselves, immerging, each, his urn
In his own well, draw solace as he may.
       Menœceus, thou hast eyes, and I can hear
Too plainly what full tides of onset sap
90 Our seven high gates, and what a weight of war
Rides on those ringing axles! jingle of bits,
Shouts, arrows, tramp of the hornfooted horse

That grind the glebe to powder! Stony showers
Of that ear-stunning hail of Arês crash
95 Along the sounding walls. Above, below,
Shock after shock, the song-built[1] towers and gates
Reel, bruised and butted with the shuddering
War-thunder of iron rams; and from within
The city comes a murmur void of joy,
100 Lest she be taken captive—maidens, wives,
And mothers with their babblers of the dawn,
And oldest age in shadow from the night,
Falling about their shrines before their Gods,
And wailing "Save us."
                       And they wail to thee!
105 These eyeless eyes, that cannot see thine own,
See this, that only in thy virtue lies
The saving of our Thebes; for, yesternight,
To me, the great God Arês, whose one bliss
Is war, and human sacrifice—himself
110 Blood-red from battle, spear and helmet tipt
With stormy light as on a mast at sea,
Stood out before a darkness, crying "Thebes,
Thy Thebes shall fall and perish, for I loathe
The seed of Cadmus—yet if one of these
115 By his own hand—if one of these—"
                                  My son,
No sound is breathed so potent to coerce,
And to conciliate, as their names who dare
For that sweet mother land which gave them birth
Nobly to do, nobly to die. Their names,
120 Graven on memorial columns, are a song
Heard in the future; few, but more than wall
And rampart, their examples reach a hand
Far through all years, and everywhere they meet
And kindle generous purpose, and the strength
125 To mould it into action pure as theirs.
       Fairer thy fate than mine, if life's best end
Be to end well! and thou refusing this,
Unvenerable will thy memory be
While men shall move the lips: but if thou dare—

---

[1] Thebes was built to the music of Amphion.

30 Thou, one of these, the race of Cadmus—then
No stone is fitted in yon marble girth
Whose echo shall not tongue thy glorious doom,
Nor in this pavement but shall ring thy name
To every hoof that clangs it, and the springs
35 Of Dircê laving yonder battle-plain,
Heard from the roofs by night, will murmur thee
To thine own Thebes, while Thebes through thee
    shall stand
Firm-based with all her Gods.
                    The Dragon's cave
Half hid, they tell me, now in flowing vines—
40 Where once he dwelt and whence he rolled himself
At dead of night—thou knowest, and that smooth
    rock
Before it, altar-fashioned, where of late
The woman-breasted Sphinx,[1] with wings drawn
    back,
Folded her lion paws, and looked to Thebes.
45 There blanch the bones of whom she slew, and these
Mixt with her own, because the fierce beast found
A wiser than herself, and dashed herself
Dead in her rage: but thou art wise enough,
Though young, to love thy wiser, blunt the curse
50 Of Pallas, hear, and though I speak the truth
Believe I speak it, let thine own hand strike
Thy youthful pulses into rest and quench
The red God's anger, fearing not to plunge
Thy torch of life in darkness, rather—thou
55 Rejoicing that the sun, the moon, the stars
Send no such light upon the ways of men
As one great deed.
              Thither, my son, and there
Thou, that hast never known the embrace of love,
Offer thy maiden life.
                  This useless hand!
60 I felt one warm tear fall upon it. Gone!
He will achieve his greatness.
                      But for me,

---

[1] The story of the Sphinx is from *Phoenissae*.

I would that I were gathered to my rest,
And mingled with the famous kings of old,
On whom about their ocean-islets flash
165 The faces of the Gods—the wise man's word,
Here trampled by the populace underfoot,
There crowned with worship—and these eyes will
    find
The men I knew, and watch the chariot whirl
About the goal again, and hunters race
170 The shadowy lion, and the warrior-kings,
In height and prowess more than human, strive
Again for glory, while the golden lyre
Is ever sounding in heroic ears
Heroic hymns, and every way the vales
175 Wind, clouded with the grateful incense-fume
Of those who mix all odour to the Gods
On one far height in one far-shining fire.
    —1885

The Epic [Morte d'Arthur] [2]

At Francis Allen's on the Christmas-eve,—
The game of forfeits done—the girls all kissed
Beneath the sacred bush and past away—
The parson Holmes, the poet Everard Hall,
5 The host, and I sat round the wassail-bowl,
Then half-way ebbed: and there we held a talk,
How all the old honour had from Christmas gone,
Or gone, or dwindled down to some odd games
In some odd nooks like this; till I, tired out
10 With cutting eights that day upon the pond,
Where, three times slipping from the outer edge,
I bumped the ice into three several stars,
Fell in a doze; and half-awake I heard
The parson taking wide and wider sweeps,

---

[2] Although published in 1842, the frames for *Morte d'Arthur* (both the introduction and conclusion—see l. 273ff.) were written some time after 1835.

15 Now harping on the church-commissioners,[1]
Now hawking at Geology and schism;
Until I woke, and found him settled down
Upon the general decay of faith
Right through the world, "at home was little left,
20 And none abroad: there was no anchor, none,
To hold by." Francis, laughing, clapt his hand
On Everard's shoulder, with "I hold by him."
"And I," quoth Everard, "by the wassail-bowl."
"Why yes," I said, "we knew your gift that way
25 At college: but another which you had,
I mean of verse (for so we held it then),
What came of that?" "You know," said Frank, "he
        burnt
His epic, his King Arthur, some twelve books"—
And then to me demanding why? "Oh, sir,
30 He thought that nothing new was said, or else
Something so said 'twas nothing—that a truth
Looks freshest in the fashion of the day:
God knows: he has a mint of reasons: ask.
It pleased *me* well enough." "Nay, nay," said Hall,
35 "Why take the style of those heroic times?
For nature brings not back the Mastodon,
Nor we those times; and why should any man
Remodel models? these twelve books of mine
Were faint Homeric echoes, nothing-worth,
40 Mere chaff and draff, much better burnt." "But I,"
Said Francis, "picked the eleventh from this hearth
And have it: keep a thing, its use will come.
I hoard it as a sugar-plum for Holmes."
He laughed, and I, though sleepy, like a horse
45 That hears the corn-bin open, pricked my ears;
For I remembered Everard's college fame
When we were Freshmen: then at my request
He brought it; and the poet little urged,
But with some prelude of disparagement,

50 Read, mouthing out his hollow oes and aes,
Deep-chested music,[2] and to this result.

MORTE D'ARTHUR [3]

So all day long the noise of battle rolled
Among the mountains by the winter sea;
Until King Arthur's table, man by man,
Had fallen in Lyonnesse[4] about their Lord,
5 King Arthur: then, because his wound was deep,
The bold Sir Bedivere uplifted him,
Sir Bedivere, the last of all his knights,
And bore him to a chapel nigh the field,
A broken chancel with a broken cross,
10 That stood on a dark strait of barren land.
On one side lay the Ocean, and on one
Lay a great water, and the moon was full.

    Then spake King Arthur to Sir Bedivere:
"The sequel of today unsolders all
15 The goodliest fellowship of famous knights
Whereof this world holds record. Such a sleep
They sleep—the men I loved. I think that we
Shall never more, at any future time,
Delight our souls with talk of knightly deeds,
20 Walking about the gardens of the halls
Of Camelot,[5] as in the days that were.
I perish by this people which I made,—
Though Merlin[6] sware that I should come again
To rule once more—but let what will be, be,
25 I am so deeply smitten through the helm

---

[2] as Tennyson himself was said to have read.

[3] written in 1833–34 under the shock of Arthur Hallam's death; later incorporated in the *Idylls of the King* as *The Passing of Arthur* (1869) where it was preceded by 169 lines and followed by 29 lines. Based largely on Malory's *Morte d'Arthur* 21.4–5.

[4] the legendary country that lay between Cornwall and the Scilly Islands.

[5] the city of Arthur's court.

[6] the magician and prophet of Arthurian romance.

---

[1] the Ecclesiastical Commission established in 1835 to administer the revenues of the Church of England.

That without help I cannot last till morn.
Thou therefore take my brand Excalibur,[1]
Which was my pride: for thou rememberest how
In those old days, one summer noon, an arm
30 Rose up from out the bosom of the lake,
Clothed in white samite,[2] mystic, wonderful,
Holding the sword—and how I rowed across
And took it, and have worn it, like a king:
And, wheresoever I am sung or told
35 In aftertime, this also shall be known:
But now delay not: take Excalibur,
And fling him far into the middle mere:
Watch what thou seëst, and lightly bring me
      word."

To him replied the bold Sir Bedivere:
40 "It is not meet, Sir King, to leave thee thus,
Aidless, alone, and smitten through the helm.
A little thing may harm a wounded man.
Yet I thy hest will all perform at full,
Watch what I see, and lightly bring thee word."

45 So saying, from the ruined shrine he stept
And in the moon athwart the place of tombs,
Where lay the mighty bones of ancient men,
Old knights, and over them the sea-wind sang
Shrill, chill, with flakes of foam. He, stepping down
50 By zig-zag paths, and juts of pointed rock,
Came on the shining levels of the lake.

There drew he forth the brand Excalibur,
And o'er him, drawing it, the winter moon,
Brightening the skirts of a long cloud, ran forth
55 And sparkled keen with frost against the hilt:
For all the haft twinkled with diamond sparks,
Myriads of topaz-lights, and jacinth-work
Of subtlest jewellery. He gazed so long
That both his eyes were dazzled, as he stood,

60 This way and that dividing the swift mind,
In act to throw: but at the last it seemed
Better to leave Excalibur concealed
There in the many-knotted waterflags,
That whistled stiff and dry about the marge.
65 So strode he back slow to the wounded King.

Then spake King Arthur to Sir Bedivere:
"Hast thou performed my mission which I gave?
What is it thou hast seen? or what hast heard?"

And answer made the bold Sir Bedivere:
70 "I heard the ripple washing in the reeds,
And the wild water lapping on the crag."

To whom replied King Arthur, faint and pale:
"Thou hast betrayed thy nature and thy name,
Not rendering true answer, as beseemed
75 Thy fëalty, nor like a noble knight:
For surer sign had followed, either hand,
Or voice, or else a motion of the mere.
This is a shameful thing for men to lie.
Yet now, I charge thee, quickly go again
80 As thou art lief and dear, and do the thing
I bad thee, watch, and lightly bring me word."

Then went Sir Bedivere the second time
Across the ridge, and paced beside the mere,
Counting the dewy pebbles, fixed in thought;
85 But when he saw the wonder of the hilt,
How curiously and strangely chased, he smote
His palms together, and he cried aloud,

"And if indeed I cast the brand away,
Surely a precious thing, one worthy note,
90 Should thus be lost for ever from the earth,
Which might have pleased the eyes of many men.
What good should follow this, if this were done?
What harm, undone? deep harm to disobey,
Seeing obedience is the bond of rule.
95 Were it well to obey then, if a king demand

---

[1] Arthur's sword, given to him by the Lady of the Lake.

[2] a rich silk material.

An act unprofitable, against himself?
The King is sick, and knows not what he does.
What record, or what relic of my lord
Should be to aftertime, but empty breath
100 And rumours of a doubt? but were this kept,
Stored in some treasure-house of mighty kings,
Some one might show it at a joust of arms,
Saying, 'King Arthur's sword, Excalibur,
Wrought by the lonely maiden of the Lake.
105 Nine years she wrought it, sitting in the deeps
Upon the hidden bases of the hills.'
So might some old man speak in the aftertime
To all the people, winning reverence.
But now much honour and much fame were lost."

110   So spake he, clouded with his own conceit,
And hid Excalibur the second time,
And so strode back slow to the wounded King.

    Then spoke King Arthur, breathing heavily:
"What is it thou hast seen? or what hast heard?"
115   And answer made the bold Sir Bedivere:
"I heard the water lapping on the crag,
And the long ripple washing in the reeds."

    To whom replied King Arthur, much in wrath:
"Ah, miserable and unkind, untrue,
120 Unknightly, traitor-hearted! Woe is me!
Authority forgets a dying king,
Laid widowed of the power in his eye
That bowed the will. I see thee what thou art,
For thou, the latest-left of all my knights,
125 In whom should meet the offices of all,
Thou wouldst betray me for the precious hilt;
Either from lust of gold, or like a girl
Valuing the giddy pleasure of the eyes.
Yet, for a man may fail in duty twice,
130 And the third time may prosper, get thee hence:
But, if thou spare to fling Excalibur,
I will arise and slay thee with my hands."

    Then quickly rose Sir Bedivere, and ran,
And, leaping down the ridges lightly, plunged
135 Among the bulrush-beds, and clutched the sword,
And strongly wheeled and threw it. The great brand
Made lightnings in the splendour of the moon,
And flashing round and round, and whirled in an
    arch,
Shot like a streamer of the northern morn,
140 Seen where the moving isles of winter shock[1]
By night, with noises of the northern sea.
So flashed and fell the brand Excalibur:
But ere he dipt the surface, rose an arm
Clothed in white samite, mystic, wonderful,
145 And caught him by the hilt, and brandished him
Three times, and drew him under in the mere.
And lightly went the other to the King.

    Then spoke King Arthur, drawing thicker breath:
"Now see I by thine eyes that this is done.
150 Speak out: what is it thou hast heard, or seen?"

    And answer made the bold Sir Bedivere:
"Sir King, I closed mine eyelids, lest the gems
Should blind my purpose, for I never saw,
Nor shall see, here or elsewhere, till I die,
155 Not though I live three lives of mortal men,
So great a miracle as yonder hilt.
Then with both hands I flung him, wheeling him;
But when I looked again, behold an arm,
Clothed in white samite, mystic, wonderful,
160 That caught him by the hilt, and brandished him
Three times, and drew him under in the mere."

    And answer made King Arthur, breathing hard:
"My end draws nigh; 'tis time that I were gone.
Make broad thy shoulders to receive my weight,
165 And bear me to the margin; yet I fear
My wound hath taken cold, and I shall die."

---

[1] icebergs.

So saying, from the pavement he half rose,
Slowly, with pain, reclining on his arm,
And looking wistfully with wide blue eyes
70 As in a picture. Him Sir Bedivere
Remorsefully regarded through his tears,
And would have spoken, but he found not words,
Then took with care, and kneeling on one knee,
O'er both his shoulders drew the languid hands,
75 And rising bore him through the place of tombs.

But, as he walked, King Arthur panted hard,
Like one that feels a nightmare on his bed
When all the house is mute. So sighed the King,
Muttering and murmuring at his ear, "Quick, quick!
80 I fear it is too late, and I shall die."
But the other swiftly strode from ridge to ridge,
Clothed with his breath, and looking, as he walked,
Larger than human on the frozen hills.
He heard the deep behind him, and a cry
85 Before. His own thought drove him, like a goad.
Dry clashed his harness in the icy caves
And barren chasms, and all to left and right
The bare black cliff clanged round him, as he based
His feet on juts of slippery crag that rang
90 Sharp-smitten with the dint of armèd heels—
And on a sudden, lo! the level lake,
And the long glories of the winter moon.
Then saw they how there hove a dusky barge,
Dark as a funeral scarf from stem to stern,
95 Beneath them; and descending they were ware
That all the decks were dense with stately forms
Black-stoled, black-hooded, like a dream—by these
Three Queens with crowns of gold—and from
        them rose
A cry that shivered to the tingling stars,
100 And, as it were one voice, an agony
Of lamentation, like a wind, that shrills
All night in a waste land, where no one comes,
Or hath come, since the making of the world.

Then murmured Arthur, "Place me in the
        barge,"
205 And to the barge they came. There those three
        Queens
Put forth their hands, and took the King, and wept.
But she, that rose the tallest of them all
And fairest, laid his head upon her lap,
And loosed the shattered casque, and chafed his
        hands,
210 And called him by his name, complaining loud,
And dropping bitter tears against his brow
Striped with dark blood: for all his face was white
And colourless, and like the withered moon
Smote by the fresh beam of the springing east;
215 And all his greaves and cuisses dashed with drops
Of onset;[1] and the light and lustrous curls—
That made his forehead like a rising sun
High from the daïs-throne—were parched with
        dust;
Or, clotted into points and hanging loose,
220 Mixed with the knightly growth that fringed his lips.
So like a shattered column lay the King;
Not like that Arthur who, with lance in rest,
From spur to plume a star of tournament,
Shot through the lists at Camelot, and charged
225 Before the eyes of ladies and of kings.

Then loudly cried the bold Sir Bedivere,
"Ah! my Lord Arthur, whither shall I go?
Where shall I hide my forehead and my eyes?
For now I see the true old times are dead,
230 When every morning brought a noble chance,
And every chance brought out a noble knight.
Such times have been not since the light that led
The holy Elders with the gift of myrrh.
But now the whole ROUND TABLE is dissolved
235 Which was an image of the mighty world;
And I, the last, go forth companionless,

---

[1] armor for shin and thigh dashed with drops of blood from battle.

And the days darken round me, and the years,
Among new men, strange faces, other minds."

    And slowly answered Arthur from the barge:
240 "The old order changeth, yielding place to new,
And God fulfils Himself in many ways,
Lest one good custom should corrupt the world.
Comfort thyself: what comfort is in me?
I have lived my life, and that which I have done
245 May He within Himself make pure! but thou,
If thou shouldst never see my face again,
Pray for my soul. More things are wrought by prayer
Than this world dreams of. Wherefore, let thy voice
Rise like a fountain for me night and day.
250 For what are men better than sheep or goats
That nourish a blind life within the brain,
If, knowing God, they lift not hands of prayer
Both for themselves and those who call them friend?
For so the whole round earth is every way
255 Bound by gold chains about the feet of God.
But now farewell. I am going a long way
With these thou seëst—if indeed I go—
(For all my mind is clouded with a doubt)
To the island-valley of Avilion;[1]
260 Where falls not hail, or rain, or any snow,
Nor ever wind blows loudly; but it lies
Deep-meadowed, happy, fair with orchard-lawns
And bowery hollows crowned with summer sea,
Where I will heal me of my grievous wound."

265   So said he, and the barge with oar and sail
Moved from the brink, like some full-breasted swan
That, fluting a wild carol ere her death,
Ruffles her pure cold plume, and takes the flood
With swarthy webs. Long stood Sir Bedivere
270 Revolving many memories, till the hull
Looked one black dot against the verge of dawn,
And on the mere the wailing died away.

----

[1] the Isle of the Blest.

[THE EPIC]

Here ended Hall, and our last light, that long
Had winked and threatened darkness, flared and fell:
275 At which the Parson, sent to sleep with sound,
And waked with silence, grunted "Good!" but we
Sat rapt: it was the tone with which he read—
Perhaps some modern touches here and there
Redeemed it from the charge of nothingness—
280 Or else we loved the man, and prized his work;
I know not: but we sitting, as I said,
The cock crew loud; as at that time of year
The lusty bird takes every hour for dawn:
Then Francis, muttering, like a man ill-used,
285 "There now—that's nothing!" drew a little back,
And drove his heel into the smouldering log,
That sent a blast of sparkles up the flue:
And so to bed; where yet in sleep I seemed
To sail with Arthur under looming shores,
290 Point after point; till on to dawn, when dreams
Begin to feel the truth and stir of day,
To me, methought, who waited with a crowd,
There came a bark that, blowing forward, bore
King Arthur, like a modern gentleman
295 Of stateliest port; and all the people cried,
"Arthur is come again: he cannot die."
Then those that stood upon the hills behind
Repeated—"Come again, and thrice as fair;"
And, further inland, voices echoed—"Come
300 With all good things, and war shall be no more."
At this a hundred bells began to peal,
That with the sound I woke, and heard indeed
The clear church-bells ring in the Christmas-morn.
—1842

"Break, break, break"

Break, break, break,
  On thy cold gray stones, O Sea!
And I would that my tongue could utter
  The thoughts that arise in me.

5   O well for the fisherman's boy,
     That he shouts with his sister at play!
   O well for the sailor lad,
     That he sings in his boat on the bay!

   And the stately ships go on
10   To their haven under the hill;
   But O for the touch of a vanished hand,
     And the sound of a voice that is still!

   Break, break, break,
     At the foot of thy crags, O Sea!
15   But the tender grace of a day that is dead
     Will never come back to me.
     —1842

Locksley Hall

Comrades, leave me here a little, while as yet 'tis
   early morn:
Leave me here, and when you want me, sound
   upon the bugle-horn.

'Tis the place, and all around it, as of old, the
   curlews call,
Dreary gleams about the moorland flying over
   Locksley Hall;[1]

5 Locksley Hall, that in the distance overlooks the
   sandy tracts,
And the hollow ocean-ridges roaring into cataracts.

Many a night from yonder ivied casement, ere I
   went to rest,
Did I look on great Orion sloping slowly to the
   West.

Many a night I saw the Pleiads, rising through the
   mellow shade,

[1] meant, said Tennyson, "to express the flying gleams of light across a dreary moorland."

10 Glitter like a swarm of fire-flies tangled in a silver
   braid.

Here about the beach I wandered, nourishing a
   youth sublime
With the fairy tales of science, and the long result
   of Time;

When the centuries behind me like a fruitful land
   reposed;
When I clung to all the present for the promise
   that it closed:

15 When I dipt into the future far as human eye could
   see;
Saw the Vision of the world, and all the wonder
   that would be.—

In the Spring a fuller crimson comes upon the
   robin's breast;
In the Spring the wanton lapwing gets himself
   another crest;

In the Spring a livelier iris changes on the
   burnished dove;
20 In the Spring a young man's fancy lightly turns to
   thoughts of love.

Then her cheek was pale and thinner than should
   be for one so young,
And her eyes on all my motions with a mute
   observance hung.

And I said, "My cousin Amy, speak, and speak the
   truth to me,
Trust me, cousin, all the current of my being sets
   to thee."

25 On her pallid cheek and forehead came a colour
   and a light,
As I have seen the rosy red flushing in the northern
   night.

And she turned—her bosom shaken with a sudden
    storm of sighs—
All the spirit deeply dawning in the dark of hazel
    eyes—

Saying, "I have hid my feelings, fearing they should
    do me wrong;"
30 Saying, "Dost thou love me, cousin?" weeping, "I
    have loved thee long."

Love took up the glass of Time, and turned it in his
    glowing hands;
Every moment, lightly shaken, ran itself in golden
    sands.

Love took up the harp of Life, and smote on all the
    chords with might;
Smote the chord of Self, that, trembling, passed in
    music out of sight.

35 Many a morning on the moorland did we hear the
    copses ring,
And her whisper thronged my pulses with the
    fulness of the Spring.

Many an evening by the waters did we watch the
    stately ships,
And our spirits rushed together at the touching of
    the lips.

O my cousin, shallow-hearted! O my Amy, mine
    no more!
40 O the dreary, dreary moorland! O the barren,
    barren shore!

Falser than all fancy fathoms, falser than all songs
    have sung,
Puppet to a father's threat, and servile to a shrewish
    tongue!

Is it well to wish thee happy?—having known
    me—to decline

On a range of lower feelings and a narrower heart
    than mine!

45 Yet it shall be: thou shalt lower to his level day by
    day,
What is fine within thee growing coarse to
    sympathise with clay.

As the husband is, the wife is: thou art mated with
    a clown,
And the grossness of his nature will have weight to
    drag thee down.

He will hold thee, when his passion shall have
    spent its novel force,
50 Something better than his dog, a little dearer than
    his horse.

What is this? his eyes are heavy: think not they are
    glazed with wine.
Go to him: it is thy duty: kiss him: take his hand in
    thine.

It may be my lord is weary, that his brain is
    overwrought:
Soothe him with thy finer fancies, touch him with
    thy lighter thought.

55 He will answer to the purpose, easy things to
    understand—
Better thou wert dead before me, though I slew
    thee with my hand!

Better thou and I were lying, hidden from the
    heart's disgrace,
Rolled in one another's arms, and silent in a last
    embrace.

Cursèd be the social wants that sin against the
    strength of youth!
60 Cursèd be the social lies that warp us from the
    living truth!

Cursèd be the sickly forms that err from honest
  Nature's rule!
Cursèd be the gold that gilds the straitened
  forehead of the fool!

Well—'tis well that I should bluster!—Hadst thou
  less unworthy proved—
Would to God—for I have loved thee more
  than ever wife was loved.

65 Am I mad, that I should cherish that which bears
  but bitter fruit?
I will pluck it from my bosom, though my heart be
  at the root.

Never, though my mortal summers to such length
  of years should come
As the many-wintered crow that leads the clanging
  rookery home.

Where is comfort? in division of the records of the
  mind?
70 Can I part her from herself, and love her, as I knew
  her, kind?

I remember one that perished: sweetly did she
  speak and move:
Such a one do I remember, whom to look at was to
  love.

Can I think of her as dead, and love her for the
  love she bore?
No—she never loved me truly: love is love for
  evermore.

75 Comfort? comfort scorned of devils! this is truth
  the poet sings,
That a sorrow's crown of sorrow is remembering
  happier things.

Drug thy memories, lest thou learn it, lest thy heart
  be put to proof,
In the dead unhappy night, and when the rain is on
  the roof.

Like a dog, he hunts in dreams, and thou art
  staring at the wall,
80 Where the dying night-lamp flickers, and the
  shadows rise and fall.

Then a hand shall pass before thee, pointing to his
  drunken sleep,
To thy widowed marriage-pillows, to the tears that
  thou wilt weep.

Thou shalt hear the "Never, never," whispered by
  the phantom years,
And a song from out the distance in the ringing of
  thine ears;

85 And an eye shall vex thee, looking ancient kindness
  on thy pain.
Turn thee, turn thee on thy pillow: get thee to thy
  rest again.

Nay, but Nature brings thee solace; for a tender
  voice will cry.
'Tis a purer life than thine; a lip to drain thy
  trouble dry.

Baby lips will laugh me down: my latest rival brings
  thee rest.
90 Baby fingers, waxen touches, press me from the
  mother's breast.

O, the child too clothes the father with a dearness
  not his due.
Half is thine and half is his: it will be worthy of the
  two.

O, I see thee old and formal, fitted to thy petty part,
With a little hoard of maxims preaching down a
daughter's heart.

95 "They were dangerous guides the feelings—she
herself was not exempt—
Truly, she herself had suffered"—Perish in thy self-
contempt!

Overlive it—lower yet—be happy! wherefore
should I care?
I myself must mix with action, lest I wither by
despair.

What is that which I should turn to, lighting upon
days like these?
100 Every door is barred with gold, and opens but to
golden keys.

Every gate is thronged with suitors, all the markets
overflow.
I have but an angry fancy: what is that which I
should do?

I had been content to perish, falling on the
foeman's ground,
When the ranks are rolled in vapour, and the winds
are laid with sound.

105 But the jingling of the guinea helps the hurt that
Honour feels,
And the nations do but murmur, snarling at each
other's heels.

Can I but relive in sadness? I will turn that earlier
page.
Hide me from my deep emotion, O thou
wondrous Mother-Age!

Make me feel the wild pulsation that I felt before
the strife,

110 When I heard my days before me, and the tumult
of my life;

Yearning for the large excitement that the coming
years would yield,
Eager-hearted as a boy when first he leaves his
father's field,

And at night along the dusky highway near and
nearer drawn,
Sees in heaven the light of London flaring like a
dreary dawn;

115 And his spirit leaps within him to be gone before
him then,
Underneath the light he looks at, in among the
throngs of men:

Men, my brothers, men the workers, ever reaping
something new:
That which they have done but earnest of the
things that they shall do:

For I dipt into the future, far as human eye could
see,
120 Saw the Vision of the world, and all the wonder
that would be;

Saw the heavens fill with commerce, argosies of
magic sails,
Pilots of the purple twilight, dropping down with
costly bales;

Heard the heavens fill with shouting, and there
rained a ghastly dew
From the nations' airy navies grappling in the
central blue;

125 Far along the world-wide whisper of the south-
wind rushing warm,
With the standards of the peoples plunging
through the thunder-storm;

Till the war-drum throbbed no longer, and the
    battle-flags were furled
In the Parliament of man, the Federation of the
    world.

There the common sense of most shall hold a
    fretful realm in awe,
30 And the kindly earth shall slumber, lapt in
    universal law.

So I triumphed ere my passion sweeping through
    me left me dry,
Left me with the palsied heart, and left me with the
    jaundiced eye;

Eye, to which all order festers, all things here are
    out of joint:
Science moves, but slowly slowly, creeping on from
    point to point:

35 Slowly comes a hungry people, as a lion creeping
    nigher,
Glares at one that nods and winks behind a slowly-
    dying fire.

Yet I doubt not through the ages one increasing
    purpose runs,
And the thoughts of men are widened with the
    process of the suns.

What is that to him that reaps not harvest of his
    youthful joys,
40 Though the deep heart of existence beat for ever
    like a boy's?

Knowledge comes, but wisdom lingers, and I linger
    on the shore,
And the individual withers, and the world is more
    and more.

Knowledge comes, but wisdom lingers, and he
    bears a laden breast,
Full of sad experience, moving toward the stillness
    of his rest.

145 Hark, my merry comrades call me, sounding on the
    bugle-horn,
They to whom my foolish passion were a target for
    their scorn:

Shall it not be scorn to me to harp on such a
    mouldered string?
I am shamed through all my nature to have loved
    so slight a thing.

Weakness to be wroth with weakness! woman's
    pleasure, woman's pain—
150 Nature made them blinder motions bounded in a
    shallower brain:

Woman is the lesser man, and all thy passions,
    matched with mine,
Are as moonlight unto sunlight, and as water unto
    wine—

Here at least, where nature sickens, nothing. Ah,
    for some retreat
Deep in yonder shining Orient, where my life
    began to beat;

155 Where in wild Mahratta-battle[1] fell my father
    evil-starred;—
I was left a trampled orphan, and a selfish uncle's
    ward.

Or to burst all links of habit—there to wander far
    away,
On from island unto island at the gateways of the
    day.

---

[1] soldiers of Bombay who were conquered in 1818.

Larger constellations burning, mellow moons and
    happy skies,
160 Breadths of tropic shade and palms in cluster,
    knots of Paradise.

Never comes the trader, never floats an European
    flag,
Slides the bird o'er lustrous woodland, swings the
    trailer from the crag;

Droops the heavy-blossomed bower, hangs the
    heavy-fruited tree—
Summer isles of Eden lying in dark-purple spheres
    of sea.

165 There methinks would be enjoyment more than in
    this march of mind,
In the steamship, in the railway, in the thoughts
    that shake mankind.

There the passions cramped no longer shall have
    scope and breathing space;
I will take some savage woman, she shall rear my
    dusky race.

Iron jointed, supple-sinewed, they shall dive, and
    they shall run,
170 Catch the wild goat by the hair, and hurl their
    lances in the sun;

Whistle back the parrot's call, and leap the
    rainbows of the brooks,
Not with blinded eyesight poring over miserable
    books—

Fool, again the dream, the fancy! but I *know* my
    words are wild,
But I count the gray barbarian lower than the
    Christian child.

175 I, to herd with narrow foreheads, vacant of our
    glorious gains,
Like a beast with lower pleasures, like a beast with
    lower pains!

Mated with a squalid savage—what to me were sun
    or clime?
I the heir of all the ages, in the foremost files of
    time—

I that rather held it better men should perish one
    by one,
180 Than that earth should stand at gaze like Joshua's
    moon in Ajalon![1]

Not in vain the distance beacons. Forward, forward
    let us range,
Let the great world spin for ever down the ringing
    grooves of change.

Through the shadow of the globe we sweep into
    the younger day:
Better fifty years of Europe than a cycle of Cathay.

185 Mother-Age (for mine I knew not) help me as
    when life begun:
Rift the hills, and roll the waters, flash the
    lightnings, weigh the Sun.

O, I see the crescent promise of my spirit hath not
    set.
Ancient founts of inspiration well through all my
    fancy yet.

Howsoever these things be, a long farewell to
    Locksley Hall!
190 Now for me the woods may wither, now for me the
    roof-tree fall.

---

[1] Joshua commanded the moon to remain stationary in the vale of
Ajalon.

Comes a vapour from the margin, blackening over
  heath and holt,
Cramming all the blast before it, in its breast a
  thunderbolt.

Let it fall on Locksley Hall, with rain or hail, or fire
  or snow;
For the mighty wind arises, roaring seaward, and I
  go.
—1842

The Vision of Sin

I

I had a vision when the night was late:
A youth came riding toward a palace-gate.
He rode a horse with wings, that would have
  flown,
But that his heavy rider kept him down.
5 And from the palace came a child of sin,
And took him by the curls, and led him in,
Where sat a company with heated eyes,
Expecting when a fountain should arise:
A sleepy light upon their brows and lips—
10 As when the sun, a crescent of eclipse,
Dreams over lake and lawn, and isles and capes—
Suffused them, sitting, lying, languid shapes,
By heaps of gourds, and skins of wine, and piles of
  grapes.

II

Then methought I heard a mellow sound,
15 Gathering up from all the lower ground;
Narrowing in to where they sat assembled
Low voluptuous music winding trembled,
Woven in circles: they that heard it sighed,
Panted hand-in-hand with faces pale,
20 Swung themselves, and in low tones replied;
Till the fountain spouted, showering wide
Sleet of diamond-drift and pearly hail;

Then the music touched the gates and died;
Rose again from where it seemed to fail,
25 Stormed in orbs of song, a growing gale;
Till thronging in and in, to where they waited,
As 'twere a hundred-throated nightingale,
The strong tempestuous treble throbbed and
  palpitated;
Ran into its giddiest whirl of sound,
30 Caught the sparkles, and in circles,
Purple gauzes, golden hazes, liquid mazes,
Flung the torrent rainbow round:
Then they started from their places,
Moved with violence, changed in hue,
35 Caught each other with wild grimaces,
Half-invisible to the view,
Wheeling with precipitate paces
To the melody, till they flew,
Hair, and eyes, and limbs, and faces,
40 Twisted hard in fierce embraces,
Like to Furies, like to Graces,
Dashed together in blinding dew:[1]
Till, killed with some luxurious agony,
The nerve-dissolving melody
45 Fluttered headlong from the sky.

III

And then I looked up toward a mountain-tract,
That girt the region with high cliff and lawn:
I saw that every morning, far withdrawn
Beyond the darkness and the cataract,
50 God made Himself an awful rose of dawn,
Unheeded: and detaching, fold by fold,
From those still heights, and, slowly drawing near,
A vapour heavy, hueless, formless, cold,
Came floating on for many a month and year,
55 Unheeded: and I thought I would have spoken,
And warned that madman ere it grew too late:
But, as in dreams, I could not. Mine was broken,
When that cold vapour touched the palace gate,

---

[1] mist.

And linked again. I saw within my head
60 A gray and gap-toothed man as lean as death,
Who slowly rode across a withered heath,
And lighted at a ruined inn, and said:

IV

"Wrinkled ostler, grim and thin!
      Here is custom come your way;
65 Take my brute, and lead him in,
      Stuff his ribs with mouldy hay.

"Bitter barmaid, waning fast!
      See that sheets are on my bed;
What! the flower of life is past:
70   It is long before you wed.

"Slip-shod waiter, lank and sour,
      At the Dragon on the heath!
Let us have a quiet hour,
      Let us hob-and-nob with Death.

75 "I am old, but let me drink;
      Bring me spices, bring me wine;
I remember, when I think,
      That my youth was half divine.

"Wine is good for shrivelled lips,
80   When a blanket wraps the day,
When the rotten woodland drips,
      And the leaf is stamped in clay.

"Sit thee down, and have no shame,
      Cheek by jowl, and knee by knee:
85 What care I for any name?
      What for order or degree?

"Let me screw thee up a peg:
      Let me loose thy tongue with wine:
Callest thou that thing a leg?
90   Which is thinnest? thine or mine?

"Thou shalt not be saved by works:
      Thou hast been a sinner too:
Ruined trunks on withered forks,
      Empty scarecrows, I and you!

95 "Fill the cup, and fill the can:
      Have a rouse[1] before the morn:
Every moment dies a man,
      Every moment one is born.

"We are men of ruined blood;
100   Therefore comes it we are wise.
Fish are we that love the mud,
      Rising to no fancy-flies.

"Name and fame! to fly sublime
      Through the courts, the camps, the schools,
105 Is to be the ball of Time,
      Bandied by the hands of fools.

"Friendship!—to be two in one—
      Let the canting liar pack!
Well I know, when I am gone,
110   How she mouths behind my back.

"Virtue!—to be good and just—
      Every heart, when sifted well,
Is a clot of warmer dust,
      Mixed with cunning sparks of hell.

115 "O! we two as well can look
      Whited thought and cleanly life
As the priest, above his book
      Leering at his neighbour's wife.

"Fill the cup, and fill the can:
120   Have a rouse before the morn:
Every moment dies a man,
      Every moment one is born.

---

[1] carouse.

"Drink, and let the parties rave:
    They are filled with idle spleen;
125 Rising, falling, like a wave,
    For they know not what they mean.

"He that roars for liberty
    Faster binds a tyrant's power;
130 And the tyrant's cruel glee
    Forces on the freer hour.

"Fill the can, and fill the cup:
    All the windy ways of men
Are but dust that rises up,
    And is lightly laid again.

135 "Greet her with applausive breath,
    Freedom, gaily doth she tread;
In her right a civic wreath,
    In her left a human head.

"No, I love not what is new;
140   She is of an ancient house:
And I think we know the hue
    Of that cap[1] upon her brows.

"Let her go! her thirst she slakes
    Where the bloody conduit runs,
145 Then her sweetest meal she makes
    On the first-born of her sons.

"Drink to lofty hopes that cool—
    Visions of a perfect State:
Drink we, last, the public fool,
150   Frantic love and frantic hate.

"Chant me now some wicked stave,
    Till thy drooping courage rise,

And the glow-worm of the grave
    Glimmer in thy rheumy eyes.

155 "Fear not thou to loose thy tongue;
    Set thy hoary fancies free;
What is loathsome to the young
    Savours well to thee and me.

"Change, reverting to the years,
160   When thy nerves could understand
What there is in loving tears,
    And the warmth of hand in hand.

"Tell me tales of thy first love—
    April hopes, the fools of chance;
165 Till the graves begin to move,
    And the dead begin to dance.

"Fill the can, and fill the cup:
    All the windy ways of men
Are but dust that rises up,
170   And is lightly laid again.

"Trooping from their mouldy dens
    The chap-fallen[2] circle spreads:
Welcome, fellow-citizens,
    Hollow hearts and empty heads!

175 "You are bones, and what of that?
    Every face, however full,
Padded round with flesh and fat,
    Is but modelled on a skull.

"Death is king, and Vivat Rex!
180   Tread a measure on the stones,
Madam—if I know your sex,
    From the fashion of your bones.

---

[1]   red cap of the French revolutionists.

[2]   gaping jaw of a skeleton.

"No, I cannot praise the fire
    In your eye—nor yet your lip:
185 All the more do I admire
    Joints of cunning workmanship.

"Lo! God's likeness—the ground-plan—
    Neither modelled, glazed, nor framed:
Buss me, thou rough sketch of man,
190   Far too naked to be shamed!

"Drink to Fortune, drink to Chance,
    While we keep a little breath!
Drink to heavy Ignorance!
    Hob-and-nob with brother Death!

195 "Thou art mazed, the night is long,
    And the longer night is near:
What! I am not all as wrong
    As a bitter jest is dear.

"Youthful hopes, by scores, to all,
200   When the locks are crisp and curled;
Unto me my maudlin gall
    And my mockeries of the world.

"Fill the cup, and fill the can:
    Mingle madness, mingle scorn!
205 Dregs of life, and lees of man:
    Yet we will not die forlorn."

v

The voice grew faint: there came a further change:
Once more uprose the mystic mountain-range:
Below were men and horses pierced with worms,
210 And slowly quickening into lower forms;
By shards and scurf of salt, and scum of dross,
Old plash[1] of rains, and refuse patched with moss.
Then some one spake: "Behold! it was a crime

Of sense avenged by sense that wore with time."[2]
215 Another said: "The crime of sense became
The crime of malice, and is equal blame."
And one: "He had not wholly quenched his power;
A little grain of conscience made him sour."
At last I heard a voice upon the slope
220 Cry to the summit, "Is there any hope?"
To which an answer pealed from that high land,
But in a tongue no man could understand;
And on the glimmering limit far withdrawn
God made Himself an awful rose of dawn.
          —1842

In Memoriam A.H.H. [3]

OBIT MDCCCXXXIII

[PROLOGUE]

Strong Son of God, immortal Love,
  Whom we, that have not seen thy face,
    By faith, and faith alone, embrace,
Believing where we cannot prove;

---

[1] puddle.

[2] "The sensualist becomes worn out by his senses." (Tennyson's note.)

[3] Tennyson's close friend, Arthur Henry Hallam, died at Vienna on 15 September 1833. As Christopher Ricks notes in his outstanding edition of Tennyson: "No event in Tennyson's life was of greater importance" (*The Poems of Tennyson*, 305). In Hallam Tennyson's *Memoir*, Tennyson is reported as saying: "It must be remembered that this is a poem, *not* an actual biography. It is founded on our friendship, on the engagement of Arthur Hallam to my sister, on his sudden death at Vienna, just before the time fixed for their marriage, and on his burial at Clevedon Church. The poem concludes with the marriage of my youngest sister Cecilia. It was meant to be a kind of *Divina Commedia*, ending with happiness. The sections were written at many different places, and as the phases of our intercourse came to my memory and suggested them. I did not write them with any view of weaving them into a whole, or for publication, until I found that I had written so many. The different moods of sorrow as in a drama are dramatically given, and my conviction that fear, doubts, and suffering will find answer and relief only through Faith in a God of Love. 'I' is not always the author speaking of himself, but the voice of the human race speaking through him. After the death of A.H.H., the divisions of the poem are made by First Xmas Eve (Section xxviii), Second Xmas (lxxviii), Third Xmas Eve (civ and cv etc.)."

5   Thine are these orbs of light and shade;
      Thou madest Life in man and brute;
      Thou madest Death; and lo, thy foot
Is on the skull which thou hast made.

Thou wilt not leave us in the dust:
10   Thou madest man, he knows not why,
      He thinks he was not made to die;
And thou hast made him: thou art just.

Thou seemest human and divine,
      The highest, holiest manhood, thou:
15   Our wills are ours, we know not how;
Our wills are ours, to make them thine.

Our little systems[1] have their day;
      They have their day and cease to be:
      They are but broken lights of thee,
20 And thou, O Lord, art more than they.

We have but faith: we cannot know;
      For knowledge is of things we see;
      And yet we trust it comes from thee,
A beam in darkness: let it grow.

25 Let knowledge grow from more to more,
      But more of reverence in us dwell;
      That mind and soul, according well,
May make one music as before,[2]

But vaster. We are fools and slight;
30   We mock thee when we do not fear:
      But help thy foolish ones to bear;
Help thy vain worlds to bear thy light.

Forgive what seemed my sin in me;
      What seemed my worth since I began;

35   For merit lives from man to man,
And not from man, O Lord, to thee.

Forgive my grief for one removed,
      Thy creature, whom I found so fair.
      I trust he lives in thee, and there
40 I find him worthier to be loved.

Forgive these wild and wandering cries,
      Confusions of a wasted youth;
      Forgive them where they fail in truth,
And in thy wisdom make me wise.
—1850 (1849)

I
I held it truth, with him[3] who sings
      To one clear harp in divers tones,
      That men may rise on stepping-stones
Of their dead selves to higher things.

5   But who shall so forecast the years
      And find in loss a gain to match?
      Or reach a hand through time to catch
The far-off interest of tears?

Let Love clasp Grief lest both be drowned,
10   Let darkness keep her raven gloss:
      Ah, sweeter to be drunk with loss,
To dance with death, to beat the ground,

Than that the victor Hours should scorn
      The long result of love, and boast,
15   "Behold the man that loved and lost,
But all he was is overworn."

---

[1] philosophy and theology.

[2] Tennyson's comment: "As in the ages of faith."

---

[3] Goethe.

II

Old Yew, which graspest at the stones
    That name the under-lying dead,
    Thy fibres net the dreamless head,
Thy roots are wrapt about the bones.

5   The seasons bring the flower again,
    And bring the firstling to the flock;
    And in the dust of thee, the clock
Beats out the little lives of men.

O not for thee the glow, the bloom,
10   Who changest not in any gale,
    Nor branding summer suns avail
To touch thy thousand years of gloom:

And gazing on thee, sullen tree,
    Sick for thy stubborn hardihood,
15   I seem to fail from out my blood
And grow incorporate into thee.

III

O Sorrow, cruel fellowship,
    O Priestess in the vaults of Death,
    O sweet and bitter in a breath,
What whispers from thy lying lip?

5   "The stars," she whispers, "blindly run;
    A web is woven across the sky;
    From out waste places comes a cry,
And murmurs from the dying sun:

"And all the phantom, Nature, stands—
10   With all the music in her tone,
    A hollow echo of my own,—
A hollow form with empty hands."

And shall I take a thing so blind,
    Embrace her as my natural good;
15   Or crush her, like a vice of blood,
Upon the threshold of the mind?

IV

To Sleep I give my powers away;
    My will is bondsman to the dark;
20   I sit within a helmless bark,
And with my heart I muse and say:

O heart, how fares it with thee now,
    That thou should'st fail from thy desire,
    Who scarcely darest to inquire,
25   "What is it makes me beat so low?"

Something it is which thou hast lost,
    Some pleasure from thine early years.
    Break, thou deep vase of chilling tears,
That grief hath shaken into frost!

30   Such clouds of nameless trouble cross
    All night below the darkened eyes;
    With morning wakes the will, and cries,
"Thou shalt not be the fool of loss."

V

I sometimes hold it half a sin
    To put in words the grief I feel;
    For words, like Nature, half reveal
And half conceal the Soul within.

5   But, for the unquiet heart and brain,
    A use in measured language lies;
    The sad mechanic exercise,
Like dull narcotics, numbing pain.

In words, like weeds,[1] I'll wrap me o'er,
10   Like coarsest clothes against the cold:
    But that large grief which these enfold
Is given in outline and no more.

---

[1] garments related to mourning.

VI

One writes, that "Other friends remain,"
   That "Loss is common to the race"—
   And common is the commonplace,
And vacant chaff well meant for grain.

5 That loss is common would not make
   My own less bitter, rather more:
   Too common! Never morning wore
To evening, but some heart did break.

O father, wheresoe'er thou be,
10   Who pledgest now thy gallant son;
   A shot, ere half thy draught be done,
Hath stilled the life that beat from thee.

O mother, praying God will save
   Thy sailor,—while thy head is bowed,
15   His heavy-shotted hammock-shroud
Drops in his vast and wandering grave.

Ye know no more than I who wrought
   At that last hour to please him well;
   Who mused on all I had to tell,
20 And something written, something thought;

Expecting still his advent home;
   And ever met him on his way
   With wishes, thinking, "here today,"
Or "here tomorrow will he come."

25 O somewhere, meek, unconscious dove,
   That sittest ranging[1] golden hair;
   And glad to find thyself so fair,
Poor child, that waitest for thy love!

For now her father's chimney glows
30   In expectation of a guest;

And thinking "this will please him best,"
   She takes a riband or a rose;

For he will see them on tonight;
   And with the thought her colour burns;
35   And, having left the glass, she turns
Once more to set a ringlet right;

And, even when she turned, the curse
   Had fallen, and her future Lord
   Was drowned in passing through the ford,
40 Or killed in falling from his horse.

O what to her shall be the end?
   And what to me remains of good?
   To her, perpetual maidenhood,
And unto me no second friend.

VII

Dark house,[2] by which once more I stand
   Here in the long unlovely street,
   Doors, where my heart was used to beat
So quickly, waiting for a hand,

5 A hand that can be clasped no more—
   Behold me, for I cannot sleep,
   And like a guilty thing I creep
At earliest morning to the door.

He is not here; but far away
10   The noise of life begins again,
   And ghastly through the drizzling rain
On the bald street breaks the blank day.

VIII

A happy lover who has come
   To look on her that loves him well,
   Who 'lights and rings the gateway bell,
And learns her gone and far from home;

---

[1] arranging.

[2] the house where Hallam lived on Wimpole St.

5　He saddens, all the magic light
　　　Dies off at once from bower and hall,
　　　And all the place is dark, and all
　　The chambers emptied of delight:

So find I every pleasant spot
10　　In which we two were wont to meet,
　　　The field, the chamber and the street,
　　For all is dark where thou art not.

Yet as that other, wandering there
　　　In those deserted walks, may find
15　　A flower beat with rain and wind,
　　Which once she fostered up with care;

So seems it in my deep regret,
　　　O my forsaken heart, with thee
　　　And this poor flower of poesy
20　Which little cared for fades not yet.

But since it pleased a vanished eye,
　　　I go to plant it on his tomb,
　　　That if it can it there may bloom,
　　Or dying, there at least may die.

　　　　　　IX
Fair ship,[1] that from the Italian shore
　　　Sailest the placid ocean-plains
　　　With my lost Arthur's loved remains,
　　Spread thy full wings, and waft him o'er.

5　So draw him home to those that mourn
　　　In vain; a favourable speed
　　　Ruffle thy mirrored mast, and lead
　　Through prosperous floods his holy urn.

All night no ruder air perplex
10　　Thy sliding keel, till Phosphor,[2] bright

As our pure love, through early light
Shall glimmer on the dewy decks.

Sphere all your lights around, above;
　　　Sleep, gentle heavens, before the prow;
15　　Sleep, gentle winds, as he sleeps now,
　　My friend, the brother of my love;

My Arthur, whom I shall not see
　　　Till all my widowed race be run;
　　　Dear as the mother to the son,
20　More than my brothers are to me.

　　　　　　X
I hear the noise about thy keel;
　　　I hear the bell struck in the night:
　　　I see the cabin-window bright;
　　I see the sailor at the wheel.

5　Thou bring'st the sailor to his wife,
　　　And travelled men from foreign lands;
　　　And letters unto trembling hands;
　　And, thy dark freight, a vanished life.

So bring him: we have idle dreams:
10　　This look of quiet flatters thus
　　　Our home-bred fancies: O to us,
　　The fools of habit, sweeter seems

To rest beneath the clover sod,
　　　That takes the sunshine and the rains,
15　　Or where the kneeling hamlet drains
　　The chalice of the grapes of God;

Than if with thee the roaring wells
　　　Should gulf him fathom-deep in brine;
　　　And hands so often clasped in mine,
20　Should toss with tangle and with shells.

---

[1]　bearing Hallam's body from Trieste to England.

[2]　star of dawn.

XI

Calm is the morn without a sound,
　　Calm as to suit a calmer grief,
　　And only through the faded leaf
The chestnut pattering to the ground:

5　Calm and deep peace on this high wold,
　　And on these dews that drench the furze,
　　And all the silvery gossamers
That twinkle into green and gold:

Calm and still light on yon great plain
10　　That sweeps with all its autumn bowers,
　　And crowded farms and lessening towers,
To mingle with the bounding main:

Calm and deep peace in this wide air,
　　These leaves that redden to the fall;
15　　And in my heart, if calm at all,
If any calm, a calm despair:

Calm on the seas, and silver sleep,
　　And waves that sway themselves in rest,
　　And dead calm in that noble breast
20　Which heaves but with the heaving deep.

XII

Lo, as a dove when up she springs
　　To bear through Heaven a tale of woe,
　　Some dolorous message knit below
The wild pulsation of her wings;

5　Like her I go; I cannot stay;
　　I leave this mortal ark behind,
　　A weight of nerves without a mind,
And leave the cliffs, and haste away

O'er ocean-mirrors rounded large,[1]
10　　And reach the glow of southern skies,

And see the sails at distance rise,
　　And linger weeping on the marge,

And saying; "Comes he thus, my friend?
　　Is this the end of all my care?"
15　　And circle moaning in the air:
"Is this the end? Is this the end?"

And forward dart again, and play
　　About the prow, and back return
　　To where the body sits, and learn
20　That I have been an hour away.

XIII

Tears of the widower, when he sees
　　A late-lost form that sleep reveals,
　　And moves his doubtful arms, and feels
Her place is empty, fall like these;

5　Which weep a loss for ever new,
　　A void where heart on heart reposed;
　　And, where warm hands have prest and closed,
Silence, till I be silent too.

Which weep the comrade of my choice,
10　　An awful thought, a life removed,
　　The human-hearted man I loved,
A Spirit, not a breathing voice.

Come Time, and teach me, many years,
　　I do not suffer in a dream;
15　　For now so strange do these things seem,
Mine eyes have leisure for their tears;

My fancies time to rise on wing,
　　And glance about the approaching sails,
　　As though they brought but merchants' bales,
20　And not the burthen that they bring.

---

[1] circular fields of vision.

XIV

If one should bring me this report,
    That thou hadst touched the land today,
    And I went down unto the quay,
And found thee lying in the port;

5   And standing, muffled round with woe,
    Should see thy passengers in rank
    Come stepping lightly down the plank,
And beckoning unto those they know;

10   And if along with these should come
    The man I held as half-divine;
    Should strike a sudden hand in mine,
And ask a thousand things of home;

And I should tell him all my pain,
15   And how my life had drooped of late,
    And he should sorrow o'er my state
And marvel what possessed my brain;

And I perceived no touch of change,
    No hint of death in all his frame,
20   But found him all in all the same,
I should not feel it to be strange.

XV

Tonight the winds begin to rise
    And roar from yonder dropping day:
    The last red leaf is whirled away,
The rooks are blown about the skies;

5   The forest cracked, the waters curled,
    The cattle huddled on the lea;
    And wildly dashed on tower and tree
The sunbeam strikes along the world:

And but for fancies, which aver
10   That all thy motions gently pass
    Athwart a plane of molten glass,
I scarce could brook the strain and stir

That makes the barren branches loud;
    And but for fear it is not so,
15   The wild unrest that lives in woe
Would dote and pore on yonder cloud

That rises upward always higher,
    And onward drags a labouring breast,
    And topples round the dreary west,
20   A looming bastion fringed with fire.

XVI

What words are these have fallen from me?
    Can calm despair and wild unrest
    Be tenants of a single breast
Or sorrow such a changeling be?

5   Or doth she only seem to take
    The touch of change in calm or storm;
    But knows no more of transient form
In her deep self, than some dead lake

That holds the shadow of a lark
10   Hung in the shadow of a heaven?
    Or has the shock, so harshly given,
Confused me like the unhappy bark

That strikes by night a craggy shelf,
    And staggers blindly ere she sink?
15   And stunned me from my power to think
And all my knowledge of myself;

And make me that delirious man
    Whose fancy fuses old and new,
    And flashes into false and true,
20   And mingled all without a plan?

XVII

Thou comest, much wept for: such a breeze
    Compelled thy canvas, and my prayer
    Was as the whisper of an air
To breathe thee over lonely seas.

5 For I in spirit see thee move
     Through circles of the bounding sky,
     Week after week: the days go by:
  Come quick, thou bringest all I love.

  Henceforth, wherever thou mayst roam,
10   My blessing, like a line of light,
     Is on the waters day and night,
  And like a beacon guards thee home.

  So may whatever tempest mars
     Mid-ocean, spare thee, sacred bark;
15   And balmy drops in summer dark
  Slide from the bosom of the stars.

  So kind an office hath been done,
     Such precious relics brought by thee;
     The dust of him I shall not see
20 Till all my widowed race be run.

XVIII

  'Tis well; 'tis something; we may stand
     Where he in English earth is laid,
     And from his ashes may be made
  The violet of his native land.

5 'Tis little; but it looks in truth
     As if the quiet bones were blest
     Among familiar names to rest
  And in the places of his youth.

  Come then, pure hands, and bear the head
10   That sleeps or wears the mask of sleep,
     And come, whatever loves to weep,
  And hear the ritual of the dead.

  Ah yet, even yet, if this might be,
     I, falling on his faithful heart,
15   Would breathing through his lips impart
  The life that almost dies in me;

  That dies not, but endures with pain,
     And slowly forms the firmer mind,
     Treasuring the look it cannot find,
20 The words that are not heard again.

XIX

  The Danube to the Severn[1] gave
     The darkened heart that beat no more;
     They laid him by the pleasant shore,
  And in the hearing of the wave.

5 There twice a day the Severn fills;
     The salt sea-water passes by,
     And hushes half the babbling Wye,
  And makes a silence in the hills.

  The Wye is hushed nor moved along,
10   And hushed my deepest grief of all,
     When filled with tears that cannot fall,
  I brim with sorrow drowning song.

  The tide flows down, the wave again
     Is vocal in its wooded walls;
15   My deeper anguish also falls,
  And I can speak a little then.

XX

  The lesser griefs that may be said,
     That breathe a thousand tender vows,
     Are but as servants in a house
  Where lies the master newly dead;

5 Who speak their feeling as it is,
     And weep the fulness from the mind:
     "It will be hard," they say, "to find
  Another service such as this."

---

[1] Hallam died at Vienna on the Danube and was buried at Clevedon on the Severn.

My lighter moods are like to these,
10   That out of words a comfort win;
    But there are other griefs within,
And tears that at their fountain freeze;

For by the hearth the children sit
    Cold in that atmosphere of Death,
15   And scarce endure to draw the breath,
Or like to noiseless phantoms flit:

But open converse is there none,
    So much the vital spirits sink
    To see the vacant chair, and think,
20 "How good! how kind! and he is gone."

XXI

I sing to him that rests below,
    And, since the grasses round me wave,
    I take the grasses of the grave,
And make them pipes whereon to blow.

5 The traveller hears me now and then,
    And sometimes harshly will he speak:
    "This fellow would make weakness weak,
And melt the waxen hearts of men."

Another answers, "Let him be,
10   He loves to make parade of pain,
    That with his piping he may gain
The praise that comes to constancy."

A third is wroth: "Is this an hour
    For private sorrow's barren song,
15   When more and more the people throng
The chairs and thrones of civil power?

"A time to sicken and to swoon,
    When Science reaches forth her arms
    To feel from world to world, and charms
20 Her secret from the latest moon?"

Behold, ye speak an idle thing:
    Ye never knew the sacred dust:
    I do but sing because I must,
And pipe but as the linnets sing:

25 And one is glad; her note is gay,
    For now her little ones have ranged;
    And one is sad: her note is changed,
Because her brood is stolen away.

XXII

The path by which we twain did go,
    Which led by tracts that pleased us well,
    Through four sweet years arose and fell,
From flower to flower, from snow to snow:

5 And we with singing cheered the way,
    And, crowned with all the season lent,
    From April on to April went,
And glad at heart from May to May:

But where the path we walked began
10   To slant the fifth autumnal slope,
    As we descended following Hope,
There sat the Shadow feared of man;

Who broke our fair companionship,
    And spread his mantle dark and cold,
15   And wrapt thee formless in the fold,
And dulled the murmur on thy lip,

And bore thee where I could not see
    Nor follow, though I walk in haste,
    And think, that somewhere in the waste
20 The Shadow sits and waits for me.

XXIII

Now, sometimes in my sorrow shut,
    Or breaking into song by fits,

Alone, alone, to where he sits,
The Shadow[1] cloaked from head to foot,

5 Who keeps the keys of all the creeds,
   I wander, often falling lame,
   And looking back to whence I came,
Or on to where the pathway leads;

And crying, How changed from where it ran
10   Through lands where not a leaf was dumb;
   But all the lavish hills would hum
The murmur of a happy Pan:[2]

When each by turns was guide to each,
   And Fancy light from Fancy caught,
15   And Thought leapt out to wed with Thought
Ere Thought could wed itself with Speech;

And all we met was fair and good,
   And all was good that Time could bring,
   And all the secret of the Spring
20 Moved in the chambers of the blood;

And many an old philosophy
   On Argive heights divinely sang,
   And round us all the thicket rang
To many a flute of Arcady.

XXIV

And was the day of my delight
   As pure and perfect as I say?
   The very source and fount of Day
Is dashed with wandering isles of night.[3]

5 If all was good and fair we met,
   This earth had been the Paradise

It never looked to human eyes
Since our first Sun arose and set.

And is it that the haze of grief
10   Makes former gladness loom so great?
   The lowness of the present state,
That sets the past in this relief?

Or that the past will always win
   A glory from its being far;
15   And orb into the perfect star
We saw not, when we moved therein?

XXV

I know that this was Life,—the track
   Whereon with equal feet we fared;
   And then, as now, the day prepared
The daily burden for the back.

5 But this it was that made me move
   As light as carrier-birds in air;
   I loved the weight I had to bear,
Because it needed help of Love:

Nor could I weary, heart or limb,
10   When mighty Love would cleave in twain
   The lading of a single pain,
And part it, giving half to him.

XXVI

Still onward winds the dreary way;
   I with it; for I long to prove
   No lapse of moons can canker Love,
Whatever fickle tongues may say.

5 And if that eye which watches guilt
   And goodness, and hath power to see
   Within the green the mouldered tree,
And towers fallen as soon as built—

---

[1] death.

[2] god of the fields and woods.

[3] sun-spots.

Oh, if indeed that eye foresee
10   Or see (in Him is no before)
    In more of life true life no more
And Love the indifference to be,

Then might I find, ere yet the morn
    Breaks hither over Indian seas,
15   That Shadow waiting with the keys,
To shroud me from my proper scorn.[1]

XXVII

I envy not in any moods
    The captive void of noble rage,
    The linnet born within the cage,
That never knew the summer woods:

5 I envy not the beast that takes
    His license in the field of time,[2]
    Unfettered by the sense of crime,
To whom a conscience never wakes;

Nor, what may count itself as blest,
10   The heart that never plighted troth
    But stagnates in the weeds of sloth;
Nor any want-begotten rest.

I hold it true, whate'er befall;
    I feel it, when I sorrow most;
15   'Tis better to have loved and lost
Than never to have loved at all.

XXVIII

The time draws near the birth of Christ:
    The moon is hid; the night is still;
    The Christmas bells from hill to hill
Answer each other in the mist.

5 Four voices of four hamlets round,
    From far and near, on mead and moor,
    Swell out and fail, as if a door
Were shut between me and the sound:

Each voice four changes on the wind,
10   That now dilate, and now decrease,
    Peace and goodwill, goodwill and peace,
Peace and goodwill, to all mankind.

This year I slept and woke with pain,
    I almost wished no more to wake,
15   And that my hold on life would break
Before I heard those bells again:

But they my troubled spirit rule,
    For they controlled me when a boy;
    They bring me sorrow touched with joy,
20 The merry merry bells of Yule.

XXIX

With such compelling cause to grieve
    As daily vexes household peace,
    And chains regret to his decrease,
How dare we keep our Christmas-eve;

5 Which brings no more a welcome guest
    To enrich the threshold of the night
    With showered largess of delight
In dance and song and game and jest?

Yet go, and while the holly boughs
10   Entwine the cold baptismal font,
    Make one wreath more for Use and Wont,
That guard the portals of the house;

Old sisters of a day gone by,
    Gray nurses, loving nothing new;
15   Why should they miss their yearly due
Before their time? They too will die.

---

[1] scorn of myself.

[2] lacking restraint in earthly life.

XXX

With trembling fingers did we weave
    The holly round the Christmas hearth;
    A rainy cloud possessed the earth,
And sadly fell our Christmas-eve.

5 At our old pastimes in the hall
    We gambolled, making vain pretence
    Of gladness, with an awful sense
Of one mute Shadow watching all.

We paused: the winds were in the beech:
10   We heard them sweep the winter land;
    And in a circle hand-in-hand
Sat silent, looking each at each.

Then echo-like our voices rang;
    We sung, though every eye was dim,
15   A merry song we sang with him
Last year: impetuously we sang:

We ceased: a gentler feeling crept
    Upon us: surely rest is meet:
    "They rest," we said, "their sleep is sweet,"
20 And silence followed, and we wept.

Our voices took a higher range;
    Once more we sang: "They do not die
    Nor lose their mortal sympathy,
Nor change to us, although they change;

25 "Rapt from the fickle and the frail
    With gathered power, yet the same,
    Pierces the keen seraphic flame
From orb to orb, from veil to veil."

Rise, happy morn, rise, holy morn,
30   Draw forth the cheerful day from night:
    O Father, touch the east, and light
The light that shone when Hope was born.

XXXI

When Lazarus left his charnel-cave,
    And home to Mary's house returned,
    Was this demanded—if he yearned
To hear her weeping by his grave?

5 "Where wert thou, brother, those four days?"
    There lives no record of reply,
    Which telling what it is to die
Had surely added praise to praise.

From every house the neighbours met,
10   The streets were filled with joyful sound,
    A solemn gladness even crowned
The purple brows of Olivet.[1]

Behold a man raised up by Christ!
    The rest remaineth unrevealed;
15   He told it not; or something sealed
The lips of that Evangelist.[2]

XXXII

Her[3] eyes are homes of silent prayer,
    Nor other thought her mind admits
    But, he was dead, and there he sits,
And he that brought him back is there.

5 Then one deep love doth supersede
    All other, when her ardent gaze
    Roves from the living brother's face,
And rests upon the Life indeed.

All subtle thought, all curious fears,
10   Borne down by gladness so complete,
    She bows, she bathes the Saviour's feet
With costly spikenard and with tears.

---

[1] Mt. Olivet near Jerusalem.

[2] St. John.

[3] Mary, sister of Lazarus.

Thrice blest whose lives are faithful prayers,
    Whose loves in higher love endure;
15   What souls possess themselves so pure,
Or is there blessedness like theirs?

XXXIII

O thou that after toil and storm
    Mayst seem to have reached a purer air,
    Whose faith has centre everywhere,
Nor cares to fix itself to form,

5 Leave thou thy sister when she prays,
    Her early Heaven,[1] her happy views;
    Nor thou with shadowed hint confuse
A life that leads melodious days.

Her faith through form is pure as thine,
10   Her hands are quicker unto good:
    Oh, sacred be the flesh and blood
To which she links a truth divine!

See thou, that countest reason ripe
    In holding by the law within,
15   Thou fail not in a world of sin,
And even for want of such a type.

XXXIV

My own dim life should teach me this,
    That life shall live for evermore,
    Else earth is darkness at the core,
And dust and ashes all that is;

5 This round of green, this orb of flame,
    Fantastic beauty; such as lurks
    In some wild Poet, when he works
Without a conscience or an aim.

What then were God to such as I?
10   'Twere hardly worth my while to choose

Of things all mortal, or to use
A little patience ere I die;

'Twere best at once to sink to peace,
    Like birds the charming serpent draws,
15   To drop head-foremost in the jaws
Of vacant darkness and to cease.

XXXV

Yet if some voice that man could trust
    Should murmur from the narrow house,
    "The cheeks drop in; the body bows;
Man dies: nor is there hope in dust:"

5 Might I not say? "Yet even here,
    But for one hour, O Love, I strive
    To keep so sweet a thing alive:"
But I should turn mine ears and hear

The moanings of the homeless sea,
10   The sound of streams that swift or slow
    Draw down Æonian[2] hills, and sow
The dust of continents to be;

And Love would answer with a sigh,
    "The sound of that forgetful shore[3]
15   Will change my sweetness more and more,
Half-dead to know that I shall die."

O me, what profits it to put
    An idle case? If Death were seen
    At first as Death, Love had not been,
20 Or been in narrowest working shut,

Mere fellowship of sluggish moods,
    Or in his coarsest Satyr[4]-shape

---

1 ideas learned in childhood.

2 ancient, aeons old.

3 the land where all things are forgotten.

4 sensual form.

Had bruised the herb and crushed the grape,
And basked and battened[1] in the woods.

XXXVI

Though truths in manhood darkly join,
 Deep-seated in our mystic frame,
 We yield all blessing to the name
Of Him that made them current coin;

5 For Wisdom dealt with mortal powers,
 Where truth in closest words shall fail,
 When truth embodied in a tale
Shall enter in at lowly doors.

And so the Word had breath, and wrought
10 With human hands the creed of creeds
 In loveliness of perfect deeds,
More strong than all poetic thought;

Which he may read that binds the sheaf,
 Or builds the house, or digs the grave,
15 And those wild eyes that watch the wave
In roarings round the coral reef.[2]

XXXVII

Urania speaks with darkened brow:
 "Thou pratest here where thou art least;
 This faith has many a purer priest,
And many an abler voice than thou.

5 "Go down beside thy native rill,
 On thy Parnassus[3] set thy feet,
 And hear thy laurel whisper sweet
About the ledges of the hill."

And my Melpomene[4] replies,
10 A touch of shame upon her cheek:
 "I am not worthy even to speak
Of thy prevailing mysteries;

"For I am but an earthly Muse,
 And owning but a little art
15 To lull with song an aching heart,
And render human love his dues;

"But brooding on the dear one dead,
 And all he said of things divine,
 (And dear to me as sacred wine
20 To dying lips is all he said),

"I murmured, as I came along,
 Of comfort clasped in truth revealed;
 And loitered in the master's field,
And darkened sanctities with song."

XXXVIII

With weary steps I loiter on,
 Though always under altered skies
 The purple from the distance dies,
My prospect and horizon gone.

5 No joy the blowing season gives,
 The herald melodies of spring,
 But in the songs I love to sing
A doubtful gleam of solace lives.

If any care for what is here
10 Survive in spirits rendered free,
 Then are these songs I sing of thee
Not all ungrateful to thine ear.

XXXIX

Old warder of these buried bones,
 And answering now my random stroke

---

[1] to feed grossly.

[2] Pacific Islanders.

[3] sacred hill of Apollo.

[4] the Muse of elegy.

With fruitful cloud and living smoke,[1]
Dark yew, that graspest at the stones

5   And dippest toward the dreamless head,
        To thee too comes the golden hour
        When flower is feeling after flower;
    But Sorrow—fixt upon the dead,

    And darkening the dark graves of men,—
10   What whispered from her lying lips?
        Thy gloom is kindled at the tips,
    And passes into gloom again.

                    XL
    Could we forget the widowed hour
        And look on Spirits breathed away,
        As on a maiden in the day
    When first she wears her orange-flower!

5   When crowned with blessing she doth rise
        To take her latest leave of home,
        And hopes and light regrets that come
    Make April of her tender eyes;

    And doubtful joys the father move,
10   And tears are on the mother's face,
        As parting with a long embrace
    She enters other realms of love;

    Her office there to rear, to teach,
        Becoming as is meet and fit
15   A link among the days, to knit
    The generations each with each;

    And, doubtless, unto thee is given
        A life that bears immortal fruit
        In those great offices that suit
20 The full-grown energies of heaven.

    ––––––––––
    [1] Tennyson's comment: "The yew, when flowering, in a wind or if
    struck sends up its pollen like smoke."

Ay me, the difference I discern!
    How often shall her old fireside
    Be cheered with tidings of the bride,
How often she herself return,

25 And tell them all they would have told,
    And bring her babe, and make her boast,
    Till even those that missed her most
Shall count new things as dear as old:

But thou and I have shaken hands,
30   Till growing winters lay me low;
        My paths are in the fields I know,
And thine in undiscovered lands.

                    XLI
Thy spirit ere our fatal loss
    Did ever rise from high to higher;
    As mounts the heavenward altar-fire,
As flies the lighter through the gross.

5   But thou art turned to something strange,
        And I have lost the links that bound
        Thy changes; here upon the ground,
No more partaker of thy change.

Deep folly! yet that this could be—
10   That I could wing my will with might
        To leap the grades of life and light,
And flash at once, my friend, to thee.

For though my nature rarely yields
        To that vague fear implied in death;
15   Nor shudders at the gulfs beneath,
The howlings from forgotten fields;

Yet oft when sundown skirts the moor
        An inner trouble I behold,
        A spectral doubt which makes me cold,
20 That I shall be thy mate no more,

Though following with an upward mind
    The wonders that have come to thee,
    Through all the secular to-be,[1]
But evermore a life behind.

XLII

I vex my heart with fancies dim:
    He still outstript me in the race;
    It was but unity of place
That made me dream I ranked with him.

5 And so may Place retain us still,
    And he the much-beloved again,
    A lord of large experience, train
To riper growth the mind and will:

And what delights can equal those
0   That stir the spirit's inner deeps,
    When one that loves but knows not, reaps
A truth from one that loves and knows?

XLIII

If Sleep and Death be truly one,
    And every spirit's folded bloom
    Through all its intervital[2] gloom
In some long trance should slumber on;

5 Unconscious of the sliding hour,
    Bare of the body, might it last,
    And silent traces of the past
Be all the colour of the flower:

So then were nothing lost to man;
0   So that still garden of the souls
    In many a figured leaf enrolls
The total world since life began;

And love will last as pure and whole
    As when he loved me here in Time,
15   And at the spiritual prime[3]
Rewaken with the dawning soul.

XLIV

How fares it with the happy dead?
    For here the man is more and more;
    But he forgets the days before
God shut the doorways of his head.[4]

5 The days have vanished, tone and tint,
    And yet perhaps the hoarding sense
    Gives out at times (he knows not whence)
A little flash, a mystic hint;

And in the long harmonious years
10   (If Death so taste Lethean springs),[5]
    May some dim touch of earthly things
Surprise thee ranging with thy peers.

If such a dreamy touch should fall,
    O turn thee round, resolve the doubt;
15   My guardian angel will speak out
In that high place, and tell thee all.

XLV

The baby new to earth and sky,
    What time his tender palm is prest
    Against the circle of the breast,
Has never thought that "this is I:"

5 But as he grows he gathers much,
    And learns the use of "I," and "me,"
    And finds "I am not what I see,
And other than the things I touch."

---

[1] aeons of the future.

[2] between lives.

---

[3] daybreak.

[4] Tennyson's comment: "Closing of the skull after babyhood."

[5] waters of forgetfulness.

So rounds he to a separate mind
    From whence clear memory may begin,
10   As through the frame that binds him in
His isolation grows defined.

This use may lie in blood and breath,
    Which else were fruitless of their due,
15   Had man to learn himself anew
Beyond the second birth of Death.

XLVI

We ranging down this lower track,
    The path we came by, thorn and flower,
    Is shadowed by the growing hour,
Lest life should fail in looking back.

5 So be it: there no shade can last
    In that deep dawn behind the tomb,
    But clear from marge to marge shall bloom
The eternal landscape of the past;

A lifelong tract of time revealed;
10   The fruitful hours of still increase;
    Days ordered in a wealthy peace,
And those five years its richest field.

O Love, thy province were not large,
    A bounded field, nor stretching far;
15   Look also, Love, a brooding star,
A rosy warmth from marge to marge.

XLVII

That each, who seems a separate whole,
    Should move his rounds, and fusing all
    The skirts of self again, should fall
Remerging in the general Soul,

5 Is faith as vague as all unsweet:
    Eternal form shall still divide
    The eternal soul from all beside;
And I shall know him when we meet:

And we shall sit at endless feast,
10   Enjoying each the other's good:
    What vaster dream can hit the mood
Of Love on earth? He seeks at least

Upon the last and sharpest height,
    Before the spirits fade away,
15   Some landing-place, to clasp and say,
"Farewell! We lose ourselves in light."

XLVIII

If these brief lays, of Sorrow born,
    Were taken to be such as closed
    Grave doubts and answers here proposed,
Then these were such as men might scorn:

5 Her care is not to part[1] and prove;
    She takes, when harsher moods remit,
    What slender shade of doubt may flit,
And makes it vassal unto love:

And hence, indeed, she sports with words,
10   But better serves a wholesome law,
    And holds it sin and shame to draw
The deepest measure from the chords:

Nor dare she trust a larger lay,
    But rather loosens from the lip
15   Short swallow-flights of song, that dip
Their wings in tears, and skim away.

XLIX

From art, from nature, from the schools,[2]
    Let random influences glance,
    Like light in many a shivered lance
That breaks about the dappled pools:

---

[1] sort out.

[2] philosophy and theology.

5   The lightest wave of thought shall lisp,
      The fancy's tenderest eddy wreathe,
      The slightest air of song shall breathe
  To make the sullen surface crisp.

  And look thy look, and go thy way,
10   But blame not thou the winds that make
      The seeming-wanton ripple break,
  The tender-pencilled shadow play.

  Beneath all fancied hopes and fears
      Ay me, the sorrow deepens down,
15   Whose muffled motions blindly drown
  The bases of my life in tears.

L

Be near me when my light is low,
    When the blood creeps, and the nerves prick
    And tingle; and the heart is sick,
And all the wheels of Being slow.

5   Be near me when the sensuous frame
     Is racked with pangs that conquer trust;
     And Time, a maniac scattering dust,
  And Life, a Fury slinging flame.

  Be near me when my faith is dry,
10   And men the flies of latter spring,
     That lay their eggs, and sting and sing
  And weave their petty cells and die.

  Be near me when I fade away,
     To point the term of human strife,
15   And on the low dark verge of life
  The twilight of eternal day.

LI

Do we indeed desire the dead
    Should still be near us at our side?
    Is there no baseness we would hide?
No inner vileness that we dread?

5   Shall he for whose applause I strove,
     I had such reverence for his blame,
     See with clear eye some hidden shame
  And I be lessened in his love?

  I wrong the grave with fears untrue:
10   Shall love be blamed for want of faith?
     There must be wisdom with great Death:
  The dead shall look me through and through.

  Be near us when we climb or fall:
     Ye watch, like God, the rolling hours
15   With larger other eyes than ours,
  To make allowance for us all.

LII

I cannot love thee as I ought,
    For love reflects the thing beloved;
    My words are only words, and moved
Upon the topmost froth of thought.

5   "Yet blame not thou thy plaintive song,"
     The Spirit of true love replied;
     "Thou canst not move me from thy side,
  Nor human frailty do me wrong.

  "What keeps a spirit wholly true
10   To that ideal which he bears?
     What record? not the sinless years
  That breathed beneath the Syrian blue:

  "So fret not, like an idle girl,
     That life is dashed with flecks of sin.
15   Abide: thy wealth is gathered in,
  When Time hath sundered shell from pearl."

LIII

How many a father have I seen,
    A sober man, among his boys,
    Whose youth was full of foolish noise,
Who wears his manhood hale and green:

5 And dare we to this fancy give,
   That had the wild oat not been sown,
   The soil, left barren, scarce had grown
The grain by which a man may live?

Or, if we held the doctrine sound
10   For life outliving heats of youth,
   Yet who would preach it as a truth
To those that eddy round and round?

Hold thou the good: define it well:
   For fear divine Philosophy
15   Should push beyond her mark, and be
Procuress to the Lords of Hell.

LIV

Oh yet we trust that somehow good
   Will be the final goal of ill,
   To pangs of nature, sins of will,
Defects of doubt, and taints of blood;

5 That nothing walks with aimless feet;
   That not one life shall be destroyed,
   Or cast as rubbish to the void,
When God hath made the pile complete;

That not a worm is cloven in vain;
10   That not a moth with vain desire
   Is shrivelled in a fruitless fire,
Or but subserves another's gain.

Behold, we know not anything;
   I can but trust that good shall fall
15   At last—far off—at last, to all,
And every winter change to spring.

So runs my dream: but what am I?
   An infant crying in the night:
   An infant crying for the light:
20 And with no language but a cry.

LV

The wish, that of the living whole
   No life may fail beyond the grave,
   Derives it not from what we have
The likest God within the soul?

5 Are God and Nature then at strife,
   That Nature lends such evil dreams?
   So careful of the type[1] she seems,
So careless of the single life;

That I, considering everywhere
10   Her secret meaning in her deeds,
   And finding that of fifty seeds
She often brings but one to bear,

I falter where I firmly trod,
   And falling with my weight of cares
15   Upon the great world's altar-stairs
That slope through darkness up to God,

I stretch lame hands of faith, and grope,
   And gather dust and chaff, and call
   To what I feel is Lord of all,
20 And faintly trust the larger hope.

LVI

"So careful of the type?" but no.
   From scarpèd cliff and quarried stone
   She cries, "A thousand types are gone:
I care for nothing, all shall go.

5 "Thou makest thine appeal to me:
   I bring to life, I bring to death:
   The spirit does but mean the breath:
I know no more." And he, shall he,

Man, her last work, who seemed so fair,
10   Such splendid purpose in his eyes,

_____
[1] species.

Who rolled the psalm to wintry skies,
Who built him fanes of fruitless prayer,

Who trusted God was love indeed
    And love Creation's final law—
15   Though Nature, red in tooth and claw
With ravine, shrieked against his creed—

Who loved, who suffered countless ills,
    Who battled for the True, the Just,
    Be blown about the desert dust,
20 Or sealed within the iron hills?

No more? A monster then, a dream,
    A discord. Dragons of the prime,
    That tare each other in their slime,
Were mellow music matched with him.

25 O life as futile, then, as frail!
    O for thy voice to soothe and bless!
    What hope of answer, or redress?
Behind the veil, behind the veil.

LVII

Peace; come away: the song of woe
    Is after all an earthly song:
    Peace; come away: we do him wrong
To sing so wildly: let us go.

5 Come; let us go: your cheeks are pale;
    But half my life I leave behind:
    Methinks my friend is richly shrined;
But I shall pass; my work will fail.

Yet in these ears, till hearing dies,
10   One set slow bell will seem to toll
    The passing of the sweetest soul
That ever looked with human eyes.

I hear it now, and o'er and o'er,
    Eternal greetings to the dead;

15 And "Ave, Ave, Ave," said,
"Adieu, adieu" for evermore.

LVIII

In those sad words I took farewell:
    Like echoes in sepulchral halls,
    As drop by drop the water falls
In vaults and catacombs, they fell;

5 And, falling, idly broke the peace
    Of hearts that beat from day to day,
    Half-conscious of their dying clay,
And those cold crypts where they shall cease.

The high Muse[1] answered: "Wherefore grieve
10   Thy brethren with a fruitless tear?
    Abide a little longer here,
And thou shalt take a nobler leave."

LIX

O Sorrow, wilt thou live with me
    No casual mistress, but a wife,
    My bosom-friend and half of life;
As I confess it needs must be;

5 O Sorrow, wilt thou rule my blood,
    Be sometimes lovely like a bride,
    And put thy harsher moods aside,
If thou wilt have me wise and good.

My centred passion cannot move,
10   Nor will it lessen from today;
    But I'll have leave at times to play
As with the creature of my love;

And set thee forth, for thou art mine,
    With so much hope for years to come,
15   That, howso'er I know thee, some
Could hardly tell what name were thine.

---

[1] Urania.

LX

He past; a soul of nobler tone:
　My spirit loved and loves him yet,
20　　Like some poor girl whose heart is set
On one whose rank exceeds her own.

He mixing with his proper sphere,
　She finds the baseness of her lot,
　Half jealous of she knows not what,
25　And envying all that meet him there.

The little village looks forlorn;
　She sighs amid her narrow days,
　Moving about the household ways,
In that dark house where she was born.

30　The foolish neighbours come and go,
　And tease her till the day draws by:
　At night she weeps, "How vain am I!
How should he love a thing so low?"

LXI

35　If, in thy second state sublime,
　Thy ransomed reason change replies
　With all the circle of the wise,
The perfect flower of human time;

And if thou cast thine eyes below,
40　　How dimly charactered and slight,
　How dwarfed a growth of cold and night,
How blanched with darkness must I grow!

Yet turn thee to the doubtful shore,
　Where thy first form was made a man;
45　　I loved thee, Spirit, and love, nor can
The soul of Shakspeare love thee more.

LXII

Though if an eye that's downward cast
　Could make thee somewhat blench or fail,

Then be my love an idle tale,
And fading legend of the past;

5　And thou, as one that once declined,
　When he was little more than boy,
　On some unworthy heart with joy,
But lives to wed an equal mind;

And breathes a novel world, the while
10　　His other passion wholly dies,
　Or in the light of deeper eyes
Is matter for a flying smile.

LXIII

Yet pity for a horse o'er-driven,
　And love in which my hound has part,
　Can hang no weight upon my heart
In its assumptions up to heaven;

5　And I am so much more than these,
　As thou, perchance, art more than I,
　And yet I spare them sympathy,
And I would set their pains at ease.

So mayst thou watch me where I weep,
10　　As, unto vaster motions bound,
　The circuits of thine orbit round
A higher height, a deeper deep.

LXIV

Dost thou look back on what hath been,
　As some divinely gifted man,
　Whose life in low estate began
And on a simple village green;

5　Who breaks his birth's invidious bar,
　And grasps the skirts of happy chance,
　And breasts the blows of circumstance,
And grapples with his evil star;

Who makes by force his merit known
    And lives to clutch the golden keys,[1]
    To mould a mighty state's decrees,
And shape the whisper of the throne;

And moving up from high to higher,
    Becomes on Fortune's crowning slope
    The pillar of a people's hope,
The centre of a world's desire;

Yet feels, as in a pensive dream,
    When all his active powers are still,
    A distant dearness in the hill,
A secret sweetness in the stream,

The limit of his narrower fate,
    While yet beside its vocal springs
    He played at counsellors and kings,
With one that was his earliest mate;

Who ploughs with pain his native lea
    And reaps the labour of his hands,
    Or in the furrow musing stands;
"Does my old friend remember me?"

LXV

Sweet soul, do with me as thou wilt;
    I lull a fancy trouble-tost
    With "Love's too precious to be lost,
A little grain shall not be spilt."

And in that solace can I sing,
    Till out of painful phases wrought
    There flutters up a happy thought,
Self-balanced on a lightsome wing:

Since we deserved the name of friends,
    And thine effect so lives in me,

A part of mine may live in thee
And move thee on to noble ends.

LXVI

You[2] thought my heart too far diseased;
    You wonder when my fancies play
    To find me gay among the gay,
Like one with any trifle pleased.

The shade by which my life was crost,
    Which makes a desert in the mind,
    Has made me kindly with my kind,
And like to him whose sight is lost;

Whose feet are guided through the land,
    Whose jest among his friends is free,
    Who takes the children on his knee,
And winds their curls about his hand:

He plays with threads, he beats his chair
    For pastime, dreaming of the sky;
    His inner day can never die,
His night of loss is always there.

LXVII

When on my bed the moonlight falls,
    I know that in thy place of rest
    By that broad water of the west,
There comes a glory on the walls;

Thy marble bright in dark appears,
    As slowly steals a silver flame
    Along the letters of thy name,
And o'er the number of thy years.

The mystic glory swims away;
    From off my bed the moonlight dies;
    And closing eaves of wearied eyes
I sleep till dusk is dipt in gray:

---

[1] symbols of civil office.

[2] Tennyson's comment: "the auditor."

And then I know the mist is drawn
    A lucid veil from coast to coast,
15   And in the dark church like a ghost
Thy tablet glimmers to the dawn.

LXVIII

When in the down I sink my head,
    Sleep, Death's twin-brother, times my breath;
    Sleep, Death's twin-brother, knows not Death,
Nor can I dream of thee as dead:

5   I walk as ere I walked forlorn,
    When all our path was fresh with dew,
    And all the bugle breezes blew
Reveillée to the breaking morn.

But what is this? I turn about,
10   I find a trouble in thine eye,
    Which makes me sad I know not why,
Nor can my dream resolve the doubt:

But ere the lark hath left the lea
    I wake, and I discern the truth;
15   It is the trouble of my youth
That foolish sleep transfers to thee.

LXIX

I dreamed there would be Spring no more,
    That Nature's ancient power was lost:
    The streets were black with smoke and frost,
They chattered trifles at the door:

5   I wandered from the noisy town,
    I found a wood with thorny boughs:
    I took the thorns to bind my brows,
I wore them like a civic crown:

I met with scoffs, I met with scorns
10   From youth and babe and hoary hairs:

They called me in the public squares
The fool that wears a crown of thorns:[1]

They called me fool, they called me child:
    I found an angel of the night;[2]
15   The voice was low, the look was bright;
He looked upon my crown and smiled:

He reached the glory of a hand,
    That seemed to touch it into leaf:
    The voice was not the voice of grief,
20 The words were hard to understand.

LXX

I cannot see the features right,
    When on the gloom I strive to paint
    The face I know; the hues are faint
And mix with hollow masks of night;

5   Cloud-towers by ghostly masons wrought,
    A gulf that ever shuts and gapes,
    A hand that points, and pallèd shapes
In shadowy thoroughfares of thought;

And crowds that stream from yawning doors,
10   And shoals of puckered faces drive;
    Dark bulks that tumble half alive,
And lazy lengths on boundless shores;

Till all at once beyond the will
    I hear a wizard music roll,
15   And through a lattice on the soul
Looks thy fair face and makes it still.

----

[1] Tennyson's comment: "To write poems about death and grief is 'to wear a crown of thorns,' which the people say ought to be laid aside." "I tried to make my grief into a crown of these poems—but it is not to be taken too closely—To write verses about sorrow grief & death is to wear a crown of thorns which ought to be put by—as people say."

[2] Tennyson's comment: "But the Divine Thing in the gloom brought comfort."

LXXI

Sleep, kinsman thou to death and trance
 And madness, thou hast forged at last
 A night-long Present of the Past
In which we went through summer France.[1]

5 Hadst thou such credit with the soul?
 Then bring an opiate trebly strong,
 Drug down the blindfold sense of wrong
That so my pleasure may be whole;

While now we talk as once we talked
10 Of men and minds, the dust of change,
 The days that grow to something strange,
In walking as of old we walked

Beside the river's wooded reach,
 The fortress, and the mountain ridge,
15 The cataract flashing from the bridge,
The breaker breaking on the beach.

LXXII

Risest thou thus, dim dawn, again,[2]
 And howlest, issuing out of night,
 With blasts that blow the poplar white,
And lash with storm the streaming pane?

5 Day, when my crowned estate begun
 To pine in that reverse of doom,
 Which sickened every living bloom,
And blurred the splendour of the sun;

Who usherest in the dolorous hour
10 With thy quick tears that make the rose
 Pull sideways, and the daisy close
Her crimson fringes to the shower;

Who might'st have heaved a windless flame
 Up the deep East, or, whispering, played
15 A chequer-work of beam and shade
Along the hills, yet looked the same,

As wan, as chill, as wild as now;
 Day, marked as with some hideous crime,
 When the dark hand struck down through time,
20 And cancelled nature's best: but thou,

Lift as thou mayst thy burthened brows
 Through clouds that drench the morning star,
 And whirl the ungarnered sheaf afar,
And sow the sky with flying boughs,

25 And up thy vault with roaring sound
 Climb thy thick noon, disastrous day;
 Touch thy dull goal of joyless gray,
And hide thy shame beneath the ground.

LXXIII

So many worlds, so much to do,
 So little done, such things to be,
 How know I what had need of thee,
For thou wert strong as thou wert true?

5 The fame is quenched that I foresaw,
 The head hath missed an earthly wreath:
 I curse not nature, no, nor death;
For nothing is that errs from law.

We pass; the path that each man trod
10 Is dim, or will be dim, with weeds:
 What fame is left for human deeds
In endless age? It rests with God.

O hollow wraith of dying fame,
 Fade wholly, while the soul exults,
15 And self-infolds the large results
Of force that would have forged a name.

---

[1] a reference to a journey to the south of France with Hallam in 1830.

[2] the first anniversary of Hallam's death.

LXXIV

As sometimes in a dead man's face,
    To those that watch it more and more,
    A likeness, hardly seen before,
Comes out—to some one of his race:

5 So, dearest, now thy brows are cold,
    I see thee what thou art, and know
    Thy likeness to the wise below,
Thy kindred with the great of old.

But there is more than I can see,
10   And what I see I leave unsaid,
    Nor speak it, knowing Death has made
His darkness beautiful with thee.

LXXV

I leave thy praises unexpressed
    In verse that brings myself relief,
    And by the measure of my grief
I leave thy greatness to be guessed;

5 What practice howso'er expert
    In fitting aptest words to things,
    Or voice the richest-toned that sings,
Hath power to give thee as thou wert?

I care not in these fading days
10   To raise a cry that lasts not long,
    And round thee with the breeze of song
To stir a little dust of praise.

Thy leaf has perished in the green,
    And, while we breathe beneath the sun,
15   The world which credits what is done
Is cold to all that might have been.

So here shall silence guard thy fame;
    But somewhere, out of human view,
    Whate'er thy hands are set to do
20 Is wrought with tumult of acclaim.

LXXVI

Take wings of fancy, and ascend,
    And in a moment set thy face
    Where all the starry heavens of space
Are sharpened to a needle's end;

5 Take wings of foresight; lighten through
    The secular abyss to come,
    And lo, thy deepest lays are dumb
Before the mouldering of a yew;

And if the matin songs, that woke
10   The darkness of our planet, last,
    Thine own shall wither in the vast,
Ere half the lifetime of an oak.

Ere these have clothed their branchy bowers
    With fifty Mays, thy songs are vain;
15   And what are they when these remain
The ruined shells of hollow towers?

LXXVII

What hope is here for modern rhyme
    To him, who turns a musing eye
    On songs, and deeds, and lives, that lie
Foreshortened in the tract of time?

5 These mortal lullabies of pain
    May bind a book, may line a box,
    May serve to curl a maiden's locks;
Or when a thousand moons shall wane

A man upon a stall may find,
10   And, passing, turn the page that tells
    A grief, then changed to something else,
Sung by a long-forgotten mind.

But what of that? My darkened ways
    Shall ring with music all the same;
15   To breathe my loss is more than fame,
To utter love more sweet than praise.

LXXVIII

Again at Christmas did we weave
    The holly round the Christmas hearth;
    The silent snow possessed the earth,
And calmly fell our Christmas-eve:

5   The yule-clog[1] sparkled keen with frost,
    No wing of wind the region swept,
    But over all things brooding slept
The quiet sense of something lost.

As in the winters left behind,
10   Again our ancient games had place,
    The mimic picture's breathing grace,[2]
And dance and song and hoodman-blind.[3]

Who showed a token of distress?
    No single tear, no mark of pain:
15   O sorrow, then can sorrow wane?
O grief, can grief be changed to less?

O last regret, regret can die!
    No—mixt with all this mystic frame,
    Her deep relations are the same,
20 But with long use her tears are dry.

LXXIX

"More than any brothers are to me,"—
    Let this not vex thee, noble heart!
    I know thee of what force thou art
To hold the costliest love in fee.

5   But thou and I are one in kind,
    As moulded like in Nature's mint;
    And hill and wood and field did print
The same sweet forms in either mind.

For us the same cold streamlet curled
10   Through all his eddying coves; the same
    All winds that roam the twilight came
In whispers of the beauteous world.

At one dear knee we proffered vows,
    One lesson from one book we learned,
15   Ere childhood's flaxen ringlet turned
To black and brown on kindred brows.

And so my wealth resembles thine,
    But he was rich where I was poor,
    And he supplied my want the more
20 As his unlikeness fitted mine.

LXXX

If any vague desire should rise,
    That holy Death ere Arthur died
    Had moved me kindly from his side,
And dropt the dust on tearless eyes;

5   Then fancy shapes, as fancy can,
    The grief my loss in him had wrought,
    A grief as deep as life or thought,
But stayed[4] in peace with God and man.

I make a picture in the brain;
10   I hear the sentence that he speaks;
    He bears the burthen of the weeks
But turns his burthen into gain.

His credit thus shall set me free;
    And, influence-rich to soothe and save,
15   Unused example from the grave
Reach out dead hands to comfort me.

LXXXI

Could I have said while he was here,
    "My love shall now no further range;

---

[1] the yule-log placed on the fire on Christmas eve.

[2] tableaux of famous paintings.

[3] blindman's bluff.

[4] endured.

There cannot come a mellower change,
For now is love mature in ear."

5 Love, then, had hope of richer store:
    What end is here to my complaint?
    This haunting whisper makes me faint,
"More years had made me love thee more."

But Death returns an answer sweet:
10   "My sudden frost was sudden gain,
    And gave all ripeness to the grain,
It might have drawn from after-heat."

LXXXII

I wage not any feud with Death
    For changes wrought on form and face;
    No lower life that earth's embrace
May breed with him, can fright my faith.

5 Eternal process moving on,
    From state to state the spirit walks;
    And these are but the shattered stalks,
Or ruined chrysalis of one.

Nor blame I Death, because he bare
10   The use of virtue out of earth:
    I know transplanted human worth
Will bloom to profit, otherwhere.

For this alone on Death I wreak
    The wrath that garners in my heart;
15   He put our lives so far apart
We cannot hear each other speak.

LXXXIII

Dip down upon the northern shore,
    O sweet new-year delaying long;
    Thou doest expectant nature wrong;
Delaying long, delay no more.

5 What stays thee from the clouded noons,
    Thy sweetness from its proper place?
    Can trouble live with April days,
Or sadness in the summer moons?

Bring orchis, bring the foxglove spire,
10   The little speedwell's darling blue,
    Deep tulips dashed with fiery dew,
Laburnums, dropping-wells of fire.

O thou, new-year, delaying long,
    Delayest the sorrow in my blood,
15   That longs to burst a frozen bud
And flood a fresher throat with song.

LXXXIV

When I contemplate all alone
    The life that had been thine below,
    And fix my thoughts on all the glow
To which thy crescent would have grown;

5 I see thee sitting crowned with good,
    A central warmth diffusing bliss
    In glance and smile, and clasp and kiss,
On all the branches of thy blood;

Thy blood, my friend, and partly mine;
10   For now the day was drawing on,
    When thou shouldst link thy life with one
Of mine own house, and boys of thine

Had babbled "Uncle" on my knee;[1]
    But that remorseless iron hour
15   Made cypress of her orange flower,
Despair of Hope, and earth of thee.

I seem to meet their least desire,
    To clap their cheeks, to call them mine.

---

[1] Hallam was engaged to the poet's sister Emily.

I see their unborn faces shine
20   Beside the never-lighted fire.

I see myself an honoured guest,
   Thy partner in the flowery walk
   Of letters, genial table-talk,
Or deep dispute, and graceful jest;

25 While now thy prosperous labour fills
   The lips of men with honest praise,
   And sun by sun the happy days
Descend below the golden hills

With promise of a morn as fair;
30   And all the train of bounteous hours
   Conduct by paths of growing powers,
To reverence and the silver hair;

Till slowly worn her earthly robe,
   Her lavish mission richly wrought,
35   Leaving great legacies of thought,
Thy spirit should fail from off the globe;

What time mine own might also flee,
   As linked with thine in love and fate,
   And, hovering o'er the dolorous strait
40 To the other shore, involved in thee,

Arrive at last the blessèd goal,
   And He that died in Holy Land
   Would reach us out the shining hand,
And take us as a single soul.

45 What reed was that on which I leant?
   Ah, backward fancy, wherefore wake
   The old bitterness again, and break
The low beginnings of content.

         LXXXV
This truth came borne with bier and pall,
   I felt it, when I sorrowed most,

'Tis better to have loved and lost,
Than never to have loved at all—

5 O true in word, and tried in deed,
   Demanding, so to bring relief
   To this which is our common grief,
What kind of life is that I lead;

And whether trust in things above
10   Be dimmed of sorrow, or sustained;
   And whether love for him have drained
My capabilities of love;

Your words have virtue such as draws
   A faithful answer from the breast,
15   Through light reproaches, half exprest,
And loyal unto kindly laws.

My blood an even tenor kept,
   Till on mine ear this message falls,
   That in Vienna's fatal wall
20 God's finger touched him, and he slept.

The great Intelligences fair
   That range above our mortal state,
   In circle round the blessèd gate,
Received and gave him welcome there;

25 And led him through the blissful climes,
   And showed him in the fountain fresh
   All knowledge that the sons of flesh
Shall gather in the cycled times.[1]

But I remained, whose hopes were dim,
30   Whose life, whose thoughts were little worth,
   To wander on a darkened earth,
Where all things round me breathed of him.

------

[1] times to come.

O friendship, equal-poised control,
    O heart, with kindliest motion warm,
35   O sacred essence, other form,
O solemn ghost, O crownèd soul!

Yet none could better know than I,
    How much of act at human hands
    The sense of human will demands
40 By which we dare to live or die.

Whatever way my days decline,
    I felt and feel, though left alone,
    His being working in mine own,
The footsteps of his life in mine;

45 A life that all the Muses decked
    With gifts of grace, that might express
    All-comprehensive tenderness,
All-subtilising intellect:

And so my passion hath not swerved
50   To works of weakness, but I find
    An image comforting the mind,
And in my grief a strength reserved.

Likewise the imaginative woe,
    That loved to handle spiritual strife,
55   Diffused the shock through all my life,
But in the present broke the blow.

My pulses therefore beat again
    For other friends that once I met;
    Nor can it suit me to forget
60 The mighty hopes that make us men.

I woo your love: I count it crime
    To mourn for any overmuch;
    I, the divided half of such
A friendship as had mastered Time;

65 Which masters Time indeed, and is
    Eternal, separate from fears:
    The all-assuming[1] months and years
Can take no part away from this:

But Summer on the steaming floods,
70   And Spring that swells the narrow brooks,
    And Autumn, with a noise of rooks,
That gather in the waning woods,

And every pulse of wind and wave
    Recalls, in change of light or gloom,
75   My old affection of the tomb,
And my prime passion in the grave:

My old affection of the tomb,
    A part of stillness, yearns to speak:
    "Arise, and get thee forth and seek
80 A friendship for the years to come.

"I watch thee from the quiet shore;
    Thy spirit up to mine can reach;
    But in dear words of human speech
We two communicate no more."

85 And I, "Can clouds of nature stain
    The starry clearness of the free?[2]
    How is it? Canst thou feel for me
Some painless sympathy with pain?"

And lightly does the whisper fall;
90   "'Tis hard for thee to fathom this;
    I triumph in conclusive bliss,
And that serene result of all."

So hold I commerce with the dead;
    Or so methinks the dead would say;

---

[1] all-consuming.

[2] the dead.

95 Or so shall grief with symbols play
And pining life be fancy-fed.

Now looking to some settled end,
    That these things pass, and I shall prove
    A meeting somewhere, love with love,
100 I crave your pardon, O my friend;

If not so fresh, with love as true,
    I, clasping brother-hands, aver
    I could not, if I would, transfer
The whole I felt for him to you.

105 For which be they that hold apart
    The promise of the golden hours?
    First love, first friendship, equal powers,
That marry with the virgin heart.

Still mine, that cannot but deplore,
110   That beats within a lonely place,
    That yet remembers his embrace,
But at his footstep leaps no more,

My heart, though widowed, may not rest
    Quite in the love of what is gone,
115   But seeks to beat in time with one
That warms another living breast.

Ah, take the imperfect gift I bring,
    Knowing the primrose yet is dear,
    The primrose of the later year,
120 As not unlike to that of Spring.

LXXXVI

Sweet after showers, ambrosial air,
    That rollest from the gorgeous gloom
    Of evening over brake and bloom
And meadow, slowly breathing bare

5 The round of space, and rapt below
    Through all the dewy-tasselled wood,

And shadowing down the hornèd flood[1]
    In ripples, fan my brows and blow

The fever from my cheek, and sigh
10   The full new life that feeds thy breath
    Throughout my frame, till Doubt and Death,
Ill brethren, let the fancy fly

From belt to belt of crimson seas
    On leagues of odour streaming far,
15   To where in yonder orient star
A hundred spirits whisper "Peace."[2]

LXXXVII

I past beside the reverend walls
    In which of old I wore the gown;[3]
    I roved at random through the town,
And saw the tumult of the halls;

5 And heard once more in college fanes
    The storm their high-built organs make,
    And thunder-music, rolling, shake
The prophet blazoned on the panes;

And caught once more the distant shout,
10   The measured pulse of racing oars
    Among the willows; paced the shores
And many a bridge, and all about

The same gray flats again, and felt
    The same, but not the same; and last
15   Up that long walk of limes I past
To see the rooms in which he dwelt.

---

[1] Tennyson's comment: "between two promontories."

[2] Tennyson's comment on the final stanza: "The west wind rolling to the Eastern seas till it meets the evening star."

[3] a reference to Trinity College, Cambridge, which Tennyson and Hallam attended.

Another name was on the door:
    I lingered; all within was noise
    Of songs, and clapping hands, and boys
20 That crashed the glass and beat the floor;

Where once we held debate, a band
    Of youthful friends,[1] on mind and art,
    And labour, and the changing mart,
And all the framework of the land;

25 When one would aim an arrow fair,
    But send it slackly from the string;
    And one would pierce an outer ring,
And one an inner, here and there;

And last the master-bowman, he,
30   Would cleave the mark. A willing ear
    We lent him. Who, but hung to hear
The rapt oration flowing free

From point to point, with power and grace
    And music in the bounds of law,
35   To those conclusions when we saw
The God within him light his face,

And seem to lift the form, and glow
    In azure orbits heavenly-wise;
    And over those ethereal eyes
40 The bar of Michael Angelo.[2]

LXXXVIII

Wild bird,[3] whose warble, liquid sweet,
    Rings Eden through the budded quicks,[4]
    O tell me where the senses mix,
O tell me where the passions meet,

5 Whence radiate: fierce extremes employ
    Thy spirits in the darkening leaf,
    And in the midmost heart of grief
Thy passion clasps a secret joy:

And I—my harp would prelude woe—
10   I cannot all command the strings;
    The glory of the sum of things
Will flash along the chords and go.

LXXXIX

Witch-elms that counterchange[5] the floor
    Of this flat lawn with dusk and bright;
    And thou, with all thy breadth and height
Of foliage, towering sycamore;

5 How often, hither wandering down,
    My Arthur found your shadows fair,
    And shook to all the liberal air
The dust and din and steam of town:

He brought an eye for all he saw;
10   He mixt in all our simple sports;
    They pleased him, fresh from brawling courts
And dusty purlieus of the law.

O joy to him in this retreat,
    Immantled in ambrosial dark,
15   To drink the cooler air, and mark
The landscape winking through the heat:

---

[1] the "Cambridge Apostles," a discussion group attended by Hallam and Tennyson.

[2] Tennyson's comment: "the broad bar of frontal bone over the eyes of Michael Angelo." "These lines I wrote from what Arthur Hallam said after reading of the prominent ridge of bone over the eyes of Michael Angelo: 'Alfred, look over my eyes; surely I have the bar of Michael Angelo!'"

---

[3] the nightingale.

[4] quickset thorn.

[5] checker.

O sound to rout the brood of cares,
    The sweep of scythe in morning dew,
    The gust that round the garden flew,
20 And tumbled half the mellowing pears!

O bliss, when all in circle drawn
    About him, heart and ear were fed
    To hear him, as he lay and read
The Tuscan[1] poets on the lawn:

25 Or in the all-golden afternoon
    A guest, or happy sister, sung,
    Or here she brought the harp and flung
A ballad to the brightening moon:

Nor less it pleased in livelier moods,
30   Beyond the bounding hill to stray,
    And break the livelong summer day
With banquet in the distant woods;

Whereat we glanced from theme to theme,
    Discussed the books to love or hate,
35   Or touched the changes of the state,
Or threaded some Socratic dream;

But if I praised the busy town,
    He loved to rail against it still,
    For "ground in yonder social mill
40 We rub each other's angles down,

"And merge" he said "in form and gloss
    The picturesque of man and man."
    We talked: the stream beneath us ran.
The wine-flask lying couched in moss,

45 Or cooled within the glooming wave;
    And last, returning from afar,

Before the crimson-circled star[2]
Had fallen into her father's grave,

And brushing ankle-deep in flowers,
50   We heard behind the woodbine veil
    The milk that bubbled in the pail,
And buzzings of the honied hours

XC

He tasted love with half his mind,
    Nor ever drank the inviolate spring
    Where nighest heaven, who first could fling
This bitter seed among mankind;

5 That could the dead, whose dying eyes
    Were closed with wail, resume their life,
    They would but find in child and wife
An iron welcome when they rise:

'Twas well, indeed, when warm with wine,
10   To pledge them with a kindly tear,
    To talk them o'er, to wish them here,
To count their memories half divine;

But if they came who past away,
    Behold their brides in other hands;
15   The hard heir strides about their lands,
And will not yield them for a day.

Yea, though their sons were none of these,
    Not less the yet-loved sire would make
    Confusion worse than death, and shake
20 The pillars of domestic peace.

Ah dear, but come thou back to me:
    Whatever change the years have wrought,
    I find not yet one lonely thought
That cries against my wish for thee.

---

[1] Dante and Petrarch.

[2] Tennyson's comment: "Before Venus, the evening star, had dipt into the sunset. The planets, according to Laplace, were evolved from the sun."

25

XCI

When rosy plumelets tuft the larch,
    And rarely pipes the mounted thrush;
    Or underneath the barren bush
Flits by the sea-blue bird of March;[1]

30 Come, wear the form by which I know
    Thy spirit in time among thy peers;
    The hope of unaccomplished years
Be large and lucid round thy brow.

When summer's hourly-mellowing change
35   May breathe, with many roses sweet,
    Upon the thousand waves of wheat,
That ripple round the lonely grange;

Come: not in watches of the night,
    But where the sunbeam broodeth warm,
40   Come, beauteous in thine after form,
And like a finer light in light.

XCII

If any vision should reveal
    Thy likeness, I might count it vain
    As but the canker of the brain;
Yea, though it spake and made appeal

5 To chances where our lots were cast
    Together in the days behind,
    I might but say, I hear a wind
Of memory murmuring the past.

Yea, though it spake and bared to view
10   A fact within the coming year;
    And though the months, revolving near,
Should prove the phantom-warning true,

They might not seem thy prophecies,
    But spiritual presentiments,

---

[1] the kingfisher.

15 And such refraction of events
As often rises ere they rise.

XCIII

I shall not see thee. Dare I say
    No spirit ever brake the band
    That stays him from the native land
Where first he walked when claspt in clay?

5 No visual shade of some one lost,
    But he, the Spirit himself, may come
    Where all the nerve of sense is numb;
Spirit to Spirit, Ghost to Ghost.

O, therefore from thy sightless[2] range
10   With gods in unconjectured bliss,
    O, from the distance of the abyss
Of tenfold-complicated change,

Descend, and touch, and enter; hear
    The wish too strong for words to name;
15   That in this blindness of the frame
My Ghost may feel that thine is near.

XCIV

How pure at heart and sound in head,
    With what divine affections bold
    Should be the man whose thought would hold
An hour's communion with the dead.

5 In vain shalt thou, or any, call
    The spirits from their golden day,
    Except, like them, thou too canst say,
My spirit is at peace with all.

They haunt the silence of the breast,
10   Imaginations calm and fair,
    The memory like a cloudless air,
The conscience as a sea at rest:

---

[2] invisible.

But when the heart is full of din,
   And doubt beside the portal waits,
15   They can but listen at the gates,
And hear the household jar within.

XCV

By night we lingered on the lawn,
   For underfoot the herb was dry;
   And genial warmth; and o'er the sky
The silvery haze of summer drawn;

5 And calm that let the tapers burn
    Unwavering: not a cricket chirred:
    The brook alone far-off was heard,
And on the board the fluttering urn:[1]

And bats went round in fragrant skies,
10   And wheeled or lit the filmy shapes
    That haunt the dusk, with ermine capes
And woolly breasts and beaded eyes;[2]

While now we sang old songs that pealed
   From knoll to knoll, where, couched at ease,
15   The white kine glimmered, and the trees
Laid their dark arms about the field.

But when those others, one by one,
   Withdrew themselves from me and night,
   And in the house light after light
20 Went out, and I was all alone,

A hunger seized my heart; I read
   Of that glad year which once had been,
   In those fallen leaves which kept their green,
The noble letters of the dead:

25 And strangely on the silence broke
   The silent-speaking words, and strange

Was love's dumb cry defying change
To test his worth; and strangely spoke

The faith, the vigour, bold to dwell
30   On doubts that drive the coward back,
   And keen through wordy snares to track
Suggestion to her inmost cell.

So word by word, and line by line,
   The dead man touched me from the past,
35   And all at once it seemed at last
The living soul was flashed on mine,

And mine in this was wound, and whirled
   About empyreal heights of thought,
   And came on that which is, and caught
40 The deep pulsations of the world,

Æonian[3] music measuring out
   The steps of Time—the shocks of Chance—
   The blows of Death. At length my trance
Was cancelled, stricken through with doubt.

45 Vague words! but ah, how hard to frame
   In matter-moulded forms of speech,
   Or even for intellect to reach
Through memory that which I became:

Till now the doubtful dusk revealed
50   The knolls once more where, couched at ease,
   The white kine glimmered, and the trees
Laid their dark arms about the field:

And sucked from out the distant gloom
   A breeze began to tremble o'er
55   The large leaves of the sycamore,
And fluctuate all the still perfume,

---

[1] a tea-urn shaking slightly because of the boiling water.

[2] moths.

[3] lasting through aeons.

And gathering freshlier overhead,
 Rocked the full-foliaged elms, and swung
 The heavy-folded rose, and flung
60 The lilies to and fro, and said

"The dawn, the dawn," and died away;
 And East and West, without a breath,
 Mixt their dim lights, like life and death,
To broaden into boundless day.

XCVI

You[1] say, but with no touch of scorn,
 Sweet-hearted, you, whose light-blue eyes
 Are tender over drowning flies,
You tell me, doubt is Devil-born.

5 I know not: one[2] indeed I knew
 In many a subtle question versed,
 Who touched a jarring lyre at first,
But ever strove to make it true:

Perplext in faith, but pure in deeds,
10 At last he beat his music out.
 There lives more faith in honest doubt,
Believe me, than in half the creeds.

He fought his doubts and gathered strength,
 He would not make his judgment blind,
15 He faced the spectres of the mind
And laid them: thus he came at length

To find a stronger faith his own;
 And Power was with him in the night,
 Which makes the darkness and the light,
20 And dwells not in the light alone,

But in the darkness and the cloud,
 As over Sinaï's peaks of old,

While Israel made their gods of gold,
Although the trumpet blew so loud.

XCVII

My love has talked with rocks and trees;
 He finds on misty mountain-ground
 His own vast shadow glory-crowned;
He sees himself in all he sees.

5 Two partners of a married life—
 I looked on these and thought of thee
 In vastness and in mystery,
And of my spirit as of a wife.

These two—they dwelt with eye on eye,
10 Their hearts of old have beat in tune,
 Their meetings made December June,
Their every parting was to die.

Their love has never past away;
 The days she never can forget
15 Are earnest[3] that he loves her yet,
Whate'er the faithless people say.

Her life is lone, he sits apart,
 He loves her yet, she will not weep,
 Though rapt in matters dark and deep
20 He seems to slight her simple heart.

He thrids the labyrinth of the mind,
 He reads the secret of the star,
 He seems so near and yet so far,
He looks so cold: she thinks him kind.

25 She keeps the gift of years before,
 A withered violet is her bliss:
 She knows not what his greatness is,
For that, for all, she loves him more.

---

[1] probably Emily Sellwood, to whom Tennyson was engaged.

[2] Arthur Hallam.

[3] assurance.

For him she plays, to him she sings
30 Of early faith and plighted vows;
  She knows but matters of the house,
And he, he knows a thousand things.

Her faith is fixt and cannot move,
  She darkly feels him great and wise,
35 She dwells on him with faithful eyes,
"I cannot understand: I love."

XCVIII

You leave us: you will see the Rhine,
  And those fair hills I sailed below,
  When I was there with him; and go
By summer belts of wheat and vine

5 To where he breathed his latest breath,
  That City.[1] All her splendour seems
  No livelier than the wisp that gleams
On Lethe in the eyes of Death.

Let her great Danube rolling fair
10 Enwind her isles, unmarked of me:
  I have not seen, I will not see
Vienna; rather dream that there,

A treble darkness, Evil haunts
  The birth, the bridal; friend from friend
15 Is oftener parted, fathers bend
Above more graves, a thousand wants

Gnarr[2] at the heels of men, and prey
  By each cold hearth, and sadness flings
  Her shadow on the blaze of kings:
20 And yet myself have heard him[3] say,

That not in any mother town[4]
  With statelier progress to and fro
  The double tides of chariots flow
By park and suburb under brown

25 Of lustier leaves; nor more content,
  He told me, lives in any crowd,
  When all is gay with lamps, and loud
With sport and song, in booth and tent,

Imperial halls, or open plain;
30 And wheels the circled dance, and breaks
  The rocket molten into flakes
Of crimson or in emerald rain.

XCIX

Risest thou thus, dim dawn, again,
  So loud with voices of the birds,
  So thick with lowings of the herds,
Day, when I lost the flower of men;

5 Who tremblest through thy darkling red
  On yon swollen brook that bubbles fast
  By meadows breathing of the past,
And woodlands holy to the dead;

Who murmurest in the foliaged eaves
10 A song that slights the coming care,
  And Autumn laying here and there
A fiery finger on the leaves;

Who wakenest with thy balmy breath
  To myriads on the genial earth,
15 Memories of bridal, or of birth,
And unto myriads more, of death.

O wheresoever those may be,
  Betwixt the slumber of the poles,

---

[1] Vienna.

[2] snarl.

[3] Hallam.

[4] metropolis.

Today they count as kindred souls;
20   They know me not, but mourn with me.

C

I climb the hill: from end to end
      Of all the landscape underneath,
      I find no place that does not breathe
Some gracious memory of my friend;

5   No gray old grange, or lonely fold,
      Or low morass and whispering reed,
      Or simple stile from mead to mead,
Or sheepwalk up the windy wold;

Nor hoary knoll of ash and haw
10   That hears the latest linnet trill,
      Nor quarry trenched along the hill
And haunted by the wrangling daw;

Nor runlet tinkling from the rock;
      Nor pastoral rivulet that swerves
15   To left and right through meadowy curves,
That feed the mothers of the flock;

But each has pleased a kindred eye,
      And each reflects a kindlier day;
      And, leaving these, to pass away,
20   I think once more he seems to die.

CI

Unwatched, the garden bough shall sway,
      The tender blossom flutter down,
      Unloved, that beech will gather brown,
This maple burn itself away;

5   Unloved, the sun-flower, shining fair,
      Ray round with flames her disk of seed,
      And many a rose-carnation feed
With summer spice the humming air;

10   Unloved, by many a sandy bar,
      The brook shall babble down the plain,
      At noon or when the lesser wain[1]
Is twisting round the polar star;

Uncared for, gird the windy grove,
15   And flood the haunts of hern and crake;[2]
      Or into silver arrows break
The sailing moon in creek and cove;

Till from the garden and the wild
      A fresh association blow,
20   And year by year the landscape grow
Familiar to the stranger's child;

As year by year the labourer tills
      His wonted glebe, or lops the glades;
      And year by year our memory fades
25   From all the circle of the hills.

CII

We leave the well-belovèd place
      Where first we gazed upon the sky;
      The roofs, that heard our earliest cry,
Will shelter one of stranger race.

5   We go, but ere we go from home,
      As down the garden-walks I move,
      Two spirits[3] of a diverse love
Contend for loving masterdom.

One whispers, "Here thy boyhood sung
10   Long since its matin song, and heard
      The low love-language of the bird
In native hazels tassel-hung."

------

[1] the Little Dipper (Ursa Minor).

[2] heron and corn crake.

[3] Tennyson's comment: "First, the love of the native place; second, this enhanced by the memory of A.H.H."

The other answers, "Yea, but here
    Thy feet have strayed in after hours
15   With thy lost friend among the bowers,
And this hath made them trebly dear."

These two have striven half the day,
    And each prefers his separate claim,
    Poor rivals in a losing game,
20 That will not yield each other way.

I turn to go: my feet are set
    To leave the pleasant fields and farms;
    They mix in one another's arms
To one pure image of regret.

CIII

On that last night before we went
    From out the doors where I was bred,
    I dreamed a vision of the dead,
Which left my after-morn content.

5   Methought I dwelt within a hall,
    And maidens[1] with me: distant hills
    From hidden summits fed with rills
A river[2] sliding by the wall.

The hall with harp and carol rang.
10   They sang of what is wise and good
    And graceful. In the centre stood
A statue veiled, to which they sang;

And which, though veiled, was known to me,
    The shape of him I loved, and love
15   For ever: then flew in a dove
And brought a summons from the sea:[3]

And when they learnt that I must go
    They wept and wailed, but led the way
    To where a little shallop lay
20 At anchor in the flood below;

And on by many a level mead,
    And shadowing bluff that made the banks,
    We glided winding under ranks
Of iris, and the golden reed;

25 And still as vaster grew the shore[4]
    And rolled the floods in grander space,
    The maidens gathered strength and grace
And presence, lordlier than before;

And I myself, who sat apart
30   And watched them, waxed in every limb;
    I felt the thews of Anakim,[5]
The pulses of a Titan's heart;

As one would sing the death of war,
    And one would chant the history
35   Of that great race, which is to be,[6]
And one the shaping of a star;

Until the forward-creeping tides
    Began to foam, and we to draw
    From deep to deep, to where we saw
40 A great ship lift her shining sides.

The man we loved was there on deck,
    But thrice as large as man he bent
    To greet us. Up the side I went,
And fell in silence on his neck:

45 Whereat those maidens with one mind
    Bewailed their lot; I did them wrong:

---

[1] Tennyson's comment: "They are the Muses, poetry, arts—all that made life beautiful here, which we hope will pass with us beyond the grave."

[2] life on earth.

[3] eternity.

---

[4] the progress of the Age.

[5] the giants of Deuteronomy.

[6] Tennyson's comment: "The great hopes of humanity and science."

"We served thee here," they said, "so long,
And wilt thou leave us now behind?"

So rapt I was, they could not win
50   An answer from my lips, but he
    Replying, "Enter likewise ye
And go with us:" they entered in.

And while the wind began to sweep
    A music out of sheet and shroud,
55   We steered her toward a crimson cloud
That landlike slept along the deep.

CIV

The time draws near the birth of Christ;
    The moon is hid, the night is still;
    A single church below the hill
Is pealing, folded in the mist.

5   A single peal of bells below,
    That wakens at this hour of rest
    A single murmur in the breast,
That these are not the bells I know.

Like strangers' voices here they sound,
10   In lands where not a memory strays,
    Nor landmark breathes of other days,
But all is new unhallowed ground.

CV

Tonight ungathered let us leave
    This laurel, let this holly stand:
    We live within the stranger's land,
And strangely falls our Christmas-eve.

5   Our father's dust is left alone
    And silent under other snows:
    There in due time the woodbine blows,
The violet comes, but we are gone.

No more shall wayward grief abuse
10   The genial hour with mask and mime;
    For change of place, like growth of time,
Has broke the bond of dying use.

Let cares that petty shadows cast,
    By which our lives are chiefly proved,
15   A little spare the night I loved,
And hold it solemn to the past.

But let no footstep beat the floor,
    Nor bowl of wassail mantle warm;[1]
    For who would keep an ancient form
20   Through which the spirit breathes no more?

Be neither song, nor game, nor feast;
    Nor harp be touched, nor flute be blown;
    No dance, no motion, save alone
What lightens in the lucid east

25   Of rising worlds by yonder wood.
    Long sleeps the summer in the seed;
    Run out your measured arcs, and lead
The closing cycle rich in good.

CVI

Ring out, wild bells, to the wild sky,
    The flying cloud, the frosty light:
    The year is dying in the night;
Ring out, wild bells, and let him die.

5   Ring out the old, ring in the new,
    Ring, happy bells, across the snow:
    The year is going, let him go;
Ring out the false, ring in the true.

Ring out the grief that saps the mind,
10   For those that here we see no more;

---

[1] warm frothing wine.

Ring out the feud of rich and poor,
Ring in redress to all mankind.

Ring out a slowly dying cause,
        And ancient forms of party strife;
15   Ring in the nobler modes of life,
With sweeter manners, purer laws.

Ring out the want, the care, the sin,
        The faithless coldness of the times;
        Ring out, ring out my mournful rhymes,
20 But ring the fuller minstrel in.

Ring out false pride in place and blood,
        The civic slander and the spite;
        Ring in the love of truth and right,
Ring in the common love of good.

25 Ring out old shapes of foul disease;
        Ring out the narrowing lust of gold;
        Ring out the thousand wars of old,
Ring in the thousand years of peace.

Ring in the valiant man and free,
30   The larger heart, the kindlier hand;
        Ring out the darkness of the land,
Ring in the Christ that is to be.

CVII

It is the day when he was born,
        A bitter day that early sank
        Behind a purple-frosty bank
Of vapour, leaving night forlorn.

5   The time admits not flowers or leaves
        To deck the banquet. Fiercely flies
        The blast of North and East, and ice
Makes daggers at the sharpened eaves,

And bristles all the brakes and thorns
10   To yon hard crescent,[1] as she hangs
        Above the wood which grides[2] and clangs
Its leafless ribs and iron horns

Together, in the drifts that pass
        To darken on the rolling brine
15   That breaks the coast. But fetch the wine,
Arrange the board and brim the glass;

Bring in great logs and let them lie,
        To make a solid core of heat;
        Be cheerful-minded, talk and treat
20 Of all things even as he were by;

We keep the day. With festal cheer,
        With books and music, surely we
        Will drink to him, whate'er he be,
And sing the songs he loved to hear.

CVIII

I will not shut me from my kind,
        And, lest I stiffen into stone,
        I will not eat my heart alone,
Nor feed with sighs a passing wind:

5   What profit lies in barren faith,
        And vacant yearning, though with might
        To scale the heaven's highest height,
Or dive below the wells of Death?

What find I in the highest place,
10   But mine own phantom chanting hymns?
        And on the depths of death there swims
The reflex of a human face.

I'll rather take what fruit may be
        Of sorrow under human skies:

---

[1] moon.

[2] crashes.

15 'Tis held that sorrow makes us wise,
Whatever wisdom sleep with thee.

CIX

Heart-affluence in discursive talk
    From household fountains never dry;
    The critic clearness of an eye,
That saw through all the Muses' walk;[1]

5 Seraphic intellect and force
    To seize and throw the doubts of man;
    Impassioned logic, which outran
The hearer in its fiery course;

High nature amorous of the good,
10   But touched with no ascetic gloom;
    And passion pure in snowy bloom
Through all the years of April blood;

A love of freedom rarely felt,
    Of freedom in her regal seat
15   Of England; not the schoolboy heat,
The blind hysterics of the Celt;

And manhood fused with female grace
    In such a sort, the child would twine
    A trustful hand, unasked, in thine,
20 And find his comfort in thy face;

All these have been, and thee mine eyes
    Have looked on: if they looked in vain,
    My shame is greater who remain,
Nor let thy wisdom make me wise.

CX

Thy converse drew us with delight,
    The men of rathe[2] and riper years:

    The feeble soul, a haunt of fears,
Forgot his weakness in thy sight.

5 On thee the loyal-hearted hung,
    The proud was half disarmed of pride,
    Nor cared the serpent at thy side
To flicker with his double tongue.

The stern were mild when thou wert by,
10   The flippant put himself to school
    And heard thee, and the brazen fool
Was softened, and he knew not why;

While I, thy nearest, sat apart,
    And felt thy triumph was as mine;
15   And loved them more, that they were thine,
The graceful tact, the Christian art;

Nor mine the sweetness or the skill,
    But mine the love that will not tire,
    And, born of love, the vague desire
20 That spurs an imitative will.

CXI

The churl in spirit, up or down
    Along the scale of ranks, through all,
    To him who grasps a golden ball,[3]
By blood a king, at heart a clown;

5 The churl in spirit, howe'er he veil
    His want in forms for fashion's sake,
    Will let his coltish nature break
At seasons through the gilded pale:[4]

For who can always act? but he,
10   To whom a thousand memories call,
    Not being less but more than all
The gentleness he seemed to be,

---

[1] where the Muses gather.

[2] early.

[3] symbol of kingship.

[4] barriers.

Best seemed the thing he was, and joined
   Each office of the social hour
15   To noble manners, as the flower
And native growth of noble mind;

Nor ever narrowness or spite,
   Or villain fancy fleeting by,
   Drew in the expression of an eye,
20 Where God and Nature met in light;

And thus he bore without abuse
   The grand old name of gentleman,
   Defamed by every charlatan,
And soiled with all ignoble use.

CXII

High wisdom holds my wisdom less,
   That I, who gaze with temperate eyes
   On glorious insufficiencies,
Set light by narrower perfectness.

5 But thou, that fillest all the room
   Of all my love, art reason why
   I seem to cast a careless eye
On souls, the lesser lords of doom.

For what wert thou? some novel power
10   Sprang up for ever at a touch,
   And hope could never hope too much,
In watching thee from hour to hour,

Large elements in order brought,
   And tracts of calm from tempest made,
15   And world-wide fluctuation swayed
In vassal tides that followed thought.

CXIII

'Tis held that sorrow makes us wise;
   Yet how much wisdom sleeps with thee
   Which not alone had guided me,
But served the seasons that may rise;

5 For can I doubt, who knew thee keen
   In intellect, with force and skill
   To strive, to fashion, to fulfil—
I doubt not what thou wouldst have been:

A life in civic action warm,
10   A soul on highest mission sent,
   A potent voice of Parliament,
A pillar steadfast in the storm,

Should licensed boldness gather force,
   Becoming, when the time has birth,
15   A lever to uplift the earth
And roll it in another course,

With thousand shocks that come and go,
   With agonies, with energies,
   With overthrowings, and with cries,
20 And undulations to and fro.

CXIV

Who loves not Knowledge? Who shall rail
   Against her beauty? May she mix
   With men and prosper! Who shall fix
Her pillars?[1] Let her work prevail.

5 But on her forehead sits a fire:
   She sets her forward countenance
   And leaps into the future chance,
Submitting all things to desire.

Half-grown as yet, a child, and vain—
10   She cannot fight the fear of death.
   What is she, cut from love and faith,
But some wild Pallas from the brain

Of Demons? fiery-hot to burst
   All barriers in her onward race

---

[1] limits.

15 For power. Let her know her place;
 She is the second, not the first.

A higher hand must make her mild,
 If all be not in vain; and guide
 Her footsteps, moving side by side
20 With wisdom, like the younger child:

For she is earthly of the mind,
 But Wisdom heavenly of the soul.
 O, friend, who camest to thy goal
So early, leaving me behind,

25 I would the great world grew like thee,
 Who grewest not alone in power
 And knowledge, but by year and hour
In reverence and in charity.

CXV

Now fades the last long streak of snow,
 Now burgeons every maze of quick[1]
 About the flowering squares, and thick
By ashen roots the violets blow.

5 Now rings the woodland loud and long,
 The distance takes a lovelier hue,
 And drowned in yonder living blue
The lark becomes a sightless song.

Now dance the lights on lawn and lea,
10   The flocks are whiter down the vale,
 And milkier every milky sail
On winding stream or distant sea;

Where now the seamew pipes, or dives
 In yonder greening gleam, and fly
15   The happy birds, that change their sky
To build and brood; that live their lives

From land to land; and in my breast
 Spring wakens too; and my regret
 Becomes an April violet,
20 And buds and blossoms like the rest.

CXVI

Is it, then, regret for buried time
 That keenlier in sweet April wakes,
 And meets the year, and gives and takes
The colours of the crescent prime?

5 Not all: the songs, the stirring air,
 The life re-orient out of dust,
 Cry through the sense to hearten trust
In that which made the world so fair.

Not all regret: the face will shine
10   Upon me, while I muse alone;
 And that dear voice, I once have known,
Still speak to me of me and mine:

Yet less of sorrow lives in me
 For days of happy commune dead;
15   Less yearning for the friendship fled,
Than some strong bond which is to be.

CXVII

O days and hours, your work is this
 To hold me from my proper place,
 A little while from his embrace,
For fuller gain of after bliss:

5 That out of distance might ensue
 Desire of nearness doubly sweet;
 And unto meeting when we meet,
Delight a hundredfold accrue,

For every grain of sand that runs,
10   And every span of shade that steals,

---

[1] quickset thorn hedge-row.

And every kiss of toothèd wheels,[1]
And all the courses of the suns.

CXVIII

Contemplate all this work of Time,
   The giant labouring in his youth;
   Nor dream of human love and truth,
As dying Nature's earth and lime;

5 But trust that those we call the dead
   Are breathers of an ampler day
   For ever nobler ends. They say,
The solid earth whereon we tread

In tracts of fluent heat began,
10   And grew to seeming-random forms,
   The seeming prey of cyclic storms,[2]
Till at the last arose the man;

Who throve and branched from clime to clime,
   The herald of a higher race,
15   And of himself in higher place,
If so he type this work of time

Within himself, from more to more;
   Or, crowned with attributes of woe
   Like glories, move his course, and show
20 That life is not as idle ore,

But iron dug from central gloom,
   And heated hot with burning fears,
   And dipt in baths of hissing tears,
And battered with the shocks of doom

25 To shape and use. Arise and fly
   The reeling Faun, the sensual feast;
   Move upward, working out the beast,
And let the ape and tiger die.

CXIX

Doors, where my heart was used to beat
   So quickly, not as one that weeps
   I come once more; the city sleeps;
I smell the meadow in the street;

5 I hear a chirp of birds; I see
   Betwixt the black fronts long-withdrawn
   A light-blue lane of early dawn,
And think of early days and thee,

And bless thee, for thy lips are bland,
10   And bright the friendship of thine eye;
   And in my thoughts with scarce a sigh
I take the pressure of thine hand.

CXX

I trust I have not wasted breath:
   I think we are not wholly brain,
   Magnetic mockeries; not in vain,
Like Paul with beasts, I fought with Death;

5 Not only cunning casts in clay:
   Let Science prove we are, and then
   What matters Science unto men,
At least to me? I would not stay.

Let him, the wiser man[3] who springs
10   Hereafter, up from childhood shape
   His action like the greater ape,
But I was *born* to other things.

CXXI

Sad Hesper o'er the buried sun
   And ready, thou, to die with him,
   Thou watchest all things ever dim
And dimmer, and a glory done:

---

[1] wheels of a clock.

[2] periodic cataclysms.

[3] ironic—one made wise by science.

5 The team is loosened from the wain,[1]
    The boat is drawn upon the shore;
    Thou listenest to the closing door,
And life is darkened in the brain.

Bright Phosphor, fresher for the night,
10   By thee the world's great work is heard
    Beginning, and the wakeful bird;
Behind thee comes the greater light:

The market boat is on the stream,
    And voices hail it from the brink;
15   Thou hear'st the village hammer clink,
And see'st the moving of the team.

Sweet Hesper-Phosphor, double name
    For what is one, the first, the last,
    Thou, like my present and my past,
20 Thy place is changed; thou art the same.

CXXII

Oh, wast thou with me, dearest, then,
    While I rose up against my doom,
    And yearned to burst the folded gloom,
To bare the eternal Heavens again,

5 To feel once more, in placid awe,
    The strong imagination roll
    A sphere of stars about my soul,
In all her motion one with law;

If thou wert with me, and the grave
10   Divide us not, be with me now,
    And enter in at breast and brow,
Till all my blood, a fuller wave,

Be quickened with a livelier breath,
    And like an inconsiderate boy,

15 As in the former flash of joy,
    I slip the thoughts of life and death;

And all the breeze of Fancy blows,
    And every dew-drop paints a bow,[2]
    The wizard lightnings deeply glow,
20 And every thought breaks out a rose.

CXXIII

There rolls the deep where grew the tree.
    O earth, what changes hast thou seen!
    There where the long street roars, hath been
The stillness of the central sea.

5 The hills are shadows, and they flow
    From form to form, and nothing stands;
    They melt like mist, the solid lands,
Like clouds they shape themselves and go.

But in my spirit will I dwell,
10   And dream my dream, and hold it true;
    For though my lips may breathe adieu,
I cannot think the thing farewell.

CXXIV

That which we dare invoke to bless;
    Our dearest faith; our ghastliest doubt;
    He, They, One, All; within, without;
The Power in darkness whom we guess;

5 I found Him not in world or sun,
    Or eagle's wing, or insect's eye;
    Nor through the questions men may try,
The petty cobwebs we have spun:

If e'er when faith had fallen asleep,
10   I heard a voice "believe no more"

---

[1] wagon.

[2] Tennyson's comment: "Every dew-drop turns into a miniature rainbow."

And heard an ever-breaking shore
That tumbled in the Godless deep;

A warmth within the breast would melt
   The freezing reason's colder part,
15   And like a man in wrath the heart
Stood up and answered "I have felt."

No, like a child in doubt and fear:
   But that blind clamour made me wise;
   Then was I as a child that cries,
20 But, crying, knows his father near;

And what I am beheld again
   What is, and no man understands;
   And out of darkness came the hands
That reach through nature, moulding men.

CXXV

Whatever I have said or sung,
   Some bitter notes my harp would give,
   Yea, though there often seemed to live
A contradiction on the tongue,

5   Yet Hope had never lost her youth;
   She did but look through dimmer eyes;
   Or Love but played with gracious lies,
Because he felt so fixed in truth:

And if the song were full of care,
10 He[1] breathed the spirit of the song;
   And if the words were sweet and strong
He set his royal signet there;

Abiding with me till I sail
   To seek thee on the mystic deeps,
15   And this electric force, that keeps
A thousand pulses dancing, fail.

CXXVI

Love is and was my Lord and King,
   And in his presence I attend
   To hear the tidings of my friend,
Which every hour his couriers bring.

5   Love is and was my King and Lord,
   And will be, though as yet I keep
   Within his court on earth, and sleep
Encompassed by his faithful guard,

And hear at times a sentinel
10 Who moves about from place to place,
   And whispers to the worlds of space,
In the deep night, that all is well.

CXXVII

And all is well, though faith and form
   Be sundered in the night of fear;
   Well roars the storm to those that hear
A deeper voice across the storm,

5   Proclaiming social truth shall spread,
   And justice, even though thrice again
   The red fool-fury of the Seine
Should pile her barricades with dead.[2]

But ill for him that wears a crown,
10 And him, the lazar, in his rags:
   They tremble, the sustaining crags;
The spires of ice are toppled down,

And molten up, and roar in flood;
   The fortress crashes from on high,
15   The brute earth lightens to the sky,
And the great Æon[3] sinks in blood,

---

[1] love.

[2] the French Revolution.

[3] great age.

And compassed by the fires of Hell;
    While thou, dear spirit, happy star,
    O'erlook'st the tumult from afar,
20 And smilest, knowing all is well.

CXXVIII

The love that rose on stronger wings,
    Unpalsied when he met with Death,
    Is comrade of the lesser faith
That sees the course of human things.

5 No doubt vast eddies in the flood
    Of onward time shall yet be made,
    And thronèd races may degrade;
Yet O ye mysteries of good,

Wild Hours that fly with Hope and Fear,
10   If all your office had to do
    With old results that look like new;
If this were all your mission here,

To draw, to sheathe a useless sword,
    To fool the crowd with glorious lies,
15   To cleave a creed in sects and cries,
To change the bearing of a word,

To shift an arbitrary power,
    To cramp the student at his desk,
    To make old bareness picturesque
20 And tuft with grass a feudal tower;

Why then my scorn might well descend
    On you and yours. I see in part
    That all, as in some piece of art,
Is toil cöoperant to an end.

CXXIX

Dear friend, far off, my lost desire,
    So far, so near in woe and weal;
    O loved the most, when most I feel
There is a lower and a higher;

5 Known and unknown; human, divine;
    Sweet human hand and lips and eye;
    Dear heavenly friend that canst not die,
Mine, mine, for ever, ever mine;

Strange friend, past, present, and to be;
10   Loved deeplier, darklier understood;
    Behold, I dream a dream of good,
And mingle all the world with thee.

CXXX

Thy voice is on the rolling air;
    I hear thee where the waters run;
    Thou standest in the rising sun,
And in the setting thou art fair.

5 What art thou then? I cannot guess;
    But though I seem in star and flower
    To feel thee some diffusive power,
I do not therefore love thee less:

My love involves the love before;
10   My love is vaster passion now;
    Though mixed with God and Nature thou,
I seem to love thee more and more.

Far off thou art, but ever nigh;
    I have thee still, and I rejoice;
15   I prosper, circled with thy voice;
I shall not lose thee though I die.

CXXXI

O living will that shalt endure[1]
    When all that seems shall suffer shock,
    Rise in the spiritual rock,
Flow through our deeds and make them pure,

5 That we may lift from out of dust
    A voice as unto him that hears,

---

[1] Tennyson's comment: "That which we know as Free-will in man."

A cry above the conquered years
To one that with us works, and trust,

With faith that comes of self-control,
10   The truths that never can be proved
Until we close with all we loved,
And all we flow from, soul in soul.

[EPILOGUE]

O true and tried, so well and long,
Demand not thou a marriage lay;
In that it is thy marriage day
Is music more than any song.

5   Nor have I felt so much of bliss
Since first he told me that he loved
A daughter of our house; nor proved
Since that dark day a day like this;

Though I since then have numbered o'er
10   Some thrice three years: they went and came,
Remade the blood and changed the frame,
And yet is love not less, but more;

No longer caring to embalm
In dying songs a dead regret,
15   But like a statue solid-set,
And moulded in colossal calm.

Regret is dead, but love is more
Than in the summers that are flown,
For I myself with these have grown
20   To something greater than before;

Which makes appear the songs I made
As echoes out of weaker times,
As half but idle brawling rhymes,
The sport of random sun and shade.

25   But where is she, the bridal flower,
That must be made a wife ere noon?
She enters, glowing like the moon
Of Eden on its bridal bower:

On me she bends her blissful eyes
30   And then on thee; they meet thy look
And brighten like the star that shook
Betwixt the palms of paradise.

O when her life was yet in bud,
He too foretold the perfect rose.
35   For thee she grew, for thee she grows
For ever, and as fair as good.

And thou art worthy; full of power;
As gentle; liberal-minded, great,
Consistent; wearing all that weight
40   Of learning lightly like a flower.

But now set out: the noon is near,
And I must give away the bride;
She fears not, or with thee beside
And me behind her, will not fear.

45   For I that danced her on my knee,
That watched her on her nurse's arm,
That shielded all her life from harm
At last must part with her to thee;

Now waiting to be made a wife,
50   Her feet, my darling, on the dead;
Their pensive tablets round her head,
And the most living words of life

Breathed in her ear. The ring is on,
The "wilt thou" answered, and again
55   The "wilt thou" asked, till out of twain
Her sweet "I will" has made you one.

Now sign your names, which shall be read,
   Mute symbols of a joyful morn,
   By village eyes as yet unborn;
60 The names are signed, and overhead

Begins the clash and clang that tells
   The joy to every wandering breeze;
   The blind wall rocks, and on the trees
The dead leaf trembles to the bells.

65 O happy hour, and happier hours
   Await them. Many a merry face
   Salutes them—maidens of the place,
That pelt us in the porch with flowers.

O happy hour, behold the bride
70   With him to whom her hand I gave.
   They leave the porch, they pass the grave
That has today its sunny side.

Today the grave is bright for me,
   For them the light of life increased,
75   Who stay to share the morning feast,
Who rest tonight beside the sea.

Let all my genial spirits advance
   To meet and greet a whiter sun;
   My drooping memory will not shun
80 The foaming grape of eastern France.[1]

It circles round, and fancy plays,
   And hearts are warmed and faces bloom,
   As drinking health to bride and groom
We wish them store of happy days.

85 Nor count me all to blame if I
   Conjecture of a stiller guest,
   Perchance, perchance, among the rest,
And, though in silence, wishing joy.

But they must go, the time draws on,
90   And those white-favoured horses wait;
   They rise, but linger; it is late;
Farewell, we kiss, and they are gone.

A shade falls on us like the dark
   From little cloudlets on the grass,
95   But sweeps away as out we pass
To range the woods, to roam the park,

Discussing how their courtship grew,
   And talk of others that are wed,
   And how she looked, and what he said,
100 And back we come at fall of dew.

Again the feast, the speech, the glee,
   The shade of passing thought, the wealth
   Of words and wit, the double health,
The crowning cup, the three-times-three,

105 And last the dance;—till I retire:
   Dumb is that tower which spake so loud,
   And high in heaven the streaming cloud,
And on the downs a rising fire:

And rise, O moon, from yonder down,
110   Till over down and over dale
   All night the shining vapour sail
And pass the silent-lighted town,

The white-faced halls, the glancing rills,
   And catch at every mountain head,
115   And o'er the friths[2] that branch and spread
Their sleeping silver through the hills;

And touch with shade the bridal doors,
   With tender gloom the roof, the wall;
   And breaking let the splendour fall
120 To spangle all the happy shores

---

[1] champagne.

[2] narrow sea inlets.

By which they rest, and ocean sounds,
    And, star and system rolling past,
    A soul shall draw from out the vast
And strike his being into bounds,

25 And, moved through life of lower phase,
    Result in man, be born and think,
    And act and love, a closer link
Betwixt us and the crowning race

30 Of those that, eye to eye, shall look
    On knowledge; under whose command
    Is Earth and Earth's, and in their hand
Is Nature like an open book;

35 No longer half-akin to brute,
    For all we thought and loved and did,
    And hoped, and suffered, is but seed
Of what in them is flower and fruit;

Whereof the man, that with me trod
    This planet, was a noble type
    Appearing ere the times were ripe,
40 That friend of mine who lives in God,

That God, which ever lives and loves,
    One God, one law, one element,
    And one far-off divine event,
To which the whole creation moves.
—1850

The Charge of the Light Brigade [1]

I

Half a league, half a league,
    Half a league onward,
All in the valley of Death
    Rode the six hundred.

5 "Forward, the Light Brigade!
    Charge for the guns!" he said:
Into the valley of Death
    Rode the six hundred.

II

"Forward, the Light Brigade!"
10 Was there a man dismayed?
Not though the soldier knew
    Some one had blundered:
Their's not to make reply,
Their's not to reason why,
15 Their's but to do and die:
Into the valley of Death
    Rode the six hundred.

III

Cannon to right of them,
Cannon to left of them,
20 Cannon in front of them
    Volleyed and thundered;
Stormed at with shot and shell,
Boldly they rode and well,
Into the jaws of Death,
25 Into the mouth of Hell
    Rode the six hundred.

IV

Flashed all their sabres bare,
Flashed as they turned in air
Sabring the gunners there,
30 Charging an army, while
    All the world wondered:
Plunged in the battery-smoke
Right through the line they broke;
Cossack and Russian
35 Reeled from the sabre-stroke
    Shattered and sundered.
Then they rode back, but not
    Not the six hundred.

---

[1] in the Crimean war. The charge took place on 25 October 1854 and Tennyson published the poem in *The Examiner* on 9 December 1854.

V

40 Cannon to right of them,
Cannon to left of them,
Cannon behind them
   Volleyed and thundered;
Stormed at with shot and shell,
While horse and hero fell,
45 They that had fought so well
Came through the jaws of Death,
Back from the mouth of Hell,
All that was left of them,
   Left of six hundred.

VI

50 When can their glory fade?
O the wild charge they made!
   All the world wondered.
Honour the charge they made!
Honour the Light Brigade,
55   Noble six hundred!
   —1854

Maud [1]

A MONODRAMA

PART I

I

I

I hate the dreadful hollow behind the little wood,
Its lips in the field above are dabbled with blood-

---

[1] Tennyson comments on the poem as follows: "This poem of *Maud or the Madness* [A.T.'s original title] is a little *Hamlet*, the history of a morbid, poetic soul, under the blighting influence of a recklessly speculative age. He is the heir of madness, an egoist with the makings of a cynic, raised to a pure and holy love which elevates his whole nature, passing from the height of triumph to the lowest depth of misery, driven into madness by the loss of her whom he has loved, and, when he has at length passed through the fiery furnace, and has recovered his reason, giving himself up to work for the good of mankind through the unselfishness born of a great passion. The peculiarity of this poem is that different phases of passion in one person take the place of different characters."

---

red heath,[2]
The red-ribbed ledges drip with a silent horror of blood,
And Echo there, whatever is asked her, answers "Death."

II

5 For there in the ghastly pit long since a body was found,
His who had given me life—O father! O God! was it well?—
Mangled, and flattened, and crushed, and dinted into the ground:
There yet lies the rock that fell with him when he fell.

III

Did he fling himself down? who knows? for a vast speculation had failed,
10 And ever he muttered and maddened, and ever wanned with despair,
And out he walked when the wind like a broken worldling wailed,
And the flying gold of the ruined woodlands drove through the air.

IV

I remember the time, for the roots of my hair were stirred
By a shuffled step, by a dead weight trailed, by a whispered fright,
15 And my pulses closed their gates with a shock on my heart as I heard
The shrill-edged shriek of a mother divide the shuddering night.

---

[2] Hallam Tennyson notes, in his *Memoir*, that "My father would say that in calling heath 'blood'-red the hero showed his extravagant fancy, which is already on the road to madness."

V

Villainy somewhere! whose? One says, we are
   villains all.
Not he: his honest fame should at least by me be
   maintained:
But that old man, now lord of the broad estate and
   the Hall,
20 Dropt off gorged from a scheme that had left us
   flaccid and drained.

VI

Why do they prate of the blessings of Peace? we
   have made them a curse,
Pickpockets, each hand lusting for all that is not its
   own;
And lust of gain, in the spirit of Cain, is it better or
   worse
Than the heart of the citizen hissing in war on his
   own hearthstone?

VII

25 But these are the days of advance, the words of the
   men of mind,
When who but a fool would have faith in a
   tradesman's ware or his word?
Is it peace or war? Civil war, as I think, and that of
   a kind
The viler, as underhand, not openly bearing the
   sword.

VIII

Sooner or later I too may passively take the print
30 Of the golden age—why not? I have neither hope
   nor trust;
May make my heart as a millstone, set my face as a
   flint,
Cheat and be cheated, and die: who knows? we are
   ashes and dust.

IX

Peace sitting under her olive, and slurring the days
   gone by,
When the poor are hovelled and hustled together,
   each sex, like swine,
35 When only the ledger lives, and when only not all
   men lie;
Peace in her vineyard—yes!—but a company forges
   the wine.

X

And the vitriol madness flushes up in the ruffian's
   head,
Till the filthy by-lane rings to the yell of the
   trampled wife,
And chalk and alum and plaster are sold to the
   poor for bread,[1]
40 And the spirit of murder works in the very means
   of life,

XI

And Sleep must lie down armed, for the villainous
   centre-bits[2]
Grind on the wakeful ear in the hush of the
   moonless nights,
While another is cheating the sick of a few last
   gasps, as he sits
To pestle a poisoned poison behind his crimson
   lights.

XII

45 When a Mammonite[3] mother kills her babe for a
   burial fee,
And Timour[4]-Mammon grins on a pile of
   children's bones,

---

[1] a notorious scandal concerning the adulteration of food.

[2] burglar's tools.

[3] a worshipper of Mammon, god of wealth.

[4] Tamerlane, the Mongol conqueror, guilty of atrocities against children.

Is it peace or war? better, war! loud war by land and
    by sea,
War with a thousand battles, and shaking a
    hundred thrones.

XIII

For I trust if an enemy's fleet came yonder round
    by the hill,
50 And the rushing battle-bolt sang from the three-
    decker out of the foam,
That the smooth-faced snubnosed rogue would
    leap from his counter and till,
And strike, if he could, were it but with his
    cheating yardwand, home.—

XIV

What! am I raging alone as my father raged in his
    mood?
Must *I* too creep to the hollow and dash myself
    down and die
55 Rather than hold by the law that I made,
    nevermore to brood
On a horror of shattered limbs and a wretched
    swindler's lie?

XV

Would there be sorrow for *me*? there was *love* in the
    passionate shriek,
Love for the silent thing that had made false haste
    to the grave—
Wrapt in a cloak, as I saw him, and thought he
    would rise and speak
60 And rave at the lie and the liar, ah God, as he used
    to rave.

XVI

I am sick of the Hall and the hill, I am sick of the
    moor and the main.
Why should I stay? can a sweeter chance ever come
    to me here?

O, having the nerves of motion as well as the
    nerves of pain,
Were it not wise if I fled from the place and the pit
    and the fear?

XVII

65 Workmen up at the Hall!—they are coming back
    from abroad;
The dark old place will be gilt by the touch of a
    millionaire:
I have heard, I know not whence, of the singular
    beauty of Maud;
I played with the girl when a child; she promised
    then to be fair.

XVIII

Maud with her venturous climbings and tumbles
    and childish escapes,
70 Maud the delight of the village, the ringing joy of
    the Hall,
Maud with her sweet purse-mouth when my father
    dangled the grapes,
Maud the beloved of my mother, the moon-faced
    darling of all,—

XIX

What is she now? My dreams are bad. She may
    bring me a curse.
No, there is fatter game on the moor; she will let
    me alone.
75 Thanks, for the fiend best knows whether woman
    or man be the worse.
I will bury myself in myself, and the Devil may
    pipe to his own.

II

Long have I sighed for a calm: God grant I may
    find it at last!
It will never be broken by Maud, she has neither
    savour nor salt,

But a cold and clear-cut face, as I found when her
    carriage past,
80 Perfectly beautiful: let it be granted her: where is
    the fault?
All that I saw (for her eyes were downcast, not to
    be seen)
Faultily faultless, icily regular, splendidly null,
Dead perfection, no more; nothing more, if it had
    not been
For a chance of travel, a paleness, an hour's defect
    of the rose,
85 Or an underlip, you may call it a little too ripe, too
    full,
Or the least little delicate aquiline curve in a
    sensitive nose,
From which I escaped heart-free, with the least
    little touch of spleen.

III

Cold and clear-cut face, why come you so cruelly
    meek,
Breaking a slumber in which all spleenful folly was
    drowned,
90 Pale with the golden beam of an eyelash dead on
    the cheek,
Passionless, pale, cold face, star-sweet on a gloom
    profound;
Womanlike, taking revenge too deep for a transient
    wrong
Done but in thought to your beauty, and ever as
    pale as before
Growing and fading and growing upon me without
    a sound,
95 Luminous, gemlike, ghostlike, deathlike, half the
    night long
Growing and fading and growing, till I could bear
    it no more,
But arose, and all by myself in my own dark garden
    ground,
Listening now to the tide in its broad-flung
    shipwrecking roar,

Now to the scream of a maddened beach dragged
    down by the wave,
100 Walked in a wintry wind by a ghastly glimmer, and
    found
The shining daffodil dead, and Orion low in his
    grave.

IV

I

A million emeralds break from the ruby-budded
    lime
In the little grove where I sit—ah, wherefore
    cannot I be
Like things of the season gay, like the bountiful
    season bland,
105 When the far-off sail is blown by the breeze of a
    softer clime,
Half-lost in the liquid azure bloom of a crescent of
    sea,
The silent sapphire-spangled marriage ring of the
    land?

II

Below me, there, is the village, and looks how quiet
    and small!
And yet bubbles o'er like a city, with gossip,
    scandal, and spite;
110 And Jack on his ale-house bench has as many lies as
    a Czar;[1]
And here on the landward side, by a red rock,
    glimmers the Hall;
And up in the high Hall-garden I see her pass like a
    light;
But sorrow seize me if ever that light be my leading
    star!

III

When have I bowed to her father, the wrinkled
    head of the race?

---

[1] Nicholas I and the Crimean war.

115 I met her today with her brother, but not to her
brother I bowed:
I bowed to his lady-sister as she rode by on the
moor;
But the fire of a foolish pride flashed over her
beautiful face.
O child, you wrong your beauty, believe it, in
being so proud;
Your father has wealth well-gotten, and I am
nameless and poor.

IV

120 I keep but a man and a maid, ever ready to slander
and steal;
I know it, and smile a hard-set smile, like a stoic, or
like
A wiser epicurean, and let the world have its way:
For nature is one with rapine, a harm no preacher
can heal;
The Mayfly is torn by the swallow, the sparrow
speared by the shrike,[1]
125 And the whole little wood where I sit is a world of
plunder and prey.

V

We are puppets, Man in his pride, and Beauty fair
in her flower;
Do we move ourselves, or are moved by an unseen
hand at a game
That pushes us off from the board, and others ever
succeed?
Ah yet, we cannot be kind to each other here for an
hour;
130 We whisper, and hint, and chuckle, and grin at a
brother's shame;
However we brave it out, we men are a little breed.

VI

A monstrous eft[2] was of old the Lord and Master of
Earth,
For him did his high sun flame, and his river
billowing ran,
And he felt himself in his force to be Nature's
crowning race.
135 As nine months go to the shaping an infant ripe for
his birth,
So many a million of ages have gone to the making
of man:
He now is first, but is he the last? is he not too
base?

VII

The man of science himself is fonder of glory, and
vain,
An eye well-practised in nature, a spirit bounded
and poor;
140 The passionate heart of the poet is whirled into
folly and vice.
I would not marvel at either, but keep a temperate
brain;
For not to desire or admire, if a man could learn it,
were more
Than to walk all day like the sultan of old in a
garden of spice.

VIII

For the drift of the Maker is dark, an Isis[3] hid by
the veil.
145 Who knows the ways of the world, how God will
bring them about?
Our planet is one, the suns are many, the world is
wide.
Shall I weep if a Poland fall? shall I shriek if a
Hungary fail?

---

[1] small predatory bird.

[2] "The great old lizards of geology." (Tennyson's note.)

[3] "The great Goddess of the Egyptians." (Tennyson's note.)

Or an infant civilisation be ruled with rod or with
    knout?
I have not made the world, and He that made it
    will guide.

IX

50 Be mine a philosopher's life in the quiet woodland
    ways,
Where if I cannot be gay let a passionless peace be
    my lot,
Far-off from the clamour of liars belied in the
    hubbub of lies;
From the long-necked geese of the world that are
    ever hissing dispraise
Because their natures are little, and, whether he
    heed it or not,
55 Where each man walks with his head in a cloud of
    poisonous flies.

X

And most of all would I flee from the cruel
    madness of love,
The honey of poison-flowers and all the
    measureless ill.
Ah Maud, you milkwhite fawn, you are all unmeet
    for a wife.
Your mother is mute in her grave as her image in
    marble above;
60 Your father is ever in London, you wander about at
    your will;
You have but fed on the roses and lain in the lilies
    of life.

V

I

A voice by the cedar tree
In the meadow under the Hall!
She is singing an air that is known to me,
5 A passionate ballad gallant and gay,
A martial song like a trumpet's call!
Singing alone in the morning of life,

In the happy morning of life and of May,
Singing of men that in battle array,
170 Ready in heart and ready in hand,
March with banner and bugle and fife
To the death, for their native land.

II

Maud with her exquisite face,
And wild voice pealing up to the sunny sky,
175 And feet like sunny gems on an English green,
Maud in the light of her youth and her grace,
Singing of Death, and of Honour that cannot die,
Till I well could weep for a time so sordid and mean,
And myself so languid and base.

III

180 Silence, beautiful voice!
Be still, for you only trouble the mind
With a joy in which I cannot rejoice,
A glory I shall not find.
Still! I will hear you no more,
185 For your sweetness hardly leaves me a choice
But to move to the meadow and fall before
Her feet on the meadow grass, and adore,
Not her, who is neither courtly nor kind,
Not her, not her, but a voice.

VI

I

190 Morning arises stormy and pale,
No sun, but a wannish glare
In fold upon fold of hueless cloud,
And the budded peaks of the wood are bowed
Caught and cuffed by the gale:
195 I had fancied it would be fair.

II

Whom but Maud should I meet
Last night, when the sunset burned
On the blossomed gable-ends
At the head of the village street,

200 Whom but Maud should I meet?
And she touched my hand with a smile so sweet,
She made me divine amends
For a courtesy not returned.

III

And thus a delicate spark
205 Of glowing and growing light
Through the livelong hours of the dark
Kept itself warm in the heart of my dreams,
Ready to burst in a coloured flame;
Till at last when the morning came
210 In a cloud, it faded, and seems
But an ashen-gray delight.

IV

What if with her sunny hair
And smile as sunny as cold,
She meant to weave me a snare
215 Of some coquettish deceit,
Cleopatra-like as of old
To entangle me when we met,
To have her lion roll in a silken net
And fawn at a victor's feet.

V

220 Ah, what shall I be at fifty
Should Nature keep me alive,
If I find the world so bitter
When I am but twenty-five?
Yet, if she were not a cheat,
225 If Maud were all that she seemed,
And her smile were all that I dreamed,
Then the world were not so bitter
But a smile could make it sweet.

VI

What if though her eye seemed full
230 Of a kind intent to me,
What if that dandy-despot, he,
That jewelled mass of millinery,

That oiled and curled Assyrian Bull[1]
Smelling of musk and of insolence,
235 Her brother, from whom I keep aloof,
Who wants the finer politic sense
To mask, though but in his own behoof,
With a glassy smile his brutal scorn—
What if he had told her yestermorn
240 How prettily for his own sweet sake
A face of tenderness might be feigned,
And a moist mirage in desert eyes,
That so, when the rotten hustings shake
In another month to his brazen lies,
245 A wretched vote may be gained.

VII

For a raven ever croaks, at my side,
Keep watch and ward, keep watch and ward,
Or thou wilt prove their tool.
Yea, too, myself from myself I guard,
250 For often a man's own angry pride
Is cap and bells for a fool.

VIII

Perhaps the smile and tender tone
Came out of her pitying womanhood,
For am I not, am I not, here alone
255 So many a summer since she died,
My mother, who was so gentle and good?
Living alone in an empty house,
Here half-hid in the gleaming wood,
Where I hear the dead at midday moan,
260 And the shrieking rush of the wainscot mouse,
And my own sad name in corners cried,
When the shiver of dancing leaves is thrown
About its echoing chambers wide,
Till a morbid hate and horror have grown
265 Of a world in which I have hardly mixt,

---

[1] "With hair curled like that of the bulls on Assyrian sculpture."
(Tennyson's note.)

And a morbid eating lichen fixt
On a heart half-turned to stone.

IX

O heart of stone, are you flesh, and caught
By that you swore to withstand?
For what was it else within me wrought
But, I fear, the new strong wine of love,
That made my tongue so stammer and trip
When I saw the treasured splendour, her hand,
Come sliding out of her sacred glove,
And the sunlight broke from her lip?

X

I have played with her when a child;
She remembers it now we meet.
Ah well, well, well I *may* be beguiled
By some coquettish deceit.
Yet, if she were not a cheat,
If Maud were all that she seemed,
And her smile had all that I dreamed,
Then the world were not so bitter
But a smile could make it sweet.

VII

I

Did I hear it half in a doze
    Long since, I know not where?
Did I dream it an hour ago,
    When asleep in this arm-chair?

II

Men were drinking together,
    Drinking and talking of me;
"Well, if it prove a girl, the boy
    Will have plenty: so let it be."

III

Is it an echo of something
    Read with a boy's delight,

295 Viziers nodding together
    In some Arabian night?

IV

Strange, that I hear two men,
    Somewhere, talking of me;
"Well, if it prove a girl, my boy
300   Will have plenty: so let it be."

VIII

She came to the village church,
And sat by a pillar alone;
An angel watching an urn
Wept over her, carved in stone;
305 And once, but once, she lifted her eyes,
And suddenly, sweetly, strangely blushed
To find they were met by my own;
And suddenly, sweetly, my heart beat stronger
And thicker, until I heard no longer
310 The snowy-banded, dilettante,
Delicate-handed priest intone;
And thought, is it pride, and mused and sighed
"No surely, now it cannot be pride."

IX

I was walking a mile,
315 More than a mile from the shore,
The sun looked out with a smile
Betwixt the cloud and the moor,
And riding at set of day
Over the dark moor land,
320 Rapidly riding far away,
She waved to me with her hand.
There were two at her side,
Something flashed in the sun,
Down by the hill I saw them ride,
325 In a moment they were gone:
Like a sudden spark
Struck vainly in the night,
Then returns the dark
With no more hope of light.

X

I

330 Sick, am I sick of a jealous dread?
Was not one of the two at her side
This new-made lord, whose splendour plucks
The slavish hat from the villager's head?
Whose old grandfather has lately died,
335 Gone to a blacker pit, for whom
Grimy nakedness dragging his trucks
And laying his trams in a poisoned gloom
Wrought, till he crept from a gutted mine
Master of half a servile shire,
340 And left his coal all turned into gold
To a grandson, first of his noble line,
Rich in the grace all women desire,
Strong in the power that all men adore,
And simper and set their voices lower,
345 And soften as if to a girl, and hold
Awe-stricken breaths at a work divine,
Seeing his gewgaw castle shine,
New as his title, built last year,
There amid perky larches and pine,
350 And over the sullen-purple moor
(Look at it) pricking a cockney ear.

II

What, has he found my jewel out?
For one of the two that rode at her side
Bound for the Hall, I am sure was he:
355 Bound for the Hall, and I think for a bride.
Blithe would her brother's acceptance be.
Maud could be gracious too, no doubt
To a lord, a captain, a padded shape,
A bought commission, a waxen face,
360 A rabbit mouth that is ever agape—
Bought? what is it he cannot buy?
And therefore splenetic, personal, base,
A wounded thing with a rancorous cry,
At war with myself and a wretched race,
365 Sick, sick to the heart of life, am I.

III

Last week came one to the county town,
To preach our poor little army down,
And play the game of the despot kings,
Though the state has done it and thrice as well:
370 This broad-brimmed hawker of holy things,
Whose ear is crammed with his cotton, and rings
Even in dreams to the chink of his pence,
This huckster put down war! can he tell
Whether war be a cause or a consequence?
375 Put down the passions that make earth Hell!
Down with ambition, avarice, pride,
Jealousy, down! cut off from the mind
The bitter springs of anger and fear;
Down too, down at your own fireside,
380 With the evil tongue and the evil ear,
For each is at war with mankind.

IV

I wish I could hear again
The chivalrous battle-song
That she warbled alone in her joy!
385 I might persuade myself then
She would not do herself this great wrong,
To take a wanton dissolute boy
For a man and leader of men.

V

Ah God, for a man with heart, head, hand,
390 Like some of the simple great ones gone
For ever and ever by,
One still strong man in a blatant land,
Whatever they call him, what care I,
Aristocrat, democrat, autocrat—one
395 Who can rule and dare not lie.

VI

And ah for a man to arise in me,
That the man I am may cease to be!

XI

I

O let the solid ground
    Not fail beneath my feet
400 Before my life has found
    What some have found so sweet;
Then let come what come may,
What matter if I go mad,
I shall have had my day.

II

405 Let the sweet heavens endure,
    Not close and darken above me
Before I am quite quite sure
    That there is one to love me;
Then let come what come may
410 To a life that has been so sad,
I shall have had my day.

XII

I

Birds in the high Hall-garden
    When twilight was falling,
Maud, Maud, Maud, Maud,
415   They were crying and calling.

II

Where was Maud? in our wood;
    And I, who else, was with her,
Gathering woodland lilies,
    Myriads blow together.

III

420 Birds in our wood sang
    Ringing through the valleys,
Maud is here, here, here
    In among the lilies.

IV

I kissed her slender hand,
425   She took the kiss sedately;

Maud is not seventeen,
    But she is tall and stately.

V

I to cry out on pride
    Who have won her favour!
430 O Maud were sure of Heaven
    If lowliness could save her.

VI

I know the way she went
    Home with her maiden posy,
For her feet have touched the meadows
435   And left the daisies rosy.[1]

VII

Birds in the high Hall-garden
    Were crying and calling to her,
Where is Maud, Maud, Maud?
    One is come to woo her.

VIII

440 Look, a horse at the door,
    And little King Charley[2] snarling,
Go back, my lord, across the moor,
    You are not her darling.

XIII

I

Scorned, to be scorned by one that I scorn,
445 Is that a matter to make me fret?
That a calamity hard to be borne?
Well, he may live to hate me yet.
Fool that I am to be vext with his pride!
I past him, I was crossing his lands;
450 He stood on the path a little aside;
His face, as I grant, in spite of spite,

---

[1] Tennyson's comment: "Because if you tread on the daisy, it turns up a rosy underside."

[2] a spaniel.

Has a broad-blown comeliness, red and white,
And six feet two, as I think, he stands;
But his essences turned the live air sick,
455 And barbarous opulence jewel-thick
Sunned itself on his breast and his hands.

II

Who shall call me ungentle, unfair,
I longed so heartily then and there
To give him the grasp of fellowship;
460 But while I past he was humming an air,
Stopt, and then with a riding-whip
Leisurely tapping a glossy boot,
And curving a contumelious lip,
Gorgonised[1] me from head to foot
465 With a stony British stare.

III

Why sits he here in his father's chair?
That old man never comes to his place:
Shall I believe him ashamed to be seen?
For only once, in the village street,
470 Last year, I caught a glimpse of his face,
A gray old wolf and a lean.
Scarcely, now, would I call him a cheat;
For then, perhaps, as a child of deceit,
She might by a true descent be untrue;
475 And Maud is as true as Maud is sweet:
Though I fancy her sweetness only due
To the sweeter blood by the other side;
Her mother has been a thing complete,
However she came to be so allied.
480 And fair without, faithful within,
Maud to him is nothing akin:
Some peculiar mystic grace
Made her only the child of her mother,
And heaped the whole inherited sin
485 On the huge scapegoat of the race,
All, all upon the brother.

IV

Peace, angry spirit, and let him be!
Has not his sister smiled on me?

XIV

I

Maud has a garden of roses
490 And lilies fair on a lawn;
There she walks in her state
And tends upon bed and bower,
And thither I climbed at dawn
And stood by her garden-gate;
495 A lion ramps at the top,
He is claspt by a passion-flower.

II

Maud's own little oak-room
(Which Maud, like a precious stone
Set in the heart of the carven gloom,
500 Lights with herself, when alone
She sits by her music and books
And her brother lingers late
With a roystering company) looks
Upon Maud's own garden-gate:
505 And I thought as I stood, if a hand, as white
As ocean-foam in the moon, were laid
On the hasp of the window, and my Delight
Had a sudden desire, like a glorious ghost, to glide,
Like a beam of the seventh Heaven, down to my
     side,
510 There were but a step to be made.

III

The fancy flattered my mind,
And again seemed overbold;
Now I thought that she cared for me,
Now I thought she was kind
515 Only because she was cold.

---

[1] turned the beholder to stone, a power of the mythical Gorgons.

IV

I heard no sound where I stood
But the rivulet on from the lawn
Running down to my own dark wood;
Or the voice of the long sea-wave as it swelled
20 Now and then in the dim-gray dawn;
But I looked, and round, all round the house I
    beheld
The death-white curtains drawn;
Felt a horror over me creep,
Prickle my skin and catch my breath,
25 Knew that the death-white curtain meant but sleep,
Yet I shuddered and thought like a fool of the sleep
    of death.

XV

So dark a mind within me dwells,
    And I make myself such evil cheer,
That if *I* be dear to some one else,
        Then some one else may have much to fear;
But if *I* be dear to some one else,
    Then I should be to myself more dear.
Shall I not take care of all that I think,
Yea even of wretched meat and drink,
  If I be dear,
  If I be dear to some one else.

XVI

I

This lump of earth has left his estate
The lighter by the loss of his weight;
And so that he find what he went to seek,
And fulsome Pleasure clog him, and drown
His heart in the gross mud-honey of town,
He may stay for a year who has gone for a week:
But this is the day when I must speak,
And I see my Oread[1] coming down,
O this is the day!
O beautiful creature, what am I

That I dare to look her way;
Think I may hold dominion sweet,
Lord of the pulse that is lord of her breast,
550 And dream of her beauty with tender dread,
From the delicate Arab arch of her feet[2]
To the grace that, bright and light as the crest
Of a peacock, sits on her shining head,
And she knows it not: O, if she knew it,
555 To know her beauty might half undo it.
I know it the one bright thing to save
My yet young life in the wilds of Time,
Perhaps from madness, perhaps from crime,
Perhaps from a selfish grave.

II

560 What, if she be fastened to this fool lord,
Dare I bid her abide by her word?
Should I love her so well if she
Had given her word to a thing so low?
Shall I love her as well if she
565 Can break her word were it even for me?
I trust that it is not so.

III

Catch not my breath, O clamorous heart,
Let not my tongue be a thrall to my eye,
For I must tell her before we part,
570 I must tell her, or die.

XVII

Go not, happy day,
    From the shining fields,
Go not, happy day,
    Till the maiden yields.
575 Rosy is the West,
    Rosy is the South,
Roses are her cheeks,
    And a rose her mouth.
When the happy Yes

---

[1] mountain nymph.

[2] curved like the neck of an Arabian horse.

580   Falters from her lips,
       Pass and blush the news
          Over glowing ships;
       Over blowing seas,
          Over seas at rest,
585   Pass the happy news,
          Blush it through the West;
       Till the red man dance
          By his red cedar-tree,
       And the red man's babe
590   Leap, beyond the sea.
       Blush from West to East,
          Blush from East to West,
       Till the West is East,
          Blush it through the West.
595   Rosy is the West,
          Rosy is the South,
       Roses are her cheeks,
          And a rose her mouth.

XVIII
I

I have led her home, my love, my only friend.
600 There is none like her, none.
And never yet so warmly ran my blood
   And sweetly, on and on
Calming itself to the long-wished-for end,
Full to the banks, close on the promised good.

II

605 None like her, none.
Just now the dry-tongued laurels' pattering talk
Seemed her light foot along the garden walk,
And shook my heart to think she comes once more;
But even then I heard her close the door,
610 The gates of Heaven are closed, and she is gone.

III

There is none like her, none.
Nor will be when our summers have decreased.
O, art thou sighing for Lebanon

In the long breeze that streams to thy delicious
    East,
615 Sighing for Lebanon,
Dark cedar, though thy limbs have here increased,
Upon a pastoral slope as fair,
And looking to the South, and fed
With honeyed rain and delicate air,
620 And haunted by the starry head
Of her whose gentle will has changed my fate,
And made my life a perfumed altar-flame;
And over whom thy darkness must have spread
With such delight as theirs of old, thy great
625 Forefathers of the thornless garden, there
Shadowing the snow-limbed Eve from whom she
    came.

IV

Here will I lie, while these long branches sway,
And you fair stars that crown a happy day
Go in and out as if at merry play,
630 Who am no more so all forlorn,
As when it seemed far better to be born
To labour and the mattock-hardened hand,
Than nursed at ease and brought to understand
A sad astrology,[1] the boundless plan
635 That makes you tyrants in your iron skies,
Innumerable, pitiless, passionless eyes,
Cold fires, yet with power to burn and brand
His nothingness into man.

V

But now shine on, and what care I,
640 Who in this stormy gulf have found a pearl
The countercharm of space and hollow sky,
And do accept my madness, and would die
To save from some slight shame one simple girl.

---

[1] Tennyson's comment: "The *sad astrology* is modern astronomy, for of old astrology was thought to sympathise with and rule man's fate. The stars are 'cold fires,' for though they emit light of the highest intensity, no perceptible warmth reaches us. His newer astrology describes them [l. 677] as 'soft splendours.'"

VI

645 Would die; for sullen-seeming Death may give
More life to Love than is or ever was
In our low world, where yet 'tis sweet to live.
Let no one ask me how it came to pass;
It seems that I am happy, that to me
650 A livelier emerald twinkles in the grass,
A purer sapphire melts into the sea.

VII

Not die; but live a life of truest breath,[1]
And teach true life to fight with mortal wrongs.
O, why should Love, like men in drinking-songs,
Spice his fair banquet with the dust of death?
655 Make answer, Maud my bliss,
Maud made my Maud by that long loving kiss,
Life of my life, wilt thou not answer this?
"The dusky strand of Death inwoven here
With dear Love's tie, makes Love himself more
        dear."

VIII

660 Is that enchanted moan only the swell
Of the long waves that roll in yonder bay?
And hark the clock within, the silver knell
Of twelve sweet hours that past in bridal white,
And died to live, long as my pulses play;
665 But now by this my love has closed her sight
And given false death her hand, and stolen away
To dreamful wastes where footless fancies dwell
Among the fragments of the golden day.
May nothing there her maiden grace affright!
670 Dear heart, I feel with thee the drowsy spell.
My bride to be, my evermore delight,
My own heart's heart, my ownest own, farewell;
It is but for a little space I go:
And ye meanwhile far over moor and fell
675 Beat to the noiseless music of the night!
Has our whole earth gone nearer to the glow

---

[1] Tennyson's comment: "This is the central idea—the holy power of Love."

Of your soft splendours that you look so bright?
I have climbed nearer out of lonely Hell.
Beat, happy stars, timing with things below,
680 Beat with my heart more blest than heart can tell,
Blest, but for some dark undercurrent woe
That seems to draw—but it shall not be so:
Let all be well, be well.

XIX

I

Her brother is coming back tonight,
685 Breaking up my dream of delight.

II

My dream? do I dream of bliss?
I have walked awake with Truth.
O when did a morning shine
So rich in atonement as this
690 For my dark-dawning youth,
Darkened watching a mother decline
And that dead man at her heart and mine:
For who was left to watch her but I?
Yet so did I let my freshness die.

III

695 I trust that I did not talk
To gentle Maud in our walk
(For often in lonely wanderings
I have cursed him even to lifeless things)
But I trust that I did not talk,
700 Not touch on her father's sin:
I am sure I did but speak
Of my mother's faded cheek
When it slowly grew so thin,
That I felt she was slowly dying
705 Vext with lawyers and harassed with debt:
For how often I caught her with eyes all wet,
Shaking her head at her son and sighing
A world of trouble within!

IV

And Maud too, Maud was moved
710　To speak of the mother she loved
As one scarce less forlorn,
Dying abroad and it seems apart
From him who had ceased to share her heart,
And ever mourning over the feud,
715　The household Fury sprinkled with blood
By which our houses are torn:
How strange was what she said,
When only Maud and the brother
Hung over her dying bed—
720　That Maud's dark father and mine
Had bound us one to the other,
Betrothed us over their wine,
On the day when Maud was born;
Sealed her mine from her first sweet breath.
725　Mine, mine by a right, from birth till death.
Mine, mine—our fathers have sworn.

V

But the true blood spilt had in it a heat
To dissolve the precious seal on a bond,
That, if left uncancelled, had been so sweet;
730　And none of us thought of a something beyond,
A desire that awoke in the heart of the child,
As it were a duty done to the tomb,
To be friends for her sake, to be reconciled;
And I was cursing them and my doom,
735　And letting a dangerous thought run wild
While often abroad in the fragrant gloom
Of foreign churches—I see her there,
Bright English lily, breathing a prayer
To be friends, to be reconciled!

VI

740　But then what a flint is he!
Abroad, at Florence, at Rome,
I find whenever she touched on me
This brother had laughed her down,
And at last, when each came home,

745　He had darkened into a frown,
Chid her, and forbid her to speak
To me, her friend of the years before;
And this was what had reddened her cheek
When I bowed to her on the moor.

VII

750　Yet Maud, although not blind
To the faults of his heart and mind,
I see she cannot but love him,
And says he is rough but kind,
And wishes me to approve him,
755　And tells me, when she lay
Sick once, with a fear of worse,
That he left his wine and horses and play,
Sat with her, read to her, night and day,
And tended her like a nurse.

VIII

760　Kind? but the deathbed desire
Spurned by this heir of the liar—
Rough by kind? yet I know
He has plotted against me in this,
That he plots against me still.
765　Kind to Maud? that were not amiss.
Well, rough but kind; why let it be so:
For shall not Maud have her will?

IX

For, Maud, so tender and true,
As long as my life endures
770　I feel I shall owe you a debt,
That I never can hope to pay;
And if ever I should forget
That I owe this debt to you
And for your sweet sake to yours;
775　O then, what then shall I say?—
If ever I *should* forget,
May God make me more wretched
Than ever I have been yet!

X

So now I have sworn to bury
780 All this dead body. of hate,
I feel so free and so clear
By the loss of that dead weight,
That I should grow light-headed, I fear,
Fantastically merry;
785 But that her brother comes, like a blight
On my fresh hope, to the Hall tonight.

XX

I

Strange, that I felt so gay,
Strange, that *I* tried today
To beguile her melancholy;
790 The Sultan, as we name him,—
She did not wish to blame him—
But he vext her and perplext her
With his worldly talk and folly:
Was it gentle to reprove her
795 For stealing out of view
From a little lazy lover
Who but claims her as his due?
Or for chilling his caresses
By the coldness of her manners,
800 Nay, the plainness of her dresses?
Now I know her but in two,
Nor can pronounce upon it
If one should ask me whether
The habit, hat, and feather,
05 Or the frock and gipsy bonnet
Be the neater and completer;
For nothing can be sweeter
Than maiden Maud in either.

II

But tomorrow, if we live,
10 Our ponderous squire will give
A grand political dinner
To half the squirelings near;
And Maud will wear her jewels,
And the bird of prey will hover,
815 And the titmouse hope to win her
With his chirrup at her ear.

III

A grand political dinner
To the men of many acres,
A gathering of the Tory,
820 A dinner and then a dance
For the maids and marriage-makers,
And every eye but mine will glance
At Maud in all her glory.

IV

For I am not invited,
825 But, with the Sultan's pardon,
I am all as well delighted,
For I know her own rose-garden,
And mean to linger in it
Till the dancing will be over;
830 And then, oh then, come out to me
For a minute, but for a minute,
Come out to your own true lover,
That your true lover may see
Your glory also, and render
835 All homage to his own darling,
Queen Maud in all her splendour.

XXI

Rivulet crossing my ground,
And bringing me down from the Hall
This garden-rose that I found,
840 Forgetful of Maud and me,
And lost in trouble and moving round
Here at the head of a tinkling fall,
And trying to pass to the sea;
O Rivulet, born at the Hall,
845 My Maud has sent it by thee
(If I read her sweet will right)
On a blushing mission to me,

Saying in odour and colour, "Ah, be
    Among the roses tonight."

XXII

I

850 Come into the garden, Maud,
    For the black bat, night, has flown,
Come into the garden, Maud,
    I am here at the gate alone;
And the woodbine spices are wafted abroad,
855   And the musk of the rose is blown.

II

For a breeze of morning moves,
    And the planet of Love is on high,
Beginning to faint in the light that she loves
    On a bed of daffodil sky,
860 To faint in the light of the sun she loves,
    To faint in his light, and to die.

III

All night have the roses heard
    The flute, violin, bassoon;
All night has the casement jessamine stirred
865   To the dancers dancing in tune;
Till a silence fell with the waking bird,
    And a hush with the setting moon.

IV

I said to the lily, "There is but one
    With whom she has heart to be gay.
870 When will the dancers leave her alone?
    She is weary of dance and play."
Now half to the setting moon are gone,
    And half to the rising day;
Low on the sand and loud on the stone
875   The last wheel echoes away.

V

I said to the rose, "The brief night goes
    In babble and revel and wine.

O young lord-lover, what sighs are those,
    For one that will never be thine?
880 But mine, but mine," so I sware to the rose,
    "For ever and ever, mine."

VI

And the soul of the rose went into my blood,
    As the music clashed in the hall;
And long by the garden lake I stood,
885   For I heard your rivulet fall
From the lake to the meadow and on to the wood,
    Our wood, that is dearer than all;

VII

From the meadow your walks have left so sweet
    That whenever a March-wind sighs
890 He sets the jewel-print of your feet
    In violets blue as your eyes,
To the woody hollows in which we meet
    And the valleys of Paradise.

VIII

The slender acacia would not shake
895   One long milk-bloom on the tree;
The white lake-blossom fell into the lake
    As the pimpernel dozed on the lea;
But the rose was awake all night for your sake,
    Knowing your promise to me;
900 The lilies and roses were all awake,
    They sighed for the dawn and thee.

IX

Queen rose of the rosebud garden of girls,
    Come hither, the dances are done,
In gloss of satin and glimmer of pearls,
905   Queen lily and rose in one;
Shine out, little head, sunning over with curls,
    To the flowers, and be their sun.

X

There has fallen a splendid tear
   From the passion-flower at the gate.
010 She is coming, my dove, my dear;
   She is coming, my life, my fate;
The red rose cries, "She is near, she is near;"
   And the white rose weeps, "She is late;"
The larkspur listens, "I hear, I hear;"
015   And the lily whispers, "I wait."

XI

She is coming, my own, my sweet;
   Were it ever so airy a tread,
My heart would hear her and beat,
   Were it earth in an earthy bed;
20 My dust would hear her and beat,
   Had I lain for a century dead;
Would start and tremble under her feet,
   And blossom in purple and red.

PART II
I
I

"The fault was mine, the fault was mine"—
Why am I sitting here so stunned and still,
Plucking the harmless wild-flower on the hill?—
It is this guilty hand!—
5 And there rises ever a passionate cry
From underneath in the darkening land—
What is it, that has been done?
O dawn of Eden bright over earth and sky,
The fires of Hell brake out of thy rising sun,
10 The fires of Hell and of Hate;
For she, sweet soul, had hardly spoken a word,
When her brother ran in his rage to the gate,
He came with the babe-faced lord;
Heaped on her terms of disgrace,
15 And while she wept, and I strove to be cool,
He fiercely gave me the lie,
Till I with as fierce an anger spoke,

And he struck me, madman, over the face,
Struck me before the languid fool,
20 Who was gaping and grinning by:
Struck for himself an evil stroke;
Wrought for his house an irredeemable woe;
For front to front in an hour we stood,
And a million horrible bellowing echoes broke
25 From the red-ribbed hollow behind the wood,
And thundered up into Heaven the Christless
   code,[1]
That must have life for a blow.
Ever and ever afresh they seemed to grow.
Was it he lay there with a fading eye?
30 "The fault was mine," he whispered, "fly!"
Then glided out of the joyous wood
The ghastly Wraith of one that I know;
And there rang on a sudden a passionate cry,
A cry for a brother's blood:
35 It will ring in my heart and my ears, till I die, till I
   die.

II

Is it gone? my pulses beat—
What was it? a lying trick of the brain?
Yet I thought I saw her stand,
A shadow there at my feet,
40 High over the shadowy land.
It is gone; and the heavens fall in a gentle rain,
When they should burst and drown with deluging
   storms
The feeble vassals of wine and anger and lust,
The little hearts that know not how to forgive:
45 Arise, my God, and strike, for we hold Thee just,
Strike dead the whole weak race of venomous worms,
That sting each other here in the dust;
We are not worthy to live.

---

[1] of duelling.

II

I

See what a lovely shell,[1]
50 Small and pure as a pearl,
Lying close to my foot,
Frail, but a work divine,
Made so fairily well
With delicate spire and whorl,
55 How exquisitely minute,
A miracle of design!

II

What is it? a learned man
Could give it a clumsy name.
Let him name it who can,
60 The beauty would be the same.

III

The tiny cell is forlorn,
Void of the little living will
That made it stir on the shore.
Did he stand at the diamond door
65 Of his house in a rainbow frill?
Did he push, when he was uncurled,
A golden foot or a fairy horn
Through his dim water-world?

IV

Slight, to be crushed with a tap
70 Of my finger-nail on the sand,
Small, but a work divine,
Frail, but of force to withstand,
Year upon year, the shock
Of cataract seas that snap
75 The three decker's oaken spine
Athwart the ledges of rock,
Here on the Breton strand!

---

[1] Tennyson's comment: "In Brittany. The shell undestroyed amid the storm perhaps symbolises to him his own first and highest nature preserved amid the storms of passion."

V

Breton, not Briton; here
Like a shipwrecked man on a coast
80 Of ancient fable and fear—
Plagued with a flitting to and fro,
A disease, a hard mechanic ghost
That never came from on high
Nor ever arose from below,
85 But only moves with the moving eye,
Flying along the land and the main—
Why should it look like Maud?
Am I to be overawed
By what I cannot but know
90 Is a juggle born of the brain?

VI

Back from the Breton coast,
Sick of a nameless fear,
Back to the dark sea-line
Looking, thinking of all I have lost;
95 An old song vexes my ear;
But that of Lamech is mine.

VII

For years, a measureless ill,
For years, for ever, to part—
But she, she would love me still;
100 And as long, O God, as she
Have a grain of love for me,
So long, no doubt, no doubt,
Shall I nurse in my dark heart,
However weary, a spark of will
105 Not to be trampled out.

VIII

Strange, that the mind, when fraught
With a passion so intense
One would think that it well
Might drown all life in the eye,—
110 That it should, by being so overwrought,
Suddenly strike on a sharper sense

For a shell, or a flower, little things
Which else would have been past by!
And now I remember, I,
15 When he lay dying there,
I noticed one of his many rings
(For he had many, poor worm) and thought
It is his mother's hair.

IX

Who knows if he be dead?
20 Whether I need have fled?
Am I guilty of blood?
However this may be,
Comfort her, comfort her, all things good,
While I am over the sea!
25 Let me and my passionate love go by,
But speak to her all things holy and high,
Whatever happen to me!
Me and my harmful love go by;
But come to her waking, find her asleep,
30 Powers of the height, Powers of the deep,
And comfort her though I die.

III

Courage, poor heart of stone!
I will not ask thee why
Thou canst not understand
35 That thou art left for ever alone:
Courage, poor stupid heart of stone.—
Or if I ask thee why,
Care not thou to reply:
She is but dead, and the time is at hand
40 When thou shalt more than die.

IV[1]

I

O that 'twere possible
After long grief and pain

To find the arms of my true love
Round me once again!

II

145 When I was wont to meet her
In the silent woody places
By the home that gave me birth,
We stood tranced in long embraces
Mixt with kisses sweeter sweeter
150 Than anything on earth.

III

A shadow flits before me,
Not thou, but like to thee:
Ah Christ, that it were possible
For one short hour to see
155 The souls we loved, that they might tell us
What and where they be.

IV

It leads me forth at evening,
It lightly winds and steals
In a cold white robe before me,
160 When all my spirit reels
At the shouts, the leagues of lights,
And the roaring of the wheels.

V

Half the night I waste in sighs,
Half in dreams I sorrow after
165 The delight of early skies;
In a wakeful doze I sorrow
For the hand, the lips, the eyes,
For the meeting of the morrow,
The delight of happy laughter,
170 The delight of low replies.

VI

'Tis a morning pure and sweet,
And a dewy splendour falls
On the little flower that clings

---

[1] This section (ll. 141–238) was written in 1833–34 and published in 1837.

To the turrets and the walls;
175   'Tis a morning pure and sweet,
And the light and shadow fleet;
She is walking in the meadow,
And the woodland echo rings;
In a moment we shall meet;
180   She is singing in the meadow
And the rivulet at her feet
Ripples on in light and shadow
To the ballad that she sings.

VII

Do I hear her sing as of old,
185   My bird with the shining head,
My own dove with the tender eye?
But there rings on a sudden a passionate cry,
There is some one dying or dead,
And a sullen thunder is rolled;
190   For a tumult shakes the city,
And I wake, my dream is fled;
In the shuddering dawn, behold,
Without knowledge, without pity,
By the curtains of my bed
195   That abiding phantom cold.

VIII

Get thee hence, nor come again,
Mix not memory with doubt,
Pass, thou deathlike type of pain,
Pass and cease to move about!
200   'Tis the blot upon the brain
That *will* show itself without.

IX

Then I rise, the eavedrops fall,
And the yellow vapours choke
The great city sounding wide;
205   The day comes, a dull red ball
Wrapt in drifts of lurid smoke
On the misty river-tide.

X

Through the hubbub of the market
I steal, a wasted frame,
210   It crosses here, it crosses there,
Through all that crowd confused and loud,
The shadow still the same;
And on my heavy eyelids
My anguish hangs like shame.

XI

215   Alas for her that met me,
That heard me softly call,
Came glimmering through the laurels
At the quiet evenfall,
In the garden by the turrets
220   Of the old manorial hall.

XII

Would the happy spirit descend,
From the realms of light and song,
In the chamber or the street,
As she looks among the blest,
225   Should I fear to greet my friend
Or to say "Forgive the wrong,"
Or to ask her, "Take me, sweet,
To the regions of thy rest"?

XIII

But the broad light glares and beats,
230   And the shadow flits and fleets
And will not let me be;
And I loathe the squares and streets,
And the faces that one meets,
Hearts with no love for me:
235   Always I long to creep
Into some still cavern deep,
There to weep, and weep, and weep
My whole soul out to thee.

V

I

Dead, long dead,
40 Long dead!
And my heart is a handful of dust,
And the wheels go over my head,
And my bones are shaken with pain,
For into a shallow grave they are thrust,
45 Only a yard beneath the street,
And the hoofs of the horses beat, beat,
The hoofs of the horses beat,
Beat into my scalp and my brain,
With never an end to the stream of passing feet,
50 Driving, hurrying, marrying, burying,
Clamour and rumble, and ringing and clatter,
And here beneath it is all as bad,
For I thought the dead had peace, but it is not so;
To have no peace in the grave, is that not sad?
55 But up and down and to and fro,
Ever about me the dead men go;
And then to hear a dead man chatter
Is enough to drive one mad.

II

Wretchedest age, since Time began,
60 They cannot even bury a man;
And though we paid our tithes in the days that are
gone,
Not a bell was rung, not a prayer was read;
It is that which makes us loud in the world of the
dead;
There is none that does his work, not one;
65 A touch of their office might have sufficed,
But the churchmen fain would kill their church,
As the churches have killed their Christ.

III

See, there is one of us sobbing,
No limit to his distress;
70 And another, a lord of all things, praying
To his own great self, as I guess;

And another, a statesman there, betraying
His party-secret, fool, to the press;
And yonder a vile physician, blabbing
275 The case of his patient—all for what?
To tickle the maggot born in an empty head,
And wheedle a world that loves him not,
For it is but a world of the dead.

IV

Nothing but idiot gabble!
280 For the prophecy given of old
And then not understood,
Has come to pass as foretold;
Not let any man think for the public good,
But babble, merely for babble.
285 For I never whispered a private affair
Within the hearing of cat or mouse,
No, not to myself in the closet alone,
But I heard it shouted at once from the top of the
house;
Everything came to be known.
290 Who told *him* we were there?

V

Not that gray old wolf,[1] for he came not back
From the wilderness, full of wolves, where he used
to lie;
He has gathered the bones for his o'ergrown whelp
to crack;
Crack them now for yourself, and howl, and die.

VI

295 Prophet, curse me the blabbing lip,
And curse me the British vermin, the rat;
I know not whether he came in the Hanover ship,[2]
But I know that he lies and listens mute
In an ancient mansion's crannies and holes:

----

[1] Maud's father.

[2] The Norwegian rat came to England in the ships of George I, House
of Hanover, in 1714.

300 Arsenic, arsenic, sure, would do it,
Except that now we poison our babes, poor souls!
It is all used up for that.

VII

Tell him now: she is standing here at my head;
Not beautiful now, not even kind;
305 He may take her now; for she never speaks her mind,
But is ever the one thing silent here.
She is not *of* us, as I divine;
She comes from another stiller world of the dead,
Stiller, not fairer than mine.

VIII

310 But I know where a garden grows,
Fairer than aught in the world beside,
All made up of the lily and rose
That blow by night, when the season is good,
To the sound of dancing music and flutes:
315 It is only flowers, they had no fruits,
And I almost fear they are not roses, but blood;
For the keeper was one, so full of pride,
He linkt a dead man there to a spectral bride;
For he, if he had not been a Sultan of brutes,
320 Would he have that hole in his side?

IX

But what will the old man[1] say?
He laid a cruel snare in a pit
To catch a friend of mine one stormy day;
Yet now I could even weep to think of it;
325 For what will the old man say
When he comes to the second corpse[2] in the pit?

X

Friend, to be struck by the public foe,
Then to strike him and lay him low,
That were a public merit, far,

330 Whatever the Quaker holds, from sin;
But the red life spilt for a private blow—
I swear to you, lawful and lawless war
Are scarcely even akin.

XI

O me, why have they not buried me deep enough?
335 Is it kind to have made me a grave so rough,
Me, that was never a quiet sleeper?
Maybe still I am but half-dead;
Then I cannot be wholly dumb;
I will cry to the steps above my head
340 And somebody, surely, some kind heart will come
To bury me, bury me
Deeper, ever so little deeper.

PART III

VI

I

My life has crept so long on a broken wing
Through cells of madness, haunts of horror and fear,
That I come to be grateful at last for a little thing:
My mood is changed, for it fell at a time of year
5 When the face of night is fair on the dewy downs,
And the shining daffodil dies, and the Charioteer
And starry Gemini hang like glorious crowns
Over Orion's grave low down in the west,
That like a silent lightning under the stars
10 She seemed to divide in a dream from a band of the
      blest,
And spoke of a hope for the world in the coming
      wars—
"And in that hope, dear soul, let trouble have rest,
Knowing I tarry for thee," and pointed to Mars
As he glowed like a ruddy shield on the Lion's[3]
      breast.

---

[1] Maud's father.

[2] Maud's brother.

[3] Mars, in the constellation Leo, which is the symbol of Britain.

II

15 And it was but a dream, yet it yielded a dear delight
To have looked, though but in a dream, upon eyes
    so fair,
That had been in a weary world my one thing bright;
And it was but a dream, yet it lightened my despair
When I thought that a war would arise in defence
    of the right,
20 That an iron tyranny now should bend or cease,
The glory of manhood stand on his ancient height,
Nor Britain's one sole God be the millionaire:
No more shall commerce be all in all, and Peace
Pipe on her pastoral hillock a languid note,
25 And watch her harvest ripen, her herd increase,
Nor the cannon-bullet rust on a slothful shore,
And the cobweb woven across the cannon's throat
Shall shake its threaded tears in the wind no more.

III

And as months ran on and rumour of battle grew,
30 "It is time, it is time, O passionate heart," said I
(For I cleaved to a cause that I felt to be pure and true),
"It is time, O passionate heart and morbid eye,
That old hysterical mock-disease should die."
And I stood on a giant deck and mixed my breath
35 With a loyal people shouting a battle cry,
Till I saw the dreary phantom arise and fly
Far into the North, and battle, and seas of death.

IV

Let it go or stay, so I wake to the higher aims
Of a land that has lost for a little her lust of gold,
40 And love of a peace that was full of wrongs and
    shames,
Horrible, hateful, monstrous, not to be told;
And hail once more to the banner of battle unrolled!
Though many a light shall darken, and many shall
    weep
For those that are crushed in the clash of jarring
    claims,

45 Yet God's just wrath shall be wreaked on a giant
    liar;[1]
And many a darkness into the light shall leap,
And shine in the sudden making of splendid names,
And noble thought be freër under the sun,
And the heart of a people beat with one desire;
50 For the peace, that I deemed no peace, is over and
    done,
And now by the side of the Black and the Baltic deep,
And deathful-grinning mouths of the fortress, flames
The blood-red blossom of war with a heart of fire.

V

Let it flame or fade, and the war roll down like a
    wind,
55 We have proved we have hearts in a cause, we are
    noble still,
And myself have awaked, as it seems, to the better
    mind;
It is better to fight for the good than to rail at the ill;
I have felt with my native land, I am one with my
    kind,
I embrace the purpose of God, and the doom
    assigned.
—1855

Tithonus [2]

The woods decay, the woods decay and fall,
The vapours weep their burthen to the ground,
Man comes and tills the field and lies beneath,
And after many a summer dies the swan.

---

[1] the Czar.

[2] Although not published until 1860, this poem was written much earlier. Tennyson says: "My friend Thackeray and his publishers had been so urgent with me to send them something, that I ferreted among my old books and found this *Tithonus*, written upwards of a quarter of a century ago....It was originally a pendent to the *Ulysses* in my former volumes." Tithonus, as Tennyson remarks, was " beloved by Aurora [goddess of the dawn], who gave him eternal life but not eternal youth. He grew old and infirm, and as he could not die, according to the legend, was turned into a grasshopper."

5 Me only cruel immortality
Consumes: I wither slowly in thine arms,
Here at the quiet limit of the world,
A white-haired shadow roaming like a dream
The ever-silent spaces of the East,
10 Far-folded mists, and gleaming halls of morn.

Alas! for this gray shadow, once a man—
So glorious in his beauty and thy choice,
Who madest him thy chosen, that he seemed
To his great heart none other than a God!
15 I asked thee, "Give me immortality."
Then didst thou grant mine asking with a smile,
Like wealthy men who care not how they give.
But thy strong Hours indignant worked their wills,
And beat me down and marred and wasted me,
20 And though they could not end me, left me maimed
To dwell in presence of immortal youth,
Immortal age beside immortal youth,
And all I was, in ashes. Can thy love,
Thy beauty, make amends, though even now,
25 Close over us, the silver star,[1] thy guide,
Shines in those tremulous eyes that fill with tears
To hear me? Let me go: take back thy gift:
Why should a man desire in any way
To vary from the kindly race of men,
30 Or pass beyond the goal of ordinance[2]
Where all should pause, as is most meet for all?

A soft air fans the cloud apart; there comes
A glimpse of that dark world where I was born.
Once more the old mysterious glimmer steals
35 From thy pure brows, and from thy shoulders pure,
And bosom beating with a heart renewed.
Thy cheek begins to redden through the gloom,
Thy sweet eyes brighten slowly close to mine,
Ere yet they blind the stars, and the wild team[3]

---

1 Venus.

2 appointed limit.

3 the horses which draw the chariot of dawn.

40 Which love thee, yearning for thy yoke, arise,
And shake the darkness from their loosened manes,
And beat the twilight into flakes of fire.

Lo! ever thus thou growest beautiful
In silence, then before thine answer given
45 Departest, and thy tears are on my cheek.

Why wilt thou ever scare me with thy tears,
And make me tremble lest a saying learnt,
In days far-off, on that dark earth, be true?
"The Gods themselves cannot recall their gifts."
50 Ay me! ay me! with what another heart
In days far-off, and with what other eyes
I used to watch—if I be he that watched—
The lucid outline forming round thee; saw
The dim curls kindle into sunny rings;
55 Changed with thy mystic change, and felt my blood
Glow with the glow that slowly crimsoned all
Thy presence and thy portals, while I lay,
Mouth, forehead, eyelids, growing dewy-warm
With kisses balmier than half-opening buds
60 Of April, and could hear the lips that kissed
Whispering I knew not what of wild and sweet,
Like that strange song I heard Apollo sing,
While Ilion like a mist rose into towers.[4]

Yet hold me not for ever in thine East:
65 How can my nature longer mix with thine?
Coldly thy rosy shadows bathe me, cold
Are all thy lights, and cold my wrinkled feet
Upon thy glimmering thresholds, when the steam
Floats up from those dim fields about the homes
70 Of happy men that have the power to die,
And grassy barrows of the happier dead.
Release me, and restore me to the ground;
Thou seëst all things, thou wilt see my grave:
Thou wilt renew thy beauty morn by morn;

---

4 Troy was built to the music of Apollo's lyre.

75 I earth in earth forget these empty courts,
And thee returning on thy silver wheels.
—1860

The Higher Pantheism

The sun, the moon, the stars, the seas, the hills
and the plains—
Are not these, O Soul, the Vision of Him who
reigns?

Is not the Vision He? though He be not that which
He seems?
Dreams are true while they last, and do we not live
in dreams?

5 Earth, these solid stars, this weight of body and
limb,
Are they not sign and symbol of thy division from
Him?

Dark is the world to thee: thyself art the reason why;
For is He not all but that which has power to feel
"I am I"?

Glory about thee, without thee; and thou fulfillest
thy doom,
10 Making Him broken gleams, and a stifled
splendour and gloom.

Speak to Him thou for He hears, and Spirit with
Spirit can meet—[1]
Closer is He than breathing, and nearer than hands
and feet.

God is law, say the wise; O Soul, and let us rejoice,
For if He thunder by law the thunder is yet His
voice.[2]

15 Law is God, say some: no God at all, says the
fool;[3]
For all we have power to see is a straight staff bent
in a pool;

And the ear of man cannot hear, and the eye of
man cannot see;
But if we could see and hear, this Vision—were it
not He?[4]
—1869

"Flower in the crannied wall"

Flower in the crannied wall,
I pluck you out of the crannies,
I hold you here, root and all, in my hand,
Little flower—but if I could understand
5 What you are, root and all, and all in all,
I should know what God and man is.
—1869

Crossing the Bar [5]

Sunset and evening star,
And one clear call for me!
And may there be no moaning of the bar,
When I put out to sea,

5 But such a tide as moving seems asleep,
Too full for sound and foam,
When that which drew from out the boundless deep
Turns again home.

Twilight and evening bell,
10 And after that the dark!

---

1 Psalm 17:6 and Romans 8:16.

2 Psalm 77:18.

3 Psalm 14:1.

4 1 Corinthians 2:9.

5 Before he died, Tennyson instructed: "Mind you put my 'Crossing the Bar' at the end of all editions of my poems." See note 2, p.280.

And may there be no sadness of farewell,
　　When I embark;

For though from out our bourne of Time and Place
　　The flood may bear me far,
15　I hope to see my Pilot[1] face to face
　　When I have crost the bar.
—1889

Idylls of the King[2]

Dedication[3]

These to His Memory—since he held them
　　dear,[4]
Perchance as finding there unconsciously
Some image of himself—I dedicate,
I dedicate, I consecrate with tears—
5　These Idylls.[5]
　　　　And indeed He seems to me
Scarce other than my king's ideal knight,
"Who reverenced his conscience as his king;
Whose glory was, redressing human wrong;
Who spake no slander, no, nor listened to it;
10　Who loved one only and who clave to her—"
Her—over all whose realms to their last isle,
Commingled with the gloom of imminent war,
The shadow of His loss drew like eclipse,
Darkening the world. We have lost him: he is gone:

15　We know him now: all narrow jealousies
Are silent; and we see him as he moved,
How modest, kindly, all-accomplished, wise,
With what sublime repression of himself,
And in what limits, and how tenderly;
20　Not swaying to this faction or to that;
Not making his high place the lawless perch
Of winged ambitions, nor a vantage-ground
For pleasure; but through all this tract of years
Wearing the white flower of a blameless life,
25　Before a thousand peering littlenesses,
In that fierce light which beats upon a throne,
And blackens every blot: for where is he,
Who dares foreshadow for an only son
A lovelier life, a more unstained, than his?
30　Or how should England dreaming of *his* sons
Hope more for these than some inheritance
Of such a life, a heart, a mind as thine,
Thou noble Father of her Kings to be,
Laborious for her people and her poor—
35　Voice in the rich dawn of an ampler day—
Far-sighted summoner of War and Waste
To fruitful strifes and rivalries of peace—[6]
Sweet nature glided by the gracious gleam
Of letters, dear to Science, dear to Art,
40　Dear to thy land[7] and ours, a Prince indeed,
Beyond all titles, and a household name,
Hereafter, through all times, Albert the Good.

　　Break not, O woman's-heart, but still endure;
Break not, for thou art Royal, but endure,
45　Remembering all the beauty of that star
Which shone so close beside Thee that ye made
One light together, but has past and leaves
The Crown a lonely splendour.

---

[1] Tennyson said that the Pilot is "that Divine and Unseen Who is always guiding us."

[2] For a detailed account of the *Idylls*, see Ricks 2.255–62. We have followed Ricks's practice of printing the *Idylls* after "Crossing the Bar."

[3] Published 1862. "To the Prince Consort" (Tennyson's note), who died on 14 December 1861.

[4] Prince Albert had asked Tennyson to inscribe a copy of the *Idylls*, 17 May 1860.

[5] Tennyson's comment: "Regarding the Greek derivation, I spelt my Idylls with two *l*'s mainly to divide them from the ordinary pastoral idyls usually spelt with one *l*. These idylls group themselves round one central figure."

[6] "The Prince Consort's work in the planning of the International Exhibitions of 1851 and 1862." (note by Tennyson's son, Hallam.)

[7] "Saxe-Coburg Gotha." (Tennyson's note.)

<pre>
                    May all love,
His love, unseen but felt, o'ershadow[1] Thee,
50 The love of all Thy sons encompass Thee,
The love of all Thy daughters cherish Thee,
The love of all Thy people comfort Thee,
Till God's love set Thee at his side again!
    —1862
</pre>

The Coming of Arthur [2]

<pre>
Leodogran, the King of Cameliard,
    Had one fair daughter, and none other child;
And she was fairest of all flesh on earth,
Guinevere, and in her his one delight.

5   For many a petty king ere Arthur came
Ruled in this isle, and ever waging war
Each upon other, wasted all the land;
And still from time to time the heathen host
Swarmed overseas, and harried what was left.
10 And so there grew great tracts of wilderness,
Wherein the beast was ever more and more,
But man was less and less, till Arthur came.
For first Aurelius[3] lived and fought and died,
And after him King Uther fought and died,
15 But either failed to make the kingdom one.
And after these King Arthur for a space,
And through the puissance of his Table Round,[4]
Drew all their petty princedoms under him,[5]
</pre>

<pre>
Their king and head, and made a realm, and
    reigned.

20   And thus the land of Cameliard was waste,
Thick with wet woods, and many a beast therein,
And none or few to scare or chase the beast;
So that wild dog, and wolf and boar and bear
Came night and day, and rooted in the fields,
25 And wallowed in the gardens of the King.
And ever and anon the wolf would steal
The children and devour, but now and then,
Her own brood lost or dead, lent her fierce teat
To human sucklings; and the children, housed
30 In her foul den, there at their meat would growl,
And mock their foster-mother on four feet,[6]
Till, straightened, they grew up to wolf-like men,[7]
Worse than the wolves. And King Leodogran
Groaned for the Roman legions here again,[8]
35 And Cæsar's eagle: then his brother king,
Urien,[9] assailed him: last a heathen horde,
Reddening the sun with smoke and earth with
    blood,
And on the spike that split the mother's heart
Spitting the child, brake on him, till, amazed,
40 He knew not whither he should turn for aid.

    But—for he heard of Arthur newly crowned,
Though not without an uproar made by those
Who cried, "He is not Uther's son"—the King
Sent to him, saying, "Arise, and help us thou!
45 For here between the man and beast we die."

    And Arthur yet had done no deed of arms,
But heard the call, and came: and Guinevere
</pre>

---

[1] to protect, (*OED*).

[2] Based on Malory's *Le Morte d'Arthur*, Bk. 1: "In this Idyll the poet lays bare the main lines of his story and of his parable." (Hallam Tennyson's note.)

[3] "Aurelius (Emrys) Ambrosius was brother of King Uther." (Tennyson's note.)

[4] "A table called King Arthur's is kept at Winchester. It was supposed to symbolise the world, being flat and round." (Tennyson's note.)

[5] "The several petty princedoms were under one head, the 'pendragon.'" (Tennyson's note.)

[6] "Imitate the wolf by going on four feet." (Tennyson's note.)

[7] "Compare what is told of in some parts of India (*Journal of Anthropological Society of Bombay*, vol. i) and of the loup-garous and were wolves of France and Germany." (Tennyson's note.)

[8] "Cf. *Groans of the Britons*, by Gildas." (Tennyson's note.)

[9] "King of North Wales." (Tennyson's note.)

Stood by the castle walls to watch him pass;
But since he neither wore on helm or shield
50 The golden symbol of his kinglihood,[1]
But rode a simple knight among his knights,
And many of these in richer arms than he,
She saw him not, or marked not, if she saw,
One among many, though his face was bare.
55 But Arthur, looking downward as he past,
Felt the light of her eyes into his life
Smite on the sudden, yet rode on, and pitched
His tents beside the forest. Then he drave
The heathen; after, slew the beast, and felled
60 The forest, letting in the sun, and made
Broad pathways for the hunter and the knight
And so returned.

> For while he lingered there,
A doubt that ever smouldered in the hearts
Of those great Lords and Barons of his realm
65 Flashed forth and into war: for most of these,
Colleaguing with a score of petty kings,
Made head against him, crying, "Who is he
That he should rule us? who hath proven him
King Uther's son? for lo! we look at him,
70 And find nor face nor bearing, limbs nor voice,
Are like to those of Uther whom we knew.
This is the son of Gorloïs, not the King;
This is the son of Anton, not the King."

And Arthur, passing thence to battle, felt
75 Travail, and throes and agonies of the life,
Desiring to be joined with Guinevere;
And thinking as he rode, "Her father said
That there between the man and beast they die.
Shall I not lift her from this land of beasts
80 Up to my throne, and side by side with me?
What happiness to reign a lonely king,
Vext—O ye stars that shudder over me,
O earth that soundest hollow under me,

Vext with waste dreams? for saving I be joined
85 To her that is the fairest under heaven,
I seem as nothing in the mighty world,
And cannot will my will, nor work my work
Wholly, nor make myself in mine own realm
Victor and lord. But were I joined with her,
90 Then might we live together as one life,
And reigning with one will in everything
Have power on this dark land to lighten it,
And power on this dead world to make it live."

Thereafter—as he speaks who tells the tale—
95 When Arthur reached a field-of-battle bright
With pitched pavilions of his foe, the world
Was all so clear about him, that he saw
The smallest rock far on the faintest hill,
And even in high day the morning star.
100 So when the King had set his banner broad,
At once from either side, with trumpet-blast,
And shouts, and clarions shrilling unto blood,
The long-lanced battle let their horses run.
And now the Barons and the kings prevailed,
105 And now the King, as here and there that war
Went swaying; but the Powers who walk the world
Made lightnings and great thunder over him,
And dazed all eyes, till Arthur by main might,
And mightier of his hands with every blow,
110 And leading all his knighthood threw the kings
Carádos, Urien, Cradlemont of Wales,
Claudias, and Clariance of Northumberland,
The King Brandagoras of Latangor,
With Anguisant of Erin, Morganore,
115 And Lot of Orkney. Then, before a voice
As dreadful as the shout of one who sees
To one who sins, and deems himself alone
And all the world asleep, they swerved and brake
Flying, and Arthur called to stay the brands
120 That hacked among the flyers, "Ho! they yield!"
So like a painted battle the war stood
Silenced, the living quiet as the dead,
And in the heart of Arthur joy was lord.

---

[1] "The golden dragon." (Tennyson's note.)

He laughed upon his warrior whom he loved
125 And honoured most. "Thou dost not doubt me
      King,
So well thine arm hath wrought for me today."
"Sir and my liege," he cried, "the fire of God
Descends upon thee in the battle-field:
I know thee for my King!" Whereat the two,
130 For each had warded either in the fight,
Sware on the field of death a deathless love.
And Arthur said, "Man's word is God in man:
Let chance what will, I trust thee to the death."

      Then quickly from the foughten field he sent
35 Ulfius, and Brastias, and Bedivere,
His new-made knights, to King Leodogran,
Saying, "If I in aught have served thee well,
Give me thy daughter Guinevere to wife."

      Whom when he heard, Leodogran in heart
40 Debating—"How should I that am a king,
However much he holp me at my need,
Give my one daughter saving to a king,
And a king's son?"—lifted his voice, and called
A hoary man, his chamberlain, to whom
45 He trusted all things, and of him required
His counsel: "Knowest thou aught of Arthur's
      birth?"

      Then spake the hoary chamberlain and said,
"Sir King, there be but two old men that know:
And each is twice as old as I; and one
50 Is Merlin, the wise man that ever served
King Uther through his magic art; and one
Is Merlin's master (so they called him) Bleys,
Who taught him magic; but the scholar ran
Before the master, and so far, that Bleys
55 Laid magic by, and sat him down, and wrote
All things and whatsoever Merlin did
In one great annal-book, where after-years
Will learn the secret of our Arthur's birth."

      To whom the King Leodogran replied,
160 "O friend, had I been holpen half as well
By this King Arthur as by thee today,
Then beast and man had had their share of me:
But summon here before us yet once more
Ulfius, and Brastias, and Bedivere."

165   Then, when they came before him, the King said,
"I have seen the cuckoo chased by lesser fowl,
And reason in the chase: but wherefore now
Do these your lords stir up the heat of war,
Some calling Arthur born of Gorloïs,
170 Others of Anton? Tell me, ye yourselves,
Hold ye this Arthur for King Uther's son?"

      And Ulfius and Brastias answered, "Ay."
Then Bedivere, the first of all his knights
Knighted by Arthur at his crowning, spake—
175 For bold in heart and act and word was he,
Whenever slander breathed against the King—

      "Sir, there be many rumours on this head:
For there be those who hate him in their hearts,
Call him baseborn, and since his ways are sweet,
180 And theirs are bestial, hold him less than man:
And there be those who deem him more than man,
And dream he dropt from heaven: but my belief
In all this matter—so ye care to learn—
Sir, for ye know that in King Uther's time
185 The prince and warrior Gorloïs, he that held
Tintagil castle by the Cornish sea,
Was wedded with a winsome wife, Ygerne:
And daughters had she borne him,—one whereof,
Lot's wife, the Queen of Orkney,[1] Bellicent,
190 Hath ever like a loyal sister cleaved
To Arthur,—but a son she had not borne.
And Uther cast upon her eyes of love:
But she, a stainless wife to Gorloïs,

---

[1] "The kingdom of Orkney and Lothian composed the North and East of Scotland." (Tennyson's note.)

So loathed the bright dishonour of his love,
195 That Gorloïs and King Uther went to war:
And overthrown was Gorloïs and slain.
Then Uther in his wrath and heat besieged
Ygerne within Tintagil, where her men,
Seeing the mighty swarm about their walls,
200 Left her and fled, and Uther entered in,
And there was none to call to but himself.
So, compassed by the power of the King,
Enforced she was to wed him in her tears,
And with a shameful swiftness: afterward,
205 Not many moons, King Uther died himself,
Moaning and wailing for an heir to rule
After him, lest the realm should go to wrack.
And that same night, the night of the new year,
By reason of the bitterness and grief
210 That vext his mother, all before his time
Was Arthur born, and all as soon as born
Delivered at a secret postern-gate
To Merlin, to be holden far apart
Until his hour should come; because the lords
215 Of that fierce day were as the lords of this,
Wild beasts, and surely would have torn the child
Piecemeal among them, had they known; for each
But sought to rule for his own self and hand,
And many hated Uther for the sake
220 Of Gorloïs. Wherefore Merlin took the child,
And gave him to Sir Anton, an old knight
And ancient friend of Uther; and his wife
Nursed the young prince, and reared him with her
    own;
And no man knew. And ever since the lords
225 Have foughten like wild beasts among themselves,
So that the realm has gone to wrack: but now,
This year, when Merlin (for his hour had come)
Brought Arthur forth, and set him in the hall,
Proclaiming, "Here is Uther's heir, your king,"
230 A hundred voices cried, "Away with him!
No king of ours! a son of Gorloïs he,
Or else the child of Anton, and no king,
Or else baseborn." Yet Merlin through his craft,

And while the people clamoured for a king,[1]
235 Had Arthur crowned; but after, the great lords
Banded, and so brake out in open war."

Then while the King debated with himself
If Arthur were the child of shamefulness,
Or born the son of Gorloïs, after death,
240 Or Uther's son, and born before his time,
Or whether there were truth in anything
Said by these three, there came to Cameliard,
With Gawain and young Modred, her two sons,
Lot's wife, the Queen of Orkney, Bellicent;
245 Whom as he could, not as he would, the King
Made feast for, saying, as they sat at meat,

"A doubtful throne is ice on summer seas.
Ye come from Arthur's court. Victor his men
Report him! Yea, but ye—think ye this king—
250 So many those that hate him, and so strong,
So few his knights, however brave they be—
Hath body enow to hold his foemen down?"

"O King," she cried, "and I will tell thee: few,
Few, but all brave, all of one mind with him;
255 For I was near him when the savage yells
Of Uther's peerage died, and Arthur sat
Crowned on the daïs, and his warriors cried,
"Be thou the king, and we will work thy will
Who love thee." Then the King in low deep tones,
260 And simple words of great authority,
Bound them by so strait vows to his own self,
That when they rose, knighted from kneeling, some
Were pale as at the passing of a ghost,
Some flushed, and others dazed, as one who wakes
265 Half-blinded at the coming of a light.

"But when he spake and cheered his Table Round
With large, divine, and comfortable words,

---

[1] Tennyson quotes Malory 1.7: "Wherefore all the commons cried at once, 'We will have Arthur unto our king.'"

Beyond my tongue to tell thee—I beheld
From eye to eye through all their Order flash
270 A momentary likeness of the King:
And ere it left their faces, through the cross
And those around it and the Crucified,
Down from the casement over Arthur, smote
Flame-colour, vert and azure, in three rays,
275 One falling upon each of three fair queens,
Who stood in silence near his throne, the friends
Of Arthur, gazing on him, tall, with bright
Sweet faces, who will help him at his need.

    "And there I saw mage Merlin, whose vast wit
280 And hundred winters are but as the hands
Of loyal vassals toiling for their liege.

    "And near him stood the Lady of the Lake,[1]
Who knows a subtler magic than his own—
Clothed in white samite, mystic, wonderful.
285 She gave the King his huge cross-hilted sword,
Whereby to drive the heathen out: a mist
Of incense curled about her, and her face
Wellnigh was hidden in the minster gloom;
But there was heard among the holy hymns
290 A voice as of the waters, for she dwells[2]
Down in a deep; calm, whatsoever storms
May shake the world, and when the surface rolls,
Hath power to walk the waters like our Lord.

    "There likewise I beheld Excalibur[3]
95 Before him at his crowning borne, the sword
That rose from out the bosom of the lake,
And Arthur rowed across and took it—rich

With jewels, elfin Urim, on the hilt,
Bewildering heart and eye—the blade so bright
300 That men are blinded by it—on one side,
Graven in the oldest tongue of all this world,
'Take me,' but turn the blade and ye shall see,
And written in the speech ye speak yourself,
'Cast me away!' And sad was Arthur's face
305 Taking it, but old Merlin counselled him,
'Take thou and strike! the time to cast away
Is yet far-off.'[4] So this great brand the king
Took, and by this will beat his foemen down."

    Thereat Leodogran rejoiced, but thought
310 To sift his doubtings to the last, and asked,
Fixing full eyes of question on her face,
"The swallow and the swift are near akin,
But thou are closer to this noble prince,
Being his own dear sister;" and she said,
315 "Daughter of Gorloïs and Ygerne am I;"
"And therefore Arthur's sister?" asked the King.
She answered, "These be secret things," and signed
To those two sons to pass, and let them be.
And Gawain went, and breaking into song
320 Sprang out, and followed by his flying hair
Ran like a colt, and leapt at all he saw:
But Modred laid his ear beside the doors,
And there half-heard; the same that afterward
Struck for the throne, and striking found his doom.

325   And then the Queen made answer, "What know
      I?
For dark my mother was in eyes and hair,
And dark in hair and eyes am I; and dark
Was Gorloïs, yea and dark was Uther too,
Wellnigh to blackness; but this King is fair
330 Beyond the race of Britons and of men.
Moreover, always in my mind I hear
A cry from out the dawning of my life,
A mother weeping, and I hear her say,

---

[1] "The Lady of the Lake in the old legends is the Church." (Tennyson's note.)

[2] Tennyson compares Revelation 14:2: "I heard a voice from heaven, as the voice of many waters."

[3] "Said to mean 'cut-steel.' In the Romance of *Merlin* the sword bore the following inscription: 'Ich am y-hote Escalabore/ Unto a king a fair tresore,' and it is added: 'On Inglis is this writing/ Kerve steel and yren and al thing.'" (Tennyson's note.)

---

[4] Ecclesiastes 3:6.

'O that ye had some brother, pretty one,
335   To guard thee on the rough ways of the world.'"

"Ay," said the King, "and hear ye such a cry?
But when did Arthur chance upon thee first?"

"O King!" she cried, "and I will tell thee true:
He found me first when yet a little maid:
340   Beaten I had been for a little fault
Whereof I was not guilty; and out I ran
And flung myself down on a bank of heath,
And hated this fair world and all therein,
And wept, and wished that I were dead; and he—
345   I know not whether of himself he came,
Or brought by Merlin, who, they say, can walk
Unseen at pleasure—he was at my side,
And spake sweet words, and comforted my heart,
And dried my tears, being a child with me.
350   And many a time he came, and evermore
As I grew greater grew with me; and sad
At times he seemed, and sad with him was I,
Stern too at times, and then I loved him not,
But sweet again, and then I loved him well.
355   And now of late I see him less and less,
But those first days had golden hours for me,
For then I surely thought he would be king.

"But let me tell thee now another tale:
For Bleys, our Merlin's master, as they say,
360   Died but of late, and sent his cry to me,
To hear him speak before he left his life.
Shrunk like a fairy changeling lay the mage;
And when I entered told me that himself
And Merlin ever served about the King,
365   Uther, before he died; and on the night
When Uther in Tintagil past away
Moaning and wailing for an heir, the two
Left the still King, and passing forth to breathe,
Then from the castle gateway by the chasm
370   Descending through the dismal night—a night
In which the bounds of heaven and earth were lost—

Beheld, so high upon the dreary deeps
It seemed in heaven, a ship, the shape thereof
A dragon winged, and all from stem to stern
375   Bright with a shining people on the decks,
And gone as soon as seen. And then the two
Dropt to the cove, and watched the great sea fall,
Wave after wave, each mightier than the last,
Till last, a ninth one,[1] gathering half the deep
380   And full of voices, slowly rose and plunged
Roaring, and all the wave was in a flame:
And down the wave and in the flame was borne
A naked babe, and rode to Merlin's feet,
Who stoopt and caught the babe, and cried 'The
     King!
385   Here is an heir for Uther!' And the fringe
Of that great breaker, sweeping up the strand,
Lashed at the wizard as he spake the word,
And all at once all round him rose in fire,
So that the child and he were clothed in fire.
390   And presently thereafter followed calm,
Free sky and stars: 'And this same child,' he said,
'Is he who reigns; nor could I part in peace
Till this were told.' And saying this the seer
Went through the strait and dreadful pass of death,
395   Not ever to be questioned any more
Save on the further side; but when I met
Merlin, and asked him if these things were truth—
The shining dragon and the naked child
Descending in the glory of the seas—
400   He laughed as is his wont, and answered me
In riddling triplets of old time, and said:

"'Rain, rain, and sun! a rainbow in the sky![2]
A young man will be wiser by and by;
An old man's wit may wander ere he die.
405   Rain, rain, and sun! a rainbow on the lea!

---

[1] "Every ninth wave is supposed by the Welsh bards to be larger than those that go before." (Hallam Tennyson's note.)

[2] "The truth appears in different guises to divers persons. The one fact is that man comes from the great deep and returns to it. This is an echo of the Welsh bards." (Tennyson's note.)

And truth is this to me, and that to thee;
And truth or clothed or naked let it be.

    Rain, sun, and rain! and the free blossoms blows:
Sun, rain, and sun! and where is he who knows?
410 From the great deep to the great deep he goes.'

    "So Merlin riddling angered me; but thou
Fear not to give this King thine only child,
Guinevere: so great bards of him will sing
Hereafter; and dark sayings from of old
415 Ranging and ringing through the minds of men,
And echoed by old folk beside their fires
For comfort after their wage-work is done,
Speak of the King; and Merlin in our time
Hath spoken also, not in jest, and sworn
420 Though men may wound him that he will not die,
But pass, again to come; and then or now
Utterly smite the heathen underfoot,
Till these and all men hail him for their king."

    She spake and King Leodogran rejoiced,
425 But musing "Shall I answer yea or nay?"
Doubted, and drowsed, nodded and slept, and saw,
Dreaming, a slope of land that ever grew,
Field after field, up to a height, the peak
Haze-hidden, and thereon a phantom king,
430 Now looming, and now lost; and on the slope
The sword rose, the hind fell, the herd was driven,
Fire glimpsed; and all the land from roof and rick,
In drifts of smoke before a rolling wind,
Streamed to the peak, and mingled with the haze
435 And made it thicker; while the phantom king
Sent out at times a voice; and here or there
Stood one who pointed toward the voice, the rest
Slew on and burnt, crying, "No king of ours,
No son of Uther, and no king of ours;"
440 Till with a wink his dream was changed, the haze
Descended, and the solid earth became
As nothing, but the King stood out in heaven,
Crowned. And Leodogran awoke, and sent

Ulfius, and Brastias and Bedivere,
445 Back to the court of Arthur answering yea.

    Then Arthur charged his warrior whom he loved
And honoured most, Sir Lancelot, to ride forth
And bring the Queen;—and watched him from the
    gates:
And Lancelot past away among the flowers,
450 (For then was latter April) and returned
Among the flowers, in May, with Guinevere.
To whom arrived, by Dubric[1] the high saint,
Chief of the church in Britain, and before
The stateliest of her altar-shrines,[2] the King
455 That morn was married, while in stainless white,
The fair beginners of a nobler time,
And glorying in their vows and him, his knights
Stood round him, and rejoicing in his joy.
Far shone the fields of May through open door,
460 The sacred altar blossomed white with May,
The Sun of May descended on their King,
They gazed on all earth's beauty in their Queen,
Rolled incense, and there past along the hymns
A voice as of the waters, while the two
465 Sware at the shrine of Christ a deathless love:
And Arthur said, "Behold, thy doom is mine.
Let chance what will, I love thee to the death!"
To whom the Queen replied with drooping eyes,
"King and my lord, I love thee to the death!"
470 And holy Dubric spread his hands and spake,
"Reign ye, and live and love, and make the world
Other, and may thy Queen be one with thee,
And all this Order of thy Table Round
Fulfil the boundless purpose of their King!"

475   So Dubric said; but when they left the shrine
Great Lords from Rome before the portal stood,

---

[1] "Archbishop of Caerleon. His crozier is said to be at St. David's."
(Tennyson's note.)

[2] "According to Malory, the Church of St. Stephen at Camelot."
(Tennyson's note.)

In scornful stillness gazing as they past;[1]
Then while they paced a city all on fire
With sun and cloth of gold, the trumpets blew,
480 And Arthur's knighthood sang before the King:—

"Blow trumpet, for the world is white with May;
Blow trumpet, the long night hath rolled away!
Blow through the living world—'Let the King
    reign.'

"Shall Rome or Heathen rule in Arthur's realm?
485 Flash brand and lance, fall battleaxe upon helm,
Fall battleaxe, and flash brand! Let the King reign.

"Strike for the King and live! his knights have
    heard
That God hath told the King a secret word.
Fall battleaxe, and flash brand! Let the King reign.

490 "Blow trumpet! he will lift us from the dust.
Blow trumpet! live the strength and die the lust!
Clang battleaxe, and clash brand! Let the King
    reign.

"Strike for the King and die! and if thou diest,
The King is King, and ever wills the highest.
495 Clang battleaxe, and clash brand! Let the King
    reign.

"Blow, for our Sun is mighty in his May!
Blow, for our Sun is mightier day by day!
Clang battleaxe, and clash brand! Let the King
    reign.

"The King will follow Christ, and we the
    King[2]
500 In whom high God hath breathed a secret thing.
Fall battleaxe, and flash brand! Let the King reign."

So sang the knighthood, moving to their hall.
There at the banquet those great Lords from Rome,
The slowly-fading mistress of the world,
505 Strode in, and claimed their tribute as of yore.
But Arthur spake, "Behold, for these have sworn
To wage my wars, and worship me their King;
The old order changeth, yielding place to new;
And we that fight for our fair father Christ,
510 Seeing that ye be grown too weak and old
To drive the heathen from your Roman wall,[3]
No tribute will we pay:" so those great lords
Drew back in wrath, and Arthur strove with Rome.

And Arthur and his knighthood for a space
Were all one will, and through that strength the
    King
510 Drew in the petty princedoms under him,
Fought, and in twelve great battles overcame
The heathen hordes, and made a realm and reigned.
—1869

Lancelot and Elaine [4]

Elaine the fair, Elaine the loveable,
Elaine, the lily maid of Astolat,
High in her chamber up a tower to the east
Guarded the sacred shield of Lancelot;
5 Which first she placed where morning's earliest ray
Might strike it, and awake her with the gleam;
Then fearing rust or soilure fashioned for it
A case of silk, and braided thereupon
All the devices blazoned on the shield
10 In their own tinct, and added, of her wit,
A border fantasy of branch and flower,
And yellow-throated nestling in the nest.
Nor rested thus content, but day by day,

---

[1] "Because Rome had been the Lord of Britain." (Tennyson's note.)

[2] 1 Corinthians 11:1.

[3] "A line of forts built by Agricola betwixt the Firth of Forth and the Clyde, forty miles long." (Tennyson's note.)

[4] when published in 1859, titled *Elaine*. The source is Malory, *Le Morte d'Arthur* 17.9–20.

Leaving her household and good father, climbed
15 That eastern tower, and entering barred her door,
Stript off the case, and read the naked shield,
Now guessed a hidden meaning in his arms,
Now made a pretty history to herself
Of every dint a sword had beaten in it,
20 And every scratch a lance had made upon it,
Conjecturing when and where: this cut is fresh;
That ten years back; this dealt him at Caerlyle;
That at Caerleon; this at Camelot:
And ah God's mercy, what a stroke was there!
25 And here a thrust that might have killed, but God
Broke the strong lance, and rolled his enemy down,
And saved him: so she lived in fantasy.

How came the lily maid by that good shield
Of Lancelot, she that knew not even his name?
30 He left it with her, when he rode to tilt
For the great diamond in the diamond jousts,
Which Arthur had ordained, and by that name
Had named them, since a diamond was the prize.

For Arthur, long before they crowned him
King,
35 Roving the trackless realms of Lyonnesse[1]
Had found a glen, gray boulder and black tarn.[2]
A horror lived about the tarn, and clave
Like its own mists to all the mountain side:
For here two brothers, one a king, had met
40 And fought together; but their names were lost;
And each had slain his brother at a blow;
And down they fell and made the glen abhorred:
And there they lay till all their bones were bleached,
And lichened into colour with the crags:
45 And he, that once was king, had on a crown
Of diamonds, one in front, and four aside.
And Arthur came, and labouring up the pass,

All in a misty moonshine, unawares
Had trodden that crowned skeleton, and the skull
50 Brake from the nape, and from the skull the crown
Rolled into light, and turning on its rims
Fled like a glittering rivulet to the tarn:
And down the shingly scaur[3] he plunged, and
caught,
And set it on his head, and in his heart
55 Heard murmurs, "Lo, thou likewise shalt be King."

Thereafter, when a King, he had the gems
Plucked from the crown, and showed them to his
knights,
Saying, "These jewels, whereupon I chanced
Divinely, are the kingdom's, not the King's—
60 For public use: henceforward let there be,
Once every year, a joust for one of these:
For so by nine years' proof we needs must learn
Which is our mightiest, and ourselves shall grow
In use of arms and manhood, till we drive
65 The heathen, who, some say, shall rule the land
Hereafter, which God hinder." Thus he spoke:
And eight years past, eight jousts had been, and still
Had Lancelot won the diamond of the year,
With purpose to present them to the Queen,
70 When all were won; but meaning all at once
To snare her royal fancy with a boon
Worth half her realm, had never spoken word.

Now for the central diamond and the last
And largest, Arthur, holding then his court
75 Hard on the river nigh the place which now
Is this world's hugest, let proclaim a joust
At Camelot, and when the time drew nigh
Spake (for she had been sick) to Guinevere,
"Are you so sick, my Queen, you cannot move
80 To these fair jousts?" "Yea, lord," she said, "ye
know it."
"Then will ye miss," he answered, "the great deeds

---

[1] "A land that is said to have stretched between Land's End and Scilly, and to have contained some of Cornwall as well." (Tennyson's note.)

[2] a small mountain lake.

[3] precipitous bank (*OED*).

Of Lancelot, and his prowess in the lists,
A sight ye love to look on." And the Queen
Lifted her eyes, and they dwelt languidly
85 On Lancelot, where he stood beside the King.
He thinking that he read her meaning there,
"Stay with me, I am sick; my love is more
Than many diamonds," yielded; and a heart
Love-loyal to the least wish of the Queen
90 (However much he yearned to make complete
The tale[1] of diamonds for his destined boon)
Urged him to speak against the truth, and say,
"Sir King, mine ancient wound[2] is hardly whole,
And lets[3] me from the saddle;" and the King
95 Glanced first at him, then her, and went his way.
No sooner gone than suddenly she began:

"To blame, my lord Sir Lancelot, much to blame!
Why go ye not to these fair jousts? the knights
Are half of them our enemies, and the crowd
100 Will murmur, 'Lo the shameless ones, who take
Their pastime now the trustful King is gone!'"
Then Lancelot vext at having lied in vain:
"Are ye so wise? ye were not once so wise,
My Queen, that summer, when ye loved me first.
105 Then of the crowd ye took no more account
Than of the myriad cricket of the mead,
When its own voice clings to each blade of grass,
And every voice is nothing. As to knights,
Them surely can I silence with all ease.
110 But now my loyal worship is allowed
Of all men: many a bard, without offence,
Has linked our names together in his lay,
Lancelot, the flower of bravery, Guinevere,
The pearl of beauty: and our knights at feast
115 Have pledged us in this union, while the King
Would listen smiling. How then? is there more?
Has Arthur spoken aught? or would yourself,

Now weary of my service and devoir,
Henceforth be truer to your faultless lord?"

120 She broke into a little scornful laugh:
"Arthur, my lord, Arthur, the faultless King,
That passionate perfection, my good lord—
But who can gaze upon the Sun in heaven?
He never spake word of reproach to me,
125 He never had a glimpse of mine untruth,
He cares not for me: only here today
There gleamed a vague suspicion in his eyes:
Some meddling rogue has tampered with him—else
Rapt in this fancy of his Table Round,
130 And swearing men to vows impossible,
To make them like himself: but, friend, to me
He is all fault who hath no fault at all:
For who loves me must have a touch of earth;
The low sun makes the colour:[4] I am yours,
135 Not Arthur's, as ye know, save by the bond.
And therefore hear my words: go to the jousts:
The tiny-trumpeting gnat can break our dream
When sweetest; and the vermin voices here
May buzz so loud—we scorn them, but they sting."

140 Then answered Lancelot, the chief of knights:
"And with what face, after my pretext made,
Shall I appear, O Queen, at Camelot, I
Before a King who honours his own word,
As if it were his God's?"

"Yea," said the Queen,
145 "A moral child without the craft to rule,
Else had he not lost me: but listen to me,
If I must find you wit: we hear it said
That men go down before your spear at a touch,
But knowing you are Lancelot; your great name,
150 This conquers: hide it therefore; go unknown:
Win! by this kiss you will: and our true King
Will then allow your pretext, O my knight,

---

[1] tally.

[2] received from Sir Mador.

[3] hinders.

[4] of sunrise and sunset.

As all for glory; for to speak him true,
Ye know right well, how meek soe'er he seem,
155 No keener hunter after glory breathes.
He love it in his knights more than himself:
They prove to him his work: win and return."

Then got Sir Lancelot suddenly to horse,
Wroth at himself. Not willing to be known,
160 He left the barren-beaten thoroughfare,
Chose the green path that showed the rarer foot,
And there among the solitary downs,
Full often lost in fancy, lost his way;
Till as he traced a faintly-shadowed track,
165 That all in loops and links among the dales
Ran to the Castle of Astolat, he saw
Fired from the west, far on a hill, the towers.
Thither he made, and blew the gateway horn.
Then came an old, dumb, myriad-wrinkled man,
170 Who let him into lodging and disarmed.
And Lancelot marvelled at the wordless man;
And issuing found the Lord of Astolat
With two strong sons, Sir Torre and Sir Lavaine,
Moving to meet him in the castle court;
175 And close behind them stept the lily maid
Elaine, his daughter: mother of the house
There was not: some light jest among them rose
With laughter dying down as the great knight
Approached them: then the Lord of Astolat:
180 "Whence comest thou, my guest, and by what name
Livest between thy lips?[1] for by thy state
And presence I might guess thee chief of those,
After the King, who eat in Arthur's halls.
Him have I seen: the rest, his Table Round,
185 Known as they are, to me they are unknown."

Then answered Lancelot, the chief of knights:
"Known am I, and of Arthur's hall, and known,
What I by mere mischance have brought, my shield.
But since I go to joust as one unknown

190 At Camelot for the diamond, ask me not,
Hereafter ye shall know me—and the shield—
I pray you lend me one, if such you have,
Blank, or at least with some device not mine."

Then said the Lord of Astolat, "Here is Torre's:
195 Hurt in his first tilt was my son, Sir Torre.
And so, God wot, his shield is blank enough.
His ye can have." Then added plain Sir Torre,
"Yea, since I cannot use it, ye may have it."
Here laughed the father saying, "Fie, Sir Churl,
200 Is that an answer for a noble knight?
Allow him! but Lavaine, my younger here,
He is so full of lustihood, he will ride,
Joust for it, and win, and bring it in an hour,
And set it in this damsel's golden hair,
205 To make her thrice as wilful as before."

"Nay, father, nay good father, shame me not
Before this noble knight," said young Lavaine,
"For nothing. Surely I but played on Torre:
He seemed so sullen, vext he could not go:
210 A jest, no more! for, knight, the maiden dreamt
That some one put this diamond in her hand,
And that it was too slippery to be held,
And slipt and fell into some pool or stream,[2]
The castle-well, belike; and then I said
215 That *if* I went and *if* I fought and won it
(But all was jest and joke among ourselves)
Then must she keep it safelier. All was jest.
But, father, give me leave, an if he will,
To ride to Camelot with this noble knight:
220 Win shall I not, but do my best to win:
Young as I am, yet would I do my best."

"So ye will grace me," answered Lancelot,
Smiling a moment, "with your fellowship
O'er these waste downs whereon I lost myself,

---

[1] an epic formula.

[2] "A vision prophetic of Guinevere hurling the diamonds into the Thames." (Tennyson's note.)

225 Then were I glad of you as guide and friend:
And you shall win this diamond,—as I hear
It is a fair large diamond,—if ye may,
And yield it to this maiden, if ye will."
"A fair large diamond," added plain Sir Torre,
230 "Such be for queens, and not for simple maids."
Then she, who held her eyes upon the ground,
Elaine, and heard her name so tost about,
Flushed slightly at the slight disparagement
Before the stranger knight, who, looking at her,
235 Full courtly, yet not falsely, thus returned:
"If what is fair be but for what is fair,
And only queens are to be counted so,
Rash were my judgment then, who deem this maid
Might wear as fair a jewel as is on earth,
240 Not violating the bond of like to like."

He spoke and ceased: the lily maid Elaine,
Won by the mellow voice before she looked,
Lifted her eyes, and read his lineaments.
The great and guilty love he bare the Queen,
245 In battle with the love he bare his lord,
Had marred his face, and marked it ere his time.
Another sinning on such heights with one,
The flower of all the west and all the world,
Had been the sleeker for it: but in him
250 His mood was often like a fiend, and rose
And drove him into wastes and solitudes
For agony, who was yet a living soul.
Marred as he was, he seemed the goodliest man
That ever among ladies ate in hall,
255 And noblest, when she lifted up her eyes.
However marred, of more than twice her years,
Seamed with an ancient swordcut on the cheek,
And bruised and bronzed, she lifted up her eyes
And loved him, with that love which was her
    doom.

260 Then the great knight, the darling of the court,
Loved of the loveliest, into that rude hall
Stept with all grace, and not with half disdain

Hid under grace, as in a smaller time,
But kindly man moving among his kind:
265 Whom they with meats and vintage of their best
And talk and minstrel melody entertained.
And much they asked of court and Table Round,
And ever well and readily answered he:
But Lancelot, when they glanced at Guinevere,
270 Suddenly speaking of the wordless man,
Heard from the Baron that, ten years before,
The heathen caught and reft him of his tongue.
"He learnt and warned me of their fierce design
Against my house, and him they caught and
    maimed;
275 But I, my sons, and little daughter fled
From bonds or death, and dwelt among the woods
By the great river in a boatman's hut.
Dull days were those, till our good Arthur broke
The Pagan yet once more on Badon hill."

280 "O there, great lord, doubtless," Lavaine said,
    rapt
By all the sweet and sudden passion of youth
Toward greatness in its elder, "you have fought.
O tell us—for we live apart—you know
Of Arthur's glorious wars." And Lancelot spoke
285 And answered him at full, as having been
With Arthur in the fight which all day long
Rang by the white mouth of the violent Glem;
And in the four loud battles by the shore
Of Duglas; that on Bassa; then the war
290 That thundered in and out the gloomy skirts
Of Celidon the forest; and again
By castle Gurnion, where the glorious King
Had on his cuirass[1] worn our Lady's Head,
Carved of one emerald centered in a sun
295 Of silver rays, that lightened as he breathed;
And at Caerleon had he helped his lord,

---

[1] breastplate on which Arthur bore the image of the Virgin Mary.

When the strong neighings of the wild white
    Horse[1]
Set every gilded parapet shuddering;
And up in Agned-Cathregonion too,
300 And down the waste sand-shores of Trath Treroit,
Where many a heathen fell; "and on the mount
Of Badon I myself beheld the King
Charge at the head of all his Table Round,
And all his legions crying Christ and him,
305 And break them; and I saw him, after, stand
High on a heap of slain, from spur to plume
Red as the rising sun with heathen blood,
And seeing me, with a great voice he cried,
'They are broken, they are broken!' for the King,
310 However mild he seems at home, nor cares
For triumph in our mimic wars, the jousts—
For if his own knight cast him down, he laughs
Saying, his knights are better men than he—
Yet in this heathen war the fire of God
315 Fills him: I never saw his like: there lives
No greater leader."

      While he uttered this,
Low to her own heart said the lily maid,
"Save your great self, fair lord:" and when he fell
From talk of war to traits of pleasantry—
320 Being mirthful he, but in a stately kind—
She still took note that when the living smile
Died from his lips, across him came a cloud
Of melancholy severe, from which again,
Whenever in her hovering to and fro
325 The lily maid had striven to make him cheer,
There brake a sudden-beaming tenderness
Of manners and of nature: and she thought
That all was nature, all, perchance, for her.
And all night long his face before her lived,
330 As when a painter, poring on a face,
Divinely through all hindrance finds the man
Behind it, and so paints him that his face,

The shape and colour of a mind and life,
Lives for his children, ever at its best
335 And fullest; so the face before her lived,
Dark-splendid, speaking in the silence, full
Of noble things, and held her from her sleep.
Till rathe[2] she rose, half-cheated in the thought
She needs must bid farewell to sweet Lavaine.
340 First as in fear, step after step, she stole
Down the long tower-stairs, hesitating:
Anon, she heard Sir Lancelot cry in the court,
"This shield, my friend, where is it?" and Lavaine
Past inward, as she came from out the tower.
345 There to his proud horse Lancelot turned, and
    smoothed
The glossy shoulder, humming to himself.
Half-envious of the flattering hand, she drew
Nearer and stood. He looked, and more amazed
Than if seven men had set upon him, saw
350 The maiden standing in the dewy light.
He had not dreamed she was so beautiful.
Then came on him a sort of sacred fear,
For silent, though he greeted her, she stood
Rapt on his face as if it were a God's.
355 Suddenly flashed on her a wild desire,
That he should wear her favour at the tilt.
She braved a riotous heart in asking for it.
"Fair lord, whose name I know not—noble it is,
I well believe, the noblest—will you wear
360 My favour at this tourney?" "Nay," said he,
"Fair lady, since I never yet have worn
Favour of any lady in the lists.
Such is my wont, as those, who know me, know."
"Yea, so," she answered; "then in wearing mine
365 Needs must be lesser likelihood, noble lord,
That those who know should know you." And he
    turned
Her counsel up and down within his mind,
And found it true, and answered, "True, my child.
Well, I will wear it: fetch it out to me:

---

1 the emblem of the Saxons.

2 "early." (Tennyson's note.)

370 What is it?" and she told him "A red sleeve
Broidered with pearls," and brought it: then he bound
Her token on his helmet, with a smile
Saying, "I never yet have done so much
For any maiden living," and the blood
375 Sprang to her face and filled her with delight;
But left her all the paler, when Lavaine
Returning brought the yet-unblazoned shield,
His brother's; which he gave to Lancelot,
Who parted with his own to fair Elaine:
380 "Do me this grace, my child, to have my shield
In keeping till I come." "A grace to me,"
She answered, "twice today. I am your squire!"
Whereat Lavaine said, laughing, "Lily maid,
For fear our people call you lily maid
385 In earnest, let me bring your colour back;
Once, twice, and thrice: now get you hence to bed:"
So kissed her, and Sir Lancelot his own hand,
And thus they moved away: she stayed a minute,
Then made a sudden step to the gate, and there—
390 Her bright hair blown about the serious face
Yet rosy-kindled with her brother's kiss—
Paused by the gateway, standing near the shield
In silence, while she watched their arms far-off
Sparkle, until they dipt below the downs.
395 Then to her tower she climbed, and took the shield,
There kept it, and so lived in fantasy.

Meanwhile the new companions past away
Far o'er the long backs of the bushless downs,
To where Sir Lancelot knew there lived a knight
400 Not far from Camelot, now for forty years
A hermit, who had prayed, laboured and prayed,
And ever labouring had scooped himself
In the white rock a chapel and a hall
On massive columns, like a shorecliff cave,
405 And cells and chambers: all were fair and dry;
The green light from the meadows underneath
Struck up and lived along the milky roofs;
And in the meadows tremulous aspen-trees

And poplars made a noise of falling showers.
410 And thither wending there that night they bode.

But when the next day broke from underground,
And shot red fire and shadows through the cave,
They rose, heard mass, broke fast, and rode away:
Then Lancelot saying, "Hear, but hold my name
415 Hidden, you ride with Lancelot of the Lake,"
Abashed Lavaine, whose instant reverence,
Dearer to true young hearts than their own praise,
But left him leave to stammer, "Is it indeed?"
And after muttering "The great Lancelot,"
420 At last he got his breath and answered, "One,
One have I seen—that other, our liege lord,
The dread Pendragon, Britain's King of kings,
Of whom the people talk mysteriously,
He will be there—then were I stricken blind
425 That minute, I might say that I had seen."

So spake Lavaine, and when they reached the lists
By Camelot in the meadow, let his eyes
Run through the peopled gallery which half round
Lay like a rainbow fallen upon the grass,
430 Until they found the clear-faced King, who sat
Robed in red samite, easily to be known,
Since to his crown the golden dragon clung,
And down his robe the dragon writhed in gold,
And from the carven-work behind him crept
435 Two dragons gilded, sloping down to make
Arms for his chair, while all the rest of them
Through knots and loops and folds innumerable
Fled ever through the woodwork, till they found
The new design wherein they lost themselves,
440 Yet with all ease, so tender was the work:
And, in the costly canopy o'er him set,
Blazed the last diamond of the nameless king.

Then Lancelot answered young Lavaine and said,
"Me you call great: mine is the firmer seat,
445 The truer lance: but there is many a youth
Now crescent, who will come to all I am

And overcome it; and in me there dwells
No greatness, save it be some far-off touch
Of greatness to know well I am not great:
450 There is the man."[1] And Lavaine gaped upon him
As on a thing miraculous, and anon
The trumpets blew; and then did either side,
They that assailed, and they that held the lists,
Set lance in rest, strike spur, suddenly move,
455 Meet in the midst, and there so furiously
Shock, that a man far-off might well perceive,
If any man that day were left afield,
The hard earth shake, and a low thunder of arms.
And Lancelot bode a little, till he saw
460 Which were the weaker; then he hurled into it
Against the stronger: little need to speak
Of Lancelot in his glory! King, duke, earl,
Count, baron—whom he smote, he overthrew.

But in the field were Lancelot's kith and kin,
465 Ranged with the Table Round that held the lists,
Strong men, and wrathful that a stranger knight
Should do and almost overdo the deeds
Of Lancelot; and one said to the other, "Lo!
What is he? I do not mean the force alone—
470 The grace and versatility of the man!
Is it not Lancelot?" "When has Lancelot worn
Favour of any lady in the lists?
Not such his wont, as we, that know him, know."
"How then? who then?" a fury seized them all,
475 A fiery family passion for the name
Of Lancelot, and a glory one with theirs.
They couched their spears and pricked their steeds,
      and thus,
Their plumes driven backward by the wind they
      made
In moving, all together down upon him
480 Bare, as a wild wave in the wide North-sea,

Green-glimmering toward the summit, bears, with
      all
Its stormy crests that smoke against the skies,
Down on a bark, and overbears the bark,[2]
And him that helms it, so they overbore
485 Sir Lancelot and his charger, and a spear
Down-glancing lamed the charger, and a spear
Pricked sharply his own cuirass, and the head
Pierced through his side, and there snapt, and
      remained.

Then Sir Lavaine did well and worshipfully;
490 He bore a knight of old repute to the earth,
And brought his horse to Lancelot where he lay.
He up the side, sweating with agony, got,
But thought to do while he might yet endure,
And being lustily holpen[3] by the rest,
495 His party,—though it seemed half-miracle
To those he fought with,—drave his kith and kin,
And all the Table Round that held the lists,
Back to the barrier; then the trumpets blew
Proclaiming his the prize, who wore the sleeve
500 Of scarlet, and the pearls; and all the knights,
His party, cried "Advance and take thy prize
The diamond;" but he answered, "Diamond me
No diamonds! for God's love, a little air!
Prize me no prizes, for my prize is death!
505 Hence will I, and I charge you, follow me not."

He spoke, and vanished suddenly from the field
With young Lavaine into the poplar grove.
There from his charger down he slid, and sat,
Gasping to Sir Lavaine, "Draw the lance-head:
510 "Ah my sweet lord Sir Lancelot," said Lavaine,
"I dread me, if I draw it, you will die."
But he, "I die already with it: draw—
Draw,"—and Lavaine drew, and Sir Lancelot gave
A marvellous great shriek and ghastly groan,

---

[1] ll. 447–50: "When I wrote that, I was thinking of Wordsworth and myself." (Tennyson's comment.)

[2] "Seen on a voyage of mine to Norway." (Tennyson's note.)

[3] archaic past participle use of "help."

515 And half his blood burst forth, and down he sank
For the pure pain, and wholly swooned away.
Then came the hermit out and bare him in,
There stanched his wound; and there, in daily doubt
Whether to live or die, for many a week
520 Hid from the wide world's rumour by the grove
Of poplars with their noise of falling showers,
And ever-tremulous aspen-trees, he lay.

But on that day when Lancelot fled the lists,
His party, knights of utmost North and West,
525 Lords of waste marches, kings of desolate isles,
Came round their great Pendragon, saying to him,
"Lo, Sire, our knight, through whom we won the
     day,
Hath gone sore wounded, and hath left his prize
Untaken, crying that his prize is death."
530 "Heaven hinder," said the King, "that such an one,
So great a knight as we have seen today—
He seemed to me another Lancelot—
Yea, twenty times I thought him Lancelot—
He must not pass uncared for. Wherefore, rise,
535 O Gawain, and ride forth and find the knight.
Wounded and wearied needs must he be near.
I charge you that you get at once to horse.
And, knights and kings, there breathes not one of
     you
Will deem this prize of ours is rashly given:
540 His prowess was too wondrous. We will do him
No customary honour: since the knight
Came not to us, of us to claim the prize,
Ourselves will send it after. Rise and take
This diamond, and deliver it, and return,
545 And bring us where he is, and how he fares,
And cease not from your quest until ye find."

So saying, from the carven flower above,
To which it made a restless heart, he took,
And gave, the diamond: then from where he sat
550 At Arthur's right, with smiling face arose,
With smiling face and frowning heart, a Prince

In the mid might and flourish of his May,
Gawain, surnamed The Courteous, fair and strong,
And after Lancelot, Tristram, and Geraint
555 And Gareth, a good knight, but therewithal
Sir Modred's brother, and the child of Lot,
Nor often loyal to his word, and now
Wroth that the King's command to sally forth
In quest of whom he knew not, made him leave
560 The banquet, and concourse of knights and kings.

So all in wrath he got to horse and went;
While Arthur to the banquet, dark in mood,
Past, thinking "Is it Lancelot who hath come
Despite the wound he spake of, all for gain
565 Of glory, and hath added wound to wound,
And ridden away to die?" So feared the King,
And, after two days' tarriance there, returned.
Then when he saw the Queen, embracing asked,
"Love, are you yet so sick?" "Nay, lord," she said.
570 "And where is Lancelot?" Then the Queen amazed,
"Was he not with you? won he not your prize?"
"Nay, but one like him." "Why that like was he."
And when the King demanded how she knew,
Said, "Lord, no sooner had ye parted from us,
575 Than Lancelot told me of a common talk
That men went down before his spear at a touch,
But knowing he was Lancelot; his great name
Conquered; and therefore would he hide his name
From all men, even the King, and to this end
580 Had made the pretext of a hindering wound,
That he might joust unknown of all, and learn
If his old prowess were in aught decayed;
And added, 'Our true Arthur, when he learns,
Will well allow my pretext, as for gain
585 Of purer glory.'"

Then replied the King:
"Far lovelier in our Lancelot had it been,
In lieu of idly dallying with the truth,
To have trusted me as he hath trusted thee.
Surely his King and most familiar friend

296

590 Might well have kept his secret. True, indeed,
Albeit I know my knights fantastical,
So fine a fear in our large Lancelot
Must needs have moved my laughter: now remains
But little cause for laughter: his own kin—
595 Ill news, my Queen, for all who love him, this!—
His kith and kin, not knowing, set upon him;
So that he went sore wounded from the field:
Yet good news too: for goodly hopes are mine
That Lancelot is no more a lonely heart.
600 He wore, against his wont, upon his helm
A sleeve of scarlet, broidered with great pearls,
Some gentle maiden's gift."

　　　　　　　　　　　　"Yea, lord," she said,
"Thy hopes are mine," and saying that, she choked,
And sharply turned about to hide her face,
605 Past to her chamber, and there flung herself
Down on the great King's couch, and writhed
　　　upon it,
And clenched her fingers till they bit the palm,
And shrieked out "Traitor" to the unhearing wall,
Then flashed into wild tears, and rose again,
610 And moved about her palace, proud and pale.

　　　Gawain the while through all the region round
Rode with his diamond, wearied of the quest,
Touched at all points, except the poplar grove,
And came at last, though late, to Astolat:
615 Whom glittering in enamelled arms the maid
Glanced at, and cried, "What news from Camelot,
　　　lord?
What of the knight with the red sleeve?" "He won."
"I knew it," she said. "But parted from the jousts
Hurt in the side," whereat she caught her breath;
620 Through her own side she felt the sharp lance go;
Thereon she smote her hand: wellnigh she swooned:
And, while he gazed wonderingly at her, came
The Lord of Astolat out, to whom the Prince
Reported who he was, and on what quest
625 Sent, that he bore the prize and could not find

The victor, but had ridden a random round
To seek him, and had wearied of the search.
To whom the Lord of Astolat, "Bide with us,
And ride no more at random, noble Prince!
630 Here was the knight, and here he left a shield;
This will he send or come for: furthermore
Our son is with him; we shall hear anon,
Needs must we hear." To this the courteous Prince
Accorded with his wonted courtesy,
635 Courtesy with a touch of traitor[1] in it,
And stayed; and cast his eyes on fair Elaine:
Where could be found face daintier? then her shape
From forehead down to foot, perfect—again
From foot to forehead exquisitely turned:
640 "Well—if I bide, lo! this wild flower for me!"
And oft they met among the garden yews,
And there he set himself to play upon her
With sallying wit, free flashes from a height
Above her, graces of the court, and songs,
645 Sighs, and slow smiles, and golden eloquence
And amorous adulation, till the maid
Rebelled against it, saying to him, "Prince,
O loyal nephew of our noble King,
Why ask you not to see the shield he left,
650 Whence you might learn his name? Why slight
　　　your King,
And lose the quest he sent you on, and prove
No surer than our falcon yesterday,
Who lost the hern[2] we slipt her at, and went
To all the winds?" "Nay, by mine head," said he,
655 "I lose it, as we lose the lark in heaven,
O damsel, in the light of your blue eyes:
But an ye will it let me see the shield."
And when the shield was brought, and Gawain saw
Sir Lancelot's azure lions, crowned with gold,
660 Ramp in the field, he smote his thigh, and mocked:
"Right was the King! our Lancelot! that true man!"

_____

[1] In Malory, however, Gawain is a loyal friend of Lancelot. Tennyson
departs from Malory throughout this episode.

[2] heron.

"And right was I," she answered merrily, "I,
Who dreamed my knight the greatest knight of all."
"And if *I* dreamed," said Gawain, "that you love
665 This greatest knight, your pardon! lo, ye know it!
Speak therefore: shall I waste myself in vain?"
Full simple was her answer, "What know I?
My brethren have been all my fellowship;
And I, when often they have talked of love,
670 Wished it had been my mother, for they talked,
Meseemed, of what they knew not; so myself—
I know not if I know what true love is,
But if I know, then, if I love not him,
I know there is none other I can love."
675 "Yea, by God's death," said he, "ye love him well,
But would not, knew ye what all others know,
And whom he loves." "So be it," cried Elaine,
And lifted her fair face and moved away:
But he pursued her, calling, "Stay a little!
680 One golden minute's grace! he wore your sleeve:
Would he break faith with one I may not name?
Must our true man change like a leaf at last?
Nay—like enow: why then, far be it from me
To cross our mighty Lancelot in his loves!
685 And, damsel, for I deem you know full well
Where your great knight is hidden, let me leave
My quest with you; the diamond also: here!
For if you love, it will be sweet to give it;
And if he love, it will be sweet to have it
690 From your own hand; and whether he love or not,
A diamond is a diamond. Fare you well
A thousand times!—a thousand times farewell!
Yet, if he love, and his love hold, we two
May meet at court hereafter: there, I think,
695 So ye will learn the courtesies of the court,
We two shall know each other."

                Then he gave,
And slightly kissed the hand to which he gave,
The diamond, and all wearied of the quest
Leapt on his horse, and carolling as he went
700 A true-love ballad, lightly rode away.

Thence to the court he past; there told the King
What the King knew, "Sir Lancelot is the knight."
And added, "Sire, my liege, so much I learnt;
But failed to find him, though I rode all round
705 The region: but I lighted on the maid
Whose sleeve he wore; she loves him; and to her,
Deeming our courtesy is the truest law,
I gave the diamond: she will render it;
For by mine head she knows his hiding-place."

710 The seldom-frowning King frowned, and replied,
"Too courteous truly! ye shall go no more
On quest of mine, seeing that ye forget
Obedience is the courtesy due to kings."

He spake and parted. Wroth, but all in awe,
715 For twenty strokes of the blood,[1] without a word,
Lingered that other, staring after him;
Then shook his hair, strode off, and buzzed abroad
About the maid of Astolat, and her love.
All ears were pricked at once, all tongues were loosed:
720 "The maid of Astolat loves Sir Lancelot,
Sir Lancelot loves the maid of Astolat."
Some read the King's face, some the Queen's, and
    all
Had marvel what the maid might be, but most
Predoomed her as unworthy. One old dame
725 Came suddenly on the Queen with the sharp news.
She, that had heard the noise of it before,
Bur sorrowing Lancelot should have stooped so low,
Marred her friend's aim with pale tranquillity.
So ran the tale like fire about the court,
730 Fire in dry stubble a nine-days' wonder flared:
Till even the knights at banquet twice or thrice
Forgot to drink to Lancelot and the Queen,
And pledging Lancelot and the lily maid
Smiled at each other, while the Queen, who sat
735 With lips severely placid, felt the knot
Climb in her throat, and with her feet unseen

---

[1] heartbeats.

Crushed the wild passion out against the floor
Beneath the banquet, where the meats became
As wormwood, and she hated all who pledged.

40   But far away the maid in Astolat,
Her guiltless rival, she that ever kept
The one-day-seen Sir Lancelot in her heart,
Crept to her father, while he mused alone,
Sat on his knee, stroked his gray face and said,
45   "Father, you call me wilful, and the fault
Is yours who let me have my will, and now,
Sweet father, will you let me lose my wits?"
"Nay," said he, "surely." "Wherefore, let me hence,"
She answered, " and find out our dear Lavaine."
50   "Ye will not lose your wits for dear Lavaine:
Bide," answered he: "we needs must hear anon
Of him, and of that other." "Ay," she said,
"And of that other, for I needs must hence
And find that other, wheresoe'er he be,
55   And with mine own hand give his diamond to him,
Lest I be found as faithless in the quest
As yon proud Prince who left the quest to me.
Sweet father, I behold him in my dreams
Gaunt as it were the skeleton of himself,
60   Death-pale, for lack of gentle maiden's aid.
The gentler-born the maiden, the more bound,
My father, to be sweet and serviceable
To noble knights in sickness, as ye know
When these have worn their tokens: let me hence
65   I pray you." Then her father nodding said,
"Ay, ay, the diamond: wit ye well, my child,
Right fain were I to learn this knight were whole,
Being our greatest: yea, and you must give it—
And sure I think this fruit is hung too high
70   For any mouth to gape for save a queen's—
Nay, I mean nothing: so then, get you gone,
Being so very wilful you must go."

Lightly, her suit allowed, she slipt away,
And while she made her ready for her ride,
75   Her father's latest word hummed in her ear,

"Being so very wilful you must go,"
And changed itself and echoed in her heart,
"Being so very wilful you must die."
But she was happy enough and shook it off,
780   As we shake off the bee that buzzes at us;
And in her heart she answered it and said,
"What matter, so I help him back to life?"
Then far away with good Sir Torre for guide
Rode o'er the long backs of the bushless downs
785   To Camelot, and before the city-gates
Came on her brother with a happy face
Making a roan horse caper and curvet
For pleasure all about a field of flowers:
Whom when she saw, "Lavaine," she cried,
"Lavaine,
790   How fares my lord Sir Lancelot?" He amazed,
"Torre and Elaine! why here? Sir Lancelot!
How know ye my lord's name is Lancelot?"
But when the maid had told him all her tale,
Then turned Sir Torre, and being in his moods
795   Left them, and under the strange-statued gate,
Where Arthur's wars were rendered mystically,
Past up the still rich city to his kin,
His own far blood, which dwelt at Camelot;
And her, Lavaine across the poplar grove
800   Led to the caves: there first she saw the casque[1]
Of Lancelot on the wall: her scarlet sleeve,
Though carved and cut, and half the pearls away,
Streamed from it still; and in her heart she laughed,
Because he had not loosed it from his helm,
805   But meant once more perchance to tourney in it.
And when they gained the cell wherein he slept,
His battle-writhen arms and mighty hands
Lay naked on the wolfskin, and a dream
Of dragging down his enemy made them move.
810   Then she that saw him lying unsleek, unshorn,
Gaunt as it were the skeleton of himself,
Uttered a little tender dolorous cry.
The sound not wonted in a place so still

---

[1] helmet.

Woke the sick knight, and while he rolled his eyes
815 Yet blank from sleep, she started to him, saying,
"Your prize the diamond sent you by the King:"
His eyes glistened: she fancied "Is it for me?"
And when the maid had told him all the tale
Of King and Prince, the diamond sent, the quest
820 Assigned to her not worthy of it, she knelt
Full lowly by the corners of his bed,
And laid the diamond in his open hand.
Her face was near, and as we kiss the child
That does the task assigned, he kissed her face.
825 At once she slipt like water to the floor.
"Alas," he said, "your ride hath wearied you.
Rest must you have." "No rest for me," she said;
"Nay, for near you, fair lord, I am at rest."
What might she mean by that? his large black eyes,
830 Yet larger through his leanness, dwelt upon her,
Till all her heart's sad secret blazed itself
In the heart's colours on her simple face;
And Lancelot looked and was perplext in mind,
And being weak in body said no more;
835 But did not love the colour; woman's love,
Save one, he not regarded, and so turned
Sighing, and feigned a sleep until he slept.

Then rose Elaine and glided through the fields,
And past beneath the weirdly-sculptured gates
840 Far up the dim rich city to her kin;
There bode the night: but woke with dawn, and past
Down through the dim rich city to the fields,
Thence to the cave: so day by day she past
In either twilight ghost-like to and fro
845 Gliding, and every day she tended him,
And likewise many a night: and Lancelot
Would, though he called his wound a little hurt
Whereof he should be quickly whole, at times
Brain-feverous in his heat and agony, seem
850 Uncourteous, even he: but the meek maid
Sweetly forbore him ever, being to him
Meeker than any child to a rough nurse,
Milder than any mother to a sick child,

And never woman yet, since man's first fall,
855 Did kindlier unto man, but her deep love
Upbore her; till the hermit, skilled in all
The simples[1] and the science of that time,
Told him that her fine care had saved his life.
And the sick man forgot her simple blush,
860 Would call her friend and sister, sweet Elaine,
Would listen for her coming and regret
Her parting step, and held her tenderly,
And loved her with all love except the love
Of man and woman when they love their best,
865 Closest and sweetest, and had died the death
In any knightly fashion for her sake.
And peradventure had he seen her first
She might have made this and that other world
Another world for the sick man; but now
870 The shackles of an old love straitened him,
His honour rooted in dishonour stood,
And faith unfaithful kept him falsely true.

Yet the great knight in his mid-sickness made
Full many a holy vow and pure resolve.
875 These, as but born of sickness, could not live:
For when the blood ran lustier in him again,
Full often the bright image of one face,
Making a treacherous quiet in his heart,
Dispersed his resolution like a cloud.
880 Then if the maiden, while that ghostly grace[2]
Beamed on his fancy, spoke, he answered not,
Or short and coldly, and she knew right well
What the rough sickness meant, but what this meant
She knew not, and the sorrow dimmed her sight,
885 And drave her ere her time across the fields
Far into the rich city, where alone
She murmured, "Vain, in vain: it cannot be.
He will not love me: how then? must I die?"
Then as a little helpless innocent bird,
890 That has but one plain passage of few notes,

---

[1] herbs and medicines.

[2] "Vision of Guinevere." (Tennyson's note.)

Will sing the simple passage o'er and o'er
For all an April morning, till the ear
Wearies to hear it, so the simple maid
Went half the night repeating, "Must I die?"
95   And now to right she turned, and now to left,
And found no ease in turning or in rest;
And "Him or death," she muttered, "death or him,"
Again and like a burthen, "Him or death."

    But when Sir Lancelot's deadly hurt was whole,
00   To Astolat returning rode the three.
There morn by morn, arraying her sweet self
In that wherein she deemed she looked her best,
She came before Sir Lancelot, for she thought
"If I be loved, these are my festal robes,
05   If not, the victim's flowers before he fall."
And Lancelot ever prest upon the maid
That she should ask some goodly gift of him
For her own self or hers; "and do not shun
To speak the wish most near to your true heart;
10   Such service have ye done me, that I make
My will of yours, and Prince and Lord am I
In mine own land, and what I will I can."
Then like a ghost she lifted up her face,
But like a ghost without the power to speak.
15   And Lancelot saw that she withheld her wish,
And bode among them yet a little space
Till he should learn it; and one morn it chanced
He found her in among the garden yews,
And said, "Delay no longer, speak your wish,
20   Seeing I go today:" then out she brake:
"Going? and we shall never see you more.
And I must die for want of one bold word."
"Speak: that I live to hear," he said, "is yours."
Then suddenly and passionately she spoke:
25   "I have gone mad. I love you: let me die."
"Ah, sister," answered Lancelot, "what is this?"
And innocently extending her white arms,
"Your love," she said, "your love—to be your wife."
And Lancelot answered, "Had I chosen to wed,
30   I had been wedded earlier, sweet Elaine:

But now there never will be wife of mine."
"No, no," she cried, "I care not to be wife,
But to be with you still, to see your face,
To serve you, and to follow you through the world."
935   And Lancelot answered, "Nay, the world, the world,
All ear and eye, with such a stupid heart
To interpret ear and eye, and such a tongue
To blare its own interpretation—nay,
Full ill then should I quit your brother's love,
940   And your good father's kindness." And she said,
"Not to be with you, not to see your face—
Alas for me then, my good days are done."
"Nay, noble maid," he answered, "ten times nay!
This is not love: but love's first flash in youth,
945   Most common: yea, I know it of mine own self:
And you yourself will smile at your own self
Hereafter, when you yield your flower of life
To one more fitly yours, not thrice your age:
And then will I, for true you are and sweet
950   Beyond mine old belief in womanhood,
More specially should your good knight be poor,
Endow you with broad land and territory
Even to the half my realm beyond the seas,
So that would make you happy: furthermore,
955   Even to the death, as though ye were my blood,
In all your quarrels will I be your knight.
This will I do, dear damsel, for your sake,
And more than this I cannot."

               While he spoke
She neither blushed nor shook, but deathly-pale
960   Stood grasping what was nearest, then replied:
"Of all this will I nothing;" and so fell,
And thus they bore her swooning to her tower.

Then spake, to whom through those black walls
    of yew
Their talk had pierced, her father: "Ay, a flash,
965   I fear me, that will strike my blossom dead.
Too courteous are ye, fair Lord Lancelot.

I pray you, use some rough discourtesy
To blunt or break her passion."

                    Lancelot said,
"That were against me: what I can I will;"
970 And there that day remained, and toward even
Sent for his shield: full meekly rose the maid,
Stript off the case, and gave the naked shield;
Then, when she heard his horse upon the stones,
Unclasping flung the casement back, and looked
975 Down on his helm, from which her sleeve had gone.
And Lancelot knew the little clinking sound;
And she by tact of love was well aware
That Lancelot knew that she was looking at him.
And yet he glanced not up, nor waved his hand,
980 Nor bad farewell, but sadly rode away.
This was the one discourtesy that he used.

   So in her tower alone the maiden sat:
His very shield was gone; only the case,
Her own poor work, her empty labour, left.
985 But still she heard him, still his picture formed
And grew between her and the pictured wall.
Then came her father, saying in low tones,
"Have comfort," whom she greeted quietly.
Then came her brethren saying, "Peace to thee,
990 Sweet sister," whom she answered with all calm.
But when they left her to herself again,
Death, like a friend's voice from a distant field
Approaching through the darkness, called; the owls
Wailing had power upon her, and she mixt
995 Her fancies with the sallow-rifted glooms
Of evening, and the moanings of the wind.

   And in those days she made a little song,
And called her song "The Song of Love and Death,"
And sang it: sweetly could she make and sing.

1000   "Sweet is true love though given in vain, in
       vain;

And sweet is death who puts an end to pain:
I know not which is sweeter, no, not I.

   "Love, art thou sweet? then bitter death must be:
Love, thou art bitter; sweet is death to me.
1005 O Love, if death be sweeter, let me die.

   "Sweet love, that seems not made to fade away,
Sweet death, that seems to make us loveless clay,
I know not which is sweeter, no, not I.

   "I fain would follow love, if that could be;
1010 I needs must follow death, who calls for me;
Call and I follow, I follow! let me die."

   High with the last line scaled her voice, and this,
All in a fiery dawning wild with wind
That shook her tower, the brothers heard, and
     thought
1015 With shuddering, "Hark the Phantom of the house
That ever shrieks before a death," and called
The father, and all three in hurry and fear
Ran to her, and lo! the blood-red light of dawn
Flared on her face, she shrilling, "Let me die!"

1020   As when we dwell upon a word we know,
Repeating, till the word we know so well
Becomes a wonder, and we know not why,
So dwelt the father on her face, and thought
"Is this Elaine?" till back the maiden fell,
1025 Then gave a languid hand to each, and lay,
Speaking a still good-morrow with her eyes.
At last she said, "Sweet brothers, yesternight
I seemed a curious little maid again,
As happy as when we dwelt among the woods,
1030 And when ye used to take me with the flood
Up the great river in the boatman's boat.
Only ye would not pass beyond the cape
That has the poplar on it: there ye fixt
Your limit, oft returning with the tide.
1035 And yet I cried because ye would not pass

Beyond it, and far up the shining flood
Until we found the palace of the King.
And yet ye would not; but this night I dreamed
That I was all alone upon the flood,
1040 And then I said, 'Now I shall have my will:'
And there I woke, but still the wish remained.
So let me hence that I may pass at last
Beyond the poplar and far up the flood,
Until I find the palace of the King.
1045 There will I enter in among them all,
And no man there will dare to mock at me;
But there the fine Gawain will wonder at me,
And there the great Sir Lancelot muse at me;
Gawain, who bad a thousand farewells to me,
1050 Lancelot, who coldly went, nor bad me one:
And there the King will know me and my love,
And there the Queen herself will pity me,
And all the gentle court will welcome me,
And after my long voyage I shall rest!"

1055   "Peace," said her father, "O my child, ye seem
Light-headed, for what force is yours to go
So far, being sick? and wherefore would ye look
On this proud fellow again, who scorns us all?"

Then the rough Torre began to heave and move,
1060 And bluster into stormy sobs and say,
"I never loved him: an I meet with him,
I care not howsoever great he be,
Then will I strike at him and strike him down,
Give me good fortune, I will strike him dead,
1065 For this discomfort he hath done the house."

To whom the gentle sister made reply,
"Fret not yourself, dear brother, nor be wroth,
Seeing it is no more Sir Lancelot's fault
Not to love me, than it is mine to love
1070 Him of all men who seems to me the highest."

"Highest?" the father answered, echoing "highest?"
(He meant to break the passion in her) "nay,

Daughter, I know not what you call the highest;
But this I know, for all the people know it,
1075 He loves the Queen, and in an open shame:
And she returns his love in open shame;
If this be high, what is it to be low?"

Then spake the lily maid of Astolat:
"Sweet father, all too faint and sick am I
1080 For anger: these are slanders: never yet
Was noble man but made ignoble talk.
He makes no friend who never made a foe.
But now it is my glory to have loved
One peerless, without stain: so let me pass,
1085 My father, howsoe'er I seem to you,
Not all unhappy, having loved God's best
And greatest, though my love had no return:
Yet, seeing you desire your child to live,
Thanks, but you work against your own desire;
1090 For if I could believe the things you say
I should but die the sooner; wherefore cease,
Sweet father, and bid call the ghostly man[1]
Hither, and let me shrive me clean, and die."

So when the ghostly man had come and gone,
1095 She with a face, bright as for sin forgiven,
Besought Lavaine to write as she devised
A letter, word for word; and when he asked
"Is it for Lancelot, is it for my dear lord?
Then will I bear it gladly;" she replied,
1100 "For Lancelot and the Queen and all the world,
But I myself must bear it." Then he wrote
The letter she devised; which being writ
And folded, "O sweet father, tender and true,
Deny me not," she said—"ye never yet
1105 Denied my fancies—this, however strange,
My latest: lay the letter in my hand
A little ere I die, and close the hand
Upon it; I shall guard it even in death.
And when the heat is gone from out my heart,

_____

[1] priest.

303

1110 Then take the little bed on which I died
For Lancelot's love, and deck it like the Queen's
For richness, and me also like the Queen
In all I have of rich, and lay me on it.
And let there be prepared a chariot-bier
1115 To take me to the river, and a barge
Be ready on the river, clothed in black.
I go in state to court, to meet the Queen.
There surely I shall speak for mine own self,
And none of you can speak for me so well.
1120 And therefore let our dumb old man alone
Go with me, he can steer and row, and he
Will guide me to that palace, to the doors."

She ceased: her father promised; whereupon
She grew so cheerful that they deemed her death
1125 Was rather in the fantasy than the blood.
But ten slow mornings past, and on the eleventh
Her father laid the letter in her hand,
And closed the hand upon it, and she died.
So that day there was dole in Astolat.

1130 But when the next sun brake from underground,
Then, those two brethren slowly with bent brows
Accompanying, the sad chariot-bier
Past like a shadow through the field, that shone
Full-summer, to that stream whereon the barge,
1135 Palled all its length in blackest samite, lay.
There sat the lifelong creature of the house,
Loyal, the dumb old servitor, on deck,
Winking his eyes, and twisted all his face.
So those two brethren from the chariot took
1140 And on the black decks laid her in her bed,
Set in her hand a lily, o'er her hung
The silken case with braided blazonings,
And kissed her quiet brows, and saying to her
"Sister, farewell for ever," and again
1145 "Farewell, sweet sister," parted all in tears.
Then rose the dumb old servitor, and the dead,
Oared by the dumb, went upward with the flood—
In her right hand the lily, in her left

The letter—all her bright hair streaming down—
1150 And all the coverlid was cloth of gold
Drawn to her waist, and she herself in white
All but her face, and that clear-featured face
Was lovely, for she did not seem as dead,
But fast asleep, and lay as though she smiled.

1155 That day Sir Lancelot at the palace craved
Audience of Guinevere, to give at last
The price of half a realm, his costly gift,
Hard-won and hardly won with bruise and blow,
With deaths of others, and almost his own
1160 The nine-years-fought-for diamonds: for he saw
One of her house, and sent him to the Queen
Bearing his wish, whereto the Queen agreed
With such and so unmoved a majesty
She might have seemed her statue, but that he,
1165 Low-drooping till he wellnigh kissed her feet
For loyal awe, saw with a sidelong eye
The shadow of some piece of pointed lace,
In the Queen's shadow, vibrate on the walls,
And parted, laughing in his courtly heart.

1170 All in an oriel on the summer side,
Vine-clad, of Arthur's palace toward the stream,
They met, and Lancelot kneeling uttered, "Queen,
Lady, my liege, in whom I have my joy,
Take, what I had not won except for you,
1175 These jewels, and make me happy, making them
An armlet for the roundest arm on earth,
Or necklace for a neck to which the swan's
Is tawnier than her cygnet's: these are words:
Your beauty is your beauty, and I sin
1180 In speaking, yet O grant my worship of it
Words, as we grant grief tears. Such sin in words
Perchance, we both can pardon: but, my Queen,
I hear of rumours flying through your court.
Our bond, as not the bond of man and wife,
1185 Should have in it an absoluter trust
To make up that defect: let rumours be:
When did not rumours fly? these, as I trust

That you trust me in your own nobleness,
I may not well believe that you believe."

90 While thus he spoke, half turned away, the
        Queen
    Brake from the vast oriel-embowering vine
    Leaf after leaf, and tore, and cast them off,
    Till all the place whereon she stood was green;
    Then, when he ceased, in one cold passive hand
95 Received at once and laid aside the gems
    There on a table near her, and replied:

    "It may be, I am quicker of belief
    Than you believe me, Lancelot of the Lake.
    Our bond is not the bond of man and wife.
00 This good is in it, whatsoe'er of ill,
    It can be broken easier. I for you
    This many a year have done despite and wrong
    To one whom ever in my heart of hearts
    I did acknowledge nobler. What are these?
05 Diamonds for me! they had been thrice their worth
    Being your gift, had you not lost your own.
    To loyal hearts the value of all gifts
    Must vary as the giver's. Not for me!
    For her! for your new fancy. Only this
10 Grant me, I pray you: have your joys apart.
    I doubt not that however changed, you keep
    So much of what is graceful: and myself
    Would shun to break those bounds of courtesy
    In which as Arthur's Queen I move and rule:
15 So cannot speak my mind. An end to this!
    A strange one! yet I take it with Amen.
    So pray you, add my diamonds to her pearls;
    Deck her with these; tell her, she shines me down:
    An armlet for an arm to which the Queen's
20 Is haggard, or a necklace for a neck
    O as much fairer—as a faith once fair
    Was richer than these diamonds—hers not mine—
    Nay, by the mother of our Lord himself,
    Or hers or mine, mine now to work my will—
25 She shall not have them."

        Saying which she seized,
    And, through the casement standing wide for heat,
    Flung them, and down they flashed, and smote the
        stream.
    Then from the smitten surface flashed, as it were,
    Diamonds to meet them, and they past away.
1230 Then while Sir Lancelot leant, in half disdain
    At love, life, all things, on the window ledge,
    Close underneath his eyes, and right across
    Where these had fallen, slowly past the barge
    Whereon the lily maid of Astolat
1235 Lay smiling, like a star in blackest night.

        But the wild Queen, who saw not, burst away
    To weep and wail in secret; and the barge,
    On to the palace-doorway sliding, paused.
    There two stood armed, and kept the door; to whom,
1240 All up the marble stair, tier over tier,
    Were added mouths that gaped, and eyes that asked
    "What is it?" but that oarsman's haggard face,
    As hard and still as is the face that men
    Shape to their fancy's eye from broken rocks
1245 On some cliff-side, appalled them, and they said,
    "He is enchanted, cannot speak—and she,
    Look how she sleeps—the Fairy Queen, so fair!
    Yea, but how pale! what are they? flesh and blood?
    Or come to take the King to Fairyland?
1250 For some do hold our Arthur cannot die,
    But that he passes into Fairyland."

        While thus they babbled of the King, the King
    Came girt with knights: then turned the tongueless
        man
    From the half-face to the full eye, and rose
1255 And pointed to the damsel, and the doors.
    So Arthur bad the meek Sir Percivale
    And pure Sir Galahad to uplift the maid;
    And reverently they bore her into the hall.
    Then came the fine Gawain and wondered at her,
1260 And Lancelot later came and mused at her,
    And last the Queen herself, and pitied her:

But Arthur spied the letter in her hand,
Stoopt, took, brake seal, and read it; this was all:

"Most noble lord, Sir Lancelot of the Lake,
1265 I, sometime called the maid of Astolat,
Come, for you left me taking no farewell,
Hither, to take my last farewell of you.
I loved you, and my love had no return,
And therefore my true love has been my death.
1270 And therefore to our Lady Guinevere,
And to all other ladies, I make moan:
Pray for my soul, and yield me burial.
Pray for my soul thou too, Sir Lancelot,
As thou art a knight peerless."

Thus he read;
1275 And ever in the reading, lords and dames
Wept, looking often from his face who read
To hers which lay so silent, and at times,
So touched were they, half-thinking that her lips,
Who had devised the letter, moved again.

1280 Then freely spoke Sir Lancelot to them all:
"My lord liege Arthur, and all ye that hear,
Know that for this most gentle maiden's death
Right heavy am I; for good she was and true,
But loved me with a love beyond all love
1285 In women, whomsoever I have known.
Yet to be loved makes not to love again;
Not at my years, however it hold in youth.
I swear by truth and knighthood that I gave
No cause, not willingly, for such a love:
1290 To this I call my friends in testimony,
Her brethren, and her father who himself
Besought me to be plain and blunt, and use,
To break her passion, some discourtesy
Against my nature: what I could, I did.
1295 I left her and I bad her no farewell;
Though, had I dreamt the damsel would have died,
I might have put my wits to some rough use,
And helped her from herself."

Then said the Queen
(Sea was her wrath, yet working after storm)
1300 "Ye might at least have done her so much grace,
Fair lord, as would have helped her from her death."
He raised his head, their eyes met and hers fell,
He adding,
"Queen, she would not be content
Save that I wedded her, which could not be.
1305 Then might she follow me through the world, she
asked;
It could not be. I told her that her love
Was but the flash of youth, would darken down
To rise hereafter in a stiller flame
Toward one more worthy of her—then would I,
1310 More specially were he, she wedded, poor,
Estate them with large land and territory
In mine own realm beyond the narrow seas,
To keep them in all joyance: more than this
I could not; this she would not, and she died."

1315 He pausing, Arthur answered, "O my knight,
It will be to thy worship, as my knight,
And mine, as head of all our Table Round,
To see that she be buried worshipfully."

So toward that shrine which then in all the realm
1320 Was richest, Arthur leading, slowly went
The marshalled Order of their Table Round,
And Lancelot sad beyond his wont, to see
The maiden buried, not as one unknown,
Nor meanly, but with gorgeous obsequies,
1325 And mass, and rolling music, like a queen.
And when the knights had laid her comely head
Low in the dust of half-forgotten kings,[1]
Then Arthur spake among them, "Let her tomb
Be costly, and her image thereupon,
1330 And let the shield of Lancelot at her feet
Be carven, and her lily in her hand.

---

[1] ll. 1319–27: "This passage and the 'tower-stair' passage [l. 341] are
among the best blank verse in *Lancelot and Elaine*, I think." (Tennyson's
comment.)

And let the story of her dolorous voyage
For all true hearts be blazoned on her tomb
In letters gold and azure!" which was wrought
335 Thereafter; but when now the lords and dames
And people, from the high door streaming, brake
Disorderly, as homeward each, the Queen,
Who marked Sir Lancelot where he moved apart,
Drew near, and sighed in passing, "Lancelot,
340 Forgive me; mine was jealousy in love."
He answered with his eyes upon the ground,
"That is love's curse; pass on, my Queen, forgiven."
But Arthur, who beheld his cloudy brows,
Approached him, and with full affection said,

345 "Lancelot, my Lancelot, thou in whom I have
Most joy and most affiance, for I know
What thou hast been in battle by my side,
And many a time have watched thee at the tilt
Strike down the lusty and long practised knight,
350 And let the younger and unskilled go by
To win his honour and to make his name,
And loved thy courtesies and thee, a man
Made to be loved; but now I would to God,
Seeing the homeless trouble in thine eyes,
355 Thou couldst have loved this maiden, shaped, it
    seems,
By God for thee alone, and from her face,
If one may judge the living by the dead,
Delicately pure and marvellously fair,
Who might have brought thee, now a lonely man
360 Wifeless and heirless, noble issue, sons
Born to the glory of thy name and fame,
My knight, the great Sir Lancelot of the Lake."

Then answered Lancelot, "Fair she was, my King,
Pure, as you ever wish your knights to be.
365 To doubt her fairness were to want an eye,
To doubt her pureness were to want a heart—
Yea, to be loved, if what is worthy love
Could bind him, but free love will not be bound."

"Free love, so bound, were freëst,"said the King.
1370 "Let love be free; free love is for the best:
And, after heaven, on our dull side of death,
What should be best, if not so pure a love
Clothed in so pure a loveliness? yet thee
She failed to bind, though being, as I think,
1375 Unbound as yet, and gentle, as I know."

And Lancelot answered nothing, but he went,
And at the inrunning of a little brook
Sat by the river in a cove, and watched
The high reed wave, and lifted up his eyes
1380 And saw the barge that brought her moving down,
Far-off, a blot upon the stream, and said
Low in himself, "Ah simple heart and sweet,
Ye loved me, damsel, surely with a love
Far tenderer than my Queen's. Pray for thy soul?
1385 Ay, that will I. Farewell too—now at last—
Farewell, fair lily. 'Jealousy in love?'
Not rather dead love's harsh heir, jealous pride?
Queen, if I grant the jealousy as of love,
May not your crescent fear for name and fame
1390 Speak, as it waxes, of a love that wanes?
Why did the King dwell on my name to me?
Mine own name shames me, seeming a reproach,
Lancelot, whom the Lady of the Lake
Caught from his mother's arms—the wondrous one
1395 Who passes through the vision of the night—
She chanted snatches of mysterious hymns
Heard on the winding waters, eve and morn
She kissed me saying, 'Thou art fair, my child,
As a king's son,' and often in her arms
1400 She bare me, pacing on the dusky mere.
Would she had drowned me in it, where'er it be!
For what am I? what profits me my name
Of greatest knight? I fought for it, and have it:
Pleasure to have it, none; to lose it, pain;
1405 Now grown a part of me: but what use in it?
To make men worse by making my sin known?
Or sin seem less, the sinner seeming great?
Alas for Arthur's greatest knight, a man

Not after Arthur's heart! I needs must break
1410 These bonds that so defame me: not without
She wills it: would I, if she willed it? nay,
Who knows? but if I would not, then may God,
I pray him, send a sudden Angel down
To seize me by the hair and bear me far,
1415 And fling me deep in that forgotten mere,
Among the tumbled fragments of the hills."

So groaned Sir Lancelot in remorseful pain,
Not knowing he should die a holy man.[1]
—1859

---

[1] "I asked my father why he did not write an Idyll 'How Sir Lancelot came unto the hermitage, and how he took the habit unto him; how he went to Almesbury and found Queen Guinevere dead, whom they brought to Glastonbury; and how Sir Lancelot died a holy man'; and he answered, 'Because it could not be done better than by Malory.' My father loved his own great imaginative knight, the Lancelot of the *Idylls*." (Hallam Tennyson's note.)

Robert Browning
1812 – 1889

Robert Browning is recognized for his poetic achievement in the dramatic monologue, especially those poems in the volumes published in 1855, *Men and Women*, and in 1864, *Dramatis Personae*. Browning received little formal education—six years of schooling from the ages of nine to fourteen, and part of one year at London University. His home education was the result of his immersion in his bank-clerk father's large and esoteric library, and the influence of his nonconformist mother's religion and her interest in nature and music. Browning's depth of learning and interest in poetic experimentation is evident in his early work—*Pauline* (1833), *Paracelsus* (1835), and *Sordello* (1840), as well as in the series *Bells and Pomegranates* (1841–46). This series also contained *Dramatic Lyrics* (1842), and *Dramatic Romances and Lyrics* (1845), the former of which included his famous "My Last Duchess," and the latter his first blank-verse dramatic monologue, "The Bishop Orders His Tomb at St. Praxed's Church." Browning met Elizabeth Barrett, whose contemporary reputation as a poet exceeded his, in 1845, and they married on 12 May 1846, after which they immediately took up residence in Italy. Browning returned to England in 1861 after Elizabeth's death, and worked on his complex multinarrative poem *The Ring and the Book* (1868–69). His poetic experimentation continued until his death in 1889.

❧❧❧

My Last Duchess [1]

FERRARA [2]

That's my last Duchess painted on the wall,
  Looking as if she were alive. I call
That piece a wonder, now: Frà Pandolf's[3] hands
Worked busily a day, and there she stands.
5 Will't please you sit and look at her? I said
"Frà Pandolf" by design, for never read
Strangers like you that pictured countenance,
The depth and passion of its earnest glance,
But to myself they turned (since none puts by
10 The curtain I have drawn for you, but I)
And seemed as they would ask me, if they durst,
How such a glance came there; so, not the first

Are you to turn and ask thus. Sir, 'twas not
Her husband's presence only, called that spot
15 Of joy into the Duchess' cheek: perhaps
Frà Pandolf chanced to say "Her mantle laps
Over my lady's wrist too much," or "Paint
Must never hope to reproduce the faint
Half-flush that dies along her throat:" such stuff
20 Was courtesy, she thought, and cause enough
For calling up that spot of joy. She had
A heart—how shall I say?—too soon made glad,
Too easily impressed; she liked whate'er
She looked on, and her looks went everywhere.
25 Sir, 'twas all one! My favour at her breast,
The dropping of the daylight in the West,
The bough of cherries some officious fool
Broke in the orchard for her, the white mule
She rode with round the terrace—all and each
30 Would draw from her alike the approving speech,
Or blush, at least. She thanked men,—good! but thanked
Somehow—I know not how—as if she ranked
My gift of a nine-hundred-years-old name
With anybody's gift. Who'd stoop to blame

---

[1] For a detailed presentation of materials related to Browning's poems, sources, annotations, textual variants, etc., see *Browning: The Poems*, ed. J. Pettigrew and T.J. Collins, 3rd ed., 2 vols. (London: Penguin, 1996).

[2] The Duke is modelled on Alfonso II, fifth Duke of Ferrara. Alfonso (b.1533) married Lucrezia de Medici, then fourteen, in 1558. She died in 1561, and poison was suspected. In 1565 the Duke married the daughter of Ferdinand I, Count of Tyrol.

[3] an imaginary painter of an imaginary painting.

35 This sort of trifling? Even had you skill
In speech—(which I have not)—to make your will
Quite clear to such an one, and say, "Just this
Or that in you disgusts me; here you miss,
Or there exceed the mark"—and if she let
40 Herself be lessoned so, nor plainly set
Her wits to yours, forsooth, and made excuse,
—E'en then would be some stooping; and I choose
Never to stoop. Oh sir, she smiled, no doubt,
Whene'er I passed her; but who passed without
45 Much the same smile? This grew; I gave commands;
Then all smiles stopped together. There she stands
As if alive. Will't please you rise? We'll meet
The company below, then. I repeat,
The Count your master's known munificence
50 Is ample warrant that no just pretence
Of mine for dowry will be disallowed;
Though his fair daughter's self, as I avowed
At starting, is my object. Nay, we'll go
Together down, sir. Notice Neptune, though,
55 Taming a sea-horse, thought a rarity,
Which Claus of Innsbruck[1] cast in bronze for me!
—1842

Soliloquy of the Spanish Cloister

I

G r-r-r—there go, my heart's abhorrence!
    Water your damned flower-pots, do!
If hate killed men, Brother Lawrence,
    God's blood, would not mine kill you!
5 What? your myrtle-bush wants trimming?
    Oh, that rose has prior claims—
Needs its leaden vase filled brimming?
    Hell dry you up with its flames!

II

At the meal we sit together:
10 *Salve tibi!*[2] I must hear
Wise talk of the kind of weather,
    Sort of season, time of year:
Not a plenteous cork-crop: scarcely
    Dare we hope oak-galls,[3] I doubt:
15 *What's the Latin name for "parsley"?*
    What's the Greek name for Swine's Snout?

III

Whew! We'll have our platter burnished,
    Laid with care on our own shelf!
With a fire-new spoon we're furnished,
20   And a goblet for ourself,
Rinsed like something sacrificial
    Ere 'tis fit to touch our chaps—[4]
Marked with L. for our initial!
    (He-he! There his lily snaps!)

IV

25 *Saint*, forsooth! While brown Dolores
    Squats outside the Convent bank
With Sanchicha, telling stories,
    Steeping tresses in the tank,
Blue-black, lustrous, thick like horsehairs,
30   —Can't I see his dead eye glow,
Bright as 'twere a Barbary corsair's?[5]
    (That is, if he'd let it show!)

V

When he finishes refection,[6]
    Knife and fork he never lays
35 Cross-wise, to my recollection,
    As do I, in Jesu's praise.

---

[1] probably Browning's invention, although the Austrian city was a centre for bronze sculpting in the sixteenth century.

[2] "Hail to thee!"

[3] growths on diseased oak-leaves.

[4] "chops": cheeks.

[5] pirate from the north-west coast of Africa.

[6] a light meal.

I the Trinity illustrate,
    Drinking watered orange-pulp—
In three sips the Arian[1] frustrate;
40   While he drains his at one gulp.

VI

Oh, those melons? If he's able
    We're to have a feast! so nice!
One goes to the Abbot's table,
    All of us get each a slice.
45 How go on your flowers? None double?
    Not one fruit-sort can you spy?
Strange!—And I, too, at such trouble,
    Keep them close-nipped on the sly!

VII

There's a great text in Galatians,[2]
50   Once you trip on it, entails
Twenty-nine distinct damnations,
    One sure, if another fails:
If I trip him just a-dying,
    Sure of heaven as sure can be,
55 Spin him round and send him flying
    Off to hell, a Manichee?[3]

VIII

Or, my scrofulous French novel
    On grey paper with blunt type!
Simply glance at it, you grovel
60   Hand and foot in Belial's gripe:[4]
If I double down its pages
    At the woeful sixteenth print,
When he gathers his greengages,
    Ope a sieve and slip it in't?

IX

65 Or, there's Satan!—one might venture
    Pledge one's soul to him, yet leave
Such a flaw in the indenture
    As he'd miss till, past retrieve,
Blasted lay that rose-acacia
70   We're so proud of! *Hy, Zy, Hine…*[5]
'St, there's Vespers![6] *Plena gratiâ*
    Ave, Virgo![7] Gr-r-r—you swine!
—1842

Johannes Agricola in Meditation[8]

There's heaven above, and night by night
  I look right through its gorgeous roof;
No suns and moons though e'er so bright
    Avail to stop me; splendour-proof
5   I keep the broods of stars aloof:
For I intend to get to God,
    For 'tis to God I speed so fast,
For in God's breast, my own abode,
    Those shoals of dazzling glory passed,
10   I lay my spirit down at last.
I lie where I have always lain,
    God smiles as he has always smiled;
Ere suns and moons could wax and wane,
    Ere stars were thundergirt, or piled
15   The heavens, God thought on me his child;
Ordained a life for me, arrayed
    Its circumstances every one
To the minutest; ay, God said
    This head this hand should rest upon

---

[1] heretical follower of the fourth-century Arius, who denied the doctrine of the Trinity.

[2] an imaginary text.

[3] a heretic who believes that the Universe reflects a constant fight between Good and Evil.

[4] the Devil's grip.

---

[5] nonsense words (?).

[6] evening prayer.

[7] "Full of grace, Hail Virgin."

[8] First published, entitled "Johannes Agricola," in the *Monthly Repository*, New Series 10, January 1836, pp. 45–46, immediately following "Porphyria," each poem signed "Z." Slightly revised, it was reprinted in *Dramatic Lyrics* in 1842, grouped with its earlier companion under the title "Madhouse Cells."

20   Thus, ere he fashioned star or sun.
And having thus created me,
       Thus rooted me, he bade me grow,
Guiltless for ever, like a tree
       That buds and blooms, nor seeks to know
25   The law by which it prospers so:
But sure that thought and word and deed
       All go to swell his love for me,
Me, made because that love had need
       Of something irreversibly
30   Pledged solely its content to be.
Yes, yes, a tree which must ascend,
       No poison-gourd foredoomed to stoop!
I have God's warrant, could I blend
       All hideous sins, as in a cup,
35   To drink the mingled venoms up;
Secure my nature will convert
       The draught to blossoming gladness fast:
While sweet dews turn to the gourd's hurt,
       And bloat, and while they bloat it, blast,
40   As from the first its lot was cast.
For as I lie, smiled on, full-fed
       By unexhausted power to bless,
I gaze below on hell's fierce bed,
       And those its waves of flame oppress,
45   Swarming in ghastly wretchedness;
Whose life on earth aspired to be
       One altar-smoke, so pure!—to win
If not love like God's love for me,
       At least to keep his anger in;
50   And all their striving turned to sin.
Priest, doctor, hermit, monk grown white
       With prayer, the broken-hearted nun,
The martyr, the wan acolyte,
       The incense-swinging child,—undone
55   Before God fashioned star or sun!
God, whom I praise; how could I praise,
       If such as I might understand,
Make out and reckon on his ways,

60   And bargain for his love, and stand,
       Paying a price, at his right hand?
—1836

Porphyria's Lover

The rain set early in tonight,
       The sullen wind was soon awake,
It tore the elm-tops down for spite,
       And did its worst to vex the lake:
5   I listened with heart fit to break.
When glided in Porphyria; straight
       She shut the cold out and the storm,
And kneeled and made the cheerless grate
       Blaze up, and all the cottage warm;
10   Which done, she rose, and from her form
Withdrew the dripping cloak and shawl,
       And laid her soiled gloves by, untied
Her hat and let the damp hair fall,
       And, last, she sat down by my side
15   And called me. When no voice replied,
She put my arm about her waist,
       And made her smooth white shoulder bare,
And all her yellow hair displaced,
       And, stooping, made my cheek lie there,
20   And spread, o'er all, her yellow hair,
Murmuring how she loved me—she
       Too weak, for all her heart's endeavour,
To set its struggling passion free
       From pride, and vainer ties dissever,
25   And give herself to me for ever.
But passion sometimes would prevail,
       Nor could tonight's gay feast restrain
A sudden thought of one so pale
       For love of her, and all in vain:
30   So, she was come through wind and rain.
Be sure I looked up at her eyes
       Happy and proud; at last I knew
Porphyria worshipped me; surprise
       Made my heart swell, and still it grew
35   While I debated what to do.

That moment she was mine, mine, fair,
    Perfectly pure and good: I found
A thing to do, and all her hair
    In one long yellow string I wound
40   Three times her little throat around,
And strangled her. No pain felt she;
    I am quite sure she felt no pain.
As a shut bud that holds a bee,
    I warily oped her lids: again
45   Laughed the blue eyes without a stain.
And I untightened next the tress
    About her neck; her cheek once more
Blushed bright beneath my burning kiss:
    I propped her head up as before,
50   Only, this time my shoulder bore
Her head, which droops upon it still:
    The smiling rosy little head,
So glad it has its utmost will,
    That all it scorned at once is fled,
55   And I, its love, am gained instead!
Porphyria's love: she guessed not how
    Her darling one wish would be heard.
And thus we sit together now,
    And all night long we have not stirred,
60   And yet God has not said a word!
    —1836

Pictor Ignotus [1]

FLORENCE, 15–

I could have painted pictures like that youth's[2]
    Ye praise so. How my soul springs up! No bar
Stayed me—ah, thought which saddens while it
      soothes!
    —Never did fate forbid me, star by star,
5 To outburst on your night with all my gift

Of fires from God: nor would my flesh have
      shrunk
From seconding my soul, with eyes uplift
    And wide to heaven, or, straight like thunder,
      sunk
To the centre, of an instant; or around
10   Turned calmly and inquisitive, to scan
The licence and the limit, space and bound,
    Allowed to truth made visible in man.
And, like that youth ye praise so, all I saw,
    Over the canvas could my hand have flung,
15 Each face obedient to its passion's law,
    Each passion clear proclaimed without a tongue;
Whether Hope rose at once in all the blood,
    A-tiptoe for the blessing of embrace,
Or Rapture drooped the eyes, as when her brood
20   Pull down the nesting dove's heart to its place;
Or Confidence lit swift the forehead up,
    And locked the mouth fast, like a castle
      braved,—[3]
O human faces, hath it spilt, my cup?
    What did ye give me that I have not saved?
25 Nor will I say I have not dreamed (how well!)
    Of going—I, in each new picture,—forth,
As, making new hearts beat and bosoms swell,
    To Pope or Kaiser, East, West, South, or North,
Bound for the calmly-satisfied great State,
30   Or glad aspiring little burgh, it went,
Flowers cast upon the car[4] which bore the freight,
    Through old streets named afresh from the event,
Till it reached home, where learned age should greet
    My face, and youth, the star not yet distinct
35 Above his hair, lie learning at my feet!—
    Oh, thus to live, I and my picture, linked
With love about, and praise, till life should end,
    And then not go to heaven, but linger here,
Here on my earth, earth's every man my friend,—
40   The thought grew frightful, 'twas so wildly dear!

---

[1] The designation "Pictor Ignotus" (Latin, "painter unknown") is used in many art museums. "Ignotus" also means "obscure."

[2] probably Raphael (1483–1520).

[3] threatened.

[4] chariot.

But a voice changed it. Glimpses of such sights
    Have scared me, like the revels through a door
Of some strange house of idols at its rites!
    This world seemed not the world it was before:
45 Mixed with my loving trusting ones, there trooped
    …Who summoned those cold faces that begun
To press on me and judge me? Though I stooped
    Shrinking, as from the soldiery a nun,
They drew me forth, and spite of me…enough!
50   These buy and sell our pictures, take and give,
Count them for garniture and household-stuff,
    And where they live needs must our pictures live
And see their faces, listen to their prate,
    Partakers of their daily pettiness,
55 Discussed of,—"This I love, or this I hate,
    This likes me more, and this affects me less!"
Wherefore I chose my portion. If at whiles
    My heart sinks, as monotonous I paint
These endless cloisters and eternal aisles
60   With the same series, Virgin, Babe and Saint,
With the same cold calm beautiful regard,—
    At least no merchant traffics in my heart;
The sanctuary's gloom at least shall ward
    Vain tongues from where my pictures stand apart:
65 Only prayer breaks the silence of the shrine
    While, blackening in the daily candle-smoke,
They moulder on the damp wall's travertine,[1]
    'Mid echoes the light footstep never woke.
So, die my pictures! surely, gently die!
70   O youth, men praise so,—holds their praise its
        worth?
Blown harshly, keeps the trump its golden cry?
    Tastes sweet the water with such specks of earth?
—1845

The Lost Leader [2]

I

Just for a handful of silver he left us,[3]
    Just for a riband to stick in his coat—
Found the one gift of which fortune bereft us,
    Lost all the others she lets us devote;
5 They, with the gold to give, doled him out silver,
    So much was theirs who so little allowed:
How all our copper had gone for his service!
    Rags—were they purple, his heart had been
        proud!
We that had loved him so, followed him, honoured
    him,
10   Lived in his mild and magnificent eye,
Learned his great language, caught his clear accents,
    Made him our pattern to live and to die!
Shakespeare was of us, Milton was for us,
    Burns, Shelley, were with us,—they watch from
        their graves!
15 He alone breaks from the van and the freeman,
    —He alone sinks to the rear and the slaves!

II

We shall march prospering,—not through his
    presence;
    Songs may inspirit us,—not from his lyre;
Deeds will be done,—while he boasts his
    quiescence,
20   Still bidding crouch whom the rest bade aspire:
Blot out his name, then, record one lost soul more,
    One task more declined, one more footpath
    untrod,
One more devils'-triumph and sorrow for angels,
    One wrong more to man, one more insult to
        God!
25 Life's night begins: let him never come back to us!

---

[2] The figure is modelled on Wordsworth.

[3] Judas's thirty pieces of silver and Wordsworth's pension and Laureate-ship.

---

[1] limestone.

There would be doubt, hesitation and pain,
Forced praise on our part—the glimmer of
    twilight,
    Never glad confident morning again!
Best fight on well, for we taught him—strike
    gallantly,
30   Menace our heart ere we master his own;
Then let him receive the new knowledge and wait
    us,
    Pardoned in heaven, the first by the throne!
—1845

The Bishop Orders His Tomb
at Saint Praxed's Church

ROME, 15–

Vanity, saith the preacher, vanity![1]
    Draw round my bed: is Anselm keeping back?
Nephews—sons mine…ah God, I know not! Well—
She, men would have to be your mother once,
5   Old Gandolf envied me, so fair she was!
What's done is done, and she is dead beside,
Dead long ago, and I am Bishop since,
And as she died so must we die ourselves,
And thence ye may perceive the world's a dream.
10   Life, how and what is it? As here I lie
In this state-chamber, dying by degrees,
Hours and long hours in the dead night, I ask
"Do I live, am I dead?" Peace, peace seems all.
Saint Praxed's ever was the church for peace;
15   And so, about this tomb of mine. I fought
With tooth and nail to save my niche, ye know:
—Old Gandolf cozened[2] me, despite my care;
Shrewd was that snatch from out the corner South
He graced his carrion with, God curse the same!
20   Yet still my niche is not so cramped but thence

One sees the pulpit o' the epistle-side,[3]
And somewhat of the choir, those silent seats,
And up into the airy dome where live
The angels, and a sunbeam's sure to lurk:
25   And I shall fill my slab of basalt[4] there,
And 'neath my tabernacle[5] take my rest,
With those nine columns round me, two and two,
The odd one at my feet where Anselm stands:
Peach-blossom marble all, the rare, the ripe
30   As fresh-poured red wine of a mighty pulse.
—Old Gandolf with his paltry onion-stone,[6]
Put me where I may look at him! True peach,
Rosy and flawless: how I earned the prize!
Draw close: that conflagration of my church
35   —What then? So much was saved if aught were
    missed!
My sons, ye would not be my death? Go dig
The white-grape vineyard where the oil-press stood,
Drop water gently till the surface sink,
And if ye find…Ah God, I know not, I!…
40   Bedded in store of rotten fig-leaves soft,
And corded up in a tight olive-frail,[7]
Some lump, ah God, of *lapis lazuli*,[8]
Big as a Jew's head cut off at the nape,
Blue as a vein o'er the Madonna's breast…
45   Sons, all have I bequeathed you, villas, all,
That brave Frascati[9] villa with its bath,
So, let the blue lump poise between my knees,
Like God the Father's globe on both his hands
Ye worship in the Jesu Church so gay,
50   For Gandolf shall not choose but see and burst!

---

[1] a version of Ecclesiates 1:2.

[2] tricked.

[3] the right side.

[4] a black stone.

[5] canopy over a tomb.

[6] a cheap marble.

[7] basket.

[8] semi-precious blue stone.

[9] town near Rome.

Swift as a weaver's shuttle fleet our years:[1]
Man goeth to the grave, and where is he?[2]
Did I say basalt for my slab, sons? Black—
'Twas ever antique-black I meant! How else
55 Shall ye contrast my frieze to come beneath?
The bas-relief in bronze ye promised me,
Those Pans[3] and Nymphs ye wot[4] of, and
    perchance
Some tripod,[5] thyrsus,[6] with a vase or so,
The Saviour at his sermon on the mount,
60 Saint Praxed in a glory,[7] and one Pan
Ready to twitch the Nymph's last garment off,
And Moses with the tables[8]...but I know
Ye mark me not! What do they whisper thee,
Child of my bowels, Anselm? Ah, ye hope
65 To revel down[9] my villas while I gasp
Bricked o'er with beggar's mouldy travertine[10]
Which Gandolf from his tomb-top chuckles at!
Nay, boys, ye love me—all of jasper,[11] then!
'Tis jasper ye stand pledged to, lest I grieve
70 My bath must needs be left behind, alas!
One block, pure green as a pistachio-nut,
There's plenty jasper somewhere in the world—
And have I not Saint Praxed's ear to pray
Horses for ye, and brown Greek manuscripts,
75 And mistresses with great smooth marbly limbs?
—That's if ye carve my epitaph aright,

Choice Latin, picked phrase, Tully's[12] every word,
No gaudy ware like Gandolf's second line—
Tully, my masters? Ulpian[13] serves his need!
80 And then how I shall lie through centuries,
And hear the blessed mutter of the mass,
And see God made and eaten all day long,
And feel the steady candle-flame, and taste
Good strong thick stupefying incense-smoke!
85 For as I lie here, hours of the dead night,
Dying in state and by such slow degrees,
I fold my arms as if they clasped a crook,[14]
And stretch my feet forth straight as stone can point,
And let the bedclothes, for a mortcloth,[15] drop
90 Into great laps and folds of sculptor's-work:
And as yon tapers dwindle, and strange thoughts
Grow, with a certain humming in my ears,
About the life before I lived this life,
And this life too, popes, cardinals and priests,
95 Saint Praxed at his sermon on the mount,
Your tall pale mother with her talking eyes,
And new-found agate urns as fresh as day,
And marble's language, Latin pure, discreet,
—Aha, ELUCESCEBAT[16] quoth our friend?
100 No Tully, said I, Ulpian at the best!
Evil and brief hath been my pilgrimage.
All *lapis*, all, sons! Else I give the Pope
My villas! Will ye ever eat my heart?
Ever your eyes were as a lizard's quick,
105 They glitter like your mother's for my soul,
Or ye would heighten my impoverished frieze,
Piece out its starved design, and fill my vase
With grapes, and add a vizor and a Term,[17]
And to the tripod ye would tie a lynx

---

[1] a version of Job 7:6.

[2] a version of Job 7:9 and 14:10.

[3] god of fields and forests.

[4] know.

[5] three-legged stool associated with the priestesses of Apollo.

[6] staff of Bacchus, god of wine.

[7] halo.

[8] tablets.

[9] squander.

[10] limestone.

[11] kind of quartz.

[12] Marcus Tullius Cicero (106–43 BC).

[13] Domitius Uelpianus (170–228), an inferior writer.

[14] Bishop's staff.

[15] pall.

[16] "He was illustrious."

[17] mask and pedestal bust.

To comfort me on my entablature[1]
Whereon I am to lie till I must ask
"Do I live, am I dead?" There, leave me, there!
For ye have stabbed me with ingratitude
115 To death—ye wish it—God, ye wish it! Stone—
Gritstone,[2] a-crumble! Clammy squares which sweat
As if the corpse they keep were oozing through—
And no more *lapis* to delight the world!
Well go! I bless ye. Fewer tapers there,
120 But in a row: and, going, turn your backs
—Ay, like departing altar-ministrants,
And leave me in my church, the church for peace,
That I may watch at leisure if he leers—
Old Gandolf, at me, from his onion-stone,
125 As still he envied me, so fair she was!
—1845

The Laboratory

ANCIEN RÉGIME [3]

I

Now that I, tying thy glass mask tightly,
May gaze through these faint smokes curling
whitely,
As thou pliest thy trade in this devil's-smithy—
Which is the poison to poison her, prithee?

II

5 He is with her, and they know that I know
Where they are, what they do: they believe my tears
flow
While they laugh, laugh at me, at me fled to the drear
Empty church, to pray God in, for them!—I am
here.

III

Grind away, moisten and mash up thy paste,
10 Pound at thy powder,—I am not in haste!
Better sit thus, and observe thy strange things,
Than go where men wait me and dance at the
King's.

IV

That in the mortar—you call it a gum?
Ah, the brave tree whence such gold oozings come!
15 And yonder soft phial, the exquisite blue,
Sure to taste sweetly,—is that poison too?

V

Had I but all of them, thee and thy treasures,
What a wild crowd of invisible pleasures!
To carry pure death in an ear-ring, a casket,
20 A signet, a fan-mount, a filigree basket!

VI

Soon, at the King's, a mere lozenge to give,
And Pauline should have just thirty minutes to live!
But to light a pastile,[4] and Elise, with her head
And her breast and her arms and her hands, should
drop dead!

VII

25 Quick—is it finished? The colour's too grim!
Why not soft like the phial's, enticing and dim?
Let it brighten her drink, let her turn it and stir,
And try it and taste, ere she fix and prefer!

VIII

What a drop! She's not little, no minion[5] like me!
30 That's why she ensnared him: this never will free
The soul from those masculine eyes,—say, "no!"
To that pulse's magnificent come-and-go.

---

[1] entablement (platform for a statue).

[2] cheap sandstone.

[3] the "Old Order" in pre-Revolution France.

[4] roll of paste, burned for perfume.

[5] delicate person.

IX

For only last night, as they whispered, I brought
My own eyes to bear on her so, that I thought
35   Could I keep them one half minute fixed, she
      would fall
Shrivelled; she fell not; yet this does it all!

X

Not that I bid you spare her the pain;
Let death be felt and the proof remain:
Brand, burn up, bite into its grace-
40 He is sure to remember her dying face!

XI

Is it done? Take my mask off! Nay, be not morose;
It kills her, and this prevents seeing it close:
The delicate droplet, my whole fortune's fee!
If it hurts her, beside, can it ever hurt me?

XII

45 Now, take all my jewels, gorge gold to your fill,
You may kiss me, old man, on my mouth if you will!
But brush this dust off me, lest horror it brings
Ere I know it—next moment I dance at the King's!
—1844

Love Among the Ruins

I

Where the quiet-coloured end of evening
    smiles,
  Miles and miles
On the solitary pastures where our sheep
  Half-asleep
5 Tinkle homeward through the twilight, stray or stop
  As they crop—
Was the site once of a city great and gay,
  (So they say)
Of our country's very capital, its prince
10   Ages since

Held his court in, gathered councils, wielding far
  Peace or war.

II

Now,—the country does not even boast a tree,
  As you see,
15 To distinguish slopes of verdure, certain rills
  From the hills
Intersect and give a name to, (else they run
  Into one)
Where the domed and daring palace shot its spires
20   Up like fires
O'er the hundred-gated circuit of a wall[1]
  Bounding all,
Made of marble, men might march on nor be
    pressed,
  Twelve abreast.

III

25 And such plenty and perfection, see, of grass
  Never was!
Such a carpet as, this summer-time, o'erspreads
  And embeds
Every vestige of the city, guessed alone,
30   Stock or stone—
Where a multitude of men breathed joy and woe
  Long ago;
Lust of glory pricked their hearts up, dread of shame
  Struck them tame;
35 And that glory and that shame alike, the gold
  Bought and sold.

IV

Now,—the single little turret that remains
  On the plains,
By the caper over-rooted, by the gourd
40   Overscored,

---

[1] Babylon and the Egyptian Thebes were reputed to have a hundred gates.

While the patching houseleek's[1] head of blossom
    winks
  Through the chinks—
Marks the basement whence a tower in ancient time
    Sprang sublime,
45 And a burning ring, all round, the chariots traced
    As they raced,
And the monarch and his minions and his dames
    Viewed the games.

V

And I know, while thus the quiet-coloured eve
50   Smiles to leave
To their folding, all our many-tinkling fleece
    In such peace,
And the slopes and rills in undistinguished grey
    Melt away—
55 That a girl with eager eyes and yellow hair
    Waits me there
In the turret whence the charioteers caught soul
    For the goal,
When the king looked, where she looks now,
    breathless, dumb
60 Till I come.

VI

But he looked upon the city, every side,
  Far and wide,
All the mountains topped with temples, all the
    glades'
  Colonnades,
65 All the causeys,[2] bridges, aqueducts,—and then,
    All the men!
When I do come, she will speak not, she will stand,
    Either hand
On my shoulder, give her eyes the first embrace
70   Of my face,

Ere we rush, ere we extinguish sight and speech
  Each on each.

VII

In one year they sent a million fighters forth
  South and North,
75 And they build their gods a brazen pillar high
    As the sky,
Yet reserved a thousand chariots in full force—
    Gold, of course.
Oh heart! oh blood that freezes, blood that burns!
80   Earth's returns
For whole centuries of folly, noise and sin!
    Shut them in,
With their triumphs and their glories and the rest!
    Love is best.
—1855

Fra Lippo Lippi [3]

I am poor brother Lippo, by your leave!
 You need not clap your torches to my face.
Zooks,[4] what's to blame? you think you see a monk!
What, 'tis past midnight, and you go the rounds,
5 And here you catch me at an alley's end
Where sportive ladies leave their doors ajar?
The Carmine's my cloister: hunt it up,
Do,—harry out, if you must show your zeal,
Whatever rat, there, haps on his wrong hole,
10 And nip each softling of a wee white mouse,
Weke, weke, that's crept to keep him company!
Aha, you know your betters! Then, you'll take
Your hand away that's fiddling on my throat,
And please to know me likewise. Who am I?
15 Why, one, sir, who is lodging with a friend
Three streets off—he's a certain...how d'ye call?

---

1 a flowering plant.

2 causeways.

3 Fra Lippo Lippi (c.1406–69), Carmelite painter and friar. His artistic creed shares much with that of Browning.

4 "Gadzooks," a mild oath.

Master—a...Cosimo of the Medici,[1]
I' the house that caps the corner. Boh! you were best!
Remember and tell me, the day you're hanged,
20   How you affected such a gullet's-gripe!
But you, sir, it concerns you that your knaves
Pick up a manner nor discredit you:
Zooks, are we pilchards,[2] that they sweep the streets
And count fair prize what comes into their net?
25   He's Judas to a tittle, that man is!
Just such a face! Why, sir, you make amends.
Lord, I'm not angry! Bid your hangdogs go
Drink out this quarter-florin to the health
Of the munificent House that harbours me
30   (And many more beside, lads! more beside!)
And all's come square again. I'd like his face—
His, elbowing on his comrade in the door
With the pike and lantern,—for the slave that holds
John Baptist's head a-dangle by the hair
35   With one hand ("Look you, now," as who should say)
And his weapon in the other, yet unwiped!
It's not your chance to have a bit of chalk,
A wood-coal or the like? or you should see!
Yes, I'm the painter, since you style me so.
40   What, brother Lippo's doings, up and down,
You know them and they take[3] you? like enough!
I saw the proper twinkle in your eye—
'Tell you, I liked your looks at very first.
Let's sit and set things straight now, hip to haunch.
45   Here's spring come, and the nights one makes up
        bands
To roam the town and sing out carnival,
And I've been three weeks shut within my mew,[4]
A-painting for the great man, saints and saints
And saints again. I could not paint all night—
50   Ouf! I leaned out of window for fresh air.
There came a hurry of feet and little feet,

A sweep of lute-strings, laughs, and whiffs of song,—
Flower o' the broom,
Take away love, and our earth is a tomb!
55   *Flower o' the quince,*
I let Lisa go, and what good in life since?
Flower o' the thyme—and so on. Round they went.
Scarce had they turned the corner when a titter
Like the skipping of rabbits by moonlight,—three
        slim shapes,
60   And a face that looked up...zooks, sir, flesh and
        blood,
That's all I'm made of! Into shreds it went,
Curtain and counterpane and coverlet,
All the bed-furniture—a dozen knots,
There was a ladder! Down I let myself,
65   Hands and feet, scrambling somehow, and so
        dropped,
And after them. I came up with the fun
Hard by Saint Laurence,[5] hail fellow, well met,—
Flower o' the rose,
If I've been merry, what matter who knows?
70   And so as I was stealing back again
To get to bed and have a bit of sleep
Ere I rise up tomorrow and go work
On Jerome[6] knocking at his poor old breast
With his great round stone to subdue the flesh,
75   You snap[7] me of the sudden. Ah, I see!
Though your eye twinkles still, you shake your
        head—
Mine's shaved—a monk, you say—the sting's in
        that!
If Master Cosimo announced himself,
Mum's the word naturally; but a monk!
80   Come, what am I a beast for? tell us, now!
I was a baby when my mother died
And father died and left me in the street.
I starved there, God knows how, a year or two

---

[1]   the Florentine ruler and patron of the arts.

[2]   small fish.

[3]   catch the fancy of.

[4]   cage.

[5]   the church of San Lorenzo.

[6]   St. Jerome (340–420), the highly ascetic saint Lippo is painting.

[7]   seize.

On fig-skins, melon-parings, rinds and shucks,
85 Refuse and rubbish. One fine frosty day,
My stomach being empty as your hat,
The wind doubled me up and down I went.
Old Aunt Lapaccia trussed me with one hand,
(Its fellow was a stinger as I knew)
90 And so along the wall, over the bridge,
By the straight cut to the convent. Six words there,
While I stood munching my first bread that month:
"So, boy, you're minded," quoth the good fat father
Wiping his own mouth, 'twas refection-time,—
95 "To quit this very miserable world?
Will you renounce"..."the mouthful of bread?"
    thought I;
By no means! Brief, they made a monk of me;
I did renounce the world, its pride and greed,
Palace, farm, villa, shop and banking-house,
100 Trash, such as these poor devils of Medici
Have given their hearts to—all at eight years old.
Well, sir, I found in time, you may be sure,
'Twas not for nothing—the good bellyful,
The warm serge and the rope that goes all round,
105 And day-long blessed idleness beside!
"Let's see what the urchin's fit for"—that came next.
Not overmuch their way, I must confess.
Such a to-do! They tried me with their books:
Lord, they'd have taught me Latin in pure waste!
110 *Flower o' the clove,*
All the Latin I construe is, "amo" I love!
But, mind you, when a boy starves in the streets
Eight years together, as my fortune was,
Watching folk's faces to know who will fling
115 The bit of half-stripped grape-bunch he desires,
And who will curse or kick him for his pains,—
Which gentleman processional and fine,
Holding a candle to the Sacrament,
Will wink and let him lift a plate and catch
120 The droppings of the wax to sell again,
Or holla for the Eight[1] and have him whipped,—

How say I?—nay, which dog bites, which lets drop
His bone from the heap of offal in the street,—
Why, soul and sense of him grow sharp alike,
125 He learns the look of things, and none the less
For admonition from the hunger-pinch.
I had a store of such remarks, be sure,
Which, after I found leisure, turned to use.
I drew men's faces on my copy-books,
130 Scrawled them within the antiphonary's marge,[2]
Joined legs and arms to the long music-notes,
Found eyes and nose and chin for A's and B's,
And made a string of pictures of the world
Betwixt the ins and outs of verb and noun,
135 On the wall, the bench, the door. The monks
    looked black.
"Nay," quoth the Prior, "turn him out, d'ye say?
In no wise. Lose a crow and catch a lark.
What if at last we get our man of parts,
We Carmelites, like those Camaldolese[3]
140 And Preaching Friars, to do our church up fine
And put the front on it that ought to be!"
And hereupon he bade me daub away.
Thank you! my head being crammed, the walls a
    blank,
Never was such prompt disemburdening.
145 First, every sort of monk, the black and white,
I drew them, fat and lean: then, folk at church,
From good old gossips waiting to confess
Their cribs[4] of barrel-droppings, candle-ends,—
To the breathless fellow at the altar-foot,
150 Fresh from his murder, safe and sitting there
With the little children round him in a row
Of admiration, half for his beard and half
For that white anger of his victim's son
Shaking a fist at him with one fierce arm,
155 Signing himself with the other because of Christ
(Whose sad face on the cross sees only this

_____

[1] the eight magistrates of Florence.

[2] the margin of a book with choral music.

[3] rival religious orders. The Camaldolese are Dominicans.

[4] petty thefts.

After the passion of a thousand years)
Till some poor girl, her apron o'er her head,
(Which the intense eyes looked through) came at eve
160 On tiptoe, said a word, dropped in a loaf,
Her pair of earrings and a bunch of flowers
(The brute took growling), prayed, and so was gone.
I painted all, then cried "'Tis ask and have;
Choose, for more's ready!"—laid the ladder flat,
165 And showed my covered bit of cloister-wall.
The monks closed in a circle and praised loud
Till checked, taught what to see and not to see,
Being simple bodies,—"That's the very man!
Look at the boy who stoops to pat the dog!
170 That woman's like the Prior's niece[1] who comes
To care about his asthma: it's the life!"
But there my triumph's straw-fire flared and
     funked;[2]
Their betters took their turn to see and say:
The Prior and the learned pulled a face
175 And stopped all that in no time. "How? what's here?
Quite from the mark of painting, bless us all!
Faces, arms, legs and bodies like the true
As much as pea and pea! it's devil's-game!
Your business is not to catch men with show,
180 With homage to the perishable clay,
But lift them over it, ignore it all,
Make them forget there's such a thing as flesh.
Your business is to paint the souls of men—
Man's soul, and it's a fire, smoke…no, it's not…
185 It's vapour done up like a new-born babe—
(In that shape when you die it leaves your mouth)[3]
It's…well, what matters talking, it's the soul!
Give us no more of body than shows soul!
Here's Giotto,[4] with his Saint a-praising God,
190 That sets us praising,—why not stop with him?

Why put all thoughts of praise out of our head
With wonder at lines, colours, and what not?
Paint the soul, never mind the legs and arms!
Rub all out, try at it a second time.
195 Oh, that white smallish female with the breasts,
She's just my niece…Herodias,[5] I would say,—
Who went and danced and got men's heads cut off!
Have it all out!" Now, is this sense, I ask?
A fine way to paint soul, by painting body
200 So ill, the eye can't stop there, must go further
And can't fare worse! Thus, yellow does for white
When what you put for yellow's simply black,
And any sort of meaning looks intense
When all beside itself means and looks naught.
205 Why can't a painter lift each foot in turn,
Left foot and right foot, go a double step,
Make his flesh liker and his soul more like,
Both in their order? Take the prettiest face,
The Prior's niece…patron-saint—is it so pretty
210 You can't discover if it means hope, fear,
Sorrow or joy? won't beauty go with these?
Suppose I've made her eyes all right and blue,
Can't I take breath and try to add life's flash,
And then add soul and heighten them threefold?
215 Or say there's beauty with no soul at all—
(I never saw it—put the case the same—)
If you get simple beauty and naught else,
You get about the best thing God invents:
That's somewhat: and you'll find the soul you have
     missed,
220 Within yourself, when you return him thanks.
"Rub all out!" Well, well, there's my life, in short,
And so the thing has gone on ever since.
I'm grown a man no doubt, I've broken bounds:
You should not take a fellow eight years old
225 And make him swear to never kiss the girls.
I'm my own master, paint now as I please—
Having a friend, you see, in the Corner-house!

---

[1] not a relation, but with whom he has relations.

[2] expired in smoke.

[3] a reference to the old doctrine that the soul leaves the body with the last breath in the form of vapour.

[4] Florentine painter and architect (1267–1337).

[5] The Prior is confused. It was Salome, daughter of Herodias, who, after dancing for Herod, asked him for the head of John the Baptist.

Lord, it's fast holding by the rings in front—
Those great rings serve more purposes than just
230 To plant a flag in, or tie up a horse!
And yet the old schooling sticks, the old grave eyes
Are peeping o'er my shoulder as I work,
The heads shake still—"It's art's decline, my son!
You're not of the true painters, great and old;
235 Brother Angelico's[1] the man, you'll find;
Brother Lorenzo[2] stands his single peer:
Fag on at flesh, you'll never make the third!"
Flower o' the pine,
You keep your mistr…manners, and I'll stick to mine!
240 I'm not the third, then: bless us, they must know!
Don't you think they're the likeliest to know,
They with their Latin? So, I swallow my rage,
Clench my teeth, suck my lips in tight, and paint
To please them—sometimes do and sometimes don't;
245 For, doing most, there's pretty sure to come
A turn, some warm eve finds me at my saints—
A laugh, a cry, the business of the world—
(Flower o' the peach,
Death for us all, and his own life for each!)
250 And my whole soul revolves, the cup runs over,
The world and life's too big to pass for a dream,
And I do these wild things in sheer despite,
And play the fooleries you catch me at,
In pure rage! The old mill-horse, out at grass
255 After hard years, throws up his stiff heels so,
Although the miller does not preach to him
The only good of grass is to make chaff.
What would men have? Do they like grass or no—
May they or mayn't they? all I want's the thing
260 Settled for ever one way. As it is,
You tell too many lies and hurt yourself:
You don't like what you only like too much,
You do like what, if given you at your word,
You find abundantly detestable.
265 For me, I think I speak as I was taught;

I always see the garden and God there
A-making man's wife: and, my lesson learned,
The value and significance of flesh,
I can't unlearn ten minutes afterwards.

270 You understand me: I'm a beast, I know.
But see, now—why, I see as certainly
As that the morning-star's about to shine,
What will hap some day. We've a youngster here
Comes to our convent, studies what I do,
275 Slouches and stares and lets no atom drop:
His name is Guidi[3]—he'll not mind the monks—
They call him Hulking Tom, he lets them talk—
He picks my practice up—he'll paint apace,
I hope so—though I never live so long,
280 I know what's sure to follow. You be judge!
You speak no Latin more than I, belike;
However, you're my man, you've seen the world
—The beauty and the wonder and the power,
The shapes of things, their colours, lights and shades,
285 Changes, surprises,—and God made it all!
—For what? Do you feel thankful, ay or no,
For this fair town's face, yonder river's line,
The mountain round it and the sky above,
Much more the figures of man, woman, child,
290 These are the frame to? What's it all about?
To be passed over, despised? or dwelt upon,
Wondered at? oh, this last of course!—you say.
But why not do as well as say,—paint these
Just as they are, careless what comes of it?
295 God's works—paint anyone, and count it crime
To let a truth slip. Don't object, "His works
Are here already; nature is complete:
Suppose you reproduce her"—(which you can't)
"There's no advantage! you must beat her, then."
300 For, don't you mark? we're made so that we love
First when we see them painted, things we have
passed
Perhaps a hundred times nor cared to see;

---

[1] Fra Angelico (1387–1455), an ethereal painter.

[2] Lorenzo Monaco (c.1370–c.1425), painter.

[3] Tomasso Guidi (1401–28?). In fact, Lippo's teacher, not his pupil.

And so they are better, painted—better to us,
Which is the same thing. Art was given for that;
305 God uses us to help each other so,
Lending our minds out. Have you noticed, now,
Your cullion's hanging face? A bit of chalk.
And trust me but you should, though! How much
    more,
If I drew higher things with the same truth!
310 That were to take the Prior's pulpit-place,
Interpret God to all of you! Oh, oh,
It makes me mad to see what men shall do
And we in our graves! This world's no blot for us,
Nor blank; it means intensely, and means good:
315 To find its meaning is my meat and drink.
"Ay, but you don't so instigate to prayer!"
Strikes in the Prior: "when your meaning's plain
It does not say to folk—remember matins,
Or, mind you fast next Friday!" Why, for this
320 What need of art at all? A skull and bones,
Two bits of stick nailed crosswise, or, what's best,
A bell to chime the hour with, does as well.
I painted a Saint Laurence[1] six months since
At Prato, splashed the fresco in fine style:
325 "How looks my painting, now the scaffold's down?"
I ask a brother: "Hugely," he returns—
"Already not one phiz[2] of your three slaves
Who turn the Deacon off his toasted side,
But's scratched and prodded to our heart's content,
330 The pious people have so eased their own
With coming to say prayers there in a rage:
We get on fast to see the bricks beneath.
Expect another job this time next year,
For pity and religion grow i' the crowd—
335 Your painting serves its purpose!" Hang the fools!

—That is—you'll not mistake an idle word
Spoke in a huff by a poor monk, Got wot,
Tasting the air this spicy night which turns

The unaccustomed head like Chianti wine!
340 Oh, the church knows! don't misreport me, now!
It's natural a poor monk out of bounds
Should have his apt word to excuse himself:
And hearken how I plot to make amends.
I have bethought me: I shall paint a piece
345 …There's for you! Give me six months, then go, see
Something in Sant' Ambrogio's![3] Bless the nuns!
They want a cast o' my office.[4] I shall paint
God in the midst, Madonna and her babe,
Ringed by a bowery flowery angel-brood,
350 Lilies and vestments and white faces, sweet
As puff on puff of grated orris-root[5]
When ladies crowd to Church at midsummer.
And then i' the front, of course a saint or two—
Saint John,[6] because he saves the Florentines,
355 Saint Ambrose, who puts down in black and white
The convent's friends and gives them a long day,
And Job, I must have him there past mistake,
The man of Uz (and Us without the z,
Painters who need his patience). Well, all these
360 Secured at their devotion, up shall come
Out of a corner when you least expect,
As one by a dark stair into a great light,
Music and talking, who but Lippo! I!—
Mazed,[7] motionless and moonstruck—I'm the man!
365 Back I shrink—what is this I see and hear?
I, caught up with my monk's-things by mistake,
My old serge gown and rope that goes all round,
I, in this presence, this pure company!
Where's a hole, where's a corner for escape?
370 Then steps a sweet angelic slip of a thing
Forward, puts out a soft palm—"Not so fast!"
—Addresses the celestial presence, "nay—
He made you and devised you, after all,

---

1   The saint was roasted to death in 258.

2   face.

3   a convent in Florence.

4   example of my work.

5   iris root, used in perfume.

6   patron saint of Florence.

7   bewildered.

Though he's none of you! Could Saint John there
    draw—
375 His camel-hair[1] make up a painting-brush?
We come to brother Lippo for all that,
Iste perfecit opus![2] So, all smile—
I shuffle sideways with my blushing face
Under the cover of a hundred wings
380 Thrown like a spread of kirtles[3] when you're gay
And play hot cockles,[4] all the doors being shut,
Till, wholly unexpected, in there pops
The hothead husband! Thus I scuttle off
To some safe bench behind, not letting go
385 The palm of her, the little lily thing
That spoke the good word for me in the nick,
Like the Prior's niece…Saint Lucy,[5] I would say.
And so all's saved for me, and for the church
A pretty picture gained. Go, six months hence!
390 Your hand, sir, and good-bye: no lights, no lights!
The street's hushed, and I know my own way back,
Don't fear me! There's the grey beginning. Zooks!
—1855

A Toccata of Galuppi's [6]

I

Oh Galuppi, Baldassaro,[7] this is very sad to
    find!
I can hardly misconceive you; it would prove
    me deaf and blind;
But although I take your meaning, 'tis with such a
    heavy mind!

II

Here you come with your old music, and here's all
    the good it brings.
5 What, they lived once thus at Venice[8] where the
    merchants were the kings,
Where Saint Mark's is, where the Doges used to
    wed the sea with rings?[9]

III

Ay, because the sea's the street there; and 'tis arched
    by…what you call
…Shylock's bridge[10] with houses on it, where they
    kept the carnival:
I was never out of England—it's as if I saw it all.

IV

10 Did young people take their pleasure when the sea
    was warm in May?
Balls and masks begun at midnight, burning ever to
    midday,
When they made up fresh adventures for the
    morrow, do you say?

V

Was a lady such a lady, cheeks so round and lips so
    red,—
On her neck the small face buoyant, like a bell-
    flower on its bed,
15 O'er the breast's superb abundance where a man
    might base his head?

VI

Well, and it was graceful of them—they'd break
    talk off and afford
—She, to bite her mask's black velvet—he, to
    finger on his sword,

---

[1] St. John wore camel hair.

[2] "This man did the work."

[3] skirts.

[4] a rustic game (here a euphemism for amorous activity).

[5] The martyr was a virgin, unlike the Prior's "niece."

[6] from *toccare*, "to touch" in Italian, a fast-moving keyboard piece.

[7] Baldassaro Galuppi (1706–85), the Venetian composer.

[8] the Cathedral of Venice.

[9] The Dukes of Venice annually celebrated the relationship of the city to the sea in a ceremony in which a ring was cast into the sea.

[10] the Rialto.

While you sat and played Toccatas, stately at the
    clavichord?[1]

VII

What? Those lesser thirds[2] so plaintive, sixths
    diminished,[3] sigh on sigh,
20 Told them something? Those suspensions,[4] those
    solutions[5]—"Must we die?"
Those commiserating sevenths[6]—"Life might last!
    we can but try!"

VIII

"Were you happy?"—"Yes."—"And are you still as
    happy?"—"Yes. And you?"
—"Then, more kisses!"—"Did *I* stop them, when a
    million seemed so few?"
Hark, the dominant's[7] persistence till it must be
    answered to!

IX

25 So, an octave[8] struck the answer. Oh, they praised
    you, I dare say!
"Brave Galuppi! that was music! good alike at grave
    and gay!

---

[1] a stringed keyboard instrument.

[2] "Lesser" means "minor"; a "third" is a chord of two notes four
semitones apart.

[3] A "sixth" is a chord made up of two notes nine semitones apart;
"diminished" (by two semitones), it becomes a chord of two notes seven
semitones apart.

[4] A suspension is a note held from one chord to another, first producing
a discord, and then resolving concordantly.

[5] resolutions, a technical term indicating a concord following a discord.

[6] chords of two notes eleven semitones apart, producing mild
dissonances.

[7] A "dominant" is "the note…which, in traditional harmonic proce-
dures, most urgently demands resolution upon the tonic" (Grove): it is
the fifth note above the tonic or key-note.

[8] The octave, being a perfect consonance, gives the "answer" to
(resolves) the dominant.

I can always leave off talking when I hear a master
    play!"

X

Then they left you for their pleasure: till in due
    time, one by one,
Some with lives that came to nothing, some with
    deeds as well undone,
30 Death stepped tacitly and took them where they
    never see the sun.

XI

But when I sit down to reason, think to take my
    stand nor swerve,
While I triumph o'er a secret wrung from nature's
    close reserve,
In you come with your cold music till I creep
    through every nerve.

XII

Yes, you, like a ghostly cricket, creaking where a
    house was burned:
35 "Dust and ashes, dead and done with, Venice spent
    what Venice earned.
The soul, doubtless, is immortal—where a soul can
    be discerned.

XIII

"Yours for instance: you know physics, something
    of geology,
Mathematics are your pastime; souls shall rise in
    their degree;
Butterflies may dread extinction,—you'll not die, it
    cannot be!

XIV

40 "As for Venice and her people, merely born to
    bloom and drop,
Here on earth they bore their fruitage, mirth and
    folly were the crop:

What of soul was left, I wonder, when the kissing
    had to stop?

XV

"Dust and ashes!" So you creak it, and I want the
    heart to scold.
Dear dead women, with such hair, too—what's
    become of all the gold
45 Used to hang and brush their bosoms? I feel chilly
    and grown old.
    —1855

By the Fire-Side [1]

I

How well I know what I mean to do
    When the long dark autumn-evenings come,
And where, my soul, is thy pleasant hue?
With the music of all thy voices, dumb
5 In life's November too!

II

I shall be found by the fire, suppose,
O'er a great wise book as beseemeth age,
While the shutters flap as the cross-wind blows
And I turn the page, and I turn the page,
10 Not verse now, only prose!

III

Till the young ones whisper, finger on lip,
"There he is at it, deep in Greek:
Now then, or never, out we slip
To cut from the hazels by the creek
15 A mainmast for our ship!"

IV

I shall be at it indeed, my friends:
Greek puts already on either side

Such a branch-work forth as soon extends
To a vista opening far and wide,
20 And I pass out where it ends.

V

The outside-frame, like your hazel-trees:
But the inside-archway widens fast,
And a rarer sort succeeds to these,
And we slope to Italy at last
25 And youth, by green degrees.

VI

I follow wherever I am led,
Knowing so well the leader's hand:
Oh woman-country, wooed not wed,
Loved all the more by earth's male-lands,
30 Laid to their hearts instead!

VII

Look at the ruined chapel again
Half-way up in the Alpine gorge!
Is that a tower, I point you plain,
Or is it a mill, or an iron-forge
35 Breaks solitude in vain?

VIII

A turn, and we stand in the heart of things;
The woods are round us, heaped and dim;
From slab to slab how it slips and springs,
The thread of water single and slim,
40 Through the ravage some torrent brings!

IX

Does it feed the little lake below?
That speck of white just on its marge
Is Pella;[2] see, in the evening-glow,
How sharp the silver spear-heads charge
45 When Alp[3] meets heaven in snow!

---

[1] one of Browning's rare personal poems; the portrait of "Leonor" is one of Mrs. Browning.

[2] village in north-west Italy.

[3] probably Monte Rosa, which can be seen from the hills around Lago d'Orta, where the poem is set.

X

On our other side is the straight-up rock;
And a path is kept 'twixt the gorge and it
By boulder-stones where lichens mock
The marks on a moth, and small ferns fit
50 Their teeth to the polished block.

XI

Oh the sense of the yellow mountain-flowers,
And thorny balls, each three in one,
The chestnuts throw on our path in showers!
For the drop of the woodland fruit's begun,
55 These early November hours,

XII

That crimson the creeper's leaf across
Like a splash of blood, intense, abrupt,
O'er a shield else gold from rim to boss,[1]
And lay it for show on the fairy-cupped
60 Elf-needled mat of moss,

XIII

By the rose-flesh mushrooms, undivulged
Last evening—nay, in today's first dew
Yon sudden coral nipple bulged,
Where a freaked[2] fawn-coloured flaky crew
65 Of toadstools peep indulged.

XIV

And yonder, at foot of the fronting ridge
That takes the turn to a range beyond,
Is the chapel reached by the one-arched bridge
Where the water is stopped in a stagnant pond
70 Danced over by the midge.

XV

The chapel and bridge are of stone alike,
Blackish-grey and mostly wet;
Cut hemp-stalks steep in the narrow dike.

See here again, how the lichens fret[3]
75 And the roots of the ivy strike!

XVI

Poor little place, where its one priest comes
On a festa-day, if he comes at all,
To the dozen folk from their scattered homes,
Gathered within that precinct small
80 By the dozen ways one roams—

XVII

To drop from the charcoal-burners' huts,
Or climb from the hemp-dressers' low shed,
Leave the grange where the woodman stores his nuts,
Or the wattled cote[4] where the fowlers spread
85 Their gear on the rock's bare juts.

XVIII

It has some pretension too, this front,
With its bit of fresco half-moon-wise
Set over the porch, Art's early wont:
'Tis John in the Desert, I surmise,
90 But has borne the weather's brunt—

XIX

Not from the fault of the builder, though,
For a pent-house[5] properly projects
Where three carved beams make a certain show,
Dating—good thought of our architect's—
95 'Five, six, nine,[6] he lets you know.

XX

And all day long a bird sings there,
And a stray sheep drinks at the pond at times;
The place is silent and aware;

---

[1] the protuberance at the centre of a shield.

[2] streaked.

[3] eat into.

[4] rough shelter of woven sticks.

[5] projecting cover.

[6] 1569.

It has had its scenes, its joys and crimes,
100　But that is its own affair.

XXI

My perfect wife, my Leonor,
Oh heart, my own, oh eyes, mine too,
Whom else could I dare look backward for,
With whom beside should I dare pursue
105　The path grey heads abhor?

XXII

For it leads to a crag's sheer edge with them;
Youth, flowery all the way, there stops-
Not they; age threatens and they contemn,
Till they reach the gulf wherein youth drops,
110　One inch from life's safe hem!

XXIII

With me, youth led...I will speak now,
No longer watch you as you sit
Reading by fire-light, that great brow
And the spirit-small hand propping it,[1]
115　Mutely, my heart knows how—

XXIV

When, if I think but deep enough,
You are wont to answer, prompt as rhyme;
And you, too, find without rebuff
Response your soul seeks many a time
120　Piercing its fine flesh-stuff.

XXV

My own, confirm me! If I tread
This path back, is it not in pride
To think how little I dreamed it led
To an age so blest that, by its side,
125　Youth seems the waste instead?

XXVI

My own, see where the years conduct!
At first, 'twas something our two souls
Should mix as mists do; each is sucked
In each now: on, the new stream rolls,
130　Whatever rocks obstruct.

XXVII

Think, when our one soul understands
The great Word which makes all things new,
When earth breaks up and heaven expands,
How will the change strike me and you
135　In the house not made with hands?[2]

XXVIII

Oh I must feel your brain prompt mine,
Your heart anticipate my heart,
You must be just before, in fine,
See and make me see, for your part,
140　New depths of the divine!

XXIX

But who could have expected this
When we two drew together first
Just for the obvious human bliss,
To satisfy life's daily thirst
145　With a thing men seldom miss?

XXX

Come back with me to the first of all,
Let us lean and love it over again,
Let us now forget and now recall,
Break the rosary in a pearly rain,
150　And gather what we let fall!

XXXI

What did I say?—that a small bird sings
All day long, save when a brown pair
Of hawks from the wood float with wide wings

---

[1] a characteristic pose of Elizabeth Barret Browning..

[2] 2 Corinthians 5:1.

Strained to a bell: 'gainst noon-day glare
155 You count the streaks and rings.

XXXII

But at afternoon or almost eve
'Tis better; then the silence grows
To that degree, you half believe
It must get rid of what it knows,
160 Its bosom does so heave.

XXXIII

Hither we walked then, side by side,
Arm in arm and cheek to cheek,
And still I questioned or replied,
While my heart, convulsed to really speak,
165 Lay choking in its pride.

XXXIV

Silent the crumbling bridge we cross,
And pity and praise the chapel sweet,
And care about the fresco's loss,
And wish for our souls a like retreat,
170 And wonder at the moss.

XXXV

Stoop and kneel on the settle[1] under,
Look through the window's grated square:
Nothing to see! For fear of plunder,
The cross is down and the altar bare,
175 As if thieves don't fear thunder.

XXXVI

We stoop and look in through the grate,
See the little porch and rustic door,
Read duly the dead builder's date;
Then cross the bridge that we crossed before,
180 Take the path again—but wait!

XXXVII

Oh moment, one and infinite!
The water slips o'er stock[2] and stone;
The West is tender, hardly bright:
How grey at once is the evening grown—
185 One star, its chrysolite![3]

XXXVIII

We two stood there with never a third,
But each by each, as each knew well:
The sights we saw and the sounds we heard,
The lights and the shades made up a spell
190 Till the trouble grew and stirred.

XXXIX

Oh, the little more, and how much it is!
And the little less, and what worlds away!
How a sound shall quicken content to bliss,
Or a breath suspend the blood's best play,
195 And life be a proof of this!

XL

Had she willed it, still had stood the screen
So slight, so sure, 'twixt my love and her:
I could fix her face with a guard between,
And find her soul as when friends confer,
200 Friends—lovers that might have been.

XLI

For my heart had a touch of the woodland-time,
Wanting to sleep now over its best.
Shake the whole tree in the summer-prime,
But bring to the last leaf no such test!
205 "Hold the last fast!" runs the rhyme.

XLII

For a chance to make your little much,
To gain a lover and lose a friend,

---

[1] bench.

[2] stump.

[3] semi-precious stone.

Venture the tree and a myriad such,
When nothing you mar but the year can mend:
210 But a last leaf—fear to touch!

XLIII

Yet should it unfasten itself and fall
Eddying down till it find your face
At some slight wind—best chance of all!
Be your heart henceforth its dwelling-place
215 You trembled to forestall!

XLIV

Worth how well, those dark grey eyes,
That hair so dark and dear, how worth
That a man should strive and agonize,
And taste a veriest hell on earth
220 For the hope of such a prize!

XLV

You might have turned and tried a man,
Set him a space to weary and wear,
And prove which suited more your plan,
His best of hope or his worst despair,
225 Yet end as he began.

XLVI

But you spared me this, like the heart you are,
And filled my empty heart at a word.
If two lives join, there is oft a scar,
They are one and one, with a shadowy third;
230 One near one is too far.

XLVII

A moment after, and hands unseen
Were hanging the night around us fast;
But we knew that a bar was broken between
Life and life: we were mixed at last
35 In spite of the mortal screen.

XLVIII

The forests had done it; there they stood;
We caught for a moment the powers at play:
They had mingled us so, for once and good,
Their work was done—we might go or stay,
240 They relapsed to their ancient mood.

XLIX

How the world is made for each of us!
How all we perceive and know in it
Tends to some moment's product thus,
When a soul declares itself—to wit,
245 By its fruit, the thing it does!

L

Be hate that fruit or love that fruit,
It forwards the general deed of man,
And each of the Many helps to recruit
The life of the race by a general plan;
250 Each living his own, to boot.

LI

I am named and known by that moment's feat;
There took my station and degree;
So grew my own small life complete,
As nature obtained her best of me—
255 One born to love you, sweet!

LII

And to watch you sink by the fire-side now
Back again, as you mutely sit
Musing by fire-light, that great brow
And the spirit-small hand propping it,
260 Yonder, my heart knows how!

LIII

So, earth has gained by one man the more,
And the gain of earth must be heaven's gain too;
And the whole is well worth thinking o'er

When autumn comes: which I mean to do
265 One day, as I said before.

—1855

An Epistle Containing the Strange Medical Experience of Karshish, the Arab Physician [1]

Karshish,[2] the picker-up of learning's crumbs,
The not-incurious in God's handiwork
(This man's-flesh he hath admirably made,
Blown like a bubble, kneaded like a paste,
5 To coop up and keep down on earth a space
That puff of vapour from his mouth , man's soul)[3]
—To Abib, all-sagacious in our art,
Breeder in me of what poor skill I boast,
Like me inquisitive how pricks and cracks
10 Befall the flesh through too much stress and strain,
Whereby the wily vapour fain would slip
Back and rejoin its source before the term,—
And aptest in contrivance (under God)
To baffle it by deftly stopping such:—
15 The vagrant Scholar to his Sage at home
Sends greeting (health and knowledge, fame with
    peace)
Three samples of true snakestone[4]—rarer still,
One of the other sort, the melon-shaped,
(But fitter, pounded fine, for charms than drugs)
20 And writeth now the twenty-second time.

My journeyings were brought to Jericho:[5]
Thus I resume. Who studious in our art
Shall count a little labour unrepaid?
I have shed sweat enough, left flesh and bone

25 On many a flinty furlong of this land.
Also, the country-side is all on fire
With rumours of a marching hitherward:
Some say Vespasian[6] cometh, some, his son.
A black lynx snarled and pricked a tufted ear;
30 Lust of my blood inflamed his yellow balls:[7]
I cried and threw my staff and he was gone.
Twice have the robbers stripped and beaten me,
And once a town declared me for a spy;
But at the end, I reach Jerusalem,
35 Since this poor covert where I pass the night,
This Bethany,[8] lies scarce the distance thence
A man with plague-sores at the third degree
Runs till he drops down dead. Thou laughest here!
'Sooth, it elates me, thus reposed and safe,
40 To void the stuffing of my travel-scrip[9]
And share with thee whatever Jewry yields.
A viscid choler[10] is observable
In tertians,[11] I was nearly bold to say;
And falling-sickness[12] hath a happier cure
45 Than our school wots of: there's a spider here
Weaves no web, watches on the ledge of tombs,
Sprinkled with mottles on an ash-grey back;
Take five and drop them...but who knows his mind,
The Syrian runagate[13] I trust this to?
50 His service payeth me a sublimate[14]
Blown up his nose to help the ailing eye.
Best wait: I reach Jerusalem at morn,
There set in order my experiences,

---

[1] Karshish and his master Abib are Browning's inventions. The story of Christ raising Lazarus from the dead is from John 11:1–44.

[2] Arabic for "one who gathers."

[3] a reference to the old doctrine that the soul leaves the body with the last breath in the form of vapour. As in "Fra Lippo Lippi," l. 186.

[4] a stone used in treating snake bites.

[5] the city east of Jerusalem.

[6] Roman Emperor (70–79). He invaded Palestine in 66; his son, Titus, did the same in 70.

[7] eyeballs.

[8] a small village near Jerusalem, the home of Lazarus.

[9] A "scrip" is a small bag.

[10] sticky bile.

[11] fevers recurring every other day.

[12] epilepsy.

[13] vagabond.

[14] product of a refining process.

Gather what most deserves, and give thee all—
55 Or I might add, Judea's gum-tragacanth[1]
Scales off in purer flakes, shines clearer-grained,
Cracks 'twixt the pestle and the porphyry,[2]
In fine exceeds our produce. Scalp-disease
Confounds me, crossing so with leprosy—
60 Thou hadst admired one sort I gained at Zoar—[3]
But zeal outruns discretion. Here I end.

Yet stay: my Syrian blinketh gratefully,
Protesteth his devotion is my price—
Suppose I write what harms not, though he steal?
65 I half resolve to tell thee, yet I blush,
What set me off a-writing first of all.
An itch I had, a sting to write, a tang![4]
For, be it this town's barrenness—or else
The Man had something in the look of him—
70 His case has struck me far more than 'tis worth.
So, pardon if—(lest presently I lose
In the great press of novelty at hand
The care and pains this somehow stole from me)
I bid thee take the thing while fresh in mind,
75 Almost in sight—for, wilt thou have the truth?
The very man is gone from me but now,
Whose ailment is the subject of discourse.
Thus then, and let thy better wit help all!

'Tis but a case of mania—subinduced[5]
80 By epilepsy, at the turning-point
Of trance prolonged unduly some three days:[6]
When by the exhibition[7] of some drug
Or spell, exorcization, stroke of art

Unknown to me and which 'twere well to know,
85 The evil thing out-breaking all at once
Left the man whole and sound of body indeed,—
But, flinging (so to speak) life's gates too wide,
Making a clear house of it too suddenly,
The first conceit[8] that entered might inscribe
90 Whatever it was minded on the wall
So plainly at that vantage, as it were,
(First come, first served) that nothing subsequent
Attaineth to erase those fancy-scrawls
The just-returned and new-established soul
95 Hath gotten now so thoroughly by heart
That henceforth she will read or these or none.
And first—the man's own firm conviction rests
That he was dead (in fact they buried him)
—That he was dead and then restored to life
100 By a Nazarene physician of his tribe:
—'Sayeth, the same bade "Rise," and he did rise.
"Such cases are diurnal," thou wilt cry.
Not so this figment!—not, that such a fume,[9]
Instead of giving way to time and health,
105 Should eat itself into the life of life,
As saffron tingeth flesh, blood, bones and all!
For see, how he takes up the after-life.
The man—it is one Lazarus a Jew,
Sanguine,[10] proportioned, fifty years of age,[11]
110 The body's habit wholly laudable,[12]
As much, indeed, beyond the common health
As he were made and put aside to show.
Think, could we penetrate by any drug
And bathe the wearied soul and worried flesh,
115 And bring it clear and fair, by three days' sleep!
Whence has the man the balm that brightens all?
This grown man eyes the world now like a child.

---

[1] a salve.

[2] a hard rock.

[3] town north of the Dead Sea.

[4] sting.

[5] brought about as a result of something else.

[6] actually four days: John 11:17, 39; an incorrect "fact."

[7] administration.

[8] fancy.

[9] hallucination.

[10] robust.

[11] Karshish's "facts" are often wrong: Lazarus would have been well over sixty.

[12] healthy.

Some elders of his tribe, I should premise,
Led in their friend, obedient as a sheep,
120 To bear my inquisition. While they spoke,
Now sharply, now with sorrow,-told the case,—
He listened not except I spoke to him,
But folded his two hands and let them talk,
Watching the flies that buzzed: and yet no fool.
125 And that's a sample how his years must go.
Look, if a beggar, in fixed middle-life,
Should find a treasure,—can he use the same
With straitened habits and with tastes starved small,
And take at once to his impoverished brain
130 The sudden element that changes things,
That sets the undreamed-of rapture at his hand
And puts the cheap old joy in the scorned dust?
Is he not such an one as moves to mirth—
Warily parsimonious, when no need,
135 Wasteful as drunkenness at undue times?
All prudent counsel as to what befits
The golden mean, is lost on such an one:
The man's fantastic will is the man's law.
So here—we call the treasure knowledge, say,
140 Increased beyond the fleshly faculty—
Heaven opened to a soul while yet on earth,
Earth forced on a soul's use while seeing heaven:
The man is witless of the size, the sum,
The value in proportion of all things,
145 Or whether it be little or be much.
Discourse to him of prodigious armaments
Assembled to besiege his city now,
And of the passing of a mule with gourds—
'Tis one! Then take it on the other side,
150 Speak of some trifling fact,—he will gaze rapt
With stupor at its very littleness,
(Far as I see) as if in that indeed
He caught prodigious import, whole results;
And so will turn to us the bystanders
155 In ever the same stupor (note this point)
That we too see not with his opened eyes.
Wonder and doubt come wrongly into play,
Preposterously, at cross-purposes.

Should his child sicken unto death,—why, look
160 For scarce abatement of his cheerfulness,
Or pretermission[1] of the daily craft!
While a word, gesture, glance from that same child
At play or in the school or laid asleep,
Will startle him to an agony of fear,
165 Exasperation, just as like. Demand
The reason why—" 'tis but a word," object—
"A gesture"—he regards thee as our lord
Who lived there in the pyramid alone,
Looked at us (dost thou mind?) when, being young,
170 We both would unadvisedly recite
Some charm's beginning, from that book of his,
Able to bid the sun throb wide and burst
All into stars, as suns grown old are wont.
Thou and the child have each a veil alike
175 Thrown o'er your heads, from under which ye both
Stretch your blind hands and trifle with a match
Over a mine of Greek fire,[2] did ye know!
He holds on firmly to some thread of life—
(It is the life to lead perforcedly)
180 Which runs across some vast distracting orb
Of glory on either side that meagre thread,
Which, conscious of, he must not enter yet—
The spiritual life around the earthly life:
The law of that is known to him as this,
185 His heart and brain move there, his feet stay here.
So is the man perplext with impulses
Sudden to start off crosswise, not straight on,
Proclaiming what is right and wrong across,
And not along, this black thread through the blaze—
190 "It should be" balked by "here it cannot be."
And oft the man's soul springs into his face
As if he saw again and heard again
His sage that bade him "Rise" and he did rise.
Something, a word, a tick[3] o' the blood within
195 Admonishes: then back he sinks at once

---

[1] neglecting.

[2] an incendiary mixture, but not used until the seventh century.

[3] pulse-beat.

To ashes, who was very fire before,
In sedulous recurrence to his trade
Whereby he earneth him the daily bread;
And studiously the humbler for that pride,
200 Professedly the faultier that he knows
God's secret, while he holds the thread of life.
Indeed the especial marking of the man
Is prone submission to the heavenly will—
Seeing it, what it is, and why it is.
205 'Sayeth, he will wait patient to the last
For that same death which must restore his being
To equilibrium, body loosening soul
Divorced even now by premature full growth:
He will live, nay, it pleaseth him to live
210 So long as God please, and just how God please.
He even seeketh not to please God more
(Which meaneth, otherwise) than as God please.
Hence, I preceive not he affects to preach
The doctrine of his sect whate'er it be,
215 Make proselytes as madmen thirst to do:
How can he give his neighbour the real ground,
His own conviction? Ardent as he is—
Call his great truth a lie, why, still the old
"Be it as God please" reassureth him.
220 I probed the sore as thy disciple should:
"How, beast," said I, "this stolid carelessness
Sufficeth[1] thee, when Rome is on her march
To stamp out like a little spark thy town,
Thy tribe, thy crazy tale and thee at once?"
225 He merely looked with his large eyes on me.
The man is apathetic, you deduce?
Contrariwise, he loves both old and young,
Able and weak, affects[2] the very brutes
And birds—how say I? flowers of the field—
230 As a wise workman recognizes tools
In a master's workshop, loving what they make.
Thus is the man, as harmless as a lamb:
Only impatient, let him do his best,

At ignorance and carelessness and sin—
235 An indignation which is promptly curbed:
As when in certain travels I have feigned
To be an ignoramus in our art
According to some preconceived design,
And happed to hear the land's practitioners
240 Steeped in conceit sublimed[3] by ignorance,
Prattle fantastically on disease,
Its cause and cure—and I must hold my peace!

Thou wilt object—Why have I not ere this
Sought out the sage himself, the Nazarene
245 Who wrought this cure, inquiring at the source,
Conferring with the frankness that befits?
Alas! it grieveth me, the learned leech
Perished in a tumult many years ago,
Accused,—our learning's fate,—of wizardry,
250 Rebellion, to the setting up a rule
And creed prodigious[4] as described to me.
His death, which happened when the earthquake fell
(Prefiguring, as soon appeared, the loss
To occult learning in our lord the sage
255 Who lived there in the pyramid alone)
Was wrought by the mad people—that's their wont!
On vain recourse, as I conjecture it,
To his tried virtue, for miraculous help—
How could he stop the earthquake? That's their way!
260 The other imputations must be lies:
But take one, though I loathe to give it thee,
In mere respect for any good man's fame.
(And after all, our patient Lazarus
Is stark mad; should we count on what he says?
265 Perhaps not: though in writing to a leech
'Tis well to keep back nothing of a case.)
This man so cured regards the curer, then,
As—God forgive me! who but God himself,
Creator and sustainer of the world,
270 That came and dwelt in flesh on it awhile!

_____
[1] may it satisfy.

[2] his affection for.

_____
[3] fancy refined by.

[4] monstrous.

—'Sayeth that such as one was born and lived,
Taught, healed the sick, broke bread at his own house,
Then died, with Lazarus by, for aught I know,
And yet was…what I said nor choose repeat,
275 And must have so avouched himself, in fact,
In hearing of this very Lazarus
Who saith—but why all this of what he saith?
Why write of trivial matters, things of price
Calling at every moment for remark?
280 I noticed on the margin of a pool
Blue-flowering borage,[1] the Aleppo[2] sort,
Aboundeth, very nitrous. It is strange!

    Thy pardon for this long and tedious case,
Which, now that I review it, needs must seem
285 Unduly dwelt on, prolixly set forth!
Nor I myself discern in what is writ
Good cause for the peculiar interest
And awe indeed this man has touched me with.
Perhaps the journey's end, the weariness
290 Had wrought upon me first. I met him thus:
I crossed a ridge of short sharp broken hills
Like an old lion's cheek teeth. Out there came
A moon made like a face with certain spots
Multiform, manifold and menacing:
295 Then a wind rose behind me. So we met
In this old sleepy town at unaware,
The man and I. I send thee what is writ.
Regard it as a chance, a matter risked
To this ambiguous Syrian—he may lose,
300 Or steal, or give it thee with equal good.
Jerusalem's repose shall make amends
For time this letter wastes, thy time and mine;
Till when, once more thy pardon and farewell!

    The very God! think, Abib; dost thou think?
305 So, the All-Great, were the All-Loving too—
So, through the thunder comes a human voice

Saying, "O heart I made, a heart beats here!
Face, my hands fashioned, see it in myself!
Thou hast no power nor mayst conceive of mine,
310 But love I gave thee, with myself to love,
And thou must love me who have died for thee!"
The madman saith He[3] said so: it is strange.
—1855

"Childe Roland to the Dark Tower Came"[4]

(See Edgar's song in *Lear*)

I

My first thought was, he lied in every word,
   That hoary cripple, with malicious eye
   Askance to watch the working of his lie
On mine, and mouth scarce able to afford
5 Suppression of the glee, that pursed and scored
   Its edge, at one more victim gained thereby.

II

What else should he be set for, with his staff?
   What, save to waylay with his lies, ensnare
   All travellers who might find him posted there,
10 And ask the road? I guessed what skull-like laugh
Would break, what crutch 'gin write my epitaph
   For pastime in the dusty thoroughfare,

III

If at his counsel I should turn aside
   Into that ominous tract which, all agree,
15   Hides the Dark Tower. Yet acquiescingly
I did turn as he pointed: neither pride

---

[1] herb, used medicinally.

[2] town in northern Syria.

[3] The capital "H" could suggest that Karshish does not (like Cleon) reject the new religion.

[4] The title quotes Edgar (playing the role of the madman, Poor Tom) in *King Lear* 3.4.186. A childe is a candidate for knighthood. Frequently questioned about the poem, Browning said that it came upon him "as a kind of dream" that had to be written, that he did not know what it meant, that he was "very fond" of it, that it was "only fantasy" with "no allegorical intention." Asked if it meant that "he that endureth to the end shall be saved," Browning replied, "Just about that." The poem and its meaning and sources, have been extensively debated.

Nor hope rekindling at the end descried,
    So much as gladness that some end might be.

IV

For, what with my whole world-wide wandering,
20   What with my search drawn out through years,
      my hope
    Dwindled into a ghost not fit to cope
With that obstreperous joy success would bring,—
I hardly tried now to rebuke the spring
    My heart made, finding failure in its scope.

V

25 As when a sick man very near to death[1]
    Seems dead indeed, and feels begin and end
    The tears and takes the farewell of each friend,
And hears one bid the other go, draw breath
Freelier outside, ("since all is o'er," he saith,
30   "And the blow fallen no grieving can amend";)

VI

While some discuss if near the other graves
    Be room enough for this, and when a day
    Suits best for carrying the corpse away,
With care about the banners, scarves and staves:
35 And still the man hears all, and only craves
    He may not shame such tender love and stay.

VII

Thus, I had so long suffered in this quest,
    Heard failure prophesied so oft, been writ
    So many times among "The Band"—to wit,
40 The knights who to the Dark Tower's search
    addressed
Their steps—that just to fail as they, seemed best,
    And all the doubt was now—should I be fit?

VIII

So, quiet as despair, I turned from him,
    That hateful cripple, out of his highway
45   Into the path he pointed. All the day
Had been a dreary one at best, and dim
Was settling to its close, yet shot one grim
    Red leer to see the plain catch its estray.[2]

IX

For mark! no sooner was I fairly found
50   Pledged to the plain, after a pace or two,
    Than, pausing to throw backward a last view
O'er the safe road, 'twas gone; grey plain all round:
Nothing but plain to the horizon's bound.
    I might go on; naught else remained to do.

X

55 So, on I went. I think I never saw
    Such starved ignoble nature; nothing throve:
    For flowers—as well expect a cedar grove!
But cockle, spurge,[3] according to their law
Might propagate their kind, with none to awe,
60   You'd think; a burr had been a treasure-trove.

XI

No! penury, inertness and grimace,
    In some strange sort, were the land's portion.
      "See
    Or shut your eyes," said Nature peevishly,
"It nothing skills:[4] I cannot help my case:
65 'Tis the Last Judgement's fire must cure this place,
    Calcine[5] its clods and set my prisoners free."

---

[1] See John Donne, "A Valediction: Forbidding Mourning," ll. 1–4.

[2] stray animal.

[3] weeds.

[4] is no use.

[5] burn to ashes.

XII

If there pushed any ragged thistle-stalk
    Above its mates, the head was chopped; the
        bents[1]
    Were jealous else. What made those holes and
        rents
70 In the dock's harsh swarth leaves, bruised as to balk
All hope of greenness? 'tis a brute must walk
    Pashing[2] their life out, with a brute's intents.

XIII

As for the grass, it grew as scant as hair
    In leprosy; thin dry blades pricked the mud
    Which underneath looked kneaded up with blood.
75
One stiff blind horse, his every bone a-stare,
Stood stupefied, however he came there:
    Thrust out past service from the devil's stud!

XIV

Alive? he might be dead for aught I know,
80   With that red gaunt and colloped[3] neck a-strain,
    And shut eyes underneath the rusty mane;
Seldom went such grotesqueness with such woe;
I never saw a brute I hated so;
    He must be wicked to deserve such pain.

XV

85 I shut my eyes and turned them on my heart.
    As a man calls for wine before he fights,
    I asked one draught of earlier, happier sights,
Ere fitly I could hope to play my part.
Think first, fight afterwards—the soldier's art:
90   One taste of the old time sets all to rights.

XVI

Not it! I fancied Cuthbert's reddening face
    Beneath its garniture of curly gold,

---

[1] coarse grasses.

[2] trampling.

[3] folds of the skin.

Dear fellow, till I almost felt him fold
An arm in mine to fix me to the place,
95 That way he used. Alas, one night's disgrace!
    Out went my heart's new fire and left it cold.

XVII

Giles then, the soul of honour—there he stands
    Frank as ten years ago when knighted first.
    What honest man should dare (he said) he durst.
100 Good—but the scene shifts—faugh! what
        hangman-hands
Pin to his breast a parchment? His own bands
    Read it. Poor traitor, spit upon and curst!

XVIII

Better this present than a past like that;
    Back therefore to my darkening path again!
105   No sound, no sight as far as eye could strain.
Will the night send a howlet[4] or a bat?
I asked: when something on the dismal flat
    Came to arrest my thoughts and change their
        train.

XIX

A sudden little river crossed my path
110   As unexpected as a serpent comes.
    No sluggish tide congenial to the glooms;
This, as it frothed by, might have been a bath
For the fiend's glowing hoof—to see the wrath
    Of its black eddy bespate with flakes and
        spumes.

XX

115 So petty yet so spiteful! All along,
    Low scrubby alders kneeled down over it;
    Drenched willows flung them headlong in a fit
Of mute despair, a suicidal throng:
The river which had done them all the wrong,
120   Whate'er that was, rolled by, deterred no whit.

---

[4] owl.

XXI

Which, while I forded,—good saints, how I feared
    To set my foot upon a dead man's cheek,
    Each step, or feel the spear I thrust to seek
For hollows, tangled in his hair or beard!
25 —It may have been a water-rat I speared,
    But, ugh! it sounded like a baby's shriek.

XXII

Glad was I when I reached the other bank.
    Now for a better country. Vain presage!
    Who were the strugglers, what war did they wage,
30 Whose savage trample thus could pad[1] the dank
Soil to a plash[2]? Toads in a poisoned tank,
    Or wild cats in a red-hot iron cage—

XXIII

The fight must so have seemed in that fell cirque.[3]
    What penned them there, with all the plain to
        choose?
35 No foot-print leading to that horrid mews,[4]
None out of it. Mad brewage set to work
    Their brains, no doubt, like galley-slaves the Turk
    Pits for his pastime, Christians against Jews.

XXIV

And more than that—a furlong on—why, there!
40   What bad use was that engine for, that wheel,
    Or brake,[5] not wheel—that harrow fit to reel
Men's bodies out like silk? with all the air
Of Tophet's[6] tool, on earth left unaware,
    Or brought to sharpen its rusty teeth of steel.

XXV

145 Then came a bit of stubbed ground, once a wood,
    Next a marsh, it would seem, and now mere earth
Desperate and done with; (so a fool finds mirth,
Makes a thing and then mars it, till his mood
Changes and off he goes!) within a rood—[7]
150   Bog, clay and rubble, sand and stark black
        dearth.

XXVI

Now blotches rankling, coloured gay and grim,
    Now patches where some leanness of the soil's
    Broke into moss or substances like boils;
Then came some palsied oak, a cleft in him
155 Like a distorted mouth that splits its rim
    Gaping at death, and dies while it recoils.

XXVII

And just as far as ever from the end!
    Naught in the distance but the evening, naught
    To point my footstep further! At the thought,
160 A great black bird, Apollyon's[8] bosom-friend,
    Sailed past, nor beat his wide wing dragon-penned[9]
    That brushed my cap—perchance the guide I
        sought.

XXVIII

For, looking up, aware I somehow grew,
    'Spite of the dusk, the plain had given place
165   All round to mountains—with such name to grace
Mere ugly heights and heaps now stolen in view.
How thus they had surprised me,—solve it, you!
    How to get from them was no clearer case.

XXIX

Yet half I seemed to recognize some trick
170   Of mischief happened to me, God knows when—

---

[1] tread down.

[2] puddle.

[3] circus or circular space.

[4] meaning a stable, but here a place of confinement.

[5] heavy harrow for crushing clods.

[6] hell.

[7] a quarter of an acre.

[8] the Devil.

[9] winged.

In a bad dream perhaps. Here ended, then,
Progress this way. When, in the very nick
Of giving up, one time more, came a click
    As when a trap shuts—you're inside the den!

XXX

175 Burningly it came on me all at once,
    This was the place! those two hills on the right,
    Crouched like two bulls locked horn in horn in
        fight;
While to the left, a tall scalped mountain...Dunce,
Dotard, a-dozing at the very nonce,
180   After a life spent training for the sight!

XXXI

What in the midst lay but the Tower itself?
    The round squat turret, blind as the fool's heart,
    Built of brown stone, without a counterpart
In the whole world. The tempest's mocking elf
185 Points to the shipman thus the unseen shelf
    He strikes on, only when the timbers start.

XXXII

Not see? because of night perhaps?—why, day
    Came back again for that! before it left,
    The dying sunset kindled through a cleft:
190 The hills, like giants at a hunting, lay,
Chin upon hand, to see the game at bay,—
    "Now stab and end the creature—to the heft!"

XXXIII

Not hear? when noise was everywhere! it tolled
    Increasingly like a bell. Names in my ears
195   Of all the lost adventurers my peers,—
How such a one was strong, and such was bold,
And such was fortunate, yet each of old
    Lost, lost! one moment knelled the woe of years.

XXXIV

There they stood, ranged along the hill-sides, met
200   To view the last of me, a living frame

For one more picture! in a sheet of flame
I saw them and I knew them all. And yet
Dauntless the slug-horn[1] to my lips I set,
    And blew. "*Childe Roland to the Dark Tower
      came.*"
—1855

The Statue and the Bust [2]

There's a palace in Florence, the world knows
    well,
And a statue watches it from the square,
And this story of both do our townsmen tell.

Ages ago, a lady there,
5 At the farthest window facing the East
Asked, "Who rides by with the royal air?"

The bridesmaids' prattle around her ceased;
She leaned forth, one on either hand;
They saw how the blush of the bride increased—

10 They felt by its beats her heart expand—
As one at each ear and both in a breath
Whispered, "The Great-Duke Ferdinand."

That self-same instant, underneath,
The Duke rode past in his idle way,
15 Empty and fine like a swordless sheath.

Gay he rode, with a friend as gay,
Till he threw his head back—"Who is she?"
—"A bride the Riccardi[3] brings home today."

---

[1] trumpet.

[2] The equestrian statue of Ferdinand de Medici (1549–1608), who became Grand-Duke of Florence in 1587, dominates the Piazza Annunziata in Florence. It is the work of John of Douay (l. 202), better known as Giovanni da Bologna (1524–1608). The bust is fictional.

[3] a leading Florentine family.

Hair in heaps lay heavily
20 Over a pale brow spirit-pure—
Carved like the heart of the coal-black tree,[1]

Crisped like a war-steed's encolure—[2]
And vainly sought to dissemble[3] her eyes
Of the blackest black our eyes endure.

25 And lo, a blade for a knight's emprise[4]
Filled the fine empty sheath of a man,—
The Duke grew straightway brave and wise.

He looked at her, as a lover can;
She looked at him, as one who awakes:
30 The past was a sleep, and her life began.

Now, love so ordered for both their sakes,
A feast was held that selfsame night
In the pile which the mighty shadow makes.

(For Via Larga is three-parts light,
35 But the palace overshadows one,
Because of a crime[5] which may God requite!

To Florence and God the wrong was done,
Through the first republic's murder there
By Cosimo and his cursèd son.)[6]

40 The Duke (with the statue's face in the square)
Turned in the midst of his multitude
At the bright approach of the bridal pair.

Face to face the lovers stood
A single minute and no more,
45 While the bridegroom bent as a man subdued—

Bowed till his bonnet brushed the floor—
For the Duke on the lady a kiss conferred,
As the courtly custom was of yore.

In a minute can lovers exchange a word?
50 In a word did pass, which I do not think,
Only one out of the thousand heard.

That was the bridegroom. At day's brink
He and his bride were alone at last
In a bedchamber by a taper's blink.

55 Calmly he said that her lot was cast,
That the door she had passed was shut on her
Till the final catafalque[7] repassed.

The world meanwhile, its noise and stir,
Through a certain window facing the East,
60 She could watch like a convent's chronicler.

Since passing the door might lead to a feast,
And a feast might lead to so much beside,
He, of many evils, chose the least.

"Freely I choose too," said the bride—
65 "Your window and its world suffice,"
Replied the tongue, while the heart replied—

"If I spend the night with that devil twice,
May his window serve as my loop[8] of hell
Whence a damned soul looks on paradise!

---

[1] ebony.

[2] mane.

[3] simulate by imitation (obsolete usage).

[4] enterprise.

[5] the suppression of Florentine liberty following the return of Cosimo de Medici in 1434.

[6] named Piero.

[7] structure supporting a coffin.

[8] loop-hole.

70 "I fly to the Duke who loves me well,
Sit by his side and laugh at sorrow
Ere I count another ave-bell.[1]

"'Tis only the coat of a page to borrow,
And tie my hair in a horse-boy's trim,
75 And I save my soul—but not tomorrow"—

(She checked herself and her eye grew dim)
"My father tarries to bless my state:
I must keep it one day more for him.

"Is one day more so long to wait?
80 Moreover the Duke rides past, I know;
We shall see each other, sure as fate."

She turned on her side and slept. Just so!
So we resolve on a thing and sleep:
So did the lady, ages ago.

85 That night the Duke said, "Dear or cheap
As the cost of this cup of bliss may prove
To body our soul, I will drain it deep."

And on the morrow, bold with love,
He beckoned the bridegroom (close on call,
90 As his duty bade, by the Duke's alcove)

And smiled "'Twas a very funeral,
Your lady will think, this feast of ours,—
A shame to efface, whate'er befall!

"What if we break from the Arno[2] bowers,
95 And try if Petraja,[3] cool and green,
Cure last night's fault with this morning's flowers?"

The bridegroom, not a thought to be seen
On his steady brow and quiet mouth,
Said, "Too much favour for me so mean!

100 "But, alas! my lady leaves[4] the South;
Each wind that comes from the Apennine
Is a menace to her tender youth:

"Nor a way exists, the wise opine,
If she quits her palace twice this year,
105 To avert the flower of life's decline."

Quoth the Duke, "A sage and a kindly fear.
Moreover Petraja is cold this spring:
Be our feast tonight as usual here!"

And then to himself—"Which night shall bring
110 Thy bride to her lover's embraces, fool—
Or I am the fool, and thou art the king!

"Yet my passion must wait a night, nor cool—
For tonight the Envoy arrives from France
Whose heart I unlock with thyself, my tool.

115 "I need thee still and might miss perchance.
Today is not wholly lost, beside,
With its hope of my lady's countenance:

"For I ride—what should I do but ride?
And passing her palace, if I list,
120 May glance at its window—well betide!"

So said, so done: nor the lady missed
One ray that broke from the ardent brow,
Nor a curl of the lips where the spirit kissed.

Be sure that each renewed the vow,
125 No morrow's sun should arise and set
And leave them then as it left them now.

---

[1] the bell calling to evening prayer.

[2] the river that runs through Florence.

[3] just north of Florence, where Ferdinand had a villa.

[4] comes from.

But next day passed, and next day yet,
With still fresh cause to wait one day more
Ere each leaped over the parapet.

30 And still, as love's brief morning wore,
With a gentle start, half smile, half sigh,
They found love not as it seemed before.

They thought it would work infallibly,
But not in despite of heaven and earth:
35 The rose would blow when the storm passed by.

Meantime they could profit in winter's dearth
By store of fruits that supplant the rose:
The world and its ways have a certain worth:

And to press a point while these oppose
40 Were simple policy; better wait:
We lose no friends and we gain no foes.

Meantime, worse fates than a lover's fate,
Who daily may ride and pass and look
Where his lady watches behind the grate!

45 And she—she watched the square like a book
Holding one picture and only one,
Which daily to find she undertook:

When the picture was reached the book was done,
And she turned from the picture at night to scheme
50 Of tearing it out for herself next sun.

So weeks grew months, years; gleam by gleam
The glory dropped from their youth and love,
And both perceived they had dreamed a dream;

Which hovered as dreams do, still above:
55 But who can take a dream for a truth?
Oh, hide our eyes from the next remove!

One day as the lady saw her youth
Depart, and the silver thread that streaked
Her hair, and, worn by the serpent's tooth,

160 The brow so puckered, the chin so peaked,—
And wondered who the woman was,
Hollow-eyed and haggard-cheeked,

Fronting[1] her silent in the glass—
"Summon here," she suddenly said,
165 "Before the rest of my old self pass,

"Him, the Carver, a hand to aid,
Who fashions the clay no love will change,
And fixes a beauty never to fade.

"Let Robbia's[2] craft so apt and strange
170 Arrest the remains of young and fair,
And rivet them while the seasons range.

"Make me a face on the window there,
Waiting as ever, mute the while,
My love to pass below in the square!

175 "And let me think that it may beguile
Dreary days which the dead must spend
Down in their darkness under the aisle,

"To say, 'What matters it at the end?
I did no more while my heart was warm
180 Than does that image, my pale-faced friend.'

"Where is the use of the lip's red charm,
The heaven of hair, the pride of the brow,
And the blood that blues the inside arm—

---

[1] confronting.

[2] name of a family of Florentine sculptors.

"Unless we turn, as the soul knows how,
185   The earthly gift to an end divine?
A lady of clay is as good, I trow."

But long ere Robbia's cornice, fine,
With flowers and fruits which leaves enlace,
Was set where now is the empty shrine—

190   (And, leaning out of a bright blue space,
As a ghost might lean from a chink of sky,
The passionate pale lady's face—

Eyeing ever, with earnest eye
And quick-turned neck at its breathless stretch,
195   Some one who ever is passing by—)

The Duke had sighed like the simplest wretch
In Florence, "Youth—my dream escapes!
Will its record stay?" And he bade them fetch

Some subtle moulder of brazen shapes—
200   "Can the soul, the will, die out of a man
Ere his body find the grave that gapes?

"John of Douay shall effect my plan,
Set me on horseback here aloft,
Alive, as the crafty sculptor can,

205   "In the very square I have crossed so oft:
That men may admire, when future suns
Shall touch the eyes to a purpose soft,

"While the mouth and the brow stay brave in
     bronze—
Admire and say, "When he was alive
210   How he would take his pleasure once!"

"And it shall go hard but I contrive
To listen the while, and laugh in my tomb
At idleness which aspires to strive."

So! While these wait the trump of doom,
215   How do their spirits pass, I wonder,
Nights and days in the narrow room?

Still, I suppose, they sit and ponder
What a gift life was, ages ago,
Six steps out of the chapel yonder.

220   Only they see not God, I know,
Nor all that chivalry[1] of his,
The soldier-saints who, row on row,

Burn upward each to his point of bliss—
Since, the end of life being manifest,
225   He had burned his way through the world to this.

I hear you reproach, "But delay was best,
For their end was a crime."—Oh, a crime will do
As well, I reply, to serve for a test,

As a virtue golden through and through,
230   Sufficient to vindicate itself
And prove its worth at a moment's view!

Must a game be played for the sake of pelf?
Where a button goes, 'twere an epigram
To offer the stamp of the very Guelph.[2]

235   The true has no value beyond the sham:
As well the counter as coin, I submit,
When your table's a hat,[3] and your prize a dram.[4]

---

[1] band of knights.

[2] A *Guelpho* was a fourteenth-century Florentine coin.

[3] for rolling dice on?

[4] a trifling stake.

Stake your counter as boldly every whit,
Venture as warily, use the same skill,
40 Do your best, whether winning or losing it,

If you choose to play!—is my principle.
Let a man contend to the uttermost
For his life's set prize, be it what it will!

The counter our lovers staked was lost
45 As surely as if it were lawful coin:
And the sin I impute to each frustrate ghost

Is—the unlit lamp and the ungirt loin,
Though the end in sight was a vice, I say.
You of the virtue (we issue join)
50 How strive you? *De te, fabula.*[1]
—1855

How It Strikes a Contemporary[2]

I only knew one poet in my life:
And this, or something like it, was his way.

You saw go up and down Valladolid,[3]
A man of mark, to know next time you saw.
5 His very serviceable suit of black
Was courtly once and conscientious still,
And many might have worn it, though none did:
The cloak, that somewhat shone and showed the
        threads,
Had purpose, and the ruff, significance.
10 He walked and tapped the pavement with his cane,
Scenting the world, looking it full in face,
An old dog, bald and blindish, at his heels.
They turned up, now, the alley by the church,
That leads nowhither; now, they breathed
        themselves
15 On the main promenade just at the wrong time:
You'd come upon his scrutinizing hat,
Making a peaked shade blacker than itself
Against the single window spared some house
Intact yet with its mouldered Moorish work,—
20 Or else surprise the ferrel of his stick
Trying the mortar's temper 'tween the chinks
Of some new shop a-building, French and fine.
He stood and watched the cobbler at his trade,
The man who slices lemons into drink,
25 The coffee-roaster's brazier, and the boys
That volunteer to help him turn its winch.
He glanced o'er books on stalls with half an eye,
And fly-leaf[4] ballads on the vendor's string,
And broad-edge bold-print posters by the wall.
30 He took such cognizance of men and things,
If any beat a horse, you felt he saw;
If any cursed a woman, he took note;
Yet stared at nobody,—you stared at him,
And found, less to your pleasure than surprise,
35 He seemed to know you and expect as much.
So, next time that a neighbour's tongue was loosed,
It marked the shameful and notorious fact,
We had among us, not so much a spy,[5]
As a recording chief-inquisitor,
40 The town's true master if the town but knew!
We merely kept a governor for form,
While this man walked about and took account
Of all thought, said and acted, then went home,
And wrote it fully to our Lord the King
45 Who has an itch to know things, he knows why,
And reads them in his bedroom of a night.
Oh, you might smile! there wanted not a touch,
A tang[6] of...well, it was not wholly ease
As back into your mind the man's look came.

---

1 "The story is about you."

2 The poem is an important poetic statement about the nature of Browning's art.

3 town about 100 miles north-west of Madrid.

---

4 printed on one sheet.

5 See *King Lear* 5.3.17.

6 sting.

50 Stricken in years a little,—such a brow
His eyes had to live under!—clear as flint
On either side the formidable nose
Curved, cut and coloured like an eagle's claw.
Had he to do with A.'s surprising fate?
55 When altogether old B. disappeared
And young C. got his mistress,—was't our friend,
His letter to the King, that did it all?
What paid the bloodless man for so much pains?
Our Lord the King has favourites manifold,
60 And shifts his ministry some once a month;
Our city gets new governors at whiles,—
But never word or sign, that I could hear,
Notified to this man about the streets
The King's approval of those letters conned
65 The last thing duly at the dead of night.
Did the man love his office? Frowned our Lord,
Exhorting when none heard—"Beseech me not!
Too far above my people,—beneath me!
I set the watch,—how should the people know?
70 Forget them, keep me all the more in mind!"
Was some such understanding 'twixt the two?

I found no truth in one report at least—
That if you tracked him to his home, down lanes
Beyond the Jewry, and as clean to pace,
75 You found he ate his supper in a room
Blazing with lights, four Titians[1] on the wall,
And twenty naked girls to change his plate!
Poor man, he lived another kind of life
In that new stuccoed third house by the bridge,
80 Fresh-painted, rather smart than otherwise!
The whole street might o'erlook him as he sat,
Leg crossing leg, one foot on the dog's back,
Playing a decent cribbage with his maid
(Jacynth, you're sure her name was) o'er the cheese
85 And fruit, three red halves of starved winter-pears,
Or treat of radishes in April. Nine,

Ten, struck the church clock, straight to bed went
he.

My father, like the man of sense he was,
Would point him out to me a dozen times;
90 "'St—'St," he'd whisper, "the Corregidor!"[2]
I had been used to think that personage
Was one with lacquered breeches, lustrous belt,
And feathers like a forest in his hat,
Who blew a trumpet and proclaimed the news,
95 Announced the bull-fights, gave each church its
turn,
And memorized[3] the miracle in vogue!
He had a great observance from us boys;
We were in error; that was not the man.

I'd like now, yet had haply been afraid,
100 To have just looked, when this man came to die,
And seen who lined the clean gay garret-sides
And stood about the neat low truckle-bed,
With the heavenly manner of relieving guard.
Here had been, mark, the general-in-chief,
105 Through a whole campaign of the world's life and
death,
Doing the King's work all the dim day long,
In his old coat and up to knees in mud,
Smoked like a herring, dining on a crust,—
And, now the day was won, relieved at once!
110 No further show or need for that old coat,
You are sure, for one thing! Bless us, all the while
How sprucely we are dressed out, you and I!
A second, and the angles alter that.
Well, I could never write a verse,—could you?
115 Let's to the Prado[4] and make the most of time.
—1855

---

[1] paintings by Titian, the Venetian artist (c. 1485–1577).

[2] Chief Magistrate.

[3] memorialized.

[4] promenade.

The Last Ride Together [1]

I

I said—Then, dearest, since 'tis so,
Since now at length my fate I know,
Since nothing all my love avails,
Since all, my life seemed meant for, fails,
5   Since this was written and needs must be—
My whole heart rises up to bless
Your name in pride and thankfulness!
Take back the hope you gave,—I claim
Only a memory of the same,
10   —And this beside, if you will not blame,
        Your leave for one more last ride with me.

II

My mistress bent that brow of hers;
Those deep dark eyes where pride demurs
When pity would be softening through,
15   Fixed me a breathing—while or two
        With life or death in the balance: right!
The blood replenished me again;
My last thought was at least not vain:
I and my mistress, side by side
20   Shall be together, breathe and ride,
        So, one day more am I deified.
            Who knows but the world may end tonight?

III

Hush! if you saw some western cloud
All billowy-bosomed, over-bowed
25   By many benedictions—sun's
And moon's and evening-star's at once—
        And so, you, looking and loving best,
Conscious grew, your passion drew
Cloud, sunset, moonrise, star-shine too,
30   Down on you, near and yet more near,
        Till flesh must fade for heaven was here!—

Thus leant she and lingered—joy and fear!
Thus lay she a moment on my breast.

IV

Then we began to ride. My soul
35   Smoothed itself out, a long-cramped scroll
Freshening and fluttering in the wind.
Fast hopes already lay behind.
        What need to strive with a life awry?
Had I said that, had I done this,
40   So might I gain, so might I miss.
Might she have loved me? just as well
She might have hated, who can tell!
Where had I been now if the worst befell?
        And here we are riding, she and I.

V

45   Fail I alone, in words and deeds?
Why, all men strive and who succeeds?
We rode; it seemed my spirit flew,
Saw other regions, cities new,
        As the world rushed by on either side.
50   I thought,—All labour, yet no less
Bear up beneath their unsuccess.
Look at the end of work, contrast
The petty done, the undone vast,
This present of theirs with the hopeful past!
55   I hoped she would love me; here we ride.

VI

What hand and brain went ever paired?
What heart alike conceived and dared?
What act proved all its thought had been?
What will but felt the fleshly screen?
60   We ride and I see her bosom heave.
There's many a crown for who can reach.
Ten lines, a statesman's life in each!
The flag stuck on a heap of bones,
A soldier's doing! what atones?

---

[1] The poem is one of Browning's most admired lyrics.

65 They scratch his name on the Abbey-stones.[1]
　My riding is better, by their leave.

VII

What does it all mean, poet? Well,
Your brains beat into rhythm, you tell
What we felt only; you expressed
70 You hold things beautiful the best,
　And pace them in rhyme so, side by side.
'Tis something, nay 'tis much: but then,
Have you yourself what's best for men?
Are you—poor, sick, old ere your time—
75 Nearer one whit your own sublime
Than we who never have turned a rhyme?
　Sing, riding's a joy! For me, I ride.

VIII

And you, great sculptor—so, you gave
A score of years to Art, her slave,
80 And that's your Venus, whence we turn
To yonder girl that fords the burn!
　You acquiesce, and shall I repine?
What, man of music, you grown grey
With notes and nothing else to say,
85 Is this your sole praise from a friend,
"Greatly his opera's strains intend,
But in music we know how fashions end!"
　I gave my youth; but we ride, in fine.

IX

Who knows what's fit for us? Had fate
90 Proposed bliss here should sublimate
My being—had I signed the bond—
Still one must lead some life beyond,
　Have a bliss to die with, dim-descried.
This foot once planted on the goal,
95 This glory-garland round my soul,
Could I descry such? Try and test!
I sink back shuddering from the quest.

Earth being so good, would heaven seem best?
　Now, heaven and she are beyond this ride.

X

100 And yet—she has not spoke so long!
What if heaven be that, fair and strong
At life's best, with our eyes upturned
Whither life's flower is first discerned,
　We, fixed so, ever should so abide?
105 What if we still ride on, we two
With life for ever old yet new,
Changed not in kind but in degree,
The instant made eternity,—
And heaven just prove that I and she
110 　Ride, ride together, for ever ride?
　　—1855

Bishop Blougram's Apology [2]

No more wine? then we'll push back chairs
　and talk.
A final glass for me, though: cool, i' faith!

---

[1] They honour him with burial in Westminster Abbey.

[2] According to Browning, Cardinal Wiseman (1801–65) served as a model for Blougram. Wiseman became Roman Catholic Archbishop of Westminster and head of the Roman Catholic Church in England in 1850; the appointment created much controversy. Elements of John Henry Newman also went into Browning's fictional Bishop. Unlike many of Browning's poems, this poem is firmly set in its contemporary time and place by a wealth of topical allusion. The names of protagonist and antagonist are suggestive. "Blougram" may refer to Lord Brougham (1778–1868), a leading nineteenth-century figure who might also have contributed to Browning's portrait. Like the Bishop in the poem, Brougham was a skilled orator and debater, as well as being arrogant and eccentric. The heavy, closed and normally four-wheeled carriage is named after him, while a "gig" is a light, open, two-wheeled carriage.

The word "Apology" in the title is probably deliberately ambiguous, meaning both a "statement of regret for error" and "justification." Among the many interpretations of the poem, the two poles are represented by one which sees the Bishop as a vulgar, fashionable priest justifying his own cowardice, and another, more widely accepted view, which presents the Bishop as an extremely clever rhetorician whose argument in the poem is dictated by the vulgar nature of his petty opponent.

We ought to have our Abbey[1] back, you see.
It's different, preaching in basilicas,
5 And doing duty in some masterpiece
Like this of brother Pugin's,[2] bless his heart!
I doubt if they're half baked, those chalk rosettes,
Ciphers and stucco-twiddlings everywhere;
It's just like breathing in a lime-kiln: eh?
10 These hot long ceremonies of our church
Cost us a little—oh, they pay the price,
You take me—amply pay it! Now, we'll talk.

So, you despise me, Mr Gigadibs.
No deprecation,—nay, I beg you, sir!
15 Beside 'tis our engagement: don't you know,
I promised, if you'd watch a dinner out,
We'd see truth dawn together?—truth that peeps
Over the glasses' edge when dinner's done,
And body gets its sop and holds its noise
20 And leaves soul free a little. Now's the time:
Truth's break of day! You do despise me then.
And if I say, "despise me,"—never fear!
I know you do not in a certain sense—
Not in my arm-chair, for example: here,
25 I well imagine you respect my place
(*Status, entourage*, worldly circumstance)
Quite to its value—very much indeed:
—Are up to the protesting eyes of you
In pride at being seated here for once—
30 You'll turn it to such capital account!
When somebody, through years and years to come,
Hints of the bishop,—names me—that's enough:
"Blougram? I knew him"—(into it you slide)
"Dined with him once, a Corpus Christi Day,[3]
35 All alone, we two; he's a clever man:
And after dinner,—why, the wine you know,—

Oh, there was wine, and good!—what with the wine...
'Faith, we began upon all sorts of talk!
He's no bad fellow, Blougram; he had seen
40 Something of mine he relished, some review:
He's quite above their humbug in his heart,
Half-said as much, indeed—the thing's his trade.
I warrant, Blougram's sceptical at times:
How otherwise? I liked him, I confess!"
45 *Che che*,[4] my dear sir, as we say at Rome,
Don't you protest now! It's fair give and take;
You have had your turn and spoken your home-
truths:
The hand's mine now, and here you follow suit.

Thus much conceded, still the first fact stays—
50 You do despise me; your ideal of life
Is not the bishop's: you would not be I.
You would like better to be Goethe, now,
Or Buonaparte, or, bless me, lower still,
Count D'Orsay,[5]—so you did what you preferred,
55 Spoke as you thought, and, as you cannot help,
Believed or disbelieved, no matter what,
So long as on that point, whate'er it was,
You loosed your mind, were whole and sole yourself.
—That, my ideal never can include,
60 Upon that element of truth and worth
Never be based! for say they make me Pope—
(They can't—suppose it for our argument!)
Why, there I'm at my tether's end, I've reached
My height, and not a height which pleases you:
65 An unbelieving Pope won't do, you say.
It's like those eerie stories nurses tell,
Of how some actor on a stage played Death,
With pasteboard crown, sham orb and tinselled dart,
And called himself the monarch of the world;
70 Then, going in the tire-room[6] afterward,
Because the play was done, to shift himself,

[1] Before being taken over by Henry VIII, Westminster Abbey was Catholic.

[2] A.W.N. Pugin (1812–52), a convert to Catholicism and an architect.

[3] the Thursday after Trinity Sunday, commemorating the celebration of the Eucharist.

[4] "come, come."

[5] Count D'Orsay (1801–52), famous Victorian dandy.

[6] dressing room.

Got touched upon the sleeve familiarly,
The moment he had shut the closet door,
By Death himself. Thus God might touch a Pope
75 At unawares, ask what his baubles mean,
And whose part he presumed to play just now.
Best be yourself, imperial, plain and true!

So, drawing comfortable breath again,
You weigh and find, whatever more or less
80 I boast of my ideal realized
Is nothing in the balance when opposed
To your ideal, your grand simple life,
Of which you will not realize one jot.
I am much, you are nothing; you would be all,
85 I would be merely much: you beat me there.

No, friend, you do not beat me: hearken why!
The common problem, yours, mine, every one's,
Is—not to fancy what were fair in life
Provided it could be,—but, finding first
90 What may be, then find how to make it fair
Up to our means: a very different thing!
No abstract intellectual plan of life
Quite irrespective of life's plainest laws,
But one, a man, who is man and nothing more,
95 May lead within a world which (by your leave)
Is Rome or London, not Fool's-paradise.
Embellish Rome, idealize away,
Make paradise of London if you can,
You're welcome, nay, you're wise.

A simile!
100 We mortals cross the ocean of this world
Each in his average cabin of a life;
The best's not big, the worst yields elbow-room.
Now for our six months' voyage—how prepare?
You come on shipboard with a landsman's list
105 Of things he calls convenient: so they are!
An India screen is pretty furniture,
A piano-forte is a fine resource,
All Balzac's novels occupy one shelf,

The new edition fifty volumes long;
110 And little Greek books, with the funny type
They get up well at Leipsic,[1] fill the next:
Go on! slabbed marble, what a bath it makes!
And Parma's pride, the Jerome,[2] let us add!
'Twere pleasant could Correggio's[3] fleeting glow
115 Hang full in face of one where'er one roams,
Since he more than the others brings with him
Italy's self,—the marvellous Modenese!—
Yet was not on your list before, perhaps.
—Alas, friend, here's the agent...is't the name?
120 The captain, or whoever's master here—
You see him screw his face up; what's his cry
Ere you set foot on shipboard? "Six feet square!"
If you won't understand what six feet mean,
Computer and purchase stores accordingly—
125 And if, in pique because he overhauls[4]
Your Jerome, piano, bath, you come on board
Bare—why, you cut a figure at the first
While sympathetic landsmen see you off;
Not afterward, when long ere half seas over,
130 You peep up from your utterly naked boards
Into some snug and well-appointed berth,
Like mine for instance (try the cooler jug—
Put back the other, but don't jog the ice!)
And mortified you mutter "Well and good;
135 He sits enjoying his sea-furniture;
'Tis stout and proper, and there's store of it:
Though I've the better notion, all agree,
Of fitting rooms up. Hang the carpenter,
Neat ship-shape fixings and contrivances—
140 I would have brought my Jerome, frame and all!"
And meantime you bring nothing: never mind—
You've proved your artist-nature: what you don't
You might bring, so despise me, as I say.

---

[1] a reference to the Teubner series of classical works which began to appear in 1849.

[2] The picture of St. Jerome is in the Ducal Academy in Parma.

[3] the Italian painter (c. 1489–1534), who studied in Modena (l. 117).

[4] throws overboard.

Now come, let's backward to the starting-place.
145 See my way: we're two college friends, suppose.
Prepare together for our voyage, then;
Each note and check the other in his work,—
Here's mine, a bishop's outfit; criticize!
What's wrong? why won't you be a bishop too?

150 Why first, you don't believe, you don't and can't,
(Not statedly, that is, and fixedly
And absolutely and exclusively)
In any revelation called divine.
No dogmas nail your faith; and what remains
155 But say so, like the honest man you are?
First, therefore, overhaul theology!
Nay, I too, not a fool, you please to think,
Must find believing every whit as hard:
And if I do not frankly say as much,
160 The ugly consequence is clear enough.

Now wait, my friend: well, I do not believe—
If you'll accept no faith that is not fixed,
Absolute and exclusive, as you say.
You're wrong,—I mean to prove it in due time.
165 Meanwhile, I know where difficulties lie
I could not, cannot solve, nor ever shall,
So give up hope accordingly to solve—
(To you, and over the wine). Our dogmas then
With both of us, though in unlike degree,
170 Missing full credence—overboard with them!
I mean to meet you on your own premise:
Good, there go mine in company with yours!

And now what are we? unbelievers both,
Calm and complete, determinately fixed
175 Today, tomorrow and for ever, pray?
You'll guarantee me that? Not so, I think!
In no wise! all we've gained is, that belief,
As unbelief before, shakes us by fits,
Confounds us like its predecessor. Where's
180 The gain? how can we guard our unbelief,
Make it bear fruit to us?—the problem here.

Just when we are safest, there's a sunset-touch,
A fancy from a flower-bell, some one's death,
A chorus-ending from Euripides,—[1]
185 And that's enough for fifty hopes and fears
As old and new at once as nature's self,
To rap and knock and enter in our soul,
Take hands and dance there, a fantastic ring,
Round the ancient idol, on his base again,—
190 The grand Perhaps![2] We look on helplessly.
There the old misgivings, crooked questions are—
This good God,—what he could do, if he would,
Would, if he could—then must have done long
      since:
If so, when, where and how? some way must be,—
195 Once feel about, and soon or late you hit
Some sense, in which it might be, after all.
Why not, "The Way, the Truth, the Life?"

                                        —That way
Over the mountain, which who stands upon
Is apt to doubt if it be meant for a road;
200 While, if he views it from the waste itself,
Up goes the line there, plain from base to brow,
Not vague, mistakable! what's a break or two
Seen from the unbroken desert either side?
And then (to bring in fresh philosophy)
205 What if the breaks themselves should prove at last
The most consummate of contrivances
To train a man's eye, teach him what is faith?
And so we stumble at truth's very test!
All we have gained then by our unbelief
210 Is a life of doubt diversified by faith,
For one of faith diversified by doubt:
We called the chess-board white,—we call it black.

"Well," you rejoin, "the end's no worse, at least;
We've reason for both colours on the board:

---

[1] Browning's favourite Greek dramatist.

[2] "I go to seek a grand perhaps," attributed to Rabelais on his death-bed.

215 Why not confess then, where I drop the faith
And you the doubt, that I'm as right as you?"

Because, friend, in the next place, this being so,
And both things even,—faith and unbelief
Left to a man's choice,—we'll proceed a step,
220 Returning to our image, which I like.

A man's choice, yes—but a cabin-passenger's—
The man made for the special life o' the world—
Do you forget him? I remember though!
Consult our ship's conditions and you find
225 One and but one choice suitable to all;
The choice, that you unluckily prefer,
Turning things topsy-turvy—they or it
Going to the ground. Belief or unbelief
Bears upon life, determines its whole course,
230 Begins at its beginning. See the world
Such as it is,—you made it not, nor I;
I mean to take it as it is,—and you,
Not so you'll take it,—though you get naught else.
I know the special kind of life I like,
235 What suits the most my idiosyncrasy,
Brings out the best of me and bears me fruit
In power, peace, pleasantness and length of days.
I find that positive belief does this
For me, and unbelief, no whit of this.
240 —For you, it does, however?—that, we'll try!
'Tis clear, I cannot lead my life, at least,
Induce the world to let me peaceably,
Without declaring at the outset, "Friends,
I absolutely and peremptorily
245 Believe!"—I say, faith is my waking life:
One sleeps, indeed, and dreams at intervals,
We know, but waking's the main point with us
And my provision's for life's waking part.
Accordingly, I use heart, head and hand
250 All day, I build, scheme, study, and make friends;
And when night overtakes me, down I lie,
Sleep, dream a little, and get done with it,
The sooner the better, to begin afresh.

What's midnight doubt before the dayspring's faith?
255 You, the philosopher, that disbelieve,
That recognize the night, give dreams their weight—
To be consistent you should keep your bed,
Abstain from healthy acts that prove you man,
For fear you drowse perhaps at unawares!
260 And certainly at night you'll sleep and dream,
Live through the day and bustle as you please.
And so you live to sleep as I to wake,
To unbelieve as I to still believe?
Well, and the common sense o' the world calls you
265 Bed-ridden,—and its good things come to me.
Its estimation, which is half the fight,
That's the first-cabin comfort I secure:
The next...but you perceive with half an eye!
Come, come, it's best believing, if we may;
270 You can't but own that!

Next, concede again,
If once we choose belief, on all accounts
We can't be too decisive in our faith,
Conclusive and exclusive in its terms,
To suit the world which gives us the good things.
275 In every man's career are certain points
Whereon he dares not be indifferent;
The world detects him clearly, if he dare,
As baffled at the game, and losing life.
He may care little or he may care much
280 For riches, honour, pleasure, work, repose,
Since various theories of life and life's
Success are extant which might easily
Comport[1] with either estimate of these;
And whoso chooses wealth or poverty,
285 Labour or quiet, is not judged a fool
Because his fellow would choose otherwise:
We let him choose upon his own account
So long as he's consistent with his choice.
But certain points, left wholly to himself,
290 When once a man has arbitrated on,

_____

[1] accord.

We say he must succeed there or go hang.
Thus, he should wed the woman he loves most
Or needs most, whatsoe'er the love or need—
For he can't wed twice. Then, he must avouch,
295 Or follow, at the least, sufficiently,
The form of faith his conscience holds the best,
Whate'er the process of conviction was:
For nothing can compensate his mistake
On such a point, the man himself being judge:
300 He cannot wed twice, nor twice lose his soul.

Well now, there's one great form of Christian
        faith
I happened to be born in—which to teach
Was given me as I grew up, on all hands,
As best and readiest means of living by;
305 The same on examination being proved
The most pronounced moreover, fixed, precise
And absolute form of faith in the whole world—
Accordingly, most potent of all forms
For working on the world. Observe, my friend!
310 Such as you know me, I am free to say,
In these hard latter days which hamper one,
Myself—by no immoderate exercise
Of intellect and learning, but the tact
To let external forces work for me,
315 —Bid the street's stones be bread and they are bread;
Bid Peter's creed, or rather, Hildebrand's,[1]
Exalt me o'er my fellows in the world
And make my life an ease and joy and pride;
It does so,—which for me's a great point gained,
320 Who have a soul and body that exact
A comfortable care in many ways.
There's power in me and will to dominate
Which I must exercise, they hurt me else:
In many ways I need mankind's respect,
325 Obedience, and the love that's born of fear:
While at the same time, there's a taste I have,

A toy of soul, a titillating thing,
Refuses to digest these dainties crude.
The naked life is gross till clothed upon:
330 I must take what men offer, with a grace
As though I would not, could I help it, take!
An uniform I wear though over-rich—
Something imposed on me, no choice of mine;
No fancy-dress worn for pure fancy's sake
335 And despicable therefore! now folk kneel
And kiss my hand—of course the Church's hand.
Thus I am made, thus life is best for me,
And thus that it should be I have procured;
And thus it could not be another way,
340 I venture to imagine.

                    You'll reply,
So far my choice, no doubt, is a success;
But were I made of better elements,
With nobler instincts, purer tastes, like you,
I hardly would account the thing success
345 Though it did all for me I say.

                        But, friend,
We speak of what is; not of what might be,
And how 'twere better if 'twere otherwise.
I am the man you see here plain enough:
Grant I'm a beast, why, beasts must lead beasts'
        lives!
350 Suppose I own at once to tail and claws;
The tailless man exceeds me: but being tailed
I'll lash out lion fashion, and leave apes
To dock their stump and dress their haunches up.
My business is not to remake myself,
355 But make the absolute best of what God made.
Or—our first simile—though you prove me doomed
To a viler berth still, to the steerage-hole,
The sheep-pen or the pig-sty, I should strive
To make what use of each were possible;
360 And as this cabin gets upholstery,
That hutch should rustle with sufficient straw.

---

[1] St. Peter was the first Pope; Hildebrand (Gregory VII, Pope 1073–85) fought for papal temporal power.

But, friend, I don't acknowledge quite so fast
I fail of all your manhood's lofty tastes
Enumerated so complacently,
365 On the mere ground that you forsooth can find
In this particular life I choose to lead
No fit provision for them. Can you not?
Say you, my fault is I address myself
To grosser estimators than should judge?
370 And that's no way of holding up the soul,
Which, nobler, needs men's praise perhaps, yet
    knows
One wise man's verdict outweighs all the fools'—
Would like the two, but, forced to choose, takes
    that.
I pine among my million imbeciles
375 (You think) aware some dozen men of sense
Eye me and know me, whether I believe
In the last winking Virgin,[1] as I vow,
And am a fool, or disbelieve in her
And am a knave,—approve in neither case,
380 Withhold their voices though I look their way:
Like Verdi[2] when, at his worst opera's end
(The thing they gave at Florence,—what's its name?)
While the mad houseful's plaudits near out-bang
His orchestra of salt-box, tongs and bones,
385 He looks through all the roaring and the wreaths
Where sits Rossini[3] patient in his stall.

    Nay, friend, I meet you with an answer here—
That even your prime men[4] who appraise their kind
Are men still, catch a wheel within a wheel,
390 See more in a truth than the truth's simple self,
Confuse themselves. You see lads walk the street
Sixty the minute; what's to note in that?

You see one lad o'erstride a chimney-stack;
Him you must watch—he's sure to fall, yet stands!
395 Our interest's on the dangerous edge of things.
The honest thief, the tender murderer,
The superstitious atheist, demirep[5]
That loves and saves her soul in new French books—
We watch while these in equilibrium keep
400 The giddy line midway: one step aside,
They're classed and done with. I, then, keep the line
Before your sages,—just the men to shrink
From the gross weights, coarse scales and labels
    broad
You offer their refinement. Fool or knave?
405 Why needs a bishop be a fool or knave
When there's a thousand diamond weights between?
So, I enlist them. Your picked twelve, you'll find,
Profess themselves indignant, scandalized
At thus being held unable to explain
410 How a superior man who disbelieves
May not believe as well: that's Schelling's[6] way!
It's through my coming in the tail of time,
Nicking the minute with a happy tact.
Had I been born three hundred years ago
415 They'd say, "What's strange? Blougram of course
    believes";
And, seventy years since, "disbelieves of course."
But now, "He may believe; and yet, and yet
How can he?" All eyes turn with interest.
Whereas, step off the line on either side—
420 You, for example, clever to a fault,
The rough and ready man who write apace,
Read somewhat seldomer, think perhaps even less—
You disbelieve! Who wonders and who cares?
Lord So-and-so—his coat bedropped with wax,
425 All Peter's chains[7] about his waist, his back

---

[1] Newman defended the belief that the Virgin's eyes move in some pictures.

[2] probably an allusion to the *Macbeth* of Verdi (1813–1901), first produced at Florence in 1847.

[3] The composer (1792–1868) was in Florence in 1847.

[4] journalists.

---

[5] woman of doubtful reputation.

[6] the German Idealist philosopher (1775–1845), who stressed the ultimate compatibility of apparently incompatible ideas.

[7] St. Peter's chains were miraculously removed by an angel: Acts 12:7.

Brave[1] with the needlework of Noodledom—[2]
Believes! Again, who wonders and who cares?
But I, the man of sense and learning too,
The able to think yet act, the this, the that,
430 I, to believe at this late time of day!
Enough; you see, I need not fear contempt.

          —Except it's yours! Admire me as these may,
You don't. But whom at least do you admire?
Present your own perfection, your ideal,
435 Your pattern man for a minute—oh, make haste,
Is it Napoleon you would have us grow?
Concede the means; allow his head and hand,
(A large concession, clever as you are)
Good! In our common primal element
440 Of unbelief (we can't believe, you know—
We're still at that admission, recollect!)
Where do you find—apart from, towering o'er
The secondary temporary aims
Which satisfy the gross taste you despise—
445 Where do you find his star?—his crazy trust
God knows through what or in what? it's alive
And shines and leads him, and that's all we want.
Have we aught in our sober night shall point
Such ends as his were, and direct the means
450 Of working out our purpose straight as his,
Nor bring a moment's trouble on success
With after-care to justify the same?
—Be a Napoleon, and yet disbelieve—
Why, the man's mad, friend, take his light away!
455 What's the vague good o' the world, for which you
          dare
With comfort to yourself blow millions up?
We neither of us see it! we do see
The blown-up millions—spatter of their brains
And writhing of their bowels and so forth,
460 In that bewildering entanglement
Of horrible eventualities

---

[1] splendid.

[2] foolish women.

Past calculation to the end of time!
Can I mistake for some clear word of God
(Which were my ample warrant for it all)
465 His puff of hazy instinct, idle talk,
"The State, that's I,"[3] quack-nonsense about crowns,
And (when one beats the man to his last hold)
A vague idea of setting things to rights,
Policing people efficaciously,
470 More to their profit, more of all to his own;
The whole to end that dismallest of ends
By an Austrian marriage,[4] cant to us the Church,
And resurrection of the old *régime*?
Would I, who hope to live a dozen years,
475 Fight Austerlitz[5] for reasons such and such?
No: for, concede me but the merest chance
Doubt may be wrong—there's judgement, life to
          come!
With just that chance, I dare not. Doubt proves
          right?
This present life is all?—you offer me
480 Its dozen noisy years, without a chance
That wedding an archduchess, wearing lace,
And getting called by divers new-coined names,
Will drive off ugly thoughts and let me dine,
Sleep, read and chat in quiet as I like!
485 Therefore I will not.

                    Take another case;
Fit up the cabin yet another way.
What say you to the poets? shall we write
Hamlet, Othello—make the world our own,
Without a risk to run of either sort?
490 I can't—to put the strongest reason first.
"But try," you urge, "the trying shall suffice;
The aim, if reached or not, makes great the life:
Try to be Shakespeare, leave the rest to fate!"
Spare my self-knowledge—there's no fooling me!

---

[3] "L'État, c'est moi" was said by Louis XIV, not Napoleon.

[4] Napoleon married Marie Louise of Austria in 1810.

[5] Napoleon's victory of 1805 over the Russians and Austrians.

495 If I prefer remaining my poor self,
I say so not in self-dispraise but praise.
If I'm a Shakespeare, let the well alone;
Why should I try to be what now I am?
If I'm no Shakespeare, as too probable,—
500 His power and consciousness and self-delight
And all we want in common, shall I find—
Trying for ever? while on points of taste
Wherewith, to speak it humbly, he and I
Are dowered alike—I'll ask you, I or he,
505 Which in our two lives realizes most?
Much, he imagined—somewhat, I possess.
He had the imagination; stick to that!
Let him say, "In the face of my soul's works
Your world is worthless and I touch it not
510 Lest I should wrong them"—I'll withdraw my plea.
But does he say so? look upon his life!
Himself, who only can, gives judgement there.
He leaves his towers and gorgeous palaces
To build the trimmest house in Stratford town;
515 Saves money, spends it, owns the worth of things,
Giulio Romano's[1] pictures, Dowland's[2] lute;
Enjoys a show, respects the puppets, too,
And none more, had he seen its entry once,
Than "Pandulph, of fair Milan cardinal."[3]
520 Why then should I who play that personage,
The very Pandulph Shakespeare's fancy made,
Be told that had the poet chanced to start
From where I stand now (some degree like mine
Being just the goal he ran his race to reach)
525 He would have run the whole race back, forsooth,
And left being Pandulph, to begin write plays?
Ah, the earth's best can be but the earth's best!
Did Shakespeare live, he could but sit at home
And get himself in dreams the Vatican,
530 Greek busts, Venetian paintings, Roman walls,

And English books, none equal to his own,
Which I read, bound in gold (he never did).
—Terni's[4] fall, Naples' bay and Gothard's top—[5]
Eh, friend? I could not fancy one of these;
535 But, as I pour this claret, there they are:
I've gained them—crossed Saint Gothard last July
With ten mules to the carriage and a bed
Slung inside; is my hap[6] the worse for that?
We want the same things, Shakespeare and myself,
540 And what I want, I have: he, gifted more,
Could fancy he too had them when he liked,
But not so thoroughly that, if fate allowed,
He would not have them also in my sense.
We play one game; I send the ball aloft
545 No less adroitly that of fifty strokes
Scarce five go o'er the wall so wide and high
Which sends them back to me: I wish and get.
He struck balls higher and with better skill,
But at a poor fence level with his head,
550 And hit—his Stratford house, a coat of arms,
Successful dealings in his grain and wool,—
While I receive heaven's incense in my nose
And style myself the cousin of Queen Bess.[7]
Ask him, if this life's all, who wins the game?

555 Believe—and our whole argument breaks up.
Enthusiasm's the best thing, I repeat;
Only, we can't command it; fire and life
Are all, dead matter's nothing, we agree:
And be it a mad dream or God's very breath,
560 The fact's the same,—belief's fire, once in us,
Makes of all else mere stuff to show itself:
We penetrate our life with such a glow
As fire lends wood and iron—this turns steel,
That burns to ash—all's one, fire proves its power
565 For good or ill, since men call flare success.

---

[1] Italian painter (c. 1492–1546).

[2] English lutanist and composer (1536–1626).

[3] a quotation from Shakespeare's Pandulph, powerful spokesman for expediency, in *King John* 3.1.138.

[4] a waterfall north of Rome.

[5] St. Gothard, the major pass between Switzerland and Italy.

[6] fate.

[7] close acquaintance of Queen Elizabeth I.

But paint a fire, it will not therefore burn.
Light one in me, I'll find it food enough!
Why, to be Luther—that's a life to lead,
Incomparably better than my own.
570 He comes, reclaims God's earth for God, he says,
Sets up God's rule again by simple means,
Re-opens a shut book,[1] and all is done.
He flared out in the flaring of mankind;
Such Luther's luck was: how shall such be mine?
575 If he succeeded, nothing's left to do:
And if he did not altogether—well,
Strauss[2] is the next advance. All Strauss should be
I might be also. But to what result?
He looks upon no future: Luther did.
580 What can I gain on the denying side?
Ice makes no conflagration. State the facts,
Read the text right, emancipate the world—
The emancipated world enjoys itself
With scarce a thank-you: Blougram told it first
585 It could not owe a farthing,—not to him
More than Saint Paul! 'twould press its pay, you
     think?
Then add there's still that plaguy hundredth chance
Strauss may be wrong. And so risk is run—
For what gain? not for Luther's, who secured
590 A real heaven in his heart throughout his life,
Supposing death a little altered things.

     "Ay, but since really you lack faith," you cry,
"You run the same risk really on all sides,
In cool indifference as bold unbelief.
595 As well be Strauss as swing 'twixt Paul and him.
It's not worth having, such imperfect faith,
No more available to do faith's work
Than unbelief like mine. Whole faith, or none!"

     Softly, my friend! I must dispute that point.
600 Once own the use of faith, I'll find you faith.
We're back on Christian ground. You call for faith:
I show you doubt, to prove that faith exists.
The more of doubt, the stronger faith, I say,
If faith o'ercomes doubt. How I know it does?
605 By life and man's free will, God gave for that!
To mould life as we choose it, shows our choice:
That's our one act, the previous work's his own.
You criticize the soil? it reared this tree—
This broad life and whatever fruit it bears!
610 What matter though I doubt at every pore,
Head-doubts, heart-doubts, doubts at any fingers'
     ends,
Doubts in the trivial work of every day,
Doubts at the very bases of my soul
In the grand moments when she probes herself—
615 If finally I have a life to show,
The thing I did, brought out in evidence
Against the thing done to me underground
By hell and all its brood, for aught I know?
I say, whence sprang this? shows it faith or
     doubt?
620 All's doubt in me; where's break of faith in this?
It is the idea, the feeling and the love,
God means mankind should strive for and show
     forth
Whatever be the process to that end,—
And not historic knowledge, logic sound,
625 And metaphysical acumen, sure!
"What think ye of Christ," friend? when all's done
     and said,
Like you this Christianity or not?
It may be false, but will you wish it true?
Has it your vote to be so if it can?
630 Trust you an instinct silenced long ago
That will break silence and enjoin you love
What mortified philosophy is hoarse,
And all in vain, with bidding you despise?
If you desire faith—then you've faith enough:
635 What else seeks God—nay, what else seek ourselves?

----

[1] has the Bible translated.

[2] David Friedrich Strauss (1808–74), the author of the *Life of Jesus*
(1835), which undermined the literal translation of the Bible.

You form a notion of me, we'll suppose,
On hearsay; it's a favourable one:
"But still" (you add), "there was no such good man,
Because of contradiction in the facts.
640 One proves, for instance, he was born in Rome,
This Blougram; yet throughout the tales of him
I see he figures as an Englishman."
Well, the two things are reconcilable.
But would I rather you discovered that,
645 Subjoining—"Still, what matter though they be?
Blougram concerns me naught, born here or
    there."

Pure faith indeed—you know not what you ask!
Naked belief in God the Omnipotent,
Omniscient, Omnipresent, sears too much
650 The sense of conscious creatures to be borne.
It were the seeing him, no flesh shall dare.
Some think, Creation's meant to show him forth:
I say it's meant to hide him all it can,
And that's what all the blessèd evil's for.
655 Its use in Time is to environ us,
Our breath, our drop of dew, with shield enough
Against that sight till we can bear its stress.
Under a vertical sun, the exposed brain
And lidless eye and disimprisoned heart
660 Less certainly would wither up at once
Than mind, confronted with the truth of him.
But time and earth case-harden us to live;
The feeblest sense is trusted most; the child
Feels God a moment, ichors[1] o'er the place,
665 Plays on and grows to be a man like us.
With me, faith means perpetual unbelief
Kept quiet like the snake 'neath Michael's foot[2]
Who stands calm just because he feels it writhe.
Or, if that's too ambitious,—here's my box—[3]

670 I need the excitation of a pinch
Threatening the torpor of the inside-nose
Nigh on the imminent sneeze that never comes.
"Leave it in peace" advise the simple folk:
Make it aware of peace by itching-fits,
675 Say I—let doubt occasion still more faith!

You'll say, once all believed, man, woman, child,
In that dear middle-age these noodles praise.
How you'd exult if I could put you back
Six hundred years, blot out cosmogony,
680 Geology, ethnology, what not,
(Greek endings, each the little passing-bell
That signifies some faith's about to die),
And set you square with Genesis again,—
When such a traveller told you his last news,
685 He saw the ark a-top of Ararat[4]
But did not climb there since 'twas getting dusk
And robber-bands infest the mountain's foot!
How should you feel, I ask, in such an age,
How act? As other people felt and did;
690 With soul more blank than this decanter's knob,
Believe—and yet lie, kill, rob, fornicate
Full in belief's face, like the beast you'd be!

No, when the fight begins within himself,
A man's worth something. God stoops o'er his head,
695 Satan looks up between his feet—both tug—
He's left, himself, i' the middle: the soul wakes
And grows. Prolong that battle through his life!
Never leave growing till the life to come!
Here, we've got callous to the Virgin's winks
700 That used to puzzle people wholesomely:
Men have outgrown the shame of being fools.
What are the laws of nature, not to bend
If the Church bid them?—brother Newman[5] asks.

---

[1] liquids issuing from wounds to help healing.

[2] The Archangel who threw Satan out of heaven is usually depicted stamping on the snake.

[3] snuff box.

---

[4] the mountain in Turkey where Noah's ark landed: Genesis 8:4.

[5] John Henry Newman, who had become a Roman Catholic in 1845, spoke strongly in favour of miracles.

Up with the Immaculate Conception,[1] then—
On to the rack with faith!—is my advice.
Will not that hurry us upon our knees,
Knocking our breasts, "It can't be—yet it shall!
Who am I, the worm, to argue with my Pope?
Low things confound the high things!" and so forth.
That's better than acquitting God with grace
As some folk do. He's tried—no case is proved,
Philosophy is lenient—he may go!

You'll say, the old system's not so obsolete
But men believe still: ay, but who and where?
King Bomba's[2] lazzaroni foster yet
The sacred flame, so Antonelli[3] writes;
But even of these, what ragamuffin saint
Believes God watches him continually,
As he believes in fire that it will burn,
Or rain that it will drench him? Break fire's law,
Sin against rain, although the penalty
Be just a singe or soaking? "No," he smiles;
"Those laws are laws that can enforce themselves."

The sum of all is—yes, my doubt is great,
My faith's still greater, then my faith's enough.
I have read much, thought much, experienced much,
Yet would die rather than avow my fear
The Naples' liquefaction[4] may be false,
When set to happen by the palace-clock
According to the clouds or dinner-time.
I hear you recommend, I might at least
Eliminate, decrassify[5] my faith

Since I adopt it; keeping what I must
And leaving what I can—such points as this.
I won't—that is, I can't throw one away.
Supposing there's no truth in what I hold
About the need of trial to man's faith,
Still, when you bid me purify the same,
To such a process I discern no end.
Clearing off one excrescence to see two,
There's ever a next in size, now grown as big,
That meets the knife: I cut and cut again!
First cut the Liquefaction, what comes last
But Fichte's clever cut[6] at God himself?
Experimentalize on sacred things!
I trust not hand nor eye nor heart nor brain
To stop betimes: they all get drunk alike.
The first step, I am master not to take.

You'd find the cutting-process to your taste
As much as leaving growths of lies unpruned,
Nor see more danger in it,—you retort.
Your taste's worth mine; but my taste proves more
    wise
When we consider that the steadfast hold
On the extreme end of the chain of faith
Gives all the advantage, makes the difference
With the rough purblind mass we seek to rule:
We are their lords, or they are free of us,
Just as we tighten or relax our hold.
So, other matters equal, we'll revert
To the first problem—which, if solved my way
And thrown into the balance, turns the scale—
How we may lead a comfortable life,
How suit our luggage to the cabin's size.

Of course you are remarking all this time
How narrowly and grossly I view life,
Respect the creature-comforts, care to rule
The masses, and regard complacently

---

[1] The Doctrine, proclaimed by the Pope in 1854, that the Virgin Mary was free from original sin when conceived.

[2] derisive nickname of Ferdinand II (1810–59), King of the Two Sicilies.

[3] Cardinal Antonelli, secretary to Pius IX.

[4] the belief that some of the crystallized blood of Saint Januarius, patron saint of Naples, liquefies regularly.

[5] purify.

[6] The German philosopher (1762–1814) thought God an idea created by man.

"The cabin," in our old phrase. Well, I do.
I act for, talk for, live for this world now,
770 As this world prizes action, life and talk:
No prejudice to what next world may prove,
Whose new laws and requirements, my best pledge
To observe then, is that I observe these now,
Shall do hereafter what I do meanwhile.
775 Let us concede (gratuitously though)
Next life relieves the soul of body, yields
Pure spiritual enjoyment: well, my friend,
Why lose this life i' the meantime, since its use
May be to make the next life more intense?

780   Do you know, I have often had a dream
(Work it up in your next month's article)
Of man's poor spirit in its progress, still
Losing true life for ever and a day
Through ever trying to be and ever being—
785 In the evolution of successive spheres—
Before its actual sphere and place of life,
Halfway into the next, which having reached,
It shoots with corresponding foolery
Halfway into the next still, on and off!
790 As when a traveller, bound from North to South,
Scouts[1] fur in Russia: what's its use in France?
In France spurns flannel: where's its need in Spain?
In Spain drops cloth, too cumbrous for Algiers!
Linen goes next, and last the skin itself,
795 A superfluity at Timbuctoo.
When, through his journey, was the fool at ease?
I'm at ease now, friend; worldly in this world,
I take and like its way of life; I think
My brothers, who administer the means,
800 Live better for my comfort—that's good too;
And God, if he pronounce upon such life,
Approves my service, which is better still.
If he keep silence,—why, for you or me
Or that brute beast pulled-up in today's "Times,"
805 What odds is't, save to ourselves, what life we lead?

---

[1] mocks at.

You meet me at this issue: you declare,—
All special-pleading done with—truth is truth,
And justifies itself by undreamed ways.
You don't fear but it's better, if we doubt,
810 To say so, act up to our truth perceived
However feebly. Do then,—act away!
'Tis there I'm on the watch for you. How one acts
Is, both of us agree, our chief concern:
And how you'll act is what I fain would see
815 If, like the candid person you appear,
You dare to make the most of your life's scheme
As I of mine, live up to its full law
Since there's no higher law that counterchecks.
Put natural religion to the test
820 You've just demolished the revealed with—quick,
Down to the root of all that checks your will,
All prohibition to lie, kill and thieve,
Or even to be an atheistic priest!
Suppose a pricking to incontinence—
825 Philosophers deduce you chastity
Or shame, from just the fact that at the first
Whoso embraced a woman in the field,
Threw club down and forewent his brains beside,
So, stood a ready victim in the reach
830 Of any brother savage, club in hand;
Hence saw the use of going out of sight
In wood or cave to prosecute his loves:
I read this in a French book t'other day.
Does law so analysed coerce you much?
835 Oh, men spin clouds of fuzz where matters end,
But you who reach where the first thread begins,
You'll soon cut that!—which means you can, but
            won't,
Through certain instincts, blind, unreasoned-out,
You dare not set aside, you can't tell why,
840 But there they are, and so you let them rule.
Then, friend, you seem as much a slave as I,
A liar, conscious coward and hypocrite,
Without the good the slave expects to get,
In case he has a master after all!
845 You own your instincts? why, what else do I,

Who want, am made for, and must have a God
Ere I can be aught, do aught?—no mere name
Want, but the true thing with what proves its truth,
To wit, a relation from that thing to me,
850 Touching from head to foot—which touch I feel,
And with it take the rest, this life of ours!
I live my life here; yours you dare not live.

—Not as I state it, who (you please subjoin)
Disfigure such a life and call it names,
855 While, to your mind, remains another way
For simple men: knowledge and power have rights,
But ignorance and weakness have rights too.
There needs no crucial effort to find truth
If here or there or anywhere about:
860 We ought to turn each side, try hard and see,
And if we can't, be glad we've earned at least
The right, by one laborious proof the more,
To graze in peace earth's pleasant pasturage.
Men are not angels, neither are they brutes:
865 Something we may see, all we cannot see.
What need of lying? I say, I see all,
And swear to each detail the most minute
In what I think a Pan's face—you, mere cloud:
I swear I hear him speak and see him wink,
870 For fear, if once I drop the emphasis,
Mankind may doubt there's any cloud at all.
You take the simple life—ready to see,
Willing to see (for no cloud's worth a face)—
And leaving quiet what no strength can move,
875 And which, who bids you move? who has the right?
I bid you; but you are God's sheep, not mine:
"*Pastor est tui Dominus.*"[1] You find
In this the pleasant pasture of our life
Much you may eat without the least offence,
880 Much you don't eat because your maw objects,
Much you would eat but that your fellow-flock
Open great eyes at you and even butt,

And thereupon you like your mates so well
You cannot please yourself, offending them;
885 Though when they seem exorbitantly sheep,
You weigh your pleasure with their butts and bleats
And strike the balance. Sometimes certain fears
Restrain you, real checks since you find them so;
Sometimes you please yourself and nothing checks:
890 And thus you graze through life with not one lie,
And like it best.

But do you, in truth's name?
If so, you beat—which means you are not I—
Who needs must make earth mine and feed my fill
Not simply unbutted at, unbickered with,
895 But motioned to the velvet of the sward
By those obsequious wethers' very selves.
Look at me, sir; my age is double yours:
At yours, I knew beforehand, so enjoyed,
What now I should be—as, permit the word,
900 I pretty well imagine your whole range
And stretch of tether twenty years to come.
We both have minds and bodies much alike:
In truth's name, don't you want my bishopric,
My daily bread, my influence and my state?
905 You're young. I'm old; you must be old one day;
Will you find then, as I do hour by hour,
Women their lovers kneel to, who cut curls
From your fat lap-dog's ear to grace a brooch—
Dukes, who petition just to kiss your ring—
910 With much beside you know or may conceive?
Suppose we die tonight: well, here am I,
Such were my gains, life bore this fruit to me,
While writing all the same my articles
On music, poetry, the fictile[2] vase
915 Found at Albano,[3] chess, Anacreon's Greek.[4]
But you—the highest honour in your life,
The thing you'll crown yourself with, all your days,

---

[1] "The Lord is your shepherd," from "The Lord is my shepherd": Psalm 23:1.

[2] moulded.

[3] site of Roman ruins a few miles south-east of Rome.

[4] Greek lyric poet of the sixth century BC.

Is—dining here and drinking this last glass
I pour you out in sign of amity
920 Before we part for ever. Of your power
And social influence, worldly worth in short,
Judge what's my estimation by the fact,
I do not condescend to enjoin, beseech,
Hint secrecy on one of all these words!
925 You're shrewd and know that should you publish
     one
The world would brand the lie—my enemies first,
Who'd sneer—"the bishop's an arch-hypocrite
And knave perhaps, but not so frank a fool."
Whereas I should not dare for both my ears
930 Breathe one such syllable, smile one such smile,
Before the chaplain who reflects myself—
My shade's so much more potent than your flesh.
What's your reward, self-abnegating friend?
Stood you confessed of those exceptional
935 And privileged great natures that dwarf mine—
A zealot with a mad ideal in reach,
A poet just about to print his ode,
A statesman with a scheme to stop this war,[1]
An artist whose religion is his art—
940 I should have nothing to object: such men
Carry the fire, all things grow warm to them,
Their drugget's[2] worth my purple, they beat me.
But you,—you're just as little those as I—
You, Gigadibs, who, thirty years of age,
945 Write stately for Blackwood's Magazine,[3]
Believe you see two points in Hamlet's soul
Unseized by the Germans yet[4]—which view you'll
     print—
Meantime the best you have to show being still
That lively lightsome article we took
950 Almost for the true Dickens,—what's its name?

———————

[1] The Crimean War began in March 1854.

[2] coarse material.

[3] an important and powerful magazine.

[4] German criticism of Shakespeare was dominant in the nineteenth
century.

"The Slum and Cellar, or Whitechapel[5] life
Limned after dark!" it made me laugh, I know,
And pleased a month, and brought you in ten
     pounds.
—Success I recognize and compliment,
955 And therefore give you, if you choose, three words
(The card and pencil-scratch is quite enough)
Which whether here, in Dublin or New York,
Will get you, prompt as at my eyebrow's wink,
Such terms as never you aspired to get
960 In all our own reviews and some not ours.
Go write your lively sketches! be the first
"Blougram, or The Eccentric Confidence"—
Or better simply say, "The Outward-bound."
Why, men as soon would throw it in my teeth
965 As copy and quote the infamy chalked broad
About me on the church-door opposite.
You will not wait for that experience though,
I fancy, howsoever you decide,
To discontinue—not detesting, not
970 Defaming, but at least—despising me!

———————

Over his wine so smiled and talked his hour
Sylvester Blougram, styled *in partibus
Episcopus, nec non*—(the deuce knows what
975 It's changed to by our novel hierarchy)
With Gigadibs the literary man,
Who played with spoons, explored his plate's design,
And ranged the olive-stones about its edge,
While the great bishop rolled him out a mind
980 Long crumpled, till creased consciousness lay
     smooth.

980 For Blougram, he believed, say, half he spoke.
The other portion, as he shaped it thus
For argumentatory purposes,
He felt his foe was foolish to dispute.
Some arbitrary accidental thoughts
985 That crossed his mind, amusing because new,

———————

[5] district in eastern London.

362

He chose to represent as fixtures there,
Invariable convictions (such they seemed
Beside his interlocutor's loose cards
Flung daily down, and not the same way twice)
990 While certain hell-deep instincts, man's weak tongue
Is never bold to utter in their truth
Because styled hell-deep ('tis an old mistake
To place hell at the bottom of the earth)
He ignored these,—not having in readiness
995 Their nomenclature and philosophy:
He said true things, but called them by wrong names.
"On the whole," he thought, "I justify myself
On every point where cavillers like this
Oppugn my life: he tries one kind of fence,[1]
1000 I close, he's worsted, that's enough for him.
He's on the ground: if ground should break away
I take my stand on, there's a firmer yet
Beneath it, both of us may sink and reach.
His ground was over mine and broke the first:
1005 So, let him sit with me this many a year!"

He did not sit five minutes. Just a week
Sufficed his sudden healthy vehemence.
Something had struck him in the "Outward-bound"
Another way than Blougram's purpose was:
1010 And having bought, not cabin-furniture
But settler's-implements (enough for three)
And started for Australia—there, I hope,
By this time he has tested his first plough,
And studied his last chapter of Saint John.[2]
—1855

Andrea del Sarto [3]

(Called "The Faultless Painter")

But do not let us quarrel any more,
No, my Lucrezia; bear with me for once:
Sit down and all shall happen as you wish.
You turn your face, but does it bring your heart?
5 I'll work then for your friend's friend, never fear,
Treat his own subject after his own way,
Fix his own time, accept too his own price,
And shut the money into this small hand
When next it takes mine. Will it? tenderly?
10 Oh, I'll content him,—but tomorrow, Love!
I often am much wearier than you think,
This evening more than usual, and it seems
As if—forgive now—should you let me sit
Here by the window with your hand in mine
15 And look a half-hour forth on Fiesole,[4]
Both of one mind, as married people use,
Quietly, quietly the evening through,
I might get up tomorrow to my work
Cheerful and fresh as ever. Let us try.
20 Tomorrow, how you shall be glad for this!
Your soft hand is a woman of itself,
And mine the man's bared breast she curls inside.
Don't count the time lost, neither; you must serve
For each of the five pictures we require:
25 It saves a model. So! keep looking so—
My serpentining beauty, rounds on rounds!
—How could you ever prick those perfect ears,
Even to put the pearl there! oh, so sweet—
My face, my moon, my everybody's moon,
30 Which everybody looks on and calls his,
And, I suppose, is looked on by in turn,

---

[1] swordsmanship.

[2] a much debated line. One popular view is that Gigadibs has given up his shallow journalism and has travelled to Australia to start a new life and to study the gospels.

[3] Andrea d'Angelo di Francesca (1486–1531), called "del Sarto" because his father was a tailor, and "The Faultless Painter" because of his technique. As with "Fra Lippo Lippi," Browning's main source for the poem was Vasari's *Lives of the Artists*, which gives most of the facts and supports the general tenor of Browning's poem.

[4] the hill-town just north-east of Florence.

While she looks—no one's: very dear, no less.
You smile? why, there's my picture ready made,
There's what we painters call our harmony!
35 A common greyness silvers everything,—
All in a twilight, you and I alike
—You, at the point of your first pride in me
(That's gone you know),—but I, at every point;
My youth, my hope, my art, being all toned down
40 To yonder sober pleasant Fiesole.
There's the bell clinking from the chapel-top;
That length of convent-wall across the way
Holds the trees safer, huddled more inside;
The last monk leaves the garden; days decrease,
45 And autumn grows, autumn in everything.
Eh? the whole seems to fall into a shape
As if I saw alike my work and self
And all that I was born to be and do,
A twilight-piece. Love, we are in God's hand.
50 How strange now, looks the life he makes us lead;
So free we seem, so fettered fast we are!
I feel he laid the fetter: let it lie!
This chamber for example—turn your head—
All that's behind us! You don't understand
55 Nor care to understand about my art,
But you can hear at least when people speak:
And that cartoon,[1] the second from the door
—It is the thing, Love! so such things should be—
Behold Madonna!—I am bold to say.
60 I can do with my pencil what I know,
What I see, what at bottom of my heart
I wish for, if I ever wish so deep—
Do easily, too—when I say, perfectly,
I do not boast, perhaps: yourself are judge,
65 Who listened to the Legate's talk last week,
And just as much they used to say in France.
At any rate 'tis easy, all of it!
No sketches first, no studies, that's long past:
I do what many dream of, all their lives,
70 —Dream? strive to do, and agonize to do,

And fail in doing. I could count twenty such
On twice your fingers, and not leave this town,
Who strive—you don't know how the others strive
To paint a little thing like that you smeared
75 Carelessly passing with your robes afloat,—
Yet do much less, so much less, Someone[2] says,
(I know his name, no matter)—so much less!
Well, less is more, Lucrezia: I am judged.
There burns a truer light of God in them,
80 In their vexed beating stuffed and stopped-up brain,
Heart, or whate'er else, than goes on to prompt
This low-pulsed forthright craftsman's hand of mine.
Their works drop groundward, but themselves, I
    know,
Reach many a time a heaven that's shut to me,
85 Enter and take their place there sure enough,
Though they come back and cannot tell the world.
My works are nearer heaven, but I sit here.
The sudden blood of these men! at a word—
Praise them, it boils, or blame them, it boils too.
90 I, painting from myself and to myself,
Know what I do, am unmoved by men's blame
Or their praise either. Somebody remarks
Morello's[3] outline there is wrongly traced,
His hue mistaken; what of that? or else,
95 Rightly traced and well ordered; what of that?
Speak as they please, what does the mountain care?
Ah, but a man's reach should exceed his grasp,
Or what's a heaven for? All is silver-grey
Placid and perfect with my art: the worse!
100 I know both what I want and what might gain,
And yet how profitless to know, to sigh
"Had I been two, another and myself,
Our head would have o'erlooked the world!" No
    doubt.
Yonder's a work now, of that famous youth
105 The Urbinate[4] who died five years ago.

----

1 sketch for a painting.

2 Michelangelo.

3 mountain north of Florence.

4 Raphael (1483–1520), born at Urbino.

('Tis copied, George Vasari[1] sent it me.)
Well, I can fancy how he did it all,
Pouring his soul, with kings and popes to see,
Reaching, that heaven might so replenish him,
110 Above and through his art—for it gives way;
That arm is wrongly put—and there again—
A fault to pardon in the drawing's lines,
Its body, so to speak: its soul is right,
He means right—that, a child may understand.
115 Still, what an arm! and I could alter it:
But all the play, the insight and the stretch—
Out of me, out of me! And wherefore out?
Had you enjoined them on me, given me soul,
We might have risen to Rafael, I and you!
120 Nay, Love, you did give all I asked, I think—
More than I merit, yes, by many times.
But had you—oh, with the same perfect brow,
And perfect eyes, and more than perfect mouth,
And the low voice my soul hears, as a bird
125 The fowler's pipe, and follows to the snare—
Had you, with these the same, but brought a mind!
Some women do so. Had the mouth there urged
"God and the glory! never care for gain.
The present by the future, what is that?
130 Live for fame, side by side with Agnolo![2]
Rafael is waiting: up to God, all three!"
I might have done it for you. So it seems:
Perhaps not. All is as God over-rules.
Beside, incentives come from the soul's self;
135 The rest avail not. Why do I need you?
What wife had Rafael, or has Agnolo?
In this world, who can do a thing, will not;
And who would do it, cannot, I perceive:
Yet the will's somewhat—somewhat, too, the
   power—
140 And thus we half-men struggle. At the end,
God, I conclude, compensates, punishes.

'Tis safer for me, if the award be strict,
That I am something underrated here,
Poor this long while, despised, to speak the truth.
145 I dared not, do you know, leave home all day,
For fear of chancing on the Paris lords.
The best is when they pass and look aside;
But they speak sometimes; I must bear it all.
Well may they speak! That Francis, that first time,
150 And that long festal year at Fontainebleau![3]
I surely then could sometimes leave the ground,
Put on the glory, Rafael's daily wear,
In that humane great monarch's golden look,—
One finger in his beard or twisted curl
155 Over his mouth's good mark that made the smile,
One arm about my shoulder, round my neck,
The jingle of his gold chain in my ear,
I painting proudly with his breath on me,
All his court round him, seeing with his eyes,
160 Such frank French eyes, and such a fire of souls
Profuse, my hand kept plying by those hearts,—
And, best of all, this, this, this face beyond,
This in the background, waiting on my work,
To crown the issue with a last reward!
165 A good time, was it not, my kingly days?
And had you not grown restless...but I know—
'Tis done and past; 'twas right, my instinct said;
Too live the life grew, golden and not grey,
And I'm the weak-eyed bat no sun should tempt
170 Out of the grange whose four walls make his world.
How could it end in any other way?
You called me, and I came home to your heart.
The triumph was—to reach and stay there; since
I reached it ere the triumph, what is lost?
175 Let my hands frame your face in your hair's gold,
You beautiful Lucrezia that are mine!
"Rafael did this, Andrea painted that;

---

[1] Giorgio Vasari (1512–74), the main source for Browning's poem, was
introduced to Andrea by Michelangelo.

[2] Michelangelo.

[3] the town south-east of Paris where Francis I built the royal palace.
Tradition suggests that Andrea was given money by the King to buy
paintings but instead used it to build a house for himself and his wife.

The Roman's[1] is the better when you pray,
But still the other's Virgin was his wife—"
180 Men will excuse me. I am glad to judge
Both pictures in your presence; clearer grows
My better fortune, I resolve to think.
For, do you know, Lucrezia, as God lives,
Said one day Agnolo, his very self,
185 To Rafael...I have known it all these years...
(When the young man was flaming out his thoughts
Upon a palace-wall for Rome to see,
Too lifted up in heart because of it)
"Friend, there's a certain sorry little scrub
190 Goes up and down our Florence, none cares how,
Who, were he set to plan and execute
As you are, pricked on by your popes and kings,
Would bring the sweat into that brow of yours!"
To Rafael's!—And indeed the arm is wrong.
195 I hardly dare...yet, only you to see,
Give the chalk here—quick, thus the line should go!
Ay, but the soul! he's Rafael! rub it out!
Still, all I care for, if he spoke the truth,
(What he? why, who but Michel Agnolo?
200 Do you forget already words like those?)
If really there was such a chance, so lost,—
Is, whether you're—not grateful—but more pleased.
Well, let me think so. And you smile indeed!
This hour has been an hour! Another smile?
205 If you would sit thus by me every night
I should work better, do you comprehend?
I mean that I should earn more, give you more.
See, it is settled dusk now; there's a star;
Morello's gone, the watch-lights show the wall,
210 The cue-owls speak the name we call them by.
Come from the window, love,—come in, at last,
Inside the melancholy little house
We built to be so gay with. God is just.
King Francis may forgive me: oft at nights
215 When I look up from painting, eyes tired out,
The walls become illumined, brick from brick

Distinct, instead of mortar, fierce bright gold,
That gold of his I did cement them with!
Let us but love each other. Must you go?
220 That Cousin[2] here again? he waits outside?
Must see you—you, and not with me? Those loans?
More gaming debts to pay? you smiled for that?
Well, let smiles buy me! have you more to spend?
While hand and eye and something of a heart
225 Are left me, work's my ware, and what's it worth?
I'll pay my fancy. Only let me sit
The grey remainder of the evening out,
Idle, you call it, and muse perfectly
How I could paint, were I but back in France,
230 One picture, just one more—the Virgin's face,
Not yours this time! I want you at my side
To hear them—that is, Michel Agnolo—
Judge all I do and tell you of its worth.
Will you? Tomorrow, satisfy your friend.
235 I take the subjects for his corridor,
Finish the portrait out of hand—there, there,
And throw him in another thing or two
If he demurs; the whole should prove enough
To pay for this same Cousin's freak. Beside,
240 What's better and what's all I care about,
Get you the thirteen scudi[3] for the ruff!
Love, does that please you? Ah, but what does he,
The Cousin! what does he to please you more?

I am grown peaceful as old age tonight.
245 I regret little, I would change still less.
Since there my past life lies, why alter it?
The very wrong to Francis!—it is true
I took his coin, was tempted and complied,
And built this house and sinned, and all is said.
250 My father and my mother died of want.[4]
Well, had I riches of my own? you see

---

[1] Raphael worked in Rome for the last twelve years of his life.

[2] Lucrezia's lover.

[3] Roman coins.

[4] Vasari says that Andrea abandoned his own parents for Lucrezia's relatives.

How one gets rich! Let each one bear his lot.
They were born poor, lived poor, and poor they
    died:
And I have laboured somewhat in my time
255 And not been paid profusely. Some good son
Paint my two hundred pictures—let him try!
No doubt, there's something strikes a balance. Yes,
You loved me quite enough, it seems tonight.
This must suffice me here. What would one have?
260 In heaven, perhaps, new chances, one more chance—
Four great walls in the New Jerusalem,
Meted on each side by the angel's reed,
For Leonard,[1] Rafael, Agnolo and me
To cover—the three first without a wife,
265 While I have mine! So—still they overcome
Because there's still Lucrezia,—as I choose.

Again the Cousin's whistle! Go, my Love.
—1855

Old Pictures in Florence

I

The morn when first it thunders in March,
    The eel in the pond gives a leap, they say:
As I leaned and looked over the aloed[2] arch
    Of the villa-gate this warm March day,
5 No flash snapped, no dumb thunder rolled
    In the valley beneath where, white and wide
And washed by the morning water gold,
    Florence lay out on the mountain-side.

II

River and bridge and street and square
10   Lay mine, as much at my beck and call,
Through the live translucent bath of air,
    As the sights in a magic crystal ball.
And of all I saw and of all I praised,

    The most to praise and the best to see
15 Was the startling bell-tower Giotto raised:[3]
    But why did it more than startle me?

III

Giotto, how, with that soul of yours,
    Could you play me false who loved you so?
Some slights if a certain heart endures
20   Yet it feels, I would have your fellows know!
I' faith, I perceive not why I should care
    To break a silence that suits them best,
But the thing grows somewhat hard to bear
    When I find a Giotto join the rest.

IV

25 On the arch where olives overhead
    Print the blue sky with twig and leaf,
(That sharp-curled leaf which they never shed)
    'Twixt the aloes, I used to lean in chief,[4]
And mark through the winter afternoons,
30   By a gift God grants me now and then,
In the mild decline of those suns like moons,
    Who walked in Florence, besides her men.

V

They might chirp and chaffer,[5] come and go
    For pleasure or profit, her men alive—
35 My business was hardly with them, I trow,
    But with empty cells of the human hive;
—With the chapter-room, the cloister-porch,
    The church's apsis,[6] aisle or nave,
Its crypt, one fingers along with a torch,
40   Its face set full for the sun to shave.

---

[1] Leonardo da Vinci (1452–1519).

[2] a kind of lily.

[3] A hundred yards high, the tower was designed by the Florentine artist Giotto Di Bondone (1267–1337).

[4] favourite spot.

[5] haggle over price.

[6] apse.

VI

Wherever a fresco peels and drops,
　　Wherever an outline weakens and wanes
Till the latest life in the painting stops,
　　Stands One whom each fainter pulse-tick pains:
45　One, wishful each scrap should clutch the brick,
　　Each tinge not wholly escape the plaster,
　—A lion who dies of an ass's kick,
　　The wronged great soul of an ancient Master.

VII

For oh, this world and the wrong it does!
50　　They are safe in heaven with their backs to it,
The Michaels[1] and Rafaels, you hum and buzz
　　Round the works of, you of the little wit!
Do their eyes contract to the earth's old scope,
　　Now that they see God face to face,
55　And have all attained to be poets, I hope?
　　'Tis their holiday now, in any case.

VIII

Much they reck of your praise and you!
　　But the wronged great souls—can they be quit
Of a world where their work is all to do,
60　　Where you style them, you of the little wit,
Old Master This and Early the Other,
　　Not dreaming that Old and New are fellows:
A younger succeeds to an elder brother,
　　Da Vincis derive in good time from Dellos.[2]

IX

65　And here where your praise might yield returns,
　　And a handsome word or two give help,
Here, after your kind, the mastiff girns[3]
　　And the puppy pack of poodles yelp.
What, not a word for Stefano there,
70　　Of brow once prominent and starry,

Called Nature's Ape and the world's despair
　　For his peerless painting? (See Vasari.)[4]

X

There stands the Master. Study, my friends,
　　What a man's work comes to! So he plans it,
75　Performs it, perfects it, makes amends
　　For the toiling and moiling, and then, *sic transit!*[5]
Happier the thrifty blind-folk labour,
　　With upturned eye while the hand is busy,
Not sidling a glance at the coin of their neighbour!
80　　'Tis looking downward that makes one dizzy.

XI

"If you knew their work you would deal your dole."
　　May I take upon me to instruct you?
When Greek Art ran and reached the goal,
　　Thus much had the world to boast *in fructu*—[6]
85　The Truth of Man, as by God first spoken,
　　Which the actual[7] generations garble,
Was re-uttered, and Soul (which Limbs betoken)
　　And Limbs (Soul informs) made new in marble.

XII

So, you saw yourself as you wished you were,
90　　As you might have been, as you cannot be;
Earth here, rebuked by Olympus there:
　　And grew content in your poor degree
With your little power, by those statues' godhead,
　　And your little scope, by their eyes' full sway,
95　And your little grace, by their grace embodied,
　　And your little date, by their forms that stay.

---

[1] Michelangelo's paintings.

[2] Dello di Niccolo Delli, a minor fifteenth-century artist.

[3] snarls.

---

[4] Stefano Fiorentino (1301–50), pupil of Vasari, known as the Ape of Nature for his realism.

[5] *sic transit gloria mundi:* "thus passes the world's glory."

[6] "as fruit."

[7] present.

XIII

You would fain be kinglier, say, than I am?
    Even so, you will not sit like Theseus.[1]
You would prove a model? The Son of Priam[2]
100   Has yet the advantage in arms' and knees' use.
You're wroth—can you slay your snake like Apollo?[3]
    You're grieved—still Niobe's[4] the grander!
You live—there's the Racers' frieze to follow:[5]
    You die—there's the dying Alexander.[6]

XIV

105 So, testing your weakness by their strength,
    Your meagre charms by their rounded beauty,
Measured by Art in your breadth and length,
    You learned—to submit is a mortal's duty.
—When I say "you" 'tis the common soul,
110   The collective, I mean: the race of Man
That receives life in parts to live in a whole,
    And grow here according to God's clear plan.

XV

Growth came when, looking your last on them all,
    You turned your eyes inwardly one fine day
115 And cried with a start—What if we so small
    Be greater and grander the while than they?
Are they perfect of lineament, perfect of stature?
    In both, of such lower types are we
Precisely because of our wider nature;
120   For time, theirs—ours, for eternity.

XVI

Today's brief passion limits their range;
    It seethes with the morrow for us and more.
They are perfect—how else? they shall never change:

We are faulty—why not? we have time in store.
125 The Artificer's hand is not arrested
    With us; we are rough-hewn, nowise polished:
They stand for our copy,[7] and, once invested
    With all they can teach, we shall see them
        abolished.

XVII

'Tis a life-long toil till our lump be leaven—
130   The better! What's come to perfection perishes.
Things learned on earth, we shall practise in heaven:
    Works done least rapidly, Art most cherishes.
Thyself shalt afford the example, Giotto!
    Thy one work, not to decrease or diminish,
135 Done at a stroke, was just (was it not?) "O!"[8]
    Thy great Campanile is still to finish.

XVIII

Is it true that we are now, and shall be hereafter,
    But what and where depend on life's minute?
Hails heavenly cheer or infernal laughter
140   Our first step out of the gulf or in it?
Shall Man, such step within his endeavour,
    Man's face, have no more play and action
Than joy which is crystallized for ever,
    Or grief, an eternal petrifaction?

XIX

145 On which I conclude, that the early painters,
    To cries of "Greek Art and what more wish you?"—
Replied, "To become now self-acquainters,
    And paint man man, whatever the issue!
Make new hopes shine through the flesh they fray,[9]
150   New fears aggrandize the rags and tatters:
To bring the invisible full into play!
    Let the visible go to the dogs—what matters?"

---

[1] mythical king of Athens.

[2] either Hector or Paris, both sons of the Trojan king.

[3] The Greek god of poetry killed the Python when a child.

[4] The Queen of Thebes grieved because the gods killed her children.

[5] the Procession of Horsemen on the Parthenon frieze.

[6] Alexander the Great.

[7] to be copied by us.

[8] Giotto, asked for a sample of his skill by a Papal envoy, drew a perfect circle with one stroke.

[9] rub away.

XX

Give these, I exhort you, their guerdon and glory
    For daring so much, before they well did it.
155 The first of the new, in our race's story,
    Beats the last of the old; 'tis no idle quiddit.[1]
The worthies began a revolution,
    Which if on earth you intend to acknowledge,
Why, honour them now! (ends my allocution)[2]
160   Nor confer your degree when the folk leave
        college.

XXI

There's a fancy some lean to and others hate—
    That, when this life is ended, begins
New work for the soul in another state,
    Where it strives and gets weary, loses and wins:
165 Where the strong and the weak, this world's congeries,
    Repeat in large what they practised in small,
Through life after life in unlimited series;
    Only the scale's to be changed, that's all.

XXII

Yet I hardly know. When a soul has seen
170   By the means of Evil that Good is best,
And, through earth and its noise, what is heaven's serene,—
    When our faith in the same has stood the test—
Why, the child grown man, you burn the rod,
    The uses of labour are surely done;
175 There remaineth a rest for the people of God:
    And I have had troubles enough, for one.

XXIII

But at any rate I have loved the season
    Of Art's spring-birth so dim and dewy;
My sculptor is Nicolo the Pisan,[3]
180   My painter—who but Cimabue?[4]

---

[1] quick turn in argument.

[2] formal address.

[3] early Italian sculptor and architect (c. 1225–c.1284).

[4] Giovanni Cimabue (1240–1302), great early Italian painter.

Nor ever was man of them all indeed,
    From these to Ghiberti[5] and Ghirlandajo,[6]
Could say that he missed my critic-meed.
    So, now to my special grievance—heigh ho!

XXIV

185 Their ghosts still stand, as I said before,
    Watching each fresco flaked and rasped,
Blocked up, knocked out, or whitewashed o'er:
    —No getting again what the church has grasped!
The works on the wall must take their chance;
190   "Works never conceded to England's thick
        clime!"
(I hope they prefer their inheritance
    Of a bucketful of Italian quick-lime.)

XXV

When they go at length, with such a shaking
    Of heads o'er the old delusion, sadly
195 Each master his way through the black streets taking,
    Where many a lost work breathes though
        badly—
Why don't they bethink them of who has merited?
    Why not reveal, while their pictures dree[7]
Such doom, how a captive might be out-ferreted?
200   Why is it they never remember me?

XXVI

Not that I expect the great Bigordi,[8]
    Nor Sandro[9] to hear me, chivalric, bellicose;
Nor the wronged Lippino;[10] and not a word I

---

[5] Lorenzo Ghiberti (1381–1455), Florentine sculptor.

[6] Domenico Bigordi or Ghirlandaio (1449–94), Florentine painter and teacher of Michelangelo.

[7] suffer.

[8] Ghirlandaio.

[9] Botticelli (Alessandro dei Filipepi) (1444–1510), Florentine painter.

[10] Filippino Lippi (1457–1504), son of Fra Lippo Lippi, painter, wronged either because he was illegitimate or because his paintings were attributed to others.

Say of a scrap of Frà Angelico's:[1]
205 But are you too fine, Taddeo Gaddi,[2]
  To grant me a taste of your intonaco,[3]
Some Jerome[4] that seeks the heaven with a sad eye?
  Not a churlish saint, Lorenzo Monaco?[5]

XXVII

Could not the ghost with the close red cap,
210   My Pollajolo,[6] the twice a craftsman,
Save me a sample, give me the hap[7]
  Of a muscular Christ that shows the
    draughtsman?[8]
No Virgin by him the somewhat petty,
  Of finical touch and tempera crumbly—
215 Could not Alesso Baldovinetti[9]
  Contribute so much, I ask him humbly?

XXVIII

Margheritone of Arezzo,[10]
  With the grave-clothes garb and swaddling
    barret[11]
220 (Why purse up mouth and beak in a pet so,
  You bald old saturnine poll-clawed parrot?)[12]
Not a poor glimmering Crucifixion,
  Where in the foreground kneels the donor?

If such remain, as is my conviction,
225   The hoarding it does you but little honour.

XXIX

225 They pass; for them the panels may thrill,
  The tempera grow alive and tinglish;
Their pictures are left to the mercies still
  Of dealers and stealers, Jews and the English,
Who, seeing mere money's worth in their prize,
230   Will sell it to somebody calm as Zeno[13]
At naked High Art, and in ecstasies
  Before some clay-cold vile Carlino![14]

XXX

No matter for these! But Giotto, you,
  Have you allowed, as the town-tongues babble
    it,—
235 Oh, never! it shall not be counted true—
  That a certain precious little tablet[15]
Which Buonarroti[16] eyed like a lover,—
  Was buried so long in oblivion's womb
And, left for another than I to discover,
240   Turns up at last! and to whom?—to whom?

XXXI

I, that have haunted the dim San Spirito,
  (Or was it rather the Ognissanti?)[17]
Patient on altar-step planting a weary toe!
  Nay, I shall have it yet! *Detur amanti*![18]
245 My Koh-i-noor[19]—or (if that's a platitude)

---

[1] Florentine painter (1387–1455).

[2] fourteenth-century Florentine painter.

[3] plaster background for fresco painting.

[4] the fourth-century saint.

[5] Florentine painter (c. 1370–c.1425).

[6] Antonio Pollaiuolo (c. 1432–98), Florentine painter, who in his self-portrait wears a red cap. "Twice a craftsman" because he was a goldsmith turned painter.

[7] chance.

[8] Pollaiuolo's depiction, *Christ at the Column.*

[9] Florentine painter (1427–99).

[10] thirteenth-century Sienese painter.

[11] biretta: a priest's flat cap.

[12] "poll clawed like a parrot": *2 Henry IV* 2.4.282.

---

[13] founder of the Stoic philosophy.

[14] a painting by Florentine Carlo Dolci (1616–86).

[15] tablet of "The Last Supper."

[16] Michelangelo.

[17] San Spirito and Ognissanti are churches in Florence.

[18] "Let it be given to the one who loves it."

[19] "Mountain of Light," famous diamond given to Queen Victoria in 1849.

Jewel of Giamschid, the Persian Sofi's[1] eye;
So, in anticipative gratitude,
    What if I take up my hope and prophesy?

XXXII

When the hour grows ripe, and a certain dotard
250   Is pitched, no parcel that needs invoicing,
To the worse side of the Mont Saint Gothard,[2]
    We shall begin by way of rejoicing;
None of that shooting the sky (blank cartridge),
    Nor a civic guard, all plumes and lacquer,
255 Hunting Radetzky's[3] soul like a partridge
    Over Morello[4] with squib and cracker.

XXXIII

This time we'll shoot better game and bag 'em hot—
    No mere display at the stone of Dante,
But a kind of sober Witanagemot[5]
260   (Ex: "Casa Guidi," *quod videas ante*)[6]
Shall ponder, once Freedom restored to Florence,
    How Art may return that departed with her.
Go, hated house, go each trace of the Lorraine's,[7]
    And bring us the days of Orgagna[8] hither!

XXXIV

265 How we shall prologize, how we shall perorate,
    Utter fit things upon art and history,
Feel truth at blood-heat and falsehood at zero rate,
    Make of the want of the age no mystery;

Contrast the fructuous[9] and sterile eras,
270   Show—monarchy ever its uncouth cub licks
Out of the bear's shape into Chimera's,[10]
    While Pure Art's birth is still the republic's.

XXXV

Then one shall propose in a speech (curt Tuscan,
    Expúrgate and sober, with scarcely an
275   "*issimo*,")[11]
To end now our half-told tale of Cambuscan,[12]
    And turn the bell-tower's *alt* to *altissimo*:[13]
And fine as the beak of a young beccaccia[14]
    The Campanile, the Duomo's fit ally,
280 Shall soar up in gold full fifty braccia,
    Completing Florence, as Florence Italy.

XXXVI

Shall I be alive that morning the scaffold
    Is broken away, and the long-pent fire,
Like the golden hope of the world, unbaffled
    Springs from its sleep, and up goes the spire
285 While "God and the People"[15] plain for its motto,
    Thence the new tricolour[16] flaps at the sky?
At least to foresee that glory of Giotto
    And Florence together, the first am I!
—1855

---

1 Giamschid: a legendary Persian king, with "Sophy" as a former title of such kings.

2 mountain in the Alps.

3 Count Radetzky (1766–1858), Austrian general.

4 mountain north of Florence.

5 governing council in Anglo-Saxon England.

6 Elizabeth Barrett Browning's long poem *Casa Guidi Windows* (1851); "which you may have seen before."

7 Austrian Emperors were of the house of Habsburg-Lorraine.

8 Andrea di Cione, fourteenth-century Florentine artist.

---

9 fruitful.

10 legendary fire-breathing monster.

11 superlative ending for Italian adjectives.

12 Chaucer's unfinished "Squire's Tale."

13 "high to highest."

14 woodcock.

15 the motto of Mazzini.

16 green, white, and red flag of Italy.

In a Balcony [1]

PERSONS
Norbert
Constance
The Queen

CONSTANCE *and* NORBERT

NORBERT: Now!

CONSTANCE: Not now!

NORBERT: Give me them again,
     those hands:
Put them upon my forehead, how it throbs!
Press them before my eyes, the fire comes through!
You cruellest, you dearest in the world,
5 Let me! The Queen must grant whate'er I ask—
How can I gain you and not ask the Queen?
There she stays waiting for me, here stand you;
Some time or other this was to be asked;
Now is the one time—what I ask, I gain:
10 Let me ask now, Love!

CONSTANCE: Do, and ruin us.

NORBERT: Let it be now, Love! All my soul breaks
     forth.
How I do love you! Give my love its way!
A man can have but one life and one death,
One heaven, one hell. Let me fulfil my fate—
15 Grant me my heaven now! Let me know you mine,
Prove you mine, write my name upon your brow,
Hold you and have you, and then die away,
If God please, with completion in my soul!

CONSTANCE: I am not yours then? How content
     this man!
20 I am not his—who change into himself,
Have passed into his heart and beat its beats,
Who give my hands to him, my eyes, my hair,
Give all that was of me away to him—

---

[1] Although written as a closet drama, the play has been performed several times. The plot and characters are Browning's own.

So well, that now, my spirit turned his own,
25 Takes part with him against the woman here,
Bids him not stumble at so mere a straw
As caring that the world be cognizant
How he loves her and how she worships him.
You have this woman, not as yet that world.
30 Go on, I bid, nor stop to care for me
By saving what I cease to care about,
The courtly name and pride of circumstance—
The name you'll pick up and be cumbered with
Just for the poor parade's sake, nothing more;
35 Just that the world may slip from under you—
Just that the world may cry "So much for him—
The man predestined to the heap of crowns:
There goes his chance of winning one, at least!"

NORBERT: The world!

CONSTANCE: You love it. Love me quite as
     well,
40 And see if I shall pray for this in vain!
Why must you ponder what it knows or thinks?

NORBERT: You pray for—what, in vain?

CONSTANCE: Oh my
     heart's heart,
How I do love you, Norbert! That is right:
But listen, or I take my hands away!
45 You say, "let it be now": you would go now
And tell the Queen, perhaps six steps from us,
You love me—so you do, thank God!

NORBERT: Thank God!

CONSTANCE: Yes, Norbert,—but you fain would
     tell your love,
And, what succeeds the telling, ask of her
50 My hand. Now take this rose and look at it,
Listening to me. You are the minister,
The Queen's first favourite, nor without a cause.
Tonight completes your wonderful year's-work
(This palace-feast is held to celebrate)
55 Made memorable by her life's success,
The junction of two crowns, on her sole head,
Her house had only dreamed of anciently:
That this mere dream is grown a stable truth,

Tonight's feast makes authentic. Whose the praise?
60 Whose genius, patience, energy, achieved
What turned the many heads and broke the hearts?
You are the fate, your minute's in the heaven.
Next comes the Queen's turn. "Name your own
reward!"
With leave to clench the past, chain the to-come,
65 Put out an arm and touch and take the sun
And fix it ever full-faced on your earth,
Possess yourself supremely of her life,—
You choose the single thing she will not grant;
Nay, very declaration of which choice
70 Will turn the scale and neutralize your work:
At best she will forgive you, if she can.
You think I'll let you choose—her cousin's hand?
NORBERT: Wait. First, do you retain your old belief
The Queen is generous,—nay, is just?
CONSTANCE: There, there!
75 So men make women love them, while they know
No more of women's hearts than…look you here,
You that are just and generous beside,
Make it your own case! For example now,
I'll say—I let you kiss me, hold my hands—
80 Why? do you know why? I'll instruct you, then—
The kiss, because you have a name at court;
This hand and this, that you may shut in each
A jewel, if you please to pick up such.
That's horrible? Apply it to the Queen—
85 Suppose I am the Queen to whom you speak:
"I was a nameless man; you needed me:
Why did I proffer you my aid? there stood
A certain pretty cousin at your side.
Why did I make such common cause with you?
90 Access to her had not been easy else.
You give my labour here abundant praise?
'Faith, labour, which she overlooked, grew play.
How shall your gratitude discharge itself?
Give me her hand!"
NORBERT: And still I urge the same.
95 Is the Queen just? just—generous or no!

CONSTANCE: Yes, just. You love a rose; no harm in
that:
But was it for the rose's sake or mine
You put it in your bosom? mine, you said—
Then, mine you still must say or else be false.
100 You told the Queen you served her for herself;
If so, to serve her was to serve yourself,
She thinks, for all your unbelieving face!
I know her. In the hall, six steps from us,
One sees the twenty pictures; there's a life
105 Better than life, and yet no life at all.
Conceive her born in such a magic dome,[1]
Pictures all round her! why, she sees the world,
Can recognize its given things and facts,
The fight of giants or the feast of gods,
110 Sages in senate, beauties at the bath,
Chases and battles, the whole earth's display,
Landscape and sea-piece, down to flowers and
fruit—
And who shall question that she knows them all,
In better semblance than the things outside?
115 Yet bring into the silent gallery
Some live thing to contrast in breath and blood,
Some lion, with the painted lion there—
You think she'll understand composedly?
—Say, "that's his fellow in the hunting-piece
120 Yonder, I've turned to praise a hundred times"?
Not so. Her knowledge of our actual earth,
Its hopes and fears, concerns and sympathies,
Must be too far, too mediate, too unreal.
The real exists for us outside, not her:
125 How should it, with that life in these four walls—
That father and that mother, first to last
No father and no mother—friends, a heap,
Lovers, no lack—a husband in due time,
And every one of them alike a lie!
130 Things painted by a Rubens[2] out of naught
Into what kindness, friendship, life should be;

_____

[1] mansion.

[2] Peter Paul Rubens (1577–1640), the great Flemish artist.

All better, all more grandiose than the life,
Only no life; mere cloth and surface-paint,
You feel, while you admire. How should she feel?
35 Yet now that she has stood thus fifty years
The sole spectator in that gallery,
You think to bring this warm real struggling love
In to her of a sudden, and suppose
She'll keep her state untroubled? Here's the truth—
40 She'll apprehend truth's value at a glance,
Prefer it to the pictured loyalty?
You only have to say, "so men are made,
For this they act; the thing has many names,
But this the right one: and now, Queen, be just!"
45 Your life slips back; you lose her at the word:
You do not even for amends gain me.
She will not understand; oh, Norbert, Norbert,
Do you not understand?
  NORBERT: The Queen's the Queen:
I am myself—no picture, but alive
50 In every nerve and every muscle, here
At the palace-window o'er the people's street,
As she in the gallery where the pictures glow:
The good of life is precious to us both.
She cannot love; what do I want with rule?
55 When first I saw your face a year ago
I knew my life's good, my soul heard one voice—
"The woman yonder, there's no use of life
But just to obtain her! heap earth's woes in one
And bear them—make a pile of all earth's joys
60 And spurn them, as they help or help not this;
Only, obtain her!" How was it to be?
I found you were the cousin of the Queen;
I must then serve the Queen to get to you.
No other way. Suppose there had been one,
65 And I, by saying prayers to some white star
With promise of my body and my soul,
Might gain you,—should I pray the star or no?
Instead, there was the Queen to serve! I served,
Helped, did what other servants failed to do.
70 Neither she sought nor I declared my end.
Her good is hers, my recompense be mine,—

I therefore name you as that recompense.
She dreamed that such a thing could never be?
Let her wake now. She thinks there was more cause
175 In love of power, high fame, pure loyalty?
Perhaps she fancies men wear out their lives
Chasing such shades. Then, I've a fancy too;
I worked because I want you with my soul:
I therefore ask your hand. Let it be now!
180 CONSTANCE: Had I not loved you from the very
      first,
Were I not yours, could we not steal out thus
So wickedly, so wildly, and so well,
You might become impatient. What's conceived
Of us without here, by the folk within?
185 Where are you now? immersed in cares of state—
Where am I now? intent on festal robes—
We two, embracing under death's spread hand!
What was this thought for, what that scruple of
      yours
Which broke the council up?—to bring about
190 One minute's meeting in the corridor!
And then the sudden sleights, strange secrecies,
Complots inscrutable, deep telegraphs,
Long-planned chance-meetings, hazards of a look.
"Does she know? does she not know? saved or lost?"
195 A year of this compression's ecstasy
All goes for nothing! you would give this up
For the old way, the open way, the world's,
His way who beats, and his who sells his wife!
What tempts you?—their notorious happiness
200 Makes you ashamed of ours? The best you'll gain
Will be—the Queen grants all that you require,
Concedes the cousin, rids herself of you
And me at once, and gives us ample leave
To live like our five hundred happy friends.
205 The world will show us with officious hand
Our chamber-entry, and stand sentinel
Where we so oft have stolen across its traps!
Get the world's warrant, ring the falcons' feet,
And make it duty to be bold and swift,
210 Which long ago was nature. Have it so!

We never hawked by rights till flung from fist?
Oh, the man's thought! no woman's such a fool.
NORBERT: Yes, the man's thought and my thought,
    which is more—
One made to love you, let the world take note!
215 Have I done worthy work? be love's the praise,
Though hampered by restrictions, barred against
By set forms, blinded by forced secrecies!
Set free my love, and see what love can do
Shown in my life—what work will spring from that!
220 The world is used to have its business done
On other grounds, find great effects produced
For power's sake, fame's sake, motives in men's
    mouth.
So, good: but let my low ground shame their high!
Truth is the strong thing. Let man's life be true!
225 And love's the truth of mine. Time prove the rest!
I choose to wear you stamped all over me,
Your name upon my forehead and my breast,
You, from the sword's blade to the ribbon's edge,
That men may see, all over, you in me—
230 That pale loves may die out of their pretence
In face of mine, shames thrown on love fall off.
Permit this, Constance! Love has been so long
Subdued in me, eating me through and through,
That now 'tis all of me and must have way.
235 Think of my work, that chaos of intrigues,
Those hopes and fears, surprises and delays,
That long endeavour, earnest, patient, slow,
Trembling at last to its assured result:
Then think of this revulsion! I resume
240 Life after death, (it is no less than life,
After such long unlovely labouring days)
And liberate to beauty life's great need
O' the beautiful, which, while it prompted work,
Suppressed itself erewhile. This eve's the time,
245 This eve intense with yon first trembling star
We seem to pant and reach; scarce aught between
The earth that rises and the heaven that bends;
All nature self-abandoned, every tree
Flung as it will, pursuing its own thoughts

250 And fixed so, every flower and every weed,
No pride, no shame, no victory, no defeat;
All under God, each measured by itself.
These statues round us stand abrupt, distinct,
The strong in strength, the weak in weakness fixed,
255 The Muse for ever wedded to her lyre,
Nymph to her fawn, and Silence to her rose:
See God's approval on his universe!
Let us do so—aspire to live as these
In harmony with truth, ourselves being true!
260 Take the first way, and let the second come!
My first is to possess myself of you;
The music sets the march-step—forward, then!
And there's the Queen, I go to claim you of,
The world to witness, wonder and applaud.
265 Our flower of life breaks open. No delay!
CONSTANCE: And so shall we be ruined, both of us.
Norbert, I know her to the skin and bone:
You do not know her, were not born to it,
To feel what she can see or cannot see.
270 Love, she is generous,—ay, despite your smile,
Generous as you are: for, in that thin frame
Pain-twisted, punctured through and through with
    cares,
There lived a lavish soul until it starved,
Debarred of healthy food. Look to the soul—
275 Pity that, stoop to that, ere you begin
(The true man's-way) on justice and your rights,
Exactions and acquittance of the past!
Begin so—see what justice she will deal!
We women hate a debt as men a gift.
280 Suppose her some poor keeper of a school
Whose business is to sit through summer months
And dole out children leave to go and play,
Herself superior to such lightness—she
In the arm-chair's state and pedagogic pomp—
285 To the life, the laughter, sun and youth outside:
We wonder such a face looks black on us?
I do not bid you wake her tenderness,
(That were vain truly—none is left to wake)
But let her think her justice is engaged

290 To take the shape of tenderness, and mark
If she'll not coldly pay its warmest debt!
Does she love me, I ask you? not a whit:
Yet, thinking that her justice was engaged
To help a kinswoman, she took me up—
295 Did more on that bare ground than other loves
Would do on greater argument. For me,
I have no equivalent of such cold kind
To pay her with, but love alone to give
If I give anything. I give her love;
300 I feel I ought to help her, and I will.
So, for her sake, as yours, I tell you twice
That women hate a debt as men a gift.
If I were you, I could obtain this grace—
Could lay the whole I did to love's account,
305 Nor yet be very false as courtiers go—
Declaring my success was recompense;
It would be so, in fact: what were it else?
And then, once loose her generosity,—
Oh, how I see it!—then, were I but you,
310 To turn it, let it seem to move itself,
And make it offer what I really take,
Accepting just, in the poor cousin's hand,
Her value as the next thing to the Queen's—
Since none love Queens directly, none dare that,
315 And a thing's shadow or a name's mere echo
Suffices those who miss the name and thing!
You pick up just a ribbon she has worn,
To keep in proof how near her breath you came.
Say, I'm so near I seem a piece of her—
320 Ask for me that way—(oh, you understand)
You'd find the same gift yielded with a grace,
Which, if you make the least show to extort…
—You'll see! and when you have ruined both of us,
Dissertate on the Queen's ingratitude!
325 NORBERT: Then, if I turn it that way, you consent?
'Tis not my way; I have more hope in truth:
Still, if you won't have truth—why, this indeed,
Were scarcely false, as I'd express the sense.
Will you remain here?

CONSTANCE: O best heart of mine,
330 How I have loved you! then, you take my way?
Are mine as you have been her minister,
Work out my thought, give it effect for me,
Paint plain my poor conceit[1] and make it serve?
I owe that withered woman everything—
335 Life, fortune, you, remember! Take my part—
Help me to pay her! Stand upon your rights?
You, with my rose, my hands, my heart on you?
Your rights are mine—you have no rights but
    mine.
NORBERT: Remain here. How you know me!
CONSTANCE: Ah, but
    still—

[*He breaks from her: she remains.*
Dance-music from within]

[*Enter the* QUEEN]
340 QUEEN: Constance? She is here as he said. Speak
    quick!
Is it so? Is it true or false? One word!
CONSTANCE: True.
QUEEN: Mercifullest Mother,[2] thanks to
    thee!
CONSTANCE: Madam?
QUEEN: I love you, Constance, from
    my soul.
Now say once more, with any words you will,
345 'Tis true, all true, as true as that I speak.
CONSTANCE: Why should you doubt it?
QUEEN: Ah, why
    doubt? why doubt?
Dear, make me see it! Do you see it so?
None see themselves; another sees them best.
You say "why doubt it?"—you see him and me.
350 It is because the Mother has such grace
That if we had but faith—wherein we fail—
Whate'er we yearn for would be granted us;

---

[1] concept.

[2] the Virgin Mary.

377

Yet still we let our whims prescribe despair,
Our fancies thwart and cramp our will and power,
355 And while, accepting life, abjure its use.
Constance, I had abjured the hope of love
And being loved, as truly as yon palm
The hope of seeing Egypt from that plot.
CONSTANCE: Heaven!
QUEEN: But it was so, Constance, it
    was so!
360 Men say—or do men say it? fancies say—
"Stop here, your life is set, you are grown old.
Too late—no love for you, too late for love—
Leave love to girls. Be queen: let Constance love."
One takes the hint—half meets it like a child,
365 Ashamed at any feelings that oppose.
"Oh love, true, never think of love again!
I am a queen: I rule, not love forsooth."
So it goes on; so a face grows like this,
Hair like this hair, poor arms as lean as these,
370 Till,—nay, it does not end so, I thank God!
CONSTANCE: I cannot understand—
QUEEN: The happier you!
Constance, I know not how it is with men:
For women (I am a woman now like you)
There is no good of life but love—but love!
375 What else looks good, is some shade flung from
    love;
Love gilds it, gives it worth. Be warned by me,
Never you cheat yourself one instant! Love,
Give love, ask only love, and leave the rest!
O Constance, how I love you!
CONSTANCE: I love you.
380 QUEEN: I do believe that all is come through you.
I took you to my heart to keep it warm
When the last chance of love seemed dead in me;
I thought your fresh youth warmed my withered
    heart.
Oh, I am very old now, am I not?
385 Not so! it is true and it shall be true!
CONSTANCE: Tell it me: let me judge if true or
    false.

QUEEN: Ah, but I fear you! you will look at me
And say, "she's old, she's grown unlovely quite
Who ne'er was beauteous: men want beauty still."
390 Well, so I feared—the curse! so I felt sure!
CONSTANCE: Be calm. And now you feel not sure,
    you say?
QUEEN: Constance, he came,—the coming was not
    strange—
Do not I stand and see men come and go?
I turned a half-look from my pedestal
395 Where I grow marble—"one young man the more!
He will love some one; that is naught to me:
What would he with my marble stateliness?"
Yet this seemed somewhat worse than heretofore;
The man more gracious, youthful, like a god,
400 And I still older, with less flesh to change—[1]
We two those dear extremes that long to touch.
It seemed still harder when he first began
To labour at those state-affairs, absorbed
The old way for the old end—interest.
405 Oh, to live with a thousand beating hearts
Around you, swift eyes, serviceable hands,
Professing they've no care but for your cause,
Thought but to help you, love but for yourself.—
And you the marble statue all the time
410 They praise and point at as preferred to life,
Yet leave for the first breathing woman's smile,
First dancer's, gypsy's or street baladine's![2]
Why, how I have ground my teeth to hear men's
    speech
Stifled for fear it should alarm my ear,
415 Their gait subdued lest step should startle me,
Their eyes declined, such queendom to respect,
Their hands alert, such treasure to preserve,
While not a man of them broke rank and spoke,
Wrote me a vulgar letter all of love,
420 Or caught my hand and pressed it like a hand!
There have been moments, if the sentinel

---

[1] give up in exchange.

[2] female public dancer.

Lowering his halbert[1] to salute the queen,
Had flung it brutally and clasped my knees,
I would have stooped and kissed him with my soul.

25 CONSTANCE: Who could have comprehended?

QUEEN: Ay,
  who—who?
Why, no one, Constance, but this one who did.
Not they, not you, not I. Even now perhaps
It comes too late—would you but tell the truth.

CONSTANCE: I wait to tell it.

QUEEN: Well, you see, he came,
30 Outfaced the others, did a work this year
Exceeds in value all was ever done,
You know—it is not I who say it—all
Say it. And so (a second pang and worse)
I grew aware not only of what he did,
35 But why so wondrously. Oh, never work
Like his was done for work's ignoble sake—
Souls need a finer aim to light and lure!
I felt, I saw, he loved—loved somebody.
And Constance, my dear Constance, do you know,
40 I did believe this while 'twas you he loved.

CONSTANCE: Me, madam?

QUEEN: It did seem to me, your face
Met him where'er he looked: and whom but you
Was such a man to love? It seemed to me,
You saw he loved you, and approved his love,
45 And both of you were in intelligence.[2]
You could not loiter in that garden, step
Into this balcony, but I straight was stung
And forced to understand. It seemed so true,
So right, so beautiful, so like you both,
50 That all this work should have been done by him
Not for the vulgar hope of recompense,
But that at last—suppose, some night like this—
Borne on to claim his due reward of me,
He might say "Give her hand and pay me so."

455 And I (O Constance, you shall love me now!)
I thought, surmounting all the bitterness,
—"And he shall have it. I will make her blest,
My flower of youth, my woman's self that was,
My happiest woman's self that might have been!
460 These two shall have their joy and leave me here."
Yes—yes!

CONSTANCE: Thanks!

QUEEN: And the word was on my lips
When he burst in upon me. I looked to hear
A mere calm statement of his just desire
For payment of his labour. When—O heaven,
465 How can I tell you? lightning on my eyes
And thunder in my ears proved that first word
Which told 'twas love of me, of me, did all—
He loved me—from the first step to the last,
Loved me!

CONSTANCE: You hardly saw, scarce heard him
  speak
470 Of love: what if you should mistake?

QUEEN: No, no—
No mistake! Ha, there shall be no mistake!
He had not dared to hint the love he felt—
You were my reflex—(how I understood!)
He said you were the ribbon I had worn,
475 He kissed my hand, he looked into my eyes,
And love, love came at end of every phrase.
Love is begun; this much is come to pass:
The rest is easy. Constance, I am yours!
I will learn, I will place my life on you,
480 Teach me but how to keep what I have won!
Am I so old? This hair was early grey;
But joy ere now has brought hair brown again,
And joy will bring the cheek's red back, I feel.
I could sing once too; that was in my youth.
485 Still, when men paint me, they declare me…yes,
Beautiful—for the last French painter did!
I know they flatter somewhat; you are frank—
I trust you. How I loved you from the first!
Some queens would hardly seek a cousin out
490 And set her by their side to take the eye:

---

[1] halberd, long-handled weapon with head combining spear-point and axe.

[2] both aware of the situation.

I must have felt that good would come from you.
I am not generous—like him—like you!
But he is not your lover after all:
It was not you he looked at. Saw you him?
495 You could not been mistaking words or looks?
He said you were the reflex of myself.
And yet he is not such a paragon
To you, to younger women who may choose
Among a thousand Norberts. Speak the truth!
500 You know you never named his name to me:
You know, I cannot give him up—ah God,
Not up now, even to you!
CONSTANCE: Then calm yourself.
QUEEN: See, I am old—look here, you happy girl!
I will not play the fool, deceive—ah, whom?
505 'Tis all gone: put your cheek beside my cheek
And what a contrast does the moon behold!
But then I set my life upon one chance,
The last chance and the best—am *I* not left,
My soul, myself? All women love great men
510 If young or old; it is in all the tales:
Young beauties love old poets who can love—
Why should not he, the poems in my soul,
The passionate faith, the pride of sacrifice,
Life-long, death-long? I throw them at his feet.
515 Who cares to see the fountain's very shape,
Whether it be a Triton's[1] or a Nymph's
That pours the foam, makes rainbows all around?
You could not praise indeed the empty conch;
But I'll pour floods of love and hide myself.
520 How I will love him! Cannot men love love?
Who was a queen and loved a poet once
Humpbacked, a dwarf? ah, women can do that!
Well, but men too; at least they tell you so.
They love so many women in their youth,
525 And even in age they all love whom they please;
And yet the best of them confide to friends
That 'tis not beauty makes the lasting love—
They spend a day with such and tire the next:

They like soul,—well then, they like phantasy,
530 Novelty even. Let us confess the truth,
Horrible though it be, that prejudice,
Prescription…curses! they will love a queen.
They will, they do: and will not, does not—he?
CONSTANCE: How can he? You are wedded: 'tis a
    name
535 We know, but still a bond. Your rank remains,
His rank remains. How can he, nobly souled
As you believe and I incline to think,
Aspire to be your favourite, shame and all?
QUEEN: Hear her! There, there now—could she
    love like me?
540 What did I say of smooth-cheeked youth and grace?
See all it does or could do! so youth loves!
Oh, tell him, Constance, you could never do
What I will—you, it was not born in! I
Will drive these difficulties far and fast
545 As yonder mists curdling before the moon.
I'll use my light too, gloriously retrieve
My youth from its enforced calamity,
Dissolve that hateful marriage, and be his,
His own in the eyes alike of God and man.
550 CONSTANCE: You will do—dare do…pause on
    what you say!
QUEEN: Hear her! I thank you, sweet, for that
    surprise.
You have the fair face: for the soul, see mine!
I have the strong soul: let me teach you, here.
I think I have borne enough and long enough,
555 And patiently enough, the world remarks,
To have my own way now, unblamed by all.
It does so happen (I rejoice for it)
This most unhoped-for issue cuts the knot.
There's not a better way of settling claims
560 Than this; God sends the accident express:
And were it for my subjects' good, no more,
'Twere best thus ordered. I am thankful now,
Mute, passive, acquiescent. I receive,
And bless God simply, or should almost fear
565 To walk so smoothly to my ends at last.

---

[1] merman-like sea-god.

Why, how I baffle obstacles, spurn fate!
How strong I am! Could Norbert see me now!
CONSTANCE: Let me consider. It is all too strange.
QUEEN: You, Constance, learn of me; do you, like
    me!
570 You are young, beautiful: my own, best girl,
You will have many lovers, and love one—
Light hair, not hair like Norbert's, to suit yours:
Taller than he is, since yourself are tall.
Love him, like me! Give all away to him;
575 Think never of yourself; throw by your pride,
Hope, fear,—your own good as you saw it once,
And love him simply for his very self.
Remember, I (and what am I to you?)
Would give up all for one, leave throne, lose life,
580 Do all but just unlove him! He loves me.
CONSTANCE: He shall.
QUEEN: You, step inside my inmost
    heart!
Give me your own heart: let us have one heart!
I'll come to you for counsel, "this he says,
This he does; what should this amount to, pray?
585 Beseech you, change it into current coin!
Is that worth kisses? Shall I please him there?"
And then we'll speak in turn of you—what else?
Your love, according to your beauty's worth,
For you shall have some noble love, all gold:
590 Whom choose you? we will get him at your choice.
—Constance, I leave you. Just a minute since,
I felt as I must die or be alone
Breathing my soul into an ear like yours:
Now, I would face the world with my new life,
595 Wear my new crown. I'll walk around the rooms,
And then come back and tell you how it feels.
How soon a smile of God can change the world!
How we are made for happiness—how work
Grows play, adversity a winning fight!
600 True, I have lost so many years: what then?
Many remain: God has been very good.
You, stay here! 'Tis as different from dreams,
From the mind's cold calm estimate of bliss,

As these stone statues from the flesh and blood,
605 The comfort thus hast caused mankind, God's
    moon![1]
    [*She goes out, leaving* CONSTANCE.
    Dance-music from within]

[NORBERT *enters*]
NORBERT: Well? we have but one minute and one
    word!
CONSTANCE: I am yours, Norbert!
NORBERT: Yes, mine.
CONSTANCE: Not till
    now!
You were mine. Now I give myself to you.
NORBERT: Constance?
CONSTANCE: Your own! I know the thriftier
    way
610 Of giving—haply, 'tis the wiser way.
Meaning to give a treasure, I might dole
Coin after coin out (each, as that were all,
With a new largess still at each despair)
And force you keep in sight the deed, preserve
615 Exhaustless till the end my part and yours,
My giving and your taking; both our joys
Dying together. Is it the wiser way?
I choose the simpler; I give all at once.
Know what you have to trust to, trade upon!
620 Use it, abuse it,—anything but think
Hereafter, "Had I known she loved me so,
And what my means, I might have thriven with it."
This is your means. I give you all myself.
NORBERT: I take you and thank God.
CONSTANCE: Look on
    through years!
625 We cannot kiss, a second day like this;
Else were this earth no earth.
NORBERT: With this day's heat
We shall go on through years of cold.

-----
[1] love.

CONSTANCE: So, best!
—I try to see those years—I think I see.
You walk quick and new warmth comes; you look
    back
630 And lay all to the first glow—not sit down
For ever brooding on a day like this
While seeing embers whiten and love die.
Yes, love lives best in its effect; and mine,
Full in its own life, yearns to live in yours.
635 NORBERT: Just so. I take and know you all at once.
Your soul is disengaged so easily,
Your face is there, I know you; give me time,
Let me be proud and think you shall know me.
My soul is slower: in a life I roll
640 The minute out whereto you condense yours—
The whole slow circle round you I must move,
To be just you. I look to a long life
To decompose this minute, prove its worth.
'Tis the sparks' long succession one by one
645 Shall show you, in the end, what fire was crammed
In that mere stone you struck: how could you
    know,
If it lay ever unproved in your sight,
As now my heart lies? your own warmth would
    hide
Its coldness, were it cold.
CONSTANCE: But how prove, how?
650 NORBERT: Prove in my life, you ask?
CONSTANCE: Quick,
    Norbert—how?
NORBERT: That's easy told. I count life just a stuff
To try the soul's strength on, educe the man.
Who keeps one end in view makes all things serve.
As with the body—he who hurls a lance
655 Or heaps up stone on stone, shows strength alike:
So must I seize and task all means to prove
And show this soul of mine, you crown as yours,
And justify us both.
CONSTANCE: Could you write books,
Paint pictures! One sits down in poverty
660 And writes or paints, with pity for the rich.

NORBERT: And loves one's painting and one's
    writing, then,
And not one's mistress! All is best, believe,
And we best as no other than we are.
We live, and they experiment on life—
665 Those poets, painters, all who stand aloof
To overlook the farther. Let us be
The thing they look at! I might take your face
And write of it and paint it—to what end?
For whom? what pale dictatress in the air
670 Feeds, smiling sadly, her fine ghost-like form
With earth's real blood and breath, the beauteous
    life
She makes despised for ever? You are mine,
Made for me, not for others in the world,
Nor yet for that which I should call my art,
675 The cold calm power to see how fair you look.
I come to you; I leave you not, to write
Or paint. You are, I am: let Rubens there
Paint us!
CONSTANCE: So, best!
NORBERT: I understand your soul.
You live, and rightly sympathize with life,
680 With action, power, success. This way is straight;
And time were short beside, to let me change
And craft my childhood learnt: my craft shall serve.
Men set me here to subjugate, enclose,
Manure their barren lives, and force thence fruit
685 First for themselves, and afterward for me
In the due tithe; the task of some one soul,
Through ways of work appointed by the world.
I am not bid create—men see no star
Transfiguring my brow to warrant that—
690 But find and bind and bring to bear their wills.
So I began: tonight sees how I end.
What if it see, too, power's first outbreak here
Amid the warmth, surprise and sympathy,
And instincts of the heart that teach the head?
695 What if the people have discerned at length
The dawn of the next nature, novel brain
Whose will they venture in the place of theirs,

Whose work, they trust, shall find them as novel ways
To untried heights which yet he only sees?
700 I felt it when you kissed me. See this Queen,
This people—in our phrase, this mass of men—
See how the mass lies passive to my hand
Now that my hand is plastic, with you by
To make the muscles iron! Oh, an end
705 Shall crown this issue as this crowns the first!
My will be on this people! then, the strain,
The grappling of the potter with his clay,
The long uncertain struggle,—the success
And consummation of the spirit-work,
710 Some vase shaped to the curl of the god's lip,
While rounded fair for human sense to see
The Graces in a dance men recognize
With turbulent applause and laughs of heart!
So triumph ever shall renew itself;
715 Ever shall end in efforts higher yet,
Ever begin...
CONSTANCE: I ever helping?
NORBERT: Thus!

[*As he embraces her, the* QUEEN *enters*]

CONSTANCE: Hist, madam! So have I performed
      my part.
You see your gratitude's true decency,
Norbert? A little slow in seeing it!
720 Begin, to end the sooner! What's a kiss?
NORBERT: Constance?
CONSTANCE: Why, must I teach it you again?
You want a witness to your dulness, sir?
What was I saying these ten minutes long?
Then I repeat—when some young handsome man
725 Like you has acted out a part like yours,
Is pleased to fall in love with one beyond,
So very far beyond him, as he says—
So hopelessly in love that but to speak
Would prove him mad,—he thinks judiciously,
730 And makes some insignificant good soul,
Like me, his friend, adviser, confidant,
And very stalking-horse to cover him

In following after what he dares not face.
When his end's gained—(sir, do you understand?)
735 When she, he dares not face, has loved him first,
—May I not say so, madam?—tops his hope,
And overpasses so his wildest dream,
With glad consent of all, and most of her
The confidant who brought the same about—
740 Why, in the moment when such joy explodes,
I do hold that the merest gentleman
Will not start rudely from the stalking-horse,
Dismiss it with a "There, enough of you!"
Forget it, show his back unmannerly:
745 But like a liberal heart will rather turn
And say, "A tingling time of hope was ours;
Betwixt the fears and falterings, we two lived
A chanceful time in waiting for the prize:
The confidant, the Constance, served not ill.
750 And though I shall forget her in due time,
Her use being answered now, as reason bids,
Nay as herself bids from her heart of hearts,—
Still, she has rights, the first thanks go to her,
The first good praise goes to the prosperous tool,
755 And the first—which is the last—rewarding kiss."
NORBERT: Constance, it is a dream—ah, see, you
      smile!
CONSTANCE: So, now his part being properly
      performed,
Madam, I turn to you and finish mine
As duly; I do justice in my turn.
760 Yes, madam, he has loved you—long and well;
He could not hope to tell you so—'twas I
Who served to prove your soul accessible,
I led his thoughts on, drew them to their place
When they had wandered else into despair,
765 And kept love constant toward its natural aim.
Enough, my part is played; you stoop half-way
And meet us royally and spare our fears:
'Tis like yourself. He thanks you, so do I.
Take him—with my full heart! my work is praised
770 By what comes of it. Be you happy, both!
Yourself—the only one on earth who can—

Do all for him, much more than a mere heart
Which though warm is not useful in its warmth
As the silk vesture of a queen! fold that
775 Around him gently, tenderly. For him—
For him,—he knows his own part!
NORBERT: Have you done?
I take the jest at last. Should I speak now?
Was yours the wager, Constance, foolish child,
Or did you but accept it? Well—at least
780 You lose by it.
CONSTANCE: Nay, madam, 'tis your turn!
Restrain him still from speech a little more,
And make him happier as more confident!
Pity him, madam, he is timid yet!
Mark, Norbert! Do not shrink now! Here I yield
785 My whole right in you to the Queen, observe!
With her go put in practice the great schemes
You teem with, follow the career else closed—
Be all you cannot be except by her!
Behold her!—Madam, say for pity's sake
790 Anything—frankly say you love him! Else
He'll not believe it: there's more earnest in
His fear than you conceive: I know the man!
NORBERT: I know the woman somewhat, and confess
I thought she had jested better: she begins
795 To overcharge[1] her part. I gravely wait
Your pleasure, madam: where is my reward?
QUEEN: Norbert, this wild girl (whom I recognize
Scarce more than you do, in her fancy-fit,
Eccentric speech and variable mirth,
800 Not very wise perhaps and somewhat bold,
Yet suitable, the whole night's work being strange)
—May still be right: I may do well to speak
And make authentic what appears a dream
To even myself. For, what she says, is true;
805 Yes, Norbert—what you spoke just now of love,
Devotion, stirred no novel sense in me,
But justified a warmth felt long before.
Yes, from the first—I loved you, I shall say:

---

[1] overact.

Strange! but I do grow stronger, now 'tis said.
810 Your courage helps mine: you did well to speak
Tonight, the night that crowns your twelvemonths'
    toil:
But still I had not waited to discern
Your heart so long, believe me! From the first
The source of so much zeal was almost plain,
815 In absence even of your own words just now
Which hazarded the truth. 'Tis very strange,
But takes a happy ending—in your love
Which mine meets: be it so! as you chose me,
So I choose you.
NORBERT: And worthily you choose.
820 I will not be unworthy your esteem,
No, madam. I do love you; I will meet
Your nature, now I know it. This was well.
I see,—you dare and you are justified:
But none had ventured such experiment,
825 Less versed than you in nobleness of heart,
Less confident of finding such in me.
I joy that thus you test me ere you grant
The dearest richest beauteousest and best
Of women to my arms: 'tis like yourself.
830 So—back again into my part's set words—
Devotion to the uttermost is yours,
But no, you cannot, madam, even you,
Create in me the love our Constance does.
Or—something truer to the tragic phrase—
835 Not yon magnolia-bell superb with scent
Invites a certain insect—that's myself—
But the small eye-flower nearer to the ground.
I take this lady.
CONSTANCE: Stay—not hers, the trap—
Stay, Norbert—that mistake were worst of all!
840 He is too cunning, madam! It was I,
I, Norbert, who...
NORBERT: You, was it, Constance? Then,
But for the grace of this divinest hour
Which gives me you, I might not pardon here!
I am the Queen's; she only knows my brain:
845 She may experiment upon my heart

And I instruct her too by the result.
But you, sweet, you who know me, who so long
Have told my heart-beats over, held my life
In those white hands of yours,—it is not well!
50 CONSTANCE: Tush! I have said it, did I not say it
    all?
The life, for her—the heart-beats, for her sake!
NORBERT: Enough! my cheek grows red, I think.
    Your test?
There's not the meanest woman in the world,
Not she I least could love in all the world,
55 Whom, did she love me, had love proved itself,
I dare insult as you insult me now.
Constance, I could say, if it must be said,
"Take back the soul you offer, I keep mine!"
But—"Take the soul still quivering on your hand,
60 The soul so offered, which I cannot use,
And, please you, give it to some playful friend,
For—what's the trifle he requites me with?"
I, tempt a woman, to amuse a man,
That two may mock her heart if it succumb?
65 No: fearing God and standing 'neath his heaven,
I would not dare insult a woman so,
Were she the meanest woman in the world,
And he, I cared to please, ten emperors!
CONSTANCE: Norbert!
NORBERT: I love once as I live but once.
70 What case is this to think or talk about?
I love you. Would it mend the case at all
If such a step as this killed love in me?
Your part were done: account to God for it!
But mine—could murdered love get up again,
75 And kneel to whom you please to designate,
And make you mirth? It is too horrible.
You did not know this, Constance? now you know
That body and soul have each one life, but one:
And here's my love, here, living, at your feet.
80 CONSTANCE: See the Queen! Norbert—this one
    more last word—
If thus you have taken jest for earnest—thus
Loved me in earnest…

NORBERT: Ah, no jest holds here!
Where is the laughter in which jests break up,
And what this horror that grows palpable?
885 Madam—why grasp you thus the balcony?
Have I done ill? Have I not spoken truth?
How could I other? Was it not your test,
To try me, what my love for Constance meant?
Madam, your royal soul itself approves,
890 The first, that I should choose thus! so one takes
A beggar,—asks him, what would buy his child?
And then approves the expected laugh of scorn
Returned as something noble from the rags.
Speak, Constance, I'm the beggar! Ha, what's this?
895 You two glare each at each like panthers now.
Constance, the world fades; only you stand there!
You did not, in tonight's wild whirl of things,
Sell me—your soul of souls, for any price?
No—no—'tis easy to believe in you!
900 Was it your love's mad trial to o'ertop
Mine by this vain self-sacrifice? well, still—
Though I might curse, I love you. I am love
And cannot change: love's self is at your feet!
            [*The* QUEEN *goes out*]
CONSTANCE: Feel my heart; let it die against your
    own!
905 NORBERT: Against my own. Explain not; let this be!
This is life's height.
CONSTANCE: Yours, yours, yours!
NORBERT: You and I—
Why care by what meanders we are here
I' the centre of the labyrinth? Men have died
Trying to find this place, which we have found.
910 CONSTANCE: Found, found!
NORBERT: Sweet, never fear what
    she can do!
We are past harm now.
CONSTANCE: On the breast of God.
I thought of men—as if you were a man.
Tempting him with a crown!
NORBERT: This must end here:
It is too perfect.

CONSTANCE: There's the music stopped.
915   What measured heavy tread? It is one blaze
About me and within me.
NORBERT: Oh, some death
Will run its sudden finger round this spark
And sever us from the rest!
CONSTANCE: And so do well.
Now the doors open.
NORBERT: 'Tis the guard comes.
CONSTANCE: Kiss![1]
—1855

Saul [2]

I

Said Abner,[3] "At last thou art come! Ere I tell,
ere thou speak,
Kiss my cheek, wish me well!" Then I wished it,
and did kiss his cheek.
And he, "Since the King, O my friend, for thy
countenance sent,
Neither drunken nor eaten have we; nor until from
his tent
5   Thou return with the joyful assurance the King
liveth yet,

Shall our lip with the honey be bright, with the
water be wet.
For out of the black mid-tent's silence, a space of
three days,
Not a sound hath escaped to thy servants, of prayer
nor of praise,
To betoken that Saul and the Spirit have ended
their strife,
10   And that, faint in his triumph, the monarch sinks
back upon life.

II

"Yet now my heart leaps, O beloved! God's child
with his dew
On thy gracious gold hair, and those lilies still
living and blue
Just broken to twine round thy harp-strings, as if
no wild heat
Were now raging to torture the desert!"

III

                      Then I, as was
meet,
Knelt down to the God of my fathers, and rose on
my feet,
And ran o'er the sand burnt to powder. The tent
was unlooped;
I pulled up the spear that obstructed, and under I
stooped;
Hands and knees on the slippery grass-patch, all
withered and gone,
That extends to the second enclosure, I groped my
way on
20   Till I felt where the foldskirts fly open. Then once
more I prayed,
And opened the foldskirts and entered, and was not
afraid
But spoke, "Here is David, thy servant!" And no
voice replied.
At the first I saw naught but the blackness; but
soon I descried

---

1 The play's conclusion has been much discussed. Browning himself said, "The queen had a large and passionate temperament, which had only once been touched and brought into intense life. She would have died, as by a knife in the heart. The guard would have come to carry away her dead body."

2 The first nine stanzas of "Saul" were first published in 1845 in *Dramatic Romances and Lyrics*. The completed poem, with an additional ten stanzas, was published in *Men and Women* in 1855. Browning could not complete the poem in 1845 because he had not at that time clearly formulated his religious/aesthetic theory. Parts of his 1845 correspondence with Miss Barrett, and his "Essay on Shelley" (1851), reflect the concerns which, once resolved, enabled him to complete the poem. The Biblical source for "Saul" is 1 Samuel 16.14–23. Smart's *Song to David* led Browning in 1845 to other of Smart's work, including the preface in which Smart writes of the "fine subject" suggested to him of "David's playing to King Saul when he was troubled with the evil spirit."

3 the captain of Saul's "host": 1 Samuel 26:5, Saul's cousin.

A something more black than the blackness—the
    vast, the upright
25 Main prop which sustains the pavilion: and slow
    into sight
Grew a figure against it, gigantic and blackest of all.
Then a sunbeam, that burst through the tent-roof,
    showed Saul.

IV

He stood as erect as that tent-prop, both arms
    stretched out wide
On the great cross-support in the centre, that goes
    to each side;
30 He relaxed not a muscle, but hung there as, caught
    in his pangs
And waiting his change, the king-serpent all heavily
    hangs,
Far away from his kind, in the pine, till deliverance
    come
With the spring-time,—so agonized Saul, drear
    and stark, blind and dumb.

V

Then I turned my harp,—took off the lilies we
    twine round its chords
35 Lest they snap 'neath the stress of the noontide—
    those sunbeams like swords!
And I first played the tune all our sheep know, as,
    one after one,
So docile they come to the pen-door till folding be
    done.
They are white and untorn by the bushes, for lo,
    they have fed
Where the long grasses stifle the water within the
    stream's bed;
40 And now one after one seeks its lodging, as star
    follows star
Into eve and the blue far above us,—so blue and so
    far!

VI

—Then the tune, for which quails on the cornland
    will each leave his mate
To fly after the player; then, what makes the
    crickets elate
Till for boldness they fight one another: and then,
    what has weight
45 To set the quick jerboa[1] a-musing outside his sand
    house—
There are none such as he for a wonder, half bird
    and half mouse!
God made all the creatures and gave them our love
    and our fear,
To give sign, we and they are his children, one
    family here.

VII

Then I played the help-tune of our reapers, their
    wine-song, when hand
50 Grasps at hand, eye lights eye in good friendship,
    and great hearts expand
And grow one in the sense of this world's life.—
    And then, the last song
When the dead man is praised on his journey—
    "Bear, bear him along
With his few faults shut up like dead flowerets! Are
    balm-seeds not here
To console us? The land has none left such as he
    on the bier.
55 Oh, would we might keep thee, my brother!"
    —And then, the glad chaunt
Of the marriage,—first go the young maidens,
    next, she whom we vaunt
As the beauty, the pride of our dwelling.—And
60   then, the great march
Wherein man runs to man to assist him and
    buttress an arch
Naught can break; who shall harm them, our
    friends?—Then, the chorus intoned

---

[1] a rodent with long back legs for leaping.

60 As the Levites[1] go up to the altar in glory enthroned.
But I stopped here: for here in the darkness Saul
groaned.

VIII

And I paused, held my breath in such silence, and
listened apart;
And the tent shook, for mighty Saul shuddered:
and sparkles 'gan dart
From the jewels that woke in his turban, at once
with a start,
65 All its lordly male[2]-sapphires, and rubies
courageous[3] at heart.
So the head: but the body still moved not, still
hung there erect.
And I bent once again to my playing, pursued it
unchecked,
As I sang,—

IX

"Oh, our manhood's prime vigour! No
spirit feels waste,
Not a muscle is stopped in its playing nor sinew
unbraced.
70 Oh, the wild joys of living! the leaping from rock
up to rock,
The strong rending of boughs from the fir-tree, the
cool silver shock
Of the plunge in a pool's living water, the hunt of
the bear,
And the sultriness showing the lion is couched in
his lair.
And the meal, the rich dates yellowed over with
gold dust divine,
75 And the locust-flesh steeped in the pitcher, the full
draught of wine,

And the sleep in the dried river-channel where
bulrushes tell
That the water was wont to go warbling so softly
and well.
How good is man's life, the mere living! how fit to
employ
All the heart and the soul and the senses for ever in
joy!
80 Hast thou loved the white locks of thy father,
whose sword thou didst guard
When he trusted thee forth with the armies, for
glorious reward?
Didst thou see the thin hands of thy mother, held
up as men sung
The low song of the nearly-departed, and hear her
faint tongue
Joining in while it could to the witness, 'Let one
more attest,
85 I have lived, seen God's hand through a lifetime,
and all was for best'?
Then they sung through their tears in strong
triumph, not much, but the rest.
And thy brothers, the help and the contest, the
working whence grew
Such results as, from seething grape-bundles, the
spirits strained true:
And the friends of thy boyhood—that boyhood of
wonder and hope,
90 Present promise and wealth of the future beyond
the eye's scope,—
Till lo, thou art grown to a monarch; a people is
thine;
And all gifts, which the world offers singly, on one
head combine!
On one head, all the beauty and strength, love and
rage (like the throe
That, a-work in the rock, helps its labour and lets
the gold go)
95 High ambition and deeds which surpass it, fame
crowning them,—all

---

[1] Those assisting the priests in the Temple were traditionally chosen
from the tribe of Levi.

[2] very blue.

[3] lively.

Brought to blaze on the head of one creature—
    King Saul!"

X

And lo, with that leap of my spirit,—heart, hand,
    harp and voice,
Each lifting Saul's name out of sorrow, each
    bidding rejoice
Saul's fame in the light it was made for—as when,
    dare I say,
100 The Lord's army, in rapture of service, strains[1]
    through its array,
And upsoareth the cherubim-chariot—"Saul!"
    cried I, and stopped,
And waited the thing that should follow. Then
    Saul, who hung propped
By the tent's cross-support in the centre, was struck
    by his name.
Have ye seen when Spring's arrowy summons goes
    right to the aim,
05 And some mountain, the last to withstand her, that
    held (he alone,
While the vale laughed in freedom and flowers) on
    a broad bust of stone
A year's snow bound about for a breastplate,—
    leaves grasp of the sheet?
Fold on fold all at once it crowds thunderously
    down to his feet,
And there fronts you, stark, black, but alive yet,
    your mountain of old,
10 With his rents, the successive bequeathings of ages
    untold—
Yea, each harm got in fighting your battles, each
    furrow and scar
Of his head thrust 'twixt you and the tempest—
    all hail, there they are!
—Now again to be softened with verdure, again
    hold the nest

Of the dove, tempt the goat and its young to the
    green on his crest
115 For their food in the ardours of summer. One long
    shudder thrilled
All the tent till the very air tingled, then sank and
    was stilled
At the King's self left standing before me, released
    and aware.
What was gone, what remained? All to traverse,
    'twixt hope and despair;
Death was past, life not come: so he waited. Awhile
    his right hand
120 Held the brow, helped the eyes left too vacant
    forthwith to remand
To their place what new objects should enter: 'twas
    Saul as before.
I looked up and dared gaze at those eyes, nor was
    hurt any more
Than by slow pallid sunsets in autumn, ye watch
    from the shore,
At their sad level gaze o'er the ocean—a sun's
    slow decline
125 Over hills which, resolved in stern silence, o'erlap
    and entwine
Base with base to knit strength more intensely: so,
    arm folded arm
O'er the chest whose slow heavings subsided.

XI

                                              What
    spell or what charm,
(For, awhile there was trouble within me) what
    next should I urge
To sustain him where song had restored him?
    —Song filled to the verge
130 His cup with the wine of this life, pressing all that
    it yields
Of mere fruitage, the strength and the beauty:
    beyond, on what fields,
Glean a vintage more potent and perfect to
    brighten the eye

---

[1] feels high tension.

And bring blood to the lip, and commend them
   the cup they put by?
He saith, "It is good"; still he drinks not: he lets me
   praise life,
135 Gives assent, yet would die for his own part.

XII

                        Then
  fancies grew rife
Which had come long ago on the pasture, when
   round me the sheep
Fed in silence—above, the one eagle wheeled slow
   as in sleep;
And I lay in my hollow and mused on the world
   that might lie
'Neath his ken, though I saw but the strip 'twixt
   the hill and the sky:
140 And I laughed—"Since my days are ordained to be
   passed with my flocks,
Let me people at least, with my fancies, the plains
   and the rocks,
Dream the life I am never to mix with, and image
   the show
Of mankind as they live in those fashions I hardly
   shall know!
Schemes of life, its best rules and right uses, the
   courage that gains,
145 And the prudence that keeps what men strive for."
   And now these old trains
Of vague thought came again; I grew surer; so,
   once more the string
Of my harp made response to my spirit,
   as thus—

XIII

"Yea, my King,"

I began—"thou dost well in rejecting mere
   comforts that spring
From the mere mortal life held in common by man
   and by brute:

150 In our flesh grows the branch of this life, in our
   soul it bears fruit.
Thou hast marked the slow rise of the tree,—how
   its stem trembled first
Till it passed the kid's lip, the stag's antler; then
   safely outburst
The fan-branches all round; and thou mindest
   when these too, in turn
Broke a-bloom and the palm-tree seemed perfect:
   yet more was to learn,
155 E'en the good that comes in with the palm-fruit.
   Our dates shall we slight,
When their juice brings a cure for all sorrow? or
   care for the plight
Of the palm's self whose slow growth produced
   them? Not so! stem and branch
Shall decay, nor be known in their place, while the
   palm-wine shall staunch
Every wound of man's spirit in winter. I pour thee
   such wine.
160 Leave the flesh to the fate it was fit for! the spirit
   be thine!
By the spirit, when age shall o'ercome thee, thou
   still shalt enjoy
More indeed, than at first when inconscious,[1] the
   life of a boy.
Crush that life, and behold its wine running! Each
   deed thou hast done
Dies, revives, goes to work in the world; until e'en
   as the sun
165 Looking down on the earth, though clouds spoil
   him, though tempests efface,
Can find nothing his own deed produced not,
   must everywhere trace
The results of his past summer-prime,—so, each
   ray of thy will,
Every flash of thy passion and prowess, long over,
   shall thrill

---

[1] unconscious.

Thy whole people, the countless, with ardour, till
    they too give forth
170 A like cheer to their sons, who in turn, fill the
    South and the North
With the radiance thy deed was the germ of.
    Carouse in the past!
But the license of age has its limit; thou diest at last:
As the lion when age dims his eyeball, the rose at
    her height
So with man—so his power and his beauty for
    ever take flight.
175 No! Again a long draught of my soul-wine! Look
    forth o'er the years!
Thou hast done now with eyes for the actual; begin
    with the seer's!
Is Saul dead? In the depth of the vale make his
    tomb—bid arise
A grey mountain of marble heaped four-square, till,
    built to the skies,
Let it mark where the great First King[1] slumbers:
    whose fame would ye know?
180 Up above see the rock's naked face, where the
    record shall go
In great characters cut by the scribe,—Such was
    Saul, so he did;
With the sages directing the work, by the populace
    chid,—
For not half, they'll affirm, is comprised there!
    Which fault to amend,
In the grove with his kind grows the cedar,
    whereon they shall spend
185 (See, in tablets 'tis level before them) their praise,
    and record
With the gold of the graver, Saul's story,—the
    statesman's great word
Side by side with the poet's sweet comment. The
    river's a-wave

With smooth paper-reeds[2] grazing each other when
    prophet-winds rave:
So the pen gives unborn generations their due and
    their part
190 In thy being! Then, first of the mighty, thank God
    that thou art!"

XIV

And behold while I sang...but O Thou who didst
    grant me that day,
And before it not seldom hast granted thy help to
    essay,
Carry on and complete an adventure,—my shield
    and my sword
In that act where my soul was thy servant, thy word
    was my word,—
195 Still be with me, who then at the summit of human
    endeavour
And scaling the highest, man's thought could,
    gazed hopeless as ever
On the new stretch of heaven above me—till,
    mighty to save,
Just one lift of thy hand cleared that distance—
    God's throne from man's grave!
Let me tell out my tale to its ending—my voice to
    my heart
200 Which can scarce dare believe in what marvels last
    night I took part,
As this morning I gather the fragments, alone with
    my sheep,
And still fear lest the terrible glory evanish like
    sleep!
For I wake in the grey dewy covert, while Hebron[3]
    upheaves
The dawn struggling with night on his shoulder,
    and Kidron[4] retrieves
205 Slow the damage of yesterday's sunshine.

---

[1] Saul was the first king of Israel.

[2] plants from which papyrus is made.

[3] mountain and city south of Jerusalem, the home of David.

[4] brook or gully near Jerusalem.

XV

I say then,—
my song
While I sang thus, assuring the monarch, and ever
more strong
Made a proffer of good to console him—he slowly
resumed
His old motions and habitudes kingly. The right-
hand replumed
His black locks to their wonted composure,
adjusted the swathes
210 Of his turban, and see—the huge sweat that his
countenance bathes,
He wipes off with the robe; and he girds now his
loins as of yore,
And feels slow for the armlets of price, with the
clasp set before.
He is Saul, ye remember in glory,—ere error[1] had
bent
The broad brow from the daily communion; and
still, though much spent
215 Be the life and the bearing that front you, the same,
God did choose,
To receive what a man may waste, desecrate, never
quite lose.
So sank he along by the tent-prop till, stayed by the
pile
Of his armour and war-cloak and garments, he
leaned there awhile,
And sat out my singing,—one arm round the tent-
prop, to raise
220 His bent head, and the other hung slack—till I
touched on the praise
I foresaw from all men in all time, to the man
patient there;
And thus ended, the harp falling forward. Then
first I was 'ware
That he sat, as I say, with my head just above his
vast knees

Which were thrust out on each side around me,
like oak-roots which please
225 To encircle a lamb when it slumbers. I looked up
to know
If the best I could do had brought solace: he spoke
not, but slow
Lifted up the hand slack at his side, till he laid it
with care
Soft and grave, but in mild settled will, on my
brow: through my hair
The large fingers were pushed, and he bent back
my head, with kind power—
230 All my face back, intent to peruse it, as men do a
flower.
Thus held he me there with his great eyes that
scrutinized mine—
And oh, all my heart how it loved him! but where
was the sign?
I yearned—"Could I help thee, my father,
inventing a bliss,
I would add, to that life of the past, both the future
and this;
235 I would give thee new life altogether, as good, ages
hence,
As this moment,—had love but the warrant, love's
heart to dispense!"

XVI

Then the truth came upon me. No harp more—
no song more! outbroke—

XVII

"I have gone the whole round of creation: I saw and
I spoke:
I, a work of God's hand for that purpose, received
in my brain
240 And pronounced on the rest of his handwork—
returned him again
His creation's approval or censure: I spoke as I saw:
I report, as a man may of God's work—all's love,
yet all's law.

---

[1] Saul has disobeyed God: 1 Samuel 15.

Now I lay down the judgeship he lent me. Each
    faculty tasked
To perceive him, has gained an abyss, where a dew-
    drop was asked.
245 Have I knowledge? confounded it shrivels at
    Wisdom laid bare.
Have I forethought? how purblind, how blank, to
    the Infinite Care!
Do I task any faculty highest, to image success?
I but open my eyes,—and perfection, no more and
    no less,
In the kind I imagined, full-fronts me, and God is
    seen God
250 In the star, in the stone, in the flesh, in the soul and
    the clod.
And thus looking within and around me, I ever
    renew
(With that stoop of the soul which in bending
    upraises it too)
The submission of man's nothing-perfect to God's
    all-complete,
As by each new obeisance in spirit, I climb to his
    feet.
255 Yet with all this abounding experience, this deity
    known,
I shall dare to discover some province, some gift of
    my own.
There's a faculty pleasant to exercise, hard to hood-
    wink,
I am fain to keep still in abeyance, (I laugh as I
    think)
Lest, insisting to claim and parade in it, wot ye, I
    worst
260 E'en the Giver in one gift.—Behold, I could love
    if I durst!
But I sink the pretension as fearing a man may
    o'ertake
God's own speed in the one way of love: I abstain
    for love's sake.
—What, my soul? see thus far and no farther?
    when doors great and small,

Nine-and-ninety flew ope at our touch, should the
    hundredth appal?
265 In the least things have faith, yet distrust in the
    greatest of all?
Do I find love so full in my nature, God's ultimate
    gift,
That I doubt his own love can compete with it?
    Here, the parts shift?
Here, the creatures surpass the Creator,—the end,
    what Began?
Would I fain in my impotent yearning do all for
    this man,
270 And dare doubt he alone shall not help him, who
    yet alone can?
Would it ever have entered my mind, the bare will,
    much less power,
To bestow on this Saul what I sang of, the
    marvellous dower
Of the life he was gifted and filled with? to make
    such a soul,
Such a body, and then such an earth for insphering
    the whole?
275 And doth it not enter my mind (as my warm tears
    attest)
These good things being given, to go on, and give
    one more, the best?
Ay, to save and redeem and restore him, maintain
    at the height
This perfection,—succeed with life's dayspring,
    death's minute of night?
Interpose at the difficult minute, snatch Saul the
    mistake,
280 Saul the failure, the ruin he seems now,—and bid
    him awake
From the dream, the probation, the prelude, to
    find himself set
Clear and safe in new light and new life,—a new
    harmony yet
To be run, and continued, and ended—who
    knows?—or endure!

The man taught enough, be life's dream, of the rest to make sure;

285 By the pain-throb, triumphantly winning intensified bliss,

And the next world's reward and repose, by the struggles in this.

XVIII

"I believe it! 'Tis thou, God, that givest, 'tis I who receive:

In the first is the last, in thy will is my power to believe.

All's one gift: thou canst grant it moreover, as prompt to my prayer

290 As I breathe out this breath, as I open these arms to the air.

From thy will, stream the worlds, life and nature, thy dread Sabaoth:[1]

I will?—the mere atoms despise me! Why am I not loth

To look that, even that in the face too? Why is it I dare

Think but lightly of such impuissance? What stops my despair?

295 This;—'tis not what man Does which exalts him, but what man Would do!

See the King—I would help him but cannot, the wishes fall through.

Could I wrestle to raise him from sorrow, grow poor to enrich,

To fill up his life, starve my own out, I would— knowing which,

I know that my service is perfect. Oh, speak through me now!

300 Would I suffer for him that I love? So wouldst thou—so wilt thou!

So shall crown thee the topmost, ineffablest, uttermost crown—

And thy love fill infinite wholly, nor leave up nor down

One spot for the creature to stand in! It is by no breath,

Turn of eye, wave of hand, that salvation joins issue with death!

305 As thy Love is discovered almighty, almighty be proved

Thy power, that exists with and for it, of being Beloved!

He who did most, shall bear most; the strongest shall stand the most weak.

'Tis the weakness in strength, that I cry for! my flesh, that I seek

In the Godhead! I seek and I find it. O Saul, it shall be

310 A Face like my face that receives thee; a Man like to me,

Thou shalt love and be loved by, for ever: a Hand like this hand

Shall throw open the gates of new life to thee! See the Christ stand!"

XIX

I know not too well how I found my way home in the night.

There were witness, cohorts about me, to left and to right,

315 Angels, powers, the unuttered, unseen, the alive, the aware:

I repressed, I got through them as hardly, as strugglingly there,

As a runner beset by the populace famished for news—

Life or death. The whole earth was awakened, hell loosed with her crews;

And the stars of night beat with emotion, and tingled and shot

320 Out in fire the strong pain of pent knowledge: but I fainted not,

---

1 hosts or armies.

For the Hand still impelled me at once and
    supported, suppressed
All the tumult, and quenched it with quiet, and
    holy behest,
Till the rapture was shut in itself, and the earth
    sank to rest.
Anon at the dawn, all that trouble had withered
    from earth—
325 Not so much, but I saw it die out in the day's
    tender birth;
In the gathered intensity brought to the grey of the
    hills;
In the shuddering forests' held breath; in the
    sudden wind-thrills;
In the startled wild beasts that bore off, each with
    eye sidling still
Though averted with wonder and dread; in the
    birds stiff and chill
330 That rose heavily, as I approached them, made
    stupid with awe:
E'en the serpent that slid away silent,—he felt the
    new law.
The same stared in the white humid faces upturned
    by the flowers;
The same worked in the heart of the cedar and
    moved the vine-bowers:
And the little brooks witnessing murmured,
    persistent and low,
335 With their obstinate, all but hushed voices—"E'en
    so, it is so!"
    —1845 (STANZAS 1–9; COMPLETE POEM: 1855)

Cleon [1]

"As certain also of your own poets have said"—[2]

Cleon the poet (from the sprinkled isles,[3]
    Lily on lily, that o'erlace the sea,
And laugh their pride when the light wave lisps
    "Greece")—
To Protus in his Tyranny:[4] much health!

5   They give thy letter to me, even now:
I read and seem as if I heard thee speak.
The master of thy galley still unlades
Gift after gift; they block my court at last
And pile themselves along its portico
10 Royal with sunset, like a thought of thee:
And one white she-slave from the group dispersed
Of black and white slaves (like the chequer-work
Pavement, at once my nation's work and gift,
Now covered with this settle-down[5] of doves),
15 One lyric woman, in her crocus vest
Woven of sea-wools,[6] with her two white hands
Commends to me the strainer and the cup
Thy lip hath bettered ere it blesses mine.

    Well-counselled, king, in thy munificence!
20 For so shall men remark, in such an act
Of love for him whose song gives life its joy,
Thy recognition of the use of life;
Nor call thy spirit barely adequate
To help on life in straight ways, broad enough

---

[1] The poem is a companion to "An Epistle...of Karshish," and was perhaps written after it.

[2] The epigraph comes from Acts 17.28: "For in him we live, and move, and have our being; as certain also of your own poets have said, For we are his offspring."

[3] The Sporades: scattered islands in the Aegean Sea.

[4] a kind of rule, but without its modern implications.

[5] flock setting down.

[6] wools dyed with sea-purple.

25 For vulgar souls, by ruling and the rest.
Thou, in the daily building of thy tower,—
Whence in fierce and sudden spasms of toil,
Or through dim lulls of unapparent growth,
Or when the general work 'mid good acclaim
30 Climbed with the eye to cheer the architect,—
Didst ne'er engage in work for mere work's sake—
Had'st ever in thy heart the luring hope
Of some eventual rest a-top of it,
Whence, all the tumult of the building hushed,
35 Thou first of men mightst look out to the East:
The vulgar saw thy tower, thou sawest the sun.
For this, I promise on thy festival
To pour libation, looking o'er the sea,
Making this slave narrate thy fortunes, speak
40 Thy great words, and describe thy royal face—
Wishing thee wholly where Zeus lives the most,
Within the eventual element of calm.

Thy letter's first requirement meets me here.
It is as thou hast heard: in one short life
45 I, Cleon, have effected all those things
Thou wonderingly dost enumerate.
That epos on thy hundred plates of gold[1]
Is mine,—and also mine the little chant,
So sure to rise from every fishing-bark
50 When, lights at prow, the seamen haul their net.
The image of the sun-god on the phare,[2]
Men turn from the sun's self to see, is mine;
The Poecile,[3] o'er-storied its whole length,
As thou didst hear, with painting, is mine too.
55 I know the true proportions of a man
And woman also, not observed before;
And I have written three books on the soul,
Proving absurd all written hitherto,
And putting us to ignorance again.

60 For music,—why, I have combined the moods,[4]
Inventing one. In brief, all arts are mine;
Thus much the people know and recognize,
Throughout our seventeen islands. Marvel not.
We of these latter days, with greater mind
65 Than our forerunners, since more composite,
Look not so great, beside their simple way,
To a judge who only sees one way at once,
One mind-point and no other at a time,—
Compares the small part of a man of us
70 With some whole man of the heroic age,
Great in his way—not ours, nor meant for ours.
And ours is greater, had we skill to know:
For, what we call this life of men on earth,
This sequence of the soul's achievements here
75 Being, as I find much reason to conceive,
Intended to be viewed eventually
As a great whole, not analysed to parts,
But each part having reference to all,—
How shall a certain part, pronounced complete,
80 Endure effacement by another part?
Was the thing done?—then, what's to do again?
See, in the chequered pavement opposite,
Suppose the artist made a perfect rhomb,[5]
And next a lozenge,[6] then a trapezoid—[7]
85 He did not overlay them, superimpose
The new upon the old and blot it out,
But laid them on a level in his work,
Making at last a picture; there it lies.
So, first the perfect separate forms were made,
90 The portions of mankind; and after, so,
Occurred the combination of the same.
For where had been a progress, otherwise?
Mankind, made up of all the single men,—
In such a synthesis the labour ends.
95 Now mark me! those divine men of old time

---

[1] an epic poem engraved on tablets of gold.

[2] statue of Apollo on the lighthouse.

[3] the painted Portico at Athens.

---

[4] modes (types of musical scale).

[5] rhombus, equilateral parallelogram.

[6] diamond-shaped figure.

[7] four-sided figure with two parallel sides.

Have reached, thou sayest well, each at one point
The outside verge that rounds our faculty;
And where they reached, who can do more than
    reach?
It takes but little water just to touch
100 At some one point the inside of a sphere,
And, as we turn the sphere, touch all the rest
In due succession: but the finer air
Which not so palpably nor obviously,
Though no less universally, can touch
105 The whole circumference of that emptied sphere,
Fills it more fully than the water did;
Holds thrice the weight of water in itself
Resolved into a subtler element.
And yet the vulgar call the sphere first full
110 Up to the visible height—and after, void;
Not knowing air's more hidden properties.
And thus our soul, misknown, cries out to Zeus
To vindicate his purpose in our life:
Why stay we on the earth unless to grow?
115 Long since, I imaged, wrote the fiction out,
That he or other god descended here
And, once for all, showed simultaneously
What, in its nature, never can be shown,
Piecemeal or in succession;—showed, I say,
120 The worth both absolute and relative
Of all his children from the birth of time,
His instruments for all appointed work.
I now go on to image,—might we hear
The judgement which should give the due to each,
125 Show where the labour lay and where the ease,
And prove Zeus' self, the latent everywhere!
This is a dream:—but no dream, let us hope,
That years and days, the summers and the springs,
Follow each other with unwaning powers.
130 The grapes which dye thy wine are richer far,
Through culture, than the wild wealth of the rock;
The suave plum than the savage-tasted drupe;[1]
The pastured honey-bee drops choicer sweet;

The flowers turn double, and the leaves turn flowers;
135 That young and tender crescent-moon, thy slave,
Sleeping above her robe as buoyed by clouds,
Refines upon the women of my youth.
What, and the soul[2] alone deteriorates?
I have not chanted verse like Homer, no—
140 Nor swept string like Terpander,[3] no—nor carved
And painted men like Phidias and his friend:[4]
I am not great as they are, point by point.
But I have entered into sympathy
With these four, running these into one soul,
145 Who, separate, ignored each other's art.
Say, is it nothing that I know them all?
The wild flower was the larger; I have dashed
Rose-blood upon its petals, pricked its cup's
Honey with wine, and driven its seed to fruit,
150 And show a better flower if not so large:
I stand myself. Refer this to the gods
Whose gift alone it is! which, shall I dare
(All pride apart) upon the absurd pretext
That such a gift by chance lay in my hand,
155 Discourse of lightly or depreciate?
It might have fallen to another's hand: what then?
I pass too surely: let at least truth stay!

    And next, of what thou followest on to ask.
This being with me as I declare, O king,
160 My works, in all these varicoloured kinds,
So done by me, accepted so by men—
Thou askest, if (my soul thus in men's hearts)
I must not be accounted to attain
The very crown and proper end of life?
165 Inquiring thence how, now life closeth up,
I face death with success in my right hand:
Whether I fear death less than dost thyself
The fortunate of men? "For" (writest thou)

---

1 wild plum.

2 in the non-Christian sense, "inner essence" or "consciousness."

3 seventh-century BC founder of Greek music.

4 the Greek sculptor of the fifth-century BC, and probably Pericles, the great Athenian statesman.

"Thou leavest much behind, while I leave naught.
170 Thy life stays in the poems men shall sing,
The pictures men shall study; while my life,
Complete and whole now in its power and joy,
Dies altogether with my brain and arm,
Is lost indeed; since, what survives myself?
175 The brazen statue to o'erlook my grave,
Set on the promontory which I named.
And that—some supple courtier of my heir
Shall use its robed and sceptred arm, perhaps,
To fix the rope to, which best drags it down.
180 I go then: triumph thou, who dost not go!"

　　　Nay, thou art worthy of hearing my whole mind.
Is this apparent, when thou turn'st to muse
Upon the scheme of earth and man in chief,
That admiration grows as knowledge grows?
185 That imperfection means perfection hid,
Reserved in part, to grace the after-time?
If, in the morning of philosophy,
Ere aught had been recorded, nay perceived,
Thou, with the light now in thee, couldst have
　　　looked
190 On all earth's tenantry, from worm to bird,
Ere man, her last, appeared upon the stage—
Thou wouldst have seen them perfect, and deduced
The perfectness of others yet unseen.
Conceding which,—had Zeus then questioned thee
195 "Shall I go on a step, improve on this,
Do more for visible creatures than is done?"
Thou wouldst have answered, "Ay, by making each
Grow conscious in himself—by that alone.
All's perfect else: the shell sucks fast the rock,
200 The fish strikes through the sea, the snake both
　　　swims
And slides, forth range the beasts, the birds take
　　　flight,
Till life's mechanics can no further go—
And all this joy in natural life is put
Like fire from off thy finger into each,
205 So exquisitely perfect is the same.

But 'tis pure fire, and they mere matter are;
It has them, not they it: and so I choose
For man, thy last premeditated work
(If I might add a glory to the scheme)
210 That a third thing should stand apart from both,
A quality arise within his soul,
Which, intro-active,[1] made to supervise
And feel the force it has, may view itself,
And so be happy." Man might live at first
215 The animal life: but is there nothing more?
In due time, let him critically learn
How he lives; and, the more he gets to know
Of his own life's adaptabilities,
The more joy-giving will his life become.
220 Thus man, who hath this quality, is best.

　　　But thou, king, hadst more reasonably said:
"Let progress end at once,—man make no step
Beyond the natural man, the better beast,
Using his senses, not the sense of sense."
225 In man there's failure, only since he left
The lower and inconscious forms of life.
We called it an advance, the rendering plain
Man's spirit might grow conscious of man's life,
And, by new lore so added to the old,
230 Take each step higher over the brute's head.
This grew the only life, the pleasure-house,
Watch-tower and treasure-fortress of the soul,
Which whole surrounding flats of natural life
Seemed only fit to yield subsistence to;
235 A tower that crowns a country. But alas,
The soul now climbs it just to perish there!
For thence we have discovered ('tis no dream—
We know this, which we had not else perceived)
That there's a world of capability
240 For joy, spread round about us, meant for us,
Inviting us; and still the soul craves all,
And still the flesh replies, "Take no jot more
Than ere thou clombst the tower to look abroad!

---

[1] internally active.

Nay, so much less as that fatigue has brought
245 Deduction to it." We struggle, fain to enlarge
Our bounded physical recipiency,[1]
Increase our power, supply fresh oil to life,
Repair the waste of age and sickness: no,
It skills not! life's inadequate to joy,
250 As the soul sees joy, tempting life to take.
They praise a fountain in my garden here
Wherein a Naiad[2] sends the water-bow
Thin from her tube; she smiles to see it rise.
What if I told her, it is just a thread
255 From that great river which the hills shut up,
And mock her with my leave to take the same?
The artificer has given her one small tube
Past power to widen or exchange—what boots[3]
To know she might spout oceans if she could?
260 She cannot lift beyond her first thin thread:
And so a man can use but a man's joy
While he sees God's. Is it for Zeus to boast,
"See, man, how happy I live, and despair—
That I may be still happier—for thy use!"
265 If this were so, we could not thank our lord,
As hearts beat on to doing; 'tis not so—
Malice it is not. Is it carelessness?
Still, no. If care—where is the sign? I ask,
And get no answer, and agree in sum,
270 O king, with thy profound discouragement,
Who seest the wider but to sigh the more.
Most progress is most failure: thou sayest well.

The last point now:—thou dost except a case—
Holding joy not impossible to one
275 With artist-gifts—to such a man as I
Who leave behind me living works indeed;
For, such a poem, such a painting lives.
What? dost thou verily trip upon a word,
Confound the accurate view of what joy is
280 (Caught somewhat clearer by my eyes than thine)
With feeling joy? confound the knowing how
And showing how to live (my faculty)
With actually living?—Otherwise
Where is the artist's vantage o'er the king?
285 Because in my great epos I display
How divers men young, strong, fair, wise, can act—
Is this as though I acted? if I paint,
Carve the young Phoebus,[4] am I therefore young?
Methinks I'm older that I bowed myself
290 The many years of pain that taught me art!
Indeed, to know is something, and to prove
How all this beauty might be enjoyed, is more:
But, knowing naught, to enjoy is something too.
Yon rower, with the moulded muscles there,
295 Lowering the sail, is nearer it than I.
I can write love-odes: thy fair slave's an ode.
I get to sing of love, when grown too grey
For being beloved: she turns to that young man,
The muscles all a-ripple on his back.
300 I know the joy of kingship: well, thou art king!

"But," sayest thou—(and I marvel, I repeat
To find thee trip on such a mere word) "what
Thou writest, paintest, stays; that does not die:
Sappho[5] survives, because we sing her songs,
305 And Aeschylus, because we read his plays!"
Why, if they live still, let them come and take
Thy slave in my despite, drink from thy cup,
Speak in my place. Thou diest while I survive?
Say rather that my fate is deadlier still,
310 In this, that every day my sense of joy
Grows more acute, my soul (intensified
By power and insight) more enlarged, more keen;
While every day my hairs fall more and more,
My hand shakes, and the heavy years increase—
315 The horror quickening still from year to year,
The consummation coming past escape

---

1 receptivity.

2 (statue of a) water-nymph.

3 use.

4 Apollo, god of sun and poetry.

5 Greek lyric poet of the seventh-century BC.

When I shall know most, and yet least enjoy—
When all my works wherein I prove my worth,
Being present still to mock me in men's mouths,
320 Alive still, in the praise of such as thou,
I, I the feeling, thinking, acting man,
The man who loved his life so over-much,
Sleep in my urn. It is so horrible,
I dare at times imagine to my need
325 Some future state revealed to us by Zeus,
Unlimited in capability
For joy, as this is in desire for joy,
—To seek which, the joy-hunger forces us:
That, stung by straitness of our life, made strait
330 On purpose to make prized the life at large—
Freed by the throbbing impulse we call death,
We burst there as the worm into the fly,[1]
Who, while a worm still, wants his wings. But no!
Zeus has not yet revealed it; and alas,
335 He must have done so, were it possible!

Live long and happy, and in that thought die:
Glad for what was! Farewell. And for the rest,
I cannot tell thy messenger aright
Where to deliver what he bears of thine
340 To one called Paulus;[2] we have heard his fame
Indeed, if Christus be not one with him—
I know not, nor am troubled much to know.
Thou canst not think a mere barbarian Jew,
As Paulus proves to be, one circumcised,
345 Hath access to a secret shut from us?
Thou wrongest our philosophy, O king,
In stooping to inquire of such an one,
As if his answer could impose at all!
He writeth, doth he? well, and he may write.
350 Oh, the Jew findeth scholars! certain slaves
Who touched on this same isle, preached him and
    Christ;

And (as I gathered from a bystander)
Their doctrine could be held by no sane man.
—1855

Two in the Campagna [3]

I

I wonder do you feel today
As I have felt since, hand in hand,
We sat down on the grass, to stray
In spirit better through the land,
5 This morn of Rome and May?

II

For me, I touched a thought, I know,
Has tantalized me many times,
(Like turns of thread the spiders throw
Mocking across our path) for rhymes
10 To catch at and let go.

III

Help me to hold it! First it left
The yellowing fennel, run to seed
There, branching from the brickwork's cleft,
Some old tomb's ruin: yonder weed
15 Took up the floating weft,[4]

IV

Where one small orange cup amassed
Five beetles,—blind and green they grope
Among the honey-meal: and last,
Everywhere on the grassy slope
20 I traced it. Hold it fast!

V

The champaign[5] with its endless fleece
Of feathery grasses everywhere!

---

[1] butterfly (emblem of the soul).

[2] St. Paul.

[3] the countryside outside Rome.

[4] web.

[5] campagna.

Silence and passion, joy and peace,
An everlasting wash of air—
25 Rome's ghost since her decease.

VI

Such life here, through such lengths of hours,
Such miracles performed in play,
Such primal naked forms of flowers,
Such letting nature have her way
30 While heaven looks from its towers!

VII

How say you? Let us, O my dove,
Let us be unashamed of soul,
As earth lies bare to heaven above!
How is it under our control
35 To love or not to love?

VIII

I would that you were all to me,
You that are just so much, no more.
Nor yours nor mine, nor slave nor free!
Where does the fault lie? What the core
40 O' the wound, since wound must be?

IX

I would I could adopt your will,
See with your eyes, and set my heart
Beating by yours, and drink my fill
At your soul's springs,—your part my part
45 In life, for good and ill.

X

No. I yearn upward, touch you close,
Then stand away. I kiss your cheek,
Catch your soul's warmth,—I pluck the rose
And love it more than tongue can speak—
50 Then the good minute goes.

XI

Already how am I so far
Out of that minute? Must I go
Still like the thistle-ball, no bar,
Onward, whenever light winds blow,
55 Fixed[1] by no friendly star?

XII

Just when I seemed about to learn!
Where is the thread now? Off again!
The old trick! Only I discern—
Infinite passion, and the pain
60 Of finite hearts that yearn.
—1855

A Grammarian's Funeral

Shortly after the Revival of Learning in Europe

Let us begin and carry up this corpse,
    Singing together.
Leave we the common crofts,[2] the vulgar thorpes[3]
    Each in its tether
5 Sleeping safe on the bosom of the plain,
    Cared-for till cock-crow:
Look out if yonder be not day again
    Rimming the rock-row!
That's the appropriate country; there, man's
        thought,
10   Rarer, intenser,
Self-gathered for an outbreak, as it ought,
    Chafes in the censer.
Leave we the unlettered plain its herd and crop;
    Seek we sepulture[4]
15 On a tall mountain, citied to the top,
    Crowded with culture!

---

[1] guided (by a "fix" on a star).

[2] small farms, or small fields.

[3] country villages.

[4] burial.

All the peaks soar, but one the rest excels;
    Clouds overcome it;
No! yonder sparkle is the citadel's
20   Circling its summit.
Thither our path lies; wind we up the heights:
    Wait ye the warning?[1]
Our low life was the level's and the night's;
    He's for the morning.
25 Step to a tune, square chests, erect each head,
    'Ware the beholders!
This is our master, famous calm and dead,
    Borne on our shoulders.
Sleep, crop and herd! sleep, darkling thorpe and
    croft,
30   Safe from the weather!
He, whom we convoy to his grave aloft,
    Singing together,
He was a man born with thy face and throat,
    Lyric Apollo!
35 Long he lived nameless: how should spring take
    note
    Winter would follow?
Till lo, the little touch, and youth was gone!
    Cramped and diminished,
Moaned he, "New measures, other feet anon!
40   My dance is finished?"
No, that's the world's way: (keep the mountain-side,
    Make for the city!)
He knew the signal, and stepped on with pride
    Over men's pity;
45 Left play for work, and grappled with the world
    Bent on escaping:
"What's in the scroll," quoth he, "thou keepest
    furled?
    Show me their shaping,
Theirs who most studied man, the bard and sage,—
50   Give!"—So, he gowned him,[2]

Straight got by heart that book to its last page:
    Learned, we found him.
Yea, but we found him bald too, eyes like lead,
    Accents uncertain:
55 "Time to taste life," another would have said,
    "Up with the curtain!"
This man said rather, "Actual life comes next?
    Patience a moment!
Grant I have mastered learning's crabbed text,
60   Still there's the comment.
Let me know all! Prate not of most or least,
    Painful or easy!
Even to the crumbs I'd fain eat up the feast,
    Ay, nor feel queasy."
65 Oh, such a life as he resolved to live,
    When he had learned it,
When he had gathered all books had to give!
    Sooner, he spurned it.
Image the whole, then execute the parts—
70   Fancy the fabric
Quite, ere you build, ere steel strike fire from quartz,
    Ere mortal dab brick!

(Here's the town-gate reached: there's the market-
    place
    Gaping before us.)
75 Yea, this in him was the peculiar grace
    (Hearten our chorus!)
That before living he'd learn how to live—
    No end to learning:
Earn the means first—God surely will contrive
80   Use for our earning.
Others mistrust and say, "But time escapes:
    Live now or never!"
He said, "What's time? Leave Now for dogs and
    apes!
    Man has Forever."
85 Back to his book then: deeper drooped his head:
    Calculus[3] racked him:

---

[1] sign to begin.

[2] dressed in the symbol (gown) of academic life.

[3] gallstones.

Leaden before, his eyes grew dross of lead:
　　Tussis[1] attacked him.
"Now, master, take a little rest!"—not he!
90　　(Caution redoubled,
Step two abreast, the way winds narrowly!)
　　Not a whit troubled
Back to his studies, fresher than at first,
　　Fierce as a dragon
95　He (soul-hydroptic[2] with a sacred thirst)
　　Sucked at the flagon.
Oh, if we draw a circle premature,
　　Heedless of far gain,
Greedy for quick returns of profit, sure
100　　Bad is our bargain!
Was it not great? did not he throw on God,
　　(He loves the burthen)—
God's task to make the heavenly period
　　Perfect the earthen?
105　Did not he magnify the mind, show clear
　　Just what it all meant?
He would not discount life, as fools do here,
　　Paid by instalment.
He ventured neck or nothing—heaven's success
110　　Found, or earth's failure:
"Wilt thou trust death or not?" He answered "Yes:
　　Hence with life's pale lure!"
That low man seeks a little thing to do,
　　Sees it and does it:
115　This high man, with a great thing to pursue,
　　Dies ere he knows it.
That low man goes on adding one to one,
　　His hundred's soon hit:
This high man, aiming at a million,
120　　Misses an unit.[3]
That, has the world here—should he need the next,
　　Let the world mind him!
This, throws himself on God, and unperplexed

Seeking shall find him.
125　So, with the throttling hands of death at strife,
　　Ground he at grammar;
Still, through the rattle,[4] parts of speech were rife:
　　While he could stammer
He settled *Hoti's*[5] business—let it be!—
130　　Properly based *Oun*[6]—
Gave us the doctrine of the enclitic *De*,[7]
　　Dead from the waist[8] down.
Well, here's the platform, here's the proper place:
　　Hail to your purlieus,[9]
135　All ye highfliers of the feathered race,
　　Swallows and curlews!
Here's the top-peak; the multitude below
　　Live, for they can, there:
This man decided not to Live but Know—
140　　Bury this man there?
Here—here's his place, where meteors shoot,
　　　clouds form,
　　Lightnings are loosened,
Stars come and go! Let joy break with the storm,
　　Peace let the dew send!
145　Lofty designs must close in like effects:
　　Loftily lying,
Leave him—still loftier than the world suspects,
　　Living and dying.
　　—1855

---

[1] bronchial coughing.

[2] extremely thirsty.

[3] misses by only a unit.

---

[4] death rattle.

[5] "that."

[6] "then."

[7] "towards." Browning wrote to Tennyson in 1863 that he wanted his grammarian working on "the biggest of the littlenesses."

[8] punning on "waste."

[9] haunts.

Dîs Aliter Visum; or, Le Byron de Nos Jours [1]

I

Stop, let me have the truth of that!
    Is that all true? I say, the day
Ten years ago when both of us
    Met on a morning, friends—as thus
5 We meet this evening, friends or what?—

II

Did you—because I took your arm
    And sillily smiled, "A mass of brass
That sea looks, blazing underneath!"
    While up the cliff-road edged with heath,
10 We took the turns nor came to harm—

III

Did you consider "Now makes twice
    That I have seen her, walked and talked
With this poor pretty thoughtful thing,
    Whose worth I weigh: she tries to sing;
15 Draws, hopes in time the eye grows nice;[2]

IV

"Reads verse and thinks she understands;
    Loves all, at any rate, that's great,
Good, beautiful; but much as we
    Down at the bath-house[3] love the sea,
20 Who breathe its salt and bruise its sands:

V

"While...do but follow the fishing-gull
    That flaps and floats from wave to cave!
There's the sea-lover, fair my friend!

What then? Be patient, mark and mend!
25 Had you the making of your skull?"

VI

And did you, when we faced the church
    With spire and sad slate roof, aloof
From human fellowship so far,
    Where a few graveyard crosses are,
30 And garlands for the swallows' perch,—

VII

Did you determine, as we stepped
    O'er the lone stone fence, "Let me get
Her for myself, and what's the earth
    With all its art, verse, music, worth—
35 Compared with love, found, gained, and kept?

VIII

"Schumann's[4] our music-maker now;
    Has his march-movement youth and mouth?
Ingres's[5] the modern man that paints;
    Which will lean on me, of his saints?
40 Heine[6] for songs; for kisses, how?"

IX

And did you, when we entered, reached
    The votive frigate,[7] soft aloft
Riding on air this hundred years,
    Safe-smiling at old hopes and fears,—
45 Did you draw profit while she preached?

X

Resolving, "Fools we wise men grow!
    Yes, I could easily blurt out curt
Some question that might find reply

---

[1] The title is from *Aeneid* 2.428: "The gods' thought was otherwise." The subtitle, "The Byron of Our Days," perhaps points to the contrast between Byron and the present "hero."

[2] discriminating.

[3] changing-room.

[4] German composer (1810–56).

[5] French painter (1780–1867).

[6] German poet (1797–1856).

[7] a ship model given to the Church to fulfill a vow.

As prompt in her stopped lips, dropped eye,
50 And rush of red to cheek and brow:

XI

"Thus were a match made, sure and fast,
    'Mid the blue weed-flowers round the mound
Where, issuing, we shall stand and stay
    For one more look at baths and bay,
55 Sands, sea-gulls, and the old church last—

XII

"A match 'twixt me, bent, wigged and lamed,
    Famous, however, for verse and worse,
Sure of the Fortieth spare Arm-chair[1]
    When gout and glory seat me there,
60 So, one whose love-freaks pass unblamed,—

XIII

"And this young beauty, round and sound
    As a mountain-apple, youth and truth
With loves and doves, at all events
    With money in the Three per Cents;[2]
65 Whose choice of me would seem profound:—

XIV

"She might take me as I take her.
    Perfect the hour would pass, alas!
Climb high, love high, what matter? Still,
    Feet, feelings, must descend the hill:
70 An hour's perfection can't recur.

XV

"Then follows Paris and full time
    For both to reason: "Thus with us!"
She'll sigh, "Thus girls give body and soul
    At first word, think they gain the goal,
75 When 'tis the starting-place they climb!

XVI

"'My friend makes verse and gets renown;
    Have they all fifty years, his peers?
He knows the world, firm, quiet and gay;
    Boys will become as much one day:
80 They're fools; he cheats, with beard less brown.

XVII

"'For boys say, *Love me or I die!*
    He did not say, *The truth is, youth*
I want, who am old and know too much;
    I'd catch youth: lend me sight and touch!
85 *Drop heart's blood where life's wheels grate dry!'*

XVIII

"While I should make rejoinder"—(then
    It was, no doubt, you ceased that least
Light pressure of my arm in yours)
    "'I can conceive of cheaper cures
90 For a yawning-fit o'er books and men.

XIX

"'What? All I am, was, and might be,
    All, books taught, art brought, life's whole strife,
Painful results since precious, just
    Were fitly exchanged, in wise disgust,
95 For two cheeks freshened by youth and sea?

XX

"'All for a nosegay!—what came first;
    With fields on flower, untried each side;
I rally, need my books and men,
    And find a nosegay': drop it, then,
100 No match yet made for best or worst!"[3]

XXI

That ended me. You judged the porch
    We left by, Norman;[4] took our look

---

[1] election to the French Academy (which has forty members).

[2] safe government bonds paying three per cent.

[3] "for better or worse" (marriage ceremony).

[4] The Pornic church was Norman (a kind of Romanesque architecture of the eleventh and twelfth centuries).

At sea and sky, wondered so few
 Find out the place for air and view;
105 Remarked the sun began to scorch;

XXII

Descended, soon regained the baths,
 And then, good-bye! Years ten since then:
Ten years! We meet: you tell me, now,
 By a window-seat for that cliff-brow,
110 On carpet-stripes for those sand-paths.

XXIII

Now I may speak: you fool, for all
 Your lore! Who made things plain in vain?
What was the sea for? What, the grey
 Sad church, that solitary day,
115 Crosses and graves and swallows' call?

XXIV

Was there naught better than to enjoy?
 No feat which, done, would make time break,
And let us pent-up creatures through
 Into eternity, our due?
120 No forcing earth teach heaven's employ?

XXV

No wise beginning, here and now,
 What cannot grow complete (earth's feat)
And heaven must finish, there and then?
 No tasting earth's true food for men,
125 Its sweet in sad, its sad in sweet?

XXVI

No grasping at love, gaining a share
 O' the sole spark from God's life at strife
With death, so, sure of range above
 The limits here? For us and love,
130 Failure; but, when God fails, despair.

XXVII

This you call wisdom? Thus you add
 Good unto good again, in vain?
You loved, with body worn and weak;
 I loved, with faculties to seek:
135 Were both loves worthless since ill-clad?

XXVIII

Let the mere star-fish in his vault
 Crawl in a wash of weed, indeed,
Rose-jacinth[1] to the finger-tips:
 He, whole in body and soul, outstrips
140 Man, found with either in default.

XXIX

But what's whole, can increase no more,
 Is dwarfed and dies, since here's its sphere.
The devil laughed at you in his sleeve!
 You knew not? That I well believe;
145 Or you had saved two souls: nay, four.

XXX

For Stephanie sprained last night her wrist,
 Ankle or something. "Pooh," cry you?
At any rate she danced, all say,
 Vilely; her vogue has had its day.
150 Here comes my husband from his whist.
—1864

---

[1] brown, red, or orange.

Abt Vogler [1]

(After he has been extemporizing upon the musical
instrument of his invention) [2]

I

Would that the structure brave,[3] the manifold
music I build,
Bidding my organ obey, calling its keys to their
work,
Claiming each slave of the sound, at a touch, as
when Solomon[4] willed
Armies of angels that soar, legions of demons
that lurk,
5 Man, brute, reptile, fly,—alien of end and of aim,
Adverse, each from the other heaven-high, hell-
deep removed,—
Should rush into sight at once as he named the
ineffable Name,
And pile him a palace straight, to pleasure the
princess he loved!

II

Would it might tarry like his, the beautiful
building of mine,
10 This which my keys in a crowd pressed and
importuned to raise!
Ah, one and all, how they helped, would dispart
now and now combine,
Zealous to hasten the work, heighten their
master his praise!
And one would bury his brow with a blind plunge
down to hell,
Burrow awhile and build, broad on the roots of
things,
15 Then up again swim into sight, having based me
my palace well,
Founded it, fearless of flame, flat on the nether
springs.[5]

III

And another would mount and march, like the
excellent minion he was,
Ay, another and yet another, one crowd but
with many a crest,
Raising my rampired[6] walls of gold as transparent
as glass,
20 Eager to do and die, yield each his place to the
rest:
For higher still and higher (as a runner tips with fire,
When a great illumination surprises a festal
night—
Outlining round and round Rome's dome[7] from
space to spire)
Up, the pinnacled glory reached, and the pride
of my soul was in sight.

IV

25 In sight? Not half? for it seemed, it was certain, to
match man's birth,
Nature in turn conceived, obeying an impulse
as I;
And the emulous heaven yearned down, made
effort to reach the earth,
As the earth had done her best, in my passion,
to scale the sky:
Novel splendours burst forth, grew familiar and
dwelt with mine,
30 Not a point nor peak but found and fixed its
wandering star;

---

1 Abbé Georg Joseph Vogler (1749–1814), German composer, organist,
theorist, teacher and noted extemporizer, had been the master of John
Relfe, Browning's music teacher.

2 the orchestrion, a kind of large organ.

3 splendid.

4 Solomon was reputed to be able to control spirits with a seal that bore
God's "ineffable name" (l. 7).

5 perhaps referring to the belief that the earth rested on a great deep.

6 strengthened against attack, ramparted.

7 St. Peter's was lighted on special occasions.

Meteor-moons, balls of blaze: and they did not pale
   nor pine,
     For earth had attained to heaven, there was no
     more near nor far.

V

Nay more; for there wanted not who walked in the
   glare and glow,
     Presences plain in the place; or, fresh from the
     Protoplast,[1]
35 Furnished for ages to come, when a kindlier wind
   should blow,
     Lured now to begin and live, in a house to their
     liking at last;
Or else the wonderful Dead who have passed
   through the body and gone,
     But were back once more to breathe in an old
     world worth their new:
What never had been, was now; what was, as it
   shall be anon;
40   And what is,—shall I say, matched both? for I
     was made perfect too.

VI

All through my keys that gave their sounds to a
   wish of my soul,
     All through my soul that praised as its wish
     flowed visibly forth,
All through music and me! For think, had I painted
   the whole,
     Why, there it had stood, to see, nor the process
     so wonder-worth:
45 Had I written the same, made verse—still, effect
   proceeds from cause,
     Ye know why the forms are fair, ye hear how
     the tale is told;
It is all triumphant art, but art in obedience to laws,
     Painter and poet are proud in the artist-list
     enrolled:—

---

[1] just created.

VII

But here is the finger of God, a flash of the will
   that can,
50   Existent behind all laws, that made them and,
     lo, they are!
And I know not if, save in this, such gift be allowed
   to man,
     That out of three sounds he frame, not a fourth
     sound, but a star.
Consider it well: each tone of our scale in itself is
   naught;
     It is everywhere in the world—loud, soft, and
     all is said:
55 Give it to me to use! I mix it with two in my
   thought:
     And, there! Ye have heard and seen: consider
     and bow the head!

VIII

Well, it is gone at last, the palace of music I reared;
     Gone! and the good tears start, the praises that
     come too slow;
For one is assured at first, one scarce can say that he
   feared,
60   That he even gave it a thought, the gone thing
     was to go.
Never to be again! But many more of the kind
     As good, nay, better perchance: is this your
     comfort to me?
To me, who must be saved because I cling with my
   mind
     To the same, same self, same love, same God:
     ay, what was, shall be.

IX

65 Therefore to whom turn I but to thee, the ineffable
   Name?
     Builder and maker, thou, of houses not made
     with hands!
What, have fear of change from thee who art ever
   the same?

Doubt that thy power can fill the heart that thy
    power expands?
There shall never be one lost good! What was, shall
    live as before;
70 The evil is null, is naught, is silence implying
    sound;
What was good shall be good, with, for evil, so
    much good more;
    On the earth the broken arcs; in the heaven, a
      perfect round.

X

All we have willed or hoped or dreamed of good
    shall exist;
    Not its semblance, but itself; no beauty, nor
    good, nor power
75 Whose voice has gone forth, but each survives for
    the melodist
    When eternity affirms the conception of an
    hour.
The high that proved too high, the heroic for earth
    too hard,
    The passion that left the ground to lose itself in
    the sky,
Are music sent up to God by the lover and the bard;
80   Enough that he heard it once: we shall hear it
    by-and-by.

XI

And what is our failure here but a triumph's
    evidence
    For the fulness of the days? Have we withered
    or agonized?
Why else was the pause prolonged but that singing
    might issue thence?
    Why rushed the discords in but that harmony
    should be prized?
85 Sorrow is hard to bear, and doubt is slow to clear,
    Each sufferer says his say, his scheme of the weal
    and woe:

But God has a few of us whom he whispers in the
    ear;
    The rest may reason and welcome: 'tis we
    musicians know.

XII

Well, it is earth with me; silence resumes her reign:
90   I will be patient and proud, and soberly
    acquiesce.
Give me the keys. I feel for the common chord[1]
    again,
    Sliding by semitones, till I sink to the minor,[2]
    —yes,
And I blunt[3] it into a ninth,[4] and I stand on alien
    ground,[5]
    Surveying awhile the heights I rolled from into
    the deep;
95 Which, hark, I have dared and done, for my
    resting-place is found,
    The C Major of this life:[6] so, now I will try to
    sleep.
—1864

---

[1] three-note chord made up of the first, third, and fifth notes in the scale.

[2] modulating from the key of the "common chord" to its relative minor key.

[3] flatten one note.

[4] one note more than the octave.

[5] the discord of the ninth. The ground is "alien" because Vogler pioneered the use of the ninth in his system of harmony.

[6] the level of ordinary living. Probably Vogler is returning to the key in which his improvisation began.

Rabbi Ben Ezra [1]

I

Grow old along with me!
    The best is yet to be,
The last of life, for which the first was made:
    Our times are in His hand
5   Who saith "A whole I planned,
Youth shows but half; trust God: see all nor be
        afraid!"

II

Not that, amassing flowers,
    Youth sighed "Which rose makes ours,
Which lily leave and then as best recall?"
10   Not that, admiring stars,
    It yearned "Nor Jove, nor Mars;
Mine be some figured flame which blends,
        transcends them all!"

III

Not for such hopes and fears
    Annulling youth's brief years,
15 Do I remonstrate: folly wide the mark!
    Rather I prize the doubt
    Low kinds exist without,
Finished and finite clods, untroubled by a spark.

IV

Poor vaunt of life indeed,
20   Were man but formed to feed
On joy, to solely seek and find and feast:
    Such feasting ended, then
    As sure an end to men;

Irks care the crop-full bird? Frets doubt the maw-
        crammed beast?

V

25 Rejoice we are allied
    To That which doth provide
And not partake, effect and not receive!
    A spark disturbs our clod;
    Nearer we hold of God
30 Who gives, than of His tribes that take, I must
        believe.

VI

Then, welcome each rebuff
    That turns earth's smoothness rough,
Each sting that bids nor sit nor stand but go!
    Be our joys three-parts pain!
35   Strive, and hold cheap the strain;
Learn, nor account the pang; dare, never grudge
        the throe!

VII

For thence,—a paradox
    Which comforts while it mocks,—
Shall life succeed in that it seems to fail:
40   What I aspired to be,
    And was not, comforts me:
A brute I might have been, but would not sink i'
        the scale.

VIII

What is he but a brute
    Whose flesh has soul to suit,
45 Whose spirit works lest arms and legs want play?
    To man, propose this test—
    Thy body at its best,
How far can that project thy soul on its lone way?

IX

Yet gifts should prove their use:
50   I own the Past profuse

---

[1] Abraham Ibn Ezra (Abenezra) (1092–1167), a Spanish Jew, spent the better part of his life travelling in exile; he was a distinguished scholar and a man of genius in several areas. It is generally agreed that the Rabbi is a spokesman for Browning himself.

Much in the poem suggests that Browning is replying to Edward FitzGerald's *Rubáiyát* (1859).

Of power each side, perfection every turn:
    Eyes, ears took in their dole,
    Brain treasured up the whole;
Should not the heart beat once "How good to live
    and learn"?

X

55   Not once beat "Praise be Thine!
    I see the whole design,
I, who saw power, see now love perfect too:
    Perfect I call Thy plan:
    Thanks that I was a man!
60   Maker, remake, complete,—I trust what Thou
    shalt do!"

XI

For pleasant is this flesh;
    Our soul, in its rose-mesh
Pulled ever to the earth, still yearns for rest;
    Would we some prize might hold
65   To match those manifold
Possessions of the brute,—gain most, as we did
    best!,

XII

Let us not always say
    "Spite of this flesh today
I strove, made head, gained ground upon the whole!"
70   As the bird wings and sings,
    Let us cry "All good things
Are ours, nor soul helps flesh more, now, than flesh
    helps soul!"

XIII

Therefore I summon age
    To grant youth's heritage,
75 Life's struggle having so far reached its term:
    Thence shall I pass, approved
    A man, for aye removed
From the developed brute; a god though in the
    germ.

XIV

And I shall thereupon
80   Take rest, ere I be gone
Once more on my adventure brave and new:
    Fearless and unperplexed,
    When I wage battle next,
What weapons to select, what armour to indue.[1]

XV

85   Youth ended, I shall try[2]
    My gain or loss thereby;
Leave the fire ashes, what survives is gold:
    And I shall weigh the same,
    Give life its praise or blame:
90   Young, all lay in dispute; I shall know, being old.

XVI

For note, when evening shuts,
    A certain moment cuts
The deed off, calls the glory from the grey:
    A whisper from the west
95   Shoots—"Add this to the rest,
Take it and try its worth: here dies another day."

XVII

So, still within this life,
    Though lifted o'er its strife,
Let me discern, compare, pronounce at last,
100   "This rage was right i' the main,
    That acquiescence vain:
The Future I may face now I have proved[3] the
    Past."

XVIII

For more is not reserved
    To man, with soul just nerved
105 To act tomorrow what he learns today:

---

[1] put on.

[2] test, or try to find out.

[3] tested.

Here, work enough to watch
The Master work, and catch
Hints of the proper craft, tricks of the tool's true
play.

XIX

As it was better, youth
110 Should strive, through acts uncouth,
Toward making, than repose on aught found made:
So, better, age, exempt
From strife, should know, than tempt[1]
Further. Thou waitedest age: wait death nor be
afraid!

XX

115 Enough now, if the Right
And Good and Infinite
Be named here, as thou callest thy hand thine own,
With knowledge absolute,
Subject to no dispute
120 From fools that crowded youth, nor let thee feel
alone.

XXI

Be there, for once and all,
Severed great minds from small,
Announced to each his station in the Past!
Was I, the world arraigned,
125 Were they, my soul disdained,
Right? Let age speak the truth and give us peace at
last!

XXII

Now, who shall arbitrate?
Ten men love what I hate,
Shun what I follow, slight what I receive;
130 Ten, who in ears and eyes
Match me: we all surmise,

They this thing, and I that: whom shall my soul
believe?

XXIII

Not on the vulgar mass
Called "work," must sentence pass,
135 Things done, that took the eye and had the price;
O'er which, from level stand,
The low world laid its hand,
Found straightway to its mind, could value in a
trice:

XXIV

But all, the world's coarse thumb
140 And finger failed to plumb,
So passed[2] in making up the main account;
All instincts immature,
All purposes unsure,
That weighed not as his work, yet swelled the
man's amount:

XXV

145 Thoughts hardly to be packed
Into a narrow act,
Fancies that broke through language and escaped;
All I could never be,
All, men ignored in me,
150 This, I was worth to God, whose wheel the pitcher
shaped.[3]

XXVI

Ay, note that Potter's wheel,
That metaphor! and feel
Why time spins fast, why passive lies our clay,—
Thou, to whom fools propound,
155 When the wine makes its round,

---

[2] ignored.

[3] The image that begins here and dominates the conclusion of the poem
is a common one: that of God as potter and man as pot. In this version,
the wheel becomes earthly time and circumstance, and the clay is man's
spiritual being. The image occurs in FitzGerald's *Rubáiyát.*

---

[1] attempt.

"Since life fleets, all is change; the Past gone, seize
    today!"[1]

XXVII

    Fool! All that is, at all,
    Lasts ever, past recall;
Earth changes, but thy soul and God stand sure:
60   What entered into thee,
    That was, is, and shall be:
Time's wheel runs back or stops: Potter and clay
    endure.

XXVIII

    He fixed thee 'mid this dance
    Of plastic[2] circumstance,
65 This Present, thou, forsooth, wouldst fain arrest:
    Machinery just meant
    To give thy soul its bent,
Try[3] thee and turn thee forth, sufficiently
    impressed.

XXIX

    What though the earlier grooves
    Which ran the laughing loves
70 Around thy base, no longer pause and press?
    What though, about thy rim,
    Skull-things in order grim
Grow out, in graver mood, obey the sterner stress?[4]

XXX

75   Look not thou down but up!
    To uses of a cup,
The festal board, lamp's flash and trumpet's peal,
    The new wine's foaming flow,
    The Master's lips a-glow!

180 Thou, heaven's consummate cup, what need'st
    thou with earth's wheel?

XXXI

    But I need, now as then,
    Thee, God, who mouldest men;
And since, not even while the whirl was worst,
    Did I,—to the wheel of life
185   With shapes and colours rife,
Bound dizzily,—mistake my end, to slake Thy
    thirst:

XXXII

    So, take and use Thy work:
    Amend what flaws may lurk,
What strain o' the stuff, what warpings past the aim!
190   My times be in Thy hand!
    Perfect the cup as planned!
Let age approve of youth, and death complete the
    same!

    —1864

---

[1] ll. 154–56 are an obvious reference to FitzGerald's *Rubáiyát*.

[2] fashioning.

[3] test.

[4] heavier pressure.

Caliban upon Setebos; or, Natural Theology in the Island [1]

"Thou thoughtest that I was altogether such a one as thyself."

[ʹWill sprawl, now that the heat of day is best,
    Flat on his belly in the pit's much mire,
With elbows wide, fists clenched to prop his chin.
And, while he kicks both feet in the cool slush,
5 And feels about his spine small eft-things[2] course,
Run in and out each arm, and make him laugh:
And while above his head a pompion[3]-plant,
Coating the cave-top as a brow its eye,
Creeps down to touch and tickle hair and beard,
10 And now a flower drops with a bee inside,
And now a fruit to snap at, catch and crunch,—
He looks out o'er yon sea which sunbeams cross
And recross till they weave a spider-web
(Meshes of fire, some great fish breaks at times)
15 And talks to his own self, howe'er he please,
Touching that other, whom his dam[4] called God.

Because to talk about Him, vexes—ha,
Could He but know! and time to vex is now,
When talk is safer than in winter-time.
20 Moreover Prosper and Miranda[5] sleep
In confidence he drudges at their task,
And it is good to cheat the pair, and gibe,
Letting the rank[6] tongue blossom into speech.]

Setebos, Setebos, and Setebos!
25 ʹThinketh, He dwelleth i' the cold o' the moon.

ʹThinketh He made it, with the sun to match,
But not the stars;[7] the stars came otherwise;
Only made clouds, winds, meteors, such as that:
Also this isle, what lives and grows thereon,
30 And snaky sea which rounds and ends the same.

ʹThinketh, it came of being ill at ease:
He hated that He cannot change His cold,
Nor cure its ache. ʹHath spied an icy fish
That longed to 'scape the rock-stream where she
    lived,
35 And thaw herself within the lukewarm brine
O' the lazy sea her stream thrusts far amid,
A crystal spike 'twixt two warm walls of wave;
Only, she ever sickened, found repulse
At the other kind of water, not her life,
40 (Green-dense and dim-delicious, bred o' the sun)
Flounced back from bliss she was not born to
    breathe,
And in her old bounds buried her despair,
Hating and loving warmth alike: so He.

ʹThinketh, He made thereat the sun, this isle,
45 Trees and the fowls here, beast and creeping thing.
Yon otter, sleek-wet, black, lithe as a leech;

---

[1] It is generally believed that the poem was to some extent triggered by Darwin's *Origin of Species* (November, 1859). Browning was interested in the furore that followed the appearance of Darwin's book, and the topical appeal of an example of the "missing link" is evident. Browning's hero is the man-monster of *The Tempest* turned theologian—at the end of the play Caliban resolves to "seek for grace" (5.1.296), and the resolve might have sparked Browning's imagination; the original Caliban's character, situation, and pronouncements lie behind almost everything in Browning's characterization. Setebos was the god of Caliban's dam, Sycorax (1.2.373); the Quiet may derive in part from the Unitarian conception of God. The "Natural Theology" of the title is Theology based on natural evidence, without revelation. The poem has generated much excellent discussion. One topic has been the poem's use of the third person (Caliban's first word—"Will"—means "he will," which means "I will") and the shifts from the third to first person. The prevailing view is that Browning had Caliban normally use the third person essentially to stress his primitiveness. The Quiet is neuter [*it*]; Setebos is third person with a capital [*He*]; Caliban, though he sometimes uses the first person, is generally third person without the capital [*he*], and frequently without the pronoun at all [*Thinketh*].

[2] newts or similar creatures.

[3] pumpkin.

[4] Sycorax in *The Tempest* 1.2.373; there her God is Setebos.

[5] the protagonist of *The Tempest* (and Caliban's master) and his daughter. In the play Prospero naps in the afternoon.

[6] rebellious.

[7] The stars are the realm of the Quiet, we learn later.

Yon auk,[1] one fire-eye in a ball of foam,
That floats and feeds; a certain badger brown
He hath watched hunt with that slant white-wedge eye
50 By moonlight; and the pie[2] with the long tongue
That pricks deep into oakwarts[3] for a worm,
And says a plain word when she finds her prize,
But will not eat the ants; the ants themselves
That build a wall of seeds and settled stalks
55 About their hole—He made all these and more,
Made all we see, and us, in spite: how else?
He could not, Himself, make a second self
To be His mate; as well have made Himself:
He would not make what he mislikes or slights,
60 An eyesore to Him, or not worth His pains:
But did, in envy, listlessness or sport,
Make what Himself would fain, in a manner, be—
Weaker in most points, stronger in a few,
Worthy, and yet mere playthings all the while,
65 Things He admires and mocks too,—that is it,
Because, so brave, so better though they be,
It nothing skills[4] if He begin to plague.
Look now, I[5] melt a gourd-fruit into mash,
Add honeycomb and pods, I have perceived,
70 Which bite like finches when they bill and kiss,—
Then, when froth rises bladdery,[6] drink up all,
Quick, quick, till maggots[7] scamper through my brain;
Last, throw me on my back i' the seeded thyme,
And wanton, wishing I were born a bird.
75 Put case, unable to be what I wish,
I yet could make a live bird out of clay:

Would not I take clay, pinch my Caliban
Able to fly?—for, there, see, he hath wings,
And great comb like the hoopoe's[8] to admire,
80 And there, a sting to do his foes offence,
There, and I will that he begin to live,
Fly to yon rock-top, nip me off the horns
Of grigs[9] high up that make the merry din,
Saucy through their veined wings, and mind me not.
85 In which feat, if his leg snapped, brittle clay,
And he lay stupid-like,—why, I should laugh;
And if he, spying me, should fall to weep,
Beseech me to be good, repair his wrong,
Bid his poor leg smart less or grow again,—
90 Well, as the chance were, this might take or else
Not take my fancy: I might hear his cry,
And give the mankin three sound legs for one,
Or pluck the other off, leave him like an egg,
And lessoned[10] he was mine and merely clay.
95 Were this no pleasure, lying in the thyme,
Drinking the mash, with brain become alive,
Making and marring clay at will? So He.

'Thinketh, such shows nor right nor wrong in Him,
Nor kind, nor cruel: He is strong and Lord.
100 'Am strong myself compared to yonder crabs
That march now from the mountain to the sea,
'Let twenty pass, and stone the twenty-first,
Loving not, hating not, just choosing so.[11]
'Say, the first straggler that boasts purple spots
105 Shall join the file, one pincer twisted off;
'Say, this bruised fellow shall receive a worm,
And two worms he whose nippers end in red;
As it likes me each time, I do: so He.

Well then, 'supposeth He is good i' the main,
110 Placable if His mind and ways were guessed,

---

[1] a kind of sea bird.

[2] magpie or the pied woodpecker (?).

[3] oak galls.

[4] avails.

[5] Caliban's first shift to the first person.

[6] bubbly.

[7] fancies.

[8] a crested colourful bird.

[9] grasshoppers or crickets.

[10] having been taught a lesson.

[11] a clear hit at doctrines of predestination.

But rougher than His handiwork, be sure!
Oh, He hath made things worthier than Himself,
And envieth that, so helped, such things do more
Than He who made them! What consoles but this?
115 That they, unless through Him, do naught at all,
And must submit: what other use in things?
'Hath cut a pipe of pithless elder-joint
That, blown through, gives exact the scream o' the
　　jay
When from her wing you twitch the feathers blue:
120 Sound this, and little birds that hate the jay
Flock within stone's throw, glad their foe is hurt:
Put case such pipe could prattle and boast forsooth
"I catch the birds, I am the crafty thing,
I make the cry my maker cannot make
125 With his great round mouth; he must blow
　　through mine!"
Would not I smash it with my foot? So He.

But wherefore rough, why cold and ill at ease?
Aha, that is a question! Ask, for that,
What knows,—the something over Setebos
130 That made Him, or He, may be, found and fought,
Worsted, drove off and did to nothing, perchance.
There may be something quiet o'er His head,
Out of His reach, that feels nor joy nor grief,
Since both derive from weakness in some way.
135 I joy because the quails come; would not joy
Could I bring quails here when I have a mind:
This Quiet, all it hath a mind to, doth.
'Esteemeth stars the outposts of its couch,
But never spends much thought nor care that way.
140 It may look up, work up,—the worse for those
It works on! 'Careth but for Setebos
The many-handed as a cuttle-fish,
Who, making Himself feared through what He does,
Looks up, first, and perceives he cannot soar
145 To what is quiet and hath happy life;
Next looks down here, and out of very spite
Makes this a bauble-world to ape yon real,

These good things to match those as hips[1] do grapes.
'Tis solace making baubles, ay, and sport.
150 Himself peeped late, eyed Prosper at his books
Careless and lofty, lord now of the isle:
Vexed, 'stitched a book of broad leaves, arrow-
　　shaped,
Wrote thereon, he knows what, prodigious words;
Has peeled a wand and called it by a name;
155 Weareth at whiles for an enchanter's robe
The eyed skin of a supple oncelot;[2]
And hath an ounce[3] sleeker than youngling mole,
A four-legged serpent he makes cower and couch,
Now snarl, now hold its breath and mind his eye,
160 And saith she is Miranda and my wife:
'Keeps for his Ariel[4] a tall pouch-bill crane
He bids go wade for fish and straight disgorge;
Also a sea-beast, lumpish, which he snared,
Blinded the eyes of, and brought somewhat tame,
165 And split its toe-webs, and now pens the drudge
In a hole o' the rock and calls him Caliban;
A bitter heart that bides its time and bites.
'Plays thus at being Prosper in a way,
Taketh his mirth with make-believes: so He.

170 His dam held that the Quiet made all things
Which Setebos vexed only: 'holds not so.
Who made them weak, meant weakness He might
　　vex.
Had He meant other, while His hand was in,
Why not make horny eyes no thorn could prick,
175 Or plate my scalp with bone against the snow,
Or overscale my flesh 'neath joint and joint,
Like an orc's[5] armour? Ay,—so spoil His sport!
He is the One now: only He doth all.

---

[1] fruit of the wild rose.

[2] ocelot or jaguar.

[3] lynx or snow-leopard or cheetah.

[4] Prospero's airy servant in *The Tempest*.

[5] probably sea monster.

'Saith, He may like, perchance, what profits Him.
80 Ay, himself loves what does him good; but why?
'Gets good no otherwise. This blinded beast
Loves whose places flesh-meat on his nose,
But, had he eyes, would want no help, but hate
Or love, just as it liked him: He hath eyes.
85 Also it pleaseth Setebos to work,
Use all His hands, and exercise much craft,
By no means for the love of what is worked.
'Tasteth, himself, no finer good i' the world
When all goes right, in this safe summer-time,
90 And he wants little, hungers, aches not much,
Than trying what to do with wit and strength.
'Falls to make something: 'piled yon pile of turfs,
And squared and stuck there squares of soft white
    chalk,
And, with a fish-tooth, scratched a moon on each,
95 And set up endwise certain spikes of tree,
And crowned the whole with a sloth's skull a-top,
Found dead i' the woods, too hard for one to kill.
No use at all i' the work, for work's sole sake;
'Shall some day knock it down again: so He.

00 'Saith He is terrible: watch His feats in proof!
One hurricane will spoil six good months' hope.
He hath a spite against me, that I know,
Just as He favours Prosper, who knows why?
So it is, all the same, as well I find.
05 'Wove wattles[1] half the winter, fenced them firm
With stone and stake to stop she-tortoises
Crawling to lay their eggs here: well, one wave,
Feeling the foot of Him upon its neck,
Gaped as a snake does, lolled out its large tongue,
10 And licked the whole labour flat: so much for spite.
'Saw a ball[2] flame down late (yonder it lies)
Where, half an hour before, I slept i' the shade:
Often they scatter sparkles: there is force!
'Dug up a newt He may have envied once

215 And turned to stone, shut up inside a stone.
Please Him and hinder this?—What Prosper does?
Aha, if He would tell me how! Not He!
There is the sport: discover how or die!
All need not die, for of the things o' the isle
220 Some flee afar, some dive, some run up trees;
Those at His mercy,—why, they please Him most
When...when...well, never try the same way twice!
Repeat what act has pleased, He may grow wroth.
You must not know His ways, and play Him off,
225 Sure of the issue. 'Doth the like himself:
'Spareth a squirrel that it nothing fears
But steals the nut from underneath my thumb,
And when I threat, bites stoutly in defence:
'Spareth an urchin[3] that contrariwise,
230 Curls up into a ball, pretending death
For fright at my approach: the two ways please.
But what would move my choler more than this,
That either creature counted on its life
Tomorrow and next day and all days to come,
235 Saying, forsooth, in the inmost of its heart,
"Because he did so yesterday with me,
And otherwise with such another brute,
So must he do henceforth and always."—Ay?
Would teach the reasoning couple what "must"
    means!
240 'Doth as he likes, or wherefore Lord? So He.

'Conceiveth all things will continue thus,
And we shall have to live in fear of Him
So long as He lives, keeps His strength: no change,
If He have done His best, make no new world
245 To please Him more, so leave off watching this,—
If He surprise not even the Quiet's self
Some strange day,—or, suppose, grow into it
As grubs grow butterflies: else, here are we,
And there is He, and nowhere help at all.

---

[1] twigs.

[2] meteor (fire ball).

[3] hedgehog.

250 'Believeth with the life, the pain shall stop.
His dam held different, that after death
He both plagued enemies and feasted friends:
Idly! He doth His worst in this our life,
Giving just respite lest we die through pain,
255 Saving last pain for worst,—with which, an end.
Meanwhile, the best way to escape His ire
Is, not to seem too happy. 'Sees, himself,
Yonder two flies, with purple films[1] and pink,
Bask on the pompion-bell above: kills both.
260 'Sees two black painful[2] beetles roll their ball
On head and tail as if to save their lives:
Moves them the stick away they strive to clear.

Even so, 'would have Him misconceive, suppose
This Caliban strives hard and ails no less,
265 And always, above all else, envies Him;
Wherefore he mainly dances on dark nights,
Moans in the sun, gets under holes to laugh,
And never speaks his mind save housed as now:
Outside, 'groans, curses. If He caught me here,
270 O'erheard this speech, and asked "What chucklest
at?"
'Would, to appease Him, cut a finger off,
Or of my three kid yearlings burn the best,
Or let the toothsome apples rot on tree,
Or push my tame beast for the orc to taste:
275 While myself lit a fire, and made a song

And sung it, *"What I hate, be consecrate*
To celebrate Thee and Thy state, no mate
For Thee; what see for envy in poor me?"
Hoping the while, since evils sometimes mend,
280 Warts rub away and sores are cured with slime,
That some strange day, will either the Quiet catch
And conquer Setebos, or likelier He
Decrepit may doze, doze, as good as die.
[What, what? A curtain[3] o'er the world at once!
285 Crickets stop hissing; not a bird—or, yes,
There scuds His raven that has told Him all!
It was fool's play, this prattling! Ha! The wind
Shoulders the pillared dust, death's house o' the
move,[4]
And fast invading fires begin! White blaze—
290 A tree's head snaps—and there, there, there, there,
there,
His thunder follows! Fool to gibe at Him!
Lo! 'Lieth flat and loveth Setebos!
'Maketh his teeth meet through his upper lip,
Will let those quails fly, will not eat this month
295 One little mess of whelks, so he may 'scape!]
—1864

---

[1] wings.

[2] taking pains.

[3] thundercloud.

[4] a whirlwind that has picked up dust.

The Ring and the Book

In June, 1860, Browning purchased an "old yellow book" from a bookstall in Florence. This collection of materials included legal briefs, pamphlets, and letters relating to a case involving a child bride, a disguised priest, a triple murder, four hangings, and the beheading of a nobleman. Browning resolved in October 1864 that he would write the twelve books of the poem that would become the *Ring and the Book* in six months, basing his work on the "pure crude fact[s]" (l. 35) of his source, but by July 1865 he had completed only 8,400 lines, about a third of the eventual total. When it was finally printed in 1868–69, its reception was better than that of any other work of Browning's published to that time. The *Athenaeum* for 20 March 1869 called it "beyond all parallel the supremest poetical achievement of our time... the most precious and profound spiritual treasure that England has produced since the days of Shakespeare."

The title of the poem contains multiple associations. It points to the poem's source, the old yellow book; to the pattern of the monologues, which is circular; to Browning's initials; and, in the ring, to the memory of Elizabeth. In the first and last books of the poem, the speaker, usually identified with Browning, addresses the British public and describes how he uncovered a book concerning a seventeenth-century Italian murder trial in a Florence bookstall. He explains why its subject attracted him, and how he has since imaginatively recreated every moment of the trial of Count Guido Franceschini, which took place in the courts of Rome in January and February 1698. The speaker portrays himself as a master craftsman who will fashion a poem out of the raw stuff of his old document.

Introducing the participants in the original case, he offers to bring them back to life through a poetic reproduction of their voices. He continually asserts the factual nature of his rendition, likening himself to a skilled goldsmith who shapes the metal (the facts), made malleable by the addition of an alloy (the poet's own fancy), until with the removal of the alloy the ring stands triumphant as a complete work of art. The speaker suggests that it is through the withdrawal of his personality that the truth emerges through the voices of the characters in the drama. While he insists upon the facts, he also indicates that the truth to be perceived by the reader lies beyond the simple factual level. Browning presents the basic material and its meaning three times in the opening book and says that he has found Guido guilty as charged; consequently, the reader is not to concern himself or herself with who is right and who is wrong but is to examine the ten monologues with a view to understanding why objective reality appears so different to different eyes.

In 1693 Guido Franceschini, a relatively poor nobleman of inferior rank, married the thirteen-year-old Francesca Pompilia, who had been raised in Rome by a couple named Comparini. When the Comparinis visited Guido's home in Arezzo three years after the marriage, they found that Guido had misrepresented his financial condition at the time of the marriage and, consequently, brought suit against him for the return of Pompilia's dowry. Violante Comparini had revealed to her husband that Pompilia was really the daughter of a prostitute, and that she had claimed her as her own in order to gain an inheritance left to them on condition of their having a child. As a result of their action, Guido became an even more impossible husband than he had been previously. Pompilia attempted to flee many times; she was eventually successful in escaping and taking flight to Rome with the assistance of a young cleric, Giuseppe Caponsacchi. Guido followed, and Pompilia and her companion were captured about fifteen miles from Rome. According to the documents, Caponsacchi was charged with "adultery," and found guilty of "seduction" and of having "carnal knowledge" of Pompilia. Pompilia was sent during further inquiry to a nunnery for penitent women. But she was pregnant, and was shortly thereafter sent to the house of the Comparinis in Rome. Eight months after her flight from Arezzo, she gave birth to a boy, who was named Gaetano. Shortly after, Guido came with four of his henchmen pretending to bear a message from Caponsacchi, murdered and mutilated the Comparinis, and left Pompilia for dead with twenty-two wounds in her body. She died four days later. Guido was captured, charged with the crime, and tried.

There was no question that Guido had committed the deed; the legal quandary was whether a husband should be allowed to kill his adulteress wife and her accomplices without incurring the ordinary penalty. This reopened the question, which the courts had never considered settled, as to whether or not Pompilia had committed adultery with Caponsacchi. Thus, the conduct and the characters of the Comparinis, Guido, Pompilia, and Caponsacchi were thrown open in order that the court might arrive at a decision as to whether Guido was justified in any way whatsoever in his triple murder. In February 1698 the court decided against Guido and condemned him to be beheaded and his fellow conspirators hanged. But Guido, who held a minor office in the church, appealed to Pope Innocent XII to set aside the judgment. The pope refused the appeal, and Guido and his companions were executed on 22 February 1698. Shortly thereafter, Pompilia was declared innocent, and Gaetano was declared the rightful heir to her property.

Browning took these materials, cast over them the light of his own imaginative power, and transmuted them into *The Ring and the Book*. Book I serves as the explanatory introduction. In Book II, "Half-Rome," the speaker is the first of three anonymous commentators upon the crime which Guido has committed. He is an older man who is having difficulty with his wife, and his sympathies are with Guido. The speaker in Book III, "The Other Half-Rome," is a younger man with finer instincts than those of "Half-Rome." He speaks on behalf of Pompilia. The speaker in Book IV, "Tertium Quid," pretends to be neutral, but there is bias beneath his apparent sophistication. He sums up, weighs, and arranges the evidence of the two speakers who have gone before him, and of the whole case. Book V, Guido's first monologue, occurs just a few days after the crime. Guido is speaking to his judges and cleverly defends himself by reviewing his life, eliciting the sympathy of the hearers, and blaming the faithlessness of his wife for his present sorry condition. In Book VI, the young priest addresses the judges about four days after the murders, while he is still in the throes of grief over the slaughter of Pompilia, his hatred of Guido, and his scorn for the judges. Book VII is "Pompilia": in her deathbed monologue, Pompilia attempts, with considerable difficulty, to reconstruct the events which have led to her present situation. She tries to explain her life to herself as well as to her confessor, Fra Celestino. Books VIII and IX present the two lawyers, Dominus Hyacinthus de Archangelis and Juris Doctor Johannes-Baptista Bottinius, the former the

defender of Guido, and the latter his prosecutor. These monologues provide some humor, striking a note of relief following the intense monologues of Pompilia and Caponsacchi, and preceding the monologue of the pope in Book X. It has been generally assumed that the pope speaks on Browning's behalf, and this is to some extent true. The judgments rendered by the pope on Guido, Pompilia, and Caponsacchi are similar to those offered by Browning's speaker in Books I and XII of the poem. In the eleventh monologue, Guido is given a second chance to defend himself immediately before his death. He sheds the hypocritical mask worn in Book V and reveals that he has, all the time, been motivated by hatred of his superiors, of the church, and above all of Pompilia. The poem's final book, "The Book and the Ring," reintroduces the speaker closely identified with Browning himself. The poem concludes with important comments on the nature of art and on the uses of indirection and obliqueness in poetry, and offers the proposition that, although the poet employs the facts, the meaning lies beyond them: "So write a book shall mean, beyond the facts,/ Suffice the eye and save the soul beside." In the final few lines the poet makes reference to his "Lyric Love," Elizabeth, and to her gold ring of verse which links England and Italy:

> And save the soul! If this intent save mine,–
> If the rough ore be rounded to a ring,
> Render all duty which good ring shall do,
> And, failing grace, succeed in guardianship,–
> Might mine but lie outside thine, Lyric Love,
> Thy rare gold ring of verse (the poet praised)
> Linking our England to his Italy!

As a working title Browning had used the name of "the collection of law-papers" (*The Old Yellow Book*), but when the poem was in type he suggested to his publishers, Smith, Elder and Company, that it be called *The Franceschini*, perhaps by analogy with Shelley's *The Cenci*. An alternative possibility, *The Book and the Ring*, he rejected as "too pretty-fairy-story-like"; Thackeray, one recalls, had published a fairy story entitled *The Rose and the Ring* in 1844. But poet and publisher ultimately agreed upon a transposition of the two nouns, and it was as *The Ring and the Book* that the poem was published in four volumes between 21 November 1868 and 27 February 1869.

The Ring and the Book: Book I

Do you see this Ring?[1]
          'T is Rome-work, made
to match
(By Castellani's[2] imitative craft)
Etrurian[3] circlets found, some happy morn,
5 After a dropping April; found alive
Spark-like 'mid unearthed slope-side figtree-roots
That roof old tombs at Chiusi:[4] soft, you see,
Yet crisp as jewel-cutting. There's one trick,[5]
(Craftsmen instruct me) one approved device
10 And but one, fits such slivers of pure gold
As this was,—such mere oozings from the mine,
Virgin as oval tawny pendent tear
At beehive-edge when ripened combs o'erflow,—
To bear the file's tooth and the hammer's tap:
15 Since hammer needs must widen out the round,
And file emboss it fine with lily-flowers,
Ere the stuff grow a ring-thing right to wear.
That trick is, the artificer melts up wax
With honey, so to speak; he mingles gold
20 With gold's alloy, and, duly tempering both,
Effects a manageable mass, then works.
But his work ended, once the thing a ring,
Oh, there's repristination![6] Just a spirt
O' the proper fiery acid o'er its face,
25 And forth the alloy unfastened flies in fume;
While, self-sufficient now, the shape remains,
The rondure brave, the lilied loveliness,
Gold as it was, is, shall be evermore:

Prime nature with an added artistry—
30 No carat lost, and you have gained a ring.
What of it? 'T is a figure, a symbol, say;
A thing's sign: now for the thing signified.

Do you see this square old yellow Book,[7] I toss
I' the air, and catch again, and twirl about
35 By the crumpled vellum covers,—pure crude fact
Secreted from man's life when hearts beat hard,
And brains, high-blooded, ticked two centuries since?
Examine it yourselves! I found this book,
Gave a *lira* for it, eightpence English just,
40 (Mark the predestination!) when a Hand,
Always above my shoulder, pushed me once,
One day still fierce 'mid many a day struck calm,
Across a Square in Florence, crammed with booths,
Buzzing and blaze, noontide and market-time;
45 Toward Baccio's marble,[8]—ay, the basement-ledge
O' the pedestal where sits and menaces
John of the Black Bands with the upright spear,
'Twixt palace and church,—Riccardi where they
    lived,
His race, and San Lorenzo where they lie.
50 This book,—precisely on that palace-step
Which, meant for lounging knaves o' the Medici,
Now serves re-venders to display their ware,—
'Monst odds and ends of ravage, picture-frames
White through the worn gilt, mirror-scones chipped,
55 Bronze angel-heads once knobs attached to chests,
(Handled when ancient dames chose forth brocade)
Modern chalk drawings, studies from the nude,
Samples of stone, jet, breccia,[9] porphyry[10]
Polished and rough, sundry amazing busts
60 In baked earth, (broken, Providence be praised!)
A wreck of tapestry, proudly-purposed web

---

[1] For the importance and meaning of the ring image, see the note above. This is also a literal reference to the ring worn by Browning's wife, who died in 1861.

[2] a firm of Roman jewellers.

[3] Etruscan rings.

[4] a town in Tuscany known for its Etruscan ruins.

[5] the gold-alloy metaphor: see above.

[6] restoration to original state.

[7] See the note above.

[8] Baccio Bandinella's statue of Giovanni della Bande Nere ("John of the Black Bands," l. 47), father of Cosimo I of Tuscany.

[9] a rock consisting of sharp cornered pieces.

[10] a hard rock containing red and white crystals.

When reds and blues were indeed red and blue,
Now offered as a mat to save bare feet
(Since carpets constitute a cruel cost)
65 Treading the chill scagliola[1] bedward: then
A pile of brown-etched prints, two *crazie*[2] each,
Stopped by a conch a-top from fluttering forth
—Sowing the Square with works of one and the
    same
Master, the imaginative Sienese[3]
70 Great in the scenic backgrounds—(name and fame
None of you know, nor does he fare the worse:)
From these…Oh, with a Lionard going cheap
If it should prove, as promised, that Joconde[4]
Whereof a copy contents the Louvre!—these
75 I picked this book from. Five compeers[5] in flank
Stood left and right of it as tempting more—
A dogseared Spicilegium,[6] the fond tale
O' the Frail One of the Flower,[7] by young Dumas,
Vulgarized Horace for the use of schools,
80 The Life, Death, Miracles of Saint Somebody,
Saint Somebody Else, his Miracles, Death and
    Life,—
With this, one glance at the lettered back of which,
And "Stall!" cried I: a *lira* made it mine.

Here it is, this I toss and take again;
85 Small-quarto size, part print part manuscript:
A book in shape but, really, pure crude fact
Secreted from man's life when hearts beat hard,
And brains, high-blooded, ticked two centuries
    since.
Give it me back! The thing's restorative
90 I' the touch and sight.

          That memorable day,
(June was the month, Lorenzo named the Square)
I leaned a little and overlooked my prize
By the low railing round the fountain-source
95 Close to the statue, where a step descends:
While clinked the cans of copper, as stooped and
    rose
Thick-ankled girls who brimmed them, and made
    place
For marketmen glad to pitch basket down,
Dip a broad melon-leaf that holds the wet,
100 And whisk their faded fresh. And on I read
Presently, though my path grew perilous
Between the outspread straw-work, piles of plait
Soon to be flapping, each o'er two black eyes
And swathe of Tuscan hair, on festas[8] fine:
105 Through fire-irons, tribes of tongs, shovels in
    sheaves,
Skeleton bedsteads, wardrobe-drawers agape,
Rows of tall slim brass lamps with dangling gear,—
And worse, cast clothes a-sweetening in the sun:
None of them took my eye from off my prize.
110 Still read I on, from written title-page
To written index, on, through street and street,
At the Strozzi, at the Pillar, at the Bridge;[9]
Till, by the time I stood at home again
In Casa Guidi[10] by Felice Church,
115 Under the doorway where the black begins
With the first stone-slab of the staircase cold,
I had mastered the contents, knew the whole truth
Gathered together, bound up in this book,
Print three-fifths,[11] written supplement the rest.
120 "*Romana Homicidiorum*"—nay,
Better translate—"A Roman murder-case:

---

[1] floor of inlaid stone.

[2] a very low domination Italian coin.

[3] See note to l. 369.

[4] Leonardo da Vinci's *La Gioconda* (*Mona Lisa*).

[5] companions.

[6] anthology.

[7] *La Dame aux Camélias* by Alexandre Dumas (1802–70).

---

[8] festival days.

[9] the Palazzo Strozzi, the column in the Piazza Santa Trinità, and the Bridge of Santa Trinità.

[10] the Brownings' home in Florence, 1847–61. Now restored, and a Browning museum, it is situated near the Pitti palace.

[11] Only about a dozen of the 262 pages in the Old Yellow Book are written; the rest are printed.

Position of the entire criminal cause
Of Guido Franceschini, nobleman,
With certain Four the cutthroats in his pay,
25 Tried, all five, and found guilty and put to death
By heading or hanging as befitted ranks,
At Rome on February Twenty Two,
Since our salvation Sixteen Ninety Eight:
Wherein it is disputed if, and when,
130 Husbands may kill adulterous wives, yet 'scape
The customary forfeit."

                Word for word,
So ran the title-page: murder, or else
Legitimate punishment of the other crime,
35 Accounted murder by mistake,—just that
And no more, in a Latin cramp enough
When the law had her eloquence to launch,
But interfilled with Italian streaks[1]
When testimony stooped to mother-tongue,—
40 That, was this old square yellow book about.
Now, as the ingot, ere the ring was forged,
Lay gold, (beseech you, hold that figure fast!)
So, in this book lay absolutely truth,
Fanciless fact, the documents indeed,
45 Primary lawyer-pleadings for, against,
The aforesaid Five; real summed-up circumstance
Adduced in proof of these on either side,
Put forth and printed, as the practice was,
At Rome, in the Apostolic Chamber's type,[2]
50 And so submitted to the eye o' the Court
Presided over by His Reverence
Rome's Governor and Criminal Judge,—the trial
Itself, to all intents, being then as now
Here in the book and nowise out of it;
55 Seeing, there properly was no judgment-bar,[3]

No bringing of accuser and accused,
And whoso judged both parties, face to face
Before some court, as we conceive of courts.
There was a Hall of Justice; that came last:
160 For justice had a chamber by the hall
Where she took evidence first, summed up the
      same,
Then sent accuser and accused alike,
In person of the advocate of each,
To weight that evidence' worth, arrange, array
165 The battle. 'T was the so-styled Fisc began,[4]
Pleaded (and since he only spoke in print
The printed voice of him lives now as then)
The public Prosecutor—"Murder's proved;
With five...what we call qualities of bad,[5]
170 Worse, worst, and yet worse still, and still worse yet;
Crest over crest crowning the cockatrice,[6]
That beggar hell's regalia to enrich
Count Guido Franceschini: punish him!"
Thus was the paper put before the court
175 In the next stage, (no noisy work at all,)
To study at ease. In due time like reply
Came from the so-styled Patron of the Poor,[7]
Official mouthpiece of the five accused
Too poor to fee a better,—Guido's luck
180 Or else his fellows', which, I hardly know,—
An outbreak as of wonder at the world,
A fury-fit of outraged innocence,
A passion of betrayed simplicity:
"Punish Count Guido? For what crime, what hint
185 O' the colour of a crime, inform us first!
Reward him rather! Recognize, we say,
In the deed done, a righteous judgment dealt!
All conscience and all courage,—there's our Count

---

[1] ll. 136–38: The legal arguments are in the late church Latin used in the Roman courts, while the testimony of witnesses is in vernacular Italian.

[2] the imprint of the papal press.

[3] In Roman practice legal arguments were presented to the court in writing. There were no "courtroom scenes" in which the two sides confronted each other. See also ll. 242–44 and ll. 1119–21.

[4] Browning errs in saying that the prosecutor began the pleading. The defence has the privilege of the first argument, as, indeed, Archangeli, in Book VIII, does.

[5] trying circumstances.

[6] a fabulous serpent with the power to kill with a look.

[7] court-appointed defence counsel.

Charactered in a word; and, what's more strange,
190 He had companionship in privilege,
Found four courageous conscientious friends:
Absolve, applaud all five, as props of law,
Sustainers of society!—perchance
A trifle over-hasty with the hand
195 To hold her tottering ark, had tumbled else;
But that's a splendid fault whereat we wink,
Wishing your cold correctness sparkled so!"
Thus paper second followed paper first,
Thus did the two join issue—nay, the four,
200 Each pleader having an adjunct. "True, he killed
—So to speak—in a certain sort—his wife,
But laudably, since thus it happed!" quoth one:
Whereat, more witness and the case postponed.
"Thus it happed not, since thus he did the deed,
205 And proved himself thereby portentousest
Of cutthroats and a prodigy of crime,
As the woman that he slaughtered was a saint,
Martyr and miracle!" quoth the other to match:
Again, more witness, and the case postponed.
210 "A miracle, ay—of lust and impudence;[1]
Hear my new reasons!" interposed the first:
"—Coupled with more of mine!" pursued his peer.
"Beside, the precedents, the authorities!"
From both at once a cry with an echo, that!
215 That was a firebrand at each fox's tail
Unleashed in a cornfield: soon spread flare enough,
As hurtled thither and there heaped themselves
From earth's four corners, all authority
And precedent for putting wives to death,
220 Or letting wives live, sinful as they seem.
How legislated, now, in this respect,
Solon and his Athenians? Quote the code
Of Romulus and Rome![2] Justinian[3] speak!

Nor modern Baldo, Bartolo[4] be dumb!
225 The Roman voice was potent, plentiful;
Cornelia de Sicariis hurried to help
Pompeia de Parricidiis;[5] *Julia de*
Something-or-other jostled *Lex* this-and-that;
King Solomon confirmed Apostle Paul:
230 That nice decision of Dolabella,[6] eh?
That pregnant instance of Theodoric,[7] oh!
Down to that choice example Aelian[8] gives
(An instance I find much insisted on)
Of the elephant who, brute-beast though he were,
235 Yet understood and punished on the spot
His master's naughty spouse and faithless friend;
A true tale which has edified each child,
Much more shall flourish favoured by our court!
Pages of proof this way, and that way proof,
240 And always—once again the case postponed.

Thus wrangled, brangled, jangled they a month,
—Only on paper, pleadings all in print,
Nor ever was, except i' the brains of men,
More noise by word of mouth than you hear now—
245 Till the court cut all short with "Judged, your cause.
Receive our sentence! Praise God! We pronounce
Count Guido devilish and damnable:
His wife Pompilia in thought, word and deed,
Was perfect pure, he murdered her for that:
250 As for the Four who helped the One, all Five—
Why, let employer and hirelings share alike
In guilt and guilt's reward, the death their due!"
So was the trial at end, do you suppose?
"Guilty you find him, death you doom him to?
255 Ay, were not Guido, more than needs, a priest,
Priest and to spare!"—this was a shot reserved;

---

[1] shamelessness.

[2] Solon (c. 640–c. 559 BC) and Romulus each included severe penalties for adultery in the legal codes of their respective societies.

[3] Byzantine emperor (482–565).

[4] famous fourteenth-century Italian jurists.

[5] legal decisions relating to murders.

[6] Roman proconsul (c. 70–43 BC).

[7] Theodoric the Great (c. 455–526), first Gothic king of Italy.

[8] Claudius Aelianus (late second, early third century AD), author of *Variae Historiae, On the Nature of Animals.*

I learn this from epistles which begin
Here where the print ends,—see the pen and ink
Of the advocate, the ready at a pinch!—
60 "My client boasts the clerkly privilege,
Has taken minor orders many enough,[1]
Shows still sufficient chrism upon his pate
To neutralize a blood-stain: *presbyter,*
Primae tonsurae, subdiaconus,
65 *Sacerdos,* so he slips from underneath
Your power, the temporal, slides inside the robe
Of mother Church: to her we make appeal
By the Pope, the Church's head!"

                  A parlous[2] plea,
70 Put in with noticeable effect, it seems;
"Since straight,"—resumes the zealous orator,
Making a friend acquainted with the facts,—
"Once the word 'clericality' let fall,
Procedure stopped and freer breath was drawn
75 By all considerate and responsible Rome."
Quality[3] took the decent part, of course;
Held by the husband, who was noble too:
Or, for the matter of that, a churl would side
With too-refined susceptibility,
80 And honour which, tender in the extreme,
Stung to the quick, must roughly right itself
At all risks, not sit still and whine for law
As a Jew would, if you squeezed him to the wall,
Brisk-trotting through the Ghetto. Nay, it seems,
85 Even the Emperor's Envoy had his say
To say on the subject; might not see, unmoved,
Civility menaced throughout Christendom
By too harsh measure dealt her champion here.
Lastly, what made all safe, the Pope was kind,
90 From his youth up, reluctant to take life,
If mercy might be just and yet show grace;
Much more unlikely then, in extreme age,

To take a life the general sense bade spare.
'T was plain that Guido would go scatheless yet.

295 But human promise, oh, how short of shine!
How topple down the piles of hope we rear!
How history proves...nay, read Herodotus![4]
Suddenly starting from a nap, as it were,
A dog-sleep with one shut, one open orb,
300 Cried the Pope's great self,—Innocent by name
And nature too, and eighty-six years old,
Antonio Pignatelli of Naples, Pope
Who had trod many lands, known many deeds,
Probed many hearts, beginning with his own,
305 And now was far in readiness for God,—
'Twas he who first bade leave those souls in peace,
Those Jansenists, re-nicknamed Molinists,[5]
('Gainst whom the cry went, like a frowsy[6] tune,
Tickling men's ears—the sect for a quarter of an
    hour
310 I' the teeth of the world which, clown-like, loves to
    chew
Be it but a straw twixt work and whistling-while,
Taste some vituperation, bite away,
Whether at marjoram-sprig or garlic-clove,
Aught it may sport with, spoil, and then spit forth)
315 "Leave them alone," bade he, "those Molinists!
Who may have other light than we perceive,
Or why is it the whole world hates them thus?"
Also he peeled off that last scandal-rag
Of Nepotism; and so observed the poor
320 That men would merrily say, "Halt, deaf and blind,
Who feed on fat things, leave the master's self
To gather up the fragments of his feast,
These be the nephews of Pope Innocent!—

---

[1] "minor" clerical orders granting immunity from civil prosecution.

[2] cunning and risky.

[3] "the superior social section," l. 927.

---

[4] Greek historian (c. 484–425 BC) who wrote stories illustrating the fall of the proud, wealthy, and mighty.

[5] heretical school of theology founded by Cornelius Jansen (1585–1638), which denied free will.

[6] untidy, musty.

His own meal costs but five carlines[1] a day,
325 Poor-priest's allowance, for he claims no more."
—He cried of a sudden, this great good old Pope,
When they appealed in last resort to him,
"I have mastered the whole matter: I nothing doubt.
Though Guido stood forth priest from head to heel,
330 Instead of, as alleged, a piece of one,—
And further, were he, from the tonsured scalp
To the sandaled sole of him, my son and Christ's,
Instead of touching us by finger-tip
As you assert, and pressing up so close
335 Only to set a blood-smutch on our robe,—
I and Christ would renounce all right in him.
Am I not Pope, and presently to die,
And busied how to render my account,
And shall I wait a day ere I decide
340 On doing or not doing justice here?
Cut off his head to-morrow by this time,
Hang up his four mates, two on either hand,
And end one business more!"

        So said, so done—
345 Rather so writ, for the old Pope bade this,
I find, with his particular chirograph,[2]
His own no such infirm hand, Friday night;
And next day, February Twenty Two,
Since our salvation Sixteen Ninety Eight,
350 —Not at the proper head-and-hanging-place
On bridge-foot close by Castle Angelo,[3]
Where custom somewhat staled the spectacle,
('Twas not so well i' the way of Rome, beside,
The noble Rome, the Rome of Guido's rank)
355 But at the city's newer gayer end,—
The cavalcading promenading place
Beside the gate and opposite the church
Under the Pincian gardens green with Spring,

'Neath the obelisk 'twixt the fountains in the
        Square,
360 Did Guido and his fellows find their fate,
All Rome for witness, and—my writer adds—
Remonstrant in its universal grief,
Since Guido had the suffrage[4] of all Rome.
This is the bookful; thus far take the truth,
365 The untempered gold, the fact untampered with,
The mere ring-metal ere the ring be made!
And what has hitherto come of it? Who preserves
The memory of this Guido, and his wife
Pompilia, more than Ademollo's[5] name,
370 The etcher of those prints, two *crazie* each,
Saved by a stone from snowing broad the Square
With scenic backgrounds? Was this truth of force?
Able to take its own part as truth should,
Sufficient, self-sustaining? Why, if so—
375 Yonder's a fire, into it goes my book,
As who shall say me nay, and what the loss?
You know the tale already: I may ask,
Rather than think to tell you, more thereof,—
Ask you not merely who were he and she,
380 Husband and wife, what manner of mankind,
But how you hold concerning this and that
Other yet-unnamed actor in the piece.
The young frank handsome courtly Canon, now,
The priest, declared the lover of the wife,
385 He who, no question, did elope with her,
For certain bring the tragedy about,
Giuseppe Caponsacchi;—his strange course
I' the matter, was it right or wrong or both?
Then the old couple, slaughtered with the wife
390 By the husband as accomplices in crime,
Those Comparini, Pietro and his spouse,—
What say you to the right or wrong of that,
When, at a known name whispered through the door
Of a lone villa on a Christmas night,
395 It opened that the joyous hearts inside

---

[1] Italian coin worth about 4 pence in Victorian money.

[2] handwriting.

[3] the Mausoleum of Hadrian, on the right bank of the Tiber.

[4] support.

[5] Luigi Ademollo (1764–1849), painter and engraver.

Might welcome as it were an angel-guest
Come in Christ's name to knock and enter, sup
And satisfy the loving ones he saved;
And so did welcome devils and their death?
400 I have been silent on that circumstance
Although the couple passed for close of kin
To wife and husband, were by some accounts
Pompilia's very parents: you know best.
Also that infant the great joy was for,
405 That Gaetano, the wife's two-weeks' babe,
The husband's first-born child, his son and heir,
Whose birth and being turned his night to day—
Why must the father kill the mother thus
Because she bore his son and saved himself?

410 Well, British Public, ye who like me not,
(God love you!) and will have your proper laugh
At the dark question, laugh it! I laugh first.
Truth must prevail, the proverb vows; and truth
—Here is it all i' the book at last, as first
415 There it was all i' the heads and hearts of Rome
Gentle and simple, never to fall nor fade
Nor be forgotten. Yet, a little while,
The passage of a century or so,
Decads thrice five, and here's time paid his tax,
420 Oblivion gone home with her harvesting,
And all left smooth again as scythe could shave.
Far from beginning with you London folk,
I took my book to Rome first, tried truth's power
On likely people. "Have you met such names?
425 Is a tradition extant of such facts?
Your law-courts stand, your records frown a-row:
What if I rove and rummage?" "—Why, you'll
        waste
Your pains and end as wise as you began!"
Everyone snickered: "names and facts thus old
430 Are newer much than Europe news we find
Down in to-day's *Diario*.[1] Records, quotha?

Why, the French burned them, what else do the
        French?
The rap-and-rending[2] nation! And it tells
Against the Church, no doubt,—another gird[3]
435 At the Temporality,[4] your Trial, of course?"
"—Quite otherwise this time," submitted I;
Clean for the Church and dead against the world,
The flesh and the devil, does it tell for once."
"—The rarer and the happier! All the same,
440 Content you with your treasure of a book,
And waive what's wanting! Take a friend's advice!
It's not the custom of the country. Mend
Your ways indeed and we may stretch a point:
Go get you manned by Manning and new-manned
445 By Newman and, mayhap, wise-manned to boot
By Wiseman,[5] and we'll see or else we won't!
Thanks meantime for the story, long and strong,
A pretty piece of narrative enough,
Which scarce ought so to drop out, one would
        think,
450 From the more curious annals of our kind.
Do you tell the story, now, in off-hand style,
Straight from the book? Or simply here and there,
(The while you vault it through the loose and large)
Hang to a hint? Or is there book at all,
455 And don't you deal in poetry, make-believe,
And the white lies it sounds like?"

                                        Yes and no!
From the book, yes; thence bit by bit I dug
The lingot[6] truth, that memorable day,
460 Assayed and knew my piecemeal gain was gold,—
Yes; but from something else surpassing that,
Something of mine which, mixed up with the mass,

---

[2] to get by snatching or stealing.

[3] attack.

[4] the papal claim to power in secular affairs.

[5] Manning, Newman, and Wiseman were three members of the Roman
Catholic hierarchy in Victorian England.

[6] ingot.

---

[1] newspaper.

Made it bear hammer and be firm to file.
Fancy with fact is just one fact the more;
465 To-wit, that fancy has informed, transpierced,
Thridded and so thrown fast[1] the facts else free,
As right through ring and ring runs the djereed[2]
And binds the loose, one bar without a break.
I fused my live soul and that inert stuff,
470 Before attempting smithcraft, on the night
After the day when,—truth thus grasped and
    gained,—
The book was shut and done with and laid by
On the cream-coloured massive agate, broad
'Neath the twin cherubs in the tarnished frame
475 O' the mirror, tall thence to the ceiling-top.
And from the reading, and that slab I leant
My elbow on, the while I read and read,
I turned, to free myself and find the world,
And stepped out on the narrow terrace, built
480 Over the street and opposite the church,
And paced its lozenge-brickwork sprinkled cool;
Because Felice-church-side stretched, a-glow
Through each square window fringed for festival,
Whence came the clear voice of the cloistered ones
485 Chanting a chant made for midsummer nights—
I know not what particular praise of God,
It always came and went with June. Beneath
I' the street, quick shown by openings of the sky
When flame fell silently from cloud to cloud,
490 Richer than that gold snow[3] Jove rained on Rhodes,
The townsmen walked by twos and threes, and
    talked,
Drinking the blackness in default of air—
A busy human sense beneath my feet:
While in and out the terrace-plants, and round
495 One branch of tall datura,[4] waxed and waned
The lamp-fly lured there, wanting the white flower.

Over the roof o' the lighted church I looked
A bowshot to the street's end, north away
Out of the Roman gate to the Roman road
500 By the river, till I felt the Apennine.[5]
And there would lie Arezzo,[6] the man's town,
The woman's trap and cage and torture-place,
Also the stage where the priest played his part,
A spectacle for angels,—ay, indeed,
505 There lay Arezzo! Farther then I fared,
Feeling my way on through the hot and dense,
Romeward, until I found the wayside inn
By Castelnuovo's[7] few mean hut-like homes
Huddled together on the hill-foot bleak,
510 Bare, broken only by that tree or two
Against the sudden bloody splendour poured
Cursewise in his departure by the day
On the low house-roof of that squalid inn
Where they three, for the first time and the last,
515 Husband and wife and priest, met face to face.
Whence I went on again, the end was near,
Step by step, missing none and marking all,
Till Rome itself, the ghastly goal, I reached.
Why, all the while,—how could it otherwise?—
520 The life in me abolished the death of things,
Deep calling unto deep: as then and there
Acted itself over again once more
The tragic piece. I saw with my own eyes
In Florence as I trod the terrace, breathed
525 The beauty and the fearfulness of night,
How it had run, this round from Rome to Rome—
Because, you are to know, they lived at Rome,
Pompilia's parents, as they thought themselves,
Two poor ignoble hearts who did their best
530 Part God's way, part the other way than God's,
To somehow make a shift and scramble through
The world's mud, careless if it splashed and spoiled,
Provided they might so hold high, keep clean

---

[1] twisted into thread.

[2] wooden javelin used in tilting at a target.

[3] wealth.

[4] plant of the nightshade family.

---

[5] sensed the Apennine mountain range.

[6] Tuscan town south-east of Florence.

[7] a hamlet fifteen miles from Rome.

Their child's soul, one soul white enough for three,
535 And lift it to whatever star should stoop,
What possible sphere of purer life than theirs
Should come in aid of whiteness hard to save.
I saw the star stoop, that they strained to touch,
And did touch and depose their treasure on,
540 As Guido Franceschini took away
Pompilia to be his for evermore,
While they sang "Now let us depart in peace,
Having beheld thy glory, Guido's wife!"
I saw the star supposed, but fog o' the fen,[1]
545 Gilded star-fashion by a glint from hell;
Having been heaved up, haled on its gross way,
By hands unguessed before, invisible help
From a dark brotherhood, and specially
Two obscure goblin creatures, fox-faced this,
550 Cat-clawed the other, called his next of kin
By Guido the main monster,—cloaked and caped,
Making as they were priests, to mock God more,—
Abate Paul, Canon Girolamo.
These who had rolled the starlike pest[2] to Rome
555 And stationed it to suck up and absorb
The sweetness of Pompilia, rolled again
That bloated bubble, with her soul inside,
Back to Arezzo and a palace there—
Or say, a fissure in the honest earth
560 Whence long ago had curled the vapour first,
Blown big by nether fires to appal day:
It touched home, broke, and blasted far and wide.
I saw the cheated couple find the cheat
And guess what foul rite they were captured for,—
565 Too fain to follow over hill and dale
That child of theirs caught up thus in the cloud
And carried by the Prince o' the Power of the Air[3]
Whither he would, to wilderness or sea.
I saw them, in the potency of fear,
570 Break somehow through the satyr-family

(For a grey mother with a monkey-mien,
Mopping and mowing,[4] was apparent too,
As, confident of capture, all took hands
And danced about the captives in a ring)
575 —Saw them break through, breathe safe, at Rome again,
Saved by the selfish instinct, losing so
Their loved one left with haters. These I saw,
In recrudescency of baffled hate,
Prepare to wring the uttermost revenge
580 From body and soul thus left them: all was sure,
Fire laid and cauldron set, the obscene ring traced,
The victim stripped and prostrate: what of God?
The cleaving of a cloud, a cry, a crash,
Quenched lay their cauldron, cowered i' the dust the crew,
585 As, in a glory of armour like Saint George,[5]
Out again sprang the young good beauteous priest
Bearing away the lady in his arms,
Saved for a splendid minute and no more.
For, whom i' the path did that priest come upon,
590 He and the poor lost lady borne so brave,
—Checking the song of praise in me, had else
Swelled to the full for God's will done on earth—
Whom but a dusk misfeatured messenger,
No other than the angel of this life,
595 Whose care is lest men see too much at once.
He made the sign, such God-glimpse must suffice,
Nor prejudice the Prince o' the Power of the Air,
Whose ministration piles us overhead
What we call, first, earth's roof and, last, heaven's floor,
600 Now grate o' the trap, then outlet of the cage:
So took the lady, left the priest alone,
And once more canopied the world with black.
But through the blackness I saw Rome again,
And where a solitary villa stood

---

[1] phosphorescence rising from decaying matter in a swamp.

[2] pestilence.

[3] Satan: Ephesians 2:2.

---

[4] grimacing.

[5] Caponsacchi is frequently referred to as a St. George figure, heroic rescuer of beleaguered women.

605 In a lone garden-quarter: it was eve,
The second of the year, and oh so cold!
Ever and anon there flittered through the air
A snow-flake, and a scanty couch of snow
Crusted the grass-walk and the garden-mould.
610 All was grave, silent, sinister,—when, ha?
Glimmeringly did a pack of were-wolves pad
The snow, those flames were Guido's eyes in front,
And all five found and footed it, the track,
To where a threshold-streak of warmth and light
615 Betrayed the villa-door with life inside,
While an inch outside were those blood-bright eyes,
And black lips wrinkling o'er the flash of teeth,
And tongues that lolled—Oh God that madest
        man!
They parleyed in their language. Then one
        whined—
620 That was the policy and master-stroke—
Deep in his throat whispered what seemed a
        name—
"Open to Caponsacchi!" Guido cried:
"Gabriel!" cried Lucifer at Eden-gate.[1]
Wide as a heart, opened the door at once,
625 Showing the joyous couple, and their child
The two-weeks' mother, to the wolves, the wolves
To them. Close eyes! And when the corpses lay
Stark-stretched, and those the wolves, their wolf-
        work done,
Were safe-embosomed by the night again,
630 I knew a necessary change in things;
As when the worst watch of the night gives way,
And there comes duly, to take cognisance,
The scrutinizing eye-point of some star—
And who despairs of a new daybreak now?
635 Lo, the first ray protruded on those five!
It reached them, and each felon writhed transfixed.
Awhile they palpitated on the spear

Motionless over Tophet:[2] stand or fall?
"I say, the spear should fall—should stand, I say!"
640 Cried the world come to judgment, granting grace
Or dealing doom according to world's wont,
Those world's-bystanders grouped on Rome's
        cross-road
At prick and summons of the primal curse
Which bids man love as well as make a lie.
645 There prattled they, discoursed the right and wrong,
Turned wrong to right, proved wolves sheep and
        sheep wolves,
So that you scarce distinguished fell[3] from fleece;
Till out spoke a great guardian of the fold,
Stood up, put forth his hand that held the crook,
650 And motioned that the arrested point decline:
Horribly off, the wriggling dead-weight reeled,
Rushed to the bottom and lay ruined there.
Though still at the pit's mouth, despite the smoke
O' the burning, tarriers turned again to talk
655 And trim the balance, and detect at least
A touch of wolf in what showed whitest sheep,
A cross of sheep redeeming the whole wolf,—
Vex truth a little longer:—less and less,
Because years came and went, and more and more
660 Brought new lies with them to be loved in turn.
Till all at once the memory of the thing,—
The fact that, wolves or sheep, such creatures
        were,—
Which hitherto, however men supposed,
Had somehow plain and pillar-like prevailed
665 I' the midst of them, indisputably fact,
Granite, time's tooth should grate against, not
        graze,—
Why, this proved sandstone, friable,[4] fast to fly
And give its grain away at wish o' the wind.
Ever and ever more diminutive,

---

[1] An analogy is drawn between Guido's use of Caponsacchi's name and Lucifer's use of Gabriel's name to gain entry to Paradise.

---

[2] Old Testament site of child sacrifice, later developed into a symbol of hell.

[3] hide.

[4] easily crumbled.

570 Base gone, shaft lost, only entablature,[1]
Dwindled into no bigger than a book,
Lay of the column; and that little, left
By the roadside 'mid the ordure, shards and weeds.
Until I haply, wandering that way,
575 Kicked it up, turned it over, and recognized,
For all the crumblement, this abacus,[2]
This square old yellow book,—could calculate
By this the lost proportions of the style.[3]

This was it from, my fancy with those facts,
580 I used to tell the tale, turned gay to grave,
But lacked a listener seldom; such alloy,
Such substance of me interfused the gold
Which, wrought into a shapely ring therewith,
Hammered and filed, fingered and favoured,[4] last
585 Lay ready for the renovating wash
O' the water. "How much of the tale was true?"
I disappeared; the book grew all in all;
The lawyer's pleadings swelled back to their size,—
Doubled in two, the crease upon them yet,
590 For more commodity of carriage,[5] see!—
And these are letters, veritable sheets
That brought posthaste the news to Florence, writ
At Rome the day Count Guido died, we find,
To stay the craving of a client there,
595 Who bound the same and so produced my book.
Lovers of dead truth, did ye fare the worse?
Lovers of live truth, found ye false my tale?

Well, now; there's nothing in nor out o' the world
Good except truth: yet this, the something else,
600 What's this then, which proves good yet seems
　　　　untrue?
This that I mixed with truth, motions of mine

That quickened, made the inertness malleolable[6]
O' the gold was not mine,—what's your name for
　　　this?
Are means to the end, themselves in part the end?
705 Is fiction which makes fact alive, fact too?
The somehow may be thishow.

　　　　　　　　　I find first
Writ down for very A.B.C. of fact,
"In the beginning God made heaven and earth;"
710 From which, no matter with what lisp, I spell
And speak you out a consequence—that man,
Man,—as befits the made, the inferior thing,—
Purposed, since made, to grow, not make in turn,
Yet forced to try and make, else fail to grow,—
715 Formed to rise, reach at, if not grasp and gain
The good beyond him,—which attempt is
　　　growth,—
Repeats God's process in man's due degree,
Attaining man's proportionate result,—
Creates, no, but resuscitates, perhaps.
720 Inalienable,[7] the arch-prerogative
Which turns thought, act—conceives, expresses
　　　too!
No less, man, bounded, yearning to be free,
May so project his surplusage of soul
In search of body, so add self to self
725 By owning what lay ownerless before,—
So find, so fill full, so appropriate forms—
That, although nothing which had never life
Shall get life from him, be, not having been,
Yet, something dead may get to live again,
730 Something with too much life or not enough,
Which, either way imperfect, ended once:
An end whereat man's impulse intervenes,
Makes new beginning, starts the dead alive,
Completes the incomplete and saves the thing.
735 Man's breath were vain to light a virgin wick,—

---

[1] topmost horizontal portion of a classic order of architecture.

[2] square-shaped top slab of a capitol in a column.

[3] column.

[4] ornamented.

[5] portability.

---

[6] capable of being hammered into shape.

[7] God's alone, not to be delegated to man.

Half-burned-out, all but quite-quenched wicks o'
    the lamp
Stationed for temple-service on this earth,
These indeed let him breathe on and relume!
For such man's feat is, in the due degree,
740 —Mimic creation, galvanism for life,[1]
But still a glory portioned in the scale.
Why did the mage[2] say,—feeling as we are wont
For truth, and stopping midway short of truth,
And resting on a lie,—"I raise a ghost?"
745 "Because", he taught adepts, "man makes not man.
Yet by a special gift, an art of arts,
More insight and more outsight and much more
Will to use both of these than boast my mates,
I can detach from me, commission forth
750 Half of my soul; which in its pilgrimage
O'er old unwandered waste ways of the world,
May chance upon some fragment of a whole,
Rag of flesh, scrap of bone in dim disuse,
Smoking flax that fed fire once: prompt therein
755 I enter, spark-like, put old powers to play,
Push lines out to the limit, lead forth last
(By a moonrise through a ruin of a crypt)
What shall be mistily seen, murmuringly heard,
Mistakenly felt: then write my name with Faust's!"
760 Oh, Faust, why Faust? Was not Elisha once?—[3]
Who bade them lay his staff on a corpse-face.
There was no voice, no hearing: he went in
Therefore, and shut the door upon them twain,
And prayed unto the Lord: and he went up
765 And lay upon the corpse, dead on the couch,
And put his mouth upon its mouth, his eyes
Upon its eyes, his hands upon its hands,
And stretched him on the flesh; the flesh waxed
    warm:
And he returned, walked to and fro the house,
770 And went up, stretched him on the flesh again,

And the eyes opened. 'Tis a credible feat
With the right man and way.

               Enough of me!
The Book! I turn its medicinable[4] leaves
775 In London now till, as in Florence erst,
A spirit laughs and leaps through every limb,
And lights my eye, and lifts me by the hair,
Letting me have my will again with these
—How title I the dead alive once more?

780 Count Guido Franceschini the Aretine,
Descended of an ancient house, though poor,
A beak-nosed bushy-bearded black-haired lord,
Lean, pallid, low of stature yet robust,
Fifty years old,—having four years ago
785 Married Pompilia Comparini, young,
Good, beautiful, at Rome, where she was born,
And brought her to Arezzo, where they lived
Unhappy lives, whatever curse the cause,—
This husband, taking four accomplices,
790 Followed this wife to Rome, where she was fled
From their Arezzo to find peace again,
In convoy, eight months earlier, of a priest,
Aretine also, of still nobler birth,
Giuseppe Caponsacchi,—and caught her there
795 Quiet in a villa on a Christmas night,
With only Pietro and Violante by,
Both her putative parents; killed the three,
Aged, they, seventy each, and she, seventeen,
And, two weeks since, the mother of his babe
800 First-born and heir to what the style[5] was worth
O' the Guido who determined, dared and did
This deed just as he purposed point by point.
Then, bent upon escape, but hotly pressed,
And captured with his co-mates that same night,
805 He, brought to trial, stood on this defence—
Injury to his honour caused the act;

---

[1] stimulation from inertia into activity.

[2] magician/poet.

[3] Faust was assisted by Satan; Elisha by God.

---

[4] healing.

[5] title.

That since his wife was false, (as manifest
By flight from home in such companionship,)
Death, punishment deserved of the false wife
810 And faithless parents who abetted her
I' the flight aforesaid, wronged nor God nor man,
"Nor false she, nor yet faithless they," replied
The accuser; "cloaked and masked this murder
glooms;
True was Pompilia, loyal too the pair;
815 Out of the man's own heart this monster curled,
This crime coiled with connivancy at crime,
His victim's breast, he tells you, hatched and
reared;
Uncoil we and stretch stark the worm of hell!"
A month the trial swayed this way and that
820 Ere judgment settled down on Guido's guilt;
Then was the Pope, that good Twelfth Innocent,
Appealed to: who well weighed what went before,
Affirmed the guilt and gave the guilty doom.

Let this old woe step on the stage again!
825 Act itself o'er anew for men to judge,
Not by the very sense and sight indeed—
(Which take at best imperfect cognizance,
Since, how heart moves brain, and how both move
hand,
What mortal ever in entirety saw?)
830 —No dose of purer truth than man digests,
But truth with falsehood, milk that feeds him now,
Not strong meat he may get to bear some day—
To-wit, by voices we call evidence,
Uproar in the echo, live fact deadened down,
835 Talked over, bruited abroad, whispered away,
Yet helping us to all we seem to hear:
For how else know we save by worth of word?

Here are the voices presently shall sound
In due succession. First, the world's outcry
840 Around the rush and ripple of any fact
Fallen stonewise, plumb on the smooth face of
things;

The world's guess, as it crowds the bank o' the
pool,
At what were figure[1] and substance, by their splash:
Then, by vibrations in the general mind,
845 At depth of deed already out of reach.
This threefold murder of the day before,—
Say, Half-Rome's feel after the vanished truth;
Honest enough, as the way is: all the same,
Harbouring in the centre of its sense
850 A hidden germ of failure, shy but sure,
Should neutralize that honesty and leave
That feel for truth at fault, as the way is too.
Some prepossession such as starts amiss,
By but a hair's breadth at the shoulder-blade,
855 The arm o' the feeler, dip he ne'er so brave;
And so leads waveringly, lets fall wide
O' the mark his finger meant to find, and fix
Truth at the bottom, that deceptive speck.
With this half-Rome, —the source of swerving, call
860 Over-belief in Guido's right and wrong
Rather than in Pompilia's wrong and right:
Who shall say how, who shall say why? 'T is there—
The instinctive theorizing whence a fact
Looks to the eye as the eye likes the look.
865 Gossip in a public place, a sample-speech.[2]
Some worthy, with his previous hint to find
A husband's side the safer, and no whit
Aware he is not Aeacus[3] the while,—
How such an one supposes and states fact
870 To whosoever of a multitude
Will listen, and perhaps prolong thereby
The not-unpleasant flutter at the breast,
Born of a certain spectacle shut in
By the church Lorenzo opposite. So, they lounge
875 Midway the mouth o' the street, on Corso[4] side,

---

[1] shape.

[2] illustrative case.

[3] King of Aegina, whose reputation for justice won him one of three judgeships in Hades.

[4] a main Roman street.

'Twixt palace Fiano and palace Ruspoli,
Linger and listen; keeping clear o' the crowd,
Yet wishful one could lend that crowd one's eyes,
(So universal is its plague of squint)
880 And make hearts beat our time that flutter false:
—All for the truth's sake, mere truth, nothing else!
How Half-Rome found for Guido much excuse.

Next, from Rome's other half, the opposite feel
For truth with a like swerve, like unsuccess,—
885 Or if success, by no more skill but luck:
This time, through rather siding with the wife,
However the fancy-fit inclined that way,
Than with the husband. One wears drab, one,
    pink;
Who wears pink, ask him "Which shall win the
    race,
890 Of coupled runners like as egg and egg?"
"—Why, if I must choose, he with the pink scarf."
Doubtless for some such reason choice fell here.
A piece of public talk to correspond
At the next stage of the story; just a day
895 Let pass and new day bring the proper change.
Another sample-speech i' the market-place
O' the Barberini by the Capucins;
Where the old Triton, at his fountain-sport,
Bernini's creature plated to the paps,
900 Puffs up steel sleet which breaks to diamond dust,
A spray of sparkles snorted from his conch,
High over the caritellas,[1] out o' the way
O' the motley merchandizing multitude.
Our murder has been done three days ago,
905 The frost is over and gone, the south wind laughs,
And, to the very tiles of each red roof
A-smoke i' the sunshine, Rome lies gold and glad:
So, listen how, to the other half of Rome,
Pompilia seemed a saint and martyr both!

910 Then, yet another day let come and go,
With pause prelusive still of novelty,
Hear a fresh speaker!—neither this nor that
Half-Rome aforesaid; something bred of both:
One and one breed the inevitable three,
915 Such is the personage harangues you next;
The elaborated product, *tertium quid:*[2]
Rome's first commotion in subsidence gives
The curd o' the cream, flower o' the wheat, as it
    were,
And finer sense o' the city. Is this plain?
920 You get a reasoned statement of the case,
Eventual verdict of the curious few
Who care to sift a business to the bran
Nor coarsely bolt it like the simpler sort.
Here, after ignorance, instruction speaks;
925 Here, clarity of candour, history's soul,
The critical mind, in short: no gossip-guess.
What the superior social section thinks,
In person of some man of quality
Who,—breathing musk from lace-work and
    brocade,
930 His solitaire amid the flow of frill,
Powdered peruke on nose, and bag at back,
And cane dependent from the ruffled wrist,—
Harangues in silvery and selectest phrase
'Neath waxlight in a glorified saloon
935 Where mirrors multiply the girandole:[3]
Courting the approbation of no mob,
But Eminence This and All-Illustrious That
Who take snuff softly, range in well-bred ring,
Card-table-quitters for observance' sake,
940 Around the argument, the rational word—
Still, spite its weight and worth, a sample-speech.
How quality dissertated on the case.

_____

[1] small figures of the Graces.

_____

[2] an indefinite thing which is related to but distinct from two other
known entities.

[3] branched candlestick.

So much for Rome and rumour; smoke comes first:
Once the smoke risen untroubled, we descry
945 Clearlier what tongues of flame may spire and spit
To eye and ear, each with appropriate tinge
According to its food, pure or impure.
The actors, no mere rumours of the act,
Intervene. First you hear Count Guido's voice,
950 In a small chamber that adjoins the court,
Where Governor and Judges, summoned thence,
Tommati, Venturini and the rest,
Find the accused ripe for declaring truth.
Soft-cushioned sits he; yet shifts seat, shirks touch,
955 As, with a twitchy brow and wincing lip
And cheek that changes to all kinds of white,
He proffers his defence, in tones subdued
Near to mock-mildness now, so mournful seems
The obtuser sense truth fails to satisfy;
960 Now, moved, from pathos at the wrong endured,
To passion; for the natural man is roused
At fools who first do wrong, then pour the blame
Of their wrong-doing, Satan-like, on Job.
Also his tongue at times is hard to curb;
965 Incisive, nigh satiric bites the phrase,
Rough-raw, yet somehow claiming privilege
—It is so hard for shrewdness[1] to admit
Folly means no harm when she calls black white!
—Eruption momentary at the most,
970 Modified forthwith by a fall o' the fire,
Sage acquiescence; for the world's the world,
And, what it errs in, Judges rectify:
He feels he has a fist, then folds his arms
Crosswise and makes his mind up to be meek.
975 And never once does he detach his eye
From those ranged there to slay him or to save,
But does his best man's-service for himself,
Despite,—what twitches brow and makes lip
    wince,—

His limbs' late taste of what was called the Cord,[2]
980 Or Vigil-torture[3] more facetiously.
Even so; they were wont to tease the truth
Out of loath witness (toying, trifling time)
By torture: 'twas a trick, a vice of the age,
Here, there and everywhere, what would you have?
985 Religion used to tell Humanity
She gave him warrant or denied him course.[4]
And since the course was much to his own mind,
Of pinching flesh and pulling bone from bone
To unhusk truth a-hiding in its hulls,
990 Nor whisper of a warning stopped the way,
He, in their joint behalf, the burly slave,
Bestirred him, mauled and maimed all recusants,[5]
While, prim in place, Religion overlooked;
And so had done till doomsday, never a sign
995 Nor sound of interference from her mouth,
But that at last the burly slave wiped brow,
Let eye give notice as if soul were there,
Muttered "'Tis a vile trick, foolish more than vile,
Should have been counted sin; I make it so:
1000 At any rate no more of it for me—
Nay, for I break the torture-engine thus!"
Then did Religion start up, stare amain,
Look round for help and see none, smile and say
"What, broken is the rack? Well done of thee!
1005 Did I forget to abrogate its use?
Be the mistake in common with us both!
—One more fault our blind age shall answer for,
Down in my book denounced though it must be
Somewhere. Henceforth find truth by milder
    means!"
1010 Ah but, Religion, did we wait for thee

---

[2] a form of torture in which the arms are twisted behind the back and tied with a rope which is then hoisted.

[3] a form of torture in which, while fastened to a stool in a sitting position, the prisoner's shoulders were tied to the wall and his legs elevated by a rod between his feet.

[4] proposed line of action.

[5] those refusing to conform.

---

[1] intelligence.

To ope the book, that serves to sit upon,
And pick such place out, we should wait indeed!
That is all history: and what is not now,
Was then, defendants found it to their cost.
1015 How Guido, after being tortured, spoke.

Also hear Caponsacchi who comes next,
Man and priest—could you comprehend the
    coil!—[1]
In days when that was rife which now is rare.
How, mingling each its multifarious wires,
1020 Now heaven, now earth, now heaven and earth at
    once,
Had plucked at and perplexed their puppet here,
Played off the young frank personable priest;
Sworn fast and tonsured plain heaven's celibate,
And yet earth's clear-accepted servitor,
1025 A courtly spiritual Cupid, squire of dames
By law of love and mandate of the mode.
The Church's own, or why parade her seal,[2]
Wherefore that chrism[3] and consecrative work?
Yet verily the world's, or why go badged
1030 A prince of sonneteers and lutanists,
Show colour of each vanity in vogue
Borne with decorum due on blameless breast?
All that is changed now, as he tells the court
How he had played the part excepted at;[4]
1035 Tells it, moreover, now the second time:
Since, for his cause of scandal, his own share
I' the flight from home and husband of the wife,
He has been censured, punished in a sort
By relegation,—exile, we should say,
1040 To a short distance for a little time,—
Whence he is summoned on a sudden now,
Informed that she, he thought to save, is lost,
And, in a breath, bidden re-tell his tale,

Since the first telling somehow missed effect,
1045 And then advise in the matter. There stands he,
While the same grim black-panelled chamber
    blinks
As though rubbed shiny with the sins of Rome
Told the same oak for ages—wave-washed wall
Whereto has set a sea of wickedness.
1050 There, where you yesterday heard Guido speak,
Speaks Caponsacchi; and there face him too
Tommati, Venturini and the rest
Who, eight months earlier, scarce repressed the
    smile,
Forewent the wink; waived recognition so
1055 Of peccadillos incident to youth,
Especially youth high-born; for youth means love,
Vows can't change nature, priests are only men,
And love needs stratagem and subterfuge:
Which age, that once was youth, should recognize,
1060 May blame, but needs not press too hard against.
Here sit the old Judges then, but with no grace
Of reverend carriage, magisterial port.
For why? The accused of eight months since,—the
    same
Who cut the conscious figure of a fool,
1065 Changed countenance, dropped bashful gaze to
    ground,
While hesitating for an answer then,—
Now is grown judge himself, terrifies now
This, now the other culprit called a judge,
Whose turn it is to stammer and look strange,
1070 As he speaks rapidly, angrily, speech that smites:
And they keep silence, bear blow after blow,
Because the seeming solitary man,
Speaking for God, may have an audience too,
Invisible, no discreet judge provokes.
1075 How the priest Caponsacchi said his say.

Then a soul sighs its lowest and its last
After the loud ones,—so much breath remains
Unused by the four-days'-dying; for she lived
Thus long, miraculously long, 't was thought,

---

[1] combination of two roles.

[2] insignia.

[3] consecrated oil.

[4] objected to.

1080 Just that Pompilia might defend herself.
How, while the hireling and the alien[1] stoop,
Comfort, yet question,—since the time is brief,
And folk, allowably inquisitive,
Encircle the low pallet where she lies
1085 In the good house that helps the poor to die,—
Pompilia tells the story of her life.
For friend and lover,—leech and man of law
Do service; busy helpful ministrants
As varied in their calling as their mind,
1090 Temper and age: and yet from all of these,
About the white bed under the arched roof,
Is somehow, as it were, evolved a one,—
Small separate sympathies combined and large,
Nothings that were, grown something very much:
1095 As if the bystanders gave each his straw,
All he had, though a trifle in itself,
Which, plaited all together, made a Cross
Fit to die looking on and praying with,
Just as well as if ivory or gold.
1100 So, to the common kindliness she speaks,
There being scarce more privacy at the last
For mind than body: but she is used to bear,
And only unused to the brotherly look.
How she endeavoured to explain her life.

1105 Then, since a Trial ensued, a touch o' the same
To sober us, flustered with frothy talk,
And teach our common sense its helplessness.
For why deal simply with divining-rod,
Scrape where we fancy secret sources flow,
1110 And ignore law, the recognized machine,
Elaborate display of pipe and wheel
Framed to unchoak, pump up and pour apace
Truth in a flowery foam shall wash the world?
The patent truth-extracting process,—ha?
1115 Let us make all that mystery turn one wheel,
Give you a single grind of law at least!

One orator, of two on either side,[2]
Shall teach us the puissance of the tongue
—That is, o' the pen which simulated tongue
1120 On paper and saved all except the sound
Which never was. Law's speech beside law's
        thought?
That were too stunning, too immense an odds:
That point of vantage, law let nobly pass.
One lawyer shall admit us to behold
1125 The manner of the making out a case,
First fashion of a speech; the chick in egg,
And masterpiece law's bosom incubates.
How Don Giacinto of the Arcangeli,
Called Procurator of the Poor at Rome,
1130 Now advocate for Guido and his mates,—
The jolly learned man of middle age,
Cheek and jowl all in laps with fat and law,
Mirthful as mighty, yet, as great hearts use,[3]
Despite the name and fame that tempt our flesh,
1135 Constant to that devotion of the hearth,
Still captive in those dear domestic ties!—
How he,—having a cause to triumph with,
All kind of interests to keep intact,
More than one efficacious[4] personage
1140 To tranquillize, conciliate and secure,
And above all, public anxiety
To quiet, show its Guido in good hands,—
Also, as if such burdens were too light,
A certain family-feast to claim his care,
1145 The birthday-banquet for the only son—
Paternity at smiling strife with law—
How he brings both to buckle in one bond;
And, thick at throat, with waterish under-eye,
Turns to his task and settles in his seat
1150 And puts his utmost means to practice now:
Wheezes out law and whiffles Latin forth,
And, just as though roast lamb would never be,

---

[1] stranger.

[2] On each side of a Roman lawsuit were two lawyers of equal status.

[3] are accustomed.

[4] influential.

Makes logic levigate[1] the big crime small:
Rubs palm on palm, rakes foot with itchy foot,
1155 Conceives and inchoates[2] the argument,
Sprinkling each flower appropriate to the time,
—Ovidian quip or Ciceronian crank,[3]
A-bubble in the larynx while he laughs,
As he had fritters deep down frying there.
1160 How he turns, twists, and tries the oily thing
Shall be—first speech for Guido 'gainst the Fisc.

Then with a skip as it were from heel to head,
Leaving yourselves fill up the middle bulk
O' the Trial, reconstruct its shape august,
1165 From such exordium[4] clap we to the close;
Give you, if we dare wing to such a height,
The absolute glory in some full-grown speech
On the other side, some finished butterfly,
Some breathing diamond-flake with leaf-gold fans,
1170 That takes the air, no trace of worm it was,
Or cabbage-bed it had production from.
Giovambattista o' the Bottini, Fisc,
Pompilia's patron by the chance of the hour,
To-morrow her persecutor,—composite, he,
1175 As becomes who must meet such various calls—
Odds of age joined in him with ends of youth.
A man of ready smile and facile tear,
Improvised hopes, despairs at nod and beck,
And language,—ah, the gift of eloquence!
1180 Language that goes as easy as a glove
O'er good and evil, smoothens both to one.
Rashness helps caution with him, fires the straw,
In free enthusiastic careless fit,
On the first proper pinnacle of rock
1185 Which happens, as reward for all that zeal,
To lure some bark to founder and bring gain:
While calm sits Caution, rapt with heavenward eye,

A true confessor's gaze amid the glare,
Beaconing to the breaker, death and hell.
1190 "Well done, thou good and faithful!" she approves:
"Hadst thou let slip a faggot to the beach,
The crew had surely spied thy precipice
And saved their boat; the simple and the slow,
Who should have prompt forestalled the wrecker's
    fee:
1195 Let the next crew be wise and hail in time!"
Just so compounded is the outside man,
Blue juvenile pure eye and pippin cheek,
And brow all prematurely soiled and seamed
With sudden age, bright devastated hair.
1200 Ah, but you miss the very tones o' the voice,
The scrannel[5] pipe that screams in heights of head,
As, in his modest studio, all alone,
The tall wight stands a-tiptoe, strives and strains,
Both eyes shut, like the cockerel that would crow,
1205 Tries to his own self amorously o'er
What never will be uttered else than so—
To the four walls, for Forum and Mars' Hill,[6]
Speaks out the poesy which, penned, turns prose.
Clavecinist[7] debarred his instrument,
1210 He yet thrums—shirking neither turn nor trill,
With desperate finger on dumb table-edge—
The sovereign rondo, shall conclude his *Suite*,
Charm an imaginary audience there,
From old Corelli to young Handel, both
1215 I' the flesh at Rome, ere he perforce go print
The cold black score, mere music for the mind—
The last speech against Guido and his gang,
With special end to prove Pompilia pure.
How the Fisc vindicates Pompilia's fame.

1220 Then comes the all but end, the ultimate
Judgment save yours. Pope Innocent the Twelfth,
Simple, sagacious, mild yet resolute,

---

[1] reduce to powder.

[2] develops.

[3] fantastic figure of speech.

[4] introduction.

[5] shrill.

[6] the Roman and Athenian assembly places.

[7] performer on the clavecin, precursor of the piano.

With prudence, probity and—what beside
From the other world he feels impress at times,
1225 Having attained to fourscore years and six,—
How, when the court found Guido and the rest
Guilty, but law supplied a subterfuge
And passed the final sentence to the Pope,
He, bringing his intelligence to bear
1230 This last time on what ball behoves him drop
In the urn, or white or black, does drop a black,
Send five souls more to just precede his own,
Stand him in stead and witness, if need were,
How he is wont to do God's work on earth.
1235 The manner of his sitting out the dim
Droop of a sombre February day
In the plain closet where he does such work,
With, from all Peter's treasury, one stool,
One table and one lathen[1] crucifix.
1240 There sits the Pope, his thoughts for company;
Grave but not sad,—nay, something like a cheer
Leaves the lips free to be benevolent,
Which, all day long, did duty firm and fast.
A cherishing there is of foot and knee,
1245 A chafing loose-skinned large-veined hand with
      hand,—
What steward but knows when stewardship earns
      its wage,
May levy praise, anticipate the lord?
He reads, notes, lays the papers down at last,
Muses, then takes a turn about the room;
1250 Unclasps a huge tome in an antique guise,
Primitive print and tongue half obsolete,
That stands him in diurnal[2] stead; opes page,
Finds place where falls the passage to be conned
According to an order long in use:
1255 And, as he comes upon the evening's chance,
Starts somewhat, solemnizes straight his smile,
Then reads aloud that portion first to last,
And at the end lets flow his own thoughts forth

Likewise aloud, for respite and relief,
1260 Till by the dreary relics of the west
Wan through the half-moon window, all his light,
He bows the head while the lips move in prayer,
Writes some three brief lines, signs and seals the
      same,
Tinkles a hand-bell, bids the obsequious Sir
1265 Who puts foot presently o' the closet-sill
He watched outside of, bear as superscribed
That mandate to the Governor forthwith:
Then heaves abroad his cares in one good sigh,
Traverses corridor with no arm's help,
1270 And so to sup as a clear conscience should.
The manner of the judgement of the Pope.

Then must speak Guido yet a second time,
Satan's old saw being apt here—skin for skin,
All a man hath that will he give for life.
1275 While life was graspable and gainable, free
To bird-like buzz her wings round Guido's brow,
Not much truth stiffened out the web of words
He wove to catch her: when away she flew
And death came, death's breath rivelled[3] up the lies,
1280 Left bare the metal thread, the fibre fine
Of truth, i' the spinning: the true words come last.
How Guido, to another purpose quite,
Speaks and despairs, the last night of his life,
In that New Prison by Castle Angelo
1285 At the bridge-foot: the same man, another voice.
On a stone bench in a close fetid cell,
Where the hot vapour of an agony,
Struck into drops on the cold wall, runs down
Horrible worms made out of sweat and tears—
1290 There crouch, well nigh to the knees in dungeon-
      straw,
Lit by the sole lamp suffered for their sake,
Two awe-struck figures, this a Cardinal,
That an Abate, both of old styled friends
Of the part-man part-monster in the midst,

---

[1] made of "latten," an alloy containing brass or bronze.

[2] daily.

[3] shrivelled.

1295 So changed is Franceschini's gentle blood.
The tiger-cat screams now, that whined before,
That pried and tried and trod so gingerly,
Till in its silkiness the trap-teeth join;
Then you know how the bristling fury foams.
1300 They listen, this wrapped in his folds of red,
While his feet fumble for the filth below;
The other, as beseems a stouter heart,
Working his best with beads and cross to ban
The enemy that comes in like a flood
1305 Spite of the standard[1] set up, verily
And in no trope[2] at all, against him there:
For at the prison-gate, just a few steps
Outside, already, in the doubtful dawn,
Thither, from this side and from that, slow sweep
1310 And settle down in silence solidly,
Crow-wise, the frightful Brotherhood of Death.
Black-hatted and black-hooded huddle they,
Black rosaries a-dangling from each waist;
So take they their grim station at the door,
1315 Torches alight and cross-bones-banner spread,
And that gigantic Christ with open arms,
Grounded. Nor lacks there aught but that the
    group
Break forth, intone the lamentable psalm,
"Out of the deeps, Lord, have I cried to thee!"—
1320 When inside, from the true profound, a sign
Shall bear intelligence that the foe is foiled,
Count Guido Franceschini has confessed,
And is absolved and reconciled with God.
Then they, intoning, may begin their march,
1325 Make by the longest way for the People's Square,
Carry the criminal to his crime's award:
A mob to cleave, a scaffolding to reach,
Two gallows and Mannaia[3] crowning all.
How Guido made defence a second time.

1330 Finally, even as thus by step and step
I led you from the level of to-day
Up to the summit of so long ago,
Here, whence I point you the wide prospect
    round—[4]
Let me, by like steps, slope you back to smooth,
1335 Land you on mother-earth, no whit the worse,
To feed o' the fat o' the furrow: free to dwell,
Taste our time's better things profusely spread
For all who love the level, corn and wine,
Much cattle and the many-folded fleece.
1340 Shall not my friends go feast again on sward,
Though cognizant of country in the clouds
Higher than wistful eagle's horny eye
Ever unclosed for, 'mid ancestral crags,
When morning broke and Spring was back once
    more,
1345 And he died, heaven, save by his heart, unreached?
Yet heaven my fancy lifts to, ladder-like,—
As Jack reached, holpen of his beanstalk-rungs!

A novel country: I might make it mine
By choosing which one aspect of the year
1350 Suited mood best, and putting solely that
On panel somewhere in the House of Fame,[5]
Landscaping[6] what I saved, not what I saw:
—Might fix you, whether frost in goblin-time
Startled the moon with his abrupt bright laugh,
1355 Or, August's hair afloat in filmy fire,
She fell, arms wide, face foremost on the world,
Swooned there and so singed out the strength of
    things.
Thus were abolished Spring and Autumn both,
The land dwarfed to one likeness of the land,
1360 Life cramped corpse-fashion. Rather learn and love
Each facet-flash of the revolving year!—
Red, green and blue that whirl into a white,

---

[1] crucifix.

[2] figure of speech.

[3] guillotine.

[4] the lay of the land.

[5] Chaucer's *House of Fame*. See the "eagle" in l. 1342.

[6] portraying.

The variance now, the eventual unity,
Which make the miracle. See it for yourselves,
1365 This man's act, changeable because alive!
Action now shrouds, now shows the informing
    thought;
Man, like a glass ball with a spark a-top,
Out of the magic fire that lurks inside,
Shows one tint at a time to take the eye:
1370 Which, let a finger touch the silent sleep,
Shifted a hair's-breadth shoots you dark for bright,
Suffuses bright with dark, and baffles so
Your sentence absolute for shine or shade.[1]
Once set such orbs,—white styled, black
    stigmatized,—
1375 A-rolling, see them once on the other side
Your good men and your bad men every one,
From Guido Franceschini to Guy Faux,[2]
Oft would you rub your eyes and change your
    names.

Such, British Public, ye who like me not,
1380 (God love you!)—whom I yet have laboured for,
Perchance more careful whoso runs may read
Than erst when all, it seemed, could read who
    ran,—
Perchance more careless[3] whoso reads may praise
Than late when he who praised and read and wrote
1385 Was apt to find himself the self-same me,—
Such labour had such issue, so I wrought
This arc, by furtherance of such alloy,
And so, by one spirt, take away its trace
Till, justifiably golden, rounds my ring.

1390 A ring without a posy, and that ring mine?

O lyric Love,[4] half-angel and half-bird
And all a wonder and a wild desire,—
Boldest of hearts that ever braved the sun,
Took sanctuary within the holier blue,
1395 And sang a kindred soul out to his face,—
Yet human at the red-ripe of the heart—[5]
When the first summons from the darkling earth
Reached thee amid thy chambers, blanched their
    blue,
And bared them of the glory—to drop down,
1400 To toil for man, to suffer or to die,—
This is the same voice: can thy soul know change?
Hail then, and hearken from the realms of help!
Never may I commence my song, my due
To God who best taught song by gift of thee,
1405 Except with bent head and beseeching hand—
That still, despite the distance and the dark,
What was, again may be; some interchange
Of grace, some splendour once thy very thought,
Some benediction anciently thy smile:
1410 —Never conclude, but raising hand and head
Thither where eyes, that cannot reach, yet yearn
For all hope, all sustainment, all reward,
Their utmost up and on,—so blessing back
In those thy realms of help, that heaven thy home,
1415 Some whiteness which, I judge, thy face makes
    proud,
Some wanness where, I think, thy foot may fall!
—1868

---

[1] ll. 1367–75: reference to an "electric egg," an instrument used to show the effect of an electric discharge in a glass vessel partially exhausted of air.

[2] instigator of the Gunpowder Plot against James I and Parliament in 1605.

[3] caring less.

[4] an invocation to Browning's "muse," Elizabeth Barrett Browning.

[5] heart of the pomegranate.

Count Guido Franceschini: Book V [1]

Thanks, Sir, but, should it please the reverend
　　Court,
I feel I can stand somehow, half sit down
Without help, make shift to even speak, you see,
Fortified by the sip of…why, 't is wine,
5　Velletri,—and not vinegar and gall,[2]
So changed and good the times grow! Thanks, kind
　　Sir!
Oh, but one sip's enough! I want my head
To save my neck, there's work awaits me still.
How cautious and considerate…aie, aie, aie,
10　Not your fault, sweet Sir! Come, you take to heart
An ordinary matter. Law is law.
Noblemen were exempt, the vulgar thought,
From racking, but, since law thinks otherwise,
I have been put to the rack: all's over now,
15　And neither wrist—what men style, out of joint:
If any harm be, 't is the shoulder-blade,
The left one, that seems wrong i' the socket,—Sirs,
Much could not happen, I was quick to faint,
Being past my prime of life, and out of health.
20　In short I thank you,—yes, and mean the word.
Needs must the Court be slow to understand
How this quite novel form of taking pain,
This getting tortured merely in the flesh,
Amounts to almost an agreeable change
25　In my case, me fastidious, plied too much
With opposite treatment, used (forgive the joke)
To the rasp-tooth toying with this brain of mine,
And, in and out my heart, the play o' the probe.
Four years have I been operated on
30　I' the soul, do you see—its tense or tremulous
　　　　part—

My self-respect, my care for a good name,
Pride in an old one, love of kindred—just
A mother, brothers, sisters, and the like,
That looked up to my face when days were dim,
35　And fancied they found light there—no one spot,
Foppishly sensitive, but has paid its pang.
That, and not this you now oblige me with,
That was the Vigil-torment,[3] if you please!
The poor old noble House that drew the rags
40　O' the Franceschini's once superb array
Close round her, hoped to slink unchallenged by,—
Pluck off these! Turn the drapery inside out
And teach the tittering town how scarlet wears!
Show men the lucklessness, the improvidence
45　Of the easy-natured Count before this Court,
The father I have some slight feeling for,
Who let the world slide, nor foresaw that friends
Then proud to cap and kiss the patron's shoe,
Would, when the purse he left held spider-webs,
50　Properly push his child to wall one day!
Mimic the tetchy humour, furtive glance
And brow where half was furious half fatigued,
O' the same son got to be of middle age,
Sour, saturnine,—your humble servant here,—
55　When things go cross and the young wife, he finds
Take to the window at a whistle's bid,
And yet demurs thereon, preposterous fool!—
Whereat the worthies judge he wants advice
And beg to civilly ask what's evil here,
60　Perhaps remonstrate on the habit they deem
He's given unduly to, of beating her
…Oh, sure he beats her—why says John so else,
Who is cousin to George who is sib[4] to Tecla's self
Who cooks the meal and combs the lady's hair?
65　What? 'T is my wrist you merely dislocate
For the future when you mean me martyrdom?
—Let the old mother's economy alone,
How the brocade-strips saved o' the seamy side

---

[1] The time is probably the third day after the murders, although the evidence is conflicting. It should also be noted that at l. 936 Guido speaks of Pompilia as having already died, but at 1687 he says she is still living. She did, in fact, die four days after his attack.

[2] Matthew 27:34, 38.

[3] See note 3, p. 435.

[4] busy-bodies, sometimes with a family relationship.

O' the wedding-gown buy raiment for a year?
70 —How she can dress and dish up—lordly dish
Fit for a duke, lamb's head and purtenance—[1]
With her proud hands, feast household so a week?
No word o' the wine rejoicing God and man
The less when three-parts water? Then, I say,
75 A trifle of torture to the flesh, like yours,
While soul is spared such foretaste of hell-fire,
Is naught. But I curtail the catalogue
Through policy,[2]—a rhetorician's trick,—
Because I would reserve some choicer points
80 O' the practice, more exactly parallel—
(Having an eye to climax) with what gift,
Eventual grace the Court may have in store
I' the way of plague—my crown of punishments.
When I am hanged or headed, time enough
85 To prove the tenderness of only that,
Mere heading, hanging,—not their counterpart,
Not demonstration public and precise
That I, having married the mongrel of a drab,
Am bound to grant that mongrel-brat, my wife,
90 Her mother's birthright-licence as is just,—
Let her sleep undisturbed, i' the family style,
Her sleep out in the embraces of a priest,
Nor disallow their bastard as my heir!
Your sole mistake,—dare I submit so much
95 To the reverend Court?—has been in all this pains
To make a stone roll down hill,—rack and wrench
And rend a man to pieces, all for what?
Why—make him ope mouth in his own defence,
Show cause for what he has done, the irregular deed,
100 (Since that he did it, scarce dispute can be)
And clear his fame a little, beside the luck
Of stopping even yet, if possible,
Discomfort to his flesh from noose or axe—
For that, out come the implements of law!
105 May it content my lords the gracious Court
To listen only half so patient-long

As I will in that sense profusely speak,
And—fie, they shall not call in screws to help!
I killed Pompilia Franceschini, Sirs;
110 Killed too the Comparini, husband, wife,
Who called themselves, by a notorious lie,
Her father and her mother to ruin me.
There's the irregular deed: you want no more
Than right interpretation of the same,
115 And truth so far—am I to understand?
To that then, with convenient speed,—because
Now I consider,—yes, despite my boast,
There is an ailing in this omoplat[3]
May clip my speech all too abruptly close,
120 Whatever the good-will in me. Now for truth!

I' the name of the indivisible Trinity!
Will my lords, in the plentitude of their light,
Weigh well that all this trouble has come on me
Through my persistent treading in the paths
125 Where I was trained to go,—wearing that yoke
My shoulder was predestined to receive,
Born to the hereditary stoop and crease?[4]
Noble, I recognized my nobler still,
The Church, my suzerain; no mock-mistress, she;
130 The secular owned the spiritual: mates of mine
Have thrown their careless hoofs up at her call
"Forsake the clover and come drag my wain!"
There they go cropping: I protruded nose
To halter, bent my back of docile beast,[5]
135 And now am whealed,[6] one wide wound all of me,
For being found at the eleventh hour o' the day
Padding the mill-track, not neck-deep in grass:
—My one fault, I am stiffened by my work,
—My one reward, I help the Court to smile!

---

[1] Exodus 12:9.

[2] shrewdness, calculation.

[3] shoulderblade.

[4] wrinkle, or possibly the furrow worn by the yoke.

[5] At the end of the preceding book Guido was portrayed as a maddened bull.

[6] flogged.

140 I am representative of a great line,
One of the first of the old families
In Arezzo, ancientest of Tuscan towns.
When my worst foe is fain to challenge this,
His worst exception runs—not first in rank
145 But second, noble in the next degree
Only; not malice 'self maligns me more.
So, my lord opposite has composed, we know,
A marvel of a book, sustains the point
That Francis boasts the primacy 'mid saints;
150 Yet not inaptly hath his argument
Obtained response from yon my other lord
In thesis published with the world's applause
—Rather 't is Dominic such post befits:
Why, at the worst, Francis stays Francis still,
155 Second in rank to Dominic it may be,
Still, very saintly, very like our Lord;[1]
And I at least descend from Guido once
Homager to the Empire,[2] nought below—
Of which account as proof that, none o' the line
160 Having a single gift beyond brave blood,
Or able to do aught but give, give, give
In blood and brain, in house and land and cash,
Not get and garner as the vulgar may,
We became poor as Francis or our Lord.
165 Be that as it likes you, Sirs,—whenever it chanced
Myself grew capable anyway of remark,
(Which was soon—penury makes wit premature)
This struck me, I was poor who should be rich
Or pay that fault[3] to the world which trifles not
170 When lineage lacks the flag yet lifts the pole:
Therefore I must make move forthwith, transfer
My stranded self, born fish with gill and fin
Fit for the deep sea, now left flap bare-backed
In slush and sand, a show to crawlers vile
175 Reared of the low-tide and aright therein.

The enviable youth with the old name,
Wide chest, stout arms, sound brown and
   pricking[4] veins,
A heartful of desire, man's natural load,
A brainful of belief, the noble's lot,—
180 All this life, cramped and gasping, high and dry
I' the wave's retreat,—the misery, good my lords,
Which made you merriment at Rome of late,—
It made me reason, rather—muse, demand
—Why our bare dropping palace, in the street
185 Where such-an-one whose grandfather sold tripe
Was adding to his purchased pile a fourth
Tall tower,[5] could hardly show a turret sound?
Why Countess Beatrice, whose son I am,
Cowered in the wintertime as she spun flax,
190 Blew on the earthen basket of live ash,
Instead of jaunting forth in coach and six
Like such-another widow who ne'er was wed?
I asked my fellows, how came this about?
"Why, Jack, the suttler's[6] child, perhaps the camp's,
195 Went to the wars, fought sturdily, took a town
And got rewarded as was natural.
She of the coach and six—excuse me there!
Why, do n't you know the story of her friend?
A clown dressed vines on somebody's estate,
200 His boy recoiled from muck, liked Latin more,
Stuck to his pen and got to be a priest,
Till one day…do n't you mind that telling tract
Against Molinos, the old Cardinal wrote?
He penned and dropped it in the patron's desk
205 Who, deep in thought and absent much of mind,
Licensed the thing, allowed it for his own;
Quick came promotion,—*suum cuique*,[7] Count!
Oh, he can pay for coach and six, be sure!"
"—Well, let me go, do likewise: war's the word—

---

[1] an allusion to the rivalry between the two religious orders of Franciscans and Dominicans.

[2] holder of an estate under the (Holy Roman) Emperor.

[3] pay for being poor.

[4] tingling with life.

[5] In Renaissance Tuscany, tall towers continued to be built as status symbols long after their military usefulness had ended.

[6] peddler trading with the army.

[7] "to each his own": Tacitus, *Annals* 4.35.4.

210 That way the Franceschini worked at first,
I'll take my turn, try soldiership."—"What, you?
The eldest son and heir and prop o' the house,
So do you see your duty? Here's your post,
Hard by the hearth and altar. (Roam from roof,
215 This youngster, play the gypsy out of doors,
And who keeps kith and kin that fall on us?)
Stand fast, stick tight, conserve your gods at home!"
"—Well then, the quiet course, the contrary trade!
We had cousin amongst us once was Pope,
220 And minor glories manifold. Try the Church,
The tonsure, and,—since heresy's but half-slain
Even by the Cardinal's tract he thought he wrote,—
Have at Molinos!"—"Have at a fool's head!
You a priest? How were marriage possible?
225 There must be Franceschini till time ends—
That's your vocation. Make your brothers priests,
Paul shall be porporate,[1] and Girolamo step
Red-stockinged[2] in the presence when you choose,
But save one Franceschini for the age!
230 Be not the vine but dig and dung its root,
Be not a priest but gird up priesthood's loins,
With one foot in Arezzo stride to Rome,
Spend yourself there and bring the purchase back!
Go hence to Rome, be guided!"

235   So I was.
I turned alike from the hill-side zig-zag thread
Of way to the table-land a soldier takes,
Alike from the low-lying pasture-place
Where churchmen graze, recline and ruminate,
240 —Ventured to mount no platform like my lords
Who judge the world, bear brain I dare not brag—
But stationed me, might thus the expression serve
As who should fetch and carry, come and go,
Meddle and make i' the cause my lords love most—
245 The public weal, which hangs to the law, which
holds

By the Church, which happens to be through God
himself.
Humbly I helped the Church till here I stand,—
Or would stand but for the omoplat, you see!
Bidden qualify for Rome, I, having a field,
250 Went, sold, it, laid the sum at Peter's foot:[3]
Which means—I settled home-accounts with speed,
Set apart just a modicum should suffice
To keep the villa's head above the waves
Of weed inundating its oil and wine,
255 And prop roof, stanchion[4] wall o' the palace so
It should keep breath i' the body, hold its own
Amid the advance of neighbouring loftiness—
(People like building where they used to beg)—
Till succoured one day,—shared the residue
260 Between my mother and brothers and sisters there,
Black-eyed babe Donna This and Donna That,
As near to starving as might decently be,
—Left myself journey-charges, change of suit,
A purse to put i' the pocket of the Groom
265 O' the Chamber of the patron, and a glove
With a ring to it for the digits of the niece
Sure to be helpful in his household,—then
Started for Rome, and led the life prescribed.
Close to the Church, though clean of it, I assumed
270 Three or four orders of no consequence,
—They cast out evil spirits and exorcise,
For example; bind a man to nothing more,
Give clerical savour to his layman's-salt,
Facilitate his claim to loaf and fish
275 Should miracle leave, beyond what feeds the flock,
Fragments to brim the basket of a friend—
While, for the world's sake, I rode, danced and
gamed,
Quitted[5] me like a courtier, measured mine

_____

[1] a wearer of cardinal's purple.

[2] in cardinal's stockings.

[3] "And Joses, who by the apostles was named Barnabas,…having land, sold it, and brought the money, and laid it at the apostles' feet": Acts 4: 36–7.

[4] "Prop" and "stanchion" are synonymous.

[5] behaved.

With whatsoever blade had fame in fence,
280 —Ready to let the basket go its round
Even though my turn was come to help myself,
Should Dives[1] count on me at dinner-time
As just the understander of a joke
And not immoderate in repartee.
285 *Utrique sic paratus*,[2] Sirs, I said
"Here," (in the fortitude of years fifteen,
So good a pedagogue is penury)
"Here wait, do service,—serving and to serve!
And, in due time, I nowise doubt at all,
290 The recognition of my service comes.
Next year I'm only sixteen. I can wait."

I waited thirty years, may it please the Court:
Saw meanwhile many a denizen o' the dung
Hop, skip, jump o'er my shoulder, make him wings
295 And fly aloft,—succeed, in the usual phrase.
Everyone soon or late comes round by Rome:
Stand still here, you'll see all in turn succeed.
Why, look you, so and so the physician here,
My father's lacquey's son we sent to school,
300 Doctored and dosed this Eminence and that,
Salved the last Pope his certain obstinate sore,
Soon bought land as became him, names it now:
I grasp bell at his griffin-guarded gate,[3]
Traverse the half-mile avenue,—a term,[4]
305 A cypress, and a statue, three and three,—
Deliver message from my Monsignor,
With varletry[5] at lounge i' the vestibule
I'm barred from, who bear mud upon my shoe.
My father's chaplain's nephew, Chamberlain,—
310 Nothing less, please you!—courteous all the same,

—He does not see me though I wait an hour
At his staircase-landing 'twixt the brace of busts,
A noseless Sylla, Marius[6] maimed to match,
My father gave him for a hexastich[7]
315 Made on my birth-day,—but he sends me down,
To make amends, that relic I prize most—
The unburnt end o' the very candle, Sirs,
Purfled[8] with paint so prettily round and round,
He carried in such state last Peter's-day,—
320 In token I, his gentleman and squire,
Had held the bridle, walked his managed mule
Without a tittup[9] the procession through.
Nay, the official,—one you know, sweet lords!—
Who drew the warrant for my transfer late
325 To the New Prisons from Tordinona,—he
Graciously had remembrance—"Francesc...ha?
His sire, now—how a thing shall come about!—
Paid me a dozen florins[10] above the fee,
For drawing deftly up a deed of sale
330 When troubles fell so thick on him, good heart,
And I was prompt and pushing! By all means!
At the New Prisons be it his son shall lie,—
Anything for an old friend!" and thereat
Signed name with triple flourish underneath.
335 These were my fellows, such their fortunes now,
While I—kept fasts and feasts innumerable,
Matins and vespers, functions to no end
I' the train of Monsignor and Eminence,
As gentleman-squire, and for my zeal's reward
340 Have rarely missed a place at the table-foot
Except when some Ambassador, or such like,
Brought his own people. Brief, one day I felt
The tick of time inside me, turning-point
And slight sense there was now enough of this:

---

[1] the rich man in Christ's parable: Luke 16.

[2] prepared for either event.

[3] guarded by statues of griffins, Greek mythological animals with the head and wings of an angel and the body of a lion.

[4] pillar surmounted by a sculptured head or bust, originally that of Terminus, god of boundaries.

[5] rabble, menials.

[6] Lucius Sulla (137–78 BC) and Gaius Marius (157–86 BC) were rival Roman generals and dictators.

[7] six-line epigram.

[8] fringed.

[9] frisk, prance.

[10] gold Florentine coins.

345 That I was near my seventh climacteric,[1]
Hard upon, if not over, the middle life,
And, although fed by the east-wind, fulsome-fine[2]
With foretaste of the Land of Promise, still
My gorge[3] gave symptom it might play me false;
350 Better not press it further,—be content
With living and dying only a nobleman,
Who merely had a father great and rich,
Who simply had one greater and richer yet,
And so on back and back till first and best
355 Began i' the night; I finish in the day.
"The mother must be getting old," I said;
"The sisters are well wedded away, our name
Can manage to pass a sister off, at need,
And do for dowry: both my brothers thrive—
360 Regular priests they are, nor, bat-like, 'bide
'Twixt flesh and fowl with neither privilege.
My spare revenue must keep me and mine.
I am tired: Arezzo's air is good to breathe;
Vittiano,—one limes[4] flocks of thrushes there;
365 A leathern coat costs little and lasts long:
Let me bid hope good-bye, content at home!"
Thus, one day, I disbosomed me and bowed.
Whereat began the little buzz and thrill
O' the gazers round me; each face brightened up:
370 As when at your Casino, deep in dawn,
A gamester says at last, "I play no more,
Forego gain, acquiesce in loss, withdraw
Anyhow:" and the watchers of his ways,
A trifle struck compunctious at the word,
375 Yet sensible of relief, breathe free once more,
Break up the ring, venture polite advice—
"How, Sir? So scant of heart and hope indeed?
Retire with neither cross nor pile[5] from play?—

So incurious, so short-casting?[6]—give your chance
380 To a younger, stronger, bolder spirit belike,
Just when luck turns and the fine throw sweeps all?"
Such was the chorus: and its goodwill meant—
"See that the loser leave door handsomely!
There's an ill look,—it's sinister, spoils sport,
385 When an old bruised and battered year-by-year
Fighter with fortune, not a penny in poke,
Reels down the steps of our establishment
And staggers on broad daylight and the world,
In shagrag[7] beard and doleful doublet, drops
390 And breaks his heart on the outside: people prate
'Such is the profit of a trip upstairs!'
Contrive he sidle forth, baulked[8] of the blow
Best dealt by way of moral, bidding down
No curse but blessings rather on our heads
395 For some poor prize he bears at tattered breast,
Some palpable sort of kind of good to set
Over and against the grievance: give him quick!"
Whereon protested Paul, "Go hang yourselves!
Leave him to me. Count Guido and brother of
        mine,
400 A word in your ear! Take courage since faint heart
Ne'er won…aha, fair lady, do n't men say?
There's a *sors*, there's a right Virgilian dip![9]
Do you see the happiness o' the hint? At worst,
If the Church want no more of you, the Court
405 No more, and the Camp as little, the ingrates,—
        come,
Count you are counted:[10] still you've coat to back,
Not cloth of gold and tissue, as we hoped,
But cloth with sparks and spangles on its frieze[11]

---

[1] the age of forty-nine.

[2] fed to satiety.

[3] stomach.

[4] catches by spreading a sticky substance on twigs.

[5] the two sides of a coin, therefore penniless.

[6] cautious.

[7] shaggy, unkempt.

[8] spared.

[9] the Roman habit of opening a copy of Virgil at random in the expectation of lighting upon a particularly appropriate and helpful passage.

[10] accounted, known.

[11] coarse, shaggy woollen fabric.

From Camp, Court, Church, enough to make a
    shine,
410 Entitle you to carry home a wife
With the proper dowry, let the worst betide!
Why, it was just a wife you meant to take!"

Now, Paul's advice was weighty: priests should
    know:
And Paul apprised me, ere the week was out,
415 That Pietro and Violante, the easy pair,
The cits enough, with stomach[1] to be more,
Had just the daughter and exact the sum
To truck[2] for the quality of myself: "She's young,
Pretty and rich: you're noble, classic, choice.
420 Is it to match?" "A match," said I.
Done! He proposed all, I accepted all,
And we performed all. So I said and did
Simply. As simply followed, not at first
But with the outbreak of misfortune, still
425 One comment on the saying and doing—"What?
No blush at the avowal you dared buy
A girl of age beseems your granddaughter,
Like ox or ass? Are flesh and blood a ware?
Are heart and soul a chattel?"
430   Softly, Sirs!
Will the Court of its charity teach poor me
Anxious to learn, of any way i' the world,
Allowed by custom and convenience, save
This same which, taught from my youth up, I trod?
435 Take me along with you; where was the wrong step?
If what I gave in barter, style and state
And all that hangs to Franceschinihood,
Were worthless,—why, society goes to ground,
Its rules are idiot's-rambling. Honour of birth,—
440 If that thing has no value, cannot buy
Something with value of another sort,
You've no reward nor punishment to give
I' the giving or the taking honour; straight

Your social fabric, pinnacle to base,
445 Comes down a-clatter like a house of cards.
Get honour, and keep honour free from flaw,
Aim at still higher honour,—gabble o' the goose!
Go bid a second blockhead like myself
Spend fifty years in guarding bubbles of breath,
450 Soapsuds with air i' the belly, gilded brave,
Guarded and guided, all to break at touch
O' the first young girl's hand and first old fool's
    purse!
All my privation and endurance, all
Love, loyalty and labour dared and did,
455 Fiddle-de-dee!—why, doer and darer both,—
Cound Guido Franceschini had hit the mark
Far better, spent his life with more effect,
As a dancer or a prizer,[3] trades that pay!
On the other hand, bid this buffoonery cease,
460 Admit that honour is a privilege,
The question follows, privilege worth what?
Why, worth the market-price,—now up, now
    down,
Just so with this as with all other ware:
Therefore essay the market, sell your name,
465 Style and condition to who buys them best!
"Does my name purchase," had I dared inquire,
"Your niece, my lord?" there would have been
    rebuff
Though courtesy, your Lordship cannot else—
"Not altogether! Rank for rank may stand:
470 But I have wealth beside, you—poverty;
Your scale flies up there: bid a second bid,
Rank too and wealth too!" Reasoned like yourself!
But was it to you I went with goods to sell?
This time 'twas my scale quietly kissed the ground,
475 Mere rank against mere wealth—some youth
    beside,
Some beauty too, thrown into the bargain, just
As the buyer likes or lets alone. I thought
To deal o' the square: others find fault, it seems:

---

[1] appetite.

[2] exchange.

[3] prizefighter.

The thing is, those my offer most concerned,
480 Pietro, Violante, cried they fair or foul?
What did they make o' the terms? Preposterous
    terms?
Why then accede so promptly, close with such
Nor take a minute to chaffer? Bargain struck,
They straight grew bilious, wished their money
    back,
485 Repented them, no doubt: why, so did I,
So did your Lordship, if town-talk be true,
Of paying a full farm's worth for that piece
By Pietro of Cortona—probably
His scholar Ciro Ferri[1] may have retouched—
490 You caring more for colour than design—
Getting a little tired of cupids too.
That's incident to all the folk who buy!
I am charged, I know, with gilding fact by fraud;
I falsified and fabricated, wrote
495 Myself down roughly richer than I prove,
Rendered a wrong revenue,—grant it all!
Mere grace, mere coquetry[2] such fraud, I say:
A flourish round the figures of a sum
For fashion's sake, that deceives nobody.
500 The veritable back-bone, understood
Essence of this same bargain, blank and bare,
Being the exchange of quality for wealth,—
What may such fancy-flights be? Flecks of oil
Flirted[3] by chapmen[4] where plain dealing grates.
505 I may have dripped a drop—"My name I sell;
Not but that I too boast my wealth"—as they,
"—We bring you riches; still our ancestor
Was hardly the rapscallion, folks saw flogged,
But heir to we know who, were rights of force!"[5]
510 They knew and I knew where the back-bone lurked

I' the writhings of the bargain, lords, believe!
I paid down all engaged for, to a doit,
Delivered them just that which, their life long,
They hungered in the hearts of them to gain—
515 Incorporation with nobility thus
In word and deed: for that they gave me wealth.
But when they came to try their gain, my gift,
Quit Rome and qualify for Arezzo, take
The tone o' the new sphere that absorbed the old,
520 Put away gossip Jack and goody Joan
And go become familiar with the Great,
Greatness to touch and taste and handle now,—
Why, then,—they found that all was vanity,
Vexation, and what Solomon describes!
525 The old abundant city-fare was best,
The kindly warmth o' the commons, the glad clap
Of the equal on the shoulder, the frank grin
Of the underling at all so many spoons
Fire-new at neighbourly treat,—best, best and best
530 Beyond compare!—down to the loll itself
O' the pot-house settle,—better such a bench
Than the stiff crucifixion by my dais
Under the piece-meal damask canopy
With the coroneted coat of arms a-top!
535 Poverty and privation for pride's sake,
All they engaged to easily brave and bear,—
With the fit upon them and their brains a-work,—
Proved unendurable to the sobered sots.
A banished prince, now, will exude a juice
540 And salamander-like[6] support the flame:
He dines on chestnuts, chucks the husks to help
The broil o' the brazier, pays the due baioc,[7]
Goes off light-hearted: his grimace begins
At the funny humours of the christening-feast
545 Of friend the money-lender,—then he's touched
By the flame and frizzles[8] at the babe to kiss!

---

[1] Pietro (1597–1669) was a celebrated baroque painter, Ferri (1634–89) his pupil.

[2] embellishment, window-dressing.

[3] sprinkled.

[4] merchants.

[5] were justice done.

---

[6] a lizard reputed in myth to live in the midst of fire.

[7] a contemporary papal coin of small value.

[8] that is, loses his salamander-like resistance to fire and burns, briskly and crisply.

Here was the converse trial, opposite mind:
Here did a petty nature split on rock
Of vulgar wants predestinate for such—
550 One dish at supper and weak wine to boot!
The prince had grinned and borne: the citizen shrieked,
Summoned the neighbourhood to attest the wrong,
Made noisy protest he was murdered,—stoned
And burned and drowned and hanged,—then broke away,
555 He and his wife, to tell their Rome the rest.
And this you admire, you men o' the world, my lords?
This moves compassion, makes you doubt my faith?
Why, I appeal to…sun and moon? Not I!
Rather to Plautus, Terence, Boccaccio's Book,[1]
560 My townsman, frank Ser Franco's merry Tales,—
To all who strip a vizard from a face,
A body from its padding, and a soul
From froth and ignorance it styles itself,—
If this be other than the daily hap
565 Of purblind[2] greed that dog-like still drops bone,
Grasps shadow, and then howls the case is hard!

So much for them so far: now for myself,
My profit or loss i' the matter: married am I:
Text whereon friendly censors burst to preach.
570 Ay, at Rome even, long ere I was left
To regulate her life for my young bride
Alone at Arezzo, friendliness outbroke
(Sifting my future to predict its fault)
"Purchase and sale being thus so plain a point,
575 How of a certain soul bound up, may-be,
I' the barter with the body and money-bags?
From the bride's soul what is it you expect?"
Why, loyalty and obedience,—wish and will
To settle and suit her fresh and plastic mind

580 To the novel, nor disadvantageous mould!
Father and mother shall the woman leave,
Cleave to the husband, be it for weal or woe:
There is the law: what sets this law aside
In my particular case? My friends submit
585 "Guide, guardian, benefactor,—fee, faw, fum,
The fact is you are forty-five years old,
Nor very comely even for that age:
Girls must have boys." Why, let girls say so then,
Nor call the boys and men, who say the same,
590 Brute this and beast the other as they do!
Come, cards on table! When you chaunt us next
Epithalamium[3] full to overflow
With praise and glory of white womanhood,
The chaste and pure—troll no such lies o'er lip!
595 Put in their stead a crudity or two,
Such short and simple statement of the case
As youth chalks on our walls at spring of year!
No! I shall still think nobler of the sex,
Believe a woman still may take a man
600 For the short period that his soul wears flesh,
And, for the soul's sake, understand the fault
Of armour frayed by fighting. Tush, it tempts
One's tongue too much! I'll say—the law's the law:
With a wife I look to find all wifeliness,
605 As when I buy, timber and twig, a tree—
I buy the song o' the nightingale inside.

Such was the pact: Pompilia from the first
Broke it, refused from the beginning day
Either in body or soul to cleave to mine,
610 And published it forthwith to all the world.
No rupture,—you must join ere you can break,—
Before we had cohabited a month
She found I was a devil and no man,—
Made common cause with those who found as much,
615 Her parents, Pietro and Violante,—moved
Heaven and earth to the rescue of all three.

---

[1] all classics of comedy, with special reference to cheating and disillusionment.

[2] stupid, uncomprehending.

[3] wedding song.

In four months' time, the time o' the parents' stay,
Arezzo was a-ringing, bells in a blaze,
With the unimaginable story rife
620 I' the mouth of man, woman and child—to-wit
My misdemeanour. First the lighter side,
Ludicrous face of things,—how very poor
The Franceschini had become at last,
The meanness and the misery of each shift
625 To save a soldo,[1] stretch and make ends meet.
Next, the more hateful aspect,—how myself
With cruelty beyond Caligula's[2]
Had stripped and beaten, robbed and murdered
     them,
The good old couple, I decoyed, abused,
630 Plundered and then cast out, and happily so,
Since,—in due course the abominable comes,—
Woe worth[3] the poor young wife left lonely here!
Repugnant in my person as my mind,
I sought,—was ever heard of such revenge?
635 —To lure and bind her to so cursed a couch,
Such co-embrace with sulphur, snake and toad,
That she was fain to rush forth, call the stones
O' the common street to save her, not from hate
Of mine merely, but…must I burn my lips
640 With the blister of the lie?…the satyr-love
Of who but my own brother, the young priest,
Too long enforced to lenten fare belike,
Now tempted by the morsel tossed him full
I' the trencher where lay bread and herbs at best.
645 Mark, this yourselves say!—this, none disallows,
Was charged to me by the universal voice
At the instigation of my four-months' wife!—
And then you ask "Such charges so preferred,
(Truly or falsely, here concerns us not)
650 Pricked you to punish now if not before?—
Did not the harshness double itself, the hate
Harden?" I answer "Have it your way and will!"

Say my resentment grew apace: what then?
Do you cry out on the marvel? When I find
655 That pure smooth egg which, laid within my nest,
Could not but hatch a comfort to us all,
Issues a cockatrice[4] for me and mine,
Do you stare to see me stamp on it? Swans are soft:
Is it not clear that she you call my wife,
660 That any wife of any husband, caught
Whetting a sting like this against his breast,—
Speckled with fragments of the fresh-broke shell,
Married a month and making outcry thus,—
Proves a plague-prodigy to God and man?
665 She married: what was it she married for,
Counted upon and meant to meet thereby?
"Love" suggest some one, "love, a little word
Whereof we have not heard one syllable."
So, the Pompilia, child, girl, wife, in one,
670 Wanted the beating pulse, the rolling eye,
The frantic gesture, the devotion due
From Thyrsis[5] to Neaera![6] Guido's love—
Why not provençal roses[7] in his shoe,
Plume to his cap, and trio of guitars
675 At casement, with a bravo[8] close beside?
Good things all these are, clearly claimable
When the fit price is paid the proper way.
Had it been some friend's wife, now, threw her fan
At my foot, with just this pretty scrap attached,
680 "Shame, death, damnation—fall these as they may,
So I find you, for a minute! Come this eve!"
—Why, at such sweet sacrifice,—who knows?
I might have fired up, found me at my post,
Ardent from head to heel, nor feared catch cough.
685 Nay, had some other friend's…say, daughter,
     tripped

---

[1] the Tuscan equivalent of the baioc (l. 542).

[2] a mad, bloodthirsty Roman emperor (12–41).

[3] woe be to.

---

[4] a fabulous serpent supposedly hatched from a cock's egg, having the power to kill with a look.

[5] stock name for a lover in pastoral poetry.

[6] name of several mistresses in classical literature.

[7] ribbon rosettes.

[8] tough bodyguard.

Upstairs and tumbled flat and frank on me,
Bareheaded and barefooted, with loose hair
And garments all at large,—cried "Take me thus!
Duke So-and-So, the greatest man in Rome—
690 To escape his hand and heart have I broke bounds,
Traversed the town and reached you!"—Then,
    indeed,
The lady had not reached a man of ice!
I would have rummaged, ransacked at the word
Those old odd corners of an empty heart
695 For remnants of dim love the long disused,
And dusty crumblings of romance! But here,
We talk of just a marriage, if you please—
The every-day conditions and no more;
Where do these bind me to bestow one drop
700 Of blood shall dye my wife's true-love-knot[1] pink?
Pompilia was no pigeon, Venus' pet,[2]
That shuffled from between her pressing paps
To sit on my rough shoulder,—but a hawk,[3]
I bought at a hawk's price and carried home
705 To do hawk's service—at the Rotunda,[4] say,
Where, six o' the callow nestlings in a row,
You pick and choose and pay the price for such.
I have paid my pound, await my penny's worth,
So, hoodwink,[5] starve and properly train my bird,
710 And, should she prove a haggard,—twist her neck!
Did I not pay my name and style, my hope
And trust, my all? Through spending these amiss
I am here! 'T is scarce the gravity of the Court
Will blame me that I never piped a tune,
715 Treated my falcon-gentle[6] like my finch.
The obligation I incurred was just
To practise mastery, prove my mastership:—

Pompilia's duty was—submit herself,
Afford me pleasure, perhaps cure my bile.
720 Am I to teach my lords what marriage means,
What God ordains thereby and man fulfils
Who, docile to the dictate, treads the house?
My lords have chosen the happier part with Paul
And neither marry nor burn,—yet priestliness
725 Can find a parallel to the marriage-bond
In its own blessed special ordinance
Whereof indeed was marriage made the type:
The Church may show her insubordinate,
As marriage her refractory. How of the Monk
730 Who finds the claustral[7] regimen too sharp
After the first month's essay? What's the mode
With the Deacon who supports indifferently[8]
The rod o' the Bishop when he tastes its smart
Full four weeks? Do you straightway slacken hold
735 Of the innocents, the all-unwary ones
Who, eager to profess,[9] mistook their mind?—
Remit a fast-day's rigour to the Monk
Who fancied Francis' manna meant roast quails,
Concede the Deacon sweet society,
740 He never thought the Levite-rule[10] renounced,—
Or rather prescribe short chain and sharp scourge
Corrective of such peccant humours?[11] This—
I take to be the Church's mode, and mine.
If I was over-harsh,—the worse i' the wife
745 Who did not win from harshness as she ought,
Wanted the patience and persuasion, lore
Of love, should cure me and console herself.
Put case that I mishandle, flurry and fright
My hawk through clumsiness in sportsmanship,

---

[1] a complicated double knot, symbolic of fidelity.

[2] In Renaissance art, a dove is often an attribute of Venus.

[3] In l. 606 Pompilia was a nightingale.

[4] the Piazza della Rotonda, site of Rome's bird market.

[5] blindfold.

[6] female falcon.

---

[7] cloistral, monastic.

[8] barely endures.

[9] take religious vows.

[10] rule for deacons.

[11] sinful self-indulgence.

750 Twitch out five pens[1] where plucking one would
        serve—
      What, shall she bite and claw to mend the case?
      And, if you find I pluck five more for that,
      Shall you weep "How he roughs the turtle[2] there?"

      Such was the starting; now of the further step.
755 In lieu of taking penance in good part,
      The Monk, with hue and cry, summons a mob
      To make a bonfire of the convent, say,—
      And the Deacon's pretty piece of virtue (save
      The ears o' the Court! I try to save my head)
760 Instructed by the ingenuous postulant,[3]
      Taxes the Bishop with adultery, (mud
      Needs must pair off with mud, and filth with
        filth)—
      Such being my next experience: who knows not—
      The couple, father and mother of my wife,
765 Returned to Rome, published before my lords,
      Put into print, made circulate far and wide
      That they had cheated me who cheated them?
      Pompilia, I supposed their daughter, drew
      Breath first 'mid Rome's worst rankness, through
        the deed
770 Of a drab and a rogue, was bye-blow bastard-babe
      Of a nameless strumpet, passed off, palmed on me
      As the daughter with the dowry. Daughter? Dirt
      O' the kennel! Dowry? Dust o' the street! Nought
        more,
      Nought less, nought else but—oh—ah—assuredly
775 A Franceschini and my very wife!
      Now take this charge as you will, for false or true,—
      This charge, preferred before your very selves
      Who judge me now,—I pray you, adjudge again,
      Classing it with the cheats or with the lies,
780 By which category I suffer most!
      But of their reckoning, theirs who dealt with me

      In either fashion,—I reserve my word,
      Justify that in its place; I am now to say,
      Whichever point o' the charge might poison most,
785 Pompilia's duty was no doubtful one.
      You put the protestation in her mouth
      "Henceforward and forevermore, avaunt
      Ye fiends, who drop disguise and glare revealed
      In your own shape, no longer father mine
790 Nor mother mine! Too nakedly you hate
      Me whom you looked as if you loved once,—me
      Whom, whether true or false, your tale now damns,
      Divulged thus to my public infamy,
      Private perdition, absolute overthrow.
795 For, hate my husband to your hearts' content,
      I, spoil and prey of you from first to last,
      I who have done you the blind service, lured
      The lion to your pit-fall,—I, thus left
      To answer for my ignorant bleating there,
800 I should have been remembered and withdrawn
      From the first o' the natural fury, not flung loose
      A proverb and a byeword men will mouth
      At the cross-way, in the corner, up and down
      Rome and Arezzo,—there, full in my face,
805 If my lord, missing them and finding me,
      Content himself with casting his reproach
      To drop i' the street where such impostors die.
      Ah, but—that husband, what the wonder were!—
      If, far from casting thus away the rag
810 Smeared with the plague, his hand had chanced
        upon,
      Sewn to his pillow by Locusta's[4] wile,—
      Far from abolishing, root, stem and branch,
      The misgrowth of infectious mistletoe
      Foisted into his stock[5] for honest graft,—
815 If he, repudiate not, renounce nowise,
      But, guarding, guiding me, maintain my cause
      By making it his own, (what other way?)
      —To keep my name for me, he call it his,

---

[1] feathers.

[2] turtledove.

[3] a candidate for admission into a religious order.

[4] a female poisoner in the time of Claudius and Nero.

[5] stem on which a graft is made, lineage.

Claim it of who would take it by their lie,—
820 To save my wealth for me—or babe of mine
Their lie was framed to beggar at the birth—
He bid them loose grasp, give our gold again:
Refuse to become partner with the pair
Even in a game which, played adroitly, gives
825 Its winner life's great wonderful new chance,—
Of marrying, to-wit, a second time,—
Ah, did he do thus, what a friend were he!
Anger he might show,—who can stamp out flame
Yet spread no black o' the brand?—yet, rough albeit
830 In the act, as whose bare feet feel embers scorch,
What grace were his, what gratitude were mine!"
Such protestation should have been my wife's.
Looking for this, do I exact too much?
Why, here's the,—word for word so much, no
    more,—
835 Avowal she made, her pure spontaneous speech
To my brother the Abate at first blush,
Ere the good impulse had begun to fade—
So did she make confession for the pair,
So pour forth praises in her own behalf.
840 "Ay, the false letter," interpose my lords—
"The simulated writing,—'t was a trick:
You traced the signs, she merely marked the same,
The product was not hers but yours." Alack,
I want no more impulsion to tell truth
845 From the other trick, the torture inside there!
I confess all—let it be understood—
And deny nothing! If I baffle you so,
Can so fence, in the plenitude of right,
That my poor lathen dagger puts aside
850 Each pass o' the Bilboa,[1] beats you all the same,—
What matters inefficiency of blade?
Mine and not hers the letter,—conceded, lords!
Impute to me that practice!—take as proved
I taught my wife her duty, made her see
855 What it behoved her see and say and do,
Feel in her heart and with her tongue declare,

_____
[1] sword made in a Spanish town famed for its steel weapons.

And, whether sluggish or recalcitrant,
Forced her to take the right step, I myself
Marching in mere marital rectitude!
860 And who finds fault here, say the tale be true?
Would not my lords commend the priest whose zeal
Seized on the sick, morose or moribund,
By the palsy-smitten finger, made it cross
His brow correctly at the critical time?
865 —Or answered for the inarticulate babe
At baptism, in its stead declared the faith,
And saved what else would perish unprofessed?
True, the incapable hand may rally yet,
Renounce the sign with renovated strength,—
870 The babe may grow up man and Molinist,—
And so Pompilia, set in the good path
And left to go alone there, soon might see
That too frank-forward, all too simple-strait
Her step was, and decline to tread the rough,
875 When here lay, tempting foot, the meadow-side,
And there the coppice called with singing-birds!
Soon she discovered she was young and fair,
That many in Arezzo knew as much,—
Yes, this next cup of bitterness, my lords,
880 Had to begin go filling, drop by drop,
Its measure up of full disgust for me,
Filtered into by every noisome drain—
Society's sink toward which all moisture runs.
Would not you prophesy—"She on whose brow is
    stamped
885 The note of the imputation that we know,—
Rightly or wrongly mothered with a whore,—
Such an one, to disprove the frightful charge,
What will she but exaggerate chastity,
Err in excess of wifehood, as it were,
890 Renounce even levities permitted youth,
Though not youth struck to age by a thunderbolt?
Cry 'wolf' i' the sheepfold, where's the sheep dares
    bleat,
Knowing the shepherd listens for a growl?"
So you expect. How did the devil decree?
895 Why, my lords, just the contrary of course!

It was in the house from the window, at the church
From the hassock,—where the theatre lent its
    lodge,[1]
Or staging for the public show left space,—
That still Pompilia needs must find herself
900 Launching her looks forth, letting looks reply
As arrows to a challenge; on all sides
Ever new contribution to her lap,
Till one day, what it is knocks at my clenched teeth
But the cup full, curse-collected all for me?
905 And I must needs drink, drink this gallant's praise,
That minion's[2] prayer, the other fop's reproach,
And come at the dregs to—Caponsacchi! Sirs,
I,—chin deep in a marsh of misery,
Struggling to extricate my name and fame
910 And fortune from the marsh would drown them all,
My face the sole unstrangled part of me,—
I must have this new gad-fly in that face,
Must free me from the attacking lover too!
Men say I battled ungracefully enough—
915 Was harsh, uncouth and ludicrous beyond
The proper part o' the husband: have it so!
Your lordships are considerate at least—
You order me to speak in my defence
Plainly, expect no quavering tuneful trills
920 As when you bid a singer solace you,—
Nor look that I shall give it, for a grace,
Stans pede in uno:[3]—you remember well
In the one case, 't is a plainsong[4] too severe,
This story of my wrongs,—and that I ache
925 And need a chair, in the other. Ask you me
Why, when I felt this trouble flap my face,
Already pricked with every shame could perch,—
When, with her parents, my wife plagued me too,—

Why I enforced not exhortation mild
930 To leave whore's-tricks and let my brows alone,
With mulct[5] of comfits, promise of perfume?

   "Far from that! No, you took the opposite course,
Breathed threatenings, rage and slaughter!" What
    you will!
And the end has come, the doom is verily here,
935 Unhindered by the threatening. See fate's flare
Full on each face of the dead guilty three!
Look at them well, and now, lords, look at this!
Tell me: if on that day when I found first
That Caponsacchi thought the nearest way
940 To his church was some half-mile round by my
    door,
And that he so admired, shall I suppose,
The manner of the swallows' come-and-go
Between the prop's o' the window over-head,—
That window happening to be my wife's—
945 As to stand gazing by the hour on high,
Of May-eves, while she sat and let him smile,—
If I,—instead of threatening, talking big,
Showing hair-powder, a prodigious pinch,
For poison in a bottle,—making believe
950 At desperate doings with a bauble-sword,
And other bugaboo-and-baby-work,—
Had, with the vulgarest household implement,
Calmly and quietly cut off, clean thro' bone,
But one joint of one finger of my wife,
955 Saying "For listening to the serenade,
Here's your ring-finger shorter a full third:
Be certain I will slice away next joint,
Next time that anybody underneath
Seems somehow to be sauntering as he hoped
960 A flower would eddy out of your hand to his
While you please fidget with the branch above
O' the rose-tree in the terrace!"—had I done so,
Why, there had followed a quick sharp scream,
    some pain,

---

[1] box, loge.

[2] servile follower.

[3] from Horace, *Satires* 1.4.10: "an easy thing, done standing on one
foot."

[4] a simple, moving chant.

[5] punishment—used ironically (so sweet and mild a punishment).

Much calling for plaister, damage to the dress,
965 A somewhat sulky countenance next day,
Perhaps reproaches,—but reflections too!
I don't hear much of harm that Malchus[1] did
After the incident of the ear, my lords!
Saint Peter took the efficacious way;
970 Malchus was sore but silenced for his life:
He did not hang himself i' the Potter's Field
Like Judas, who was trusted with the bag
And treated to sops after he proved a thief.
So, by this time, my true and obedient wife
975 Might have been telling beads with a gloved hand;
Awkward a little at pricking hearts and darts
On sampler possibly, but well otherwise:
Not where Rome shudders now to see her lie.
I give that for the course a wise man takes;
980 I took the other however, tried the fool's,
The lighter remedy, brandished rapier dread
With cork-ball at the tip, boxed Malchus' ear
Instead of severing the cartilage,
Called her a terrible nickname, and the like
985 And there an end: and what was the end of that?
What was the good effect o' the gentle course?
Why, one night I went drowsily to bed,
Dropped asleep suddenly, not suddenly woke,
But did wake with rough rousing and loud cry,
990 To find noon in my face, a crowd in my room,
Fumes in my brain, fire in my throat, my wife
Gone God knows whither,—rifled vesture-chest,
And ransacked money-coffer. "What does it mean?"
The servants had been drugged too, stared and
    yawned,
995 "It must be that our lady has eloped!"
—"Whither and with whom?"—"With whom but
    the Canon's self?
One recognizes Caponsacchi there!"—
(By this time the admiring[2] neighbourhood
Joined chorus round me while I rubbed my eyes)

1000 "'T is months since their intelligence[3] began,—
A comedy the town was privy to,—
He wrote and she wrote, she spoke, he replied,
And going in and out your house last night
Was easy work for one…to be plain with you…
1005 Accustomed to do both, at dusk and dawn
When you were absent,—at the villa, you know,
Where husbandry required the master-mind.
Did not you know? Why, we all knew, you see!"
And presently, bit by bit, the full and true
1010 Particulars of the tale were volunteered
With all the breathless zeal of friendship—"Thus
Matters were managed: at the seventh hour of
    night"…
—"Later, at daybreak"…"Caponsacchi came"…
—"While you and all your household slept like
    death,
1015 Drugged as your supper was with drowsy stuff"…
—"And your own cousin Guillichini too—
Either or both entered your dwelling-place,
Plundered it at their pleasure, made prize of all,
Including your wife…"—"Oh, your wife led the
    way,
1020 Out of doors, on to the gate…"—"But gates are
    shut,
In a decent town, to darkness and such deeds:
They climbed the wall—your lady must be lithe—
At the gap, the broken bit…"—"Torrione,[4] true!
To escape the questioning guard at the proper gate,
1025 Clemente, where at the inn, hard by, 'the Horse,'
Just outside, a calash[5] in readiness
Took the two principals, all alone at last,
To gate San Spirito, which o'erlooks the road,
Leads to Perugia, Rome and liberty."
1030 Bit by bit thus made-up mosaic-wise,
Flat lay my fortune,—tesselated[6] floor,

---

[1] John 17:10–11.

[2] wondering, excited.

[3] secret communications.

[4] the Great Tower in Arezzo.

[5] carriage.

[6] mosaic.

Imperishable tracery devils should foot
And frolic it on, around my broken gods,
Over my desecrated hearth.
                                        So much
1035 For the terrible effect of threatening, Sirs!

Well, this way I was shaken wide awake,
Doctored and drenched,[1] somewhat unpoisoned so;
Then, set on horseback and bid seek the lost
1040 I started alone, head of me, heart of me
Fire, and each limb as languid…ah, sweet lords,
Bethink you!—poison-torture, try persuade
The next refractory Molinist with that!…
Floundered thro' day and night, another day
1045 And yet another night, and so at last,
As Lucifer kept falling to find hell,
Tumbled into the court-yard of an inn
At the end, and fell on whom I thought to find,
Even Caponsacchi,—what part once was priest,
1050 Cast to the winds now with the cassock-rags:
In cape and sword a cavalier confessed,[2]
There stood he chiding dilatory grooms,
Chafing that only horseflesh and no team
Of eagles would supply the last relay,
1055 Whirl him along the league, the one post more
Between the couple and Rome and liberty.
'T was dawn, the couple were rested in a sort,
And though the lady, tired,—the tenderer sex,—
Still lingered in her chamber,—to adjust
1060 The limp hair, look for any blush astray,—
She would descend in a twinkling,—"Have you out
The horses therefore!"
                                        So did I find my wife.
Is the case complete? Do your eyes here see with
          mine?
1065 Even the parties dared deny no one
Point out of all these points.
                                        What follows next?

---

[1] given a large dose of purgative medicine.

[2] manifest, avowed.

"Why, that then was the time," you interpose,
"Or then or never, while the fact was fresh,
1070 To take the natural vengeance: there and thus
They and you,—somebody had stuck a sword
Beside you while he pushed you on your horse,—
'T was requisite to slay the couple, Count!"
Just so my friends say—"Kill!" they cry in a breath,
1075 Who presently, when matters grow to a head
And I do kill the offending ones indeed,—
When crime of theirs, only surmised before,
Is patent, proved indisputably now,—
When remedy for wrong, untried at the time,
1080 Which law professes shall not fail a friend,
Is thrice tried now, found threefold worse than
          null,—
When what might turn to transient shade, who
          knows?
Solidifies into a blot which breaks
Hell's black off in pale flakes for fear of mine,—
1085 Then, when I claim and take revenge—"So rash?"
They cry—"so little reverence for the law?"

Listen, my masters, and distinguish here!
At first, I called in law to act and help:
Seeing I did so, "Why, 'tis clear," they cry,
1090 "You shrank from gallant readiness and risk,
Were coward: the thing's inexplicable else."
Sweet my lords, let the thing be! I fall flat,
Play the reed, not the oak, to breath of man.
Only, inform my ignorance! Say I stand
1095 Convicted of the having been afraid,
Proved a poltroon,[3] no lion but a lamb,—
Does that deprive me of my right of lamb
And give my fleece and flesh to the first wolf?
Are eunuchs, women, children, shieldless quite
1100 Against attack their own timidity tempts?
Cowardice were misfortune and no crime!
—Take it that way, since I am fallen so low
I scarce dare brush the fly that blows my face,

---

[3] coward.

And thank the man who simply spits not there,—
1105 Unless the Court be generous, comprehend
How one brought up at the very feet of law
As I, awaits the grave Gamaliel's nod
Ere he clench fist at outrage,—much less, stab!
—How, ready enough to rise at the right time,
1110 I still could recognise no time mature
Unsanctioned by a move o' the judgment-seat,
So, mute in misery, eyed my masters here
Motionless till the authoritative word
Pronounced amercement.[1] There's the riddle solved:
1115 This is just why I slew nor her nor him,
But called in law, law's delegate in the place,
And bade arrest the guilty couple, Sirs!
We had some trouble to do so—you have heard
They braved me,—he with arrogance and scorn,
1120 She, with a volubility of curse,
A conversancy[2] in the skill of tooth
And claw to make suspicion seem absurd,
Nay, an alacrity to put to proof
At my own throat my own sword, teach me so
1125 To try conclusions better the next time,—
Which did the proper service with the mob.
They never tried to put on mask at all:
Two avowed lovers forcibly torn apart,
Upbraid the tyrant as in a playhouse scene,
1130 Ay, and with proper clapping and applause
From the audience that enjoys the bold and free.
I kept still, said to myself, "There's law!" Anon
We searched the chamber where they passed the
    night,
Found what confirmed the worst was feared before,
1135 However needless confirmation now—
The witches' circle intact, charms undisturbed
That raised the spirit and succubus,[3]—letters,
    to-wit,
Love-laden, each the bag o' the bee that bore

Honey from lily and rose to Cupid's hive,—
1140 Now, poetry in some rank blossom-burst,
Now, prose,—"Come here, go there, wait such a
    while,
He's at the villa, now he's back again:
We are saved, we are lost, we are lovers all the same!"
All in order, all complete,—even to a clue
1145 To the drowsiness that happed so opportune—
No mystery, when I read "Of all things, find
What wine Sir Jealousy decides to drink—
Red wine? Because a sleeping-potion, dust
Dropped into white, discolours wine and shows."

1150 —"Oh, but we did not write a single word!
Somebody forged the letters in our name!—"
Both in a breath protested presently.
Aha, Sacchetti again!—"Dame,"—quoth the Duke,
"What meaneth this epistle, counsel me,
1155 I pick from out thy placket[4] and peruse,
Wherein my page averreth thou are white
And warm and wonderful 'twixt pap and pap?"
"Sir," laughed the Lady "'t is a counterfeit!
Thy page did never stroke but Dian's breast,
1160 The pretty hound I nurture for thy sake:
To lie were losel,[5]—by my fay, no more!"
And no more say I too, and spare the Court.

Ah, the Court! yes, I come to the Court's self;
Such the case, so complete in fact and proof
1165 I laid at the feet of law,—there sat my lords,
Here sit they now, so may they ever sit
In easier attitude than suits my haunch!
In this same chamber did I bare my sores
O' the soul and not the body,—shun no shame,
1170 Shrink from no probing of the ulcerous part,
Since confident in Nature,—which is God,—
That she who, for wise ends, concocts a plague,
Curbs, at the right time, the plague's virulence too:

---

[1] penalty.

[2] familiarity with.

[3] female demon.

[4] either her petticoat or a pocket in her skirt.

[5] futile.

Law renovates even Lazarus,—cures me!
175 Caesar thou seekest? To Caesar thou shalt go!
Caesar's at Rome; to Rome accordingly!

The case was soon decided: both weights, cast
I' the balance, vibrate, neither kicks the beam,
Here away, there away, this now and now that.
180 To every one o' my grievances law gave
Redress, could purblind eye but see the point.
The wife stood a convicted runagate[1]
From house and husband,—driven to such a course
By what she somehow took for cruelty
185 Oppression and imperilment of life—
Not that such things were, but that so they seemed:
Therefore, the end conceded lawful, (since
To save life there's no risk should stay our leap)
It follows that all means to the lawful end
190 Are lawful likewise,—poison, theft and flight.
As for the priest's part, did he meddle or make,
Enough that he too thought life jeopardised;
Concede him then the colour charity
Cast on a doubtful course,—if blackish white
195 Or whitish black, will charity hesitate?
What did he else but act the precept out,
Leave, like a provident shepherd, his safe flock
To follow the single lamb and strayaway?
Best hope so and think so,—that the ticklish time
200 I' the carriage, the tempting privacy, the last
Somewhat ambiguous accident at the inn,
—All may bear explanation: may? then, must!
The letters,—do they so incriminate?
Bu what if the whole prove a prank o' the pen,
205 Flight of the fancy, none of theirs at all,
Bred of the vapours of my brain belike,
Or at worst mere exercise of scholar's-wit
In the courtly Caponsacchi: verse, convict?
Did not Catullus write less seemly once?
210 Yet *doctus*[2] and unblemished he abides.

Wherefore so ready to infer the worst?
Still, I did righteously in bringing doubts
For the law to solve,—take the solution now!
"Seeing that the said associates, wife and priest,
1215 Bear themselves not without some touch of blame
—Else why the pother, scandal and outcry
Which trouble our peace and require chastisement?
We, for complicity in Pompilia's flight
And deviation,[3] and carnal intercourse
1220 With the same, do set aside and relegate
The Canon Caponsacchi for three years
At Civita in the neighbourhood of Rome:
And we consign Pompilia to the care
Of a certain Sisterhood of penitents
1225 I' the city's self, expert to deal with such."
Word for word, there's your judgment! Read it,
lords,
Re-utter your deliberate penalty
For the crime yourselves establish![4] Your award—
Who chop a man's right-hand off at the wrist
1230 For tracing with forefinger words in wine
O' the table of a drinking-booth that bear
Interpretation as they mocked the Church!
—Who brand a woman black between the breasts
For sinning by connection[5] with a Jew:
1235 While for the Jew's self—pudency[6] be dumb!
You mete out punishment such and such, yet so
Punish the adultery of wife and priest!
Take note of that, before the Molinists do,
And read me right the riddle, since right must be!
1240 While I stood rapt away with wonderment,
Voices broke in upon my mood and muse.
"Do you sleep?" began the friends at either ear,
"The case is settled,—you willed it should be so—
None of our counsel, always recollect!
1245 With law's award, budge! Back into your place!

---

[1] runaway.

[2] learned, wise.

---

[3] departure from the path of virtue.

[4] accept as true.

[5] sexual intercourse.

[6] shame, modesty.

Your betters shall arrange the rest for you.
We'll enter a new action, claim divorce:
Your marriage was a cheat themselves allow:
You erred i' the person,—might have married thus
1250 Your sister or your daughter unaware.
We'll gain you, that way, liberty at least,
Sure of so much by law's own showing. Up
And off with you and your unluckiness—
Leave us to bury the blunder, sweep things smooth!"
1255 I was in humble frame of mind, be sure!
I bowed, betook me to my place again.
Station by station I retraced the road,
Touched at this hostel, passed this post-house by,
Where, fresh-remembered yet, the fugitives
1260 Had risen to the heroic stature: still—
"That was the bench they sat on,—there's the board
They took the meal at,—yonder garden-ground
They leaned across the gate of,"—ever a word
O' the Helen and the Paris, with "Ha! You're he,
1265 The...much-commiserated husband?"[1] Step
By step, across the pelting, did I reach
Arezzo, underwent the archway's grin,
Traversed the length of sarcasm in the street,
Found myself in my horrible house once more,
1270 And after a colloquy...no word assists!
With the mother and the brothers, stiffened me
Strait out from head to foot as dead man does,
And, thus prepared for life as he for hell,
Marched to the public Square and met the world.
1275 Apologise for the pincers, palliate screws?
Ply me with such toy-trifles, I entreat!
Trust who has tried both sulphur and sops-in-wine!

I played the man as I best might, bade friends
Put non-essentials by and face the fact.
1280 "What need to hang myself as you advise?
The paramour is banished,—the ocean's width,

Or the suburb's length,—to Ultima Thule,[2] say,
Or Proxima Civitas,[3] what's the odds of name
And place? He's banished, and the fact's the thing.
1285 Why should law banish innocence an inch?
Here's guilt then, what else do I care to know?
The adulteress lies imprisoned,—whether in a well
With bricks above and a snake for company,
Or tied by a garter to a bed-post,—much
1290 I mind what's little,—least's enough and to spare!
The little fillip[4] on the coward's cheek
Serves as though crab-tree cudgel broke his pate.
Law has pronounced there's punishment, less or
        more:
And I take note o' the fact and use it thus—
1295 For the first flaw in the original bond,
I claim release. My contract was to wed
The daughter of Pietro and Violante. Both
Protest they never had a child at all.
Then I have never made a contract: good!
1300 Cancel me quick the thing pretended one.
I shall be free. What matter if hurried over
The harbour-boom[5] by a great favouring tide,
Or the last of a spent ripple that lifts and leaves?
The Abate is about it. Laugh who wins!
1305 You shall not laugh me out of faith in law!
I listen, through all your noise, to Rome!"
                                        Rome spoke.
In three months letters thence admonished me,
"Your plan for the divorce is all mistake.
1310 It would hold, now, had you, taking thought to
        wed
Rachel of the blue eye and golden hair,
Found swarth-skinned Leah cumber couch next day:
But Rachel, blue-eyed golden hair aright,

---

[1] Menelaus.

[2] a locale vaguely placed in the far north by Virgil and other ancient writers.

[3] nearby town—Civita Vecchia, thirty-five miles from Rome.

[4] tap.

[5] barrier, often of logs roped or chained together.

Proving to be only Laban's child, not Lot's,[1]
1315 Remains yours all the same for ever more.
No whit to the purpose is your plea: you err
I' the person and the quality—nowise
In the individual,—that's the case in point!
You go to the ground,—are met by a cross-suit
1320 For separation, of the Rachel here,
From bed and board,—she is the injured one,
You did the wrong and have to answer it.
As for the circumstance of imprisonment
And colour[2] it lends to this your new attack,
1325 Never fear, that point is considered too!
The durance is already at an end;
The convent-quiet preyed upon her health,
She is transferred now to her parents' house
—No-parents, when that cheats and plunders you,
1330 But parentage again confessed in full,
When such confession pricks and plagues you
        more—
As now—for, this their house is not the house
In Via Vittoria wherein neighbours' watch
Might incommode the freedom of your wife,
1335 But a certain villa smothered up in vines
At the town's edge by the gate i' the Pauline way,
Out of eye-reach, out of ear-shot, little and lone,
Whither a friend,—at Civita, we hope,
A good half-dozen-hours' ride off,—might, some
        eve,
1340 Betake himself, and whence ride back, some morn,
Nobody the wiser: but be that as it may,
Do not afflict your brains with trifles now.
You have still three suits to manage, all and each
Ruinous truly should the event play false.
1345 It is indeed the likelier so to do,
That brother Paul, your single prop and stay,
After a vain attempt to bring the Pope

To set aside procedures, sit himself
And summarily use prerogative,
1350 Afford us the infallible finger's tact
To disentwine your tangle of affairs,
Paul,—finding it moreover past his strength
To stem the irruption,[3] bear Rome's ridicule
Of...since friends must speak...to be round with
        you...
1355 Of the old outwitted husband, wronged and wroth,
Pitted against a brace of juveniles—
A brisk priest who is versed in Ovid's art
More than his Summa,[4] and a gamesome wife
Able to act Corinna[5] without book,
1360 Beside the waggish parents who played dupes
To dupe the duper—(and truly divers scenes
Of the Arezzo palace, tickle rib
And teaze eye till the tears come, so we laugh;
Nor wants the shock at the inn its comic force,
1365 And then the letters and poetry—*merum sal!*)[6]
—Paul, finally, in such a state of things,
After a brief temptation to go jump
And join the fishes in the Tiber, drowns
Sorrow another and a wiser way:
1370 House and goods, he has sold all off, is gone,
Leaves Rome,—whether for France or Spain, who
        knows?
Or Britain almost divided from our orb.
You have lost him anyhow."
                                Now,—I see my lords
1375 Shift in their seat,—would I could do the same!
They probably please expect my bile was moved
To purpose, nor much blame me: now, they judge,
The fiery titillation[7] urged my flesh

---

1 a fusion of two separate episodes, Laban's tricking Jacob into marrying
Leah instead of Rachel and Lot's incest with his two daughters: Genesis
29:16–25 and Genesis 19:30–35 respectively.

2 justification, legal authority.

3 sudden breaking in, incursion.

4 "Ovid's art" is his *Ars Amatoria*: the "Summa" is the *Summa Theologiae*
of St. Thomas Aquinas.

5 Ovid's mistress.

6 "very spicy."

7 sensation, excitement.

Break through the bonds. By your pardon, no,
    sweet Sirs!
1380 I got such missives in the public place;
When I sought home,—with such news, mounted
    stair
And sat at last in the sombre gallery,
('T was Autumn, the old mother in bed betimes,
Having to bear that cold, the finer frame
1385 Of her daughter-in-law had found intolerable—
The brother, walking misery away
O' the mountain-side with dog and gun belike)
As I supped, ate the coarse bread, drank the wine
Weak once, now acrid with the toad's-head-
    squeeze,[1]
1390 My wife's bestowment,—I broke silence thus:
"Let me, a man, manfully meet the fact,
Confront the worst o' the truth, end, and have
    peace!
I am irremediably beaten here,—
The gross illiterate vulgar couple,—bah!
1395 Why, they have measured forces, mastered mine,
Made me their spoil and prey from first to last.
They have got my name,—'t is nailed now fast to
    theirs,
The child or changeling is anyway my wife;
Point by point as they plan they execute,
1400 They gain all, and I lose all—even to the lure
That led to loss,—they have the wealth again
They hazarded awhile to hook me with,
Have caught the fish and find the bait entire:
They even have their child or changeling back
1405 To trade with, turn to account a second time.
The brother, presumably might tell a tale
Or give a warning,—he, too, flies the field,
And with him vanish help and hope of help.
They have caught me in the cavern where I fell,
1410 Covered my loudest cry for human aid
With this enormous paving-stone of shame.

Well, are we demigods or merely clay?
Is success still attendant on desert?
Is this, we live on, heaven and the final state,
1415 Or earth which means probation to the end?
Why claim escape from man's predestined lot
Of being beaten and baffled?—God's decree,
In which I, bowing bruised head, acquiesce.
One of us Franceschini fell long since
1420 I' the Holy Land, betrayed, tradition runs,
To Paynims[2] by the feigning of a girl
He rushed to free from ravisher, and found
Lay safe enough with friends in ambuscade
Who flayed him while she clapped her hands and
    laughed:
1425 Let me end, falling by a like device.
It will not be so hard. I am the last
O' my line which will not suffer any more.
I have attained to my full fifty years,
(About the average of us all, 'tis said,
1430 Though it seems longer to the unlucky man)
—Lived through my share of life; let all end here,
Me and the house and grief and shame at once.
Friends my informants,—I can bear your blow!"
And I believe 't was in no unmeet match
1435 For the stoic's mood, with something like a smile,
That, when morose December roused me next,
I took into my hand, broke seal to read
The new epistle from Rome. "All to no use!
Whate'er the turn next injury take," smiled I,
1440 "Here's one has chosen his part and knows his cue.
I am done with, dead now; strike away, good
    friends!
Are the three suits decided in a trice?
Against me,—there's no question! How does it go?
Is the parentage of my wife demonstrated
1445 Infamous to her wish? Parades she now
Loosed of the cincture that so irked the loin?
Is the last penny extracted from my purse
To mulct me for demanding the first pound

---

[1] A poison often referred to in literature, it was especially favoured by adulterous wives who wanted to kill their husbands.

[2] pagans.

Was promised in return for value paid?
450 Has the priest, with nobody to court beside,
Courted the Muse in exile, hitched my hap
Into a rattling ballad-rhyme which, bawled
At tavern-doors, wakes rapture everywhere,
And helps cheap wine down throat this Christmas
time,
455 Beating the bagpipes? Any or all of these!
As well, good friends, you cursed my palace here
To its old cold stone face,—stuck your cap for crest
Over the shield that's extant in the Square,—
Or spat on the statue's cheek, the impatient world
460 Sees cumber tomb-top in our family church:
Let him creep under covert as I shall do,
Half below-ground already indeed. Good-bye!
My brothers are priests, and childless so; that's
well—
And, thank God most for this, no child leave I—
465 None after me to bear till his heart break
The being a Franceschini and my son!"

"Nay," said the letter, "but you have just that!
A babe, your veritable son and heir—
Lawful,—'t is only eight months since your wife
470 Left you,—so, son and heir, your babe was born
Last Wednesday in the villa,—you see the cause
For quitting Convent without beat of drum,
Stealing a hurried march to this retreat
That's not so savage as the Sisterhood
475 To slips and stumbles: Pietro's heart is soft,
Violante leans to pity's side,—the pair
Ushered you into life a bouncing boy:
And he's already hidden away and safe
From any claim on him you mean to make—
480 They need him for themselves,—don't fear, they
know
The use o' the bantling,[1]—the nerve thus laid bare
To nip at, new and nice, with finger-nail!"

Then I rose up like fire, and fire-like roared.
What, all is only beginning not ending now?
1485 The worm which wormed its way from skin
through flesh
To the bone and there lay biting, did its best,
What, it goes on to scrape at the bone's self,
Will wind to inmost marrow and madden me?
There's to be yet my representative,
1490 Another of the name shall keep displayed
The flag with the ordure on it, brandish still
The broken sword has served to stir a jakes?[2]
Who will he be, how will you call the man?
A Franceschini,—when who cut my purse,
1495 Filched my name, hemmed me round, hustled me
hard
As rogues at a fair some fool they strip i' the midst,
When these count gains, vaunt pillage presently:—
But a Caponsacchi, oh, be very sure!
When what demands its tribute of applause
1500 Is the cunning and impudence o' the pair of cheats,
The lies and lust o' the mother, and the brave
Bold carriage[3] of the priest, worthily crowned
By a witness to his feat i' the following age,—
And how this three-fold cord could hook and fetch
1505 And land leviathan[4] that king of pride!
Or say, by some mad miracle of chance,
Is he indeed my flesh and blood, this babe?
Was it because fate forged a link at last
Betwixt my wife and me, and both alike
1510 Found we had henceforth some one thing to love,
Was it when she could damn my soul indeed
She unlatched door, let all the devils o' the dark
Dance in on me to cover her escape?
Why then, the surplusage of disgrace, the spilth
1515 Over and above the measure of infamy,
Failing to take effect on my coarse flesh
Seasoned with scorn now, saturate with shame,—

---

[1] illegitimate brat.

[2] privy.

[3] conduct.

[4] the sea monster in Job 41.

Is saved to instil on and corrode the brow,
The baby-softness of my first-born child—
1520 The child I had died to see though in a dream,
The child I was bid strike out for, beat the wave
And baffle the tide of troubles where I swam,
So I might touch shore, lay down life at last
At the feet so dim and distant and divine
1525 Of the apparition, as 't were Mary's babe
Had held, through night and storm, the torch
      aloft,—
Born now in very deed to bear this brand
On forehead and curse me who could not save!
Rather be the town-talk true, Square's jest, street's
      jeer
1530 True, my own inmost heart's confession true,
And he's the priest's bastard and none of mine!
Ay, there was cause for flight, swift flight and sure!
The husband gets unruly, breaks all bounds
When he encounters some familiar face,
1535 Fashion of feature, brow and eyes and lips
Where he least looked to find them,—time to fly!
This bastard then, a nest for him is made,
As the manner is of vermin, in my flesh—
Shall I let the filthy pest buzz, flap and sting,
1540 Busy at my vitals and, nor hand nor foot
Lift, but let be, lie still and rot resigned?
No, I appeal to God,—what says Himself,
How lessons Nature when I look to learn?
Why, that I am alive, am still a man
1545 With brain and heart and tongue and right-hand
      too—
Nay, even with friends, in such cause as this,
To right me if I fail to take my right.
No more of law; a voice beyond the law
Enters my heart, *Quis est pro Domino?*[1]

1550 Myself, in my own Vittiano, told the tale
To my own serving-people summoned there:
Told the first half of it, scarce heard to end

By judges who got done with judgment quick
And clamoured to go execute her 'hest—
1555 Who cried "Not one of us that dig your soil
And dress your vineyard, prune your olive-trees,
But would have brained the man debauched our
      wife,
And staked the wife whose lust allured the man,
And paunched the Duke, had it been possible,
1560 Who ruled the land, yet barred us such revenge!"
I fixed on the first whose eyes caught mine, some
      four,
Resolute youngsters with the heart still fresh,
Filled my purse with the residue o' the coin
Uncaught-up by my wife whom haste made blind,
1565 Donned the first rough and rural garb I found,
Took whatsoever weapon came to hand,
And out we flung and on we ran or reeled
Romeward, I have no memory of our way,
Only that, when at intervals the cloud
1570 Of horror about me opened to let in life,
I listened to some song in the ear, some snatch
Of legend, relic of religion, stray
Fragment of record very strong and old
Of the first conscience, the anterior[2] right,
1575 The God's-gift to mankind, impulse to quench
The antagonistic spark of hell and tread
Satan and all his malice into dust,
Declare to the world the one law, right is right.
Then the cloud re-encompassed me, and so
1580 I found myself, as on the wings of winds,
Arrived: I was at Rome on Christmas Eve.

Festive bells—everywhere the Feast o' the Babe,
Joy upon earth, peace and good will to man!
I am baptized. I started and let drop
1585 The dagger. "Where is it, His promised peace?"
Nine days o' the Birth-Feast did I pause and pray
To enter into no temptation more.
I bore the hateful house, my brother's once,

---

[1] "Who is on the Lord's side?": Exodus 32:26.

[2] early, primitive.

Deserted,—let the ghost of social joy
590 Mock and make mouths at me from empty room
And idle door that missed the master's step,—
Bore the frank wonder of incredulous eyes,
As my own people watched without a word,
Waited, from where they huddled round the hearth
595 Black like all else, that nod so slow to come—
I stoped my ears even to the inner call
Of the dread duty, heard only the song
"Peace upon earth," saw nothing but the face
O' the Holy Infant and the halo there
600 Able to cover yet another face
Behind it, Satan's which I else should see.
But, day by day, joy waned and withered off:
The Babe's face, premature with peak and pine,
Sank into wrinkled ruinous old age,
605 Suffering and death, then mist-like disappeared,
And showed only the Cross at end of all,
Left nothing more to interpose 'twixt me
And the dread duty,—for the angel's song,
"Peace upon earth," louder and louder pealed
610 "O Lord, how long, how long be unavenged?"
On the ninth day, this grew too much for man.
I started up—"Some end must be!" At once,
Silence: then, scratching like a death-watch-tick,[1]
Slowly within my brain was syllabled,
615 "One more concession, one decisive way
And but one, to determine thee the truth,—
This way, in fine, I whisper in thy ear:
Now doubt, anon decide, thereupon act!"

"That is a way, thou whisperest in my ear!
620 I doubt, I will decide, then act," said I—
Then beckoned my companions: "Time is come!"

And so, all yet uncertain save the will
To do right, and the daring aught save leave
Right undone, I did find myself at last
625 I' the dark before the villa with my friends,

And made the experiment, the final test,
Ultimate chance that ever was to be
For the wretchedness inside. I knocked—
    pronounced
The name, the predetermined touch for truth,
1630 "What welcome for the wanderer? Open straight—"
To the friend, physician, friar upon his rounds,
Traveller belated, beggar lame and blind?—
No, but—"to Caponsacchi!" And the door
Opened.
1635   And then,—why, even then, I think,
I' the minute that confirmed my worst of fears,
Surely,—I pray God that I think aright!—
Had but Pompilia's self, the tender thing
Who once was good and pure, was once my lamb
1640 And lay in my bosom, had the well-known shape
Fronted me in the door-way,—stood there faint
With the recent pang, perhaps, of giving birth
To what might, though by miracle, seem my
    child,—
Nay more, I will say, had even the aged fool
1645 Pietro, the dotard, in whom folly and age
Wrought, more than enmity or malevolence,
To practice and conspire against my peace,—
Had either of these but opened, I had paused.
But it was she the hag, she that brought hell
1650 For a dowry with her to her husband's house,
She the mock-mother, she that made the match
And married me to perdition, spring and source
O' the fire inside me that boiled up from heart
To brain and hailed the Fury gave it birth,—
1655 Violante Comparini, she it was,
With the old grin amid the wrinkles yet,
Opened: as if in turning from the Cross,
With trust to keep the sight and save my soul,
I had stumbled, first thing, on the serpent's head
1660 Coiled with a leer at foot of it.
                        There was the end!
Then was I rapt away by the impulse, one
Immeasurable everlasting wave of a need
To abolish that detested life. 'T was done:

---

[1] the sound of a death-watch beetle.

1665 You know the rest and how the folds o' the thing,
Twisting for help, involved the other two
More or less serpent-like: how I was mad,
Blind, stamped on all, the earth-worms with the
    asp,
And ended so.

1670   You came on me that night,
Your officers of justice,—caught the crime
In the first natural frenzy of remorse?
Twenty miles off, sound sleeping as a child
On a cloak i' the straw which promised shelter first,
1675 With the bloody arms beside me,—was it not so?
Wherefore not? Why, how else should I be found?
I was my own self, had my sense again,
My soul safe from the serpents. I could sleep:
Indeed and, dear my lords, I shall sleep now,
1680 Spite of my shoulder, in five minutes' space,
When you dismiss me, having truth enough!
It is but a few days are passed, I find,
Since this adventure. Do you tell me, four?
Then the dead are scarce quiet where they lie,
1685 Old Pietro, old Violante, side by side
At the church Lorenzo,—oh, they know it well!
So do I. But my wife is still alive,
Has breath enough to tell her story yet,
Her way, which is not mine, no doubt at all.
1690 And Caponsacchi, you have summoned him,—
Was he so far to send for? Not at hand?
I thought some few o' the stabs were in his heart,
Or had not been so lavish,—less had served.
Well, he too tells his story,—florid prose
1695 As smooth as mind is rough. You see, my lords,
There will be a lying intoxicating smoke
Born of the blood,—confusion probably,—
For lies breed lies—but all that rests with you!
The trial is no concern of mine; with me
1700 The main of the care is over: I at least
Recognise who took that huge burthen off,
Let me begin to live again. I did
God's bidding and man's duty, so, breathe free;
Look you to the rest! I heard Himself prescribe,

1705 That great Physician, and dared lance the core
Of the bad ulcer; and the rage abates,
I am myself and whole now: I prove cured
By the eyes that see, the ears that hear again,
The limbs that have relearned their youthful play,
1710 The healthy taste of food and feel of clothes
And taking to our common life once more,
All that now urges my defence from death.
The willingness to live, what means it else?
Before,—but let the very action speak!
1715 Judge for yourselves, what life seemed worth to me
Who, not by proxy but in person, pitched
Head-foremost into danger as a fool
That never cares if he can swim or no—
So he but find the bottom, braves the brook.
1720 No man omits precaution, quite neglects
Secrecy, safety, schemes not how retreat,
Having schemed he might advance. Did I so
    scheme?
Why, with a warrant which 't is ask and have,
With horse thereby made mine without a word,
1725 I had gained the frontier and slept safe that night.
Then, my companions,—call them what you
    please,
Slave or stipendiary,[1]—what need of one
To me whose right-hand did its owner's work?
Hire an assassin yet expose yourself?
1730 As well buy glove and then thrust naked hand
I' the thorn-bush. No, the wise man stays at home,
Sends only agents out, with pay to earn:
At home, when they come back,—he straight
    discards[2]
Or else disowns. Why use such tools at all
1735 When a man's foes are of his house, like mine,
Sit at his board, sleep in his bed? Why noise,
When there's the *acquetta* and the silent way?
Clearly my life was valueless.

---

[1] paid employee, hireling.

[2] disposes of (by killing).

But now

1740 Health is returned, and sanity of soul
Nowise indifferent to the body's harm.
I find the instinct bids me save my life;
My wits, too, rally round me; I pick up
And use the arms that strewed the ground before,
1745 Unnoticed or spurned aside: I take my stand
Make my defence. God shall not lose life
May do Him further service, while I speak
And you hear, you my judges and last hope!
You are the law: 't is to the law I look.
1750 I began life by hanging to the law,
To the law it is I hang till life shall end.
My brother made appeal to the Pope, 't is true,
To stay proceedings, judge my cause himself
Nor trouble law,—some fondness of conceit[1]
1755 That rectitude, sagacity sufficed
The investigator in a case like mine,
Dispensed with the machine of law. The Pope
Knew better, set aside my brother's plea
And put me back to law,—referred the cause
1760 *Ad judices meos,*—doubtlessly did well.
Here, then, I clutch my judges,—I claim law—
Cry, by the higher law whereof your law
O' the land is humbly representative,—
Cry, on what points is it, where either accuse,
1765 I fail to furnish you defence? I stand
Acquitted, actually or virtually,
By every intermediate kind of court
That takes account of right or wrong in man,
Each unit in the series that begins
1770 With God's throne, ends with the tribunal here.
God breathes, not speaks, his verdicts, felt not
        heard,
Passed on successively to each court I call
Man's conscience, custom, manners, all that make
More and more effort to promulgate, mark
1775 God's verdict in determinable[2] words,

Till last come human jurists—solidify
Fluid result,—what's fixable lies forged,
Statute,[3]—the residue escapes in fume,
Yet hangs aloft, a cloud, as palpable
1780 To the finer sense as word the legist[4] welds.
Justinian's Pandects[5] only make precise
What simply sparkled in men's eyes before,
Twitched in their brow or quivered on their lip,
Waited the speech they called but would not come.
1785 These courts then, whose decree your own
        confirms,—
Take my whole life, not this last act alone,
Look on it by the light reflected thence!
What has Society to charge me with?
Come, unreservedly,—favour nor fear,—
1790 I am Guido Franceschini, am I not?
You know the courses I was free to take?
I took just that which let me serve the Church,
I gave it all my labour in body and soul
Till these broke down i' the service. "Specify?"
1795 Well, my last patron was a Cardinal.
I left him unconvicted of a fault—
Was even helped, by way of gratitude,
Into the new life that I left him for,
This very misery of the marriage,—he
1800 Made it, kind soul, so far as in him lay—
Signed the deed where you yet may see his name.
He is gone to his reward,—dead, being my friend
Who could have helped here also,—that, of course!
So far, there's my acquittal, I suppose.
1805 Then comes the marriage itself—no question, lords,
Of the entire validity of that!
In the extreme distress, 't is true,
For after-reasons, furnished abundantly,
I wished the thing invalid, went to you
1810 Only some months since, set you duly forth

---

[1] silly idea.

[2] explicit.

[3] fixed by law.

[4] lawyer.

[5] the collection of legal codes and decisions which still served as the basis of Roman law at this time.

My wrong and prayed your remedy, that a cheat
Should not have force to cheat my whole life long.
"Annul a marriage? 'T is impossible!
Though ring about your neck be brass not gold,
1815 Needs must it clasp, gangrene you all the same!"
Well, let me have the benefit, just so far,
O' the fact announced,—my wife then is my wife,
I have allowance for a husband's right.
I am charged with passing right's due
          bound,—such acts
1820 As I thought just, my wife called cruelty,
Complained of in due form,—convoked no court
Of common gossipry, but took her wrongs—
And not once, but so long as patience served—
To the town's top, jurisdiction's pride of place,
1825 To the Archbishop and the Governor,
These heard her charge with my reply, and found
That futile, this sufficient: they dismissed
The hysteric querulous rebel, and confirmed
Authority in its wholesome exercise,
1830 They, with directest access to the facts.
"—Ay, for it was their friendship favoured you,
Hereditary alliance against a breach
I' the social order: prejudice for the name
Of Franceschini!"—So I hear it said:
1835 But not here. You, lords, never will you say
"Such is the nullity of grace and truth,
Such the corruption of the faith, such lapse
Of law, such warrant have the Molinists
For daring reprehend us as they do,—
1840 That we pronounce it just a common case,
Two dignitaries, each in his degree
First, foremost, this the spiritual head, and that
The secular arm o' the body politic,
Should, for mere wrongs' love and injustice' sake,
1845 Side with, aid and abet in cruelty
This broken beggarly noble,—bribed perhaps
By his watered wine and mouldy crust of bread—
Rather than that sweet tremulous flower-like wife
Who kissed their hands and curled about their feet
1850 Looking the irresistible loveliness

In tears that takes man captive, turns"…enough!
Do you blast your predecessors? What forbids
Posterity to trebly blast yourselves
Who set the example and instruct their tongue?
1855 You dreaded the crowd, succumbed to the popular
          cry,
Or else, would nowise seem defer thereto
And yield to public clamour though i' the right!
You ridded your eye of my unseemliness,
The noble whose misfortune wearied you,—
1860 Or, what's more probable, made common cause
With the cleric section, punished in myself
Maladroit uncomplaisant laity,
Defective in behaviour to a priest
Who claimed the customary partnership
1865 I' the house and the wife. Lords, any lie will serve!
Look to it,—or allow me freed so far!

Then I proceed a step, come with clean hands
Thus far, re-tell the tale told eight months since.
The wife, you allow so far, I have not wronged,
1870 Has fled my roof, plundered me and decamped
In company with the priest her paramour:
And I gave chace, came up with, caught the two
At the wayside inn where both had spent the night,
Found them in flagrant fault, and found as well,
1875 By documents with name and plan and date,
The fault was furtive then that's flagrant now,
Their intercourse a long established crime.
I did not take the license law's self gives
To slay both criminals o' the spot at the time,
1880 But held my hand,—preferred play prodigy
Of patience which the world calls cowardice,
Rather than seem anticipate the law
And cast discredit on its organs,—you—
So, to your bar I brought both criminals,
1885 And made my statement: heard their counter-charge
Nay,—their corroboration of my tale,
Nowise disputing its allegements, not
I' the main, not more than nature's decency
Compels men to keep silence in this kind,—

890 Only contending that the deeds avowed
Would take another colour and bear excuse.
You were to judge between us; so you did.
You disregard the excuse, you breathe away
The colour of innocence and leave guilt black,
895 "Guilty" is the decision of the court,
And that I stand in consequence untouched,
One white integrity from head to heel.
Not guilty? Why then did you punish them?
True, punishment has been inadequate—
900 'T is not I only, not my friends that joke,
My foes that jeer, who echo "inadequate"—
For, by a chance that comes to help for once,
The same case simultaneously was judged
At Arezzo, in the province of the Court
905 Where the crime had beginning but not end.
They then, deciding on but half o' the crime,
The effraction,[1] robbery,—features of the fault
I never cared to dwell upon at Rome,—
What was it they adjudged as penalty
910 To Pompilia,—the one criminal o' the pair
Amenable[2] to their judgment, not the priest
Who is Rome's? Why, just imprisonment for life
I' the Stinche. There was Tuscany's award
To a wife that robs her husband: you at Rome
915 Having to deal with adultery in a wife
And, in a priest, breach of the priestly vow,
Give gentle sequestration for a month
In a manageable Convent, then release,
You call imprisonment, in the very house
920 O' the very couple, the sole aim and end
Of the culprits' crime was—there to reach and rest
And there take solace and defy me: well,—
This difference 'twixt their penalty and yours
Is immaterial: make your penalty less—
925 Merely that she should henceforth wear black gloves
And white fan, she who wore the opposite—
Why, all the same the fact o' the thing subsists.

_____

[1] burglary.

[2] subject.

Reconcile to your conscience as you may,
Be it on your own heads, you pronounced one half
1930 O' the penalty for heinousness like hers
And his, that's for a fault at Carnival
Of comfit-pelting past discretion's law,
Or accident to handkerchief in Lent
Which falls perversely as a lady kneels
1935 Abruptly, and but half conceals her neck!
I acquiesce for my part,—punished, though
By a pin-point scratch, means guilty: guilty means
—What have I been but innocent hitherto?
Anyhow, here the offence, being punished, ends.

1940 Ends?—for you deemed so, did you not, sweet
lords?
That was throughout the veritable aim
O' the sentence light or heavy,—to redress
Recognised wrong? You righted me, I think?
Well then,—what if I, at this last of all,
1945 Demonstrate you, as my whole pleading proves,
No particle of wrong received thereby
One atom of right?—that cure grew worse disease?
That in the process you call "justice done"
All along you have nipped away just inch
1950 By inch the creeping climbing length of plague
Breaking my tree of life from root to branch,
And left me, after all and every act
Of your interference,—lightened of what load?
At liberty wherein? Mere words and wind!
1955 "Now I was saved, now I should feel no more
The hot breath, find a respite from fixed eye
And vibrant tongue!" Why, scarce your back was
turned,
There was the reptile, that feigned death at first,
Renewing its detested spire and spire
1960 Around me, rising to such heights of hate
That, so far from mere purpose now to crush
And coil itself on the remains of me,
Body and mind, and there flesh fang content,
Its aim is now to evoke life from death,
1965 Make me anew, satisfy in my son

The hunger I may feed but never sate,
Tormented on to perpetuity,—
My son, whom, dead, I shall know, understand,
Feel, hear, see, never more escape the sight
1970 In heaven that's turned to hell, or hell returned
(So, rather, say) to this same earth again,—
Moulded into the image and made one,
Fashioned of soul as featured like in face,
First taught to laugh and lisp and stand and go
1975 By that thief, poisoner and adulteress
I call Pompilia, he calls...sacred name,
Be unpronounced, be unpolluted here!
And last led up to the glory and prize of hate
By his...foster-father, Caponsacchi's self,
1980 The perjured priest, pink[1] of conspirators,
Tricksters and knaves, yet polished, superfine,
Manhood to model adolescence by...
Lords, look on me, declare,—when, what I show,
Is nothing more nor less than what you deemed
1985 And doled me out for justice,—what did you say?
For reparation, restitution and more,—
Will you not thank, praise, bid me to your breasts
For having done the thing you thought to do,
And thoroughly trampled out sin's life at last?
1990 I have heightened phrase to make your soft speech
        serve,
Doubled the blow you but essayed to strike,
Carried into effect your mandate here
That else had fallen to ground: mere duty done,
Oversight of the master just supplied
1995 By zeal i' the servant: I, being used to serve,
Have simply...what is it they charge me with?
Blackened again, made legible once more
Your own decree, not permanently writ,
Rightly conceived but all too faintly traced,—
2000 It reads efficient,[2] now, comminatory,[3]
A terror to the wicked, answers so

The mood o' the magistrate, the mind of law.
Absolve, then, me, law's mere executant!
Protect your own defender,—save me, Sirs!
2005 Give me my life, give me my liberty,
My good name and my civic rights again!
It would be too fond, too complacent play
Into the hands o' the devil, should we lose
The game here, I for God: a soldier-bee
2010 That yields his life, exenterate[4] with the stroke
O' the sting that saves the hive. I need that life,
Oh, never fear! I'll find life plenty use
Though it should last five years more, aches and all!
For, first thing, there's the mother's age to help—
2015 Let her come break her heart upon my breast,
Not on the blank stone of my nameless tomb!
The fugitive brother has to be bidden back
To the old routine, repugnant to the tread,
Of daily suit and service to the Church,—
2020 Thro' gibe and jest, those stones that Shimei[5]
        flung!
Ay, and the spirit-broken youth at home,
The awe-struck altar-ministrant, shall make
Amends for faith now palsied at the source,
Shall see truth yet triumphant, justice yet
2025 A victor in the battle of this world!
Give me—for last, best gift, my son again,
Whom law makes mine,—I take him at your word,
Mine be he, by miraculous mercy, lords!
Let me lift up his youth and innocence
2030 To purify my palace, room by room
Purged of the memories, lend from his bright brow
Light to the old proud paladin[6] my sire
Shrunk now for same into the darkest shade
O' the tapestry, showed him once and shrouds him
        now!
2035 Then may we,—strong from that rekindled smile,—
Go forward, face new times, the better day.

---

[1] the flower of, perfection.

[2] effective, productive of results.

[3] threatening.

[4] disemboweled.

[5] 2 Samuel 2:5–13—the stones were thrown at David.

[6] perfect knight.

And when, in times made better through your brave
Decision now,—might but Utopia be!—
Rome rife with honest women and strong men,
1040 Manners reformed, old habits back once more,
Customs that recognize the standard worth,—
The wholesome household rule in force again,
Husbands once more God's representative,
Wives like the typical Spouse once more, and Priests
1045 No longer men of Belial,[1] with no aim
At leading silly women captive, but
Of rising to such duties as yours now,—
Then will I set my son at my right-hand
And tell his father's story to this point,
1050 Adding "The task seemed superhuman, still
I dared and did it, trusting God and law:
And they approved of me: give praise to both!"
And if, for answer, he shall stoop to kiss
My hand, and peradventure start thereat,—
1055 I engage to smile "That was an accident
I' the necessary process,—just a trip
O' the torture-irons in their search for truth,—
Hardly misfortune, and no fault at all."
—1868-69

Pompilia: Book VII [2]

I am just seventeen years and five months old,
And, if I lived one day more, three full weeks;
'T is writ so in the church's register,
Lorenzo in Lucina, all my names
5 At length, so many names for one poor child,
—Francesca Camilla Vittoria Angela
Pompilia Comparini,—laughable!
Also 't is writ that I was married there
Four years ago: and they will add, I hope,
10 When they insert my death, a word or two,—

Omitting all about the mode of death,—
This, in its place, this which one cares to know,
That I had been a mother of a son
Exactly two weeks. It will be through grace
15 O' the Curate, not through any claim I have;
Because the boy was born at, so baptized
Close to, the Villa, in the proper church:
A pretty church, I say no word against,
Yet stranger-like,—while this Lorenzo seems
20 My own particular place, I always say.
I used to wonder, when I stood scarce high
As the bed here, what the marble lion[3] meant,
With half his body rushing from the wall,
Eating the figure of a prostrate man—
25 (To the right, it is, of entry by the door)
An ominous sign to one baptized like me,
Married, and to be buried there, I hope.
And they should add, to have my life complete,
He is a boy and Gaetan by name—
30 Gaetano, for a reason,[4]—if the friar
Don Celestine will ask this grace for me
Of Curate Ottoboni: he it was
Baptized me: he remembers my whole life
As I do his grey hair.

35   All these few things
I know are true,—will you remember them?
Because time flies. The surgeon cared for me,
To count my wounds,—twenty-two dagger-
     wounds,
Five deadly, but I do not suffer much—
40 Or too much pain,—and am to die to-night.

Oh, how good God is that my babe was born,
—Better than born, baptized and hid away
Before this happened, safe from being hurt!
That had been sin God could not well forgive:
45 He was too young to smile and save himself.

---

[1] "they knew not the Lord": 1 Samuel 2:12, 22.

[2] the time is the fourth day after the murders, the same day Caponsacchi appeared before the court.

[3] There were two lions in the portico of the church of San Lorenzo.

[4] See the next note.

When they took, two days after he was born,
My babe away from me to be baptized
And hidden awhile, for fear his foe should find,—
The country-woman, used to nursing babes,
50 Said "Why take on so? where is the great loss?
These next three weeks he will but sleep and feed,
Only begin to smile at the month's end;
He would not know you, if you kept him here,
Sooner than that; so, spend three merry weeks
55 Snug in the Villa, getting strong and stout,
And then I bring him back to be your own,
And both of you may steal to—we know where!"
The month—there wants of it two weeks this day!
Still, I half fancied when I heard the knock
60 At the Villa in the dusk, it might prove she—
Come to say "Since he smiles before the time,
Why should I cheat you out of one good hour?
Back I have brought him; speak to him and judge!"
Now I shall never see him; what is worse,
65 When he grows up and gets to be my age,
He will seem hardly more than a great boy;
And if he asks "What was my mother like?"
People may answer "Like girls of seventeen"—
And how can he but think of this and that,
70 Lucias, Marias, Sofias, who titter or blush
When he regards them as such boys may do?
Therefore I wish some one will please to say
I looked already old though I was young;
Do I not…say, if you are by to speak…
75 Look nearer twenty? No more like, at least,
Girls who look arch or redden when boys laugh,
Than the poor Virgin that I used to know
At our street-corner in a lonely niche,—
The babe, that sat upon her knees, broke off,—
80 Thin white glazed clay, you pitied her the more:
She, not the gay ones, always got my rose.

How happy those are who know how to write!
Such could write what their son should read in
    time,
Had they a whole day to live out like me.

85 Also my name is not a common name,
"Pompilia," and may help to keep apart
A little the thing I am from what girls are.
But then how far away, how hard to find
Will anything about me have become,
90 Even if the boy bethink himself and ask!
No father that he ever knew at all,
Nor ever had—no, never had, I say!
That is the truth,—nor any mother left,
Out of the little two weeks that she lived,
95 Fit for such memory as might assist:
As good too as no family, no name,
Not even poor old Pietro's name, nor hers,
Poor kind unwise Violante, since it seems
They must not be my parents any more.
100 That is why something put it in my head
To call the boy "Gaetano"—no old name
For sorrow's sake; I looked up to the sky
And took a new saint to begin anew.[1]
One who has only been made saint—how long?
105 Twenty-five years: so, carefuller, perhaps,
To guard a namesake than those old saints grow,
Tired out by this time,—see my own five saints![2]

On second thoughts, I hope he will regard
The history of me as what someone dreamed,
110 And get to disbelieve it at the last:
Since to myself it dwindles fast to that,
Sheer dreaming and impossibility,—
Just in four days too! All the seventeen years,
Not once did a suspicion visit me
115 How very different a lot is mine
From any other woman's in the world.
The reason must be, 't was by step and step
It got to grow so terrible and strange:
These strange woes stole on tiptoe, as it were,
120 Into my neighbourhood and privacy,
Sat down where I sat, laid them where I lay;

---

[1] St. Gaetano, canonized in 1671.

[2] See ll. 6–7.

And I was found familiarised with fear,
When friends broke in, held up a torch and cried
"Why, you Pompilia in the cavern thus,
125 How comes that arm of yours about a wolf?
And the soft length,—lies in and out your feet
And laps you round the knee,—a snake it is!"
And so on.

        Well, and they are right enough,
130 By the torch they hold up now: for first, observe,
I never had a father,—no, nor yet
A mother: my own boy can say at least
"I had a mother whom I kept two weeks!"
Not I, who little used to doubt—*I* doubt
135 Good Pietro, kind Violante, gave me birth?
They loved me always as I love my babe
(—Nearly so, that is—quite so could not be—)
Did for me all I meant to do for him,
Till one surprising day, three years ago,
140 They both declared, at Rome, before some judge
In some court where the people flocked to hear,
That really I had never been their child,
Was a mere castaway, the careless crime
Of an unknown man, the crime and care too much
145 Of a woman known too well,—little to these,
Therefore, of whom I was the flesh and blood:
What then to Pietro and Violante, both
No more my relatives than you or you?
Nothing to them! You know what they declared.

150 So with my husband,—just such a surprise,
Such a mistake, in that relationship!
Everyone says that husbands love their wives,
Guard them and guide them, give them happiness;
'Tis duty, law, pleasure, religion: well,
155 You see how much of this comes true in mine!
People indeed would fain have somehow proved
He was no husband: but he did not hear,
Or would not wait, and so has killed us all.
Then there is…only let me name one more!
160 There is the friend,—men will not ask about,

But tell untruths of, and give nicknames to,
And think my lover, most surprise of all!
Do only hear, it is the priest they mean,
Giuseppe Caponsacchi: a priest—love,
165 And love me! Well, yet people think he did.
I am married, he has taken priestly vows,
They know that, and yet go on, say, the same,
"Yes, how he loves you!" "That was love"—they say,
When anything is answered that they ask:
170 Or else "No wonder you love him"—they say.
Then they shake heads, pity much, scarcely blame—
As if we neither of us lacked excuse,
And anyhow are punished to the full,
And downright love atones for everything!
175 Nay, I heard read-out in the public court
Before the judge, in presence of my friends,
Letters 't was said the priest had sent to me,
And other letters sent him by myself,
We being lovers!

180   Listen what this is like!
When I was a mere child, my mother…that's
Violante, you must let me call her so
Nor waste time, trying to unlearn the word,…
She brought a neighbour's child of my own age
185 To play with me of rainy afternoons;
And, since there hung a tapestry on the wall,
We two agreed to find each other out
Among the figures. "Tisbe,[1] that is you,
With half-moon on your hair-knot, spear in hand,
190 Flying, but no wings, only the great scarf
Blown to a bluish rainbow at your back:
Call off your hound and leave the stag alone!"
"—And there are you, Pompilia, such green leaves
Flourishing out of your five finger-ends,
195 And all the rest of you so brown and rough:

---

[1] Diana the huntress.

Why is it you are turned a sort of tree?"[1]
You know the figures never were ourselves
Though we nicknamed them so. Thus, all my
    life,—
As well what was, as what, like this, was not,—
200 Looks old, fantastic and impossible:
I touch a fairy thing that fades and fades,
—Even to my babe! I thought, when he was born,
Something began for once that would not end,
Nor change into a laugh at me, but stay
205 For evermore, eternally quite mine.
    Well, so he is,—but yet they bore him off,
The third day, lest my husband should lay traps
And catch him, and by means of him catch me.
Since they have saved him so, it was well done:
210 Yet thence comes such confusion of what was
With what will be,—that late seems long ago,
And, what years should bring round, already come,
Till even he withdraws into a dream
As the rest do: I fancy him grown great,
215 Strong, stern, a tall young man who tutors me,
Frowns with the others "Poor imprudent child!
Why did you venture out of the safe street?
Why go so far from help to that lone house?
Why open at the whisper and the knock?"

220 Six days ago when it was New Year's-day,
We bent above the fire and talked of him,
What he should do when he was grown and great.
Violante, Pietro, each had given the arm
I leant on, to walk by, from couch to chair
225 And fireside,—laughed, as I lay safe at last,
"Pompilia's march from bed to board is made,
Pompilia back again and with a babe,
Shall one day lend his arm and help her walk!"
Then we all wished each other more New Years.
230 Pietro began to scheme—"Our cause is gained;
The law is stronger than a wicked man:

Let him henceforth go his way, leave us ours!
We will avoid the city, tempt no more
The greedy ones by feasting and parade,—
235 Live at the other villa, we know where,
Still farther off, and we can watch the babe
Grow fast in the good air; and wood is cheap
And wine sincere[2] outside the city gate.
I still have two or three old friends will grope
240 Their way along the mere half-mile of road,
With staff and lantern on a moonless night
When one needs talk: they'll find me, never fear,
And I'll find them a flash of the old sort yet!"
Violante said "You chatter like a crow:
245 Pompilia tires o' the tattle, and shall to-bed:
Do not too much the first day,—somewhat more
To-morrow, and, the next, begin the cape
And hood and coat! I have spun wool enough."
Oh what a happy friendly eve was that!

250 And, next day, about noon, out Pietro went—
He was so happy and would talk so much,
Until Violante pushed and laughed him forth
Sight-seeing in the cold,—"So much to see
I' the churches! Swathe your throat three times!"
    she cried,
255 "And, above all, beware the slippery ways,
And bring us all the news by supper-time!"
He came back late, laid by cloak, staff and hat,
Powdered so thick with snow it made us laugh,
Rolled a great log upon the ash o' the hearth,
260 And bade Violante treat us to a flask,
Because he had obeyed her faithfully,
Gone sight-see through the seven, and found no
    church
To his mind like San Giovanni—"There's the fold,
And all the sheep together, big as cats!
265 And such a shepherd, half the size of life,
Starts up and hears the angel"—when, at the door,
A tap: we started up: you know the rest.

---

[1] an allusion to the story of Daphne who, when chased by Apollo, was turned into a laurel tree.

[2] genuine.

Pietro at least had done no harm, I know;
Nor even Violante, so much harm as makes
270 Such revenge lawful. Certainly she erred—
Did wrong, how shall I dare say otherwise?—
In telling that first falsehood, buying me
From my poor faulty mother at a price,
To pass off upon Pietro as his child:
275 If one should take my babe, give him a name,
Say he was not Gaetano and my own,
But that some other woman made his mouth
And hands and feet,—how very false were that!
No good could come of that; and all harm did.
280 Yet if a stranger were to represent
"Needs must you either give your babe to me
And let me call him mine for ever more,
Or let your husband get him"—ah, my God,
That were a trial I refuse to face!
285 Well, just so here: it proved wrong but seemed
        right
To poor Violante—for there lay, she said,
My poor real dying mother in her rags,
Who put me from her with the life and all,
Poverty, pain, shame and disease at once,
290 To die the easier by what price I fetched—
Also (I hope) because I should be spared
Sorrow and sin,—why may not that have helped?
My father,—he was no one, any one,—
The worse, the likelier,—call him,—he who came,
295 Was wicked for his pleasure, went his way,
And left no trace to track by; there remained
Nothing but me, the unnecessary life,
To catch up or let fall,—and yet a thing
She could make happy, be made happy with,
300 This poor Violante,—who would frown thereat?

Well, God, you see! God plants us where we grow.
It is not that, because a bud is born
At a wild briar's end, full i' the wild beast's way,
We ought to pluck and put it out of reach
305 On the oak-tree top,—say, "There the bud
        belongs!"

She thought, moreover, real lies were—lies told
For harm's sake; whereas this had good at heart,
Good for my mother, good for me, and good
For Pietro who was meant to love a babe,
310 And needed one to make his life of use,
Receive his house and land when he should die.
Wrong, wrong and always wrong! how plainly
        wrong!
For see, this fault kept pricking, as faults do,
All the same at her heart,—this falsehood hatched,
315 She could not let it go nor keep it fast.
She told me so,—the first time I was found
Locked in her arms once more after the pain,
When the nuns let me leave them and go home,
And both of us cried all the cares away,—
320 This it was set her on to make amends,
This brought about the marriage—simply this!
Do let me speak for her you blame so much!
When Paul, my husband's brother, found me out,
Heard there was wealth for who should marry me,
325 So, came and made a speech to ask my hand
For Guido,—she, instead of piercing straight
Through the pretence to the ignoble truth,
Fancied she saw God's very finger point,
Designate just the time for planting me,
330 (The wild briar-slip she plucked to love and wear)
In soil where I could strike real root, and grow,
And get to be the thing I called myself:
For, wife and husband are one flesh, God says,
And I, whose parents seemed such and were none,
335 Should in a husband have a husband now,
Find nothing, this time, but was what it seemed,
—All truth and no confusion any more.
I know she meant all good to me, all pain
To herself,—since how could it be aught but pain,
340 To give me up, so, from her very breast,
The wilding flower-tree-branch that, all those years,
She had got used to feel for and find fixed?
She meant well: has it been so ill i' the main?
That is but fair to ask: one cannot judge
345 Of what has been the ill or well of life,

The day that one is dying,—sorrows change
Into not altogether sorrow-like;
I do see strangeness but scarce misery,
Now it is over, and no danger more.
350 My child is safe; there seems not so much pain.
It comes, most like, that I am just absolved,
Purged of the past, the foul in me, washed fair,—
One cannot both have and not have, you know,—
Being right now, I am happy and colour things.
355 Yes, every body that leaves life sees all
Softened and bettered: so with other sights:
To me at least was never evening yet
But seemed far beautifuller than its day,
For past is past.

360   There was a fancy came,
When somewhere, in the journey with my friend,
We stepped into a hovel to get food;
And there began a yelp here, a bark there,—
Misunderstanding creatures that were wroth
365 And vexed themselves and us till we retired.
The hovel is life: no matter what dogs bit
Or cats scratched in the hovel I break from,
All outside is lone field, moon and such peace—
Flowing in, filling up as with a sea
370 Whereon comes Someone, walks fast on the white,
Jesus Christ's self, Don Celestine declares,
To meet me and calm all things back again.

Beside, up to my marriage, thirteen years
Were, each day, happy as the day was long:
375 This may have made the change too terrible.
I know that when Violante told me first
The cavalier,—she meant to bring next morn,
Whom I must also let take, kiss my hand,—
Would be at San Lorenzo the same eve
380 And marry me,—which over, we should go
Home both of us without him as before,
And, till she bade speak, I must hold my tongue,
Such being the correct way with girl-brides,

From whom one word would make a father
      blush,—
385 I know, I say, that when she told me this,
—Well, I no more saw sense in what she said
Than a lamb does in people clipping wool;
Only lay down and let myself be clipped.
And when next day the cavalier who came
390 (Tisbe had told me that the slim young man[1]
With wings at head, and wings at feet, and sword
Threatening a monster, in our tapestry,
Would eat a girl else,—was a cavalier)
When he proved Guido Franceschini,—old
395 And nothing like so tall as I myself,
Hook-nosed and yellow in a bush of beard,
Much like a thing I saw on a boy's wrist,
He called an owl and used for catching birds,—
And when he took my hand and made a smile—
400 Why, the uncomfortableness of it all
Seemed hardly more important in the case
Than,—when one gives you, say, a coin to
      spend,—
Its newness or its oldness; if the piece
Weigh properly and buy you what you wish,
405 No matter whether you get grime or glare!
Men take the coin, return you grapes and figs.
Here, marriage was the coin, a dirty piece
Would purchase me the praise of those I loved:
About what else should I concern myself?

410 So, hardly knowing what a husband meant,
I supposed this or any man would serve,
No whit the worse for being so uncouth:
For I was ill once and a doctor came
With a great ugly hat, no plume thereto,
415 Black jerkin and black buckles and black sword,
And white sharp beard over the ruff in front,
And oh so lean, so sour-faced and austere!—
Who felt my pulse, made me put out my tongue,
Then oped a phial, dripped a drop or two

_____
[1] Perseus, rescuer of Andromeda.

476

420 Of a black bitter something,—I was cured!
What mattered the fierce beard or the grim face?
It was the physic beautified the man,
Master Malpichi,[1]—never met his match
In Rome, they said,—so ugly all the same!

425 However, I was hurried through a storm,
Next dark eve of December's deadest day—
How it rained!—through our street and the Lion's-
    mouth
And the bit of Corso,—cloaked round, covered
    close,
I was like something strange or contraband,—
430 Into blank San Lorenzo, up the aisle,
My mother keeping hold of me so tight,
I fancied we were come to see a corpse
Before the altar which she pulled me toward.
There we found waiting an unpleasant priest
435 Who proved the brother, not our parish friend,
But one with mischief-making mouth and eye,
Paul, whom I know since to my cost. And then
I heard the heavy church-door lock out help
Behind us: for the customary warmth,
440 Two tapers shivered on the altar. "Quick—
Lose no time!"—cried the priest. And straightway
    down
From…what's behind the altar where he hid—
Hawk-nose and yellowness and bush and all,
Stepped Guido, caught my hand, and there was I
445 O' the chancel, and the priest had opened book,
Read here and there, made me say that and this,
And after, told me I was now a wife,
Honoured indeed, since Christ thus weds the
    Church,
And therefore turned he water into wine,
450 To show I should obey my spouse like Christ.
Then the two slipped aside and talked apart,
And I, silent and scared, got down again

And joined my mother who was weeping now.
Nobody seemed to mind us any more,
455 And both of us on tiptoe found our way
To the door which was unlocked by this, and wide.
When we were in the street, the rain had stopped,
All things looked better. At our own house-door,
Violante whispered "No one syllable
460 To Pietro! Girl-brides never breathe a word!"
"—Well treated to a wetting, draggle-tails!"
Laughed Pietro as he opened—"Very near
You made me brave the gutter's roaring sea
To carry off from roost old dove and young,
465 Trussed up in church, the cote, by me, the kite!
What do these priests mean, praying folk to death
On stormy afternoons, with Christmas close
To wash our sins off nor require the rain?"
Violante gave my hand a timely squeeze,
470 Madonna saved me from immodest speech,
I kissed him and was quiet, being a bride.

When I saw nothing more, the next three weeks,
Of Guido—"Nor the Church sees Christ" thought I:
"Nothing is changed however, wine is wine
475 And water only water in our house.
Nor did I see that ugly doctor since
The cure of the illness: just as I was cured,
I am married,—neither scarecrow will return."

Three weeks, I chuckled—"How would Giulia
    stare,
480 And Tecla smile and Tisbe laugh outright,
Were it not impudent[2] for brides to talk!"—
Until one morning, as I sat and sang
At the broidery-frame alone i' the chamber,—loud
Voices, two, three together, sobbings too,
485 And my name, "Guido," "Paolo," flung like stones
From each to the other! In I ran to see.
There stood the very Guido and the priest
With sly face,—formal but nowise afraid,—

---

[1] Marcello Malpighi (1628–94), biologist and physician to the Pope from 1691 to 1694.

[2] immodest.

While Pietro seemed all red and angry, scarce
490 Able to stutter out his wrath in words;
And this it was that made my mother sob,
As he reproached her—"You have murdered us,
Me and yourself and this our child beside!"
Then Guido interposed "Murdered or not,
495 Be it enough your child is now my wife!
I claim and come to take her." Paul put in,
"Consider—kinsman, dare I term you so?—
What is the good of your sagacity
Except to counsel in a strait like this?
500 I guarantee the parties man and wife
Whether you like or loathe it, bless or ban.
May spilt milk be put back within the bowl—
The done thing, undone? You, it is, we look
For counsel to, you fitliest will advise!
505 Since milk, though spilt and spoilt, does marble
        good,
Better we down on knees and scrub the floor,
Than sigh, 'the waste would make a syllabub!'[1]
Help us so turn disaster to account,
So predispose the groom, he needs shall grace
510 The bride with favour from the very first,
Not begin marriage an embittered man!"
He smiled,—the game so wholly in his hands!
While fast and faster sobbed Violante—"Ay,
All of us murdered, past averting now!
515 O my sin, O my secret!" and such like.

Then I began to half surmise the truth;
Something had happened, low, mean, underhand,
False, and my mother was to blame, and I
To pity, whom all spoke of, none addressed:
520 I was the chattel that had caused a crime.
I stood mute,—those who tangled must untie
The embroilment. Pietro cried "Withdraw, my
        child!
She is not helpful to the sacrifice

<hr>

[1] a beverage made of sweetened milk mixed with wine or cider and beaten into a froth.

At this stage,—do you want the victim by
525 While you discuss the value of her blood?
For her sake, I consent to hear you talk:
Go, child, and pray God help the innocent!"

I did go and was praying God, when came
Violante, with eyes swollen and red enough,
530 But movement on her mouth for make-believe
Matters were somehow getting right again.
She bade me sit down by her side and hear.
"You are too young and cannot understand,
Nor did your father understand at first.
535 I wished to benefit all three of us,
And when he failed to take my meaning,—why,
I tried to have my way at unaware—
Obtained him the advantage he refused.
As if I put before him wholesome food
540 Instead of broken victual,—he finds change
I' the viands, never cares to reason why,
But falls to blaming me, would fling the plate
From window, scandalize the neighbourhood,
Even while he smacks his lips,—men's way, my
        child!
545 But either you have prayed him unperverse
Or I have talked him back into his wits:
And Paolo was a help in time of need,—
Guido, not much—my child, the way of men!
A priest is more a woman than a man,
550 And Paul did wonders to persuade. In short,
Yes, he was wrong, your father sees and says;
My scheme was worth attempting: and bears fruit,
Gives you a husband and a noble name,
A palace and no end of pleasant things.
555 What do you care about a handsome youth?
They are so volatile, and teaze their wives!
This is the kind of man to keep the house.
We lose no daughter,—gain a son, that's all:
For 'tis arranged we never separate,
560 Nor miss, in our grey time of life, the tints
Of you that colour eve to match with morn.
In good or ill, we share and share alike,

And cast our lots into a common lap,
And all three die together as we lived!
565 Only, at Arezzo,—that's a Tuscan town,
Not so large as this noisy Rome, no doubt,
But older far and finer much, say folks,—
In a great palace where you will be queen,
Know the Archbishop and the Governor,
570 And we see homage done you ere we die.
Therefore, be good and pardon!"—"Pardon what?
You know things, I am very ignorant:
All is right if you only will not cry!"

And so an end! Because a blank begins
575 From when, at the word, she kissed me hard and
    hot,
And took me back to where my father leaned
Opposite Guido—who stood eyeing him,
As eyes the butcher the cast panting ox
That feels his fate is come, nor struggles more,—
580 While Paul looked archly on, pricked brow at
    whiles
With the pen-point as to punish triumph there,—
And said "Count Guido, take your lawful wife
Until death part you!"

                    All since is one blank,
585 Over and ended; a terrific dream.
It is the good of dreams—so soon they go!
Wake in a horror of heart-beats, you may—
Cry, "The dread thing will never from my
    thoughts!"
Still, a few daylight doses of plain life,
590 Cock-crow and sparrow-chirp, or bleat and bell
Of goats that trot by, tinkling, to be milked;
And when you rub your eyes awake and wide,
Where is the harm o' the horror? Gone! So here.
I know I wake,—but from what? Blank, I say!
595 This is the note of evil: for good lasts.
Even when Don Celestine bade "Search and find!
For your soul's sake, remember what is past,
The better to forgive it,"—all in vain!

What was fast getting indistinct before,
600 Vanished outright. By special grace perhaps,
Between that first calm and this last, four years
Vanish,—one quarter of my life, you know.
I am held up, amid the nothingness,
By one or two truths only—thence I hang,
605 And there I live,—the rest is death or dream,
All but those points of my support. I think
Of what I saw at Rome once in the Square
O' the Spaniards, opposite the Spanish House:[1]
There was a foreigner had trained a goat,
610 A shuddering white woman of a beast,
To climb up, stand straight on a pile of sticks
Put close, which gave the creature room enough:
When she was settled there he, one by one,
Took away all the sticks, left just the four
615 Whereon the little hoofs did really rest,
There she kept firm, all underneath was air.
So, what I hold by, are my prayer to God,
My hope, that came in answer to the prayer,
Some hand would interpose and save me—hand
620 Which proved to be my friend's hand: and,—best
    bliss,—
That fancy which began so faint at first,
That thrill of dawn's suffusion through my dark,
Which I perceive was promise of my child,
The light his unborn face sent long before,—
625 God's way of breaking the good news to flesh.
That is all left now of those four bad years.
Don Celestine urged "But remember more!
Other men's faults may help me find your own.
I need the cruelty exposed, explained,
630 Or how can I advise you to forgive?"
He thought I could not properly forgive
Unless I ceased forgetting,—which is true:
For, bringing back reluctantly to mind
My husband's treatment of me,—by a light
635 That's later than my life-time, I review
And comprehend much and imagine more,

_____
[1] embassy.

479

And have but little to forgive at last.
For now,—be fair and say,—is it not true
He was ill-used and cheated of his hope
640　To get enriched by marriage? Marriage gave
Me and no money, broke the compact so:
He had a right to ask me on those terms,
As Pietro and Violante to declare
They would not give me: so the bargain stood:
645　They broke it, and he felt himself aggrieved,
Became unkind with me to punish them.
They said 't was he began deception first,
Nor, in one point whereto he pledged himself,
Kept promise: what of that, suppose it were?
650　Echoes die off, scarcely reverberate
For ever,—why should ill keep echoing ill,
And never let our ears have done with noise?
Then my poor parents took the violent way
To thwart him,—he must needs retaliate,—wrong,
655　Wrong, and all wrong,—better say, all blind!
As I myself was, that is sure, who else
Had understood the mystery: for his wife
Was bound in some sort to help somehow there.
It seems as if I might have interposed,
660　Blunted the edge of their resentment so,
Since he vexed me because they first vexed him;
"I will entreat them to desist, submit,
Give him the money and be poor in peace,—
Certainly not go tell the world: perhaps
665　He will grow quiet with his gains."

　　　　　　　　　　　　　Yes, say
Something to this effect and you do well!
But then you have to see first: I was blind.
That is the fruit of all such wormy ways,
670　The indirect, the unapproved of God:
You cannot find their author's end and aim,
Not even to substitute your good for bad,
Your open for the irregular; you stand
Stupefied, profitless, as cow or sheep
675　That miss a man's mind; anger him just twice
By trial at repairing the first fault.

Thus, when he blamed me, "You are a coquette,
A lure-owl posturing to attract birds,
You look love-lures at theatre and church,
680　In walk, at window!"—that, I knew, was false:
But why he charged me falsely, whither sought
To drive me by such charge,—how could I know?
So, unaware, I only made things worse.
I tried to soothe him by abjuring walk,
685　Window, church, theatre, for good and all,
As if he had been in earnest: that, you know,
Was nothing like the object of his charge.
Yes, when I got my maid to supplicate
The priest, whose name she read when she would
　　　read
690　Those feigned false letters I was forced to hear
Though I could read no words of,—he should
　　　cease
Writing,—nay, if he minded prayer of mine,
Cease from so much as even pass the street
Whereon our house looked,—in my ignorance
695　I was just thwarting Guido's true intent;
Which was, to bring about a wicked change
Of sport to earnest, tempt a thoughtless man
To write indeed, and pass the house, and more,
Till both of us were taken in a crime.
700　He ought not to have wished me thus act lies,
Simulate folly,—but,—wrong or right, the wish,—
I failed to apprehend its drift. How plain
It follows,—if I fell into such fault,
He also may have overreached the mark,
705　Made mistake, by perversity of brain,
In the whole sad strange plot, this same intrigue
To make me and my friend unself ourselves,
Be other man and woman than we were!
Think it out, you who have the time! for me,—
710　I cannot say less; more I will not say.
Leave it to God to cover and undo!
Only, my dulness should not prove too much!
—Not prove that in a certain other point
Wherein my husband blamed me,—and you
　　　blame,

If I interpret smiles and shakes of head,—
I was dull too. Oh, if I dared but speak!
Must I speak? I am blamed that I forwent
A way to make my husband's favour come.
That is true: I was firm, withstood, refused...
720   —Women as you are, how can I find the words?

I felt there was just one thing Guido claimed
I had no right to give nor he to take;
We being in estrangement, soul from soul:
Till, when I sought help, the Archbishop smiled,
725   Inquiring into privacies of life,
—Said I was blameable—(he stands for God)
Nowise entitled to exemption there.
Then I obeyed,—as surely had obeyed
Were the injunction "Since your husband bids,
730   Swallow the burning coal he proffers you!"
But I did wrong, and he gave wrong advice
Though he were thrice Archbishop,—that, I
        know!—
Now I have got to die and see things clear.
Remember I was barely twelve years old—
735   A child at marriage: I was let alone
For weeks, I told you, lived my child-life still
Even at Arezzo, when I woke and found
First...but I need not think of that again—
Over and ended! Try and take the sense
740   Of what I signify, if it must be so.
After the first, my husband, for hate's sake,
Said one eve, when the simpler cruelty
Seemed somewhat dull at edge and fit to bear,
"We have been man and wife six months almost:
745   How long is this your comedy to last?
Go this night to my chamber, not your own!"
At which word, I did rush—most true the charge—
And gain the Archbishop's house—he stands for
        God—
And fall upon my knees and clasp his feet,
750   Praying him hinder what my estranged soul
Refused to bear, though patient of the rest:
"Place me within a convent," I implored—

"Let me henceforward lead the virgin life
You praise in Her you bid me imitate!"
755   What did he answer? "Folly of ignorance!
Know, daughter, circumstances make or mar
Virginity,—'t is virtue or 't is vice.
That which was glory in the Mother of God
Had been, for instance, damnable in Eve
760   Created to be mother of mankind.
Had Eve, in answer to her Maker's speech
"Be fruitful, multiply, replenish earth"—
Pouted "But I choose rather to remain
Single"—why, she had spared herself forthwith
765   Further probation by the apple and snake,
Been pushed straight out of Paradise! For see—
If motherhood be qualified[1] impure,
I catch you making God command Eve sin!
—A blasphemy so like these Molinists',
770   I must suspect you dip into their books."
Then he pursued "'T was in your covenant!"

No! There my husband never used deceit.
He never did by speech nor act imply
"Because of our souls' yearning that we meet
775   And mix in soul through flesh, which yours and
        mine
Wear and impress, and make their visible selves,
—All which means, for the love of you and me,
Let us became one flesh, being one soul!"
He only stipulated for the wealth;
780   Honest so far. But when he spoke as plain—
Dreadfully honest also—"Since our souls
Stand each from each, a whole world's width
        between,
Give me the fleshy vesture I can reach
And rend and leave just fit for hell to burn!"—
785   Why, in God's name, for Guido's soul's own sake
Imperilled by polluting mine,—I say,
I did resist; would I had overcome!

---

[1] seen as.

My heart died out at the Archbishop's smile;
—It seemed so stale and worn a way o' the world,
790 As though 't were nature frowning—"Here is
     Spring,
The sun shines as he shone at Adam's fall,
The earth requires that warmth reach everywhere:
What, must your patch of snow be saved forsooth
Because you rather fancy snow than flowers?"
795 Something in this style he began with me.
Last he said, savagely for a good man,
"This explains why you call your husband harsh,
Harsh to you, harsh to whom you love. God's
     Bread!
The poor Count has to manage a mere child
800 Whose parents leave untaught the simplest things
Their duty was and privilege to teach,—
Goodwives' instruction, gossips' lore: they laugh
And leave the Count the task,—or leave it me!"
Then I resolved to tell a frightful thing.
805 "I am not ignorant,—know what I say,
Declaring this is sought for hate, not love.
Sir, you may hear things like almighty God.
I tell you that my housemate, yes—the priest
My husband's brother, Canon Girolamo—
810 Has taught me what depraved and misnamed love
Means, and what outward signs denote the sin,
For he solicits me and says he loves,
The idle young priest with nought else to do.
My husband sees this, knows this, and lets be.
815 Is it your counsel I bear this beside?"
"—More scandal, and against a priest this time!
What, 't is the Canon now?"—less snappishly—
"Rise up, my child, for such a child you are,
The rod were too advanced a punishment!
820 Let's try the honeyed cake. A parable!
'Without a parable spake He not to them.'
There was a ripe round long black toothsome fruit,
Even a flower-fig, the prime boast of May:
And, to the tree, said...either the spirit o' the fig,
825 Or, if we bring in men, the gardener,
Archbishop of the orchard—had I time

To try o' the two which fits in best: indeed
It might be the Creator's self, but then
The tree should bear an apple, I suppose,—
830 Well, anyhow, one with authority said
'Ripe fig, burst skin, regale the fig-pecker—
The bird whereof thou art a perquisite!'[1]
'Nay,' with a flounce, replied the restif[2] fig,
'I much prefer to keep my pulp myself:
835 He may go breakfastless and dinnerless,
Supperless of one crimson seed, for me!'
So, back she flopped into her bunch of leaves.
He flew off, left her,—did the natural lord,—
And lo, three hundred thousand bees and wasps
840 Found her out, feasted on her to the shuck:
Such gain the fig's that gave its bird no bite!
The moral,—fools elude their proper lot,
Tempt other fools, get ruined all alike.
Therefore go home, embrace your husband quick!
845 Which if his Canon brother chance to see,
He will the sooner back to book again."

So, home I did go; so, the worst befell:
So, I had proof the Archbishop was just man,
And hardly that, and certainly no more.
850 For, miserable consequence to me,
My husband's hatred waxed nor waned at all,
His brother's boldness grew effrontery soon,
And my last stay and comfort in myself
Was forced from me: henceforth I looked to God
855 Only, nor cared my desecrated soul
Should have fair walls, gay windows for the world.
God's glimmer, that came through the ruin-top,
Was witness why all lights were quenched inside:
Henceforth I asked God counsel, not mankind.

860 So, when I made the effort, saved myself,
They said—"No care to save appearance here!
How cynic,—when, how wanton, were enough!"

---

[1] having sole right to.

[2] perverse.

—Adding, it all came of my mother's life—
My own real mother, whom I never knew,
865 Who did wrong (if she needs must have done wrong)
Through being all her life, not my four years,
At mercy of the hateful,—every beast
O' the field was wont to break that fountain-fence,
Trample the silver into mud so murk
870 Heaven could not find itself reflected there,—
Now they cry "Out on her, who, plashy pool,
Bequeathed turbidity and bitterness
To the daughter-stream where Guido dipt and drank!"

Well, since she had to bear this brand—let me!
875 The rather do I understand her now,—
From my experience of what hate calls love,—
Much love might be in what their love called hate.
If she sold…what they call, sold…me her child—
I shall believe she hoped in her poor heart
880 That I at least might try be good and pure,
Begin to live untempted, not go doomed
And done with ere once found in fault, as she.
Oh and, my mother, it all came to this?
Why should I trust those that speak ill of you,
885 When I mistrust who speaks even well of them?
Why, since all bound to do me good, did harm,
May not you, seeming as you harmed me most,
Have meant to do most good—and feed your child
From bramble-bush, whom not one orchard-tree
890 But drew-back bough from, nor let one fruit fall?
This it was for you sacrificed your babe?
Gained just this, giving your heart's hope away
As I might give mine, loving it as you,
If…but that never could be asked of me!

895 There, enough! I have my support again,
Again the knowledge that my babe was, is,
Will be mine only. Him, by death, I give
Outright to God, without a further care,—
But not to any parent in the world,—

900 So to be safe: why is it we repine?
What guardianship were safer could we choose?
All human plans and projects come to nought,
My life, and what I know of other lives,
Prove that: no plan nor project! God shall care!

905 And now you are not tired? How patient then
All of you,—Oh yes, patient this long while
Listening, and understanding, I am sure!
Four days ago, when I was sound and well
And like to live, no one would understand.
910 People were kind, but smiled "And what of him,
Your friend, whose tonsure, the rich dark-brown hides?
There, there!—your lover, do we dream he was?
A priest too—never were such naughtiness!
Still, he thinks many a long think, never fear,
915 After the shy pale lady,—lay so light
For a moment in his arms, the lucky one!"
And so on: wherefore should I blame you much?
So we are made, such difference in minds,
Such difference too in eyes that see the minds!
920 That man, you misinterpret and misprise—
The glory of his nature, I had thought,
Shot itself out in white light, blazed the truth
Through every atom of his act with me:
Yet where I point you, through the chrystal shrine,
925 Purity in quintessence, one dew-drop,
You all descry a spider in the midst.
One says, "The head of it is plain to see,"
And one, "They are the feet by which I judge,"
All say, "Those films were spun by nothing else."

930 Then, I must lay my babe away with God,
Nor think of him again, for gratitude.
Yes, my last breath shall wholly spend itself
In one attempt more to disperse the stain,
The mist from other breath fond mouths have made,
935 About a lustrous and pellucid soul:
So that, when I am gone but sorrow stays,

And people need assurance in their doubt
If God yet have a servant, man a friend,
The weak a saviour and the vile a foe,—
940 Let him be present, by the name invoked,
Giuseppe-Maria Caponsacchi!

                              There,
Strength comes already with the utterance!
I will remember once more for his sake
945 The sorrow: for he lives and is belied.
Could he be here, how he would speak for me!

I had been miserable three drear years
In that dread palace and lay passive now,
When I first learned there could be such a man.
950 Thus it fell: I was at a public play,
In the last days of Carnival last March,
Brought there I knew not why, but now know well.
My husband put me where I sat, in front;
Then crouched down, breathed cold through me
        from behind,
955 Stationed i' the shadow,—none in front could
        see,—
I, it was, faced the stranger-throng beneath,
The crowd with upturned faces, eyes one stare,
Voices one buzz. I looked but to the stage,
Whereupon two lovers sang and interchanged
960 "True life is only love, love only bliss:
I love thee—thee I love!" then they embraced.
I looked thence to the ceiling and the walls,—
Over the crowd, those voices and those eyes,—
My thoughts went through the roof and out, to
        Rome
965 On wings of music, waft of measured words,—
Set me down there, a happy child again,
Sure that to-morrow would be festa-day,
Hearing my parents praise past festas more,
And seeing they were old if I was young,
970 Yet wondering why they still would end discourse
With "We must soon go, you abide your time,

And,—might we haply see the proper friend
Throw his arm over you and make you safe!"

Sudden I saw him; into my lap there fell
975 A foolish twist of comfits, broke my dream
And brought me from the air and laid me low,
As ruined as the soaring bee that's reached
(So Pietro told me at the Villa once)
By the dust-handful. There the comfits lay:
980 I looked to see who flung them, and I faced
This Caponsacchi, looking up in turn.
Ere I could reason out why, I felt sure,
Whoever flung them, his was not the hand,—
Up rose the round face and good-natured grin
985 Of him who, in effect, had played the prank,
From covert close beside the earnest face,—
Fat waggish Conti, friend of all the world.
He was my husband's cousin, privileged
To throw the thing: the other, silent, grave,
990 Solemn almost, saw me, as I saw him.

There is a psalm Don Celestine recites,
"Had I a dove's wings, how I fain would flee!"
The psalm runs not "I hope, I pray for wings,"—
Not "If wings fall from heaven, I fix them fast,"—
995 Simply "How good it were to fly and rest,
Have hope now, and one day expect content!
How well to do what I shall never do!"
So I said "Had there been a man like that,
To lift me with his strength out of all strife
1000 Into the calm, how I could fly and rest!
I have a keeper in the garden here
Whose sole employment is to strike me low
If ever I, for solace, seek the sun.
Life means with me successful feigning death,
1005 Lying stone-like, eluding notice so,
Forgoing here the turf and there the sky.
Suppose that man had been instead of this!"

Presently Conti laughed into my ear,
—Had tripped up to the raised place where I sat—

1010 "Cousin, I flung them brutishly and hard!
Because you must be hurt, to look austere
As Caponsacchi yonder, my tall friend
A-gazing now. Ah, Guido, you so close?
Keep on your knees, do! Beg her to forgive!
1015 My cornet[1] battered like a cannon-ball.
Good bye, I'm gone!"—nor waited the reply.

That night at supper, out my husband broke,
"Why was that throwing, that buffoonery?
Do you think I am your dupe? What man would
    dare
1020 Throw comfits in a stranger lady's lap?
'Twas knowledge of you bred such insolence
In Caponsacchi; he dared shoot the bolt,
Using that Conti for his stalking-horse.
How could you see him this once and no more,
1025 When he is always haunting hereabout
At the street-corner or the palace-side,
Publishing my shame and your impudence?
You are a wanton,—I a dupe, you think?
O Christ, what hinders that I kill her quick?"
1030 Whereat he drew his sword and feigned a thrust.

All this, now,—being not so strange to me,
Used to such misconception day by day
And broken-in to bear,—I bore, this time,
More quietly than woman should perhaps;
1035 Repeated the mere truth and held my tongue.

Then he said, "Since you play the ignorant,
I shall instruct you. This amour,—commenced
Or finished or midway in act, all's one,—
'Tis the town-talk; so my revenge shall be.
1040 Does he presume because he is a priest?
I warn him that the sword I wear shall pink
His lily-scented cassock through and through,
Next time I catch him underneath your eaves!"

_____

[1] a piece of paper twisted like a cone.

But he had threatened with the sword so oft
1045 And, after all, not kept his promise. All
I said was, "Let God save the innocent!
Moreover, death is far from a bad fate.
I shall go pray for you and me, not him;
And then I look to sleep, come death or, worse,
1050 Life." So, I slept.

There may have elapsed a week,
When Margherita,—called my waiting-maid,
Whom it is said my husband found too fair—
Who stood and heard the charge and the reply,
1055 Who never once would let the matter rest
From that night forward, but rang changes still
On this the thrust and that the shame, and how
Good cause for jealousy cures jealous fools,
And what a paragon was this same priest
1060 She talked about until I stopped my ears,—
She said, "A week is gone; you comb your hair,
Then go mope in a corner, cheek on palm,
Till night comes round again,—so, waste a week
As if your husband menaced you in sport.
1065 Have not I some acquaintance with his tricks?
Oh no, he did not stab the serving-man
Who made and sang the rhymes about me once!
For why? They sent him to the wars next day.
Nor poisoned he the foreigner, my friend,
1070 Who wagered on the whiteness of my breast,—
The swarth skins of our city in dispute:
For, though he paid me proper compliment,
The Count well knew he was besotted with
Somebody else, a skin as black as ink,
1075 (As all the town knew save my foreigner)
He found and wedded presently,—"Why need
Better revenge?"—the Count asked. But what's here?
A priest, that does not fight, and cannot wed,
Yet must be dealt with! If the Count took fire
1080 For the poor pastime of a minute,—me—
What were the conflagration for yourself,
Countess and lady-wife and all the rest?
The priest will perish; you will grieve too late:

So shall the city-ladies' handsomest
1085 Frankest and liberalest gentleman
Die for you, to appease a scurvy dog
Hanging's too good for. Is there no escape?
Were it not simple Christian charity
To warn the priest be on his guard,—save him
1090 Assured death, save yourself from causing it?
I meet him in the street. Give me a glove,
A ring to show for token! Mum's the word!"

I answered, "If you were, as styled, my maid,
I would command you: as you are, you say,
1095 My husband's intimate,—assist his wife
Who can do nothing but entreat 'Be still!'
Even if you speak truth and a crime is planned,
Leave help to God as I am forced to do!
There is no other course, or we should craze,
1100 Seeing such evil with no human cure.
Reflect that God, who makes the storm desist,
Can make an angry violent heart subside.
Why should we venture teach Him governance?
Never address me on this subject more!"

1105 Next night she said, "But I went, all the same,
—Ay, saw your Caponsacchi in his house,
And come back stuffed with news I must outpour.
I told him, 'Sir, my mistress is a stone:
Why should you harm her for no good you get?
1110 For you do harm her—prowl about our place
With the Count never distant half the street,
Lurking at ever corner, would you look!
'Tis certain she has witched you with a spell.
Are there not other beauties at your beck?
1115 We all know, Donna This and Monna That
Die for a glance of yours, yet here you gaze!
Go make them grateful, leave the stone its cold!'
And he—oh, he turned first white and then red,
And then—'To her behest I bow myself,
1120 Whom I love with my body and my soul:
Only, a word i' the bowing! See, I write
One little word, no harm to see or hear!

Then, fear no further!' This is what he wrote.
I know you cannot read,—therefore, let me!
1125 *'My idol!'*"…

But I took it from her hand
And tore it into shreds. "Why join the rest
Who harm me? Have I ever done you wrong?
People have told me 't is you wrong myself:
1130 Let it suffice I either feel no wrong
Or else forgive it,—yet you turn my foe!
The others hunt me and you throw a noose!"

She muttered, "Have your wilful way!" I slept.

Whereupon…no, I leave my husband out!
1135 It is not to do him more hurt, I speak.
Let it suffice, when misery was most,
One day, I swooned and got a respite so.
She stooped as I was slowly coming to,
This Margherita, ever on my trace,
1140 And whispered—"Caponsacchi!"

If I drowned,
But woke afloat i' the wave with upturned eyes,
And found their first sight was a star! I turned—
For the first time, I let her have her will,
1145 Heard passively,—"The imposthume[1] at such head,
One touch, one lancet-puncture would relieve,—
And still no glance the good physician's way
Who rids you of the torment in a trice!
Still he writes letters you refuse to hear.
1150 He may prevent[2] your husband, kill himself,
So desperate and all fordone is he!
Just hear the pretty verse he made to-day!
A sonnet from Mirtillo. *'Peerless fair…'*
All poetry is difficult to read,
1155 —The sense of it is, anyhow, he seeks
Leave to contrive you an escape from hell,

---

[1] abscess.

[2] anticipate.

And for that purpose asks an interview.
I can write, I can grant it in your name,
Or, what is better, lead you to his house.
1160 Your husband dashes you against the stones;
This man would place each fragment in a shrine:
You hate him, love your husband!"

I returned,
"It is not true I love my husband,—no,
1165 Nor hate this man. I listen while you speak,
—Assured that what you say is false, the same:
Much as when once, to me a little child,
A rough gaunt man in rags, with eyes on fire,
A crowd of boys and idlers at his heels,
1170 Rushed as I crossed the Square, and held my head
In his two hands, 'Here's she will let me speak!
You little girl, whose eyes do good to mine,
I am the Pope, am Sextus, now the Sixth;
And that Twelfth Innocent, proclaimed to-day,
1175 Is Lucifer disguised in human flesh!
The angels, met in conclave, crowned me!'—thus
He gibbered and I listened; but I knew
All was delusion, ere folks interposed
'Unfasten him, the maniac!' Thus I know
1180 All your report of Caponsacchi false,
Folly or dreaming; I have seen so much
By that adventure at the spectacle,
The face I fronted that one first, last time:
He would belie it by such words and thoughts.
1185 Therefore while you profess to show him me,
I ever see his own face. Get you gone!"

"—That will I, nor once open mouth again,—
No, by Saint Joseph and the Holy Ghost!
On your head be the damage, so adieu!"
1190 And so more days, more deeds I must forget,
Till…what a strange thing now is to declare!
Since I say anything, say all if true!
And how my life seems lengthened as to serve!
It may be idle or inopportune,
1195 But, true?—why, what was all I said but truth,

Even when I found that such as are untrue
Could only take the truth in through a lie?
Now—I am speaking truth to the Truth's self:
God will lend credit to my words this time.

1200 It had got half through April. I arose
One vivid daybreak,—who had gone to bed
In the old way my wont those last three years,
Careless until, the cup drained, I should die.
The last sound in my ear, the over-night,
1205 Had been a something let drop on the sly
In prattle by Margherita, "Soon enough
Gaieties end, now Easter's past: a week,
And the Archbishop gets him back to Rome,—
Everyone leaves the town for Rome, this Spring,—
1210 Even Caponsacchi, out of heart and hope,
Resigns himself and follows with the flock."
I heard this drop and drop like rain outside
Fast-falling through the darkness while she spoke:
So had I heard with like indifference,
1215 "And Michael's pair of wings will arrive first
At Rome to introduce the company,
Will bear him from our picture where he fights
Satan,—expect to have that dragon loose
And never a defender!"[1]—my sole thought
1220 Being still, as night came, "Done, another day!
How good to sleep and so get nearer death!"—
When, what, first thing at daybreak, pierced the sleep
With a summons to me? Up I sprang alive,
Light in me, light without me, everywhere
1225 Change! A broad yellow sun-beam was let fall
From heaven to earth,—a sudden drawbridge lay,
Along which marched a myriad merry motes,
Mocking the flies that crossed them and recrossed
In rival dance, companions new-born too.
1230 On the house-eaves, a dripping shag of weed
Shook diamonds on each dull grey lattice-square,

---

[1] an allusion to the painting of St. Michael fighting the dragon by the Italian Spinello Aretino (c. 1346–1410), in the church of San Francesco, Arezzo.

As first one, then another bird leapt by,
And light was off, and lo was back again,
Always with one voice,—where are two such
    joys?—
1235 The blessed building-sparrow! I stepped forth,
Stood on the terrace,—o'er the roofs, such sky!
My heart sang, "I too am to go away,
I too have something I must care about,
Carry away with me to Rome, to Rome!
1240 The bird brings hither sticks and hairs and wool,
And nowhere else i' the world; what fly breaks
    rank,
Falls out of the procession that befits,
From window here to window there, with all
The world to choose,—so well he knows his
    course?
1245 I have my purpose and my motive too,
My march to Rome, like any bird or fly!
Had I been dead! How right to be alive!
Last night I almost prayed for leave to die,
Wished Guido all his pleasure with the sword
1250 Or the poison,—poison, sword, was but a trick,
Harmless, may God forgive him the poor jest!
My life is charmed, will last till I reach Rome!
Yesterday, but for the sin,—ah, nameless be
The deed I could have dared against myself!
1255 Now—see if I will touch an unripe fruit,
And risk the health I want to have and use!
Not to live, now, would be the wickedness,—
For life means to make haste and go to Rome
And leave Arezzo, leave all woes at once!"

1260 Now, understand here, by no means mistake!
Long ago had I tried to leave that house
When it seemed such procedure would stop sin;
And still failed more the more I tried—at first
The Archbishop, as I told you,—next, our lord
1265 The Governor,—indeed I found my way,
I went to the great palace where he rules,
Though I knew well 't was he who,—when I gave
A jewel or two, themselves had given me,

Back to my parents,—since they wanted bread,
1270 They who had never let me want a nosegay,—he
Spoke of the jail for felons, if they kept
What was first theirs, then mine, so doubly theirs,
Though all the while my husband's most of all!
I knew well who had spoke the word wrought this:
1275 Yet, being in extremity, I fled
To the Governor, as I say,—scarce opened lip
When—the cold cruel snicker close behind—
Guido was on my trace, already there,
Exchanging nod and wink for shrug and smile,
1280 And I—pushed back to him and, for my pains,
Paid with…but why remember what is past?
I sought out a poor friar the people call
The Roman, and confessed my sin which came
Of their sin,—that fact could not be repressed,—
1285 The frightfulness of my despair in God:
And, feeling, through the grate, his horror shake,
Implored him, "Write for me who cannot write,
Apprise my parents; make them rescue me!
You bid me be courageous and trust God:
1290 Do you in turn dare somewhat, trust and write
'Dear friends, who used to be my parents once,
And now declare you have no part in me,
This is some riddle I want wit to solve,
Since you must love me with no difference.
1295 Even suppose you altered,—there's your hate,
To ask for: hate of you two dearest ones
I shall find liker love than love found here,
If husbands love their wives. Take me away
And hate me as you do the gnats and fleas,
1300 Even the scorpions! How I shall rejoice!'
Write that and save me!" And he promised—wrote
Or did not write; things never changed at all:
He was not like the Augustinian here!
Last, in a desperation I appealed
1305 To friends, whoever wished me better days,
To Guillichini, that's of kin,—"What, I—
Travel to Rome with you? A flying[1] gout

---

[1] passing from one part of the body to another.

Bids me deny my heart and mind my leg!"
Then I tried Conti, used to brave—laugh back
1310 The louring thunder when his cousin scowled
At me protected by his presence: "You—
Who well know what you cannot save me from,—
Carry me off! What frightens you, a priest?"
He shook his head, looked grave—"Above my
    strength!
1315 Guido has claws that scratch, shows feline teeth;
A formidabler foe than I dare fret:
Give me a dog to deal with, twice the size!
Of course I am a priest and Canon too,
But…by the bye…though both, not quite so bold,
1320 As he, my fellow-Canon, brother-priest,
The personage in such ill odour here
Because of the reports—pure birth o' the brain—
Our Caponsacchi, he's your true Saint George
To slay the monster, set the Princess free,
1325 And have the whole High-Altar to himself:
I always think so when I see that piece
I' the Pieve, that's his church and mine, you know:
Though you drop eyes at mention of his name!"

That name had got to take a half-grotesque
1330 Half-ominous, wholly enigmatic sense,
Like any bye-word, broken bit of song
Born with a meaning, changed by mouth and
    mouth
That mix it in a sneer or smile, as chance
Bids, till it now means nought but ugliness
1335 And perhaps shame.

            —All this intends to say,
That, over-night, the notion of escape
Had seemed distemper, dreaming; and the name,—
Not the man, but the name of him, thus made
1340 Into a mockery and disgrace,—why, she
Who uttered it persistently, had laughed,
"I name his name, and there you start and wince
As criminal from the red tongs' touch!"—yet now,
Now, as I stood letting morn bathe me bright,

1345 Choosing which butterfly should bear my news,—
The white, the brown one, or that tinier blue,—
The Margherita, I detested so,
In she came—"The fine day, the good Spring time!
What, up and out at window? That is best.
1350 No thought of Caponsacchi?—who stood there
All night on one leg, like the sentry crane,
Under the pelting of your water-spout—
Looked last look at your lattice ere he leave
Our city, bury his dead hope at Rome?
1355 Ay, go to looking-glass and make you fine,
While he may die ere touch one least loose hair
You drag at with the comb in such a rage!"

I turned—"Tell Caponsacchi he may come!"

"Tell him to come? Ah, but, for charity,
1360 A truce to fooling! Come? What,—come this eve?
Peter and Paul! But I see through the trick—
Yes, come, and take a flower-pot on his head
Flung from your terrace! No joke, sincere truth?"

How plainly I perceived hell flash and fade
1365 O' the face of her,—the doubt that first paled joy,
Then, final reassurance I indeed
Was caught now, never to be free again!
What did I care?—who felt myself of force[1]
To play with the silk, and spurn the horsehair-
    springe.

1370 "But—do you know that I have bade him come,
And in your own name? I presumed so much,
Knowing the thing you needed in your heart.
But somehow—what had I to show in proof?
He would not come: half-promised, that was all,
1375 And wrote the letters you refused to read.
What is the message that shall move him now?"

------

[1] required.

489

"After the Ave Maria, at first dark,
I will be standing on the terrace, say!
I would I had a good long lock of hair
1380 Should prove I was not lying! Never mind!"

Off she went—"May he not refuse, that's all—
Fearing a trick!"

        I answered, "He will come."
And, all day, I sent prayer like incense up
1385 To God the strong, God the beneficent,
God ever mindful in all strife and strait,
Who, for our own good, makes the need extreme,
Till at the last He puts forth might and saves.
An old rhyme came into my head and rang
1390 Of how a virgin, for the faith of God,
Hid herself, from the Paynims that pursued,
In a cave's heart; until a thunderstone,
Wrapped in a flame, revealed the couch and prey:
And they laughed—Thanks to lightning, ours at
        last!"
1395 And she cried "Wrath of God, assert His love!
Servant of God, thou fire, befriend His child!"
And lo, the fire she grasped at, fixed its flash,
Lay in her hand a calm cold dreadful sword
She brandished till pursuers strewed the ground,
1400 So did the souls within them die away,
As o'er the prostrate bodies, sworded, safe,
She walked forth to the solitudes and Christ:
So should I grasp the lightning and be saved!

And still, as the day wore, the trouble grew
1405 Whereby I guessed there would be born a star,
Until at an intense throe of the dusk,
I started up, was pushed, I dare to say,
Out on the terrace, leaned and looked at last
Where the deliverer waited me: the same
1410 Silent and solemn face, I first descried
At the spectacle, confronted mine once more.

So was that minute twice vouchsafed me, so
The manhood, wasted then, was still at watch
To save me yet a second time: no change
1415 Here, though all else changed in the changing
        world!

I spoke on the instant, as my duty bade,
In some such sense as this, whatever the phrase.
"Friend, foolish words were borne from you to me;
Your soul behind them is the pure strong wind,
1420 Not dust and feathers which its breath may bear:
These to the witless seem the wind itself,
Since proving thus the first of it they feel.
If by mischance you blew offence my way,
The straws are dropt, the wind desists no whit,
1425 And how such strays were caught up in the street
And took a motion from you, why inquire?
I speak to the strong soul, no weak disguise.
If it be truth,—why should I doubt it truth?—
You serve God specially, as priests are bound,
1430 And care about me, stranger as I am,
So far as wish my good,—that miracle
I take to intimate He wills you serve
By saving me,—what else can He direct?
Here is the service. Since a long while now,
1435 I am in course of being put to death:
While death concerned nothing but me, I bowed
The head and bade, in heart, my husband strike.
Now I imperil something more, it seems,
Something that's trulier me than this myself,
1440 Something I trust in God and you to save.
You go to Rome, they tell me: take me there,
Put me back with my people!"

        He replied—
The first word I heard ever from his lips,
1445 All himself in it,—an eternity
Of speech, to match the immeasurable depths
O' the soul that then broke silence—"I am yours."

So did the star rise, soon to lead my step,
Lead on, nor pause before it should stand still
450 Above the House o' the Babe,—my babe to be,
That knew me first and thus made me know him,
That had his right of life and claim on mine,
And would not let me die till he was born,
But pricked me at the heart to save us both,
455 Saying "Have you the will? Leave God the way!"
And the way was Caponsacchi—"mine," thank
God!
He was mine, he is mine, he will be mine.

No pause i' the leading and the light! I know,
Next night there was a cloud came, and not he:
460 But I prayed through the darkness till it broke
And let him shine. The second night, he came.

"The plan is rash; the project desperate:
In such a flight needs must I risk your life,
Give food for falsehood, folly or mistake,
465 Ground for your husband's rancour and
revenge"—
So he began again, with the same face.
I felt that, the same loyalty—one star
Turning now red that was so white before—
One service apprehended newly: just
470 A word of mine and there the white was back!

"No, friend, for you will take me! 'Tis yourself
Risk all, not I,—who let you, for I trust
In the compensating great God: enough!
I know you: when is it that you will come?"

475 "To-morrow at the day's dawn." Then I heard
What I should do: how to prepare for flight
And where to fly.

            That night my husband bade
"—You, whom I loathe, beware you break my sleep
480 This whole night! Couch beside me like the corpse

I would you were!" The rest you know, I think—
How I found Caponsacchi and escaped.

And this man, men call sinner? Jesus Christ!
Of whom men said, with mouths Thyself mad'st
once,
1485 "He hath a devil"—say he was Thy saint,
My Caponsacchi! Shield and show—unshroud
In Thine own time the glory of the soul
If aught obscure,—if ink-spot, from vile pens
Scribbling a charge against him—(I was glad
1490 Then, for the first time, that I could not write)—
Flirted his way, have flecked the blaze!

                                    For me,
'Tis otherwise: let men take, sift my thoughts
—Thoughts I throw like the flax for sun to bleach!
1495 I did think, do think, in the thought shall die,
That to have Caponsacchi for my guide,
Ever the face upturned to mine, the hand
Holding my hand across the world,—a sense
That reads, as only such can read, the mark
1500 God sets on woman, signifying so
She should—shall peradventure—be divine;
Yet 'ware, the while, how weakness mars the print
And makes confusion, leaves the thing men see,
—Not this man,—who from his own soul, re-
writes
1505 The obliterated charter,—love and strength
Mending what's marred: "So kneels a votarist,
Weeds some poor waste traditionary[1] plot
Where shrine once was, where temple yet may be,
Purging the place but worshipping the while,
1510 By faith and not by sight, sight clearest so,—
Such way the saints work,"—says Don Celestine.
But I, not privileged to see a saint
Of old when such walked earth with crown and
palm,
If I call "saint" what saints call something else—

---

[1] by tradition.

1515 The saints must bear with me, impute the fault
To a soul i' the bud, so starved by ignorance,
Stinted of warmth, it will not blow this year
Nor recognize the orb which Spring-flowers know.
But if meanwhile some insect with a heart
1520 Worth floods of lazy music, spendthrift joy—
Some fire-fly renounced Spring for my dwarfed
      cup,
Crept close to me with lustre for the dark,
Comfort against the cold,—what though excess
Of comfort should miscall the creature—sun?
1525 What did the sun to hinder while harsh hands
Petal by petal, crude and colourless,
Tore me? This one heart brought me all the Spring!

Is all told? There's the journey: and where's time
To tell you how that heart burst out in shine?
1530 Yet certain points do press on me too hard.
Each place must have a name, though I forget:
How strange it was—there where the plain begins
And the small river mitigates[1] its flow—
When eve was fading fast, and my soul sank,
1535 And he divined what surge of bitterness,
In overtaking me, would float me back
Whence I was carried by the striding day—
So,—"This grey place was famous once," said he—
And he began that legend of the place
1540 As if in answer to the unspoken fear,
And told me all about a brave man dead,
Which lifted me and let my soul go on!
How did he know too,—at that town's approach
By the rock-side,—that in coming near the signs,
1545 Of life, the house-roofs and the church and tower,
I saw the old boundary and wall o' the world
Rise plain as ever round me, hard and cold,
As if the broken circlet joined again,
Tightened itself about me with no break,—
1550 As if the town would turn Arezzo's self,—
The husband there,—the friends my enemies,

All ranged against me, not an avenue
I try, but would be blocked and drive me back
On him,—this other,...oh the heart in that!
1555 Did not he find, bring, put into my arms,
A new-born babe?—and I saw faces beam
Of the young mother proud to teach me joy,
And gossips round expecting my surprise
At the sudden hole through earth that lets in
      heaven.
1560 I could believe himself by his strong will
Had woven around me what I thought the world
We went along in, every circumstance,
Towns, flowers and faces, all things helped so well!
For, through the journey, was it natural
1565 Such comfort should arise from first to last?
As I look back, all is one milky way;
Still bettered more, the more remembered, so
Do new stars bud while I but search for old,
And fill all gaps i' the glory, and grow him—
1570 Him I now see make the shine everywhere.
Even at the last when the bewildered flesh,
The cloud of weariness about my soul
Clogging too heavily, sucked down all sense,—
Still its last voice was, "He will watch and care;
1575 Let the strength go, I am content: he stays!"
I doubt not he did stay and care for all—
From that sick minute when the head swam round,
And the eyes looked their last and died on him,
As in his arms he caught me and, you say,
1580 Carried me in, that tragical red eve,
And laid me where I next returned to life
In the other red of morning, two red plates
That crushed together, crushed the time between,
And are since then a solid fire to me,—
1585 When in, my dreadful husband and the world
Broke,—and I saw him, master, by hell's right,
And saw my angel helplessly held back
By guards that helped the malice—the lamb prone,
The serpent towering and triumphant—then
1590 Came all the strength back in a sudden swell,
I did for once see right, do right, give tongue

---
[1] checks.

492

The adequate protest: for a worm must turn
If it would have its wrong observed by God.
I did spring up, attempt to thrust aside
595 That ice-block 'twixt the sun and me, lay low
The neutralizer of all good and truth.
If I sinned so,—never obey voice more
O' the Just and Terrible, who bids us—"Bear!"
Not—""Stand by, bear to see my angels bear!"
600 I am clear it was on impulse to serve God
Not save myself,—no—nor my child unborn!
Had I else waited patiently till now?—
Who saw my old kind parents, silly-sooth
And too much trustful, for their worst of faults,
605 Cheated, brow-beaten, stripped and starved, cast
      out
Into the kennel: I remonstrated,
Then sank to silence, for,—their woes at end,
Themselves gone,—only I was left to plague.
If only I was threatened and belied,
610 What matter? I could bear it and did bear;
It was a comfort, still one lot for all:
They were not persecuted for my sake
And I, estranged, the single happy one.
But when at last, all by myself I stood
615 Obeying the clear voice which bade me rise,
Not for my own sake but my babe unborn,
And take the angel's hand was sent to help—
And found the old adversary athwart the path—
Not my hand simply struck from the angel's, but
620 The very angel's self made foul i' the face
By the fiend who struck there,—that I would not
      bear,
That only I resisted! So, my first
And last resistance was invincible.
Prayers move God; threats, and nothing else, move
      men!
625 I must have prayed a man as he were God
When I implored the Governor to right
My parents' wrongs: the answer was a smile.
The Archbishop,—did I clasp his feet enough,
Hide my face hotly on them, while I told

1630 More than I dared make my own mother know?
The profit was—compassion and a jest.
This time, the foolish prayers were done with, right
Used might, and solemnized the sport at once.
All was against the combat: vantage, mine?
1635 The runaway avowed, the accomplice-wife,
In company with the plan-contriving priest?
Yet, shame thus rank and patent, I struck, bare,
At foe from head to foot in magic mail,
And off it withered, cobweb-armoury
1640 Against the lightning! 'T was truth singed the lies
And saved me, not the vain sword nor weak speech!

You see, I will not have the service fail!
I say, the angel saved me: I am safe!
Others may want and wish, I wish nor want
1645 One point o' the circle plainer, where I stand
Traced round about with white to front the world.
What of the calumny I came across,
What o' the way to the end?—the end crowns all.
The judges judged aright i' the main, gave me
1650 The uttermost of my heart's desire, a truce
From torture and Arezzo, balm for hurt
With the quiet nuns,—God recompense the good!
Who said and sang away the ugly past.
And, when my final fortune was revealed,
1655 What safety while, amid my parents' arms,
My babe was given me! Yes, he saved my babe:
It would not have peeped forth, the bird-like thing,
Through that Arezzo noise and trouble: back
Had it returned nor ever let me see!
1660 But the sweet peace cured all, and let me live
And give my bird the life among the leaves
God meant him! Weeks and months of quietude,
I could lie in such peace and learn so much—
Begin the task, I see how needful now,
1665 Of understanding somewhat of my past,—
Know life a little, I should leave so soon.
Therefore, because this man restored my soul,
All has been right; I have gained my gain, enjoyed
As well as suffered,—nay, got foretaste too

1670 Of better life beginning where this ends—
All through the breathing-while allowed me thus,
Which let good premonitions reach my soul
Unthwarted, and benignant influence flow
And interpenetrate and change my heart,
1675 Uncrossed by what was wicked,—nay, unkind.
For, as the weakness of my time drew nigh,
Nobody did me one disservice more,
Spoke coldly or looked strangely, broke the love
I lay in the arms of, till my boy was born,
1680 Born all in love, with nought to spoil the bliss
A whole long fortnight: in a life like mine
A fortnight filled with bliss is long and much.
All women are not mothers of a boy,
Though they live twice the length of my whole life,
1685 And, as they fancy, happily all the same.
There I lay, then, all my great fortnight long,
As if it would continue, broaden out
Happily more and more, and lead to heaven:
Christmas before me,—was not that a chance?
1690 I never realized God's birth before—
How he grew likest God in being born.
This time I felt like Mary, had my babe
Lying a little on my breast like hers.
So all went on till, just four days ago—
1695 The night and the tap.

                    O it shall be success
To the whole of our poor family! My friends
…Nay, father and mother,—give me back my
    word!
They have been rudely stripped of life, disgraced
1700 Like children who must needs go clothed too fine,
Carry the garb of Carnival in Lent:
If they too much affected frippery,
They have been punished and submit themselves,
Say no word: all is over, they see God
1705 Who will not be extreme to mark their fault
Or He had granted respite: they are safe.

For that most woeful man my husband once,
Who, needing respite, still draws vital breath,
I—pardon him? So far as lies in me,
1710 I give him for his good the life he takes,
Praying the world will therefore acquiesce.
Let him make God amends,—none, none to me
Who thank him rather that, whereas strange fate
Mockingly styled him husband and me wife,
1715 Himself this way at least pronounced divorce,
Blotted the marriage-bond: this blood of mine
Flies forth exultingly at any door,
Washes the parchment white, and thanks the blow.
We shall not meet in this world nor the next,
1720 But where will God be absent? In His face
Is light, but in His shadow healing too:
Let Guido touch the shadow and be healed!
And as my presence was importunate,[1]—
My earthly good, temptation and a snare,—
1725 Nothing about me but drew somehow down
His hate upon me,—somewhat so excused
Therefore, since hate was thus the truth of him,—
May my evanishment for evermore
Help further to relieve the heart that cast
1730 Such object of its natural loathing forth!
So he was made; he nowise made himself:
I could not love him, but his mother did.
His soul has never lain beside my soul;
But for the unresisting body,—thanks!
1735 He burned that garment spotted by the flesh!
Whatever he touched is rightly ruined: plague
It caught, and disinfection it had craved
Still but for Guido; I am saved through him
So as by fire; to him—thanks and farewell!

1740 Even for my babe, my boy, there's safety thence—
From the sudden death of me, I mean: we poor
Weak souls, how we endeavour to be strong!
I was already using up my life,—
This portion, now, should do him such a good,

------

[1] troublesome.

745 This other go to keep off such an ill!
The great life; see, a breath and it is gone!
So is detached, so left all by itself
The little life, the fact which means so much.
Shall not God stoop the kindlier to His work,
750 His marvel of creation, foot would crush,
Now that the hand He trusted to receive
And hold it, lets the treasure fall perforce?
The better; He shall have in orphanage
His own way all the clearlier: if my babe
755 Outlive the hour—and he has lived two weeks—
It is through God who knows I am not by.
Who is it makes the soft gold hair turn black,
And sets the tongue, might lie so long at rest,
Trying to talk? Let us leave God alone!
760 Why should I doubt He will explain in time
What I feel now, but fail to find the words?
My babe nor was, nor is, nor yet shall be
Count Guido Franceschini's child at all—
Only his mother's, born of love not hate!
765 So shall I have my rights in after-time.
It seems absurd, impossible to-day;
So seems so much else not explained but known.

Ah! Friends, I thank and bless you every one!
No more now: I withdraw from earth and man
770 To my own soul, compose myself for God.

Well, and there is more! Yes, my end of breath
Shall bear away my soul in being true!
He is still here, not outside with the world,
Here, here, I have him in his rightful place!
775 'T is now, when I am most upon the move,
I feel for what I verily find—again
The face, again the eyes, again, through all,
The heart and its immeasurable love
Of my one friend, my only, all my own,
780 Who put his breast between the spears and me.
Ever with Caponsacchi! Otherwise
Here alone would be failure, loss to me—
How much more loss to him, with life debarred

From giving life, love locked from love's display,
1785 The day-star stopped its task that makes night
        morn!
O lover of my life, O soldier-saint,
No work begun shall ever pause for death!
Love will be helpful to me more and more
I' the coming course, the new path I must tread,
1790 My weak hand in thy strong hand, strong for that!
Tell him that if I seem without him now,
That's the world's insight! Oh, he understands!
He is at Civita—do I once doubt
The world again is holding us apart?
1795 He had been here, displayed in my behalf
The broad brow that reverberates the truth,
And flashed the word God gave him, back to man!
I know where the free soul is flown! My fate
Will have been hard for even him to bear:
1800 Let it confirm him in the trust of God,
Showing how holily he dared the deed!
And, for the rest,—say, from the deed, no touch
Of harm came, but all good, all happiness,
Not one faint fleck of failure! Why explain?
1805 What I see, oh, he sees and how much more!
Tell him,—I know not wherefore the true word
Should fade and fall unuttered at the last—
It was the name of him I sprang to meet
When came the knock, the summons and the end.
1810 "My great heart, my strong hand are back again!"
I would have sprung to these, beckoning across
Murder and hell gigantic and distinct
O' the threshold, posted to exclude me heaven:
He is ordained to call and I to come!
1815 Do not the dead wear flowers when dressed for
        God?
Say,—I am all in flowers from head to foot!
Say,—not one flower of all he said and did,
Might seem to flit unnoticed, fade unknown,
But dropped a seed has grown a balsam-tree
1820 Whereof the blossoming perfumes the place
At this supreme of moments! He is a priest;
He cannot marry therefore, which is right:

I think he would not marry if he could.
Marriage on earth seems such a counterfeit,
1825 Mere imitation of the inimitable:
In heaven we have the real and true and sure.
'T is there they neither marry nor are given
In marriage but are as the angels: right,
Oh how right that is, how like Jesus Christ
1830 To say that! Marriage-making for the earth,
With gold so much,—birth, power, repute so
      much,
Or beauty, youth so much, in lack of these!
Be as the angels rather, who, apart,
Know themselves into one, are found at length
1835 Married, but marry never, no, nor give
In marriage; they are man and wife at once
When the true time is: here we have to wait
Not so long neither! Could we by a wish
Have what we will and get the future now,
1840 Would we wish aught done undone in the past?
So, let him wait God's instant men call years;
Meantime hold hard by truth and his great soul,
Do out the duty! Through such souls alone
God stooping shows sufficient of His light
1845 For us i' the dark to rise by. And I rise.
      —1868–69

Guido: Book XI [1]

You are the Cardinal Acciaiuoli, and you,
  Abate Panciatichi—two good Tuscan names;
Acciaiuoli—ah, your ancestor it was,
Built the huge battlemented convent-block
5 Over the little forky flashing Greve
That takes the quick turn at the foot o' the hill
Just as one first sees Florence: oh those days!
'T is Ema, though, the other rivulet,

The one-arched, brown brick bridge yawns
      over,—yes,
10 Gallop and go five minutes, and you gain
The Roman Gate from where the Ema's bridged:
Kingfishers fly there: how I see the bend
O'erturreted by Certosa [2] which he built,
That Senescal [3] (we styled him) of your House!
15 I do adjure you, help me, Sirs! My blood
Comes from as far a source: ought it to end
This way, by leakage through their scaffold-planks
Into Rome's sink where her red refuse runs?
Sirs, I beseech you by blood-sympathy,
20 If there be any vile experiment
In the air,—if this your visit simply prove,
When all's done, just a well-intentioned trick,
That tries for truth truer than truth itself,
By startling up a man, ere break of day,
25 To tell him he must die at sunset,—pshaw!
That man's a Franceschini; feel his pulse,
Laugh at your folly, and let's all go sleep!
You have my last word,—innocent am I
As Innocent my Pope and murderer,
30 Innocent as a babe, as Mary's own,
As Mary's self,—I said, say and repeat,—
And why, then, should I die twelve hours hence?
      I—
Whom, not twelve hours ago, the gaoler bade
Turn to my straw-truss, settle and sleep sound
35 That I might wake the sooner, promptlier pay
His dues of meat-and-drink-indulgence, cross
His palm with fee of the good-hand, [4] beside,
As gallants use who go at large again!
For why? All honest Rome approved my part;
40 Whoever owned wife, sister, daughter,—nay,
Mistress,—had any shadow of any right
That looks like right, and, all the more resolved,
Held it with tooth and nail,—these manly men

---

[1] The time is before dawn on the day following the Pope's rejection of Guido's appeal.

[2] Carthusian monastery near Florence.

[3] official in charge of feasting and ceremonies in a medieval household.

[4] tip.

Approved! I being for Rome, Rome was for me!
45 Then, there's the point reserved, the subterfuge
My lawyers held by, kept for last resource,
Firm should all else,—the impossible fancy!—
    fail,—
And sneaking burgess-spirit win the day:
The knaves! One plea at least would hold, they
    laughed,
50 One grappling-iron scratch the bottom-rock
Even should the middle mud let anchor go—
And hook my cause on to the Clergy's,—plea
Which, even if law tipped off my hat and plume,
Would show my priestly tonsure, save me so,—
55 The Pope moreover, this old Innocent,
Being so meek and mild and merciful,
So fond o' the poor and so fatigued of earth,
So…fifty thousand devils in deepest hell!
Why must he cure us of our strange conceit
60 Of the angel in man's likeness, that we loved
And looked should help us at a pinch? He help?
He pardon? Here's his mind and message—death,
Thank the good Pope! Now, is he good in this,
Never mind, Christian,—no such stuff's extant,—
65 But will my death do credit to his reign,
Show he both lived and let live, so was good?
Cannot I live if he but like? "The law!"
Why, just the law gives him the very chance,
The precise leave to let my life alone,
70 Which the angelic soul of him (he says)
Yearns after! Here they drop it in his palm,
My lawyers, capital o' the cursed kind,—
A life to take and hold and keep: but no!
He sighs, shakes head, refuses to shut hand,
75 Motions away the gift they bid him grasp,
And of the coyness[1] comes that off I run
And down I go, he best knows whither,—mind,
He knows, and sets me rolling all the same!
Disinterested Vicar of our Lord,
80 This way he abrogates and disallows,

Nullifies and ignores,—reverts in fine
To the good and right, in detriment of me!
Talk away! Will you have the naked truth?
He's sick of his life's supper,—swallowed lies:
85 So, hobbling bedward, needs must ease his maw
Just where I sit o' the door-sill. Sir Abate,
Can you do nothing? Friends, we used to frisk:
What of this sudden slash in a friend's face,
This cut across our good companionship
90 That showed its front so gay when both were
    young?
Were not we put into a beaten path,
Bid pace the world, we nobles born and bred,
The body of friends with each his scutcheon full
Of old achievement and impunity,—
95 Taking the laugh of morn and Sol's salute
As forth we fared, pricked[2] on to breathe[3] our steeds
And take equestrian sport over the green
Under the blue, across the crop,—what care?
So we went prancing up hill and down dale,
100 In and out of the level and the straight,
By the bit of pleasant byeway, where was harm?
Still Sol salutes me and the morning laughs:
I see my grandsire's hoof-prints,—point the spot
Where he drew rein, slipped saddle, and stabbed
    knave
105 For daring throw gibe—much less, stone—from
    pale,[4]
Then back, and on, and up with the cavalcade;
Just so wend we, now canter, now converse,
Till, 'mid the jauncing[5] pride and jaunty port,[6]
Something of a sudden jerks at somebody—
110 A dagger is out, a flashing cut and thrust,
Because I play some prank my grandsire played,
And here I sprawl: where is the company? Gone!

---

[1] reserve.

[2] galloped.

[3] exercise.

[4] fence.

[5] prancing.

[6] elegant, well-bred manner.

A trot and a trample! only I lie trapped,
Writhe in a certain novel springe just set
115 By the good old Pope: I'm first prize. Warn me?
     Why?
Apprize me that the law o' the game is changed?
Enough that I'm a warning, as I writhe,
To all and each my fellows of the file,
And make law plain henceforward past mistake,
120 "For such a prank, death is the penalty!"
Pope the Five Hundredth…what do I know or care?
Deputes your Eminence and Abateship
To announce that, twelve hours from this time, he
     needs
I just essay upon my body and soul
125 The virtue of his bran-new engine,[1] prove
Represser of the pranksome! I'm the first!
Thanks. Do you know what teeth you mean to try
The sharpness of, on this soft neck and throat?
I know it,—I have seen and hate it,—ay,
130 As you shall, while I tell you: let me talk,
Or leave me, at your pleasure! talk I must:
What is your visit but my lure to talk?
You have a something to disclose?—a smile,
At end of the forced sternness, means to mock
135 The heart-beats here? I call your two hearts stone!
Is your charge to stay with me till I die?
Be tacit[2] as your bench, then! Use your ears,
I use my tongue: how glibly yours will run
At pleasant supper-time…God's curse!…to-night
140 When all the guests jump up, begin so brisk
"Welcome, his Eminence who shrived the wretch!
Now we shall have the Abate's story!"

                                        Life!
How I could spill this overplus of mine
145 Among those hoar-haired, shrunk-shanked, odds
     and ends
Of body and soul, old age is chewing dry!

Those windle-straws[3] that stare while purblind
     death
Mows here, mows there, makes hay of juicy me,
And misses, just the bunch of withered weed,
150 Would brighten hell and streak its smoke with flame!
How the life I could shed yet never shrink,
Would drench their stalks with sap like grass in
     May!
Is it not terrible, I entreat you, Sirs?
Such manifold and plenitudinous life,
155 Prompt at death's menace to give blow for threat,
Answer his "Be thou not!" by "Thus I am!"—
Terrible so to be alive yet die?

How I live, how I see! so,—how I speak!
Lucidity of soul unlocks the lips:
160 I never had the words at will before.
How I see all my folly at a glance!
"A man requires a woman and a wife:"
There was my folly; I believed the saw:
I knew that just myself concerned myself,
165 Yet needs must look for what I seemed to lack,
In a woman,—why, the woman's in the man!
Fools we are, how we learn things when too late!
Overmuch life turns round my woman-side;
The male and female in me, mixed before,
170 Settle of a sudden: I'm my wife outright
In this unmanly appetite for truth,
This careless courage as to consequence,
This instantaneous sight through things and
     through,
This voluble rhetoric, if you please,—'t is she!
175 Here you have that Pompilia whom I slew,
Also the folly for which I slew her!

                                        Fool!
And, fool-like, what is it I wander from?
What, of the sharpness of your iron tooth?

---

[1] the guillotine.

[2] taciturn, silent.

---

[3] literally, dried stalks of grass; here used also in the figurative sense of
feeble, scrawny old men.

180　Ah,—that I know the hateful thing: this way.
　　I chanced to stroll forth, many a good year gone,
　　One warm Spring eve in Rome, and unaware
　　Looking, mayhap, to count what stars were out,
　　Came on your huge axe in a frame, that falls
185　And so cuts off a man's head underneath,
　　Mannaia,—thus we made acquaintance first,
　　Out of the way, in a bye-part o' the town,
　　At the Mouth-of-Truth[1] o' the river-side, you
　　　　know:
　　One goes by the Capitol: and wherefore coy,
190　Retiring out of crowded noisy Rome?
　　Because a very little time ago
　　It had done service, chopped off head from trunk,
　　Belonging to a fellow whose poor house
　　The thing had made a point to stand before.
195　Felice Whatsoever-was-the-name
　　Who stabled buffaloes and so gained bread,
　　(Our clowns unyoke them in the ground hard by)
　　And, after use of much improper speech,
　　Had struck at Duke Some-title-or-other's face,
200　Because he kidnapped, carried away and kept
　　Felice's sister that would sit and sing
　　I' the filthy doorway while she plaited fringe
　　To deck the brutes with,—on their gear it goes,—
　　The good girl with the velvet in her voice.
205　So did the Duke, so did Felice, so
　　Did Justice, intervening with her axe.
　　There the man-mutilating engine stood
　　At ease, both gay and grim, like a Swiss guard
　　Off duty,—purified itself as well,
210　Getting dry, sweet and proper for next week,—
　　And doing incidental good, 't was hoped
　　To the rough lesson-lacking populace
　　Who now and then, forsooth, must right their
　　　　wrongs!
　　There stood the twelve-foot-square of scaffold,
　　　　railed

215　Considerately round to elbow-height:
　　(Suppose an officer should tumble thence
　　And sprain his ankle and be lame a month,
　　Through starting when the axe fell and head too?)
　　Railed likewise were the steps whereby 't was
　　　　reached.
220　All of it painted red: red, in the midst,
　　Ran up two narrow tall beams barred across,
　　Since from the summit, some twelve feet to reach,
　　The iron plate with the sharp shearing edge
　　Had…slammed, jerked, shot or slid,—I shall find
　　　　which!
225　There it lay quiet, fast in its fit place,
　　The wooden half-moon collar, now eclipsed
　　By the blade which blocked its curvature: apart,
　　The other half,—the under half-moon board
　　Which, helped by this, completes a neck's
　　　　embrace,—
230　Joined to a sort of desk that wheels aside
　　Out of the way when done with,—down you kneel,
　　In you're wheeled, over you the other drops,
　　Tight you are clipped, whiz, there's the blade on you,
　　Out trundles body, down flops head on floor,
235　And where's your soul gone? That, too, I shall find!
　　This kneeling-place was red, red, never fear!
　　But only slimy-like with paint, not blood,
　　For why? a decent pitcher stood at hand,
　　A broad dish to hold sawdust, and a broom
240　By some unnamed utensil,—scraper-rake,—
　　Each with a conscious air of duty done.
　　Underneath, loungers,—boys and some few men,—
　　Discoursed[2] this platter and the other tool,
　　Just as, when grooms tie up and dress a steed,
245　Boys lounge and look on, and elucubrate[3]
　　What the round brush is used for, what the
　　　　square,—
　　So was explained—to me the skill-less man—
　　The manner of the grooming for next world

---

[1] a marble head of an open-mouthed Triton in the church of Santa Maria in Cosmedin.

[2] discussed.

[3] learnedly explain.

Undergone by Felice What's-his-name.
250 There's no such lovely month in Rome as May—
May's crescent is no half-moon of red plank,
And came now tilting o'er the wave i' the west,
One greenish-golden sea, right 'twixt those bars
Of the engine—I began acquaintance with,
255 Understood, hated, hurried from before,
To have it out of sight and cleanse my soul!
Here it is all again, conserved for use:
Twelve hours hence I may know more, not hate
    worse.
That young May-moon-month! Devils of the deep!
260 Was not a Pope then Pope as much as now?
Used not he chirrup o'er the Merry Tales,
Chuckle,—his nephew so exact the wag
To play a jealous cullion[1] such a trick
As wins the wife i' the pleasant story! Well?
265 Why do things change? Wherefore is Rome
    un-Romed?
I tell you, ere Felice's corpse was cold,
The Duke, that night, threw wide his palace-doors,
Received the compliments o' the quality,
For justice done him,—bowed and smirked his best,
270 And in return passed round a pretty thing,
A portrait of Felice's sister's self,
Florid old rogue Albano's[2] masterpiece,
As—better than virginity in rags—
Bouncing Europa on the back o' the bull:
275 They laughed and took their road the safelier home.
Ah, but times change, there's quite another Pope,
I do the Duke's deed, take Felice's place,
And, being no Felice, lout and clout,[3]
Stomach but ill the phrase "I lose my head!"
280 How euphemistic! Lose what? Lose your ring,
Your snuff-box, tablets,[4] kerchief!—but, your
    head?

I learnt the process at an early age;
'T was useful knowledge in those same old days,
To know the way a head is set on neck.
285 My fencing master urged "Would you excel?
Rest not content with mere bold give-and-guard,
Nor pink the antagonist somehow-anyhow,—
See me dissect a little, and know your game!
Only anatomy makes a thrust the thing."
290 Oh Cardinal, those lithe live necks of ours!
Here go the vertebrae, here's *Atlas*, here
Axis,[5] and here the symphyses[6] stop short,
So wisely and well,—as, o'er a corpse, we cant,—[7]
And here's the silver cord which…what's our word?
295 Depends from the gold bowl, which loosed
    (not "lost")
Lets us from heaven to hell,—one chop, we're
    loose!
"And not much pain i' the process," quoth the sage:
Who told him? Not Felice's ghost, I think!
Such "losing" is scarce Mother Nature's mode.
300 She fain would have cord ease itself away,
Worn to a thread by threescore years and ten,
Snap while we slumber: that seems bearable:
I'm told one clot of blood extravasate[8]
Ends one as certainly as Roland's[9] sword,—
305 One drop of lymph[10] suffused proves Oliver's
    mace,—[11]
Intruding, either of the pleasant pair,
On the arachnoid tunic[12] of my brain.
That's Nature's way of loosing cord!—but Art,
How of Art's process with the engine here?

---

[1] dupe.

[2] Francesco Albano, Bolognese painter (1578–1660).

[3] clod.

[4] memorandum books.

[5] the top vertebrae.

[6] the unions of bones.

[7] chant (with suggestion of affected piety).

[8] escaped from the proper vessel, such as an artery.

[9] Charlemagne's nephew.

[10] body fluid which flows into the blood stream.

[11] fatal (Oliver was Roland's companion in arms).

[12] membrane coating.

310 When bowl and cord alike are crushed across,
Bored between, bruised through? Why, if Fagon's
self,[1]
The French Court's pride, that famed practitioner,
Would pass his cold pale lightning of a knife,
Pistoja-ware,[2] adroit 'twixt joint and joint,
315 With just a "See how facile, gentlefolks!"—
The thing were not so bad to bear! Brute force
Cuts as he comes, breaks in, breaks on, breaks out
O' the hard and soft of you: is that the same?
A lithe snake thrids the hedge, makes throb no leaf:
320 A heavy ox sets chest to brier and branch,
Bursts somehow through, and leaves one hideous
hole
Behind him!

      And why, why must this needs be?
Oh, if men were but good! They are not good,
325 Nowise like Peter: people called him rough,
But if, as I left Rome, I spoke the Saint,
—"*Petrus, quo vadis?*"[3]—doubtless, I should hear,
"To free the prisoner and forgive his fault!
I plucked the absolute dead from God's own bar,
330 And raised up Dorcas,—why not rescue thee?"
What would cost one such nullifying word?
If Innocent succeeds to Peter's place,
Let him think Peter's thought, speak Peter's speech!
I say, he is bound to it: friends, how say you?
335 Concede I be all one bloodguiltiness
And mystery of murder in the flesh,[4]
Why should that fact keep the Pope's mouth shut
fast?
He execrates my crime,—good!—sees hell yawn

One inch from the red plank's end which I press,—
340 Nothing is better! What's the consequence?
How does a Pope proceed that knows his cue?
Why, leaves me linger out my minute here,
Since close on death come judgment and the doom,
Nor cribs at dawn its pittance from a sheep
345 Destined ere dewfall to be butcher's-meat!
Think, Sirs, if I had done you any harm,
And you require the natural revenge,
Suppose, and so intend to poison me,
—Just as you take and slip into my draught
350 The paperful of powder that clears scores,
You notice on my brow a certain blue:
How you both overset the wine at once!
How you both smile! "Our enemy has the plague!
Twelve hours hence he'll be scraping his bones bare
355 Of that intolerable flesh, and die,
Frenzied with pain: no need for poison here!
Step aside and enjoy the spectacle!"
Tender for souls are you, Pope Innocent!
Christ's maxim is—one soul outweighs the world:
360 Respite me, save a soul, then, curse the world!
"No," venerable sire, I hear you smirk,
"No: for Christ's gospel changes names, not things,
Renews the obsolete, does nothing more!
Our fire-new gospel is retinkered law,
365 Our mercy, justice,—Jove's rechristened God,—
Nay, whereas, in the popular conceit,
'T is pity that old harsh Law somehow limps,
Lingers on earth, although Law's day be done,—
Else would benignant Gospel interpose,
370 Not furtively as now, but bold and frank
O'erflutter us with healing in her wings,—
Law is all harshness, Gospel were all love!—
We like to put it, on the contrary,—
Gospel takes up the rod which Law lets fall;
375 Mercy is vigilant when justice sleeps;
Does Law let Guido taste the Gospel-grace?
The secular arm allow the spiritual power
To act for once?—what compliment so fine
As that the Gospel handsomely be harsh,

---

[1] chief physician to Louis XIV.

[2] fine cutlery (including weapons) made at Pistoia, near Florence.

[3] Fleeing Nero's persecution, St. Peter met Jesus on the Appian Way and inquired "*Domine quo vadis?*" ("Lord, whither goest thou?"). Jesus replied "*Venio iterum crucifigi*" ("I am on my way to be crucified"), whereupon St. Peter returned to be martyred. This is the legend as told by St. Ambrose.

[4] the very embodiment of the art of murder.

380 Thrust back Law's victim on the nice and coy?"[1]
Yes, you do say so,—else you would forgive
Me, whom Law dares not touch but tosses you!
Don't think to put on the professional face!
You know what I know,—casuists as you are,
385 Each nerve must creep, each hair start, sting and
    stand,
At such illogical inconsequence!
Dear my friends, do but see! A murder's tried,
There are two parties to the cause: I'm one,
—Defend myself, as somebody must do:
390 I have the best o' the battle: that's a fact,
Simple fact,—fancies find no place beside:
What though half Rome condemned me? Half
    approved:
And, none disputes, the luck is mine at last,
All Rome, i' the main, acquits me: whereupon
395 What has the Pope to ask but "How finds Law?"
"I find," replies Law, "I have erred this while:
Guilty or guiltless, Guido proves a priest,
No layman: he is therefore yours, not mine:
I bound him: loose him, you whose will is Christ's!"
400 And now what does this Vicar of the Lord,
Shepherd o' the flock,—one of whose charge bleats
    sore
For crook's help from the quag wherein it drowns?
Law suffers him put forth the crumpled end,—
His pleasure is to turn staff, use the point,
405 And thrust the shuddering sheep he calls a wolf,
Back and back, down and down to where hell
    gapes!
"Guiltless," cries Law—"Guilty" corrects the Pope!
"Guilty," for the whim's sake! "Guilty," he
    somehow thinks,
And anyhow says: 't is truth; he dares not lie!
410 Others should do the lying. That's the cause
Brings you both here: I ought in decency
Confess to you that I deserve my fate,
Am guilty, as the Pope thinks,—ay, to the end,

Keep up the jest, lie on, lie ever, lie
415 I' the latest gasp of me! What reason, Sirs?
Because to-morrow will succeed to-day
For you, though not for me: and if I stick
Still to the truth, declare with my last breath,
I die an innocent and murdered man,—
420 Why, there's the tongue of Rome will wag a-pace
This time to-morrow,—do n't I hear the talk!
"So, to the last he proved impenitent?
Pagans have said as much of martyred saints!
Law demurred, washed her hands of the whole case.
425 Prince Somebody said this, Duke Something, that.
Doubtless the man's dead, dead enough, do n't fear!
But, hang it, what if there have been a spice,
A touch of…eh?[2] You see, the Pope's so old,
Some of us add, obtuse,—age never slips
430 The chance of shoving youth to face death first!"
And so on. Therefore to suppress such talk
You two come here, entreat I tell you lies,
And end, the edifying way. I end,
Telling the truth! Your self-styled shepherd thieves!
435 A thief—and how thieves hate the wolves we know:
Damage to theft, damage to thrift, all's one!
The red hand is sworn foe of the black jaw!
That's only natural, that's right enough:
But why the wolf should compliment the thief
440 With the shepherd's title, bark out life in thanks,
And, spiteless, lick the prong that spits him,—eh,
Cardinal? My Abate, scarcely thus!
There, let my sheepskin-garb, a curse on 't, go—
Leave my teeth free if I must show my shag!
445 Repent? What good shall follow? If I pass
Twelve hours repenting, will that fact hook fast
The thirteenth at the horrid dozen's end?
If I fall forthwith at your feet, gnash, tear,
Foam, rave, to give your story the due grace,[3]
450 Will that assist the engine half-way back

---

[1] reserved, reluctant.

[2] The suppressed word probably is "doubt": see below, l. 721, "a spice
of doubt."

[3] credibility.

Into its hiding-house?—boards, shaking now,
Bone against bone, like some old skeleton bat
That wants, now winter 's dead, to wake and prey!
Will howling put the spectre back to sleep?
455 Ah, but I misconceive your object, Sirs!
Since I want new life like the creature,—life
Being done with here, begins i' the world away:
I shall next have "Come, mortals, and be judged!"
There's but a minute betwixt this and then:
460 So, quick, be sorry since it saves my soul!
Sirs, truth shall save it, since no lies assist!
Hear the truth, you, whatever you style yourselves,
Civilization and society!
Come, one good grapple, I with all the world!
465 Dying in cold blood is the desperate thing;
The angry heart explodes, bears off in blaze
The indignant soul, and I'm combustion-ripe.
Why, you intend to do your worst with me!
That's in your eyes! You dare no more than death,
470 And mean no less. I must make up my mind!
So Pietro,—when I chased him here and there,
Morsel by morsel cut away the life
I loathed,—cried for just respite to confess
And save his soul: much respite did I grant!
475 Why grant me respite who deserve my doom?
Me—who engaged to play a prize, fight you,
Knowing your arms, and foil you, trick for trick,
At rapier-fence, your match and, may be, more.
I knew that if I chose sin certain sins,
480 Solace my lusts out of the regular way
Prescribed me, I should find you in the path,
Have to try skill with a redoubted foe;
You would lunge, I would parry, and make end.
At last, occasion of a murder comes:
485 We cross blades, I, for all my brag, break guard,
And in goes the cold iron at my breast,
Out at my back, and end is made of me.
You stand confessed the adroiter swordsman,—ay,
But on your triumph you increase, it seems,
490 Want more of me than lying flat on face:
I ought to raise my ruined head, allege

Not simply I pushed worse blade o' the pair,
But my antagonist dispensed with steel!
There was no passage of arms, you looked me low,
495 With brow and eye abolished cut-and-thrust
Nor used the vulgar weapon! This chance scratch,
This incidental hurt, this sort of hole
I' the heart of me? I stumbled, got it so!
Fell on my own sword as a bungler may!
500 Yourself proscribe such heathen tools, and trust
To the naked virtue: it was virtue stood
Unarmed and awed me,—on my brow there
    burned
Crime out so plainly, intolerably, red,
That I was fain to cry—"Down to the dust
505 With me, and bury there brow, brand and all!"
Law had essayed the adventure,—but what's Law?
Morality exposed the Gorgon-shield![1]
Morality and Religion conquer me.
If Law sufficed would you come here, entreat
510 I supplement law, and confess forsooth?
Did not the Trial show things plain enough?
"Ah, but a word of the man's very self
Would somehow put the keystone in its place
And crown the arch!" Then take the word you
    want!

515 I say that, long ago, when things began,
All the world made agreement, such and such
Were pleasure-giving profit-bearing acts,
But henceforth extra-legal, nor to be:
You must not kill the man whose death would
    please
520 And profit you, unless his life stop yours
Plainly, and need so be put aside:
Get the thing by a public course, by law,
Only no private bloodshed as of old!
All of us, for the good of every one,
525 Renounced such licence and conformed to law:

---

[1] Athene's shield with the Gorgon's head in the centre; whoever looked
on it was turned to stone.

503

Who breaks law, breaks pact, therefore, helps himself
To pleasure and profit over and above the due,
And must pay forfeit,—pain beyond his share:
For pleasure is the sole good in the world,
530 Anyone's pleasure turns to someone's pain,
So, let law watch for everyone,—say we,
Who call things wicked that give too much joy,
And nickname the reprisal, envy makes,
Punishment: quite right! thus the world goes round.
535 I, being well aware such pact there was,
Who in my time have found advantage too
In law's observance and crime's penalty,—
Who, but for wholesome fear law bred in friends,
Had doubtless given example long ago,
540 Furnished forth some friend's pleasure with my pain,
And, by my death, pieced out his scanty life,—
I could not, for that foolish life of me,
Help risking law's infringement,—I broke bond,
And needs must pay price,—wherefore, here's my head,
545 Flung with a flourish! But, repentance too?
But pure and simple sorrow for law's breach
Rather than blunderer's-ineptitude?
Cardinal, no! Abate, scarcely thus!
'T is the fault, not that I dared try a fall
550 With Law and straightway am found undermost,
But that I fail to see, above man's law,
God's precept you, the Christians recognize?
Colly my cow![1] Do n't fidget, Cardinal!
Abate, cross your breast and count your beads
555 And exorcize the devil, for here he stands
And stiffens in the bristly nape of neck,
Daring you drive him hence! You, Christians both?
I say, if ever was such faith at all
Born in the world, by your community
560 Suffered to live its little tick of time,
'T is dead of age now, ludicrously dead;

Honour its ashes, if you be discreet,
In epitaph only! For, concede its death,
Allow extinction, you may boast unchecked
565 What feats the thing did in a crazy land
At a fabulous epoch,—treat your faith, that way,
Just as you treat your relics: "Here's a shred
Of saintly flesh, a scrap of blessed bone,
Raised King Cophetua,[2] who was dead, to life
570 In Mesopotamy twelve centuries since,
Such was its virtue!"—twangs the Sacristan,
Holding the shrine-box up, with hands like feet
Because of gout in every finger-joint:
Does he bethink him to reduce one knob,
575 Allay one twinge by touching what he vaunts?
I think he half uncrooks fist to catch fee,
But, for the grace, the quality of cure,—
Cophetua was the man put that to proof!
Not otherwise, your faith is shrined and shown
580 And shamed at once: you banter while you bow!
Do you dispute this? Come, a monster-laugh,
A madman's laugh, allowed his Carnival
Later ten days than when all Rome, but he,
Laughed at the candle-contest:[3] mine's alight,
585 'T is just it sputter till the puff o' the Pope
End it to-morrow and the world turn Ash.
Come, thus I wave a wand and bring to pass
In a moment, in the twinkle of an eye,
What but that—feigning everywhere grows fact,
590 Professors turn possessors, realize
The faith they play with as a fancy now,
And bid it operate, have full effect
On every circumstance of life, to-day,
In Rome,—faith's flow set free at fountain-head!
595 Now, you'll own, at this present when I speak,
Before I work the wonder, there's no man
Woman or child in Rome, faith's fountain-head,

---

1 a mild expletive.

2 legendary Ethiopian king.

3 To mark the end of Carnival, everyone in the streets sought to extinguish the others' lighted tapers, which were relighted as often as they were put out until they were utterly consumed.

But might, if each were minded, realize
Conversely unbelief, faith's opposite—
500 Set it to work on life unflinchingly,
Yet give no symptom of an outward change:
Why should things change because men disbelieve?
What's incompatible, in the whited tomb,
With bones and rottenness one inch below?
505 What saintly act is done in Rome to-day
But might be prompted by the devil,—"is"
I say not,—"has been and again may be,"—
I do say, full i' the face o' the crucifix
You try to stop my mouth with! Off with it!
510 Look in your own heart, if your soul have eyes!
You shall see reason why, though faith were fled,
Unbelief still might work the wires and move
Man, the machine, to play a faithful part.
Preside your college, Cardinal, in your cape,
515 Or,—having got above his head, grown Pope,—
Abate, gird your loins and wash my feet!
Do you suppose I am at loss at all
Why you crook, why you cringe, why fast or feast?
Praise, blame, sit, stand, lie or go!—all of it,
520 In each of you, purest unbelief may prompt,
And wit explain to who has eyes to see.
But, lo, I wave wand, make the false the true!
Here's Rome believes in Christianity!
What an explosion, how the fragments fly
525 Of what was surface, mask and make-believe!
Begin now,—look at this Pope's-halberdier[1]
In wasp-like black and yellow foolery!
He, doing duty at the corridor,
Wakes from a muse and stands convinced of sin!
530 Down he flings halbert, leaps the passage-length,
Pushes into the presence, pantingly
Submits the extreme peril of the case
To the Pope's self,—whom in the world beside?—
And the Pope breaks talk with ambassador,
535 Bids aside bishop, wills the whole world wait

Till he secure that prize, outweighs the world,
A soul, relieve the sentry of his qualm!
His Altitude the Referendary,—[2]
Robed right, and ready for the usher's word
640 To pay devoir,—is, of all times, just then
'Ware of a master-stroke of argument
Will cut the spinal cord...ugh, ugh!...I mean,
Paralyse Molinism for evermore!
Straight he leaves lobby, trundles, two and two,
645 Down steps, to reach home, write if but a word
Shall end the impudence: he leaves who likes
Go pacify the Pope: there's Christ to serve!
How otherwise would men display their zeal?
If the same sentry had the least surmise
650 A powder-barrel 'neath the pavement lay
In neighbourhood with what might prove a match,
Meant to blow sky-high Pope and presence both—
Would he not break through courtiers, rank and file,
Bundle up, bear off and save body so,
655 O' the Pope, no matter for his priceless soul?
There's no fool's-freak here, nought to soundly
    swinge,
Only a man in earnest, you'll so praise
And pay and prate about, that earth shall ring!
Had thought possessed the Referendary
660 His jewel-case at home was left ajar,
What would be wrong in running, robes awry,
To be beforehand with the pilferer?
What talk then of indecent haste? Which means,
That both these, each in his degree, would do
665 Just that,—for a comparative nothing's sake,
And thereby gain approval and reward,—
Which, done for what Christ says is worth the
    world,[3]
Procures the doer curses, cuffs and kicks.
I call such difference 'twixt act and act,
670 Sheer lunacy unless your truth on lip
Be recognized a lie in heart of you!

---

[1] a member of the Swiss guard (above, l. 208) who carried an eight-foot-long halberd (combination of axe and spear).

[2] important Vatican official.

[3] that is, the saving of a soul: Matthew 16:26.

How do you all act, promptly or in doubt,
When there's a guest poisoned at supper-time
And he sits chatting on with spot on cheek?
675 "Pluck him by the skirt, and round him in the ears,
Have at him by the beard, warn anyhow!"
Good, and this other friend that's cheat and thief
And dissolute,—go stop the devil's feast,
Withdraw him from the imminent hell-fire!
680 Why, for your life, you dare not tell your friend
"You lie, and I admonish you for Christ!"
Who yet dare seek that same man at the Mass
To warn him—on his knees, and tinkle near,—[1]
He left a cask a-tilt, a tap unturned,
685 The Trebbian[2] running: what a grateful jump
Out of the Church rewards your vigilance!
Perform that self-same service just a thought
More maladroitly,—since a bishop sits
At function!—and he budges not, bites lip,—
690 "You see my case: how can I quit my post?
He has an eye to any such default.
See to it, neighbour, I beseech your love!"
He and you know the relative worth of things,
What is permissible or inopportune.
695 Contort your brows! You know I speak the truth:
Gold is called gold, and dross called dross, i' the
Book:
Gold you let lie and dross pick up and prize!
—Despite your muster of some fifty monks
And nuns a-maundering here and mumping
there,[3]
700 Who could, and on occasion would, spurn dross,
Clutch gold, and prove their faith a fact so far,—
I grant you! Fifty times the number squeak
And gibber in the madhouse—firm of faith,
This fellow, that his nose supports the moon,
705 The other, that his straw hat crowns him Pope:
Does that prove all the world outside insane?

Do fifty miracle-mongers match the mob
That acts on the frank faithless principle,
Born-baptized-and-bred Christian-atheists, each
710 With just as much a right to judge as you,—
As many senses in his soul, or nerves
I' neck of him as I,—whom, soul or sense,
Neck and nerve, you abolish presently,—
I being the unit in creation now
715 Who pay the Maker, in this speech of mine,
A creature's duty, spend my last of breath
In bearing witness, even by my worst fault
To the creature's obligation, absolute,
Perpetual: my worst fault protests, "The faith
720 Claims all of me: I would give all she claims,
But for a spice of doubt: the risk's too rash:
Double or quits, I play, but, all or nought,
Exceeds my courage: therefore, I descend
To the next faith with no dubiety—
725 Faith in the present life, made last as long
And prove as full of pleasure as may hap,
Whatever pain it cause the world." I'm wrong?
I've had my life, whate'er I lose: I'm right?
I've got the single good there was to gain.
730 Entire faith, or else complete unbelief,—
Aught between has my loathing and contempt,
Mine and God's also, doubtless: ask yourself,
Cardinal, where and how you like a man!
Why, either with your feet upon his head,
735 Confessed your caudatory,[4] or at large
The stranger in the crowd who caps to you
But keeps his distance,—why should he presume?
You want no hanger-on and dropper-off,
Now yours, and now not yours but quite his own,
740 According as the sky looks black or bright.
Just so I capped to and kept off from faith—
You promised trudge behind through fair and foul,
Yet leave i' the lurch at the first spit of rain.
Who holds to faith whenever rain begins?
745 What does the father when his son lies dead,

---

[1] the ringing of the bell at the elevation of the Host.

[2] a wine from north-western Italy.

[3] Both verbs mean "muttering."

[4] train bearer (literally, "tail"; Browning's invention).

The merchant when his money-bags take wing,
The politician whom a rival ousts?
No case but has its conduct, faith prescribes:
Where's the obedience that shall edify?
750 Why, they laugh frankly in the face of faith
And take the natural course,—this rends his hair
Because his child is taken to God's breast,
That gnashes teeth and raves at loss of trash
Which rust corrupts and thieves break through and
        steal,
755 And this, enabled to inherit earth
Through meekness, curses till your blood runs cold!
Down they all drop to my low level, ease
Heart upon dungy earth that's warm and soft,
And let who will, attempt the altitudes.
760 We have the prodigal son of heavenly sire,
Turning his nose up at the fatted calf,
Fain to fill belly with the husks we swine
Did eat by born depravity of taste!

Enough of the hypocrites. But you, Sirs, you—
765 Who never budged from litter where I lay,
And buried snout i' the draff-box[1] while I fed,
Cried amen to my creed's one article—
"Get pleasure, 'scape pain,—give your preference
To the immediate good, for time is brief,
770 And death ends good and ill and everything:
What's got is gained, what's gained soon is gained
        twice,
And,—inasmuch as faith gains most,—feign faith!"
So did we brother-like pass word about:
—You, now,—like bloody drunkards but
        half-drunk,
775 Who fool men yet perceive men find them fools,
And that a titter gains the gravest mouth,—
O' the sudden you must needs re-introduce
Solemnity, must sober undue mirth
By a blow dealt your boon companion here
780 Who, using the old licence, dreamed of harm

No more than snow in harvest: yet it falls!
You check the merriment effectually
By pushing your abrupt machine i' the midst,
Making me Rome's example: blood for wine!
785 The general good needs that you chop and change!
I may dislike the hocus-pocus,—Rome,
The laughter-loving people, won't they stare
Chap-fallen![2]—while serious natures sermonize
"The magistrate, he beareth not the sword
790 In vain; who sins may taste its edge, we see!"
Why my sin, drunkards? Where have I abused
Liberty, scandalized you all so much?
Who called me, who crooked finger till I came,
Fool that I was, to join companionship?
795 I knew my own mind, meant to live my life,
Elude your envy, or else make a stand,
Take my own part and sell you my life dear:
But it was "Fie! No prejudice in the world
To the proper manly instinct! Cast your lot
800 Into our lap, one genius[3] ruled our births,
We'll compass joy by concert;[4] take with us
The regular irregular way i' the wood;
You'll miss no game through riding breast by breast,
In this preserve, the Church's park and pale,
805 Rather than outside where the world is waste!"
Come, if you said not that, did you say this?
Give plain and terrible warning, "Live, enjoy?
Such life begins in death and ends in hell!
Dare you bid us assist you to your sins
810 Who hurry sin and sinners from the earth?
No such delight for us, why then for you?
Leave earth, seek heaven or find its opposite!"
Had you so warned me, not in lying words
But veritable deeds with tongues of flame,
815 That had been fair, that might have struck a man,
Silenced the squabble between soul and sense,
Compelled him make his mind up, take one course

---

[1] trough of refuse, swill.

[2] slack-jawed, crestfallen.

[3] presiding spirit, "good angel."

[4] find pleasure together.

Or the other, peradventure!—wrong or right,
Foolish or wise, you would have been at least
820   Sincere, no question,—forced me choose, indulge
Or else renounce my instincts, still play wolf
Or find my way submissive to the fold,
Be red-crossed on the fleece, one sheep the more.
But you as good as bade me wear sheep's wool
825   Over wolf's skin, suck blood and hide the noise
By mimicry of something like a bleat,—
Whence it comes that because, despite my care,
Because I smack my tongue too loud for once,
Drop baaing, here's the village up in arms!
830   Have at the wolf's throat, you who hate the breed!
Oh, were it only open yet to choose—
One little time more—whether I'd be free
Your foe, or subsidized your friend forsooth!
Should not you get a growl through the white fangs
835   In answer to your beckoning! Cardinal,
Abate, managers o' the multitude,
I'd turn your gloved hands to account, be sure!
You should manipulate the coarse rough mob:
'T is you I'd deal directly with, not them,—
840   Using your fears: why touch the thing myself
When I could see you hunt and then cry "Shares!
Quarter the carcass or we quarrel; come,
Here's the world ready to see justice done!"
Oh, it had been a desperate game, but game
845   Wherein the winner's chance were worth the pains
To try conclusions!—at the worst, what's worse
Than this Mannaia-machine, each minute's talk,
Helps push an inch the nearer me? Fool, fool!

You understand me and forgive, sweet Sirs?
850   I blame you, tear my hair and tell my woe—
All's but a flourish, figure of rhetoric!
One must try each expedient to save life.
One makes fools look foolisher fifty-fold
By putting in their place the wise like you
855   To take the full force of an argument
Would buffet their stolidity in vain.
If you should feel aggrieved by the mere wind

O' the blow that means to miss you and maul them,
That's my success! Is it not folly, now,
860   To say with folks, "A plausible defence—
We see through notwithstanding, and reject?"
Reject the plausible they do, these fools,
Who never even make pretence to show
One point beyond its plausibility
865   In favour of the best belief they hold!
"Saint Somebody-or-other raised the dead:"
Did he? How do you come to know as much?
"Know it, what need? The story's plausible,
Avouched for by a martyrologist,
870   And why should good men sup on cheese and leeks
On such a saint's day, if there were no saint?"
I praise the wisdom of these fools, and straight
Tell them my story—"plausible, but false!"
False, to be sure! What else can story be
875   That runs—a young wife tired of an old spouse,
Found a priest whom she fled away with,—both
Took their full pleasure in the two-days' flight,
Which a grey-headed greyer-hearted pair,
(Whose best boast was, their life had been a lie)
880   Helped for the love they bore all liars. Oh,
Here incredulity begins! Indeed?
Allow then, were no one point strictly true,
There's that i' the tale might seem like truth at least
To the unlucky husband,—jaundiced patch,—[1]
885   Jealousy maddens people, why not him?
Say, he was maddened, so, forgivable!
Humanity pleads that though the wife were true,
The priest true, and the pair of liars true,
They might seem false to one man in the world!
890   A thousand gnats make up a serpent's sting,
And many sly soft stimulants to wrath
Compose a formidable wrong at last,
That gets called easily by some one name
Not applicable to the single parts,
895   And so draws down a general revenge,
Excessive if you take crime, fault by fault.

---

[1] jealous fool.

Jealousy! I have known a score of plays,
Were listened to and laughed at in my time
As like the everyday-life on all sides,
900 Wherein the husband, mad as a March hare,
Suspected all the world contrived his shame;
What did the wife? The wife kissed both eyes
    blind,[1]
Explained away ambiguous circumstance,
And while she held him captive by the hand,
905 Crowned his head,[2]—you know what's the
    mockery,—
By half her body behind the curtain. That's
Nature now! That's the subject of a piece
I saw in Vallombrosa Convent,[3] made
Expressly to teach men what marriage was!
910 But say "Just so did I misapprehend!"
Or "Just so she deceived me to my face!"
And that's pretence too easily seen through!
All those eyes of all husbands in all plays,
At stare like one expanded peacock-tail,
915 Are laughed at for pretending to be keen
While horn-blind: but the moment I step forth—
Oh, I must needs o' the sudden prove a lynx[4]
And look the heart, that stone-wall, through and
    through!
Such an eye, God's may be,—not yours nor mine.

920 Yes, presently…what hour is fleeting now?
When you cut earth away from under me,
I shall be left alone with, pushed beneath
Some such an apparitional[5] dread orb;
I fancy it go filling up the void
925 Above my mote-self it devours, or what
Immensity please wreak on nothingness.

Just so I felt once, couching through the dark,
Hard by Vittiano; young I was, and gay,
And wanting to trap fieldfares:[6] first a spark
930 Tipped a bent,[7] as a mere dew-globule might
Any stiff grass-stalk on the meadow,—this
Grew fiercer, flamed out full, and proved the sun.
What do I want with proverbs, precepts here?
Away with man! What shall I say to God?
935 This, if I find the tongue and keep the mind—
"Do Thou wipe out the being of me, and smear
This soul from off Thy white of things, I blot!
I am one huge and sheer mistake,—whose fault?
Not mine at least, who did not make myself!"
940 Someone declares my wife excused me so!
Perhaps she knew what argument to use.
Grind your teeth, Cardinal, Abate, writhe!
What else am I to cry out in my rage,
Unable to repent one particle
945 O' the past? Oh, how I wish some cold wise man
Would dig beneath the surface which you scrape,
Deal with the depths, pronounce on my desert
Groundedly! I want simple sober sense,
That asks, before it finishes with a dog,
950 Who taught the dog that trick you hang him for?
You both persist to call that act a crime,
Sense would call…yes, I do assure you, Sirs,…
A blunder! At the worst, I stood in doubt
On cross-road, took one path of many paths:
955 It leads to the red thing, we all see now,
But nobody at first saw one primrose
In bank, one singing-bird in bush, the less,
To warn from wayfare: let me prove you that!
Put me back to the cross-road, start afresh!
960 Advise me when I take the first false step!
Give me my wife: how should I use my wife,
Love her or hate her? Prompt my action now!
There she stands, there she is alive and pale,
The thirteen-years'-old child, with milk for blood,

---

[1] The kiss of an adulterous wife was said to blind her husband to her infidelity.

[2] that is, with the horns of a cuckold.

[3] monastery near Florence.

[4] to have the ability to see through solid substances.

[5] a phantasm.

[6] thrushes.

[7] stiff stalk of grass.

965 Pompilia Comparini, as at first,
Which first is only four brief years ago!
I stand too in the little ground-floor room
O' the father's house in Via Vittoria: see!
Her so-called mother,—one arm round the waist
970 O' the child to keep her from the toys—let fall,
At wonder I can live yet look so grim,—
Ushers her in, with deprecating wave
Of the other,—there she fronts me loose, at large,
Held only by the mother's fingertip—
975 Struck dumb, for she was white enough before!
She eyes me with those frightened balls of black,
As heifer—the old simile comes pat—
Eyes tremblingly the altar and the priest:
The amazed look, all one insuppressive prayer,—
980 Might she but be set free as heretofore,
Have this cup leave her lips unblistered, bear
Any cross anywhither anyhow,
So but alone, so but apart from me!
You are touched? So am I, quite otherwise,
985 If 't is with pity. I resent my wrong,
Being a man: we only show man's soul
Through man's flesh, she sees mine, it strikes her
    thus!
Is that attractive? To a youth perhaps—
Calf-creature, one-part boy to three-parts girl,
990 To whom it is a flattering novelty
That he, men use to motion from their path,
Can thus impose, thus terrify in turn
A chit whose terror shall be changed apace
To bliss unbearable when, grace and glow,
995 Prowess and pride descend the throne and touch
Esther in all that pretty tremble,[1] cured
By the dove o' the sceptre! But myself am old,
O' the wane at least, in all things: what do you say
To her who frankly thus confirms my doubt?
1000 I am past the prime, I scare the woman-world,
Done-with that way: you like this piece of news?

A little saucy rose-bud minx can strike
Death-damp in the breast of doughty king
Though 't were French Louis,[2]—soul I
    understand,—
1005 Saying, by gesture of repugnance, just
"Sire, you are regal, puissant and so forth,
But—young you have been, are not, nor will be!"
In vain the mother nods, winks, bustles up
"Count, girls incline to mature worth like you!"
1010 As for Pompilia, what's flesh, fish or fowl
To one who apprehends no difference,
And would accept you even were you old
As you are…youngish by her father's side?
Trim but your beard a little, thin your bush
1015 Of eyebrow; and for presence, portliness[3]
And decent gravity, you beat a boy!"
Deceive you for a second, if you may,
In presence of the child that so loves age,
Whose neck writhes, cords itself against your kiss,
1020 Whose hand you wring stark, rigid with despair!
Well, I resent this; I am young in soul,
Nor old in body,—thews and sinews here,—
Though the vile surface be not smooth as once,—
Far beyond the first wheelwork[4] that went wrong
1025 Through the untempered iron ere 't was proof:[5]
I am the steel man worth ten times the crude,—
Would woman see what this declines to see,
Declines to say "I see,"—the officious[6] word
That makes the thing, pricks on the soul to shoot
1030 New fire into the half-used cinder, flesh!
Therefore 't is she begins with wronging me,
Who cannot but begin with hating her.
Our marriage follows: there we stand again!
Why do I laugh? Why, in the very gripe

---

[1] Esther 15:5–16 (Apocrypha), where Esther is repeatedly so portrayed as she petitions Ahasuerus for her countrymen.

[2] See note to ll. 2277–78 below.

[3] dignity.

[4] clockwork.

[5] of tested strength, impenetrable.

[6] efficacious, with an overtone of "officious lie": one told as an act of kindness to further another's interests (*OED*).

035 O' the jaws of death's gigantic skull do I
Grin back his grin, make sport of my own pangs?
Why from each clashing of his molars, ground
To make the devil bread from out my grist,
Leaps out a spark of mirth, a hellish toy?
040 Take notice we are lovers in a church,
Waiting the sacrament to make us one
And happy! Just as bid, she bears herself,
Comes and kneels, rises, speaks, is silent,—goes:
So have I brought my horse, by word and blow,
045 To stand stock-still and front the fire he dreads.
How can I other than remember this,
Resent the very obedience? Gain thereby?
Yes, I do gain my end and have my will,—
Thanks to whom? When the mother speaks the
   word,
050 She obeys it—even to enduring me!
There had been compensation in revolt—
Revolt's to quell: but martyrdom rehearsed,
But predetermined saintship for the sake
O' the mother?—"Go!" thought I, "we meet again!"
055 Pass the next weeks of dumb contented death,
She lives,—wakes up, installed in house and home,
Is mine, mine all day long, all night-long mine.
Good folks begin at me with open mouth
"Now, at least, reconcile the child to life!
060 Study and make her love…that is, endure
The…hem! the…all of you though somewhat old,
Till it amount to something, in her eye,
As good as love, better a thousand times,—
Since nature helps the woman in such strait,
065 Makes passiveness her pleasure: failing which,
What if you give up boys' and girls' fools'-play
And go on to wise friendship all at once?
Those boys and girls kiss themselves cold, you
   know,
Toy themselves tired and slink aside full soon
070 To friendship, as they name satiety:
Thither go you and wait their coming!" Thanks,
Considerate advisers,—but, fair play!
Had you and I but started fair at first,

We, keeping fair, might reach it, neck by neck,
1075 This blessed goal, whenever fate so please:
But why am I to miss the daisied mile
The course begins with, why obtain the dust
Of the end precisely at the starting-point?
Why quaff life's cup blown free of all the beads,
1080 The bright red froth wherein our beard should
   steep
Before our mouth essay the black o' the wine?
Foolish, the love-fit? Let me prove it such
Like you, before like you I puff things clear!
"The best's to come, no rapture but content!
1085 Not the first glory but a sober glow,
Nor a spontaneous outburst in pure boon,
So much as, gained by patience, care and toil!"
Go preach that to your nephews, not to me
Who, tired i' the midway of my life, would stop
1090 And take my first refreshment in a rose:
What's this coarse woolly hip, worn smooth of leaf,
You counsel I go plant in garden-pot,
Water with tears, manure with sweat and blood,
In confidence the seed shall germinate
1095 And for its very best, some far-off day,
Grow big, and blow me out a dog-rose[1] bell?
Why must your nephews begin breathing spice
O' the hundred-petalled Provence prodigy?[2]
Nay, more and worse,—would such my root bear
   rose—
1100 Prove really flower and favourite, not the kind
That's queen, but those three leaves that make one
   cup
And hold the hedge-bird's breakfast,—then indeed
The prize though poor would pay the care and toil!
Respect we Nature that makes least as most,
1105 Marvellous in the minim! But this bud,
Bit through and burned black by the tempter's
   tooth,
This bloom whose best grace was the slug outside

---

[1] small flower of the wild brier in hedges and thickets.

[2] a large rose.

And the wasp inside its bosom,—call you "rose?"
Claim no immunity from a weed's fate
1110 For the horrible present! What you call my wife
I call a nullity in female shape,
Vapid disgust, soon to be pungent plague,
When mixed with, made confusion and a curse
By two abominable nondescripts,
1115 That father and that mother: think you see
The dreadful bronze our boast, we Aretines,
The Etruscan monster,[1] the three-headed thing,
Bellerophon's foe! How name you the whole beast?
You choose to name the body from one head,
1120 That of the simple kid which droops the eye,
Hangs the neck and dies tenderly enough:
I rather see the griesly lion belch
Flame out i' the midst, the serpent writhe her rings,
Grafted into the common stock for tail,
1125 And name the brute, Chimaera, which I slew!
How was there ever more to be—(concede
My wife's insipid harmless nullity)—
Dissociation from that pair of plagues—
That mother with her cunning and her cant—[2]
1130 The eyes with first their twinkle of conceit,
Then, dropped to earth in mock-demureness,
      —now,
The smile self-satisfied from ear to ear,
Now, the prim pursed-up mouth's protruded lips,
With deferential duck, slow swing of head,
1135 Tempting the sudden fist of man too much,—
That owl-like screw of lid and rock of ruff![3]
As for the father,—Cardinal, you know,
The kind of idiot!—rife are such in Rome,
But they wear velvet commonly, such fools,
1140 At the end of life, can furnish forth young folk
Who grin and bear with imbecility,
Since the stalled ass, the joker, sheds from jaw
Corn, in the joke, for those who laugh or starve:

But what say we to the same solemn beast
1145 Wagging his ears and wishful of our pat,
When turned, with hide in holes and bones laid
      bare,
To forage for himself i' the waste o' the world,
Sir Dignity i' the dumps?[4] Pat him? We drub
Self-knowledge, rather, into frowzy pate,
1150 Teach Pietro to get trappings[5] or go hang!
Fancy this quondam[6] oracle in vogue
At Via Vittoria, this personified
Authority when time was,—Pantaloon[7]
Flaunting his tom-fool tawdry just the same
1155 As if Ash-Wednesday were mid-Carnival!
That's the extreme and unforgiveable
Of sins, as I account such. Have you stooped
For your own ends to bestialize yourself
By flattery of a fellow of this stamp?
1160 The ends obtained, or else shown out of reach,
He goes on, takes the flattery for pure truth,—
"You love and honour me, of course: what next?"
What, but the trifle of the stabbing, friend?—
Which taught you how one worships when the
      shrine
1165 Has lost the relic that we bent before.
Angry? And how could I be otherwise?
'T is plain: this pair of old pretentious fools,
Meant to fool me: it happens, I fooled them.
Why could not these who sought to buy and sell
1170 Me,—when they found themselves were bought
      and sold,
Make up their mind to the proved rule of right,
Be chattel and not chapman any more?
Miscalculation has its consequence;
But when the shepherd crooks a sheep-like thing
1175 And meaning to get wool, dislodges fleece
And finds the veritable wolf beneath,

---

[1] Chimaera, l. 1125.

[2] whining.

[3] sway of its collar of feathers.

[4] gloomy.

[5] harness.

[6] former.

[7] foolish old man in Italian pantomine.

(How that staunch image serves at every turn!)
Does he, by way of being politic,
Pluck the first whisker grimly visible?—
1180 Or rather grow in a trice all gratitude,
Protest this sort-of-what-one-might-name sheep
Beats the old other curly-coated kind,
And shall share board and bed, if so it deign,
With its discoverer, like a royal ram?
1185 Ay, thus, with chattering teeth and knocking knees,
Would wisdom treat the adventure: these, forsooth,
Tried whisker-plucking, and so found what trap
The whisker kept perdue, two rows of teeth—
Sharp, as too late the prying fingers felt.
1190 What would you have? The fools transgress, the
      fools
Forthwith receive appropriate punishment:
They first insult me, I return the blow,
There follows noise enough: four hubbub months,
Now hue and cry, now whimpering and wail—
1195 A perfect goose-yard cackle of complaint
Because I do not gild the geese their oats,—
I have enough of noise, ope wicket wide,
Sweep out the couple to go whine elsewhere,
Frightened a little, hurt in no respect,
1200 And am just taking thought to breathe again,
Taste the sweet sudden silence all about,
When, there they are at it, the old noise I know,
At Rome i' the distance! "What, begun once more?
Whine on, wail ever, 't is the loser's right!"
1205 But eh, what sort of voice grows on the wind?
Triumph it sounds and no complaint at all!
And triumph it is! My boast was premature:
The creatures, I turned forth, clapped wing and crew
Fighting-cock-fashion,—they had filched a pearl
1210 From dung-heap, and might boast with cause
      enough!
I was defrauded of all bargained for,—
You know, the Pope knows, not a soul but knows
My dowry was derision, my gain—muck,
My wife, (the Church declared my flesh and blood)
1215 The nameless bastard of a common whore:

My old name turned henceforth to…shall I say
"He that received the ordure in his face?"
And they who planned this wrong, performed this
      wrong,
And then revealed this wrong to the wide world,
1220 Rounded myself in the ears with my own wrong,—
Why, these were…note hell's lucky malice, now!…
These were just they, and they alone, could act
And publish in this wise their infamy,
Secure that men would in a breath believe
1225 Compassionate and pardon them,—for why?
They plainly were too stupid to invent,
Too simple to distinguish wrong from right,—
Inconscious agents they, the silly-sooth,
Of heaven's retributive justice on the strong
1230 Proud cunning violent oppressor—me!
Follow them to their fate and help your best,
You Rome, Arezzo, foes called friends of mine,
They gave the good long laugh to at my cost!
Defray your share o' the cost since you partook
1235 The entertainment! Do!—assured the while,
That not one stab, I dealt to right and left,
But went the deeper for a fancy—this—
That each might do me two-fold service, find
A friend's face at the bottom of each wound,
1240 And scratch its smirk a little!

                              Panciatichi!
There's a report at Florence,—is it true?—
That when your relative the Cardinal
Built, only the other day, that barrack-bulk,
1245 The palace in Via Larga, someone picked
From out the street a saucy quip enough
That fell there from its day's flight through the
      town,
About the flat front and the windows wide
And ugly heap of cornice,—hitched the joke
1250 Into a sonnet, signed his name thereto,
And forthwith pinned on post the pleasantry.
For which he's at the galleys, rowing now
Up to his waist in water,—just because
Panciatic and *lymphatic* rhymed so pat:

1255 I hope, Sir, those who passed this joke on me
Were not unduly punished? What say you,
Prince of the Church, my patron? Nay, indeed!
I shall not dare insult your wits so much
As think this problem difficult to solve!
1260 This Pietro and Violante, then, I say,
These two ambiguous insects, changing name
And nature with the season's warmth or chill,—
Now, grovelled, grubbing toiling moiling ants,
A very synonym of thrift and peace,—
1265 Anon, with lusty June to prick their heart,
Soared i' the air, winged flies for more offence,
Circled me, buzzed me deaf and stung me blind,
And stunk me dead with fetor in the face
Until I stopped the nuisance: there's my crime!
1270 Pity I did not suffer them subside
Into some further shape and final form
Of execrable life? My masters, no!
I, by one blow, wisely cut short at once
Them and their transformations of disgust[1]
1275 In the snug little Villa out of hand.
"Grant me confession, give bare time for that!"—
Shouted the sinner till his mouth was stopped.
His life confessed!—that was enough for me,
Who came to see that he did penance. 'S death!
1280 Here's a coil raised, a pother and for what?
Because strength, being provoked by weakness,
        fought
And conquered,—the world never heard the like!
Pah, how I spend my breath on them, as if
'T was their fate troubled me, too hard to range
1285 Among the right and fit and proper things!

Ay, but Pompilia,—I await your word,—
She, unimpeached of crime, unimplicate
In folly, one of alien blood to these
I punish, why extend my claim, exact
1290 Her portion of the penalty? Yes, friends,
I go too fast: the orator's at fault:

Yes, ere I lay her, with your leave, by them
As she was laid at San Lorenzo late,
I ought to step back, lead her by degrees,
1295 Recounting at each step some fresh offence,
Up to the red bed,—never fear, I will!
Gaze at her, where you place her, to begin,
Confound me with her gentleness and worth!
The horrible pair have fled and left her now,
1300 She has her husband for her sole concern,
His wife, the woman fashioned for his help,
Flesh of his flesh, bone of his bone, the bride
To groom as is the Church and Spouse, to Christ:
There she stands in his presence,—"Thy desire
1305 Shall be to the husband, o'er thee shall he rule!"
—"Pompilia, who declare that you love God,
You know who said that: then, desire my love,
Yield me contentment and be ruled aright!"
She sits up, she lies down, she comes and goes,
1310 Kneels at the couch-side, overleans the sill
O' the window, cold and pale and mute as stone,
Strong as stone also. "Well, are they not fled?
Am I not left, am I not one for all?
Speak a word, drop a tear, detach a glance,
1315 Bless me or curse me of your own accord!
Is it the ceiling only wants your soul,
Is worth your eyes?" And then the eyes descend
And do look at me. Is it at the meal?
"Speak!" she obeys, "Be silent!" she obeys,
1320 Counting the minutes till I cry "Depart,"
As brood-bird when you saunter past her eggs.
Departed, just the same through door and wall
I see the same stone strength of white despair.
And all this will be never otherwise!
1325 Before, the parents' presence lent her life:
She could play off her sex's armoury,
Intreat, reproach, be female to my male,
Try all the shrieking doubles[2] of the hare,
Go clamour to the Commissary, bid

---

[1] disgusting metamorphoses.

[2] sharp or backward turns.

330 The Archbishop hold my hands and stop my
    tongue,
And yield fair sport so: but the tactics change,
The hare stands stock-still to enrage the hound!
Since that day when she learned she was no child
Of those she thought her parents,—that their trick
335 Had tricked me whom she thought sole trickster
    late,—
Why, I suppose she said within herself
"Then, no more struggle for my parents' sake,
And, for my own sake, why needs struggle be?"
But is there no third party to the pact?
340 What of her husband's relish or dislike
For this new game of giving up the game,
This worst offence of not offending more?
I'll not believe but instinct wrought in this,
Set her on to conceive and execute
345 The preferable plague…how sure they probe,—
These jades, the sensitivest soft of man!
The long black hair was wound now in a wisp,—
Crowned sorrow better than the wild web late:
No more soiled dress, 'tis trimness triumphs now,
350 For how should malice go with negligence?
The frayed silk looked the fresher for her spite!
There was an end to springing out of bed,
Praying me, with face buried on my feet,
Be hindered of my pastime,—so an end
355 To my rejoinder, "What, on the ground at last?
Vanquished in fight, a supplicant for life?
What if I raise you? 'Ware the casting down
When next you fight me!" Then, she lay there, mine:
Now, mine she is if I please wring her neck,—
360 A moment of disquiet, working eyes,
Protruding tongue, a long sigh, then no more—
As if one killed the horse one could not ride!
Had I enjoined "Cut off the hair!"—why, snap
The scissors, and at once a yard or so
365 Had fluttered in black serpents to the floor:
But till I did enjoin it, how she combs,
Uncurls and draws out to the complete length,
Plaits, places the insulting rope on head

To be an eyesore past dishevelment!
1370 Is all done? Then sit still again and stare!
I advise—no one think to bear that look
Of steady wrong, endured as steadily,
—Through what sustainment of deluding hope?
Who is the friend i' the background that notes all?
1375 Who may come presently and close accounts?
This self-possession to the uttermost,
How does it differ in aught, save degree,
From the terrible patience of God?
                    "All which just means,
1380 She did not love you!" Again the word is launched
And the fact fronts me! What, you try the wards[1]
With the true key and the dead lock flies ope?
No, it sticks fast and leaves you fumbling still!
You have some fifty servants, Cardinal,—
1385 Which of them loves you? Which subordinate
But makes parade of such officiousness[2]
That,—if there's no love prompts it,—love, the
    sham,
Does twice the service done by love, the true.
God bless us liars, where's one touch of truth
1390 In what we tell the world, or world tells us,
Of how we like each other? All the same,
We calculate on word and deed, nor err,—
Bid such a man do such a loving act,
Sure of effect and negligent of cause,
1395 Just as we bid a horse, with cluck of tongue,
Stretch his legs arch-wise, crouch his saddled back
To foot-reach of the stirrup—all for love,
And some for memory of the smart of switch
On the inside of the foreleg—what care we?
1400 Yet where's the bond obliges horse to man
Like that which binds fast wife to husband? God
Laid down the law: gave man the brawny arm
And ball of fist—woman the beardless cheek
And proper place to suffer in the side:
1405 Since it is he can strike, let her obey!

---

[1] projections inside a lock.

[2] servility.

Can she feel no love? Let her show the more,
Sham the worse, damn herself praiseworthily!
Who's that soprano Rome went mad about
Last week while I lay rotting in my straw?
1410 The very jailor gossiped in his praise—
How,—dressed up like Armida,[1] though a man;
And painted to look pretty, though a fright,—
He still made love so that the ladies swooned,
Being an eunuch. "Ah, Rinaldo[2] mine!
1415 But to breathe by thee while Jove slays us both!"
All the poor bloodless creature never felt,
Si, do, re, me, fa, squeak and squall—for what?
Two gold zecchines the evening! Here's my slave,
Whose body and soul depend upon my nod,
1420 Can't falter out the first note in the scale
For her life! Why blame me if I take the life?
All women cannot give men love, forsooth!
No, nor all pullets lay the henwife eggs—
Whereat she bids them remedy the fault,
1425 Brood on a chalk-ball: soon the nest is stocked—
Otherwise, to the plucking and the spit!
This wife of mine was of another mood—
Would not begin the lie that ends with truth,
Nor feign the love that brings real love about:
1430 Wherefore I judged, sentenced and punished her.
But why particularize, defend the deed?
Say that I hated her for no one cause
Beyond my pleasure so to do,—what then?
Just on as much incitement acts the world,
1435 All of you! Look and like! You favour one,
Brow-beat another, leave alone a third,—
Why should you master natural caprice?
Pure nature! Try—plant elm by ash in file;
Both unexceptionable trees enough,
1440 They ought to overlean each other, pair
At top and arch across the avenue
The whole path to the pleasaunce:[3] do they so—

Or loathe, lie off abhorrent each from each?
Lay the fault elsewhere, since we must have faults:
1445 Mine shall have been,—seeing there's ill in the end
Come of my course,—that I fare somehow worse
For the way I took,—my fault…as God's my judge
I see not where the fault lies, that's the truth!
I ought…oh, ought in my own interest
1450 Have let the whole adventure go untried,
This chance by marriage,—or else, trying it,
Ought to have turned it to account some one
O' the hundred otherwises? Ay, my friend,
Easy to say, easy to do,—step right
1455 Now you've stepped left and stumbled on the thing,
—The red thing! Doubt I any more than you
That practice makes man perfect? Give again
The chance,—same marriage and no other wife,
Be sure I'll edify you! That's because
1460 I'm practised, grown fit guide for Guido's self.
You proffered guidance,—I know, none so well,—
You laid down law and rolled decorum out,
From pulpit-corner on the gospel-side,—[4]
Wanted to make your great experience mine,
1465 Save me the personal search and pains so: thanks!
Take your word on life's use? When I take his—
The muzzled ox that treadeth out the corn,
Gone blind in padding round and round one
        path,—
As to the taste of green grass in the field!
1470 What do you know o' the world that 's trodden flat
And salted sterile with your daily dung,
Leavened into a lump of loathsomeness?
Take your opinion of the modes of life,
The aims of life, life's triumph or defeat,
1475 How to feel, how to scheme and how to do
Or else leave undone? You preached long and loud
On high-days, "Take our doctrine upon trust!
Into the mill-house with you! Grind our corn,
Relish our chaff, and let the green grass grow!"
1480 I tried chaff, found I famished on such fare,

---

[1] character in an opera based on Tasso's *Gerusalemme Liberata*.

[2] also a character in an opera based on Tasso's *Gerusalemme Liberata*.

[3] secluded garden.

[4] the left side as one faces the altar.

So made this mad rush at the mill-house-door,
Buried my head up to the ears in dew,
Browzed on the best, for which you brain me, Sirs!
Be it so! I conceived of life that way,
1485 And still declare—life, without absolute use
Of the actual sweet therein, is death, not life.
Give me,—pay down,—not promise, which is
        air,—
Something that's out of life and better still,
Make sure reward, make certain punishment,
1490 Entice me, scare me,—I'll forego this life;
Otherwise, no!—the less that words, mere wind,
Would cheat me of some minutes while they plague.
The fulness of revenge here,—blame yourselves
For this eruption of the pent-up soul
1495 You prisoned first and played with afterward!
"Deny myself" meant simply pleasure you,
The sacred and superior, save the mark!
You—whose stupidity and insolence
I must defer to, soothe at every turn,—
1500 Whose swine-like snuffling greed and grunting lust
I had to wink at or help gratify,—
While the same passions,—dared they perk in me,
Me, the immeasurably marked, by God,
Master of the whole world of such as you,—
1505 I, boast such passions? 'T was "Suppress them
        straight!
Or stay, we'll pick and choose before destroy:
Here's wrath in you,—a serviceable sword,—
Beat it into a ploughshare! What's this long
Lance-like ambition? Forge a pruning-hook,
1510 May be of service when our vines grow tall!
But—sword used swordwise, spear thrust out as
        spear?
Anathema![1] Suppression is the word!"
My nature, when the outrage was too gross,
Widened itself an outlet over-wide
1515 By way of answer?—sought its own relief

With more of fire and brimstone than you wished?
All your own doing: preachers, blame yourselves!

'Tis I preach while the hourglass runs and runs!
God keep me patient! All I say just means—
1520 My wife proved, whether by her fault or mine,—
That's immaterial,—a true stumbling-block
I' the way of me her husband: I but plied
The hatchet yourselves use to clear a path,
Was politic, played the game you warrant wins,
1525 Plucked at law's robe a-rustle through the courts,
Bowed down to kiss divinity's buckled shoe
Cushioned i' the church: efforts all wide the aim!
Procedures to no purpose! Then flashed truth!
The letter kills, the spirit keeps alive
1530 In law and gospel: there be nods and winks
Instruct a wise man to assist himself
In certain matters nor seek aid at all.
"Ask money of me,:—quoth the clownish saw,—
"And take my purse! But,—speaking with
        respect,—
1535 Need you solace for the troubled nose?
Let everybody wipe his own himself!"
Sirs, tell me free and fair! Had things gone well
At the wayside inn: had I surprised asleep
The runaways, as was so probable,
1540 And pinned them each to other partridge-wise,
Through back and breast to breast and back, then
        bade
Bystanders witness if the spit, my sword,
Were loaded with unlawful game for once—
Would you have interposed to damp the glow
1545 Applauding me on every husband's cheek?
Would you have checked the cry "A judgment, see!
A warning, note! Be henceforth chaste, ye wives,
Nor stray beyond your proper precinct, priests!"
If you had, then your house against itself
1550 Divides, nor stands your kingdom any more!
Oh, why, why was it not ordained just so?
Why fell not things out so nor otherwise?
Ask that particular devil whose task it is

---

[1] a curse upon it!

To trip the all-but-at perfection,—slur
1555 The line o' the painter just where paint leaves off
And life begins,—puts ice into the ode
O' the poet while he cries "Next stanza—fire!"
Inscribes all human effort with one word,
Artistry's haunting curse, the Incomplete!
1560 Being incomplete, the act escaped success.
Easy to blame now! Every fool can swear
To hole in net that held and slipped the fish.
But, treat my act with fair unjaundiced eye,
What was there wanting to a masterpiece
1565 Except the luck that lies beyond a man?
My way with the woman, now proved grossly
    wrong,
Just missed of being gravely grandly right
And making critics laugh o' the other side.
Do, for the poor obstructed artist's sake,
1570 Go with him over that spoiled work once more!
Take only its first flower, the ended act
Now in the dusty pod, dry and defunct!
I march to the Villa, and my men with me,
That evening, and we reach the door and stand.
1575 I say...no, it shoots through me lightning-like
While I pause, breathe, my hand upon the latch,
"Let me forebode! Thus far, too much success:
I want the natural failure—find it where?
Which thread will have to break and leave a loop
1580 I' the meshy combination, my brain's loom
Wove this long while and now next minute tests?
Of three that are to catch, two should go free,
One must: all three surprised,—impossible!
Beside, I seek three and may chance on six,—
1585 This neighbour, t' other gossip,—the babe's birth
Brings such to fireside and folks give them wine,—
'T is late: but when I break in presently
One will be found outlingering the rest
For promise of a posset,—one whose shout
1590 Would raise the dead down in the catacombs,
Much more the city-watch that goes its round.
When did I ever turn adroitly up
To sun some brick embedded in the soil,

And with one blow crush all three scorpions there?
1595 Or Pietro or Violante shambles off—
It cannot be but I surprise my wife—
If only she is stopped and stamped on, good!
That shall suffice: more is improbable.
Now I may knock!" And this once for my sake
1600 The impossible was effected: I called king,
Queen and knave in a sequence, and cards came,
All three, three only! So, I had my way,
Did my deed: so, unbrokenly lay bare
Each taenia[1] that had sucked me dry of juice,
1605 At last outside me, not an inch of ring
Left now to writhe about and root itself
I' the heart all powerless for revenge! Henceforth
I might thrive: these were drawn and dead and
    damned.
Oh Cardinal, the deep long sigh you heave
1610 When the load's off you, ringing as it runs
All the way down the serpent-stair to hell!
No doubt the fine delirium flustered me,
Turned my brain with the influx of success
As if the sole need now were to wave wand
1615 And find doors fly wide,—wish and have my will,—
The rest o' the scheme would care for itself: escape?
Easy enough were that, and poor beside!
It all but proved so,—ought to quite have proved,
Since, half the chances had sufficed, set free
1620 Anyone, with his senses at command,
From thrice the danger of my flight. But, drunk,
Redundantly triumphant,—some reverse
Was sure to follow! There's no other way
Accounts for such prompt perfect failure then
1625 And there on the instant. Any day o' the week,
A ducat slid discreetly into palm
O' the mute post-master, while you whisper him—
How you the Count and certain four your knaves,
Have just been mauling who was malapert,[2]
1630 Suspect the kindred may prove troublesome,

---

[1] tapeworm.

[2] impudent.

Therefore, want horses in a hurry,—that
And nothing more secures you any day
The pick o' the stable! Yet I try the trick,
Double the bribe, call myself Duke for Count,
635 And say the dead man only was a Jew,
And for my pains find I am dealing just
With the one scrupulous fellow in all Rome—
Just this immaculate official stares,
Sees I want hat on head and sword in sheath,
640 Am splashed with other sort of wet than wine,
Shrugs shoulder, puts my hand by, gold and all,
Stands on the strictness of the rule o' the road!
"Where's the Permission?" Where's the wretched
        rag
With the due seal and sign of Rome's Police,
645 To be had for asking, half-an-hour ago?
"Gone? Get another, or no horses hence!"
He dares not stop me, we five glare too grim,
But hinders,—hacks and hamstrings[1] sure enough,
Gives me some twenty miles of miry road
650 More to march in the middle of that night
Whereof the rough beginning taxed the strength
O' the youngsters, much more mine, such as you
        see,
Who had to think as well as act: dead-beat,
We gave in ere we reached the boundary
655 And safe spot out of this irrational Rome,—
Where, on dismounting from our steeds next day,
We had snapped our fingers at you, safe and sound,
Tuscans once more in blessed Tuscany,
Where the laws make allowance, understand
660 Civilized life and do its champions right!
Witness the sentence of the Rota there,
Arezzo uttered, the Granduke confirmed,
One week before I acted on its hint,—
Giving friend Guillichini, for his love,
665 The galleys, and my wife your saint, Rome's
        saint,—
Rome manufactures saints enough to know,—

---

[1] disables (by cutting tendons).

Seclusion at the Stinche for her life.
All this, that all but was, might all have been,
Yet was not! baulked by just a scrupulous knave
1670 Whose palm was horn through handling horses'
        hoofs
And could not close upon my proffered gold!
What say you to the spite of fortune? Well,
The worst's in store: thus hindered, haled this way
To Rome again by hangdogs, whom find I
1675 Here, still to fight with, but my pale frail wife?
—Riddled with wounds by one not like to waste
The blows he dealt,—knowing anatomy,—
(I think I told you) one to pick and choose
The vital parts! 'T was learning all in vain!
1680 She too must shimmer through the gloom o' the
        grave,
Come and confront me—not at judgment-seat
Where I could twist her soul, as erst her flesh,
And turn her truth into a lie,—but there,
O' the death-bed, with God's hand between us both,
1685 Striking me dumb, and helping her to speak,
Tell her own story her own way, and turn
My plausibility to nothingness!
Four whole days did Pompilia keep alive,
With the best surgery of Rome agape
1690 At the miracle,—this cut, the other slash,
And yet the life refusing to dislodge,
Four whole extravagant impossible days,
Till she had time to finish and persuade
Every man, every woman, every child
1695 In Rome of what she would: the selfsame she
Who, but a year ago, had wrung her hands
Reddened her eyes and beat her breasts, rehearsed
The whole game at Arezzo, nor availed
Thereby to move one heart or raise one hand!
1700 When destiny intends you cards like these,
What good of skill and preconcerted play?
Had she been found dead, as I left her dead,
I should have told a tale brooked no reply:
You scarcely will suppose me found at fault
1705 With that advantage! "What brings me to Rome?

Necessity to claim and take my wife:
Better, to claim and take my new-born babe,—
Strong in paternity a fortnight old,
When 't is at strongest: warily I work,
1710 Knowing the machinations of my foe;
I have companionship and use the night:
I seek my wife and child,—I find—no child
But wife, in the embraces of that priest
Who caused her to elope from me. These two,
1715 Backed by the pander-pair who watch the while,
Spring on me like so many tiger-cats,
Glad of the chance to end the intruder. I—
What should I do but stand on my defence,
Strike right, strike left, strike thick and threefold,
        slay,
1720 Not all—because the coward priest escapes.
Last, I escape, in fear of evil tongues,
And having had my taste of Roman law."
What's disputable, refutable here?—
Save by just this one ghost-thing half on earth,
1725 Half out of it,—as if she held God's hand
While she leant back and looked her last at me,
Forgiving me (here monks begin to weep)
Oh, from her very soul, commending mine
To heavenly mercies which are infinite,—
1730 While fixing fast my head beneath your knife!
'T is fate not fortune! All is of a piece!
What was it you informed me of my youths?
My rustic four o' the family, soft swains,
What sweet surprise had they in store for me,
1735 Those of my very household,—what did Law
Twist with her rack-and-cord-contrivance late
From out their bones and marrow? What but this—
Had no one of these several stumbling-blocks
Stopped me, they yet were cherishing a scheme,
1740 All of their honest country homespun wit,
To quietly next day at crow of cock,
Cut my own throat too, for their own behoof,
Seeing I had forgot to clear accounts
O' the instant, nowise slackened speed for that,—
1745 And somehow never might find memory,

Once safe back in Arezzo, where things change,
And a court-lord needs mind no country lout.
Well, being the arch-offender, I die last,—
May, ere my head falls, have my eyesight free,
1750 Nor miss them dangling high on either hand,
Like scarecrows in a hemp-field; for their pains!

And then my Trial,—'t is my Trial that bites
Like a corrosive, so the cards are packed,
Dice loaded, and my life-stake tricked away!
1755 Look at my lawyers, lacked they grace of law,
Latin or logic? Were not they fools to the height,
Fools to the depth, fools to the level between,
O' the foolishness set to decide the case?
They feign, they flatter; nowise does it skill,
1760 Everything goes against me: deal each judge
His dole of flattery and feigning,—why,
He turns and tries and snuffs and savours it,
As an old fly the sugar-grain, your gift;
Then eyes your thumb and finger, brushes clean
1765 The absurd old head of him, and whisks away,
Leaving your thumb and finger dirty. Faugh!

And finally, after this long-drawn range
Of affront, failure, failure and affront,—
This path, twixt crosses leading to a skull,[1]
1770 Paced by me barefoot, bloodied by my palms
From the entry to the end,—there's light at length,
A cranny of escape,—appeal may be
To the old man, to the father, to the Pope,
For a little life—from one whose life is spent,
1775 A little pity—from pity's source and seat,
A little indulgence to rank, privilege,
From one who is the thing personified,
Rank, privilege, indulgence, grown beyond
Earth's bearing, even, ask Jansenius[2] else!
1780 Still the same answer, still no other tune

---

[1] the road to Calvary.

[2] heretical school of theology founded by Cornelius Jansen (1585–1638), which denied free will.

From the cicala perched at the tree-top
Than crickets noisy round the root,—'t is "Die!"
Bids Law—"Be damned!" adds Gospel,—nay,
No word so frank,—'t is rather, "Save yourself!"
1785 The Pope subjoins—"Confess and be absolved!
So shall my credit countervail[1] your shame,
And the world see I have not lost the knack
Of trying all the spirits,—yours, my son,
Wants but a fiery washing to emerge
1790 In clarity! Come, cleanse you, ease the ache
Of these old bones, refresh our bowels, boy!"
Do I mistake your mission from the Pope?
Then, bear his Holiness the mind of me!
I do get strength from being thrust to wall,
1795 Successively wrenched from pillar and from post
By this tenacious hate of fortune, hate
Of all things in, under, and above earth.
Warfare, begun this mean unmanly mode,
Does best to end so,—gives earth spectacle
1800 Of a brave fighter who succumbs to odds
That turn defeat to victory. Stab, I fold
My mantle round me! Rome approves my act:
Applauds the blow which costs me life but keeps
My honour spotless: Rome would praise no more
1805 Had I fallen, say, some fifteen years ago,
Helping Vienna when our Aretines
Flocked to Duke Charles and fought Turk
    Mustafa;[2]
Nor would you two be trembling o'er my corpse
With all this exquisite solicitude.
1810 Why is it that I make such suit to live?
The popular sympathy that's round me now
Would break like bubble that o'er-domes a fly—
Pretty enough while he lies quiet there,
But let him want the air and ply the wing,
1815 Why, it breaks and bespatters him, what else?

Cardinal, if the Pope had pardoned me,
And I walked out of prison through the crowd,
It would not be your arm I should dare press!
Then, if I got safe to my place again,
1820 How sad and sapless were the years to come!
I go my old ways and find things grown grey;
You priests leer at me, old friends look askance;
The mob's in love, I'll wager, to a man,
With my poor young good beauteous murdered
    wife:
1825 For hearts require instruction how to beat,
And eyes, on warrant of the story, wax
Wanton[3] at portraiture in white and black
Of dead Pompilia gracing ballad-sheet,
Which, had she died unmurdered and unsung,
1830 Would never turn though she paced street as bare
As the mad penitent ladies do in France.
My brothers quietly would edge me out
Of use and management of things called mine;
Do I command? "You stretched command before!"
1835 Show anger? "Anger little helped you once!"
Advise? "How managed you affairs of old?"
My very mother, all the while they gird,[4]
Turns eye up, gives confirmatory groan,—
For unsuccess, explain it how you will,
1840 Disqualifies you, makes you doubt yourself,
—Much more, is found decisive by your friends.
Beside, am I not fifty years of age?
What new leap would a life take, checked like mine
I' the spring at outset? Where's my second chance?
1845 Ay, but the babe...I had forgot my son,
My heir! Now for a burst of gratitude!
There's some appropriate service to intone,
Some *gaudeamus*[5] and thanksgiving-psalm!
Old, I renew my youth in him, and poor
1850 Possess a treasure,—is not that the phrase?
Only I must wait patient twenty years—

---

[1] offset, compensate for.

[2] In 1683 Duke Charles of Lorraine was one of the leaders assisting John Sobieski when he marched to relieve Vienna from the siege of the Turks.

[3] gloat.

[4] taunt, gibe.

[5] let us rejoice.

Nourishing all the while, as father ought,
The excrescence with my daily blood of life.
Does it respond to hope, such sacrifice,—
1855 Grows the wen plump while I myself grow lean?
Why, here's my son and heir in evidence,
Who stronger, wiser, handsomer than I
By fifty years, relieves me of each load,—
Tames my hot horse, carries my heavy gun,
1860 Courts my coy mistress,—has his apt advice
On house-economy, expenditure,
And what not? All which good gifts and great
   growth
Because of my decline, he brings to bear
On Guido, but half apprehensive how
1865 He cumbers earth, crosses the brisk young Count,
Who civilly would thrust him from the scene.
Contrariwise, does the blood-offering fail?
There's an ineptitude, one blank the more
Added to earth in semblance of my child?
1870 Then, this has been a costly piece of work,
My life exchanged for his!—why, he, not I,
Enjoy the world, if no more grace accrue?
Dwarf me, what giant have you made of him?
I do not dread the disobedient son—
1875 I know how to suppress rebellion there,
Being not quite the fool my father was.
But grant the medium measure of a man,
The usual compromise 'twixt fool and sage,
—You know—the tolerably-obstinate,
1880 The not-so-much-perverse but you may train,
The true son-servant that, when parent bids
"Go work, son, in my vineyard!" makes reply
"I go, Sir!"—Why, what profit in your son
Beyond the drudges you might subsidize,
1885 Have the same work from at a paul the head?
Look at those four young precious olive-plants
Reared at Vittiano,—not on flesh and blood,
These twenty years, but black bread and sour wine!
I bade them put forth tender branch, and hook
1890 And hurt three enemies I had in Rome:
They did my hest as unreluctantly,

At promise of a dollar, as a son
Adjured by mumping memories of the past!
No, nothing repays youth expended so—
1895 Youth, I say, who am young still,—give but leave
To live my life out, to the last I'd live
And die conceding age no right of youth!
It is the will runs the renewing nerve
Through flaccid flesh, would faint before the time.
1900 Therefore no sort of use for son have I—
Sick, not of life's feast but of steps to climb
To the house where life prepares her feast,—of
   means
To the end: for make the end attainable
Without the means,—my relish were like yours.
1905 A man may have an appetite enough
For a whole dish of robins ready cooked,
And yet lack courage to face sleet, pad snow,
And snare sufficiency for supper.

                       Thus
1910 The time's arrived when, ancient Roman-like,
I am bound to fall on my own sword,—why not
Say—Tuscan-like, more ancient, better still?
Will you hear truth can do no harm nor good?
I think I never was at any time
1915 A Christian, as you nickname all the world,
Me among others: truce to nonsense now!
Name me, a primitive religionist—
As should the aboriginary be
I boast myself, Etruscan, Aretine,
1920 One sprung,—your frigid Virgil's fiercest word,—[1]
From fauns and nymphs, trunks and the heart of
   oak,
With,—for a visible divinity,—
The portent of a Jove Aegiochus[2]
Descried 'mid clouds, lightning and thunder,
   couched
1925 On topmost crag of your Capitoline—

---

[1] It is "indigenae": *Aeneid* 8.314.

[2] the bearer of a goatskin breastplate.

'Tis in the Seventh Aeneid,—what, the Eighth?
Right,—thanks, Abate,—though the Christian's
    dumb,
The Latinist's vivacious in you yet!
I know my grandsire had our tapestry
930 Marked with the motto, 'neath a certain shield
His grandson presently will give some gules[1]
To vary azure. First we fight for faiths,
But get to shake hands at the last of all:
Mine's your faith too,—in Jove Aegiochus!
935 Nor do Greek gods, that serve as supplement,
Jar with the simpler scheme, if understood.
We want such intermediary race
To make communication possible;
The real thing were too lofty, we too low,
940 Midway hang these: we feel their use so plain
In linking height to depth, that we doff hat
And put no question nor pry narrowly
Into the nature hid behind the names.
We grudge no rite the fancy may demand;
945 But never, more than needs, invent, refine,
Improve upon requirement, idly wise
Beyond the letter, teaching gods their trade,
Which is to teach us: we'll obey when taught.
Why should we do our duty past the due?
950 When the sky darkens, Jove is wroth,—say prayer!
When the sun shines and Jove is glad,—sing psalm!
But wherefore pass prescription and devise
Blood-offering for sweat-service, lend the rod
A pungency through pickle of our own?
955 Learned Abate,—no one teaches you
What Venus means and who's Apollo here!
I spare you, Cardinal,—but, though you wince,
You know me, I know you, and both know that!
So, if Apollo bids us fast, we fast:
960 But where does Venus order we stop sense[2]
When Master Pietro[3] rhymes a pleasantry?

Give alms prescribed on Friday,—but, hold hand
Because your foe lies prostrate,—where's the word
Explicit in the book debars revenge?
1965 The rationale of your scheme is just
"Pay toll here, there pursue your pleasure free!"
So do you turn to use the medium-powers,[4]
Mars and Minerva, Bacchus and the rest,
And so are saved propitiating—what?
1970 What all good, all wise and all potent Jove
Vexed by the very sins in man, himself
Made life's necessity when man he made?
Irrational bunglers! So, the living truth
Revealed to strike Pan dead,[5] ducks low at last,
1975 Prays leave to hold its own and live good days
Provided it go masque grotesquely, called
Christian not Pagan? Oh, you purged the sky
Of all gods save the One, the great and good,
Clapped hands and triumphed! But the change
    came fast:
1980 The inexorable need in man for life—
Life,—you may mulct[6] and minish to a grain
Out of the lump, so the grain left but live,—
Laughed at your substituting death for life,
And bade you do your worst,—which worst was
    done
1985 —Pass that age styled the primitive and pure
When Saint this, Saint that, dutifully starved,
Froze, fought with beasts, was beaten and abused
And finally ridded of his flesh by fire,
Keeping the while unspotted from the world!—
1990 Good: but next age, how goes the game, who gives
His life and emulates Saint that and this?
They mutiny, mutter who knows what excuse?
In fine make up their minds to leave the new,

---

[1] red (in heraldry).

[2] close our ears or eyes.

[3] Pietro Aretino (1492–1556), author of lascivious sonnets.

---

[4] intercessory gods, the "intermediary race" of l. 1937.

[5] According to legend, during the reign of Tiberius—perhaps at the very moment of the crucifixion—voyagers at sea between Greece and Italy heard a voice from shore proclaiming that Pan was dead: Plutarch, *De Oracularum Defectu* 17.

[6] reduce.

Stick to the old,—enjoy old liberty,
1995 No prejudice, all the same, if so it please,
To the new profession: sin o' the sly, henceforth!
Let the law stand: the letter kills, what then?
The spirit saves as unmistakeably.
Omniscience sees, Omnipotence could stop,
2000 All-mercifulness pardons,—it must be,
Frown law its fiercest, there's a wink somewhere.

Such was the logic in this head of mine:
I, like the rest, wrote "poison" on my bread;
But broke and ate:—said "those that use the sword
2005 Shall perish by the same;" then stabbed my foe.
I stand on solid earth, not empty air:
Dislodge me, let your Pope's crook hale me hence!
Not he, nor you! And I so pity both,
I'll make the speech you want the wit to make:
2010 "Count Guido, who reveal our mystery,[1]
You trace all issues to the love of life:
We have a life to love and guard, like you.
Why did you put us upon self-defence?
You well knew what prompt pass-word would
        appease
2015 The sentry's ire when folk infringe his bounds,
And yet kept mouth shut: do you wonder then
If, in mere decency, he shot you dead?
He can't have people play such pranks as you
Beneath his nose at noonday, who disdain
2020 To give him an excuse before the world,
By crying 'I break rule to save our camp!'
Under the old rule, such offence were death;
And so had you heard Pontifex pronounce
'Since you slay foe and violate the form,
2025 That turns to murder, which were sacrifice
Had you, while, say, law-suiting him to death,
But raised an altar to the Unknown God,
Or else the Genius of the Vatican.'
Why then this pother?—all because the Pope
2030 Doing his duty, cries 'A foreigner,

You scandalize the natives: here at Rome
Romano vivitur more:[2] wise men, here,
Put the Church forward and efface themselves.
The fit defence had been,—you stamped on wheat,
2035 Intending all the time to trample tares,—
Were fain extirpate, then, the heretic,
And now find, in your haste you slew a fool:
Nor Pietro, nor Violante, nor your wife
Meant to breed up your babe a Molinist!
2040 Whence you are duly contrite. Not one word
Of all this wisdom did you urge!—which slip
Death must atone for!'"
                    So, let death atone!
So ends mistake, so end mistakers!—end
2045 Perhaps to recommence,—how should I know?
Only, be sure, no punishment, no pain
Childish, preposterous, impossible,
But some such fate as Ovid could foresee,—
Byblis in fluvium, let the weak soul end
2050 In water, *sed Lycaon in lupum*,[3] but
The strong become a wolf for evermore!
Change that Pompilia to a puny stream
Fit to reflect the daisies on its bank!
Let me turn wolf, be whole, and sate, for once,—
2055 Wallow in what is now a wolfishness
Coerced[4] too much by the humanity
That's half of me as well! Grow out of man,
Glut the wolf-nature,—what remains but grow
Into the man again, be man indeed
2060 And all man? Do I ring the changes right?
Deformed, transformed, reformed, informed,
        conformed!
The honest instinct, pent and crossed[5] through life,
Let surge by death into a visible flow

---

[1] tricks of the trade.

[2] "When in Rome, do as the Romans do."

[3] The tearful Byblis, in love with her own brother, was transformed into a fountain: Ovid, *Metamorphoses* 9.663–65. The cruel Lycaon was turned into a wolf: ll. 237–39.

[4] restrained, curbed.

[5] dammed up.

Of rapture: as the strangled thread of flame
2065 Painfully winds, annoying and annoyed,
Malignant and maligned, thro' stone and ore,
Till earth exclude the stranger:[1] vented once,
It finds full play, is recognized a-top
Some mountain as no such abnormal birth.
2070 Fire for the mount, the streamlet for the vale!
Ay, of the water was that wife of mine—
Be it for good, be it for ill, no run
O' the red thread through that insignificance!
Again, how she is at me with those eyes!
2075 Away with the empty stare! Be holy still,
And stupid ever! Occupy your patch
Of private snow that's somewhere in what world
May now be growing icy round your head,
And aguish at your foot-print,—freeze not me,
2080 Dare follow not another step I take,
Not with so much as those detested eyes,
No, though they follow but to pray me pause
On the incline, earth's edge that's next to hell!
None of your abnegation of revenge!
2085 Fly at me frank, tug while I tear again!
There's God, go tell Him, testify your worst!
Not she! There was no touch in her of hate:
And it would prove her hell, if I reached mine!
To know I suffered, would still sadden her,
2090 Do what the angels might to make amends!
Therefore there's either no such place as hell,
Or thence shall I be thrust forth, for her sake,
And thereby undergo three hells, not one—
I who, with outlet for escape to heaven,
2095 Would tarry if such flight allowed my foe
To raise his head, relieved of that firm foot
Had pinned him to the fiery pavement else!
So am I made, "Who did not make myself:"
(How dared she rob my own lip of the word?)
2100 Beware me in what other world may be!—
Pompilia, who have brought me to this pass!
All I know here, will I say there, and go

Beyond the saying with the deed. Some use
There cannot but be for a mood like mine,
2105 Implacable, persistent in revenge.
She maundered, "All is over and at end:
I go my own road, go you where God will!
Forgive you! I forget you!" There's the saint
That takes your taste, you other kind of men!
2110 How you had loved her! Guido wanted skill
To value such a woman at her worth!
Properly the instructed criticize
"What's here, you simpleton have tossed to take
Its chance i' the gutter? This a daub, indeed?
2115 Why, 't is a Rafael that you kicked to rags!"
Perhaps so: some prefer the pure design:
Give me my gorge of colour, glut of gold
In a glory round the Virgin made for me!
Titian's the man, not Monk Angelico
2120 Who traces you some timid chalky ghost
That turns the church into a charnel: ay,
Just such a pencil might depict my wife!
She,—since she, also, would not change herself,—
Why could not she come in some heart-shaped
   cloud,
2125 Rainbowed about with riches, royalty
Rimming her round, as round the tintless lawn
Guardingly runs the selvage cloth of gold?
I would have left the faint fine gauze untouched,
Needle-worked over with its lily and rose,
2130 Let her bleach unmolested in the midst,
Chill that selected solitary spot
Of quietude she pleased to think was life:
Purity, pallor grace the lawn no doubt
When there's the costly bordure to unthread
2135 And make again an ingot: but what's grace
When you want[2] meat and drink and clothes and
   fire?
A tale comes to my mind that's apposite—
Possibly true, probably false, a truth
Such as all truths we live by, Cardinal!

[1] alien element.

[2] lack.

2140 'T is said, a certain ancestor of mine
Followed—whoever was the potentate,
To Paynimrie,[1] and in some battle, broke
Through more than due allowance of the foe
And, risking much his own life, saved the lord's.
2145 Battered and bruised, the Emperor scrambles up,
Rubs his eyes and looks round and sees my sire,
Picks a furze-sprig from out his hauberk-joint,
(Token how near the ground went majesty)
And says "Take this, and, if thou get safe home,
2150 Plant the same in thy garden-ground to grow:
Run thence an hour in a straight line, and stop:
Describe a circle round (for central point)
The furze aforesaid, reaching every way
The length of that hour's run: I give it thee,—
2155 The central point, to build a castle there,
The circumjacent[2] space, for fit demesne,[3]
The whole to be thy children's heritage,—
Whom, for my sake, bid thou wear furze on cap!"
Those are my arms: we turned the furze a tree
2160 To show more, and the greyhound tied thereto,
Straining to start, means swift and greedy both;
He stands upon a triple mount of gold—
By Jove, then, he's escaping from true gold
And trying to arrive at empty air!
2165 Aha! the fancy never crossed my mind!
My father used to tell me, and subjoin
"As for the castle, that took wings and flew:
The broad lands,—why, to traverse them to-day
Would task my gouty feet, and though in my prime
2170 I doubt not I could stand and spit so far:
But for the furze, boy, fear no lack of that,
So long as fortune leaves one field to grub!
Wherefore hurra for furze and loyalty!"
What may I mean, where may the lesson lurk?
2175 "Do not bestow on man by way of gift
Furze without some substantial framework,—grace

Of purity, a furze-sprig of a wife,
To me, i' the thick of battle for my bread,
Without some better dowry,—house and land!"
2180 No other gift than sordid muck? Yes, Sir!
Many more and much better. Give them me!
O those Olimpias bold, those Biancas brave,[4]
That brought a husband will worth Ormuz'[5]
wealth!
Cried "Thou being mine, why, what but thine
am I?
2185 Be thou to me law, right, wrong, heaven and hell!
Let us blend souls, be thou in me to bid
Two bodies work one pleasure! What are these
Called king, priest, father, mother, stranger, friend?
They fret thee or they frustrate? Give the word—
2190 Be certain they shall frustrate nothing more!
And who is this young florid foolishness
That holds thy fortune in his pigmy clutch,
—Being a prince and potency, forsooth!—
And hesitates to let the trifle go?
2195 Let me but seal up eye, sing ear to sleep
Sounder than Samson,—pounce thou on the prize
Shall slip from off my breast, and down couch-side
And on to floor, and far as my lord's feet—
Where he stands in the shadow with the sword
2200 Waiting to see what Delilah dares do!
Is the youth fair? What is a man to me
Who am thy call-bird?[6] Twist his neck—my
dupe's,—
Then take the breast shall turn a breast indeed!"
Such women are there; and they marry whom?
2205 Why, when a man has gone and hanged himself
Because of what he calls a wicked wife,—
See, if the turpitude, he makes his moan,
Be not mere excellence the fool ignores!

---

[1] heathen land.

[2] surrounding.

[3] estate.

[4] heroines of Italian romance.

[5] diamond market on an island at the mouth of the Persian Gulf.

[6] decoy bird.

His monster is perfection, Circe,[1] sent
2210 Straight from the sun, with rod the idiot blames
As not an honest distaff[2] to spin wool!
O thou Lucrezia,[3] is it long to wait
Yonder where all the gloom is in a glow
With thy suspected presence?—virgin yet,
2215 Virtuous again in face of what's to teach—
Sin unimagined, unimaginable,—
I come to claim my bride,—thy Borgia's self
Not half the burning bridegroom I shall be!
Cardinal, take away your crucifix!
2220 Abate, leave my lips alone, they bite!
'T is vain you try to change, what should not
        change,
And cannot. I have bared, you bathe my heart—
It grows the stonier for your saving dew!
You steep the substance, you would lubricate,
2225 In waters that but touch to petrify!

You too are petrifactions of a kind:
Move not a muscle that shows mercy; rave
Another twelve hours, every word were waste!
I thought you would not slay impenitence,—
2230 Teazed first contrition from the man you slew,—
I thought you had a conscience. Cardinal,
You know I am wronged!—wronged, say, and
        wronged maintain.
Was this strict inquisition made for blood
When first you showed us scarlet on your back,
2235 Called to the College? That straightforward way
To that legitimate end,—I think it passed
Over a scantling[4] of heads brained, hearts broke,
Lives trodden into dust,—how otherwise?

Such is the way o' the world, and so you walk:
2240 Does memory haunt your pillow? Not a whit.
God wills you never pace your garden-path
One appetizing hour ere dinner-time
But your intrusion there treads out of life
An universe of happy innocent things:
2245 Feel you remorse about that damsel-fly[5]
Which buzzed so near your mouth and flapped
        your face,
You blotted it from being at a blow?
It was a fly, you were a man, and more,
Lord of created things, so took your course.
2250 Manliness, mind,—these are things fit to save,
Fit to brush fly from: why, because I take
My course, must needs the Pope kill me?—kill you!
Because this instrument he throws away
Is strong to serve a master: it were yours
2255 To have and hold and get such good from out!
The Pope who dooms me, needs must die next year;
I'll tell you how the chances are supposed
For his successor: first the Chamberlain,
Old San Cesario,—Colloredo, next,—
2260 Then, one, two, three, four, I refuse to name,
After these, comes Altieri; then come you—
Seventh on the list you are, unless…ha, ha,
How can a dead hand give a friend a lift?
Are you the person to despise the help
2265 O' the head shall drop in pannier presently?
So a child seesaws on or kicks away
The fulcrum-stone that's all the sage requires
To fit his lever to and move the world.
Cardinal, I adjure you in God's name,
2270 Save my life, fall at the Pope's feet, set forth
Things your own fashion, not in words like these
Made for a sense like yours who apprehend!
Translate into the court-conventional
"Count Guido must not die, is innocent!
2275 Fair, be assured! But what an he were foul,
Blood-drenched and murder-crusted head to foot?

---

[1] the sorceress in the *Odyssey* 10. 237–396, daughter of Helios (the sun), who turned Odysseus's companions into swine with her wand.

[2] staff used by women in spinning.

[3] Lucrezia Borgia, daughter of Pope Alexander VI, formerly credited with "picturesque crimes" and sexual licentiousness but now rehabilitated by historians.

[4] beam of wood, trestle.

[5] dragon-fly.

Spare one whose death insults the Emperor,
And outrages the Louis[1] you so love!
He has friends who will avenge him; enemies
2280 Who hate the church now with impunity
Missing the old coercive:[2] would you send
A soul straight to perdition, dying frank
An atheist?" Go and say this, for God's sake!
—Why, you don't think I hope you'll say one
    word?
2285 Neither shall I persuade you from your stand
Nor you persuade me from my station: take
Your crucifix away, I tell you twice!

Come, I am tired of silence! Pause enough!
You have prayed: I have gone inside my soul
2290 And shut its door behind me: 't is your torch
Makes the place dark,—the darkness let alone
Grows tolerable twilight,—one may grope
And get to guess at length and breadth and depth.
What is this fact I feel persuaded of—
2295 This something like a foothold in the sea,
Although Saint Peter's bark scuds, billow-borne,
Leaves me to founder where it flung me first?
Spite of your splashing, I am high and dry!
God takes his own part in each thing he made;
2300 Made for a reason, he conserves his work,
Gives each its proper instinct of defence.
My lamblike wife could neither bark nor bite,
She bleated, bleated, till for pity pure,
The village roused it, ran with pole and prong
2305 To the rescue, and behold the wolf's at bay!
Shall he try bleating?—or take turn or two,
Since the wolf owns to kinship with the fox,
And failing to escape the foe by these,
Give up attempt, die fighting quietly?
2310 The last bad blow that strikes fire in at eye

And on to brain, and so out, life and all,
How can it but be cheated of a pang
While, fighting quietly, the jaws enjoy
Their re-embrace in mid back-bone they break,
2315 After their weary work thro' the foes' flesh?
That's the wolf-nature. Do n't mistake my trope!
The Cardinal is qualmish! Eminence,
My fight is figurative, blows i' the air,
Brain-war with powers and principalities,[3]
2320 Spirit-bravado, no real fisticuffs!
I shall not presently, when the knock comes,
Cling to this bench nor flee the hangman's face,
No, trust me! I conceive worse lots than mine.
Whether it be the old contagious fit[4]
2325 And plague o' the prison have surprised me too,
The appropriate drunkenness of the death-hour
Creep on my sense, the work o' the wine and
    myrrh,—
I know not,—I begin to taste my strength,
Careless, gay even: what's the worth of life?
2330 The Pope is dead, my murderous old man,
For Tozzi[5] told me so: and you, forsooth—
Why, you do n't think, Abate, do your best,
You'll live a year more with that hacking cough
And blotch of crimson where the cheek's a pit?
2335 Tozzi has got you also down in book.
Cardinal, only seventh of seventy near,[6]
Is not one called Albano[7] in the lot?
Go eat your heart, you'll never be a Pope!
Inform me, is it true you left your love,
2340 A Pucci, for promotion in the church?
She's more than in the church,—in the churchyard!
Plautilla Pucci, your affianced bride,
Has dust now in the eyes that held the love,—

---

[1] There is some evidence that the Holy Roman Emperor attempted to exert his influence to spare Guido's life. It is doubtful whether his death would have "outraged" Louis XIV.

[2] compelling force.

[3] a frequent phrase in the Pauline epistles.

[4] sudden attack of illness, with a suggestion of madness.

[5] physician to the Pope.

[6] the number of cardinals.

[7] In his last hours, Guido had the voice of prophecy; Innocent's successor was Cardinal Albano.

And Martinez,[1] suppose they make you Pope,
2345 Stops that with *veto*,—so, enjoy yourself!
I see you all reel to the rock, you waves—
Some forthright, some describe a sinuous track,
Some crested, brilliantly with heads above,
Some in a strangled swirl sunk who knows how,
2350 But all bound whither the main-current sets,
Rockward, an end in foam for all of you!
What if I am o'ertaken, pushed to the front
By all you crowding smoother souls behind,
And reach, a minute sooner than was meant,
2355 The boundary, whereon I break to mist?
Go to! the smoothest safest of you all,
Most perfect and compact wave in my train,
Spite of the blue tranquillity above,
Spite of the breadth before of lapsing peace
2360 Where broods the halcyon[2] and the fish leaps free,
Will presently begin to feel the prick
At lazy heart, the push at torpid brain,
Will rock vertiginously[3] in turn, and reel,
And, emulative, rush to death like me:
2365 Later or sooner by a minute then,
So much for the untimeliness of death,—
And, as regards the manner that offends,
The rude and rough, I count the same for gain—
Be the act harsh and quick! Undoubtedly
2370 The soul's condensed and, twice itself, expands
To burst thro' life, in alteration due,
Into the other state whate'er it prove.
You never know what life means till you die:
Even throughout life, 't is death that makes life live,
2375 Gives it whatever the significance.
For see, on your own ground and argument,
Suppose life had no death to fear, how find
A possibility of nobleness
In man, prevented daring any more?
2380 What's love, what's faith without a worst to dread?

Lack-lustre jewelry; but faith and love
With death behind them bidding do or die—
Put such a foil at back, the sparkle's born!
From out myself how the strange colours come!
2385 Is there a new rule in another world?
Be sure I shall resign myself: as here
I recognized no law I could not see,
There, what I see, I shall acknowledge too:
On earth I never took the Pope for God,
2390 In heaven I shall scarce take God for the Pope.
Unmanned, remade: I hold it probable—
With something changeless at the heart of me
To know me by, some nucleus that's myself:
Accretions did it wrong? Away with them—
2395 You soon shall see the use of fire!

                Till when,
All that was, is; and must for ever be.
Nor is it in me to unhate my hates,—
I use up my last strength to strike once more
2400 Old Pietro in the wine-house-gossip-face,
To trample underfoot the whine and wile
Of that Violante,—and I grow one gorge
To loathingly reject Pompilia's pale
Poison my hasty hunger took for food.
2405 A strong tree wants no wreaths about its trunk,
No cloying cups, no sickly sweet of scent,
But sustenance at root, a bucketful.
How else lived that Athenian[4] who died so,
Drinking hot bull's-blood, fit for men like me?
2410 I lived and died a man, and take man's chance,
Honest and bold: right will be done to such.
Who are these you have let descend my stair?
Ha, their accursed psalm![5] Lights at the sill!
Is it "Open" they dare bid you? Treachery!
2415 Sirs, have I spoken one word all this while
Out of the world of words I had to say?

---

[1] the emperor's ambassador to Rome.

[2] kingfisher.

[3] dizzily.

[4] Themistocles, the Athenian statesman who was rumoured to have poisoned himself.

[5] "Out of the depths Lord, have I cried to thee": Psalm 130:1.

Not one word! All was folly; I laughed and mocked!
Sirs, my first true word, all truth and no lie,
Is—save me notwithstanding! Life is all!
2420 I was just stark mad,—let the madman live
Pressed by as many chains as you please pile!
Do n't open! Hold me from them! I am yours,
I am the Granduke's—no, I am the Pope's!
Abate,—Cardinal,—Christ,—Maria,—God,…
2425 Pompilia, will you let them murder me?
—1869

Prologue (to Asolondo) [1]

"The Poet's age is sad: for why?
  In youth, the natural world could show
No common object but his eye
  At once involved with alien glow—
5 His own soul's iris-bow. [2]

"And now a flower is just a flower:
  Man, bird, beast are but beast, bird, man—
Simply themselves, uncinct [3] by dower
  Of dyes which, when life's day began,
10 Round each in glory [4] ran."

Friend, did you need an optic glass,
  Which were your choice? A lens to drape
In ruby, emerald, chrysopras, [5]
  Each object—or reveal its shape
15 Clear outlined, past escape,

The naked very thing?—so clear
  That, when you had the chance to gaze,
You found its inmost self appear
  Through outer seeming—truth ablaze,
20 Not falsehood's fancy-haze?

How many a year, my Asolo,
  Since—one step just from sea to land— [6]
I found you, loved yet feared you so—
  For natural objects seemed to stand
25 Palpably fire-clothed! No—

No mastery of mine o'er these!
  Terror with beauty, like the Bush
Burning but unconsumed. Bend knees,
  Drop eyes to earthward! Language? Tush!
30 Silence 'tis awe decrees.

And now? The lambent flame is—where?
  Lost from the naked world: earth, sky,
Hill, vale, tree, flower,—Italia's rare
  O'er-running beauty crowds the eye—
35 But flame? The Bush is bare.

Hill, vale, tree, flower—they stand distinct,
  Nature to know and name. What then?
A Voice spoke thence which straight unlinked
  Fancy from fact: see, all's in ken: [7]
40 Has once my eyelid winked?

No, for the purged ear apprehends
  Earth's import, not the eye late dazed:
The Voice said "Call my works thy friends!
  At Nature dost thou shrink amazed?
45 God is it who transcends."

Asolo: 6 September 1889
—1889

---

[1] Browning visited Asolo in 1838 and again in 1878. In a letter of 14 October Browning wrote: "it is a strange experience that the impression I had in my first visit to this delightful place near fifty years ago… —strange that this impression of beauty should be confirmed if not heightened."

[2] rainbow (Iris was the goddess of the rainbow).

[3] uncircled.

[4] splendor and halo.

[5] golden-green precious stone.

[6] an easy journey to Venice, about thirty miles distant.

[7] sight.

Development

My Father was a scholar and knew Greek.
When I was five years old, I asked him once
"What do you read about?"
                    "The siege of Troy."
"What is a siege and what is Troy?"
                              Whereat

5 He piled up chairs and tables for a town,
Set me a-top for Priam,[1] called our cat
—Helen, enticed away from home (he said)
By wicked Paris,[2] who couched somewhere close
Under the footstool, being cowardly,
10 But whom—since she was worth the pains, poor
        puss—
Towzer and Tray,—our dogs, the Atreidai,[3]—sought
By taking Troy to get possession of
—Always when great Achilles[4] ceased to sulk,
(My pony in the stable)—forth would prance
15 And put to flight Hector[5]—our page-boy's self.
This taught me who was who and what was what:
So far I rightly understood the case
At five years old: a huge delight it proved
And still proves—thanks to that instructor sage
20 My Father, who knew better than turn straight
Learning's full flare on weak-eyed ignorance,
Or, worse yet, leave weak eyes to grow sand-blind,
Content with darkness and vacuity.

It happened, two or three years afterward,
25 That—I and playmates playing at Troy's Siege—
My Father came upon our make-believe.
"How would you like to read yourself the tale
Properly told, of which I gave you first

Merely such notion as a boy could bear?
30 Pope,[6] now, would give you the precise account
Of what, some day, by dint of scholarship,
You'll hear—who knows?—from Homer's very
        mouth.
Learn Greek by all means, read the 'Blind Old
        Man,
Sweetest of Singers'—*tuphlos* which means 'blind,'
35 *Hedistos* which means 'sweetest.' Time enough!
Try, anyhow, to master him some day;
Until when, take what serves for substitute,
Read Pope, by all means!"
                    So I ran through Pope,
Enjoyed the tale—what history so true?
40 Also attacked my Primer, duly drudged,
Grew fitter thus for what was promised next—
The very thing itself, the actual words,
When I could turn—say, Buttman[7] to account.

Time passed, I ripened somewhat: one fine day,
45 "Quite ready for the Iliad, nothing less?
There's Heine,[8] where the big books block the
        shelf:
Don't skip a word, thumb well the Lexicon!"

I thumbed well and skipped nowise till I learned
Who was who, what was what, from Homer's
        tongue,
50 And there an end of learning. Had you asked
The all-accomplished scholar, twelve years old,
"Who was it wrote the Iliad?"—what a laugh!
"Why, Homer, all the world knows: of his life
Doubtless some facts exist: it's everywhere:
55 We have not settled, though, his place of birth:
He begged, for certain, and was blind beside:

[1] king of Troy.

[2] Helen...Paris: Paris, son of Priam, abducted Helen, wife of Menelaus, and precipitated the Trojan War.

[3] sons of Atreus: Menelaus, and Agamemnon king of Mycenae.

[4] The greatest Greek warrior sulks in his tent through much of the *Iliad*.

[5] the greatest Trojan warrior, killed by Achilles.

[6] Alexander Pope's translation of the *Iliad* appeared in 1715–20.

[7] Philipp Karl Buttman (1764–1829), German scholar and author of a Greek Grammar.

[8] Christian Gottlob Heyne (1729–1812), editor of a standard *Iliad* (1802).

Seven cities claimed him—Sico, with best right,
Thinks Byron.[1] What he wrote? Those Hymns[2]
    we have.
Then there's the 'Battle of the Frogs and Mice,'[3]
60   That's all—unless they dig 'Margites' up[4]
(I'd like that) nothing more remains to know."
Thus did youth spend a comfortable time;
Until—"What's this the Germans say is fact
That Wolf[5] found out first? It's unpleasant work
65   Their chop and change, unsettling one's belief:
All the same, while we live, we learn, that's sure."
So, I bent brow o'er *Prolegomena*.

And, after Wolf, a dozen of his like
Proved there was never any Troy at all,
70   Neither Besiegers nor Besieged,—nay, worse,—
No actual Homer, no authentic text,
No warrant for the fiction I, as fact,
Had treasured in my heart and soul so long—
Ay, mark you! and as fact held still, still hold,
75   Spite of new knowledge, in my heart of hearts
And soul of souls, fact's essence freed and fixed
From accidental fancy's guardian sheath.
Assuredly thenceforward—thank my stars!—
However it got there, deprive who could—
80   Wring from the shrine my precious tenantry,
Helen, Ulysses, Hector and his Spouse,[6]
Achilles and his Friend?[7]—though Wolf—ah, Wolf!
Why must he needs come doubting, spoil a dream?

But then "No dream's worth waking"—Browning
    says:
85   And here's the reason why I tell thus much.
I, now mature man, you anticipate,
May blame my Father justifiably
For letting me dream out my nonage thus,
And only by such slow and sure degrees
90   Permitting me to sift the grain from chaff,
Get truth and falsehood known and named as such.
Why did he ever let me dream at all,
Not bid me taste the story in its strength?
Suppose my childhood was scarce qualified
95   To rightly understand mythology,
Silence at least was in his power to keep:
I might have—somehow—correspondingly—
Well, who knows by what method, gained my gains,
Been taught, by forthrights[8] not meanderings,
100   My aim should be to loathe, like Peleus'[9] son,
A lie as Hell's Gate, love my wedded wife,
Like Hector, and so on with all the rest.
Could not I have excogitated this
Without believing such men really were?

105   That is—he might have put into my hand
The "Ethics"?[10] In translation, if you please,
Exact, no pretty lying that improves,
To suit the modern taste: no more, no less—
The "Ethics": 'tis a treatise I find hard
110   To read aright now that my hair is grey,
And I can manage the original.
At five years old—how ill had fared its leaves!
Now, growing double o'er the Stagirite,[11]
At least I soil no page with bread and milk,
115   Nor crumple, dogsear and deface—boys' way.
    —1889

---

[1] Scio...Byron: Scio is one of the traditional seven cities. In *The Bride of Abydos* 2.27, Byron refers to the "blind old man of Scio's rocky isle."

[2] The *Homeric Hymns* are now known not to be by Homer.

[3] mock-heroic Greek poem, involving burlesques of the *Iliad*, at one time attributed to Homer.

[4] The lost Greek comic poem was thought by Aristotle to be Homer's.

[5] Friedrich August Wolf (1759–1824), author of the *Prolegomena in Homerum* (1795), argued that the *Iliad* and *Odyssey* were handed down in an oral tradition and that multiple authorship was involved.

[6] Andromache.

[7] Patroclus.

[8] straight course.

[9] Achilles.

[10] Aristotle's *Nicomachean Ethics*.

[11] Aristotle, born at Stagira.

Edward Lear
1812 – 1888

Edward Lear was an artist and poet. He is known for his landscapes and natural history drawings, as well as for his nonsense poems and limericks.

❧❧❧

The Owl and the Pussy-Cat

The Owl and the Pussy-Cat went to sea
  In a beautiful pea-green boat,
They took some honey, and plenty of money,
  Wrapped up in a five-pound note.
5 The Owl looked up to the stars above,
    And sang to a small guitar,
"O lovely Pussy! O Pussy, my love,
    What a beautiful Pussy you are,
      You are,
10   You are!
    What a beautiful Pussy you are!"

Pussy said to the Owl, "You elegant fowl!
  How charmingly sweet you sing!
O let us be married! too long we have tarried:
15   But what shall we do for a ring?"
They sailed away for a year and a day,
  To the land where the Bong-tree grows
And there in a wood a Piggy-wig stood
  With a ring at the end of his nose,
20   His nose,
    His nose,
  With a ring at the end of his nose.

"Dear Pig, are you willing to sell for one shilling
25 Your ring?" Said the Piggy, "I will."
So they took it away, and were married next day
  By the Turkey who lives on the hill.
They dinèd on mince, and slices of quince,

Which they ate with a runcible spoon;[1]
30 And hand in hand, on the edge of the sand,
  They danced by the light of the moon,
    The moon,
    The moon,
  They danced by the light of the moon.
—1871

The Dong with a Luminous Nose

When awful darkness and silence reign
  Over the Great Gromboolian plain,
    Through the long, long wintry nights;—
When the angry breakers roar
5 As they beat on the rocky shore;—
    When Storm-clouds brood on the towering heights
Of the Hills of the Chankly Bore:—

Then, through the vast and gloomy dark,
There moves what seems a fiery spark,
10 A lonely spark with silvery rays
    Piercing the coal-black night,—
  A meteor strange and bright:—
Hither and thither the vision strays,
  A single lurid light.

15 Slowly it wanders,—pauses,—creeps,—
Anon it sparkles,—flashes and leaps;
And ever as onward it gleaming goes

---

[1] as coined by Lear, a fork with three prongs, two of which are broad, the third curved and sharp-edged.

A light on the Bong-tree stems it throws.
And those who watch at that midnight hour
20 From Hall or Terrace, or lofty Tower,
Cry, as the wild light passes along,—
    "The Dong!—the Dong!
    "The wandering Dong through the forest goes!
    "The Dong! the Dong!
25   "The Dong with a luminous Nose!"

    Long years ago
    The Dong was happy and gay,
Till he fell in love with a Jumbly Girl
    Who came to those shores one day.
30 For the Jumblies came in a Sieve, they did,—
Landing at eve near the Zemmery Fidd
    Where the Oblong Oysters grow,
    And the rocks are smooth and gray.
And all the woods and the valleys rang
35 With the Chorus they daily and nightly sang,—
    "Far and few, far and few,
    Are the lands where the Jumblies live;
    Their heads are green, and their hands are
      blue
    And they went to sea in a Sieve."

40 Happily, happily passed those days!
    While the cheerful Jumblies staid;
    They danced in circlets all night long,
To the plaintive pipe of the lively Dong,
    In the moonlight, shine, or shade.
45 For day and night he was always there
By the side of the Jumbly Girl so fair,
With her sky-blue hands, and her sea-green hair.
Till the morning came of that hateful day
When the Jumblies sailed in their Sieve away,
50 And the Dong was left on the cruel shore
Gazing—gazing for evermore,—
Ever keeping his weary eyes on
That pea-green sail on the far horizon,—
Singing the Jumbly Chorus still
55 As he sate all day on the grassy hill,—

    "Far and few, far and few,
    Are the lands where the Jumblies live;
    Their heads are green, and their hands are blue
    And they went to sea in a Sieve."

60 But when the sun was low in the West,
    The Dong arose and said,
"What little sense I once possessed
    Has quite gone out of my head!"
And since that day he wanders still
65 By lake and forest, marsh and hill,
Singing—"O somewhere, in valley or plain
"Might I find my Jumbly Girl again!
"For ever I'll seek by lake and shore
"Till I find my Jumbly Girl once more!"

70   Playing a pipe with silvery squeaks,
    Since then his Jumbly Girl he seeks,
    And because by night he could not see,
    He gathered the bark of the Twangum Tree
      On the flowery plain that grows.
75   And he wove him a wondrous Nose,—
    A Nose as strange as a Nose could be!
Of vast proportions and painted red,
And tied with cords to the back of his head.
    —In a hollow rounded space it ended
80   With a luminous Lamp within suspended,
      All fenced about
      With a bandage stout
      To prevent the wind from blowing it
        out;—
    And with holes all round to send the light,
85   In gleaming rays on the dismal night.

And now each night, and all night long,
Over those plains still roams the Dong;
And above the wail of the Chimp and Snipe
You may hear the squeak of his plaintive pipe
90 While ever he seeks, but seeks in vain
To meet with his Jumbly Girl again;
Lonely and wild—all night he goes,—

The Dong with a luminous Nose!
And all who watch at the midnight hour,
95 From Hall or Terrace, or lofty Tower,
Cry, as they trace the Meteor bright,
Moving along through the dreary night,—
    "This is the hour when forth he goes,
    "The Dong with the luminous Nose!
100   "Yonder—over the plain he goes;
      "He goes!
      "He goes;
    "The Dong with the luminous Nose!"
—1877

How Pleasant to Know Mr. Lear

The Self-Portrait of the Laureate of Nonsense

"How pleasant to know Mr. Lear!"
  Who has written such volumes of stuff!
Some think him ill-tempered and queer,
  But a few think him pleasant enough.

5 His mind is concrete and fastidious,
  His nose is remarkably big;
His visage is more or less hideous,
  His beard it resembles a wig.

He has ears, and two eyes, and ten fingers,
10   Leastways if you reckon two thumbs;
Long ago he was one of the singers,
  But now he is one of the dumbs.

He sits in a beautiful parlour,
  With hundreds of books on the wall;
15 He drinks a great deal of Marsala,
  But never gets tipsy at all.

He has many friends, laymen and clerical,
  Old Foss is the name of his cat:[1]
His body is perfectly spherical,
20   He weareth a runcible hat.

When he walks in a waterproof white,
  The children run after him so!
Calling out, "He's come out in his night-
  gown, that crazy old Englishman, oh!"

25 He weeps by the side of the ocean,
  He weeps on the top of the hill;
He purchases pancakes and lotion,
  And chocolate shrimps from the mill.

He reads but he cannot speak Spanish,
30   He cannot abide ginger beer:
Ere the days of his pilgrimage vanish,
  How pleasant to know Mr. Lear!
—1894 (1879)

---

[1] It was; Lear's beloved feline companion died in 1887 at the age of 17.

Charlotte Brontë
1816 – 1855

Charlotte Brontë was the third daughter of Patrick Brontë and Maria Branwell and the eldest of the three famous sisters. After the traumatic experience of the Clergy Daughters' School (fictionalized in *Jane Eyre*), Charlotte attended school at Roe Head near Mirfield and later taught there; like her sister Anne, she worked as a governess to help support the family. The sisters decided to open their own school and, hoping to increase their facility with languages, Charlotte and Emily attended the Pensionnat Heger in Brussels in 1842. While Charlotte is remembered primarily as a novelist, her poems, and especially her poems on the deaths of her sisters, have a haunting quality. Charlotte survived all of her siblings and married in 1854, but died in the winter of 1855 of consumption and complications arising from pregnancy.

❦

The Missionary

Plough, vessel, plough the British main,
  Seek the free ocean's wider plain;
Leave English scenes and English skies,
Unbind, dissever English ties;
5 Bear me to climes remote and strange,
Where altered life, fast-following change,
Hot action, never-ceasing toil,
Shall stir, turn, dig, the spirit's soil;
Fresh roots shall plant, fresh seed shall sow,
10 Till a new garden there shall grow,
Cleared of the weeds that fill it now,—
Mere human love, mere selfish yearning,
Which, cherished, would arrest me yet.
I grasp the plough, there's no returning,
15 Let me, then, struggle to forget.

But England's shores are yet in view,
And England's skies of tender blue
Are arched above her guardian sea.
I cannot yet Remembrance flee;
20 I must again, then, firmly face
That task of anguish, to retrace.
Wedded to home—I home forsake;
Fearful of change—I changes make;
Too fond of ease—I plunge in toil;
25 Lover of calm—I seek turmoil:

Nature and hostile Destiny
Stir in my heart a conflict wild;
And long and fierce the war will be
Ere duty both has reconciled.

30 What other tie yet holds me fast
To the divorced, abandoned past?
Smouldering, on my heart's altar lies
The fire of some great sacrifice,
Not yet half quenched. The sacred steel
35 But lately struck my carnal will,
My life-long hope, first joy and last,
What I loved well, and clung to fast;
What I wished wildly to retain,
What I renounced with soul-felt pain;
40 What—when I saw it, axe-struck, perish—
Left me no joy on earth to cherish;
A man bereft—yet sternly now
I do confirm that Jephtha[1] vow:
Shall I retract, or fear, or flee?
45 Did Christ, when rose the fatal tree
Before Him, on Mount Calvary?[2]
'Twas a long fight, hard fought, but won,
And what I did was justly done.

---

[1] the biblical judge who killed his only daughter because he had declared to God that if he conquered in battle he would sacrifice the first thing he met on returning home: Judges 11:30–40.

[2] the mount near Jerusalem where Christ was crucified.

Yet, Helen! from thy love I turned,
50 When my heart most for thy heart burned;
I dared thy tears, I dared thy scorn—
Easier the death-pang had been borne.
Helen, thou might'st not go with me,
I could not—dared not stay for thee!
55 I heard afar, in bonds complain
The savage from beyond the main;
And that wild sound rose o'er the cry
Wrung out by passion's agony;
And even when, with the bitterest tear
60 I ever shed, mine eyes were dim,
Still, with the spirit's vision clear,
I saw Hell's empire, vast and grim,
Spread on each Indian river's shore,
Each realm of Asia covering o'er.
65 There the weak, trampled by the strong,
Live but to suffer—hopeless die;
There pagan-priests, whose creed is Wrong,
Extortion, Lust, and Cruelty,
Crush our lost race—and brimming fill
70 The bitter cup of human ill;
And I—who have the healing creed,
The faith benign of Mary's Son,
Shall I behold my brother's need,
And selfishly to aid him shun?
75 I—who upon my mother's knees,
In childhood, read Christ's written word,
Received His legacy of peace,
His holy rule of action heard;
I—in whose heart the sacred sense
80 Of Jesus' love was early felt;
Of His pure, full benevolence,
His pitying tenderness for guilt;
His shepherd-care for wandering sheep,
For all weak, sorrowing, trembling things,
85 His mercy vast, His passion deep
Of anguish for man's sufferings;
I—schooled from childhood in such lore—
Dared I draw back or hesitate,
When called to heal the sickness sore

90 Of those far off and desolate?
Dark, in the realm and shades of Death,
Nations, and tribes, and empires lie,
But even to them the light of Faith
Is breaking on their sombre sky:
95 And be it mine to bid them raise
Their drooped heads to the kindling scene,
And know and hail the sunrise blaze
Which heralds Christ the Nazarene.
I know how Hell the veil will spread
100 Over their brows and filmy eyes,
And earthward crush the lifted head
That would look up and seek the skies;
I know what war the fiend will wage
Against that soldier of the Cross,
105 Who comes to dare his demon—rage,
And work his kingdom shame and loss.
Yes, hard and terrible the toil
Of him who steps on foreign soil,
Resolved to plant the gospel vine,
110 Where tyrants rule and slaves repine;
Eager to lift Religion's light
Where thickest shades of mental night
Screen the false god and fiendish rite;
Reckless that missionary blood,
115 Shed in wild wilderness and wood,
Has left, upon the unblest air,
The man's deep moan—the martyr's prayer.
I know my lot—I only ask
Power to fulfil the glorious task;
120 Willing the spirit, may the flesh
Strength for the day receive afresh.
May burning sun or deadly wind
Prevail not o'er an earnest mind;
May torments strange or direst death
125 Nor trample truth, nor baffle faith.
Though such blood-drops should fall from me
As fell in old Gethsemane,[1]

---

[1] the garden outside Jerusalem where the agony, betrayal, and arrest of Christ took place: Matthew 26:36.

Welcome the anguish, so it gave
More strength to work—more skill to save.
130 And, oh! if brief must be my time,
If hostile hand or fatal clime
Cut short my course—still o'er my grave,
Lord, may Thy harvest whitening wave.
So I the culture may begin,
135 Let others thrust the sickle in;
If but the seed will faster grow,
May my blood water what I sow!
What! have I ever trembling stood,
And feared to give to God that blood?
140 What! has the coward love of life
Made me shrink from the righteous strife?
Have human passions, human fears
Severed me from those Pioneers
Whose task is to march first, and trace
145 Paths for the progress of our race?
It has been so; but grant me, Lord,
Now to stand steadfast by Thy word!
Protected by salvation's helm,
Shielded by faith, with truth begirt,
150 To smile when trials seek to whelm
And stand 'mid testing fires unhurt
Hurling Hell's strongest bulwarks down,
Even when the last pang thrills my breast,
When Death bestows the Martyr's crown,
155 And calls me into Jesus' rest.
Then for my ultimate reward—
Then for the world-rejoicing word—
The voice from Father—Spirit—Son:
"Servant of God, well hast thou done!"
—1846

Master and Pupil [1]

I gave, at first, attention close;
 Then interest warm ensued;

From interest, as improvement rose,
    Succeeded gratitude.

5 Obedience was no effort soon,
    And labour was no pain;
If tired, a word, a glance alone
    Would give me strength again.

From others of the studious band
10   Ere long he singled me;
But only by more close demand
    And sterner urgency.

The task he from another took,
    From me he did reject;
15 He would no slight omission brook,
    And suffer no defect.

If my companions went astray,
    He scarce their wanderings blamed;
If I but faltered in the way,
20   His anger fiercely flamed.

When sickness stayed awhile my course,
    He seemed impatient still,
Because his pupil's flagging force
    Could not obey his will.

25 One day when summoned to the bed
    Where pain and I did strive,
I heard him, as he bent his head,
    Say, "God, she must revive!"

I felt his hand, with gentle stress,
30   A moment laid on mine,
And wished to mark my consciousness
    By some responsive sign.

But powerless then to speak or move,
    I only felt, within,

---

[1] The original draft of the above poem is in an exercise-book used by Charlotte Brontë in Brussels, 1843.

35 The sense of Hope, the strength of Love,
　　Their healing work begin.

And as he from the room withdrew,
　　My heart his steps pursued;
I longed to prove, by efforts new,
40　　My speechless gratitude.

When once again I took my place,
　　Long vacant, in the class,
Th' unfrequent smile across his face
　　Did for one moment pass.

45 The lessons done; the signal made
　　Of glad release and play,
He, as he passed, an instant stayed,
　　One kindly word to say.

"Jane, till to-morrow you are free
50　　From tedious task and rule;
This afternoon I must not see
　　That yet pale face in school.

"Seek in the garden-shades a seat,
　　Far from the playground din;
55 The sun is warm, the air is sweet:
　　Stay till I call you in."

A long and pleasant afternoon
　　I passed in those green bowers;
All silent, tranquil, and alone
60　　With birds, and bees, and flowers.

Yet, when my master's voice I heard
　　Call, from the window, "Jane!"
I entered, joyful, at the word,
　　The busy house again.

65 He, in the hall, paced up and down;
　　He paused as I passed by;

His forehead stern relaxed its frown;
　　He raised his deep-set eye.

"Not quite so pale," he murmured low.
70　　"Now, Jane, go rest awhile,"
And as I smiled his smoothened brow
　　Returned as glad a smile.

My perfect health restored, he took
　　His mien austere again;
75 And, as before, he would not brook
　　The slightest fault from Jane.

The longest task, the hardest theme
　　Fell to my share as erst,
And still I toiled to place my name
80　　In every study first.

He yet begrudged and stinted praise,
　　But I had learnt to read
The secret meaning of his face,
　　And that was my best meed.

85 Even when his hasty temper spoke
　　In tones that sorrow stirred,
My grief was lulled as soon as woke
　　By some relenting word.

And when he lent some precious book,
90　　Or gave some fragrant flower,
I did not quail to Envy's look,
　　Upheld by Pleasure's power.

At last our school ranks took their ground,
　　The hard-fought field I won;
95 The prize, a laurel-wreath, was bound
　　My throbbing forehead on.

Low at my master's knee I bent,
　　The offered crown to meet;

Its green leaves through my temples sent
100   A thrill as wild as sweet.

The strong pulse of Ambition struck
    In every vein I owned;
At the same instant, bleeding broke
    A secret, inward wound.

105 The hour of triumph was to me
    The hour of sorrow sore;
A day hence I must cross the sea,
    Ne'er to recross it more.

An hour hence, in my master's room,
110   I with him sat alone,
And told him what a dreary gloom
    O'er joy had parting thrown.

He little said; the time was brief,
    The ship was soon to sail;
115 And while I sobbed in bitter grief
    My master but looked pale.

They called in haste: he bade me go,
    Then snatched me back again;
He held me fast and murmured low,
120   "Why will they part us, Jane?

"Were you not happy in my care?
    Did I not faithful prove?
Will others to my darling bear
    As true, as deep a love?

125 "O God, watch o'er my foster-child!
    Oh, guard her gentle head!
When winds are high and tempests wild
    Protection round her spread!

"They call again: leave then my breast;
130   Quit thy true shelter, Jane;

But when deceived, repulsed, opprest,
    Come home to me again!"
—1857 (1845?)

On the Death of Emily Jane Brontë [1]

My darling, thou wilt never know
    The grinding agony of woe
      That we have borne for thee.
Thus may we consolation tear
5 E'en from the depth of our despair
      And wasting misery.

The nightly anguish thou art spared
When all the crushing truth is bared
      To the awakening mind,
10 When the galled heart is pierced with grief,
Till wildly it implores relief,
      But small relief can find.

Nor know'st thou what it is to lie
Looking forth with streaming eye
15   On life's lone wilderness.
"Weary, weary, dark and drear,
How shall I the journey bear,
      The burden and distress?"

Then since thou art spared such pain
20 We will not wish thee here again;
      He that lives must mourn.
God help us through our misery
And give us rest and joy with thee
      When we reach our bourne!
—1896 (DECEMBER 24, 1848)

---

[1] Emily Jane Brontë died on 19 December 1848.

On the Death of Anne Brontë [1]

There's little joy in life for me,
   And little terror in the grave;
I've lived the parting hour to see
   Of one I would have died to save.

5 Calmly to watch the failing breath,
   Wishing each sigh might be the last;
Longing to see the shade of death
   O'er those belovèd features cast.

The cloud, the stillness that must part
10   The darling of my life from me;
And then to thank God from my heart,
   To thank Him well and fervently;

Although I knew that we had lost
   The hope and glory of our life;
15 And now, benighted, tempest-tossed,
   Must bear alone the weary strife.
     —1896 (JUNE 21, 1849)

Reason

Unloved I love, unwept I weep,
   Grief I restrain, hope I repress;
Vain is this anguish, fixed and deep,
   Vainer desires or means of bliss.

5 My life is cold, love's fire being dead;
   That fire self-kindled, self-consumed;
What living warmth erewhile it shed,
   Now to how drear extinction doomed!

Devoid of charm how could I dream
10   My unasked love would e'er return?
What fate, what influence lit the flame
   I still feel inly, deeply burn?

---

[1] Anne Brontë died at Scarborough on 28 May 1849.

Alas! there are those who should not love;
   I to this dreary band belong;
15 This knowing let me henceforth prove
   Too wise to list delusion's song.

No, Syren! Beauty is not mine;
   Affection's joy I ne'er shall know;
Lonely will be my life's decline,
20   Even as my youth is lonely now.

Come Reason—Science—Learning—Thought—
   To you my heart I dedicate;
I have a faithful subject brought:
   Faithful because most desolate.

25 Fear not a wandering, feeble mind:
   Stern Sovereign, it is all your own
To crush, to cheer, to loose, to bind;
   Unclaimed, unshared, it seeks your throne.

Soft may the breeze of summer blow,
30   Sweetly its sun in valleys shine;
All earth around with love may glow,--
   No warmth shall reach this heart of mine.

Vain boast and false! Even now the fire
   Though smothered, slacked, repelled, is burning
35 At my life's source; and stronger, higher,
   Waxes the spirit's trampled yearning.

It wakes but to be crushed again:
   Faint I will not, nor yield to sorrow;
Conflict and force will quell the brain;
40   Doubt not I shall be strong to-morrow.

Have I not fled that I may conquer?
   Crost the dark sea in firmest faith
That I at last might plant my anchor
   Where love cannot prevail to death?
     —1913 (JANUARY 1836)

"The house was still—the room was still"

The house was still—the room was still
'Twas eventide in June
A caged canary to the sun
Then setting—trilled a tune

5 A free bird on that lilac bush
Outside the lattice heard
He listened long—there came a hush
He dropped an answering word—

The prisoner to the free replied
—1915 (1846–47)

The Lonely Lady

She was alone that evening—and alone
  She had been all that heavenly summer day.
She scarce had seen a face, or heard a tone
  And quietly the hours had slipped away,
5 Their passage through the silence hardly known
  Save when the clock with silver chime did say
The number of the hour, and all in peace
Listened to hear its own vibration cease.

Wearied with airy task, with tracing flowers
10   Of snow on lace, with singing hymn or song
With trying all her harp's symphonious powers
  By striking full its quivering strings along,
And drawing out deep chords, and shaking showers
  Of brilliant sound, from shell and wires among,
15 Wearied with reading books, weary with weeping,
Heart-sick of Life, she sought for death in sleeping.

She lay down on her couch—but could she sleep?
  Could she forget existence in a dream
That blotting out reality might sweep
20   Over her weariness, the healing stream
Of hope and hope's fruition?—Lo the deep

And amber glow of that departing beam
Shot from that blood-red sun—points to her brow
Straight like a silent index, mark it now

25 Kindling her perfect features, bringing bloom
  Into the living marble, smooth and bright
As sculptured effigy on hallowed tomb
  Glimmering amid the dimmed and solemn light
Native to Gothic pile—so wan, so white
30 In shadow gleamed that face, in rosy flush
Of setting sun, rich with a living blush.

Up rose the lonely lady, and her eyes
  Instinctive raised their fringe of raven shade
And fixed upon those vast and glorious skies
35   Their lustre that in death alone might fade.
Skies fired with crimson clouds, burning with dyes
  Intense as blood—they arched above and rayed
The firmament with broad and vivid beams
That seemed to bend towards her all their gleams.

40 It was the arc of battle, leagues away
  In the direction of that setting sun
An army saw that livid summer day
  Closing their serried[1] ranks and squared upon,
Saw it with awe, so deeply was the ray,
45   The last ray tinged with blood—so wild it shone,
So strange the semblance gory, burning, given
To pool and stream and sea by that red heaven.
—1934 (MAY, 1837)

"Is this my tomb, this humble stone"

Is this my tomb, this humble stone
  Above this narrow mound?
Is this my resting place, so lone,
  So green, so quiet round?
5 Not even a stately tree to shade

---

[1] crowded.

The sunbeam from my bed,
Not even a flower in tribute laid
As sacred to the dead.

I look along those evening hills,
10   As mute as earth may be,
I hear not even the voice of rills—
Not even a cloud I see.
How long is it since human tread
Was heard on that dim track
15 Which, through the shadowy valleys led,
Winds far, and farther back?

And was I not a lady once,
My home a princely hall?
And did not hundreds make response
20   Whene'er I deigned to call?
Methinks, as in a doubtful dream,
That dwelling proud I see
Where I caught first the early beam
Of being's day's spring face.

25 Methinks the flash is round me still
Of mirrors broad and bright;
Methinks I see the torches fill
My chambers with their light,
And o'er my limbs the draperies flow
30   All gloss and silken shine,
On my cold brow the jewels glow
As bright as festal wine.

Who then disrobed that worshipped form?
Who wound this winding sheet?
35 Who turned the blood that ran so warm
To Winter's frozen sleet?
O can it be that many a sun
Has set, as that sets now,
Since last its fervid lustre shone
40   Upon my living brow?

Have all the wild dark clouds of night
Each eve for years drawn on
While I interred so far from light
Have slumbered thus alone?
45 Has this green mound been wet with rain—
Such rain as storms distil
When the wind's high and warning strain
Swells loud on sunless hill?

And I have slept where roughest hind
50   Had shuddered to pass by,
And no dread did my spirit find
In all that snow-racked sky,
Though shook the iron-rails around
As, swept by deepened breeze,
55 They gave a strange and hollow sound
That living veins might freeze.

O was that music like my own?—
Such as I used to play
When soft and clear and holy shone
60   The summer moon's first ray,
And saw me lingering still to feel
The influence of that sky?
O words may not the peace reveal
That filled its concave high,

65 As rose and bower how far beneath
Hung down o'ercharged with dew,
And sighed their sweet and fragrant breath
To every gale that blew
The hour for music, but in vain,
70   Each ancient stanza rose
To lips that could not with their strain
Break Earth's and Heaven's repose.

Yet first a note and then a line
The fettered tongue would say,
75 And then the whole rich song divine

Found free a gushing way.
Past, lost, forgotten, I am here,
    They dug my chamber deep,
I know no hope, I feel no fear,
80   I sleep—how calm I sleep!
     —1934 (JUNE 4, 1837)

"Obscure and little seen my way"

Obscure and little seen my way
    Through life has ever been,
But winding from my earliest day
    Through many a wondrous scene.
5 None ever asked what feelings moved
    My heart, or flushed my cheek,

And if I hoped, or feared or loved
    No voice was heard to speak.

I watched, I thought, I studied long,
10 The crowds I moved unmarked among,
I nought to them and they to me
But shapes of strange variety.
The Great with all the elusive shine
Of power and wealth and lofty line
15 I long have marked and well I know.
     —1934 (NOVEMBER 1837)

Emily Jane Brontë
1818 – 1848

Emily Brontë was the fourth daughter of Patrick Brontë and Maria Branwell. Emily is justly considered the most intense of the sisters and expresses in her work a passionate and, at times, violent gothic sensibility. The extraordinary creative exertion, on the part of Emily, Anne, and Charlotte, that followed their unsuccessful plan to open a school, produced the enigmatic *Wuthering Heights*, which was published with Anne's *Agnes Grey* in 1847. Though Emily is best remembered for this startling novel, her poetry—honest, impassioned, and vigorous—equally declares its composer "[n]o trembler in the world's storm-troubled sphere" ("No Coward Soul is Mine"). The success, or at least notoriety, of *Wuthering Heights* was followed less than one year later by the death of Emily's brother Branwell. It is said that Emily caught a cold at Branwell's funeral and that she subsequently became consumptive. After having refused to see a doctor, Emily died at Haworth in December of 1848.

❦

"Riches I hold in light esteem"

Riches I hold in light esteem
And Love I laugh to scorn
And lust of Fame was but a dream
That vanished with the morn—

5 And if I pray, the only prayer
That moves my lips for me
Is—"Leave the heart that now I bear
And give me liberty."

Yes, as my swift days near their goal
10 'Tis all that I implore—
Through life and death, a chainless soul
With courage to endure!
—(MARCH 1, 1841)

To Imagination

When weary with the long day's care,
And earthly change from pain to pain,
And lost, and ready to despair,
Thy kind voice calls me back again—
5 O my true friend, I am not lone
While thou canst speak with such a tone!

So hopeless is the world without,
The world within I doubly prize;
Thy world where guile and hate and doubt
10 And cold suspicion never rise;
Where thou and I and Liberty
Have undisputed sovereignty.

What matters it that all around
Danger and grief and darkness lie,
15 If but within our bosom's bound
We hold a bright unsullied sky,
Warm with ten thousand mingled rays
Of suns that know no winter days?

Reason indeed may oft complain
20 For Nature's sad reality,
And tell the suffering heart how vain
Its cherished dreams must always be;
And Truth may rudely trample down
The flowers of Fancy newly blown.

25 But thou art ever there to bring
The hovering visions back and breathe
New glories o'er the blighted spring
And call a lovelier life from death,
And whisper with a voice divine
30 Of real worlds as bright as thine.

I trust not to thy phantom bliss,
Yet still in evening's quiet hour
With never-failing thankfulness
I welcome thee, benignant power,
35   Sure solacer of human cares
And brighter hope when hope despairs.
—1846 (SEPTEMBER 3, 1844)

Plead For Me

O thy bright eyes must answer now,
When Reason, with a scornful brow,
Is mocking at my overthrow;
O thy sweet tongue must plead for me
5   And tell why I have chosen thee!

Stern Reason is to judgement come
Arrayed in all her forms of gloom:
Wilt thou my advocate be dumb?
No, radiant angel, speak and say
10   Why I did cast the world away;

Why I have persevered to shun
The common paths that others run;
And on a strange road journeyed on
Heedless alike of Wealth and Power—
15   Of Glory's wreath and Pleasure's flower.

These once indeed seemed Beings divine,
And they perchance heard vows of mine
And saw my offerings on their shrine—
But, careless gifts are seldom prized,
20   And mine were worthily despised;

So with a ready heart I swore
To seek their altar-stone no more,
And gave my spirit to adore
Thee, ever present, phantom thing—
25   My slave, my comrade, and my King!

A slave because I rule thee still;
Incline thee to my changeful will
And make thy influence good or ill—
A comrade, for by day and night
30   Thou art my intimate delight—

My Darling Pain that wounds and sears
And wrings a blessing out from tears
By deadening me to real cares;
And yet, a king—though prudence well
35   Have taught thy subject to rebel.

And am I wrong to worship where
Faith cannot doubt nor Hope despair
Since my own soul can grant my prayer?
Speak, God of Visions, plead for me
40   And tell why I have chosen thee!
—1846 (OCTOBER 14, 1844)

Remembrance

Cold in the earth, and the deep snow piled
above thee!
Far, far removed, cold in the dreary grave!
Have I forgot, my Only Love, to love thee,
Severed at last by Time's all-wearing wave?

5   Now, when alone, do my thoughts no longer hover
Over the mountains on Angora's[1] shore;
Resting their wings where heath and fern-leaves
cover
That noble heart for ever, ever more?

Cold in the earth, and fifteen wild Decembers
10   From those brown hills have melted into spring—
Faithful indeed is the spirit that remembers
After such years of change and suffering!

---

[1] Ankara, a city in Asia Minor.

Sweet Love of youth, forgive if I forget thee
While the World's tide is bearing me along:
15 Sterner desires and darker hopes beset me,
Hopes which obscure but cannot do thee wrong.

No other Sun has lightened up my heaven;
No other Star has ever shone for me:
All my life's bliss from thy dear life was given—
20 All my life's bliss is in the grave with thee.

But when the days of golden dreams had perished
And even Despair was powerless to destroy,
Then did I learn how existence could be cherished,
Strengthened and fed without the aid of joy;

25 Then did I check the tears of useless passion,
Weaned my young soul from yearning after thine;
Sternly denied its burning wish to hasten
Down to that tomb already more than mine!

And even yet, I dare not let it languish,
30 Dare not indulge in Memory's rapturous pain;
Once drinking deep of that divinest anguish,
How could I seek the empty world again?
    —1846 (1845)

The Prisoner
A Fragment

In the dungeon-crypts, idly did I stray,
Reckless of the lives wasting there away;
"Draw the ponderous bars! open, Warder stern!"
He dared not say me nay—the hinges harshly turn.

5 "Our guests are darkly lodged," I whisper'd, gazing
    through
The vault, whose grated eye showed heaven more
    grey than blue;
(This was when glad spring laughed in awaking
    pride;)

"Aye, darkly lodged enough!" returned my sullen
    guide.

Then, God forgive my youth; forgive my careless
    tongue;
10 I scoffed, as the chill chains on the damp
    flag-stones rung:
"Confined in triple walls, art thou so much to fear,
That we must bind thee down and clench thy
    fetters here?"

The captive raised her face, it was as soft and mild
As sculptured marble saint, or slumbering
    unwean'd child;
15 It was so soft and mild, it was so sweet and fair,
Pain could not trace a line, nor grief a shadow
    there!

The captive raised her hand and pressed it to her
    brow;
"I have been struck," she said, "and I am suffering
    now;
Yet these are little worth, your bolts and irons
    strong,
20 And, were they forged in steel, they could not hold
    me long."

Hoarse laughed the jailor grim: "Shall I be won to
    hear;
Dost think, fond, dreaming wretch, that *I* shall
    grant thy prayer?
Or, better still, wilt melt my master's heart with
    groans?
Ah! sooner might the sun thaw down these granite
    stones.

25 "My master's voice is low, his aspect bland and
    kind,
But hard as hardest flint, the soul that lurks
    behind;

And I am rough and rude, yet not more rough to
    see
Than is the hidden ghost that has its home in me."

About her lips there played a smile of almost scorn,
30 "My friend," she gently said, "you have not heard
    me mourn;
When you my kindred's lives, *my* lost life, can
    restore,
Then may I weep and sue,—but never, friend,
    before!

Still, let my tyrants know, I am not doomed to wear
Year after year in gloom, and desolate despair;
35 A messenger of Hope, comes every night to me,
And offers for short life, eternal liberty.

He comes with western winds, with evening's
    wandering airs,
With that clear dusk of heaven that brings the
    thickest stars.
Winds take a pensive tone, and stars a tender fire,
40 And visions rise, and change, that kill me with
    desire.

Desire for nothing known in my maturer years,
When Joy grew mad with awe, at counting future
    tears.
When, if my spirit's sky was full of flashes warm,
I knew not whence they came, from sun, or
    thunder storm.

45 But, first, a hush of peace—a soundless calm
    descends;
The struggle of distress, and fierce impatience ends.
Mute music soothes my breast, unuttered harmony,
That I could never dream, till Earth was lost to me.

Then dawns the Invisible; the Unseen its truth
    reveals;
50 My outward sense is gone, my inward essence feels:

Its wings are almost free—its home, its harbour
    found,
Measuring the gulf, it stoops, and dares the final
    bound.

Oh, dreadful is the check—intense the agony—
When the ear begins to hear, and the eye begins to
    see;
55 When the pulse begins to throb, the brain to think
    again,
The soul to feel the flesh, and the flesh to feel the
    chain.

Yet I would lose no sting, would wish no torture
    less,
The more that anguish racks, the earlier it will bless;
And robed in fires of hell, or bright with heavenly
    shine,
60 If it but herald death, the vision is divine!"

She ceased to speak, and we, unanswering, turned
    to go—
We had no further power to work the captive woe:
Her cheek, her gleaming eye, declared that man
    had given
A sentence, unapproved, and overruled by Heaven.
    —1846 (1845)

"No coward soul is mine" [1]

No coward soul is mine
No trembler in the world's storm-troubled
    sphere
I see Heaven's glories shine
And Faith shines equal arming me from Fear

5 O God within my breast
Almighty ever-present Deity

---

[1] "The following are the last lines my sister Emily ever wrote."
(Charlotte Brontë's note.)

Life, that in me hast rest
As I Undying Life, have power in Thee

Vain are the thousand creeds
10 That move men's hearts, unutterably vain,
Worthless as withered weeds
Or idlest froth amid the boundless main

To waken doubt in one
Holding so fast by thy infinity
15 So surely anchored on
The steadfast rock of Immortality

With wide-embracing love
Thy spirit animates eternal years
Pervades and broods above,
20 Changes, sustains, dissolves, creates and rears

Though Earth and moon were gone
And suns and universes ceased to be
And thou wert left alone
Every Existence would exist in thee

25 There is not room for Death
Nor atom that his might could render void
Since thou art Being and Breath
And what thou art may never be destroyed.
—1850 (JANUARY 2, 1846)

Stanzas—"Often rebuked, yet always back returning"[1]

Often rebuked, yet always back returning
To those first feelings that were born with me,
And leaving busy chase of wealth and learning
For idle dreams of things which cannot be:

5 To-day, I will seek not the shadowy region;
Its unsustaining vastness waxes drear;
And visions rising, legion after legion,
Bring the unreal world too strangely near.

I'll walk, but not in old heroic traces,
10 And not in paths of high morality,
And not among the half-distinguished faces,
The clouded forms of long-past history.

I'll walk where my own nature would be leading:
It vexes me to choose another guide:
15 Where the gray flocks in ferny glens are feeding;
Where the wild wind blows on the mountain
side.

What have those lonely mountains worth revealing?
More glory and more grief than I can tell:
The earth that wakes *one* human heart to feeling
20 Can centre both the worlds of Heaven and Hell.
—1850

A Farewell to Alexandria[2]

I've seen this dell in July's shine
As lovely as an angel's dream;
Above, heaven's depth of blue divine;
Around, the evening's golden beam.

5 I've seen the purple heather-bell
Look out by many a storm-worn stone;
And oh, I've seen such music swell,
Such wild notes wake these passes lone—

So soft, yet so intensely felt,
10 So low, yet so distinctly heard,
My breath would pause, my eyes would melt,
And my tears dew the green heath-sward.

---

[1] The authorship of this poem has alternately been credited to Charlotte and Emily Brontë; there is no firm evidence for either claim.

[2] This poem was given the title of "The Outcast Mother" in *The Cornhill Magazine*, May, 1860, where it was initially published.

I'd linger here a summer day,
Nor care how fast the hours flew by,
15 Nor mark the sun's departing ray
Smile sadly glorious from the sky.

Then, then I might have laid thee down
And deemed thy sleep would gentle be;
I might have left thee, darling one,
20 And thought thy God was guarding thee!

But now there is no wandering glow,
No gleam to say that God is nigh;
And coldly spreads thy couch of snow,
And harshly sounds thy lullaby.

25 Forests of heather, dark and long,
Wave their brown, branching arms above,
And they must soothe thee with their song,
And they must shield my child of love!

Alas, the flakes are heavily falling;
30 They cover fast each guardian crest;
And chilly white their shroud is palling
Thy frozen limbs and freezing breast.

Wakes up the storm more madly wild,
The mountain drifts are tossed on high—
35 Farewell, unblessed, unfriended child,
I cannot bear to watch thee die!
—1860 (JULY 12, 1839)

"Long neglect has worn away"

Long neglect has worn away
Half the sweet enchanting smile;
Time has turned the bloom to grey;
Mould and damp the face defile.

5 But that lock of silky hair,
Still beneath the picture twined,

Tells what once those features were,
Paints their image on the mind.

Fair the hand that traced that line,
10 "Dearest, ever deem me true";
Swiftly flew the fingers fine
When the pen that motto drew.
—1902 (1837)

"The night is darkening round me"

The night is darkening round me,
The wild winds coldly blow;
But a tyrant spell has bound me
And I cannot, cannot go.

5 The giant trees are bending
Their bare boughs weighed with snow,
And the storm is fast descending
And yet I cannot go.

Clouds beyond clouds above me,
10 Wastes beyond wastes below
But nothing drear can move me;
I will not, cannot go.
—1902 (1837)

"What winter floods, what showers of spring"

What winter floods, what showers of spring
Have drenched the grass by night and day;
And yet, beneath, that spectre ring,
Unmoved and undiscovered lay

5 A mute remembrancer of crime,
Long lost, concealed, forgot for years,
It comes at last to cancel time,
And waken unavailing tears.
—1910 (1839)

"She dried her tears, and they did smile"

She dried her tears, and they did smile
To see her cheeks' returning glow;
Nor did discern how all the while
That full heart throbbed to overflow.

5 With that sweet look and lively tone,
And bright eye shining all the day,
They could not guess, at midnight lone
How she would weep the time away.
—1910 (1839?)

Eliza Cook
1818 – 1889

First publishing at the age of seventeen, Eliza Cook gained an early reputation for unpretentiously moral and humane verse, focussing on domesticity and social issues concerning women and children. Prolific in her personal publications (*Lays of the Wild Harp* [1835],

Melaia and Other Poems [1838], *Poems, Second Series* [1845], and *New Echoes, and Other Poems* [1864]), Cook also contributed to London periodicals such as *The Weekly Dispatch*, and edited and contributed to her biweekly periodical, *Eliza Cook's Journal* (1849–54).

❦

Lines

Written at Midnight, in the Anticipation of a Dreaded Bereavement

Though to the passing world my heart
    A quiet, untouched thing may seem,
It bleeds, my Mother, bleeds for *thee*;
    My love, my sorrow, and my theme.

5 How many a night these aching eyes
    Have watched beside thy wasting form;
Watched, like the anxious mariner,
    Who marks and dreads the coming storm.

How many a time I've bent mine ear,
10   To catch thy low and fainting breath;
And trembled lest thy soul had fled,
    Unnoticed, to the realms of death.

My Mother! thou wilt die, and leave
    The world, with life and grief, to me;
15 Oh! would the human branch might fade,
    When severed from its parent tree!

I do adore thee! such my first
    Fond, broken lisping did proclaim;
And all I suffer now but proves
20   My shrine and homage still the same.

Time, that will alter breast and brow
    So strangely that we know them not:
That sponges out all trace of truth,
    Or darkens it with many a blot!

25 In me hath wrought its changes too,
    Alike in bosom, lip, and brain;
And taught me much, much that, alas!
    Is learnt but in the school of Pain.

I'm strangely warped from what I was,
30   For some few years, in Life's fresh morn;
When Thought, scarce linked with Reason's chain,
    Nor dared to question, doubt, or scorn.

Though young in years, I've learnt to look
    With trustless eye on all and each;
35 And shudder that I find so oft
    The coldest heart with gentlest speech.

But one deep stream of feeling flows
    With warm devoted love for thee;
A stream whose tide, without an ebb
40   Will reach Eternity's vast sea.

Time has not dimmed, nor will it dim,
    One ray of that bright, glowing flame
Which constant burns, like Allah's[1] fire
    Upon the altar of thy name.

---

[1] the term for "God" in Islam.

45 But, ah! that name, so dearly prized,
    So fondly cherished, soon must be
A beacon quenched; a treasure wrecked
    To live but in the memory.

Father of Mercy, is there naught
50   Of tribulation Thou canst send
Upon my heart but this dire stroke,
    To scathe, to sadden, and to rend?

Wilt Thou not spare, at least awhile,
    The only one I care to call
55 My own? Oh! wilt thou launch the bolt,
    And crush at once my earthly all?

But this is impious. Faith and Hope
    Will teach me how to bear my lot;
To think Almighty Wisdom best,
60   To bow my head, and murmur not.

The chastening hand of One above
    Falls heavy; but I'll kiss the rod;[1]
He gives the wound, and I must trust
    Its healing to the self-same God.
    —1835

The Waters

What was it that I loved so well about my
    childhood's home?
It was the wide and wave-lashed shore, the black
    rocks, crowned with foam
It was the sea-gull's flapping wing, all trackless in
    its flight;
Its screaming note that welcomed on the fierce and
    stormy night.
5 The wild heath had its flowers and moss, the forest
    had its trees,

Which, bending to the evening wind, made music
    in the breeze:
But earth, ha! ha! I laugh e'en now, earth had no
    charms for *me*;
No scene half bright enough to win my young
    heart from the sea!
No! 'twas the ocean, vast and deep, the fathomless,
    the free!
10 The mighty, rushing waters that were ever dear to
    me!

My earliest steps would wander, from the green
    and fertile land,
Down where the clear, blue ocean rolled, to pace
    the rugged strand;
I'd proudly fling the proffered bribe and gilded toy
    away,
To gather up the salt sea weeds, or dabble in the
    spray!
15 I shouted to the distant crew, or launched my
    mimic bark;
I met the morning's freshness there, and lingered
    till the dark:
When dark, I climbed, with bounding step, the
    steep and jutting cliff,
To see them trim the beacon-light to guide the
    fisher's skiff!
Oh! how I loved the Waters, and even longed to be
20 A bird, or boat, or anything that dwelt upon the
    Sea.

The moon! the moon! oh, tell me, do ye love her
    placid ray?
Do ye love the shining, starry train that gathers
    round her way?
Oh! if ye do, go watch her when she climbs above
    the main,
While her full transcript lives below, upon the
    crystal plain.
25 While her soft light serenely falls; and rising billows
    seem

---

[1] the reprimanding rod of the Old Testament God.

Like sheets of silver spreading forth to meet her
    hallowed beam;
Look! and thy soul will own the spell; thou'lt feel as
    I have felt;
Thou'lt love the waves as I have loved, and kneel as
    I have knelt;
And, well I know, the prayer of saint or martyr
    ne'er could be
30 More fervent in its faith than mine, beside the
    moon-lit Sea.

I liked not those who nurtured me; they gave my
    bosom pain;
They strove to fix their shackles on a soul that
    spurned the chain:
I grew rebellious to their hope, disdainful of their
    care;
And all they dreaded most, my spirit loved the
    most to dare.
35 And am I changed? have I become a tame and
    fashioned thing?
Have I yet learned to sing the joys that Pleasure's
    minions sing?
Is there a smile upon my brow, when mixed with
    Folly's crowd?
Is the false whisper dearer than the storm-wail,
    shrill and loud?
No! no! my soul is as it was, and as it e'er will be—
40 Loving, and free as what it loves, the curbless,
    mighty Sea.
—1835

The Ploughshare of Old England

The sailor boasts his stately ship, the bulwark of
    the isle;
The soldier loves his sword, and sings of tented
    plains the while;
But we will hang the ploughshare up within our
    fathers' halls,
And guard it as the deity of plenteous festivals.
5 We'll pluck the brilliant poppies, and the far-famed
    barley-corn,
To wreathe with bursting wheat-ears that outshine
    the saffron morn;
We'll crown it with a glowing heart, and pledge
    our fertile land:
The Ploughshare of Old England, and the sturdy
    peasant band.

The work it does is good and blest, and may be
    proudly told;
10 We see it in the teeming barns, and fields of waving
    gold;
Its metal is unsullied, no blood-stain lingers there:
God speed it well, and let it thrive unshackled
    everywhere.
The bark may rest upon the wave, the spear may
    gather dust,
But never may the prow that cuts the furrow lie
    and rust.
15 Fill up, fill up, with glowing heart, and pledge our
    fertile land:
The Ploughshare of Old England, and the sturdy
    peasant band.
—1838

The Old Arm-Chair

I love it, I love it; and who shall dare
To chide me for loving that old Arm-chair?
I've treasured it long as a sainted prize:
I've bedewed it with tears, and embalmed it with
    sighs.
5 'Tis bound by a thousand bands to my heart;
Not a tie will break, not a link will start.
Would ye learn the spell?—a mother sat there;
And a sacred thing is that old Arm-chair.

In Childhood's hour I lingered near
10 The hallowed seat with listening ear;
And gentle words that mother would give;
To fit me to die, and teach me to live.
She told me shame would never betide,
With truth for my creed and God for my guide;
15 She taught me to lisp my earliest prayer;
As I knelt beside that old Arm-chair.

I sat and watched her many a day,
When her eye grew dim, and her locks were grey:
And I almost worshipped her when she smiled,
20 And turned from her Bible to bless her child.
Years rolled on; but the last one sped—
My idol was shattered; my earth-star fled:
I learnt how much the heart can bear,
When I saw her die in that old Arm-chair.

25 'Tis past, 'tis past, but I gaze on it now
With quivering breath and throbbing brow:
'Twas there she nursed me; 'twas there she died:
And Memory flows with lava tide.
Say it is folly, and deem me weak,
30 While the scalding drops start down my cheek;
But I love it, I love it; and cannot tear
My soul from a mother's old Arm-chair.
—1838

Song of the Red Indian

Oh! why does the white man hang on my path,
    Like the hound on the tiger's track?
Does the flush of my dark skin awaken his wrath?
    Does he covet the bow at my back?
5 He has rivers and seas where the billow and breeze
    Bear riches for him alone;
And the sons of the wood never plunge in the flood
    That the white man calls his own.
Then why should he covet the streams where none
10   But the red-skin dare to swim?

Oh! why should he wrong the hunter one
    Who never did harm to him?

The Father above thought fit to give
    To the white man corn and wine;
15 There are golden fields where he may live,
    But the forest shades are mine.
The eagle has its place of rest,
    The wild horse where to dwell;
And the Spirit who gave the bird its nest,
20   Made me a home as well.
Then back, go back from the red-skin's track
    For the hunter's eyes grow dim,
To find the white man wrongs the one
    Who never did harm to him.

25 Oh! why does the pale-face always call
    The red man "heathen brute?"
He does not bend where the dark knees fall,
    But the tawny lip is mute.
We cast no blame on his creed or name,
30   Or his temples, fine and high;
But he mocks at us with a laughing word
    When we worship a star-lit sky.
Yet, white man, what has thy good faith done
    And where can its mercy be,
35 If it teach thee to hate the hunter one
    Who never did harm to thee?

We need no book to tell us how
    Our lives shall pass away;
For we see the onward torrent flow,
40   And the mighty tree decay.
"Let thy tongue be true and thy heart be brave,"
    Is among the red-skins' lore;
We can bring down the swift wing and dive in the
        wave,
    And we seek to know no more.
45 Then back, go back, and let us run
    With strong, unfettered limb;

For why should the white man wrong the one
    Who never did harm to him?

We know there's a hand that has fixed the hill
50   And planted the prairie plain;
That can fling the lightnings when it will,
    And pour out the torrent rain.
Far away and alone, where the headlong tide
    Dashes on with our bold canoe.
55 We ask and trust that hand to guide
    And carry us safely through.
The Great Spirit dwells in the beautiful sun,
    And while we kneel in its light,
Who will not own that the hunter one
60   Has an altar pure and bright?

The painted streak on a warrior's cheek
    Appears a wondrous thing;
The white man stares at a wampum[1] belt,
    And a plume from the heron's wing.
65 But the red man wins the panthers' skins
    To cover his dauntless form;
While the pale-face hides his breast in a garb
    That he takes from the crawling worm.
And your lady fair, with her gems so rare,
70   Her ruby, gold, and pearl,
Would be as strange to other eyes
    As the bone-decked Indian girl.

Then why does the cruel, white man come
    With the war-whoop's yelling sound?
75 Oh! why does he take our wigwam home,
    And the jungled hunting-ground?
The wolf-cub has its lair of rest,
    And the wild horse where to dwell,
And the Spirit who gave the bird its nest
80   Made me a place as well.
Then back, go back, from the red-skin's track;

---

[1] small beads made of shells, used by North American Indians for ornament, money, etc.

For the hunter's eyes grow dim,
To find that the white man wrongs the one
    Who never did harm to him.
—1845

Song of the Ugly Maiden

Oh! the world gives little of love or light,
    Though my spirit pants for much;
For I have no beauty for the sight,
    No riches for the touch.
5 I hear men sing o'er the flowing cup
    Of woman's magic spell;
And vows of zeal they offer up,
    And eloquent tales they tell.
They bravely swear to guard the fair
10   With strong, protecting arms;
But will they worship woman's worth
    Unblent with woman's charms?
No! ah, no! 'tis little they prize
Crookbacked forms and rayless eyes.

15 Oh! 'tis a saddening thing to be
    A poor and Ugly one;
In the sand Time puts in his glass for me,
    Few sparkling atoms run.
For my drawn lids bear no shadowing fringe,
20   My locks are thin and dry;
My teeth wear not the rich pearl tinge,
    Nor my lips the henna dye.
I know full well I have naught of grace
    That maketh woman "divine;"
25 The wooer's praise and doting gaze
    Have never yet been mine.
Where'er I go all eyes will shun
The loveless mien of the Ugly one.

I join the crowd where merry feet
30   Keep pace with the merry strain;
I note the earnest words that greet

The fair ones in the train.
The stripling youth has passed me by;
    He leads another out!
35 She has a light and laughing eye,
    Like sunshine playing about.
The wise man scanneth calmly round,
    But his gaze stops not with me;
It has fixed on a head whose curls, unbound,
40   Are bright as curls can be;
And he watches her through the winding dance
With smiling care and tender glance.

The gay cavalier has thrust me aside;
    Whom does he hurry to seek?
45 One with a curving lip of pride,
    And a forehead white and sleek.
The grey-haired veteran, young with wine,
    Would head the dance once more;
He looks for a hand, but passes mine.
50   As all have passed before.
The pale, scarred face may sit alone,
    The unsightly brow may mope;
There cometh no tongue with winning tone
    To flatter Affection's hope.
55 O Ugliness! thy desolate pain
Had served to set the stamp on Cain.[1]

My quick brain hears the thoughtless jeers
    That are whispered with laughing grin;
As though I had fashioned my own dull orbs,
60   And chosen my own seared skin.
Who shall dream of the withering pang,
    As I find myself forlorn—
Sitting apart, with lonely heart,
    'Mid cold neglect and scorn?
65 I could be glad as others are,
    For my soul is young and warm;
And kind it had been to darken and mar
    My feelings with my form;

For fondly and strong as my spirit may yearn,
70 It gains no sweet love in return.

Man, just Man! I know thine eye
    Delighteth to dwell on those
Whose tresses shade, with curl or braid,
    Cheeks soft and round as the rose.
75 I know thou wilt ever gladly turn
    To the beautiful and bright;
But is it well that thou shouldst spurn
    The one GOD chose to blight?
Oh! why shouldst thou trace my shrinking face
80   With coarse, deriding jest?
Oh! why forget that a charmless brow
    May abide with a gentle breast?
Oh! why forget that gold is found
    Hidden beneath the roughest ground?

85 Would that I had passed away
    Ere I knew that I was born;
For I stand in the blessed light of day
    Like a weed among the corn,—
The black rock in the wide, blue sea—
90   The snake in the jungle green,
Oh! who will stay in the fearful way
    Where such ugly things are seen?
Yet mine is the fate of lonelier state
    Than that of the snake or rock;
95 For those who behold me in their path
    Not only shun, but mock.
O Ugliness! thy desolate pain
Had served to set the stamp on Cain.
—1845

My Old Straw Hat

Farewell, old friend,—we part at last;
Fruits, flowers, and summer, all are past;
And when the beech-leaves bid adieu,
My Old Straw Hat must vanish too.

---

[1] the oldest son of Adam and Eve, who killed his brother Abel: Genesis 4.

5 We've been together many an hour,
   In grassy dell, and garden bower;
   And plait and riband, scorched and torn,
   Proclaim how well thou hast been worn.
   We've had a time, gay, bright, and long;
10 So let me sing a grateful song,—
   And if one bay-leaf falls to me,
   I'll stick it firm and fast in thee,
                     My Old Straw Hat.

   Thy flapping shades and flying strings
15 Are worth a thousand close-tied things.
   I love thy easy-fitting crown,
   Thrust lightly back, or slouching down.
   I cannot brook a muffled ear,
   When lark and blackbird whistle near;
20 And dearly like to meet and seek
   The fresh wind with unguarded cheek.
   Tossed in a tree, thou'lt bear no harm;
   Flung on the moss, thou'lt lose no charm;
   Like many a real friend on earth,
25 Rough usage only proves thy worth,
                     My Old Straw Hat.

   The world will stare at those who wear
   Rich, snowy pearls in raven hair;
   And diamonds flash bravely out
30 In chestnut tresses wreathed about:
   The golden bands may twine and twirl,
   Like shining snakes through each fair curl;
   And soft down with imperial grace
   May bend o'er Beauty's blushing face:
35 But much I doubt if brows that bear
   The jewelled clasp and plumage rare,
   Or temples bound with crescent wreath,
   Are half so cool as mine beneath
                     My Old Straw Hat.

40 Minerva's helmet![1] what of that?
   Thou'rt quite as good, my Old Straw Hat!
   For I can think! and muse, and dream,
   With poring brain and busy scheme;
   I can inform my craving soul
45 How wild bees work and planets roll;
   And be all silent, grave and grim,
   Beneath the shelter of thy brim.
   The cap of Liberty, forsooth!
   Thou art the thing to me in truth;
50 For slavish fashion ne'er can break
   Into the green path where I take
                     My Old Straw Hat.

   My Old Straw Hat, my conscience tells
   Thou hast been hung with Folly's bells;
55 Yet Folly rings a pleasant chime,
   If the rogue will but "mind his time,"
   And not come jingling on the way
   When sober minstrels ought to play.
   For oft when hearts and eyes are light,
60 Old Wisdom *should* keep out of sight.
   But now the rustic bench is left,
   The tree of every leaf bereft,
   The merry voices, all are still,
   That welcomed to the well-known hill
65   My Old Straw Hat.

   Farewell, old friend, thy work is done;
   The misty clouds shut out the sun;
   The grapes are plucked, the hops are off,
   The woods are stark, and I must doff
70 My Old Straw Hat—but "bide a wee,"
   Fair skies we've seen, yet we may see
   Skies full as fair as those of yore,
   And then we'll wander forth once more.
   Farewell, till drooping bluebells blow,
75 And violets stud the warm hedgerow—

---

[1] the Roman goddess of wisdom, technical skill, and invention. She traditionally wears armour and a helmet.

Farewell, till daisies deck the plain—
Farewell, till spring days come again—
                    My Old Straw Hat!
—1845

Lines Written for the Sheffield Mechanics Exhibition, 1846

The ice-bound tide, with currents pent beneath,
    Is stagnant, dreary, dull, and sad as Death:
Black, frowning clouds hang like a pall unfurled
Above the source whose Commerce aids a world.
5   The *River's frozen*—and the "outward bound"
Lies like a coffin in the ice-grave round.

The stripling boy with dust-polluted skin,
Hears no soft bubble-plash to tempt him in;
The famished curlew,[1] fluttering far to seek
10 For water, falls with stiff, unmoistened beak;
And vernal bloom that vain would deck the bank,
Crushed by the chill breath, leaves a cheerless
        blank.

But see; the summer sun with glowing beam
Flings radiant warmth upon the torpid stream;
15 The dense and blackened mass is seen no more—
Life stirs the waters—Joy is on the shore;
And fast and fresh the tide goes rolling by,
Beneath the glory of a cloudless sky.

The laden bark hastes onward with her freight:
20 Destined to cheer some lone and distant state:
The growing children loiter by the side,
Watching the waves that sparkle as they glide;
Wading knee-deep to touch the lily's brim.
Till bold in Hope—they plunge—strike out—and
        swim.

25 The bird, whose soft notes hail Affection's nest,
Comes nigh to drink, and lave[2] its downy breast;
The buds that spring, burst forth with deeper hue,
With sweeter perfume, and a richer dew;
And the pure River, spreading as it goes;
30 Bears Health and Loveliness where'er it flows.

Knowledge, bright Knowledge, so *thy* sun must
        shine,
And leave unchanged the Spirit-stream divine
Knowledge, fair Knowledge, 'tis alone thy ray
Can melt the bars of mortal ice away;
35 Thy honest sunshine only can unbind
The hard, cold fetters freezing up the *Mind*;
Letting the tide of Intellect run free
With clear strong gush to the Eternal Sea.

Fair Knowledge pleads the Universal Cause;
40 Truth in her language—Justice in her laws:
Leading rude Ignorance with gentle hand,
To join Creation's highest, noblest band,
Loudly proclaiming that her humblest halls
Aid Peace and Virtue more than prison walls,
45 There we do list the teachings that impart
Strength to the brain, and Goodness to the heart;—
There do we gain the wisdom that bestows
Balm for our own, and care for others' woes.
There do we learn to prize the mercies sent,
50 And hail the Giver with a glad content;
And *all* must bless the Temple that is raised
Where Man grows happier, while God is praised.
—1849

A Song For The Workers
Written for the Early Closing Movement

Let man toil to win his living,
    Work is not a task to spurn:

---

[1] any variety of large, brownish wading birds with downward curving
bills.

[2] bathe.

Poor is gold of others' giving,
    To the silver that we earn.

5 Let Man proudly take his station
    At the smithy, loom, or plough;
The richest crown-pearls in a nation
    Hang from Labor's reeking brow.

Though her hand grows hard with duty,
10   Filling up the common Fate;
Let fair Woman's cheek of beauty
    Never blush to own its state.

Let fond Woman's heart of feeling
    Never be ashamed to spread
15 Industry and honest dealing
    As a barter for her bread.

Work on bravely, GOD's own daughters!
    Work on stanchly, GOD's own sons!
But when Life has too rough waters,
20   Truth must fire her minute guns.

Shall ye be *unceasing* drudges?
    Shall the cry upon your lips
Never make your selfish judges
    Less severe with Despot-whips?

25 Shall the mercy that we cherish,
    As old England's primest boast,
See no slaves but those who perish
    On a far and foreign coast?

When we reckon hives of money,
30   Owned by Luxury and Ease,
Is it just to grasp the honey
    While Oppression chokes the bees?

Is it just the poor the lowly
    Should be held as soulless things?

35 Have they not a claim as holy
    As rich men, to angel's wings?

Shall we burden boyhood's muscle?
    Shall the young girl mope and lean,
Till we hear the dead leaves rustle
40   On a tree that should be green?

Shall we bar the brain from thinking
    Of aught else than work and woe?
Shall we keep parched lips from drinking
    Where refreshing waters flow?

45 Shall we strive to shut out Reason
    Knowledge, Liberty, and Health?
Shall all Spirit-light be treason
    To the mighty King of Wealth?

Shall we stint with niggard measure,
50   Human joy, and human rest?
Leave no profit—give no pleasure
    To the toiler's human breast?

Shall our men, fatigued to loathing,
    Plod on sickly, worn, and bowed?
55 Shall our maidens sew fine clothing,
    Dreaming of their own white shroud?

No! for Right is up and asking
    Loudly for a juster lot;
And Commerce must not let her tasking
60   Form a nation's canker-spot.

Work on bravely, GOD's own daughters!
    Work on stanchly, GOD's own sons!
But, till ye have smoother waters,
    Let Truth fire her minute guns!
—1853

My Ladye Love

See, my longing eyes behold her;
  She has come, and I am blest;
Nearer, nearer still I fold her
  To my faithful, doting breast.

5 Never yet was maiden truer
  At the olden, trysting shine;
Never maiden met a wooer
  With a love surpassing mine.

What a winsome, dainty creature
10 Is my charming, darling one;
See, she dresses her fair tresses
  With the gold braids of the sun.

See how gaily she is wreathing
  Green, with white and purple bloom;
15 Till my veins beat high with breathing
  Such a sweet and fresh perfume.

Hark! she speaks—soft winds are coming—
  Rich and varied music floats
Now below in brooklets humming;
20 Then above in woodlark's notes.

Look upon her dimpled fingers
  Gemmed with apple-blossom ring;
Wonder not my fond kiss lingers
  On the hawthorn pearls that cling

25 Round her neck with tender lustre,
  Adding fairness to the fair;
While the young bees swarm and cluster;
  Feasting on the beauty there.

Hand in hand we gaily ramble;
30 She may lead me where she will;

Tripping now o'er pink-eyed bramble;
  Resting then on turf-clad hill.

Beautiful she seems when sitting,
  With her face one happy flush;
35 Till her gauzy cloud-veil flitting,
  Softly shadows down the blush.

Wistfully I watch her treading,
  Where beneath each step she takes
Deeper tints of green are spreading,
40 And a brighter earth-star wakes.

See, her lovely eyes are beaming
  Where the woodland runnel plays;
And the ripples now are gleaming
  In a flash of sparkling rays.

45 On she wanders—all who meet her
  Pouring welcome in her ear;
Every bud becoming sweeter,
  As it feels her presence near.

Worshipped one! I bend before thee
50 With a homage saints might own;
Blest and blessing, I adore thee,—
  Messenger from God's high throne.

I am yet thy constant wooer,
  Bending with a fervent zeal;
55 Never wilt thou have a truer
  Devotee to serve and kneel.

Never will my soul's affiance
  To a fairer idol cling;
Never own more pure alliance;
60 For *my* "Ladye Love" is *Spring.*"
—1870

Arthur Hugh Clough
1819 – 1861

Arthur Hugh Clough was educated at Rugby and Balliol College, Oxford. He became a fellow of Oriel and then principal of University Hall, London. His poems appeared in *Ambarvalia* (1849), *Dipsychus* (1850), *Amours de Voyage* (1858), and *Mari Magno or Tales On Board* (1861). Clough and Matthew Arnold were friends and poetic rivals; after Clough's premature death in 1861 Arnold wrote the problematic elegy "Thyrsis" in his memory. Clough's short verse reveals his clear-sighted cynicism about social conventions; his longer works, such as the novel-in-verse *Amours de Voyage*, combine social commentary with ambitious formal experimentation.

Duty—that's to say complying

Duty—that's to say complying
　　With whate'er's expected here;
On your unknown cousin's dying,
　　Straight be ready with the tear;
5　Upon etiquette relying,
Unto usage naught denying,
Lend your waist to be embraced,
　　Blush not even, never fear;
Claims of kith and kin connection,
10　　Claims of manners honour still,
Ready money of affection
　　Pay, whoever drew the bill.
With the form conforming duly,
Senseless what it meaneth truly,
15　Go to church—the world require you,
　　To balls—the world require you too,
And marry—papa and mamma desire you,
　　And your sisters and schoolfellows do.
Duty—'tis to take on trust
20　What things are good, and right, and just;
　　And whether indeed they be or be not,
　　Try not, test not, feel not, see not:
　　'Tis walk and dance, sit down and rise
　　By leading, opening ne'er your eyes;
25　Stunt sturdy limbs that Nature gave,
And be drawn in a Bath chair[1] along to the grave.

'Tis the stern and prompt suppressing,
　　As an obvious deadly sin,
All the questing and the guessing
30　　Of the soul's own soul within:
　　　'Tis the coward acquiescence
　　　　In a destiny's behest,
　　　To a shade by terror made
　　　Sacrificing aye the essence
35　　　Of all that's truest, noblest, best;
'Tis the blind non-recognition
　　Or of goodness, truth, or beauty,
Save by precept and submission;
　　Moral blank, and moral void,
40　　Life at very birth destroyed,
Atrophy, exinanition![2]
Duty!—
Yea, by duty's prime condition,
　　Pure nonentity of duty!
—1849

Qui Laborat, Orat [3]

O only Source of all our light and life,
　　Whom as our truth, our strength, we see and
　　　feel,

---
[1] a wheeled chair first used at Bath, a city popular with invalids because of its hot springs.

[2] utter emptiness.

[3] This poem is dated Oxford, 1845, in *Poems* (Norton, 1862), but Thomas Arnold dated it 1847. Published 1849. "He who works, prays."

But whom the hours of mortal moral strife
    Alone aright reveal!

5 Mine inmost soul, before Thee inly brought,
    Thy presence owns ineffable, divine;
Chastised each rebel self-encentered thought,
    My will adoreth Thine.

With eye down-dropt, if then this earthly mind
10 Speechless remain, or speechless e'en depart,
Nor seek to see (for what of earthly kind
    Can see Thee as Thou art?)—

If sure assured 'tis but profanely bold
    In thought's abstractest forms to seem to see,
15 It dare not dare thee dread communion hold
    In ways unworthy Thee,—

O not unowned, Thou shalt unnamed forgive,
    In worldly walks the prayerless heart prepare,
And if in work its life it seem to live,
20 Shalt make that work be prayer.

Nor times shall lack, when, while the work it plies,
    Unsummoned powers the blinding film shall
      part,
And scarce by happy tears made dim, the eyes
    In recognition start.

25 As wills Thy will, or give or e'en forbear
    The beatific supersensual sight,
So, with Thy blessing blest, that humbler prayer
    Approach Thee morn and night.
    —1849

The Latest Decalogue [1]

Thou shalt have one God only; who
  Would be at the expense of two?
No graven images may be
Worshipped, except the currency:
5 Swear not at all; for thy curse
Thine enemy is none the worse:
At church on Sunday to attend
Will serve to keep the world thy friend:
Honour thy parents; that is, all
10 From whom advancement may befall:
Thou shalt not kill; but need'st not strive
Officiously to keep alive:
Do not adultery commit;
Advantage rarely comes of it:
15 Thou shalt not steal; an empty feat,
When it's so lucrative to cheat:
Bear not false witness; let the lie
Have time on its own wings to fly:
Thou shalt not covet; but tradition
20 Approves all forms of competition.

The sum of all is, thou shalt love,
If any body, God above:
At any rate shall never labour
More than thyself to love thy neighbour. [2]
—1850

"Say not the struggle nought availeth"

Say not the struggle nought availeth,
  The labour and the wounds are vain,
The enemy faints not, nor faileth,
    And as things have been, things remain.

---

[1] The original decalogue was the ten commandments given to Moses by God on Mount Sinai.

[2] These last four lines were not originally published with the poem. Discovered in one of the poet's manuscripts, they were appended to the poem in 1951.

5　If hopes were dupes, fears may be liars;
　　　It may be, in yon smoke concealed,
　　Your comrades chase e'en now the fliers,
　　　And, but for you, possess the field.

　　For while the tired waves, vainly breaking,
10　　Seem here no painful inch to gain,
　　Far back through creeks and inlets making
　　　Came, silent, flooding in, the main,

　　And not by eastern windows only,
　　　When daylight comes, comes in the light,
15　In front the sun climbs slow, how slowly,
　　　But westward, look, the land is bright.
　　　　　—1855 (1849)

Amours de Voyage

Oh, you are sick of self-love, Malvolio,
And taste with a distempered appetite!
　　　　—Shakspeare[1]

Il doutait de tout, même de l'amour.
　　　　—French Novel[2]

Solvitur ambulando.
　　　　—Solutio Sophismatum[3]

Flevit amores
Non elaboratum ad pedem.
　　　　—Horace[4]

CANTO I

*O**ver the great windy waters, and over the clear*
　　crested summits,

---

[1]　Shakespeare, *Twelfth Night* 1.5.87–88.

[2]　"He doubted everything, even love." The "French novel" is unknown.

[3]　"It is explained by walking. The answer to sophists." A common-sense reply to over-elaborate theorists such as Zeno, who declared that there was no such thing as motion.

[4]　"[Anacreon] sang his plaintive stains of love in simple measure." Horace, *Epodes* 15.11–12.

Unto the sun and the sky, and unto the perfecter
　　earth,
Come, let us go,—to a land wherein gods of the old
　　time wandered,
　　Where every breath even now changes to ether
　　divine.
5　*Come, let us go; though withal a voice whisper, "The*
　　world that we live in,
　　Whithersoever we turn, still is the same narrow
　　crib;
'Tis but to prove limitation, and measure a cord, that
　　we travel;
　　Let who would 'scape and be free go to his
　　chamber and think;
'Tis but to change idle fancies for memories wilfully
　　falser;
10　*'Tis but to go and have been."—Come, little bark!*
　　let us go.

1 CLAUDE TO EUSTACE

*D*ear Eustatio, I write that you may write me an
　　answer,
Or at the least to put us again *en rapport* with each
　　other.
Rome disappoints me much,—St. Peter's,[5]
　　perhaps, in especial;
Only the Arch of Titus and view from the Lateran[6]
　　please me:
15　This, however, perhaps, is the weather, which truly
　　is horrid.
Greece must be better, surely; and yet I am feeling
　　so spiteful,
That I could travel to Athens, to Delphi,[7] and
　　Troy,[8] and Mount Sinai,

---

[5]　St. Peter's Basilica.

[6]　the Church of St. John Lateran overlooking the Campagna, the great plain outside Rome.

[7]　a town at the foot of Mt. Parnassus, famous for a temple of Apollo and for a celebrated oracle.

[8]　the fortress city of Homer's *Iliad*.

Though but to see with my eyes that these are
    vanity also.
    Rome disappoints me much; I hardly as yet
      understand, but
20 *Rubbishy* seems the word that most exactly would
    suit it.
All the foolish destructions, and all the sillier
    savings,
All the incongruous things of past incompatible
    ages,
Seem to be treasured up here to make fools of
    present and future.
Would to Heaven the old Goths[1] had made a
    cleaner sweep of it!
25 Would to Heaven some new ones would come and
    destroy these churches!
However, one can live in Rome as also in London.
Rome is better than London, because it is other
    than London.
It is a blessing, no doubt, to be rid, at least for a
    time, of
All one's friends and relations,—yourself (forgive
    me!) included,—
30 All the *assujettissement*[2] of having been what one
    has been,
What one thinks one is, or thinks that others
    suppose one;
Yet, in despite of all, we turn like fools to the
    English.
Vernon has been my fate; who is here the same that
    you knew him,—
Making the tour, it seems, with friends of the name
    of Trevellyn.

II CLAUDE TO EUSTACE

35 Rome disappoints me still; but I shrink and adapt
    myself to it.

Somehow a tyrannous sense of a superincumbent
    oppression
Still, wherever I go, accompanies ever, and makes
    me
Feel like a tree (shall I say?) buried under a ruin of
    brick-work.
Rome, believe me, my friend, is like its own Monte
    Testaceo,[3]
40 Merely a marvellous mass of broken and castaway
    wine-pots.
Ye gods! what do I want with this rubbish of ages
    departed,
Things that Nature abhors, the experiments that
    she has failed in?
What do I find in the Forum? An archway and two
    or three pillars.
Well, but St. Peter's? Alas, Bernini[4] has filled it
    with sculpture!
45 No one can cavil, I grant, at the size of the great
    Coliseum.
Doubtless the notion of grand and capacious and
    massive amusement,
This the old Romans had; but tell me, is this an
    idea?
Yet of solidity much, but of splendour little is
    extant:
"Brickwork I found thee, and marble I left thee!"[5]
    their Emperor vaunted;
50 "Marble I thought thee, and brickwork I find
    thee!" the Tourist may answer.

III GEORGINA TREVELLYN TO LOUISA

At last, dearest Louisa, I take up my pen to address
    you.

---

[1] a Germanic tribe which invaded and devastated Europe in the third
and fifth centuries.

[2] constraint or subjection.

[3] a 100-foot high mound consisting of broken pieces of pottery from
ancient warehouses.

[4] seventeenth-century Baroque sculptor.

[5] The quotation is from Suetonius in his biography of Augustus Caesar
(63 BC–14 AD): "he so improved the city that he justly boasted that he
found it brick and left it marble." The principle architect was Agrippa.

Here we are, you see, with the seven-and-seventy
    boxes,
Courier, Papa and Mamma, the children, and
    Mary and Susan:
Here we all are at Rome, and delighted of course
    with St. Peter's,
55 And very pleasantly lodged in the famous Piazza di
    Spagna.
Rome is a wonderful place, but Mary shall tell you
    about it;
Not very gay, however; the English are mostly at
    Naples;[1]
There are the A.s, we hear, and most of the W.
    party.
George, however, is come; did I tell you about his
    mustachios?
60 Dear, I must really stop, for the carriage, they tell
    me, is waiting.
Mary will finish; and Susan is writing, they say, to
    Sophia.
Adieu, dearest Louise,—evermore your faithful
    Georgina.
Who can a Mr. Claude be whom George has taken
    to be with?
Very stupid, I think, but George says so *very* clever.

IV CLAUDE TO EUSTACE

65 No, the Christian faith, as at any rate I understood
    it,
With its humiliations and exaltations combining,
Exaltations sublime, and yet diviner abasements,
Aspirations from something most shameful here
    upon earth and
In our poor selves to something most perfect above
    in the heavens,—
70 No, the Christian faith, as I, at least, understood it,
Is not here, O Rome, in any of these thy churches;

Is not here, but in Freiburg,[2] or Rheims,[3] or
    Westminster Abbey.[4]
What in thy Dome[5] I find, in all thy recenter efforts,
Is a something, I think, more *rational* far, more
    earthly,
75 Actual, less ideal, devout not in scorn and refusal,
But in a positive, calm, Stoic-Epicurean acceptance.
This I begin to detect in St. Peter's and some of the
    churches,
Mostly in all that I see of the sixteenth-century
    masters;
Overlaid of course with infinite gauds and
    gewgaws,
80 Innocent, playful follies, the toys and trinkets of
    childhood,
Forced on maturer years, as the serious one thing
    needful,
By the barbarian will of the rigid and ignorant
    Spaniard.[6]
    Curious work, meantime, re-entering society;
    how we
Walk a livelong day, great Heaven, and watch our
    shadows!
85 What our shadows seem, forsooth, we will
    ourselves be.
Do I look like that? you think me that: then I am
    that.

---

[1] the third largest city in Italy, located in the central part of the country, 120 miles southeast of Rome.

[2] a town in South Baden, Germany, on the western slope of the Black Forest. It is a cultural and tourist centre noted for its cathedral.

[3] a city in northern France; the centre of the champagne industry.

[4] the premier church of Great Britain and the burial place of notable English men and women since the fourteenth century. An abbey has stood on this site since 616 AD.

[5] of St. Peter's Basilica, designed by Michelangelo.

[6] Italy was annexed to the Spanish Empire in 1530.

v CLAUDE TO EUSTACE

Luther,[1] they say, was unwise; like a half-taught
    German, he could not
See that old follies were passing most tranquilly out
    of remembrance;
Leo the Tenth[2] was employing all efforts to clear
    out abuses;
90 Jupiter, Juno, and Venus, Fine Arts, and Fine
    Letters, the Poets,
Scholars, and Sculptors, and Painters, were quietly
    clearing away the
Martyrs, and Virgins, and Saints, or at any rate
    Thomas Aquinas:
He must forsooth make a fuss and distend his huge
    Wittenberg[3] lungs, and
Bring back Theology once yet again in a flood
    upon Europe:
95 Lo you, for forty days from the windows of heaven
    it fell; the
Waters prevail on the earth yet more for a hundred
    and fifty;
Are they abating at last? the doves that are sent to
    explore are
Wearily fain to return, at the best with a leaflet of
    promise,—
Fain to return, as they went, to the wandering
    wave-tost vessel,—

100 Fain to re-enter the roof which covers the clean and
    the unclean,—
Luther, they say, was unwise; he didn't see how
    things were going;
Luther was foolish,—but, O great God! what call
    you Ignatius?[4]
O my tolerant soul, be still! but you talk of
    barbarians,
Alaric, Attila,[5] Genseric;—why, they came, they
    killed, they
105 Ravaged, and went on their way; but these vile,
    tyrannous Spaniards,[6]
These are here still,—how long, O ye Heavens,[7] in
    the country of Dante?
These, that fanaticized Europe, which now can
    forget them, release not
This, their choicest of prey, this Italy; here you see
    them,—
Here, with emasculate pupils and gimcrack
    churches of Gesu,[8]
110 Pseudo-learning and lies, confessional-boxes and
    postures,—
Here, with metallic beliefs and regimental
    devotions,—
Here, overcrusting with slime, perverting, defacing,
    debasing,

---

[1] Martin Luther (1483–1546), was one of the founders of Protestantism. Originally a student of law, he later became a monk and a Doctor of Theology. On 31 October 1517, Luther nailed his Ninety-Five Theses to a Wittenberg church door in protest against the financial corruption and moral debasement inherent in the practice of granting indulgences (a financial contribution to the church made in order to gain absolution from sins). Luther subsequently opposed the infallibility of the Pope and was ordered in a Papal Bull to recant or face excommunication. Luther burned the Bull and was brought before the imperial Diet of Worms and given another opportunity to recant, but he refused. He spent the rest of his life under special protection.

[2] the Pope at the time when Luther started the Reformation (1517). His family, the Medicis, were renowned patrons of the arts.

[3] a city in central Germany; Luther's home town and burial place.

[4] St. Ignatius of Loyola (1491–1556), founder of the Jesuits, Spanish soldier and priest, and a leader of the Counter-Reformation.

[5] King of the Huns (d. 453).

[6] During the sixteenth and seventeenth centuries, Spain ruled much of western Europe and was the principal Catholic country which opposed the Reformation (notably with the Inquisition). In 1849 Spain still controlled Sicily.

[7] Isaiah 6:11: the prophet Isaiah has a vision of the Lord speaking to him and describing the punishment of the idolatrous people of Israel. Isaiah asks how long their suffering will endure. In Revelation 6:9–11, "How long, O Lord, how long" is the cry of the martyrs who were slain for the word of God. See D.G. Rossetti's poem "Vox Ecclesiae Vox Christi."

[8] the principal Jesuit church in Rome.

Michel Angelo's dome,[1] that had hung the
    Pantheon in heaven,
Raphael's Joys and Graces,[2] and thy clear stars,
    Galileo![3]

VI CLAUDE TO EUSTACE

115 Which of three Misses Trevellyn is it that Vernon
    shall marry
Is not a thing to be known; for our friend is one of
    those natures
Which have their perfect delight in the general
    tender-domestic,
So that he trifles with Mary's shawl, ties Susan's
    bonnet,
Dances with all, but at home is most, they say, with
    Georgina,
120 Who is, however, *too* silly in my apprehension for
    Vernon.
I, as before when I wrote, continue to see them a
    little;
Not that I like them much or care a *bajocco*[4] for
    Vernon,
But I am slow at Italian, have not many English
    acquaintance,
And I am asked, in short, and am not good at
    excuses.
125 Middle-class people these, bankers very likely, not
    wholly
Pure of the taint of the shop; will at table d'hôte[5]
    and restaurant
Have their shilling's worth, their penny's
    pennyworth even:
Neither man's aristocracy this, nor God's, God
    knoweth!

---

[1] the dome of St. Peter's Basilica.

[2] the paintings of Raphael.

[3] the first astronomer to use a telescope to view the stars.

[4] a small coin worth less than a cent.

[5] a set restaurant meal offered at a fixed price.

Yet they are fairly descended, they give you to
    know, well connected;
130 Doubtless somewhere in some neighbourhood
    have, and are careful to keep, some
Threadbare-genteel relations, who in their turn are
    enchanted
Grandly among county people to introduce at
    assemblies
To the unpennied cadets our cousins with excellent
    fortunes.
Neither man's aristocracy this, nor God's, God
    knoweth!

VII CLAUDE TO EUSTACE

135 Ah, what a shame, indeed, to abuse these most
    worthy people!
Ah, what a sin to have sneered at their innocent
    rustic pretensions!
Is it not laudable really, this reverent worship of
    station?
Is it not fitting that wealth should tender this
    homage to culture?
Is it not touching to witness these efforts, if little
    availing,
140 Painfully made, to perform the old ritual service of
    manners?
Shall not devotion atone for the absence of
    knowledge? and fervour
Palliate, cover, the fault of a superstitious
    observance?
Dear, dear, what do I say? but, alas! just now, like
    Iago,[6]
I can be nothing at all, if it is not critical wholly;
145 So in fantastic height, in coxcomb exaltation,
Here in the Garden I can walk, can freely concede
    to the Maker[7]
That the works of his hand are all very good: his
    creatures,

---

[6] *Othello.*

[7] the Garden of Eden; God is the Maker.

Beast of the field and fowl, he brings them before
    me; I name them;
That which I name them, they are,—the bird, the
    beast, and the cattle.
150 But for Adam,—alas, poor critical coxcomb Adam!
But for Adam there is not found an help-meet for
    him.[1]

VIII CLAUDE TO EUSTACE

No, great Dome of Agrippa,[2] thou art not
    Christian! canst not,
Strip and replaster and daub and do what they will
    with thee, be so!
Here underneath the great porch of colossal
    Corinthian columns,
155 Here as I walk, do I dream of the Christian belfries
    above them?
Or on a bench as I sit and abide for long hours, till
    thy whole vast
Round grows dim as in dreams to my eyes, I
    repeople thy niches,
Not with the Martyrs, and Saints, and Confessors,
    and Virgins, and children,
But with the mightier forms of an older, austerer
    worship;
160 And I recite to myself, how
                    Eager for battle here
    Stood Vulcan, here matronal Juno,
       And with the bow to his shoulder faithful
    He who with pure dew laveth of Castaly
165   His flowing locks, who holdeth of Lycia
    The oak forest and the wood that bore him,
      Delos' and Patara's own Apollo.[3]

IX CLAUDE TO EUSTACE

Yet it is pleasant, I own it, to be in their company;
    pleasant,
Whatever else it may be, to abide in the feminine
    presence.
170 Pleasant, but wrong, will you say? But this happy,
    serene coexistence
Is to some poor soft souls, I fear, a necessity simple,
Meat and drink and life, and music, filling with
    sweetness,
Thrilling with melody sweet, with harmonies
    strange overwhelming,
All the long-silent strings of an awkward,
    meaningless fabric.
175 Yet as for that, I could live, I believe, with children;
    to have those
Pure and delicate forms encompassing, moving
    about you,
This were enough, I could think; and truly with
    glad resignation
Could from the dream of romance, from the fever
    of flushed adolescence,
Look to escape and subside into peaceful avuncular
    functions.
180 Nephews and nieces! alas, for as yet I have none!
    and, moreover,
Mothers are jealous, I fear me, too often, too
    rightfully; fathers
Think they have title exclusive to spoiling their
    own little darlings;
And by the law of the land, in despite of
    Malthusian doctrine,[4]
No sort of proper provision is made for that most
    patriotic,

---

[1] See Genesis 2:20. Line 151 is a direct quotation from the Bible.

[2] the Pantheon, which was built in 27 AD under the rule of Agrippa. The centre of pantheism, it was later used as a Christian church.

[3] Hic avidus stetit
  Vulcanus, hic matrona Juno, et
    Nunquam humeris positurus arcum,
  Qui rore puro Castaliæ lavit
  Crines solutos, qui Lyciæ tenet

    Dumeta natalemque silvam,
      Delius et Patareus Apollo. [C.'s note]
Claude (and Clough) have translated Horace, *Odes* 3.4.58–64.

[4] T.R. Malthus (1766–1834), in his *Essay on Population* (1798), argued that population increases geometrically while the means of subsistence increase linearly; hence, population tends to outrun the available food supply.

185 Most meritorious subject, the childless and
  bachelor uncle.

X CLAUDE TO EUSTACE

Ye, too, marvellous Twain,[1] that erect on the
  Monte Cavallo

Stand by your rearing steeds in the grace of your
  motionless movement,

Stand with your upstretched arms and tranquil
  regardant faces,

Stand as instinct with life in the might of
  immutable manhood,—

190 O ye mighty and strange, ye ancient divine ones of
  Hellas,

Are ye Christian too? to convert and redeem and
  renew you,

Will the brief form have sufficed, that a Pope has
  set up on the apex

Of the Egyptian stone that o'ertops you, the
  Christian symbol?

And ye, silent, supreme in serene and victorious
  marble,

195 Ye that encircle the walls of the stately Vatican
  chambers,

Juno and Ceres, Minerva, Apollo, the Muses and
  Bacchus,[2]

Ye unto whom far and near come posting the
  Christian pilgrims,

Ye that are ranged in the halls of the mystic
  Christian pontiff,

Are ye also baptized? are ye of the Kingdom of
  Heaven?

200 Utter, O some one, the word that shall reconcile
  Ancient and Modern!

Am I to turn me for this unto thee, great Chapel of
  Sixtus?[3]

---

[1] Castor and Pollux, twin brothers from Greek and Roman legend, the
sons of Jupiter (Zeus) and Leda.

[2] statues in the Vatican.

[3] the Sistine Chapel, built for Pope Sixtus IV between 1472–81.

XI CLAUDE TO EUSTACE

These are the facts. The uncle, the elder brother,
  the squire (a

Little embarrassed, I fancy), resides in a family
  place in

Cornwall,[4] of course; "Papa is in business," Mary
  informs me;

205 He's a good sensible man, whatever his trade is.
  The mother

Is—shall I call it fine?—herself she would tell you
  refined, and

Greatly, I fear me, looks down on my bookish and
  maladroit manners;

Somewhat affecteth the blue;[5] would talk to me
  often of poets;

Quotes, which I hate, Childe Harold;[6] but also
  appreciates Wordsworth;[7]

210 Sometimes adventures on Schiller;[8] and then to
  religion diverges;

Questions me much about Oxford;[9] and yet, in her
  loftiest flights, still

---

[4] the county located at the extreme southwestern tip of England.
Trevellyn is a typical Cornish name; the popular saying runs "By Tre,
Pol, and Pen/ Ye well shall know all Cornishmen."

[5] A "blue-stocking" woman is a woman with strong intellectual interests.
A society of bluestockings was founded in England in 1750 by a Mrs.
Montagu; the name originated in Venice in 1400.

[6] "Childe" is a young man of noble birth. "Childe Harold" is a popular
poem by Byron, published 1812–18; the poem describes the travels and
reflections of the hero.

[7] William Wordsworth, Romantic poet (1770–1850). "The Prelude" is
a semi-autobiographical work.

[8] Johann Christoph Friedrich von Schiller (1759–1805), German
dramatist and poet. In *Kabale und Liebe* (Intrigue and Love), 1784,
Schiller depicts the tragic love affair between a young middle-class
woman and an aristocratic youth.

[9] site of the famous university, founded in the twelfth century, and the
centre of the Oxford Movement of the Victorian period, which sought
to revive the Church of England as a divine institution, separate from the
state and with independent spiritual status, and to reinstate seventeenth-
century High Church rituals. The movement was also known as Tractar-
ianism because its aims and beliefs were published in pamphlets or tracts.

Grates the fastidious ear with the slightly
    mercantile accent.

Is it contemptible, Eustace,—I'm perfectly
    ready to think so,—
Is it,—the horrible pleasure of pleasing inferior
    people?
215 I am ashamed my own self; and yet true it is, if
    disgraceful,
That for the first time in life I am living and
    moving with freedom.
I, who never could talk to the people I meet with
    my uncle,—
I, who have always failed,—I, trust me, can suit the
    Trevellyns;
I, believe me,—great conquest,—am liked by the
    country bankers.
220 And I am glad to be liked, and like in return very
    kindly.
So it proceeds; *Laissez faire, laissez aller,*[1]—such is
    the watchword.
Well, I know there are thousands as pretty and
    hundreds as pleasant,
Girls by the dozen as good, and girls in abundance
    with polish
Higher and manners more perfect than Susan or
    Mary Trevellyn.
225 Well, I know, after all, it is only juxtaposition,—
Juxtaposition, in short; and what is juxtaposition?

XII CLAUDE TO EUSTACE

But I am in for it now,—*laissez faire,* of a truth,
    laissez aller.
Yes, I am going,—I feel it, I feel and cannot recall
    it,—
Fusing with this thing and that, entering into all
    sorts of relations,

230 Tying I know not what ties, which, whatever they
    are, I know one thing,
Will, and must, woe is me, be one day painfully
    broken,—
Broken with painful remorses, with shrinkings of
    soul, and relentings,
Foolish delays, more foolish evasions, most foolish
    renewals.
But I have made the step, have quitted the ship of
    Ulysses;[2]
235 Quitted the sea and the shore, passed into the
    magical island;
Yet on my lips is the *moly,* medicinal, offered of
    Hermes.[3]
I have come into the precinct, the labyrinth closes
    around me,
Path into path rounding slyly; I pace slowly on,
    and the fancy,
Struggling awhile to sustain the long sequences,
    weary, bewildered,
240 Fain must collapse in despair; I yield, I am lost and
    know nothing;
Yet in my bosom unbroken remaineth the clew; I
    shall use it.
Lo, with the rope on my loins I descend through
    the fissure; I sink, yet
Inly secure in the strength of invisible arms up
    above me;
Still, wheresoever I swing, wherever to shore, or to
    shelf, or
245 Floor of cavern untrodden, shell-sprinkled,
    enchanting, I know I
Yet shall one time feel the strong cord tighten
    about me,—
Feel it, relentless, upbear me from spots I would
    rest in; and though the

---

[1] the principle of allowing things to look after themselves, specifically used to mean non-interference by government in economic affairs.

[2] king of Ithaca, to which he returns, after ten years' wandering, from Troy: see Homer's *Odyssey.*

[3] *moly* is a mythical herb with magic powers which, in the *Odyssey,* is given by Hermes (the messenger god) to Odysseus to protect him from Circe's incantation.

Rope sway wildly, I faint, crags wound me, from
    crag unto crag re-
Bounding, or, wide in the void, I die ten deaths,
    ere the end I
250 Yet shall plant firm foot on the broad lofty spaces I
    quit, shall
Feel underneath me again the great massy strengths
    of abstraction,
Look yet abroad from the height o'er the sea whose
    salt wave I have tasted.

       XIII GEORGINA TREVELLYN TO LOUISA—

Dearest Louisa,—Inquire, if you please, about
    Mr. Claude—.
He has been once at R., and remembers meeting
    the H.s.
255 Harriet L., perhaps, may be able to tell you about
    him.
It is an awkward youth, but still with very good
    manners;
Not without prospects, we hear; and, George says,
    highly connected.
Georgy declares it absurd, but Mamma is alarmed,
    and insists he has
Taken up strange opinions and may be turning a
    Papist.[1]
260 Certainly once he spoke of a daily service he went to.
"Where?" we asked, and he laughed and answered,
    "At the Pantheon."
This was a temple, you know, and now is a
    Catholic church; and
Though it is said that Mazzini has sold it for
    Protestant service,
Yet I suppose the change can hardly as yet be
    effected.
265 Adieu again,—evermore, my dearest, your loving
    Georgina.

       P.S. BY MARY TREVELLYN

I am to tell you, you say, what I think of our last
    new acquaintance.
Well, then, I think that George has a very fair right
    to be jealous.
I do not like him much, though I do not dislike
    being with him.
He is what people call, I suppose, a superior man,
    and
270 Certainly seems so to me; but I think he is frightfully
    selfish.

Alba, thou findest me still, and, Alba,[2] thou findest
    me ever,
    Now from the Capitol steps, now over Titus's
       Arch,
Here from the large grassy spaces that spread from the
    Lateran portal,
    Towering o'er aqueduct lines lost in perspective
       between,
275 *Or from a Vatican window, or bridge, or the high*
    Coliseum,
    Clear by the garlanded line cut of the Flavian
       ring.[3]
Beautiful can I not call thee, and yet thou hast
    power to o'ermaster,
    Power of mere beauty; in dreams, Alba, thou
       hauntest me still.
Is it religion? I ask me; or is it a vain superstition?
280   *Slavery abject and gross? service, too feeble, of*
       truth?
Is it an idol I bow to, or is it a god that I worship?
    Do I sink back on the old, or do I soar from the
       mean?

---

[1] a Catholic.

[2] Alba Longa, the original city of Rome and the birthplace of Romulus and Remus; here, the ancient spirit of Rome.

[3] In these lines the speaker gives a bird's-eye view of Rome, identifying several famous buildings and monuments. The Flavian ring or Amphitheatre is another name for the Coliseum.

So through the city I wander and question,
    unsatisfied ever,
  Reverent so I accept, doubtful because I revere.

CANTO II

Is it illusion? or does there a spirit from perfecter ages,
  Here, even yet, amid loss, change, and corruption,
    abide?
Does there a spirit we know not, though seek, though
  we find, comprehend not
  Here to entice and confuse, tempt and evade us,
    abide?
5 *Lives in the exquisite grace of the column disjointed*
  and single,
  Haunts the rude masses of brick garlanded gayly
    with vine,
E'en in the turret fantastic surviving that springs from
  the ruin,
  E'en in the people itself? is it illusion or not?
Is it illusion or not that attracteth the pilgrim
  transalpine,
10   *Brings him a dullard and dunce hither to pry and*
    to stare?
Is it illusion or not that allures the barbarian stranger,
  Brings him with gold to the shrine, brings him in
    arms to the gate?

I CLAUDE TO EUSTACE

What do the people say, and what does the
  government do?—you
Ask, and I know not at all. Yet fortune will favour
  your hopes; and
15 I, who avoided it all, am fated, it seems, to describe
  it.
I, who nor meddle nor make in politics,—I who
  sincerely
Put not my trust in leagues nor any suffrage by
  ballot,

Never predicted Parisian millenniums, never
  beheld a
New Jerusalem coming down dressed like a bride
  out of heaven
20 Right on the Place de la Concorde,—I,
  nevertheless, let me say it,
Could in my soul of souls, this day, with the Gaul
  at the gates, shed
One true tear for thee, thou poor little Roman
  republic!
France, it is foully done! and you, my stupid old
  England,—
You, who a twelvemonth ago said nations must
  choose for themselves, you
25 Could not, of course, interfere,—you, now, when a
  nation has chosen—
Pardon this folly! *The Times*[1] will, of course, have
  announced the occasion,
Told you the news of to-day; and although it was
  slightly in error
When it proclaimed as a fact the Apollo was sold to
  a Yankee,
You may believe when it tells you the French are at
  Civita Vecchia.[2]

II CLAUDE TO EUSTACE

30 Dulce it is, and *decorum*,[3] no doubt, for the
  country to fall,—to
Offer one's blood an oblation to Freedom, and die
  for the Cause; yet
Still, individual culture is also something, and no
  man
Finds quite distinct the assurance that he of all
  others is called on,
Or would be justified, even, in taking away from
  the world that

---

[1] *The Times* of London, a daily newspaper.

[2] a Roman seaport north of the city.

[3] "It is sweet and becoming to die for one's country." Horace, *Odes* 3.2.13.

35 Precious creature, himself. Nature sent him here to
abide here;
Else why sent him at all? Nature wants him still, it
is likely.
On the whole, we are meant to look after ourselves;
it is certain
Each has to eat for himself, digest for himself, and
in general
Care for his own dear life, and see to his own
preservation;
40 Nature's intentions, in most things uncertain, in
this most plain, are decisive;
These, on the whole, I conjecture the Romans will
follow, and I shall.
    So we cling to our rocks like limpets; Ocean
may bluster,
Over and under and round us; we open our shells
to imbibe our
Nourishment, close them again, and are safe,
fulfilling the purpose
45 Nature intended,—a wise one, of course, and a
noble, we doubt not.
Sweet it may be and decorous, perhaps, for the
country to die; but,
On the whole, we conclude the Romans won't do
it, and I sha'n't.

III CLAUDE TO EUSTACE

Will they fight? They say so. And will the French? I
can hardly,
Hardly think so; and yet—He is come,[1] they say, to
Palo,
50 He is passed from Monterone, at Santa Severa
He hath laid up his guns. But the Virgin, the
Daughter of Roma,
She hath despised thee and laughed thee to
scorn,—the Daughter of Tiber,

She hath shaken her head and built barricades
against thee!
Will they fight? I believe it. Alas! 'tis ephemeral
folly,
55 Vain and ephemeral folly, of course, compared
with pictures,
Statues, and antique gems!—Indeed: and yet
indeed too,
Yet methought, in broad day did I dream,—tell it
not in St. James's,[2]
Whisper it not in thy courts, O Christ
Church![3]—yet did I, waking,
Dream of a cadence that sings, *Si tombent nos jeunes
héros, la*
60 *Terre en produit de nouveaux contre vous tous prêts à
se battre;*[4]
Dreamt of great indignations and angers
transcendental,
Dreamt of a sword at my side and a battle-horse
underneath me.

IV CLAUDE TO EUSTACE

Now supposing the French or the Neapolitan
soldier
Should by some evil chance come exploring the
Maison Serny
65 (Where the family English are all to assembly for
safety),
Am I prepared to lay down my life for the British
female?
Really, who knows? One has bowed and talked, till,
little by little,
All the natural heat has escaped of the chivalrous
spirit.

---

[1] Claude refers to the invasion of Rome by the French Commander, Marshal Oudinot, who had arrived at the request of Pope Pius IX to help overthrow the newly formed Roman Republic.

[2] possibly St. James's Square in London, a place frequented by sophisticated society; also possibly the Court of St. James, the British court where foreign ambassadors are based and site of many diplomatic functions.

[3] Christ Church College, Oxford.

[4] the *Marseillaise*, hymn of the French Revolution and the national anthem of France.

Oh, one conformed, of course; but one doesn't die
for good manners,
70 Stab or shoot, or be shot, by way of graceful
attention.
No, if it should be at all, it should be on the
barricades there;
Should I incarnadine ever this inky pacifical finger,
Sooner far should it be for this vapour of Italy's
freedom,
Sooner far by the side of the d——d and dirty
plebeians.
75 Ah, for a child in the street I would strike; for the
full-blown lady—
Somehow, Eustace, alas! I have not felt the vocation.
Yet these people of course will expect, as of course,
my protection,
Vernon in radiant arms stand forth for the lovely
Georgina,
And to appear, I suppose, were but common
civility. Yes, and
80 Truly I do not desire they should either be killed or
offended.
Oh, and of course you will say, "When the time
comes, you will be ready."
Ah, but before it comes, am I to presume it will be
so?
What I cannot feel now, am I to suppose that I
shall feel?
Am I not free to attend for the ripe and indubious
instinct?
85 Am I forbidden to wait for the clear and lawful
perception?
Is it the calling of man to surrender his knowledge
and insight,
For the mere venture of what may, perhaps, be the
virtuous action?
Must we, walking our earth, discerning a little, and
hoping
Some plain visible task shall yet for our hands be
assigned us,—

90 Must we abandon the future for fear of omitting
the present,
Quit our own fireside hopes at the alien call of a
neighbour,
To the mere possible shadow of Deity offer the
victim?
And is all this, my friend, but a weak and ignoble
refining,
Wholly unworthy the head or the heart of Your
Own Correspondent?

v Claude to Eustace

95 Yes, we are fighting at last, it appears. This
morning as usual,
Murray,[1] as usual, in hand, I enter the Caffè Nuovo;
Seating myself with a sense as it were of a change in
the weather,
Not understanding, however, but thinking mostly
of Murray,
And, for to-day is their day, of the Campidoglio
Marbles,
100 *Caffè-latte!* I call to the waiter,—and *Non c' è latte*,
This is the answer he makes me, and this the sign
of a battle.
So I sit; and truly they seem to think any one else
more
Worthy than me of attention. I wait for my
milkless *nero*,
Free to observe undistracted all sorts and sizes of
persons,
105 Blending civilian and soldier in strangest costume,
coming in, and
Gulping in hottest haste, still standing, their
coffee,—withdrawing
Eagerly, jangling a sword on the steps, or jogging a
musket
Slung to the shoulder behind. They are fewer,
moreover, than usual,

---

[1] a standard travel guide. The Campidoglio Marbles are the statues in
the Campidoglio Museum behind the Forum.

Much, and silenter far; and so I begin to imagine
110 Something is really afloat. Ere I leave, the Caffè is
    empty,
Empty too the streets, in all its length the Corso
Empty, and empty I see to my right and left the
    Condotti.[1]
    Twelve o'clock, on the Pincian Hill,[2] with lots
      of English,
Germans, Americans, French,—the Frenchmen,
    too, are protected,—
115 So we stand in the sun, but afraid of a probable
    shower;
So we stand and stare, and see, to the left of
    St. Peter's,
Smoke, from the cannon, white,—but that is at
    intervals only,—
Black, from a burning house, we suppose, by the
    Cavalleggieri;[3]
And we believe we discern some lines of men
    descending
120 Down through the vineyard-slopes, and catch a
    bayonet gleaming.
Every ten minutes, however,—in this there is no
    misconception,—
Comes a great white puff from behind Michel
    Angelo's dome, and
After a space the report of a real big gun,—not the
    Frenchman's?—
That must be doing some work. And so we watch
    and conjecture.
125   Shortly, an Englishman comes, who says he has
      been to St. Peter's,
Seen the Piazza and troops, but that is all he can
    tell us;
So we watch and sit, and, indeed, it begins to be
    tiresome.—

All this smoke is outside;[4] when it has come to the
    inside,
It will be time, perhaps, to descend and retreat to
    our houses.
130   Half past one, or two. The report of small arms
    frequent,
Sharp and savage indeed; that cannot all be for
    nothing:
So we watch and wonder; but guessing is tiresome,
    very.
Weary of wondering, watching, and guessing, and
    gossiping idly,
Down I go, and pass through the quiet streets with
    the knots of
135 National Guards patrolling, and flags hanging out
    at the windows,
English, American, Danish,—and, after offering to
    help an
Irish family moving *en masse* to the Maison Serny,
After endeavouring idly to minister balm to the
    trembling
Quinquagenarian[5] fears of two lone British spinsters,
140 Go to make sure of my dinner before the enemy
    enter.
But by this there are signs of stragglers returning;
    and voices
Talk, though you don't believe it, of guns and
    prisoners taken;
And on the walls you read the first bulletin of the
    morning,—
This is all that I saw, and all I know of the battle.

VI CLAUDE TO EUSTACE
145 Victory! Victory!—Yes! ah, yes, thou republican
    Zion,[6]

---

[1] The Corso and Condotti are main streets of Rome.

[2] overlooks the city, site of a public park.

[3] The Porta Cavalleggieri near St. Peter's was the centre of the French attack on Rome.

[4] outside the walls of Rome.

[5] fifty-year-old.

[6] a hill in Jerusalem, site of the Temple and the City of David; a symbol of the true Church of God and the Kingdom of Heaven.

Truly the kings of the earth are gathered and gone by together;
Doubtless they marvelled to witness such things, were astonished, and so forth.
Victory! Victory! Victory!—Ah, but it is, believe me,
Easier, easier far, to intone the chant of the martyr
150 Than to indite any pæan of any victory. Death may
Sometimes be noble; but life, at the best, will appear an illusion.
While the great pain is upon us, it is great; when it is over,
Why, it is over. The smoke of the sacrifice rises to heaven,
Of a sweet savour, no doubt, to Somebody; but on the altar,
155 Lo, there is nothing remaining but ashes and dirt and ill odour.
So it stands, you perceive; the labial muscles, that swelled with
Vehement evolution of yesterday Marseillaises,
Articulations sublime of defiance and scorning, to-day col-
Lapse and languidly mumble, while men and women and papers
160 Scream and re-scream to each other the chorus of Victory. Well, but
I am thankful they fought, and glad that the Frenchmen were beaten.[1]

VII Claude to Eustace

So, I have seen a man killed! An experience that, among others!
Yes, I suppose I have; although I can hardly be certain,
And in a court of justice could never declare I had seen it.

165 But a man was killed, I am told, in a place where I saw
Something; a man was killed, I am told, and I saw something.
I was returning home from St. Peter's; Murray, as usual,
Under my arm, I remember; had crossed the St. Angelo bridge; and
Moving towards the Condotti, had got to the first barricade, when
170 Gradually, thinking still of St. Peter's, I became conscious
Of a sensation of movement opposing me,—tendency this way
(Such as one fancies may be in a stream when the wave of the tide is
Coming and not yet come,—a sort of poise and retention);
So I turned, and, before I turned, caught sight of stragglers
175 Heading a crowd, it is plain, that is coming behind that corner.
Looking up, I see windows filled with heads; the Piazza,
Into which you remember the Ponte St. Angelo enters,
Since I passed, has thickened with curious groups; and now the
Crowd is coming, has turned, has crossed that last barricade, is
180 Here at my side. In the middle they drag at something. What is it?
Ha! bare swords in the air, held up! There seems to be voices
Pleading and hands putting back; official, perhaps; but the swords are
Many, and bare in the air. In the air? They descend; they are smiting,

---

[1] beaten by Garibaldi, with Mazzini one of the leaders of the Roman Republic.

Hewing, chopping—At what? In the air once more
    upstretched! And
185 Is it blood that's on them? Yes, certainly blood! Of
    whom, then?
Over whom is the cry of this furor of exultation?
    While they are skipping and screaming, and
        dancing their caps on the points of
Swords and bayonets, I to the outskirts back, and
    ask a
Mercantile-seeming by-stander, "What is it?" and
    he, looking always
190 That way, makes me answer, "A Priest, who was
    trying to fly to
The Neapolitan army,"—and thus explains the
    proceeding.
    You didn't see the dead man? No;—I began to
      be doubtful;
I was in black myself, and didn't know what
    mightn't happen;—
But a National Guard close by me, outside of the
    hubbub,
195 Broke his sword with slashing a broad hat covered
    with dust,—and
Passing away from the place with Murray under my
    arm, and
Stooping, I saw through the legs of the people the
      legs of a body.
    You are the first, do you know, to whom I have
      mentioned the matter.
Whom should I tell it to, else?—these girls?—the
    Heavens forbid it!—
200 Quidnuncs at Monaldini's?[1]—idlers upon the
    Pincian?
    If I rightly remember, it happened on that
      afternoon when
Word of the nearer approach of a new Neapolitan
    army

First was spread. I began to bethink me of Paris
    Septembers,[2]
Thought I could fancy the look of the old 'Ninety-
    two. On that evening
205 Three or four, or, it may be, five, of these people
    were slaughtered.
Some declare they had, one of them, fired on a
    sentinel; others
Say they were only escaping; a Priest, it is currently
    stated,
Stabbed a National Guard on the very Piazza
    Colonna:
History, Rumour of Rumours, I leave it to thee to
    determine!
210 But I am thankful to say the government seems
    to have strength to
Put it down; it has vanished, at least; the place is
    most peaceful.
Through the Trastevere[3] walking last night, at nine
    of the clock, I
Found no sort of disorder; I crossed by the
    Island-bridges,
So by the narrow streets to the Ponte Rotto, and
    onwards
215 Thence, by the Temple of Vesta, away to the great
    Coliseum,
Which at the full of the moon is an object worthy a
    visit.

VIII Georgina Trevellyn to Louisa—
Only think, dearest Louisa, what fearful scenes we
have witnessed!

    *   *   *   *   *

George has just seen Garibaldi, dressed up in a long
white cloak, on

---

[1] news-sellers at a reading room where the London daily papers could
be borrowed. "Quidnunc" means literally "what now."

[2] the September Massacres of royalists in the French Revolution, 1792.

[3] a working-class area of Rome.

Horseback, riding by, with his mounted negro
   behind him:
220 This is a man, you know, who came from America
   with him,
Out of the woods, I suppose, and uses a *lasso* in
   fighting,
Which is, I don't quite know, but a sort of noose, I
   imagine;
This he throws on the heads of the enemy's men in
   a battle,
Pulls them into his reach, and then most cruelly
   kills them:
225 Mary does not believe, but we heard it from an
   Italian.
Mary allows she was wrong about Mr. Claude
   being selfish;
He was *most* useful and kind on the terrible
   thirtieth of April.[1]
Do not write here any more; we are starting
   directly for Florence:
We should be off to-morrow, if only Papa could
   get horses;
230 All have been seized everywhere for the use of this
   dreadful Mazzini.

P.S.
   Mary has seen thus far.—I am really so angry,
      Louisa,—
Quite out of patience, my dearest! What can the
   man be intending!
I am quite tired; and Mary, who might bring him
   to in a moment,
Lets him go on as he likes, and neither will help
   nor dismiss him.

IX CLAUDE TO EUSTACE

235 It is most curious to see what a power a few calm
   words (in

Merely a brief proclamation) appear to possess on
   the people.
Order is perfect, and peace; the city is utterly
   tranquil;
And one cannot conceive that this easy and
   nonchalant crowd, that
Flows like a quiet stream through street and
   market-place, entering
240 Shady recesses and bays of church, *osteria*,[2] and
   caffè,
Could in a moment be changed to a flood as of
   molten lava,
Boil into deadly wrath and wild homicidal delusion.
     Ah, 'tis an excellent race,—and even in old
     degradation,
Under a rule that enforces to flattery, lying, and
   cheating,
245 E'en under Pope and Priest, a nice and natural
   people.
Oh, could they but be allowed this chance of
   redemption!—but clearly
That is not likely to be. Meantime,
   notwithstanding all journals,
Honour for once to the tongue and the pen of the
   eloquent writer!
Honour to speech! and all honour to thee, thou
   noble Mazzini!

X CLAUDE TO EUSTACE

250 I am in love meantime, you think; no doubt you
   would think so.
I am in love, you say; with those letters, of course,
   you would say so.
I am in love, you declare. I think not so; yet I grant
   you
It is a pleasure, indeed, to converse with this girl.
     Oh, rare gift,
Rare felicity, this! she can talk in a rational way, can

---

[1] the day of the French invasion of Rome, described by Claude in Letter V.

[2] inn or hotel.

255 Speak upon subjects that really are matters of mind
and of thinking,
Yet in perfection retain her simplicity; never, one
moment,
Never, however you urge it, however you tempt
her, consents to
Step from ideas and fancies and loving sensations
to those vain
Conscious understandings that vex the minds of
man-kind.
260 No, though she talk, it is music; her fingers desert
not the keys; 'tis
Song, though you hear in the song the articulate
vocables sounded,
Syllabled singly and sweetly the words of
melodious meaning.
I am in love, you say; I do not think so exactly.

XI CLAUDE TO EUSTACE

There are two different kinds, I believe, of human
attraction:
265 One which simply disturbs, unsettles, and makes
you uneasy,
And another that poises, retains, and fixes and
holds you.
I have no doubt, for myself, in giving my voice for
the latter.
I do not wish to be moved, but growing where I
was growing,
There more truly to grow, to live where as yet I had
languished.
270 I do not like being moved: for the will is excited;
and action
Is a most dangerous thing; I tremble for something
factitious,
Some malpractice of heart and illegitimate process;
We are so prone to these things with our terrible
notions of duty.

XII CLAUDE TO EUSTACE

Ah, let me look, let me watch, let me wait,
unhurried, unprompted!
275 Bid me not venture on aught that could alter or
end what is present!
Say not, Time flies, and Occasion, that never
returns, is departing!
Drive me not out, ye ill angels with fiery swords,
from my Eden,
Waiting, and watching, and looking! Let love be its
own inspiration!
Shall not a voice, if a voice there must be, from the
airs that environ,
280 Yea, from the conscious heavens, without our
knowledge or effort,
Break into audible words? and love be its own
inspiration?

XIII CLAUDE TO EUSTACE

Wherefore and how I am certain, I hardly can tell;
but it *is* so.
She doesn't like me, Eustace; I think she never will
like me.
Is it my fault, as it is my misfortune, my ways are
not her ways?
285 Is it my fault, that my habits and modes are
dissimilar wholly?
'Tis not her fault, 'tis her nature, her virtue, to
misapprehend them:
'Tis not her fault, 'tis her beautiful nature, not ever
to know me.
Hopeless it seems,—yet I cannot, though hopeless,
determine to leave it:
She goes,—therefore I go; she moves,—I move, not
to lose her.

XIV CLAUDE TO EUSTACE

290 Oh, 'tisn't manly, of course, 'tisn't manly, this
method of wooing;
'Tisn't the way very likely to win. For the woman,
they tell you,

Ever prefers the audacious, the wilful, the
    vehement hero;
She has no heart for the timid, the sensitive soul;
    and for knowledge,—
Knowledge, O ye Gods!—when did they appreciate
    knowledge?
295 Wherefore should they, either? I am sure I do not
      desire it.
    Ah, and I feel too, Eustace, she cares not a tittle
      about me!
(Care about me, indeed! and do I really expect it?)
But my manner offends; my ways are wholly
    repugnant;
Every word that I utter estranges, hurts, and repels
    her;
300 Every moment of bliss that I gain, in her exquisite
      presence,
Slowly, surely, withdraws her, removes her, and
    severs her from me.
Not that I care very much!—any way, I escape
    from the boy's own
Folly, to which I am prone, of loving where it is
    easy.
Not that I mind very much! Why should I? I am
    not in love, and
305 Am prepared, I think, if not by previous habit,
Yet in the spirit beforehand for this and all that is
    like it;
It is an easier matter for us contemplative creatures,
Us, upon whom the pressure of action is laid so
    lightly;
We discontented indeed with things in particular,
    idle,
310 Sickly, complaining, by faith in the vision of things
    in general,
Manage to hold on our way without, like others
    around us,
Seizing the nearest arm to comfort, help, and
    support us.
Yet, after all, my Eustace, I know but little about it.

All I can say for myself, for present alike and for
    past, is,
315 Mary Trevellyn, Eustace, is certainly worth your
    acquaintance.
You couldn't come, I suppose, as far as Florence, to
    see her?

      XV GEORGINA TREVELLYN TO LOUISA—
. . . . . . To-morrow we're starting for Florence,
Truly rejoiced, you may guess, to escape from
    republican terrors;
Mr. C. and Papa to escort us; we by *vettura*[1]
320 Through Siena, and Georgy to follow and join us
    by Leghorn.
Then—Ah, what shall I say, my dearest? I tremble
    in thinking!
You will imagine my feelings,—the blending of
    hope and of sorrow!
How can I bear to abandon Papa and Mamma and
    my Sisters?
Dearest Louisa, indeed it is very alarming; but trust
    me
325 Ever, whatever may change, to remain your loving
    Georgina.

      P.S. BY MARY TREVELLYN
. . . . . . "Do I like Mr. Claude any better?"
I am to tell you,—and, "Pray, is it Susan or I that
    attract him?"
This he never has told, but Georgina could
    certainly ask him.
All I can say for myself is, alas! that he rather repels
    me.
330 There! I think him agreeable, but also a little
    repulsive.
So be content, dear Louisa; for one satisfactory
    marriage
Surely will do in one year for the family you would
    establish;

----

[1] a horse-drawn carriage.

Neither Susan nor I shall afford you the joy of a
    second.

P.S. BY GEORGINA TREVELLYN

Mr. Claude, you must know, is behaving a little bit
    better;
335 He and Papa are great friends; but he really is too
    shilly-shally,—
So unlike George! Yet I hope that the matter is
    going on fairly.
I shall, however, get George, before he goes, to say
    something.
Dearest Louisa, how delightful, to bring young
    people together!

————————

Is it to Florence we follow, or are we to tarry yet
    longer,
340   *E'en amid clamour of arms, here in the city of old,*
Seeking from clamour of arms in the Past and the Arts
    to be hidden,
    Vainly 'mid Arts and the Past seeking one life to
    forget?
Ah, fair shadow, scarce seen, go forth! for anon he
    shall follow,—
    He that beheld thee, anon, whither thou leadest,
    must go!
345 *Go, and the wise, loving Muse, she also will follow*
    and find thee!
    She, should she linger is Rome, were not dissevered
    from thee!

CANTO III

Yet to the wondrous St. Peter's, and yet to the solemn
    Rotonda,
    Mingling with heroes and gods, yet to the Vatican
    walls,
Yet may we go, and recline, while a whole mighty
    world seems above us

Gathered and fixed to all time into one roofing
    supreme;
5 *Yet may we, thinking on these things, exclude what is*
    meaner around us;
    Yet, at the worst of the worst, books and a chamber
    remain;
Yet may we think, and forget, and possess our souls in
    resistance,—
    Ah, but away from the stir, shouting, and gossip of
    war,
Where, upon Apennine slope, with the chestnut the
    oak-trees immingle,
10   *Where amid odorous copse bridle-paths wander*
    and wind,
Where under mulberry-branches the diligent rivulet
    sparkles,
    Or amid cotton and maize peasants their
    waterworks ply,
Where, over fig-tree and orange in tier upon tier still
    repeated,
    Garden on garden upreared, balconies step to the
    sky,—
15 *Ah, that I were, far away from the crowd and the*
    streets of the city,
    Under the vine-trellis laid, O my beloved, with
    thee!

1 MARY TREVELLYN TO MISS ROPER,—*on the way to*
    Florence

Why doesn't Mr. Claude come with us? you
    ask.—We don't know.
You should know better than we. He talked of the
    Vatican marbles;
But I can't wholly believe that this was the actual
    reason,—
20 He was so ready before, when we asked him to
    come and escort us.
Certainly he is odd, my dear Miss Roper. To
    change so
Suddenly, just for a whim, was not quite fair to the
    party,—

Not quite right. I declare, I really almost am
 offended:
I, his great friend, as you say, have doubtless a title
 to be so.
25 Not that I greatly regret it, for dear Georgina
 distinctly
Wishes for nothing so much as to show her
 adroitness. But, oh, my
Pen will not write any more;—let us say nothing
 further about it.

* * * * *

Yes, my dear Miss Roper, I certainly called him
 repulsive;
So, I think him, but cannot be sure I have used the
 expression
30 Quite as your pupil should; yet he does most truly
 repel me.
Was it to you I made use of the word? or who was
 it told you?
Yes, repulsive; observe, it is but when he talks of
 ideas,
That he is quite unaffected, and free, and
 expansive, and easy;
I could pronounce him simply a cold intellectual
 being.—
35 When does he make advances?—He thinks that
 women should woo him;
Yet, if a girl should do so, would be but alarmed
 and disgusted.
She that should love him must look for small love
 in return,—like the ivy
On the stone wall, must expect but a rigid and
 niggard support, and
E'en to get that must go searching all round with
 her humble embraces.

II CLAUDE TO EUSTACE,—*from Rome*
40 Tell me, my friend, do you think that the grain
 would sprout in the furrow,

Did it not truly accept as its *summum* and *ultimum*
 bonum[1]
That mere common and may-be indifferent soil it
 is set in?
Would it have force to develop and open its young
 cotyledons,
Could it compare, and reflect, and examine one
 thing with another?
45 Would it endure to accomplish the round of its
 natural functions,
Were it endowed with a sense of the general
 scheme of existence?
 While from Marseilles in the steamer we
 voyaged to Civita Vecchia,
Vexed in the squally seas as we lay by Capraja and
 Elba,[2]
Standing, uplifted, alone on the heaving poop of
 the vessel,
50 Looking around on the waste of the rushing
 incurious billows,
"This is Nature," I said: "we are born as it were
 from her waters,
Over her billows that buffet and beat us, her
 offspring uncared-for,
Casting one single regard of a painful victorious
 knowledge,
Into her billows that buffet and beat us we sink and
 are swallowed."
55 This was the sense in my soul, as I swayed with the
 poop of the steamer;
And as unthinking I sat in the hall of the famed
 Ariadne,[3]
Lo, it looked at me there from the face of a Triton
 in marble.[4]

---

[1] "the highest and ultimate goal."

[2] islands off the northwestern coast of Italy.

[3] a statue of the sleeping Ariadne in the Vatican Museum.

[4] Triton is a sea-god, the son of Poseidon and Amphitrite, represented
as a fish with a human head.

It is the simpler thought, and I can believe it the
    truer.
Let us not talk of growth; we are still in our
    Aqueous Ages.

III CLAUDE TO EUSTACE

60 Farewell, Politics, utterly! What can I do? I cannot
Fight, you know; and to talk I am wholly ashamed.
    And although I
Gnash my teeth when I look in your French or
    your English papers,
What is the good of that? Will swearing, I wonder,
    mend matters?
Cursing and scolding repel the assailants? No, it is
    idle;
65 No, whatever befalls, I will hide, will ignore or
    forget it.
Let the tail shift for itself; I will bury my head. And
    what's the
Roman Republic to me, or I to the Roman
    Republic?[1]
    Why not fight?—In the first place, I haven't so
      much as a musket.
In the next, if I had, I shouldn't know how I
    should use it.
70 In the third, just at present I'm studying ancient
    marbles.
In the fourth, I consider I owe my life to my
    country.
In the fifth,—I forget, but four good reasons are
    ample.
Meantime, pray, let 'em fight, and be killed. I
    delight in devotion.
So that I 'list not, hurrah for the glorious army of
    martyrs!
75 *Sanguis martyrum semen Ecclesiæ*;[2] though it would
    seem this

---

[1] See *Hamlet* 2.2.593.

[2] Tertullian, *Apologeticus* 50.13: "The blood of martyrs is the seed [or vital spirit] of the Church."

Church is indeed of the purely Invisible, Kingdom-
    come kind:
Militant here on earth! Triumphant, of course,
    then, elsewhere!
Ah, good Heaven, but I would I were out far away
    from the pother!

IV CLAUDE TO EUSTACE

Not, as we read in the words of the olden-time
    inspiration,
80 Are there two several trees in the place we are set to
    abide in;
But on the apex most high of the Tree of Life in
    the Garden,
Budding, unfolding, and falling, decaying and
    flowering ever,
Flowering is set and decaying the transient blossom
    of Knowledge,—
Flowering alone, and decaying, the needless,
    unfruitful blossom.
85   Or as the cypress-spires by the fair-flowing
      stream Hellespontine,
Which from the mythical tomb of the godlike
    Protesilaüs[3]
Rose sympathetic in grief to his lovelorn Laodamia,[4]
Evermore growing, and, when in their growth to
    the prospect attaining,
Over the low sea-banks, of the fatal Ilian city,
90 Withering still at the sight which still they upgrow
    to encounter.
    Ah, but ye that extrude from the ocean your
      helpless faces,
Ye over stormy seas leading long and dreary
    processions,
Ye, too, brood of the wind, whose coming is
    whence we discern not,
Making your nest on the wave, and your bed on
    the crested billow,

---

[3] a Thessalian hero, suitor of Helen, participant in the Trojan War.

[4] the daughter of Acastus, wife of Protesilaüs.

95 Skimming rough waters, and crowding wet sands
  that the tide shall return to,
Cormorants, ducks, and gulls, fill ye my
  imagination!
Let us not talk of growth; we are still in our
  Aqueous Ages.

V MARY TREVELLYN TO MISS ROPER,—*from Florence*
Dearest Miss Roper,—Alas! we are all at Florence
  quite safe, and
You, we hear, are shut up! indeed, it is sadly
  distressing!
100 We were most lucky, they say, to get off when we
  did from the troubles.
Now you are really besieged! they tell us it soon
  will be over;
Only I hope and trust without any fight in the city.
Do you see Mr. Claude?—I thought he might do
  something for you.
I am quite sure on occasion he really would wish to
  be useful.
105 What is he doing? I wonder;—still studying
  Vatican marbles?
Letters, I hope, pass through. We trust your
  brother is better.

VI CLAUDE TO EUSTACE
Juxtaposition, in fine; and what is juxtaposition?
Look you, we travel along in the railway-carriage,
  or steamer,
And, *pour passer le temps*,[1] till the tedious journey
  be ended,
110 Lay aside paper or book, to talk with the girl that is
  next one;
And, *pour passer le temps*, with the terminus all but
  in prospect,
Talk of eternal ties and marriages made in heaven.
  Ah, did we really accept with a perfect heart the
  illusion!

─────
[1] "to pass the time."

Ah, did we really believe that the Present indeed is
  the Only!
115 Or through all transmutation, all shock and
  convulsion of passion,
Feel we could carry undimmed, unextinguished,
  the light of our knowledge!
  But for his funeral train which the bridegroom
  sees in the distance,
Would he so joyfully, think you, fall in with the
  marriage-procession?
But for that final discharge, would he dare to enlist
  in that service?
120 But for that certain release, ever sign to that
  perilous contract?
But for that exit secure, ever bend to that
  treacherous doorway?—
Ah, but the bride, meantime,—do you think she
  sees it as he does?
  But for the steady fore-sense of a freer and
  larger existence,
Think you that man could consent to be
  circumscribed here into action?
125 But for assurance within of a limitless ocean divine,
  o'er
Whose great tranquil depths unconscious the wind-
  tost surface
Breaks into ripples of trouble that come and change
  and endure not,—
But that in this, of a truth, we have our being, and
  know it,
Think you we men could submit to live and move
  as we do here?
130 Ah, but the women,—God bless them!—they don't
  think at all about it.
  Yet we must eat and drink, as you say. And as
  limited beings
Scarcely can hope to attain upon earth to an Actual
  Abstract,
Leaving to God contemplation, to His hands
  knowledge confiding,

Sure that in us if it perish, in Him it abideth and
    dies not,
135 Let us in His sight accomplish our petty particular
    doings,—
Yes, and contented sit down to the victual that He
    has provided.
Allah[1] is great, no doubt, and Juxtaposition his
    prophet.
Ah, but the women, alas! they don't look at it in
    that way.
    Juxtaposition is great;—but, my friend, I fear
    me, the maiden
140 Hardly would thank or acknowledge the lover that
    sought to obtain her,
Not as the thing he would wish, but the thing he
    must even put up with,—
Hardly would tender her hand to the wooer that
    candidly told her
That she is but for a space, an *ad-interim*[2] solace
    and pleasure,—
That in the end she shall yield to a perfect and
    absolute something,
145 Which I then for myself shall behold, and not
    another,—
Which, amid fondest endearments, meantime I
    forget not, forsake not.
Ah, ye feminine souls, so loving and so exacting,
Since we cannot escape, must we even submit to
    deceive you?
Since, so cruel is truth, sincerity shocks and revolts
    you,
150 Will you have us your slaves to lie to you, flatter
    and—leave you?

        VII CLAUDE TO EUSTACE
Juxtaposition is great,—but, you tell me, affinity
    greater.

Ah, my friend, there are many affinities, greater
    and lesser,
Stronger and weaker; and each, by the favour of
    juxtaposition,
Potent, efficient, in force,—for a time; but none,
    let me tell you,
155 Save by the law of the land and the ruinous force of
    the will, ah,
None, I fear me, at last quite sure to be final and
    perfect.
Lo, as I pace in the street, from the peasant-girl to
    the princess,
Homo sum, nihil humani a me alienum puto,—
Vir sum, nihil fœminei,[3]—and e'en to the uttermost
    circle,
160 All that is Nature's is I, and I all things that are
    Nature's.
Yes, as I walk, I behold, in a luminous, large
    intuition,
That I can be and become anything that I meet
    with or look at:
I am the ox in the dray, the ass with the garden-
    stuff panniers;
I am the dog in the doorway, the kitten that plays
    in the window,
165 On sunny slab of the ruin the furtive and fugitive
    lizard,
Swallow above me that twitters, and fly that is
    buzzing about me;
Yea, and detect, as I go, by a faint but a faithful
    assurance,
E'en from the stones of the street, as from rocks or
    trees of the forest,
Something of kindred, a common, though latent
    vitality, greet me;
170 And, to escape from our strivings, mistakings,
    misgrowths, and perversions,

---

[1] Arabic name of God.

[2] for the time being; "meanwhile" is an archaic usage.

---

[3] Terence, *Heauton Timorumenos (The Self-Tormentor)*, l. 77: "I am a man; I count nothing that concerns man foreign to me." Claude's variation may be translated: "I am a man; I count nothing that concerns women foreign to me."

Fain could demand to return to that perfect and
    primitive silence,
Fain be enfolded and fixed, as of old, in their rigid
    embraces.

VIII CLAUDE TO EUSTACE

And as I walk on my way, I behold them
    consorting and coupling;
Faithful it seemeth, and fond, very fond, very
    probably faithful;
175 All as I go on my way, with a pleasure sincere and
      unmingled.
    Life is beautiful, Eustace, entrancing,
      enchanting to look at;
As are the streets of a city we pace while the
    carriage is changing,
As a chamber filled-in with harmonious, exquisite
    pictures,
Even so beautiful Earth; and could we eliminate
    only
180 This vile hungering impulse, this demon within us
    of craving,
Life were beatitude, living a perfect divine
    satisfaction.

IX CLAUDE TO EUSTACE

Mild monastic faces in quiet collegiate cloisters:
So let me offer a single and celibatarian phrase, a
Tribute to those whom perhaps you do not believe
    I can honour.
185 But, from the tumult escaping, 'tis pleasant, of
    drumming and shouting,
Hither, oblivious awhile, to withdraw, of the fact
    or the falsehood,
And amid placid regards and mildly courteous
    greetings
Yield to the calm and composure and gentle
    abstraction that reign o'er
Mild monastic faces in quiet collegiate cloisters.
190   Terrible word, Obligation! You should not,
      Eustace, you should not,

No, you should not have used it. But, O great
    Heavens! I repel it.
Oh, I cancel, reject, disavow, and repudiate wholly
Every debt in this kind, disclaim every claim, and
    dishonour,
Yea, my own heart's own writing, my soul's own
    signature! Ah, no!
195 I will be free in this; you shall not, none shall, bind
    me.
No, my friend, if you wish to be told, it was this
    above all things,
This that charmed me, ah, yes, even this, that she
    held me to nothing.
No, I could talk as I pleased; come close; fasten
    ties, as I fancied;
Bind and engage myself deep;—and lo, on the
    following morning
200 It was all e'en as before, like losings in games
    played for nothing.
Yes, when I came, with mean fears in my soul, with
    a semi-performance
At the first step breaking down in its pitiful rôle of
    evasion,
When to shuffle I came, to compromise, not meet,
    engagements,
Lo, with her calm eyes there she met me and knew
    nothing of it,—
205 Stood unexpecting, unconscious. *She* spoke not of
    obligations,
Knew not of debt,—ah, no, I believe you, for
    excellent reasons.

X CLAUDE TO EUSTACE

Hang this thinking, at last! what good is it? oh, and
    what evil!
Oh, what mischief and pain! like a clock in a sick
    man's chamber,
Ticking and ticking, and still through every covert
    of slumber pursuing.
210   What shall I do to thee, O thou Preserver of
      Men? Have compassion;

Be favourable, and hear! Take from me this regal
    knowledge;
Let me, contented and mute, with the beasts of the
    field, my brothers,
Tranquilly, happily lie,—and eat grass, like
    Nebuchadnezzar![1]

XI CLAUDE TO EUSTACE

Tibur is beautiful, too, and the orchard slopes, and
    the Anio[2]
215 Falling, falling yet, to the ancient lyrical cadence;
Tibur and Anio's tide; and cool from Lucretilis ever,
With the Digentian stream, and with the
    Bandusian fountain,
Folded in Sabine recesses, the valley and villa of
    Horace:—
So not seeing I sung; so seeing and listening say I,
220 Here as I sit by the stream, as I gave at the cell of
    the Sibyl,
Here with Albunea's home and the grove of
    Tiburnus beside me;
Tivoli beautiful is, and musical, O Teverone,
Dashing from mountain to plain, thy parted
    impetuous waters!
Tivoli's waters and rocks; and fair under Monte
    Gennaro
225 (Haunt even yet, I must think, as I wander and
    gaze, of the shadows,

Faded and pale, yet immortal, of Faunus,[3] the
    Nymphs,[4] and the Graces[5]),
Fair in itself, and yet fairer with human completing
    creations,
Folded in Sabine recesses the valley and villa of
    Horace:—
So not seeing I sung; so now—Nor seeing, nor
    hearing,
230 Neither by waterfall lulled, nor folded in sylvan
    embraces,
Neither by cell of the Sibyl, nor stepping the
    Monte Gennaro,
Seated on Anio's bank, nor sipping Bandusian
    waters,
But on Montorio's height,[6] looking down on the
    tile-clad streets, the
Cupolas, crosses, and domes, the bushes and
    kitchen-gardens,
235 Which, by the grace of the Tiber, proclaim
    themselves Rome of the Romans,—
But on Montorio's height, looking forth to the
    vapoury mountains,
Cheating the prisoner Hope with illusions of vision
    and fancy,—
But on Montorio's height, with these weary
    soldiers by me,
Waiting till Oudinot enter, to reinstate Pope and
    Tourist.

XII MARY TREVELLYN TO MISS ROPER

240 Dear Miss Roper,—It seems, George Vernon,
    before we left Rome, said

---

[1] a corruption of Nebuchadrezzar: Jeremiah 21:2; the greatest king of Babylon, probably responsible for building the famous Hanging Gardens. Ruled 604–561 BC: see Daniel 4:25–33.

[2] In a footnote, Clough quoted Horace's *Odes* 1.7.12–14, celebrating the ancient town of Tibur, now called Tivoli. The Anio, or Teverone, is the river, which forms a waterfall there. Clough also mentions rivers and waterfalls named by Horace in *Odes* 1.7 and 3.13. The temple of the Sibyl Albunea was near Tibur.

[3] the Roman version of Pan, grandson of Saturn, a rustic god and a prophet.

[4] in classical mythology, minor female deities of woods, streams, rivers, etc. They were young and beautiful maidens.

[5] three sister-goddesses who bestowed beauty and charm; their names were Aglaea, Thalia, and Euphrosyne.

[6] a hill in Rome also know as the Janiculum.

Something to Mr. Claude about what they call his
    attentions.
Susan, two nights ago, for the first time, heard this
    from Georgina.
It is *so* disagreeable and *so* annoying to think of!
If it could only be known, though we may never
    meet him again, that
245 It was all George's doing, and we were entirely
    unconscious,
It would extremely relieve—Your ever affectionate
    Mary.

P.S. (1)
    Here is your letter arrived this moment, just as I
        wanted.
So you have seen him,—indeed,—and
    guessed,—how dreadfully clever!
What did he really say? and what was your answer
    exactly?
250 Charming!—but wait for a moment, I haven't read
    through the letter.

P.S. (2)
    Ah, my dearest Miss Roper, do just as you fancy
        about it.
If you think it sincerer to tell him I know of it, do
    so.
Though I should most extremely dislike it, I know
    I could manage.
It is the simplest thing, but surely wholly uncalled
    for.
255 Do as you please; you know I trust implicitly to you.
Say whatever is right and needful for ending the
    matter.
Only don't tell Mr. Claude, what I will tell you as a
    secret,
That I should like very well to show him myself I
    forget it.

P.S. (3)
    I am to say that the wedding is finally settled for
    Tuesday.
260 Ah, my dear Miss Roper, you surely, surely can
    manage
Not to let it appear that I know of that odious
    matter.
It would be pleasanter far for myself to treat it
    exactly
As if it had not occurred; and I do not think he
    would like it.
I must remember to add, that as soon as the
    wedding is over
265 We shall be off, I believe, in a hurry, and travel to
    Milan,
There to meet friends of Papa's, I am told, at the
    Croce di Malta;[1]
Then I cannot say whither, but not at present to
    England.

XIII CLAUDE TO EUSTACE
Yes, on Montorio's height for a last farewell of the
    city,—
So it appears; though then I was quite uncertain
    about it.
270 So, however, it was. And now to explain the
    proceeding.
    I was to go, as I told you, I think, with the
        people to Florence.
Only the day before, the foolish family Vernon
Made some uneasy remarks, as we walked to our
    lodging together,
As to intentions, forsooth, and so forth. I was
    astounded,
275 Horrified quite; and obtaining just then, as it
    happened, an offer
(No common favour) of seeing the great Ludovisi
    collection,

---

[1] possibly a hotel in Milan.

Why, I made this a pretence, and wrote that they
    must excuse me.
How could I go? Great Heaven! to conduct a
    permitted flirtation
Under those vulgar eyes, the observed of such
    observers![1]

280 Well, but I now, by a series of fine diplomatic
    inquiries,
Find from a sort of relation, a good and sensible
    woman,
Who is remaining at Rome with a brother too ill
    for removal,
That it was wholly unsanctioned, unknown,—not,
    I think, by Georgina:
She, however, ere this,—and that is the best of the
    story,—
285 She and the Vernon, thank Heaven, are wedded
    and gone—honey-mooning.
So—on Montorio's height for a last farewell of the
    city.
Tibur I have not seen, nor the lakes that of old I
    had dreamt of;
Tiber I shall not see, nor Anio's waters, nor deep
    en-
Folded in Sabine recesses the valley and villa of
    Horace;
290 Tibur I shall not see;—but something better I shall
    see.
    Twice I have tried before, and failed in getting
      the horses;
    Twice I have tried and failed: this time it shall not
      be a failure.

Therefore farewell, ye hills, and ye, ye envineyarded
    ruins.
    Therefore farewell, ye walls, palaces, pillars, and
      domes!
295 *Therefore farewell, far seen, ye peaks of the mythic*
    Albano,

Seen from Montorio's height, Tibur and Æsula's[2]
    hills!
Ah, could we once, ere we go, could we stand, while,
    to ocean descending,
    Sinks o'er the yellow dark plain slowly the yellow
      broad sun,
Stand, from the forest emerging at sunset, at once in
    the champaign,
300 *Open, but studded with trees, chestnuts*
      umbrageous and old,
E'en in those fair open fields that incurve to thy
    beautiful hollow,
    Nemi, imbedded in wood, Nemi, inurned in the
      hill!—[3]
Therefore farewell, ye plains, and ye hills, and the
    City Eternal!
Therefore farewell! We depart, but to behold you
    again!

CANTO IV

Eastward, or Northward, or West? I wander and ask
    as I wander,
    Weary, yet eager and sure, Where shall I come to
      my love?
Whitherward hasten to seek her? Ye daughters of Italy,
    tell me,
    Graceful and tender and dark, is she consorting
      with you?
5 *Thou that out-climbest the torrent, that tendest thy*
    goats to the summit,
    Call to me, child of the Alp, has she been seen on
      the heights?
Italy, farewell I bid thee! for whither she leads me, I
    follow.
    Farewell the vineyard! for I, where I but guess her,
      must go.

---

[1] *Hamlet* 3.1.163.

[2] a mountain and town, both near Tibur.

[3] a town and a lake south of Rome.

Weariness welcome, and labour, wherever it be, if at
    last it
10   *Bring me in mountain or plain into the sight of*
    my love.

I CLAUDE TO EUSTACE,—*from Florence*

Gone from Florence; indeed; and that is truly
    provoking;—
Gone to Milan, it seems; then I go also to Milan.
Five days now departed; but they can travel but
    slowly;—
I quicker far; and I know, as it happens, the house
    they will go to.—
15 Why, what else should I do? Stay here and look at
    the pictures,
Statues, and churches? Alack, I am sick of the
    statues and pictures!—
No, to Bologna, Parma, Piacenza, Lodi, and Milan,
Off go we to-night,—and the Venus go to the
    Devil!

II CLAUDE TO EUSTACE,—*from Bellaggio*

Gone to Como, they said; and I have posted to
    Como.[1]
20 There was a letter left; but the *cameriere*[2] had lost it.
Could it have been for me? They came, however, to
    Como,
And from Como went by the boat,—perhaps to the
    Splügen,—
Or to the Stelvio, say, and the Tyrol; also it might
    be
By Porlezza across to Lugano, and so to the
    Simplon
25 Possibly, or the St. Gothard,—or possibly, too, to
    Baveno,
Orta, Turin, and elsewhere. Indeed, I am greatly
    bewildered.

III CLAUDE TO EUSTACE,—*from Bellaggio*

I have been up the Splügen, and on the Stelvio also:
Neither of these can I find they have followed; in
    no one inn, and
This would be odd, have they written their names.
    I have been to Porlezza;
30 There they have not been seen, and therefore not at
    Lugano.
What shall I do? Go on through the Tyrol,
    Switzerland, Deutschland,
Seeking, an inverse Saul,[3] a kingdom, to find only
    asses?
There is a tide,[4] at least in the *love* affairs of
    mortals,
Which, when taken at flood, leads on to the
    happiest fortune,—
35 Leads to the marriage-morn and the orange-flowers
    and the altar,
And the long lawful line of crowned joys to
    crowned joys succeeding.—
Ah, it has ebbed with me! Ye gods, and when it was
    flowing,
Pitiful fool that I was, to stand fiddle-faddling in
    that way!

IV CLAUDE TO EUSTACE,—from *Bellaggio*

I have returned and found their names in the book
    at Como.
40 Certain it is I was right, and yet I am also in error.
Added in feminine hand, I read, *By the boat to*
    Bellaggio.—
So to Bellaggio again, with the words of her writing
    to aid me.
Yet at Bellaggio I find no trace, no sort of
    remembrance.
So I am here, and wait, and know every hour will
    remove them.

---

[1] references here and in the following lines are to towns, lakes, and
mountain passes in Northern Italy and Switzerland.

[2] hotel clerk.

[3] I Samuel 9–10.

[4] *Julius Caesar* 4.3.217–20.

V CLAUDE TO EUSTACE,—*from Bellaggio*

45 I have but one chance left,—and that is going to
Florence.
But it is cruel to turn. The mountains seem to
demand me,—
Peak and valley from far to beckon and motion me
onward.
Somewhere amid their folds she passes whom fain I
would follow;
Somewhere among those heights she haply calls me
to seek her.
50 Ah, could I hear her call! could I catch the glimpse
of her raiment!
Turn, however, I must, though it seem I turn to
desert her;
For the sense of thing is simply to hurry to Florence,
Where the certainty yet may be learnt, I suppose,
from the Ropers.

VI MARY TREVELLYN, *from Lucerne,*
TO MISS ROPER, *at Florence*

Dear Miss Roper,—By this you are safely away, we
are hoping,
55 Many a league from Rome; erelong we trust we
shall see you.
How have you travelled? I wonder;—was Mr.
Claude your companion?
As for ourselves, we went from Como straight to
Lugano;
So by the Mount St. Gothard; we meant to go by
Porlezza,
Taking the steamer, and stopping, as you had
advised, at Bellaggio,
60 Two or three days or more; but this was suddenly
altered,
After we left the hotel, on the very way to the
steamer.
So we have seen, I fear, not one of the lakes in
perfection.
Well, he is not come; and now, I suppose, he
will not come.

What will you think, meantime?—and yet I must
really confess it;—
65 What will you say? I wrote him a note. We left in a
hurry,
Went from Milan to Como, three days before we
expected.
But I thought, if he came all the way to Milan, he
really
Ought not to be disappointed; and so I wrote three
lines to
Say I had heard he was coming, desirous of joining
our party;—
70 If so, then I said, we had started for Como, and
meant to
Cross the St. Gothard, and stay, we believed, at
Lucerne, for the summer.
Was it wrong? and why, if it was, has it failed to
bring him?
Did he not think it worth while to come to Milan?
He knew (you
Told him) the house we should go to. Or may it,
perhaps, have miscarried?
75 Any way, now, I repent, and am heartily vexed that
I wrote it.

*There is a home on the shore of the Alpine sea,[1] that
upswelling
    High up the mountain-sides spreads in the hollow
    between;
Wilderness, mountain, and snow from the land of the
olive conceal it;
    Under Pilatus's hill[2] low by its river it lies:*
80 *Italy, utter the word, and the olive and vine will
allure not,—
    Wilderness, forest, and snow will not the passage
    impede;
Italy, unto thy cities receding, the clew to recover,
    Hither, recovered the clew, shall not the traveller
    haste?*

---

[1] Lake Lucerne, Switzerland.

[2] mountain in Switzerland near Lucerne.

CANTO V

There is a city, upbuilt on the quays of the turbulent
      Arno,[1]
   Under Fiesole's[2] *heights,—thither are we to return?*
There is a city that fringes the curve of the inflowing
      waters,
   Under the perilous hill fringes the beautiful
      bay,—
5 *Parthenope*[3] *do they call thee?—the Siren, Neapolis,*
      seated
   Under Vesevus's[4] *hill,—are we receding to thee?—*
Sicily, Greece, will invite, and the Orient;—or are we
      to turn to
   England, which may after all be for its children
      the best?

I MARY TREVELLYN, *at Lucerne*, To MISS ROPER, *at Florence*

So you are really free, and living in quiet at
      Florence;
10 That is delightful news;—you travelled slowly and
      safely;
Mr. Claude got you out; took rooms at Florence
      before you;
Wrote from Milan to say so; had left directly for
      Milan,
Hoping to find us soon;—*if he could, he would, you*
      are certain.—
Dear Miss Roper, your letter has made me
      exceedingly happy.
15   You are quite sure, you say, he asked you about
      our intentions;

You had not heard as yet of Lucerne, but told him
      of Como.—
Well, perhaps he will come;—however, I will not
      expect it.
Though you say you are sure,—*if he can, he will,*
      you are certain.
O my dear, many thanks from your ever
      affectionate Mary.

II CLAUDE TO EUSTACE

Florence.

20 *Action will furnish belief,*[5]—but will that belief be
            the true one?
This is the point, you know. However, it doesn't
      much matter.
What one wants, I suppose, is to predetermine the
      action,
So as to make it entail, not a chance-belief, but the
      true one.
Out of the question, you say; if a thing isn't wrong,
      we may do it.
25 Ah! but this *wrong*, you see—but I do not know
            that it matters.
      Eustace, the Ropers are gone, and no one can
            tell me about them.

Pisa.

Pisa, they say they think; and so I follow to Pisa,
Hither and thither inquiring. I weary of making
      inquiries;
I am ashamed, I declare, of asking people about
      it.—
30 Who are your friends? You said you had friends
            who would certainly know them.

---

[1] the river Arno in Florence.

[2] a town on a hillside overlooking Florence.

[3] The ancient site of Naples was named Parthenope, after one of the sirens. The Sirens were mythical monsters, half woman and half bird, said to entice sailors to their deaths by their beautiful singing.

[4] Mount Vesuvius.

---

[5] presumably Eustace's conventionally Victorian advice to Claude. Compare "Experience is the child of Thought, and Thought is the child of Action. We cannot learn men from books" (Disraeli, *Vivian Gray*, 1826).

Florence.

But it is idle, moping, and thinking, and trying to
fix her
Image more and more in, to write the old perfect
inscription
Over and over again upon every page of
remembrance.
    I have settled to stay at Florence to wait for your
answer.
35 Who are your friends? Write quickly and tell me. I
wait for your answer.

III MARY TREVELLYN TO MISS ROPER, *at Lucca Baths*

You are at Lucca Baths, you tell me, to stay for the
summer;
Florence was quite too hot; you can't move further
at present.
Will you not come, do you think, before the
summer is over?
    Mr. C. got you out with very considerable
trouble;
40 And he was useful and kind, and seemed so happy
to serve you;
Didn't stay with you long, but talked very openly
to you;
Made you almost his confessor, without appearing
to know it,—
What about?—and you say you didn't need his
confessions.
O my dear Miss Roper, I dare not trust what you
tell me!
45   Will he come, do you think? I am really so sorry
for him!
They didn't give him my letter at Milan, I feel
pretty certain.
You had told him Bellaggio. We didn't go to
Bellaggio;
So he would miss our track, and perhaps never
come to Lugano,
Where we were written in full, *To Lucerne across the
St. Gothard.*

50 But he could write to you;—you would tell him
where you were going.

IV CLAUDE TO EUSTACE

Let me, then, bear to forget her. I will not cling to
her falsely;
Nothing factitious or forced shall impair the old
happy relation.
I will let myself go, forget, not try to remember;
I will walk on my way, accept the chances that
meet me,
55 Freely encounter the world, imbibe these alien airs,
and
Never ask if new feelings and thoughts are of her or
of others.
Is she not changing, herself?—the old image would
only delude me.
I will be bold, too, and change,—if it must be. Yet
if in all things,
Yet if I do but aspire evermore to the Absolute
only,
60 I shall be doing, I think, somehow, what she will be
doing;—
I shall be thine, O my child, some way, though I
know not in what way.
Let me submit to forget her; I must; I already
forget her.

V CLAUDE TO EUSTACE

Utterly vain is, alas! this attempt at the
Absolute,—wholly!
I, who believed not in her, because I would fain
believe nothing,
65 Have to believe as I may, with a wilful, unmeaning
acceptance.
I, who refused to enfasten the roots of my floating
existence
In the rich earth, cling now to the hard, naked rock
that is left me.—
Ah, she was worthy, Eustace,—and that, indeed, is
my comfort,—

Worthy a nobler heart than a fool such as I could
    have given.

———————

70 Yes, it relieves me to write, though I do not send,
    and the chance that
Takes may destroy my fragments. But as men pray,
    without asking
Whether One really exist to hear or do anything for
    them,—
Simply impelled by the need of the moment to
    turn to a Being
In a conception of whom there is freedom from all
    limitation,—
75 So in your image I turn to an *ens rationis*[1] of
    friendship.
Even so write in your name I know not to whom
    nor in what wise.

———————

There was a time, methought it was but lately
    departed,
When, if a thing was denied me, I felt I was bound
    to attempt it;
Choice alone should take, and choice alone should
    surrender.
80 There was a time, indeed, when I had not retired
    thus early,
Languidly thus, from pursuit of a purpose I once
    had adopted.
But it is over, all that! I have slunk from the
    perilous field in
Whose wild struggle of forces the prizes of life are
    contested.
It is over, all that! I am a coward, and know it.
85 Courage in me could be only factitious, unnatural,
    useless.

———————

Comfort has come to me here in the dreary streets
    of the city,

Comfort—how do you think?—with a barrel-
    organ to bring it.
Moping along the streets, and cursing my day as I
    wandered,
All of a sudden my ear met the sound of an English
    psalm-tune.
90 Comfort me it did, till indeed I was very near crying.
Ah, there is some great truth, partial, very likely,
    but needful,
Lodged, I am strangely sure, in the tones of the
    English psalm-tune.
Comfort it was at least; and I must take without
    question
Comfort, however it come, in the dreary streets of
    the city.

———————

95 What with trusting myself, and seeking support
    from within me,
Almost I could believe I had gained a religious
    assurance,
Formed in my own poor soul a great moral basis to
    rest on.
Ah, but indeed I see, I feel it factitious entirely;
I refuse, reject, and put it utterly from me;
100 I will look straight out, see things, not try to evade
    them;
Fact shall be fact for me; and the Truth the Truth
    as ever,
Flexible, changeable, vague, and multiform, and
    doubtful.—
Off, and depart to the void, thou subtle, fanatical
    tempter!

———————

I shall behold thee again (is it so?) at a new
    visitation,
105 O ill genius thou! I shall, at my life's dissolution,
(When the pulses are weak, and the feeble light of
    the reason
Flickers, an unfed flame retiring slow from the
    socket),

———————

[1] literally, an "entity of reason"—an idea that exists in the mind only,
as opposed to an *ens reale* which exists in the world, independently of the
mind.

Low on a sick-bed laid, hear one, as it were, at the
    doorway,
And, looking up, see thee, standing by, looking
    emptily at me;
110 I shall entreat thee then, though now I dare to
    refuse thee,—
Pale and pitiful now, but terrible then to the
    dying.—
Well, I will see thee again, and while I can, will
    repel thee.

VI Claude to Eustace

Rome is fallen, I hear, the gallant Medici taken,
Noble Manara slain, and Garibaldi has lost *il*
    Moro;[1]—
115 Rome is fallen; and fallen, or falling, heroical Venice.
I, meanwhile, for the loss of a single small chit of a
    girl, sit
Moping and mourning here,—for her, and myself
    much smaller.
    Whither depart the souls of the brave that die in
      the battle,
Die in the lost, lost fight, for the cause that perishes
    with them?
120 Are they upborne from the field on the slumberous
    pinions of angels
Unto a far-off home, where the weary rest from
    their labour,
And the deep wounds are healed, and the bitter and
    burning moisture
Wiped from the generous eye? or do they linger,
    unhappy,
Pining, and haunting the grave of their by-gone
    hope and endeavour?
125   All declamation, alas! though I talk, I care not
      for Rome, nor
Italy; feebly and faintly, and but with the lips, can
    lament the

---

[1] Il Moro, the Moor, was the name of Garibaldi's Negro servant.
Giacomo de Medici and Luciano Manara were leaders of the Republican
movement.

Wreck of the Lombard youth and the victory of the
    oppressor.
Whither depart the brave?—God knows; I certainly
    do not.

VII Mary Trevellyn to Miss Roper

He has not come as yet; and now I must not expect
    it.
130 You have written, you say, to friends at Florence, to
    see him,
If he perhaps should return;—but that is surely
    unlikely.
Has he not written to you?—he did not know your
    direction.
Oh, how strange never once to have told him
    where you were going!
Yet if he only wrote to Florence, that would have
    reached you.
135 If what you say he said was true, why has he not
    done so?
Is he gone back to Rome, do you think, to his
    Vatican marbles?—
O my dear Miss Roper, forgive me! do not be
    angry!—
You have written to Florence;—your friends would
    certainly find him.
Might you not write to him?—but yet it is so little
    likely!
140 I shall expect nothing more.—Ever yours, your
    affectionate Mary.

VIII Claude to Eustace

I cannot stay at Florence, not even to wait for a
    letter.
Galleries only oppress me. Remembrance of hope I
    had cherished
(Almost more than as hope, when I passed through
    Florence the first time)
Lies like a sword in my soul. I am more a coward
    than ever,

145 Chicken-hearted, past thought. The *caffès* and
    waiters distress me.
All is unkind, and, alas! I am ready for any one's
    kindness.
Oh, I knew it of old, and knew it, I thought, to
    perfection,
If there is any one thing in the world to preclude all
    kindness,
It is the need of it,—it is this sad, self-defeating
    dependence.
150 Why is this, Eustace? Myself, were I stronger, I
    think I could tell you.
But it is odd when it comes. So plumb I the deeps
    of depression,
Daily in deeper, and find no support, no will, no
    purpose.
All my old strengths are gone. And yet I shall have
    to do something.
Ah, the key of our life, that passes all wards, opens
    all locks,
155 Is not *I will*, but *I must*. I must,—I must,—and I
    do it.

————————

After all, do I know that I really cared so about her?
Do whatever I will, I cannot call up her image;
For when I close my eyes, I see, very likely,
    St. Peter's,
Or the Pantheon façade, or Michel Angelo's figures,
160 Or, at a wish, when I please, the Alban hills and the
    Forum,—
But that face, those eyes,—ah no, never anything
    like them;
Only, try as I will, a sort of featureless outline,
And a pale blank orb, which no recollection will
    add to.
After all perhaps there was something factitious
    about it:
165 I have had pain, it is true; I have wept; and so have
    the actors.[1]

————————

1 *Hamlet* 2.2.589.

At the last moment I have your letter, for which I
    was waiting.
I have taken my place, and see no good in inquiries.
Do nothing more, good Eustace, I pray you. It
    only will vex me.
Take no measures. Indeed, should we meet, I could
    not be certain;
170 All might be changed, you know. Or perhaps there
    was nothing to be changed.
It is a curious history, this; and yet I foresaw it;
I could have told it before. The Fates, it is clear, are
    against us;
For it is certain enough that I met with the people
    you mention;
They were at Florence the day I returned there, and
    spoke to me even;
175 Stayed a week, saw me often; departed, and whither
    I know not.
Great is Fate, and is best. I believe in Providence
    partly.
What is ordained is right, and all that happens is
    ordered.
Ah, no, that isn't it. But yet I retain my conclusion.
I will go where I am led, and will not dictate to the
    chances.
180 Do nothing more, I beg. If you love me, forbear
    interfering.

IX CLAUDE TO EUSTACE

Shall we come out of it all, some day, as one does
    from a tunnel?
Will it be all at once, without our doing or asking,
We shall behold clear day, the trees and meadows
    about us,
And the faces of friends, and the eyes we loved
    looking at us?
185 Who knows? Who can say? It will not do to
    suppose it.

x CLAUDE TO EUSTACE,—*from Rome*

Rome will not suit me, Eustace; the priests and
    soldiers possess it;
Priests and soldiers;—and, ah! which is worst, the
      priest or the soldier?
    Politics, farewell, however! For what could I do?
      with inquiring,
Talking, collating the journals, go fever my brain
    about things o'er
190 Which I can have no control. No, happen whatever
    may happen,
Time, I suppose, will subsist; the earth will revolve
    on its axis;
People will travel; the stranger will wander as now
    in the city;
Rome will be here, and the Pope the *custode* of
    Vatican marbles.[1]
    I have no heart, however, for any marble or
      fresco;
195 I have essayed it in vain; 'tis vain as yet to essay it:
But I may haply resume some day my studies in
    this kind;
Not as the Scripture says, is, I think, the fact. Ere
    our death-day,
Faith, I think, does pass, and Love; but Knowledge[2]
    abideth.
Let us seek Knowledge;—the rest must come and
    go as it happens.
200 Knowledge is hard to seek, and harder yet to adhere
    to.
Knowledge is painful often; and yet when we
    know, we are happy.
Seek it, and leave mere Faith and Love to come
    with the chances.
As for Hope,—to-morrow I hope to be starting for
    Naples.
Rome will not do, I see, for many very good
    reasons.

205 Eastward, then, I suppose, with the coming of
    winter, to Egypt.

xi MARY TREVELLYN TO MISS ROPER

You have heard nothing; of course, I know you can
    have heard nothing.
Ah, well, more than once I have broken my
    purpose, and sometimes,
Only too often, have looked for the little lake-
    steamer to bring him.
But it is only fancy,—I do not really expect it.
210 Oh, and you see I know so exactly how he would
    take it:
Finding the chances prevail against meeting again,
    he would banish
Forthwith every thought of the poor little possible
    hope, which
I myself could not help, perhaps, thinking only too
    much of;
He would resign himself, and go. I see it exactly.
215 So I also submit, although in a different manner.
    Can you not really come? We go very shortly to
    England.

———————

So go forth to the world, to the good report and the
    evil!
    Go, little book![3] thy tale, is it not evil and good?
Go, and if strangers revile, pass quietly by without
    answer.
    Go, and if curious friends ask of thy rearing and
    age,
Say, "I am flitting about many years from brain unto
    brain of
    Feeble and restless youths born to inglorious days;
But," so finish the word, "I was writ in a Roman
    chamber,
    "When from Janiculan heights[4] thundered the
    cannon of France."
—1858

---

1 custodian or caretaker.

2 "Faith…Love…Knowledge": I Corinthians 13:8.

3 Cf. Chaucer, *Troilus and Criseyde* l. 1786. This type of conven-
tionalized stanza at the end of a poem is called the envoy.

4 See note to Canto III, Letter XI.

George Eliot
1819 – 1880

George Eliot was the pseudonym of Mary Anne (also spelled Mary Ann and Marian) Evans. Although she wrote lyrics and longer dramatic pieces (both represented in this collection), she is primarily known for her realistic fiction: e.g. *Adam Bede* (1859), *Silas Marner* (1861), *Middlemarch* (1871–72), and *Daniel Deronda* (1876). In her early twenties Eliot rejected religious orthodoxies and became interested in non-doctrinal interpretation of the scriptures. This led to her translation of Strauss's *Life of Jesus, Critically Examined* (1846), and Feuerbach's *Essence of Christianity* (1854). Eliot became an anonymous editor of the *Westminster Review* (1851–54); from 1854 until his death in 1878 she lived with the writer and scholar George Henry Lewes, whose previous marriage prevented their legal union.

ↀↀↀ

"O, May I Join the Choir Invisible"

Longum illud tempus, quum non ero, magis me movet, quam hoc exiguum.—Cicero, ad Att., 12.18.[1]

O, may I join the choir invisible
Of those immortal dead who live again
In minds made better by their presence: live
In pulses stirred to generosity,
5 In deeds of daring rectitude, in scorn
For miserable aims that end with self,
In thoughts sublime that pierce the night like stars,
And with their mild persistence urge man's search
To vaster issues.
       So to live is heaven:
10 To make undying music in the world,
Breathing as beauteous order that controls
With growing sway the growing life of man.
So we inherit that sweet purity
For which we struggled, failed, and agonised
15 With widening retrospect that bred despair.
Rebellious flesh that would not be subdued,
A vicious parent shaming still its child,
Poor anxious penitence, is quick dissolved;
Its discords, quenched by meeting harmonies,

20 Die in the large and charitable air.
And all our rarer, better, truer self,
That sobbed religiously in yearning song,
That watched to ease the burthen of the world,
Laboriously tracing what must be,
25 And what may yet be better—saw within
A worthier image for the sanctuary,
And shaped it forth before the multitude
Divinely human, raising worship so
To higher reverence more mixed with love—
30 That better self shall live till human Time
Shall fold its eyelids, and the human sky
Be gathered like a scroll within the tomb
Unread for ever.
       This is life to come,
Which martyred men have made more glorious
35 For us who strive to follow. May I reach
That purest heaven, be to other souls
The cup of strength in some great agony,
Enkindle generous ardour, feed pure love,
Beget the smiles that have no cruelty—
40 Be the sweet presence of a good diffused,
And in diffusion ever more intense.
So shall I join the choir invisible,
Whose music is the gladness of the world.
—1867

---

[1] "And the long expense of time after I shall cease to be is of more account to me than this little span."

The Spanish Gypsy

BOOK I

*   *   *   *

A HANDSOME ROOM IN THE CASTLE

On a table a rich jewel-casket

Silva had doffed his mail and with it all
The heavier harness of his warlike cares.
He had not seen Fedalma; miser-like
He hoarded through the hour a costlier joy
5 By longing oft-repressed. Now it was earned;
And with observance wonted he would send
To ask admission. Spanish gentlemen
Who wooed fair dames of noble ancestry
Did homage with rich tunics and slashed sleeves
10 And outward-surging linen's costly snow;
With broidered scarf transverse, and rosary
Handsomely wrought to fit high-blooded prayer;
So hinting in how deep respect they held
That self they threw before their lady's feet.
15 And Silva—that Fedalma's rate should stand
No jot below the highest, that her love
Might seem to all the royal gift it was—
Turned every trifle in his mien and garb
To scrupulous language, uttering to the world
20 That since she loved him he went carefully,
Bearing a thing so precious in his hand.
A man of high-wrought strain, fastidious
In his acceptance, dreading all delight
That speedy dies and turns to carrion:
25 His senses much exacting, deep instilled
With keen imagination's airy needs;—
Like strong-limbed monsters studded o'er with eyes,
Their hunger checked by overwhelming vision,
Or that fierce lion in symbolic dream
30 Snatched from the ground by wings and new-
        endowed
With a man's thought-propelled relenting heart.

Silva was both the lion and the man;
First hesitating shrank, then fiercely sprang,
Or having sprung, turned pallid at his deed
35 And loosed the prize, paying his blood for nought.
A nature half-transformed, with qualities
That oft bewrayed each other, elements
Not blent but struggling, breeding strange effects,
Passing the reckoning of his friends or foes.
40 Haughty and generous, grave and passionate;
With tidal moments of devoutest awe,
Sinking anon to farthest ebb of doubt;
Deliberating ever, till the sting
Of a recurrent ardour made him rush
45 Right against reasons that himself had drilled
And marshalled painfully. A spirit framed
Too proudly special for obedience,
Too subtly pondering for mastery:
Born of a goddess with a mortal sire,
50 Heir of flesh-fettered, weak divinity,
Doom-gifted with long resonant consciousness
And perilous heightening of the sentient soul.
But look less curiously: life itself
May not express us all, may leave the worst
55 And the best too, like tunes in mechanism
Never awaked. In various catalogues
Objects stand variously. Silva stands
As a young Spaniard, handsome, noble, brave,
With titles many, high in pedigree;
60 Or, as a nature quiveringly poised
In reach of storms, whose qualities may turn
To murdered virtues that still walk as ghosts
Within the shuddering soul and shriek remorse;
Or, as a lover—In the screening time
65 Of purple blossoms, when the petals crowd
And softly crush like cherub cheeks in heaven,
Who thinks of greenly withered fruit and worms?
O the warm southern spring is beauteous!
And in love's spring all good seems possible:
70 No threats, all promise, brooklets ripple full
And bathe the rushes, vicious crawling things
Are pretty eggs, the sun shines graciously

And parches not, the silent rain beats warm
As childhood's kisses, days are young and grow,
75 And earth seems in its sweet beginning time
Fresh made for two who live in Paradise.
Silva is in love's spring, its freshness breathed
Within his soul along the dusty ways
While marching homeward; 't is around him now
80 As in a garden fenced in for delight,—
And he may seek delight. Smiling he lifts
A whistle from his belt, but lets it fall
Ere it has reached his lips, jarred by the sound
Of ushers' knocking, and a voice that craves
85 Admission for the Prior of San Domingo.

PRIOR (*entering*)
You look perturbed, my son. I thrust myself
Between you and some beckoning intent
That wears a face more smiling than my own.

DON SILVA
Father, enough that you are here. I wait,
90 As always, your commands—nay, should have sought
An early audience.

PRIOR
                    To give, I trust,
Good reasons for your change of policy?

DON SILVA
Strong reasons, father.

PRIOR
                    Ay, but are they good?
I have known reasons strong, but strongly evil.

DON SILVA
95 'T is possible. I but deliver mine
To your strict judgment. Late despatches sent
With urgence by the Count of Bavien,
No hint on my part prompting, with besides

The testified concurrence of the king
100 And our Grand Master, have made peremptory
The course which else had been but rational.
Without the forces furnished by allies
The siege of Guadix would be madness. More,
El Zagal has his eyes upon Bedmár:
105 Let him attempt it: in three weeks from hence
The Master and the Lord of Aguilar
Will bring their forces. We shall catch the Moors,
The last gleaned clusters of their bravest men,
As in a trap. You have my reasons, father.

PRIOR
110 And they sound well. But free-tongued rumour adds
A pregnant supplement—in substance this:
That inclination snatches arguments
To make indulgence seem judicious choice;
That you, commanding in God's Holy War,[1]
115 Lift prayers to Satan to retard the fight
And give you time for feasting—wait a siege,
Call daring enterprise impossible,
Because you'd marry! You, a Spanish duke,
Christ's general, would marry like a clown,
120 Who, selling fodder dearer for the war,
Is all the merrier; nay, like the brutes,
Who know no awe to check their appetite,
Coupling 'mid heaps of slain, while still in front
The battle rages.

DON SILVA
                    Rumour on your lips
125 Is eloquent, father.

PRIOR
                    Is she true?

DON SILVA
                                        Perhaps.
I seek to justify my public acts

---
[1] the Crusades.

And not my private joy. Before the world
Enough if I am faithful in command,
Betray not by my deeds, swerve from no task
130   My knightly vows constrain me to: herein
I ask all men to test me.

PRIOR
          Knightly vows?
Is it by their constraint that you must marry?

DON SILVA
Marriage is not a breach of them. I use
A sanctioned liberty—your pardon, father,
135   I need not teach you what the Church decrees.
But facts may weaken texts, and so dry up
The fount of eloquence. The Church relaxed
Our Order's rule before I took the vows.

PRIOR
Ignoble liberty! you snatch your rule
140   From what God tolerates, not what he loves?—
Inquire what lowest offering may suffice,
Cheapen it meanly to an obolus,[1]
Buy, and then count the coin left in your purse
For your debauch? —Measure obedience
145   By scantest powers of brethren whose frail flesh
Our Holy Church indulges?—Ask great Law,
The rightful Sovereign of the human soul,
For what it pardons, not what it commands?
O fallen knighthood, penitent of high vows,
150   Asking a charter to degrade itself!
Such poor apology of rules relaxed
Blunts not suspicion of that doubleness
Your enemies tax you with.

DON SILVA
             Oh, for the rest,
Conscience is harder than our enemies,
155   Knows more, accuses with more nicety,

---
[1] small coins.

Nor needs to question Rumour if we fall
Below the perfect model of our thought.
I fear no outward arbiter.—You smile?

PRIOR
Ay, at the contrast 'twixt your portraiture
160   And the true image of your conscience, shown
As now I see it in your acts. I see
A drunken sentinel who gives alarm
At his own shadow, but when scalers snatch
His weapon from his hand smiles idiot-like
165   At games he's dreaming of.

DON SILVA
           A parable!
The husk is rough—holds something bitter,
    doubtless.

PRIOR
Oh, the husk gapes with meaning over-ripe.
You boast a conscience that controls your deeds,
Watches your knightly armour, guards your rank
170   From stain of treachery—you, helpless slave,
Whose will lies nerveless in the clutch of lust—
Of blind mad passion—passion itself most helpless,
Storm-driven, like the monsters of the sea.
O famous conscience!

DON SILVA
          Pause there! Leave unsaid
175   Aught that will match that text. More were too
    much,
Even from holy lips. I own no love
But such as guards my honour, since it guards
Hers whom I love! I suffer no foul words
To stain the gift I lay before her feet;
180   And, being hers, my honour is more safe.

PRIOR
Versemakers' talk! fit for a world of rhymes,
Where facts are feigned to tickle idle ears,

Where good and evil play at tournament
And end in amity—a world of lies—
185 A carnival of words where every year
Stale falsehoods serve fresh men. Your honour safe?
What honour has a man with double bonds?
Honour is shifting as the shadows are
To souls that turn their passions into laws.
190 A Christian knight who weds an infidel—

DON SILVA (*fiercely*)
An infidel!

PRIOR
          May one day spurn the Cross,
And call that honour!—one day find his sword
Stained with his brother's blood, and call that honour!
Apostates'[1] honour?—harlots' chastity!
195 Renegades' faithfulness?—Iscariot's![2]

DON SILVA
Strong words and burning; but they scorch not me.
Fedalma is a daughter of the Church—
Has been baptised and nurtured in the faith.

PRIOR
Ay, as a thousand Jewesses, who yet
200 Are brides of Satan in a robe of flames.

DON SILVA
Fedalma is no Jewess, bears no marks
That tell of Hebrew blood.

PRIOR
          She bears the marks
Of races unbaptised, that never bowed
Before the holy signs, were never moved
205 By stirrings of the sacramental gifts.

_____
[1] renegade.
[2] the surname of Judas, the apostle who betrayed Christ: Luke 22:3.

DON SILVA (*scornfully*)
Holy accusers practise palmistry,
And, other witness lacking, read the skin.

PRIOR
I read a record deeper than the skin.
What! Shall the trick of nostrils and of lips
210 Descend through generations, and the soul
That moves within our frame like God in worlds—
Convulsing, urging, melting, withering—
Imprint no record, leave no documents,
Of her great history? Shall men bequeath
215 The fancies of their palate to their sons,
And shall the shudder of restraining awe,
The slow-wept tears of contrite memory,
Faith's prayerful labour, and the food divine
Of fasts ecstatic—shall these pass away
220 Like wind upon the waters, tracklessly?
Shall the mere curl of eyelashes remain,
And god-enshrining symbols leave no trace
Of tremors reverent?—That maiden's blood
Is as unchristian as the leopard's.

DON SILVA
          Say,
225 Unchristian as the Blessed Virgin's blood
Before the angel spoke the word, "All hail!"

PRIOR (*smiling bitterly*)
Said I not truly? See, your passion weaves
Already blasphemies!

DON SILVA
          'T is you provoke them.

PRIOR
I strive, as still the Holy Spirit strives,
230 To move the will perverse. But, failing this,
God commands other means to save our blood,
To save Castilian glory—nay, to save
The name of Christ from blot of traitorous deeds.

DON SILVA

Of traitorous deeds! Age, kindred, and your cowl,
235 Give an ignoble licence to your tongue.
As for your threats, fulfil them at your peril.
'T is you, not I, will gibbet our great name
To rot in infamy. If I am strong
In patience now, trust me, I can be strong
240 Then in defiance.

PRIOR

Miserable man!
Your strength will turn to anguish, like the strength
Of fallen angels. Can you change your blood?
You are a Christian, with the Christian awe
In every vein. A Spanish noble, born
245 To serve your people and your people's faith.
Strong, are you? Turn your back upon the Cross—
Its shadow is before you. Leave your place:
Quit the great ranks of knighthood: you will walk
For ever with a tortured double self,
250 A self that will be hungry while you feast,
Will blush with shame while you are glorified,
Will feel the ache and chill of desolation,
Even in the very bosom of your love.
Mate yourself with this woman, fit for what?
255 To make the sport of Moorish palaces,
A lewd Herodias[1]—

DON SILVA

Stop! no other man,
Priest though he were, had had his throat left free
For passage of those words. I would have clutched
His serpent's neck, and flung him out to hell!
260 A monk must needs defile the name of love:
He knows it but as tempting devils paint it.
You think to scare my love from its resolve
With arbitrary consequences, strained
By rancorous effort from the thinnest motes
265 Of possibility?—cite hideous lists

Of sins irrelevant, to frighten me
With bugbears' names, as women fright a child?
Poor pallid wisdom, taught by inference
From blood-drained life, where phantom terrors
        rule,
270 And all achievement is to leave undone!
Paint the day dark, make sunshine cold to me,
Abolish the earth's fairness, prove it all
A fiction of my eyes—then, after that,
Profane Fedalma.

PRIOR

O there is no need:
275 She has profaned herself. Go, raving man,
And see her dancing now. Go, see your bride
Flaunting her beauties grossly in the gaze
Of vulgar idlers—eking out the show
Made in the Plaça by a mountebank.[2]
280 I hinder you no farther.

DON SILVA

It is false!

PRIOR

Go, prove it false, then.

[Father Isidor
Drew on his cowl and turned away. The face
That flashed anathemas,[3] in swift eclipse
Seemed Silva's vanished confidence. In haste
285 He rushed unsignalled through the corridor
To where the Duchess once, Fedalma now,
Had residence retired from din of arms—
Knocked, opened, found all empty—said
With muffled voice, "Fedalma!"—called more loud,
290 More oft on Iñez, the old trusted nurse—
Then searched the terrace-garden, calling still,
But heard no answering sound, and saw no face

[1] Herod's second wife; she told her daughter Salome to ask Herod for the head of John the Baptist after she danced for him.

[2] a charlatan who sells quack medicines in public upon a platform.

[3] strong curses.

Save painted faces staring all unmoved
By agitated tones. He hurried back,
295 Giving half-conscious orders as he went
To page and usher, that they straight should seek
Lady Fedalma; then with stinging shame
Wished himself silent; reached again the room
Where still the Father's menace seemed to hang
300 Thickening the air; snatched cloak and plumèd hat,
And grasped, not knowing why, his poniard's[1] hilt;
Then checked himself and said:—]

                              If he spoke truth!
To know were wound enough—to see the truth
Were fire upon the wound. It must be false!
305 His hatred saw amiss, or snatched mistake
In other men's report. I am a fool!
But where can she be gone? gone secretly?
And in my absence? Oh, she meant no wrong!
I am a fool!—But where can she be gone?
310 With only Iñez? Oh, she meant no wrong!
I swear she never meant it. There's no wrong
But she would make it momentary right
By innocence in doing it.—
                              And yet,
What is our certainty? Why, knowing all
315 That is not secret. Mighty confidence!
One pulse of Time makes the base hollow—sends
The towering certainty we built so high
Toppling in fragments meaningless. What is—
What will be—must be—pooh! they wait the key
320 Of that which is not yet; all other keys
Are made of our conjectures, take their sense
From humours fooled by hope, or by despair.
Know what is good? O God, we know not yet
If bliss itself is not young misery
325 With fangs swift growing.—
                              But some outward harm,
May even now be hurting, grieving her.
Oh! I must search—face shame—if shame be there.

_____
[1] dagger.

Here, Perez! hasten to Don Alvar—tell him
Lady Fedalma must be sought—is lost—
330 Has met, I fear, some mischance. He must send
Towards divers points. I go myself to seek
First in the town.—

                    [As Perez oped the door,
Then moved aside for passage of the Duke,
Fedalma entered, cast away the cloud
335 Of serge and linen, and outbeaming bright,
Advanced a pace towards Silva—but then paused,
For he had started and retreated; she,
Quick and responsive as the subtle air
To change in him, divined that she must wait
340 Until they were alone: they stood and looked.
Within the Duke was struggling confluence
Of feelings manifold—pride, anger, dread,
Meeting in stormy rush with sense secure
That she was present, with the new-stilled thirst
345 Of gazing love, with trust inevitable
As in beneficent virtues of the light
And all earth's sweetness, that Fedalma's soul
Was free from blemishing purpose. Yet proud wrath
Leaped in dark flood above the purer stream
350 That strove to drown it: Anger seeks its prey—
Something to tear with sharp-edged tooth and claw,
Likes not to go off hungry, leaving Love
To feast on milk and honeycomb at will.
Silva's heart said, he must be happy soon,
355 She being there; but to be happy—first
He must be angry, having cause. Yet love
Shot like a stifled cry of tenderness
All through the harshness he would fain have given
To the dear word,]

DON SILVA
Fedalma!

FEDALMA
                              O my lord!
360 You are come back, and I was wandering!

DON SILVA (*coldly, but with suppressed agitation*)
You meant I should be ignorant.

FEDALMA
Oh no,
I should have told you after—not before,
Lest you should hinder me.

DON SILVA
Then my known wish
Can make no hindrance?

FEDALMA (*archly*)
That depends
365 On what the wish may be. You wished me once
Not to uncage the birds. I meant to obey:
But in a moment something—something stronger,
Forced me to let them out. It did no harm.
They all came back again—the silly birds!
370 I told you, after.

DON SILVA (*with haughty coldness*)
Will you tell me now
What was the prompting stronger than my wish
That made you wander?

FEDALMA (*advancing a step towards him,
with a sudden look of anxiety*)
Are you angry?

DON SILVA (*smiling bitterly*)
Angry?
A man deep-wounded may feel too much pain
To feel much anger.

FEDALMA (*still more anxiously*)
You—deep wounded?

DON SILVA
Yes!
375 Have I not made your place and dignity

The very heart of my ambition? You—
No enemy could do it—you alone
Can strike it mortally.

FEDALMA
Nay, Silva, nay.
Has some one told you false? I only went
380 To see the world with Iñez—see the town,
The people, everything. It was no harm.
I did not mean to dance: it happened so
At last—

DON SILVA
O God, it's true then!—true that you,
A maiden nurtured as rare flowers are,
385 The very air of heaven sifted fine
Lest any mote should mar your purity,
Have flung yourself out on the dusty way
For common eyes to see your beauty soiled!
You own it true—you danced upon the Plaça?

FEDALMA (*proudly*)
390 Yes, it is true. I was not wrong to dance.
The air was filled with music, with a song
That seemed the voice of the sweet eventide—
The glowing light entering through eye and ear—
That seemed our love—mine, yours—they are but
one—
395 Trembling through all my limbs, as fervent words
Tremble within my soul and must be spoken.
And all the people felt a common joy
And shouted for the dance. A brightness soft
As of the angels moving down to see
400 Illumined the broad space. The joy, the life
Around, within me, were one heaven: I longed
To blend them visibly: I longed to dance
Before the people—be as mounting flame
To all that burned within them! Nay, I danced;
405 There was no longing: I but did the deed
Being moved to do it.

(*As* FEDALMA *speaks, she and* DON SILVA *are
gradually drawn nearer to each other.*)
                                    Oh! I seemed new-waked
To life in unison with a multitude—
Feeling my soul upborne by all their souls,
Floating within their gladness! Soon I lost
410 All sense of separateness: Fedalma died
As a star dies, and melts into the light.
I was not, but joy was, and love and triumph
Nay, my dear lord, I never could do aught
But I must feel you present. And once done,
415 Why, you must love it better than your wish.
I pray you, say so—say, it was not wrong!
        (*While* FEDALMA *has been making this last
        appeal, they have gradually come close together,
        and at last embrace.*)

              DON SILVA (*holding her hands*)
Dangerous rebel! if the world without
Were pure as that within—but 't is a book
Wherein you only read the poesy
420 And miss all wicked meanings. Hence the need
For trust—obedience—call it what you will—
Towards him whose life will be your guard—
        towards me
Who now am soon to be your husband.

                    FEDALMA
                                    Yes!
That very thing that when I am your wife
425 I shall be something different,—shall be
I know not what, a Duchess with new thoughts—
For nobles never think like common men,
Nor wives like maidens (Oh, you wot not yet
How much I note, with all my ignorance)—
430 That very thing has made me more resolve
To have my will before I am your wife.
How can the Duchess ever satisfy
Fedalma's unwed eyes? and so to-day
I scolded Iñez till she cried and went.

                    DON SILVA
435 It was a guilty weakness: she knows well
That since you pleaded to be left more free
From tedious tendance and control of dames
Whose rank matched better with your destiny,
Her charge—my trust—was weightier.

                    FEDALMA
                                    Nay, my lord,
440 You must not blame her, dear old nurse. She cried.
Why, you would have consented too, at last.
I said such things! I was resolved to go,
And see the streets, the shops, the men at work,
The women, little children—everything,
445 Just as it is when nobody looks on.
And I have done it! We were out four hours.
I feel so wise.

                    DON SILVA
                    Had you but seen the town,
You innocent naughtiness, not shown yourself—
Shown yourself dancing—you bewilder me!—
450 Frustrate my judgment with strange negatives
That seem like poverty, and yet are wealth
In precious womanliness, beyond the dower
Of other women: wealth in virgin gold,
Outweighing all their petty currency.
455 You daring modesty! You shrink no more
From gazing men than from the gazing flowers
That, dreaming sunshine, open as you pass.

                    FEDALMA
No, I should like the world to look at me
With eyes of love that make a second day.
460 I think your eyes would keep the life in me
Though I had nought to feed on else. Their blue
Is better than the heavens'—holds more love
For me, Fedalma—is a little heaven
For this one little world that looks up now.

DON SILVA

465 O precious little world! you make the heaven
As the earth makes the sky. But, dear, all eyes,
Though looking even on you, have not a glance
That cherishes—

FEDALMA

Ah no, I meant to tell you—
Tell how my dancing ended with a pang.
470 There came a man, one among many more,
But *he* came first, with iron in his limbs.
And when the bell tolled, and the people prayed,
And I stood pausing—then he looked at me.
O Silva, such a man! I thought he rose
475 From the dark place of long-imprisoned souls,
To say that Christ had never come to them.
It was a look to shame a seraph's joy,
And make him sad in heaven. It found me there—
Seemed to have travelled far to find me there
480 And grasp me—claim this festal life of mine
As heritage of sorrow, chill my blood
With the cold iron of some unknown bonds.
The gladness hurrying full within my veins
Was sudden frozen, and I danced no more.
485 But seeing you let loose the stream of joy,
Mingling the present with the sweetest past.
Yet, Silva, still I see him. Who is he?
Who are those prisoners with him? Are they
        Moors?

DON SILVA

No, they are Gypsies, strong and cunning knaves,
490 A double gain to us by the Moors' loss:
The man you mean—their chief—is an ally
The infidel will miss. His look might chase
A herd of monks, and make them fly more swift
Than from St. Jerome's lion.[1] Such vague fear,
495 Such bird-like tremors when that savage glance

Turned full upon you in your height of joy
Was natural, was not worth emphasis.
Forget it, dear. This hour is worth whole days
When we are sundered. Danger urges us
500 To quick resolve.

FEDALMA

What danger? what resolve?
I never felt chill shadow in my heart
Until this sunset.

DON SILVA

A dark enmity
Plots how to sever us. And our defence
Is speedy marriage, secretly achieved,
505 Then publicly declared. Beseech you, dear,
Grant me this confidence; do my will in this,
Trusting the reasons why I overset
All my own airy building raised so high
Of bridal honours, marking when you step
510 From off your maiden throne to come to me
And bear the yoke of love. There is great need.
I hastened home, carrying this prayer to you
Within my heart. The bishop is my friend,
Furthers our marriage, holds in enmity—
515 Some whom we love not and who love not us.
By this night's moon our priest will be despatched
From Jaën.[2] I shall march an escort strong
To meet him. Ere a second sun from this
Has risen—you consenting—we may wed.

FEDALMA

520 None knowing that we wed?

DON SILVA

Beforehand none
Save Iñez and Don Alvar. But the vows
Once safely binding us, my household all
Shall know you as their Duchess. No man then

---

[1] A monk and scholar (340–420), who led the life of a hermit in Chalcis near Antioch, Jerome is often depicted with a lion at his feet according to the legend that recounts how he removed a thorn from a lion's paw.

[2] a southern Spanish town.

Can aim a blow at you but through my breast,
525 And what stains you must stain our ancient name;
If any hate you I will take his hate,
And wear it as a glove upon my helm;
Nay, God himself will never have the power
To strike you solely and leave me unhurt,
530 He having made us one. Now put the seal
Of your dear lips on that.

FEDALMA

A solemn kiss?—
Such as I gave you when you came that day
From Córdova,[1] when first we said we loved?
When you had left the ladies of the Court
535 For thirst to see me; and you told me so,
And then I seemed to know why I had lived.
I never knew before. A kiss like that?

DON SILVA

Yes, yes, you face divine! When was our kiss
Like any other?

FEDALMA

Nay, I cannot tell
540 What other kisses are. But that one kiss
Remains upon my lips. The angels, spirits,
Creatures with finer sense, may see it there.
And now another kiss that will not die,
Saying, To-morrow I shall be your wife!
(*They kiss, and pause a moment, looking earnestly
in each other's eyes. Then* FEDALMA, *breaking away
from* DON SILVA, *stands at a little distance from
him with a look of roguish delight.*)
545 Now I am glad I saw the town to-day
Before I am a Duchess—glad I gave
This poor Fedalma all her wish. For once,
Long years ago, I cried when Iñez said,
"You are no more a little girl"; I grieved
550 To part for ever from that little girl

And all her happy world so near the ground.
It must be sad to outlive aught we love.
So I shall grieve a little for these days
Of poor unwed Fedalma. Oh, they are sweet,
555 And none will come just like them. Perhaps the wind
Wails so in winter for the summers dead,
And all sad sounds are nature's funeral cries
For what has been and is not. Are they, Silva?
(*She comes nearer to him again, and lays her hand
on his arm, looking up at him with melancholy.*)

DON SILVA

Why, dearest, you began in merriment,
560 And end as sadly as a widowed bird.
Some touch mysterious has new-tuned your soul
To melancholy sequence. You soared high
In that wild flight of rapture when you danced,
And now you droop. 'T is arbitrary grief,
565 Surfeit of happiness, that mourns for loss
Of unwed love, which does but die like seed
For fuller harvest of our tenderness.
We in our wedded life shall know no loss.
We shall new-date our years. What went before
570 Will be the time of promise, shadows, dreams;
But this, full revelation of great love.
For rivers blent take in a broader heaven,
And we shall blend our souls. Away with grief!

*   *   *   *

A LARGE CHAMBER

*Richly furnished, opening on a terrace-garden, the
trees visible through the window in faint
moonlight. Flowers hanging about the window, lit
up by the tapers. The casket of jewels open on a
table. The gold necklace lying near.* FEDALMA,
*splendidly dressed and adorned with pearls and
rubies, is walking up and down.*

---

[1] Córdoba, a city in southern Spain.

FEDALMA

So soft a night was never made for sleep,
But for the waking of the finer sense
To every murmuring and gentle sound,
To subtlest odours, pulses, visitings
5   That touch our frames with wings too delicate
To be discerned amid the blare of day.
    (*She pauses near the window to gather some
    jasmine: then walks again.*)
Surely these flowers keep happy watch—their
    breath
Is their fond memory of the loving light.
I often rue the hours I lose in sleep:
10 It is a bliss too brief, only to see
This glorious world, to hear the voice of love,
To feel the touch, the breath of tenderness,
And then to rest as from a spectacle.
I need the curtained stillness of the night
15 To live through all my happy hours again
With more selection—cull them quite away
From blemished moments. Then in loneliness
The face that bent before me in the day
Rises in its own light, more vivid seems
20 Painted upon the dark, and ceaseless glows
With sweet solemnity of gazing love,
Till like the heavenly blue it seems to grow
Nearer, more kindred, and more cherishing,
Mingling with all my being. Then the words,
25 The tender low-toned words come back again,
With repetition welcome as the chime
Of softly hurrying brooks—"My only love—
My love while life shall last—my own Fedalma!"
Oh it is mine—the joy that once has been!
30 Poor eager hope is but a stammerer,
Must listen dumbly to great memory,
Who makes our bliss the sweeter by her telling.
    (*She pauses a moment musingly.*)
But that dumb hope is still a sleeping guard
Whose quiet rhythmic breath saves me from dread
35 In this fair paradise. For if the earth
Broke off with flower-fringed edge, visibly sheer,

Leaving no footing for my forward step
But empty blackness—
                    Nay, there is no fear—
They will renew themselves, day and my joy,
40 And all that past which is securely mine,
Will be the hidden root that nourishes
Our still unfolding, ever-ripening love!
    (*While she is uttering the last words, a little bird
    falls softly on the floor behind her; she hears the
    light sound of its fall, and turns round.*)
Did something enter?—
                    Yes, this little bird—
    (*She lifts it.*)
Dead and yet warm; 't was seeking sanctuary,
45 And died, perhaps of fright, at the altar foot.
Stay, there is something tied beneath the wing!
A strip of linen, streaked with blood—what blood?
The streaks are written words—are sent to me—
O God, are sent to me! *Dear child, Fedalma,*
50 *Be brave, give no alarm—your Father comes!*
    (*She lets the bird fall again.*)
My Father—comes—my Father—
    (*She turns in quivering expectation toward the
    window. There is perfect stillness a few moments
    until* ZARCA *appears at the window. He enters
    quickly and noiselessly; then stands still at his full
    height, and at a distance from* FEDALMA.)

FEDALMA (*in a low distinct tone of terror*)
                    It is he!
I said his fate had laid its hold on mine.

ZARCA (*advancing a step or two*)
You know, then, who I am?

FEDALMA
            The prisoner—
He whom I saw in fetters—and this necklace—

ZARCA

55 Was played with by your fingers when it hung
About my neck, full fifteen years ago.

FEDALMA (*looking at the necklace and handling it,*
then speaking, as if unconsciously)
Full fifteen years ago!

ZARCA
The very day
I lost you, when you wore a tiny gown
Of scarlet cloth with golden broidery:
60 'T was clasped in front by coins—two golden coins.
The one upon the left was split in two
Across the king's head, right from brow to nape,
A dent i' the middle nicking in the cheek.
You see I know the little gown by heart.

FEDALMA (*growing paler and more tremulous*)
65 Yes. It is true—I have the gown—the clasps—
The braid—sore tarnished:—it is long ago!

ZARCA
But yesterday to me; for till to-day
I saw you always as that little child.
And when they took my necklace from me, still
70 Your fingers played about it on my neck,
And still those buds of fingers on your feet
Caught in its meshes as you seemed to climb
Up to my shoulder. You were not stolen all.
You had a double life fed from my heart.—
(FEDALMA, *letting fall the necklace, makes an*
impulsive movement towards him, with
out-stretched hands.)
75 The Gypsy father loves his children well.

FEDALMA (*shrinking, trembling, and letting*
fall her hands)
How came it that you sought me—no—I mean
How came it that you knew me—that you lost me?

ZARCA
Poor child! I see—your father and his rags
Are welcome as the piercing wintry wind
80 Within this silken chamber. It is well.
I would not have a child who stooped to feign,
And aped a sudden love. Better, true hate.

FEDALMA (*raising her eyes towards him, with a flash*
of admiration, and looking at him fixedly)
Father, how is it that we lost each other?

ZARCA
I lost you as a man may lose a gem
85 Wherein he has compressed his total wealth,
Or the right hand whose cunning makes him great:
I lost you by a trivial accident.
Marauding Spaniards, sweeping like a storm
Over a spot within the Moorish bounds,
90 Near where our camp lay, doubtless snatched you
up,
When Zind, your nurse, as she confessed, was urged
By burning thirst to wander toward the stream,
And leave you on the sand some paces off
Playing with pebbles, while she dog-like lapped.
95 'T was so I lost you—never saw you more
Until to-day I saw you dancing! Saw
The daughter of the Zíncalo make sport
For those who spit upon her people's name.

FEDALMA (*vehemently*)
It was not sport. What if the world looked on?—
95 I danced for joy—for love of all the world.
But when you looked at me my joy was stabbed—
Stabbed with your pain. I wondered—now I
know—
It was my father's pain.
(*She pauses a moment with eyes bent down-ward,*
during which ZARCA *examines her face. Then she*
says quickly,)
How were you sure
At once I was your child?

ZARCA

          I had witness strong

100 As any Cadi[1] needs, before I saw you!
I fitted all my memories with the chat
Of one named Juan—one whose rapid talk
Showers like the blossoms from a light-twigged
    shrub,
If you but cough beside it. I learned all
105 The story of your Spanish nurture—all
The promise of your fortune. When at last
I fronted you, my little maid full-grown,
Belief was turned to vision: then I saw
That she whom Spaniards called the bright
    Fedalma—
110 The little red-frocked foundling three years old—
Grown to such perfection the Spanish Duke
Had wooed her for his Duchess—was the child,
Sole offspring of my flesh, that Lambra bore
One hour before the Christian, hunting us,
115 Hurried her on to death. Therefore I sought—
Therefore I come to claim you—claim my child,
Not from the Spaniard, not from him who robbed,
But from herself.
    (FEDALMA *has gradually approached close to*
    ZARCA, *and with a low sob sinks on her knees*
    before him. He stoops to kiss her brow, and lays his
    hands on her head.)

ZARCA (*with solemn tenderness*)
Then my child owns her father?

FEDALMA

             Father! yes.
120 I will eat dust before I will deny
The flesh I spring from.

ZARCA

         There my daughter spoke.
Away then with these rubies!

---

[1] a minor Moslem magistrate or judge.

(*He seizes the circlet of rubies and flings it on the*
ground. FEDALMA, *starting from the ground*
with strong emotion, shrinks backward.)
         Such a crown
Is infamy around a Zíncala's brow.
It is her people's blood, decking her shame.

FEDALMA (*after a moment, slowly and distinctly,*
    as if accepting a doom)
125 Then—I was born—a Zíncala?

ZARCA

             Of a blood
Unmixed as virgin wine-juice.

FEDALMA

            Of a race
More outcast and despised than Moor or Jew?

ZARCA

Yes: wanderers whom no God took knowledge of
To give them laws, to fight for them, or blight
130 Another race to make them ampler room;
Who have no Whence or Whither in their souls,
No dimmest lore of glorious ancestors
To make a common hearth for piety.

FEDALMA

A race that lives on prey as foxes do
135 With stealthy, petty rapine: so despised,
It is not persecuted, only spurned,
Crushed underfoot, warred on by chance like rats,
Or swarming flies, or reptiles of the sea
Dragged in the net unsought, and flung far off
140 To perish as they may?

ZARCA

         You paint us well.
So abject are the men whose blood we share:
Untutored, unbefriended, unendowed;
No favourites of heaven or of men.

Therefore I cling to them! Therefore no lure
145 Shall draw me to disown them, or forsake
The meagre wandering herd that lows for help
And needs me for its guide, to seek my pasture
Among the well-fed beeves that graze at will.
Because our race has no great memories,
150 I will so live, it shall remember me
For deeds of such divine beneficence
As rivers have, that teach men what is good
By blessing them. I have been schooled—have
    caught
Lore from the Hebrew, deftness from the Moor—
155 Know the rich heritage, the milder life,
Of nations fathered by a mighty Past;
But were our race accursed (as they who make
Good luck a god count all unlucky men)
I would espouse their curse sooner than take
160 My gifts from brethren naked of all good,
And lend them to the rich for usury.
        (FEDALMA *again advances, and putting forth her
        right hand grasps* ZARCA'S *left. He places his other
        hand on her shoulder. They stand so, looking at
        each other.*)

                    ZARCA
And you, my child? are you of the other mind,
Choosing forgetfulness, hating the truth
That says you are akin to needy men?—
165 Wishing your father were some Christian Duke,
Who could hang Gypsies when their task was done,
While you, his daughter, were not bound to care?

        FEDALMA (*in a troubled eager voice*)
No, I should always care—I cared for you—
For all, before I dreamed—

                    ZARCA
                        Before you dreamed
170 That you were born a Zíncala—your flesh
Stamped with your people's faith.

        FEDALMA (*bitterly*)
                    The Gypsies' faith?
Men say they have none.

                    ZARCA
                    Oh, it is a faith
Taught by no priest, but by their beating hearts:
Faith to each other: the fidelity
175 Of fellow-wanderers in a desert place
Who share the same dire thirst, and therefore share
The scanty water: the fidelity
Of men whose pulses leap with kindred fire,
Who in the flash of eyes, the clasp of hands,
180 The speech that even in lying tells the truth
Of heritage inevitable as birth,
Nay, in the silent bodily presence feel
The mystic stirring of a common life
Which makes the many one: fidelity
185 To the consecrating oath our sponsor Fate
Made through our infant breath when we were born
The fellow-heirs of that small island, Life,
Where we must dig and sow and reap with brothers.
Fear thou that oath, my daughter—nay, not fear,
190 But love it; for the sanctity of oaths
Lies not in lightning that avenges them,
But in the injury wrought by broken bonds
And in the garnered good of human trust.
And you have sworn—even with your infant breath
195 You too were pledged—

        FEDALMA (*letting go* ZARCA'S *hand, and sinking back-
            ward on her knees, with bent head, as if
            before some impending crushing weight*)
                    To what? what have I sworn?

                    ZARCA
To take the heirship of the Gypsy's child:
The child of him who, being chief, will be
The saviour of his tribe, or if he fail
Will choose to fail rather than basely win
200 The prize of renegades. Nay, will not choose—

Is there a choice for strong souls to be weak?
For men erect to crawl like hissing snakes?
I choose not—I *am* Zarca. Let him choose
Who halts and wavers, having appetite
205 To feed on garbage. You, my child—are you
Halting and wavering?

FEDALMA (*raising her head*)
                Say what is my task.

ZARCA
To be the angel of a homeless tribe:
To help me bless a race taught by no prophet
And make their name, now but a badge of scorn,
210 A glorious banner floating in their midst,
Stirring the air they breathe with impulses
Of generous pride, exalting fellowship
Until it soars to magnanimity.
I'll guide my brethren forth to their new land,
215 Where they shall plant and sow and reap their own,
Serving each other's needs, and so be spurred
To skill in all the arts that succour life;
Where we may kindle our first altar-fire
From settled hearths, and call our Holy Place
220 The hearth that binds us in one family.
That land awaits them: they await their chief—
Me who am prisoned. All depends on you.

FEDALMA (*rising to her full height, and looking
solemnly at* ZARCA)
Father, your child is ready! She will not
Forsake her kindred: she will brave all scorn
225 Sooner than scorn herself. Let Spaniards all,
Christians, Jews, Moors, shoot out the lip and say,
"Lo, the first hero in a tribe of thieves."
Is it not written so of them? They, too,
Were slaves, lost, wandering, sunk beneath a curse,
230 Till Moses, Christ, and Mahomet[1] were born,
Till beings lonely in their greatness lived,

And lived to save their people. Father, listen.
The Duke to-morrow weds me secretly:
But straight he will present me as his wife
235 To all his household, cavaliers and dames
And noble pages. Then I will declare
Before them all, "I am his daughter, his,
The Gypsy's, owner of this golden badge."
Then I shall win your freedom; then the Duke—
240 Why, he will be your son!—will send you forth
With aid and honours. Then, before all eyes
I'll clasp this badge on you, and lift my brow
For you to kiss it, saying by that sign,
"I glory in my father." This, to-morrow.

ZARCA
245 A woman's dream—who thinks by smiling well
To ripen figs in frost. What! marry first,
And then proclaim your birth? Enslave yourself
To use your freedom? Share another's name,
Then treat it as you will? How will that tune
250 Ring in your bridegroom's ears—that sudden song
Of triumph in your Gypsy father?

FEDELMA (*discouraged*)
                      Nay,
I meant not so. We marry hastily—
Yet there is time—there will be:—in less space
Than he can take to look at me, I'll speak
255 And tell him all. Oh, I am not afraid!
His love for me is stronger than all hate;
Nay, stronger than my love, which cannot sway
Demons that haunt me—tempt me to rebel.
Were he Fedalma and I Silva, he
260 Could love confession, prayers, and tonsured monks
If my soul craved them. He will never hate
The race that bore him what he loves the most.
I shall but do more strongly what I will,
Having his will to help me. And to-morrow,
265 Father, as surely as this heart shall beat,
You—every Gypsy chained, shall be set free.

---

[1] Muhammad.

ZARCA (*coming nearer to her, and laying
his hand on her shoulder*)
Too late, too poor a service that, my child!
Not so the woman who would save her tribe
Must help its heroes—not by wordy breath,
270　By easy prayers strong in a lover's ear,
By showering wreaths and sweets and wafted kisses,
And then, when all the smiling work is done,
Turning to rest upon her down again,
And whisper languid pity for her race
275　Upon the bosom of her alien spouse.
Not to such petty mercies as can fall
'Twixt stitch and stitch of silken broidery,
Such miracles of mitred[1] saints who pause
Beneath their gilded canopy to heal
280　A man sun-stricken: not to such trim merit
As soils its dainty shoes for charity
And simpers meekly at the pious stain,
But never trod with naked bleeding feet
Where no man praised it, and where no Church
　　blessed:
285　Not to such almsdeeds fit for holidays
Were you, my daughter, consecrated—bound
By laws that, breaking, you will dip your bread
In murdered brother's blood and call it sweet—
When you were born beneath the dark man's tent,
290　And lifted up in sight of all your tribe,
Who greeted you with shouts of loyal joy,
Sole offspring of the chief in whom they trust
As in the oft-tried never-failing flint
They strike their fire from. Other work is yours.

FEDALMA
295　What work?—what is it that you ask of me?

ZARCA
A work as pregnant as the act of men
Who set their ships aflame and spring to land,
A fatal deed—

FEDALMA
Stay! never utter it!
If it can part my lot from his whose love
300　Has chosen me. Talk not of oaths, of birth,
Of men as numerous as the dim white stars—
As cold and distant, too, for my heart's pulse.
No ills on earth, though you should count them up
With grains to make a mountain, can outweigh
305　For me, his ill who is my supreme love.
All sorrows else are but imagined flames,
Making me shudder at an unfelt smart;
But his imagined sorrow is a fire
That scorches me.

ZARCA
I know, I know it well—
310　The first young passionate wail of spirits called
To some great destiny. In vain, my daughter!
Lay the young eagle in what nest you will,
The cry and swoop of eagles overhead
Vibrate prophetic in its kindred frame,
315　And make it spread its wings and poise itself
For the eagle's flight. Hear what you have to do.
　　(FEDALMA *stands half averted, as if she dreaded
　　the effect of his looks and words.*)
My comrades even now file off their chains
In a low turret by the battlements,
Where we were locked with slight and sleepy
　　guard—
320　We who had files hid in our shaggy hair,
And possible ropes that waited but our will
In half our garments. Oh, the Moorish blood
Runs thick and warm to us, though thinned by
　　chrism.[2]
I found a friend among our gaolers—one
325　Who loves the Gypsy as the Moor's ally.
I know the secrets of this fortress. Listen.
Hard by yon terrace is a narrow stair,
Cut in the living rock, and at one point

---

[1] A mitre is a tall, deeply cleft headdress worn by bishops and abbots as a symbol of office.

[2] consecrated oil used in baptism.

In its slow straggling course it branches off
330 Towards a low wooden door, that art has bossed
To such unevenness, it seems one piece
With the rough-hewn rock. Open that door, it leads
Through a broad passage burrowed under-ground
A good half-mile out to the open plain:
335 Made for escape, in dire extremity
From siege of burning, of the house's wealth
In women or in gold. To find that door
Needs one who knows the number of the steps
Just to the turning-point; to open it,
340 Needs one who knows the secret of the bolt.
You have that secret: you will ope that door,
And fly with us.

FEDALMA (*receding a little, and gathering herself
up in an attitude of resolve opposite to* ZARCA)
No, I will never fly!
Never forsake that chief half of my soul
Where lies my love. I swear to set you free.
345 Ask for no more; it is not possible.
Father, my soul is not too base to ring
At touch of your great thoughts; nay, in my blood
There streams the sense unspeakable of kind,
As leopard feels at ease with leopard. But—
350 Look at these hands! You say when they were little
They played about the gold upon your neck.
I do believe it, for their tiny pulse
Made record of it in the inmost coil
Of growing memory. But see them now!
355 Oh, they have made fresh record; twined themselves
With other throbbing hands whose pulses feed
Not memories only but a blended life—
Life that will bleed to death if it be severed.
Have pity on me, father! Wait the morning;
360 Say you will wait the morning. I will win
Your freedom openly: you shall go forth
With aid and honours. Silva will deny
Nought to my asking—

ZARCA (*with contemptuous decision*)
Till you ask him aught
Wherein he is powerless. Soldiers even now
365 Murmur against him that he risks the town,
And forfeits all the prizes of a foray,
To get his bridal pleasure with a bride
Too low for him. They'll murmur more and louder
If captives of our pith and sinew, fit
370 For all the work the Spaniard hates, are freed—
Now, too, when Spanish hands are scanty. What,
Turn Gypsies loose instead of hanging them!
'T is flat against the edict. Nay, perchance
Murmurs aloud may turn to silent threats
375 Of some well-sharpened dagger; for your Duke
Has to his heir a pious cousin, who deems
The Cross were better served if he were Duke.
Such good you'll work your lover by your prayers.

FEDALMA
Then, I will free you now! You shall be safe,
380 Nor he be blamed, save for his love to me.
I will declare what I have done: the deed
May put our marriage off—

ZARCA
Ay, till the time
When you shall be a queen in Africa,
And he be prince enough to sue for you.
385 You cannot free us and come back to him.

FEDALMA
And why?

ZARCA
I would compel you to go forth.

FEDALMA
You tell me that?

ZARCA
Yes, for I'd have you choose;
Though, being of the blood you are—my blood—
You have no right to choose.

FEDALMA

         I only owe
390 A daughter's debt; I was not born a slave.

ZARCA

No, not a slave; but you were born to reign,
'T is a compulsion of a higher sort,
Whose fetters are the net invisible
That holds all life together. Royal deeds
395 May make long destinies for multitudes,
And you are called to do them. You belong
Not to the petty round of circumstance
That makes a woman's lot, but to your tribe,
Who trust in me and in my blood with trust
400 That men call blind; but it is only blind
As unyeaned reason is, that grows and stirs
Within the womb of superstition.

FEDALMA

         No!
I belong to him who loves me—whom I love—
Who chose me—whom I chose—to whom I pledged
405 A woman's truth. And that is nature too,
Issuing a fresher law than laws of birth.

ZARCA

Unmake yourself, then, from a Zíncala—
Unmake yourself from being child of mine!
Take holy water, cross your dark skin white;
410 Round your proud eyes to foolish kitten looks;
Walk mincingly, and smirk, and twitch your robe:
Unmake yourself—doff all the eagle plumes
And be a parrot, chained to a ring that slips
Upon a Spaniard's thumb, at will of his
415 That you should prattle o'er his words again!
Get a small heart that flutters at the smiles
Of that plump penitent, that greedy saint
Who breaks all treaties in the name of God,
Saves souls by confiscation, sends to heaven
420 The altar-fumes of burning heretics,

And chaffers with the Levite[1] for the gold:
Holds Gypsies beasts unfit for sacrifice,
So sweeps them out like worms alive or dead.
Go, trail your gold and velvet in her court!—
425 A conscious Zíncala, smile at your rare luck,
While half your brethren—

FEDALMA

         I am not so vile!
It is not to such mockeries that I cling,
Not to the flaring tow of gala-lights;
It is to him—my love—the face of day.

ZARCA

430 What, will you part him from the air he breathes,
Never inhale with him although you kiss him?
Will you adopt a soul without its thoughts,
Or grasp a life apart from flesh and blood?
Till then you cannot wed a Spanish Duke
435 And not wed shame at mention of your race,
And not wed hardness to their miseries—
Nay, not wed murder. Would you save my life
Yet stab my purpose? maim my every limb,
Put out my eyes, and turn me loose to feed?
440 Is that salvation? rather drink my blood.
That child of mine who weds my enemy—
Adores a God who took no heed of Gypsies—
Forsakes her people, leaves their poverty
To join the luckier crowd that mocks their woes—
445 That child of mine is doubly murderess,
Murdering her father's hope, her people's trust.
Such draughts are mingled in your cup of love!
And when you have become a thing so poor,
Your life is all a fashion without law
450 Save frail conjecture of a changing wish,
Your worshipped sun, your smiling face of day,
Will turn to cloudiness, and you will shiver
In your thin finery of vain desire.

----

[1] any member of the Levi tribe, who were the chosen assistants of Jewish priests.

Men call his passion madness; and he, too,
455 May learn to think it madness: 't is a thought
Of ducal sanity.

FEDALMA

No, he is true!
And if I part from him I part from joy.
Oh, it was morning with us—I seemed young.
But now I know I am an aged sorrow—
460 My people's sorrow. Father, since I am yours—
Since I must walk an unslain sacrifice,
Carrying the knife within me, quivering—
Put cords upon me, drag me to the doom
My birth has laid upon me. See, I kneel:
465 I cannot will to go.

ZARCA

Will then to stay!
Say you will take your better, painted such
By blind desire, and choose the hideous worse
For thousands who were happier but for you.
My thirty followers are assembled now
470 Without this terrace: I your father wait
That you may lead us forth to liberty—
Restore me to my tribe—five hundred men
Whom I alone can save, alone can rule,
And plant them as a mighty nation's seed.
475 Why, vagabonds who clustered round one man,
Their voice of God, their prophet and their king,
Twice grew to empire on the teeming shores
Of Africa, and sent new royalties
To feed afresh the Arab sway in Spain.
480 My vagabonds are a seed more generous,
Quick as the serpent, loving as the hound,
And beautiful as disinherited gods.
They have a promised land beyond the sea:
There I may lead them, raise my standard, call
485 The wandering Zíncali to that new home,
And make a nation—bring light, order, law,
Instead of chaos. You, my only heir,
Are called to reign for me when I am gone.

Now choose your deed: to save or to destroy.
490 You, a born Zíncala, you, fortunate
Above your fellows—you who hold a curse
Or blessing in the hollow of your hand—
Say you will loose that hand from fellowship,
Let go the rescuing rope, hurl all the tribes,
495 Children and countless beings yet to come,
Down from the upward path of light and joy,
Back to the dark and marshy wilderness
Where life is nought but blind tenacity
Of that which is. Say you will curse your race!

FEDALMA (*rising and stretching out her arms*
in deprecation)

500 No, no—I will not say it—I will go!
Father, I choose! I will not take a heaven
Haunted by shrieks of far-off misery.
This deed and I have ripened with the hours:
It is a part of me—a wakened thought
505 That, rising like a giant, masters me,
And grows into a doom. O mother life,
That seemed to nourish me so tenderly,
Even in the womb you vowed me to the fire,
Hung on my soul the burden of men's hopes,
510 And pledged me to redeem!—I'll pay the debt.
You gave me strength that I should pour it all
Into this anguish. I can never shrink
Back into bliss—my heart has grown too big
With things that might be. Father, I will go.
515 I will strip off these gems. Some happier bride
Shall wear them, since Fedalma would be dowered
With nought but curses, dowered with misery
Of men—of women, who have hearts to bleed
As hers is bleeding.
(*She sinks on a seat, and begins to take off her jewels.*)
Now, good gems, we part.
520 Speak of me always tenderly to Silva.
(*She pauses, turning to* ZARCA.)
O father, will the women of our tribe
Suffer as I do, in the years to come

When you have made them great in Africa?
Redeemed from ignorant ills only to feel
525 A conscious woe? Then—is it worth the pains?
Were it not better when we reach that shore
To raise a funeral-pile and perish all,
So closing up a myriad avenues
To misery yet unwrought? My soul is faint—
530 Will these sharp pangs buy any certain good?

ZARCA

Nay, never falter: no great deed is done
By falterers who ask for certainty.
No good is certain, but the steadfast mind,
The undivided will to seek the good:
535 'T is that compels the elements, and wrings
A human music from the indifferent air.
The greatest gift the hero leaves his race
Is to have been a hero. Say we fail!—
We feed the high tradition of the world,
540 And leave our spirit in our children's breasts.

FEDALMA (*unclasping her jewelled belt,
and throwing it down*)

Yes, say that we shall fail! I will not count
On aught but being faithful. I will take
This yearning self of mine and strangle it.
I will not be half-hearted: never yet
545 Fedalma did aught with a wavering soul.
Die, my young joy—die, all my hungry hopes—
The milk you cry for from the breast of life
Is thick with curses. Oh, all fatness here
Snatches its meat from leanness—feeds on graves.
550 I will seek nothing but to shun base joy.
The saints were cowards who stood by to see
Christ crucified: they should have flung themselves
Upon the Roman spears, and died in vain—
The grandest death, to die in vain—for love
555 Greater than sways the forces of the world!
That death shall be my bridegroom. I will wed
The curse that blights my people. Father, come!

ZARCA

No curse has fallen on us till we cease
To help each other. You, if you are false
560 To that first fellowship, lay on the curse.
But write now to the Spaniard: briefly say
That I, your father, came; that you obeyed
The fate which made you Zíncala, as his fate
Made him a Spanish duke and Christian knight.
565 He must not think—

FEDALMA

                      Yes, I will write, but he—
Oh, he would know it—he would never think
The chain that dragged me from him could be aught
But scorching iron entering in my soul.
                      (*She writes.*)
Silva, sole love—he came—my father came.
570 *I am the daughter of the Gypsy chief*
Who means to be the Saviour of our tribe.
He calls on me to live for his great end.
To live? nay, die for it. Fedalma dies
In leaving Silva: all that lives henceforth
575 *Is the poor Zíncala.*   (*She rises.*)
                      Father, now I go
To wed my people's lot.

ZARCA

                      To wed a crown.
Our people's lowly lot we will make royal—
Give it a country, homes, and monuments
Held sacred through the lofty memories
580 That we shall leave behind us. Come, my Queen!

FEDALMA

Stay, my betrothal ring!—one kiss—farewell!
O love, you were my crown. No other crown
Is aught but thorns on my poor woman's brow.

BOOK III

*　　*　　*　　*

FEDALMA (*letting one hand fall and moving a little from him with a look of sudden terror, while he clasps her more firmly by the other arm*)
　　　　　Silva!

DON SILVA
　　　　　It is nought.
Enough that I am here. Now we will cling.
What power shall hinder us? You left me once
To set your father free. That task is done,
5　And you are mine again. I have braved all
That I might find you, see your father, win
His furtherance in bearing you away
To some safe refuge. Are we not betrothed?

FEDALMA
Oh, I am trembling 'neath the rush of thoughts
10　That come like griefs at morning—look at me
With awful faces, from the vanishing haze
That momently had hidden them.

DON SILVA
　　　　　　　What thoughts?

FEDALMA
Forgotten burials. There lies a grave
Between this visionary present and the past.
15　Our joy is dead, and only smiles on us
A loving shade from out the place of tombs.

DON SILVA
Your love is faint, else aught that parted us
Would seem but superstition. Love supreme
Defies dream-terrors—risks avenging fires.
20　I have risked all things. But your love is faint.

FEDALMA (*retreating a little, but keeping his hand*)
Silva, if now between us came a sword,
Severed my arm, and left our two hands clasped,

This poor maimed arm would feel the clasp till death.
What parts us is a sword—
　　　(ZARCA *has been advancing in the background.*
　　　He has drawn his sword, and now thrusts the
　　　naked blade between them. DON SILVA *lets*
　　　go FEDALMA's *hand, and grasps his sword.*
　　　FEDALMA, *startled at first, stands firmly, as if*
　　　prepared to interpose between her Father and
　　　the Duke.)

ZARCA
　　　　　Ay, 't is a sword
25　That parts the Spaniard and the Zíncala:
A sword that was baptised in Christian blood,
When once a band, cloaking with Spanish law
Their brutal rapine, would have butchered us,
And outraged then our women.
　　　(*Resting the point of his sword on the ground.*)
　　　　　　　My lord Duke,
30　I was a guest within your fortress once
Against my will; had entertainment too—
Much like a galley-slave's. Pray, have you sought
The Zíncalo's camp, to find a fit return
For that Castilian courtesy? or rather
35　To make amends for all our prisoned toil
By free bestowal of your presence here?

DON SILVA
Chief, I have brought no scorn to meet your scorn.
I came because love urged me—that deep love
I bear to her whom you call daughter—her
40　Whom I reclaim as my betrothèd bride.

ZARCA
Doubtless you bring for final argument
Your men-at-arms who will escort your bride?

DON SILVA
I came alone. The only force I bring
Is tenderness. Nay, I will trust besides
45　In all the pleadings of a father's care

To wed his daughter as her nurture bids.
And for your tribe—whatever purposed good
Your thoughts may cherish, I will make secure
With the strong surety of a noble's power:
50 My wealth shall be your treasury.

ZARCA (*with irony*)
                              My thanks!
To me you offer liberal price; for her
Your love's beseeching will be force supreme.
She will go with you as a willing slave,
Will give a word of parting to her father,
55 Wave farewells to her tribe, then turn and say,
"Now, my lord, I am nothing but your bride;
I am quite culled, have neither root nor trunk,
Now wear me with your plume!"

DON SILVA
                              Yours is the wrong
Feigning in me one thought of her below
60 The highest homage. I would make my rank
The pedestal of her worth; a noble's sword,
A noble's honour, her defence; his love
The life-long sanctuary of her womanhood.

ZARCA
I tell you, were you King of Aragon,
65 And won my daughter's hand, your higher rank
Would blacken her dishonour. 'T were excuse
If you were beggared, homeless, spit upon,
And so made even with her people's lot;
For then she would be lured by want, not wealth,
70 To be a wife amongst an alien race
To whom her tribe owes curses.

DON SILVA
                              Such blind hate
Is fit for beasts of prey, but not for men.
My hostile acts against you should but count
As ignorant strokes against a friend unknown;
75 And for the wrongs inflicted on your tribe

By Spanish edicts or the cruelty
Of Spanish vassals, am I criminal?
Love comes to cancel all ancestral hate,
Subdues all heritage, proves that in mankind
80 Union is deeper than division.

ZARCA
                              Ay,
Such love is common: I have seen it oft—
Seen many women rend the sacred ties
That bind them in high fellowship with men,
Making them mothers of a people's virtue:
85 Seen them so levelled to a handsome steed
That yesterday was Moorish property,
To-day is Christian—wears new-fashioned gear,
Neighs to feeders, and will prance alike
Under all banners, so the banner be
90 A master's who caresses. Such light change
You call conversion; but we Zíncali call
Conversion infamy. Our people's faith
Is faithfulness; not the rote-learned belief
That we are heaven's highest favourites,
95 But the resolve that being most forsaken
Among the sons of men, we will be true
Each to the other, and our common lot.
You Christians burn men for their heresy:
Our vilest heretic is that Zíncala
100 Who, choosing ease, forsakes her people's woes.
The dowry of my daughter is to be
Chief woman of her tribe, and rescue it.
A bride with such a dowry has no match
Among the subjects of that Catholic Queen
105 Who would have Gypsies swept into the sea
Or else would have them gibbeted.[1]

DON SILVA
                              And you,
Fedalma's father—you who claim the dues
Of fatherhood—will offer up her youth

----
[1] put to death by hanging.

To mere grim idols of your phantasy!
110 Worse than all Pagans, with no oracle
To bid you murder, no sure good to win,
Will sacrifice your daughter—to no god,
But to a ravenous fire within your soul,
Mad hopes, blind hate, that like possessing fiends
115 Shriek at a name! This sweetest virgin, reared
As garden flowers, to give the sordid world
Glimpses of perfectness, you snatch and thrust
On dreary wilds; in visions mad, proclaim
Semiramis[1] of Gypsy wanderers;
120 Doom, with a broken arrow in her heart,
To wait for death 'mid squalid savages:
For what? You would be saviour of your tribe;
So said Fedalma's letter; rather say,
You have the will to save by ruling men,
125 But first to rule; and with that flinty will
You cut your way, though the first cut you give
Gash you child's bosom.

> (*While* DON SILVA *has been speaking, with
> growing passion,* FEDALMA *has placed herself
> between him and her father.*)

ZARCA (*with calm irony*)
                    You are loud, my lord!
You only are the reasonable man;
You have a heart, I none. Fedalma's good
130 Is what you see, you care for; while I seek
No good, not even my own, urged on by nought
But hellish hunger, which must still be fed
Though in the feeding it I suffer throes.
Fume at your own opinion as you will:
135 I speak not now to you, but to my daughter.
If she still calls it good to mate with you,
To be a Spanish duchess, kneel at court,
And hope her beauty is excuse to men
When women whisper, "A mere Zíncala!"
140 If she still calls it good to take a lot

That measures joy for her as she forgets
Her kindred and her kindred's misery,
Nor feels the softness of her downy couch
Marred by remembrance that she once forsook
145 The place that she was born to—let her go!
If life for her still lies in alien love,
That forces her to shut her soul from truth
As men in shameful pleasures shut out day;
And death, for her, is to do rarest deeds,
150 Which, even failing, leave new faith to men,
The faith in human hearts—then, let her go!
She is my only offspring; in her veins
She bears the blood her tribe has trusted in;
Her heritage is their obedience,
155 And if I died, she might still lead them forth
To plant the race her lover now reviles
Where they may make a nation, and may rise
To grander manhood than his race can show;
Then live a goddess, sanctifying oaths,
160 Enforcing right, and ruling consciences,
By law deep-graven in exalting deeds,
Through the long ages of her people's life.
If she can leave that lot for silken shame,
For kisses honeyed by oblivion—
165 The bliss of drunkards or the blank of fools—
Then let her go! You Spanish Catholics,
When you are cruel, base, and treacherous,
For ends not pious, tender gifts to God,
And for men's wounds offer much oil to churches:
170 We have no altars for such healing gifts
As soothe the heavens for outrage done on earth.
We have no priesthood and no creed to teach
That she—the Zíncala—who might save her race
And yet abandons it, may cleanse that blot,
175 And mend the curse her life has been to men,
By saving her own soul. Her one base choice
Is wrong unchangeable, is poison shed
Where men must drink, shed by her poisoning will.
Now choose, Fedalma!

---

[1] the legendary Assyrian queen and founder of Babylon, celebrated for
her beauty, sexual exploits, and wisdom.

[But her choice was made.
180 Slowly, while yet her father spoke, she moved
From where oblique with deprecating arms
She stood between the two who swayed her heart:
Slowly she moved to choose sublimer pain;
Yearning, yet shrinking; wrought upon by awe,
185 Her own brief life seeming a little isle
Remote through visions of a wider world
With fates close-crowded; firm to slay her joy
That cut her heart with smiles beneath the knife,
Like a sweet babe foredoomed by prophecy.
190 She stood apart, yet near her father: stood
Hand clutching hand, her limbs all tense with will
That strove 'gainst anguish, eyes that seemed a soul
Yearning in death towards him she loved and left.
He faced her, pale with passion and a will
195 Fierce to resist whatever might seem strong
And ask him to submit: he saw one end—
He must be conqueror; monarch of his lot
And not its tributary. But she spoke
Tenderly, pleadingly.]

FEDALMA

My lord, farewell!
200 'T was well we met once more; now we must part.
I think we had the chief of all love's joys
Only in knowing that we loved each other.

DON SILVA

I thought we loved with love that clings till death,
Clings as brute mothers bleeding to their young,
205 Still sheltering, clutching it, though it were dead;
Taking the death-wound sooner than divide.
I thought we loved so.

FEDALMA

Silva, it is fate.
Great Fate has made me heiress of this woe.
You must forgive Fedalma all her debt:
210 She is quite beggared: if she gave herself,
'T would be a self corrupt with stifled thoughts

Of a forsaken better. It is truth
My father speaks: the Spanish noble's wife
Were a false Zíncala. No! I will bear
215 The heavy trust of my inheritance.
See, 't was my people's life that throbbed in me:
An unknown need stirred darkly in my soul,
And made me restless even in my bliss.
Oh, all my bliss was in our love; but now
220 I may not taste it: some deep energy
Compels me to choose hunger. Dear, farewell!
I must go with my people.

[She stretched forth
Her tender hands, that oft had lain in his,
The hands he knew so well, that sight of them
225 Seemed like their touch. But he stood still as death;
Locked motionless by forces opposite:
His frustrate hopes still battled with despair;
His will was prisoner to the double grasp
Of rage and hesitancy. All the way
230 Behind him he had trodden confident,
Ruling munificently in his thought
This Gypsy father. Now the father stood
Present and silent and unchangeable
As a celestial portent. Backward lay
235 The traversed road, the town's forsaken wall,
The risk, the daring; all around him now
Was obstacle, save where the rising flood
Of love close pressed by anguish of denial
Was sweeping him resistless; save where she
240 Gazing stretched forth her tender hands, that hurt
Like parting kisses. Then at last he spoke.]

DON SILVA

No, I can never take those hands in mine
Then let them go for ever!

FEDALMA

It must be.
We may not make this world a paradise
245 By walking it together hand in hand,

623

With eyes that meeting feed a double strength.
We must be only joined by pains divine
Of spirits blent in mutual memories.
Silva, our joy is dead.

DON SILVA
                    But love still lives,
250 And has a safer guard in wretchedness.
Fedalma, women know no perfect love:
Loving the strong, they can forsake the strong;
Man clings because the being whom he loves
Is weak and needs him. I can never turn
255 And leave you to your difficult wandering;
Know that you tread the desert, bear the storm,
Shed tears, see terrors, faint with weariness,
Yet live away from you. I should feel nought
But your imagined pains: in my own steps
260 See your feet bleeding, taste your silent tears,
And feel no presence but your loneliness.
No, I will never leave you!

ZARCA
                    My lord Duke,
I have been patient, given room for speech,
Bent not to move my daughter by command,
265 Save that of her own faithfulness. But now,
All further words are idle elegies
Unfitting times of action. You are here
With the safe-conduct of that trust you showed
Coming unguarded to the Gypsy's camp.
270 I would fain meet all trust with courtesy
As well as honour; but my utmost power
Is to afford you Gypsy guard to-night
Within the tents that keep the northward lines,
And for the morrow, escort on your way
275 Back to the Moorish bounds.

DON SILVA
                    What if my words
Were meant for deeds, decisive as a leap
Into the current? It is not my wont

To utter hollow words, and speak resolves
Like verses bandied in a madrigal.[1]
280 I spoke in action first: I faced all risks
To find Fedalma. Action speaks again
When I, a Spanish noble, here declare
That I abide with her, adopt her lot,
Claiming alone fulfilment of her vows
285 As my betrothèd wife.

FEDALMA (*wresting herself from him, and
standing opposite with a look of terror*)
                    Nay, Silva, nay!
You could not live so—spring from your high
          place—

DON SILVA
Yes, I have said it. And you, chief, are bound
By her strict vows, no stronger fealty
Being left to cancel them.

ZARCA
                    Strong words, my lord!
290 Sounds fatal as the hammer-strokes that shape
The glowing metal: they must shape your life.
That you will claim my daughter is to say
That you will leave your Spanish dignities,
Your home, your wealth, your people, to become
295 Wholly a Zíncalo: share our wanderings,
And be a match meet for my daughter's dower
By living for her tribe; take the deep oath
That binds you to us; rest within our camp,
Nevermore hold command of Spanish men,
300 And keep my orders. See, my lord, you lock
A many-winding chain—a heavy chain.

DON SILVA
I have but one resolve: let the rest follow.
What is my rank? To-morrow it will be filled
By one who eyes it like a carrion bird,

---

[1] a short love poem that is often set to music.

624

305 Waiting for death. I shall be no more missed
Than waves are missed that leaping on the rock
Find there a bed and rest. Life's a vast sea
That does its mighty errand without fail,
Panting in unchanged strength though waves are
    changing.
310 And I have said it: she shall be my people,
And where she gives her life I will give mine.
She shall not live alone, nor die alone.
I will elect my deeds, and be the liege
Not of my birth, but of that good alone
315 I have discerned and chosen.

              ZARCA
                    Our poor faith
Allows not rightful choice, save of the right
Our birth has made for us. And you, my lord,
Can still defer your choice, for some days' space.
I march perforce to-night; you, if you will,
320 Under a Gypsy guard, can keep the heights
With silent Time that slowly opes the scroll
Of change inevitable—take no oath
Till my accomplished task leave me at large
To see you keep your purpose or renounce it.

            DON SILVA
325 Chief, do I hear amiss, or does your speech
Ring with a doubleness which I had held
Most alien to you? You would put me off,
And cloak evasion with allowance? No!
We will complete our pledges. I will take
330 That oath which binds not me alone, but you,
To join my life for ever with Fedalma's.

              ZARCA
I wrangle not—time presses. But the oath
Will leave you that same post upon the heights;
Pledged to remain there while my absence lasts.
335 You are agreed, my lord?

            DON SILVA
            Agreed to all.

              ZARCA
Then I will give the summons to our camp.
We will adopt you as a brother now,
After our wonted fashion.
                    [*Exit* ZARCA.

(SILVA *takes* FEDALMA's *hands*.)

              FEDALMA
            O my lord!
I think the earth is trembling: nought is firm.
340 Some terror chills me with a shadowy grasp.
Am I about to wake, or do you breathe
Here in this valley? Did the outer air
Vibrate to fatal words, or did they shake
Only my dreaming soul? You—join—our tribe?

            DON SILVA
345 Is then your love too faint to raise belief
Up to that height?

             FEDALMA
             Silva, had you but said
That you would die—that were an easy task
For you who oft have fronted death in war.
But so to live for me—you, used to rule—
350 You could not breathe the air my father breathes:
His presence is subjection. Go, my lord!
Fly, while there yet is time. Wait not to speak.
I will declare that I refused your love—
Would keep no vows to you—

            DON SILVA
               It is too late.
355 You shall not thrust me back to seek a good
Apart from you. And what good? Why, to face
Your absence—all the want that drove me forth—
To work the will of a more tyrannous friend
That any uncowled father. Life at least
360 Gives choice of ills; forces me to defy,
But shall not force me to a weak defiance.

The power that threatened you, to master me,
That scorches like a cave-hid dragon's breath,
Sure of its victory in spite of hate,
365 Is what I last will bend to—most defy.
Your father has a chieftain's ends, befitting
A soldier's eye and arm: were he as strong
As the Moors' prophet, yet the prophet too
Had younger captains of illustrious fame
370 Among the infidels. Let him command,
For when your father speaks, I shall hear you.
Life were no gain if you were lost to me:
I would straight go and seek the Moorish walls,
Challenge their bravest, and embrace swift death.
375 The Glorious Mother and her pitying Son
Are not Inquisitors, else their heaven were hell.
Perhaps they hate their cruel worshippers.
And let them feed on lies. I'll rather trust
They love you and have sent me to defend you.

FEDALMA

380 I made my creed so, just to suit my mood
And smooth all hardship, till my father came
And taught my soul by ruling it. Since then
I cannot weave a dreaming happy creed
Where our love's happiness is not accursed.
385 My father shook my soul awake. And you—
The bonds Fedalma may not break for you,
I cannot joy that you should break for her.

DON SILVA

Oh, Spanish men are not a petty band
Where one deserter makes a fatal breach.
390 Men, even nobles, are more plenteous
Than steeds and armour; and my weapons left
Will find new hands to wield them. Arrogance
Makes itself champion of mankind, and holds
God's purpose maimed for one hidalgo[1] lost.

395 See where your father comes and brings a crowd
Of witnesses to hear my oath of love;
The low red sun glows on them like a fire.
This seems a valley in some strange new world,
Where we have found each other, my Fedalma.
—1868

Armgart

SCENE 1

A Salon lit with lamps and ornamented with green plants. An open piano, with many scattered sheets of music. Bronze busts of Beethoven and Gluck[2] on pillars opposite each other. A small table spread with supper. To FRÄULEIN WALPURGA, *who advances with a slight lameness of gait from an adjoining room, enters* GRAF DORNBERG *at the opposite door in a travelling dress.*

GRAF

Good morning, Fräulein!

WALPURGA

          What, so soon returned?
I feared your mission kept you still at Prague.

GRAF

But now arrived! You see my travelling dress.
I hurried from the panting, roaring steam
5 Like any courier of embassy
Who hides the fiends of war within his bag.

WALPURGA

You know that Armgart sings to-night?

GRAF

          Has sung!

---

[1] a Spanish nobleman of secondary rank, inferior to a grandee.

[2] Christopher Willibald Gluck (1714–87), German composer.

'T is close on half-past nine. The *Orpheus*[1]
Lasts not so long. Her spirits—were they high?
10 Was Leo confident?

WALPURGA

He only feared
Some tameness at beginning. Let the house
Once ring, he said, with plaudits,[2] she is safe.

GRAF

And Armgart?

WALPURGA

She was stiller than her wont.
But once, at some such trivial word of mine,
15 As that the highest prize might yet be won
By her who took the second—she was roused.
"For me," she said, "I triumph or I fail.
I never strove for any second prize."

GRAF

Poor human-hearted singing-bird! She bears
20 Caesar's ambition in her delicate breast,
And nought to still it with but quivering song!

WALPURGA

I had not for the world been there to-night:
Unreasonable dread oft chills me more
Than any reasonable hope can warm.

GRAF

25 You have a rare affection for your cousin;
As tender as a sister's.

WALPURGA

Nay, I fear
My love is little more than what I felt
For happy stories when I was a child.
She fills my life that would be empty else,
30 And lifts my nought to value by her side.

GRAF

She is reason good enough, or seems to be,
Why all were born whose being ministers
To her completeness. Is it most her voice
Subdues us? or her instinct exquisite,
35 Informing each old strain with some new grace
Which takes our sense like any natural good?
Or most her spiritual energy
That sweeps us in the current of her song?

WALPURGA

I know not. Losing either, we should lose
40 That whole we call our Armgart. For herself,
She often wonders what her life had been
Without that voice for channel to her soul.
She says, it must have leaped through all her
    limbs—
Made her a Maenad[3]—made her snatch a brand
45 And fire some forest, that her rage might mount
In crashing roaring flames through half a land,
Leaving her still and patient for a while.
"Poor wretch!" she says, of any murderess—
"The world was cruel, and she could not sing:
50 I carry my revenges in my throat;
I love in singing, and am loved again."

GRAF

Mere mood! I cannot yet believe it more.
Too much ambition has unwomaned her;
But only for a while. Her nature hides
55 One half its treasures by its very wealth,
Taxing the hours to show it.

---

[1] a mythological musician whose ability to enchant via the lyre influenced beasts, trees and even rocks. When his wife Eurydice died, he gained her release from the underworld with the promise that he would not look upon her until they had reached the upperworld. At the final moment, he failed. His story is the subject of operas by Gluck and Monteverdi.

[2] applause.

---

[3] a female attendant of Dionysus.

WALPURGA
          Hark! She comes.
Enter LEO *with a wreath in his hand, holding the*
door open for ARMGART, *who wears a furred mantle*
and hood. She is followed by her maid, carrying
an armful of bouquets.

LEO
Place for the queen of song!

GRAF (*advancing towards* ARMGART, *who throws*
     off her hood and mantle, and shows a
       star of brilliants in her hair)
                    A triumph, then.
You will not be a niggard of your joy
And chide the eagerness that came to share it.

ARMGART
60 O kind! You hastened your return for me.
    I would you had been there to hear me sing!
    Walpurga, kiss me: never tremble more
    Lest Armgart's wing should fail her. She has found
    This night the region where her rapture breathes—
65 Pouring her passion on the air made live
    With human heart-throbs. Tell them, Leo, tell them
    How I outsang your hope and made you cry
    Because Gluck could not hear me. That was folly!
    He sang, not listened: every linkèd note
70 Was his immortal pulse that stirred in mine,
    And all my gladness is but part of him.
    Give me the wreath.
                    [*She crowns the bust of* GLUCK.

LEO (*sardonically*)
              Ay, ay, but mark you this:
It was not part of him—that trill you made
In spite of me and reason!

ARMGART
              You were wrong—
75 Dear Leo, you were wrong: the house was held

As if a storm were listening with delight
And hushed its thunder.

LEO
              Will you ask the house
To teach you singing? Quit your *Orpheus* then,
And sing in farces grown to operas,
80 Where all the prurience[1] of the full-fed mob
Is tickled with melodic impudence:
Jerk forth burlesque bravuras, square your arms
Akimbo with a tavern wench's grace,
And set the splendid compass of your voice
85 To lyric jigs. Go to! I thought you meant
To be an artist—lift your audience
To see your vision, not trick forth a show
To please the grossest taste of grossest numbers.

ARMGART (*taking up* LEO's *hand, and kissing it*)
Pardon, good Leo, I am penitent.
90 I will do penance: sing a hundred trills
Into a deep-dug grave, then burying them
As one did Midas'[2] secret, rid myself
Of naughty exultation. O I trilled
At nature's prompting, like the nightingales.
95 Go scold them, dearest Leo.

LEO
              I stop my ears.
Nature in Gluck inspiring Orpheus,
Has done with nightingales. Are bird-beaks lips?

GRAF
Truce to rebukes! Tell us—who were not there—
The double drama: how the expectant house
100 Took the first notes.

---

[1] lasciviousness.

[2] Midas, the king of Phrygia, who was given the power to turn everything he touched into gold by Dionysus. When he turned his daughter into gold he begged to have the power revoked.

WALPURGA (*turning from her occupation of decking
the room with the flowers*)
　　　　　　Yes, tell us all, dear Armgart.
Did you feel tremors? Leo, how did she look?
Was there a cheer to greet her?

LEO
　　　　　　　　Not a sound.
She walked like Orpheus in his solitude,
And seemed to see nought but what no man saw.
105 'T was famous. Not the Schroeder-Devrient
Had done it better. But your blessed public
Had never any judgment in cold blood—
Thinks all perhaps were better otherwise,
Till Nature brings a reason.

ARMGART (*scornfully*)
　　　　　　　　I knew that!
110 The women whispered, "Not a pretty face!"
The men, "Well, well, a goodly length of limb:
She bears the chiton."—It were all the same
Were I the Virgin Mother and my stage
The opening heavens at the Judgment-day:
115 Gossips would peep, jog elbows, rate the price
Of such a woman in the social mart.
What were the drama of the world to them,
Unless they felt the hell-prong?

LEO
　　　　　　Peace, now, peace!
I hate my phrases to be smothered o'er
120 With sauce of paraphrase, my sober tune
Made bass to rambling trebles, showering down
In endless demi-semi-quavers.

ARMGART (*taking a bon-bon from the table, uplifting
it before putting it into her mouth, and turning away*)
　　　　　　　　Mum!

GRAF
Yes, tell us all the glory, leave the blame.

WALPURGA
You first, dear Leo—what you saw and heard;
125 Then Armgart—she must tell us what she felt.

LEO
Well! The first notes came clearly firmly forth.
And I was easy, for behind those rills
I knew there was a fountain. I could see
The house was breathing gently, heads were still;
130 Parrot opinion was struck meekly mute,
And human hearts were swelling. Armgart stood
As if she had been new-created there
And found her voice which found a melody.
The minx! Gluck had not written, nor I taught:
135 Orpheus was Armgart, Armgart Orpheus.
Well, well, all through the *scena* I could feel
The silence tremble now, now poise itself
With added weight of feeling, till at last
Delight o'er-toppled it. The final note
140 Had happy drowning in the unloosed roar
That surged and ebbed and ever surged again,
Till expectation kept it pent awhile
Ere Orpheus returned. Pfui! He was changed:
My demi-god was pale, had downcast eyes
145 That quivered like a bride's who fain would send
Backward the rising tear.

ARMGART (*advancing, but then turning away, as if to
check her speech*)
　　　　　　　　I *was* a bride,
As nuns are at their spousals.

LEO
　　　　　　　Ay, my lady,
That moment will not come again: applause
May come and plenty; but the first, first draught!
(*Snaps his fingers.*)
150 Music has sounds for it—I know no words.
I felt it once myself when they performed
My overture to Sintram. Well! 't is strange,
We know not pain from pleasure in such joy.

ARMGART (*turning quickly*)
Oh, pleasure has cramped dwelling in our souls,
155 And when full Being comes must call on pain
To lend it liberal space.

WALPURGA
I hope the house
Kept a reserve of plaudits: I am jealous
Lest they had dulled themselves for coming good
That should have seemed the better and the best.

LEO
160 No, 't was a revel where they had but quaffed
Their opening cup. I thank the artist's star,
His audience keeps not sober: once afire,
They flame towards climax, though his merit hold
But fairly even.

ARMGART (*her hand on* LEO's *arm*)
Now, now, confess the truth:
165 I sang still better to the very end—
All save the trill; I give that up to you,
To bite and growl at. Why, you said yourself,
Each time I sang, it seemed new doors were oped
That you might hear heaven clearer.

LEO (*shaking his finger*)
I was raving.

ARMGART
170 I am not glad with that mean vanity
Which knows no good beyond its appetite
Full feasting upon praise! I am only glad,
Being praised for what I know is worth the praise;
Glad of the proof that I myself have part
175 In what I worship! At the last applause—
Seeming a roar of tropic winds that tossed
The handkerchiefs and many-coloured flowers,
Falling like shattered rainbows all around—
Think you I felt myself a *prima donna*?
180 No, but a happy spiritual star

Such as old Dante[1] saw, wrought in a rose
Of light in paradise, whose only self
Was consciousness of glory wide-diffused,
Music, life, power—I moving in the midst
185 With a sublime necessity of good.

LEO (*with a shrug*)
I thought it was a *prima donna* came
Within the side-scenes; ay, and she was proud
To find the bouquet from the royal box
Enclosed a jewel-case, and proud to wear
190 A star of brilliants, quite an earthly star,
Valued by thalers.[2] Come, my lady, own
Ambition has five senses, and a self
That gives it good warm lodging when it sinks
Plump down from ecstasy.

ARMGART
Own it? why not?
195 Am I a sage whose words must fall like seed
Silently buried toward a far-off spring?
I sing to living men and my effect
Is like the summer's sun, that ripens corn
Or now or never. If the world brings me gifts,
200 Gold, incense, myrrh—'t will be the needful sign
That I have stirred it as the high year stirs
Before I sink to winter.

GRAF
Ecstasies
Are short—most happily! We should but lose
Were Armgart borne too commonly and long
205 Out of the self that charms us. Could I choose,
She were less apt to soar beyond the reach
Of woman's foibles, innocent vanities,
Fondness for trifles like that pretty star
Twinkling beside her cloud of ebon hair.

---

[1] Dante Alighieri, Italian poet of the *Divine Comedy* (1265–1321).

[2] German silver coins no longer in use.

ARMGART (*taking out the gem and looking at it*)
210 This little star! I would it were the seed
Of a whole Milky Way, if such bright shimmer
Were the sole speech men told their rapture with
At Armgart's music. Shall I turn aside
From splendours which flash out the glow I make,
215 And live to make, in all the chosen breasts
Of half a Continent? No, may it come,
That splendour! May the day be near when men
Think much to let my horses draw me home,
And new lands welcome me upon their beach,
220 Loving me for my fame. That is the truth
Of what I wish, nay, yearn for. Shall I lie?
Pretend to seek obscurity—to sing
In hope of disregard? A vile pretence!
And blasphemy besides. For what is fame
225 But the benignant strength of One, transformed
To joy of Many? Tributes, plaudits come
As necessary breathing of such joy;
And may they come to me!

GRAF
    The auguries[1]
Point clearly that way. Is it no offence
230 To wish the eagle's wing may find repose,
As feebler wings do, in a quiet nest?
Or has the taste of fame already turned
The Woman to a Muse—

LEO (*going to the table*)
        Who needs no supper.
I am her priest, ready to eat her share
235 Of good Walpurga's offerings.

WALPURGA
        Armgart, come.
Graf, will you come?

---

[1] the priests of ancient Rome who prophesized via the interpretation of omens, such as the motions of birds when in flight.

GRAF
    Thanks, I play truant here,
And must receive my self-indulged delay.
But will the Muse receive a votary
At any hour to-morrow?

ARMGART
    Any hour
240 After rehearsal, after twelve at noon.

SCENE 2

The same Salon, morning. ARMGART *seated, in her bonnet and walking dress. The* GRAF *standing near her against the piano.*

GRAF
Armgart, to many minds the first success
Is reason for desisting. I have known
A man so versatile, he tried all arts,
But when in each by turns he had achieved
5 Just so much mastery as made men say,
"He could be king here if he would," he threw
The lauded skill aside. He hates, said one,
The level of achieved preëminence,
He must be conquering still; but others said—

ARMGART
10 The truth, I hope: he had a meagre soul,
Holding no depth where love could root itself.
"Could if he would?" True greatness ever wills—
It lives in wholeness if it live at all,
And all its strength is knit with constancy.

GRAF
15 He used to say himself he was too sane
To give his life away for excellence
Which yet must stand, an ivory statuette
Wrought to perfection through long lonely years,
Huddled in the mart of mediocrities.

20 He said, the very finest doing wins
The admiring only; but to leave undone,
Promise and not fulfil, like buried youth,
Wins all the envious, makes them sigh your name
As that fair Absent, blameless Possible,
25 Which could alone impassion them; and thus,
Serene negation has free gift of all,
Panting achievement struggles, is denied,
Or wins to lose again. What say you, Armgart?
Truth has rough flavours if we bite it through;
30 I think this sarcasm came from out its core
Of bitter irony.

ARMGART

It is the truth
Mean souls select to feed upon. What then?
Their meanness is a truth, which I will spurn.
The praise I seek lives not in envious breath
35 Using my name to blight another's deed.
I sing for love of song and that renown
Which is the spreading act, the world-wide share,
Of good that I was born with. Had I failed—
Well, that had been a truth most pitiable;
40 I cannot bear to think what life would be
With high hope shrunk to endurance, stunted aims
Like broken lances ground to eating-knives,
A self sunk down to look with level eyes
At low achievement, doomed from day to day
45 To distaste of its consciousness. But I—

GRAF

Have won, not lost, in your decisive throw.
And I too glory in this issue; yet,
The public verdict has no potency
To sway my judgment of what Armgart is:
50 My pure delight in her would be but sullied,
If it o'erflowed with mixture of men's praise.
And had she failed, I should have said, "The pearl
Remains a pearl for me, reflects the light
With the same fitness that first charmed my gaze—
55 Is worth as fine a setting now as then."

ARMGART (rising)

Oh, you are good! But why will you rehearse
The talk of cynics, who with insect eyes
Explore the secrets of the rubbish-heap?
I hate your epigrams and pointed saws
60 Whose narrow truth is but broad falsity.
Confess your friend was shallow.

GRAF

I confess
Life is not rounded in an epigram,
And saying aught, we leave a world unsaid.
I quoted, merely to shape forth my thought
65 That high success has terrors when achieved—
Like preternatural spouses whose dire love
Hangs perilous on slight observances:
Whence it were possible that Armgart crowned
Might turn and listen to a pleading voice,
70 Though Armgart striving in the race was deaf.
You said you dared not think what life had been
Without the stamp of eminence; have you thought
How you will bear the poise of eminence
With dread of sliding? Paint the future out
75 As an unchecked and glorious career,
'T will grow more strenuous by the very love
You bear to excellence, the very fate
Of human powers, which tread at every step
On possible verges.

ARMGART

I accept the peril.
80 I choose to walk high with sublimer tread
Rather than crawl in safety. And, besides,
I am an artist as you are a noble:
I ought to bear the burthen of my rank.

GRAF

Such parallels, dear Armgart, are but snares
85 To catch the mind with seeming argument—
Small baits of likeness 'mid disparity.
Men rise the higher as their task is high,

The task being well achieved. A woman's rank
Lies in the fulness of her womanhood:
90 Therein alone she is royal.

ARMGART
                    Yes, I know
The oft-taught Gospel: "Woman, thy desire
Shall be that all superlatives on earth
Belong to men, save the one highest kind—
To be a mother. Thou shalt not desire
95 To do aught best save pure subservience:
Nature has willed it so!" O blessed Nature!
Let her be arbitress; she gave me voice
Such as she only gives a woman child,
Best of its kind, gave me ambition too,
100 That sense transcendent which can taste the joy
Of swaying multitudes, of being adored
For such achievement, needed excellence,
As man's best art must wait for, or be dumb.
Men did not say, when I had sung last night,
105 "'T was good, nay, wonderful, considering
She is a woman"—and then turn to add,
"Tenor or baritone had sung her songs
Better, of course: she's but a woman spoiled."
I beg your pardon, Graf, you said it.

GRAF
                    No!
110 How should I say it, Armgart? I who own
The magic of your nature-given art
As sweetest effluence of your womanhood
Which, being to my choice the best, must find
The best of utterance. But this I say:
115 Your fervid youth beguiles you; you mistake
A strain of lyric passion for a life
Which in the spending is a chronicle
With ugly pages. Trust me, Armgart, trust me;
Ambition exquisite as yours which soars
120 Toward something quintessential you call fame,
Is not robust enough for this gross world
Whose fame is dense with false and foolish breath.

Ardour, a-twin with nice refining thought,
Prepares a double pain. Pain had been saved,
125 Nay, purer glory reached, had you been throned
As woman only, holding all your art
As attribute to that dear sovereignty—
Concentering your power in home delights
Which penetrate and purify the world.

ARMGART
130 What! leave the opera with part ill-sung
While I was warbling in a drawing-room?
Sing in a chimney-corner to inspire
My husband reading news? Let the world hear
My music only in his morning speech
135 Less stammering than most honourable men's?
No! tell me that my song is poor, my art
The piteous feat of weakness aping strength—
That were fit proem[1] to your argument.
Till then, I am an artist by my birth—
140 By the same warrant that I am a woman:
Nay, in the added rarer gift I see
Supreme vocation: if a conflict comes,
Perish—no, not the woman, but the joys
Which men make narrow by their narrowness.
145 Oh, I am happy! The great masters write
For women's voices, and great Music wants me!
I need not crush myself within a mould
Of theory called Nature: I have room
To breathe and grow unstunted.

GRAF
                    Armgart, hear me.
150 I meant not that our talk should hurry on
To such collision. Foresight of the ills
Thick shadowing your path, drew on my speech
Beyond intention. True, I came to ask
A great renunciation, but not this
155 Towards which my words at first perversely strayed,
As if in memory of their earlier suit,

---

[1] introduction, preface.

Forgetful…
Armgart, do you remember too? the suit
Had but postponement, was not quite disdained—
160 Was told to wait and learn—what it has learned—
A more submissive speech.

ARMGART (*with some agitation*)
                          Then it forgot
Its lesson cruelly. As I remember,
'T was not to speak save to the artist crowned,
Nor speak to her of casting off her crown.

GRAF
165 Nor will it, Armgart. I come not to seek
Any renunciations save the wife's,
Which turns away from other possible love
Future and worthier, to take his love
Who asks the name of husband. He who sought
170 Armgart obscure, and heard her answer, "Wait"—
May come without suspicion now to seek
Armgart applauded.

ARMGART (*turning towards him*)
                          Yes, without suspicion
Of aught save what consists with faithfulness
In all expressed intent. Forgive me, Graf—
175 I am ungrateful to no soul that loves me—
To you most grateful. Yet the best intent
Grasps but a living present which may grow
Like any unfledged bird. You are a noble,
And have a high career; just now you said
180 'T was higher far than aught a woman seeks
Beyond mere womanhood. You claim to be
More than a husband, but could not rejoice
That I were more than wife. What follows, then?
You choosing me with such persistency
185 As is but stretched-out rashness, soon must find
Our marriage asks concessions, asks resolve
To share renunciation or demand it.
Either we both renounce a mutual ease,
As in a nation's need both man and wife

190 Do public services, or one of us
Must yield that something else for which each lives
Besides the other. Men are reasoners:
That premiss of superior claims perforce
Urges conclusion—"Armgart, it is you."

GRAF
195 But if I say I have considered this
With strict prevision, counted all the cost
Which that great good of loving you demands—
Questioned my stores of patience, half resolved
To live resigned without a bliss whose threat
200 Touched you as well as me—and finally,
With impetus of undivided will
Returned to say, "You shall be free as now;
Only accept the refuge, shelter, guard,
My love will give your freedom"—then your words
205 Are hard accusal.

ARMGART
                          Well, I accuse myself.
My love would be accomplice of your will.

GRAF
Again—my will?

ARMGART
                          Oh, your unspoken will.
Your silent tolerance would torture me,
And on that rack I should deny the good
210 I yet believed in.

GRAF
                          Then I am the man
Whom you would love?

ARMGART
                          Whom I refuse to love!
No; I will live alone and pour my pain
With passion into music, where it turns
To what is best within my better self.

215 I will not take for husband one who deems
The thing my soul acknowledges as good—
The thing I hold worth striving, suffering for,
To be a thing dispensed with easily,
Or else the idol of a mind infirm.

GRAF

220 Armgart, you are ungenerous; you strain
My thought beyond its mark. Our difference
Lies not so deep as love—as union
Through a mysterious fitness that transcends
Formal agreement.

ARMGART

It lies deep enough
225 To chafe the union. If many a man
Refrains, degraded, from the utmost right,
Because the pleadings of his wife's small fears
Are little serpents biting at his heel,—
How shall a woman keep her steadfastness
230 Beneath a frost within her husband's eyes
Where coldness scorches? Graf, it is your sorrow
That you love Armgart. Nay, it is her sorrow
That she may not love you.

GRAF

Woman, it seems,
Has enviable power to love or not
235 According to her will.

ARMGART

She has the will—
I have—who am one woman—not to take
Disloyal pledges that divide her will.
The man who marries me must wed my Art—
Honour and cherish it, not tolerate.

GRAF

240 The man is yet to come whose theory
Will weigh as nought with you against his love.

ARMGART

Whose theory will plead beside his love.

GRAF

Himself a singer, then? who knows no life
Out of the opera books, where tenor parts
245 Are found to suit him?

ARMGART

You are bitter, Graf.
Forgive me; seek the woman you deserve,
All grace, all goodness, who has not yet found
A meaning in her life, nor any end
Beyond fulfilling yours. The type abounds.

GRAF

250 And happily, for the world.

ARMGART

Yes, happily.
Let it excuse me that my kind is rare:
Commonness is its own security.

GRAF

Armgart, I would with all my soul I knew
The man so rare that he could make your life
255 As woman sweet to you, as artist safe.

ARMGART

Oh, I can live unmated, but not live
Without the bliss of singing to the world,
And feeling all my world respond to me.

GRAF

May it be lasting. Then, we two must part?

ARMGART

260 I thank you from my heart for all. Farewell!

SCENE 3

A YEAR LATER

The same Salon. WALPURGA *is standing looking
towards the window with an air of uneasiness.*
DOCTOR GRAHN.

DOCTOR
Where is my patient, Fräulein?

WALPURGA
           Fled! Escaped!
Gone to rehearsal. Is it dangerous?

DOCTOR
No, no; her throat is cured. I only came
To hear her try her voice. Had she yet sung?

WALPURGA
5 No; she had meant to wait for you. She said,
"The Doctor has a right to my first song."
Her gratitude was full of little plans,
But all were swept away like gathered flowers
By sudden storm. She saw this opera bill—
10 It was a wasp to sting her: she turned pale,
Snatched up her hat and mufflers, said in haste,
"I go to Leo—to rehearsal—none
Shall sing Fidelio[1] to-night but me!"
Then rushed down-stairs.

DOCTOR (*looking at his watch*)
           And this, not long ago?

WALPURGA
15 Barely an hour.

DOCTOR
I will come again,
Returning from Charlottenburg[2] at one.

WALPURGA
Doctor, I feel a strange presentiment.
Are you quite easy?

DOCTOR
         She can take no harm.
'T was time for her to sing: her throat is well.
20 It was a fierce attack, and dangerous;
I had to use strong remedies, but—well!
At one, dear Fräulein, we shall meet again.

SCENE 4

TWO HOURS LATER

WALPURGA *starts up, looking towards the door.*
ARMGART *enters, followed by* LEO. *She throws
herself on a chair which stands with its back
towards the door, not seeming to see anything.*
WALPURGA *casts a questioning terrified look at* LEO.
*He shrugs his shoulders, and lifts up his hands
behind* ARMGART, *who sits like a helpless image,
while* WALPURGA *takes off her hat and mantle.*

WALPURGA
Armgart, dear Armgart (*kneeling and taking her
    hands*), only speak to me,
Your poor Walpurga. Oh, your hands are cold.
Clasp mine, and warm them! I will kiss them warm.
    (ARMGART *looks at her an instant, then draws
    away her hands, and, turning aside, buries her
    face against the back of the chair,* WALPURGA
    rising and standing near.*)
          (DOCTOR GRAHN *enters.*)

---

[1] an opera written by Beethoven.

[2] a city in Brandenburg, Germany.

DOCTOR

News! stirring news to-day! wonders come thick.

ARMGART (*starting up at the first sound of his voice,*
and speaking vehemently)

5 Yes, thick, thick, thick! and you have murdered it!
Murdered my voice—poisoned the soul in me,
And kept me living.
You never told me that your cruel cures
Were clogging films—a mouldy, dead'ning blight—
10 A lava-mud to crust and bury me,
Yet hold me living in a deep, deep tomb,
Crying unheard forever! Oh, your cures
Are devil's triumphs: you can rob, maim, slay,
And keep a hell on the other side your cure
15 Where you can see your victim quivering
Between the teeth of torture—see a soul
Made keen by loss—all anguish with a good
Once known and gone!
      (*Turns and sinks back on her chair.*)
          O misery, misery!
You might have killed me, might have let me sleep
20 After my happy day and wake—not here!
In some new unremembered world,—not here,
Where all is faded, flat—a feast broke off—
Banners all meaningless—exulting words
Dull, dull—a drum that lingers in the air
25 Beating to melody which no man hears.

DOCTOR (*after a moment's silence*)

A sudden check has shaken you, poor child!
All things seem livid, tottering to your sense,
From inward tumult. Stricken by a threat
You see your terrors only. Tell me, Leo:
30 'T is not such utter loss.
      (LEO, *with a shrug, goes quietly out.*)
          The freshest bloom
Merely, has left the fruit; the fruit itself—

ARMGART

Is ruined, withered, is a thing to hide

Away from scorn or pity. Oh, you stand
And look compassionate now, but when Death came
35 With mercy in his hands, you hindered him.
I did not choose to live and have your pity.
You never told me, never gave me choice
To die a singer, lightning-struck, unmaimed,
Or live what you would make me with your cures—
40 A self accursed with consciousness of change,
A mind that lives in nought but members lopped,
A power turned to pain—as meaningless
As letters fallen asunder that once made
A hymn of rapture. Oh, I had meaning once,
45 Like day and sweetest air. What am I now?
The millionth woman in superfluous herds.
Why should I be, do, think? 'Tis thistle-seed,
That grows and grows to feed the rubbish-heap.
Leave me alone!

DOCTOR

      Well, I will come again;
50 Send for me when you will, though but to rate me.
That is medicinal—a letting blood.

ARMGART

Oh, there is one physician, only one,
Who cures and never spoils. Him shall I send for;
He comes readily.

DOCTOR (*to* WALPURGA)

One word, dear Fräulein.

SCENE 5

ARMGART, WALPURGA

ARMGART

Walpurga, have you walked this morning?

WALPURGA

               No.

ARMGART

Go, then, and walk; I wish to be alone.

WALPURGA

I will not leave you.

ARMGART

Will not, at my wish?

WALPURGA

Will not, because you wish it. Say no more,
5   But take this draught.

ARMGART

                    The Doctor gave it you?
It is an anodyne. Put it away.
He cured me of my voice, and now he wants
To cure me of my vision and resolve—
Drug me to sleep that I may wake again
10 Without a purpose, abject as the rest
To bear the yoke of life. He shall not cheat me
Of that fresh strength which anguish gives the soul,
The inspiration of revolt, ere rage
Slackens to faltering. Now I see the truth.

WALPURGA (setting down the glass)

15 Then you must see a future in your reach,
With happiness enough to make a dower
For two of modest claims.

ARMGART

                    Oh, you intone
That chant of consolation wherewith ease
Makes itself easier in the sight of pain.

WALPURGA

20 No: I would not console you, but rebuke.

ARMGART

That is more bearable. Forgive me, dear.
Say what you will. But now I want to write.
                (She rises and moves towards a table.)

WALPURGA

I say then, you are simply fevered, mad;
You cry aloud at horrors that would vanish
25 If you would change the light, throw into shade
The loss you aggrandise, and let day fall
On good remaining, nay on good refused
Which may be gain now. Did you not reject
A woman's lot more brilliant, as some held,
30 Than any singer's? It may still be yours.
Graf Dornberg loved you well.

ARMGART

                    Not me, not me.
He loved one well who was like me in all
Save in voice which made that All unlike
As diamond is to charcoal. Oh, a man's love!
35 Think you he loves a woman's inner self
Aching with loss of loveliness?—as mothers
Cleave to the palpitating pain that dwells
Within their misformed offspring?

WALPURGA

                    But the Graf
Chose you as simple Armgart—had preferred
40 That you should never seek for any fame
But such as matrons have who rear great sons.
And therefore you rejected him; but now—

ARMGART

Ay, now—now he would see me as I am,
                (She takes up a hand-mirror.)
Russet and songless as a missel-thrush.[1]
45 An ordinary girl—a plain brown girl,
Who, if some meaning flash from out her words,
Shocks as a disproportioned thing—a Will
That, like an arm astretch and broken off,
Has nought to hurl—the torso of a soul.
50 I sang him into love of me: my song
Was consecration, lifted me apart

_____

[1] a European thrush that eats mistletoe berries.

From the crowd chiselled like me, sister forms,
But empty of divineness. Nay, my charm
Was half that I could win fame yet renounce!
55 A wife with glory possible absorbed
Into her husband's actual.

WALPURGA
For shame!
Armgart, you slander him. What would you say
If now he came to you and asked again
That you would be his wife?

ARMGART
No, and thrice no!
60 It would be pitying constancy, not love,
That brought him to me now. I will not be
A pensioner in marriage. Sacraments
Are not to feed the paupers of the world.
If he were generous—I am generous too.

WALPURGA
65 Proud, Armgart, but not generous.

ARMGART
Say no more.
He will not know until—

WALPURGA
He knows already.

ARMGART (quickly)
Is he come back?

WALPURGA
Yes, and will soon be here.
The Doctor had twice seen him and would go
From hence again to see him.

ARMGART
Well, he knows.
70 It is all one.

WALPURGA
What if he were outside?
I hear a footstep in the ante-room.

ARMGART (raising herself and assuming calmness)
Why let him come, of course. I shall behave
Like what I am, a common personage
Who looks for nothing but civility.
75 I shall not play the fallen heroine,
Assume a tragic part and throw out cues
For a beseeching lover.

WALPURGA
Some one raps.
(Goes to the door.)
A letter—from the Graf.

ARMGART
Then open it.
(WALPURGA still offers it.)
Nay, my head swims. Read it. I cannot see.
(WALPURGA opens it, reads and pauses.)
80 Read it. Have done! No matter what it is.

WALPURGA (reads in a low, hesitating voice)
"I am deeply moved—my heart is rent, to hear
of your illness and its cruel result, just now
communicated to me by Dr. Grahn. But surely it
is possible that this result may not be permanent.
85 For youth such as yours, Time may hold in store
something more than resignation: who shall say
that it does not hold renewal? I have not dared to
ask admission to you in the hours of a recent shock,
but I cannot depart on a long mission without
90 tendering my sympathy and my farewell. I start
this evening for the Caucasus[1], and thence I pro-
ceed to India, where I am intrusted by the Govern-
ment with business which may be of long duration."

---
[1] a mountain range in southeastern Europe.

639

(WALPURGA *sits down dejectedly.*)

ARMGART (*after a slight shudder, bitterly*)
The Graf has much discretion. I am glad.
95 He spares us both a pain, not seeing me.
What I like least is that consoling hope—
That empty cup, so neatly ciphered "Time,"
Handed me as a cordial for despair.
(*Slowly and dreamily*) Time—what a word to fling
     as charity!
100 Bland neutral word for slow, dull-beating pain—
Days, months, and years!—If I would wait for them.
     (*She takes up her hat and puts it on, then wraps*
     her mantle round her. WALPURGA *leaves the room.*)
Why, this is but beginning. (WALP. *reënters.*) Kiss
     me, dear
I am going now—alone—out—for a walk.
Say you will never wound me any more
105 With such cajolery as nurses use
To patients amorous of a crippled life.
Flatter the blind: I see.

WALPURGA
     Well, I was wrong.
In haste to soothe, I snatched at flickers merely.
Believe me, I will flatter you no more.

ARMGART
110 Bear witness, I am calm. I read my lot
As soberly as if it were a tale
Writ by a creeping feuilletonist[1] and called
"The Woman's Lot: a Tale of Everyday":
A middling woman's, to impress the world
115 With high superfluousness; her thoughts a crop
Of chick-weed errors or of pot-herb facts,
Smiled at like some child's drawing on a slate.
"Genteel?" "O yes, gives lessons; not so good
As any man's would be, but cheaper far."

120 "Pretty?" "No; yet she makes a figure fit
For good society. Poor thing, she sews
Both late and early, turns and alters all
To suit the changing mode. Some widower
Might do well, marrying her; but in these days!—
125 Well, she can somewhat eke her narrow gains
By writing, just to furnish her with gloves
And droschkies[2] in the rain. They print her things
Often for charity."—Oh, a dog's life!
A harnessed dog's, that draws a little cart
130 Voted a nuisance! I am going now.

WALPURGA
Not now, the door is locked.

ARMGART
          Give me the key!

WALPURGA
Locked on the outside. Gretchen has the key:
She is gone on errands.

ARMGART
               What, you dare to keep me
Your prisoner?

WALPURGA
          And have I not been yours?
135 Your wish has been a bolt to keep me in.
Perhaps that middling woman whom you paint
With far-off scorn—

ARMGART
               I paint what I must be!
What is my soul to me without the voice
That gave it freedom?—gave it one grand touch
140 And made it nobly human?—Prisoned now,
Prisoned in all the petty mimicries
Called woman's knowledge, that will fit the world
As doll-clothes fit a man. I can do nought

---

[1] the writer of stories that appear in the literary section of a French newspaper.

[2] carriages.

Better than what a million women do—
145 Must drudge among the crowd and feel my life
Beating upon the world without response,
Beating with passion through an insect's horn
That moves a millet-seed[1] laboriously.
If I *would* do it!

WALPURGA (*coldly*)
And why should you not?

ARMGART (*turning quickly*)
150 Because Heaven made me royal—wrought me out
With subtle finish towards pre-eminence,
Made every channel of my soul converge
To one high function, and then flung me down,
That breaking I might turn to subtlest pain.
155 An inborn passion gives a rebel's right:
I would rebel and die in twenty worlds
Sooner than bear the yoke of thwarted life,
Each keenest sense turned into keen distaste,
Hunger not satisfied but kept alive
160 Breathing in languor half a century.
All the world now is but a rack of threads
To twist and dwarf me into pettiness
And basely feigned content, the placid mask
Of woman's misery.

WALPURGA (*indignantly*)
Ay, such a mask
165 As the few born like you to easy joy,
Cradled in privilege, take for natural
On all the lowly faces that must look
Upward to you! What revelation now
Shows you the mask or gives presentiment
170 Of sadness hidden? You who every day
These five years saw me limp to wait on you,
And thought the order perfect which gave *me*,
The girl without pretension to be aught,
A splendid cousin for my happiness:

_____
[1] cereal grass.

175 To watch the night through when her brain was fired
With too much gladness—listen, always listen
To what *she* felt, who having power had right
To feel exorbitantly, and submerge
The souls around her with the poured-out flood
180 Of what must be ere she were satisfied!
That was feigned patience, was it? Why not love,
Love nurtured even with that strength of self
Which found no room save in another's life?
Oh, such as I know joy by negatives,
185 And all their deepest passion is a pang
Till they accept their pauper's heritage,
And meekly live from out the general store
Of joy they were born stripped of. I accept—
Nay, now would sooner choose it than the wealth
190 Of natures you call royal, who can live
In mere mock knowledge of their fellows' woe,
Thinking their smiles may heal it.

ARMGART (*tremulously*)
Nay, Walpurga,
I did not make a palace of my joy
To shut the world's truth from me. All my good
195 Was that I touched the world and made a part
In the world's dower of beauty, strength, and bliss;
It was the glimpse of consciousness divine
Which pours out day and sees the day is good.
Now I am fallen dark; I sit in gloom,
200 Remembering bitterly. Yet you speak truth;
I wearied you, it seems; took all your help
As cushioned nobles use a weary serf,
Not looking at his face.

WALPURGA
Oh, I but stand
As a small symbol for the mighty sum
205 Of claims unpaid to needy myriads;
I think you never set your loss beside
That mighty deficit. Is your work gone—
The prouder queenly work that paid itself
And yet was overpaid with men's applause?

210 Are you no longer chartered, privileged,
But sunk to simple woman's penury,
To ruthless Nature's chary average—
Where is the rebel's right for you alone?
Noble rebellion lifts a common load;
215 But what is he who flings his own load off
And leaves his fellows toiling? Rebel's right?
Say rather, the deserter's. Oh, you smiled
From your clear height on all the million lots
Which yet you brand as abject.

ARMGART
                I was blind
220 With too much happiness: true vision comes
Only, it seems, with sorrow. Were there one
This moment near me, suffering what I feel,
And needing me for comfort in her pang—
Then it were worth the while to live; not else.

WALPURGA
225 One—near you—why, they throng! you hardly stir
But your act touches them. We touch afar.
For did not swarthy slaves of yesterday
Leap in their bondage at the Hebrews' flight,[1]
Which touched them through the thrice millennial dark?
230 But you can find the sufferer you need
With touch less subtle.

ARMGART
Who has need of me?

WALPURGA
Love finds the need it fills. But you are hard.

ARMGART
Is it not you, Walpurga, who are hard?
You humoured all my wishes till to-day,
235 When fate has blighted me.

_____

[1] from Egypt, and thus, enslavement.

WALPURGA
             You would not hear
The "chant of consolation": words of hope
Only embittered you. Then hear the truth—
A lame girl's truth, whom no one ever praised
For being cheerful. "It is well," they said:
240 "Were she cross-grained she could not be endured."
A word of truth from her had startled you;
But you—you claimed the universe; nought less
Than all existence working in sure tracks
Towards your supremacy. The wheels might scathe
245 A myriad destinies—nay, must perforce;
But yours they must keep clear of; just for you
The seething atoms through the firmament
Must bear a human heart—which you had not!
For what is it to you that women, men,
250 Plod, faint, are weary, and espouse despair
Of aught but fellowship? Save that you spurn
To be among them? Now, then, you are lame—
Maimed, as you said, and levelled with the crowd:
Call it new birth—birth from that monstrous Self
255 Which, smiling down upon a race oppressed,
Says, "All is good, for I am throned at ease."
Dear Armgart—nay, you tremble—I am cruel.

ARMGART
O no! hark! Some one knocks. Come in!—come in!
                       (_Enter_ LEO.)

LEO
See, Gretchen let me in. I could not rest
260 Longer away from you.

ARMGART
             Sit down, dear Leo.
Walpurga, I would speak with him alone.
                (WALPURGA _goes out._)

LEO (_hesitatingly_)
You mean to walk?

ARMGART

No, I shall stay within.
(*She takes off her hat and mantle, and sits down
immediately. After a pause, speaking in a subdued
tone to* LEO.)
How old are you?

LEO

Threescore and five.

ARMGART

That's old.
I never thought till now how you have lived.
265 They hardly ever play your music?

LEO (*raising his eyebrows and throwing out his lip*)
No!
Schubert too wrote for silence: half his work
Lay like a frozen Rhine till summers came
That warmed the grass above him. Even so!
His music lives now with a mighty youth!

ARMGART
270 Do you think yours will live when you are dead?

LEO

Pfui! The time was, I drank that home-brewed wine
And found it heady, while my blood was young:
Now it scarce warms me. Tipple it as I may,
I am sober still, and say: "My old friend Leo,
275 Much grain is wasted in the world and rots;
Why not thy handful?"

ARMGART

Strange! since I have known you
Till not I never wondered how you lived.
When I sang well—that was your jubilee.
But you were old already.

LEO

Yes, child, yes:

280 Youth thinks itself the goal of each old life;
Age has but travelled from a far-off time
Just to be ready for youth's service. Well!
It was my chief delight to perfect you.

ARMGART

Good Leo! You have lived on little joys.
285 But your delight in me is crushed forever.
Your pains, where are they now? They shaped intent
Which action frustrates; shaped an inward sense
Which is but keen despair, the agony
Of highest vision in the lowest pit.

LEO

290 Nay, nay, I have a thought: keep to the stage,
To drama without song; for you can act—
Who knows how well, when all the soul is poured
Into that sluice alone?

ARMGART

I know, and you:
The second or third best in tragedies
295 That cease to touch the fibre of the time.
No; song is gone, but nature's other gift,
Self-judgment, is not gone. Song was my speech,
And with its impulse only, action came:
Song was the battle's onset, when cool purpose
300 Glows into rage, becomes a warring god
And moves the limbs with miracle. But now—
Oh, I should stand hemmed in with thoughts and
rules—
Say "This way passion acts," yet never feel
The might of passion. How should I declaim?
305 As monsters write with feet instead of hands.
I will not feed on doing great tasks ill,
Dull the world's sense with mediocrity,
And live by trash that smothers excellence.
One gift I had that ranked me with the best—
310 The secret of my frame—and that is gone.
For all life now I am a broken thing.
But silence there! Good Leo, advise me now.

I would take humble work and do it well—
Teach music, singing—what I can—not here,
315 But in some smaller town where I may bring
The method you have taught me, pass your gift
To others who can use it for delight.
You think I can do that?
> (*She pauses with a sob in her voice.*)

LEO
                    Yes, yes, dear child!
And it were well, perhaps, to change the place—
320 Begin afresh as I did when I left
Vienna with a heart half broken.

ARMGART (*roused by surprise*)
                    You?

LEO
Well, it is long ago. But I had lost—
No matter! We must bury our dead joys
And live above them with a living world.
325 But whither, think you, you would like to go?

ARMGART
To Freiburg.[1]

LEO
                    In the Breisgau?[2] And why there?
It is too small.

ARMGART
                    Walpurga was born there,
And loves the place. She quitted it for me
These five years past. Now I will take her there.
330 Dear Leo, I will bury my dead joy.

LEO
Mothers do so, bereaved; then learn to love
Another's living child.

---

[1] a city in Baden.

[2] Breslau, a formerly German city in southwest Poland.

ARMGART
                    Oh, it is hard
To take the little corpse, and lay it low,
And say, "None misses it but me."
335 She sings...
I mean Paulina sings Fidelio,
And they will welcome her to-night.

LEO
                    Well, well,
'T is better that our griefs should not spread far.
—1870

Brother and Sister Sonnets [3]

I

I cannot choose but think upon the time
When our two lives grew like two buds that kiss
At lightest thrill from the bee's swinging chime,
Because the one so near the other is.

5 He was the elder and a little man
Of forty inches, bound to show no dread,
And I the girl that puppy-like now ran,
Now lagged behind my brother's larger tread.

I held him wise, and when he talked to me
10 Of snakes and birds, and which God loved the best,
I thought his knowledge marked the boundary
Where men grew blind, though angels knew the
    rest.

---

[3] "I hope that the brother and sister love each other very dearly: life might be so enriched if that relation were made the most of, as one of the highest forms of friendship. A good while ago I made a poem, in the form of sonnets after the Shakspeare[sic] type, on the childhood of a brother and sister...little descriptive bits on the mutual influences in their small lives. This was always one of my best-loved subjects. And I was proportionately enraged about that execrable discussion raised in relation to Byron. The deliberate insistence on the subject was a worse crime against society than the reputed fact." (Eliot's note.)

If he said "Hush!" I tried to hold my breath.
Wherever he said "Come!" I stepped in faith.

II

15 Long years have left their writing on my brow,
But yet the freshness and the dew-fed beam
Of those young mornings are about me now,
When we two wandered toward the far-off stream

With rod and line. Our basket held a store
20 Baked for us only, and I thought with joy
That I should have my share, though he had more,
Because he was the elder and a boy

The firmaments of daisies since to me
Have had those mornings in their opening eyes,
25 The bunchèd cowslip's pale transparency
Carries that sunshine of sweet memories,

And wild-rose branches take their finest scent
From those blest hours of infantine content.

III

Our mother bade us keep the trodden ways,
30 Stroked down my tippet,[1] set my brother's frill,
Then with the benediction of her gaze
Clung to us lessening, and pursued us still

Across the homestead to the rookery elms,
Whose tall old trunks had each a grassy mound,
35 So rich for us, we counted them as realms
With varied products: here were earth-nuts found,

And here the Lady-fingers in deep shade;
Here sloping toward the Moat the rushes grew,
The large to split for pith, the small to braid:
40 While over all the dark rooks cawing flew,

And made a happy strange solemnity,
A deep-toned chant from life unknown to me.

---

[1] the long narrow strip of cloth as part of an attachment to a hood.

IV

Our meadow-path had memorable spots:
One where it bridged a tiny rivulet,
45 Deep hid by tangled blue Forget-me-nots;
And all along the waving grasses met

My little palm, or nodded to my cheek,
When flowers with upturned faces gazing drew
My wonder downward, seeming all to speak
50 With eyes of souls that dumbly heard and knew.

Then came the copse, where wild things rushed
        unseen,
And black-scathed grass betrayed the past abode
Of mystic gypsies, who still lurked between
Me and each hidden distance of the road.

55 A gypsy once had startled me at play,
Blotting with her dark smile my sunny day.

V

Thus rambling we were schooled in deepest lore,
And learned the meanings that give words a soul,
The fear, the love, the primal passionate store,
60 Whose shaping impulses make manhood whole.

Those hours were seed to all my after good;
My infant gladness, through eye, ear, and touch,
Took easily as warmth a various food
To nourish the sweet skill of loving much.

65 For who in age shall roam the earth and find
Reasons for loving that will strike out love
With sudden rod from the hard year-pressed mind?
Were reasons sown as thick as stars above,

'Tis love must see them, as the eye sees light:
70 Day is but Number to the darkened sight.

VI

Our brown canal was endless to my thought;
And on its banks I sat in dreamy peace,
Unknowing how the good I loved was wrought,
Untroubled by the fear that it would cease.

75 Slowly the barges floated into view
Rounding a grassy hill to me sublime
With some Unknown beyond it, whither flew
The parting cuckoo toward a fresh spring-time.

The wide-arched bridge, the scented elder-flowers,
80 The wondrous watery rings that died too soon,
The echoes of the quarry, the still hours
With white robe sweeping-on the shadeless noon,

Were but my growing self, are part of me,
My present Past, my root of piety.

VII

85 Those long days measured by my little feet
Had chronicles which yield me many a text;
Where irony still finds an image meet
Of full-grown judgements in this world perplext.

One day my brother left me in high charge,
90 To mind the rod, while he went seeking bait,
And bade me, when I saw a nearing barge,
Snatch out the line, lest he should come too late.

Proud of the task, I watched with all my might
For one whole minute, till my eyes grew wide,
95 Till sky and earth took on a strange new light
And seemed a dream-world floating on some
        tide—

A fair pavilioned boat for me alone
Bearing me onward through the vast unknown.

VIII

But sudden came the barge's pitch-black prow,
100 Nearer and angrier came my brother's cry,
And all my soul was quivering fear, when lo!
Upon the imperilled line, suspended high,

A silver perch! My guilt that won the prey,
Now turned to merit, had a guerdon[1] rich
105 Of hugs and praises, and made merry play,
Until my triumph reached its highest pitch

When all at home were told the wondrous feat,
And how the little sister had fished well.
In secret, though my fortune tasted sweet,
110 I wondered why this happiness befell.

"The little lass had luck," the gardener said:
And so I learned, luck was with glory wed.

IX

We had the selfsame world enlarged for each
By loving difference of girl and boy:
115 The fruit that hung on high beyond my reach
He plucked for me, and oft he must employ

A measuring glance to guide my tiny shoe
Where lay firm stepping-stones, or call to mind
"This thing I like my sister may not do,
120 For she is little, and I must be kind."

Thus boyish Will the nobler mastery learned
Where inward vision over impulse reigns,
Widening its life with separate life discerned,
A Like unlike, a Self that self restrains.

125 His years with others must the sweeter be
For those brief days he spent in loving me.

---

[1] reward, recompense.

X

His sorrow was my sorrow, and his joy
Sent little leaps and laughs through all my frame;
My doll seemed lifeless and no girlish toy
130 Had any reason when my brother came.

I knelt with him at marbles, marked his fling
Cut the ringed stem and make the apple drop,
Of watched him winding close the spiral string
That looped the orbits of the humming top.

135 Grasped by such fellowship my vagrant thought
Ceased with dream-fruit dream-wished to fulfil;
My aëry-picturing fantasy was taught
Subjection to the harder, truer skill

That seeks with deeds to grave a thought-
tracked line,
140 And by "What is," "What will be" to define.

XI

School parted us; we never found again
That childish world where our two spirits mingled
Like scents from varying roses that remain
One sweetness, nor can evermore be singled.

145 Yet the twin habit of that early time
Lingered for long about the heart and tongue:
We had been natives of one happy clime,
And its dear accent to our utterance clung.

Till the dire years whose awful name is Change
150 Had grasped our souls still yearning in divorce,
And pitiless shaped them in two forms that range
Two elements which sever their life's course.

But were another childhood-world my share,
I would be born a little sister there.
—1874 (1869)

Anne Brontë
1820 — 1849

Anne Brontë was the fifth and youngest daughter of Patrick Brontë and Maria Branwell. Because of her young age, Anne did not attend the ill-managed Clergy Daughters' School at Cowan Bridge. Anne was forced to help support the family as a governess between 1839 and 1845 and, after an unsuccessful attempt to open their own school in 1844, Charlotte, Emily, and Anne published, at their own expense, a volume of poetry under the pseudonyms Currer, Ellis, and Acton Bell. The volume attracted some positive critical notice but sold dismally. Anne had a history of respiratory problems; mere days after relocating to Scarborough in hopes of a "sea cure," Anne died on May 28, 1849.

cσℓσ

A Fragment—"Maiden, thou wert thoughtless once"

"Maiden, thou wert thoughtless once
    Of beauty or of grace,
Simple and homely in attire
    Careless of form and face.
5 Then whence this change, and why so oft
    Dost smooth thy hazel hair?
And wherefore deck thy youthful form
    With such unwearied care?

"Tell us—and cease to tire our ears
10   With yonder hackneyed strain—
Why wilt thou play those simple tunes
    So often o'er again?"
"Nay, gentle friends, I can but say
    That childhood's thoughts are gone.
15 Each year its own new feelings brings
    And years move swiftly on,

And for those little simple airs,
    I love to play them o'er—
So much I dare not promise now
20   To play them never more."
I answered and it was enough;
    They turned them to depart;

They could not read my secret thoughts
    Nor see my throbbing heart.

25 I've noticed many a youthful form
    Upon whose changeful face
The inmost workings of the soul
    The gazer's eye might trace.
The speaking eye, the changing lip,
30   The ready blushing cheek,
The smiling or beclouded brow
    Their different feelings speak.

But, thank God! you might gaze on mine
    For hours and never know
35 The secret changes of my soul
    From joy to bitter woe.
Last night as we sat round the fire
    Conversing merrily,
We heard without approaching steps
40   Of one well known to me.

There was no trembling in my voice,
    No blush upon my cheek,
No lustrous sparkle in my eyes
    Of hope or joy to speak.
45 But O my spirit burned within,
    My heart beat thick and fast.
He came not nigh—he went away
    And then my joy was past.

And yet my comrades marked it not,
50   My voice was still the same;
They saw me smile, and o'er my face—
    No signs of sadness came;
They little knew my hidden thoughts
    And they will never know
55 The anguish of my drooping heart,
    The bitter aching woe!
—1846 (JANUARY 1, 1840)

Lines Written at Thorp Green

O! I am very weary
    Though tears no longer flow;
My eyes are tired of weeping,
    My heart is sick of woe.

5   My life is very lonely,
    My days pass heavily;
I'm weary of repining,
    Wilt thou not come to me?

Oh didst thou know my longings
10   For thee from day to day,
My hopes so often blighted,
    Thou wouldst not thus delay.
—1846 (AUGUST 28, 1840)

"My soul is awakened, my spirit is soaring"

My soul is awakened, my spirit is soaring,
    And carried aloft on the wings of the breeze;
For, above, and around me, the wild wind is roaring
Arousing to rapture the earth and the seas.

5   The long withered grass in the sunshine is glancing,
The bare trees are tossing their branches on high;
The dead leaves beneath them are merrily dancing,
The white clouds are scudding across the blue sky.

I wish I could see how the ocean is lashing
10 The foam of its billows to whirlwinds of spray,
I wish I could see how its proud waves are dashing
And hear the wild roar of their thunder today!
—1846 (DECEMBER 30, 1842)

A Word to the Calvinists

You may rejoice to think yourselves secure,
    You may be grateful for the gift divine,
That grace unsought which made your black hearts
    pure
And fits your earthborn souls in Heaven to shine.

5   But is it sweet to look around and view
Thousands excluded from that happiness,
Which they deserve at least as much as you,
Their faults not greater nor their virtues less?

And wherefore should you love your God the more
10 Because to you alone his smiles are given,
Because He chose to pass the many o'er
And only bring the favoured few to Heaven?

And wherefore should your hearts more grateful
    prove
Because for *all* the Saviour did not die?
15 Is yours the God of justice and of love
And are your bosoms warm with charity?

Say does your heart expand to all mankind
And would you ever to your neighbour do,
—The weak, the strong, the enlightened and the
    blind—
20 As you would have your neighbour do to you?

And when you looking on your fellow men
Behold them doomed to endless misery,
How can you talk of joy and rapture then?
May God withold such cruel joy from me!

25 That none *deserve* eternal bliss I know:
    Unmerited the grace in mercy given,
    But none shall sink to everlasting woe
    That have not well deserved the wrath of Heaven.

    And O! there lives within my heart
30 A hope long nursed by me,
    (And should its cheering ray depart
    How dark my soul would be)

    That as in Adam all have died
    In Christ shall all men live
35 And ever round his throne abide
    Eternal praise to give;

    That even the wicked shall at last
    Be fitted for the skies
    And when their dreadful doom is past
40 To light and life arise.

    I ask not how remote the day
    Nor what the sinner's woe
    Before their dross[1] is purged away,
    Enough for me to know

45 That when the cup of wrath is drained,
    The metal purified,
    They'll cling to what they once disdained
    And live by him that died.
    —1846 (MAY 28, 1843)

The Captive Dove

Poor restless Dove, I pity thee,
    And when I hear thy plaintive moan
I'll mourn for thy captivity
And in thy woes forget mine own.

---

[1] worthless or trivial matter.

5 To see thee stand prepared to fly,
    And flap those useless wings of thine,
    And gaze into the distant sky
    Would melt a harder heart than mine.

    In vain! In vain! Thou canst not rise—
10 Thy prison roof confines thee there;
    Its slender wires delude thine eyes,
    And quench thy longing with despair.

    O! thou wert made to wander free
    In sunny mead and shady grove,
15 And far beyond the rolling sea
    In distant climes at will to rove.

    Yet hadst thou but one gentle mate
    Thy little drooping heart to cheer
    And share with thee thy captive state,
20 Thou couldst be happy even there.

    Yes, even there, if listening by
    One faithful dear companion stood,
    While gazing on her full bright eye
    Thou mightst forget thy native wood.

25 But thou, poor solitary dove,
    Must make unheard thy joyless moan;
    The heart that nature formed to love
    Must pine neglected and alone.
    —1846 (OCTOBER 31, 1843)

Views of Life

When sinks my heart in hopeless gloom,
    When life can shew no joy for me,
And I behold a yawning tomb
Where bowers and palaces should be,

5 In vain, you talk of morbid dreams,
    In vain, you gaily smiling say

That what to me so dreary seems
The healthy mind deems bright and gay.

I too have smiled, and thought like you,
10 But madly smiled, and falsely deemed:
My present thoughts I know are true,
I'm waking now, 'twas then I dreamed.

I lately saw a sunset sky,
And stood enraptured to behold
15 Its varied hues of glorious dye:
First, fleecy clouds of shining gold;

These blushing took a rosy hue;
Beneath them shone a flood of green,
Nor less divine the glorious blue
20 That smiled above them and between:

I cannot name each lovely shade,
I cannot say how bright they shone;
But one by one I saw them fade,
And what remained when they were gone?

25 Dull clouds remained of sombre hue,
And when their borrowed charm was o'er,
The sky grew dull and charmless too
That smiled so softly bright before.

So gilded by the glow of youth
30 Our varied life looks fair and gay,
And so remains the naked truth
When that false light is past away.

Why blame ye, then, my keener sight
That clearly sees a world of woes
35 Through all the haze of golden light
That flattering Falsehood round it throws?

When the young mother smiles above
The first born darling of her heart

Her bosom glows with earnest love
40 While tears of speechless rapture start.

Fond dreamer! little does she know
The anxious toil, the suffering,
The blasted hopes, the burning woe,
The object of her joy will bring.

45 Her blinded eyes behold not now
What soon or late must be his doom,
The anguish that will cloud his brow,
The bed of death, the dreary tomb.

As little know the youthful pair
50 In mutual love supremely blest
What weariness and cold despair
Ere long will seize the aching breast.

And even should love and faith remain
(The greatest blessings life can show)
55 Amid adversity and pain
To shine throughout with cheering glow,

They do not see how cruel death
Comes on, their loving hearts to part;
One feels not now the gasping breath,
60 The rending of the earthbound heart,

The soul's and body's agony,
Ere she may sink to her repose;
The sad survivor cannot see
The grave above his darling close,

65 Nor how, despairing and alone,
He then must wear his life away
And linger feebly toiling on,
And fainting sink into decay.

O, youth may listen patiently,
70 While sad experience tells her tale;

But doubt sits smiling in his eye,
For ardent hope will still prevail.

He hears how feeble Pleasure dies,
By guilt destroyed, and pain and woe;
75 He turns to Hope—and she replies
"Believe it not—it is not so!"

"O! heed her not," experience says,
"For thus she whispered once to me;
She told me in my youthful days
80 How glorious manhood's prime would be.

"When in the time of early Spring
Too chill the winds that o'er me passed,
She said each coming day would bring
A fairer heaven, a gentler blast.

85 "And when the sun too seldom beamed,
The sky o'ercast too darkly frowned,
The frequent rain too constant streamed,
And mists too dreary gathered round,

"She told me summer's glorious ray
90 Would chase those vapours all away,
        And scatter glories round,
With sweetest music fill the trees,
Load with rich scent the gentle breeze
        And strew with flowers the ground.

95 "But when beneath that scorching sky
I languished weary through the day
        While birds refused to sing,
Verdure decayed from field and tree,
And panting nature mourned with me
100   The freshness of the spring.

"Wait but a little while," she said,
"Till summer's burning days are fled,
        And Autumn shall restore
With golden riches of her own,

105 And summer's glories mellowed down
        The freshness you deplore."

"And long I waited, but in vain;
That freshness never came again,
        Though summer passed away,
110 Though Autumn's mists hung cold and chill
And drooping nature languished still,
        And sank into decay;

"Till wintry blasts foreboding blew
Through leafless trees—and then I knew
115   That hope was all a dream.
But thus, fond youth, she cheated me,
And she will prove as false to thee,
        Though sweet her words may seem."

Stern prophet! cease thy bodings dire—
120 Thou canst not quench the ardent fire
        That warms the breast of youth.
O! let it cheer him while it may,
And gently, gently, die away
        Chilled by the damps of truth.

125 Tell him that earth is not our rest,
Its joys are empty, frail at best;
        And point beyond the sky;
But gleams of light may reach us here,
And hope the *roughest* path can cheer:
130   Then do not bid it fly.

Though hope may promise joys that still
Unkindly time will ne'er fulfil;
        Or if they come at all,
We never find them unalloyed—
135 Hurtful perchance, or soon destroyed,
        They vanish or they pall.

Yet hope itself a brightness throws
O'er all our labours and our woes,
        While dark foreboding care

140   A thousand ills will oft portend
     That Providence may ne'er intend
         The trembling heart to bear.

     Or if they come, it oft appears,
     Our woes are lighter than our fears,
145   And far more strongly borne.
     Then let us not enhance our doom,
     But e'en in midnight's blackest gloom
        Expect the rising morn.

     Because the road is rough and long,
150   Shall we despise the skylark's song,
        That cheers the wanderer's way?
     Or trample down, with reckless feet
     The smiling flowerets bright and sweet
        Because they soon decay?

155   Pass pleasant scenes unnoticed by,
     Because the next is bleak and drear;
     Or not enjoy a smiling sky
     Because a tempest may be near?

     No! while we journey on our way,
160   We'll notice every lovely thing,
     And ever as they pass away,
     To memory and hope we'll cling.

     And though that awful river flows
     Before us when the journey's past,
165   Perchance of all the pilgrim's woes
     Most dreadful, shrink not—'tis the last!

     Though icy cold, and dark, and deep;
     Beyond it smiles that blessed shore
     Where none shall suffer, none shall weep,
170   And bliss shall reign for evermore.
     —1846 (1845)

Self-Communion

"The mist is resting on the hill;
   The smoke is hanging in the air;
The very clouds are standing still;
A breathless calm broods everywhere.
5   Thou pilgrim through this vale of tears
Thou, too, a little moment cease
Thy anxious toil and fluttering fears,
And rest thee, for a while, in peace."

   "I would, but Time keeps working still
10 And moving on for good or ill:
     He will not rest nor stay.
In pain or ease, in smiles or tears,
     He still keeps adding to my years
     And stealing life away.
15 His footsteps in the ceaseless sound
     Of yonder clock, I seem to hear,
That through this stillness so profound
     Distinctly strikes the vacant ear.
     For ever striding on and on
20 He pauses not by night or day;
And all my life will soon be gone
As these past years have slipped away.
He took my childhood long ago,
And then my early youth; and lo,
25   He steals away my prime!
I cannot see how fast it goes,
But well my inward spirit knows
     The wasting power of time."

   "Time steals thy moments, drinks thy breath,
30 Changes and wastes thy mortal frame;
But though he gives the clay to death,
He cannot touch the inward flame.
Nay, though he steals thy years away,
Their memory is left thee still,
35 And every month and every day
Leaves some effect of good or ill.

The wise will find in Memory's store
A help for that which lies before
    To guide their course aright;
40 Then, hush thy plaints and calm thy fears;
Look back on these departed years,
    And, say, what meets thy sight?"

"I see, far back, a helpless child,
Feeble and full of causeless fears,
45 Simple and easily beguiled
    To credit all it hears.
More timid than the wild wood-dove
Yet trusting to another's care,
And finding in protecting love
50 Its only refuge from despair,—
Its only balm for every woe,
The only bliss its soul can know:—
    Still hiding in its breast
A tender heart too prone to weep,
55 A love so earnest, strong and deep
    It could not be expressed.

Poor helpless thing! what can it do
Life's stormy cares and toils among;—
How tread this weary desert through
60 That awes the brave and tires the strong?
Where shall it centre so much trust
Where truth maintains so little sway,
Where seeming fruit is bitter dust,
And kisses oft to death betray?
65 How oft must sin and falsehood grieve
A heart so ready to believe
    And willing to admire!
With strength so feeble, fears so strong,
Amid this selfish bustling throng,
70   How will it faint and tire!

That tender love so warm and deep,
    How can it flourish here below?
What bitter floods of tears must steep
The strong soil where it would grow!

75 O earth! a rocky breast is thine—
A hard soil and a cruel clime,
Where tender plants must droop and pine,
Or alter with transforming time.
That soul, that clings to sympathy
80 As ivy clasps the forest tree,
    How can it stand alone?
That heart so prone to overflow
E'en at the *thought* of other's woe,
    How will it bear its own?

85 How, if a sparrow's death can wring
Such bitter tearfloods from the eye,
Will it behold the suffering
Of struggling, lost humanity?
The torturing pain, the pining grief,
90 The sin-degraded misery,
The anguish that defies relief?"

"Look back again—What dost thou see?"

"I see one kneeling on the sod,
With infant hands upraised to Heaven,
95 A young heart feeling after God,
Oft baffled, never backward driven.
Mistaken oft, and oft astray,
It strives to find the narrow way
    But gropes and toils alone:
100 That inner life of strife and tears,
Of kindling hopes and lowering fears,
    To none but God is known.
'Tis better thus: for *man* would scorn
Those childish prayers, those artless cries,
105 That darkling spirit tossed and torn,
    But *God* will not despise!
We may regret such waste of tears,
Such darkly toiling misery,
Such wildering doubts and harrowing fears,
110 Where joy and thankfulness should be;
But wait, and Heaven will send relief.

Let patience have her perfect work:
Lo, strength and wisdom spring from grief
And joys behind afflictions lurk!

115 It asked for light, and it is heard;
God grants that struggling soul repose;
And, guided by his holy word,
It wiser than its teachers grows.
It gains the upward path at length,
120 And passes on from strength to strength,
⠀⠀⠀Leaning on Heaven the while:
Night's shades departing one by one,
It sees at last the rising sun,
And feels his cheering smile.
125 In all its darkness and distress
For light it sought, to God it cried;
And through the pathless wilderness,
He was its comfort and its guide."

"So was it, and so will it be;
130 Thy God will guide and strengthen thee;
⠀⠀⠀His goodness cannot fail.
The sun that on thy morning rose
Will light thee to the evening's close,
⠀⠀⠀Whatever storms assail."

135 "*God* alters not; but Time on me
A wide and wondrous change has wrought;
And in these parted years I see
Cause for grave care and saddening thought.
I see that time, and toil, and truth
140 And inward hardness can impart,—
Can freeze the generous blood of youth,
And steel full fast the tender heart."

"Bless God for that divine decree!—
That hardness comes with misery,
145 And suffering deadens pain;
That at the frequent sight of woe
E'en pity's tears forget to flow,
If reason still remain!

Reason, with conscience by her side
150 But gathers strength from toil and truth;
And she will prove a surer guide
Than those sweet instincts of our youth.
Thou that hast known such anguish sore
In weeping where thou couldst not bless,
155 Canst *thou* that softness so deplore—
That suffering, shrinking tenderness?
Thou that hast felt what cankering care
A loving heart is doomed to bear,
⠀⠀⠀Say, how canst *thou* regret
160 That fires unfed must fall away,
Long droughts can dry the softest clay,
⠀⠀⠀And cold will cold beget?"

"Nay, but 'tis hard to *feel* that chill
Come creeping o'er the shuddering heart,
165 Love may be full of pain, but still,
'Tis sad to see it so depart,—
To watch that fire, whose genial glow
Was formed to comfort and to cheer,
For want of fuel, fading so,
170 Sinking to embers dull and drear,—
To see the soft soil turned to stone
⠀⠀⠀For lack of kindly showers,—
To see those yearnings of the breast,
Pining to bless and to be blessed,
175 Drop withered, frozen one by one,
Till centred in itself alone,
⠀⠀⠀It wastes its blighted powers.

Oh, I have known a wondrous joy
In early friendship's pure delight,—
180 A genial bliss that could not cloy—
My sun by day, my moon by night.
Absence, indeed, was sore distress,
And thought of death was anguish keen,
And there was cruel bitterness
185 When jarring discords rose between;
And sometimes it was grief to know

My fondness was but half returned.
But this was nothing to the woe
With which another truth was learned:—
190 That I must check, or nurse apart
Full many an impulse of the heart
        And many a darling thought:
What my soul worshipped, sought, and prized,
Were slighted, questioned, or despised;—
195   this pained me more than aught.
And as my love the warmer glowed
The deeper would that anguish sink,
That this dark stream between us flowed,
Though both stood bending o'er its brink.
200 Until, at last, I learned to bear
A colder heart within my breast;
To share such thoughts as I could share,
        And calmly keep the rest.
I saw that they were sundered now,
205 The trees that at the root were one:
They yet might mingle leaf and bough,
But still the stems must stand alone.

O love is sweet of every kind!
'Tis sweet the helpless to befriend,
210 To watch the young unfolding mind,
To guide, to shelter, and defend;
To lavish tender toil and care,
And ask for nothing back again,
But that our smiles a blessing bear,
215 And all our toil be not in vain.
And sweeter far than words can tell
Their love whose ardent bosoms swell
        With thoughts they need not hide;
Where fortune frowns not on their joy,
220 And Prudence seeks not to destroy,
        Nor Reason to deride.
Whose love may freely gush and flow,
Unchecked, unchilled by doubt or fear,
For in their inmost hearts they know
225 It is not vainly nourished there.
They know that in a kindred breast

Their long desires have found a home
Where heart and soul may kindly rest
Weary and lorn no more to roam.
230 Their dreams of bliss were not in vain,
As they love they are loved again,
And they can bless as they are blessed.

O vainly might I seek to show
The joys from happy love that flow!
235 The warmest words are all too cold
The secret transports to unfold
Of simplest word or softest sigh,
Or from the glancing of an eye
        To say what rapture beams;
240 One look that bids our fears depart,
And well assures the trusting heart
It beats not in the world alone—
Such speechless raptures I have known,
        But only in my dreams.

245 My life has been a morning sky
Where Hope her rainbow glories cast
O'er kindling vapours far and nigh:
And, if the colours faded fast
Ere one bright hue had died away
250 Another o'er its ashes gleamed;
And if the lower clouds were grey,
The mists above more brightly beamed.
But not for long;—at length, behold,
Those tints less warm, less radiant grew,
255 Till but one streak of paly gold
Glimmered through clouds of saddening hue.
And I am calmly waiting, now,
To see that also pass away,
And leave, above the dark hill's brow
260 A rayless arch of sombre grey."

"So must it fare with all thy race
Who seek in earthly things their joy:
So fading hopes lost hopes shall chase,
        Till Disappointment all destroy.

265 But they that fix their hopes on high
Shall, in the blue refulgent sky,
　　　The sun's transcendent light,
Behold a purer, deeper glow
Than these uncertain gleams shall show,
270 　　　However fair or bright.
O weak of heart! why thus deplore
That Truth will Fancy's dreams destroy?
Did I not tell thee, years before,
Life was for labour, not for joy?
275 Cease, selfish spirit, to repine;
O'er thine own ills no longer grieve;
Lo, there are sufferings worse than thine,
Which thou mayst labour to relieve.
If Time indeed too swiftly flies,
280 Gird on thine armour, haste, arise,
　　　For thou hast much to do;—
To lighten woe, to trample sin,
And foes without and foes within
　　　To combat and subdue.
285 Earth hath too much of sin and pain:
The bitter cup—the binding chain
　　　Dost thou indeed lament?
Let not thy weary spirit sink;
But strive—not by one drop or link
290 　　　The evil to augment.
Strive rather thou, by peace and joy,
The bitter poison to destroy,
　　　The cruel chain to break,
O strive! and if thy strength be small,
295 Strive yet the more, and spend it all
　　　For Love and Wisdom's sake!"

"O I have striven both hard and long
But many are my foes and strong,
My gains are light—my progress slow;
300 For hard's the way I have to go,
And my worst enemies, I know
　　　Are those within my breast;
And it is hard to toil for aye,—

Through sultry noon and twilight grey
305 　　　To toil and never rest."

"There is a rest beyond the grave,
A lasting rest from pain and sin,
Where dwell the faithful and the brave;
But they must strive who seek to win."
310 "Show me that rest—I ask no more.
O drive these gloomy mists away;
And let me see that sunny shore,
　　　However far away!
However wide this rolling sea,
315 However wild my passage be,
Howe'er my bark be tempest tossed,
May it but reach that haven fair,
May I but land and wander there,
With those that I have loved and lost;
320 With such a glorious hope in view,
I'll gladly toil and suffer too.
Rest *without* toil I would not ask;
I would not shun the hardest task:
Toil is my glory—Grief my gain,
325 If God's approval they obtain.
Could I but hear my Saviour say,—
'I know thy patience and thy love;
How thou has held the narrow way,
For my sake laboured night and day,
330 And watched, and striven with them that strove;
And still hast borne, and didst not faint,'—
Oh, this would be reward indeed!"

"Press forward, then, without complaint;
Labour and love—and such shall be thy meed."
—1900 (1847–1848)

The Bluebell

A fine and subtle spirit dwells
In every little flower,

Each one its own sweet feeling breathes
With more or less of power.

5　There is a silent eloquence
In every wild bluebell
That fills my softened heart with bliss
That words could never tell.

Yet I recall not long ago
10　A bright and sunny day,
'Twas when I led a toilsome life
So many leagues away;

That day along a sunny road
All carelessly I strayed,
15　Between two banks where smiling flowers
Their varied hues displayed.

Before me rose a lofty hill,
Behind me lay the sea,
My heart was not so heavy then
20　As it was wont to be.

Less harassed than at other times
I saw the scene was fair,
And spoke and laughed to those around,
As if I knew no care.

25　But when I looked upon the bank
My wandering glances fell
Upon a little trembling flower,
A single sweet bluebell.

Whence came that rising in my throat,
30　That dimness in my eye?
Why did those burning drops distil—
Those bitter feelings rise?

O, that lone flower recalled to me
My happy childhood's hours
35　When bluebells seemed like fairy gifts
A prize among the flowers,

Those sunny days of merriment
When heart and soul were free,
And when I dwelt with kindred hearts
40　That loved and cared for me.

I had not then mid heartless crowds
To spend a thankless life
In seeking after others' weal
With anxious toil and strife.

45　"Sad wanderer, weep those blissful times
That never may return!"
The lovely floweret seemed to say,
And thus it made me mourn.
—1902 (AUGUST 22, 1840)

Dreams

While on my lonely couch I lie
I seldom feel myself alone,
For fancy fills my dreaming eye
With scenes and pleasures of its own.

5　Then I may cherish at my breast
An infant's form beloved and fair,
May smile, and soothe it into rest
With all a mother's fondest care.

How sweet to feel its helpless form
10　Depending thus on me alone;
And while I hold it safe and warm,
What bliss to think it is my own!

And glances then may meet my eyes
That daylight never showed to me,
15　What raptures in my bosom rise
Those earnest looks of love to see!

To feel my hand so kindly pressed,
To know myself beloved at last,

To think my heart has found a rest,
20 My life of solitude is past.

But then to wake and find it flown,
The dream of happiness destroyed,
To find myself unloved, alone,
What tongue can speak the dreary void?

25 A heart whence warm affections flow,
Creator, thou hast given to me,
And am I only thus to know
How sweet the joys of love would be?
—1915 (1845)

A Voice from the Dungeon

I'm buried now; I've done with life;
I've done with hate, revenge and strife;
I've done with joy, and hope and love
And all the bustling world above.

5 Long have I dwelt forgotten here
In pining woe and dull despair;
This place of solitude and gloom
Must be my dungeon and my tomb.

No hope, no pleasure can I find;
10 I am grown weary of my mind;
Often in balmy sleep I try
To gain a rest from misery,

And in one hour of calm repose
To find a respite from my woes,
15 But dreamless sleep is not for me
And I am still in misery.

I dream of liberty, 'tis true,
But then I dream of sorrow too,
Of blood and guilt and horrid woes,
20 Of tortured friends and happy foes;

I dream about the world, but then
I dream of fiends instead of men;
Each smiling hope so quickly fades
And such a lurid gloom pervades

25 That world—that when I wake and see
Those dreary phantoms fade and flee,
Even in my dungeon I can smile,
And taste of joy a little while.

And yet it is not always so;
30 I dreamt a little while ago
That all was as it used to be:
A fresh free wind passed over me;

It was a pleasant summer's day,
The sun shone forth with cheering ray,
35 Methought a little lovely child
Looked up into my face and smiled.

My heart was full, I wept for joy,
It was my own, my darling boy;
I clasped him to my breast and he
40 Kissed me and laughed in childish glee.

Just then I heard in whisper sweet
A well known voice my name repeat.
His father stood before my eyes;
I gazed at him in mute surprise,

45 I thought he smiled and spoke to me,
But still in silent ecstasy
I gazed at him; I could not speak;
I uttered one long piercing shriek.

Alas! Alas! That cursed scream
50 Aroused me from my heavenly dream;
I looked around in wild despair,
I called them, but they were not there;
The father and the child are gone,
And I must live and die alone.
—1934 (OCTOBER 1837)

Jean Ingelow
1820 — 1897

Jean Ingelow was educated by her Evangelical parents at home. Her initial publications were stories featured in *Youth's Magazine* under the pseudonym, Orris. Best remembered for her children's books, and the fairy tale, *Mopsa the Fairy* (1869), Ingelow was, in her time, celebrated as one of the major lyric poets of the Victorian period, and considered as a possible candidate for poet laureate at the age of seventy-two. Although her poetry has not satisfied modern literary tastes, Ingelow's popularity reflected the age's appreciation for nature, sentiment, and rather conventional religiosity.

❧❧❧

Supper At The Mill

Mother

Well, Frances.

     Frances

Well, good mother, how are you?

 M. I'm hearty, lass, but warm; the weather's
    warm:

I think 'tis mostly warm on market days.

5 I met with George behind the mill: said he,

"Mother, go in and rest awhile."

 F.   Ay, do.

And stay to supper; put your basket down.

 M. Why, now, it is not heavy?

 F.   Willie, man

Get up and kiss your Granny. Heavy, no!

10 Some call good churning luck; but, luck or skill,

Your butter mostly comes as firm and sweet

As if 'twas Christmas. So you sold it all?

 M. All but this pat that I put by for George;

He always loved my butter.

 F.   That he did.

15 *M.* And has your speckled hen brought off her
    brood?

 F. Not yet; but that old duck I told you of,

She hatched eleven out of twelve to-day.

 Child. And Granny, they're so yellow.

 M.   Ah, my lad,

Yellow as gold—yellow as Willie's hair.

20 *C.* They're all mine, Granny—father says
    they're mine.

 M. To think of that!

 F.   Yes. Granny, only think!

Why, father means to sell them when they're fat,

And put the money in the savings bank,

And all against our Willie goes to school:

25 But Willie would not touch them—no, not he;

He knows that father would be angry else.

 C. But I want one to play with—O, I want

A little yellow duck to take to bed!

 M. What! would you rob the poor old mother,
    then?

30 *F.* Now, Granny, if you'll hold the babe awhile;

'Tis time I took up Willie to his crib.

         [*Exit Frances.*

[*Mother sings to the infant.*]

 Playing on the virginals,[1]

  Who but I? Sae glad, sae free,

 Smelling for all cordials,

  The green mint and marjorie;

35 Set among the budding broom,

  Kingcup and daffodilly,

 By my side I made him room:

  O love my Willie!

---

[1] a small rectangular harpsichord.

40   "Like me, love me, girl o' gowd,"
     Sang he to my nimble strain;
  Sweet his ruddy lips o'erflowed
     Till my heartstrings rang again:
  By the broom, the bonny broom,
45   Kingcup and daffodilly,
  In my heart I made him room:
     O love my Willie!

  "Pipe and play, dear heart,"sang he,
     "I must go, yet pipe and play;
50   Soon I'll come and ask of thee
     For an answer yea or nay;"
  And I waited till the flocks
     Panted in yon waters stilly,
  And the corn stood in the shocks:
55   O love my Willie!

  I thought first when thou didst come
     I would wear the ring for thee,
  But the year told out its sum
     Ere again thou sat'st by me;
60   Thou hadst nought to ask that day
     By kingcup and daffodilly;
  I said neither yea nor nay:
     O love my Willie!

     Enter George.
  G. Well, mother, 'tis a fortnight now, or more,
65 Since I set eyes on you.
  M.   Ay, George, my dear,
I reckon you've been busy: so have we.
  G. And how does father?
  M.   He gets through his
  work,
But he grows stiff, a little stiff, my dear;
He's not so young, you know, by twenty years,
70 As I am—not so young by twenty years,
And I'm past sixty.
  G.   Yet he's hale and stout,
And seems to take a pleasure in his pipe;

And seems to take a pleasure in his cows,
And a pride, too.
  M.   And well he may, my dear.
75   *G.* Give me the little one, he tires your arm;
He's such a kicking, crowing, wakeful rogue,
He almost wears our lives out with his noise
Just at day-dawning, when we wish to sleep.
What! you young villain, would you clench your fist
80 In father's curls? a dusty father, sure,
And you're as clean as wax.
                Ah, you may laugh;
But if you live a seven years more or so,
These hands of yours will all be brown and scratched
With climbing after nest-eggs. They'll go down
85 As many rat-holes as are round the mere;[1]
And you'll love mud, all manner of mud and dirt,
As your father did afore you, and you'll wade
After young water-birds; and you'll get bogged
Setting of eel-traps, and you'll spoil your clothes,
90 And come home torn and dripping: then, you know
You'll feel the stick—you'll feel the stick, my lad!

     Enter Frances.
  F. You should not talk so to the blessed babe—
How can you, George? why, he may be in heaven
Before the time you tell of.
  M.   Look at him:
So earnest, such an eager pair of eyes!
95 He thrives, my dear.
  F. Yes, that he does, thank God!
My children are all strong.
  M.   'Tis much to say:
Sick children fret their mothers' hearts to shreds,
And do no credit to their keep nor care.
100 Where is your little lass?
  F.   Your daughter came
And begged her of us for a week or so.
  M. Well, well, she might be wiser, that she might,
For she can sit at ease and pay her way;

---

[1] a lake or pond.

A sober husband, too—a cheerful man—
105 Honest as ever stepped, and fond of her;
Yet she is never easy, never glad,
Because she has not children. Well-a-day!
If she could know how hard her mother worked,
And what ado I had, and what a moil[1]
110 With my half-dozen! Children, ay, forsooth,
They bring their own love with them when they come,
But if they come not there is peace and rest;
The pretty lambs! and yet she cries for more:
Why, the world's full of them, and so is heaven—
115 They are not rare.
     G.   No, mother, not at all;
But Hannah must not keep our Fanny long—
She spoils her.
     M.   Ah! folks spoil their children now;
When I was a young woman 'twas not so;
We made our children fear us, made them work,
120 Kept them in order.
     G.   Were not proud of them—
Eh, mother?
     M.   I set store by mine, 'tis true,
But then I had good cause.
     G.   My lad, d'ye hear?
Your Granny was not proud, by no means proud!
She never spoilt your father—no, not she,
125 Nor ever made him sing at harvest-home,
Nor at the forge, nor at the baker's shop,
Nor to the doctor while she lay abed
Sick, and he crept upstairs to share her broth.
     M. Well, well, you were my youngest, and, what's
          more,
130 Your father loved to hear you sing—he did,
Although, good man, he could not tell one tune
From the other.
     F.   No he got his voice from you:
Do use it, George, and send the child to sleep.
     G.   What must I sing?
     F. The Ballad of the man

135 That is so shy he cannot speak his mind.
     G. Ay, of the purple grapes and crimson leaves;
But, mother, put your shawl and bonnet off.
And, Frances, lass, I brought some cresses in:
Just wash them, toast the bacon, break some eggs,
140 And let us to supper shortly.

            [*Sings.*]
My neighbor White—we met to-day—
He always had a cheerful way.
     As if he breathed at ease;
My neighbor White lives down the glade,
145 And I live higher, in the shade
     Of my old walnut-trees.

So many lads and lasses small,
To feed them all, to clothe them all,
     Must surely tax his wit;
150 I see his thatch when I look out,
His branching roses creep about,
     And vines half smother it.

There white-haired urchins climb his eaves,
And little watch-fires heap with leaves,
155   And milky filberts[2] hoard;
And there his oldest daughter stands
With downcast eyes and skilful hands
     Before her ironing-board.

She comforts all her mother's days,
160 And with her sweet obedient ways
     She makes her labor light
So sweet to hear, so fair to see!
O, she is much too good for me,
     That lovely Lettice White!

165 'Tis hard to feel one's self a fool!
With that same lass I went to school—
     I then was great and wise;

---

[1] hard work; drudgery.

[2] hazel-nut.

She read upon an easier book,
And I—I never cared to look
    Into her shy blue eyes.
170

And now I know they must be there,
Sweet eyes, behind those lashes fair
    That will not raise their rim:
If maids be shy, he cures who can;
175
But if a man be shy—a man—
    Why then, the worse for him!

My mother cries, "For such a lad
A wife is easy to be had
    And always to be found;
180
A finer scholar scarce can be,
And for a foot and leg," says she,
    "He beats the country round!"

"My handsome boy must stoop his head
To clear her door whom he would wed."
185
    Weak praise, but fondly sung!
"O mother! scholars sometimes fail—
And what can foot and leg avail
    To him that wants a tongue?"

When by her ironing-board I sit,
190
Her little sisters round me flit,
    And bring me forth their store;
Dark cluster grapes of dusty-blue,
And small sweet apples, bright of hue
    And crimson to the core.

195
But she abideth silent, fair;
All shaded by her flaxen hair
    The blushes come and go;
I look, and I no more can speak
Than the red sun that on her cheek
200
    Smiles as he lieth low.

Sometimes the roses by the latch,
Or scarlet vine-leaves from her thatch,

Come sailing down like birds;
When from their drifts her board I clear,
205
She thanks me, but I scarce can hear
    The shyly uttered words.

Oft have I wooed sweet Lettice White
By daylight and by candlelight
    When we two were apart.
210
Some better day come on apace,
And let me tell her face to face,
    "Maiden, thou hast my heart."

How gently rock yon poplars high
Against the reach of primrose sky
215
    With heaven's pale candles stored!
She sees them all, sweet Lettice White;
I'll ev'n go sit again to-night
    Beside her ironing-board!

Why, you young rascal! who would think it, now?
220 No sooner do I stop than you look up.
What would you have your poor old father do?
'Twas a brave song, long-winded, and not loud.
    M. He heard the bacon sputter on the fork,
And heard his mother's step across the floor.
225 Where did you get that song?—'tis new to me.
    G. I bought it of a pedlar.
    M.   Did you so?
Well, you were always for the love-songs, George.
    F. My dear, just lay his head upon your arm,
And if you'll pace and sing two minutes more
230 He needs must sleep—his eyes are full of sleep.
    G. Do you sing, mother.
    F.   Ay, good mother, do;
'Tis long since we have heard you.
    M.   Like enough;
I'm an old woman, and the girls and lads
I used to sing to sleep e'ertop me now.
235 What should I sing for?
    G.   Why, to pleasure us.

Sing in the chimney corner, where you sit
And I'll pace gently with the little one.

[*Mother sings.*]
When sparrows build, and the leaves break forth,
    My old sorrow wakes and cries,
240 For I know there is dawn in the far, far north,
    And a scarlet sun doth rise;
Like a scarlet fleece the snow-field spreads,
    And icy founts run free,
And the bergs begin to bow their heads,
245   And plunge, and sail in the sea.

O my lost love, and my own, own love,
    And my love that loved me so!
Is there never a chink in the world above
    Where they listen for words from below?
250 Nay, I spoke once, and I grieved thee sore,
    I remember all that I said,
And now thou wilt hear me no more—no more
    Till the sea gives up her dead.

Thou didst set thy foot on the ship, and sail
255   To the ice-fields and the snow;
Thou wert sad, for thy love did naught avail,
    And the end I could not know;
How could I tell I should love thee to-day,
    Whom that day I held not dear?
260 How could I know I should love thee away
    When I did not love thee anear?

We shall walk no more through the sodden plain
    With the faded bents o'erspread,
We shall stand no more by the seething main
265   While the dark wrack drives o'erhead;
We shall part no more in the wind and the rain,
    Where thy last farewell was said:
But perhaps I shall meet thee and know thee again
    When the sea gives up her dead.

270 *F.* Asleep at last, and time he was, indeed.
Turn back the cradle-quilt, and lay him in;
And, mother, will you please to draw your chair?—
The supper's ready.
     —1863

Remonstrance

Daughters of Eve! your mother did not well:
    She laid the apple in your father's hand,
And we have read, O wonder! what befell—
    The man was not deceived, nor yet could stand;
5 He chose to lose, for love of her, his throne,—
With her could die, but could not live alone.

Daughters of Eve! he did not fall so low,
    Nor fall so far, as that sweet woman fell:
For something better, than as gods to know,
10   That husband in that home left off to dwell:
For this, till love be reckoned less than lore,
Shall man be first and best for evermore.

Daughters of Eve! it was for your dear sake
    The world's first hero died an uncrowned king;
15 But God's great pity touched the grand mistake,
    And made his married love a sacred thing:
For yet his nobler sons, if aught be true,
Find the lost Eden in their love to you.
    —1867

A Lily And A Lute

(*Song of the uncommunicated Ideal*)

I

I opened the eyes of my soul.
               And behold,
A white river-lily: a lily awake, and aware,—
For she set her face upward,—aware how in scarlet
    and gold

A long wrinkled cloud, left behind of the
        wandering air,
5   Lay over with fold upon fold,
    With fold upon fold.

And the blushing sweet shame of the cloud made
    her also ashamed,
The white river-lily, that suddenly knew she was fair;
And over the far-away mountains that no man hath
    named,
10 And that no foot hath trod,
Flung down out of heavenly places, there fell, as it
    were,
A rose-bloom, a token of love, that should make
    them endure,
Withdrawn in snow-silence forever, who keep
    themselves pure,
And look up to God.

15   Then I said, "In rosy air,
    Cradled on thy reaches fair,
    While the blushing early ray
    Whitens into perfect day,
    River-lily, sweetest known,
20 Art thou set for me alone?
    Nay, but I will bear thee far,
    Where yon clustering steeples are,
    And the bells ring out o'erhead,
    And the stated prayers are said;
25 And the busy farmer's pace,
    Trading in the market-place;
    And the country lasses sit
    By their butter, praising it;
    And the latest news is told,
30 While the fruit and cream are sold;
    And the friendly gossips greet,
    Up and down the sunny street.
    For," I said, "I have not met,
    White one, any folk as yet
35 Who would send no blessing up,
    Looking on a face like thine;

For thou art as Joseph's cup,[1]
And by thee might they divine.

"Nay! but thou a spirit art;
40 Men shall take thee in the mart
For the ghost of their best thought,
Raised at noon, and near them brought;
Or the prayer they made last night,
Set before them all in white."

45 And I put out my rash hand,
For I thought to draw to land
The white lily. Was it fit
Such a blossom should expand,
Fair enough for a world's wonder,
50 And no mortal gather it?
No. I strove, and it went under,
And I drew, but it went down;
And the water-weeds' long tresses,
And the overlapping cresses,
55 Sullied its admired crown.
Then along the river strand,
Trailing, wrecked, it came to land,
Of its beauty half despoiled,
And its snowy pureness soiled:
60 O! I took it in my hand,—
You will never see it now,
White and golden as it grew:
No, I cannot show it you,
Nor the cheerful town endow
65 With the freshness of its brow.
If a royal painter, great
With the colors dedicate
To a dove's neck, a sea-bight
And the flickerings over white
70 Mountain summits far away,—
One content to give his mind
To the enrichment of mankind,

---

[1] the cup from which Christ is said to have drunk at the Last Supper,
also used by Joseph of Arimithea to catch drops of Christ's blood at the
Crucifixion. Linked, in Arthurian Legend, with the object of the
quest—the holy grail.

And the laying up of light
In men's houses,—on that day,
75　Could have passed in kingly mood,
Would he ever have endued
Canvas with the peerless thing,
In the grace that it did bring,
And the light that o'er it flowed,
80　With the pureness that it showed,
And the pureness that it meant?
Could he skill to make it seen
As he saw? For this, I ween,
He were likewise impotent.

II

I opened the doors of my heart.
　　　　　　　　And behold,
There was music within and a song,
And echoes did feed on the sweetness, repeating it long.
I opened the doors of my heart. And behold,
5　There was music that played itself out in aeolian notes;
Then was heard, as a far-away bell at long intervals
　　tolled,
　　That murmurs and floats,
And presently dieth, forgotten of forest and wold.
And comes in all passion again and a tremblement soft,
10　　That maketh the listener full oft
To whisper, "Ah! would I might hear it forever and
　　aye,
　　When I toil in the heat of the day,
　　When I walk in the cold."

　　I opened the door of my heart. And behold,
15　　There was music within, and a song.
But while I was hearkening, lo, blackness without,
　　thick and strong,
Came up and came over, and all that sweet fluting
　　was drowned,
　　I could hear it no more;
For the welkin[1] was moaning, the waters were stirred
　　on the shore,

_____
[1] the sky or upper air.

20　And trees in the dark all around
Were shaken. It thundered. "Hark, hark! there is
　　thunder to-night!
The sullen long wave rears her head, and comes
　　down with a will;
The awful white tongues are let loose, and the stars
　　are all dead;—
There is thunder! it thunders! and ladders of light
25　　Run up. There is thunder!" I said,
"Loud thunder! it thunders! and up in the dark overhead,
A down-pouring cloud (there is thunder!), a down-
　　pouring cloud
Hails out her fierce message, and quivers the deep in
　　its bed,
And cowers the earth held at bay; and they mutter
　　aloud,
30　And pause with an ominous tremble, till, great in
　　their rage,
The heavens and earth come together, and meet with
　　a crash;
And the fight is so fell as if Time had come down
　　with the flash.
　　And the story of life was all read,
And the Giver had turned the last page.

35　　Now their bar the pent waterfloods lash,
And the forest trees give out their language austere
　　with great age;
　　And there flieth o'er moor and o'er hill,
　　And there heaveth at intervals wide,
The long sob of nature's great passion, as loath to
　　subside,
40　　Until quiet drop down on the tide,
　　And mad echo hath moaned herself still.

　　　　Lo! or ever I was 'ware,
　　　　In the silence of the air,
　　　Through my heart's wide-open door,
　　　Music floated forth once more,
45　　　Floated to the world's dark rim,
　　　And looked over with a hymn;

Then came home with flutings fine,
And discoursed in tones divine
50 Of a certain grief of mine;
And went downward and went in,
Glimpses of my soul to win,
And discovered such a deep
That I could not choose but weep,
55 For it lay, a land-locked sea,
Fathomless and dim to me.

O the song! It came and went,
Went and came.

             I have not learned.
Half the lore whereto it yearned,
60 Half the magic that it meant.
Water booming in a cave;
Or the swell of some long wave,
Setting in from unrevealed
Countries; or a foreign tongue,
65 Sweetly talked and deftly sung,
While the meaning is half sealed;
May be like it. You have heard
Also;—can you find a word
For the naming of such song?
70 No; a name would do it wrong.
You have heard it in the night,
In the dropping rain's despite.
In the midnight darkness deep,
When the children were asleep,
75 And the wife—no, let that be;
SHE asleep! She knows right well
What the song to you and me,
While we breathe, can never tell;
She hath heard its faultless flow,
80 Where the roots of music grow.

While I listened, like young birds,
Hints were fluttering; almost words,—
Leaned and leaned, and nearer came;—
Everything had changed its name.

85 Sorrow was a ship, I found,
Wrecked with them that in her are,
On an island richer far
Than the port where they were bound.
Fear was but the awful boom
90 Of the old great bell of doom,
Tolling, far from earthly air,
For all worlds to go to prayer.
Pain, that to us mortal clings,
But the pushing of our wings,
95 That we have no use for yet,
And the uprooting of our feet
From the soil where they are set,
And the land we reckon sweet.
Love in growth, the grand deceit
100 Whereby men the perfect greet;
Love in wane, the blessing sent
To be (howsoe'er it went)
Nevermore with earth content.

O, full sweet, and O, full high,
105 Ran that music up the sky;
But I cannot sing it you,
More than I can make you view,
With my paintings labial,
Sitting up in awful row,
110 White old men majestical,
Mountains, in their gowns of snow,
Ghosts of kings; as my two eyes,
Looking over speckled skies,
See them now. About their knees,
115 Half in haze, there stands at ease
A great army of green hills,
Some bareheaded; and, behold,
Small green mosses creep on some.
Those be mighty forests old;
120 And white avalanches come
Through yon rents, where now distils
Sheeny silver, pouring down
To a tune of old renown,
Cutting narrow pathways through

125 Gentian[1] belts of airy blue,
To a zone where starwort blows,
And long reaches of the rose.

So, that haze all left behind,
130 Down the chestnut forests wind,
Pass yon jagged spires, where yet
Foot of man was never set;
Past a castle yawning wide,
With a great breach in its side,
135 To a nest-like valley, where,
Like a sparrow's egg in hue,
Lie two lakes, and teach the true
Color of the sea-maid's hair.

What beside? The world beside!
Drawing down and down to greet
140 Cottage clusters at our feet,—
Every scent of summer tide,—
Flowery pastures all aglow
(Men and women mowing go
Up and down them); also soft,
145 Floating of the film aloft,
Fluttering of the leaves alow.
Is this told? It is not told.
Where's the danger? where's the cold
Slippery danger up the steep?
150 Where yon shadow fallen asleep?
Chirping bird and tumbling spray,
Light, work, laughter, scent of hay,
Peace, and echo, where are they?

Ah, they sleep, sleep all untold;
155 Memory must their grace unfold
Silently; and that high song
Of the heart, it doth belong
To the hearers. Not a whit,

160 Though a chief musician heard,
Could he make a tune for it.

Though a lute full deftly strung,
And the sweetest bird e'er sung,
Could have tried it,—O, the lute
165 For that wondrous song were mute,
And the bird would do her part,
Falter, fail, and break her heart,—
Break her heart, and furl her wings,
On the unexpressive strings.

—1867

Gladys And Her Island

(On the Advantages of the Poetical Temperament)

An Imperfect Fable with a Doubtful Moral

.   .   .   .   .

She mowed at her, but Gladys took the helm:
"Peace, peace!" she said; "be good: you shall not steer,
735 For I am your liege lady." Then she sang
The sweetest song she knew all the way home.

So Gladys set her feet upon the sand;
While in the sunset glory died away
The peaks of that blest island.
                              "Fare you well,
740 My country, my own kingdom," then she said,
"Till I go visit you again, farewell."

She looked toward their house with whom she dwelt,—
The carriages were coming. Hastening up,
She was in time to meet them at the door,
745 And lead the sleepy little ones within;
And some were cross and shivered, and her dames
Were weary and right hard to please; but she
Felt like a beggar suddenly endowed
With a warm cloak to 'fend her from the cold.
750 "For, come what will." she said, "I had *to-day*,
There is an island."

---

[1] mountainous plant usually having violet or vivid blue trumpet-shaped flowers.

THE MORAL

What is the moral? Let us think awhile,
Taking the editorial WE to help,
It sounds respectable.

                The moral; yes,
We always read, when any fable ends,
5   "Hence we may learn." A moral must be found.
What do you think of this: "Hence we may learn
That dolphins swim about the coast of Wales,
And Admiralty maps should now be drawn
By teacher-girls, because their sight is keen,
10 And they can spy out islands." Will that do?
No, that is far too plain,—too evident.

Perhaps a general moralizing vein—
(We know we have a happy knack that way.
We have observed, moreover, that young men
15 Are fond of good advice, and so are girls;
Especially of that meandering kind
Which, winding on so sweetly, treats of all
They ought to be and do and think and wear,
As one may say, from creeds to comforters.
20 Indeed, we much prefer that sort ourselves,
So soothing). Good, a moralizing vein:
That is the thing; but how to manage it?
"*Hence we may learn,*" if we be so inclined,
That life goes best with those who take it best;
25 That wit can spin from work a golden robe
To queen it in; that who can paint at will
A private picture-gallery, should not cry
For shillings that will let him in to look
At some by others painted. Furthermore,
30 Hence we may learn, you poets—(*and we count*
For poets all who ever felt that such
They were, and all who secretly have known
That such they could be; ay, moreover, all
Who wind the robes of ideality
35 *About the bareness of their lives, and hang*

Comforting curtains, knit of fancy's yarn,
Nightly betwixt them and the frosty world),—
Hence we may learn, you poets, that of all
We should be most content. The earth is given
40 To us: we reign by virtue of a sense
Which lets us hear the rhythm of that old verse,
The ring of that old tune whereto she spins.
Humanity is given to us: we reign
By virtue of a sense which lets us in
45 To know its troubles ere they have been told,
And take them home and lull them into rest
With mournfullest music. Time is given to us,—
Time past, time future. Who, good sooth, beside
Have seen it well, have walked this empty world
50 When she went steaming, and from pulpy hills
Have marked the spurting of their flamy crowns?

    Have not we seen the tabernacle pitched,
And peered between the linen curtains, blue,
Purple, and scarlet, at the dimness there,
55 And, frighted, have not dared to look again?
But, quaint antiquity! beheld, we thought,
A chest that might have held the manna pot,
And Aaron's rod[1] that budded. Ay, we leaned
Over the edge of Britain, while the fleet
60 Of Cæsar loomed and neared; then, afterwards,
We saw fair Venice looking at herself
In the glass below her, while her Doge[2] went forth
In all his bravery to the wedding.

                    This,
However, counts for nothing to the grace
65 We wot of in time future:—therefore add,
And afterwards have done: "*Hence we may learn,*"
That though it be a grand and comely thing
To be unhappy—(and we think it is,
Because so many grand and clever folk

---

[1] the rod used by Aaron to perform miracles: Numbers 17:8.

[2] the chief magistrate of the former republics of Venice and Genoa.

70 Have found out reasons for unhappiness,
And talked about uncomfortable things,—
Low motives, bores, and shams, and hollowness,
The hollowness o' the world, till we at last
Have scarcely dared to jump or stamp, for fear,
75 Being so hollow, it should break some day,
And let us in),—yet, since we are not grand,
O, not at all, and as for cleverness,
That may be or may not be,—it is well
For us to be as happy as we can!

80 Agreed; and with a word to the nobler sex,
As thus: We pray you carry not your guns
On the full cock; we pray you set your pride
In its proper place, and never be ashamed
Of any honest calling,—let us add,
85 And end: For all the rest, hold up your heads
And mind your English.
—1867

On The Borders of Cannock Chase

A cottager leaned whispering by her hives,
Telling the bees some news, as they lit down,
And entered one by one their waxen town.
Larks passioning hung o'er their brooding wives,
5 And all the sunny hills where heather thrives
Lay satisfied with peace. A stately crown
Of trees enringed the upper headland brown,
And reedy pools, wherein the moor-hen dives,
Glittered and gleamed.

A resting-place for light,
10 They that were bred here love it; but they say,
"We shall not have it long; in three years' time
A hundred pits will cast out fires by night,
Down yon still glen their smoke shall trail its way,
And the white ash lie thick in lieu of rime."[1]
—?1880

[1] hoarfrost.

Dora Greenwell
1821 — 1882

Dorothy (Dora) Greenwell was born in Lanchester. She published her first volume of poetry in 1848 (entitled, economically, *Poems*), and this volume was reprinted in 1850. She wrote prolifically, producing volumes of poetry in 1861 and 1867 (entitling both, as before, *Poems*), 1869 (*Carmina Crucis*), 1873 (*Songs of Salvation*), and 1876 (*Camera Obscura*). Greenwell published prose on matters theological and political, and she wrote two biographies. A collection of short essays was published in 1866, including the notable "Our Single Women." Greenwell was physically weak most of her life (and an opium addict in older age), but, as her editor of 1889 puts it, she was passionate and forceful "when moved with indignation against some huge moral wrong." In 1881 Greenwell was injured in an accident from which she never fully recovered. She died in 1882 at her brother's home in Clifton.

∾∾∾

The Singer

Before the loud acclaim that rose
    To greet her as she came,
She bent with lowly grace that seemed
    Such tribute to disclaim;
5 With arms meek-folded on her breast
    And drooping head, she stood;
Then raised a glance that seemed to plead
    For youth and womanhood;
A soft, beseeching smile, a look,
10   As if all silently
The kindness to her heart she took,
    And put the homage by.

She stood dejected then, methought,
    A Captive, though a Queen,
15 Before the throng—when sudden passed
    A change across her mien;
Unto her full dilating eye,
    Unto her slender hand,
There came a light of sovereignty,
20   A gesture of command:
And to her lip an eager flow
    Of song, that seemed to bear
Her soul away on rushing wings
    Unto its native air;

25 Her eyes was fixed, her cheek flushed bright
    With power; she seemed to call
On spirits duteous to her voice
    At every rise and fall;
There was no triumph on her brow,
30   No tumult in her breast,
Her soaring soul had won its home,
    And smiled there as at rest;
She felt no more those countless eyes
    Upon her; she had gained
35 A region where they troubled not
    The joy she had attained;
Now, now, she spoke her native speech,
    An utterance fraught with spells,
The echoes of the heart to reach
40   Within their slumber-cells:
And many a quick unbidden sigh,
    And starting tear, revealed
How surely at her touch the springs
    Of feeling were unsealed;
45 The Present seemed unto the Past
    For one sweet moment bound,
With all its broken ties made fast,
    And all its lost ones found;
They who were always loved, seemed now
50   Yet more than ever dear;
Yet closer to the heart they came:

That always were so near:
And trembling back unto the lips
   As if they ne'er had changed,
55 Old names returned that had been thence
   Long severed, long estranged;
For in the strain, like those that fall
   On wanderers as they roam,
The exiled spirit found once more
60   Its country and its home!

She ceased, yet on her parted lips
   A happy smile abode,
As if the sweetness of her song
   Yet lingered whence it flowed;
65 But for a while—her bosom heaved,
   She was the same no more,
The light and spirit fled; she stood
   As she had stood before;
Unheard, unheeded to her ear
70   The shouts of rapture came,
A voice had once more power to thrill,
   That only spoke her name;
Unseen, unheeded, at her feet
   Fell many a bright bouquet,
75 A single flower, in silence given,
   Was once more sweet than they;
For link by link, her own wild strain
   Had drawn her spirit back,
By windings of a silver chain
80   Upon a long-lost track.
And with her song her heart returned,
   To days for ever gone,
Ere Woman's gift of Fame was hers,
   The Many for the One!

85 E'en thus, Oh Earth! before thee still
   Thy Poet-Singers stand,
And bear the soul upon their songs
   Unto its native land;
And even thus, with loud acclaim
90   The praise of skill, of art,

Is dealt to those who only speak
   The language of the heart!
While they who love and listen best
   Can little guess or know,
95 The wounds that from the Singer's breast
   Have let such sweetness flow;
They guess not whence it gushing, starts
   The clear and piercing tone,
That wins it way to other hearts,
100   Through anguish of its own!
They know not Mastery must spring
   From conflict and from strife;
These are not only Songs they sing,
   They are the Singer's Life!
—1850

The Railway Station

Not well nor wisely some have said, "Among us
   Once moved a spirit fair, that now hath fled,"
And deemed, that at the hurrying sounds which
     throng us,
   Its shining wings for sudden flight were spread;

5 Not all the turmoil of the Age of Iron[1]
   Can scare that Spirit hence; like some sweet bird
That loud harsh voices in its cage environ,
   It sings above them all, and will be heard!

Not for the noise of axes or of hammers,
10   Will that sweet bird forsake her chosen nest;
Her warblings pierce through all those deafening
     clamours,
   But surer to their echoes in the breast.

And not the Past alone, with all its guerdon[2]
   Of twilight sounds and shadows, bids them rise;

[1] the final and worst age of humanity, according to Greek myth, fraught with wickedness, greed, and overall degeneracy.

[2] recompense.

15 But soft, above the noontide heat and burden
        Of the stern present, float those melodies;

For not with Baron bold, with Minstrel tender,
        Not with the ringing sound of shield and lance,
Not with the Field of Gold in all its splendour,
20   Died out the generous flame of old Romance:

Still, on a nobler strife than tilt or tourney,
        Rides forth the errant-knight, with brow elate;
Still patient pilgrims take, in hope, their journey;
        Still meek and cloistered spirits stand and wait:

25 Still hath the living, moving world around us,
        Its legends, fair with honour, bright with truth;
Still, as in tales that in our childhood bound us,
        Love holds the fond traditions of its youth!

We need not linger o'er the fading traces
30   Of lost Divinities; or seek to hold
Their serious converse 'mid Earth's green, waste
        places,
        Or by her lonely fountains, as of old:

For, far remote from Nature's fair creations,
        Within the busy mart, the crowded street,
35 With sudden, sweet, unlooked-for revelations
        Of a bright Presence we may chance to meet;

E'en *now*, beside a restless tide's commotion,
        I stand and hear, in broken music swell,
Above the ebb and flow of Life's great ocean,
40   An under-song of greeting and farewell.

For here are Meetings: moments that inherit
        The hopes and wishes, that through months
        and years

Have held such anxious converse with the spirit,
        That now its joy can only speak in tears;

45 And here are Partings: hands that soon must sever,
        Yet clasp the firmer; heart, that unto heart,
Was ne'er so closely bound before, nor ever
        So near the other as when now they part;

And here Time holds his steady pace unbroken,
50   For all that crowds within his narrow scope;
For all the language, uttered and unspoken,
        That will return when Memory comforts Hope!

One short and hurried moment, and for ever
        Flies, like a dream, its sweetness and its pain;
55 And, for the hearts that love, the hands that sever,
        Who knows what meetings are in store again?

They who are left, unto their homes returning,
        With musing step, trace o'er each by-gone
            scene;
And they upon their journey—doth no yearning,
60   No backward glance revert to what hath been?

Yes! for a while, perchance, a tear-drop starting,
        Dims the bright scenes that greet the eye and
            mind;
But here—as ever in Life's cup of Parting—
        Theirs is the bitterness who stay behind!

65 So in Life's sternest, last Farewell, may waken
        A yearning thought, a backward glance be thrown
By them who leave: but oh! how blest the Taken—
        To those who stay behind when THEY are gone!
—1850

The Picture and the Scroll

"Oh, mes amis! lisez-vous quelquefois mes vers;
mon âme y est empreinte."[1]

A bride looked long upon her picture: "Thou
  Art left among the things I held most dear,
A dearer love is calling me; yet now
  These to my heart have never been so near;
5 And I shall not be by when they are gay;
They will be sad, and I shall be away;
Yet thou wilt look upon them night and day,
  As once I looked, so now I leave upon
Thy silent lips a kiss to bide alway;
10   Smile on them, smile on them when I am
    gone!"

A Singer looked in silence on a scroll,
  Her eyes were dark with eloquent fire, her soul
Smiled through them bride-like, yet the hand was
  cold
That locked her slender palm within its hold,
15 And set the spousal wreath upon her brow;
  She said, "I go from all that has been dear,
For dearer love is calling me; yet now
  These to my heart have never been so near,
So will I leave my kiss this scroll upon,
20   That they may find it, while I whisper clear,
'Smile on them, smile on them when I am gone!'"
—1861

The Broken Chain

Captives, bound in iron bands,
  Half have learned to love their chain,
Slaves have held up ransomed hands,
  Praying to be slaves again:
5 So doth custom reconcile,

Soothing even pain to smile;
So a sadness will remain
  In the breaking of the chain.

But if chain were wove of flower,
10   Linked and looped to sister free,
With a Name and with an Hour,
  Running down its Rosary,
Light as gossamers on green,
  By their shining only seen;
15 Would not something sad remain
  In the breaking of the chain?

But if chain were woven shining,
  Firm as gold and fine as hair,
20 Twisting round the heart and twining,
  Binding all that centres there
In a knot, that like the olden
  May be cut, yet ne'er unfolden,
Would not something sharp remain
25   In the breaking of the chain?
—1861

Old Letters

Within an ancient hall,
  Where oft I love to wander, once I found
  An antique casket, that without a sound
Flew open quick, and as a Rose will fall
5 To pieces at a touch when overblown,
So was the floor around me thickly strown
  With yellow leaves, the letters of the Dead:
Oh, hands that wrote these words! oh, loving eyes
That brightened over them! oh, hearts whose prize
10 And treasure once were these, by Time made Heir
To this your sometime wealth, with pious care
I gather in my hoards; for this is dust
Of human hearts that now I hold in trust,
And while I muse above it, spirits flown
15 Come back and commune with me, till the fled

---

[1] "Oh, my friends, sometimes read my verses; my spirit is imprinted there."

Pale ink reveals two names that now have grown
Familiar to my soul, as I had known
And pitied them in youth; in parley soft
I win their secrets forth from them, and oft
20 Make question of their Past! Did Love find rest
And fold its wing where it had made its nest
So warm and deep, or were these of the strong
And patient souls, condemned, though wedded long,
To serve for the other duteously, and wait
25 Upon a harsher Laban,[1]—Life, that proves
With grievous, stern delays each heart that loves?
O gentle spirits, all your lives on high
Are written fair, but mortal history
Is traced upon the sand that may not keep
30 The dint of wave, so quick the dash and leap
        That follows on—a picture on the wall—
A name upon the stone—a leaf whose green
Less quickly fades, because it once hath been
        Within the Dove's soft beak, and this is all.

                            I
                    (*Written in Cipher.*)
35 I write to thee in cypher, even so
        Doth not the heart write ever? being proud,
It careth not to boast its wealth, nor show
        Where lie its precious things by speaking loud.
And here, upon my page an uncouth sign
40   Would say, "I love thee;" farther down this
            mark
        Shows plain, "for ever," yet the sense is dark
To every eye that looks on it but thine.
So is it ever with my heart, thine ear
        Can catch each broken whisper it hath used;
45 So even with my life, thou makest clear
        Its meaning, ofttimes to myself confused;
The souls that use one mother-tongue are free
To mould their rapid speech, but when from thee
        I turn to others, straight I have to choose
50 My words, as one who in a foreign dress

_____
[1] the biblical father of Rachel and Leah.

Must clothe his thought, speak slow in fear to err,
Interpreting himself;

                    We do but guess
At one another darkly, 'mid the stir
That thickens round us; in this life of ours
55 We are like players, knowing not the powers
Nor compass of the instruments we vex,
And by our rash, unskilful touch perplex
To straining discord, needing still the key
To seek, and all our being heedfully
60 To tune to one another's:

                            Ours were set
Together at the first; each hand could move
Like a skilled master's, knowing well each fret
        And chord of the sweet viol he doth love,
All up and down each other's soul, and yet
65   Call forth new concords,—now with softer kiss
I move o'er other souls in fear to miss
        Their latent charm; these too, if better known
Were worthier prizing; Love's great charity
        Hath taught this lesson, as beside her knee
70 I stand, and child-like con it o'er and o'er,
        "Through loving one so much love all the
            more."

                            II
How much, dear friend, how much
        Wouldst thou from me? Oh, nothing but the
            whole
I give or take: what good is in the touch
75   Of hands that for awhile the other fold,
Of eyes that read in each Life's unexpressed
Deep hint of ecstasy to each confessed,
Of hearts that for awhile are warm and blest
        Within the other, yet into the cold
80 Must pass again, while fading from the West.
Pale gleams withdraw, and grieving winds molest?
        Content, content! within a quiet room
        All warm and lit we meet, the outward gloom

Is like a folding arm about us pressed;
85   A space to love in, and a space to pray
    We find; content, content! until the Day
Go down we quit not our belovèd rest.

III

    Oft have I bent my gaze
Adown our Life's steep edge with eyeballs dim
90   And thirsting soul, aweary of the day's
Hot parching dust and glare; this well is deep,
    Too seldom rise the waters to its brim,
And I had nought to draw with! oft in sleep
I felt them touch my very lips, and flow
95 All o'er my forehead and my hands, but, lo
I waked and thirsted; looking down, I knew
Each pebble lying at the base, that drew
    A glimmer from the sunbeam; round the rim
I knew each flower, each forkèd fern that through
100 The stone did thrust its tongue, each moss that grew
Far down its cool and slippery sides—I knew
All but the water's freshness.

    Now I yearn
No more in vain, no longer need I stoop
    So wistful o'er the well, for like an urn
105 Is thy pure soul to me, wherein I scoop
    The waters as I list, and still return.

IV

    We broke no piece of gold,
We took no pledge of lock nor picture slid
    Within the breast; our faith was not so cold
110 That it should ask for any sign! We date
    Our marriage from our meeting day, and hold
These spousals of the soul inviolate
As they are secret; for no friends were bid
    To grace out banquet, yet a guest Divine
115 Was there, who from that hour did consecrate
Life's water, turning it for us to wine.

V

    Stern voices say, "Too much
Thou givest unto one thy soul in trust;
To frame such covenants with things of dust
120   Is but idolatry, that to decay
Doth quickly tend." I answer not to such,
But turning from them proudly, I appeal
Unto my equals, none but those that feel
    Shall be my judges in this question; nay!
125 I will not unto these my cause unseal,
But bear it to a Court where I shall find
A yet more patient hearing; far more kind
The Father than the Brethren! He who made
    The heart doth know its need, but what are we,
130 And whence have we our wisdom, unafraid
    With hands unskilled to vex a mystery
We cannot disentangle?

    Yet I speak
Too harshly in this matter, silence best
Becometh happy spirits; hearts at rest;—
135 O Love, thy gentleness hath made me meek!

VI

    Upon thy lips this name
Of mine so softly taken, first became
That which it is in very deed, the name
Most Christian and most kind, by which I claim
140 A wide inheritance;—and I have borne
This name so long, and only yester morn
Have learned its sweetness! so doth life, our field
Redeemed for us, but slowly, slowly yield
The treasure hid within it! all our less
145   Would grow to more, and this our Earth to Heaven,
Might we but pierce unto the blessedness
That lies so near us, might we but possess
    The things that are our own, as they were given!

VII

    I turn from things behind;
150 They lose their savour! now that on the core

Of Life content I feed, I fling the rind,
That once looked fair, aside for evermore,
For I have pierced beneath it. Since my eyes
Have looked upon thy face, to all things wise,
155 And pure, and noble they have clearer grown;
But careless are they to the vanities
    That once could hold them chained. I stood alone
To watch the long procession that yestreen
    Moved through our city stately to the flow
160 Of martial music; then I saw thee lean
    From out a balcony, and all the show
Went by unmarked of me, as we had been
    Alone beside the river winding slow;—
So doth this world's fair Pageant pass me by,
165   I see but thee! yet do not therefore grow
Unmindful of its goodly company:
I tracked those glittering ranks until they stayed
    Within the square, and passing through the door
Of the great Minster, took within its shade
170 The sunshine after them; like One that prayed
    In silence, seemed that multitude, before
So bright and jubilant, now only made
The stiller for its vastness, as the sea
Doth soothe the sense with wide monotony
175 Of quiet waves unstirred. I saw thee kneel
    Afar; the organ, as it were the Soul
Of many human souls, that did reveal
    Their secrets, sighed, as on its stormy roll
It gathered them; my silent spirit drew
180 More close to those who prayed with me; I knew
That each of these still faces, where I see
No charm to bid me look again, doth make
The sunshine of some eye, and for its sake
The heavens and earth look fairer: each that here
185 Doth kneel, is loved of some, or hath been dear,
    The treasure of some heart beneath the sod.
Oh, we are held unto the other near
    When each is dear to one—and all to God!
—1861

To Elizabeth Barrett Browning
in 1851

I lose myself within thy mind—from room
    To goodly room thou leadest me, and still
    Dost show me of thy glory more, until
My soul, like Sheba's[1] Queen, faints, overcome,
5 And all my spirit dies within me, numb,
    Sucked in by thine, a larger star, at will;
    And hasting like thy bee, my hive to fill,
I "swoon for very joy" amid thy bloom;
Till—not like that poor bird (as poets feign)
10   That tried against the Lutanist's[2] her skill,
    Crowding her thick precipitate notes, until
Her weak heart break above the contest vain—
    Did not thy strength a nobler thought instil,
I feel as if I ne'er could sing again!
—1851

To Elizabeth Barrett Browning
in 1861 [3]

I praised thee not while living; what to thee
    Was praise of mine? I mourned thee not when
        dead;
    I only love thee,—love thee! oh thou fled
Fair spirit, free at last where all are free,
5 I only thee, bless thee, that to me
    For ever thou hast made the rose more red,
    More sweet each word by olden singers said
In sadness, or by children in their glee;
    Once, only once in life I heard thee speak,
10   Once, only once I kissed thee on the cheek,
And met thy kiss and blessing; scarce I knew
Thy smile, I only loved thee, only grew,

---

[1] an ancient kingdom of southwestern Arabia (now the Republic of Yemen). For the biblical story about the meeting between King Solomon and the queen of Sheba, see 1 Kings 10:1–13.

[2] lute-player.

[3] Elizabeth Barrett Browning died in Italy, 1861.

Through wealth, through strength of thine, less
    poor, less weak;
  Oh, what hath death with souls like thine to do?
—1861

One Flower

"Farewell, my flowers," I said,
  The sweet Rose as I passed
Blushed to its core, its last
Warm tear the Lily shed,
5 The Violet hid its head
Among its leaves, and sighed,
"Oh thou, my flower, my pride,
Sweet Summer's sweetest bride,
The rest are fair, but dear
10 Art thou, hast thou no tear?
    What givest thou?" "The whole,"
The glowing Pink replied,
    "Blush, tear, and smile, and sigh I gave
    In giving thee my soul."
15   "The summer, wandering by,
Hath breathed in thee her sigh,
Hath wooed thee from the South,
With kisses of her mouth;
Hath wooed thee from the West,
20 Hath blest thee with the best
    Warm blessings of the sun;
And yet a heavy dower
Is thine, my joy, my flower,
Thy soul hath burst its sheath,
25 Oh, is it love or death,
    Sweet flower, that thou hast won?
Oh, is it love or death
That breathes from this thy breath,
That kindles in thine eye?"
30 Then won I for reply,

"I have made sweet mine hour;
As dies the flower, I die,
  I lived as lives the flower."
—1867

A Scherzo

(A Shy Person's Wishes)

With the wasp at the innermost heart of a peach,
  On a sunny wall out of tip-toe reach,
With the trout in the darkest summer pool,
With the fern-seed clinging behind its cool
5 Smooth frond, in the chink of an aged tree,
In the woodbine's horn with the drunken bee,
With the mouse in its nest in a furrow old,
With the chrysalis wrapt in its gauzy fold;
With things that are hidden, and safe, and bold:
10 With things that are timid, and shy, and free,
Wishing to be;
With the nut in its shell, with the seed in its pod,
With the corn as it sprouts in the kindly clod,
Far down where the secret of beauty shows
15 In the bulb of the tulip, before it blows;
With things that are rooted, and firm, and deep,
Quiet to lie, and dreamless to sleep;
With things that are chainless, and tameless, and proud,
With the fire in the jagged thunder-cloud,
20 With the wind in its sleep, with the wind in its waking,
With the drops that go to the rainbow's making,
Wishing to be with the light leaves shaking,
Or stones on some desolate highway breaking;
Far up on the hills, where no foot surprises
25 The dew as it falls, or the dust as it rises;
To be couched with the beast in its torrid lair,
Or drifting on ice with the polar bear,
With the weaver at work at his quiet loom:
Anywhere, anywhere, out of this room!
—1867

A Song to Call to Remembrance

A Plea for the Coventry Ribbon-Weavers.

I heard a little maiden sing, "What can the matter
 be?"
A simple song, a merry song, yet sad it seemed to
 me,
"Oh, my love is coming from the town, he is
 coming from the fair,
And he will bring me ribbons blue to tie my bonny
 hair!"

5   O lasses fair, that love to wear—O lads that love to
 see
The ribbons bright, the ribbons rare—what can the
 matter be?
At Christmas-tide, when all beside are merry and
 are glad,
How many English hearts are sore, how many
 homes are sad!

The looms are stopped, the hands are still that
 wrought the ribbons gay;
10 When anxious fathers have no work, the children
 dare not play;
No cheerful noise around the board; oh! little to
 prepare!
The mother's work is quickly o'er, but not the
 mother's care!

And all is dull and all is chill within the humble
 room;
Beside his black and fireless hearth, beside his idle
 loom,
15 The poor man sits from day to day in garments
 worn and thin,
And sees the homely comforts go he toiled so hard
 to win.

The icicle hangs on the eaves, and silent as a stone
All Nature lies in sleep or death, chilled through
 unto the bone;

The earth below is white and cold, the skies are
 cold and grey,
20 The grave seems very near, and Heaven seems very
 far away.

Oh sad and short the wintry day, oh sad and long
 the night,
When in the heart there is no hope, and in the
 house no light,
No fire, no food! yet goodly gifts, yet words of
 Christian cheer,
Can make the grave seem farther off, can make the
 heavens more near.

25 Ye merry hearts, that meet to laugh and dance the
 hours away,
Ye gentle hearts, that better love in sheltered homes
 to pray,
Think on the homes whose Christmas guests are
 only Want and Care,
Think on the hearts too sad for mirth, too sad
 perchance for prayer;

For Want and Care are dreary mates, and where
 they enter in
30 There Love should follow after quick, for
 Discontent and Sin
Without the door are knocking loud—oh! keep
 them waiting there,
And hold at bay the prowling wolf of savage, gaunt
 despair!

A little while and skies will clear that now are
 overcast;
Our ship that rides 'mid heavy seas will right itself
 at last;
35 Come, loving hearts, come, open hands, with
 bounty warm and wide,
Come, lend our struggling friends a lift, till the
 turning of the tide.
—1867

Speranza (Lady Wilde)
1821? – 1896

The writer known as Speranza was born Jane Francesca (or possibly just Frances) Elgee in Wexford to Charles Elgee and Sarah Kingsbury. A titanic personality herself, she begat another in the form of her son, Oscar Wilde. She was highly politicized and given, in the name of Irish independence, to anti-British, sometimes incendiary rhetoric in her writing (an Irish periodical to which she contributed was suppressed for sedition in 1848). In 1864 Speranza published a collection of verse entitled *Poems*, and in 1867 she published *Poems: Second Series: Translations*. In 1851 she married an Irish surgeon, antiquary, and nationalist. Together they collected ancient Irish myths and legends, participating (with friend W. B. Yeats) in the Celtic cultural renaissance of the late nineteenth and early twentieth centuries. When her husband died in 1876, Speranza relocated to London and became there, as in Dublin, the centre of a devoted artistic salon. She continued to write, and the influence of the women's movement is evident in her collections of essays, *Notes on Men, Women, and Books* (1891) and *Social Studies* (1893).

❧❧❧

The Voice of the Poor

I

Was sorrow ever like to our sorrow?
    Oh, God above!
Will our night never change into a morrow
    Of joy and love?
5 A deadly gloom is on us waking, sleeping,
    Like the darkness at noontide,
That fell upon the pallid mother, weeping
    By the Crucified.

II

Before us die our brothers of starvation:
10   Around are cries of famine and despair
Where is hope for us, or comfort, or salvation—
    Where—oh! where?
If the angels ever hearken, downward bending,
    They are weeping, we are sure,
15 At the litanies of human groans ascending
    From the crushed hearts of the poor.

III

When the human rests in love upon the human,
    All grief is light;
But who bends one kind glance to illumine
20   Our life-long night?
The air around is ringing with their laughter—
    God has only made the rich to smile;
But we—in our rags, and want, and woe—we
    follow after,
25   Weeping the while.

IV

And the laughter seems but uttered to deride us.
    When—oh! when
Will fall the frozen barriers that divide us
    From other men?
30 Will ignorance for ever thus enslave us?
    Will misery for ever lay us low?
All are eager with their insults, but to save us,
    None, none, we know.

V

We never knew a childhood's mirth and gladness,
35   Nor the proud heart of youth, free and brave;
Oh! a deathlike dream of wretchedness and sadness,
    Is life's weary journey to the grave.
Day by day we lower sink and lower,
    Till the Godlike soul within,

40 Falls crushed, beneath the fearful demon power
    Of poverty and sin.

VI

So we toil on, on with fever burning
    In heart and brain;
So we toil on, on through bitter scorning,
45   Want, woe, and pain:
We dare not raise our eyes to the blue heaven,
    Or the toil must cease—
We dare not breathe the fresh air God has given
    One hour in peace.

VII

50 We must toil, though the light of life is burning,
    Oh, how dim!
We must toil on our sick bed, feebly turning
    Our eyes to Him,
Who alone can hear the pale lip faintly saying,
55   With scarce moved breath
While the paler hands, uplifted, aid the praying—
    "Lord, grant us *Death!*"
—1864

A Remonstrance

Addressed to D. Florence M'Carthy, M.R.I.A. [1]

Stand on the heights, O Poet! nor come down
  Amid the wise old serpents, coiled around
The Tree of Knowledge in Academies.
The Poet's place is by the Tree of Life,
5 Whose fruit turns men to Gods, and makes them
    live,
Not seeking buried treasure in the tombs.
Leave the dim records of a by-gone age
To those great Archivists, who flash the torch
10 Of Truth along Time's mouldering records,

[1] "On reading his Essay on the Collation of Certain Ancient Spanish Manuscripts, printed from the proceedings of the Royal Irish Academy." (Speranza's note.)

Illuminating all the fading Past,
Like golden letters on an ancient scroll.
The Poet soars with eagles, breathes pure ether,
Basks in the light that suns the mountain peak,
15 And sings, from spirit altitudes, such strains,
That all the toilers in life's rugged furrows
Are forced, for once, to lift the bow'd-down head,
And look on Heaven. Flashes from Poet's words
Electric light, strong, swift, and sudden, like
20 The clash of thunder-clouds, by which men read
God's writing legibly on human hearts.

O Poet-Prophets! God hath sent ye forth
With lips made consecrate by altar fire,
To guide the Future, not to tread the Past;
25 To chaunt, in glorious music, man's great hymn,
The watchword of humanity—Advance!
Advance in Wisdom, Nobleness, and Truth,
High aims, high purposes, and self-control,
Which is self-reverence, knowing we shall stand
30 With crownéd angels before God's great throne
The Poet nerves the arm to do great deeds,
Inspires great thoughts, flings o'er the tears of life
The rainbow arch, to save us from despair;
Quickens the stagnant energies to act,
35 Bears the advancing banner of the age,
Full in the van of all Humanity;
And, with a strength, God-given, rolls the stone,
As angels may, from off the Sepulchre
Where souls lie bound, bidding them rise and live.

40 O Poet! preach this Gospel once again—
True Life, true Liberty, God's gifts to man;
Freedom from servile aims and selfish ends,
That swathe and bind the kingly spirit down,
Like Egypt's grave-clothes on the royal dead;
45 Scatter the golden grain of lofty thoughts
From which spring hero-deeds—that so, in truth,
Our Future may be nobler than our Past,

In all that makes a nation's life divine—
This is the Poet's mission, therefore—THINE.
—1864

A Lament For the Potato

A.D. 1739.
(From the Irish)

There is woe, there is clamour, in our desolated
    land,
And wailing lamentation from a famine-stricken
    band;
And weeping are the multitudes in sorrow and
    despair,
For the green fields of Munster[1] lying desolate and
    bare.

5 Woe for Lorc's[2] ancient kingdom, sunk in slavery
    and grief;
Plundered, ruined, are our gentry, our people, and
    their Chief;
For the harvest lieth scattered, more worth to us
    than gold,
All the kindly food that nourished both the young
    and the old.

Well I mind me of the cosherings,[3] where princes
    might dine,
10 And we drank until nightfall the best seven sorts of
    wine;
Yet was ever the Potato our old, familiar dish,
And the best of all sauces with the beeves and the
    fish.

But the harp now is silent, no one careth for the
    sound;
No flowers, no sweet honey, and no beauty can be
    found;
15 Not a bird its music thrilling though the leaves of
    the wood,
Nought but weeping and hands wringing in
    despair for our food.

And the Heavens, all in darkness, seem lamenting
    our doom,
No brightness in the sunlight, not a ray to pierce
    the gloom;
The cataract comes rushing with a fearful deepened
    roar,
20 And ocean bursts its boundaries, dashing wildly on
    the shore.

Yet, in misery and want, we have one protecting
    man,
Kindly Barry,[4] of Fitzstephen's old hospitable clan;
By mount and river working deeds of charity and
    grace:
Blessings ever on our champion, best hero of his
    race!

25 Save us, God! In Thy mercy bend to hear the
    people's cry,
From the famine-stricken fields, rising bitterly on
    high;
Let the mourning and the clamour cease in Lorc's
    ancient land,

---

[1] a south-western province of Ireland.

[2] "Lorc, or Lorcan, an ancient King of Munster, the grandfather of the great King Brian Boru." (Speranza's note.) Brian Boru (c. 941–1014 AD), hero and high-king of Ireland from 1002 until his death.

[3] rich banquets and feasts.

[4] not identified.

And shield us in the death-hour by Thy strong,
  protecting hand![1]
—1864

Fatality

From the German

I

One glance from thy dark eyes is all I pray for,
  One word from thy lips breathed on mine,
One clasp of thy dear hand as a last favour—
  Then go—I'll never more repine.

II

5   Yet, thought of thee will dim my eyes with
      weeping,
  In the noon-day's glorious light,
And dreams of thee will haunt my troubled sleeping,
  'Neath the shadows of the night.

III

A fatal gulf for ever lies between us,
10 I know we dare not speak of love,
Yet angels, purest angels, had they seen us,
  Might well have pardoned from above.

IV

The future is too dark for my sad seeing;
  I gaze, but, weeping, turn away—
15 No hope, alas! of our ever being
  Less sad than we are here this day.
—1864

---

[1] "This Irish poem, so pathetic and expressive in its simplicity, first appeared in the *Dublin University Magazine*, in the Essay on 'The Food of the Irish,' by Sir William Wilde. It is quoted by him as 'highly characteristic both of the feelings of the people and the extent of the calamity of that time; besides being a good specimen of the native poetry of the Irish more than a hundred years ago.'" (Speranza's note.)

Corinne's Last Love-Song

I

How beautiful, how beautiful you streamed
  upon my sight,
In glory and in grandeur, as a gorgeous sunset-light!
How softly, soul-subduing, fell your words upon
  mine ear,
Like low aerial music when some angel hovers near!
5   What tremulous, faint ecstacy to clasp your hand
      in mine,
Till the darkness fell upon me of a glory too divine!
The air around grew languid with our intermingled
  breath,
And in your beauty's shadow I sank motionless as
  death.
I saw you not, I heard not, for a mist was on my
  brain—
10 I only felt that life could give no joy like that again.

II

And this was Love—I knew it not, but blindly
  floated on,
And now I'm on the ocean waste, dark, desolate,
  alone;
The waves are raging round me—I'm reckless
  where they guide;
No hope is left to light me, no strength to stem the
  tide.
15 As a leaf along the torrent, a cloud across the sky,
As dust upon the whirlwind, so my life is drifting
  by.
The dream that drank the meteor's light—the form
  from Heav'n has flown—
The vision and the glory, they are passing—they
  are gone.
Oh! love is frantic agony, and life one throb of pain;
20 Yet I would bear its darkest woes to dream that
      dream again.
—1864

Tristan and Isolde [1]

The Love Sin.

None, unless the saints above,
Knew the secret of their love;
For with calm and stately grace
Isolde held her queenly place,
5   Tho' the courtiers' hundred eyes
Sought the lovers to surprise,
Or to read the mysteries
Of a love—so rumour said—
By a magic philtre fed,
10 Which for ever in their veins
Burn'd with love's consuming pains.

Yet their hands would twine unseen,
    In a clasp 'twere hard to sever;
And whoso watched their glances meet,
15   Gazing as they'd gaze for ever,
Might have marked the sudden heat
Crims'ning on each flushing cheek,
As the tell-tale blood would speak
Of love that never should have been—
20 The love of Tristan and his Queen.

But, what hinders that the two,
    In the spring of their young life,
Love each other as they do?
Thus the tempting thoughts begin—
25 Little recked they of the sin;
Nature joined them hand in hand,
Is not that a truer band
    Than the formal name of wife?

Ah! what happy hours were theirs!
30   One might note them at the feast

Laughing low to loving airs,
    Loving airs that pleased them best;
Or interchanging the swift glance
In the mazes of the dance.
35 So the sunny moments rolled,
And they wove bright threads of gold
    Through the common web of life;
Never dreaming of annoy,
    Or the wild world's wicked strife;
40 Painting earth and heaven above
    In the light of their own joy,
In the purple light of love.

Happy moments, which again
Brought sweet torments in their train:
45 All love's petulance and fears,
Wayward doubts and tender tears;
Little jealousies and pride,
That can loving hearts divide:
Murmured vow and clinging kiss,
50 Working often bane as bliss;
All the wild, capricious changes
Through which lovers' passion ranges.

Yet would love, in every mood,
Find Heaven's manna for its food;
55 For love will grow wan and cold,
And die ere ever it is old,
That is never assailed by fears,
Or steeped in repentant tears,
Or passed through the fire like gold.

60 So loved Tristan and Isolde,
In youth's sunny, golden time,
In the brightness of their prime;
Little dreaming hours would come,
Like pale shadows from the tomb,
65 When an open death of doom
Had been still less hard to bear,
Than the ghastly, cold despair

---

[1] a medieval legend in which Tristan is sent to Ireland by king Mark of Cornwall to bring back the princess Isolde to become the king's bride. Unbeknownst to either of them, Tristan and Isolde drink a love potion and eventually die together.

Of those hidden vows, whose smart
Pale the cheek, and break the heart.
—1864

The Poet's Destiny

The Priest of Beauty, the Anointed One,
Through the wide world passes the Poet on.
All that is noble by his word is crown'd,
But on his brow th' Acanthus[1] wreath is bound.
5 Eternal temples rise beneath his hand,
While his own griefs are written in the sand;
He plants the blooming gardens, trails the vine—
But others wear the flowers, drink the wine;
He plunges in the depths of life to seek
10 Rich joys for other hearts—his own may break.
Like the poor diver beneath Indian skies,
He flings the pearl upon the shore—and dies.
—1864

An Appeal to Ireland

I

The sin of our race is upon us,
The pitiless, cruel disdain
Of brother for brother, tho' coiling
Round both is the one fatal chain;
5 And aimless and reckless and useless
Our lives pass along to the grave
In tumults of words that bewilder,
And the conflicts of slave with slave.

II

Yet shadows are heavy around us,
10 The darkness of sin and of shame,
While the souls of the Nation to slumber
Are lulled by vain visions of fame;
True hearts, passion-wasted, and breaking

With sense of our infinite wrong,
15 Oh! wake them, nor dread the awaking,
We need all the strength of the strong.

III

For we rage with senseless endeavours
In a fever of wild unrest,
While glory lies trampled, dishonoured,
20 Death-pale, with a wound in her breast;
Had we loosened one chain from the spirit,
Had we strove from the ruin of things
To build up a Temple of Concord,
More fair than the palace of Kings;

IV

25 Our name might be heard where the Nations
Press on to the van of the fight,
Where Progress makes war upon Evil,
And Darkness is scattered by Light.
They have gold and frankincense and myrrh
30 To lay at the feet of their King,
But we—what have we but the wine-cup
Of wrath and of sorrow to bring?

V

Let us ask of our souls, lying under
The doom of this bondage and ban,
35 Why we, made by God high as Angels,
Should fall so much lower than man;
Some indeed have been with us would scale
Heav'n's heights for life-fire if they dare—
But the vultures now gnaw at their hearts
40 Evermore on the rocks of Despair.

VI

Let us think, when we stand before God,
On the Day of the Judgment roll,
And He asks of the work we have done
In the strength of each God-like soul;
45 Can we answer—"Our prayers have gone up
As light from the stars and the sun,

---

[1] a plant with large leaves found in the Mediterranean region.

And Thy blessing came down on our deeds
   As a crown when the victory's won.

VII

"We fought with wild beasts, wilder passions,
50   As of old did the saints of God,
Tho' our life-blood ran red in the dust
   Of the fierce arena we trod;
We led up Thy people triumphant
   From Egypt's dark bondage of sin,
55 And made the fair land which Thou gavest
   All glorious without and within.

VIII

"We changed to a measure of music
   The discord and wail of her days,
For sorrow gave garments of gladness,
60   For scorn of her enemies praise;
We crowned her a Queen in the triumph
   Of noble and beautiful lives,
While her chariot of Freedom rolled on
   Through the crash of her fallen gyves."[1]

IX

65 I ask of you, Princes, and Rulers,
   I ask of you, Brothers around,
Can ye thus make reply for our people
   When the Nations are judged or crowned?
If not, give the reins of the chariot
70   To men who can curb the wild steeds—
They are nearing the gulf, in this hour
   We appeal by our wrongs and our needs.

X

Stand back and give place to new leaders;
   We need them—some strong gifted souls,
75 From whose lips, never touched by a falsehood,
   The heart's richest eloquence rolls.
True Patriots by grandeur of purpose,

True men by the power of the brain:
The chosen of God to lift upward
80   His Ark[2] with hands clear of all stain.

XI

We need them to tend the Lord's vineyard,
   As shepherds to watch round His fold,
With brave words from pure hearts outpouring,
   As wine from a chalice of gold;
85 That the souls of the Nation uplifted,
   May shine in new radiance of light,
As of old stood the Prophets transfigured
   In glory with Christ on the height.

XII

Far out, where the grand western sunsets
90   Flush crimson the mountain and sea,
And the echoes of Liberty mingle
   With the roar of the waves on the lea;
Where over the dim shrouded passes
   The clouds fling a rainbow-hued arch,
95 And through giant-rent portals a people
   Go forth on their sad, solemn march:

XIII

I had dreams of a future of glory
   For this fair motherland of mine,
When knowledge would bring with its splendours
100   The Human more near the Divine.
And as flash follows flash on the mountains,
   When lightnings and thunders are hurled,
So would throb in electrical union
   Her soul with the soul of the world.

XIV

105 For we stand too apart in our darkness,
   As plants long rent from the sun,
And the mystical breath of the spirit
   Scarce touches our hearts sweeping on.

---

[1] shackles.

[2] the ark of the covenant.

I appeal from this drear isolation
110 To earth, to the mountains, and sky—
Must we die as of thirst in a desert,
 While full tides of life pass us by?

xv

Yet still, through the darkness and sorrow,
115 I dream of a time yet to be,

When from mountain and ocean to Heaven
 Will rise up the Hymn of the Free.
When our Country, made perfect through trial,
 White-robed, myrtle-crowned, as a Bride,
120 Will stand forth, "a Lady of Kingdoms,"
 Through Light and through Love glorified.
 —1864

Matthew Arnold
1822 – 1888

Matthew Arnold, son of Thomas Arnold, headmaster of the famous public school Rugby from 1828 to 1842, was a poet and prose writer, traditionally ranked with Browning and Tennyson as one of the most important poets of the Victorian age. But unlike Browning and Tennyson, Arnold could not sustain his poetic impulse. His poetry, which he began publishing early in his career, reflected a deep sense of personal insecurity, barrenness, and even a note of resigned despair. These traits are evident in *The Strayed Reveller and Other Poems* (1849), *Empedocles on Etna and Other Poems* (1852), and "Thyrsis" (1866), an elegy on the death of his friend Arthur Hugh Clough. After 1855 Arnold wrote very little poetry, turning instead to the production of a great deal of high quality prose including literary criticism, political and cultural commentary, and religious writings. His most important work in cultural commentary is *Culture and Anarchy* (1869).

∽∾∽

To a Gipsy Child by the Sea-Shore

Douglas, Isle of Man[1]

Who taught this pleading to unpractised eyes?
  Who hid such import in an infant's gloom?
Who lent thee, child, this meditative guise?
  Who massed, round that slight brow, these clouds of doom?

5 Lo! sails that gleam a moment and are gone;
  The swinging waters, and the clustered pier.
Not idly Earth and Ocean labour on,
  Nor idly do these sea-birds hover near.

But thou, whom superfluity of joy[2]
10 Wafts not from thine own thoughts, nor longings vain,
  Nor weariness, the full-fed soul's annoy—
Remaining in thy hunger and thy pain;

Thou, drugging pain by patience; half averse
  From thine own mother's breast, that knows not thee;

15 With eyes which sought thine eyes thou didst converse,
  And that soul-searching vision fell on me.

Glooms that go deep as thine I have not known:
  Moods of fantastic sadness, nothing worth.
Thy sorrow and thy calmness are thine own:
20 Glooms that enhance and glorify this earth.

What mood wears like complexion to thy woe?
  His, who in mountain glens, at noon of day,
Sits rapt, and hears the battle break below?
  —Ah! thine was not the shelter, but the fray.

25 Some exile's, mindful how the past was glad?
  Some angel's, in an alien planet born?
—No exile's dream was ever half so sad,
  Not any angel's sorrow so forlorn.

Is the calm thine of stoic souls, who weigh
30 Life well, and find it wanting, nor deplore;
But in disdainful silence turn away,
  Stand mute, self-centred, stern, and dream no more?

Or do I wait, to hear some gray-haired king
  Unravel all his many-coloured lore;

---

[1] probably written August 1843 or 1844, after the Arnold family passed part of the long vacation at Douglas on the Isle of Man.

[2] Cf. stanza 3 and 4 of Wordsworth's "Immortality Ode."

35   Whose mind hath known all arts of governing,
    Mused much, loved life a little, loathed it more?

    Down the pale cheek long lines of shadow slope,
    Which years, and curious thought, and suffering
      give.
    —Thou hast foreknown the vanity of hope,
40   Foreseen thy harvest—yet proceed'st to live.

    O meek anticipant of that sure pain
    Whose sureness gray-haired scholars hardly learn!
    What wonder shall time breed, to swell thy strain?
    What heavens, what earth, what sun shalt thou
      discern?

45   Ere the long night, whose stillness brooks no star,
    Match that funereal aspect with her pall,
    I think thou wilt have fathomed life too far,
    Have known too much—or else forgotten all.

    The Guide of our dark steps a triple veil
50   Betwixt our senses and our sorrow keeps;
    Hath sown with cloudless passages the tale
    Of grief, and eased us with a thousand sleeps.

    Ah! not the nectarous poppy lovers use,
    Not daily labour's dull, Lethæan spring,
55   Oblivion in lost angels can infuse
    Of the soiled glory and the trailing wing.

    And though thou glean, what strenuous gleaners
      may,
    In the thronged fields where winning comes by
      strife;
    And though the just sun gild, as mortals pray,
60   Some reaches of thy storm-vext stream of life;[1]

    Though that blank sunshine blind thee; though the
      cloud

    That severed the world's march and thine be gone;
    Though ease dulls grace, and Wisdom be too proud
    To halve a lodging that was all her own—

65   Once, ere the day decline, thou shalt discern,
    Oh once, ere night, in thy success, thy chain!
    Ere the long evening close, thou shalt return,
    And wear this majesty of grief again.
    —1849[2]

The Strayed Reveller

THE PORTICO OF CIRCE'S PALACE, EVENING

A Youth. Circe.

THE YOUTH

Faster, faster,
O Circe, Goddess,
Let the wild, thronging train,
The bright procession
5 Of eddying forms,
Sweep through my soul!

Thou standest, smiling
Down on me! thy right arm,
Leaned up against the column there,
10 Props thy soft cheek;
Thy left holds, hanging loosely,
The deep cup, ivy-cinctured,
I held but now.

  Is it, then, evening
15 So soon? I see the night-dews,
Clustered in thick beads, dim
The agate brooch-stones
On thy white shoulder;
The cool night-wind, too,

---

[1] a figure favoured by Romantic poets, and Arnold.

[2] We are following Kenneth and Miriam Allott in arranging the poems by date of composition as far as that can be determined. For a detailed presentation of materials related to Arnold's poems, sources, annotations, textural variants, etc., see *The Poems of Matthew Arnold*, ed. Kenneth and Miriam Allott, 2nd ed. (London: Longmans, 1979).

20 Blows through the portico,
Stirs thy hair, Goddess,
Waves thy white robe!

CIRCE

Whence art thou, sleeper?

THE YOUTH

When the white dawn first
25 Through the rough fir-planks
Of my hut, by the chestnuts,
Up at the valley-head,
Came breaking. Goddess!
I sprang up, I threw round me
30 My dappled fawn-skin;
Passing out, from the wet turf,
Where they lay, by the hut door,
I snatched up my vine-crown, my fir-staff,
All drenched in dew—
35 Came swift down to join
The rout early gathered
In the town, round the temple,
Iacchus'[1] white fane
On yonder hill.

40 Quick I passed, following
The wood-cutters' cart-track
Down the dark valley; I saw
On my left, through the beeches,
Thy palace, Goddess,
45 Smokeless, empty!
Trembling, I entered; beheld
The court all silent,
The lions sleeping,
On the altar this bowl.
50 I drank, Goddess!
And sank down here, sleeping,
On the steps of thy portico.

CIRCE

Foolish boy! Why tremblest thou?
Thou lovest it, then, my wine?
55 Wouldst more of it? See, how glows.
Through the delicate, flushed marble,
The red, creaming liquor,
Strown with dark seeds!
Drink, then! I chide thee not,
60 Deny thee not my bowl.
Come, stretch forth thy hand, then—so!
Drink—drink again!

THE YOUTH

Thanks, gracious one!
Ah, the sweet fumes again!
65 More soft, ah me,
More subtle-winding
Than Pan's flute-music!
Faint—faint! Ah me,
Again the sweet sleep!

CIRCE

70 Hist! Thou—within there!
Come forth, Ulysses!
Art tired with hunting?
While we range the woodland,
See what the day brings.

ULYSSES

75 Ever new magic!
Hast thou then lured hither,
Wonderful Goddess, by thy art,
The young, languid-eyed Ampelus,[2]
Iacchus' darling—
80 Or some youth beloved of Pan,
Of Pan and the Nymphs?
That he sits, bending downward
His white, delicate neck
To the ivy-wreathed marge
85 Of thy cup; the bright, glancing vine-leaves

---

[1] a minor deity identified with Dionysus.

[2] son of a nymph and satyr.

That crown his hair,
Falling forward, mingling
With the dark ivy-plants—
His fawn-skin, half untied,
90 Smeared with red wine-stains? Who is he,
That he sits, overweighed
By fumes of wine and sleep,
So late, in thy portico?
What youth, Goddess, what guest
95 Of Gods or mortals?

CIRCE

Hist! he wakes!
I lured him not hither, Ulysses.
Nay, ask him!

THE YOUTH

Who speaks? Ah, who comes forth
100 To thy side, Goddess, from within?
How shall I name him?
This spare, dark-featured,
Quick-eyed stranger?
Ah, and I see too
105 His sailor's bonnet,
His short-coat, travel-tarnished,
With one arm bare!—
Art thou not he, whom fame
This long time rumours
110 The favoured guest of Circe, brought by the waves?
Art thou he, stranger?
The wise Ulysses,
Laertes' son?

ULYSSES

I am Ulysses.
115 And thou, too, sleeper?
Thy voice is sweet.
It may be thou hast followed
Through the islands some divine bard,
By age taught many things,
120 Age and the Muses;

And heard him delighting
The chiefs and people
In the banquet, and learned his songs,
Of Gods and Heroes,
125 Of war and arts,
And peopled cities,
Inland, or built
By the grey sea.—If so, then hail!
I honour and welcome thee.

THE YOUTH

130 The Gods are happy.
They turn on all sides
Their shining eyes,
And see below them
The earth and men.

135 They see Tiresias[1]
Sitting, staff in hand,
On the warm, grassy
Asopus bank,
His robe drawn over
140 His old, sightless head,
Revolving inly
The doom of Thebes.

They see the Centaurs[2]
In the upper glens
145 Of Pelion, in the streams,
Where red-berried ashes fringe
The clear-brown shallow pools,
With streaming flanks, and heads
Reared proudly, snuffing
150 The mountain wind.

They see the Indian
Drifting, knife in hand,
His frail boat moored to

---

[1] the blind soothsayer who foresaw the "doom of Thebes."

[2] savage inhabitants of Mt. Pelion in Thessaly, often depicted as half man, half horse.

A floating isle thick-matted
155 With large-leaved, low-creeping melon-plants,
And the dark cucumber.
He reaps, and stows them,
Drifting—drifting; round him,
Round his green harvest-plot,
160 Flow the cool lake-waves,
The mountains ring them.

They see the Scythian[1]
On the wide steppe, unharnessing
His wheeled house at noon.
165 He tethers his beast down, and makes his meal—
Mares' milk, and bread
Baked on the embers: all around
The boundless, waving grass-plains stretch, thick-
          starred
With saffron and the yellow hollyhock
170 And flag-leaved iris-flowers.
Sitting in his cart
He makes his meal; before him, for long miles,
Alive with bright green lizards,
And the springing bustard-fowl,
175 The track, a straight black line,
Furrows the rich soil; here and there
Clusters of lonely mounds
Topped with rough-hewn,
Grey, rain-bleared statues, overpeer
180 The sunny waste.

They see the ferry
On the broad, clay-laden
Lone Chorasmian stream;[2] thereon,
With snort and strain,
185 Two horses, strongly swimming, tow
The ferry-boat, with woven ropes
To either bow
Firm harnessed by the mane; a chief,

With shout and shaken spear,
190 Stands at the prow, and guides them; but astern
The cowering merchants, in long robes,
Sit pale beside their wealth
Of silk-bales, and of balsam-drops,
Of gold and ivory,
195 Of turquoise-earth and amethyst,
Jasper and chalcedony,
And milk-barred onyx-stones.
The loaded boat swings groaning
In the yellow eddies;
200 The Gods behold them.

They see the Heroes
Sitting in the dark ship
On the foamless, long-heaving.
Violet sea,
205 At sunset nearing
The Happy Islands.[3]

    These things, Ulysses,
The wise bards also
Behold and sing.
210 But oh, what labour!
O prince, what pain!
They too can see
Tiresias; but the Gods,
Who give them vision,
215 Added this law:
That they should bear too
His groping blindness,
His dark foreboding,
His scorned white hairs;
220 Bear Hera's anger
Through a life lengthened
To seven ages.[4]

_____

[1] nomadic northern tribe.

[2] the river Oxus.

[3] Greek paradise for heroes.

[4] Tiresias was blinded by Hera as a result of a dispute, and Zeus lengthened his life to seven generations.

They see the Centaurs
On Pelion; then they feel,
225 They too, the maddening wine
Swell their large veins to bursting; in wild pain
They feel the biting spears
Of the grim Lapithæ, and Theseus, drive,
Drive crashing through their bones; they feel
230 High on a jutting rock in the red stream
Alcmena's dreadful son[1]
Ply his bow; such a price
The Gods exact for song:
To become what we sing.

235 They see the Indian
On his mountain lake; but squalls
Make their skiff reel, and worms
In the unkind spring have gnawn
Their melon-harvest to the heart.—They see
240 The Scythian; but long frosts
Parch them in winter-time on the bare steppe,
Till they too fade like grass; they crawl
Like shadows forth in spring.

They see the merchants
245 On the Oxus stream; but care
Must visit first them too, and make them pale.
Whether, through whirling sand,
A cloud of desert robber-horse have burst
Upon their caravan; or greedy kings,
250 In the walled cities the way passes through,
Crushed them with tolls; or fever-airs,
On some great river's marge,
Mown them down, far from home.

They see the Heroes
255 Near harbour; but they share
Their lives, and former violent toil in Thebes,
Seven-gated Thebes, or Troy;
Or where the echoing oars

Of Argo first
260 Startled the unknown sea.

The old Silenus[2]
Came, lolling in the sunshine,
From the dewy forest-coverts,
This way, at noon.
265 Sitting by me, while his Fauns
Down at the water-side
Sprinkled and smoothed
His drooping garland,
He told me these things.

270 But I, Ulysses,
Sitting on the warm steps,
Looking over the valley,
All day long, have seen,
Without pain, without labour,
275 Sometimes a wild-haired Mænad—[3]
Sometimes a Faun with torches—
And sometimes, for a moment,
Passing through the dark stems
Flowing-robed, the beloved,
280 The desired, the divine,
Beloved Iacchus.

Ah, cool night-wind, tremulous stars!
Ah, glimmering water,
Fitful earth-murmur,
285 Dreaming woods!
Ah, golden-haired, strangely smiling Goddess,
And thou, proved, much enduring,
Wave-tossed Wanderer!
Who can stand still?
290 Ye fade, ye swim, ye waver before me—
The cup again!

---

[1] Hercules also fought the Centaurs.

[2] Silenus, satyr teacher and companion of the youthful Dionysus.

[3] female worshipper of Iacchus.

Faster, faster,
O Circe, Goddess,
Let the wild, thronging train,
295   The bright procession
Of eddying forms,
Sweep through my soul!
—1849 (1847–48?)

Resignation

To Fausta[1]

*T*o *die be given us, or attain!*
  Fierce work it were, to do again.
So pilgrims, bound for Mecca, prayed
At burning noon; so warriors said,
5   Scarfed with the cross, who watched the miles
Of dust which wreathed their struggling files
Down Lydian mountains; so, when snows
Round Alpine summits, eddying, rose,
The Goth, bound Rome-wards; so the Hun,
10   Crouched on his saddle, while the sun
Went lurid down o'er flooded plains
Through which the groaning Danube strains
To the drear Euxine;—so pray all,
Whom labours, self-ordained, enthrall;
15   Because they to themselves propose
On this side the all-common close
A goal which, gained, may give repose.
So pray they; and to stand again
Where they stood once, to them were pain;
20   Pain to thread back and to renew
Past straits, and currents long steered through.

But milder natures, and more free—
Whom an unblamed serenity
Hath freed from passions, and the state
25   Of struggle these necessitate;

Whom schooling of the stubborn mind
Hath made, or birth hath found, resigned—
These mourn not, that their goings pay
Obedience to the passing day.
30   These claim not every laughing Hour
For handmaid to their striding power;
Each in her turn, with torch upreared,
To await their march; and when appeared,
Through the cold gloom, with measured race,
35   To usher for a destined space
(Her own sweet errands all foregone)
The too imperious traveller on.
These, Fausta, ask not this; nor thou,
Time's chafing prisoner, ask it now!

40   We left, just ten years since, you say,
That wayside inn we left to-day.[2]
Our jovial host, as forth we fare,
Shouts greeting from his easy chair.
High on a bank our leader stands,
45   Reviews and ranks his motley bands,
Makes clear our goal to every eye—
The valley's western boundary.
A gate swings to! our tide hath flowed
Already from the silent road.
50   The valley-pastures, one by one,
Are threaded, quiet in the sun;
And now beyond the rude stone bridge
Slopes gracious up the western ridge.
Its woody border, and the last
55   Of its dark upland farms is past—
Cool farms, with open-lying stores,
Under their burnish'd sycamores;
All past! and through the trees we glide,
Emerging on the green hill-side.
60   There climbing hangs, a far-seen sign,
Our wavering, many-coloured line;
There winds, upstreaming slowly still
Over the summit of the hill.

---

[1] Arnold's elder sister Jane with whom he walked in the Lake District in the period 1847–49. She is named a female Faust because she is uneasy with inaction and desires a life of accomplishment.

[2] the inn at Wythburn, Cumberland.

And now, in front, behold outspread
65 Those upper regions we must tread!
Mild hollows, and clear heathy swells,
The cheerful silence of the fells.
Some two hours' march with serious air,
Through the deep noontide heats we fare;
70 The red-grouse, springing at our sound,
Skims, now and then, the shining ground;
No life, save his and ours, intrudes
Upon these breathless solitudes.
O joy! again the farms appear.
75 Cool shade is there, and rustic cheer;
There springs the brook will guide us down,
Bright comrade, to the noisy town.
Lingering, we follow down; we gain
The town, the highway, and the plain.
80 And many a mile of dusty way,
Parched and road-worn, we made that day;
But, Fausta, I remember well,
That as the balmy darkness fell
We bathed our hands with speechless glee,
85 That night, in the wide-glimmering sea.

Once more we tread this self-same road,
Fausta, which ten years since we trod;
Alone we tread it, you and I,
Ghosts of that boisterous company.
90 Here, where the brook shines, near its head,
In its clear, shallow, turf-fringed bed;
Here, whence the eye first sees, far down,
Capped with faint smoke, the noisy town;
Here sit we, and again unroll,
95 Though slowly, the familiar whole.
The solemn wastes of healthy hill
Sleep in the July sunshine still;
The self-same shadows now, as then,
Play through this grassy upland glen;
100 The loose dark stones on the green way
Lie strewn, it seems, where then they lay;
On this mild bank above the stream,
(You crush them!) the blue gentians gleam.

Still this wild brook, the rushes cool,
105 The sailing foam, the shining pool!
These are not changed; and we, you say,
Are scarce more changed, in truth, than they.

The gipsies, whom we met below,
They, too, have long roamed to and fro;
110 They ramble, leaving, where they pass,
Their fragments on the cumbered grass.
And often to some kindly place
Chance guides the migratory race,
Where, though long wanderings intervene,
115 They recognise a former scene.
The dingy tents are pitched; the fires
Give to the wind their wavering spires;
In dark knots crouch round the wild flame
Their children, as when first they came;
120 They see their shackled beasts again
Move, browsing, up the gray-walled lane.
Signs are not wanting, which might raise
The ghost in them of former days—
Signs are not wanting, if they would;
125 Suggestions to disquietude.
For them, for all, time's busy touch,
While it mends little, troubles much.
Their joints grow stiffer—but the year
Runs his old round of dubious cheer;
130 Chilly they grow—yet winds in March,
Still, sharp as ever, freeze and parch;
They must live still—and yet, God knows,
Crowded and keen the country grows;
It seems as if, in their decay,
135 The law grew stronger every day.[1]
So might they reason, so compare,
Fausta, times past with times that are.
But no!—they rubbed through yesterday
In their hereditary way,
140 And they will rub through, if they can,
To-morrow on the self-same plan,

---

[1] laws against trespassing become more strictly enforced.

Till death arrive to supersede,
For them, vicissitude and need.

The poet, to whose mighty heart
145 Heaven doth a quicker pulse impart,
Subdues that energy to scan
Not his own course, but that of man.
Though he move mountains, though his day
Be passed on the proud heights of sway,
150 Though he hath loosed a thousand chains,
Though he hath borne immortal pains,
Action and suffering though he know—
He hath not lived, if he lives so.
He sees, in some great-historied land,
155 A ruler of the people stand,
Sees his strong thought in fiery flood
Roll through the heaving multitude;
Exults—yet for no moment's space
Envies the all-regarded place.
160 Beautiful eyes meet his—and he
Bears to admire uncravingly;[1]
They pass—he, mingled with the crowd,
Is in their far-off triumphs proud.
From some high station he looks down,
165 At sunset, on a populous town;
Surveys each happy group which fleets,
Toil ended, through the shining streets,
Each with some errand of its own—
And does not say: *I am alone.*
170 He sees the gentle stir of birth
When morning purifies the earth;
He leans upon a gate and sees
The pastures, and the quiet trees.
Low, woody hill, with gracious bound,
175 Folds the still valley almost round;
The cuckoo, loud on some high lawn,
Is answered from the depth of dawn;
In the hedge straggling to the stream,
Pale, dew-drenched, half-shut roses gleam;

---

[1] emotionally detached.

180 But, where the farther side slopes down,
He sees the drowsy new-waked clown
In his white quaint-embroidered frock
Make, whistling, tow'rd his mist-wreathed flock—
Slowly, behind his heavy tread,
185 The wet, flowered grass heaves up its head.
Leaned on his gate, he gazes—tears
Are in his eyes, and in his ears
The murmur of a thousand years.
Before him he sees life unroll,
190 A placid and continuous whole—
That general life, which does not cease,
Whose secret is not joy, but peace;
That life, whose dumb wish is not missed
If birth proceeds, if things subsist;
195 The life of plants, and stones, and rain,
The life he craves—if not in vain
Fate gave, what chance shall not control,
His sad lucidity of soul.

You listen—but that wandering smile,
200 Fausta, betrays you cold the while!
Your eyes pursue the bells of foam
Washed, eddying, from this bank, their home.
Those gipsies, so your thoughts I scan,
Are less, the poet more, than man.
205 *They feel not, though they move and see;*
Deeper the poet feels; but he
Breathes, when he will, immortal air,
Where Orpheus and where Homer are.
In the day's life, whose iron round
210 *Hems us all in, he is not bound;*
He leaves his kind, o'erleaps their pen,
And flees the common life of men.
He escapes thence, but we abide—
Not deep the poet sees, but wide.
215 The world in which we live and move
Outlasts aversion, outlasts love,
Outlasts each effort, interest, hope,
Remorse, grief, joy;—and were the scope
Of these affections wider made,

220 Man still would see, and see dismayed,
Beyond his passion's widest range,
Far regions of eternal change.
Nay, and since death, which wipes out man,
Finds him with many an unsolved plan,
225 With much unknown, and much untried,
Wonder not dead, and thirst not dried,
Still gazing on the ever full
Eternal mundane spectacle—
This world in which we draw our breath,
230 In some sense, Fausta, outlasts death.

Blame thou not, therefore, him who dares
Judge vain beforehand human cares;
Whose natural insight can discern
What through experience others learn;
235 Who needs not love and power, to know
Love transient, power an unreal show;
Who treads at ease life's uncheered ways—
Him blame not, Fausta, rather praise!
Rather thyself for some aim pray
240 Nobler than this, to fill the day;
Rather that heart, which burns in thee,
Ask, not to amuse, but to set free;
Be passionate hopes not ill resigned
For quiet, and a fearless mind.
245 And though fate grudge to thee and me
The poet's rapt security,
Yet they, believe me, who await
No gifts from chance, have conquered fate.
They, winning room to see and hear,
250 And to men's business not too near,
Through clouds of individual strife
Draw homeward to the general life.
Like leaves by suns not yet uncurled;
To the wise, foolish; to the world,
255 Weak; yet not weak, I might reply,
Not foolish, Fausta, in His eye,
To whom each moment in its race,
Crowd as we will its neutral space,

Is but a quiet watershed
260 Whence, equally, the seas of life and death are fed.

Enough, we live!—and if a life,
With large results so little rife,
Though bearable, seem hardly worth
This pomp of words, this pain of birth;
265 Yet, Fausta, the mute turf we tread,
The solemn hills around us spread,
This stream which falls incessantly,
The strange-scrawled rocks,[1] the lonely sky,
If I might lend their life a voice,
270 Seem to bear rather than rejoice.
And even could the intemperate prayer
Man iterates, while these forbear,
For movement, for an ampler sphere,
Pierce Fate's impenetrable ear;
275 Not milder is the general lot
Because our spirits have forgot,
In action's dizzying eddy whirled,
The something that infects the world.
—1849 (1843–48?)

The Forsaken Merman

Come, dear children, let us away;
Down and away below!
Now my brothers call from the bay,
Now the great winds shoreward blow,
5 Now the salt tides seaward flow;
Now the wild white horses play,
Champ and chafe and toss in the spray.
Children dear, let us away!
This way, this way!

10 Call her once before you go—
Call once yet!
In a voice that she will know:

---

[1] striations on boulders transported by glacial action in the Lake District.

"Margaret! Margaret!"
Children's voices should be dear
15 (Call once more) to a mother's ear;
Children's voices, wild with pain—
Surely she will come again!
Call her once and come away;
This way, this way!
20 "Mother dear, we cannot stay!
The wild white horses foam and fret."
Margaret! Margaret!

Come, dear children, come away down;
Call no more!
25 One last look at the white-walled town,
And the little grey church on the windy shore,
Then come down!
She will not come though you call all day;
Come away, come away!
30 Children dear, was it yesterday
We heard the sweet bells over the bay?
In the caverns where we lay,
Through the surf and through the swell,
The far-off sound of a silver bell?
35 Sand-strewn caverns, cool and deep,
Where the winds are all asleep;
Where the spent lights quiver and gleam,
Where the salt weed sways in the stream,
Where the sea-beasts, ranged all round,
40 Feed in the ooze of their pasture-ground;
Where the sea-snakes coil and twine,
Dry their mail and and bask in the brine;
Where great whales come sailing by,
Sail and sail, with unshut eye,
45 Round the world for ever and aye?
When did music come this way?
Children dear, was it yesterday?
Children dear, was it yesterday
(Call yet once) that she went away?
50 Once she sate with you and me,
On a red gold throne in the heart of the sea,
And the youngest sate on her knee.

She combed its bright hair, and she tended it well,
When down swung the sound of a far-off bell.
55 She sighed, she looked up through the clear green
sea;
She said: "I must go, for my kinfolk pray
In the little grey church on the shore to-day.
'Twill be Easter-time in the world—ah me!
And I lose my poor soul, Merman! here with thee."
60 I said: "Go up, dear heart, through the waves;
Say thy prayer, and come back to the kind
sea-caves!"
She smiled, she went up through the surf in the bay.
Children dear, was it yesterday?

Children dear, were we long alone?
65 "The sea grows stormy, the little ones moan;
Long prayers," I said, "in the world they say;
Come!" I said; and we rose through the surf in the
bay.
We went up the beach, by the sandy down
Where the sea-stocks bloom, to the white-walled
town;
70 Through the narrow paved streets, where all was
still,
To the little grey church on the windy hill.
From the church came a murmur of folk at their
prayers,
But we stood without in the cold blowing airs.
We climbed on the graves, on the stones worn with
rains,
75 And we gazed up the aisle through the small leaded
panes.
She sate by the pillar; we saw her clear:
"Margaret, hist! come quick, we are here!
Dear heart," I said, "we are long alone;
The sea grows stormy, the little ones moan."
80 But, ah, she gave me never a look,
For her eyes were sealed to the holy book!
Loud prays the priest; shut stands the door.
Come away, children, call no more!
Come away, come down, call no more!

85   Down, down, down!
Down to the depths of the sea!
She sits at her wheel in the humming town,
Singing most joyfully.
Hark what she sings: "O joy, O joy,
90 For the humming street, and the child with its toy!
For the priest, and the bell, and the holy well;[1]
For the wheel where I spun,
And the blessed light of the sun!"
And so she sings her fill,
95 Singing most joyfully,
Till the spindle drops from her hand,
And the whizzing wheel stands still.
She steals to the window, and looks at the sand,
And over the sand at the sea;
100 And her eyes are set in a stare;
And anon there breaks a sigh,
And anon there drops a tear,
From a sorrow-clouded eye,
And a heart sorrow-laden,
105 A long, long sigh;
For the cold strange eyes of a little Mermaiden
And the gleam of her golden hair.

     Come away, away children:
Come children, come down!
110 The hoarse wind blows coldly;
Lights shine in the town.
She will start from her slumber
When gusts shake the door;
She will hear the winds howling,
115 Will hear the waves roar.
We shall see, while above us
The waves roar and whirl,
A ceiling of amber,
A pavement of pearl.
120 Singing: "Here came a mortal,
But faithless was she!

And alone dwell for ever
The kings of the sea."

But, children, at midnight,
125 When soft the winds blow,
When clear falls the moonlight,
When spring-tides are low;
When sweet airs come seaward
From heaths starred with broom,
130 And high rocks throw mildly
On the blanched sands a gloom;
Up the still, glistening beaches,
Up the creeks we will hie,
Over banks of bright seaweed
135 The ebb-tide leaves dry.
We will gaze, from the sand-hills,
At the white, sleeping town;
At the church on the hill-side—
And then come back down.
140 Singing: "There dwells a loved one,
But cruel is she!
She left lonely for ever
The kings of the sea."
    —1849 (1847–49?)

To Marguerite—Continued

Yes! in the sea of life enisled,
  With echoing[2] straits between us thrown,
Dotting the shoreless watery wild,
We mortal millions live *alone*.
5 The islands feel the enclasping flow,
And then their endless bounds they know.

But when the moon their hollows lights,
And they are swept by balms of spring,
And in their glens, on starry nights,
10 The nightingales divinely sing;

---

[1] holy water font.

[2] to make communication difficult.

And lovely notes, from shore to shore,
Across the sounds and channels pour—

Oh! then a longing like despair
Is to their farthest caverns sent;
15 For surely once, they feel, we were
Parts of a single continent!
Now round us spreads the watery plain—
Oh might our marges meet again!

Who ordered, that their longing's fire
20 Should be, as soon as kindled, cooled?
Who renders vain their deep desire?—
A God, a God their severance ruled!
And bade betwixt their shores to be
The unplumbed, salt, estranging sea.
—1852 (1849)

Stanzas in Memory
of the Author of "Obermann"[1]

November, 1849

In front the awful Alpine track
Crawls up its rocky stair;

The autumn storm-winds drive the rack,
Close o'er it, in the air.

5 Behind are the abandon'd baths[2]
Mute in their meadows lone;
The leaves are on the valley paths,
The mists are on the Rhone—

The white mists rolling like a sea!
10 I hear the torrents roar.
—Yes, Obermann, all speaks of thee;
I feel thee near once more!

I turn thy leaves! I feel their breath
Once more upon me roll;
15 That air of languor, cold, and death,
Which brooded o'er thy soul.

Fly hence, poor wretch, whoe'er thou art,
Condemned to cast about,[3]
All shipwreck in thy own weak heart,
20 For comfort from without!

---

[1] The following note on Senancour was first attached to the poem in 1869: "The author of *Obermann*, Étienne Pivert de Senancour, has little celebrity in France, his own country; and out of France he is almost unknown. But the profound inwardness, the austere sincerity, of his principal work, *Obermann*, the delicate feeling for nature which it exhibits, and the melancholy eloquence of many passages of it, have attracted and charmed some of the most remarkable spirits of this century, such as George Sand and Sainte-Beuve, and will probably always find a certain number of spirits whom they touch and interest.

Senancour was born in 1770. He was educated for the priesthood, and passed some time in the seminary of St. Sulpice; broke away from the Seminary and from France itself, and passed some years in Switzerland, where he married; returned to France in middle life, and followed thenceforward the career of a man of letters, but with hardly any fame or success. He died an old man in 1846, desiring that on his grave might be placed these words only: *Éternité, deviens mon asile!*

The influence of Rousseau, and certain affinities with more famous and fortunate authors of his own day,—Chateaubriand and Madame de Staël,—are everywhere visible in Senancour. But though, like these eminent personages, he may be called a sentimental writer, and though

Obermann, a collection of letters from Switzerland treating almost entirely of nature and of the human soul, may be called a work of sentiment, Senancour has a gravity and severity which distinguish him from all other writers of the sentimental school. The world is with him in his solitude far less than it is with them; of all writers he is the most perfectly isolated and the least attitudinising. His chief work, too, has a value and power of its own, apart from these merits of its author. The stir of all the main forces, by which modern life is and has been impelled, lives in the letters of *Obermann*; the dissolving agencies of the eighteenth century, the fiery storm of the French Revolution, the first faint promise and dawn of that new world which our own time is but now more fully bringing to light—all these are to be felt, almost to be touched, there. To me, indeed, it will always seems that the impressiveness of this production can hardly be rated too high.

Besides *Obermann* there is one other of Senancour's works which, for those spirits who feel his attraction, is very interesting; its title is *Libres Méditations d'un Solitaire Inconnu*."

[2] "The baths of Leuk. This poem was conceived, and partly composed, in the valley going down from the foot of the Gemmi Pass towards the Rhone." (Arnold's note, first added in 1869.)

[3] turning the ship away from the wind to ease its passage.

A fever in these pages burns
Beneath the calm they feign;
A wounded human spirit turns,
Here, on its bed of pain.

25 Yes, though the virgin mountain-air
Fresh through these pages blows;
Though to these leaves the glaciers spare
The soul of their white snows;

Though here a mountain-murmur swells
30 Of many a dark-boughed pine;
Though, as you read, you hear the bells
Of the high-pasturing kine—

Yet, through the hum of torrent lone,
And brooding mountain-bee,
35 There sobs I know not what ground-tone
Of human agony.

Is it for this, because the sound
Is fraught too deep with pain,
That Obermann! the world around
40 So little loves thy strain?

Some secrets may the poet tell,
For the world loves new ways;
To tell too deep ones is not well—
It knows not what he says.

45 Yet, of the spirits who have reigned
In this our troubled day,
I know but two,[1] who have attained,
Save thee, to see their way.

By England's lakes, in grey old age,
50 His quiet home one keeps;
And one, the strong much-toiling sage,
In German Weimar sleeps.

But Wordsworth's eyes avert their ken
From half of human fate;
55 And Goethe's course few sons of men
May think to emulate.

For he pursued a lonely road,
His eyes on Nature's plan;
Neither made man too much a God,
60 Nor God too much a man.

Strong was he, with a spirit free
From mists, and sane, and clear;
Clearer, how much! than ours—yet we
Have a worse course to steer.

65 For though his manhood bore the blast
Of a tremendous time,
Yet in a tranquil world was passed
His tenderer youthful prime.

But we, brought forth and reared in hours
70 Of change, alarm, surprise—
What shelter to grow ripe is ours?
What leisure to grow wise?

Like children bathing on the shore,
Buried a wave beneath,
75 The second wave succeeds, before
We have had time to breathe.

Too fast we live, too much are tried,
Too harassed, to attain
Wordsworth's sweet calm, or Goethe's wide
80 And luminous view to gain.

And then we turn, thou sadder sage,
To thee! we feel thy spell!
—The hopeless tangle of our age,
Thou too hast scanned it well!

---

[1] Wordsworth died in 1850 and Goethe in 1832 (see ll. 49–56).

85 Immoveable thou sittest, still
As death, composed to bear!
Thy head is clear, thy feeling chill,
And icy thy despair.

Yes, as the son of Thetis said,
90 I hear thee saying now:
Greater by far than thou are dead;
Strive not! die also thou!

Ah! two desires toss about
The poet's feverish blood.
95 One drives him to the world without,
And one to solitude.

The glow, he cries, *the thrill of life,*
Where, where do these abound?
Not in the world, not in the strife
100 Of men, shall they be found.

He who hath watched, not shared, the strife,
Knows how the day hath gone.
He only lives with the world's life,
Who hath renounced his own.

105 To thee we come, then! Clouds are rolled
Where thou, O seer! art set;
Thy realm of thought is drear and cold—
The world is colder yet!

And thou hast pleasures, too, to share
110 With those who come to thee—
Balms floating on thy mountain-air,
And healing sights to see.

How often, where the slopes are green
On Jaman,[1] has thou sate
115 By some high chalet-door, and seen
The summer-day grow late;

And darkness steal o'er the wet grass
With the pale crocus starred,

And reach that glimmering sheet of glass
120 Beneath the piny sward,

Lake Leman's[2] waters, far below!
And watched the rosy light
Fade from the distant peaks of snow;
And on the air of night

125 Heard accents of the eternal tongue
Through the pine branches play—
Listened, and felt thyself grow young!
Listened and wept—Away!

Away the dreams that but deceive
130 And thou, sad guide, adieu!
I go, fate drives me; but I leave
Half of my life with you.

We, in some unknown Power's employ,
Move on a rigorous line;
135 Can neither, when we will, enjoy,
Nor, when we will, resign.

I in the world must live; but thou,
Thou melancholy shade!
Wilt not, if thou canst see me now,
140 Condemn me, nor upbraid.

For thou art gone away from earth,
And place with those dost claim,
The Children of the Second Birth,
Whom the world could not tame;

145 And with that small, transfigured band,
Whom many a different way
Conducted to their common land,
Thou learn'st to think as they.

Christian and pagan, king and slave,
150 Soldier and anchorite,

---

[1] overlooking Vevey on the Lake of Geneva.

[2] Lake Geneva.

Distinctions we esteem so grave,
Are nothing in their sight.

They do not ask, who pined unseen,
Who was on action hurled,
155 Whose one bond is, that all have been
Unspotted by the world.

There without anger thou wilt see
Him who obeys thy spell
No more, so he but rest, like thee,
160 Unsoiled!—and so, farewell.

Farewell!—Whether thou now liest near
That much-loved inland sea,
The ripples of whose blue waves cheer
Vevey and Meillerie;

165 And in that gracious region bland,
Where with clear-rustling wave
The scented pines of Switzerland
Stand dark round thy green grave,

Between the dusty vineyard-walls
170 Issuing on that green place
The early peasant still recalls
The pensive stranger's face,

And stoops to clear thy moss-grown date
Ere he plods on again;
175 Or whether, by maligner fate,
Among the swarms of men,

Where between granite terraces
The blue Seine rolls her wave,
The Capital of Pleasure sees
180 The hardly-heard-of grave;

Farewell! Under the sky we part,
In this stern Alpine dell.
O unstrung will! O broken heart!
A last, a last farewell!
—1852 (1849)

Empedocles on Etna[1]

A DRAMATIC POEM

PERSONS

EMPEDOCLES
PAUSANIAS, *a Physician.*
CALLICLES, *a young Harp-player.*

The Scene of the Poem is on Mount Etna; at first in the forest region, afterwards on the summit of the mountain.

ACT 1. SCENE 1

Morning. A Pass in the forest region of Etna.

---

[1] See the opening paragraphs of Arnold's "Preface to *Poems*, 1853" for the poet's (after) thoughts on the poem. The following are Arnold's notes on the poem, preserved in the Yale MS:

"He is a philosopher.

He has not the religious consolation of other men, facile because adapted to their weaknesses, or because shared by all around and charging the atmosphere they breathe.

He sees things as they are—the world as it is—God as he is: in their stern simplicity.

The sight is a severe and mind-tasking one: to know the mysteries which are communicated to others by fragments, in parables.

But he started towards it in hope: his first glimpses of it filled him with joy; he had friends who shared his hope and joy and communicated to him theirs: even now he does not deny that the sight is capable of affording rapture and the purest peace.

But his friends are dead: the world is all against him, and incredulous of the truth: his mind is overtasked by the effort to hold fast so great and severe a truth in solitude: the atmosphere he breathes not being modified by the presence of human life, is too rare for him. He perceives still the truth of the truth, but cannot be transported and rapturously agitated by his [*for* its] grandeur: his spring and elasticity of mind are gone: he is clouded, oppressed, dispirited, without hope and energy.

Before he becomes the victim of depression and overtension of mind, to the utter deadness to joy, grandeur, spirit, and animated life, he desires to die; to be reunited with the universe, before by exaggerating his human side he has become utterly estranged from it."

Act I concerns "modern thought"—essentially Stoic and empty of meaningful ethical values—and Act II presents "modern feelings"—depression and ennui ("Preface").

CALLICLES

(*Alone, resting on a rock by the path.*)

The mules, I think, will not be here this hour;
They feel the cool wet turf under their feet
By the stream-side, after the dusty lanes
In which they have toiled all night from Catana,[1]
5   And scarcely will they budge a yard. O Pan,
How gracious is the mountain at this hour!
A thousand times have I been here alone,
Or with the revellers from the mountain-towns,
But never on so fair a morn; the sun
10   Is shining on the brilliant mountain-crests,
And on the highest pines; but farther down,
Here in the valley, is in shade; the sward
Is dark, and on the stream the mist still hangs;
One sees one's footprints crushed in the wet grass,
15   One's breath curls in the air; and on these pines
That climb from the stream's edge, the long grey
        tufts,
Which the goats love, are jewelled thick with dew.
Here will I stay till the slow litter comes.
I have my harp too—that is well. Apollo!
20   What mortal could be sick or sorry here?
I know not in what mind Empedocles,
Whose mules I followed, may be coming up,
But if, as most men say, he is half mad
With exile, and with brooding on his wrongs,
25   Pausanias, his sage friend, who mounts with him,
Could scarce have lighted on a lovelier cure.
The mules must be below, far down. I hear
Their tinkling bells, mixed with the song of birds,
Rise faintly to me—now it stops! Who's here?
30   Pausanias! and on foot? alone?

PAUSANIAS
                    And thou, then?
I left thee supping with Peisianax,
With thy head full of wine, and thy hair crowned,
Touching thy harp as the whim came on thee,

And praised and spoiled by master and by guests
35   Almost as much as the new dancing-girl.
Why hast thou followed us?

CALLICLES
                    The night was hot,
And the feast past its prime; so we slipped out
Some of us, to the portico to breathe—
Peisianax, thou know'st, drinks late; and then,
40   As I was lifting my soiled garland off,
I saw the mules and litter in the court,
And in the litter sate Empedocles;
Thou, too, wast with him. Straightway I sped home;
I saddled my white mule, and all night long
45   Through the cool lovely country followed you,
Passed you a little since as morning dawned,
And have this hour sate by the torrent here,
Till the slow mules should climb in sight again.
And now?

PAUSANIAS
            And now, back to the town with speed!
50   Crouch in the wood first, till the mules have passed;
They do but halt, they will be here anon.
Thou must be viewless to Empedocles;
Save mine, he must not meet a human eye.
One of his moods is on him that thou know'st;
55   I think, thou wouldst not vex him.

CALLICLES
                    No—and yet
I would fain stay, and help thee tend him. Once
He knew me well, and would oft notice me;
And still, I know not how, he draws me to him,
And I could watch him with his proud sad face,
60   His flowing locks and gold-encircled brow
And kingly gait, for ever; such a spell
In his severe looks, such a majesty
As drew of old the people after him,
In Agrigentum and Olympia,
65   When his star reigned, before his banishment,

---

[1] town at the foot of Mt. Etna.

Is potent still on me in his decline.
But oh! Pausanias, he is changed of late;
There is a settled trouble in his air
Admits no momentary brightening now,
70 And when he comes among his friends at feasts,
'Tis as an orphan among prosperous boys.
Thou know'st of old he loved this harp of mine,
When first he sojourned with Peisianax;
He is now always moody, and I fear him;
75 But I would serve him, soothe him, if I could,
Dared one but try.

PAUSANIAS
Thou wast a kind child ever!
He loves thee, but he must not see thee now.
Thou hast indeed a rare touch on thy harp,
He loves that in thee, too; there was a time
80 (But that is passed), he would have paid[1] thy strain
With music to have drawn the stars from heaven.
He hath his harp and laurel with him still,
But he has laid the use of music by,
And all which might relax his settled gloom.
85 Yet thou may'st try thy playing, if thou wilt—
But thou must keep unseen; follow us on,
But at a distance! in these solitudes,
In this clear mountain-air, a voice will rise,
Though from afar, distinctly; it may soothe him.
90 Play when we halt, and, when the evening comes
And I must leave him (for his pleasure is
To be left musing these soft nights alone
In the high unfrequented mountain-spots),
Then watch him, for he ranges swift and far,
95 Sometimes to Etna's top, and to the cone;
But hide thee in the rocks a great way down,
And try thy noblest strains, my Callicles,
With the sweet night to help thy harmony!
Thou wilt earn my thanks sure, and perhaps his.

CALLICLES
100 More than a day and night, Pausanias,
Of this fair summer-weather, on these hills,
Would I bestow to help Empedocles.
That needs no thanks; one is far better here
Than in the broiling city in these heats.
105 But tell me, how hast thou persuaded him
In this his present fierce, man-hating mood,
To bring thee out with him alone on Etna?

PAUSANIAS
Thou hast heard all men speaking of Pantheia,
The woman who at Agrigentum lay
110 Thirty long days in a cold trance of death,
And whom Empedocles called back to life.
Thou art too young to note it, but his power
Swells with the swelling evil of this time,
And holds men mute to see where it will rise.
115 He could stay swift diseases in old days,
Chain madmen by the music of his lyre,
Cleanse to sweet airs the breath of poisonous
streams,
And in the mountain-chinks inter the winds.
This he could do of old; but now, since all
120 Clouds and grows daily worse in Sicily,
Since broils tear us in twain, since this new swarm
Of sophists[2] has got empire in our schools
Where he was paramount, since he is banished
And lives a lonely man in triple gloom—
125 He grasps the very reins of life and death.
I asked him of Pantheia yesterday,
When we were gathered with Peisianax,
And he made answer, I should come at night
On Etna here, and be alone with him,
130 And he would tell me, as his old, tried friend,
Who still was faithful, what might profit me;
That is, the secret of this miracle.

---

[1] rewarded.

[2] the proponents of specious (sophistical) reasoning.

CALLICLES

Bah! Thou a doctor! Thou art superstitious.
Simple Pausanias, 'twas no miracle!
135 Pantheia, for I know her kinsmen well,
Was subject to these trances from a girl.
Empedocles would say so, did he deign;
But he still lets the people, whom he scorns,
Gape and cry *wizard* at him, if they list.
40 But thou, thou art no company for him!
Thou art as cross, as soured as himself!
Thou hast some wrong from thine own citizens,
And then thy friend is banished, and on that,
Straightway thou fallest to arraign the times,
45 As if the sky was impious not to fall.
The sophists are no enemies of his;
I hear, Gorgias, their chief, speaks nobly of him,
As of his gifted master, and once friend.
He is too scornful, too high-wrought, too bitter.
150 'Tis not the times, 'tis not the sophists vex him;
There is some root of suffering in himself,
Some secret and unfollowed vein of woe,
Which makes the time look black and sad to him.
Pester him not in this his sombre mood
55 With questionings about an idle tale,
But lead him through the lovely mountain-paths,
And keep his mind from preying on itself,
And talk to him of things at hand and common,
Not miracles! thou art a learned man,
60 But credulous of fables as a girl.

PAUSANIAS

And thou, a boy whose tongue outruns his
    knowledge,
And on whose lightness blame is thrown away.
Enough of this! I see the litter wind
Up by the torrent-side, under the pines.
65 I must rejoin Empedocles. Do thou
Crouch in the brushwood till the mules have passed;
Then play thy kind part well. Farewell till night!

SCENE II
*Noon. A Glen on the highest skirts of the woody region
of Etna.*
EMPEDOCLES — PAUSANIAS

PAUSANIAS

The noon is hot. When we have crossed the stream,
We shall have left the woody tract, and come
Upon the open shoulder of the hill.
See how the giant spires of yellow bloom
5 Of the sun-loving gentian, in the heat,
Are shining on those naked slopes like flame!
Let us rest here; and now, Empedocles,
Pantheia's history!

[*A harp-note below is heard.*

EMPEDOCLES

Hark! what sound was that
Rose from below? If it were possible,
10 And we were not so far from human haunt,
I should have said that some one touched a harp.
Hark! there again!

PAUSANIAS

'Tis the boy Callicles,
The sweetest harp-player in Cantana.
He is for ever coming on these hills,
15 In summer, to all country-festivals,
With a gay revelling band; he breaks from them
Sometimes, and wanders far among the glens.
But heed him not, he will not mount to us;
I spoke with him this morning. Once more,
    therefore,
20 Instruct me of Pantheia's story, Master,
As I have prayed thee.

EMPEDOCLES

That? and to what end?

PAUSANIAS

It is enough that all men speak of it.
But I will also say, that when the Gods
Visit us as they do with sign and plague,
25 To know those spells of thine which stay their hand
Were to live free from terror.

EMPEDOCLES

              Spells? Mistrust them!
Mind is the spell which governs earth and heaven.
Man has a mind with which to plan his safety;
Know that, and help thyself!

PAUSANIAS

              But thine own words?
30 "The wit and counsel of man was never clear,
Troubles confound the little wit he has."
Mind is a light which the Gods mock us with,
To lead those false who trust it.
                     [*The harp sounds again.*

EMPEDOCLES

              Hist! once more!
Listen, Pausanias! —Ay, 'tis Callicles;
35 I know these notes among a thousand. Hark!

CALLICLES

(Sings unseen, from below)
The track winds down to the clear stream,
To cross the sparkling shallows; there
The cattle love to gather, on their way
To the high mountain-pastures, and to stay,
40 Till the rough cow-herds drive them past,
Knee-deep in the cool ford; for 'tis the last
Of all the woody, high, well-watered dells
On Etna; and the beam
Of noon is broken there by chestnut-boughs
45 Down its steep verdant sides; the air
Is freshened by the leaping stream, which throws
Eternal showers of spray on the mossed roots
Of trees, and veins of turf, and long dark shoots

Of ivy-plants, and fragrant hanging bells
50 Of hyacinths, and on late anemones,
That muffle its wet banks; but glade,
And stream, and sward, and chestnut-trees,
End here; Etna beyond, in the broad glare
Of the hot noon, without a shade,
55 Slope beyond slope, up to the peak, lies bare;
The peak, round which the white clouds play.

    In such a glen, on such a day,
    On Pelion, on the grassy ground,
    Chiron, the aged Centaur lay,
60   The young Achilles standing by.
    The Centaur taught him to explore
    The mountains; where the glens are dry
    And the tired Centaurs come to rest,
    And where the soaking springs abound
65   And the straight ashes grow for spears,
    And where the hill-goats come to feed,
    And the sea-eagles build their nest.
    He showed him Phthia far away,
    And said: O boy, I taught this lore
70   To Peleus, in long distant years!
    He told him of the Gods, the stars,
    The tides; and then of mortal wars,
    And of the life which heroes lead
    Before they reach the Elysian place
75   And rest in the immortal mead;
    And all the wisdom of his race.

The music below ceases, and EMPEDOCLES *speaks,
accompanying himself in a solemn manner on his
harp.*

    The out-spread world to span
    A cord the Gods first slung,
    And then the soul of man
80   There, like a mirror, hung,
And bade the winds through space impel the gusty
    toy.

Hither and thither spins
The wind-borne, mirroring soul,
A thousand glimpses wins,
85 And never sees a whole;
Looks once, and drives elsewhere, and leaves its last
  employ.

The Gods laugh in their sleeve
To watch man doubt and fear,
Who knows not what to believe
90 Since he sees nothing clear,
And dares stamp nothing false where he finds
  nothing sure.

Is this, Pausanias, so?
And can our souls not strive,
But with the winds must go,
95 And hurry where they drive?
Is fate indeed so strong, man's strength indeed so
  poor?

I will not judge. That man,
Howbeit, I judge as lost,
Whose mind allows a plan,
100 Which would degrade it most;
And he treats doubt the best who tries to see least
  ill.

Be not, then, fear's blind slave!
Thou art my friend; to thee,
All knowledge that I have,
105 All skill I wield, are free.
Ask not the latest news of the last miracle.

Ask not what days and nights
In trance Pantheia lay,
But ask how thou such sights
110 May'st see without dismay;
Ask what most helps when known, thou son of
  Anchitus!

What? hate, and awe, and shame
Fill thee to see our time;
Thou feelest thy soul's frame
115 Shaken and out of chime?
What? life and chance go hard with thee too, as
  with us;

Thy citizens, 'tis said,
Envy thee and oppress,
Thy goodness no men aid,
120 All strive to make it less;
Tyranny, pride, and lust, fill Sicily's abodes;

Heaven is with earth at strife,
Signs make thy soul afraid,
The dead return to life,
125 Rivers are dried, winds stayed;
Scarce can one think in calm, so threatening are the
  Gods;

And we feel, day and night,
The burden of ourselves—
Well, then, the wiser wight
130 In his own bosom delves,
And asks what ails him so, and gets what cure he
  can.

The sophist sneers: Fool, take
Thy pleasure, right or wrong.
The pious wail: Forsake
135 A world these sophists throng.
Be neither saint nor sophist-led, but be a man!

These hundred doctors try
To preach thee to their school.
We have the truth! they cry;
140 And yet their oracle,
Trumpet it as they will, is but the same as thine.

Once read thy own breast right,
And thou hast done with fears;

Man gets no other light,
145   Search he a thousand years.
Sink in thyself! there ask what ails thee, at that
      shrine!

What makes thee struggle and rave?
Why are men ill at ease?
'Tis that the lot they have
150   Fails their own will to please;
For man would make no murmuring, were his will
      obeyed.

And why is it, that still
Man with his lot thus fights?
'Tis that he makes this *will*
155   The measure of his *rights*,
And believes Nature outraged if his will's gainsaid.

Couldst thou, Pausanias, learn
How deep a fault is this;
Couldst thou but once discern
160   Thou hast no *right* to bliss,
No title from the Gods to welfare and repose;

Then thou wouldst look less mazed
Whene'er of bliss debarred,
Nor think the Gods were crazed
165   When thy own lot went hard.
But we are all the same—the fools of our own
      woes!

For, from the first faint morn
Of life, the thirst for bliss
Deep in man's heart is born;
170   And, sceptic as he is,
He fails not to judge clear if this be quenched or
      no.

Nor is the thirst to blame.
Man errs not that he deems

His welfare his true aim,
175   He errs because he dreams
The world does but exist that welfare to bestow.

We mortals are no kings
For each of whom to sway
A new-made world up-springs,
180   Meant merely for his play;
No, we are strangers here; the world is from of old.

In vain our pent wills fret,
And would the world subdue,
Limits we did not set
185   Condition we all do;
Born into life we are, and life must be our mould.

Born into life! man grows
Forth from his parents' stem,
And blends their bloods, as those
190   Of theirs are blent in them;
So each new man strikes root into a far fore-time.

Born into life! we bring
A bias with us here,
And, when here, each new thing
195   Affects us we come near;
To tunes we did not call our being must keep
      chime.

Born into life! in vain,
Opinions, those or these,
Unaltered to retain
200   The obstinate mind decrees;
Experience, like a sea, soaks all-effacing in.

Born into life! who lists
May what is false hold dear,
And for himself make mists
205   Through which to see less clear;
The world is what it is, for all our dust and din.

Born into life! 'tis we,
And not the world, are new;
Our cry for bliss, our plea,
210   Others have urged it too—
Our wants have all been felt, our errors made
  before.

No eye could be too sound
To observe a world so vast,
No patience too profound
215   To sort what's here amassed;
How man may here best live no care too great to
  explore.

But we—as some rude guest
Would change, where'er he roam,
The manners there professed
220   To those he brings from home—
We mark not the world's course, but would have *it*
  take *ours*.

The world's course proves the terms
On which man wins content;
Reason the proof confirms—
225   We spurn it, and invent
A false course for the world, and for ourselves, false
  powers.

Riches we wish to get,
Yet remain spendthrifts still;
We would have health, and yet
230   Still use our bodies ill;
Bafflers of our own prayers, from youth to life's last
  scenes.

We would have inward peace,
Yet will not look within;
We would have misery cease,
235   Yet will not cease from sin;
We want all pleasant ends, but will use no harsh
  means;

We do not what we ought,
What we ought not, we do,
And lean upon the thought
240   That chance will bring us through;
But our own acts, for good or ill, are mightier
  powers.

Yet, even when man forsakes
All sin—is just, is pure,
Abandons all which makes
245   His welfare insecure—
Other existences there are, that clash with ours.

Like us, the lightning-fires
Love to have scope and play;
The stream, like us, desires
250   An unimpeded way;
Like us, the Libyan wind delights to roam at large.

Streams will not curb their pride
The just man not to entomb,
Nor lightnings go aside
255   To give his virtues room;
Now is that wind less rough which blows a good
  man's barge.

Nature, with equal mind,
Sees all her sons at play;
Sees man control the wind,
260   The wind sweep man away;
Allows the proudly-riding and the foundering bark.

And, lastly, though of ours
No weakness spoil our lot,
Though the non-human powers
265   Of Nature harm us not,
The ill deeds of other men make often *our* life dark.

What were the wise man's plan?
Through this sharp, toil-set life,
To work as best he can,

270 And win what's won by strife.
But we an easier way to cheat our pains have
found.

Scratched by a fall, with moans
As children of weak age
Lend life to the dumb stones
275 Whereon to vent their rage,
And bend their little fists, and rate the senseless
ground;

So, loth to suffer mute,
We, peopling the void air,
Make Gods to whom to impute
280 The ills we ought to bear;
With God and Fate to rail at, suffering easily.

Yet grant—as sense long missed
Things that are now perceived,
And much may still exist
285 Which is not yet believed—
Grant that the world were full of Gods we cannot
see;

All things the world which fill
Of but one stuff are spun,
That we who rail are still,
290 With what we rail at, one;
One with the o'erlaboured Power that through the
breadth and length

Of earth, and air, and sea,
In men, and plants, and stones,
Hath toil perpetually,
295 And travails, pants, and moans
Fain would do all things well, but sometimes fails
in strength.

And patiently exact
This universal God
Alike to any act

300 Proceeds at any nod,
And quietly declaims the cursings of himself.

This is not what man hates,
Yet he can curse but this.
Harsh Gods and hostile Fates
305 Are dreams! this only *is*—
Is everywhere; sustains the wise, the foolish elf.

Nor only, in the intent
To attach blame elsewhere,
Do we at will invent
310 Stern Powers who make their care
To embitter human life, malignant Deities;

But, next, we would reverse
The scheme ourselves have spun,
And what we made to curse
315 We now would lean upon,
And feign kind Gods who perfect what man vainly
tries.

Look, the world tempts our eye,
And we would know it all!
We map the starry sky,
320 We mine this earthen ball,
We measure the sea-tides, we number the sea-
sands;

We scrutinise the dates
Of long-past human things,
The bounds of effaced states,
325 The lines of deceased kings;
We search out dead men's words, and works of
dead men's hands;

We shut our eyes, and muse
How our own minds are made.
What springs of thought they use,
330 How rightened, how betrayed—

And spend our wit to name what most employ
  unnamed.

But still, as we proceed
The mass swells more and more
Of volumes yet to read,
335   Of secrets yet to explore.
Our hair grows grey, our eyes are dimmed, our heat
  is tamed;

We rest our faculties,
And thus address the Gods:
"True science if there is,
340   It stays in your abodes!
Man's measures cannot mete the immeasurable All.

"You only can take in
The world's immense design.
Our desperate search was sin,
345   Which henceforth we resign,
Sure only that your mind sees all things which
  befall."

Fools! That in man's brief term
He cannot all things view,
Affords no ground to affirm
350   That there are Gods who do;
Nor does being weary prove that he has where to
  rest.

Again. Our youthful blood
Claims rapture as its right;
The world, a rolling flood
355   Of newness and delight,
Draws in the enamoured gazer to its shining breast;

Pleasure, to our hot grasp,
Gives flowers after flowers;
With passionate warmth we clasp
360   Hand after hand in ours;

Nor do we soon perceive how fast our youth is
  spent.

At once our eyes grow clear!
We see, in blank dismay,
Year posting after year,
365   Sense after sense decay;
Our shivering heart is mined by secret discontent;

Yet still, in spite of truth,
In spite of hopes entombed,
That longing of our youth
370   Burns ever unconsumed,
Still hungrier for delight as delights grow more
  rare.

We pause; we hush our heart,
And thus address the Gods:
"The world hath failed to impart
375   The joy our youth forebodes,
Failed to fill up the void which in our breasts we
  bear.

"Changeful till now, we still
Looked on to something new;
Let us, with changeless will,
380   Henceforth look on to you,
To find with you the joy we in vain here require!"

Fools! That so often here
Happiness mocked our prayer,
I think, might make us fear
385   A like event elsewhere;
Make us, not fly to dreams, but moderate desire.

And yet, for those who know
Themselves, who wisely take
Their way through life, and bow
390   To what they cannot break,
Why should I say that life need yield but *moderate*
  bliss?

Shall we, with temper spoiled,
Health sapped by living ill,
And judgment all embroiled
395 By sadness and self-will
Shall *we* judge what for man is not true bliss or is?

Is it so small a thing
To have enjoyed the sun,
To have lived light in the spring,
400 To have loved, to have thought, to have done;
To have advanced true friends, and beat down
baffling foes—

That we must feign a bliss
Of doubtful future date,
And, while we dream on this,
405 Lose all our present state,
And relegate to worlds yet distant our repose?

Not much, I know, you prize
What pleasures may be had,
Who look on life with eyes
410 Estranged, like mine, and sad;
And yet the village-churl feels the truth more than
you,

Who's loth to leave this life
Which to him little yields—
His hard-tasked sunburnt wife,
415 His often-laboured fields,
The boors with whom he talked, the country-spots
he knew.

But thou, because thou hear'st
Men scoff at Heaven and Fate,
Because the Gods thou fear'st
420 Fail to make blest thy state,
Tremblest, and wilt not dare to trust the joys there
are!

I say: Fear not! Life still
Leaves human effort scope.
But, since life teems with ill,
425 Nurse no extravagant hope;
Because thou must not dream, thou need'st not
then despair!

*A long pause. At the end of it the notes of a harp
below are again heard, and* CALLICLES *sings:—*

Far, far from here,
The Adriatic breaks in a warm bay
Among the green Illyrian hills; and there
430 The sunshine in the happy glens is fair,
And by the sea, and in the brakes.
The grass is cool, the sea-side air
Buoyant and fresh, the mountain flowers
More virginal and sweet than ours.
435 And there, they say, two bright and aged snakes,
Who once were Cadmus and Harmonia,[1]
Bask in the glens or on the warm sea-shore,
In breathless quiet, after all their ills;
Nor do they see their country, nor the place
440 Where the Sphinx lived among the frowning hills,
Nor the unhappy palace of their race,
Nor Thebes, nor the Ismenus, any more.

There those two live, far in the Illyrian brakes!
They had stayed long enough to see,
445 In Thebes, the billow of calamity
Over their own dear children rolled,
Curse upon curse, pang upon pang,
For years, they sitting helpless in their home,
A grey old man and woman; yet of old
450 The Gods had to their marriage come,
And at the banquet all the Muses sang.

Therefore they did not end their days
In sight of blood; but were rapt, far away,

---

[1] Cadmus, the founder of Thebes, and Harmonia, his wife.

To where the west-wind plays,
455 And murmurs of the Adriatic come
To those untrodden mountain-lawns; and there
Placed safely in changed forms, the pair
Wholly forget their first sad life, and home,
And all that Theban woe, and stray
460 For ever through the glens, placid and dumb.

EMPEDOCLES

That was my harp-player again! —where is he?
Down by the stream?

PAUSANIAS
Yes, Master, in the wood.

EMPEDOCLES

He ever loved the Theban story well!
But the day wears. Go now, Pausanias,
465 For I must be alone. Leave me one mule;
Take down with thee the rest to Catana.
And for young Callicles, thank him from me;
Tell him, I never failed to love his lyre—
But he must follow me no more to-night.

PAUSANIAS
470 Thou wilt return to-morrow to the city?

EMPEDOCLES

Either to-morrow or some other day,
In the sure revolutions of the world,
Good friend, I shall revisit Catana.
I have seen many cities in my time,
475 Till mine eyes ache with the long spectacle,
And I shall doubtless see them all again;
Thou know'st me for a wanderer from of old.
Meanwhile, stay me not now. Farewell, Pausanias!
He departs on his way up the mountain.

PAUSANIAS (*alone*)

I dare not urge him further—he must go;
480 But he is strangely wrought! I will speed back

And bring Peisianax to him from the city;
His counsel could once soothe him. But, Apollo!
How his brow lightened as the music rose!
Callicles must wait here, and play to him;
485 I saw him through the chestnuts far below,
Just since, down at the stream. Ho! Callicles!
He descends, calling.

ACT II
Evening. The Summit of Etna.

EMPEDOCLES

Alone!—
On this charred, blackened, melancholy waste,
Crowned by the awful peak, Etna's great mouth,
Round which the sullen vapour rolls—alone!
5 Pausanias is far hence, and that is well,
For I must henceforth speak no more with man.
He hath his lesson too, and that debt's paid;
And the good, learned, friendly, quiet man
May bravelier front his life, and in himself
10 Find henceforth energy and heart. But I—
The weary man, the banished citizen,
Whose banishment is not his greatest ill,
Whose weariness no energy can reach,
And for whose hurt courage is not the cure—
15 What should I do with life and living more?

No, thou art come too late, Empedocles!
And the world hath the day, and must break thee,
Not thou the world. With men thou canst not live,
Their thoughts, their ways, their wishes, are not
thine;
20 And being lonely thou art miserable,
For something has impaired thy spirit's strength,
And dried its self-sufficing fount of joy.
Thou canst not live with men nor with thyself—
O sage! O sage! Take then the one way left;
25 And turn thee to the elements, thy friends,
Thy well-tried friends, thy willing ministers,

And say: Ye helpers, hear Empedocles,
Who asks this final service at your hands!
Before the sophist-brood hath overlaid
30 The last spark of man's consciousness with words—
Ere quite the being of man, ere quite the world
Be disarrayed of their divinity—
Before the soul lose all her solemn joys,
And awe be dead, and hope impossible,
35 And the soul's deep eternal night come on—
Receive me, hide me, quench me, take me home!

He advances to the edge of the crater. Smoke and fire
break forth with a loud noise, and CALLICLES *is heard*
below singing:—

The lyre's voice is lovely everywhere;
In the court of Gods, in the city of men,
And in the lonely rock-strewn mountain-glen,
40 In the still mountain air.
Only to Typho[1] it sounds hatefully;
To Typho only, the rebel o'erthrown,
Through whose heart Etna drives her roots of stone
To imbed them in the sea.

45 Wherefore dost thou groan so loud?
Wherefore do thy nostrils flash,
Through the dark night, suddenly,
Typho, such red jets of flame?
Is thy tortured heart still proud?
50 Is thy fire-scathed arm still rash?
Still alert thy stone-crushed frame?
Doth thy fierce soul still deplore
Thine ancient rout by the Cilician hills,
And that cursed treachery on the Mount of Gore?[2]
55 Do thy bloodshot eyes still weep
The fight which crowned thine ills,

---

[1] Typho, one of the giants who warred on the Olympian gods, was
pinned by Jove under Mt. Etna, from where he spews lava and fire.

[2] Mt. Haemus, so called, from Typho's blood spilt on it in his last battle
with Zeus.

Thy last mischance on this Sicilian deep?
Hast thou sworn, in thy sad lair,
Where erst the strong sea-currents sucked thee
    down,
60 Never to cease to writhe, and try to rest,
Letting the sea-stream wander through thy hair?
That thy groans, like thunder pressed,
Begin to roll, and almost drown
The sweet notes whose lulling spell
65 Gods and the race of mortals love so well,
When through thy caves thou hearest music swell?

But an awful pleasure bland
Spreading o'er the Thunderer's face,
When the sound climbs near his seat,
70 The Olympian council sees;
As he lets his lax right hand,
Which the lightnings doth embrace,
Sink upon his mighty knees.
And the eagle, at the beck
75 Of the appeasing, gracious harmony,
Droops all his sheeny, brown, deep-feathered neck,
Nestling nearer to Jove's feet;
While o'er his sovran eye
The curtains of the blue films slowly meet.

80 And the white Olympus-peaks
Rosily brighten, and the soothed Gods smile
At one another from their golden chairs,
And no one round the charméd circle speaks.
Only the loved Hebe bears
85 The cup about, whose draughts beguile
Pain and care, with a dark store
Of fresh-pulled violets wreathed and nodding o'er;
And her flushed feet glow on the marble floor.

EMPEDOCLES

He fables, yet speaks truth!
90 The brave, impetuous heart yields everywhere
To the subtle, contriving head;
Great qualities are trodden down,

And littleness united
Is become invincible.
95   These rumblings are not Typho's groans, I know!
These angry smoke-bursts
Are not the passionate breath
Of the mountain-crushed, tortured, intractable
     Titan king—
But over all the world
100   What suffering is there not seen
Of plainness oppressed by cunning,
As the well-counselled Zeus oppressed
That self-helping son of earth!
What anguish of greatness,
105   Railed and hunted from the world,
Because its simplicity rebukes
This envious, miserable age!

I am weary of it.
—Lie there, ye ensigns
110   Of my unloved preëminence
In an age like this!
Among a people of children,
Who thronged me in their cities,
Who worshipped me in their houses,
115   And asked, not wisdom,
But drugs to charm with,
But spells to mutter—
All the fool's-armoury of magic! Lie there,
My golden circlet,
120   My purple robe![1]

CALLICLES (*from below*)
As the sky-brightening south-wind clears the day,
And makes the massed clouds roll,
The music of the lyre blows away
The clouds which wrap the soul.
125   Oh! that Fate had let me see
That triumph of the sweet persuasive lyre,
That famous, final victory,
When jealous Pan with Marsyas did conspire;[2]

When, from far Parnassus' side,
130   Young Apollo, all the pride
Of the Phrygian flutes to tame,
To the Phrygian highlands came;
Where the long green reed-beds sway
In the rippled waters grey
135   Of that solitary lake
Where Mæander's springs are born;
Whence the ridged pine-wooded roots
Of Messogis westward break,
Mounting westward, high and higher.
140   There was held the famous strife;
There the Phyrgian brought his flutes,
And Apollo brought his lyre;
And, when now the westering sun
Touched the hills, the strife was done,
145   And the attentive Muses said:
"Marsyas, thou art vanquishéd!"
Then Apollo's minister
Hanged upon a branching fir
Marsyas, that unhappy Faun,
150   And began to whet his knife.
But the Mænads,[3] who were there,
Left their friend, and with robes flowing
In the wind, and loose dark hair
O'er their polished bosoms blowing,
155   Each her ribboned tambourine
Flinging on the mountain-sod,
With a lovely frightened mien
Came about the youthful God.
But he turned his beauteous face
160   Haughtily another way,
From the grassy sun-warmed place

---

[1]   symbols of civic power.

[2]   Marsyas, a satyr, foolishly challenged Apollo to a musical contest. The winner could do as he wished with the vanquished. Apollo won and had Marsyas flayed alive.

[3]   female followers of Bacchus.

Where in proud repose he lay,
With one arm over his head,
Watching how the whetting sped.

165   But aloof, on the lake-strand,
Did the young Olympus stand,
Weeping at his master's end;
For the Faun had been his friend.
For he taught him how to sing,
170 And he taught him flute-playing.
Many a morning had they gone
To the glimmering mountain-lakes,
And had torn up by the roots
The tall crested water-reeds
175 With long plumes and soft brown seeds,
And had carved them into flutes,
Sitting on a tabled stone
Where the shoreward ripple breaks.
And he taught him how to please
180 The red-snooded Phrygian girls,
Whom the summer evening sees
Flashing in the dance's whirls
Underneath the starlit trees
In the mountain-villages.
185 Therefore now Olympus stands,
At his master's piteous cries
Pressing fast with both his hands
His white garment to his eyes,
Not to see Apollo's scorn;
190 Ah, poor Faun, poor Faun! ah, poor Faun!

EMPEDOCLES

And lie thou there,
My laurel bough![1]
Scornful Apollo's ensign, lie thou there!
Though thou hast been my shade in the world's
    heat—
195 Though I have loved thee, lived in honouring
    thee—

Yet lie thou there,
My laurel bough!
I am weary of thee.
I am weary of the solitude
200 Where he who bears thee must abide—
Of the rocks of Parnassus,
Of the gorge of Delphi,
Of the moonlit peaks, and the caves.
Thou guardest them, Apollo!
205 Over the grave of the slain Pytho,[2]
Though young, intolerably severe!
Thou keepest aloof the profane,
But the solitude oppresses thy votary!
The jars of men reach him not in thy valley—
210 But can life reach him?
Thou fencest him from the multitude—
Who will fence him from himself?
He hears nothing but the cry of the torrents,
And the beating of his own heart.
215 The air is thin, the veins swell,
The temples tighten and throb there—
Air! air!

Take thy bough, set me free from my solitude;
I have been enough alone!

220 Where shall thy votary fly them? back to men?
But they will gladly welcome him once more,
And help him to unbend his too tense thought,
And rid him of the presence of himself,
And keep their friendly chatter at his ear,
225 And haunt him, till the absence from himself,
That other torment, grow unbearable;
And he will fly to solitude again,
And he will find its air too keen for him,
And so change back; and many thousand times
230 Be miserably bandied to and fro
Like a sea-wave, betwixt the world and thee,
Thou young, implacable God! and only death

---

[1] sign of his poetic life.

[2] serpent which guarded Delphi, slain by Apollo.

Can cut his oscillations short, and so
Bring him to poise. There is no other way.

235 And yet what days were those, Parmenides!
When we were young, when we could number
    friends
In all the Italian cities like ourselves,
When with elated hearts we joined your train,
Ye Sun-born Virgins! on the road of truth.
240 Then we could still enjoy, then neither thought
Nor outward things were closed and dead to us;
But we received the shock of mighty thoughts
On simple minds with a pure natural joy;
And if the sacred load oppressed our brain,
245 We had the power to feel the pressure eased,
The brow unbound, the thoughts flow free again,
In the delightful commerce of the world.
We had not lost our balance then, nor grown
Thought's slaves, and dead to every natural joy.
250 The smallest thing could give us pleasure then—
The sports of the country-people,
A flute-note from the woods,
Sunset over the sea;
Seed-time and harvest,
255 The reapers in the corn,
The vinedresser in his vineyard,
The village-girl at her wheel.

Fullness of life and power of feeling, ye
Are for the happy, for the souls at ease,
260 Who dwell on a firm basis of content!
But he, who has outlived his prosperous days—
But he, whose youth fell on a different world
From that on which his exiled age is thrown—
Whose mind was fed on other food, was trained
265 By other rules than are in vogue to-day—
Whose habit of thought is fixed, who will not
    change,
But, in a world he loves not, must subsist
In ceaseless opposition, be the guard
Of his own breast, fettered to what he guards,

270 That the world win no mastery over him—
Who has no friend, no fellow left, not one;
Who has no minute's breathing space allowed
To nurse his dwindling faculty of joy—
Joy and the outward world must die to him,
275 As they are dead to me.

A long pause, during which EMPEDOCLES *remains
motionless, plunged in thought. The night deepens. He
moves forward and gazes round him, and proceeds:—*

And you, ye stars,
Who slowly begin to marshal,
As of old, the fields of heaven,
Your distant, melancholy lines!
280 Have you, too, survived yourselves?
Are you, too, what I fear to become?
You, too, once lived;
You, too, moved joyfully
Among august companions,
285 In an older world, peopled by Gods,
In a mightier order,
The radiant, rejoicing, intelligent Sons of Heaven.
But now, ye kindle
Your lonely, cold-shining lights,
290 Unwilling lingerers
In the heavenly wilderness,
For a younger, ignoble world;
And renew, by necessity,
Night after night your courses,
295 In echoing, unneared silence,
Above a race you know not—
Uncaring and undelighted,
Without friend and without home;
Weary like us, though not
300 Weary with our weariness.

No, no, ye stars! there is no death with you,
No languor, no decay! languor and death,
They are with me, not you! ye are alive—
Ye, and the pure dark ether where ye ride

305 Brilliant above me! And thou, fiery world.
That sapp'st the vitals of this terrible mount
Upon whose charred and quaking crust I stand—
Thou, too, brimmest with life! —the sea of cloud,
That heaves its white and billowy vapours up
310 To moat this isle of ashes from the world,
Lives; and that other fainter sea, far down,
O'er whose lit floor a road of moonbeams leads
To Etna's Liparëan sister-fires
And the long dusky line of Italy—
315 That mild and luminous floor of waters lives,
With held-in joy swelling its heart; I only,
Whose spring of hope is dried, whose spirit has
    failed,
I, who have not, like these, in solitude
Maintained courage and force, and in myself
320 Nursed an immortal vigour—I alone
Am dead to life and joy, therefore I read
In all things my own deadness.
                A long silence. He continues:—

Oh, that I could glow like this mountain!
Oh, that my heart bounded with the swell of the
    sea!
325 Oh, that my soul were full of light as the stars!
Oh, that it brooded over the world like the air!

But no, this heart will glow no more; thou art
A living man no more, Empedocles!
Nothing but a devouring flame of thought—
330 But a naked, eternally restless mind!
                After a pause:—

To the elements it came from
Everything will return—
Our bodies to earth,
Our blood to water,
335 Heat to fire,
Breath to air,
They were well born, they will be well entombed—
But mind?...

And we might gladly share the fruitful stir
340 Down in our mother earth's miraculous womb;
Well would it be
With what rolled of us in the stormy main;
We might have joy, blent with the all-bathing air,
Or with the nimble, radiant life of fire.

345 But mind, but thought—
If these have been the master part of us—
Where will *they* find their parent element?
What will receive *them*, who will call *them* home?
But we shall still be in them, and they in us,
350 And we shall be the strangers of the world,
And they will be our lords, as they are now;
And keep us prisoners of our consciousness,
And never let us clasp and feel the All
But through their forms, and modes, and stifling
    veils.
355 And we shall be unsatisfied as now;
And we shall feel the agony of thirst,
The ineffable longing for the life of life
Baffled for ever; and still thought and mind
Will hurry us with them on their homeless march,
360 Over the unallied unopening earth,
Over the unrecognising sea; while air
Will blow us fiercely back to sea and earth,
And fire repel us from its living waves.
And then we shall unwillingly return
365 Back to this meadow of calamity,
This uncongenial place, this human life;
And in our individual human state
Go through the sad probation all again,
To see if we will poise our life at last,
370 To see if we will now at last be true
To our own only true, deep-buried selves,
Being one with which we are one with the whole
    world;
Or whether we will once more fall away
Into some bondage of the flesh or mind,
375 Some slough of sense, or some fantastic maze
Forged by the imperious lonely thinking-power.

And each succeeding age in which we are born
Will have more peril for us than the last;
Will goad our senses with a sharper spur,
380 Will fret our minds to an intenser play,
Will make ourselves harder to be discerned.
And we shall struggle awhile, gasp and rebel—
And we shall fly for refuge to past times,
Their soul of unworn youth, their breath of
    greatness;
385 And the reality will pluck us back,
Knead us in its hot hand, and change our nature.
And we shall feel our powers of effort flag,
And rally them for one last fight—and fail;
And we shall sink in the impossible strife,
390 And be astray for ever.

        Slave of sense
I have in no wise been; but slave of thought?...
And who can say: I have been always free,
Lived ever in the light of my own soul?—
I cannot; I have lived in wrath and gloom,
395 Fierce, disputatious, ever at war with man,
Far from my own soul, far from warmth and light.
But I have not grown easy in these bonds—
But I have not denied what bonds these were.
Yea, I take myself to witness,
400 That I have loved no darkness,
Sophisticated no truth,
Nursed no delusion,
Allowed no fear!

    And therefore, O ye elements! I know—
405 Ye know it too—it hath been granted me
Not to die wholly, not to be all enslaved.
I feel it in this hour. The numbing cloud
Mounts off my soul; I feel it, I breathe free.

Is it but for a moment?
410 —Ah, boil up, ye vapours!
Leap and roar, thou sea of fire!
My soul glows to meet you.

Ere it flag, ere the mists
Of despondency and gloom
415 Rush over it again,
Receive me, save me!

               [*He plunges into the crater.*

      CALLICLES (*from below*)
Through the black, rushing smoke-bursts,
Thick breaks the red flame;
All Etna heaves fiercely
420 Her forest-clothed frame.

Not here, O Apollo!
Are haunts meet for thee.
But, where Helicon breaks down
In cliff to the sea,

425 Where the moon-silvered inlets
Send far their light voice
Up the still vale of Thisbe,[1]
O speed, and rejoice!

On the sward at the cliff-top
430 Lie strewn the white flocks,
On the cliff-sides the pigeons
Roost deep in the rocks.

In the moonlight the shepherds,
Soft lulled by the rills,
435 Lie wrapped in their blankets
Asleep on the hills.

—What forms are these coming
So white through the gloom?
What garments out-glistening
440 The gold-flowered broom?

What sweet-breathing presence
Out-perfumes the thyme?

---

1 a village in the valley below Mt. Helicon, the mountain of the muses
("the Nine" of l. 446).

What voice enrapture
The night's balmy prime?

445 'Tis Apollo comes leading
His choir, the Nine.
—The leader is fairest,
But all are divine.

They are lost in the hollows!
450 They stream up again!
What seeks on this mountain
The glorified train?

They bathe on this mountain,
In the spring by their road;
455 Then on to Olympus,
Their endless abode.

—What praise do they mention?
Of what is it told?
What will be for ever;
460 That was from of old.

First hymn they the Father
Of all things; and then,
The rest of immortals,
The action of men.

465 The day in his hotness,
The strife with the palm;
The night in her silence,
The stars in their calm.
—1852 (1849–52)

Memorial Verses

April, 1850

Goethe in Weimer sleeps, and Greece,
Long since, saw Byron's struggle cease.[1]
But one such death remained to come;

The last poetic voice is dumb—
5 We stand to-day by Wordsworth's tomb.

When Byron's eyes were shut in death,
We bowed our head and held our breath.
He taught us little; but our soul
Had *felt* him like the thunder's roll.
10 With shivering heart the strife we saw
Of passion with eternal law;
And yet with reverential awe
We watched the fount of fiery life
Which served for that Titanic strife.

15 When Goethe's death was told, we said:
Sunk, then, is Europe's sagest head.
Physician of the iron age,
Goethe has done his pilgrimage.
He took the suffering human race,
20 He read each wound, each weakness clear;
And struck his finger on the place,
And said: *Thou ailest here, and here!*
He looked on Europe's dying hour[2]
Of fitful dream and feverish power;
25 His eye plunged down the weltering strife,
The turmoil of expiring life—
He said: *The end is everywhere,*
Art still has truth, take refuge there!
And he was happy, if to know
30 Causes of things, and far below
His feet to see the lurid flow
Of terror, and insane distress,
And headlong fate, be happiness.

And Wordsworth!—Ah, pale ghosts, rejoice!
35 For never has such soothing voice
Been to your shadowy world conveyed,
Since erst, at morn, some wandering shade
Heard the clear song of Orpheus come

---

[1] Goethe died in 1832, Byron in Greece in 1824.

[2] the industrial and political revolutions of the eighteenth and nineteenth centuries, undermining basic Christian values.

Through Hades, and the mournful gloom.
40 Wordsworth has gone from us—and ye,
Ah, may ye feel his voice as we!
He too upon a wintry clime
Had fallen—on this iron time
Of doubts, disputes, distractions, fears.
45 He found us when the age had bound
Our souls in its benumbing round;
He spoke, and loosed our heart in tears.
He laid us as we lay at birth
On the cool flowery lap of earth,
50 Smiles broke from us and we had ease;
The hills were round us, and the breeze
Went o'er the sun-lit fields again;
Our foreheads felt the wind and rain.
Our youth returned; for there was shed
55 On spirits that had long been dead,
Spirits dried up and closely furled,
The freshness of the early world.

Ah! since dark days still bring to light
Man's prudence and man's fiery might,
60 Time may restore us in his course
Goethe's sage mind and Byron's force;
But where will Europe's latter hour
Again find Wordsworth's healing power?
Others will teach us how to dare,
65 And against fear our breast to steel;
Others will strengthen us to bear—
But who, ah! who, will make us feel?
The cloud of mortal destiny,
Others will front it fearlessly—
70 But who, like him, will put it by?

Keep fresh the grass upon his grave,
O Rotha,[1] with thy living wave!
Sing him thy best! For few or none
Hears thy voice right, now he is gone.
—1852 (1850)

_____

[1] stream near Grasmere, Wordsworth's burial site.

Dover Beach

The sea is calm to-night.
The tide is full, the moon lies fair
Upon the straits; on the French coast the light
Gleams and is gone; the cliffs of England stand,
5 Glimmering and vast, out in the tranquil bay.
Come to the window, sweet is the night-air!
Only, from the long line of spray
Where the sea meets the moon-blanched land,
Listen! you hear the grating roar
10 Of pebbles which the waves draw back, and fling,
At their return, up the high strand,
Begin, and cease, and then again begin,
With tremulous cadence slow, and bring
The eternal note of sadness in.

15 Sophocles long ago
Heard it on the Ægæan, and it brought
Into his mind the turbid ebb and flow
Of human misery; we
Find also in the sound a thought,
20 Hearing it by this distant northern sea.

The Sea of Faith
Was once, too, at the full, and round earth's shore
Lay like the folds of a bright girdle furled.
But now I only hear
25 Its melancholy, long, withdrawing roar,
Retreating, to the breath
Of the night-wind, down the vast edges drear
And naked shingles[2] of the world.

Ah, love, let us be true
30 To one another! for the world, which seems
To lie before us like a land of dreams,
So various, so beautiful, so new,
Hath really neither joy, nor love, nor light,
Nor certitude, nor peace, nor help for pain;

_____

[2] pebbled beaches.

35 And we are here as on a darkling plain
Swept with confused alarms of struggle and flight,
Where ignorant armies clash by night.
—1867 (1851)

The Buried Life

Light flows our war of mocking words, and yet,
Behold, with tears mine eyes are wet!
I feel a nameless sadness o'er me roll.
Yes, yes, we know that we can jest,
5 We know, we know that we can smile!
But there's a something in this breast,
To which thy light words bring no rest,
And thy gay smiles no anodyne.[1]
Give me thy hand, and hush awhile,
10 And turn those limpid eyes on mine,
And let me read there, love! thy inmost soul.

Alas! is even love too weak
To unlock the heart, and let it speak?
Are even lovers powerless to reveal
15 To one another what indeed they feel?
I knew the mass of men concealed
Their thoughts, for fear that if revealed
They would by other men be met
With blank indifference, or with blame reproved;
20 I knew they lived and moved
Tricked in disguises, alien to the rest
Of men, and alien to themselves—and yet
The same heart beats in every human breast!

But we, my love!—doth a like spell benumb
25 Our hearts, our voices? must we too be dumb?

Ah! well for us, if even we,
Even for a moment, can get free
Our heart, and have our lips unchained;
For that which seals them hath been deep-ordained!

Fate, which foresaw
30 How frivolous a baby man would be—
By what distractions he would be possessed,
How he would pour himself in every strife,
And well-nigh change his own identity—
35 That it might keep from his capricious play
His genuine self, and force him to obey

Even in his own despite his being's law,
Bade through the deep recesses of our breast
The unregarded river of our life
40 Pursue with indiscernible flow its way;
And that we should not see
The buried stream, and seem to be
Eddying at large in blind uncertainty,
Though driving on with it eternally.

45 But often, in the world's most crowded streets,
But often, in the din of strife,
There rises an unspeakable desire
After the knowledge of our buried life;
A thirst to spend our fire and restless force
50 In tracking out our true, original course;

A longing to inquire
Into the mystery of this heart which beats
So wild, so deep in us—to know
Whence our lives come and where they go.
55 And many a man in his own breast then delves,
But deep enough, alas! none ever mines.
And we have been on many thousand lines,[2]
And we have shown, on each, spirit and power;
But hardly have we, for one little hour,
60 Been on our own line, have we been ourselves—
Hardly had skill to utter one of all
The nameless feelings that course through our
breast,

[1] that which relieves pain.

[2] Arnold's note on ll. 57–60 in the Yale MS: "We have been on a thousand lines and on each have shown spirit talent even geniality but hardly for an hour between birth and death have we been on our own one natural line, have we been ourselves, have we breathed freely."

But they course on for ever unexpressed.
And long we try in vain to speak and act
65 Our hidden self, and what we say and do
Is eloquent, is well—but 'tis not true!
And then we will no more be racked
With inward striving, and demand
Of all the thousand nothings of the hour
70 Their stupefying power;
Ah yes, and they benumb us at our call!
Yet still, from time to time, vague and forlorn,
From the soul's subterranean depth upborne
As from an infinitely distant land,
75 Come airs, and floating echoes, and convey
A melancholy into all our day.
Only—but this is rare—
When a belovéd hand is laid in ours,
When, jaded with the rush and glare
80 Of the interminable hours,
Our eyes can in another's eyes read clear,
When our world-deafened ear
Is by the tones of a loved voice caressed—
A bolt is shot back somewhere in our breast,
85 And a lost pulse of feeling stirs again.
The eye sinks inward, and the heart lies plain,
And what we mean, we say, and what we would,
    we know.
A man becomes aware of his life's flow,
And hears its winding murmur; and he sees
90 The meadows where it glides, the sun, the breeze.

And there arrives a lull in the hot race
Wherein he doth for ever chase
That flying and elusive shadow, rest.
An air of coolness plays upon his face,
95 And an unwonted calm pervades his breast.
And then he thinks he knows
The hills where his life rose,
And the sea where it goes.
    —1852 (1849–52)

Stanzas from the Grande Chartreuse [1]

Through Alpine meadows soft-suffused
With rain, where thick the crocus blows,
Past the dark forges long disused,
The mule-track from Saint Laurent [2] goes.
5 The bridge is crossed, and slow we ride,
Through forest, up the mountain-side.

The autumnal evening darkens round,
The wind is up, and drives the rain;
While, hark! far down, with strangled sound
10 Doth the Dead Guier's stream [3] complain,
Where that wet smoke, among the woods,
Over his boiling cauldron broods.

Swift rush the spectral vapours white
Past limestone scars with ragged pines,
15 Showing—then blotting from our sight!
Halt—through the cloud-drift something shines!
High in the valley, wet and drear,
The huts of Courrerie [4] appear.

Strike leftward! cries our guide; and higher
20 Mounts up the stony forest-way.
At last the encircling trees retire;
Look! through the showery twilight grey
What pointed roofs are these advance?
A palace of the Kings of France?

25 Approach, for what we seek is here!
Alight, and sparely sup, and wait
For rest in this outbuilding near;
Then cross the sward and reach that gate.

----

[1] Carthusian monastery in the French Alps which Arnold visited in
1851 on his way from Grenoble to Chambéry.

[2] a village near the monastery.

[3] a river near the monastery.

[4] another nearby village.

Knock; pass the wicket! Thou art come
30 To the Carthusians' world-famed home.

The silent courts, where night and day
Into their stone-carved basins cold
The splashing icy fountains play—
The humid corridors behold!
35 Where, ghostlike in the deepening night,
Cowled forms brush by in gleaming white.

The chapel, where no organ's peal
Invests the stern and naked prayer—
With penitential cries they kneel
40 And wrestle; rising then, with bare
And white uplifted faces stand,
Passing the Host from hand to hand;[1]

Each takes, and then his visage wan
Is buried in his cowl once more.
45 The cells! —the suffering Son of Man
Upon the wall—the knee-worn floor—
And where they sleep, that wooden bed,
Which shall their coffin be, when dead!

The library, where tract and tome
50 Not to feed priestly pride are there,
To hymn the conquering march of Rome,
Nor yet to amuse, as ours are!
They paint of souls the inner strife,
Their drops of blood, their death in life.

55 The garden, overgrown—yet mild,
See, fragrant herbs are flowering there!
Strong children of the Alpine wild
Whose culture is the brethren's care;
Of human tasks their only one,
60 And cheerful works beneath the sun.

Those halls, too, destined to contain
Each its own pilgrim-host of old,
From England, Germany, or Spain—
All are before me! I behold
65 The House, the Brotherhood austere!
—And what am I, that I am here?

For rigorous teachers seized my youth,
And purged its faith, and trimmed its fire,
Showed me the high, white star of Truth,
70 There bade me gaze, and there aspire.
Even now their whispers pierce the gloom
What dost thou in this living tomb?

Forgive me, masters of the mind!
At whose behest I long ago
75 So much unlearnt, so much resigned—
I come not here to be your foe!
I seek these anchorites, not in ruth,
To curse and to deny your truth;

Not as their friend, or child, I speak!
80 But as, on some far northern strand,
Thinking of his own Gods, a Greek
In pity and mournful awe might stand
Before some fallen Runic stone—[2]
For both were faiths, and both are gone.

85 Wandering between two worlds, one dead,
The other powerless to be born,
With nowhere yet to rest my head,
Like these, on earth I wait forlorn.
Their faith, my tears, the world deride—
90 I come to shed them at their side.

Oh, hide me in your gloom profound,
Ye solemn seats of holy pain!
Take me, cowled forms, and fence me round,
Till I possess my soul again;

----

[1] The host (the consecrated bread) is not passed from hand to hand during mass. Arnold is probably referring to the Pax (a small tablet), which was kissed by the priest and then passed through the congregation.

[2] an inscribed religious tablet.

95 Till free my thoughts before me roll,
Not chafed by hourly false control!

For the world cries your faith is now
But a dead time's exploded dream;
My melancholy, sciolists say,
100 Is a past mode, an outworn theme—
As if the world had ever had
A faith, or sciolists[1] been sad!

Ah, if it *be* passed, take away,
At least, the restlessness, the pain;
105 Be man henceforth no more a prey
To these out-dated stings again!
The nobleness of grief is gone—
Ah, leave us not the fret alone!

But—if you cannot give us ease—
110 Last of the race of them who grieve,
Here leave us to die out with these
Last of the people who believe!
Silent, while years engrave the brow;
Silent—the best are silent now.

115 Achilles[2] ponders in his tent,
The kings of modern thought are dumb;
Silent they are, though not content,
And wait to see the future come.
They have the grief men had of yore,
120 But they contend and cry no more.

Our fathers watered with their tears
This sea of time whereon we sail,
Their voices were in all men's ears
Who passed within their puissant hail.
125 Still the same ocean round us raves,
But we stand mute, and watch the waves.

For what availed it, all the noise
And outcry of the former men?
Say, have their sons achieved more joys,
130 Say, is life lighter now than then?
The sufferers died, they left their pain—
The pangs which tortured them remain.

What helps it now, that Byron bore,
With haughty scorn which mocked the smart,
135 Through Europe to the Ætolian shore[3]
The pageant of his bleeding heart?
That thousands counted every groan,
And Europe made his woe her own?

What boots it, Shelley! that the breeze
140 Carried thy lovely wail away,
Musical through Italian trees
Which fringe thy soft blue Spezzian bay?[4]
Inheritors of thy distress
Have restless hearts one throb the less?

145 Or are we easier, to have read,
O Obermann![5] the sad, stern page,
Which tells us how thou hidd'st thy head
From the fierce tempest of thine age
In the lone brakes of Fontainebleau
150 Or chalets near the Alpine snow?

Ye slumber in your silent grave!
The world, which for an idle day
Grace to your mood of sadness gave,
Long since hath flung her weeds away.
155 The eternal trifler breaks your spell;
But we—we learnt your lore too well!

Years hence, perhaps, may dawn an age,
More fortunate, alas! than we,

---

[1] a pretender to knowledge.

[2] the hero whose potential is thwarted by indecision.

[3] the Greek province where Byron died.

[4] on the Gulf of Spezia, where Shelley spent his final days.

[5] an imaginary recluse created by Étienne Pivert de Senancour (1770–1846).

Which without hardness will be sage,
160 And gay without frivolity.
Sons of the world, oh, speed those years;
But, while we wait, allow our tears!

Allow them! We admire with awe
The exulting thunder of your race;
165 You give the universe your law,
You triumph over time and space!
Your pride of life, your tireless powers,
We laud them, but they are not ours.

We are like children reared in shade
170 Beneath some old-world abbey wall,
Forgotten in a forest-glade,
And secret from the eyes of all.
Deep, deep the greenwood round them waves,
Their abbey, and its close of graves!

175 But, where the road runs near the stream,
Oft through the trees they catch a glance
Of passing troops in the sun's beam—
Pennon, and plume, and flashing lance!
Forth to the world those soldiers fare,
180 To life, to cities, and to war!

And through the wood, another way,
Faint bugle-notes from far are borne,
Where hunters gather, staghounds bay,
Round some fair forest-lodge at morn.
185 Gay dames are there, in sylvan green;
Laughter and cries—those notes between!

The banners flashing through the trees
Make their blood dance and chain their eyes;
That bugle-music on the breeze
190 Arrests them with a charmed surprise.
Banner by turns and bugle woo:
Ye shy recluses, follow too!

O children, what do ye reply?—
"Action and pleasure, will ye roam

195 Through these secluded dells to cry
And call us?—but too late ye come!
Too late for us your call ye blow,
Whose bent was taken long ago.

"Long since we pace this shadowed nave;
200 We watch those yellow tapers shine,
Emblems of hope over the grave,
In the high altar's depth divine;
The organ carries to our ear
Its accents of another sphere.

205 "Fenced early in this cloistral round
Of reverie, of shade, of prayer,
How should we grow in other ground?
How can we flower in foreign air?
—Pass, banners, pass, and bugles, cease;
210 And leave our desert to its peace!"
—1855 (1851–55)

The Scholar-Gipsy [1]

Go, for they call you, shepherd, from the hill;
Go, shepherd, and untie the wattled cotes! [2]
No longer leave thy wistful flock unfed,

[1] The tale of the Scholar-Gipsy is from Joseph Glanvill's *The Vanity of Dogmatizing* (1661). Arnold's note to the poem is a collection of sentences from Glanvill: "There was very lately a lad in the University at Oxford, who was by his poverty forced to leave his studies there; and at last to join himself to a company of vagabond gipsies. Among these extravagant people, by the insinuating subtilty of his carriage, he quickly got so much of their love and esteem as that they discovered to him their mystery. After he had been a pretty while well exercised in the trade, there chanced to ride by a couple of scholars, who had formerly been of his acquaintance. They quickly spied out their old friend among the gipsies; and he gave them an account of the necessity which drove him to that kind of life, and told them that the people he went with were not such imposters as they were taken for, but that they had a traditional kind of learning among them, and could do wonders by the power of imagination, their fancy binding that of others; that himself had learned much of their art, and when he had compassed the whole secret, he intended, he said, to leave their company, and give the world an account of what he had learned."

[2] sheepfolds made of interwoven twigs.

Nor let thy bawling fellows rack their throats,
  5   Nor the cropped herbage shoot another head.
       But when the fields are still,
     And the tired men and dogs all gone to rest,
     And only the white sheep are sometimes
           seen
       Cross and recross the strips of moon-
           blanched green,
  10   Come, shepherd, and again begin the quest!¹

     Here, where the reaper was at work of late—
       In this high field's dark corner, where he leaves
         His coat, his basket, and his earthen cruse,
       And in the sun all morning binds the sheaves,
  15   Then here, at noon, comes back his stores to
             use—
           Here will I sit and wait,
     While to my ear from uplands far away
       The bleating of the folded flocks is borne,
       With distant cries of reapers in the corn—
  20   All the live murmur of a summer's day.

     Screened is this nook o'er the high, half-reaped
           field,
       And here till sun-down, shepherd! will I be.
         Through the thick corn the scarlet poppies
             peep,
       And round green roots and yellowing stalks I
           see
  25   Pale pink convolvulus in tendrils creep;
         And air-swept lindens yield
     Their scent, and rustle down their perfumed
           showers
         Of bloom on the bent grass where I am laid,
         And bower me from the August sun with
             shade;
  30   And the eye travels down to Oxford's towers.

     And near me on the grass lies Glanvil's book—
       Come, let me read the oft-read tale again!

The story of the Oxford scholar poor,
     Of pregnant parts and quick inventive brain,
  35   Who, tired of knocking at preferment's door,
         One summer-morn forsook
     His friends, and went to learn the gipsy-lore,
       And roamed the world with that wild
           brotherhood,
       And came, as most men deemed, to little
           good,
  40   But came to Oxford and his friends no more.

     But once, years after, in the country-lanes,
       Two scholars, whom at college erst he knew,
         Met him, and of his way of life enquired;
       Whereat he answered, that the gipsy-crew,
  45   His mates, had arts to rule as they desired
           The workings of men's brains,
     And they can bind them to what thoughts they
           will.²
         "And I," he said, "the secret of their art,
         When fully learned, will to the world impart;
  50   But it needs heaven-sent moments for this
           skill."

     This said, he left them, and returned no more.
       But rumours hung about the country-side,
         That the lost Scholar long was seen to stray,
       Seen by rare glimpses, pensive and tongue-tied,
  55   In hat of antique shape, and cloak of grey,
           The same the gipsies wore.
     Shepherds had met him on the Hurst³ in spring;
       At some lone alehouse in the Berkshire
           moors,
         On the warm ingle-bench,⁴ the smock-
             frocked boors⁵
  60   Had found him seated at their entering,

¹ for the Scholar-Gipsy.

² in Glanvill, by hypnotism.

³ hill outside Oxford.

⁴ bench by a fireplace.

⁵ peasants.

But, 'mid their drink and clatter, he would fly.
    And I myself seem half to know thy looks,
        And put the shepherds, wanderer! on thy
           trace;
    And boys who in lone wheatfields scare the
        rooks
65   I ask if thou hast passed their quiet place;
        Or in my boat I lie
    Moored to the cool bank in the summer-heats,
        'Mid wide grass meadows which the
           sunshine fills,
        And watch the warm, green-muffled
           Cumner hills,
70   And wonder if thou haunt'st their shy retreats.

For most, I know, thou lov'st retiréd ground!
    Thee at the ferry Oxford riders blithe,
        Returning home on summer-nights, have
           met
    Crossing the stripling Thames at Bab-lock-
        hithe,
75   Trailing in the cool stream thy fingers wet,
        As the punt's rope chops round;
    And leaning backward in a pensive dream,
        And fostering in thy lap a heap of flowers
        Plucked in shy fields and distant Wychwood
           bowers,
80   And thine eyes resting on the moonlit stream.

And then they land, and thou art seen no more!
    Maidens, who from the distant hamlets come
        To dance around the Fyfield elm in May,
    Oft through the darkening fields have seen thee
        roam,
85   Or cross a stile into the public way.
        Oft thou hast given them store
    Of flowers—the frail-leafed, white anemone,
        Dark bluebells drenched with dews of
           summer eves,
        And purple orchises with spotted leaves—
90   But none hath words she can report of thee.

And, above Godstow Bridge, when hay-time's here
    In June, and many a scythe in sunshine flames,
        Men who through those wide fields of
           breezy grass
    Where black-winged swallows haunt the
        glittering Thames,
95   To bathe in the abandoned lasher pass,[1]
        Have often passed thee near
    Sitting upon the river bank o'ergrown;
        Marked thine outlandish garb, thy figure
           spare,
        Thy dark vague eyes, and soft abstracted
           air—
100   But, when they came from bathing, thou wast
        gone!

At some lone homestead in the Cumner hills,
    Where at her open door the housewife darns,
        Thou hast been seen, or hanging on a gate
    To watch the threshers in the mossy barns.
105   Children, who early range these slopes and
        late
        For cresses from the rills,
    Have known thee eying, all an April-day,
        The springing pastures and the feeding kine;
        And marked thee, when the stars come out
           and shine,
110   Through the long dewy grass move slow away.

In autumn, on the skirts of Bagley Wood—
    Where most the gipsies by the turf-edged way
        Pitch their smoked tents, and every bush
           you see
    With scarlet patches tagged and shreds of grey,
115   Above the forest-ground called Thessaly—
        The blackbird, picking food,
    Sees thee, nor stops his meal, nor fears at all;
        So often has he known thee past him stray,

---

[1] pool below a dam.

Rapt, twirling in thy hand a withered spray,
120 And waiting for the spark from heaven to fall.

And once, in winter, on the causeway chill
Where home through flooded fields foot-
travellers go,
Have I not passed thee on the wooden
bridge,
Wrapped in thy cloak and battling with the
snow,
125 Thy face tow'rd Hinksey and its wintry
ridge?
And thou hast climbed the hill,
And gained the white brow of the Cumner
range;
Turned once to watch, while thick the
snowflakes fall,
The line of festal light in Christ-Church
hall—
130 Then sought thy straw in some sequestered
grange.

But what—I dream! Two hundred years are flown
Since first thy story ran through Oxford halls,
And the grave Glanvil did the tale inscribe
That thou wert wandered from the studious
walls
135 To learn strange arts, and join a gipsy-tribe;
And thou from earth art gone
Long since, and in some quiet churchyard laid—
Some country-nook, where o'er thy
unknown grave
Tall grasses and white flowering nettles wave,
140 Under a dark, red-fruited yew-tree's shade.

—No, no, thou hast not felt the lapse of hours!
For what wears out the life of mortal men?
'Tis that from change to change their being
rolls;
'Tis that repeated shocks, again, again,
145 Exhaust the energy of strongest souls

And numb the elastic powers.
Till having used our nerves with bliss and teen,[1]
And tired upon a thousand schemes our wit,
To the just-pausing Genius we remit
150 Our worn-out life, and are—what we have
been.

Thou hast not lived, why should'st thou perish, so?
Thou hadst *one* aim, *one* business, *one* desire;
Else wert thou long since numbered with the
dead!
Else hadst thou spent, like other men, thy fire!
155 The generations of thy peers are fled,
And we ourselves shall go;
But thou possessest an immortal lot,
And we imagine thee exempt from age
And living as thou liv'st on Glanvil's page,
160 Because thou hadst—what we, alas! have not.

For early didst thou leave the world, with powers
Fresh, undiverted to the world without,
Firm to their mark, not spent on other
things;
Free from the sick fatigue, the languid doubt,
165 Which much to have tried, in much been
baffled, brings.
O life unlike to ours!
Who fluctuate idly without term or scope,
Of whom each strives, nor knows for what
he strives,
And each half-lives a hundred different lives;
170 Who wait like thee, but not, like thee, in hope.

Thou waitest for the spark from heaven! and we,
Light half-believers of our casual creeds,
Who never deeply felt, nor clearly willed,
Whose insight never has borne fruit in deeds,
175 Whose vague resolves never have been
fulfilled;
For whom each year we see

_____
[1] grief or woe.

Breeds new beginnings, disappointments new;
  Who hesitate and falter life away,
    And lose to-morrow the ground won
      to-day—
180 Ah! do not we, wanderer! await it too?

Yes, we await it!—but it still delays,
  And then we suffer! and amongst us one,
    Who most has suffered, takes dejectedly
    His seat upon the intellectual throne;
185   And all his store of sad experience he
        Lays bare of wretched days;
      Tells us his misery's birth and growth and signs,
      And how the dying spark of hope was fed,
      And how the breast was soothed, and how
        the head,
190 And all his hourly varied anodynes.[1]

This for our wisest! and we others pine,
  And wish the long unhappy dream would end,
    And waive all claim to bliss, and try to bear;
  With close-lipped patience for our only friend,
195   Sad patience, too near neighbour to despair—
        But none has hope like thine!
      Thou through the fields and through the woods
        dost stray,
      Roaming the country-side, a truant boy,
      Nursing thy project in unclouded joy,
200 And every doubt long blown by time away.

O born in days when wits were fresh and clear,
  And life ran gaily as the sparkling Thames;
    Before this strange disease of modern life,
  With its sick hurry, its divided aims,
205   Its heads o'ertaxed, its palsied hearts, was
        rife—
      Fly hence, our contact fear!
    Still fly, plunge deeper in the bowering wood!
      Averse, as Dido did with gesture stern

From her false friend's approach in Hades
  turn,[2]
210 Wave us away, and keep thy solitude!

Still nursing the unconquerable hope,
  Still clutching the inviolable shade,
    With a free, onward impulse brushing
      through,
    By night, the silvered branches of the glade—
215   Far on the forest-skirts, where none pursue,
        On some mild pastoral slope
      Emerge, and resting on the moonlit pales
      Freshen thy flowers as in former years
      With dew, or listen with enchanted ears,
220 From the dark dingles,[3] to the nightingales!

But fly our paths, our feverish contact fly!
  For strong the infection of our mental strife,
    Which, though it gives no bliss, yet spoils
      for rest;
    And we should win thee from thy own fair life,
225   Like us distracted, and like us unblest.
        Soon, soon thy cheer would die,
      Thy hopes grow timorous, and unfixed thy
        powers,
        And thy clear aims be cross and shifting
          made;
        And then thy glad perennial youth would
          fade,
230 Fade, and grow old at last, and die like ours.

Then fly our greetings, fly our speech and smiles!
  —As some grave Tyrian[4] trader, from the sea,
    Descried at sunrise an emerging prow
    Lifting the cool-haired creepers stealthily,
235   The fringes of a southward-facing brow

---

[2] Dido killed herself when Aeneas deserted her, and she turned away from him "with gesture stern" when he visited Hades.

[3] wooded dells.

[4] traders from Tyre, in Asia Minor, who fled from the aggressive Greeks.

---

[1] relieving pain.

Among the Ægean isles;
And saw the merry Grecian coaster come,
   Freighted with amber grapes, and Chian
      wine,
   Green, bursting figs, and tunnies[1] steeped in
      brine—
240 And knew the intruders on his ancient home,

The young light-hearted masters of the waves—
   And snatched his rudder, and shook out more
      sail;
   And day and night held on indignantly
   O'er the blue Midland waters with the gale,
245   Betwixt the Syrtes[2] and soft Sicily,
      To where the Atlantic raves[3]
   Outside the western straits; and unbent sails
      There, where down cloudy cliffs, through
         sheets of foam,
      Shy traffickers, the dark Iberians come;
250 And on the beach undid his corded bales.
   —1853 (1852–53)

Philomela [4]

Hark! Ah, the nightingale—
   The tawny-throated!
Hark, from that moonlit cedar what a burst!
What triumph! hark!—what pain!
5 O wanderer from a Grecian shore,
Still, after many years, in distant lands,
Still nourishing in thy bewildered brain

That wild, unquenched, deep-sunken, old-world
   pain—
Say, will it never heal?
10 And can this fragrant lawn
With its cool trees, and night,
And the sweet, tranquil Thames,
And moonshine, and the dew,
To thy racked heart and brain
15 Afford no balm?
Dost thou to-night behold,
Here, through the moonlight on this English grass,
The unfriendly palace in the Thracian wild?
Dost thou again peruse
20 With hot cheeks and seared eyes
The too clear web, and thy dumb sister's shame?
Dost thou once more assay
Thy flight, and feel come over thee,
Poor fugitive, the feathery change
25 Once more, and once more seem to make resound
With love and hate, triumph and agony,
Lone Daulis, and the high Cephissian vale?[5]
Listen, Eugenia—
How thick the bursts come crowding through the
   leaves!
30 Again—thou hearest?
Eternal passion!
Eternal pain!
   —1853 (1852–53)

---

[1] fish.

[2] Gulf of Sidra on the northern coast of Africa.

[3] beyond the Straits of Gibraltar.

[4] Arnold's version of the Greek myth has Tereus, a Thracian king, husband of Philomela, fall in love with and rape Procne, Philomela's sister. To conceal his conduct he cuts out her tongue. But Procne communicates with Philomela via a piece of embroidery. Philomela then kills the king's son Itys, and the two sisters flee. As a result of their prayer to the gods to be changed into birds, Philomela becomes a nightingale and Procne a swallow.

---

[5] the valley of the River Cephisus.

Thyrsis [1]

A MONODY, to commemorate the author's friend, ARTHUR
HUGH CLOUGH, who died at Florence, 1861

How changed is here each spot man makes or
    fills!
  In the two Hinkseys [2] nothing keeps the same;
    The village street its haunted mansion lacks,
  And from the sign is gone Sibylla's [3] name,
5   And from the roofs the twisted chimney-
        stacks—
      Are ye too changed, ye hills?
  See, 'tis no foot of unfamiliar men
    To-night from Oxford up your pathway
      strays!
  Here came I often, often, in old days—
10 Thyrsis and I; we still had Thyrsis then.

Runs it not here, the track by Childsworth Farm,
  Past the high wood, to where the elm-tree
    crowns
    The hill behind whose ridge the sunset
      flames?
  The signal-elm, that looks on Ilsley Downs,
15   The Vale, the three lone weirs, the youthful
      Thames? [4]
      This winter-eve is warm,
  Humid the air! leafless, yet soft as spring,
    The tender purple spray on copse and briers!
  And that sweet city with her dreaming spires,
20 She needs not June for beauty's heightening,

Lovely all times she lies, lovely to-night!—
  Only, methinks, some loss of habit's power

Befalls me wandering through this upland
    dim.
  Once passed I blindfold here, at any hour;
25   Now seldom come I, since I came with him.
      That single elm-tree bright
  Against the west—I miss it! is it gone?
    We prized it dearly; while it stood, we said,
    Our friend, the Gipsy-Scholar, was not dead;
30 While the tree lived, he in these fields lived on.

Too rare, too rare, grow now my visits here,
  But once I knew each field, each flower, each
    stick;
    And with the country-folk acquaintance
      made
  By barn in threshing time, by new-built rick.
35   Here, too, our shepherd-pipes we first
      assayed.
      Ah me! this many a year
  My pipe is lost, my shepherd's holiday!
    Needs must I lose them, needs with heavy
      heart
    Into the world and wave of men depart;
40 But Thyrsis of his own will went away. [5]

It irked him to be here, he could not rest.
  He loved each simple joy the country yields,
    He loved his mates; but yet he could not
      keep, [6]
  For that a shadow loured on the fields,
45   Here with the shepherds and the silly [7] sheep.
      Some life of men unblest
  He knew, which made him droop, and filled his
    head.
    He went; his piping took a troubled sound

---

[1] modelled on the form of the pastoral elegy originally written in Greek by Theocritus. Especially appropriate for this poem because Arnold and Clough had spent much time walking in the Cumner countryside near Oxford as undergraduates.

[2] villages of North and South Hinksey.

[3] Sybella Curr, keeper of an inn in South Hinksey, who died in 1860.

[4] that is, near its source.

---

[5] a reference to Clough's resignation of his Oriel fellowship in 1848 and his departure from Oxford. But he did not leave, as Arnold suggests (ll. 46–47), for reasons of social conscience.

[6] stay.

[7] innocent.

Of storms that rage outside our happy
    ground;
50   He could not wait their passing, he is dead.

So, some tempestuous morn in early June,
    When the year's primal burst of bloom is o'er,
        Before the roses and the longest day—
    When garden-walks and all the grassy floor
55   With blossoms red and white of fallen May
        And chestnut-flowers are strewn—
    So have I heard the cuckoo's parting cry,
        From the wet field, through the vexed
            garden-trees,
        Come with the volleying rain and tossing
            breeze;
60   *The bloom is gone, and with the bloom go I!*

Too quick despairer, wherefore wilt thou go?
    Soon will the high Midsummer pomps come on,
        Soon will the musk carnations break and
            swell,
    Soon shall we have gold-dusted snapdragon,
65   Sweet-William with his homely cottage-
            smell,
        And stocks in fragrant blow;
    Roses that down the alleys shine afar,
        And open, jasmine-muffled lattices,
        And groups under the dreaming garden-trees,
70   And the full moon, and the white evening-star.

He hearkens not! light comer, he is flown!
    What matters it? next year he will return,
        And we shall have him in the sweet spring-
            days,
    With whitening hedges, and uncrumpling fern,
75   And blue-bells trembling by the forest-ways,
        And scent of hay new-mown.
    But Thyrsis never more we swains shall see;
        See him come back and cut a smoother reed,

And blow a strain the world at last shall
    heed—
80   For Time, not Corydon,[1] hath conquered thee!

Alack, for Corydon no rival now!
    But when Sicilian shepherds lost a mate,
        Some good survivor with his flute would go,
    Piping a ditty sad for Bion's[2] fate;
85   And cross the unpermitted ferry's flow,[3]
        And relax Pluto's[4] brow,
    And make leap up with joy the beauteous head
        Of Proserpine, among whose crownéd hair
        Are flowers first opened on Sicilian air,
90   And flute his friend, like Orpheus,[5] from the
        dead.

O easy access to the hearer's grace
    When Dorian shepherds sang to Proserpine!
        For she herself had trod Sicilian fields,
    She knew the Dorian water's gush divine,
95   She knew each lily white which Enna yields,
        Each rose with blushing face;
    She loved the Dorian pipe, the Dorian strain.
        But ah, of our poor Thames she never heard!
        Her foot the Cumner cowslips never stirred;
100   And we should tease her with our plaint in vain!

Well! wind-dispersed and vain the words will be,
    Yet, Thyrsis, let me give my grief its hour
        In the old haunt, and find our tree-topped
            hill!
    Who, if not I, for questing here hath power?

---

[1] Corydon wins over Thyrsis in a musical contest in Virgil's seventh
Eclogue.

[2] from Moschus's pastoral elegy, "Lament for Bion."

[3] The crossing of the river Styx to the underworld could be made only
by the dead.

[4] king of the underworld and Proserpine, his queen.

[5] Orpheus won the release of his wife Eurydice with the beauty of his
playing.

105   I know the wood which hides the daffodil,
        I know the Fyfield tree,[1]
    I know what white, what purple fritillaries[2]
        The grassy harvest of the river-fields,
        Above by Ensham, down by Sandford, yields,
110   And what sedged brooks are Thames's tributaries;

I know these slopes; who knows them if not I?
    But many a dingle on the loved hill-side,
        With thorns once studded, old, white-blossomed trees,
    Where thick the cowslips grew, and far descried
115   High towered the spikes of purple orchises,
        Hath since our day put by
    The coronals of that forgotten time;
        Down each green bank hath gone the ploughboy's team,
    And only in the hidden brookside gleam
120   Primroses, orphans of the flowery prime.

Where is the girl, who by the boatman's door,
    Above the locks, above the boating throng,
        Unmoored our skiff when through the Wytham flats,
    Red loosestrife and blond meadow-sweet among
125   And darting swallows and light water-gnats,
        We tracked the shy Thames shore?
    Where are the mowers, who, as the tiny swell
        Of our boat passing heaved the river-grass,
        Stood with suspended scythe to see us pass?
130   They are all gone, and thou art gone as well!

Yes, thou art gone! and round me too the night
    In ever-nearing circle weaves her shade.
        I see her veil draw soft across the day,
    I feel her slowly chilling breath invade

135   The cheek grown thin, the brown hair sprent[3] with grey;
        I feel her finger light
    Laid pausefully upon life's headlong train;
        The foot less prompt to meet the morning dew,
    The heart less bounding at emotion new,
140   And hope, once crushed, less quick to spring again.

And long the way appears, which seemed so short
    To the less practised eye of sanguine youth;
        And high the mountain-tops, in cloudy air,
    The mountain-tops where is the throne of Truth,
145   Tops in life's morning-sun so bright and bare!
        Unbreachable the fort
    Of the long-battered world uplifts its wall;
        And strange and vain the earthly turmoil grows,
    And near and real the charm of thy repose,
150   And night as welcome as a friend would fall.

But hush! the upland hath a sudden loss
    Of quiet!—Look, adown the dusk hill-side,
        A troop of Oxford hunters going home,
    As in old days, jovial and talking, ride!
155   From hunting with the Berkshire hounds they come.
        Quick! let me fly, and cross
    Into yon farther field!—'Tis done; and see,
        Backed by the sunset, which doth glorify
        The orange and pale violet evening-sky,
160   Bare on its lonely ridge, the Tree! the Tree!

I take the omen! Eve lets down her veil,
    The white fog creeps from bush to bush about,

---

[1] elm tree near the village of Fyfield.

[2] lily-like flower.

[3] sprinkled.

The west unflushes, the high stars grow
    bright,
And in the scattered farms the lights come out.
165   I cannot reach the signal-tree to-night,
      Yet, happy omen, hail!
Hear it from thy broad lucent Arno-vale[1]
    (For there thine earth-forgetting eyelids keep
    The morningless and unawakening sleep
170   Under the flowery oleanders pale),

Hear it, O Thyrsis, still our tree is there!
    Ah, vain! These English fields, this upland dim,
      These brambles pale with mist engarlanded,
    That lone, sky-pointing tree, are not for him;
175   To a boon southern country he is fled,
        And now in happier air,
    Wandering with the great Mother's[2] train divine
      (And purer or more subtle soul than thee,
      I trow, the mighty Mother doth not see)
180   Within a folding of the Apennine,[3]

Thou hearest the immortal chants of old!
    Putting his sickle to the perilous grain
      In the hot cornfield of the Phrygian king,
    For thee the Lityerses-song again
185   Young Daphnis with his silver voice doth
        sing;
      Sings his Sicilian fold,
    His sheep, his hapless love, his blinded eyes—
    And how a call celestial round him rang,
    And heavenward from the fountain-brink he
      sprang,
190   And all the marvel of the golden skies.[4]

There thou art gone, and me thou leavest here
    Sole in these fields! yet will I not despair.
      Despair I will not, while I yet descry
    'Neath the mild canopy of English air
195   That lonely tree against the western sky.
      Still, still these slopes, 'tis clear,
    Our Gipsy-Scholar haunts, outliving thee!
      Fields where soft sheep from cages pull the
        hay,
    Woods with anemones in flower till May,
200   Know him a wanderer still; then why not me?

A fugitive and gracious light he seeks,
    Shy to illumine; and I seek it too.
      This does not come with houses or with gold,
    With place, with honour, and a flattering crew;
205   'Tis not in the world's market bought and
        sold—
      But the smooth-slipping weeks
    Drop by, and leave its seeker still untired;
      Out of the heed of mortals he is gone,
      He wends unfollowed, he must house alone;
210   Yet on he fares, by his own heart inspired.

Thou too, O Thyrsis, on like quest wast bound;
    Thou wanderedst with me for a little hour!
      Men gave thee nothing; but this happy quest,
    If men esteemed thee feeble, gave thee power,
215   If men procured thee trouble, gave thee rest.
      And this rude Cumner ground,

---

[1] Florence, in the Arno valley, where Clough is buried.

[2] goddess of nature, Cybele.

[3] mountain range near Florence.

[4] Arnold's note to this stanza is from Servius's commentary on Virgil's *Eclogues*: "Daphnis, the ideal Sicilian shepherd of Greek pastoral poetry, was said to have followed into Phrygia his mistress Piplea, who had been carried off by robbers, and to have found her in the power of the king of Phrygia, Lityerses. Lityerses used to make strangers try a contest with

him in reaping corn and to put them to death if he overcame them. Hercules arrived in time to save Daphnis, took upon himself the reaping-contest with Lityerses, overcame him, and slew him. The Lityerses-song connected with this tradition was, like the Linus-song, one of the early plaintive strains of Greek popular poetry, and used to be sung by corn-reapers. Other traditions represented Daphnis as beloved by a nymph who exacted from him an oath to love no one else. He fell in love with a princess, and was struck blind by the jealous nymph. Mercury, who was his father, raised him to heaven, and made a fountain spring up in the place from which he ascended. At this fountain the Sicilians offered yearly sacrifices."

Its fir-topped Hurst, its farms, its quiet fields,
    Here cam'st thou in thy jocund youthful
        time,
    Here was thine height of strength, thy
        golden prime!
220   And still the haunt beloved a virtue yields.

What though the music of thy rustic flute
    Kept not for long its happy, country tone;
        Lost it too soon, and learnt a stormy note
Of men contention-tossed, of men who groan,
225   Which tasked thy pipe too sore, and tired
        thy throat
        It failed, and thou wast mute![1]
    Yet hadst thou always visions of our light,
        And long with men of care thou couldst not
        stay,
        And soon thy foot resumed its wandering
        way,
230   Left human haunt, and on alone till night.

Too rare, too rare, grow now my visits here!
    'Mid city-noise, not, as with thee of yore,
        Thyrsis! in reach of sheep-bells is my home.
    —Then through the great town's harsh, heart-
        wearying roar,
235   Let in thy voice a whisper often come,
        To chase fatigue and fear:
Why faintest thou? I wandered till I died.
    Roam on! The light we sought is shining
    still.
    Dost thou ask proof? Our tree yet crowns
    the hill,
240   *Our Scholar travels yet the loved hill-side.*
    —1866 (1864–65)

---

[1] Clough published no new poems in England after 1849.

Coventry Patmore
1823 – 1896

A Roman Catholic poet, essayist, and critic, Coventry Kersey Dighton Patmore was the author of *The Angel in the House* (1854–56), *The Unknown Eros* (1877), *Amelia* (1878), and *The Rod, the Root and the Flower* (1895). A central voice in the Catholic literary revival, Patmore was intimately associated with the Pre-Raphaelites and a variety of other literary personages. Born in a literary family, Patmore was privately educated and developed sophisticated religious and aesthetic theories that were further fortified upon a visit to Rome in 1864. Leaving his position in the printed book department of the British Museum, Patmore relaxed into a private life that ended with a close friendship with Alice Meynell. A friend and correspondent of Gerard Manley Hopkins, Patmore embarked on a private discourse that is reflected in work that actively explores the boundaries of meter and language.

ഇൟ

The Toys

My little Son, who look'd from thoughtful eyes
And moved and spoke in quiet grown-up wise,
Having my law the seventh time disobey'd,
I struck him, and dismiss'd
5 With hard words and unkiss'd,
His Mother, who was patient, being dead.
Then, fearing lest his grief should hinder sleep,
I visited his bed,
But found him slumbering deep,
10 With darken'd eyelids, and their lashes yet
From his late sobbing wet.
And I, with moan,
Kissing away his tears, left others of my own;
For, on a table drawn beside his head,
15 He had put, within his reach,
A box of counters and a red-vein'd stone,
A piece of glass abraded by the beach
And six or seven shells,
A bottle with bluebells
20 And two French copper coins, ranged there with
    careful art,
To comfort his sad heart.
So when that night I pray'd
To God, I wept, and said:

Ah, when at last we lie with tranced breath,
25 Not vexing Thee in death,
And Thou rememberest of what toys
We made our joys,
How weakly understood,
Thy great commanded good,
30 Then, fatherly not less
Than I whom Thou hast moulded from the clay,
Thou'lt leave Thy wrath, and say,
"I will be sorry for their childishness."
—1876

Magna est Veritas

Here, in this little Bay,
Full of tumultuous life and great repose,
Where, twice a day,
The purposeless, glad ocean comes and goes,
5 Under high cliffs, and far from the huge town,
I sit me down.
For want of me the world's course will not fail:
When all its work is done, the lie shall rot;
The truth is great, and shall prevail,
10 When none cares whether it prevail or not.
—1877

The Angel in the House [1]

BOOK I

THE PROLOGUE

"Mine is no horse with wings, to gain
    The region of the spheral chime;
He does but drag a rumbling wain,
    Cheer'd by the silver bells of rhyme;
5 And if at Fame's bewitching note
    My homely Pegasus [2] pricks an ear,
The world's cart-collar hugs his throat,
    And he's too wise to kick or rear."

Thus ever answer'd Vaughan his wife,
10   Who, more than he, desired his fame;
But, in his heart, his thoughts were rife
    How for her sake to earn a name.
With bays poetic three times crown'd,
    And other college honours won,
15 He, if he chose, might be renown'd,
    He had but little doubt, she none;
And in a loftier phrase he talk'd
    With her, upon their Wedding-Day,
(The eighth), while through the fields they walk'd,
20   Their children shouting by the way.

"Not careless of the gift of song,
    Nor out of love with noble fame,
I, meditating much and long
    What I should sing, how win a name,
25 Considering well what theme unsung,
    What reason worth the cost of rhyme,
Remains to loose the poet's tongue

In these last days, the dregs of time,
    Learn that to me, though born so late,
30 There does, beyond desert, befall
    (May my great fortune make me great!)
    The first of themes sung last of all.
In green and undiscover'd ground,
    Yet near where many others sing,
35 I have the very well-head found
    Whence gushes the Pierian Spring." [3]

Then she: "What is it, Dear? The Life
    Of Arthur, or Jerusalem's Fall?"
"Neither: your gentle self, my wife,
40   And love, that grows from one to all.
And if I faithfully proclaim
    Of these the exceeding worthiness,
Surely the sweetest wreath of Fame
    Shall, to your hope, my brows caress;
45 And if, by virtue of my choice
    Of this, the most heart-touching theme
That ever tuned a poet's voice,
    I live, as I am bold to dream,
To be delight to future days,
50   And into silence only cease
When those are still, who shared their bays
    With Laura and with Beatrice. [4]
Imagine, Dear, how learned men
    Will deep-conceived devices find,
55 Beyond my purpose and my ken,
    An ancient bard of simple mind!
You, Sweet, his Mistress, Wife, and Muse,
    Were you for mortal woman meant?
Your praises give a hundred clues
60   To mythological intent!
And, severing thus the truth from trope,
    In you the Commentators see,

---

[1] We are printing the text of the last separately printed edition, published by Harrap in 1923, containing the final versions of Books I and II.

[2] in Greek mythology, the winged horse ridden by Bellerophon. When Mount Helicon, the home of the Muses, began to rise up into heaven, Pegasus kicked it, thus releasing the inspirational river Hippocrene.

[3] Pieria was reputedly the home of the Muses; to drink of the Pierian spring is to be poetically inspired.

[4] the women who inspired the love poetry of Petrarch and Dante, respectively.

Some Faith, some Charity, some Hope,
    Some, wiser, think you all the three."
65 She laugh'd. How proud she always was
    To see how proud he was of her!
But he had grown distraught, because
    The Muse's mood began to stir.

The Cathedral Close

PRELUDE

Love's Reality

I walk, I trust, with open eyes;
70   I've travell'd half my worldly course;
And in the way behind me lies
    Much vanity and some remorse;
I've lived to feel how pride may part
    Spirits, tho' match'd like hand and glove;
75 I've blush'd for love's abode, the heart;
    But have not disbelieved in love;
Nor unto love, sole mortal thing
    Of worth immortal, done the wrong
To count it, with the rest that sing,
80   Unworthy of a serious song;
And love is my reward; for now,
    When most of dead'ning time complain,
The myrtle blooms upon my brow,
    Its odour quickens all my brain.

Love's Immortality

85 How vilely 'twere to misdeserve
    The poet's gift of perfect speech,
In song to try, with trembling nerve,
    The limit of its utmost reach,
Only to sound the wretched praise
90   Of what to-morrow shall not be,
So mocking with immortal bays
    The cross-bones of mortality!
I do not thus. My faith is fast

That all the loveliness I sing
95 Is made to bear the mortal blast,
    And blossom in a better Spring.

The Poet's Humility

From love's abysmal ether rare
    If I to men have here made known
New truths, they, like new stars, were there.
100   But only not yet written down.
Nor verse, nor art, nor plot, nor plan,
    Nor aught of mine here's worth a toy:
Quit praise and blame, and, if you can,
    Do, brother, for the nonce, enjoy.
105 Moving but as the feelings move,
    I run, or loiter with delight,
Or stop to mark where gentle Love
    Persuades the soul from height to height.
Yet, know, that, though my words are gay
110   As David's dance, which Michael scorn'd,
If rightly you peruse the Lay,
    You shall be sweetly help'd and warn'd.

The Impossibility

Of all the impossibilities
    Of love's achieving, surely none
115 So hopeless as to speak it is.
    By love, in me, may this be done!
Lo, love's obey'd by all. 'Tis right
    That all should know what they obey,
Lest erring conscience damp delight,
120   And folly laugh our joys away.
Thou Primal Love, who grantest wings
    And voices to the woodland birds,
Grant me the power of saying things
    Too simple and too sweet for words!

Heaven and Earth

125 How long shall men deny the flower
    Because its roots are in the earth,

And crave with tears from God the dower
    They have, and have despised as dearth.

The Cathedral Close

Once more I came to Sarum Close
130   With joy half memory, half desire,
And breathed the sunny wind that rose
    And blew the shadows o'er the Spire,
And toss'd the lilac's scented plumes,
    And sway'd the chestnut's thousand cones,
135 And fill'd my nostrils with perfumes,
    And shaped the clouds in waifs and zones,
And wafted down the serious strain
    Of Sarum bells, when, true to time,
I reach'd the Dean's, with heart and brain
140   That trembled to the trembling chime.

'Twas half my home six years ago.
    The six years had not alter'd it:
Red-brick and ashlar, long and low,
    With dormers and with oriels lit.
145 Geranium, lychnis, rose array'd
    The windows, all wide open thrown;
And some one in the Study play'd
    The Wedding-March of Mendelssohn.[1]
And there it was I last took leave:
150   'Twas Christmas: I remember'd now
The cruel girls, who feign'd to grieve,
    Took down the evergreens; and how
The laurel into blazes woke
    The fire, lighting the large, low room,
155 A dim, rich lustre of old oak
    And crimson velvet's glowing gloom.

No change had touch'd Dean Churchill: kind,
    By widowhood more than winters bent,
And settled in a cheerful mind,
160   As still forecasting heaven's content.

Well might his thoughts be fixed on high,
    Now she was there! Within her face
Humility and dignity
    Were met in a most sweet embrace.
165 She seem'd expressly sent below
    To teach our erring minds to see
The rhythmic change of time's swift flow
    As part of still eternity.
Her life, all honour, observed, with awe
170   Which cross experience could not mar,
The fiction of the Christian law
    That all men honourable are;
And so her smile at once conferr'd
    High flattery and benign reproof;
175 And I, a rude boy, strangely stirr'd,
    Grew courtly in my own behoof.

Was this her eldest, Honor; prude,
    Who would not let me pull the swing;
Who, kiss'd at Christmas, called me rude,
180   And sobb'd alone, and would not sing?
How changed! In shape no slender Grace,[2]
    But Venus;[3] milder than the dove;
Her mother's air; her Norman face;
    Her large sweet eyes, clear lakes of love.
185 Mary I knew. In former time
    Ailing and pale, she thought that bliss
Was only for a better clime,
    And, heavenly overmuch, scorn'd this.
I, rash with theories of the right,
190   Which stretch'd the tether of my Creed,
But did not break it, held delight
    Half discipline. We disagreed.
She told the Dean I wanted grace.
    Now she was kindest of the three,
195 And two wild roses deck'd her face.

---

[1] Felix Mendelssohn (1809–47), German composer.

[2] alluding to the three Graces, sister-goddesses who bestowed beauty and charm. Their names were Aglaia, Thalia, and Euphrosyne.

[3] the Roman goddess of beauty and sensual love; perhaps also the statue Venus de Medici in the Uffizi Gallery, Florence.

And, what, was this my Mildred, she
To herself and all a sweet surprise?
    My Pet, who romp'd and roll'd a hoop?
I wonder'd where those daisy eyes
200   Had found their touching curve and droop.
Unmannerly times! But now we sat
    Stranger than strangers; till I caught
And answer'd Mildred's smile; and that
    Spread to the rest, and freedom brought.
205 By Honor I was kindly task'd
    To explain my never coming down
From Cambridge; Mary smiled and ask'd
    Were Kant and Goethe[1] yet outgrown?
And, pleased, we talk'd the old days o'er;
210   And, parting, I for pleasure sigh'd.
To be there as a friend, (since more!)
    Seem'd then, seems still, excuse for pride;
For something that abode endued
    With temple-like repose, an air
215 Of life's kind purposes pursued
    With order'd freedom sweet and fair.

Mary and Mildred

PRELUDE

The Paragon

When I behold the skies aloft
    Passing the pageantry of dreams,
The cloud whose bosom, cygnet-soft,

220 A couch for nuptial Juno[2] seems,
    The ocean broad, the mountains bright,
     The shadowy vales with feeding herds,
I from my lyre the music smite,
    Nor want for justly matching words.
225 All powers of the sea and air,
    All interests of hill and plain,
I so can sing, in seasons fair,
    That who hath felt may feel again;
Nay more, the gracious Muses bless
230   At times my tongue until I can,
With moving emphasis, express
    The likeness of the perfect man.
Elated oft by such free songs,
    I think with utterance free to raise
235 That hymn for which the whole world longs,
    A worthy hymn in woman's praise;
A hymn bright-noted like a bird's,
    Arousing these song-sleepy times
With rhapsodies of perfect words,
240   Ruled by returning kiss of rhymes.
But when I look on her and hope
    To tell with joy what I admire,
My thoughts lie cramp'd in narrow scope,
    Or in the feeble birth expire;
245 No skill'd complexity of speech,
    No simple phrase of tenderest fall,
No liken'd excellence can reach
    Her, the most excellent of all.
The best half of creation's best,
250   Its heart to feel, its eye to see,
The crown and complex of the rest,
    Its aim and its epitome.
Nay, might I utter my conceit,
    'Twere after all a vulgar song,
255 For she's so simply, subtly sweet,
    My deepest rapture does her wrong.
Yet it is now my chosen task

---

[1] Immanuel Kant (1724–1804); German professor of logic and metaphysics, his influential works include the *Critique of Pure Reason* (1781). Johann Wolfgang von Goethe (1749–1832) lived and worked in Weimar; in 1791 he was appointed director of the Weimar court theatre. Author of many influential works including *Faust* (1832), *The Sorrows of Young Werther* (1774), and *Wilhelm Meister's Apprenticeship* (1795–96). The latter two works were translated by Thomas Carlyle, who introduced Goethe's thought to English intellectuals. The speaker here has been reading (studying) philosophy at Cambridge University.

[2] the queen of heaven, wife and sister of Jupiter; the special protector of marriage and of women.

To sing her worth as Maid and Wife;
Nor happier post than this I ask,
260   To live her laureate all my life.
On wings of love uplifted free,
   And by her gentleness made great,
I'll teach how noble man should be
   To match her with such a lovely mate;
265 And then in her will move the more
   The woman's wish to be desired,
(By praise increased,) till both shall soar,
   With blissful emulations fired.
And, as geranium, pink, or rose
270   Is thrice itself through power of art,
So may my happy skill disclose
   New fairness even in her fair heart;
Until that churl shall nowhere be,
   Who bends not, awed, before the throne
275 Of her affecting majesty,
   So meek, so far unlike our own;
Until, (for who may hope too much
   From her who wields the powers of love?)
Our lifted lives at last shall touch
280   That happy goal to which they move;
Until, we find, as darkness rolls
   Away, and evil mist dissolve,
That nuptial contrasts are the poles
   On which the heavenly spheres revolve.

MARY AND MILDRED

285 One morning, after Church, I walk'd
   Alone with Mary on the Lawn,
And felt myself, howe'er we talked,
   To grave themes delicately drawn.
When she, delighted, found I knew
290   More of her peace than she supposed,
Our confidences heavenwards grew,
   Like fox-glove buds, in pairs disclosed
Our former faults did we confess,
   Our ancient feud was more than heal'd,
295 And, with the woman's eagerness

For amity full-sign'd and seal'd,
She, offering up for sacrifice
   Her heart's reserve, brought out to show
Some verses, made when she was ice
300   To all but Heaven, six years ago;
Since happier grown! I took and read
   The neat-writ lines. She, void of guile,
Too late repenting, blush'd and said,
   I must not think about the style.

.   .   .   .   .

305 She from a rose-tree shook the blight;
   And well she knew that I knew well
Her grace with silence to requite.

Honoria

PRELUDE

The Lover

He meets, by heavenly chance express,
   The destined maid; some hidden hand
310 Unveils to him that loveliness
   Which others cannot understand.
No songs of love, no summer dreams
   Did e'er his longing fancy fire
With vision like to this; she seems
315   In all things better than desire!
His merits in her presence grow,
   To match the promise in her eyes,
And round her happy footsteps blow
   The authentic airs of Paradise.
320 For joy of her he cannot sleep;
   Her beauty haunts him all the night.
It melts his heart, it makes him weep
   For wonder, worship, and delight.

No smallest boon were bought too dear,
325   Though barter'd for his love-sick life;
Yet trusts he, with undaunted cheer,

To vanquish heaven and call her wife.
He notes how queens of sweetness still
    Neglect their crowns, and stoop to mate;
330 How, self-consign'd with lavish will,
    They ask but love proportionate;
How swift pursuit by small degrees,
    Love's tactic, works like miracle;
How valour, clothed in courtesies,
335   Brings down the haughtiest citadel;
And therefore, though he merits not
    To kiss the braid upon her skirt,
His hope, discouraged ne'er a jot,
    Out-soars all possible desert.

The Attainment

340 You love? That's high as you shall go
    For 'tis as true as Gospel text,[1]
Not noble then is never so,
    Either in this world or the next.

Honoria

She was all mildness; yet 'twas writ
345   Upon her beauty legibly,
"He that's for heaven itself unfit,
    Let him not hope to merit me."

If question were of her for wife,
    Ill might be mended, hope increased.
350 Not that I soar'd so far above
    Myself, as this great hope to dare;
And yet I well foresaw that love
    Might hope where reason must despair;
And, half-resenting the sweet pride
355   Which would not ask me to admire,
"Oh," to my secret heart I sigh'd,
    "That I were worthy to desire!"

---

[1] specifically, the lives of Christ told by the Evangelists in the New Testament, but the phrase also refers to the entire Christian message.

The Morning Call

PRELUDE

The Rose of the World

Lo, when the Lord made North and South
    And sun and moon ordained, He,
360 Forthbringing each by word of mouth
    In order of its dignity,
Did man from the crude clay express
    By sequence, and, all else decreed,
He form'd the woman; nor might less
365   Than Sabbath such a work succeed.
And still with favour singled out,
    Marr'd less than man by mortal fall,
Her disposition is devout,
    Her countenance angelical;
370 The best things that the best believe
    Are in her face so kindly writ
The faithless, seeing her, conceive,
    Not only heaven, but hope of it;
No idle thought her instinct shrouds,
375   But fancy chequers settled sense,
Like alteration of the clouds
    On noonday's azure permanence;
Pure dignity, composure, ease,
    Declare affections nobly fix'd,
380 And impulse sprung from due degrees
    Of sense and spirit sweetly mix'd;
Her modesty, her chiefest grace,
    The cestus[2] clasping Venus's side,
Is potent to deject the face
385   Of him who would affront its pride;
Wrong dares not in her presence speak,
    Nor spotted thought its taint disclose
Under the protest of a cheek
    Outbragging Nature's boast the rose.
390 In mind and manners how discreet!

---

[2] a belt or girdle, particularly that worn by a bride in ancient times.

How artless in her very art;
How candid in discourse; how sweet
    The concord of her lips and heart;
How simple and how circumspect;
395   How subtle and how fancy-free;
Though sacred to her love, how deck'd
    With unexclusive courtesy;
How quick in talk to see from far
    The way to vanquish or evade;
400 How able her persuasions are
    To prove, her reasons to persuade;
How, (not to call true instinct's bent
    And woman's very nature, harm,)
How amiable and innocent
405   Her pleasure in her power to charm;
How humbly careful to attract,
    Though crown'd with all the soul desires,
Connubial aptitude exact,
    Diversity that never tires.

The Tribute

410 Boon Nature to the woman bows.
    She walks in all its glory clad,
And, chief herself of earthly shows,
    Each other helps her, and is glad,
No splendour 'neath the sky's proud dome
415   But serves for her familiar wear;
The far-fetched diamond finds its home
    Flashing and smouldering in her hair;
For her the seas their pearls reveal;
    Art and strange lands her pomp supply
420 With purple, chrome, and cochineal,
    Ochre, and lapis lazuli;
The worm its golden woof presents;
    Whatever runs, flies, dives, or delves,
All doff for her their ornaments,
425   Which suit her better than themselves;
And all, by this their power to give,
    Proving her right to take, proclaim

Her beauty's clear prerogative
    To profit so by Eden's blame.

Compensation

430 That nothing here may want its praise,
    Know, she who in her dress reveals
A fine and modest taste, displays
    More loveliness than she conceals.

THE MORNING CALL

"Full many a lady has ere now
435   My apprehensive fancy fired,
And woven may a transient chain;
    But never lady like to this,
Who holds me as the weather-vane
    Is held by yonder clematis.
440 She seems the life of nature's powers;
    Her beauty is the genial thought
Which makes the sunshine bright; the flowers,
    But for hint of her, were nought."
A voice, the sweeter for the grace
445   Of suddenness, while thus I dream'd,
"Good morning!" said or sang. Her face
    The mirror of the morning seem'd.
Her sisters in the garden walk'd,
    And would I come? Across the Hall
450 She took me; and we laugh'd and talk'd
    About the Flower-show and the Ball.
The sweet hour lapsed, and left my breast
    A load of joy and tender care;
And this delight, which life oppress'd,
455   To fix'd aims grew, that ask'd for pray'r.

I went, and closed and lock'd the door,
    And cast myself down on my bed,
    And there, with many a blissful tear,
I vow'd to love and pray'd to wed
460   The maiden who grown so dear;
Thank'd God who had set her in my path;

And promised, as I hoped to win,
I never would sully my faith
　　By the least selfishness or sin.

The Violets

PRELUDE

The Parallel

465　I know not how to her it seems,
　　Or how to a perfect judging eye,
But, as my loving thought esteems,
　　Man misdeserves his sweet ally.
Where she succeeds with cloudless brow,
470　　In common and in holy course,
He fails, in spite of prayer and vow
　　And agonies of faith and force;
Or, if his suit with Heaven prevails
　　To righteous life, his virtuous deeds
475　Lack beauty, virtue's badge; she fails
　　More graciously than he succeeds.
Her spirit, compact of gentleness,
　　If Heaven postpones or grants her prayer,
Conceives no pride in its success,
480　　And in its failure no despair.

Prospective Faith

They safely walk in darkest ways
　　Whose youth is lighted from above,
Where, through the senses' silvery haze,
　　Dawns the veil'd moon of nuptial love.
485　Who is the happy husband? He
　　Who, scanning his unwedded life,
Thanks Heaven, with a conscience free,
　　'Twas faithful to his future wife.

THE VIOLETS

I went not to the Dean's unbid,
490　　For I'd not have my mystery,

From her so delicately hid,
　　Discuss'd by gossips at their tea.
A long, long week, and not once there,
　　Had made my spirit sick and faint,
495　And lack-love, foul as love is fair,
　　Perverted all things to complaint.
How vain the world had grown to be!
　　How mean all people and their ways,
How ignorant their sympathy,
500　　And how impertinent their praise;
To my necessity how strange
　　The sunshine and the song of birds;
How dull the clouds' continual change,
　　How foolishly content the herds;
505　How unaccountable the law
　　Which bade me sit in blindness here,
While she, the sun by which I saw,
　　Shed splendour in an idle sphere!
And then I kiss'd her stolen glove,
510　　And sigh'd to reckon and define
The modes of martyrdom in love,
　　And how far each one might be mine.
Wretched were life, if the end were now!
　　But this gives tears to dry despair,
515　Faith shall be blest, we know not how,
　　And love fulfill'd, we know not where.

While thus I grieved, and kiss'd her glove,
　　My man brought in her note to say,
Papa had bid her send his love,
520　　And would I dine with them next day?
They had learn'd and practised Purcell's glee,[1]
　　To sing it by to-morrow night.
The Postscript was: Her sisters and she
　　Inclosed some violets, blue and white;
525　She and her sisters found them where
　　I wager'd once no violets grew;

---

[1] Henry Purcell (1659–95), English composer and organist at Westminster Abbey.

So they had won the gloves. And there
    The violets lay, two white, one blue.

The Dean

PRELUDE

Perfect Love rare

Most rare is still most noble found,
530   Most noble still most incomplete;
Sad law, which leaves King Love uncrown'd
    In this obscure, terrestrial seat!
With bale more sweet than others' bliss,
    And bliss more wise than others' bale,
535 The secrets of the world are his,
    And freedom without let or pale.

Love Justified

This little germ of nuptial love,
    Which springs so simply from the sod,
The root is, as my song shall prove,
540   Of all our love to man and God.

Love Serviceable

What measure Fate to him shall mete
    Is not the noble Lover's care;
He's heart-sick with a longing sweet
    To make her happy as she's fair.
545 And, holding life as so much pelf
    To buy her posies, learns this lore:
He does not rightly love himself
    Who does not love another more.

Love a Virtue

Strong passions mean weak will, and he
550   Who truly knows the strength and bliss
Which are in love, will own with me

No passion but a virtue 'tis.
Ice-cold strikes heaven's noble glow
    To spirits whose vital heat is hell;
555 And to corrupt hearts even so
    The songs I sing, the tale I tell.
These cannot see the robes of white
    In which I sing of love. Alack,
But darkness shows in heavenly light,
560   Though whiteness, in the dark, is black!

THE DEAN

The Ladies rose. I held the door,
    And sigh'd, as her departing grace
Assured me that she alway wore
    A heart as happy as her face;

565 Towards my mark the Dean's talk set:
    He praised my "Notes on Abury,"
Read when the Association met
    At Sarum; he was glad to see
I had not stopp'd, as some men had,
570   At Wrangler[1] and Prize Poet; last,
He hoped the business was not bad
    I came about: then the wine pass'd.

A full glass prefaced my reply:
    I loved his daughter, Honor; he knew
575 My estate and prospects; might I try
    To win her? To mine eyes tears flew.
He thought 'twas that. I might. He gave
    His true consent, if I could get
Her love. A dear, good Girl! she'd have
580   Only three thousand pounds as yet;
More bye and bye. Yes, his good will
    Should go with me; he would not stir;
He and my father in old time still
    Wish'd I should one day marry her;

---

[1] at Cambridge University, a student who has achieved the highest standing in the mathematical tripos (a series of examinations).

585 That, though his blessing and his prayer
    Had help'd, should help, my suit, yet he
Left all to me, his passive share
    Consent and opportunity.
My chance, he hoped, was good: I'd won
590   Some name already; friends and place
Appear'd within my reach, but none
    Her mind and manners would not grace.

Ætna and the Moon[1]

PRELUDE

The Prodigal

To heroism and holiness
    How hard it is for man to soar
595 But how much harder to be less
    Than what his mistress loves him for!
There is no man so full of pride,
    And none so intimate with shame,
And none to manhood so denied,
600   As not to mend if women blame.
He does with ease what do he must,
    Or merit this, and nought's debarr'd
From man, when woman shall be just
    In yielding her desired regard.
605 Ah wasteful woman, she who may
    On her sweet self set her own price,
Knowing he cannot choose but pay,
    How has she cheapen'd paradise;
How given for nought her priceless gift,
610   How spoil'd the bread and spill'd the wine,
Which, spent with due, respective thrift,
    Had made brutes men, and men divine.

The Metamorphosis

Maid, choosing man, remember this:
    You take his nature with his name.

---

[1] Aetna, or Etna, in Sicily, is the highest active volcano in Europe.

615 Ask, too, what his religion is,
    For you will soon be of the same.

ÆTNA AND THE MOON

To ease my heart, I feigning, seized
    A pen, and, showering tears, declared
My unfeign'd passion; sadly pleased
620   Only to dream that so I dared.
Thus was the fervid truth confess'd,
    But wild with paradox ran the plea,
As wilfully in hope depress'd,
    Yet bold beyond hope's warranty:

625 "O, more than dear, be more than just,
    And do not deafly shut the door!
I claim no right to speak; I trust
    Mercy, not right; yet who has more?
Your name pronounced brings to my heart
630   A feeling like the violet's breath,
Which does so much of heaven impart
    It makes me yearn with tears for death;
The winds that in the garden toss
    The Guelder-roses give me pain,
635 Alarm me with the dread of loss,
    Exhaust me with the dream of gain;
I'm troubled by the clouds that move;
    Thrill'd by the breath which I respire;
And ever, like a torch, my love,
640   Thus agitated, flames the higher;
All's hard that has not you for goal;
    I scarce can move my hand to write,
For love engages all my soul,
    And leaves the body void of might;
645 The wings of will spread idly as do
    The bird's that in a vacuum lies;
My breast, asleep with dreams of you,
    Forgets to breathe, and bursts in sighs;
I see no rest this side the grave,
650   No rest or hope from you apart;
Your life is in the rose you gave,

Its perfume suffocates my heart;
There's no refreshment in the breeze;
    The heaven o'erwhelms me with its blue;
655 I faint beside the dancing seas;
    Winds, skies, and waves are only you;
The thought or act which not intends
    You service, seems a sin and shame;
In that one only object ends
660   Conscience, religion, honour, fame.
Yet think not, Dear, that, thus engaged,
    These drop their heavenly function; no,
They simply bow where Heaven's presaged
    In semblance of the liveliest show.
665 Ah, could I put off love! Could we
    Never have met! What calm, what ease
Nay, but, alas, this remedy
    Were ten times worse than the disease;
For when, indifferent, I pursue
670   The world's best pleasures for relief,
My heart, still sickening back to you,
    Finds none like memory of its grief;
And, though 'twere very hell to hear
    You felt such misery as I,
675 All good, save you, were far less dear
    Than is that ill with which I die!
Where'er I go, wandering forlorn,
    You are the world's love, life and glee:
O, wretchedness not to be borne
680   If she that's Love should not love me!"

I could not write another word,
    Through pity for my own distress;
And forth I went, untimely stirr'd
    To make my misery more or less.
685 I went, beneath the heated noon,
    To where, in her simplicity,
She sat at work; and, as the Moon
    On Ætna smiles, she smiled on me;
But, now and then, in cheek and eyes,
690   I saw, or fancied, such a glow

As when, in summer-evening skies,
Some say "It lightens," some say "No."

Sarum Plain[1]

PRELUDE

The Revelation

An idle poet, here and there,
    Looks round him, but, for all the rest,
695 The world, unfathomably fair,
    Is duller than a witling's jest.
Love wakes men, once a life-time each;
    They life their heavy lids, and look;
And, lo, what one sweet page can teach
700   They read with joy, then shut the book.
And some give thanks, and some blaspheme,
    And most forget; but, either way,
That and the Child's unheeded dream
    Is all the light of all their day.

The Spirit's Epochs

705 Not in the crises of events,
    Of compass'd hopes, or fears fulfill'd,
Or acts of gravest consequence,
    Are life's delight and depth reveal'd.
I drew my bride, beneath the moon,
710   Across my threshold; happy hour!
But, ah, the walk that afternoon
    We saw the water-flags in flower!

The Prototype

Lo, there, whence love, life, light are pour'd,
    Veil'd with impenetrable rays,
715 Amidst the presence of the Lord

---

[1] Salisbury Plain; the location of Stonehenge, a prehistoric circle of massive stones at one time thought to have been built by the Druids.

749

Co-equal Wisdom laughs and plays.
Female and male God made the man;
His image is the whole, not half;
And in our love we dimly scan
720   The love which is between Himself.

SARUM PLAIN

Brief worship done, which still endows
    The day with beauty not its own;
Breakfast enjoy'd, 'mid hush of boughs
    And perfumes thro' the windows blown;
725 With intervening pause, that paints
    Each act with honour, life with calm,
(As old processions of the Saints
    At every step have wands of palm),
We rose; the ladies went to dress,
730   And soon return'd with smiles; and then,
Plans fix'd, to which the Dean said Yes,
    Once more we drove to Salisbury Plain.
We past my house, (observed with praise
    By Mildred, Mary acquiesced),
735 And left the old and lazy greys
    Below the hill, and walk'd the rest.
The moods of love are like the wind,
    And none knows whence or why they rise,
I ne'er before felt heart and mind
740   So much affected through mine eyes.
How cognate with the flatter'd air,
    How form'd for earth's familiar zone,
She moved; how feeling and how fair
    For others' pleasure and her own;
745 And, ah, the heaven of her face!
    How, when she laugh'd, I seem'd to see
The gladness of the primal grace,
    And how, when grave, its dignity!
Of all she was, the least not less
750   Delighted the devoted eye;
No fold or fashion of her dress
    Her fairness did not sanctify;
Better it seem'd as now to walk,

And humbly by her gentle side
755 Observe her smile and hear her talk,
    Then call the world's next best my bride.

By the great stones we chose our ground
    For shade; and there, in converse sweet,
Took luncheon. On a little mound
760   Sat the three ladies; at their feet,
I sat; and smelt the heathy smell,
    Pluck'd hare-bells, turn'd the telescope
To the country round. My life went well,
    For once, without the wheels of hope;
765 And I despised the Druid rocks
    That scowled their chill gloom from above,
Like churls whose stolid wisdom mocks
    The lightness of immortal love.
And, as we talk'd, my spirit quaff'd
770   The sparkling winds; the candid skies
At our untruthful strangeness laugh'd;
    I kill'd with mine her smiling eyes;
And sweet familiarness and awe
    Prevail'd that hour on either part.

Sahara

PRELUDE

The Wife's Tragedy

775 Man must be pleased; but him to please
    Is woman's pleasure; down the gulf
Of his condoled necessities
    She casts her best, she flings herself.
How often flings for nought! and yokes
780   Her heart to an icicle or whim,
Whose each impatient word provokes
    Another, not from her, but him;
While she, too gentle even to force
    His penitence by kind replies,
785 Waits by, expecting his remorse,

With pardon in her pitying eyes;
And if he once, by shame oppress'd,
    A comfortable word confers,
She leans and weeps against his breast,
790   And seems to think the sin was hers;
And whilst his love has any life,
    Or any eye to see her charms,
At any time, she's still his wife,
    Dearly devoted to his arms;
795 She loves with love that cannot tire;
    And when, ah woe, she loves alone,
Through passionate duty love flames higher,
    As grass grows taller round a stone.

Common Graces

O man, (and Legion is thy name,)
800   Who hadst for dowry with thy wife
A conduct void of outward blame,
    The beauty of a loyal life,
Is nature in thee too spiritless,
    Ignoble, impotent, and dead,
805 To prize her love and loveliness
    The more for being thy daily bread?
And art thou one of that vile crew
    Which see no splendour in the sun,
Praising alone the good that's new,
810   Or over, or not yet begun?
And has it dawn'd on thy dull wits
    That love warms many as soft a nest,
That, though swathed round with benefits,
    Thou art not singularly blest?
815 And fail thy thanks for gifts divine,
    The common food of many a heart,
Because they are not only thine?
    Beware lest in the end thou art
Cast as a goat forth from the fold,
820   Too proud to feel the common grace
Of blissful myriads who behold
    For evermore the Father's face.

SAHARA

I stood by Honor and the Dean,
    They seated in the London train.
825 A month from her! yet this had been,
    Ere now, without such bitter pain.
But neighbourhood makes parting light,
    And distance remedy has none;
Alone, she near, I felt as might
830   A blind man sitting in the sun;
She near, all for the time was well;
    Hope's self, when we were far apart,
With lonely feeling, like the smell
    Of heath on mountains, fill'd my heart.

835 The bell rang, and, with shrieks like death,
    Link catching link, the long array,
With ponderous pulse and fiery breath,
    Proud of its burthen, swept away;
And through the lingering crowd I broke,
840   Sought the hill-side, and thence, heart-sick,
Beheld, far off, the little smoke
    Along the landscape kindling quick.
Life without her was vain and gross,
    The glory from the world was gone,
845 And on the gardens of the Close
    As on Sahara shone the sun.

Going to Church

I woke at three; for I was bid
    To breakfast with the Dean at nine,
And thence to Church. My curtain slid,
850   I found the dawning Sunday fine.

My prayers for her being done, I took
    Occasion by the quiet hour
To find and know, by Rule and Book,
    The rights of love's beloved power.

855 My giddiest hope allow'd
No selfish thought, or earthly smirch;
And forth I went, in peace, and proud
    To take my passion into Church.
I found them, with exactest grace
860   And fresh as Spring, for Spring attired;
And by the radiance in her face
    I saw she felt she was admired;
And, through the common luck of love,
    A moment's fortunate delay,
865 To fit the little lilac glove,
    Gave me her arm; and I and they,
(They true to this and every hour,
    As if attended on by Time),
Went into Church while yet the tower
870   Was noisy with the finish'd chime.

Her soft voice, singularly heard
    Beside me, in the Psalms, withstood
The roar of voices, like a bird
    Sole warbling in a windy wood;
875 And, when we knelt, she seem'd to be
    An angel teaching me to pray;
And all through the high Liturgy
    My spirit rejoiced without allay.

The Dance

PRELUDE

The Daughter of Eve

The woman's gentle mood o'er-stept
880   Withers my love, that lightly scans
The rest, and does in her accept
    All her own faults, but none of man's.

As man I cannot judge her ill,
    Or honour her fair station less,
885 Who with a woman's errors, still
    Preserves a woman's gentleness.

Aurea Dicta

Child, would you shun the vulgar doom,.
    In love disgust, in death despair?
Know, death must come and love must come,
890   And so for each your soul prepare.

Lest sacred love your soul ensnare,
    With pious fancy still infer
"How loving and how lovely fair
    Must he be who has fashioned her!"

895 Love's perfect blossom only blows
    Where noble manners veil defect.
Angels may be familiar; those
    Who err each other must respect.

Love blabb'd of is a great decline;
900   A careless word unsanctions sense;
But he who casts Heaven's truth to swine
    Consummates all incontinence.

THE DANCE

"My memory of heaven awakes!
    She's not of the earth, although her light,
905 As lantern'd by her body, makes
    A piece of it past bearing bright.
So innocently proud and fair
    She is, that Wisdom sings for glee
And Folly dies, breathing one air
910   With such a bright-cheek'd chastity;
And though her charms are a strong law
    Compelling all men to admire,
They go so clad with lovely awe
    None but the noble dares desire."

915 This learn'd I, watching where she danced,
    Native to melody and light,
And now and then toward me glanced,
    Pleased, as I hoped, to please my sight.

Ah, love to speak was impotent,
    920   Till music did a tongue confer,
And I ne'er knew what music meant,
    Until I danced to it with her.
I press'd her hand, by will or chance
    I know not, but I saw the rays
925 Withdrawn, which did till then enhance
    Her fairness with its thanks for praise.
I knew my spirit's vague offence
    Was patent to the dreaming eye
And heavenly tact of innocence,
930   And did for fear my fear defy,
And ask'd her for the next dance.
    "Yes."

I saw she saw; and, O sweet Heaven,
    Could my glad mind have credited
935 That influence had to me been given
    To affect her so, I should have said
That, though she from herself conceal'd
    Love's felt delight and fancied harm,
They made her face the jousting field
940   Of joy and beautiful alarm.

The Abdication

From little signs, like little stars,
    Whose faint impression on the sense
The very looking straight at mars,
    Or only seen by confluence;
945 From instinct of a mutual thought,
    Whence sanctity of manners flow'd;
From chance unconscious, and from what
    Concealment, overconscious, show'd;
Her hand's less weight upon my arm,
950   Her lowlier mien; that match'd with this;
I found, and felt with strange alarm,
    I stood committed to my bliss.

I grew assur'd, before I ask'd,
    That she'd be mine without reserve,

955 And in her unclaim'd graces bask'd,
    At leisure, till the time should serve,
With just enough of dread to thrill
    The hope, and make it trebly dear;
Thus loth to speak the word to kill
960   Either the hope or happy fear.
Till once, through lanes returning late,
    Her laughing sisters lagg'd behind;
And, ere we reach'd her father's gate,
    We paused with one presentient mind;
965 And, in the dim and perfumed mist,
    Their coming stay'd, who, friends to me,
And very women, loved to assist
    Love's timid opportunity.

Twice rose, twice died my trembling word;
970   The faint and frail Cathedral chimes
Spake time in music, and we heard
    The chafers rustling in the limes.
Her dress, that touch'd me where I stood,
    The warmth of her confided arm,
975 Her bosom's gentle neighbourhood,
    Her pleasure in her power to charm;
Her look, her love, her form, her touch,
    The least seem'd most by blissful turn,
Blissful but that it pleased too much,
980   And taught the wayward soul to yearn.
It was as if a harp with wires
    Was traversed by the breath I drew;
And, oh, sweet meeting of desires,
    She, answering, own'd that she loved too.

985 Honoria was to be my bride!
    The hopeless heights of hope were scaled;
The summit won, I paused and sigh'd,
    As if success itself had fail'd.
It seem'd as if my lips approach'd
990   To touch at Tantalus'[1] reward,

---

[1] the son of Zeus and a nymph. As punishment for divulging the secrets of the gods, he was submerged up to the chin in a river; water and fruit moved away from him whenever he attempted to eat or drink.

And rashly on Eden life encroach'd,
    Half-blinded by the flaming sword.
The whole world's wealthiest and its best,
    So fiercely sought, appear'd, when found,
995 Poor in its need to be possess'd,
    Poor from its very want of bound.
By that consenting scared and shock'd,
    Such change came o'er her mien and mood
That I felt startled and half-mock'd,
1000   As winning what I had not woo'd.

My queen was crouching at my side,
    By love unscepter'd and brought low,
Her awful garb of maiden pride
    All melted into tears like snow;
1005 The mistress of my reverent thought,
    Whose praise was all I ask'd of fame,
In my close-watch'd approval sought
    Protection as from danger and blame;
Her soul, which late I loved to invest
1010   With pity for my poor desert,
Buried its face within my breast,
    Like a pet fawn by hunters hurt.

BOOK II

Accepted

What fortune did my heart foretell?
    What shook my spirit, as I woke,
Like the vibration of a bell
    Of which I had not heard the stroke?
5 Was it some happy vision shut
    From memory by the sun's fresh ray?
Was it that linnet's song; or but
    A natural gratitude for day?
Or the mere joy the senses weave,
10   A wayward ecstasy of life?

Then I remember'd, yester-eve
    I won Honoria for my wife.

The Course of True Love

PRELUDE

The Changed Allegiance

Watch how a bird, that captived sings,
    The cage set open, first looks out,
15 Yet fears the freedom of his wings,
    And now withdraws, and flits about,
The maiden so, from love's free sky
    In chaste and prudent counsels caged,
But longing to be loosen'd by
20   Her suitor's faith declared and gaged,
When blest with that release desired,
    First doubts if truly she is free,
Then pauses, restlessly retired,
    Alarm'd at too much liberty;
25 But after that, habitual faith,
    Divorced from self, where late 'twas due,
Walks nobly in its novel path,
    And she's to changed allegiance true;
And, prizing what she can't prevent,
30   (Right wisdom, often misdeem'd whim,)
Her will's indomitably bent
    On mere submissiveness to him;
To him she'll cleave, for him forsake
    Father's and mother's fond command!
35 He is her lord, for he can take
    Hold of her faint heart with his hand.

THE COURSE OF TRUE LOVE

Oh, beating heart of sweet alarm,
    Which stays the lover's step when near
His mistress and her awful charm
40   Of grace and innocence sincere!

I held the half-shut door and heard
    The voice of my betrothed wife,
Who sang my verses, every word
    By music taught its latent life.

      .   .   .   .

45   "Go, Child, and see him out yourself,"
    The Dean said, after tea, "and shew
The place, upon that upper shelf,
    Where Tasso[1] stands, lent long ago."

A rose in ruin, from her breast,
50   Fell, as I took a fond adieu,
"Those rose-leaves to my heart be press'd,
    Honoria, while it aches for you!"
"You must go now, Love!" "See, the air
    Is thick with starlight!" "Let me tie
55 This scarf on. Oh, your Tasso! There!
    I'm coming, Aunt!" "Sweet, Sweet!" "Good-bye!"
With love's bright arrows from her eyes,
    And balm on her permissive lips,
She pass'd, and night was a surprise,
60   As when the sun at Quito[2] dips.

The County Ball

PRELUDE

Love Ceremonious

Keep your undrest, familiar style
    For strangers, but respect your friend,
Her most, whose matrimonial smile
    Is and asks honour without end.
65 'Tis found, and needs it must so be,
    That life from love's allegiance flags,
When love forgets his majesty

---

[1] Torquato Tasso (1544–95), Italian poet.

[2] a city in north central Ecuador, high in the Andes mountains; a noted
Roman Catholic centre.

In sloth's unceremonious rags.
Let love make home a gracious Court;
70   There let the world's rude, hasty ways
Be fashion'd to a loftier port,
    And learn to bow and stand at gaze;
And let the sweet, respective sphere
    Of personal worship there obtain
75 Circumference for moving clear,
    None treading on another's train.
This makes that pleasures do not cloy,
    And dignifies our mortal strife
With calmness and considerate joy,
80   Befitting our immortal life.

The County Ball

Well, Heaven be thank'd my first-love fail'd,
    And, Heaven be thank'd, our first-loves do!
Thought I, when Fanny past me sail'd,
    Loved once, for what I never knew.

85 But there danced she, who from the leaven
    Of ill preserved my heart and wit
All unawares, for she was heaven,
    Others at best but fit for it.
One of those lovely things she was
90   In whose least action there can be
Nothing so transient but it has
    An air of immortality.
Her motion, feeling 'twas beloved,
    The pensive soul of tune express'd,
95 And, oh, what perfume, as she moved,
    Came from the flowers in her breast!
Ah, none but I discern'd her looks,
    When in the throng she pass'd me by,
For love is like a ghost, and brooks
100   Only the chosen seer's eye.
Whilst so her beauty fed my sight,
    And whilst I lived in what she said,

Accordant airs, like all delight
    Most sweet when noted least, were play'd;
105 I held my breath, and thought "how bright!"
    That guileless beauty in its noon,
Compelling tribute of desires
    Ardent as day when Sirius[1] reigns,
Pure as the permeating fires
110   That smoulder in the opal's veins.

The Koh-i-Noor [2]

PRELUDE

Love Thinking

What lifts her in my thoughts so far
    Beyond all else? Let Love not err!
'Tis that which all right women are,
    But which I'll know in none but her.
115 She is to me the only Ark[3]
    Of that high mystery which locks
The lips of joy, or speaks in dark
    Enigmas and in paradox;
That potent charm, which none can fly,
120   Nor would, which makes me bond and free,
Nor can I tell it first 'twas I
    Chose it, or it elected me.

THE KOH-I-NOOR

"Be man's hard virtues highly wrought,
    But let my gentle Mistress be,
125 In every look, word, deed, and thought,
    Nothing but sweet and womanly!
Her virtues please my virtuous mood,
    But what at all times I admire

Is, not that she is wise or good,
130   But just the thing which I desire.
With versatility to bring
    Her mental tone to any strain,
If oft'nest she is anything,
    Be it thoughtless, talkative, and vain.
135 That seems in her supremest grace
    Which, virtue or not, apprises me
That my familiar thoughts embrace
    Unfathomable mystery."

I answer'd thus; for she desired
140   To know what mind I most approved
Partly to learn what she inquired,
    Partly to get the praise she loved.
I praised her, but no praise could fill
    The depths of her desire to please,
145 Though dull to others as a Will
    To them that have no legacies.
The more I praised the more she shone,
    Her eyes incredulously bright,
And all her happy beauty blown
150   Beneath the beams of my delight.
Sweet rivalry was thus begot;
    By turns, my speech, in passion's style,
With flatteries the truth o'ershot,
    And she surpass'd them with her smile.

155 "Dear Felix!" "Sweet, sweet Love!" But there
    Was Aunt Maude's noisy ring and knock!
"Stay, Felix; you have caught my hair.
    Stoop! Thank you!" "May I have that lock?"
"Not now. Good morning, Aunt!" "Why, Puss,
160   "You look magnificent to-day."
"Here's Felix, Aunt." "Fox and green goose!
    Who handsome gets should handsome pay."
"Aunt, you are friends!" "Ah, to be sure!
    Good morning! Go on flattering, Sir;
165 A woman's like the Koh-i-noor,
    Worth just the price that's put on her."

---

[1] the Dog-Star, thought to be scorchingly hot.

[2] a famous diamond presented to Queen Victoria in 1849; reputed to bring bad luck to its possessor.

[3] the Ark of the Covenant.

The Epitaph

The Last Night at Home

Oh, Muse, who dost to me reveal
  The mystery of the woman's life,
Relate how 'tis a maid might feel,
170   The night before she's crown'd a wife!
Lo, sleepless in her little bed,
  She lies and counts the hours till noon.
Ere this, to-morrow, she'll be wed
  Ere this? Alas, how strangely soon!
175 A fearful blank of ignorance
  Lies manifest across her way,
And shadows, cast from unknown chance,
  Make sad and dim the coming day.
Her faithless dread she now discards,
180 And now remorseful memory flings
Its glory round the last regards
  Of home and all accustom'd things.
Her father's voice, her mother's eyes
  Accuse her treason; 'tis in vain
185 She thinks herself a wife, and tries
  To comprehend the greater gain;
Her unknown fortune nothing cheers
  Her loving heart's familiar loss,
And torrents of repentant tears
190 Their hot and smarting threshold cross.
When first within her bosom Love
  Took birth, and beat his blissful wings,
It seem'd to lift her mind above
  All care for other earthly things;
195 But, oh, too lightly did she vow
  To leave for aye her happy nest;
And dreadful is the thought that now
  Assaults her weak and shaken breast:
Ah, should her lover's love abate;
200 Ah, should she, miserable, lose
All dear regards of maiden state,

Dissolved by time and marriage dues!
And so her fears increase, till fear
  O'erfilms her apprehensive eye
205 That she may swoon, with no one near,
  And haply so, unmarried, die.
With instinct of her ignorance,
  (The virgin's strength and veiled guide,)
She prays, and casts the reins of chance
210 To Love, nor recks what shall betide.

    .   .   .   .

The gentle wife, who decks his board
  And makes his day to have no night,
Whose wishes wait upon her lord,
  Who finds her own in his delight,
215 Is she another now than she
  Who, mistress of her maiden charms,
At his wild prayer, incredibly
  Committed them to his proud arms?
Unless her choice of him's a slur
220 Which makes her proper credit dim,
He never enough can honour her
  Who past all speech has honour'd him.

The Foreign Land

A woman is a foreign land,
  Of which, though there he settle young
225 A man will ne'er quite understand
  The customs, politics, and tongue.
The foolish hie them post-haste through,
  See fashions odd, and prospects fair,
Learn of the language, "How-d'ye do,"
230 And go and brag that they've been there.
The most for leave to trade apply,
  For once, at Empire's seat her heart,
Then get what knowledge ear and eye
  Glean chancewise in the life-long mart.
235 And certain others few and fit,
  Attach them to the Court, and see
The Country's best, its accent hit,
  And partly sound its polity.

The Epitaph

"At Church in twelve hours more, we meet!
240   This Dearest, is our last farewell."
"Oh, Felix, do you love me?" "Sweet,
    Why do you ask?" "I cannot tell."

And was it no vain fantasy
    That raised me from the earth with pride?
245 Should I to-morrow verily
    Be Bridegroom, and Honoria Bride?
Should I, in simple fact, henceforth
    Live unconditionally lord
Of her whose smile for brightest worth
250   Seem'd all too bountiful reward?
If now to part with her could make
    Her pleasure greater, sorrow less,
I for my epitaph would take
    "To serve seem'd more than to possess."
255 And I perceived, (the vision sweet
    Dimming with happy dew mine eyes,)
That love and joy are torches lit
    From altar-fires of sacrifice.

Across the sky the daylight crept,
260   And birds grew garrulous in the grove,
And on my marriage-morn I slept
    A soft sleep, undisturb'd by love.

The Wedding

PRELUDE

Constancy rewarded

I vow'd unvarying faith, and she,
    To whom in full I pay that vow,
265 Rewards me with variety
    Which men who change can never know.

THE WEDDING

Life smitten with a feverish chill,
    The brain too tired to understand,
In apathy of heart and will,
270   I took the woman from the hand
Of him who stood for God, and heard
    Of Christ, and of the Church his Bride;
The Feast, by presence of the Lord
    And his first Wonder, beautified;
275 The mystic sense to Christian men;
    The bonds in innocency made,
And gravely to be enter'd then
    For children, godliness, and aid,
And honour'd, and kept free from smirch;
280   And how a man must love his wife
No less than Christ did love his Church,
    If need be, giving her his life;
And, vowing then the mutual vow,
    The tongue spake, but intention slept.
285 'Tis well for us Heaven asks not how
    This oath is sworn, but how 'tis kept.

O, bold seal of a bashful bond,
    Which makes the marriage-day to be,
To those before it and beyond,
290   An ice-berg in an Indian sea!

"Now, while she's changing," said the Dean,
    "Her bridal for her travelling dress,
I'll preach allegiance to your queen!
    Preaching's the trade which I profess;
295 And one more minute's mine! You know
    I've paid my girl a father's debt,
And this last charge is all I owe.
    She's yours; but I love more than yet
You can; such fondness only wakes
300   When time has raised the heart above
The prejudice of youth, which makes
    Beauty conditional to love.
Prepare to meet the weak alarms

Of novel nearness; recollect
305 The eye which magnifies her charms
     Is microscopic for defect.
Fear comes at first; but soon, rejoiced,
     You'll find your strong and tender loves
Like holy rocks by Druids poised,
310   The least force shakes, but none removes.
Although you smile, there's much to mend!
     Yet never girl, I think, had less.
Her worst point is, she's apt to spend
     Too much on alms-deeds and on dress.
315 Her strength is your esteem; beware
     Of finding fault; her will's unnerv'd
By blame; from you 'twould be despair;
     But praise that is not quite deserv'd
Will all her noble nature move
320   To make your utmost wishes true.
Yet think, while mending thus your Love,
     Of matching her ideal too!
The death of nuptial joy is sloth:
     To keep you mistress in your wife,
325 Keep to the very height your oath,
     And honour her with arduous life.
Lastly, no personal reverence doff.
     Life's all externals unto those
Who pluck the blushing petals off,
330   To find the secret of the rose.—
How long she's staying! Green's Hotel
     I'm sure you'll like. The charge is fair,
The wines good. I remember well
     I stopp'd once, with her mother, there.
335 A tender conscience of her vow
     That mother had! She is so like her!"
But Mrs Fife, much flurried, now
     Whisper'd, "Miss Honor's ready, Sir."

Husband and Wife

PRELUDE

The Married Lover

Why, having won her, do I woo?
340   Because her spirit's vestal grace
Provokes me always to pursue,
     But, spirit-like, eludes embrace;
Because her womanhood is such
     That, as on court-days subjects kiss
345 The Queen's hand, yet so near a touch
     Affirms no mean familiarness,
Because although in act and word
     As lowly as a wife can be,
Her manners, when they call me Lord,
350   Remind me 'tis by courtesy;
Because, though free of the outer court
     I am, this Temple keeps its shrine
Sacred to Heaven; because, in short,
     She's not and never shall be mine.

HUSBAND AND WIFE

355 As souls, ambitious, but low-born,
     If raised past hope by luck or wit,
All pride of place will proudly scorn,
     And live as they'd been used to it,
So we two wore our strange estate;
360   Familiar, unaffected, free,
We talk'd, until the dusk grew late,
     Of this and that; but, after tea,
As doubtful if a lot so sweet
     As ours was ours in very sooth,
365 Like children, to promote conceit,
     We feign'd that it was not the truth;
And she assumed the maiden coy,
     And I adored remorseless charms,
And then we clapp'd our hands for joy
370   And ran into each other's arms.

The Epilogue

"Ah, dearest wife, a fresh-lit fire
    Sends forth to heaven great shows of fume,
And watchers, far away, admire;
    But when the flames their power assume,
375 The more they burn the less they show,
    The clouds no longer smirch the sky,
And then the flames intensest glow
    When far-off watchers think they die.
The fumes of early love my verse
380   Has figured—" "You must paint the flame!"
"'Twould merit the Promethean curse![1]
    But now, Sweet, for your praise and blame."
"You speak too boldly; veils are due
    To women's feelings," "Fear not this!
385 Women will vow I say not true,
    And men believe the lips they kiss."
"I did not call you 'Dear' or 'Love,'
    I think, till after Frank was born."
"That fault I cannot well remove;
390   The rhymes"—but Frank now blew his horn,
And Walter bark'd on hands and knees,
    At Baby in the mignonette,
And all made, full-cry, for the trees
    Where Felix and his wife were set.
395 Again disturb'd, (crickets have cares!)
    True to their annual use they rose,
To offer thanks at Evening Prayers
    In three times sacred Sarum Close.
—COMPLETELY PUB. 1905

---

[1] Prometheus stole fire from the gods to give to man; as a punishment
he was chained to a rock, where an eagle gnawed at his liver each day
until he was finally released by Hercules.

William Allingham

1824 – 1889

William Allingham was an Anglo-Irish poet who published a dozen volumes of verse between 1850 and 1887. Allingham worked in Northern Ireland, but visited London almost every year and was acquainted with Leigh Hunt, Thomas Carlyle, the Pre-Raphaelite group, and Coventry Patmore. In the early 1850s he met Alfred Tennyson, with whom he formed a lifelong friendship. His *Diary* (1907) is an important record of that friendship and of his innumerable conversations with and about Tennyson.

∽∾∽

The Fairies

Up the airy mountain,
   Down the rushy glen,
We daren't go a-hunting
   For fear of little men;
5 Wee folk, good folk,
   Trooping all together;
Green jacket, red cap,
   And white owl's feather!

Down along the rocky shore
10 Some make their home,
They live on crispy pancakes
   Of yellow tide-foam;
Some in the reeds
   Of the black mountain lake,
15 With frogs for their watch-dogs,
   All night awake.

High on the hill-top
   The old King sits;
He is now so old and gray
20 He's nigh lost his wits.
With a bridge of white mist
   Columbkill he crosses,
On his stately journeys
   From Slieveleague to Rosses;
25 Or going up with music
   On cold starry nights,

To sup with the Queen
   Of the gay Northern Lights.

They stole little Bridget
30 For seven years long;
When she came down again
   Her friends were all gone.
They took her lightly back,
   Between the night and morrow,
35 They thought that she was fast asleep,
   But she was dead with sorrow.
They have kept her ever since
   Deep within the lake,
On a bed of flag-leaves,
40 Watching till she wake.

By the craggy hill-side,
   Through the mosses bare,
They have planted thorn-trees
   For pleasure here and there.
45 Is any man so daring
   As dig them up in spite,
He shall find their sharpest thorns
   In his bed at night.

Up the airy mountain,
50 Down the rushy glen,
We daren't go a-hunting
   For fear of little men;
Wee folk, good folk,

Trooping all together;
55 Green jacket, red cap,
And white owl's feather!
—1850

"Four Ducks on a Pond"

Four ducks on a pond,
A grass-bank beyond,
A blue sky of spring,
White clouds on the wing;
5 What a little thing
To remember for years—
To remember with tears!
—1882

Writing

A man who keeps a diary, pays
Due toll to many tedious days;
But life becomes eventful—then
His busy hand forgets the pen.
5 Most books, indeed, are records less
Of fulness than of emptiness.
—1884

Express
(From Liverpool, Southwards)

We move in elephantine row,
The faces of our friends retire,
The roof withdraws, and curtsying flow
The message-bearing lines of wire;
5 With doubling, redoubling beat,
Smoother we run and more fleet.

By flow'r-knots, shrubs, and slopes of grass,
Cut walls of rock with ivy-stains,
Thro' winking arches swift we pass,
10 And flying, meet the flying trains,

Whirr—whirr—gone!
And still we hurry on;

By orchards, kine[1] in pleasant leas,
A hamlet-lane,[2] a spire, a pond,
15 Long hedgerows, counter-changing trees,
With blue and steady hills beyond;
(House, platform, post,
Flash—and are lost!)

Smooth-edged canals, and mills on brooks;
20 Old farmsteads, busier than they seem,
Rose-crusted or of graver looks,
Rich with old tile and motley beam;
Clay-cutting, slope, and ridge,
The hollow rumbling bridge.

25 Gray vapour-surges, whirl'd in the wind
Of roaring tunnels, dark and long,
Then sky and landscape unconfined,
Then streets again where workers throng
Come—go. The whistle shrill
30 Controls us to its will.

Broad vents, and chimneys tall as masts,
With heavy flags of streaming smoke;
Brick mazes, fiery furnace-blasts,
Walls, waggons, gritty heaps of coke;
35 Through these our ponderous rank
Glides in with hiss and clank.

So have we sped our wondrous course
Amid a peaceful busy land,
Subdued by long and painful force
40 Of planning head and plodding hand.
How much by labour can
The feeble race of man!
—1889

---

[1] cattle.

[2] A hamlet is a small village.

Sydney Dobell
1824 – 1874

Sydney Dobell [with Alexander Smith (1830–1867)] was a so-called "Spasmodic" poet. He wrote *The Roman* (1850), *Balder* (1854), *England in a Time of War* (1856), and other poems. His style is over-excited, often to the point of incoherence. The work of Dobell and Smith was satirized in W.E. Aytoun's parody, *Firmilian: a Spasmodic Tragedy* (1854).

෴

The Botanist's Vision

The sun that in Breadalbane's[1] lake doth fall
  Was melting to the sea down golden Tay,[2]
When a cry came along the peopled way,
"Sebastopol[3] is ours!" From that wild call
5 I turned, and leaning on a time-worn wall
Quaint with the touch of many an ancient day,
The mappèd mould and mildewed marquetry
Knew with my focussed soul; which bent down all
Its sense, power, passion, to the sole regard
10 Of each green minim, as it were but born
To that one use. I strode home stern and hard;
In my hot hands I laid my throbbing head,
And all the living world and all the dead
Began a march which did not end at morn.
—1856

To the Authoress of "Aurora Leigh"[4]

Were Shakspeare born a twin, his lunar twin
  (Not of the golden but the silver bow)
Should be like thee: so, with such eyes and brow,
Sweeten his looks, so, with her dear sex in
5 His voice, (a king's words writ out by the queen)

Unman his bearded English, and, with flow
Of breastfull robes about her female snow,
Present the lordly brother. Oh Last-of-kin
There be ambitious Women here on earth
10 Who will not thank thee to have sung so well!
Apollo[5] and Diana[6] are one birth,
Pollux[7] and Helen[8] break a single shell.
Who now may hope? While Adam was alone
Eve was to come. She came; God's work was done.
—1860

Perhaps

Ten heads and twenty hearts! so that this me,
  Having more room and verge, and striking less
The cage that galls us into consciousness,
Might drown the rings and ripples of to be
5 In the smooth deep of being: plenary
Round hours; great days, as if two days should press
Together, and their wine-press'd night accresce
The next night to so dead a parody
Of death as cures such living: of these ordain

---

[1] Breadalbane is a mountainous region of Perthshire, Scotland.

[2] the largest river in Scotland, mainly in Perthshire.

[3] port and naval base on the Black Sea in Russia. During the Crimean war, the city was finally seized and destroyed by British, French, and Turkish troops following an eleven-month siege (1854–55).

[4] Elizabeth Barrett Browning (1806–61).

[5] in Greek mythology, also called Helios, the sun-god and the god of music, poetry, archery, prophecy, and medicine. Represented as the perfection of youthful manhood, Apollo is the twin brother of Diana.

[6] also called Artemis; associated with the moon; the goddess of hunting and fertility.

[7] son of Jupiter (the Roman equivalent of Zeus) and Leda; the twin brother of Castor.

[8] sister of Castor and Pollux; the archetype of female beauty. While married to Menelaus, Helen eloped with Paris, bringing about the siege of Troy.

10 My years; of those large years grant me not seven,
Nor seventy, no, nor only seventy sevens!
And then, perhaps, I might stand well in even
This rain of things; down-rain, up-rain, side-rain;
This rain from Earth and Ocean, air and heaven,
15 And from the Heaven within the Heaven of Heavens.
—1875

Two Sonnets on the Death of Prince Albert [1]

I

In a great house by the wide Sea I sat,
And down slow fleets and waves that never cease
Looked back to the first keels of War and Peace;
I saw the Ark,[2] what time the shoreless flat
5 Began to rock to rising Ararat;[3]
Or Argo,[4] surging home, with templed Greece
To leeward, while, mast-high, the lurching fleece
Swung morn from deep to deep. Then in a plat
Of tamarisk a bird called me. When again
10 My soul looked forth I ponder'd not the main
Of waters but of time; and from our fast
Sure Now, with Pagan joy, beheld the pain

Of tossing heroes on the triremed Past
Obtest the festive Gods and silent stars in vain.

II

And as I mused on all we call our own,
And (in words their passionate hope had taught
Expressing this late world for which they fought
And prayed) said, lifting up my head to the sun,
5 "Ne quibus diis immortalibus,"[5]—one
Ran with fear's feet, and lo! a voice distraught
"The Prince" and "Dead." And at the sound methought
The bulwark of my great house thunder'd down.
And, for an instant,—as some spell were sapping
10 All place—the hilly billows and billowy hills
Heaved through my breast the lapping wave that kills
The heart; around me the floor rises and falls
And jabbling stones of the unsteady walls
Ebb and flow together, lapping, lapping.
—1875 (1861)

---

[1] Prince Albert (1819–61), titled Prince Consort, was the beloved and popular husband of Queen Victoria. Known as Albert the Good after Tennyson's "Dedication" to *Idylls of the King* (1891): "Beyond all titles, and a household name,/ Hereafter, thro' all times, Albert the Good."

[2] the vessel built, according to God's instructions, by Noah in order to save himself, his family, and representatives of all the animals from the flood: see Genesis 8:4.

[3] a mountainous district in Armenia, said to be the resting place for the Ark after the flood subsided: see Genesis 8:4.

[4] in Greek mythology, Jason's sailing ship, used on the voyage to seek the golden fleece. Its sailors were called the Argonauts. Phryxus, son of Athamus and Ino, had been ordered to be sacrificed because his mother believed him to be the cause of a famine. Phryxus escaped on the winged ram Chrysomallus, which had a golden fleece. After his escape the ram was sacrificed and the fleece given to King Aeëtes, who hung it on a sacred oak tree. Jason set out to recover it.

---

[5] probably a misquotation. The literal translation is "not to which immortal Gods."

George MacDonald
1824 – 1905

Scottish born, George MacDonald wrote poetry, fiction, children's stories, sermons, and literary criticism. He was an avid and wide-ranging reader, fluent in eight languages, and disparate in his use of sources.

∾∾

Professor Noctutus

Nobody knows the world but me.
The rest go to bed; I sit up and see.
I'm a better observer than any of you all,
For I never look out till the twilight fall,
5 And never then without the green glasses,
And that is how my wisdom passes.

I never think, for that is not fit:
I observe. I have seen the white moon sit
On her nest, the sea, like a fluffy owl,
10 Hatching the boats and the long-legged fowl!
When the oysters gape—you may make a note—
She drops a pearl into every throat.

I can see the wind: can you do that?
I see the dreams he has in his hat,
15 I see him shaking them out as he goes,
I see them rush in at man's snoring nose.
Ten thousand things you could not think,
I can write down plain with pen and ink!

You know that I know; therefore pull off your hat,
20 Whether round and tall, or square and flat:
You cannot do better than trust in me;
You may shut your eyes in fact—*I see!*
Lifelong I will lead you, and then, like the owl,
I will bury you nicely with my spade and showl.
—1871

No End of No-Story

There is a river
whose waters run asleep
run run ever
singing in the shallows
5 dumb in the hollows
sleeping so deep
and all the swallows
that dip their feathers
in the hollows
10 or in the shallows
are the merriest swallows
and the nests they make
with the clay they cake
with the water they shake
15 from their wings that rake
the water out of the shallows
or out of the hollows
will hold together
in any weather
20 and the swallows
are the merriest fellows
and have the merriest children
and are built very narrow
like the head of an arrow
25 to cut the air
and go just where
the nicest water is flowing
and the nicest dust is blowing
and each so narrow
30 like the head of an arrow
is a wonderful barrow

to carry the mud he makes
for his children's sakes
from the wet water flowing
35 and the dry dust blowing
to build his nest
for her he loves best
and the wind cakes it
the sun bakes it
40 into a nest
for the rest
of her he loves best
and all their merry children
each little fellow
45 with a beak as yellow
as the buttercups growing
beside the flowing
of the singing river
always and ever
50 growing and blowing
as fast as the sheep
awake or asleep
crop them and crop
and cannot stop
55 their yellowness blowing
nor yet the growing
of the obstinate daisies
the little white praises
they grow and they blow
60 they spread out their crown
and they praise the sun
and when he goes down
their praising is done
they fold up their crown
65 and sleep every one
till over the plain
he is shining amain
and they're at it again
praising and praising
70 such low songs raising
that no one can hear them
but the sun so near them

and the sheep that bite them
but do not fright them
75 are the quietest sheep
awake or asleep
with the merriest bleat
and the little lambs
are the merriest lambs
80 forgetting to eat
for the frolic in their feet
and the lambs and their dams
are the whitest sheep
with the woolliest wool
85 for the swallow to pull
when he makes his nest
for her he loves best
and they shine like snow
in the grasses that grow
90 by the singing river
that sings for ever
and the sheep and the lambs
are merry for ever
because the river
95 sings and they drink it
and the lambs and their dams
would any one think it
are bright and white
because of their diet
100 which gladdens them quiet
for what they bite
is buttercups yellow
and daisies white
and grass as green
105 as the river can make it
with wind as mellow
to kiss it and shake it
as never was known
but here in the hollows
110 beside the river
where all the swallows
are the merriest fellows
and the nests they make

with the clay they cake
115 in the sunshine bake
till they are like bone
and as dry in the wind
as a marble stone
dried in the wind
120 the sweetest wind
that blows by the river
flowing for ever
and who shall find
whence comes the wind
125 that blows on the hollows
and over the shallows
where dip the swallows
and comes and goes
and the sweet life blows
130 into the river
that sings as it flows
and the sweet life blows
into the sheep
awake or asleep
135 with the woolliest wool
and the trailingest tails
and never fails
gentle and cool
to wave the wool
140 and to toss the grass
as the lambs and the sheep
over it pass
and tug and bite
with their teeth so white
145 and then with the sweep
of their trailing tails
smooth it again
and it grows amain
and amain it grows
150 and the wind that blows
tosses the swallows
over the hollows
and over the shallows
and blows the sweet life

155 and the joy so rife
into the swallows
that skim the shallows
and have the yellowest children
and the wind that blows
160 is the life of the river
that flows for ever
and washes the grasses
still as it passes
and feeds the daisies
165 the little white praises
and buttercups sunny
with butter and honey
that whiten the sheep
awake or asleep
170 that nibble and bite
and grow whiter than white
and merry and quiet
on such good diet
watered by the river
175 and tossed for ever
by the wind that tosses
the wool and the grasses
and the swallow that crosses
with all the swallows
180 over the shallows
dipping their wings
to gather the water
and bake the cake
for the wind to make
185 as hard as a bone
and as dry as a stone
and who shall find
whence comes the wind
that blows from behind
190 and ripples the river
that flows for ever
and still as it passes
waves the grasses
and cools the daisies
195 the white sun-praises

that feed the sheep
awake or asleep
and give them their wool
for the swallows to pull
200 a little away
to mix with the clay
that cakes to a nest
for those they love best
and all the yellow children
205 soon to go trying

their wings at the flying
over the hollows
and over the shallows
with all the swallows
210 that do not know
whence the wind doth blow
that comes from behind
a blowing wind
—1893

Adelaide Anne Procter
1825 – 1864

Immensely popular during her career, Adelaide Anne Procter's poetry reflects the causes that she strived for in her lifetime—feminism, philanthropy, and religion. The daughter of a playwright and poet, Procter submitted her first poems to *Household Words* under a pseudonym at the age of twenty-eight, winning the support of Charles Dickens. Publishing under her own name, Procter continued to win praise with *Legends and Lyrics* (2 series, 1858 and 1861), the anthology *Victoria Regia* (1861), and *A Chaplet of Verses* (1862), selling more copies of her poems than any of her contemporaries except for Tennyson.

ↄ◦ↄ

The Cradle Song of the Poor

Hush! I cannot bear to see thee
    Stretch thy tiny hands in vain;
Dear, I have no bread to give thee,
    Nothing, child, to ease thy pain!
5   When God sent thee first to bless me,
    Proud, and thankful too, was I;
Now, my darling, I, thy mother,
    Almost long to see thee die.
       Sleep, my darling, thou art weary;
10   God is good, but life is dreary.

I have watched thy beauty fading,
    And thy strength sink day by day;
Soon, I know, will Want and Fever
15   Take thy little life away.
Famine makes thy father reckless,
    Hope has left both him and me;
We could suffer all, my baby,
    Had we but a crust for thee.
20   Sleep, my darling, thou art weary;
       God is good, but life is dreary.

Better thou shouldst perish early,
    Starve so soon, my darling one,
Than in helpless sin and sorrow
25   Vainly live, as I have done.
Better that thy angel spirit

With my joy, my peace, were flown,
Than thy heart grew cold and careless,
    Reckless, hopeless, like my own.
30   Sleep, my darling, thou art weary;
       God is good, but life is dreary.

I am wasted, dear, with hunger,
    And my brain is all opprest,
I have scarcely strength to press thee,
35   Wan and feeble, to my breast.
Patience, baby, God will help us,
    Death will come to thee and me,
He will take us to his Heaven,
    Where no want or pain can be.
40   Sleep, my darling, thou art weary;
       God is good, but life is dreary.

Such the plaint that, late and early,
    Did we listen, we might hear
Close beside us,—but the thunder
45   Of a city dulls our ear.
Every heart, as God's bright Angel,
    Can bid one such sorrow cease;
God has glory when his children
    Bring his poor ones joy and peace!
50   Listen, nearer while she sings
       Sounds the fluttering of wings!
—1858

Incompleteness

Nothing resting in its own completeness
Can have worth or beauty: but alone
Because it leads and tends to farther sweetness,
Fuller, higher, deeper than its own.

5 Spring's real glory dwells not in the meaning,
Gracious though it be, of her blue hours;
But is hidden in her tender leaning
To the Summer's richer wealth of flowers.

Dawn is fair, because the mists fade slowly
10 Into Day, which floods the world with light;
Twilight's mystery is so sweet and holy
Just because it ends in starry Night.

Childhood's smiles unconscious graces borrow
From Strife, that in a far-off future lies;
15 And angel glances (veiled now by Life's sorrow)
Draw our hearts to some belovèd eyes.

Life is only bright when it proceedeth
Towards a truer, deeper Life above;
Human Love is sweetest when it leadeth
20 To a more divine and perfect Love.

Learn the mystery of Progression duly:
Do not call each glorious change, Decay;
But know we only hold our treasures truly,
When it seems as if they passed away.

25 Nor dare to blame God's gifts for incompleteness;
In that want their beauty lies: they roll
Towards some infinite depth of love and sweetness,
Bearing onward man's reluctant soul.
—1858

My Picture Gallery

I

You write and think of me, my friend, with pity;
While you are basking in the light of Rome,
Shut up within the heart of this great city,
Too busy and too poor to leave my home.

II

5 You think my life debarred all rest or pleasure,
Chained all day to my ledger and my pen;
Too sickly even to use my little leisure
To bear me from the strife and din of men.

III

Well, it is true; yet, now the days are longer,
10 At sunset I can lay my writing down,
And slowly crawl (summer has made me stronger)
Just to the nearest outskirt of the town.

IV

There a wide Common, blackened though and
    dreary
With factory smoke, spreads outward to the West;
15 I lie down on the parched-up grass, if weary,
Or lean against a broken wall to rest.

V

So might a King, turning to Art's rich treasure,
At evening, when the cares of state were done,
Enter his royal gallery, drinking pleasure
20 Slowly from each great picture, one by one.

VI

Towards the West I turn my weary spirit,
And watch my pictures: one each night is mine.
Earth and my soul, sick of day's toil, inherit
A portion of that luminous peace divine.

VII

25 There I have seen a sunset's crimson glory,
Burn as if earth were one great Altar's blaze;
Or, like the closing of a piteous story,
Light up the misty world with dying rays.

VIII

There I have seen the Clouds, in pomp and
splendour,
30 Their gold and purple banners all unfurl;
There I have watched colours, more faint and
tender
Than pure and delicate tints upon a pearl.

IX

Skies strewn with roses fading, fading slowly,
While one star trembling watched the daylight die;
35 Or deep in gloom a sunset, hidden wholly,
Save through gold rents torn in a violet sky.

X

Or parted clouds, as if asunder riven
By some great angel—and beyond a space
Of far-off tranquil light; the gates of Heaven
40 Will lead us grandly to as calm a place.

XI

Or stern dark walls of cloudy mountain ranges
Hid all the wonders that we knew must be;
While, far on high, some little white clouds' changes
Revealed the glory they alone could see.

XII

45 Or in wild wrath the affrighted clouds lay
shattered,
Like treasures of the lost Hesperides,[1]
All in a wealth of ruined splendour scattered,
Save one strange light on distant silver sea.

XIII

What land or time can claim the Master Painter,
50 Whose art could teach him half such gorgeous dyes?
Or skill so rare, but purer hues and fainter
Melt every evening in my western skies.

XIV

So there I wait, until the shade has lengthened,
And night's blue misty curtain floated down;
55 Then, with my heart calmed, and my spirit
strengthened,
I crawl once more back to the sultry town.

XV

What Monarch, then, has nobler recreations
Than mine? Or where the great and classic Land
Whose wealth of Art delights the gathered nations
60 That owns a Picture Gallery half as grand?
—1858

An Appeal

"The Irish Church Mission for Converting
the Catholics."

Spare her, oh cruel England!
Thy Sister lieth low;
Chained and oppressed she lieth,
Spare her that cruel blow.

5 We ask not for the freedom
Heaven has vouchsafed to thee,
Nor bid thee share with Ireland
The empire of the sea;
Her children ask no shelter—
10 Leave them the stormy sky;
They ask not for thy harvests,
For they know how to die:
Deny them, if it please thee,
A grave beneath the sod—

---

[1] the nymphs who guarded the golden apples that Gaea gave as a
wedding present to Hera.

15 But we do cry, oh England,
   Leave them their faith in God!
Take, if thou wilt, the earnings
   Of the poor peasant's toil,
Take all the scanty produce
20   That grows on Irish soil,
To pay the alien preachers
   Whom Ireland will not hear,
To pay the scoffers at a Creed
   Which Irish hearts hold dear:
25 But leave them, cruel England,
   The gift their God has given,
Leave them their ancient worship,
   Leave them their faith in Heaven.

You come and offer Learning—
30   A mighty gift, 'tis true;
Perchance the greatest blessing
   That now is known to you—
But not to see the wonders
   Sages of old beheld
35 Can they peril a priceless treasure,
   The Faith their Fathers held;
For in learning and in science
   They may forget to pray—
God will not ask for knowledge
40   On the great judgment day.
When, in their wretched cabins,
   Racked by the fever pain,
And the weak cries of their children
   Who ask for food in vain;
45 When starving, naked, helpless,
   From the shed that keeps them warm
Man has driven them forth to perish,
   In a less cruel storm;
Then, then, we plead for mercy,
50   Then, Sister, hear our cry!
For all we ask, oh England,
   Is—leave them there to die!
Cursed is the food and raiment
   For which a soul is sold;

55 Tempt not another Judas[1]
   To barter God for gold.
You offer food and shelter
   If they their faith deny:—
What do you gain, oh England,
60   By such a shallow lie?…
We will not judge the tempted,
   May God blot out their shame,
He sees the misery round them,
   He knows man's feeble frame;
65 His pity still may save them,
   In His strength they must trust
Who calls us all His children,
   Yet knows we are but dust.

Then leave them the kind tending
70   Which helped their childish years;
Leave them the gracious comfort
   Which dries the mourner's tears;
Leave them to that great mother
   In whose bosom they were born;
75 Leave them the holy mysteries
   That comfort the forlorn:
And, amid all their trials,
   Let the Great Gift abide,
Which you, oh prosperous England,
80   Have dared to cast aside.
Leave them the pitying Angels,
   And Mary's gentle aid,
For which earth's dearest treasures
   Were not too dearly paid.
85 Take back your bribes, then, England.
   Your gold is black and dim,
And if God sends plague and famine
   They can die and go to Him.
—1858

---

[1] Judas Iscariot, the disciple who betrayed Jesus for money: Matthew 26:14,48.

The Jubilee of 1850

The titles of the "Island of Saints"
and the "Dower of Our Lady," though
more frequently applied to Ireland, were
often given to England in former times.

Bless God, ye happy Lands,
    For your more favoured lot:
Our England dwells apart,
    Yet oh, forget her not.
5   While, with united joy,
    This day you all adore,
Remember what she was,
    Though her voice is heard no more.
        Pray for our desolate land,
10   Left in her pride and power:—
        She was the Isle of Saints,
        She was Our Lady's Dower.

Look on her ruined Altars;
    He dwelleth there no more:
15 Think what her empty churches
    Have been in times of yore;
She knows the names no longer
    Of her own sainted dead,
Denies the faith they held,
20   And the cause for which they bled.
        Then pray for our desolate land,
        Left in her pride and power:—
        She was the Isle of Saints,
        She was Our Lady's Dower.

25 Pray that her vast Cathedrals,
    Deserted, empty, bare,
May once more echo accents
    Of Love, and Faith, and Prayer;
That the holy sign may bless us,
30   On wood, and field, and plain,
And Jesus, Mary, Joseph,
    May dwell with us again.

Pray, ye more faithful nations
    In this most happy hour:—
35   She was the Isle of Saints,
        She was Our Lady's Dower.

Beg of our Lord to give her
    The gift she cast aside,
And in His mercy pardon
40   Her faithlessness and pride:
Pray to her Saints, who worship
    Before God's mercy Throne;
Look where our Queen is dwelling,
    Ask her to claim her own,
45   To give her the proud titles
        Lost in an evil hour—
        She was the Isle of Saints,
        She was Our Lady's Dower.
—1858

Homeless

It is cold dark midnight, yet listen
    To that patter of tiny feet!
Is it one of your dogs, fair lady,
    Who whines in the bleak cold street?—
5   Is it one of your silken spaniels
    Shut out in the snow and the sleet?

My dogs sleep warm in their baskets,
    Safe from the darkness and snow;
All the beasts in our Christian England,
10   Find pity wherever they go—
(Those are only the homeless children
    Who are wandering to and fro.)

Look out in the gusty darkness—
    I have seen it again and again,
15 That shadow, that flits so slowly
    Up and down past the window pane:—
It is surely some criminal lurking
    Out there in the frozen rain?

Nay, our Criminals all are sheltered,
20   They are pitied and taught and fed:
That is only a sister-woman
        Who has got neither food nor bed—
And the Night cries "sin to be living,"
        And the River cries "sin to be dead."

25 Look out at that farthest corner
        Where the wall stands blank and bare:—
Can that be a pack which a Pedlar
        Has left and forgotten there?
His goods lying out unsheltered
30   Will be spoilt by the damp night air.

Nay;—goods in our thrifty England
        Are not left to lie and grow rotten,
For each man knows the market value
        Of silk or woollen or cotton...
35 But in counting the riches of England
        I think our Poor are forgotten.

Our Beasts and our Thieves and our Chattels
        Have weight for good or for ill;
But the Poor are only His image,
40   His presence, His word, His will—
And so Lazarus[1] lies at our doorstep
        And Dives[2] neglects him still.
        —1858

A Woman's Question

Before I trust my Fate to thee,
        Or place my hand in thine,
Before I let thy Future give
        Colour and form to mine,
5 Before I peril all for thee, question thy soul to-
        night for me.

I break all slighter bonds, nor feel
        A shadow of regret:
Is there one link within the Past,
        That holds thy spirit yet?
10 Or is thy Faith as clear and free as that which I can
        pledge to thee?

Does there within thy dimmest dreams
        A possible future shine,
Wherein thy life could henceforth breathe,
        Untouched, unshared by mine?
15 If so, at any pain or cost, oh, tell me before all is
        lost.

Look deeper still. If thou canst feel
        Within thy inmost soul,
That thou hast kept a portion back,
        While I have staked the whole;
20 Let no false pity spare the blow, but in true mercy
        tell me so.

Is there within thy heart a need
        That mine cannot fulfil?
One chord that any other hand
        Could better wake or still?
25 Speak now—lest at some future day my whole life
        wither and decay.

Lives there within thy nature hid
        The demon-spirit Change,
Shedding a passing glory still
        On all things new and strange?—
30 It may not be thy fault alone—but shield my heart
        against thy own.

Couldst thou withdraw thy hand one day
        And answer to my claim,
That Fate, and that to-day's mistake,
        Not thou—had been to blame?
35 Some soothe their conscience thus: but thou, wilt
        surely warn and save me now.

---

[1] the brother of Mary and Martha who was raised from the dead by
Christ: John 11.

[2] the rich man of biblical parable: Luke 16:19–31.

Nay, answer *not*—I dare not hear,
    The words would come too late;
Yet I would spare thee all remorse,
    So, comfort thee, my Fate—
40 Whatever on my heart may fall—remember, I
    would risk it all!
—1858

A Woman's Answer

I will not let you say a Woman's part
    Must be to give exclusive love alone;
Dearest, although I love you so, my heart
    Answers a thousand claims besides your own.

5 I love—what do I not love? earth and air
    Find space within my heart, and myriad things
You would not deign to heed, are cherished there,
    And vibrate on its very inmost strings.

I love the summer with her ebb and flow
10   Of light, and warmth, and music that have nurst
Her tender buds to blossoms…and you know
    It was in summer that I saw you first.

I love the winter dearly too,…but then
    I owe it so much; on a winter's day,
15 Bleak, cold, and storm, you returned again,
    When you had been those weary months away.

I love the Stars like friends; so many nights
    I gazed at them, when you were far from me,
Till I grew blind with tears…those far off lights
20   Could watch you, whom I longed in vain to see.

I love the Flowers; happy hours lie
    Shut up within their petals close and fast:
You have forgotten, dear: but they and I
    Keep every fragment of the golden Past.

25 I love, too, to be loved; all loving praise
    Seems like a crown upon my Life,—to make
It better worth the giving, and to raise
    Still nearer to your own the heart you take.

I love all good and noble souls;—I heard
30   One speak of you but lately, and for days
Only to think of it, my soul was stirred
    In tender memory of such generous praise.

I love all those who love you; all who owe
    Comfort to you: and I can find regret
35 Even for those poorer hearts who once could know,
    And once could love you, and can now forget.

Well, is my heart so narrow—I, who spare
    Love for all these? Do I not even hold
My favourite books in special tender care,
40   And prize them as a miser does his gold?

The Poets that you used to read to me
    While summer twilights faded in the sky;
But most of all I think Aurora Leigh,[1]
    Because—because—do you remember why?

45 Will you be jealous? Did you guess before
    I loved so many things?—Still you the best:—
Dearest, remember that I love you more,
    Oh, more a thousand times than all the rest!
—1858

A Woman's Last Word

Well—the links are broken,
    All is past;
This farewell, when spoken,
    Is the last.
5 I have tried and striven

---

[1] Elizabeth Barrett Browning's popular verse-novel, which discussed the role of poetry, and the "Woman Question" debate.

All in vain;
Such bonds must be riven,
    Spite of pain,
And never, never, never
10   Knit again.

So I tell you plainly,
    It must be:
I shall try, not vainly,
    To be free;
15 Truer, happier chances
    Wait me yet,
While you, through fresh fancies,
    Can forget;—
And life has nobler uses
20   Than Regret.

All past words retracing,
    One by one,
Does not help effacing
    What is done.
25 Let it be. Oh, stronger
    Links can break!
Had we dreamed still longer
    We could wake,—
Yet let us part in kindness
30   For Love's sake.

Bitterness and sorrow
    Will at last,
In some bright to-morrow,
    Heal their past;
35 But future hearts will never
    Be as true
As mine was—is ever,
    Dear, for you…
Then must we part, when loving
40   As we do?
    —1858

Envy

He was the first always: Fortune
    Shone bright in his face.
I fought for years; with no effort
    He conquered the place:
5 We ran; my feet were bleeding,
    But he won the race.

Spite of his many successes
    Men loved him the same;
My one pale ray of good fortune
10   Met scoffing and blame.
When we erred, they gave him pity,
    But me—only shame.

My home was still in the shadow,
    His lay in the sun:
15 I longed in vain: what he asked for
    It straightway was done.
Once I staked all my heart's treasure,
    We played—and he won.

Yes; and just now I have seen him
20   Cold, smiling, and blest,
Laid in his coffin. God help me!
    While he is at rest,
I am cursed still to live:—even
    Death loved him the best.
—1858

A Legend of Provence

The lights extinguished, by the hearth I leant,
    Half weary with a listless discontent.
The flickering giant-shadows, gathering near,
Closed round me with a dim and silent fear.
5 All dull, all dark; save when the leaping flame,
Glancing, lit up a Picture's ancient frame.
Above the hearth it hung. Perhaps the night,

My foolish tremors, or the gleaming light,
Lent power to that Portrait dark and quaint—
10 A Portrait such as Rembrandt[1] loved to paint—
The likeness of a Nun. I seemed to trace
A world of sorrow in the patient face,
In the thin hands folded across her breast—
Its own and the room's shadow hid the rest.
15 I gazed and dreamed, and the dull embers stirred,
Till an old legend that I once had heard
Came back to me; linked to the mystic gloom
Of that dark Picture in the ghostly room.

In the far south, where clustering vines are hung;
20 Where first the old chivalric lays were sung,
Where earliest smiled that gracious child of France,
Angel and knight and fairy, called Romance,
I stood one day. The warm blue June was spread
Upon the earth; blue summer overhead,
25 Without a cloud to fleck its radiant glare,
Without a breath to stir its sultry air.
All still, all silent, save the sobbing rush
Of rippling waves, that lapsed in silver hush
Upon the beach; where, glittering towards the
     strand,
30 The purple Mediterranean kissed the land.

All still, all peaceful; when a convent chime
Broke on the mid-day silence for a time,
Then trembling into quiet, seemed to cease,
In deeper silence and more utter peace.
35 So as I turned to gaze, where gleaming white,
Half hid by shadowy trees from passers' sight,
The Convent lay, one who had dwelt for long
In that fair home of ancient tale and song,
Who knew the story of each cave and hill,
40 And every haunting fancy lingering still
Within the land, spake thus to me, and told
The Convent's treasured Legend, quaint and old:

Long years ago, a dense and flowering wood,
Still more concealed where the white convent stood,
45 Borne on its perfumed wings the title came:
"Our Lady of the Hawthorns" is its name.
Then did that bell, which still rings out to-day,
Bid all the country rise, or eat, or pray.
Before that convent shrine, the haughty knight
50 Passed the long vigil of his perilous fight;
For humbler cottage strife or village brawl,
The Abbess listened, prayed, and settled all.
Young hearts that came, weighed down by love or
     wrong,
Left her kind presence comforted and strong.
55 Each passing pilgrim, and each beggar's right
Was food, and rest, and shelter for the night.
But, more than this, the Nuns could well impart
The deepest mysteries of the healing art;
Their store of herbs and simples[2] was renowned,
60 And held in wondering faith for miles around.
Thus strife, love, sorrow, good and evil fate,
Found help and blessing at the convent gate.
Of all the nuns, no heart was half so light,
No eyelids veiling glances half as bright,
65 No step that glided with such noiseless feet,
No face that looked so tender or so sweet,
No voice that rose in choir so pure, so clear,
No heart to all the others half so dear,
So surely touched by others' pain or woe,
70 (Guessing the grief her young life could not know,)
No soul in childlike faith so undefiled,
As Sister Angela's, the "Convent Child."
For thus they loved to call her. She had known
No home, no love, no kindred, save their own.
75 An orphan, to their tender nursing given,
Child, plaything, pupil, now the Bride of Heaven.
And she it was who trimmed the lamp's red light
That swung before the altar, day and night;
Her hands it was whose patient skill could trace

---

[1] Dutch painter, Rembrandt van Rijn (1606–69).

[2] medicines.

80 The finest broidery, weave the costliest lace;
But most of all, her first and dearest care,
The office she would never miss or share,
Was every day to weave fresh garlands sweet,
To place before the shrine at Mary's feet.
85 Nature is bounteous in that region fair,
For even winter has her blossoms there.
Thus Angela loved to count each feast the best,
By telling with what flowers the shrine was dressed.
In pomp supreme the countless Roses passed,
90 Battalion on battalion thronging fast
Each with a different banner, flaming bright,
Damask, or striped, or crimson, pink, or white,
Until they bowed before a new born queen,
And the pure virgin Lily rose serene.
95 Though Angela always thought the Mother blest
Must love the time of her own hawthorn best,
Each evening through the year, with equal care,
She placed her flowers; then kneeling down in
        prayer,
As their faint perfume rose before the shrine,
100 So rose her thoughts, as pure and as divine.
She knelt until the shades grew dim without,
Till one by one the altar lights shone out,
Till one by one the Nuns, like shadows dim,
Gathered around to chant their vesper hymn;
105 Her voice then led the music's wingèd flight,
And "Ave, Maris Stella" filled the night.

But wherefore linger on those days of peace?
When storms draw near, then quiet hours must
        cease.
War, cruel war, defaced the land, and came
110 So near the convent with its breath of flame,
That, seeking shelter, frightened peasants fled,
Sobbing out tales of coming fear and dread.
Till after a fierce skirmish, down the road,
One night came straggling soldiers, with their load
115 Of wounded, dying comrades; and the band,
Half pleading, yet as if they could command,
Summoned the trembling Sisters, craved their care,

Then rode away, and left the wounded there.
But soon compassion bade all fear depart,
120 And bidding every Sister do her part,
Some prepare simples, healing salves, or bands
The Abbess chose the more experienced hands,
To dress the wounds needing most skilful care;
Yet even the youngest Novice took her share
125 To Angela, who had but ready will
And tender pity, yet no special skill,
Was given the charge of a young foreign Knight,
Whose wounds were painful, but whose danger
        slight
Day after day she watched beside his bed,
130 And first in hushed repose the hours fled:
His feverish moans alone the silence stirred,
Or her soft voice, uttering some pious word.
At last the fever left him; day by day
The hours, no longer silent, passed away.
135 What could she speak of? First, to still his plaints,
She told him legends of the martyred Saints;
Described the pangs, which, through God's
        plenteous grace,
Had gained their souls so high and bright a place.
This pious artifice soon found success—
140 Or so she fancied—for he murmured less.
So she described the glorious pomp sublime,
In which the chapel shone at Easter time,
The Banners, Vestments, gold, and colours bright,
Counted how many tapers gave their light;
145 Then, in minute detail went on to say,
How the High Altar looked on Christmas-day:
The kings and shepherds, all in green and red,
And a bright star of jewels overhead.
Then told the sign by which they all had seen,
150 How even nature loved to greet her Queen
For, when Our Lady's last procession went
Down the long garden, every head was bent,
And, rosary in hand, each Sister prayed;
As the long floating banners were displayed,
155 They struck the hawthorn boughs, and showers
        and showers

Of buds and blossoms strewed her way with flowers.
The Knight unwearied listened; till at last,
He too described the glories of his past;
Tourney, and joust, and pageant bright and fair,
160 And all the lovely ladies who were there.
But half incredulous she heard. Could this—
This be the world? this place of love and bliss!
Where then was hid the strange and hideous charm,
That never failed to bring the gazer harm?
165 She crossed herself, yet asked, and listened still,
And still the Knight described with all his skill
The glorious world of joy, all joys above,
Transfigured in the golden mist of love.
Spread, spread your wings, ye angel guardians
        bright,
170 And shield these dazzling phantoms from her sight!
But no; days passed, matins and vespers rang,
And still the quiet Nuns toiled, prayed, and sang,
And never guessed the fatal, coiling net
Which every day drew near, and nearer yet,
175 Around their darling; for she went and came
About her duties, outwardly the same.
The same? ah, no! even when she knelt to pray,
Some charmèd dream kept all her heart away.
So days went on, until the convent gate
180 Opened one night. Who durst go forth so late?
Across the moonlit grass, with stealthy tread,
Two silent, shrouded figures passed and fled.
And all was silent, save the moaning seas,
That sobbed and pleaded, and a wailing breeze
185 That sighed among the perfumed hawthorn trees.

What need to tell that dream so bright and brief,
Of joy unchequered by a dread of grief?
What need to tell how all such dreams must fade,
Before the slow, foreboding, dreaded shade,
190 That floated nearer, until pomp and pride,
Pleasure and wealth, were summoned to her side,
To bid, at least, the noisy hours forget,
And clamour down the whispers of regret.
Still Angela strove to dream, and strove in vain;

195 Awakened once, she could not sleep again.
She saw, each day and hour, more worthless grown
The heart for which she cast away her own;
And her soul learnt, through bitterest inward strife,
The slight, frail love for which she wrecked her life,
200 The phantom for which all her hope was given,
The cold bleak earth for which she bartered heaven
But all in vain; would even the tenderest heart
Now stoop to take so poor an outcast's part?

Years fled, and she grew reckless more and more,
205 Until the humblest peasant closed his door,
And where she passed, fair dames, in scorn and pride,
Shuddered, and drew their rustling robes aside.
At last a yearning seemed to fill her soul,
A longing that was stronger than control:
210 Once more, just once again, to see the place
That knew her young and innocent; to retrace
The long and weary southern path; to gaze
Upon the haven of her childish days;
Once more beneath the convent roof to lie;
215 Once more to look upon her home—and die!

Weary and worn—her comrades, chill remorse
And black despair, yet a strange silent force
Within her heart, that drew her more and more—
Onward she crawled, and begged from door to door.
220 Weighed down with weary days, her failing strength
Grew less each hour, till one day's dawn at length,
As first its rays flooded the world with light,
Showed the broad waters, glittering blue and bright,
And where, amid the leafy hawthorn wood,
225 Just as of old the quiet cloister stood.
Would any know her? Nay, no fear. Her face
Had lost all trace of youth, of joy, of grace,
Of the pure happy soul they used to know—
The novice Angela—so long ago.
230 She rang the convent bell. The well-known sound
Smote on her heart, and bowed her to the ground,
And she, who had not wept for long dry years,
Felt the strange rush of unaccustomed tears;

Terror and anguish seemed to check her breath,
235 And stop her heart. Oh God! could this be death?
Crouching against the iron gate, she laid
Her weary head against the bars, and prayed:
But nearer footsteps drew, then seemed to wait;
And then she heard the opening of the grate,
240 And saw the withered face, on which awoke
Pity and sorrow, as the portress spoke,
And asked the stranger's bidding: "Take me in,"
She faltered, "Sister Monica, from sin,
And sorrow, and despair, that will not cease;
245 Oh, take me in, and let me die in peace!"
With soothing words the Sister bade her wait,
Until she brought the key to unbar the gate.
The beggar tried to thank her as she lay,
And heard the echoing footsteps die away.
250 But what soft voice was that which sounded near,
And stirred strange trouble in her heart to hear?
She raised her head; she saw—she seemed to
            know—
A face that came from long, long years ago:
Herself; yet not as when she fled away,
255 The young and blooming novice, fair and gay,
But a grave woman, gentle and serene:
The outcast knew it—*what she might have been.*
But, as she gazed and gazed, a radiance bright
Filled all the place with strange and sudden light;
260 The Nun was there no longer, but instead,
A figure with a circle round its head,
A ring of glory; and a face, so meek,
So soft, so tender…Angela strove to speak,
And stretched her hands out, crying, "Mary mild,
265 Mother of mercy, help me!—help your child!"
And Mary answered, "From thy bitter past,
Welcome, my child! oh, welcome home at last!
I filled thy place. Thy flight is known to none,
For all thy daily duties I have done;
270 Gathered thy flowers, and prayed, and sung, and
            slept;
Didst thou not know, poor child, *thy place was
            kept?*

Kind hearts are here; yet would the tenderest one
Have limits to its mercy: God has none.
And man's forgiveness may be true and sweet,
275 But yet he stoops to give it. More complete
Is Love that lays forgiveness at thy feet,
And pleads with thee to raise it. Only Heaven
Means *crowned*, not *vanquished*, when it says
            'Forgiven!'"
Back hurried Sister Monica; but where
280 Was the poor beggar she left lying there?
Gone; she searched in vain, and sought the place
For that wan woman, with the piteous face:
But only Angela at the gateway stood,
Laden with hawthorn blossoms from the wood.
285 And never did a day pass by again,
But the old portress, with a sigh of pain,
Would sorrow for her loitering: with a prayer
That the poor beggar, in her wild despair,
Might not have come to any ill; and when
290 She ended, "God forgive her!" humbly then
Did Angela bow her head, and say "Amen!"
How pitiful her heart was! all could trace
Something that dimmed the brightness of her face
After that day, which none had seen before;
295 Not trouble—but a shadow—nothing more.

Years passed away. Then, one dark day of dread
Saw all the sisters kneeling round a bed,
Where Angela lay dying; every breath
Struggling beneath the heavy hand of death.
300 But suddenly a flush lit up her cheek,
She raised her wan right hand, and strove to speak.
In sorrowing love they listened; not a sound
Or sigh disturbed the utter silence round.
The very tapers' flames were scarcely stirred,
305 In such hushed awe the sisters knelt and heard.
And through that silence Angela told her life:
Her sin, her flight; the sorrow and the strife,
And the return; and then clear, low and calm,
"Praise God for me, my sisters;" and the psalm
310 Rang up to heaven, far and clear and wide,

Again and yet again, then sank and died;
While her white face had such a smile of peace.
They saw she never heard the music cease;
And weeping sisters laid her in her tomb,
315 Crowned with a wreath of perfumed hawthorn
       bloom.

And thus the Legend ended. It may be
Something is hidden in the mystery,
Besides the lesson of God's pardon shown,
Never enough believed, or asked or known.
320 Have we not all, amid life's petty strife,
Some pure ideal of a noble life
That once seemed possible? Did we not hear
The flutter of its wings, and feel it near,
And just within our reach? It was. And yet
325 We lost it in this daily jar and fret,
And now live idle in a vague regret.
But still *our place is kept*, and it will wait.
Ready for us to fill it, soon or late:
No star is ever lost we once have seen,
330 We always may be what we might have been.
Since Good, though only thought, has life and
       breath,
God's life—can always be redeemed from death;
And evil, in its nature, is decay,
And any hour can blot it all away;
335 The hopes that lost in some far distance seem,
May be the truer life, and this the dream.
       —1858

Philip and Mildred

Lingering fade the rays of daylight, and the
       listening air is chilly;
   Voice of bird and forest murmur, insect hum
       and quivering spray,
Stir not in that quiet hour: through the valley, calm
   and stilly,

All in hushed and loving silence watch the slow
   departing Day.

5   Till the last faint western cloudlet, faint and rosy,
       ceases blushing,
   And the blue grows deep and deeper where one
       trembling planet shines,
And the day has gone for ever—then, like some
       great ocean rushing,
   The sad night wind wails lamenting, sobbing
       through the moaning pines.

Such, of all day's changing hours, is the fittest and
       the meetest
10   For a farewell hour—and parting looks less
       bitter and more blest;
Earth seems like a shrine for sorrow, Nature's
       mother-voice is sweetest,
   And her hand seems laid in chiding on the
       unquiet throbbing breast.

Words are lower, for the twilight seems rebuking
       sad repining,
   And wild murmur and rebellion, as all childish
       and in vain;
15   Breaking through dark future hours clustering
       starry hopes seem shining,
   Then the calm and tender midnight folds her
       shadow round the pain.

So they paced the shady lime-walk in that twilight
       dim and holy,
   Still the last farewell deferring, she could hear or
       he should say;
Every word, weighed down by sorrow, fell more
       tenderly and slowly—
20   This, which now beheld their parting, should
       have been their wedding-day.

Should have been: her dreams of childhood, never
       straying, never faltering,

Still had needed Philip's image to make future
    life complete;
Philip's young hopes of ambition, ever changing,
    ever altering,
Needed Mildred's gentle presence even to make
    successes sweet.

25 This day should have seen their marriage; the calm
    crowning and assurance
Of two hearts, fulfilling rather, and not
    changing, either life:
Now they must be rent asunder, and her heart
    must learn endurance,
For he leaves their home, and enters on a world
    of work and strife.

But her gentle spirit long had learnt,
    unquestioning, submitting,
30   To revere his youthful longings, and to marvel
    at the fate
That gave such a humble office, all unworthy and
    unfitting,
    To the genius of the village, who was born for
    something great.

When the learnèd Traveller came there who had
    gained renown at college,
Whose abstruse research had won him even
    European fame,
35 Questioned Philip, praised his genius, marvelled at
    his self-taught knowledge,
Could she murmur if he called him up to
    London and to fame?

Could she waver when he bade her take the burden
    of decision,
Since his troth to her was plighted, and his life
    was now her own?
Could she doom him to inaction? could she, when
    a newborn vision

40 Rose in glory for his future, check it for her sake
    alone?

So her little trembling fingers, that had toiled with
    such fond pleasure,
    Paused, and laid aside, and folded the
    unfinished wedding gown;
Faltering earnestly assurance, that she too could, in
    her measure,
    Prize for him the present honour, and the
    future's sure renown.

45 Now they pace the shady lime-walk, now the last
    words must be spoken,
    Words of trust, for neither dreaded more than
    waiting and delay;
Was not love still called eternal—could a plighted
    vow be broken?—
    See the crimson light of sunset fades in purple
    mist away.

"Yes, my Mildred," Philip told her, "one calm
    thought of joy and blessing,
50   Like a guardian spirit by me, through the
    world's tumultuous stir,
Still will spread its wings above me, and now
    urging, now repressing,
    With my Mildred's voice will murmur thoughts
    of home, and love, and her.

"It will charm my peaceful leisure, sanctify my
    daily toiling,
    With a right none else possesses, touching my
    heart's inmost string;
55 And to keep its pure wings spotless I shall fly the
    world's touch, soiling
    Even in thought this Angel Guardian of my
    Mildred's Wedding Ring.

"Take it, dear; this little circlet is the first link,
    strong and holy,

Of a life-long chain, and holds me from all
    other love apart;
Till the day when you may wear it as my wife—my
    own—mine wholly—
60 Let me know it rests for ever near the beating of
    your heart."

Dawn of day saw Philip speeding on his road to the
    Great City,
    Thinking how the stars gazed downward just
      with Mildred's patient eyes;
Dreams of work, and fame, and honour, struggling
    with a tender pity,
    Till the loving Past receding saw the conquering
      Future rise.

65 Daybreak still found Mildred watching, with the
    wonder of first sorrow,
    How the outward world unaltered shone the
      same this very day;
How unpitying and relentless busy life met this
    new morrow,
    Earth, and sky, and man unheeding that her joy
      had passed away.

Then the round of weary duties, cold and formal,
    came to meet her,
70   With the life within departed that had given
      them each a soul;
And her sick heart even slighted gentle words that
    came to greet her;
    For Grief spread its shadowy pinions, like a
      blight upon the whole.

Jar one chord, the harp is silent; move one stone,
    the arch is shattered;
    One small clarion-cry of sorrow bids an armèd
      host awake;
75 One dark cloud can hide the sunlight; loose one
    string the pearls are scattered;

Think one thought, a soul may perish; say one
    word, a heart may break!

Life went on, the two lives running side by side; the
    outward seeming,
    And the truer and diviner hidden in the heart
      and brain;
Dreams grow holy, put in action; work grows fair
    through starry dreaming;
80   But where each flows on unmingling, both are
      fruitless and in vain.

Such was Mildred's life; her dreaming lay in some
    far-distant region,
    All the fairer, all the brighter, that its glories
      were but guessed;
And the daily round of duties seemed an unreal,
    airy legion—
    Nothing true save Philip's letters and the ring
      upon her breast.

85 Letters telling how he struggled, for some plan or
    vision aiming,
    And at last how he just grasped it as a fresh one
      spread its wings;
How the honour or the learning, once the climax,
    now were claiming,
    Only more and more, becoming merely steps to
      higher things.

Telling her of foreign countries: little store had she
    of learning,
90   So her earnest, simple spirit answered as he
      touched the string;
Day by day, to these bright fancies all her silent
    thoughts were turning,
    Seeing every radiant picture framed within her
      golden Ring.

Oh, poor heart—love, if thou willest; but, thine
    own soul still possessing,

Live thy life: not a reflection or a shadow of his
    own:
95 Lean as fondly, as completely, as thou willest but
    confessing
    That thy strength is God's, and therefore can at
      need be, stand alone.

Little means were there around her to make farther
    wider ranges,
    Where her loving gentle spirit could try any
      stronger flight;
And she turned aside, half fearing that fresh
    thoughts were fickle changes—
100   That she *must* stay as he left her on that farewell
      summer night.

Love should still be guide and leader, like a herald
    should have risen,
    Lighting up the long dark vistas, conquering
      opposing fates;
But new claims, new thoughts, new duties found
    her heart a silent prison,
    And found Love, with folded pinions, like a
      jailer by the gates.

105 Yet why blame her? it had needed greater strength
    than she was given
    To have gone against the current that so calmly
      flowed along;
Nothing fresh came near the village save the rain
    and dew of heaven,
    And her nature was too passive, and her love
      perhaps too strong.

The great world of thought, that rushes down the
    years, and onward sweeping
110   Bears upon its mighty billows in its progress
      each and all,
Flowed so far away, its murmur did not rouse them
    from their sleeping;

Life and Time and Truth were speaking, but
    they did not hear their call.

Years flowed on; and every morning heard her
    prayer grow lower, deeper,
    As she called all blessings on him, and bade
      every ill depart,
115 And each night when the cold moonlight shone
    upon that quiet sleeper,
    It would show her ring that glittered with each
      throbbing of her heart.

Years passed on. Fame came for Philip in a full,
    o'erflowing measure;
    He was spoken of and honoured through the
      breadth of many lands,
And he wrote it all to Mildred, as if praise were
    only pleasure,
120   As if fame were only honour, when he laid them
      in her hands.

Mildred heard it without wonder, as a sure result
    expected,
    For how could it fail, since merit and renown
      go side by side:
And the neighbours who first fancied genius ought
    to be suspected,
    Might at last give up their caution, and could
      own him now with pride.

125 Years flowed on. These empty honours led to others
    they called better,
    He had saved some slender fortune, and might
      claim his bride at last:
Mildred, grown so used to waiting, felt half startled
    by the letter
    That now made her future certain, and would
      consecrate her past.

And he came: grown sterner, older—changed
    indeed a grave reliance

130   Had replaced his eager manner, and the quick
        short speech of old:
    He had gone forth with a spirit half of hope and
        half defiance;
    He returned with proud assurance half
        disdainful and half cold.

    Yet his old self seemed returning while he stood
        sometimes, and listened
    To her calm soft voice, relating all the thoughts
        of these long years;
135   And if Mildred's heart was heavy, and at times her
        blue eyes glistened,
    Still in thought she would not whisper aught of
        sorrow or of fears.

    Autumn with its golden corn-fields, autumn with
        its storms and showers,
    Had been there to greet his coming with its
        forests gold and brown;
    And the last leaves still were falling, fading still the
        year's last flowers,
140   When he left the quiet village, and took back
        his bride to town.

    Home—the home that she had pictured many a
        time in twilight, dwelling
    On that tender gentle fancy, folded round with
        loving care;
    Here was home—the end, the haven; and what
        spirit voice seemed telling,
    That she only held the casket, with the gem no
        longer there?

145   Sad it may be to be longing, with a patience faint
        and weary,
    For a hope deferred—and sadder still to see it
        fade and fall;
    Yet to grasp the thing we long for, and, with
        sorrow sick and dreary,

    Then to find how it can fail us, is the saddest
        pain of all.

    What was wanting? He was gentle, kind, and
        generous still, deferring
150   To her wishes always; nothing seemed to mar
        their tranquil life:
    There are skies so calm and leaden that we long for
        storm-winds stirring,
    There is peace so cold and bitter, that we almost
        welcome strife.

    Darker grew the clouds above her, and the slow
        conviction clearer,
    That he gave her home and pity, but that heart,
        and soul, and mind
155   Were beyond her now; he loved her, and in youth
        he had been near her,
    But he now had gone far onward, and had left
        her there behind.

    Yes, beyond her: yes, quick-hearted, her Love
        helped her in revealing
    It was worthless, while so mighty; was too weak,
        although so strong;
    There were courts she could not enter; depths she
        could not sound; yet feeling
160   It was vain to strive or struggle, vainer still to
        mourn or long.

    He would give her words of kindness, he would
        talk of home, but seeming
    With an absent look, forgetting if he held or
        dropped her hand;
    And then turn with eager pleasure to his writing,
        reading, dreaming,
    Or to speak of things with others that she could
        not understand.

165   He had paid, and paid most nobly, all he owed; no
        need of blaming;

It had cost him something, may be, that no
    future could restore:
In her heart of hearts she knew it; Love and
    Sorrow, not complaining,
      Only suffered all the deeper, only loved him all
      the more.

Sometimes then a stronger anguish, and more cruel,
    weighed upon her,
170   That through all those years of waiting, he had
    slowly learnt the truth;
He had known himself mistaken, but that, bound
    to her in honour,
      He renounced his life, to pay her for the
      patience of her youth.

But a star was slowly rising from that mist of grief,
    and brighter
      Grew her eyes, for each slow hour surer comfort
      seemed to bring;
175 And she watched with strange sad smiling, how her
    trembling hands grew slighter,
      And how thin her slender finger, and how large
      her wedding-ring.

And the tears dropped slowly on it, as she kissed
    that golden token
      With a deeper love, it may be, than was in the
      far off past;
And remembering Philip's fancy, that so long ago
    was spoken,

180 Thought her Ring's bright angel guardian had
    stayed near her to the last.

Grieving sorely, grieving truly, with a tender care
    and sorrow,
      Philip watched the slow, sure fading of his gentle
      patient wife;
Could he guess with what a yearning she was
    longing for the morrow,
      Could he guess the bitter knowledge that had
      wearied her of life?

185 Now with violets strewn upon her, Mildred lies in
    peaceful sleeping;
      All unbound her long, bright tresses, and her
      throbbing heart at rest,
And the cold, blue rays of moonlight, through the
    open casement creeping,
      Show the Ring upon her finger, and her hands
      crossed on her breast.

Peace at last. Of peace eternal is her calm sweet
    smile a token.
190 Has some angel lingering near her let a radiant
    promise fall?
Has he told her Heaven unites again the links that
    Earth has broken?
      For on Earth so much is needed, but in Heaven
      Love is all!

—1858

Mortimer Collins
1827 – 1876

Mortimer Collins began his professional life as a teacher of mathematics at Queen Elizabeth's College, Guernsey, but left in 1856 to become a full-time writer. Collins was a prolific journalist, novelist, and poet with a vibrant sense of humour; he loved dogs, was a first-rate amateur naturalist and a good chess-player.

ၐၐၐ

Lotos Eating [1]

I

Who would care to pass his life away
    Of the Lotos-land a dreamful denizen—
Lotos-islands in a waveless bay,
    Sung by Alfred Tennyson?

II

5 Who would care to be a dull new-comer
    Far across the wild sea's wide abysses,
Where, about the earth's 3000th summer
    Passed divine Ulysses? [2]

III

Rather give me coffee, art, a book,
10   From my windows a delicious sea-view,

Southdown mutton, somebody to cook—
    "Music?" I believe you.

IV

Strawberry icebergs in the summer time—
    But of elmwood many a massive splinter,
15 Good ghost stories, and a classic rhyme,
    For the nights of winter.

V

Now and then a friend and some sauterne,
    Now and then a haunch of Highland venison:
And for Lotos-lands I'll never yearn
20   Maugre [3] Alfred Tennyson.
   —1855

---

[1] The reference is to Alfred Tennyson's poem, "The Lotos-Eaters."

[2] the mythical king of Ithaca (a Greek island) and the hero of Homer's *Odyssey*; see also Tennyson's poem, "Ulysses."

[3] in spite of.

J. Stanyan Bigg
1828 – 1865

J. Stanyan Bigg was a poet, novelist, and journalist. He lived in Ireland for a number of years as editor of the *Dowshire Protestant*. With the publication of his poem "Night and the Soul" in 1854, he became identified with the Spasmodic movement. (See also Sydney Dobell, p. 763.)

അ

An Irish Picture

A smoking swamp before a cottage door;
  A drowned dog bobbing to a soleless shoe;
A broken wash-tub, with its ragged staves
Swimming and ducking to a battered hat,
5 Whenever the wind stirs the reedy slime;
A tumbled peat-stack, dripping in the rain;
A long, lank pig, with dissipated eyes,
Leading a vagrant life among the moors;
A rotting paling, and a plot of ground,
10 With fifteen cabbage-stalks amid lush weeds;

A moss-grown pathway, and a worn-out gate,
Its broken bars down-dangling from the nails;
A windy cottage, with a leaky thatch,
And two dim windows set like eyes asquint;
15 A bulging doorway, with a drunken lean;
Two half-nude children dabbling in the mire,
And scrambling eagerly for bottle-necks;
A man akimbo at the open door,
His battered hat slouched o'er his sottish eyes,
20 Smoking contented in the falling rain.
—1862

Gerald Massey
1828 – 1907

Gerald Massey was a poet of humble origins: he was born in a hut at Gamble Wharf on the canal near Tring. After only a few years of schooling, he was put to work at the age of eight in a silk mill. He then tried straw-plaiting and at the age of fifteen he became an errand boy in London. Massey published *Poems and Chansons* in 1848 and *Voices of Freedom and Lyrics of Love* in 1850. His position as a poet of liberty, labour, and the people was established in 1854 with his third volume, *The Ballad of Babe Christabel and Other Poems*, which went through five editions in one year.

☙☙☙

Hope On, Hope Ever

Hope on, hope ever! though to-day be dark,
    The sweet sunburst may smile on thee
        to-morrow:
Tho' thou art lonely, there's an eye will mark
    Thy loneliness, and guerdon all thy sorrow!
5 Tho' thou must toil 'mong cold and sordid men,
    With none to echo back thy thought, or love
        thee,
Cheer up, poor heart! thou dost not beat in vain,
    For God is over all, and heaven above thee—
        Hope on, hope ever.

10 The iron may enter in and pierce thy soul,[1]
    But cannot kill the love within thee burning:
The tears of misery, thy bitter dole,
    Can never quench thy true heart's seraph
        yearning
For better things: nor crush thy ardour's trust,
15   That Error from the mind shall be uprooted,
That Truths shall dawn as flowers spring from the
        dust,
    And Love be cherisht where Hate was
        embruted!
        Hope on, hope ever.

I know 'tis hard to bear the sneer and taunt,—
20   With the heart's honest pride at midnight
        wrestle;
To feel the killing canker-worm of Want,
    While rich rogues in their stolen luxury nestle;
For I have felt it. Yet from Earth's cold Real
    My soul looks out on coming things, and
        cheerful
25 The warm Sunrise floods all the land Ideal,
    And still it whispers to the worn and tearful,
        Hope on, hope ever.

Hope on, hope ever! after darkest night,
    Comes, full of loving life, the laughing Morning;
30 Hope on, hope ever! Spring-tide, flusht with light,
    Aye crowns old Winter with her rich adorning.
Hope on, hope ever! yet the time shall come,
    When man to man shall be a friend and brother;
And this old world shall be a happy home,
35   And all Earth's family love one another!
        Hope on, hope ever.

—1861

The Cry of the Unemployed

'Tis hard, 'tis hard to wander on through this
    bright world of ours,
Beneath a sky of smiling blue, on velvet paths of
    flowers,

---

[1] to experience the pangs of anguish and bitterness; from the Prayer Book version of Psalm 105:18; a mistranslation of Hebrew, included in the Vulgate Bible.

With music in the woods, as there were nought but
    joyaunce known,
Or Angels walkt earth's solitudes, and yet with
    want to groan,
5 To see no beauty in the stars, nor in God's radiant
    smile,
To wail and wander misery-curst! willing, but
    cannot toil.
There's burning sickness at my heart, I sink down
    famishéd!
God of the wretched, hear my prayer: I would that
    I were dead!

Heaven droppeth down with manna[1] still in many
    a golden show'r,
10 And feeds the leaves with fragrant breath, with
    silver dew the flow'r.
There's honey'd fruit for bee and bird, with bloom
    laughs out the tree,
And food for all God's happy things; but none
    gives food to me.
Earth, deck'd with Plenty's garland-crown, smiles
    on my aching eye,
The purse-proud,—swathed in luxury,—disdainful
    pass me by:
15 I've eager hands, and earnest heart—but may not
    work for bread!
God of the wretched, hear my prayer: I would that
    I were dead!

Gold, art thou not a blessed thing, a charm above
    all other,
To shut up hearts to Nature's cry, when brother
    pleads with brother?
Hast thou a music sweeter than the voice of loving
    kindness?
20 No! curse thee, thou'rt a mist 'twixt God and men
    in outer blindness.

"Father, come back!" my children cry; their voices,
    once so sweet,
Now quiver lance-like in my bleeding heart! I
    cannot meet
The looks that make the brain go mad, for dear
    ones asking bread—
God of the wretched, hear my prayer: I would that
    I were dead!

25 Lord! what right have the poor to wed? Love's for
    the gilded great:
Are they not form'd of nobler clay, who dine off
    golden plate?
'Tis the worst curse of Poverty to have a feeling
    heart:
Why can I not, with iron-grasp, tear out the tender
    part?
I cannot slave in yon Bastile![2] ah no, 'twere bitterer
    pain,
30 To wear the Pauper's iron within, than drag the
    Convict's chain.
I'd work but cannot, starve I may, but will not beg
    for bread:
God of the wretched, hear my prayer: I would that
    I were dead!
—1861

A Song in the City

Coining the heart, brain, and sinew, to gold,
  Till we sink in the dark, on the pauper's dole;
Feeling for ever the flowerless mould,
    Growing about the uncrownéd soul!
5 O, God! O God! must this evermore be
The lot of the Children of Poverty?
    The Spring is calling from brae and bower,
    In the twinkling sheen of the sunny hour,

---

[1] Manna was the miraculous food provided for the children of Israel on
their journey from Egypt to the Holy Land: Exodus 16:15, 31.

[2] the State Prison in Paris, built as a castle by Charles V (1370–83);
seized by the mob 14 July 1778 at the beginning of the French Revo-
lution. The term is generally used to mean a prison or prison-like place.

Earth smiles in her golden green;
10　There's music below, in the glistering leaves,
There's music above, and heaven's blue bosom
　　heaves
　　The silvery clouds between;
The boughs of the woodland are nodding in
　　play;
And wooingly beckon my spirit away—
15　　I hear the dreamy hum
Of bees in the bloom, and birds on the spray;
And they, too, are calling my thinking away;
　　But I cannot—cannot come.
Visions of verdant and heart-cooling places
20　　Will steal on my soul like a golden spring-rain,
Bringing the lost light of brave, vanisht faces;
　　Till all my life blossoms with beauty again.
But O, for a glimpse of the flower-laden Morning,
　　That makes the heart leap up, and knock at
　　heaven's door!
25　O for the green lane, the green field, the green
　　wood,
　　To take in, by heartfuls, their greenness once
　　more!
How I yearn to lie down and just roll in the
　　meadows,
And nestle in leaves, and the sleep of the shadows,
　　Where primroses in their green chambers are
　　waking,
30　There, let my soul out from its cavern of clay,
To float down the warm spring, away and away!
　　FOR I WAS NOT MADE MERELY FOR
　　MONEY-MAKING.

At this wearisome work I oftentimes turn,
　　From my bride, and my monitress, Duty,
35　Forgetting the strife, and the wrestle of life,
　　To talk with the spirit of beauty.
The multitude's hum, and the chinking of gold,
　　Grow hush as the dying of day,
For on wings, making music, with joy untold,
40　　My heart is up, and away!

Glad as the bird in the tree-top chanting
　　Its anthem to Liberty;
With its heart all in musical gratitude panting,
　　And O, 'tis a bliss to be!
45　Once more to drink in the life-breathing air,
　　Lapt in luxurious flowers—
To recall again the pleasures that were
　　In Infancy's innocent hours—
To wash the earth-stains and the dust from my soul,
50　　In nature's reviving tears, once more;
To feast at her banquet, and drink from her bowl
　　Rich dew, for the heart's hot core.
Ah me! ah me! it is heavenly then,
　　And hints of the spirit-world, near alway,
55　Are stirring, and stirr'd, in my heart again,
　　Like leaves at the kiss of May:
It is but a dream, yet 'tis passing sweet,
　　And when from its spells my spirit is
　　waking,
Dark is my heart, and the wild tears start;
60　　FOR I WAS NOT MADE MERELY FOR
　　MONEY-MAKING.

My soul leaneth out, to the whisperings
　　Of the mighty, the marvellous spirits of old;
And heavenward soareth to strengthen her wings,
　　When Labour relapseth its earthly hold;
65　And breathless with awfullest beauty—it listens,
　　To catch the Night's deep, starry mystery;
Or in mine eyes, dissolved, it glistens,
　　Big, for the moan of Humanity.
Much that is written within its chamber,
70　Much that is shrined in the mind's living amber,
　　Much of this thought of mine,—
I fain would struggle and give to birth;
For I would not pass away from earth,
　　And make no sign!
75　I yearn to utter, what might live on,
In the world's heart, when I am gone.
I would not plod on, like these slaves of gold,
　　Who darken their souls, in a dusky cave:

I would see the world better, and nobler-soul'd,
80   Ere I lay me down in my green turf-grave.
I may toil till my life is filled with dreariness,
Toil till my heart is a wreck in its weariness,
Toil for ever, for tear-steept bread,
Till I go down to the silent dead.
85   But, by this yearning, this hoping, this aching,
I WAS NOT MADE MERELY FOR MONEY-MAKING.
    —1861

"As proper mode of quenching legal lust..."

As proper mode of quenching legal lust,
A Roué takes unto Himself a Wife:
'Tis Cheaper when the bones begin to rust,
And there's no other Woman you can trust;
5   But, mind you, in return, Law says you must
    Provide her with the physical means of life:
And then the blindest beast may wallow and roll;

The twain are One flesh, never mind the Soul:
You may not cruelly beat her, but are free
10   To violate the life in sanctuary;
In virgin soil renew old seeds of Crime
To blast eternity as well as time:
    She must show black and blue, or no divorce
    Is granted by the Law of Physical Force.
—1889

Womankind

Dear things! we would not have you learn too
    much—
    Your Ignorance is so charming! We've a notion
That greater knowledge might not lend you such
    Sure aid to blind obedience and devotion.
—1889

George Meredith
1828 – 1909

Born the son of a tailor and naval outfitter in Portsmouth, George Meredith was educated in Germany. On returning to England, Meredith initially set out to study law, but soon turned to literature. A novelist, poet, journalist, and reader for major publishers, Meredith is one of the major literary figures of late Victorian England, though his direct influence was subtle and circumscribed. Although Meredith was publishing by 1851, he did not win admirers until writing his novel, *The Ordeal of Richard Feverel* (1859), and producing his most famous volume of poems, *Modern Love* (1862). His reputation this century has probably suffered more than those of other major Victorian figures. But his interest in psychological exploration, his provocative character depictions (especially of women), and his support from other Victorians (Thomas Hardy, William Ernest Henley, and Robert Louis Stevenson) clearly indicate that Meredith was an influential and important figure of his age.

❧❧❧

Modern Love

I

By this he knew she wept with waking eyes:
That, at his hand's light quiver by her head,
The strange low sobs that shook their common bed,
Were called into her with a sharp surprise,
5 And strangled mute, like little gaping snakes,
Dreadfully venomous to him. She lay
Stone-still, and the long darkness flowed away
With muffled pulses. Then, as midnight makes
Her giant heart of Memory and Tears
10 Drink the pale drug of silence, and so beat
Sleep's heavy measure, they from head to feet
Were moveless, looking through their dead black
        years,
By vain regret scrawled over the blank wall.
Like sculptured effigies they might be seen
15 Upon their marriage-tomb, the sword between;
Each wishing for the sword that severs all.

II

It ended, and the morrow brought the task.
Her eyes were guilty gates, that let him in
By shutting all too zealous for their sin:
Each sucked a secret, and each wore a mask.
5 But, oh, the bitter taste her beauty had!
He sickened as at breath of poison-flowers:
A languid humour stole among the hours,
And if their smiles encountered, he went mad
And raged deep inward, till the light was brown
10 Before his vision, and the world forgot,
Looked wicked as some old dull murder-spot.
A star with lurid beams, she seemed to crown
The pit of infamy: and then again
He fainted on his vengefulness, and strove
15 To ape the magnanimity of love,
And smote himself, a shuddering heap of pain.

III

This was the woman; what now of the man?
But pass him. If he comes beneath a heel,
He shall be crushed until he cannot feel,
Or, being callous, haply till he can.
5 But he is nothing:—nothing? Only mark
The rich light striking out from her on him!
Ha! what a sense it is when her eyes swim
Across the man she singles, leaving dark
All else! Lord God, who mad'st the thing so fair,
10 See that I am drawn to her even now!
It cannot be such harm on her cool brow
To put a kiss? Yet if I meet him there!

But she is mine! Ah, no! I know too well
I claim a star whose light is overcast:
15 I claim a phantom-woman in the Past.
The hour has struck, though I heard not the bell!

IV

All other joys of life he strove to warm,
And magnify, and catch them to his lip:
But they had suffered shipwreck with the ship,
And gazed upon him sallow from the storm.
5 Or if Delusion came, 'twas but to show
The coming minute mock the one that went.
Cold as a mountain in its star-pitched tent,
Stood high Philosophy, less friend than foe:
Whom self-caged Passion, from its prison-bars,
10 Is always watching with a wondering hate.
Not till the fire is dying in the grate,
Look we for any kinship with the stars.
Oh, wisdom never comes when it is gold,
And the great price we pay for it full worth:
15 We have it only when we are half-earth.
Little avails that coinage to the old!

V

A message from her set his brain aflame.
A world of household matters filled her mind,
Wherein he saw hypocrisy designed:
She treated him as something that is tame,
5 And but at other provocation bites.
Familiar was her shoulder in the glass,
Through that dark rain: yet it may come to pass
That a changed eye finds such familiar sights
More keenly tempting than new loveliness.
10 The "What has been" a moment seemed to his own:
The splendours, mysteries, dearer because known,
Nor less divine: Love's inmost sacredness,
Called to him, "Come!"—In his restraining start,
Eyes nurtured to be looked at, scarce could see
15 A wave of the great waves of Destiny
Convulsed at a checked impulse of the heart.

VI

It chanced his lips did meet her forehead cool.
She had no blush, but slanted down her eye.
20 Shamed nature, then, confesses love can die:
And most she punishes the tender fool
Who will believe what honours her the most!
Dead! is it dead? She has a pulse, and flow
Of tears, the price of blood-drops, as I know,
25 For whom the midnight sobs around Love's ghost,
Since then I heard her, and so will sob on.
The love is here; it has but changed its aim.
O bitter barren woman! what's the name?
The name, the name, the new name thou hast won?
30 Behold me striking the world's coward stroke!
That will I not do, though the sting is dire.
—Beneath the surface this, while by the fire
They sat, she laughing at a quiet joke.

VII

She issues radiant from her dressing-room,
Like one prepared to scale an upper sphere:
—By stirring up a lower, much I fear!
How deftly that oiled barber lays his bloom!
5 That long-shanked dapper Cupid[1] with frisked
     curls,
Can make known women torturingly fair;
The gold-eyed serpent dwelling in rich hair,
Awakes beneath his magic whisks and twirls.
His art can take the eyes from out my head,
10 Until I see with eyes of other men;
While deeper knowledge crouches in its den,
And sends a spark up:—is it true we are wed?
Yea! filthiness of body is most vile,
But faithlessness of heart I do hold worse.
15 The former, it were not so great a curse
To read on the steel-mirror of her smile.

---

[1] the Roman god of love, usually depicted as a young boy.

VIII

Yet it was plain she struggled, and that salt
Of righteous feeling made her pitiful.
Poor twisting worm, so queenly beautiful!
Where came the cleft between us? whose the fault?
5 My tears are on thee, that have rarely dropped
As balm for any bitter wound of mine:
My breast will open for thee at a sign!
But, no: we are two reed-pipes, coarsely stopped:
The God once filled them with his mellow breath;
10 And they were music till he flung them down,
Used! used! Hear now the discord-loving clown
Puff his gross spirit in them, worse than death!
I do not know myself without thee more:
In this unholy battle I grow base:
15 If the same soul be under the same face,
Speak, and a taste of that old time restore!

IX

He felt the wild beast in him betweenwhiles
So masterfully rude, that he would grieve
To see the helpless delicate thing receive
His guardianship through certain dark defiles.
5 Had he not teeth to rend, and hunger too?
But still he spared her. Once: "Have you no fear?"
He said; 'twas dusk; she in his grasp; none near.
She laughed: "No, surely; am I not with you?"
And uttering that soft starry "you," she leaned
10 Her gentle body near him, looking up;
And from her eyes, as from a poison-cup,
He drank until the flittering eyelids screened.
Devilish malignant witch! and oh, young beam
Of heaven's circle-glory! Here thy shape
15 To squeeze like an intoxicating grape—
I might, and yet thou goest safe, supreme.

X

But where began the change; and what's my crime?
The wretch condemned, who has not been arraigned,
Chafes at his sentence. Shall I, unsustained,
Drag on Love's nerveless body thro' all time?

5 I must have slept, since now I wake. Prepare,
You lovers, to know Love a thing of moods:
Not like hard life, of laws. In Love's deep woods,
I dreamt of loyal Life:—the offence is there!
Love's jealous woods about the sun are curled;
10 At least, the sun far brighter there did beam.—
My crime is, that the puppet of a dream,
I plotted to be worthy of the world.
Oh, had I with my darling helped to mince
The facts of life, you still had seen me go
15 With hindward feather and with forward toe,
Her much-adored delightful Fairy Prince!

XI

Out in the yellow meadows, where the bee
Hums by us with the honey of the Spring,
And showers of sweet notes from the larks on wing,
Are dropping like a noon-dew, wander we.
5 Or is it now? or was it then? for now,
As then, the larks from running rings pour showers:
The golden foot of May is on the flowers,
And friendly shadows dance upon her brow.
What's this, when Nature swears there is no change
10 To challenge eyesight? Now, as then, the grace
Of heaven seems holding earth in its embrace.
Nor eyes, nor heart, has she to feel it strange?
Look, woman, in the West. There wilt thou see
An amber cradle near the sun's decline:
15 Within it, featured even in death divine,
Is lying a dead infant, slain by thee.

XII

Not solely that the Future she destroys,
And the fair life which in the distance lies
For all men, beckoning out from dim rich skies:
Nor that the passing hour's supporting joys
5 Have lost the keen-edged flavour, which begat
Distinction in old times, and still should breed
Sweet Memory, and Hope,—earth's modest seed,
And heaven's high-prompting: not that the world is
  flat

Since that soft-luring creature I embraced,
10 Among the children of Illusion went:
Methinks with all this loss I were content,
If the mad Past, on which my foot is based,
Were firm, or might be blotted; but the whole
Of life is mixed: the mocking Past will stay:
15 And if I drink oblivion of a day,
So shorten I the stature of my soul.

XIII

"I play for Seasons; not Eternities!"
Says Nature, laughing on her way. "So must
All those whose stake is nothing more than dust!"
And lo, she wins, and of her harmonies
5 She is full sure! Upon her dying rose,
She drops a look of fondness, and goes by,
Scarce any retrospection in her eye;
For she the laws of growth most deeply knows,
Whose hands bear, here, a seed-bag—there, an urn.
10 Pledged she herself to aught, 'twould mark her end!
This lesson of our only visible friend,
Can we not teach our foolish hearts to learn?
Yes! yes!—but, oh, our human rose is fair
Surpassingly! Lose calmly Love's great bliss,
15 When the renewed for ever of a kiss
Whirls life within the shower of loosened hair!

XIV

What soul would bargain for a cure that brings
Contempt the nobler agony to kill?
Rather let me bear on the bitter ill,
And strike this rusty bosom with new stings!
5 It seems there is another veering fit,
Since on a gold-haired lady's eyeballs pure,
I looked with little prospect of a cure,
The while her mouth's red bow loosed shafts of wit.
Just heaven! can it be true that jealousy
10 Has decked the woman thus? and does her head
Swim somewhat for possession forfeited?
Madam, you teach me many things that be.
I open an old book, and there I find,

That "Women still may love whom they deceive."
15 Such love I prize not, madam: by your leave,
The game you play at is not to my mind.

XV

I think she sleeps: it must be sleep, when low
Hangs that abandoned arm toward the floor;
The face turned with it. Now make fast the door.
Sleep on: it is your husband, not your foe.
5 The Poet's black stage-lion of wronged love,
Frights not our modern dames:—well if he did!
Now will I pour new light upon that lid,
Full-sloping like the breasts beneath. "Sweet dove,
Your sleep is pure. Nay, pardon: I disturb.
10 I do not? good!" Her waking infant-stare
Grows woman to the burden my hands bear:
Her own handwriting to me when no curb
Was left on Passion's tongue. She trembles through;
A woman's tremble—the whole instrument:—
15 I show another letter lately sent.
The words are very like: the name is new.

XVI

In our old shipwrecked days there was an hour,
When in the firelight steadily aglow,
Joined slackly, we beheld the red chasm grow
Among the clicking coals. Our library-bower
5 That eve was left to us: and hushed we sat
As lovers to whom Time is whispering.
From sudden-opened doors we heard them sing:
The nodding elders mixed good wine with chat.
Well knew we that Life's greatest treasure lay
10 With us, and of it was our talk. "Ah, yes!
Love dies!" I said: I never thought it less.
She yearned to me that sentence to unsay.
Then when the fire domed blackening, I found
Her cheek was salt against my kiss, and swift
15 Up the sharp scale of sobs her breast did lift:—
Now am I haunted by that taste! that sound!

XVII

At dinner, she is hostess, I am host.
Went the feast ever cheerfuller? She keeps
The Topic over intellectual deeps
In buoyancy afloat. They see no ghost.
5 With sparkling surface-eyes we ply the ball:
It is in truth a most contagious game:
HIDING THE SKELETON, shall be its name.
Such play as this, the devils might appal!
But here's the greater wonder; in that we
10 Enamoured of an acting nought can tire,
Each other, like true hypocrites, admire;
Warm-lighted looks, Love's ephemerioe,[1]
Shoot gaily o'er the dishes and the wine.
We waken envy of our happy lot.
15 Fast, sweet, and golden, shows the marriage-knot.
Dear guests, you now have seen Love's corpse-light
   shine.

XVIII

Here Jack and Tom are paired with Moll and Meg.
Curved open to the river-reach is seen
A country merry-making on the green.
Fair space for signal shakings of the leg.
5 That little screwy fiddler from his booth,
Whence flows one nut-brown stream, commands
   the joints
Of all who caper here at various points.
I have known rustic revels in my youth:
The May-fly[2] pleasures of a mind at ease.
10 An early goddess was a country lass:
A charmed Amphion-oak[3] she tripped the grass.
What life was that I lived? The life of these?
Heaven keep them happy! Nature they seem near.
They must, I think, be wiser than I am;

---

[1] ephemera, or fleeting aspects.

[2] a short-lived insect.

[3] Amphion was the son of Zeus and Antiope, whose lyre-playing caused
the stones and trees to dance spontaneously. The city of Thebes is said
to have been built by stones forming themselves into walls and buildings
as Amphion played.

15 They have the secret of the bull and lamb.
'Tis true that when we trace its source, 'tis beer.

XIX

No state is enviable. To the luck alone
Of some few favoured men I would put claim.
I bleed, but her who wounds I will not blame.
Have I not felt her heart as 'twere my own
5 Beat thro' me? could I hurt her? heaven and hell!
But I could hurt her cruelly! Can I let
My Love's old time-piece to another set,
Swear it can't stop, and must for ever swell?
Sure, that's one way Love drifts into the mart
10 Where goat-legged buyers throng. I see not plain:—
My meaning is, it must not be again.
Great God! the maddest gambler throws his heart.
If any state be enviable on earth,
'Tis yon born idiot's, who, as days go by,
15 Still rubs his hands before him, like a fly,
In a queer sort of meditative mirth.

XX

I am not of those miserable males
Who sniff at vice and, daring not to snap,
Do therefore hope for heaven. I take the hap
Of all my deeds. The wind that fills my sails,
5 Propels; but I am helmsman. Am I wrecked,
I know the devil has sufficient weight
To bear: I lay it not on him, or fate.
Besides, he's damned. That man I do suspect
A coward, who would burden the poor deuce
10 With what ensues from his own slipperiness.
I have just found a wanton-scented tress
In an old desk, dusty for lack of use.
Of days and nights it is demonstrative,
That, like some aged star, gleam luridly.
15 If for those times I must ask charity,
Have I not any charity to give?

XXI

We three are on the cedar-shadowed lawn;
My friend being third. He who at love once laughed,
Is in the weak rib by a fatal shaft
Struck through, and tells his passion's bashful dawn
5 And radiant culmination, glorious crown,
When "this" she said: went "thus": most wondrous
    she.
Our eyes grow white, encountering: that we are
    three,
Forgetful; then together we look down.
But he demands our blessing; is convinced
10 That words of wedded lovers must bring good.
We question; if we dare! or if we should!
And pat him, with light laugh. We have not winced.
Next, she has fallen. Fainting points the sign
To happy things in wedlock. When she wakes,
15 She looks the star that thro' the cedar shakes:
Her lost moist hand clings mortally to mine.

XXII

What may the woman labour to confess?
There is about her mouth a nervous twitch.
'Tis something to be told, or hidden:—which?
I get a glimpse of hell in this mild guess.
5 She has desires of touch, as if to feel
That all the household things are things she knew.
She stops before the glass. What sight in view?
A face that seems the latest to reveal!
For she turns from it hastily, and tossed
10 Irresolute, steals shadow-like to where
I stand; and wavering pale before me there,
Her tears fall still as oak-leaves after frost.
She will not speak. I will not ask. We are
League-sundered by the silent gulf between.
15 You burly lovers on the village green,
Yours is a lower, and a happier star!

XXIII

'Tis Christmas weather, and a country house
Receives us: rooms are full: we can but get
An attic-crib. Such lovers will not fret
At that, it is half-said. The great carouse
5 Knocks hard upon the midnight's hollow door,
But when I knock at hers, I see the pit.
Why did I come here in that dullard fit?
I enter, and lie couched upon the floor.
Passing, I caught the coverlet's quick beat:—
10 Come, Shame, burn to my soul! and Pride, and
    Pain—
Foul demons that have tortured me, enchain!
Out in the freezing darkness the lambs bleat.
The small bird stiffens in the low starlight.
I know not how, but shuddering as I slept,
15 I dreamed a banished angel to me crept:
My feet were nourished on her breasts all night.

XXIV

The misery is greater, as I live!
To know her flesh so pure, so keen her sense,
That she does penance now for no offence,
Save against Love. The less can I forgive!
5 The less can I forgive, though I adore
That cruel lovely pallor which surrounds
Her footsteps; and the low vibrating sounds
That come on me, as from a magic shore.
Low are they, but most subtle to find out
10 The shrinking soul. Madam, 'tis understood
When women play upon their womanhood;
It means, a Season gone. And yet I doubt
But I am duped. That nun-like look waylays
My fancy. Oh! I do but wait a sign!
15 Pluck out the eyes of pride! thy mouth to mine!
Never! though I die thirsting. Go thy ways!

XXV

You like not that French novel? Tell me why.
You think it quite unnatural. Let us see.
The actors are, it seems, the usual three:
Husband, and wife, and lover. She—but fie!
5 In England we'll not hear of it. Edmond,
The lover, her devout chagrin doth share;

Blanc-mange and absinthe are his penitent fare,
Till his pale aspect makes her over-fond:
So, to preclude fresh sin, he tries rosbif.[1]
10 Meantime the husband is no more abused:
Auguste forgives her ere the tear is used.
Then hangeth all on one tremendous IF:—
If she will choose between them. She does choose;
And takes her husband, like a proper wife.
15 Unnatural? My dear, these things are life:
And life, some think, is worthy of the Muse.

XXVI

Love ere he bleeds, an eagle in high skies,
Has earth beneath his wings: from reddened eve
He views the rosy dawn. In vain they weave
The fatal web below while far he flies.
5 But when the arrow strikes him, there's a change.
He moves but in the track of his spent pain,
Whose red drops are the links of a harsh chain,
Binding him to the ground, with narrow range.
A subtle serpent then has Love become.
10 I had the eagle in my bosom erst:
Henceforward with the serpent I am cursed.
I can interpret where the mouth is dumb.
Speak, and I see the side-lie of a truth.
Perchance my heart may pardon you this deed:
15 But be no coward:—you that made Love bleed,
You must bear all the venom of his tooth!

XXVII

Distraction is the panacea, Sir!
I hear my oracle of Medicine say.
Doctor! that same specific yesterday
I tried, and the result will not deter
5 A second trial. Is the devil's line
Of golden hair, or raven black, composed?
And does a cheek, like any sea-shell rosed,
Or clear as widowed sky, seem most divine?
No matter, so I taste forgetfulness.

_____
[1] the French name for roast beef.

10 And if the devil snare me, body and mind,
Here gratefully I score:—he seemëd kind,
When not a soul would comfort my distress!
O sweet new world, in which I rise new made!
O Lady, once I gave love: now I take!
15 Lady, I must be flattered. Shouldst thou wake
The passion of a demon, be not afraid.

XXVIII

I must be flattered. The imperious
Desire speaks out. Lady, I am content
To play with you the game of Sentiment,
And with you enter on paths perilous;
5 But if across your beauty I throw light,
To make it threefold, it must be all mine.
First secret; then avowed. For I must shine
Envied,—I, lessened in my proper sight!
Be watchful of your beauty, Lady dear!
10 How much hangs on that lamp you cannot tell.
Most earnestly I pray you, tend it well:
And men shall see me as a burning sphere;
And men shall mark you eyeing me, and groan
To be the God of such a grand sunflower!
15 I feel the promptings of Satanic power,
While you do homage unto me alone.

XXIX

Am I failing? For no longer can I cast
A glory round about this head of gold.
Glory she wears, but springing from the mould;
Not like the consecration of the Past!
5 Is my soul beggared? Something more than earth
I cry for still: I cannot be at peace
In having Love upon a mortal lease.
I cannot take the woman at her worth!
Where is the ancient wealth wherewith I clothed
10 Our human nakedness, and could endow
With spiritual splendour a white brow
That else had grinned at me the fact I loathed?
A kiss is but a kiss now! and no wave
Of a great flood that whirls me to the sea.

15 But, as you will! we'll sit contentedly,
    And eat our pot of honey on the grave.

                    XXX

    What are we first? First, animals; and next
    Intelligences at a leap; on whom
    Pale lies the distant shadow of the tomb,
    And all that draweth on the tomb for text.
5   Into which state comes Love, the crowning sun:
    Beneath whose light the shadow loses form.
    We are the lords of life, and life is warm.
    Intelligence and instinct now are one.
    But Nature says: "My children most they seem
10 When they least know me: therefore I decree
    That they shall suffer." Swift doth young Love flee,
    And we stand wakened, shivering from our dream.
    Then if we study Nature we are wise.
    Thus do the few who live but with the day:
15 The scientific animals are they.—
    Lady, this is my sonnet to your eyes.

                    XXXI

    This golden head has wit in it. I live
    Again, and a far higher life, near her.
    Some women like a young philosopher;
    Perchance because he is diminutive.
5   For woman's manly god must not exceed
    Proportions of the natural nursing size.
    Great poets and great sages draw no prize
    With women: but the little lap-dog breed,
    Who can be hugged, or on a mantel-piece
10 Perched up for adoration, these obtain
    Her homage. And of this we men are vain?
    Of this! 'Tis ordered for the world's increase!
    Small flattery! Yet she has that rare gift
    To beauty, Common Sense. I am approved.
15 It is not half so nice as being loved,
    And yet I do prefer it. What's my drift?

                    XXXII

    Full faith I have she holds that rarest gift
    To beauty, Common Sense. To see her lie
    With her fair visage an inverted sky
    Bloom-covered, while the underlids uplift,
5   Would almost wreck the faith; but when her mouth
    (Can it kiss sweetly? sweetly!) would address
    The inner me that thirsts for her no less,
    And has so long been languishing in drouth,
    I feel that I am matched; that I am man!
10 One restless corner of my heart or head,
    That holds a dying something never dead,
    Still frets, though Nature giveth all she can.
    It means, that woman is not, I opine,
    Her sex's antidote. Who seeks the asp
15 For serpents' bites? 'Twould calm me could I clasp
    Shrieking Bacchantes[1] with their souls of wine!

                    XXXIII

    "In Paris, at the Louvre, there have I seen
    The sumptuously-feathered angel pierce
    Prone Lucifer, descending.[2] Looked he fierce,
    Showing the fight a fair one? Too serene!
5   The young Pharsalians[3] did not disarray
    Less willingly their locks of floating silk:
    That suckling mouth of his, upon the milk
    Of heaven might still be feasting through the fray.
    Oh, Raphael! when men the Fiend do fight,
10 They conquer not upon such easy terms.
    Half serpent in the struggle grow these worms.
    And does he grow half human, all is right."
    This to my Lady in a distant spot,
    Upon the theme: *While mind is mastering clay,*

---

[1] the female followers of Bacchus, god of wine, whose revelries included shrieking and uninhibited dancing.

[2] The painting referred to is "St. Michael," by Raphael (1483–1520). Although Lucifer means "lightbringer," and referred originally to Venus, the morning star, the name has come to be applied to Satan, whose pride prompted him to set himself up as a star in heaven.

[3] the followers of Julius Caesar at the Battle of Pharsalia in which Caesar claimed a decisive victory despite being outnumbered.

15 *Gross clay invades it.* If the spy you play,
My wife, read this! Strange love talk, is it not?

xxxiv

Madam would speak with me. So, now it comes:
The Deluge or else Fire! She's well; she thanks
My husbandship. Our chain on silence clanks.
Time leers between, above his twiddling thumbs.
5 Am I quite well? Most excellent in health!
The journals, too, I diligently peruse.
Vesuvius[1] is expected to give news:
Niagara[2] is no noisier. By stealth
Our eyes dart scrutinizing snakes. She's glad
10 I'm happy, says her quivering under-lip.
"And are not you?' "How can I be?" "Take ship!
For happiness is somewhere to be had."
"Nowhere for me!" Her voice is barely heard.
I am not melted, and make no pretence.
15 With commonplace I freeze her, tongue and sense.
Niagara or Vesuvius is deferred.

xxxv

It is no vulgar nature I have wived.
Secretive, sensitive, she takes a wound
Deep to her soul, as if the sense had swooned,
And not a thought of vengeance had survived.
5 No confidences has she: but relief
Must come to one whose suffering is acute.
O have a care of natures that are mute!
They punish you in acts: their steps are brief.
What is she doing? What does she demand
10 From Providence or me? She is not one
Long to endure this torpidly, and shun
The drugs that crowd about a woman's hand.
At Forfeits during snow we played, and I
Must kiss her. "Well performed!" I said: then she:
15 "'Tis hardly worth the money, you agree?"
Save her? What for? To act this wedded lie!

---

1 Mt. Vesuvius, a volcano near Naples.

2 Niagara Falls, in Ontario, Canada and New York state.

xxxvi

My Lady unto Madam makes her bow.
The charm of women is, that even while
You're probed by them for tears, you yet may smile,
Nay, laugh outright, as I have done just now.
5 The interview was gracious: they anoint
(To me aside) each other with fine praise:
Discriminating compliments they raise,
That hit with wondrous aim on the weak point:
My Lady's nose of Nature might complain.
10 It is not fashioned aptly to express
Her character of large-browed steadfastness.
But Madam says: Thereof she may be vain!
Now, Madam's faulty feature is a glazed
And inaccessible eye, that has soft fires,
15 Wide gates, at love-time only. This admires
My Lady. At the two I stand amazed.

xxxvii

Along the garden terrace, under which
A purple valley (lighted at its edge
By smoky torch-flame on the long cloud-ledge
Whereunder dropped the chariot), glimmers rich,
5 A quiet company we pace, and wait
The dinner-bell in prae-digestive calm.
So sweet up violet banks the Southern balm
Breathes round, we care not if the bell be late:
Though here and there grey seniors question Time
10 In irritable coughings. With slow foot
The low rosed moon, the face of Music mute,
Begins among her silent bars to climb.
As in and out, in silvery dusk, we thread,
I hear the laugh of Madam, and discern
15 My Lady's heel before me at each turn.
Our tragedy, is it alive or dead?

xxxviii

Give to imagination some pure light
In human form to fix it, or you shame
The devils with that hideous human game:—
Imagination urging appetite!

5 Thus fallen have earth's greatest Gogmagogs,[1]
Who dazzle us, whom we can not revere:
Imagination is the charioteer
That, in default of better, drives the hogs.
So, therefore, my dear Lady, let me love!
10 My soul is arrowy to the light in you.
You know me that I never can renew
The bond that woman broke: what would you have?
'Tis Love, or Vileness! not a choice between,
Save petrifaction! What does Pity here?
15 She killed a thing, and now it's dead, 'tis dear.
Oh, when you counsel me, think what you mean!

XXXIX

She yields: my Lady in her noblest mood
Has yielded: she, my golden-crownëd rose!
The bride of every sense! more sweet than those
Who breathe the violet breath of maidenhood.
5 O visage of still music in the sky!
Soft moon! I feel thy song, my fairest friend!
True harmony within can apprehend
Dumb harmony without. And hark! 'tis nigh!
Belief has struck the note of sound: a gleam
10 Of living silver shows me where she shook
Her long white fingers down the shadowy brook,
That sings her song, half-waking, half in dream.
What two come here to mar this heavenly tune?
A man is one: the woman bears my name,
15 And honour. Their hands touch! Am I still tame?
God, what a dancing spectre seems the moon!

XL

I bade my Lady think what she might mean.
Know I my meaning, I? Can I love one,

---

[1] In British legend, Gog and Magog were monstrous giants who were taken prisoner and forced to act as porters at the royal palace. Their statues have stood at the Guildhall since the time of Henry V. The figures carved in 1708 by Richard Saunders (to replace a pair destroyed in the Great Fire of London, September 1666) would have been known by Meredith, but were themselves destroyed in an air raid in 1940. In Revelation 20:8, Gog and Magog represent all future enemies of the Kingdom of God.

And yet be jealous of another? None
Commits such folly. Terrible Love, I ween,
5 Has might, even dead, half sighing to upheave
The lightless seas of selfishness amain:
Seas that in a man's heart have no rain
To fall and still them. Peace can I achieve,
By turning to this fountain-source of woe,
10 This woman, who's to Love as fire to wood?
She breathed the violet breath of maidenhood
Against my kisses once! but I say, No!
The thing is mocked at! Helplessly afloat,
I know not what I do, whereto I strive,
15 The dread that my old love may be alive,
Has seized my nursling new love by the throat.

XLI

How many a thing which we cast to the ground,
When others pick it up becomes a gem!
We grasp at all the wealth it is to them;
And by reflected light its worth is found.
5 Yet for us still 'tis nothing! and that zeal
Of false appreciation quickly fades.
This truth is little known to human shades,
How rare from their own instinct 'tis to feel!
They waste the soul with spurious desire,
10 That is not the ripe flame upon the bough.
We two have taken up a lifeless vow
To rob a living passion: dust for fire!
Madam is grave, and eyes the clock that tells
Approaching midnight. We have struck despair
15 Into two hearts. O, look we like a pair
Who for fresh nuptials joyfully yield all else?

XLII

I am to follow her. There is much grace
In women when thus bent on martyrdom.
They think that dignity of soul may come,
Perchance, with dignity of body. Base!
5 But I was taken by that air of cold
And statuesque sedateness, when she said
"I'm going"; lit a taper, bowed her head,

And went, as with the stride of Pallas[1] bold.
Fleshly indifference horrible! The hands
10 Of Time now signal: O, she's safe from me!
Within those secret walls what do I see?
Where first she set the taper down she stands:
Not Pallas: Hebe[2] shamed! Thoughts black as death,
Like a stirred pool in sunshine break. Her wrists
15 I catch: she faltering, as she half resists,
"You love...? love...? love...?" all on an indrawn
        breath.

XLIII

Mark where the pressing wind shoots javelin-like,
Its skeleton shadow on the broad-backed wave!
Here is a fitting spot to dig Love's grave;
Here where the ponderous breakers plunge and
        strike,
5 And dart their hissing tongues high up the sand:
In hearing of the ocean, and in sight
Of those ribbed wind-streaks running into white.
If I the death of Love had deeply planned,
I never could have made is half so sure,
10 As by the unblest kisses which upbraid
The full-waked sense; or failing that, degrade!
'Tis morning: but no morning can restore
What we have forfeited. I see no sin:
The wrong is mixed. In tragic life, God wot,
15 No villain need be! Passions spin the plot:
We are betrayed by what is false within.

XLIV

They say, that Pity in Love's service dwells,
A porter at the rosy temple's gate.
I missed him going: but it is my fate
To come upon him now beside his wells;
5 Whereby I know that I Love's temple leave,

And that the purple doors have closed behind.
Poor soul! if in those early days unkind,
Thy power to sting had been but power to grieve,
We now might with an equal spirit meet,
10 And not be matched like innocence and vice.
She for the Temple's worship has paid price,
And takes the coin of Pity as a cheat.
She sees through simulation to the bone:
What's best in her impels her to the worst:
15 Never, she cries, shall Pity soothe Love's thirst,
Or foul hypocrisy for truth atone!

XLV

It is the season of the sweet wild rose,
My Lady's emblem in the heart of me!
So golden-crownëd shines she gloriously,
And with that softest dream of blood she glows:
5 Mild as an evening heaven round Hesper[3] bright!
I pluck the flower, and smell it, and revive
The time when in her eyes I stood alive.
I seem to look upon it out of Night.
Here's Madam, stepping hastily. Her whims
10 Bid her demand the flower, which I let drop.
As I proceed, I feel her sharply stop,
And crush it under heel with trembling limbs.
She joins me in a cat-like way, and talks
Of company, and even condescends
15 To utter laughing scandal of old friends.
These are the summer days, and these our walks.

XLVI

At last we parley: we so strangely dumb
In such a close communion! It befell
About the sounding of the Matin-bell,[4]
And lo! her place was vacant, and the hum
5 Of loneliness was round me. Then I rose,
And my disordered brain did guide my foot
To that old wood where our first love-salute

---

[1] Pallas Athene, another name for Minerva, the Roman goddess of
wisdom and the arts. She is said to have sprung fully armed from the
head of Jupiter.

[2] the goddess of youth, accused of immodesty by Jupiter and
consequently deprived of her role of cupbearer to the gods.

[3] Venus, the evening star.

[4] the bell announcing the start of Morning Prayer.

Was interchanged: the source of many throes!
There did I see her, not alone. I moved
10 Toward her, and made proffer of my arm.
She took it simply, with no rude alarm;
And that disturbing shadow passed reproved.
I felt the pained speech coming, and declared
My firm belief in her, ere she could speak.
15 A ghastly morning came into her cheek,
While with a widening soul on me she stared.

XLVII

We saw the swallows gathering in the sky,
And in the osier-isle we heard them noise.
We had not to look back on summer joys,
Or forward to a summer of bright dye:
5 But in the largeness of the evening earth
Our spirits grew as we went side by side.
The hour became her husband and my bride.
Love that had robbed us so, thus blessed our dearth!
The pilgrims of the year waxed very loud
10 In multitudinous chatterings, as the flood
Full brown came from the West, and like pale blood
Expanded to the upper crimson cloud.
Love that had robbed us of immortal things,
This little moment mercifully gave,
15 Where I have seen across the twilight wave
The swan sail with her young beneath her wings.

XLVIII

Their sense is with their senses all mixed in,
Destroyed by subtleties these women are!
More brain, O Lord, more brain! or we shall mar
Utterly this fair garden we might win.
5 Behold! I looked for peace, and thought it near.
Our inmost hearts had opened, each to each.
We drank the pure daylight of honest speech.
Alas! that was the fatal draught, I fear.
For when of my lost Lady came the word,
10 This woman, O this agony of flesh!
Jealous devotion bade her break the mesh,
That I might seek that other like a bird.

I do adore the nobleness! despise
The act! She has gone forth, I know not where.
15 Will the hard world my sentience of her share?
I feel the truth; so let the world surmise.

XLIX

He found her by the ocean's moaning verge,
Nor any wicked change in her discerned;
And she believed his old love had returned,
Which was her exultation, and her scourge.
5 She took her hand, and walked with him, and seemed
The wife he sought, though shadow-like and dry.
She had one terror, lest her heart should sigh,
And tell her loudly she no longer dreamed.
She dared not say, "This is my breast: look in."
10 But there's a strength to help the desperate weak.
That night he learned how silence best can speak
The awful things when Pity pleads for Sin.
About the middle of the night her call
Was heard, and he came wondering to the bed.
15 "Now kiss me, dear! it may be, now!" she said.
Lethe[1] had passed those lips, and he knew all.

L

Thus piteously Love closed what he begat:
The union of this ever-diverse pair!
These two were rapid falcons in a snare,
Condemned to do the flitting of the bat.
5 Lovers beneath the singing sky of May,
They wandered once; clear as the dew on flowers:
But they fed not on the advancing hours:
Their hearts held cravings for the buried day.
Then each applied to each that fatal knife,
10 Deep questioning, which probes to endless dole.
Ah, what a dusty answer gets the soul
When hot for certainties in this our life!—
In tragic hints here see what evermore
Moves dark as yonder midnight ocean's force,

---

[1] one of the rivers of Hades, from which the souls of the dead drink in
order to forget their earthly lives.

15 Thundering like ramping hosts of warrior horse,
To throw that faint thin line upon the shore!
—1862

Lucifer in Starlight [1]

On a starred night Prince Lucifer uprose.
Tired of his dark dominion, swung the fiend
Above the rolling ball, in cloud part screened,
Where sinners hugged their specter of repose.
5 Poor prey to his hot fit of pride were those.

And now upon his western wing he leaned,
Now his huge bulk o'er Afric's sands careened,
Now the black planet shadowed Arctic snows.
Soaring through wider zones that pricked his scars
10 With memory of the old revolt from Awe,
He reached a middle height, and at the stars,
Which are the brain of heaven, he looked, and sank.
Around the ancient track marched, rank on rank,
The army of unalterable law.
—1883

---

[1] Lucifer ("light-bringer"), the morning-star, is a name given to Satan. The "scars" (1. 9) are those which resulted from the wounds suffered by Satan during his rebellion against God and his expulsion from Heaven.

Dante Gabriel Rossetti
1828 – 1882

Although he was the son of an Italian political refugee, Dante Gabriel Rossetti (born Gabriel Charles) never pursued a political life, preferring instead to concentrate on artistic endeavours. Rossetti demonstrated extraordinary talent in both painting and poetry. His interest in art developed, in part, from his study of Keats's poems and letters, in which a sensuous response to beauty, through colour, texture, words, and women, functioned as a source of inspiration. With Ford Madox Brown, John Everett Millais, and William Holman Hunt, Rossetti formed the Pre-Raphaelite Brotherhood in 1848 in a concerted effort to reject neoclassical conventions in favour of the simplicity and purity of pre-Renaissance art. While the diverse interests of each artist led to the break-up of the circle within a few years, the group's presence and ideas aroused immense interest and opposition during its formation and after its dissolution. Rossetti's personal view of art is one that connects the heavenly with the earthly and implicitly earthly, an artistic approach which is reflected in his poetry. "The Blessed Damozel" was first published in the Pre-Raphaelite journal *The Germ* in 1850. *Poems by D.G. Rossetti*, containing the original version of *The House of Life* sonnet sequence, was published in 1871.

❧❧❧

The Blessed Damozel [1]

The blessed damozel leaned out
    From the gold bar of Heaven;
Her eyes were deeper than the depth
    Of waters stilled at even;
5 She had three lilies in her hand,
    And the stars in her hair were seven.

Her robe, ungirt from clasp to hem,
    No wrought flowers did adorn,
But a white rose of Mary's gift,
10   For service meetly worn;
Her hair that lay along her back
    Was yellow like ripe corn.

Herseemed [2] she scarce had been a day
    One of God's choristers;
15 The wonder was not yet quite gone
    From that still look of hers;

Albeit, to them she left, her day
    Had counted as ten years.

(To one, it is ten years of years.
20   …Yet now, and in this place,
Surely she leaned o'er me—her hair
    Fell all about my face…
Nothing: the autumn-fall of leaves.
    The whole years sets apace.)

25 It was the rampart of God's house
    That she was standing on;
By God built over the sheer depth
    The which is Space begun;
So high, that looking downward thence
30   She scarce could see the sun.

It lies in Heaven, across the flood
    Of ether, [3] as a bridge.
Beneath, the tides of day and night
    With flame and darkness ridge

---

[1] the Anglo-Norman form of damsel—a young unmarried woman, a maiden, a virgin.

[2] it seemed to her.

---

[3] hypothetical substance which was supposed to be diffused in space beyond the earth's atmosphere.

35 The void, as low as where this earth
    Spins like a fretful midge.[1]

Around her, lovers, newly met
    'Mid deathless love's acclaims,
Spoke evermore among themselves
40   Their heart-remembered names;
And the souls mounting up to God
    Went by her like thin flames.

And still she bowed herself and stooped
    Out of the circling charm;
45 Until her bosom must have made
    The bar she leaned on warm,
And the lilies lay as if asleep
    Along her bended arm.

From the fixed place of Heaven she saw
50   Time like a pulse shake fierce
Through all the worlds. Her gaze still strove
    Within the gulf to pierce
Its path; and now she spoke as when
    The stars sang in their spheres.

55 The sun was gone now; the curled moon
    Was like a little feather
Fluttering far down the gulf; and now
    She spoke through the still weather.
Her voice was like the voice the stars
60   Had when they sang together.[2]

(Ah sweet! Even now, in that bird's song,
    Strove not her accents there,
Fain to be hearkened? When those bells
    Possessed the mid-day air,
65 Strove not her steps to reach my side
    Down all the echoing stair?)

"I wish that he were come to me,
    For he will come," she said.
"Have I not prayed in Heaven?—on earth,
70   Lord, Lord, has he not pray'd?
Are not two prayers a perfect strength?
    And shall I feel afraid?

"When round his head the aureole clings,
    And he is clothed in white,
75 I'll take his hand and go with him
    To the deep wells of light;
As unto a stream we will step down,
    And bathe there in God's sight.

"We two will stand beside that shrine,
80   Occult, withheld, untrod,
Whose lamps are stirred continually
    With prayer sent up to God;
And see our old prayers, granted, melt
    Each like a little cloud.

85 "We two will lie i' the shadow of
    That living mystic tree[3]
Within whose secret growth the Dove[4]
    Is sometimes felt to be,
While every leaf that His plumes touch
90   Saith His Name audibly.

"And I myself will teach to him,
    I myself, lying so,
The songs I sing here; which his voice
    Shall pause in, hushed and slow,
95 And find some knowledge at each pause,
    Or some new thing to know."

(Alas! we two, we two, thou say'st!
    Yea, one wast thou with me
That once of old. But shall God lift

---

[1] common name for a variety of small flies and insects.

[2] See Job 38.7: "When the morning stars sang together, and all the sons of God shouted for joy."

[3] See Revelation 22.2: "the tree of life" in Heaven.

[4] the Holy Spirit, Holy Ghost.

100 To endless unity
The soul whose likeness with thy soul
Was but its love for thee?)

"We two," she said, "will seek the groves
Where the lady Mary is,
105 With her five handmaidens, whose names
Are five sweet symphonies,
Cecily, Gertrude, Magdalen,
Margaret and Rosalys.

"Circlewise sit they, with bound locks
110 And foreheads garlanded;
Into the fine cloth white like flame
Weaving the golden thread,
To fashion the birth-robes for them
Who are just born, being dead.

115 "He shall fear, haply, and be dumb:
Then will I lay my cheek
To his, and tell about our love,
Not once abashed or weak:
And the dear Mother will approve
120 My pride, and let me speak.

"Herself shall bring us, hand in hand,
To Him round whom all souls
Kneel, the clear-ranged unnumbered heads
Bowed with their aureoles:
125 And angels meeting us shall sing
To their citherns and citoles.[1]

"There will I ask of Christ the Lord
Thus much for him and me:—
Only to live as once on earth
130 With Love,—only to be,
As then awhile, for ever now
Together, I and he."

She gazed and listened and then said,
Less sad of speech than mild,—
135 "All this is when he comes." She ceased.
The light thrilled towards her, fill'd
With angels in strong level flight.
Her eyes prayed, and she smil'd.

(I saw her smile.) But soon their path
140 Was vague in distant spheres:
And then she cast her arms along
The golden barriers,
And laid her face between her hands,
And wept. (I heard her tears.)
—1850 (1847)

My Sister's Sleep [2]

She fell asleep on Christmas Eve:
At length the long-ungranted shade
Of weary eyelids overweigh'd
The pain nought else might yet relieve.

5 Our mother, who had leaned all day
Over the bed from chime to chime,
Then raised herself for the first time,
And as she sat her down, did pray.

Her little work-table was spread
10 With work to finish. For the glare
Made by her candle, she had care
To work some distance from the bed.

Without, there was a cold moon up,
Of winter radiance sheer and thin;

---

[1] antique stringed instruments.

[2] The Margaret of the poem is fictive; neither of Rossetti's two sisters had died when the poem was first written and published.

15　The hollow halo it was in
　　Was like an icy crystal cup.[1]

　　Through the small room, with subtle sound
　　　　Of flame, by vents the fireshine drove[2]
　　　　And reddened. In its dim alcove
20　The mirror shed a clearness round.

　　I had been sitting up some nights,
　　　　And my tired mind felt weak and blank;
　　　　Like a sharp strengthening wine it drank
　　The stillness and the broken lights.

25　Twelve struck. That sound, by dwindling years
　　　　Heard in each hour, crept off; and then
　　　　The ruffled silence spread again,
　　Like water that a pebble stirs.

　　Our mother rose from where she sat:
30　　　Her needles, as she laid them down,
　　　　Met lightly, and her silken gown
　　Settled: no other noise than that.

　　"Glory unto the Newly Born!"[3]
　　　　So, as said angels, she did say;
35　　　Because we were in Christmas Day,
　　Though it would still be long till morn.

　　Just then in the room over us
　　　　There was a pushing back of chairs,
　　　　As some who had sat unawares
40　So late, now heard the hour, and rose.

---

[1] In early versions of the poem, the moon is "hollow, like an altar cup."
This and other revisions were made to the poem in 1869 in an attempt,
as Rossetti said in a letter, to "eliminate the religious element altogether"
from the poem.

[2] was fanned.

[3] a reference, perhaps, to the Christmas hymn "Hark, the Herald Angels
Sing."

　　With anxious softly-stepping haste
　　　　Our mother went where Margaret lay,
　　　　Fearing the sounds o'erhead—should they
　　Have broken her long watched-for rest!

45　She stooped an instant, calm, and turned;
　　　　But suddenly turned back again;
　　　　And all her features seemed in pain
　　With woe, and her eyes gazed and yearned.

　　For my part, I but hid my face,
50　　　And held my breath, and spoke no word:
　　　　There was none spoken; but I heard
　　The silence for a little space.

　　Our mother bowed herself and wept:
　　　　And both my arms fell, and I said,
55　　　"God knows I knew that she was dead."
　　And there, all white, my sister slept.

　　Then kneeling, upon Christmas morn
　　　　A little after twelve o'clock,
　　　　We said, ere the first quarter struck,
60　"Christ's blessing on the newly born!"
　　　　—1850; 1870 (1847; 1869)

Jenny

*Vengeance of Jenny's case! Fie on her! Never name
her, child!*—(Mrs. Quickly)

Lazy laughing languid Jenny,
　　Fond of a kiss and fond of a guinea,
Whose head upon my knee to-night
Rests for while, as if grown light
5　With all our dances and the sound
To which the wild tunes spun you round:
Fair Jenny mine, the thoughtless queen
Of kisses which the blush between
Could hardly make much daintier;
10　Whose eyes are as blue skies, whose hair

Is countless gold incomparable:
Fresh flower, scarce touched with signs that tell
Of Love's exuberant hotbed:—Nay,
Poor flower left torn since yesterday
15   Until to-morrow leave you bare;
Poor handful of bright spring-water
Flung in the whirlpool's shrieking face;
Poor shameful Jenny, full of grace
Thus with your head upon my knee;—
20   Whose person or whose purse may be
The lodestar of your reverie?

This room of yours, my Jenny, looks
A change from mine so full of books,
Whose serried ranks hold fast, forsooth,
25   So many captive hours of youth,—
The hours they thieve from day and night
To make one's cherished work come right,
And leave it wrong for all their theft,
Even as to-night my work was left:
30   Until I vowed that since my brain
And eyes of dancing seemed so fain,
My feet should have some dancing too:—
And thus it was I met with you.
Well, I suppose 'twas hard to part,
35   For here I am. And now, sweetheart,
You seem too tired to get to bed.

It was a careless life I led
When rooms like this were scarce so strange
Not long ago. What breeds the change,—
40   The many aims or the few years?
Because to-night it all appears
Something I do not know again.

The cloud's not danced out of my brain,—
The cloud that made it turn and swim
45   While hour by hour the books grew dim.
Why, Jenny, as I watch you there,—
For all your wealth of loosened hair,
Your silk ungirdled and unlac'd

And warm sweets open to the waist,
50   All golden in the lamplight's gleam,—
You know not what a book you seem,
Half-read by lightning in a dream!
How should you know, my Jenny? Nay,
And I should be ashamed to say:—
55   Poor beauty, so well worth a kiss!
But while my thought runs on like this
With wasteful whims more than enough,
I wonder what you're thinking of.

If of myself you think at all,
60   What is the thought?—conjectural
On sorry matters best unsolved?—
Or inly is each grace revolved
To fit me with a lure?—or (sad
To think!) perhaps you're merely glad
65   That I'm not drunk or ruffianly
And let you rest upon my knee.

For sometimes, were the truth confess'd,
You're thankful for a little rest,—
Glad from the crush to rest within,
70   From the heart-sickness and the din
Where envy's voice at virtue's pitch
Mocks you because your gown is rich;
And from the pale girl's dumb rebuke,
Whose ill-clad grace and toil-worn look
75   Proclaim the strength that keeps her weak,
And other nights than yours bespeak;
And from the wise unchildish elf,
To schoolmate lesser than himself
Pointing you out, what thing you are:—
80   Yes, from the daily jeer and jar,
From shame and shame's outbraving too,
Is rest not sometimes sweet to you?—
But most from the hatefulness of man,
Who spares not to end what he began,
85   Whose acts are ill and his speech ill,
Who, having used you at his will,

Thrusts you aside, as when I dine
I serve the dishes and the wine.

Well, handsome Jenny mine, sit up:
90 I've filled our glasses, let us sup,
And do not let me think of you,
Lest shame of yours suffice for two.
What, still so tired? Well, well then, keep
Your head there, so you do not sleep;
95 But that the weariness may pass
And leave you merry, take this glass.
Ah! lazy lily hand, more bless'd
If ne'er in rings it had been dress'd
Nor ever by a glove conceal'd!

100 Behold the lilies of the field,
They toil not neither do they spin;
(So doth the ancient text[1] begin,—
Not of such rest as one of these
Can share.) Another rest and ease
105 Along each summer-sated hath
From its new lord the garden hath
Than that whose spring in blessings ran
Which praised the bounteous husbandman,
Ere yet, in days of hankering breath,
110 The lilies sickened unto death.

What, Jenny, are your lilies dead?
Aye, and the snow-white leaves are spread
Like winter on the garden-bed.
But you had roses left in May,—
115 They were not gone too. Jenny, nay,
But must your roses die, and those
Their purfled buds that should unclose?
Even so; the leaves are curled apart,
Still red as from the broken heart,
120 And here's the naked stem of thorns.

Nay, nay, mere words. Here nothing warns
As yet of winter. Sickness here
Or want alone could waken fear,—
Nothing but passion wrings a tear.
125 Except when there may rise unsought
Haply at times a passing thought
Of the old days which seem to be
Much older than any history
That is written in any book;
130 When she would lie in fields and look
Along the ground through the blown grass,
And wonder where the city was,
Far out of sight, whose broil and bale
They told her then for a child's tale.

135 Jenny, you know the city now.
A child can tell the tale there, how
Some things which are not yet enroll'd
In market-lists are bought and sold
Even till the early Sunday light,
140 When Saturday night is market-night
Everywhere, be it dry or wet,
And market-night in the Haymarket.[2]
Our learned London children know,
Poor Jenny, all your pride and woe;
145 Have seen your lifted silken skirt
Advertise dainties through the dirt;
Have seen your coach-wheels splash rebuke
On virtue; and have learned your look
When, wealth and health slipped past, you stare
150 Along the streets alone, and there,
Round the long park, across the bridge,
The cold lamps at the pavement's edge
Wind on together and apart,
A fiery serpent for your heart.

155 Let the thoughts pass, an empty cloud!
Suppose I were to think aloud,—

---

[1] Matthew 6:28–9.

[2] a street in the theatre district of London, in this period a notorious haunt of prostitutes.

What if to her all this were said?
Why, as a volume seldom read
Being opened halfway shuts again,
160 So might the pages of her brain
Be parted at such words, and thence
Close back upon the dusty sense.
For is there hue or shape defin'd
In Jenny's desecrated mind,
165 Where all contagious currents meet,
A Lethe of the middle street?[1]
Nay, it reflects not any face,
Nor sound is in its sluggish pace,
But as they coil those eddies clot,
170 And night and day remember not.

    Why, Jenny, you're asleep at last!—
Asleep, poor Jenny, hard and fast,—
So young and soft and tired; so fair,
With chin thus nestled in your hair,
175 Mouth quiet, eyelids almost blue
As if some sky of dreams shone through!

    Just as another woman sleeps!
Enough to throw one's thoughts in heaps
Of doubt and horror,—what to say
180 Or think,—this awful secret sway,
The potter's power over the clay![2]
Of the same lump (it has been said)
For honour and dishonour made,
Two sister vessels. Here is one.

185   My cousin Nell is fond of fun,
And fond of dress, and change, and praise,
So mere a woman in her ways:
And if her sweet eyes rich in youth
Are like her lips that tell the truth,
190 My cousin Nell is fond of love.

And she's the girl I'm proudest of.
Who does not prize her, guard her well?
The love of change, in cousin Nell,
Shall find the best and hold it dear:
195 The unconquered mirth turn quieter
Not through her own, through others' woe:
The conscious pride of beauty glow
Beside another's pride in her,
One little part of all they share.
200 For Love himself shall ripen these
In a kind soil to just increase
Through years of fertilizing peace.

    Of the same lump (as it is said)
For honour and dishonour made,
205 Two sister vessels. Here is one.

    It makes a goblin of the sun.

    So pure,—so fall'n! How dare to think
Of the first common kindred link?
Yet, Jenny, till the world shall burn
210 It seems that all things take their turn;
And who shall say but this fair tree
May need, in changes that may be,
Your children's children's charity?
Scorned then, no doubt, as you are scorn'd!
215 Shall no man hold his pride forewarn'd
Till in the end, the Day of Days,
At Judgment, one of his own race,
As frail and lost as you, shall rise,—
His daughter, with his mother's eyes?

220   How Jenny's clock ticks on the shelf!
Might not the dial scorn itself
That has such hours to register?
Yet as to me, even so to her
Are golden sun and silver moon,
225 In daily largesse of earth's boon,
Counted for life-coins to one tune.
And if, as blindfold fates are toss'd,

---

[1] Gutters—often containing sewage—used to flow down the middle of the street. Lethe is the river of forgetfulness in Hades.

[2] Romans 9:21.

Through some one man this life be lost,
Shall soul not somehow pay for soul?

230   Fair shines the gilded aureole
In which our highest painters place
Some living woman's simple face.
And the stilled features thus descried
As Jenny's long throat droops aside,—
235 The shadows where the cheeks are thin,
And pure wide curve from ear to chin,—
With Raffael's, Leonardo's hand[1]
To show them to men's souls, might stand,
Whole ages long, the whole world through,
240 For preachings of what God can do.
What has man done here? How atone,
Great God, for this which man has done?
And for the body and soul which by
Man's pitiless doom must now comply
245 With lifelong hell, what lullaby
Of sweet forgetful second birth
Remains? All dark. No sign on earth
What measure of God's rest endows
The many mansions of his house.[2]

250   If but a woman's heart might see
Such erring heart unerringly
For once! But that can never be.

Like a rose shut in a book
In which pure women may not look,
255 For its base pages claim control
To crush the flower within the soul;
Where through each dead rose-leaf that clings,
Pale as transparent Psyche-wings,[3]
To the vile text, are traced such things

260 As might make lady's cheek indeed
More than a living rose to read;
So nought save foolish foulness may
Watch with hard eyes the sure decay;
And so the life-blood of this rose,
265 Puddled with shameful knowledge, flows
Through leaves no chaste hand may unclose:
Yet still it keeps such faded show
Of when 'twas gathered long ago,
That the crushed petals' lovely grain,
270 The sweetness of the sanguine stain,
Seen of a woman's eyes, must make
Her pitiful heart, so prone to ache,
Love roses better for its sake:—
Only that this can never be:—
275 Even so unto her sex is she.

Yet, Jenny, looking long at you,
The woman almost fades from view.
A cipher of man's changeless sum
Of lust, past, present, and to come,
280 Is left. A riddle that one shrinks
To challenge from the scornful sphinx.[4]

Like a toad within a stone[5]
Seated while Time crumbles on;
Which sits there since the earth was curs'd
285 For Man's transgression at the first;
Which, living through all centuries,
Not once has seen the sun arise;
Whose life, to its cold circle charmed,
The earth's whole summers have not warmed;
290 Which always—whitherso the stone
Be flung—sits there, deaf, blind, alone;—
Aye, and shall not be driven out

---

[1] the painters Raphael (1483–1520) and Leonardo da Vinci (1452–1519).

[2] John 14:2.

[3] Psyche means the soul; Psyche was also a beautiful maiden beloved but then spurned by Cupid.

[4] in Greek mythology, a monster with the head and breasts of a woman, the body of a lion, the wings of a bird, and the tail of a serpent. The sphinx spoke in a human voice, setting riddles and devouring those who could not find answers.

[5] It was thought that a toad confined within a cave or rock could live indefinitely without sustenance.

Till that which shuts him round about
Break at the very Master's stroke,
295 And the dust thereof vanish as smoke,
And the seed of Man vanish as dust:—
Even so within this world is Lust.

Come, come, what use in thoughts like this?
Poor little Jenny, good to kiss,—
300 You'd not believe by what strange roads
Thought travels, when your beauty goads
A man to-night to think of toads!
Jenny, wake up…Why, there's the dawn!

And there's an early waggon drawn
305 To market, and some sheep that jog
Bleating before a barking dog;
And the old streets come peering through
Another night that London knew;
And all as ghostlike as the lamps.

310 So on the wings of day decamps
My last night's frolic. Glooms begin
To shiver off as lights creep in
Past the gauze curtains half drawn-to,
And the lamp's doubled shade grows blue,—
315 Your lamp, my Jenny, kept alight,
Like a wise virgin's, all one night!
And in the alcove coolly spread
Glimmers with dawn your empty bed;
And yonder your fair face I see
320 Reflected lying on my knee,
Where teems with first foreshadowings
Your pier-glass scrawled with diamond rings:[1]
And on your bosom all night worn
Yesterday's rose now droops forlorn,
325 But dies not yet this summer morn.

And now without, as if some word
Had called upon them that they heard,
The London sparrows far and nigh
Clamour together suddenly;
330 And Jenny's cage-bird grown awake
Here in their song his part must take,
Because here too the day doth break.

And somehow in myself the dawn
Among stirred clouds and veils withdrawn
335 Strikes greyly on her. Let her sleep.
But will I wake her if I heap
These cushions thus beneath her head
Where my knee was? No,—there's your bed,
My Jenny, while you dream. And there
340 I lay among your golden hair
Perhaps the subject of your dreams,
These golden coins.
                                    For still one deems
That Jenny's flattering sleep confers
New magic on the magic purse,—
345 Grim web, how clogged with shrivelled flies!
Between the threads fine fumes arise
And shape their pictures in the brain.
There roll no streets in glare and rain,
Nor flagrant man-swine whets his tusk;
350 But delicately sighs in musk
The homage of the dim boudoir;
Or like a palpitating star
Thrilled into song, the opera-night
Breathes faint in the quick pulse of light;
355 Or at the carriage-window shine
Rich wares for choice; or, free to dine,
Whirls through its hour of health (divine
For her) the concourse of the Park.
And though in the discounted dark
360 Her functions there and here are one,
Beneath the lamps and in the sun
There reigns at least the acknowledged belle
Apparelled beyond parallel.
Ah Jenny, yes, we know your dreams.

---

[1] A pier-glass is a mirror; the names of Jenny's lovers have been
scratched on the mirror with a diamond ring.

365   For even the Paphian Venus[1] seems
A goddess o'er the realms of love,
When silver-shrined in shadowy grove:
Aye, or let offerings nicely plac'd
But hide Priapus[2] to the waist,
370 And whoso looks on him shall see
An eligible deity.

    Why, Jenny, waking here alone
May help you to remember one,
Though all the memory's long outworn
375 Of many a double-pillowed morn.
I think I see you when you wake,
And rub your eyes for me, and shake
My gold, in rising, from your hair,
A Danaë[3] for a moment there.

380   Jenny, my love rang true! for still
Love at first sight is vague, until
That tinkling makes him audible.

    And must I mock you to the last,
Ashamed of my own shame,—aghast
385 Because some thoughts not born amiss
Rose at a poor fair face like this?
Well, of such thoughts so much I know:
In my life, as in hers, they show,
By a far gleam which I may near,
390 A dark path I can strive to clear.

    Only one kiss. Good-bye, my dear.
—1870 (1848–50; 1869–70)

---

[1] Paphos is a city on Cyprus where Venus was worshipped in orgiastic rites. The Paphian Venus represents sexual love, and "Paphian" can mean prostitute.

[2] in Greek mythology, the god of reproductive power, fertility, and gardens, represented by a phallic statue.

[3] daughter of Acrisius, King of Argos, who locked her up in a tower to prevent her marrying. In order to seduce Danae, Zeus transformed himself into a shower of gold.

The Portrait

This is her picture as she was:
    It seems a thing to wonder on,
As though mine image in the glass
    Should tarry when myself am gone.
5 I gaze until she seems to stir,—
Until mine eyes almost aver
    That now, even now, the sweet lips part
    To breathe the words of the sweet heart:—
And yet the earth is over her.

10 Alas! even such the thin-drawn ray
    That makes the prison-depths more rude,—
The drip of water night and day
    Giving a tongue to solitude.
Yet only this, of love's whole prize,
15 Remains; save what in mournful guise
    Takes counsel with my soul alone,—
    Save what is secret and unknown,
Below the earth, above the skies.

In painting her I shrined her face
20   'Mid mystic trees, where light falls in
Hardly at all; a covert place
    Where you might think to find a din
Of doubtful talk, and a live flame
Wandering, and many a shape whose name
25   Not itself knoweth, and old dew,
    And your own footsteps meeting you,
And all things going as they came.

A deep dim wood; and there she stands
    As in that wood that day: for so
30 Was the still movement of her hands
    And such the pure line's gracious flow.
And passing fair the type must seem,
Unknown the presence and the dream.
    'T is she: though of herself, alas!

35 Less than her shadow on the grass
Or than her image in the stream.

That day we met there, I and she
    One with the other all alone;
And we were blithe; yet memory
40   Saddens those hours, as when the moon
Looks upon daylight. And with her
I stooped to drink the spring-water,
    Athirst where other waters sprang:
    And where the echo is, she sang,—
45 My soul another echo there.

But when that hour my soul won strength
    For words whose silence wastes and kills,
Dull raindrops smote us, and at length
    Thundered the heat within the hills.
50 That eve I spoke those words again
Beside the pelted window-pane;
    And there she hearkened what I said,
    With under-glances that surveyed
The empty pastures blind with rain.

55 Next day the memories of these things,
    Like leaves through which a bird has flown,
Still vibrated with Love's warm wings;
    Till I must make them all my own
And paint this picture. So, 'twixt ease
60 Of talk and sweet long silences,
    She stood among the plants in bloom
    At windows of a summer room,
To feign the shadow of the trees.

And as I wrought, while all above
65   And all around was fragrant air,
In the sick burthen of my love
    It seemed each sun-thrilled blossom there
Beat like a heart among the leaves.
O heart that never beats nor heaves,
70   In that one darkness lying still,

What now to thee my love's great will
Or the fine web the sunshine weaves?

For now doth daylight disavow
    Those days—nought left to see or hear.
75 Only in solemn whispers now
    At night-time these things reach mine ear;
When the leaf-shadows at a breath
Shrink in the road, and all the heath,
    Forest and water, far and wide,
80   In limpid starlight glorified,
Lie like the mystery of death.

Last night at last I could have slept,
    And yet delayed my sleep till dawn,
Still wandering. Then it was I wept:
85   For unawares I came upon
Those glades where once she walked with me:
And as I stood there suddenly,
    All wan with traversing the night,
    Upon the desolate verge of light
90 Yearned loud the iron-bosomed sea.

Even so, where Heaven holds breath and hears
    The beating heart of Love's own breast,—
Where round the secret of all secret of all spheres
    All angels lay their wings to rest,—
95 How shall my soul stand rapt and awed,
When, by the new birth borne abroad
    Throughout the music of the suns,
    It enters in her soul at once
And knows the silence there for God!

100 Here with her face doth memory sit
    Meanwhile, and wait the day's decline,
Till other eyes shall look from it,
    Eyes of the spirit's Palestine,[1]
Even than the old gaze tenderer:
105 While hopes and aims long lost with her

---

[1] Palestine, the holy land.

Stand round her image side by side,
Like tombs of pilgrims that have died
About the Holy Sepulchre.[1]
—1870 (1847–70)

The Woodspurge

The wind flapped loose, the wind was still,
Shaken out dead from tree and hill:
I had walked on at the wind's will,—
I sat now, for the wind was still.

5 Between my knees my forehead was,—
My lips, drawn in, said not Alas!
My hair was over in the grass,
My naked ears heard the day pass.

My eyes, wide open, had the run
10 Of some ten weeds to fix upon;
Among those few, out of the sun,
The woodspurge flowered, three cups in one.

From perfect grief there need not be
Wisdom or even memory:
15 One thing then learnt remains to me,—
The woodspurge has a cup of three.
—1870 (1856)

The Ballad of Dead Ladies [2]

(translation from François Villon)

Tell me now in what hidden way is
Lady Flora the lovely Roman?
Where's Hipparchia, and where is Thais,[3]

5 Neither of them the fairer woman?
Where is Echo,[4] beheld of no man,
Only heard on river and mere,—
She whose beauty was more than human?…
But where are the snows of yester-year?

Where's Héloise, the learned nun,
10 For whose sake Abeillard,[5] I ween,
Lost manhood and put priesthood on?
(From Love he won such dule and teen!)
And where, I pray you, is the Queen[6]
Who willed that Buridan should steer
15 Sewed in a sack's mouth down the Seine?…
But where are the snows of yester-year?

White Queen Blanche,[7] like a queen of lilies,
With a voice like any mermaiden,—
Bertha Broadfoot, Beatrice, Alice,[8]
20 And Ermengarde the lady of Maine,[9]—
And that good Joan[10] whom Englishmen
At Rouen doomed and burned her there,—
Mother of God, where are they then?…
But where are the snows of yester-year?

---

[1] the cave in Jerusalem where Christ's body was entombed.

[2] a translation of François Villon's "Balade des dames du temps jadis" (1450).

[3] Flora, Hipparchis, and Thais were famous courtesans of Rome, Greece, and Athens respectively.

[4] In classical mythology, Echo was a nymph in love with Narcissus. When her love was not returned she pined away until only her voice remained.

[5] The beautiful and accomplished Heloise fell in love with her tutor, the eminent scholar and theologian Peter Abelard (1079–1142). She gave birth to a son and they were secretly married; however, Heloise's guardian, a Canon of Notre Dame, was furious and had Abelard castrated. Abelard entered a monastery and Heloise became a nun. They are buried together in Pere-Lachaise Cemetery in Paris.

[6] Margaret of Burgundy, who had her former lovers (including the scholar Buridan) sewn up in sacks and tossed into the Seine.

[7] possibly Blanche of Castille.

[8] Bertha Broadfoot was the mother of Charlemagne (742–814), ruler of Europe and hero of chivalric romances. Beatrice is possibly an allusion to the woman who inspired the poetry of Dante Alighieri (1265–1321). Alice is unknown.

[9] a countess of the French region of Anjou.

[10] Joan of Arc (1412–31), who was burned at the stake.

25 Nay, never ask this week, fair lord,
    Where they are gone, nor yet this year,
Except with this for an overword,—
    But where are the snows of yester-year?
    —1870 (1869)

A Last Confession

(Regno Lombardo-Veneto, 1848)[1]

*   *   *   *   *

Our Lombard country-girls along the coast
    Wear daggers in their garters: for they know
That they might hate another girl to death
Or meet a German lover. Such a knife
5 I bought her, with a hilt of horn and pearl.

    Father, you cannot know of all my thoughts
That day in going to meet her,—that last day
For the last time, she said;—of all the love
And all the hopeless hope that she might change
10 And go back with me. Ah! and everywhere,
At places we both knew along the road,
Some fresh shape of herself as once she was
Grew present at my side; until it seemed—
So close they gathered round me—they would all
15 Be with me when I reached the spot at last,
To plead my cause with her against herself
So changed. O Father, if you knew all this
You cannot know, then you would know too, Father.
And only then, if God can pardon me.
20 What can be told I'll tell, if you will hear.

    I passed a village-fair upon my road,
And thought, being empty-handed, I would take
Some little present: such might prove, I said,
Either a pledge between us, or (God help me!)

25 A parting gift. And there it was I bought
The knife I spoke of, such as women wear.

    That day, some three hours afterwards, I found
For certain, it must be a parting gift.
And, standing silent not at last, I looked
30 Into her scornful face; and heard the sea
Still trying hard to din into my ears
Some speech it knew which still might change her
    heart,
If only it could make me understand.
One moment thus. Another, and her face
35 Seemed further off than the last line of sea,
So that I thought, if now she were to speak
I could not hear her. Then again I knew
All, as we stood together on the sand
At Iglio,[2] in the first thin shade o' the hills.

40   "Take it," I said, and held it out to her,
While the hilt glanced within my trembling hold;
"Take it and keep it for my sake," I said.
Her neck unbent not, neither did her eyes
Move, nor her foot left beating of the sand;
45 Only she put it by from her and laughed.

    Father, you hear my speech and not her laugh;
But God heard that. Will God remember all?

    It was another laugh than the sweet sound
50 Which rose from her sweet childish heart, that day
Eleven years before, when first I found her
Alone upon the hill-side; and her curls
Shook down in the warm grass as she looked up
Out of her curls in my eyes bent to hers.
55 She might have served a painter to pourtray
That heavenly child which in the latter days
Shall walk between the lion and the lamb.
I had been for nights in hiding, worn and sick

[1] In 1848, Italian nationalists rose in revolt against their Austrian oppressors; open war broke out in the duchies of Lombardy and Venetia in northern Italy. The speaker is an Italian patriot fatally wounded by the Austrians and making his deathbed confession to his priest.

[2] Notes by William Michael Rossetti, Dante Gabriel's younger brother, say that the poet invented this place-name.

And hardly fed; and so her words at first
60 Seemed fitful like the talking of the trees
And voices in the air that knew my name.
And I remember that I sat me down
Upon the slope with her, and thought the world
Must be all over or had never been,
65 We seemed there so alone. And soon she told me
Her parents both were gone away from her.
I though perhaps she meant that they had died;
But when I asked her this, she looked again
Into my face and said that yestereve
70 They kissed her long, and wept and made her weep,
And gave her all the bread they had with them,
And then had gone together up the hill
Where we were sitting now, and had walked on
Into the great red light; "and so," she said,
75 "I have come up here too; and when this evening
They step out of the light as they stepped in,
I shall be here to kiss them." And she laughed.

Then I bethought me suddenly of the famine;
And how the church-steps throughout all the town,
80 When last I had been there a month ago,
Swarmed with starved folk; and how the bread was
        weighed
By Austrians armed; and women that I knew
For wives and mothers walked the public street,
85 Saying aloud that if their husbands feared
To snatch the children's food, themselves would
        stay
85 Till they had earned it there. So then this child
Was piteous to me; for all told me then
Her parents must have left her to God's chance,
To man's or to the Church's charity,
Because of the great famine, rather than
90 To watch her growing thin between their knees.
With that, God took my mother's voice and spoke,
And sights and sounds came back and things long
        since,
And all my childhood found me on the hills;
And so I took her with me.

                                    I was young,
95 Scarce man then, Father: but the cause which gave
The wounds I die of now had brought me then
Some wounds already; and I lived alone,
As any hiding hunted man must live.
It was no easy thing to keep a child
100 In safety; for herself it was not safe,
And doubled my own danger: but I knew
That God would help me.

                                    Yet a little while
Pardon me, Father, if I pause. I think
I have been speaking to you of some matters
105 There was no need to speak of, have I not?
You do not know how clearly those things stood
Within my mind, which I have spoken of,
Nor how they strove for utterance. Life all past
Is like the sky when the sun sets in it,
110 Clearest where furthest off.

                                    I told you how
She scorned my parting gift and laughed. And yet
A woman's laugh's another thing sometimes:
I think they laugh in Heaven. I know last night
I dreamed I saw into the garden of God,
115 Where women walked whose painted images
I have seen with candles round them in the church.
They bent this way and that, one to another,
Playing: and over the long golden hair
Of each there floated like a ring of fire
120 Which when she stooped stooped with her, and
        when she rose
Rose with her. Then a breeze flew in among them,
As if a window had been opened in Heaven
For God to give His blessing from, before
This world of ours should set; (for in my dream
125 I thought our world was setting, and the sun
Flared, a spent taper;) and beneath that gust
The rings of light quivered like forest-leaves.
Then all the blessed maidens who were there
Stood up together, as it were a voice
130 That called them; and they threw their tresses back,
And smote their palms, and all laughed up at once,

For the strong heavenly joy they had in them
To hear God bless the world. Wherewith I woke:
And looking round, I saw as usual
135 That she was standing there with her long locks
Pressed to her side; and her laugh ended theirs.

    For always when I see her now, she laughs.
And yet her childish laughter haunts me too,
The life of this dead terror; as in days
140 When she, a child, dwelt with me. I must tell
Something of those days yet before the end.

    I brought her from the city—one such day
When she was still a merry loving child,—
The earliest gift I mind my giving her;
145 A little image of a flying Love[1]
Made of our coloured glass-ware, in his hands
A dart of gilded metal and a torch.
And him she kissed and me, and fain would know
Why were his poor eyes blindfold, why the wings
150 And why the arrow. What I knew I told
Of Venus[2] and of Cupid,—strange old tales.
And when she heard that he could rule the loves
Of men and women, still she shook her head
And wondered; and, "Nay, nay," she murmured
        still,
155 "So strong, and he a younger child than I!"
And then she'd have me fix him on the wall
Fronting her little bed; and then again
She needs must fix him there herself, because
I gave him to her and she loved him so,
160 And he should make her love me better yet,
If women loved the more, the more they grew.
But the fit place upon the wall was high
For her, and so I held her in my arms:
And each time that the heavy pruning-hook
165 I gave her for a hammer slipped away
As it would often, still she laughed and laughed,

And kissed and kissed me. But amid her mirth,
Just as she hung the image on the nail,
It slipped and all its fragments strewed the ground:
170 And as it fell she screamed, for in her hand
The dart had entered deeply and drawn blood.
And so her laughter turned to tears: and "Oh!"
I said, the while I bandaged the small hand,—
"That I should be the first to make you bleed,
175 Who love and love and love you!"—kissing still
The fingers till I got her safe to bed.
And still she sobbed,—"not for the pain at all,"
She said, "but for the Love, the poor good Love
You gave me." So she cried herself to sleep.

180   Another later thing comes back to me.
'T was in those hardest foulest days of all,
When still from his shut palace, sitting clean
Above the splash of blood, old Metternich[3]
(May his soul die, and never-dying worms
185 Feast on its pain for ever!) used to thin
His year's doomed hundreds daintily, each month
Thirties and fifties. This time, as I think,
Was when his thrift forbad the poor to take
That evil brackish salt which the dry rocks
190 Keep all through winter when the sea draws in.
The first I heard of it was a chance shot
In the street here and there, and on the stones
A stumbling clatter as of horse hemmed round.
Then, when she saw me hurry out of doors,
195 My gun slung at my shoulder and my knife
Stuck in my girdle, she smoothed down my hair
And laughed to see me look so brave, and leaped
Up to my neck and kissed me. She was still
A child; and yet that kiss was on my lips
200 So hot all day where the smoke shut us in.

    For now, being always with her, the first love
I had—the father's, brother's love—was changed,
I think, in somewise; like a holy thought

---

[1] Cupid, the Roman god of love, usually depicted as a young boy.

[2] the Roman goddess of beauty and sensual love.

---

[3] chancellor of the Austrian Empire.

Which is a prayer before one knows of it.
205 The first time I perceived this, I remember,
Was once when after hunting I came home
Weary, and she brought food and fruit for me,
And sat down at my feet upon the floor
Leaning against my side. But when I felt
210 Her sweet head reach from that low seat of hers
So high as to be laid upon my heart,
I turned and looked upon my darling there
And marked for the first time how tall she was;
And my heart beat with so much violence
215 Under her cheek, I though she could not choose
But wonder at it soon and ask me why;
And so I bade her rise and eat with me.
And when, remembering all and counting back
The time, I made out fourteen years for her
220 And told her so, she gazed at me with eyes
As of the sky and sea on a grey day,
And drew her long hands through her hair, and
    asked me
If she was not a woman; and then laughed:
And as she stooped in laughing, I could see
225 Beneath the growing throat the breasts half-globed
Like folded lilies deepset in the stream.

Yes, let me think of her as then; for so
Her image, Father, is not like the sights
Which come when you are gone. She had a mouth
230 Made to bring death to life,—the underlip
Sucked in, as if it strove to kiss itself.
Her face was pearly pale, as when one stoops
Over wan water; and the dark crisped hair
And the hair's shadow made it paler still:—
235 Deep-serried locks, the dimness of the cloud
Where the moon's gaze is set in eddying gloom.
Her body bore her neck as the tree's stem
Bears the top branch; and as the branch sustains
The flower of the year's pride, her high neck bore
240 That face made wonderful with night and day.
Her voice was swift, yet ever the last words
Fell lingeringly; and rounded finger-tips

She had, that clung a little where they touched
And then were gone o' the instant. Her great eyes,
245 That sometimes turned half dizzily beneath
The passionate lids, as faint, when she would speak,
Had also in them hidden springs of mirth,
Which under the dark lashes evermore
Shook to her laugh, as when a bird flies low
250 Between the water and the willow-leaves,
And the shade quivers till he wins the light.

I was a moody comrade to her then,
For all the love I bore her. Italy,
The weeping desolate mother, long has claimed
255 Her sons' strong arms to lean on, and their hands
To lop the poisonous thicket from her path,
Cleaving her way to light. And from her need
Had grown the fashion of my whole poor life
Which I was proud to yield her, as my father
260 Had yielded his. And this had come to be
A game to play, a love to clasp, a hate
To wreak, all things together that a man
Needs for his blood to ripen; till at times
All else seemed shadows, and I wondered still
265 To see such life pass muster and be deemed
Times's bodily substance. In those hours, no doubt,
To the young girl my eyes were like my soul,—
Dark wells of death-in-life that yearned for day.
And though she ruled me always, I remember
270 That once when I was thus and she still kept
Leaping about the place and laughing, I
Did almost chide her; whereupon she knelt
And putting her two hands into my breast
Sang me a song. Are these tears in my eyes?
275 'T is long since I have wept for anything.
I thought that song forgotten out of mind;
And now, just as I spoke of it, it came
All back. It is but a rude thing, ill rhymed,
Such as a blind man chaunts and his dog hears
280 Holding the platter, when the children run
To merrier sport and leave him. Thus it goes:—

La bella donna
Piangendo disse:
"Come son fisse
285 Le stelle in cielo!
Quel fiato anelo
Dello stanco sole,
Quanto m' assonna!
E la luna, macchiata
290 Come uno specchio
Logoro e vecchio,—
Faccia affannata,
Che cosa vuole?

"Chè stelle, luna, e sole,
295 Ciascun m' annoja
E m' annojano insieme;
Non me ne preme
Nè ci prendo gioja.
E veramente,
300 Che le spalle sien franche
E le braccia blanche
E il seno caldo e tondo,
Non mi fa niente.
Chè cosa al mondo
305 Posso più far di questi
Se non piacciono a te, come dicesti?"

La donna rise
E riprese ridendo:—
"Questo mano che prendo
310 E dunque mia?
Tu m' ami dunque?
Dimmelo ancora,
Non in modo qualunque,
Ma le parole
315 Belle e precise
Che dicesti pria.

'Siccome suole
La state talora
(Dicesti) un qualche istante

320 Tornare innanze inverno,
Così tu fai ch' io scerno
Le foglie tutte quante,
Ben ch' io certo tenessi
Per passato l'autunno.'

325 "Eccolo il mio alunno!
Io debbo insegnargli
Quei cari detti istessi
Ch' ei mi disse una volta!
Oimè! Che cosa dargli,"
330 (Ma ridea piano piano
Dei baci in sulla mano,)
"Ch' ei non m'abbia da lungo tempo tolta?"

————

She wept, sweet lady,
And said in weeping:
"What spell is keeping
The stars so steady?
Why does the power
Of the sun's noon-hour
To sleep so move me?
And the moon in heaven,
Stained where she passes
As a worn-out glass is,—
Wearily driven,
Why walks she above me?

"Stars, moon, and sun too,
I'm tired of either
And all together!
Whom speak they unto
That I should listen?
For very surely,
Though my arms and shoulders
Dazzle beholders,
And my eyes glisten,
All's nothing purely!
What are words said for
At all about them,
If he they are made for
Can do without them?"

She laughed, sweet lady,
And said in laughing:
"His hand clings half in
My own already!
Oh! do you love me?
Oh! speak of passion
In no new fashion,
No loud inveighings,
But the old sayings
You once said of me.

      "You said: 'As summer,
Through boughs grown brittle,
Comes back a little
Ere frosts benumb her,—
So bring'st thou to me
All leaves and flowers,
Though autumn's gloomy
To-day in the bowers.'

      "Oh! does he love me,
When my voice teaches
The very speeches
He then spoke of me?
Alas! what flavour
Still with me lingers?"
(But she laughed as my kisses
Glowed in her fingers
With love's old blisses.)
"Oh! what one favour
Remains to woo him,
Whose whole poor savour
Belongs not to him?"

————

      That I should sing upon this bed!—with you
To listen, and such words still left to say!
335 Yet was it I that sang? The voice seemed hers,
As on the very day she sang to me;
When, having done, she took out of my hand
Something that I had played with all the while
And laid it down beyond my reach; and so

340 Turning my face round till it fronted hers,—
"Weeping or laughing, which was best?" she said.

      But these are foolish tales. How should I show
The heart that glowed then with love's heat, each
      day
More and more brightly?—when for long years now
345 The very flame that flew about the heart,
And gave it fiery wings, has come to be
The lapping blaze of hell's environment
Whose tongues all bid the molten heart despair.

      Yet one more thing comes back on me to-night
350 Which I may tell you: for it bore my soul
Dread firstlings of the brood that rend it now.
It chanced that in our last year's wanderings
We dwelt at Monza, far away from home,
If home we had: and in the Duomo there
355 I sometimes entered with her when she prayed.

      An image of Our Lady[1] stands there, wrought
In marble by some great Italian hand
In the great days when She and Italy
Sat on one throne together: and to Her
360 And to none else my loved one told her heart.
She was a woman then; and as she knelt,—
Her sweet brow in the sweet brow's shadow there,—
They seemed two kindred forms whereby our land
(Whose work still serves the world for miracle)
365 Made manifest herself in womanhood.
Father, the day I speak of was the first
For weeks that I had borne her company
Into the Duomo; and those weeks had been
Much troubled, for then first the glimpses came
370 Of some impenetrable restlessness
Growing in her to make her changed and cold.
And as we entered there that day, I bent
My eyes on the fair Image, and I said
Within my heart, "Oh turn her heart to me!"

————

[1] the Virgin Mary, mother of Christ.

375 And so I left her to her prayers, and went
To gaze upon the pride of Monza's shrine,
Where in the sacristy the light still falls
Upon the Iron Crown of Italy,[1]
On whose crowned heads the day has closed, nor
    yet
380 The daybreak gilds another head to crown.
But coming back, I wondered when I saw
That the sweet Lady of her prayers now stood
Alone without her; until further off,
Before some new Madonna gaily decked,
385 Tinselled and gewgawed, a slight German toy,
I saw her kneel, still praying. At my step
She rose, and side by side we left the church.
I was much moved, and sharply questioned her
Of her transferred devotion; but she seemed
390 Stubborn and heedless; till she lightly laughed
And said: "The old Madonna? Aye indeed,
She had my old thoughts,—this one has my new."
Then silent to the soul I held my way:
And from the fountains of the public place
395 Unto the pigeon-haunted pinnacles,
Bright wings and water winnowed the bright air;
And stately with her laugh's subsiding smile
She went, with clear-swayed waist and towering
    neck
And hands held light before her; and the face
400 Which long had made a day in my life's night
Was night in day to me; as all men's eyes
Turned on her beauty, and she seemed to tread
Beyond my heart to the world made for her.

    Ah, there! my wounds will snatch my sense again:
405 The pain comes billowing on like a full cloud
Of thunder, and the flash that breaks from it
Leaves my brain burning. That's the wound he gave,
The Austrian whose white coat I still made match

With his white face, only the two grew red
410 As suits his trade. The devil makes them wear
White for a livery, that the blood may show
Braver that brings them to him. So he looks
Sheer o'er the field and knows his own at once.

    Give me a draught of water in that cup;
415 My voice feels thick; perhaps you do not hear;
But you *must* hear. If you mistake my words
And so absolve me, I am sure the blessing
Will burn my soul. If you mistake my words
And so absolve me, Father, the great sin
420 Is yours, not mine: mark this: your soul shall burn
With mine for it. I have seen pictures where
Souls burned with Latin shriekings in their mouths:
Shall my end be as theirs? Nay, but I know
'T is you shall shriek in Latin. Some bell rings,
425 Rings through my brain: it strikes the hour in hell.

    You see I cannot, Father; I have tried,
But cannot, as you see. These twenty times
Beginning, I have come to the same point
And stopped. Beyond, there are but broken words
430 Which will not let you understand my tale.
It is that then we have her with us here,
As when she wrung her hair out in my dream
To-night, till all the darkness reeked of it.
Her hair is always wet, for she has kept
435 Its tresses wrapped about her side for years;
And when she wrung them round over the floor,
I heard the blood between her fingers hiss;
So that I sat up in my bed and screamed
Once and again; and once to once, she laughed.
440 Look that you turn not now,—she's at your back:
Gather your robe up, Father, and keep close,
Or she'll sit down on it and send you mad.

    At Iglio in the first thin shade o' the hills
The sand is black and red. The black was black
445 When what was spilt that day sank into it,

---

[1] the crown of the ancient Lombardic kings, said to have been bestowed
by Pope Gregory the Great (in office 590–604). It was restored to the
King of Italy by the Emperor of Austria in 1866 and housed in the
Cathedral at Monza.

And the red scarcely darkened. There I stood
This night with her, and saw the sand the same.

.   .   .   .

What would you have me tell you? Father, Father,
How shall I make you know? You have not known
450 The dreadful soul of woman, who one day
Forgets the old and takes the new to heart,
Forgets what man remembers, and therewith
Forgets the man. Nor can I clearly tell
How the change happened between her and me.
455 Her eyes looked on me from an emptied heart
When most my heart was full of her; and still
In every corner of myself I sought
To find what service failed her; and no less
Than in the good time past, there all was hers.
460 What do you love? Your Heaven? Conceive it spread
For one first year of all eternity
All round you with all joys and gifts of God;
And then when most your soul is blent with it
And all yields song together,—then it stands
465 O' the sudden like a pool that once gave back
Your image, but now drowns it and is clear
Again,—or like a sun bewitched, that burns
Your shadow from you, and still shines in sight.
How could you bear it? Would you not cry out,
470 Among those eyes grown blind to you, those ears
That hear no more your voice you hear the same,—
"God! what is left but hell for company,
But hell, hell, hell?"—until the name so breathed
Whirled with hot wind and sucked you down in fire?
475 Even so I stood the day her empty heart
Left her place empty in our home, while yet
I knew not why she went nor where she went
Nor how to reach her: so I stood the day
When to my prayers at last one sight of her
480 Was granted, and I looked on Heaven made pale
With scorn, and heard Heaven mock me in that
    laugh.

O sweet, long sweet! Was that some ghost of you,
Even as your ghost that haunts me now,—twin
    shapes
Of fear and hatred? May I find you yet
485 Mine when death wakes? Ah! be it even in flame,
We may have sweetness yet, if you but say
As once in childish sorrow: "Not my pain,
My pain was nothing: oh your poor poor love,
Your broken love!"
            My Father, have I not
490 Yet told you the last things of that last day
On which I went to meet her by the sea?
O God, O God! but I must tell you all.

Midway upon my journey, when I stopped
To buy the dagger at the village fair,
495 I saw two cursed rats about the place
I knew for spies—blood-sellers both. That day
Was not yet over; for three hours to come
I prized my life: and so I looked around
For safety. A poor painted mountebank
500 Was playing tricks and shouting in a crowd.
I knew he must have heard my name, so I
Pushed past and whispered to him who I was,
And of my danger. Straight he hustled me
Into his booth, as it were in the trick,
505 And brought me out next minute with my face
All smeared in patches and a zany's gown;
And there I handed him his cups and balls
And swung the sand-bags round to clear the ring
For half an hour. The spies came once and looked;
510 And while they stopped, and made all sights and
    sounds
Sharp to my startled senses, I remember
A woman laughed above me. I looked up
And saw where a brown-shouldered harlot leaned
Half through a tavern window thick with vine.
515 Some man had come behind her in the room
And caught her by her arms, and she had turned
With that coarse empty laugh on him, as now
He munched her neck with kisses, while the vine

Crawled in her back.
              And three hours afterwards,
520 When she that I had run all risks to meet
Laughed as I told you, my life burned to death
Within me, for I thought it like the laugh
Heard at the fair. She had not left me long;
But all she might have changed to, or might change
    to,
525 (I know nought since—she never speaks a word—)
Seemed in that laugh. Have I not told you yet,
Not told you all this time what happened, Father,
When I had offered her the little knife,
And bade her keep it for my sake that loved her,
530 And she laughed? Have I not told you yet?

    "Take it," I said to her the second time,
"Take it and keep it." And then came a fire
That burnt my hand; and then the fire was blood,
And sea and sky were blood and fire, and all
535 The day was one red blindness; till it seemed,
Within the whirling brain's eclipse, that she
Or I or all things bled or burned to death.
And then I found her laid against my feet
And knew that I had stabbed her, and saw still
540 Her look in falling. For she took the knife
Deep in her heart, even as I bade her then,
And fell; and her stiff bodice scooped the sand
Into her bosom.
              And she keeps it, see,
Do you not see she keeps it?—there, beneath
545 Wet fingers and wet tresses, in her heart.
For look you, when she stirs her hand, it shows
The little hilt of horn and pearl,—even such
A dagger as our women of the coast
Twist in their garters.
              Father, I have done:
550 And from her side she now unwinds the thick
Dark hair; all round her side it is wet through,
But, like the sand at Iglio, does not change.
Now you may see the dagger clearly. Father,
I have told all: tell me at once what hope

555 Can reach me still. For now she draws it out
Slowly, and only smiles as yet: look, Father,
She scarcely smiles: but I shall hear her laugh
Soon, when she shows the crimson steel to God.
—1870 (1849, 1869–70)

The Sea-Limits

Consider the sea's listless chime:
    Time's self it is, made audible,—
    The murmur of the earth's own shell.
Secret continuance sublime
5   Is the sea's end: our sight may pass
    No furlong further. Since time was,
This sound hath told the lapse of time.

No quiet, which is death's,—it hath
10   The mournfulness of ancient life,
    Enduring always at dull strife.
As the world's heart of rest and wrath,
    Its painful pulse is in the sands.
    Last utterly, the whole sky stands,
15 Grey and not known, along its path.

Listen alone beside the sea,
    Listen alone among the woods;
    Those voices of twin solitudes
Shall have one sound alike to thee:
20   Hark where the murmurs of thronged men
    Surge and sink back and surge again,—
Still the one voice of wave and tree.

Gather a shell from the strown beach
    And listen at its lips: they sigh
25   The same desire and mystery,
The echo of the whole sea's speech.
    And all mankind is thus at heart
    Not anything but what thou art:
And Earth, Sea, Man, are all in each.
—1870 (1849)

Found

For a Picture

"There is a budding morrow in midnight:"—
   So sang our Keats, our English nightingale.
And here, as lamps across the bridge turn pale
In London's smokeless resurrection-light,
5 Dark breaks to dawn. But o'er the deadly blight
   Of Love deflowered and sorrow of none avail,
   Which makes this man gasp and this woman
        quail,
Can day from darkness ever again take flight?

Ah! gave not these two hearts their mutual pledge,
10 Under one mantle sheltered 'neath the hedge
   In gloaming courtship? And, O God! to-day
He only knows he holds her;—but what part
Can life now take? She cries in her locked heart,—
   "Leave me—I do not know you—go away!"
       —1881

At the Sunrise in 1848 [1]

God said, Let there be light; and there was
   light.[2]
   Then heard we sounds as though the Earth did
      sing
And the Earth's angel cried upon the wing:
We saw priests fall together and turn white:
5 And covered in the dust from the sun's sight,
   A king was spied, and yet another king.
   We said: "The round world keeps its balancing;
On this globe, they and we are opposite,—
If it is day with us, with them 't is night.
10   Still, Man, in thy just pride, remember this:—
    Thou hadst not made that thy sons' sons
       shall ask

What the word *king* may mean in their day's
      task,
   But for the light that led: and if light is,
It is because God said, Let there be light.
—1886 (1848)

The House of Life:

A Sonnet-Sequence [3]

"A Sonnet is a moment's monument,—"
INTRODUCTORY SONNET

A Sonnet is a moment's monument,—
   Memorial from the Soul's eternity
   To one dead deathless hour. Look that it be,
Whether for lustral[4] rite or dire portent,
Of its own arduous fulness reverent:
   Carve it in ivory or in ebony,
   As Day or Night may rule; and let Time see
Its flowering crest impearled and orient.[5]

A Sonnet is a coin: its face reveals
   The soul,—its converse, to what Power 'tis due:—
Whether for tribute to the august appeals
   Of Life, or dower in Love's high retinue,
It serve; or, 'mid the dark wharf's cavernous breath,
In Charon's palm it pay the toll to Death.[6]
—1881 (1880)

---

[1] 1848 was a year of many revolutions in Europe as people in many nations attempted to overthrow their oppressors.

[2] Genesis 1:3.

[3] The work is a collection of sonnets which were composed from 1848–81, and published from 1863–81. The number of sonnets is 102 (if the "Introductory Sonnet" is included) or 103 (if "Nuptial Sleep" is included). Rossetti first published 50 sonnets in *Poems* (1870), with his final version appearing in *Ballads and Sonnets* (1881).

[4] cleansing, purificatory.

[5] precious, shining.

[6] In Greek myth, Charon was the ferryman who conveyed the dead in his boat across the river Styx to Hades, a task for which each passenger paid him a coin. The dead were buried with a coin in their mouths to pay Charon's fee.

Nuptial Sleep
SONNET VIa [1]

At length their long kiss severed, with sweet
    smart:
    And as the last slow sudden drops are shed
    From sparkling eaves when all the storm has fled,
So singly flagged the pulses of each heart.
5 Their bosoms sundered, with the opening start
    Of married flowers to either side outspread
    From the knit stem; yet still their mouths, burnt
        red,
Fawned on each other where they lay apart.

Sleep sank them lower than the tide of dreams,
10   And their dreams watched them sink, and slid
        away.
Slowly their souls swam up again, through gleams
    Of watered light and dull drowned waifs of day;
Till from some wonder of new woods and streams
    He woke, and wondered more: for there she lay.
—1870

The Portrait
SONNET X

O Lord of all compassionate control,
    O Love! let this my lady's picture glow
    Under my hand to praise her name, and show
Even of her inner self the perfect whole:
5 That he who seeks her beauty's furthest goal,
    Beyond the light that the sweet glances throw
    And refluent wave of the sweet smile, may know
The very sky and sea-line of her soul.

Lo! it is done. Above the enthroning throat
10   The mouth's mould testifies of voice and kiss,

The shadowed eyes remember and foresee.
Her face is made her shrine. Let all men note
    That in all years (O Love, thy gift is this!)
    They that would look on her must come to
        me.
—1870 (1869)

Silent Noon
SONNET XIX

Your hands lie open in the long fresh grass,—
    The finger-points look through like rosy
        blooms:
    Your eyes smile peace. The pasture gleams and
        glooms
'Neath billowing skies that scatter and amass.
All round our nest, far as the eye can pass,
    Are golden kingcup-fields with silver edge
    Where the cow-parsley skirts the hawthorn-
        hedge.
5 'Tis visible silence, still as the hour-glass.

Deep in the sun-searched growths the dragon-fly
Hangs like a blue thread loosened from the sky:—
    So this wing'd hour is dropt to us from above.
Oh! clasp we to our hearts, for deathless dower,
This close-companioned inarticulate hour
    When twofold silence was the song of love.
—1870

Willowwood
SONNETS XLIX, L, LI, LII

I

I sat with Love upon a woodside well,
    Leaning across the water, I and he;
    Nor ever did he speak nor looked at me,
But touched his lute wherein was audible
5 The certain secret thing he had to tell:
    Only our mirrored eyes met silently

---

[1] Distressed by Robert Buchanan's criticism in "The Fleshly School of Poetry," Rossetti removed "Nuptial Sleep" from the sequence after its initial publication in 1870.

In the low wave; and that sound came to be
The passionate voice I knew; and my tears fell.

And at their fall, his eyes beneath grew hers;
10 And with his foot and with his wing-feathers
    He swept the spring that watered my heart's
      drouth.
Then the dark ripples spread to waving hair,
And as I stooped, her own lips rising there
    Bubbled with brimming kisses at my mouth.

II

And now Love sang: but his was such a song,
So meshed with half-remembrance hard to free,
    As souls disused in death's sterility
May sing when the new birthday tarries long.
5 And I was made aware of dumb throng
    That stood aloof, one form by every tree,
    All mournful forms, for each was I or she,
The shades of those our days that had no tongue.

They looked on us, and knew us and were known;
10   While fast together, alive from the abyss,
    Clung the soul-wrung implacable close kiss;
And pity of self through all made broken moan
Which said, "For once, for once, for once alone!"
    And still Love sang, and what he sang was
      this:—

III

"O YE, all ye that walk in Willowwood,
That walk with hollow faces burning white;
What fathom-depth of soul-struck widowhood,
    What long, what longer hours, one lifelong
      night,
5 Ere ye again, who so in vain have wooed
    Your last hope lost, who so in vain invite
Your lips to that their unforgotten food,
    Ere ye, ere ye again shall see the light!

Alas! the bitter banks in Willowwood,
10   With tear-spurge wan, with blood-wort burning
      red:
Alas! if ever such a pillow could
    Steep deep the soul in sleep till she were dead,—
Better all life forget her than this thing,
That Willowwood should hold her wandering!"

IV

So sang he: and as meeting rose and rose
    Together cling through the wind's wellaway
    Nor change at once, yet near the end of day
The leaves drop loosened where the heart-stain
    glows,—
5 So when the song died did the kiss unclose;
    And her face fell back drowned, and was as grey
    As its grey eyes; and if it ever may
Meet mine again I know not if Love knows.

Only I know that I leaned low and drank
10 A long draught from the water where she sank,
    Her breath and all her tears and all her soul:
And as I leaned, I know I felt Love's face
Pressed on my neck with moan of pity and grace,
    Till both our heads were in his aureole.
—1869 (1869)

The Soul's Sphere
SONNET LXII

Some prisoned moon in steep cloud-fastnesses,—
  Throned queen and thralled; some dying sun
    whose pyre
Blazed with momentous memorable fire;—
Who hath not yearned and fed his heart with these?
5 Who, sleepless, hath not anguished to appease
    Tragical shadow's realm of sound and sight
    Conjectured in the lamentable night?...
Lo! the soul's sphere of infinite images!

What sense shall count them? Whether it forecast
10   The rose-winged hours that flutter in the van
      Of Love's unquestioning unrevealèd span,—
Visions of golden futures: or that last
Wild pageant of the accumulated past
      That clangs and flashes for a drowning man.
—1881 (1873)

The Landmark
SONNET LXVII

Was *that* the landmark? What,—the foolish well
      Whose wave, low down, I did not stoop to drink,
      But sat and flung the pebbles from its brink
In sport to send its imaged skies pell-mell,
5   (And mine own image, had I noted well!)—
      Was that my point of turning?—I had thought
      The stations of my course should rise unsought,
As altar-stone or ensigned citadel.

But lo! the path is missed, I must go back,
10   And thirst to drink when next I reach the spring
Which once I stained, which since may have grown black.
      Yet though no light be left nor bird now sing
      As here I turn, I'll thank God, hastening,
That the same goal is still on the same track.
—1869 (1854)

Autumn Idleness
SONNET LXIX

This sunlight shames November where he grieves
      In dead red leaves, and will not let him shun
      The day, though bough with bough be over-run.
But with a blessing every glade receives
5   High salutation; while from hillock-eaves
      The deer gaze calling, dappled white and dun,

As if, being foresters of old, the sun
Had marked them with the shade of forest-leaves.

Here dawn to-day unveiled her magic glass;
10   Here noon now gives the thirst and takes the dew;
Till eve bring rest when other good things pass.
      And here the lost hours the lost hours renew
While I still lead my shadow o'er the grass,
      Nor know, for longing, that which I should do.
—1870 (1850)

The Hill Summit
SONNET LXX

This feast-day of the sun, his altar there
      In the broad west has blazed for vesper-song;
      And I have loitered in the vale too long
And gaze now a belated worshiper.
5   Yet may I not forget that I was 'ware,
      So journeying, of his face at intervals
      Transfigured where the fringed horizon falls,—
A fiery bush with coruscating hair.

And not that I have climbed and won this height,
10   I must tread downward through the sloping shade
And travel the bewildered tracks till night.
      Yet for this hour I still may here be stayed
      And see the gold air and the silver fade
And the last bird fly into the last light.
—1870 (1853)

Old and New Art

SONNETS LXXIV, LXXV, LXXVI

I. ST. LUKE THE PAINTER [1]

Give honour unto Luke Evangelist;
  For he it was (the aged legends say)
  Who first taught Art to fold her hands and pray.
Scarcely at once she dared to rend the mist
5 Of devious symbols: but soon having wist
  How sky-breadth and field-silence and this day
  Are symbols also in some deeper way,
She looked through these to God and was God's
  priest.

And if, past noon, her toil began to irk,
10 And she sought talismans, and turned in vain
  To soulless self-reflections of man's skill,—
  Yet now, in this the twilight, she might still
  Kneel in the latter grass to pray again,
Ere the night cometh and she may not work. [2]

II. NOT AS THESE

"I am not as these are," the poet saith
  In youth's pride, and the painter, among men
  At bay, where never pencil comes nor pen,
And shut about with his own frozen breath.
5 To others, for whom only rhyme wins faith
  As poets,—only paint as painters,—then
  He turns in the cold silence; and again
Shrinking, "I am not as these are," he saith.

And say that this is so, what follows it?
10 For were thine eyes set backwards in thine head,
  Such words were well; but they see on, and
    far.

Unto the lights of the great Past, new-lit
  Fair for the Future's track, look thou instead,—
  Say thou instead, "I am not as *these* are."

III. THE HUSBANDMEN

Though God, as one that is an householder,
  Called these to labour in His vineyard first,
  Before the husk of darkness was well burst
Bidding them grope their way out and bestir,
5 (Who, questioned of their wages, answered, "Sir,
  Unto each man a penny:") though the worst
  Burthen of heat was theirs and the dry thirst:
Though God has since found none such as these
  were
To do their work like them:—Because of this
10 Stand not ye idle in the market-place.
    Which of ye knoweth *he* is not that last
Who may be first by faith and will?—yea, his
  The hand which after the appointed days
    And hours shall give a Future to their Past?
—1870 (1849)

Soul's Beauty

SONNET LXXVII

Under the arch of Life, where love and death,
  Terror and mystery, guard her shrine, I saw
  Beauty enthroned; and though her gaze struck
    awe,
I drew it in as simply as my breath.
5 Hers are the eyes which, over and beneath,
  The sky and sea bend on thee,—which can draw,
  By sea or sky or woman, to one law,
The allotted bondman of her palm and wreath.

This is that Lady Beauty, in whose praise
10 Thy voice and hand shake still,—long known to
    thee
    By flying hair and fluttering hem,—the beat

---

[1] Luke, the Evangelist, is also the patron saint of artists (and physicians). Tradition says that he painted a portrait of the Virgin Mary.

[2] John 9:4.

Following her daily of thy heart and feet,
How passionately and irretrievably,
In what fond flight, how many ways and days!
—1868 (1867)

Body's Beauty
SONNET LXXVIII

Of Adam's first wife, Lilith,[1] it is told
(The witch he loved before the gift of Eve,)
That, ere the snake's, her sweet tongue could deceive,
And her enchanted hair was the first gold.
5 And still she sits, young while the earth is old,
And, subtly of herself contemplative,
Draws men to watch the bright web she can weave,
Till heart and body and life are in its hold.

The rose and poppy are her flowers; for where
10 Is he not found, O Lilith, whom shed scent
And soft-shed kisses and soft sleep shall snare?
Lo! as that youth's eyes burned at thine, so went
Thy spell through him, and left his straight neck bent
And round his heart one strangling golden hair.
—1868 (1867)

A Superscription
SONNET XCVII

Look in my face; my name is Might-have-been;
I am also called No-more, Too-late, Farewell;
Unto thine ear I hold the dead-sea shell
Cast up thy Life's foam-fretted feet between;
5 Unto thine eyes the glass where that is seen
Which had Life's form and Love's, but by my spell
Is now a shaken shadow intolerable,
Of ultimate things unuttered the frail screen.

Mark me, how still I am! But should there dart
10 One moment through thy soul the soft surprise
Of that winged Peace which lulls the breath of sighs,—
Then shalt thou see me smile, and turn apart
Thy visage to mine ambush at thy heart
Sleepless with cold commemorative eyes.
—1869 (1868)

The One Hope
SONNET CI

When vain desire at last and vain regret
Go hand in hand to death, and all is vain,
What shall assuage the unforgotten pain
And teach the unforgetful to forget?
5 Shall Peace be still a sunk stream long unmet,—
Or may the soul at once in a green plain
Stoop through the spray of some sweet life-fountain
And cull the dew-drenched flowering amulet?

Ah! when the wan soul in that golden air
10 Between the scriptured petals softly blown
Peers breathless for the gift of grace unknown,—
Ah! let none other alien spell soe'er
But only the one Hope's one name be there,—
Not less nor more, but even that word alone.
—1870 (1870)

---

[1] In Rabbinical writings, Lilith is said to have been the first wife of Adam.

Arthur Munby
1828 – 1910

Arthur Munby was a civil servant, diarist, and minor poet. He was obsessed with working-class women, and his verse concerns that group and country life. Munby's diaries reveal that his obsession was partly sexual in nature, and his interest in working-class women led him to pursue, interview, record, and photograph them. In 1873 he secretly married his maidservant, Hannah Cullwick (1833–1909).

❧❧❧

The Serving Maid

When you go out at early morn,
　Your busy hands, sweet drudge, are bare;
　For you must work, and none are there
To see with scorn—to feel with scorn.

5　And when the weekly wars begin,
　Your arms are naked to the hilt,
　And many a sturdy pail's a-tilt
To sheathe them in—to plunge them in.

For you at least can understand
10　That daily work is hard and stern,
　That those who toil for bread must learn
To bare the hand—to spoil the hand.

But in the evening, when they dine,
　And you behind each frequent chair
15　Are flitting lightly here and there
To bring them wine—to pour them wine;

Oh then, from every dainty eye
　That may not so be shock'd or grieved,
　Your hands are hid, your arms are sleeved:
20　We ask not why—we tell not why.

Ah fools! Though you for workday scours,
　And they for show, unveil their charms,
　Love is not bound to snowy arms,
He thinks of yours—he speaks of yours:

25　To me his weighted shaft has come;
　Though hand and arm are both unseen,
　Your rosy wrist peeps out between
And sends it home—and speeds it home.
—1865

Post Mortem[1]

I lay in my coffin under the sod;
　But the rooks they caw'd, and the sheep they trod
And munch'd and bleated, and made such a noise—
What with the feet of the charity boys[2]
5　Trampling over the old grave-stones—
That it loosen'd my inarticulate bones,
　And chased my sleep away.

So I turn'd (for the coffin is not so full
As it was, you know) my aching skull;
10　And said to my wife—and it's not my fault
If she *does* lie next to me in the vault—
Said to her kindly, "My love, my dear,
How do you like these sounds we hear
　Over our heads to-day?"

15　My wife had always a good strong voice;
But I'm not so sure that I did rejoice
When I found it as strong as it used to be,
And so unexpectedly close to me:

---

[1] "after death"; the term was introduced into English in the nineteenth century.

[2] residents of an orphanage.

I thought, if her temper *should* set in,
20 Why, the boards between us are very thin,
And whenever the bearers come one by one
To deposit the corpse of my eldest son,
Who is spending the earnings of his papa
With such sumptuous ease and such great *éclât*,[1]
25 They may think it more pleasant, perhaps, than I
    did,
To find that in death we were not divided.
However, I trusted to time and the worms;
And I kept myself to the mildest terms
    Of a conjugal How d'ye do.

30 "John," said my wife, "you're a Body, like me;
At least if you ain't, why you ought to be;
And I really don't think, when I reflect,
That I ought to pay as much respect
To a rattling prattling skeleton
35 As I did to a man of sixteen stone.
However (says she), I shall just remark
That this here place is so cool and dark,
I'm certain sure, if you hadn't have spoke,
My slumber'd never have thus been broke;
40 So I wish you'd keep your—voice in your head;
For I don't see the good of being dead,
    If one mayn't be quiet too."

She spoke so clear and she spoke so loud,
I thank'd my stars that a linen shroud
45 And a pair of boards (though they *were* but thin)
Kept out some part of that well-known din:
And, talking of shrouds, the very next word
That my empty echoing orbits heard
Was, "Gracious me, I can tell by the feel
50 That I'm all over rags from head to heel!
Here's jobs for needle and thread without ending,
For there's ever-so-many holes wants mending!"
"My love," I ventured to say, "I fear
It's not much use, your mending 'em here;
55 For, as fast as you do, there's worse than moth,

And worse than mice, or rats, or both,
Will eat up the work of your cotton ball
And leave you never a shroud at all—
    No more than they have to me."

60 Now, whether it was that she took it ill
My seeming to question her feminine skill,
Or whether 'twas simply that we were wedded—
The very thing happen'd that most I dreaded:
For, by way of reply, on the coffin-side,
65 Just where the planks had started wide,
There came a blow so straight and true
That it shook my vertebral column in two;
And what more might have follow'd I cannot tell,
But that very minute ('twas just as well)
70 The flagstone was lifted overhead,
And the red-nosed buriers of the dead
Let down a load on my coffin-plate
That stunn'd me quite with the shock of its weight.
'Twas the corpse, of course, of my eldest son,
75 Who had injured his brain (a little one)
By many a spirituous brain-dissolver,
And finish'd it off with a Colt's revolver.[2]
Well—when they had gone and the noise had ceased,
I look'd for one other attack, at least:
80 But, would you believe it? The place was quiet,
And the worms had resumed their usual diet!
Nay, everything else was silent too;
The rooks they neither caw'd nor flew,
And the sheep slept sound by footstone and head,
85 And the charity boys had been whipp'd to bed.
So I turn'd again, and I said to myself—
"Now, as sure as I'm laid on this sordid shelf
Away from the living that smile or weep,
I'll sleep if I can, and let *her* too sleep:
90 And I will not once, for pleasure or pain,
Unhinge my jaws to speak again,
    No, not if she speaks to me."
—1865

---

[1] brilliance, dazzling effect, conspicuous success.

[2] The revolver was invented by the American Samuel Colt in 1835.

A Husband's Episodes

I heard a note in my garden bower;
   A note of cooing, and kisses of love.
My fair young wife was abroad at that hour:
   I saw the cedar branches move,

5 And two shadows, one of a man,
   Certainly pass'd across the lawn
Into the place where *our* kisses began,
   When the chamber was still and the curtains
     drawn.

At last I said, when the morning came,
10   And she was as sleek as a sunning dove,
"Shall we go forth, my dainty dame,
   From the jonquil-nests and the cedar grove,

"And seek the open air of the sea,
   Where the blue waves gallop against the shore
15 Just as the heart of a man, set free,
   Bounds toward the steadfast things of yore?"

We went; for she did not spy my drift:
   She only saw, that down by the sea
There would be many a change and shift,
20   And many a chance of escape from me.

But I was 'ware of a certain walk,
   Close to the edge of the cliffs so tall,
Where ledges and lumps of the crafty chalk
   Break off to the deep, that swallows them all.

25 We walk'd there once, and not in vain;
   For ever so long it had not slid,
But the rock was loosen'd now by rain,
   And I thought it would slide that day. It did.

So she went down with it into the foam;
30   And, the crowner's 'quest absolving me,

I turn'd (with crape on my hat) toward home,
   And waited awhile till the end should be.

I had not long to wait for him:
   He came, with malice shut up in his eyes,
35 With his tongue so trite, and his smile so trim,
   And gave me comfort, and gave me sighs:

But, when I went with him back to the train—
   Just as a friend should do, you know—
We talk'd the sad tale over again;
40   And, whether I let his damp hand go

A little too sharply, who can tell?
   But down, with a ghastly groan and grim,
Under the griding[1] wheels he fell;
   And the train went over him, limb by limb.

45 As I drove home that glorious night,
   I did not laugh; for you see, my groom
Was sitting behind with his face so white;
   And he *could* tell tales to the housemaids' room.

But I gave my leader the lightest touch
50   Of a whip that would hardly bear control,
And I whistled a few sweet bars—not much—
   Of the merry tune that fill'd my soul.

Ah well! The work of my life is done:
   But I should be rather glad, d'ye know,
55 To get away from the shining sun,
   And hide my triumph beneath my woe.
—1865

T' Runawaa Lass

"Wah, Mary! sittin' lawnsum of a bench,
   Wi' leean white fingers clasp'd, an'
     soonken ah,

---

[1] a poetical term, meaning to pierce through or scrape.

835

A' doin' nowt! Thoo wast a bonny wench,
    Loosty an' strong; wativer's coom'd te tha'?

5 "Ah mahnd, when Maason tonnops was te haw,
    Hoo well thruff t' lands thah foot kept oop wi'
      mahn,
Friv end te end; an' when wa'd dun t' last raw,
    Ah said Ah'd swop mah weary airms for thahn.

"Ther's neer a wonn was fit te match wi' thee
10   Them happy daas, i' t' field or farm or byre;
As brant and lissum as a poplar tree,
    As brisk and cheery as thah moother fire.

"An' noo, thah faace has lossen t' sunbonn glaw,
    Thah stoot yoong limbs ha' getten shroonk an'
      small!
15 Ther's summat worrkin' i' thah mahnd, Ah knaw:
    Speeak oop, me lass, an' tell auld Philip all!"

Then she, with grave affection in her eyes,
    Toss'd back her batter'd bonnet and her hair,
And look'd at him; who saw her wan face rise
20   Again to beauty, sorrow being there.

"Aye, Philip, them was happy daas, indeed!
    Ah mahnd 'em well: sich bonny crops as yon
Oor maaster ow'd, Ah seer Ah niver seed
    I' t' sooth; an' him a joggin' oot upon

25 "His gallowaa, te watch us all agaat—
    Me, an' oor Jaan, an' Jack (wat's getten Jack?)
An' thee, auld lad! Bud wat, it's ovver laat
    For sich as me te fet them good things back!

"Philip, wat said tha' when Ah runn'd awaa?
30   Thaa knaw'd Ah *did*; Ah'd shaam te ax it else;
Bud weer Ah went tha' knawna; an' Ah laa
    Tha' reckon nowt: they're too well off thersels.

"It's all along o' *him*—Ah darna naam
    His awesum naam, for all Ah've said it scoors
35 An' scoors o' tahms, when fost mah trooble caam:
    His faather land, thoo knaws, wer floosh wi'
      oors,

"An' oft an' oft, when Ah've been fettlin' t' coos,
    Or oot i' t' sta'ala'd, maybe, be mesen,
He used te coom, an' dawdle oop te t'hoose,
40   An' stan' an' leeak at ma' lahk owt; an' then

"He'd ax, Was t' maaster in? an sich as that;
    An' keep on axin', when Ah'd tell'd him Naw:
Fond wench! Ah might ha' seen wat he'd be at—
    Bud Ah wer daft te think he luved ma' saw.

45 "Ah thowt, fost tahm Ah foond me 'and iv his,
    Hoo roogh an' bad wer mahn; bud he says,
     'Seah,'
He says, 'me lass, tha' weean't be long lahk this;
    Thoo'lt live a laady, an' ha' nowt te deah.'

"A *laady!* Sitha—this here hand, 'at's tonn'd
50   As white as white, Ah'd fling it, blud an' baan
(That would E too, an' welcum), into t' pond,
    If Ah mud hev mah broon un back agaan.

"Aye, lad! Ah's wander'd oop an' doon a year,
    Be slaape rooads an' be slooshy rooads, si' then,
55 An' larnt wat fawks is maad on; an' Ah seer
    A vast o' laadies is as bad as t' men.

"Bud this backend, when things was got te t' wost
    Wi' me, an' t' babby hingin' at ma' breast,
Ah thowt Ah'd gang te weer Ah lived at fost,
60   An' beg for meeat an' drink, an' maybe rest.

"Well, an' Ah coom'd te' t' farm; bud chap at door
    Says 'Naw,' an' bangs it reet agin me faace;
Sae then Ah gaed tiv oor 'oose; an' mah poor

Auld moother's deead, an' faather's lossen t'
    plaace

65 "An' left, along o' me! When Ah heerd that,
    Ah'd lahk to swound; bud summat kept ma' oop
Wahl Ah gat here; an' here Ah sat an' sat,
    An' t' lahl un hoddin' up it mooth for t' sup

"Ah couldna give. Sae then, at last, Ah says,
70   'Mah baabe,' Ah says, 'there's nowt for thee an'
      me
I' this wolld; bud ther's happen better daas
    Wi' granny, oop i' heaven: saw wa'll dee!'

"Aa, 'twer' a job te do it—still, it's dun:
    Leeaksta, lad, leeaksta! T' boondle o' mah knee,
75 It's noan a thing 'at sich as you mud shun,—
    It's mah dead baabe: an' noo then, *Ah* mun dee!"

He was a poor man, Philip: do you think
    He led her to the workhouse, or, mayhap,
Fetch'd out the constable, to get a blink
80   Of that cold infant chilling all her lap?

Such pious folks as you, and I, and they,
    Of course had done it: so perhaps, you know,
Perhaps, he did! At least, I cannot say,
    For fear of men, I dare not answer, No.
—1865

"Followers Not Allowed"

Ædis nobis AREA *est.* [1]
    Plaut. Asin.

Now lithe and listen, ladies, if you please;
  Here are the words of Hannah Cullender, [2]

[1] Literal translation: "Our house is a place for catching things," from the
Comedy of Asses by Plautus.

[2] presumably a thinly veiled reference to Hannah Cullwick, the
domestic servant whom Munby secretly married.

A maid-of-all-work. You that sit at ease,
    You don't see much that's beautiful in her,
5 Who never sits at all, except at meals,
    And then so awkwardly. You know, her face
Is coarse and homely, and from head to heels,
    Through all her clumsy frame, the lines of grace
Are shockingly distorted. If her hand
10   Be placed against your own, you needn't grudge
The pain of touching it; you'll understand,
    Just by the look, that she's a very drudge,
A mere hard-working servant.
                Well! and yet,
    I say again, you laughing light-o'-loves,
15 Before you clasp the last new carcanet
    About your arm, or fit your last new gloves,
Listen to Hannah. This is what she said,
    Once on a time, when she had holiday,
And, for a wonder, left off earning bread
20   To go a-pleasuring. She was as gay,
All by herself, as if she'd had, like you,
    Duenna, flaming footmen, cavalier;
Her tastes being humble, and her fetters few,
    She walk'd about, and gazed, and drank her beer,
25 And chatted, too, with strangers; for, you see,
    One must have folks to talk to, and the girl
Has not a friend in all the town but me,
    That was her mistress once. Perhaps the whirl
Of London life had got into her brain;
30   But this is what she said to me; and mind,
She said it meekly.
             I had tried in vain
    To warn her of the men: "You're very kind;
But, ma'am," she said, "although it's fifteen year
    I've been in service, if you come to *age*,
35 I doubt I'm younger than my missis were
    When she were married. It's the taking wage,
And doing work, and bothering, that tells,
    And makes one coarse. But still, it makes us
      strong,
And very good at fending for oursels;
40   And that's the main thing, too.

It's not so long
Since Miss Jemima, that was wed last spring,
    First courted with the brewer; and, my word!
But they was free to court, like anything:
    Why, things was left o' purpose, as I heard,
45 For them to meet, and get acquaint, and be
    Match'd, like, and so have done with it. But
        what!
When Jim and me was keeping company,
    My missis play'd a different game to that:
'Twas, 'Oh, no! There's no followers allow'd
50   In this house.' So my Jim, next time he come,
I show'd him my charackter (I was proud,
    And so was he), and, 'Jim,' I says, 'go home;
We've been a-courting now this goodish while,
    And here's the end o't; for I can't afford,'
55 I says (and then I made-believe to smile),
    'I can't afford to lose my place.' My word!
It went again me; he did look so smart
    And nice, and were a tidy chap, you see,
As could be: still, I settled we must part,
60   And part we did.
                                But, ma'am, I think 'twould be
A rare good job, to let a servant maid
    Live honest, then, and have her sweethearts free,
Like ladies have; and not be so afraid,
    And run out sneaking to the area-gate,
65 And whispering on the sly. There's many a lass
    Takes up with lads and finds 'em out too late,
For want of leave to know 'em. It do pass
    My wits, to reckon what a man is like,
When he just meets you, maybe, on a spree,
70   Or brings the milk, and that. There's Bickerdike
Our butcher; bless you, ma'am, he bothers me
    Week after week, with every joint of meat,
To have him: have him? Why, I canna tell,
    No more than you can, if he means deceit,
75 With seeing him a that way. He might well
    Be on with other girls, all unbeknown,
One to a street, or better. But to come
    Right open and above-board, and sit down,

And show hisself, and tell what sort of home
80   He'd give a wife, and say out, like a man,
Before our master, what he say to me;
    Why, then it would be different."
                                            I began
To find this babble tedious. Generally
    One thinks of servants as a race who live
85 By labour and new bonnets; and, indeed,
    How could our households be at peace and thrive,
If they had sweethearts too? So, there was need
    To warn our Hannah against courting. Still—
These lonely maidens, fretting in their dens
90   Against each other, full of foolish will,
Forlorn of nobler women's and of men's
    Companionship and counsel—after all,
Perhaps there may be found within their souls
    Some frozen germ that represents in small
95 The full-grown love which fashions and controls
    The hearts of us fair ladies.—Well: if so,
    I think we ought to cherish it, you know.
—1865

Woman's Rights

One must take the rough with the smooth.
Nec crimen duras esset habere manus.

Some say, that women should be weak;
    That sunburnt throat and roughen'd cheek
        Are wholly out of place
For that sweet sex, whose duty lies
5   In having lovely lips and eyes,
        And attitudes all grace.

And some, with difference, are agreed
That women should be weak, indeed,
        Of body and of limb;
10 But, *en revanche,*[1] in brain and mind

—————
[1] in return; as a retaliation. The term was introduced into English in the nineteenth century.

They may and ought to be a kind
   Of stronger seraphim.

Weak? cries another; why, they are!
No talk of 'should be:' you're aware
15   That much diversity
Of ways, of frame, and, in a word,
Of nature, makes it quite absurd
   For them to work as we.

"Of course!" says one; "it's not our trade:
20 Our little hands were never made
   To wipe another's dust;
So here's the formula I use:
'Let women work because they choose,
   And men because they must.'

25 "That is, at handiwork. But brains!
I shall not waste (says she) much pains
   To prove and prove again
That women needn't stay at home
To use them; they may go and come,
30   A better sort of men,

"At mart and meeting, church and bar:
Wherever fame and fortune are
   There I (she says) believe
That woman shortly will resort;
35 Till every Adam finds in court
   An opposition Eve."

Alas, my lively learned friends!
This child but feebly comprehends
   The meaning of it all:
40 What with your speeches and your sections,
Your arguments and grave objections,
   Your—well, I won't say gall;

Your pamphlets, letters to the *Times*,
Smart magazines, and ready rhymes
45   On everything but love;

And papers too by high-soul'd men,
Whose bosoms bleed for Lydia, when
   She soils her dainty glove;

I tell you, what with this and that,
50 We plain ones can't think what you're at;
   Indeed we really can't:
And therefore, in the name of sense,
Eschew negation and pretence,
   And say the thing you want!

55 Look here: you strive, and nobly too,
To find employment for that crew
   Of hapless imbeciles
(Excuse the word) whose lot in life
Lies 'twixt the needle and the knife,
60   Unless they sell their smiles:

You trust them with a watch's works;
You make them prentices and clerks;
   Put pens behind their ears;
Or bid them tell the feeling cords,
65 In vivid music of dumb words,
   Our triumphs and our fears:

'Tis new; but who will interfere?
For me, I trust that every year
   Your telegraphic maids,
70 Your girls who copy briefs and wills
Or set up circulars and bills,
   May flourish in their trades.

Et puis, mesdames?[1] These quiet duties
May do for sedentary beauties;
75   But, you yourselves must own,
All women don't like sitting still;
All are not competent to fill
   A clerkly seat in town.

---

[1] "And then, ladies?"

Some lasses, neither slim nor fair,
80 Live mostly in the open air,
   And rather like it, too:
Their faces and their hands are brown;
Their fists, perchance, might knock you down,
   If they were minded to!

85 What say you then of such as these?
May they continue, if they please,
   To swing the pail, to scrub,
To make the cheese, to warm the cruds,
And lash the storm of steaming suds
90   Within the washing-tub?

"Well, yes," say you; "undoubtedly:
We meddle not with them; you see
   Our business is with wrong:
We wish to set the balance straight,
95 And somewhat equalize in fate
   The feeble and the strong.

"We seek the *middle* classes' good:
Their overflowing womanhood
   Exactly suits our plan;
100 Which is, to prove the latent might
Of women, and assert their right
   To work abreast of man."

Good: and a blessing on the deed!
Since then you're anxious to succeed,
105   I gladly make it known
That Nature, in her wiser hours,
Has seconded this plan of yours
   By teachings of her own.

"Whene'er you take your walks abroad,"
110 You'll haply see along the road,
   In field, or yard, or farm,
Those girls of whom I spoke just now:
You'll see them lift a sweating brow,
   Or bare a rough red arm

115 Right up through all its brawny length;
And do with ease such feats of strength
   As make you ladies stare;
Or, pausing in their toil, they'll stand
And hold you out a harden'd hand,
120   And ask you how you are.

Is it not comfort, then, to know
These wenches have such thews to show,
   And work with such a will?
What health there is in every face!
125 And, if with a Herculean grace,[1]
   Are they not graceful still?

"Oh no!" you scream, "good gracious, no!
You *wicked* man! How dare you so
   Distort our publish'd views?
130 We *hate* what is unfeminine;
We can't see anything divine
   In muscles or in thews!

"Hard hands! and oh, a dirty face!
What sad indelible disgrace
135   For this soft sex of ours!
We want them to be nice and clean;
With tasteful dress and gentle mien,
   Like nymphs among the flowers!

"If these poor souls are so degraded
140 They fancy they can work, unaided
   By our wise counsellings,
We must, we really must, present
And pass a Bill through Parliament
   To stop such dreadful things!

145 "Why were they never, never taught
To scorn their labour as they ought,
   And feel that it is wrong

---

[1] In Greek mythology, Hercules was a hero of superhuman physical strength, the son of Zeus and Alcmene.

Thus to use strength and gain by it?
It doesn't signify one bit
150   That they *are* well and strong:

"We're bound to *show* them what they want;
To say they mustn't and they shan't
    Destroy their fair complexions
By doing work that *men* should do:
155   Great, big, ungrateful men like you,
    Who raise these weak objections!"

I raise objections? Nay, my dears:
'Tis true, I've watch'd their work for years
    With no unfriendly eye;
160   Because, alas! in every point
My facts are somewhat out of joint
    With half your theory.

But now, you see, you're caught at last:
Women, whose powers are so vast,
165   Are *children*, after all!
They mustn't give, as men may give,
Their sweat and brains, nor freely live
    In great things and in small:

They must be guided from above,
170   By quips of patronizing love,
    To do or not to do:
Though they be made of stalwart stuff,
Buxom and brave and stout enough,
    And full of spirit too,

175   Yet they may never seek, forsooth,
To enterprize their lusty youth
    In labours or commands
Which, while they leave unfetter'd course
To native energy and force,
180   Might spoil their pretty hands!

"Nay, spoil their woman's heart," say you.
What! Then you think it isn't true
    That every woman dims
The moon-like lustre of her kind
185   As much by manliness of mind
    As manliness of limbs?

Or else—and this is what you mean—
You simply seek a grander scene,
    A more sublime display,
190   For female talents of the brain:
You strive (I hope 'tis not in vain)
    To find your sex a way

To share our honours and our fame—
The civic or forensic name
195   On which your fancy lingers;
But, when it comes to rough hard work,
You will not help us with a fork—
    Much less with your white fingers.

There is a game that schoolboys use,
200   Called "Heads I win, and tails you lose";
    And this smart game of shares,
Wherein we men are to be drudges,
And you both *élégantes*[1] and Judges,
    Seems very much like theirs.

205   Why don't you drop it, and be frank?
For our part, we must say point-blank,
    With much respectful moan,
That we'll oppose you tooth and nail,
Unless you'll swallow *all* the whale,
210   Or let the beast alone.

Either agree, you stand apart,
As much by nature as by art,
    In power of the mind—
In grasp of knowledge—in the right

---

[1] elegant women.

215 Of work—in such inferior might
  As differs kind from kind;

Either confess (and Truth forbid
We should allow it, if you did)
  That you are born to serve:
220 Slight creatures, only fit to stand
The smaller tasks of head and hand:
  Weaklings in every nerve:

Or else, take heart of grace, and say,
"You men, we'll meet you any day
225   On all the field of life;
Save only to our bounded sex
The matron care that guards and checks
  A mother, or a wife."

Since there is work for all and each,
230 Rough or refined in frame and speech,
  Rudely or gently nurst,—
Take it; and if you need defence,
Cry, *Honi soit qui mal y pense,*[1]
  And let them think their worst.

235 But don't come forth, with hand on hip
And such grand airs of championship
  To battle for your right,
And then turn round on half your troops
With these terrific howls and whoops,
240   Because they love to fight

In ways less ladylike than yours:
Don't say your Amazons[2] are boors,
  And mustn't seek to ride,
Because, when they have tighten'd girth,
245 Like half the women of the earth
  They choose to mount astride.

Don't practise, in your noble rage,
To stint an honest maiden's wage
  And dwarf her vigour too,
250 Whene'er her daily labours fall
'Mid scenes which you think bad for all,
  Because they startle *you.*

Weaklings, indeed! Yon stunted girl
Who minds the bobbins as they twirl
255   Or plies the flashing loom,
She is a weakling, if you will:
And yet, because she works on still
  Shut up inside a room,

You let her work; you don't pretend
260 That *that* degrades her in the end:
  But, if she dares to go
And brace her muscles in the fields,
Till with a sinewy arm she wields
  The hayfork or the hoe,

265 Straight you lift up your prudish eyes,
Affect a feminine surprise,
  And do your best to spoil
The hearty health, the bluff content,
That Nature's righteous self hath sent
270   To bless her sunburnt toil!

Weaklings? I chanced to be of late
Where young Tom Prentiss and his mate
  Were working side by side:
Who was his mate? A *woman*, dears!
275 A lass whom he has loved for years;
  His sweetheart, Ellen Hyde.

Ah, Ellen is a girl to see;
She has not sacrificed—not she—
  Her massive breadth of limb:
280 If any lad less kind and good

---

[1] literally, "evil to him who evil thinks." The motto of the "Most Noble Order of the Garter," the highest order of knighthood in Great Britain.

[2] in Greek mythology, a race of female warriors living in Scythia.

Than Tom, should happen to be rude,
    She'd make short work of him!

Yet with her strength she is most fair;
Fairest of all the women there,
285   When summer morns are rathe
She seeks her labour, and her large
Lithe form is hail'd by every barge
    That lies along the staith.

Save the red beads about her neck
290 (Tom's gift) her beauty has no speck
    Of gawds and coquetries:
Her bonnet tilted o'er her brow
Is set there, not to guard its snow,
    But just to shade her eyes.

295 Beneath a sleeveless vest of say
Her ample shoulders freely play,
    Her bosom beats at ease;
And, veil'd by half her kilted gown,
The lindsey kirtle[1] loiters down
300   Not far below her knees.

Her hosen? Yes, their warm grey strands
Were knitted by her own true hands
    Beside the cottage fire;
And ankle-boots of size and weight,
305 Nail-studded, shoed with iron plate,
    Complete her brave attire.

Thus have I seen her ply her trade,
With Tom at hand to cheer and aid—
    Though aid she needed none:
310 Who should compare her frame with his
Might fairly doubt, if that or this
    Could better work alone:

And sometimes, when a pause was made,
Leaning on pickaxe or on spade
315   She smiled and whisper'd low,
Whilst, with long labour grown too warm
She drew her firm and freckled arm
    Across her beaded brow.

Thus too, within her mother's home
320 I've seen her frankly go and come—
    So bonny, and so tall;
And seen her sleek her chestnut hair,
And mend her things of workday wear,
    And smooth her Sunday shawl,

325 And sew, in hope of leisure hours,
Her bonnet with the wee bit flowers
    That Tom would most approve;
And in her broken looking-glass
Behold unmoved as sweet a lass
330   As man could wish to love.

Ah Virtue, what a sight was here!
A sight for those to whom is dear
    The substance, not the show:
A woman strong to dare and do,
335 Yet soft towards suffering, and true
    In welfare and in woe:

Whose woman's nature is not lost,
Nor marr'd, nor even tempest-tost,
    But strengthen'd and controll'd:
340 Who, working thus with sinewy hands,
Grows deaf to Folly's fond commands,
    Grows calm and solemn-soul'd.

Yes, ladies of the Yankee creed,[2]
We scruple not to see you bleed—
345   With lancets—if you will,
Or show the pulpit and the bar

---

[1] "Kilted" means "tucked up"; "kirtle" is a woman's gown or outer petticoat. The term was archaic in the nineteenth century.

[2] Yankee refers to a citizen of the U.S.A.; to be precise, of New England.

How worthy of ourselves you are
  In subtlety and skill;

But, leave your stronger mates alone:
They, tense of thews and stout of bone,
  Rejoice to work amain;

And so they shall, in breadth and length:
As free to use their woman's strength
  As you your woman's brain.
—1865

Elizabeth Siddal
1829 – 1862

Elizabeth Siddal met one of the young Pre-Raphaelites, Walter Deverell, when she was working in a milliner's shop near Leicester Square in London when she was about twenty. Attracted by her unusual beauty, Deverell asked her to model for one of his pictures. She later modelled for Holman Hunt, Dante Gabriel Rossetti, and Millais— for whom she posed, in one of the most popular of Victorian depictions, as the drowned Ophelia (in a bath of cooling water, as a result of which she caught a bad cold). In 1852 she became exclusively Rossetti's model; they were married in May 1860. On 10 February, 1862, she took an overdose of laudanum, whether accidentally or intentionally, and died the next morning. Her poems invite interesting comparison with the lyrics of Christina Rossetti.

❧❧

The Lust of the Eyes

I care not for my Lady's soul
  Though I worship before her smile;
I care not where be my Lady's goal
  When her beauty shall lose its wile.

5 Low sit I down at my Lady's feet
  Gazing through her wild eyes
Smiling to think how my love will fleet
  When their starlike beauty dies.

I care not if my Lady pray
10   To our Father which is in Heaven
But for joy my heart's quick pulses play
  For to me her love is given.

Then who shall close my Lady's eyes
  And who shall fold her hands?
15 Will any hearken if she cries
  Up to the unknown lands?
—1899

Worn Out

Thy strong arms are around me, love,
  My head is on thy breast:

Though words of comfort come from thee,
  My soul is not at rest:

5 For I am but a startled thing,
  Nor can I ever be
Aught save a bird whose broken wing
  Must fly away from thee.

I cannot give to thee the love
10   I gave so long ago—
The love that turned and struck me down
  Amid the blinding snow.

I can but give a sinking heart
  And weary eyes of pain,
15 A faded mouth that cannot smile
  And may not laugh again.

Yet keep thine arms around me, love,
  Until I drop to sleep:
Then leave me—saying no good-bye,
20   Lest I might fall and weep.
—1899 (1856)

At Last

O mother, open the window wide
    And let the daylight in;
The hills grow darker to my sight
    And thoughts begin to swim.

5 And mother dear, take my young son,
    (Since I was born of thee)
And care for all his little ways
    And nurse him on thy knee.

And mother, wash my pale pale hands
10   And then bind up my feet;
My body may no longer rest
    Out of its winding sheet.

And mother dear, take a sapling twig
    And green grass newly mown,
15 And lay them on my empty bed
    That my sorrow be not known.

And mother, find three berries red
    And pluck them from the stalk,
And burn them at the first cockcrow
20   That my spirit may not walk.

And mother dear, break a willow wand,
    And if the sap be even,
Then save it for sweet Robert's sake
    And he'll know my soul's in heaven.

25 And mother, when the big tears fall,
    (And fall, God knows, they may)
Tell him I died of my great love
    And my dying heart was gay.

And mother dear, when the sun has set
30   And the pale kirk grass waves,
Then carry me through the dim twilight
    And hide me among the graves.
                —1899 (1861)

Love and Hate

O pe not thy lips, thou foolish one,
    Nor turn to me thy face:
The blasts of heaven shall strike me down
    Ere I will give thee grace.

5 Take thou thy shadow from my path,
    Nor turn to me and pray:
The wild, wild winds thy dirge may sing
    Ere I will bid thee stay.

Lift up thy false brow from the dust,
10   Nor wild thine hands entwine
Among the golden summer-leaves
    To mock the gay sunshine.

And turn away thy false dark eyes,
    Nor gaze into my face:
15 Great love I bore thee; now great hate
    Sits grimly in its place.

All changes pass me like a dream,
    I neither sing nor pray;
And thou art like the poisonous tree
20   That stole my life away.
                —1906 (1857)

T.E. Brown
1830 – 1897

Thomas Edward Brown was, like William Barnes, a regionalist poet. He wrote narrative and lyrical verse, some in standard English, much in the Manx dialect (a form of Gaelic spoken on the Isle of Man).

※※※

A Sermon at Clevedon[1]

Good Friday [2]

Go on! Go on!
　Don't wait for me!
Isaac was Abraham's son—[3]
Yes, certainly—
5　*And as they clomb Moriah—*
I know! I know!
A type of the Messiah—
Just so! just so!
Perfectly right; and then the ram
10　Caught in the—*listening?* Why of course I am!
Wherefore, my brethren, that was counted—yes—
To Abraham for righteousness—[4]
Exactly, so I said—
At least—but go a-head!
15　*Now mark*
The conduct of the Patriarch—
"Behold the wood!"
Isaac exclaimed—By Jove, an Oxford hood![5]
"But where"—
20　What long straight hair!

"Where is the lamb?"
You mean—the ram:
No, no! I beg your pardon!
There's the Churchwarden,
25　In the Clerk's pew—
Stick tipped with blue—
Now Justification—
"By Faith?"[6] I fancy; Aye, the old equation;
Go it, Justice! Go it, Mercy!
30　Go it, Douglas! Go it, Percy!
I back the winner,
And have the vague conception of the sinner—
Limbs nude,
Horatian attitude,[7]
35　Nursing his foot in Sublapsarian mood—[8]
More power
To you my friend! you're good for half-an-hour.
Dry bones! dry bones!
But in my ear the long-drawn west wind moans,
40　Sweet voices seem to murmur from the wave;
And I can sit, and look upon the stones
That cover Hallam's grave.

—1900

---

[1] Clevedon is a town in Somerset and the burial-place of Arthur Henry Hallam.

[2] the Friday preceding Easter Day; the anniversary of the Crucifixion of Christ. "Good" here means "holy."

[3] See Genesis 22 for the background to this section of the poem.

[4] See Romans 4:3.

[5] robes worn by a member of Oxford University.

[6] to gain one's righteousness from believing in Jesus Christ, not from one's own works. This doctrine was central to the Reformation controversy, as Martin Luther held that humans were saved by faith alone.

[7] Quintus Horatius Flaccus—Horace (65–8 BC).

[8] a Calvinist belief, holding that humans are already fallen despite the election of some individuals.

Christina Rossetti
1830 – 1894

The youngest child in the Rossetti family, Christina Georgina Rossetti was educated at home, in an environment where the men were political, academic, and artistic, and the women were intensely religious. Her father, Gabriele, was an Italian political refugee; her brothers were the poet, painter, and critic, Dante Gabriel, and the critic, William Michael; her sister, Maria Francesca, was a nun. Christina herself was a devout Anglo-Catholic, influenced by the Oxford Movement which attempted to bring early Catholic doctrines and rites into the Anglican church. Associated with the Pre-Raphaelite Brotherhood, Christina contributed to its journal, *The Germ*, and published works which reflected both her devout religiosity and the artistic and poetic influences of the PRB. Gaining immediate recognition with *Goblin Market and Other Poems* (1862) and continued praise with *The Prince's Progress and Other Poems* (1866), Rossetti's works are distinctive in their remarkably simple diction and beautiful, languid imagery.

❧❧❧

Goblin Market

Morning and evening
Maids heard the goblins cry:
"Come buy our orchard fruits,
Come buy, come buy:
5   Apples and quinces,
Lemons and oranges,
Plump unpecked cherries,
Melons and raspberries,
Bloom-down-cheeked peaches,
10   Swart-headed mulberries,
Wild free-born cranberries,
Crab-apples, dewberries,
Pine-apples, blackberries,
Apricots, strawberries;—
15   All ripe together
In summer weather,—
Morns that pass by,
Fair eves that fly;
Come buy, come buy:
20   Our grapes fresh from the vine,
Pomegranates full and fine,
Dates and sharp bullaces,
Rare pears and greengages,

Damsons[1] and bilberries,
25   Taste them and try:
Currants and gooseberries,
Bright-fire-like barberries,
Figs to fill your mouth,
Citrons from the South,
30   Sweet to tongue and sound to eye;
Come buy, come buy."

Evening by evening
Among the brookside rushes,
Laura bowed her head to hear,
35   Lizzie veiled her blushes:
Crouching close together
In the cooling weather,
With clasping arms and cautioning lips,
With tingling cheeks and finger tips.
40   "Lie close," Laura said,
Pricking up her golden head:
"We must not look at goblin men,
We must not buy their fruits:
Who knows upon what soil they fed
45   Their hungry thirsty roots?"
"Come buy," call the goblins

---

[1] a variety of plum, as are bullaces and greengages.

Hobbling down the glen.
"Oh," cried Lizzie, "Laura, Laura,
You should not peep at goblin men."
50 Lizzie covered up her eyes,
Covered close lest they should look;
Laura reared her glossy head,
And whispered like the restless brook:
"Look, Lizzie, look, Lizzie,
55 Down the glen tramp little men.
One hauls a basket,
One bears a plate,
One lugs a golden dish
Of many pounds' weight.
60 How fair the vine must grow
Whose grapes are so luscious;
How warm the wind must blow
Through those fruit bushes."
"No," said Lizzie: "No, no, no;
65 Their offers should not charm us,
Their evil gifts would harm us."
She thrust a dimpled finger
In each ear, shut eyes and ran:
Curious Laura chose to linger
70 Wondering at each merchant man.
One had a cat's face,
One whisked a tail,
One tramped at a rat's pace,
One crawled like a snail,
75 One like a wombat prowled obtuse and furry,
One like a ratel[1] tumbled hurry skurry.
She heard a voice like voice of doves
Cooing all together:
They sounded kind and full of loves
80 In the pleasant weather.

Laura stretched her gleaming neck
Like a rush-imbedded swan,
Like a lily from the beck,[2]

Like a moonlit poplar branch,
85 Like a vessel at the launch
When its last restraint is gone.

Backwards up the mossy glen
Turned and trooped the goblin men,
With their shrill repeated cry,
90 "Come buy, come buy."
When they reached where Laura was
They stood stock still upon the moss,
Leering at each other,
Brother with queer brother;
95 Signalling each other,
Brother with sly brother.
One set his basket down,
One reared his plate;
One began to weave a crown
100 Of tendrils, leaves, and rough nuts brown
(Men sell not such in any town);
One heaved the golden weight
Of dish and fruit to offer her:
"Come buy, come buy," was still their cry.

105 Laura stared but did not stir,
Longed but had no money.
The whisk-tailed merchant bade her taste
In tones as smooth as honey,
The cat-faced purr'd,
110 The rat-paced spoke a word
Of welcome, and the snail-paced even was heard;
One parrot-voiced and jolly
Cried "Pretty Goblin" still for "Pretty Polly";
One whistled like a bird.

115 But sweet-tooth Laura spoke in haste:
"Good Folk, I have no coin;
To take were to purloin:
I have no copper in my purse,
I have no silver either,

---

[1] South African animal, much like a badger.

[2] small brook.

120 And all my gold is on the furze[1]
   That shakes in windy weather
   Above the rusty heather."
"You have much gold upon your head,"
   They answered all together:
125 "Buy from us with a golden curl."
She clipped a precious golden lock,
She dropped a tear more rare than pearl,
Then sucked their fruit globes fair or red.
Sweeter than honey from the rock,
130 Stronger than man-rejoicing wine,
Clearer than water flowed that juice;
She never tasted such before,
How should it cloy with length of use?
She sucked and sucked and sucked the more
135 Fruits which that unknown orchard bore;
She sucked until her lips were sore;
Then flung the emptied rinds away
But gathered up one kernel stone,
And knew not was it night or day
140 As she turned home alone.

   Lizzie met her at the gate
   Full of wise upbraidings:
"Dear, you should not stay so late,
   Twilight is not good for maidens;
145 Should not loiter in the glen
   In the haunts of goblin men.
Do you not remember Jeanie,
How she met them in the moonlight,
Took their gifts both choice and many,
150 Ate their fruits and wore their flowers
   Plucked from bowers
Where summer ripens at all hours?
But ever in the noonlight
   She pined and pined away;
155 Sought them by night and day,
Found them no more but dwindled and grew grey;
   Then fell with the first snow,

While to this day no grass will grow
   Where she lies low:
160 I planted daisies there a year ago
   That never blow.
   You should not loiter so."
"Nay, hush," said Laura:
   "Nay, hush, my sister:
165 I ate and ate my fill,
Yet my mouth waters still;
Tomorrow night I will
   Buy more:" and kissed her:
"Have done with sorrow;
170 I'll bring you plums tomorrow
Fresh on their mother twigs,
   Cherries worth getting;
You cannot think what figs
   My teeth have met in,
175 What melons icy-cold
Piled on a dish of gold
Too huge for me to hold,
What peaches with a velvet nap,
Pellucid[2] grapes without one seed:
180 Odorous indeed must be the mead
Whereon they grow, and pure the wave they drink
   With lilies at the brink,
   And sugar-sweet their sap."

   Golden head by golden head,
185 Like two pigeons in one nest
   Folded in each other's wings,
They lay down in their curtained bed:
Like two blossoms on one stem,
Like two flakes of new-fall'n snow,
190 Like two wands of ivory
   Tipped with gold for awful kings.
Moon and stars gazed in at them,
Wind sang to them lullaby,
Lumbering owls forbore to fly,
195 Not a bat flapped to and fro

---

[1] a prickly evergreen shrub with dark-green spines and yellow flowers.

[2] translucent.

Round their nest:
Cheek to cheek and breast to breast
Locked together in one nest.

Early in the morning
200 When the first cock crowed his warning,
Neat like bees, as sweet and busy,
Laura rose with Lizzie:
Fetched in honey, milked the cows,
Aired and set to rights the house,
205 Kneaded cakes of whitest wheat,
Cakes for dainty mouths to eat,
Next churned butter, whipped up cream,
Fed their poultry, sat and sewed;
Talked as modest maidens should:
210 Lizzie with an open heart,
Laura in an absent dream,
One content, one sick in part;
One warbling for the mere bright day's delight,
One longing for the night.

215 At length slow evening came:
They went with pitchers to the reedy brooks;
Lizzie most placid in her look,
Laura most like a leaping flame.
They drew the gurgling water from its deep.
220 Lizzie plucked purple and rich golden flags,
Then turning homeward said: "The sunset flushes
Those furthest loftiest crags;
Come Laura, not another maiden lags.
No wilful squirrel wags,
225 The beasts and birds are fast asleep."
But Laura loitered still among the rushes,
And said the bank was steep.

And said the hour was early still,
The dew not fall'n, the wind not chill;
230 Listening ever, but not catching
The customary cry,
"Come buy, come buy,"
With its iterated jingle

Of sugar-baited words:
235 Not for all her watching
Once discerning even one goblin
Racing, whisking, tumbling, hobbling—
Let alone the herds
That used to tramp along the glen,
240 In groups or single,
Of brisk fruit-merchant men.

Till Lizzie urged, "O Laura, come;
I hear the fruit-call, but I dare not look:
You should not loiter longer at this brook:
245 Come with me home.
The stars rise, the moon bends her arc,
Each glow-worm winks her spark,
Let us get home before the night grows dark:
For clouds may gather
250 Though this is summer weather,
Put out the lights and drench us through;
Then if we lost our way what should we do?"

Laura turned cold as stone
To find her sister heard that cry alone,
255 That goblin cry,
"Come buy our fruits, come buy."
Must she then buy no more such dainty fruit?
Must she no more such succous[1] pasture find,
Gone deaf and blind?
260 Her tree of life drooped from the root:
She said not one word in her heart's sore ache:
But peering thro' the dimness, nought discerning,
Trudged home, her pitcher dripping all the way;
So crept to bed, and lay
265 Silent till Lizzie slept;
Then sat up in a passionate yearning,
And gnashed her teeth for baulked desire, and wept
As if her heart would break.

---

[1] succulent.

Day after day, night after night,
270 Laura kept watch in vain
In sullen silence of exceeding pain.
She never caught again the goblin cry,
"Come buy, come buy;"—
She never spied the goblin men
275 Hawking their fruits along the glen:
But when the noon waxed bright
Her hair grew thin and grey;
She dwindled, as the fair full moon doth turn
To swift decay and burn
280 Her fire away.

One day remembering her kernel-stone
She set it by a wall that faced the south;
Dewed it with tears, hoped for a root,
Watched for a waxing shoot,
285 But there came none.
It never saw the sun,
It never felt the trickling moisture run:
While with sunk eyes and faded mouth
She dreamed of melons, as a traveller sees
290 False waves in desert drouth
With shade of leaf-crowned trees,
And burns the thirstier in the sandful breeze.

She no more swept the house,
Tended the fowl or cows,
295 Fetched honey, kneaded cakes of wheat,
Brought water from the brook:
But sat down listless in the chimney-nook
And would not eat.

Tender Lizzie could not bear
300 To watch her sister's cankerous care,
Yet not to share.
She night and morning
Caught the goblins' cry:
"Come buy our orchard fruits,
305 Come buy, come buy:"—
Beside the brook, along the glen,

She heard the tramp of goblin men,
The voice and stir
Poor Laura could not hear;
310 Longed to buy fruit to comfort her,
But feared to pay too dear.
She thought of Jeanie in her grave,
Who should have been a bride;
But who for joys brides hope to have
315 Fell sick and died
In her gay prime,
In earliest winter time,
With the first glazing rime,
With the first snow-fall of crisp winter time.

320 Till Laura dwindling
Seemed knocking at Death's door.
Then Lizzie weighed no more
Better and worse;
But put a silver penny in her purse,
325 Kissed Laura, crossed the heath with clumps of furze
At twilight, halted by the brook:
And for the first time in her life
Began to listen and look.

Laughed every goblin
330 When they spied her peeping:
Came towards her hobbling,
Flying, running, leaping,
Puffing and blowing,
Chuckling, clapping, crowing.

335 Clucking and gobbling,
Mopping and mowing,
Full of airs and graces,
Pulling wry faces,
Demure grimaces,
340 Cat-like and rat-like,
Ratel- and wombat-like,
Snail-paced in a hurry,
Parrot-voiced and whistler,
Helter skelter, hurry skurry,

345 Chattering like magpies,
Fluttering like pigeons,
Gliding like fishes,—
Hugged her and kissed her:
Squeezed and caressed her:
350 Stretched up their dishes,
Panniers,[1] and plates:
"Look at our apples
Russet and dun,
Bob at our cherries,
355 Bite at our peaches,
Citrons and dates,
Grapes for the asking,
Pears red with basking
Out in the sun,
360 Plums on their twigs;
Pluck them and suck them,—
Pomegranates, figs."

"Good folk," said Lizzie,
Mindful of Jeanie:
365 "Give me much and many:"
Held out her apron,
Tossed them her penny.
"Nay, take a seat with us,
Honour and eat with us,"
370 They answered grinning:
"Our feast is but beginning.
Night yet is early,
Warm and dew-pearly,
Wakeful and starry:
375 Such fruits as these
No man can carry;
Half their bloom would fly,
Half their dew would dry,
Half their flavour would pass by.
380 Sit down and feast with us,
Be welcome guest with us,
Cheer you and rest with us."—

"Thank you," said Lizzie: "But one waits
At home alone for me:
385 So without further parleying,
If you will not sell me any
Of your fruits though much and many,
Give me back my silver penny
I tossed you for a fee."—
390 They began to scratch their pates,
No longer wagging, purring,
But visibly demurring,
Grunting and snarling.
One called her proud,
395 Cross-grained, uncivil;
Their tones waxed loud,
Their looks were evil.
Lashing their tails
They trod and hustled her,
400 Elbowed and jostled her,
Clawed with their nails,
Barking, mewing, hissing, mocking,
Tore her gown and soiled her stocking,
Twitched her hair out by the roots,
405 Stamped upon her tender feet,
Held her hands and squeezed their fruits
Against her mouth to make her eat.

White and golden Lizzie stood,
Like a lily in a flood,—
410 Like a rock of blue-veined stone
Lashed by tides obstreperously,—
Like a beacon left alone
In a hoary roaring sea,
Sending up a golden fire,—
415 Like a fruit-crowned orange-tree
White with blossoms honey-sweet
Sore beset by wasp and bee,—
Like a royal virgin town
Topped with gilded dome and spire
420 Close beleaguered by a fleet
Mad to tug her standard down.

---

[1] large wicker baskets.

One may lead a horse to water,
Twenty cannot make him drink.
Though the goblins cuffed and caught her,
425 Coaxed and fought her,
Bullied and besought her,
Scratched her, pinched her black as ink,
Kicked and knocked her,
Mauled and mocked her,
430 Lizzie uttered not a word;
Would not open lip from lip
Lest they should cram a mouthful in:
But laughed in heart to feel the drip
Of juice that syruped all her face,
435 And lodged in dimples of her chin,
And streaked her neck which quaked like curd.
At last the evil people,
Worn out by her resistance,
Flung back her penny, kicked their fruit
440 Along whichever road they took,
Not leaving root or stone or shoot;
Some writhed into the ground,
Some dived into the brook
With ring and ripple,
445 Some scudded on the gale without a sound,
Some vanished in the distance.

In a smart, ache, tingle,
Lizzie went her way;
Knew not was it night or day;
450 Sprang up the bank, tore thro' the furze,
Threaded copse and dingle,
And heard her penny jingle
Bouncing in her purse,—
Its bounce was music to her ear.
455 She ran and ran
As if she feared some goblin man
Dogged her with gibe or curse
Or something worse:
But not one goblin skurried after,
460 Nor was she pricked by fear;
The kind heart made her windy-paced

That urged her home quite out of breath with haste
And inward laughter.

She cried, "Laura," up the garden,
465 "Did you miss me?
Come and kiss me.
Never mind my bruises,
Hug me, kiss me, suck my juices
Squeezed from goblin fruits for you,
470 Goblin pulp and goblin dew.
Eat me, drink me, love me;
Laura, make much of me;
For your sake I have braved the glen
And had to do with goblin merchant men."

475 Laura started from her chair,
Flung her arms up in the air,
Clutched her hair:
"Lizzie, Lizzie, have you tasted
For my sake the fruit forbidden?
480 Must your light like mine be hidden,
Your young life like mine be wasted,
Undone in mine undoing,
And ruined in my ruin,
Thirsty, cankered, goblin-ridden?"—
485 She clung about her sister,
Kissed and kissed and kissed her:
Tears once again
Refreshed her shrunken eyes,
Dropping like rain
490 After long sultry drouth;
Shaking with aguish fear, and pain,
She kissed and kissed her with a hungry mouth.

Her lips began to scorch,
That juice was wormwood to her tongue,
495 She loathed the feast:
Writhing as one possessed she leaped and sung,
Rent all her robe, and wrung
Her hands in lamentable haste,
And beat her breast.

500 Her locks streamed like the torch
Borne by a racer at full speed,
Or like the mane of horses in their flight,
Or like an eagle when she stems[1] the light
Straight toward the sun,
505 Or like a caged thing freed,
Or like a flying flag when armies run.

Swift fire spread through her veins, knocked at her
    heart,
Met the fire smouldering there
510 And overbore its lesser flame;
She gorged on bitterness without a name:
Ah fool, to choose such part
510 Of soul-consuming care!
Sense failed in the mortal strife:
Like the watch-tower of a town
Which an earthquake shatters down,
Like a lightning-stricken mast,
515 Like a wind-uprooted tree
Spun about,
Like a foam-topped waterspout
Cast down headlong in the sea,
She fell at last;
520 Pleasure past and anguish past,
Is it death or is it life?

Life out of death.
That night long Lizzie watched by her,
Counted her pulse's flagging stir,
525 Felt for her breath,
Held water to her lips, and cooled her face
With tears and fanning leaves.
But when the first birds chirped about their eaves,
And early reapers plodded to the place
530 Of golden sheaves,
And dew-wet grass
Bowed in the morning winds so brisk to pass,
And new buds with new day
Opened of cup-like lilies on the stream,

535 Laura awoke as from a dream,
Laughed in the innocent old way,
Hugged Lizzie but not twice or thrice;
Her gleaming locks showed not one thread of grey,
Her breath was sweet as May,
540 And light danced in her eyes.

Days, weeks, months, years
Afterwards, when both were wives
With children of their own;
Their mother-hearts beset with fears,
545 Their lives bound up in tender lives;
Laura would call the little ones
And tell them of her early prime,
Those pleasant days long gone
Of not-returning time:
550 Would talk about the haunted glen,
The wicked quaint fruit-merchant men,
Their fruits like honey to the throat
But poison in the blood
(Men sell not such in any town):
555 Would tell them how her sister stood
In deadly peril to do her good,
And win the fiery antidote:
Then joining hands to little hands
Would bid them cling together,—
560 "For there is no friend like a sister
In calm or stormy weather;
To cheer one on the tedious way,
To fetch one if one goes astray,
To lift one if one totters down,
565 To strengthen whilst one stands."
—1862 (APRIL 27, 1859)

A Birthday

My heart is like a singing bird
  Whose nest is in a watered shoot:
My heart is like an apple tree
  Whose boughs are bent with thickset fruit;

---

[1] makes headway against.

5 My heart is like a rainbow shell
    That paddles in a halcyon[1] sea;
My heart is gladder than all these
    Because my love is come to me.

Raise me a dais of silk and down;
10   Hang it with vair[2] and purple dyes;
Carve it in doves and pomegranates,
    And peacocks with a hundred eyes;
Work it in gold and silver grapes,
    In leaves and silver fleurs-de-lys;
15 Because the birthday of my life
    Is come, my love is come to me.
    —1862

After Death

The curtains were half drawn; the floor was
    swept
    And strewn with rushes; rosemary and may[3]
Lay thick upon the bed on which I lay,
Where, through the lattice, ivy-shadows crept.
5 He leaned above me, thinking that I slept
    And could not hear him; but I heard him say,
    "Poor child, poor child"; and as he turned away
Came a deep silence, and I knew he wept.
He did not touch the shroud, or raise the fold
10   That hid my face, or take my hand in his,
        Or ruffle the smooth pillows for my head.
        He did not love me living; but once dead
    He pitied me; and very sweet it is
To know he still is warm though I am cold.
    —1862

---

[1] tranquil.

[2] a kind of squirrel fur, bluish-grey and white, represented heraldically by rows of blue and white shields or bells.

[3] hawthorn flowers.

An Apple Gathering

I plucked pink blossoms from mine apple tree
    And wore them all that evening in my hair:
Then in due season when I went to see
    I found no apples there.

5 With dangling basket all along the grass
    As I had come I went the selfsame track:
My neighbors mocked me while they saw me pass
    So empty-handed back.

Lilian and Lilias smiled in trudging by,
10   Their heaped-up basket teased me like a jeer;
Sweet-voiced they sang beneath the sunset sky,
    Their mother's home was near.

Plump Gertrude passed me with her basket full,
    A stronger hand than hers helped it along;
15 A voice talked with her through the shadows cool
    More sweet to me than song.

Ah Willie, Willie, was my love less worth
    Than apples with their green leaves piled above?
I counted rosiest apples on the earth
20   Of far less worth than love.

So once it was with me you stooped to talk
    Laughing and listening in this very lane;
To think that by this way we used to walk
    We shall not walk again!

25 I let my neighbors pass me, ones and twos
    And groups; the latest said the night grew chill,
And hastened: but I loitered; while the dews
    Fell fast I loitered still.
    —1862

Echo [1]

Come to me in the silence of the night;
    Come in the speaking silence of a dream;
Come with soft rounded cheeks and eyes as bright
        As sunlight on a stream;
5   Come back in tears,
O memory, hope, love of finished years.

Oh dream how sweet, too sweet, too bitter sweet,
    Whose wakening should have been in Paradise,
Where souls brimfull of love abide and meet;
10   Where thirsting longing eyes
            Watch the slow door
That opening, letting in, lets out no more.

Yet come to me in dreams, that I may live
    My very life again tho' cold in death:
15 Come back to me in dreams, that I may give
        Pulse for pulse, breath for breath:
            Speak low, lean low,
As long ago, my love, how long ago.
—1862

"No, Thank you, John"

I never said I loved you, John:
    Why will you teaze me day by day,
And wax a weariness to think upon
        With always "do" and "pray"?

5 You know I never loved you, John;
        No fault of mine made me your toast:
Why will you haunt me with a face as wan
        As shows an hour-old ghost?

I dare say Meg or Moll would take
10   Pity upon you, if you'd ask:

And pray don't remain single for my sake
        Who can't perform that task.

I have no heart?—Perhaps I have not;
        But then you're mad to take offence
15 That I don't give you what I have not got:
        Use your own common sense.

Let bygones be bygones:
        Don't call me false, who owed not to be true:
I'd rather answer "No" to fifty Johns
20   Than answer "Yes" to you.

Let's mar our pleasant days no more,
        Song-birds of passage, days of youth:
Catch at today, forget the days before:
        I'll wink at your untruth.

25 Let us strike hands as hearty friends;
        No more, no less; and friendship's good:
Only don't keep in view ulterior ends,
        And points not understood

In open treaty. Rise above
30   Quibbles and shuffling off and on:
Here's friendship for you if you like; but love,—
        No, thank you, John.
—1862

Song

When I am dead, my dearest,
        Sing no sad songs for me;
Plant thou no roses at my head,
        Nor shady cypress tree.
5 Be the green grass above me
        With showers and dewdrops wet;
And if thou wilt, remember,
        And if thou wilt, forget.

---

[1] the nymph who, because of her unrequited lover for Narcissus, pined away until only her voice remained.

I shall not see the shadows,
10   I shall not feel the rain;
I shall not hear the nightingale
      Sing on as if in pain.[1]
And dreaming through the twilight
      That doth not rise nor set,
15 Haply I may remember,
      And haply may forget.
—1862

Uphill

Does the road wind uphill all the way?
      Yes, to the very end.
Will the day's journey take the whole long day?
      From morn to night, my friend.

5   But is there for the night a resting place?
      A roof for when the slow dark hours begin.
May not the darkness hide it from my face?
      You cannot miss that inn.

Shall I meet other wayfarers at night?
10   Those who have gone before.
Then must I knock, or call when just in sight?
      They will not keep you standing at that door.

Shall I find comfort, travel-sore and weak?
      Of labor you shall find the sum.
15 Will there be beds for me and all who seek?
      Yea, beds for all who come.
—1862

---

[1] Tereus, a Thracian king, husband of Procne, fell in love with and raped Philomela, Procne's sister. To conceal his conduct he cut out her tongue. But Philomela communicated with Procne via a piece of embroidery. Procne killed the king's son Itys, and the two sisters fled. As a result of their prayer to the gods to be changed into birds, Philomela became a nightingale and Procne a swallow.

A Better Resurrection

I have no wit, no words, no tears;
      My heart within me like a stone
Is numbed too much for hopes or fears;
      Look right, look left, I dwell alone;
5   I lift mine eyes, but dimmed with grief
      No everlasting hills I see;
My life is in the falling leaf:
      O Jesus, quicken me.

My life is like a faded leaf,
10   My harvest dwindled to a husk;
Truly my life is void and brief
      And tedious in the barren dusk;
My life is like a frozen thing,
      No bud nor greenness can I see:
15 Yet rise it shall—the sap of Spring;
      O Jesus, rise in me.

My life is like a broken bowl,
      A broken bowl that cannot hold
One drop of water for my soul
20   Or cordial in the searching cold;
Cast in the fire the perished thing,
      Melt and remould it, till it be
A royal cup for Him my King:
      O Jesus, drink of me.
—1862

"The Iniquity of the Fathers Upon the Children"

Oh the rose of keenest thorn!
      One hidden summer morn
Under the rose I was born.

I do not guess his name
5   Who wrought my Mother's shame,
And gave me life forlorn,

But my Mother, Mother, Mother,
I know her from all other.
My Mother pale and mild,
10 Fair as ever was seen,
She was but scarce sixteen,
Little more than a child,
When I was born
To work her scorn.
15 With secret bitter throes,
In a passion of secret woes,
She bore me under the rose.

One who my Mother nursed
Took me from the first:—
20 "O nurse, let me look upon
This babe that costs so dear;
Tomorrow she will be gone:
Other mothers may keep
Their babes awake and asleep,
25 But I must not keep her here."—
Whether I know or guess,
I know this not the less.

So I was sent away
That none might spy the truth:
30 And my childhood waxed to youth
And I left off childish play.
I never cared to play
With the village boys and girls;
And I think they thought me proud,
35 I found so little to say
And kept so from the crowd:
But I had the longest curls
And I had the largest eyes,
And my teeth were small like pearls;
40 The girls might flout and scout me,
But the boys would hang about me
In sheepish mooning wise.

Our one-street village stood
A long mile from the town,

45 A mile of windy down
And bleak one-sided wood,
With not a single house.
Our town itself was small,
With just the common shops,
50 And throve in its small way.
Our neighbouring gentry reared
The good old-fashioned crops,
And made old-fashioned boasts
Of what John Bull would do
55 If Frenchman Frog appeared,
And drank old-fashioned toasts,
And made old-fashioned bows
To my Lady at the Hall.

My Lady at the Hall
60 Is grander than they all:
Hers is the oldest name
In all the neighbourhood;
But the race must die with her
Tho' she's a lofty dame,
65 For she's unmarried still.

Poor people say she's good
And has an open hand
As any in the land,
And she's the comforter
70 Of many sick and sad;
My nurse once said to me
That everything she had
Came of my Lady's bounty:
"Tho' she's greatest in the county
75 She's humble to the poor,
No beggar seeks her door
But finds help presently.
I pray both night and day
For her, and you must pray:
80 But she'll never feel distress
If needy folk can bless."

I was a little maid
When here we came to live
From somewhere by the sea.
85 Men spoke a foreign tongue
There where we used to be
When I was merry and young,
Too young to feel afraid;
The fisher-folk would give
90 A kind strange word to me,
There by the foreign sea:
I don't know where it was,
But I remember still
Our cottage on a hill,
95 And fields of flowering grass
On that fair foreign shore.

I like my old home best,
But this was pleasant too:
So here we made our nest
100 And here I grew.
And now and then my Lady
In riding past our door
Would nod to Nurse and speak,
Or stoop and pat my cheek;
105 And I was always ready
To hold the field-gate wide
For my Lady to go thro';
My Lady in her veil
So seldom put aside,
110 My Lady grave and pale.

I often sat to wonder
Who might my parents be,
For I knew of something under
My simple-seeming state.
115 Nurse never talked to me
Of mother or of father,
But watched me early and late
With kind suspicious cares:
Or not suspicious, rather
120 Anxious, as if she knew

Some secret I might gather
And smart for unawares.
Thus I grew.

But Nurse waxed old and grey,
125 Bent and weak with years.
There came a certain day
That she lay upon her bed
Shaking her palsied head,
With words she gasped to say
130 Which had to stay unsaid.
Then with a jerking hand
Held out so piteously
She gave a ring to me
Of gold wrought curiously,
135 A ring which she had worn
Since the day that I was born,
She once had said to me:
I slipped it on my finger;
Her eyes were keen to linger
140 On my hand that slipped it on;
Then she sighed one rattling sigh
And stared on with sightless eyes:—
The one who loved me was gone.

How long I stayed alone
145 With the corpse, I never knew,
For I fainted dead as stone:
When I came to life once more
I was down upon the floor,
With neighbours making ado
150 To bring me back to life.
I heard the sexton's wife
Say: "Up, my lad, and run
To tell it at the Hall;
She was my Lady's nurse,
155 And done can't be undone.
I'll watch by this poor lamb.
I guess my Lady's purse
Is always open to such:
I'd run up on my crutch

A cripple as I am,"
(For cramps had vexed her much)
"Rather than this dear heart
Lack one to take her part."

For days day after day
On my weary bed I lay
Wishing the time would pass;
Oh, so wishing that I was
Likely to pass away:
For the one friend whom I knew
Was dead, I knew no other,
Neither father nor mother;
And I, what should I do?

One day the sexton's wife
Said: "Rouse yourself, my dear:
My Lady has driven down
From the Hall into the town,
And we think she's coming here.
Cheer up, for life is life."

But I would not look or speak,
Would not cheer up at all.
My tears were like to fall,
So I turned round to the wall
And hid my hollow cheek
Making as if I slept,
As silent as a stone,
And no one knew I wept.
What was my Lady to me,
The grand lady from the Hall?
She might come, or stay away,
I was sick at heart that day:
The whole world seemed to be
Nothing, just nothing to me,
For aught that I could see.

Yet I listened where I lay:
A bustle came below,
A clear voice said: "I know;

I will see her first alone,
It may be less of a shock
If she's so weak today:"—
A light hand turned the lock,
A light step crossed the floor,
One sat beside my bed:
But never a word she said.

For me, my shyness grew
Each moment more and more:
So I said never a word
And neither looked nor stirred;
I think she must have heard
My heart go pit-a-pat:
Thus I lay, my Lady sat,
More than a mortal hour—
(I counted one and two
By the house-clock while I lay):
I seemed to have no power
To think of a thing to say,
Or do what I ought to do,
Or rouse myself to a choice.

At last she said: "Margaret,
Won't you even look at me?"
A something in her voice
Forced my tears to fall at last,
Forced sobs from me thick and fast;
Something not of the past,
Yet stirring memory;
A something new, and yet
Not new, too sweet to last,
Which I never can forget.

I turned and stared at her:
Her cheek showed hollow-pale;
Her hair like mine was fair,
A wonderful fall of hair
That screened her like a veil;
But her height was statelier,
Her eyes had depth more deep;

235 I think they must have had
Always a something sad,
Unless they were asleep.

While I stared, my Lady took
My hand in her spare hand
240 Jewelled and soft and grand,
And looked with a long long look
Of hunger in my face;
As if she tried to trace
Features she ought to know,
245 And half hoped, half feared, to find.
Whatever was in her mind
She heaved a sigh at last,
And began to talk to me.

"Your nurse was my dear nurse,
250 And her nursling's dear," said she:
"No one told me a word
Of her getting worse and worse,
Till her poor life was past"
(Here my Lady's tears dropped fast):
255 "I might have been with her,
I might have promised and heard,
But she had no comforter.
She might have told me much
Which now I shall never know,
260 Never never shall know."
She sat by me sobbing so,
And seemed so woe-begone,
That I laid one hand upon
Hers with a timid touch,
265 Scarce thinking what I did,
Not knowing what to say:
That moment her face was hid
In the pillow close by mine,
Her arm was flung over me,
270 She hugged me, sobbing so
As if her heart would break,
And kissed me where I lay.

After this she often came
To bring me fruit or wine,
275 Or sometimes hothouse flowers.
And at nights I lay awake
Often and often thinking
What to do for her sake.
Wet or dry it was the same:
280 She would come in at all hours,
Set me eating and drinking
And say I must grow strong;
At last the day seemed long
And home seemed scarcely home
285 If she did not come.

Well, I grew strong again:
In time of primroses,
I went to pluck them in the lane;
In time of nestling birds,
290 I heard them chirping round the house;
And all the herds
Were out at grass when I grew strong,
And days were waxen long,
And there was work for bees
295 Among the May-bush boughs,
And I had shot up tall,
And life felt after all
Pleasant, and not so long
When I grew strong.

300 I was going to the Hall
To be my Lady's maid:
"Her little friend," she said to me,
"Almost her child,"
She said and smiled
305 Sighing painfully;
Blushing, with a second flush
As if she blushed to blush.

Friend, servant, child: just this
My standing at the Hall;
310 The other servants call me "Miss,"

My Lady calls me "Margaret,"
With her clear voice musical.
She never chides when I forget
This or that; she never chides.
315 Except when people come to stay,
(And that's not often) at the Hall,
I sit with her all day
And ride out when she rides.
She sings to me and makes me sing;
320 Sometimes I read to her,
Sometimes we merely sit and talk.
She noticed once my ring
And made me tell its history:
That evening in our garden walk
325 She said she should infer
The ring had been my father's first,
Then my mother's, given for me
To the nurse who nursed
My mother in her misery,
330 That so quite certainly
Some one might know me, who...
Then she was silent, and I too.

I hate when people come:
The women speak and stare
335 And mean to be so civil.
This one will stroke my hair,
That one will pat my cheek
And praise my Lady's kindness,
Expecting me to speak;
340 I like the proud ones best
Who sit as struck with blindness,
As if I wasn't there.
But if any gentleman
Is staying at the Hall
345 (Tho' few come prying here),
My Lady seems to fear
Some downright dreadful evil,
And makes me keep my room
As closely as she can:
350 So I hate when people come,

It is so troublesome.
In spite of all her care,
Sometimes to keep alive
I sometimes do contrive
355 To get out in the grounds
For a whiff of wholesome air,
Under the rose you know:
It's charming to break bounds,
Stolen waters are sweet,
360 And what's the good of feet
If for days they mustn't go?
Give me a longer tether,
Or I may break from it.

Now I have eyes and ears
365 And just some little wit:
"Almost my Lady's child;"
I recollect she smiled,
Sighed and blushed together;
Then her story of the ring
370 Sounds not improbable,
She told it me so well
It seemed the actual thing:—
Oh, keep your counsel close,
But I guess under the rose,
375 In long past summer weather
When the world was blossoming,
And the rose upon its thorn:
I guess not who he was
Flawed honour like a glass
380 And made my life forlorn,
But my Mother, Mother, Mother,
Oh, I know her from all other.

My Lady, you might trust
Your daughter with your fame.
385 Trust me, I would not shame
Our honourable name,
For I have noble blood
Tho' I was bred in dust
And brought up in the mud.

390   I will not press my claim,
Just leave me where you will:
But you might trust your daughter,
For blood is thicker than water
And you're my mother still.

395   So my Lady holds her own
With condescending grace,
And fills her lofty place
With an untroubled face
As a queen may fill a throne.
400   While I could hint a tale—
(But then I am her child)—
Would make her quail;
Would set her in the dust,
Lorn with no comforter,
405   Her glorious hair defiled
And ashes on her cheek:
The decent world would thrust
Its finger out at her,
Not much displeased I think
410   To make a nine days' stir;
The decent world would sink
Its voice to speak of her.

Now this is what I mean
To do, no more, no less:
415   Never to speak, or show
Bare sign of what I know.
Let the blot pass unseen;
Yea, let her never guess
I hold the tangled clue
420   She huddles out of view.
Friend, servant, almost child,
So be it and nothing more
On this side of the grave.
Mother, in Paradise,
425   You'll see with clearer eyes;
Perhaps in this world even
When you are like to die
And face to face with Heaven

You'll drop for once the lie:
430   But you must drop the mask, not I.

My Lady promises
Two hundred pounds with me
Whenever I may wed
A man she can approve:
435   And since besides her bounty
I'm fairest in the county
(For so I've heard it said,
Tho' I don't vouch for this),
Her promised pounds may move
440   Some honest man to see
My virtues and my beauties;
Perhaps the rising grazier,
Or temperance publican,
May claim my wifely duties.
445   Meanwhile I wait their leisure
And grace-bestowing pleasure,
I wait the happy man;
But if I hold my head
And pitch my expectations
450   Just higher than their level,
They must fall back on patience:
I may not mean to wed,
Yet I'll be civil.

Now sometimes in a dream
455   My heart goes out of me
To build and scheme,
Till I sob after things that seem
So pleasant in a dream:
A home such as I see
460   My blessed neighbours live in
With father and with mother,
All proud of one another,
Named by one common name
From baby in the bud
465   To full-blown workman father;
It's little short of Heaven.
I'd give my gentle blood

To wash my special shame
And drown my private grudge;
470 I'd toil and moil much rather
The dingiest cottage drudge
Whose mother need not blush,
Than live here like a lady
And see my Mother flush
475 And hear her voice unsteady
Sometimes, yet never dare
Ask to share her care.

Of course the servants sneer
Behind my back at me;
480 Of course the village girls,
Who envy me my curls
And gowns and idleness,
Take comfort in a jeer;
Of course the ladies guess
485 Just so much of my history
As points the emphatic stress
With which they laud my Lady;
The gentlemen who catch
A casual glimpse of me
490 And turn again to see,
Their valets on the watch
To speak a word with me,
All know and sting me wild;
Till I am almost ready
495 To wish that I were dead,
No faces more to see,
No more words to be said,
My Mother safe at last
Disburdened of her child,
500 And the past past.

"All equal before God"—
Our Rector has it so,
And sundry sleepers nod:
It may be so; I know
505 All are not equal here,
And when the sleepers wake

They make a difference.
"All equal in the grave"—
That shows an obvious sense:
510 Yet something which I crave
Not death itself brings near;
How should death half atone
For all my past; or make
The name I bear my own?

515 I love my dear old Nurse
Who loved me without gains;
I love my mistress even,
Friend, Mother, what you will:
But I could almost curse
520 My Father for his pains;
And sometimes at my prayer
Kneeling in sight of Heaven
I almost curse him still:
Why did he set his snare
525 To catch at unaware
My Mother's foolish youth;
Load me with shame that's hers,
And her with something worse,
A lifelong lie for truth?

530 I think my mind is fixed
On one point and made up:
To accept my lot unmixed;
Never to drug the cup
But drink it by myself.
535 I'll not be wooed for pelf;[1]
I'll not blot out my shame
With any man's good name;
But nameless as I stand,
My hand is my own hand,
540 And nameless as I came
I go to the dark land.

---

[1] money, wealth.

"All equal in the grave"—
I bide my time till then:
"All equal before God"—
545 Today I feel His rod,
Tomorrow He may save:
   Amen.
—1866

Monna Innominata

A Sonnet of Sonnets

Beatrice, immortalized by "altissimo poeta…cotanto amante"; Laura, celebrated by a great though an inferior bard,—have alike paid the exceptional penalty of exceptional honour, and have come down to us resplendent with charms, but (at least, to my apprehension) scant of attractiveness.

 These heroines of world-wide fame were preceded by a bevy of unnamed ladies, "donne innominate," sung by a school of less conspicuous poets; and in that land and that period which gave simultaneous birth to Catholics, to Albigenses, and to Troubadours, one can imagine many a lady as sharing her lover's poetic aptitude, while the barrier between them might be one held sacred by both, yet not such as to render mutual love incompatible with mutual honour.

 Had such a lady spoken for herself, the portrait left us might have appeared more tender, if less dignified, than any drawn even by a devoted friend. Or had the Great Poetess of our own day and nation only been unhappy instead of happy, her circumstances would have invited her to bequeath to us, in lieu of the "Portuguese Sonnets," an inimitable "donna innominata" drawn not from fancy but from feeling, and worthy to occupy a niche beside Beatrice and Laura.

I

Lo di che han detto a' dolci amici addio. [1]—DANTE.
Amor, con quanto sforzo oggi mi vinci! [2]—PETRARCA.

Come back to me, who wait and watch for
 you:—
 Or come not yet, for it is over then,
 And long it is before you come again,
So far between my pleasures are and few.
5 While, when you come not, what I do I do
 Thinking "Now when he comes," my sweetest
  "when":
 For one man is my world of all the men
This wide world holds; O love, my world is you.
Howbeit, to meet you grows almost a pang
10 Because the pang of parting comes so soon;
 My hope hangs waning, waxing, like a moon
  Between the heavenly days on which we meet:
Ah me, but where are now the songs I sang
  When life was sweet because you called them
   sweet?

2

Era già l'ora che volge il desio. [3]—DANTE.
Ricorro al tempo ch' io vi vidi prima. [4]—PETRARCA.

I wish I could remember that first day,
 First hour, first moment of your meeting me,
 If bright or dim the season, it might be
Summer or Winter for aught I can say;
5 So unrecorded did it slip away,
 So blind was I to see and to foresee,
 So dull to mark the budding of my tree
That would not blossom yet for many a May.
If only I could recollect it, such
10 A day of days! I let it come and go
 As traceless as a thaw of bygone snow;

---

[1] "The day they have said to their sweet friends farewell." Translations by Emilia Spoldi.

[2] "Love, today with great effort you have overcome me!"

[3] "It was now the hour that turneth back desire."

[4] "I have recourse to the time when I first saw you."

It seemed to mean so little, meant so much;
If only now I could recall that touch,
    First touch of hand in hand—Did one but
        know!

3

O ombre vane, fuor che ne l'aspetto![1]—DANTE.
Immaginata guida la conduce.[2]—PETRARCA.

I dream of you to wake: would that I might
  Dream of you and not wake but slumber on;
    Nor find with dreams the dear companion gone,
As Summer ended Summer birds take flight.
5 In happy dreams I hold you full in sight,
    I blush again who waking look so wan;
    Brighter than sunniest day that ever shone,
In happy dreams your smile makes day of night.
Thus only in a dream we are at one,
10   Thus only in a dream we give and take
      The faith that maketh rich who take or give;
    If thus to sleep is sweeter than to wake,
      To die were surely sweeter than to live,
Though there be nothing new beneath the sun.

4

Poca favilla gran fiamma seconda.[3]—DANTE.
Ogni altra cosa, ogni pensier va fore,
E sol ivi con voi rimansi amore.[4]—PETRARCA.

I loved you first: but afterwards your love,
  Outsoaring mine, sang such a loftier song
As drowned the friendly cooings of my dove.
    Which owes the other most? My love was long,
5   And yours one moment seemed to wax more
      strong;
I loved and guessed at you, you construed me
And loved me for what might or might not be—

---

[1] "O empty shadows, save in aspect only!"

[2] "Imaginary guide leads her."

[3] "A little spark is followed by great flame."

[4] "Every other thing, every thought disappears
    And here alone with you I stay."

Nay, weights and measures do us both a wrong.
For verily love knows not "mine" or "thine";
10   With separate "I" and "thou" free love has done,
      For one is both and both are one in love:
Rich love knows nought of "thine that is not mine";
    Both have the strength and both the length
      thereof,
    Both of us, of the love which makes us one.

5

Amor che a nullo amato amar perdona.[5]—DANTE.
Amor m'addusse in sì gioiosa spene.[6]—PETRARCA.

O my heart's heart, and you who are to me
  More than myself myself, God be with you,
    Keep you in strong obedience leal[7] and true
To Him whose noble service setteth free;
5 Give you all good we see or can foresee,
    Make your joys many and your sorrows few,
    Bless you in what you bear and what you do,
Yea, perfect you as He would have you be.
So much for you; but what for me, dear friend?
10   To love you without stint and all I can
Today, tomorrow, world without an end;
      To love you much and yet to love you more,
    As Jordan[8] at his flood sweeps either shore;
Since woman is the helpmeet made for man.

6

Or puoi la quantitate
Comprender de l'amor che a te mi scalda.[9]—DANTE.
Non vo'che da tal nodo amor mi scioglia.[10]—PETRARCA.

Trust me, I have not earned your dear rebuke,—
  I love, as you would have me, God the most;

---

[5] "Love which exempts no one beloved from loving."

[6] "Love roused in me such joyful hope."

[7] loyal.

[8] a river flowing into the Dead Sea.

[9] "Now canst thou the sum of love which
    Warms me to thee comprehend."

[10] "I don't want love to release me from such knot."

Would lose not Him, but you, must one be lost,
Nor with Lot's wife[1] cast back a faithless look,
5   Unready to forego what I forsook;
    This say I, having counted up the cost,
    This, though I be the feeblest of God's host,
The sorriest sheep Christ shepherds with His crook.
Yet while I love my God the most, I deem
10   That I can never love you overmuch;
    I love Him more, so let me love you too;
    Yea, as I apprehend it, love is such
I cannot love you if I love not Him,
    I cannot love Him if I love not you.

7

Qui primavera sempre ed ogni frutto.[2]—DANTE.
Ragionando con meco ed io con lui.[3]—PETRARCA.

"Love me, for I love you"—and answer me,
    "Love me, for I love you": so shall we stand
    As happy equals in the flowering land
Of love, that knows not a dividing sea.
5   Love builds the house on rock and not on sand,
    Love laughs what while the winds rave
      desperately;
And who hath found love's citadel unmanned?
    And who hath held in bonds love's liberty?—
My heart's a coward though my words are brave—
10   We meet so seldom, yet we surely part
    So often; there's a problem for your art!
      Still I find comfort in his Book, who saith,
Though jealousy be cruel as the grave,
    And death be strong, yet love is strong as
      death.

8

Come dicesse a Dio, D'altro non calme.[4]—DANTE.
Spero trovar pietà non che perdono.[5]—PETRARCA.

"I, if I perish, perish"—Esther[6] spake:
    And bride of life or death she made her fair
    In all the lustre of her perfumed hair
And smiles that kindle longing but to slake.
5   She put on pomp of loveliness, to take
    Her husband through his eyes at unaware;
    She spread abroad her beauty for a snare,
Harmless as doves and subtle as a snake.
She trapped him with one mesh of silken hair,
10   She vanquished him by wisdom of her wit,
    And built her people's house that it should
      stand:—
    If I might take my life so in my hand,
And for my love to Love put up my prayer,
    And for love's sake by Love be granted it!

9

O dignitosa coscienza e netta![7]—DANTE.
Spirto più acceso di virtuti ardenti.[8]—PETRARCA.

Thinking of you, and all that was, and all
    That might have been and now can never be,
    I feel your honoured excellence, and see
Myself unworthy of the happier call:
5   For woe is me who walk so apt to fall,
    So apt to shrink afraid, so apt to flee,
    Apt to lie down and die (ah woe is me!)
Faithless and hopeless turning to the wall.
And yet not hopeless quite nor faithless quite,
10 Because not loveless; love may toil all night,

---

[1] Glancing back at the doomed city of Sodom, she turned into a pillar of salt.

[2] "Here evermore was Spring and every fruit."

[3] "Reasoning with me and I with him."

---

[4] "As if it said to God, nothing else I care for."

[5] "I hope to find not only pardon, but pity."

[6] the Jewish wife of the Persian King, Ahasuerus (Xerxes), who delivered her people from Haman's slaughter.

[7] "O noble conscience and without a stain!"

[8] "More vivid spirit of ardent virtues."

But take at morning; wrestle till the break
   Of day, but then wield power with God and
      man:—
   So take I heart of grace as best I can,
Ready to spend and be spent for your sake.

10

Con miglior corso e con migliore stella.[1]—DANTE.
La vita fugge e non s'arresta un' ora.[2]—PETRARCA.

Time flies, hope flags, life plies a wearied wing;
   Death following hard on life gains ground apace;
   Faith runs with each and rears an eager face,
Outruns the rest, makes light of everything,
5 Spurns earth, and still finds breath to pray and sing;
   While love ahead of all uplifts his praise,
   Still asks for grace and still gives thanks for grace,
Content with all day brings and night will bring.
Life wanes; and when love folds his wings above
10   Tired hope, and less we feel his conscious pulse,
     Let us go fall asleep, dear friend, in peace:
     A little while, and age and sorrow cease;
   A little while, and life reborn annuls
Loss and decay and death, and all is love.

11

Vien dietro a me e lascia dir le genti.[3]—DANTE.
Contando i casi della vita nostra.[4]—PETRARCA.

Many in aftertimes will say of you
   "He loved her"—while of me what will they
     say?
   Not that I loved you more than just in play,
For fashion's sake as idle women do.
5 Even let them prate; who know not what we knew
   Of love and parting in exceeding pain,

Of parting hopeless here to meet again,
Hopeless on earth, and heaven is out of view.
But by my heart of love laid bare to you,
10   My love that you can make not void nor vain,
Love that foregoes you but to claim anew
     Beyond this passage of the gate of death,
   I charge you at the Judgment make it plain
     My love of you was life and not a breath.

12

Amor che ne la mente mi ragiona.[5]—DANTE.
Amor vien nel bel viso di costei.[6]—PETRARCA.

If there be any one can take my place
   And make you happy whom I grieve to grieve,
   Think not that I can grudge it, but believe
I do commend you to that nobler grace,
5 That readier wit than mine, that sweeter face;
   Yea, since your riches make me rich, conceive
   I too am crowned, while bridal crowns I weave,
And thread the bridal dance with jocund pace.
For if I did not love you, it might be
10   That I should grudge you some one dear delight;
     But since the heart is yours that was mine
       own,
   Your pleasure is my pleasure, right my right,
Your honourable freedom makes me free,
     And you companioned I am not alone.

13

E drizzeremo glí occhi al Primo Amore.[7]—DANTE.
Ma trovo peso non da le mie braccia.[8]—PETRARCA.

If I could trust mine own self with your fate,
   Shall I not rather trust it in God's hand?
   Without Whose Will one lily doth not stand,

---

[1] "With better course and with a better star."

[2] "Life is flying from me, not stopping an hour."

[3] "Come after me and let the people talk."

[4] "Telling over the events of our life."

[5] "Love that within my mind discourses with me."

[6] "Love appears in her lovely face."

[7] "And unto the First Love will turn our eyes."

[8] "But I find a burden, not for my arms (to bear)."

Nor sparrow fall at his appointed date;
5   Who numbereth the innumerable sand,
Who weighs the wind and water with a weight,
To Whom the world is neither small nor great,
    Whose knowledge foreknew every plan we
        planned.
Searching my heart for all that touches you,
    I find there only love and love's goodwill
10 Helpless to help and impotent to do,
Of understanding dull, of sight most dim;
And therefore I commend you back to Him
    Whose love your love's capacity can fill.

14

E la Sua Volontade è nostra pace.[1]—DANTE.
Sol con questi pensier, con altre chiome.[2]—PETRARCA.

Youth gone, and beauty gone if ever there
    Dwelt beauty in so poor a face as this;
    Youth gone and beauty, what remains of bliss?
I will not bind fresh roses in my hair,
5 To shame a cheek at best but little fair,—
    Leave youth his roses, who can bear a thorn,—
I will not seek for blossoms anywhere,
    Except such common flowers as blow with corn.
Youth gone and beauty gone, what doth remain?
10   The longing of a heart pent up forlorn,
      A silent heart whose silence loves and longs;
      The silence of a heart which sang its songs
    While youth and beauty made a summer morn,
Silence of love that cannot sing again.
—1881

"For Thine Own Sake, O My God"

Wearied of sinning, wearied of repentance,
    Wearied of self, I turn, my God, to Thee;

To Thee, my Judge, on Whose all-righteous
      sentence
    Hangs mine eternity:
5 I turn to Thee, I plead Thyself with Thee,—
    Be pitiful to me.

Wearied I loathe myself, I loathe my sinning,
    My stains, my festering sores, my misery:
Thou the Beginning, Thou ere my beginning
10   Didst see and didst foresee
Me miserable, me sinful, ruined me,—
    I plead Thyself with Thee.

I plead Thyself with Thee Who art my Maker,
    Regard Thy handiwork that cries to Thee;
15 I plead Thyself with Thee Who wast partaker
    Of mine infirmity,
Love made Thee what Thou art, the love of me,—
    I plead Thyself with Thee.
—1882

In an Artist's Studio

One face looks out from all his canvasses,
    One selfsame figure sits or walks or leans;
    We found her hidden just behind those screens,
That mirror gave back all her loveliness.
5 A queen in opal or in ruby dress,
    A nameless girl in freshest summer greens,
    A saint, an angel;—every canvass means
The same one meaning, neither more nor less.
He feeds upon her face by day and night,
10   And she with true kind eyes looks back on him
Fair as the moon and joyful as the light:
    Not wan with waiting, not with sorrow dim;
Not as she is, but was when hope shone bright;
    Not as she is, but as she fills his dream.
—1896

---

[1] "And his will is our peace."

[2] "Alone with these thoughts, with different tresses."

Lewis Carroll
1832 – 1898

Lewis Carroll was the pseudonym of Charles Lutwidge Dodgson, a professor of mathematics at Oxford. His major achievements are the famous works of fantasy, *Alice's Adventures in Wonderland* (1865), and its sequel, *Through the Looking Glass* (1872). Carroll was also the author of many humorous poems, most notably *The Hunting of the Snark* (1876). Some of his best poems, "Jabberwocky" and "The Walrus and the Carpenter," were included in the Alice books.

⁊⊰⊱⁊

Jabberwocky

'Twas brillig and the slithy toves
    Did gyre and gimble in the wabe;
All mimsy were the borogroves,
    And the mome raths outgrabe.

5 "Beware the Jabberwock, my son!
    The jaws that bite, the claws that catch!
Beware the Jubjub bird, and shun
    The frumious Bandersnatch!"

He took his vorpal sword in hand:
10   Long time the manxome foe he sought—
So rested he by the Tumtum tree.
    And stood awhile in thought.

And as in uffish thought he stood,
    The Jabberwock, with eyes of flame,
15 Came whiffling through the tulgey wood,
    And burbled as it came!

One, two! One, two! And though and through
    The vorpal blade went snicker-snack!
He left it dead, and with its head
20   He went galumphing back.

"And hast thou slain the Jabberwock?
    Come to my arms, my beamish boy!

O frabjous day! Callooh! Callay!"
    He chortled in his joy.

25 "Twas brillig and the slithy toves
    Did gyre and gimble in the wabe;
All mimsy were the borogroves,
    And the mome raths outgrabe.
—1872 (1855)

The Walrus and the Carpenter

The sun was shining on the sea,
    Shining with all his might:
He did his very best to make
    The billows smooth and bright—
5 And this was odd, because it was
    The middle of the night.

The moon was shining sulkily,
    Because she thought the sun
Had got no business to be there
10   After the day was done—
"It's very rude of him," she said,
    "To come and spoil the fun!"

The sea was wet as wet could be,
    The sands were dry as dry.
15 You could not see a cloud, because
    No cloud was in the sky:

No birds were flying overhead—
   There were no birds to fly.

The Walrus and the Carpenter
20   Were walking close at hand:
They wept like anything to see
   Such quantities of sand:
"If this were only cleared away,"
   They said, "it would be grand!"

25 "If seven maids with seven mops
   Swept it for half a year,
Do you suppose," the Walrus said,
   "That they could get it clear?"
"I doubt it," said the Carpenter,
30   And shed a bitter tear.

"O Oysters, come and walk with us!"
   The Walrus did beseech.
"A pleasant walk, a pleasant talk,
   Along the briny beach:
35 We cannot do with more than four,
   To give a hand to each."

The eldest Oyster looked at him,
   But never a word he said:
The eldest Oyster winked his eye,
40   And shook his heavy head—
Meaning to say he did not choose
   To leave the oyster-bed.

But four young Oysters hurried up,
   All eager for the treat:
45 Their coats were brushed, their faces washed,
   Their shoes were clean and neat—
And this was odd, because you know,
   They hadn't any feet.

Four other Oysters followed them,
50   And yet another four;
And thick and fast they came at last,

And more, and more, and more—
   All hopping through the frothy waves,
   And scrambling to the shore.

55 The Walrus and the Carpenter
   Walked on a mile or so,
And then they rested on a rock
   Conveniently low:
And all the little Oysters stood
60   And waited in a row.

"The time has come," the Walrus said,
   "To talk of many things:
Of shoes—and ships—and sealing wax—
   Of cabbages—and kings—
65 And why the sea is boiling hot—
   And whether pigs have wings."

"But wait a bit," the Oysters cried,
   "Before we have our chat;
For some of us are out of breath,
70   And all of us are fat!"
"No hurry!" said the Carpenter.
   They thanked him much for that.

"A loaf of bread," the Walrus said,
   "Is what we chiefly need:
75 Pepper and vinegar besides
   Are very good indeed—
Now, if you're ready, Oysters dear,
   We can begin to feed."

"But not on us!" the Oysters cried,
80   Turning a little blue.
"After such kindness, that would be
   A dismal thing to do!"
"The night is fine," the Walrus said.
   "Do you admire the view?

85 "It was so kind of you to come!
   And you are very nice!"

The carpenter said nothing but
    "Cut us another slice.
I wish you were not quite so deaf—
90   I've had to ask you twice!"

"It seems a shame," the Walrus said,
    "To play them such a trick.
After we've brought them out so far,
    And made them trot so quick!"
95 The Carpenter said nothing but
    "The butter's spread too thick!"

"I weep for you," the Walrus said:
    "I deeply sympathize."
With sobs and tears he sorted out
100   Those of the largest size,
Holding his pocket-handkerchief
    Before his streaming eyes.

"O Oysters," said the Carpenter,
    "You've had a pleasant run!
105 Shall we be trotting home again?"
    But answer came there none—
And this was scarcely odd, because
    They'd eaten every one.
        —1872 (1869)

The Hunting of the Snark [1]

An Agony, in Eight Fits [2]

FIT THE FIRST

The Landing

"Just the place for a Snark!" [3] the Bellman [4] cried,
    As he landed his crew with care;
Supporting each man on the top of the tide
    By a finger entwined in his hair.

5   "Just the place for a Snark! I have said it twice:
    That alone should encourage the crew.
Just the place for a Snark! I have said it thrice:
    What I tell you three times is true."

---

[1] "As this poem is to some extent connected with the lay of the Jabberwock, let me take this opportunity of answering a question that has often been asked me, how to pronounce 'slithy toves.' The 'i' in 'slithy' is long, as in 'writhe'; and 'toves' is pronounced so as to rhyme with 'groves.' Again, the first 'o' in 'borogoves' is pronounced like the 'o' in 'borrow.' I have heard people try to give it the sound of the 'o' in 'worry.' Such is Human Perversity.

This also seems a fitting occasion to notice the other hard words in that poem. Humpty-Dumpty's theory, of two meanings packed into one word like a portmanteau, seems to me the right explanation for all.

For instance, take the two words, 'fuming' and 'furious.' Make up your mind that you will say both words, but leave it unsettled which you will say first. Now open your mouth and speak. If your thoughts incline ever so little towards 'fuming,' you will say 'fuming-furious'; if they turn, by even a hair's breadth, towards 'furious,' you will say 'furious-fuming'; but if you have that rarest of gifts, a perfectly balanced mind, you will say 'frumious.'" (Carroll's note.)

Readers are referred to Martin Gardner's brilliant and delightful edition, *The Annotated Snark* (Bramwell House, 1962; Penguin, 1967).

[2] Agony is used here in the old sense of a struggle that involves great anguish, bodily pain, or death. Fit has the double meaning of a convulsion or a canto (Gardner).

[3] a word invented by Carroll.

[4] a town crier or nightwatchman who walked through the streets at night and called out the hours.

The crew was complete: it included a Boots[1]—
    A maker of Bonnets and Hoods—
A Barrister, brought to arrange their disputes—
    And a Broker,[2] to value their goods.

A Billiard-marker,[3] whose skill was immense,
    Might perhaps have won more than his share—
But a Banker, engaged at enormous expense,
    Had the whole of their cash in his care.

There was also a Beaver, that paced on the deck,
    Or would sit making lace in the bow;
And had often (the Bellman said) saved them from wreck
    Though none of the sailors knew how.

There was one who was famed for the number of things
    He forgot when he entered the ship:
His umbrella, his watch, all his jewels and rings,
    And the clothes he had bought for the trip.

He had forty-two boxes, all carefully packed,
    With his name painted clearly on each:
But, since he omitted to mention the fact,
    They were all left behind on the beach.

The loss of his clothes hardly mattered, because
    He had seven coats on when he came,
With three pairs of boots—but the worst of it was,
    He had wholly forgotten his name.

He would answer to "Hi!" or to any loud cry,
    Such as "Fry me!" or "Fritter my wig!"

To "What-you-may-call-um!" or "What-was-his-name!"
    But especially "Thing-um-a-jig!"

While, for those who preferred a more forcible word,
    He had different names from these:
His intimate friends called him "Candle-ends,"
    And his enemies "Toasted-cheese."

"His form is ungainly—his intellect small—"
    (So the Bellman would often remark)—
"But his courage is perfect! And that, after all,
    Is the thing that one needs with a Snark."

He would joke with hyænas, returning their stare
    With an impudent wag of the head:
And he once went a walk, paw-in-paw, with a bear,
    "Just to keep up its spirits," he said.

He came as a Baker: but owned, when too late—
    And it drove the poor Bellman half-mad—
He could only bake Bride-cake[4]—for which, I may state,
    No materials were to be had.

The last of the crew needs especial remark,
    Though he looked an incredible dunce:
He had just one idea—but, that one being "Snark,"
    The good Bellman engaged him at once.

He came as a Butcher: but gravely declared,
    When the ship had been sailing a week,
He could only kill Beavers. The Bellman looked scared
    And was almost too frightened to speak.

But at length he explained, in a tremulous tone,
    There was only one Beaver on board;

---

[1] a hotel-servant who cleans boots and shoes.

[2] a man licensed to appraise and sell household goods (Gardner).

[3] the employee of a billiard-parlour who keeps a record of the game by marking the points made by each player (Gardner).

[4] wedding cake.

And that was a tame one he had of his own,
    Whose death would be deeply deplored.

65 The Beaver, who happened to hear the remark,
    Protested, with tears in its eyes,
That not even the rapture of hunting the Snark
    Could atone for that dismal surprise!

It strongly advised that the Butcher should be
70   Conveyed in a separate ship:
But the Bellman declared that would never agree
    With the plans he had made for the trip:

Navigation was always a difficult art,
    Though with only one ship and one bell:
75 And he feared he must really decline, for his part,
    Undertaking another as well.

The Beaver's best course was, no doubt, to procure
    A second-hand dagger-proof coat—
So the Baker advised it—and next, to insure
80   Its life in some Office of note:[1]

This Banker suggested, and offered for hire
    (On moderate terms) or for sale,
Two excellent policies, one Against Fire,
    And one Against Damage From Hail.

85 Yet still, ever after that sorrowful day,
    Whenever the Butcher was by,
The Beaver kept looking the opposite way,
    And appeared unaccountably shy.

FIT THE SECOND

The Bellman's Speech

The Bellman himself they all praised to the skies—
    Such a carriage, such ease, and such grace!
Such solemnity, too! One could see he was wise,
    The moment one looked in his face!

5 He had bought a large map representing the sea,
    Without the least vestige of land:
And the crew were much pleased when they found
    it to be
    A map they could all understand.

"What's the good of Mercator's North Poles and
    Equators,
10   Tropics, Zones and Meridian Lines?"[2]
So the Bellman would cry: and the crew would
    reply
    "They are merely conventional signs!

"Other maps are such shapes, with their islands and
    capes!
    But we've got our brave Captain to thank"
15 (So the crew would protest) "That he's bought *us*
    the best—
    A perfect and absolute blank!"

This was charming, no doubt: but they shortly
    found out
    That the Captain they trusted so well
Had only one notion for crossing the ocean,
20   And that was to tingle his bell.

He was thoughtful and grave—but the orders he
    gave
    Were enough to bewilder a crew.

---

[1] In England, a life insurance company is commonly called an office. "Office of note" is a company of good repute. "Hire" in the next line means "rent" (Gardner).

[2] Gerhardus Mercator, sixteenth-century Flemish mathematician and cartographer. He devised a method, known as "Mercator's projection," of projecting a spherical map of the earth on a flat rectangle (Gardner).

When he cried "Steer to starboard, but keep her
    head larboard!"
    What on earth was the helmsman to do?

25 Then the bowsprit got mixed with the rudder
    sometimes,
    A thing, as the Bellman remarked,
That frequently happens in tropical climes,
    When a vessel is, so to speak, "snarked."

But the principal failing occurred in the sailing,
30   And the Bellman, perplexed and distressed,
Said he *had* hoped, at least, when the wind blew
    due East,
    That the ship would *not* travel due West!

But the danger was past—they had landed at last,
    With their boxes, portmanteaus, and bags:
35 Yet at first sight the crew were not pleased with the
    view,
    Which consisted of chasms and crags.

The Bellman perceived that their spirits were low,
    And repeated in musical tone
Some jokes he had kept for a season of woe—
40   But the crew would do nothing but groan.

He served out some grog with a liberal hand,
    And bade them sit down on the beach:
And they could not but own that their Captain
    looked grand,
    As he stood and delivered his speech.

45 "Friends, Romans, and countrymen, lend me your
    ears!"[1]
    (They were all of them fond of quotations:
So they drank to his health, and they gave him
    three cheers,
    While he served out additional rations.)

"We have sailed many months, we have sailed
    many weeks,
50   (Four weeks to the month you may mark),
But never as yet ('tis your captain who speaks)
    Have we had the least glimpse of a Snark!

"We have sailed many weeks, we have sailed many
    days,
    (Seven days to the week, I allow),
55 But a Snark, on the which we might lovingly gaze,
    We have never beheld until now.

"Come, listen, my men, while I tell you again
    The five unmistakable marks
By which you may know, wheresoever you go,
60   The warranted genuine Snarks.

"Let us take them in order. The first is the taste,
    Which is meagre and hollow, but crisp:
Like a coat that is rather too tight in the waist,
    With a flavour of Will-o'-the-wisp.

65 "Its habit of getting up late, you'll agree
    That it carries too far, when I say
That it frequently breakfasts at five-o'clock tea,
    And dines on the following day.

"The third is its slowness in taking a jest,
70   Should you happen to venture on one,
It will sigh like a thing that is deeply distressed:
    And it always looks grave at a pun.

"The fourth is its fondness for bathing machines,[2]
    Which it constantly carries about,
75 And believes that they add to the beauty of scenes—
    A sentiment open to doubt.

---

[1] Shakespeare, *Julius Caesar* 3.2.75.

[2] individual wooden locker rooms on wheels, which would be drawn into the sea by horses when the Victorian bather was ready to take the plunge (adapted from Gardner).

"The fifth is ambition. It next will be right
    To describe each particular batch:
Distinguishing those that have feathers, and bite,
80   From those that have whiskers, and scratch.

"For, although common Snarks do no manner of
    harm,
    Yet I feel it my duty to say
Some are Boojums——" The Bellman broke off in
    alarm,
    For the Baker had fainted away.

FIT THE THIRD

The Baker's Tale

They roused him with muffins—they roused him
    with ice—
    They roused him with mustard and cress—
They roused him with jam and judicious advice—
    They set him conundrums to guess.

5   When at length he sat up and was able to speak,
    His sad story he offered to tell;
And the Bellman cried "Silence! Not even a shriek!"
    And excitedly tingled his bell.

There was silence supreme! Not a shriek, not a
    scream,
10   Scarcely even a howl or a groan,
As the man they called "Ho!" told his story of woe
    In an antediluvian tone.

"My father and mother were honest, though poor——"
    "Skip all that!" cried the Bellman in haste.
15   "If it once becomes dark, there's no chance for a
    Snark—
    We have hardly a minute to waste!"

"I skip forty years," said the Baker, in tears,
    "And proceed without further remark
To the day when you took me aboard of your ship
20   To help you in hunting the Snark.

"A dear uncle of mine (after whom I was named)
    Remarked, when I bade him farewell——"
"Oh, skip your dear uncle!" the Bellman exclaimed,
    As he angrily tingled his bell.

25   "He remarked to me then," said that mildest of men,
    "'If your Snark be a Snark, that is right:
Fetch it home by all means—you may serve it with
    greens
    And it's handy for striking a light.

"'You may seek it with thimbles—and seek it with
    care;
30   You may hunt it with forks and hope;
You may threaten its life with a railway-share;[1]
    You may charm it with smiles and soap—'"

("That's exactly the method," the Bellman bold
    In a hasty parenthesis cried,
35   "That's exactly the way I've always been told
    That the capture of Snarks should be tried!")

"'But oh, beamish nephew, beware of the day,
    If your Snark be a Boojum! For then
You will softly and suddenly vanish away,
40   And never be met with again!'

"It is this, it is this that oppresses my soul,
    When I think of my uncle's last words:
And my heart is like nothing so much as a bowl
    Brimming over with quivering curds!

45   "It is this, it is this——" "We have had that before!"
    The Bellman indignantly said.

---

[1] a share in a railway company.

And the Baker replied, "Let me say it once more.
   "It is this, it is this that I dread!

"I engage with the Snark—each night after dark—
50   In a dreamy delirious fight:
I serve it with greens in those shadowy scenes,
   And I use it for striking a light:

"But if ever I meet with a Boojum, that day,
   In a moment, (of this I am sure),
55 I shall softly and suddenly vanish away—
   And the notion I cannot endure!"

FIT THE FOURTH

The Hunting

The Bellman looked uffish, and wrinkled his brow.
   "If only you'd spoken before!
It's excessively awkward to mention it now,
   With the Snark, so to speak, at the door.

5   "We should all of us grieve, as you may well believe,
   If you never were met with again—
But surely, my man, when the voyage began,
   You might have suggested it then?

"It's excessively awkward to mention it now—
10   As I think I've already remarked."
And the man they called "Hi!" replied with a sigh,
   "I informed you the day we embarked.

"You may charge me with murder—or want of
     sense—
   (We are all of us weak at times):
15 But the slightest approach to a false pretence
   Was never among my crimes!

"I said it in Hebrew—I said it in Dutch—
   I said it in German and Greek:

But I wholly forgot (and it vexes me much)
20   That English is what you speak!"

"'Tis a pitiful tale," said the Bellman, whose face
   Had grown longer at every word:
"But now that you've stated the whole of your case,
   More debate would be simply absurd.

25 "The rest of my speech," (he explained to his men)
   "You shall hear when I've leisure to speak it.
But the Snark is at hand, let me tell you again!
   'Tis your glorious duty to seek it!

"To seek it with thimbles, to seek it with care;
30   To pursue it with forks and hope;
To threaten its life with a railway-share;
   To charm it with smiles and soap!

"For the Snark's a peculiar creature, that won't
   Be caught in a commonplace way.
35 Do all that you know, and try all that you don't:
   Not a chance must be wasted to-day!

"For England expects[1]—I forbear to proceed:
   'Tis a maxim tremendous, but trite:
And you'd best be unpacking the things that you
     need
40   To rig yourselves out for the fight."

Then the Banker endorsed a blank cheque (which
   he crossed),
   And changed his loose silver for notes:
The Baker with care combed his whiskers and hair,
   And shook the dust out of his coats:

45 The Boots and the Broker were sharpening a spade—
   Each working the grindstone in turn:

---

[1] "England expects every man to do his duty." This was a flag signal to the fleet, ordered by Horatio Nelson shortly before he was killed at the battle of Trafalgar in 1805 (Gardner).

But the Beaver went on making lace, and displayed
　　No interest in the concern:

Though the Barrister tried to appeal to its pride,
50　　And vainly proceeded to cite
A number of cases, in which making laces
　　Had proved an infringement of right.

The maker of Bonnets ferociously planned
　　A novel arrangement of bows:
55 While the Billiard-marker with quivering hand
　　Was chalking the tip of his nose.

But the Butcher turned nervous, and dressed
　　　himself fine,
　　With yellow kid gloves and a ruff—
Said he felt it exactly like going to dine,
60　　Which the Bellman declared was all "stuff."

"Introduce me, now there's a good fellow," he said.
　　"If we happen to meet it together!"
And the Bellman, sagaciously nodding his head,
　　Said "That must depend on the weather."

65 The Beaver went simply galumphing about,
　　At seeing the Butcher so shy:
And even the Baker, though stupid and stout,
　　Made an effort to wink with one eye.

"Be a man!" cried the Bellman in wrath, as he heard
70　　The Butcher beginning to sob.
"Should we meet with a Jubjub, that desperate bird,
　　We shall need all our strength for the job!"

FIT THE FIFTH

The Beaver's Lesson

They sought it with thimbles, they sought it with
　　care;

They pursued it with forks and hope;
They threatened its life with a railway-share;
　　They charmed it with smiles and soap.

5 Then the Butcher contrived an ingenious plan
　　For making a separate sally;
And had fixed on a spot unfrequented by man,
　　A dismal and desolate valley.

But the very same plan to the Beaver occurred:
10　　It had chosen the very same place:
Yet neither betrayed, by a sign or a word,
　　The disgust that appeared in his face.

Each thought he was thinking of nothing but
　　　"Snark"
　　And the glorious work of the day;
15 And each tried to pretend that he did not remark
　　That the other was going that way.

But the valley grew narrow and narrower still,
　　And the evening got darker and colder,
Till (merely from nervousness, not from good will)
20　　They marched along shoulder to shoulder.

Then a scream, shrill and high, rent the shuddering
　　　sky
　　And they knew that some danger was near:
The Beaver turned pale to the tip of his tail,
　　And even the Butcher felt queer.

25 He thought of his childhood, left far behind—
　　That blissful and innocent state—
The sound so exactly recalled to his mind
　　A pencil that squeaks on a slate!

"'Tis the voice of the Jubjub!" he suddenly cried,
30　　(This man, that they used to call "Dunce.")
"As the Bellman would tell you," he added with
　　　pride,
　　"I have uttered that sentiment once.

"'Tis the note of the Jubjub! Keep count, I entreat.
　　You will find I have told it you twice.
35　'Tis the song of the Jubjub! The proof is complete,
　　If only I've stated it thrice."

The Beaver had counted with scrupulous care,
　　Attending to every word:
But it fairly lost heart, and outgrabe in despair,
40　When the third repetition occurred.

It felt that, in spite of all possible pains,
　　It had somehow contrived to lose count,
And the only thing now was to rack its poor brains
　　By reckoning up the amount.

45　"Two added to one—if that could but be done,"
　　It said, "with one's fingers and thumbs!"
Recollecting with tears how, in earlier years,
　　It had taken no pains with its sums.

"The thing can be done," said the Butcher, "I think.
50　The thing must be done, I am sure.
The thing shall be done! Bring me paper and ink,
　　The best there is time to procure."

The Beaver brought paper, portfolio, pens,
　　And ink in unfailing supplies:
55　While strange creepy creatures came out of their
　　　dens,
　　And watched them with wondering eyes.

So engrossed was the Butcher, he heeded them not,
　　As he wrote with a pen in each hand,
And explained all the while in a popular style
60　Which the Beaver could well understand.

"Taking Three as the subject to reason about—
　　A convenient number to state—
We add Seven, and Ten, and then multiply out
　　By One Thousand diminished by Eight.

65　"The result we proceed to divide, as you see,
　　By Nine Hundred and Ninety and Two:
Then subtract Seventeen and the answer must be
　　Exactly and perfectly true.

"The method employed I would gladly explain,
70　While I have it so clear in my head,
If I had but the time and you had but the brain—
　　But much remains yet to be said.

"In one moment I've seen what has hitherto been
　　Enveloped in absolute mystery,
75　And without extra charge I will give you at large
　　A Lesson in Natural History."

In his genial way he proceeded to say
　　(Forgetting all laws of propriety,
And that giving instruction, without introduction,
80　Would have caused quite a thrill in Society),

"As to temper the Jubjub's a desperate bird,
　　Since it lives in perpetual passion:
Its taste in costume is entirely absurd—
　　It is ages ahead of the fashion:

85　"But it knows any friend it has met once before:
　　It never will look at a bribe:
And in charity meetings it stands at the door,
　　And collects—though it does not subscribe.

"Its flavour when cooked is more exquisite far
90　Than mutton, or oysters, or eggs:
(Some think it keeps best in an ivory jar,
　　And some in mahogany kegs:)

"You boil it in sawdust: you salt it in glue:
　　You condense it with locusts and tape:
95　Still keeping one principal object in view—
　　To preserve its symmetrical shape."

The Butcher would gladly have talked till next day,
    But he felt that the Lesson must end,
100 And he wept with delight in attempting to say
    He considered the Beaver his friend:

While the Beaver confessed, with affectionate
    looks,
    More eloquent even than tears,
It had learnt in ten minutes far more than all books
    Would have taught it in seventy years.

105 They returned hand-in-hand, and the Bellman,
    unmanned,
    (For a moment) with noble emotion,
Said "This amply repays all the wearisome days
    We have spent on the billowy ocean!"

Such friends, as the Beaver and Butcher became,
110   Have seldom if ever been known;
In winter or summer, 'twas always the same—
    You could never meet either alone.

And when quarrels arose—as one frequently finds
    Quarrels will, spite of every endeavour—
115 The song of the Jubjub recurred to their minds,
    And cemented their friendship for ever!

FIT THE SIXTH

The Barrister's Dream

They sought it with thimbles, they sought it with
    care;
    They pursued it with forks and hope;
They threatened its life with a railway-share;
    They charmed it with smiles and soap.

5 But the Barrister, weary of proving in vain
    That the Beaver's lace-making was wrong,

Fell asleep, and in dreams saw the creature quite
    plain
    That his fancy had dwelt on so long.

He dreamed that he stood in a shadowy Court,
10   Where the Snark, with a glass in its eye,
Dressed in gown, bands, and wig, was defending a
    pig
    On a charge of deserting its sty.

The witness proved, without error or flaw,
    That the sty was deserted when found:
15 And the Judge kept explaining the state of the law
    In a soft undercurrent of sound.

The indictment had never been clearly expressed,
    And it seemed that the Snark had begun,
And had spoken three hours, before anyone guessed
20   What the pig was supposed to have done.

The Jury had each formed a different view
    (Long before the indictment was read),
And they all spoke at once, so that none of them
    knew
    One word that the others had said.

25 "You must know—" said the Judge; but the Snark
    exclaimed "Fudge!
    That statute is obsolete quite!
Let me tell you, my friends, the whole question
    depends
    On an ancient manorial right.

"In the manner of Treason the pig would appear
30   To have aided but scarcely abetted:
While the charge of Insolvency fails, it is clear,
    If you grant the plea 'never indebted.'[1]

---

[1] Never indebted, or *nil debet*, is a legal term meaning "he owes
nothing." It is the plea of the defendant, in a common-law action of
debt, by which he denies completely the actions of the plaintiff
(Gardner).

"The fact of Desertion I will not dispute:
　　But its guilt, as I trust, is removed
35　(So far as relates to the costs of this suit)
　　By the Alibi which has been proved.

"My poor client's fate now depends on your votes."
　　Here the speaker sat down in his place,
And directed the Judge to refer to his notes,
40　And briefly to sum up the case.

But the Judge said he never had summed up before;
　　So the Snark undertook it instead;
And summed it so well that it came to far more
　　Than the Witnesses ever had said!

45　When the verdict was called for, the Jury declined,
　　As the word was so puzzling to spell;
But they ventured to hope that the Snark wouldn't
　　mind
　　Undertaking that duty as well.

So the Snark found the verdict, although, as it
　　owned,
50　It was spent with the toils of the day:
When it said the word "GUILTY!" the Jury all
　　groaned
　　And some of them fainted away.

Then the Snark pronounced sentence, the Judge
　　being quite
　　Too nervous to utter a word:
55　When it rose to its feet, there was silence like night,
　　And the fall of a pin might be heard.

"Transportation for life"[1] was the sentence it gave,
　　"And *then* to be fined forty pound."

----

[1] the practice of shipping convicts overseas, originally to America and subsequently to Australia and Van Diemen's Land. The sentence of transportation was abolished in 1857 and the last convict ship sailed in 1868.

The Jury all cheered, though the Judge said he
　　feared
60　That the phrase was not legally sound.

But their wild exultation was suddenly checked
　　When the jailer informed them, with tears,
Such a sentence would not have the slightest effect,
　　As the pig had been dead for some years.

65　The Judge left the Court, looking deeply disgusted:
　　But the Snark, though a little aghast,
As the lawyer to whom the defence was intrusted,
　　Went bellowing on to the last.

Thus the Barrister dreamed, while the bellowing
　　seemed
70　To grow every moment more clear;
Till he woke to the knell of a furious bell,
　　Which the Bellman rang close at his ear.

FIT THE SEVENTH

The Banker's Fate

They sought it with thimbles, they sought it with
　　care;
　　They pursued it with forks and hope;
They threatened its life with a railway-share;
　　They charmed it with smiles and soap.

5　And the Banker, inspired with a courage so new
　　It was matter for general remark,
Rushed madly ahead and was lost to their view
　　In his zeal to discover the Snark.

But while he was seeking with thimbles and care,
10　A Bandersnatch swiftly drew nigh
And grabbed at the Banker, who shrieked in despair,
　　For he knew it was useless to fly.

He offered large discount—he offered a cheque
    (Drawn "to bearer") for seven-pounds-ten:
15 But the Bandersnatch merely extended its neck
    And grabbed at the Banker again.

Without pause or rest—while those frumious jaws
    Went savagely snapping around—
He skipped and he hopped, and he floundered and
    flopped,
20   Till fainting he fell to the ground.

The Bandersnatch fled as the others appeared
    Led on by that fear-stricken yell:
And the Bellman remarked: "It is just as I feared!"
    And solemnly tolled on his bell.

25 He was black in the face, and they scarcely could
    trace
    The least likeness to what he had been:
While so great was his fright that his waistcoat
    turned white—
    A wonderful thing to be seen!

To the horror of all who were present that day,
30   He uprose in full evening dress,
And with senseless grimaces endeavoured to say
    What his tongue could no longer express.

Down he sank in a chair—ran his hands through
    his hair—
    And chanted in mimsiest tones
35 Words whose utter inanity proved his insanity,
    As he rattled a couple of bones.

"Leave him here to his fate—it is getting so late!"
    The Bellman exclaimed in a fright.
"We have lost half the day. Any further delay,
40   And we shan't catch a Snark before night!"

FIT THE EIGHTH

The Vanishing

They sought it with thimbles, they sought it with
    care;
    They pursued it with forks and hope;
They threatened its life with a railway-share;
    They charmed it with smiles and soap.

5 They shuddered to think that the chase might fail,
    And the Beaver, excited at last,
Went bounding along on the tip of its tail,
    For the daylight was nearly past.

"There is Thingumbob shouting!" the Bellman said,
10   "He is shouting like mad, only hark!
He is waving his hands, he is wagging his head,
    He has certainly found a Snark!"

They gazed in delight, while the Butcher exclaimed
    "He was always a desperate wag!"
15 They beheld him—their Baker—their hero
    unnamed
    On the top of a neighbouring crag.

Erect and sublime, for one moment of time.
    In the next, that wild figure they saw
(As if stung by a spasm) plunge into a chasm,
20   While they waited and listened in awe.

"It's a Snark!" was the sound that first came to their
    ears,
    And seemed almost too good to be true.
Then followed a torrent of laughter and cheers:
    Then the ominous words "It's a Boo—— "

25 Then silence. Some fancied they heard in the air
    A weary and wandering sigh
That sounded like "—jum!" but the others declare
    It was only a breeze that went by.

They hunted till darkness came on, but they found
30   Not a button, or feather, or mark,
By which they could tell that they stood on the
     ground
     Where the Baker had met with the Snark.

In the midst of the word he was trying to say,
     In the midst of his laughter and glee,
35   He had softly and suddenly vanished away—
     For the Snark *was* a Boojum, you see.
—1876

William Morris
1834 – 1896

Educated at Marlborough College (1848–51), and Exeter College, Oxford (1853–56), Morris was the author of prose romances and verse narratives. In addition, he was a pioneering designer, a translator, and a leader of the early British socialist movement. Morris's major works include a volume of lyric and dramatic verse, *The Defence of Guenevere and other Poems* (1858), and *The Earthly Paradise* (1868–70), twenty-four verse narratives derived from classical and medieval tales.

❧❧❧

The Defence of Guenevere [1]

But, knowing now that they would have her
    speak,
She threw her wet hair backward from her brow,
Her hand close to her mouth touching her cheek,

As though she had had there a shameful blow,
5 And feeling it shameful to feel aught but shame
All through her heart, yet felt her cheek burned so,

She must a little touch it; like one lame
She walked away from Gauwaine,[2] with her head
Still lifted up; and on her cheek of flame

10 The tears dried quick; she stopped at last and said:
"O knights and lords, it seems but little skill
To talk of well-known things past now and dead.

"God wot[3] I ought to say, I have done ill,
And pray you all forgiveness heartily!
15 Because you must be right, such great lords—still

"Listen, suppose your time were come to die,
And you were quite alone and very weak;
Yea, laid a dying while very mightily

"The wind was ruffling up the narrow streak
20 Of river through your broad lands running well:
Suppose a hush should come, then some one speak:

"'One of these cloths is heaven, and one is hell,
Now choose one cloth for ever; which they be,
I will not tell you, you must somehow tell

25 "'Of your own strength and mightiness; here, see!'
Yea, yea, my lord, and you to ope your eyes,
At foot of your familiar bed to see

"A great God's angel standing, with such dyes,
Not known on earth, on his great wings, and hands
30 Held out two ways, light from the inner skies

"Showing him well, and making his commands
Seem to be God's commands, moreover, too,
Holding within his hands the cloths on wands;

"And one of these strange choosing cloths was blue,
35 Wavy and long, and one cut short and red;
No man could tell the better of the two.

---

[1] Guenevere, the wife of King Arthur, was accused of adultery with the knight Sir Lancelot. In this dramatic monologue she speaks in self-defence at her trial. The story is recounted in Malory's *Morte d'Arthur*.

[2] a knight of Arthur's Round Table, and Guenevere's chief accuser.

[3] God knows.

"After a shivering half-hour you said:
'God help! heaven's colour, the blue'; and he said,
  'hell.'
Perhaps you then would roll upon your bed,

40 "And cry to all good men that loved you well,
'Ah Christ! if only I had known, known, known;'
Launcelot went away, then I could tell,

"Like wisest man how all things would be, moan,
And roll and hurt myself, and long to die,
45 And yet fear much to die for what was sown.

"Nevertheless you, O Sir Gauwaine, lie,
Whatever may have happened through these years,
God knows I speak truth, saying that you lie."

Her voice was low at first, being full of tears,
50 But as it cleared, it grew full loud and shrill,
Growing a windy shriek in all men's ears,

A ringing in their startled brains, until
She said that Gauwaine lied, then her voice sunk,
And her great eyes began again to fill,

55 Though still she stood right up, and never shrunk,
But spoke on bravely, glorious lady fair!
Whatever tears her full lips may have drunk,

She stood, and seemed to think, and wrung her hair,
Spoke out at last with no more trace of shame,
60 With passionate twisting of her body there:

"It chanced upon a day that Launcelot came
To dwell at Arthur's court: at Christmas-time
This happened; when the heralds sung his name,

"'Son of King Ban of Benwick,' seemed to chime
65 Along with all the bells that rang that day,
O'er the white roofs, with little change of rhyme.

"Christmas and whitened winter passed away,
And over me the April sunshine came,
Made very awful with black hail-clouds, yea

70 "And in the Summer I grew white with flame,
And bowed my head down—Autumn, and the sick
Sure knowledge things would never be the same,

"However often Spring might be most thick
Of blossoms and buds, smote on me, and I grew
75 Careless of most things, let the clock tick, tick,

"To my unhappy pulse, that beat right through
My eager body; while I laughed out loud,
And let my lips curl up at false or true,

"Seemed cold and shallow without any cloud.
80 Behold my judges, then the cloths were brought:
While I was dizzied thus, old thoughts would
  crowd,

"Belonging to the time ere I was bought
By Arthur's great name and his little love;
Must I give up for ever then, I thought,

85 "That which I deemed would ever round me move
Glorifying all things; for a little word,
Scarce ever meant at all, must I now prove

"Stone-cold for ever? Pray you, does the Lord
Will that all folks should be quite happy and good?
90 I love God now a little, if this cord

"Were broken, once for all what striving could
Make me love anything in earth or heaven?
So day by day it grew, as if one should

"Slip slowly down some path worn smooth and
  even,
95 Down to a cool sea on a summer day;
Yet still in slipping there was some small leaven

"Of stretched hands catching small stones by the
    way,
Until one surely reached the sea at last,
And felt strange new joy as the worn head lay

100 "Back, with the hair like sea-weed; yea all past
Sweat of the forehead, dryness of the lips,
Washed utterly out by the dear waves o'ercast

"In the lone sea, far off from any ships!
Do I not know now of a day in Spring?
105 No minute of that wild day ever slips

"From out my memory; I hear thrushes sing,
And wheresoever I may be, straightway
Thoughts of it all come up with the most fresh
    sting;

"I was half mad with beauty on that day,
110 And went without my ladies all alone,
In a quiet garden walled round every way;

"I was right joyful of that wall of stone,
That shut the flowers and trees up with the sky,
And trebled all the beauty: to the bone,

115 "Yea right through to my heart, grown very shy
With weary thoughts, it pierced, and made me glad;
Exceedingly glad, and I knew verily,

"A little thing just then had made me mad;
I dared not think, as I was wont to do,
120 Sometimes, upon my beauty; if I had

"Held out my long hand up against the blue,
And, looking on the tenderly darken'd fingers,
Thought that by rights one ought to see quite
    through,

"There, see you, where the soft still light yet lingers,
125 Round by the edges; what should I have done,
If this had joined with yellow spotted singers,

"And startling green drawn upward by the sun?
But shouting, loosed out, see now! all my hair,
And trancedly stood watching the west wind run

130 "With faintest half-heard breathing sound—why
    there
I lose my head e'en now in doing this;
But shortly listen—In that garden fair

"Came Launcelot walking; this is true, the kiss
Wherewith we kissed in meeting that spring day,
135 I scarce dare talk of the remember'd bliss,

"When both our mouths went wandering in one
    way,
And aching sorely, met among the leaves;
Our hands being left behind strained far away.

"Never within a yard of my bright sleeves
140 Had Launcelot come before—and now, so nigh!
After that day why is it Guenevere grieves?

"Nevertheless you, O Sir Gauwaine, lie,
Whatever happened on through all those years,
God knows I speak truth, saying that you lie.

145 "Being such a lady could I weep these tears
If this were true? A great queen such as I
Having sinn'd this way, straight her conscience
    sears;

"And afterwards she liveth hatefully,
Slaying and poisoning, certes never weeps,—
150 Gauwaine be friends now, speak me lovingly.

"Do I not see how God's dear pity creeps
All through your frame, and trembles in your
    mouth?
Remember in what grave your mother sleeps,

"Buried in some place far down in the south,
155 Men are forgetting as I speak to you;
By her head sever'd in that awful drouth

"Of pity that drew Agravaine's[1] fell blow,
I pray your pity! let me not scream out
For ever after, when the shrill winds blow

160 "Through half your castle-locks! let me not shout
For ever after in the winter night
When you ride out alone! in battle-rout

"Let not my rusting tears make your sword light!
Ah! God of mercy, how he turns away!
165 So, ever must I dress me to the fight;

"So—let God's justice work! Gauwaine, I say,
See me hew down your proofs: yea, all men know
Even as you said how Mellyagraunce[2] one day,

"One bitter day in *la Fausse Garde*,[3] for so
170 All good knights held it after, saw—
Yea, sirs, by cursed unknightly outrage; though

"You, Gauwaine, held his word without a flaw,
This Mellyagraunce saw blood upon my bed—
Whose blood then pray you? is there any law

175 "To make a queen say why some spots of red
Lie on her coverlet? or will you say,
'Your hands are white, lady, as when you wed,

"'Where did you bleed?' and must I stammer
    out—'Nay,
I blush indeed, fair lord, only to rend
180 My sleeve up to my shoulder, where there lay

"'A knife-point last night': so must I defend
The honour of the lady Guenevere?
Not so, fair lords, even if the world should end

"This very day, and you were judges here
185 Instead of God. Did you see Mellyagraunce
When Launcelot stood by him? what white fear

"Curdled his blood, and how his teeth did dance,
His side sink in? as my knight cried and said,
'Slayer of unarm'd men, here is a chance!

190 "'Setter of traps,[4] I pray you guard your head,
By God I am so glad to fight with you,
Stripper of ladies, that my hand feels lead

"'For driving weight; hurrah now! draw and do,
For all my wounds are moving in my breast,
195 And I am getting mad with waiting so.'

"He struck his hands together o'er the beast,
Who fell down flat, and grovell'd at his feet,
And groan'd at being slain so young—'at least.'

"My knight said: 'Rise you, sir, who are so fleet
200 At catching ladies, half-arm'd will I fight,
My left side all uncovered!' then I weet,

---

[1] Gauwaine's brother, who accused his mother of infidelity and murdered her.

[2] Mellyagraunce had charged Guenevere with adultery after he found blood on her sheets while she was staying at his castle. The blood was actually Lancelot's, who had cut his arm climbing through Guenevere's window, but Lancelot defended her honour, saying that it came from wounded knights who had been placed in her rooms.

[3] the False Castle, the phrase expressing Guenevere's contempt.

---

[4] Mellyagraunce attempted to prevent Lancelot from defending Guenevere's honour in a duel by making him fall through a trapdoor into a dungeon.

"Up sprang Sir Mellyagraunce with great delight
Upon his knave's face; not until just then
Did I quite hate him, as I saw my knight

205 "Along the lists look to my stake and pen
With such a joyous smile, it made me sigh
From agony beneath my waist-chain,[1] when

"The fight began, and to me they drew nigh;
Ever Sir Launcelot kept him on the right,
210 And traversed warily, and ever high

"And fast leapt caitiff's sword, until my knight
Sudden threw up his sword to his left hand,
Caught it, and swung it; that was all the fight.

"Except a spout of blood on the hot land;
215 For it was hottest summer; and I know
I wonder'd how the fire, while I should stand,

"And burn, against the heat, would quiver so,
Yards above my head; thus these matters went;
Which things were only warnings of the woe

220 "That fell on me. Yet Mellyagraunce was shent,[2]
For Mellyagraunce had fought against the Lord;
Therefore, my lords, take heed lest you be blent[3]

"With all this wickedness; say no rash word
Against me, being so beautiful; my eyes,
225 Wept all away to grey, may bring some sword

"To drown you in your blood; see my breast rise,
Like waves of purple sea, as here I stand;
And how my arms are moved in wonderful wise,

"Yea also at my full heart's strong command,
230 See through my long throat how the words go up
In ripples to my mouth; how in my hand

"The shadow lies like wine within a cup
Of marvellously colour'd gold; yea now
This little wind is rising, look you up,

235 "And wonder how the light is falling so
Within my moving tresses: will you dare,
When you have looked a little on my brow,

"To say this thing is vile? or will you care
For any plausible lies of cunning woof,
240 When you can see my face with no lie there

"For ever? am I not a gracious proof—
'But in your chamber Launcelot was found'—
Is there a good knight then would stand aloof,

"When a queen says with gentle queenly sound:
245 'O true as steel, come now and talk with me,
I love to see your step upon the ground

"'Unwavering, also well I love to see
That gracious smile light up your face, and hear
Your wonderful words, that all mean verily

250 "'The thing they seem to mean: good friend, so
    dear
To me in everything, come here to-night,
Or else the hours will pass most dull and drear;

"'If you come not, I fear this time I might
Get thinking over much of times gone by,
255 When I was young, and green hope was in sight:

"'For no man cares now to know why I sigh;
And no man comes to sing me pleasant songs,
Nor any brings me the sweet flowers that lie

---

[1] Guenevere is chained to a stake where she will be burned.

[2] disgraced, ruined.

[3] blended with or blinded by.

260 "'So thick in the gardens; therefore one so longs
To see you, Launcelot; that we may be
Like children once again, free from all wrongs

"'Just for one night.' Did he not come to me?
What thing could keep true Launcelot away
If I said 'Come'? there was one less than three

265 "In my quiet room that night, and we were gay;
Till sudden I rose up, weak, pale, and sick,
Because a bawling broke our dream up, yea

"I looked at Launcelot's face and could not speak,
For he looked helpless too, for a little while;
270 Then I remember how I tried to shriek,

"And could not, but fell down; from tile to tile
The stones they threw up rattled o'er my head
And made me dizzier; till within a while

"My maids were all about me, and my head
275 On Launcelot's breast was being soothed away
From its white chattering, until Launcelot said—

"By God! I will not tell you more to-day,
Judge any way you will—what matters it?
You know quite well the story of that fray,

280 "How Launcelot still'd their bawling, the mad fit
That caught up Gauwaine—all, all, verily,
But just that which would save me; these things
    flit.

"Nevertheless you, O Sir Gauwaine, lie,
Whatever may have happen'd these long years,
285 God knows I speak truth, saying that you lie!

"All I have said is truth, by Christ's dear tears."
She would not speak another word, but stood
Turn'd sideways; listening, like a man who hears

His brother's trumpet sounding through the wood
290 Of his foes' lances. She lean'd eagerly,
And gave a slight spring sometimes, as she could

At last hear something really; joyfully
Her cheek grew crimson, as the headlong speed
Of the roan charger drew all men to see,
295 The knight who came was Launcelot at good need.
    —1858

The Haystack in the Floods [1]

Had she come all the way for this,
To part at last without a kiss?
Yea, had she borne the dirt and rain
That her own eyes might see him slain
5 Beside the haystack in the floods?

Along the dripping leafless woods,
The stirrup touching either shoe,
She rode astride as troopers do;
With kirtle kilted [2] to her knee,
10 To which the mud splash'd wretchedly;
And the wet dripp'd from every tree
Upon her head and heavy hair,
And on her eyelids broad and fair;
The tears and rain ran down her face.
15 By fits and starts they rode apace,
And very often was his place
Far off from her; he had to ride
Ahead, to see what might betide
When the roads cross'd; and sometimes, when
20 There rose a murmuring from his men,
Had to turn back with promises;

_____

[1] After the defeat of the French at Poitiers in 1356, Sir Robert de
Marny, an English knight, and his mistress Jehane are travelling through
France, intent on reaching the frontier of Gascony, which is in English
hands. They are confronted by a traitorous French knight, Godmar, who
intends to murder Robert and seize Jehane.

[2] skirt tucked up.

Ah me! she had but little ease;
And often for pure doubt and dread
She sobb'd, made giddy in the head
25 By the swift riding; while, for cold,
Her slender fingers scarce could hold
The wet reins; yea, and scarcely, too,
She felt the foot within her shoe
Against the stirrup: all for this,
30 To part at last without a kiss
Beside the haystack in the floods.

For when they near'd that old soak'd hay,
They saw across the only way
That Judas, Godmar, and the three
35 Red running lions dismally
Grinn'd from his pennon,[1] under which,
In one straight line along the ditch,
The counted thirty heads.
                                    So then,
While Robert turn'd round to his men,
40 She saw at once the wretched end,
And, stooping down, tried hard to rend
Her coif the wrong way from her head,
And hid her eyes; while Robert said:
"Nay, love, 'tis scarcely two to one,
45 At Poictiers where we made them run[2]
So fast—why, sweet my love, good cheer.
The Gascon frontier is so near,
Nought after this."

                        But, "O," she said,
"My God! my God! I have to tread
50 The long way back without you; then
The court at Paris;[3] those six men;

The gratings of the Chatelet;
The swift Seine on some rainy day
Like this, and people standing by,
55 And laughing, while my weak hands try
To recollect how strong men swim.
All this, or else a life with him,
For which I should be damned at last,
Would God that this next hour were past!"

60 He answer'd not, but cried his cry,
"St. George for Marny!"[4] cheerily;
And laid his hand upon her rein.
Alas! no man of all his train
Gave back that cheery cry again;
65 And, while for rage his thumb beat fast
Upon his sword-hilt, some one cast
About his neck a kerchief long,
And bound him.

                        Then they went along
To Godmar; who said: "Now, Jehane,
70 Your lover's life is on the wane
So fast, that, if this very hour
You yield not as my paramour,
He will not see the rain leave off—
Nay, keep your tongue from gibe and scoff,
75 Sir Robert, or I slay you now."

She laid her hand upon her brow,
Then gazed upon the palm, as though
She thought her forehead bled, and—"No!"
She said, and turn'd her head away,
80 As there were nothing else to say,
And everything were settled: red
Grew Godmar's face from chin to head:
"Jehane, on yonder hill there stands
My castle, guarding well my lands:
85 What hinders me from taking you,
And doing that I list to do

---

[1] pennant or banner.

[2] The English won the Battle of Poitiers despite being outnumbered five to one; Gascony was English territory at this time.

[3] Jehane fears being tried as a witch and imprisoned in the Grand Chatelet prison. Women accused of being witches were thrown into a river as a test of their innocence: if they sank and drowned they were deemed innocent, but if they swam they were found guilty.

[4] Robert calls on St. George, the patron saint of England.

To your fair wilful body, while
Your knight lies dead?"

                    A wicked smile
Wrinkled her face, her lips grew thin,
90 A long way out she thrust her chin:
"You know that I should strangle you
While you were sleeping; or bite through
Your throat, by God's help—ah!" she said,
"Lord Jesus, pity your poor maid!
95 For in such wise they hem me in,
I cannot choose but sin and sin,
Whatever happens: yet I think
They could not make me eat or drink,
And so should I just reach my rest."
100 "Nay, if you do not my behest,
O Jehane! though I love you well,"
Said Godmar, "would I fail to tell
All that I know?" "Foul lies," she said.
"Eh? lies, my Jehane? by God's head,
105 At Paris folks would deem them true!
Do you know, Jehane, they cry for you,
'Jehane the brown! Jehane the brown!
Give us Jehane to burn or drown!'—
Eh—gag me Robert!—sweet my friend,
110 This were indeed a piteous end
For those long fingers, and long feet,
And long neck, and smooth shoulders sweet;
An end that few men would forget
That saw it—So, an hour yet:
115 Consider, Jehane, which to take
Of life or death!"

                    So, scarce awake,
Dismounting, did she leave that place,
And totter some yards: with her face
Turn'd upward to the sky she lay,
120 Her head on a wet heap of hay,
And fell asleep: and while she slept,
And did not dream, the minutes crept
Round to the twelve again; but she,
Being waked at last, sigh'd quietly,
125 And strangely childlike came, and said:

"I will not." Straightway Godmar's head,
As though it hung on strong wires, turn'd
Most sharply round, and his face burn'd.

For Robert—both his eyes were dry,
130 He could not weep, but gloomily
He seem'd to watch the rain; yea, too,
His lips were firm; he tried once more
To touch her lips, she reach'd out, sore
And vain desire so tortured them,
135 The poor grey lips, and now the hem
Of his sleeve brush'd them.

                    With a start
Up Godmar rose, thrust them apart;
From Robert's throat he loosed the bands
Of silk and mail; with empty hands
140 Held out, she stood and gazed, and saw,
The long bright blade without a flaw
Glide out from Godmar's sheath, his hand
In Robert's hair; she saw him bend
Back Robert's head; she saw him send
145 The thin steel down; the blow told well,
Right backward the knight Robert fell,
And moan'd as dogs do, being half dead,
Unwitting, as I deem: so then
Godmar turn'd grinning to his men,
150 Who ran, some five or six, and beat
His head to pieces at their feet.

Then Godmar turn'd again and said:
"So, Jehane, the first fitte[1] is read!
Take note, my lady, that your way
155 Lies backward to the Chatelet!"
She shook her head and gazed awhile
At her cold hands with a rueful smile,
As though this thing had made her mad.

This was the parting that they had
160 Beside the haystack in the floods.
    —1858

_____

[1] section or canto of a poem.

Riding Together

For many, many days together
  The wind blew steady from the East;
For many days hot grew the weather,
  About the time of our Lady's Feast.[1]

5 For many days we rode together,
  Yet met we neither friend nor foe;
Hotter and clearer grew the weather,
  Steadily did the East wind blow.

We saw the trees in the hot, bright weather,
10 Clear-cut, with shadows very black,
As freely we rode on together
  With helms unlaced and bridles slack.

And often, as we rode together,
  We, looking down the green bank'd stream,
15 Saw flowers in the sunny weather,
  And saw the bubble-making bream.

And in the night lay down together,
  And hung above our heads the rood,[2]
Or watch'd night-long in the dewy weather,
20 The while the moon did watch the wood.

Our spears stood bright and thick together,
  Straight out the banners stream'd behind,
As we gallop'd on in the sunny weather,
  With faces turn'd towards the wind.

25 Down sank our threescore spears together,
  As thick we saw the pagans ride;
His eager face in the clear fresh weather,
  Shone out that last time by my side.

Up the sweep of the bridge we dash'd together,
30 It rock'd to the crash of the meeting spears,

Down rain'd the buds of the dear spring weather,
  The elm-tree flowers fell like tears.

There, as we roll'd and writhed together,
  I threw my arms above my head,
35 For close by my side, in the lovely weather,
  I saw him reel and fall back dead.

I and the slayer met together,
  He waited the death-stroke there in his place,
With thoughts of death, in the lovely weather,
40 Gapingly mazed at my madden'd face.

Madly I fought as we fought together;
  In vain: the little Christian band
The pagans drown'd, as in stormy weather,
  The river drowns low-lying land.

45 They bound my blood-stain'd hands together,
  They bound his corpse to nod by my side:
Then on we rode, in the bright March weather,
  With clash of cymbals did we ride.

We ride no more, no more together;
50 My prison-bars are thick and strong,
I take no heed of any weather,
  The sweet Saints grant I live not long.
—1856

Near Avalon[3]

A ship with shields before the sun,
  Six maidens round the mast,
A red-gold crown on every one,
A green gown on the last.

5 The fluttering green banners there
Are wrought with ladies' heads most fair,

[1] the Feast of Annunciation, March 25.

[2] the cross.

[3] an island Paradise in the west where King Arthur and other heroes supposedly went after death.

And a portraiture of Guenevere
The middle of each sail doth bear.

A ship with sails before the wind,
10 And round the helm six knights,
Their heaumes are on, whereby, half blind,
They pass by many sights.

The tatter'd scarlet banners there,
Right soon will leave the spear-heads bare,
15 Those six knights sorrowfully bear
In all their heaumes some yellow hair.
—1858

An Apology

Of Heaven or Hell I have no power to sing,
I cannot ease the burden of your fears,
Or make quick-coming death a little thing,
Or bring again the pleasure of past years,
5 Nor for my words shall ye forget your tears,
Or hope again for aught that I can say,
The idle singer of an empty day.

But rather, when aweary of your mirth,
From full hearts still unsatisfied ye sigh,
10 And, feeling kindly unto all the earth,
Grudge every minute as it passes by,
Made the more mindful that the sweet days die—
—Remember me a little then I pray,
The idle singer of an empty day.

15 The heavy trouble, the bewildering care
That weighs us down who live and earn our bread,
These idle verses have no power to bear;
So let me sing of names rememberèd,
Because they, living not, can ne'er be dead,
20 Or long time take their memory quite away
From us poor singers of an empty day.

Dreamer of dreams, born out of my due time,
Why should I strive to set the crooked straight?
Let it suffice me that my murmuring rhyme
25 Beats with light wing against the ivory gate,[1]
Telling a tale not too importunate
To those who in the sleepy region stay,
Lulled by the singer of an empty day.

Folk say, a wizard to a northern king
30 At Christmas-tide such wondrous things did show,
That through one window men beheld the spring,
And through another saw the summer glow,
And through a third the fruited vines a-row,
While still, unheard, but in its wonted way,
35 Piped the drear wind of that December day.

So with this Earthly Paradise it is,
If ye will read aright, and pardon me,
Who strive to build a shadowy isle of bliss
Midmost the beating of the steely sea,
40 Where tossed about all hearts of men must be;
Whose ravening monsters mighty men shall slay,
Not the poor singer of an empty day.
—1868

A Garden by the Sea

I know a little garden-close,
Set thick with lily and red rose,
Where I would wander if I might
From dewy morn to dewy night,
5 And have one with me wandering.

And though within it no birds sing,
And though no pillared house is there,
And though the apple-boughs are bare
Of fruit and blossom, would to God

---

[1] In Homer, false dreams emerge from the Gates of Ivory of the Cave of Sleep, and true dreams issue from the Gates of Horn.

10   Her feet upon the green grass trod,
     And I beheld them as before.

     There comes a murmur from the shore,
     And in the close two fair streams are,
     Drawn from the purple hills afar,
15   Drawn down unto the restless sea:
     Dark hills whose heath-bloom feeds no bee,
     Dark shore no ship has ever seen,
     Tormented by the billows green
     Whose murmur comes unceasingly
20   Unto the place for which I cry.

     For which I cry both day and night,
     For which I let slip all delight,
     Whereby I grow both deaf and blind,
     Careless to win, unskilled to find,
25   And quick to lose what all men seek.

     Yet tottering as I am and weak,
     Still have I left a little breath
     To seek within the jaws of death
     An entrance to that happy place,
30   To seek the unforgotten face,
     Once seen, once kissed, once reft from me
     Anigh the murmuring of the sea.
     —1891 (1867)

The End of May

How the wind howls this morn
   About the end of May,
And drives June on apace
To mock the world forlorn
5   And the world's joy passed away
And my unlonged-for face!
The world's joy passed away;
For no more may I deem
That any folk are glad
10 To see the dawn of day
Sunder the tangled dream
Wherein no grief they had.
Ah, through the tangled dream
Where others have no grief
15 Ever it fares with me
That fears and treasons stream
And dumb sleep slays belief
Whatso therein may be.
Sleep slayeth all belief
20 Until the hopeless light
Wakes at the birth of June
More lying tales to weave,
More love in woe's despite,
More hope to perish soon.
    —1891

James Thomson
1834 – 1882

Born in Glasgow, the son of a dressmaker and merchant seaman, Thomson moved to London in 1840, where at the age of eight he was placed in a London Scottish asylum upon his mother's illness and certain death. Having been employed as an army schoolmaster from 1854 until 1862, Thomson then worked as a secretary in the merchant's office of Charles Bradlaugh. It was in Bradlaugh's weekly *National Reformer* that Thomson's poetry and prose were initially published. Self-educated in French, German, and Italian, Thomson translated Heine, Novalis, and Leopardi. After spending some time travelling in Colorado, and acting as a war correspondent in Spain, Thomson ended his association with Bradlaugh in 1875 and began work as a freelance writer. An intimate of the Rossettis and George Meredith, Thomson published two collections of poetry in 1880 and 1881 before dying in poverty and alcoholism in 1882.

❧❧❧

The City of Dreadful Night

Per me si va nella città dolente.—DANTE.[1]

Poi di tanto adoprar, di tanti moti
D'ogni celeste, ogni terrena cosa,
Girando senza posa,
Per tornar sempre là donde son mosse;
Uso alcuno, alcun frutto
Indovinar non so.[2]

Sola nel mondo eterna, a cui si volve
Ogni creata cosa,
In te, morte, si posa
Nostra ignuda natura;
Lieta no, ma sicura
Dell' antico dolor...
Però ch' esser beato
Nega ai mortali e nega a' morti il fato.—LEOPARDI.[3]

Proem

Lo, thus, as prostrate, "In the dust I write
    My heart's deep languor and my soul's sad
        tears."[4]
Yet why evoke the spectres of black night
    To blot the sunshine of exultant years?
5 Why disinter dead faith from mouldering hidden?
Why break the seals of mute despair unbidden,
    And wail life's discords into careless ears?

Because a cold rage seizes one at whiles
    To show the bitter old and wrinkled truth
10 Stripped naked of all vesture that beguiles,
    False dreams, false hopes, false masks and
        modes of youth;
Because it gives some sense of power and passion
In helpless impotence to try to fashion
    Our woe in living words howe'er uncouth.

15 Surely I write not for the hopeful young,
    Or those who deem their happiness of worth,
Or such as pasture and grow fat among
    The shows of life and feel nor doubt nor dearth,

---

[1] Dante, *Inferno* 3.1: "Through me is the way into the city of pain." The first line of the nine-line inscription above the gate that leads into the hell of eternal pain (*eterno dolore*), the hell of the lost (*perduta gente*).

[2] Giacomo Leopardi (1798–1837), "*Canti* 23: Canto notturno di un pastore errante dell'Asia," ll. 93–98: "Then out of such endless working, so many movements of everything in heaven and earth, revolving incessantly, only to return to the point from which they were moved: from all this I can imagine neither purpose nor gain."

[3] Leopardi, *Operette Morali*, "Coro di morti" from "Dialogo di Federico Ruysch e delle sue mummie," ll. 1–6, ll. 31–32: "Eternal alone in the world, receiver of all created things, in you, death, our naked being comes to rest; joyful no, but safe from the age-old pain…For happiness is denied by fate to the living and denied to the dead."

[4] Shakespeare, *Titus Andronicus* 3.1.12–13.

896

Or pious spirits with a God above them
20 To sanctify and glorify and love them,
    Or sages who foresee a heaven on earth.

For none of these I write, and none of these
    Could read the writing if they deigned to try:
So may they flourish, in their due degrees,
25   On our sweet earth and in their unplaced sky.
If any cares for the weak words here written,
It must be some one desolate, Fate-smitten,
    Whose faith and hope are dead, and who would
        die.

Yes, here and there some weary wanderer
30   In that same city of tremendous night,
Will understand the speech, and feel a stir
    Of fellowship in all-disastrous fight;
"I suffer mute and lonely, yet another
Uplifts his voice to let me know a brother
35   Travels the same wild paths though out of
        sight."

O sad Fraternity, do I unfold
    Your dolorous mysteries shrouded from of yore?
Nay, be assured; no secret can be told
    To any who divined it not before:
40 None uninitiate by many a presage
Will comprehend the language of the message,
    Although proclaimed aloud for evermore.

I

The City is of Night; perchance of Death,
    But certainly of Night; for never there
Can come the lucid morning's fragrant breath
    After the dewy dawning's cold grey air;
5 The moon and stars may shine with scorn or pity;
The sun has never visited that city,
    For it dissolveth in the daylight fair.

Dissolveth like a dream of night away;
    Though present in distempered gloom of
        thought
10 And deadly weariness of heart all day.
    But when a dream night after night is brought
Throughout a week, and such weeks few or many
Recur each year for several years, can any
    Discern that dream from real life in aught?

15 For life is but a dream whose shapes return,
    Some frequently, some seldom, some by night
And some by day, some night and day: we learn,
    The while all change and many vanish quite,
In their recurrence with recurrent changes
20 A certain seeming order; where this ranges
    We count things real; such is memory's might.

A river girds the city west and south,
    The main north channel of a broad lagoon,
Regurging with the salt tides from the mouth;
25   Waste marshes shine and glister to the moon
For leagues, then moorland black, then stony ridges;
Great piers and causeways, many noble bridges,
    Connect the town and islet suburbs strewn.

Upon an easy slope it lies at large,
30   And scarcely overlaps the long curved crest
Which swells out two leagues from the river marge.
    A trackless wilderness rolls north and west,
Savannahs, savage woods, enormous mountains,
Bleak uplands, black ravines with torrent fountains;
35   And eastward rolls the shipless sea's unrest.

The city is not ruinous, although
    Great ruins of an unremembered past,
With others of a few short years ago
    More sad, are found within its precincts vast.
40 The street-lamps always burn; but scarce a casement
In house or palace front from roof to basement
    Doth glow or gleam athwart the mirk air cast.

The street-lamps burn amidst the baleful glooms,
    Amidst the soundless solitudes immense
45 Of rangèd mansions dark and still as tombs.
    The silence which benumbs or strains the sense
Fulfils with awe the soul's despair unweeping:
Myriads of habitants are ever sleeping,
    Or dead, or fled from nameless pestilence!

50 Yet as in some necropolis you find
    Perchance one mourner to a thousand dead,
So there; worn faces that look deaf and blind
    Like tragic masks of stone. With weary tread,
Each wrapt in his own doom, they wander, wander,
55 Or sit foredone and desolately ponder
    Through sleepless hours with heavy drooping
       head.

Mature men chiefly, few in age or youth,
    A woman rarely, now and then a child:
A child! If here the heart turns sick with ruth
60   To see a little one from birth defiled,
Or lame or blind, as preordained to languish
Through youthless life, think how it bleeds with
      anguish
    To meet one erring in that homeless wild.

They often murmur to themselves, they speak
65   To one another seldom, for their woe
Broods maddening inwardly and scorns to wreak
    Itself abroad; and if at whiles it grow
To frenzy which must rave, none heeds the clamour,
Unless there waits some victim of like glamour,
70   To rave in turn, who lends attentive show.

The City is of Night, but not of Sleep;
    There sweet sleep is not for the weary brain;
The pitiless hours like years and ages creep,
    A night seems termless hell. This dreadful strain
75 Of thought and consciousness which never ceases,
Or which some moments' stupor but increases,

This, worse than woe, makes wretches there
    insane.

They leave all hope behind who enter there:[1]
    One certitude while sane they cannot leave,
80 One anodyne for torture and despair;
    The certitude of Death, which no reprieve
Can put off long; and which, divinely tender,
But waits the outstretched hand to promptly render
    That draught whose slumber nothing can
      bereave.

II

Because he seemed to walk with an intent
    I followed him; who, shadowlike and frail,
Unswervingly though slowly onward went,
    Regardless, wrapt in thought as in a veil:
5 Thus step for step with lonely sounding feet
We travelled many a long dim silent street.

At length he paused: a black mass in the gloom,
    A tower that merged into the heavy sky;
Around, the huddled stones of grave and tomb:
10   Some old God's-acre now corruption's sty:
He murmured to himself with dull despair,
Here Faith died, poisoned by this charnel air.

Then turning to the right went on once more,
    And travelled weary roads without suspense;
15 And reached at last a low wall's open door,
    Whose villa gleamed beyond the foliage dense:
He gazed, and muttered with a hard despair,
Here Love died, stabbed by its own worshipped
    pair.

Then turning to the right resumed his march,
20   And travelled streets and lanes with wondrous
      strength,
Until on stooping through a narrow arch

---

[1] Dante, *Inferno* 3.9: "Leave all hope behind, you who enter."

We stood before a squalid house at length:
He gazed, and whispered with a cold despair,
Here Hope died, starved out in its utmost lair.

25 When he had spoken thus, before he stirred,
    I spoke, perplexed by something in the signs
Of desolation I had seen and heard
    In this drear pilgrimage to ruined shrines:
When Faith and Love and Hope are dead indeed,
30 Can Life still live? By what doth it proceed?

As whom his one intense thought overpowers,
    He answered coldly, Take a watch, erase
The signs and figures of the circling hours,
    Detach the hands, remove the dial-face;
35 The works proceed until run down; although
Bereft of purpose, void of use, still go.

Then turning to the right paced on again,
    And traversed squares and travelled streets
      whose glooms
Seemed more and more familiar to my ken;
    And reached that sullen temple of the tombs;
40 And paused to murmur with the old despair,
Here Faith died, poisoned by this charnel air.

I ceased to follow, for the knot of doubt
    Was severed sharply with a cruel knife:
45 He circled thus for ever tracing out
    The series of the fraction left of Life;
Perpetual recurrence in the scope
Of but three terms, dead Faith, dead Love, dead
    Hope.

III

Although lamps burn along the silent streets,
    Even when moonlight silvers empty squares
The dark holds countless lanes and close retreats;
    But when the night its sphereless mantle wears
5 The open spaces yawn with gloom abysmal,

The sombre mansions loom immense and dismal,
    The lanes are black as subterranean lairs.

And soon the eye a strange new vision learns:
    The night remains for it as dark and dense,
10 Yet clearly in this darkness it discerns
    As in the daylight with its natural sense;
Perceives a shade in shadow not obscurely,
Pursues a stir of black in blackness surely,
    Sees spectres also in the gloom intense.

15 The ear, too, with the silence vast and deep
    Becomes familiar though unreconciled;
Hears breathings as of hidden life asleep,
    And muffled throbs as of pent passions wild,
Far murmurs, speech of pity or derision;
20 But all more dubious than the things of vision,
    So that it knows not when it is beguiled.

No time abates the first despair and awe,
    But wonder ceases soon; the weirdest thing
Is felt least strange beneath the lawless law
    Where Death-in-Life is the eternal king;
25 Crushed impotent beneath this reign of terror,
Dazed with such mysteries of woe and error,
    The soul is too outworn for wondering.

IV

He stood alone within the spacious square
    Declaiming from the central grassy mound,
With head uncovered and with streaming hair,
    As if large multitudes were gathered round:
5 A stalwart shape, the gestures full of might,
The glances burning with unnatural light:—

As I came through the desert thus it was,
As I came through the desert: All was black,
In heaven no single star, on earth no track;
10 A brooding hush without a stir or note,
The air so thick it clotted in my throat;
And thus for hours; then some enormous things

Swooped past with savage cries and clanking wings:
　　　But I strode on austere;
15　　　No hope could have no fear.

As I came through the desert thus it was,
As I came through the desert: Eyes of fire
Glared at me throbbing with a starved desire;
The hoarse and heavy and carnivorous breath
20　Was hot upon me from deep jaws of death;
Sharp claws, swift talons, fleshless fingers cold
Plucked at me from the bushes, tried to hold:
　　　But I strode on austere;
　　　No hope could have no fear.

25　As I came through the desert thus it was,
As I came through the desert: Lo you, there,
That hillock burning with a brazen glare;
Those myriad dusky flames with points a-glow
Which writhed and hissed and darted to and fro;
30　A Sabbath of the Serpents, heaped pell-mell
For Devil's roll-call and some *fête* of Hell:
　　　Yet I strode on austere;
　　　No hope could have no fear.

As I came through the desert thus it was,
35　As I came through the desert: Meteors ran
And crossed their javelins on the black sky-span;
The zenith opened to a gulf of flame,
The dreadful thunderbolts jarred earth's fixed frame;
The ground all heaved in waves of fire that surged
40　And weltered round me sole there unsubmerged:
　　　Yet I strode on austere;
　　　No hope could have no fear.

As I came through the desert thus it was,
As I came through the desert: Air once more,
45　And I was close upon a wild sea-shore;
Enormous cliffs arose on either hand,
The deep tide thundered up a league-broad strand;
White foambelts seethed there, wan spray swept
　　and flew;

The sky broke, moon and stars and clouds and blue:
50　　　And I strode on austere;
　　　No hope could have no fear.

As I came through the desert thus it was,
As I came through the desert: On the left
The sun arose and crowned a broad crag-cleft;
55　There stopped and burned out black, except a rim,
A bleeding eyeless socket, red and dim;
Whereon the moon fell suddenly south-west,
And stood above the right-hand cliffs at rest:
　　　Still I strode on austere;
60　　　No hope could have no fear.

As I came through the desert thus it was,
As I came through the desert: From the right
A shape came slowly with a ruddy light;
A woman with a red lamp in her hand,
65　Bareheaded and barefooted on that strand;
O desolation moving with such grace!
O anguish with such beauty in thy face!
　　　I fell as on my bier,
　　　Hope travailed with such fear.

70　As I came through the desert thus it was,
As I came through the desert: I was twain,
Two selves distinct that cannot join again;
One stood apart and knew but could not stir,
And watched the other stark in swoon and her;
75　And she came on, and never turned aside,
Between such sun and moon and roaring tide:
　　　And as she came more near
　　　My soul grew mad with fear.

As I came through the desert thus it was,
80　As I came through the desert: Hell is mild
And piteous matched with that accursèd wild;
A large black sign was on her breast that bowed,
A broad black band ran down her snow-white shroud;
That lamp she held was her own burning heart,
85　Whose blood-drops trickled step by step apart:

The mystery was clear;
Mad rage had swallowed fear.

As I came through the desert thus it was,
As I came through the desert: By the sea
90 She knelt and bent above that senseless me;
Those lamp-drops fell upon my white brow there,
She tried to cleanse them with her tears and hair;
She murmured words of pity, love, and woe,
She heeded not the level rushing flow:
95   And mad with rage and fear,
    I stood stonebound so near.

As I came through the desert thus it was,
As I came through the desert: When the tide
Swept up to her there kneeling by my side,
100 She clasped that corpse-like me, and they were borne
Away, and this vile me was left forlorn;
I know the whole sea cannot quench that heart,
Or cleanse that brow, or wash those two apart:
    They love; their doom is drear,
105   Yet they nor hope nor fear;
    But I, what do I here?

V

How he arrives there none can clearly know;
    Athwart the mountains and immense wild tracts,
Or flung a waif upon that vast sea-flow,
    Or down the river's boiling cataracts:
5 To reach it is as dying fever-stricken;
To leave it, slow faint birth intense pangs quicken;
    And memory swoons in both the tragic acts.

But being there one feels a citizen;
    Escape seems hopeless to the heart forlorn:
10 Can Death-in-Life be brought to life again?
    And yet release does come; there comes a morn
When he awakes from slumbering so sweetly
That all the world is changed for him completely,
    And he is verily as if new-born.

15 He scarcely can believe the blissful change,
    He weeps perchance who wept not while accurst;
Never again will he approach the range
    Infected by that evil spell now burst:
Poor wretch! who once hath paced that dolent city
20 Shall pace it often, doomed beyond all pity,
    With horror ever deepening from the first.

Though he possess sweet babes and loving wife,
    A home of peace by loyal friendships cheered,
And love them more than death or happy life,
25   They shall avail not; he must dree his weird;[1]
Renounce all blessings for that imprecation,
Steal forth and haunt that builded desolation,
    Of woe and terrors and thick darkness reared.

VI

I sat forlornly by the river-side,
    And watched the bridge-lamps glow like golden
        stars
Above the blackness of the swelling tide,
    Down which they struck rough gold in ruddier
        bars;
5 And heard the heave and plashing of the flow
Against the wall a dozen feet below.

Large elm-trees stood along that river-walk;
    And under one, a few steps from my seat,
I heard strange voices join in stranger talk,
10   Although I had not heard approaching feet:
These bodiless voices in my waking dream
Flowed dark words blending with the sombre
        stream:—

And you have after all come back; come back.
I was about to follow on your track.
15 And you have failed: our spark of hope is black.

_____

[1] a Scottish expression meaning "endure his fate."

That I have failed is proved by my return:
The spark is quenched, nor ever more will burn,
But listen; and the story you shall learn.

I reached the portal common spirits fear,
20 And read the words above it, dark yet clear,
"Leave hope behind, all ye who enter here:"

And would have passed in, gratified to gain
That positive eternity of pain,
Instead of this insufferable inane.

25 A demon warder clutched me, Not so fast;
First leave your hopes behind!—But years have
        passed
Since I left all behind me, to the last:

You cannot count for hope, with all your wit,
This bleak despair that drives me to the Pit:
30 How could I seek to enter void of it?

He snarled, What thing is this which apes a soul,
And would find entrance to our gulf of dole
Without the payment of the settled toll?

Outside the gate he showed an open chest:
35 Here pay their entrance fees the souls unblest;
Cast in some hope, you enter with the rest.

This is Pandora's box;[1] whose lid shall shut,
And Hell-gate too, when hopes have filled it; but
They are so thin that it will never glut.

40 I stood a few steps backwards, desolate;
And watched the spirits pass me to their fate,
And fling off hope, and enter at the gate.

_____

[1] In Greek mythology, Pandora's box contained all human misfortunes
and evils, which were unleashed on the world when her husband,
Epimetheus, opened the box.

When one casts off a load he springs upright,
Squares back his shoulders, breathes with all his
        might,
45 And briskly paces forward strong and light:

But these, as if they took some burden, bowed;
The whole frame sank; however strong and proud
Before, they crept in quite infirm and cowed.

And as they passed me, earnestly from each
50 A morsel of his hope I did beseech,
To pay my entrance; but all mocked my speech.

Not one would cede a tittle of his store,
Though knowing that in instants three or four
He must resign the whole for evermore.

55 So I returned. Our destiny is fell;
For in this Limbo we must ever dwell,
Shut out alike from Heaven and Earth and Hell.

The other sighed back, Yea; but if we grope
With care through all this Limbo's dreary scope,
60 We yet may pick up some minute lost hope;

And, sharing it between us, entrance win,
In spite of fiends so jealous for gross sin:
Let us without delay our search begin.

VII

Some say that phantoms haunt those shadowy
        streets,
    And mingle freely there with sparse mankind;
And tell of ancient woes and black defeats,
    And murmur mysteries in the grave enshrined:
5 But others think them visions of illusion,
Or even men gone far in self-confusion;
    No man there being wholly sane in mind.

And yet a man who raves, however mad,
    Who bares his heart and tells of his own fall,

10 Reserves some inmost secret good or bad:
 The phantoms have no reticence at all:
The nudity of flesh will blush though tameless,
The extreme nudity of bone grins shameless,
 The unsexed skeleton mocks shroud and pall.

15 I have seen phantoms there that were as men
 And men that were as phantoms flit and roam;
Marked shapes that were not living to my ken,
 Caught breathings acrid as with Dead Sea foam:
The City rests for man so weird and awful,
20 That his intrusion there might seem unlawful,
 And phantoms there may have their proper
  home.

VIII

While I still lingered on that river-walk,
 And watched the tide as black as our black doom,
I heard another couple join in talk,
 And saw them to the left hand in the gloom
5 Seated against an elm bole on the ground,
Their eyes intent upon the stream profound.

"I never knew another man on earth
 But had some joy and solace in his life,
 Some chance of triumph in the dreadful strife:
10 My doom has been unmitigated dearth."

"We gaze upon the river, and we note
The various vessels large and small that float,
Ignoring each wrecked and sunken boat."

"And yet I asked no splendid dower, no spoil
15 Of sway or fame or rank or even wealth;
 But homely love with common food and health,
And nightly sleep to balance daily toil."

"This all-too humble soul would arrogate
Unto itself some signalising hate
20 From the supreme indifference of Fate!"

"Who is most wretched in this dolorous place?
 I think myself; yet I would rather be
 My miserable self than He, than He
Who formed such creatures to His own disgrace.

25 "The vilest thing must be less vile than Thou
 From whom it had its being, God and Lord!
 Creator of all woe and sin! abhorred,
Malignant and implacable! I vow

"That not for all Thy power furled and unfurled,
30 For all the temples to Thy glory built,
 Would I assume the ignominious guilt
Of having made such men in such a world."

"As if a Being, God or Fiend, could reign,
At once so wicked, foolish, and insane,
35 As to produce men when He might refrain!

"The world rolls round for ever like a mill;
It grinds out death and life and good and ill;
It has no purpose, heart or mind or will.

"While air of Space and Time's full river flow
40 The mill must blindly whirl unresting so:
It may be wearing out, but who can know?

"Man might know one thing were his sight less dim;
That it whirls not to suit his petty whim,
That it is quite indifferent to him.

45 "Nay, does it treat him harshly as he saith?
It grinds him some slow years of bitter breath,
Then grinds him back into eternal death."

IX

It is full strange to him who hears and feels,
 When wandering there in some deserted street,
The booming and the jar of ponderous wheels,
 The trampling clash of heavy ironshod feet:

5 Who in this Venice of the Black Sea rideth?[1]
Who in this city of the stars abideth
    To buy or sell as those in daylight sweet?

The rolling thunder seems to fill the sky
    As it comes on; the horses snort and strain,
10 The harness jingles, as it passes by;
    The hugeness of an overburthened wain:
A man sits nodding on the shaft or trudges
Three parts asleep beside his fellow-drudges:
    And so it rolls into the night again.

15 What merchandise? whence, whither, and for
      whom?
    Perchance it is a Fate-appointed hearse,
Bearing away to some mysterious tomb
    Or Limbo of the scornful universe
The joy, the peace, the life-hope, the abortions
20 Of all things good which should have been our
      portions,
    But have been strangled by that City's curse.

x

The mansion stood apart in its own ground;
    In front thereof a fragrant garden-lawn,
High trees about it, and the whole walled round:
    The massy iron gates were both withdrawn;
5 And every window of its front shed light,
Portentous in that City of the Night.

But though thus lighted it was deadly still
    As all the countless bulks of solid gloom;
Perchance a congregation to fulfil
10   Solemnities of silence in this doom,
Mysterious rites of dolour and despair
Permitting not a breath of chant or prayer?

Broad steps ascended to a terrace broad
    Whereon lay still light from the open door;
15 The hall was noble, and its aspect awed,
    Hung round with heavy black from dome to
      floor;
And ample stairways rose to left and right
Whose balustrades were also draped with night.

I paced from room to room, from hall to hall,
20   Nor any life throughout the maze discerned;
But each was hung with its funereal pall,
    And held a shrine, around which tapers burned,
With picture or with statue or with bust,
All copied from the same fair form of dust:

25 A woman very young and very fair;
    Beloved by bounteous life and joy and youth,
And loving these sweet lovers, so that care
    And age and death seemed not for her in sooth:
Alike as stars, all beautiful and bright,
30 These shapes lit up that mausoléan night.

At length I heard a murmur as of lips,
    And reached an open oratory hung
With heaviest blackness of the whole eclipse;
    Beneath the dome a fuming censer swung;
35 And one lay there upon a low white bed,
With tapers burning at the foot and head:

The Lady of the images: supine,
    Deathstill, lifesweet, with folded palms she lay:
And kneeling there as at a sacred shrine
40   A young man wan and worn who seemed to pray:
A crucifix of dim and ghostly white
Surmounted the large altar left in night:—

The chambers of the mansion of my heart,
In every one whereof thine image dwells,
45 Are black with grief eternal for thy sake.

---

[1] Venice is a city in north Italy built on 118 small islands connected by
canals. The Black Sea is a large inland sea between Europe and Asia.

The inmost oratory of my soul,
Wherein thou ever dwellest quick or dead,
Is black with grief eternal for thy sake.

I kneel beside thee and I clasp the cross,
50 With eyes for ever fixed upon that face,
So beautiful and dreadful in its calm.

I kneel here patient as thou liest there;
As patient as a statue carved in stone,
Of adoration and eternal grief.

55 While thou dost not awake I cannot move;
And something tells me thou wilt never wake,
And I alive feel turning into stone.

Most beautiful were Death to end my grief,
Most hateful to destroy the sight of thee,
60 Dear vision better than all death or life.

But I renounce all choice of life or death,
For either shall be ever at thy side,
And thus in bliss or woe be ever well.—

He murmured thus and thus in monotone,
65   Intent upon that uncorrupted face,
Entranced except his moving lips alone:
   I glided with hushed footsteps from the place.
This was the festival that filled with light
That palace in the City of the Night.

XI

What men are they who haunt these fatal glooms,
   And fill their living mouths with dust of death,
And make their habitations in the tombs,
   And breathe eternal sighs with mortal breath,
5 And pierce life's pleasant veil of various error
To reach that void of darkness and old terror
   Wherein expire the lamps of hope and faith?

They have much wisdom yet they are not wise,
   They have much goodness yet they do not well,
10 (The fools we know have their own Paradise,
   The wicked also have their proper Hell);
They have much strength but still their doom is
   stronger,
Much patience but their time endureth longer,
   Much valour but life mocks it with some spell.

15 They are most rational and yet insane:
   An outward madness not to be controlled;
A perfect reason in the central brain,
   Which has no power, but sitteth wan and cold,
And sees the madness, and foresees as plainly
20 The ruin in its path, and trieth vainly
   To cheat itself refusing to behold.

And some are great in rank and wealth and power,
   And some renowned for genius and for worth;
And some are poor and mean, who brood and cower
25   And shrink from notice, and accept all dearth
Of body, heart and soul, and leave to others
All boons of life: yet these and those are brothers,
   The saddest and the weariest men on earth.

XII

Our isolated units could be brought
   To act together for some common end?
For one by one, each silent with his thought,
   I marked a long loose line approach and wend
5 Athwart the great cathedral's cloistered square,
And slowly vanish from the moonlit air.

Then I would follow in among the last:
   And in the porch a shrouded figure stood,
Who challenged each one pausing ere he passed,
10   With deep eyes burning through a blank white
   hood:
Whence come you in the world of life and light
To this our City of Tremendous Night?—

From pleading in a senate of rich lords
For some scant justice to our countless hordes
15 Who toil half-starved with scarce a human right:
I wake from daydreams to this real night.

From wandering through many a solemn scene
Of opium visions, with a heart serene
And intellect miraculously bright:
20 I wake from daydreams to this real night.

From making hundreds laugh and roar with glee
By my transcendent feats of mimicry,
And humour wanton as an elfish sprite:
I wake from daydreams to this real night.

25 From prayer and fasting in a lonely cell,
Which brought an ecstasy ineffable
Of love and adoration and delight:
I wake from daydreams to this real night.

From ruling on a splendid kingly throne
30 A nation which beneath my rule has grown
Year after year in wealth and arts and might:
I wake from daydreams to this real night.

From preaching to an audience fired with faith
The Lamb[1] who died to save our souls from death,
35 Whose blood hath washed our scarlet sins wool-
    white:
I wake from daydreams to this real night.

From drinking fiery poison in a den
Crowded with tawdry girls and squalid men,
Who hoarsely laugh and curse and brawl and fight:
40 I wake from daydreams to this real night.

From picturing with all beauty and all grace
First Eden[2] and the parents of our race,

A luminous rapture unto all men's sight:
I wake from daydreams to this real night.

45 From writing a great work[3] with patient plan
To justify the ways of God to man,
And show how ill must fade and perish quite:
I wake from daydreams to this real night.

From desperate fighting with a little band
50 Against the powerful tyrants of our land,
To free our brethren in their own despite:
I wake from daydreams to this real night.

Thus, challenged by that warder sad and stern,
    Each one responded with his own countersign,
55 Then entered the cathedral; and in turn
    I entered also, having given mine;
But lingered near until I heard no more,
And marked the closing of the massive door.

XIII

Of all things human which are strange and wild
    This is perchance the wildest and most strange,
And showeth man most utterly beguiled,
    To those who haunt that sunless City's range;
5 That he bemoans himself for aye, repeating
How Time is deadly swift, how life is fleeting,
    How naught is constant on the earth but
       change.

The hours are heavy on him and the days;
    The burden of the months he scarce can bear;
10 And often in his secret soul he prays
    To sleep through barren periods unaware,
Arousing at some longed-for date of pleasure;
Which having passed and yielded him small treasure,
    He would outsleep another term of care.

---

[1] Christ.

[2] the Garden of Eden.

[3] Milton's *Paradise Lost* 1.26: "To justify the ways of God to man."

15 Yet in his marvellous fancy he must make
   Quick wings for Time, and see it fly from us;
This Time which crawleth like a monstrous snake,
   Wounded and slow and very venomous;
Which creeps blindwormlike round the earth and
   ocean,
20 Distilling poison at each painful motion,
   And seems condemned to circle ever thus.

And since he cannot spend and use aright
   The little time here given him in trust,
But wasteth it in weary undelight
   Of foolish toil and trouble, strife and lust,
25 He naturally claimeth to inherit
The everlasting Future, that his merit
   May have full scope; as surely is most just.

O length of the intolerable hours,
30   O nights that are as æons of slow pain,
O Time, too ample for our vital powers,
   O Life, whose woeful vanities remain
Immutable for all of all our legions
Through all the centuries and in all the regions,
35   Not of your speed and variance *we* complain.

We do not ask a longer term of strife,
   Weakness and weariness and nameless woes;
We do not claim renewed and endless life
   When this which is our torment here shall close,
40 An everlasting conscious inanition!
We yearn for speedy death in full fruition,
   Dateless oblivion and divine repose.

XIV

Large glooms were gathered in the mighty fane,
   With tinted moongleams slanting here and there;
And all was hush: no swelling organ-strain,
   No chant, no voice or murmuring of prayer;
5 No priests came forth, no tinkling censers fumed,
And the high altar space was unillumed.

Around the pillars and against the walls
   Leaned men and shadows; others seemed to
      brood
Bent or recumbent in secluded stalls.
10   Perchance they were not a great multitude
Save in that city of so lonely streets
Where one may count up every face he meets.

All patiently awaited the event
   Without a stir or sound, as if no less
15 Self-occupied, doomstricken while attent.
   And then we heard a voice of solemn stress
From the dark pulpit, and our gaze there met
Two eyes which burned as never eyes burned yet:

Two steadfast and intolerable eyes
20   Burning beneath a broad and rugged brow;
The head behind it of enormous size.
   And as black fir-groves in a large wind bow,
Our rooted congregation, gloom-arrayed,
By that great sad voice deep and full were
   swayed:—

25 O melancholy Brothers, dark, dark, dark!
O battling in black floods without an ark![1]
   O spectral wanderers of unholy Night!
My soul hath bled for you these sunless years,
With bitter blood-drops running down like tears:
30   Oh dark, dark, dark, withdrawn from joy and
      light!

My heart is sick with anguish for your bale;
Your woe hath been my anguish; yea, I quail
   And perish in your perishing unblest.
And I have searched the highths and depths, the
   scope
35 Of all our universe, with desperate hope
   To find some solace for your wild unrest.

_____

[1] The allusion is to the story of Noah and the Flood: Genesis 7 and 8.

And now at last authentic word I bring,
Witnessed by every dead and living thing;
   Good tidings of great joy for you, for all:[1]
40 There is no God; no Fiend with names divine
Made us and tortures us; if we must pine,
   It is to satiate no Being's gall.

It was the dark delusion of dream,
That living Person conscious and supreme,
45   Whom we must curse for cursing us with life;
Whom we must curse because the life He gave
Could not be buried in the quiet grave,
   Could not be killed by poison or by knife.

This little life is all we must endure,
50 The grave's most holy peace is ever sure,
   We fall asleep and never wake again;
Nothing is of us but the mouldering flesh,
Whose elements dissolve and merge afresh
   In earth, air, water, plants, and other men.

55 We finish thus; and all our wretched race
Shall finish with its cycle, and give place
   To other beings, with their own time-doom:
Infinite æons ere our kind began;
Infinite æons after the last man
60   Has joined the mammoth in earth's tomb and
      womb.

We bow down to the universal laws,
Which never had for man a special clause
   Of cruelty or kindness, love or hate:
If toads and vultures are obscene to sight,
65 If tigers burn with beauty and with might,[2]
   Is it by favour or by wrath of Fate?

All substance lives and struggles evermore
Through countless shapes continually at war,
   By countless interactions interknit:
70 If one is born a certain day on earth,
All times and forces tended to that birth,
   Not all the world could change or hinder it.

I find no hint throughout the Universe
Of good or ill, of blessing or of curse;
75   I find alone Necessity Supreme;
With infinite Mystery, abysmal, dark,
Unlighted ever by the faintest spark
   For us the flitting shadows of a dream.

O Brothers of sad lives! they are so brief;
80 A few short years must bring us all relief:
   Can we not bear these years of labouring breath?
But if you would not this poor life fulfil,
Lo, you are free to end it when you will,
   Without the fear of waking after death.—

The organ-like vibrations of his voice
   Thrilled through the vaulted aisles and died away;
The yearning of the tones which bade rejoice
   Was sad and tender as a requiem lay:
Our shadowy congregation rested still
As brooding on that "End it when you will."

xv
Wherever men are gathered, all the air
   Is charged with human feeling, human thought;
Each shout and cry and laugh, each curse and prayer,
   Are into its vibrations surely wrought;
5 Unspoken passion, wordless meditation,
Are breathed into it with our respiration;
   It is with our life fraught and overfraught.

So that no man there breathes earth's simple breath,
   As if alone on mountains or wide seas;
10 But nourishes warm life or hastens death
   With joys and sorrows, health and foul disease,

---

[1] Luke 2:10.

[2] Cf. William Blake's "The Tyger," which begins "Tyger, tyger, burning
bright/ In the forests of the night."

Wisdom and folly, good and evil labours,
Incessant of his multitudinous neighbours;
   He in his turn affecting all of these.

15 That City's atmosphere is dark and dense,
   Although not many exiles wander there,
With many a potent evil influence,
   Each adding poison to the poisoned air;
Infections of unutterable sadness,
20 Infections of incalculable madness,
   Infections of incurable despair.

XVI

Our shadowy congregation rested still,
   As musing on that message we had heard
And brooding on that "End it when you will;"
   Perchance awaiting yet some other word;
5 When keen as lightning through a muffled sky
Sprang forth a shrill and lamentable cry:—

The man speaks sooth, alas! the man speaks sooth:
   We have no personal life beyond the grave;
There is no God; Fate knows nor wrath nor ruth:
10   Can I find here the comfort which I crave?

In all eternity I had one chance,
   One few years' term of gracious human life:
The splendours of the intellect's advance,
   The sweetness of the home with babes and wife;

15 The social pleasures with their genial wit;
   The fascination of the worlds of art,
The glories of the worlds of nature, lit
   By large imagination's glowing heart;

The rapture of mere being, full of health;
20   The careless childhood and the ardent youth,
The strenuous manhood winning various wealth,
   The reverend age serene with life's long truth:

All the sublime prerogatives of Man;
   The storied memories of the times of old,
25 The patient tracking of the world's great plan
   Through sequences and changes myriadfold.

This chance was never offered me before;
   For me the infinite Past is blank and dumb:
This chance recurreth never, nevermore;
30   Blank, blank for me the infinite To-come.

And this sole chance was frustrate from my birth,
   A mockery, a delusion; and my breath
Of noble human life upon this earth
   So racks me that I sigh for senseless death.

35 My wine of life is poison mixed with gall,
   My noonday passes in a nightmare dream,
I worse than lose the years which are my all:
   What can console me for the loss supreme?

Speak not of comfort where no comfort is,
40   Speak not at all: can words make foul things fair?
Our life's a cheat, our death a black abyss:
   Hush and be mute envisaging despair.—

This vehement voice came from the northern aisle
   Rapid and shrill to its abrupt harsh close;
45 And none gave answer for a certain while,
   For words must shrink from these most
      wordless woes;
At last the pulpit speaker simply said,
With humid eyes and thoughtful drooping head:—

My Brother, my poor Brothers, it is thus;
50 This life itself holds nothing good for us,
   But it ends soon and nevermore can be;
And we knew nothing of it ere our birth,
And shall know nothing when consigned to earth:
   I ponder these thoughts and they comfort me.

XVII

How the moon triumphs through the endless
    nights!
    How the stars throb and glitter as they wheel
Their thick processions of supernal lights
    Around the blue vault obdurate as steel!
5 And men regard with passionate awe and yearning
The mighty marching and the golden burning,
    And think the heavens respond to what they
      feel.

Boats gliding like dark shadows of a dream,
    Are glorified from vision as they pass
10 The quivering moonbridge on the deep black stream;
    Cold windows kindle their dead glooms of glass
To restless crystals; cornice, dome, and column
Emerge from chaos in the splendour solemn;
    Like faëry lakes gleam lawns of dewy grass.

15 With such a living light these dead eyes shine,
    These eyes of sightless heaven, that as we gaze
We read a pity, tremulous, divine,
    Or cold majestic scorn in their pure rays:
Fond man! they are not haughty, are not tender;
20 There is no heart or mind in all their splendour,
    They thread mere puppets all their marvellous
      maze.

If we could near them with the flight unflown,
    We should but find them worlds as sad as this,
Or suns all self-consuming like our own
25   Enringed by planet worlds as much amiss:
They wax and wane through fusion and confusion;
The spheres eternal are a grand illusion,
    The empyréan is a void abyss.

XVIII

I wandered in a suburb of the north,
    And reached a spot whence three close lanes led
      down,
Beneath thick trees and hedgerows winding forth

Like deep brook channels, deep and dark and
    lown:[1]
5 The air above was wan with misty light,
The dull grey south showed one vague blur of
    white.

I took the left-hand lane and slowly trod
    Its earthen footpath, brushing as I went
The humid leafage; and my feet were shod
10   With heavy languor, and my frame downbent,
With infinite sleepless weariness outworn,
So many nights I thus had paced forlorn.

After a hundred steps I grew aware
    Of something crawling in the lane below;
15 It seemed a wounded creature prostrate there
    That sobbed with pangs in making progress
      slow,
The hind limbs stretched to push, the fore limbs
    then
To drag; for it would die in its own den.

But coming level with it I discerned
20   That it had been a man; for at my tread
It stopped in its sore travail and half-turned,
    Leaning upon its right, and raised its head,
And with the left hand twitched back as in ire
Long grey unreverend locks befouled with mire.

25 A haggard filthy face with bloodshot eyes,
    An infamy for manhood to behold.
He gasped all trembling, What, you want my prize?
    You leave, to rob me, wine and lust and gold
And all that men go mad upon, since you
30 Have traced my sacred secret of the clue?

You think that I am weak and must submit;
    Yet I but scratch you with this poisoned blade,
And you are dead as if I clove with it

---

[1] a Scottish word meaning "sheltered."

That false fierce greedy heart. Betrayed! betrayed!
35   I fling this phial if you seek to pass,
And you are forthwith shrivelled up like grass.

And then with sudden change, Take thought! take
        thought!
    Have pity on me! it is mine alone.
If you could find, it would avail you naught;
40   Seek elsewhere on the pathway of your own:
For who of mortal or immortal race
The lifetrack of another can retrace?

Did you but know my agony and toil!
    Two lanes diverge up yonder from this lane;
45   My thin blood marks the long length of their soil;
    Such clue I left, who sought my clue in vain:
My hands and knees are worn both flesh and bone;
I cannot move but with continual moan.

But I am in the very way at last
50   To find the long-lost broken golden thread
Which reunites my present with my past,
        If you but go your own way. And I said,
I will retire as soon as you have told
Whereunto leadeth this lost thread of gold.

55   And so you know it not! he hissed with scorn;
        I feared you, imbecile! It leads me back
From this accursed night without a morn,
        And through the deserts which have else no track,
And through vast wastes of horror-haunted time,
60   To Eden innocence in Eden's clime:

And I become a nursling soft and pure,
    An infant cradled on its mother's knee,
Without a past, love-cherished and secure;
    Which if it saw this loathsome present Me,
65   Would plunge its face into the pillowing breast,
And scream abhorrence hard to lull to rest.

He turned to grope; and I retiring brushed
        Thin shreds of gossamer from off my face,
And mused, His life would grow, the germ
            uncrushed;
70   He should to antenatal night retrace,
And hide his elements in that large womb
Beyond the reach of man-evolving Doom.

And even thus, what weary way were planned,
        To seek oblivion through the far-off gate
75   Of birth, when that of death is close at hand!
        For this is law, if law there be in Fate:
What never has been, yet may have its when;
The thing which has been, never is again.

                    XIX
The mighty river flowing dark and deep,
        With ebb and flood from the remote sea-tides
Vague-sounding through the City's sleepless sleep,
        Is named the River of the Suicides;
5   For night by night some lorn wretch overweary,
And shuddering from the future yet more dreary,
        Within its cold secure oblivion hides.

One plunges from a bridge's parapet,
        As by some blind and sudden frenzy hurled;
10   Another wades in slow with purpose set
        Until the waters are above him furled;
Another in a boat with dreamlike motion
Glides drifting down into the desert ocean,
        To starve or sink from out the desert world.

15   They perish from their suffering surely thus,
        For none beholding them attempts to save,
The while each thinks how soon, solicitous,
        He may seek refuge in the self-same wave;
Some hour when tired of ever-vain endurance
20   Impatience will forerun the sweet assurance
        Of perfect peace eventual in the grave.

When this poor tragic-farce has palled us long,
    Why actors and spectators do we stay?—
To fill our so-short *rôles* out right or wrong;[1]
25   To see what shifts are yet in the dull play
For our illusion; to refrain from grieving
Dear foolish friends by our untimely leaving:
    But those asleep at home, how blest are they!

Yet it is but for one night after all:
    What matters one brief night of dreary pain?
When after it the weary eyelids fall
    Upon the weary eyes and wasted brain;
And all sad scenes and thoughts and feelings vanish
In that sweet sleep no power can ever banish,
    That one best sleep which never wakes again.

                    xx
I sat me weary on a pillar's base,
    And leaned against the shaft; for broad moonlight
O'erflowed the peacefulness of cloistered space,
    A shore of shadow slanting from the right:
5   The great cathedral's western front stood there,
A wave-worn rock in that calm sea of air.

Before it, opposite my place of rest,
    Two figures faced each other, large, austere;
A couchant sphinx[2] in shadow to the breast,
10   An angel standing in the moonlight clear;
So mighty by magnificence of form,
They were not dwarfed beneath that mass enorm.

Upon the cross-hilt of a naked sword
    The angel's hands, as prompt to smite, were held;
15 His vigilant intense regard was poured
    Upon the creature placidly unquelled,

Whose front was set at level gaze which took
No heed of aught, a solemn trance-like look.

And as I pondered these opposèd shapes
20   My eyelids sank in stupor, that dull swoon
Which drugs and with a leaden mantle drapes
    The outworn to worse weariness. But soon
A sharp and clashing noise the stillness broke,
And from the evil lethargy I awoke.

25 The angel's wings had fallen, stone on stone,
    And lay there shattered; hence the sudden sound:
A warrior leaning on his sword alone
    Now watched the sphinx with that regard
        profound;
The sphinx unchanged looked forthright, as aware
30 Of nothing in the vast abyss of air.

Again I sank in that repose unsweet,
    Again a clashing noise my slumber rent;
The warrior's sword lay broken at his feet:
    An unarmed man with raised hands impotent
35 Now stood before the sphinx, which ever kept
Such mien as if with open eyes it slept.

My eyelids sank in spite of wonder grown;
    A louder crash upstartled me in dread:
The man had fallen forward, stone on stone,
40   And lay there shattered, with his trunkless head
Between the monster's large quiescent paws,
Beneath its grand front changeless as life's laws.

The moon had circled westward full and bright,
    And made the temple-front a mystic dream,
45 And bathed the whole enclosure with its light,
    The sworded angel's wrecks, the sphinx supreme:
I pondered long that cold majestic face
Whose vision seemed of infinite void space.

---

[1] Shakespeare, *As You Like It* 2.7.139–66.

[2] in Greek mythology, a monster with the head and breasts of a woman, the body of a lion, the wings of a bird and the tail of a serpent. The sphinx spoke in a human voice, setting riddles and devouring those who could not find answers.

XXI

Anear the centre of that northern crest
    Stands out a level upland bleak and bare,
From which the city east and south and west
    Sinks gently in long waves; and thronèd there
5 An Image sits, stupendous, superhuman,
The bronze colossus of a wingèd Woman,
    Upon a graded granite base foursquare.

Low-seated she leans forward massively,
    With cheek on clenched left hand, the forearm's
        might
10 Erect, its elbow on her rounded knee;
    Across a clasped book in her lap the right
Upholds a pair of compasses; she gazes
With full set eyes, but wandering in thick mazes
    Of sombre thought beholds no outward sight.

15 Words cannot picture her; but all men know
    That solemn sketch the pure sad artist[1] wrought
Three centuries and threescore years ago,
    With phantasies of his peculiar thought:
The instruments of carpentry and science
20 Scattered about her feet, in strange alliance
    With the keen wolf-hound sleeping
        undistraught;

Scales, hour-glass, bell, and magic-square[2] above;
    The grave and solid infant perched beside,
With open winglets that might bear a dove,
25   Intent upon its tablets, heavy-eyed;
Her folded wings as of a mighty eagle,
But all too impotent to lift the regal
    Robustness of her earth-born strength and
        pride;

And with those wings, and that light wreath which
    seems
30   To mock her grand head and the knotted frown
Of forehead charged with baleful thoughts and
    dreams,
    The household bunch of keys, the housewife's
    gown
Voluminous, indented, and yet rigid
As if a shell of burnished metal frigid,
35   The feet thick-shod to tread all weakness down;

The comet hanging o'er the waste dark seas,
    The massy rainbow curved in front of it
Beyond the village with the masts and trees;
    The snaky imp, dog-headed, from the Pit,
40 Bearing upon its batlike leathern pinions
Her name unfolded in the sun's dominions,
    The "MELENCOLIA" that transcends all wit.

Thus has the artist copied her, and thus
    Surrounded to expound her form sublime,
45 Her fate heroic and calamitous;
    Fronting the dreadful mysteries of Time,
Unvanquished in defeat and desolation,
Undaunted in the hopeless conflagration
    Of the day setting on her baffled prime.

50 Baffled and beaten back she works on still,
    Weary and sick of soul she works the more,
Sustained by her indomitable will:
    The hands shall fashion and the brain shall pore,
And all her sorrow shall be turned to labour,
55 Till Death the friend-foe piercing with his sabre
    That mighty heart of hearts ends bitter war.

But as if blacker night could dawn on night,
    With tenfold gloom on moonless night unstarred,
A sense more tragic than defeat and blight,
60   More desperate than strife with hope debarred,
More fatal than the adamantine Never

---

[1] Albrecht Dürer (1471–1528): the "solemn sketch" in the poem is
Dürer's engraving *Melancolia I*.

[2] an ancient astrological device in which the numbers in each line of the
square—horizontal, vertical, or diagonal—add up to the same total.

Encompassing her passionate endeavour,
  Dawns glooming in her tenebrous regard:

The sense that every struggle brings defeat
65   Because Fate holds no prize to crown success;
That all the oracles are dumb or cheat
  Because they have no secret to express;
That none can pierce the vast black veil uncertain
Because there is no light beyond the curtain;
70   That all is vanity and nothingness.

Titanic¹ from her high throne in the north,
  That City's sombre Patroness and Queen,
In bronze sublimity she gazes forth
  Over her Capital of teen and threne,²
75 Over the river with its isles and bridges,
The marsh and moorland, to the stern rock-ridges,
  Confronting them with a coëval³ mien.

The moving moon and stars from east to west
  Circle before her in the sea of air;
80 Shadows and gleams glide round her solemn rest.
  Her subjects often gaze up to her there:
The strong to drink new strength of iron endurance,
The weak new terrors; all, renewed assurance
  And confirmation of the old despair.
—1874

E.B.B. ⁴

1861

I

The white-rose garland at her feet,
  The crown of laurel at her head,
Her noble life on earth complete,
  Lay her in the last low bed
5 For the slumber calm and deep:
"He giveth His belovèd sleep."

II

Soldiers find their fittest grave
  In the field whereon they died;
So her spirit pure and brave
10   Leaves the clay it glorified
To the land for which she fought
With such grand impassioned thought.

III

Keats and Shelley⁵ sleep at Rome,
  She in well-loved Tuscan⁶ earth;
15 Finding all their death's long home
  Far from their old home of birth.
Italy, you hold in trust
Very sacred English dust.

III

Therefore this one prayer I breathe,—
20   That you yet may worthy prove
Of the heirlooms they bequeath
  Who have loved you with such love:
Fairest land while land of slaves
Yields their free souls no fit graves.
—1880

---

¹ In Greek mythology, the Titans were giants of enormous size and strength.

² affliction and lamentation.

³ of equal antiquity.

⁴ The poet Elizabeth Barrett Browning died in Florence, Italy, June 29, 1861.

⁵ The Romantic poets John Keats (1795–1821) and Percy Bysshe Shelley (1792–1822); both died in Italy.

⁶ of Tuscany, a region of central Italy.

A Real Vision of Sin [1]

Like a soaking blanket overhead
Spongy and lax the sky was spread,
Opaque as the eye of a fish long dead.

Like trees in a drawing gummed together
5   Some trees stood dim in the drizzling weather;
Sweating mere blood-flowers gloomed the heather.

Like a festering gash left gaping wide
That foul canal, long swooned from tide,
The marshy moorland did divide.

10   In a slushy hollow near its bank,
Where noisome weeds grew thick and dank,
And the very soil like an old corpse stank,

They cowered together, the man and crone,
Two old bags of carious bone;
15   They and a mangy cur alone:

Ragged, haggard, filthy, both;
Viewing each the other loath;
Growling now and then an oath.

She at length with a spasm raised
20   Her strong grey eyes, still strong tho' glazed;
And thus her meditations phrased:

"No mite left of all our treasure;
Sin itself has no more pleasure:
Drained out, drained out, our full measure!"

25   He quavered back: "It does seem so:
The sun 'e died out long ago;
The earth and the sky are a-rottin' slow?"

She writhed her thick brows, dirty grey:
"Then take at once my easy way
30   Of swamping misery from our clay.

"No trembling, dear red-rat-eyes! Come!
We slip together through that green scum,
And then with the world here rot on dumb."

He sat still, nipping spiteful blows
35   On the snarling cur's amorphous nose;
Relishing faintly her propose.

"Well *you* look lovely, so you do,
To call *me* names: a-drowndin' you
Would go to spoil this pleasant view!

40   "This 'ere damned life is bad enough;
But, say we smother in that stuff,
Our next life's only worse, you muff!"

The woman thereto coldly sneered:
"Of course, as usual all afeared,
45   Old slaver-dewy stubble-beard.

"Idiot and coward! hell-flames feed
On certain fuel; but, indeed,
A used-up soul won't sate their greed.

"When Earth once gets us cold and stark
50   She'll keep us safely in the dark:
No fear of rousing with the lark!

"Full long ago in grim despair,
She growled, *How those two witch-fires flare!
They'll get no second chance I swear!*"

55   She laught this truth out 'gainst the man;
Who shuffling, ill at ease, began:
"You can be devilish sore, you can.

---

[1] a response to Tennyson's "A Vision of Sin."

"Suppose you're right; this life's a one
That's cursèd bad, but better than none…
60 I wish they'd light another Sun.

"We used to spree and we don't spree now;
A screw is loose in the world, allow,
We didn't make it, anyhow.

"Say Life's hard-up, No-life's more glum:
65 Just think—a lashing lot of rum,
And a night with you and a cool old chum!"

She fingered a toad from its love-work sweet,
And flung to the cur with a "Mangy, eat;
They say there's poison in the meat;

70 "And so the next time you bite this dear
He'll die off mad; for else I fear
He'd fester for ever and ever here."

Its loose fangs squashed through the nectarous lump;
Then it went and crouched on a doddered stump,
75 With an evil eye on the Male Sin's hump.

He blinked and shuffled and swore and groaned:
Rasping the bristly beard she owned,
She thought drear thoughts until she too moaned.

"I see the truth," with a scornful laugh,
80 "I have starved abroad on the swine-fouled draff,
While sleek at home sucked the fatt'ning calf.

"Too late, too late! Yet it's good to see,
If only damnation, thoroughly;
My Life has never met with me.

85 "And *you*, you never loved me, *you!*
A heart that never once beat true,
How could it love? I loved for two.

"This dirty crumpled rag of a breast
Was globed with milk once; I possest
90 The means of being grandly blest!

"Did the babe of mine suck luscious sips,
Soothing the nipple with rose-soft lips
While her eyes drooped mild in a dear eclipse?

"A babe!—could I now squeeze out three drops
95 Between that poor cur's ulcerous chaps,
He'd die as livid as yon tree-tops.

"You know where it rests, that child-dream gone?
Come, grope in this charming water-lawn,
Through ooze and slime and filth and spawn:

100 "Perhaps we shall find a shudderous feel,
Neither of eft, nor toad, nor eel;
May hear a long long stifled squeal:

"Touch the rotten bones of a murdered brat
Whose flesh was daynt to the water-rat,—
105 If it *does* gnaw flesh, it would relish that!"

He ventured, "Curse all memory!
It's more than thirty years:" but she
Continued fierce, unheedingly.

"Come, and this loathsome life out-smother,
110 No fear that we'll ever have another:
The rain may beat and the wind may wuther,

"But we shall rot with the rotting soil,
Safe in sleep from the whole sad coil;
Sleep's better than corn and wine and oil.

115 "Here's a kiss; now at once!" effused the witch,
And dragged the wildered male to the ditch,
And plunged there prone by a bladdery bitch.

Drowned dead, stone dead...and still her grasp
Clawed *him*: but with a frenzied gasp
120   He shuddered off the scranny clasp.

Up the soddened bank in a fury of funk
He sprawled; "She's awful! but she's sunk;
I daren't die except dead drunk."

He managed at length the hollow to win;
125   And was gulping down with a pang-writhed grin
The black bottle's last of vitriol gin,

When his gorge was choked by a sudden blight:
The cur growled mad with venom and fright,
And its blotches of hair all bristled upright.

130   Its frenzy burst out in a wolfish yell;
It leapt at his throat like an imp of hell;
In a spasm of horror the bottle fell:

It griped up his flaccid throat with a force
That made his terrorment gurgle hoarse,
135   While he turned as blue as a cholera-corse.

It haled him into the festering dike;
So all sank dead in its clam alike,—
The Man, the Woman, the virtuous Tyke.

And the dense rain crooned in its sullen flow
140   From the sodden sky-stretch drooping low
To the sodden earth; and to and fro

Crept a maundering wind too weak to blow;
And the dim world murmured dismal woe:
For the earth and the sky *were* a-rotting slow.
—1880

John Leicester Warren (Lord de Tabley)
1835 – 1895

John Leicester Warren was one of a number of late-Victorian poets who expressed the pessimism and skepticism of the period. His collected works, in *Poems* *Dramatic and Lyrical* (1893–95), reveal a sad dignity untouched by "Decadence."

෴

The Strange Parable [1]

I think it left me when the sun was great.
I cannot tell the very point of time
When the cure wrought and I was free of this.
What drave[2] it from me less and least I know.
5 Was it some word compelling from without,
Some royal accent potent to expel
This tribe of thing? It rent my soul, and fled,
Upon the waste wind, down the void. Who knows?
Let me consider, I had no pain then.
10 Only a kind of echo-pain remained.
And yet my soul ached with the loss of this,
My old abhorrence. It had wrought its roots
And worked its fibres round my nature so,
That I was lost without the thing I loathed;
15 Painless, I seemed to hanker for old pain;
To crave a presence necessary long
Thro' custom, rather than that new unrest
Which had replaced the banished agony.

Well, it was gone at last and plucked away.
20 The day it went resembled other days
So much. The latest conflict with the thing
Was so like others, where I always sank
Worsted. I thought as little it would go,
As that the sun would blacken his round orb.
25 I had grown feebler every day with it,
Cared, strove, and hated less, when like a clap
My soul was empty and the spirit gone.

Strangely I rose, felt myself sound and free,
But so belated; as a man that dreams,
30 And knows that he is dreaming in a land
Of phantoms, and he thinks; "My dream must break
This moment or the next. I will lie still
And only watch. All here is smoke, and dream."
So nature seemed a filmy veil of sleep,
35 The hills delusion, the firm fields as mist,
The cloud-cones vapour, mirage the bright woods.
The languor and the vacancy of change
Replaced the antagonistic element,
That gave a substance to my life erewhile,
40 And stung my native energies from sleep,
To war against this noxious demon's way
And push of still encroaching filaments.
All this indeed had found most sudden end.
The ferment as by miracle withdrew.
45 The tyranny was gone and left no wound.
The agony's vibration smoothed itself
To apathetic calm. And I remained
A painless naked thing without a soul.

Then I fared forth alone beneath the skies
50 Without a will to guide me on my way,
In automatic motion like a drift;
Or as a feather teased by some side-breeze
Athwart the master-current of the wind.
So nerveless and chaotic was my life.

55 My stagnant heart was empty save of fear.
A little eddying influx strangely stirred
Of barren dread beneath my barren heart.

---

[1] Luke 11:24.

[2] drove.

Oh, but indeed this thing is pitiful,
When fear, in dearth of any purpose, rules;
60 When the man, wretched beyond wretchedness,
Has still the primal instinct left of fear;
Why should he fear, poor brute? yet he fears still.
And this ignoble thing usurps the seat
Of purpose, and her vacant function fills,
65 And, save one dreamy fear, the man is nought.

After this fashion I fared aimless then;
The sting that stood for purpose drave me on.
I wound along the roots of battered crags,
Arid as death; and jumbled as a dream
70 Of ruin driving thro' a sick man's brain,
Who doubts and wearies on his fevered bed.
Then, as I clomb, rose yawning heights, abrupt,
Broken in flanks and ledges of great flags,
Immeasurable levels of smooth death;
75 Tilted in pinnacles among the clouds,
Where the hill-raven faltered in the mist.
My mood was calmer in these solitudes,
I loathed to look upon the valley world,
Fat, with slow smoke, grey crowded homes, and
       squares
80 Of meadow, rank with juicy undermath,
And languid cropping kine dwarfed into bees;
And the faint sprinkle of the water-wheels,
And each mill-torrent's shudder-gleam below.
Weary was I of all my fellows' ways;
85 And lonely on the summits I was best.
Sometimes a peat-tarn capped the giant chain;
A waste of ice, pale grass, and sodden sedge
And rotten fangs of rush; whose trembling floor
Festered in moss, and darkened to decay.
90 Yet here I shuddered, as the star-time came,
To see the evil spirits of the fen
Trimming their lamps to lure me. And I sighed,
Knowing how fiends had marred the under vales,
To find new demons herded in the snows
95 Up in the eternal solitudes of God,
Therefore I wandered on, and still no peace:

And still I paced the uplands dry and drear.
And still the curse stung burning at my heart.

Then to myself I spake and spake with heed,—
100 The isolation and the restless feet
Of Cain[1] are mine for always. Shall I choose
To roam for ever, with no living voice
Save mine own sighing, hear no word of love?
Love, tho' a lie on lying lips, still sweet—
105 To wander till God blind me and I cease.
This is the desolation of the grave.
My pain erewhile to this was almost peace.
Is my gloom shaken with one rift of morn,
Is my verge radiant with one hint of sun?
110 Is this a phantom or a wreath of cloud
Eyed like a death, that beckons as I move?

And I with heedful steps devised return;
My slow blood sickened in the weary ways;
And all the evil I had ever done
115 Came crowding on me in slow loathsome shapes,
Saying, behold thy deed, changed, thy deed still,
In its corruption. 'Twas a merry deed
In thine old careless season. Mark it now;
For time is great to find things in their truth,
120 And this was foul beneath its shining hide
In those days even; but the taint has spread
And bloated it and shown the world its core.
And then came others, reaching out foul hands,
Distorted from young faces I had known,
125 Until I fled along the barren hills
And prayed to find death with a bitter prayer:
I loathed myself too greatly to endure
The hateful and irrevocable past.

What then sustained me through? No hand of
       heaven.
130 No death sat waiting by the granite slab,

---

[1] Cain, Adam and Eve's first-born son, murdered his brother Abel: see
Genesis 4:1–14.

Or in the cracks of that dread violet lake
Frozen and fast since God created snow.
The greedy chasm refused me: at my tread
The snows yelled downwards, loosened ere my feet
135   Had made two onward steps. The crazy shales
Withheld me by an inch of crumbling ledge
From the abysmal silence leagues below.

At last the plain, O God: the bitter heights
Are whistling long behind. This rooted flower
140   Comes on me like the voices of my friends.
There is my place, last of the level plain:
The mist had masked it wholly yet I know
The faintest border of the filmy wall,
And nearer, nearer drawn, my weary feet
145   Pause on the empty precinct of my race.

Ay me, returning. This is no return.
The core of desolation, where no rest
Shall come for ever, or one eyelid fall
In that sweet pure oblivion of the just.
150   Empty and swept and garnished tho' it be,
This is no home, but some sepulchral den
Set round with urn and ashes of the dead;
Death breathes about its chambers like a blight,
The hearth is darkened with a phantom curse;
155   I think no child will play there any more,
And I am lonelier here than on the void.

So went I forth, and took unto my need
Seven former comrades in the naked walls;
They came and dwelt there, souls that mock the
    light,
160   And banter with the melancholy time,
Unheeding the to-morrow; drowning sense
And foresight down; contented to maintain
A grim carousal with a staring death,
And imminent destruction, in an hour
165   Ready to touch the cup and put away
From all pale lips for ever lust of wine.
Therefore the drift and end I do not know;

Only this thing is certain in my soul,
That man with men must change his words or die.
170   And this I hold, man lonely is not man,
Dowered with the curse and need of social bond,
And leavened by his fellows into sin,
Because he cannot take his path alone.
The fretful ache of living goads him on.
175   Tho' he pry vainly thro' the secret doors
Of future, only gloom and cloud within
Are seen for answer; joy before his feet
Fades, and sweet rest retires in rainbow foam;
Perilous instincts lure him and mislead.
180   Tho' for a season he may conquer down
And put to flight the traitor legion well,
Yet with to-morrow's light they will return;
And if he yield, relapsing to their rule,
Relapse is worse perdition to the man,
185   Than to have never left his sin at all.
Ay me, mysterious doom; what help is mine?
—1870

A Song of Faith Forsworn

Take back your suit.
  It came when I was weary and distraught
With hunger. Could I guess the fruit you brought?
I ate in mere desire of any food,
5   Nibbled its edge and nowhere found it good.
Take back your suit.

Take back your love,
It is a bird poached from my neighbour's wood:
Its wings are wet with tears, its beak with blood.
10   'Tis a strange fowl with feathers like a crow:
Death's raven, it may be, for all we know.
Take back your love.

Take back your gifts.
False is the hand that gave them; and the mind
15   That planned them, as a hawk spread in the wind

To poise and snatch the trembling mouse below.
To ruin where it dares—and then to go.
Take back your gifts.

Take back your vows.
20 Elsewhere you trimmed and taught these lamps to
        burn;
You bring them stale and dim to serve my turn.
You lit those candles in another shrine,
Guttered and cold you offer them on mine.
Take back your vows.

25 Take back your words.
What is your love? Leaves on a woodland plain,
Where some are running and where some remain:
What is your faith? Straws on a mountain height,
Dancing like demons on Walpurgis night.[1]
30 Take back your words.

Take back your lies.
Have them again: they wore a rainbow face,
Hollow with sin and leprous with disgrace;
Their tongue was like a mellow turret bell
35 To toll hearts burning into wide-lipped hell.
Take back your lies.

Take back your kiss.
Shall I be meek, and lend my lips again
To let this adder daub them with his stain?
40 Shall I turn cheek to answer, when I hate?
You kiss like Judas[2] in the garden gate!
Take back your kiss.

Take back delight,
A paper boat launched on a heaving pool
45 To please a child, and folded by a fool;
The wild elms roared: it sailed—a yard or more.

Out went our ship but never came to shore.
Take back delight.

Take back your wreath.
50 Has it done service on a fairer brow?
Fresh, was it folded round her bosom snow?
Her cast-off weed my breast will never wear:
Your word is "love me." My reply "despair!"
Take back your wreath.
—1893

Echoes of Hellas [3]

O choir of Tempe mute these many years,
    O fountain lutes of lyric Hippocrene,[4]
On whose polluted brink no Muse is seen.
No more, between the gleaming vales, one hears

5   Apollo's footfall or the sobbing tears
Of Daphne budding finger-tips of green.[5]
No nymphs are bathing with their huntress Queen[6]
In the warm shallows of the mountain meres.

Great Pan[7] is dead: he perished long ago:
10 His reedy pipes these uplands never heard.
What trembling sounds from yonder coppice
        come?

---

[1] the eve of May Day, when witches and demons engage in revelries.

[2] an insincere or deceitful act of affection; see Matthew 26:49.

---

[3] The ancient Greeks called their country Hellas. This poem is probably a response to Elizabeth Barrett Browning's "The Dead Pan."

[4] the fountain of the Muses—goddesses of the arts and sciences—on Mount Helicon, and hence the source of poetic inspiration.

[5] Apollo was the god of music, poetry, medicine, and manhood. He fell in love with Daphne, but she fled from him, having vowed perpetual chastity. In protection, the gods changed her into a bay tree.

[6] Diana, the goddess of hunting, fertility, and the moon, who was predominantly worshipped by women.

[7] Pan was the Greek god of pastures, flocks, and forests, associated with music, particularly the shepherd's flute or pipe. He was part man and part goat.

Some ravished queen, who tells the dale her woe?
Nay, since the maids Pierian[1] here are dumb,
The nightingale[2] is nothing but a bird.
—1893

L'Envoi [3]

Thou askest overmuch of song to bid its
    trammelled numbers
    Arouse from graves long undisturbed, dead
      memories that have lain,
To bid it with exorcist spell break through their
    hallowed slumbers,
    And raise a crowd of spectres thou shalt never
      still again.

5 Thou askest for those lays to which thine ear once
    loved to listen,
    Ah me! the harp is all unstrung! its golden tones
      are fled
No more the pearl-drop at its sound in sympathy
    shall glisten
    Upon thine eyelash, telling more than ever
      words have said.

Those strains that sank into our ears, those words
    our hearts have noted!
10   Ah me, the harp is broken, all its golden chords
      unstrung!

There was a time its melody our trancéd souls has
    floated
    On amber streams, by emerald meads—that
      dreamland of the young.
—1903

Conclusion

'Tis gone, the land of dreams! A greyer sky
    Has leadened all the beaming sunrise zone;
The hard world wakes in cold reality,
    Romance hath still'd her music, touch and tone.

5 It was a land of heroes, and of streams
    Rolling gigantic music; dreadful heights
Beetled beneath the thunder clouds, with gleams
    Of a wild sunset spread in flying lights.

Or emerald valleys, myrtle growths embayed,
10   Whereby the masted streamers fluttering ride,
Where wakeful fountains rippled on, nor stayed
    The night-long murmur of their lisping tide.

The maiden waits by some enchanted spring:
    His charger watches by a bleeding knight:
15 The fairy princess leads her elves a ring:
    The ogre crashes down the pinewood's height.

Gone? all shall go, the fable and the truth:
    Ambrosial glimpses of an antique day,
Lost, as the love dream of a withered youth
20   In wintry eyes where charmèd laughter lay.
—1903

---

[1] Pieria was reputedly the home of the Muses, the "maids Pierean."

[2] Philomela was raped by her brother-in-law Tereus, who then cut out her tongue to prevent her telling of the assault; the gods subsequently turned Philomela into a nightingale, and the bird has become associated with music and poetry, as in Keats's "To a Nightingale."

[3] An envoy, or "l'envoi," is a conventionalized stanza placed at the end of a ballad.

Mary Elizabeth Braddon
1837 – 1915

To support her family, Mary Elizabeth Braddon initially took to the stage before turning to writing. From 1861 to 1874, Braddon led a rather scandalous existence, living with the publisher John Maxwell until his insane wife died in an Irish asylum and they could marry. Raising five children and five step-children, Braddon also managed to write the extremely successful and notorious sensation novel, *Lady Audley's Secret* (1861). Producing over seventy novels, writing poems, plays, and anonymous tales for penny dreadfuls, Braddon also edited and contributed to magazines such as *Temple Bar* and *Belgravia*.

ↄ҉ↄ

Queen Guinevere [1]

I wear a crown of gems upon my brow,
    Bright gems drop down upon my yellow hair,
And none can tell beneath their grandeur, how
    My brain is racked with care:

5 How wicked love my lost soul is enchaining,—
    As sinful men are chained to torture's wheel,
So I, the prisoner of my griefs remaining,
    My own dark doom do seal.

There is a figure that I should not fashion,
10   Whose form I shape from every changing shade;
The shadow of my wild and wicked passion,
    I meet in grove and glade.

There is a voice, whose music ever changing,
    I hear in ev'ry murmur of the sea,
15 In ev'ry wind o'er moor and mountain ranging,
    In ev'ry rustling tree.

There is a face I see in mournful splendour,
    In each star-jewel of the crown of night,
Whose lineaments all nature's beauties render,
20   In shadow and in light.

There is a dream that I should perish, dreaming,
    A dream that haunts me still by night and day;
But yet so subtle am I in fair seeming,
    None dare my fame gainsay.

25 And thus I murmur: Oh, my Lancelot! [2]
    First of all warriors breathing heaven's breath,
I pray to die, that thou mayst be forgot;
    If we forget in death.

Oh, my lost soul! Oh, my loved Lancelot!
30   My broken faith! Those deep and dreaming eyes!
I cannot hide me where thou comest not,
    To shut me from the skies.

Oh, weary earth without my Lancelot!
    Oh, dreary life bereft of end or aim!
35 Save to seek out some solitary spot,
    Wherein to hide my shame.

Oh, fatal passion, that absorbs my life!
    Oh, dreadful madness, that consumes my soul!
A queen, aye, worse; oh, misery, a wife!
40   God give me self-control!

God give me strength to bear, and silence keep;
    Angels, once women, pity woman's pain,

---

[1] the wife of King Arthur and lover of Lancelot du Lac.

[2] in Arthurian legend, the bravest and most lauded of the knights of the Round Table.

And hush me to that slumber, calm and deep,
    From which none wake again!
—1861

At Last

He

At last, at last! My hand rests on your hair,
    Through the deep shadows in your eyes, I look,
    There was a time I read them as a book;
Life drifts away, and all life's long despair,
5   And lo, I rest my hand upon your hair.

At last! How should you guess that it was so?
    I poring at my studies in the shade,
    You, in the sunshine, glitteringly arrayed,
Flitting, embodied brightness, to and fro;
10   I say, how should you guess it could be so?

How should you know I loved you? there was not
    One link between us; not a thought of mine
    That had one shade in harmony with thine;
In your bright mission, and my quiet lot,
15   One unison, one concord, there was not.

And yet, and yet—apart from all the rest,
    I've watched you till the watching grew a pain,
    And yet I lingered, watching you again,—
Love, a dull anguish, stifled in my breast,
20   But in all outward seeming, as the rest.

So I grew mad, not what the world calls mad,
    But that slow madness of the soul, that broods
    Under the gravest and the stillest moods;
And some have called me churlish, others, sad,
25   They all were wrong, they should have called me
      mad.

If there had been a hope, a thought, a chance
    Of your love, I had, hand to hand with fate,
    Fought that great battle which makes manhood
      great,
And walked through fire to win one gentle glance;
30   But oh, my Nemesis,[1] there was no chance.

And so my life ebbed, purposeless, away,
    As some slow river through a desert flowing;
    Enough to me that weary life was going;
The pall of night fell dark on every day,
35   And I was happy, so life ebbed away.

Life held no purpose underneath the skies,
    Earth held no prize but one, and that was you,
    And that could not be mine,—I knew, I knew,
I was not born to win so great a prize,
40   Then what was there for me, below the skies?

At last, at last! My hand is on your hair,
    Deep, deep, I gaze into those tender eyes;
    Low in their depths some hidden sorrow lies;
Tell me, whose life has been one long despair,
45   Speak, as I rest my hand upon your hair.

She

At last, at last! That sorrow in my eyes
    Has brooded there for melancholy years;
    At first their light was drowned in hopeless tears,
50   But there was comfort in loud agonies;
It is the quiet grief has dimmed my eyes.

At last, at last! And yet you cannot read
    The sorrow that has shadowed all my youth:
    What! can the soul not fathom the soul's truth,
55   With the same sorrow could your true heart bleed,
And yet the pain in my heart never read?

---

[1] the Greek goddess of retributive justive.

I loved you. With that wondering regard
    I scarce dared own unto myself; I thought
    My pride debased, to love, and love unfought;
60 Where others knelt, where others prayed, 'twas hard
    Never to win one wandering regard.

And yet, and yet—how often have I turned
    To the still shade, where bending o'er some book,
    You, the grave scholar sat, with earnest look
65 That never answered mine? my cheek has burned
    That my heart owned a passion unreturned—

And so I married, and have been—I'll not
    Reproach you with that misery! My chain
    Wore its slow length, though every link was pain.
70 Let the dead past be buried and forgot,
    But, oh, to have been loved, yet known it not!

I do reproach you with a blighted life,
    I do accuse you for our wasted years,
    Your ruined manhood, all my hidden tears,
75 My life-long lie as an unloving wife,
    These on your head, with all a wretched life.

Dying, you send for me, to tell me this,
    Which told before—I might have been. Oh,
      God!
    Teach me to bow beneath the bitter rod;[1]
80 It was Thy will to hold me from such bliss,
    So, from his dying lips I gather this.

Yet, by Love's immortality, we may,
    In some serener sphere united yet,
    This lower loss, these lower griefs, forget
85 In the great glory of eternal day.
    The fulness of the soul responds, "We may."

So rest thine hand in blessing on my hair;
    I have been loved, I have been loved—at last!

---

[1] the biblical rod, symbolic of punishment and rule.

This wondrous present blots out all the past;
90 Life drifts away, and all a life's despair—
    So die, beloved, thine hand upon my hair.
    —1861

Waiting

Two women stood upon the yellow sand,
    The waves and sea-weeds curling round their
      feet,—
One shaded with a brown but slender hand
    Her dark eyes from the heat.

5 I asked, "Why watch ye thus beside the deep,
    Whose rise and fall the hidden moon controls?"
"We wait a touch shall wake us from our sleep;
    We're waiting for our souls."

"Are not your souls within your breasts?" I cried,
10   A bitter laugh ran down the stretching sands;
"My soul went forth," one said, "with him who died
    Far off in unknown lands.

"And from that day I've been the shadow only,
    Of what I was before that day came down;
15 The dead, than I, could never be more lonely,
    In yonder peopled town."

I wept to hear her. "You are broken-hearted,
    By loss of him you loved so well!" I said.
"Not so, both heart and soul with him departed,
20   And I am only—dead.

"I knew his death-hour, though none other knew,—
    The world between us; but I felt him die—
A shiver pierced my inmost being through—
    That was his parting sigh!

25 "His comrades waited for the ship's return,
    And hoping, fearing, lingered on the shore;

I had no fear, no hope,—'Go back and mourn,
　　You will not meet him more.'

"I said—they called me mad, and went their way;
30　　I watched the waves come up, and rave, and roll,
But never saw his face unto this day;
　　And thus I lost my soul."

The other woman neither spoke nor moved.
　　"And she?" I asked. "I know her not," she said,
35 "I only know that she has lost and loved,
　　And she like me, seems—dead."

"Love comes not once," I said, "but till the last,
　　The soul's dead winters change to living springs,
God wakes the lyre to music of the Past—"
40　　But not the broken strings!

"But not the broken strings," she cried, "Go to,
　　Why do you stand to argue with a ghost?
We see not these things as they seem to you
　　Because our *souls are lost*.

45 "Leave us; why waste your comfort on the dead?
　　We with our hopes were wrecked on yonder
　　　tide;
We ask no pity, neither tears," she said,
　　"We did not weep—we died!"

And so I left them—more I could not learn:
50　　Still stood they where the surges round them
　　　broke,
But evermore my memory would return
　　To her who never spoke.
　　—1861

Under Ground

Oh, let the scornful lip be loud,
　Though every word were once a wound;

Rail on, beloved! be cold, be proud;
　　I can defy you—under ground!

5 Pass by my grave with careless tread,
　　Spurn the low grass and crush the weed:
The turf may fade above my head,
　　The heart beneath will never bleed.

I loved you, as men love, who stake
10　　Their soul upon one cast,—I lost.
Your common hearts can only break,
　　And life was all my madness cost.

I did not curse you when you sold
　　Your wicked heart; and when you lied,
15 And bartered all your soul for gold,
　　I let you go, and only—died.

So laugh, and tell them how I threw
　　Name, honour, creed, beneath your feet;
Tell all I lost in loving you,
20　　And how you flung me off, my sweet!

But keep this in your memory:
　　When all is told, when all is said,
The triumph still remains with me,
　　And I am victor—being dead!

25 So laugh your loudest!—say your worst!—
　　Ring o'er my grave the silver sound!
Through you in life and death accurst,
　　I yet escape you—under ground!
　—1861

Waking

My life is over ere my days are done,
The crown is withered ere the race is won,
The veil hath fallen ere the shrine is neared,

926

And the fair statue which my love had reared
         Is shattered to the ground.

Thy beauty was the beauty of my mind,
Which with thine outward image I entwined,
Till every thought that God made fair in me
I shaped and sublimated into thee,
         And with thy likeness bound.

I made thee all the purest tell of truth,
About the glowing beauty of thy youth,

I shed the light of every lovely dream,
And seeing thee in that reflected beam,
         Beheld thee more than fair.

Thou wert to me, th'incarnate Beautiful,
Beside which all the stars of Heaven were dull;
I set thee high above all earthly strife;
Into one dream of thee I made my life,
         And waking, I despair.

—1861

Algernon Charles Swinburne

1837 – 1909

Algernon Charles Swinburne's family background was aristocratic (his father was an admiral and his grandfather a baronet), and his education was privileged—he was educated at Eton and Oxford. Beginning his writing at Oxford (1856–60), he met Dante Gabriel Rossetti and was briefly associated with the Pre-Raphaelite circle. Swinburne led a dissolute, wild life (his predilection for flagellation pornography is infamous), attaining literary notoriety with *Atalanta in Calydon* (1865) and *Poems and Ballads, First Series #1* (1866). In an age that prided itself on middle-class values and religiosity, Swinburne's works were blasphemous, erotic, and subversive, rebelling against the moral repressiveness of his time as he asserted a doctrine of "l'art pour l'art." Engaged in literary debates with Thomas Carlyle, John Ruskin, and Ralph Waldo Emerson over the value of morality in art, his essay "Under the Microscope" (1872) is a response, parodic as it is, to Robert Buchanan's "The Fleshly School of Poetry" (1871), which attacked both Swinburne and Rossetti's sensuous, poetic impulses. A liberal republican, in the *Song of Italy* (1867) and *Songs before Sunrise* (1871) he sided with Italian political revolt against oppression. Swinburne was also a respected scholar, publishing studies of William Blake (1868), William Shakespeare (1880), and essays on French and English contemporaries. With an aesthetic vision that influenced younger generations, Swinburne was a poet who drew on a wide range of interests, and was willing to pursue his own beliefs against the prejudices of his time.

❦❦❦

Atalanta in Calydon

A TRAGEDY

Τοὺς ξῶντας εὖ δρᾶν· κατθανὼν δὲ πᾶς ἀνὴρ
Γῆ καὶ σκιά· τὸ μηδὲν εἰς οὐδὲν ῥέπει.
—EUR. *Fr. Mel* 20 (537)[1]

THE ARGUMENT

Althæa, daughter of Thestius and Eurythemis, queen of Calydon, being with child of Meleager her first-born son, dreamed that she brought forth a brand burning; and upon his birth came the three Fates and prophesied of him three things, namely these; that he should have great strength of his hands, and good fortune in this life, and that he should live no longer when the brand then in the fire were consumed: wherefore his mother plucked it forth and kept it by her. And the child being a man grown sailed with Jason after the fleece of gold, and won himself great praise of all men living; and when the tribes of the north and west made war upon Ætolia, he fought against their army and scattered it. But Artemis, having at the first stirred up these tribes to war against Œneus king of Calydon, because he had offered sacrifice to all the gods saving her alone, but her he had forgotten to honour, was yet more wroth because of the destruction of this army, and sent upon the land of Calydon a wild boar which slew many and wasted all their increase, but him could none slay, and many went against him and perished. Then were all the chief men of Greece gathered together, and among then Atalanta, daughter of Iasius the Arcadian, a virgin; for whose sake Artemis let slay the boar, seeing she favoured the maiden greatly; and Meleager having despatched it gave the spoil thereof to Atalanta, as one beyond measure enamoured of her; but the brethren of Althæa his mother, Toxeus and Plexippus, with such others as

---

[1] "The living treat well; for, dying, every man is earth and shadow; nothing to nothing descends."

misliked that she only should bear off the praise whereas many had borne the labour, laid wait for her to take away her spoil; but Meleager fought against them and slew them: whom when Althæa their sister beheld and knew to be slain of her son, she waxed for wrath and sorrow like as one mad, and taking the brand whereby the measure of her son's life was meted to him, she cast it upon a fire; and with the wasting thereof his life likewise wasted away, that being brought back to his father's house he died in a brief space; and his mother also endured not long after for very sorrow; and this was his end, and the end of that hunting.

THE PERSONS

CHIEF HUNTSMAN	TOXEUS
CHORUS	PLEXIPPUS
ALTHÆA	HERALD
MELEAGER	MESSENGER
ŒNEUS	SECOND MESSENGER
ATALANTA	

CHIEF HUNSTMAN

Maiden,[1] and mistress of the months and stars
Now folded in the flowerless fields of heaven,
Goddess whom all gods love with threefold heart,
Being treble in thy divided deity,
5 A light for dead men and dark hours, a foot
Swift on the hills as morning, and a hand
To all things fierce and fleet that roar and range
Mortal, with gentler shafts than snow or sleep;
Hear now and help and lift no violent hand,
10 But favourable and fair as thine eye's beam
Hidden and shown in heaven; for I all night
Amid the king's hounds and the hunting men
Have wrought and worshipped toward thee; nor
    shall men

See goodlier hounds or deadlier edge of spears;
15 But for the end, that lies unreached at yet
Between the hands and on the knees of gods.
O fair-faced sun, killing the stars and dews
And dreams and desolation of the night!
Rise up, shine, stretch thine hand out, with thy bow
20 Touch the most dimmest height of trembling
    heaven,
And burn and break the dark about thy ways,
Shot through and through with arrows; let thine
    hair
Lighten as flame above that flameless shell
Which was the moon, and thine eyes fill the world
25 And thy lips kindle with swift beams; let earth
Laugh, and the long sea fiery from thy feet
Through all the roar and ripple of streaming springs
And foam in reddening flakes and flying flowers
Shaken from hands and blown from lips of nymphs
30 Whose hair or breast divides the wandering wave
With salt close tresses cleaving lock to lock,
All gold, or shuddering and unfurrowed snow;
And all the winds about thee with their wings,
And fountain-heads of all the watered world;
35 Each horn of Acheloüs,[2] and the green
Euenus, wedded with the straitening sea.
For in fair time thou comest; come also thou,
Twin-born with him, and virgin, Artemis,
And give our spears their spoil, the wild boar's hide,
40 Sent in thine anger against us for sin done
And bloodless altars without wine or fire.
Him now consume thou; for thy sacrifice
With sanguine-shining steam divides the dawn,
And one, the maiden rose of all thy maids,
45 Arcadian Atalanta, snowy-souled,
Fair as the snow and footed as the wind,
From Ladon and well-wooded Mænalus
Over the firm hills and the fleeting sea
Hast thou drawn hither, and many an armèd king,

---

[1] Artemis, who combined three identities: Diana, goddess of chastity and the hunt; Luna, mother of months; Hecate, goddess of the dead.

[2] the river-god, who appeared in three forms: as a bull, as a serpent, and as a bull-headed man.

50 Heroes, the crown of men, like gods in fight.
Moreover out of all the Ætolian land,
From the full-flowered Lelantian pasturage
To what of fruitful field the son of Zeus[1]
Won from the roaring river and labouring sea
55 When the wild god shrank in his horn and fled
And foamed and lessened through his wrathful fords,
Leaving clear lands that steamed with sudden sun,
These virgins with the lightening of the day
Bring thee fresh wreaths and their own sweeter hair,
60 Luxurious locks and flower-like mixed with flowers,
Clean offering, and chaste hymns; but me the time
Divides from these things; whom do thou not less
Help and give honour, and to mine hounds good
   speed,
And edge to spears, and luck to each man's hand.

CHORUS

65 When the hounds of spring are on winter's traces,
   The mother of months in meadow or plain
Fills the shadows and windy places
   With lisp of leaves and ripple of rain;
And the brown bright nightingale amorous
70 Is half assuaged for Itylus,[2]
For the Thracian ships and the foreign faces,
   The tongueless vigil, and all the pain.

Come with bows bent and with emptying of quivers,
   Maiden most perfect, lady of light,
75 With a noise of winds and many rivers,
   With a clamour of waters, and with might;
Bind on thy sandals, O thou most fleet,
Over the splendour and speed of thy feet;
For the faint east quickens, the wan west shivers,
80   Round the feet of the day and the feet of the
     night.

---

[1] Hercules, who had defeated Achelous and cut off one of his horns.

[2] or Itys, son of Tereus, who was killed by his mother, Procne, and fed to his unknowing father in revenge for Tereus's rape of Procne's sister, Philomela, and the subsequent cutting out of her tongue to prevent her from accusing him.

Where shall we find her, how shall we sing to her,
   Fold our hands round her knees, and cling?
O that man's heart were as fire and could spring to
   her,
   Fire, or the strength of the streams that spring!
85 For the stars and the winds are unto her
As raiment, as songs of the harp-player;
For the risen stars and the fallen cling to her,
   And the southwest-wind and the west-wind
     sing.

For winter's rains and ruins are over,
90   And all the season of snows and sins;
The days dividing lover and lover,
   The light that loses, the night that wins;
And time remembered is grief forgotten,
And frosts are slain and flowers begotten,
95 And in green underwood and cover
   Blossom by blossom the spring begins.

The full streams feed on flower of rushes,
   Ripe grasses trammel a travelling foot,
The faint fresh flame of the young year flushes
100   From leaf to flower and flower to fruit;
And fruit and leaf are as gold and fire,
And the oat is heard above the lyre,
And the hoofèd heel of a satyr crushes
   The chestnut-husk at the chestnut-root.

105 And Pan[3] by noon and Bacchus[4] by night,
   Fleeter of foot than the fleet-foot kid,
Follows with dancing and fills with delight
   The Mænad and the Bassarid;[5]
And soft as lips that laugh and hide
110 The laughing leaves of the trees divide,
And screen from seeing and leave in sight
   The god pursuing, the maiden hid.

---

[3] in Greek mythology the god of pastures, forests, flocks and herds.

[4] in Roman mythology, the god of wine.

[5] followers of Bacchus.

The ivy falls with the Bacchanal's hair
    Over her eyebrows hiding her eyes;
115 The wild vine slipping down leaves bare
    Her bright breast shortening into sighs;
The wild vine slips with the weight of its leaves,
But the berried ivy catches and cleaves
To the limbs that glitter, the feet that scare
120   The wolf that follows, the fawn that flies.

ALTHÆA

What do ye singing? what is this ye sing?

CHORUS

Flowers bring we, and pure lips that please the gods,
And raiment meet for service: lest the day
Turn sharp with all its honey in our lips.

ALTHÆA

125 Night, a black hound, follows the white fawn day,
Swifter than dreams the white flown feet of sleep;
Will ye pray back the night with any prayers?
And though the spring put back a little while
Winter, and snows that plague all men for sin,
130 And the iron time of cursing, yet I know
Spring shall be ruined with the rain, and storm
Eat up like fire the ashen autumn days.
I marvel what men do with prayers awake
Who dream and die with dreaming; any god,
135 Yea the least god of all things called divine,
Is more than sleep and waking; yet we say,
Perchance by praying a man shall match his god.
For if sleep have no mercy, and man's dreams
Bite to the blood and burn into the bone,
140 What shall this man do waking? By the gods,
He shall not pray to dream sweet things to-night,
Having dreamt once more bitter things than death.

CHORUS

Queen, but what is it that hath burnt thine heart?
For thy speech flickers like a blown-out flame.

ALTHÆA

145 Look, ye say well, and know not what ye say;
For all my sleep is turned into a fire,
And all my dreams to stuff that kindles it.

CHORUS

Yet one doth well being patient of the gods.

ALTHÆA

Yea, lest they smite us with some four-foot plague.

CHORUS

150 But when time spreads find out some herb for it.

ALTHÆA

And with their healing herbs infect our blood.

CHORUS

What ails thee to be jealous of their ways?

ALTHÆA

What if they give us poisonous drinks for wine?

CHORUS

They have their will; much talking mends it not.

ALTHÆA

155 And gall for milk, and cursing for a prayer?

CHORUS

Have they not given life, and the end of life?

ALTHÆA

Lo, where they heal, they help not; thus they do,
They mock us with a little piteousness,
And we say prayers, and weep; but at the last,
160 Sparing awhile, they smite and spare no whit.

CHORUS

Small praise man gets dispraising the high gods:
What have they done that thou dishonourest them?

ALTHÆA

First Artemis for all this harried land
I praise not, and for wasting of the boar
165 That mars with tooth and tusk and fiery feet
Green pasturage and the grace of standing corn
And meadow and marsh with springs and unblown
  leaves,
Flocks and swift herds and all that bite sweet grass,
I praise her not; what things are these to praise?

CHORUS

170 But when the king did sacrifice, and gave
Each god fair dues of wheat and blood and wine,
Her not with bloodshed nor burnt-offering
Revered he, nor with salt or cloven cake;
Wherefore being wroth she plagued the land; but
  now
175 Takes off from us fate and her heavy things.
Which deed of these twain were not good to praise?
For a just deed looks always either way
With blameless eyes, and mercy is no fault.

ALTHÆA

Yea, but a curse she hath sent above all these
180 To hurt us where she healed us; and hath lit
Fire where the old fire went out, and where the wind
Slackened, hath blown on us with deadlier air.

CHORUS

What storm is this that tightens all our sail?

ALTHÆA

Love, a thwart sea-wind full of rain and foam.

CHORUS

185 Whence blown, and born under what stormier star?

ALTHÆA

Southward across Euenus from the sea.

CHORUS

Thy speech turns toward Arcadia like blown wind.

ALTHÆA

Sharp as the north sets when the snows are out.

CHORUS

Nay, for this maiden hath no touch of love.

ALTHÆA

190 I would she had sought in some cold gulf of sea
Love, or in dens where strange beasts lurk, or fire,
Or snows on the extreme hills, or iron land
Where no spring is; I would she had sought therein
And found, or ever love had found her here.

CHORUS

195 She is holier than all holy days or things,
The sprinkled water or fume of perfect fire;
Chaste, dedicated to pure prayers, and filled
With higher thoughts than heaven; a maiden clean,
Pure iron, fashioned for a sword; and man
200 She loves not; what should one such do with love?

ALTHÆA

Look you, I speak not as one light of wit,
But as a queen speaks, being heart-vexed; for oft
I heard my brothers wrangling in mid hall,
And am not moved; and my son chiding them,
205 And these things nowise move me, but I know
Foolish and wise men must be to the end,
And feed myself with patience; but this most,
This moves me, that for wise men as for fools
Love is one thing, an evil thing, and turns
210 Choice words and wisdom into fire and air.
And in the end shall no joy come, but grief,
Sharp words and soul's division and fresh tears
Flower-wise upon the old root of tears brought
  forth,
Fruit-wise upon the old flower of tears sprung up,
215 Pitiful sighs, and much regrafted pain.

These things are in my presage, and myself
Am part of them and know not; but in dreams
The gods are heavy on me, and all the fates
Shed fire across my eyelids mixed with night,
220 And burn me blind, and disilluminate
My sense of seeing, and my perspicuous soul
Darken with vision; seeing I see not, hear
And hearing am not holpen, but mine eyes
Stain many tender broideries in the bed
225 Drawn up about my face that I may weep
And the king wake not; and my brows and lips
Tremble and sob in sleeping, like swift flames
That tremble, or water when it sobs with heat
Kindled from under; and my tears fill my breast
230 And speck the fair dyed pillows round the king
With barren showers and salter than the sea,
Such dreams divide me dreaming; for long since
I dreamed that out of this my womb had sprung
Fire and firebrand; this was ere my son,
235 Meleager, a goodly flower in fields of fight,
Felt the light touch him coming forth, and wailed
Childlike; but yet he was not; and in time
I bare him, and my heart was great; for yet
So royally was never strong man born,
240 Nor queen so nobly bore as noble a thing
As this my son was: such a birth God sent
And such a grace to bear it. Then came in
Three weaving women, and span each a thread,
Saying This for strength and That for luck, and one
245 Saying Till the brand upon the hearth burn down,
So long shall this man see good days and live.
And I with gathered raiment from the bed
Sprang, and drew forth the brand, and cast on it
Water, and trod the flame bare-foot, and crushed
250 With naked hand spark beaten out of spark
And blew against and quenched it; for I said,
These are the most high Fates that dwell with us,
And we find favour a little in their sight,
A little, and more we miss of, and much time
255 Foils us; howbeit they have pitied me, O son,
And thee most piteous, thee a tenderer thing

Than any flower of fleshly seed alive.
Wherefore I kissed and hid him with my hands,
And covered under arms and hair, and wept,
260 And feared to touch him with my tears, and laughed;
So light a thing was this man, grown so great
Men cast their heads back, seeing against the sun
Blaze the armed man carven on his shield, and hear
The laughter of little bells along the brace
265 Ring, as birds singing or flutes blown, and watch,
High up, the cloven shadow of either plume
Divide the bright light of the brass, and make
His helmet as a windy and wintering moon
Seen through blown cloud and plume-like drift,
     when ships
270 Drive, and men strive with all the sea, and oars
Break, and the beaks dip under, drinking death;
Yet was he then but a span long, and moaned
With inarticulate mouth inseparate words,
And with blind lips and fingers wrung my breast
275 Hard, and thrust out with foolish hands and feet,
Murmuring; but those grey women with bound hair
Who fright the gods frighted not him; he laughed
Seeing them, and pushed out hands to feel and haul
Distaff and thread, intangible; but they
280 Passed, and I hid the brand, and in my heart
Laughed likewise, having all my will of heaven.
But now I know not if to left or right
The gods have drawn us hither; for again
I dreamt, and saw the black brand burst on fire
285 As a branch bursts in flower, and saw the flame
Fade flower-wise, and Death came and with dry lips
Blew the charred ash into my breast; and Love
Trampled the ember and crushed it with swift feet.
This I have also at heart; that not for me,
290 Not for me only or son of mine, O girls,
The gods have wrought life, and desire of life,
Heart's love and heart's division; but for all
There shines one sun and one wind blows till night.
And when night comes the wind sinks and the sun,
295 And there is no light after, and no storm,
But sleep and much forgetfulness of things.

In such wise I gat knowledge of the gods
Years hence, and heard high sayings of one most
   wise,
Eurythemis my mother, who beheld
300 With eyes alive and spake with lips of these
As one on earth disfleshed and disallied
From breath or blood corruptible; such gifts
Time gave her, and an equal soul to these
And equal face to all things; thus she said.
305 But whatsoever intolerable or glad
The swift hours weave and unweave, I go hence
Full of mine own soul, perfect of myself,
Toward mine and me sufficient; and what chance
The gods cast lots for and shake out on us,
310 That shall we take, and that much bear withal.
And now, before these gather to the hunt,
I will go arm my son and bring him forth,
Lest love or some man's anger work him harm.

CHORUS

Before the beginning of years
315   There came to the making of man
Time, with a gift of tears;
   Grief, with a glass that ran;
Pleasure, with pain for leaven;
   Summer, with flowers that fell;
320 Remembrance fallen from heaven,
   And madness risen from hell;
Strength without hands to smite;
   Love that endures for a breath:
Night, the shadow of light,
325   And life, the shadow of death.
And the high gods took in hand
   Fire, and the falling of tears,
And a measure of sliding sand
   From under the feet of the years;
330 And froth and drift of the sea;
   And dust of the labouring earth;
And bodies of things to be
   In the houses of death and birth;
And wrought with weeping and laughter,

335   And fashioned with loathing and love
With life before and after
   And death beneath and above,
For a day and a night and a morrow,
   That his strength might endure for a span
340 With travail and heavy sorrow,
   The holy spirit of man.
From the winds of the north and the south
   They gathered as unto strife;
They breathed upon his mouth,
345   They filled his body with life;
Eyesight and speech they wrought
   For the veils of the soul therein,
A time for labour and thought,
   A time to serve and to sin;[1]
350 They gave him light in his ways,
   And love, and a space for delight,
And beauty and length of days,
   And night, and sleep in the night.
His speech is a burning fire;
355   With his lips he travaileth;
In his heart is a blind desire,
   In his eyes foreknowledge of death;
He weaves, and is clothed with derision;
   Sows, and he shall not reap;
360 His life is a watch or a vision
   Between a sleep and a sleep.

MELEAGER

O sweet new heaven and air without a star,
Fair day, be fair and welcome, as to men
With deeds to do and praise to pluck from thee.
365 Come forth a child, born with clear sound and light,
With laughter and swift limbs and prosperous looks;
That this great hunt with heroes for the hounds
May leave thee memorable and us well sped.

ALTHÆA

Son, first I praise thy prayer, then bid thee speed;
370 But the gods hear men's hands before their lips,

---

[1] Cf. Ecclesiastes 3:1–4.

And heed beyond all crying and sacrifice
Light of things done and noise of labouring men.
But thou, being armed and perfect for the deed,
Abide; for like rain-flakes in a wind they grow,
375 The men thy fellows, and the choice of the world,
Bound to root out the tuskèd plague, and leave
Thanks and safe days and peace in Calydon.

MELEAGER

For the whole city and all the low-lying land
Flames, and the soft air sounds with them that come;
380 The gods give all these fruit of all their works.

ALTHÆA

Set thine eye thither and fix thy spirit and say
Whom there thou knowest; for sharp mixed shadow
    and wind
Blown up between the morning and the mist,
With steam of steeds and flash of bridle or wheel,
385 And fire, and parcels of the broken dawn,
And dust divided by hard light, and spears
That shine and shift as the edge of wild beasts' eyes,
Smite upon mine; so fiery their blind edge
Burns, and bright points break up and baffle day.

MELEAGER

390 The first, for many I know not, being far off,
Peleus the Larissæan, couched with whom
Sleeps the white sea-bred wife and silver-shod,
Fair as fled foam, a goddess; and their son
Most swift and splendid of men's children born,
395 Most like a god, full of the future fame.

ALTHÆA

Who are these shining like one sundered star?

MELEAGER

Thy sister's sons, a double flower of men.

ALTHÆA

O sweetest kin to me in all the world,

O twin-born blood of Leda, gracious heads
400 Like kindled lights in untempestuous heaven,
Fair flower-like stars on the iron foam of fight,
With what glad heart and kindliness of soul,
Even to the staining of both eyes with tears
And kindling of warm eyelids with desire,
405 A great way off I greet you, and rejoice
Seeing you so fair, and moulded like as gods.
Far off ye come, and least in years of these,
But lordliest, but worth love to look upon.

MELEAGER

Even such (for sailing hither I saw far hence,
410 And where Eurotas hollows his moist rock
Nigh Sparta with a strenuous-hearted stream)
Even such I saw their sisters; one swan-white,
The little Helen, and less fair than she
Fair Clytæmnestra, grave as pasturing fawns
415 Who feed and fear some arrow; but at whiles,
As one smitten with love or wrung with joy,
She laughs and lightens with her eyes, and then
Weeps; whereat Helen, having laughed, weeps too,
And the other chides her, and she being chid speaks
    nought,
420 But cheeks and lips and eyelids kisses her,
Laughing; so fare they, as in their bloomless bud
And full of unblown life, the blood of gods.

ALTHÆA

Sweet days befall them and good loves and lords,
And tender and temperate honours of the hearth,
425 Peace, and a perfect life and blameless bed.
But who shows next an eagle wrought in gold,
That flames and beats broad wings against the sun
And with void mouth gapes after emptier prey?

MELEAGER

Know by that sign the reign of Telamon
430 Between the fierce mouths of the encountering brine
On the strait reefs of twice-washed Salamis.

ALTHÆA

For like one great of hand he bears himself,
Vine-chapleted, with savours of the sea,
Glittering as wine and moving as a wave.
435 But who girt round there roughly follows him?

MELEAGER

Ancæus, great of hand, an iron bulk,
Two-edged for fight as the axe against his arm,
Who drives against the surge of stormy spears
Full-sailed; him Cepheus follows, his twin-born,
440 Chief name next his of all Arcadian men.

ALTHÆA

Praise be with men abroad; chaste lives with us,
Home-keeping days and household reverences.

MELEAGER

Next by the left unsandalled foot know thou
The sail and oar of this Ætolian land,
445 Thy brethren, Toxeus and the violent-souled
Plexippus, over-swift with hand and tongue;
For hands are fruitful, but the ignorant mouth
Blows and corrupts their work with barren breath.

ALTHÆA

Speech too bears fruit, being worthy; and air blows
down
450 Things poisonous, and high-seated violences,
And with charmed words and songs have men put
out
Wild evil, and the fire of tyrannies.

MELEAGER

Yea, all things have they, save the gods and love.

ALTHÆA

Love thou the law and cleave to things ordained.

MELEAGER

455 Law lives upon their lips whom these applaud.

ALTHÆA

How sayest thou these? what god applauds new
things?

MELEAGER

Zeus, who hath fear and custom under foot.

ALTHÆA

But loves not laws thrown down and lives awry.

MELEAGER

Yet is not less himself than his own law.

ALTHÆA

460 Nor shifts and shuffles old things up and down.

MELEAGER

But what he will remoulds and discreates.

ALTHÆA

Much, but not this, that each thing live its life.

MELEAGER

Nor only live, but lighten and lift up higher.

ALTHÆA

Pride breaks itself, and too much gained is gone.

MELEAGER

465 Things gained are gone, but great things done
endure.

ALTHÆA

Child, if a man serve law through all his life
And with his whole heart worship, him all gods
Praise; but who loves it only with his lips,
And not in heart and deed desiring it
470 Hides a perverse will with obsequious words,
Him heaven infatuates and his twin-born fate
Tracks, and gains on him, scenting sins far off,
And the swift hounds of violent death devour.
Be man at one with equal-minded gods,

475 So shall he prosper; not through laws torn up,
Violated rule and a new face of things.
A woman armed makes war upon herself,
Unwomanlike, and treads down use and wont
And the sweet common honour that she hath,
480 Love, and the cry of children, and the hand
Trothplight and mutual mouth of marriages.
This doth she, being unloved; whom if one love,
Not fire nor iron and the wide-mouthed wars
Are deadlier than her lips or braided hair.
485 For of the one comes poison, and a curse
Falls from the other and burns the lives of men.
But thou, son, be not filled with evil dreams,
Nor with desire of these things; for with time
Blind love burns out; but if one feed it full
490 Till some discolouring stain dyes all his life,
He shall keep nothing praiseworthy, nor die
The sweet wise death of old men honourable,
Who have lived out all the length of all their years
Blameless, and seen well-pleased the face of gods,
495 And without shame and without fear have wrought
Things memorable, and while their days held out
In sight of all men and the sun's great light
Have gat them glory and given of their own praise
To the earth that bare them and the day that bred,
500 Home friends and far-off hospitalities,
And filled with gracious and memorial fame
Lands loved of summer washed by violent seas,
Towns populous and many unfooted ways,
And alien lips and native with their own.
505 But when white age and venerable death
Mow down the strength and life within their limbs,
Drain out the blood and darken their clear eyes,
Immortal honour is on them, having past
Through splendid life and death desirable
510 To the clear seat and remote throne of souls,
Lands indiscoverable in the unheard-of west,
Round which the strong stream of a sacred sea
Rolls without wind for ever, and the snow
There shows not her white wings and windy feet,
515 Nor thunder nor swift rain saith anything,

Nor the sun burns, but all things rest and thrive;
And these, filled full of days, divine and dead,
Sages and singers fiery from the god,
And such as loved their land and all things good
520 And, best beloved of best men, liberty,
Free lives and lips, free hands of men free-born,
And whatsoever on earth was honourable
And whosoever of all the ephemeral seed,
Live there a life no liker to the gods
525 But nearer than their life of terrene days.
Love thou such life and look for such a death.
But from the light and fiery dreams of love
Spring heavy sorrows and a sleepless life,
Visions not dreams, whose lids no charm shall close
530 Nor song assuage them waking; and swift death
Crushes with sterile feet the unripening ear,
Treads out the timeless vintage; whom do thou
Eschewing embrace the luck of this thy life,
Not without honour; and it shall bear to thee
535 Such fruit as men reap from spent hours and wear,
Few men, but happy; of whom be thou, O son,
Happiest, if thou submit thy soul to fate,
And set thine eyes and heart on hopes high-born
And divine deeds and abstinence divine.
540 So shalt thou be toward all men all thy days
As light and might communicable, and burn
From heaven among the stars above the hours,
And break not as a man breaks nor burn down:
For to whom other of all heroic names
545 Have the gods given his life in hand as thine?
And gloriously hast thou lived, and made thy life
To me that bare thee and to all men born
Thankworthy, a praise for ever; and hast won fame
When wild wars broke all round thy father's house,
550 And the mad people of windy mountain ways
Laid spears against us like a sea, and all
Ætolia thundered with Thessalian hoofs;
Yet these, as wind baffles the foam, and beats
Straight back the relaxed ripple, didst thou break
555 And loosen all their lances, till undone
And man from man they fell; for ye twain stood

God against god, Ares and Artemis,
And thou the mightier; wherefore she unleashed
A sharp-toothed curse thou too shalt overcome;
560 For in the greater blossom of thy life
Ere the full blade caught flower, and when time
 gave
Respite, thou didst not slacken soul nor sleep,
But with great hand and heart seek praise of men
Out of sharp straits and many a grievous thing,
565 Seeing the strange foam of undivided seas
On channels never sailed in, and by shores
Where the old winds cease not blowing, and all the
 night
Thunders, and day is no delight to men.

CHORUS

Meleager, a noble wisdom and fair words
570 The gods have given this woman; hear thou these.

MELEAGER

O mother, I am not fain to strive in speech
Nor set my mouth against thee, who art wise
Even as they say and full of sacred words.
But one thing I know surely, and cleave to this;
575 That though I be not subtle of wit as thou
Nor womanlike to weave sweet words, and melt
Mutable minds of wise men as with fire,
I too, doing justly and reverencing the gods,
Shall not want wit to see what things be right.
580 For whom they love and whom reject, being gods,
There is no man but seeth, and in good time
Submits himself, refraining all his heart.
And I too as thou sayest have seen great things;
Seen otherwhere, but chiefly when the sail
585 First caught between stretched ropes the roaring
 west,
And all our oars smote eastward, and the wind
First flung round faces of seafaring men
White splendid snow-flakes of the sundering foam,
And the first furrow in virginal green sea
590 Followed the plunging ploughshare of hewn pine,

And closed, as when deep sleep subdues man's
 breath
Lips close and heart subsides; and closing, shone
Sunlike with many a Nereid's hair,[1] and moved
Round many a trembling mouth of doubtful gods,
595 Risen out of sunless and sonorous gulfs
Through waning water and into shallow light,
That watched us; and when flying the dove was
 snared
As with men's hands, but we shot after and sped
Clear through the irremeable Symplegades;[2]
600 And chiefliest when hoar beach and herbless cliff
Stood out ahead from Colchis, and we heard
Clefts hoarse with wind, and saw through
 narrowing reefs
The lightning of the intolerable wave
Flash, and the white wet flame of breakers burn
605 Far under a kindling south-wind, as a lamp
Burns and bends all its blowing flame one way;
Wild heights untravelled of the wind, and vales
Cloven seaward by their violent streams, and white
With bitter flowers and bright salt scurf of brine;
610 Heard sweep their sharp swift gales, and bowing
 birdwise
Shriek with birds' voices, and with furious feet
Tread loose the long skirts of a storm; and saw
The whole white Euxine[3] clash together and fall
Full-mouthed, and thunderous from a thousand
 throats:
615 Yet we drew thither and won the fleece and won
Medea, deadlier than the sea; but there
Seeing many a wonder and fearful things to men
I saw not one thing like this one seen here,
Most fair and fearful, feminine, a god,
620 Faultless; whom I that love not, being unlike,

---

[1] Nereids are sea-nymphs of Greek myth, the fifty daughters of Nereus and Doris.

[2] "irremeable," allowing no return; "Symplegades," two massive rocks that perpetually clashed against each other.

[3] the Euxine Sea, now known—oddly, in this context—as the Black Sea.

Fear, and give honour, and choose from all the
    gods.

ŒNEUS

Lady, the daughter of Thestius, and thou, son,
Not ignorant of your strife nor light of wit,
Scared with vain dreams and fluttering like spent
    fire,
625 I come to judge between you, but a king
Full of past days and wise from years endured.
Nor thee I praise, who art fain to undo things done:
Nor thee, who art swift to esteem them overmuch.
For what the hours have given is given, and this
630 Changeless; howbeit these change, and in good time
Devise new things and good, not one thing still.
Us have they sent now at our need for help
Among men armed a woman, foreign born,
Virgin, not like the natural flower of things
635 That grows and bears and brings forth fruit and dies;
Unlovable, no light for a husband's house,
Espoused; a glory among unwedded girls,
And chosen of gods who reverence maidenhood.
These too we honour in honouring her; but thou,
640 Abstain thy feet from following, and thine eyes
From amorous touch; nor set toward hers thine
    heart,
Son, lest hate bear no deadlier fruit than love.

ALTHÆA

O king, thou art wise, but wisdom halts; and just,
But the gods love not justice more than fate,
645 And smite the righteous and the violent mouth,
And mix with insolent blood the reverent man's,
And bruise the holier as the lying lips.
Enough; for wise words fail me, and my heart
Takes fire and trembles flamewise, O my son,
650 O child, for thine head's sake; mine eyes wax thick,
Turning toward thee, so goodly a weaponed man,
So glorious; and for love of thine own eyes
They are darkened, and tears burn them, fierce as
    fire,

And my lips pause and my soul sinks with love.
655 But by thine hand, by thy sweet life and eyes,
By thy great heart and these clasped knees, O son,
I pray thee that thou slay me not with thee.
For there was never a mother woman-born
Loved her sons better; and never a queen of men
660 More perfect in her heart toward whom she loved.
For what lies light on many and they forget,
Small things and transitory as a wind o' the sea,
I forget never; I have seen thee all thine years
A man in arms, strong and a joy to men,
665 Seeing thine head glitter and thine hand burn its
    way
Through a heavy and iron furrow of sundering
    spears;
But always also a flower of three suns old,
The small one thing that lying drew down my life
To lie with thee and feed thee; a child and weak,
670 Mine, a delight to no man, sweet to me.
Who then sought to thee? who gat help? who knew
If thou wert goodly? nay, no man at all.
Or what sea saw thee, or sounded with thine oar,
Child? or what strange land shone with war
    through thee?
675 But fair for me thou wert, O little life,
Fruitless, the fruit of mine own flesh, and blind,
More than much gold, ungrown, a foolish flower.
For silver nor bright snow nor feather of foam
Was whiter, and no gold yellower than thine hair,
680 O child, my child; and now thou art lordlier grown,
Not lovelier, nor a new thing in mine eyes,
I charge thee by thy soul and this my breast,
Fear thou the gods and me and thine own heart,
Lest all these turn against thee; for who knows
685 What wind upon what wave of altering time
Shall speak a storm and blow calamity?
And there is nothing stabile in the world
But the gods break it; yet not less, fair son,
If but one thing be stronger, if one endure,
690 Surely the bitter and the rooted love
That burns between us, going from me to thee,

Shall more endure than all things. What dost thou,
Following strange loves? why wilt thou kill mine
    heart?
Lo, I talk wild and windy words, and fall
695 From my clear wits, and seem of mine own self
Dethroned, dispraised, disseated; and my mind,
That was my crown, breaks, and mine heart is gone,
And I am naked of my soul, and stand
Ashamed, as a mean woman; take thou thought:
700 Live if thou wilt, and if thou wilt not, look,
The gods have given thee life to lose or keep,
Thou shalt not die as men die, but thine end
Fallen upon thee shall break me unaware.

MELEAGER

Queen, my whole heart is molten with thy tears,
705 And my limbs yearn with pity of thee, and love
Compels with grief mine eyes and labouring breath;
For what thou art I know thee, and this thy breast
And thy fair eyes I worship, and am bound
Toward thee in spirit and love thee in all my soul.
710 For there is nothing terribler to men
Than the sweet face of mothers, and the might.
But what shall be let be; for us the day
Once only lives a little, and is not found.
Time and the fruitful hour are more than we,
715 And these lay hold upon us; but thou, God,
Zeus, the sole steersman of the helm of things,
Father, be swift to see us, and as thou wilt
Help: or if adverse, as thou wilt, refrain.

CHORUS

We have seen thee, O Love, thou art fair; thou art
    goodly, O Love;
720 Thy wings make light in the air as the wings of a
    dove.[1]
Thy feet are as winds that divide the stream of the
    sea;
Earth is thy covering to hide thee, the garment of
    thee.

---

[1] Cf. Song of Solomon 4:1.

Thou art swift and subtle and blind as a flame of
    fire;
Before thee the laughter, behind thee the tears of
    desire;
725 And twain go forth beside thee, a man with a maid;
Her eyes are the eyes of a bride whom delight
    makes afraid;
As the breath in the buds that stir is her bridal
    breath:
But Fate is the name of her; and his name is Death.

For an evil blossom was born
730   Of sea-foam and the frothing of blood,
      Blood-red and bitter of fruit,
        And the seed of it laughter and tears,
And the leaves of it madness and scorn;
    A bitter flower from the bud,
735   Sprung of the sea without root,
        Sprung without graft from the years.

The weft of the world was untorn
    That is woven of the day on the night,
    The hair of the hours was not white
740 Nor the raiment of time overworn,
    When a wonder, a world's delight,
A perilous goddess was born;
    And the waves of the sea as she came
Clove, and the foam at her feet,
745   Fawning, rejoiced to bring forth
A fleshly blossom, a flame
Filling the heavens with heat
    To the cold white ends of the north.

And in air the clamorous birds,
750   And men upon earth that hear
Sweet articulate words
    Sweetly divided apart,
    And in shallow and channel and mere
The rapid and footless herds,
755   Rejoiced, being foolish of heart.

For all they said upon earth,
 She is fair, she is white like a dove,
  And the life of the world in her breath
Breathes, and is born at her birth;
760 For they knew thee for mother of love,
  And knew thee not mother of death.

What hadst thou to do being born,
 Mother, when winds were at ease,
As a flower of the springtime of corn,
765 A flower of the foam of the seas?
For bitter thou wast from thy birth,
 Aphrodite, a mother of strife;
For before thee some rest was on earth,
 A little respite from tears,
770 A little pleasure of life;
For life was not then as thou art,
  But as one that waxeth in years
Sweet-spoken, a fruitful wife;
  Earth had no thorn, and desire
775 No string, neither death any dart;
  What hadst thou to do among these,
  Thou, clothed with a burning fire,
Thou, girt with sorrow of heart,
  Thou, sprung of the seed of the seas
780 As an ear from a seed of corn,
  As a brand plucked forth of a pyre,
As a ray shed forth of the morn,
  For division of soul and disease,
For a dart and a sting and a thorn?
785 What ailed thee then to be born?

Was there not evil enough,
 Mother, and anguish on earth
 Born with a man at his birth,
Wastes underfoot, and above
790 Storm out of heaven, and dearth
Shaken down from the shining thereof,
  Wrecks from afar overseas
And peril of shallow and firth,
  And tears that spring and increase

795 In the barren places of mirth,
That thou, having wings as a dove,
 Being girt with desire for a girth,
  That thou must come after these,
That thou must lay on him love?

800 Thou shouldst not so have been born:
  But death should have risen with thee,
 Mother, and visible fear,
  Grief, and the wringing of hands,
And noise of many that mourn;
805 The smitten bosom, the knee
  Bowed, and in each man's ear
  A cry as of perishing lands,
A moan as of people in prison,
 A tumult of infinite griefs;
810 And thunder of storm on the sands,
  And wailing of waves on the shore;
And under thee newly arisen
 Loud shoals and shipwrecking reefs,
  Fierce air and violent light;
815 Sail rent and sundering oar,
  Darkness, and noises of night;
Clashing of streams in the sea,
 Wave against wave as a sword,
  Clamour of currents, and foam;
820 Rains making ruin on earth,
  Winds that wax ravenous and roam
As wolves in a wolfish horde;
Fruits growing faint in the tree,
  And blind things dead in their birth;
825 Famine, and blighting of corn,
  When thy time was come to be born.

All these we know of; but thee
 Who shall discern or declare?
In the uttermost ends of the sea
830 The light of thine eyelids and hair,
  The light of thy bosom as fire
  Between the wheel of the sun
And the flying flames of the air?

Wilt thou turn thee not yet nor have pity,
835 But abide with despair and desire
And the crying of armies undone,
Lamentation of one with another
And breaking of city by city;
The dividing of friend against friend,
840 The severing of brother and brother;
Wilt thou utterly bring to an end?
Have mercy, mother!

For against all men from of old
Thou hast set thine hand as a curse,
845 And cast out gods from their places.
These things are spoken of thee.

Strong kings and goodly with gold
Thou hast found out arrows to pierce,
And made their kingdoms and races
850 As dust and surf of the sea.
All these, overburdened with woes
And with length of their days waxen weak,
Thou slewest; and sentest moreover
Upon Tyro[1] an evil thing,
855 Rent hair and a fetter and blows
Making bloody the flower of the cheek,
Though she lay by a god as a lover,
Though fair, and the seed of a king.
For of old, being full of thy fire,
860 She endured not longer to wear
On her bosom a saffron vest,
On her shoulder an ashwood quiver;
Being mixed and made one through desire
With Enipeus, and all her hair
865 Made moist with his mouth, and her
breast
Filled full of the foam of the river.

----

[1] Tyro fell in love with Poseidon, who had taken the form of the river-god Enipeus; she gave birth to twin sons, but abandoned them out of fear and was later in turn rejected by her husband.

ATALANTA

Sun, and clear light among green hills, and day
Late risen and long sought after, and you just gods
Whose hands divide anguish and recompense,
870 But first the sun's white sister, a maid in heaven,
On earth of all maids worshipped—hail, and hear,
And witness with me if not without sign sent,
Not without rule and reverence, I a maid
Hallowed, and huntress holy as whom I serve,
875 Here in your sight and eyeshot of these men
Stand, girt as they toward hunting, and my shafts
Drawn; wherefore all ye stand up on my side,
If I be pure and all ye righteous gods,
Lest one revile me, a woman, yet no wife,
880 That bear a spear for spindle, and this bow strung
For a web woven; and with pure lips salute
Heaven, and the face of all the gods, and dawn
Filling with maiden flames and maiden flowers
The starless fold o' the stars, and making sweet
885 The warm wan heights of the air, moon-trodden
ways
And breathless gates and extreme hills of heaven.
Whom, having offered water and bloodless gifts,
Flowers, and a golden circlet of pure hair,
Next Artemis I bid be favourable
890 And make this day all golden, hers and ours,
Gracious and good and white to the unblamed end.
But thou, O well-beloved, of all my days
Bid it be fruitful, and a crown for all,
To bring forth leaves and bind round all my hair
895 With perfect chaplets woven for thine of thee.
For not without the word of thy chaste mouth,
For not without law given and clean command,
Across the white straits of the running sea
From Elis even to the Acheloïan horn,
900 I with clear winds came hither and gentle gods,
Far off my father's house, and left uncheered
Iasius, and uncheered the Arcadian hills
And all their green-haired waters, and all woods
Disconsolate, to hear no horn of mine
905 Blown, and behold no flash of swift white feet.

942

MELEAGER

For thy name's sake and awe toward thy chaste head,
O holiest Atalanta, no man dares
Praise thee, though fairer than whom all men praise,
And godlike for thy grace of hallowed hair
910 And holy habit of thine eyes, and feet
That make the blown foam neither swift nor white
Though the wind winnow and whirl it; yet we praise
Gods, found because of thee adorable
And for thy sake praiseworthiest from all men:
915 Thee therefore we praise also, thee as these,
Pure, and a light lit at the hands of gods.

TOXEUS

How long will ye whet spears with eloquence,
Fight, and kill beasts dry-handed with sweet words?
Cease, or talk still and slay thy boars at home.

PLEXIPPUS

920 Why, if she ride among us for a man,
Sit thou for her and spin; a man grown girl
Is worth a woman weaponed; sit thou here.

MELEAGER

Peace, and be wise; no gods love idle speech.

PLEXIPPUS

Nor any man a man's mouth woman-tongued.

MELEAGER

925 For my lips bite not sharper than mine hands.

PLEXIPPUS

Nay, both bite soft, but no whit softly mine.

MELEAGER

Keep thine hands clean; they have time enough to
    stain.

PLEXIPPUS

For thine shall rest and wax not red to-day.

MELEAGER

Have all thy will of words; talk out thine heart.

ALTHÆA

930 Refrain your lips, O brethren, and my son,
Lest words turn snakes and bite you uttering them.

TOXEUS

Except she give her blood before the gods,
What profit shall a maid be among men?

PLEXIPPUS

Let her come crowned and stretch her throat for a
    knife,
935 Bleat out her spirit and die, and so shall men
Through her too prosper and through prosperous
    gods,
But nowise through her living; shall she live
A flower-bud of the flower bed, or sweet fruit
For kisses and the honey-making mouth,
940 And play the shield for strong men and the spear?
Then shall the heifer and her mate lock horns,
And the bride overbear the groom, and men
Gods; for no less division sunders these;
Since all things made are seasonable in time,
945 But if one alter unseasonable are all.
But thou, O Zeus, hear me that I may slay
This beast before thee and no man halve with me
Nor woman, lest these mock thee, though a god,
Who hast made men strong, and thou being wise
    be held
950 Foolish; for wise is that thing which endures.

ATALANTA

Men, and the chosen of all this people, and thou,
King, I beseech you a little bear with me.
For if my life be shameful that I live,
Let the gods witness and their wrath; but these
955 Cast no such word against me. Thou, O mine,
O holy, O happy goddess, if I sin
Changing the words of women and the works

943

For spears and strange men's faces, hast not thou
One shaft of all thy sudden seven that pierced
960 Seven through the bosom[1] or shining throat or side,
All couched about one mother's loosening knees,
All holy born, engraffed of Tantalus?
But if toward any of you I am overbold
That take thus much upon me, let him think
965 How I, for all my forest holiness,
Fame, and this armed and iron maidenhood,
Pay thus much also; I shall have no man's love
For ever, and no face of children born
Or feeding lips upon me or fastening eyes
970 For ever, nor being dead shall kings my sons
Mourn me and bury, and tears on daughters' cheeks
Burn; but a cold and sacred life, but strange,
But far from dances and the back-blowing torch,
Far off from flowers or any bed of man,
975 Shall my life be for ever: me the snows
That face the first o' the morning, and cold hills
Full of the land-wind and sea-travelling storms
And many a wandering wing of noisy nights
That know the thunder and hear the thickening
        wolves—
980 Me the utmost pine and footless frost of woods
That talk with many winds and gods, the hours
Re-risen, and white divisions of the dawn,
Springs thousand-tongued with the intermitting
        reed
And streams that murmur of the mother snow—
985 Me these allure, and know me; but no man
Knows, and my goddess only. Lo now, see
If one of all you these things vex at all.
Would God that any of you had all the praise
And I no manner of memory when I die,
990 So might I show before her perfect eyes
Pure, whom I follow, a maiden to my death.
But for the rest let all have all they will;
For is it a grief to you that I have part,

Being woman merely, in your male might and deeds
995 Done by main strength? yet in my body is throned
As great a heart, and in my spirit, O men,
I have not less of godlike. Evil it were
That one coward should mix with you, one hand
Fearful, one eye abase itself; and these
1000 Well might ye hate and well revile, not me.
For not the difference of the several flesh
Being vile or noble or beautiful or base
Makes praiseworthy, but purer spirit and heart
Higher than these meaner mouths and limbs, that
        feed,
1005 Rise, rest, and are and are not; and for me,
What should I say? but by the gods of the world
And this my maiden body, by all oaths
That bind the tongue of men and the evil will,
I am not mighty-minded, nor desire
1010 Crowns, nor the spoil of slain things nor the fame;
Feed ye on these, eat and wax fat; cry out,
Laugh, having eaten, and leap without a lyre,
Sing, mix the wind with clamour, smite and shake
Sonorous timbrels and tumultuous hair,
1015 And fill the dance up with tempestuous feet,
For I will none; but having prayed my prayers
And made thank-offering for prosperities,
I shall go hence and no man see me more.
What thing is this for you to shout me down,
1020 What, for a man to grudge me this my life
As it were envious of all yours, and I
A thief of reputations? nay, for now,
If there be any highest in heaven, a god
Above all thrones and thunders of the gods
1025 Throned, and the wheel of the world roll under him,
Judge he between me and all of you, and see
If I transgress at all: but ye, refrain
Transgressing hands and reinless mouths, and keep
Silence, lest by much foam of violent words
1030 And proper poison of your lips ye die.

CŒNEUS

O flower of Tegea, maiden, fleetest foot

---

[1] Seven of Niobe's children were killed by Artemis and seven by Apollo when Niobe, daughter of Tantalus, boasted of them to Leto, the mother of Artemis and Apollo.

And holiest head of women, have good cheer
Of thy good words: but ye, depart with her
In peace and reverence, each with blameless eye
1035 Following his fate; exalt your hands and hearts,
Strike, cease not, arrow on arrow and wound on
    wound,
And go with gods and with the gods return.

CHORUS

Who hath given man speech? or who hath set
    therein
A thorn for peril and a snare for sin?
1040 For in the word his life is and his breath,
    And in the word his death,
That madness and the infatuate heart may breed
    From the word's womb the deed
And life bring one thing forth ere all pass by,
1045 Even one thing which is ours yet cannot die—
Death. Hast thou seen him ever anywhere,
Time's twin-born brother, imperishable as he
Is perishable and plaintive, clothed with care
    And mutable as sand,
1050 But death is strong and full of blood and fair
And perdurable and like the lord of land?
Nay, time thou seest not, death thou wilt not see
Till life's right hand be loosened from thine hand
    And thy life-days from thee.

1055 For the gods very subtly fashion
    Madness with sadness upon earth:
Not knowing in any wise compassion,
    Nor holding pity of any worth;
And many things they have given and taken,
1060   And wrought and ruined many things;
The firm land have they loosed and shaken,
    And sealed the sea with all her springs;
They have wearied time with heavy burdens
    And vexed the lips of life with breath:
1065 Set men to labour and given them guerdons,
    Death, and great darkness after death:
Put moans into the bridal measure

And on the bridal wools a stain;
And circled pain about with pleasure,
1070   And girdled pleasure about with pain;
And strewed one marriage-bed with tears and fire
For extreme loathing and supreme desire.

What shall be done with all these tears of ours?
    Shall they make watersprings in the fair heaven
1075 To bathe the brows of morning? or like flowers
Be shed and shine before the starriest hours,
    Or made the raiment of the weeping Seven?
Or rather, O our masters, shall they be
Food for the famine of the grievous sea,
1080   A great well-head of lamentation
Satiating the sad gods? or fall and flow
Among the years and seasons to and fro,
    And wash their feet with tribulation
And fill them full with grieving ere they go?
1085   Alas, our lords, and yet alas again,
Seeing all your iron heaven is gilt as gold
    But all we smite thereat in vain;
Smite the gates barred with groanings manifold,
    But all the floors are paven with our pain.
1090 Yea, and with weariness of lips and eyes,
With breaking of the bosom, and with sighs,
    We labour, and are clad and fed with grief
And filled with days we would not fain behold
And nights we would not hear of; we wax old,
1095   All we wax old and wither like a leaf.
We are outcast, strayed between bright sun and
    moon;
    Our light and darkness are as leaves of flowers,
Black flowers and white, that perish; and the noon
    As midnight, and the night as daylight hours.
1100   A little fruit a little while is ours,
    And the worm finds it soon.

But up in heaven the high gods one by one
    Lay hands upon the draught that quickeneth,
Fulfilled with all tears shed and all things done,
1105   And stir with soft imperishable breath

The bubbling bitterness of life and death,
And hold it to our lips and laugh; but they
Preserve their lips from tasting night or day,
    Lest they too change and sleep, the fates that
        spun,
1110 The lips that made us and the hands that slay;
    Lest all these change, and heaven bow down to
        none,
Change and be subject to the secular sway
    And terrene revolution of the sun.
Therefore they thrust it from them, putting time
    away.

1115 I would the wine of time, made sharp and sweet
    With multitudinous days and nights and tears
    And many mixing savours of strange years,
Were no more trodden of them under feet,
    Cast out and spilt about their holy places:
1120 That life were given them as a fruit to eat
And death to drink as water; that the light
Might ebb, drawn backward from their eyes, and
    night
    Hide for one hour the imperishable faces.
That they might rise up sad in heaven, and know
1125 Sorrow and sleep, one paler than young snow,
    One cold as blight of dew and ruinous rain;
Rise up and rest and suffer a little, and be
Awhile as all things born with us and we,
    And grieve as men, and like slain men be slain.

1130 For now we know not of them; but one saith
    The gods are gracious, praising God; and one,
When hast thou seen? or hast thou felt his breath
    Touch, nor consume thine eyelids as the sun,
Nor fill thee to the lips with fiery death?
1135   None hath beheld him, none
Seen above other gods and shapes of things,
Swift without feet and flying without wings,
Intolerable, not clad with death or life,
    Insatiable, not known of night or day,
1140 The lord of love and loathing and of strife

Who gives a star and takes a sun away;
Who shapes the soul, and makes her a barren wife
    To the earthly body and grievous growth of clay;
Who turns the large limbs to a little flame
1145   And binds the great sea with a little sand;
Who makes desire, and slays desire with shame;
    Who shakes the heaven as ashes in his hand;
Who, seeing the light and shadow for the same,
    Bids day waste night as fire devours a brand,
1150 Smites without sword, and scourges without rod;
    The supreme evil, God.
    Yea, with thine hate, O God, thou hast covered us,
    One saith, and hidden our eyes away from sight,
And made us transitory and hazardous,
1155   Light things and slight;
Yet have men praised thee, saying, He hath made
    man thus,
    And he doeth right.
Thou hast kissed us, and hast smitten; thou hast laid
Upon us with thy left hand life, and said,
1160 Live: and again thou hast said, Yield up your breath,
And with thy right hand laid upon us death.
Thou hast sent us sleep, and stricken sleep with
    dreams,
    Saying, Joy is not, but love of joy shall be;
Thou hast made sweet springs for all the pleasant
    streams,
1165   In the end thou hast made them bitter with the
    sea.
Thou hast fed one rose with dust of many men;
    Thou hast marred one face with fire of many
    tears;
Thou hast taken love, and given us sorrow again;
    With pain thou hast filled us full to the eyes and
    ears.
1170 Therefore because thou art strong, our father, and we
    Feeble; and thou art against us, and thine hand
Constrains us in the shallows of the sea
    And breaks us at the limits of the land;
Because thou hast bent thy lightnings as a bow,
1175   And loosed the hours like arrows; and let fall

Sins and wild words and many a wingèd woe
　　And wars among us, and one end of all;
Because thou hast made the thunder, and thy feet
　　Are as a rushing water when the skies
1180 Break, but thy face as an exceeding heat
　　And flames of fire the eyelids of thine eyes;
Because thou art over all who are over us;
　　Because thy name is life and our name death;
Because thou art cruel and men are piteous,
1185　　And our hands labour and thine hand scattereth;
Lo, with hearts rent and knees made tremulous,
　　Lo, with ephemeral lips and casual breath,
　　　At least we witness of thee ere we die
That these things are not otherwise, but thus;
1190　　That each man in his heart sigheth, and saith,
　　　That all men even as I,
All we are against thee, against thee, O God most
　　high.

　　But ye, keep ye on earth
　　Your lips from over-speech,
1195 Loud words and longing are so little worth;
　　And the end is hard to reach.
For silence after grievous things is good,
　　And reverence, and the fear that makes men
　　　whole,
And shame, and righteous governance of blood,
1200　　And lordship of the soul.
But from sharp words and wits men pluck no fruit,
And gathering thorns they shake the tree at root;
　　For words divide and rend;
　　But silence is most noble till the end.

ALTHÆA

1205 I heard within the house a cry of news
And came forth eastward hither, where the dawn
Cheers first these warder gods that face the sun
And next our eyes unrisen; for unaware
Came clashes of swift hoofs and trampling feet
1210 And through the windy pillared corridor
Light sharper than the frequent flames of day

That daily fill it from the fiery dawn;
Gleams, and a thunder of people that cried out,
And dust and hurrying horsemen; lo their chief,
1215 That rode with Œneus rein by rein, returned.
What cheer, O herald of my lord the king?

HERALD

Lady, good cheer and great; the boar is slain.

CHORUS

Praised be all gods that look toward Calydon.

ALTHÆA

Good news and brief; but by whose happier hand?

HERALD

1220 A maiden's and a prophet's and thy son's.

ALTHÆA

Well fare the spear that severed him and life.

HERALD

Thine own, and not an alien, hast thou blest.

ALTHÆA

Twice be thou too for my sake blest and his.

HERALD

At the king's word I rode afoam for thine.

ALTHÆA

1225 Thou sayest he tarrieth till they bring the spoil?

HERALD

Hard by the quarry, where they breathe, O queen.

ALTHÆA

Speak thou their chance; but some bring flowers
　　and crown
These gods and all the lintel, and shed wine,
Fetch sacrifice and slay; for heaven is good.

HERALD

1230 Some furlongs northward where the brakes begin
West of that narrowing range of warrior hills
Whose brooks have bled with battle when thy son
Smote Acarnania, there all they made halt,
And with keen eye took note of spear and hound,
1235 Royally ranked; Laertes island-born,
The young Gerenian Nestor, Panopeus,
And Cepheus and Ancæus, mightiest thewed,
Arcadians; next, and evil-eyed of these,
Arcadian Atalanta, with twain hounds
1240 Lengthening the leash, and under nose and brow
Glittering with lipless tooth and fire-swift eye;
But from her white braced shoulder the plumed
    shafts
Rang, and the bow shone from her side; next her
Meleager, like a sun in spring that strikes
1245 Branch into leaf and bloom into the world,
A glory among men meaner; Iphicles,
And following him that slew the biform bull
Pirithous, and divine Eurytion,
And, bride-bound to the gods, Æacides,
1250 Then Telamon his brother, and Argive-born
The seer and sayer of visions and of truth,
Amphiaraus; and a four-fold strength,
Thine, even thy mother's and thy sister's sons.
And recent from the roar of foreign foams
1255 Jason, and Dryas twin-begot with war,
A blossom of bright battle, sword and man
Shining; and Idas, and the keenest eye
Of Lynceus, and Admetus twice-espoused,
And Hippasus and Hyleus, great in heart.
1260 These having halted bade blow horns, and rode
Though woods and waste lands cleft by stormy
    streams,
Past yew-trees and the heavy hair of pines,
And where the dew is thickest under oaks,
This way and that; but questing up and down
1265 They saw no trail nor scented; and one said,
Plexippus, Help, or help not, Artemis,
And we will flay thy boarskin with male hands;

But saying, he ceased and said not that he would,
Seeing where the green ooze of a sun-struck marsh
1270 Shook with a thousand reeds untunable,
And in their moist and multitudinous flower
Slept no soft sleep, with violent visions fed,
The blind bulk of the immeasurable beast.
And seeing, he shuddered with sharp lust of praise
1275 Through all his limbs, and launched a double dart.
And missed; for much desire divided him,
Too hot of spirit and feebler than his will,
That his hand failed, though fervent; and the shaft,
Sundering the rushes, in a tamarisk stem
1280 Shook, and stuck fast; then all abode save one,
The Arcadian Atalanta; from her side
Sprang her hounds, labouring at the leash, and
    slipped,
And plashed ear-deep with plunging feet; but she
Saying, Speed it as I send it for thy sake,
1285 Goddess, drew bow and loosed; the sudden string
Rang, and sprang inward, and the waterish air
Hissed, and the moist plumes of the songless reeds
Moved as a wave which the wind moves no more.
But the boar heaved half out of ooze and slime
1290 His tense flank trembling round the barbèd wound,
Hateful; and fiery with invasive eyes
And bristling with intolerable hair
Plunged, and the hounds clung, and green flowers
    and white
Reddened and broke all round them where they
    came.
1295 And charging with sheer tusk he drove, and smote
Hyleus; and sharp death caught his sudden soul,
And violent sleep shed night upon his eyes.
Then Peleus, with strong strain of hand and heart,
Shot; but the sidelong arrow slid, and slew
1300 His comrade born and loving countryman,
Under the left arm smitten, as he no less
Poised a like arrow; and bright blood brake afoam,
And falling, and weighed back by clamorous arms,
Sharp rang the dead limbs of Eurytion.
1305 Then one shot happier, the Cadmean seer,

Amphiaraus; for his sacred shaft
Pierced the red circlet of one ravening eye
Beneath the brute brows of the sanguine boar,
Now bloodier from one slain; but he so galled
1310 Sprang straight, and rearing cried no lesser cry
Than thunder and the roar of wintering streams
That mix their own foam with the yellower sea;
And as a tower that falls by fire in fight
With ruin of walls and all its archery,
1315 And breaks the iron flower of war beneath,
Crushing charred limbs and molten arms of men;
So through crushed branches and the reddening
    brake
Clamoured and crashed the fervour of his feet,
And trampled, springing sideways from the tusk,
1320 Too tardy a moving mould of heavy strength,
Ancæus; and as flakes of weak-winged snow
Break, all the hard thews of his heaving limbs
Broke, and rent flesh fell every way, and blood
Flew, and fierce fragments of no more a man.
1325 Then all the heroes drew sharp breath, and gazed,
And smote not; but Meleager, but thy son,
Right in the wild way of the coming curse
Rock-rooted, fair with fierce and fastened lips,
Clear eyes, and springing muscle and shortening
    limb—
1330 With chin aslant indrawn to a tightening throat,
Grave, and with gathered sinews, like a god,—
Aimed on the left side his well-handled spear
Grasped where the ash was knottiest hewn, and
    smote,
And with no missile wound, the monstrous boar
1335 Right in the hairiest hollow of his hide
Under the last rib, sheer through bulk and bone,
Deep in; and deeply smitten, and to death,
The heavy horror with his hanging shafts
Leapt, and fell furiously, and from raging lips
1340 Foamed out the latest wrath of all his life.
And all they praised the gods with mightier heart,
Zeus and all gods, but chiefliest Artemis,
Seeing; but Meleager bade whet knives and flay,

Strip and stretch out the splendour of the spoil;
1345 And hot and horrid from the work all these
Sat, and drew breath and drank and made great
    cheer
And washed the hard sweat off their calmer brows.
For much sweet grass grew higher than grew the
    reed,
And good for slumber, and every holier herb,
1350 Narcissus, and the low-lying melilote,
And all of goodliest blade and bloom that springs
Where, hid by heavier hyacinth, violet buds
Blossom and burn; and fire of yellower flowers
And light of crescent lilies, and such leaves
1355 As fear the Faun's[1] and know the Dryad's[2] foot;
Olive and ivy and poplar dedicate,
And many a well-spring overwatched of these.
There now they rest; but me the king bade bear
Good tidings to rejoice this town and thee.
1360 Wherefore be glad, and all ye give much thanks,
For fallen is all the trouble of Calydon.

ALTHÆA
Laud ye the gods; for this they have given is good,
And what shall be they hide until their time.
Much good and somewhat grievous hast thou said,
1365 And either well; but let all sad things be,
Till all have made before the prosperous gods
Burnt-offering, and poured out the floral wine.
Look fair, O gods, and favourable; for we
Praise you with no false heart or flattering mouth,
1370 Being merciful, but with pure souls and prayer.

HERALD
Thou hast prayed well; for whoso fears not these,
But once being prosperous waxes huge of heart,
Him shall some new thing unaware destroy.

CHORUS
O that I now, I too were

---

[1] satyrs, or rural gods with horns and tails.

[2] tree-nymphs.

1375 By deep wells and water-floods,
Streams of ancient hills, and where
All the wan green places bear
Blossoms cleaving to the sod,
Fruitless fruit, and grasses fair,
1380 Or such darkest ivy-buds
As divide thy yellow hair,
Bacchus, and their leaves that nod
Round thy fawnskin brush the bare
Snow-soft shoulders of a god;
1385 There the year is sweet, and there
Earth is full of secret springs,
And the fervent rose-cheeked hours,
Those that marry dawn and noon,
There are sunless, there look pale
1390 In dim leaves and hidden air,
Pale as grass or latter flowers
Or the wild vine's wan wet rings
Full of dew beneath the moon,
And all day the nightingale
1395 Sleeps, and all night sings;
There in cold remote recesses
That nor alien eyes assail,
Feet, nor imminence of wings,
Nor a wind nor any tune,
1400 Thou, O queen and holiest,
Flower the whitest of all things,
With reluctant lengthening tresses
And with sudden splendid breast
Save of maidens unbeholden,
1405 There art wont to enter, there
Thy divine swift limbs and golden
Maiden growth of unbound hair,
Bathed in waters white,
Shine, and many a maid's by thee
1410 In moist woodland or the hilly
Flowerless brakes where wells abound
Out of all men's sight;
Or in lower pools that see
All their marges clothed all round
1415 With the innumerable lily,

Whence the golden-girdled bee
Flits through flowering rush to fret
White or duskier violet,
Fair as those that in far years
1420 With their buds left luminous
And their little leaves made wet,
From the warmer dew of tears,
Mother's tears in extreme need,
Hid the limbs of Iamus,
1425 Of thy brother's seed;
For his heart was piteous
Toward him, even as thine heart now
Pitiful toward us;
Thine, O goddess, turning hither
1430 A benignant blameless brow;
Seeing enough of evil done
And lives withered as leaves wither
In the blasting of the sun;
Seeing enough of hunters dead,
1435 Ruin enough of all our year,
Herds and harvests slain and shed,
Herdsmen stricken many an one,
Fruits and flocks consumed together,
And great length of deadly days.
1440 Yet with reverent lips and fear
Turn we toward thee, turn and praise
For this lightening of clear weather
And prosperities begun.
For not seldom, when all air
1445 As bright water without breath
Shines, and when men fear not, fate
Without thunder unaware
Breaks, and brings down death.
Joy with grief ye great gods give,
1450 Good with bad, and overbear
All the pride of us that live,
All the high estate,
As ye long since overbore,
As in old time long before,
1455 Many a strong man and a great,
All that were.

But do thou, sweet, otherwise,
Having heed of all our prayer,
Taking note of all our sighs;
1460 We beseech thee by thy light,
By thy bow, and thy sweet eyes,
And the kingdom of the night,
Be thou favourable and fair;
By thine arrows and thy might
1465 And Orion overthrown;
By the maiden thy delight,
By the indissoluble zone
And the sacred hair.

MESSENGER

Maidens, if ye will sing now, shift your song,
1470 Bow down, cry, wail for pity; is this a time
For singing? nay, for strewing of dust and ash,
Rent raiment, and for bruising of the breast.

CHORUS

What new thing wolf-like lurks behind thy words?
What snake's tongue in thy lips? what fire in the
        eyes?

MESSENGER

1475 Bring me before the queen and I will speak.

CHORUS

Lo, she comes forth as from thank-offering made.

MESSENGER

A barren offering for a bitter gift.

ALTHÆA

What are these borne on branches, and the face
Covered? no mean men living, but now slain
1480 Such honour have they, if any dwell with death.

MESSENGER

Queen, thy twain brethren and thy mother's sons.

ALTHÆA

Lay down your dead till I behold their blood
If it be mine indeed, and I will weep.

MESSENGER

Weep if thou wilt, for these men shall no more.

ALTHÆA

1485 O brethren, O my father's sons, of me
Well loved and well reputed, I should weep
Tears dearer than the dear blood drawn from you
But that I know you not uncomforted,
Sleeping no shameful sleep, however slain,
1490 For my son surely hath avenged you dead.

MESSENGER

Nay, should thine own seed slay himself, O queen?

ALTHÆA

Thy double word brings forth a double death.

MESSENGER

Know this then singly, by one hand they fell.

ALTHÆA

What mutterest thou with thine ambiguous
        mouth?

MESSENGER

1495 Slain by thy son's hand; is that saying so hard?

ALTHÆA

Our time is come upon us: it is here.

CHORUS

O miserable, and spoiled at thine own hand.

ALTHÆA

Wert thou not called Meleager from this womb?

CHORUS

A grievous huntsman hath it bred to thee.

ALTHÆA

1500 Wert thou born fire, and shalt thou not devour?

CHORUS

The fire thou madest, will it consume even thee?

ALTHÆA

My dreams are fallen upon me; burn thou too.

CHORUS

Not without God are visions born and die.

ALTHÆA

The gods are many about me; I am one.

CHORUS

1505 She groans as men wrestling with heavier gods.

ALTHÆA

They rend me, they divide me, they destroy.

CHORUS

Or one labouring in travail of strange births.

ALTHÆA

They are strong, they are strong; I am broken, and
    these prevail.

CHORUS

The god is great against her; she will die.

ALTHÆA

1510 Yea, but not now; for my heart too is great.
I would I were not here in sight of the sun,
But thou, speak all thou sawest, and I will die.

MESSENGER

O queen, for queenlike hast thou borne thyself,
A little word may hold so great mischance.
1515 For in division of the sanguine spoil
These men thy brethren wrangling bade yield up

The boar's head and the horror of the hide
That this might stand a wonder in Calydon,
Hallowed; and some drew toward them; but thy son
1520 With great hands grasping all that weight of hair
Cast down the dead heap clanging and collapsed
At female feet, saying This thy spoil not mine,
Maiden, thine own hand for thyself hath reaped,
And all this praise God gives thee: she thereat
1525 Laughed, as when dawn touches the sacred night
The sky sees laugh and redden and divide
Dim lips and eyelids virgin of the sun,
Hers, and the warm slow breasts of morning heave,
Fruitful, and flushed with flame from lamp-lit hours,
1530 And maiden undulation of clear hair
Colour the clouds; so laughed she from pure heart,
Lit with a low blush to the braided hair,
And rose-coloured and cold like very dawn,
Golden and godlike, chastely with chaste lips,
1535 A faint grave laugh; and all they held their peace,
And she passed by them. Then one cried Lo now,
Shall not the Arcadian shoot out lips at us,
Saying all we were despoiled by this one girl?
And all they rode against her violently
1540 And cast the fresh crown from her hair, and now
They had rent her spoil away, dishonouring her,
Save that Meleager, as a tame lion chafed,
Bore on them, broke them, and as fire cleaves wood
So clove and drove them, smitten in twain; but she
1545 Smote not nor heaved up hand; and this man first,
Plexippus, crying out This for love's sake, sweet,
Drove at Meleager, who with spear straightening
Pierced his cheek through; then Toxeus made for
    him,
Dumb, but his spear spake; vain and violent words.
1550 Fruitless; for him too stricken through both sides
The earth felt falling, and his horse's foam
Blanched thy son's face, his slayer; and these being
    slain,
None moved nor spake; but Œneus bade bear hence
These made of heaven infatuate in their deaths,
1555 Foolish; for these would baffle fate, and fell.

And they passed on, and all men honoured her,
Being honourable, as one revered of heaven.

ALTHÆA

What say you, women? is all this not well done?

CHORUS

No man doth well but God hath part in him.

ALTHÆA

1560 But no part here; for these my brethren born
Ye have no part in, these ye know not of
As I that was their sister, a sacrifice
Slain in their slaying. I would I had died for these;
For this man dead walked with me, child by child,
1565 And made a weak staff for my feebler feet
With his own tender wrist and hand, and held
And led me softly and shewed me gold and steel
And shining shapes of mirror and bright crown
And all things fair; and threw light spears, and
    brought
1570 Young hounds to huddle at my feet and thrust
Tame heads against my little maiden breasts
And please me with great eyes; and those days went
And these are bitter and I a barren queen
And sister miserable, a grievous thing
1575 And mother of many curses; and she too,
My sister Leda, sitting overseas
With fair fruits round her, and her faultless lord,
Shall curse me, saying A sorrow and not a son,
Sister, thou barest, even a burning fire,
1580 A brand consuming thine own soul and me.
But ye now, sons of Thestius, make good cheer,
For ye shall have such wood to funeral fire
As no king hath; and flame that once burnt down
Oil shall not quicken or breath relume or wine
1585 Refresh again; much costlier than fine gold,
And more than many lives of wandering men.

CHORUS

O queen, thou hast yet with thee love-worthy things,
Thine husband, and the great strength of thy son.

ALTHÆA

Who shall get brothers for me while I live?
1590 Who bear them? who bring forth in lieu of these?
Are not our fathers and our brethren one,
And no man like them? are not mine here slain?
Have we not hung together, he and I,
Flowerwise feeding as the feeding bees,
1595 With mother-milk for honey? and this man too,
Dead, with my son's spear thrust between his sides,
Hath he not seen us, later born than he,
Laugh with lips filled, and laughed again for love?
There were no sons then in the world, nor spears,
1600 Nor deadly births of women; but the gods
Allowed us, and our days were clear of these.
I would I had died unwedded, and brought forth
No swords to vex the world; for these that spake
Sweet words long since and loved me will not speak
1605 Nor love nor look upon me; and all my life
I shall not hear nor see them living men.
But I too living, how shall I now live?
What life shall this be with my son, to know
What hath been and desire what will not be,
1610 Look for dead eyes and listen for dead lips,
And kill mine own heart with remembering them,
And with those eyes that see their slayer alive
Weep, and wring hands that clasp him by the hand?
How shall I bear my dreams of them, to hear
1615 False voices, feel the kisses of false mouths
And footless sound of perished feet, and then
Wake and hear only it may be their own hounds
Whine masterless in miserable sleep,
And see their boar-spears and their beds and seats
1620 And all the gear and housings of their lives
And not the men? shall hounds and horses mourn,
Pine with strange eyes, and prick up hungry ears,

Famish and fail at heart for their dear lords,
And I not heed at all? and those blind things
1625 Fall off from life for love's sake, and I live?
Surely some death is better than some life,
Better one death for him and these and me
For if the gods had slain them it may be
I had endured it; if they had fallen by war
1630 Or by the nets and knives of privy death
And by hired hands while sleeping, this thing too
I had set my soul to suffer; or this hunt,
Had this despatched them, under tusk or tooth
Torn, sanguine, trodden, broken; for all deaths
1635 Or honourable or with facile feet avenged
And hands of swift gods following, all save this,
Are bearable; but not for their sweet land
Fighting, but not a sacrifice, lo these
Dead; for I had not then shed all mine heart
1640 Out at mine eyes: then either with good speed,
Being just, I had slain their slayer atoningly,
Or strewn with flowers their fire and on their tombs
Hung crowns, and over them a song, and seen
Their praise outflame their ashes: for all men,
1645 All maidens, had come thither, and from pure lips
Shed songs upon them, from heroic eyes
Tears; and their death had been a deathless life;
But now, by no man hired nor alien sword,
By their own kindred are they fallen, in peace,
1650 After much peril, friendless among friends,
By hateful hands they loved; and how shall mine
Touch these returning red and not from war,
These fatal from the vintage of men's veins,
Dead men my brethren? how shall these wash off
1655 No festal stains of undelightful wine,
How mix the blood, my blood on them, with me,
Holding mine hand? or how shall I say, son,
That am no sister? but by night and day
Shall we not sit and hate each other, and think
1660 Things hate-worthy? not live with shamefast eyes,
Brow-beaten, treading soft with fearful feet,
Each unupbraided, each without rebuke
Convicted, and without a word reviled

Each of another? and I shall let thee live
1665 And see thee strong and hear men for thy sake
Praise me, but these thou wouldest not let live
No man shall praise for ever? these shall lie
Dead, unbeloved, unholpen, all through thee?
Sweet were they toward me living, and mine heart
1670 Desired them, but was then well satisfied,
That now is as men hungered; and these dead
I shall want always to the day I die.
For all things else and all men may renew;
Yea, son for son the gods may give and take,
1675 But never a brother or sister any more.

CHORUS

Nay, for the son lies close about thine heart,
Full of thy milk, warm from thy womb, and drains
Life and the blood of life and all thy fruit,
Eats thee and drinks thee as who breaks bread and
    eats,
1680 Treads wine and drinks, thyself, a sect of thee;
And if he feed not, shall not thy flesh faint?
Or drink not, are not thy lips dead for thirst?
This thing moves more than all things, even thy son,
That thou cleave to him; and he shall honour thee,
1685 Thy womb that bare him and the breasts he knew,
Reverencing most for thy sake all his gods.

ALTHÆA

But these the gods too gave me, and these my son,
Not reverencing his gods nor mine own heart
Nor the old sweet years nor all venerable things,
1690 But cruel, and in his ravin like a beast,
Hath taken away to slay them: yea, and she,
She the strange woman, she the flower, the sword,
Red from spilt blood, a mortal flower to men,
Adorable, detestable—even she
1695 Saw with strange eyes and with strange lips rejoiced,
Seeing these mine own slain of mine own, and me
Made miserable above all miseries made,
A grief among all women in the world,
A name to be washed out with all men's tears.

CHORUS

1700 Strengthen thy spirit; is this not also a god,
Chance, and the wheel of all necessities?
Hard things have fallen upon us from harsh gods,
Whom lest worse hap rebuke we not for these.

ALTHÆA

My spirit is strong against itself, and I
1705 For these things' sake cry out on mine own soul
That it endures outrage, and dolorous days,
And life, and this inexpiable impotence.
Weak am I, weak and shameful; my breath drawn
Shames me, and monstrous things and violent gods.
1710 What shall atone? what heal me? what bring back
Strength to the foot, light to the face? what herb
Assuage me? what restore me? what release?
What strange thing eaten or drunken, O great gods,
Make me as you or as the beasts that feed,
1715 Slay and divide and cherish their own hearts?
For these ye show us; and we less than these
Have not wherewith to live as all these things
Which all their lives fare after their own kind
As who doth well rejoicing; but we ill,
1720 Weeping or laughing, we whom eyesight fails,
Knowledge and light of face and perfect heart,
And hands we lack, and wit; and all our days
Sin, and have hunger, and die infatuated.
For madness have ye given us and not health,
1725 And sins whereof we know not; and for these
Death, and sudden destruction unaware.
What shall we say now? what thing comes of us?

CHORUS

Alas, for all this all men undergo.

ALTHÆA

Wherefore I will not that these twain, O gods,
1730 Die as a dog dies, eaten of creeping things,
Abominable, a loathing; but though dead
Shall they have honour and such funereal flame
As strews men's ashes in their enemies' face

And blinds their eyes who hate them: lest men say,
1735 "Lo how they lie, and living had great kin,
And none of these hath pity of them, and none
Regards them lying, and none is wrung at heart,
None moved in spirit for them, naked and slain,
Abhorred, abased, and no tears comfort them":
1740 And in the dark this grieve Eurythemis,
Hearing how these her sons come down to her
Unburied, unavenged, as kinless men,
And had a queen their sister. That were shame
Worse than this grief. Yet how to atone at all
1745 I know not; seeing the love of my born son,
A new-made mother's new-born love, that grows
From the soft child to the strong man, now soft
Now strong as either, and still one sole same love,
Strives with me, no light thing to strive withal;
1750 This love is deep, and natural to man's blood,
And ineffaceable with many tears.
Yet shall not these rebuke me though I die,
Nor she in that waste world with all her dead,
My mother, among the pale flocks fallen as leaves,
1755 Folds of dead people, and alien from the sun;
Nor lack some bitter comfort, some poor praise,
Being queen, to have borne her daughter like a
    queen,
Righteous; and though mine own fire burn me too,
She shall have honour and these her sons, though
    dead.
1760 But all the gods will, all they do, and we
Not all we would, yet somewhat; and one choice
We have, to live and do just deeds and die.

CHORUS

Terrible words she communes with, and turns
Swift fiery eyes in doubt against herself,
1765 And murmurs as who talks in dreams with death.

ALTHÆA

For the unjust also dieth, and him all men
Hate, and himself abhors the unrighteousness,
And seeth his own dishonour intolerable.

But I being just, doing right upon myself,
1770 Slay mine own soul, and no man born shames me.
For none constrains nor shall rebuke, being done,
What none compelled me doing; thus these things
    fare.
Ah, ah, that such things should so fare; ah me,
That I am found to do them and endure,
1775 Chosen and constrained to choose, and bear myself
Mine own wound through mine own flesh to the
    heart
Violently stricken, a spoiler and a spoil,
A ruin ruinous, fallen on mine own son.
Ah, ah, for me too as for these; alas,
1780 For that is done that shall be, and mine hand
Full of the deed, and full of blood mine eyes,
That shall see never nor touch anything
Save blood unstanched and fire unquenchable.

CHORUS
What wilt thou do? what ails thee? for the house
1785 Shakes ruinously; wilt thou bring fire for it?

ALTHÆA
Fire in the roofs, and on the lintels fire.
Lo ye, who stand and weave, between the doors,
There; and blood drips from hand and thread, and
    stains
Threshold and raiment and me passing in
1790 Flecked with the sudden sanguine drops of death.

CHORUS
Alas that time is stronger than strong men,
Fate than all gods: and these are fallen on us.

ALTHÆA
A little since and I was glad; and now
I never shall be glad or sad again.

CHORUS
1795 Between two joys a grief grows unaware.

ALTHÆA
A little while and I shall laugh; and then
I shall weep never and laugh not any more.

CHORUS
What shall be said? for words are thorns to grief.
Withhold thyself a little and fear the gods.

ALTHÆA
1800 Fear died when these were slain; and I am as dead,
And fear is of the living; these fear none.

CHORUS
Have pity upon all people for their sake.

ALTHÆA
It is done now; shall I put back my day?

CHORUS
An end is come, an end; this is of God.

ALTHÆA
1805 I am fire, and burn myself; keep clear of fire.

CHORUS
The house is broken, is broken; it shall not stand.

ALTHÆA
Woe, woe for him that breaketh; and a rod
Smote it of old, and now the axe is here.

CHORUS
Not as with sundering of the earth
1810   Nor as with cleaving of the sea
Nor fierce foreshadowings of a birth
    Nor flying dreams of death to be
Nor loosening of the large world's girth
And quickening of the body of night,
1815   And sound of thunder in men's ears
And fire of lightning in men's sight,
    Fate, mother of desires and fears,
    Bore unto men the law of tears;

But sudden, an unfathered flame,
1820   And broken out of night, she shone,
She, without body, without name,
    In days forgotten and foregone;
And heaven rang round her as she came
Like smitten cymbals, and lay bare;
1825   Clouds and great stars, thunders and snows,
The blue sad fields and folds of air,
    The life that breathes, the life that grows,
    All wind, all fire, that burns or blows,
Even all these knew her: for she is great;
1830   The daughter of doom, the mother of death,
The sister of sorrow; a lifelong weight
    That no man's finger lighteneth,
Nor any god can lighten fate;
A landmark seen across the way
1835   Where one race treads as the other trod;
An evil sceptre, an evil stay,
    Wrought for a staff, wrought for a rod,
    The bitter jealousy of God.

For death is deep as the sea,
1840   And fate as the waves thereof.
Shall the waves take pity on thee
    Or the southwind offer thee love?
Wilt thou take the night for thy day
Or the darkness for light on thy way,
1845   Till thou say in thine heart Enough?
Behold, thou art over fair, thou art over wise;
The sweetness of spring in thine hair, and the light
    in thine eyes.
The light of the spring in thine eyes, and the sound
    in thine ears;
Yet thine heart shall wax heavy with sighs and thine
    eyelids with tears.
1850 Wilt thou cover thine hair with gold, and with
    silver thy feet?
Hast thou taken the purple to fold thee, and made
    thy mouth sweet?
Behold, when thy face is made bare, he that loved
    thee shall hate;

Thy face shall be no more fair at the fall of thy fate.
For thy life shall fall as a leaf and be shed as the rain;
1855 And the veil of thine head shall be grief; and the
    crown shall be pain.

ALTHÆA

Ho, ye that wail, and ye that sing, make way
Till I be come among you. Hide your tears,
Ye little weepers, and your laughing lips,
Ye laughers for a little; lo mine eyes
1860 That outweep heaven at rainiest, and my mouth
That laughs as gods laugh at us. Fate's are we,
Yet fate is ours a breathing-space; yea, mine,
Fate is made mine for ever; he is my son,
My bedfellow, my brother. You strong gods,
1865 Give place unto me; I am as any of you,
To give life and to take life. Thou, old earth,
That hast made man and unmade; thou whose
    mouth
Looks red from the eaten fruits of thine own womb;
Behold me with what lips upon what food
1870 I feed and fill my body; even with flesh
Made of my body. Lo, the fire I lit
I burn with fire to quench it; yea, with flame
I burn up even the dust and ash thereof.

CHORUS

Woman, what fire is this thou burnest with?

ALTHÆA

1875 Yea to the bone, yea to the blood and all.

CHORUS

For this thy face and hair are as one fire.

ALTHÆA

A tongue that licks and beats upon the dust.

CHORUS

And in thine eyes are hollow light and heat.

ALTHÆA

Of flame not fed with hand or frankincense.

CHORUS

1880 I fear thee for the trembling of thine eyes,

ALTHÆA

Neither with love they tremble nor for fear.

CHORUS

And thy mouth shuddering like a shot bird.

ALTHÆA

Not as the bride's mouth when man kisses it.

CHORUS

Nay, but what thing is this thing thou hast done?

ALTHÆA

1885 Look, I am silent, speak your eyes for me.

CHORUS

I see a faint fire lightening from the hall.

ALTHÆA

Gaze, stretch your eyes, strain till the lids drop off.

CHORUS

Flushed pillars down the flickering vestibule.

ALTHÆA

Stretch with your necks like birds: cry, chirp as
    they.

CHORUS

1890 And a long brand that blackens: and white dust.

ALTHÆA

O children, what is this ye see? your eyes
Are blinder than night's face at fall of moon.
That is my son, my flesh, my fruit of life,
My travail, and the year's weight of my womb.

1895 Meleager, a fire enkindled of mine hands
And of mine hands extinguished; this is he.

CHORUS

O gods, what word has flown out at thy mouth?

ALTHÆA

I did this and I say this and I die.

CHORUS

Death stands upon the doorway of thy lips,
1900 And in thy mouth has death set up his house.

ALTHÆA

O death, a little, a little while, sweet death,
Until I see the brand burnt down and die.

CHORUS

She reels as any reed under the wind,
And cleaves unto the ground with staggering feet.

ALTHÆA

1905 Girls, one thine will I say and hold my peace.
I that did this will weep not nor cry out,
Cry ye and weep: I will not call on gods,
Call ye on them; I will not pity man,
Shew ye your pity. I know not if I live;
1910 Save that I feel the fire upon my face
And on my cheek the burning of a brand.
Yea the smoke bites me, yea I drink the steam
With nostril and with eyelid and with lip
Insatiate and intolerant; and mine hands
1915 Burn, and fire feeds upon mine eyes; I reel
As one made drunk with living, whence he draws
Drunken delight; yet I, though mad for joy,
Loathe my long living and am waxen red
As with the shadow of shed blood; behold,
1920 I am kindled with the flames that fade in him,
I am swollen with subsiding of his veins,
I am flooded with his ebbing; my lit eyes
Flame with the falling fire that leaves his lids

1925 Bloodless; my cheek is luminous with blood
Because his face is ashen. Yet, O child,
Son, first-born, fairest—O sweet mouth, sweet eyes,
That drew my life out through my suckling breast,
That shone and clove mine heart through—O soft knees
Clinging, O tender treadings of soft feet,
1930 Cheeks warm with little kissings—O child, child,
What have we made each other? Lo, I felt
Thy weight cleave to me, a burden of beauty, O son,
Thy cradled brows and loveliest loving lips,
The floral hair, the little lightening eyes,
1935 And all thy goodly glory; with mine hands
Delicately I fed thee, with my tongue
Tenderly spake, saying, Verily in God's time,
For all the little likeness of thy limbs,
Son, I shall make thee a kingly man to fight,
1940 A lordly leader; and hear before I die,
"She bore the goodliest sword of all the world."
Oh! oh! For all my life turns round on me;
I am severed from myself, my name is gone,
My name that was a healing, it is changed,
1945 My name is a consuming. From this time,
Though mine eyes reach to the end of all these things,
My lips shall not unfasten till I die.

SEMICHORUS

She has filled with sighing the city,
And the ways thereof with tears;
1950 She arose, she girdled her sides,
She set her face as a bride's;
She wept, and she had no pity;
Trembled, and felt no fears.

SEMICHORUS

Her eyes were clear as the sun,
1955 Her brows were fresh as the day;
She girdled herself with gold,
Her robes were manifold;
But the days of her worship are done,
Her praise is taken away.

SEMICHORUS

1960 For she set her hand to the fire,
With her mouth she kindled the same;
As the mouth of a flute-player,
So was the mouth of her;
With the might of her strong desire
1965 She blew the breath of the flame.

SEMICHORUS

She set her hand to the wood,
She took the fire in her hand;
As one who is nigh to death,
She panted with strange breath;
1970 She opened her lips unto blood,
She breathed and kindled the brand.

SEMICHORUS

As a wood-dove newly shot,
She sobbed and lifted her breast;
She sighed and covered her eyes,
1975 Filling her lips with sighs;
She sighed, she withdrew herself not,
She refrained not, taking not rest;

SEMICHORUS

But as the wind which is drouth,
And as the air which is death,
1980 As storm that severeth ships,
Her breath severing her lips,
The breath came forth of her mouth
And the fire came forth of her breath.

SECOND MESSENGER

Queen, and you maidens, there is come on us
1985 A thing more deadly than the face of death;
Meleager the good lord is as one slain.

SEMICHORUS

Without sword, without sword is he stricken;
Slain, and slain without hand.

SECOND MESSENGER

For as keen ice divided of the sun
1990 His limbs divide, and as thawed snow the flesh
Thaws from off all his body to the hair.

SEMICHORUS

He wastes as the embers quicken;
With the brand he fades as a brand.

SECOND MESSENGER

Even while they sang and all drew hither and he
1995 Lifted both hands to crown the Arcadian's hair
And fix the looser leaves, both hands fell down.

SEMICHORUS

With rending of cheek and of hair
Lament ye, mourn for him, weep.

SECOND MESSENGER

Straightway the crown slid off and smote on earth,
2000 First fallen; and he, grasping his own hair, groaned
And cast his raiment round his face and fell.

SEMICHORUS

Alas for visions that were,
And soothsayings spoken in sleep.

SECOND MESSENGER

But the king twitched his reins in and leapt down
2005 And caught him, crying out twice "O child" and
thrice,
So that men's eyelids thickened with their tears.

SEMICHORUS

Lament with a long lamentation,
Cry, for an end is at hand.

SECOND MESSENGER

O son, he said, son, lift thine eyes, draw breath,
2010 Pity me; but Meleager with sharp lips
Gasped, and his face waxed like as sunburnt grass.

SEMICHORUS

Cry aloud, O thou kingdom, O nation,
O stricken, a ruinous land.

SECOND MESSENGER

Whereat king Œneus, straightening feeble knees,
2015 With feeble hands heaved up a lessening weight,
And laid him sadly in strange hands, and wept.

SEMICHORUS

Thou art smitten, her lord, her desire,
Thy dear blood wasted as rain.

SECOND MESSENGER

And they with tears and rendings of the beard
2020 Bear hither a breathing body, wept upon
And lightening at each footfall, sick to death.

SEMICHORUS

Thou madest thy sword as a fire,
With fire for a sword thou art slain.

SECOND MESSENGER

And lo, the feast turned funeral, and the crowns
2025 Fallen; and the huntress and the hunter trapped;
And weeping and changed faces and veiled hair.

MELEAGER

Let your hands meet
Round the weight of my head;
Lift ye my feet
2030 As the feet of the dead;
For the flesh of my body is molten, the limbs of it
molten as lead.

CHORUS

O thy luminous face,

Thine imperious eyes!
O the grief, O the grace,
As of day when it dies!
2035 Who is this bending over thee, lord, with tears and
suppression of sighs?

MELEAGER

Is a bride so fair?
Is a maid so meek?
With unchapleted hair,
2040 With unfilleted cheek,
Atalanta, the pure among women, whose name is as
blessing to speak.

ATALANTA

I would that with feet
Unsandalled, unshod,
Overbold, overfleet,
2045 I had swum not nor trod
From Arcadia to Calydon northward, a blast of the
envy of God.

MELEAGER

Unto each man his fate;
Unto each as he saith
In whose fingers the weight
2050 Of the world is as breath;
Yet I would that in clamour of battle mine hands
had laid hold upon death.

CHORUS

Not with cleaving of shields
And their clash in thine ear,
When the lord of fought fields
2055 Breaketh spearshaft from spear,
Thou art broken, our lord, thou art broken, with
travail and labour and fear.

MELEAGER

Would God he had found me
Beneath fresh boughs!

Would God he had bound me
2060 Unawares in mine house,
With light in mine eyes, and songs in my lips, and
a crown on my brows!

CHORUS

Whence art thou sent from us?
Whither thy goal?
How art thou rent from us,
2065 Thou that wert whole,
As with severing of eyelids and eyes, as with
sundering of body and soul!

MELEAGER

My heart is within me
As an ash in the fire;
Whosoever hath seen me,
2070 Without lute, without lyre,
Shall sing of me grievous things, even things that
were ill to desire.

CHORUS

Who shall raise thee
From the house of the dead?
Or what man praise thee
2075 That thy praise may be said?
Alas thy beauty! alas thy body! alas thine head!

MELEAGER

But thou, O mother,
The dreamer of dreams,
Wilt thou bring forth another
2080 To feel the sun's beams
When I move among shadows a shadow, and wail
by impassable streams?

ŒNEUS

What thing wilt thou leave me
Now this thing is done?
A man wilt thou give me,
2085 A son for my son,

For the light of mine eyes, the desire of my life, the
   desirable one?

CHORUS

Thou wert glad above others,
   Yea, fair beyond word;
Thou wert glad among mothers;
2090   For each man that heard
Of thee, praise there was added unto thee, as wings
   to the feet of a bird.

ŒNEUS

Who shall give back
   Thy face of old years,
With travail made black,
2095   Grown grey among fears,
Mother of sorrow, mother of cursing, mother of
   tears?

MELEAGER

Though thou art as fire
   Fed with fuel in vain,
My delight, my desire,
2100   Is more chaste than the rain,
More pure than the dewfall, more holy than stars
   are that live without stain.

ATALANTA

I would that as water
   My life's blood had thawn,
Or as winter's wan daughter
2105   Leaves lowland and lawn
Spring-stricken, or ever mine eyes had beheld thee
   made dark in thy dawn.

CHORUS

When thou dravest the men
   Of the chosen of Thrace,
None turned him again
2110   Nor endured he thy face

Clothed round with the blush of the battle, with
   light from a terrible place.

ŒNEUS

Thou shouldst die as he dies
   For whom none sheddeth tears;
Filling thine eyes
2115   And fulfilling thine ears
With the brilliance of battle, the bloom and the
   beauty, the splendour of spears.

CHORUS

In the ears of the world
   It is sung, it is told,
And the light thereof hurled
2120   And the noise thereof rolled
From the Acroceraunian snow to the ford of the
   fleece of gold.

MELEAGER

Would God ye could carry me
   Forth of all these;
Heap sand and bury me
2125   By the Chersonese
Where the thundering Bosphorus answers the
   thunder of Pontic seas.

ŒNEUS

Dost thou mock at our praise
   And the singing begun
And the men of strange days
2130   Praising my son
In the folds of the hills of home, high places of
   Calydon?

MELEAGER

For the dead man no home is;
   Ah, better to be
What the flower of the foam is
2135   In fields of the sea,

That the sea-waves might be as my raiment, the
    gulf-stream a garment for me.

CHORUS

    Who shall seek thee and bring
        And restore thee thy day,
    When the dove dipt her wing
2140   And the oars won their way
Where the narrowing Symplegades whitened the
    straits of Propontis with spray?

MELEAGER

    Will ye crown me my tomb
        Or exalt me my name,
    Now my spirits consume,
2145   Now my flesh is a flame?
Let the sea slake it once, and men speak of me
    sleeping to praise me or shame.

CHORUS

    Turn back now, turn thee,
        As who turns him to wake;
    Though the life in thee burn thee,
2150   Couldst thou bathe it and slake
Where the sea-ridge of Helle hangs heavier, and
    east upon west waters break?

MELEAGER

    Would the winds blow me back
        Or the waves hurl me home?
    Ah, to touch in the track
2155   Where the pine learnt to roam
Cold girdles and crowns of the sea-gods, cool
    blossoms of water and foam!

CHORUS

    The gods may release
        That they made fast;
    Thy soul shall have ease
2160   In thy limbs at the last;

But what shall they give thee for life, sweet life that
    is overpast?

MELEAGER

    Not the life of men's veins,
        Not of flesh that conceives;
    But the grace that remains,
2165   The fair beauty that cleaves
To the life of the rains in the grasses, the life of the
    dews on the leaves.

CHORUS

    Thou wert helmsman and chief
        Wilt thou turn in an hour,
    Thy limbs to the leaf,
2170   Thy face to the flower,
Thy blood to the water, thy soul to the gods who
    divide and devour?

MELEAGER

    The years are hungry,
        They wail all their days;
    The gods wax angry
2175   And weary of praise;
And who shall bridle their lips? and who shall
    straiten their ways?

CHORUS

    The gods guard over us
        With sword and with rod;
    Weaving shadow to cover us,
2180   Heaping the sod,
That law may fulfil herself wholly, to darken man's
    face before God.

MELEAGER

O holy head of Œneus, lo thy son
Guiltless, yet red from alien guilt, yet foul
With kinship of contaminated lives,
2185 Lo, for their blood I die; and mine own blood
For bloodshedding of mine is mixed therewith,

That death may not discern me from my kin.
Yet with clean heart I die and faultless hand,
Not shamefully; thou therefore of thy love
2190 Salute me, and bid fare among the dead
Well, as the dead fare; for the best man dead
Fares sadly; nathless I now faring well
Pass without fear where nothing is to fear
Having thy love about me and thy goodwill,
2195 O father, among dark places and men dead.

ŒNEUS

Child, I salute thee with sad heart and tears,
And bid thee comfort, being a perfect man
In fight, and honourable in the house of peace.
The gods give thee fair wage and dues of death,
2200 And me brief days and ways to come at thee.

MELEAGER

Pray thou thy days be long before thy death,
And full of ease and kingdom; seeing in death
There is no comfort and none aftergrowth,
Nor shall one thence look up and see day's dawn
2205 Nor light upon the land whither I go.
Live thou and take thy fill of days and die
When thy day comes; and make not much of death
Lest ere thy day thou reap an evil thing.
Thou too, the bitter mother and mother-plague
2210 Of this my weary body—thou too, queen,
The source and end, the sower and the scythe,
The rain that ripens and the drought that slays,
The sand that swallows and the spring that feeds,
To make me and unmake me—thou, I say,
2215 Althæa, since my father's ploughshare, drawn
Through fatal seedland of a female field,
Furrowed thy body, whence a wheaten ear
Strong from the sun and fragrant from the rains
I sprang and cleft the closure of thy womb,
2220 Mother, I dying with unforgetful tongue
Hail thee as holy and worship thee as just
Who art unjust and unholy; and with my knees
Would worship, but thy fire and subtlety,

Dissundering them, devour me; for these limbs
2225 Are as light dust and crumblings from mine urn
Before the fire has touched them; and my face
As a dead leaf or dead foot's mark on snow,
And all this body a broken barren tree
That was so strong, and all this flower of life
2230 Disbranched and desecrated miserably,
And minished all that god-like muscle and might
And lesser than a man's: for all my veins
Fail me, and all mine ashen life burns down.
I would thou hadst let me live; but gods averse,
2235 But fortune, and the fiery feet of change,
And time, these would not, these tread out my life,
These and not thou; me too thou hast loved, and I
Thee; but this death was mixed with all my life,
Mine end with my beginning: and this law,
2240 This only, slays me, and not my mother at all.
And let no brother or sister grieve too sore,
Nor melt their hearts out on me with their tears,
Since extreme love and sorrowing overmuch
Vex the great gods, and overloving men
2245 Slay and are slain for love's sake; and this house
Shall bear much better children; why should these
Weep? but in patience let them live their lives
And mine pass by forgotten: thou alone,
Mother, thou sole and only, thou not these,
2250 Keep me in mind a little when I die
Because I was thy first-born; let thy soul
Pity me, pity even me gone hence and dead,
Though thou wert wroth, and though thou bear
        again
Much happier sons, and all men later born
2255 Exceedingly excel me; yet do thou
Forget not, nor think shame; I was thy son.
Time was I did not shame thee; and time was
I thought to live and make thee honourable
With deeds as great as these men's; but they live,
2260 These, and I die; and what things should have been
Surely I know not; yet I charge thee, seeing
I am dead already, love me not the less,
Me, O my mother; I charge thee by these gods,

My father's, and that holier breast of thine,
2265 By these that see me dying, and that which nursed,
Love me not less, thy first-born: though grief come,
Grief only, of me, and of all these great joy,
And shall come always to thee; for thou knowest,
O mother, O breasts that bare me, for ye know,
2270 O sweet head of my mother, sacred eyes,
Ye know my soul albeit I sinned, ye know
Albeit I kneel not neither touch thy knees,
But with my lips I kneel, and with my heart
I fall about thy feet and worship thee.
2275 And ye farewell now, all my friends; and ye,
Kinsmen, much younger and glorious more than I,
Sons of my mother's sister; and all farewell
That were in Colchis with me, and bare down
The waves and wars that met us: and though times
2280 Change, and though now I be not anything,
Forget not me among you, what I did
In my good time; for even by all those days,
Those days and this, and your own living souls,
And by the light and luck of you that live,
2285 And by this miserable spoil, and me
Dying, I beseech you, let my name not die.
But thou, dear, touch me with thy rose-like hands.
And fasten up mine eyelids with thy mouth,
A bitter kiss; and grasp me with thine arms,
2290 Printing with heavy lips my light waste flesh,
Made light and thin by heavy-handed fate,
And with thine holy maiden eyes drop dew,
Drop tears for dew upon me who am dead,
Me who have loved thee; seeing without sin done
2295 I am gone down to the empty weary house
Where no flesh is nor beauty nor swift eyes
Nor sound of mouth nor might of hands and feet.
But thou, dear, hide my body with thy veil,
And with thy raiment cover foot and head,
2300 And stretch thyself upon me and touch hands
With hands and lips with lips: be pitiful
As thou art maiden perfect; let no man
Defile me to despise me, saying, This man
Died woman-wise, a woman's offering, slain

2305 Through female fingers in his woof of life,
Dishonourable; for thou hast honoured me.
And now for God's sake kiss me once and twice
And let me go; for the night gathers me,
And in the night shall no man gather fruit.

ATALANTA

2310 Hail thou: but I with heavy face and feet
Turn homeward and am gone out of thine eyes.

CHORUS

Who shall contend with his lords
    Or cross them or do them wrong?
Who shall bind them as with cords?
2315   Who shall tame them as with song?
Who shall smite them as with swords?
        For the hands of their kingdom are strong.
—1865

Laus Veneris [1]

Asleep or waking is it? for her neck,
    Kissed over close, wears yet a purple speck
        Wherein the pained blood falters and goes out;
Soft, and stung softly—fairer for a fleck.

5 But though my lips shut sucking on the place,
There is no vein at work upon her face;
    Her eyelids are so peaceable, no doubt
Deep sleep has warmed her blood through all its
    ways.

Lo, this is she that was the world's delight;
10 The old grey years were parcels of her might;
    The strewings of the ways wherein she trod
Were the twain seasons of the day and night.

Lo, she was thus when her clear limbs enticed
All lips that now grow sad with kissing Christ,

_____
[1] "Praise of Venus."

15 Stained with blood fallen from the feet of God,
The feet and hands whereat our souls were priced.

Alas, Lord, surely thou art great and fair.
But lo her wonderfully woven hair!
    And thou didst heal us with thy piteous kiss;
20 But see now, Lord; her mouth is lovelier.

She is right fair; what hath she done to thee?
Nay, fair Lord Christ, lift up thine eyes and see;
    Had now thy mother such a lip—like this?
Thou knowest how sweet a thing it is to me.

25 Inside the Horsel[1] here the air is hot;
Right little peace one hath for it, God wot;
    The scented dusty daylight burns the air,
And my heart chokes me till I hear it not.

Behold, my Venus,[2] my soul's body, lies
30 With my love laid upon her garment-wise,
    Feeling my love in all her limbs and hair
And shed between her eyelids through her eyes.

She holds my heart in her sweet open hands
Hanging asleep; hard by her head there stands,
35   Crowned with gilt thorns and clothed with flesh
            like fire,
Love,[3] wan as foam blown up the salt burnt
        sands—

Hot as the brackish waifs of yellow spume
That shift and steam—loose clots of arid fume
    From the sea's panting mouth of dry desire;
40 There stands he, like one labouring at a loom.

The warp holds fast across; and every thread
That makes the woof up has dry specks of red;
    Always the shuttle cleaves clean through, and he
Weaves with the hair of many a ruined head.

45 Love is not glad nor sorry, as I deem;
Labouring he dreams, and labours in the dream,
    Till when the spool is finished, lo I see
His web, reeled off, curls and goes out like steam.

Night falls like fire; the heavy lights run low,
50 And as they drop, my blood and body so
    Shake as the flame shakes, full of days and hours
That sleep not neither weep they as they go.

Ah yet would God this flesh of mine might be
Where air might wash and long leaves cover me,
55   Where tides of grass break into foam of flowers,
Or where the wind's feet shine along the sea.

Ah yet would God that stems and roots were bred
Out of my weary body and my head,
    That sleep were sealed upon me with a seal,
60 And I were as the least of all his dead.

Would God my blood were dew to feed the grass,
Mine ears made deaf and mine eyes blind as glass,
    My body broken as a turning wheel,
And my mouth stricken ere it saith Alas!

65 Ah God, that love were as a flower or flame,
That life were as the naming of a name,
    That death were not more pitiful than desire,
That these things were not one thing and the same!

Behold now, surely somewhere there is death:
70 For each man hath some space of years, he saith,
    A little space of time ere time expire,
A little day, a little way of breath.

---

[1] Mt. Horsel, the legendary mountain of Venus in Germany.

[2] the goddess of love and beauty.

[3] Cupid, the Roman god of love, usually represented as a beautiful youth.

And lo, between the sundawn and the sun,
His day's work and his night's work are undone;
　　And lo, between the nightfall and the light,
75 He is not, and none knoweth of such an one.

Ah God, that I were as all souls that be,
As any herb or leaf of any tree,
　　As men that toil through hours of labouring
　　　night,
80 As bones of men under the deep sharp sea.

Outside it must be winter among men;
For at the gold bars of the gates again
　　I heard all night and all the hours of it
The wind's wet wings and fingers drip with rain.

85 Knights gather, riding sharp for cold; I know
The ways and woods are strangled with the snow;
　　And with short song the maidens spin and sit
Until Christ's birthnight, lily-like, arow.

The scent and shadow shed about me make
90 The very soul in all my senses ache;
　　The hot hard night is fed upon my breath,
And sleep beholds me from afar awake.

Alas, but surely where the hills grow deep,
Or where the wild ways of the sea are steep,
95 　　Or in strange places somewhere there is death,
And on death's face the scattered hair of sleep.

There lover-like with lips and limbs that meet
They lie, they pluck sweet fruit of life and eat;
　　But me the hot and hungry days devour,
100 And in my mouth no fruit of theirs is sweet.

No fruit of theirs, but fruit of my desire,
For her love's sake whose lips through mine respire;
　　Her eyelids on her eyes like flower on flower,
Mine eyelids on mine eyes like fire on fire.

105 So lie we, not as sleep that lies by death,
With heavy kisses and with happy breath;
　　Not as man lies by woman, when the bride
Laughs low for love's sake and the words he saith.

For she lies, laughing low with love; she lies
110 And turns his kisses on her lips to sighs,
　　To sighing sound of lips unsatisfied,
And the sweet tears are tender with her eyes.

Ah, not as they, but as the souls that were
Slain in the old time, having found her fair;
115 　　Who, sleeping with her lips upon their eyes,
Heard sudden serpents hiss across her hair.

Their blood runs round the roots of time like rain:
She casts them forth and gathers them again;
　　With nerve and bone she weaves and multiplies
120 Exceeding pleasure out of extreme pain.

Her little chambers drip with flower-like red,
Her girdles, and the chaplets of her head,
　　Her armlets and her anklets; with her feet
She tramples all that wine-press of the dead.

125 Her gateways smoke with fume of flowers and fires,
With loves burnt out and unassuaged desires;
　　Between her lips the steam of them is sweet,
The languor on her ears of many lyres.

Her beds are full of perfume and sad sound,
130 Her doors are made with music, and barred round
　　With sighing and with laughter and with tears,
With tears whereby strong souls of men are bound.

There is the knight Adonis[1] that was slain;
With flesh and blood she chains him for a chain

---

[1] the beloved of Venus, a beautiful youth who preferred hunting to love;
he was killed by a wild boar.

135 The body and the spirit in her ears
Cry, for her lips divide him vein by vein.

Yea, all she slayeth; yea, every man save me;
Me, love, thy lover that must cleave to thee
    Till the ending of the days and ways of earth,
140 The shaking of the sources of the sea.

Me, most forsaken of all souls that fell;
Me, satiated with things insatiable;
    Me, for whose sake the extreme hell makes mirth,
Yea, laughter kindles at the heart of hell.

145 Alas thy beauty! for thy mouth's sweet sake
My soul is bitter to me, my limbs quake
    As water, as the flesh of men that weep,
As their heart's vein whose heart goes nigh to
    break.

Ah God, that sleep with flower-sweet finger-tips
150 Would crush the fruit of death upon my lips;
    Ah God, that death would tread the grapes of
      sleep
And wring their juice upon me as it drips.

There is no change of cheer for many days,
But change of chimes high up in the air, that sways
    155 Rung by the running fingers of the wind;
And singing sorrows heard on hidden ways.

Day smiteth day in twain, night sundereth night,
And on mine eyes the dark sits as the light;
    Yea, Lord, thou knowest I know not, having
      sinned,
160 If heaven be clean or unclean in thy sight.

Yea, as if earth were sprinkled over me,
Such chafed harsh earth as chokes a sandy sea,
    Each pore doth yearn, and the dried blood
      thereof
Gasps by sick fits, my heart swims heavily,

165 There is a feverish famine in my veins;
Below her bosom, where a crushed grape stains
    The white and blue, there my lips caught and
      clove
An hour since, and what mark of me remains?

I dare not always touch her, lest the kiss
170 Leave my lips charred. Yea, Lord, a little bliss,
    Brief bitter bliss, one hath for a great sin;
Nathless thou knowest how sweet a thing it is.

Sin, is it sin whereby men's souls are thrust
Into the pit? yet had I a good trust
175   To save my soul before it slipped therein,
Trod under by the fire-shod feet of lust.

For if mine eyes fail and my soul takes breath,
I look between the iron sides of death
    Into sad hell where all sweet love hath end,
180 All but the pain that never finisheth.

There are the naked faces of great kings,
The singing folk with all their lute-playings;
    There when one cometh he shall have to friend
The grave that covets and the worm that clings.

185 There sit the knights that were so great of hand,
The ladies that were queens of fair green land,
    Grown grey and black now, brought unto the
      dust,
Soiled, without raiment, clad about with sand.

There is one end for all of them; they sit
190 Naked and sad, they drink the dregs of it,
    Trodden as grapes in the wine-press of lust,
Trampled and trodden by the fiery feet.

I see the marvellous mouth whereby there fell
Cities and people whom the gods loved well,

195 Yet for her sake on them the fire gat hold,
And for their sakes on her the fire of hell.[1]

And softer than the Egyptian lote-leaf is,
The queen[2] whose face was worth the world to kiss
 Wearing at breast a suckling snake of gold;
200 And large pale lips of strong Semiramis,[3]

Curled like a tiger's that curl back to feed;
Red only where the last kiss made them bleed;
 Her hair most thick with many a carven gem,
Deep in the mane, great-chested, like a steed.

205 Yea, with red sin the faces of them shine;
But in all these there was no sin like mine;
 No, not in all the strange great sins of them
That made the wine-press froth and foam with
  wine.

For I was of Christ's choosing, I God's knight,
210 No blinkard heathen stumbling for scant light;
 I can well see, for all the dusty days
Gone past, the clean great time of goodly fight.

I smell the breathing battle sharp with blows,
With shrieks of shafts and snapping short of bows;
215 The fair pure sword smites out in subtle ways,
Sounds and long lights are shed between the rows

Of beautiful mailed men; the edged light slips,
Most like a snake that takes short breath and dips
 Sharp from the beautifully bending head,
220 With all its gracious body lithe as lips

That curl in touching you; right in this wise
My sword doth, seeming fire in mine own eyes,
 Leaving all colours in them brown and red

---

[1] probably an allusion to Helen of Troy.

[2] Cleopatra.

[3] a legendary queen of Assyria, founder of the city of Nineveh (ninth
century BC).

And flecked with death; then the keen breaths like
 sighs,
225 The caught-up choked dry laughters following
 them,
When all the fighting face is grown aflame
 For pleasure, and the pulse that stuns the ears,
And the heart's gladness of the goodly game.

Let me think yet a little; I do know
230 These things were sweet, but sweet such years ago
 Their savour is all turned now into tears;
Yea, ten years since, where the blue ripples blow,

The blue curled eddies of the blowing Rhine,
I felt the sharp wind shaking grass and vine
235 Touch my blood too, and sting me with delight
Through all this waste and weary body of mine

That never feels clear air; right gladly then
I rode alone, a great way off my men,
 And heard the chiming bridle smite and smite,
240 And gave each rhyme thereof some rhyme again,

Till my song shifted to that iron one;
Seeing there rode up between me and the sun
 Some certain of my foe's men, for his three
White wolves across their painted coats did run.

245

The first red-bearded, with square cheeks—alack,
I made my knave's blood turn his beard to black;
 The slaying of him was a joy to see:
Perchance too, when at night he came not back,

250 Some woman fell a-weeping, whom this thief
Would beat when he had drunken; yet small grief
 Hath any for the ridding of such knaves;
Yea, if one wept, I doubt her teen was brief.

This bitter love is sorrow in all lands,
255 Draining of eyelids, wringing of drenched hands,

Sighing of hearts and filling up of graves;
A sign across the head of the world he stands,

As one that hath a plague-mark on his brows;
Dust and spilt blood do track him to his house
260   Down under earth; sweet smells of lip and cheek,
Like a sweet snake's breath made more poisonous

With chewing of some perfumed deadly grass,
Are shed all round his passage if he pass,
    And their quenched savour leaves the whole
        soul weak,
Sick with keen guessing whence the perfume was.

265 As one who hidden in deep sedge and reeds
Smells the rare scent made where a panther feeds,
    And tracking ever slotwise the warm smell
Is snapped upon by the sweet mouth and bleeds,

His head far down the hot sweet throat of her—
270 So one tracks love, whose breath is deadlier,
    And lo, one springe and you are fast in hell,
Fast as the gin's grip of a wayfarer.

I think now, as the heavy hours decrease
One after one, and bitter thoughts increase
275   One upon one, of all sweet finished things;
The breaking of the battle; the long peace

Wherein we sat clothed softly, each man's hair
Crowned with green leaves beneath white hoods of
        vair;
    The sounds of sharp spears at great tourneyings,
280 And noise of singing in the late sweet air.

I sang of love too, knowing nought thereof;
"Sweeter," I said, "the little laugh of love

Than tears out of the eyes of Magdalen,[1]
Or any fallen feather of the Dove.[2]

285 "The broken little laugh that spoils a kiss,
The ache of purple pulses, and the bliss
    Of blinded eyelids that expand again—
Love draws them open with those lips of his,

"Lips that cling hard till the kissed face has grown
290 Of one same fire and colour with their own;
    Then ere one sleep, appeased with sacrifice,
Where his lips wounded, there his lips atone."

I sang these things long since and knew them not;
"Lo, here is love, or there is love, God wot,
295   This man and that finds favour in his eyes."
I said, "but I, what guerdon have I got?

"The dust of praise that is blown everywhere
In all men's faces with the common air;
    The bay-leaf[3] that wants chafing to be sweet
300 Before they wind it in a singer's hair."

So that one dawn I rode forth sorrowing;
I had no hope but of some evil thing,
    And so rode slowly past the windy wheat,
And past the vineyard and the water-spring,

305 Up to the Horsel. A great elder-tree
Held back its heaps of flowers to let me see
    The ripe tall grass, and one that walked therein,
Naked, with hair shed over to the knee.

---

[1] Mary Magdalen, a reformed prostitute who was present at Christ's crucifixion.

[2] the Holy Spirit.

[3] A crown of bay leaves, or laurel, was traditionally given to poets in ancient Greece; the custom arose at the Pythian games, held in honour of Apollo, the god of poetry.

She walked between the blossom and the grass;
310 I knew the beauty of her, what she was,
    The beauty of her body and her sin,
And in my flesh the sin of hers, alas!

Alas! for sorrow is all the end of this.
O sad kissed mouth, how sorrowful it is!
315   O breast whereat some suckling sorrow clings,
Red with the bitter blossom of a kiss!

Ah, with blind lips I felt for you, and found
About my neck your hands and hair enwound,
    The hands that stifle and the hair that stings,
320 I felt them fasten sharply without sound.

Yea, for my sin I had great store of bliss:
Rise up, make answer for me, let thy kiss
    Seal my lips hard from speaking of my sin,
Lest one go mad to hear how sweet it is.

325 Yet I waxed faint with fume of barren bowers,
And murmuring of the heavy-headed hours;
    And let the dove's beak fret and peck within
My lips in vain, and Love shed fruitless flowers.

So that God looked upon me when your hands
330 Were hot about me; yea, God brake my bands
    To save my soul alive, and I came forth
Like a man blind and naked in strange lands

That hears men laugh and weep, and knows not
    whence
Nor wherefore, but is broken in his sense;
335   Howbeit I met folk riding from the north
Towards Rome,[1] to purge them of their souls'
    offence,

And rode with them, and spake to none; the day
Stunned me like lights upon some wizard way,

And ate like fire mine eyes and mine eyesight;
340 So rode I, hearing all these chant and pray,

And marvelled; till before us rose and fell
White cursed hills, like outer skirts of hell
    Seen where men's eyes look through the day to
        night,
Like a jagged shell's lips, harsh, untunable,

345 Blown in between by devils' wrangling breath;
Nathless we won well past that hell and death,
    Down to the sweet land where all airs are good,
Even unto Rome where God's grace tarrieth.

Then came each man and worshipped at his knees
350 Who in the Lord God's likeness bears the keys
    To bind or loose, and called on Christ's shed
        blood,
And so the sweet-souled father gave him ease.[2]

But when I came I fell down at his feet,
Saying, "Father, though the Lord's blood be right
    sweet,
355   The spot it takes not off the panther's skin,
Nor shall an Ethiop's stain be bleached with it.[3]

"Lo, I have sinned and have spat out at God,
Wherefore his hand is heavier and his rod
    More sharp because of mine exceeding sin,
360 And all his raiment redder than bright blood

"Before mine eyes; yea, for my sake I wot
The heat of hell is waxen seven times hot
    Through my great sin." Then spake he some
        sweet word,
Giving me cheer; which thing availed me not;

---

[1] a common destination for medieval pilgrims.

[2] according to the Tannhauser legend, Pope Urban IV (1261–64). The apostle Peter, who was given the keys to the kingdom of heaven by Christ, is traditionally believed to have founded the papacy.

[3] Ethiop is a generic term for an African: cf. also Jeremiah 13:23.

365 Yea, scarce I wist if such indeed were said;
For when I ceased—lo, as one newly dead
   Who hears a great cry out of hell, I heard
The crying of his voice across my head.

"Until this dry shred staff, that hath no whit
370 Of leaf nor bark, bear blossom and smell sweet,
   Seek thou not any mercy in God's sight,
For so long shalt thou be cast out from it."

Yea, what if dried-up stems wax red and green,
Shall that thing be which is not nor has been?
375   Yea, what if sapless bark wax green and white,
Shall any good fruit grow upon my sin?

Nay, though sweet fruit were plucked of a dry tree,
And though men drew sweet waters of the sea,
   There should not grow sweet leaves on this dead
     stem,
380 This waste wan body and shaken soul of me.

Yea, though God search it warily enough,
There is not one sound thing in all thereof;
   Though he search all my veins through,
     searching them
He shall find nothing whole therein but love.

385 For I came home right heavy, with small cheer,
And lo my love, mine own soul's heart, more dear
   Than mine own soul, more beautiful than God,
Who hath my being between the hands of her—

Fair still, but fair for no man saving me,
390 As when she came out of the naked sea[1]
   Making the foam as fire whereon she trod,
And as the inner flower of fire was she.

Yea, she laid hold upon me, and her mouth
Clove unto mine as soul to body doth,
395   And, laughing, made her lips luxurious;
Her hair had smells of all the sunburnt south,

Strange spice and flower, strange savour of crushed
   fruit,
And perfume the swart kings tread underfoot
   For pleasure when their minds wax amorous
400 Charred frankincense and grated sandal-root.

And I forgot fear and all weary things,
All ended prayers and perished thanksgivings,
   Feeling her face with all her eager hair
Cleave to me, clinging as a fire that clings

405 To the body and to the raiment, burning them;
As after death I know that such-like flame
   Shall cleave to me for ever; yea, what care,
Albeit I burn then, having felt the same?

Ah love, there is no better life than this;
410 To have known love, how bitter a thing it is,
   And afterward be cast out of God's sight;
Yea, these that know not, shall they have such bliss

High up in barren heaven before his face
As we twain in the heavy-hearted place,
415   Remembering love and all the dead delight,
And all that time was sweet with for a space?

For till the thunder in the trumpet[2] be,
Soul may divide from body, but not we
   One from another; I hold thee with my hand,
420 I let mine eyes have all their will of thee,

I seal[3] myself upon thee with my might,
Abiding alway out of all men's sight
   Until God loosen over sea and land
The thunder of the trumpets of the night.

       EXPLICIT LAUS VENERIS.[4]

—1866

---

[2] the trumpet announcing the Last Judgement.

[3] Cf. Song of Solomon 8:6.

[4] "Here ends the praise of Venus"; a formulaic phrase used in medieval manuscripts.

---

[1] Aphrodite (or Venus) was born in the foam of the sea.

The Triumph of Time

Before our lives divide for ever,
While time is with us and hands are free
(Time, swift to fasten and swift to sever
　　Hand from hand, as we stand by the sea),
5　I will say no word that a man might say
Whose whole life's love goes down in a day;
For this could never have been; and never,
　　Though the gods and the years relent, shall be.

Is it worth a tear, is it worth an hour
10　　To think of things that are well outworn?
Of fruitless husk and fugitive flower,
　　The dream foregone and the deed forborne?
Though joy be done with and grief be vain,
Time shall not sever us wholly in twain;
15　Earth is not spoilt for a single shower;
　　But the rain has ruined the ungrown corn.

It will grow not again, this fruit of my heart,
　　Smitten with sunbeams, ruined with rain.
The singing seasons divide and depart,
20　　Winter and summer depart in twain.
It will grow not again, it is ruined at root,
The bloodlike blossom, the dull red fruit;
Though the heart yet sickens, the lips yet smart,
　　With sullen savour of poisonous pain.

25　I have given no man of my fruit to eat;
　　I trod the grapes, I have drunken the wine.
Had you eaten and drunken and found it sweet,
　　This wild new growth of the corn and vine,
This wine and bread without lees or leaven,
30　We had grown as gods, as the gods in heaven,
Souls fair to look upon, goodly to greet,
　　One splendid spirit, your soul and mine.

In the change of years, in the coil of things,
　　In the clamour and rumour of life to be,

35　We, drinking love at the furthest springs,
　　Covered with love as a covering tree,
We had grown as gods, as the gods above,
Filled from the heart to the lips with love,
Held fast in his hands, clothed warm with his wings,
40　　O love, my love, had you loved but me!

We had stood as the sure stars stand, and moved
　　As the moon moves, loving the world; and seen
Grief collapse as a thing disproved,
　　Death consume as a thing unclean.
45　Twain halves of a perfect heart, made fast
Soul to soul while the years fell past;
Had you loved me once, as you have not loved;
　　Had the chance been with us that has not been.

I have put my days and dreams out of mind,
50　　Days that are over, dreams that are done.
Though we seek life through, we shall surely find
　　There is none of them clear to us now, not one.
But clear are these things; the grass and the sand,
Where, sure as the eyes reach, ever at hand,
55　With lips wide open and face burnt blind,
　　The strong sea-daisies feast on the sun.

The low downs lean to the sea; the stream,
　　One loose thin pulseless tremulous vein,
Rapid and vivid and dumb as a dream,
60　　Works downward, sick of the sun and the rain;
No wind is rough with the rank rare flowers;
The sweet sea, mother of loves and hours,
Shudders and shines as the grey winds gleam,
　　Turning her smile to a fugitive pain.

65　Mother of loves that are swift to fade,
　　Mother of mutable winds and hours.
A barren mother, a mother-maid,
　　Cold and clean as her faint salt flowers.
I would we twain were even as she,
70　Lost in the night and the light of the sea,

Where faint sounds falter and wan beams wade,
    Break, and are broken, and shed into showers.

The loves and hours of the life of a man,
    They are swift and sad, being born of the sea,
75 Hours that rejoice and regret for a span,
    Born with a man's breath, mortal as he;
Loves that are lost ere they come to birth,
Weeds of the wave, without fruit upon earth.
I lose what I long for, save what I can,
80   My love, my love, and no love for me!

It is not much that a man can save
    On the sands of life, in the straits of time,
Who swims in sight of the great third wave
    That never a swimmer shall cross or climb.
85 Some waif washed up with the strays and spars
That ebb-tide shows to the shore and the stars;
Weed from the water, grass from a grave,
    A broken blossom, a ruined rhyme.

There will no man do for your sake, I think,
90   What I would have done for the least word said.
I had wrung life dry for your lips to drink,
    Broken it up for your daily bread:
Body for body and blood for blood,
As the flow of the full sea risen to flood
95 That yearns and trembles before it sink,
    I had given, and lain down for you, glad and
        dead.

Yea, hope at highest and all her fruit,
    And time at fullest and all his dower,
I had given you surely, and life to boot,
100   Were we once made one for a single hour.
But now, you are twain, you are cloven apart,
Flesh of his flesh, but heart of my heart;
And deep in one is the bitter root,
    And sweet for one is the lifelong flower.

105 To have died if you cared I should die for you,
    clung
    To my life if you bade me, played my part
As it pleased you—these were the thoughts that
    stung,
    The dreams that smote with a keener dart
Than shafts of love or arrows of death;
110 These were but as fire is, dust, or breath,
Or poisonous foam on the tender tongue
    Of the little snakes that eat my heart.

I wish we were dead together to-day,
    Lost sight of, hidden away out of sight,
115 Clasped and clothed in the cloven clay,
    Out of the world's way, out of the light,
Out of the ages of worldly weather,
Forgotten of all men altogether,
As the world's first dead, taken wholly away,
120   Made one with death, filled full of the night.

How we should slumber, how we should sleep,
    Far in the dark with the dreams and the dews!
And dreaming, grow to each other, and weep,
    Laugh low, live softly, murmur and muse;
125 Yea, and it may be, struck through by the dream,
Feel the dust quicken and quiver, and seem
Alive as of old to the lips, and leap
    Spirit to spirit as lovers use.

Sick dreams and sad of a dull delight;
130   For what shall it profit when men are dead
To have dreamed, to have loved with the whole
    soul's might,
    To have looked for day when the day was fled?
Let come what will, there is one thing worth,
To have had fair love in the life upon earth:
135 To have held love safe till the day grew night,
    While skies had colour and lips were red.

Would I lose you now? would I take you then,
    If I lose you now that my heart has need?

And come what may after death to men,
140   What thing worth this will the dead years breed?
Lose life, lose all; but at least I know,
O sweet life's love, having loved you so,
Had I reached you on earth, I should lose not again,
    In death nor life, nor in dream or deed.

145   Yea, I know this well: were you once sealed mine,
    Mine in the blood's beat, mine in the breath,
Mixed into me as honey in wine,
    Not time, that sayeth and gainsayeth,
Nor all strong things had severed us then;
150   Not wrath of gods, nor wisdom of men,
Nor all things earthly, nor all divine,
    Nor joy nor sorrow, nor life nor death.

I had grown pure as the dawn and the dew,
    You had grown strong as the sun or the sea,
155   But none shall triumph a whole life through:
    For death is one, and the fates are three.[1]
At the door of life, by the gate of breath,
There are worse things waiting for men than death;
Death could not sever my soul and you,
160   As these have severed your soul from me.

You have chosen and clung to the chance they sent
        you,
    Life sweet as perfume and pure as prayer.
But will it not one day in heaven repent you?
    Will they solace you wholly, the days that were?
165   Will you lift up your eyes between sadness and bliss,
Meet mine, and see where the great love is,
And tremble and turn and be changed? Content you;
    The gate is strait; I shall not be there.

But you, had you chosen, had you stretched hand,
170   Had you seen good such a thing were done,
I too might have stood with the souls that stand

_____
[1] in Greek mythology, the goddesses Clotho, Lachesis, and Atropos.
Clotho spins the thread of life, Lachesis determines the length of life,
and Atropos cuts the thread of life.

In the sun's sight, clothed with the light of the
        sun;
But who now on earth need care how I live?
Have the high gods anything left to give,
175   Save dust and laurels and gold and sand?
    Which gifts are goodly; but I will none.

O all fair lovers about the world,
    There is none of you, none, that shall comfort
        me.
My thoughts are as dead things, wrecked and
        whirled
180   Round and round in a gulf of the sea;
And still, through the sound and the straining stream,
Through the coil and chafe, they gleam in a dream,
The bright fine lips so cruelly curled,
    And strange swift eyes where the soul sits free.

185   Free, without pity, withheld from woe,
    Ignorant; fair as the eyes are fair.
Would I have you change now, change at a blow,
    Startled and stricken, awake and aware?
Yea, if I could, would I have you see
190   My very love of you filling me,
And know my soul to the quick, as I know
    The likeness and look of your throat and hair?

I shall not change you. Nay, though I might,
    Would I change my sweet one love with a word?
195   I had rather your hair should change in a night,
    Clear now as the plume of a black bright bird;
Your face fail suddenly, cease, turn grey,
Die as a leaf that dies in a day.
I will keep my soul in a place out of sight,
200   Far off, where the pulse of it is not heard.

Far off it walks, in a bleak blown space,
    Full of the sound of the sorrow of years.
I have woven a veil for the weeping face,
    Whose lips have drunken the wine of tears;
205   I have found a way for the failing feet,

A place for slumber and sorrow to meet;
There is no rumour about the place,
    Nor light, nor any that sees or hears.

I have hidden my soul out of sight, and said
210   "Let none take pity upon thee, none
Comfort thy crying: for lo, thou art dead,
    Lie still now, safe out of sight of the sun.
Have I not built thee a grave, and wrought
Thy grave-clothes on thee of grievous thought
215 With soft spun verses and tears unshed,
    And sweet light visions of things undone?

"I have given thee garments and balm and myrrh,
    And gold, and beautiful burial things.
But thou, be at peace now, make no stir;
220   Is not thy grave as a royal king's?
Fret not thyself though the end were sore;
Sleep, be patient, vex me no more.
Sleep; what hast thou to do with her?
    The eyes that weep, with the mouth that sings?"

225 Where the dead red leaves of the years lie rotten,
    The cold old crimes and the deeds thrown by,
The misconceived and the misbegotten,
    I would find a sin to do ere I die,
Sure to dissolve and destroy me all through,
230 That would set you higher in heaven, serve you
And leave you happy, when clean forgotten,
    As a dead man out of mind, am I.

Your lithe hands draw me, your face burns through
    me,
    I am swift to follow you, keen to see;
235 But love lacks might to redeem or undo me;
    As I have been, I know I shall surely be;
"What should such fellows as I do?"[1] Nay,
My part were worse if I chose to play;

For the worst is this after all; if they knew me,
240   Not a soul upon earth would pity me.

And I play not for pity of these; but you,
    If you saw with your soul what man am I,
You would praise me at least that my soul all
        through
    Clove to you, loathing the lives that lie;
245 The souls and lips that are bought and sold,
The smiles of silver and kisses of gold,
The lapdog loves that whine as they chew,
    The little lovers that curse and cry.

There are fairer women, I hear; that may be;
250   But I, that I love you and find you fair,
Who are more than fair in my eyes if they be,
    Do the high gods know or the great gods care?
Though the swords in my heart for one were
        seven,[2]
Would the iron hollow of doubtful heaven,
255 That knows not itself whether night-time or day be,
    Reverberate words and a foolish prayer?

I will go back to the great sweet mother,
    Mother and lover of men, the sea.
I will go down to her, I and none other,
260   Close with her, kiss her and mix her with me;
Cling to her, strive with her, hold her fast:
O fair white mother, in days long past
Born without sister, born without brother,
    Set free my soul as thy soul is free.

265 O fair green-girdled mother of mine,
    Sea, that art clothed with the sun and the rain,
Thy sweet hard kisses are strong like wine,
    Thy large embraces are keen like pain.
Save me and hide me with all thy waves,
270 Find me one grave of thy thousand graves,
Those pure cold populous graves of thine

[1] *Hamlet* 3.1.128–29.

[2] the Seven Sorrows of Mary.

Wrought without hand in a world without
    stain.

I shall sleep, and move with the moving ships,
    Change as the winds change, veer in the tide;
275 My lips will feast on the foam of thy lips,
    I shall rise with thy rising, with thee subside;
Sleep, and not know if she be, if she were,
Filled full with life to the eyes and hair,
As a rose is fulfilled to the roseleaf tips
280   With splendid summer and perfume and pride.

This woven raiment of nights and days,
    Were it once cast off and unwound from me,
Naked and glad would I walk in thy ways,
    Alive and aware of thy ways and thee;
285 Clear of the whole world, hidden at home,
Clothed with the green and crowned with the foam,
A pulse of the life of thy straits and bays,
    A vein in the heart of the streams of the sea.

Fair mother, fed with the lives of men,
290   Thou art subtle and cruel of heart, men say.
Thou hast taken, and shalt not render again;
    Thou art full of thy dead, and cold as they.
But death is the worst that comes of thee;
Thou art fed with our dead, O mother, O sea,
295 But when hast thou fed on our hearts? or when,
    Having given us love, hast thou taken away?

O tender-hearted, O perfect lover,
    Thy lips are bitter, and sweet thine heart.
The hopes that hurt and the dreams that hover,
300   Shall they not vanish away and apart?
But thou, thou art sure, thou art older than earth;
Thou art strong for death and fruitful of birth;
Thy depths conceal and thy gulfs discover;
    From the first thou wert; in the end thou art.

305 And grief shall endure not for ever, I know.
    As things that are not shall these things be;

We shall live through seasons of sun and of snow,
    And none be grievous as this to me.
We shall hear, as one in a trance that hears,
310 The sound of time, the rhyme of the years;
Wrecked hope and passionate pain will grow
    As tender things of a spring-tide sea.

Sea-fruit that swings in the waves that hiss,
    Drowned gold and purple and royal rings.
315 And all time past, was it all for this?
    Times unforgotten, and treasures of things?
Swift years of liking and sweet long laughter,
That wist not well of the years thereafter
Till love woke, smitten at heart by a kiss,
320   With lips that trembled and trailing wings?

There lived a singer in France of old
    By the tideless dolorous midland sea.
In a land of sand and ruin and gold
    There shone one woman, and none but she.
325 And finding life for her love's sake fail,
Being fain to see her, he bade set sail,
Touched land, and saw her as life grew cold,
    And praised God, seeing; and so died he.

Died, praising God for his gift and grace:
330   For she bowed down to him weeping, and said
"Live"; and her tears were shed on his face
    Or ever the life in his face was shed.
The sharp tears fell through her hair, and stung
Once, and her close lips touched him and clung
335 Once, and grew one with his lips for a space;
    And so drew back, and the man was dead.[1]

O brother, the gods were good to you.
    Sleep, and be glad while the world endures.

---

[1] The legend of Geoffrey Rudel, a twelfth-century troubadour of Provence, who fell in love with the princess of Tripoli, whom he had never seen. He sailed across the Mediterranean Sea to visit her but fell ill on the voyage and was believed dead when the ship arrived. The princess came to see his body; Rudel revived for a few moments and then died.

Be well content as the years wear through;
340   Give thanks for life, and the loves and lures;
Give thanks for life, O brother, and death,
For the sweet last sound of her feet, her breath,
For gifts she gave you, gracious and few,
      Tears and kisses, that lady of yours.

345 Rest, and be glad of the gods; but I,
      How shall I praise them, or how take rest?
There is not room under all the sky
      For me that knows not of worst or best,
Dream or desire of the days before,
350 Sweet things or bitterness, any more.
Love will not come to me now though I die,
      As love came close to you, breast to breast.

I shall never be friends again with roses;
      I shall loathe sweet tunes, where a note grown
         strong
355 Relents and recoils, and climbs and closes,
      As a wave of the sea turned back by song.
There are sounds where the soul's delight takes fire,
      Face to face with its own desire;
A delight that rebels, a desire that reposes;
360   I shall hate sweet music my whole life long.

The pulse of war and passion of wonder,
      The heavens that murmur, the sounds that shine,
The stars that sing and the loves that thunder,
      The music burning at heart like wine,
365 An armed archangel whose hands raise up
All senses mixed in the spirit's cup
Till flesh and spirit are molten in sunder—
      These things are over, and no more mine.

These were a part of the playing I heard
370   Once, ere my love and my heart were at strife:
Love that sings and hath wings as a bird,
      Balm of the wound and heft of the knife.
Fairer than earth is the sea, and sleep
Than overwatching of eyes that weep,

375 Now time has done with his one sweet word,
      The wine and leaven of lovely life.

I shall go my ways, tread out my measure,
      Fill the days of my daily breath
With fugitive things not good to treasure,
380   Do as the world doth, say as it saith;
But if we had loved each other—O sweet,
Had you felt, lying under the palms of your feet,
The heart of my heart, beating harder with pleasure
      To feel you tread it to dust and death—

385 Ah, had I not taken my life up and given
      All that life gives and the years let go,
The wine and honey, the balm and leaven,
      The dreams reared high and the hopes brought
         low?
Come life, come death, not a word be said;
390 Should I lose you living, and vex you dead?
I never shall tell you on earth; and in heaven,
      If I cry to you then, will you hear or know?
—1866

Itylus [1]

Swallow, my sister, O sister swallow,
  How can thine heart be full of the spring?
      A thousand summers are over and dead.
What hast thou found in the spring to follow?
5   What hast thou found in thine heart to sing?
      What wilt thou do when the summer is
         shed?

O swallow, sister, O fair swift swallow,
  Why wilt thou fly after spring to the south,

---

[1] Tereus, king of Thrace, raped his sister-in-law Philomela and cut out her tongue to prevent her from accusing him. Philomela wove the story into a tapestry which she gave to her sister, Tereus's wife Procne. In revenge, Procne killed her son Itylus (or Itys) and fed his body to Tereus. The sisters then fled, transformed into birds: Philomela into a nightingale and Procne into a swallow. Cf. Arnold's "Philomela."

The soft south whither thine heart is set?
10 Shall not the grief of the old time follow?
Shall not the song thereof cleave to thy mouth?
Hast thou forgotten ere I forget?

Sister, my sister, O fleet sweet swallow,
Thy way is long to the sun and the south;
15 But I, fulfilled of my heart's desire,
Shedding my song upon height, upon hollow,
From tawny body and sweet small mouth
Feed the heart of the night with fire.

I the nightingale all spring through,
20 O swallow, sister, O changing swallow,
All spring through till the spring be done,
Clothed with the light of the night on the dew,
Sing, while the hours and the wild birds follow,
Take flight and follow and find the sun.

25 Sister, my sister, O soft light swallow,
Though all things feast in the spring's
guest-chamber,
How hast thou heart to be glad thereof yet?
For where thou fliest I shall not follow,
Till life forget and death remember,
30 Till thou remember and I forget.

Swallow, my sister, O singing swallow,
I know not how thou hast heart to sing.
Hast thou the heart? is it all past over?
Thy lord the summer is good to follow,
35 And fair the feet of thy lover the spring:
But what wilt thou say to the spring thy
lover?

O swallow, sister, O fleeting swallow,
My heart in me is a molten ember
And over my head the waves have met.
40 But thou wouldst tarry or I would follow,
Could I forget or thou remember,
Couldst thou remember and I forget.

O sweet stray sister, O shifting swallow,
The heart's division divideth us.
45 Thy heart is light as a leaf of a tree;
But mine goes forth among sea-gulfs hollow
To the place of the slaying of Itylus,
The feast of Daulis,[1] the Thracian sea.

O swallow, sister, O rapid swallow,
50 I pray thee sing not a little space.
Are not the roofs and the lintels wet?
The woven web that was plain to follow,
The small slain body, the flowerlike face,
Can I remember if thou forget?

55 O sister, sister, thy first-begotten!
The hands that cling and the feet that follow,
The voice of the child's blood crying yet
Who hath remembered me? who hath forgotten?
Thou hast forgotten, O summer swallow,
60 But the world shall end when I forget.
—1866

Anactoria

τίνος αὖ τὺ πειθοῖ
μὰψ σαγηνεύσας φιλότατα[2]—SAPPHO.[3]

My life is bitter with thy love; thine eyes
Blind me, thy tresses burn me, thy sharp sighs
Divide my flesh and spirit with soft sound,
And my blood strengthens, and my veins abound.
5 I pray thee sigh not, speak not, draw not breath;
Let life burn down, and dream it is not death.
I would the sea had hidden us, the fire

---

[1] the feast in the city of Daulis, Greece, at which Tereus ate the flesh of his son Itys.

[2] "Of whom by persuasion hast thou vainly caught love?" A mistranslation of Sappho's "Ode to Aphrodite," ll. 18–19. The correct version is "Whom shall I make to give thee room in her heart's love?"

[3] Sappho of Lesbos was a Greek lyric poet of the seventh-century BC. Anactoria was one of her lovers.

(Wilt thou fear that, and fear not my desire?)
Severed the bones that bleach, the flesh that cleaves,
10 And let our sifted ashes drop like leaves.
I feel thy blood against my blood: my pain
Pains thee, and lips bruise lips, and vein stings vein.
Let fruit be crushed on fruit, let flower on flower,
Breast kindle breast, and either burn one hour.
15 Why wilt thou follow lesser loves? are thine
Too weak to bear these hands and lips of mine?
I charge thee for my life's sake, O too sweet
To crush love with thy cruel faultless feet,
I charge thee keep thy lips from hers or his,
20 Sweetest, till theirs be sweeter than my kiss:
Lest I too lure, a swallow for a dove,
Erotion or Erinna[1] to my love.
I would my love could kill thee; I am satiated
With seeing thee live, and fain would have thee
    dead.
25 I would earth had thy body as fruit to eat,
And no mouth but some serpent's found thee sweet.
I would find grievous ways to have thee slain,
Intense device, and superflux of pain;
Vex thee with amorous agonies, and shake
30 Life at thy lips, and leave it there to ache;
Strain out thy soul with pangs too soft to kill,
Intolerable interludes, and infinite ill;
Relapse and reluctation of the breath,
Dumb tunes and shuddering semitones of death.
35 I am weary of all thy words and soft strange ways,
Of all love's fiery nights and all his days,
And all the broken kisses salt as brine
That shuddering lips make moist with waterish
    wine,
And eyes the bluer for all those hidden hours
40 That pleasure fills with tears and feeds from flowers,
Fierce at the heart with fire that half comes through,
But all the flowerlike white stained round with blue;
The fervent underlid, and that above
Lifted with laughter or abashed with love;

45 Thine amorous girdle, full of thee and fair,
And leavings of the lilies in thine hair.
Yea, all sweet words of thine and all thy ways,
And all the fruit of nights and flower of days,
And stinging lips wherein the hot sweet brine
50 That Love was born of burns and foams like wine,
And eyes insatiable of amorous hours,
Fervent as fire and delicate as flowers,
Coloured like night at heart, but cloven through
Like night with flame, dyed round like night with
    blue,
55 Clothed with deep eyelids under and above—
Yea, all thy beauty sickens me with love;
Thy girdle empty of thee and now not fair,
And ruinous lilies in thy languid hair.
Ah, take no thought for Love's sake; shall this be,
60 And she who loves thy lover not love thee?
Sweet soul, sweet mouth of all that laughs and lives,
Mine is she, very mine; and she forgives.
For I beheld in sleep the light that is
In her high place in Paphos,[2] heard the kiss
65 Of body and soul that mix with eager tears
And laughter stinging through the eyes and ears;
Saw Love, as burning flame from crown to feet,
Imperishable, upon her storied seat;
Clear eyelids lifted toward the north and south,
70 A mind of many colours, and a mouth
Of many tunes and kisses; and she bowed,
With all her subtle face laughing aloud,
Bowed down upon me, saying, "Who doth thee
    wrong,
Sappho?" but thou—thy body is the song,
75 Thy mouth the music; thou art more than I,
Though my voice die not till the whole world die;
Though men that hear it madden; though love
    weep,
Though nature change, though shame be charmed
    to sleep.
Ah, wilt thou slay me lest I kiss thee dead?

---

[1] Erotion is a Greek male name. Erinna was another of Sappho's lovers.

[2] Cyprus, a centre for the worship of Aphrodite.

80 Yet the queen laughed from her sweet heart and said:
"Even she that flies shall follow for thy sake,
And she shall give thee gifts that would not take,
Shall kiss that would not kiss thee" (yea, kiss me)
"When thou wouldst not"—when I would not kiss
    thee!
85 Ah, more to me than all men as thou art,
Shall not my songs assuage her at the heart?
Ah, sweet to me as life seems sweet to death,
Why should her wrath fill thee with fearful breath?
Nay, sweet, for is she God alone? hath she
90 Made earth and all the centuries of the sea,
Taught the sun ways to travel, woven most fine
The moonbeams, shed the starbeams forth as wine,
Bound with her myrtles, beaten with her rods,
The young men and the maidens and the gods?
95 Have we not lips to love with, eyes for tears,
And summer and flower of women and of years?
Stars for the foot of morning, and for noon
Sunlight, and exaltation of the moon;
Waters that answer waters, fields that wear
100 Lilies, and languor of the Lesbian[1] air?
Beyond those flying feet of fluttered doves,
Are there not other gods for other loves?
Yea, though she scourge thee, sweetest, for my sake,
Blossom not thorns and flowers not blood should
    break.
105 Ah that my lips were tuneless lips, but pressed
To the bruised blossom of thy scourged white
    breast!
Ah that my mouth for Muses'[2] milk were fed
On the sweet blood thy sweet small wounds had
    bled!
That with my tongue I felt them, and could taste
110 The faint flakes from thy bosom to the waist!
That I could drink thy veins as wine, and eat
Thy breasts like honey! that from face to feet
Thy body were abolished and consumed,

And in my flesh thy very flesh entombed!
115 Ah, ah, thy beauty! like a beast it bites,
Stings like an adder, like an arrow smites.
Ah sweet, and sweet again, and seven times sweet
The paces and the pauses of thy feet!
Ah sweeter than all sleep or summer air
120 The fallen fillets fragrant from thine hair!
Yea, though their alien kisses do me wrong,
Sweeter thy lips than mine with all their song;
Thy shoulders whiter than a fleece of white,
And flower-sweet fingers, good to bruise or bite
125 As honeycomb of the inmost honey-cells,
With almond-shaped and roseleaf-coloured shells,
And blood like purple blossom at the tips
Quivering; and pain made perfect in thy lips
For my sake when I hurt thee; O that I
130 Durst crush thee out of life with love, and die,
Die of thy pain and my delight, and be
Mixed with thy blood and molten into thee!
Would I not plague thee dying overmuch?
Would I not hurt thee perfectly? not touch
135 Thy pores of sense with torture, and make bright,
Thine eyes with bloodlike tears and grievous light
Strike pang from pang as note is struck from note,
Catch the sob's middle music in thy throat,
Take thy limbs living, and new-mould with these
140 A lyre of many faultless agonies?
Feed thee with fever and famine and fine drouth,
With perfect pangs convulse thy perfect mouth,
Make thy life shudder in thee and burn afresh,
And wring thy very spirit through the flesh?
145 Cruel? but love makes all that love him well
As wise as heaven and crueller than hell.
Me hath love made more bitter toward thee
Than death toward man; but were I made as he
Who hath made all things to break them one by
    one,
150 If my feet trod upon the stars and sun
And souls of men as his have always trod,
God knows I might be crueller than God.
For who shall change with prayers or thanksgivings

---

[1] from Lesbos.

[2] goddesses of poetry and the other arts.

The mystery of the cruelty of things?
155 Or say what God above all gods and years
With offering and blood-sacrifice of tears,
With lamentation from strange lands, from graves
Where the snake pastures, from scarred mouth of
slaves
From prison, and from plunging prows of ships
160 Through flamelike foam of the sea's closing lips—
With thwartings of strange signs, and wind-blown
hair
Of comets, desolating the dim air,
When darkness is made fast with seals and bars,
And fierce reluctance of disastrous stars,
165 Eclipse, and sound of shaken hills, and wings
Darkening, and blind inexpiable things—
With sorrow of labouring moons, and altering light
And travail of the planets of the night,
And weeping of the weary Pleiads seven,[1]
170 Feeds the mute melancholy lust of heaven?
Is not his incense bitterness, his meat
Murder? his hidden face and iron feet
Hath not man known, and felt them on their way
Threaten and trample all things and every day?
175 Hath he not sent us hunger? who hath cursed
Spirit and flesh with longing? filled with thirst
Their lips who cried unto him? who bade exceed
The fervid will, fall short the feeble deed,
Bade sink the spirit and the flesh aspire,
180 Pain animate the dust of dead desire,
And life yield up her flower to violent fate?
Him would I reach, him smite, him desecrate,
Pierce the cold lips of God with human breath,
And mix his immortality with death.
185 Why hath he made us? what had all we done
That we should live and loathe the sterile sun,
And with the moon wax paler as she wanes,
And pulse by pulse feel time grow through our
veins?

Thee too the years shall cover; thou shalt be
190 As the rose born of one same blood with thee,
As a song sung, as a word said, and fall
Flower-wise, and be not any more at all,
Nor any memory of thee anywhere;
For never Muse has bound above thine hair
195 The high Pierian flower[2] whose graft outgrows
All summer kinship of the mortal rose
And colour of deciduous days, nor shed
Reflex and flush of heaven about thine head,
Nor reddened brows made pale by floral grief
200 With splendid shadow from that lordlier leaf.
Yea, thou shalt be forgotten like spilt wine,
Except these kisses of my lips on thine
Brand them with immortality; but me—
Men shall not see bright fire nor hear the sea,
205 Nor mix their hearts with music, nor behold
Cast forth of heaven, with feet of awful gold
And plumeless wings that make the bright air blind,
Lightning, with thunder for a hound behind
Hunting through fields unfurrowed and unsown,
210 But in the light and laughter, in the moan
And music, and in grasp of lip and hand
And shudder of water that makes felt on land
The immeasurable tremor of all the sea,
Memories shall mix and metaphors of me.
215 Like me shall be the shuddering calm of night,
When all the winds of the world for pure delight
Close lips that quiver and fold up wings that ache;
When nightingales are louder for love's sake,
And leaves tremble like lute-strings or like fire;
220 Like me the one star swooning with desire
Even at the cold lips of the sleepless moon,
As I at thine; like me the waste white noon,
Burnt through with barren sunlight; and like me
The land-stream and the tide-stream in the sea.
225 I am sick with time as these with ebb and flow,
And by the yearning in my veins I know

---

[1] in Greek mythology, the seven daughters of Atlas and Pleione who were transformed into stars when Orion pursued them.

[2] Pieria was a region on the slopes of Mt. Olympus where the Muses lived and were worshipped.

The yearning sound of waters; and mine eyes
Burn as that beamless fire which fills the skies
With troubled stars and travailing things of flame;
230 And in my heart the grief consuming them
Labours, and in my veins the thirst of these,
And all the summer travail of the trees
And all the winter sickness; and the earth,
Filled full with deadly works of death and birth,
235 Sore spent with hungry lusts of birth and death,
Has pain like mine in her divided breath;
Her spring of leaves is barren, and her fruit
Ashes; her boughs are burdened, and her root
Fibrous and gnarled with poison; underneath
240 Serpents have gnawn it through with tortuous teeth
Made sharp upon the bones of all the dead,
And wild birds rend her branches overhead.
These, woven as raiment for his word and thought,
These hath God made, and me as these, and
        wrought
245 Song, and hath lit it at my lips; and me
Earth shall not gather though she feed on thee.
As a shed tear shalt thou be shed; but I—
Lo, earth may labour, men live long and die,
Years change and stars, and the high God devise
250 New things, and old things wane before his eyes
Who wields and wrecks them, being more strong
        than they—
But, having made me, me he shall not slay.
Nor slay nor satiate, like those herds of his
Who laugh and live a little, and their kiss
255 Contents them, and their loves are swift and sweet,
And sure death grasps and gains them with slow
        feet,
Love they or hate they, strive or bow their knees—
And all these ends he hath his will of these.
Yea, but albeit he slay me, hating me—
260 Albeit he hide me in the deep dear sea
And cover me with cool wan foam, and ease
This soul of mine as any soul of these,
And give me water and great sweet waves, and make
The very sea's name lordlier for my sake,

265 The whole sea sweeter—albeit I die indeed
And hide myself and sleep and no man heed,
Of me the high God hath not all his will.
Blossom of branches, and on each high hill
Clear air and wind, and under in clamorous vales
270 Fierce noises of the fiery nightingales,
Buds burning in the sudden spring like fire,
The wan washed sand and the waves' vain desire,
Sails seen like blown white flowers at sea, and words
That bring tears swiftest, and long notes of birds
275 Violently singing till the whole world sings—
I Sappho shall be one with all these things,
With all high things for ever; and my face
Seen once, my songs once heard in a strange place,
Cleave to men's lives, and waste the days thereof
280 With gladness and much sadness and long love.
Yea, they shall say, earth's womb has borne in vain
New things, and never this best thing again;
Borne days and men, borne fruits and wars and
        wine,
Seasons and songs, but no song more like mine.
285 And they shall know me as ye who have known me
        here,
Last year when I loved Atthis, and this year
When I love thee; and they shall praise me, and say
"She hath all time as all we have our day,
Shall she not live and have her will"—even I?
290 Yea, though thou diest, I say I shall not die.
For these shall give me of their souls, shall give
Life, and the days and loves wherewith I live,
Shall quicken me with loving, fill with breath,
Save me and serve me, strive for me with death.
295 Alas, that neither moon nor snow nor dew
Nor all cold things can purge me wholly through,
Assuage me nor allay me nor appease,
Till supreme sleep shall bring me bloodless ease;
Till time wax faint in all his periods;
300 Till fate undo the bondage of the gods,
And lay, to slake and satiate me all through,

Lotus[1] and Lethe[2] on my lips like dew,
And shed around and over and under me
Thick darkness and the insuperable sea.
—1866

Hymn to Proserpine [3]

(After the Proclamation in Rome
of the Christian Faith) [4]

Vicisti, Galilæe [5]

I have lived long enough, having seen one thing,
  that love hath an end;
Goddess and maiden and queen, be near me now
  and befriend.
Thou art more than the day or the morrow, the
  seasons that laugh or that weep;
For these give joy and sorrow; but thou,
  Proserpina, sleep.
5 Sweet is the treading of wine, and sweet the feet of
  the dove;
But a goodlier gift is thine than foam of the grapes
  or love.
Yea, is not even Apollo, with hair and harpstring of
  gold,
A bitter God to follow, a beautiful God to behold?
I am sick of singing: the bays burn deep and chafe:
  I am fain
10 To rest a little from praise and grievous pleasure
  and pain.
For the Gods we know not of, who give us our
  daily breath,

We know they are cruel as love or life, and lovely as
  death.
O Gods dethroned and deceased, cast forth, wiped
  out in a day!
From your wrath is the world released, redeemed
  from your chains, men say.
15 New Gods are crowned in the city; their flowers
  have broken your rods;
They are merciful, clothed with pity, the young
  compassionate Gods.
But for me their new device is barren, the days are
  bare;
Things long past over suffice, and men forgotten
  that were.
Time and the Gods are at strife; ye dwell in the
  midst thereof,
20 Draining a little life from the barren breasts of love.
I say to you, cease, take rest; yea, I say to you all, be
  at peace,
Till the bitter milk of her breast and the barren
  bosom shall cease.
Wilt thou yet take all, Galilean? but these thou
  shalt not take,
The laurel, the palms and the pæan, the breast of
  the nymphs in the brake;
25 Breasts more soft than a dove's that tremble with
  tenderer breath;
And all the wings of the Loves, and all the joy
  before death;
All the feet of the hours that sound as a single lyre,
Dropped and deep in the flowers, with strings that
  flicker like fire.
More than these wilt thou give, things fairer than
  all these things?
30 Nay, for a little we live, and life hath mutable
  wings.
A little while and we die; shall life not thrive as it
  may?
For no man under the sky lives twice, outliving his
  day.

---

[1] The lotus is said to induce forgetfulness.

[2] Lethe is the river of forgetfulness in Hades.

[3] the Roman counterpart of the Greek goddess Persephone, Queen of
the underworld.

[4] the Edict of Milan, passed by Constantine in 313 AD, which officially
recognized Christianity.

[5] "Thou hast conquered, Galilean": reported to be the dying words of
the Emperor Julian (331–63 AD), who had renounced Christianity
during his lifetime.

And grief is a grievous thing, and a man hath
    enough of his tears:
Why should he labour, and bring fresh grief to
    blacken his years?
35 Thou hast conquered, O pale Galilean; the world
    has grown grey from thy breath;
We have drunken of things Lethean, and fed on
    the fulness of death.
Laurel is green for a season, and love is sweet for a
    day;
But love grows bitter with treason, and laurel
    outlives not May.
Sleep, shall we sleep after all? for the world is not
    sweet in the end;
40 For the old faiths loosen and fall, the new years
    ruin and rend.
Fate is a sea without shore, and the soul is a rock
    that abides;
But her ears are vexed with the roar and her face
    with the foam of the tides.
O lips that the live blood faints in, the leavings of
    racks and rods!
O ghastly glories of saints, dead limbs of gibbeted
    Gods!
45 Though all men abase them before you in spirit,
    and all knees bend,
I kneel not neither adore you, but standing, look to
    the end.
All delicate days and pleasant, all spirits and
    sorrows are cast
Far out with the foam of the present that sweeps to
    the surf of the past:
Where beyond the extreme sea-wall, and between
    the remote sea-gates,
50 Waste water washes, and tall ships founder, and
    deep death waits:
Where, mighty with deepening sides, clad about
    with the seas as with wings,
And impelled of invisible tides, and fulfilled of
    unspeakable things,

White-eyed and poisonous-finned, shark-toothed
    and serpentine-curled,
Rolls, under the whitening wind of the future, the
    wave of the world.
55 The depths stand naked in sunder behind it, the
    storms flee away;
In the hollow before it the thunder is taken and
    snared as a prey;
In its sides is the north-wind bound; and its salt is
    of all men's tears;
With light of ruin, and sound of changes, and pulse
    of years:
With travail of day after day, and with trouble of
    hour upon hour;
60 And bitter as blood is the spray; and the crests are
    as fangs that devour:
And its vapour and storm of its steam as the
    sighing of spirits to be;
And its noise as the noise in a dream; and its depth
    as the roots of the sea:
And the height of its heads as the height of the
    utmost stars of the air:
And the ends of the earth at the might thereof
    tremble, and time is made bare.
65 Will ye bridle the deep sea with reins, will ye
    chasten the high sea with rods?
Will ye take her to chain her with chains, who is
    older than all ye Gods?[1]
All ye as a wind shall go by, as a fire shall ye pass
    and be past;
Ye are Gods, and behold, ye shall die, and the
    waves be upon you at last.
In the darkness of time, in the deeps of the years, in
    the changes of things,
70 Ye shall sleep as a slain man sleeps, and the world
    shall forget you for kings.
Though the feet of thine high priests tread where
    thy lords and our forefathers trod,

---

[1] Cf. Job 38–41.

Though these that were Gods are dead, and thou
    being dead art a God,
Though before thee the throned Cytherean[5] be
    fallen, and hidden her head,
Yet thy kingdom shall pass, Galilean, thy dead shall
    go down to thee dead.
75 Of the maiden thy mother men sing as a goddess
    with grace clad around;
Thou art throned where another was king; where
    another was queen she is crowned.
Yea, once we had sight of another: but now she is
    queen, say these.
Not as thine, not as thine was our mother, a
    blossom of flowering seas,
Clothed round with the world's desire as with
    raiment, and fair as the foam,
80 And fleeter than kindled fire, and a goddess, and
    mother of Rome.[6]
For thine came pale and a maiden, and sister to
    sorrow; but ours,
Her deep hair heavily laden with odour and colour
    of flowers,
White rose of the rose-white water, a silver
    splendour, a flame,
Bent down unto us that besought her, and earth
    grew sweet with her name.
85 For thine came weeping, a slave among slaves, and
    rejected; but she
Came flushed from the full-flushed wave, and
    imperial, her foot on the sea.
And the wonderful waters knew her, the winds and
    the viewless ways,
And the roses grew rosier, and bluer the sea-blue
    stream of the bays.
Ye are fallen, our lords, by what token? we wist that
    ye should not fall.
90 Ye were all so fair that are broken; and one more
    fair than ye all.

But I turn to her still, having seen she shall surely
    abide in the end;
Goddess and maiden and queen, be near me now
    and befriend.
O daughter of earth, of my mother, her crown and
    blossom of birth,
I am also, I also, thy brother; I go as I came unto
    earth.
95 In the night where thine eyes are as moons are in
    heaven, the night where thou art,
Where the silence is more than all tunes, where
    sleep overflows from the heart,
Where the poppies[7] are sweet as the rose in our
    world, and the red rose is white,
And the wind falls faint as it blows with the fume
    of the flowers of the night.
And the murmur of spirits that sleep in the shadow
    of Gods from afar
100 Grows dim in thine ears and deep as the deep dim
    soul of a star,
In the sweet low light of thy face, under heavens
    untrod by the sun,
Let my soul with their souls find place, and forget
    what is done and undone.
Thou art more than the Gods who number the
    days of our temporal breath;
For these give labour and slumber; but thou,
    Proserpina, death.
105 Therefore now at thy feet I abide for a season in
    silence. I know
I shall die as my fathers died, and sleep as they
    sleep; even so.
For the glass of the years is brittle wherein we gaze
    for a span;
A little soul for a little bears up this corpse which is
    man.
So long I endure, no longer; and laugh not again,
    neither weep.

---

[5] Aphrodite, who came ashore at Cythera after her birth in the sea.

[6] Aeneas, the founder of Rome, was protected by his mother Venus.

---

[7] the flowers of sleep and oblivion, traditionally associated with Proserpine.

110 For there is no God found stronger than death; and
　　death is a sleep.

—1866

The Leper [1]

Nothing is better, I well think,
　　Than love; the hidden well-water
Is not so delicate to drink:
　　This was well seen of me and her.

5 I served her in a royal house;
　　I served her wine and curious meat.
For will to kiss between her brows,
　　I had no heart to sleep or eat.

Mere scorn God knows she had of me,
10 　　A poor scribe, nowise great or fair,
Who plucked his clerk's hood back to see
　　Her curled-up lips and amorous hair.

I vex my head with thinking this.
　　Yea, though God always hated me,
15 And hates me now that I can kiss
　　Her eyes, plait up her hair to see

How she then wore it on the brows,
　　Yet am I glad to have her dead
Here in this wretched wattled house
20 　　Where I can kiss her eyes and head.

Nothing is better, I well know,
　　Than love; no amber in cold sea
Or gathered berries under snow:
　　That is well seen of her and me.

25 Three thoughts I make my pleasure of:
　　First I take heart and think of this:
That knight's gold hair she chose to love,
　　His mouth she had such will to kiss.

Then I remember that sundawn
30 　　I brought him by a privy way
Out at her lattice, and thereon
　　What gracious words she found to say.

(Cold rushes for such little feet—
　　Both feet could lie into my hand.
35 A marvel was it of my sweet
　　Her upright body could so stand.)

"Sweet friend, God give you thank and grace;
　　Now am I clean and whole of shame,
Nor shall men burn me in the face
40 　　For my sweet fault that scandals them."

I tell you over word by word.
　　She, sitting edgewise on her bed,
Holding her feet, said thus. The third,
　　A sweeter thing than these, I said.

---

[1] Swinburne appended a fraudulent note, purporting to be from the
Grandes Chroniques de France (1505) but actually in his own approx-
imation of sixteenth-century French, to *The Leper*; it translates as follows:
"In those days the country was full of unclean persons and lepers. This
caused the King great dismay, seeing that God must be greatly offended.
Now it came to pass that a noble woman, Yolande de Sallières by name,
was afflicted and sorely wasted by this ugly disease; all her friends and
relations having before their very eyes the anger of God thrust her forth
from their homes, resolving never to shelter or succour a body cursed by
God and an abomination to all men. In former days, this lady had been
a beauty most pleasing to behold, generous with her body and of easy
virtue. However, none of those lovers who had frequently embraced and
tenderly kissed her wanted now to shelter so hideous a woman and so
detestable a sinner. A clerk who had once served her in the office of
lackey and go-between in matters venereal took her in and hid her in a
little hut. There the poor woman died a cruel and wretched death; and
after her died the said clerk who had cared for her out of true love for six
months, washing her, clothing her, and unclothing her every day with his
own hands. They even say that the naughty man, the cursed clerk,
remembering the great former loveliness of this ruined beauty pleasured
himself aplenty in kissing her on her dreadful, leprous lips and pressing
her gently to him with lover's hands. Wherefore, he died of the same
awful disease. This took place in Gastinois near Fontainebellant. And
when King Philippe heard of this happening he was greatly amazed by
it" (trans. Robin F. Jones).

45 God, that makes time and ruins it
    And alters not, abiding God,
Changed with disease her body sweet,
    The body of love wherein she abode.

Love is more sweet and comelier
50   Than a dove's throat strained out to sing.
All they spat out and cursed at her
    And cast her forth for a base thing.

They cursed her, seeing how God had wrought
    This curse to plague her, a curse of his.
55 Fools were they surely, seeing not
    How sweeter than all sweet she is.

He that had held her by the hair,
    With kissing lips blinding her eyes,
Felt her bright bosom, strained and bare,
60   Sigh under him, with short mad cries

Out of her throat and sobbing mouth
    And body broken up with love,
With sweet hot tears his lips were loth
    Her own should taste the savour of,

65 Yea, he inside whose grasp all night
    Her fervent body leapt or lay,
Stained with sharp kisses red and white,
    Found her a plague to spurn away.

I hid her in this wattled house,
70   I served her water and poor bread.
For joy to kiss between her brows
    Time upon time I was nigh dead.

Bread failed; we got but well-water
    And gathered grass with dropping seed;
75 I had such joy of kissing her,
    I had small care to sleep or feed.

Sometimes when service made me glad
    The sharp tears leapt between my lids,

Falling on her, such joy I had
80   To do the service God forbids.

"I pray you let me be at peace,
    Get hence, make room for me to die."
She said that: her poor lip would cease,
    Put up to mine, and turn to cry.

85 I said, "Bethink yourself how love
    Fared in us twain, what either did;
Shall I unclothe my soul thereof?
    That I should do this, God forbid."

Yea, though God hateth us, he knows
90   That hardly in a little thing
Love faileth of the work it does
    Till it grow ripe for gathering.

Six months, and now my sweet is dead
    A trouble takes me; I know not
95 If all were done well, all well said,
    No word or tender deed forgot.

Too sweet, for the least part in her,
    To have shed life out by fragments; yet,
Could the close mouth catch breath and stir,
100   I might see something I forget.

Six months, and I sit still and hold
    In two cold palms her cold two feet.
Her hair, half grey half ruined gold,
    Thrills me and burns me in kissing it.

105 Love bites and stings me through, to see
    Her keen face made of sunken bones.
Her worn-off eyelids madden me,
    That were shot through with purple once.

She said, "Be good with me; I grow
110   So tired for shame's sake, I shall die

If you say nothing": even so.
    And she is dead now, and shame put by.

Yea, and the scorn she had of me
    In the old time, doubtless vexed her then.
115 I never should have kissed her. See
    What fools God's anger makes of men!

She might have loved me a little too,
    Had I been humbler for her sake.
But that new shame could make love new
120   She saw not—yet her shame did make.

I took too much upon my love,
    Having for such mean service done
Her beauty and all the ways thereof,
    Her face and all the sweet thereon.

125 Yea, all this while I tended her,
    I know the old love held fast his part,
I know the old scorn waxed heavier,
    Mixed with sad wonder, in her heart.

It may be all my love went wrong—
130   A scribe's work writ awry and blurred,
Scrawled after the blind evensong—
    Spoilt music with no perfect word.

But surely I would fain have done
    All things the best I could. Perchance
135 Because I failed, came short of one,
    She kept at heart that other man's.

I am grown blind with all these things:
    It may be now she hath in sight
Some better knowledge; still there clings
140   The old question. Will not God do right?
—1866

Dolores [1]

(Notre-Dame des Sept Douleurs) [2]

Cold eyelids that hide like a jewel
    Hard eyes that grow soft for an hour;
The heavy white limbs, and the cruel
    Red mouth like a venomous flower;
5 When these are gone by with their glories,
    What shall rest of thee then, what remain,
O mystic and sombre Dolores,
    Our Lady of Pain?

Seven sorrows the priests give their Virgin;
10   But thy sins, which are seventy times seven,
Seven ages would fail thee to purge in,
    And then they would haunt thee in heaven:
Fierce midnights and famishing morrows,
    And the loves that complete and control
15 All the joys of the flesh, all the sorrows
    That wear out the soul.

O garment not golden but gilded,[3]
    O garden where all men may dwell,
O tower not of ivory, but builded
20   By hands that reach heaven from hell;
O mystical rose of the mire,
    O house not of gold but of gain,
O house of unquenchable fire,
    Our Lady of Pain!

25 O lips full of lust and of laughter,
    Curled snakes that are fed from my breast,
Bite hard, lest remembrance come after
    And press with new lips where you pressed.
For my heart too springs up at the pressure,
30   Mine eyelids too moisten and burn;

---

[1] from the Latin *dolor*, meaning pain.

[2] Our Lady of the Seven Sorrows.

[3] Cf. the Litany of the Blessed Virgin and the Song of Solomon 7:4.

Ah, feed me and fill me with pleasure,
    Ere pain come in turn.

In yesterday's reach and to-morrow's,
    Out of sight though they lie of to-day,
35 There have been and there yet shall be sorrows
    That smite not and bite not in play.
The life and the love thou despisest,
    These hurt us indeed, and in vain,
O wise among women, and wisest,
40   Our Lady of Pain.

Who gave thee thy wisdom? what stories
    That stung thee, what visions that smote?
Wert thou pure and a maiden, Dolores,
    When desire took thee first by the throat?
45 What bud was the shell of a blossom
    That all men may smell to and pluck?
What milk fed thee first at what bosom?
    What sins gave thee suck?

We shift and bedeck and bedrape us,
50   Thou art noble and nude and antique;
Libitina[1] thy mother, Priapus
    Thy father, a Tuscan and Greek.
We play with light loves in the portal,
    And wince and relent and refrain;
55 Loves die and we know thee immortal,
    Our Lady of Pain.

Fruits fail and love dies and time ranges;
    Thou art fed with perpetual breath,
And alive after infinite changes,
60   And fresh from the kisses of death;
Of languors rekindled and rallied,
    Of barren delights and unclean,
Things monstrous and fruitless, a pallid
    And poisonous queen.

---

[1] Roman goddess of gardens, sexual pleasure, fertility and death—the female Roman equivalent to the Greek god Priapus.

65 Could you hurt me, sweet lips, though I hurt you?
    Men touch them, and change in a trice
The lilies and languors of virtue
    For the raptures and roses of vice;
Those lie where thy foot on the floor is,
70   These crown and caress thee and chain,
O splendid and sterile Dolores,
    Our Lady of Pain.

There are sins it may be to discover,
    There are deeds it may be to delight.
75 What new work wilt thou find for thy lover,
    What new passions for daytime or night?
What spells that they know not a word of
    Whose lives are as leaves overblown?
What tortures undreamt of, unheard of,
80   Unwritten, unknown?

Ah beautiful passionate body
    That never has ached with a heart!
On thy mouth though the kisses are bloody,
    Though they sting till it shudder and smart,
85 More kind than the love we adore is,
    They hurt not the heart or the brain
O bitter and tender Dolores,
    Our Lady of Pain.

As our kisses relax and redouble,
90   From the lips and the foam and the fangs
Shall no new sin be born for men's trouble,
    No dream of impossible pangs?
With the sweet of the sins of old ages
    Wilt thou satiate thy soul as of yore?
95 Too sweet is the rind, say the sages,
    Too bitter the core.

Hast thou told all thy secrets the last time,
    And bared all thy beauties to one?
Ah, where shall we go then for pastime,
100   If the worst that can be has been done?
But sweet as the rind was the core is;

We are fain of thee still, we are fain,
  O sanguine and subtle Dolores,
    Our Lady of Pain.

105 By the hunger of change and emotion,
  By the thirst of unbearable things,
By despair, the twin-born of devotion,
  By the pleasure that winces and stings,
The delight that consumes the desire,
110   The desire that outruns the delight,
By the cruelty deaf as a fire
    And blind as the night,

By the ravenous teeth that have smitten
  Through the kisses that blossom and bud,
115 By the lips intertwisted and bitten
  Till the foam has a savour of blood,
By the pulse as it rises and falters,
  By the hands as they slacken and strain,
I adjure thee, respond from thine altars,
120   Our Lady of Pain.

Wilt thou smile as a woman disdaining
  The light fire in the veins of a boy?
But he comes to thee sad, without feigning,
  Who has wearied of sorrow and joy;
125 Less careful of labour and glory
  Than the elders whose hair has uncurled;
And young, but with fancies as hoary
    And grey as the world.

I have passed from the outermost portal
130   To the shrine where a sin is a prayer;
What care though the service be mortal?
  O our lady of Torture, what care?
All thine the last wine that I pour is,
  The last in the chalice we drain,
135 O fierce and luxurious Dolores,
    Our Lady of Pain.

All thine the new wine of desire,
  The fruit of four lips as they clung
Till the hair and the eyelids took fire,
140   The foam of a serpentine tongue,
The froth of the serpents of pleasure,
  More salt than the foam of the sea,
Now felt as a flame, now at leisure
    As wine shed for me.

145 Ah thy people, thy children, thy chosen,
  Marked cross from the womb and perverse,
They have found out the secret to cozen
  The gods that constrain us and curse;
They alone, they are wise, and none other;
150   Give me place, even me, in their train,
O my sister, my spouse, and my mother,
    Our Lady of Pain.

For the crown of our life as it closes
  Is darkness, the fruit thereof dust;
155 No thorns go as deep as a rose's,
  And love is more cruel than lust.
Time turns the old days to derision,
  Our loves into corpses or wives;
And marriage and death and division
160   Make barren our lives.

And pale from the past we draw nigh thee,
  And satiate with comfortless hours;
And we know thee, how all men belie thee,
  And we gather the fruit of thy flowers;
165 The passion that slays and recovers,
  The pangs and the kisses that rain
On the lips and the limbs of thy lovers,
    Our Lady of Pain.

The desire of thy furious embraces
170   Is more than the wisdom of years,
On the blossom though blood lie in traces,
  Though the foliage be sodden with tears.
For the lords in whose keeping the door is

That opens on all who draw breath
175　Gave the cypress to love, my Dolores,
　　　The myrtle to death.

And they laughed, changing hands in the measure,
　　　And they mixed and made peace after strife;
Pain melted in tears, and was pleasure;
180　　Death tingled with blood, and was life.
Like lovers they melted and tingled,
　　　In the dusk of thine innermost fane;
In the darkness they murmured and mingled,
　　　Our Lady of Pain.

185　In a twilight where virtues are vices,
　　　In thy chapels, unknown of the sun,
To a tune that enthralls and entices,
　　　They were wed, and the twain were as one.
For the tune from thine altar hath sounded
190　　Since God bade the world's work begin,
And the fume of thine incense abounded,
　　　To sweeten the sin.

Love listens, and paler than ashes,
　　　Through his curls as the crown on them slips
195　Lifts languid wet eyelids and lashes,
　　　And laughs with insatiable lips.
Thou shalt hush him with heavy caresses,
　　　With music that scares the profane;
Thou shalt darken his eyes with thy tresses,
200　　Our Lady of Pain.

Thou shalt blind his bright eyes though he wrestle,
　　　Thou shalt chain his light limbs though he strive;
In his lips all thy serpents shall nestle,
　　　In his hands all thy cruelties thrive.
205　In the daytime thy voice shall go through him,
　　　In his dreams he shall feel thee and ache;
Thou shalt kindle by night and subdue him
　　　Asleep and awake.

Thou shalt touch and make redder his roses
210　　With juice not of fruit nor of bud;
When the sense in the spirit reposes,
　　　Thou shalt quicken the soul though the blood.
Thine, thine the one grace we implore is,
　　　Who would live and not languish or feign,
215　O sleepless and deadly Dolores,
　　　Our Lady of Pain.

Dost thou dream, in a respite of slumber,
　　　In a lull of the fires of thy life,
Of the days without name, without number,
220　　When thy will stung the world into strife;
When, a goddess, the pulse of thy passion
　　　Smote kings as they revelled in Rome;
And they hailed thee re-risen, O Thalassian,[1]
　　　Foam-white, from the foam?

225　When thy lips had such lovers to flatter,
　　　When the city lay red from thy rods,
And thine hands were as arrows to scatter
　　　The children of change and their gods;
When the blood of thy foemen made fervent
230　　A sand never moist from the main,
As one smote them, their lord and thy servant,
　　　Our Lady of Pain.

On sands by the storm never shaken,
　　　Nor wet from the washing of tides;
235　Nor by foam of the waves overtaken,
　　　Nor winds that the thunder bestrides;
But red from the print of thy paces,
　　　Made smooth for the world and its lords,
Ringed round with a flame of fair faces,
240　　And splendid with swords.

There the gladiator, pale for thy pleasure,
　　　Drew bitter and perilous breath;
There torments laid hold on the treasure

---

[1] an epithet applied to Venus, meaning "born from the sea."

Of limbs too delicious for death;
245 When thy gardens were lit with live torches;
When the world was a steed for thy rein;
When the nations lay prone in thy porches,
Our Lady of Pain.

When, with flame all around him aspirant,
250 Stood flushed, as a harp-player stands,
The implacable beautiful tyrant,[1]
Rose-crowned, having death in his hands;
And a sound as the sound of loud water
Smote far through the flight of the fires,
255 And mixed with the lightning of slaughter
A thunder of lyres.

Dost thou dream of what was and no more is,
The old kingdoms of earth and the kings?
Dost thou hunger for these things, Dolores,
260 For these, in a world of new things?
But thy bosom no fasts could emaciate,
No hunger compel to complain
Those lips that no bloodshed could satiate,
Our Lady of Pain.

265 As of old when the world's heart was lighter,
Through thy garments the grace of thee glows,
The white wealth of thy body made whiter
By the blushes of amorous blows,
And seamed with sharp lips and fierce fingers,
270 And branded by kisses that bruise;
When all shall be gone that now lingers,
Ah, what shall we lose?

Thou wert fair in the fearless old fashion,
And thy limbs are as melodies yet,
275 And move to the music of passion
With lithe and lascivious regret.
What ailed us, O gods, to desert you

For creeds that refuse and restrain?
Come down and redeem us from virtue,
280 Our Lady of Pain.

All shrines that were Vestal[2] are flameless;
But the flame has not fallen from this;
Though obscure be the god, and though nameless
The eyes and the hair that we kiss;
285 Low fires that love sits by and forges
Fresh heads for his arrows and thine;
Hair loosened and soiled in mid orgies
With kisses and wine.

Thy skin changes country and colour,
290 And shrivels or swells to a snake's.
Let it brighten and bloat and grow duller,
We know it, the flames and the flakes,
Red brands on it smitten and bitten,
Round skies where a star is a stain,
295 And the leaves with thy litanies written,
Our Lady of Pain.

On thy bosom though many a kiss be,
There are none such as knew it of old.
Was it Alciphron[3] once or Arisbe,[4]
300 Male ringlets or feminine gold,
That thy lips met with under the statue,
Whence a look shot out sharp after thieves
From the eyes of the garden-god[5] at you
Across the fig-leaves?

305 Then still, through dry seasons and moister,
One god had a wreath to his shrine;

---

[1] the Emperor Nero, who is said to have illuminated his gardens with the bodies of burning Christians.

[2] the Virgin priestesses of Vesta, the Greek and Roman goddess of the hearth and home.

[3] the author of letters supposedly written by famous courtesans.

[4] a wife of King Priam of Troy.

[5] Priapus.

Then love was a pearl of his oyster,[1]
    And Venus rose red out of wine.
We have all done amiss, choosing rather
310   Such loves as the wise gods disdain;
Intercede for us thou with thy father,
    Our Lady of Pain.

In spring he had crowns of his garden,
    Red corn in the heat of the year,
315 Then hoary green olives that harden
    When the grape-blossom freezes with fear;
And milk-budded myrtles with Venus
    And vine-leaves with Bacchus he trod;
And ye said, "We have seen, he hath seen us,
320   A visible God."

What broke off the garlands that girt you?
    What sundered you spirit and clay?
Weak sins yet alive are as virtue
    To the strength of the sins of that day.
325 For dried is the blood of thy lover,
    Ipsithilla,[2] contracted the vein;
Cry aloud, "Will he rise and recover,
    Our Lady of Pain?"

Cry aloud; for the old world is broken:
330   Cry out; for the Phrygian[3] is priest,
And rears not the bountiful token
    And spreads not the fatherly feast.
From the midmost of Ida,[4] from shady
    Recesses that murmur at morn,
335 They have brought and baptized her, Our Lady,
    A goddess new-born.

---

[1] "*Nam te præcipuè in suis urbibus colit ora Hellespontia, cæteris ostreosior oris.*—CATULL. *Carm.* xviii." (Swinburne's note.) "For the Hellespont shore especially worships you in its cities being oysterier than the other coasts."

[2] a lover mentioned by Catullus in *Carmina* 32.

[3] Cybele, the goddess of nature and generation, was worshipped at Phrygia.

[4] a high mountain near Mt. Olympus (and the scene of the judgement of Paris).

And the chaplets of old are above us,
    And the oyster-bed teems out of reach;
Old poets outsing and outlove us,
340   And Catullus makes mouths at our speech.
Who shall kiss, in thy father's own city,
    With such lips as he sang with, again?
Intercede for us all of thy pity,
    Our Lady of Pain.

345 Out of Dindymus[5] heavily laden
    Her lions draw bound and unfed
A mother, a mortal, a maiden,
    A queen over death and the dead.
She is cold, and her habit is lowly,
350   Her temple of branches and sods;
Most fruitful and virginal, holy,
    A mother of gods.

She hath wasted with fire thine high places,
    She hath hidden and marred and made sad
355 The fair limbs of the Loves, the fair faces
    Of gods that were goodly and glad.
She slays, and her hands are not bloody;
    She moves as a moon in the wane,
White-robed, and thy raiment is ruddy,
360   Our Lady of Pain.

They shall pass and their places be taken,
    The gods and the priests that are pure.
They shall pass, and shalt thou not be shaken?
    They shall perish, and shalt thou endure?
365 Death laughs, breathing close and relentless
    In the nostrils and eyelids of lust,
With a pinch in his fingers of scentless
    And delicate dust.

But the worm shall revive thee with kisses;
370   Thou shalt change and transmute as a god,

---

[5] Mt. Dindymus was the centre of worship of Cybele. Her chariot was drawn by lions.

As the rod to a serpent that hisses,
　　As the serpent again to a rod.
Thy life shall not cease though thou doff it;
　　Thou shalt live until evil be slain,
375 And good shall die first, said thy prophet,
　　Our Lady of Pain.

Did he lie? did he laugh? does he know it,
　　Now he lies out of reach, out of breath,
Thy prophet, thy preacher, thy poet,
380　　Sin's child by incestuous Death?
Did he find out in fire at his waking,
　　Or discern as his eyelids lost light,
When the bands of the body were breaking
　　And all came in sight?

385 Who has known all the evil before us,
　　Or the tyrannous secrets of time?
Though we match not the dead men that bore us
　　At a song, at a kiss, at a crime—
Though the heathen outface and outlive us,
390　　And our lives and our longings are twain—
Ah, forgive us our virtues, forgive us,
　　Our Lady of Pain.

Who are we that embalm and embrace thee
　　With spices and savours of song?
395 What is time, and his children should face thee?
　　What am I, that my lips do thee wrong?
I could hurt thee—but pain would delight thee;
　　Or caress thee—but love would repel;
And the lovers whose lips would excite thee
400　　Are serpents in hell.

Who now shall content thee as they did,
　　Thy lovers, when temples were built
And the hair of the sacrifice braided
　　And the blood of the sacrifice spilt,
405 In Lampsacus[1] fervent with faces,

In Aphaca[2] red from thy reign,
　　Who embraced thee with awful embraces,
　　　Our Lady of Pain?

Where are they, Cotytto[3] or Venus,
410　　Astarte or Ashtaroth,[4] where?
Do their hands as we touch come between us?
　　Is the breath of them hot in thy hair?
From their lips have thy lips taken fever,
　　With the blood of their bodies grown red?
415 Hast thou left upon earth a believer
　　If these men are dead?

They were purple of raiment and golden,
　　Filled full of thee, fiery with wine,
Thy lovers, in haunts unbeholden,
420　　In marvellous chambers of thine.
They are fled, and their footprints escape us,
　　Who appraise thee, adore, and abstain,
O daughter of Death and Priapus,
　　Our Lady of Pain.

425 What ails us to fear overmeasure,
　　To praise thee with timorous breath,
O mistress and mother of pleasure,
　　The one thing as certain as death?
We shall change as the things that we cherish,
430　　Shall fade as they faded before,
As foam upon water shall perish,
　　As sand upon shore.

We shall know what the darkness discovers
　　If the grave-pit be shallow or deep;
435 And our fathers of old, and our lovers,
　　We shall know if they sleep not or sleep.
We shall see whether hell be not heaven,

1　centre of worship of Priapus.

2　centre of worship of Venus.

3　a Thracian goddess, worshipped with sexual orgies.

4　two versions of the same name; a middle-Eastern counterpart to Venus.

Find out whether tares be not grain,
And the joys of thee seventy times seven,
440   Our Lady of Pain.
—1866

The Garden of Proserpine [1]

Here, where the world is quiet;
    Here, where all trouble seems
Dead winds' and spent waves' riot
    In doubtful dreams of dreams;
5 I watch the green field growing
For reaping folk and sowing,
For harvest-time and mowing,
    A sleepy world of streams.

I am tired of tears and laughter,
10   And men that laugh and weep;
Of what may come hereafter
    For men that sow to reap:
I am weary of days and hours,
Blown buds of barren flowers,
15 Desires and dreams and powers
    And everything but sleep.

Here life has death for neighbour,
    And far from eye or ear
Wan waves and wet winds labour,
20   Weak ships and spirits steer;
They drive adrift, and whither
They wot not who make thither;
But no such winds blow hither,
    And no such things grow here.

25 No growth of moor or coppice,
    No heather-flower or vine,
But bloomless buds of poppies,
    Green grapes of Proserpine,

Pale beds of blowing rushes
30 Where no leaf blooms or blushes
Save this whereout she crushes
    For dead men deadly wine.

Pale, without name or number,
    In fruitless fields of corn,
35 They bow themselves and slumber
    All night till light is born;
And like a soul belated,
In hell and heaven unmated,
By cloud and mist abated
40   Comes out of darkness morn.

Though one were strong as seven,
    He too with death shall dwell,
Nor wake with wings in heaven,
    Nor weep for pains in hell;
45 Though one were fair as roses,
His beauty clouds and closes;
And well though love reposes,
    In the end it is not well.

Pale, beyond porch and portal,
50   Crowned with calm leaves, she stands
Who gathers all things mortal
    With cold immortal hands;
Her languid lips are sweeter
Than love's who fears to greet her
55 To men that mix and meet her
    From many times and lands.

She waits for each and other,
    She waits for all men born;
Forgets the earth her mother,
60   The life of fruits and corn;
And spring and seed and swallow
Take wing for her and follow
Where summer song rings hollow
    And flowers are put to scorn.

---

1. The garden is the underworld, ruled by Proserpine, daughter of Ceres (or Demeter) the Earth Mother.

65 There go the loves that wither,
      The old loves with wearier wings;
   And all dead years draw thither,
      And all disastrous things;
   Dead dreams of days forsaken,
70 Blind buds that snows have shaken,
   Wild leaves that winds have taken,
      Red strays of ruined springs.

   We are not sure of sorrow,
      And joy was never sure;
75 To-day will die to-morrow;
      Time stoops to no man's lure;
   And love, grown faint and fretful,
   With lips but half regretful
   Sighs, and with eyes forgetful
80   Weeps that no loves endure.

   From too much love of living,
      From hope and fear set free,
   We thank with brief thanksgiving
      Whatever gods may be
85 That no life lives for ever;
   That dead men rise up never;
   That even the weariest river
      Winds somewhere safe to sea.

   Then star nor sun shall waken,
90   Nor any change of light:
   Nor sound of waters shaken,
      Nor any sound or sight:
   Nor wintry leaves or vernal,
   Nor days nor things diurnal;
95 Only the sleep eternal
      In an eternal night.
   —1866

Hertha [1]

I am that which began;
   Out of me the years roll;
Out of me God and man;
   I am equal and whole;
5 God changes, and man, and the form of them
   bodily; I am the soul.

   Before ever land was,
      Before ever the sea,
   Or soft hair of the grass,
      Or fair limbs of the tree,
10 Or the flesh-coloured fruit of my branches, I was,
   and thy soul was in me.

   First life on my sources
      First drifted and swam;
   Out of me are the forces
      That save it or damn;
15 Out of me man and woman, and wild-beast and
   bird; before God was, I am. [2]

   Beside or above me
      Nought is there to go;
   Love or unlove me,
      Unknow me or know,
20 I am that which unloves me and loves; I am
   stricken, and I am the blow.

   I the mark that is missed
      And the arrows that miss,
   I the mouth that is kissed
      And the breath in the kiss,
25 The search, and the sought, and the seeker, the soul
   and the body that is.

---

[1] The speaker of this poem is the ancient Germanic goddess of the earth, fertility and growth, whom Swinburne here regards as the source of all creation.

[2] Cf. Exodus 3:14 and John 8:58.

I am that thing which blesses
  My spirit elate;
That which caresses
  With hands uncreate
30 My limbs unbegotten that measure the length of
  the measure of fate.

But what thing dost thou now,
  Looking Godward, to cry
"I am I, thou art thou,
  I am low, thou art high"?
35 I am thou, whom thou seekest to find him; find
  thou but thyself, thou art I.

I the grain and the furrow,
  The plough-cloven clod
And the ploughshare drawn thorough,
  The germ and the sod,
40 The deed and the doer, the seed and the sower, the
  dust which is God.

Hast thou known how I fashioned thee,
  Child, underground?
Fire that impassioned thee,
  Iron that bound,
45 Dim changes of water, what thing of all these hast
  thou known of or found?

Canst thou say in thine heart
  Thou hast seen with thine eyes
With what cunning of art
  Thou wast wrought in what wise,
50 But what force of what stuff thou wast shapen, and
  shown on my breast to the skies?

Who hath given, who hath sold it thee,
  Knowledge of me?
Hath the wilderness told it thee?
  Hast thou learnt of the sea?
55 Hast thou communed in spirit with night? have the
  winds taken counsel with thee?

Have I set such a star
  To show light on thy brow
That thou sawest from afar
  What I show to thee now?
60 Have ye spoken as brethren together, the sun and
  the mountains and thou?

What is here, dost thou know it?
  What was, hast thou known?
Prophet nor poet
  Nor tripod[1] nor throne
65 Nor spirit nor flesh can make answer, but only thy
  mother alone.

Mother, not maker,
  Born, and not made;
Though her children forsake her,
  Allured or afraid,
70 Praying prayers to the God of their fashion, she
  stirs not for all that have prayed.

A creed is a rod,
  And a crown is of night;
But this thing is God,
  To be man with thy might,
75 To grow straight in the strength of thy spirit, and
  live out thy life as the light.

I am in thee to save thee,
  As my soul in thee saith;
Give thou as I gave thee,
  Thy life-blood and breath,
80 Green leaves of thy labour, white flowers of thy
  thought, and red fruit of thy death.

Be the ways of thy giving
  As mine were to thee;
The free life of thy living,

---

[1] The tripod was the three-legged altar on which the oracular priestesses of Apollo at Delphi sat.

Be the gift of it free;
85 Not as servant to lord, nor as master to slave, shalt
thou give thee to me.

O children of banishment,
Souls overcast,
Were the lights ye see vanish meant
Always to last,
90 Ye would know not the sun overshining the
shadows and stars overpast.

I that saw where ye trod
The dim paths of the night
Set the shadow called God
In your skies to give light;
95 But the morning of manhood is risen, and the
shadowless soul is in sight.

The tree many-rooted[1]
That swells to the sky
With frondage red-fruited,
The life-tree am I;
100 In the buds of your lives is the sap of my leaves: ye
shall live and not die.

But the Gods of your fashion
That take and that give,
In their pity and passion
That scourge and forgive,
105 They are worms that are bred in the bark that falls
off; they shall die and not live.

My own blood is what stanches
The wounds in my bark;
Stars caught in my branches
Make day of the dark,
110 And are worshipped as suns till the sunrise shall
tread out their fires as a spark.

---

[1] in Norse mythology, the tree Yggdrasil.

Where dead ages hide under
The live roots of the tree,
In my darkness the thunder
Makes utterance of me;
115 In the clash of my boughs with each other ye hear
the waves sound of the sea.

That noise is of Time,
As his feathers are spread
And his feet set to climb
Through the boughs overhead,
120 And my foliage rings round him and rustles, and
branches are bent with his tread.

The storm-winds of ages
Blow through me and cease,
The war-wind that rages,
The spring-wind of peace,
125 Ere the breath of them roughen my tresses, ere one
of my blossoms increase.

All sounds of all changes,
All shadows and lights
On the world's mountain-ranges
And stream-riven heights,
130 Whose tongue is the wind's tongue and language of
storm-clouds on earth-shaking nights;

All forms of all faces,
All works of all hands
In unsearchable places
Of time-stricken lands,
135 All death and all life, and all reigns and all ruins,
drop through me as sands.

Though sore be my burden
And more than ye know,
And my growth have no guerdon
But only to grow,
140 Yet I fail not of growing for lightnings above me or
deathworms below.

These too have their part in me,
As I too in these;
Such fire is at heart in me,
Such sap is this tree's,
145 Which hath in it all sounds and all secrets of
infinite lands and of seas.

In the spring-coloured hours
When my mind was as May's,
There brake forth of me flowers
By centuries of days,
150 Strong blossoms with perfume of manhood, shot
out from my spirit as rays.

And the sound of them springing
And smell of their shoots
Were as warmth and sweet singing
And strength to my roots;
155 And the lives of my children made perfect with
freedom of soul were my fruits.

I bid you but be;
I have need not of prayer;
I have need of you free
As your mouths of mine air;
160 That my heart may be greater within me,
beholding the fruits of me fair.

More fair than strange fruit is
Of faiths ye espouse;
In me only the root is
That blooms in your boughs;
165 Behold now your God that ye made you, to feed
him with faith of your vows.

In the darkening and whitening
Abysses adored,
With dayspring and lightning
For lamp and for sword,
170 God thunders in heaven, and his angels are red
with the wrath of the Lord.

O my sons, O too dutiful
Toward Gods not of me,
Was not I enough beautiful?
Was it hard to be free?
175 For behold, I am with you, am in you and of you;
look forth now and see.

Lo, winged with world's wonders,
With miracles shod,
With the fires of his thunders
For raiment and rod,
180 God trembles in heaven, and his angels are white
with the terror of God.

For his twilight is come on him,[1]
His anguish is here;
And his spirits gaze dumb on him,
Grown grey from his fear;
185 And his hour taketh hold of him stricken, the last
of his infinite year.

Thought made him and breaks him,
Truth slays and forgives;
But to you, as time takes him,
This new thing it gives,
190 Even love, the beloved Republic, that feeds upon
freedom and lives.

For truth only is living,
Truth only is whole,
And the love of his giving
Man's polestar and pole;
195 Man, pulse of my centre, and fruit of my body, and
seed of my soul.

One birth of my bosom;
One beam of mine eye;
One topmost blossom

---

[1] in Norse mythology, the period of Ragnarok or universal destruction, after which a new world will emerge.

That scales the sky;
200 Man, equal and one with me, man that is made of
    me, man that is I.
    —1871

A Forsaken Garden

In a coign of the cliff between lowland and
    highland,
    At the sea-down's edge between windward and
      lee,
Walled round with rocks as an inland island,
    The ghost of a garden fronts the sea.
5 A girdle of brushwood and thorn encloses
    The steep square slope of the blossomless bed
Where the weeds that grew green from the graves
    of its roses
      Now lie dead.

The fields fall southward, abrupt and broken,
10   To the low last edge of the long lone land.
If a step should sound or a word be spoken,
    Would a ghost not rise at the strange guest's
      hand?
So long have the grey bare walks lain guestless,
    Through branches and briars if a man make way,
15 He shall find no life but the sea-wind's, restless
      Night and day.

The dense hard passage is blind and stifled
    That crawls by a track none turn to climb
To the strait waste place that the years have rifled
20   Of all but the thorns that are touched not of time.
The thorns he spares when the rose is taken;
    The rocks are left when he wastes the plain.
The wind that wanders, the weeds wind-shaken,
      These remain.

25 Not a flower to be pressed of the foot that falls not;
    As the heart of a dead man the seed-plots are dry;

From the thicket of thorns whence the nightingale
    calls not,
    Could she call, there were never a rose to reply.
Over the meadows that blossom and wither
30   Rings but the note of a sea-bird's song;
Only the sun and the rain come hither
      All year long.

The sun burns sere and the rain dishevels
    One gaunt bleak blossom of scentless breath.
35 Only the wind here hovers and revels
    In a round where life seems barren as death.
Here there was laughing of old, there was weeping,
    Haply, of lovers none ever will know,
Whose eyes went seaward a hundred sleeping
40   Years ago.

Heart handfast in heart as they stood, "Look thither,"
    Did he whisper? "look forth from the flowers to
      the sea;
For the foam-flowers endure when the rose-
    blossoms wither,
    And men that love lightly may die—but we?"
45 And the same wind sang and the same waves
    whitened,
    And or ever the garden's last petals were shed,
In the lips that had whispered, the eyes that had
    lightened,
      Love was dead.

Or they loved their life through, and then went
    whither?
    And were one to the end—but what end who
50   knows?
Love deep as the sea as a rose must wither,
    As the rose-red seaweed that mocks the rose.
Shall the dead take thought for the dead to love
    them?
    What love was ever as deep as a grave?
55 They are loveless now as the grass above them
      Or the wave.

All are at one now, roses and lovers,
    Not known of the cliffs and the fields and the
        sea.
Not a breath of the time that has been hovers
60   In the air now soft with a summer to be.
Not a breath shall there sweeten the seasons
        hereafter
    Of the flowers or the lovers that laugh now or
        weep,
When as they that are free now of weeping and
        laughter
    We shall sleep.

65 Here death may deal not again for ever;
    Here change may come not till all change end.
From the graves they have made they shall rise up
        never,
    Who have left nought living to ravage and rend.
Earth, stones, and thorns of the wild ground
        growing,
70   While the sun and the rain live, these shall be;
Till a last wind's breath upon all these blowing
    Roll the sea.

Till the slow sea rise and the sheer cliff crumble,
    Till terrace and meadow the deep gulfs drink,
75 Till the strength of the waves of the high tides
        humble
    The fields that lessen, the rocks that shrink,
Here now in his triumph where all things falter,
    Stretched out on the spoils that his own hand
        spread,
As a god self-slain on his own strange altar,
80   Death lies dead.
—1878

At A Month's End

The night last night was strange and shaken:
    More strange the change of you and me.

Once more, for the old love's love forsaken,
    We went out once more toward the sea.

5 For the old love's love-sake dead and buried,
    One last time, one more and no more,
We watched the waves set in, the serried
    Spears of the tide storming the shore.

Hardly we saw the high moon hanging,
10   Heard hardly through the windy night
Far waters ringing, low reefs clanging,
    Under wan skies and waste white light.

With chafe and change of surges chiming,
    The clashing channels rocked and rang
15 Large music, wave to wild wave timing,
    And all the choral water sang.

Faint lights fell this way, that way floated,
    Quick sparks of sea-fire keen like eyes
From the rolled surf that flashed, and noted
20   Shores and faint cliffs and bays and skies.

The ghost of sea that shrank up sighing
    At the sand's edge, a short sad breath
Trembling to touch the goal, and dying
    With weak heart heaved up once in death—

25 The rustling sand and shingle shaken
    With light sweet touches and small sound—
These could not move us, could not waken
    Hearts to look forth, eyes to look round.

Silent we went an hour together,
30   Under grey skies by waters white.
Our hearts were full of windy weather,
    Clouds and blown stars and broken light.

Full of cold clouds and moonbeams drifted
    And streaming storms and straying fires,

35 Our souls in us were stirred and shifted
    By doubts and dreams and foiled desires.

Across, aslant, a scudding sea-mew
    Swam, dipped, and dropped, and grazed the sea:
And one with me I could not dream you;
40   And one with you I could not be.

As the white wing the white wave's fringes
    Touched and slid over and flashed past—
As a pale cloud a pale flame tinges
    From the moon's lowest light and last—

45 As a star feels the sun and falters,
    Touched to death by diviner eyes—
As on the old gods' untended altars
    The old fire of withered worship dies—

(Once only, once the shrine relighted
50   Sees the last fiery shadow shine,
Last shadow of flame and faith benighted,
    Sees falter and flutter and fail the shrine)

So once with fiery breath and flying
    Your winged heart touched mine and went,
55 And the swift spirits kissed, and sighing,
    Sundered and smiled and were content.

That only touch, that feeling only,
    Enough we found, we found too much;
For the unlit shrine is hardly lonely
60   As one the old fire forgets to touch.

Slight as the sea's sight of the sea-mew,
    Slight as the sun's sight of the star:
Enough to show one must not deem you
    For love's sake other than you are.

65 Who snares and tames with fear and danger
    A bright beast of a fiery kin,

Only to mar, only to change her
    Sleek supple soul and splendid skin?

Easy with blows to mar and maim her,
70   Easy with bonds to bind and bruise;
What profit, if she yield her tamer
    The limbs to mar, the soul to lose?

Best leave or take the perfect creature,
    Take all she is or leave complete;
75 Transmute you will not form or feature,
    Change feet for wings or wings for feet.

Strange eyes, new limbs, can no man give her;
    Sweet is the sweet thing as it is.
No soul she hath, we see, to outlive her;
80   Hath she for that no lips to kiss?

So may one read his weird, and reason,
    And with vain drugs assuage no pain.
For each man in his loving season
    Fools and is fooled of these in vain.

85 Charms that allay not any longing,
    Spells that appease not any grief,
Time brings us all by handfuls, wronging
    All hurts with nothing of relief.

Ah, too soon shot, the fool's bolt misses!
90   What help? the world is full of loves;
Night after night of running kisses,
    Chirp after chirp of changing doves.

Should Love disown or disesteem you
    For loving one man more or less?
95 You could not tame your light white sea-mew,
    Nor I my sleek black pantheress.

For a new soul let whoso please pray,
    We are what life made us, and shall be.

For you the jungle and me the sea-spray,
    And south for you and north for me.

But this one broken foam-white feather
    I throw you off the hither wing,
Splashed stiff with sea-scurf and salt weather,
    This song for sleep to learn and sing—

Sing in your ear when, daytime over,
    You, couched at long length on hot sand
With some sleek sun-discoloured lover,
    Wince from his breath as from a brand:

Till the acrid hour aches out and ceases,
    And the sheathed eyeball sleepier swims,
The deep flank smoothes its dimpling creases,
    And passion loosens all the limbs:

Till dreams of sharp grey north-sea weather
    Fall faint upon your fiery sleep,
As on strange sands a strayed bird's feather
    The wind may choose to lose or keep.

But I, who leave my queen of panthers,
    As a tired honey-heavy bee
Gilt with sweet dust from gold-grained anthers
    Leaves the rose-chalice, what for me?

From the ardours of the chaliced centre,
    From the amorous anthers' golden grime,
That scorch and smutch all wings that enter,
    I fly forth hot from honey-time.

But as to a bee's gilt thighs and winglets
    The flower-dust with the flower-smell clings;
As a snake's mobile rampant ringlets
    Leave the sand marked with print of rings;

So to my soul in surer fashion
    Your savage stamp and savour hangs;

100
105
110
115
120
125
130

The print and perfume of old passion,
    The wild-beast mark of panther's fangs.
—1878

Ave Atque Vale [1]

In Memory of Charles Baudelaire [2]

Nous devrions pourtant lui porter quelques fleurs;
Les morts, les pauvres morts, ont de grandes douleurs,
Et quand Octobre souffle, émondeur des vieux arbres,
Son vent mélancolique à l'entour de leurs marbres,
Certe, ils doivent trouver les vivants bien ingrats.
        —"Les Fleurs du Mal."

I

Shall I strew on thee rose or rue or laurel,
  Brother, on this that was the veil of thee?
    Or quiet sea-flower moulded by the sea,
Or simplest growth of meadow-sweet or sorrel,
    Such as the summer-sleepy Dryads [3] weave,
    Waked up by snow-soft sudden rains at eve?
Or wilt thou rather, as on earth before,
    Half-faded fiery blossoms, pale with heat
    And full of bitter summer, but more sweet
To thee than gleanings of a northern shore
    Trod by no tropic feet?

II

For always thee the fervid languid glories
    Allured of heavier suns in mightier skies;
    Thine ears knew all the wandering watery sighs
Where the sea sobs round Lesbian promontories,
    The barren kiss of piteous wave to wave
    That knows not where is that Leucadian grave

5
10
15

---

[1] "Hail and Farewell." From Catullus's lament for his dead brother, "Frater ave atque vale."

[2] The French poet Charles Baudelaire (1821–67) was enormously admired by Swinburne, who wrote this elegy on receiving an account of Baudelaire's death. The report was untrue.

[3] tree-nymphs.

Which hides too deep the supreme head of song.
　　Ah, salt and sterile as her kisses were,
20　　The wild sea winds her and the green gulfs bear
Hither and thither, and vex and work her wrong,
　　Blind gods that cannot spare.[1]

III

Thou sawest, in thine old singing season, brother,
　　Secrets and sorrows unbeheld of us:
25　　Fierce loves, and lovely leaf-buds poisonous,
Bare to thy subtler eye, but for none other
　　Blowing by night in some unbreathed-in clime;
　　The hidden harvest of luxurious time,
Sin without shape, and pleasure without speech;
30　　And where strange dreams in a tumultuous sleep
　　Make the shut eyes of stricken spirits weep;
And with each face thou sawest the shadow on each,
　　Seeing as men sow men reap.[2]

IV

O sleepless heart and sombre soul unsleeping,
35　　That were athirst for sleep and no more life
　　And no more love, for peace and no more strife!
Now the dim gods of death have in their keeping
　　Spirit and body and all the springs of song,
　　Is it well now where love can do no wrong,
40　Where stingless pleasure has no foam or fang
　　Behind the unopening closure of her lips?
　　Is it not well where soul from body slips
And flesh from bone divides without a pang
　　As dew from flower-bell drips?

V

45　It is enough; the end and the beginning
　　Are one thing to thee, who art past the end.
　　O hand unclasped of unbeholden friend,
For thee no fruits to pluck, no palms for winning,

No triumph and no labour and no lust,
50　　Only dead yew-leaves and a little dust.
O quiet eyes wherein the light saith nought,
　　Whereto the day is dumb, nor any night
　　With obscure finger silences your sight,
Nor in your speech the sudden soul speaks thought,
55　　Sleep, and have sleep for light.

VI

Now all strange hours and all strange loves are over,
　　Dreams and desires and sombre songs and sweet,
　　Hast thou found place at the great knees and feet
Of some pale Titan-woman[3] like a lover,
60　　Such as thy vision here solicited,
　　Under the shadow of her fair vast head,
The deep division of prodigious breasts,
　　The solemn slope of mighty limbs asleep,
　　The weight of awful tresses that still keep
65　The savour and shade of old-world pine-forests
　　Where the wet hill-winds weep?

VII

Hast thou found any likeness for thy vision?
　　O gardener of strange flowers, what bud, what
　　　bloom,
　　Hast thou found sown, what gathered in the
　　　gloom?
70　What of despair, of rapture, of derision,
　　What of life is there, what of ill or good?
　　Are the fruits grey like dust or bright like blood?
Does the dim ground grow any seed of ours,
　　The faint fields quicken any terrene root,
75　　In low lands where the sun and moon are mute
And all the stars keep silence? Are there flowers
　　At all, or any fruit?

---

[1] Lines 14–22 refer to the tradition that the Greek poet Sappho of Lesbos was supposed to have drowned herself off the island of Leucas. Baudelaire refers to Sappho in his poem "Lesbos."

[2] Cf. Galatians 6:7.

---

[3] a reference to Baudelaire's poem "La Géante" ("The Giantess"). In Greek mythology the Titans were giants.

VIII

Alas, but though my flying song flies after,
 O sweet strange elder singer, thy more fleet
80   Singing, and footprints of thy fleeter feet,
Some dim derision of mysterious laughter
 From the blind tongueless warders of the dead,
 Some gainless glimpse of Proserpine's[1] veiled
   head,
Some little sound of unregarded tears
85 Wept by effaced unprofitable eyes,
  And from pale mouths some cadence of dead
   sighs—
These only, these the hearkening spirit hears,
 Sees only such things rise.

IX

Thou art far too far for wings of words to follow,
90 Far too far off for thought or any prayer.
  What ails us with thee, who art wind and air?
What ails us gazing where all seen is hollow?
 Yet with some fancy, yet with some desire,
  Dreams pursue death as winds a flying fire,
95 Our dreams pursue our dead and do not find.
  Still, and more swift than they, the thin flame
   flies,
  The low light fails us in elusive skies,
Still the foiled earnest ear is deaf, and blind
 Are still the eluded eyes.

X

100 Not thee, O never thee, in all time's changes,
 Not thee, but this the sound of thy sad soul,
  The shadow of thy swift spirit, this shut scroll
I lay my hand on, and not death estranges
 My spirit from communion of thy song—
105   These memories and these melodies that throng
Veiled porches of a Muse funereal—[2]
 These I salute, these touch, these clasp and fold

As though a hand were in my hand to hold,
Or through mine ears a mourning musical
110 Of many mourners rolled.

XI

I among these, I also, in such station
 As when the pyre was charred, and piled the sods,
  And offering to the dead made, and their gods,
The old mourners had, standing to make libation,
115 I stand, and to the gods and to the dead
  Do reverence without prayer or praise, and shed
Offering to these unknown, the gods of gloom,
 And what of honey and spice my seedlands bear,
 And what I may of fruits in this chilled air,
120 And lay, Orestes-like, across the tomb
 A curl of severed hair.[3]

XII

But by no hand nor any treason stricken,
 Not like the low-lying head of Him, the King,
  The flame that made of Troy a ruinous thing,
125 Thou liest, and on this dust no tears could quicken
 There fall no tears like theirs that all men hear
 Fall tear by sweet imperishable tear
Down the opening leaves of holy poets' pages.
 Thee not Orestes, not Electra mourns;
130 But bending us-ward with memorial urns
The most high Muses that fulfil all ages
 Weep, and our God's heart yearns.

XIII

For, sparing of his sacred strength, not often
 Among us darkling here the lord of light[4]
135 Makes manifest his music and his might
In hearts that open and in lips that soften

---

1   queen of the underworld.

2   Melpomene, the muse of tragedy.

3   King Agamemnon (l. 123) was murdered by his wife and her lover. After a long absence from home, Orestes returns and lays a lock of his hair on his father's tomb as a sacrifice. Orestes meets his sister, Electra, at Agamemnon's tomb. The story is recounted in Aeschylus's (525–456 BC) drama the *Choëphori*.

4   Apollo, god of the sun and of poetry.

With the soft flame and heat of songs that shine.
Thy lips indeed he touched with bitter wine,
And nourished them indeed with bitter bread;
140   Yet surely from his hand thy soul's food came,
The fire that scarred thy spirit at his flame
Was lighted, and thine hungering heart he fed
    Who feeds our hearts with fame.

XIV

Therefore he too now at thy soul's sunsetting,
145   God of all suns and songs, he too bends down
    To mix his laurel with thy cypress crown,
And save thy dust from blame and from forgetting.
    Therefore he too, seeing all thou wert and art,
    Compassionate, with sad and sacred heart,
150 Mourns thee of many his children the last dead,
    And hallows with strange tears and alien sighs
    Thine unmelodious mouth and sunless eyes,
And over thine irrevocable head
    Sheds light from the under skies.

XV

155 And one weeps with him in the ways Lethean,
    And stains with tears her changing bosom chill:
    That obscure Venus of the hollow hill,[1]
That thing transformed which was the Cytherean,
    With lips that lost their Grecian laugh divine
160   Long since, and face no more called Erycine;
A ghost, a bitter and luxurious god.
    Thee also with fair flesh and singing spell
    Did she, a sad and second prey, compel
Into the footless places once more trod,
165   And shadows hot from hell.

XVI

And now no sacred staff shall break in blossom,
    No choral salutation lure to light
    A spirit sick with perfume and sweet night

And love's tired eyes and hands and barren bosom.
170   There is no help for these things; none to mend
    And none to mar; not all our songs, O friend,
Will make death clear or make life durable.
    Howbeit with rose and ivy and wild vine
    And with wild notes about this dust of thine
175 At least I fill the place where white dreams dwell
    And wreathe an unseen shrine.

XVII

Sleep; and if life was bitter to thee, pardon,
    If sweet, give thanks; thou hast no more to live;
    And to give thanks is good, and to forgive.
180 Out of the mystic and the mournful garden
    Where all day through thine hands in barren
        braid
    Wove the sick flowers of secrecy and shade,
Green buds of sorrow and sin, and remnants grey,
    Sweet-smelling, pale with poison, sanguine-
        hearted,
185   Passions that sprang from sleep and thoughts
        that started,
Shall death not bring us all as thee one day
    Among the days departed?

XVIII

For thee, O now a silent soul, my brother,
    Take at my hands this garland, and farewell.
190   Thin is the leaf, and chill the wintry smell,
And chill the solemn earth, a fatal mother,
    With sadder than the Niobean womb,[2]
    And in the hollow of her breasts a tomb.
Content thee, howsoe'er, whose days are done;
195   There lies not any troublous thing before,
    Nor sight nor sound to war against thee more,
For whom all winds are quiet as the sun,
    All waters as the shore.
—1878 (1868)

---

[1] In the legend of Tannhäuser, Venus the Cytherean, or Erycine, appears as an enchantress who entices victims into the caverns of Horselberg, the Mountain of Venus.

[2] Niobe's excessive pride in the number of children that she had led her to boast of them to Leto, the mother of Artemis and Apollo. Subsequently seven of her children were killed by Artemis and seven by Apollo.

A Jacobite's Farewell

1716 [1]

There 's nae mair lands to tyne,[2] my dear,
　　And nae mair lives to gie:
Though a man think sair to live nae mair,
　　There 's but one day to die.

5　For a' things come and a' days gane,
　　What needs ye rend your hair?
But kiss me till the morn's morrow,
　　Then I 'll kiss ye nae mair.

O lands are lost and life's losing,
10　　And what were they to gie?
Fu' mony a man gives all he can,
　　But nae man else gives ye.

Our king wons[3] ower the sea's water,
　　And I in prison sair:
15　But I 'll win out the morn's morrow,
　　And ye 'll see me nae mair.
　　　　　—1889

The Lake of Gaube

The sun is lord and god, sublime, serene,
　　And sovereign on the mountains: earth and air
Lie prone in passion, blind with bliss unseen
　　By force of sight and might of rapture, fair
5　　As dreams that die and know not what they were.
The lawns, the gorges, and the peaks, are one
Glad glory, thrilled with sense of unison
In strong compulsive silence of the sun.

Flowers dense and keen as midnight stars aflame
10　　And living things of light like flames in flower
That glance and flash as though no hand might tame
　　Lightnings whose life outshone their stormlit
　　　　hour
　　And played and laughed on earth, with all their
　　　　power
Gone, and with all their joy of life made long
15　And harmless as the lightning life of song,
Shine sweet like stars when darkness feels them
　　　　strong.

The deep mild purple flaked with moonbright gold
　　That makes the scales seem flowers of hardened
　　　　light,
The flamelike tongue, the feet that noon leaves cold,
20　　The kindly trust in man, when once the sight
　　Grew less than strange, and faith bade fear take
　　　　flight,
Outlive the little harmless life that shone
And gladdened eyes that loved it, and was gone
Ere love might fear that fear had looked thereon.

25　Fear held the bright thing hateful, even as fear,
　　Whose name is one with hate and horror, saith
That heaven, the dark deep heaven of water near,
　　Is deadly deep as hell and dark as death.
　　　The rapturous plunge that quickens blood and
　　　　breath
30　With pause more sweet than passion, ere they strive
To raise again the limbs that yet would dive
Deeper, should there have slain the soul alive.

As the bright salamander in fire of the noonshine
　　exults and is glad of his day,
The spirit that quickens my body rejoices to pass
　　from the sunlight away,
35　To pass from the glow of the mountainous
　　　flowerage, the high multitudinous bloom,
Far down through the fathomless night of the
　　water, the gladness of silence and gloom.

---

[1] 1716 marked the end of the unsuccessful attempt of the Old Pretender, James Stewart (1688–1766), to secure the English throne. Swinburne's family was notably sympathetic to the Jacobite cause.

[2] to lose.

[3] lives.

Death-dark and delicious as death in the dream of a
    lover and dreamer may be,
It clasps and encompasses body and soul with
    delight to be living and free:
Free utterly now, though the freedom endure but
    the space of a perilous breath,
40 And living, though girdled about with the darkness
    and coldness and strangeness of death:
Each limb and each pulse of the body rejoicing,
    each nerve of the spirit at rest,
All sense of the soul's life rapture, a passionate
    peace in its blindness blest.
So plunges the downward swimmer, embraced of
    the water unfathomed of man,
The darkness unplummeted, icier than seas in mid-
    winter, for blessing or ban;
45 And swiftly and sweetly, when strength and breath
    fall short, and the dive is done,
Shoots up as a shaft from the dark depth shot, sped
    straight into sight of the sun;
And sheer through the snow-soft water, more dark
    than the roof of the pines above,
Strikes forth, and is glad as a bird whose flight is
    impelled and sustained of love.
As a sea-mew's love of the sea-wind breasted and
    ridden for rapture's sake
50 Is the love of his body and soul for the darkling
    delight of the soundless lake:

As the silent speed of a dream too living to live for
    a thought's space more
Is the flight of his limbs through the still strong
    chill of the darkness from shore to shore.
Might life be as this is and death be as life that casts
    off time as a robe,
The likeness of infinite heaven were a symbol
    revealed of the lake of Gaube.

55 Whose thought has fathomed and measured
    The darkness of life and of death,
The secret within them treasured,
    The spirit that is not breath?
Whose vision has yet beholden
60   The splendour of death and of life?
Though sunset as dawn be golden,
    Is the word of them peace, not strife?
Deep silence answers: the glory
    We dream of may be but a dream,
65 And the sun of the soul wax hoary
    As ashes that show not a gleam.
But well shall it be with us ever
    Who drive through the darkness here,
If the soul that we live by never,
70   For aught that a lie saith, fear.
—1904

Augusta Webster
1837 – 1894

Augusta Webster is remembered as a poet, dramatist, and essayist. She published a three-volume novel in 1864 under the name of Cecil Home; her first volume of poetry, *Blanche Lisle and Other Poems*, was also issued under this pen-name. Her dramatic works are *The Auspicious Day* (1872), *Disguises* (1879), *In a Day* (1882), and *The Sentence* (1887). The first volume of poetry to be published under Webster's own name was *Dramatic Studies* in 1866. This volume was followed by *A Woman Sold and Other Poems* in 1867, *Portraits* in 1870, *A Book of Rhyme* in 1881, and *Mother and Daughter* in 1895. The latter volume contains an unfinished and unsentimentalized sonnet cycle on the experience of motherhood. Webster advocated women's suffrage and offered her thoughts on topics relevant to married women in a collection of essays called *A Housewife's Opinions* (1878). Webster was sometimes accused of indelicacy, perhaps never more intensely than when she published her poetic consideration of the lot of the "fallen woman" in "A Castaway" (1870), but she never compromised her imaginative vision and energy.

❧❧❧

Circe [1]

The sun drops luridly into the west;
Darkness has raised her arms to draw him down
Before the time, not waiting as of wont
Till he has come to her behind the sea;
5 And the smooth waves grow sullen in the gloom
And wear their threatening purple; more and more
The plain of waters sways and seems to rise
Convexly from its level of the shores;
And low dull thunder rolls along the beach:
10 There will be storm at last, storm, glorious storm!

   Oh welcome, welcome, though it rend my
      bowers,
Scattering my blossomed roses like the dust,
Splitting the shrieking branches, tossing down
My riotous vines with their young half-tinged
      grapes
15 Like small round amethysts or beryls strung
Tumultuously in clusters; though it sate
Its ravenous spite among my goodliest pines
Standing there round and still against the sky
That makes blue lakes between their sombre tufts,
20 Or harry from my silvery olive slopes
Some hoary king whose gnarled fantastic limbs
Wear rugged armour of a thousand years;
Though it will hurl high on my flowery shores
The hostile wave that rives[2] at the poor sward[3]
25 And drags it down the slants, that swirls its foam
Over my terraces, shakes their firm blocks
Of great bright marbles into tumbled heaps,
And makes my pleached[4] and mossy labyrinths,
Where the small odorous blossoms grow like stars
30 Strewn in the milky way, a briny marsh.
What matter? let it come and bring me change,
Breaking the sickly sweet monotony.

   I am too weary of this long bright calm;
Always the same blue sky, always the sea
35 The same blue perfect likeness of the sky,
One rose to match the other that has waned,
To-morrow's dawn the twin of yesterday's;
And every night the ceaseless crickets chirp

---

[1] the enchantress in Homer's *Odyssey*, who turned men into swine.

[2] to split or tear apart.

[3] turf.

[4] plaited.

The same long joy and the late strain of birds
40 Repeats their strain of all the even month;
And changelessly the petty plashing surfs
Bubble their chiming burden round the stones;
Dusk after dusk brings the same languid trance
Upon the shadowy hills, and in the fields
45 The waves of fireflies come and go the same,
Making the very flash of light and stir
Vex one like dronings of the shuttles at task.

   Give me some change. Must life be only sweet,
All honey-pap as babes would have their food?
50 And, if my heart must always be adrowse
In a hush of stagnant sunshine, give me, then,
Something outside me stirring; let the storm
Break up the sluggish beauty, let it fall
Beaten below the feet of passionate winds,
55 And then to-morrow waken jubilant
In a new birth; let me see subtle joy
Of anguish and of hopes, of change and growth.

   What fate is mine, who, far apart from pains
And fears and turmoils of the cross-grained world,
60 Dwell like a lonely god in a charmed isle
Where I am first and only, and, like one
Who should love poisonous savours more than
     mead,
Long for a tempest on me and grow sick
Of rest and of divine free carelessness!
65 Oh me, I am a woman, not a god;
Yea, those who tend me, even, are more than I,
My nymphs[1] who have the souls of flowers and
     birds
Singing and blossoming immortally.

   Ah me! these love a day and laugh again,
70 And loving, laughing, find a full content;
But I know nought of peace, and have not loved.

Where is my love? Does someone cry for me
Not knowing whom he calls? Does his soul cry
For mine to grow beside it, grow in it?
75 Does he beseech the gods to give him me,
The one unknown rare woman by whose side
No other woman thrice as beautiful
Could once seem fair to him; to whose voice heard
In any common tones no sweetest sound
80 Of love made melody on silver lutes,
Or singing like Apollo's[2] when the gods
Grow pale with happy listening, might be peered
For making music to him; whom once found
There will be no more seeking anything?

85   Oh love, oh love, oh love, art not yet come
Out of the waiting shadows into life?
Art not yet come after so many years
That I have longed for thee? Come! I am here.

   Not yet. For surely I should feel a sound
90 Of his far answer if now in the world
He sought me who will seek me—Oh, ye gods,
Will he not seek me? Is it all a dream?
Will there be only these, these bestial things
Who wallow in their styes, or mop and mow
95 Among the trees, or munch in pens and byres,
Or snarl and filch behind their wattled coops;
These things who had believed that they were men?

   Nay, but he *will* come. Why am I so fair,
And marvellously minded, and with sight
100 Which flashes suddenly on hidden things,
As the gods see, who do not need to look?
Why wear I in my eyes that stronger power
Than basilisks,[3] whose gaze can only kill,
To draw men's souls to me to live or die
105 As I would have them? Why am I given pride

---

[1] any of a group of minor nature goddesses in Greek mythology.

[2] the Greek and Roman sun-god, patron of music and poetry.

[3] a mythical reptile with a lethal breath and look, supposedly hatched from a cock's egg.

Which yet longs to be broken, and this scorn,
Cruel and vengeful, for the lesser men
Who meet the smiles I waste for lack of him,
And grow too glad? Why am I who I am?
110 But for the sake of him whom fate will send
One day to be my master utterly,
That he should take me, the desire of all,
Whom only he in the world could bow to him.

Oh, sunlike glory of pale glittering hairs,
115 Bright as the filmy wires my weavers take
To make me golden gauzes—Oh, deep eyes,
Darker and softer than the bluest dusk
Of August violets, darker and deep
Like crystal fathomless lakes in summer noons—
120 Oh, sad sweet longing smile—Oh, lips that tempt
My very self to kisses—oh, round cheeks
Tenderly radiant with the even flush
Of pale smoothed coral—perfect lovely face
Answering my gaze from out this fleckless pool—
125 Wonder of glossy shoulders, chiselled limbs—
Should I be so your lover as I am,
Drinking an exquisite joy to watch you thus
In all a hundred changes through the day,
But that I love you for him till he comes,
130 But that my beauty means his loving it?

Oh, look! a speck on this side of the sun,
Coming—yes, coming with the rising wind
That frays the darkening cloud-wrack on the verge
And in a little while will leap abroad,
135 Spattering the sky with rushing blacknesses,
Dashing the hissing mountainous waves at the stars.
'Twill drive me that black speck a shuddering hulk
Caught in the buffeting waves, dashed impotent
From ridge to ridge, will drive it in the night
140 With that dull jarring crash upon the beach,
And the cries for help and the cries of fear and
        hope.

And then to-morrow they will thoughtfully,
With grave low voices, count their perils up,
And thank the gods for having let them live
145 And tell of wives and mothers in their homes,
And children, who would have such loss in them
That they must weep (and maybe I weep too)
With fancy of the weepings had they died.
And the next morrow they will feel their ease
150 And sigh with sleek content, or laugh elate,
Tasting delight of rest and revelling,
Music and perfumes, joyaunce for the eyes
Of rosy faces and luxurious pomps,
The savour of the banquet and the glow
155 And fragrance of the wine-cup; and they'll talk
How good it is to house in palaces
Out of the storms and struggles, and what luck
Strewed their good ship on our accessless coast.
Then the next day the beast in them will wake,
160 And one will strike and bicker, and one swell
With puffed-up greatness, and one gibe and strut
In apish pranks, and one will line his sleeve
With pilfered booties, and one snatch the gems
Out of the carven goblets as they pass,
165 One will grow mad with fever of the wine,
And one will sluggishly besot himself,
And one be lewd, and one be gluttonous;
And I shall sickly look and loathe them all.

Oh my rare cup! my pure and crystal cup,
170 With not one speck of colour to make false
The entering lights, or flaw to make them swerve!
My cup of Truth! How the lost fools will laugh
And thank me for my boon, as if I gave
Some momentary flash of the gods' joy,
175 To drink where *I* have drunk and touch the touch
Of *my* lips with their own! Aye, let them touch.

Too cruel, am I? And the silly beasts,
Crowding around me when I pass their way,
Glower on me and, although they love me still,
180 (With their poor sorts of love such as they could)

Call wrath and vengeance to their humid eyes
To scare me into mercy, or creep near
With piteous fawnings, supplicating bleats.
Too cruel? Did I choose them what they are?
185 Or change them from themselves by poisonous
    charms?
But any draught, pure water, natural wine,
Out of my cup, revealed them to themselves
And to each other. Change? there was no change;
Only disguise gone from them unawares:
190 And had there been one true right man of them
He would have drunk the draught as I had drunk,
And stood unharmed and looked me in the eyes,
Abashing me before him. But these things—
Why, which of them has even shown the kind
195 Of some one nobler beast? Pah! yapping wolves,
And pitiless stealthy wild-cats, curs, and apes,
And gorging swine, and slinking venomous snakes—
All false and ravenous and sensual brutes
That shame the Earth that bore them, these they
    are.

200 Lo, lo! the shivering blueness darting forth
On half the heavens, and the forked thin fire
Strikes to the sea: and hark, the sudden voice
That rushes through the trees before the storm,
And shuddering of the branches. Yet the sky
205 Is blue against them still, and early stars
Sparkle above the pine-tops; and the air
Clings faint and motionless around me here.

Another burst of flame—and the black speck
210 Shows in the glare, lashed onwards. It were well
I bade make ready for our guests to-night.
—1870

A Castaway

Poor little diary, with its simple thoughts,
Its good resolves, its "Studied French an hour,"

"Read Modern History," "Trimmed up my grey
    hat,"
"Darned stockings," "Tatted," "Practised my new
    song,"
5 "Went to the daily service," "Took Bess soup,"
"Went out to tea." Poor simple diary!
And did *I* write it? Was I this good girl,
This budding colourless young rose of home?
Did I so live content in such a life,
10 Seeing no larger scope, nor asking it,
Than this small constant round—old clothes to
    mend,
New clothes to make, then go and say my prayers,
Or carry soup, or take a little walk
And pick the ragged-robins in the hedge?
15 Then, for ambition, (was there ever life
That could forego that?) to improve my mind
And know French better and sing harder songs;
For gaiety, to go, in my best white
Well washed and starched and freshened with new
    bows,
20 And take tea out to meet the clergyman.
No wishes and no cares, almost no hopes,
Only the young girl's hazed and golden dreams
That veil the Future from her.

                So long since:
And now it seems a jest to talk of me
25 As if I could be one with her, of me
Who am...me.

              And what is that? My looking-glass
Answers it passably; a woman sure,
No fiend, no slimy thing out of the pools,
A woman with a ripe and smiling lip
30 That has no venom in its touch I think,
With a white brow on which there is no brand;
A woman none dare call not beautiful,
Not womanly in every woman's grace.

Aye, let me feed upon my beauty thus,
35 Be glad in it like painters when they see
At last the face they dreamed but could not find
Look from their canvas on them, triumph in it,
The dearest thing I have. Why, 'tis my all,
Let me make much of it: is it not this,
40 This beauty, my own curse at once and tool
To snare men's souls, (I know what the good say
Of beauty in such creatures) is it not this
That makes me feel myself a woman still,
With still some little pride, some little—

                         Stop!
45 "Some little pride, some little"—Here's a jest!
What word will fit the sense but modesty?
A wanton I, but modest!

                    Modest, true;
I'm not drunk in the streets, ply not for hire
At infamous corners with my likenesses
50 Of the humbler kind; yes, modesty's my word—
'Twould shape my mouth well too, I think I'll try:
"Sir, Mr What-you-will, Lord Who-knows-what,
My present lover or my next to come,
Value me at my worth, fill your purse full,
55 For I am modest; yes, and honour me
As though your schoolgirl sister or your wife
Could let her skirts brush mine or talk of me;
For I am modest."

              Well, I flout myself:
But yet, but yet—

              Fie, poor fantastic fool,
60 Why do I play the hypocrite alone,
Who am no hypocrite with others by?
Where should be my "But yet"? I am that thing
Called half a dozen dainty names, and none
Dainty enough to serve the turn and hide
65 The one coarse English worst that lurks beneath:
Just that, no worse, no better.

                  And, for me,
I say let no one be above her trade;

I own my kindredship with any drab
Who sells herself as I, although she crouch
70 In fetid garrets and I have a home
All velvet and marqueterie[1] and pastilles,[2]
Although she hide her skeleton in rags
And I set fashions and wear cobweb lace:
The difference lies but in my choicer ware,
75 That I sell beauty and she ugliness;
Our traffic's one—I'm no sweet slaver-tongue
To gloze[3] upon it and explain myself
A sort of fractious angel misconceived—
Our traffic's one: I own it. And what then?
80 I know of worse that are called honourable.
Our lawyers, who with noble eloquence
And virtuous outbursts lie to hang a man,
Or lie to save him, which way goes the fee:
Our preachers, gloating on your future hell
85 For not believing what they doubt themselves:
Our doctors, who sort poisons out by chance
And wonder how they'll answer, and grow rich:
Our journalists, whose business is to fib
And juggle truths and falsehoods to and fro:
90 Our tradesmen, who must keep unspotted names
And cheat the least like stealing that they can:
Our—all of them, the virtuous worthy men
Who feed on the world's follies, vices, wants,
And do their businesses of lies and shams
95 Honestly, reputably, while the world
Claps hands and cried "good luck," which of their
        trades,
Their honourable trades, barefaced like mine,
All secrets brazened out, would shew more white?

        And whom do I hurt more than they? as much?
100 The wives? Poor fools, what do I take from them
Worth crying for or keeping? If they knew

---

[1] ornamental inlaid work of wood or ivory, most often used in furniture and flooring.

[2] French from Latin *pastillus* "little loaf, lozenge."

[3] to fawn over.

What their fine husbands look like seen by eyes
That may perceive there are more men than one!
But, if they can, let them just take the pains
105　To keep them: 'tis not such a mighty task
To pin an idiot to your apron-string;
And wives have an advantage over us,
(The good and blind ones have) the smile or pout
Leaves them no secret nausea at odd times.
110　Oh, they could keep their husbands if they cared,
But 'tis an easier life to let them go,
And whimper at it for morality.

　　　Oh! those shrill carping virtues, safely housed
From reach of even a smile that should put red
115　On a decorous cheek, who rail at us
With such a spiteful scorn and rancorousness,
(Which maybe is half envy at the heart)
And boast themselves so measurelessly good
And us so measurelessly unlike them,
120　What is their wondrous merit that they stay
In comfortable homes whence not a soul
Has ever thought of tempting them, and wear
No kisses but a husband's upon lips
There is no other man desires to kiss—
125　Refrain in fact from sin impossible?
How dare they hate us so? what have they done,
What borne, to prove them other than we are?
What right have they to scorn us—glass-case saints,
Dianas[1] under lock and key—what right
130　More than the well-fed helpless barn-door fowl
To scorn the larcenous wild-birds?

　　　　　　　Pshaw, let be!
Scorn or no scorn, what matter for their scorn?
I have outfaced my own—that's harder work.
Aye, let their virtuous malice dribble on—
135　Mock snowstorms on the stage—I'm proof long
　　since:

I have looked coolly on my what and why,
And I accept myself.

　　　　　　　Oh I'll endorse
The shamefullest revilings mouthed at me,
Cry "True! Oh perfect picture! Yes, that's I!"
140　And add a telling blackness here and there,
And then dare swear you, every nine of ten,
My judges and accusers, I'd not change
My conscience against yours, you who tread out
Your devil's pilgrimage along the roads
145　That take in church and chapel, and arrange
A roundabout and decent way to hell.

　　　Well, mine's a short way and a merry one:
So says my pious hash of ohs and ahs,
Choice texts and choicer threats, appropriate names,
150　(Rahabs[2] and Jezebels[3]) some fierce Tartuffe[4]
Hurled at me through the post. We had rare fun
Over that tract digested with champagne.
Where is it? where's my rich repertory
Of insults Biblical? "I prey on souls"—
155　Only my men have oftenest none I think:
"I snare the simple ones"—but in these days
There seem to be none simple and none snared
And most men have their favourite sinnings planned
To do them civilly and sensibly:
160　"I braid my hair"—but braids are out of date:
"I paint my cheeks"—I always wear them pale:
"I—"

　　　Pshaw! the trash is savourless to-day:
One cannot laugh alone. There, let it burn.
What, does the windy dullard think one needs

---

[1]　the Roman goddess of the moon, hunting, and virginity.

[2]　a prostitute who played an important role in the Israelites' success in the battle for Jericho.

[3]　the shameless and wicked woman who married Ahab, king of Israel: 1 Kings 16, 19; 2 Kings 9:7–10, 30–37.

[4]　the titular hero of Molière's satirical comedy; he was a religious hypocrite.

165　His wisdom dove-tailed on to Solomon's,[1]
　　His threats out-threatening God's, to teach the news
　　That those who need not sin have safer souls?
　　We know it, but we've bodies to save too;
　　And so we earn our living.

　　　　　　　　　　　Well lit, tract!
170　At least you've made me a good leaping blaze.
　　Up, up, how the flame shoots! and now 'tis dead.
　　Oh proper finish, preaching to the last—
　　No such bad omen either; sudden end,
　　And no sad withering horrible old age.
175　How one would clutch at youth to hold it tight!
　　And then to know it gone, to see it gone,
　　Be taught its absence by harsh careless looks,
　　To live forgotten, solitary, old—
　　The cruellest word that ever woman learns.
180　Old—that's to be nothing, or to be at best
　　A blurred memorial that in better days
　　There was a woman once with such a name.
　　No, no, I could not bear it: death itself
　　Shows kinder promise...even death itself,
185　Since it must come one day—

　　　　　　　　　　　Oh this grey gloom!
　　This rain, rain, rain, what wretched thoughts it
　　　　brings!
　　Death: I'll not think of it.

　　　　　　　　　　　Will no one come?
　　'Tis dreary work alone.

　　　　　　　　　　　Why did I read
　　That silly diary? Now, sing-song, ding-dong,
190　Come the old vexing echoes back again,
　　Church bells and nursery good-books, back again
　　Upon my shrinking ears that had forgotten—
　　I hate the useless memories: 'tis fools' work
　　Singing the hacknied dirge of "better days":

195　Best take Now kindly, give the past good-bye,
　　Whether it were a better or a worse.

　　　　　Yes, yes, I listened to the echoes once,
　　The echoes and the thoughts from the old days.
　　The worse for me: I lost my richest friend,
200　And that was all the difference. For the world,
　　I would not have that flight known. How they'd
　　　　roar:
　　"What! Eulalie, when she refused us all,
　　'Ill' and 'away,' was doing Magdalene,[2]
　　Tears, ashes, and her Bible, and then off
205　To hide her in a Refuge...for a week!"

　　　　　A wild whim that, to fancy I could change
　　My new self for my old because I wished!
　　Since then, when in my languid days there comes
　　That craving, like homesickness, to go back
210　To the good days, the dear old stupid days,
　　To the quiet and the innocence, I know
　　'Tis a sick fancy and try palliatives.[3]

　　　　　What is it? You go back to the old home,
　　And 'tis not *your* home, has no place for you,
215　And, if it had, you could not fit you in it.
　　And could I fit me to my former self?
　　If I had had the wit, like some of us,
　　To sow my wild-oats into three per cents,
　　Could I not find me shelter in the peace
220　Of some far nook where none of them would come,
　　Nor whisper travel from this scurrilous world
　　(That gloats, and moralizes through its leers)
　　To blast me with my fashionable shame?
　　There I might—oh my castle in the clouds!
225　And where's its rent?—but there, were there a there,
　　I might again live the grave blameless life
　　Among such simple pleasures, simple cares:

---

[1]　the son of David and King of Israel, famed for his wisdom.

[2]　Mary Magdalene: Luke 8:2, and also identified with the repentant woman in Luke 7:37—commonly regarded as the reformed prostitute.

[3]　used to alleviate pain or anxiety.

But could they be my pleasures, be my cares?
The blameless life, but never the content—
230 Never. How could I henceforth be content
With any life but one that sets the brain
In a hot merry fever with its stir?
What would there be in quiet rustic days,
Each like the other, full of time to think,
235 To keep one bold enough to live at all?
Quiet is hell, I say—as if a woman
Could bear to sit alone, quiet all day,
And loathe herself and sicken on her thoughts.

They tried it at the Refuge,[1] and I failed:
240 I could not bear it. Dreary hideous room,
Coarse pittance, prison rules, one might bear these
And keep one's purpose; but so much alone,
And then made faint and weak and fanciful
By change from pampering to half-famishing—
245 Good God, what thoughts come! Only one week
     more
And 'twould have ended: but in one day more
I must have killed myself. And I loathe death,
The dreadful foul corruption with who knows
What future after it.

          Well, I came back,
250 Back to my slough. Who says I had my choice?
Could I stay there to die of some mad death?
And if I rambled out into the world
Sinless but penniless, what else were that
But slower death, slow pining shivering death
255 By misery and hunger? Choice! What choice
Of living well or ill? could I have that?
And who would give it me? I think indeed
If some kind hand, a woman's—I hate men—
Had stretched itself to help me to firm ground,
260 Taken a chance and risked my falling back,
I could have gone my way not falling back:

But, let her be all brave, all charitable,
How could she do it? Such a trifling boon—
A little work to live by, 'tis not much—
265 And I might have found will enough to last:
But where's the work? More sempstresses[2] than
     shirts;
And defter hands at white work than are mine
Drop starved at last: dressmakers, milliners,
Too many too they say; and then their trades
270 Need skill, apprenticeship. And why so bold
As hire me for their humblest drudgery?
Not even for scullery slut; not even, I think,
For governess although they'd get me cheap.
And after all it would be something hard,
275 With the marts for decent women overfull,
If I could elbow in and snatch a chance
And oust some good girl so, who then perforce
Must come and snatch her chance among our
     crowd.

Why, if the worthy men who think all's done
280 If we'll but come where we can hear them preach,
Could bring us all, or any half of us,
Into their fold, teach all us wandering sheep,
Or only half of us, to stand in rows
And baa them hymns and moral songs, good lack,
285 What would they do with us? what could they do?
Just think! with were't but half of us on hand
To find work for...or husbands. Would they try
To ship us to the colonies for wives?

Well, well, I know the wise ones talk and talk:
290 "Here's cause, here's cure:" "No, here it is, and here:"
And find society to blame, or law,
The Church, the men, the women, too few schools,
Too many schools, too much, too little taught:
Somewhere or somehow someone is to blame:
295 But I say all the fault's with God himself
Who puts too many women in the world.

---

[1] usually, shelters set up for "fallen women" and prostitutes who wished to reform.

[2] variation of "seamstress."

We ought to die off reasonably and leave
As many as the men want, none to waste.
Here's cause; the woman's superfluity:
300 And for the cure, why, if it were the law,
Say, every year, in due percentages,
Balancing them with males as the times need,
To kill off female infants, 'twould make room;
And some of us would not have lost too much,
305 Losing life ere we know what it *can* mean.

The other day I saw a woman weep
Beside her dead child's bed: the little thing
Lay smiling, and the mother wailed half mad,
Shrieking to God to give it back again.
310 I could have laughed aloud: the little girl
Living had but her mother's life to live;
There she lay smiling, and her mother wept
To know her gone!

My mother would have wept.

Oh, mother, mother, did you ever dream,
315 You good grave simple mother, you pure soul
No evil could come nigh, did you once dream
In all your dying cares for your lone girl
Left to fight out her fortune helplessly
That there would be *this* danger?—for *your* girl,
320 Taught by you, lapped in a sweet ignorance,
Scarcely more wise of what things sin could be
Than some young child a summer six months old,
Where in the north the summer makes a day,
Of what is darkness…darkness that will come
325 To-morrow suddenly. Thank God at least
For this much of my life, that when you died,
That when you kissed me dying, not a thought
Of this made sorrow for you, that I too
Was pure of even fear.

Oh yes, I thought,
330 Still new in my insipid treadmill life,

(My father so late dead), and hopeful still,
There might be something pleasant somewhere in
    it,
Some sudden fairy come, no doubt, to turn
My pumpkin to a chariot, I thought then
335 That I might plod and plod and drum the sounds
Of useless facts into unwilling ears,
Tease children with dull questions half the day
Then con dull answers in my room at night
Ready for next day's questions, mend quill pens
340 And cut my fingers, add up sums done wrong
And never get them right; teach, teach, and teach—
What I half knew, or not at all—teach, teach
For years, a lifetime—*I!*

And yet, who knows?
It might have been, for I was patient once,
345 And willing, and meant well; it might have been
Had I but still clung on in my first place—
A safe dull place, where mostly there were smiles
But never merry-makings; where all days
Jogged on sedately busy, with no haste;
350 Where all seemed measured out, but margins broad:
A dull home but a peaceful, where I felt
My pupils would be dear young sisters soon,
And felt their mother take me to her heart,
Motherly to all lonely harmless things.
355 But I must have a conscience, must blurt out
My great discovery of my ignorance!
And who required it of me? And who gained?
What did it matter for a more or less
The girls learnt in their schoolbooks, to forget
360 In their first season? We did well together:
They loved me and I them: but I went off
To housemaid's pay, six crossgrained brats to teach,
Wrangles and jangles, doubts, disgráce…then this;
And they had a perfection found for them,
365 Who has all ladies' learning in her head
Abridged and scheduled, speaks five languages,

Knows botany and conchology[1] and globes,
Draws, paints, plays, sings, embroiders, teaches all
On a patent method never known to fail:
370 And now they're finished and, I hear, poor things,
Are the worst dancers and worst dressers out.
And where's their profit of those prison years
All gone to make them wise in lesson-books?
Who wants his wife to know weeds' Latin names?
375 Who ever chose a girl for saying dates?
Or asked if she had learned to trace a map?

Well, well, the silly rules this silly world
Makes about women! This is one of them.
Why must there be pretence of teaching them
380 What no one ever cares that they should know,
What, grown out of the schoolroom, they cast off
Like the schoolroom pinafore,[2] no better fit
For any use of real grown-up life,
For any use to her who seeks or waits
385 The husband and the home, for any use,
For any shallowest pretence of use,
To her who has them? Do I not know this,
I, like my betters, that a woman's life,
Her natural life, her good life, her one life,
390 Is in her husband, God on earth to her,
And what she knows, and what she can and is
Is only good as it brings good to him?

Oh God, do I not know it? I the thing
Of shame and rottenness, the animal
395 That feed men's lusts and prey on them, I, I,
Who should not dare to take the name of wife
On my polluted lips, who in the word
Hear but my own reviling, I know that.
I could have lived by that rule, how content:
400 My pleasure to make him some pleasure, pride
To be as he would have me, duty, care,
To fit all to his taste, rule my small sphere

To his intention; then to lean on him,
Be guided, tutored, loved—no, not that word,
405 That *loved* which between men and women means
All selfishness, all cloying talk, all lust,
All vanity, all idiocy—not loved,
But cared for. I've been loved myself, I think,
Some once or twice since my poor mother died,
410 But *cared for*, never:—that's a word for homes,
Kind homes, good homes, where simple children come
And ask their mother is this right or wrong,
Because they know she's perfect, cannot err;
Their father told them so, and he knows all,
415 Being so wise and good and wonderful,
Even enough to scold even her at times
And tell her everything she does not know.
Ah the sweet nursery logic!

Fool! thrice fool!
Do I hanker after that too? Fancy me
420 Infallible nursery saint, live code of law!
Me preaching! teaching innocence to be good!—
A mother!

Yet the baby thing that woke
And wailed an hour or two, and then was dead,
Was mine, and had he lived...why then my name
425 Would have been mother. But 'twas well he died:
I could have been no mother, I, lost then
Beyond his saving. Had he come before
And lived, come to me in the doubtful days
When shame and boldness had not grown one sense,
430 For his sake, with the courage come of him,
I might have struggled back.

But how? But how?
His father would not then have let me go:
His time had not yet come to make an end
Of my "for ever" with a hireling's fee
435 And civil light dismissal. None but him
To claim a bit of bread of if I went,

---

[1] a branch of zoology that centres on mollusks and shells.

[2] a sleeveless apron-like garment worn primarily by girls.

Child or no child: would he have given it me?
He! no; he had not done with me. No help,
No help, no help. Some ways can be trodden back,
440 But never our way, we who one wild day
Have given goodbye to what in our deep hearts
The lowest woman still holds best in life,
Good name—good name though given by the
    world
That mouths and garbles with its decent prate,
445 And wraps it in respectable grave shams,
And patches conscience partly by the rule
Of what one's neighbour thinks, but something
    more
By what his eyes are sharp enough to see.
How I could scorn it with its Pharisees,[1]
450 If it could not scorn me: but yet, but yet—
Oh God, if I could look it in the face!

Oh I am wild, am ill, I think, to-night:
Will no one come and laugh with me? No feast,
No merriment to-night. So long alone!
455 Will no one come?

At least there's a new dress
To try, and grumble at—they never fit
To one's ideal. Yes, a new rich dress,
With lace like this too, that's a soothing balm
For any fretting woman, cannot fail;
460 I've heard men say it…and they know so well
What's in all women's hearts, especially
Women like me.

No help! no help! no help!
How could it be? It was too late long since—
Even at the first too late. Whose blame is that?
465 There are some kindly people in the world,
But what can *they* do? If one hurls oneself

Into a quicksand, what can be the end,
But that one sinks and sinks? Cry out for help?
Ah yes, and, if it came, who is so strong
470 To strain from the firm ground and lift one out?
And how, so firmly clutching the stretched hand
As death's pursuing terror bids, even so,
How can one reach firm land, having to foot
The treacherous crumbling soil that slides and gives
475 And sucks one in again? Impossible path!
No, why waste struggles, I or any one?
What is must be. What then? I where I am,
Sinking and sinking; let the wise pass by
And keep their wisdom for an apter use,
480 Let me sink merrily as I best may.

Only, I think my brother—I forgot;
He stopped his brotherhood some years ago—
But if he had been just so much less good
As to remember mercy. Did he think
485 How once I was his sister, prizing him
As sisters do, content to learn for him
The lesson girls with brothers all must learn,
To do without?

I have heard girls lament
That doing so without all things one would,
490 But I saw never aught to murmur at,
For men must be made ready for their work
And women all have more or less their chance
Of husbands to work for them, keep them safe
Like summer roses in soft greenhouse air
495 That never guess 'tis winter out of doors:
No, I saw never aught to murmur at,
Content with stinted fare and shabby clothes
And cloistered silent life to save expense,
Teaching myself out of my borrowed books,
500 While he for some one pastime, (needful, true,
To keep him of his rank; 'twas not his fault)
Spent in a month what could have given me
My teachers for a year.

---

[1] an ancient Jewish sect that strictly observed the written law, but
simultaneously insisted on the importance of the oral law that had
evolved out of common usage. In this modern context, the term is a
negative epithet: self-serving hypocrites.

'Twas no one's fault:
For could he be launched forth on the rude sea
505 Of this contentious world and left to find
Oars and the boatman's skill by some good chance?
'Twas no one's fault: yet still he might have thought
Of our so different youths and owned at least
'Tis pitiful when a mere nerveless girl
510 Untutored must put forth upon that sea,
Not in the woman's true place, the wife's place,
To trust a husband and be borne along,
But impotent blind pilot to herself.

Merciless, merciless—like the prudent world
515 That will not have the flawed soul prank itself
With a hoped second virtue, will not have
The woman fallen once lift up herself…
Lest she should fall again. Oh how his taunts,
His loathing fierce reproaches, scarred and seared
520 Like branding iron hissing in a wound!
And it was true—*that* killed me: and I felt
A hideous hopeless shame burn out my heart,
And knew myself for ever that he said,
That which I was—Oh it was true, true, true.

525 No, not true then. I was not all that then.
Oh, I have drifted on before mad winds
And made ignoble shipwreck; not to-day
Could any breeze of heaven prosper me
Into the track again, nor any hand
530 Snatch me out of the whirlpool I have reached;
But then?

Nay, he judged very well: he knew
Repentance was too dear a luxury
For a beggar's buying, knew it earns no bread—
And knew me a too base and nerveless thing
535 To bear my first fault's sequel and just die.
And how could he have helped me? Held my hand,
Owned me for his, fronted the angry world
Clothed with my ignominy? Or maybe
Taken me to his home to damn him worse?

540 What did I look for? for what less would serve
That he could do, a man without a purse?
He meant me well, he sent me that five pounds,
Much to him then; and, if he bade me work
And never vex him more with news of me,
545 We both knew him too poor for pensioners.
I see he did his best; I could wish now
Sending it back I had professed some thanks.

But there! I was too wretched to be meek:
It seemed to me as if he, every one,
550 The whole great world, were guilty of my guilt,
Abettors and avengers: in my heart
I gibed them back their gibings; I was wild.

I see clear now and know one has one's life
In hand at first to spend or spare or give
555 Like any other coin; spend it, or give,
Or drop it in the mire, can the world see
You get your value for it, or bar off
The hurrying of its marts to grope it up
And give it back to you for better use?
560 And if you spend or give, that is your choice;
And if you let it slip, that's your choice too,
You should have held it firmer. Yours the blame,
And not another's, not the indifferent world's
Which goes on steadily, statistically,
565 And count by censuses not separate souls—
And if it somehow needs to its worst use
So many lives of women, useless else,
It buys us of ourselves; we could hold back,
Free all of us to starve, and some of us,
570 (Those who have done no ill, and are in luck)
To slave their lives out and have food and clothes
Until they grow unserviceably old.

Oh, I blame no one—scarcely even myself.
It was to be: the very good in me
575 Has always turned to hurt; all I thought right
At the hot moment, judged of afterwards,
Shows reckless.

Why, look at it, had I taken
The pay my dead child's father offered me
For having been its mother, I could then
580 Have kept life in me—many have to do it,
That swarm in the back alleys, on no more,
Cold sometimes, mostly hungry, but they live—
I could have gained a respite trying it,
And maybe found at last some humble work
585 To eke the pittance out. Not I, forsooth,
I must have spirit, must have womanly pride,
Must dash back his contemptuous wages, I
Who had not scorned to earn them, dash them back
The fiercer that he dared to count our boy
590 In my appraising: and yet now I think
I might have taken it for my dead boy's sake;
It would have been *his* gift.

                    But I went forth
With my fine scorn, and whither did it lead?
Money's the root of evil do they say?
595 Money is virtue, strength: money to me
Would then have been repentance: could I live
Upon my idiot's pride?

                    Well, it fell soon.
I had prayed Clement might believe me dead,
And yet I begged of him—That's like me too,
600 Beg of him and then send him back his alms!
What if he gave as to a whining wretch
That holds her hand and lies? I am less to him
Than such a one; her rags do him no wrong,
But I, I wrong him merely that I live,
605 Being his sister. Could I not at least
Have still let him forget me? But 'tis past:
And naturally he may hope I am long dead.

    Good God! to think that we were what we were
One to the other…and now!

                    He has done well;
610 Married a sort of heiress, I have heard,

A dapper little madam dimple cheeked
And dimple brained, who makes him a good wife—
No doubt she'd never own but just to him,
And in a whisper, she can even suspect
615 That we exist, we other women things:
What would she say if she could learn one day
She has a sister-in-law? So he and I
Must stand apart till doomsday.

                    But the jest,
To think how she would look!—Her fright, poor
    thing!
620 The notion!—I could laugh outright…or else,
For I feel near it, roll on the ground and sob.

    Well, after all, there's not much difference
Between the two sometimes.

                    Was that the bell?
Someone at last, thank goodness. There's a voice,
625 And that's a pleasure. Whose though? Ah, I know.
Why did she come alone, the cackling goose?
Why not have brought her sister?—she tells more
And titters less. No matter; half a loaf
Is better than no bread.

                    Oh, is it you?
630 Most welcome, dear: one gets so moped alone.
—1870

Mother and Daughter Sonnets

VI

Sometimes, as young things will, she vexes me,
    Wayward, or too unheeding, or too blind.
    Like aimless birds that, flying on a wind,
Strike slant against their own familiar tree;
5 Like venturous children pacing with the sea,
    That turn but when the breaker spurts behind
    Outreaching them with spray: she in such kind
Is borne against some fault, or does not flee.

And so, may be, I blame her for her wrong,
10   And she will frown and lightly plead her part,
And then I bid her go. But 'tis not long:
    Then comes she lip to ear and heart to heart.
And thus forgiven her love seems newly strong,
And, oh my penitent, how dear thou art!
—1895

VII

H er father lessons me I at times am hard,
    Chiding a moment's fault as too grave ill,
    And let some little blot my vision fill,
Scanning her with a narrow near regard.
5 True. Love's unresting gaze is self-debarred
    From all sweet ignorance, and learns a skill,
    Not painless, of such signs as hurt love's will,
That would not have its prize one tittle[1] marred.

Alas! Who rears and loves a dawning rose
10   Starts at a speck upon one petal's rim:
Who sees a dusk creep in the shrined pearl's glows,
    Is ruined at once: "My jewel growing dim!"
I watch one bud that on my bosom blows,
    I watch one treasured pearl for me and him.
—1895

IX

O h weary hearts! Poor mothers that look back!
    So outcasts from the vale where they were
        born
    Turn on their road and, with a joy forlorn,
See the far roofs below their arid track:
5 So in chill buffets while the sea grows black
    And windy skies, once blue, are tost and torn,
    We are not yet forgetful of the morn,
And praise anew the sunshine that we lack.

Oh, sadder than pale sufferers by a tomb
10   That say "My dead is happier, and is more,"
    Are they who dare no "is" but tell what's o'er—
Thus the frank childhood, those the lovable
    ways—
    Stirring the ashes of remembered days
For yet some sparks to warm the livelong gloom.
—1895

XII

S he has made me wayside posies: here they stand,
    Bringing fresh memories of where they grew.
    As new-come travellers from a world we knew
Wake every while some image of their land,
5 So these whose buds our woodland breezes fanned
    Bring to my room the meadow where they blew,
    The brook-side cliff, the elms where wood-
        doves coo—
And every flower is dearer for her hand.

Oh blossoms of the paths she loves to tread,
10   Some grace of her is in all thoughts you bear:
    For in my memories of your homes that were,
The old sweet loneliness they kept is fled,
And would I think it back I find instead
    A presence of my darling mingling there.
—1895

XIII

M y darling scarce thinks music sweet save
    mine:
    'Tis that she does but love me more than hear.
    She'll not believe my voice to stranger ear
Is merely measure to the note and line;
5 "Not so," she says; "Thou hast a secret thine:
    The others' singing's only rich, or clear,
    But something in thy tones brings music near;
As though thy song could search me and divine."

---

[1] iota.

Oh voice of mine that in some day not far
10   Time, the strong creditor, will call his debt,
Will dull—and even to her—will rasp and mar,
    Sing Time asleep because of her regret,
Be twice thy life the thing her fancies are,
    Thou echo to the self she knows not yet.
—1895

XIV

To love her as to-day is so great bliss
    I needs must think of morrows almost loth,
    Morrows wherein the flower's unclosing growth
Shall make my darling other than she is.
5 The breathing rose excels the bud I wis,
    Yet bud that will be rose is sweet for both;
    And by-and-by seems like some later troth
Named in the moment of a lover's kiss.

Yes, I am jealous, as of one now strange
10   That shall instead of her possess my thought,
Of her own self made new by any change,
    Of her to be by ripening morrows brought.
My rose of women under later skies!
Yet, ah! my child with the child's trustful eyes!
—1895

XV

That some day Death who has us all for jest
    Shall hide me in the dark and voiceless mould,
    And him whose living hand has mine in hold,
Where loving comes not nor the looks that rest,
5 Shall make us nought where we are known the best,
    Forgotten things that leave their track untold
    As in the August night the sky's dropped gold—
This seems no strangeness, but Death's natural
    hest.

But looking on the dawn that is her face
10   To know she too is Death's seems misbelief;
She should not find decay, but, as the sun

Moves mightier from the veil that hides his place,
Keep ceaseless radiance. Life is Death begun:
    But Death and her! That's strangeness passing
      grief.
—1895

XVI

She will not have it that my day wanes low,
    Poor of the fire its drooping sun denies,
    That on my brow the thin lines write good-byes
Which soon may be read plain for all to know,
5 Telling that I have done with youth's brave show;
    Alas! and done with youth in heart and eyes,
    With wonder and with far expectancies,
Save but to say "I knew such long ago."

She will not have it. Loverlike to me,
10   She with her happy gaze finds all that's best,
She sees this fair and that unfretted still,
    And her own sunshine over all the rest:
So she half keeps me as she'd have me be,
And I forget to age, through her sweet will.
—1895

XVII

And how could I grow old while she's so young?
    Methinks her heart sets time for mine to beat,
    We are so near; her new thoughts, incomplete,
Find their shaped wording happen on my tongue;
5 Like bloom on last year's winterings newly sprung
    My youth upflowers with hers, and must repeat
    Old joyaunces in me nigh obsolete.
Could I grow older while my child's so young?

And there are tales how youthful blood instilled
10   Thawing frore[1] Age's veins gave life new course,
And quavering limbs and eyes made indolent
    Grew freshly eager with beginning force:

_____
[1] frozen.

She so breathes impulse. Were my years twice spent,
Not burdening Age, with her, could make me
    chilled.
—1870

The Wind's Tidings In August 1870 [1]

"Oh voice of summer winds among the trees,
    What soft news art thou bringing to us
      here?
Dost thou come whispering of hushed scenes like
    these,
    Languid in sunlight, while the drowsy deer
5 Couch placidly at rest, and from the brake
    The song of fearless wild birds rings out clear,
And groves and meadows and this baby lake
    Are dreaming to thy dreaming lullaby?
Art telling of hushed scenes like these? Awake,
10   Answer, sweet dying wind, and do not die."

And the voice of the faint winds, dying away,
    Answered me, "Nay."

"Oh voice of summer winds, then art thou come
    From fluttering in the tangles of the vines
15 Beside the blue blue seas, in the far home
    Of the dim olives and the dusky pines,
And from the cypress bosks, and where the air
    Grows lush and heavy 'twixt the dark starred
      lines
Of orange hedge a-bloom, and the wide glare
20   Floods soft round hills with southern perfect
      day?
Answer again, low voice, hast thou been there?
    Art telling of the dreamland far away?"

And the voice of the winds sighed over my head,
    "Nay, nay," it said.

---

[1] probably a reference to the Franco-Prussian war (1870–71).

25 "Oh sweet low voice of winds, whose wavering
      flights
    Smoothly, like flickering swallows, come and go,
What, is thy tale of where the ceaseless heights
    Rest white and cloudlike in their virgin snow?
Hast thou been wandering round the scented firs,
30   And where the dauntless shrub-flowers bud and
      blow
Against the pale chill sea that never stirs,
    And where the midway foam hangs o'er the
      cleft?
Speak, slumbrous voice, to slumbrous listeners,
    Art telling us of these that thou hast left?"

35 And the voice of the dying winds breathed low,
    "Nay, nay; not so."

"Oh voice of dying winds, make sweet reply,
    Whence hast thou come? What does thy
      whisper say?
Answer, oh dying voice, and do not die."
40   It whispered in a hush, "The dead men lay
Fallen together like the sickled grain;
    Onward still dashed the whirlwind and the fray;
The thunders and the tramplings shook the plain;
    There was the crash and clash of host to host,
45 Throes, and the blood-pools widening, death and
      pain."
    And waning in a murmur it was lost.
—1881

To-Day

Oh God, where hast thou hidden Truth? Oh
    Truth,
    Where is the road to God?
Lo, we, that should be old, have learned our youth;
    We are not manly ripe; we have not dower
5 Of all the wisdom that a world can gain
In the centuries of work, peace, war, hope, pain;

We are not strong with all the gathered power
From age to age left our inheritance;
We stand not near the goal, there by the advance
10   Of step on step, though mire and blood and
          tears,
      Forgotten fathers trod;
We are new in a new world; where shall we know,
      Where in the ancient years,
Sign-marks to guide us on the way we go?

15   We are new in a new world. As children learn
          Life by surprise and doubt,
So life must learn itself at each return
      Of the upsoaring Phoenix[1] birth from sleep
Among the ashes of an ended Past.
20   In its own strength, and singly from the last,
          Each age's long To-day begins to creep
In baby paces whitherward it goes.
And from too far with too unsure a close,
          Like void sonorous echoes in the hill,
25   Yesterday's voice rings out,
So gives the questioning turmoil of our cries
          Answer such as we will.
Has Past writ Present in its histories?

Our fathers saw, we see not with their eyes,
30   Knew, and we learned in vain:
We seek old wisdoms in a novel wise;
      We toil beginners of the things that are;
Like lessons which we early get by rote,
Heedless of meaning in the words we quote,
35   And by and by, the schoolroom left afar,
Discern at last their sense or find a new,
The just, the unjust, the counterfeit, the true,
          We said from books upon our fathers' shelves,
          All must be learned again:
40   We, children-like, still wondering as we grow,

Change, and become ourselves,
And only as ourselves can henceforth know.

How shall we know? what must we do? what be?
          Answer us, Life, instead:
45   Past speaks us a dead tongue, we look to thee
          And know thee teacher—yet a tardy one;
For now we labour, fearing to what end;
We journey, dimly seeing where we tend;
          We do, and question was it rightly done;
50   Doubt and distrust of self beside us stand;
And who will find us Truth? where is her hand
          To guide us on or back by the round path,
          Leading but whence it led,
She travels on from God to reach him by?
55   What is the name she hath
To find her by to-day? Life, make reply.
—1881

Her Memories

Not by her grave: thither I bid them take
      Fresh garlands of the flowers that pleased her
          best,
And lay them by the headstone, for my sake,
      My token and remembrance with the rest:
5   But here, where in the brightening of the west
I see her mountains grow into the sky,
      Her native world, and mine because of her,
      Here, where that low sigh of the pinewood's
          stir,
That was her dearest music, fills all sound,
10   I am with her;
And always, always, past comes passing by,
Lost in her grave, but here as if half found.

Not by her grave: it is too still, too cold,
      And save my loss is nothing with me there.
15   What memories have I there of her of old?
      They came not there, the dear lost days that
          were;

---

[1] in Egyptian myth, a beautiful, lone bird that resided in the Arabian desert for 500 to 600 years before consuming itself in fire, and rising from the ashes to start a new life.

Not *she* lies there, but only my despair;
Not *she*, but death and all my loneliness.
  What memories save all memories love must
    shun?
20 I would not think of death and her as one;
She shall be only life-ful in my mind,
  With life's self one;
A name of glad remindings and old bliss,
So something of her presence left behind.

25 Not by her grave: some day will I return,
  When sorrow keeps its wont unvexed by place,
And, sitting on the turf beside, will learn
  To call before me there her waking face,
  Not that white face that slept and took no trace
30 Of change because I kissed it, nor for tears.
  Some day; for now I should forget her so,
  Lose the fair happy woman and but know
The coldness and the silence when she died,
  Lose her all so,
35 My love that was my life of all for years.
She loved this music when the pinewoods sighed.
—1881

A Coarse Morning

Oh the yellow boisterous sea,
The surging, chafing, murderous sea!
And the wind-gusts hurtle the torn clouds by,
On to the south through a shuddering sky,
5 And the bare black ships scud aloof from the land.
  'Tis as like the day as can be,
When the ship came in sight that came never to
  strand,
The ship that was blown on the sunken sand—
  And he coming back to me!

10   Oh the great white snake of foam,
  The coiling, writhing, snake of white foam,
Hissing and huddering out in the bay,
Over the banks where the wrecked ship lay,

Over the sands where the dead may lie deep!
15   There are some in the churchyard loam,[1]
Some two or three the sea flung to our keep:
Their mothers can sit by a grave to weep,
  But *my* son never came home.

  Never, never, living or dead—
20 Oh, never, Willie, living or dead,
Could you keep your word and come back to me!
Oh, my darling! As like this day as can be,
When the ship came in sight that came never to
  strand,
  When the ship came rounding the head,
25 Close to the haven and close to the sand.—
And their graves are long green that were tossed to
  land.
  Ah, "Sure to come back," he said!
—1881

Not To Be

The rose said "Let but this long rain be past,
And I shall feel my sweetness in the sun
And pour its fullness into life at last."
  But when the rain was done,
5 But when dawn sparkled through unclouded air,
  She was not there.

The lark said "Let but winter be away,
  And blossoms come, and light, and I will soar,
And lose the earth, and be the voice of day."
10   But when the snows were o'er,
But when spring broke in blueness overhead,
  The lark was dead.

And myriad roses made the garden glow,
  And skylarks carolled all the summer long—
15 What lack of birds to sing and flowers to blow?
  Yet, ah, lost scent, lost song!

---

[1] rich fertile soil.

Poor empty rose, poor lark that never trilled!
    Dead unfulfilled!
—1881

Once

I set a lily long ago;
  I watched it whiten in the sun;
  I loved it well, I had but one.
  Then summer-time was done,
5 The wind came and the rain,
    My lily bent, lay low.
Only the night-time sees my pain—
    Alas, my lily long ago!

    I had a rose-tree born in May;
10   I watched it burgeon and grow red,
  I breathed the perfume that it shed.
  Then summer-time had sped,
The frost came with its sleep,
    My rose-tree died away.
15 Only the silence hears me weep—
    Alas, lost rose-tree! lost, lost May!

    The garden's lily blows once more;
  The buried rose will wake and climb;
  There is no thought of rain and rime
20   After, next summer-time.
But the heart's blooms are weak;
    Once dead for ever o'er.
Not night, not silence knows me seek
    My joy that waned and blooms no more.
—1881

The Old Dream

Nay, tell me not. I will not know.
  Because of her my life is bare,
A waste where blow-seeds spring and grow
Then die because the soil is spent,
5   And leave no token they were there;
A soddened mere where marsh-lights gleam,
But no star sees the ray it lent:
  Because of her despoiled and bare.
What then? she did a wrong unmeant.
10   Leave me my dream.

Tell me no more. I will not know.
  My life, if she had harsher eyes,
Did her sweet voice not deepen so,
Had maybe missed this bitterness;
15   Maybe I should have been more wise
If she were sterner, or could seem,
If she could have been pitiless.
  Too sweet low voice! too trustful eyes!
What then? she could not judge their stress.
20   Leave me my dream.

I will not know. Rob not my heart:
  It is too poor to lose yet more.
Leave the old dream where she was part:
Are all smiles ill, all sweetness lies?
25   One blossom once my life-time bore,
It wakened at her April beam,
Then froze; yet dead 'tis still some prize:
  It shows me blossoms were of yore.
Let be: I need some memories:
30   Leave me my dream.
—1881

Thomas Hardy
1840 – 1928

Thomas Hardy was born and lived most of his life in rural Dorsetshire. Although now best known for his fiction (e.g. *The Return of the Native* [1878], *The Mayor of Casterbridge* [1886], *Tess of the d'Urbervilles* [1891], and *Jude the Obscure* [1895]), Hardy began and ended his career as a poet. His early poetry and some new works were published in *Wessex Poems* (1898), followed over the years by seven volumes of lyrics and narratives.

❧❧❧

Hap

If but some vengeful god would call to me
From up the sky, and laugh: "Thou suffering
    thing,
Know that thy sorrow is my ecstasy,
That thy love's loss is my hate's profiting!"

5 Then would I bear it, clench myself, and die,
Steeled by the sense of ire unmerited;
Half-eased in that a Powerfuller than I
Had willed and meted me the tears I shed.

But not so. How arrives it joy lies slain,
10 And why unblooms the best hope ever sown?
—Crass Casualty obstructs the sun and rain,
And dicing Time for gladness casts a moan....
These purblind Doomsters had as readily strown
Blisses about my pilgrimage as pain.
  —(1866)[1]

Neutral Tones

We stood by a pond that winter day,
  And the sun was white, as though chidden of
    God,
And a few leaves lay on the starving sod;
  —They had fallen from an ash, and were gray.

5 Your eyes on me were as eyes that rove
Over tedious riddles of years ago;
And some words played between us to and fro
  On which lost the more by our love.

The smile on your mouth was the deadest thing
10 Alive enough to have strength to die;
And a grin of bitterness swept thereby
  Like an ominous bird a-wing…

Since then, keen lessons that love deceives,
And wrings with wrong, have shaped to me
15 Your face, and the God-curst sun, and a tree,
  And a pond edged with grayish leaves.
  —(1867)

A Broken Appointment

You did not come,
And marching Time drew on, and wore me
  numb.—
Yet less for loss of your dear presence there
Than that I thus found lacking in your make
5 That high compassion which can overbear
Reluctance for pure lovingkindness' sake
Grieved I, when, as the hope-hour stroked its sum,
  You did not come.

You love not me,
10 And love alone can lend you loyalty;

---

[1] dates of composition given, if known. The order is that of *Collected Poems* (1926).

—I know and knew it. But, unto the store
Of human deeds divine in all but name,
Was it not worth a little hour or more
To add yet this: Once you, a woman, came
15 To soothe a time-torn man; even though it be
    You love not me?

The Darkling Thrush

I leant upon a coppice gate
    When Frost was spectre-gray,
And Winter's dregs made desolate
    The weakening eye of day.
5 The tangled bine-stems scored the sky
    Like strings of broken lyres,
And all mankind that haunted nigh
    Had sought their household fires.

The land's sharp features seemed to be
10   The Century's corpse outleant,
His crypt the cloudy canopy,
    The wind his death-lament.
The ancient pulse of germ and birth
    Was shrunken hard and dry,
15 And every spirit upon earth
    Seemed fervourless as I.

At once a voice arose among
    The bleak twigs overhead
In a full-hearted evensong
20   Of joy illimited;
An aged thrush, frail, gaunt, and small,
    In blast-beruffled plume,
Had chosen thus to fling his soul
    Upon the growing gloom.

25 So little cause for carolings
    Of such ecstatic sound
Was written on terrestrial things
    Afar or nigh around,

That I could think there trembled through
30   His happy good-night air
Some blessed Hope, whereof he knew
    And I was unaware.
—(1900)

The Self-Unseeing

Here is the ancient floor,
    Footworn and hollowed and thin,
Here was the former door
Where the dead feet walked in.

5 She sat here in her chair,
Smiling into the fire;
He who played stood there,
Bowing it higher and higher.

Childlike, I danced in a dream;
10 Blessings emblazoned that day;
Everything glowed with a gleam;
Yet we were looking away!

In Tenebris [1]

II

Considerabam ad dexteram, et videbam; et non erat
qui cognosceret me....Non est qui requirat animam
meam.—Ps. CXLI. [2]

When the clouds' swoln bosoms echo back the
    shouts of the many and strong
That things are all as they best may be, save a few
    to be right ere long,

---

[1] "In darkness" or "in gloom." Vulgate version, Psalm 141.

[2] "I looked on my right hand, and beheld, but there was no man that
would know me...no man cared for my soul." King James version, Psalm
142.

And my eyes have not the vision in them to discern
    what to these is so clear,
The blot seems straightway in me alone; one better
    he were not here.

5   The stout upstanders say, All's well with us: ruers
    have nought to rue!
And what the potent say so oft, can it fail to be
    somewhat true?
Breezily go they, breezily come; their dust smokes
    around their career,
Till I think I am one born out of due time, who
    has no calling here.

Their dawns bring lusty joys, it seems; their
    evenings all that is sweet;
10   Our times are blessed times, they cry: Life shapes it
    as is most meet,
And nothing is much the matter; there are many
    smiles to a tear;
Then what is the matter is I, I say. Why should
    such an one be here?…

Let him in whose ears the low-voiced Best is killed
    by the clash of the First,
Who holds that if way to the Better there be, it
    exacts a full look at the Worst,
15   Who feels that delight is a delicate growth cramped
    by crookedness, custom, and fear,
Get him up and be gone as one shaped awry; he
    disturbs the order here.
—(1895–96)

The Minute Before Meeting

The grey gaunt days dividing us in twain
    Seemed hopeless hills my strength must faint
    to climb,
But they are gone; and now I would detain
The few clock-beats that part us; rein back Time,

5   And live in close expectance never closed
In change for far expectance closed at last,
So harshly has expectance been imposed
On my long need while these slow blank months
    passed.

And knowing that what is now about to be
10   Will all *have been* in O, so short a space!
I read beyond it my despondency
When more dividing months shall take its place,
Thereby denying to this hour of grace
A full-up measure of felicity.
—(1871)

Night in the Old Home

When the wasting embers redden the chimney-
    breast,
And Life's bare pathway looms like a desert track to
    me,
And from hall and parlour the living have gone to
    their rest,
My perished people who housed them here come
    back to me.

5   They come and seat them around in their mouldy
    places,
Now and then bending towards me a glance of
    wistfulness,
A strange upbraiding smile upon all their faces,
And in the bearing of each a passive tristfulness.

"Do you uphold me, lingering and languishing here,
A pale late plant of your once strong stock?" I say
    to them;
"A thinker of crooked thoughts upon Life in the
    sere,
And on That which consigns men to night after
    showing the day to them?"

"—O let be the Wherefore! We fevered our years
   not thus:
Take of Life what it grants, without question!" they
   answer me seemingly.
15 "Enjoy, suffer, wait: spread the table here freely like
   us,
And, satisfied, placid, unfretting, watch Time away
   beamingly!"

The Something that Saved Him

It was when
Whirls of thick waters laved me
   Again and again,
That something arose and saved me;
5   Yea, it was then.

   In that day
Unseeing the azure went I
   On my way,
And to white winter bent I,
10   Knowing no May.

   Reft of renown,
Under the night clouds beating
   Up and down,
In my needfulness greeting
15   Cit and clown.

   Long there had been
Much of a murky colour
   In the scene,
Dull prospects meeting duller;
20   Nought between.

   Last, there loomed
A closing-in blind alley,
   Though there boomed

   A feeble summons to rally
25   Where it gloomed.

   The clock rang;
The hour brought a hand to deliver;
   I upsprang,
And looked back at den, ditch and river,
30   And sang.

Afterwards

When the Present has latched its postern
   behind my tremulous stay,
  And the May month flaps its glad green leaves
   like wings,
Delicate-filmed as new-spun silk, will the
   neighbours say,
  "He was a man who used to notice such
   things"?

5 If it be in the dusk when, like an eyelid's soundless
   blink,
  The dewfall-hawk comes crossing the shades to
   alight
Upon the wind-warped upland thorn, a gazer may
   think,
  "To him this must have been a familiar sight."

If I pass during some nocturnal blackness, mothy
   and warm,
10 When the hedgehog travels furtively over the
   lawn,
One may say, "He strove that such innocent
   creatures should come to no harm,
  But he could do little for them; and now he is
   gone."

If, when hearing that I have been stilled at last, they
   stand at the door,

Watching the full-starred heavens that winter
     sees,
15 Will this thought rise on those who will meet my
     face no more,
    "He was one who had an eye for such
     mysteries"?

And will any say when my bell of quittance is heard
     in the gloom,
    And a crossing breeze cuts a pause in its
     outrollings,
Till they rise again, as they were a new bell's boom,
20   "He hears it not now, but used to notice such
     things"?

A Young Man's Exhortation

Call off your eyes from care
By some determined deftness; put forth joys
Dear as excess without the core that cloys,
    And charm Life's lourings fair.

5   Exalt and crown the hour
That girdles us, and fill it full with glee,
Blind glee, excelling aught could ever be
    Were heedfulness in power.

    Send up such touching strains
10 That limitless recruits from Fancy's pack
Shall rush upon your tongue, and tender back
    All that your soul contains.

    For what do we know best?
That a fresh love-leaf crumpled soon will dry,
15 And that men moment after moment die,
    Of all scope dispossest.

    If I have seen one thing
It is the passing preciousness of dreams;
That aspects are within us; and who seems
20   Most kingly is the King.
—(1867)

Snow in the Suburbs

Every branch big with it,
    Bent every twig with it;
Every fork like a white web-foot;
Every street and pavement mute:
5 Some flakes have lost their way, and grope back
    upward, when
Meeting those meandering down they turn and
    descend again.
    The palings are glued together like a wall,
    And there is no waft of wind with the
     fleecy fall.

    A sparrow enters the tree,
10   Whereon immediately
A snow-lump thrice his own slight size
Descends on him and showers his head and eyes,
    And overturns him,
    And near inurns him,
15 And lights on a nether twig, when its brush
Starts off a volley of other lodging lumps with a
    rush.

    The steps are a blanched slope,
    Up which, with feeble hope,
    A black cat comes, wide-eyed and thin;
20   And we take him in.

In a Wood

From *The Woodlanders*

Pale beech and pine so blue,
    Set in one clay,
Bough to bough cannot you
    Live out your day?
5 When the rains skim and skip,
Why mar sweet comradeship,
Blighting with poison-drip
    Neighbourly spray?

Heart-halt and spirit-lame,
10   City-opprest,
Unto this wood I came
    As to a nest;
Dreaming that sylvan peace
Offered the harrowed ease—
15 Nature a soft release
    From men's unrest.

But, having entered in,
    Great growths and small
Show them to men akin—
20   Combatants all!

Sycamore shoulders oak,
Bines the slim sapling yoke,
Ivy-spun halters choke
    Elms stout and tall.

25 Touches from ash, O wych,
    Sting you like scorn!
You, too, brave hollies, twitch
    Sidelong from thorn.
Even the rank poplars bear
30 Lothly a rival's air,
Cankering in blank despair
    If overborne.

Since, then, no grace I find
    Taught me of trees,
35 Turn I back to my kind,
    Worthy as these.
These at least smiles abound,
There discourse trills around,
There, now and then, are found
40   Life-loyalties.
  —1877

Edward Dowden
1843 – 1913

A critic and occasional poet, Dowden wrote a number of miscellaneous critical essays, but is perhaps best known for *Shakespeare: His Mind and Art*, a subjective treatment in which the author professed an ability to discern in the plays evidence of Shakespeare's own intellectual, moral, and spiritual experiences.

⁘

Burdens

Are sorrows hard to bear,—the ruin
Of flowers, the rotting of red fruit,
A love's decease, a life's undoing,
    And summer slain, and song-birds mute,
5 And skies of snow and bitter air?
These things, you deem, are hard to bear.

But ah the burden, the delight
    Of dreadful joys! Noon opening wide,
Golden and great; the gulfs of night,
10   Fair deaths, and rent veils cast aside,
Strong soul to strong soul rendered up,
And silence filling like a cup.
—1876 (1872)

Leonardo's "Monna Lisa"[1]

Make thyself known, Sibyl,[2] or let despair
Of knowing thee be absolute; I wait
Hour-long and waste a soul. What word of fate
Hides 'twixt the lips which smile and still forbear?
5 Secret perfection! Mystery too fair!
Tangle the sense no more lest I should hate
Thy delicate tyranny, the inviolate
Poise of thy folded hands, thy fallen hair.
Nay, nay,—I wrong thee with rough words; still be
10 Serene, victorious, inaccessible;

Still smile but speak not; lightest irony
Lurk ever 'neath thine eyelids' shadow; still
O'ertop our knowledge; Sphinx[3] of Italy,
Allure us and reject us at thy will!
—1876

Europa[4]

"He stood with head erect fronting the herd;
    At the first sight of him I knew the God
And had no fear. The grass is sweet and long
Up the east land backed by a pale blue heaven:
5 Gray, shining gravel shelves toward the sea
Which sang and sparkled; between these he stood,
Beautiful, with imperious head, firm foot,
And eyes resolved on present victory,
Which swerved not from the full acquist of joy,
10 Calmly triumphant. Did I see at all
The creamy hide, deep dewlap, little horns,
Or hear the girls describe them? I beheld
Zeus,[5] and the law of my completed life.
Therefore the ravishment of some great calm
15 Possessed me, and I could not basely start
Or scream; if there was terror in my breast
It was to see the inevitable bliss

---

[1] painted in 1504; featured in the Louvre, Paris.

[2] a female prophet of classical legend.

[3] in Greek mythology, a monster with the head and breasts of a woman, the body of a lion, the wings of a bird, and the tail of a serpent. The sphinx spoke in a human voice, setting riddles and devouring those who could not find answers.

[4] the daughter of Agenor and sister of Cadmus, king of Thebes, taken by Zeus in the form of a bull from Tyre to Crete where she bore Minos.

[5] the supreme god of Greek myth; his Roman equivalent is Jupiter.

In prone descent from heaven; apart I lived
Held in some solitude, intense and clear,
20 Even while amid the frolic girls I stooped
And praised the flowers we gathered, they and I.
Pink-streaked convolvulus the warm sand bears,
Orchids, dark poppies with the crumpled leaf,
And reeds and giant rushes from a pond
25 Where the blue dragon-fly shimmers and shifts.
All these were notes of music, harmonies
Fashioned to underlie a resonant song,
Which sang how no more days of flower-culling
Little Europa must desire; henceforth
30 The large needs of the world resumed her life,
So her least joy must be no trivial thing,
But ordered as the motion of the stars,
Or grand incline of sun-flower to the sun.

By this the God was near; my soul waxed strong,
35 And wider orbed the vision of the world
As fate drew nigh. He stooped, all gentleness,
Inviting touches of the tender hands,
And wore the wreaths they twisted round his horns
In lordly-playful wise, me all this while
40 Summoning by great mandates at my heart,
Which silenced every less authentic call,
Away, away, from girlhood, home, sweet friends,
The daily dictates of my mother's will,
Agenor's[1] cherishing hand, and all the ways
45 Of the calm household. I would fain have felt
Some ruth to part from these, the tender ties
Severing with thrills of passion. Can I blame
My heart for light surrender of things dear,
And hardness of a little selfish soul?
50 Nay: the decree of joy was over me,
There was the altar, I, the sacrifice
Foredoomed to life, not death; the victim bound
Looked for the stroke, the world's one fact for her,
The blissful consummation: straight to this
55 Her course had tended from the hour of birth,

---

[1] King of Tyre, son of Poseidon, father of Europa.

Even till this careless morn of maidenhood
A sudden splendour changed to life's high noon:
For this my mother taught me gracious things,
My father's thoughts had dealt with me, for this
60 The least flower blossomed, the least cloud went by,
All things conspired for this; the glad event
Summed my full past and held it, as the fruit
Holds the fair sequence of the bud and flower
In soft matureness.

                    Now he bent the knee;
65 I never doubted of my part to do,
Nor lingered idly, since to veil command
In tender invitation pleased my lord;
I sat, and round his neck one arm I laid
Beyond all chance secure. Whether my weight
70 Or the soft pressure of the encircling arm
Quickened in him some unexpected bliss
I know not, but his flight was one steep rush.
Oh uncontrollable and joyous rage!
O splendour of the multitudinous sea!
75 Swift foam about my feet, the eager stroke
Of the strong swimmer, new sea-creatures brave,
And uproar of blown conch, and shouting lips
Under the open heaven; till Crete[2] rose fair
With stedfast shining peak, and promontories.

80 Shed not a leaf, O plane-tree, not a leaf,
Let sacred shadow, and slumbrous sound remain
Alway, where Zeus looked down upon his bride.
—1876

Seeking God

I said "I will find God," and forth I went
To seek Him in the clearness of the sky,
But over me stood unendurably
Only a pitiless, sapphire firmament

---

[2] the fourth largest island in the Mediterranean Sea, and site of one of the world's earliest civilizations, the Minoan (c. 1500 BC).

5 Ringing the world,—blank splendour; yet intent
Still to find God, "I will go seek," said I,
"His way upon the waters," and drew nigh
An ocean marge weed-strewn, and foam-besprent;
And the waves dashed on idle sand and stone,
10 And very vacant was the long, blue sea;
But in the evening as I sat alone,
My window open to the vanishing day,
Dear God! I could not choose but kneel and pray,
And it sufficed that I was found of Thee.
—1876

In a June Night

(*A Study in the manner of Robert Browning.*)

I

See, the door opens of this alcove,
Here we are now in the cool night air
Out of the heat and smother; above
    The stars are a wonder, alive and fair,
5 It is a perfect night,—your hand,—
    Down these steps and we reach the garden,
An odorous, dim, enchanted land,
    With the dusk stone-god for only warden.

II

Was I not right to bring you here?
10   We might have seen slip the hours within
Till God's new day in the East were clear,
    And His silence abashed the dancer's din,
Then each have gone away, the pain
    And longing greatened, not satisfied,
15 By a hand's slight touch or a glance's gain,—
    And now we are standing side by side!

III

Come to the garden's end,—not so,
    Not by the grass, it would drench your feet;
See, here is a path where the trees o'ergrow

And the fireflies flicker; but, my sweet,
20 Lean on me now, for one cannot see
    Here where the great leaves lie unfurled
To take the whole soul and the mystery
    Of a summer night poured out for the world.

IV

25 Into the open air once more!
    Yonder's the edge of the garden-wall
Where we may sit and talk,—deplore
    This half-hour lost from so bright a ball,
Or praise my partner with the eyes
30   And the raven hair, or the other one
With her flaxen curls, and slow replies
    As near asleep in the Tuscan sun.

V[1]

Hush! do you hear on the beach's cirque
    Just below, though the lake is dim,
35 How the little ripples do their work,
    Fall and faint on the pebbled rim,
So they say what they want, and then
    Break at the marge's feet and die;
It is so different with us men
40   Who never can once speak perfectly.

VI

Yet hear me,—trust that they mean indeed
    Oh, so much more than the words will say,
Or shall it be 'twixt us two agreed
    That all we might spend a night and day
45 In striving to put in a word or thought,
    Which were then from ourselves a thing apart,
Shall be just believed and quite forgot,
    When my heart is felt against your heart.

VII

Ah, but that will not tell you all,
50   How I am yours not thus alone,

---

[1] Compare with Matthew Arnold's "Dover Beach."

To find how your pulses rise and fall,
    And winning you wholly be your own,
But yours to be humble, could you grow
    The Queen that you are, remote and proud.
55 And I with only a life to throw
    Where the others' flowers for your feet were
        strowed.

VIII

Well, you have faults too! I can blame
    If you choose: this hand is not so white
Or round as a little one that came
60   On my shoulder once or twice to-night
Like a soft white dove. Envy her now!
    And when you talked to that padded thing

And I passed you leisurely by, your bow
    Was cold, not a flush nor fluttering.

IX

65 Such foolish talk! while that one star still
    Dwells o'er the mountain's margin-line
Till the dawn takes all; one may drink one's fill
    Of such quiet; there's a whisper fine
In the leaves a-tremble, and now 'tis dumb;
70   We have lived long years, love, you and I,
And the heart grows faint, your lips, then: come,—
    It were not so very hard to die.
—1876

Robert Bridges
1844 – 1930

Educated at Eton and Corpus Christi College, Oxford, Bridges went to London as a medical student in 1869. His major interest, however, was poetry: he wrote several long poems, including *Prometheus the Firegiver* (1883) and *Eros and Psyche* (1885). His major contribution to literature was *The Shorter Poems* (1890), which contained some of the following selections. He was named Poet Laureate in 1913. Bridges was accomplished as a prosodist and as a poet, but is best known today as the friend and early editor of Gerard Manley Hopkins.

❧❧❧

London Snow

When men were all asleep the snow came flying,
In large white flakes falling on the city brown,
Stealthily and perpetually settling and loosely lying,
    Hushing the latest traffic of the drowsy town;
5 Deadening, muffling, stifling its murmurs failing;
Lazily and incessantly floating down and down:
    Silently sifting and veiling road, roof and railing;
Hiding difference, making unevenness even,
Into angles and crevices softly drifting and sailing.
10   All night it fell, and when full inches seven
It lay in the depth of its uncompacted lightness,
The clouds blew off from a high and frosty heaven;
    And all woke earlier for the unaccustomed brightness
Of the winter dawning, the strange unheavenly glare:
15 The eye marvelled—marvelled at the dazzling whiteness;
    The ear hearkened to the stillness of the solemn air;
No sound of wheel rumbling nor of foot falling,
And the busy morning cries came thin and spare.
    Then boys I heard, as they went to school, calling,
20 They gathered up the crystal manna to freeze
Their tongues with tasting, their hands with snowballing;
    Or rioted in a drift, plunging up to the knees;

Or peering up from under the white-mossed wonder,
    "O look at the trees!" they cried, "O look at the trees!"
25   With lessened load a few carts creak and blunder,
Following along the white deserted way,
A country company long dispersed asunder:
    When now already the sun, in pale display
Standing by Paul's high dome,[1] spread forth below
30 His sparkling beams, and awoke the stir of the day.
    For now doors open, and war is waged with the snow;
And trains of sombre men, past tale of number,
Tread long brown paths, as toward their toil they go:
    But even for them awhile no cares encumber
35 Their minds diverted; the daily word is unspoken,
The daily thoughts of labour and sorrow slumber
At the sight of the beauty that greets them, for the charm they have broken.
—1880

On a Dead Child

Perfect little body, without fault or stain on thee,
    With promise of strength and manhood full and fair!
        Though cold and stark and bare,

---
[1] St. Paul's Cathedral.

The bloom and the charm of life doth awhile
    remain on thee.

5 Thy mother's treasure wert thou;—alas! no longer
    To visit her heart with wondrous joy; to be
        Thy father's pride;—ah, he
Must gather his faith together, and his strength
    make stronger.

To me, as I move thee now in the last duty,
10   Dost thou with a turn or gesture anon respond;
        Startling my fancy fond
With a chance attitude of the head, a freak of
    beauty.

Thy hand clasps, as 'twas wont, my finger, and
    holds it:
    But the grasp is the clasp of Death,
          heartbreaking and stiff;
15   Yet feels to my hand as if
'Twas still thy will, thy pleasure and trust that
    enfolds it.

So I lay thee there, thy sunken eyelids closing,—
    Go lie thou there in thy coffin, thy last little
        bed!—
        Propping thy wise, sad head,
20 Thy firm, pale hands across thy chest disposing.

So quiet! doth the change content thee?—Death,
    whither hath he taken thee?
    To a world, do I think, that rights the disaster
        of this?
        The vision of which I miss,
Who weep for the body, and wish but to warm
    thee and awaken thee?

25 Ah! little at best can all our hopes avail us
    To lift this sorrow, or cheer us, when in the dark,
        Unwilling, alone we embark,
And the things we have seen and have known and
    have heard of, fail us.
—1880

Gerard Manley Hopkins
1844 – 1889

Gerard Manley Hopkins, the Oxford-educated English poet and Roman Catholic priest, was an innovative technician who applied his art to the dual themes of nature and religion. Converting to Catholicism in 1866 under the guidance of the Tractarians, Hopkins joined the Society of Jesus in 1868. Encouraged to eulogize the loss of five nuns at sea, Hopkins wrote *The Wreck of the Deutschland* (1875–76). Representing Hopkins's first successful experiment with "sprung rhythm," the poem eschews the accentual-syllabic measures conventionally associated with modern English verse. Poems such as "The Windhover" (1877) and the "terrible sonnets" (1885–89) have garnered Hopkins recognition as a poet of stunning originality.

❧❧❧

The Wreck of the Deutschland

*To the
happy memory of five Franciscan nuns
exiles by the Falck Laws*[1]
*drowned between midnight and morning of
Dec. 7th, 1875*

PART THE FIRST

1

THOU mastering me
    God! giver of breath and bread;
  World's strand, sway of the sea;
    Lord of living and dead;
5 Thou hast bound bones and veins in me,
      fastened me flesh,
  And after it is almost unmade, what with dread,
      Thy doing: and dost thou touch me afresh?
  Over again I feel thy finger and find thee.

2

    I did say yes
10   O at lightning and lashed rod;
  Thou heardst me truer than tongue confess
    Thy terror, O Christ, O God;

Thou knowest the walls, altar and hour and night:
  The swoon of a heart that the sweep and the
      hurl of thee trod
15   Hard down with a horror of height:
And the midriff astrain with leaning of, laced with
    fire of stress.

3

    The frown of his face
    Before me, the hurtle of hell
  Behind, where, where was a, where was a place?
20   I whirled out wings that spell
And fled with a fling of the heart to the heart of
    the Host.
  My heart, but you were dovewinged, I can tell,
    Carrier-witted, I am bold to boast,
To flash from the flame to the flame then, tower
    from the grace to the grace.

4

25   I am soft sift
    In an hourglass—at the wall
  Fast, but mined with a motion, a drift,
    And it crowds and it combs to the fall;
I steady as a water in a well, to a poise, to a pane,
30 But roped with, always, all the way down from
    the tall
    Fells or flanks of the voel,[2] a vein

---

[1] The Falk Laws, so-called after the Prussian minister of education, Adalbert Falk, were a series of anti-Catholic decrees passed in Germany in 1873. The *Deutschland* sank in the mouth of the Thames as over 200 German Catholics were attempting to find refuge in America.

[2] a Welsh word meaning a bare hill or mountain.

Of the gospel proffer, a pressure, a principle,
    Christ's gift.

5

    I kiss my hand
      To the stars, lovely-asunder
35   Starlight, wafting him out of it; and
      Glow, glory in thunder;
Kiss my hand to the dappled-with-damson west:
Since, tho' he is under the world's splendour
    and wonder,
    His mystery must be instressed, stressed;
40 For I greet him the days I meet him, and bless
    when I understand.

6

    Not out of his bliss
      Springs the stress felt
    Nor first from heaven (and few know this)
      Swings the stroke dealt—
45 Stroke and a stress that stars and storms deliver,
That guilt is hushed by, hearts are flushed by
    and melt—
    But it rides time like riding a river
(And here the faithful waver, the faithless fable and
    miss).

7

    It dates from day
50   Of his going in Galilee;[1]
    Warm-laid grave of a womb-life grey;
      Manger, maiden's knee;
The dense and the driven Passion,[2] and frightful
    sweat:
    Thence the discharge of it, there its swelling to
    be,
55   Though felt before, though in high flood
    yet—

---

[1] the homeland of Christ, who was called "The Galilean."

[2] the sufferings of Christ.

What none would have known of it, only the heart,
    being hard at bay.

8

    Is out with it! Oh,
      We lash with the best or worst
60   Word last! How a lush-kept plush-capped sloe
      Will, mouthed to flesh-burst,
Gush!—flush the man, the being with it, sour
    or sweet,
    Brim, in a flash, full!—Hither then, last or first,
    To hero of Calvary,[3] Christ,'s feet—
Never ask if meaning it, wanting it, warned of
    it—men go.

9

65   Be adored among men,
      God, three-numberèd form;
    Wring thy rebel, dogged in den,
      Man's malice, with wrecking and storm.
    Beyond saying sweet, past telling of tongue,
70   Thou art lightning and love, I found it, a winter
    and warm;
    Farther and fondler of heart thou hast wrung:
Hast thy dark descending and most art merciful
    then.

10

    With an anvil-ding
      And with fire in him forge thy will
75   Or rather, rather then, stealing as Spring
      Through him, melt him but master him
      still:
    Whether at once, as once at a crash Paul,[4]
    Or as Austin, a lingering-out swéet skíll,
    Make mercy in all of us, out of us all
80 Mastery, but be adored, but be adored King.

---

[3] the place of Christ's crucifixion.

[4] The sudden conversion of St. Paul: Acts 22:6–16; "Austin" is St. Augustine of Hippo (354–430), whose conversion, described in his *Confessions*, was gradual.

PART THE SECOND

11

"Some find me a sword; some
The flange and the rail; flame,
Fang, or flood" goes Death on drum,
And storms bugle his fame.
85 But wé dream we are rooted in earth—Dust!
Flesh falls within sight of us, we, though our
flower the same,
Wave with the meadow, forget that there must
The sour scythe cringe, and the blear share come.

12

On Saturday sailed from Bremen,[1]
90 American-outward-bound,
Take settler and seamen, tell men with
women,
Two hundred souls in the round—
O Father, not under thy feathers nor ever as
guessing
The goal was a shoal, of a fourth the doom to
be drowned;
95 Yet did the dark side of the bay of thy blessing
Not vault them, the million of rounds of thy mercy
not reeve even them in?

13

Into the snow she sweeps,
Hurling the haven behind,
The Deutschland, on Sunday; and so the sky
keeps,
100 For the infinite air is unkind,
And the sea flint-flake, black-backed in the
regular blow,
Sitting Eastnortheast, in cursed quarter, the wind;
Wiry and white-fiery and whirlwind-
swivellèd snow
Spins to the widow-making unchilding unfathering
deeps.

[1] a seaport of Germany.

14

105 She drove in the dark to leeward,
She struck—not a reef or a rock
But the combs[2] of a smother of sand: night
drew her
Dead to the Kentish Knock;[3]
And she beat the bank down with her bows and
the ride of her keel:
110 The breakers rolled on her beam with ruinous
shock;
And canvas and compass, the whorl and the
wheel
Idle for ever to waft her or wind her with, these she
endured.

15

Hope had grown grey hairs,
Hope had mourning on,
115 Trenched with tears, carved with cares,
Hope was twelve hours gone;
And frightful a nightfall folded rueful a day
Nor rescue, only rocket and lightship, shone,
And lives at last were washing away:
120 To the shrouds they took,—they shook in the
hurling and horrible airs.

16

One stirred from the rigging to save
The wild woman-kind below,
With a rope's end round the man, handy
and brave—
He was pitched to his death at a blow,
125 For all his dreadnought breast and braids of thew:
They could tell him for hours, dandled the to
and fro
Through the cobbled foam-fleece. What
could he do
With the burl of the fountains of air, buck and the
flood of the wave?

[2] ridges

[3] a sandbank near the mouth of Thames.

17

They fought with God's cold—
130   And they could not and fell to the deck
      (Crushed them) or water (and drowned
        them) or rolled
    With the sea-romp over the wreck,
Night roared, with the heart-break hearing a
    heart-broke rabble,
The woman's wailing, the crying of child
    without check—
135   Till a lioness arose breasting the babble,
A prophetess towered in the tumult, a virginal
    tongue told.

18

    Ah, touched in your bower of bone,
    Are you! turned for an exquisite smart,
    Have you! make words break from me here
      all alone,
140   Do you!—mother of being in me, heart.
O unteachably after evil, but uttering truth,
    Why, tears! is it? tears; such a melting, a
    madrigal start!
    Never-eldering revel and river of youth,
What can it be, this glee? the good you have there
    of your own?

19

145   Sister, a sister calling
    A master, her master and mine!—
    And the inboard seas run swirling and
      hawling;
    The rash smart sloggering brine
Blinds her; but she that weather sees one thing,
    one;
150 Has one fetch in her: she rears herself to divine
    Ears, and the call of the tall nun
To the men in the tops and the tackle rode over the
    storm's brawling.

20

    She was first of a five and came
    Of a coifèd sisterhood.
155   (O Deutschland, double a desperate name!
    O world wide of its good!
But Gertrude,[1] lily, and Luther, are two of a town,
    Christ's lily and beast of the waste wood:
    From life's dawn it is drawn down,
160 Abel is Cain's brother[2] and the breasts they have
    sucked the same.)

21

    Loathed for a love men knew in them,
    Banned by the land of their birth,
    Rhine refused them, Thames would ruin them;
    Surf, snow, river and earth
165 Gnashed: but thou art above, thou Orion[3] of light;
    Thy unchancelling poising palms were weighing
      the worth,
    Thou martyr-master: in thy sight
Storm flakes were scroll-leaved flowers, lily
    showers—sweet heaven was astrew in them.

22

    Five! the finding and sake
170   And cipher of suffering Christ.
    Mark, the mark is of man's make
    And the word of it Sacrificed.
But he scores it in scarlet himself on his own
    bespoken,
    Before-time-taken, dearest prizèd and priced—
175   Stigma, signal, cinquefoil token
For lettering of the lamb's fleece, ruddying of the
    rose-flake.

---

[1] St. Gertrude (1256–1302), lived near Eisleben, Germany, the birth-place of Martin Luther.

[2] Cain, the first-born son of Adam and Eve, murdered his brother Abel.

[3] the constellation named after the giant hunter of Greek mythology.

23

Joy fall to thee, father Francis,
   Drawn to the Life that died;
With the gnarl of the nails in thee, niche of
      the lance, his
      Lovescape crucified[1]
180 And seal of his seraph-arrival! and these thy
      daughters
And five-livèd and leavèd favour and pride,
      Are sisterly sealed in wild waters,
To bathe in his fall-gold mercies, to breathe in his
   all-fire glances.

24

185   Away in the loveable west,
      On a pastoral forehead of Wales,[2]
   I was under a roof here, I was at rest,
      And they the prey of the gales;
She to the black-about air, to the breaker, the
      thickly
190 Falling flakes, to the throng that catches and
      quails
      Was calling "O Christ, Christ, come
      quickly":[3]
The cross to her she calls Christ to her, christens
   her wild-worst Best.

25

      The majesty! what did she mean?
      Breathe, arch and original Breath.[4]
195   Is it love in her of the being as her lover had
      been?
      Breathe, body of lovely Death.
      They were else-minded then, altogether, the men

Woke thee with a *We are perishing* in the
      weather of Gennesareth.[5]
   Or is it that she cried for the crown then,
200 The keener to come at the comfort for feeling the
      combating keen?

26

      For how to the heart's cheering
      The down-dugged ground-hugged grey
   Hovers off, the jay-blue heavens appearing
      Of pied and peeled May!
205 Blue-beating and hoary-glow height; or night,
      still higher,
   With belled fire and the moth-soft Milky Way,
      What by your measure is the heaven of desire,
The treasure never eyesight got, nor was ever
   guessed what for the hearing?

27

      No, but it was not these.
210   The jading and jar of the cart,
   Time's tasking, it is fathers that asking for ease
      Of the sodden-with-its-sorrowing heart,
   Not danger, electrical horror; then further it finds
   The appealing of the Passion is tenderer in
      prayer apart:
215   Other, I gather, in measure her mind's
Burden, in wind's burly and beat of endragonèd
   seas.

28

      But how shall I...make me room there:
      Reach me a...Fancy, come faster—
   Strike you the sight of it? look at it loom there,
220   Thing that she...There then! the Master,
Ipse,[6] the only one, Christ, King, Head:
   He was to cure the extremity where he had cast
      her;

---

[1] Christ's five wounds, described as the Lovescape, are reproduced in the stigmata received by St. Francis.

[2] Hopkins was studying theology at St. Beuno's College in Wales.

[3] *The Times* of London reported that these were the last words of one of the nuns.

[4] the Holy Spirit.

[5] See Matthew 14:22–23.

[6] "He himself."

Do, deal, lord it with living and dead;
Let him ride, her pride, in his triumph, despatch
and have done with his doom there.

29

225   Ah! there was a heart right!
There was single eye!
Read the unshapeable shock night
And knew the who and the why;
Wording it how but by him that present and
past,
230 Heaven and earth are word of, worded by?—
The Simon Peter[1] of a soul! to the blast
Tarpeïan-fast,[2] but a blown beacon of light.

30

Jesu, heart's light,
Jesu, maid's son,
235   What was the feast followed the night
Thou hadst glory of this nun?—
Feast of the one woman without stain.[3]
For so conceivèd, so to conceive thee is done;
But here was heart-throe, birth of a brain,
240 Word, that heard and kept thee and uttered thee
outright.

31

Well, she has thee for the pain, for the
Patience; but pity of the rest of them!
Heart, go and bleed at a bitterer vein for the
Comfortless unconfessed of them—
245 No not uncomforted: lovely felicitous
Providence
Finger of a tender of, O of a feathery delicacy,
the breast of the

Maiden could obey so, be a bell to, ring of
it, and
Startle the poor sheep back! is the shipwrack then a
harvest, does tempest carry the grain for thee?

32

I admire thee, master of the tides,
250   Of the Yore-flood,[4] of the year's fall;
The recurb and the recovery of the gulf's sides,
The girth of it and the wharf of it and
the wall;
Stanching, quenching ocean of a motionable
mind;
Ground of being, and granite of it: past all
255   Grasp God, throned behind
Death with a sovereignty that heeds but hides,
bodes but abides;

33

With a mercy that outrides
The all of water, an ark
For the listener; for the lingerer with a love
glides
260   Lower than death and the dark;
A vein for the visiting of the past-prayer, pent in
prison,
The-last-breath penitent spirits—the uttermost
mark
Our passion-plungèd giant risen,
The Christ of the Father compassionate, fetched in
the storm of his strides.

34

265   Now burn, new born to the world,
Double-naturèd name,
The heaven-flung, heart-fleshed, maiden-
furled
Miracle-in-Mary-of-flame,
Mid-numberèd he in three of the thunder-throne!

---

[1] See Matthew 14:28.

[2] possibly a reference to the Tarpeian women, warlike female attendants in Virgil's *Aeneid* 11.

[3] the Feast of the Immaculate Conception of the Virgin Mary, December 8.

---

[4] Genesis 1.1–10: the primordial waters; Genesis 6–8: Noah's flood:

270 Not a dooms-day dazzle in his coming nor dark
    as he came;
  Kind, but royally reclaiming his own;
A released shower, let flash to the shire, not a
  lightning of fire hard-hurled.

35

    Dame, at our door
    Drowned, and among our shoals,
275   Remember us in the roads, the heaven-haven
    of the reward:
      Our King back, Oh, upon English souls!
Let him easter in us, be a dayspring to the
  dimness of us, be a crimson-cresseted east,
More brightening her, rare-dear Britain, as his
  reign rolls,
Pride, rose, prince, hero of us, high-priest,
280 Our hearts' charity's hearth's fire, our thoughts'
  chivalry's throng's Lord.
    —1918 (1876)

God's Grandeur

The world is charged with the grandeur of God.
  It will flame out, like shining from shook foil;
  It gathers to a greatness, like the ooze of oil
Crushed. Why do men then now not reck his rod?
5 Generations have trod, have trod, have trod;
  And all is seared with trade; bleared, smeared
    with toil;
  And wears man's smudge and shares man's
    smell: the soil
Is bare now, nor can foot feel, being shod.

And for all this, nature is never spent;
10   There lives the dearest freshness deep down
    things;
And though the last lights off the black West went
  Oh, morning, at the brown brink eastward,
    springs—

Because the Holy Ghost[1] over the bent
  World broods with warm breast and with ah!
    bright wings.
  —1895 (1877)

The Windhover

To Christ our Lord

I caught this morning morning's minion, king-
  dom of daylight's dauphin, dapple-dawn-
    drawn Falcon, in his riding
  Of the rolling level underneath him steady air,
    and striding
High there, how he rung upon the rein of a
  wimpling wing
5 In his ecstasy! then off, off forth on swing,
  As a skate's heel sweeps smooth on a bow-bend:
    the hurl and gliding
  Rebuffed the big wind. My heart in hiding
Stirred for a bird,—the achieve of, the mastery of
  the thing!

Brute beauty and valour and act, oh, air, pride,
  plume, here
10   Buckle! AND the fire that breaks from thee then,
    a billion
Times told lovelier, more dangerous, O my
  chevalier!

  No wonder of it: shéer plód makes plough
    down sillion
Shine, and blue-bleak embers, ah my dear,
  Fall, gall themselves, and gash gold-vermilion.
  —1918 (1877)

Pied Beauty

Glory be to God for dappled things—
  For skies of couple-colour as a brinded cow;

---

[1] the third person of the Christian Trinity; the Divine or Holy Spirit.

For rose-moles all in stipple upon trout that
    swim;
Fresh-firecoal chestnut-falls; finches' wings;
5   Landscape plotted and pieced—fold, fallow,
      and plough;
    And áll trádes, their gear and tackle and
      trim.

All things counter, original, spare, strange;
    Whatever is fickle, freckled (who knows how?)
      With swift, slow; sweet, sour; adazzle, dim;
10 He fathers-forth whose beauty is past change:
                          Praise him.

—1918 (1877)

Hurrahing in Harvest

Summer ends now; now, barbarous in beauty,
  the stooks rise
Around; up above, what wind-walks! what lovely
    behaviour
Of silk-sack clouds! has wilder, wilful-wavier
Meal-drift moulded ever and melted across skies?

5   I walk, I lift up, I lift up heart, eyes,
    Down all that glory in the heavens to glean our
      Saviour;
    And, éyes, heárt, what looks, what lips yet gave
      you a
    Rapturous love's greeting of realer, of rounder
      replies?

    And the azurous hung hills are his world-wielding
      shoulder
10 Majestic—as a stallion stalwart, very-violet-
      sweet!—
    These things, these things were here and but the
      beholder
    Wanting; which two when they once meet,
    The heart rears wings bold and bolder

And hurls for him, O half hurls earth for him off
    under his feet.
—1918 (1877)

The Caged Skylark

As a dare-gale skylark scanted in a dull cage
  Man's mounting spirit in his bone-house,
    mean house, dwells—
    That bird beyond the remembering his free fells;
This in drudgery, day-labouring-out life's age.

5   Though aloft on turf or perch or poor low stage,
    Both sing sometímes the sweetest, sweetest spells,
    Yet both droop deadly sómetimes in their cells
Or wring their barriers in bursts of fear or rage.

Not that the sweet-fowl, song-fowl, needs no rest—
10 Why, hear him, hear him babble and drop down to
    his nest,
    But his own nest, wild nest, no prison.

Man's spirit will be flesh-bound when found at best,
But uncumberèd: meadow-down is not distressed
    For a rainbow footing it nor he for his bónes
      rísen.
—(1918) 1877

Peace

When will you ever, Peace, wild wooddove, shy
  wings shut,
Your round me roaming end, and under be my
    boughs?
When, when, Peace, will you, Peace? I'll not play
    hypocrite
To own my heart: I yield you do come sometimes;
    but

5 That piecemeal peace is poor peace. What pure
peace allows
Alarms of wars, the daunting wars, the death of it?

O surely, reaving Peace, my Lord should leave in lieu
Some good! And so he does leave Patience exquisite,
That plumes to Peace thereafter. And when Peace
here does house
10 He comes with work to do, he does not come to coo,
He comes to brood and sit.
—1918 (1879)

Felix Randal

Felix Randal the farrier, O is he dead then? my
duty all ended,
Who have watched his mould of man, big-boned
and hardy-handsome
Pining, pining, till time when reason rambled in it
and some
Fatal four disorders, fleshed there, all contended?

5 Sickness broke him. Impatient, he cursed at first,
but mended
Being anointed and all; though a heavenlier heart
began some
Months earlier, since I had our sweet reprieve and
ransom
Tendered to him. Ah well, God rest him all road
ever he offended!

This seeing the sick endears them to us, us too it
endears.
10 My tongue had taught thee comfort, touch had
quenched thy tears,
Thy tears that touched my heart, child, Felix, poor
Felix Randal;

How far from then forethought of, all thy more
boisterous years,
When thou at the random grim forge, powerful
amidst peers,

Didst fettle for the great grey drayhorse his bright
and battering sandal!
—1918 (1880)

"As kingfishers catch fire, dragonflies draw flame"

As kingfishers catch fire, dragonflies draw flame;
As tumbled over rim in roundy wells
Stones ring; like each tucked string tells, each
hung bell's
Bow swung finds tongue to fling out broad its
name;
5 Each mortal thing does one thing and the same:
Deals out that being indoors each one dwells;
Selves—goes itself; *myself* it speaks and spells,
Crying *What I do is me: for that I came.*

I say more: the just man justices;
10 Keeps gráce: thát keeps all his goings graces;
Acts in God's eye what in God's eye he is—
Christ. For Christ plays in ten thousand places,
Lovely in limbs, and lovely in eyes not his
To the Father through the features of men's
faces.
—1918 (1881 OR 1882)

The Leaden Echo and the Golden Echo

(*Maidens' song from St. Winefred's Well*) [1]

THE LEADEN ECHO

How to kéep—is there ány any, is there none
such, nowhere known some, bow or brooch

---

[1] St. Winifred, a virgin martyr, is the patron saint of North Wales.
Prince Caradoc made violent advances to her and struck off her head,
but it was replaced by St. Beuno who brought her back to life. On the
spot where her head had lain, the healing spring of Holywell gushed
forth.

or braid or brace, láce, latch or catch or key to
    keep
Back beauty, keep it, beauty, beauty, beauty,…from
    vanishing away?
Ó is there no frowning of these wrinkles, rankèd
    wrinkles deep,
Down? no waving off of these most mournful
    messengers, still messengers, sad and stealing
    messengers of grey?—
No there 's none, there 's none, O no there 's none,
5 Nor can you long be, what you now are, called fair,
Do what you may do, what, do what you may,
And wisdom is early to despair:
Be beginning; since, no, nothing can be done
To keep at bay
10 Age and age's evils, hoar hair,
Ruck and wrinkle, drooping, dying, death's worst,
    winding sheets, tombs and worms and tumbling
    to decay;
So be beginning, be beginning to despair.
O there 's none; no no no there 's none:
Be beginning to despair, to despair,
Despair, despair, despair, despair.

THE GOLDEN ECHO

                Spare!
There ís one, yes I have one (Hush there!),
Only not within seeing of the sun.
Not within the singeing of the strong sun,
5 Tall sun's tingeing, or treacherous the tainting of
    the earth's air,
Somewhere elsewhere there is ah well where! one,
Óne. Yes I cán tell such a key, I dó know such a place,
Where whatever's prizèd and passes of us,
    everything that's fresh and fast flying of us,
    seems to us sweet of us and swiftly away with,
    done away with, undone,
Undone, done with, soon done with, and yet dearly
    and dangerously sweet

10 Of us, the wimpled-water-dimpled, not-by-
    morning-matchèd face,
The flower of beauty, fleece of beauty, too too apt
    to, ah! to fleet,
Never fleets móre, fastened with the tenderest truth
To its own best being and its loveliness of youth: it
    is an ever-lastingness of, O it is an all youth!
Come then, your ways and airs and looks, locks,
    maidengear, gallantry and gaiety and grace,
15 Winning ways, airs innocent, maiden manners,
    sweet looks, loose locks, long locks, lovelocks,
    gaygear, going gallant, girlgrace—
Resign them, sign them, seal them, send them,
    motion them with breath,
And with sighs soaring, soaring síghs, deliver
Them; beauty-in-the-ghost, deliver it, early now,
    long before death
Give beauty back, beauty, beauty, beauty, back to
    God, beauty's self and beauty's giver.
20 See; not a hair is, not an eyelash, not the least lash
    lost; every hair
Is, hair of the head, numbered.
Nay, what we had lighthanded left in surly the
    mere mould
Will have waked and have waxed and have walked
    with the wind what while we slept,
This side, that side hurling a heavyheaded
    hundredfold
25 What while we, while we slumbered.
O then, weary then whý should we tread? O why
    are we so haggard at the heart, so care-coiled,
    care-killed, so fagged, so fashed, so cogged, so
    cumbered,
When the thing we freely fórfeit is kept with fonder
    a care,
Fonder a care kept than we could have kept it, kept
Far with fonder a care (and we, we should have lost
    it) finer, fonder
30 A care kept.—What kept? do but tell us where
    kept, where.—

Yonder.—What high as that! We follow, now we
    follow.—Yonder, yes yonder, yonder,
Yonder.
—1918 (1882)

Spelt from Sibyl's Leaves [1]

Earnest, earthless, equal, attuneable, | vaulty,
    voluminous,…stupendous
Evening strains to be tíme's vást, | womb-of-all,
    home-of-all, hearse-of-all night.
Her fond yellow hornlight wound to the west, |
    her wild hollow hoarlight hung to the height
Waste; her earliest stars, earlstars, | stárs principal,
    overbend us,
5 Fíre-féaturing heaven. For earth | her being has
    unbound; her dapple is at an end, as-
tray or aswarm, all throughther, in throngs; | self
    ín self steepèd and páshed—qúite
Disremembering, dísmémbering | áll now. Heart,
    you round me right
With: Óur évening is over us; óur night | whélms,
    whélms, ánd will end us.
Only the beakleaved boughs dragonish | damask
    the tool-smooth bleak light; black,
10 Ever so black on it. Óur tale, O óur oracle! | Lét
    life, wáned, ah lét life wind
Off hér once skéined stained véined varíety |
    upon, áll on twó spools; párt, pen, páck
Now her áll in twó flocks, twó folds—black, white;
    | right, wrong; reckon but, reck but, mind
But thése two; wáre of a wórld where bút these |
    twó tell, each off the óther; of a rack
Where, selfwrung, selfstrung, sheathe-and
    shelterless, | thóughts agaínst thoughts ín
    groans grínd.
—1918 (1885)

---

[1] Sibyl, a female prophet of Greek and Roman mythology. The
Cumaean Sibyl, described in Virgil's *Aeneid*, wrote down her prophecies
on leaves.

Carrion Comfort

Not, I'll not, carrion comfort, Despair, not feast
    on thee;
Not untwist—slack they may be—these last strands
    of man
In me ór, most weary, cry *I can no more.* I can;
Can something, hope, wish day come, not choose
    not to be.

5 But ah, but O thou terrible, why wouldst thou
    rude on me
Thy wring-world right foot rock? lay a lionlimb
    against me? scan
With darksome devouring eyes my bruisèd bones?
    and fan,
O in turns of tempest, me heaped there; me frantic
    to avoid thee and flee?

Why? That my chaff might fly; my grain lie, sheer
    and clear.
10 Nay in all that toil, that coil, since (seems) I kissed
    the rod,
Hand rather, my heart lo! lapped strength, stole
    joy, would laugh, chéer.
Cheer whom though? The hero whose heaven-
    handling flung me, fóot tród
Me? or me that fought him? O which one? is it
    each one? That night, that year
Of now done darkness I wretch lay wrestling with
    (my God!) my God.
—1918 (1855)

"No worst, there is none"

No worst, there is none. Pitched past pitch of
    grief,
More pangs will, schooled at forepangs, wilder wring.
Comforter, where, where is your comforting?

Mary,[1] mother of us, where is your relief?
5 My cries heave, herds-long; huddle in a main; a chief-
woe, world-sorrow; on an age-old anvil wince and sing—
Then lull, then leave off. Fury[2] had shrieked "No ling-
ering! Let me be fell: force I must be brief."
O the mind, mind has mountains; cliffs of fall
10 Frightful, sheer, no-man-fathomed. Hold them cheap
May who ne'er hung there. Nor does long our small
Durance deal with that steep or deep. Here! creep,
Wretch, under a comfort serves in a whirlwind: all
Life death does end and each day dies with sleep.
—1918 (1885?)

"To seem the stranger lies my lot, my life"

To seem the stranger lies my lot, my life
Among strangers. Father and mother dear,
Brothers and sisters are in Christ not near
And he my peace / my parting, sword and strife.

5 England, whose honour O all my heart woos, wife
To my creating thought, would neither hear
Me, were I pleading, plead nor do I; I wear-
y of idle a being but by where wars are rife.

I am in Ireland now; now I am at a third
10 Remove. Not but in all removes I can
Kind love both give and get. Only what word

Wisest my heart breeds dark heaven's baffling ban
Bars or hell's spell thwarts. This to hoard unheard,
Heard unheeded, leaves me a lonely began.
—1893 (1885)

---

[1] the Virgin Mary, mother of Christ.

[2] The Roman Furies were merciless goddesses of vengeance whose punishments continued after death.

"I wake and feel the fell of dark, not day"

I wake and feel the fell of dark, not day.
What hours, O what black hoürs we have spent
This night! what sights you, heart, saw; ways you went!
And more must, in yet longer light's delay.

5 With witness I speak this. But where I say
Hours I mean years, mean life. And my lament
Is cries countless, cries like dead letters sent
To dearest him that lives alas! away.

I am gall, I am heartburn. God's most deep decree
10 Bitter would have me taste: my taste was me;
Bones built in me, flesh filled, blood brimmed the curse.

Selfyeast of spirit a dull dough sours. I see
The lost are like this, and their scourge to be
As I am mine, their sweating selves; but worse.
—1918 (1885?)

"Patience, hard thing! the hard thing but to pray"

Patience, hard thing! the hard thing but to pray,
But bid for, Patience is! Patience who asks
Wants war, wants wounds; weary his times, his tasks;
To do without, take tosses, and obey.

5 Rare patience roots in these, and, these away,
Nowhere. Natural heart's ivy, Patience masks
Our ruins of wrecked past purpose. There she basks
Purple eyes and seas of liquid leaves all day.

We hear our hearts grate on themselves: it kills
10 To bruise them dearer. Yet the rebellious wills
Of us we do bid God bend to him even so.

And where is he who more and more distills
Delicious kindness?—He is patient. Patience fills
His crisp combs, and that comes those ways we
    know.
  —1918 (1885)

"My own heart let me more have pity on"

My own heart let me more have pity on; let
  Me live to my sad self hereafter kind,
Charitable; not live this tormented mind
With this tormented mind tormenting yet.

5   I cast for comfort I can no more get
By groping round my comfortless, than blind
Eyes in their dark can day or thirst can find
Thirst's all-in-all in all a world of wet.

Soul, self; come, poor Jackself, I do advise
10   You, jaded, let be; call off thoughts awhile
Elsewhere; leave comfort root-room; let joy size

At God knows when to God knows what; whose
    smile
's not wrung, see you; unforeseen times rather—as
    skies
Betweenpie mountains—lights a lovely mile.
  —1918 (1885)

Tom's Garland

upon the Unemployed

Tom—garlanded with squat and surly steel
  Tom; then Tom's fallowbootfellow piles pick
By him and rips out rockfire homeforth—sturdy
    Dick;
Tom Heart-at-ease, Tom Navvy: he is all for his
    meal
5   Sure, 's bed now. Low be it: lustily he his low lot
    (feel

That ne'er need hunger, Tom; Tom seldom sick,
Seldomer heartsore; that treads through,
    prickproof, thick
Thousands of thorns, thoughts) swings though.
    Commonweal
Little Í reck ho! lacklevel in, if all had bread:
10 What! Country is honour enough in all us—lordly
    head,
With heaven's lights high hung round, or,
    mother-ground
That mammocks, might foot. But nó way sped,
Nor mind nor mainstrength; gold go garlanded
With, perilous, O nó; nor yet plod safe shod sound;
15   Undenizened, beyond bound
Of earth's glory, earth's ease, all; no one, nowhere,
In wide the world's weal; rare gold, bold steel, bare
          In both; care, but share care—
This, by Despair, bred Hangdog dull; by Rage,
20 Manwolf, worse; and their packs infest the age.
  —1918 (1887)

Harry Ploughman

Hard as hurdle arms, with a broth of goldish
  flue
Breathed round; the rack of ribs; the scooped flank;
    lank
Rope-over thigh; knee-nave; and barrelled shank—
    Head and foot, shoulder and shank—
5   By a grey eye's heed steered well, one crew, fall to;
Stand at stress. Each limb's barrowy brawn, his thew
That onewhere curded, onewhere sucked or sank—
    Soared ór sánk—,
Though as a beechbole firm, find his, as at a
    rollcall, rank
10 And features, in flesh, what deed he each must do—
    His sinew-service where do.

He leans to it, Harry bends, look. Back, elbow, and
    liquid waist

In him, all quail to the wallowing o' the plough. 'S
    cheek crimsons; curls
Wag or crossbridle, in a wind lifted, windlaced—
15   See his wind- lilylocks -laced;
Churlsgrace, too, child of Amansstrength, how it
    hangs or hurls
Them—broad in bluff hide his frowning feet
    lashed! raced
With, along them, cragiron under and cold furls—
        With-a-fountain's shining-shot
        furls.
    —1918 (1887)

It was a hard thing to undo this knot

It was a hard thing to undo this knot.
The rainbow shines, but only in the thought
Of him that looks. Yet not in that alone,
For who makes rainbows by invention?
5 And many standing round a waterfall
See one bow each, yet not the same to all,
But each a hand's breadth further than the next.
The sun on falling waters writes the text
Which yet is in the eye or in the thought.
10 It was a hard thing to undo this knot.
    —1937 (1864)

Eugene Lee-Hamilton
1845 – 1907

Eugene Lee-Hamilton was a poet of considerable accomplishment, although undeservedly neglected in the twentieth century. His most noteworthy volumes are *Imaginary Sonnets* (1891)—dramatic monologues on themes from the German and Italian Renaissance—and the more mature *Sonnets of the Wingless Hours* (1894), written during years of illness.

ᕙᕗ

The Keys of the Convent

I

The night had closed, and all reposed
    Within the Convent's walls,
The cloisters fair now empty were,
    And silent were the halls.

5 And undisturbed, with passions curbed
    The Nuns to rest had gone;
The moonbeams peeping could see them sleeping,
    Each in her cell of stone.

But there was one, the portress nun,
10   Whom mighty struggles tried;
With breathing bated, awaked she waited
    A well-known step outside.

She crouched with shame, where burnt the flame
    Before the Virgin's figure;
15 And, as she knelt, each moment felt
    Her bursting heart grow bigger.

"O Mary[1] mild, and Holy Child,"
    She cried with burning brow,
"Oh give me power, this bitter hour,
20   To keep my convent vow;

"See how I fight, this live-long night
    With fierce temptation near;

Which Love shall call, prevent my fall,
    Vouchsafe my prayer to hear."

25 And at the feet of Mary sweet
    The sister portress lay
Convulsed and pale, with groan and wail,
    Nor ceased for help to pray.

But soon outside was heard a stride
30   Distinctly more and more,
And there was heard a whispered word,
    Athrough the grated door:

"Away, away, 'tis almost day,
    My steed hard by is waiting;
35 I cannot wait; 'tis late, 'tis late,
    Unfasten quick the grating."

She gave a start, loud thumped her heart
    And to her feet she leapt;
By passion urged, by conscience scourged,
40   Half to the door she stept.

There, all unnerved, she now observed
    The door, and now the shrine,
Where fair and mild, the Virgin smiled
    Her smile of love Divine.

45 "Once gone with *him*, oh who will trim
    Thy lamp that's ever burning,

---

[1] the Virgin Mary, Mother of Christ.

Or wreathe thy flowers in noon-tide hours,
    When once there's no returning?"

"I've not the strength," she gasped at length,
50   "I've not the strength to stay;"
As more and more outside the door,
    Was heard the call "Away!"

But ere she fled, with muffled head,
    She kissed the Virgin's knees,
55 And in her charge, she left the large
    And heavy Convent keys.

II
She drank her measure of sinful pleasure;
    At last the dregs were met,
The more they thickened the more she sickened,
60   But thicker grew they yet.

She looked around; no help she found,
    She dared not look above;
She could no more to Heaven soar
    Than a bespattered dove.

65 But from her life with scandal rife,
    She now with loathing turned,
And for the end, which God should send,
    From dawn to eve she yearned.

At last one day she tore away
70   The jewelled chain she wore;
The silken dress which did oppress,
    From off her limbs she tore;

And donned again her old and plain
    And cherished Nun's attire
75 Hid in her trunk, and which she'd shrunk
    From giving to the fire.

And courage rallied and firmly sallied
    When Day was nearly spent;

On, on, she flew, though well she knew
80   What was the punishment.

She sighted late the Convent gate,
    Sound slept the pious flock;
And lo, the door revolved before
    Her hand had time to knock.

85 What could it mean? Had she been seen?
    She shyly stepped within,
No soul was there? The Portress where?
    And who had let her in?

But in the shrine, the lamp did shine
90   Before the Virgin's figure,
In whose white hand the keys did stand.
    Her awe grew ever bigger.

She knelt again in fear and pain,
    As on that fatal night,
95 And the Mother of God appeared to nod
    By the uncertain light.

And there she stay'd, and humbly prayed
    Until the matins rang,
Then, pale of face, she took her place
100   Among the nuns who sang.

But in their eyes was no surprise,
    As if they'd never missed her;
None seemed amazed; no cry was raised,
    That 'twas their erring sister.

105 She asked of one: Which was the nun
    Who now was Portress there?
But, stranger yet, her words were met
    By Wonder's gaping stare.

Ye Saints above! Her sinful love,
110   Had it been nought but dreaming?

And was her flight that fatal night,
    And her return, mere seeming?

"But no, but no," she murmured low,
    "Her sin was but too real,"
115 When a sudden thought at which she caught,
    Brought light in her ordeal.

When she had fled with muffled head,
    While all in peace did sleep,
Had she not given the Queen of Heaven
120   The Convent keys to keep?

And could it be, that even she
    Had done the sinner's duty,
And service done to save the nun
    Betrayed by Youth and Beauty.

125 She knelt again, but not in pain;
    Oh, had she guessed aright?
And the mother of God, appeared to nod
    In the uncertain light.
    —1880

Introduction

(*Picciola*)

There was a captive once at Fenestrèl,[1]
    To whom there came an unexpected love
In the dim light which reached his narrow cell
    From high above.

5 No hinge had turned, no gaoler seen her pass;
But when once there, she undisturbed remained;
For who would grudge a harmless blade of grass
    To one long chained?

Between the flagstones of his prison floor
10 He saw one day a pale green shoot peep out,

And with a rapture never felt before
    He watched it sprout.

The shoot became a flower: on its life
He fixed all hope, and ceased of self to think;
15 Striving to widen with his pointless knife
    The cruel chink.

He bore great thirst when, parched, she drooped
    her head
In that close cell, to give her of his cup;
And when it froze, he stripped his wretched bed
20   To wrap her up.

Naming her Picciola; and week by week
Grew so enamoured as her leaves unfurled
That his fierce spirit almost ceased to seek
    The outer world.

25 Oh such another Picciola hast thou,
My prison-nurtured Poetry, long been;
Sprung up between the stones, I know not how,
    From seed unseen!

This book is all a plant of prison growth,
30 Watered with prison water, not sweet rain;
The writer's limbs and mind are laden both
    By heavy chains.

Not by steel shackles, riveted by men,
But by the clankless shackles of disease;
35 Which Death's own hand alone can sever, when
    He so shall please.

What work I do, I do with numbed, chained hand,
With scanty light, and seeing ill the whole,
And each small part, once traced, must changeless
    stand
40   Beyond control.

---

[1] name of a prison.

The thoughts come peeping, like the small black
    mice
Which in the dusk approach the prisoner's bed,
Until they even nibble at his slice
    Of mouldy bread.

45 The whole is prison work: the human shapes
Are such fantastic figures, one and all,
As with a rusty nail the captive scrapes
    Upon his wall.

But if some shape of horror makes you shrink,
50 It is perchance some outline he has got
From nightmare's magic lantern. Do you think
    He knows it not?

Scratched on that prison stone-work you will find
Some things more bold than men are wont to read.
55 The sentenced captive does not hide his mind;
    He has no need.

Oh, would my prison were of solid stone
That knows no change, for habit might do much,
And men have grown to love their dungeons lone;
60   But 'tis not such.

It is that iron room whose four walls crept
On silent screws, and came each night more near
By steady inches while the victim slept,
    And had no fear.

65 At dawn he wakes; there somehow seems a change;
The cell seems smaller; less apart the beams.
He sets it down to fancy; yet 'tis strange
    How close it seems!

The next day comes; his narrow strip of sky
70 Seems narrower still: all day his strained eyes sweep
Floor, walls, and roof. He's sure the roof's less high:
    He dares not sleep.

The third day breaks. He sees—he wildly calls
On God and man, who care not to attend;
75 He maims his hands against the conscious walls
    That seek his end.

All day he fights, unarmed and all alone,
Against the closing walls, the shrinking floor,
Till Nature, ceasing to demand her own,
80   Rebels no more.

Then waits in silence, noting the degrees—
Perhaps with hair grown white from that dread
    doubt—
Till those inexorable walls shall squeeze
    His strong soul out.

SIENA, *July,* 1882
—1882

The New Medusa [1]

A.D. 1620

Grown strangely pale? Grown silent and morose
In my three years of travel? Brother John,
    Oh, once for all, why watch me thus so close?
When since my childhood was my cheek not wan,
5   My soul not moody, and my speech not short?
    As Nature made me, let me then live on.
Spare me thy questions; seek such noisy sport
    As suits thy stronger frame and happier mood,
    And cease thy preaching of this irksome sort.
10 It suits my whim to hold aloof and brood;
    Go, medler, go! Forgive me, I recall
    The word; it was too harsh, for thou art good.
O cruel Heaven, shall I tell him all?
    God knows I need a hand to cling to tight,

---

[1] In classical mythology, Medusa is the chief of the three Gorgons, who had serpents on their heads instead of hair. Originally a beautiful woman, Medusa was transformed into a Gorgon by Minerva as punishment for violating Minerva's temple.

15 For on my path all Horror's shadows fall.
I am like one who's dogged, and who, as night
   Is closing in, must cross a lonely spot,
   And needs some staunch companion in his flight.
My enemy is Madness: I have got
20   His stealthy step behind me, ever near,
   And he will clutch me if thou help me not.
Oh, I have sailed across a sea of fear,
   And met new lands to add to Horror's realms,
   And shores of Guilt whence none may
      scatheless steer.
25 A very world of jarring thoughts o'erwhelms
   My cowering soul when I would tell what's been
   Since last I saw this Hall, these English elms.
Yet must the tale be told, and every scene
   Gone o'er again. I fear some monstrous thing
30   From my own self, and on thy strength must
      lean.

So listen. I had spent the early spring
   In Venice, till Ascension Feast[1]—the day
   On which the Doge[2] casts in his bridal ring;
And had embarked, with pleasant winds of May
35   And gentle seas, on a Venetian ship
   Bound for Palermo,[3] where I meant to stay.
All gave us promise of a prosperous trip;
   Yet, by the second day, mishap began,
   And 'tween two Turkish sail we had to slip.
40 From dawn to dusk before the Turk we ran,
   Till, safe and breathless off Illyria's[4] coast,
   We each thanked God to be a chainless man.
'Twas but the respite of an hour at most;
   The weather changed with dread rapidity.

45 As in rebuke of Safety's hasty boast,
God laid His mighty hand upon the sea,
   Moulding at once a million liquid peaks
   That ever round us tossed more furiously.
For three whole days the tempest blanched the cheeks
50   Of men whom years of storm had ill enriched,
   And long familiar with the petrel's shrieks.
It was as if the maddened ocean itched
   Beneath the ship; so desperately it tried
   To shake it off, and bounded, roared, and
      pitched,
55 And, like a lion in whose quivering hide
   An insect burrows, wasted strength and wrath,
   In rush on rush, by littleness defied.
At last, like one who no more hoping hath,
   It ceased the strife; and we, at dawn of day,
60   Had set the helm to seek our long-lost path,
When in the offing, on the lurid grey,
   Where tossed black waves, as if of ire still full,
   We saw a something looming far away.
It proved to be a small dismasted hull,
65   To all appearance empty, which remained
   Upon one spot, just like a sea-rocked gull.
On closer search we found that it contained
   A woman, lashed to remnants of a mast,
   Who seemed a corpse, but, slowly, life regained.
70 Her black, wet, rope-like locks she backward cast,
   And in her troubled memory seemed to seek;
   Then strangely, doggedly, concealed the past.
Her garb, her features, said she was a Greek,
   But Tuscan[5] she spoke well; and 'tis that tongue
75   Which she and I in aftertimes did speak.
And as she stood amid the wondering throng,
   And no account of home or kindred gave,
   A murmur 'mong the sailors ran along.
"Keep her," they cried; "we'll sell her as a slave;
80   She owns no kin that she should be exempt;

---

[1] In the Christian religion, Ascension Day commemorates the ascent of Jesus from earth to heaven.

[2] the chief magistrate of the Venetian Republic. Venice is a city in north Italy built on 118 small islands connected by canals. It was occupied by Napoleon in 1797 and united with the Kingdom of Italy in 1866.

[3] the largest city of Sicily.

[4] an ancient region on the north and east shores of the Adriatic Sea.

[5] from Tuscany, a region of central Italy; from 1569 to 1860 it was a Grand Duchy, and united with Italy in 1861.

She's common prize tossed up by wind and
　　wave."
She caught the words, but made no vain attempt
　　To melt their hearts by prayer and sobs and
　　sighs,
　　And looked around her with a queen's contempt.
85　And then it was that suddenly her eyes,
　　Singling me out, were fastened upon mine
　　So searchingly, that all felt huge surprise;
And that, like one who by some secret sign
　　Knows that a strange command will be obeyed,
90　She cried, "Lord, buy me;" and I paid her fine.
So she my slave, and I her slave was made,
　　She taking eager bondage from that hour,
　　And binding me in chains that never weighed.
She seemed contented with a latent power,
95　Keeping slave garb, and took small gifts alone,
　　As might an empress from some love below her.
She bade me name her, and I named her Joan,
　　Feeling no wish to pry within her breast,
　　Or learn what name her former life might own.
100　With all the strong lithe beauty, she possessed
　　The noiseless tread of a tame leopardess,
　　Docile, majestic, holding strength repressed.
With wondrous insight soon she learned to guess
　　My gloomy temper's ever-shifting mood,
105　And, fierce in love, was chary of caress.
Now wisely silent, she would let me brood
　　Until the fit was over; now she cheered
　　With such fantastic tales as tribes still rude
Delight to hear, the night till dawn appeared;
110　Now sang unto the lute some old Greek air,
　　Like gusts of moaning tempest wild and weird.
And other gifts she had, and arts more rare;
　　For when at Syracuse[1] I once fell ill
　　Of a malignant fever, and her care
115　Preserved my life, she showed a leech's[2] skill
　　In mingling drugs, and knew how to extract

From long-sought herbs a juice for ague's cure.
Oh she was strangely dowered, and she lacked
　　Nought that can rivet man to woman's side,
120　Nought that can win, or on the senses act.
But there were moments when a fear would glide
　　Across my heart, I knew not well of what,
　　And on the secret which her life might hide
My mind would work; and yet she daily got
125　A firmer tenure of the love she'd won,
　　And felt each day my kisses grow more hot,
Even as those of the Sicilian sun,
　　Which made of winter spring, with fiery love,
　　Long ere the thaw had in our clime begun.

130　She loved, like me, from place to place to move,
　　And seldom we long lingered where mere chance
　　Had made us stop, but sought some lovelier
　　grove,
Where, from deep shade, we saw the sunshine dance
　　On the blue sea which lapped the tideless coast,
135　And watched the sails which specked the blue
　　expanse.
But when that happened which I dread to reach,
　　We were abiding where the owlet made
　　The night oft sleepless with his lonesome screech
It was a sea-girt castle much decayed,
140　Belonging to an old Sicilian prince
　　With whom, when at Palermo, I had stayed.
He loathed the place, would go to no expense
　　To keep it up; but, loving town resorts,
　　Had left it in his youth, nor seen it since.
145　It suited well my mood. The weird reports,
　　The legends which the peasants loved to tell
　　About its empty halls and grass-grown courts;
Its garden paths where unpicked flowers fell;
　　Its silent rooms where many echoes woke
150　And fancies came—all made me love it well.
Its furniture of carved and blackened oak
　　Looked ghostly in the twilight; while the walls
　　Were hung with shields and swords of mighty
　　stroke.

---

[1] a city in south-east Sicily, site of the ruins of the Temple of Apollo.

[2] a doctor.

Of mighty stroke? Ay, ay, my tongue forestalls
155 My hesitating thoughts as I related,
And every item that I name appals,
As I retread in mind where monstrous Fate
Changed love to horror; every look I cast
Makes me all love, all horror, re-create.

160 One night—O John, I come to it at last—
One night I had a nightmare in my sleep
For vividness and terror unsurpassed.
Methought I felt a snake's cold body creep
About my hand and throat, entwine them tight,
165 And o'er my breast a hideous mastery keep.
Awhile I lay all helpless, in despite
Of agony, and felt the pressed veins swell,
Then forced a smothered cry into the night.
My cry awoke me, waking Joan as well,
170 When panting still with nightmare fear, I found
That the black locks that on her bosom fell
Had crept about my throat and girt it round
So tightly as awhile to stop the breath,
While other locks about my arms had wound.
175 We laughed away my ugly dream of death,
And in the silence of the night that waned
We heaped up kisses, burying fear beneath.
I gave the thing no thought; but Hell ordained
That this same dream, before a week was out,
180 Should be repeated, and its horror strained.
Once more the snakes encompassed me about,
Once more I woke her with my strangled cry,
Once more I found her locks around my throat.

Then I began to brood; and by and by
185 Strange things of God's strong chastisement of
crime
Recurred all vaguely to my memory.
I seemed to recollect from olden rhymes
Some tale about the hair of those who take
A many lives through poison; how at times,
190 When guilt haunts sleep, each lock becomes a snake,
While they remain unconscious of the change;

And turns again to hair so soon they wake.
Smile not, or I will throttle thee. The range
Of Nature is so vast that it hath room
195 For things more strange than what we call most
strange.
I am not mad. I thought with growing gloom
How we had met her, tossed alone at sea,
And how the Turks who rule those coasts oft
doom
Their women to strange punishments. Might she,
200 For some great crime, not have been made to
brave
The winds and waves by some such strange
decree?
And then I thought what proof she often gave
Of skill in medicine and botanic lore;
And how that serves to kill that serves to save.
205 I struggled with these thoughts—I struggled sore:
With shame and self-contempt I cast them out,
And, looking on her beauty, loved her more.
But listen, John. A month or thereabout
Went by unmarked, and then there came a night
210 Which seemed to put an end to every doubt.

I was awake; there was no sound, no light.
Yes, there was sound: her breathing met my ear,
The breath of dreamless sleep—low, smooth,
and slight.
But suddenly it quickened, as in fear,
215 And broken words whose sense I could not tell
Escaped her lips; my name I seemed to hear.
Now listen, John. Methought she lay not well,
I stretched my hand to slightly raise her head;
But what my hand encountered was, O hell!
220 No locks of silky hair: it met instead
A something cold which whipt around my wrist
Unholdable, and through my fingers fled.
I groped again and felt two others twist
About my arm;—a score of vipers twined
225 Beneath my hand, and, as I touched them, hissed.
There is a horror which leaves free the mind

But glues the tongue. Without a word I slipt
    From out the bed, and struck a light behind
Its ample curtain; then, unheard, I crept
230   Close up and let the light's faint radiance hover
    Over the Gorgon's features as she slept.
The snakes were gone. But long I bent me over
    Her placid face with searching, sickened glance,
    Like one who in deep waters would discover
235 A corpse, and can see nothing save, perchance,
    The landscape's fair reflected shapes, which keep
    Balking the vision with their endless dance.
It seemed to me that in that placid sleep,
    Beneath that splendid surface lay concealed
240   Unutterable horror sunken deep.
And, seeking not to have the whole revealed,
    I fled that fatal room without a sound,
    And sought the breeze of night with brain that
        reeled.

How long I wandered 'mid the rocks around,
245   Like some priced outlaw—whether one, or two,
    Or three whole days I know not—fever bound
A veil across my brain, and I've no clue
    To guide my memory through those days accurst,
    Or show me what my misery found to do.
250 I recollect intolerable thirst,
    And nothing more; until the night again
    Enwrapped the earth, and with it brought the
        worst.
A mighty wish, with which I fought in vain,
    Came o'er my soul to see once more her face,
255   And dragged me back, as by an unseen chain.
Where love and horror struggle, there is place
    For countless fierce and contradict'ry tides
    Of Will and Sense within one short day's space.
With every hour the gale has shifted sides;
260   The needle of Thought's compass will have leapt
    From pole to pole, and chance at last decides.
So I returned, and like a thief I crept
    Into the house, where every light was out,
    And sought the silent chamber where she slept.

265 O brother, brother! I'm in awful doubt.
    If what I saw, and what shall now be told,
    Was a mere figment of the brain throughout,
Then will the sickened Heaven ne'er behold
    A deed more monstrous than the deed I've done,
270   Though this old earth should grow again as old.
But if the thing was real, if 'twas one
    Of hell's corroborations of great guilt,
    My hand was an avenger's hand alone.
So wonder not, if, with the blood I've spilt
275   Still on my hand, I fain would have thee think
    That the great wall, which God Himself hath
        built
Between this world and hell, may have a chink
    Through which some horror, yet unknown to
        earth,
    And over great for us, may sometimes slink.
280 May not such strays from Hell have given birth
    To poets' fancies which the wise deride,
    And olden saws of which we now make mirth.
Oh who shall have the courage to decide
    Between the things that are and those that seem,
285   And tell the spirit that the eyes have lied?
Watch thy own face reflected in the stream;
    Is that a figment? Who shall dare to call
    That unsubstantial form a madman's dream?
Or watch the shadow on the sunlit wall,
290   If thou could'st clutch it great would be thy skill;
    Thou'lt feel a chilly spot—and that is all.
So may the spectres which, more subtle still,
    Elude the feeble intellect of man,
    And leave us empty-handed with a chill,
295 Be just as much reality. We spend
    Life 'mid familiar spectres, while the soul
    In fear denies the rest. But hear the end.

The moon was at the full; but o'er the whole
    Vast vault of heaven was stretched a fleecy tent,
300   Through which her baffled light but dimly stole,
Save where the breezes of the night had rent
    On some few points that subtle woof o'erhead,

That men might catch her glances as she went.
And as once more I trod with stealthy tread
305   Each silent, vast, and solitary room,
  Where, through the tiny panes, encased in lead,
Of Gothic windows,[1] moonlight broke the gloom
  So dimly that I scarce could thread my way,
  I seemed a ghost returning to its tomb.
310 I neared the fatal bed in which she lay;
  Its sculptured columns had a ghostly look;
  Its heavy daïs, of faded silk by day,
Looked stony in its tintlessness, and took
  The semblance of the marble canopy
315   Above some Templar's tomb.[2] Yea, every nook
Of this strange room bred awe, I know not why,
  While dim mysterious gleamings seemed to thrill
  From swords and shields that decked the walls
    on high.
With soundless step, approaching nearer still,
320   I touched the sculptured oak, while love and fear
  Contesting in my breast suspended will.
I saw her shape but vaguely, but could hear
  Her placid breath attesting, if aught could,
  A dreamless sleep and conscience wholly clear.
325 Love in my breast was winning, as I stood
  And watched her thus some moments in her sleep;
  Her tranquil breathing seemed to do me good.
But suddenly it quickened with a leap,
  Becoming like the fierce and panting breath
330   Of one in flight, who climbs a rocky steep.
The soul seemed struggling with the fear of death,
  While broken utterings in a tongue unknown
  Escaped at moments through her tightened teeth.
I was about to wake her, when the moon
335   Lit up the bed, and let me see a sight
  Which for a while changed flesh and blood to
    stone.

---

1 Gothic architecture was common in western Europe from the twelfth to the sixteenth centuries.

2 The Knights Templar were founded in France in 1119 to protect pilgrims travelling to holy sites; they were suppressed in 1312.

All round the face, convulsed in sleep and white,
  Innumerable snakes—some large and slow,
  Some lithe and small—writhed bluish in the
    light,
340 Each striving with a sort of ceaseless flow
  To quit the head, and groping as in doubt;
  Then, fast retained, returning to the brow.
They glided on her pillow; all about
  The moonlit sheet in endless turn and coil,
345   And all about her bosom, in and out;
While round her temples, pale as leaden foil,
  And fast closed lids, live curls of vipers twined,
  Whose endless writhe had made all hell recoil.
Long I stood petrified; both limbs and mind
350   Refusing in the presence of that face
  The customary work to each assigned.
But, all at once, I felt a fire replace
  My frozen blood, and unseen spirits seemed
  To call for an Avenger, and to brace
355 My arm for one great blow. Above me gleamed
  A double-handed sword upon the wall,
  Whose weight, till then, beyond my strength I
    deemed.
I seized it, swung it high, and let it fall
  Like thunder on the sleeping Gorgon's neck
360   Before her eye could see or tongue could call.
And, O my God! as if herself a snake
  Which, stricken of a sudden in its sleep,
  Coils up and writhes all round the injuring stake,
She coiled about the weapon in a heap,
365   But gave no sound, while all the sheet soaked red,
  Except a sort of gurgle hoarse and deep,
Which made me strike again, until the head,
  Whose beauty death's convulsion seemed to
    spare,
  Rolled like a heavy ball from off the bed.
370 I held the dripping trophy by the hair,
  Which now no more was snakes, but long black
    locks,
  And scanned the features with a haggard stare.
And, like to one around whose spirit flocks

375 Too great a crowd of thoughts for thought to act,
 I fled once more along the moonlit rocks.
 Then Doubt, with his tormentors, came and racked.
 —1882

The Raft

He shook his head. "No, no," he said, "a man
 Need neither be insane nor wholly bad
Who does that kind of thing. I say again,
That there are minutes in the lives of all
5 When Satan seems to pass across the heart
Just as a shadow flits across the path;
And if it happen that we be possessed
Of power in such minutes, woe betide
Ourselves and others. Bring not yet the lamp,
10 But let the twilight have its way; the fire
Is light enough; I have a tale to tell,
And care not, as I tell it, to be watched.
My children, you shall hear what made me leave,
Some fifty years ago, my native land,
15 And seek this colony, then barely formed.
I speak at last; for I am old, so old
That human justice, even if it cared,
Could scarce o'ertake me on the final brink.
But human justice cares not; I am safe.
20 All has been long forgotten in that land
Whose very language I have long unlearned.
I would to God I could forget as well
A desperate shriek, which ever and anon
Rings in my ears.

Now listen. I was born
25 In the Black Forest,[1] on the Upper Murg,[2]
A noble torrent, which with rush and roar
Fights its way out through many a fir-crowned
 gorge

And rocky pass, till, with diminished strength
And slackened pace, it falls into the Rhine.[3]
30 A noble torrent truly: not pale green
With silvery shallows, like the rivers here,
But with clear coppery gleamings and a grand
Voluminous impulsion. Fast as light
Across the rapids, down the watery slopes
35 Swoop many rafts—long, narrow, supple—
Which men with pikes, one standing at each end,
Guide past projecting rocks, to right and left,
With perilous dexterity. And then
There are the shoots of timber. Once a year
40 All that the ever-sounding axe has felled
Of giant trunks for miles and miles around
Stored in a mighty mountain reservoir
Is hurled into the stream, and rushes down
In one terrific and tumultuous race.
45 Ten thousand struggling, rolling, tossing trunks
Press like a routed army through the gorge,
And, hampered by their number and the rocks,
O'erride each other in their desperate flight,
Sing, reappear, and sink o'erwhelmed once more;
50 Crashing with splintery crunchings and a roar
Like never-ending thunder. So for hours
The furious rush continues, and the stream
Appears alive with logs. Then by degrees
The numbers thin, the crowd contends no more,
55 And single stragglers, leaving far behind
Their stranded comrades, gently make their way
To distant saw-mills. On the lower Murg,
At Ottenau[4] and Gernsbach, where the deal
Is stored and sold and floated down the Rhine
60 To Rotterdam,[5] the timber merchants drive

---

[1] a heavily forested mountain range in southern Germany; a popular tourist destination.

[2] a river in the Black Forest region.

---

[3] a major German river (and also a province of Germany).

[4] Ottenheim and Ottenhofen are both villages in South Baden, Germany; Ottenhofen is a popular tourist destination in the Black Forest.

[5] a city in the western Netherlands, connected with Germany by several branches of the Rhine River.

A busy commerce—or at least they did;
All may have altered.

When I did the thing
Which changed my life, and made me, like a thief,
Desert the country, I was twenty-five.
65 My father was the owner of a mill
And well-to-do. We sawed a many plank.
The heaps of sawdust in the wide mill yard
Grew year by year, the income keeping pace;
For sawing is a profitable trade,
70 With small fatigue: the water does the work.
I had obtained the liking of a girl,
The daughter of a miller higher up,
And we were to be married. All men thought
That I was over lucky, as my bride
75 Was heiress to her father's mill, and I
Would thus inherit two. As I have said,
I had a deal of leisure—far too much.
My uncle was a ranger of the Duke's;
He gave me shooting in the neighbouring hills,
80 And many a roebuck fell beneath my gun.
And then I left the fish but little peace.
The fish abounded in the shallow runs;
You saw the greyling turning on their sides
In shoals, like flashing mirrors, and the trout,
85 Large, yellow-bellied trout, leapt at the flies
By scores at dusk.

It was an August night—
Warm, moonlit, still, and breezeless. I had spent
The evening at the miller's, and had met,
On my way home, a village chum, with whom,
90 Before we parted company, I took
A glass of spirits at the village inn.
I fear it was not much: I say *I fear*,
Because each single drop that I can plead,
When I shall answer for that evening's work,
95 Will be of value at the bar of Heaven.
O God Almighty! would I had gone home
And sought my bed as usual! But instead

The evil powers which obstruct our fate
Made me pass on along the riverside,
100 And seek a certain spot, there to rebait
Some night-lines which I'd sunk the day before.
It was a quiet pool, in which a raft
Would sometimes moor and wait for break of day
Before it crossed a longish stretch of stream
105 Of ticklish navigation just beyond,
Where long, dark slopes of water, which were split
By tooth-like points, sucked down the rafts like
     straws,
And called for proven skill, for ready wits,
And for good light. Woe to the luckless raft
110 Which lacking these passed in: its fate was sealed.

Well to resume. I reached the shallow pool
Above the entrance of the gorge—the place
Where I had laid the night-lines; there I found
What I had not expected on that night,
115 A raft, with men asleep; three lay curled up,
While, in the middle of the raft, a sort
Of little cabin served, perhaps, to shield
Women or children from the dew; the poles
With which they steered the raft were on the bank,
120 Together with an axe; and by ill luck
The raft was moored upon the very spot
Where I had sunk the night-lines. What to do?
The men were fast asleep; the river's roar,
Monotonous and ceaseless, drowned my step.
125 I bared my arm, and tried to find the lines
Beneath the raft; it was of no avail;
Then with the axe I tried to fish them up,
But with no more success. Then by the raft
I sat me down. I think my mind at first
130 Was with the lines; then by degrees my thoughts
Passed to the sleeping men, on whom my eyes
Mechanically rested; and I thought
How wondrously unconscious were these men
Of my existence and my presence there;
135 In what security they slept; while I
Was moving, watching, thinking not two yards

From where they lay. Something like
A sense of power over them began to grow
Upon me as I looked. And then it was
140 That Satan's shadow passed across my heart:
Together with the power came the wish
To play them, in their false security,
A sort of monster trick. The single rope
Which held the raft was close beside my knee,
145 The axe within my hand. Within myself
I heard a voice which seemed to say,
"Cut it, and send them spinning. Cut it quick.
Thou hast enormous power in thy hands;
Thou need'st but raise a finger. What, afraid?
150 They are unconscious: see how sound they sleep,
The careless fools. On thee alone depends
A mighty wakening. Never will these hills
Have seen so great a scamper. Cut it quick;
Cut it, I say!" And with a single stroke
155 I cut the tether, and I pushed the raft.
It drifted slowly out into the light
And left me in the shadow. Suddenly
The current caught it, swung it sharply round,
So that it struck a rock, and off it shot.
160 There was a shout of men, a woman's shriek,
Some figures flitted wildly to and fro upon it
As it vanished. I was free
To find my lines at leisure.

                              But I stood
Upon the bank and trembled. Long I looked
165 Adown the stream, and tried to see and hear;
But all was hushed except the water's roar,
Monotonous and ceaseless. Then I turned,
And, like a man who bears a crushing weight
Which may not be set down, and who succeeds
170 Only by rapid staggering straight ahead
In reaching to his goal, I staggered home,
Crushed and pushed forward and deprived of
        thought
By the great weight of crime which was to rest
Upon my head until I reached the grave.

175 What roundabout untrodden path I took
I have no notion, nor how long I walked:
Next day I found red clay upon my clothes,
And there was none for miles. And yet I doubt
If what I felt in that first great recoil
180 Was what you call remorse; what crushed my soul
Was not the horror of the new-done thing,
But its enormity: I was as yet
A culprit, not a criminal, and felt
Responsible to men, and not to God.
185 Whether or not I slept I cannot tell.
I think I must have slept, for I have heard
That the first sleep of murderers is deep.
A sudden crime exhausts. 'Tis later on,
When Fear begins to sit beside your bed,
190 And makes a danger of each sound of night,
And at each moment twitches you and cries,
"Awake! awake! they come!" 'Tis later on,
When from behind your pillow sharp remorse
Whispers, "Not yet to sleep, not yet, not yet!"
195 And fills you with self-horror, that you hear
The weary striking of the tardy hours.
And pray for dawn. I think that when I woke
And slowly dressed I had alone a sense
That a misfortune had o'ertaken me, that now
200 I had an awful secret to preserve,
And that my life was changed. The daily hum,
The clatter, and the sawing of the mill,
The cackling of the poultry, and the song
Of lighter-hearted neighbours, hurt my ear.
205 Then thought began, and I surveyed the deed,
But only as we measure the extent
Of some great accident. Beyond a doubt
Whoever passed the rapids unprepared
(Even supposing that the raft should stick,
210 And not be shivered by repeated shocks),
Would be swung off or washed away at once.
Below the rapids, both to right and left,
The banks were high and rocky: no escape.
An ugly job, a very ugly job,
215 And inconceivable. But it was done.

What most was to be feared was that my looks,
When men began to talk, would let it out,
And then I prayed an impious prayer to God,
That this even might vanish and be lost,
220 Just as the raft had vanished into night;
That none might seek or mourn, and that the
      flood
Into whose awful keeping I had given
These unknown men and women in their sleep
Might be for ever dumb.

                    I heard a step:
225 It was my father bidding me get up,
And seek a distant village, down the stream,
To settle some transaction for the mill.
Down stream! I thought—Oh not for worlds down
      stream!
But he insisted, and I feared to rouse
230 Suspicion by refusal; so I went.
The road, at first, was not along the bank,
It met it only nearly two miles off
Below the rapids, when both road and stream
Passed through a gorge. On entering this gorge
235 There fell upon my heart, I know not why,
Together with the shadow of the place,
A sudden fear: I feared to be alone
With this dark river, even as a man
May fear to be alone with one whose hand
240 For price of gold had served him over well.
The aspect of the gorge was sinister,
The road and river both were tightly squeezed
To half their width, in Nature's rocky gripe:
A sunless home of echoes, where you saw,
245 On looking up, a narrow strip of sky,
On which the kites, which circled round and round,
Were sharply printed. Rapid, deep, and black,
The stream, between two cruel walls of rock,
Formed whirling pools, and ever and anon
250 Rolled some huge root, which in the distant gloom
Looked like a drowning wretch that none could help.
I stopped in doubt; but to retrace my steps

Was dangerous; and so I hurried on,
Not looking at the river by my side.
255 Half through the gorge, just where it made a bend,
The banks were less abrupt; some ridge-like rocks
Ran out into the water, shelving down
To meet the current. On the first of these
Lay something dark. I had to pass close by,
260 And had to look, it was a human form;
The body of a woman lately drowned.
She lay half in, half out; the circling flood,
Which still retained possession of her feet,
Gave her strange tugs and twitches, and kept up
265 A lapping and a flapping of her clothes
Beyond all measure horrible. Her eyes,
Wide open like her mouth, seemed fixed on mine,
Drawing me onwards by resistless force.
She seemed to be still young—thirty at most.
270 I dared not turn, and yet I dared not pass;
At last I passed her quickly, and I fled;
And as I fled I shrank as one pursued
Who feels a hand descending on his back.
I seemed to feel at every step I took
275 Her clammy hand upon me, and to hear
Her ever louder and more threatening voice
Claim back her stolen life.

                   Beyond the gorge
There was a little village, where I heard
That fragments of a raft had floated down,
280 And that the body of a man, fresh drowned,
Had just been found. I dared not let them know
What I myself had seen upon the rock,
Lest they should make me lead them to the spot.
They'll find the body soon enough, I thought.
285 Not all the riches that the world contained
Would have induced me, quaking still with fear,
To face that sight or pass that gorge again;
And when the business which I had to do
Was settled (how I did it Heaven knows),
290 And I returned, it was by rugged paths,

Which passed not near the river, but which went
Across the fir-clad mountains.

                    One by one
The bodies were recovered; they were six:
Three men, two women, and a little girl.
295 All went to see them, I alone held back.
And soon a rumour spread from door to door
That the catastrophe was not the work
Of accident; that where the raft had moored,
And where the poles were lying with an axe,
300 A bit of rope, sharp severed, had been found,
Which tallied with another severed rope,
Still dangling from a piece of shivered raft
Upon the rocks. But who had done the deed?
There was no evidence, and I was safe.
305 If altered looks and habits could convict,
I think you might have hung me; for in truth
Whate'er I was, I was no hypocrite;
And great as was the need, I hid but ill
The gloom of guilt. To smile and seem at ease
310 And live as usual was beyond my strength;
I held aloof from all my village friends;
As you may think, I left the trout in peace;
And if, at times, I still would take my gun
And wander in the hills, it was because
315 It took me from the river. I was changed.
And yet the neighbours, strange as it may seem,
Had no suspicion; men are sometimes blind.
One person only, almost from the first,
Suspected me, and that was my betrothed.
320 I saw it, and I writhed. When once or twice
The raft was spoken of, I caught her eye
Rest on me for one moment in a way
That made me turn aside; and when anon
She told me that the match was broken off,
325 I bowed my head, although I loved her still,
And asked no explanation.

                    Oh God's hand
Was heavy on me then, and I believe,

By all that is most holy upon earth,
That those whom I had hurried unprepared
330 Into destruction were well avenged
As if the Law had held me in its gripe.
Nay, there were moments when the Law's revenge
Seemed lighter in the balance; and the dread
Of heaping shame upon my father's home
335 Alone withheld me, hounded by remorse,
From giving myself up; and there were times
(I shudder at the memory) when the stream,
Desisting from its old accusing roar,
Made wild seductive music in my ears
340 And lured me to its brink. Then, bending o'er
Some dark and whirling pool, about to leap,
A hideous fear would seize me that the corpse
Of the drowned woman might be in its depth
Awaiting my embrace. Oh, I repeat,
345 God's hand was heavy on me. When, at night,
Great storms would shake the hills, and dazzling
        shafts
Would fall with rattling simultaneous crash
Of thunder near the mill, and make it quake
Even to its foundations, I would start
350 And, cowering like a craven in my bed,
Would think, "It is the messenger of God
Who seeks me in the darkness."

                    Such a life,
Had it gone on much longer, would have led
Either to madness or to further crime.
355 There came a moment when I felt that nought
Could save me but departure and a life
Of all engrossing enterprise. And so,
Within six months of that most fatal night,
And unconvicted, save by God above,
360 I fled my country like a hunted thief,
Without a blessing or a farewell wish,
Nor have I seen it since. For fifty years,
Out here beyond the ocean, I have lived
A life of work, acquiring by degrees
365 Both wealth and influence; and have obtained

With bitter satisfaction the respect
Of men unstained by crime; and I believe
That what a man can do to purchase back
His self-respect and win a smile from Heaven
370 I have not left undone. But the schools
And all the hospitals which I could found
Would not bring back again the dead to life.
And, like the captives who in former days
Were fettered to a heavy cannon ball,
375 Which, if they wished to move from place to place,
They had to raise and carry, I am chained
To one great load of guilt; the cannon ball
Which I have dragged through life has been unseen;
But not the less immense has been its weight.
—1882

To the Muse

To keep in life the posture of the grave
    While others walk and run and dance and leap;
    To keep it ever, waking or asleep,
While shrink the limbs that Nature goodly gave:

5 In summer's heat no more to breast the wave;
    No more to wade through tangled grasses deep;
    Nor tread the cornfield where the reapers reap;
Nor stretch the worn limbs beneath a leafy nave:

'Tis hard; 'tis hard. And so in winter, too,
10   'Tis hard to hear no more the sweet faint creak
Of the crisp snow, the frozen earth's clear ring,

Where ripe blue sloes and crimson berries woo
    The hopping robin. But when thou dost seek
My lonely room, sweet Muse, Despair takes wing.
—1894

River Babble
II

And yet I think—if ever years awoke
    My limbs to motion, so that I could stand
    Again beside a river, rod in hand,
As Evening spreads his solitary cloak—

5 That I would leave the little speckled folk
    Their happy life—their marvellous command
    Of stream's wild ways—and break the cruel
        wand,
To let them cleave the current at a stroke,

As I myself once could. Oh, it were sweet
    To ride the running ripple of the wave,
As long ago, when wanes the long day's heat;

Or search, in daring headers, what gems pave
    The river-bed, until the bold hands meet,
In the depths of beryl, what the tricked eyes crave!
—1894

Twilight

A sudden pang contracts the heart of Day,
    As fades the glory of the sunken sun.
    The bats replace the swallows one by one;
The cries of playing children die away.

5 Like one in pain, a bell begins to sway;
    A few white oxen, from their labour done,
    Pass ghostly through the dusk; the crone that
        spun
Beside her door, turns in, and all grows grey.

And still I lie, as I all day have lain,
10   Here in this garden, thinking of the time
Before the years of helplessness and pain;

Or playing with the fringes of a rhyme,
    Until the yellow moon, amid her train
Of throbbing stars, appears o'er yonder lime.
—1894

What the Sonnet Is

Fourteen small broidered berries on the hem
    Of Circe's[1] mantle, each of magic gold;
    Fourteen of lone Calypso's[2] tears that rolled
Into the sea, for pearls to come of them;

5 Fourteen clear signs of omen in the gem
    With which Medea[3] human fate foretold;
    Fourteen small drops, which Faustus,[4] growing old,
Craved of the Fiend, to water Life's dry stem.

It is the pure white diamond Dante brought
10   To Beatrice;[5] the sapphire Laura wore
When Petrarch[6] cut it sparkling out of thought;

The ruby Shakespeare[7] hewed from his heart's core;
    The dark deep emerald that Rossetti[8] wrought
For his own soul, to wear for evermore.
—1894

Sunken Gold

In dim green depths rot ingot-laden ships;
    And gold doubloons, that from the drowned
        hand fell,
    Lie nestled in the ocean-flower's bell
With love's old gifts, once kissed by long-drowned
    lips.

5 And round some wrought gold cup the sea-grass
        whips,
    And hides lost pearls, near pearls still in their
        shell,
    Where sea-weed forests fill each ocean dell
And seek dim twilight with their restless tips.

So lie the wasted gifts, the long-lost hopes,
10   Beneath the now hushed surface of myself,
In lonelier depths than where the diver gropes;

They lie deep, deep; but I at times behold
    In doubtful glimpses, on some reefy shelf,
The gleam of irrecoverable gold.
—1894

The Ever Young
I

There are round lips that once obtained a
    draught
    From the deep sapphire of the Fount of Youth;[9]

---

[1] in Greek myth, a sorceress, responsible for turning the companions of Ulysses into swine.

[2] Queen of the island of Ogygia on which Ulysses was shipwrecked. Ulysses stayed with her for seven years; when he left she was broken-hearted.

[3] the daughter of Aeëtes, wife and helper of Jason, priestess, sorceress, and murderer.

[4] the hero of Marlowe's *Tragical History of Dr. Faustus* (1592) and Goethe's *Faust* (1832); he sold his soul to the devil in exchange for 24 more years of life.

[5] The poet, Dante Alighieri (1265–1321), fell idealistically in love with Beatrice, although she married someone else. Beatrice is celebrated in Dante's great poems *Vita Nuova* and the *Divina Commedia* (*The Divine Comedy*).

[6] another famous pair of lovers. Petrarch was an Italian poet (1304–74); Laura, whose true identity is unknown, inspired his love poetry. Petrarch is also known for his sonnet sequences and was a major influence on early English poets.

[7] English poet and playwright (1564–1616), notable for his sonnets.

[8] Dante Gabriel Rossetti (1828–82). Pre-Raphaelite poet, critic, and painter; author of the sonnet sequence *The House of Life*.

[9] in popular legend, a fountain with the power of restoring youth.

Lips old, lips young, whose smile attests the truth
Of that great dream at which the wise have
    laughed;

5 And there are brows, which still, by magic craft,
       Defy the years that know nor rest nor ruth,
       And which remain, in spite of Time's sharp
          tooth,
   As radiant as the wondrous waters quaffed.

10 But not of living flesh and blood are they;
       And Art alone can give their long youth birth,
   And bid them keep it while mere men grow grey.

   Art makes the only ever-young on earth;
       Shapes which can keep, till crumbled quite away,
   A young saint's rapture or a young faun's mirth.
   —1894

The Ever Young
II

What impious wrinkle ever marred the cheek
   Of that proud beauty, armless from of old,[1]
   Who stands, though twenty centuries are scroll'd,
Young as when first she smiled upon the Greek?

5 What thread of silver ever dared to streak
       The wavy wonder of the wanton gold
       Round Titian's[2] Magdalen, while men behold
   Each other whiten, as their lives grow bleak?

   And those more breathing beings that the pen
10   Creates of subtler substance than the brush
   Or chisel ever dealt with,—what of them?

   Are Juliet's[3] eyes less bright in those of men,

---

[1] the Venus de Milo (second-century BC); now in the Louvre, Paris.

[2] Tiziano Vecellio (Titian) (c. 1488–1576); Venetian painter.

[3] the teenage tragic heroine of Shakespeare's *Romeo and Juliet*.

Her cheek less oval; and will ages crush
The youth from out Pompilia's[4] frail cut stem?
—1894

The Ever Young
III

And yet Art's wonders are at last Death's prize;
   The shattered marble crumbles into lime;
   Canvas and fresco perish into grime;
The pen's great shapes will die when language dies.

5 The Milo stone[5] will go where lime's dust flies,
       And Titian's Magdalen grow black with time;
       Juliet will end with England's tongue and rhyme,
   Pompilia too, that other shapes may rise.

   But not a wrinkle will o'ercreep their brow,
10   Nor thread of silver mar the locks we love,
   However oft a century's knell has rung;

   And when they die they will be fair as now;
       For they are cherished by the gods above;
   And those the gods are fond of, perish young.
—1894

The Mandolin

[A.D. 1559]

Sit nearer to my bed.
   Have I been rambling? I can ill command
The sequence of my thoughts, though words come
    fast.
   A fire is in my head

---

[4] the tragic young mother of Robert Browning's *The Ring and the Book*, a long poem relating a seventeenth-century Roman murder. Pompilia, married unwillingly to an ageing nobleman, is stabbed to death by her husband, who suspects her of infidelity. In Book 7, Pompilia speaks from her deathbed.

[5] statue of Venus de Milo.

5 And in my veins, like hell's own flame fast fanned.
No sleep for eighty nights. It cannot last.
    The Pope ere long, perhaps ere close of day,
    Will have a scarlet hat to give away.[1]

    Good priest, dost hear a sound,
10 A faint far sound as of a mandolin?
Thou hearest naught? Well, well it matters not.
    I, who was to be crowned
At the next Conclave![2] I was safe to win;
And 'twill be soon: Caraffa's[3] step has got
15   So tottering. O God, that I should miss
    The prize within my grasp, and end like this!

    Three little months ago
What cardinal was so robust as I?
And now the rings drop off my fingers lean!
20   I have a deadly foe,
Who steals away my life till I shall die;
A foe whom well I know, though all unseen,
    Unseizable, unstrikable; he lurks
    Ever at hand, and my destruction works.
25   Thou thinkest I am mad?
Not mad; no, no; but kept awake to death,
And sent by daily inches into hell.
    Slow starving were less bad,
Or measured poison, or the hard-drawn breath
30 And shrivelling muscles of a wasting spell.
    I tell thee, Father, I've been months awake,
    Spent with the thirst that sleep alone can slake.

    O holy, holy Sleep,
Thou sweet but over-frightenable power!
35 Thou whom a tinkle scares or whispered word!
    Return, return and creep
Over my sense, and in this final hour

Lay on my lids the kiss so long deferred.
    But, ah! it cannot be; and I shall die
40   Awake, I know; the foe is hovering nigh.

    Attend: I'll tell thee all—
I tried to steal his life; and, in return,
Night after night he steals my sleep away.
    Oh, I would slowly maul
45 His body with the pincers, or would burn
His limbs upon red embers, or would flay
    The skin from off him slowly, if he fell
    Into my hands, though I should sicken hell!

    The mischief all began
50 With Claudia, whom thou knewest; my own niece,
My dowered ward, brought up in my own home.
    I had an old pet plan
That she should wed Duke Philip, and increase
The number of my partisans in Rome.
55   Oh, they were matched; for he had rank and
        power,
    And she rare beauty and a princely dower.

    With infinite delight
I saw her beauty come, and watched its growth
With greater rapture than a miser knows,
60   Who in the silent night
Counts up his growing treasure, and is loath
To close the lid, and seek his lone repose.
    And, long before her beauty was full-blown,
    Men called her worthy of a ducal crown.

65   But as her beauty grew,
Her lip would often curl, her brow contract,
With ominous impatience of control;
    The least compulsion drew
Rebellious answers; all respect she lacked;
70 The spirit of resistance filled her soul:
    She took not to Duke Philip, as the year
    For marriage neared; and I began to fear.

---

[1] In the Catholic Church, a Cardinal wears a red hat.

[2] an assembly of Cardinals after the death of a Pope for the purpose of electing a successor.

[3] evidently the present Pope.

Give me again to drink:
There is a fierce excitement in my brain,
75 And speech relieves me; but my strength sinks fast.
    The end is near, I think.
And I would tell thee all, that not in vain
May be thy absolution at the last.
    Where was it I had got? I lose the thread
80   Of thought at times, and know not what I've
        said.

    Ay, now I recollect.
There was a man who hung about me ever,
One Hannibal Petroni, bastard born,
    Whom I did half suspect
85 Of making love to Claudia. He was clever,
And had the arts and ways that should adorn
    A better birth; but from the first I hated
    His very sight; and hatred ne'er abated.

    He played with rare, rare skill
90 Upon the mandolin; his wrist was stronger
Than that of any player I have known;
    And with his quivering quill
He could sustain the thrilling high notes longer
Than others could, and drew a voice-like tone
95   Of unexampled clearness from the wire,
    Which often made me, while I loathed, admire.

    For 'tis a wondrous thing,
The mandolin, when played with cunning hand,
And charms the nerves till pleasure grows too sharp;
100   Now mimicking the string
Of a guitar, now aping at command
The viol or the weird Æolian harp.[1]
    The sound now tinkles, now vibrates, now
        comes
    Faint, thin, and thread-like; 'tis a gnat that
        hums.

105 And he would often come
On breezeless moonlit nights of May and June,
And play beneath these windows, or quite near,
    When every sound in Rome
Had died away, and I abhorred his tune;
110 For well I knew it was for Claudia's ear;
    And I would pace my chamber while he played,
    And, in my heart, curse moon and serenade.

    How came this thing about?
My mind grows hazy and my temples swell.
115 Give me more drink! Oh, I remember now.
    One morning I found out
That they were corresponding—letters fell
Into my hands. It was a crushing blow;
    My plans were crumbling. In my fear and wrath
120 I said, "Why wait? Remove him from thy path."

    It's easy here in Rome,
Provided you are liberal with the price;
The willing Tiber[2] sweeps all trace away.
    Yet, ere I sent him home
125 To heaven or hell, I think I warned him twice
To go his ways; but he preferred to stay.
    He braved me in his rashness, and I said,
    "Let his destruction be on his own head."

    When Claudia learned his death,
130 What a young tigress! I can see her now
With eyes illumined by a haggard flame,
    And feel her withering breath,
As in a hissing, never-ending flow
She poured her awful curses on my name.
135 'Twas well I kept her close; for she had proofs,
    And would have howled them from the very
        roofs.

    It is an ugly tale,
And must be told; but what was I to do?

---

[1] a type of harp that produces music when the strings are blown by the wind; often used as a symbol of poetic inspiration.

[2] a river in central Italy.

I wanted peace, not war; but one by one
140   I saw my efforts fail.
She was unmanageable; and she drew
Her fate upon herself—ay, she alone.
    I placed her in a convent, where they tried
All means in vain. She spurned her food, and
    died.

145   But he, the cause of all,
I know not how, has risen from the dead,
And takes my life by stealing sleep away.
    No sooner do I fall
Asleep each night, than, creeping light of tread
150 Beneath my window, he begins to play.
    How well I know his touch! It takes my life
    Less quickly, but more surely, than a knife.

    Now 'tis a rapid burst
Of high and brilliant melody, which ceases
155 As soon as it has waked me with a leap;
    And now a sound, at first
As faint as a gnat's humming, which increases
And creeps between the folded thoughts of sleep,
    Tickling the brain, and keeping in suspense,
160   Through night's long hours, the o'er-excited
    sense.

    Oh, I have placed my spies
All round the house, and offered huge rewards
To any that may see him; but in vain.
    The cunning rogue defies
165 The best-laid plan, and fears nor traps nor swords;
But, scarce my eyes are closed, begins again
    His artful serenade. Oh, he is sly,
    And loves to fool the watchman and the spy!

    But I should find a way
170 To catch him yet, if my retainers had
A little faith, and helped me as they ought.
    I overheard one say,
"Mark me: the Cardinal is going mad;

He hears a mandolin where there is naught."
175   Ay, that's Petroni's skill. He sends the sound
    Straight to my ear, unheard by those around!

    Once, on a moonlit night,
I caught a glimpse of him; the villain sat
Beneath my window, on the garden wall;
180   And in the silvery light
I saw his mandolin. Then, like a cat,
I crept downstairs, with fierce intent to fall
    Upon and throttle him. I made a rush;
    I seized him by the throat. It was a bush.

185   But I have talked o'ermuch;
And something like a drowsiness descends
Upon my eyelids with a languid weight.
    Oh, would it were the touch
Of sweet returning sleep, to make amends
190 For long desertion, ere it be too late!
    My fevered pulse grows calm; my heated brow
    Aches less and less, and throbs no longer now.

    O Sleep, O gentle Sleep,
I feel thee near; thou hast returned at last.
195 It was that draught of soothing hellebore.
    I feel sweet slumber creep
Across each aching sense, as in the past,
And consciousness is fading more and more.
    I care not to awake again; let Death,
200   Whenever Sleep shall leave me, take my breath.

    Give ear! give ear! give ear!
I hear him; he is coming; it is he!
He plays triumphant strains, faint, far away.
    Ye fools, do ye not hear?
205 Oh, we shall catch him yet, and you shall see
A year of hell compressed into a day.
    Bring me my clothes, and help me out of bed.
    Oh, I can stand; I'm weak, but not yet dead.

Bring me my scarlet cloak
210 And scarlet stockings.—No, they're dyed with blood.
Oh, you may laugh! but it's beyond a doubt:
    The dyers let them soak,
In every street, in murder-reddened mud.
It is the only dye that won't wash out.
215   The Pope is dead; Caraffa's dead at last.
    I'm wanted at the Conclave. Dress me fast.

    Who dares to hold me down?
I'm papable.[1] By noon we must convene;
Bring me my clothes, and help me quick to rise.
220   When I've the triple crown[2]
Safe on my head, I'll sweep the cesspool clean.
What's all that muttering? Speak out loud, ye spies!

There's a conspiracy at work, I know,
To keep me from the Conclave—but I'll go.

225   The Papacy is lost.
    Lost, wholly lost. The Papal keys, all black
With rust and dirt, won't turn the lock of heaven.
        What's that? What's that? The Host?[3]
    There's poison in the Wafer[4]—take it back!
230 I'll spit it out! I'll rather die unshriven!
    Help, Claudia, help! Where's Claudia? Where's
        she fled?
    They're smothering me with pillows in my bed!
—1894

---

[1] eligible to the Papacy.

[2] the Pope's tiara.

[3] the consecrated bread of the Eucharist, regarded as the sacrifice of the body of Christ.

[4] a thin disk of unleavened bread used in the Eucharist (communion or mass).

Michael Field

1846 – 1914 (Katherine Bradley) and 1862 – 1913 (Edith Cooper)

Katherine Bradley and her niece, Edith Cooper, formed one of the most remarkable relationships in the history of English letters. Enjoying a common passion for classical art, they developed a strong emotional and intellectual bond. Bradley and Cooper first collaborated under the names Arran and Isla Leigh; together they produced a volume of poetry entitled *Bellerophon and Other Poems* (1881). Their first efforts under the masculine pseudonym Michael Field were two tragic dramas published in 1884 entitled *Callirrhoe* and *Fair Rosamund*. The former was extremely well received until the true identity of Michael Field was revealed. They produced, over the course of their lives, 27 verse tragedies and numerous volumes of poems, among them *Long Ago* (1889), *Sight and Song* (1892), and *Underneath the Bough* (1893). Bradley and Cooper converted to Roman Catholicism near the end of their lives; they died of the same disease (cancer) within nine months of one another.

⌘⌘⌘

Preface

The aim of this little volume is, as far as may be, to translate into verse what the lines and colours of certain chosen pictures sing in themselves; to express not so much what these pictures are to the poet, but rather what poetry they objectively incarnate. Such an attempt demands patient, continuous sight as pure as the gazer can refine it of theory, fancies, or his mere subjective enjoyment.

"Il faut, par un effort d'esprit, se transporter dans les personnages et non les attirer à soi."[1] For *personnages* substitute *peintures*,[2] and this sentence from Gustave Flaubert's "Correspondence" resumes the method of art-study from which these poems arose.

Not even "le grand Gustave" could ultimately illude himself as a formative power in his work—not after the pain of a lifetime directed to no other end. Yet the effort to see things from their own centre, by suppressing the habitual centralisation of the visible in ourselves, is a process by which we eliminate our idiosyncrasies and obtain an impression clearer, less passive, more intimate.

When such effort has been made, honestly and with persistence, even then the inevitable force of individuality must still have play and a temperament mould the purified impression:—

> "When your eyes have done their part,
> Thought must length it in the heart."

M. F.

—(FEBRUARY 15, 1892)

Drawing of Roses and Violets

Leonardo Da Vinci [3]

The Accademia of Venice

Leonardo saw the spring
    Centuries ago,
Saw the spring and loved it in its flowers—
    Violet, rose:
    One that grows
Mystic, shining on the tufted bowers,
And burns its incense to the summer hours;
    And one that hiding low,
    Half-face, half-wing,

5

---

[1] "It is necessary, by an effort of spirit, to transport oneself into the personages and not to draw them to oneself."

[2] paintings.

[3] Italian Renaissance painter, sculptor, scientist, musician, architect, and natural philosopher (1452–1519).

10 With shaded wiles
Hides and yet smiles.

Leonardo drew the blooms
On an April day:
How his subtle pencil loved its toil,
15 Loved to draw!
For he saw
In the rose's amorous, open coil
Women's placid temples that would foil
Hearts in the luring way
20 That checks and dooms
Men with reserve
Of limpid curve.

Leonardo loved the still
Violet as it blows,
25 Plucked it from the darkness of its leaves,
Where it shoots
From wet roots;
Found in it the precious smile that weaves
Sweetness round Madonna's mouth and heaves
30 Her secret lips, then goes,
At its fine will,
About her face
He loved to trace.

Leonardo drew in spring,
35 Restless spring gone by,
Flowers he chose should never after fade
For the wealth
Of strange stealth
In the rose, the violet's half-displayed,
40 Mysterious smile within the petals' shade
That season did not die,
Like everything,
Of ruin's blight
And April's flight.
—1892

La Gioconda [1]

Leonardo Da Vinci

The Louvre

Historic, side-long, implicating eyes;
A smile of velvet's lustre on the cheek;
Calm lips the smile leads upward; hand that lies
Glowing and soft, the patience in its rest
5 Of cruelty that waits and doth not seek
For prey; a dusky forehead and a breast
Where twilight touches ripeness amorously:
Behind her, crystal rocks, a sea and skies
Of evanescent blue on cloud and creek;
10 Landscape that shines suppressive of its zest
For those vicissitudes by which men die.
—1892

The Birth of Venus

Sandro Botticelli [2]

The Uffizi

Frills of brimming wavelets lap
Round a shell that is a boat;
Roses fly like birds and float
Down the crisp air; garments flap:
5 Midmost of the breeze, with locks
In possession of the wind,
Coiling hair in loosened shocks,
Sways a girl who seeks to bind
New-born beauty with a tress
10 Gold about her nakedness.

And her chilled, wan body sweet
Greets the ruffled cloak of rose,
Daisy-stitched, that Flora [3] throws

---

[1] the portrait by Leonardo da Vinci, also known as the *Mona Lisa*.

[2] Italian Renaissance painter (1444?–1510).

[3] the Roman goddess of flowers.

Toward her ere she set her feet
15　On the green verge of the world:
Flora, with the corn-flower dressed,
Round her neck a rose-spray curled
Flowerless, wild-rose at her breast,
To her goddess hastes to bring
20　The wide chiton[1] of the spring.

While from ocean, breathing hard,
With sole pressure toward the bay,—
Olive raiment, pinions grey
By clipt rose-stems thinly starred,
25　Zephyrus[2] and Boreas[3] pass,
One in wonder, one desire:
And the cool sea's dawnlit mass
Boreas' foot has lifted higher,
As he blows the shell to land,
30　Where the reed invades the sand.

She who treads the rocking shell—
Tearful shadow in her eyes
Of reluctant sympathies,
On her mouth a pause, a spell,
35　Candour far too lone to speak
And no knowledge on her brows;
Virgin stranger, come to seek
Covert of strong orange-boughs
By the sea-wind scarcely moved,—
40　She is Love that hath not loved.
　　—1892

---

[1]　a loose garment of varied length, worn by both men and women in ancient Greece.

[2]　the personification of the west wind in Greek mythology. Zephyrus was perceived as the most gentle and warming of all sylvan deities.

[3]　in Greek myth, the god of the north wind.

A Portrait

Bartolommeo Veneto[4]

The Städel'sche Institut at Frankfurt

A crystal, flawless beauty on the brows
　　Where neither love nor time has conquered space
On which to live; her leftward smile endows
　　The gazer with no tidings from the face;
5　About the clear mounds of the lip it winds with
　　　　silvery pace
　　And in the umber eyes it is a light
Chill as a glowworm's when the moon embrowns
　　　　an August night.

　　She saw her beauty often in the glass,
　　　　Sharp on the dazzling surface, and she knew
10　　The haughty custom of her grace must pass:
　　　　Though more persistent in all charm it grew
As with a desperate joy her hair across her throat
　　　　she drew
　　In crinkled locks stiff as dead, yellow snakes...
Until at last within her soul the resolution wakes.

15　　She will be painted, she who is so strong
　　　　In loveliness, so fugitive in years:
　　Forth to the field she goes and questions long
　　　　Which flowers to choose of those the summer
　　　　　　bears;
She plucks a violet larkspur,—then a columbine
　　　　appears
20　　Of perfect yellow,—daisies choicely wide;
These simple things with finest touch she gathers in
　　　　her pride.

　　Next on her head, veiled with well-bleachen
　　　　white
　　And bound across the brow with azure-blue,

---

[4]　an Italian painter noted for his portraits, particularly *Portrait of a Young Woman*, which is reputed to be of Lucrezia Borgia.

She sets the box-tree leaf and coils it tight
25 In spiky wreath of green, immortal hue;
Then, to the prompting of her strange, emphatic
        insight true,
    She bares one breast, half-freeing it of robe,
And hangs green-water gem and cord beside the
        naked globe.

    So was she painted and for centuries
30 Has held the fading field-flowers in her hand
    Austerely as a sign. O fearful eyes
And soft lips of the courtesan who planned
To give her fragile shapeliness to art, whose reason
        spanned
    Her doom, who bade her beauty in its cold
35 And vacant eminence persist for all men to behold!

    She had no memories save of herself
    And her slow-fostered graces, naught to say
    Of love in gift or boon; her cruel pelf[1]
    Had left her with no hopes that grow and stay;
40 She found default in everything that happened
        night or day,
    Yet stooped in calm to passion's dizziest strife
And gave to art a fair, blank form, unverified by
        life.

    Thus has she conquered death: her eyes are fresh,
    Clear as her frontlet jewel, firm in shade
45 And definite as on the linen mesh
    Of her white hood the box-tree's sombre braid,
That glitters leaf by leaf and with the year's waste
        will not fade.
    The small, close mouth, leaving no room for
        breath,
In perfect, still pollution smiles—Lo, she has
        conquered death!
—1892

---

[1] a contemptuous term denoting wealth.

A "Sant' Imagine"

Fiorenzo di Lorenzo[2]

The Städel'sche Institut at Frankfurt

A Holy Picture—variably fair
  In colour and fantastic in device!
        With what an ecstasy is laid
        The pattern of this red brocade,
5 Blood-red above Madonna's seat for glory;
        But gold and black behind the victor-two
            Who, full in view
        Of the great, central form, in thought
        Live through the martyrdom they wrought;
10 Afresh, with finer senses, suffer and despair.
            Why is their story
    Set in such splendour one must note the nice
    Edge of the arras[3] and the glancing tone
    Of jacinth[4] floor, pale rose before the Virgin's
        throne?

15 A young St. Christopher,[5] with Umbria's[6] blue
    Clear in his eyes, stands nobly to the right
        And questions how the thing may hap
        The little, curious, curled-up chap,
    That clings almost astride upon his shoulder
20   And with uncertain baby-fingers lays
            A pat of praise
        On the crisp, propping head, should press
        Upon him to acute distress.
    Vainly he turns; within the child's eyes is no clue;

---

[2] an Italian Renaissance painter (c.1445–1525).

[3] a type of tapestry.

[4] a reddish-orange precious stone.

[5] the patron saint of ferry-workers and travellers. He was believed to carry people across a bridgeless river. Once, carrying a child who became heavier with each step, the saint remarked that he felt as though he were weighed down with the burdens of the world, to which the Christ-child replied, "Thou hast borne upon thy back the world and Him who created it."

[6] a region of central Italy.

25   And he with colder
Heart must give succour to the sad in plight:
To him no secrets of his doom are known;
Who suffers fate to load must bear the load alone.

And wherefore doth Madonna thus look down
30 So wistful toward the book upon her knees?
Has she no comfort? Is there need
Within the Scriptures she should read
    Who to the living Word her bosom presses?
With bliss of her young Babe so near,
35   Is it not drear
    Darkly from books to understand
    What bodes his coming to the land?
Alas, as any other child he catches at her gown
    And, with caresses,
40 Breaks on her still *Magnificat*:[1] to ease
And give air to her spirit with her own
Christ she must hold communion in great songs
    alone.

She bows and sheds no comfort on the boy
Whose face turns on her full of bleeding tears,
45   Sebastian,[2] with the arrows' thrill
    Intolerable to him still,
    Full of an agony that has no measure,
    That cannot rise, grow to the height and wane,
    Being simple pain
50   That to his nature is as bound
    As anguish to the viol's sound:
    He suffers as the sensitive enjoy;
    And, as their pleasure,
His pain is hid from common eyes and ears.
55 Wide-gaping as for air, breathing no moan,
His delicate, exhausted lips are open thrown.

---

[1] the hymn of the Virgin Mary in Luke 1:46–55.

[2] An early defender of the Christian faith, St. Sebastian entered the Roman army, but was condemned to death by Emperor Diocletian when his religious faith was discovered. A troop of soldiers tied him to a tree and shot him with arrows.

And now back to the picture's self we come,
Its subtle, glowing spirit; turn our eyes
60   From those grave, isolated, strange
    Figures, to feel how sweet the range
Of colour in the marbles, with what grace is
Sebastian's porphyry-column reared aloft!
    How waving, soft
And fringed the palm-branch of the stave
65 Saint Christopher exalts!—they must have all
    things brave
About them who are born for martyrdom:
    The fine, stern faces
Refuse so steadily what they despise;
The world will never mix them with her own—
70 They choose the best, and with the best are left
    alone.
—1892

The Magdalen

Timoteo Viti[3]

The Accademia at Bologna

This tender sylph[4] of a maid
Is the Magdalen—this figure lone:
    Her attitude is swayed
    By the very breath she breathes,
5 The prayer of her being that takes no voice.
    Boulders, the grass enwreathes,
    Arch over her as a cave
    That of old an earthquake clave
    And filled with stagnant gloom:
10 Yet a woman has strength to choose it for her
    room.

    Her long, fair hair is allowed
To wander in its thick simpleness;
    The graceful tresses crowd

---

[3] teacher of the Renaissance painter Raphael.

[4] a slender, graceful woman or girl.

Unequal, yet close enough
15   To have woven about her neck and breast
      A wimple of golden stuff.
      Though the rock behind is rude,
      The sweetness of solitude
      Is on her face, the soft
20   Withdrawal that in wild-flowers we have loved so
      oft.

      Her mantle is scarlet-red
In folds of severe resplendency;
      Her hair beneath is spread
      Full-length; from its lower flakes
25 Her feet come forth in their naked charm:
      A wind discreetly shakes
      The scarlet raiment, the hair.
      Her small hands, a tranquil pair,
      Are laid together; her book
30 And cup of ointment furnish scantily her nook.

      She is happy the livelong day,
Yet her thoughts are often with the past;
      Her sins are done away,
      They can give her no annoy.
35 She is white—oh! infinitely clean
      And her heart throbs with joy;
      Besides, there is joy in heaven
      That her sins are thus forgiven;
      And she thinks till even-fall
40 Of the grace, the strangeness, the wonder of it all.

      She is shut from fellowship;
How she loved to mingle with her friends!
      To give them eyes and lip;
      She lived for their sake alone;
45 Not a braid of her hair, not a rose
      Of her cheek was her own:
      And she loved to minister
      To any in want of her,
      All service was so sweet:

50 Now she must stand all day on lithe, unsummoned
      feet.

      Among the untrodden weeds
And moss she is glad to be remote;
      She knows that when God needs
      From the sinning world relief,
55 He will find her thus with the wild bees,
      The doves and the plantain-leaf,
      Waiting in a perfect peace
      For His kingdom's sure increase,
      Waiting with a deeper glow
60 Of patience every day, because He tarrieth so.

      By her side the box of nard[1]
Unbroken…God is a great way off;
      She loves Him: it is hard
      That she may not now even spread
65 The burial-spice, who would gladly keep
      The tomb where He lay dead,
      As it were her rocky cave;
      And fold the linen and lave
      The napkin that once bound
70 His head; no place for her pure arts is longer
      found.

      And these are the things that hurt;
For the rest she gives herself no pain:
      She wears no camel shirt,
      She uses nor scourge, nor rod;
75 But bathes her fair body in the well
      And keeps it pure for God:
      The beauty, that He hath made
      So bright, she guards in the shade,
      For, as an angel's dress,
80 Spotless she must preserve her new-born loveliness.

      Day by day and week by week,
She lives and muses and makes no sound;

---

[1] an aromatic plant.

She has no words to speak
The joy that her desert brings:
85 In her heart there is a song
And yet no song she sings.
Since the word *Rabboni*[1] came
Straightway at the call of her name
And the Master reproved,
90 It seems she has no choice—her lips have never
moved.

She stole away when the pale
Light was trembling on the garden-ground
And others told the tale,
Christ was risen; she roamed the wide,
95 Fearful countries of the wilderness
And many a river-side,
Till she found her destined grot,[2]
South, in France, a woody spot,
Where she is often glad,
100 Musing on those great days when she at first grew
sad.
—1892

A Pen-Drawing of Leda

Sodoma[3]

The Grand Duke's Palace at Weimar[4]

'Tis Leda[5] lovely, wild and free,
Drawing her gracious Swan down
through the grass to see
Certain round eggs without a speck:

One hand plunged in the reeds and one dinting the
downy neck,
5 Although his hectoring bill
Gapes toward her tresses,
She draws the fondled creature to her will.

She joys to bend in the live light
Her glistening body toward her love, how much
more bright!
10 Though on her breast the sunshine lies
And spreads its affluence on the wide curves of her
waist and thighs,
To her meek, smitten gaze
Where her hand presses
The Swan's white neck sink Heaven's concentred
rays.
—1892

"Death, men say, is like a sea"

Death, men say, is like a sea
That engulfs mortality,
Treacherous, dreadful, blindingly
Full of storm and terror.

5 Death is like the deep, warm sand
Pleasant when we come to land,
Covering up with tender hand
The wave's drifted error.

Life's a tortured, booming gurge
10 Winds of passion strike and urge,
And transmute to broken surge
Foam-crests of ambition.

Death's a couch of golden ground,
Warm, soft, permeable mound,
15 Where from even memory's sound
We shall have remission.
—1893

---

[1] "master" or "teacher."

[2] grotto.

[3] A contemporary of Raphael, the Sienese painter Sodoma (1477–1549), painted frescos in the Vatican that were later replaced by those of the master.

[4] a city in central Germany.

[5] A Spartan queen and wife of Tyndareus, Leda was the mother of Clytemnestra (by Tyndareus), Helen, Castor, and Pollux (by Zeus, who came to her as a swan).

"Ah, Eros doth not always smite"

A h, Eros[1] doth not always smite
   With cruel, shining dart,
Whose bitter point with sudden might
   Rends the unhappy heart—
5 Not thus forever purple-stained,
   And sore with steely touch,
Else were its living fountain drained
   Too oft and overmuch.
O'er it sometimes the boy will deign
10   Sweep the shaft's feathered end;
And friendship rises without pain
   Where the white plumes descend.
   —1893

"Sometimes I do despatch my heart"

S ometimes I do despatch my heart
  Among the graves to dwell apart:
On some the tablets are erased,
Some earthquake-tumbled, some defaced,
5 And some that have forgotten lain
A fall of tears makes green again;
And my brave heart can overtread
Her brood of hopes, her infant dead,
And pass with quickened footsteps by
10 The headstone of hoar memory,
   Till she hath found
   One swelling mound
With just her name writ and *beloved*;
From that she cannot be removed.
   —1893

An Apple-Flower

I felt my leaves fall free,
  I felt the wind and sun,

At my heart a honey-bee:
  And life was done.
—1893

"Solitary Death, make me thine own"

S olitary Death, make me thine own,
  And let us wander the bare fields together;
   Yea, thou and I alone,
Roving in unembittered unison forever.

5   I will not harry thy treasure-graves,
I do not ask at thy still hands a lover;
   My heart within me craves
To travel till we twain Time's wilderness discover.

   To sojourn with thee my soul was bred,
10 And I, the courtly sights of life refusing,
   To the wide shadows fled,
And mused upon thee often as I fell a-musing.

   Escaped from chaos, thy mother Night,
In her maiden breast a burthen that awed her,
15   By cavern waters white
Drew thee her first-born, her unfathered off-spring,
   toward her.

   On dewy plats, near twilight dingle,
She oft, to still thee from men's sobs and curses
   In thine ears a-tingle,
20 Pours her cool charms, her weird, reviving chaunt
   rehearses.

   Though mortals menace thee or elude,
And from thy confines break in swift transgression.
   Thou for thyself art sued
Of me, I claim thy cloudy purlieus[2] my possession.

---

[1] the god of love, and son of Aphrodite.

[2] environs.

25   To a lone freshwater, where the sea
    Stirs the silver flux of the reeds and willows,
        Come thou, and beckon me
    To lie in the lull of the sand-sequestered billows:

    Then take the life I have called my own
30   And to the liquid universe deliver;
        Loosening my spirit's zone,
    Wrap round me as thy limbs the wind, the light,
      the river.
    —1893

"A curling thread"

    A curling thread
    Uncoils overhead—
    From the chimney-stack
    A replenished track
5   Of vapour, in haste
    To increase and waste,
    Growing wings as it grows
    Of amber and rose,
    With an upward flight
10   To the frosty light.
    Puff on puff
    Of the soft breath-stuff,
    Till the cloudy fleece
    Thickens its feathers; its rounds increase,
15   Mingle and widen, and lose the line
    Of their dull confine,
    Thinning mote by mote[1]
    As they upward float,
    And by-and-bye
20   Are effaced on the sky.

    To evoke,
    Like the smoke,
    Dower on dower

---

[1] a speck of dust.

    By the power
25   Of our art:
    To have part
    In the air and the sun,
    Till our course be run,
    Till the sigh be breathed,
30   Till the wreath be wreathed,
    And we disappear,
    Leaving heaven clear!
    —1893

A Spring Morning By the Sea

    I did not take me to the sea,
    When the winged morning wakened me
    With beamy plumes: I used them right
    To bear me in an Eastern flight
5   Of arrowy swiftness to the bed
    Where my beloved still slumberèd,
    Lying half poet and half child,
    The twin divineness reconciled.
    And I, who scarce could breathe to see
10   Her spirit in its secrecy
    So innocent, drew back in awe
    That I should give such creature law;
    Then looked and found God standing near,
    And to His Rule resigned my Dear.
    —1893

Love's Sour Leisure

    As a poem in my mind
    Thy sweet lineaments are shrined:
    From the memory, alas!
    Sweetest, sweetest verse will pass;
5   And the fragments I must piece
    Lest the fair tradition cease.
    There is balmy air I trow
    On the uplands of thy brow,

But the temple's veinèd mound
10 Is the Muses' sacred ground;
While the tresses pale are groves
That the laurelled godhead loves.
There is something in the cheek
Like a dimple still to seek,
15 As my poet timidly
Love's incarnate kiss would flee.
But the mouth! That land to own
Long did Aphroditè[1] moan,
Ere the virgin goddess grave
20 From the temptress of the wave
That most noble clime did win;
Who, retreating to the chin,
Took her boy's bow for a line,
The sweet boundary to define,
25 And about the beauteous bays
Still in orbèd queenship plays.
I have all the charact'ry
Of thy features, yet lack thee;
And by couplets to confess
30 What I wholly would possess
Doth but whet the appetite
Of my too long-famished sight:
Vainly if my eyes entreat,
Tears will be their daily meat.
—1893

"It was deep April, and the morn"

It was deep April, and the morn
    Shakspere was born;
The world was on us, pressing sore;
My Love and I took hands and swore,
5   Against the world, to be
Poets and lovers evermore,
To laugh and dream on Lethe's[2] shore,

To sing to Charon[3] in his boat,
Heartening the timid souls afloat;
10 Of judgment never to take heed,
But to those fast-locked souls to speed,
Who never from Apollo[4] fled,
Who spent no hour among the dead;
    Continually
15   With them to dwell,
Indifferent to heaven and hell.
—1893

Noon

Full summer and at noon; from a waste bed
Convolvulus,[5] musk-mallow, poppies spread
The triumph of the sunshine overhead.

Blue on refulgent[6] ash-trees lies the heat;
5 It tingles on the hedge-rows; the young wheat
Sleeps, warm in golden verdure,[7] at my feet.

The pale, sweet grasses of the hayfield blink;
The heath-moors, as the bees of honey drink,
Suck the deep bosom of the day. To think

10 Of all that beauty by the light defined
None shares my vision! Sharply on my mind
Presses the sorrow: fern and flower are blind.
—1893

---

[1] Greek goddess of love.

[2] the river of forgetfulness in Hades.

---

[3] the boatman who ferries dead souls across the river Styx to Hades.

[4] in Greek and Roman myth, the god of poetry, music, prophecy, and medicine. Epitomizing manly beauty and youth, Apollo is also associated with Helios, the sun god.

[5] a plant with trumpet-shaped flowers.

[6] gloriously bright.

[7] freshness, vegetation.

An Aeolian Harp

Dost thou not hear? Amid dun, lonely hills
Far off a melancholy music shrills,
As for a joy that no fruition fills.

Who live in that far country of the wind?
5 The unclaimed hopes, the powers but half-divined,
The shy, heroic passions of mankind.

And all are young in those reverberant bands;
None marshalls them, no mellow voice commands;
They whirl and eddy as the shifting sands.

10 There, there is ruin, and no ivy clings;
There pass the mourners for untimely things,
There breaks the stricken cry of crownless kings.

But ever and anon there spreads a boom
Of wonder through the air, arraigning doom
15 With ineffectual plaint as from a tomb.
—1893

Cyclamens

They are terribly white:
There is snow on the ground,
And a moon on the snow at night;
The sky is cut by the winter light;
5 Yet I, who have all these things in ken,
Am struck to the heart by the chiselled white
Of this handful of cyclamen.
—1893

Alice Meynell
1847 – 1922

Alice Meynell was a poet, journalist, and political activist, particularly in support of the non-militant suffragists. Her first volume of poetry, *Preludes* (1875), was admired by Tennyson and Ruskin, and through her later work she became friends with fellow-poets Francis Thomp-son, Coventry Patmore, and George Meredith. Her best poems, reflecting the Victorian themes of the ambiguity of motherhood, the fallen woman, and the social and political ramifications of motherhood (she bore eight children), are personal lyrics.

❧❧❧

A Letter from a Girl to Her Own Old Age

Listen, and when thy hand this paper presses,
O time-worn woman, think of her who blesses
What thy thin fingers touch, with her caresses.

O mother, for the weight of years that break thee!
5 O daughter, for slow time must yet awake thee,
And from the changes of my heart must make thee!

O fainting traveler, morn is gray in heaven.
Dost thou remember how the clouds were driven?
And are they calm about the fall of even?

10 Pause near the ending of thy long migration,
For this one sudden hour of desolation
Appeals to one hour of thy meditation.

Suffer, O silent one, that I remind thee
Of the great hills that stormed the sky behind thee,
15 Of the wild winds of power that have resigned
      thee.

Know that the mournful plain where thou must
      wander
Is but a gray and silent world, but ponder
The misty mountains of the morning yonder.

Listen:—the mountain winds with rain were
      fretting,

20 And sudden gleams the mountain-tops besetting.
I cannot let thee fade to death, forgetting.

What part of this wild heart of mine, I know not,
Will follow with thee where the great winds blow
      not,
And where the young flowers of the mountain
      grow not.

25 Yet let my letter with my lost thoughts in it
Tell what the way was when thou didst begin it
And win with thee the goal when thou shalt win it.

Oh, in some hour of thine, my thoughts shall guide
      thee.
Suddenly, though time, darkness, silence, hide thee,
30 This wind from thy lost country flits beside thee,—

Telling thee: all thy memories moved the maiden,
With thy regrets was morning overshaden;
With sorrow, thou hast left, her life was laden.

But whether shall my thoughts turn to pursue thee?
35 Life changes, and the years and days renew thee.
Oh, Nature brings my straying heart unto thee.

Her winds will join us, with their constant kisses
Upon the evening as the morning tresses,
Her summers breathe the same unchanging blisses.

40 And we, so altered in our shifting phases,
Track one another 'mid the many mazes
By the eternal child-breath of the daisies.

I have not writ this letter of divining
To make a glory of thy silent pining,
45 A triumph of thy mute and strange declining.

Only one youth, and the bright life was shrouded.
Only one morning, and the day was clouded.
And one old age with regrets is crowded.

O hush, O hush! Thy tears my words are steeping.
50 O hush, hush, hush! So full, the fount of weeping?
Poor eyes, so quickly moved, so near to sleeping?

Pardon the girl; such strange desires beset her.
Poor woman, lay aside the mournful letter
That breaks thy heart; the one who wrote, forget
        her:

55 The one who now thy faded features guesses,
With filial fingers thy gray hair caresses,
With morning tears thy mournful twilight blesses.
—1875

In February

Rich meanings of the prophet-Spring adorn,
Unseen, this colourless sky of folded showers,
    And folded winds; no blossom in the bowers;
A poet's face asleep in this grey morn.

5 Now in the midst of the old world forlorn
    A mystic child is set in these still hours.
    I keep this time, even before the flowers,
Sacred to all the young and the unborn:

To all the miles and miles of unsprung wheat,
10   And to the Spring waiting beyond the portal,
        And to the future of my own young art,

And, among all these things, to you, my sweet,
    My friend, to your calm face and the immortal
        Child tarrying all your life-time in your heart.
—1875

A Poet's Fancies

I
The Love of Narcissus [1]

Like him who met his own eyes in the river,
    The poet trembles at his own long gaze
That meets him through the changing nights and days
From out great Nature; all her waters quiver
5 With his fair image facing him for ever;
        The music that he listens to betrays
        His own heart to his ears; by trackless ways
His wild thoughts tend to him in long endeavour.

His dreams are far among the silent hills;
10   His vague voice calls him from the darkened
        plain
With winds at night; strange recognition thrills
    His lonely heart with piercing love and pain;
He knows again his mirth in mountain rills,
    His weary tears that touch him with the rain.

II
To Any Poet

Thou who singest through the earth
    All the earth's wild creatures fly thee;
Everywhere thou marrest mirth,—

---

[1] in Greek myth, a beautiful youth who inspired the unrequited love of
the nymph, Echo, who subsequently died; as punishment, Nemesis
caused Narcissus to pine away for love of his own reflection, changing
him into the narcissus flower.

Dumbly they defy thee;
5   There is something they deny thee.

Pines thy fallen nature ever
For the unfallen Nature sweet.
But she shuns thy long endeavour,
    Though her flowers and wheat
10   Throng and press thy pausing feet.

Though thou tame a bird to love thee,
Press thy face to grass and flowers,
All these things reserve above thee
    Secrets in the bowers,
15   Secrets in the sun and showers.

Sing thy sorrow, sing thy gladness,
In thy songs must wind and tree
Bear the fictions of thy sadness,
    Thy humanity.
20   For their truth is not for thee.

Wait, and many a secret nest,
Many a hoarded winter-store
Will be hidden on thy breast.
    Things thou longest for
25   Will not fear or shun thee more.

Thou shalt intimately lie
In the roots of flowers that thrust
Upwards from thee to the sky,
    With no more distrust
30   When they blossom from thy dust.

Silent labours of the rain
Shall be near thee, reconciled;
Little lives of leaves and grain,
    All things shy and wild,
35   Tell thee secrets, quiet child.

Earth, set free from thy fair fancies
And the art thou shalt resign,

Will bring forth her rue and pansies
    Unto more divine
40   Thoughts than any thoughts of thine.

Nought will fear thee, humbled creature.
There will lie thy mortal burden
Pressed unto the heart of Nature,
    Songless in a garden,
45   With a long embrace of pardon.

Then the truth all creatures tell,
And His will Whom thou entreatest
Shall absorb thee; there shall dwell
    Silence, the completest
50   Of thy poems, last and sweetest.

X
Unlinked

If I should quit thee, sacrifice, forswear,
    To what, my art, shall I give thee in keeping?
        To the long winds of heaven? Shall these come
            sweeping
My songs forgone against my face and hair?

5   Or shall the mountain streams my lost joys bear,
        My past poetic pain be weeping?
        No, I shall live a poet waking, sleeping,
And I shall die a poet unaware.

From me, my art, thou canst not pass away;
10   And I, a singer though I cease to sing,
            Shall own thee without joy in thee or woe.

Through my indifferent words of every day,
        Scattered and all unlinked the rhymes shall ring,
            And make my poem; and I shall not know.
—1893

The Shepherdess

She walks—the lady of my delight—
   A shepherdess of sheep.
Her flocks are thoughts. She keeps them white;
   She guards them from the steep;
5   She feeds them on the fragrant height,
   And folds them in for sleep.

She roams maternal hills and bright,
   Dark valleys safe and deep.
Into that tender breast at night
10   The chastest stars may peep.
She walks—the lady of my delight—
   A shepherdess of sheep.

She holds her little thoughts in sight,
   Though gay they run and leap.
15 She is so circumspect and right;
   She has her soul to keep.
She walks—the lady of my delight—
   A shepherdess of sheep.
—1895

Parentage

*"When Augustus Caesar legislated against the unmarried
citizens of Rome, he declared them to be, in some sort, slayers
of the people."*

Ah! no, not these!
These, who were childless, are not they who gave
So many dead unto the journeying wave,
The helpless nurslings of the cradling seas;
5 Not they who doomed by infallible decrees
Unnumbered man to the innumerable grave.

   But those who slay
Are fathers. Theirs are armies. Death is theirs—

The death of innocences and despairs;
10 The dying of the golden and the grey.
The sentence, when these speak it, has no Nay.
And she who slays is she who bears, who bears.
—1896

Cradle-Song at Twilight

The child not yet is lulled to rest.
   Too young a nurse, the slender Night
So laxly holds him to her breast
   That throbs with flight.

5 He plays with her, and will not sleep.
   For other playfellows she sighs;
An unmaternal fondness keep
   Her alien eyes.
—1896

In Manchester Square

(In Memoriam T. H.)

The paralytic man has dropped in death
   The crossing-sweeper's brush to which he clung,
One-handed, twisted, dwarfed, scanted of breath,
   Although his hair was young.

5 I saw this year the winter vines of France,
   Dwarfed, twisted, goblins in the frosty drouth—
Gnarled, crippled, blackened little stems askance
   On long hills to the South.

Great green and golden hands of leaves ere long
10   Shall proffer clusters in that vineyard wide.
And O his might, his sweet, his wine, his song,
   His stature, since he died!
—1913

Maternity

One wept whose only child was dead,
　　New-born, ten years ago.
"Weep not; he is in bliss," they said.
　　She answered, "Even so,

5　"Ten years ago was born in pain
　　A child, not now forlorn.
But oh, ten years ago, in vain,
　　A mother, a mother was born."
—1913

A Study

In three monologues, with interruptions

I

Before Light

Among the first to wake. What wakes with me?
　A blind wind and a few birds and a star.
With tremor of darkened flowers and whisper of birds,
Oh, with a tremor, with a tremor of heart—
5　Begins the day i' the dark. I, newly waked,
Grope backwards for my dreams, thinking to slide
Back unawares to dreams, in vain, in vain.
There is a sorrow for me in this day.
It watched me from afar the livelong night,
10　And now draws near, but has not touched me yet.
In from my garden flits the secret wind,—
My garden.—This great day with all its hours
(Its hours, my soul!) will be like other days
Among my flowers. The morning will awake,
15　Like to the lonely waking of a child
Who grows uneasily to a sense of tears,
Because his mother had come and wept and gone;
The morning grass and lilies will be wet,
In all their happiness, with mysterious dews.
20　And I shall leave the high noon in my garden,

The sun enthroned and all his court my flowers,
And go my journey as I live,—alone.
Then in the ripe rays of the later day
All the small blades of thin grass one by one,
25　Looked through with sun, will make each a long shade,
And daisies' heads will bend with butterflies.
And one will come with secrets at her heart,
Evening, whose darkening eyes hide all her heart,
And poppy-crowned move 'mid my lonely flowers.
30　And shall another, I wonder, come with her,—
I, with a heavy secret at my heart,
Uncrowned of all crowns to my garden and flowers?
Thou little home of mine, fair be thy day.
These things will be, but oh, across the hills,
35　Behind me in the dark, what things will be?
—Well, even if sorrow fills me through and through
Until my life be pain and pain my life,
Shall I not bear myself and my own life?
—A little life, O Lord, a little sorrow.
40　And I remember once when I was ill
That the whole world seemed breaking through with
　　me,
Who lay so light and still; stillness availed not,
My weakness being a thing of power, I thought.

"Come to the Port to-morrow," says the letter,
45　And little more, except a few calm words,
Intended to prepare me (and I guess,
I guess for what). He never was too kind,
This man, the one i' the world, kin to my son,
Who knew my crime, who watched me with cold eyes,
50　And stayed me with calm hands, and hid the thing,
For horror more than pity; and took my son;
And mercifully let me ebb away
In this grey town of undesigned grey lives,
Five years already. To-day he sends for me.
55　And now I will prevent the dawn with prayers.

II
About Noon

She shut her five years up within the house.
And towards the noon she lifted up her eyes,
Looked to the gentle hills with a stirred heart,
Moved with the mystery of unknown places
60 Near to a long-known home; smiled, as she could,
A difficult smile that hurt half of her mouth,
Until she passed the streets and all sharp looks.

"Sharp looks, and since I was a child, sharp looks!
These know not, certainly, who scan me so,
65 That not a girl of all their brightest girls
Has such an eager heart for smiles as I.
It is no doubt the fault of my cold face
And reticent eyes that never make appeal,
Or plead for the small pale bewildered soul.
70 If they but knew what a poor child I am!
—Oh, born of all the past, what a poor child!
I could waste golden days and showers of words,
And laugh for nothing, and read my poets again,
And tend a voice I had, songless for ever;—
75 I would not if I might. I would not cease,
Not if I might, the penance and the pain
For that lost soul down somewhere in the past,,
That soul of mine that did and knew such things,
If I could choose; and yet I wish, I wish,
80 Such little wishes, and so longingly.
Who would believe me, knowing what I am?

"Now from these noontide hills my home, my time,
My life for years lies underneath mine eyes,
And all the years that led up to these years.
85 I can judge now, and not the world for me.
And I, being what I am, and having done
What I have done, look back upon my youth
—Before my crime, I mean,—and testify:
It was not happy, no, it was not white,
90 It was not innocent, no, the young fair time.
The people and the years passed in my glass;

And all the insincerity of my thoughts
I laid upon the pure and simple Nature
(Now all the hills and fields are free of me),
95 Smiling at my elaborate sigh the smile
Of any Greek composing sunny gods.
And now begins my one true white child-time,
This time of desolate altars and all ruins.
For Pan is dead and the altars are in ruins.

100 "The world is full of endings for me, I find,
Emotions lost, and words and thoughts forgotten.
Yet amid all these *last* things, there is one,
But one Beginning, a seed within my soul.
Come quickly! and go by quickly, O my years!
105 Strip me of things and thoughts; as I have seen
The ilex changing leaves; for day by day
A little innocent life grows in my life,
A little ignorant life i' the world-worn life;
And I become a child with a world to learn,
110 Timorous, with another world to learn,
Timorous, younger, whiter towards my death."

She turned to the strange sea that five long years
Had sent her letters of his misty winds,
Bearing a cry of storms in other lands,
115 And songs of mariners singing over seas;
And having long conjectured of his face,
Seeing his face, paused, thinking of the past.
Down the hills came she to the town and sea,
And met her child's friend where he waited her.
120 She swayed to his words unsaid, as the green canes
Murmur i' the quiet unto a wind that comes:

"I sent for you, mind, for your sake alone.
—No, my dear ward is well. But it has chanced
(I know it's a hard thing for you to bear,
125 But you are strong, I know) that he has learnt
What I had faithfully kept,—your life, your past,
Your secret. Well, we hope that you repent,
At least, your son and I."

         "God bless my son,
My little son hopes I repent at least."

130 "When he had read the papers—by mischance—
I would have kept them from him, broken down,
Beside himself at first, though the young heart
Recovered and is calm now, he resolved
On the completest parting, for he thinks
135 He could not live under one sky with you.
But being unwilling to disturb you now
And vex you in your harmless life, gives up
His hopes in England, his career, and sails
To-night to make a new life in the States.
140 As to the question of your seeing him
(He is in the town here), I persuaded him
To let you choose, this being probably
The last time in this world. It rests with you."

"I pray you, as we pray morning and night,
145 Save me from the sick eyes of my one child;
But let me see my one child once. Amen.

"I never came across the hills before
In all these years; now all these years are done.
Who would have said it, yesterday at this hour?
150 Now my son knows, and I have crossed the hills,
And sure my poor face faces other things.
Not back! not home! anything, anything,
Anything—no, don't turn, I am very calm.
Not back the way I came to-day, not home.
155 Oh, anything but home and a long life."

"Am I the arbiter? Besides, what fate
Can you desire more merciful than home
And hidden life? And then remember him.
You have borne the separation as it seems
160 With the most perfect patience. And your life
Ending (as to the world), owes this at least—
It is not much—to his bright beginning life,
Absence and perfect silence till you die.
I've done my duty, as I think, to both.

165 If you seemed in the least to ask for pity
I well could pity you. I hope that time
Will bring you a softer heart. Good-bye."

        "Good-bye."

III
At Twilight

Gone, O my child forsaking me, my flower.
Yet I forsaken pity you with tears,
170 Gone while I learn a world to learn a world.
I am to have no part with you again,
And you have many things to share; it's keen,—
I love you, I love you; but more keen is this,—
That you will have no part with me again;
175 And what have I to share? Pain, happy child.
Gone, gone into the west, for ever gone,
O little one, my flower; not you alone,
My son who are leaving me, but he, the child
Of five years back. That is the worst farewell.
180 I had not thought him lost until to-day.
But he had kept with me until to-day;—
Never seen, never heard; but he was there,
Behind the door on which I laid my hand,
Out in the garden when I sat within,
185 A turn of road before me in my walks.
As others greet a presence I did greet
An absence, O my sweet, my sweet surprise!
How will it be now? for he is so changed
I hardly knew the face I saw pass by.
190 And yet it is the one that must of needs
Grow from that long ago face innocent,
Grave with the presage of a human life.
So, child, giving again in thought my kiss,
My last, long since, I kiss you tall and changed
195 In that one kiss, and kiss you a man and old,
And so I kiss you dead. And yet, O child,
O child, a certain soul goes from my days;
They fall together like a rosary told,
Not aves now, but beads,—you being gone.

200 I was not worthy to be comfortless,
I find, and feasts broke in upon my fasts;
And innocent distractions and desires
Surprised me in my penitential tears.
For my absent child God gives me a child in Spring;
205 New seasons and the fresh and innocent earth,
Ever new years and children of the years,
Kin to the young thoughts of my weary heart,
Chime with the young thoughts of my weary heart,
My kin in all the world. And He Himself
210 Is young i' the quiet time of cold and snows.
(Mary! who fledst to Egypt with Him; Joseph!
And thou whose tomb I kissed in Padua,
Protect this perilous childhood in my heart!)
But oh, to-night, I know not why, to-night
215 Out of the earth and sky, out of the sea
My consolations fade. These empty arms
I stretch no more unto the beautiful world,
But clasp them close about the lonely heart
No other arms will clasp. What is thy pain,
220 What is thy pain, inexplicable heart?
Sorrow for ruined and for desolate days.
Failing in penitence, I, who fail in all,
Leave all my thoughts alone, and life mine eyes
Quietly to One who makes amends for me.
225 Peace, O my soul, for thou hast failed in all:
(One thought, at last, that I might take to Heaven!)
It's well I never guessed this thing before,
I mean the weakness and the littleness
Of that which by God's grace begins in me.
230 Oh, earthly hopes and wishes, stay with me
(He will be patent); linger, O my loves
And phases of myself, and play with this
New life of grace (as He whose gift it is
Played with the children, a child). How could I bear
235 To see how little is perfect yet—a speck
If all things else should suddenly wither away?
(And yet they wither away, they wither away.)
Less than I knew, less than I know am I,
Returning childless, but, O Father, a child.

240 She therefore turned unto the Eastern hills,
Thrilled with a west wind sowing stars. She saw
Her lonely upward way climb to the verge
And ending of the day-time; and she knew
The downward way in presence of the night.
245 She heard the fitful sheep-bells in the glen
Move like a child's thoughts. There she felt the earth
Lonely in space. And all things suddenly
Shook with her tears. She went with shadowless feet,
Moving along the shadow of the world,
250 Faring alone to home and a long life,
Setting a twilight face to meet the stars.
—1913?

A Father of Women

AD SROROREM E.B. [1]
"Thy father was transfused into thy blood."
Dryden: Ode to Mrs. Killigrew [2]

Our father works in us,
The daughters of his manhood. Not undone
Is he, not wasted, though transmuted thus,
    And though he left no son.

5   Therefore on him I cry
To arm me: "For my delicate mind a casque,
A breastplate for my heart, courage to die,
    Of thee, captain, I ask.

        "Nor strengthen only; press
10 A finger on this violent blood and pale,
Over this rash will let thy tenderness
    A while pause, and prevail.

---

[1] "To my sister."

[2] Dryden's "Ode to Anne Killigrew" is not an expression of his private grief, but an extremely ornate gesture which raises the deceased poet artist to the heights of symbolism, in which she comes to embody the arts themselves.

"And shepherd-father, thou
Whose staff folded my thoughts before my birth,
15 Control them now I am of earth, and now
    Thou art no more of earth.

"O liberal, constant, dear,
Crush in my nature the ungenerous art
Of the inferior; set me high, and here,
20   Here garner up thy heart!"

Like to him now are they,
The million living fathers of the War—
Mourning the crippled world, the bitter day—
    Whose striplings are no more.

25   The crippled world! Come then,
Fathers of women with your honour in trust;
Approve, accept, know them daughters of men,
    Now that your sons are dust.
          —1917

The Threshing Machine

No "fan is in his hand" for these
Young villagers beneath the trees,
    Watching the wheels. But I recall
    The rhythm of rods that rise and fall,
5 Purging the harvest, over-seas.

No fan, no flail, no threshing-floor!
And all their symbols evermore
    Forgone in England now—the sign,
    The visible pledge, the threat divine,
10 The chaff dispersed, the wheat in store.

The unbreathing engine marks no tune,
Steady at sunrise, steady at noon,
    Inhuman, perfect, saving time,

And saving measure, and saving rhyme—
15 And did our Ruskin[1] speak too soon?

"No noble strength on earth" he sees
"Save Hercules'[2] arm"; his grave decrees
    Curse wheel and steam. As the wheels ran
    I saw the other strength of man,
20 I knew the brain of Hercules.
          —1923

Reflections

(I) In Ireland

A mirror faced a mirror: ire and hate
Opposite ire and hate; the multiplied,
The complex charge rejected, intricate,
    From side to sullen side;

5 One plot, one crime, one treachery, nay, one name,
    Assumed, denounced, in echoes of replies.
The doubt, exchanged, lit thousands of one flame
    Within those mutual eyes.

(II) In "Othello"[3]

A mirror faced a mirror: in sweet pain
    His dangers with her pity did she track,
Received her pity with his love again,
    And these she wafted back.

5 That masculine passion in her little breast
    She bandied with him; her compassion he

---

[1] John Ruskin (1819–1900), English writer, art critic, and social reformer.

[2] in Greek and Roman myth, the son of Zeus and the mortal, Alcmene, lauded and immortalized for feats of strength, especially the twelve labours imposed on him by Hera, Zeus's wife.

[3] a Shakespearean tragedy in which the title character, a noble and celebrated Moor, is made madly jealous by Iago. Duped, Othello kills his faithful and beloved wife, Desdemona.

Bandied with her. What tender sport! No rest
  Had love's infinity.

(III) *In Two Poets*

A mirror faced a mirror: O thy word,
  Thou lord of images, did lodge in me,

Locked to my heart, homing from home, a bird,
  A carrier, bound for thee.

5 Thy migratory greatness, greater far
    For that return, returns; now grow divine
By endlessness my visiting thoughts, that are
  Those visiting thoughts of thine.

—1923

Digby Mackworth Dolben
1848 – 1867

Digby Mackworth Dolben, a young poet with religious inclinations and a love of beauty, was befriended and influenced by Robert Bridges, a distant cousin.

❧❧❧

A Song

The world is young today:
  Forget the gods are old,
  Forget the years of gold
When all the months were May.

5 A little flower of Love
  Is ours, without a root,
  Without the end of fruit,
Yet—take the scent thereof.

There may be hope above,
10 There may be rest beneath;
  We see them not, but Death
Is palpable—and Love.
  —1880 (1867)

A Poem Without A Name [1]

I

Surely before the time my Sun has set:
The evening had not come, it was but noon,
The gladness passed from all my Pleasant Land;
And, through the night that knows nor star nor
    moon,
5 Among clean souls who all but Heaven forget,
Alone remembering I wander on.
They sing of triumph, and a Mighty Hand
Locked fast in theirs through sorrow's Mystery;
They sing of glimpses of another Land,
10 Whose purples gleam through all their agony.

---

[1] Dolben's works were published posthumously by Robert Bridges.

But I—I did not choose like them, I chose
The summer roses, and the red, red wine,
The juice of earth's wild grapes, to drink with those
Whose glories yet thro' saddest memories shine.
15 I will not tell of them, of him who came;
I will not tell you what men call my land.
They speak half-choked in fogs of scorn and sin.
I turn from all their pitiless human din
To voices that can feel and understand.
20 O ever-laughing rivers, sing his name
To all your lilies;—tell it out, O chime,
In hourly four-fold voices;—western breeze
Among the avenues of scented lime
Murmur it softly to the summer night; —
25 O sunlight, water, music, flowers and trees,
Heart-beats of nature's infinite delight,
Love him for ever, all things beautiful!
A little while it was he stayed with me,
And taught me knowledge sweet and wonderful,
30 And satisfied my soul with poetry:
But soon, too soon, there sounded from above
Innumerable clapping of white hands,
And countless laughing voices sang of love,
And called my friend away to other lands.
35 Well—I am very glad they were so fair,
For whom the lightening east and morning skies;
For me the sunset of his golden hair,
Fading among the hills of Paradise.
  Weed-grown is all my garden of delight;—
40 Most tired, most cold without the Eden-gate,
With eyes still good for ache, tho' not for sight,
Among the briers and thorns I weep and wait.
Now first I catch the meaning of a strife,

A great soul-battle fought for death or life.
45 Nearing me come the rumours of a war,
And blood and dust sweep cloudy from afar,
And, surging round, the sobbing of the sea
Choked with the weepings of humanity.
    Alas! no armour have I fashioned me,
50 And, having lived on honey in the past,
Have gained no strength. From the unfathomed sea
I draw no food, for all the nets I cast.
I am not strong enough to fight beneath,
I am not clean enough to mount above;
55 Oh let me dream, although to dream is death,
Beside the hills where last I saw my Love.
    —1911

After Reading Aeschylus [1]

I will not sing my little puny songs.
 It is more blessed for the rippling pool
To be absorbed in the great ocean-wave
Than even to kiss the sea-weeds on its breast.
5 Therefore in passiveness I will lie still,
And let the multitudinous music of the Greek
Pass into me, till I am musical.
    —1911

Good Friday [2]

W as it a dream—the outline of that Face,
 Which seemed to lighten from the Holy
        Place,
Meeting all want, fulfilling all desire?
A dream—the music of that Voice most sweet,
5 Which seemed to rise above the chanting choir?
A dream—the treadings of those wounded Feet,
Pacing about the Altar still and slow?

Illusion—all I thought to love and know?
    Strong Sorrow-wrestler of Mount Calvary, [3]
10 Speak through the blackness of Thine Agony,
Say, have I ever known Thee? answer me!
Speak, Merciful and Mighty, lifted up
To draw those to Thee who have power to will
The roseate Baptism, and the bitter Cup, [4]
15 The Royal Graces of the Cross-crowned Hill. [5]
    Terrible Golgotha—among the bones
Which whiten thee, as thick as splintered stones
Where headlong rocks have crushed themselves away,
I stumble on—Is it too dark to pray?
    —1911

Sister Death

M y sister Death! I pray thee come to me
 Of thy sweet charity,
And be my nurse but for a little while;
    I will indeed lie still,
5 And not detain thee long, when once is spread,
    Beneath the yew, my bed:
I will not ask for lilies or for roses;
    But when the evening closes,
Just take from any brook a single knot
10   Of pale Forget-me-not,
And lay them in my hand, until I wake,
    For his dear sake;
(For should he ever pass and by me stand,
    He yet might understand—)
15 Then heal the passion and the fever
    With one cool kiss, for ever.
    —1911

---

[1] Greek tragic dramatist (525–456 BC); author of over 80 plays, of which only 7 are extant.

[2] in the Christian religion, the Friday before Easter, anniversary of the Crucifixion of Christ. "Good" here means holy.

[3] the place of Christ's crucifixion.

[4] Baptism is a sacrament of the Christian church dating back to pre-Apostolic times. The cup can also symbolize affliction; when in agony in the garden of Gethsemane, Christ prayed "remove this cup from me": see Matthew 26:39.

[5] Golgotha, the place outside Jerusalem where Christ was crucified.

Pro Castitate [1]

Virgin born of Virgin,[2]
　　To Thy shelter take me:
Purest, holiest Jesu,
　　Chaste and holy make me.

5　Wisdom, power and beauty,
　　These are not for me;
Give me, give me only
　　Perfect Chastity.

By Thy Flagellation,
10　　Flesh immaculate—
By Thine endless glory,
　　Manhood consummate—

By Thy Mother Mary,
　　By Thine Angel-host,
15　By the Monks and Maidens
　　Who have loved Thee most,

Keep my flesh and spirit,
　　Eyes and ears and speech,
Taste and touch and feeling,
20　　Sanctify them each.

Through the fiery furnace
　　Walk, O Love, beside me;
In the provocation
　　From the tempter hide me.

25　When they come about me,
　　Dreams of earthly passion,
Drive O drive them from me,
　　Of Thy sweet compassion:

For to feed beside Thee
30　　With the Virgin choir,
In the vale of lilies,
　　Is my one desire.

Not for might and glory
　　Do I ask above,
35　Seeking of Thee only
　　Love and love and love.
　　　　　—1911

---

[1] "In praise of chastity."

[2] Jesus Christ and his mother Mary.

William Ernest Henley
1849 – 1903

William Ernest Henley was a poet, critic, and dramatist. He collaborated with Robert Louis Stevenson on five dramas, and published quite traditional verse, in contrast to the work of his contemporary decadents, in *A Book of Verses* (1888) and *For England's Sake* (1890).

೧೦೯

Waiting

A square, squat room (a cellar on promotion),
   Drab to the soul, drab to the very daylight;
Plasters astray in unnatural-looking tinware;
Scissors and lint and apothecary's jars.

5 Here, on a bench a skeleton would writhe from,
   Angry and sore, I wait to be admitted:

Wait till my heart is lead upon my stomach,
While at their ease two dressers do their chores.

One has a probe—it feels to me a crowbar.
10   A small boy sniffs and shudders after bluestone.[1]
   A poor old tramp explains his poor old ulcers.
   Life is (I think) a blunder and a shame.
—1888 (1873)

---

[1] copper sulphate.

William H. Mallock
1849 – 1923

William H. Mallock caricatured the aesthetic doctrines of Walter Pater in *The New Republic* (1877). Pater responded with *Marius The Epicurean* (1885).

Mallock was generally adverse to contemporary developments, including democracy and socialism.

ℰↃℰↄ

Christmas Thoughts, by a Modern Thinker

(*After Mr Matthew Arnold*)

The windows of the church are bright;
    'Tis Christmas Eve; a low wind breathes;
And girls with happy eyes to-night
    Are hanging up the Christmas wreaths;

5 And village voices by-and-by
    Will reach my windows through the trees,
With wild, sweet music: "Praise on high
    To God: on earth, good-will and peace."

Oh, happy girls, that hang the wreaths!
10   Oh, village fiddlers, happy ye!
Christmas to you still truly breathes
    Good-will and peace; but not to me.

Yes, gladness is your simple rôle,
    Ye foolish girls, ye labouring poor;
15 But joy would ill beseem my soul—
    To sigh, my part is, and endure.

For once as Rousseau[1] stood, I stand
    Apart, made picturesque by grief—
One of a small world-weary band,
20   The orphans of a dead belief.

Through graveyards lone we love to stray,
    And sadly the sad tombs explore,
And contradict the texts which say
    That we shall rise once more.

25 Our faith is dead, of course; and grief
    Fills its room up; and Christmas pie
And turkey cannot bring relief
    To such as Obermann[2] and I.

Ah, Obermann, and might I pass
30   This English Christmas-tide with thee,
Far by those inland waves whose glass
    Brightens and breaks by Meillerie;

Or else amongst the sternest dells
    Alp shags with pine, we'd mix our sighs,
35 Mourn at the sound of Christmas bells,
    Sniff at the smell of Christmas pies.

But thou art dead; and long, dank grass
    And wet mould cool thy tired, hot brain;
Thou art lain down, and now, alas!
40   Of course you won't get up again.

Yet, Obermann, 'tis better so;
    For if, sad slumberer, after all
You were to re-arise, you know
    'Twould make us feel so very small.

---

[1] Jean-Jacques Rousseau (1712–78), unconventional and controversial philosopher who viewed civilization as corrupt and advocated a return to natural innocence. Notable works include *Emile* (1762) and the revealingly autobiographical *Confessions* (1781–88).

[2] See Matthew Arnold's poem, "Stanzas in Memory of the Author of 'Obermann,'" and Étienne Pivert de Senancour's book, *Obermann* (1804). The eponymous hero is the author of a series of letters written from Switzerland.

45 Best bear our grief this manlier way,
    And make our grief be balm to grief;
For if in faith sweet comfort lay,
    There lurks sweet pride in unbelief.

Wherefore, remembering this, once more
50   Unto my childhood's church I'll go,
And bow my head at that low door
    I passed through standing, long ago.

I'll sit in the accustomed place,
    And make, while all the unlearnèd stare,
55 A mournful, atheistic face
    At their vain noise of unheard prayer.

Then, while they hymn the heavenly birth
    And angel voices from the skies,

My thoughts shall go where Weimar's earth
60   For ever darkens Goethe's[1] eyes;

Till sweet girls' glances from their books
    Shall steal towards me, and they sigh:
"How intellectual he looks,
    And yet how wistful! And his eye

65 Has that vain look of baffled prayer!"
    And then when church is o'er I'll run,
Comb misery into all my hair,
    And go and get my portrait done.
—1893

---

[1] Johann Wolfgang von Goethe (1749–1832), lived and worked in Weimar; in 1791 he was appointed director of the Weimar court theatre. He was the author of many influential works, including *Faust* (1832), *The Sorrows of Young Werther* (1774), and *Wilhelm Meister's Apprenticeship* (1795–96). The latter two works were translated by Thomas Carlyle, who introduced Goethe's thought to English intellectuals.

Robert Louis Stevenson
1850 – 1894

A late-Victorian figure of considerable prominence, Stevenson was a novelist, short-story writer, essayist, and poet. Born in Edinburgh, he lived and travelled abroad until the early 1880s when he settled in the South Pacific. Stevenson's most notable works include *Treasure Island* (1883), *A Child's Garden of Verses* (1885), *Kidnapped* (1886) and *The Strange Case of Dr. Jekyll and Mr. Hyde* (1886).

ᘓᕓᘓ

Bed in Summer

In winter I get up at night
And dress by yellow candle-light.
In summer, quite the other way,
I have to go to bed by day.

5   I have to go to bed and see
The birds still hopping on the tree,
Or hear the grown-up people's feet
Still going past me in the street.

And does it not seem hard to you,
10 When all the sky is clear and blue,
And I should like so much to play
To have to go to bed by day?
—1885

Travel

I should like to rise and go
Where the golden apples grow;
Where below another sky
Parrot islands anchored lie,
5 And, watched by cockatoos and goats,
Lonely Crusoes[1] building boats;
Where in sunshine reaching out
Eastern cities, miles about,
Are with mosque and minaret

10 Among sandy gardens set,
And the rich goods from near and far
Hang for sale in the bazaar;
Where the Great Wall round China goes,
And on one side the desert blows,
15 And with bell and voice and drum,
Cities on the other hum;
Where are forests, hot as fire,
Wide as England, tall as a spire,
Full of apes and cocoa-nuts
20 And the negro hunters' huts;
Where the knotty crocodile
Lies and blinks in the Nile,
And the red flamingo flies
Hunting fish before his eyes;
25 Where in jungles, near and far,
Man-devouring tigers are,
Lying close and giving ear
Lest the hunt be drawing near,
Or a comer-by be seen
30 Swinging in a palanquin;
Where among the desert sands
Some deserted city stands,
All its children, sweep and prince,
Grown to manhood ages since,
35 Not a foot in street or house,
Not a stir of child or mouse,
And when kindly falls the night,
In all the town no spark of light.
There I'll come when I'm a man
40 With a camel caravan;

---

[1] an allusion to Daniel Defoe's novel *Robinson Crusoe* (1719).

Light a fire in the gloom
Of some dusty dining-room;
See the pictures on the walls,
Heroes, fights and festivals;
45 And in the corner find the toys
Of the old Egyptian boys.
—1885

The Land of Counterpane

When I was sick and lay a-bed,
I had two pillows at my head,
And all my toys beside me lay
To keep me happy all the day.

5 And sometimes for an hour or so
I watched my leaden soldiers go,
With different uniforms and drills,
Among the bed-clothes, through the hills;

And sometimes sent my ships in fleets
10 All up and down among the sheets;
Or brought my trees and houses out,
And planted cities all about.

I was the giant great and still
That sits upon the pillow-hill,
15 And sees him before him, dale and plain,
The pleasant land of counterpane.
—1885

The Land of Story-books

At evening, when the lamp is lit,
Around the fire my parents sit;
They sit at home and talk and sing,
And do not play at anything.

5 Now, with my little gun, I crawl
All in the dark along the wall,
And follow round the forest track
Away behind the sofa back.

There, in the night, where none can spy,
10 All in my hunter's camp I lie,
And play at books that I have read
Till it is time to go to bed.

These are the hills, these are the woods,
These are my starry solitudes;
15 And there the river by whose brink
The roaring lions come to drink.

I see the others far away
As if in firelit camp they lay,
And I, like to an Indian scout,
20 Around their party prowled about.

So, when my nurse comes in for me,
Home I return across the sea,
And go to bed with backward looks
At my dear land of Story-books.
—1885

Requiem

Under the wide and starry sky,
Dig the grave and let me lie.
Glad did I live and gladly die,
    And I laid me down with a will.

5 This be the verse you grave for me:
Here he lies where he longed to be;
Home is the sailor, home from the sea,
    And the hunter home from the hill.
—1887 (1880-84)

The Celestial Surgeon

If I have faltered more or less
In my great task of happiness;
If I have moved among my race
And shown no glorious morning face;
5 If beams from happy human eyes
Have moved me not; if morning skies,
Books, and my food, and summer rain
Knocked on my sullen heart in vain:
Lord, thy most pointed pleasure take
10 And stab my spirit broad awake;
Or, Lord, if too obdurate I,
Choose thou, before that spirit die,
A piercing pain, a killing sin,
And to my dead heart run them in!
—1887 (1882?)

"I have trod the upward
and the downward slope"

I have trod the upward and the downward slope;
I have endured and done in days before;
I have longed for all, and bid farewell to hope;
And I have lived and loved, and closed the door.
—1895

"So live, so love, so use that fragile hour"

So live, so love, so use that fragile hour,
That when the dark hand of the shining power
Shall one from other, wife or husband, take,
The poor survivor may not weep and wake.
—1916 (1885)

"I saw red evening through the rain"

I saw red evening through the rain
Lower above the steaming plain;
I heard the hour strike small and still,
From the black belfry on the hill.

5 Thought is driven out of doors to-night
By bitter memory of delight;
The sharp constraint of finger tips,
Or the shuddering touch of lips.

I heard the hour strike small and still,
10 From the black belfry on the hill.
Behind me I could still look down
On the outspread monstrous town.

The sharp constraint of finger tips
Or the shuddering touch of lips,
15 And all old memories of delight
Crowd upon my soul to-night.

Behind me I could still look down
On the outspread feverish town;
But before me still and grey
20 And lonely was the forward way.
—1921 (1875)

Oscar Wilde
1854 — 1900

Oscar Wilde was born in Ireland, attended Trinity College, Dublin, and graduated from Oxford in 1878. Wilde was an adherent of the "art for art's sake" movement (see Walter Pater), a position articulated in the essay, "The Critic as Artist" (1890). His major works include *The Picture of Dorian Gray* (1890), essays such as "The Soul of Man Under Socialism" (1891), and a number of plays such as *Lady Windermere's Fan* (1892), *Salomé* (1894), and *The Importance of Being Earnest* (1895). Wilde's homosexuality led to a series of trials and in 1895 he was sentenced to two years in jail. He died in Paris.

❧❧❧

Requiescat [1]

Tread lightly, she is near
    Under the snow,
Speak gently, she can hear
    The daisies grow.

5 All her bright golden hair
    Tarnished with rust,
She that was young and fair
    Fallen to dust.

Lily-like, white as snow,
10   She hardly knew
She was a woman, so
    Sweetly she grew.

Coffin-board, heavy stone,
    Lie on her breast,
15 I vex my heart alone,
    She is at rest.

Peace, Peace, she cannot hear
    Lyre or sonnet,
All my life's buried here,
20   Heap earth upon it.

AVIGNON
—1881, REV. 1882

Hélas! [2]

To drift with every passion till my soul
  Is a stringed lute on which all winds can play,
Is it for this that I have given away
Mine ancient wisdom, and austere control?
5 Methinks my life is a twice-written scroll
Scrawled over on some boyish holiday
With idle songs for pipe and virelay,
Which do but mar the secret of the whole.
Surely there was a time I might have trod
10 The sunlight heights, and from life's dissonance
Struck one clear chord to reach the ears of God:
Is that time dead? lo! with a little rod
I did but touch the honey of romance—
And must I lose a soul's inheritance?
—1881

---

[1] "May s/he rest." The expression "R.I.P." means rest in peace, or *requiescat in pace.*

[2] "Alas."

Impressions

I
LE JARDIN [1]

The lily's withered chalice falls
  Around its rod of dusty gold,
  And from the beech-trees on the wold
The last wood-pigeon coos and calls.

5   The gaudy leonine sunflower
  Hangs black and barren on its stalk,
  And down the windy garden walk
The dead leaves scatter,—hour by hour.

Pale privet-petals white as milk
10   Are blown into a snowy mass:
  The roses lie upon the grass
Like little shreds of crimson silk.

II
LA MER [2]

A white mist drifts across the shrouds,
  A wild moon in this wintry sky
  Gleams like an angry lion's eye
Out of a mane of tawny clouds.

5   The muffled steersman at the wheel
  Is but a shadow in the gloom;—

And in the throbbing engine-room
Leap the long rods of polished steel.

The shattered storm has left its trace
10   Upon this huge and heaving dome,
  For the thin threads of yellow foam
Float on the waves like ravelled lace.
—1882

Symphony in Yellow

An omnibus across the bridge
  Crawls like a yellow butterfly,
  And, here and there, a passer-by
Shows like a little restless midge.

5   Big barges full of yellow hay
  Are moved against the shadowy wharf,
  And, like a yellow silken scarf,
The thick fog hangs along the quay.

The yellow leaves begin to fade
10   And flutter from the Temple elms,[3]
  And at my feet the pale green Thames
Lies like a rod of rippled jade.
—1889

---

[1] the garden.

[2] the sea.

[3] the part of London known as the Temple lies between Fleet Street and the Thames River. Originally the site of the Templar's headquarters, the area is now given over to law courts and offices.

John Davidson
1857 – 1909

A playwright and novelist as well as a poet, John Davidson came to London from a Scotch Calvinistic milieu. One of the first Englishmen to be influenced by Nietzsche, Davidson gave a new turn to romantic subjects by introducing vigorous modern ideas of self-expression and the fulfillment of desires.

❧

Thirty Bob a Week [1]

I couldn't touch a stop and turn a screw,
   And set the blooming[2] world a-work for me,
Like such as cut their teeth—I hope, like you—
   On the handle of a skeleton gold key;
5 I cut mine on a leek, which I eat it every week:
   I'm a clerk at thirty bob as you can see.

But I don't allow it's luck and all a toss;
   There's no such thing as being starred and
      crossed;
It's just the power of some to be a boss,
10   And the bally power of others to be bossed:
I face the music, sir; you bet I ain't a cur;
   Strike me lucky if I don't believe I'm lost!

For like a mole I journey in the dark,
   A-travelling along the underground
15 From my Pillar'd Halls and broad Suburbean Park,
   To come the daily dull official round;
And home again at night with my pipe all alight,
   A-scheming how to count ten bob a pound.

And it's often very cold and very wet,
20   And my missis stitches towels for a hunks;
And the Pillar'd Halls is half of it to let—
   Three rooms about the size of travelling trunks.

And we cough, my wife and I, to dislocate a sigh,
   When the noisy little kids are in their bunks.

25 But you never hear her do a growl or whine,
   For she's made of flint and roses, very odd;
And I've got to cut my meaning rather fine,
   Or I'd blubber, for I'm made of greens and sod:
So p'r'aps we are in Hell for all that I can tell,
30   And lost and damn'd and served up hot to God.

I ain't blaspheming, Mr. Silver-tongue;
   I'm saying things a bit beyond your art:
Of all the rummy starts you ever sprung,
   Thirty bob a week's the rummiest start!
35 With your science and your books and your the'ries
      about spooks,
   Did you ever hear of looking in your heart?

I didn't mean your pocket, Mr., no:
   I mean that having children and a wife,
With thirty bob on which to come and go,
40   Isn't dancing to the tabor and the fife:
When it doesn't make you drink, by Heaven! it
      makes you think,
   And notice curious items about life.

I step into my heart and there I meet
   A god-almighty devil singing small,
45 Who would like to shout and whistle in the street,
   And squelch the passers flat against the wall;
If the whole world was a cake he had the power to
      take,

---

[1] slang for a shilling (equivalent to 10 New Pence); this usage in effect from about 1800.

[2] euphemism for "bloody."

He would take it, ask for more, and eat them
    all.

And I meet a sort of simpleton beside,
50   The kind that life is always giving beans;
With thirty bob a week to keep a bride
    He fell in love and married in his teens:
At thirty bob he stuck; but he knows it isn't luck:
    He knows the seas are deeper than tureens.

55 And the god-almighty devil and the fool
    That meet me in the High Street on the strike,
When I walk about my heart a-gathering wool,
    Are my good and evil angels if you like.
And both of them together in every kind of weather
60   Ride me like a double-seated bike.

That's rough a bit and needs its meaning curled.
    But I have a high old hot un in my mind—
A most engrugious[1] notion of the world,
    That leaves your lightning 'rithmetic behind:
65 I give it at a glance when I say "There ain't no
      chance,
    Nor nothing of the lucky-lottery kind."

And it's this way that I make it out to be:
    No fathers, mothers, countries, climates—none;
No Adam was responsible for me,
70   Nor society, nor systems, nary one:
A little sleeping seed, I woke—I did, indeed—
    A million years before the blooming sun.

I woke because I thought the time had come;
    Beyond my will there was no other cause;
75 And everywhere I found myself at home,
    Because I chose to be the thing I was;
And in whatever shape of mollusc or of ape
    I always went according to the laws.

I was the love that chose my mother out;
80   I joined two lives and from the union burst;
My weakness and my strength without a doubt
    Are mine alone for ever from the first:
It's just the very same with a difference in the name
    As "Thy will be done." You say it if you durst!

85 They say it daily up and down the land
    As easy as you take a drink, it's true;
But the difficultest go to understand,
    And the difficultest job a man can do,
Is to come it brave and meek with thirty bob a week,
90   And feel that that's the proper thing for you.

It's a naked child against a hungry wolf;
    It's playing bowls upon a splitting wreck;
It's walking on a string across a gulf
    With millstones fore-and-aft about your neck;
95 But the thing is daily done by many and many a
      one;
    And we fall, face forward, fighting, on the deck.
—1894

A Ballad of a Nun

From Eastertide to Eastertide
    For ten long years her patient knees
Engraved the stones—the fittest bride
    Of Christ in all the diocese.

5 She conquered every earthly lust;
    The abbess loved her more and more;
And, as a mark of perfect trust,
    Made her the keeper of the door.

High on a hill the convent hung,
10   Across a duchy looking down,
Where everlasting mountains flung
    Their shadows over tower and town.

---

[1] a coinage of Davidson's, presumably from "egregious."

The jewels of their lofty snows
  In constellations flashed at night;
15 Above their crests the moon arose;
  The deep earth shuddered with delight.

Long ere she left her cloudy bed,
  Still dreaming in the orient land,
On many a mountain's happy head
20   Dawn lightly laid her rosy hand.

The adventurous sun took Heaven by storm;
  Clouds scattered largesses of rain;
The sounding cities, rich and warm,
  Smouldered and glittered in the plain.

25 Sometimes it was a wandering wind,
  Sometimes the fragrance of the pine,
Sometimes the thought how others sinned,
  That turned her sweet blood into wine.

Sometimes she heard a serenade
30   Complaining sweetly far away:
She said, "A young man woos a maid;"
  And dreamt of love till break of day.

Then would she ply her knotted scourge
  Until she swooned; but evermore
35 She had the same red sin to purge,
  Poor, passionate keeper of the door!

For still night's starry scroll unfurled,
  And still the day came like a flood;
It was the greatness of the world
40   That made her long to use her blood.

In winter-time when Lent drew nigh,
  And hill and plain were wrapped in snow,
She watched beneath the frosty sky
  The nearest city nightly glow.

45 Like peals of airy bells outworn
  Faint laughter died above her head
In gusts of broken music borne:
  "They keep the Carnival," she said.

Her hungry heart devoured the town:
50   "Heaven save me by a miracle!
Unless God sends an angel down,
  Thither I go though it were Hell."

She dug her nails deep in her breast,
  Sobbed, shrieked, and straight withdrew the bar:
55 A fledgling flying from the nest,
  A pale moth rushing to a star.

Fillet and veil in strips she tore;
  Her golden tresses floated wide;
The ring and bracelet that she wore
60   As Christ's betrothed, she cast aside.

"Life's dearest meaning I shall probe;
  Lo! I shall taste of love at last!
Away!" She doffed her outer robe,
  And sent it sailing down the blast.

65 Her body seemed to warm the wind;
  With bleeding feet o'er ice she ran:
"I leave the righteous God behind;
  I go to worship sinful man."

She reached the sounding city's gate;
70   No question did the warder ask:
He passed her in: "Welcome, wild mate!"
  He thought her some fantastic mask.

Half-naked through the town she went;
  Each footstep left a bloody mark;
75 Crowds followed her with looks intent;
  Her bright eyes made the torches dark.

Alone and watching in the street
    There stood a grave youth nobly dressed;
To him she knelt and kissed his feet;
80   Her face her great desire confessed.

Straight to his house the nun he led:
    "Strange lady, what would you with me?"
"Your love, your love, sweet lord," she said;
    "I bring you my virginity."

85 He healed her bosom with a kiss;
    She gave him all her passion's hoard;
And sobbed and murmured ever, "This
    Is life's great meaning, dear, my lord.

"I care not for my broken vow;
90   Though God should come in thunder soon,
I am sister to the mountains now,
    And sister to the sun and moon."

Through all the towns of Belmarie
    She made a progress like a queen.
95 "She is," they said, "whate'er she be,
    The strangest woman ever seen.

"From fairyland she must have come,
    Or else she is a mermaiden."
Some said she was a ghoul, and some
100   A heathen goddess born again.

But soon her fire to ashes burned;
    Her beauty changed to haggardness;
Her golden hair to silver turned;
    The hour came of her last caress.

105 At midnight from her lonely bed
    She rose, and said, "I have had my will."
The old ragged robe she donned, and fled
    Back to the convent on the hill.

Half-naked as she went before,
110   She hurried to the city wall,
Unnoticed in the rush and roar
    And splendour of the carnival.

No question did the warder ask:
    Her ragged robe, her shrunken limb,
115 Her dreadful eyes! "It is no mask;
    It is a she-wolf, gaunt and grim!"

She ran across the icy plain;
    Her worn blood curdled in the blast;
Each footstep left a crimson stain;
120   The white-faced moon looked on aghast.

She said between her chattering jaws,
    "Deep peace is mine, I cease to strive;
Oh, comfortable convent laws,
    That bury foolish nuns alive!

125 "A trowel for my passing-bell,
    A little bed within the wall,
A coverlet of stones; how well
    I there shall keep the Carnival!"

Like tired bells chiming in their sleep,
130   The wind faint peals of laughter bore;
She stopped her ears and climbed the steep,
    And thundered at the convent door.

It opened straight: she entered in,
    And at the wardress' feet fell prone:
135 "I come to purge away my sin;
    Bury me, close me up in stone."

The wardress raised her tenderly;
    She touched her wet and fast-shut eyes:
"Look, sister; sister, look at me;
140   Look; can you see through my disguise?"

She looked and saw her own sad face,
    And trembled, wondering, "Who art thou?"
"God sent me down to fill your place:
    I am the Virgin Mary now."

145 And with the word, God's mother shone:
    The wanderer whispered, "Mary, hail!"
The vision helped her to put on
    Bracelet and fillet, ring and veil.

"You are sister to the mountains now,
150   And sister to the day and night;
Sister to God." And on the brow
    She kissed her thrice, and left her sight.

While dreaming in her cloudy bed,
    Far in the crimson orient land,
155 On many a mountain's happy head
    Dawn lightly laid her rosy hand.
    —1894

A Ballad in Blank Verse

His father's house looked out across a firth
Broad-bosomed like a mere, beside a town[1]
Far in the North, where Time could take his ease,
And Change hold holiday; where Old and New
5 Weltered upon the border of the world.

"Oh now," he thought—a youth whose sultry eyes,
Bold brown and wanton mouth were not all lust,
But haunted from within and from without
By memories, visions, hopes, divine desires—
10 "Now may my life beat out upon this shore
A prouder music than the winds and waves
Can compass in their haughtiest moods. I need
No world more spacious than the region here:
The foam-embroidered firth, a purple path
15 For argosies that still on pinions speed,

Or fiery-hearted cleave with iron limbs
And bows precipitous the pliant sea;
The sloping shores that fringe the velvet tides
With heavy bullion and with golden lace
20 Of restless pebble woven and fine spun sand;
The villages that sleep the winter through,
And, wakening with the spring, keep festival
All summer and all autumn: this grey town
That pipes the morning up before the lark
25 With shrieking steam, and from a hundred stalks
Lacquers the sooty sky; where hammers clang
On iron hulls, and cranes in harbours creak
Rattle and swing, whole cargoes on their necks;
Where men sweat gold that others hoard or spend,
30 And lurk like vermin in their narrow streets:
This old grey town, this firth, the further strand
Spangled with hamlets, and the wooded steeps,
Whose rocky tops behind each other press,
Fantastically carved like antique helms
35 High-hung in heaven's cloudy armoury,
Is world enough for me. Here daily dawn
Burns through the smoky east; with fire-shod feet
The sun treads heaven, and steps from hill to hill
Downward before the night that still pursues
40 His crimson wake; here winter plies his craft,
Soldering the years with ice; here spring appears,
Caught in a leafless brake, her garland torn,
Breathless with wonder, and the tears half-dried
Upon her rosy cheek; here summer comes
45 And wastes his passion like a prodigal
Right royally; and here her golden gains
Free-handed as a harlot autumn spends;
And here are men to know, women to love."
His father, woman-hearted, great of soul,
50 Wilful and proud, save for one little shrine
That held a pinch-beck cross, had closed and
    barred
The many mansions[2] of his intellect.

---

[1] perhaps the town of Greenock.

[2] John 14:2.

"My son," he said—to him, fresh from his firth
And dreams at evening; while his mother sat,
55 She also with her dingy crucifix
And feeble rushlight, praying for her boy—
"My son, have you decided for the Lord?
Your mother's heart and mine are exercised
For your salvation. Will you turn to Christ?
60 Now, young and strong, you hanker for the world;
But think: the longest life must end at last,
And then come Death and Judgment. Are you fit
To meet your God before the great white throne?
If on the instant Death should summon you,
65 What doom would the Eternal Judge[1] pronounce—
'Depart from me' or 'Sit on My right hand'?
In life it is your privilege to choose,
But after death you have no choice at all.
Die unbelieving, and in endless woe
70 You must believe throughout eternity.
My son, reject not Christ; he pleads through me;
The Holy Spirit uses my poor words.
How it would fill your mother's heart and mine,
And God's great heart with joy unspeakable,
75 Were you, a helpless sinner, now to cry,
'Lord I believe: help Thou mine unbelief'."[2]
He clenched his teeth; his blood, fulfilled of brine,
Of sunset, and his dreams, boomed in his ears.
A vision rose before him; and the sound
80 Husky and plaintive of his father's voice
Seemed unintelligible and afar.
He saw Apollo on the Dardan beach:[3]
The waves lay still; the winds hung motionless,
And held their breath to hear the rebel god,
85 Conquered and doomed, with stormy sobbing song,
And crashing discords of his golden lyre,

Reluctantly compel the walls of Troy,[4]
Unquarried and unhewn, in supple lines
And massive strength to rise about the town.

90 A quavering voice shattered his fantasy:
His father's pleading done, his mother cried,
With twitching forehead, scalding tears that broke
The seal of wrinkled eyelids, mortised hands
Where knuckles jutted white: "Almighty God!—
95 Almighty God!—Oh, save my foolish boy."
He glanced about the dreary parlour, clenched
His teeth, and once again his blood, fulfilled
Of brine, of sunset, and his dreams, exhaled
A vision. While his parents clutched their hearts,
100 Expecting his conversion instantly,
And listened if perchance they might o'erhear
The silent heavens burst into applause
Over one lost repentant, he beheld
The Cyprian Aphrodite,[5] all one blush
105 And glance of passion, from the violet sea
Step inland, fastening as she went her zone.[6]
She reached a gulf that opened in the ground
Deep in a leafless wood and waited there,
Battling the darkness with her wistful eyes.
110 Then suddenly she blanched and blushed again,
And her divinely pulsing body bowed
With outstretched arms over the yawning earth.
Straightway Adonis,[7] wonderstruck and pale,
Stole from the sepulchre, a moonbeam wraith.
115 But Aphrodite with a golden cry

---

[4] In Homer's *Iliad* (eighth century BC), Troy was a fortress city in the northwest corner of Asia Minor.

[5] Aphrodite is the Greek name for Venus, the goddess of love who sprang from the foam of the sea. Cyprus was a major centre for the worship of Aphrodite.

[6] the girdle of Aphrodite, which magically made everyone fall in love with its wearer.

[7] in classical mythology, the lover of Aphrodite (or Venus). A beautiful young man, Adonis was killed by the jealous Ares in the form of a wild boar, and descended to the underworld. Aphrodite begged Zeus to allow Adonis to return to her during the summer months.

---

[1] God.

[2] Mark 9:24.

[3] "Dardan" means Trojan; Apollo and Poseidon were sent by Zeus as servants to King Laomedon, for whom they built the city of Troy.

That echoed round the world and shook the stars,
Caught him and thawed him in her warm embrace,
And murmuring kisses bore him to her bower.
Then all the trees were lit with budding flames
120 Of emerald, and all the meads and leas,
Coverts and shady places, glades and dells,
Odoured and dimly stained with opening flowers,
And loud with love-songs of impassioned birds,
Became the shrine and hostel of the spring.

125 His wanton face grew sweet and wonderful,
Beholding Aphrodite. But they thought—
His father and his mother, sick with hope—
It was the Holy Ghost's effectual call.[1]
Entranced he rose and glided from the room;
130 They, undeceived, like little children sobbed.

Slowly he broke his mother's tender heart,
Until she died in anguish for his sins.
His father then besought him on his knees,
With tears and broken speech and pleading hands

135 "My son," he said, "you open all the wounds
Daily and nightly of the Lord of Heaven:
You killed your mother, you are killing me:
Is it not sin enough, poor foolish boy?"

For this was in the North, where Time stands still
140 And Change holds holiday, where Old and New
Welter upon the border of the world,
And savage faith works woe.

                                  "Oh, let me be!"
The dreamer cried, and rushing from the house
He sought the outcast Aphrodite, dull,
145 Tawdry, unbeautiful, but still divine
Even in the dark streets of a noisome port.

At times he wrote his dreams, rebellious still
That he should be constrained to please himself
As one is eased by roaring on the rack.
150 Desperate he grew, and wandering by his firth,
Exclaimed against the literature he loved.
"Lies, lies!" he muttered. "And the noblest, lies!
Why should we lie? what penalty is this—
To write, and sing, and think, and speculate,
155 Hag-ridden by ideas, or 'twixt the shafts
Like broken horses, blinded, bitted, reined,
And whipped about the world by steel-tagged
    creeds!"

Wasted and sad with wantonness, and wan
With fantasy—a furnace seven times hot,
160 Wherein he tried all things; and wrung with woe
To see his father dying for his sake,
And by the memory of his mother's death,
He yielded tamely and professed himself
Convinced of sin but confident in Christ.

165 Then to the table of the Lord he went,
Ghastly, with haunted eyes that shone, and limbs
That scarcely bore him, like a heretic
Led to the chamber where tormentors stood
Muffled and silent, earnest to explore,
170 With cunning flames and cords and engines dire,
The sunken wells of pain, the gloomy gulfs
Obscurely wallowing in the souls of men.

In solemn tones the grey-haired presbyter—
"This is My body which is given for you,
175 This do in memory of Me."[2]

                                  The boy,
Whose blood within him clamoured like a storm,
Uttered a smothered cry and rose, but lo!
The happy triumph on his father's face!
"Why do I not die now? like husks of corn,

---

[1] a term from Calvinist theology, meaning the work of God's spirit that persuades believers to follow Jesus Christ.

[2] Matthew 26:26.

180 The bread, like vitriol the sip of wine!
I eat and drink damnation to myself
To give my father's troubled spirit of peace."[1]
The stealthy elders creaked about the floor,
Guiding the cup and platter; looking down,
185 The children in the gallery smirked and watched
Who took the deepest draught; and ancient dames
Crumpled their folded handerchiefs, and pressed
With knuckly fingers sprays of southernwood.

Ah! down no silver beam the Holy Grail[2]
190 Glided from Heaven, a crimson cup that throbbed
As throbs the heart divine; no aching sounds
Of scarce-heard music stole into the aisle,
Like disembodied pulses beating love.

But in the evening by the purple firth
195 He walked, and saw brown locks upon the brine,
And pale hands beckon him to come away,
Where mermaids, with their harps and golden
        combs,
Sit throned upon the carven antique poops
Of treasure-ships, and soft sea-dirges sing
200 Over the green-gilt bones of mariners.
He saw vast forms and dreadful draw aside
The flowing crimson curtains of the west
With far-off thundrous rustle, and threaten him
From heaven's porch; beneath his feet the earth
205 Quaked like a flame-sapped bridge that spans the
        wave
Of fiery Phlegethon;[3] and in the wind
An icy voice was borne from some waste place,
Piercing him to the marrow. Night came down,
And still he wandered helpless by the firth,

210 That under clouded skies gleamed black and smooth
Like cooling pitch. But when the moon broke out
And poured athwart the glittering ebony
Torrents of molten silver, hurtling thoughts
Trooped forth disorderly.

                              "I'll have no creed,"
215 He said. "Though I be weakest of my kind,
I'll have no creed. Lo! there is but one creed,
The vulture-phoenix[4] that for ever tears
The soul of man in chains of flesh and blood
Rivetted to the earth; the clime, the time,
220 Change but its plumage. Gluttonous bird of prey,
More fatal than all famines, plagues and wars,
I wrench you off, although my soul go too!
With bloody claws and dripping beak unfleshed,
Spread out your crackling vans that darken heaven;
225 Rabid and curst, fly yelping where you list!
Henceforth I shall be God; for consciousness
Is God: I suffer; I am God: this Self,
That all the universe combines to quell,
Is greater than the universe; and *I*
230 Am that I am.[5] To think and not be God?—
It cannot be! Lo! I shall spread this news,
And gather to myself a band of Gods—
An army, and go forth against the world,
Conquering and to conquer. Snowy steppes
235 Of Muscovy,[6] frost-bound Siberian plains,
And scalding sands of Ethiopia,
Where groans oppress the bosom of the wind,
And men in gangs are driven to icy graves,

---

[1] Cf. 1 Corinthians 11:28–9.

[2] the cup or chalice traditionally used by Christ at the Last Supper; the subject of much medieval legend, romance, and allegory. According to legend its whereabouts are unknown; in Arthurian romances, the Knights of the Round Table are involved in a series of quests for the Holy Grail.

[3] a river of liquid fire in Hades; see Milton, *Paradise Lost* 2.580.

---

[4] In Greek mythology, the phoenix is a fabulous bird which lives only a certain number of years, after which it burns itself to ashes and is reborn. The phoenix is associated with alchemy; the sign of the phoenix is used by chemists' shops. The vulture is a carnivorous bird; these lines probably also allude to the myth of Prometheus, who stole fire from the god Hephaestus in order to save humankind. Zeus punished Prometheus by chaining him to a rock where an eagle preyed on his liver all day, the liver being renewed each night.

[5] Cf. Exodus 3:14.

[6] Moscow.

Or lashed to brutish slavery under suns
240 Whose sheer beams scorch and flay like burning
blades,
Shall ring, enfranchised, with divine delight.
At home, where millions mope, in labyrinths
Of hideous streets astray without a clue,
Unfed, unsexed, unsoulled, unhelped, I bring
245 Life, with the gospel, 'Up, quit you like Gods!'"

Possessed with this, upon his father's hour
Of new-found happiness he burst, and cried,
"Father, my father, I have news to tell!
I know the word that shall uproot the thrones
250 Of oldest monarchs, and for ever lay
The doting phantom with the triple crown:
A word dynamic with the power of doom
To blast conventicles and parliaments,
Unsolder federations, crumble states,
255 And in the fining pot cast continents.
A word that shall a new beginning be,
And out of chaos make the world again.
Behold, my father! we, who heretofore,
Fearful and weak, deep-dyed in Stygian creeds
260 Against the shafts of pain and woe, have walked
The throbbing earth, most vulnerable still
In every pore and nerve: we, trembling things,
Who but an hour ago in frantic dread
Burned palsied women, and with awe beheld
265 A shaven pate mutter a latin spell
Over a biscuit: we, even we are Gods!
Nothing beneath, about us, or above
Is higher than ourselves. Henceforth degree,
Authority, religion, government,
270 Employer and employed are obsolete
As penal torture or astrology.
The mighty spirit of the universe,
Conscious in us, shall"…

                        Suddenly aware
Of gaping horror on his father's face,
275 He paused; and he, the old man, white as death,

With eyes like stars upon the crack of doom,
Rose quaking; and "The unpardonable sin!—
The unpardonable sin!" he whispered hoarse.
"This was the sin of Lucifer[1]—to make
280 Himself God's equal. If I may, my son—
If it be God's will, I shall go to hell
To be beside you. I shall be there first:
I have not many hours to live. I thought—
Here as I sat beside your mother's chair—
285 I—my boy!—I wander somewhat. Let me—
I'll sit again.—Let me remember now
How happy I have been to-day, my son
A member of the Church of Christ, and I
Beside him at Communion,[2] seeing him
290 And seeing at the window of heaven the face
Of her who bore him, sweet and glorified.
At home I sit and think that, as he lived
Most absolute in sin, he shall, like Paul[3]
Be as insatiable in doing well.
295 I think how, when my time comes, I shall go
And tell his mother of his holy life
Of labour for the Lord; and then I see
My boy at last appear before the Throne.
'By what right com'st thou here?' the Judge
demands.
300 He hangs his head; but round about him throng
A crowd of souls, who cry 'He was our staff;
He led us here.' 'Sit thou on My right hand,'
The sentence falls; and we, my wife and I,
Awaiting you.…There came a devil in
305 Wearing the likeness of my boy, and said
He was predestined for a reprobate,

---

[1] in Latin, means "light-bearer." The name was first applied to Jesus (2 Peter 1:19) and to Venus, the morning star. In Isaiah 14:12 it is applied to the King of Babylon, who boasted that he would ascend to the heavens and make himself the equal of God, but who was fated to be cast down to the uttermost recesses of the pit. St. Jerome and other Fathers applied the name Lucifer to Satan, and it has been used in this way by poets ever since.

[2] Holy Communion.

[3] St. Paul.

A special vessel of the wrath of God.
Holy he was begotten; holy born;
With tearful prayers attended all his life;
310 Cherished with scrupulous love, and shown the path
To heaven by her who ne'er shall see him there;
For out of this there comes but blasphemy
And everlasting Hell…Ah! who are these?
My soul is hustled by a multitude
315 Of wild-eyed prodigals and wrenched about.
Boy, help me to blaspheme. I cannot face
Without you her that nursed you at her breast.
Let us curse God together and going forth
Plunge headlong in the waves, and be at rest
320 In Hell for evermore. Some end to this!—
This awful gnawing pain in every part!
Or certainty that this will never end!
This, now, is Hell!…There was a paltry way
Of fooling God some casuists hit upon.
325 How went it! Yes, that God did fore-ordain
And so foreknew that those who should believe
Should enter glory of their own free-will.
Ah! pink of blasphemies that makes of God
An impotent spectator! Let us two
330 Believe in this, and that shall damn us best!…
I dare, but cannot; for the Lord of Hosts,[1]
The God of my salvation, is my God:
He, ere the world began, predestined me
To life eternal: to the bitter end
335 Against my will I persevere, a saint;
And find my will at length the will of God.
What is my son, and what the hopes and fears
Of my dead wife and me before the flame
Of God's pure purpose, His, from whose dread eyes
340 The earth and heaven fled and found no place!
Beside the crystal river[2] I shall walk
For ever with the Lord. The city of gold,[3]
The jasper walls thereof, the gates of pearl,

The bright foundation-stones of emerald,
345 Of sapphire, chrysoprase, of every gem,
And the high triumph of unending day
Shall be but wildfire on a summer eve
Beside the exceeding glory of delight,
That shall entrance me with the constant thought
350 Of how in Hell through all eternity
My son performs the perfect will of God.
Amen. I come, Lord Jesus. If his sin
Be not to death…Heaven opens!"…

                                    Thus he died;
For this was in the North where Time stands still,
355 And Change holds holiday; where Old and New
Welter upon the border of the world,
And savage creeds can kill.

                              The trembling boy
Knelt down, but dared to think, "A dreadful death!
To die believing in so dull a God,
360 A useless Hell, a jewel-huckster's Heaven!"
Forthwith it flashed like light across his mind,
"If it be terrible into the hands
Of the living God to fall, how much more dire
To sicken face to face, like our sad age,
365 Chained to an icy corpse of deity,
Decked though it be and painted and embalmed!"

He took his father's hand and kissed his brow
And, weeping like a woman, watched him long;
Then softly rose and stepped into the night.
370 He stood beside the house a little space,
Hearing the wind speak low in whispers quaint,
An irresponsible and wandering voice.
But soon he hastened to the water's edge;
For from the shore there came sea-minstrelsy
375 Of waves that broke upon the hollow beach,
With liquid sound of pearling surges blent,
Cymbals, and muffled drums and dulcimers.

---

[1] God.

[2] Revelation 21:18–21.

[3] Revelation 21:21.

Sparse diamonds in the dead-black dome of night,
A few stars lit the moon-deserted air
380 And swarthy heaving of the firth obscure.
He, knowing every rock and sandy reach,
All night unfalteringly walked the shore,
While tempest after tempest rose and fell
Within his soul, that like an o'er-wrought sea
385 Laboured to burst its continent and hang
Some glittering trophy high among the stars.
At last the fugal music of the tide,
With cymbals, muffled drums, and dulcimers,
Into his blood a rhythmic measure beat,
390 And gave his passion scope and way in words.

"How unintelligent, how blind am I,
How vain!" he cried. "A God? a mole, a worm!
An engine frail, of brittle bones conjoined;
With tissue packed; with nerves, transmitting force;
395 And driven by water, thick and coloured red:
That may for some few pence a day be hired
In thousands to be shot at! Oh, a God,
That lies and steals and murders! Such a God
Passionate, dissolute, incontinent!
400 A God that starves in thousands, and ashamed,
Or shameless in the workhouse lurks; that sweats
In mines and foundries! An enchanted God,
Whose nostrils in a palace breathe perfume,
Whose cracking shoulders hold the palace up,
405 Whose shoeless feet are rotting in the mire!
A God who said a little while ago,
'I'll have no creed;' and of his Godhood straight
Patched up a creed unwittingly—with which
He went and killed his father. Subtle lie
410 That tempts our weakness always; magical,
And magically changed to suit the time!
'Lo, ye shall be as Gods!'—the serpent's cry—
Rose up again, 'Ye shall be sons of God;'
And now the glosing word is in the air,
415 'Thou shalt be God by simply taking thought.'
And if one could, believing this, convert

A million to be upright, chaste and strong,
Gentle and tolerant, it were but to found
A new religion, bringing new offence,
420 Setting child against the father still.
Some thought imprisons us; we set about
To bring the world within the woven spell:
Our ruthless creeds that bathe the earth in blood
Are moods by alchemy made dogmas of—
425 The petrifaction of a metaphor.
No creed for me! I am a man apart:
A mouthpiece for the creeds of all the world;
A soulless life that angels may possess
Or demons haunt, wherein the foulest things
430 May loll at ease beside the loveliest;
A martyr for all mundane moods to tear;
The slave of every passion; and the slave
Of heat and cold, of darkness and of light;
A trembling lyre for every wind to sound.
435 I am a man set by to overhear
The inner harmony, the very tune
Of Nature's heart; to be a thoroughfare
For all the pageantry of Time; to catch
The mutterings of the Spirit of the Hour
440 And make them known; and of the lowliest
To be the minister, and therefore reign
Prince of the powers of the air, lord of the world
And master of the sea. Within my heart
I'll gather all the universe, and sing
445 As sweetly as the spheres; and I shall be
The first of men to understand himself…
And lo! to give me courage comes the dawn,
Crimsoning the smoky east; and still the sun
With fire-shod feet shall step from hill to hill
450 Downward before the night; winter shall ply
His ancient craft, soldering the years with ice;
And spring appear, caught in a leafless brake,
Breathless with wonder and the tears half-dried
Upon her rosy cheek; summer shall come
455 And waste his passion like a prodigal
Right royally; and autumn spend her gold

Free-handed as a harlot; men to know,
Women to love are waiting everywhere."
—1894

A Northern Suburb

Nature selects the longest way,
    And winds about in tortuous grooves;
A thousand years the oaks decay;
    The wrinkled glacier hardly moves.

5 But here the whetted fangs of change
        Daily devour the old demesne—
    The busy farm, the quiet grange,
        The wayside inn, the village green.

    In gaudy yellow brick and red,
10   With rooting pipes, like creepers rank,
    The shoddy terraces o'erspread
        Meadow, and garth, and daisied bank.

    With shelves for rooms the houses crowd,
        Like draughty cupboards in a row—
15 Ice-chests when wintry winds are loud,
        Ovens when summer breezes blow.

    Roused by the fee'd policeman's knock,
        And sad that day should come again,
    Under the stars the workmen flock
20   In haste to reach the workmen's train.

    For here dwell those who must fulfil
        Dull tasks in uncongenial spheres,
    Who toil through dread of coming ill,
        And not with hope of happier years—

25 The lowly folk who scarcely dare
        Conceive themselves perhaps misplaced,
    Whose prize for unremitting care
        Is only not to be disgraced.
        —1897

A Woman and Her Son

"Has he come yet?" the dying woman asked.
    "No," said the nurse. "Be quiet."
                                "When he
                                    comes
Bring him to me: I may not live an hour."
"Not if you talk. Be quiet."
                    "When he comes
5 Bring him to me."
                "Hush, will you!"
                            Night came down.
    The cries of children playing in the street
    Suddenly rose more voluble and shrill;
    Ceased, and broke out again; and ceased and broke
    In eager prate; then dwindled and expired.
10 "Across the dreary common once I saw
    The moon rise out of London like a ghost.
    Has the moon risen? Is he come?"
                                "Not yet.
    Be still, or you will die before he comes."

    The working-men with heavy iron tread,
15 The thin-shod clerks, the shopmen neat and plump
    Home from the city came. On muddy beer
    The melancholy mean suburban street
    Grew maudlin for an hour; pianos waked
    In dissonance from dreams of rusty peace,
20 And unpitched voices quavered tedious songs
    Of sentiment infirm or nerveless mirth.

    "Has he come yet?"
                    "Be still or you will die!"

    And when the hour of gaiety had passed,
    And the poor revellers were gone to bed,
25 The moon among the chimneys wandering long
    Escaped at last, and sadly overlooked
    The waste raw land where doleful suburbs thrive.

Then came a firm quick step—measured but quick;
And then a triple knock that shook the house
30 And brought the plaster down.

                 "My son!" she cried.
"Bring him to me!"
            He came; the nurse went out.

"Mother, I thought to spare myself this pain,"
He said at once, "but that was cowardly.
And so I come to bid you try to think,
35 To understand at last."
               "Still hard, my son?"
"Hard as the nether millstone."[1]
                  "But I hope
To soften you," she said, "before I die."

"And I to see you harden with a hiss
As life goes out in the cold bath of death.
40 Oh, surely now your creed will set you free
For one great moment, and the universe
Flash on your intellect as power, power, power,
Knowing not good or evil, God or sin,
But only everlasting yea and nay.
45 Is weakness greatness? No, a thousand times!
Is force the greatest? Yes, for ever yes!
Be strong, be great, now you have come to die."
"My son, you seem to me a kind of prig."

"How can I get it said? Think, mother, think!
50 Look back upon your fifty wretched years
And show me anywhere the hand of God.
Your husband saving souls—O, paltry souls
That need salvation!—lost the grip of things,
And left you penniless with none to aid
55 But me the prodigal. Back to the start!
An orphan girl, hurt, melancholy, frail,
Before you learned to play, your toil began:
That might have been your making, had the weight

Of drudgery, the unsheathed fire of woe
60 Borne down and beat on your defenceless life:
Souls shrivel up in these extremes of pain,
Or issue diamonds to engrave the world;
But yours before it could be made or marred,
Plucked from the burning, saved by faith,[2] became
65 Inferior as a thing of paste that hopes
To pass for real in heaven's enduring light.
You married then a crude evangelist,
Whose soul was like a wafer that can take
One single impress only."

                  "Oh, my son!
70 Your father!"

              "He, my father! These are times
When all must to the crucible—no thought,
Practice, or use, or custom sacro-sanct
But shall be violable now. And first
If ever we evade the wonted round,
75 The stagnant vortex of the eddying years,
The child must take the father by the beard,
And say, 'What did you in begetting me?'"

"I will not listen!"

             "But you shall, you must—
You cannot help yourself. Death in your eyes
80 And voice, and I to torture you with truth,
Even as your preachers for a thousand years
Pestered with falsehood souls of dying folk.
Look at the man, your husband. Of the soil;
Broad, strong, adust; head, massive; eyes of steel;
85 Yet some way ailing, for he understood
But one idea, and he married you."

The dying woman sat up straight in bed;
A ghastly blush glowed on her yellow cheek,
And flame broke from her eyes, but words came not.

---

[1] Cf. Job 41:24.

[2] Cf. Amos 4:11.

90 The son's pent wrath burnt on. "He married you;
    You were his wife, his servant; cheerfully
    You bore him children; and your house was hell.
    Unwell, half-starved, and clad in cast-off clothes,
    We had no room, no sport; nothing but fear
95 Of our evangelist, whose little purse
    Opened to all save us; who squandered smiles
    On wily proselytes, and gloomed at home.
    You had eight children; only three grew up:
    Of these, one died bedrid, and one insane,
100 And I alone am left you. Think of it!
    It matters nothing if a fish, a plant
    Teem with waste offspring, but conscious womb!
    Eight times you bore a child, and in fierce throes,
    For you were frail and small: of all your love,
105 Your hopes, your passion, not a memory steals
    To smooth your dying pillow, only I
    Am here to rack you. Where does God appear!"

    "God shall appear," the dying woman said.
    "God has appeared; my heart is in his hand.
110 Were there no God, no Heaven!—Oh, foolish boy!
    You foolish fellow! Pain and trouble here
    Are God's benignest providence—the whip
    And spur to Heaven. But joy was mine below—
    I am unjust to God—great joy was mine:
115 Which makes Heaven sweeter too; because if earth
    Afford such pleasure in mortality
    What must immortal happiness be like!
    Eight times I was a mother. Frail and small?
    Yes; but the passionate, courageous mate
120 Of a strong man. Oh, boy! You paltry boy!
    Hush! Think! Think—you! Eight times I bore a
        child,
    Eight souls for God! In Heaven they wait for me—
    My husband and the seven. I see them all!
    And two are children still—my little ones!
125 While I have sorrowed here, shrinking sometimes
    From that which was decreed, my Father, God,
    Was storing Heaven with treasure for me. Hush!
    My dowry in the skies! God's thoughtfulness!

    I see it all! Lest Heaven might, unalloyed,
130 Distress my shy soul, I leave earth in doubt
    Of your salvation: something to hope and fear
    Until I get accustomed to the peace
    That passeth understanding. When you come—
    For you will come, my son…"

                                Her strength gave out;
135 She sank down panting, bathed in tears and sweat.

    "Could I but touch your intellect," he cried,
    "Before you die! Mother, the world is mad:
    This castle in the air, this Heaven of yours,
    Is the lewd dream of morbid vanity.
140 For each of us death is the end of all;
    And when the sun goes out the race of men
    Shall cease for ever. It is ours to make
    This farce of fate a splendid tragedy:
    Since we must be the sport of circumstance,
145 We should be sportsmen, and produce a breed
    Of gallant creatures, conscious of their doom,
    Marching with lofty brows, game to the last.
    Oh good and evil, heaven and hell are lies!
    But strength is great: there is no other truth:
150 This is the yea-and-nay that makes men hard.
    Mother, be hard and happy in your death."
    "What do you say? I hear the waters roll…"
    Then, with a faint cry, striving to arise—
    "After I die I shall come back to you,
155 And then you must believe; you must believe,
    For I shall bring you news of God and Heaven!"

    He set his teeth, and saw his mother die.
    Outside a city-reveller's tipsy tread
    Severed the silence with a jagged rent;
160 The tall lamps flickered through the sombre street,
    With yellow light hiding the stainless stars:
    In the next house a child awoke and cried;
    Far off a clank and clash of shunting trains
    Broke out and ceased, as if the fettered world
165 Started and shook its irons in the night;

Across the dreary common citywards,
The moon, among the chimneys sunk again,
Cast on the clouds a shade of smoky pearl.

And when her funeral day had come, her son,
170   Before they fastened down the coffin lid,
Shut himself in the chamber, there to gaze
Upon her dead face, hardening his heart.
But as he gazed, into the smooth wan cheek
Life with its wrinkles shot again; the eyes
175   Bust open, and the bony fingers clutched
The coffin sides; the woman raised herself,
And owl-like in her shroud blinked on the light.

"Mother, what news of God and Heaven?" he
    asked.

Feeble and strange, her voice came from afar:
180   "I am not dead: I must have been asleep."

"Do not imagine that. You lay here dead—
Three days and nights, a corpse. Life has come back:
Often it does, although faint-hearted folk
Fear to admit it: none of those who die,
185   And come to life again, can ever tell
Of any bourne from which they have returned:
Therefore they were not dead, your casuists say.
The ancient jugglery that tricks the world!
You lay here dead, three days and nights. What
    news?
190   'After I die I shall come back to you,
And then you must believe'—these were your
    words—
'For I shall bring you news of God and Heaven.'"
She cast a look forlorn about the room:
The door was shut; the worn venetian, down;
195   And stuffy sunlight through the dusty slats
Spotted the floor, and smeared the faded walls.
He with his strident voice and eyes of steel
Stood by relentless.

        "I remember, dear,"
She whispered, "very little. When I died
200   I saw my children dimly bending down,
The little ones in front, to beckon me,
A moment in the dark; and that is all."

"That was before you died—the last attempt
Of fancy to create the heart's desire.
205   Now mother, be courageous, now, be hard."

"What must I say or do, my dearest son?
Oh me, the deep discomfort of my mind!
Come to me, hold me, help me to be brave,
And I shall make you happy if I can,
210   For I have none but you—none anywhere...
Mary, the youngest,, whom you never saw
Looked out of Heaven first: her little hands...
Three days and nights, dead, and no memory!...
A poor old creature dying a second death,
215   I understand the settled treachery,
The plot of love and hope against the world.
Fearless, I gave myself at nature's call;
And when they died, my children, one by one,
All sweetly in my heart I buried them.
220   Who stole them while I slept? Where are they all?
My heart is eerie, like a rifled grave
Where silent spiders spin among the dust,
And the wind moans and laughs under its breath.
But in a drawer...What is there in the drawer?
225   No pressure of a little rosy hand
Upon a faded cheek—nor anywhere
The seven fair stars I made. Oh love the cheat!
And hope, the radiant devil pointing up,
Lest men should cease to give the couple sport
230   And end the world at once! For three days dead—
Here in my coffin; and no memory!
Oh, it is hard! But I—I, too, am hard...
Be hard, my son, and steep your heart of flesh
In stony waters till it grows a stone,
235   Or love and hope will hack it with blunt knives
As long as it can feel."

He, holding her,
With sobs and laughter spoke: his mind had snapped
Like a frayed string o'erstretched: "Mother, rejoice;
For I shall make you glad. There is no heaven.
240 Your children are resolved to dust and dew:
But, mother, I am God. I shall create
The heaven of your desires. There must be heaven
For mothers and their babes. Let heaven be now!"

They found him conjuring chaos with mad words
245 And brandished hands across his mother's corpse.

Thus did he see her harden with a hiss
As life went out in the cold bath of death;
Thus did she soften him before she died:
For both were bigots—fateful souls that plague
250 The gentle world.
—1897

Yuletide

Now wheel and hoof and horn
In every street
Stunned to its chimney-tops,
In every murky street—
5 Each lamp-lit gorge by traffic rent
Asunder,
Ravines of serried shops
By business tempests torn—
In every echoing street,
10 From early morn
Till jaded night falls dead,
Wheel, hoof, and horn
Tumultuous thunder
Beat
15 Under
A noteless firmament
Of lead.

When the winds list
A fallen cloud
20 Where yellow dregs of light
Befouled remain,
The woven gloom
Of smoke and mist,
The soot-entangled rain
25 That jumbles day and night
In city and town,
An umber-emerald shroud
Rehearsing doom,
The London fog comes down.

30 But sometimes silken beams,
As bright
As adamant on fire,
Of the uplifted sun's august attire,
With frosty fibrous light
35 Magnetic shine
On happier dreams
That abrogate despair,
When all the sparkling air
Of smoke and sulphur shriven,
40 Like an iced wine
Fills the high cup
Of heaven;
For urban park and lawn,
The city's scenery,
45 Heaths, commons, dells
That compass London rich
In greenery,
With diamond-dust of rime
Empowdered, flash
50 At dawn;
And tossing bells
Of stealthy hansome chime
With silvery crash
In radiant ways

55 Attuned and frozen up
To concert pitch—
In resonant ways,
Where wheels and hoofs inwrought,
Cars, omnibuses, wains,
60 Beat, boom, and clash
Discordant fugal strains
Of cymbals, trumpets, drums;
While careless to arrive,

The nerved pedestrian comes
65 Exulting in the splendour overhead,
And in the live
Elastic ground,
The pavement, tense and taut,
That yields a twangling sound
70 At every tread.
—1906

A. Mary F. Robinson
1857 – 1944

Agnes Mary Frances Robinson was born in Leamington and educated herself reading in her father's library until she went to school in Brussels in 1870. She later studied in Italy and at University College, London, where she focussed on Greek literature. Her first book of verse,

A Handful of Honeysuckle, was privately printed in 1878. She subsequently published many volumes of verse, a novel, and a biography of Emily Brontë (1883). Robinson believed that the ballad was a special woman's form, valuable for its authenticity of experience.

❧❧❧

The Scape-Goat [1]

She lived in the hovel alone, the beautiful child.
 Alas, that it should have been so!
But her father died of the drink, and the sons were
  wild,
 And where was the girl to go?

5 Her brothers left her alone in the lonely hut.
 Ah, it was dreary at night
When the wind whistled right thro' the door that
  never would shut,
 And sent her sobbing with fright.

She never had slept alone; when the stifling room
10 Held her, brothers, father—all.
Ah, better their violence, better their threats, than
  the gloom
 That now hung close as a pall!

When the hard day's washing was done, it was
  sweeter to stand
 Hearkening praises and vows,
15 To feel her cold fingers kept warm in a sheltering
  hand,
 Than crouch in the desolate house.

Ah, me! she was only a child; and yet so aware
 Of the shame which follows on sin.
A poor, lost, terrified child! she stept in the snare,
20 Knowing the toils she was in.

Yet, now, when I watch her pass with a heavy reel,
 Shouting her villainous song,
It is only pity or shame, do you think, that I feel
 For the infinite sorrow and wrong?

25 With a sick, strange wonder I ask, Who shall
  answer the sin,
 Thou, lover, brothers of thine?
Or he who left standing thy hovel to perish in?
 Or I, who gave no sign?
—1884

The Idea

Beneath this world of stars and flowers
 That rolls in visible deity,
I dream another world is ours
 And is the soul of all we see.

5 It hath no form, it hath no spirit;
 It is perchance the Eternal Mind;
Beyond the sense that we inherit
 I feel it dim and undefined.

---

[1] a person bearing the blame for the sins and shortcomings of others; biblically, a goat sent into the wild after the Jewish chief priest symbolically laid the sins of the people on it: Leviticus 16.

How far below the depth of being,
10   How wide beyond the starry bound
It rolls unconscious and unseeing,
    And is as Number or as Sound.

And through the vast fantastic visions
    Of all this actual universe,
15 It moves unswerved by our decisions,
    And is the play that we rehearse.
    —1886

Darwinism [1]

When first the unflowering Fern-forest
    Shadowed the dim lagoons of old,
A vague, unconscious, long unrest
    Swayed the great fronds of green and gold.

5   Until the flexible stem grew rude,
    The fronds began to branch and bower,
And lo! upon the unblossoming wood
    There breaks a dawn of apple-flower.

Then on the fruitful forest-boughs
10   For ages long the unquiet ape
Swung happy in his airy house
    And plucked the apple, and sucked the grape.

Until at length in him there stirred
    The old, unchanged, remote distress,
15 That pierced his world of wind and bird
    With some divine unhappiness.

Not love, nor the wild fruits he sought,
    Nor the fierce battles of his clan

Could still the unborn and aching thought,
20   Until the brute became the man.

Long since; and now the same unrest
    Goads to the same invisible goal,
Till some new gift, undream'd, unguess'd,
    End the new travail of the soul.
—1888

An Orchard at Avignon [2]

The hills are white, but not with snow:
    They are as pale in summer time,
For herb or grass may never grow
    Upon their slopes of lime.

5   Within the circle of the hills
    A ring, all flowering in a round,
An orchard-ring of almond fills
    The plot of stony ground.

More fair than happier trees, I think,
10   Grown in well-watered pasture land
These parched and stunted branches, pink
    Above the stones and sand.

O white, austere, ideal place,
    Where very few will care to come,
15 Where spring hath lost the waving grace
    She wears for us at home!

Fain would I sit and watch for hours
    The holy whiteness of thy hills,
Their wreath of pale auroral flowers,
20   Their peace the silence fills.

A place of secret peace thou art,
    Such peace as in an hour of pain

---

[1] a theory of biological evolution developed by Charles Darwin and
others, stating that species of organisms arise and develop through the
natural selection of inherited variations that increase the individual's
ability to survive and reproduce.

[2] a southern French city situated by the Rhone river; formerly the papal
seat (1309–77).

One moment fills the amazèd heart,
   And never comes again.
—1888

Love, Death, and Art

Lord, give me Love! give me the silent bliss
  Of meeting souls, of answering eyes and hands;
The comfort of one heart that understands;
The thrill and rapture of Love's sealing kiss.

5 Or grant me—lest I weary of all this—
The quiet of Death's unimagined lands,
Wherein the longed-for Tree of Knowledge stands
Where Thou art, Lord—and the great mysteries.

Nay, let me sing, my God, and I'll forego,
10 Love's smiling mouth, Death's sweetlier smiling eyes.
Better my life long mourn in glorious woe,
Than love unheard in a mute Paradise—

For no grief, no despair, can quail me long,
While I can make these sweet to me in song.
—1891

Art and Life

A Sonnet

When autumn come, my orchard trees alone,
  Shall bear no fruit to deck the reddening
     year—
  When apple gatherers climb the branches sere
Only on mine no harvest shall be grown.
5 For when the pearly blossom first was blown,
  I filled my hands with delicate buds and dear,
  I dipped them in thine icy waters clear,
O well of Art! and tuned them all to stone.

Therefore, when winter comes, I shall not eat
10 Of mellow apples such as others prize:
  I shall go hungry in a magic spring!—
All round my head and bright before mine eyes
The barren, strange, eternal blossoms meet,
  While I, not less an-hungered, gaze and sing.
—1891

Song

Oh for the wings of a dove,
  To fly far away from my own soul,
  Reach and be merged in the vast whole
Heaven of infinite Love!

5 Oh that I were as the rain,
  To fall and be lost in the great sea,
  One with the waves, till the drowned Me
Might not be severed again!

Infinite arms of the air,
10 Surrounding the stars and without strife
  Blending our life with their large life,
Lift me and carry me there!
—1891

Neurasthenia [1]

I watch the happier people of the house
  Come in and out, and talk, and go their ways;
I sit and gaze at them; I cannot rouse
  My heavy mind to share their busy days.

5 I watch them glide, like skaters on a stream,
  Across the brilliant surface of the world.

---

[1] a form of neurosis, typically arising from emotional trauma and indicated by depression, exhaustion, excessive worrying and inexplicable pain.

But I am underneath: they do not dream
    How deep below the eddying flood is whirl'd.

They cannot come to me, nor I to them;
10   But, if a mightier arm could reach and save,
Should I forget the tide I had to stem?
    Should I, like these, ignore the abysmal wave?

Yes! in the radiant air how could I know
How black it is, how fast it is, below?
—1902

To My Muse

The vast Parnassus[1] never knew thy face,
  O Muse of mine, O frail and tender elf
  That dancest in a moonbeam to thyself
Where olives rustle in a lonely place!

5 And yet…thou hast a sort of Tuscan[2] grace;
    Thou may'st outlive me! Some unborn Filelf
    One day may range thee on his studious shelf
With Lenau,[3] Leopardi,[4] and their race.

And so, some time, the sole sad scholar's friend,
    The melancholy comrade of his dreams,
10   Thou may'st, O Muse, escape a little while
The none the less inevitable end:
    Take heart, therefore, and sing the thing that
      seems,
      And watch the world's disaster with a smile.
—1902

---

[1] the mountain in central Greece which, in antiquity, was sacred to the Muses.

[2] referring to the northern region of Italy.

[3] Nikolaus Lenau (1802–50), German poet.

[4] Giacomo Leopardi (1798–1837), Italian poet.

J.K. Stephen
1859 – 1892

J ames K. Stephen was a minor poet, who, in *Lapsus Calami* (1891), parodies the work of D.G. Rossetti, Robert Browning, and others.

ↂↃↄ

In the Backs [1]

As I was strolling lonely in the Backs,
I met a woman whom I did not like.
I did not like the way the woman walked:
Loose-hipped, big-boned, disjointed, angular.
5   If her anatomy comprised a waist,
I did not notice it: she had a face
With eyes and lips adjusted thereunto,
But round her mouth no pleasing shadows stirred,
Nor did her eyes invite a second glance.
10   Her dress was absolutely colourless,
Devoid of taste or shape or character;
Her boots were rather old, and rather large,
And rather shabby, not precisely matched.
Her hair was very far from beautiful

15   And not abundant: she had such a hat
As neither merits nor expects remark.
She was not clever, I am very sure,
Nor witty nor amusing; well-informed
She may have been, and kind, perhaps, of heart;
20   But gossip was writ plain upon her face.
And so she stalked her dull unthinking way;
Or, if she thought of anything, it was
That such a one had got a second class,
Or Mrs So-and-So a second child.
25   I do not want to see that girl again:
I do not like her: and I should not mind
If she were done away with, killed, or ploughed.
She did not seem to serve a useful end:
And certainly she was not beautiful.
—1891

---

[1]   the grounds beside the river Cam at the back of several Cambridge colleges—a famously beautiful place to walk.

Francis Thompson
1859 – 1907

Along with Coventry Patmore and Gerard Manley Hopkins, Francis Thompson forms Victorian England's triumvirate of Catholic poets. Born to a physician and Catholic convert, Thompson initially sought to emulate his father's work, but then realized that his years of ill health and nervousness rendered him unsuitable for medical practice. After years of mental and economic depression, Thompson, the poet, began to flourish; Thompson's three volumes of poetry are *Poems* (1893), *Sister Songs* (1895), and *New Poems* (1897).

ℰℐℰℐ

The Hound of Heaven

I fled Him, down the nights and down the days;
  I fled Him, down the arches of the years;
I fled Him, down the labyrinthine ways
    Of my own mind; and in the mist of tears
5 I hid from Him, and under running laughter.
      Up vistaed hopes I sped;
      And shot, precipitated,
Adown Titanic[1] glooms of chasméd fears,
  From those strong Feet that followed, followed after.
10   But with unhurrying chase,
      And unperturbéd pace,
    Deliberate speed, majestic instancy,
      They beat—and a Voice beat
      More instant than the Feet—
15   "All things betray thee, who betrayest Me."

      I pleaded, outlaw-wise,
By many a hearted casement, curtained red,
    Trellised with intertwining charities
(For, though I knew His love Who followed,
20   Yet was I sore adread
Lest, having Him, I must have naught beside);
But, if one little casement parted wide,
    The gust of His approach would clash it to.

Fear wist[2] not to evade, as Love wist to pursue.
25 Across the margent[3] of the world I fled,
    And troubled the gold gateways of the stars,
    Smiting for shelter on their clangéd bars,
      Fretted to dulcet jars
And silvern chatter the pale ports o' the moon.
30 I said to dawn, Be sudden; to eve, Be soon;
    With thy young skyey blossoms heap me over
      From this tremendous Lover!
Float thy vague veil about me, lest He see!
    I tempted all His servitors, but to find
35 My own betrayal in their constancy,
In faith to Him their fickleness to me,
    Their traitorous trueness, and their loyal deceit.
To all swift things for swiftness did I sue;
    Clung to the whistling mane of every wind.
40   But whether they swept, smoothly flect,
      The long savannahs of the blue;
        Or whether, Thunder-driven,
      They clanged his chariot 'thwart a heaven,
Plashy with flying lightnings round the spurn o'
    their feet—
45 Fear wist not to evade as Love wist to pursue.
      Still with unhurrying chase,
      And unperturbéd pace,
    Deliberate speed, majestic instancy,
      Came on the following Feet,
50   And a Voice above their beat—

---

[1] In Greek mythology, the Titans were giants of enormous size and strength.

[2] archaic form of "to wit," meaning "know."

[3] margin.

"Naught shelters thee, who wilt not shelter
    Me."

I sought no more that after which I strayed
    In face of man or maid;
But still within the little children's eyes
55   Seems something, something that replies:
They at least are for me, surely for me!
I turned me to them very wistfully;
But, just as their young eyes grew sudden fair
    With dawning answers there,
60 Their angel plucked them from me by the hair.
"Come then, ye other children, Nature's—share
With me" (said I) "your delicate fellowship;
    Let me greet you lip to lip,
    Let me twine with you caresses,
65   Wantoning
    With our Lady-Mother's vagrant tresses.
        Banqueting
    With her in her wind-walled palace,
    Underneath her azured dais,
70   Quaffing, as your taintless way is,
        From a chalice
Lucent-weeping out of the dayspring."
        So it was done;
I in their delicate fellowship was one—
75 Drew the bolt of Nature's secrecies.
    I knew all the swift importings
    On the willful face of skies;
    I knew how the clouds arise
    Spuméd of the wild sea-snortings;
80   All that's born or dies
    Rose and drooped with—made them shapers
Of mine own moods, or wailful or divine—
    With them joyed and was bereaven.
    I was heavy with the even,
85   When she lit her glimmering tapers
    Round the day's dead sanctities.
    I laughed in the morning's eyes.
I triumphed and I saddened with all weather,

    Heaven and I wept together,
90 And its sweet tears were salt with mortal mine;
Against the red throb of its sunset-heart
    I laid my own to beat,
    And share commingling heat;
But not by that, by that, was eased my human smart.
95 In vain my tears were wet on Heaven's gray cheek.
For ah! we know not what each other says,
    These things and I; in sound *I* speak—
Their sound is but their stir, they speak by silences.
Nature, poor stepdame, cannot slake my drouth;
100   Let her, if she would owe me,
Drop yon blue bosom-veil of sky, and show me
    The breasts o' her tenderness;
Never did any milk of hers once bless
    My thirsting mouth.
105   Nigh and nigh draws the chase,
    With unperturbéd pace,
    Deliberate speed, majestic instancy;
        And past those noiséd Feet
        A voice comes yet more fleet—
110 "Lo! naught contents thee, who content'st
    not Me."

Naked I wait Thy love's uplifted stroke!
My harness piece by piece Thou hast hewn from
    me,
    And smitten me to my knee;
    I am defenseless utterly.
115   I slept, me thinks, and woke,
And, slowly gazing, find me stripped in sleep.
In the rash lustihead of my young powers,
    I shook the pillaring hours
And pulled my life upon me; grimed with smears,
120 I stand amid the dust o' the mounded years—
My mangled youth lies dead beneath the heap.
My days have crackled and gone up in smoke,
Have puffed and burst as sun-starts on a stream.
    Yea, faileth now even dream
125 The dreamer, and the lute the lutanist;
Even the linked fantasies, in whose blossomy twist

I swung the earth a trinket at my wrist,
Are yielding; cords of all too weak account
For earth with heavy griefs so overplussed.
130   Ah! is Thy love indeed
A weed, albeit an amaranthine weed,
Suffering no flowers except its own to mount?
        Ah! must—
        Designer infinite!—
135   Ah! must Thou char the wood ere Thou canst limn
        with it?
My freshness spent its wavering shower i' the dust;
And now my heart is as a broken fount,
Wherein tear-drippings stagnate, spilt down ever
        From the dank thoughts that shiver
140   Upon the sightful branches of my mind.
        Such is; what is to be?
The pulp so bitter, how shall taste the rind?
I dimly guess what Time in mists confounds;
Yet ever and anon a trumpet sounds
145   From the hid battlements of Eternity;
Those shaken mists a space unsettle, then
Round the half-glimpséd turrets slowly wash again.
        But not ere him who summoneth
        I first have seen, enwound
150   With glooming robes purpureal, cypress-crowned;
His name I know, and what his trumpet saith.
Whether man's heart or life it be which yields
        Thee harvest, must Thy harvest fields
        Be dunged with rotten death?

155   Now of that long pursuit
        Comes on at hand the bruit;
        That Voice is round me like a bursting
            sea;

        "And is thy earth so marred,
        Shattered in shard on shard?
160   Lo, all things fly thee, for thou fliest Me!
        Strange, piteous, futile thing,
Wherefore should any set thee love apart?
Seeing none but I makes much of naught" (He
        said),
"And human love needs human meriting,
165   How has thou merited—
Of all man's clotted clay the dingiest clot?
        Alack, thou knowest not
How little worthy of any love thou art!
Whom wilt thou find to love ignoble thee
170   Save Me, save only Me?
All which I took from thee I did but take,
        Not for thy harms,
But just that thou might'st seek it in My arms.
        All which thy child's mistake
175   Fancies as lost, I have stored for thee at home;
        Rise, clasp My hand, and come!"

        Halts by me that footfall;
        Is my gloom, after all,
        Shade of His hand, outstretched caressingly?
180   "Ah, fondest, blindest, weakest,
        I am He Whom thou seekest!
Thou dravest[1] love from thee, who dravest Me."
—1893 (1891)

---

[1] archaic past tense of drive.

Mary Coleridge
1861 – 1907

Mary Elizabeth Coleridge, a descendant of Samuel Taylor Coleridge, was born in London. A number of her essays, collected under the title *Non Sequitur*, were published in 1900, and she continued to compose pieces for the *Times Literary Supplement* from 1902 until her death. Coleridge wrote a number of novels between 1893 and 1906, and began her career as a poet reluctantly. Some of her efforts were submitted by a friend to Robert Bridges, who so admired her ability that he became her poetic mentor. In 1897 Coleridge published *Fancy's Guerdon*. In this volume, as in *Fancy's Following* (1896), Coleridge's imagistic lyrics participate in the shift from Victorian to early Modernist aesthetics. Coleridge worked as a teacher at the Working Woman's College from 1895 until her death of acute appendicitis at age 45.

❧❧❧

IX

The Other Side of a Mirror

I sat before my glass one day,
   And conjured up a vision bare,
Unlike the aspects glad and gay,
   That erst were found reflected there—
5 The vision of a woman, wild
   With more than womanly despair.

Her hair stood back on either side
   A face bereft of loveliness.
It had no envy now to hide
10 What once no man on earth could guess.
It formed the thorny aureole
   Of hard unsanctified distress.

Her lips were open—not a sound
   Came through the parted lines of red.
15 Whate'er it was, the hideous wound
   In silence and in secret bled.
No sigh relieved her speechless woe,
   She had no voice to speak her dread.

And in her lurid eyes there shone
20 The dying flame of life's desire,
Made mad because its hope was gone,
   And kindled at the leaping fire
Of jealousy, and fierce revenge,
   And strength that could not change nor tire.

25 Shade of a shadow in the glass,
   O set the crystal surface free!
Pass—as the fairer visions pass—
   Nor ever more return, to be
The ghost of a distracted hour,
30 That heard me whisper, "I am she!"
—1896

XIV

Regina

My Queen her sceptre did lay down,
   She took from her head the golden crown
Worn by right of her royal birth.
Her purple robe she cast aside,
5 And the scarlet vestures of her pride,
That was the pride of the earth.
In her nakedness was she
Queen of the world, herself and me.

My Queen took up her sceptre bright,
10 Her crown more radiant than the light,
The rubies gleaming out of the gold.

She donned her robe of purple rare,
And did a deed that none may dare,
That makes the blood run cold.
15 And in her bravery is she
Queen of herself, the world and me.
—1896

XXVII

Winged Words

As darting swallows swim across a pool,
Whose tranquil depths reflect a tranquil sky,
So, o'er the depths of silence, dark and cool,
    Our winged words dart playfully,
5   And seldom break
    The quiet surface of the lake,
        As they flit by.
—1896

LX

Marriage

No more alone sleeping, no more alone waking,
Thy dreams divided, thy prayers in twain;
Thy merry sisters to-night forsaking,
    Never shall we see thee, maiden, again.

5 Never shall we see thee, thine eyes glancing,
    Flashing with laughter and wild in glee,
Under the mistletoe kissing and dancing,
    Wantonly free.

There shall come a matron walking sedately,
10   Low-voiced, gentle, wise in reply.
Tell me, O tell me, can I love her greatly?
    All for her sake must the maiden die!
—1899

LXIII

In Dispraise of the Moon

I would not be the Moon, the sickly thing,
To summon owls and bats upon the wing;
For when the noble Sun is gone away,
She turns his night into a pallid day.

5 She hath no air, no radiance of her own,
That world unmusical of earth and stone.
She wakes her dim, uncoloured, voiceless hosts,
Ghost of the Sun, herself the sun of ghosts.

The mortal eyes that gaze too long on her
10 Of Reason's piercing ray defrauded are.
Light in itself doth feed the living brain;
That light, reflected, but makes darkness plain.
—1899

LXXVI

The White Women [1]

Where dwell the lovely, wild white women folk,
        Mortal to man?
They never bowed their necks beneath the yoke,
They dwelt alone when the first morning broke
5   And Time began.

Taller are they than man, and very fair,
        Their cheeks are pale,
At sight of them the tiger in his lair,
The falcon hanging in the azure air,
10   The eagles quail.

The deadly shafts their nervous hands let fly
    Are stronger than our strongest—in their form
Larger, more beauteous, carved amazingly,

---
[1] "From a legend of Malay, told by Hugh Clifford." (Coleridge's note.)

And when they fight, the wild white women cry
15   The war-cry of the storm.

Their words are not as ours. If man might go
      Among the waves of Ocean when they break
And hear them—hear the language of the snow
Falling on torrents—he might also know
20   The tongue they speak.

Pure are they as the light; they never sinned,
      But when the rays of the eternal fire
Kindle the West, their tresses they unbind
And fling their girdles to the Western wind,
25   Swept by desire.

Lo, maidens to the maidens then are born.
      Strong children of the maidens and the breeze,
Dreams are not—in the glory of the morn,
Seen through the gates of ivory and horn—
30   More fair than these.

And none may find their dwelling. In the shade
      Primeval of the forest oaks they hide.
One of our race, lost in an awful glade,
Saw with his human eyes a wild white maid,
35   And gazing, died.

—1900

XCVII

The Fire Lamp

The fire, the lamp, and I, were alone together.
      Out in the street it was wild and windy
            weather.

The fire said, "Once I lived, and now I shine.
I was a wood once, and the wind was mine."

5   The lamp said, "Once I lived and was the Sun.
The fire and I, in those old days, were one."

The fire said, "Once I lived and saw the Spring.
I die in smoke to warm this mortal thing."

The lamp said, "I was once alive and free.
10 In smoke I die to let this mortal see."

Then I remembered all the beasts that died
That I might eat and might be satisfied.

Then I remembered how my feet were shod,
Thought of the myriad lives on which I trod,

15 And sighed to feel that as I went my way,
I was a murderer ninety times a day.
—1908

CXIV

To the writer of a poem on a bridge

Dear builder of the Bridge, with thee I stood
      And watched the waters flow
And heard thy cry of "Onward" o'er the flood,
      Between two skies, one over, one below.

5   Whether it was the outward eye that thought,
      The inward eye that saw,
I know not; into harmony were brought
      The floating image and abiding law.
—1908

CXCI

Tar Ublia Chi Bien Eima [1]

To me realities but seem
      The offspring of a foolish dream.
The things that were, alone are true,
The Past is Present here with you.
5   With you among the flowers I stray,

---

[1] from old Catalan: "The one who has a deep love never forgets."

That grow not here but far away,
And gazing from your eyes I see
A soul for ever lost to me.
—1908

CCVI

A Clever Woman

You thought I had the strength of men,
  Because with men I dared to speak,
And courted Science now and then,
  And studied Latin for a week;
5 But woman's woman, even when
  She reads her Ethics in the Greek.

You thought me wiser than my kind;
  You thought me "more than common tall;"
You thought because I had a mind,
10 That I could have no heart at all;
But woman's woman you will find,
  Whether she be great or small.

And then you needs must die—ah, well!
  I knew you not, you loved not me.
15 'Twas not because that darkness fell,
  You saw not what there was to see.
But I that saw and could not tell—
  O evil Angel, set me free!
—1908

Amy Levy
1861 – 1889

Amy Levy was born in London into an upper-middle-class Anglo-Jewish family, and was the first Jewish woman to matriculate at Newnham College, Cambridge. Her first publication was the ballad "Ida Grey" (1875), published in the journal *The Pelican*. This poem was followed by the short story "Euphemia, A Sketch" (1880), and various work that appeared in the literary magazines *Temple Bar*, *The Gentleman's Magazine*, and *The Jewish Chronicle*. She contributed also to *Woman's World*, developing a friendship with its editor, Oscar Wilde. Levy published her first volume of poetry, entitled *Xantippe and Other Verse*, in 1881. Levy wrote three novels; *Miss Meredith* was serialized in 1886, and *The Romance of a Shop* was published in book form in 1888. *Reuben Sachs* (1888), by some considered her most important work, addresses the cultural and personal complexities of Jewish assimilation. The book was critically well-received, but it was rejected by those members of the Anglo-Jewish community who felt that Levy was unsympathetic to them. Levy's promise as a writer was abruptly cut short when, just before her twenty-eighth birthday and for reasons that remained undisclosed, she committed suicide at her parents' home in London.

❧❧❧

Xantippe

A Fragment

What, have I waked again? I never thought
   To see the rosy dawn, or ev'n this grey,
Dull, solemn stillness, ere the dawn has come.
The lamp burns low; low burns the lamp of life:
5 The still morn stays expectant, and my soul,
All weighted with a passive wonderment,
Waiteth and watcheth, waiteth for the dawn.
Come hither, maids; too soundly have ye slept
That should have watched me; nay, I would not
   chide—
10 Oft have I chidden, yet I would not chide
In this last hour;—now all should be at peace.
I have been dreaming in a troubled sleep
Of weary days I thought not to recall;
Of stormy days, whose storms are hushed long
   since;
15 Of gladsome days, of sunny days; alas!
In dreaming, all their sunshine seem'd so sad,
As though the current of the dark To-Be
Had flow'd, prophetic, through the happy hours.

And yet, full well, I know it was not thus;
20 I mind me sweetly of the summer days,
When, leaning from the lattice, I have caught
The fair, far glimpses of a shining sea:
And nearer, of tall ships which thronged the bay,
And stood out blackly from a tender sky
25 All flecked with sulphur, azure, and bright gold;
And in the still, clear air have heard the hum
Of distant voices; and methinks there rose
No darker fount to mar or stain the joy
Which sprang ecstatic in my maiden breast
30 Than just those vague desires, those hopes and
     fears,
Those eager longings, strong, though undefined,
Whose very sadness makes them seem so sweet.
What cared I for the merry mockeries
Of other maidens sitting at the loom?
35 Or for sharp voices, bidding me return
To maiden labour? Were we not apart—
I and my high thoughts, and my golden dreams,
My soul which yearned for knowledge, for a tongue
That should proclaim the stately mysteries
40 Of this fair world, and of the holy gods?
Then followed days of sadness, as I grew

To learn my woman-mind had gone astray,
And I was sinning in those very thoughts—
For maidens, mark, such are not woman's
   thoughts—
45 (And yet, 'tis strange, the gods who fashion us
Have given us such promptings)....
                       Fled the years,
Till seventeen had found me tall and strong,
And fairer, runs it, than Athenian maids
Are wont to seem; I had not learnt it well—
50 My lesson of dumb patience—and I stood
At Life's great threshold with a beating heart,
And soul resolved to conquer and attain....
Once, walking 'thwart the crowded market-place,
With other maidens, bearing in the twigs,
55 White doves for Aphrodite's sacrifice,
I saw him, all ungainly and uncouth,
Yet many gathered round to hear his words,
Tall youths and stranger-maidens—Sokrates[1]—
I saw his face and marked it, half with awe,
60 Half with a quick repulsion at the shape....
The richest gem lies hidden furthest down,
And is the dearer for the weary search;
We grasp the shining shells which strew the shore,
Yet swift we fling them from us; but the gem
65 We keep for aye and cherish. So a soul,
Found after weary searching in the flesh
Which half repelled our senses, is more dear,
For that same seeking, than the sunny mind
Which lavish Nature marks with thousand hints
70 Upon a brow of beauty. We are prone
To overweigh such subtle hints, then deem,
In after disappointment, we are fooled....
And when, at length, my father told me all,
That I should wed me with great Sokrates,
75 I, foolish, wept to see at once cast down
The maiden image of a future love,
Where perfect body matched the perfect soul.
But slowly, softly did I cease to weep;

---

[1] Socrates, the Athenian philosopher and teacher (470–399 BC).

Slowly I 'gan to mark the magic flash
80 Leap to the eyes, to watch the sudden smile
Break round the mouth, and linger in the eyes;
To listen for the voice's lightest tone—
Great voice, whose cunning modulations seemed
Like to the notes of some sweet instrument.
85 So did I reach and strain, until at last
I caught the soul athwart the grosser flesh.
Again of thee, sweet Hope, my spirit dreamed!
I, guided by his wisdom and his love,
Led by his words, and counselled by his care,
90 Should lift the shrouding veil from things which be,
And at the flowing fountain of his soul
Refresh my thirsting spirit....
                    And indeed,
In those long days which followed that strange day
When rites and song, and sacrifice and flow'rs,
95 Proclaimed that we were wedded, did I learn,
In sooth, a-many lessons; bitter ones
Which sorrow taught me, and not love inspired,
Which deeper knowledge of my kind impressed
With dark insistence on reluctant brain;—
100 But that great wisdom, deeper, which dispels
Narrowed conclusions of a half-grown mind,
And sees athwart the littleness of life
Nature's divineness and her harmony,
Was never poor Xantippe's....
                       I would pause
105 And would recall no more, no more of life,
Than just the incomplete, imperfect dream
Of early summers, with their light and shade,
Their blossom-hopes, whose fruit was never ripe;
But something strong within me, some sad chord
110 Which loudly echoes to the later life,
Me to unfold the after-misery
Urges, with plaintive wailing in my heart.
Yet, maidens, mark; I would not that ye thought
I blame my lord departed, for he meant
115 No evil, so I take it, to his wife.
'Twas only that the high philosopher,
Pregnant with noble theories and great thoughts,

Deigned not to stoop to touch so slight a thing
As the fine fabric of a woman's brain—
120 So subtle as a passionate woman's soul.
I think, if he had stooped a little, and cared
I might have risen nearer to his height,
And not lain shattered, neither fit for use
As goodly household vessel, nor for that
125 Far finer thing which I had hoped to be....
Death, holding high his retrospective lamp,
Shows me those first, far years of wedded life,
Ere I had learnt to grasp the barren shape
Of what the Fates had destined for my life.
130 Then, as all youthful spirits are, was I
Wholly incredulous that Nature meant
So little, who had promised me so much.
At first I fought my fate with gentle words,
With high endeavours after greater things;
135 Striving to win the soul of Sokrates,
Like some slight bird, who sings her burning love
To human master, till at length she finds
Her tender language wholly misconceived,
And that same hand whose kind caress she sought,
140 With fingers flippant flings the careless corn....
I do remember how, one summer's eve,
He, seated in an arbour's leafy shade,
Had bade me bring fresh wine-skins....
                                   As I stood
Ling'ring upon the threshold, half concealed
145 By tender foliage, and my spirit light
With draughts of sunny weather, did I mark
An instant the gay group before mine eyes.
Deepest in shade, and facing where I stood,
Sat Plato, with his calm face and low brows
150 Which met above the narrow Grecian eyes,
The pale, thin lips just parted to the smile,
Which dimpled that smooth olive of his cheek.
His head a little bent, sat Sokrates,
With one swart finger raised admonishing,
155 And on the air were borne his changing tones.
Low lounging at his feet, one fair arm thrown
Around his knee (the other, high in air

Brandish'd a brazen amphor,[1] which yet rained
Bright drops of ruby on the golden locks
160 And temples with their fillets of the vine),
Lay Alkibiades[2] the beautiful.
And thus, with solemn tone, spake Sokrates:
"This fair Aspasia,[3] which our Perikles[4]
Hath brought from realms afar, and set on high
165 In our Athenian city, hath a mind,
I doubt not, of a strength beyond her race;
And makes employ of it, beyond the way
Of women nobly gifted: woman's frail—
Her body rarely stands the test of soul;
170 She grows intoxicate with knowledge; throws
The laws of custom, order, 'neath her feet,
Feasting at life's great banquet with wide throat."
Then sudden, stepping from my leafy screen,
Holding the swelling wine-skin o'er my head,
175 With breast that heaved, and eyes and cheeks
        aflame,
Lit by a fury and a thought, I spake:
"By all great powers around us! can it be
That we poor women are empirical?[5]
That gods who fashioned us did strive to make
180 Beings too fine, too subtly delicate,
With sense that thrilled response to ev'ry touch
Of nature's, and their task is not complete?
That they have sent their half-completed work
To bleed and quiver here upon the earth?
185 To bleed and quiver, and to weep and weep,
To beat its soul against the marble walls
Of men's cold hearts, and then at last to sin!"
I ceased, the first hot passion stayed and stemmed
And frighted by the silence: I could see,

---

[1] a tall jar with a narrow neck.

[2] Alcibiades (c. 450–404 BC), an Athenian politician and general in the Peloponnesian war; he plays a role in Plato's *Symposium*.

[3] the clever and influential Greek woman who was the mistress of Pericles; (470?–410 BC).

[4] an Athenian statesman and general of great renown (?–429 BC).

[5] that is, guided by experience rather than principles.

190 Framed by the arbour foliage, which the sun
In setting softly gilded with rich gold,
Those upturned faces, and those placid limbs;
Saw Plato's narrow eyes and niggard mouth,
Which half did smile and half did criticise,
195 One hand held up, the shapely fingers framed
To gesture of entreaty—"Hush, I pray,
Do not disturb her; let us hear the rest;
Follow her mood, for here's another phase
Of your black-browed Xantippe...."
                                        Then I saw
200 Young Alkibiades, with laughing lips
And half-shut eyes, contemptuous shrugging up
Soft, snowy shoulders, till he brought the gold
Of flowing ringlets round about his breasts.
But Sokrates, all slow and solemnly,
205 Raised, calm, his face to mine, and sudden spake:
"I thank thee for the wisdom which thy lips
Have thus let fall among us: prythee tell
From what high source, from what philosophies
Didst cull the sapient notion of thy words?"
210 Then stood I straight and silent for a breath,
Dumb, crushed with all the weight of cold
    contempt;
But swiftly in my bosom there uprose
A sudden flame, a merciful fury sent
To save me; with both angry hands I flung
215 The skin upon the marble, where it lay
Spouting red rills and fountains on the white;
Then, all unheeding faces, voices, eyes,
I fled across the threshold, hair unbound—
White garment stained to redness—beating heart
220 Flooded with all the flowing tide of hopes
Which once had gushed out golden, now sent back
Swift to their sources, never more to rise....
I think I could have borne the weary life,
The narrow life within the narrow walls,
225 If he had loved me; but he kept his love
For this Athenian city and her sons;
And, haply, for some stranger-woman, bold
With freedom, thought, and glib philosophy....

Ah me! the long, long weeping through the nights,
230 The weary watching for the pale-eyed dawn
Which only brought fresh grieving: then I grew
Fiercer, and cursed from out my inmost heart
The Fates which marked me an Athenian maid.
Then faded that vain fury; hope died out;
235 A huge despair was stealing on my soul,
A sort of fierce acceptance of my fate,—
He wished a household vessel—well 'twas good,
For he should have it! He should have no more
The yearning treasure of a woman's love,
240 But just the baser treasure which he sought.
I called my maidens, ordered out the loom,
And spun unceasing from the morn till eve;
Watching all keenly over warp[1] and woof,[2]
Weighing the white wool with a jealous hand.
245 I spun until, methinks, I spun away
The soul from out my body, the high thoughts
From out my spirit; till at last I grew
As ye have known me,—eye exact to mark
The texture of the spinning; ear all keen
250 For aimless talking when the moon is up,
And ye should be a-sleeping; tongue to cut
With quick incision, 'thwart the merry words
Of idle maidens....
                        Only yesterday
My hands did cease from spinning; I have wrought
255 My dreary duties, patient till the last.
The gods reward me! Nay, I will not tell
The after years of sorrow; wretched strife
With grimmest foes—sad Want and Poverty;—
Nor yet the time of horror, when they bore
260 My husband from the threshold; nay, nor when
The subtle weed had wrought its deadly work.
Alas! alas! I was not there to soothe
The last great moment; never any thought
Of her that loved him—save at least the charge,

---

[1] in weaving, the threads running lengthwise in the loom.

[2] the threads that are woven back and forth across the fixed threads in a loom.

265 All earthly, that her body should not starve....
You weep, you weep; I would not that ye wept;
Such tears are idle; with the young, such grief
Soon grows to gratulation, as, "her love
Was withered by misfortune; mine shall grow
270 All nurtured by the loving," or, "her life
Was wrecked and shattered—mine shall smoothly
    sail."
Enough, enough. In vain, in vain, in vain!
The gods forgive me! Sorely have I sinned
In all my life. A fairer fate befall
275 You all that stand there....
                        Ha! the dawn has come;
I see a rosy glimmer—nay! it grows dark;
Why stand ye so in silence? throw it wide,
The casement, quick; why tarry?—give me air—
O fling it wide, I say, and give me light!
—1881

Felo De Se [1]

With Apologies to Mr. Swinburne [2]

For repose I have sighed and have struggled; have
    sigh'd and have struggled in vain;
I am held in the Circle of Being and caught in the
    Circle of Pain.
I was wan and weary with life; my sick soul yearned
    for death;
I was weary of women and war and the sea and the
    wind's wild breath;
5 I cull'd sweet poppies and crush'd them, the blood
    ran rich and red:—
And I cast it in crystal chalice and drank of it till I
    was dead.
And the mould of the man was mute, pulseless in
    ev'ry part,
The long limbs lay on the sand with an eagle eating
    the heart.

Repose for the rotting head and peace for the
    putrid breast,
10 But for that which is "I" indeed the gods have
    decreed no rest;
No rest but an endless aching, a sorrow which
    grows amain:—
I am caught in the Circle of Being and held in the
    Circle of Pain.
Bitter indeed is Life, and bitter of Life the breath,
But give me life and its ways and its men, if this be
    Death.
15 Wearied I once of the Sun and the voices which
    clamour'd around:
Give them me back—in the sightless depths there
    is neither light nor sound.
Sick is my soul, and sad and feeble and faint as it
    felt
When (far, dim day) in the fair flesh-fane of the
    body it dwelt.
But then I could run to the shore, weeping and
    weary and weak;
20 See the waves' blue sheen and feel the breath of the
    breeze on my cheek:
Could wail with the wailing wind; strike sharply
    the hands in despair;
Could shriek with the shrieking blast, grow
    frenzied and tear the hair;
Could fight fierce fights with the foe or clutch at a
    human hand;
And weary could lie at length on the soft, sweet,
    saffron sand....
25 I have neither a voice nor hands, nor any friend nor
    a foe;
I am I—just a Pulse of Pain—I am I, that is all I
    know.
For Life, and the sickness of Life, and Death and
    desire to die;—
They have passed away like the smoke, here is
    nothing but Pain and I.
—1881

---

1 "a crime against oneself," i.e. suicide.

2 Algernon Charles Swinburne (1837–1909), Victorian poet.

To a Dead Poet[1]

I knew not if to laugh or weep;
  They sat and talked of you—
"'Twas here he sat; 'twas this he said!
  'Twas that he used to do."

5 "Here is the book wherein he read,
  The room wherein he dwelt;
And he" (they said) "was such a man
  Such things he thought and felt."

I sat and sat, I did not stir;
10 They talked and talked away.
I was as mute as any stone,
  I had no word to say.

They talked and talked; like to a stone
  My heart grew in my breast—
15 I, who had never seen your face,
  Perhaps I knew you best.
  —1884

A Minor Poet

What should such fellows as I do,
Crawling between earth and heaven?[2]

Here is the phial; here I turn the key
  Sharp in the lock. Click!—there's no doubt it
    turned.
This is the third time; there is luck in threes—
Queen Luck, that rules the world, befriend me now
5 And freely I'll forgive you many wrongs!
Just as the draught began to work, first time,
Tom Leigh, my friend (as friends go in the world),
Burst in, and drew the phial from my hand,
(Ah, Tom! ah, Tom! that was a sorry turn!)
10 And lectured me a lecture, all compact

Of neatest, newest phrases, freshly culled
From works of newest culture: "common good";
"The world's great harmonies"; "must be content
With knowing God works all things for the best,
15 And Nature never stumbles." Then again,
"The common good," and still, "the common,
    good";
And what a small thing was our joy or grief
When weigh'd with that of thousands. Gentle Tom,
But you might wag your philosophic tongue
20 From morn till eve, and still the thing's the same:
I am myself, as each man is himself—
Feels his own pain, joys his own joy, and loves
With his own love, no other's. Friend, the world
Is but one man; one man is but the world.
25 And I am I, and you are Tom, that bleeds
When needles prick your flesh (mark, yours, not
    mine).
I must confess it; I can feel the pulse
A-beating at my heart, yet never knew
The throb of cosmic pulses. I lament
30 The death of youth's ideal in my heart;
And, to be honest, never yet rejoiced
In the world's progress—scarce, indeed, discerned;
(For still it seems that God's a Sisyphus[3]
With the world for stone).
                          You shake your head.
                          I'm base,
35 Ignoble? Who is noble—you or I?
I was not once thus! Ah, my friend, we are
As the Fates make us.
                  This time is the third;
The second time the flask fell from my hand,
Its drowsy juices spilt upon the board;
40 And there my face fell flat, and all the life
Crept from my limbs, and hand and foot were
    bound
With mighty chains, subtle, intangible;

----

1 Levy's "dead poet" is believed to be James Thomson (1843–82).

2 Shakespeare, *Hamlet* 3.1.127.

3 the king of Corinth who, in Greek myth, was doomed in Hades to push uphill a heavy stone that would always roll back down.

While still the mind held to its wonted use,
Or rather grew intense and keen with dread,
45 An awful dread—I thought I was in Hell.
In Hell, in Hell! Was ever Hell conceived
By mortal brain, by brain Divine devised,
Darker, more fraught with torment, than the world
For such as I? A creature maimed and marr'd
50 From very birth. A blot, a blur, a note
All out of tune in this world's instrument.
A base thing, yet not knowing to fulfil
Base functions. A high thing, yet all unmeet
For work that's high. A dweller on the earth,
55 Yet not content to dig with other men
Because of certain sudden sights and sounds
(Bars of broken music; furtive, fleeting glimpse
Of angel faces 'thwart the grating seen)
Perceived in Heaven. Yet when I approach
60 To catch the sound's completeness, to absorb
The faces' full perfection, Heaven's gate,
Which then had stood ajar, sudden falls to,
And I, a-shiver in the dark and cold,
Scarce hear afar the mocking tones of men:
65 "He would not dig, forsooth; but he must strive
For higher fruits than what our tillage yields;
Behold what comes, my brothers, of vain pride!"
Why play with figures? trifle prettily
With this my grief which very simply 's said,
70 "There is no place for me in all the world"?
The world's a rock, and I will beat no more
A breast of flesh and blood against a rock....
A stride across the planks for old time's sake.
Ah, bare, small room that I have sorrowed in;
75 Ay, and on sunny days, haply, rejoiced;
We know some things together, you and I!
Hold there, you rangéd row of books! In vain
You beckon from your shelf. You've stood my
    friends
Where all things else were foes; yet now I'll turn
80 My back upon you, even as the world
Turns it on me. And yet—farewell, farewell!
You, lofty Shakespeare, with the tattered leaves

And fathomless great heart, your binding's bruised
Yet did I love you less? Goethe,[1] farewell;
85 Farewell, triumphant smile and tragic eyes,
And pitiless world-wisdom!
                                  For all men
These two. And 'tis farewell with you, my friends,
More dear because more near: Theokritus;[2]
Heine[3] that stings and smiles; Prometheus'[4] bard;
90 (I've grown too coarse for Shelley latterly:)
And one wild singer of to-day, whose song
Is all aflame with passionate bard's blood
Lash'd into foam by pain and the world's wrong.
At least, he has a voice to cry his pain;
95 For him, no silent writhing in the dark,
No muttering of mute lips, no straining out
Of a weak throat a-choke with pent-up sound,
A-throb with pent-up passion....
                                  Ah, my sun!
That's you, then, at the window, looking in
100 To beam farewell on one who's loved you long
And very truly. Up, you creaking thing,
You squinting, cobwebbed casement!
                                  So, at last,
I can drink in the sunlight. How it falls
Across that endless sea of London roofs,
105 Weaving such golden wonders on the grey,
That almost for the moment we forget—
The world of woe beneath them.
                                  Underneath,
For all the sunset glory, Pain is king.
Yet, the sun's there, and very sweet withal;
110 And I'll not grumble that it's only sun,
But open wide my lips—thus—drink it in;

---

[1] Johann Wolfgang von Goethe (1749–1832), the German poet and
dramatist.

[2] Theocritus, the Greek pastoral poet who lived during the third century
BC.

[3] Heinrich Heine, the German poet and prose writer (1797–1856).

[4] the Greek god who stole fire from heaven and gave it to humankind.
As punishment, Prometheus was chained to a rock where a vulture, each
day, ate his liver which was restored during the night.

Turn up my face to the sweet evening sky
(What royal wealth of scarlet on the blue
So tender-toned, you'd almost think it green)
115 And stretch my hands out—so—to grasp it tight.
Ha, ha! 'tis sweet awhile to cheat the Fates,
And be as happy as another man.
The sun works in my veins like wine, like wine!
'Tis a fair world: if dark, indeed, with woe,
120 Yet having hope and hint of such a joy,
That a man, winning, well might turn aside,
Careless of Heaven…

         O enough; I turn
From the sun's light, or haply I shall hope.
I have hoped enough; I would not hope again;
125 'Tis hope that is most cruel.

         Tom, my friend,
You very sorry philosophic fool;
'Tis you, I think, that bid me be resign'd,
Trust, and be thankful.

         Out on you! Resign'd?
I'm not resign'd, not patient, not school'd in
130 To take my starveling's portion and pretend
I'm grateful for it. I want all, all, all;
I've appetite for all. I want the best:
Love, beauty, sunlight, nameless joy of life.
There's too much patience in the world, I think.
135 We have grown base with crooking of the knee.
Mankind—say—God has bidden to a feast;
The board is spread, and groans with cates[1] and
    drinks;
In troop the guests; each man with appetite
Keen-whetted with expectance.

         In they troop,
140 Struggle for seats, jostle and push and seize.
What's this? what's this? There are not seats for all!
Some men must stand without the gates; and some
Must linger by the table, ill-supplied
With broken meats. One man gets meat for two,
145 The while another hungers. If I stand

---

[1] delicacies.

Without the portals, seeing others eat
Where I had thought to satiate the pangs
Of mine own hunger; shall I then come forth
When all is done, and drink my Lord's good health
150 In my Lord's water? Shall I not rather turn
And curse him, curse him for a niggard host?
O, I have hungered, hungered, through the years,
Till appetite grows craving, then disease;
I am starved, wither'd shrivelled.

         Peace, O peace!
155 This rage is idle; what avails to curse
The nameless forces, the vast silences
That work in all things

         This time is the third,
I wrought before in heat, stung mad with pain,
Blind, scarcely understanding; now I know
160 What thing I do.

         There was a woman once;
Deep eyes she had, white hands, a subtle smile,
Soft speaking tones: she did not break my heart,
Yet haply had her heart been otherwise
Mine had not now been broken. Yet, who knows?
165 My life was jarring discord from the first:
Tho' here and there brief hints of melody,
Of melody unutterable, clove the air.
From this bleak world, into the heart of night,
The dim, deep bosom of the universe,
170 I cast myself. I only crave for rest;
Too heavy is the load. I fling it down.

EPILOGUE

We knocked and knocked; at last, burst in the
    door,
And found him as you know—the outstretched
    arms
Propping the hidden face. The sun had set,
175 And all the place was dim with lurking shade.
There was no written word to say farewell,
Or make more clear the deed.

         I search'd and search'd;
The room held little: just a row of books

Much scrawl'd and noted; sketches on the wall,
180 Done rough in charcoal; the old instrument
(A violin, no Stradivarius)
He played so ill on; in the table drawer
Large schemes of undone work. Poems half-writ;
Wild drafts of symphonies; big plans of fugues;[1]
185 Some scraps of writing in a woman's hand:
No more—the scattered pages of a tale,
A sorry tale that no man cared to read.
Alas, my friend, I lov'd him well, tho' he
Held me a cold and stagnant-blooded fool,
190 Because I am content to watch, and wait
With a calm mind the issue of all things.
Certain it is my blood's no turbid stream;
Yet, for all that, haply I understood
More than he ever deem'd; nor held so light
195 The poet in him. Nay, I sometimes doubt
If they have not, indeed, the better part—
These poets, who get drunk with sun, and weep
Because the night or a woman's face is fair.
Meantime there is much talk about my friend.
200 The women say, of course, he died for love;
The men, for lack of gold, or cavilling
Of carping critics. I, Tom Leigh, his friend,
I have no word at all to say of this.
Nay, I had deem'd him more philosopher;
205 For did he think by this one paltry deed
To cut the knot of circumstance, and snap
The chain which binds all being?
—1884

Magdalen

All things I can endure, save one.
The bare, blank room where is no sun;
The parcelled hours; the pallet hard;
The dreary faces here within;

5 The outer women's cold regard;
The Pastor's iterated "sin";—
These things could I endure, and count
No overstrain'd, unjust amount;
No undue payment for such bliss—
10 Yea, all things bear, save only this:
That you, who knew what thing would be,
Have wrought this evil unto me.
It is so strange to think on still—
That you, that *you* should do me ill!
15 Not as one ignorant or blind,
But seeing clearly in your mind
How this must be which now has been,
Nothing aghast at what was seen.
Now that the tale is told and done,
20 It is so strange to think upon.

You were so tender with me, too!
One summer's night a cold blast blew,
Closer about my throat you drew
The half-slipt shawl of dusky blue.
25 And once my hand, on a summer's morn,
I stretched to pluck a rose; a thorn
Struck through the flesh and made it bleed
(A little drop of blood indeed!)
Pale grew your cheek; you stoopt and bound
30 Your handkerchief about the wound;
Your voice came with a broken sound;
With the deep breath your breast was riven;
I wonder, did God laugh in Heaven?

How strange, that *you* should work my woe!
35 How strange! I wonder, do you know
How gladly, gladly I had died
(And life was very sweet that tide)
To save you from the least, light ill?
How gladly I had borne your pain.
40 With one great pulse we seem'd to thrill,—
Nay, but we thrill'd with pulses twain.

---

[1] musical compositions that focus on and develop a theme through various instruments/voices placed in succession in accordance with the laws of counterpoint.

Even if one had told me this,
"A poison lurks within your kiss,
Gall that shall turn to night his day":
45   Thereon I straight had turned away—
Ay, tho' my heart had crack'd with pain—
And never kiss'd your lips again.

At night, or when the daylight nears,
I hear the other women weep;
50   My own heart's anguish lies too deep
For the soft rain and pain of tears.
I think my heart has turn'd to stone.
A dull, dead weight that hurts my breast;
Here, on my pallet-bed alone,
55   I keep apart from all the rest.
Wide-eyed I lie upon my bed,
I often cannot sleep all night;
The future and the past are dead,
There is no thought can bring delight.
60   All night I lie and think and think;
If my heart were not made of stone,
But flesh and blood, it needs must shrink
Before such thoughts. Was ever known
A woman with a heart of stone?

65   The doctor says that I shall die.
It may be so, yet what care I?
Endless reposing from the strife,
Death do I trust no more than life.
For one thing is like one arrayed,
70   And there is neither false nor true;
But in a hideous masquerade
All things dance on, the ages through.
And good is evil, evil good;
Nothing is known or understood
75   Save only Pain. I have no faith
In God or Devil, Life or Death.

The doctor says that I shall die.
You, that I knew in days gone by,
I fain would see your face once more,

80   Con well its features o'er and o'er;
And touch your hand and feel your kiss,
Look in your eyes and tell you this:
That all is done, that I am free;
That you, through all eternity,
85   Have neither part nor lot in me.
—1884

A London Plane-Tree

Green is the plane-tree in the square,
The other trees are brown;
They droop and pine for country air;
The plane-tree loves the town.

5   Here from my garret-pane, I mark
The plane-tree bud and blow,
Shed her recuperative bark,
And spread her shade below.

Among her branches, in and out,
10   The city breezes play;
The dun fog wraps her round about;
Above, the smoke curls grey.

Others the country take for choice,
And hold the town in scorn;
15   But she has listened to the voice
On city breezes borne.
—1889

London Poets

(In Memoriam)

They trod the streets and squares where now I
tread,
With weary hearts, a little while ago;
When, thin and grey, the melancholy snow
Clung to the leafless branches overhead;
5   Or when the smoke-veiled sky grew stormy-red

In autumn; with a re-arisen woe
Wrestled, what time the passionate spring winds
    blow;
And paced scorched stones in summer:—they are
    dead.

The sorrow of their souls to them did seem
10 As real as mine to me, as permanent.
To-day, it is the shadow of a dream,
The half-forgotten breath of breezes spent.
So shall another soothe his woe supreme—
"No more he comes, who this way came and
    went."
—1889

On The Threshold

O God, my dream! I dreamed that you were dead;
  Your mother hung above the couch and wept
Whereon you lay all white, and garlanded
With blooms of waxen whiteness. I had crept
5 Up to your chamber-door, which stood ajar,
And in the doorway watched you from afar,
Nor dared advance to kiss your lips and brow.
I had no part nor lot in you, as now;
Death had not broken between us the old bar;
10 Nor torn from out my heart the old, cold sense
Of your misprision and my impotence.
—1889

In The Black Forest

I lay beneath the pine trees,
  And looked aloft, where, through
The dusky, clustered tree-tops,
  Gleamed rent, gay rifts of blue.

5 I shut my eyes, and a fancy
  Fluttered my sense around:

"I lie here dead and buried,
  And this is churchyard ground.

I am at rest for ever;
10 Ended the stress and strife."
Straight I fell to and sorrowed
  For the pitiful past life.

Right wronged, and knowledge wasted;
  Wise labour spurned for ease;
15 The sloth and the sin and the failure;
  Did I grow sad for these?

They had made me sad so often;
  Not now they made me sad;
My heart was full of sorrow
20 For joy it never had.
—1889

To Vernon Lee [1]

On Bellosguardo,[2] when the year was young,
  We wandered, seeking for the daffodil
And dark anemone, whose purples fill
The peasant's plot, between the corn-shoots
    sprung.

5 Over the grey, low wall the olive flung
Her deeper greyness; far off, hill on hill
Sloped to the sky, which, pearly-pale and still,
Above the large and luminous landscape hung.

A snowy blackthorn flowered beyond my reach;
10 You broke a branch and gave it to me there;
I found for you a scarlet blossom rare.

---

[1] "Vernon Lee" is the pen name for author and scholar, Violet Page (1856–1935).

[2] a hill in Florence.

Thereby ran on of Art and Life our speech;
And of the gifts the gods had given to each—
Hope unto you, and unto me Despair.
—1889

To E. [1]

The mountains in fantastic lines
    Sweep, blue-white, to the sky, which shines
Blue as blue gems; athwart the pines
        The lake gleams blue.

5   We three were here, three years gone by;
Our Poet, with fine-frenzied eye,
You, steeped in learned lore, and I,
        A poet too.

Our Poet brought us books and flowers,
10 He read us *Faust*;[2] he talked for hours
Philosophy (sad Schopenhauer's)[3]
        Beneath the trees:

And do you mind that sunny day,
When he, as on the sward he lay,
15 Told of Lassalle[4] who bore away
        The false Louise?

Thrice-favoured bard! to him alone
That green and snug retreat was shown,

Where to the vulgar herd unknown,
20   Our pens we plied.

(For, in those distant days, it seems,
We cherished sundry idle dreams,
And with our flowing foolscap reams
        The Fates defied.)

25 And after, when the day was gone,
And the hushed, silver night came on,
He showed us where the glow-worm shone;—
        We stooped to see.

There, too, by yonder moon we swore
30 Platonic friendship o'er and o'er;
No folk, we deemed, had been before
        So wise and free.

            *   *   *

And do I sigh or smile to-day?
Dead love or dead ambition, say,
35 Which mourn we most? Not much we weigh
        Platonic friends.

On you the sun is shining free;
Our Poet sleeps in Italy,
Beneath an alien sod; on me
40   The cloud descends.
    —1889

---

[1] The identity of E. is unknown.

[2] The subject of many literary and operatic works, Faust sells his soul to
the devil in return for knowledge and power.

[3] Arthur Schopenhauer, German philosopher (1788–1860).

[4] Ferdinand Lassalle, German socialist (1825–64).

Rudyard Kipling
1865 – 1936

Rudyard Kipling was a poet, novelist, and short story writer. He was born in Bombay, but was placed in a foster home in England in 1871. He returned to live in India in 1882, then settled in England in 1889. Kipling's work includes a volume of poetry, *Departmental Ditties* (1886), short stories, *Plain Tales From The Hills* (1888), and his masterpiece based on his Indian experience, the novel *Kim* (1901).

☙☙☙

Gentlemen-Rankers

To the legion of the lost ones, to the cohort of
    the damned,
  To my brethren in their sorrow overseas,
Sings a gentleman of England cleanly bred,
    machinely crammed,
  And a trooper of the Empress, if you please.
5 Yes, a trooper of the forces who has run his own six
    horses,
  And faith he went the pace and went it blind,
And the world was more than kin while he held the
    ready tin,
  But to-day the Sergeant's something less than
    kind.
    We're poor little lambs who've lost our way,
      Baa! Baa! Baa!
10   We're little black sheep who've gone astray,
      Baa—aa—aa!
    Gentlemen-rankers out on the spree,
    Damned from here to Eternity,
15   God ha' mercy on such as we,
      Baa! Yah! Bah!

Oh, it's sweet to sweat through stables, sweet to
    empty kitchen slops,
  And it's sweet to hear the tales the troopers tell,
To dance with blowzy housemaids at the
    regimental hops
20   And thrash the cad who says you waltz too well.

Yes, it makes you cock-a-hoop to be "Rider" to
    your troop,
  And branded with a blasted worsted spur,
When you envy, O how keenly, one poor Tommy[1]
    living cleanly
  Who blacks your boots and sometimes calls you
    "Sir."

25 If the home we never write to, and the oaths we
    never keep,
  And all we know most distant and most dear,
Across the snoring barrack-room return to break
    our sleep,
  Can you blame us if we soak ourselves in beer?
When the drunken comrade mutters and the great
    guard-lantern gutters
30   And the horror of our fall is written plain,
Every secret, self-revealing on the aching
    whitewashed ceiling,
  Do you wonder that we drug ourselves from
    pain?

We have done with Hope and Honour, we are lost
    to Love and Truth,
  We are dropping down the ladder rung by
    rung,
35 And the measure of our torment is the measure of
    our youth.
    God help us, for we knew the worst too young!

---
[1] a British soldier.

Our shame is clean repentance for the crime that
    brought the sentence,
    Our pride it is to know no spur of pride,
And the Curse of Reuben holds us till an alien turf
    enfolds us
40   And we die, and none can tell Them where we
        died.
    We're poor little lambs who've lost our way,
        Baa! Baa! Baa!
    We're little black sheep who've gone astray,
        Baa—aa—aa!
45   Gentlemen-rankers out on the spree,
    Damned from here to Eternity,
    God ha' mercy on such as we,
        Baa! Yah! Bah!

—1892

In the Neolithic Age [1]

In the Neolithic Age savage warfare did I wage
   For food and fame and woolly horses' pelt.
I was singer to my clan in that dim, red Dawn of
    Man,
    And I sang of all we fought and feared and felt.

5   Yea, I sang as now I sing, when the Prehistoric
     spring
    Made the piled Biscayan ice-pack split and shove;
And the troll and gnome and dwerg, and the Gods
    of Cliff and Berg
    Were about me and beneath me and above.

But a rival of Solutré, told the tribe my style was
    outré [2]—
10   'Neath a tomahawk, of diorite, he fell.

And I left my views on Art, barbed and tanged,
    below the heart
    Of a mammothistic etcher at Grenelle. [3]

Then I stripped them, scalp from skull, and my
    hunting-dogs fed full,
    And their teeth I threaded neatly on a thong;
15 And I wiped my mouth and said, "It is well that
    they are dead,
    "For I know my work is right and theirs was
    wrong."

But my Totem [4] saw the shame; from his ridgepole-
    shrine he came,
    And he told me in a vision of the night:—
"There are nine and sixty ways of constructing
    tribal lays,
20   "And every single one of them is right!"

    . . . .

Then the silence closed upon me till They put new
    clothing on me
    Of whiter, weaker flesh and bone more frail;
And I stepped beneath Time's finger, once again a
    tribal singer,
    And a minor poet certified by Traill! [5]

25 Still they skirmish to and fro, men my messmates
    on the snow,
    When we headed off the aurochs [6] turn for turn;
When the rich Allobrogenses never kept
    amanuenses,
    And our only plots were piled in lakes at Berne. [7]

---

[1] the later stone age.

[2] outside the bounds of propriety.

[3] a district of Paris, on the left band of the Seine.

[4] A totem is a natural object, usually an animal, taken as the emblem of
a person or clan.

[5] Henry Duff Traill (1842–1900).

[6] extinct wild ox.

[7] city in Switzerland, founded in the twelfth century.

Still a cultured Christian age sees us scuffle, squeak,
    and rage,
30   Still we pinch and slap and jabber, scratch and
      dirk;
Still we let our business slide—as we dropped the
    half-dressed hide—
    To show a fellow-savage how to work.

Still the world is wondrous large,—seven seas from
    marge to marge—
    And it holds a vast of various kinds of man;
35 And the wildest dreams of Kew[1] are the facts of
      Khatmandhu,[2]
    And the crimes of Clapham[3] chaste in
      Martaban.[4]

Here's my wisdom for your use, as I learned it
    when the moose
    And the reindeer roared where Paris roars
    to-night:—
"*There are nine and sixty ways of constructing tribal*
    lays,
40   "*And—every—single—one—of—them—is—*
      right!"
—1892

Recessional[5]
1897

G od of our fathers, known of old,
  Lord of our far-flung battle-line,

Beneath whose awful Hand we hold
    Dominion over palm and pine—
5 Lord God of Hosts, be with us yet,
Lest we forget—lest we forget![6]

The tumult and the shouting dies;
    The Captains and the Kings depart:
Still stands Thine ancient sacrifice,
10   An humble and a contrite heart.[7]
Lord God of Hosts, be with us yet,
Lest we forget—lest we forget!

Far-called, our navies melt away;
    On dune and headland sinks the fire:
15 Lo, all our pomp of yesterday
    Is one with Nineveh and Tyre![8]
Judge of the Nations, spare us yet,
Lest we forget—lest we forget!

If, drunk with sight of power, we loose
20   Wild tongues that have not Thee in awe,
Such boastings as the Gentiles[9] use,
    Or lesser breeds without the Law—
Lord God of Hosts, be with us yet,
Lest we forget—lest we forget!

25 For heathen heart that puts her trust
    In reeking tube and iron shard,
All valiant dust that builds on dust,
    And guarding, calls not Thee to guard,
For frantic boast and foolish word—
30 Thy mercy on Thy People, Lord!
—1897 (1897)

---

[1] an affluent district of Richmond, west of London.

[2] Katmandu or Kathmandu, the capital city of Nepal.

[3] a residential district of London.

[4] a village in Lower Burma, invaded by British troops during the Anglo-Burmese wars of 1824 and 1852.

[5] A recessional is a hymn sung while the clergy and the choir leave the church in procession at the end of a service. Kipling's poem was written as the year of Queen Victoria's Diamond Jubilee, celebrating her sixtieth year on the throne, was ending.

[6] Deuteronomy 6:12.

[7] Psalms 51:17.

[8] Nineveh was the capital of ancient Assyria, now buried under sand. Tyre, in Phoenicia, was once an important maritime city but has fallen from greatness.

[9] Romans 2:14.

The White Man's Burden [1]

Take up the White Man's burden—
    Send forth the best ye breed—
Go bind your sons to exile
    To serve your captives' need;
5 To wait in heavy harness,
    On fluttered folk and wild—
Your new-caught, sullen peoples,
    Half-devil and half-child.

Take up the White Man's burden—
10   In patience to abide,
To veil the threat of terror
    And check the show of pride;
By open speech and simple,
    An hundred times made plain,
15 To seek another's profit,
    And work another's gain.

Take up the White Man's burden—
    The savage wars of peace—
Fill full the mouth of Famine
20   And bid the sickness cease;
And when your goal is nearest
    The end for others sought,
Watch Sloth and heathen Folly
    Bring all your hope to nought.

25 Take up the White Man's burden—
    No tawdry rule of kings,
But toil of serf and sweeper—
    The tale of common things.
The ports ye shall not enter,
30   The roads ye shall not tread,
Go make them with your living,
    And mark them with your dead!

Take up the White Man's burden—
    And reap his old reward:
35 The blame of those ye better,
    The hate of those ye guard—
The cry of hosts ye humour
    (Ah, slowly!) toward the light:—
"Why brought ye us from bondage,
40   "Our loved Egyptian night?" [2]

Take up the White Man's burden—
    Ye dare not stoop to less—
Nor call too loud on Freedom
    To cloak your weariness;
45 By all ye cry or whisper,
    By all ye leave or do,
The silent, sullen peoples
    Shall weigh your Gods and you.

Take up the White Man's burden—
50   Have done with childish days—
The lightly proffered laurel.
    The easy, ungrudged praise.
Comes now, to search your manhood
    Through all the thankless years,
55 Cold, edged with dear-bought wisdom,
    The judgment of your peers!
        —1899

If

If you can keep your head when all about you
    Are losing theirs and blaming it on you,
If you can trust yourself when all men doubt you,
    But make allowance for their doubting too;
5 If you can wait and not be tired by waiting,
    Or being lied about, don't deal in lies,

---

[1] This phrase, used to describe the United States's responsibility for Cuba and the Philippines, became popular towards the end of the Spanish-American War in 1898.

[2] Exodus 16:2–3: when the Israelites were hungry in the wilderness, journeying from Egypt, they cried against Moses and Aaron: "Would to God we had died by the hand of the Lord in the land of Egypt, where we sat by the flesh pots, and when we did eat bread to the full."

Or being hated, don't give way to hating,
    And yet don't look too good, nor talk too wise:

If you can dream—and not make dreams your
    master;
10   If you can think—and not make thoughts your
      aim;
If you can meet with Triumph and Disaster
    And treat those two impostors just the same;
If you can bear to hear the truth you've spoken
    Twisted by knaves to make a trap for fools,
15 Or watch the things you gave your life to, broken,
    And stoop and build 'em up with worn-out
      tools:

If you can make one heap of all your winnings
    And risk it on one turn of pitch-and-toss,

20 And lose, and start again at your beginnings
    And never breath a word about your loss;
If you can force your heart and nerve and sinew
    To serve your turn long after they are gone,
And so hold on when there is nothing in you
    Except the Will which says to them: "Hold on!"

25 If you can talk with crowds and keep your virtue,
    Or walk with Kings—nor lose the common touch,
If neither foes nor loving friends can hurt you,
    If all men count with you, but none too much;
If you can fill the unforgiving minute
30   With sixty seconds' worth of distance run,
Yours is the Earth and everything that's in it,
    And—which is more—you'll be a Man, my son!
—1910

John Gray
1866 – 1934

The autodidact John Gray was a Symbolist poet and member of the Rhymer's Club with Ernest Dowson, John Davidson, Lionel Johnson, and Arthur Symons. He also knew Oscar Wilde, who agreed to finance Gray's volume *Silverpoints* (1893). Gray converted to Roman Catholicism in 1890 and was ordained in 1901, after which he wrote predominantly religious poetry. He lived in Edinburgh, where he was for many years rector of St. Peter's.

❧❧❧

The Barber

I

I dreamed I was a barber; and there went
Beneath my hand, oh! manes extravagant.
Beneath my trembling fingers, many a mask
Of many a pleasant girl. It was my task
5 To gild their hair, carefully, strand by strand;
To paint their eyebrows with a timid hand;
To draw a bodkin, from a vase of kohl,
Through the closed lashes; pencils from a bowl
Of sepia to paint them underneath;
10 To blow upon their eyes with a soft breath.
They lay them back and watched the leaping
   bands.

II

The dream grew vague. I moulded with my hands
The mobile breasts, the valley; and the waist
I touched; and pigments reverently placed
15 Upon their thighs in sapient spots and stains,
Beryls and crysolites and diaphanes,
And gems whose hot harsh names are never said.
I was a masseur; and my fingers bled
With wonder as I touched their awful limbs.

III

20 Suddenly, in the marble trough, there seems
O, last of my pale mistresses, Sweetness!

A twy-lipped[1] scarlet pansie. My caress
Tinges thy steelgray eyes to violet.
Adown thy body skips the pit-a-pat
25 Of treatment once heard in a hospital
For plagues that fascinate, but half appal.

IV

So, at the sound, the blood of me stood cold.
The chaste hair ripened into sullen gold.
The throat, the shoulders, swelled and were uncouth.
30 The breasts rose up and offered each a mouth.
And on the belly pallid blushes crept,
That maddened me, until I laughed and wept.
—1893

Poem

To Arthur Edmonds

Geranium, houseleek, lain in oblong beds
On the trim grass. The daisies' leprous stain
Is fresh. Each night the daisies burst again,
Though every day the gardener crops their heads.

5 A wistful child, in foul unwholesome shreds,
Recalls some legend of a daisy chain
That makes a pretty necklace. She would fain
Make one, and wear it, if she had some threads.

---

[1] double-lipped.

Sun, leprous flowers, foul child. The asphalt burns,
10 The garrulous sparrows perch on metal Burns.
Sing! Sing! they say, and flutter with their wings.
He does not sing, he only wonders why

He is sitting there. The sparrows sing. And I
Yield to the strait allure of simple things.
—1893

Ernest Dowson
1867 – 1900

Ernest Dowson was a participant in the so-called "Aesthetic" or "Decadent Movement" (or "art for art's sake movement"), with Walter Pater, Oscar Wilde, and Lionel Johnson. He led a lonely, dissipated, and short life, typified by depression and spiritual unrest. He excluded from his poetry all moral and intellectual concerns, offering instead a combination of delicate sounds and carefully realized images. Influences from Swinburne, Verlaine, and Catullus are intertwined in his poetry, with others from the Roman Catholic liturgy and hymnology.

ↄ⊃ↄ

Nuns of the Perpetual Adoration

Calm, sad, secure; behind high convent walls,
    These watch the sacred lamp, these watch and
        pray:
And it is one with them when evening falls,
    And one with them the cold return of day.

5 These heed not time; their nights and days they
        make
    Into a long, returning rosary,
Whereon their lives are threaded for Christ's sake;
    Meekness and vigilance and chastity.

A vowed patrol, in silent companies,
10   Life-long they keep before the living Christ.
In the dim church, their prayers and penances
    Are fragrant incense to the Sacrificed.

Outside, the world is wild and passionate;
    Man's weary laughter and his sick despair
15 Entreat at their impenetrable gate:
    They heed no voices in their dream of prayer.

They saw the glory of the world displayed;
    They saw the bitter of it, and the sweet;
They knew the roses of the world should fade,
20   And be trod under by the hurrying feet.

Therefore they rather put away desire,
    And crossed their hands and came to sanctuary;
And veiled their heads and put on coarse attire:
    Because their comeliness was vanity.

25 And there they rest; they have serene insight
    Of the illuminating dawn to be:
Mary's sweet Star[1] dispels for them the night,
    The proper darkness of humanity.

Calm, sad, secure; with faces worn and mild:
30   Surely their choice of vigil is the best?
Yea! for our roses fade, the world is wild;
    But there, beside the altar, there, is rest.
—1891

Non Sum Qualis Eram Bonae Sub Regno Cynarae [2]

Last night, ah, yesternight, betwixt her lips and
    mine
There fell thy shadow, Cynara! thy breath was shed
Upon my soul between the kisses and the wine;
And I was desolate and sick of an old passion,
5   Yea, I was desolate and bowed my head:
I have been faithful to thee, Cynara! in my fashion.

---

[1] presumably the star announcing the birth of Jesus.

[2] "I am not what I once was under the spell of kind Cynara": Horace, *Odes* 4.1.3.

All night upon mine heart I felt her warm heart beat,
Night-long within mine arms in love and sleep she
    lay;
Surely the kisses of her bought red mouth were
    sweet;
10 But I was desolate and sick of an old passion,
    When I awoke and found the dawn was gray:
I have been faithful to thee, Cynara! in my fashion.

I have forgot much, Cynara! gone with the wind,
Flung roses, roses riotously with the throng,
15 Dancing, to put thy pale, lost lilies out of mind;
But I was desolate and sick of an old passion,
    Yea, all the time, because the dance was long:
I have been faithful to thee, Cynara! in my fashion.

I cried for madder music and for stronger wine,
20 But when the feast is finished and the lamps expire,
Then falls thy shadow, Cynara! the night is thine;
And I am desolate and sick of an old passion,
    Yea, hungry for the lips of my desire:
I have been faithful to thee, Cynara! in my fashion.
—1891

Villanelle of Sunset [1]

Come hither, Child! and rest:
    This is the end of day,
Behold the weary West!

    Sleep rounds with equal zest
5   Man's toil and children's play:
Come hither, Child! and rest.

    My white bird, seek thy nest,
    Thy drooping head down lay:
Behold the weary West!

---

10   Now are the flowers confest
    Of slumber: sleep, as they!
Come hither, Child! and rest.

    Now eve is manifest,
    And homeward lies our way:
15 Behold the weary West!

    Tired flower! upon my breast,
    I would wear thee alway:
Come hither, Child! and rest;
Behold, the weary West!
—1892

To One in Bedlam [2]

With delicate, mad hands, behind his sordid bars,
    Surely he hath his posies, which they tear and
twine;
Those scentless wisps of straw, that miserably line
His strait, caged universe, whereat the dull world
    stares,

5 Pedant and pitiful. O, how his rapt gaze wars
With their stupidity! Know they what dreams
    divine
Lift his long, laughing reveries like enchaunted wine,
And make his melancholy germane to the stars?

O lamentable brother! if those pity thee,
10 Am I not fain of all thy lone eyes promise me;
Half a fool's kingdom, far from men who sow and
    reap,
All their days, vanity? Better than mortal flowers,

---

[1] a pastoral or lyric poem consisting of five three-line stanzas and a final quatrain, with only two rhymes throughout.

[2] from "bethlem," a contraction of Bethlehem. It means a lunatic asylum or madhouse, hence a place of hubbub and confusion. The original "Bedlam" was the priory of St. Mary of Bethlehem outside Bishopsgate, London; it was founded in 1247 and began to take in "lunatics" in 1377.

Thy moon-kissed roses seem: better than love or
    sleep,
The star-crowned solitude of thine oblivious hours!
—1892

Benedictio Domini

Without, the sullen noises of the street!
    The voice of London, inarticulate,
Hoarse and blaspheming, surges in to meet
    The silent blessing of the Immaculate.[1]

5 Dark is the church, and dim the worshippers,
    Hushed with bowed heads as though by some
        old spell,
While through the incense-laden air there stirs
    The admonition of a silver bell.

Dark is the church, save where the altar stands,
10   Dressed like a bride, illustrious with light,
Where one old priest exalts with tremulous hands
    The one true solace of man's fallen plight.

Strange silence here: without, the sounding street
    Heralds the world's swift passage to the fire:
15 O Benediction,[2] perfect and complete!
    When shall men cease to suffer and desire?
—1896

Ad Manus Puellae [3]

I was always a lover of ladies' hands!
    Or ever mine heart came here to tryst,
For the sake of your carved white hands' commands;

    The tapering fingers, the dainty wrist;
5   The hands of a girl were what I kissed.

I remember an hand like a *fleur-de-lys*
    When it slid from its silken sheath, her glove;
With its odours passing ambergris:[4]
    And that was the empty husk of a love.
10   Oh, how shall I kiss your hands enough?

They are pale with the pallor of ivories;
    But they blush to the tips like a curled sea-shell:
What treasure, in kingly treasuries,
    Of gold, and spice for the thurible,[5]
15   Is sweet as her hands to hoard and tell?

I know not the way from your finger-tips,
    Nor how I shall gain the higher lands,
The citadel of your sacred lips:
    I am captive still of my pleasant bands,
20   The hands of a girl, and most your hands.
—1896

Terre Promise

Even now the fragrant darkness of her hair
  Had brushed my cheek; and once, in passing by,
Her hand upon my hand lay tranquilly:
What things unspoken trembled in the air!

5 Always I know, how little severs me
From mine heart's country, that is yet so far;
And must I lean and long across a bar,
That half a word would shatter utterly?

Ah might it be, that just by touch of hand,
10 Or speaking silence, shall the barrier fall;

---

[1] Mary, Mother of Christ. This appellation refers to the Immaculate Conception—the dogma that the Virgin Mary was free of original sin from the moment of her conception.

[2] the uttering of a blessing; the name for a Roman Catholic service in which the congregation receives the Blessed Sacrament.

[3] "To (In Praise of) the Hands of a Girl."

[4] a strong-smelling waxlike secretion of the intestine of the sperm whale, used in perfume manufacture.

[5] a censer, a sometimes ornate metal container in which incense is burnt on glowing charcoal at religious ceremonies.

And she shall pass, with no vain words at all,
But droop into mine arms, and understand!
—1896 (1893)

Spleen [1]

For Arthur Symons

I was not sorrowful, I could not weep,
And all my memories were put to sleep.

I watched the river grow more white and strange,
All day till evening I watched it change.

5   All day till evening I watched the rain
Beat wearily upon the window pane.

I was not sorrowful, but only tired
Of everything that ever I desired.

Her lips, her eyes, all day became to me
10 The shadow of a shadow utterly.

All day mine hunger for her heart became
Oblivion, until the evening came,

And left me sorrowful, inclined to weep,
With all my memories that could not sleep.
—1896

Vitae summa brevis spem nos vetat incohare longam [2]

(They are not long, the weeping and the laughter)

They are not long, the weeping and the laughter,
Love and desire and hate:
I think they have no portion in us after
We pass the gate.

5   They are not long, the days of wine and roses:
Out of a misty dream
Our path emerges for a while, then closes
Within a dream.
—1896

---

[1] the organ once believed to be the source of melancholy and ill humour; also part of the title of a volume of prose poems by Charles Baudelaire, *Paris Spleen* (1869).

[2] "How should a mortal's hopes be long, when the span of life is so short?": Horace, *Odes* 1.4.15.

Lionel Johnson
1867 – 1902

Lionel Johnson was another member of the "Aesthetic Movement" (see Ernest Dowson). His poetry reflects his sensitivity to beauty (he was tutored by Walter Pater at Oxford), and a desire for intense experience.

୧୨୧

The Dark Angel

Dark Angel, with thine aching lust
To rid the world of penitence:
Malicious Angel, who still dost
My soul such subtile violence!

5 Because of thee, no thought, no thing,
Abides for me undesecrate:
Dark Angel, ever on the wing,
Who never reachest me too late!

When music sounds, then changest thou
10 Its silvery to a sultry fire:
Nor will thine envious heart allow
Delight untortured by desire.

Through thee, the gracious Muses[1] turn
To Furies,[2] O mine Enemy!
15 And all the things of beauty burn
With flames of evil ecstasy.

Because of thee, the land of dreams
Becomes a gathering place of fears:
Until tormented slumber seems
20 One vehemence of useless tears.

When sunlight glows upon the flowers,
Or ripples down the dancing sea:
Thou, with thy troop of passionate powers,
Beleaguerest, bewilderest, me.

25 Within the breath of autumn woods,
Within the winter silences:
Thy venomous spirit stirs and broods,
O Master of impieties!

The ardour of red flame is thine,
30 And thine the steely soul of ice:
Thou poisonest the fair design
Of nature, with unfair device.

Apples of ashes, golden bright;
Waters of bitterness, how sweet!
35 O banquet of a foul delight,
Prepared by thee, dark Paraclete![3]

Thou art the whisper in the gloom,
The hinting tone, the haunting laugh:
Thou art the adorner of my tomb,
40 The minstrel of mine epitaph.

I fight thee, in the Holy Name!
Yet, what thou dost, is what God saith:
Tempter! should I escape thy flame,
Thou wilt have helped my soul from Death:

45 The second Death, that never dies,
That cannot die, when time is dead:

---

[1] in Greek mythology, the nine daughters of Zeus and Mnemosyne. Originally goddesses of memory, the Muses were later identified with individual arts and sciences.

[2] the Roman name for the Greek *erinyes*, three goddesses. Accounts of their origin vary; they were said to be the daughters of night, or of Earth and Darkness. They were merciless goddesses of vengeance who punished all transgressors, especially those who neglected filial duty or the claims of kinship.

[3] a title of the Holy Spirit; literally, "the advocate" or comforter.

Live Death, wherein the lost soul cries,
Eternally uncomforted.

Dark Angel, with thine aching lust!
50 Of two defeats, of two despairs:
Less dread, a change to drifting dust,
Than thine eternity of cares.

Do what thou wilt, thou shalt not so,
Dark Angel! triumph over me:
Lonely, unto the Lone I go;
Divine, to the Divinity.
—1894 (1893)

Summer Storm

To Harold Child

The wind, hark! the wind in the angry woods:
And how clouds purple the west: there broods
Thunder, thunder; and rain will fall;
Fresh fragrance cling to the wind from all
5   Roses holding water wells,
Laurels gleaming to the gusty air;
    Wilding mosses of the dells,
Drenched hayfields, and dripping hedgerows fair.

The wind, hark! the wind dying again:
10 The wind's voice matches the far-off main,
In sighing cadences: Pan[1] will wake,
Pan in the forest, whose rich pipes make
    Music to the folding flowers,
In the pure eve, where no hot spells are:
15   Those be favourable hours
Hymned by Pan beneath the shepherd star.
—1895 (1887)

---

[1] Greek "all" or "everything." In Greek mythology, the god of pastures, forests, flocks, and herds; the universal deity, Pan, had the torso of a man and the body and legs of a goat. Legend has it that the cry "Great Pan is dead" was heard at the moment of Christ's crucifixion.

Dead

To Olivier Georges Destrée

In Merioneth,[2] over the sad moor
Drives the rain, the cold wind blows:
    Past the ruinous church door,
The poor procession without music goes.

5 Lonely she wandered out her hour, and died.
    Now the mournful curlew cries
    Over her, laid down beside
Death's lonely people: lightly down she lies.

In Merioneth, the wind lives and wails,
10   On from hill to lonely hill:
    Down the loud, triumphant gales,
A spirit cries *Be strong!* and cries *Be still!*
—1895 (1887)

The End

To Austin Ferrand

I gave you more than love: many times more:
I gave mine honour into your fair keeping.
You lost mine honour: wherefore now restore
The love, I gave; not dead, but cold and sleeping.
5 You loveless, I dishonoured, go our ways:
Dead is the past: dead must be all my days.

Death and the shadows tarry not: fulfil
Your years with folly and love's imitation.
You had mine all: mine only now, to kill
10 All trembling memories of mine adoration.
That done, to lie me down, and die, and dream,
What once, I thought you were: what still, you seem.
—1897 (1887)

---

[2] English for Meirionnydd, a region of Wales. It was the territory of Meirion, grandson of Cunedda, who conquered northern and western Wales in the fifth century AD.

Nihilism

To Samuel Smith

Among immortal things not made with hands;
Among immortal things, dead hands have made:
Under the Heavens, upon the Earth, there stands
Man's life, my life: of life I am afraid.

5 Where silent things, and unimpassioned things,
Where things of nought, and things decaying, are:
I shall be calm soon, with the calm, death brings.
The skies are gray there, without any star.

Only the rest! the rest! Only the gloom,
10 Soft and long gloom! The pausing from all thought!
My life, I cannot taste: the eternal tomb
Brings me the peace, which life has never brought.

For all the things I do, and do not well;
All the forced drawings of a mortal breath:
15 Are as the hollow music of a bell,
That times the slow approach of perfect death.
　　　　　　　　　　　　—1897 (1888)

The Darkness

To the Rev. Fr. Dover, S.J.

Master of spirits! hear me: King of souls!
I kneel before Thine altar, the long night,
Besieging Thee with penetrable prayers;
And all I ask, light from the Face of God.
5 Thy darkness Thou hast given me enough,
The dark clouds of Thine angry majesty:
Now give me light! I cannot always walk
Surely beneath the full and starless night.
Lighten me, fallen down, I know not where,
10 Save, to the shadows and the fear of death.
Thy Saints in light see light, and sing for joy:
Safe from the dark, safe from the dark and cold.
But from my dark comes only doubt of light:

Disloyalty, that trembles to despair.
15 Now bring me out of night, and with the sun
Clothe me, and crown me with Thy seven stars,[1]
Thy spirits in the hollow of Thine hand.
Thou from the still throne of Thy tabernacle
Wilt come to me in glory, O Lord God!
20 Thou wilt, I doubt Thee not: I worship Thee
Before Thine holy altar, the long night.
Else have I nothing in the world, but death:
Thine hounding winds rush by me day and night,
Thy seas roar in mine ears: I have no rest,
25 No peace, but am afflicted constantly,
Driven from wilderness to wilderness.
And yet Thou hast a perfect house of light,
Above the four great winds, an house of peace:
Its beauty of the crystal and the dew,
30 Guard Angels and Archangels, in their hands
The blade of a sword shaken. Thither bring
Thy servant: when the black night falls on me,
With bitter voices tempting in the gloom,
Send out Thine armies, flaming ministers,
35 And shine upon the night: for what I would,
I cannot, save these help me. O Lord God!
Now, when my prayers upon Thine altar lie,
When Thy dark anger is too hard for me:
Through vision of Thyself, through flying fire,
40 Have mercy, and give light, and stablish me!
　　　　　　　　　　　　—1897 (1889)

In a Workhouse

To Hartley Withers

Old hopes I saw there: and perchance I saw
Other old passions in their trembling age,
Withered, and desolate, but not yet dead:
And I had rather seen an house of death,
5 Than those live men, unmanned, wasted, forlorn,
Looking toward death out of their empty lives.

---

[1] the planets, or the constellation of the Pleiades or the Great Bear; see
King Lear 1.5.1605.

They could not with the sad comfort of thought
Fill up the miserable day; nor muse
Upon the shadowy nature of the world,
10 And on that meditation stay themselves.
Nor wisdom of bright dreaming came there back
To these dulled minds, that never had the time,
The hard day's labour done, to do with dreams.
Nought theirs, but sullen waiting for no end;
15 Nought, but surrender to necessity.
No solemn faith, nor no impassioned trust,
Mastered their wills: here were no pagan souls,
Grandly enduring dooms, mighty to bear
Stern visitation of majestic fates,
20 Proudly alone and strong: these had no wills,
These were none else, than worn and haggard things,
Nor men, nor brutes, nor shades: and yet alive.
Bruised victims of the trampling years, hurt souls,
They fell before the march of their own kind:
25 Now, scarred memorials of laborious war,
Tragic and monumental live these men.
—1897 (1889)

Bagley Wood

To Percy Addleshaw

The night is full of stars, full of magnificence:
  Nightingales hold the wood, and fragrance
    loads the dark.
Behold, what fires august, what lights eternal! Hark,
What passionate music poured in passionate love's
    defence!
5 Breathe but the wafting wind's nocturnal
    frankincense!
Only to feel this night's great heart, only to mark
The splendours and the glooms, brings back the
    patriarch,
Who on Chaldæan wastes found God through
    reverence.

Could we but live at will upon this perfect height,
10 Could we but always keep the passion of this peace,
Could we but face unshamed the look of this pure
    light,
Could we but win earth's heart, and give desire
    release:
Then were we all divine, and then were ours by
    right
These stars, these nightingales, these scents: then
    shame would cease.
—(1890)

The Destroyer of a Soul

I hate you with a necessary hate.
  First, I sought patience: passionate was she:
My patience turned in very scorn of me,
That I should dare forgive a sin so great,
5 As this, through which I sit disconsolate;
Mourning for that live soul, I used to see;
Soul of a saint, whose friend I used to be:
Till you came by! a cold, corrupting, fate.

Why come you now? You, whom I cannot cease
10 With pure and perfect hate to hate? Go, ring
The death-bell with a deep, triumphant toll!
Say you, my friend sits by me still? Ah, peace!
Call you this thing my friend? this nameless thing?
This living body, hiding its dead soul?
—(1892)

The Precept of Silence

I know you: solitary griefs,
  Desolate passions, aching hours!
I know you: tremulous beliefs,
Agonized hopes, and ashen flowers!

5 The winds are sometimes sad to me;
The starry spaces, full of fear:

Mine is the sorrow on the sea,
And mine the sigh of places drear.

Some players upon plaintive strings
10 Publish their wistfulness abroad:
I have not spoken of these things,
Save to one man, and unto God.
—(1893)

A Proselyte

Heart of magnificent desire:
O equal of the lordly sun!
Since thou hast cast on me thy fire,
My cloistral peace, so hardly won,
5   Breaks from its trance:
          One glance
From thee hath all its joy undone.

Of lonely quiet was my dream;
Day gliding into fellow day,
10 With the mere motion of a stream:
But now in vehement disarray

Go time and thought,
          Distraught
With passion kindled at thy ray.

15 Heart of tumultuary might,
O greater than the mountain flame,
That leaps upon the fearful night!
On me thy devastation came,
          Sudden and swift;
20   A gift
Of joyous torment without name.

Thy spirit stings my spirit: thou
Takest by storm and ecstasy
The cloister of my soul. And now,
25 With ardour that is agony,
          I do thy will;
               Yet still
Hear voices of calm memory.
—(1894)

Charlotte Mew
1869 – 1928

Charlotte Mew was born in London into a middle-class family that witnessed the early death of three children and the institutionalization of two others due to insanity. Mew's first publication, a short story, appeared in *The Yellow Book* in 1894. Her first collection of poetry was not published until 1916. *The Farmer's Bride*, as the collection was called, did not sell well, but it was well-received in literary circles. Eschewing marriage, Mew formed a pas-

sionate yet unrequited regard for her friend May Sinclair. Mew wrote very little after 1916, producing one volume of poetry entitled *Saturday Market* in 1921 and producing another entitled *The Rambling Sailor*, which was post-humously published in 1929. Suffering from what was diagnosed as neurasthenia, she was admitted in 1928 to a nursing home, where she ultimately ended her own life.

ꕔꕔꕔ

The Farmer's Bride

To—
He asked life of thee, and thou gavest him a long life:
even for ever and ever…

Three Summers since I chose a maid,
  Too young maybe—but more's to do
At harvest-time than bide and woo.
    When us was wed she turned afraid
5 Of love and me and all things human;
Like the shut of a winter's day.
Her smile went out, and 'twasn't a woman—
    More like a little frightened fay.[1]
      One night, in the Fall, she runned away.

10 "Out 'mong the sheep, her be," they said,
  'Should properly have been abed;
But sure enough she wasn't there
Lying awake with her wide brown stare.
So over seven-acre field and up-along across the
    down
15 We chased her, flying like a hare
Before our lanterns. To Church-Town
    All in a shiver and a scare
We caught her, fetched her home at last
    And turned the key upon her, fast.

20 She does the work about the house
As well as most, but like a mouse:
    Happy enough to chat and play
    With birds and rabbits and such as they,
    So long as men-folk keep away.
25 "Not near, not near!" her eyes beseech
When one of us comes within reach.
    The women say that beasts in stall
    Look round like children at her call.
    I've hardly heard her speak at all.

30 Shy as a leveret,[2] swift as he,
Straight and slight as a young larch tree,
Sweet as the first wild violets, she,
To her wild self. But what to me?

The short days shorten and the oaks are brown,
35   The blue smoke rises to the low grey sky,
One leaf in the still air falls slowly down,
    A magpie's spotted feathers lie
On the black earth spread white with rime,
The berries redden up to Christmas-time.
40   What's Christmas-time without there be
    Some other in the house than we!

---

[1] fairy.

[2] a hare during its first year.

She sleeps up in the attic there
    Alone, poor maid. 'Tis but a stair
Betwixt us. Oh! my God! the down,
45 The soft young down of her, the brown,
  The brown of her—her eyes, her hair, her hair!
      —1916

The Fête

To-night again the moon's white mat
  Stretches across the dormitory floor
While outside, like an evil cat
  The *pion*[1] prowls down the dark corridor,
5 Planning, I know, to pounce on me, in spite
For getting leave to sleep in town last night.
But it was none of us who make that noise,
  Only the old brown owl that hoots and flies
Out of the ivy—he will say it was us boys—
10 *Seigneur mon Dieu!* the *sacré*[2] soul of spies!
  He would like to catch each dream that lies
    Hidden behind our sleepy eyes:
Their dream? But mine—it is the moon and the
    wood that sees;
All my long life how I shall hate the trees!

15 In the *Place d'Armes*, the dusty planes, all Summer
    through
Dozed with the market women in the sun and
    scarcely stirred
    To see the quiet things that crossed the
    Square—,
A tiny funeral, the flying shadow of a bird,
  The hump-backed barber Célestin Lemaire,
20   Old madame Michel in her three-wheeled chair,
    And filing past to Vespers,[3] two and two,
    The *demoiselles* of the *pensionnat*.[4]

Towed like a ship through the harbour bar,
  Safe into port, where *le petit Jésus*
25 Perhaps makes nothing of the look they shot at
    you:
    Si, c'est défendu, mais que voulez-vous?[5]
It was the sun. The sunshine weaves
A pattern on dull stones: the sunshine leaves
    The portraiture of dreams upon the eyes
30   Before it dies:
    All Summer through
The dust hung white upon the drowsy planes
Till suddenly they woke with the Autumn rains.

    It is not only the little boys
    Who have hardly got away from toys,
35 But I, who am seventeen next year,
Some nights, in bed, have grown cold to hear
    That lonely passion of the rain
Which makes you think of being dead,
40 And of somewhere living to lay your head
    As if you were a child again,
Crying for one thing, known and near
Your empty heart, to still the hunger and the fear
    That pelts and beats with it against the pane.
45   But I remember smiling too
At all the sun's soft tricks and those Autumn dreads
    In winter time, when the grey light broke slowly
    through
The frosted window-lace to drag us shivering from
    our beds.
    And when at dusk the singing wind swung
    down
50 Straight from the stars to the dark country roads
    Beyond the twinkling town,
    Striking the leafless poplar boughs as he went
    by,
Like some poor, stray dog by the wayside lying
    dead,
We left behind us the old world of dread,

---

1 supervisor.

2 "[O] Lord my God!" the "accursed."

3 a church service taking place late in the afternoon or early evening.

4 "girls" of the "boarding-school."

5 "Yes, it's forbidden, but what can one do?"

55 I and the wind as we strode whistling on under the
        Winter sky.

    And then in Spring for three days came the Fair
        Just as the planes were starting into bud
    Above the caravans: you saw the dancing bear
        Pass on his chain; and heard the jingle and the
            thud.
60   Only four days ago
        They let you out of this dull show
    To slither down the *montagne russe*[1] and chaff the
        man *à la tête de veau*[2]—
            Hit, slick, the bull's eye at the *tir*,[3]
    Spin round and round till your head went queer
65 On the *porcs-roulants*.[4] *Oh! là là! la fête!*
    Va pour du vin, et le tête-à-tête[5]
    With the girl who sugars the *gaufres!*[6] *Pauvrette*,[7]
        How thin she was; but she smiled, you bet,
        As she took your tip—"One does not forget
70 The good days, Monsieur." Said with a grace,
    But *sacré bleu!*[8] what a ghost of a face!
        And no fun too for the *demoiselles*
    Of the *pensionnat*, who were hurried past,
        With their "*Oh, que c'est beau—Ah, qu'elle est
            belle!*"[9]
75 A lap-dog's life from first to last!
    The good nights are not made for sleep, nor the
        good days for dreaming in,
        And at the end in the big Circus tent we sat and
            shook and stewed like sin!

Some children there had got—but where?
Sent from the south, perhaps—a red bouquet
80   Of roses, sweetening the fetid air
With scent from gardens by some far away blue bay.
    They threw one at the dancing bear;
The white clown caught it. From St. Rémy's tower
    The deep, slow bell tolled out the hour;
85 The black clown, with his dirty grin
    Lay, sprawling in the dust, as She rode in.

    She stood on a white horse—and suddenly you saw
        the bend
    Of a far-off road at dawn, with knights riding
        by,
A field of spears—and then the gallant day
90 Go out in storm, with ragged clouds low down,
        sullen and grey
    Against red heavens: wild and awful, such a sky
    As witnesses against you at the end
Of a great battle; bugles blowing, blood and dust—
The old *Morte d'Arthur*,[10] fight you must—
95   It died in anger. But it was not death
    That had you by the throat, stopping your breath.
She looked like Victory. She rode my way.

She laughed at the black clown and then she flew
    A bird above us, on the wing
100 Of her white arms; and you saw through
A rent in the old tent, a patch of sky
With one dim star. She flew, but not so high—
    And then she did not fly;
She stood in the bright moonlight at the door
105 Of a strange room, she threw her slippers to the
        floor—
        Again, again
    You heard the patter of the rain,
        The starving rain—it was this Thing,
Summer was this, the gold mist in your eyes;—

---

[1] "Russian mountain."

[2] the man "with the calf's head."

[3] "firing."

[4] "the rides."

[5] "Oh! la, la! the festival! / Go for wine, and the private interview."

[6] "waffles."

[7] "Poor little thing."

[8] "[by] holy heaven!"

[9] "Oh, how beautiful it is—Ah, how lovely it is!"

---

[10] alluding to Sir Thomas Malory's collected tales of King Arthur and his knights of the Round Table.

The starving rain—it was this Thing,
Summer was this, the gold mist in your eyes;—
110   Oh God! it dies,
              But after death—,
To-night the splendour and the sting
    Blows back and catches at your breath,
The smell of beasts, the smell of dust, the scent of
    all the roses in the world, the sea, the Spring,
115 The beat of drums, the pad of hoofs, music, the
    dream, the dream, the Enchanted Thing!

In the *Place d'Armes* all afternoon
125   The building birds had sung "Soon, soon,"
The shuttered streets slept sound that night,
          It was full moon:
The path into the wood was almost white,
The trees were very still and seemed to stare:
130   Not far before your soul the Dream flits on,
        But when you touch it, it is gone
And quite alone your soul stands there.

At first you scarcely saw her face,
You knew the maddening feet were there,
What called was that half-hidden, white unrest
To which now and then she pressed
120   Her finger-tips; but as she slackened pace
And turned and looked at you it grew quite bare:
        There was not anything you did not dare:—
Like trumpeters the hours passed until the last day
    of the Fair.

Mother of Christ, no one has seen your eyes: how
    can men pray
          Even unto you?
135 There were only wolves' eyes in the wood—
          My Mother is a woman too:
Nothing is true that is not good,
With that quick smile of hers, I have heard her
    say;—
I wish I had gone back home to-day;
140   I should have watched the light that so gently
          dies

From our high window, in the Paris skies,
          The long, straight chain
          Of lamps hung out along the Seine:
I would have turned to her and let the rain
145 Beat on her breast as it does against the pane;—
          Nothing will be the same again;—
There is something strange in my little Mother's
    eyes,
There is something new in the old heavenly air of
    Spring
The smell of beasts, the smell of dust—*The
    Enchanted Thing!*

150 All my life long I shall see moonlight on the fern
          And the black trunks of trees. Only the hair
Of any woman can belong to God.
The stalks are cruelly broken where we trod,
          There had been violets there,
155   I shall not care
As I used to do when I see the bracken burn.
—1916

In Nunhead Cemetery

It is the clay that makes the earth stick to his
          spade;
    He fills in holes like this year after year;
The others have gone; they were tired, and half afraid
    But I would rather be standing here;

5 There is nowhere else to go. I have seen this place
          From the windows of the train that's going past
Against the sky. This is rain on my face—
    It was raining here when I saw it last.

There is something horrible about a flower;
10   This, broken in my hand, is one of those
He threw in just now: it will not live another hour;
    There are thousands more: you do not miss a
          rose.

One of the children hanging about
    Pointed at the whole dreadful heap and smiled
15 This morning, after THAT was carried out;
    There is something terrible about a child.

We were like children, last week, in the Strand;
    That was the day you laughed at me
Because I tried to make you understand
20   The cheap, stale chap I used to be
    Before I saw the things you make me see.

This is not a real place; perhaps by-and-by
    I shall wake—I am getting drenched with all
        this rain:
To-morrow I will tell you about the eyes of the
    Crystal Palace train
25   Looking down on us, and you will laugh and I
        shall see what you see again.

    Not here, not now. We said "Not yet
    Across our low stone parapet
Will the quick shadows of the sparrows fall."

30   But still it was a lovely thing
    Through the grey months to wait for Spring
    With the birds that go a-gypsying
In the parks till the blue seas call.
    And next to these, you used to care
35   For the lions in Trafalgar Square,
Who'll stand and speak for London when her bell
    of Judgment tolls—
    And the gulls at Westminster that were
    The old sea-captains' souls.
40 To-day again the brown tide splashes, step by step,
    the river stair,
    And the gulls are there!

By a month we have missed our Day:
    The children would have hung about
Round the carriage and over the way
45   As you and I came out.

We should have stood on the gulls' black cliffs and
    heard the sea
    And seen the moon's white track,
I would have called, you would have come to me
    And kissed me back.

50 You have never done that: I do not know
    Why I stood staring at your bed
And heard you, though you spoke so low,
    But could not reach your hands, your little head.
There was nothing we could not do, you said,
55   And you went, and I let you go!

Now I will burn you back, I will burn you through,
    Though I am damned for it we two will lie
    And burn, here where the starlings fly
    To these white stones from the wet sky—;
60   Dear, you will say this is not I—
It would not be you, it would not be you!

If for only a little while
    You will think of it you will understand,
    If you will touch my sleeve and smile
65   As you did that morning in the Strand
    I can wait quietly with you
    Or go away if you want me to—
God! What is God? but you face has gone and
    your hand!
    Let me stay here too.

70   When I was quite a little lad
    At Christmas time we went half mad
    For joy of all the toys we had,
And then we used to sing about the sheep
    The shepherds watched by night;
75 We used to pray to Christ to keep
    Our small souls safe till morning light—;
I am scared, I am staying with you to-night—
    Put me to sleep.

I shall stay here: here you can see the sky;
80 The houses in the streets are much too high;
   There is no one left to speak to there;
   Here they are everywhere,
And just above them fields and fields of roses lie—
If he would dig it all up again they would not die.
   —1916

Ken

The town is old and very steep,
   A place of bells and cloisters and grey towers,
And black clad people walking in their sleep—
   A nun, a priest, a woman taking flowers
5   To her new grave; and watched from end to end
   By the great Church above, through the still
         hours:
      But in the morning and the early dark
The children wake to dart from doors and call
Down the wide, crooked street, where, at the bend,
10   Before it climbs up to the park,
Ken's is the gabled house facing the Castle wall.

When first I came upon him there
Suddenly, on the half-lit stair,
I think I hardly found a trace
15 Of likeness to a human face
      In his. And I said then
If in His image God made men,
Some other must have made poor Ken—
But for his eyes which looked at you
20 As two red, wounded stars might do.

He scarcely spoke, you scarcely heard,
      His voice broke off in little jars
To tears sometimes. An uncouth bird
      He seemed as he ploughed up the street,
25 Groping, with knarred, high-lifted feet
      And arms thrust out as if to beat
         Always against a threat of bars.

And oftener than not there'd be
   A child just higher than his knee
30 Trotting beside him. Through his dim
   Long twilight this, at least, shone clear,
   That all the children and the deer,
      Whom every day he went to see
Out in the park, belonged to him.

35 "God help the folk that next him sits
   He fidgets so, with his poor wits."
The neighbours said on Sunday nights
When he would go to Church to "see the lights!"
   Although for these he used to fix
40 His eyes upon a crucifix
   In a dark corner, staring on
   Till everybody else had gone.
   And sometimes, in his evil fits,
You could not move him from his chair—
45 You did not look at him as he sat there,
   Biting his rosary to bits.
While pointing to the Christ he tried to say
   "Take it away."

      Nothing was dead:
50 He said "a bird" if he picked up a broken wing,
   A perished leaf or any such thing
      Was just "a rose"; and once when I had said
   He must not stand and knock there any more,
   He left a twig on the mat outside my door.

55   Not long ago
The last thrush stiffened in the snow,
   While black against a sullen sky
      The sighing pines stood by.
But now the wind has left our rattled pane
60 To flutter the hedge-sparrow's wing,
   The birches in the wood are red again
      And only yesterday
The larks went up a little way to sing
      What lovers say
65   Who loiter in the lanes to-day;

The buds begin to talk of May
  With learned rooks on city trees,
    And if God please
    With all of these
70 We too, shall see another Spring.

But in that red brick barn upon the hill
  I wonder—can one own the deer,
And does one walk with children still
    As one did here—
75   Do roses grow
Beneath those twenty windows in a row—
    And if some night
When you have not seen any light
They cannot move you from your chair
80   What happens there?
    I do not know.

    So, when they took
Ken to that place, I did not look
    After he called and turned on me
85   His eyes. These I shall see—
—1916

Madeleine In Church

Here, in the darkness, where this plaster saint
  Stands nearer than God stands to our distress,
And one small candle shines, but not so faint
  As the far lights of everlastingness
5 I'd rather kneel than over there, in open day
    Where Christ is hanging, rather pray
      To something more like my own clay,
      Not too divine;
    For, once, perhaps my little saint
10   Before he got his niche and crown,
Had one short stroll about the town;
It brings him closer, just that taint
      And anyone can wash the paint
Off our poor faces, his and mine!

15 Is that why I see Monty now? equal to any saint,
    poor boy, as good as gold,
But still, with just the proper trace
Of earthliness on his shining wedding face;
And then gone suddenly blank and old
The hateful day of the divorce:
20 Stuart got his, hands down, of course
Crowing like twenty cocks and grinning like a
    horse:
But Monty took it hard. All said and done I liked
    him best,—
He was the first, he stands out clearer than the rest.
      It seems too funny all we other rips
25   Should have immortal souls; Monty and Redge
    quite damnably
Keeps theirs afloat while we go down like
    scuttled ships.—
      It's funny too, how easily we sink,
      One might put up a monument, I
      think
    To half the world and cut across it "Lost at
    Sea!"
30 I should drown Jim, poor little sparrow, if I netted
    him to-night—
      No, it's no use this penny light—
      Or my poor saint with his tin-pot
      crown—
      The trees of Calvary[1] are where they were,
      When we are sure that we can spare
35   The tallest, let us go and strike it down
And leave the other two standing there.
      I, too, would ask him to remember me
If there were any Paradise beyond this earth that I
    could see.

      Oh! quiet Christ who never knew
40   The poisonous fangs that bite us through
      And make us do the things we do,

---

[1] the place near Jerusalem where Christ was crucified: Luke 23:33,
Matthew 27:33.

See how we suffer and fight and die,
How helpless and how low we lie,
God holds You, and You hang so high,
45 Though no one looking long at You,
Can think you do not suffer too,
But, up there, from your still, star-lighted tree
What can You know, what can You really see
Of this dark ditch, the soul of me!

50 We are what we are: when I was half a child
I could not sit
Watching black shadows on green lawns and red
carnations burning in the sun,
Without paying so heavily for it
That joy and pain, like any mother and her
unborn child were almost one.
I could hardly bear
55 The dreams upon the eyes of white
geraniums in the dusk,
The thick, close voice of musk,
The jessamine music on the thin
night air,
Or, sometimes, my own hands about me
anywhere—
The sight of my own face (for it was lovely then)
even the scent of my own hair,
60 Oh! there was nothing, nothing that did not
sweep to the high seat
Of laughing gods, and then blow down and
beat
My soul into the highway dust, as hoofs do the
dropped roses of the street.
I think my body was my soul,
And when we are made thus
65 Who shall control
Our hands, our eyes, the wandering passion
of our feet,
Who shall teach us
To thrust the world out of our heart; to say, till
perhaps in death,
When the race is run,

70 And it is forced from us with our last breath
"Thy will be done"?
If it is Your will that we should be content with the
tame, bloodless things,
As pale as angels smirking by, with folded
wings.
Oh! I know Virtue, and the peace it
brings!
75 The temperate, well-worn smile
The one man gives you, when you are
evermore his own:
And afterwards the child's, for a little
while,
With its unknowing and all-seeing
eyes
So soon to change, and make you feel
how quick
80 The clock goes round. If one had learned the
trick—
(How does one though?) quite
early on,
Of long green pastures under placid skies,
One might be walking now with patient
truth.
What did we ever care for it, who have asked for
youth,
85 When, oh! my God! this is going or has
gone?

There is a portrait of my mother, at
nineteen,
With the black spaniel, standing by the
garden seat,
The dainty head held high against the
painted green
And throwing out the youngest smile, shy, but half
haughty and half sweet.
90 Her picture then: but simply Youth, or
simply Spring
To me to-day: a radiance on the wall,
So exquisite, so heart-breaking a thing

Beside the mask that I remember, shrunk
and small,
Sapless and lined like a dead leaf,
95 All that was left of oh! the loveliest face, by time
and grief!

And in the glass, last night, I saw a ghost behind
my chair—
Yet why remember it, when one can still go
moderately gay—?
Or could—with any one of the old crew,
But oh! these boys! the solemn way
100 They take you, and the things they say—
This "I have only as long as you"
When you remind them you are not precisely
twenty-two—
Although at heart perhaps—God! if it were
Only the face, only the hair!
105 If Jim had written to me as he did to-day
A year ago—and now it leaves me cold—
I know what this means, old, old, *old!*
Et avec ça—mais on a vécu, tout se paie.[1]

That is not always true: there was my Mother—
(well at least the dead are free!)
110 Yoked to the man that Father was; yoked to the
woman I am, Monty too;
The little portress at the Convent School,
stewing in hell so patiently;
The poor, fair boy who shot himself at Aix.[2] And
what of me—and what of me?
But I, I paid for what I had, and they for
nothing. No, one cannot see
How it shall be made up to them is some
serene eternity.
115 If there were fifty heavens God could not give us
back the child who went or never came;

---

[1] "And this granted—whoever has lived knows that everything has its consequences."

[2] city in southern France, near Marseilles.

Here, on our little patch of this great earth,
the sun of any darkened day,
Not one of all the starry buds hung on the
hawthorn trees of last year's May,
No shadow from the sloping fields of
yesterday;
For every hour they slant across the hedge a
different way,
120 The shadows are never the same.

"Find rest in Him" One knows the
parsons' tags—
Back to the fold, across the evening fields,
like any flock of baa-ing sheep:
Yes, it may be, when He has shorn, led us to
slaughter, torn the bleating soul in us to rags,
For so He giveth His belovèd sleep.
125 Oh! He will take us stripped and done,
Driven into His heart. So we are won:
Then safe, safe are we? in the shelter of His
everlasting wings—
I do not envy Him his victories. His arms are
full of broken things.

But I shall not be in them. Let Him take
130 The finer ones, the easier to break.
And they are not gone, yet, for me, the lights, the
colours, the perfumes,
Though now they speak rather in
sumptuous rooms,
In silks and in gem-like wines;
Here, even, in this corner where my little
candle shines
135 And overhead the lancet-window
glows
With golds and crimsons you could
almost drink
To know how jewels taste, just as I used to think
There was the scent in every red and yellow rose
Of all the sunsets. But this place is
grey,

140 And much too quiet. No one here,
Why, this is awful, this is fear!
Nothing to see, no face,
Nothing to hear except your heart
beating in space
As if the world was ended. Dead
at last!
145 Dead soul, dead body, tied
together fast.
These to go on with and alone, to the
slow end:
No one to sit with, really, or to speak to, friend
to friend:
Out of the long procession, black or
white or red
Not one left now to say "Still I am here, then see
you, dear, lay here your head."
150 Only the doll's house looking on the
Park
To-night, all nights, I know, when the man
puts the lights out, very dark.
With, upstairs, in the blue and gold box of a room,
just the maids' footsteps overhead,
Then utter silence and the empty world—the
room—the bed—
The corpse! No, not quite dead, while
this cries out in me,
155 But nearly: very soon to be
A handful of forgotten dust—
There must be someone. Christ! there
must,
Tell me there *will* be some one. Who?
If there were no one else, could it be
You?

160 How old was Mary out of whom you cast
So many devils? Was she young or perhaps for
years
She had sat staring, with dry eyes, at this and that
man going past

Till suddenly she saw You on the steps of
Simon's[1] house
And stood and looked at you through
tears.
165 I think she must have known by
those
The thing, for what it was that had come
to her.
For some of us there is a passion, I
suppose
So far from earthly cares and earthly fears
That in its stillness you can hardly stir
170 Or in its nearness, lift your hand,
So great that you have simply got to stand
Looking at it though tears, through tears.
Then straight from these there broke the
kiss,
I think You must have known by
this
175 The thing for what it was, that had come
to You:
She did not love You like the rest,
It was in her own way, but at the worst,
the best,
She gave you something altogether
new.
And through it all, from her, no word,
She scarcely saw You, scarcely heard:
180 Surely You knew when she so touched
You with her hair,
Or by the wet cheek lying there,
And while her perfume clung to You from head to
feet all through the day
185 That You can change the things for
which we care,
But even You, unless You kill us, not the
way.

---

[1] Simon Peter, one of the twelve apostles, the reputed author of two
books of the New Testament that carry his name; considered the first
Pope and founder of the Christian church.

This, then was peace for her, but passion
    too.
    I wonder was it like a kiss that once I
        knew,
        The only one that I would care to
            take

190 Into the grave with me, to which if there were
        afterwards, to wake.
          Almost as happy as the carven dead
        In some dim chancel[1] lying head by
           head
    We slept with it, but face to face, the whole
      night through—
One breath, one throbbing quietness, as if the
    thing behind our lips was endless life,

195 Lost, as I woke, to hear in the strange earthly
        dawn, his "Are you there?"
        And lie still, listening to the wind
        outside, among the firs.

So Mary chose the dream of Him for what was
    left to her of night and day,
It is the only truth: it is the dream in us that
    neither life nor death nor any other thing
    can take away:
    But if she had not touched Him in the doorway
    of the dream could she have cared so much?

200 She was a sinner, we are what we are: the spirit
    afterwards, but first, the touch.
And He has never shared with me my haunted
    house beneath the trees
Of Eden and Calvary, with its ghosts that have not
    any eyes for tears,
And the happier guests who would not see, or if
      they did, remember these,
      Though they lived there a thousand
      years.

205 Outside, too gravely looking at me, He
    seems to stand,
    And looking at Him, if my forgotten
      spirit came
        Unwillingly back, what could it claim
        Of those calm eyes, that quiet speech,
      Breaking like a slow tide upon the beach,

210   The scarred, not quite human hand?—
    Unwillingly back to the burden of old
    imaginings
    When it has learned so long not to think,
    not to be,
Again, again it would speak as it has spoken to
      me of things
      That I shall not see!

215 I cannot bear to look at this divinely bent and
    gracious head:
    When I was small I never quite believed that
    He was dead:
    And at the Convent school I used to lie
    awake in bed
Thinking about His hands. It did not matter
    what they said,
He was alive to me, so hurt, so hurt! And most of
    all in Holy Week

220   When there was no one else to see
    I used to think it would not hurt me too,
    so terribly,
    If He had ever seemed to notice me
    Or, if, for once, He would only speak.

—1916

The Road To Kérity

Do you remember the two old people we passed
    on the road to Kérity,
Resting their sack on the stones, by the drenched
    wayside,

---

[1] the end of the church around the altar, normally reserved for the use
of the clergy and the choir.

Looking at us with their lightless eyes through the
   driving rain, and then out again
To the rocks, and the long white line of the tide:
5 Frozen ghosts that were children once, husband
   and wife, father, and mother,
Looking at us with those frozen eyes; have you ever
         seen anything quite so chilled or
            so old?
         But we—with our arms about each
            other,
         We did not feel the cold!
—1916

I Have Been Through The Gates

His heart, to me, was a place of palaces and
   pinnacles and shining towers;
I saw it then as we see things in dreams,—I do not
   remember how long I slept;
I remember the trees, and the high, white walls,
   and how the sun was always on the towers;
The walls are standing to-day, and the gates: I have
   been through the gates, I have groped, I have
   crept
5 Back, back. There is dust in the streets, and blood;
   they are empty; darkness is over them;
His heart is a place with the lights gone out,
   forsaken by great winds and the heavenly rain,
   unclean and unswept,
Like the heart of the holy city, old, blind, beautiful
      Jerusalem,
         Over which Christ wept.
—1916

The Cenotaph [1]

Not yet will those measureless fields be green
   again

Where only yesterday the wild, sweet, blood of
   wonderful youth was shed;
There is a grave whose earth must hold too long,
   too deep a stain,
Though for ever over it we may speak as proudly as
   we may tread.
5 But here, where the watchers by lonely hearths
   from the thrust of an inward sword have more
   slowly bled,
We shall build the Cenotaph: Victory, winged,
   with Peace, winged too, at the column's head.
And over the stairway, at the foot—oh! here, leave
   desolate, passionate hands to spread
Violets, roses, and laurel, with the small, sweet,
   twinkling country things
Speaking so wistfully of other Springs,
10 From the little gardens of little places where son or
   sweetheart was born and bred.
In splendid sleep, with a thousand brothers
         To lovers—to mothers
         Here, too, lies he:
Under the purple, the green, the red,
15 It is all young life: it must break some women's
   hearts to see
Such a brave, gay coverlet to such a bed!
Only, when all is done and said,
God is not mocked and neither are the dead.

For this will stand in our Market-place—
20   Who'll sell, who'll buy
         (Will you or I
Lie each to each with the better grace)?
While looking into every busy whore's and
   huckster's face
As they drive their bargains, is the Face
25 Of God: and some young, piteous, murdered face.
—1916

---

[1] an empty tomb or monument honouring someone whose body is elsewhere.

V. R. I. [1]

I. *January 22nd, 1901* [2]

" A Nation's Sorrow." No. In that strange hour
   We did but note the flagging pulse of day,
The sudden pause of Time, and turn away
Incredulous of grief; beyond the power
5 Of question or of tears. Thy people's pain
   Was their perplexity: Thou could'st not be
God's and not England's. Let Thy spirit reign,
   For England is not England without Thee.
Still Thine, Immortal Dead, she still shall stake
10   Thy fame against the world, and hold supreme
Thy unsuspended sway. Then lay not down
   Thy sceptre, lest her Empire prove a dream
Of Thine, great, gentle Sleeper, who shalt wake
   When God doth please, to claim another
     crown.

II. *February 2nd, 1901* [3]

When, wrapped in the calm majesty of sleep,
   She passes through her people to her rest,
   Has she no smile in slumber? Is her breast,
Even to their sorrow, pulseless? Shall they weep
5 And She not with them? Nothing is so strange
   As this, that England's passion, be it pain,
   Or joy, or triumph, never shall again
Find voice in her. No change is like this change.
For all this mute indifference of death,
10   More dear She is than She has ever been.
   The dark crowd gathers: not "The Queen! The
     Queen!"
Upon its lips to-day. A quickened breath—
   She passes—through the hush, the straining
     gaze,
   The vast, sweet silence of its love and praise.
  —1916

---

[1] "Victoria Regina Imperatrix."

[2] the date of Queen Victoria's death.

[3] the date of Queen Victoria's funeral.

POETIC THEORY

∽∾∽

William Johnson Fox
1786 – 1864

William J. Fox was a Unitarian minister, a man of letters, and a politician. He already had some reputation as a drama critic when, with the establishment of the *Westminster Review* in 1824, he published his first article. By 1830 he was co-editor of the *Monthly Repository*, the leading organ of the Unitarians. In 1831 he purchased the journal's copyright and made it an organ of social reform and literary criticism. Fox's astute interest in promising young authors is demonstrated in his 1831 Tennyson article printed here, as well as in his 1833 review of Robert Browning's first published work, *Pauline*. Fox subsequently established a life-long friendship with Browning.

ᎨᏄᏇ

Tennyson – Poems, Chiefly Lyrical – 1830

It would be a pity that poetry should be an exception to the great law of progression that obtains in human affairs; and it is not. The machinery of a poem is not less susceptible of improvement than the machinery of a cotton-mill; nor is there any better reason why the one should retrograde from the days of Milton, than the other from those of Arkwright. Of course we do not mean that the cases are precisely parallel, but the difference is not so much in favour of the perfectibility of the cotton-mill as is often imagined. Man cannot be less progressive than his own works and contrivances; in fact it is by his improvement that they are improved; and the mechanical arts are continually becoming superior to what they were, just because the men who are occupied in or about those arts have grown wiser than their predecessors, and have the advantage of a clearer knowledge of principles, an experience more extended or more accurately recorded, and perhaps a stronger stimulus to invention. Their progressiveness is merely a consequence from, a sort of reflection of, the progressiveness of his nature; but poetry is far nearer and dearer; it is essential to that nature itself; it is part and parcel of his constitution; and can only retrograde in the retrogradation of humanity.

There is nothing mysterious, or anomalous, in the power of producing poetry, or in that of its enjoyment; neither the one nor the other is a supernatural gift bestowed capriciously nobody knows how, when, or why. It may be a compound, but it is not incapable of analysis; and although our detection of the component parts may not enable us to effect their combination at pleasure, it may yet guide us to many useful conclusions and well-grounded anticipations. The elements of poetry are universal. The exercise of the organs of sight and sense stimulates man to some degree of descriptive poetry; wherever there is passion, there is dramatic poetry; wherever enthusiasm, there is lyric poetry; wherever reflection, there is metaphysical poetry. It is as widely diffused as the electric fluid.[1] It may be seen flashing out by fits and starts all the world over. The most ignorant talk poetry when they are in a state of excitement, the firmly-organized think and feel poetry with every breeze of sensation that sweeps over their well-tuned nerves. There is an unfathomable store of it in human nature; the species must fail before that can be exhausted; the only question is, whether there be any reason why these permanent elements should not be wrought into their combined form, in the future,

---

[1] a reference to the widely held nineteenth-century theory that an electric fluid pervaded the entire universe and was present in all material bodies.

with a facility and power which bear some direct ratio to the progress of society.

So far as poetry is dependent upon physical organization; and doubtless it is to some extent so dependent; there is no reason why it should deteriorate. Eyes and ears are organs which nature finishes off with very different gradations of excellence. Nervous systems vary from the finest degree of susceptibility down to the toughness of a coil of hempen cable. *Poeta nascitur*[1] in a frame the most favourable to acute perception and intense enjoyment of the objects of sense; and it would be difficult to show that poets are not, and will not continue to be, produced as excellent as they have been, and as frequently. Why, then, should not those species of poetry which may be termed its music and its painting, which spring from, and appeal to, our sense of the beautiful in form or colour and of harmonious modulation, abound as much as heretofore? He is no lover of nature who has any notion that the half of her loveliness has ever yet been told. Descriptive poetry is the most exhaustible; but our coal mines will fail us much sooner. No man ever yet saw all the beauty of a landscape. He may have watched it from the rising to the setting sun, and through the twilight, and the moonlight, and the starlight, and all round the seasons, but he is deceived if he thinks then that it has nothing more for him. Indeed it is not he who ever will think so, but the man who drove down one day and back the next because he found the place so dull. The world has tired of descriptive poetry because it has been deluged with what was neither poetical nor descriptive. The world was quite right to be no longer tolerant of the repetition of conventional, traditionary, unfelt, and unmeaning phrases. But Cowper[2] did not find the ground preoccupied. Bucolics, and Georgics, and

Eclogues, and Pastorals, all made reverential room for his honest verses; and the shelf on which they took their stand is far from crowded. Nature will never cease to be poetical, nor society either. Spears and shields; gods, goddesses, and muses; and all the old scenery and machinery may indeed wear out. That is of little consequence. The age of chivalry was but one, and poetry has many ages. The classical and romantic schools are both but sects of a religion which is universal. Even the fields which have been most frequently reaped will still bear harvests; and rich ones too. Bards began with battles some thousands of years ago, and yet nobody ever wrote the Fight of Flodden field till it was indited by Scott,[3] nor did any one anticipate Campbell's glorious ballad of the battle of Hohenlinden.[4] Genius is never anticipated. No wit ever complained that all the good things had been said; nor will any poet, to the world's end, find that all worthy themes have been sung. Is not the French Revolution as good as the siege of Troy? And the landing of the Pilgrim Fathers on the shores of America, as that of the Trojan fugitives on the coast of Italy? The world has never been more disposed to make the want of a hero "an uncommon want" than in these supposed unpoetical days on which we are fallen. And were they not provided, poetry might do without them. The old epics will probably never be surpassed, any more than the old coats of mail; and for the same reason; nobody wants the article; its object is accomplished by other means; they are become mere curiosities. A long story, with a plot to be ravelled and unravelled, and characters to be developed, and descriptions to be introduced, and a great moral lesson at the end of it, is now always done, and best done, in prose. A large portion always was prose in fact, and necessarily so; but literary

---

[1] "a poet is born."

[2] William Cowper (1731–1800), an important pastoral poet of the second half of the eighteenth century.

[3] Sir Walter Scott (1771–1832), poet and novelist, author of *The Waverly Novels*. His highly successful poem, *Marmion* (1808), featured the historical battle of Flodden field.

[4] Thomas Campbell (1777–1844), author of martial lyrics, and poems expressing both the heroism and futility of battle, such as *Hohenlinden*.

superstition kept up the old forms after every body felt them intolerably wearisome and soporific, though few dared be so heretical as to say so, until the utilitarian spirit showed itself even in poetical criticism, and then the dull farce ended. This we take to be a great reformation. We have left off singing what ought only to be said, but the singing is neither the less nor the worse on that account. Nor will it be. The great principle of human improvement is at work in poetry as well as everywhere else. What is it that is reforming our criminal jurisprudence? What is shedding its lights over legislation? What purifies religions? What makes all arts and sciences more available for human comfort and enjoyment? Even that which will secure a succession of creations out of the unbounded and everlasting materials of poetry, our ever-growing acquaintance with the philosophy of mind and of man, and the increasing facility with which that philosophy is applied. This is the essence of poetic power, and he who possesses it never need furbish up ancient armour, or go to the East Kehama-hunting, or bulbul-catching.[1] Poetry, like charity, begins at home. Poetry, like morality, is founded on the precept, know thyself. Poetry, like happiness, is in the human heart. Its inspiration is of that which is in man, and it will never fail because there are changes in costume and grouping. What is the vitality of the *Iliad*? Character; nothing else. All the rest is only read either out of antiquarianism or of affectation. Why is Shakespeare the greatest of poets? Because he was one of the greatest of philosophers. We reason on the conduct of his characters with as little hesitation as if they were real living human beings. Extent of observation, accuracy of thought, and depth of reflection, were the qualities which won the prize of sovereignty for his imagination, and the effect of these qualities was practically to anticipate, so far as was needful for his purposes, the mental philosophy of a future age. Metaphysics must be the

stem of poetry for the plant to thrive; but if the stem flourishes we are not likely to be at a loss for leaves, flowers, and fruit. Now whatever theories may have come into fashion, and gone out of fashion, the real science of mind advances with the progress of society like all other sciences. The poetry of the last forty years already shows symptoms of life in exact proportion as it is imbued with this science. There is least of it in the exotic legends of Southey,[2] and the feudal romances of Scott. More of it, though in different ways, in Byron and Campbell. In Shelley there would have been more still, had he not devoted himself to unsound and mystical theories. Most of all in Coleridge and Wordsworth. They are all going or gone; but here is a little book as thoroughly and unitedly metaphysical and poetical in its spirit as any of them; and sorely shall we be disappointed in its author if it be not the precursor of a series of productions which shall beautifully illustrate our speculations, and convincingly prove their soundness.

Do not let our readers be alarmed. These poems are any thing but heavy; anything but stiff and pedantic, except in one particular, which shall be noticed before we conclude; anything but cold and logical. They are graceful, very graceful; they are animated, touching, and impassioned. And they are so, precisely because they are philosophical; because they are not made up of metrical cant and conventional phraseology; because there is sincerity where the author writes from experience, and accuracy whether he writes from experience or observation; and he only writes from experience or observation, because he has felt and thought, and learned to analyze thought and feeling; because his own mind is rich in poetical associations, and he has wisely been content with its riches; and because, in his composition, he has not sought to construct an elaborate and artificial harmony, but only to pour forth his thoughts in those expressive and simple melodies

---

[1] animal and song-bird of Persia.

[2] the poet Robert Southey (1774–1843).

whose meaning, truth, and power, are the soonest recognized and the longest felt.

The most important department in which metaphysical science has been a pioneer for poetry is in the analysis of particular states of mind; a work which is now performed with ease, power, and utility as much increased, as in the grosser dissections of the anatomical lecturer. Hence the poet, more fortunate than the physician, has provision made for an inexhaustible supply of subjects. A new world is discovered for him to conquer. The poets of antiquity rarely did more than incidentally touch this class of topics; the external world had not yet lost its freshness; situations, and the outward expression of the thoughts, feelings and passions generated by those situations, were a province so much nearer at hand, and presented so much to be done and enjoyed, that they rested there content, like the two tribes and a half of Israel, who sought not to cross the narrow boundary that separated them from a better and richer country.[1] Nor let them be blamed; it was for the philosophers to be the first discoverers and settlers, and for poetry afterwards to reap the advantage of their labours. This has only been done recently, or rather is only beginning to be done at all. Metaphysical systems and discussions in verse, there have been indeed, from Lucretius down to Akenside.[2] But they have generally had just argument enough to spoil the poetry, and just poetry enough to spoil the argument. They resembled paintings of the bones, arteries, veins, and muscles; very bad as a substitute to the anatomist for the real substances in the human body, and still worse for the artist as the materials for a pleasant picture. Science, mental or physical, cannot be taught poetically; but the power derived from science may be used poetically; and metaphysics may do as much for the poet as anatomy has done for

the painter, in truth, more, for the painter's knowledge of the human frame does not furnish him with distinct subjects for the exercise of his art; we have just remarked the unfitness. The benefit which the painter derives is that of being able to delineate the external appearances of the living body with greater truth and effect. And while the poet has an analogous advantage from mental science in the greater truth and effect of his delineations of external action, character, passion, and all that belongs to situation and grouping; he also finds in the phenomena exhibited in moral dissection (though not in the operation itself, in the application of the logical scalpel) some of the finest originals for his pictures; and they exist in infinite variety.

Mr Tennyson has some excellent specimens of this class. He seems to obtain entrance into a mind as he would make his way into a landscape; he climbs the pineal gland as if it were a hill in the centre of the scene; looks around on all objects with their varieties of form, their movements, their shades of colour, and their mutual relations and influences; and forthwith produces as graphic a delineation in the one case as Wilson or Gainsborough[3] could have done in the other, to the great enrichment of our gallery of intellectual scenery. In the "Supposed Confessions of a second-rate sensitive mind not in unity with itself," there is an extraordinary combination of deep reflection, metaphysical analysis, picturesque description, dramatic transition, and strong emotion. The author personates (he can personate anything he pleases from an angel to a grasshopper) a timid sceptic, but who must evidently always remain such, and yet be miserable in his scepticism; whose early associations, and whose sympathies, make religion a necessity to his heart; yet who has not lost his pride in the prowess of his youthful infidelity; who is tossed hither and thither on the conflicting currents of feeling and doubt, without that vigorous intellectual decision

---

[1] a reference to the flight of the Jews from Egypt: Exodus 14:5–30.

[2] from the ancients (Lucretius, Roman poet and philosopher [96?–55 BC]), to the moderns (Mark Akenside, poet [1721–70]).

[3] eighteenth-century English painters.

which alone could "ride in the whirlwind and direct the storm," until at last he disappears with an exclamation which remains on the ear like

> the bubbling cry
> Of some strong swimmer in his agony.

Now without intruding any irreverent comparison or critical profanity we do honestly think this state of mind as good a subject for poetical description as even the shield of Achilles itself. Such topics are more in accordance with the spirit and intellect of the age than those about which poetry has been accustomed to be conversant; their adoption will effectually redeem it from the reproach of being frivolous and enervating; and of their affinity with the best pictorial qualities of poetry we have conclusive evidence in this very composition. The delineations of the trustful infant, the praying mother, the dying lamb, are as good as anything of the kind can be; while those of the supposed author's emotions as he gazes on "Christians with happy countenances," or stands by the Christian grave, or realizes again, with a mixture of self-admiration and self-reproach, "the unsunned freshness of his strength," when he "went forth in quest of truth," are of a higher order, and are more powerfully, though not less gracefully finished.

Our author has the secret of the transmigration of the soul. He can cast his own spirit into any living thing, real or imaginary. Scarcely Vishnu[1] himself becomes incarnate more easily, frequently, or perfectly. And there is singular refinement, as well as solid truth, in his impersonations, whether they be of inferior creatures or of such elemental beings as Syrens, as mermen and mermaidens. He does not merely assume their external shape, and exhibit his own mind masquerading. He takes their senses, feelings, nerves, and brain, along with their names and local habitations; still it is himself in them,

modified but not absorbed by their peculiar constitution and mode of being. In "The Merman" one seems to feel the principle of thought injected by a strong volition into the cranium of the finny worthy, and coming under all the influences, as thinking principles do, of the physical organization to which it is for the time allied: for a moment the identification is complete; and then a consciousness of contrast springs up between the reports of external objects brought to the mind by the senses and those which it has been accustomed to receive; and this consciousness gives to the description a most poetical colouring:

> There would be neither moon nor star;
> But the wave would make music above us afar—
> Low thunder and light in the magic night—
>   Neither moon nor star.
> We would call aloud in the dreary dells, &c.

The Mermaid is beautifully discriminated, and most delicately drawn. She is the younger sister of Undine; or Undine herself before she had a soul.[2] And the Syrens, who could resist these Sea Fairies, as the author prefers calling them? We must introduce a fragment of their song, though it is barbarous to break such a piece of coral for a specimen:

> Day and night to the billow the fountain calls
> …
> Whither away, whither away, whither away with
>   the sail and the oar?

The poet has here done, in the character of the Sea-Fairies, that which he has several times done in his own person, and always admirably; he has created a scene out of the character, and made the feeling within generate an appropriate assemblage of external objects. Every mood of the mind has its own outward

---

[1] the second member of the trinity in Hindu theology, popularly believed to have had several human incarnations.

[2] a female water spirit who could acquire a soul by marrying, and having a child by, a mortal.

world, or rather makes its own outward world. But it is not always, perhaps with sensitive and imaginative minds it is seldom, that the external objects, and their qualities will be seen through the medium of congeniality. It is thus in "L'Allegro" and "Il Penseroso"; but Milton was a happy man; the visions of both those poems were seen with the eyes of happiness, the only difference being that the one depicts a state of light-hearted, and the other of sober-minded enjoyment. There is not less truth, perhaps a more refined observation, in the opposite course which our author has taken in the two poems "Nothing Will Die," and "All Things Will Die." The outward objects, at the commencement of each, are precisely the same; the states of mind, are in contrast; and each seizes with avidity on some appearance which is uncongenial with itself. He who thinks that nothing will die, yet looks with wondering, and almost wearied eye on the ever-flowing stream, &c.; and he, who feels that all things must die, gazes mournfully on those same objects in the "gayest, happiest attitude," which his own fancy has unconsciously compelled them to assume. There is this difference, however, that the felicitous conviction, in the first poem, enables the mind to recover itself with a sort of elastic bound; while in the second the external beauty and enjoyment, being at permanent variance with the tone of feeling, the mind after a melancholy recognition of their loveliness sinks into unmixed gloom, and surrounds itself with objects of deeper and darker shade. We shall be better understood by quoting the commencement of each.

NOTHING WILL DIE

ALL THINGS WILL DIE

Both poems conclude nearly in the same terms, with the exception of a discriminative epithet or two; but expressing in the one case an exulting joyousness, "So let the wind range"; and in the other a reckless

and desperate gaiety, just as religion and infidelity sometimes approximate, in terms, to the inculcation of the same moral; and while the preacher of immortality cries "rejoice evermore," the expectant of annihilation shouts, "Let us eat and drink, for tomorrow we die."

"Mariana" is, we are disposed to think, although there are several poems which rise up reproachfully in our recollection as we say so, altogether, the most perfect composition in the volume. The whole of this poem, of eighty-four lines, is generated by the legitimate process of poetical creation, as that process is conducted in a philosophical mind, from a half sentence in Shakespeare. There is no mere amplification; it is all production; and production from that single germ. That must be a rich intellect, in which thoughts thus take root and grow. Mariana, the forsaken betrothed of Angelo, is described in *Measure for Measure*, as living in seclusion at "the moated grange." Mr Tennyson knows the place well; the ruinous, old, lonely house, the neglected garden, the forlorn stagnation of the locality.

> About a stonecast from the wall
> …
> The level waste, the rounding grey.

And here it was, that the deserted one lingered day after day in that "hope deferred which maketh the heart sick." The dreariness of the abode and the surrounding scenery was nothing to her;

> She only said, "My life is dreary,
>   He cometh not," she said;
> She said, "I am aweary, aweary,
>   I would that I were dead!"

The poem takes us through the circuit of four-and-twenty hours of this dreary life. Through all the changes of the night and day she has but one feeling, the variation of which is only by different degrees of acuteness and intensity in the misery it produces; and again and again we feel, before its repetition, the coming of the melancholy burthen,

> And ever when the moon was low
> …
> I would that I were dead.

The day, by its keener expectancy, was more harassing and agitating than the night; and by its sights and sounds, in that lonely place, and under the strange interpretations of a morbid fancy and a breaking heart, did yet more "confound her sense." Her deserted parents, the greyheaded domestics that had nursed her infancy in her father's house, seemed to be there; she recognized them, and what would they with her?

> Old faces glimmered through the doors,
> Old footsteps trod the upper floors,
> Old voices called her from without.

Again the hour passed at which Angelo used to arrive; again the evening is come when he used to be there, where he never would be again; the bright sunshiny evening, blazing and fading; and

> —most she loathed the hour
> …
> Oh God, that I were dead!"

A considerable number of the poems are amatory; they are the expression not of heartless sensuality, nor of a sickly refinement, nor of fantastic devotion, but of manly love; and they illustrate the philosophy of the passion while they exhibit the various phases of its existence, and embody its power. An arrangement of them might be made which should depict the whole history of passion from its birth to its apotheosis, or its death. We have seen

THE BURIAL OF LOVE

Had we space we should discuss this topic. It is of incalculable importance to society. Upon what love is, depends what woman is, and upon what woman is, depends what the world is, both in the present and the future. There is not a greater moral necessity in England than that of a reformation in female education. The boy is a son; the youth is a lover; and the man who thinks lightly of the elevation of character and the extension of happiness which woman's influence is capable of producing, and ought to be directed to the production of, in society, is neither the wisest of philosophers nor the best of patriots. How long will it be before we shall have read to better purpose the eloquent lessons, and the yet more eloquent history, of that gifted and glorious being, Mary Wollstonecraft? [1]

Mr Tennyson sketches females as well as ever did Sir Thomas Lawrence. [2] His portraits are delicate, his likenesses (we will answer for them) perfect, and they have life, character, and individuality. They are nicely assorted also to all the different gradations of emotion and passion which are expressed in common with the descriptions of them. There is an appropriate object for every shade of feeling, from the light touch of a passing admiration, to the triumphant madness of soul and sense, or the deep and everlasting anguish of survivorship.

Lilian is the heroine of the first stage:

> Airy, fairy Lilian,
> …
> Cruel little Lilian.

Madeline indicates that another degree has been taken in the freemasonry of love, "smiling frowning evermore." And so we are conducted, through various gradations, to Isabel, "the stately flower of female

---

[1] Mary Wollstonecraft (1759–97), author of *A Vindication of the Rights of Women* (1792).

[2] (1769–1830), English portrait painter, successor to Sir Joshua Reynolds as principal painter to the King in 1792.

fortitude, and perfect wifehood," to the intense and splendid passion of "Hero," and to the deep pathos of the ballad and dirge of "Oriana."

We had noted many other passages for extract or remark, but our limits are prescribed and almost arrived at. We should also have illustrated the felicitous effect often produced by the iteration of a word or sentence so posited that it conveys a different meaning or shade of meaning, excites a varied kind of emotion, and is involuntarily uttered in a different tone. There are many beautiful instances of this kind. In the ballad of Oriana, and in the songs, repetition, with a slight variation of epithet, is also practised with great power. Rousseau's[1] *air des trois notes* is only a curiosity; Mr Tennyson has made some very touching, and some very animating melodies, of little more than that number of words. He is a master of musical combinations. His songs set themselves, and generate their own tunes, as all songs do which are good for anything; but they are not many. Perhaps our author is only surpassed, among recent poets, by Coleridge, in the harmony of his versification.

It would also have been pleasant to have transcribed and analyzed such pictures as those of the Dying Swan, the Sleeping Beauty, Adeline, &c.; and to have shown how the author can breathe his own spirit into unconscious things, making them instinct with life and feeling. One stanza of an autumnal song may intimate to some readers the facility and grace with which he identifies himself with nature.

> A spirit haunts the year's last hours
> …
> Heavily hangs the tigerlily.

We must protest against the irregularities of measure, and the use of antiquated words and obsolete pronunciation, in which our author indulges so freely. He exposes himself thereby to the charge, and

---

[1] Jean Jacques Rousseau (1712–78), French philosopher and writer.

we think not unfairly, of indolence and affectation. There are few variations of effect which a skilful artist cannot produce, if he will but take the pains, without deviating from that regularity of measure which is one of the original elements of poetical enjoyment; made so by the tendency of the human frame to periodical movements; and the continued sacrifice of which is but ill compensated to the disappointed ear by any occasional, and not otherwise attainable correspondence between the movement of a verse and the sense which it is intended to convey. Nor certainly is any thing gained by a song's being studded with words which to most readers may require a glossary.

Mr Tennyson has the propensity which Shelley had, to use a word or two which young ladies of the present day are not accustomed to read or sing in the parlour; in singing, we believe, the toleration is greater than in reading or conversation; sentences, avoiding the words, but meaning much worse, are not generally proscribed.

That these poems will have a very rapid and extensive popularity we do not anticipate. Their very originality will prevent their being generally appreciated for a time. But that time will come, we hope, to a not far distant end. They demonstrate the possession of powers, to the future direction of which we look with some anxiety. A genuine poet has deep responsibilities to his country and the world, to the present and future generations, to earth and heaven. He, of all men, should have distinct and worthy objects before him, and consecrate himself to their promotion. It is thus that he best consults the glory of his art, and his own lasting fame. Mr Tennyson has a dangerous quality in that facility of impersonation on which we have remarked, and by which he enters so thoroughly into the most strange and wayward idiosyncrasies of other men. It must not degrade him into a poetical harlequin. He has higher work to do than that of disporting himself amongst "mystics" and "flowing philosophers." He knows that "the poet's mind is holy ground"; he knows that the poet's portion is to be

> Dower'd with the hate of love, the scorn of scorn,
> The love of love;

he has shown, in the lines from which we quote, his own just conception of the grandeur of a poet's destiny; and we look to him for its fulfilment. It is not for such men to sink into mere verse-makers for the amusement of themselves or others. They can influence the associations of unnumbered minds; they can command the sympathies of unnumbered hearts; they can disseminate principles; they can give those principles power over men's imaginations; they can excite in a good cause the sustained enthusiasm that is sure to conquer; they can blast the laurels of the tyrants, and hallow the memories of the martyrs of patriotism; they can act with a force, the extent of which it is difficult to estimate, upon national feelings and character, and consequently upon national happiness. If our estimate of Mr Tennyson be correct, he too is a poet; and many years hence may be read his juvenile description of that character with the proud consciousness that it has become the description and history of his own work:

> So many minds did gird their orbs with beams
> …
> Her beautiful bold brow.

—1831

Arthur Henry Hallam
1811 – 1833

Arthur Henry Hallam, a young man of great talent and potential, entered Trinity College, Cambridge, in 1828 and became a close friend of Tennyson, probably beginning in 1829. With Tennyson, Hallam was a member of the "Cambridge Apostles," an undergraduate debating and discussion society. In August, 1831, Hallam published a review of Tennyson's 1830 *Poems, Chiefly Lyrical* in the *Englishman's Magazine*. Hallam died from a haemorrhage while visiting Vienna in September, 1833, and Tennyson began composing some sections of his elegiac *In Memoriam A.H.H.* as early as October, 1833. It was published in 1850, the year that Tennyson became Poet Laureate.

❧❧❧

On Some of the Characteristics of Modern Poetry

AND ON THE LYRICAL POEMS OF ALFRED TENNYSON [1]

So Mr. Montgomery's[2] *Oxford*, by the help of some pretty illustrations, has contrived to prolong its miserable existence to a second edition! But this is slow work, compared to that triumphant progress of the *Omnipresence,* which, we concede to the author's friends, was "truly astonishing." We understand, moreover, that a new light has broken upon this "desolator desolate;" and since the "columns" have begun to follow the example of "men and gods," by whom our poetaster has long been condemned, "it is the fate of genius," he begins to discover, "to be unpopular." Now, strongly as we protest against Mr. Montgomery's application of this maxim to his own case, we are much disposed to agree with him as to its abstract correctness. Indeed, the truth which it involves seems to afford the only solution of so curious a phenomenon as the success, partial and transient though it be, of himself, and other of his calibre.

When Mr. Wordsworth, in his celebrated Preface to the *Lyrical Ballads*, asserted that immediate or rapid popularity was not the test of poetry, great was the consternation and clamour among those farmers of public favour, the established critics. Never had so audacious an attack been made upon their undoubted privileges and hereditary charter of oppression.

"What! *The Edinburgh Review* not infallible!" shrieked the amiable petulance of Mr. Jeffrey.

"*The Gentleman's Magazine* incapable of decision!" faltered the feeble garrulity of Silvanus Urban.[3]

And straightway the whole sciolist herd, men of rank, men of letters, men of wealth, men of business, all the "mob of gentlemen who think with ease,"[4] and a terrible number of old ladies and boarding-school misses began to scream in chorus, and prolonged the notes of execration with which they overwhelmed the new doctrine, until their wits and their voices fairly gave in from exhaustion. Much, no doubt, they did, for much persons will do when they fight for their dear selves; but there was one thing they could not do, and unfortunately it was the only one of any importance. They could not put down Mr. Words-

---

[1] This review of Tennyson's *Poems, Chiefly Lyrical* (1830), appeared in *The Englishman's Magazine* in August, 1831. Because of the close friendship between Hallam and Tennyson, it is generally accepted that the essay reflects Tennyson's own view of his early work.

[2] Robert Montgomery (1807–55), a third-rate contemporary poetaster.

[3] Francis Jeffrey, the editor of *The Edinburgh Review* from 1802–29; Sylvanus Urban was the pseudonym used by successive editors of *The Gentleman's Magazine.*

[4] Pope's satiric description of the Cavalier and Court poets who "wrote with ease" in the reign of Charles I and Charles II.

worth by clamour, or prevent his doctrine, once uttered, and enforced by his example, from awakening the minds of men, and giving a fresh impulse to art. It was the truth, and it prevailed; not only against the exasperation of that hydra, the Reading Public, whose vanity was hurt, and the blustering of its keepers, whose delusion was exposed, but even against the false glosses and narrow apprehensions of the Wordsworthians themselves. It is the madness of all who loosen some great principle, long buried under a snow-heap of custom and superstition, to imagine that they can restrain its operation, or circumscribe it by their purposes. But the right of private judgment was stronger than the will of Luther; and even the genius of Wordsworth cannot expand itself to the full periphery of poetic art.

It is not true, as his exclusive admirers would have it, that the highest species of poetry is the reflective; it is a gross fallacy, that because certain opinions are acute or profound, the expression of them by the imagination must be eminently beautiful. Whenever the mind of the artist suffers itself to be occupied, during its periods of creation, by any other predominant motive than the desire of beauty, the result is false in art.

Now there is undoubtedly no reason why he may not find beauty in those moods of emotion, which arise from the combinations of reflective thought; and it is possible that he may delineate these with fidelity, and not be led astray by any suggestions of an unpoetical mood. But though possible, it is hardly probable; for a man whose reveries take a reasoning turn, and who is accustomed to measure his ideas by their logical relations rather than the congruity of the sentiments to which they refer, will be apt to mistake the pleasure he has in knowing a thing to be true, for the pleasure he would have in knowing it to be beautiful, and so will pile his thoughts in a rhetorical battery, that they may convince, instead of letting them flow in a natural course of contemplation, that they may enrapture.

It would not be difficult to shew, by reference to the most admired poems of Wordsworth, that he is frequently chargeable with this error; and that much has been said by him which is good as philosophy, powerful as rhetoric, but false as poetry. Perhaps this very distortion of the truth did more in the peculiar juncture of our literary affairs to enlarge and liberalize the genius of our age, than could have been effected by a less sectarian temper.

However this may be, a new school of reformers soon began to attract attention, who, professing the same independence of immediate favor, took their stand on a different region of Parnassus from that occupied by the Lakers,[1] and one, in our opinion, much less liable to perturbing currents of air from ungenial climates. We shall not hesitate to express our conviction, that the cockney school (as it was termed in derision from a cursory view of its accidental circumstances) contained more genuine inspiration, and adhered more steadily to that portion of truth which it embraced, than any *form* of art that has existed in this country since the days of Milton. Their *caposetta*[2] was Mr. Leigh Hunt, who did little more than point the way, and was diverted from his aim by a thousand personal predilections and political habits of thought.

But he was followed by two men of very superior make; men who were born poets, lived poets, and went poets to their untimely graves. Shelley and Keats were indeed of opposite genius; that of the one was vast, impetuous, and sublime, the other seemed to be "fed with honeydew," and to have "drunk the

---

[1] "This cant term was justly ridiculed by Mr. Wordsworth's supporters; but it was not so easy to substitute an inoffensive denomination. We are not at all events the first who have used it without a contemptuous intention, for we remember to have heard a disciple quote Aristophanes in its behalf:—Ουτος ου τοιυ ηδαδων τωνδ ᾽ ὦν ὁρᾶυ᾽ ὑμεῖς ἀεὶ ἀλλὰ ΑΙΜΝΑΙΟΣ. 'This is no common, no barn-door fowl: No, but a Lakist.'" (Hallam's note.)

[2] head of a sect.

milk of Paradise."[1] Even the softness of Shelley comes out in bold, rapid, comprehensive strokes; he has no patience for minute beauties, unless they can be massed into a general effect of grandeur. On the other hand, the tenderness of Keats cannot sustain a lofty flight; he does not generalize or allegorize Nature; his imagination works with few symbols, and reposes willingly on what is given freely.

Yet in this formal opposition of character there is, it seems to us, a groundwork of similarity sufficient for the purposes of classification, and constituting a remarkable point in the progress of literature. They are both poets of sensation rather than reflection. Susceptible of the slightest impulse from external nature, their fine organs trembled into emotion at colors, and sounds, and movements, unperceived or unregarded by duller temperaments. Rich and clear were their perceptions of visible forms; full and deep their feelings of music. So vivid was the delight attending the simple exertions of eye and ear, that it became mingled more and more with their trains of active thought, and tended to absorb their whole being into the energy of sense. Other poets *seek* for images to illustrate their conceptions; these men had no need to seek; they lived in a world of images; for the most important and extensive portion of their life consisted in those emotions which are immediately conversant with the sensation. Like the hero of Goethe's novel, they would hardly have been affected by what is called the pathetic parts of a book; but the *merely beautiful* passages, "those from which the spirit of the author looks clearly and mildly forth," would have melted them to tears.[2] Hence they are not descriptive, they are picturesque. They are not smooth and *negatively* harmonious; they are full of deep and varied melodies.

This powerful tendency of imagination to a life of immediate sympathy with the external universe, is not nearly so liable to false views of art as the opposite disposition of purely intellectual contemplation. For where beauty is constantly passing before "that inward eye, which is the bliss of solitude;"[3] where the soul seeks it as a perpetual and necessary refreshment to the sources of activity and intuition; where all the other sacred ideas of our nature, the idea of good, the idea of perfection, the idea of truth, are habitually contemplated through the medium of this predominant mood, so that they assume its colour, and are subject to its peculiar laws, there is little danger that the ruling passion of the whole mind will cease to direct its creative operations, or the energetic principle of love for the beautiful sink, even for a brief period, to the level of a mere notion in the understanding.

We do not deny that it is, on other accounts, dangerous for frail humanity to linger with fond attachment in the vicinity of sense. Minds of this description are especially liable to moral temptations; and upon them, more than any, it is incumbent to remember, that their mission as men, which they share with their fellow-beings, is of infinitely higher interest than their mission as artists, which they possess by rare and exclusive privilege. But it is obvious that, critically speaking, such temptations are of slight moment. Not the gross and evident passions of our nature, but the elevated and less separable desires, are the dangerous enemies which misguide the poetic spirit in its attempts at self-cultivation. That delicate sense of fitness which grows with the growth of artist feelings, and strengthens with their strength, until it acquires a celerity and weight of decision hardly inferior to the correspondent judgments of conscience, is weakened by every indulgence of heterogeneous aspirations, however pure they may be, however lofty, however suitable to human nature.

We are therefore decidedly of opinion that the heights and depths of art are most within the reach of

---

[1] from Coleridge's "Kubla Khan."

[2] *Wilhelm Meisters Lehrjahre* 5.6.

[3] Wordsworth, "I Wandered Lonely as a Cloud."

those who have received from nature the "fearful and wonderful" constitution we have described, whose poetry is a sort of magic, producing a number of impressions, too multiplied, too minute, and too diversified to allow of our tracing them to their causes, because just such was the effect, even so boundless and so bewildering, produced on their imaginations by the real appearance of Nature.

These things being so, our friends of the new school had evidently much reason to recur to the maxim laid down by Mr. Wordsworth, and to appeal from the immediate judgment of lettered or unlettered contemporaries to the decision of a more equitable posterity. How should they be popular, whose senses told them a richer and ampler tale than most men could understand, and who constantly expressed, because they constantly felt, sentiments of exquisite pleasure or pain, which most men were not permitted to experience? The public very naturally derided them as visionaries, and gibbeted *in terrorem*[1] those inaccuracies of diction occasioned sometimes by the speed of their conceptions, sometimes by the inadequacy of language to their peculiar conditions of thought.

But it may be asked, does not this line of argument prove too much? Does it not prove that there is a barrier between these poets and all other persons so strong and immovable, that, as has been said of the Supreme Essence, we must be themselves before we can understand them in the least? Not only are they not liable to sudden and vulgar estimation, but the lapse of ages, it seems, will not consolidate their fame, nor the suffrages of the wise few produce any impression, however remote or slow matured, on the judgment of the incapacitated many.

We answer, this is not the import of our argument. Undoubtedly the true poet addresses himself, in all his conceptions, to the common nature of us all. Art is a lofty tree, and may shoot up far beyond our grasp, but its roots are in daily life and experience. Every bosom contains the elements of those complex emotions which the artist feels, and every head can, to a certain extent, go over in itself the process of their combination, so as to understand his expressions and sympathize with his state. But this requires exertion; more or less, indeed, according to the difference of occasion, but always some degree of exertion. For since the emotions of the poet, during composition, follow a regular law of association, it follows that to accompany their progress up to the harmonious prospect of the whole, and to perceive the proper dependence of every step on that which preceded, it is absolutely necessary *to start from the same point*, i.e. clearly to apprehend that leading sentiment of the poet's mind, by their conformity to which the host of suggestions are arranged.

Now this requisite exertion is not willingly made by the large majority of readers. It is so easy to judge capriciously, and according to indolent impulse! For very many, therefore, it has become *morally* impossible to attain the author's point of vision, on account of their habits, or their prejudices, or their circumstances; but it is never *physically* impossible, because nature has placed in every man the simple elements, of which art is the sublimation. Since then this demand on the reader for activity, when he wants to peruse his author in a luxurious passiveness, is the very thing that moves his bile, it is obvious that those writers will be always most popular who require the least degree of exertion. Hence, whatever is mixed up with art, and appears under its semblance, is always more favorably regarded than art free and unalloyed. Hence, half the fashionable poems in the world are mere rhetoric, and half the remainder are, perhaps, not liked by the generality for their substantial merits. Hence, likewise, of the really pure compositions, those are most universally agreeable which take for their primary subject the *usual* passions of the heart, and deal with them in a simple state, without

---

[1] as a warning.

applying the transforming powers of high imagination. Love, friendship, ambition, religion, &c., are matters of daily experience even amongst unimaginative tempers. The forces of association, therefore, are ready to work in these directions, and little effort of will is necessary to follow the artist.

For the same reason, such subjects often excite a partial power of composition, which is no sign of a truly poetic organization. We are very far from wishing to depreciate this class of poems, whose influence is so extensive, and communicates so refined a pleasure. We contend only that the facility with which its impressions are communicated is no proof of its elevation as a form of art, but rather the contrary.

What, then, some may be ready to exclaim, is the pleasure derived by most men, from Shakespeare, or Dante, or Homer, entirely false and factitious? If these are really masters of their art, must not the energy required of the ordinary intelligences that come in contact with their mighty genius, be the greatest possible? How comes it then, that they are popular? Shall we not say, after all, that the difference is in the power of the author, not in the tenor of his meditations? Those eminent spirits find no difficulty in conveying to common apprehensions their lofty sense and profound observation of Nature. They keep no aristocratic state, apart from the sentiments of society at large; they speak to the hearts of all, and by the magnetic force of their conceptions, elevate inferior intellects into a higher and purer atmosphere.

The truth contained in this observation is undoubtedly important; geniuses of the most universal order, and assigned by destiny to the most propitious era of a nation's literary development, have a clearer and a larger access to the minds of their compatriots than can ever open to those who are circumscribed by less fortunate circumstances. In the youthful periods of any literature there is an expansive and communicative tendency in mind which produces unreserved-

ness of communion, and reciprocity of vigor between different orders of intelligence.

Without abandoning the ground which has always been defended by the partizans of Mr. Wordsworth, who declare with perfect truth, that the number of real admirers of what is really admirable in Shakespeare and Milton is much fewer than the number of apparent admirers might lead one to imagine, we may safely assert that the intense thoughts set in circulation by those "orbs of song" and their noble satellites "in great Eliza's golden time," did not fail to awaken a proportionable intensity of the nature of numberless auditors. Some might feel feebly, some strongly; the effect would vary according to the character of the recipient; but upon none was the stirring influence entirely unimpressive. The knowledge and power thus imbibed became a part of national existence; it was ours as Englishmen; and amid the flux of generations and customs we retain unimpaired this privilege of intercourse with greatness.

But the age in which we live comes late in our national progress. That first raciness and juvenile vigor of literature, when nature "wandered as in her prime, and played at will her virgin fancies" is gone, never to return.[1] Since that day we have undergone a period of degradation. "Every handicraftsman has worn the mask of Poesy."[2] It would be tedious to repeat the tale so often related of the French contagion and the heresies of the Popian school.

With the close of the last century came an era of reaction, an era of painful struggle to bring our over-civilised condition of thought into union with the fresh productive spirit that brightened the morning of our literature. But repentance is unlike innocence; the laborious endeavor to restore has more complicated methods of action than the freedom of un-

---

[1] Hallam's synthesis of l. 40 and l. 784 from Wordsworth's "Descriptive Sketches" (1793 ed.).

[2] Keats, "Sleep and Poetry," ll. 200–01.

tainted nature. Those different powers of poetic disposition, the energies of Sensitive,[1] of Reflective, of Passionate Emotion, which in former times were intermingled, and derived from mutual support an extensive empire over the feelings of men, were now restrained within separate spheres of agency. The whole system no longer worked harmoniously, and by intrinsic harmony acquired external freedom; but there arose a violent and unusual action in the several component functions, each for itself, all striving to reproduce the regular power which the whole had once enjoyed.

Hence the melancholy which so evidently characterises the spirit of modern poetry; hence that return of the mind upon itself and the habit of seeking relief in idiosyncrasies rather than community of interest. In the old times the poetic impulse went along with the general impulse of the nation; in these it is a reaction against it, a check acting for conservation against a propulsion towards change.

We have indeed seen it urged in some of our fashionable publications, that the diffusion of poetry must be in the direct ratio of the diffusion of machinery, because a highly civilized people must have new objects of interest, and thus a new field will be open to description. But this notable argument forgets that against this *objective* amelioration may be set the decrease of *subjective* power, arising from a prevalence of social activity, and a continual absorption of the higher feelings into the palpable interests of ordinary life. The French Revolution may be a finer theme than the war of Troy; but it does not so evidently follow that Homer is to find his superior.

Our inference, therefore, from this change in the relative position of artists to the rest of the community is, that modern poetry in proportion to its depth and truth is likely to have little immediate authority over public opinion. Admirers it will have; sects consequently it will form; and these strong undercurrents will in time sensibly affect the principal stream. Those writers whose genius, though great, is not strictly and essentially poetic, become mediators between the votaries of art and the careless cravers for excitement.[2] Art herself, less manifestly glorious than in her periods of undisputed supremacy, retains her essential prerogatives, and forgets not to raise up chosen spirits who may minister to her state and vindicate her title.

One of the faithful Islâm, a poet in the truest and highest sense, we are anxious to present to our readers. He has yet written little and published less; but in these "preludes of a loftier strain"[3] we recognize the inspiring god. Mr. Tennyson belongs decidedly to the class we have already described as Poets of Sensation. He sees all the forms of nature with the "eruditus oculus," and his ear has a fairy fineness. There is a strange earnestness in his worship of beauty which throws a charm over his impassioned song, more easily felt than described, and not to be escaped by those who have once felt it. We think he has more definiteness and roundness of general conception than the late Mr. Keats, and is much more free from blemishes of diction and hasty capriccios of fancy. He has also this advantage over that poet and his friend Shelley, that he comes before the public unconnected with any political party or peculiar system of opinions. Nevertheless, true to the theory we have stated, we believe his participation in their characteristic excellences is sufficient to secure him a share of their unpopularity.

---

[1] "We are aware that this is not the right word, being appropriated by common use to a different signification. Those who think the caution given by Caesar should not stand in the way of urgent occasion, may substitute 'sensuous'; a word in use amongst our elder divines, and revived by a few bold writers in our own time." (Hallam's note.)

[2] "May we not compare them to the bright but unsubstantial clouds which, in still evenings, girdle the side of lofty mountains, and seem to form a natural connexion between the lowly vallies spread out beneath, and those isolated peaks that hold the 'last parley with the setting sun'?" (Hallam's note.)

[3] Shelley's *The Revolt of Islam*, "Dedication" 10.83.

The volume of "Poems, chiefly Lyrical," does not contain above 154 pages; but it shews us much more of the character of its parent mind, than many books we have known of much larger compass and more boastful pretensions. The features of original genius are clearly and strongly marked. The author imitates nobody; we recognise the spirit of his age, but not the individual form of this or that writer. His thoughts bear no more resemblance to Byron or Scott, Shelley or Coleridge, than to Homer or Calderon, Firdúsí or Calidasa.[1]

We have remarked five distinctive excellencies of his own manner. First, his luxuriance of imagination, and at the same time his control over it. Secondly his power of embodying himself in ideal characters, or rather moods of character, with such extreme accuracy of adjustment, that the circumstances of the narration seem to have a natural correspondence with the predominant feeling, and, as it were, to be evolved from it by assimilative force. Thirdly his vivid, picturesque delineation of objects, and the peculiar skill with which he holds all of them *fused*, to borrow a metaphor from science, in a medium of strong emotion. Fourthly, the variety of his lyrical measures, and exquisite modulation of harmonious words and cadences to the swell and fall of the feelings expressed. Fifthly, the elevated habits of thought, implied in these compositions, and imparting a mellow soberness of tone, more impressive, to our minds, than if the author had drawn up a set of opinions in verse, and sought to instruct the understanding rather than to communicate the love of beauty to the heart.

We shall proceed to give our readers some specimens in illustration of these remarks, and, if possible, we will give them entire; for no poet can be fairly judged of by fragments, least of all, a poet like Mr. Tennyson, whose mind conceives nothing isolated, nothing abrupt, but every part with reference to some other part, and in subservience to the idea of the whole.

Recollections of the Arabian Nights!—What a delightful, endearing title! How we pity those to whom it calls up no reminiscence of early enjoyment, no sentiment of kindliness as towards one who sings a song they have loved, or mentions with affection a departed friend! But let nobody expect a multifarious enumeration of Viziers, Barmecides, Fireworshippers, and Cadis;[2] trees that sing, horses that fly, and Goules that eat rice-pudding!

Our author knows what he is about; he has, with great judgment, selected our old acquaintance, "the good Haroun Alraschid," as the most prominent object of our childish interest, and with him has called up one of those luxurious garden scenes, the account of which, in plain prose, used to make our mouth water for sherbet, since luckily we were too young to think much about Zobeide![3] We think this poem will be the favourite among Mr. Tennyson's admirers; perhaps upon the whole it is our own; at least we find ourselves recurring to it oftener than to any other, and every time we read it, we feel the freshness of its beauty increase, and are inclined to exclaim with Madame de Sévigné, "*à force d'être ancien, il m'est nouveau.*"[4] But let us draw the curtain.

RECOLLECTIONS OF THE ARABIAN NIGHTS

> When the breeze of a joyful dawn blew free
> In the silken sail of infancy,
> The tide of time flow'd back with me,
>   The forward-flowing tide of time;
> 5 And many a sheeny summer-morn,

---

[1] Calderón (1600–81), Spanish dramatist; Firdúsí (c. 950–1020), Persian poet; Calidasa (third century AD.?), Indian poet and dramatist.

[2] characters in the *Arabian Nights*.

[3] Haroun-al-Raschid (763–809), caliph of Baghdad, appears in many of the tales. Zobeide was his wife.

[4] "Because it is old, it is new to me." Madame de Sévigny (1626–96), famous letter-writer.

Adown the Tigris I was borne,
By Bagdat's shrines of fretted gold,
High-walled gardens green and old;
True Mussulman was I and sworn,
10   For it was in the golden prime
       Of good Haroun Alraschid.

Anight my shallop, rustling thro'
The low and bloomed foliage, drove
The fragrant, glistening deeps, and clove
15 The citron-shadows in the blue;
By garden porches on the brim,
The costly doors flung open wide,
Gold glittering thro' lamplight dim,
And broider'd sofas on each side.
20   In sooth it was a goodly time,
     For it was in the golden prime
       Of good Haroun Alraschid.

Often, where clear-stemm'd platans guard
The outlet, did I turn away
25 The boat-head down a broad canal
From the main river sluiced, where all
The sloping of the moonlit sward
Was damask-work, and deep inlay
Of braided blooms unmown, which crept
30 Adown to where the water slept.
     A goodly place, a goodly time,
     For it was in the golden prime
       Of good Haroun Alraschid.

A motion from the river won
35 Ridged the smooth level, bearing on
My shallop thro' the star-strown calm,
Until another night in night
I enter'd, from the clearer light,
Imbower'd vaults of pillar'd palm,
40 Imprisoning sweets, which, as they clomb
Heavenward, were stay'd beneath the dome
     Of hollow boughs. A goodly time,
     For it was in the golden prime
       Of good Haroun Alraschid.

45 Still onward; and the clear canal
Is rounded to as clear a lake.
From the green rivage many a fall
Of diamond rillets musical,
Thro' little crystal arches low
50 Down from the central fountain's flow
Fallen silver-chiming, seemed to shake
The sparkling flints beneath the prow.
     A goodly place, a goodly time,
     For it was in the golden prime
55   Of good Haroun Alraschid.

Above thro' many a bowery turn
A walk with vari-colored shells
Wander'd engrain'd. On either side
All round about the fragrant marge
60 From fluted vase, and brazen urn
In order, eastern flowers large,
Some dropping low their crimson bells
Half-closed, and others studded wide
     With disks and tiars, fed the time
65   With odor in the golden prime
       Of good Haroun Alraschid.

Far off, and where the lemon grove
In closest coverture upsprung,
The living airs of middle night
70 Died round the bulbul as he sung;
Not he, but something which possess'd
The darkness of the world, delight,
Life, anguish, death, immortal love,
Ceasing not, mingled, unrepress'd,
75   Apart from place, withholding time,
     But flattering the golden prime
       Of good Haroun Alraschid.

Black the garden-bowers and grots
Slumber'd; the solemn palms were ranged
80 Above, unwoo'd of summer wind;
A sudden splendor from behind
Flush'd all the leaves with rich gold-green,
And, flowing rapidly between
Their interspaces, counterchanged
85 The level lake with diamond-plots

Of dark and bright. A lovely time,
For it was in the golden prime
    Of good Haroun Alraschid.

Dark-blue the deep sphere overhead,
90   Distinct with vivid stars inlaid,
Grew darker from that under-flame;
So, leaping lightly from the boat,
With silver anchor left afloat,
In marvel whence that glory came
95   Upon me, as in sleep I sank
In cool soft turf upon the bank,
    Entranced with that place and time,
    So worthy of the golden prime
      Of good Haroun Alraschid.

100 Thence thro' the garden I was drawn—
A realm of pleasance, many a mound,
And many a shadow-chequer'd lawn
Full of the city's stilly sound,
And deep myrrh-thickets blowing round
105 The stately cedar, tamarisks,
Thick rosaries of scented thorn,
Tall orient shrubs, and obelisks
    Graven with emblems of the time,
    In honor of the golden prime
110   Of good Haroun Alraschid.

With dazed vision unawares
From the long alley's latticed shade
Emerged, I came upon the great
Pavilion of the Caliphat.
115 Right to the carven cedarn doors,
Flung inward over spangled floors,
Broad-based flights of marble stairs
Ran up with golden balustrade,
    After the fashion of the time,
120   And humor of the golden prime
      Of good Haroun Alraschid.

The fourscore windows all alight
As with the quintessence of flame,
A million tapers flaring bright
125 From twisted silvers look'd to shame

The hollow-vaulted dark, and stream'd
Upon the mooned domes aloof
In inmost Bagdat, till there seem'd
Hundreds of crescents on the roof
130   Of night new-risen, that marvellous time
    To celebrate the golden prime
      Of good Haroun Alraschid.

Then stole I up, and trancedly
Gazed on the Persian girl alone,
135 Serene with argent-lidded eyes
Amorous, and lashes like to rays
Of darkness, and a brow of pearl
Tressed with redolent ebony,
In many a dark delicious curl,
140 Flowing beneath her rose-hued zone;
    The sweetest lady of the time,
    Well worthy of the golden prime
      Of good Haroun Alraschid.

Six columns, three on either side,
145 Pure silver, underpropt a rich
Throne of the massive ore, from which
Down-droop'd, in many a floating fold,
Engarlanded and diaper'd
With inwrought flowers, a cloth of gold.
150 Thereon, his deep eye laughter-stirr'd
With merriment of kingly pride,
    Sole star of all that place and time,
    I saw him—in his golden prime,
      THE GOOD HAROUN ALRASCHID

Criticism will sound but poorly after this; yet we cannot give silent votes. The first stanza, we beg leave to observe, places us at once in the position of feeling, which the poem requires. The scene is before us, around us; we cannot mistake its localities, or blind ourselves to its colours. That happy ductility of childhood returns for the moment; "true Mussulmans are we, and sworn," and yet there is a latent knowledge, which heightens the pleasure, that to our change from really childish thought we owe the capacities by which we enjoy the recollection.

As the poem proceeds, all is in perfect keeping. There is a solemn distinctness in every image, a majesty of slow motion in every cadence, that aids the illusion of thought, and steadies its contemplation of the complete picture. Originality of observation seems to cost nothing to our author's liberal genius; he lavishes images of exquisite accuracy and elaborate splendour, as a common writer throws about metaphorical truisms, and exhausted tropes. Amidst all the varied luxuriance of the sensations described, we are never permitted to lose sight of the idea which gives unity to this variety, and by the recurrence of which, as a sort of mysterious influence, at the close of every stanza, the mind is wrought up, with consummate art, to the final disclosure. This poem is a perfect gallery of pictures; and the concise boldness, with which in a few words an object is clearly painted, is sometimes (see the 6th stanza) majestic as Milton, sometimes (see the 12th) sublime as Aeschylus.

We have not, however, so far forgot our vocation as critics, that we would leave without notice the slight faults which adhere to this precious work. In the 8th stanza, we doubt the propriety of using the bold compound "black-green," at least in such close vicinity to "gold-green;" nor is it perfectly clear by the term, although indicated by the context, that "diamond plots" relates to shape rather than colour. We are perhaps very stupid, but "vivid stars unrayed" does not convey to us a very precise notion. "*Rosaries* of scented thorn," in the 10th stanza is, we believe, an entirely unauthorized use of the word. Would our author translate "*biferique rosaria Paesti*"—"And *rosaries* of Paestum, twice in bloom? [1]

To the beautiful 13th stanza we are sorry to find any objection; but even the bewitching loveliness of that "Persian girl" shall not prevent our performing the rigid duty we have undertaken, and we must hint to Mr. Tennyson that "redolent" is no synonyme for

"fragrant." Bees may be redolent *of* honey; spring may be "redolent *of* youth and love;" but the absolute use of the word has, we fear, neither in Latin nor English any better authority than the monastic epitaph on Fair Rosamund: "*Hic jacet in tombâ Rosa Mundi, non Rosa Munda, non redolet, sed olet, quae redolere solet.*"[2]

We are disposed to agree with Mr. Coleridge when he says "no adequate compensation can be made for the mischief a writer does by confounding the distinct senses of words."[3] At the same time our feelings in this instance rebel strongly in behalf of "redolent;" for the melody of the passage, as it stands, is beyond the possibility of improvement, and unless he should chance to light upon a word very nearly resembling this in consonants and vowels, we can hardly quarrel with Mr. Tennyson if, in spite of our judgment, he retains the offender in his service.

Our next specimen is of a totally different character, but not less complete, we think, in its kind. Have we among our readers any who delight in the heroic poems of Old England, the inimitable ballads? Any to whom Sir Patrick Spens, and Clym of the Clough, and Glorious Robin are consecrated names? Any who sigh with disgust at the miserable abortions of simpleness mistaken for simplicity, or florid weakness substituted for plain energy which they may often have seen dignified with the title of Modern Ballads?

Let such draw near and read *The Ballad of Oriana*. We know no more happy seizure of the antique spirit in the whole compass of our literature; yet there is no foolish self-desertion, no attempt at obliterating the present, but everywhere a full discrimination of how

---

[1] The translation is, in fact, correct.

[2] Rosamund Clifford, mistress of Henry II. "Here in this tomb lies the Rose of the World, not the lovely Rosa; she is no longer fragrant as she used to be but gives forth an offensive odor." Hallam's pedantic point is that this is the only authority one could cite for using "redolent" with the proposition "of" as a synonym for "fragrant."

[3] probably not a direct quotation, but a paraphrase of a familiar Coleridgian idea. "See "Aphorism 1" in "Prudential Aphorisms," *Aids to Reflection*.

much ought to be yielded and how much retained. The author is well aware that the art of one generation cannot *become* that of another by any will or skill; but the artist may transfer the spirit of the past, making it a temporary form for his own spirit, and so effect, by idealizing power, a new and legitimate combination. If we were asked to name among the real antiques that which bears greatest resemblance to this gem, we should refer to the ballad of *Fair Helen of Kirkconnel Lea* in the *Minstrelsy of the Scottish Border.*[1] It is a resemblance of mood, not of execution. They are both highly wrought lyrical expressions of pathos; and it is very remarkable with what intuitive art every expression and cadence in *Fair Helen* is accorded to the main feeling.

The characters that distinguish the language of our *lyrical* from that of our *epic* ballads have never yet been examined with the accuracy they deserve. But, beyond question, the class of poems which in point of harmonious combination *Oriana* most resembles, is the Italian. Just thus the meditative tenderness of Dante and Petrarch is embodied in the clear, searching notes of Tuscan song. These mighty masters produce two-thirds of their effect by *sound.* Not that they sacrifice sense to sound, but that sound conveys their meaning where words would not. There are innumerable shades of fine emotion in the human heart, especially when the senses are keen and vigilant, which are too subtle and too rapid to admit of corresponding phrases. The understanding takes no definite note of them; how then can they leave signatures in language? Yet they exist; in plenitude of being and beauty they exist; and in music they find a medium through which they pass from heart to heart. The tone becomes the sign of the feeling; and they reciprocally suggest each other.

Analogous to this suggestive power may be reckoned, perhaps, in a sister art, the effects of Venetian colouring. Titian *explains* by tints, as

Petrarch by tones. Words would not have done the business of the one, nor any groupings or *narration by form,* that of the other. But, shame upon us! we are going back to our metaphysics, when that "sweet, meek face" is waiting to be admitted.

THE BALLAD OF ORIANA

My heart is wasted with my woe,
    Oriana.
There is no rest for me below,
    Oriana.
5 When the long dun wolds are ribb'd with snow,
And loud the Norland whirlwinds blow,
    Oriana,
Alone I wander to and fro,
    Oriana.

10 Ere the light on dark was growing,
    Oriana,
At midnight the cock was crowing,
    Oriana;
Winds were blowing, waters flowing,
15 We heard the steeds to battle going,
    Oriana,
Aloud the hollow bugle blowing,
    Oriana.

In the yew-wood black as night,
20   Oriana,
Ere I rode into the fight,
    Oriana,
While blissful tears blinded my sight
By star-shine and by moonlight,
25   Oriana,
I to thee my troth did plight,
    Oriana.

She stood upon the castle wall,
    Oriana;
30 She watch'd my crest among them all,
    Oriana;
She saw me fight, she heard me call,

---

[1] edited by Sir Walter Scott, 1802–03.

When forth there stept a foeman tall,
    Oriana,
35 Atween me and the castle wall,
    Oriana.

The bitter arrow went aside,
    Oriana;
The false, false arrow went aside,
40   Oriana;
The damned arrow glanced aside,
And pierced thy heart, my love, my bride,
    Oriana!
Thy heart, my life, my love, my bride,
45   Oriana!

O, narrow, narrow was the space,
    Oriana!
Loud, loud rung out the bugle's brays,
    Oriana.
50 O, deathful stabs were dealt apace.
The battle deepen'd in its place,
    Oriana;
But I was down upon my face,
    Oriana.

55 They should have stabb'd me where I lay,
    Oriana!
How could I rise and come away,
    Oriana?
How could I look upon the day?
60 They should have stabb'd me where I lay,
    Oriana—
They should have trod me into clay,
    Oriana.

O breaking heart that will not break,
65   Oriana!
O pale, pale face so sweet and meek,
    Oriana!
Thou smilest, but thou dost not speak,
And then the tears run down my cheek,
70   Oriana.
What wantest thou? whom dost thou seek,
    Oriana?

I cry aloud; none hear my cries,
    Oriana.
75 Thou comest atween me and the skies,
    Oriana
I feel the tears of blood arise
Up from my heart unto my eyes,
    Oriana.
80 Within thy heart my arrow lies,
    Oriana!

O cursed hand! O cursed blow!
    Oriana!
O happy thou that liest low,
85   Oriana!
All night the silence seems to flow
Beside me in my utter woe,
    Oriana.
A weary, weary way I go,
90   Oriana!

When Norland winds pipe down the sea,
    Oriana,
I walk, I dare not think of thee,
    Oriana.
95 Thou liest beneath the greenwood tree,
I dare not die and come to thee,
    Oriana.
I hear the roaring of the sea,
    Oriana.

We have heard it objected to this poem that the name occurs once too often in every stanza. We have taken the plea into our judicial consideration, and the result is that we overrule it and pronounce that the proportion of the melodious cadences to the pathetic parts of the narration could not be diminished without materially affecting the rich lyrical impression of the ballad.

For what is the author's intention? To gratify our curiosity with a strange adventure? To shake our nerves with a painful story? Very far from it. Tears indeed may "blind our sight" as we read; but they are "blissful tears." The strong musical delight prevails over every painful feeling and mingles them all in its deep swell until they attain a composure of exalted sorrow, a mood in which the latest repose of agitation becomes visible, and the influence of beauty spreads like light over the surface of the mind.

The last line, with its dreamy wildness, reveals the design of the whole. It is transferred, if we mistake not, from an old ballad (a freedom of immemorial usage with ballad-mongers, as our readers doubtless know) but the merit lies in the abrupt application of it to the leading sentiment, so as to flash upon us in a few little words a world of meaning, and to consecrate the passion that was beyond cure or hope by resigning it to the accordance of inanimate Nature, who, like man, has her tempests and occasions of horror, but august in their largeness of operation, awful by their dependence on a fixed and perpetual necessity.

We must give one more extract, and we are almost tempted to choose by lot among many that crowd on our recollection, and solicit our preference with such witchery as it is not easy to withstand. The poems towards the middle of the volume seem to have been written at an earlier period than the rest. They display more unrestrained fancy and are less evidently proportioned to their ruling ideas than those which we think of later date. Yet in the *Ode to Memory*—the only one which we have the poet's authority for referring to early life—there is a majesty of expression, united to a truth of thought, which almost confounds our preconceived distinctions.

The *Confessions of a Second-rate, Sensitive Mind* are full of deep insight into human nature, and into those particular trials which are sure to beset men who think and feel for themselves at this epoch of social development. The title is perhaps ill-chosen. Not only has it an appearance of quaintness which has no sufficient reason, but it seems to us incorrect. The mood portrayed in this poem, unless the admirable skill of delineation has deceived us, is rather the

clouded season of a strong mind than the habitual condition of one feeble and "second-rate." Ordinary tempers build up fortresses of opinion on one side or another; they will see only what they choose to see. The distant glimpse of such agony as is here brought out to view is sufficient to keep them for ever in illusions, voluntarily raised at first, but soon trusted in with full reliance as inseparable parts of self.

Mr. Tennyson's mode of "rating" is different from ours. He may esteem none worthy of the first order who has not attained a complete universality of thought, and such trustful reliance on a principle of repose which lies beyond the war of conflicting opinions, that the grand ideas, "*qui planent sans cesse au dessus de l'humanité,*"[1] cease to affect him with bewildering impulses of hope and fear. We have not space to enter further into this topic; but we should not despair of convincing Mr. Tennyson that such a position of intellect would not be the most elevated, nor even the most conducive to perfection of art.

The "How" and the "Why" appears to present the reverse of the same picture. It is the same mind still: the sensitive sceptic, whom we have looked upon in his hour of distress, now scoffing at his own state with an earnest mirth that borders on sorrow. It is exquisitely beautiful to see in this, as in the former portrait, how the feeling of art is kept ascendant in our minds over distressful realities, by constant reference to images of tranquil beauty, whether touched pathetically, as the Ox and the Lamb in the first piece, or with fine humour, as the "great bird" and "little bird" in the second.

The Sea Fairies is another strange title; but those who turn to it with the very natural curiosity of discovering who these new births of mythology may be, will be unpardonable if they do not linger over it with higher feelings. A stretch of lyrical power is here exhibited which we did not think the English language had possessed. The proud swell of verse as the

---

[1] ideas "which soar forever above humanity."

harp tones "run up the ridged sea," and the soft and melancholy lapse as the sounds die along the widening space of water, are instances of that right imitation which is becoming to art, but which in the hands of the unskilful, or the affecters of easy popularity, is often converted into a degrading mimicry, detrimental to the best interests of the imagination.

A considerable portion of this book is taken up with a very singular and very beautiful class of poems on which the author has evidently bestowed much thought and elaboration. We allude to the female characters, every trait of which presumes an uncommon degree of observation and reflection. Mr. Tennyson's way of proceeding seems to be this. He collects the most striking phenomena of individual minds until he arrives at some leading fact, which allows him to lay down an axiom or law; and then, working on the law thus attained, he clearly discerns the tendency of what new particulars his invention suggests, and is enabled to impress an individual freshness and unity on ideal combinations. These expressions of character are brief and coherent; nothing extraneous to the dominant fact is admitted, nothing illustrative of it, and, as it were, growing out of it, is rejected. They are like summaries of mighty dramas. We do not say this method admits of such large luxuriance of power as that of our real dramatists; but we contend that it is a new species of poetry, a graft of the lyric on the dramatic, and Mr. Tennyson deserves the laurel of an inventor, an enlarger of our modes of knowledge and power.

We must hasten to make our election; so, passing by the "airy, fairy Lilian," who "clasps her hands" in vain to retain us; the "stately flower" of matronly fortitude, "revered Isabel"; Madeline, with her voluptuous alternation of smile and frown; Mariana, last, but oh not least—we swear by the memory of Shakespeare, to whom a monument of observant love has here been raised by simply expanding all the latent meanings and beauties contained in one stray

thought of his genius[1]—we shall fix on a lovely, albeit somewhat mysterious lady, who has fairly taken our "heart from out our breast."

ADELINE

I

Mystery of mysteries,
    Faintly smiling Adeline,
    Scarce of earth nor all divine,
Nor unhappy, nor at rest,
    But beyond expression fair
    With thy floating flaxen hair;
Thy rose-lips and full blue eyes
    Take the heart from out my breast.
    Wherefore those dim looks of thine,
    Shadowy, dreaming Adeline?

II

Whence that aery bloom of thine,
    Like a lily which the sun
Looks thro' in his sad decline,
    And a rose-bush leans upon,
Thou that faintly smilest still,
    As a Naiad in a well,
    Looking at the set of day,
Or a phantom two hours old
    Of a maiden past away,
Ere the placid lips be cold?
Wherefore those faint smiles of thine,
    Spiritual Adeline?

III

What hope or fear or joy is thine?
Who talketh with thee, Adeline?
    For sure thou art not all alone.
      Do beating hearts of salient springs
    Keep measure with thine own?
    Hast thou heard the butterflies

---

[1] Tennyson's epigraph under the title of "Mariana" is from Shakespeare's *Measure for Measure* 3.1.277: "Mariana in the moated grange."

What they say betwixt their wings?
     Or in stillest evenings
With what voice the violet woos
To his heart the silver dews?
     Or when little airs arise,
     How the merry bluebell rings
To the mosses underneath?
     Hast thou look'd upon the breath
     Of the lilies at sunrise?
Wherefore that faint smile of thine,
Shadowy, dreaming Adeline?

IV

Some honey-converse feeds thy mind,
     Some spirit of a crimson rose
     In love with thee forgets to close
     His curtains, wasting odorous sighs
All night long on darkness blind.
What aileth thee? whom waitest thou
With thy soften'd, shadow'd brow,
          And those dew-lit eyes of thine,
          Thou faint smiler, Adeline?

V

Lovest thou the doleful wind
     When thou gazest at the skies?
Doth the low tongued Orient
     Wander from the side of the morn
     Dripping with Sabæan spice
On thy pillow, lowly bent
     With melodious airs lovelorn,
Breathing Light against thy face,
While his locks a-drooping twined
Round thy neck in subtle ring
Make a carcanet of rays,
     And ye talk together still,
In the language wherewith Spring
     Letters cowslips on the hill?
Hence that look and smile of thine,
     Spiritual Adeline.

Is not this beautiful? When this Poet dies, will not the Graces and the Loves mourn over him,

"*fortunatâque favilla nascentur violae.*[1] How original is the imagery, and how delicate! How wonderful the new world thus created for us, the region between real and unreal! The gardens of Armida[2] were but poorly musical compared with the roses and lillies that bloom around thee, thou faint smiler, Adeline, on whom the glory of imagination reposes, endowing all thou lookest on with sudden and mysterious life. We could expatiate on the deep meaning of this poem, but it is time to twitch our critical mantles; and, as our trade is not that of mere enthusiasm, we shall take our leave with an objection (perhaps a cavil) to the language of the cowslips, which we think too ambiguously spoken of for a subject on which nobody, except Mr. Tennyson, can have any information. The "ringing bluebell," too, if it be not a pun, suggests one, and might probably be altered to advantage.

One word more before we have done, and it shall be a word of praise. The language of this book, with one or two rare exceptions, is thorough and sterling English. A little more respect, perhaps, was due to the "*jus et norma loquendi*";[3] but we are inclined to consider as venial a fault arising from generous enthusiasm for the principles of sound analogy, and for that Saxon element, which constituted the intrinsic freedom and nervousness of our native tongue. We see no signs in what Mr. Tennyson has written of the Quixotic spirit which has led some persons to desire the reduction of English to a single form, by excluding nearly the whole of Latin and Roman derivatives. Ours is necessarily a compound language; as such alone it can flourish and increase; nor will the author of the poems we have extracted be likely to barter for a barren appearance of symmetrical structure that fertility of expression and variety of har-

---

[1] "Violets will be born from these blest ashes": Persius, *Satires* 1. 39–40

[2] Armida, in Tasso's *Jerusalem Delivered*, lured Christians who were attacking the Holy City into gardens.

[3] "the right and rule of speech" from Horace, *Ars Poetica*, l. 72.

mony which "the speech that Shakspeare spoke" derived from the sources of southern phraseology.

In presenting this young poet to the public as one not studious of instant popularity, nor likely to obtain it, we may be thought to play the part of a fashionable lady who deludes her refractory mate into doing what she chooses by pretending to wish the exact contrary; or of a cunning pedagogue who practises a similar manoeuvre on some self-willed Flibbertigibbet[1] of the school room. But the supposition would do us wrong. We have spoken in good faith, commending this volume to feeling hearts and imaginative tempers, not to the stupid readers, or the voracious readers, or the malignant readers, or the readers after dinner!

We confess, indeed, we never knew an instance in which the theoretical abjurers of popularity have shewn themselves very reluctant to admit its actual advances. So much virtue is not, perhaps, in human nature; and if the world should take a fancy to buy up these poems, in order to be revenged on the *Englishman's Magazine,*[2] who knows whether even we might not disappoint its malice by a cheerful adaptation of our theory to "existing circumstances?"
—1831

---

[1] devil.

[2] the periodical in which this review appeared.

Letitia E. Landon
L.E.L.
1802 – 1838

Letitia Elizabeth Landon, the poet and novelist well known in her own time as L.E.L., was born in Chelsea. She wrote to support her family, producing, tirelessly, five volumes of poetry in seven years: *The Fate of Adelaide* (1821), *The Improvisatrice* (1824), *The Troubadour* (1825), *The Golden Violet* (1827), and *The Venetian Bracelet, the Lost Pleiad, A History of the Lyre, and Other Poems* (1828). Landon embraces the Romantic aesthetic of spontaneity, yet tends to elaborate typically Victorian topics (indulging at times in excesses of Victorian sentimentality). As well as poetry, she published four novels between 1831 and 1838. She married George Maclean, the colonial governor of Cape Coast Castle in Ghana, and accompanied him back to the Gold Coast despite rumours that Maclean was a bigamist. Four months later, L.E.L. was found dead in her room with a bottle of prussic acid in her hand.

&c&c&c

On the Ancient and Modern Influence of Poetry [1]

It is curious to observe how little one period resembles another. Centuries are the children of one mighty family, but there is no family-likeness between them. We ourselves are standing on the threshold of a new era, and we are already hastening to make as wide a space, mark as vast a difference as possible, between our own age and its predecessor. Whatever follies we may go back upon, whatever opinions we may re-adopt, they are never those which have gone *immediately* before us. Already there is a wide gulph between the last century and the present. In religion, in philosophy, in politics, in manners, there has passed a great change; but in none has been worked a greater change than in poetry, whether as it regards the art itself, or the general feeling towards it. The decline and fall of that Roman empire of the mind seems now advanced as an historical fact; while we are equally ready to admit that some twenty years since the republic was in its plenitude of power. In the meantime a new set of aspirants have arisen, and a new set of opinions are to be won. But it is from the past that we best judge of the present; and perhaps we shall more accurately say what poetry is by referring to what it has been.

Poetry in every country has had its origin in three sources, connected with the strongest feelings belonging to the human mind—Religion, War, and Love. The mysteries of the present; the still greater mysteries of the future; the confession of some superior power so deeply felt; higher impulses speaking so strongly of some spiritual influence of a purer order than those of our common wants and wishes;—these all found words and existence in poetry. The vainest fictions of mythology were the strongest possible evidence how necessary to the ignorance of humanity was the belief of a superior power; so entire was the interior conviction, that sooner than believe in nothing no belief was too absurd for adoption. The imagination, which is the source of poetry, has in every country been the beginning as well as the ornament of civilization. It civilizes because it refines. A general view of its influence in the various quarters of the globe will place this in the most striking point of view.

Africa is the least civilized quarter of the globe, not so much from its savage as from its apathetic

[1] from *New Monthly Magazine* Vol. 35, November 1832.

state; one could almost believe that it had been formed from the dregs of the other parts. Now, the distinguishing mark of its deficiency in that soil of mind wherewith the intellect works, is its total want of imagination. It is the only great portion of the world which is not emphatically made known to us by its own peculiar religion. Her mythology was the earthly immortality of Greece. Greece is indelibly linked with the idea of civilization; but all those fine and graceful beliefs which made its springs holy places, and haunted the fragrant life of every flower and leaf, were the creations of its earliest time. Look from thence to the fierce regions of the North,—how full is the Scandinavian faith of the wild and wonderful! or to the East, how gorgeous their tales of enchantment, with their delicate Peris, and the fallen and fearful spirits in their subterranean caverns! —again, the faith of Brahma, with its thousand deities. Or, to cross the wide Atlantic, there are the vestiges of a terrible creed yet touched with something of spiritual loveliness, in their singing-birds bringing tidings of the departed, and in the green hunting-grounds which made their future hope. Each and all these creeds are the work and wonder of the imagination—but in these Africa has no part. No august belief fills with beauty or terror the depths of her forests, and no fallen temple makes its site sacred though in ruins. Her creeds have neither beauty nor grandeur. The Devil is their principal Deity, and their devotion is born of physical fear. Other nations have had their various faiths, created and coloured by the scenes which gave them birth. The religion of Greece was beautiful as her own myrtle and olive groves. The Scandinavian was like its own wild mountains and snowy wastes, with just gleams of beauty from its starry nights and meteors. The Arabian was glowing and magnificent as the summer earth and radiant sky of its believers; while that of the American Indian was terrible as the huge serpents and the interminable forests which gave shelter to its mysteries. But in Africa the sunny

sky, the noble rivers, the woods, splendid in size and foliage, have been without their wonted effect. Slaves from the earliest period, the very superstitions of her sable sons are mean fears caught from their masters; all about them is earthly, utterly unredeemed by those spiritual awakenings which are as lights from another world. We might believe that some great original curse has been said over them, and that they are given over into the hand of man and not of God. And in simple truth that curse has been slavery. The Helots[1] even of Greece were uninspired. "A slave cannot be eloquent," said Longinus;[2] nor poetical either—the wells of his enthusiasm are dried up. What some ancient writer says of iron may be applied to Poetry—its use is the first step to civilization, and civilization is freedom.

Next to Religion War was the great source of poetry; and the deeds of the brave were sung in that spirit of encouragement which one man will ever receive from the praise bestowed on the deeds of another, when he meditates similar achievements of his own. And here we may be permitted a few words on what we cannot but consider an unjust and erroneous opinion, now much insisted upon,—that poets and conquerors have been equal enemies of the human race—the one but acting what the other praised; and that the sin of encouragement was equal, if not greater, than that of commission. In answer to this we must observe that it is not fair to judge of former actions by our present standard. Our first view of society is always the same: we see the human race dwelling in small dispersed sets, with rude habits, the results of hardships and of dangers. A more favourable situation, or, more commonly, the influence of some superior mind, which from the wonderful effects produced by a single man is often a nation's history: these or similar causes first placed some of the tribes in positions of comparative

---

[1] a member of the lowest class of serfs in ancient Sparta.

[2] Greek philosopher and rhetorician (213?–73 AD).

comfort and advancement. This position would of course be envied by their savage and starving neighbours, who would consider brute force the only means of sharing their advantages. Single motives never last: ambition, aggrandisement, conquest with a view to security, soon gave a thousand motives to warfare that had originally began in want and self-defence. It has required centuries so to consolidate kingdoms that now a breathing space is allowed for reflection on the sin of sacrificing man's most valuable possession—life. But what part has the poet taken in these scenes of bloodshed? One certainly of amelioration. If he has sung of conquerors, the qualities held up to admiration were those of magnanimity and generosity. He has spoken of the love and liberty as holding light the love of life; and the highest eulogium of a warrior was that he died in defence of his native country. But to give our assertion the support of an example.—Perhaps the spirit which animates, the desire which excites, the power which supports, a conqueror, were never more entirely personified than in Xerxes.[1] He possessed to the utmost that grasping ambition, that carelessness of human blood, which characterize the mere conqueror; yet with all the purple pomp of his power, we are not aware of his having been held up otherwise than in reprobation, while the whole world has been filled with the fame of his brave opposers; and the names of those who fell at Marathon are still the watchwords of freedom. Again, in the days of chivalry, what were the qualities the minstrel lauded in the knight?—his valour, certainly, but still more his courtesy, his protection of the weak against the strong, his devotion, his truth;—till the "ungentle knight" was almost as much a phrase of disgrace as that of the "recreant."

Love was the third great fountain of poetry's inspiration; and who that has ever loved will deny the necessity of a language, beyond the working-day

tongue of our ordinary run of hopes and fears, to express feelings which have so little in common with them. What has been the most popular love-poetry in all countries?—that which gave expression to its spiritual and better part—constancy kept like a holy thing—blessings on the beloved one, though in that blessing we have ourselves no share; or sad and affectionate regrets in whose communion our own nature grows more kindly from its sympathy. We are always the better for entering into other's sorrow or other's joy.

The whole origin and use of poetry may be expressed in a few brief words: it originates in that idea of superior beauty and excellence inherent in every nature—and it is employed to keep that idea alive; and the very belief in excellence is one cause of its existence. When we speak of poetry as the fountain whence youth draws enthusiasm for its hopes,— where the warrior strengthens his courage, and the lover his faith,—the treasury where the noblest thoughts are garnered,—the archives where the noblest deeds are recorded,—we but express an old belief. One of our great reviews—the "Westminster"—in speaking of the fine arts, &c. says, "The aristocracy do well to encourage poetry: it is by fiction themselves exist—and what is poetry but fiction?" We deny that poetry is fiction; its merit and its power lie alike in its truth: to one heart the aspiring and elevated will come home; to another the simple and natural: the key-note to one will be the voice of memory, which brings back young affections—early confidence,—hill and valley yet glad with the buoyant step which once past over them,—flowers thrice lovely from thoughts indelibly associated with their leaf or breath: such as these are touched by all that restores, while it recalls, days whose enjoyment would have been happiness, could they but have had the knowledge of experience without its weariness. To another, poetry will be a vision and a delight, because the virtue of which he dreams is there realized—and because the "love

---

[1] king of Persia (486–65 BC).

which his spirit has painted" is to be found in its pages. But in each and all cases the deep well of sympathy is only to be found when the hazel rod is poised by the hand of truth. And, till some moral steam is discovered as potent as that now so active in the physical world, vain will be the effort to regulate mankind like machinery: there will ever be spiritual awakenings, and deep and tender thoughts, to turn away from the hurry and highways of life, and whose place of refuge will still be the green paths and pleasant waters of poesy. That tribes of worse than idle followers have crowded the temple, and cast the dust they brought around the soiled altar,—that many have profaned their high gift to base use—that poetry has often turned aside from its divine origin and diviner end,—is what must be equally admitted and lamented; but who will deny that our best and most popular (indeed in this case best and popular are equivalent terms) poetry makes its appeal to the higher and better feelings of our nature, and not a poet but owes his fame to that which best deserves it? What a code of pure and beautiful morality, applicable to almost every circumstance, might be drawn from Shakspeare!

The influence of poetry has two eras,—first as it tends to civilize; secondly as it tends to prevent that very civilization from growing too cold and too selfish. Its first is its period of action; its second is that of feeling and reflection: it is that second period which at present exists. On the mere principle of utility, in our wide and weary world, with its many sorrows and more cares, how anxiously we ought to keep open every source of happiness! and who among us does not recollect some hour when a favourite poet spread before us a page like that of a magician's; when some expression has seemed like the very echo of our feelings; how often and with what a sensation of pleasure have long-remembered passages sprang to our lips; how every natural beauty has caught a fresh charm from being linked with some associate verse! Who that has these or similar recollections but would

keep the ear open, and the heart alive, to the "song that lightens the languid way!"

Why one age should be more productive in poetry than another is one of those questions—a calculation of the mental longitude—likely to remain unanswered. That peculiar circumstances do not create the poet is proved by the fact, that only one individual is so affected: if it were mere circumstance, it would affect alike all who are brought within its contact. What confirmation of this theory (if theory it be) is to be found in the history of all poets!—where are we to seek the cause which made them such, if not in their own minds? We daily see men living amid beautiful scenery; and scenery is much dwelt upon by the advocates of circumstance. Switzerland is a most beautiful country, yet what great poet has it ever produced? The spirit which in ancient days peopled grove and mountain with Dryad and Oread,[1] or, in modern times, with associations, must be in him who sees, not in the object seen. How many there are, leading a life of literary leisure, living in a romantic country, and writing poetry all their days, who yet go down to their unremembered graves no more poets than if they had never turned a stanza! While, on the other hand, we see men with every obstacle before them, with little leisure and less encouragement, yet force their upward way, make their voice heard, and leave their memory in imperishable song. Take Burns for an example: much stress has been laid on the legendary ballads he was accustomed to hear from infancy; but if these were so potent, why did they not inspire his brother as well as himself? Mr. Gilbert Burns is recorded, by every biographer, to have been a sensible, and even a superior man; he dwelt in the same country—he heard the same songs—why was he not a poet too? There can be but one answer, —there was not that inherent quality in his mind which there was in his brother's. Many young men

---

[1]   in Greek mythology, wood nymph and mountain nymph.

are born to a higher name than fortune—many spend their youth amid the most exciting scenes—yet why do none of these turn out a Byron, but for some innate first cause? What made Milton in old age,—in sickness, in poverty—depressed by all that would have weighed to the very dust an ordinary man—without one of man's ordinary encouragements,—what could have made him turn to the future as to a home, collect his glorious energies, and finish a work, the noblest aid ever given to the immortality of a language? What, but that indefinable spirit, whose enthusiasm is nature's own gift to the poet. *Poeta nascitur non fit*[1] is, like many other old truths, the very truth after all.

We cannot but consider that, though some be still among us, our own great poets belong to another age. Their fame is established, and their horde of imitators have dispersed; those wearying followers who, to use the happy expression of a contemporary writer, "think that breaking the string is bending the bow of Ulysses." We hear the daily complaints of the want of present taste and talent for poetry: we are more prepared to admit the latter than the former. In the most sterile times of the imagination, love of poetry has never been lacking; the taste may have been bad, but still the taste existed. Wordsworth truly says, "that, with the young, poetry is a passion;" and there will always be youth in the world to indulge the hopes, and feel the warm and fresh emotions, which their fathers have found to be vain, or have utterly exhausted. To these, poetry will ever be a natural language; and it is the young who make the reputation of a poet. We soon lose that keen delight, which marvels if others share not in it: the faculty of appreciation is the first which leaves us. It is tact rather than feeling which enables experience to foresee the popularity of a new poet. As to the alleged want of taste, we only refer to the editions of established authors which still find purchasers: one

has just appeared of Scott, another of Byron. With what enthusiasm do some set up Wordsworth for an idol, and others Shelley! But this taste is quite another feeling to that which creates; and the little now written possesses beauty not originality. The writers do not set their own mark on their property: one might have put forth the work of the other, or it might be that of their predecessors. This was not the case some few years ago. Who could have mistaken the picturesque and chivalric page of Scott for the impassioned one of Byron? or who could for a moment have hesitated as to whether a poem was marked with the actual and benevolent philosophy of Wordsworth, or the beautiful but ideal theory of Shelley? We are now producing no great or original (the words are synonymous) poet. We have graceful singing in the bower, but no voice that startles us into wonder, and hurries us forth to see whose trumpet is awakening the land. We know that when the snow has long lain, warming and fertilizing the ground, and when the late summer comes, hot and clear, the rich harvest will be abundant under such genial influences. Perhaps poetry too may have its atmosphere; and a long cold winter may be needed for its glad and glorious summer. The soil of song, like that of earth, may need rest for renewal. Again we repeat, that though the taste be not, the spirit of the day is, adverse to the production of poetry. Selfishness is its principle, indifference its affectation, and ridicule its commonplace. We allow no appeals save to our reason, or to our fear of laughter. We must either be convinced or sneered into things. Neither calculation nor sarcasm are the elements for poetry. A remark made by Scott to one of his great compeers shows how he knew the age in which he was fated to end his glorious career:—"Ah—it is well that we have made our reputation!" The personal is the destroyer of the spiritual; and to the former everything is now referred. We talk of the author's self more than his works, and we know his name rather than his writings. There is a base maca-

---

[1] a poet is born, not made.

damizing spirit in literature; we seek to level all the high places of old. But till we can deny that fine "farther looking hope" which gives such a charm to Shakspeare's confessional sonnets; till we can deny that "The Paradise Lost" was the work of old age, poverty, and neglect, roused into delightful exertion by a bright futurity; till we can deny the existence of those redeemers of humanity—we must admit, also, the existence of a higher, more prophetic, more devoted and self-relying spirit than is to be accounted for on the principles either of vanity or of lucre: we shall be compelled to admit that its inspiration is, indeed,

> "A heavenly breath
> Along an earthly lyre." [1]

Methinks there are some mysteries in the soul on whose precincts it were well to "tread with unsandalled foot." [2] Poetry like religion requires faith, and we are the better and happier for yielding it. The imagination is to the mind what life is to the body—its vivifying and active part. In antiquity, poetry had to create, it now has to preserve. Its first effort was against barbarism, its last is against selfishness. A world of generous emotions, of kindly awakenings, those

> "Which bid the perished pleasures move
> In mournful mockery o'er the soul of love;" [3]

a world of thought and feeling, now lies in the guardianship of the poet. These are they who sit in the gate called the beautiful, which leads to the temple. Its meanest priests should feel that their office is sacred. Enthusiasm is no passion of the drawing-room, or of the pence-table: its home is the heart, and its hope is afar. This is too little the creed of our generation; yet, without such creed, poetry has neither present life nor future immortality. As Whitehead [4] finely says in his poem of "The Solitary,"—

> "Not for herself, not for the wealth she brings,
> Is the muse wooed and won, but for the deep,
>   Occult, profound, unfathomable things,—
> The engine of our tears whene'er we weep,
> The impulse of our dreams whene'er we sleep,
>   The mysteries that our sad hearts possess,
> Which, and the keys whereof, the Muse doth keep,—
>   Oh! to kindle soft humanity, to raise,
> With gentle strength infused, the spirit bowed;
>   To pour a second sunlight on our days,
> And draw the restless lightning from our cloud;
> To cheer the humble and to dash the proud.
>   Besought in peace to live, in peace to die,—
>   The poet's task is done—Oh, Immortality!"

He is only a true poet, who can say, in the words of Coleridge, "My task has been my delight; I have not looked either to guerdon or praise, and to me Poetry is its own exceeding great reward." [5]

—1832

---

[1] not identified.

[2] not identified.

[3] not identified.

---

[4] William Whitehead (1715–85), a minor eighteenth-century poet.

[5] source in Coleridge not identified.

John Stuart Mill
1806 – 1873

John Stuart Mill was born in London and was educated at home by his father, James Mill. He began studying Greek at the age of three, and before entering his teens he was intensely involved with the study of calculus, political economy, and logic. In 1820–21 he lived in France, attending university lectures at Montpellier. When he returned to London, he joined his father in the Examiner's Office of the East India Company which, like his father, he eventually headed. Mill was one of the leading British philosophers of the nineteenth century. His works include the two-volume *System of Logic* (1843), *Principles of Political Economy* (1848), *On Liberty* (1859), *Utilitarianism* (1863), and *The Subjection of Women* (1869). Raised by his father to believe in the Benthamite principles of Utilitarianism, Mill later realized that such a rationalistic upbringing sorely neglected emotional development (see his *Autobiography* [1873]). In "What is Poetry?" (1833), Mill argues for the importance of poetry, which appeals to the senses, in contrast to science, which addresses belief.

❦

"What is Poetry?" [1]

It has often been asked, what is poetry? And many and various are the answers which have been returned. The vulgarest of all—one with which no person possessed of the faculties to which poetry addresses itself can ever have been satisfied—is that which confounds poetry with metrical composition: yet to this wretched mockery of a definition, many have been led back, by the failure of all their attempts to find any other that would distinguish what they have been accustomed to call poetry, from much which they have known only under other names.

That, however, the word *poetry* does import something quite peculiar in its nature, something which may exist in what is called prose as well as in verse, something which does not even require the instrument of words, but can speak, through those other audible symbols called musical sounds, and even through the visible ones, which are the language of sculpture, painting, and architecture; all this, as we believe, is and must be felt, though perhaps indistinctly, by all upon whom poetry in any of its shapes produces any impression beyond that of tickling the ear. To the mind, poetry is either nothing, or it is the better part of all art whatever, and of real life too; and the distinction between poetry and what is not poetry, whether explained or not, is felt to be fundamental.

Where everyone feels a difference, a difference there must be. All other appearance may be fallacious, but the appearance of a difference is itself a real difference. Appearances too, like other things, must have a cause, and that which can cause anything, even an illusion, must be a reality. And hence, while a half-philosophy disdains the classifications and distinctions indicated by popular language, philosophy carried to its highest point may frame new ones, but never sets aside the old, content with correcting and regularizing them. It cuts fresh channels for thought, but it does not fill up such as it finds ready-made, but traces, on the contrary, more deeply, broadly, and distinctly, those into which the current has spontaneously flowed.

Let us then attempt, in the way of modest inquiry, not to coerce and confine nature within the bounds of an arbitrary definition, but rather to find the boundaries which she herself has set, and erect a barrier round them; not calling mankind to account

---

[1] first published in January 1833, in the *Monthly Repository*. This, and the article which follows, were signed "Antiquus." They were revised and published together in 1867 under the title "Poetry and Its Varieties."

for having misapplied the word *poetry*, but attempting to clear up to them the conception which they already attach to it, and to bring before their minds as a distinct principle that which, as a vague feeling, has really guided them in their actual employment of the term.

The object of poetry is confessedly to act upon the emotions; and therein is poetry sufficiently distinguished from what Wordsworth affirms to be its logical opposite, namely, not prose, but matter of fact or science.[1] The one addresses itself to the belief, the other to the feelings. The one does its work by convincing or persuading, the other by moving. The one acts by presenting a proposition to the understanding, the other by offering interesting objects of contemplation to the sensibilities.

This, however, leaves us very far from a definition of poetry. We have distinguished it from one thing, but we are bound to distinguish it from everything. To present thoughts or images to the mind for the purpose of acting upon the emotions, does not belong to poetry alone. It is equally the province (for example) of the novelist: and yet the faculty of the poet and the faculty of the novelist are as distinct as any other two faculties; as the faculty of the novelist and of the orator, or of the poet and the metaphysician. The two characters may be united, as characters the most disparate may; but they have no natural connection.

Many of the finest poems are in the form of novels, and in almost all good novels there is true poetry. But there is a radical distinction between the interest felt in a novel as such, and the interest excited by poetry; for the one is derived from incident, the other from the representation of feeling. In one, the source of the emotion excited is the exhibition of a state or states of human sensibility; in the other, of a series of states of mere outward circumstances. Now, all minds are capable of being affected more or less by

representations of the latter kind, and all, or almost all, by those of the former; yet the two sources of interest correspond to two distinct and (as respects their greatest development) mutually exclusive characters of mind. So much is the nature of poetry dissimilar to the nature of fictitious narrative, that to have a really strong passion for either of the two, seems to presuppose or to superinduce a comparative indifference to the other.

At what age is the passion for a story, for almost any kind of story, merely as a story, the most intense? In childhood. But that also is the age at which poetry, even of the simplest description, is least relished and least understood; because the feelings with which it is especially conversant are yet undeveloped, and not having been even in the slightest degree experienced, cannot be sympathized with. In what stage of the progress of society, again, is storytelling most valued, and the storyteller in greatest request and honor? In a rude state; like that of the Tartars and Arabs at this day, and of almost all nations in the earliest ages. But in this state of society there is little poetry except ballads, which are mostly narrative, that is, essentially stories, and derive their principal interest from the incidents. Considered as poetry, they are of the lowest and most elementary kind: the feelings depicted, or rather indicated, are the simplest our nature has; such joys and griefs as the immediate pressure of some outward event excites in rude minds, which live wholly immersed in outward things, and have never, either from choice or a force they could not resist, turned themselves to the contemplation of the world within. Passing now from childhood, and from the childhood of society, to the grown-up men and women of this most grown-up and unchildlike age—the minds and hearts of greatest depth and elevation are commonly those which take greatest delight in poetry; the shallowest and emptiest, on the contrary, are, by universal remark, the most addicted to novel reading. This accords, too, with all analogous experience of human

---

[1] in his "Preface" to the *Lyrical Ballads*.

nature. The sort of persons whom not merely in books but in their lives, we find perpetually engaged in hunting for excitement from without, are invariably those who do not possess, either in the vigor of their intellectual powers or in the depth of their sensibilities, that which would enable them to find ample excitement nearer at home. The same persons whose time is divided between sightseeing, gossip, and fashionable dissipation, take a natural delight in fictitious narrative; the excitement it affords is of the kind which comes from without. Such persons are rarely lovers of poetry, though they may fancy themselves so, because they relish novels in verse. But poetry, which is the delineation of the deeper and more secret workings of the human heart, is interesting only to those to whom it recalls what they have felt, or whose imagination it stirs up to conceive what they could feel, or what they might have been able to feel, had their outward circumstances been different.

Poetry, when it is really such, is truth; and fiction also, if it is good for anything, is truth: but they are different truths. The truth of poetry is to paint the human soul truly: the truth of fiction is to give a true picture of life. The two kinds of knowledge are different, and come by different ways, come mostly to different persons. Great poets are often proverbially ignorant of life. What they know has come by observation of themselves; they have found there one highly delicate, and sensitive, and refined specimen of human nature, on which the laws of human emotion are written in large characters, such as can be read off without much study: and other knowledge of mankind, such as comes to men of the world by outward experience, is not indispensable to them as poets: but to the novelist such knowledge is all in all; he has to describe outward things, not the inward man; actions and events, not feelings; and it will not do for him to

be numbered among those who, as Madame Roland said of Brissot,[1] know man but not men.

All this is no bar to the possibility of combining both elements, poetry and narrative or incident, in the same work, and calling it either a novel or a poem; but so may red and white combine on the same human features, or on the same canvas; and so may oil and vinegar, though opposite natures, blend together in the same composite taste. There is one order of composition which requires the union of poetry and incident, each in its highest kind—the dramatic. Even there the two elements are perfectly distinguishable, and may exist of unequal quality, and in the most various proportion. The incidents of a dramatic poem may be scant and ineffective, though the delineation of passion and character may be of the highest order; as in Goethe's glorious *Torquato Tasso*; or again, the story as a mere story may be well got up for effect, as is the case with some of the most trashy productions of the Minerva press:[2] it may even be, what those are not, a coherent and probable series of events, though there be scarcely a feeling exhibited which is not exhibited falsely, or in a manner absolutely commonplace. The combination of the two excellencies is what renders Shakespeare so generally acceptable, each sort of readers finding in him what is suitable to their faculties. To the many he is great as a storyteller, to the few as a poet.

In limiting poetry to the delineation of states of feeling, and denying the name where nothing is delineated but outward objects, we may be thought to have done what we promised to avoid—to have not found, but made a definition, in opposition to the usage of the English language, since it is established by common consent that there is a poetry called descriptive. We deny the charge. Description

---

[1] Marie Jeanne Phlipon Roland de la Platière, in *Appel à l'impartiale postérité*, 1795.

[2] publishing house, from 1790 to 1820, of William Lane, a busy caterer to popular taste.

is not poetry because there is descriptive poetry, no more than science is poetry because there is such a thing as a didactic poem; no more, we might almost say, than Greek or Latin is poetry because there are Greek and Latin poems. But an object which admits of being described, or a truth which may fill a place in a scientific treatise, may also furnish an occasion for the generation of poetry, which we thereupon choose to call descriptive or didactic. The poetry is not in the object itself, nor in the scientific truth itself, but in the state of mind in which the one and the other may be contemplated. The mere delineation of the dimensions and colors of external objects is not poetry, no more than a geometrical ground plan of St. Peter's or Westminster Abbey is painting. Descriptive poetry consists, no doubt, in description, but in description of things as they appear, not as they are; and it paints them not in their bare and natural lineaments, but arranged in the colors and seen through the medium of the imagination set in action by the feelings. If a poet is to describe a lion, he will not set about describing him as a naturalist would, nor even as a traveler would, who was intent upon stating the truth, the whole truth, and nothing but the truth. He will describe him by imagery, that is, by suggesting the most striking likenesses and contrasts which might occur to a mind contemplating the lion, in the state of awe, wonder, or terror, which the spectacle naturally excites, or is, on the occasion, supposed to excite. Now this is describing the lion professedly, but the state of excitement of the spectator really. The lion may be described falsely or in exaggerated colors, and the poetry be all the better; but if the human emotion be not painted with the most scrupulous truth, the poetry is bad poetry, i.e., is not poetry at all, but a failure.

Thus far our progress towards a clear view of the essentials of poetry has brought us very close to the last two attempts at a definition of poetry which we happen to have seen in print, both of them by poets and men of genius. The one is by Ebenezer Elliott,[1] the author of *Corn-Law Rhymes*, and other poems of still greater merit. "Poetry," says he, "is impassioned truth." The other is by a writer in *Blackwood's Magazine*, and comes, we think, still nearer the mark. We forget his exact words, but in substance he defined poetry as "man's thoughts tinged by his feelings." There is in either definition a near approximation to what we are in search of. Every truth which man can announce, every thought, even every outward impression, which can enter into his consciousness, may become poetry when shown through any impassioned medium, when invested with the coloring of joy, or grief, or pity, or affection, or admiration, or reverence, or awe, or even hatred or terror: and, unless so colored, nothing, be it as interesting as it may, is poetry. But both these definitions fail to discriminate between poetry and eloquence. Eloquence, as well as poetry, is impassioned truth; eloquence, as well as poetry, is thoughts colored by the feelings. Yet common apprehension and philosophic criticism alike recognize a distinction between the two: there is much that everyone would call eloquence, which no one would think of classing as poetry. A question will sometimes arise, whether some particular author is a poet; and those who maintain the negative commonly allow, that though not a poet, he is a highly eloquent writer.

The distinction between poetry and eloquence appears to us to be equally fundamental with the distinction between poetry and narrative, or between poetry and description. It is still farther from having been satisfactorily cleared up than either of the others, unless, which is highly probable, the German artists and critics have thrown some light upon it which has not yet reached us. Without a perfect knowledge of what they have written, it is something like presumption to write upon such subjects at all, and we shall be the foremost to urge that, whatever

---

[1] (1781–1849), working-class poet.

we may be about to submit, may be received, subject to correction from them.

Poetry and eloquence are both alike the expression or uttering forth of feeling. But if we may be excused the seeming affectation of the antithesis, we should say that eloquence is *heard*, poetry is *overheard*. Eloquence supposes an audience; the peculiarity of poetry appears to us to lie in the poet's utter unconsciousness of a listener. Poetry is feeling confessing itself to itself, in moments of solitude, and bodying itself forth in symbols which are the nearest possible representations of the feeling in the exact shape in which it exists in the poet's mind. Eloquence is feeling pouring itself forth to other minds, courting their sympathy, or endeavoring to influence their belief, or move them to passion or to action.

All poetry is of the nature of soliloquy. It may be said that poetry, which is printed on hot-pressed paper, and sold at a bookseller's shop, is a soliloquy in full dress, and upon the stage. But there is nothing absurd in the idea of such a mode of soliloquizing. What we have said to ourselves, we may tell to others afterwards; what we have said or done in solitude, we may voluntarily reproduce when we know that other eyes are upon us. But no trace of consciousness that any eyes are upon us must be visible in the work itself. The actor knows that there is an audience present; but if he act as though he knew it, he acts ill. A poet may write poetry with the intention of publishing it; he may write it even for the express purpose of being paid for it; that it should be poetry, being written under any such influences, is far less probable; not, however, impossible; but not otherwise possible than if he can succeed in excluding from his work every vestige of such lookings-forth into the outward and everyday world, and can express his feelings exactly as he has felt them in solitude, or as he feels that he should feel them, though they were to remain forever unuttered. But when he turns round and addresses himself to another person; when the act of utterance is not itself the end, but a means to an end—viz., by the feelings he himself expresses to work upon the feelings, or upon the belief, or the will of another—when the expression of his emotions, or of his thoughts, tinged by his emotions, is tinged also by that purpose, by that desire of making an impression upon another mind, then it ceases to be poetry, and becomes eloquence.

Poetry, accordingly, is the natural fruit of solitude and meditation; eloquence, of intercourse with the world. The persons who have most feeling of their own, if intellectual culture have given them a language in which to express it, have the highest faculty of poetry; those who best understand the feelings of others, are the most eloquent. The persons, and the nations, who commonly excel in poetry, are those whose character and tastes render them least dependent for their happiness upon the applause, or sympathy, or concurrence of the world in general. Those to whom that applause, that sympathy, that concurrence are most necessary, generally excel most in eloquence. And hence, perhaps, the French, who are the least poetical of all great and refined nations, are among the most eloquent: the French, also, being the most sociable, the vainest, and the least self-dependent.

If the above be, as we believe, the true theory of the distinction commonly admitted between eloquence and poetry; or though it be not that, yet if, as we cannot doubt, the distinction above stated be a real bona fide distinction, it will be found to hold, not merely in the language of words, but in all other language, and to intersect the whole domain of art.

Take, for example, music: we shall find in that art, so peculiarly the expression of passion, two perfectly distinct styles; one of which may be called the poetry, the other the oratory of music. This difference being seized would put an end to much musical sectarianism. There has been much contention whether the character of Rossini's music—the music, we mean, which is characteristic of that composer—is compatible with the expression of passion. Without doubt, the passion it expresses is not the musing, meditative tenderness, or pathos, or grief of Mozart, the great poet of his art. Yet it is passion, but garrulous passion—the passion which pours itself into other ears; and therein the better calculated for dramatic effect, having a natural adaptation for dialogue. Mozart also is great in musical oratory; but his most touching compositions are in the opposite style—that of soliloquy. Who can imagine *"Dove sono"*[1] *heard?* We imagine it *over*-heard. The same is the case with many of the finest national airs. Who can hear those words, which speak so touchingly the sorrows of a mountaineer in exile:

> My heart's in the Highlands—my heart is not
>   here;
> My heart's in the Highlands, a-chasing the deer,
> A-chasing the wild-deer, and following the roe—
> My heart's in the Highlands, wherever I go.

Who can hear those affecting words, married to as affecting an air, and fancy that he sees the singer? That song has always seemed to us like the lament of a prisoner in a solitary cell, ourselves listening, unseen, in the next. As the direct opposite of this, take "Scots wha hae wi' Wallace bled,"[2] where the music is as oratorical as the poetry.

Purely pathetic music commonly partakes of soliloquy. The soul is absorbed in its distress, and though there may be bystanders, it is not thinking of them. When the mind is looking within and not without, its state does not often or rapidly vary; and hence the even, uninterrupted flow, approaching almost to monotony, which a good reader, or a good singer, will give to words or music of a pensive or melancholy cast. But grief, taking the form of a prayer, or of a complaint becomes oratorical; no longer low, and even, and subdued, it assumes a more emphatic rhythm, a more rapidly returning accent;

instead of a few slow, equal notes, following one after another at regular intervals, it crowds note upon note, and ofttimes assumes a hurry and bustle like joy. Those who are familiar with some of the best of Rossini's serious compositions, such as the air *"Tu che i miseri conforti,"* in the opera of *Tancredi,* or the duet *"Ebben per mia memoria,"* in *La Gazza Ladra,* will at once understand and feel our meaning. Both are highly tragic and passionate; the passion of both is that of oratory, not poetry. The like may be said of that most moving prayer in Beethoven's *Fidelio* *"Komm, Hoffnung, lass das letzte Stern/Der Müde nicht erbleichen"*;[3] in which Madam Devrient, last summer, exhibited such consummate powers of pathetic expression. How different from Winter's beautiful *"Paga pii,"* the very soul of melancholy exhaling itself in solitude; fuller of meaning, and, therefore, more profoundly poetical than the words for which it was composed—for it seems to express not simply melancholy, but the melancholy of remorse.

If, from vocal music, we now pass to instrumental, we may have a specimen of musical oratory in any fine military symphony or march: while the poetry of music seems to have attained its consummation in Beethoven's Overture to *Egmont.* We question whether so deep an expression of mixed grandeur and melancholy was ever in any other instance produced by mere sounds.

In the arts which speak to the eye, the same distinctions will be found to hold, not only between poetry and oratory, but between poetry, oratory, narrative, and simple imitation or description.

Pure description is exemplified in a mere portrait or a mere landscape—productions of art, it is true, but of the mechanical rather than of the fine arts, being works of simple imitation, not creation. We say, a mere portrait, or a mere landscape, because it is possible for a portrait or a landscape, without ceasing to be such, to be also a picture. A portrait by

---

[1] Wolfgang Amadeus Mozart, *Le Nozze di Figaro.*

[2] two songs by Robert Burns.

[3] "Come, Hope, do not let the last star of the tired ones fade away."

Lawrence, or one of Turner's views, is not a mere copy from nature: the one combines with the given features that particular expression (among all good and pleasing ones) which those features are most capable of wearing, and which, therefore, in combination with them, is capable of producing the greatest positive beauty. Turner, again, unites the objects of the given landscape with whatever sky, and whatever light and shade, enable those particular objects to impress the imagination most strongly. In both, there is creative art—not working after an actual model, but realizing an idea.

Whatever in painting or sculpture expresses human feeling, or character, which is only a certain state of feeling grown habitual, may be called, according to circumstances, the poetry or the eloquence of the painter's or the sculptor's art; the poetry, if the feeling declares itself by such signs as escape from us when we are unconscious of being seen; the oratory, if the signs are those we use for the purpose of voluntary communication.

The poetry of painting seems to be carried to its highest perfection in the *Peasant Girl* of Rembrandt, or in any Madonna or Magdalen of Guido;[1] that of sculpture, in almost any of the Greek statues of the gods; not considering these in respect to the mere physical beauty, of which they are such perfect models, not undertaking either to vindicate or to contest the opinion of philosophers, that even physical beauty is ultimately resolvable into expression; we may safely affirm, that in no other of man's works did so much of soul ever shine through mere inanimate matter.

The narrative style answers to what is called historical painting, which it is the fashion among connoisseurs to treat as the climax of the pictorial art. That it is the most difficult branch of the art, we do not doubt, because, in its perfection, it includes the perfection of all the other branches: as in like manner

an epic poem, though, insofar as it is epic (i.e., narrative), it is not poetry at all, is yet esteemed the greatest effort of poetic genius, because there is no kind whatever of poetry which may not appropriately find a place in it. But a historical picture, as such, that is, as the representation of an incident, must necessarily, as it seems to us, be poor and ineffective. The narrative powers of painting are extremely limited. Scarcely any picture, scarcely any series even of pictures, which we know of, tells its own story without the aid of an interpreter; you must know the story beforehand; then, indeed, you may see great beauty and appropriateness in the painting. But it is the single figures which, to us, are the great charm even of a historical picture. It is in these that the power of the art is really seen: in the attempt to narrate, visible and permanent signs are far behind the fugitive audible ones which follow so fast one after another, while the faces and figures in a narrative picture, even though they be Titian's, stand still. Who would not prefer one *Virgin and Child* of Raphael, to all the pictures which Rubens, with his fat, frowzy Dutch Venuses, ever painted? Though Rubens, besides excelling almost everyone in his mastery over all the mechanical parts of his art, often shows real genius in grouping his figures, the peculiar problem of historical painting. But, then, who, except a mere student of drawing and coloring, ever cared to look twice at any of the figures themselves? The power of painting lies in poetry, of which Rubens had not the slightest tincture—not in narrative, where he might have excelled.

The single figures, however, in an historical picture, are rather the eloquence of painting than the poetry: they mostly (unless they are quite out of place in the picture) express the feelings of one person as modified by the presence of others. Accordingly the minds whose bent leads them rather to eloquence than to poetry, rush to historical painting. The French painters, for instance, seldom attempt, because they could make nothing of, single heads, like

---

[1] Guido Reni (1575–1642), Italian painter of sacred objects.

those glorious ones of the Italian masters, with which they might glut themselves day after day in their own Louvre. They must all be historical; and they are, almost to a man, attitudinizers. If we wished to give to any young artist the most impressive warning our imaginations could devise, against that kind of vice in the pictorial, which corresponds to rant in the histrionic art, we would advise him to walk once up and once down the gallery of the Luxembourg; even now when David, the great corrupter of taste, has been translated from this world to the next, and from the Luxembourg, consequently, into the more elevated sphere of the Louvre. Every figure in French painting or statuary seems to be showing itself off before spectators: they are in the worst style of corrupted eloquence, but in no style of poetry at all. The best are stiff and unnatural; the worst resemble figures of cataleptic patients. The French artists fancy themselves imitators of the classics, yet they seem to have no understanding and no feeling of that repose which was the peculiar and pervading character of Grecian art, until it began to decline: a repose tenfold more indicative of strength than all their stretching and straining; for strength, as Thomas Carlyle says, does not manifest itself in spasms.

There are some productions of art which it seems at first difficult to arrange in any of the classes above illustrated. The direct aim of art as such, is the production of the beautiful; and as there are other things beautiful besides states of mind, there is much of art which may seem to have nothing to do with either poetry or eloquence as we have defined them. Take for instance a composition of Claude, or Salvator Rosa.[1] There is here creation of new beauty: by the grouping of natural scenery, conformably indeed to the laws of outward nature, but not after any actual model; the result being a beauty more perfect and faultless than is perhaps to be found in

---

[1] Claude (le) Lorrain (1604–05[?]–82), French painter, draughtsman, and etcher, noted as an ideal landscape artist, and Salvator Rosa (1615–72), Italian landscape painter.

any actual landscape. Yet there is a character of poetry even in these, without which they could not be so beautiful. The unity, and wholeness, and aesthetic congruity of the picture still lies in singleness of expression; but it is expression in a different sense from that in which we have hitherto employed the term. The objects in an imaginary landscape cannot be said, like the words of a poem or the notes of a melody, to be the actual utterance of a feeling; but there must be some feeling with which they harmonize, and which they have a tendency to raise up in the spectator's mind. They must inspire a feeling of grandeur, a loveliness, a cheerfulness, a wildness, a melancholy, a terror. The painter must surround his principal objects with such imagery as would spontaneously arise in a highly imaginative mind, when contemplating those objects under the impression of the feelings which they are intended to inspire. This, if it be not poetry, is so nearly allied to it, as scarcely to require being distinguished.

In this sense we may speak of the poetry of architecture. All architecture, to be impressive, must be the expression or symbol of some interesting idea; some thought, which has power over the emotions. The reason why modern architecture is so paltry, is simply that it is not the expression of any idea; it is a mere parroting of the architectural tongue of the Greeks, or of our Teutonic ancestors, without any conception of a meaning.

To confine ourselves, for the present, to religious edifices: these partake of poetry, in proportion as they express, or harmonize with, the feelings of devotion. But those feelings are different according to the conception entertained of the beings, by whose supposed nature they are called forth. To the Greek, these beings were incarnations of the greatest conceivable physical beauty, combined with supernatural power: and the Greek temples express this, their predominant character being graceful strength; in other words, solidity, which is power, and lightness which is also power, accomplishing with small means what seemed to require great; to combine all in one word, *majesty*. To the Catholic, again, the Deity was something far less clear and definite; a being of still more resistless power than the heathen divinities; greatly to be loved; still more greatly to be feared; and wrapped up in vagueness, mystery, and incomprehensibility. A certain solemnity, a feeling of doubting and trembling hope, like that of one lost in a boundless forest who thinks he knows his way but is not sure, mixes in all the genuine expressions of Catholic devotion. This is eminently the expression of the pure Gothic cathedral; conspicuous equally in the mingled majesty and gloom of its vaulted roofs and stately aisles, and in the "dim religious light" [1] which steals through its painted windows.

There is no generic distinction between the imagery which is the expression of feeling and the imagery which is felt to harmonize with feeling. They are identical. The imagery in which feeling utters itself forth from within, is also that in which it delights when presented to it from without. All art, therefore, in proportion as it produces its effects by an appeal to the emotions partakes of poetry, unless it partakes of oratory, or of narrative. And the distinction which these three words indicate, runs through the whole field of the fine arts.

The above hints have no pretension to the character of a theory. They are merely thrown out for the consideration of thinkers, in the hope that if they do not contain the truth, they may do somewhat to suggest it. Nor would they, crude as they are, have been deemed worthy of publication, in any country but one in which the philosophy of art is so completely neglected, that whatever may serve to put any inquiring mind upon this kind of investigation, cannot well, however imperfect in itself, fail altogether to be of use.

—JANUARY 1833

---

[1] from Milton's "Il Penseroso."

"*Two Kinds of Poetry*" [2]

"NASCITUR POËTA" [3] is a maxim of classical antiquity, which has passed to these latter days with less questioning than most of the doctrines of that early age. When it originated, the human faculties were occupied, fortunately for posterity, less in examining how the works of genius are created than in creating them; and the adage probably had no higher source than the tendency common among mankind to consider all power which is not visibly the effect of practice, all skill which is not capable of being reduced to mechanical rules, as the result of a peculiar gift. Yet this aphorism, born in the infancy of psychology, will perhaps be found, now when that science is in its adolescence, to be as true as an epigram ever is; that is, to contain some truth, —truth, however, which has been so compressed, and bent out of shape, in order to tie it up into so small a knot of only two words, that it requires an almost infinite amount of unrolling and laying straight before it will resume its just proportions

We are not now intending to remark upon the grosser misapplications of this ancient maxim, which have engendered so many races of poetasters. The days are gone by, when every raw youth, whose borrowed phantasies have set themselves to a borrowed tune, mistaking, as Coleridge says, an ardent desire of poetic reputation for poetic genius, [4] while unable to disguise from himself that he had taken no means whereby he might *become* a poet, could fancy himself a born one. Those who would reap without sowing, and gain the victory without fighting the battle, are ambitious now of another sort of distinction, and are born novelists or public speakers, not poets; and the wiser thinkers understand and acknowledge that poetic excellence is subject to the

---

[2] first published in October 1833, in the *Monthly Repository*.

[3] a poet is born.

[4] in the *Biographia Literaria* 2.15.

same necessary conditions with any other mental endowment, and that to no one of the spiritual benefactors of mankind is a higher or a more assiduous intellectual culture needful than to the poet. It is true, he possesses this advantage over others who use the "instrument of words,"—that, of the truths which he utters, a larger proportion are derived from personal consciousness and a smaller from philosophic investigation. But the power itself of discriminating between what really is consciousness and what is only a process of inference completed in a single instant, and the capacity of distinguishing whether that of which the mind is conscious be an eternal truth or but a dream, are among the last results of the most matured and perfect intellect. Not to mention that the poet, no more than any other person who writes, confines himself altogether to intuitive truths, nor has any means of communicating even these but by words, every one of which derives all its power of conveying a meaning from a whole host of acquired notions and facts learnt by study and experience.

Nevertheless, it seems undeniable in point of fact, and consistent with the principles of a sound metaphysics, that there are poetic *natures.* There is a mental and physical constitution or temperament peculiarly fitted for poetry. This temperament will not of itself make a poet, no more than the soil will the fruit; and as good fruit may be raised by culture from indifferent soils, so may good poetry from naturally unpoetical minds. But the poetry of one who is a poet by nature will be clearly and broadly distinguishable from the poetry of mere culture. It may not be truer, it may not be more useful; but it will be different: fewer will appreciate it, even though many should affect to do so, but in those few it will find a keener sympathy, and will yield them a deeper enjoyment.

One may write genuine poetry, and not be a poet, for whosoever writes out truly any human feeling, writes poetry. All persons, even the most unimaginative, in moments of strong emotion, speak poetry;

and hence the drama is poetry, which else were always prose, except when a poet is one of the characters. What *is* poetry but the thoughts and words in which emotion spontaneously embodies itself? As there are few who are not, at least for some moments and in some situations, capable of some strong feeling, poetry is natural to most persons at some period of their lives; and any one whose feelings are genuine, though but of the average strength,—if he be not diverted by uncongenial thoughts or occupations from the indulgence of them, and if he acquire by culture, as all persons may, the faculty of delineating them correctly,—has it in his power to be a poet, so far as a life passed in writing unquestionable poetry may be considered to confer that title. But *ought* it to do so? Yes, perhaps, in a collection of "British poets." But "poet" is the name also of a variety of man, not solely of the author of a particular variety of book. Now, to have written whole volumes of real poetry is possible to almost all kinds of characters, and implies no greater peculiarity of mental construction than to be the author of a history or a novel.

Whom, then, shall we call poets? Those who are so constituted, that emotions are the links of association by which their ideas, both sensuous and spiritual, are connected together. This constitution belongs (within certain limits) to all in whom poetry is a pervading principle. In all others, poetry is something extraneous and superinduced; something out of themselves, foreign to the habitual course of their every-day lives and characters; a world to which they may make occasional visits, but where they are sojourners, not dwellers, and which, when out of it, or even when in it, they think of, peradventure, but as a phantom-world,—a place of *ignes fatui*[1] and spectral illusions. Those only who have the peculiarity of association which we have mentioned, and which is a natural though not an universal conse-

---

[1] false illuminations.

quence of intense sensibility, instead of seeming not themselves when they are uttering poetry, scarcely seem themselves when uttering any thing to which poetry is foreign. Whatever be the thing which they are contemplating, if it be capable of connecting itself with their emotions, the aspect under which it first and most naturally paints itself to them is its poetic aspect. The poet of culture sees his object in prose, and describes it in poetry: the poet of nature actually sees it in poetry.

This point is perhaps worth some little illustration; the rather as metaphysicians (the ultimate arbiters of all philosophical criticism), while they have busied themselves for two thousand years, more or less, about the few *universal* laws of human nature, have strangely neglected the analysis of its *diversities.* Of these, none lie deeper or reach further than the varieties which difference of nature and of education makes in what may be termed the habitual bond of association. In a mind entirely uncultivated, which is also without any strong feelings, objects whether of sense or of intellect arrange themselves in the mere casual order in which they have been seen, heard, or otherwise perceived. Persons of this sort may be said to think chronologically. If they remember a fact, it is by reason of a fortuitous coincidence with some trifling incident or circumstance which took place at the very time. If they have a story to tell, or testimony to deliver in a witness-box, their narrative must follow the exact order in which the events took place: *dodge* them, and the thread of association is broken; they cannot go on. Their associations, to use the language of philosophers, are chiefly of the successive, not the synchronous kind; and, whether successive or synchronous, are mostly casual.

To the man of science, again, or of business, objects group themselves according to the artificial classifications which the understanding has voluntarily made for the convenience of thought or of practice. But, where any of the impressions are vivid

and intense, the associations into which these enter are the ruling ones; it being a well-known law of association, that, the stronger a feeling is, the more quickly and strongly it associates itself with any other object or feeling. Where, therefore, nature has given strong feelings, and education has not created factitious tendencies stronger than the natural ones, the prevailing associations will be those which connect objects and ideas with emotions, and with each other through the intervention of emotions. Thoughts and images will be linked together according to the similarity of the feelings which cling to them. A thought will introduce a thought by first introducing a feeling which is allied with it. At the centre of each group of thoughts or images will be found a feeling; and the thoughts or images will be there, only because the feeling was there. The combinations which the mind puts together, the pictures which it paints, the wholes which Imagination constructs out of the materials supplied by Fancy, will be indebted to some dominant *feeling,* not, as in other natures, to a dominant *thought,* for their unity and consistency of character,—for what distinguishes them from incoherences.

The difference, then, between the poetry of a poet, and the poetry of a cultivated but not naturally poetic mind, is, that in the latter, with however bright a halo of feeling the thought may be surrounded and glorified, the thought itself is always the conspicuous object; while the poetry of a poet is Feeling itself, employing Thought only as the medium of its expression. In the one, feeling waits upon thought; in the other, thought upon feeling. The one writer has a distinct aim, common to him with any other didactic author: he desires to convey the thought, and he conveys it clothed in the feelings which it excites in himself, or which he deems most appropriate to it. The other merely pours forth the overflowing of his feelings; and all the thoughts which those feelings suggest are floated promiscuously along the stream.

It may assist in rendering our meaning intelligible if we illustrate it by a parallel between the two English authors of our own day who have produced the greatest quantity of true and enduring poetry, —Wordsworth and Shelley. Apter instances could not be wished for: the one might be cited as the type, the *exemplar,* of what the poetry of culture may accomplish; the other, as perhaps the most striking example ever known of the poetic temperament. How different, accordingly, is the poetry of these two great writers! In Wordsworth, the poetry is almost always the mere setting of a thought. The thought may be more valuable than the setting, or it may be less valuable; but there can be no question as to which was first in his mind. What he is impressed with, and what he is anxious to impress, is some proposition more or less distinctly conceived; some truth, or something which he deems such. He lets the thought dwell in his mind, till it excites, as is the nature of thought, other thoughts, and also such feelings as the measure of his sensibility is adequate to supply. Among these thoughts and feelings, had he chosen a different walk of authorship (and there are many in which he might equally have excelled), he would probably have made a different selection of media for enforcing the parent thought: his habits, however, being those of poetic composition, he selects in preference the strongest feelings, and the thoughts with which most of feeling is naturally or habitually connected. His poetry, therefore, may be defined to be his thoughts, colored by, and impressing themselves by means of, emotions. Such poetry, Wordsworth has occupied a long life in producing; and well and wisely has he so done. Criticisms, no doubt, may be made occasionally both upon the thoughts themselves, and upon the skill he has demonstrated in the choice of his media; for an affair of skill and study, in the most rigorous sense, it evidently was. But he has not labored in vain: he has

exercised, and continues to exercise, a powerful, and mostly a highly beneficial influence over the formation and growth of not a few of the most cultivated and vigorous of the youthful minds of our time, over whose heads poetry of the opposite description would have flown, for want of an original organization, physical or mental, in sympathy with it.

On the other hand, Wordsworth's poetry is never bounding, never ebullient; has little even of the appearance of spontaneousness: the well is never so full that it overflows. There is an air of calm deliberateness about all he writes which is not characteristic of the poetic temperament. His poetry seems one thing; himself, another. He seems to be poetical because he wills to be so, not because he cannot help it. Did he will to dismiss poetry, he need never again, it might almost seem, have a poetical thought. He never seems possessed by any feeling: no emotion seems ever so strong as to have entire sway, for the time being, over the current of his thoughts. He never, even for the space of a few stanzas, appears entirely given up to exultation, or grief, or pity, or love, or admiration, or devotion, or even animal spirits. He now and then, though seldom, attempts to write as if he were; and never, we think, without leaving an impression of poverty: as the brook, which, on nearly level ground, quite fills its banks, appears but a thread when running rapidly down a precipitous declivity. He has feeling enough to form a decent, graceful, even beautiful, decoration to a thought which is in itself interesting and moving; but not so much as suffices to stir up the soul by mere sympathy with itself in its simplest manifestation, nor enough to summon up that array of "thoughts of power," which, in a richly stored mind, always attends the call of really intense feeling. It is for this reason, doubtless, that the genius of Wordsworth is essentially unlyrical. Lyric poetry, as it was the earliest kind, is also, if the view we are now taking of poetry be correct, more eminently and peculiarly poetry than any other: it is the poetry most natural to a really poetic temperament, and least capable of being successfully imitated by one not so endowed by nature.

Shelley is the very reverse of all this. Where Wordsworth is strong, he is weak: where Wordsworth is weak, he is strong. Culture, that culture by which Wordsworth has reared from his own inward nature the richest harvest ever brought forth by a soil of so little depth, is precisely what was wanting to Shelley; or let us rather say, he had not, at the period of his deplorably early death, reached sufficiently far in that intellectual progression of which he was capable, and which, if it has done so much for greatly inferior natures, might have made of him the most perfect, as he was already the most gifted, of our poets. For him, voluntary mental discipline had done little: the vividness of his emotions and of his sensations had done all. He seldom follows up an idea: it starts into life, summons from the fairy-land of his inexhaustible fancy some three or four bold images, then vanishes, and straight he is off on the wings of some casual association into quite another sphere. He had scarcely yet acquired the consecutiveness of thought necessary for a long poem. His more ambitious compositions too often resemble the scattered fragments of a mirror,—colors brilliant as life, single images without end, but no picture. It is only when under the overruling influence of some one state of feeling, either actually experienced, or summoned up in the vividness of reality by a fervid imagination, that he writes as a great poet; unity of feeling being to him the harmonizing principle which a central idea is to minds of another class, and supplying the coherency and consistency which would else have been wanting. Thus it is in many of his smaller, and especially his lyrical poems. They are obviously written to exhale, perhaps to relieve, a state of feeling, or of conception of feeling, almost oppressive from its vividness. The thoughts and imagery are suggested by the feeling, and are such as it finds unsought. The state of feeling may be either of soul or of sense, or

oftener (might we not say invariably?) of both; for the poetic temperament is usually, perhaps always, accompanied by exquisite senses. The exciting cause may be either an object or an idea. But whatever of sensation enters into the feeling must not be local, or consciously organic: it is a condition of the whole frame, not of a part only. Like the state of sensation produced by a fine climate, or indeed like all strongly pleasurable or painful sensations in an impassioned nature, it pervades the entire nervous system. States of feeling, whether sensuous or spiritual, which thus possess the whole being, are the fountains of that which we have called the poetry of poets, and which is little else than a pouring-forth of the thoughts and images that pass across the mind while some permanent state of feeling is occupying it.

To the same original fineness of organization, Shelley was doubtless indebted for another of his rarest gifts,—that exuberance of imagery, which, when unrepressed, as in many of his poems it is, amounts to a fault. The susceptibility of his nervous system, which made his emotions intense, made also the impressions of his external senses deep and clear; and agreeably to the law of association, by which, as already remarked, the strongest impressions are those which associate themselves the most easily and strongly, these vivid sensations were readily recalled to mind by all objects or thoughts which had co-existed with them, and by all feelings which in any degree resembled them. Never did a fancy so teem with sensuous imagery as Shelley's. Wordsworth economizes an image, and detains it until he has distilled all the poetry out of it, and it will not yield a drop more: Shelley lavishes his with a profusion which is unconscious because it is inexhaustible.

If, then, the maxim "Nascitur poëta" means, either that the power of producing poetical compositions is a peculiar faculty which the poet brings into the world with him, which grows like any of his bodily powers, and is as independent of culture as his height and his complexion; or that any natural peculiarity whatever is implied in producing poetry, real poetry, and in any quantity,—such poetry too, as, to the majority of educated and intelligent readers, shall appear quite as good as, or even better than, any other,—in either sense the doctrine is false. And, nevertheless, there *is* poetry which could not emanate but from a mental and physical constitution, peculiar, not in the kind, but in the degree, of its susceptibility; a constitution which makes its possessor capable of greater happiness than mankind in general, and also of greater unhappiness; and because greater, so also more various. And such poetry, to all who know enough of nature to own it as being in nature, is much more poetry, is poetry in a far higher sense, than any other; since the common element of all poetry, that which constitutes poetry,—human feeling,—enters far more largely into this than into the poetry of culture; not only because the natures which we have called poetical really feel more, and consequently have more feeling to express, but because, the capacity of feeling being so great, feeling, when excited and not voluntarily resisted, seizes the helm of their thoughts, and the succession of ideas and images becomes the mere utterance of an emotion; not, as in other natures, the emotion a mere ornamental coloring of the thought.

Ordinary education and the ordinary course of life are constantly at work counteracting this quality of mind, and substituting habits more suitable to their own ends: if, instead of substituting, they were content to superadd, there would be nothing to complain of. But when will education consist, not in repressing any mental faculty or power, from the uncontrolled action of which danger is apprehended, but in training up to its proper strength the corrective and antagonist power?

In whomsoever the quality which we have described exists, and is not stifled, that person is a poet.

Doubtless he is a greater poet in proportion as the fineness of his perceptions, whether of sense or of internal consciousness, furnishes him with an ampler supply of lovely images, the vigor and richness of his intellect with a greater abundance of moving thoughts. For it is through these thoughts and images that the feeling speaks, and through their impressiveness that it impresses itself, and finds response in other hearts; and, from these media of transmitting it (contrary to the laws of physical nature), increase of intensity is reflected back upon the feeling itself. But all these it is possible to have, and not be a poet: they are mere materials, which the poet shares in common with other people. What constitutes the poet is not the imagery, nor the thoughts, nor even the feelings, but the law according to which they are called up. He is a poet, not because he has ideas of any particular kind, but because the succession of his ideas is subordinate to the course of his emotions.

Many who have never acknowledged this in theory bear testimony to it in their particular judgments. In listening to an oration, or reading a written discourse, not professedly poetical, when do we begin to feel that the speaker or author is putting off the character of the orator or the prose-writer, and is passing into the poet? Not when he begins to show strong feeling; *then* we merely say, he is in earnest; he feels what he says: still less when he expresses himself in imagery; then, unless illustration be manifestly his sole object, we are apt to say, this is affectation. It is when the feeling (instead of passing away, or, if it continue, letting the train of thoughts run on exactly as they would have done if there were no influence at work but the mere intellect) becomes itself the originator of another train of association, which expels, or blends with, the former; when (for example) either his words, or the mode of their arrangement, are such as we spontaneously use only when in a state of excitement, proving that the mind is at least as much occupied by a passive state of its own feelings as by the desire of attaining the premeditated end which the discourse has in view.[1]

Our judgments of authors who lay actual claim to the title of poets follow the same principle. Whenever, after a writer's meaning is fully understood, it is still matter of reasoning and discussion whether he is a poet or not, he will be found to be wanting in the characteristic peculiarity of association so often adverted to. When, on the contrary, after reading or hearing one or two passages, we instinctively and without hesitation cry out, "This is a poet!" the probability is that the passages are strongly marked with this peculiar quality. And we may add, that, in such case, a critic, who, not having sufficient feeling to respond to the poetry, is also without sufficient philosophy to understand it though he feel it not, will be apt to pronounce, not "This is prose," but "This is exaggeration," "This is mysticism," or "This is nonsense."

Although a philosopher cannot, by culture, make himself, in the peculiar sense in which we now use the term, a poet,—unless at least he have that peculiarity of nature which would probably have made poetry his earliest pursuit,—a poet may always, by culture, make himself a philosopher. The poetic laws of association are by no means such as *must* have their course, even though a deliberate purpose require their suspension. If the peculiarities of the poetic temperament were uncontrollable in any poet, they might be supposed so in Shelley; yet how powerfully, in the "Cenci," does he coerce and restrain all the characteristic qualities of his genius! what severe simplicity, in place of his usual barbaric splendor! how rigidly does he keep the feelings and the imagery in subordination to the thought!

The investigation of nature requires no habits or qualities of mind but such as may always be acquired by industry and mental activity. Because, at one time, the mind may be so given up to a state of feeling, that the succession of its ideas is determined by the present enjoyment or suffering which pervades it, this is no reason but that in the calm retirement of study, when under no peculiar excitement either of the outward or of the inward sense, it may form any combinations, or pursue any trains of ideas, which are most conducive to the purposes of philosophic inquiry; and may, while in that state, form deliberate convictions, from which no excitement will afterwards make it swerve. Might we not go even further than this? We shall not pause to ask whether it be not a misunderstanding of the nature of passionate feeling to imagine that it is inconsistent with calmness; whether they who so deem of it do not mistake passion, in the militant or antagonistic state, for the type of passion universally,—do not confound passion struggling towards an outward object, with passion brooding over itself. But, without entering into this deeper investigation, that capacity of strong feeling which is supposed necessarily to disturb the judgment is also the material out of which all *motives* are made,—the motives, consequently, which lead human beings to the pursuit of truth. The greater the individual's capability of happiness and of misery, the stronger interest has that individual in arriving at truth; and, when once that interest is felt, an impassioned nature is sure to pursue this, as to pursue any other object, with greater ardor: for energy of character is commonly the offspring of strong feeling. If, therefore, the most impassioned natures do not ripen into the most powerful intellects, it is always from defect of culture, or something wrong in the circumstances by which the being has originally or succes-

---

[1] "And this, we may remark by the way, seems to point to the true theory of poetic diction, and to suggest the true answer to as much as is erroneous of Wordsworth's celebrated doctrine on that subject. For, on the one hand, *all* language which is the natural expression of feeling is really poetical, and will be felt as such, apart from conventional associations; but, on the other, whenever intellectual culture has afforded a choice between several modes of expressing the same emotion, the stronger the feeling is, the more naturally and certainly will it prefer the language which is most peculiarly appropriated to itself, and kept sacred from the contact of more vulgar objects of contemplation." (Mill's note.)

sively been surrounded. Undoubtedly, strong feelings require a strong intellect to carry them, as more sail requires more ballast; and when, from neglect or bad education, that strength is wanting, no wonder if the grandest and swiftest vessels make the most utter wreck.

Where, as in some of our older poets, a poetic nature has been united with logical and scientific culture, the peculiarity of association arising from the finer nature so perpetually alternates with the associations attainable by commoner natures trained to high perfection, that its own particular law is not so conspicuously characteristic of the result produced, as in a poet like Shelley, to whom systematic intellectual culture, in a measure proportioned to the intensity of his own nature, has been wanting. Whether the superiority will naturally be on the side of the philosopher-poet, or of the mere poet; whether the writings of the one ought, as a whole, to be truer, and their influence more beneficent, than those of the other,— is too obvious in principle to need statement: it would be absurd to doubt whether two endowments are better than one; whether truth is more certainly arrived at by two processes, verifying and correcting each other, than by one alone. Unfortunately, in practice, the matter is not quite so simple: there the question often is, Which is least prejudicial to the intellect,—uncultivation or malcultivation? For, as long as education consists chiefly of the mere inculcation of traditional opinions, many of which, from the mere fact that the human intellect has not yet reached perfection, must necessarily be false; so long as even those who are best taught are rather taught to know the thoughts of others than to think,—it is not always clear that the poet of acquired ideas has the advantage over him whose feeling has been his sole teacher. For the depth and durability of wrong as well as right impressions is proportional to the fineness of the material; and they who have the greatest capacity of natural feeling are generally those whose artificial feelings are the strongest. Hence, doubtless, among other reasons, it is, that, in an age of revolutions in opinion, the contemporary poets, those at least who deserve the name, those who have any individuality of character, if they are not before their age, are almost sure to be behind it; an observation curiously verified all over Europe in the present century. Nor let it be thought disparaging. However urgent may be the necessity for a breaking-up of old modes of belief, the most strong-minded and discerning, next to those who head the movement, are generally those who bring up the rear of it.

—1833

Sir Henry Taylor
1800 – 1886

Sir Henry Taylor was a minor literary figure, author of a number of plays and poems. A collected edition of his work was published in five volumes in 1877–78. He is best known for his closet drama *Philip Van Artevelde* and

for his "Preface" to that work. His classical anti-romantic stance contrasts with the 1831 essay of Arthur Henry Hallam.

∽∾∾

Preface to *Philip Van Artevelde* [1]

As this work, consisting of two Plays and an Interlude, is equal in length to about six such plays as are adapted to representation, it is almost unnecessary to say that it was not intended for the stage. It is properly an Historical Romance, cast in a dramatic and rhythmical form. Historic truth is preserved in it, as far as the material events are concerned—of course with the usual exception of such occasional dilatations and compressions of time as are required in dramatic composition.

This is, perhaps, all the explanation which is absolutely required in this place; but as there may be readers who feel an inclination to learn something of an author's tastes in poetry before they proceed to the perusal of what he has written, I will take the opportunity which a preface affords me of expressing my opinions upon two or three of the most prominent features in the present state of poetical literature; and I shall do so the more gladly, because I am apprehensive that without some previous intimations of the kind, my work might occasion disappointment to the admirers of that highly- coloured poetry which has been popular in these later years. If in the strictures which, with this object, I may be led to make upon authors of great reputation, I should appear to be wanting in the respect due to prevalent opinions, —opinions which, from the very circumstances of their prevalence, must be assumed to be partaken by

many to whom deference is owing, I trust that it will be attributed, not to any spirit of dogmatism, far less to a love of disparagement, but simply to the desire of exercising, with a discreet freedom, that humble independence of judgment in matters of taste which it is for the advantage of literature that every man of letters should maintain.

My views have not, in truth, been founded upon any predisposition to depreciate the popular poetry of the times. It will always produce a powerful impression upon very young readers, and I scarcely think that it can have been more admired by any than by myself when I was included in that category. I have not ceased to admire this poetry in its degree; and the interlude which I have inserted between these plays will show that, to a limited extent, I have been desirous even to cultivate and employ it; but I am unable to concur in opinion with those who would place it in the foremost ranks of the art; nor does it seem to have been capable of sustaining itself quite firmly in the very high degree of public estimation in which it was held at its first appearance and for some years afterwards. The poetical taste to which some of the popular poets of this century gave birth, appears at present to maintain a more unshaken dominion over the writers of poetry than over its readers.

These poets were characterized by great sensibility and fervour, by a profusion of imagery, by force and beauty of language, and by a versification peculiarly easy and adroit and abounding in that sort of melody which, by its very obvious cadences, makes itself most

---

[1] Taylor published his poetic drama, *Philip Van Artevelde*, in 1834.

pleasing to an unpractised ear. They exhibit, therefore, many of the most attractive graces and charms of poetry—its vital warmth not less than its external embellishments—and had not the admiration which they excited tended to produce an indifference to higher, graver, and more various endowments, no one would have said that it was, in any evil sense, excessive. But from this unbounded indulgence in the mere luxuries of poetry, has there not ensued a want of adequate appreciation for its intellectual and immortal part? I confess that such seems to me to have been both the actual and the natural result; and I can hardly believe the public taste to have been in a healthy state whilst the most approved poetry of past times was almost unread. We may now perhaps be turning back to it; but it was not, as far as I can judge, till more than a quarter of a century had expired, that any signs of reaction could be discerned. Till then, the elder luminaries of our poetical literature were obscured or little regarded; and we sate with dazzled eyes at a high festival of poetry, where, as at the funeral of Arvalan,[1] the torch-light put out the star-light.

So keen was the sense of what the new poets possessed, that it never seemed to be felt that anything was deficient in them. Yet their deficiencies were not unimportant. They wanted, in the first place, subject-matter. A feeling came more easily to them than a reflection, and an image was always at hand when a thought was not forthcoming. Either they did not look upon mankind with observant eyes, or they did not feel it to be any part of their vocation to turn what they saw to account. It did not belong to poetry, in their apprehension, to thread the mazes of life in all its classes and under all its circumstances, common as well as romantic, and, seeing all things, to infer and to instruct: on the contrary, it was to stand aloof from everything that is plain and true; to have little concern with what is rational or wise; it

was to be, like music, a moving and enchanting art, acting upon the fancy, the affections, the passions, but scarcely connected with the exercise of the intellectual faculties. These writers had, indeed, adopted a tone of language which is hardly consistent with the state of mind in which a man makes use of his understanding. The realities of nature, and the truths which they suggest, would have seemed cold and incongruous if suffered to mix with the strains of impassioned sentiment and glowing imagery in which they poured themselves forth. Spirit was not to be debased by any union with matter in their effusions, dwelling, as they did, in a region of poetical sentiment which did not permit them to walk upon the common earth or to breath the common air.

Writers, however, whose appeal is made so exclusively to the excitabilities of mankind, will not find it possible to work upon them continuously without a diminishing effect. Poetry of which sense is not the basis,—sense rapt or inspired by passion, not bewildered or subverted,—poetry over which the passionate reason of Man does not preside in all its strength as well as all its ardours,—though it may be excellent of its kind, will not long be reputed to be poetry of the highest order. It may move the feelings and charm the fancy; but failing to satisfy the understanding, it will not take permanent possession of the strongholds of fame.[2] Lord Byron, in giving the most admirable example of this species of poetry, undoubtedly gave the strongest impulse to the appetite for it. Yet this impulse is losing its force; and even Lord

---

[1] a character in Robert Southey's "Curse of Kehama."

[2] "Till this moment, when recurring for another purpose to Mr. Wordsworth's preface to his poems and to Mr. Coleridge's remarks upon them in his 'Biographia Literaria,' I was not aware for how many of my tenets I was indebted to those admirable specimens of philosophical criticism. The root of the matter is to be found in them.

In the first and second editions this note ended here. I have since been informed by a friend who was once a visitor at Rydal Mount at the same time as myself, that some parts of my preface have been borrowed from Mr. Wordsworth's conversation. I dare say this is the case. I can only wish that my mind and writings were as much enriched as they ought to be by the abundant opportunities I have enjoyed of drawing from the same source." (Taylor's note.)

Byron himself repudiated in the latter years of his life the poetical taste which he had espoused and propagated. The constitution of this writer's mind is not difficult to understand, and sufficiently explains the growth of his taste.

Had he united a cultivated and capacious intellect with his peculiarly poetical temperament, he would probably have been the greatest poet of his age. But no man can be a very great poet who is not also a great philosopher. Whatever Lord Byron's natural powers may have been, idleness and light reading, an early acquisition of popularity by the exercise of a single talent, and an absorbing and contracting self-love, confined the field of his operations within narrow limits. He was in knowledge merely a man of *belles-lettres;* nor does he appear at any time to have betaken himself to such studies as would have tended to the cultivation and discipline of his reasoning powers or the enlargement of his mind. He had, however, not only an ardent and brilliant imagination, but a clear understanding; and the signs both of what he had and of what he wanted are apparent in his poetry. There is apparent in it a working and moulding spirit, with a want of material to work up,—a great command of language, with a want of any views or reflections which, if unembellished by imagery or unassociated with passionate feelings, it would be very much worth while to express. Page after page throughout his earlier poems, there is the same uninformed energy at work upon the same old feelings; and when at last he became conscious that a theme was wanting, it was at a period of life when no man will consent to put himself to school; he could change his style and manner, but he could not change his moral and intellectual being, nor extend the sphere of his contemplations to subjects which were alien in *spirit* from those with which he had been hitherto, whether in life or in literature, exclusively conversant: in short, his mind was past the period of growth; there was to use a phrase of Ben Jonson's an

ingenistitium, or wit-stand: he felt, apparently, that the food on which he had fed his mind had not been invigorating; but he could no longer bear a stronger diet, and he turned his genius loose to rove over the surface of society, content with such slight observations upon life and manners as any acute man of the world might collect upon his travels, and conscious that he could recommend them to attention by such wit, brilliancy, dexterity of phrase and versatility of fancy, as no one but himself could command.

His misanthropy was probably, like his tenderness, not practical, but merely matter of imagination, assumed for purposes of effect. But whilst his ignorance of the better elements of human nature may be believed to have been in a great measure affected, it is not to be supposed that he knew of them with a large and appreciating knowledge. Yet that knowledge of human nature which is exclusive of what is good in it, is to say the least, as shallow and imperfect as that which is exclusive of what is evil. There is no such thing as philosophical misanthropy; and if a misanthropical spirit, be it genuine or affected, be found to pervade a man's writings, that spirit may be poetical as far as it goes, but, being at fault in its philosophy, it will never, in the long run of time, approve itself equal to the institution of a poetical fame of the highest and most durable order.

These imperfections are especially observable in the portraitures of human character (if such it can be called) which are most prominent in Lord Byron's works. There is nothing in them of the mixture and modification,—nothing of the composite fabric which Nature has assigned to Man. They exhibit rather passions personified than persons impassioned. But there is yet a worse defect in them. Lord Byron's conception of a hero is an evidence, not only of scanty materials of knowledge from which to construct the ideal of a human being, but also of a want of perception of what is great or noble in our nature. His heroes are creatures abandoned to their passions, and essentially, therefore, weak of mind. Strip them of the veil of mystery and the trappings of poetry, resolve them into their plain realities, and they are such beings as, in the eyes of a reader of masculine judgment, would certainly excite no sentiment of admiration, even if they did not provoke contempt. When the conduct and feelings attributed to them are reduced into prose and brought to the test of a rational consideration, they must be perceived to be beings in whom there is no strength except that of their intensely selfish passions,—in whom all is vanity, their exertions being for vanity under the name of love or revenge, and their sufferings for vanity under the name of pride. If such beings as these are to be regarded as heroical, where in human nature are we to look for what is low in sentiment or infirm in character?

How nobly opposite to Lord Byron's ideal was that conception of an heroical character which took life and immortality from the hand of Shakespeare:—

> "Give me that man
> That is not passion's slave, and I will wear him
> In my heart's core; aye, in my heart of heart." [1]

Lord Byron's genius, however, was powerful enough to cast a highly romantic colouring over these puerile creations, and to impart the charms of forcible expression, fervid feeling, and beautiful imagery, to thoughts in themselves not more remarkable for novelty than for soundness. The public required nothing more; and if he himself was brought latterly to a sense of his deficiencies of knowledge and general intellectual cultivation, it must have been more by the effect of time in so far maturing his very vigorous understanding than by any correction from without. No writer of his age has had less of the benefits of adverse criticism. His own judgment and that of his readers have been left equally without check or guidance; and the decline in popular estimation which he has suffered for these last few years may be rather attributed to a satiated appetite on the part of the public than to a rectified taste; for those who have ceased to admire his poetry so ardently as they did, do not appear in general to have transferred their admiration to any worthier object.

Nor can it be said that anything better, or indeed anything half so good, has been subsequently produced. The poetry of the day, whilst it is greatly inferior in quality, continues to be like his in kind. It consists of little more than a poetical diction, an arrangement of words implying a sensitive state of mind and therefore more or less calculated to excite corresponding associations, though, for the most part, not pertinently to any matter in hand; a diction which addresses itself to the sentient, not the percipient properties of the mind, and displays merely symbols or types of feelings which might exist with equal force in a being the most barren of understanding.

It may be proper, however, to make a distinction between the ordinary Byronian poetry, and that which may be considered as the offspring, either in the first or second generation, of the genius of Mr. Shelley. Mr. Shelley was a person of a more powerful and expansive imagination than Lord Byron, but he was inferior to him in those practical abilities which (unacceptable as such an opinion may be to those who believe themselves to be writing under the guidance of inspiration) are essential to the production of consummate poetry. The editor of Mr. Shelley's posthumous poems apologizes for the publication of some fragments in a very incomplete state, by remarking how much "more than every other poet of the present day, every line and word he wrote is instinct with peculiar beauty." Let no man sit down to write with the purpose of making every line and word beautiful and peculiar. The only effect of such an endeavour will be to corrupt his judgment and confound his understanding. In Mr. Shelley's case, besides an endeavour of this kind, there seems to

---

[1] *Hamlet* 3.2.77.

have been an attempt to unrealize every object in nature, presenting them under forms and combinations in which they are never to be seen through the mere medium of our eye-sight. Mr. Shelley seems to have written under the notion that no phenomena can be perfectly poetical until they shall have been so decomposed from their natural order and coherency as to be brought before the reader in the likeness of a phantasma or a vision. A poet is, in his estimation (if I may venture to infer his principles from his practice), purely and pre-eminently a visionary. Much beauty, exceeding splendour of diction and imagery, cannot but be perceived in his poetry, as well as exquisite charms of versification; and a reader of an apprehensive fancy will doubtless be entranced whilst he reads; but when he shall have closed the volume and considered within himself what it has added to his stock of permanent impressions, of recurring thoughts, of pregnant recollections, he will probably find his stores in this kind no more enriched by having read Mr. Shelley's poems, than by having gazed on so many gorgeously-coloured clouds in an evening sky. Surpassingly beautiful they were whilst before his eyes; but forasmuch as they had no relevancy to his life, past or future, the impression upon the memory barely survived that upon the senses.

I would by no means wish to be understood as saying that a poet can be too imaginative, provided that his other faculties be exercised in due proportion to his imagination. I would have no man depress his imagination, but I would have him raise his reason to be its equipoise. What I would be understood to oppugn is the strange opinion which seems to prevail amongst certain of our writers and readers of poetry, that reason stands in a species of antagonism to poetical genius, instead of being one of its most essential constituents. The maxim that a poet should be "of imagination all compact,"[1] is not, I think, to be adopted thus literally. That predominance of the

imaginative faculty, or of impassioned temperament, which is incompatible with the attributes of a sound understanding and a just judgment, may make a rhapsodist, a melodist, or a visionary, each of whom may produce what may be admired for the particular talent and beauty belonging to it: but imagination and passion thus unsupported will never make a poet in the largest and highest sense of the appellation:—

> "For Poetry is Reason's self sublimed;
> 'Tis Reason's sovereignty, whereunto
> All properties of sense, all dues of wit,
> All fancies, images, perceptions, passions,
> All intellectual ordinance grown up
> From accident, necessity, or custom,
> Seen to be good, and after made authentic;
> All ordinance aforethought that from science
> Doth prescience take, and from experience law;
> All lights and institutes of digested knowledge,
> Gifts and endowments of intelligence,
> From sources living, from the dead bequests,—
> Subserve and minister."[2]

Mr. Shelley and his disciples, however,—the followers (if I may so call them) of the phantastic school, labour to effect a revolution in this order of things. They would transfer the domicile of poetry to regions where reason, far from having any supremacy or rule, is all but unknown, an alien and an outcast; to seats of anarchy and abstraction, where imagination exercises the shadow of an authority, over a people of phantoms, in a land of dreams.

In bringing these cursory criticisms to an end, I must beg leave to warn the reader against any expectation that he will find my work free either from the faults which I attribute to others, or from faults which may be worse and more peculiarly my own. The actual works of men will not bear to be measured by their ideal standards in any case; and I may observe, in reference to my own, that my critical

---

[1] *Midsummer Night's Dream* 5.1.8.

[2] Taylor's own verse, from an unpublished MS.

views have rather resulted from composition than directed it. If, however, I have been unable to avoid the errors which I condemn, or errors not less censurable, I trust that, on the other hand, I shall not be found to have deprived myself, by any narrowness or perversity of judgment, of the advantage which the study of these writers, exceptionable though they be, may undoubtedly afford to one who, whilst duly taking note of their general defects, shall not have closed his mind to a perception of their particular excellences. I feel, and have already expressed, a most genuine and I hope not an inadequate admiration for the powers which they respectively possess; and wherever it might occur to me that the exercise of those powers would be appropriate and consistent, I should not fail to benefit by their example to the extent of my capabilities. To say, indeed, that I admire them, is to admit that I owe them much; for admiration is never thrown away upon the mind of him who feels it, except when it is misdirected or blindly indulged. There is perhaps nothing which more enlarges or enriches the mind than the disposition to lay it genially open to impressions of pleasure from the exercise of every species of power; nothing by which it is more impoverished than the habit of undue depreciation. What is puerile, pusillanimous, or wicked, it can do us no good to admire; but let us admire all that can be admired without debasing the dispositions or stultifying the understanding.

—LONDON, MAY, 1834.

Dante Gabriel Rossetti
1828 – 1882

Although he was the son of an Italian political refugee, Dante Gabriel Rossetti (born Gabriel Charles) never pursued a political life, preferring instead to concentrate on artistic endeavours. Demonstrating extraordinary talent in both painting and poetry, Rossetti's interest in art developed, in part, from his study of Keats' poems and letters, in which a sensuous response to beauty, through colour, texture, words, and women, functioned as a source of inspiration. With Ford Madox Brown, John Everett Millais, and William Holman Hunt, Rossetti formed the Pre-Raphaelite Brotherhood in 1848 in a concerted effort to reject neoclassical conventions in favour of the simpli-city and purity of pre-Renaissance art. While the diverse interests of each artist led to the break-up of the circle within a few years, the group's presence and ideas aroused immense interest and opposition during its formation and after its dissolution. Rossetti's personal view of art is one that connects the heavenly with the earthly and implicitly earthly, an artistic approach which is reflected in his poetry. Initially better known for his paintings, his poem "The Blessed Damozel" was published in the Pre-Raphaelite journal *The Germ* in 1850. *Poems by D.G. Rossetti*, containing the original version of *The House of Life* sonnet sequence, was published in 1871.

⌒⌒⌒

Hand and Soul [1]

Rivolsimi in quel lato
Là nde venìa la voce,
E parvemi una luce
Che lucea quanto stella:
La mia mente era quella. [2]
—Bonaggiunta Urbiciani (1250)

Before any knowledge of painting was brought to Florence, there were already painters in Lucca, and Pisa, and Arezzo, who feared God and loved the art. The keen, grave workmen from Greece, whose trade it was to sell their own works in Italy and teach Italians to imitate them, had already found rivals of the soil with skill that could forestall their lessons and cheapen their crucifixes and *addolorate*, more years than is supposed before the art came at all into Florence. The pre-eminence to which Cimabue [3] was raised at once by his contemporaries, and which he still retains to a wide extent even in the modern mind, is to be accounted for, partly by the circumstances under which he arose, and partly by that extraordinary *purpose of fortune* born with the lives of some few, and through which it is not a little thing for any who went before, if they are even remembered as the shadows of the coming of such an one, and the voices which prepared his way in the wilderness. It is thus, almost exclusively, that the painters of whom I speak are now known. They have left little, and but little heed is taken of that which men hold to have been surpassed; it is gone like time gone—a track of dust and dead leaves that merely led to the fountain.

Nevertheless, of very late years, and in very rare instances, some signs of a better understanding have become manifest. A case in point is that of the tryptic and two cruciform pictures at Dresden, by Chiaro di Messer Bello dell' Erma, to which the eloquent

---

[1] The text is based on the version which appeared in *The Germ* in January, 1850.

[2] "I turned in that direction
From where the voice came,
And it seemed to me [to be] a light:
That was my mind."

[3] Giovanni Cimabue (c. 1240–c. 1302), Florentine painter, traditionally thought of as the innovator of Italian art.

pamphlet of Dr. Aemmster [1] has at length succeeded in attracting the students. There is another still more solemn and beautiful work, now proved to be by the same hand, in the gallery at Florence. It is the one to which my narrative will relate.

———————

This Chiaro dell' Erma was a young man of very honorable family in Arezzo; where, conceiving art almost, as it were, for himself, and loving it deeply, he endeavoured from early boyhood towards the imitation of any objects offered in nature. The extreme longing after a visible embodiment of his thoughts strengthened as his years increased, more even than his sinews or the blood of his life; until he would feel faint in sunsets and at the sight of stately persons. When he had lived nineteen years, he heard of the famous Giunta Pisano, [2] and, feeling much of admiration, with, perhaps, a little of that envy which youth always feels until it has learned to measure success by time and opportunity, he determined that he would seek out Giunta, and, if possible, become his pupil.

Having arrived in Pisa, he clothed himself in humble apparel, being unwilling that any other thing than the desire he had for knowledge should be his plea with the great painter; and then, leaving his baggage at a house of entertainment, he took his way along the street, asking whom he met for the lodging of Giunta. It soon chanced that one of that city, conceiving him to be a stranger and poor, took him into his house, and refreshed him; afterwards directing him on his way.

When he was brought to speech of Giunta, he said merely that he was a student, and that nothing in the world was so much at his heart as to become that which he had heard told of him with whom he was speaking. He was received with courtesy and consid-

eration, and shewn into the study of the famous artist. But the forms he saw there were lifeless and incomplete; and a sudden exultation possessed him as he said with himself, "I am the master of this man." The blood came at first into his face, but the next moment he was quite pale and fell to trembling. He was able, however, to conceal his emotion; speaking very little to Giunta, but, when he took his leave, thanking him respectfully.

After this, Chiaro's first resolve was, that he would work out thoroughly some one of his thoughts, and let the world know him. But the lesson which he had now learned, of how small a greatness might win fame, and how little there was to strive against, served to make him torpid, and rendered his exertions less continual. Also Pisa was a larger and more luxurious city than Arezzo; and, when, in his walks, he saw the great gardens laid out for pleasure, and the beautiful women who passed to and fro, and heard the music that was in the groves of the city at evening, he was taken with wonder that he had never claimed his share of the inheritance of those years in which his youth was cast. And women loved Chiaro; for, in despite of the burthen of study, he was well-favoured and very manly in his walking; and, seeing his face in front, there was a glory upon it, as upon the face of one who feels a light round his hair.

So he put thought from him, and partook of his life. But, one night, being in a certain company of ladies, a gentleman that was there with him began to speak of the paintings of a youth named Bonaventura, which he had seen in Lucca; adding that Giunta Pisano might now look for a rival. When Chiaro heard this, the lamps shook before him, and the music beat in his ears and made him giddy. He rose up, alleging a sudden sickness, and went out of that house with his teeth set.

He now took to work diligently; not returning to Arezzo, but remaining in Pisa, that no day more might be lost; only living entirely to himself. Sometimes, after nightfall, he would walk abroad in the

———————

[1] not identified.

[2] Giunta Pisano (1202?–58), Italian painter of great influence.

most solitary places he could find; hardly feeling the ground under him, because of the thoughts of the day which held him in fever.

The lodging he had chosen was in a house that looked upon gardens fast by the Church of San Rocco. During the offices, as he sat at work, he could hear the music of the organ and the long murmur that the chanting left; and if his window were open, sometimes, at those parts of the mass where there is silence throughout the church, his ear caught faintly the single voice of the priest. Beside the matters of his art and a very few books, almost the only object to be noticed in Chiaro's room was a small consecrated image of St. Mary Virgin wrought out of silver, before which stood always, in summer-time, a glass containing a lily and a rose.

It was here, and at this time, that Chiaro painted the Dresden pictures; as also, in all likelihood, the one—inferior in merit, but certainly his—which is now at Munich. For the most part, he was calm and regular in his manner of study; though often he would remain at work through the whole of a day, not resting once so long as the light lasted; flushed, and with the hair from his face. Or, at times, when he could not paint, he would sit for hours in thought of all the greatness the world had known from of old; until he was weak with yearning, like one who gazes upon a path of stars.

He continued in this patient endeavour for about three years, at the end of which his name was spoken throughout all Tuscany. As his fame waxed, he began to be employed, besides easel-pictures, upon paintings in fresco: but I believe that no traces remain to us of any of these latter. He is said to have painted in the Duomo: and D'Agincourt[1] mentions having seen some portions of a fresco by him which originally had its place above the high altar in the Church of the Certosa; but which, at the time he saw it, being

___
[1] Jean-Baptiste Seroux D'Agincourt (1730–1814), art historian and critic of architecture.

very dilapidated, had been hewn out of the wall, and was preserved in the stores of the convent. Before the period of Dr. Aemmster's researches, however, it had been entirely destroyed.

Chiaro was now famous. It was for the race of fame that he had girded up his loins; and he had not paused until fame was reached: yet now, in taking breath, he found that the weight was still at his heart. The years of his labour had fallen from him, and his life was still in its first painful desire.

With all that Chiaro had done during these three years, and even before, with the studies of his early youth, there had always been a feeling of worship and service. It was the peace-offering that he made to God and to his own soul for the eager selfishness of his aim. There was earth, indeed, upon the hem of his raiment; but *this* was of the heaven, heavenly. He had seasons when he could endure to think of no other feature of his hope than this: and sometimes, in the ecstacy of prayer, it had even seemed to him to behold that day when his mistress—his mystical lady (now hardly in her ninth year, but whose solemn smile at meeting had already lighted on his soul like the dove of the Trinity)—even she, his own gracious and holy Italian art—with her virginal bosom, and her unfathomable eyes, and the thread of sunlight round her brows—should pass, through the sun that never sets into the circle of the shadow of the tree of life, and be seen of God, and found good: and then it had seemed to him, that he, with many who, since his coming, had joined the band of whom he was one (for, in his dream, the body he had worn on earth had been dead an hundred years), were permitted to gather round the blessed maiden, and to worship with her through all ages and ages, saying, Holy, holy, holy. This thing he had seen with the eyes of his spirit; and in this thing had trusted, believing that it would surely come to pass.

But now (being at length led to enquire closely into himself), even as, in the pursuit of fame, the unrest abiding after attainment had proved to him that he had misinterpreted the craving of his own spirit—so also, now that he would willingly have fallen back on devotion, he became aware that much of that reverence which he had mistaken for faith had been no more than the worship of beauty. Therefore, after certain days passed in perplexity, Chiaro said within himself, "My life and my will are yet before me: I will take another aim to my life."

From the moment Chiaro set a watch on his soul, and put his hand to no other works but only to such as had for their end the presentment of some moral greatness that should impress the beholder: and, in doing this, he did not choose for his medium the action and passion of human life, but cold symbolism and abstract impersonation. So the people ceased to throng about his pictures as heretofore; and, when they were carried through town and town to their destination, they were no longer delayed by the crowds eager to gaze and admire: and no prayers or offerings were brought to them on their path, as to his Madonnas, and his Saints, and his Holy Children. Only the critical audience remained to him; and these, in default of more worthy matter, would have turned their scrutiny on a puppet or a mantle. Meanwhile, he had no more of fever upon him; but was calm and pale each day in all that he did and in his goings in and out. The works he produced at this time have perished—in all likelihood, not unjustly. It is said (and we may easily believe it) that, though more laboured than his former pictures, they were cold and unemphatic; bearing marked out upon them, as they must certainly have done, the measure of that boundary to which they were made to conform.

And the weight was still close to Chiaro's heart: but he held in his breath, never resting (for he was afraid), and would not know it.

Now it happened, within these days, that there fell a great feast in Pisa, for holy matters: and each man left his occupation; and all the guilds and companies of the city were got together for games and rejoicings. And there were scarcely any that stayed in the houses, except ladies who lay or sat along their balconies between open windows which let the breeze beat through the rooms and over the spread tables from end to end. And the golden cloths that their arms lay upon drew all eyes upward to see their beauty; and the day was long; and every hour of the day was bright with the sun.

So Chiaro's model, when he awoke that morning on the hot pavement of the Piazza Nunziata, and saw the hurry of people that passed him, got up and went along with them; and Chiaro waited for him in vain.

For the whole of that morning, the music was in Chiaro's room from the Church close at hand: and he could hear the sounds that the crowd made in the streets; hushed only at long intervals while the processions for the feast-day changed in going under his windows. Also, more than once, there was a high clamour from the meeting of factious persons: for the ladies of both leagues were looking down; and he who encountered his enemy could not choose but draw upon him. Chiaro waited a long time idle; and then knew that his model was gone elsewhere. When at his work, he was blind and deaf to all else; but he feared sloth: for then his stealthy thoughts would begin, as it were, to beat round and round him, seeking a point for attack. He now rose, therefore, and went to the window. It was within a short space of noon; and underneath him a throng of people was coming out through the porch of San Rocco.

The two greatest houses of the feud in Pisa had filled the church for that mass. The first to leave had been the Gherghiotti; who, stopping on the threshold, had fallen back in ranks along each side of the archway: so that now, in passing outward, the Marotoli had to walk between two files of men whom they hated, and whose fathers had hated theirs. All the chiefs were there and their whole adherence; and each knew the name of each. Every man of the Marotoli, as he came forth and saw his foes, laid back his hood and gazed about him, to show the badge upon the close cap that held his hair. And of the Gherghiotti there were some who tightened their girdles; and some shrilled and threw up their wrists scornfully, as who flies a falcon; for that was the crest of their house.

On the walls within the entry were a number of tall, narrow frescoes, presenting a moral allegory of Peace, which Chiaro had painted that year for the Church. The Gherghiotti stood with their backs to these frescoes: and among them Golzo Ninuccio, the youngest noble of the faction, called by the people Golaghiotta, for his debased life. This youth had remained for some while talking listlessly to his fellows, though with his sleepy sunken eyes fixed on them who passed: but now, seeing that no man jostled another, he drew the long silver shoe off his foot, and struck the dust out of it on the cloak of him who was going by, asking how far the tides rose at Viderza. And he said so because it was three months since, at that place, the Gherghiotti had beaten the Marotoli to the sands, and held them there while the sea came in; whereby many had been drowned. And, when he had spoken, at once the whole archway was dazzling with the light of confused swords; and they who had left turned back; and they who were still behind made haste to come forth: and there was so much blood cast up the walls on a sudden that it ran in long streams down Chiaro's paintings.

Chiaro turned himself from the window; for the light felt dry between his lids, and he could not look. He sat down, and heard the noise of contention driven out of the church-porch and a great way through the streets; and soon there was a deep murmur that heaved and waxed from the other side of the city, where those of both parties were gathering to join in the tumult.

Chiaro sat with his face in his open hands. Once again he had wished to set his foot on a place that looked green and fertile; and once again it seemed to him that the thin rank mask was about to spread away, and that this time the chill of the water must leave leprosy in his flesh. The light still swam in his head, and bewildered him at first; but when he knew his thoughts, they were these:—

"Fame failed me: faith failed me: and now this also,—the hope that I nourished in this my generation of man,—shall pass from me, and leave my feet and my hands groping. Yet, because of this, are my feet become slow and my hands thin. I am as one who, through the whole night, holding his way diligently, hath smitten the steel unto the flint, to lead some whom he knew darkling; who hath kept his eyes always on the sparks that himself made, lest they should fail; and who, towards dawn, turning to bid them that he had guided God speed, sees the wet grass untrodden except of his own feet. I am as the last hour of the day, whose chimes are a perfect number; whom the next followeth not, nor light ensueth from him; but in the same darkness is the old order begun afresh. Men say, 'This is not God nor man; he is not as we are, neither above us: let him sit beneath us, for we are many.' Where I write Peace, in that spot is the drawing of swords, and there men's footprints are red. When I would sow, another harvest is ripe. Nay, it is much worse with me than thus much. Am I not as a cloth drawn before the light, that the looker may not be blinded; but which sheweth thereby the grain of its own coarseness; so that the light seems defiled, and men say, 'We will not walk by it.' Wherefore through me they shall be doubly accursed, seeing that through me they reject the light. May one be a devil and not know it?"

As Chiaro was in these thoughts, the fever encroached slowly on his veins, till he could sit no longer, and would have risen; but suddenly he found awe within him, and held his head bowed, without stirring. The warmth of the air was not shaken; but there seemed a pulse in the light, and a living freshness, like rain. The silence was a painful music, that made the blood ache in his temples; and he lifted his face and his deep eyes.

A woman was present in his room, clad to the hands and feet with a green and grey raiment, fashioned to that time. It seemed that the first thoughts he had ever known were given him as at first from her eyes, and he knew her hair to be the golden veil through which he beheld his dreams. Though her hands were joined, her face was not lifted, but set forward; and though the gaze was austere, yet her mouth was supreme in gentleness. And as he looked, Chiaro's spirit appeared abashed of its own intimate presence, and his lips shook with the thrill of tears; it seemed such a bitter while till the spirit might be indeed alone.

She did not move closer towards him, but he felt her to be as much with him as his breath. He was like one who, scaling a great steepness, hears his own voice echoed in some place much higher than he can see, and the name of which is not known to him. As the woman stood, her speech was with Chiaro: not, as it were, from her mouth or in his ears; but distinctly between them.

"I am an image, Chiaro, of thine own soul within thee. See me, and know me as I am. Thou sayest that fame has failed thee, and faith failed thee; but because at least thou hast not laid thy life unto riches, therefore, though thus late, I am suffered to come into thy knowledge. Fame suffced not, for that thou didst seek fame: seek thine own conscience (not thy mind's conscience, but thine heart's), and all shall approve and suffice. For Fame, in noble soils, is a fruit of the Spring: but not therefore should it be said: 'Lo! my garden that I planted is barren: the crocus is here, but the lily is dead in the dry ground, and shall not lift the earth that covers it: therefore I will fling my garden together, and give it unto the builders.' Take heed rather that thou trouble not the wise secret earth; for in the mould that thou throwest up shall the first tender growth lie to waste; which else had been made strong in its season. Yea, and even if the year fall past in all its months, and the soil be indeed, to thee, peevish and incapable, and though thou

indeed gather all thy harvest, and it suffice for others, and thou remain vext with emptiness; and others drink of thy streams, and the drouth rasp thy throat;—let it be enough that these have found the feast good, and thanked the giver: remembering that, when the winter is striven through, there is another year, whose wind is meek, and whose sun fulfilleth all."

While he heard, Chiaro went slowly on his knees. It was not to her that spoke, for the speech seemed with him and his own. The air brooded in sunshine, and though the turmoil was great outside, the air within was at peace. But when he looked in her eyes, he wept. And she came to him, and cast her hair over him, and, took her hands above his forehead, and spoke again:

"Thou has said," she continued, gently, "that faith failed thee. This cannot be so. Either thou hadst it not, or thou hast it. But who bade thee strike the point betwixt love and faith? Wouldst thou sift the warm breeze from the sun that quickens it? Who bade thee turn upon God and say: 'Behold, my offering is of earth, and not worthy: thy fire comes not upon it: therefore, though I slay not my brother whom thou acceptest, I will depart before thou smite me.' Why shouldst thou rise up and tell God He is not content? Had He, of His warrant, certified so to thee? Be not nice to seek out division; but possess thy love in sufficiency: assuredly this is faith, for the heart must believe first. What He hath set in thine heart to do, that do thou; and even though thou do it without thought of Him, it shall be well done: it is this sacrifice that He asketh of thee, and His flame is upon it for a sign. Think not of Him; but of His love and thy love. For God is no morbid exactor: He hath no hand to bow beneath, for a foot, that thou shouldst kiss it."

And Chiaro held silence, and wept into her hair which covered his face; and the salt tears that he shed ran through her hair upon his lips; and he tasted the bitterness of shame.

Then the fair woman, that was his soul, spoke again to him saying:

"And for this thy last purpose, and for those unprofitable truths of thy teaching,—thine heart hath already put them away, and it needs not that I lay my bidding upon thee. How is that thou, a man, wouldst say coldly to the mind what God hath said to the heart warmly? Thy will was honest and wholesome; but look well lest this also be folly,—to say, 'I, in doing this, do strengthen God among men.' When at any time hath he cried unto thee, saying, 'My son, lend me thy shoulder, for I fall?' Deemest thou that the men who enter God's temper in malice, to the provoking of blood, and neither for his love nor for his wrath will abate their purpose,—shall afterwards stand with thee in the porch, midway between Him and themselves, to give ear unto thy thin voice, which merely the fall of their visors can drown, and to see thy hands, stretched feebly, tremble among their swords? Give thou to God no more than he asketh of thee; but to man also, that which is man's. In all that thou doest, work from thine own heart, simply; for his heart is as thine, when thine is wise and humble; and he shall have understanding of thee. One drop of rain is as another, and the sun's prism in all: and shalt not thou be as he, whose lives are the breath of One? Only by making thyself his equal can he learn to hold communion with thee, and at last own thee above him. Not till thou lean over the water shalt thou see thine image therein: stand erect, and it shall slope from thy feet and be lost. Know that there is but this means whereby thou may'st serve God with man:— Set thine hand and thy soul to serve man with God."

And when she that spoke had said these words within Chiaro's spirit, she left his side quietly, and stood up as he had first seen her; with her fingers laid together, and her eyes steadfast, and with the breadth of her long dress covering her feet on the floor. And, speaking again, she said:

"Chiaro, servant of God, take now thine Art unto thee, and paint me thus, as I am, to know me: weak, as I am, and in the weeds of this time; only with eyes which seek out labour, and with a faith, not learned, yet jealous of prayer. Do this; so shall thy soul stand before thee always, and perplex thee no more."

And Chiaro did as she bade him. While he worked, his face grew solemn with knowledge: and before the shadows had turned, his work was done. Having finished, he lay back where he sat, and was asleep immediately: for the growth of that strong sunset was heavy about him, and he felt weak and haggard; like one just come out of a dusk, hollow country, bewildered with echoes, where he had lost himself, and who has not slept for many days and nights. And when she saw him lie back, the beautiful woman came to him, and sat at his head, gazing, and quieted his sleep with her voice.

The tumult of the factions had endured all that day through all Pisa, though Chiaro had not heard it: and the last service of that Feast was a mass sung at midnight from the windows of all the churches for the many dead who lay about the city, and who had to be buried before morning, because of the extreme heats.

In the Spring of 1847 I was at Florence. Such as were there at the same time with myself—those, at least to whom Art is something,—will certainly recollect how many rooms of the Pitti Gallery were closed through that season, in order that some of the picture they contained might be examined and repaired without the necessity of removal. The hall, the staircase, and the vast central suite of apartments, were the only accessible portions: and in these such paintings as they could admit from the sealed *penetralia* were profanely huddled together, without respect of dates, schools, or persons.

I fear that, through this interdict, I may have missed seeing many of the best pictures. I do not mean *only* the most talked of: for these, as they were restored, generally found their way somehow into the open rooms, owing to the clamours raised by the students; and I remember how old Ercoli's, the curator's, spectacles used to be mirrored in the reclaimed surface, as he leaned mysteriously over these works with some of the visitors, to scrutinize and elucidate.

One picture, that I saw that Spring, I shall not easily forget. It was among those, I believe, brought from the other rooms, and had been hung, obviously out of all chronology, immediately beneath that head by Raphael[1] so long known as the "Berrettino," and now said to be the portrait of Cecco Ciulli.

The picture I speak of is a small one, and represents merely the figure of a woman, clad to the hands and feet with a green and grey raiment, chaste and early in its fashion, but exceedingly simple. She is standing: her hands are held together lightly, and her eyes set earnestly open.

The face and hands in this picture, though wrought with great delicacy, have the appearance of being painted at once, in a single sitting: the drapery is unfinished. As soon as I saw the figure, it drew an awe upon me, like water in shadow. I shall not attempt to describe it more than I have already done; for the most absorbing wonder of it was its literality. You knew that figure, when painted, had been seen; yet it was not a thing to be seen of men. This language will appear ridiculous to such as have never looked on the work; and it may be even to some among those who have. On examining it closely, I perceived in one corner of the canvass the words *Manus Animam pinxit,*[2] and the date 1239.

I turned to my Catalogue, but that was useless, for the pictures were all displaced. I then stepped up to the Cavaliere Ercoli, who was in the room at the moment, and asked him regarding the subject and authorship of the painting. He treated the matter, I thought, somewhat slightingly, and said that he could show me the reference in the Catalogue, which he had compiled. This, when found, was not of much value, as it merely said, "Schizzo d'autore incerto,"[3] adding the inscription. I could willingly have prolonged my inquiry, in the hope that it might somehow lead to some result; but I had disturbed the curator from certain yards of Guido, and he was not communicative. I went back therefore, and stood before the picture till it grew dusk.

The next day I was there again; but this time a circle of students was round the spot, all copying the "Berrettino." I contrived, however, to find a place whence I could see *my* picture, and where I seemed to be in nobody's way. For some minutes I remained undisturbed; and then I heard, in an English voice: "Might I beg of you, sir, to stand a little more to this side, as you interrupt my view."

I felt vext, for, standing where he asked me, a glare struck on the picture from the windows, and I could not see it. However, the request was reasonably made, and from a countryman; so I complied, and turning away, stood by his easel. I knew it was not worth while; yet I referred in some way to the work underneath the one he was copying. He did not laugh, but he smiled as we do in England: "Very odd, is it not?" said he.

The other students near us were all continental; and seeing an Englishman select an Englishman to speak with, conceived, I suppose, that he could understand no language but his own. They had evidently been noticing the interest which the little picture appeared to excite in me.

One of them, an Italian, said something to another who stood next to him. He spoke with a Genoese accent, and I lost the sense in the villanous dialect. "Che so?" replied the other, lifting his eyebrows towards the figure; "Roba mistica: 'st' Inglesi

---

[1] Raphael (1483–1520), Italian painter, definer of High Renaissance style.

[2] "Hand painted Soul."

[3] "The sketch of the author is uncertain."

1241

son matti sul misticismo: somiglia alle nebbie di là. Li fa pensare alla patria,

> E intenerisce il core
> Lo dì ch'han detto ai dolci amici adio."

"La notte, vuoi dire,"[1] said a third.

There was a general laugh. My compatriot was evidently a novice in the language, and did not take in what was said. I remained silent, being amused.

"Et toi donc?" said he who had quoted Dante, turning to a student, whose birthplace was unmistakable even had he been addressed in any other language: "que dis-tu de ce genre-la?"

"Moi?" returned the Frenchman, standing back from his easel, and looking at me and at the figure, quite politely, though with an evident reservation: "Je dis, mon cher, que c'est une specialite dont je me fiche pas mal. Je tiens que quand on ne comprend pas une chose, c'est qu'elle ne signifie rien."[2]

My reader thinks possibly that the French student was right.

—1850

---

[1] "What am I?" "Mystical clothing: the English are crazy about mysticism. It's like the fog from there. It makes them think about their nation,

> The inner part of their heart

I'm saying what others have said, goodbye to the dear friend."
"At night, I mean to say."

[2] "And you then…what do you have to say about this style?" "Me?…I say, my dear, that it's a specialty that I don't much care for. I believe that when there is something that we don't understand, it's because it means nothing."

Robert Browning

1812 – 1889

Robert Browning is recognized for his poetic achievement in the dramatic monologue, especially those poems in the volumes published in 1855, *Men and Women*, and 1864, *Dramatis Personae*. Browning received little formal education—six years of schooling from the ages of nine to fourteen, and part of one year at London University. His home education was the result of his immersion in his bank-clerk father's large and esoteric library, and the influence of his nonconformist mother's religion and her interest in nature and music. Browning's depth of learning and interest in poetic experimentation is evident in his early work—*Pauline* (1833), *Paracelsus* (1835), and *Sordello* (1840), as well as in the series *Bells and Pomegranates* (1841–46). This series also contained *Dramatic Lyrics* (1842), and *Dramatic Romances and Lyrics* (1845), the former of which included his famous "My Last Duchess," and the latter his first blank-verse dramatic monologue, "The Bishop Orders His Tomb at St. Praxed's Church." Browning met Elizabeth Barrett, whose contemporary reputation as a poet exceeded his, in 1845, and they married on 12 May 1846, after which they immediately took up residence in Italy. Browning returned to England in 1861 after Elizabeth's death, and worked on his complex multinarrative poem *The Ring and the Book* (1868–69). His poetic experimentation continued until his death in 1889.

❦

"Introductory Essay" ["Essay on Shelley"] [1]

An opportunity having presented itself for the acquisition of a series of unedited letters by Shelley, all more or less directly supplementary to and illustrative of the collection already published by Mr. Moxon, that gentleman has decided on securing them. They will prove an acceptable addition to a body of correspondence, the value of which towards a right understanding of its author's purpose and work, may be said to exceed that of any similar contribution exhibiting the worldly relations of a poet whose genius has operated by a different law.

Doubtless we accept gladly the biography of an objective poet, as the phrase now goes; one whose endeavour has been to reproduce things external (whether the phenomena of the scenic universe, or the manifested action of the human heart and brain) with an immediate reference, in every case, to the common eye and apprehension of his fellow men, assumed capable of receiving and profiting by this reproduction. It has been obtained through the poet's double faculty of seeing external objects more clearly, widely, and deeply, than is possible to the average mind, at the same time that he is so acquainted and in sympathy with its narrower comprehension as to be careful to supply it with no other materials than it can combine into an intelligible whole. The auditory of such a poet will include, not only the intelligences which, save for such assistance, would have missed the deeper meaning and enjoyment of the original objects, but also the spirits of a like endowment with his own, who, by means of his abstract, can forthwith pass to the reality it was made from, and either corroborate their impressions of things known already, or supply themselves with new from whatever shows in the inexhaustible variety of existence may have hitherto escaped their knowledge. Such a poet is properly the ποιητης, the fashioner; and the thing fashioned, his poetry, will of necessity be substantive, projected from himself and distinct. We

---

[1] The "Introductory Essay" to the *Letters of Percy Bysshe Shelley* was published early in 1852 by Edward Moxon, Browning's friend and the publisher of the *Bells and Pomegranates* (1841–46) series. The letters were found to be spurious before the book was distributed, and it was immediately withdrawn from circulation.

are ignorant what the inventor of *Othello* conceived of that fact as he beheld it in completeness, how he accounted for it, under what known law he registered its nature, or to what unknown law he traced its coincidence. We learn only what he intended we should learn by that particular exercise of his power,—the fact itself,—which, with its infinite significances, each of us receives for the first time as a creation, and is hereafter left to deal with, as, in proportion to his own intelligence, he best may. We are ignorant, and would fain be otherwise.

Doubtless, with respect to such a poet, we covet his biography. We desire to look back upon the process of gathering together in a lifetime, the materials of the work we behold entire; of elaborating, perhaps under difficulty and with hindrance, all that is familiar to our admiration in the apparent facility of success. And the inner impulse of this effort and operation, what induced it? Did a soul's delight in its own extended sphere of vision set it, for the gratification of an insuppressible power, on labour, as other men are set on rest? Or did a sense of duty or of love lead it to communicate its own sensations to mankind? Did an irresistible sympathy with men compel it to bring down and suit its own provision of knowledge and beauty to their narrow scope? Did the personality of such an one stand like an open watchtower in the midst of the territory it is erected to gaze on, and were the storms and calms, the stars and meteors, its watchman was wont to report of, the habitual variegation of his every-day life, as they glanced across its open roof or lay reflected on its four-square parapet? Or did some sunken and darkened chamber of imagery witness, in the artificial illumination of every storied compartment we are permitted to contemplate, how rare and precious were the outlooks through here and there an embrasure upon a world beyond, and how blankly would have pressed on the artificer the boundary of his daily life, except for the amorous diligence with which he had rendered permanent by art whatever came to

diversify the gloom? Still, fraught with instruction and interest as such details undoubtedly are, we can, if needs be, dispense with them. The man passes, the work remains. The work speaks for itself, as we say: and the biography of the worker is no more necessary to an understanding or enjoyment of it, than is a model or anatomy of some tropical tree, to the right tasting of the fruit we are familiar with on the market-stall,—or a geologist's map and stratification, to the prompt recognition of the hill-top, our landmark of every day.

We turn with stronger needs to the genius of an opposite tendency—the subjective poet of modern classification. He, gifted like the objective poet with the fuller perception of nature and man, is impelled to embody the thing he perceives, not so much with reference to the many below as to the one above him, the supreme Intelligence which apprehends all things in their absolute truth,—an ultimate view ever aspired to, if but partially attained, by the poet's own soul. Not what man sees, but what God sees—the *Ideas* of Plato, seeds of creation lying burningly on the Divine Hand—it is toward these that he struggles. Not with the combination of humanity in action, but with the primal elements of humanity he has to do; and he digs where he stands,—preferring to seek them in his own soul as the nearest reflex of that absolute Mind, according to the intuitions of which he desires to perceive and speak. Such a poet does not deal habitually with the picturesque groupings and tempestuous tossings of the forest-trees, but with their roots and fibres naked to the chalk and stone. He does not paint pictures and hang them on the walls, but rather carries them on the retina of his own eyes: we must look deep into his human eyes, to see those pictures on them. He is rather a seer, accordingly, than a fashioner, and what he produces will be less a work than an effluence. That effluence cannot be easily considered in abstraction from his personality,—being indeed the very radiance and aroma of his personality, projected from it but not separated. Therefore, in our approach to the poetry, we necessarily approach the personality of the poet; in apprehending it we apprehend him, and certainly we cannot love it without loving him. Both for love's and for understanding's sake we desire to know him, and as readers of his poetry must be readers of his biography also.

I shall observe, in passing, that it seems not so much from any essential distinction in the faculty of the two poets or in the nature of the objects contemplated by either, as in the more immediate adaptability of these objects to the distinct purpose of each, that the objective poet, in his appeal to the aggregate human mind, chooses to deal with the doings of men, (the result of which dealing, in its pure form, when even description, as suggesting a describer, is dispensed with, is what we call dramatic poetry), while the subjective poet, whose study has been himself, appealing through himself to the absolute Divine mind, prefers to dwell upon those external scenic appearances which strike out most abundantly and uninterruptedly his inner light and power, selects that silence of the earth and sea in which he can best hear the beating of his individual heart, and leaves the noisy, complex, yet imperfect exhibitions of nature in the manifold experience of man around him, which serve only to distract and suppress the working of his brain. These opposite tendencies of genius will be more readily descried in their artistic effect than in their moral spring and cause. Pushed to an extreme and manifested as a deformity, they will be seen plainest of all in the fault of either artist, when subsidiarily to the human interest of his work his occasional illustrations from scenic nature are introduced as in the earlier works of the originative painters—men and women filling the foreground with consummate mastery, while mountain, grove and rivulet show like an anticipatory revenge on that succeeding race of landscape-painters whose "figures" disturb the perfection of their earth and sky. It would be idle to inquire, of these two kinds of poetic faculty

in operation, which is the higher or even rarer endowment. If the subjective might seem to be the ultimate requirement of every age, the objective, in the strictest state, must still retain its original value. For it is with this world, as starting point and basis alike, that we shall always have to concern ourselves: the world is not to be learned and thrown aside, but reverted to and relearned. The spiritual comprehension may be infinitely subtilized, but the raw material it operates upon, must remain. There may be no end of the poets who communicate to us what they see in an object with reference to their own individuality; what it was before they saw it, in reference to the aggregate human mind, will be as desirable to know as ever. Nor is there any reason why these two modes of poetic faculty may not issue hereafter from the same poet in successive perfect works, examples of which, according to what are now considered the exigences of art, we have hitherto possessed in distinct individuals only. A mere running-in of the one faculty upon the other, is, of course, the ordinary circumstance. Far more rarely it happens that either is found so decidedly prominent and superior, as to be pronounced comparatively pure: while of the perfect shield, with the gold and the silver side set up for all comers to challenge, there has yet been no instance. Either faculty in its eminent state is doubtless conceded by Providence as a best gift to men, according to their especial want. There is a time when the general eye has, so to speak, absorbed its fill of the phenomena around it, whether spiritual or material, and desires rather to learn the exacter significance of what it possesses, than to receive any augmentation of what is possessed. Then is the opportunity for the poet of loftier vision, to lift his fellows, with their half-apprehensions, up to his own sphere, by intensifying the import of details and rounding the universal meaning. The influence of such an achievement will not soon die out. A tribe of successors (Homerides) working more or less in the same spirit, dwell on his discoveries and reinforce his doctrine; till, at unawares, the world is found to be subsisting wholly on the shadow of a reality, on sentiments diluted from passions, on the tradition of a fact, the convention of a moral, the straw of last year's harvest. Then is the imperative call for the appearance of another sort of poet, who shall at once replace this intellectual rumination of food swallowed long ago, by a supply of the fresh and living swathe; getting at new substance by breaking up the assumed wholes into parts of independent and unclassed value, careless of the unknown laws for re-combining them (it will be the business of yet another poet to suggest those hereafter), prodigal of objects for men's outer and not inner sight, shaping for their uses a new and different creation from the last, which it displaces by the right of life over death,—to endure until, in the inevitable process, its very sufficiency to itself shall require, at length, an exposition of its affinity to something higher,—when the positive yet conflicting facts shall again precipitate themselves under a harmonizing law, and one more degree will be apparent for a poet to climb in that mighty ladder, of which, however cloud-involved and undefined may glimmer the topmost step, the world dares no longer doubt that its gradations ascend.

Such being the two kinds of artists, it is naturally, as I have shown, with the biography of the subjective poet that we have the deeper concern. Apart from his recorded life altogether, we might fail to determine with satisfactory precision to what class his productions belong, and what amount of praise is assignable to the producer. Certainly, in the face of any conspicuous achievement of genius, philosophy, no less than sympathetic instinct, warrants our belief in a great moral purpose having mainly inspired even where it does not visibly look out of the same. Greatness in a work suggests an adequate instrumentality; and none of the lower incitements, however they may avail to initiate or even effect many considerable displays of power, simulating the nobler inspiration to which they are mistakenly referred, have been found able,

under the ordinary conditions of humanity, to task themselves to the end of so exacting a performance as a poet's complete work. As soon will the galvanism that provokes to violent action the muscles of a corpse, induce it to cross the chamber steadily: sooner. The love of displaying power for the display's sake, the love of riches, of distinction, of notoriety,—the desire of a triumph over rivals, and the vanity in the applause of friends,—each and all of such whetted appetites grow intenser by exercise and increasingly sagacious as to the best and readiest means of self-appeasement,—while for any of their ends, whether the money or the pointed finger of the crowd, or the flattery and hate to heart's content, there are cheaper prices to pay, they will all find soon enough, than the bestowment of a life upon a labour, hard, slow, and not sure. Also, assuming the proper moral aim to have produced a work, there are many and various states of an aim: it may be more intense than clear-sighted, or too easily satisfied with a lower field of activity than a steadier aspiration would reach. All the bad poetry in the world (accounted poetry, that is, by its affinities) will be found to result from some one of the infinite degrees of discrepancy between the attributes of the poet's soul, occasioning a want of correspondency between his work and the verities of nature,—issuing in poetry, false under whatever form, which shows a thing not as it is to mankind generally, nor as it is to the particular describer, but as it is supposed to be for some unreal neutral mood, midway between both and of value to neither, and living its brief minute simply through the indolence of whatever accepts it or his incapacity to denounce a cheat. Although of such depths of failure there can be no question here we must in every case betake ourselves to the review of a poet's life ere we determine some of the nicer questions concerning his poetry,—more especially if the performance we seek to estimate aright, has been obstructed and cut short of completion by circumstances,—a disastrous youth or a premature death. We may learn from the biography whether his spirit invariably saw and spoke from the last height to which it had attained. An absolute vision is not for this world, but we are permitted a continual approximation to it, every degree of which in the individual, provided it exceed the attainment of the masses, must procure him a clear advantage. Did the poet ever attain to a higher platform than where he rested and exhibited a result? Did he know more than he spoke of?

I concede however, in respect to the subject of our study as well as some few other illustrious examples, that the unmistakable quality of the verse would be evidence enough, under usual circumstances, not only of the kind and degree of the intellectual but of the moral constitution of Shelley: the whole personality of the poet shining forward from the poems, without much need of going further to seek it. The "Remains"—produced within a period of ten years, and at a season of life when other men of at all comparable genius have hardly done more than prepare the eye for future sight and the tongue for speech—present us with the complete enginery of a poet, as signal in the excellence of its several adaptitudes as transcendent in the combination of effects,—examples, in fact, of the whole poet's function of beholding with an understanding keenness the universe, nature and man, in their actual state of perfection in imperfection,—of the whole poet's virtue of being untempted by the manifold partial developments of beauty and good on every side, into leaving them the ultimates he found them,—induced by the facility of the gratification of his own sense of those qualities, or by the pleasure of acquiescence in the shortcomings of his predecessors in art, and the pain of disturbing their conventionalisms,—the whole poet's virtue, I repeat, of looking higher than any manifestation yet made of both beauty and good, in order to suggest from the utmost actual realization of the one a corresponding capability in the other, and out of the calm, purity and energy of nature, to reconstitute and store up for the forthcoming stage of

man's being, a gift in repayment of that former gift, in which man's own thought and passion had been lavished by the poet on the else-incompleted magnificence of the sunrise, the else-uninterpreted mystery of the lake,—so drawing out, lifting up, and assimilating this ideal of a future man, thus descried as possible, to the present reality of the poet's soul already arrived at the higher state of development, and still aspirant to elevate and extend itself in conformity with its still-improving perceptions of, no longer the eventual Human, but the actual Divine. In conjunction with which noble and rare powers, came the subordinate power of delivering these attained results to the world in an embodiment of verse more closely answering to and indicative of the process of the informing spirit, (failing as it occasionally does, in art, only to succeed in highest art),—with a diction more adequate to the task in its natural and acquired richness, its material colour and spiritual transparency,—the whole being moved by and suffused with a music at once of the soul and the sense, expressive both of an external might of sincere passion and an internal fitness and consonancy,—than can be attributed to any other writer whose record is among us. Such was the spheric poetical faculty of Shelley, as its own self-sufficing central light, radiating equally through immaturity and accomplishment, through many fragments and occasional completion, reveals it to a competent judgement.

But the acceptance of this truth by the public, has been retarded by certain objections which cast us back on the evidence of biography, even with Shelley's poetry in our hands. Except for the particular character of these objections, indeed, the non-appreciation of his contemporaries would simply class, now that it is over, with a series of experiences which have necessarily happened and needlessly been wondered at, ever since the world began, and concerning which any present anger may well be moderated, no less in justice to our forerunners than in policy to ourselves. For the misapprehensiveness of his age is exactly what a poet is sent to remedy; and the interval between his operation and the generally perceptibly effect of it, is no greater, less indeed, than in many other departments of the great human effort. The *E pur si muove*[1] of the astronomer was as bitter a word as any uttered before or since by a poet over his rejected living work, in that depth of conviction which is so like despair.

But in this respect was the experience of Shelley peculiarly unfortunate—that the disbelief in him as a man, even preceded the disbelief in him as a writer; the misconstruction of his moral nature preparing the way for the misappreciation of his intellectual labours. There existed from the beginning,—simultaneous with, indeed anterior to his earliest noticeable works, and not brought forward to counteract any impression they had succeeded in making, —certain charges against his private character and life, which, if substantiated to their whole breadth, would materially disturb, I do not attempt to deny, our reception and enjoyment of his works, however wonderful the artistic qualities of these. For we are not sufficiently supplied with instances of genius of his order, to be able to pronounce certainly how many of its constituent parts have been tasked and strained to the production of a given lie, and how high and pure a mood of the creative mind may be dramatically simulated as the poet's habitual and exclusive one. The doubts, therefore, arising from such a question, required to be set at rest, as they were effectually, by those early authentic notices of Shelley's career and the corroborative accompaniment of his letters, in which not only the main tenor and principal result of his life, but the purity and beauty of many of the processes which had conduced to them, were made apparent enough for the general reader's purpose,—whoever lightly condemned Shelley first, on the evidence of reviews and gossip, as

lightly acquitting him now, on that of memoirs and correspondence. Still, it is advisable to lose no opportunity of strengthening and completing the chain of biographical testimony; much more, of course, for the sake of the poet's original lovers, whose volunteered sacrifice of particular principle in favour of absorbing sympathy we might desire to dispense with, than for the sake of his foolish haters, who have long since diverted upon other objects their obtuseness or malignancy. A full life of Shelley should be written at once, while the materials for it continue in reach; not to minister to the curiosity of the public, but to obliterate the last stain of that false life which was forced on the public's attention before it had any curiosity on the matter,—a biography, composed in harmony with the present general disposition to have faith in him, yet not shrinking from a candid statement of all ambiguous passages, through a reasonable confidence that the most doubtful of them will be found consistent with a belief in the eventual perfection of his character, according to the poor limits of our humanity. Nor will men persist in confounding, any more than God confounds, with genuine infidelity and an atheism of the heart, those passionate, impatient struggles of a boy towards distant truth and love, made in the dark, and ended by one sweep of the natural seas before the full moral sunrise could shine out on him. Crude convictions of boyhood, conveyed in imperfect and inapt forms of speech,— for such things all boys have been pardoned. There are growing-pains, accompanied by temporary distortion, of the soul also. And it would be hard indeed upon this young Titan of genius, murmuring in divine music his human ignorances, through his very thirst for knowledge, and his rebellion, in mere aspiration to law, if the melody itself substantiated the error, and the tragic cutting short of life perpetuated into sins, such faults as, under happier circumstances, would have been left behind by the consent of the most arrogant moralist, forgotten on the lowest steps of youth.

---

[1] the words of Galileo, spoken (quietly?) after recanting his assertion of the earth's movement: "And yet it does move."

The responsibility of presenting to the public a biography of Shelley, does not, however, lie with me: I have only to make it a little easier by arranging these few supplementary letters, with a recognition of the value of the whole collection. This value I take to consist in a most truthful conformity of the Correspondence, in its limited degree, with the moral and intellectual character of the writer as displayed in the highest manifestations of his genius. Letters and poems are obviously an act of the same mind, produced by the same law, only differing in the application to the individual or collective understanding. Letters and poems may be used indifferently as the basement of our opinion upon the writer's character; the finished expression of a sentiment in the poems, giving light and significance to the rudiments of the same in the letters, and these, again, in their incipiency and unripeness, authenticating the exalted mood and reattaching it to the personality of the writer. The musician speaks on the note he sings with; there is no change in the scale, as he diminishes the volume into familiar intercourse. There is nothing of that jarring between the man and the author, which has been found so amusing or so melancholy; no dropping of the tragic mask, as the crowd melts away; no mean discovery of the real motives of a life's achievement, often, in other lives, laid bare as pitifully as when, at the close of a holiday, we catch sight of the internal lead-pipes and wood-valves, to which, and not to the ostensible conch and dominant Triton of the fountain, we have owed our admired water-work. No breaking out, in household privacy, of hatred, anger and scorn, incongruous with the higher mood and suppressed artistically in the book: no brutal return to self-delighting, when the audience of philanthropic schemes is out of hearing: no indecent stripping off the grander feeling and rule of life as too costly and cumbrous for every-day wear. Whatever Shelley was, he was with an admirable sincerity. It was not always truth that he thought and spoke; but in the purity of truth he spoke and thought always.

Everywhere is apparent his belief in the existence of Good, to which Evil is an accident; his faithful holding by what he assumed to be the former, going everywhere in company with the tenderest pity for those acting or suffering on the opposite hypothesis. For he was tender, though tenderness is not always the characteristic of very sincere natures; he was eminently both tender and sincere. And not only do the same affection and yearning after the well-being of his kind, appear in the letters as in the poems, but they express themselves by the same theories and plans, however crude and unsound. There is no reservation of a subtler, less costly, more serviceable remedy for his own ill, than he has proposed for the general one; nor does he ever contemplate an object on his own account, from a less elevation than he uses in exhibiting it to the world. How shall we help believing Shelley to have been, in his ultimate attainment, the splendid spirit of his own best poetry, when we find even his carnal speech to agree faithfully, at faintest as at strongest, with the tone and rhythm of his most oracular utterances?

For the rest, these new letters are not offered as presenting any new feature of the poet's character. Regarded in themselves, and as the substantive productions of a man, their importance would be slight. But they possess interest beyond their limits, in confirming the evidence just dwelt on, of the poetical mood of Shelley being only the intensification of his habitual mood; the same tongue only speaking, for want of the special excitement to sing. The very first letter, as one instance for all, strikes the key-note of the predominating sentiment of Shelley throughout his whole life—his sympathy with the oppressed. And when we see him at so early an age, casting out, under the influence of such a sympathy, letters and pamphlets on every side, we accept it as the simple exemplification of the sincerity, with which, at the close of his life, he spoke of himself, as—

One whose heart a stranger's tear might wear
As water-drops the sandy fountain stone;
Who loved and pitied all things, and could moan
For woes which others hear not, and could see
The absent with the glass of phantasy,
And near the poor and trampled sit and weep,
Following the captive to his dungeon deep—
One who was as a nerve o'er which do creep
The else-unfelt oppressions of this earth. [1]

Such sympathy with his kind was evidently developed in him to an extraordinary and even morbid degree, at a period when the general intellectual powers it was impatient to put in motion, were immature or deficient.

I conjecture, from a review of the various publications of Shelley's youth, that one of the causes of his failure at the outset, was the peculiar *practicalness* of his mind, which was not without a determinate effect on his progress in theorizing. An ordinary youth, who turns his attention to similar subjects, discovers falsities, incongruities, and various points for amendment, and, in the natural advance of the purely critical spirit unchecked by considerations of remedy, keeps up before his young eyes so many instances of the same error and wrong, that he finds himself unawares arrived at the startling conclusion that all must be changed—or nothing: in the face of which plainly impossible achievement, he is apt (looking perhaps a little more serious by the time he touches at the decisive issue), to feel, either carelessly or considerately, that his own attempting a single piece of service would be worse than useless even, and to refer the whole task to another age and person—safe in proportion to his incapacity. Wanting words to speak, he has never made a fool of himself by speaking. But, in Shelley's case, the early fervour and power to *see*, was accompanied by as precocious a fertility to *contrive*: he endeavoured to realize as he went on idealizing; every wrong had simultaneously

[1] *Julian and Maddelo*, ll. 442–50.

its remedy, and, out of the strength of his hatred for the former, he took the strength of his confidence in the latter—till suddenly he stood pledged to the defence of a set of miserable little expedients, just as if they represented great principles, and to an attack upon various great principles, really so, without leaving himself time to examine whether, because they were antagonistical to the remedy he had suggested, they must therefore be identical or even essentially connected with the wrong he sought to cure,—playing with blind passion into the hands of his enemies, and dashing at whatever red cloak was held forth to him, as the cause of the fireball he had last been stung with—mistaking Churchdom for Christianity, and for marriage, "the sale of love" and the law of sexual oppression.

Gradually, however he was leaving behind him this low practical dexterity, unable to keep up with his widening intellectual perception; and, in exact proportion as he did so, his true power strengthened and proved itself. Gradually he was raised above the contemplation of spots and the attempt at effacing them, to the great Abstract Light, and, through the discrepancy of the creation, to the sufficiency of the First Cause. Gradually he was learning that the best way of removing abuses is to stand fast by truth. Truth is one, as they are manifold; and innumerable negative effects are produced by the upholding of one positive principle. I shall say what I think,—had Shelley lived he would have finally ranged himself with the Christians; his very instinct for helping the weaker side (if numbers make strength), his very "hate of hate," which at first mistranslated itself into delirious Queen Mab notes and the like, would have got clearer-sighted by exercise. The preliminary step to following Christ, is the leaving the dead to bury their dead—not clamouring on His doctrine for an especial solution of difficulties which are referable to the general problem of the universe. Already he had attained to a profession of "a worship to the Spirit of good within, which requires (before it sends that inspiration forth, which impresses its likeness upon all it creates) devoted and disinterested homage, *as Coleridge says*,"—and Paul likewise. And we find in one of his last exquisite fragments, avowedly a record of one of his own mornings and its experience, as it dawned on him at his soul and body's best in his boat on the Serchio—that as surely as

> The stars burnt out in the pale blue air,
> And the thin white moon lay withering there—
> Day had kindled the dewy woods,
> And the rocks above, and the stream below,
> And the vapours in their multitudes,
> And the Apennine's shroud of summer snow—
> Day had awakened all things that be; [1]

just so surely, he tells us (stepping forward from this delicious dance-music, choragus-like, into the grander measure befitting the final enunciation),

> All rose to do the task He set to each,
> Who shaped us to his ends and not our own;
> The million rose to learn, and One to teach
> What none yet ever knew or can be known. [2]

No more difference than this, from David's pregnant conclusion so long ago!

Meantime, as I call Shelley a moral man, because he was true, simple-hearted, and brave, and because what he acted corresponded to what he knew, so I call him a man of religious mind, because every audacious negative cast up by him against the Divine, was interpenetrated with a mood of reverence and adoration,—and because I find him everywhere taking for granted some of the capital dogmas of Christianity, while most vehemently denying their historical basement. There is such a thing as an efficacious knowledge of and belief in the politics of Junius, or the poetry of Rowley, though a man

should at the same time dispute the title of Chatterton to the one, and consider the author of the other, as Byron wittily did, "really, truly, nobody at all."[3] There is even such a thing, we come to learn wonderingly in these very letters, as a profound sensibility and adaptitude for art, while the science of the percipient is so little advanced as to admit of his stronger admiration for Guido (and Carlo Dolce!) than for Michael Angelo. A Divine Being has Himself said, that "a word against the Son of man shall be forgiven to a man," while "a word against the Spirit of God" (implying a general deliberate preference of perceived evil to perceived good) "shall not be forgiven to a man." Also, in religion, one earnest and unextorted assertion of belief should outweigh, as a matter of testimony, many assertions of unbelief. The fact that there is a gold-region is established by the finding of one lump, though you miss the vein never so often.

He died before his youth ended. In taking the measure of him as a man, he must be considered on the whole and at his ultimate spiritual stature, and not be judged of at the immaturity and by the mistakes of ten years before: that, indeed, would be to judge of the author of "Julian and Maddalo" by "Zastrozzi." Let the whole truth be told of his worst mistake. I believe, for my own part, that if anything could now shame or grieve Shelley, it would be an attempt to vindicate him at the expense of another.

In forming a judgement, I would, however, press on the reader the simple justice of considering ten-

---

[1] "The Boat on the Serchio," ll. 7–13.

[2] ll. 30–33.

[3] "Or, to take our illustrations from the writings of Shelley himself, there is such a thing as admirably appreciating a work by Andrea Verocchio,—and fancifully characterising the Pisan Torre Guelfa by the Ponte a Mare, black against the sunsets,—and consummately painting the islet of San Clemente with its penitentiary for rebellious priests, to the west between Venice and the Lido—while you believe the first to be a fragment of an antique sarcophagus,—the second, Ugolino's Tower of Famine (the vestiges of which should be sought for in the Piazza de' Cavalieri)—and the third (as I convinced myself last summer at Venice), San Servolo with its madhouse—which, far from being "windowless," is as full of windows as a barrack." (Browning's note.)

derly his constitution of body as well as mind, and how unfavourable it was to the steady symmetries of conventional life; the body, in the torture of incurable disease, refusing to give repose to the bewildered soul, tossing in its hot fever of the fancy,—and the laudanum-bottle making but a perilous and pitiful truce between these two. He was constantly subject to "that state of mind" (I quote his own note to "Hellas") "in which ideas may be supposed to assume the force of sensation, through the confusion of thought with the objects of thought, and excess of passion animating the creations of the imagination": in other words, he was liable to remarkable delusions and hallucinations. The nocturnal attack in Wales, for instance, was assuredly a delusion; and I venture to express my own conviction derived from a little attention to the circumstances of either story, that the idea of the enamoured lady following him to Naples, and of the "man in the cloak" who struck him at the Pisan post-office, were equally illusory,—the mere projection, in fact, from himself, of the image of his own love and hate.

> To thirst and find no fill—to wail and wander
> With short unsteady steps—to pause and ponder—
> To feel the blood run through the veins and tingle
> When busy thought and blind sensation mingle,—
> To nurse the image of *unfelt caresses*
> Till dim imagination just possesses
> The half-created shadow— [1]

of unfelt caresses,—and of unfelt blows as well: to such conditions was his genius subject. It was not at Rome only (where he heard a mystic voice exclaiming, "Cenci, Cenci," in reference to the tragic theme which occupied him at the time),—it was not at Rome only that he mistook the cry of "old rags." The habit of somnambulism is said to have extended to the very last days of his life.

Let me conclude with a thought of Shelley as a poet. In the hierarchy of creative minds, it is the presence of the highest faculty that gives first rank, in virtue of its kind, not degree; no pretension of a lower nature, whatever the completeness of development or variety of effect, impeding the precedency of the rarer endowment though only in the germ. The contrary is sometimes maintained; it is attempted to make the lower gifts (which are potentially included in the higher faculty) of independent value, and equal to some exercise of the special function. For instance, should not a poet possess common sense? Then the possession of abundant common sense implies a step towards becoming a poet. Yes; such a step as the lapidary's, when, strong in the fact of carbon entering largely into the composition of the diamond, he heaps up a sack of charcoal in order to compete with the Koh-i-noor. I pass at once, therefore, from Shelley's minor excellencies to his noblest and predominating characteristics.

This I call his simultaneous perception of Power and Love in the absolute, and of Beauty and Good in the concrete, while he throws, from his poet's station between both, swifter, subtler, and more numerous films for the connexion of each with each, than have been thrown by any modern artificer of whom I have knowledge; proving how, as he says,

> The spirit of the worm within the sod,
> In love and worship blends itself with God. [2]

I would rather consider Shelley's poetry as a sublime fragmentary essay towards a presentment of the correspondency of the universe to Deity, of the natural to the spiritual, and of the actual to the ideal, than I would isolate and separately appraise the worth of many detachable portions which might be acknowledged as utterly perfect in a lower moral point of view, under the mere conditions of art. It

---

[1] "To thirst and find no fill," ll. 1–7.

[2] *Epipsychidion*, ll. 128–29.

would be easy to take my stand on successful instances of objectivity in Shelley: there is the unrivalled "Cenci"; there is the "Julian and Maddalo" too; there is the magnificent "Ode to Naples": why not regard, it may be said, the less organized matter as the radiant elemental foam and solution, out of which would have been evolved, eventually, creations as perfect even as those? But I prefer to look for the highest attainment, not simply the high,—and, seeing it, I hold by it. There is surely enough of the work "Shelley" to be known enduringly among men, and, I believe, to be accepted of God, as human work may; and around the imperfect proportions of such, the most elaborated productions of ordinary art must arrange themselves as inferior illustrations.

It is because I have long held these opinions in assurance and gratitude, that I catch at the opportunity offered to me of expressing them here; knowing that the alacrity to fulfil an humble office conveys more love than the acceptance of the honour of a higher one, and that better, therefore, than the signal service it was the dream of my boyhood to render to his fame and memory, may be the saying of a few, inadequate words upon these scarcely more important supplementary letters of SHELLEY.

—Paris, December 4, 1851.

Arthur Hugh Clough
1819 – 1861

Arthur Hugh Clough was educated at Rugby and Balliol College, Oxford. He became a fellow of Oriel and then principal of University Hall, London. His poems appeared in *Ambarvalia* (1849), *Amours de Voyage* (1849), *Dipsychus* (1850), and *Mari Magno or Tales On Board* (1861). Clough and Matthew Arnold were friends and poetic rivals; after Clough's premature death in 1861 Arnold wrote the problematic elegy "Thyrsis" in his memory. Clough's short verse reveals his clear-sighted cynicism about social conventions; his longer works, such as the novel-in-verse *Amours de Voyage*, combine social commentary with ambitious formal experimentation.

❧❧❧

Recent English Poetry: A Review of Several Volumes of Poems by Alexander Smith, Matthew Arnold, and Others [1]

Poems by Alexander Smith,[2] a volume recently published in London, and by this time reprinted in Boston, deserve attention. They have obtained in England a good deal more notice than is usually accorded there to first volumes of verse; nor is this by any means to be ascribed to the mere fact that the writer is, as we are told, a mechanic; though undoubtedly that does add to their external interest, and perhaps also enhances their intrinsic merit. It is to this, perhaps, that they owe a force of purpose and character which makes them a grateful contrast to the ordinary languid collectanea published by young men of literary habits; and which, on the whole, may be accepted as more than compensation for many imperfections of style and taste.

The models, whom this young poet has followed, have been, it would appear, predominantly, if not exclusively, the writers of his own immediate time, *plus* Shakspeare. The antecedents of the Life-Drama, the one long poem which occupies almost the whole of his volume, are to be found in the Princess, in parts of Mrs. Browning, in the love of Keats, and the *habit* of Shakspeare. There is no Pope, or Dryden,[3] or even Milton; no Wordsworth, Scott, or even Byron to speak of. We have before us, we may say, the latest disciple of the school of Keats, who was indeed no well of English undefiled, though doubtless the fountain-head of a true poetic stream. Alexander Smith is young enough to free himself from his present manner, which does not seem his simple and natural own. He has given us, so to say, his Endymion; it is certainly as imperfect, and as mere a promise of something wholly different as was that of the master he has followed.

We are not sorry, in the mean time, that this Endymion is not upon Mount Latmos.[4] The natural man does pant within us after *flumina silvasque;*[5] yet really, and truth to tell, is it not, upon the whole, an easy matter to sit under a green tree by a purling brook, and indite pleasing stanzas on the beauties of Nature and fresh air? Or is it, we incline to ask, so very great an exploit to wander out into the pleasant field of Greek or Latin mythology, and reproduce, with more or less of modern adaptation,—

---

[1] first published in the *North American Review*, July, 1853.

[2] Smith (1830–67), whose first book of poems was published in 1853, was a member of the so-called Spasmodic School.

[3] "The word *spoom*, which Dryden uses as the verb of the substantive *spume*, occurs also in Beaumont and Fletcher. Has Keats employed it? It seems hardly to deserve reimpatriation." (Clough's note.)

[4] frequented by the mythological Endymion.

[5] streams and woods.

the shadows
Faded and pale, yet immortal, of Faunus, the
Nymphs, and the Graces? [1]

Studies of the literature of any distant age, or country; all the imitations and *quasi*-translations which help to bring together into a single focus, the scattered rays of human intelligence; poems after classical models, poems from Oriental sources, and the like, have undoubtedly a great literary value. Yet there is no question, it is plain and patent enough, that people much prefer Vanity Fair and Bleak House. Why so? Is it simply because we have grown prudent and prosaic, and should not welcome, as our fathers did, the Marmions and the Rokebys, the Childe Harolds, and the Corsairs?[2] Or is it, that to be wildly popular, to gain the ear of multitudes, to shake the hearts of men, poetry should deal more than at present it usually does, with general wants, ordinary feelings, the obvious rather than the rare facts of human nature? Could it not attempt to convert into beauty and thankfulness, or at least into some form and shape, some feeling, at any rate, of content—the actual, palpable things with which our every-day life is concerned; introduce into business and weary task-work a character and a soul of purpose and reality; intimate to us relations which, in our unchosen, peremptorily-appointed posts, in our grievously narrow and limited spheres of action, we still, in and through all, retain to some central, celestial fact? Could it not console us with a sense of significance, if not of dignity, in that often dirty, or at least dingy, work which it is the lot of so many of us to have to do, and which some one or other, after all, must do? Might it not divinely condescend to all infirmities; be in all points tempted as we are; exclude nothing, least of all guilt and distress, from its wide fraternization; not content itself merely with talking of what may be better elsewhere, but seek also to deal with what *is* here? We could each one of us, alas, be so much that somehow we find we are not; we have all of us fallen away from so much that we still long to call ours. Cannot the Divine Song in some way indicate to us our unity, though from a great way off, with those happier things; inform us, and prove to us, that though we are what we are, we may yet, in some way, even in our abasement, even by and through our daily work, be related to the purer existence.

The modern novel is preferred to the modern poem, because we do here feel an attempt to include these indispensable latest addenda—these phenomena which, if we forget on Sunday, we must remember on Monday—these positive matters of fact, which people, who are not verse-writers, are obliged to have to do with.

Et fortasse cupressum
Scis simulare; quid hoc, si fractis enatat expes
Navibus, aere dato qui pingitur? [3]

The novelist does try to build us a real house to be lived in; and this common builder, with no notion of the orders, is more to our purpose than the student of ancient art who proposes to lodge us under an Ionic portico. We are, unhappily, not gods, nor even marble statues. While the poets, like the architects, are—a good thing enough in its way—studying ancient art, comparing, thinking, theorizing, the common novelist tells a plain tale, often trivial enough, about this, that, and the other, and obtains one reading at any rate; is thrown away indeed tomorrow, but is devoured to-day.

We do not at all mean to prepare the reader for finding the great poetic desideratum in this present Life-Drama. But it has at least the advantage, such as it is, of not showing much of the *littérateur* or con-

---

[1] from Clough's *Amours de Voyage* 3.225–26.

[2] heroes of poetic romances by Scott and Byron.

[3] Horace, *Ars Poetica*, ll. 19–21: "Perhaps you know how to draw a cypress; but what good is that if you are hired by a sailor to paint his portrait struggling to shore after a wreck?"

noisseur, or indeed the student; nor is it, as we have said, mere pastoral sweet piping from the country. These poems were not written among books and busts, nor yet

> By shallow rivers, to whose falls
> Melodious birds sing madrigals.[1]

They have something substantive and lifelike, immediate and firsthand, about them. There is a charm, for example, in finding, as we do, continual images drawn from the busy seats of industry; it seems to satisfy a want that we have long been conscious of, when we see the black streams that welter out of factories, the dreary lengths of urban and suburban dustiness,

> the squares and streets,
> And the faces that one meets,[2]

irradiated with a gleam of divine purity. There are moods when one is prone to believe that, in these last days, no longer by "clear spring or shady grove," no more upon any Pindus or Parnassus, or by the side of any Castaly,[3] are the true and lawful haunts of the poetic powers: but, we could believe it, if anywhere, in the blank and desolate streets, and upon the solitary bridges of the midnight city, where Guilt is, and wild Temptation, and the dire Compulsion of what has once been done—there, with these tragic sisters around him, and with Pity also, and pure Compassion, and pale Hope, that looks like Despair, and Faith in the garb of Doubt, there walks the discrowned Apollo, with unstrung lyre; nay, and could he sound it, those mournful Muses would

scarcely be able as of old, to respond and "sing in turn with their beautiful voices."[4]

To such moods, and in such states of feeling, this Life-Drama will be an acceptable poem. Under the guise of a different story, a story unskilful enough in its construction, we have seemed continually to recognize the ingenuous, yet passionate, youthful spirit, struggling after something like right and purity amidst the unnumbered difficulties, contradictions, and corruptions of the heated and crowded, busy, vicious, and inhuman town. Eager for action, incapable of action without some support, yet knowing not on what arm to dare lean; not untainted; hard-pressed; in some sort, at times, overcome,—still we seem to see the young combatant, half combatant half martyr, resolute to fight it out, and not to quit this for some easier field of battle,—one way or other to make something of it.

The story, such as we have it, is inartificial enough. Walter, a boy of poetic temperament and endowment, has, it appears, in the society of a poet friend now deceased, grown up with the ambition of achieving something great in the highest form of human speech. Unable to find or make a way, he is diverted from his lofty purposes by a romantic love-adventure, obscurely told, with a "Lady" who finds him asleep, Endymion-like, under a tree. The fervor and force of youth wastes itself here in vain; a quick disappointment,—for the lady is betrothed to another,—sends him back enfeebled, exhausted, and embittered, to essay once again his task. Disappointed affections, and baffled ambition, contending henceforward in unequal strife with the temptations of scepticism, indifference, apathetic submission, base indulgence, and the like;—the sickened, and defeated, yet only too strong, too powerful man, turning desperately off, and recklessly at last plunging in mid-unbelief into joys to which only belief and moral purpose can give reality;—out of horror-stricken

---

[1] from Christopher Marlowe's "The Passionate Shepherd to His Love," ll. 7–8.

[2] from Tennyson's *Maud* 2.4.232–33. *Maud* was first published in 1855, but these lines appeared in an annual in 1834.

[3] two mountains and a fountain sacred to Apollo and the Muses.

[4] not identified.

guilt, the new birth of clearer and surer, though humbler, conviction, trust, resolution;—these happy changes met, perhaps a little prematurely and almost more than halfway, by success in the aims of a purified ambition, and crowned too, at last, by the blessings of a regenerate affection,—such is the argument of the latter half of the poem; and there is something of a current and tide, so to say, of poetic intention in it, which carries on the reader, (after the first few scenes,) perforce, in spite of criticism and himself, through faulty imagery, turgid periods, occasional bad versification and even grammar, to the close. Certainly, there is something of a real flesh-and-blood heart and soul in the case, or this could not be so.

Of the first four or five scenes, perhaps the less said the better. There are frequent fine lines, occasional beautiful passages; but the tenor of the narrative is impeded and obstructed to the last degree, not only by accumulations of imagery, but by episode, and episode within episode, of the most embarrassing form. It is really discouraging to turn page upon page, while Walter is quoting the poems of his lost friend, and wooing the unknown lady of the wood with a story of another lady and an Indian page. We could almost recommend the reader to begin with the close of scene IV., where the hero's first love-disappointment is decided, and the lady quits her young poet.

<blockquote>
"I must go,
Nay, nay, I go alone! Yet one word more.
Strive for the Poet's crown, but ne'er forget,
How poor are fancy's blooms to thoughtful fruits:
That gold and crimson mornings, though more bright
Than soft blue days, are scarcely half their worth.
Walter 'farewell,' the world shall hear of thee.
                    [She still lingers.
"I have a strange sweet thought. I do believe
I shall be dead in spring, and that the soul
Which animates and doth inform these limbs,
</blockquote>

<blockquote>
Will pass into the daisies of my grave:
If memory shall ever lead thee there,
Through daisies I'll look up into thy face,
And feel a dim sweet joy; and if they move
As in a little wind, thou'lt know 'tis I."
</blockquote>

The ensuing scene, between Walter and a Peasant, is also obscurely and indecisively given; and before Part VI., it would have been well, we think, to place some mark of the lapse of time. The second division of the poem here commences. We are reintroduced to the hero in a room in London, reading a poetical manuscript. Edward, a friend, enters and interrupts. We quote from a speech of Walter's.

<blockquote>
                  "Thou mock'st at much;
And he who sneers at any living hope,
Or aspiration of a human heart,
Is just so many stages less than God,
That universal and all-sided Love.
I'm wretched, Edward, to the very heart:
I see an unreached heaven of young desire
Shine through my hopeless tears. My drooping sails
Flap idly 'gainst the mast of my intent.
I rot upon the waters, when my prow
Should grate the golden isles.
    Edward.   What wouldst thou do?
Thy train did teem with vapors wild and vast.
    Walter. But since my younger and my hotter days,
(As nebula condenses to an orb,)
These vapors gathered to one shining hope
Sole hanging in my sky.
    Edward.   What hope is that?
    Walter. To set this age to music—the great work
Before the poet now—I do believe
When it is fully sung, its great complaint,
Its hope, its yearning, told to earth and heaven,
Our troubled age shall pass, as doth a day
That leaves the west all crimson with the promise
Of the diviner morrow, which even then
Is hurrying up the great world's side with light."
</blockquote>

Two scenes of conversation are given between Walter and this friend, Edward, cold, clear-sighted, a little cynical, but patient, calm, resigned, and moral. He as it happens is going on the morrow to Bedfordshire to visit

"Old Mr. Wilmott, nothing in himself,
But rich as ocean. He has in his hand
Sea-marge and moor, and miles of stream and grove,
Dull flats, scream-startled, as the exulting train
Streams like a meteor through the frighted night,
Wind-billowed plains of wheat, and marshy fens,
Unto whose reeds on midnights blue and cold,
Long strings of geese come clanging from the stars,
Yet wealthier in one child than all of these."

Thither Walter accompanies him. We subjoin part of a dialogue between him and the "one child," in whom, more than in all his land, old Mr. Wilmott was blest. Walter had been describing his own story under the name of another person.

"*Violet.* Did you know well that youth of whom you
spake?
Walter. Know him! Oh yes; I knew him as myself,—
Two passions dwelt at once within his soul,

.   .   .   .

The dead was Love, the living, Poetry.
Violet. Alas! if Love rose never from the dead.
Walter. Between him and the lady of his love
There stood a wrinkled worldling.

.   .   .   .

                    And when she died,
The rivers of his heart ran all to waste;
They found no ocean; dry sands sucked them up.
Lady! he was a fool, a pitiful fool!
She said she loved him, would be dead in spring—
She asked him but to stand beside her grave—
She said she would be daisies—and she thought
'T would give her joy to feel that he was near.
She died, like music; and would you believe it?
He kept her foolish words within his heart,

As ceremonious as a chapel keeps
A relic of a saint. And in the spring
The doting idiot went.
Violet. What found he there?
Walter. Laugh till your sides ache! oh, he went, poor
fool,
But he found nothing, save red-trampled clay,
And a dull, sobbing rain. Do you not laugh?
Amid the comfortless rain he stood and wept;
Bareheaded in the mocking, pelting rain.
He might have known 't was ever so on earth.
Violet. You cannot laugh yourself, sir, nor can I.
Her unpolluted corse[1] doth sleep in earth
Like a pure thought within a sinful soul.
Dearer is Earth to God for her sweet sake.["]

The issue and catastrophe of a new love-adventure here, in this unhappy and distempered period of baffled and disappointed ambition, and power struggling vainly for a vent, may be conjectured from the commencement of a scene, which perhaps might be more distinctly marked as the opening of the third part.

[*A bridge in a City. Midnight. Walter alone.*]
"Adam lost Paradise—eternal tale,
Repeated in the lives of all his sons.
I had a shining orb of happiness,—
God gave it me, but sin passed over it
As smallpox passes o'er a lovely face,
Leaving it hideous. I have lost for ever
The paradise of young and happy thoughts,
And now stand in the middle of my life
Looking back through my tears, ne'er to return.
I've a stern tryst with death, and must go on,
Though with slow steps and oft-reverted eyes.
'Tis a thick, rich-hazed, sumptuous autumn night;
The moon grows like a white flower in the sky;
The stars are dim. The tired year rests content
Among her sheaves, as a fond mother rests
Among her children—all her work is done,

---

[1] archaic form of corpse.

There is a weight of peace upon the world;
It sleeps; God's blessing on it. Not on me.

    .   .   .   .   .

                   Good men have said,
That sometimes God leaves sinners to their sin,—
He has left me to mine, and I am changed;
My worst part is insurgent, and my will
Is weak and powerless as a trembling king
When millions rise up hungry. Woe is me!
My soul breeds sins as a dead body worms,—
They swarm and feed upon me.["]

Three years appear to have gone by, when Walter,
like a stag sorehunted, returns to the home of his
childhood.

"'Twas here I spent my youth, as far removed
From the great heavings, hopes and fears of man,
As unknown isle asleep in unknown seas.
Gone my pure heart, and with it happy days;
No manna falls around me from on high,
Barely from off the desert of my life
I gather patience and severe content.
God is a worker. He has thickly strewn
Infinity with grandeur. God is Love;
He yet shall wipe away creation's tears,
And all the worlds shall summer in his smile.
Why work I not. The veriest mote that sports
Its one-day life within the sunny beam,
Has its stern duties. Wherefore have I none?
I will throw off this dead and useless past,
As a strong runner, straining for his life,
Unclasps a mantle to the hungry winds.
A mighty purpose rises large and slow
From out the fluctuations of my soul,
As ghostlike from the dim and trembling sea
Starts the completed moon.["]

Here, in this determination, he writes his poem,
—attains in this spirit the object which had formerly
been his ambition. And here, in the last scene, we
find him happy, or peaceful at least, with Violet.

"*Violet.* I always pictured you in such a place
Writing your book, and hurrying on, as if
You had a long and wondrous tale to tell,
And felt Death's cold hand closing round your heart.
  Walter. Have you read my book?
  Violet. I have.
  Walter.   It is enough.
The book was only written for two souls,
And they are thine and mine.
  Violet.   For many weeks,
When I was dwelling by the moaning sea,
Your name was blown to me on every wind,
And I was glad; for by that sign I knew
You had fulfilled your heart, and hoped you would
Put off the robes of sorrow, and put on
The singing crown of Fame."

Again, below, she resumes,—

                   "Walter! dost thou believe
Love will redeem all errors? Oh, my friend,
This gospel saves you! doubt it, you are lost.
Deep in the mists of sorrow long I lay,
Hopeless and still, when suddenly this truth
Like a slant sunbeam quivered through the mist,
And turned it into radiance. In the light
I wrote these words, while you were far away,
Fighting with shadows. Oh, Walter, in one boat
We floated o'er the smooth, moon-silvered sea;
The sky was smiling with its orbs of bliss;
And while we lived within each other's eyes,
We struck and split, and all the world was lost
In one wild whirl of horror darkening down.
At last I gained a deep and silent isle,
Moaned on by a dim sea, and wandered round,
Week after week, the happy-mournful shore,
Wondering if you had 'scaped.
  Walter.   Thou noble soul,
Teach me, if thou art nearer God than I!
My life was one long dream; when I awoke,
Duty stood like an angel in my path,
And seemed so terrible, I could have turned
Into my yesterdays, and wandered back
To distant childhood, and gone out to God

By the gate of birth, not death. Life, lift me up
By thy sweet inspiration, as the tide
Lifts up a stranded boat upon the beach.
I will go forth 'mong men, not mailed in scorn,
But in the armor of a pure intent.
Great duties are before me, and great songs,
And whether crowned or crownless, when I fall,
It matters not, so as God's work is done.
I've learned to prize the quiet lightning deed,
Not the applauding thunder at its heels,
Which men call Fame. Our night is past;
We stand in precious sunrise; and beyond,
A long day stretches to the very end."

So be it, O young Poet; Poet, perhaps it is early to affirm; but so be it, at any rate, O young man. While you go forth in that "armor of pure intent," the hearts of some readers, be assured, will go with you.

Empedocles on Etna and other Poems, with its earlier companion volume, The Strayed Reveller and other Poems, are, it would seem, the productions (as is, or was, the English phrase) of a scholar and a gentleman; a man who has received a refined education, seen refined "society," and been more, we dare say, in the world, which is called the world, than in all likelihood has a Glasgow mechanic. More refined, therefore, and more highly educated sensibilities,—too delicate, are they, for common service?—a calmer judgment also, a more poised and steady intellect, the *siccum lumen* of the soul; a finer and rarer aim perhaps, and certainly a keener sense of difficulty, in life;—these are the characteristics of him whom we are to call "A." Empedocles, the sublime Sicilian philosopher, the fragments of whose moral and philosophic poems testify to his genius and character,—Empedocles, in the Poem before us, weary of misdirected effort, weary of imperfect thought, impatient of a life which appears to him a miserable failure, and incapable, as he conceives, of doing any thing that shall be true to that proper interior self,

"Being one with which we are one with the whole
world,"

wandering forth, with no determined purpose, into the mountain solitudes, followed for a while by Pausanias, the eager and laborious physician, and at a distance by Callicles, the boy-musician, flings himself at last, upon a sudden impulse and apparent inspiration of the intellect, into the boiling crater of Etna; rejoins there the elements. "Slave of sense," he was saying, pondering near the verge,

"Slave of sense
I have in no wise been: but slave of thought?
And who can say, he has been always free,
Lived ever in the light of his own soul?
I cannot:—

. . . .

But I have not grown easy in these bonds,
But I have not denied what bonds these were.
Yea, I take myself to witness
That I have loved no darkness,
Sophisticated no truth,
Nursed no delusion,
Allowed no fear.
And therefore, O ye Elements, I know—
Ye know it too—it hath been granted me,
Not to die wholly, not to be all enslaved.
I feel it in this hour. The numbing cloud
Mounts off my soul: I feel it, I breathe free.

Is it but for a moment?
Ah, boil up, ye vapors!
Leap and roar, thou sea of Fire!
My soul glows to meet you.
Ere it flag, ere the mists
Of despondency and gloom
Rush over it again,
Receive me! save me!["]
[*He plunges into the crater.*]

The music of the boy Callicles, to which he chants his happy mythic stories, somewhat frigidly perhaps, relieves, as it sounds in the distance, the gloomy catastrophe.

Tristram and Iseult (these names form the title of the next and only other considerable poem) are, in the old romantic cycle of North-France and Germany, the hero and the heroine of a mournful tale. Tristram of Lyonness[e], the famed companion of King Arthur, received in youth a commission to bring from across the sea the Princess Iseult of Ireland, the destined bride of the King of Cornwall. The mother of the beautiful princess gave her, as a parting gift, a cup of a magic wine, which she and her royal husband should drink together on their marriage-day in their palace at Tyntagil; so they should love each other perfectly and forever. But on the voyage it befell—

> The calm sea shines, loose hang the vessel's sails,
> Before us are the sweet green fields of Wales,
> And overhead the cloudless sky of May.
> 'Ah, would I were'—

(saith Iseult)

> "Ah, would I were in those green fields at play,
> Not pent on shipboard this delicious day.
> Tristram, I pray thee of thy courtesy,
> Reach me my golden cup that stands by thee,
> And pledge me in it first for courtesy.'

On the dreamy seas it so befell, that Iseult and Tristram drank together of the golden cup. Tristram, therefore, and Iseult should love each other perfectly and for ever. Yet nothing the less for this must Iseult be wedded to the King of Cornwall; and Tristram, vainly lingering, fly and go forth upon his way.

But it so chanced that, after long and weary years of passion vainly contended with, years of travel and hard fighting, Tristram, lying wounded in Brittany, was tended by another, a youthful, innocent Iseult, in whose face he seemed to see the look of that Iseult of the past, that was, and yet could not be, his. Weary, and in his sad despondency, Tristram wedded Iseult of Brittany, whose heart, in his stately deep distress, he had moved to a sweet and tender affection. The modern poem opens with the wedded knight come home again, after other long years, and other wars, in which he had fought at King Arthur's side with the Roman emperor, and subdued the heathen Saxons on the Rhine, lying once more sick and sad at heart, upon what ere long he feels shall be his deathbed. Ere he die, he would see, once yet again, her with whom in his youth he drank of that fatal cup.

> *Tristram.* Is she not come? the messenger was sure.
> Prop me upon the pillows once again—
> Raise me, my page: this cannot long endure.
> Christ! what a night! how the sleet whips the pane!
> What lights will those out to the northward be?
> *The Page.* The lanterns of the fishing-boats at sea.

And so through the whole of Part I. of our poem, lies the sick and weary knight upon his bed, reviewing sadly, while sadly near him stands his timid and loving younger Iseult, reviewing, half sleeping, half awake, those old times, that hapless voyage, and all that thence ensued; and still in all his thought recurring to the proud Cornish Queen, who, it seems, will let him die unsolaced. He speaks again, now broad awake.

> Is my page here? Come turn me to the fire.
> Upon the window panes the moon shines bright;
> The wind is down; but she'll not come to-night.
> Ah no,—she is asleep in Tyntagil—
>
> . . . .
>
> My princess, art thou there? Sweet, 'tis too late.
> To bed and sleep; my fever is gone by;
> To-night my page shall keep me company.
> Where do the children sleep? kiss them for me.
> Poor child, thou art almost as pale as I;
> This comes of nursing long and watching late.
> To bed—good night.

And so, (our poet passing without notice from Tristram's semi-dramatic musings and talkings, to his own not more coherent narrative)—

> She left the gleam-lit fireplace,
> She came to the bed-side;
> She took his hands in hers; her tears
> Down on her slender fingers rained.
> She raised her eyes upon his face—
> Not with a look of wounded pride—
> A look as if the heart complained;—
> Her look was like a sad embrace;
> The gaze of one who can divine
> A grief, and sympathize.
> Sweet flower, thy children's eyes
> Are not more innocent than thine.

Sleeping with her little ones, and, it may be, dreaming too, though less happily than they, lies Iseult of Brittany. And now—

> What voices are those on the clear night air?
> What lights in the courts? what steps on the stair?

PART II

> *Tristram.* Raise the light, my page, that I may see her.
> —Thou art come at last, then, haughty Queen!
> Long I've waited, long have fought my fever,
> Late thou comest, cruel thou hast been.
> *Iseult.* Blame me not, poor sufferer, that I tarried.
> I was bound; I could not break the band,
> Chide not with the past, but feel the present;
> I am here—we meet—I hold thy hand.

Yes, the Queen Iseult of Cornwall, Iseult that was of Ireland, Iseult of the ship upon the dreamy seas long since, has crossed these stormy seas to-night, is here, holds his hand. And so proceeds, through some six or seven pages of Part II., the fine colloquy of the two sad, world-worn, late-reunited lovers. When we open upon Part III.,

> A year had flown, and in the chapel old
> Lay Tristram and Queen Iseult dead and cold.

Beautiful, simple old mediaeval story! We have followed it, led on as much by its own intrinsic charm as by the form and coloring—beautiful too, but indistinct—which our modern poet has given it. He is obscure at times, and hesitates and falters in it; the knights and dames, we fear, of old North-France and Western Germany would have been grievously put to it to make him out. Only upon a fourth re-reading, and by the grace of a happy moment, did we satisfy our critical conscience that, when the two lovers have sunk together in death, the knight on his pillows, and Queen Iseult kneeling at his side, the poet, after passing to the Cornish court where she was yesternight, returns to address himself to a hunter with his dogs, worked in the tapestry of the chamber here, whom he conceives to be pausing in the pictured chase, and staring, with eyes of wonder, on the real scene of the pale knight on the pillows and the kneeling lady fair. But

> Cheer, cheer thy dogs into the brake,
> O hunter! and without a fear
> Thy golden-tasselled bugle blow,
> And through the glade thy pastime take!
> For thou wilt rouse no sleepers here,
> For these thou seest are unmoved;
> Cold, cold as those who lived and loved
> A thousand years ago."

Fortunately, indeed, with the commencement of Part III., the most matter-of-fact quarterly conscience may feel itself pretty well set at ease by the unusually explicit statements that

> A year had fled; and in the chapel old
> Lay Tristram and Queen Iseult dead and cold.
> The young surviving Iseult, one bright day
> Had wandered forth; her children were at play
> In a green circular hollow in the heath

Which borders the sea shore; a country path
Creeps over it from the tilled fields behind.

Yet anon, again and thicker now perhaps than ever, the mist of more than poetic dubiousness closes over and around us. And as he sings to us about the widowed lady Iseult, sitting upon the sea-banks of Brittany, watching her bright-eyed children, talking with them and telling them old Breton stories, while still, in all her talk and her story, her own dreamy memories of the past, and perplexed thought of the present, mournfully mingle, it is really all but impossible to ascertain her, or rather his, real meanings. We listen, indeed, not quite unpleased, to a sort of faint musical mumble, conveying at times a kind of subdued half-sense, or intimating, perhaps, a three-quarters-implied question; Is any thing real?—is love any thing?—what is any thing?—is there substance enough even in sorrow to mark the lapse of time?—is not passion a diseased unrest?—did not the fairy Vivian, when the wise Merlin forgot his craft to fall in love with her, wave her wimple over her sleeping adorer?

Nine times she waved the fluttering wimple round,
And made a little plot of magic ground;
And in that daisied circle, as men say,
Is Merlin prisoner to the judgment day,
But she herself whither she will can rove,
For she was passing weary of his love.

Why or wherefore, or with what purport, who will venture exactly to say?—but such, however, was the tale which, while Tristram and his first Iseult lay in their graves, the second Iseult, on the sea-banks of Brittany, told her little ones.

And yet, dim and faint as is the sound of it, we still prefer this dreamy patience, the soft submissive endurance of the Breton lady, and the human passions and sorrows of the Knight and the Queen, to the high, and shall we say, pseudo-Greek inflation of the philosopher musing above the crater, and the boy Callicles, singing myths upon the mountain.

Does the reader require morals and meanings to these stories? What shall they be, then?—the deceitfulness of knowledge, and the illusiveness of the affections, the hardiness and roughness and contrariousness of the world, the difficulty of living at all, the impossibility of doing any thing,—*voilà tout?* A charitable and patient reader, we believe, (such as is the present reviewer.) will find in the minor poems that accompany these pieces, intimations—what more can reader or reviewer ask?—of some better and further thing than these; some approximations to a kind of confidence, some incipiences of a degree of hope, some roots, retaining some vitality, of conviction and moral purpose.

And though we wear out life, alas,
Distracted as a homeless wind,
In beating where we must not pass,
And seeking what we shall not find,

Yet shall we one day gain, life past,
Clear prospect o'er our being's whole
Shall we ourselves, and learn at last
Our true affinities of soul.

We shall not then deny a course
To every thought the mass ignore,
We shall not then call hardness force,
Nor lightness wisdom any more.[1]

In the future, it seems, there is something for us; and for the present also, which is more germane to our matter, we have discovered some precepts about "hope, light and *persistence*,"[2] which we intend to make the most of. Meantime, it is one promising point in our author of the initial, that his second is certainly on the whole an improvement upon his first

---

[1] from "A Farewell," ll. 49–60.

[2] from "The Second Best," l. 23. Emphasis added by Clough.

volume. There is less obvious study of effect; upon the whole, a plainer and simpler and less factitious manner and method of treatment. This, he may be sure, is the only safe course. Not by turning and twisting his eyes, in the hope of seeing things as Homer, Sophocles, Virgil, or Milton saw them; but by seeing them, by accepting them as he sees them, and faithfully depicting accordingly, will he attain the object he desires.

In the earlier volume, one of the most generally admired pieces was "The Forsaken Merman."

> Come, dear children, let us away
> Down, and away below,

says the Merman, standing upon the sea-shore, whither he and his children came up to call back the human Margaret, their mother, who had left them to go, for one day—for Easterday—to say her prayers with her kinsfolk in the little gray church on the shore:

> ' 'Twill be Easter-time in the world—ah me,
> And I lose my poor soul, Merman, here with thee.'

And when she staid, and staid on, and it seemed a long while, and the little ones began to moan, at last, up went the Merman with the little ones to the shore, and so on into the town, and to the little gray church, and there looked in through the small leaded panes of the window. There she sits in the aisle; but she does not look up, her eyes are fixed upon the holy page; it is in vain we try to catch her attention.

> Come away, children, call no more,
> Come away, come down, call no more.

Down, down to the depths of the sea. She will live up there and be happy, among the things she had known before. Yet sometimes a thought will come across her; there will be times when she will

> Steal to the window and look at the sand;
> And over the sand at the sea;
> And anon there breaks a sigh,
> And anon there drops a tear,
> From a sorrow-clouded eye,
> And a heart sorrow-laden,
>   A long, long sigh,
> For the cold strange eyes of a little mermaiden,
> And the gleam of her golden hair.

Come away, children, come down. We will be happy in our bright home under the sea—happy, though the cruel one leaves us lonely for ever. Yet we too, sometimes at midnight, when winds blow softly, and the moonlight falls clear,

> Up the still glistening beaches,
> Up the creeks we will hie,
> Over banks of bright sea-weed
> The ebb-tide leaves dry.
> We will gaze from the sand hills
> At the white sleeping town,
> At the church on the hill side;
>   And then come back down,—
> Singing, 'there dwells a loved one,
> But cruel is she,
> She left lonely for ever
> The Kings of the Sea.'

It is a beautiful poem, certainly; and deserves to have been given at full length. "The Strayed Reveller" itself is more ambitious, perhaps a little strained. It is a pleasing and significant imagination, however, to present to us Circe and Ulysses in colloquy with a stray youth from the train of Bacchus, who drinks eagerly the cup of the enchantress, not as did the sailors of the Ithacan king, for gross pleasure, but for the sake of the glorious and superhuman vision and knowledge it imparts.

> 'But I, Ulysses,
> Sitting on the warm steps,

Looking over the valley,
All day long have seen,
Without pain, without labor,
Sometimes a wild-haired maenad,
Sometimes a Faun with torches."

But now, we are fain to ask, where are we, and whither are we unconsciously come? Were we not going forth to battle in the armor of a righteous purpose, with our first friend, with Alexander Smith? How is it we find ourselves here, reflecting, pondering, hesitating, musing, complaining, with "A." As the wanderer at night, standing under a stormy sky, listening to the wild harmonies of winds, and watching the wild movements of the clouds, the tree-tops, or possibly the waves, may, with a few steps, very likely, pass into a lighted sitting-room, and a family circle, with pictures and books, and literary leisure, and ornaments, and elegant small employments,—a scene how dissimilar to that other, and yet how entirely natural also;—so it often happens too with books. You have been reading Burns, and you take up Cowper. You feel at home, how strangely! in both of them. Can both be the true thing? and if so, in what new form can we express the relation, the harmony, between them? Such a discrepancy there certainly does exist between the two books that have been before us here. We close the one and open the other, and feel ourselves moving to and fro between two totally different, repugnant, and hostile theories of life. Are we to try and reconcile them, or judge between them?

May we escape from all the difficulty by a mere quotation, and pronounce with the shepherd of Virgil,

"Non nostrum inter vos tantas componere lites
Et vitulâ tu dignus, et hic." [1]

Or will the reader be content to bow down with us in this place, and acknowledge the presence of that highest object of worship among the modern Germans, an *antinomy*.[2] (That is, O unlearned reader, ignorant, not impossibly, of Kant and the modern German religion,—in brief, a contradiction in terms, the ordinary *phenomenal* form of a *noumenal*[3] Verity; as, for example, *the world must have had a beginning*, and, *the world cannot have had a beginning*, in the transcendental fusion or confusion of which consists the Intelligible or unintelligible truth.) Will you be content, O reader, to plod in German manner over miles of a straight road, that seems to lead somewhere, with the prospect of arriving at last at some point where it will divide at equal angles, and lead equally in two opposite directions, where you may therefore safely pause, and thankfully set up your rest, and adore in sacred doubt the Supreme Bifurcation? Or do you hold, with Voltaire, who said (*apropos* of the question then debated among the French wits, whether there were or were not a God) that "after all, one must take a side"?

With all respect for the Antinomies and Germans, and "most distinguished consideration" for Voltaire and Parisian persiflage, still, it may not be quite necessary for us, on the present occasion, either to stand still in transcendental doubt, or toss up, as it were, for our side. Individuals differ in character, capacity, and positions; and, according to their circumstances, will combine, in every possible variety of degree, the two elements of thoughtful discriminating selection and rejection, and frank and bold acceptance of what lies around them. Between the extremes of ascetic and timid self-culture, and of unquestioning, unhesitating confidence, we may

---

[1] *Eclogues* 3.108–09: "It is not within our power to determine the strife between you: you are both worthy of the heifer."

[2] a contradiction or inconsistency between two apparently reasonable principles or laws.

[3] In the transcendental philosophy of Immanuel Kant (1724–1804), the noumenon is essence beyond human comprehension; the phenomenon is the form of the noumenon apprehensible to humans through the senses and reason.

consent to see and tolerate every kind and gradation of intermixture. Nevertheless, upon the whole, for the present age, the lessons of reflectiveness and the maxims of caution do not appear to be more needful or more appropriate than exhortations to steady courage and calls to action. There is something certainly of an over-educated weakness of purpose in Western Europe—not in Germany only, or France, but also in more busy England. There is a disposition to press too far the finer and subtler intellectual and moral susceptibilities; to insist upon following out, as they say, to their logical consequences, the notices of some single organ of the spiritual nature; a proceeding which perhaps is hardly more sensible in the grown man than it would be in the infant to refuse to correct the sensations of sight by those of the touch. Upon the whole, we are disposed to follow out, if we must follow out at all, the analogy of the bodily senses; we are inclined to accept rather than investigate; and to put our confidence less in arithmetic and antinomies, than in

A few strong instincts and a few plain rules.[1]

Let us remark also in the minor Poems, which accompany Empedocles, a disposition, perhaps, to assign too high a place to what is called Nature. It may indeed be true, as the astronomers say, though after all it is no very great piece of knowledge, that the heavenly bodies describe ellipses; and go on, from and to all the ages, performing that self-repeating, unattaining curve. But does it, therefore, of necessity follow that human souls do something analogous in the spiritual spaces? Number is a wonderful thing, and the laws of nature sublime; nevertheless, have we not a sort of intuition of the existence, even in our own poor human selves, of something akin to a Power superior to, and transcending, all manifesta-

tions of Nature, all intelligible forms of Number and Law. We quote one set of verses, in which our author does appear to have escaped for once from the dismal cycle of his rehabilitated Hindoo-Greek theosophy—

MORALITY.

We cannot kindle when we will
The fire that in the heart resides,
The spirit bloweth and is still,
In mystery our soul abides;—
    But tasks, in hours of insight willed,
Can be through hours of gloom fulfilled.

With aching hands and bleeding feet
We dig and heap, lay stone on stone;
We bear the burden and the heat
Of the long day, and wish 'twere done.
    Not till the hours of light return,
All we have built do we discern.

Then when the clouds are off the soul,
When thou dost look in Nature's eye,
Ask how *she* viewed thy self-control,
Thy struggling tasked morality—
    Nature whose free, light, cheerful air,
Oft made thee, in thy gloom despair.

And she, whose censure thou dost dread,
Whose eye thou wert afraid to seek,—
See, on her face a glow is spread,
A strong emotion on her cheek.
    'Ah child,' she cries, 'that strife divine,
Whence was it, for it is not mine?

There is no effort on my brow—
I do not strive, I do not weep;
I rush with the swift spheres, and glow
In joy, and when I will, I sleep,—
    Yet that severe, that earnest air,
I saw, I felt it once more, but where?

---

[1] from Wordsworth's sonnet, "Alas, what boots the long laborious quest."

I knew not yet the gauge of Time,
Nor wore the manacles of space,—
I felt it in some other clime,
I saw it in some other place.
 'T was when the heavenly house I trod,
And lay upon the breast of God.'

It is wonderful what stores of really valuable thought may lie neglected in a book, simply because they are not put in that form which serves our present occasions. But if we have been inclined to yield to a preference for the picture of simple, strong, and certain, rather than of subtle, shifting, and dubious feelings, and in point of tone and matter to go along with the young mechanic, in point of diction and manner, we must certainly assign the palm to "A," in spite of a straining after the rounded Greek form, such as, to some extent, vitiates even the style of Milton. Alexander Smith lies open to much graver critical carping. He writes, it would almost seem, under the impression that the one business of the poet is to coin metaphors and similes. He tells them out as a clerk might sovereigns at the Bank of England. So many comparisons, so much poetry; it is the sterling currency of the realm. Yet he is most pleased, perhaps, when he can double or treble a similitude; speaking of A, he will call it a B, which is, as it were, the C of a D. By some maturer effort we may expect to be thus conducted even to Z. But simile within simile, after the manner of Chinese boxes, are more curious than beautiful; nor is it the true aim of the poet, as of the Italian boy in the street, to poise upon his head, for public exhibition, a board crowded as thick as they can stand with images, big and little, black and white, of anybody and everybody, in any possible order of disorder, as they happen to pack. *Tanquam scopulum, insolens verbum,*[1] says the precept of ancient taste, which our author seems to accept freely, with the modern comment of—

In youth from rock to rock I went
With pleasure high and turbulent,—
 Most pleased, when most uneasy.[2]

The movement of his poem is indeed rapid enough; there is a sufficient impetus to carry us over a good deal of rough and "rocky" ground; there is a real continuity of poetic purpose;—but it is so perpetually presumed upon; the attention, which the reader desires to devote to the pursuit of the main drift of what calls itself a single poem, *simplex et unum,* is so incessantly called off to look at this [and look at] that; when, for example, we would fain follow the thought and feeling of Violet and Walter, we are with such peremptory and frequent eagerness summoned to observe how like the sky is to *x* and the stars are to *y,* that on the whole, though there is a real continuity of purpose, we cannot be surprised that the critic of the London Examiner failed to detect it. Keats and Shelley, and Coleridge, perhaps, before them, with their extravagant love for Elizabethan phraseology, have led to this mischief. Has not Tennyson followed a little too much in their train? Coleridge, we suppose, would have maintained it to be an excellence in the "myriad-minded" dramatist, that he so often diverts us from the natural course of thought, feeling, and narrative, to see how curiously two trifles resemble each other, or that, in a passage of deep pathos, he still finds time to apprise us of a paronomasia.[3] But faults which disfigure Shakespeare are not beauties in a modern volume.

 I rot upon the waters when my prow
 Should *grate* the golden isles

may be a very Elizabethan, but is certainly rather a vicious expression. Force and condensation are good, but it is possible to combine them with purity of

---

[1] a saying of Julius Caesar: "Avoid an unusual word as a pilot would a dangerous rock."

[2] from Wordsworth's "To a Daisy."

[3] the act of punning.

phrase. One of the most successful delineations in the whole poem is contained in the following passage, which introduces scene VII.

> [A balcony overlooking the sea.]
> The lark is singing in the blinding sky,—
> Hedges are white with May. The bridegroom sea
> Is toying with the shore, his wedded bride,
> And in the fulness of his marriage joy,
> He decorates her tawny front with shells—
> Retires a space to see how fair she looks,
> Then proud, runs up to kiss her. All is fair,—
> All glad, from grass to sun. Yet more I love
> Than this, the shrinking day that sometimes comes
> In winter's front, so fair 'mongst its dark peers,
> It seems a straggler from the files of June,
> Which in its wanderings had lost its wits,
> And half its beauty, and when it returned,
> Finding its old companions gone away,
> It joined November's troop, then marching past;
> And so the frail thing comes, and greets the world
> With a thin crazy smile, then bursts in tears—
> And all the while it holds within its hand
> A few half-withered flowers;—I love and pity it.

It may be the fault of our point of view; but certainly we do not find even here that happy, unimpeded sequence which is the charm of really good writers. Is there not something incongruous in the effect of the immediate juxtaposition of these two images? We have lost, it may be, that impetuosity, that *élan*, which lifts the young reader over hedge and ditch at flying leaps, across country,—or we should not perhaps entertain any offence, or even surprise, at being transferred *per saltum*[1] from the one field to the other. But we could almost ask, was the passage, so beautiful, though perhaps a little prolonged, about the June day in November, written consecutively, and in one flow, with the previous, and also beautiful one about ocean and his bride. We dare say it was;

but it does not read, somehow, in the same straight line with it,—

> Tantum series juncturaque pollet.[2]

We venture, too, to record a perhaps hypercritical objection to "the *blinding* sky" in this particular collocation. Perhaps in the first line of a scene, while the reader has not yet warmed to his duty, simplicity should be especially observed;—a single image, without any repeated reflection, so to speak, in a second mirror, should suffice. The following, which open scene XI., are better.

> "Summer hath murmured with her leafy lips
> Around my home, and I have heard her not;
> I've missed the process of three several years
> From shaking wind flowers to the tarnished gold
> That rustles sere on Autumn's aged limbs."

Except the last two lines. Our author will not keep his eye steady upon the thing before him; he goes off, and distracts us, and breaks the impression he had begun to succeed in giving, by bidding us look now at something else. Some simpler epithets that *shaking*, and some plainer language than *tarnished gold* or *aged limbs*, would have done the work better. We are quite prepared to believe that these faults and these *disagreeables* have personally been necessities to the writer, are awkwardnesses of growth, of which the full stature may show no trace. He should be assured, however, that though the rude vigor of the style of his Life-Drama may attract upon the first reading, yet in any case, it is not the sort of writing which people recur to with pleasure and fall back upon with satisfaction. It may be a groundless fancy, yet we do fancy, that there is a whole hemisphere, so to say, of the English language which he has left unvisited. His diction feels to us, as if between Milton and Burns he

---

[1] at a bound.

[2] Horace, *Ars Poetica*, l. 242: Clough's point is that everything must be part of a simple whole.

had not read, and between Shakespeare and Keats had seldom admired. Certainly there is but little inspiration in the compositions of the last century; yet English was really best and most naturally written, when there was, perhaps, least to write about. To obtain a real command of the language, some familiarity with the prose writers, at any rate, of that period, is almost essential; and to write out, as a mere daily task, passages, for example, of Goldsmith, would do a verse-composer of the nineteenth century as much good, we believe, as the study of Beaumont and Fletcher.[1]

—1855

---

[1] Clough's concluding remarks on two minor poets are omitted here.

Matthew Arnold

1822 – 1888

Matthew Arnold, son of Thomas Arnold, headmaster of the famous public school Rugby from 1828 to 1842, was a poet and prose writer, traditionally ranked with Browning and Tennyson as one of the most important poets of the Victorian age. But unlike Browning and Tennyson, Arnold could not sustain his poetic impulse. His poetry, which he began publishing early in his career, reflected a deep sense of personal insecurity, barrenness, and even a note of resigned despair. These traits are evident in *The Strayed Reveller and Other Poems* (1849), *Empedocles on Etna and Other Poems* (1852), and "Thyrsis" (1866), an elegy on the death of his friend Arthur Hugh Clough. After 1855 Arnold wrote very little poetry, turning instead to the production of a great deal of high quality prose including literary criticism, political and cultural commentary, and religious writings. His most important work in cultural commentary is *Culture and Anarchy* (1869).

☙❧☙

Preface to the First Edition of Poems

(1853)

In two small volumes of Poems, published anonymously, one in 1849, the other in 1852, many of the Poems which compose the present volume have already appeared. The rest are now published for the first time.

I have, in the present collection, omitted the Poem from which the volume published in 1852 took its title.[1] I have done so, not because the subject of it was a Sicilian Greek born between two and three thousand years ago, although many persons would think this a sufficient reason. Neither have I done so because I had, in my own opinion, failed in the delineation which I intended to effect. I intended to delineate the feelings of one of the last of the Greek religious philosophers, one of the family of Orpheus and Musaeus,[2] having survived his fellows, living on into a time when the habits of Greek thought and feeling had begun fast to change, character to dwindle, the influence of the Sophists[3] to prevail. Into the feelings of a man so situated there entered much that we are accustomed to consider as exclusively modern; how much, the fragments of Empedocles himself which remain to us are sufficient at least to indicate. What those who are familiar only with the great monuments of early Greek genius suppose to be its exclusive characteristics, have disappeared; the calm, the cheerfulness, the disinterested objectivity have disappeared; the dialogue of the mind with itself has commenced; modern problems have presented themselves; we hear already the doubts, we witness the discouragement, of Hamlet and of Faust.

The representations of such a man's feelings must be interesting, if consistently drawn. We all naturally take pleasure, says Aristotle,[4] in any imitation or representation whatever: this is the basis of our love of Poetry: and we take pleasure in them, he adds, because all knowledge is naturally agreeable to us; not to the philosopher only, but to mankind at large. Every representation therefore which is consistently drawn may be supposed to be interesting, inasmuch as it gratifies this natural interest in knowledge of all

---

[1] "Empedocles on Etna." Arnold's "Preface" is extremely important and self-revealing, as Arnold uses it to rationalize his exclusion of his most important poem from the 1853 volume.

[2] legendary Greek poets and musicians. Orpheus was the father of Musaeus.

[3] Greek teachers of philosophy who were masters of sophistical reasoning.

[4] *Poetics* 4.2–5.

kinds. What is *not* interesting, is that which does not add to our knowledge of any kind; that which is vaguely conceived and loosely drawn; a representation which is general, indeterminate, and faint, instead of being particular, precise, and firm.

Any accurate representation may therefore be expected to be interesting; but, if the representation be a poetical one, more than this is demanded. It is demanded, not only that it shall interest, but also that it shall inspirit and rejoice the reader: that it shall convey a charm, and infuse delight. For the Muses, as Hesiod says,[1] were born that they might be "a forgetfulness of evils, and a truce from cares": and it is not enough that the Poet should add to the knowledge of men, it is required of him also that he should add to their happiness. "All Art," says Schiller,[2] "is dedicated to Joy, and there is no higher and no more serious problem, than how to make men happy. The right Art is that alone, which creates the highest enjoyment."

A poetical work, therefore, is not yet justified when it has been shown to be an accurate, and therefore interesting representation; it has to be shown also that it is a representation from which men can derive enjoyment. In presence of the most tragic circumstances, represented in a work of Art, the feeling of enjoyment, as is well known, may still subsist: the representation of the most utter calamity, of the liveliest anguish, is not sufficient to destroy it: the more tragic the situation, the deeper becomes the enjoyment; and the situation is more tragic in proportion as it becomes more terrible.

What then are the situations, from the representation of which, though accurate, no poetical enjoyment can be derived? They are those in which the suffering finds no vent in action; in which a continuous state of mental distress is prolonged, unrelieved by incident, hope, or resistance; in which there is everything to be endured, nothing to be done. In such situations there is inevitably something morbid, in the description of them something monotonous. When they occur in actual life, they are painful, not tragic; the representation of them in poetry is painful also.

To this class of situations, poetically faulty as it appears to me, that of Empedocles, as I have endeavored to represent him, belongs; and I have therefore excluded the Poem from the present collection.

And why, it may be asked, have I entered into this explanation respecting a matter so unimportant as the admission or exclusion of the Poem in question? I have done so, because I was anxious to avow that the sole reason for its exclusion was that which has been stated above; and that it has not been excluded in deference to the opinion which many critics of the present day appear to entertain against subjects chosen from distant times and countries: against the choice, in short, of any subjects but modern ones.

"The Poet," it is said,[3] and by an intelligent critic, "the Poet who would really fix the public attention must leave the exhausted past, and draw his subjects from matters of present import, and *therefore* both of interest and novelty."

Now this view I believe to be completely false. It is worth examining, inasmuch as it is a fair sample of a class of critical dicta everywhere current at the present day, having a philosophical form and air, but no real basis in fact; and which are calculated to vitiate the judgment of readers of poetry, while they exert, so far as they are adopted, a misleading influence on the practice of those who make it.

What are the eternal objects of Poetry, among all nations and at all times? They are actions; human actions; possessing an inherent interest in themselves, and which are to be communicated in an interesting manner by the art of the Poet. Vainly will the latter

---

[1] early Greek poet in his *Theogony*, ll. 54–56.

[2] German poet and critic of the Romantic period.

[3] "In *The Spectator* of April 2nd, 1853. The words quoted were not used with reference to poems of mine." (Arnold's note.) The critic was R.S. Rintoul, the editor of the magazine.

imagine that he has everything in his own power; that he can make an intrinsically inferior action equally delightful with a more excellent one by his treatment of it; he may indeed compel us to admire his skill, but his work will possess, within itself, an incurable defect.

The Poet, then, has in the first place to select an excellent action; and what actions are the most excellent? Those, certainly, which most powerfully appeal to the great primary human affections: to those elementary feelings which subsist permanently in the race, and which are independent of time. These feelings are permanent and the same; that which interests them is permanent and the same also. The modernness or antiquity of an action, therefore, has nothing to do with its fitness for poetical representation; this depends upon its inherent qualities. To the elementary part of our nature, to our passions, that which is great and passionate is eternally interesting; and interesting solely in proportion to its greatness and to its passion. A great human action of a thousand years ago is more interesting to it than a smaller human action of to-day, even though upon the representation of this last the most consummate skill may have been expended, and though it has the advantage of appealing by its modern language, familiar manners, and contemporary allusions, to all our transient feelings and interests. These, however, have no right to demand of a poetical work that it shall satisfy them; their claims are to be directed elsewhere. Poetical works belong to the domain of our permanent passions: let them interest these, and the voice of all subordinate claims upon them is at once silenced.

Achilles, Prometheus, Clytemnestra, Dido—what modern poem presents personages as interesting, even to us moderns, as these personages of an "exhausted past"? We have the domestic epic dealing with the details of modern life which pass daily under our eyes; we have poems representing modern personages in contact with the problems of modern life, moral, intellectual, and social; these works have been produced by poets the most distinguished of their nation and time; yet I fearlessly assert that *Hermann and Dorothea, Childe Harold, Jocelyn,* the *Excursion,*[1] leave the reader cold in comparison with the effect produced upon him by the later books of the *Iliad,* by the *Oresteia,* or by the episode of Dido.[2] And why is this? Simply because in the three last-named cases the action is greater, the personages nobler, the situations more intense: and this is the true basis of the interest in a poetical work, and this alone.

It may be urged, however, that past actions may be interesting in themselves, but that they are not to be adopted by the modern Poet, because it is impossible for him to have them clearly present to his own mind, and he cannot therefore feel them deeply, nor represent them forcibly. But this is not necessarily the case. The externals of a past action, indeed, he cannot know with the precision of a contemporary; but his business is with its essentials. The outward man of Oedipus[3] or of Macbeth, the houses in which they lived, the ceremonies of their courts, he cannot accurately figure to himself; but neither do they essentially concern him. His business is with their inward man; with their feelings and behaviour in certain tragic situations, which engage their passions as men; these have in them nothing local and casual; they are as accessible to the modern Poet as to a contemporary.

The date of an action, then, signifies nothing: the action itself, its selection and construction, this is what is all-important. This the Greeks understood far more clearly than we do. The radical difference between their poetical theory and ours consists, as it appears to me, in this: that, with them, the poetical

---

[1] narrative and philosophical poems by Goethe, Byron, Lamartine, and Wordsworth.

[2] Clytemnestra, the wife of Agamemnon, is in Aeschylus's *Oresteia*; Dido in Virgil's *Aeneid*, Book 4.

[3] king of Thebes and hero of Sophocles's *Oedipus Tyrannus*.

character of the action in itself, and the conduct of it, was the first consideration; with us, attention is fixed mainly on the value of the separate thoughts and images which occur in the treatment of an action. They regarded the whole; we regard the parts. With them, the action predominated over the expression of it; with us, the expression predominates over the action. Not that they failed in expression or were inattentive to it; on the contrary, they are the highest models of expression, the unapproached masters of the *grand style*:[1] but their expression is so excellent because it is so admirably kept in its right degree of prominence; because it is so simple and so well subordinated; because it draws its force directly from the pregnancy of the matter which it conveys. For what reason was the Greek tragic poet confined to so limited a range of subjects? Because there are so few actions which unite in themselves, in the highest degree, the conditions of excellence: and it was not thought that on any but an excellent subject could an excellent Poem be constructed. A few actions, therefore, eminently adapted for tragedy, maintained almost exclusive possession of the Greek tragic stage; their significance appeared inexhaustible; they were as permanent problems, perpetually offered to the genius of every fresh poet. This too is the reason of what appears to us moderns a certain baldness of expression in Greek tragedy; of the triviality with which we often reproach the remarks of the chorus, where it takes part in the dialogue: that the action itself, the situation of Orestes, or Merope, or Alcmaeon,[2] was to stand the central point of interest, unforgotten, absorbing, principal; that no accessories were for a moment to distract the spectator's attention from this; that the tone of the parts was to be perpetually kept down, in order not to impair the grandiose effect of the whole. The terrible old mythic

story on which the drama was founded stood, before he entered the theatre, traced in its bare outlines upon the spectator's mind; it stood in his memory, as a group of statuary, faintly seen, at the end of a long and dark vista: then came the Poet, embodying outlines, developing situations, not a word wasted, not a sentiment capriciously thrown in: stroke upon stroke, the drama proceeded: the light deepened upon the group; more and more it revealed itself to the rivetted gaze of the spectator: until at last, when the final words were spoken, it stood before him in broad sunlight, a model of immortal beauty.

This was what a Greek critic demanded; this was what a Greek poet endeavored to effect. It signified nothing to what time an action belonged; we do not find that the *Persae*[3] occupied a particularly high rank among the dramas of Aeschylus because it represented a matter of contemporary interest: this was not what a cultivated Athenian required; he required that the permanent elements of his nature should be moved; and dramas of which the action, though taken from a long-distant mythic time, yet was calculated to accomplish this in a higher degree than that of the *Persae*, stood higher in his estimation accordingly. The Greeks felt, no doubt, with their exquisite sagacity of taste, that an action of present times was too near them, too much mixed up with what was accidental and passing, to form a sufficiently grand, detached, and self-subsistent object for a tragic poem: such objects belonged to the domain of the comic poet, and of the lighter kinds of poetry. For the more serious kinds, for *pragmatic* poetry, to use an excellent expression of Polybius,[4] they were more difficult and severe in the range of subjects which they permitted. Their theory and practice alike, the admirable treatise of Aristotle, and the unrivalled works of their poets, exclaim with a

---

[1] noble, heroic, or great.

[2] three heroic characters in Greek tragedies, each of whom avenged the murder of some member of his family.

[3] a tragedy written by Aeschylus, produced in 472 BC.

[4] Greek historian. Pragmatic poetry is poetry concerned with matters of everyday life.

thousand tongues—"All depends upon the subject; choose a fitting action, penetrate yourself with the feeling of its situations; this done, everything else will follow."

But for all kinds of poetry alike there was one point on which they were rigidly exacting; the adaptability of the subject to the kind of poetry selected, and the careful construction of the poem.

How different a way of thinking from this is ours! We can hardly at the present day understand what Menander[1] meant, when he told a man who inquired as to the progress of his comedy that he had finished it, not having yet written a single line, because he had constructed the action of it in his mind. A modern critic would have assured him that the merit of his piece depended on the brilliant things which arose under his pen as he went along. We have poems which seem to exist merely for the sake of single lines and passages; not for the sake of producing any total-impression. We have critics who seem to direct their attention merely to detached expressions, to the language about the action, not to the action itself. I verily think that the majority of them do not in their hearts believe that there is such a thing as a total-impression to be derived from a poem at all, or to be demanded from a poet; they think the term a common-place of metaphysical criticism. They will permit the Poet to select any action he pleases, and to suffer that action to go as it will, provided he gratifies them with occasional bursts of fine writing, and with a shower of isolated thoughts and images. That is, they permit him to leave their poetical sense ungratified, provided that he gratifies their rhetorical sense and their curiosity. Of his neglecting to gratify these, there is little danger; he needs rather to be warned against the danger of attempting to gratify these alone; he needs rather to be perpetually reminded to prefer his action to everything else; so to treat this, as to permit its inherent excellences to develop themselves, without interruption from the intrusion of his personal peculiarities: most fortunate, when he most entirely succeeds in effacing himself, and in enabling a noble action to subsist as it did in nature.

But the modern critic not only permits a false practice; he absolutely prescribes false aims.—"A true allegory of the state of one's own mind in a representative history," the Poet is told, "is perhaps the highest thing that one can attempt in the way of poetry."[2]—And accordingly he attempts it. An allegory of the state of one's own mind, the highest problem of an art which imitates actions! No assuredly, it is not, it never can be so: no great poetical work has ever been produced with such an aim. *Faust* itself, in which something of the kind is attempted, wonderful passages as it contains, and in spite of the unsurpassed beauty of the scenes which relate to Margaret, *Faust* itself, judged as a whole, and judged strictly as a poetical work, is defective: its illustrious author, the greatest poet of modern times, the greatest critic of all times, would have been the first to acknowledge it; he only defended his work, indeed, by asserting it to be "something incommensurable."

The confusion of the present times is great, the multitude of voices counselling different things bewildering, the number of existing works capable of attracting a young writer's attention and of becoming his models, immense: what he wants is a hand to guide him through the confusion, a voice to prescribe to him the aim which he should keep in view, and to explain to him that the value of the literary works which offer themselves to his attention is relative to their power of helping him forward on his road towards this aim. Such a guide the English writer at the present day will nowhere find. Failing this, all that can be looked for, all indeed that can be desired, is, that his attention should be fixed on excellent models; that he may reproduce, at any rate, something of their excellence, by penetrating himself with

---

[1] Greek comic dramatist (342?–292 BC).

[2] David Masson, in the *North British Review*, August, 1853.

their works and by catching their spirit, if he cannot be taught to produce what is excellent independently.

Foremost among these models for the English writer stands Shakespeare: a name the greatest perhaps of all poetical names; a name never to be mentioned without reverence. I will venture, however, to express a doubt whether the influence of his works, excellent and fruitful for the readers of poetry, for the great majority, has been of unmixed advantage to the writers of it. Shakespeare indeed chose excellent subjects—the world could afford no better than *Macbeth,* or *Romeo and Juliet,* or *Othello*: he had no theory respecting the necessity of choosing subjects of present import, or the paramount interest attaching to allegories of the state of one's own mind; like all great poets, he knew well what constituted a poetical action; like them, wherever he found such an action, he took it; like them, too, he found his best in past times. But to these general characteristics of all great poets he added a special one of his own; a gift, namely, of happy, abundant, and ingenious expression, eminent and unrivalled: so eminent as irresistibly to strike the attention first in him, and even to throw into comparative shade his other excellences as a poet. Here has been the mischief. These other excellences were his fundamental excellences *as a poet;* what distinguishes the artist from the mere amateur, says Goethe, is *Architectonicè* in the highest sense; that power of execution, which creates, forms, and constitutes: not the profoundness of single thoughts, not the richness of imagery, not the abundance of illustration. But these attractive accessories of a poetical work being more easily seized than the spirit of the whole, and these accessories being possessed by Shakespeare in an unequalled degree, a young writer having recourse to Shakespeare as his model runs great risk of being vanquished and absorbed by them, and, in consequence, of reproducing, according to the measure of his power, these, and these alone. Of this preponderating quality of Shakespeare's genius,

accordingly, almost the whole of modern English poetry has, it appears to me, felt the influence. To the exclusive attention on the part of his imitators to this it is in a great degree owing, that of the majority of modern poetical works the details alone are valuable, the composition worthless. In reading them one is perpetually reminded of that terrible sentence on a modern French poet—*il dit tout ce qu'il veut, mais malheureusement il n'a rien à dire.*[1]

Let me give an instance of what I mean. I will take it from the works of the very chief among those who seem to have been formed in the school of Shakespeare: of one whose exquisite genius and pathetic death render him for ever interesting. I will take the poem of *Isabella, or the Pot of Basil,* by Keats. I choose this rather than the *Endymion,* because the latter work (which a modern critic has classed with the *Fairy Queen!*), although undoubtedly there blows through it the breath of genius, is yet as a whole so utterly incoherent, as not strictly to merit the name of a poem at all. The poem of *Isabella,* then, is a perfect treasure-house of graceful and felicitous words and images: almost in every stanza there occurs one of those vivid and picturesque turns of expression, by which the object is made to flash upon the eye of the mind, and which thrill the reader with a sudden delight. This one short poem contains, perhaps, a greater number of happy single expressions which one could quote than all the extant tragedies of Sophocles. But the action, the story? The action in itself is an excellent one; but so feebly is it conceived by the Poet, so loosely constructed, that the effect produced by it, in and for itself, is absolutely null. Let the reader, after he has finished the poem of Keats, turn to the same story in the *Decameron:*[2] he will then feel how pregnant and interesting the same

---

[1] "He says all he wishes to, but unfortunately he has nothing to say." The poet referred to is Théophile Gautier, the leader of the French school of Art for Art's Sake.

[2] by Boccaccio.

action has become in the hands of a great artist, who above all things delineates his object; who subordinates expression to that which it is designed to express.

I have said that the imitators of Shakespeare, fixing their attention on his wonderful gift of expression, have directed their imitation to this, neglecting his other excellences. These excellences, the fundamental excellences of poetical art, Shakespeare no doubt possessed them—possessed many of them in a splendid degree; but it may perhaps be doubted whether even he himself did not sometimes give scope to his faculty of expression to the prejudice of a higher poetical duty. For we must never forget that Shakespeare is the great poet he is from his skill in discerning and firmly conceiving an excellent action, from his power of intensely feeling a situation, of intimately associating himself with a character; not from his gift of expression, which rather even leads him astray, degenerating sometimes into a fondness for curiosity of expression, into an irritability of fancy, which seems to make it impossible for him to say a thing plainly, even when the press of the action demands the very directest language, or its level character the very simplest. Mr. Hallam,[1] than whom it is impossible to find a saner and more judicious critic, has had the courage (for at the present day it needs courage) to remark, how extremely and faultily difficult Shakespeare's language often is. It is so: you may find main scenes in some of his greatest tragedies, *King Lear* for instance, where the language is so artificial, so curiously tortured, and so difficult, that every speech has to be read two or three times before its meaning can be comprehended. This over-curiousness of expression is indeed but the excessive employment of a wonderful gift—of the power of saying a thing in a happier way than any other man; nevertheless, it is carried so far that one understands

what M. Guizot[2] meant, when he said that Shakespeare appears in his language to have tried all styles except that of simplicity. He has not the severe and scrupulous self-restraint of the ancients, partly no doubt, because he had a far less cultivated and exacting audience: he has indeed a far wider range than they had, a far richer fertility of thought; in this respect he rises above them: in his strong conception of his subject, in the genuine way in which he is penetrated with it, he resembles them, and is unlike the moderns: but in the accurate limitation of it, the conscientious rejection of superfluities, the simple and rigorous development of it from the first line of his work to the last, he falls below them, and comes nearer to the moderns. In his chief works, besides what he has of his own, he has the elementary soundness of the ancients; he has their important action and their large and broad manner: but he has not their purity of method. He is therefore a less safe model; for what he has of his own is personal, and inseparable from his own rich nature; it may be imitated and exaggerated, it cannot be learned or applied as an art; he is above all suggestive; more valuable, therefore, to young writers as men than as artists. But clearness of arrangement, rigour of development, simplicity of style—these may to a certain extent be learned: and these may, I am convinced, be learned best from the ancients, who although infinitely less suggestive than Shakespeare, are thus, to the artist, more instructive.

What then, it will be asked, are the ancients to be our sole models? the ancients with their comparatively narrow range of experience, and their widely different circumstances? Not, certainly, that which is narrow in the ancients, nor that in which we can no longer sympathize. An action like the action of the *Antigone* of Sophocles, which turns upon the conflict between the heroine's duty to her brother's corpse

---

[1] Henry Hallam (1777–1859), in his *Introduction to the Literature of Europe in the Fifteenth, Sixteenth, and Seventeenth Centuries.*

[2] French historian (1787–1874), in his preface to *Shakespeare and His Time.*

and that to the laws of her country, is no longer one in which it is possible that we should feel a deep interest. I am speaking too, it will be remembered, not of the best sources of intellectual stimulus for the general reader, but of the best models of instruction for the individual writer. This last may certainly learn of the ancients, better than anywhere else, three things which it is vitally important for him to know:—the all-importance of the choice of a subject; the necessity of accurate construction; and the subordinate character of expression. He will learn from them how unspeakably superior is the effect of the one moral impression left by a great action treated as a whole, to the effect produced by the most striking single thought or by the happiest image. As he penetrates into the spirit of the great classical works, as he becomes gradually aware of their intense significance, their noble simplicity, and their calm pathos, he will be convinced that it is this effect, unity and profoundness of moral impression, at which the ancient Poets aimed; that it is this which constitutes the grandeur of their works, and which makes them immortal. He will desire to direct his own efforts towards producing the same effect. Above all, he will deliver himself from the jargon of modern criticism, and escape the danger of producing poetical works conceived in the spirit of the passing time, and which partake of its transitoriness.

The present age makes great claims upon us: we owe it service, it will not be satisfied without our admiration. I know not how it is, but their commerce with the ancients appears to me to produce, in those who constantly practise it, a steadying and composing effect upon their judgment, not of literary works only, but of men and events in general. They are like persons who have had a very weighty and impressive experience; they are more truly than others under the empire of facts, and more independent of the language current among those with whom they live. They wish neither to applaud nor to revile their age: they wish to know what it is, what it can give them,

and whether this is what they want. What they want, they know very well; they want to educe and cultivate what is best and noblest in themselves: they know, too, that this is no easy task—χαλεπὸν as Pittacus said, χαλεπὸν ἐσθλὸν ἔμμεαι[1]—and they ask themselves sincerely whether their age and its literature can assist them in the attempt. If they are endeavouring to practise any art, they remember the plain and simple proceedings of the old artists, who attained their grand results by penetrating themselves with some noble and significant action, not by inflating themselves with a belief in the pre-eminent importance and greatness of their own times. They do not talk of their mission, nor of interpreting their age, nor of the coming Poet; all this, they know, is the mere delirium of vanity; their business is not to praise their age, but to afford to the men who live in it the highest pleasure which they are capable of feeling. If asked to afford this by means of subjects drawn from the age itself, they ask what special fitness the present age has for supplying them: they are told that it is an era of progress, an age commissioned to carry out the great ideas of industrial development and social amelioration. They reply that with all this they can do nothing; that the elements they need for the exercise of their art are great actions, calculated powerfully and delightfully to affect what is permanent in the human soul; that so far as the present age can supply such actions, they will gladly make use of them; but that an age wanting in moral grandeur can with difficulty supply such, and an age of spiritual discomfort with difficulty be powerfully and delightfully affected by them.

A host of voices will indignantly rejoin that the present age is inferior to the past neither in moral grandeur nor in spiritual health. He who possesses the discipline I speak of will content himself with remembering the judgements passed upon the pres-

---

[1] "It is hard to be excellent." Pittacus (seventh century BC) was one of the so-called Seven Sages of Greece.

ent age, in this respect, by the two men, the one of strongest head, the other of widest culture, whom it has produced; by Goethe and by Niebuhr.[1] It will be sufficient for him that he knows the opinions held by these two great men respecting the present age and its literature; and that he feels assured in his own mind that their aims and demands upon life were such as he would wish, at any rate, his own to be; and their judgement as to what is impeding and disabling such as he may safely follow. He will not, however, maintain a hostile attitude towards the false pretensions of his age; he will content himself with not being overwhelmed by them. He will esteem himself fortunate if he can succeed in banishing from his mind all feelings of contradiction, and irritation, and impatience; in order to delight himself with the contemplation of some noble action of a heroic time, and to enable others, through his representation of it, to delight in it also.

I am far indeed from making any claim, for myself, that I possess this discipline; or for the following Poems, that they breathe its spirit. But I say, that in the sincere endeavour to learn and practise, amid the bewildering confusion of our times, what is sound and true in poetical art, I seemed to myself to find the only sure guidance, the only solid footing, among the ancients. They, at any rate, knew what they wanted in Art, and we do not. It is this uncertainty which is disheartening, and not hostile criticism. How often have I felt this when reading words of disparagement or of cavil: that it is the uncertainty as to what is really to be aimed at which makes our difficulty, not the dissatisfaction of the critic, who himself suffers from the same uncertainty. *Non me tua fervida terrent Dicta: Dii me terrent, et Jupiter hostis.*[2]

Two kinds of *dilettanti*, says Goethe, there are in poetry: he who neglects the indispensable mechanical part, and thinks he has done enough if he shows spirituality and feeling; and he who seeks to arrive at poetry merely by mechanism, in which he can acquire an artisan's readiness, and is without soul and matter. And he adds, that the first does most harm to Art, and the last to himself. If we must be *dilettanti*: if it is impossible for us, under the circumstances amidst which we live, to think clearly, to feel nobly, and to delineate firmly: if we cannot attain to the mastery of the great artists—let us, at least, have so much respect for our Art as to prefer it to ourselves: let us not bewilder our successors: let us transmit to them the practice of Poetry, with its boundaries and wholesome regulative laws, under which excellent works may again, perhaps, at some future time, be produced, not yet fallen into oblivion through our neglect, not yet condemned and cancelled by the influence of their eternal enemy, Caprice.

—1853

---

[1] the German historian of Rome (1776–1831).

[2] "Your hot words do not frighten me....The gods frighten me, and Jupiter as my enemy": *Aeneid* 12.894–95.

Gerald Massey
1828 – 1907

Gerald Massey was a poet of humble origins: he was born in a hut at Gamble Wharf on the canal near Tring. After only a few years of schooling, he was put to work at the age of eight in a silk mill. He then tried straw-plaiting and at the age of fifteen he became an errand boy in London. Massey published *Poems and Chansons* in 1848 and *Voices of Freedom and Lyrics of Love* in 1850. His position as a poet of liberty, labour, and the people was established in 1854 with the third volume, *The Ballad of Babe Christabel and Other Poems*, which went through five editions in one year.

⁜⁜⁜

Preface to the Third Edition of Babe Christabel

I do not think a volume of verse should need a Preface. But as my Book has reached a Third Edition, and as almost as much has been said about myself as about my Book, perhaps I may be excused, even by the Preface-hater, if I do take this opportunity of writing a few words. I have been considerably censured for the political opinions which it contains,—as I expected to be. Before printing, I was advised not to include the political pieces, as, it was urged, they would prove an obstacle to the success of my Poetry, and close the drawing-room door against me. And if I had looked on the success of my Book in a poetical light alone, I should not have printed the greater portion of the political verses. But that was not the sole point of view. Those verses do not adequately express what I think and feel now, since they were written some five or six years ago: yet they express what I thought and felt then, and what thousands beside me have thought and felt, and what thousands still think and feel. They were the outcome of a peculiar and marked experience. I printed the "Memoir," so that they might be read in the light, or gloom, of that experience, and the Book contain its own excuse. They have not read me aright, who have not thus interpreted it. I have been blamed for the rebellious feelings to which the political pieces give utterance; but they were perfectly natural under the circumstances. Indeed, I look upon those same rebellious feelings as my very deliverance from a fatal slough. There are conditions in which many of the poor exist, where humanity must be either rebel or slave. For the slave, degradation and moral death are certain; but for the rebel there is always a chance of becoming conqueror; and the force to resist is far better than the faculty to succumb.

It is not that I seek to sow dissension between class and class, or fling firebrands among the combustibles of society; for when I smite the hearts of my fellows, I would rather they should gush with the healing waters of love, than with the fearful fires of hatred. I yearn to raise them into loveable beings. I would kindle in the hearts of the masses a sense of the beauty and grandeur of the universe, call forth the lineaments of Divinity in their poor worn faces, give them glimpses of the grace and glory of Love and the marvellous significance of Life, and elevate the standard of Humanity for all. But strange wrongs are daily done in the land, bitter feelings are felt, and wild words will be spoken. It was not for myself alone that I wrote these things: it was always the condition of others that so often made the mist rise up and cloud my vision. Nor was it for myself that I have uncurtained some scenes of my life to the public gaze, but as an illustration of the lives of others, who suffer and toil on, "die, and make no sign;" and because one's own personal experience is of more value than that of others taken upon hearsay.

So I keep my political verses as memorials of my past, as one might keep some worn-out garment because he had passed through the furnace in it, nothing doubting that in the future they will often prove my passport to the hearts and homes of thousands of the poor, when the minstrel comes to their door with something better to bring them. They will know that I have suffered their sufferings, wept their tears, thought their thoughts, and felt their feelings; and they will trust me.

I have been congratulated by some correspondents on the uses of suffering, and the riches I have wrung from Poverty: as though it were a blessed thing to be born in the condition in which I was, and surrounded with untoward circumstances as I have been. My experience tells me that Poverty is inimical to the development of Humanity's noblest attributes. Poverty is a never-ceasing struggle for the means of living, and it makes one hard and selfish. To be sure, noble lives have been wrought out in the sternest poverty. Many such are being wrought out now, by the unknown heroes and martyrs of the Poor. I have known men and women in the very worst circumstances, to whom heroism seemed a heritage, and to be noble a natural way of living. But they were so in spite of their poverty, and not because of it. What they might have been if the world had done better by them, I cannot tell; but if their minds had been enriched by culture, the world would have been the gainer. When Christ said, "Blessed are they who suffer," he did not speak of those who suffer from want and hunger, and who always see the Bastille looming up and blotting out the sky of their future. Such suffering brutalizes. True,—natures ripen and strengthen in suffering; but it is that suffering which chastens and ennobles,—that which clears the spiritual sight,—not the anxiety lest work should fail, and the want of daily bread. The beauty of Suffering is not to be read in the face of Hunger.

Above all, Poverty is a cold place to write Poetry in. It is not attractive to poetical influences. The Muses do not like entertainment which is not fit for man or beast. Nor do the best fruits of Poetry ripen in the rain and shade and wind alone: they want sunshine, warmth, and the open sky. And should the heart of a poor man break into song, it is likely that his poverty may turn into hailstones that which might have fallen on the world in fructifying rain. A poor man, fighting his battle of life, has little time for the rapture of repose which Poetry demands. He cannot take Poetry like a Bride to his heart and home, and devote a life to her service. He can only keep some innermost chamber of his heart sacred for her, from whence he gets occasional glimpses of her wondrous beauty, when he can steal away from the outward strife, like some child who has found a treasure, and steals aside to look on it in secret and alone, lest rude and importunate companions should snatch it from the possessor's hands. Considering all things, it may appear madness for a poor man to attempt Poetry in the face of the barriers that surround him. So many hearts have been broken, so many lives have been wasted, so many lions are in the way of the Gate Beautiful, and so many wrecks lie by the path! And so it is,—a diseased madness, or a divine one. If the disease, then there is no help for a man: if the divine, then there is no hindrance for him.

Who would not pity the poor versifier at the outset of his career? But who would not also rejoice with him in the end, when the world crowns him a Poet with paeans of acclaim? And, in spite of all things, there will be poetry in the midst of poverty. Even as there is scarcely a space in the world so barren but some plot of natural richness will be running all to flowers,—some type of loveliness will be starting up from Earth's inner Sea of Beauty, even in waste and wilderness, on rock and ruin, in Alpine snows and sandy solitudes,—so is it with Poetry, the Flower of Humanity. It will continually be springing, in its own natural way, in the most bleak and barren byways of the world, as well as in the richest and most cultivated pastures. The winds of heaven, or the birds of God, will drop the seed, and the flower will follow, even though sown amid the bushes and brambles of the obscurest hamlet, or in the crevices of the city pavement. Not that the wilderness, or the rock, or the snows are the fittest places to rear flowers of the most exquisite fragrance and beauty; neither are Poverty and Penury, with their hell of torture, and daily wrestle with grim Death, the fittest soil to grow and perfect the flower of Poetry. The greatest original Genius can only develop itself according to the circumstances which environ it. It needs food to nourish it, and time and opportunity to unfold it. If it lack these, it must remain dwarfed and stunted, and perhaps wither and die.

Besides, it is not while the fight is raging, and the struggle is sore, that the Poet can sing. He must first do battle and overcome, climb from the stir and strife, and be able to watch from his mountain where he dwells apart. The fullest and rarest streams of Poetry only flow through a mind at peace. The mirror of the Poet's soul must be calm and clear: else it will give forth distorted reflections and false imaginings.

Had I known, when I began to write verses, what I know now, I think I should have been intimidated, and not have begun at all. So many and so glorious are the luminaries already up and shining, that one would pause before hoisting a rushlight. But I was ignorant of these things. And as I have begun, and conquered some preliminary difficulties,—as I have been sweated down to the proper jockey-weight at which I can ride Pegasus with little danger of spraining his wings,—and as a purpose has gradually and unconsciously grown upon me,—I dare say I shall go on, making the best of my limited materials, with the view of writing some songs that may become dear to the hearts of the people, cheering them in their sorrows, voicing their aspirations, lighting them on the way up which they are groping darkly after better things, and saluting their triumphs with hymns of victory!

I cannot conclude without thanking those Critics who have given me so generous a welcome. And I would also thank those who have not spared my faults, or dwelt tenderly on my failings. They, also, have done me good, and I am grateful for it. Friendly praise is somewhat like a warm bath,—apt to enervate, especially if we stay in too long; but friendly censure is like a cold bath, bracing and healthful, though we are always glad to get out of it. Some of the Critics have called me a "Poet;" but that word is much too lightly spoken, much too freely bandied about. I know what a Poet is too well to fancy that I am one yet. It is a high standard that I set up myself, and I do not ask it to be lowered to reach my stature; nor would I have the Poet's awful crown diminished to mete my lesser brow. I may have that something within which kindles flame-like at the breath of Love, or mounts into song in the presence of Beauty; but, alas! mine is a "jarring lyre."

I have only entered the lists, and inscribed my name: the race has yet to be run. Whether I shall run it, and win the Poet's crown, or not, time alone will prove, and not the prediction of friend or foe. The crowns of Poetry are not in the keeping of Critics. At most they can only give us paper credit. There have been many who have given some sign of promise,—just set a rainbow of hope in the dark cloud of their life,—and never fulfilled their promise: and the world has wondered why. But it might not have been matter of wonder if the world could have read what was written behind the cloud. Others, again, are songful in youth, like the nightingales in spring, who soon cease to sing, because they have to build nests, rear their young, and provide for them; and so the songs grow silent,—the heart is full of cares, and the dreamer has no time to dream. I hope that my future holds some happier fate.

—1854

John Ruskin
1819 – 1900

John Ruskin was one of the most prolific and important social and aesthetic theorists and critics of the Victorian period. His major early interests were painting and architecture, in part inspired by his youthful travels and his encounters with Italian painting and Gothic architecture. Ruskin's first major work, *Modern Painters* (in five volumes [1834–60]), began as a defence of J.M.W. Turner (1775–1851), the only "Modern" painter, Ruskin be-lieved, who accurately depicted nature in terms of the energy infusing natural form. "Of the Pathetic Fallacy" offers examples of those who deviate from such accuracy. His work on architecture, *The Seven Lamps of Architecture* (1849) and *The Stones of Venice* (1851–53), and his wide-ranging social commentary, e.g. *Unto This Last* (1862) and *Fors Clavigera* (1871–84), continued to articulate his aesthetic and moral concerns.

എഃ

Of the Pathetic Fallacy [1]

1. German dullness and English affectation, have of late much multiplied among us the use of two of the most objectionable words that were ever coined by the troublesomeness of metaphysicians—namely, *objective,* and *subjective.*

No words can be more exquisitely, and in all points, useless; and I merely speak of them that I may, at once and for ever, get them out of my way and out of my readers's. But to get that done, they must be explained.

The word *blue,* say certain philosophers, means the sensation of color which the human eye receives in looking at the open sky, or at a bell gentian.

Now, say they farther, as this sensation can only be felt when the eye is turned to the object, and as, therefore, no such sensation is produced by the object when nobody looks at it, therefore the thing, when it is not looked at, is not blue; and thus (say they) there are many qualities of things which depend as much on something else as on themselves. To be sweet, a thing must have a taster; it is only sweet while it is being tasted, and if the tongue had not capacity of taste, then the sugar would not have the quality of sweetness.

And then they agree that the qualities of things which thus depend upon our perception of them, and upon our human nature as affected by them, shall be called subjective; and the qualities of things which they always have, irrespective of any other nature, as roundness or squareness, shall be called objective.

From these ingenious views the step is very easy to a farther opinion, that it does not much matter what things are in themselves, but only what they are to us; and that the only real truth of them is their appear-ance to, or effect upon, us. From which position, with a hearty desire for mystification, and much egotism, selfishness, shallowness, and impertinence, a philosopher may easily go so far as to believe, and say, that everything in the world depends upon his seeing or thinking of it, and that nothing, therefore, exists, but what he sees or thinks of.

2. Now, to get rid of all these ambiguities and troublesome words at once, be it observed that the word *blue* does *not* mean the *sensation* caused by a gentian on the human eye; but it means the *power* of producing that sensation: and this power is always there, in the thing, whether we are there to experi-ence it or not, and would remain there though there were not left a man on the face of the earth. Precisely

---

[1] Ruskin's "Of the Pathetic Fallacy" was first published in 1856 in his *Modern Painters*, Vol. 3, Part 4, Chapter 12.

in the same way gunpowder has a power of exploding. It will not explode if you put no match to it. But it has always the power of so exploding, and is therefore called an explosive compound, which it very positively and assuredly is, whatever philosophy may say to the contrary.

In like manner, a gentian does not produce the sensation of blueness if you don't look at it. But it has always the power of doing so; its particles being everlastingly so arranged by its Maker. And, therefore, the gentian and the sky are always verily blue, whatever philosophy may say to the contrary; and if you do not see them blue when you look at them, it is not their fault, but yours.[1]

3. Hence I would say to these philosophers: If, instead of using the sonorous phrase, *It is objectively so,* you will use the plain old phrase, *It is so,* and if instead of the sonorous phrase, *It is subjectively so,* you will say, in plain old English, *It does so,* or *It seems so to me,* you will, on the whole, be more intelligible to your fellow creatures; and besides, if you find that a thing which generally *does so* to other people (as a gentian looks blue to most men) does *not* so to you, on any particular occasion, you will not fall into the impertinence of saying, that the thing is not so, or did not so, but you will say simply (what you will be all the better for speedily finding out), that something is the matter with you. If you find that you cannot explode the gunpowder, you will not declare that all gunpowder is subjective, and all explosion imaginary, but you will simply suspect and declare yourself to be an ill-made match. Which, on

the whole, though there may be a distant chance of a mistake about it, is, nevertheless, the wisest conclusion you can come to until further experiment.[2]

4. Now, therefore, putting these tiresome and absurd words quite out of our way, we may go on at our ease to examine the point in question—namely, the difference between the ordinary, proper, and true appearances of things to us; and the extraordinary, or false appearances, when we are under the influence of emotion, or contemplative fancy;[3] false appearances, I say, as being entirely unconnected with any real power or character in the object, and only imputed to it by us.

For instance, "The spendthrift crocus, bursting through the mold/Naked and shivering, with his cup of gold."[4]

This is very beautiful and yet very untrue. The crocus is not a spendthrift, but a hardy plant; its yellow is not gold, but saffron. How is it that we enjoy so much the having it put into our heads that it is anything else than a plain crocus?

---

[1] "It is quite true, that in all qualities involving sensation, there may be a doubt whether different people receive the same sensation from the same thing (compare [*Modern Painters*] Part 2, Section 1, Chapter 5); but, though this makes such facts not distinctly explicable, it does not alter the facts themselves. I derive a certain sensation, which I call sweetness, from sugar. That is a fact. Another person feels a sensation, which *he* also calls sweetness, from sugar. That is also a fact. The sugar's power to produce these two sensations, which we suppose to be, and which are, in all probability, very nearly the same in both of us, and, on the whole, in the human race, is its sweetness." (Ruskin's note.)

[2] "In fact (for I may as well, for once, meet our German friends in their own style), all that has been subjected to us on the subject seems object to this great objection; that the subjection of all things (subject to no exceptions) to senses which are, in us, both subject and object, and objects of perpetual contempt, cannot but make it our ultimate object to subject ourselves to the sense, and to remove whatever objections existed to such subjection. So that, finally, that which is the subject of examination or object of attention, uniting thus in itself the characters of subness and obness (so that, that which has no obness in it should be subsubjective, or a subsubject, and that which has no subness in it should be called upper or oberobjective, or an obobject); and we also, who suppose ourselves the objects of every arrangement, and are certainly the subjects of every sensual impression, thus uniting in ourselves, in an obverse or adverse manner, the characters of obness and subness, must both become metaphysically dejected or rejected, nothing remaining in *us* objective, but subjectivity, and the very objectivity of the object being lost in the abyss of this subjectivity of the human.

There is, however, some meaning in the above sentence, if the reader cares to make it out; but in a pure German sentence of the highest style there is often none whatever." (Ruskin's note.)

[3] "Contemplative, in the sense explained in [*Modern Painters*] Part 3, Section 2, Chapter 4." (Ruskin's note.)

[4] "Holmes (Oliver Wendell), quoted by Miss Mitford in her *Recollections of a Literary Life*." (Ruskin's note.)

It is an important question. For, throughout our past reasonings about art, we have always found that nothing could be good or useful, or ultimately pleasurable, which was untrue. But here is something pleasurable in written poetry, which is nevertheless *untrue*. And what is more, if we think over our favorite poetry, we shall find it full of this kind of fallacy, and that we like it all the more for being so.

5. It will appear also, on consideration of the matter, that this fallacy is of two principal kinds. Either, as in this case of the crocus, it is the fallacy of willful fancy, which involves no real expectation that it will be believed; or else it is a fallacy caused by an excited state of the feelings, making us, for the time, more or less irrational. Of the cheating of the fancy we shall have to speak presently; but in this chapter, I want to examine the nature of the other error, that which the mind admits when affected strongly by emotion. Thus, for instance, in *Alton Locke*,[1] "They rowed her in across the rolling foam—/The cruel, crawling foam."

The foam is not cruel, neither does it crawl. The state of mind which attributes to it these characters of a living creature is one in which the reason is unhinged by grief. All violent feelings have the same effect. They produce in us a falseness in all our impressions of external things, which I would generally characterize as the "pathetic fallacy."

6. Now we are in the habit of considering this fallacy as eminently a character of poetical description, and the temper of mind in which we allow it, as one eminently poetical, because passionate. But I believe, if we look well into the matter, that we shall find the greatest poets do not often admit this kind of falseness—that it is only the second order of poets who much delight in it.[2]

Thus, when Dante describes the spirits falling from the bank of Acheron "as dead leaves flutter from a bough,"[3] he gives the most perfect image possible of their utter lightness, feebleness, passiveness, and scattering agony of despair, without, however, for an instant losing his own clear perception that *these* are souls, and *those* are leaves; he makes no confusion of one with the other. But when Coleridge speaks of "the one red leaf, the last of its clan,/That dances as often as dance it can,"[4] he has a morbid, that is to say, a so far false, idea about the leaf; he fancies a life in it, and will, which there are not; confuses its powerlessness with choice, its fading death with merriment, and the wind that shakes it with music. Here, however, there is some beauty, even in the morbid passage; but take an instance in Homer and Pope. Without the knowledge of Ulysses, Elpenor, his youngest follower, has fallen from an upper chamber in the Circean palace, and has been left dead, unmissed by his leader or companions, in the

---

[1] by Charles Kingsley (1819–75).

[2] "I admit two orders of poets, but no third; and by these two orders I mean the creative (Shakespeare, Homer, Dante), and reflective or perceptive (Wordsworth, Keats, Tennyson). But both of these must be *first*-rate in their range, though their range is different; and with poetry second-rate in *quality* no one ought to be allowed to trouble mankind. There is quite enough of the best—much more than we can ever read or enjoy in the length of a life; and it is a literal wrong or sin in any person to encumber us with inferior work. I have no patience with apologies made by young pseudopoets, "that they believe there is *some* good in what they have written: that they hope to do better in time," etc. *Some* good! If there is not *all* good, there is no good. If they ever hope to do better, why do they trouble us now? Let them rather courageously burn all they have done, and wait for the better days. There are few men, ordinarily educated, who in moments of strong feeling could not strike out a poetical thought, and afterwards polish it so as to be presentable. But men of sense know better than so to waste their time; and those who sincerely love poetry, know the touch of the master's hand on the chords too well to fumble among them after him. Nay, more than this, all inferior poetry is an injury to the good, inasmuch as it takes away the freshness of rhymes, blunders upon and gives a wretched commonalty to good thoughts; and, in general, adds to the weight of human weariness in a most woeful and culpable manner. There are few thoughts likely to come across ordinary men, which have not already been expressed by greater men in the best possible way; and it is a wiser, more generous, more noble thing to remember and point out the perfect words, than to invent poorer ones, wherewith to encumber temporarily the world." (Ruskin's note.)

[3] *The Divine Comedy*, "Inferno" 3.112.

[4] *Christabel* 1.49–50.

haste of their departure. They cross the sea to the Cimmerian land; and Ulysses summons the shades from Tartarus. The first which appears is that of the lost Elpenor. Ulysses, amazed, and in exactly the spirit of bitter and terrified lightness which is seen in Hamlet,[1] addresses the spirit with the simple, startled words: "Elpenor! How camest thou under the shadowy darkness? Hast thou come faster on foot than I in my black ship?"[2] Which Pope renders thus:

O, say, what angry power Elpenor led
To glide in shades, and wander with the dead?
How could thy soul, by realms and seas disjoined,
Outfly the nimble sail, and leave the lagging wind?

I sincerely hope the reader finds no pleasure here, either in the nimbleness of the sail, or the laziness of the wind! And yet how is it that these conceits are so painful now, when they have been pleasant to us in the other instances?

7. For a very simple reason. They are not a *pathetic* fallacy at all, for they are put into the mouth of the wrong passion—a passion which never could possibly have spoken them—agonized curiosity. Ulysses wants to know the facts of the matter; and the very last thing his mind could do at the moment would be to pause, or suggest in any wise what was *not* a fact. The delay in the first three lines, and conceit in the last, jar upon us instantly like the most frightful discord in music. No poet of true imaginative power could possibly have written the passage.[3]

Therefore, we see that the spirit of truth must guide us in some sort, even in our enjoyment of fallacy. Coleridge's fallacy has no discord in it, but Pope's has set our teeth on edge. Without farther questioning, I will endeavor to state the main bearings of this matter.

8. The temperament which admits the pathetic fallacy, is, as I said above, that of a mind and body in some sort too weak to deal fully with what is before them or upon them; borne away, or overclouded, or overdazzled by emotion; and it is a more or less noble state, according to the force of the emotion which had induced it. For it is no credit to a man that he is not morbid or inaccurate in his perceptions, when he has no strength of feeling to warp them; and it is in general a sign of higher capacity and stand in the ranks of being, that the emotions should be strong enough to vanquish, partly, the intellect, and make it believe what they choose. But it is still a grander condition when the intellect also rises, till it is strong enough to assert its rule against, or together with, the utmost efforts of the passions; and the whole man stands in an iron glow, white hot, perhaps, but still strong, and in no wise evaporating; even if he melts, losing none of his weight.

So, then, we have the three ranks: the man who perceives rightly, because he does not feel, and to whom the primrose is very accurately the primrose, because he does not love it. Then, secondly, the man who perceives wrongly, because he feels, and to whom the primrose is anything else than a primrose: a star, or a sun, or a fairy's shield, or a forsaken maiden. And then, lastly, there is the man who perceives rightly in spite of his feelings, and to whom the primrose is forever nothing else than itself—a

---

[1] "Well said, old mole! canst work i' the ground so fast?" [*Hamlet* 1.5.162.] (Ruskin's note.)

[2] *Odyssey* 11.56–57.

[3] "It is worth while comparing the way a similar question is put by the exquisite sincerity of Keats:

'He wept, and his bright tears
Went trickling down the golden bow he held.
Thus, with half-shut, suffused eyes, he stood;
While from beneath some cumbrous boughs hard by
With a solemn step an awful goddess came,

And there was purport in her looks for him,
Which he with eager guess began to read
Perplexed, the while melodiously he said,
"How camest thou over the unfooted sea?"

[*Hyperion* 3.42–50.]"
(Ruskin's note.)

little flower, apprehended in the very plain and leafy fact of it, whatever and how many soever the associations and passions may be that crowd around it. And, in general, these three classes may be rated in comparative order, as the men who are not poets at all, and the poets of the second order, and the poets of the first; only however great a man may be, there are always some subjects which *ought* to throw him off his balance; some, by which his poor human capacity of thought should be conquered, and brought into the inaccurate and vague state of perception, so that the language of the highest inspiration becomes broken, obscure, and wild in metaphor, resembling that of the weaker man, overborne by weaker things.

9. And thus, in full, there are four classes: the men who feel nothing, and therefore see truly; the men who feel strongly, think weakly, and see untruly (second order of poets); the men who feel strongly, think strongly, and see truly (first order of poets); and the men who, strong as human creatures can be, are yet submitted to influences stronger than they, and see in a sort untruly, because what they see is inconceivably above them. This last is the usual condition of prophetic inspiration.

10. I separate these classes, in order that their character may be clearly understood; but of course they are united each to the other by imperceptible transitions, and the same mind, according to the influences to which it is subjected, passes at different times into the various states. Still, the difference between the great and less man is, on the whole, chiefly is the point of *alterability*. That is to say, the one knows too much, and perceives and feels too much of the past and future, and of all things beside and around that which immediately affects him, to be in any wise shaken by it. His mind is made up; his thoughts have an accustomed current; his ways are steadfast; it is not this or that new sight which will at once unbalance him. He is tender to impression at the surface, like a rock with deep moss upon it; but there is too much mass of him to be moved. The

smaller man, with the same degree of sensibility, is at once carried off his feet; he wants to do something he did not want to do before; he views all the universe in a new light through his tears; he is gay or enthusiastic, melancholy or passionate, as things come and go to him. Therefore the high creative poet might even be thought, to a great extent, impassive (as shallow people think Dante stern), receiving indeed all feelings to the full, but having a great center of reflection and knowledge in which he stands serene, and watches the feeling, as it were, from far off.

Dante, in his most intense moods, has entire command of himself, and can look around calmly, at all moments, for the image or the word that will best tell what he sees to the upper or lower world. But Keats and Tennyson, and the poets of the second order, are generally themselves subdued by the feelings under which they write, or, at least, write as choosing to be so; and therefore admit certain expressions and modes of thought which are in some sort diseased or false.

11. Now so long as we see that the *feeling* is true, we pardon, or are even pleased by, the confessed fallacy of sight which it induces: we are pleased, for instance, with those lines of Kingsley's above quoted, not because they fallaciously describe foam, but because they faithfully describe sorrow. But the moment the mind of the speaker becomes cold, that moment every such expression becomes untrue, as being forever untrue in the external facts. And there is no greater baseness in literature than the habit of using these metaphorical expressions in cold blood. An inspired writer, in full impetuosity of passion, may speak wisely and truly of "raging waves of the sea foaming out their own shame"; but it is only the basest writer who cannot speak of the sea without talking of "raging waves," "remorseless floods," "ravenous billows," etc.; and it is one of the signs of the highest power in a writer to check all such habits of thought, and to keep his eyes fixed firmly on the

pure fact, out of which if any feeling comes to him or his reader, he knows it must be a true one.

To keep to the waves, I forget who it is who represents a man in despair desiring that his body may be cast into the sea, "Whose changing mound, and foam that passed away,/Might mock the eyes that questioned where I lay."

Observe, there is not a single false, or even over-charged, expression. *Mound* of the sea wave is per-fectly simply and true; *changing* is as familiar as may be; *foam that passed away,* strictly literal; and the whole line descriptive of the reality with a degree of accuracy which I know not any other verse, in the range of poetry, that altogether equals. For most people have not a distinct idea of the clumsiness and massiveness of a large wave. The word *wave* is used too generally of ripples and breakers, and bendings in light drapery or grass: it does not by itself convey a perfect image. But the word *mound* is heavy, large, dark, definite; there is no mistaking the kind of wave meant, nor missing the sight of it. Then the term *changing* has a peculiar force also. Most people think of waves as rising and falling. But if they look at the sea carefully, they will perceive that the waves do not rise and fall. They change. Change both place and form, but they do not fall; one wave goes on, and on, and still on; now lower, now higher, now tossing its mane like a horse, now building itself together like a wall, now shaking, now steady, but still the same wave, till at last it seems struck by something, and changes, one knows not how—becomes another wave.

The close of the line insists on this image, and paints it still more perfectly—*foam that passed away.* Not merely melting, disappearing, but passing on, out of sight, on the career of the wave. Then, having put the absolute ocean fact as far as he may before our eyes, the poet leaves us to feel about it as we may, and to trace for ourselves the opposite fact—the image of the green mounds that do not change, and the white and written stones that do not pass away; and thence to follow out also the associated images of the calm life with the quiet grave, and the despairing life with the fading foam—"Let no man move his bones."[1] "As for Samaria, her king is cut off like the foam upon the water."[2]

But nothing of this is actually told or pointed out, and the expressions, as they stand, are perfectly severe and accurate, utterly uninfluenced by the firmly governed emotion of the writer. Even the word *mock* is hardly an exception, as it may stand merely for *deceive* or *defeat,* without implying any impersonation of the waves.

12. It may be well, perhaps, to give one or two more instances to show the peculiar dignity possessed by all passages, which thus limit their expression to the pure fact, and leave the hearer to gather what he can from it. Here is a notable one from the *Iliad.* Helen, looking from the Scaean gate of Troy over the Grecian host, and telling Priam the names of its captains, says at last:

I see all the other dark-eyed Greeks; but two I cannot see—Castor and Pollux—whom one mother bore with me. Have they not followed from fair Lacedaemon, or have they indeed come in their sea-wandering ships, but now will not enter into the battle of men, fearing the shame and the scorn that is in me?

Then Homer: "So she spoke. But them, already, the life-giving earth possessed, there in Lacedaemon, in the dear fatherland."[3]

Note, here, the high poetical truth carried to the extreme. The poet has to speak of the earth in sad-ness, but he will not let that sadness affect or change his thoughts of it. No; though Castor and Pollux be

---

[1] 2 Kings 23:18.

[2] Hosea 10:7.

[3] *Iliad* 3.243–44.

dead, yet the earth is our mother still, fruitful, life-giving. These are the facts of the thing. I see nothing else than these. Make what you will of them.

13. Take another very notable instance from Casimir de la Vigne's terrible ballad, *La Toilette de Constance.* I must quote a few lines out of it here and there, to enable the reader who has not the book by him, to understand its close.[1]

> *Adieu, bal, plaisir, amour!*
> *On disait, Pauvre Constance!*
> *Et on dansait, jusqu'au jour,*
> *Chez l'ambassadeur de France.*

Yes, that is the fact of it. Right or wrong, the poet does not say. What you may think about it, he does not know. He has nothing to do with that. There lie the ashes of the dead girl in her chamber. There they danced, till the morning, at the Ambassador's of France. Make what you will of it.

If the reader will look through the ballad, of which I have quoted only about the third part, he will find that there is not, from beginning to end of it, a single poetical (so called) expression, except in one stanza. The girl speaks as simple prose as may be; there is not a word she would not have actually used as she was dressing. The poet stands by, impassive as a statue, recording her words just as they come. At last the doom seizes her, and in the very presence of death, for an instant, his own emotions conquer him. He records no longer the facts only, but the facts as they seem to him. The fire gnaws with *voluptuousness—without pity.* It is soon past. The fate is fixed forever; and he retires into his pale and crystalline atmosphere of truth. He closes all with the calm veracity, "They said, 'Poor Constance!'"

14. Now in this there is the exact type of the consummate poetical temperament. For, be it clearly and constantly remembered, that the greatness of a poet depends upon the two facilities, acuteness of feeling, and command of it. A poet is great, first in proportion to the strength of his passion, and then, that strength being granted, in proportion to his government of it; there being, however, always a point beyond which it would be inhuman and monstrous if he pushed this government, and, therefore, a point at which all feverish and wild fancy becomes just and true. Thus the destruction of the kingdom of Assyria cannot be contemplated firmly by a prophet of Israel. The fact is too great, too wonderful. It overthrows him, dashes him into a confused element of dreams. All the world is to his stunned thought, full of strange voices. "Yea, the fir trees rejoice at thee, and the cedars of Lebanon, saying, 'Since thou art gone down to the grave, no feller is come up against us.'"[2] So, still more, the thought of the presence of deity cannot be borne without this great astonishment. "The mountains and the hills shall break forth before you into singing, and all the trees of the fields shall clap their hands."[3]

15. But by how much this feeling is noble when it is justified by the strength of its cause, by so much it is ignoble when there is not cause enough for it; and beyond all other ignobleness is the mere affectation of it, in hardness of heart. Simply bad writing may almost always, as above noticed, be known by its adoption of these fanciful metaphorical expressions as a sort of current coin; yet there is even a worse, at least a more harmful condition of writing than this, in which such expressions are not ignorantly and feelinglessly caught up, but, by some master, skillful in handling, yet insincere, deliberately wrought out with chill and studied fancy; as if we should try to make an old lava stream look red-hot again, by covering it with dead leaves, or white-hot, with hoar-frost.

---

[1] Here Ruskin quotes part of the poem; the last four lines of the quote are included here.

[2] Isaiah 14:8.

[3] Isaiah 55:12.

When Young is lost in veneration, as he dwells on the character of truly good and holy man, he permits himself for a moment to be overborne by the feeling so far as to exclaim—

Where shall I find him? Angels, tell me where.
You know him; he is near you; point him out.
Shall I see glories beaming from his brow,
Or trace his footsteps by the rising flowers? [1]

This emotion has a worthy cause, and is thus true and right. But now hear the coldhearted Pope say to a shepherd girl—

Where'er you walk, cool gales shall fan the glade;
Trees, where you sit, shall crowd into a shade;
Your praise the birds shall chant in every grove,
And winds shall waft it to the powers above.
But would you sing, and rival Orpheus' strain,
The wondering forests soon should dance again;
The moving mountains hear the powerful call,
And headlong streams hang, listening, in their fall. [2]

This is not, nor could it for a moment be mistaken for, the language of passion. It is simple falsehood, uttered by hypocrisy in definite absurdity, rooted in affectation, and coldly asserted in the teeth of nature and fact. Passion will indeed go far in deceiving itself; but it must be a strong passion, not the simple wish of a lover to tempt his mistress to sing. Compare a very closely parallel passage in Wordsworth, in which the lover has lost his mistress:

Three years had Barbara in her grave been laid,
When thus his moan he made:

"Oh, move, thou cottage, from beyond yon oak,
Or let the ancient tree uprooted lie,

That in some other way yon smoke
May mount into the sky.

If still behind yon pine tree's ragged bough,
Headlong, the waterfall must come,
Oh, let it, then, be dumb—
Be anything, sweet stream, but that which thou art
now." [3]

Here is a cottage to be moved, if not a mountain, and a waterfall to be silent, if it is not to hang listening: but with what different relation to the mind that contemplates them! Here, in the extremity of its agony, the soul cries out wildly for relief, which at the same moment it partly knows to be impossible, but partly believes possible, in a vague impression that a miracle *might* be wrought to give relief even to a less sore distress—that nature is kind, and God is kind, and that grief is strong: it knows not well what *is* possible to such grief. To silence a stream, to move a cottage wall—one might think it could do as much as that!

16. I believe these instances are enough to illustrate the main point I insist upon respecting the pathetic fallacy—that so far as it *is* a fallacy, it is always the sign of a morbid state of mind, and comparatively of a weak one. Even in the most inspired prophet it is a sign of the incapacity of his human sight or thought to bear what has been revealed to it. In ordinary poetry, if it is found in the thoughts of the poet himself, it is at once a sign of his belonging to the inferior school; if in the thoughts of the characters imagined by him, it is right or wrong according to the genuineness of the emotion from which it springs; always, however, implying necessarily *some* degree of weakness in the character.

Take two most exquisite instances from master hands. The Jessy of Shenstone, and the Ellen of Wordsworth, have both been betrayed and deserted.

---

[1] *Night Thoughts* 2.345.

[2] *Summer: The Second Pastoral, or Alexis*, ll. 78–84. Ruskin has omitted four lines following the first couplet.

---

[3] *'Tis Said, that Some Have Died for Love*, but somewhat misquoted.

Jessy, in the course of her most touching complaint, says:

> If through the garden's flowery tribes I stray,
>   Where bloom the jasmines that could once allure,
> "Hope not to find delight in us," they say,
>   "For we are spotless, Jessy; we are pure."[1]

Compare this with some of the words of Ellen:

> "Ah, why," said Ellen, sighing to herself,
> "Why do not words, and kiss, and solemn pledge,
> And nature, that is kind in woman's breast,
> And reason, that in man is wise and good,
> And fear of Him who is a righteous Judge,
> Why do not these prevail for human life,
> To keep two hearts together, that began
> Their springtime with one love, and that have need
> Of mutual pity and forgiveness sweet
> To grant, or be received; while that poor bird—
> O, come and hear him! Thou who hast to me
> Been faithless, hear him—though a lowly creature,
> One of God's simple children, that yet know not
> The Universal Parent, *how* he sings!
> As if he wished the firmament of heaven
> Should listen, and give back to him the voice
> Of his triumphant constancy and love;
> The proclamation that he makes, how far
> His darkness doth transcend our fickle light."[2]

The perfection of both these passages, as far as regards truth and tenderness of imagination in the two poets, is quite insuperable. But of the two characters imagined, Jessy is weaker than Ellen, exactly in so far as something appears to her to be in nature which is not. The flowers do not really reproach her. God meant them to comfort her, not to taunt her; they would do so if she saw them rightly.

Ellen, on the other hand, is quite above the slightest erring emotion. There is not the barest film of fallacy in all her thoughts. She reasons as calmly as if she did not feel. And, although the singing of the bird suggests to her the idea of its desiring to be heard in heaven, she does not for an instant admit any veracity in the thought. "As if," she says, "I know he means nothing of the kind; but it does verily seem as if." The reader will find, by examining the rest of the poem, that Ellen's character is throughout consistent in this clear though passionate strength.

It then being, I hope, now made clear to the reader in all respects that the pathetic fallacy is powerful only so far as it is pathetic, feeble so far as it is fallacious, and, therefore, that the dominion of truth is entire, over this, as over every other natural and just state of the human mind, we may go on to the subject for the dealing with which this prefatory inquiry became necessary; and why necessary, we shall see forthwith.[3]

—1856

---

[1] *Elegy* 26.

[2] *The Excursion* 6.869–87.

[3] "I cannot quit this subject without giving two more instances, both exquisite, of the pathetic fallacy, which I have just come upon, in *Maud*:

> 'For a great speculation had failed;
> And ever he muttered and maddened, and ever wanned with despair;
> And out he walked when the wind like a broken worlding wailed,
> And the *flying gold of the ruined woodlands drove through the air.*

> There has fallen a splendid tear
> From the passion-flower at the gate.

> *The red rose cries, "She is near, she is near";*
> *And the white rose weeps, "She is late."*
> The larkspur listens, "I hear, I hear";
> And the lily whispers, "I wait."'"

(Ruskin's note.)
Tennyson 1.9–12, 908–09, and 912–15, but l. 9 is misquoted.

Matthew Arnold
1822 – 1888

(See previous biographical note on page 1270.)

ↄ৩ৎↄ

The Function of Criticism at the Present Time [1]

Many objections have been made to a proposition which, in some remarks of mine on translating Homer, I ventured to put forth; a proposition about criticism, and its importance at the present day. I said: "Of the literature of France and Germany, as of the intellect of Europe in general, the main effort, for now many years, has been a critical effort; the endeavour, in all branches of knowledge, theology, philosophy, history, art, science, to see the object as in itself it really is." I added, that owing to the operation in English literature of certain causes, "almost the last thing for which one would come to English literature is just that very thing which now Europe most desires,—criticism;" [2] and that the power and value of English literature was thereby impaired. More than one rejoinder declared that the importance I here assigned to criticism was excessive, and asserted the inherent superiority of the creative effort of the human spirit over its critical effort. And the other day, having been led by a Mr. Shairp's excellent notice of Wordsworth[3] to turn again to his biogra-

phy, I found, in the words of this great man, whom I, for one, must always listen to with the profoundest respect, a sentence passed on the critic's business, which seems to justify every possible disparagement of it. Wordsworth says in one of his letters:

"The writers in these publications" (the Reviews), "while they prosecute their inglorious employment, can not be supposed to be in a state of mind very favourable for being affected by the finer influences of a thing so pure as genuine poetry." [4]

And a trustworthy reporter of his conversation quotes a more elaborate judgment to the same effect:

"Wordsworth holds the critical power very low, infinitely lower than the inventive; and he said to-day that if the quantity of time consumed in writing critiques on the works of others were given to original composition, of whatever kind it might be, it would be much better employed; it would make a man find out sooner his own level, and it would do infinitely less mischief. A false or malicious criticism may do much injury to the minds of others, a stupid invention, either in prose or verse, is quite harmless." [5]

It is almost too much to expect of poor human nature, that a man capable of producing some effect in one line of literature, should, for the greater good of society, voluntarily doom himself to impotence

---

[1] published in November, 1864.

[2] in "On Translating Homer," lectures given at Oxford 1860–61.

[3] J.C. Shairp, Scots critic, wrote "Wordsworth: The Man and Poet" which appeared in *North British Review* 61 (1864), pp. 1–54. Arnold inserted the following footnote: " I cannot help thinking that a practice, common in England during the last century, and still followed in France, of printing a notice of this kind,—a notice by a competent critic,—to serve as an introduction to an eminent author's works, might be revived among us with advantage. To introduce all succeeding editions of Wordsworth, Mr. Shairp's notice might, it seems to me, excellently serve; it is written from the point of view of an admirer, nay, of a

disciple, and that is right; but then the disciple must be also, as in this case he is, a critic, a man of letters, not, as too often happens, some relation or friend with no qualification for his task except affection for his author."

[4] letter to Bernard Barton (1816) in Christopher Wordsworth, *Memoirs of William Wordsworth* (1851), 2.53.

[5] William Knight, *The Life of Wordsworth* (1880), 3.438.

and obscurity in another. Still less is this to be expected from men addicted to the composition of the "false or malicious criticism" of which Wordsworth speaks. However, everybody would admit that a false or malicious criticism had better never been written. Everybody, too, would be willing to admit, as a general proposition, that the critical faculty is lower than the inventive. But is it true that criticism is really, in itself, a baneful and injurious employment; is it true that all time given to writing critiques on the works of others would be much better employed if it were given to original composition of whatever kind this may be? Is it true Johnson had better have gone on producing more *Irenes*[1] instead of writing his *Lives of the Poets*; nay, is it certain that Wordsworth himself was better employed in making his Ecclesiastical Sonnets than when he made his celebrated Preface, so full of criticism, and criticism of the works of others?[2] Wordsworth was himself a great critic, and it is to be sincerely regretted that he has not left us more criticism; Goethe was one of the greatest of critics, and we may sincerely congratulate ourselves that he has left us so much criticism. Without wasting time over the exaggeration which Wordsworth's judgment on criticism clearly contains, or over an attempt to trace the causes,—not difficult, I think, to be traced,—which may have led Wordsworth to this exaggeration, a critic may with advantage seize an occasion for trying his own conscience, and for asking himself of what real service at any given moment the practice of criticism either is or may be made to his own mind and spirit, and to the minds and spirits of others.

The critical power is of lower rank than the creative. True; but in assenting to this proposition, one or two things are to be kept in mind. It is undeniable that the exercise of a creative power, that a free creative activity, is the highest function of man; it is

proved to be so by man's finding in it his true happiness. But it is undeniable, also, that men may have the sense of exercising this free creative activity in other ways than in producing great words of literature or art; if it were not so, all but a very few men would be shut out from the true happiness of all men. They may have it in well-doing, they may have it in learning, they may have it even in criticising. This is one thing to be kept in mind. Another is, that the exercise of the creative power in the production of great works of literature or art, however high this exercise of it may rank, is not at all epochs and under all conditions possible; and that therefore labour may be vainly spent in attempting it, which might with more fruit be used in preparing for it, in rendering it possible. This creative power works with elements, with materials; what if it has not those materials, those elements, ready for its use? In that case it must surely wait till they are ready. Now in literature,—I will limit myself to literature, for it is about literature that the question arises,—the elements with which the creative power works are ideas; the best ideas, on every matter which literature touches, current at the time. At any rate we may lay it down as certain that in modern literature no manifestation of the creative power not working with these can be very important or fruitful. And I say *current* at the time, not merely accessible at the time; for creative literary genius does not principally show itself in discovering new ideas; that is rather the business of the philosopher. The grand work of literary genius is a work of synthesis and exposition, not of analysis and discovery; its gift lies in the faculty of being happily inspired by a certain intellectual and spiritual atmosphere, by a certain order of ideas, when it finds itself in them; of dealing divinely with these ideas, presenting them in the most effective and attractive combinations,—making beautiful works with them, in short. But it must have the atmosphere, it must find itself amidst the order of ideas, in order to work freely; and these it is not so easy to command. This is why great

---

[1] *Irene* (1749), an unsuccessful play by Samuel Johnson.

[2] "Preface" to the second edition (1800) of the *Lyrical Ballads*.

creative epochs in literature are so rare, this is why there is so much that is unsatisfactory in the productions of many men of real genius; because, for the creation of a masterwork of literature two powers must concur, the power of the man and the power of the moment, and the man is not enough without the moment; the creative power has, for its happy exercise, appointed elements, and those elements are not in its own control.

Nay, they are more within the control of the critical power. It is the business of the critical power, as I said in the words already quoted, "in all branches of knowledge, theology, philosophy, history, art, science, to see the object as in itself it really is." Thus it tends, at last, to make an intellectual situation of which the creative power can profitably avail itself. It tends to establish an order of ideas, if not absolutely true, yet true by comparison with that which it displaces; to make the best ideas prevail. Presently these new ideas reach society, the touch of truth is the touch of life, and there is a stir and growth everywhere; out of this stir and growth come the creative epochs of literature.

Or, to narrow our range, and quit these considerations of the general march of genius and of society—considerations which are apt to become too abstract and impalpable,—every one can see that a poet, for instance, ought to know life and the world before dealing with them in poetry; and life and the world being in modern times very complex things, the creation of a modern poet, to be worth much, implies a great critical effort behind it; else it must be a comparatively poor, barren, and short-lived affair. This is why Byron's poetry had so little endurance in it, and Goethe's so much; both Byron and Goethe had a great productive power, but Goethe's was nourished by a great critical effort providing the true materials for it, and Byron's was not; Goethe knew life and the world, the poet's necessary subjects, much more comprehensively and thoroughly than

Byron. He knew a great deal more of them, and he knew them much more as they really are.

It has long seemed to me that the burst of creative activity in our literature, through the first quarter of this century, had about it in fact something premature; and that from this cause its productions are doomed, most of them, in spite of the sanguine hopes which accompanied and do still accompany them, to prove hardly more lasting than the productions of far less splendid epochs. And this prematureness comes from its having proceeded without having its proper data, without sufficient materials to work with. In other words, the English poetry of the first quarter of this century, with plenty of energy, plenty of creative force, did not know enough. This makes Byron so empty of matter, Shelley so incoherent, Wordsworth even, profound as he is, yet so wanting in completeness and variety. Wordsworth cared little for books, and disparaged Goethe. I admire Wordsworth, as he is, so much that I cannot wish him different; and it is vain, no doubt, to imagine such a man different from what he is, to suppose that he *could* have been different. But surely the one thing wanting to make Wordsworth an even greater poet than he is,—his thought richer, and his influence of wider application,—was that he should have read more books, among them, no doubt, those of that Goethe whom he disparaged without reading him.

But to speak of books and reading may easily lead to a misunderstanding here. It was not really books and reading that lacked to our poetry at this epoch; Shelley had plenty of reading, Coleridge had immense reading. Pindar and Sophocles—as we all say so glibly, and often with so little discernment of the real import of what we are saying—had not many books; Shakspeare was no deep reader. True; but in the Greece of Pindar and Sophocles, in the England of Shakspeare, the poet lived in a current of ideas in the highest degree animating and nourishing to the creative power; society was, in the fullest measure, permeated by fresh thought, intelligent and alive.

And this state of things is the true basis for the creative power's exercise, in this it finds its data, its materials, truly ready for its hand; all the books and reading in the world are only valuable as they are helps to this. Even when this does not actually exist, books and reading may enable a man to construct a kind of semblance of it in his own mind, a world of knowledge and intelligence in which he may live and work. This is by no means an equivalent to the artist for the nationally diffused life and thought of the epochs of Sophocles or Shakspeare; but, besides that it may be a means of preparation for such epochs, it does really constitute, if many share in it, a quickening and sustaining atmosphere of great value. Such an atmosphere the many-sided learning and the long and widely combined critical effort of Germany formed for Goethe, when he lived and worked. There was no national glow of life and thought there, as in the Athens of Pericles or the England of Elizabeth. That was the poet's weakness. But there was a sort of equivalent for it in the complete culture and unfettered thinking of a large body of Germans. That was his strength. In the England of the first quarter of this century there was neither a national glow of life and thought, such as we had in the age of Elizabeth, nor yet a culture and a force of learning and criticism such as were to be found in Germany. Therefore the creative power of poetry wanted, for success in the highest sense, materials and a basis; a thorough interpretation of the world was necessarily denied to it.

At first sight it seems strange that out of the immense stir of the French Revolution and its age should not have come a crop of works of genius equal to that which came out of the stir of the great productive time of Greece, or out of that of the Renascence, with its powerful episode the Reformation. But the truth is that the stir of the French Revolution took a character which essentially distinguished it from such movements as these. These were, in the main, disinterestedly intellectual and spiritual movements; movements in which the human spirit looked for its satisfaction in itself and in the increased play of its own activity. The French Revolution took a political, practical character. The movement which went on in France under the old *régime,* from 1700 to 1789, was far more really akin than that of the Revolution itself to the movement of the Renascence; the France of Voltaire and Rousseau told far more powerfully upon the mind of Europe than the France of the Revolution. Goethe reproached this last expressly with having "thrown quiet culture back."[1] Nay, and the true key to how much in our Byron, even in our Wordsworth, is this!—that they had their source in a great movement of feeling, not in a great movement of mind. The French Revolution, however,—that object of so much blind love and so much blind hatred,—found undoubtedly its motive-power in the intelligence of men, and not in their practical sense; this is what distinguishes it from the English Revolution of Charles the First's time. This is what makes it a more spiritual event than our Revolution, an event of much more powerful and worldwide interest, though practically less successful; it appeals to an order of ideas which are universal, certain, permanent. 1789 asked of a thing, Is it rational? 1642 asked of a thing, Is it legal? or, when it went furthest, Is it according to conscience? This is the English fashion, a fashion to be treated, within its own sphere, with the highest respect; for its success, within its own sphere, has been prodigious. But what is law in one place is not law in another; what is law here to-day is not law even here to-morrow; and as for conscience, what is binding on one man's conscience is not binding on another's. The old woman who threw her stool at the head of the surpliced minister in St. Giles's Church at Edinburgh[2] obeyed an impulse to which millions of the human race may be permitted to remain strangers. But the prescrip-

---

[1] in "The Four Seasons: Spring."

[2] Janet Geddes threw the stool on July 25, 1637, in protest against the effort by Charles I to impose the English liturgy on the Scottish Church.

tions of reason are absolute, unchanging, of universal validity; *to count by tens is the easiest way of counting*—that is a proposition of which every one, from here to the Antipodes, feels the force; at least I should say so if we did not live in a country where it is not impossible that any morning we may find a letter in *The Times* declaring that a decimal coinage is an absurdity.[1] That a whole nation should have been penetrated with an enthusiasm for pure reason, and with an ardent zeal for making its prescriptions triumph, is a very remarkable thing, when we consider how little of mind or anything so worthy and quickening as mind, comes into the motives which alone, in general, impel great masses of men. In spite of the extravagant direction given to this enthusiasm, in spite of the crimes and follies in which it lost itself, the French Revolution derives from the force, truth, and universality of the ideas which it took for its law, and from the passion with which it could inspire a multitude for these ideas, a unique and still living power; it is—it will probably long remain—the greatest, the most animating event in history. And as no sincere passion for the things of the mind, even though it turn out in many respects an unfortunate passion, is ever quite thrown away and quite barren of good, France has reaped from hers one fruit—the natural and legitimate fruit, though not precisely the grand fruit she expected: she is the country in Europe where *the people* is most alive.

But the mania for giving an immediate political and practical application to all these fine ideas of the reason was fatal. Here an Englishman is in his element: on this theme we can all go on for hours. And all we are in the habit of saying on it has undoubtedly a great deal of truth. Ideas cannot be too much prized in and for themselves, cannot be too much lived with; but to transport them abruptly into the world of politics and practice, violently to revolutionise this world to their bidding—that is quite another thing.

There is the world of ideas and there is the world of practice; the French are often for suppressing the one and the English the other; but neither is to be suppressed. A member of the House of Commons said to me the other day: "That a thing is an anomaly, I consider to be no objection to whatever." I venture to think he was wrong; that a thing is an anomaly *is* an objection to it, but absolutely and in the sphere of ideas: it is not necessarily, under such and such circumstances, or at such and such a moment, an objection to it in the sphere of politics and practice. Joubert has said beautifully: "C'est la force et la droit qui règlent toutes choses dans le monde; la force en attendant le droit."[2] (Force and right are the governors of the this world; force till right is ready.) *Force till right is ready*; and till right is ready, force, the existing order of things, is justified, is the legitimate ruler. But right is something moral, and implies inward recognition, free assent of the will; we are not ready for right,—*right, so far as we are concerned, is not ready,*—until we have attained this sense of seeing it and willing it. The way in which for us it may change and transform force, the existing order of things, and become, in its turn, the legitimate ruler of the world, should depend on the way in which, when our time comes, we see it and will it. Therefore for other people enamoured of their own newly discerned right, to attempt to impose it upon us as ours, and violently to substitute their right for our force, is an act of tyranny, and to be resisted. It sets at nought the second great half of our maxim, *force till right is ready*. This was the grand error of the French Revolution; and its movement of ideas, by quitting the intellectual sphere and rushing furiously into the political sphere, ran, indeed, a prodigious and memorable course, but produced no such intellectual fruit as the movement of ideas of the Renascence, and created, in opposition to itself, what I may call an *epoch of concentration*. The great force of that epoch

---

[1] A decimal coinage bill was introduced and withdrawn in 1863.

[2] Joseph Joubert (1754–1824), *Pensées* (Paris, 1874).

of concentration was England; and the great voice of that epoch of concentration was Burke. It is the fashion to treat Burke's writings on the French Revolution as superannuated and conquered by the event; as the eloquent but unphilosophical tirades of bigotry and prejudice. I will not deny that they are often disfigured by the violence and passion of the moment, and that in some directions Burke's view was bounded, and his observation therefore at fault. But on the whole, and for those who can make the needful corrections, what distinguishes these writings is their profound, permanent, fruitful, philosophical truth. They contain the true philosophy of an epoch of concentration, dissipate the heavy atmosphere which its own nature is apt to engender round it, and make its resistance rational instead of mechanical.

But Burke is so great because, almost alone in England, he brings thought to bear upon politics, he saturates politics with thought. It is his accident that his ideas were at the service of an epoch of concentration, not of an epoch of expansion; it is his characteristic that he so lived by ideas, and had such a source of them welling up within him, that he could float even an epoch of concentration and English Tory politics with them. It does not hurt him that Dr. Price[1] and the Liberals were enraged with him; it does not even hurt him that George the Third and the Tories were enchanted with him. His greatness is that he lived in a world which neither English Liberalism nor English Toryism is apt to enter;—the world of ideas, not the world of catchwords and party habits. So far is it from being really true of him that he "to party gave up what was meant for mankind,"[2] that at the very end of his fierce struggle with the French Revolution, after all his invectives against its false pretensions, hollowness, and madness, with his

sincere conviction of its mischievousness, he can close a memorandum on the best means of combating it, some of the last pages he ever wrote,—the *Thoughts on French Affairs*, in December 1791,—with these striking words:

"The evil is stated, in my opinion, as it exists. The remedy must be where power, wisdom, and information, I hope, are more united with good intentions than they can be with me. I have done with this subject, I believe, for ever. It has given me many anxious moments for the last two years. *If a great change is to be made in human affairs, the minds of men will be fitted to it; the general opinions and feelings will draw that way. Every fear, every hope will forward it; and then they who persist in opposing this mighty current in human affairs, will appear rather to resist the decrees of Providence itself, than the mere designs of men. They will not be resolute and firm, but perverse and obstinate.*"

That return of Burke upon himself has always seemed to me one of the finest things in English literature, or indeed in any literature. That is what I call living by ideas; when one side of a question has long had your earnest support, when all your feelings are engaged, when you hear all round you no language but one, when your party talks this language like a steam-engine and can imagine no other,—still to be able to think, still to be irresistibly carried, if so it be, by the current of thought to the opposite side of the question, and, like Balaam, to be unable to speak anything *but what the Lord has put in your mouth*.[3] I know nothing more striking, and I must add that I know nothing more un-English.

For the Englishman in general is like my friend the Member of Parliament, and believes, point-blank, that for a thing to be an anomaly is absolutely no objection to it whatever. He is like the Lord Auckland of Burke's day, who, in a memorandum on the French Revolution, talks of "certain miscreants,

---

[1] Richard Price (1723–91), a Nonconformist minister, preached a sermon in praise of the French Revolution which Burke attacked in his *Reflections on the French Revolution* (1790).

[2] Goldsmith in his "Retaliation."

[3] Numbers 22:35,38.

assuming the name of philosophers, who have presumed themselves capable of establishing a new system of society."[1] The Englishman has been called a political animal, and he values what is political and practical so much that ideas easily become objects of dislike in his eyes, and thinkers "miscreants," because ideas and thinkers have rashly meddled with politics and practice. This would be all very well if the dislike and neglect confined themselves to ideas transported out of their own sphere, and meddling rashly with practice; but they are inevitably extended to ideas as such, and to the whole life of intelligence; practice is everything, a free play of the mind is nothing. The notion of the free play of the mind upon all subjects being a pleasure in itself, being an object of desire, being an essential provider of elements without which a nation's spirit, whatever compensations it may have for them, must, in the long run, die of inanition,[2] hardly enters into an Englishman's thoughts. It is noticeable that the word *curiosity*, which in other languages is used in a good sense, to mean, as a high and fine quality of man's nature, just this disinterested love of a free play of the mind on all subjects, for its own sake,—it is noticeable, I say, that this word has in our language no sense of the kind, no sense but a rather bad and disparaging one. But criticism, real criticism, is essentially the exercise of this very quality. It obeys an instinct prompting it to try to know the best that is known and thought in the world, irrespectively of practice, politics, and everything of the kind; and to value knowledge and thought as they approach this best, without the intrusion of any other considerations whatever. This is an instinct for which there is, I think, little original sympathy in the practical English nature, and what there was of it had undergone a long benumbing

period of blight and suppression in the epoch of concentration which followed the French Revolution.

But epochs of concentration cannot well endure for ever; epochs of expansion, in the due course of things, follow them. Such an epoch of expansion seems to be opening in this country. In the first place all danger of a hostile forcible pressure of foreign ideas upon our practice has long disappeared; like the traveller in the fable,[3] therefore, we begin to wear our cloak a little more loosely. Then, with a long peace, the ideas of Europe steal gradually and amicably in, and mingle, though in infinitesimally small quantities at a time, with our own notions. Then, too, in spite of all that is said about the absorbing and brutalising influence of our passionate material progress, it seems to me indisputable that this progress is likely, though not certain, to lead in the end to an apparition of intellectual life; and that man, after he has made himself perfectly comfortable and has now to determine what to do with himself next, may begin to remember that he has a mind, and that the mind may be made the source of great pleasure. I grant it is mainly the privilege of faith, at present, to discern this end to our railways, our business, and our fortune-making; but we shall see if, here as elsewhere, faith is not in the end the true prophet. Our ease, our travelling, and our unbounded liberty to hold just as hard and securely as we please to the practice to which our notions have given birth, all tend to beget an inclination to deal a little more freely with these notions themselves, to canvass them a little, to penetrate a little into their real nature. Flutterings of curiosity, in the foreign sense of the word, appear amongst us, and it is in these that criticism must look to find its account. Criticism first; a time of true creative activity, perhaps,—which, as I have said, must inevitably be preceded amongst us by a time of criticism,—hereafter, when criticism has done its work.

---

[1] William Eden, Lord Auckland (1744–1814), English diplomat.

[2] emptiness.

[3] in Aesop's fable of the wind and the sun.

It is of the last importance that English criticism should clearly discern what rule for its course, in order to avail itself of the field now opening to it, and to produce fruit for the future, it ought to take. The rule may be summed up in one word,—*disinterestedness*. And how is criticism to show disinterestedness? By keeping aloof from what is called "the practical view of things;" by resolutely following the law of its own nature, which is to be a free play of the mind on all subjects which it touches. By steadily refusing to lend itself to any of those ulterior, political, practical considerations about ideas, which plenty of people will be sure to attach to them, which perhaps ought often to be attached to them, which in this country at any rate are certain to be attached to them quite sufficiently, but which criticism has really nothing to do with. Its business is, as I have said, simply to know the best that is known and thought in the world, and by in its turn making this known, to create a current of true and fresh ideas. Its business is to do this with inflexible honesty, with due ability; but its business is to do no more, and to leave alone all questions of practical consequences and applications, questions which will never fail to have due prominence given to them. Else criticism, besides being really false to its own nature, merely continues in the old rut which it has hitherto followed in this country, and will certainly miss the chance now given to it.

For what is at present the bane of criticism in this country? It is that practical considerations cling to it and stifle it. It subserves interests not its own. Our organs of criticism are organs of men and parties having practical ends to serve, and with them those practical ends are the first thing and the play of the mind the second; so much play of mind as is compatible with the prosecution of those practical ends is all that is wanted. An organ like the *Revue des Deux Mondes*, having for its main function to understand and utter the best that is known and thought in the world, existing, it may be said, as just an organ for a free play of the mind, we have not. But we have the *Edinburgh Review*, existing as an organ of the old Whigs, and for as much play of the mind as may suit its being that; we have the *Quarterly Review*, existing as an organ of the Tories, and for as much play of mind as may suit its being that; we have the *British Quarterly Review*, existing as an organ of the political Dissenters, and for as much play of mind as may suit its being that; we have *The Times*, existing as an organ of the common, satisfied, well-to-do Englishman, and for as much play of mind as may suit its being that. And so on through all the various fractions, political and religious, of our society; every fraction has, as such, its organ of criticism, but the notion of combining all fractions in the common pleasure of a free disinterested play of mind meets with no favour. Directly this play of mind wants to have more scope, and to forget the pressure of practical considerations a little, it is checked, it is made to feel the chain. We saw this the other day in the extinction, so much to be regretted, of the *Home and Foreign Review*. Perhaps in no organ of criticism in this country was there so much knowledge, so much play of mind; but these could not save it. The *Dublin Review* subordinates play of mind to the practical business of English and Irish Catholicism, and lives. It must needs be that men should act in sects and parties, that each of these sects and parties should have its organ, and should make this organ subserve the interests of its action; but it would be well, too, that there should be a criticism, not the minister of these interests, not their enemy, but absolutely and entirely independent of them. No other criticism will ever attain any real authority or make any real way towards its end,—the creating a current of true and fresh ideas.

It is because criticism has so little kept in the pure intellectual sphere, has so little detached itself from practice, has been so directly polemical and controversial, that it has so ill accomplished, in this country, its best spiritual work; which is to keep man from a self-satisfaction which is retarding and vulgarizing, to lead him towards perfection, by making his mind dwell upon what is excellent in itself, and the absolute beauty and fitness of things. A polemical practical criticism makes men blind even to the ideal imperfection of their practice, makes them willingly assert its ideal perfection, in order the better to secure it against attack; and clearly this is narrowing and baneful for them. If they were reassured on the practical side, speculative considerations of ideal perfection they might be brought to entertain, and their spiritual horizon would thus gradually widen. Sir Charles Adderley[1] says to the Warwickshire farmers:—

"Talk of the improvement of breed! Why, the race we ourselves represent, the men and women, the old Anglo-Saxon race, are the best breed in the whole world...The absence of a too enervating climate, too unclouded skies, and a too luxurious nature, has produced so vigorous a race of people, and has rendered us so superior to all the world."

Mr. Roebuck[2] says to the Sheffeld cutlers:—

"I look around me and ask what is the state of England? Is not property safe? Is not every man able to say what he likes? Can you not walk from one end of England to the other in perfect security? I ask you whether, the world over or in past history, there in anything like it? Nothing. I pray that our unrivaled happiness may last."[3]

Now obviously there is a peril for poor human nature in words and thoughts of such exuberant self-satisfaction, until we find ourselves safe in the streets of the Celestial City.

---

[1] Conservative statesman (1814–1905).

[2] John Arthur Roebuck (1801–79), was a Benthamite and member of Parliament from Sheffield.

[3] speeches reported in the London *Times* on 17 September 1863, and 19 August 1864.

Das wenige verschwindet leicht dem Blicke
Der vorwärts sieht, wie viel noch übrig bleibt—

says Goethe; "the little that is done seems nothing when we look forward and see how much we have yet to do."[4] Clearly this is a better line of reflection for weak humanity, so long as it remains on this earthly field of labour and trial.

But neither Sir Charles Adderley nor Mr. Roebuck is by nature inaccessible to considerations of this sort. They only lose sight of them owing to the controversial life we all lead, and the practical from which all speculation takes with us. They have in view opponents whose aim is not ideal, but practical; and in their zeal to uphold their own practice against these innovators, they go so far as even to attribute to this practice an ideal perfection. Somebody has been wanting to introduce a six-pound franchise, or to abolish church-rates, or to collect agricultural statistics by force, or to diminish local self-government. How natural, in reply to such proposals, very likely improper or ill-timed, to go a little beyond the mark and to say stoutly, "such a race of people as we stand, so superior to all the world! The Old Anglo-Saxon race, the best breed in the whole world! I pray that our unrivaled happiness may last! I ask you whether, the world over or in past history, there is anything like it?" And so long as criticism answers this dithyramb by insisting that the old Anglo-Saxon race would be still more superior to all others if it had no church-rates, or that our unrivalled happiness would last yet longer with a six-pound franchise, so long will the strain, "The best breed in the whole world!" swell louder and louder, everything ideal and refining will be lost out of sight, and both the assailed and their critics will remain in a sphere, to say the truth, perfectly unvital, a sphere in which spiritual progression is impossible. But let criticism leave church-rates and the franchise alone, and in the most candid

---

[4] in *Iphigenia in Tauris* 1.2.91–92.

spirit, without a single lurking thought of practical innovation, confront with our dithyramb this paragraph on which I stumbled in a newspaper immediately after reading Mr. Roebuck:—

"A shocking child murder has just been committed at Nottingham. A girl named Wragg left the workhouse there on Saturday morning with her young illegitimate child. The child was soon afterwards found dead on Mapperly Hills, having been strangled. Wragg is in custody."

Nothing but that; but, in juxtaposition with the absolute eulogies of Sir Charles Adderley and Mr. Roebuck, how eloquent, how suggestive are those few lines! "Our old Anglo-Saxon breed, the best in the whole world!"—how much that is harsh and ill-favoured there is in this best! *Wragg!* If we are to talk of ideal perfection of "the best in the whole world," has any one reflected what a touch of grossness in our race, what an original shortcoming in the more delicate spiritual perceptions, is shown by the natural growth amongst us of such hideous names—Higginbottom, Stiggins, Bugg! In Ionia and Attica they were luckier in this respect that "the best race in the world;" by the Ilissus there was no Wragg, poor thing![1] And "our unrivaled happiness";—what an element of grimness, bareness, and hideousness mixes with it and blurs it; the workhouse, the dismal Mapperly Hills,—how dismal those who have seen them will remember;—the gloom, the smoke, the cold, the strangled illegitimate child! "I ask you whether, the world over or in past history, there is anything like it?" Perhaps not, one is inclined to answer; but at any rate, in that case, the world is very much to be pitied. And the final touch,—short, bleak, and inhuman: *Wragg is in custody.* The sex lost in the confusion of our unrivalled happiness; or (shall I say?) the superfluous Christian name lopped off by the straightforward vigour of our old Anglo-Saxon breed! There is profit for the spirit in such contrasts

as this; criticism serves the cause of perfection by establishing them. By eluding sterile conflict, by refusing to remain in the sphere where alone narrow and relative conceptions have any worth and validity, criticism may diminish its momentary importance, but only in this way has it a chance of gaining admittance for those wider and more perfect conceptions to which all its duty is really owed. Mr. Roebuck will have a poor opinion of an adversary who replies to his defiant songs of triumph only by murmuring under his breath, *Wragg is in custody;* but in no other way will these songs of triumph be induced gradually to moderate themselves, to get rid of what in them is excessive and offensive, and to fall into a softer and truer key.

It will be said that it is a very subtle and indirect action which I am thus prescribing for criticism, and that, by embracing in this manner the Indian virtue of detachment and abandoning the sphere of practical life, it condemns itself to a slow and obscure work. Slow and obscure it may be, but it is the only proper work of criticism. The mass of mankind will never have any ardent zeal for seeing things as they are; very inadequate ideas will always satisfy them. On these inadequate ideas reposes, and must repose, the general practice of the world. That is as much as saying that whoever sets himself to see things as they are will find himself one of a very small circle; but it is only by this small circle resolutely doing its own work that adequate ideas will ever get current at all. The rush and roar of practical life will always have a dizzying and attracting effect upon the most collected spectator, and tend to draw him into its vortex; most of all will this be the case where that life is so powerful as it is in England. But it is only by remaining collected, and refusing to lend himself to the point of view of the practical man, that the critic can do the practical man any service; and it is only by the greatest sincerity in pursuing his own course, and by at last convincing even the practical man of his

---

[1] a famous river near Athens.

sincerity, that he can escape misunderstandings which perpetually threaten him.

For the practical man is not apt for fine distinctions, and yet in these distinctions truth and the highest culture greatly find their account. But it is not easy to lead a practical man,—unless you reassure him as to your practical intentions, you have no chance of leading him,—to see a thing which he has always been used to look at from one side only, which he greatly values, and which, looked at from that side, quite deserves, perhaps, all the prizing and admiring which he bestows upon it,—that this thing, looked at from another side, may appear much less beneficent and beautiful, and yet retain all its claims to our practical allegiance. Where shall we find language innocent enough, how shall we make the spotless purity of our intentions evident enough, to enable us to say to the political Englishman that the British Constitution itself, which, seen from the practical side, looks such a magnificent organ of progress and virtue, seen from the speculative side,—with its compromises, its love of facts, its horror of theory, its studied avoidance of clear thoughts,—that, seen from this side, our august Constitution sometimes looks,—forgive me, shade of Lord Somers![1]—a colossal machine for the manufacture of Philistines? How is Cobbett[2] to say this and not be misunderstood, blackened as he is with the smoke of a lifelong conflict in the field of political practice? How is Mr. Carlyle to say it and not be misunderstood, after his furious raid into this field with his *Latter-day Pamphlets?* how is Mr. Ruskin, after his pugnacious political economy? I say, the critic must keep out of the region of immediate practice in the political, social, humanitarian sphere, if he wants to make a beginning for that more free

speculative treatment of things, which may perhaps one day make its benefits felt even in this sphere, but in a natural and thence irresistible manner.

Do what he will, however, the critic will still remain exposed to frequent misunderstandings, and nowhere so much as in this country. For here people are particularly indisposed even to comprehend that without this free disinterested treatment of things, truth and the highest culture are out of the question. So immersed are they in practical life, so accustomed to take all their notions from this life and its processes, that they are apt to think that truth and culture themselves can be reached by the processes of this life, and that it is an impertinent singularity to think of reaching them in any other. "We are all *terrae filii*,"[3] cries their eloquent advocate; "all Philistines together. Away with the notion of proceeding by any other course than the course dear to the Philistines; let us have a social movement, let us organise and combine a party to pursue truth and new thought, let us call it *the liberal party*, and let us all stick to each other, and back each other up. Let us have no nonsense about independent criticism, and intellectual delicacy, and the few and the many. Don't let us trouble ourselves about foreign thought; we shall invent the whole thing for ourselves as we go along. If one of us speaks well, applaud him; if one of us speaks ill, applaud him too; we are all in the same movement, we are all liberals, we are all in pursuit of truth." In this way the pursuit of truth becomes really a social, practical, pleasurable affair, almost requiring a chairman, a secretary, and advertisements; with the excitement of an occasional scandal, a little resistance, to give the happy sense of difficulty overcome; but, in general, plenty of bustle and very little thought. To act is so easy, as Goethe says: to think is so hard! It is true that the critic has many temptations to go with the stream, to make one of the party movement, one of these *terrae filii*; it seems ungracious to refuse to be

---

[1] chair of the committee which drew up the *Declaration of Rights* in 1689.

[2] William Cobbett (1762–1835), a radical journalist with an abrasive style.

[3] "sons of the earth."

a *terrae filius*, when so many excellent people are; but the critic's duty is to refuse, or, if resistance is vain, at least to cry with Obermann: "*Périssons en résistant.*"[1]

How serious a matter it is to try and resist, I had ample opportunity of experiencing when I ventured some time ago to criticise the celebrated first volume of Bishop Colenso.[2] The echoes of the storm which was then raised I still, from time to time, hear grumbling around me. That storm arose out of a misunderstanding almost inevitable. It is result of no little culture to attain to a clear perception that science and religion are two wholly different things. The multitude will for ever confuse them; but happily that is of no great real importance, for while the multitude imagines itself to live by its false science, it does really live by its true religion. Dr. Colenso, however, in his first volume did all he could to strengthen the confusion,[3] and to make it dangerous. He did this with the best intentions, I freely admit, and with the most candid ignorance that this was the natural effect of what he was doing; but, says Joubert, "Ignorance, which in matters of morals extenuates the crime, is itself, in intellectual matters, a crime of the first order."[4] I criticised Bishop Colenso's speculative

confusion. Immediately there was a cry raised: "What is this? here is a liberal attacking a liberal. Do you not belong to the movement? are not you a friend of truth? Is not Bishop Colenso in pursuit of truth? then speak with proper respect of his book. Dr. Stanley[5] is another friend of truth, and you speak with proper respect of his book; why make these invidious differences? both books are excellent, admirable, liberal; Bishop Colenso's perhaps the most so, because it is the boldest, and will have the best practical consequences for the liberal cause. Do you want to encourage to the attack of a brother liberal his, and your, and our implacable enemies, the *Church and State Review* or the *Record*,—the High Church rhinoceros and the Evangelical hyæna? Be silent, therefore; or rather speak, speak as loud as ever you can! and go into ecstacies over the eighty and odd pigeons."

But criticism cannot follow this coarse and indiscriminate method. It is unfortunately possible for a man in pursuit of truth to write a book which reposes upon a false conception. Even the practical consequences of a book are to genuine criticism no recommendation of it, if the book is, in the highest sense, blundering. I see that a lady who herself, too, is in pursuit of truth, and who writes with great ability, but a little too much, perhaps, under the influence of the practical spirit of the English liberal movement, classes Bishop Colenso's book and M. Renan's together, in her survey of the religious state of Europe, as facts of the same order, works, both of them, of "great importance"; "great ability, power, and skill;" Bishop Colenso's, perhaps, the most powerful; at least, Miss Cobbe gives special expression to her gratitude that to Bishop Colenso "has been given the strength to grasp, and the courage to teach, truths of such deep import."[6] In the same way,

---

[1] "Let us perish resisting," from Senancour's *Obermann*.

[2] "So sincere is my dislike to all personal attack and controversy, that I abstain from reprinting, at this distance of time form the occasion which called them forth, the essays in which I criticised Dr. Colenso's book; I feel bound, however, after all that has passed, to make here a final declaration, of my sincere impenitence for having published them. Nay, I cannot forbear repeating yet once more, for his benefit and that of his readers, this sentence from my original remarks upon him: 'There is truth of science and truth of religion; truth of science does not become truth of religion till it is made religious.' And I will add: Let us have all the science there is from the men of science; from the men of religion let us have religion." (Arnold's note.) Arnold thought that John William Colenso's (1814–83) *The Pentateuch and Book of Joshua Critically Examined* (1862), was superficial.

[3] "It has been said I make it 'a crime against literary criticism and the higher culture to attempt to inform the ignorant.' Need I point out that the ignorant are not informed by being confirmed in a confusion?" (Arnold's note.)

[4] *Pensées.*

[5] Arthur P. Stanley. Arnold had compared his *The Bible: Its Form and Substance* (1863), favorably to Colenso's.

[6] Frances Power Cobbe, *Broken Lights* (1864). Ernest Renan's the *Vie de Jésus* (1863), and D.F. Strauss's book, mentioned below, was *Das Leben Jesu* (1835).

more than one popular writer has compared him to Luther. Now it is just this kind of false estimate which the critical spirit is, it seems to me, bound to resist. It is really the strongest possible proof of the low ebb at which, in England, the critical spirit is, that while the critical hit in the religious literature of Germany is Dr. Strauss's book, in that of France M. Renan's book, the book of Bishop Colenso is the critical hit in the religious literature of England. Bishop Colenso's book reposes on a total misconception of the essential elements of the religious problem, as that problem is now presented for solution. To criticism, therefore, which seeks to have the best that is known and thought on this problem, it is, however well meant, of no importance whatever. M. Renan's book attempts a new synthesis of the elements furnished to us by the Four Gospels. It attempts, in my opinion, a synthesis, perhaps premature, perhaps impossible, certainly not successful. Up to the present time, at any rate, we must acquiesce in Fleury's sentence on such recastings of the Gospel-story: "*Quiconque s'imagine la pouvoir mieux écrire, ne l'entend pas.*"[1] M. Renan had himself passed by anticipation a like sentence on his own work, when he said: "If a new presentation of the character of Jesus were offered to me, I would not have it; its very clearness would be, in my opinion, the best proof of its insufficiency." His friends may with perfect justice rejoin that at the sight of the Holy Land, and of the actual scene of the Gospel-story, all the current of M. Renan's thoughts may have naturally changed, and a new casting of that story irresistibly suggested itself to him; and that this is just a case for applying Cicero's maxim: Change of mind is not inconsistency—*nemo doctus unquam mutationem consilii inconstantiam dixit esse.*"[2] Nevertheless, for criticism, M. Renan's first thought must still be the truer one, as long as his new

casting so fails more fully to commend itself, more fully (to use Coleridge's happy phrase about the Bible) to *find* us.[3] Still M. Renan's attempt is, for criticism, of the most real interest and importance, since, with all its difficulty, a fresh synthesis of the New Testament *data,*—not a making war on them, in Voltaire's fashion, not a leaving them out of mind, in the world's fashion, but the putting a new construction upon them, the taking them from under the old, traditional, conventional point of view and placing them under a new one,—is the very essence of the religious problem, as now presented; and only by efforts in this direction can it receive a solution.

Again, in the same spirit in which she judges Bishop Colenso, Miss Cobbe, like so many earnest liberals of our practical race, both here and in America, herself sets vigorously about a positive re-construction of religion, about making a religion of the future out of hand, or at least setting about making it. We must not rest, she and they are always thinking and saying, in negative criticism, we must be creative and constructive; hence we have such works as her recent *Religious Duty*, and works still more considerable, perhaps, by others, which will be in every one's mind. These works often have much ability; they often spring out of sincere convictions, and a sincere wish to do good; and they sometimes, perhaps, do good. Their fault is (if I may be permitted to say so) one which they have in common with the British College of Health, in the New Road. Everyone knows the British College of Health; it is that building with the lion and the statue of the Goddess Hygeia before it; at least I am sure about the lion, though I am not absolutely certain about the Goddess Hygeia. This building does credit, perhaps, to the resources of Dr. Morrison[4] and his disciples; but

---

[1] "Whoever imagines that he can write it better, does not understand it," from Claude Fleury's *Discours sur l'histoire ecclésiastique* (1691–1720).

[2] *Letters to Atticus* 15.7: "No learned man has said it to be inconsistent to change his mind."

[3] in his *Confessions of an Inquiring Spirit*.

[4] James Morrison, a self-styled "Hygeist" who sold "Morrison's Pills" as a universal cure-all. The British College of Health was the name of his pharmacy.

it falls a good deal short of one's idea of what a British College of Health ought to be. In England, where we hate public interference and love individual enterprise, we have a whole crop of places like the British College of Health; the grand name without the grand thing. Unluckily, creditable to individual enterprise as they are, they tend to impair our taste by making us forget what more grandiose, noble, or beautiful character properly belongs to a public institution. The same may be said of the religions of the future of Miss Cobbe and others. Creditable, like the British College of Health, to the resources of their authors, they yet tend to make us forget what more grandiose, noble, or beautiful character properly belongs to religious constructions. The historic religions, with all their faults, have had this; it certainly belongs to the religious sentiment, when it truly flowers, to have this; and we impoverish our spirit if we allow a religion of the future without it. What then is the duty of criticism here? To take the practical point of view, to applaud the liberal movement and all its works,—its New Road religions of the future into the bargain,—for their general utility's sake? By no means; but to be perpetually dissatisfied with these works, while they perpetually fall short of a high and perfect ideal.

In criticism, these are elementary laws; but they never can be popular, and in this country they have been very little followed, and one meets with immense obstacles in following them. That is a reason for asserting them again and again. Criticism must maintain its independence of the practical spirit and its aims. Even with well-meant efforts of the practical spirit it must express dissatisfaction, if in the sphere of the ideal they seem impoverishing and limiting. It must not hurry on to the goal because of its practical importance. It must be patient, and know how to wait; and flexible, and know how to attach itself to things and how to withdraw from them. It must be apt to study and praise elements that for the fulness of spiritual perfection are wanted, even though they

belong to a power which in the practical sphere may be maleficent. It must be apt to discern the spiritual shortcomings or illusions of powers that in the practical sphere may be beneficent. And this without any notion of favouring or injuring, in the practical sphere, one power or the other; without any notion of playing off, in this sphere, one power against the other. When one looks, for instance, at the English Divorce Court,—an institution which perhaps has its practical conveniences, but which in the ideal sphere is so hideous; an institution which neither makes divorce impossible nor makes it decent, which allows a man to get rid of his wife, or a wife of her husband, but makes them drag one another first, for the public edification, through a mire of unutterable infamy,—when one looks at this charming institution, I say, with its crowded trials, its newspaper reports, and its money compensations, this institution in which the gross unregenerate British Philistine has indeed stamped an image of himself,—one may be permitted to find the marriage theory of Catholicism refreshing and elevating. Or when Protestantism, in virtue of its supposed rational and intellectual origin, gives the law to criticism too magisterially, criticism may and must remind it that its pretensions, in this respect, are illusive and do it harm; that the Reformation was a moral rather than an intellectual event; that Luther's theory of grace no more exactly reflects the mind of the spirit than Bossuet's philosophy of history reflects it;[1] and that there is no more antecedent probability of the Bishop of Durham's stock of ideas being agreeable to perfect reason than of Pope Pius the Ninth's. But criticism will not on that account forget the achievements of Protestantism in the practical and moral sphere; nor that, even in the intellectual sphere, Protestantism, though in a blind and stumbling manner, carried forward the Rena-

---

[1] In his *Discourse on Universal History* (1681), Jacques Bossuet explains history as divinely guided for the benefit of Catholicism.

scence, while Catholicism threw itself violently across its path.

I lately heard a man of thought and energy contrasting the want of ardour and movement which he now found amongst young men in this country with what he remembered in his own youth, twenty years ago. "What reformers we were then!" he exclaimed; "what a zeal we had! how we canvassed every institution in Church and State, and were prepared to remodel them all on first principles!" He was inclined to regret, as a spiritual flagging, the lull which he saw. I am disposed rather to regard it as a pause in which the turn to a new mode of spiritual progress is being accomplished. Everything was long seen, by the young and ardent amongst us, in inseparable connection with politics and practical life. We have pretty well exhausted the benefits of seeing things in this connection, we have got all that can be got by so seeing them. Let us try a more disinterested mode of seeing them; let us betake ourselves more to the serener life of the mind and spirit. This life too, may have its excesses and dangers; but they are not for us at present. Let us think of quietly enlarging our stock of true and fresh ideas, and not, as soon as we get an idea or half an idea, be running out with it into the street, and trying to make it rule there. Our ideas will, in the end, shape the world all the better for maturing a little. Perhaps in fifty years' time it will in the English House of Commons be an objection to an institution that it is an anomaly, and my friend the Member of Parliament will shudder in his grave. But let us in the meanwhile rather endeavour that in twenty years' time it may, in English literature, be an objection to a proposition that it is absurd. That will be a change so vast, that the imagination almost fails to grasp it. *Ab integro saeclorum nascitur ordo.*[1]

If I have insisted so much on the course which criticism must take where politics and religion are concerned, it is because, where these burning matters are in question, it is most likely to go astray. I have wished, above all, to insist on the attitude which criticism should adopt towards things in general; on its right tone and temper of mind. But then comes another question as to the subject-matter which literary criticism should most seek. Here, in general, its course is determined for it by the idea which is the law of its being; the idea of a disinterested endeavour to learn and propagate the best that is known and thought in the world, and thus to establish a current of fresh and true ideas. By the very nature of things, as England is not all the world, much of the best that is known and thought in the world cannot be of English growth, must be foreign; by the nature of things, again, it is just this that we are least likely to know, while English thought is streaming in upon us from all sides, and takes excellent care that we shall not be ignorant of its existence. The English critic of literature, therefore, must dwell much on foreign thought, and with particular heed on any part of it, which, while significant and fruitful in itself, is for any reason specially likely to escape him. Again, judging is often spoken of as the critic's one business, and so in some sense it is; but the judgment which almost insensibly forms itself in a fair and clear mind, along with fresh knowledge, is the valuable one; and thus knowledge, and ever fresh knowledge, must be the critic's great concern for himself. And it is by communicating fresh knowledge, and letting his own judgment pass along with it,—but insensibly, and in the second place, not the first, as a sort of companion and clue, not as an abstract lawgiver,—that the critic will generally do most good to his readers. Sometimes, no doubt, for the sake of establishing an author's place in literature, and his relation to a central standard (and if this is not done, how are we to get at our *best in the world*?) criticism may have to deal with a subject-matter so familiar that fresh knowledge is out of the question, and then it must be all judgment; an enunciation and detailed application of principles. Here the great safeguard is never to let

---

[1] "Order is born from the renewal of generations": Virgil, *Eclogues* 4.5.

oneself become abstract, always to retain an intimate and lively consciousness of the truth of what one is saying, and, the moment this fails us, to be sure that something is wrong. Still, under all circumstances, this mere judgment and application of principles is, in itself, not the most satisfactory work to the critic; like mathematics, it is tautological, and cannot well give us, like fresh learning, the sense of creative activity.

But stop, someone will say; all this talk is of no practical use to us whatever; this criticism of yours is not what we have in our minds when we speak of criticism; when we speak of critics and criticism, we mean critics and criticism of the current English literature of the day; when you offer to tell criticism of its function, it is to this criticism that we expect you to address yourself. I am sorry for it, for I am afraid I must disappoint these expectations. I am bound by my own definition of criticism: *a disinterested endeavour to learn and propagate the best that is known and thought in the world*. How much of current English literature comes into this "best that is known and thought in the world"? Not very much, I fear; certainly less, at this moment, than of the current literature of France or Germany. Well, then, am I to alter my definition of criticism, in order to meet the requirements of a number of practising English critics, who, after all, are free in their choice of a business? That would be making criticism lend itself just to one of those alien practical considerations, which, I have said, are so fatal to it. One may say, indeed, to those who have to deal with the mass—so much better disregarded—of current English literature, that they may at all events endeavour, in dealing with this, to try it, so far as they can, by the standard of the best that is known and thought in the world; one may say, that to get anywhere near this standard, every critic should try and possess one great literature, at least, besides his own; and the more unlike his own, the better. But, after

all, the criticism I am really concerned with,—the criticism which alone can much help us for the future, the criticism which, throughout Europe, is at the present day meant, when so much stress is laid on the importance of criticism and the critical spirit,—is a criticism which regards Europe as being, for intellectual and spiritual purposes, one great confederation, bound to a joint action and working to a common result; and whose members have, for their proper outfit, a knowledge of Greek, Roman, and Eastern antiquity, and of one another. Special, local, and temporary advantages being put out of account, that modern nation will in the intellectual and spiritual sphere make most progress, which most thoroughly carries out this programme. And what is that but saying that we too, all of us, as individuals, the more thoroughly we carry it out, shall make the more progress?

There is so much inviting us!—what are we to take? what will nourish us in growth towards perfection? That is the question which, with the immense field of life and of literature lying before him, the critic has to answer; for himself first, and afterwards for others. In this idea of the critic's business the essays brought together in the following pages have had their origin; in this idea, widely different as are their subjects, they have, perhaps, their unity.

I conclude with what I said at the beginning: to have the sense of creative activity is the great happiness and the great proof of being alive, and it is not denied to criticism to have it; but then criticism must be sincere, simple, flexible, ardent, ever widening its knowledge. Then it may have, in no contemptible measure, a joyful sense of creative activity; a sense which a man of insight and conscience will prefer to what he might derive from a poor, starved, fragmentary, inadequate creation. And at some epochs no other creation is possible.

Still, in full measure, the sense of creative activity belongs only to genuine creation; in literature we must never forget that. But what true man of letters ever can forget it? It is no such common matter for a gifted nature to come into possession of a current of true and living ideas, and to produce amidst the inspiration of them, that we are likely to underrate it. The epochs of Aeschylus and Shakespeare make us feel their pre-eminence. In an epoch like those is, no doubt, the true life of literature; there is the promised land, towards which criticism can only beckon. That promised land it will not be ours to enter, and we shall die in the wilderness: but to have desired to enter it, to have saluted it from afar, is already, perhaps, the best distinction among contemporaries; it will certainly be the best title to esteem with posterity.

—1864

Walter Bagehot
1826 – 1877

Walter Bagehot was a businessman, economist, historian, and literary critic. Among Bagehot's literary studies, his essay "Wordsworth, Tennyson and Browning; or Pure, Ornate, and Grotesque Art in English Poetry" relates the poetry of Milton and Wordsworth to "Pure" or classical art, that of Tennyson to "Ornate" or Romantic art, and the poetry of Browning to "Grotesque" (i.e. ugly) or medieval art.

✺✺✺

Wordsworth, Tennyson, and Browning; or, Pure, Ornate, and Grotesque Art in English Poetry [1]

We couple these two books together, not because of their likeness, for they are as dissimilar as books can be; nor on account of the eminence of their authors, for in general two great authors are too much for one essay; but because they are the best possible illustration of something we have to say upon poetical art—because they may give to it life and freshness. The accident of contemporaneous publication has here brought together two books very characteristic of modern art, and we want to show how they are characteristic.

Neither English poetry nor English criticism have ever recovered the *eruption* which they both made at the beginning of this century into the fashionable world. The poems of Lord Byron were received with an avidity that resembles our present avidity for sensation novels, and were read by a class which at present reads little but such novels. Old men who remember those days may be heard to say, "We hear nothing of poetry now-a-days; it seems quite down." And "down" it certainly is, if for poetry it be a descent to be no longer the favourite excitement of the more frivolous part of the "upper" world. That stimulating poetry is now little read. A stray school-boy may still be detected in a wild admiration for the *Giaour* or the *Corsair* (and it is suitable to his age, and he should not be reproached for it), but the *real* posterity—the quiet students of a past literature—never read them or think of them. A line or two linger on the memory; a few telling strokes of occasional and felicitous energy are quoted, but this is all. As wholes, these exaggerated stories were worthless; they taught nothing, and, therefore, they are forgotten. If now-a-days a dismal poet were, like Byron, to lament the fact of his birth, and to hint that he was too good for the world, the *Saturday Review* would say that "they doubted if he *was* too good; that a sulky poet was a questionable addition to a tolerable world; that he need not have been born, as far as they were concerned." Doubtless, there is much in Byron besides his dismal exaggeration, but it was that exaggeration which made "the sensation," which gave him a wild moment of dangerous fame. As so often happens, the cause of his momentary fashion is the cause also of his lasting oblivion. Moore's [2] former reputation was less excessive, yet it has not been more permanent. The prettiness of a few songs preserves the memory of his name, but as a poet to *read* he is forgotten. There is nothing to read in him; no exquisite thought, no sublime feeling, no consummate description of true character. Almost the sole result of the poetry of that time is the harm which it has done. It degraded for a time the whole character of the art. It said by practice, by a most efficient and

---

[1] This essay first appeared in the *National Review*, November 1864, Vol. 1 (New Series), pp. 27–66, prompted by the publication of Tennyson's *Enoch Arden* volume and Browning's *Dramatis Personae*.

[2] Thomas Moore (1779–1852), Irish poet and friend of Byron.

successful practice, that it was the aim, the *duty* of poets, to catch the attention of the passing, the fashionable, the busy world. If a poem "fell dead," it was nothing; it was composed to please the "London" of the year, and if that London did not like it, why, it had failed. It fixed upon the minds of a whole generation, it engraved in popular memory and tradition, a vague conviction that poetry is but one of the many *amusements* for the light classes, for the lighter hours of all classes. The mere notion, the bare idea, that poetry is a deep thing, a teaching thing, the most surely and wisely elevating of human things, is even now to the coarse public mind nearly unknown.

As was the fate of poetry, so inevitably was that of criticism. The science that expounds which poetry is good and which is bad is dependent for its popular reputation on the popular estimate of poetry itself. The critics of that day had *a* day, which is more than can be said for some since; they professed to tell the fashionable world in what books it would find new pleasure, and therefore they were read by the fashionable world. Byron counted the critic and poet equal. The *Edinburgh Review* penetrated among the young, and into places of female resort where it does not go now. As people ask, "Have you read *Henry Dunbar*? and what do you think of it?" so they then asked, "Have you read the *Giaour*? and what do you think of it?" Lord Jeffrey, a shrewd judge of the world, employed himself in telling it what to think; not so much what it ought to think, as what at bottom it did think; and so by dexterous sympathy with current society he gained contemporary fame and power. Such fame no critic must hope for now. His articles will not penetrate where the poems themselves do not penetrate. When poetry was noisy, criticism was loud; now poetry is a still small voice, and criticism must be smaller and stiller. As the function of such criticism was limited, so was its subject. For the great and (as time now proves) the *permanent* part of the poetry of his time—for Shelley and for Words-

worth—Lord Jeffrey had but one word. He said[1] "It won't do." And it will not do to amuse a drawing-room.

The doctrine that poetry is a light amusement for idle hours, a metrical species of sensational novel, has not indeed been without gainsayers wildly popular. Thirty years ago, Mr. Carlyle most rudely contradicted it. But perhaps this is about all that he has done. He has denied, but he has not disproved. He has contradicted the floating paganism, but he has not founded the deep religion. All about and around us a *faith* in poetry struggles to be extricated, but it is not extricated. Some day, at the touch of the true word, the whole confusion will by magic cease; the broken and shapeless notions cohere and crystallise into a bright and true theory. But this cannot be yet.

But though no complete theory of the poetic art as yet be possible for us, though perhaps only our children's children will be able to speak on this subject with the assured confidence which belongs to accepted truth, yet something of some certainty may be stated on the easier elements, and something that will throw light on these two new books. But it will be necessary to assign reasons, and the assigning of reasons is a dry task. Years ago, when criticism only tried to show how poetry could be made a *good* amusement, it was not impossible that criticism itself should be amusing. But now it must at least be serious, for we believe that poetry is a serious and a deep thing.

There should be a word in the language of literary art to express what the word "picturesque" expresses for the fine arts. *Picturesque* means fit to be put into a picture; we want a word *literatesque*, "fit to be put into a book."

. . . .

There are an infinite number of classes of human beings, but in each of these classes there is a distinc-

---

[1] The first words in Lord Jeffrey's celebrated review of "The Excursion" were "This will never do."

tive type which, if we could expand it out in words, would define the class. We cannot expand it in formal terms any more than a landscape, or a species of landscapes; but we have an art, an art of words, which can draw it. Travellers and others often bring home, in addition to their long journals—which, though so living to them, are so dead, so inanimate, so undescriptive to all else—a pen-and-ink sketch, rudely done very likely, but which, perhaps, even the more for the blots and strokes, gives a distinct notion, an emphatic image, to all who see it. They say at once, *now* we know the sort of thing. The sketch has *hit* the mind. True literature does the same. It describes sorts, varieties, and permutations, by delineating the type of each sort, the ideal of each variety, the central, the marking trait of each permutation.

On this account, the greatest artists of the world have ever shown an enthusiasm for reality. To care for notions and abstractions; to philosophise; to reason out conclusions; to care for schemes of thought, are signs in the artistic mind of secondary excellence. A Schiller, an Euripides,[1] a Ben Jonson cares for *ideas*—for the parings of the intellect, and the distillation of the mind; a Shakespeare, a Homer, a Goethe finds his mental occupation, the true home of his natural thoughts, in the real world—"which is the world of all of us"—where the face of nature, the moving masses of men and women, are ever changing, ever multiplying, ever mixing one with the other. The reason is plain—the business of the poet, of the artist, is with *types*; and those types are mirrored in reality. As a painter must not only have a hand to execute, but an eye to distinguish—as he must go here and then there through the real world to catch the picturesque man, the picturesque scene, which are to live on his canvas—so the poet must find in that reality, the *literatesque* man, the *literatesque* scene

which nature intends for him, and which will live in his page. Even in reality he will not find this type complete, or the characteristics perfect; but there, he will find at least *something*, some hint, some intimation, some suggestion; whereas, in the stagnant home of his own thoughts he will find nothing pure, nothing *as it is,* nothing which does not bear his own mark, which is not somehow altered by a mixture with himself.

. . . .

But in these delicate matters, it is easy to misapprehend. There is, undoubtedly, a sort of poetry which is produced as it were out of the author's mind. The description of the poet's own moods and feelings is a common sort of poetry—perhaps the commonest sort. But the peculiarity of such cases is that the poet does not describe himself *as* himself: autobiography is not his subject; he takes himself as a specimen of human nature; he describes, not himself, but a distillation of himself : he takes such of his moods as are most characteristic, as most typify certain moods of certain men, or certain moods of all men; he chooses preponderant feelings of special sorts of men, or occasional feelings of men of all sorts; but with whatever other difference and diversity, the essence is that such self-describing poets describe what is *in* them, but not *peculiar* to them,—what is generic, not what is special and individual. Gray's *Elegy* describes a mood which Gray felt more than other men, but which most others, perhaps all others, feel too. It is more popular, perhaps, than any English poem, because that sort of feeling is the most diffused of high feelings, and because Gray added to a singular nicety of fancy an habitual proneness to a *contemplative*—a discerning but unbiased—meditation on death and on life. Other poets cannot hope for such success: a subject, so popular, so grave, so wise, and yet so suitable to the writer's nature, is hardly to be found. But the same ideal, the same unautobiographical character, is to be found in the

---

[1] Johann Cristoph Friedrich von Schiller (1759–1805), German philosopher. Euripedes (480–406 BC), Greek tragedian.

writings of meaner men. Take sonnets of Hartley Coleridge, for example:—

I

TO A FRIEND

When we were idlers with the loitering rills,
The need of human love we little noted:
Our love was nature; and the peace that floated
On the white mist, and dwelt upon the hills,
To sweet accord subdued our wayward wills:
One soul was ours, one mind, one heart devoted,
That, wisely doating, ask'd not why it doated,
And ours the unknown joy, which knowing kills.
But now I find, how dear thou wert to me;
That man is more than half of nature's treasure,
Of that fair Beauty which no eye can see,
Of that sweet music which no ear can measure;
And now the streams may sing for others' pleasure,
The hills sleep on in their eternity.

II

TO THE SAME

In the great city we are met again,
Where many souls there are, that breathe and die,
Scarce knowing more of nature's potency,
Than what they learn from heat, or cold, or rain,
The sad vicissitude of weary pain:
For busy man is lord of ear and eye,
And what hath nature, but the vast, void sky,
And the throng'd river toiling to the main?
Oh! say not so, for she shall have her part
In every smile, in every tear that falls;
And she shall hide her in the secret heart,
Where love persuades, and sterner duty calls:
But worse it were than death, or sorrow's smart
To live without a friend within these walls.

III

TO THE SAME

We part'd on the mountains, as two streams
From one clear spring pursue their several ways;
And thy fleet course hath been through many a maze
In foreign lands, where silvery Padus gleams
To that delicious sky, whose glowing beams
Brighten'd the tresses that old Poets praise;
Where Petrarch's patient love, and artful lays,
And Ariosto's song of many themes,
Moved the soft air. But I, a lazy brook,
As close pent up within my native dell,
Have crept along from nook to shady nook,
Where flowrets blow, and whispering Naiads dwell.
Yet now we meet, that parted were so wide,
O'er rough and smooth to travel side by side.

The contrast of instructive and enviable locomotion with refining but instructive meditation is not special and peculiar to these two, but general and universal. It was set down by Hartley Coleridge because he was the most meditative and refining of men.

What sort of literatesque types are fit to be described in the sort of literature called poetry, is a matter on which much might be written. Mr. Arnold, some years since, put forth a theory that the art of poetry could only delineate *great actions*. But though, rightly interpreted and understood—using the word action so as to include high and sound activity in contemplation—this definition may suit the highest poetry, it certainly cannot be stretched to include many inferior sorts and even many good sorts. Nobody in their senses would describe Gray's *Elegy* as the delineation of a "great action;" some kinds of mental contemplation may be energetic enough to deserve this name, but Gray would have been frightened at the very word. He loved scholar-like calm and quiet inaction; his very greatness depended on his *not* acting, on his "wise passiveness," on his indulging the grave idleness which so well appreciates so much of human life. But the best answer—the *reductio ad absurdum*—of Mr. Arnold's doctrine, is the mutilation which it has caused him to make of his own writings. It has forbidden him, he tells us, to reprint *Empedocles*—a poem undoubtedly containing defects and even excesses, but containing also these lines:—

And yet what days were those, Parmenides!
When we were young, when we could number friends
In all the Italian cities like ourselves,
When with elated hearts we join'd your train,
Ye Sun-born virgins! on the road of truth.
Then we could still enjoy, then neither thought
Nor outward things were clos'd and dead to us,
But we received the shock of mighty thoughts
On simple minds with a pure natural joy;
And if the sacred load oppress'd our brain,
We had the power to feel the pressure eased,
The brow unbound, the thoughts flow free again,
In the delightful commerce of the world.
We had not lost our balance then, nor grown
Thought's slaves, and dead to every natural joy.
The smallest thing could give us pleasure then—
The sports of the country—people,
A flute note from the woods,
Sunset over the sea;
Seed-time and harvest,
The reapers in the corn,
The vinedresser in his vineyard,
The village-girl at her wheel.
Fullness of life and power of feeling, ye
Are for the happy, for the souls at ease,
Who dwell on a firm basis of content!
But he, who has outlived his prosperous days—
But he, whose youth fell on a different world
From that on which his exiled age is thrown—
Whose mind was fed on other food, was train'd
By other rules than are in vogue to-day—
Whose habit of thought is fix'd, who will not change,
But in a world he loves not, must subsist
In ceaseless opposition, be the guard

Of his own breast, fetter'd to what he guards,
That the world win no mastery over him—
Who has no friend, no fellow left, not one;
Who has no minute's breathing space allow'd
To nurse his dwindling faculty of joy—
Joy and the outward world must die to him,
As they are dead to me.

(235–75)

What freak of criticism can induce a man who has written such poetry as this, to discard it, and say it is not poetry? Mr. Arnold is privileged to speak of his own poems, but no other critic could speak so and not be laughed at.

We are disposed to believe that no very sharp definition can be given—at least in the present state of the critical art—of the boundary line between poetry and other sorts of imaginative delineation. Between the undoubted dominions of the two kinds there is a debateable land; everybody is agreed that the *Œdipus at Colonus is* poetry: everyone is agreed that the wonderful appearance of Mrs. Veal is *not* poetry. But the exact line which separates grave novels in verse, like *Aylmer's Field* or *Enoch Arden*, from grave novels not in verse, like *Silas Marner* or *Adam Bede*, we own we cannot draw with any confidence. Nor, perhaps, is it very important; whether a narrative is thrown into verse or not certainly depends in part on the taste of the age, and in part on its mechanical helps. Verse is the only mechanical help to the memory in rude times, and there is little writing till a cheap something is found to write upon, and a cheap something to write with. Poetry—verse, at least—is the literature of *all work* in early ages; it is only later ages which write in what *they* think a natural and simple prose. There are other casual influences in the matter too; but they are not material now. We need only say here that poetry, because it has a more marked rhythm than prose, must be more intense in meaning and more concise in style than prose. People expect a "marked rhythm" to imply something worth marking; if it fails to do so they are disappointed. They are displeased at the visible waste of a powerful instrument; they call it "doggerel," and rightly call it, for the metrical expression of full thought and eager feeling—the burst of metre—incident to high imagination, should not be wasted on petty matters which prose does as well,—which it does better—which it suits by its very limpness and weakness, whose small changes it follows more easily, and to whose lowest details it can fully and without effort degrade itself. Verse, too, should be *more concise*, for long continued rhythm tends to jade the mind, just as brief rhythm tends to attract the attention. Poetry should be memorable and emphatic, intense, and *soon over*.

The great divisions of poetry, and of all other literary art, arise from the different modes in which these *types*—these characteristic men, these characteristic feelings—may be variously described. There are three principal modes which we shall attempt to describe—the *pure*, which is sometimes, but not very wisely, called the classical; the *ornate*, which is also unwisely called romantic; and the *grotesque*, which might be called the mediæval. We will describe the nature of these a little. Criticism, we know, must be brief—not, like poetry, because its charm is too intense to be sustained—but on the contrary, because its interest is too weak to be prolonged; but elementary criticism, if an evil, is a necessary evil; a little while spent among the simple principles of art is the first condition, the absolute pre-requisite, for surely apprehending and wisely judging the complete embodiments and miscellaneous forms of actual literature.

The definition of *pure* literature is that it describes the type in its simplicity; we mean, with the exact amount of accessory circumstance which is necessary to bring it before the mind in finished perfection, and *no more* than that amount. The *type* needs some accessories from its nature—a picturesque landscape does not consist wholly of picturesque features. There is a setting of surroundings—as the Americans would say, of *fixings*—without which the reality is not itself. By a traditional mode of speech, as soon as we see a picture in which a complete effect is produced by detail so rare and so harmonised as to escape us, we say how "classical." The whole which is to be seen appears at once and through the detail, but the detail itself is not seen: we do not think of that which gives us the idea; we are absorbed in the idea itself. Just so in literature, the pure art is that which works with the fewest strokes; the fewest, that is, for its purpose, for its aim is to call up and bring home to men an idea, a form, a character; and if that idea be twisted, that form be involved, that character perplexed, many strokes of literary art will be needful. Pure art does not mutilate its object: it represents it as fully as is possible with the slightest effort which is possible: it shrinks from no needful circumstances, as little as it inserts any which are needless. The precise peculiarity is not merely that no incidental circumstance is inserted which does not tell on the main design:—no art is fit to be called *art* which permits a stroke to be put in without an object;—but that only the minimum of such circumstance is inserted at all. The form is sometimes said to be bare, the accessories are sometimes said to be invisible, because the appendages are so choice that the shape only is perceived.

.   .   .   .

The extreme opposite to this pure art is what may be called ornate art. This species of art aims also at giving a delineation of the typical idea in its perfection and its fulness, but it aims at so doing in a manner most different. It wishes to surround the type with the greatest number of circumstances which it will *bear*. It works not by choice and selection, but by accumulation and aggregation. The idea is not, as in the pure style, presented with the least clothing which it will endure, but with the richest and most involved clothing that it will admit.

We are fortunate in not having to hunt out of past literature an illustrative specimen of the ornate style. Mr. Tennyson has just given one, admirable in itself, and most characteristic of the defects and the merits of this style. The story of *Enoch Arden*, as he has enhanced and presented it, is a rich and splendid composite of imagery and illustration. Yet how simple that story is in itself. A sailor who sells fish, breaks his leg, gets dismal, gives up selling fish, goes to sea, is wrecked on a desert island, stays there some years, on his return finds his wife married to a miller, speaks to a landlady on the subject, and dies. Told in the pure and simple, the unadorned and classical style, this story would not have taken three pages, but Mr. Tennyson has been able to make it the principal, the largest, tale in his new volume. He has done so only by giving to every event and incident in the volume an accompanying commentary. He tells a great deal about the torrid zone which a rough sailor like Enoch Arden certainly would not have perceived; and he gives to the fishing village, to which all the characters belong, a softness and a fascination which such villages scarcely possess in reality.

The description of the tropical island, on which the sailor is thrown, is an absolute model of adorned art:—

> This mountain wooded to the peak, the lawns
> And winding glades high up like ways to Heaven,
> The slender coco's drooping crown of plumes,
> The lightning flash of insect and of bird,
> The lustre of the long convolvuluses
> That coil'd around the stately stems, and ran
> Ev'n to the limit of the land, the glows
> And glories of the broad belt of the world,
> All these he saw; but what he fain had seen
> He could not see, the kindly human face,
> Nor ever hear a kindly voice, but heard
> The myriad shriek of wheeling ocean-fowl,
> The league-long roller thundering on the reef,
> The moving whisper of huge trees that branch'd
> And blossom'd in the zenith, or the sweep

> Of some precipitous rivulet to the wave,
> As down the shore he ranged, or all day long
> Sat often in the seaward-gazing gorge,
> A shipwreck'd sailor, waiting for a sail:
> No sail from day to day, but every day
> The sunrise broken into scarlet shafts
> Among the palms and ferns and precipices;
> The blaze upon the waters to the east;
> The blaze upon his island overhead;
> The blaze upon the waters to the west;
> Then the great stars that globed themselves in Heaven,
> The hollower-bellowing ocean, and again
> The scarlet shafts of sunrise—but no sail.
>
> (568–95)

No expressive circumstance can be added to this description, no enhancing detail suggested. A much less happy instance is the description of Enoch's life before he sailed:—

> While Enoch was abroad on wrathful seas,
> Or often journeying landward; for in truth
> Enoch's white horse, and Enoch's ocean spoil
> In ocean-smelling osier, and his face,
> Rough-redden'd with a thousand winter gales,
> Not only to the market-cross were known,
> But in the leafy lanes behind the down,
> Far as the portal-warding lion-whelp,
> And peacock yew-tree of the lonely Hall,
> Whose Friday fare was Enoch's ministering.
>
> (90–100)

So much has not often been made of selling fish.

The essence of ornate art is in this manner to accumulate round the typical object, everything which can be said about it, every associated thought that can be connected with it, without impairing the essence of the delineation.

The first defect which strikes a student of ornate art—the first which arrests the mere reader of it—is what is called a want of simplicity. Nothing is described as it is, everything has about it an atmosphere of *something else*. The combined and associated thoughts, though they set off and heighten particular ideas and aspects of the central and typical conception, yet complicate it: a simple thing—"a daisy by the river's brim"—is never left by itself, something else is put with it; something not more connected with it than "lion-whelp" and the "peacock yew-tree" are with the "fresh fish for sale" the Enoch carries past them. Even in the highest cases, ornate art leaves upon a cultured and delicate taste the conviction that it is not the highest art, that it is somehow excessive and overrich, that it is not chaste in itself or chastening to the mind that sees it—that it is in an unexplained manner unsatisfactory, "a thing in which we feel there is some hidden want!"

That want is a want of "definition." We must all know landscapes, river landscapes especially, which are in the highest sense beautiful, which when we first see them give us a delicate pleasure; which in some—and these the best cases—give even a gentle sense of surprise that such things should be so beautiful, and yet when we come to live in them, to spend even a few hours in them, we seem stifled and oppressed. On the other hand, there are people to whom the sea-shore is a companion, an exhilaration; and not so much for the brawl of the shore as for the *limited* vastness, the finite infinite, of the ocean as they see it. Such people often come home braced and nerved, and if they spoke out the truth, would have only to say "We have seen the horizon line;" if they were let alone, indeed, they would gaze on it hour after hour, so great to them is the fascination, so full the sustaining calm, which they gain from that union of form and greatness. To a very inferior extent, but still, perhaps, to an extent which most people understand better, a common arch will have the same effect. A bridge completes a river landscape; if of the old and many-arched sort, it regulates by a long series of defined forms the vague outline of wood and river which before had nothing to measure it; if of the new scientific sort, it introduces still more strictly a geometrical element; it stiffens the scenery which was

before too soft, too delicate, too vegetable. Just such is the effect of pure style in literary art. It calms by conciseness; while the ornate style leaves on the mind a mist of beauty, an excess of fascination, a complication of charm, the pure style leaves behind it the simple, defined, measured idea, as it is, and by itself. That which is chaste chastens; there is a poised energy—a state half thrill, and half tranquillity—which pure art gives; which no other can give; a pleasure justified as well as felt; an ennobled satisfaction at what ought to satisfy us, and must ennoble us.

Ornate art is to pure art what a painted statue is to an unpainted. It is impossible to deny that a touch of colour *does* bring out certain parts, does convey certain expressions, does heighten certain features, but it leaves on the work as a whole, a want, as we say, "of something;" a want of that inseparable chasteness which clings to simple sculpture, an impairing predominance of alluring details which impairs our satisfaction with our own satisfaction; which makes us doubt whether a higher being than ourselves will be satisfied even though we are so. In the very same manner, though the *rouge* of ornate literature excites our eye, it also impairs our confidence.

.   .   .   .

It will be said, if ornate art be, as you say, an inferior species of art, why should it ever be used? If pure art be the best sort of art, why should it not always be used?

The reason is this: literary art, as we just now explained, is concerned with literatesque characters in literatesque situations; and the *best* art is concerned with the *most* literatesque characters in the *most* literatesque situations. Such are the subjects of pure art; it embodies with the fewest touches, and under the most select and choice circumstances, the highest conceptions; but it does not follow that only the best subjects are to be treated by art, and then only in the very best way. Human nature could not endure such a critical commandment as that, and it would be an erroneous criticism which gave it. *Any* literatesque character may be described in literature under *any* circumstances which exhibit its literatesqueness.

. . . .

For these reasons ornate art is within the limits as legitimate as pure art. It does what pure art could not do. The very excellence of pure art confines its employment. Precisely because it gives the best things by themselves and exactly as they are, it fails when it is necessary to describe inferior things among other things, with a list of enhancements and a crowd of accompaniments that in reality do not belong to it. Illusion, half belief, unpleasant types, imperfect types, are as much the proper sphere of ornate art, as an inferior landscape is the proper sphere for the true efficacy of moonlight. A really great landscape needs sunlight and bears sunlight; but moonlight is an equaliser of beauties; it gives a romantic unreality to what will not stand the bare truth. And just so does romantic art.

There is, however, a third kind of art which differs from these on the point in which they most resemble one another. Ornate art and pure art have this in common, that they paint the types of litera-ture in as good perfection as they can. Ornate art, indeed, uses undue disguises and unreal enhance-ments; it does not confine itself to the best types; on the contrary it is its office to make the best of imper-fect types and lame approximations; but ornate art, as much as pure art, catches its subject in the best light it can, takes the most developed aspect of it which it can find, and throws upon it the most congruous colours it can use. But grotesque art does just the contrary. It takes the type, so to say, *in difficulties*. It gives a representation of it in its minimum develop-ment, amid the circumstances least favourable to it, just while it is struggling with obstacles, just where it is encumbered with incongruities. It deals, to use the language of science, not with normal types but with abnormal specimens; to use the language of old philosophy, not with what nature is striving to be, but with what by some lapse she has happened to become.

This art works by contrast. It enables you to see, it makes you see, the perfect type by painting the opposite deviation. It shows you what ought to be by what ought not to be; when complete, it reminds you of the perfect image by showing you the distorted and imperfect image. Of this art we possess in the present generation one prolific master. Mr. Browning is an artist working by incongruity. Possibly hardly one of his most considerable efforts can be found which is not great because of its odd mixture. He puts together things which no one else would have put together, and produces on our minds a result which no one else would have produced, or tried to produce. His admirers may not like all we may have to say of him. But in our way we too are among his admirers. No one ever read him without seeing not only his great ability but his great *mind*. He not only possesses superficial useable talents, but the strong something, the inner secret something, which uses them and controls them; he is great, not in mere accomplishments, but in himself. He has applied a hard strong intellect to real life; he has applied the same intellect to the problems of his age. He has striven to know what *is*: he has endeavoured not to be cheated by counterfeits, not to be infatuated with illusions. His heart is in what he says. He has battered his brain against his creed till he believes it. He has accomplishments too, the more effective because they are mixed. He is at once a student of mysticism and a citizen of the world. He brings to the club sofa distinct visions of old creeds, intense images of strange thoughts: he takes to the bookish student tidings of wild Bohemia, and little traces of the *demi-monde*. He puts down what is good for the naughty and what is naughty for the good. Over women his easier writings exercise that imperious power which belongs to the writings of a great man of the world upon such matters. He knows women, and therefore they wish to know him. If we blame many of Browning's efforts, it is in the interest of art, and not from a wish to hurt or degrade him.

If we wanted to illustrate the nature of grotesque art by an exaggerated instance, we should have selected a poem which the chance of late publication brings us in this new volume. Mr. Browning has undertaken to describe what may be called *mind in difficulties*—mind set to make out the universe under the worst and hardest circumstances. He takes "Caliban," not perhaps exactly Shakespeare's Caliban, but an analogous and worse creature; a strong thinking power, but a nasty creature—a gross animal, uncontrolled and unelevated by any feeling of religion or duty. The delineation of him will show that Mr. Browning does not wish to take undue advantage of his readers by a choice of nice subjects.

> 'Will sprawl, now that the heat of day is best,
> Flat on his belly in the pit's much mire,
> With elbows wide, fists clenched to prop his chin.
> And, while he kicks both feet in the cool slush,
> And feels about his spine small eft-things course,
> Run in and out each arm, and make him laugh;
> And while above his head a pompion-plant,
> Coating the cave-top as a brow its eye,
> Creeps down to touch and tickle hair and beard,
> And now a flower drops with a bee inside,
> And now a fruit to snap at, catch and crunch,—
>
> (1–11)

This pleasant creature proceeds to give his idea of the origin of the universe, and it is as follows. Caliban speaks in the third person, and is of opinion that the maker of the universe took to making it on account of his personal discomfort:—

> Setebos, Setebos, and Setebos!
> 'Thinketh, He dwelleth i' the cold o' the moon.
> 'Thinketh He made it, with the sun to match,

> But not the stars; the stars came otherwise;
> Only made clouds, winds, meteors, such as that;
> Also this isle, what lives and grows thereon,
> And snaky sea which rounds and ends the same.
>
> 'Thinketh, it came of being ill at ease:
> He hated that He cannot change His cold,
> Nor cure its ache. 'Hath spied an icy fish
> That longed to 'scape the rock-stream where she lived,
> And thaw herself within the lukewarm brine
> O' the lazy sea her stream thrusts far amid,
> A crystal spike 'twixt two warm walls of wave;
> Only she ever sickened, found repulse
> At the other kind of water, not her life,
> (Green-dense and dim-delicious, bred o' the sun)
> Flounced back from bliss she was not born to breathe,
> And in her old bounds buried her despair,
> Hating and loving warmth alike: so He.
>
> 'Thinketh, He made thereat the sun, this isle,
> Trees and the fowls here, beast and creeping thing.
> Yon otter, sleek-wet, black, lithe as a leech;
> Yon auk, one fire-eye, in a ball of foam,
> That floats and feeds; a certain badger brown
> He hath watched hunt with that slant white-wedge eye
> By moonlight; and the pie with the long tongue
> That pricks deep into oakwarts for a worm,
> And says a plain word when she finds her prize,
> But will not eat the ants; the ants themselves
> That build a wall of seeds and settled stalks
> About their hole—He made all these and more,
> Made all we see, and us, in spite: how else?
>
> (24–56)

It may seem perhaps to most readers that these lines are very difficult, and that they are unpleasant. And so they are. We quote them to illustrate, not the *success* of grotesque art, but the *nature* of grotesque art. It shows the end at which this species of art aims, and if it fails it is from over-boldness in the choice of a subject by the artist, or from the defects of its execution. A thinking faculty more in difficulties—a great type—an inquisitive, searching intellect under more disagreeable conditions, with worse helps, more likely to find falsehood, less likely to find truth, can scarcely be imagined. Nor is the mere description of the thought at all bad: on the contrary, if we closely examine it, it is very clever. Hardly anyone could have amassed so many ideas at once nasty and suitable. But scarcely any readers—any casual readers—who are not of the sect of Mr. Browning's admirers will be able to examine it enough to appreciate it. From a defect, partly of subject, and partly of style, many of Mr. Browning's works make a demand upon the reader's zeal and sense of duty to which the nature of most readers is unequal. They have on the turf the convenient expression "staying power": some horses can hold on and others cannot. But hardly any reader not of especial and peculiar nature can hold on through such composition. There is not enough of "staying power" in human nature. One of his greatest admirers once owned to us that he seldom or never began a new poem without looking on in advance, and foreseeing with caution what length of intellectual adventure he was about to commence. Whoever will work hard at such poems will find much mind in them: they are a sort of quarry of ideas, but whoever goes there will find these ideas in such a jagged, ugly, useless shape that he can hardly bear them.

. . . .

It is very natural that a poet whose wishes incline, or whose genius conducts him, to a grotesque art, should be attracted towards mediæval subjects. There is no age whose legends are so full of grotesque subjects, and no age where real life was so fit to suggest them. Then, more than at any other time, good principles have been under great hardships. The vestiges of ancient civilisation, the germs of modern civilisation, the little remains of what had been, the small beginnings of what is, were buried under a cumbrous mass of barbarism and cruelty. Good elements hidden in horrid accompaniments are the special theme of grotesque art, and these mediæval

life and legends afford more copiously than could have been furnished before Christianity gave its new elements of good, or since modern civilisation has removed some few at least of the old elements of destruction. A *buried* life like the spiritual mediæval was Mr. Browning's natural element, and he was right to be attracted by it. His mistake has been, that he has not made it pleasant; that he has forced his art to topics on which no one could charm, or on which he, at any rate, could not; that on these occasions and in these poems he has failed in fascinating men and women of sane taste.

. . . .

Something more we had to say of Mr. Browning, but we must stop. It is singularly characteristic of this age that the poems which rise to the surface should be examples of ornate art and grotesque art, not of pure art. We live in the realm of the *half* educated. The number of readers grows daily, but the quality of readers does not improve rapidly. The middle class is scattered, headless; it is well-meaning, but aimless; wishing to be wise, but ignorant how to be wise. The aristocracy of England never was a literary aristocracy, never even in the days of its full power, of its unquestioned predominance, did it guide—did it even seriously try to guide—the taste of England. Without guidance young men, and tired men, are thrown amongst a mass of books; they have to choose which they like; many of them would much like to improve their culture, to chasten their taste, if they knew how. But left to themselves they take, not pure art, but showy art; not that which permanently relieves the eye and makes it happy whenever it looks, and as long as it looks, but *glaring* art which catches and arrests the eye for a moment, but which in the end fatigues it. But before the wholesome remedy of nature—the fatigue—arrives, the hasty reader has passed on to some new excitement, which in its turn stimulates for an instant, and then is passed by for ever. These conditions are not favourable to the due appreciation of pure art—of that art which must be known before it is admired—which must have fastened irrevocably on the brain before you appreciate it—which you must love ere it will seem worthy of your love. Women, too, whose voice in literature counts as well as that of men—and in a light literature counts for more than that of men—women, such as we know them, such as they are likely to be, ever prefer a delicate unreality to a true or firm art. A dressy literature, an exaggerated literature, seem to be fated to us. These are our curses, as other times had theirs.

.   .   .   .

—1864

John Morley
1838 – 1923

John Morley was a man of letters and a politician. He edited the *Fortnightly Review,* the *Pall Mall Gazette,* and *Macmillan's Magazine.* Morley wrote biographies of John Cobden (1881), Burke (1889), and Gladstone (1903), and became an elected member of Parliament in 1883. He was normally more judicious and liberal than his heated discussion of Swinburne would suggest.

⟲⟳⟲

Mr. Swinburne's New Poems: Poems and Ballads [1]

It is mere waste of time, and shows a curiously mistaken conception of human character, to blame an artist of any kind for working at a certain set of subjects rather than at some other set which the critic may happen to prefer. An artist, at all events an artist of such power and individuality as Mr. Swinburne, works as his character compels him. If the character of his genius drives him pretty exclusively in the direction of libidinous song, we may be very sorry, but it is of no use to advise him and to preach to him. What comes of discoursing to a fiery tropical flower of the pleasant fragrance of the rose or the fruitfulness of the fig-tree? Mr. Swinburne is much too stoutly bent on taking his own course to pay any attention to critical monitions as to the duty of the poet, or any warnings of the worse than barrenness of the field in which he has chosen to labour. He is so firmly and avowedly fixed in an attitude of revolt against the current notions of decency and dignity and social duty that to beg of him to become a little more decent, to fly a little less persistently and gleefully to the animal side of human nature, is simply to beg him to be something different from Mr. Swinburne. It is a kind of protest which his whole position makes it impossible for him to receive with anything but laughter and contempt. A rebel of his calibre is not to be brought to a better mind by solemn little sermons on the loyalty which a man owes to virtue. His warmest prayer to the gods is that they should

> Come down and redeem us from virtue.

His warmest hope for men is that they should change

> The lilies and languors of virtue
> For the raptures and roses of vice. [2]

It is of no use, therefore, to scold Mr. Swinburne for grovelling down among the nameless shameless abominations which inspire him with such frenzied delight. They excite his imagination to its most vigorous efforts, they seem to him the themes most proper for poetic treatment, and they suggest ideas which, in his opinion, it is highly to be wished that English men and women should brood upon and make their own. He finds that these fleshly things are his strong part, so he sticks to them. Is it wonderful that he should? And at all events he deserves credit for the audacious courage with which he has revealed to the world a mind all aflame with the feverish carnality of a schoolboy over the dirtiest passages in Lemprière. [3] It is not every poet who would ask us all to go hear him tuning his lyre in a stye. It is not

---

[1] published in the *Saturday Review* in August, 1866. Swinburne answered Morley in a pamphlet, *Notes on "Poems and Ballads."*

[2] "Dolores," l. 279 and ll. 67–68.

[3] John Lemprière, *Bibliotheca Classica,* a handbook to classical mythology widely used in the nineteenth century.

everybody who would care to let the world know that he found the most delicious food for poetic reflection in the practices of the great island of the Ægean, in the habits of Messalina, of Faustina, of Pasiphaë.[1] Yet these make up Mr. Swinburne's version of the dreams of fair women, and he would scorn to throw any veil over pictures which kindle, as these do, all the fires of his imagination in their intensest heat and glow. It is not merely "the noble, the nude, the antique" which he strives to reproduce. If he were a rebel against the fat-headed Philistines and poor-blooded Puritans who insist that all poetry should be such as may be wisely placed in the hands of girls of eighteen, and is fit for the use of Sunday schools, he would have all wise and enlarged readers on his side. But there is an enormous difference between an attempt to revivify among us the grand old pagan conceptions of Joy, and attempt to glorify all the bestial delights that the subtleness of Greek depravity was able to contrive. It is a good thing to vindicate passion, and the strong and large and rightful pleasures of sense, against the narrow and inhuman tyranny of shrivelled anchorites. It is a very bad and silly thing to try to set up the pleasures of sense in the seat of the reason they have dethroned. And no language is too strong to condemn the mixed vileness and childishness of depicting the spurious passion of a putrescent imagination, the unnamed lusts of sated wantons, as if they were the crown of character and their enjoyment the great glory of human life. The only comfort about the present volume is that such a piece as "Anactoria" will be unintelligible to a great many people, and so will the fevered folly of "Hermaphroditus," as well as much else that is nameless and abominable. Perhaps if Mr. Swinburne can a second and a third time find a respectable

publisher willing to issue a volume of the same stamp, crammed with pieces which many a professional vendor of filthy prints might blush to sell if he only knew what they meant, English readers will gradually acquire a truly delightful familiarity with these unspeakable foulnesses; and a lover will be able to present to his mistress a copy of Mr. Swinburne's latest verses with a happy confidence that she will have no difficulty in seeing the point of every allusion to Sappho or the pleasing Hermaphroditus, or the embodiment of anything else that is loathsome and horrible. It will be very charming to hear a drawing-room discussion on such verses as these, for example:—

> Stray breaths of Sapphic song that blew
>   Through Mitylene
> Shook the fierce quivering blood in you
>   By night, Faustine.
> The shameless nameless love that makes
>   Hell's iron gin
> Shut on you like a trap that breaks
>   The soul, Faustine.
> And when your veins were void and dead,
>   What ghosts unclean
> Swarmed round the straitened barren bed
>   That hid Faustine?
> What sterile growths of sexless root
>   Or epicene?
> What flower of kisses without fruit
>   Of love, Faustine?[2]

We should be sorry to be guilty of anything so offensive to Mr. Swinburne as we are quite sure an appeal to the morality of all the wisest and best men would be. The passionate votary of the goddess whom he hails as "Daughter of Death and Priapus"[3] has got too high for this. But it may be presumed that common sense is not too insulting a standard by

---

[1] The island is Lesbos, the home of Sappho and her circle of Lesbians. Messalina and Faustina, both notorious for licentiousness, were the wives of the emperors Claudius and Antonius. Pasiphaë, daughter of Helios and wife of Minos, gave birth to Minotaurus as a result of her passion for Minotaur.

[2] "Faustine," ll. 117–32.

[3] The goddess is Dolores.

which to measure the worth and place of his new volume. Starting from this sufficiently modest point, we may ask him whether there is really nothing in women worth singing about except "quivering flanks" and "splendid supple thighs," "hot sweet throats" and "hotter hands than fire," and their blood as "hot wan wine of love"? Is purity to be expunged from the catalogue of desirable qualities? Does a poet show respect to his own genius by gloating, as Mr. Swinburne does, page after page and poem after poem, upon a single subject, and that subject kept steadily in a single light? Are we to believe that having exhausted hot lustfulness, and wearied the reader with a luscious and nauseating iteration of the same fervid scenes and fervid ideas, he has got to the end of his tether? Has he nothing more to say, no further poetic task but to go on again and again about

> The white wealth of thy body made whiter
>   By the blushes of amorous blows,
> And seamed with sharp lips and fierce fingers,
>   And branded by kisses that bruise.

And to invite new Félises to

> Kiss me once hard, as though a flame
>   Lay on my lips and made them fire. [1]

Mr. Swinburne's most fanatical admirers must long for something newer than a thousand times repeated talk of

> Stinging lips wherein the hot sweet brine
> That Love was born of burns and foams like wine.

And

> Hands that sting like fire,

And of all those women,

>   Swift and white,
> And subtly warm and half perverse,
> And sweet like sharp soft fruit to bite,
> And like a snake's love lithe and fierce. [2]

This stinging and biting, all these "lithe lascivious regrets," all this talk of snakes and fire, of blood and wine and brine, of perfumes and poisons and ashes, grows sickly and oppressive on the senses. Every picture is hot and garish with this excess of flaming violent colour. Consider the following two stanzas:—

> From boy's pierced throat and girl's pierced bosom
> Drips, reddening round the blood-red blossom,
>   The slow delicious bright soft blood,
> Bathing the spices and the pyre,
> Bathing the flowers and fallen fire,
>   Bathing the blossom by the bud.

> Roses whose lips the flame has deadened
> Drink till the lapping leaves are reddened
>   And warm wet inner petals weep;
> The flower whereof sick sleep gets leisure,
> Barren of balm and purple pleasure,
>   Fumes with no native steam of sleep. [3]

Or these, from the verses to Dolores, so admirable for their sustained power and their music, if hateful on other grounds:— [4]

It was too rashly said, when *Atalanta in Calydon* appeared, that Mr. Swinburne had drunk deep at the springs of Greek poetry, and had profoundly conceived and assimilated the divine spirit of Greek art. *Chastelard* was enough to show that this had been

---

[1] "Dolores," ll. 267–70; "Félise," ll. 136–37.

[2] The second and third quotations are from "Before Dawn" l. 45, and "Félise," ll. 101–04. The first has not been identified.

[3] "Ilicet," ll. 73–84.

[4] Morley quotes here extensively.

very premature.[1] But the new volume shows with still greater plainness how far removed Mr. Swinburne's tone of mind is from that of the Greek poets. Their most remarkable distinction is their scrupulous moderation and sobriety in colour. Mr. Swinburne riots in the profusion of colour of the most garish and heated kind. He is like a composer who should fill his orchestra with trumpets, or a painter who should exclude every colour but a blaring red, and a green as of sour fruit. There are not twenty stanzas in the whole book which have the faintest tincture of soberness. We are in the midst of fire and serpents, wine and ashes, blood and foam, and a hundred lurid horrors. Unsparing use of the most violent colours and the most intoxicated ideas and images is Mr. Swinburne's prime characteristic. Fascinated as everybody must be by the music of his verse, it is doubtful whether part of the effect may not be traced to something like a trick of words and letters, to which he resorts in season and out of season with a persistency that any sense of artistic moderation must have stayed. The Greek poets in their most impetuous moods never allowed themselves to be carried on by the swing of words, instead of by the steady, though buoyant, flow of thoughts. Mr. Swinburne's hunting of letters, his hunting of the same word, to death is ceaseless. We shall have occasion by and by to quote a long passage in which several lines will be found to illustrate this. Then, again, there is something of a trick in such turns as these:—

Came flushed from the full-flushed wave.
Grows dim in thine ears and deep as the deep
    dim soul of a star.
White rose of the rose-white water, a silver
    splendour and flame.[2]

There are few pages in the volume where we do not find conceits of this stamp doing duty for thoughts. The Greeks did not wholly disdain them, but they never allowed them to count for more than they were worth. Let anybody who compares Mr. Swinburne to the Greeks read his ode to "Our Lady of Pain," and then read the well-known scene in the *Antigone* between Antigone and the Chorus, beginning *zowc avizars puxov,* or any of the famous choruses in the *Agamemnon,* or an ode of Pindar.[3] In the height of all their passion there is an infinite soberness of which Mr. Swinburne has not a conception.

Yet, in spite of its atrocities, the present volume gives new examples of Mr. Swinburne's forcible and vigorous imagination. The "Hymn to Proserpine" on the proclamation of the Christian faith in Rome, full as it is of much that many persons may dislike, contains passages of rare vigour:

Where beyond the extreme sea-wall, and be-
    tween the remote sea-gates,
Waste water washes, and tall ships founder,
    and deep death waits:
Where, mighty with deepening sides, clad
    about with the seas as with wings,
And impelled of invisible tides, and fulfilled of
    unspeakable things,
White-eyed and poisonous-finned, shark-
    toothed and serpentine-curled,
Rolls, under the whitening wind of the future,
    the wave of the world.
The depths stand naked in sunder behind it,
    the storms flee away;
In the hollow before it the thunder is taken and
    snared as a prey;
In its sides is the north-wind bound; and its
    salt is of all men's tears;
With light of ruin, and sound of changes, and
    pulse of years:

---

[1] *Atalanta* (1865), a drama in the Greek form with choruses; *Chastelard,* published later in the same year, was a romantic play about Mary Queen of Scots.

[2] "Hymn to Proserpine," l. 86, l. 100, and l. 83.

---

[3] The scene from Sophodes's *Antigone* is at ll. 781 ff. The *Agamemnon* is by Aeschylus. Morley erroneously transliterates the Greek: Ἔρως ἀνίκατε μάχαν.

With travail of day after day, and with trouble
    of hour upon hour;
And bitter as blood is the spray; and the crests
    are as fangs that devour:
And its vapour and storm of its steam as the
    sighing of spirits to be;
And its noise as the noise in a dream; and its
    depth as the roots of the sea:
And the height of its heads as the height of the
    utmost stars of the air:
And the ends of the earth at the might thereof
    tremble, and time is made bare. [1]

The variety and rapidity and sustention, the revelling in power, are not more remarkable here than in many other passages, though even here it is not variety and rapidity of thought. The anapæst to which Mr. Swinburne so habitually resorts is the only foot that suffices for his never-staying impetuosity. In the "Song in Time of Revolution" he employs it appropriately, and with a sweeping force as of the elements:—

The heart of the rulers is sick, and the high priest
    covers his head!
For this is the song of the quick that is heard
    in the ears of the dead.
The poor and the halt and the blind are keen and
    mighty and fleet:
Like the noise of the blowing of wind is the sound
    of the noise of their feet

There are, too, sweet and picturesque lines scattered in the midst of this red fire which the poet tosses to and fro about his verses. Most of the poems, in his wearisomely iterated phrase, are meant "to sting the senses like wine," but to some stray pictures one may apply his own exquisite phrases on certain of Victor Hugo's songs, which, he says,

Fell more soft than dew or snow by night,
    Or wailed as in some flooded cave
Sobs the strong broken spirit of a wave. [2]

For instance, there is a perfect delicacy and beauty in four lines of the hendecasyllabics—a metre that is familiar in the Latin line often found on clocks and sundials, *Horæ nam pereunt et imputantur:*—[3]

When low light was upon the windy reaches,
Where the flower of foam was blown, a lily
Dropt among the sonorous fruitless furrows
And green fields of the sea that make no pasture.

Nothing can be more simple and exquisite than

For the glass of the years is brittle wherein we
    gaze for a span.

Or than this:—

In deep wet ways by grey old gardens
Fed with sharp spring the sweet fruit hardens;
    They know not what fruits wane or grow;
Red summer burns to the utmost ember;
They know not, neither can remember,
    The old years and flowers they used to know.

Or again:—

With stars and sea-winds for her raiment
    Night sinks on the sea. [4]

Up to a certain point, one of the deepest and most really poetical pieces is that called the "Sundew." A couple of verses may be quoted to illustrate the graver side of the poet's mind:—

---

[1] ll. 47–64.

[2] "To Victor Hugo," ll. 46–48.

[3] "For the hours slip by and are charged to our account."

[4] The passages quoted are, respectively, from "Hendecasyllabics," ll. 32–35; "Hymn to Proserpine," l. 107; "Ilicet," ll. 115–20; "Dedication" to *Poems and Ballads,* last lines.

The deep scent of the heather burns
About it; breathless though it be,
Bow down and worship; more than we
Is the least flower whose life returns,
Least weed renascent in the sea.

*   *   *   *

You call it sundew: how it grows,
If with its colour it have breath,
If life taste sweet to it, if death
Pain its soft petal, no man knows:
Man has no right or sense that saith.

There is no finer effect of poetry than to recall to the minds of men the bounds that have been set to the scope of their sight and senses, to inspire their imaginations with a vivid consciousness of the size and the wonders and the strange remote companionships of the world of force and growth and form outside of man. "*Qui se considérera de la sorte*," said Pascal, "*s'effraiera, sans doute, de se voir comme suspendu dans la masse que la nature lui a donnée entre ces deux abîmes de l'infini et du néant.*"[1] And there are two ways in which a man can treat this affright that seizes his fellows as they catch interrupted glimpses of their position. He can transfigure their baseness of fear into true poetic awe, which shall underlie their lives as a lasting record of solemn rapture. Or else he can jeer and mock at them, like an unclean fiery imp from the pit. Mr. Swinburne does not at all events treat the lot of mankind in the former spirit. In his best mood, he can only brood over "the exceeding weight of God's intolerable scorn, not to be borne;" he can only ask of us, "O fools and blind, what seek ye there high up in the air," or "Will ye beat always at the Gate, Ye fools of fate."[2] If he is not in his best mood he is in his worst—a mood of schoolboy lustfulness. The bottomless pit encompasses us on one side, and stews and bagnios on the other.[3] He is either the vindictive and scornful apostle of a crushing ironshod despair, or else he is the libidinous laureate of a pack of satyrs. Not all the fervour of his imagination, the beauty of his melody, the splendour of many phrases and pictures, can blind us to the absence of judgment and reason, the reckless contempt for anything like a balance, and the audacious counterfeiting of strong and noble passion by mad intoxicated sensuality. The lurid clouds of lust or of fiery despair and defiance never lift to let us see the pure and peaceful and bounteous kindly aspects of the great landscape of human life. Of enlarged *meditation*, the note of the highest poetry, there is not a trace, and there are too many signs that Mr. Swinburne is without any faculty in that direction. Never have such bountifulness of imagination, such mastery of the music of verse, been yoked with such thinness of contemplation and such poverty of genuinely impassioned thought.

—1866

---

[1] From the *Pensées* (1670), sec. 43: "If a man will look at himself in this way, he will no doubt be terrified to see himself suspended in the material form given him by nature between the two abysses of infinity and nothingness."

[2] See "Félise," ll. 221–35.

[3] Stews and bagnios are brothels.

Eneas Sweetland Dallas
1828 – 1879

A journalist and author, Dallas was educated at Edinburgh University, where he was especially interested in applying ideas derived from eclectic psychology to the analysis of aesthetic effects in poetry, rhetoric, and the fine arts. His literary commentaries include "Poetics, an Essay on Poetry" (1852), and *The Gay Science* (1866), from which the "The Secrecy of Art" is taken. In *The Gay Science*, Dallas attempts to explain the manner in which the human mind participates in and responds to the pleasures of poetry.

༼༽

"The Secrecy of Art"
from *The Gay Science*, Chapter 9.

We ought now to proceed at once to the consideration of pleasure. I began by showing that pleasure is the end of art. I brought forward a cloud of witnesses to prove that this has always been acknowledged. And after showing that all these witnesses, in their several ways, define and limit the pleasure which art seeks, we discovered that the English school of critics has, more than any other, the habit of insisting on a limitation to it, which is more full of meaning as a principle in art than all else that has been advanced by the various schools of criticism. That the pleasure of art is the pleasure of imagination is the one grand doctrine of English criticism, and the most pregnant doctrine of all criticism. But it was difficult to find out what imagination really is; and therefore the last three chapters were allotted to an inquiry into the nature of it. The result at which we have arrived is that imagination is but another name for that unconscious action of the mind which may be called the Hidden Soul. And with this understanding, we ought now to proceed to the scrutiny of pleasure. I will, however, ask the reader to halt for a few minutes, that I may point out how this understanding as to the nature of imagination bears on the definition with which we started— that pleasure is the end of art. Few are willing to acknowledge pleasure as the end of art. I took some pains to defend pleasure in this connection as a fit object of pursuit, and if I have not satisfied every mind, I hope now to do so by the increased light which the analysis of imagination will have thrown upon the subject.

We started with the common doctrine, that art is the opposite of science, and that, as the object of science is knowledge, so that of art is pleasure. But if the reader has apprehended what I have tried to convey to him as to the existence within us of two great worlds of thought—a double life, the one known or knowable, the other unknown and for the most part unknowable, he will be prepared, if not to accept, yet to understand this further conception of the difference between science and art that the field of science is the known and knowable, while the field of art is the unknown and the unknowable. It is a strange paradox that the mind should be described as possessing and compassing the unknown. But my whole argument has been working up to this point, and, I trust, rendering it credible—that the mind may possess and be possessed by thoughts of which nevertheless it is ignorant.

Now, because such a statement as this will appear to be a paradox to those who have not considered it; also, because to say that the field of art is the unknown, is like saying that the object of art is a negation, it is fit that in ordinary speech we should avoid such phrases, and be content with the less paradoxical expression—that the object of art is pleasure. The object of science, we say, is knowledge—a perfect grasp of all the facts which lie within the sphere of consciousness. The object of art is pleasure—a sensible possession or enjoyment of the world beyond consciousness. We do not know that world, yet we feel it—feel it chiefly in pleasure, but sometimes in pain, which is the shadow of pleasure. It is a vast world we have seen; of not less importance to us than the world of knowledge. It is in the hidden sphere of thought, even more than in the open one, that we live, and move, and have our being; and it is in this sense that the idea of art is always a secret. We hear much of the existence of such a secret, and people are apt to say—If a secret exist, and if the artist convey it in his art, why does he not plainly tell us what it is? But here at once we fall into contradictions, for as all language refers to the known, the moment we begin to apply it to the unknown, it fails. Until the existence of an unknown hidden life within us be thoroughly well accepted, not only felt, but also to some extent understood, there will always be an esoteric mode of stating the doctrine, which is not for the multitude.

Although at first sight it may appear absurd to speak of the unknown as the domain of art, and to describe the artist as communicating to the world, through his works, a secret that he and it will never unravel, yet there is a common phrase which, if we consider it well, may help to render this paradox less difficult of belief. Montesquieu[1] has a profound sentence at which I have often wondered: "Si notre âme n'avait point été unié au corps, elle aurait connu; mais il y a apparence qu'elle aurait aimé ce qu'elle aurait connu: à présent nous n'aimons presque que ce que nous ne connaissons pas."[2] I have wondered by what process of thought a man of the last century

arrived at such a conclusion. It scarcely fits into the thinking of his time; and I imagine he must have worked it out of the phrase— Je ne sais quoi.[3] It was

[3] "Montesquieu's remark will be found in his *Essai sur le Goût*, where, indeed, he dwells so much upon the je ne sais quoi, as to make one nearly certain that by some subtle process of hidden thought, unknown to himself, it suggested the remark. The curious thing is, that he attempts to explain in measured language the je ne sais quoi; and his explanation robs it of its richness of meaning. Nothing can be more flat; and one is puzzled to understand how the thinker who could make the remark which I have quoted above, should give us the following definition of the je ne sais quoi: 'Il y a quelquefois dans les personnes ou dans les choses un charme invisible, une grâce naturelle, qu'on n'a pu définir, et qu'on a été forcé d'appeler le *je ne sais quoi*. Il me semble que c'est un effet principalement fondé sur la surprise. Nous sommes touchés de ce qu'une personne nous plaît plus qu'elle ne nous a paru d'abord devoir nous plaire, et nous sommes agréablement surpris de ce qu'elle a su vaincre des défauts que nos yeux nous montrent, et que le cœur ne croit plus. Voilà pourquoi les femmes laides ont très-souvent des grâces, et qu'il est rare que les belles en aient. Car une belle personne fait ordinairement le contraire de ce que nous avions attendu; elle parvient à nous paroître moins amiable; après nous avoir surpris en bien, elle nous surprend en mal; mais l'impression du bien est ancienne, celle du mal nouvelle: aussi les belles personnes font-elles rarement les grandes passions, presque toujours réservées à celles qui ont des grâces, c'est-à-dire des agrémens que nous n'attendions point, et que nous n'avions pas sujet d'attendre. Les grandes parures ont rarement de la grâce, et souvent l'habillement des bergères en a. Nous admirons la majesté des draperies de Paul Véronèse; mais nous sommes touchés de la simplicité de Raphaël et de la pureté du Corrége. Paul Véronèse promet beaucoup, et paye ce qu'il promet. Raphaël et le Corrége promettent peu, et payent beaucoup; et cela nous plaît davantage.'" (Dallas's note.)

"We find sometimes, in certain persons, and in certain objects, an invisible charm, a natural gracefulness, which has not been hitherto defined, and which we have been obliged to express by the vague epithet *Je ne sais quoi*. It appears to me highly probable, that this secret charm is principally the effect of surprise. We are sensibly touched, when we find certain persons more agreeable than at first sight we imagined them to be; and we are filled with a pleasing kind of surprise, when we see them triumph over those defects which the eye still perceives, but which the heart no longer feels. Hence we find often, among the female sex, those inexpressible graces adorn the ugly, which are very seldom lavished upon the fair and beautiful. A beautiful nymph generally disappoints our expectations, and appears, after some little time, less amiable than at first sight; after having surprised us first by her charms, she falls greatly off, and surprises us at length by her defects: but the first surprise is a part of pleasure, which is become faint and languid, and is almost effaced; whereas the second is a fresh and lively sensation of disgust. Hence it rarely happens, that the beautiful are the objects of a violent and durable

---

[1] Robert de Montesquieu (1855–1921), French poet, critic, and essayist.

[2] "If our soul had not been joined to our body, it would have known; but apparently it would have loved what it knew; at present we love almost exclusively what we do not know."

in the last century a commonplace of French criticism and conversation, that what is most lovely, most attractive, in man, in nature, in art, is a certain je ne sais quoi. And adopting this phrase, it will not be much of a paradox to assert that, while the object of science is to know and to make known, the object of art is to appropriate and to communicate the nameless grace, the ineffable secret of the know-not-what. If the object of art were to make known and to explain its ideas, it would no longer be art, but science. Its object is very different. The true artist recognises, however dimly, the existence within us of a double world of thought, and his object is, by subtle forms, tones, words, allusions, associations, to establish a connection with the unconscious hemisphere of the mind, and to make us feel a mysterious energy there in the hidden soul. For this purpose he doubtless makes use of the known. He paints what we have seen, he describes what we have heard; but his use of knowledge is ever to suggest something beyond knowledge. If he be merely dealing with the known and making it better known, then it becomes necessary to ask wherein does his work differ from science? Through knowledge, through consciousness, the artist appeals to the unconscious part of us. The poet's words, the artist's touches, are electric; and we feel those words, and the shock of those touches, going through us in a way we cannot define, but always giving us a thrill of pleasure, awakening distant associations, and filling us with the sense of a mental possession beyond that of which we are daily and hourly conscious. Art is poetical in proportion as it has this power of appealing to what I may call the absent mind, as distant from the present mind, on which falls the great glare of consciousness, and to which alone science appeals. On the temple of art, as on the temple of Isis, might be inscribed—"I am whatsoever is, whatsoever has been, whatsoever shall be; and the veil which is over my face no mortal hand has ever raised."

—1866

passion; which seems rather reserved for the *agreeable*; than for the *fair*; for those graces which strike us unexpectedly, and which indeed we had no reason to expect. Sumptuous and magnificent robes are generally destitute of that graceful air which we often find in the simplicity of the shepherd's habit. We admire the air of majesty that reigns in the draperies of Paul Veronese; but we are also most agreeably touched with the simplicity of Raphael, and the graces that flow from the pencil of Corregio. Paul Veronese promises much, and performs what he promises. Raphael and Corregio promise little, but perform a great deal; and this is doubly pleasing to the surprised spectator."

Robert Buchanan
1841 – 1901

"The Fleshly School of Poetry: Mr. D.G. Rossetti," signed "Thomas Maitland" (published in the *Contemporary Review* for October, 1871), was a review of the fifth edition of Rossetti's *Poems*. Buchanan was a minor poet, critic, and novelist. He took sides in the literary squabbles of the 1860s against Swinburne and the Rossettis, and his attack in this essay reflects his personal as well as his literary animosity. Rossetti answered him in "The Stealthy School of Criticism" and Swinburne in *Under the Microscope*, both of which follow.

ↄ⁀ↄↄↄ⁀ↄ

The Fleshly School of Poetry: Mr. D.G. Rossetti

If, on the occasion of any public performance of Shakespeare's great tragedy, the actors who perform the parts of Rosencranz and Guildenstern were, by a preconcerted arrangement and by means of what is technically known as "gagging," to make themselves fully as prominent as the leading character, and to indulge in soliloquies and business strictly belonging to Hamlet himself, the result would be, to say the least of it, astonishing; yet a very similar effect is produced on the unprejudiced mind when the "walking gentlemen"[1] of the fleshly school of poetry, who bear precisely the same relation to Mr. Tennyson as Rosencranz and Guildenstern do to the prince of Denmark in the play, obtrude their lesser identities and parade their smaller idiosyncrasies in the front rank of leading performers. In their own place, the gentlemen are interesting and useful. Pursuing still the theatrical analogy, the present drama of poetry might be cast as follows: Mr. Tennyson supporting the part of Hamlet, Mr. Matthew Arnold that of Horatio, Mr. Bailey that of Voltimand, Mr. Buchanan that of Cornelius, Messrs. Swinburne and Morris the parts of Rosencranz and Guildenstern, Mr. Rossetti that of Osric, and Mr. Robert Lytton

that of "A Gentleman."[2] It will be seen that we have left no place for Mr. Browning, who may be said, however, to play the leading character in his own peculiar fashion on alternate nights.

This may seem a frivolous and inadequate way of opening our remarks on a school of verse-writers which some people regard as possessing great merits; but in good truth, it is scarcely possible to discuss with any seriousness the pretensions with which foolish friends and small critics have surrounded the fleshly school, which, in spite of its spasmodic[3] ramifications in the erotic direction, is merely one of the many sub-Tennysonian schools expanded to supernatural dimensions, and endeavouring by affectations all its own to overshadow its connection with the great original. In the sweep of one single poem, the weird and doubtful "Vivien,"[4] Mr. Tennyson has concentrated all the epicene force which, wearisomely expanded, constitutes the characteristic of the writers at present under consideration; and if in "Vivien" he has indicated for them the bounds of sensualism in art, he has in *Maud*, in the dramatic person of the hero, afforded distinct precedent for the hysteric tone and overloaded style which is now so familiar to readers of Mr. Swinburne. The fleshliness

---

[1] actors who simply walk on and off stage.

[2] Philip Bailey, founder of the Spasmodic School, and author of *Festus* (1830 and 1845). Lytton was the son of Edward Bulwer-Lytton (1803–73), novelist.

[3] "by fits and starts," and as related to the Spasmodic School.

[4] later called "Merlin and Vivien," one of the *Idylls of the King*.

of "Vivien" may indeed be described as the distinct quality held in common by all the members of the last sub-Tennysonian school, and it is a quality which becomes unwholesome when there is no moral or intellectual quality to temper and control it. Fully conscious of this themselves, the fleshly gentlemen have bound themselves by solemn league and covenant to extol fleshliness as the distinct and supreme end of poetic and pictorial art; to aver that poetic expression is greater than poetic thought, and by inference that the body is greater than the soul, and sound superior to sense; and that the poet, properly to develop his poetic faculty, must be an intellectual hermaphrodite, to whom the very facts of day and night are lost in a whirl of aesthetic terminology. After Mr. Tennyson has probed the depths of modern speculation in a series of commanding moods, all right and interesting in him as the reigning personage, the walking gentlemen, knowing that something of the sort is expected from all leading performers, bare their roseate bosoms and aver that *they* are creedless; the only possible question here being, if any disinterested person cares twopence whether Rosencranz, Guildenstern, and Osric are creedless or not—their self-revelation on that score being so perfectly gratuitous? But having gone so far, it was and is too late to retreat. Rosencranz, Guildenstern, and Osric, finding it impossible to risk an individual bid for the leading business, have arranged all to play leading business together, and mutually to praise, extol, and imitate each other; and although by these measures they have fairly earned for themselves the title of the Mutual Admiration School, they have in a great measure succeeded in their object—to the general stupefaction of a British audience. It is time, therefore, to ascertain whether any of these gentlemen has actually in himself the making of a leading performer. When the *Athenæum*—once more cautious in such matters—advertised nearly every week some interesting particular about Mr. Swinburne's health, Mr. Morris's holiday-making, or Mr. Rossetti's genealogy, varied with such startling statements as "We are informed that Mr. Swinburne dashed off his noble ode *at a sitting*," or "Mr. Swinburne's songs have already reached a second edition," or "Good poetry seems to be in demand; the first edition of Mr. O'Shaughnessy's[1] poems is exhausted;" when the *Academy* informed us that "During the past year or two Mr. Swinburne has written several novels" (!), and that some review or other is to be praised for giving Mr. Rossetti's poems "the attentive study which they demand"—when we read these things we might or might not know pretty well how and where they originated; but to a provincial eye, perhaps, the whole thing really looked like leading business. It would be scarcely worth while, however, to inquire into the pretensions of the writers on merely literary grounds, because sooner or later all literature finds its own level, whatever criticism may say or do in the matter; but it unfortunately happens in the present case that the fleshly school of verse-writers are, so to speak, public offenders, because they are diligently spreading the seeds of disease broadcast wherever they are read and understood. Their complaint too is catching, and carries off many young persons. What the complaint is, and how it works, may be seen on a very slight examination of the works of Mr. Dante Gabriel Rossetti, to whom we shall confine our attention in the present article.

Mr. Rossetti has been known for many years as a painter of exceptional powers, who, for reasons best known to himself, has shrunk from publicly exhibiting his pictures, and from allowing anything like a popular estimate to be formed of their qualities. He belongs, or is said to belong, to the so-called Pre-Raphaelite school, a school which is generally considered to exhibit much genius for colour, and great indifference to perspective. It would be unfair to

---

[1] Arthur William O'Shaughnessy (1844–81), a minor poet related to the Pre-Raphaelite circle.

judge the painter by the glimpses we have had of his works, or by the photographs which are sold of the principal paintings. Judged by the photographs, he is an artist who conceives unpleasantly, and draws ill. Like Mr. Simeon Solomon,[1] however, with whom he seems to have many points in common, he is distinctively a colourist, and of his capabilities in colour we cannot speak, though we should guess that they are great; for if there is any good quality by which his poems are specially marked, it is a great sensitiveness to hues and tints as conveyed in poetic epithet. These qualities, which impress the casual spectator of the photographs from his pictures, are to be found abundantly among his verses. There is the same thinness and transparence of design, the same combination of the simple and the grotesque, the same morbid deviation from healthy forms of life, the same sense of weary, wasting, yet exquisite sensuality; nothing virile, nothing tender, nothing completely sane; a superfluity of extreme sensibility, of delight in beautiful forms, hues, and tints, and a deep-seated indifference to all agitating forces and agencies, all tumultuous griefs and sorrows, all the thunderous stress of life, and all the straining storm of speculation. Mr. Morris is often pure, fresh, and wholesome as his own great model; Mr. Swinburne startles us more than once by some fine flash of insight; but the mind of Mr. Rossetti is like a glassy mere, broken only by the dive of some water-bird or the hum of winged insects, and brooded over by an atmosphere of insufferable closeness, with a light blue sky above it, sultry depths mirrored within it, and a surface so thickly sown with waterlilies that it retains its glassy smoothness even in the strongest wind. Judged relatively to his poetic associates, Mr. Rossetti must be pronounced inferior to either. He cannot tell a pleasant story like Mr. Morris, nor forge alliterative thunderbolts like Mr. Swinburne. It must be conceded, nevertheless, that he is neither so glibly imitative as the one, nor so transcendently superficial as the other.

Although he has been known for many years as a poet as well as a painter—as a painter and poet idolized by his own family and personal associates—and although he has once or twice appeared in print as a contributor to magazines, Mr. Rossetti did not formally appeal to the public until rather more than a year ago, when he published a copious volume of poems, with the announcement that the book, although it contained pieces composed at intervals during a period of many years, "included nothing which the author believes to be immature." This work was inscribed to his brother, Mr. William Rossetti, who, having written much both in poetry and criticism, will perhaps be known to bibliographers as the editor of the worst edition of Shelley which has yet seen the light. No sooner had the work appeared than the chorus of eulogy began. "The book is satisfactory from end to end," wrote Mr. Morris in the *Academy*; "I think these lyrics, with all their other merits, the most complete of their time; nor do I know what lyrics of any time are to be called *great*, if we are to deny the title to these." On the same subject Mr. Swinburne went into a hysteria of admiration: "golden affluence," "jewel-coloured words," "chastity of form," "harmonious nakedness," "consummate fleshly sculpture," and so on in Mr. Swinburne's well-known manner when reviewing his friends.[2] Other critics, with a singular similarity of phrase, followed suit. Strange to say, moreover, no one accused Mr. Rossetti of naughtiness. What had been heinous in Mr. Swinburne was majestic exquisiteness in Mr. Rossetti. Yet we question if there is anything in the unfortunate *Poems and Ballads* quite so questionable on the score of thorough naughtiness as many pieces in Mr. Rossetti's collection. Mr. Swinburne was wilder, more outrageous, more

---

[1] Pre-Raphaelite painter.

[2] a reference to Swinburne's 1870 *Fortnightly Review* article on Rossetti's poems.

blasphemous, and his subjects were more atrocious in themselves; yet the hysterical tone slew the animalism, the furiousness of epithet lowered the sensation; and the first feeling of disgust at such themes as "Laus Veneris" and "Anactoria," faded away into comic amazement. It was only a little mad boy letting off squibs; not a great strong man, who might be really dangerous to society. "I *will* be naughty!" screamed the little boy; but, after all, what did it matter? It is quite different, however, when a grown man, with the self-control and easy audacity of actual experience, comes forward to chronicle his amorous sensations, and, first proclaiming in a loud voice his literary maturity, and consequent responsibility, shamelessly prints and publishes such a piece of writing as this sonnet on "Nuptial Sleep;"—

At length their long kiss severed, with sweet smart:
    And as the last slow sudden drops are shed
    From sparkling eaves when all the storm has fled,
So singly flagged the pulses of each heart.
Their bosoms sundered, with the opening start
    Of married flowers to either side outspread
    From the knit stem; yet still their mouths, burnt red,
Fawned on each other where they lay apart.
Sleep sank them lower than the tide of dreams,
    And their dreams watched them sink, and slid away.
Slowly their souls swam up again, through gleams
    Of watered light and dull drowned waifs of day;
Till from some wonder of new woods and streams
    He woke, and wondered more: for there she lay.

This, then, is "the golden affluence of words, the firm outline, the justice and chastity of form." Here is a full-grown man, presumably intelligent and cultivated, putting on record for other full-grown men to read, the most secret mysteries of sexual connection, and that with so sickening a desire to reproduce the sensual mood, so careful a choice of epithet to convey mere animal sensations, that we merely shudder at the shameless nakedness. We are no purists in such matters. We hold the sensual part of our nature to be

as holy as the spiritual or intellectual part, and we believe that such things must find their equivalent in all; but it is neither poetic, nor manly, nor even human, to obtrude such things as the themes of whole poems. It is simply nasty. Nasty as it is, we are very mistaken if many readers do not think it nice. English society of one kind purchases the *Day's Doings.*[1] English society of another kind goes into ecstasy over Mr. Solomon's pictures—pretty pieces of morality, such as "Love dying by the breath of Lust." There is not much to choose between the two objects of admiration, except that painters like Mr. Solomon lend actual genius to worthless subjects, and thereby produce veritable monsters—like the lovely devils that danced round Saint Anthony.[2] Mr. Rossetti owes his so-called success to the same causes. In poems like "Nuptial Sleep," the man who is too sensitive to exhibit his pictures, and so modest that it takes him years to make up his mind to publish his poems, parades his private sensations before a coarse public, and is gratified by their applause.

It must not be supposed that all Mr. Rossetti's poems are made up of trash like this. Some of them are as noteworthy for delicacy of touch as others are for shamelessness of exposition. They contain some exquisite pictures of nature, occasional passages of real meaning, much beautiful phraseology, lines of peculiar sweetness, and epithets chosen with true literary cunning. But the fleshly feeling is everywhere. Sometimes, as in "The Stream's Secret," it is deliciously modulated, and adds greatly to our emotion of pleasure at perusing a finely-wrought poem; at other times, as in the "Last Confession," it is fiercely held in check by the exigencies of a powerful situation and the strength of a dramatic speaker; but it is generally in the foreground, flushing the whole poem with unhealthy rose-colour, stifling the senses with

---

[1] a popular *Illustrated Journal* of daily events.

[2] a reference to the temptations of St. Anthony depicted in the painting by Joachim Patinir (1485–1524).

overpowering sickliness, as of too much civet. Mr. Rossetti is never dramatic, never impersonal—always attitudinizing, posturing, and describing his own exquisite emotions. He is the Blessed Damozel, leaning over the "gold bar of heaven," and seeing

> Time like a pulse shake fierce
> Thro' all the worlds.

he is "heaven-born Helen, Sparta's queen," whose "each twin breast is an apple sweet;" he is Lilith the first wife of Adam; he is the rosy Virgin of the poem called "Ave," and the Queen in the "Staff and Scrip;" he is "Sister Helen" melting her waxen man; he is all these, just as surely as he is Mr. Rossetti soliloquizing over Jenny in her London lodging, or the very nuptial person writing erotic sonnets to his wife.[1] In petticoats or pantaloons, in modern times or in the middle ages, he is just Mr. Rossetti, a fleshly person, with nothing particular to tell us or teach us, with extreme self-control, a strong sense of colour, and a careful choice of diction. Amid all his "affluence of jewel-coloured words," he has not given us one rounded and noteworthy piece of art, though his verses are all art; not one poem which is memorable for its own sake, and quite separate from the displeasing identity of the composer. The nearest approach to a perfect whole is the "Blessed Damozel," a peculiar poem, placed first in the book, perhaps by accident, perhaps because it is a key to the poems which follow. This poem appeared in a rough shape many years ago in the *Germ*, an unwholesome periodical started by the Pre-Raphaelites, and suffered, after gasping through a few feeble numbers, to die the death of all such publications. In spite of its affected title, and of numberless affectations throughout the text, the "Blessed Damozel" has great merits of its own, and a few lines of real genius. We have heard it described as the record of actual grief and love, or, in

simple words, the apotheosis of one actually lost by the writer; but, without having any private knowledge of the circumstance of its composition, we feel that such an account of the poem is inadmissible. It does not contain one single note of sorrow. It is a "composition," and a clever one. Read the opening stanzas:—

> The blessed damozel leaned out
>   From the gold bar of Heaven;
> Her eyes were deeper than the depth
>   Of water stilled at even;
> She had three lilies in her hand,
>   And the stars in her hair were seven.
>
> Her robe, ungirt from clasp to hem,
>   No wrought flowers did adorn,
> But a white rose of Mary's gift,
>   For service meetly worn;
> Her hair that lay along her back
>   Was yellow like ripe corn.

This is a careful sketch for a picture, which, worked into actual colour by a master, might have been worth seeing. The steadiness of hand lessens as the poem proceeds, and although there are several passages of considerable power,—such as that where, far down the void,

>   this earth
>   Spins like a fretful midge

or that other, describing how

>   the curled moon
>   Was like a little feather
>   Fluttering far down the gulf—

the general effect is that of a queer old painting in a missal, very affected and very odd. What moved the British critic to ecstacy in this poem seems to us very sad nonsense indeed, or, if not sad nonsense, very

---

[1] his sonnet sequence "The House of Life."

meretricious affectation. Thus, we have seen the following verses quoted with enthusiasm, as italicized—

And still she bowed herself and stooped
    Out of the circling charm;
Until her bosom must have made
    The bar she leaned on warm,
And the lilies lay as if asleep
    Along her bended arm.

From the fixed place of Heaven she saw
    Time like a pulse shake fierce
Thro' all the worlds. Her gaze still strove
    Within the gulf to pierce
Its path; and now she spoke as when
    The stars sang in their spheres.

It seems to us that all these lines are very bad, with the exception of the two admirable lines ending the first verse, and that the italicized portions are quite without merit, and almost without meaning. On the whole, one feels disheartened and amazed at the poet who, in the nineteenth century, talks about "damozels," "citherns," and "citoles," and addresses the mother of Christ as the "Lady Mary,"—

With her five handmaidens, whose names
    Are five sweet symphonies,
Cecily, Gertrude, Magdalen,
    Margaret and Rosalys.

A suspicion is awakened that the writer is laughing at us. We hover uncertainly between picturesqueness and namby-pamby, and the effect, as Artemus Ward[1] would express it, is "weakening to the intellect." The thing would have been almost too much in the shape of a picture, though the workmanship might have made amends. The truth is that literature, and more particularly poetry, is in a very bad way when one art

gets hold of another, and imposes upon it its conditions and limitations. In the first few verses of the "Damozel" we have the subject, or part of the subject, of a picture, and the inventor should either have painted it or left it alone altogether; and, had he done the latter, the world would have lost nothing. Poetry is something more than painting; and an idea will not become a poem, because it is too smudgy for a picture.

In a short notice from a well-known pen, giving the best estimate we have seen of Mr. Rossetti's powers as a poet, the *North American Review* offers a certain explanation for affectation such as that of Mr. Rossetti. The writer suggests that "it may probably be the expression of genuine moods of mind in natures too little comprehensive."[2] We would rather believe that Mr. Rossetti lacks comprehension than that he is deficient in sincerity; yet really, to paraphrase the words which Johnson applied to Thomas Sheridan, Mr. Rossetti is affected, naturally affected, but it must have taken him a great deal of trouble to become what we now see him—such an excess of affectation is not in nature.[3] There is very little writing in the volume spontaneous in the sense that some of Swinburne's verses are spontaneous; the poems all look as if they had taken a great deal of trouble. The grotesque mediævalism of "Stratton Water" and "Sister Helen," the mediaeval classicism of "Troy Town," the false and shallow mysticism of "Eden Bower," are one and all essentially imitative, and must have cost the writer much pains. It is time, indeed, to point out that Mr. Rossetti is a poet possessing great powers of assimilation and some faculty for concealing the nutriment on which he feeds. Setting aside the *Vita Nuova* and the early Italian poems, which are familiar to many readers by

---

[1] American humorist Charles F. Browne, who wrote under this pseudonym for *Punch*.

[2] J.R. Dennett, "Rossetti's Poems," *North American Review* (October, 1870), 473.

[3] "Why, sir, Sherry is dull, *naturally* dull; but it must have taken him a *great deal of trouble* to become what we now see him—such an excess of stupidity is not in nature.—*Boswell's Life*." (Buchanan's note.)

his own excellent translations,[1] Mr. Rossetti may be described as a writer who has yielded to an unusual extent to the complex influences of the literature surrounding him at the present moment. He has the painter's imitative power developed in proportion to his lack of the poet's conceiving imagination. He reproduces to a nicety the manner of an old ballad, a trick in which Mr. Swinburne is also an adept. Cultivated readers, moreover, will recognise in every one of these poems the tone of Mr. Tennyson broken up by the style of Mr. and Mrs. Browning, and disguised here and there by the eccentricities of the pre-Raphaelites. The "Burden of Nineveh" is a philosophical edition of "Recollections of the Arabian Nights;" "A Last Confession" and "Dante at Verona" are, in the minutest trick and form of thought, suggestive of Mr. Browning; and that the sonnets have been largely moulded and inspired by Mrs. Browning can be ascertained by any critic who will compare them with the *Sonnets from the Portuguese*. Much remains, nevertheless, that is Mr. Rossetti's own. We at once recognise as his own property such passages as this:—

> I looked up
> And saw where a brown-shouldered harlot leaned
> Half through a tavern window thick with vine.
> Some man had come behind her in the room
> And caught her by her arms, and she had turned
> With that coarse empty laugh on him, as now
> *He munched her neck with kisses, while the vine*
> *Crawled in her back.*

Or this:—

> As I stooped, her own lips rising there
> *Bubbled with brimming kisses at my mouth*

Or this:—

> Have seen your lifted silken skirt
> Advertise dainties through the dirt!

Or this:—

> What more prize than love to impel thee,
> *Grip* and *lip* my limbs as I tell thee. [2]

Passages like these are the common stock of the walking gentlemen of the fleshly school. We cannot forbear expressing our wonder, by the way, at the kind of women whom it seems the unhappy lot of these gentlemen to encounter. We have lived as long in the world as they have, but never yet came across persons of the other sex who conduct themselves in the manner described. Females who bite, scratch, scream, bubble, munch, sweat, writhe, twist, wriggle, foam, and in a general way slaver over their lovers, must surely possess some extraordinary qualities to counteract their otherwise most offensive mode of conducting themselves. It appears, however, on examination, that their poet-lovers conduct themselves in a similar manner. They, too, bite, scratch, scream, bubble, munch, sweat, writhe, twist, wriggle, foam, and slaver, in a style frightful to hear of. Let us hope that it is only their fun, and that they don't mean half they say. At times, in reading such books as this, one cannot help wishing that things had remained for ever in the asexual state described in Mr. Darwin's great chapter on Palingenesis.[3] We get very weary of this protracted hankering after a person of the other sex; it seems meat, drink, thought, sinew, religion for the fleshly school. There is no limit to the fleshliness, and Mr. Rossetti finds in it its own religious justification much in the same way as Holy Willie:—

---

[1] *The Early Italian Poets* (1861).

[2] quotations from "A Last Confession," "The House of Life," "Jenny," and "Eden Bower."

[3] probably a reference to *The Descent of Man* (1871).

Maybe thou let'st this fleshly thorn
Perplex thy servant night and morn,
    'Cause he's so gifted.
If so, thy hand must e'en be borne,
    Until thou lift it. [1]

Whether he is writing of the holy Damozel, or of the Virgin herself, or of Lilith, or Helen, or of Dante, or of Jenny the street-walker, he is fleshly all over, from the roots of his hair to the tip of his toes; never a true lover merging his identity into that of the beloved one; never spiritual, never tender; always self-conscious and aesthetic. "Nothing," says a modern writer, "in human life is so utterly remorseless—not love, not hate, not ambition, not vanity—as the artistic or æsthetic instinct morbidly developed to the suppression of conscience and feeling;" and at no time do we feel more fully impressed with this truth than after the perusal of "Jenny," in some respects the finest poem in the volume, and in all respects the poem best indicative of the true quality of the writer's humanity. It is a production which bears signs of having been suggested by Mr. Buchanan's quasi-lyrical poems, which it copies in the style of title, and particularly by "Artist and Model;" but certainly Mr. Rossetti cannot be accused, as the Scottish writer has been accused, of maudlin sentiment and affected tenderness. The first two lines are perfect:—

Lazy laughing languid Jenny,
Fond of a kiss and fond of a guinea;

And the poem is a soliloquy of the poet—who has been spending the evening in dancing at a casino—over his partner, whom he has accompanied home to the usual style of lodgings occupied by such ladies, and who has fallen asleep with her head upon his knee, while he wonders, in a wretched pun—

Whose person or whose purse may be
The lodestar of your reverie?

The soliloquy is long, and in some parts beautiful, despite a very constant suspicion that we are listening to an emasculated Mr. Browning, whose whole tone and gesture, so to speak, is occasionally introduced with startling fidelity; and there are here and there glimpses of actual thought and insight, over and above the picturesque touches which belong to the writer's true profession, such as that where, at daybreak—

    lights creep in
Past the gauze curtains half drawn to,
And *the Lamp's doubled shade grows blue.*

What we object to in this poem is not the subject, which any writer may be fairly left to choose for himself; nor anything particularly vicious in the poetic treatment of it; nor any bad blood bursting through in special passages. But the whole tone, without being more than usually coarse, seems heartless. There is not a drop of piteousness in Mr. Rossetti. He is just to the outcast, even generous; severe to the seducer; sad even at the spectacle of lust in dimity and fine ribbons. Notwithstanding all this, and a certain delicacy and refinement of treatment unusual with this poet, the poem repels and revolts us, and we like Mr. Rossetti least after its perusal. We are angry with the fleshly person at last. The "Blessed Damozel" puzzled us, the "Song of the Bower" amused us, the love-sonnet depressed and sickened us, but "Jenny," though distinguished by less special viciousness of thought and style than any of these, fairly makes us lose patience. We detect its fleshliness at a glance; we perceive that the scene was fascinating less through its human tenderness than because it, like all the others, possessed an inherent quality of animalism. "The whole work" ("Jenny,") writes Mr. Swinburne, "is worthy to fill its place for ever as one

---

[1] incorrectly quoted stanza from Burns's "Holy Willie's Prayer."

of the most perfect poems of an age or generation. There is just the same life-blood and breadth of poetic interest in this episode of a London street and lodging as in the song of 'Troy Town' and the song of 'Eden Bower;' just as much, and no jot more,"—to which last statement we cordially assent; for there is bad blood in all, and breadth of poetic interest in none. "Vengeance of Jenny's case," indeed!—when such a poet as this comes fawning over her, with tender compassion in one eye and aesthetic enjoyment in the other!

It is time that we permitted Mr. Rossetti to speak for himself, which we will do by quoting a fairly representative poem entire:—

LOVE-LILY.

Between the hands, between the brows,
Between the lips of Love-Lily,
A spirit is born whose birth endows
My blood with fire to burn through me;
Who breathes upon my gazing eyes,
Who laughs and murmurs in mine ear,
At whose least touch my colour flies,
And whom my life grows faint to hear.

Within the voice, within the heart,
Within the mind of Love-Lily,
A spirit is born who lifts apart
His tremulous wings and looks at me;
Who on my mouth his finger lays,
And shows, while whispering lutes confer,
That Eden of Love's watered ways
Whose winds and spirits worship her.

Brows, hands, and lips, heart, mind, and voice,
Kisses and words of Love-Lily,—
Oh! bid me with your joy rejoice
Till *riotous longing rest in me!*
Ah! let not hope be still distraught,
But find in her its gracious goal,
Whose speech Truth knows not from her thought,
Nor Love her body from her soul.

With the exception of the usual "riotous longing," which seems to make Mr. Rossetti a burthen to himself, there is nothing to find fault with in the extreme fleshliness of these verses, and to many people who live in the country they may even appear beautiful. Without pausing to criticise a thing so trifling—as well might we dissect a cobweb or anatomize a medusa—let us ask the reader's attention to a peculiarity to which all the students of the fleshly school must sooner or later give their attention—we mean the habit of accenting the last syllable in words which in ordinary speech are accentuated on the penultimate:—

Between the hands, between the brows,
Between the lips of Love-Lil*ee!*

which may be said to give to the speaker's voice a sort of cooing tenderness just bordering on a loving whistle. Still better as an illustration are the lines:—

Saturday night is market night
Everywhere, be it dry or wet,
And market night in the Haymar-*ket!*

which the reader may advantageously compare with Mr. Morris's

Then said the king
Thanked be thou; *neither for nothing*
Shalt thou this good deed do to me;

or Mr. Swinburne's

In either of the twain
Red roses full of rain;
She hath for bond*women*
All kinds of flowers. [1]

It is unnecessary to multiply examples of an affectation which disfigures all these writers—Guildenstern, Rosencranz, and Osric; who, in the same spirit which prompts the ambitious nobodies that rent London theatres in the "empty" season to make up for their

---

[1] "Madonna Mia," ll. 5–8.

dullness by fearfully original "new readings," distinguish their attempt at leading business by affecting the construction of their grandfathers and great-grandfathers, and the accentuation of the poets of the court of James I. It is in all respects a sign of remarkable genius, from this point of view, to rhyme "was" with "grass," "death" with "lièth," "love" with "of," "once" with "suns," and so on *ad nauseam*. We are far from disputing the value of bad rhymes used occasionally to break up the monotony of verse, but the case is hard when such blunders become the rule and not the exception, when writers deliberately lay themselves out to be as archaic and affected as possible. Poetry is perfect human speech, and these archaisms are the mere fiddlededeeing of empty heads and hollow hearts. Bad as they are, they are the true indication of falser tricks and affectations which lie far deeper. They are trifles, light as air, showing how the wind blows. The soul's speech and the heart's speech are clear, simple, natural, and beautiful, and reject the meretricious tricks to which we have drawn attention.

It is on the score that these tricks and affectations have procured the professors a number of imitators, that the fleshly school deliver their formula that great poets are always to be known because their manner is immediately reproduced by small poets, and that a poet who finds few imitators is probably of inferior rank—by which they mean to infer that they themselves are very great poets indeed. It is quite true that they are imitated. On the stage, twenty provincial "stars" copy Charles Kean, while not one copies his father; there are dozens of actors who reproduce Mr. Charles Dillon, and not one who attempts to reproduce Macready.[1] When we take up the poems of Mr. O'Shaughnessy, we are face to face with a second-hand Mr. Swinburne; when we read Mr. Payne's queer allegories, we remember Mr. Morris's early

stage; and every poem of Mr. Marston's reminds us of Mr. Rossetti.[2] But what is really most droll and puzzling in the matter is, that these imitators seem to have no difficulty whatever in writing nearly, if not quite, as well as their masters. It is not bad imitations they offer us, but poems which read just like the originals; the fact being that it is easy to reproduce sound when it has no strict connection with sense, and simple enough to cull phraseology not hopelessly interwoven with thought and spirit. The fact that these gentlemen are so easily imitated is the most damning proof of their inferiority. What merits they have lie with their faults on the surface, and can be caught by any young gentleman as easily as the measles, only they are rather more difficult to get rid of. All young gentlemen have animal faculties, though few have brains; and if animal faculties without brains will make poems, nothing is easier in the world. A great and good poet, however, is great and good irrespective of manner, and often in spite of manner; he is great because he brings great ideas and new light, because his thought is a revelation; and, although it is true that a great manner generally accompanies great matter, the manner of great matter is almost inimitable. The great poet is not Cowley,[3] imitated and idolized and reproduced by every scribbler of his time; nor Pope, whose trick of style was so easily copied that to this day we cannot trace his own hand with any certainty in the *Iliad*; nor Donne, nor Sylvester,[4] nor the Della Cruscans.[5] Shakespeare's blank verse is the most difficult and Jonson's the most easy to imitate, of all the Elizabethan stock and Shakespeare's verse is the best verse, because it combines the great qualities of all contem-

---

[1] Charles Kean, actor son of the famous Edmund Kean, Charles Dixon, Victorian actor, and W.C. Macready, another actor of great stature.

[2] Buchanan refers to Arthur W.E. O'Shaughnessy's *An Epic of Women* (1820), John Payne's *The Masque of Shadows* (1870), and Philip B. Marston's *Songtide and Other Poems* (1871).

[3] Abraham Cowley (1618–87).

[4] Joshua Sylvester (1563–1618), translator.

[5] a group of pretentious later eighteenth-century English poets.

porary verse, with no individual affectations; and so perfectly does this verse, with all its splendour, intersect with the style of contemporaries *at their best*, that we would undertake to select passage after passage which would puzzle a good judge to tell which of the Elizabethans was the author—Marlowe, Beaumont, Dekker, Marston, Webster, or Shakespeare himself. The great poet is Dante, full of the thunder of a great Idea; and Milton, unapproachable in the serene white light of thought and sumptuous wealth of style; and Shakespeare, all poets by turns, and all men in succession; and Goethe, always innovating, and ever indifferent to innovation for its own sake; and Wordsworth, clear as crystal and deep as the sea; and Tennyson, with his vivid range, far-piercing sight, and perfect speech; and Browning, great, not by virtue of his eccentricities, but because of his close intellectual grasp. Tell *Paradise Lost*, the *Divine Comedy*, in naked prose; so the same by *Hamlet*, *Macbeth*, and *Lear*; read Mr. Hayward's translation of *Faust*; take up the *Excursion*, a great poem, though its speech is nearly prose already; turn the "Guinevere" into a mere story; reproduce Pompilia's last dying speech without a line of rhythm. Reduced to bald English, all these poems, and all great poems, lose much; but how much do they not retain? They are poems to the very roots and depths of being, poems born and delivered from the soul, and treat them as cruelly as you may, poems they will remain. So it is with all good and thorough creations, however low in their rank; so it is with the "Ballot in a Wedding" and "Clever Tom Clinch," just as much as with the "Epistle of Karsheesh," or Goethe's torso of "Prometheus;" with Shelley's "Skylark," or Alfred de Musset's "A la Lune," as well as Racine's "Athalie," Victor Hugo's "Parricide," or Hood's "Last Man." A poem is a poem, first as to the soul, next as to the form. The fleshly persons who wish to create form for its own sake are merely pronouncing their own doom. But *such* form! If the Pre-Raphaelite

fervour gains ground, we shall soon have popular songs like this:—

> When winds do roar, and rains do pour,
> Hard is the life of the sail*or*;
> He scarcely as he reels can tell
> The side-lights from the binn*acle*;
> He looketh on the wild wa*ter*, &c.,

and so on, till the English speech seems the speech of raving madmen. Of a piece with other affectations is the device of a burthen, of which the fleshly persons are very fond for its own sake, quite apart from its relevancy. Thus Mr. Rossetti sings:—

> Why did you melt your waxen man,
> > Sister Helen?
> To-day is the third since you began.
> The time was long, yet the time ran,
> > Little brother.
> (*O mother, Mary mother,*
> *Three days to-day between Heaven and Hell*)

This burthen is repeated, with little or no alteration, through thirty-four verses, and might with as much music, and far more point, run as follows:—

> Why did you melt your waxen man,
> > Sister Helen?
> To-day is the third since you began.
> The time was long, yet the time ran,
> > Little brother.
> (*O Mr. Dante Rossetti,*
> *What stuff is this about Heaven and Hell?*)

About as much to the point is a burthen of Mr. Swinburne's, something to the following effect:—

> We were three maidens in the green corn,
> *Hey chickaleerie, the red cock and gray,*
> Fairer maidens were never born,
> *One o'clock, two o'clock, off and away.* [1]

---

[1] Buchanan's parody of "The King's Daughter," opening lines.

We are not quite certain of the words, as we quote from memory, but we are sure our version fairly represents the original, and is quite as expressive. Productions of this sort are "silly sooth" in good earnest, though they delight some newspaper critics of the day, and are copied by young gentlemen with animal faculties morbidly developed by too much tobacco and too little exercise. Such indulgence, however, would ruin the strongest poetical constitution; and it unfortunately happens that neither masters nor pupils were naturally very healthy. In such a poem as "Eden Bower" there is not one scrap of imagination, properly so-called. It is a clever grotesque in the worst manner of Callot,[1] unredeemed by a gleam of true poetry or humour. No good poet would have wrought into a poem the absurd tradition about Lilith; Goethe was content to glance at it merely, with a grim smile, in the great scene in the Brocken.[2] We may remark here that poems of this unnatural and morbid kind are only tolerable when they embody a profound meaning, as do Coleridge's "Ancient Mariner" and "Cristabel." Not that we would insult the memory of Coleridge by comparing his exquisitely conscientious work with this affected rubbish about "Eden Bower" and "Sister Helen," though his influence in their composition is unmistakable. Still more unmistakable is the influence of that most unwholesome poet, Beddoes,[3] who, with all his great powers, treated his subjects in a thoroughly insincere manner, and is now justly forgotten.

The great strong current of English poetry rolls on, ever mirroring in its bosom new prospects of fair and wholesome thought. Morbid deviations are endless and inevitable; there must be marsh and stagnant mere as well as mountain and wood. Glancing backward into the shady places of the obscure, we see the once prosperous nonsense-writers each now consigned to his own little limbo—Skelton and Gower still playing fantastic tricks with the mother-tongue; Gascoigne outlasting the applause of all, and living to see his own works buried before him; Sylvester doomed to oblivion by his own fame as a translator; Carew the idol of the courts, and Donne the beloved of the schoolmen, both buried in the same oblivion; the fantastic Fletchers winning the wonder of collegians, and fading out through sheer poetic impotence; Cowley shaking all England with his pindarics, and perishing with them; Waller,[4] the famous, saved from oblivion by the natural note of one single song—and so on, through league after league of a flat and desolate country which once was prosperous, till we come again to these fantastic figures of the fleshly school, with their droll mediaeval garments, their funny archaic speech, and the fatal marks of literary consumption in every pale and delicate visage. Our judgment on Mr. Rossetti, to whom we in the meantime confine our judgment, is substantially that of the *North American Reviewer*, who believes that "we have in him another poetical man, and a man markedly poetical, and of a kind apparently, though not radically, different from any of our secondary writers of poetry, but that we have not in him a new poet of any weight;" and that he is "so affected, sentimental, and painfully self-conscious, that the best to be done in his case is to hope that this book of his, having unpacked his bosom of so much that is unhealthy, may have done him more good than it has given others pleasure." Such, we say, is our opinion, which might very well be wrong, and have to undergo modification, if Mr. Rossetti was younger and less self-possessed. His "maturity" is fatal.

—1871

---

[1] Jacques Callot (1592–1635), French painter and engraver.

[2] the scene called "Walpurgis Night," the night of the witches.

[3] Thomas Lovell Beddoes (1803–49), late Romantic poet.

[4] fifteenth-, sixteenth-, and seventeenth-century English poets.

Dante Gabriel Rossetti
1828 – 1882

(See previous biographical note on page 1234.)

༄

The Stealthy School Of Criticism

Your paragraph, a fortnight ago, relating to the pseudonymous authorship of an article, violently assailing myself and other writers of poetry, in the *Contemporary Review* for October last, reveals a species of critical masquerade which I have expressed in the heading given to this letter. Since then, Mr. Sidney Colvin's note, qualifying the report that he intends to "answer" that article, has appeared in your pages; and my own view as to the absolute forfeit, under such conditions, of all claim to honourable reply, is precisely the same as Mr. Colvin's. For here a critical organ, professedly adopting the principle of open signature, would seem, in reality, to assert (by silent practice, however, not by enunciation,) that if the anonymous in criticism was—as itself originally inculcated—but an early caterpillar stage, the nominate too is found to be no better than a homely transitional chrysalis, and that the ultimate butterfly form for a critic who likes to sport in sunlight and yet to elude the grasp, is after all the pseudonymous. But, indeed, what I may call the "Siamese" aspect of the entertainment provided by the *Review* will elicit but one verdict. Yet I may, perhaps, as the individual chiefly attacked, be excused for asking your assistance now in giving a specific denial to specific charges which, if unrefuted, may still continue, in spite of their author's strategic *fiasco*, to serve his purpose against me to some extent.

The primary accusation, on which this writer grounds all the rest, seems to be that others and myself "extol fleshliness as the distinct and supreme end of poetic and pictorial art; aver that poetic expression is greater than poetic thought; and, by inference, that the body is greater than the soul, and sound superior to sense."

As my own writings are alone formally dealt with in the article, I shall confine my answer to myself; and this must first take unavoidably the form of a challenge to prove so broad a statement. It is true, some fragmentary pretence at proof is put in here and there throughout the attack, and thus far an opportunity is given of contesting the assertion.

A Sonnet entitled *Nuptial Sleep* is quoted and abused at page 338 of the *Review*, and is there dwelt upon as a "whole poem," describing "merely animal sensations." It is no more a whole poem, in reality, than is any single stanza of any poem throughout the book. The poem, written chiefly in sonnets, and of which this is one sonnet-stanza, is entitled *The House of Life*; and even in my first published instalment of the whole work (as contained in the volume under notice) ample evidence is included that no such passing phase of description as the one headed *Nuptial Sleep* could possibly be put forward by the author of *The House of Life* as his own representative view of the subject of love. In proof of this, I will direct attention (among the love-sonnets of this poem) to Nos. 2, 8, 11, 17, 28, and more especially 13, which, indeed, I had better print here.

LOVE-SWEETNESS

"Sweet dimness of her loosened hair's downfall
    About thy face; her sweet hands round thy head
    In gracious fostering union garlanded;
Her tremulous smiles; her glances' sweet recall

Of love; her murmuring sighs memorial;
    Her mouth's culled sweetness by thy kisses shed
    On cheeks and neck and eyelids, and so led
Back to her mouth which answers there for all:—

"What sweeter than these things, except the thing
    In lacking which all these would lose their sweet:—
    The confident heart's still fervour; the swift beat
And soft subsidence of the spirit's wing
Then when it feels, in cloud-girt wayfaring,
    The breath of kindred plumes against its feet?"

Any reader may bring any artistic charge he pleases against the above sonnet; but one charge it would be impossible to maintain against the writer of the series in which it occurs, and that is, the wish on his part to assert that the body is greater than the soul. For here all the passionate and just delights of the body are declared—somewhat figuratively, it is true, but unmistakably—to be as naught if not ennobled by the concurrence of the soul at all times. Moreover, nearly one half of this series of sonnets has nothing to do with love, but treats of quite other life-influences. I would defy any one to couple with fair quotation of Sonnets 29, 30, 31, 39, 40, 41, 43, or others, the slander that their author was not impressed, like all other thinking men, with the responsibilities and higher mysteries of life; while Sonnets 35, 36, and 37, entitled *The Choice*, sum up the general view taken in a manner only to be evaded by conscious insincerity. Thus much for *The House of Life*, of which the sonnet *Nuptial Sleep* is one stanza, embodying, for its small constituent share, a beauty of natural universal function, only to be reprobated in art if dwelt on (as I have shown that it is not here) to the exclusion of those other highest things of which it is the harmonious concomitant.

At page 342, an attempt is made to stigmatize four short quotations as being specially "my own property," that is, (for the context shows the meaning,) as being grossly sensual; though all guiding reference to any precise page or poem in my book is avoided here. The first of these unspecified quotations is from the *Last Confession*; and is the description referring to the harlot's laugh, the hideous character of which, together with its real or imagined resemblance to the laugh heard soon afterwards from the lips of one long cherished as an ideal, is the immediate cause which makes the maddened hero of the poem a murderer. Assailants may say what they please; but no poet or poetic reader will blame me for making the incident recorded in these seven lines as repulsive to the reader as it was to the hearer and beholder. Without this, the chain of motive and result would remain obviously incomplete. Observe also that these are but seven lines in a poem of some five hundred, not one other of which could be classed with them.

A second quotation gives the last two lines *only* of the following sonnet, which is the first of four sonnets in *The House Of Life* jointly entitled *Willow-wood*:—

"I sat with Love upon a woodside well,
    Leaning across the water, I and he;
    Nor ever did he speak nor looked at me,
But touched his lute wherein was audible
The certain secret thing he had to tell:
    Only our mirrored eyes met silently
    In the low wave; and that sound seemed to be
The passionate voice I knew; and my tears fell.

"And at their fall, his eyes beneath grew hers;
And with his foot and with his wing-feathers
    He swept the spring that watered my heart's drouth.
Then the dark ripples spread to waving hair,
And as I stooped, her own lips rising there
    Bubbled with brimming kisses at my mouth."

The critic has quoted (as I said) only the last two lines, and he has italicized the second as something unbearable and ridiculous. Of course the inference would be that this was really my own absurd bubble-

and-squeak notion of an actual kiss. The reader will perceive at once, from the whole sonnet transcribed above, how untrue such an inference would be. The sonnet describes a dream or trance of divided love momentarily re-united by the longing fancy; and in the imagery of the dream, the face of the beloved rises through deep dark waters to kiss the lover. Thus the phrase, "Bubbled with brimming kisses," etc., bears purely on the special symbolism employed, and from that point of view will be found, I believe, perfectly simple and just.

A third quotation is from *Eden Bower*, and says,

> "What more prize than love to impel thee?
> Grip and lip my limbs as I tell thee!"

Here again no reference is given, and naturally the reader would suppose that a human embrace is described. The embrace, on the contrary, is that of a fabled snake-woman and a snake. It would be possible still, no doubt, to object on other grounds to this conception; but the ground inferred and relied on for full effect by the critic is none the less an absolute misrepresentation. These three extracts, it will be admitted, are virtually, though not verbally, garbled with malicious intention; and the same is the case, as I have shown, with the sonnet called *Nuptial Sleep* when purposely treated as a "whole poem."

The last of the four quotations grouped by the critic as conclusive examples consists of two lines from *Jenny*. Neither some thirteen years ago, when I wrote this poem, nor last year when I published it, did I fail to foresee impending charges of recklessness and aggressiveness, or to perceive that even some among those who could really *read* the poem, and acquit me on these grounds, might still hold that the thought in it had better have dispensed with the situation which serves it for framework. Nor did I omit to consider how far a treatment from without might here be possible. But the motive powers of art reverse the requirement of science, and demand first of all an *inner* standing-point. The heart of such a mystery as this must be plucked from the very world in which it beats or bleeds; and the beauty and pity, the self-questionings and all-questionings which it brings with it, can come with full force only from the mouth of one alive to its whole appeal, such as the speaker put forward in the poem,—that is, of a young and thoughtful man of the world. To such a speaker, many half-cynical revulsions of feeling and reverie, and a recurrent presence of the impressions of beauty (however artificial) which first brought him within such a circle of influence, would be inevitable features of the dramatic relations portrayed. Here again I can give the lie, in hearing of honest readers, to the base or trivial ideas which my critic labours to connect with the poem. There is another little charge, however, which this minstrel in mufti brings against *Jenny*, namely, one of plagiarism from that very poetic self of his which the tutelary prose does but enshroud for the moment. This question can, fortunately, be settled with ease by others who have read my critic's poems; and thus I need the less regret that, not happening myself to be in that position, I must be content to rank with those who cannot pretend to an opinion on the subject.

It would be humiliating, need one come to serious detail, to have to refute such an accusation as that of "binding oneself by solemn league and covenant to extol fleshliness as the distinct and supreme end of poetic and pictorial art"; and one cannot but feel that here every one will think it allowable merely to pass by with a smile the foolish fellow who has brought a charge thus framed against any reasonable man. Indeed, what I have said already is substantially enough to refute it, even did I not feel sure that a fair balance of my poetry must, of itself, do so in the eyes of every candid reader. I say nothing of my pictures; but those who know them will laugh at the idea. That I may, nevertheless, take a wider view than some poets or critics, of how much, in the material conditions absolutely given to man to deal with as distinct from his spiritual aspirations, is admissible within the limits of Art,—this, I say, is possible enough; nor do I wish to shrink from such responsibility. But to state that I do so to the ignoring or overshadowing of spiritual beauty, is an absolute falsehood, impossible to be put forward except in the indulgence of prejudice or rancour.

I have selected, amid much railing on my critic's part, what seemed the most representative indictment against me, and have, so far, answered it. Its remaining clauses set forth how others and myself "aver that poetic expression is greater than poetic thought... and sound superior to sense"—an accusation elsewhere, I observe, expressed by saying that we "wish to create form for its own sake." If writers of verse are to be listened to in such arraignment of each other, it might be quite competent of me to prove, from the works of my friends in question, that no such thing is the case with them; but my present function is to confine myself to my own defence. This, again, it is difficult to do quite seriously. It is no part of my undertaking to dispute the verdict of any "contemporary," however contemptuous or contemptible, on my own measure of executive success; but the accusation cited above is not against the poetic value of certain work, but against its primary and (by assumption) its admitted aim. And to this I must reply that so far, assuredly, not even Shakespeare himself could desire more arduous human tragedy for development in Art than belongs to the themes I venture to embody, however incalculably higher might be his power of dealing with them. What more inspiring for poetic effort than the terrible Love turned to Hate,—perhaps the deadliest of all passion-woven complexities,—which is the theme of *Sister Helen*, and, in a more fantastic form, of *Eden Bower*—the surroundings of both poems being the mere machinery of a central universal meaning? What, again, more so than the savage penalty exacted for a lost ideal, as expressed in the *Last Confession*;—than the outraged love for man and burning compensations in art and memory of *Dante at Verona*;—than the baffling problems which the face of *Jenny* conjures up;—or than the analysis of passion and feeling attempted in *The House of Life*, and others among the more purely lyrical poems? I speak here, as does my critic in the clause adduced, of *aim*, not of *achievement*; and so far, the mere summary is instantly subversive of the preposterous imputation. To assert that the poet whose matter is such as this aims chiefly at "creating form for its own sake," is, in fact, almost an ingenuous kind of dishonesty; for surely it delivers up the asserter at once, bound hand and foot, to the tender mercies of contradictory proof. Yet this may fairly be taken as an example of the spirit in which a constant effort is here made against me to appeal to those who either are ignorant of what I write, or else belong to the large class too easily influenced by an assumption of authority in addressing them. The false name appended to the article must, as is evident, aid this position vastly; for who, after all, would not be apt to laugh at seeing one poet confessedly come forward as aggressor against another in the field of criticism?

It would not be worth while to lose time and patience in noticing minutely how the system of misrepresentation is carried into points of artistic detail,—giving us, for example, such statements as that the burthen employed in the ballad of *Sister Helen* "is repeated with little or no alteration through thirty-four verses," whereas the fact is, that the alteration of it in every verse is the very scheme of the poem. But these are minor matters quite thrown into the shade by the critic's more daring sallies. In addition to the class of attack I have answered above, the article contains, of course, an immense amount of personal paltriness; as, for instance, attributions of my work to this, that, or the other absurd derivative source; or again, pure nonsense (which can have no real meaning even to the writer) about "one art getting hold of another, and imposing on it its conditions and limitations"; or, indeed, what not besides? However, to such antics as this, no more attention is possible than that which Virgil enjoined Dante to bestow on the meaner phenomena of his pilgrimage.

Thus far, then, let me thank you for the opportunity afforded me to join issue with the Stealthy School of Criticism. As for any literary justice to be done on this particular Mr. Robert-Thomas, I will merely ask the reader whether, once identified, he does not become manifestly his own best "sworn tormentor"? For who will then fail to discern all the palpitations which preceded his final resolve in the great question whether to be or not to be his acknowledged self when he became an assailant? And yet this is he who, from behind his mask, ventures to charge another with "bad blood," with "insincerity," and the rest of it (and that where poetic fancies are alone in question); while every word on his own tongue is covert rancour, and every stroke from his pen perversion of truth. Yet, after all, there is nothing wonderful in the lengths to which a fretful poet-critic will carry such grudges as he may bear, while publisher and editor can both be found who are willing to consider such means admissible, even to the clear subversion of first professed tenets in the *Review* which they conduct.

In many phases of outward nature, the principle of chaff and grain holds good,—the base enveloping the precious continually; but an untruth was never yet the husk of a truth. Thresh and riddle and winnow it as you may,—let it fly in shreds to the four winds,—falsehood only will be that which flies and that which stays. And thus the sheath of deceit which this pseudonymous undertaking presents at the outset insures in fact what will be found to be its real character to the core.

—1871

Algernon Charles Swinburne

1837 – 1909

Algernon Charles Swinburne's family background was aristocratic (his father was an admiral and his grandfather a baronet), and his education was privileged—he was educated at Eton and Oxford. Beginning his writing at Oxford (1856–60), he met Dante Gabriel Rossetti and was briefly associated with the Pre-Raphaelite circle. Swinburne led a dissolute, wild life (his predilection for flagellation pornography is infamous), attaining literary notoriety with *Atalanta in Calydon* (1865), and *Poems and Ballads, Series #1* (1866). In an age that prided itself on middle-class values and religiosity, Swinburne's works were blasphemous, erotic, and subversive, rebelling against the moral repressiveness of his time as he asserted a doctrine of "l'art pour l'art." Engaged in literary debates with Thomas Carlyle, John Ruskin, and Ralph Waldo Emerson over the value of morality in art, his essay "Under the Microscope" (1872), is a response, parodic as it is, to Robert Buchanan's "The Fleshly School of Poetry" (1871), which attacked both Swinburne's and Rossetti's sensuous, poetic impulses. A liberal republican, in the *Song of Italy* (1867) and *Songs before Sunrise* (1871) he sided with Italian political revolt against oppression. Swinburne was also a respected scholar, publishing studies of William Blake (1868), William Shakespeare (1880), and essays on French and English contemporaries. With an aesthetic vision that influenced younger generations, Swinburne was a poet who drew on a wide range of interests, and was willing to pursue his own beliefs against the prejudices of his time.

◦◦◦

From *Under The Microscope*

It seems to me that the moral tone of the Arthurian story has been on the whole lowered and degraded by Mr. Tennyson's mode of treatment.[1] Wishing to make his central figure the noble and perfect symbol of an ideal man, he has removed not merely the excuse but the explanation of the fatal and tragic loves of Launcelot and Guenevere. The hinge of the whole legend of the Round Table, from its first glory to its final fall, is the incestuous birth of Mordred from the connexion of Arthur with his half-sister, unknowing and unknown; as surely as the hinge of the Oresteia[2] from first to last is the sacrifice at Aulis. From the immolation of Iphigenia springs the wrath of Clytæmnestra, with all its train of evils ensuing; from the sin of Arthur's youth proceeds the ruin of his reign and realm through the falsehood of his wife, a wife unloving and unloved. Remove in either case the plea which leaves the heroine less sinned against indeed than sinning, but yet not too base for tragic compassion and interest, and there remains merely the presentation of a vulgar adulteress. From the background of the one story the ignoble figure of Ægisthus starts into the foreground, and we see in place of the terrible and patient mother, perilous and piteous as a lioness bereaved, the congenial harlot of a coward and traitor. A poet undertaking to rewrite the Agamemnon, who should open his poem with some scene of dalliance or conspiracy between Ægisthus and Clytæmnestra and proceed to make of their common household intrigue the mainspring of his plan, would not more depress the design and lower the keynote of the Æschylean drama, than Mr. Tennyson has lowered the note and deformed the outline of the Arthurian story, by reducing Arthur to the level of a wittol, Guenevere to the level of a woman of intrigue, and Launcelot to the level of a "co-respondent." Treated as he has

---

[1] Swinburne refers to Alfred Lord Tennyson's *Idylls of the King* (1869).

[2] The *Oresteia* trilogy by the ancient Greek dramatist Aeschylus (525–456 BC), consists of *Agamemnon*, *Choephori*, and *Eumenides*.

treated it, the story is rather a case for the divorce-court than for poetry. At the utmost it might serve the recent censor of his countrymen, the champion of morals so dear to President Thiers[1] and the virtuous journalist[2] who draws a contrast in favour of his chastity between him and other French or English authors, for a new study of the worn and wearisome old topic of domestic intrigue; but such "camelias" should be left to blow in the common hotbeds of the lower kind of novelist. Adultery must be tragic and exceptional to afford stuff for art to work upon; and the debased preference of Mr. Tennyson's heroine for a lover so much beneath her noble and faithful husband is as mean an instance as any day can show in its newspaper reports of a common woman's common sin. In the old story, the king, with the doom denounced in the beginning by Merlin hanging over all his toils and triumphs as a tragic shadow, stands apart in no undignified patience to await the end in its own good time of all his work and glory, with no eye for the pain and passion of the woman who sits beside him as queen rather than as wife. Such a figure is not unfit for the centre of a tragic action; it is neither ignoble nor inconceivable; but the besotted blindness of Mr. Tennyson's "blameless king" to the treason of a woman who has had the first and last of his love and the whole devotion of his blameless life is nothing more or less than pitiful and ridiculous. All the studious care and exquisite eloquence of the poet can throw no genuine halo round the sprouting brows of a royal husband who remains to the very last the one man in his kingdom insensible of his disgrace. The unclean taunt of the hateful Vivien is simply the expression in vile language of an undeniable truth; such a man as this king is indeed hardly "man at all;" either fool or coward he must surely be. Thus it is that by the very excision of what may have seemed in his eyes a moral blemish Mr. Tennyson has blemished the whole story; by the very exaltation of his hero as something more than man he has left him in the end something less. The keystone of the whole building is removed, and in place of a tragic house of song where even sin had all the dignity and beauty that sin can retain, and without which it can afford no fit material for tragedy, we find an incongruous edifice of tradition and invention where even virtue is made to seem either imbecile or vile. The story as it stood of old had in it something almost of Hellenic dignity and significance; in it as in the great Greek legends we could trace from a seemingly small root of evil the birth and growth of a calamitous fate, not sent by mere malevolence of heaven, yet in its awful weight and mystery of darkness apparently out of all due retributive proportion to the careless sin or folly of presumptuous weakness which first incurred its infliction; so that by mere hasty resistance and return of violence for violence a noble man may unwittingly bring on himself and all his house the curse denounced on parricide, by mere casual indulgence of light love and passing wantonness a hero king may unknowingly bring on himself and all his kingdom the doom imposed on incest. This presence and imminence of Fate inevitable as invisible throughout the tragic course of action can alone confer on such a story the proper significance and the necessary dignity; without it the action would want meaning and the passion would want nobility; with it, we may hear in the high funereal homily which concludes as with dirge-music the great old book of Sir Thomas Mallory some echo not utterly unworthy of that supreme lament of wondering and wailing spirits—

---

1 Louis Adolphe Thiers (1797–1877), French historian and statesman, first president of the Third Republic.

2 Robert Buchanan (1841–1901), poet, novelist, and dramatist; anonymous author of "The Fleshly School of Poetry" (1872).

ποῖ δῆτα κρανεῖ, ποῖ καταλήξει
μετακοιμισθὲν μένος ἄτης; [1]

The fatal consequence or corollary of this original flaw in his scheme is that the modern poet has been obliged to degrade all the other figures of the legend in order to bring them into due harmony with the degraded figures of Arthur and Guenevere. The courteous and loyal Gawain of the old romancers, already deformed and maligned in the version of Mallory himself, is here a vulgar traitor; the benignant Lady of the Lake, foster-mother of Launcelot, redeemer and comforter of Pelleas, becomes the very vilest figure in all that cycle of more or less symbolic agents and patients which Mr. Tennyson has set revolving round the figure of his central wittol. I certainly do not share the objection of the virtuous journalist to the presentation in art of an unchaste woman; but I certainly desire that the creature presented should retain some trace of human or if need be of devilish dignity. The Vivien of Mr. Tennyson's idyl seems to me, to speak frankly, about the most base and repulsive person ever set forth in serious literature. Her impurity is actually eclipsed by her incredible and incomparable vulgarity—("*O ay,*" *said Vivien, "that were likely too*"). She is such a sordid creature as plucks men passing by the sleeve. I am of course aware that this figure appears the very type and model of a beautiful and fearful temptress of the flesh, the very embodied and ennobled ideal of danger and desire, in the chaster eyes of the virtuous journalist who grows sick with horror and disgust at

the license of other French and English writers; but I have yet to find the French or English contemporary poem containing a passage that can be matched against the loathsome dialogue in which Merlin and Vivien discuss the nightly transgressions against chastity, within doors and without, of the various knights of Arthur's court. I do not remember that any modern poet whose fame has been assailed on the score of sensual immorality—say for instance the author of "Mademoiselle de Maupin" or the author of the "Fleurs du Mal" [2]—has ever devoted an elaborate poem to describing the erotic fluctuations and vacillations of a dotard under the moral and physical manipulation of a prostitute. The conversation of Vivien is exactly described in the poet's own phrase—it is "as the poached filth that floods the middle street." Nothing like it can be cited from the verse which embodies other poetic personations of unchaste women. From the Cleopatra of Shakespeare and the Dalilah of Milton to the Phraxanor of Wells, a figure worthy to be ranked not far in design below the highest of theirs, we may pass without fear of finding any such pollution. Those heroines of sin are evil, but noble in their evil way; it is the utterly ignoble quality of Vivien which makes her so unspeakably repulsive and unfit for artistic treatment. "Smiling saucily," she is simply a subject for the police-court.

—1872

---

[1] "Where will the doom come to fulfillment?
Where will the rage of calamity be lulled to rest and cease?"

[2] Théophile Gautier published *Mademoiselle de Maupin* in 1835–36, and Charles Baudelaire published *Les Fleurs du mal* in 1857.

Walter Pater
1839 – 1894

Walter Pater was educated at King's School, Canterbury, and Queen's College, Oxford. After receiving a fellowship at Oxford in 1865, he established himself in rooms at Brasenose College and devoted himself to his lectures, particularly on Plato and Platonics, and the study of art. In his influential *Studies in the History of the* *Renaissance* (1873), he argues for the concept of nondiscursive, nonutilitarian art, epitomized by his phrase, "art for art's sake," which became a slogan for the aesthetic movement of the 1870s and 1880s and the subsequent "decadence" of the 1890s.

❧❧❧

Preface and Conclusion to
The Renaissance: Studies in Art and Poetry

PREFACE

Many attempts have been made by writers on art and poetry to define beauty in the abstract, to express it in the most general terms, to find some universal formula for it. The value of these attempts has most often been in the suggestive and penetrating things said by the way. Such discussions help us very little to enjoy what has been well done in art or poetry, to discriminate between what is more and what is less excellent in them, or to use words like beauty, excellence, art, poetry, with a more precise meaning than they would otherwise have. Beauty, like all other qualities presented to human experience, is relative; and the definition of it becomes unmeaning and useless in proportion to its abstractness. To define beauty, not in the most abstract but in the most concrete terms possible, to find not its universal formula, but the formula which expresses most adequately this or that special manifestation of it, is the aim of the true student of aesthetics.

"To see the object as in itself it really is," has been justly said to be the aim of all true criticism whatever; and in aesthetic criticism the first step towards seeing one's object as it really is, is to know one's own impression as it really is, to discriminate it, to realise it distinctly. The objects with which aesthetic criticism deals—music, poetry, artistic and accomplished forms of human life—are indeed receptacles of so many powers or forces: they possess, like the products of nature, so many virtues or qualities. What is this song or picture, this engaging personality presented in life or in a book, to *me*? What effect does it really produce on me? Does it give me pleasure? and if so, what sort or degree of pleasure? How is my nature modified by its presence, and under its influence? The answers to these questions are the original facts with which the aesthetic critic has to do; and, as in the study of light, of morals, of number, one must realise such primary data for one's self, or not at all. And he who experiences these impressions strongly, and drives directly at the discrimination and analysis of them, has no need to trouble himself with the abstract question what beauty is in itself, or what its exact relation to truth or experience—metaphysical questions, as unprofitable as metaphysical questions elsewhere. He may pass them all by as being, answerable or not, of no interest to him.

The aesthetic critic, then, regards all the objects with which he has to do, all works of art, and the fairer forms of nature and human life, as powers or forces producing pleasurable sensations, each of a more or less peculiar or unique kind. This influence he feels, and wishes to explain, by analysing and reducing it to its elements. To him, the picture, the landscape, the engaging personality in life or in a book, *La Gioconda*, the hills of Carrara, Pico of Mirandola,[1] are valuable for their virtues, as we say, in speaking of a herb, a wine, a gem; for the property each has of affecting one with a special, a unique, impression of pleasure. Our education becomes complete in proportion as our susceptibility to these impressions increases in depth and variety. And the function of the aesthetic critic is to distinguish, to analyse, and separate from its adjuncts, the virtue by which a picture, a landscape, a fair personality in life or in a book, produces this special impression of beauty or pleasure, to indicate what the source of that impression is, and under what conditions it is experienced. His end is reached when he has disengaged that virtue, and noted it, as a chemist notes some natural element, for himself and others; and the rule for those who would reach this end is stated with great exactness in the words of a recent critic of Sainte-Beuve;—*De se borner à connaître de près les belles choses, et à s'en nourrir en exquis amateurs, en humanistes accomplis.*[2]

What is important, then, is not that the critic should possess a correct abstract definition of beauty for the intellect, but a certain kind of temperament, the power of being deeply moved by the presence of beautiful objects. He will remember always that beauty exists in many forms. To him all periods, types, schools of taste, are in themselves equal. In all ages there have been some excellent workmen, and some excellent work done. The question he asks is always:—in whom did the stir, the genius, the sentiment of the period find itself? where was the receptacle of its refinement, its elevation, its taste?

"The ages are all equal," says William Blake, "but genius is always above its age."[3]

Often it will require great nicety to disengage this virtue from the commoner elements with which it may be found in combination. Few artists, not Goethe or Byron even, work quite cleanly, casting off all *débris*, and leaving us only what the heat of their imagination has wholly fused and transformed. Take, for instance, the writings of Wordsworth. The heat of his genius, entering into the substance of his work, has crystallised a part, but only a part, of it; and in that great mass of verse there is much which might well be forgotten. But scattered up and down it, sometimes fusing and transforming entire compositions, like the Stanzas on *Resolution and Independence*, or the *Ode on the Recollections of Childhood*, sometimes, as if at random, depositing a fine crystal here or there, in a matter it does not wholly search through and transmute, we trace the action of his unique, incommunicable faculty, that strange, mystical sense of a life in natural things, and of man's life as a part of nature, drawing strength and colour and character from local influences, from the hills and streams, and from natural sights and sounds. Well! that is the *virtue*, the active principle in Wordsworth's poetry, and then the function of the critic of Wordsworth is to follow up that active principle, to disengage it, to mark the degree in which it penetrates his verse.

The subjects of the following studies are taken from the history of the *Renaissance*, and touch what I think the chief points in that complex, many-sided movement. I have explained in the first of them what I understand by the word, giving it a much wider scope than was intended by those who originally used it to denote that revival of classical antiquity in the fifteenth century which was only one of many results of a general excitement and enlightening of the

---

[1] "La Gioconda" refers to Leonardo da Vinci's Mona Lisa; marble is quarried from the "hills of Carrara"; Pico of Mirandola (1463–94) was an Italian philosopher about whom Pater wrote an essay included in *The Renaissance*.

[2] "To confine themselves to knowing beautiful things intimately, and to sustain themselves by these, as sensitive amateurs and accomplished humanists do."

[3] Blake makes this comment in an annotation of *The Works of Sir Joshua Reynolds*.

human mind, but of which the great aim and achievements of what, as Christian art, is often falsely opposed to the Renaissance, were another result. This outbreak of the human spirit may be traced far into the middle age itself, with its motives already clearly pronounced, the care for physical beauty, the worship of the body, the breaking down of those limits which the religious system of the middle age imposed on the heart and the imagination. I have taken as an example of this movement, this earlier Renaissance within the middle age itself, and as an expression of its qualities, two little compositions in early French; not because they constitute the best possible expression of them, but because they help the unity of my series, inasmuch as the Renaissance ends also in France, in French poetry, in a phase of which the writings of Joachim du Bellay[1] are in many ways the most perfect illustration. The Renaissance, in truth, put forth in France an aftermath, a wonderful later growth, the products of which have to the full that subtle and delicate sweetness which belongs to a refined and comely decadence, just as its earliest phases have the freshness which belongs to all periods of growth in art, the charm of *ascêsis*,[2] of the austere and serious girding of the loins in youth.

But it is in Italy, in the fifteenth century, that the interest of the Renaissance mainly lies,—in that solemn fifteenth century which can hardly be studied too much, not merely for its positive results in the things of the intellect and the imagination, its concrete works of art, its special and prominent personalities, with their profound aesthetic charm, but for its general spirit and character, for the ethical qualities of which it is a consummate type.

The various forms of intellectual activity which together make up the culture of an age, move for the most part from different starting points, and by unconnected roads. As products of the same generation they partake indeed of a common character, and unconsciously illustrate each other; but of the producers themselves, each group is solitary, gaining what advantage or disadvantage there may be in intellectual isolation. Art and poetry, philosophy and the religious life, and that other life of refined pleasure and action in the conspicuous places of the world, are each of them confined to its own circle of ideas, and those who prosecute either of them are generally little curious of the thoughts of others. There come, however, from time to time, eras of more favourable conditions, in which the thoughts of men draw nearer together than is their wont, and the many interests of the intellectual world combine in one complete type of general culture. The fifteenth century in Italy is one of these happier eras, and what is sometimes said of the age of Pericles is true of that of Lorenzo:—it is an age productive in personalities, many-sided, centralised, complete. Here, artists and philosophers and those whom the action of the world has elevated and made keen, do not live in isolation, but breathe a common air, and catch light and heat from each other's thoughts. There is a spirit of general elevation and enlightenment in which all alike communicate. The unity of this spirit gives unity to all the various products of the Renaissance; and it is to this intimate alliance with mind, this participation in the best thoughts which that age produced, that the art of Italy in the fifteenth century owes much of its grave dignity and influence.

I have added an essay on Winckelmann,[3] as not incongruous with the studies which precede it, because Winckelmann, coming in the eighteenth century, really belongs in spirit to an earlier age. By his enthusiasm for the things of the intellect and the imagination for their own sake, by his Hellenism, his life-long struggle to atcain to the Greek spirit, he is in sympathy with the humanists of a previous century.

---

[1] du Bellay (1524–60), a French poet about whom Pater wrote an essay in *The Renaissance*.

[2] asceticism.

[3] Johann Joachim Winckelmann (1717–68), a German classical scholar.

He is the last fruit of the Renaissance, and explains in a striking way its motive and tendencies.

CONCLUSION

To regard all things and principles of things as inconstant modes or fashions has more and more become the tendency of modern thought. Let us begin with that which is without—our physical life. Fix upon it in one of its more exquisite intervals, the moment, for instance, of delicious recoil from the flood of water in summer heat. What is the whole physical life in that moment but a combination of natural elements to which science gives their names? But those elements, phosphorus and lime and delicate fibres, are present not in the human body alone: we detect them in places most remote from it. Our physical life in perpetual motion of them—the passage of the blood, the waste and repairing of the lenses of the eye, the modification of the tissues of the brain under every ray of light and sound—processes which science reduces to simpler and more elementary forces. Like the elements of which we are composed, the action of these forces extends beyond us: it rusts iron and ripens corn. Far out on every side of us those elements are broadcast, driven in many currents; and birth and gesture and death and the springing of violets from the grave are but a few out of ten thousand resultant combinations. That clear, perpetual outline of face and limb is but an image of ours, under which we group them—a design in a web, the actual threads of which pass out beyond it. This at least of flame-like our life has, that it is but the concurrence, renewed from moment to moment, of forces parting sooner or later on their ways.

Or, if we begin with the inward world of thought and feeling, the whirlpool is still more rapid, the flame more eager and devouring. There it is no longer the gradual darkening of the eye, the gradual fading of colour from the wall—movements of the shoreside, where the water flows down indeed, though in apparent rest—but the race of the midstream, a drift of momentary acts of sight and passion and thought. At first sight experience seems to bury us under a flood of external objects, pressing upon us with a sharp and importunate reality, calling us out of ourselves in a thousand forms of action. But when reflexion begins to play upon those objects they are dissipated under its influence; the cohesive force seems suspended like some trick of magic; each object is loosed into a group of impressions—colour, odour, texture—in the mind of the observer. And if we continue to dwell in thought on this world, not of objects in the solidity with which language invests them, but of impressions, unstable, flickering, inconsistent, which burn and are extinguished with our consciousness of them, it contracts still further: the whole scope of observation is dwarfed into the narrow chamber of the individual mind. Experience, already reduced to a group of impressions, is ringed round for each one of us by that thick wall of personality through which no real voice has ever pierced on its way to us, or from us to that which we can only conjecture to be without. Every one of those impressions is the impression of the individual in his isolation, each mind keeping as a solitary prisoner its own dream of a world. Analysis goes a step farther still, and assures us that those impressions of the individual mind to which, for each one of us, experience dwindles down, are in perpetual flight; that each of them is limited by time, and that as time is infinitely divisible, each of them is infinitely divisible also; all that is actual in it being a single moment, gone while we try to apprehend it, of which it may ever be more truly said that it has ceased to be than that it is. To such a tremulous wisp constantly reforming itself on the stream, to a single sharp impression, with a sense in it, a relic more or less fleeting, of such moments gone by, what is real in our life fines itself down. It is with this movement, with the passage and dissolution of impressions, images, sensations, that analysis leaves off—that continual vanishing away, that strange, perpetual weaving and unweaving of ourselves.

Philosophiren, says Novalis, *ist dephlegmatisiren, vivificiren*.[1] The service of philosophy, of speculative culture, towards the human spirit, is to rouse, to startle it to a life of constant and eager observation. Every moment some form grows perfect in hand or face; some tone on the hills or the sea is choicer than the rest; some mood of passion or insight or intellectual excitement is irresistibly real and attractive to us,—for that moment only. Not the fruit of experience, but experience itself, is the end. A counted number of pulses only is given to us of a variegated, dramatic life. How may we see in them all that is to be seen in them by the finest senses? How shall we pass most swiftly from point to point, and be present always at the focus where the greatest number of vital forces unite in their purest energy?

To burn always with this hard, gemlike flame, to maintain this ecstasy, is success in life. In a sense it might even be said that our failure is to form habits: for, after all, habit is relative to a stereotyped world, and meantime it is only the roughness of the eye that makes any two persons, things, situations, seem alike. While all melts under our feet, we may well grasp at any exquisite passion, or any contribution to knowledge that seems by a lifted horizon to set the spirit free for a moment, or any stirring of the senses, strange dyes, strange colours, and curious odours, or work of the artist's hands, or the face of one's friend. Not to discriminate every moment some passionate attitude in those about us, and in the very brilliancy of their gifts some tragic dividing of forces on their ways, is, on this short day of frost and sun, to sleep before evening. With this sense of the splendour of our experience and of its awful brevity, gathering all we are into one desperate effort to see and touch, we shall hardly have time to make theories about the things we see and touch. What we have to do is to be for ever curiously testing new opinions and courting new impressions, never acquiescing in a facile orthodoxy of Comte,[2] or of Hegel,[3] or of our own. Philosophical theories or ideas, as points of view, instruments of criticism, may help us to gather up what might otherwise pass unregarded by us. "Philosophy is the microscope of thought." The theory or idea or system which requires of us the sacrifice of any part of this experience, in consideration of some interest into which we cannot enter, or some abstract theory we have not identified with ourselves, or of what is only conventional, has no real claim upon us.

One of the most beautiful passages of Rousseau[4] is that in the sixth book of the *Confessions*, where he describes the awakening in him of the literary sense. An undefinable taint of death had clung always about him, and now in early manhood he believed himself smitten by mortal disease. He asked himself how he might make as much as possible of the interval that remained; and he was not biassed by anything in his previous life when he decided that it must be by intellectual excitement, which he found just then in the clear, fresh writings of Voltaire. Well! we are all *condamnés*[5] as Victor Hugo says: we are all under sentence of death but with a sort of indefinite reprieve—*les hommes sont tous condamnés à mort avec des sursis indéfinis*: we have an interval and then our place knows us no more. Some spend this interval in listlessness, some in high passions, the wisest, at least among "the children of this world,"[6] in art and song. For our one chance lies in expanding that interval, in getting as many pulsations as possible into the given time. Great passions may give us this quickened sense

---

[1] "To philosophize is to cast off inertia, to make oneself alive."
Novalis (Friedrich von Hardenberg [1772–1801]) was a German Romantic.

[2] Auguste Compte (1798–1857), French Positivist.

[3] Georg W.F. Hegel (1770–1831), German Idealist.

[4] Jean-Jacques Rousseau (1712–78), French philosopher and writer.

[5] condemned.

[6] Luke 16:8.

of life, ecstasy and sorrow of love, the various forms of enthusiastic activity, disinterested or otherwise, which come naturally to many of us. Only be sure it is passion—that it does yield you this fruit of a quickened, multiplied consciousness. Of such wisdom, the poetic passion, the desire of beauty, the love of art for its own sake, has most. For art comes to you proposing frankly to give nothing but the highest quality to your moments as they pass, and simply for those moments' sake.

—1873

Gerard Manley Hopkins
1844 – 1889

Gerard Manley Hopkins, the Oxford-educated English poet and Roman Catholic priest, was an innovative technician who applied his art to the dual themes of nature and religion. Converting to Catholicism in 1866 under the guidance of the Tractarians, Hopkins joined the Society of Jesus in 1868. Encouraged to eulogize the loss of five nuns at sea, Hopkins wrote *The Wreck of the Deutschland* (1875–76). Representing Hopkins's first successful experiment with "sprung rhythm," the poem eschews the accentual-syllabic measures conventionally associated with modern English verse. Poems such as "The Windhover" (1877) and the "terrible sonnets" (1885–89) have garnered Hopkins recognition as a poet of stunning originality.

⌘⌘⌘

Author's Preface [1]

The poems in this book are written some in Running Rhythm, the common rhythm in English use, some in Sprung Rhythm, and some in a mixture of the two. And those in the common rhythm are some counterpointed, some not.

Common English rhythm, called Running Rhythm above, is measured by feet of either two or three syllables and (putting aside the imperfect feet at the beginning and end of lines and also some unusual measures in which feet seem to be paired together and double or composite feet to arise) never more or less.

Every foot has one principal stress or accent, and this or the syllable it falls on may be called the Stress of the foot and the other part, the one or two unaccented syllables, the Slack. Feet (and the rhythms made out of them) in which the stress comes first are called Falling Feet and Falling Rhythms, feet and rhythm in which the slack comes first are called Rising Feet and Rhythms, and if the stress is between two slacks there will be Rocking Feet and Rhythms. These distinctions are real and true to nature; but for purposes of scanning it is a great convenience to follow the example of music and take the stress always first, as the accent or the chief accent always comes first in a musical bar. If this is done there will be in common English verse only two possible feet—the so-called accentual Trochee and Dactyl, and correspondingly only two possible uniform rhythms, the so-called Trochaic and Dactylic. But they may be mixed and then what the Greeks called a Logaoedic Rhythm arises. These are the facts and according to these the scanning of ordinary regularly-written English verse is very simple indeed and to bring in other principles is here unnecessary.

But because verse written strictly in these feet and by these principles will become same and tame the poets have brought in licences and departures from rule to give variety, and especially when the natural rhythm is rising, as in the common ten- syllable or five-foot verse, rhymed or blank. These irregularities are chiefly Reversed Feet and Reversed or Counterpoint Rhythm, which two things are two steps or degrees of licence in the same kind. By a reversed foot I mean the putting the stress where, to judge by the rest of the measure, the slack should be and the slack where the stress, and this is done freely at the beginning of a line and, in the course of a line, after a pause; only scarcely ever in the second foot or place and never in the last, unless when the poet designs some extraordinary effect; for these places are characteristic and sensitive and cannot well be touched. But the reversal of the first foot and of some middle foot

---

[1] written about 1883, prefatory to Hopkins's manuscript poems kept by Robert Bridges.

after a strong pause is a thing so natural that our poets have generally done it, from Chaucer down, without remark and it commonly passes unnoticed and cannot be said to amount to a formal change of rhythm, but rather is that irregularity which all natural growth and motion shews. If however the reversal is repeated in two feet running, especially so as to include the sensitive second foot, it must be due either to great want of ear or else is a calculated effect, the super-inducing or *mounting* of a new rhythm upon the old; and since the new or mounted rhythm is actually heard and at the same time the mind naturally supplies the natural or standard foregoing rhythm, for we do not forget what the rhythm is that by rights we should be hearing, two rhythms are in some manner running at once and we have something answerable to counterpoint in music, which is two or more strains of tune going on together, and this is Counterpoint Rhythm. Of this kind of verse Milton is the great master and the choruses of *Samson Agonistes* are written throughout in it—but with the disadvantage that he does not let the reader clearly know what the ground-rhythm is meant to be and so they have struck most readers as merely irregular. And in fact if you counterpoint throughout, since only one of the counter rhythms is actually heard, the other is really destroyed or cannot come to exist, and what is written is one rhythm only and probably Sprung Rhythm, of which I now speak.

Sprung Rhythm, as used in this book, is measured by feet of from one to four syllables, regularly, and for particular effects any number of weak or slack syllables may be used. It has one stress, which falls on the only syllable, if there is only one, or, if there are more, then scanning as above, on the first, and so gives rise to four sorts of feet, a monosyllable and the so-called accentual Trochee, Dactyl, and the First Paeon. And there will be four corresponding natural rhythms; but nominally the feet are mixed and any

one may follow any other. And hence Sprung Rhythm differs from Running Rhythm in having or being only one nominal rhythm, a mixed or "logaoedic" one, instead of three, but on the other hand in having twice the flexibility of foot, so that any two stresses may either follow one another running or be divided by one, two, or three slack syllables. But strict Sprung Rhythm cannot be counterpointed. In Sprung Rhythm, as in logaoedic rhythm generally, the feet are assumed to be equally long or strong and their seeming inequality is made up by pause or stressing.

Remark also that it is natural in Sprung Rhythm for the lines to be *rove over*, that is for the scanning of each line immediately to take up that of the one before, so that if the first has one or more syllables at its end the other must have so many the less at its beginning; and in fact the scanning runs on without break from the beginning, say, of a stanza to the end and all the stanza is one long strain, though written in lines asunder.

Two licences are natural to Sprung Rhythm. The one is rests, as in music; but of this an example is scarcely to be found in this book, unless in the *Echos*, second line. The other is *hangers* or *outrides*, that is one, two, or three slack syllables added to a foot and not counting in the nominal scanning. They are so called because they seem to hang below the line or ride forward or backward from it in another dimension than the line itself, according to a principle needless to explain here. These outriding half feet or hangers are marked by a loop underneath them, and plenty of them will be found.

The other marks are easily understood, namely accents, where the reader might be in doubt which syllable should have the stress; slurs, that is loops *over* syllables, to tie them together into the time of one; little loops at the end of a line to shew that the rhyme goes on to the first letter of the next line; what in music are called pauses ⌢, to shew that the syllable should be dwelt on; and twirls ~, to mark reversed or counterpointed rhythm.

Note on the nature and history of Sprung Rhythm—Sprung Rhythm is the most natural of things. For (1) it is the rhythm of common speech and of written prose, when rhythm is perceived in them. (2) It is the rhythm of all but the most monotonously regular music, so that in the words of choruses and refrains and in songs written closely to music it arises. (3) It is found in nursery rhymes, weather saws, and so on; because, however these may have been once made in running rhythm, the terminations having dropped off by the change of language, the stresses come together and so the rhythm is sprung. (4) It arises in common verse when reversed or counterpointed, for the same reason.

But nevertheless in spite of all this and though Greek and Latin lyric verse, which is well known, and the old English verse seen in "Pierce Ploughman" are in sprung rhythm, it has in fact ceased to be used since the Elizabethan age, Greene being the last writer who can be said to have recognized it. For perhaps there was not, down to our days, a single, even short, poem in English in which sprung rhythm is employed—not for single effects or in fixed places—but as the governing principle of the scansion. I say this because the contrary has been asserted: if it is otherwise the poem should be cited.

Some of the sonnets in this book are in five-foot, some in six-foot or Alexandrine lines.

Nos. 13 and 22 are Curtal-Sonnets, that is they are constructed in proportions resembling those of the sonnet proper, namely, 6 + 4 instead of 8 + 6, with however a half-line tailpiece (so that the equation is rather $\frac{12}{2} + \frac{9}{2} = \frac{21}{2} = 10\frac{1}{2}$).

—1883

Amy Levy
1861 – 1889

Amy Levy was born in London into an upper-middle-class Anglo-Jewish family, and was the first Jewish woman to matriculate at Newnham College, Cambridge. Her first publication was the ballad "Ida Grey" (1875), published in the journal *The Pelican*. This poem was followed by the short story "Euphemia, A Sketch" (1880), and various work that appeared in the literary magazines *Temple Bar*, *The Gentleman's Magazine*, and *The Jewish Chronicle*. She contributed also to *Woman's World*, developing a friendship with its editor, Oscar Wilde. Levy published her first volume of poetry, entitled *Xantippe and Other Verse*, in 1881. Levy wrote three novels; *Miss Meredith* was serialized in 1886, and *The Romance of a Shop* was published in book form in 1888. *Reuben Sachs* (1888), by some considered her most important work, addresses the cultural and personal complexities of Jewish assimilation. The book was critically well-received, but it was rejected by those members of the Anglo-Jewish community who felt that Levy was unsympathetic to them. Levy's promise as a writer was abruptly cut short when, just before her twenty-eighth birthday and for reasons that remained undisclosed, she committed suicide at her parents' home in London.

❧❧❧

James Thomson: A Minor Poet [1]

1

A few months ago there died very miserably in London a poet called James Thomson.[2] He was neither the idol of a literary clique nor the darling of society's drawing-rooms; he was only a poet of wonderful originality and power, and his death created but little stir.

There is nothing very remarkable in this; Homer, we know, had to beg his bread; contemporary cavaliers held Milton not too highly; and I claim for James Thomson the genius of a Homer or a Milton. He is distinctly what in our loose phraseology we call a minor poet; no prophet, standing above and outside things, to whom all sides of a truth (more or less foreshortened, certainly) are visible; but a passionately subjective being, with intense eyes fixed on one side of the solid polygon[3] of truth, and realising that one side with a fervour and intensity to which the philosopher with his birdseye view rarely attains.

Had circumstances been otherwise, I cannot say what might have been the development of a nature so large and strong; with due allowance of sunshine, who knows what fruit might have ripened on a soil so rich and deep? But James Thomson was a poor Scotchman, of humble origin, of straightened means, with every social disadvantage. From first to last, his life was a bitter and sordid struggle; the Fates had given him to fight one of the dreariest, weariest fights in which man has ever drawn sword. The Fates were cruel; but the result of their cruelty is a product so moving, so wonderful, so unique, that we do not cry out against them; rather are we dumb before the horrible complexity of their workings.

James Thomson is essentially the poet of mood; he has symbolised, as no poet has done before him, a certain phase of modern feeling, I was going to say of modern pessimism, but the word scarcely covers the sense.

The City of Dreadful Night, his masterpiece, as it is a poem quite unique in our literature, stands forth as the very sign and symbol of that attitude of mind

[1] first published in two parts in *The Cambridge Review*, 21 February 1883, and 28 February 1883.

[2] See biographical note on Thomson in the Poetry section.

[3] a plane figure with several angles or sides.

which we call Weltschmerz, Pessimism, what you will; i.e., the almost perfect expression of a form of mental suffering which I can convey by no other means than by the use of a very awkward figure—by calling it "grey pain," "the insufferable inane" which makes a man long for the "positive pain." Most of us at some time or other of our lives have wandered in the City of Dreadful Night; the shadowy forms, the dim streets, the monotonous tones are familiar to us; but to those who have never trod its streets, the poet's words can be little else than "a tale of little meaning tho' the words are strong."

> If any cares for the weak words here written,
> It must be someone desolate, fate-smitten....
> Yes, here and there some weary wanderer
>   In that same city of tremendous night,
> Will understand the speech, and feel a stir
>   Of fellowship in all disastrous flight.
>   [ll. 26–27, 29–32]

The poet recognises his own limits. These limits, it may be objected, are very narrow. He dwells on a view of things which is morbid, nay false, which does not exist for the perfectly healthy human being.

But philosophy teaches us that all things are as real as one another, and as unreal.

> ὁρῶ γὰρ ἡμᾶς οὐδὲν ὄντας ἄλλο πλὴν
> εἴδωλ᾽ ὅσοιπερ ζῶμεν ἢ κούφην σκιάν.[1]

The fact that such a state of mind exists is enough; it is one of the phenomena of our world, as true, as false, as worthy, as unworthy of consideration as any other:

> For life is but a dream, whose shapes return,
>   Some frequently, some seldom, some by night,
> Some by day, some night and day; we learn,

While all things change and many vanish quite,
In their recurrence with recurrent changes
A certain seeming order; where this ranges
    We count things real.
                                [ll. 57–63]

The city, with its dark lagoon, its waste of glistening marshes, its boundary where "rolls the shipless sea's unrest" [l. 77], its vast unruined streets where the lamps always burn tho' there is no light in the houses, rises before us, a picture distinct, real in itself, real in the force of its symbolic meaning. The wanderer goes down into the city; all is dim and shadowy; the dismal inhabitants, whose faces are "like to tragic masks of stone" [l. 95], are few and far between, holding little intercourse with one another, communing each man with himself, "for their woe / Broods maddening inwardly and scorns to wreak / Itself abroad"[ll. 107–9]. The wanderer follows in the footsteps of one sad being who appears to be walking with some intent, and presently stands successively before the spots where Faith and Hope and Love have died. Then the perplexed question escapes him: "When Faith and Love and Hope are dead indeed, / Can life still live?"[ll. 155–56].

The answer is a striking example of the wonderful blending of sound and meaning, of outward and inward sense, which marks the poem.

> As one whom his intense thought overpowers,
>   He answered coldly; "Take a watch, erase
> The signs and figures of the circling hours:
>   Detach the hands, remove the dial face;
> The works proceed until run down: altho'
> Bereft of purpose, void of use, still go."
>   [ll. 157–62]

The wanderer passes on, leaving his guide pursuing the self-same dismal round, and makes his way to a spacious square (the insistence on the great size of

---

[1] from Sophocles, *Ajax* 2.125–26, spoken by Odysseus: "Alas! we living mortals, what are we/But phantoms all or unsubstantial shades."

the city is noteworthy) where a man is standing alone and declaiming aloud with mighty gestures.

"No hope can have no fear" [ll. 217ff.] is the text of the speech; the lonely soul can go on its way indifferent, hardened, through the glooms and terrors of this world; it is only when love comes that death and the fear of death can move and sway us. I quote one of the earlier verses of this tragic recital:

As I came through the desert thus it was
As I came through the desert, eyes of fire
Glared at me, throbbing with a starved desire:
The hoarse, and heavy, and carnivorous breath
Was hot upon me from deep jaws of death;
Sharp claws, swift talons, fleshless fingers cold
Plucked at me from the bushes, tried to hold:
　　　But I strode on austere,
　　　No hope could have no fear.
　　　　　　　　　　　[ll. 218–26]

The wanderer goes on his way finding everywhere the same brooding shadow of nameless horror. Hell itself is eagerly sought, a much-desired goal, as a refuge from the void agony of the city. He makes his way into a vast cathedral, where a preacher is addressing the shadowy multitude with words of good cheer. Yes, here in the City of Dreadful Night these are good-tidings that he brings: there is no God; no "fiend with names Divine" made and tortured us; "we bow down to the universal laws"; there is no life beyond the grave, and each man is free to end his life at will [ll. 724ff.].

Silence follows the speaker's words; then suddenly breaks forth a shrill and terrible cry:

In all eternity I had one chance,
　　One few years' term of gracious human life,
The splendour of the intellect's advance,
　　The sweetness of the home with babes and wife.

The social pleasures with their genial wit,
　　The fascination of the worlds of art,

The glories the worlds of nature lit
　　By large imagination's glowing heart…

All the sublime prerogatives of man.…

This chance was never offered me before,
　　For me the infinite Past is blank and dumb,
This chance recurreth never, never more,
　　Blank, blank for me, the infinite to-come:

And this sole chance was frustrate from my birth,
　　A mockery, a delusion.
　　　　　　　　　　[ll. 807–14, 819, 823–28]

There is no mistaking such writing as this; it goes to the very heart of things; it is for all time and all humanity.

I will not attempt to follow further the course of the poem. The passage which closes it on Dürer's[1] "Melancolia" is worthy of its text; I can say no more.

The value of the poem does not lie in isolated passages, in pregnant lines which catch the ear and eye and linger in the memory; it is as a complete conception, as a marvellously truthful expression of what it is almost impossible to express at all, that we must value it. And the truthfulness is none the less that it has been expressed to a great extent by means of symbols; the nature of the subject is such that it is only by resorting to such means that it can be adequately represented. Mood, seen through the medium of such draughtsmanship and painter's skill, is no longer a dream, a shadow which the sunbeams shall disperse, but one side of a truth.

The City of Dreadful Night is always standing; ceaselessly one or other human soul visits and revisits the graves of Faith and Hope and Love; ceaselessly in the vast cathedral does the preacher give forth his good tidings to that shadowy congregation, and ever and anon rises up the shrill sound of agonised protest from their midst.

---

[1] Albrecht Dürer (1471–1528), German painter and wood engraver.

From the aesthetic point of view this poem is the consummation of James Thomson's art; but there is much work of his full of infinite possibilities and half-frustrated fulfillment to which the student of human nature will turn with ever greater interest. For the nature of James Thomson was so wide and rich, his intellect so quick and far reaching, and there is, moreover, such great chastity of thought, such large nobleness about the man. Here is no mere poetic weakling kicking against the pricks, but a great human soul, horribly vital and sensitive in all its pans, struggling with a great agony.

2

From Homer downwards poets have received but sorry treatment at the hands of the Fates, and James Thomson's life was a terribly hard one even for a poet. Here was a man of great powers, of great passions, hemmed in and thwarted on every side by circumstances petty in themselves, but, like Mercutio's wound, "enough."[1] It was many years before he could publish the volume containing the *City of Dreadful Night,* for the prosaic reason of want of money. His considerable knowledge of Italian, German, and Spanish were acquired painfully and in after life, and yet he has caught the spirit of his spiritual kinsmen Heine and of Leopardi,[2] as no other poet has succeeded in doing.

"Only once," says one of his friends, "did I see Thomson smile with purely personal pleasure. It was when he received a letter beginning 'dear fellow-poet,' and signed 'George Eliot.' I never thought there was a spark of vanity in him till then."[3]

"The talent," says Emerson, "sucks the substance." Such a talent as that of James Thomson must have been a heavy burden for any but the strongest to bear under the most favourable circumstances; and when we consider the dark and narrow circumstances of his lonely life we can only stand aghast. For, if one comes to think of it, it is appalling what infinite and exquisite anguish can be suffered by a single human being who is perhaps sitting quietly in his chair before us, or crosses our path in the sunny street and fields. The human organism is so complex; there are so many strings to vibrate to the touch of pain; the body and soul of man are such perfect pain-conductors. And all through the work of James Thomson we hear one note, one cry, muffled sometimes, but always there; a passionate, hungry cry for life, for the things of this human, flesh and blood life; for love and praise, for mere sunlight and sun's warmth.

> Sweet is to sing, but believe me this,
> Lips only sing when they cannot kiss.[4]

No, this is not the highest utterance, the word of the great artist struggling towards completion; rather is it the under, coarser cry of the imperfect human being, crushed beneath a load which he is not formed to bear.

> Statues and pictures and art may be grand,
> But they are not the life for which they stand,[5]

he sings; and Grillparzer, saddest of poets, whose substance the talent sucked like a very vampire, strikes the same note when he makes his Sappho say: "Und Leben ist ja doch des Lebens höchstes Ziel."[6]

In the two groups of lyrics, *Sunday at Hampstead* and *Sunday up the River*, this intensely human side of the poet comes out in a marked degree; the verses, which show distinctly his kinship with Heine, are so

---

[1] *Romeo and Juliet* 3.1.96–97.

[2] Heinrich Heine, German poet and prose writer (1797–1856), and Italian poet Giacomo Leopardi (1798–1837).

[3] letter from Eliot dated 30 May 1874.

[4] the opening couplet of part 3 of Thomson's "Art."

[5] the concluding couplet.

[6] Franz Grillparzer (1791–1872), Austrian poet and dramatist. Levy quotes his 1817 drama, *Sappho*: "Life is, after all, life's highest aim."

full of sunshine and beauty and a most exquisite love. And here I would remark that as regards love James Thomson desired only the best. In youth he loved a woman. She died early, and he loved her memory till the end of his own life. There is a little poem called "Mater Tenebrarum," not very remarkable for artistic beauty, in which the poet lies sleepless on his bed at night "famished with an uttermost famine for love," which is startling with excess of truth, absolutely rough with pain; we seem to see the blood and sweat on the page as we read.

In the poem called "Our Ladies of Death," the poet stands aloof from the strife; the weary nerves and muscles are for awhile relaxed; he looks around with the wide, sad gaze of deeper knowledge, and asks for nothing save perfect, dreamless rest. It is no longer the passionate rebel against fate, stung to agony by the thousand petty shafts of circumstance, who is speaking; for a moment a voice stronger and fuller issues from the weary lips. Only a few months ago the group gathered round James Thomson's grave and heard these words, the utterance of him they mourned, read out in the dreary grave-yard.

> Weary of erring in this desert life,
> Weary of hoping hopes for ever vain,
> Weary of struggling in all-sterile strife,
> Weary of thought which maketh nothing plain,
> I close my eyes and calm my panting breath,
> And pray to thee, O ever-quiet Death,
> To come and soothe away my bitter pain.[1]

The rest, so long sought, so long desired, had come at last.

And for us, what is there for us to do now that the great agony is over? We read the books of the dead man, close them, and away. They are books over which one wrings the hands in despair. There is so much and yet so little. As we read them, the old question, the old plaint rises to our lips:

> Who shall change with tears and thanksgivings
> The mystery of the cruelty of things?[2]

But there is another question, less vast and vague, though perhaps not much easier to answer, which must occur to us at the same time. How comes it that in a day like our own, when the shrill, small voices of a legion of bepraised versifiers are heard all around— how comes it that this man of such large powers, such truth, such force of passion and intellect, such originality, should have been entirely overlooked for the greater part of his life, and even at its close so scantily recognised? Certainly he lacked one graceful finish of our latter-day bards; the pretty modern-classical trick, the prettier trick of old-French forms were unknown to him. We know that the mingled odours of livery -stables and surgery, said to linger about Keats, have stunk in the nostrils of one fastidious critic.[3] James Thomson, says report, did not speak the Queen's English with the precision that one would desire; it is certain that he began life as an army schoolmaster, and never rose to be anything higher than a commis-voyageur.[4] And it is certain also that here and there in his verse (and very often in his prose) he breaks out into absolute vulgarity— into a nudity of expression which he has neither the wit nor the taste to drape in the garb of ancient Greece or mediaeval France.

Rough and unequal he certainly is, but that he understood the meaning of perfect work he has shown us in the few gem-like translations from Heine, and in some of his own lyrics, written in Heine's vein. And the weird, powerful poem, "In the Room," is almost perfect as it stands.

But even his warmest admirers cannot claim for James Thomson a light touch, a fine taste, a delicate

---

[1] stanza 1 of Thomson's "To Our Ladies of Death."

[2] source unknown.

[3] probably either John Gibson Lockhart or John Wilson Crocker, both severely critical of Keats's work.

[4] a commercial traveller.

wit. "When he laughs," says one critic, "it is a guf-faw." To tell the truth, he is always terribly in earnest. The hot-house emotions of "culture" are entirely unknown to him, and I cannot help thinking that it is because of this very earnestness, this absolute truthfulness of feeling and expression, that James Thomson will take a recognised place among our poets, when the mass of our minor bards shall have been consigned by a ruthless posterity to oblivion.

James Thomson, as we know, died miserably. Respectable people shook their heads over him in death, as they had done in life. It was not to be expected that they could feel much sorrow for a man who, it was averred, had drunk himself to death.

But his few friends speak of the genial and loving spirit; the wit, the chastity, the modesty and tenderness of the dead man. To us, who never saw his face nor touched his living hand, his image stands out large and clear, unutterably tragic: the image of a great mind and a great soul thwarted in their development by circumstance; of a nature struggling with itself and Fate; of an existence doomed to bear a twofold burden.

—1883

James McNeill Whistler
1834 – 1903

One of the most prominent painters of the Victorian era, Whistler was born in Lowell, Massachusetts, and resided in Paris (1855–60), and then London (1869– 1903). Whistler did much to promote the cause of the visual arts, and art in general. The "Ten O'Clock" lecture stresses the primacy of art and the artist.

ოჳო

Ten O'Clock [1]

Ladies and Gentlemen:
It is with great hesitation and much misgiving that I appear before you, in the character of The Preacher.

If timidity be at all allied to the virtue modesty, and can find favour in your eyes, I pray you, for the sake of that virtue, accord me your utmost indulgence.

I would plead for my want of habit, did it not seem preposterous, judging from precedent, that aught save the most efficient effrontery could be ever expected in connection with my subject—for I will not conceal from you that I mean to talk about Art. Yes, Art—that has of late become, as far as much discussion and writing can make it, a sort of common topic for the tea-table.

Art is upon the Town!—to be chucked under the chin by the passing gallant—to be enticed within the gates of the householder—to be coaxed into company, as a proof of culture and refinement.

If familiarity can breed contempt, certainly Art—or what is currently taken for it—has been brought to its lowest stage of intimacy.

The people have been harassed with Art in every guise, and vexed with many methods as to its endurance. They have been told how they shall love Art, and live with it. Their homes have been invaded, their walls covered with paper, their very dress taken to task—until, roused at last, bewildered and filled with the doubts and discomforts of senseless suggestion, they resent such intrusion, and cast forth the false prophets, who have brought the very name of the beautiful into disrepute, and derision upon themselves.

Alas! ladies and gentlemen, Art has been maligned. She has naught in common with such practices. She is a goddess of dainty thought—reticent of habit, abjuring all obtrusiveness, purposing in no way to better others.

She is, withal, selfishly occupied with her own perfection only—having no desire to teach—seeking and finding the beautiful in all conditions and in all times, as did her high priest, Rembrandt, when he saw picturesque grandeur and noble dignity in the Jews' quarter of Amsterdam, and lamented not that its inhabitants were not Greeks.

As did Tintoret and Paul Veronese, among the Venetians, while not halting to change the brocaded silks for the classic draperies of Athens.

As did, at the Court of Philip, Velasquez, whose Infantas, clad in inæsthetic hoops, are, as works of Art, of the same quality as the Elgin marbles.

No reformers were these great men—no improvers of the way of others! Their productions alone were their occupation, and, filled with the poetry of their science, they required not to alter their surroundings—for, as the laws of their Art were revealed to them they saw, in the development of their work,

---

[1] "Ten O'Clock" was originally given as a lecture at St. James' Hall, Piccadilly, in 1885.

that real beauty which, to them, was as much a matter of certainty and triumph as is to the astronomer the verification of the result, foreseen with the light given to him alone. In all this, their world was completely severed from that of their fellow-creatures with whom sentiment is mistaken for poetry; and for whom there is no perfect work that shall not be explained by the benefit conferred upon themselves.

Humanity takes the place of Art, and God's creations are excused by their usefulness. Beauty is confounded with virtue, and, before a work of Art, it is asked: "What good shall it do?"

Hence it is that nobility of action, in this life, is hopelessly linked with the merit of the work that portrays it; and thus the people have acquired the habit of looking, as who should say, not *at* a picture, but *through* it, at some human fact, that shall, or shall not, from a social point of view, better their mental or moral state. So we have come to hear of the painting that elevates, and of the duty of the painter—of the picture that is full of thought, and of the panel that merely decorates.

A favourite faith, dear to those who teach, is that certain periods were especially artistic, and that nations, readily named, were notably lovers of Art.

So we are told that the Greeks were, as a people, worshippers of the beautiful, and that in the fifteenth century Art was engrained in the multitude.

That the great masters lived in common understanding with their patrons—that the early Italians were artists—all—and that the demand for the lovely thing produced it.

That we, of to-day, in gross contrast to this Arcadian purity, call for the ungainly, and obtain the ugly.

That, could we but change our habits and climate—were we willing to wander in groves— could we be roasted out of broadcloth—were we to do without haste, and journey without speed, we should again *require* the spoon of Queen Anne, and pick at our peas with the fork of two prongs. And so, for the flock, little hamlets grow near Hammersmith, and the steam horse is scorned.

Useless! quite hopeless and false is the effort!— built upon fable, and all because "a wise man has uttered a vain thing and filled his belly with the East wind."

Listen! There never was an artistic period.

There never was an Art-loving nation.

In the beginning, man went forth each day— some to do battle, some to the chase; others, again, to dig and to delve in the field—all that they might gain and live, or lose and die. Until there was found among them one, differing from the rest, whose pursuits attracted him not, and so he stayed by the tents with the women, and traced strange devices with a burnt stick upon a gourd.

This man, who took no joy in the ways of his brethren—who cared not for conquest, and fretted in the field—this designer of quaint patterns—this deviser of the beautiful—who perceived in Nature about him curious curvings, as faces are seen in the fire—this dreamer apart, was the first artist.

And when, from the field and from afar, there came back the people, they took the gourd—and drank from out of it.

And presently there came to this man another —and, in time, others—of like nature, chosen by the Gods—and so they worked together; and soon they fashioned, from the moistened earth, forms resembling the gourd. And with the power of creation, the heirloom of the artist, presently they went beyond the slovenly suggestion of Nature, and the first vase was born, in beautiful proportion.

And the toilers tilled, and were athirst; and the heroes returned from fresh victories, to rejoice and to feast; and all drank alike from the artists' goblets, fashioned cunningly, taking no note the while of the craftsman's pride, and understanding not his glory in his work; drinking at the cup, not from choice, not from a consciousness that it was beautiful, but because, forsooth, there was none other!

And time, with more state, brought more capacity for luxury, and it became well that men should dwell in large houses, and rest upon couches, and eat at tables; whereupon the artist, with his artificers, built palaces, and filled them with furniture, beautiful in proportion and lovely to look upon.

And the people lived in marvels of art—and ate and drank out of masterpieces—for there was nothing else to eat and to drink out of, and no bad building to live in; no article of daily life, of luxury, or of necessity, that had not been handed down from the design of the master, and made by his workmen.

And the people questioned not, *and had nothing to say in the matter*.

So Greece was in its splendour, and Art reigned supreme—by force of fact, not by election—and there was no meddling from the outsider. The mighty warrior would no more have ventured to offer a design for the temple of Pallas Athene than would the sacred poet have proffered a plan for constructing the catapult.

And the Amateur was unknown—and the Dilettante undreamed of!

And history wrote on, and conquest accompanied civilisation, and Art spread, or rather its products were carried by the victors among the vanquished from one country to another. And the customs of cultivation covered the face of the earth, so that all peoples continued to use what *the artist alone produced*.

And centuries passed in this using, and the world was flooded with all that was beautiful, until there arose a new class, who discovered the cheap, and foresaw the fortune in the facture of the sham.

Then sprang into existence the tawdry, the common, the gewgaw.

The taste of the tradesman supplanted the science of the artist, and what was born of the million went

back to them, and charmed them, for it was after their own heart; and the great and the small, the statesman and the slave, took to themselves the abomination that was tendered, and preferred it—and have lived with it ever since!

And the artist's occupation was gone, and the manufacturer and the huckster took his place.

And now the heroes filled from the jugs and drank from the bowls—with understanding—noting the glare of their new bravery, and taking pride in its worth.

And the people—this time—had much to say in the matter—and all were satisfied. And Birmingham and Manchester arose in their might—and Art was relegated to the curiosity shop.

Nature contains the elements, in colour and form, of all pictures, as the keyboard contains the notes of all music.

But the artist is born to pick, and choose, and group with science, these elements, that the result may be beautiful—as the musician gathers his notes, and forms his chords, until he bring forth from chaos glorious harmony.

To say to the painter, that Nature is to be taken as she is, is to say to the player, that he may sit on the piano.

That Nature is always right, is an assertion, artistically, as untrue, as it is one whose truth is universally taken for granted. Nature is very rarely right, to such an extent even, that it might almost be said that Nature is usually wrong; that is to say, the condition of things that shall bring about the perfection of harmony worthy a picture is rare, and not common at all.

This would seem, to even the most intelligent, a doctrine almost blasphemous. So incorporated with our education has the supposed aphorism become, that its belief is held to be part of our moral being, and the words themselves have, in our ear, the ring of religion. Still, seldom does Nature succeed in producing a picture.

The sun blares, the wind blows from the east, the sky is bereft of cloud, and without, all is of iron. The windows of the Crystal Palace are seen from all points of London. The holiday-maker rejoices in the glorious day, and the painter turns aside to shut his eyes.

How little this is understood, and how dutifully the casual in Nature is accepted as sublime, may be gathered from the unlimited admiration daily produced by a very foolish sunset.

The dignity of the snow-capped mountain is lost in distinctness, but the joy of the tourist is to recognise the traveller on the top. The desire to see, for the sake of seeing it, is, with the mass, alone the one to be gratified, hence the delight in detail.

And when the evening mist clothes the riverside with poetry, as with a veil, and the poor buildings lose themselves in the dim sky, and the tall chimneys become campanili, and the warehouses are palaces in the night, and the whole city hangs in the heavens, and fairy-land is before us—then the wayfarer hastens home; the working man and the cultured one, the wise man and the one of pleasure, cease to understand, as they have ceased to see, and Nature, who, for once, has sung in tune, sings her exquisite song to the artist alone, her son and her master—her son in that he loves her, her master in that he knows her.

To him her secrets are unfolded, to him her lessons have become gradually clear. He looks at her flower, not with the enlarging lens, that he may gather facts for the botanist, but with the light of the one who sees in her choice selection of brilliant tones and delicate tints, suggestions of future harmonies.

He does not confine himself to purposeless copying, without thought, each blade of grass, as commended by the inconsequent, but, in the long curve of the narrow leaf, corrected by the straight tall stem, he learns how grace is wedded to dignity, how

strength enhances sweetness, that elegance shall be the result.

In the citron wing of the pale butterfly, with its dainty spots of orange, he sees before him the stately halls of fair gold, with their slender saffron pillars, and is taught how the delicate drawing high upon the walls shall be traced in tender tones of orpiment, and repeated by the base in notes of graver hue.

In all that is dainty and lovable he finds hints for his own combinations, and *thus* is Nature ever his resource and always at his service, and to him is naught refused.

Through his brain, as through the last alembic,[1] is distilled the refined essence of that thought which began with the Gods, and which they left him to carry out.

Set apart by them to complete their works, he produces that wondrous thing called the masterpiece, which surpasses in perfection all that they have contrived in what is called Nature; and the Gods stand by and marvel, and perceive how far away more beautiful is the Venus of Melos than was their own Eve.

For some time past, the unattached writer has become the middleman in this matter of Art, and his influence, while it has widened the gulf between the people and the painter, has brought about the most complete misunderstanding as to the aim of the picture.

For him a picture is more or less a hieroglyph or symbol of story. Apart from a few technical terms, for the display of which he finds an occasion, the work is considered absolutely from a literary point of view; indeed, from what other can he consider it? And in his essays he deals with it as with a novel—a history—or an anecdote. He fails entirely and most naturally to see its excellences, or demerits—

---

[1] anything that refines, changes or purifies.

artistic—and so degrades Art, by supposing it a method of bringing about a literary climax.

It thus, in his hands, becomes merely a means of perpetrating something further, and its mission is made a secondary one, even as a means is second to an end.

The thoughts emphasised, noble or other, are inevitably attached to the incident, and become more or less noble, according to the eloquence or mental quality of the writer, who looks the while, with disdain, upon what he holds as "mere execution"—a matter belonging, he believes, to the training of the schools, and the reward of assiduity. So that, as he goes on with his translation from canvas to paper, the work becomes his own. He finds poetry where he would feel it were he himself transcribing the event, invention in the intricacy of the *mise en scène*, and noble philosophy in some detail of philanthropy, courage, modesty, or virtue, suggested to him by the occurrence.

All this might be brought before him, and his imagination be appealed to, by a very poor picture—indeed, I might safely say that it generally is.

Meanwhile, the *painter's* poetry is quite lost to him—the amazing invention that shall have put form and colour into such perfect harmony, that exquisiteness is the result, he is without understanding—the nobility of thought, that shall have given the artist's dignity to the whole, says to him absolutely nothing.

So that his praises are published, for virtues we would blush to possess—while the great qualities, that distinguish the one work from the thousand, that make of the masterpiece the thing of beauty that it is—have never been seen at all.

That this is so, we can make sure of, by looking back at old reviews upon past exhibitions, and reading the flatteries lavished upon men who have since been forgotten altogether—but, upon whose works, the language has been exhausted, in rhapsodies—that left nothing for the National Gallery.

A curious matter, in its effect upon the judgment of these gentlemen, is the accepted vocabulary of poetic symbolism, that helps them, by habit, in dealing with Nature: a mountain, to them, is synonymous with height—a lake, with depth—the ocean, with vastness—the sun, with glory.

So that a picture with a mountain, a lake, and an ocean—however poor in paint—is inevitably "lofty," "vast," "infinite," and "glorious"—on paper.

There are those also, sombre of mien, and wise with the wisdom of books, who frequent museums and burrow in crypts; collecting—comparing—compiling—classifying—contradicting.

Experts these—for whom a date is an accomplishment—a hall-mark, success!

Careful in scrutiny are they, and conscientious of judgment—establishing, with due weight, unimportant reputations—discovering the picture, by the stain on the back—testing the torso, by the leg that is missing—filling folios with doubts on the way of that limb—disputations and dictatorial, concerning the birthplace of inferior persons—speculating, in much writing, upon the great worth of bad work.

True clerks of the collection, they mix memoranda with ambition, and, reducing Art to statistics, they "file" the fifteenth century, and "pigeon-hole" the antique!

Then the Preacher "appointed"!

He stands in high places—harangues and holds forth.

Sage of the Universities—learned in many matters, and of much experience in all, save his subject.

Exhorting—denouncing—directing.

Filled with wrath and earnestness.

Bringing powers of persuasion, and polish of language, to prove—nothing.

Torn with much teaching—having naught to impart.

Impressive—important—shallow.

Defiant—distressed—desperate.

Crying out, and cutting himself—while the gods hear not.

Gentle priest of the Philistine withal, again he ambles pleasantly from all point, and through many volumes, escaping scientific assertion—"babbles of green fields."

So Art has become foolishly confounded with education—that all should be equally qualified.

Whereas, while polish, refinement, culture, and breeding, are in no way arguments for artistic result, it is also no reproach to the most finished scholar or greatest gentleman in the land that he be absolutely without eye for painting or ear for music—that in his heart he prefers the popular print to the scratch of Rembrandt's needle, or the songs of the hall to Beethoven's "C minor Symphony."

Let him have but the wit to say so, and not feel the admission a proof of inferiority.

Art happens—no hovel is safe from it, no Prince may depend upon it, the vastest intelligence cannot bring it about, and puny efforts to make it universal end in quaint comedy, and coarse farce.

This is as it should be—and all attempts to make it otherwise are due to the eloquence of the ignorant, the zeal of the conceited.

The boundary-line is clear. Far from me to propose to bridge it over—that the pestered people be pushed across. No! I would save them from further fatigue. I would come to their relief, and would lift from their shoulders this incubus of Art.

Why, after centuries of freedom from it, and indifference to it, should it now be thrust upon them by the blind—until wearied and puzzled, they know no longer how they shall eat or drink—how they shall sit or stand—or wherewithal they shall clothe themselves—without afflicting Art.

But, lo! there is much talk without!

Triumphantly they cry, "Beware! This matter does indeed concern us. We also have our part in all true Art!—for, remember the 'the one touch of Nature' that 'makes the whole world kin.'"

True, indeed. But let not the unwary jauntily suppose that Shakespeare herewith hands him his passport to Paradise, and thus permits him speech among the chosen. Rather, learn that, in this very sentence, he is condemned to remain without—to continue with the common.

This one chord that vibrates with all—this "one touch of Nature" that calls aloud to the response of each—that explains the popularity of the "Bull" of Paul Potter—that excuses the price of Murillo's "Conception"—this one unspoken sympathy that pervades humanity, is—Vulgarity!

Vulgarity—under whose fascinating influence "the many" have elbowed "the few," and the gentle circle of Art swarms with the intoxicated mob of mediocrity, whose leaders prate and counsel, and call aloud, where the Gods once spoke in whisper!

And now from their midst the Dilettante stalks abroad. The amateur is loosed. The voice of the aesthete is heard in the land, and catastrophe is heard in the land, and catastrophe is upon us.

The meddler beckons the vengeance of the Gods, and ridicule threatens the fair daughters of the land.

And there are curious converts to a weird *culte*, in which all instinct for attractiveness—all freshness and sparkle—all woman's winsomeness—is to give way to a strange vocation for the unlovely—and this desecration in the name of the Graces!

Shall this gaunt, ill-at-ease, distressed, abashed mixture of *mauvaise honte*[1] and desperate assertion call itself artistic, and claim cousinship with the artist—who delights in the dainty, the sharp, the bright gaiety of beauty?

No!—a thousand times no! Here are no connections of ours.

---

[1] "self-consciousness."

We will have nothing to do with them.

Forced to seriousness, that emptiness may be hidden, they dare not smile—

While the artist, in fulness of heart and head, is glad, and laughs aloud, and is happy in his strength, and is merry at the pompous pretension—the solemn silliness that surrounds him.

For Art and Joy go together, with bold openness, and high head, and ready hand—fearing naught, and dreading no exposure.

Know, then, all beautiful women, that we are with you. Pay no heed, we pray you, to this outcry of the unbecoming—this last plea for the plain.

It concerns you not.

Your own instinct is near the truth—your own wit far surer guide than the untaught ventures of thick-heeled Apollos.

What! will you up and follow the first piper that leads you down Petticoat Lane, there, on a Sabbath, to gather, for the week, from the dull rags of ages wherewith to bedeck yourselves? that, beneath your travestied awkwardness, we have trouble to find your own dainty selves? Oh, fie! Is the world, then, exhausted? and must we go back because the thumb of the mountebank jerks the other way?

Costume is not dress.

And the wearers of wardrobes may not be doctors of taste!

For by what authority shall these be pretty masters? Look well, and nothing have they invented —nothing put together for comeliness' sake.

Haphazard from their shoulders hang the garments of the hawker—combining in their person the motley of many manners with the medley of the mummers' closet.

Set up as a warning, and a finger-post of danger, they point to the disastrous effect of Art upon the middle classes.

Why this lifting of the brow in deprecation of the present—this pathos in reference to the past?

If Art be rare to-day, it was seldom heretofore.

It is false, this teaching of decay.

The master stands in no relation to the moment at which he occurs—a monument of isolation —hinting at sadness—having no part in the progress of his fellow-men.

He is also no more the product of civilisation than is the scientific truth asserted dependent upon the wisdom of a period. The assertion itself requires the *man* to make it. The truth was from the beginning.

So Art is limited to the infinite, and beginning there cannot progress.

A silent indication of its wayward independence from all extraneous advance, is in the absolutely unchanged condition and form of implement since the beginning of things.

The painter has but the same pencil—the sculptor the chisel of centuries.

Colours are not more since the heavy hangings of night were first drawn aside, and the loveliness of light revealed.

Neither chemist or engineer can offer new elements of the masterpiece.

False again, the fabled link between the grandeur of Art and the glories and virtues of the State, for Art feeds not upon nations, and peoples may be wiped from the face of the earth, but Art *is*.

It is indeed high time that we cast aside the weary weight of responsibility and co-partnership, and know that, in no way, do our virtues minister to its worth, in no way do our vices impede its triumph!

How irksome! how hopeless! how superhuman the self-imposed task of the nation! How sublimely vain the belief that it shall live nobly or art perish.

Let us reassure ourselves, at our own option is our virtue. Art we in no way affect.

A whimsical goddess, and a capricious, her strong sense of joy tolerates no dulness, and, live we never so spotlessly, still may she turn her back upon us.

As, from time immemorial, she has done upon the Swiss in their mountains.

What more worthy people! Whose every Alpine gap yawns with tradition, and is stocked with noble story; yet, the perverse and scornful one will none of it, and the sons of patriots are left with the clock that turns the mill, and the sudden cuckoo, with difficulty restrained in its box.

For this was Tell a hero! For this did Gessler die!

Art, the cruel jade, cares not, and hardens her heart, and hies her off to the East, to find, among the opium-eaters of Nankin, a favourite with whom she lingers fondly—caressing his blue porcelain, and painting his coy maidens, and marking his plates with her six marks of choice—indifferent in her companionship with him, to all save the virtue of his refinement!

He it is who calls her—he who holds her!

And again to the West, that her next lover may bring together the Gallery at Madrid, and show to the world how the Master[1] towers above all; and in their intimacy they revel, he and she, in this knowledge; and he knows the happiness untasted by other mortal.

She is proud of her comrade, and promises that in after-years, others shall pass that way, and understand.

So in all time does this superb one cast about for the man worthy her love—and Art seeks the Artist alone.

Where he is, there she appears, and remains with him—loving and fruitful—turning never aside in moments of hope deferred—of insult—and of ribald misunderstanding; and when he dies she sadly takes her flight, though loitering yet in the land, from fond association, but refusing to be consoled.[2]

---

[1] Velasquez.

[2] "And so have we the ephemeral influence of the Master's memory—the afterglow, in which are warmed, for a while, the worker and disciple." (Whistler's note.)

With the man, then, and not with the multitude, are her intimacies; and in the book of her life the names inscribed are few—scant, indeed, the list of those who have helped to write her story of love and beauty.

From the sunny morning, when, with her glorious Greek relenting, she yielded up the secret of repeated line, as, with his hand in hers, together they marked in marble, the measured rhyme of lovely limb and draperies flowing in unison, to the day when she dipped the Spaniard's brush in light and air, and made his people live within their frames, and *stand upon their legs*, that all nobility and sweetness, and tenderness, and magnificence should be theirs by right, ages had gone by, and few had been her choice.

Countless, indeed, the horde of pretenders! But she knew them not.

A teeming, seething, busy mass, whose virtue was industry, and whose industry was vice!

Their names go to fill the catalogue of the collection at home, of the gallery abroad, for the delectation of the bagman and the critic.

Therefore have we cause to be merry!—and to cast away all care—resolved that all is well—as it ever was—and that it is not meet that we should be cried at, and urged to take measures!

Enough have we endured of dulness! Surely are we weary of weeping, and our tears have been cozened from us falsely, for they have called out woe! when there was no grief!—and, alas! where all is fair!

We have then but to wait—until, with the mark of the Gods upon him—there come among us again the chosen—who shall continue what has gone before. Satisfied that, even were he never to appear, the story of the beautiful is already complete—hewn in the marbles of the Parthenon—and broidered, with the birds, upon the fan of Hokusai—at the foot of Fusiyama.

—1890

William Morris

1834 – 1896

Educated at Marlborough College (1848–51), and Exeter College, Oxford (1853–56), Morris was the author of prose romances and verse narratives. In addition, he was a pioneering designer, a translator, and a leader of the early British socialist movement. Morris' major works include a volume of lyric and dramatic verse, *The Defence of Guenevere and other Poems* (1858), and *The Earthly Paradise* (1868–70), twenty-four verse narratives derived from classical and medieval tales.

ↄↄↄ

Of the Origins of Ornamental Art [1]

Perhaps it may at first sight seem to some of you that ornamental art is no very important subject, and that it is no great matter what its origins were: but I hope to show you before I have done that it is a subject of very great importance, and that it is well worth while to consider what its origins were, since it may lead us to finding out what its aims are, or should be; which in its turn may lead us to thinking of matters of the deepest importance.

First of all I must say that though the phrase is generally accepted it is not a good or descriptive one; for all art should be ornamental, and when it is not ornamental, and in the degree in which it is not, it fails of a part of its purpose: however, the phrase is used, and understood to mean a certain kind of art other than pictures or sculptures which tell a definite story and are meant to represent according to some standard or another certain facts of external nature.

What then is this body of art which is something different from what we nowadays call pictures and sculpture?

It is the art of the people: the art produced by the daily labour of all kinds of men for the daily use of all kinds of men: surely therefore we may at the outset suppose that it is of importance to the race of man, since on all sides it surrounds our life and our work.

What is the end and aim of human labour? Is it not first the continuance, and next the elevation of the human race? If therefore it has gone astray at any time from its due aim, and no one surely will be so rash as to say that it never has, it has erred in turning its force to the production of things which are not useful either for the continuance or the elevation of the race of man.

Let us consider then what things human labour produces for the service of the world. Broadly speaking they may be divided into two kinds first those which serve the needs of the body, and second those which serve the needs of the mind: such things as food, raiment, and shelter, and the tools for obtaining these on the one hand, and on the other, poetry, music, the stored-up knowledge of the fashion of the universe which we call science, and of the deeds of men on the earth which we call history, and also the pictured representations of that history however wrought.

These two kinds of productions, between them make up the wealth of the world; the things that are made to satisfy the necessities of a healthy body and a healthy mind.

But furthermore the wealth made for the service of the body can again definitely be divided into those things which perish at once in the using, as food and

---

[1] first delivered as a lecture on 24 November 1883, at Eton College. A much revised version, the opening paragraphs of which were probably a reply to Whistler's 1885 "Ten O'Clock," was delivered at Kelmscott House on 19 May 1886. The 1886 lecture, printed here, is from *The Unpublished Lectures of William Morris*, ed. and compiled by Eugene D. Le Mire, Wayne State University Press, 1969.

fuel and the like, and those which are made to last some time and serve our needs day after day or year after year, as raiment and houses and so forth.

Here then you see between the rude arts, whose end is the production of mere food and raw material, and the exalted arts, which should satisfy the cravings of our minds, lies a mass of wealth-producing labour of a special character, which is that side of human labour to which I wish specially to draw your attention tonight; this labour is called in what I should almost venture to name our modern jargon the Industrial Arts.

Now all the things produced by these arts or crafts might be made without any reference to anything but their first obvious use: the house might have been just so many walls and so much roof: so much stone and timber, uncarved, unmoulded, unpainted (except for weather-defense); the cup might have taken the first convenient form it would from the potter's hand; the cloth might have remained undyed, unfigured, and in all this men's bodies would have felt no lack; while their minds would have been free to exercise themselves with music and poetry and pictured images of the past, or with the gathering of the knowledge of what is and what has been.

But men would not have it so; from the very first they have striven to make their household and personal goods beautiful as well as useful; the rudest savage no sooner learns how to make anything than he learns also how to ornament it: before the earliest dawn of history this instinct for ornament existed as clearly as it did in the palmy days of Italian art: as you know implements exist of men who dwelt in Europe ages before any of the races we name now, on which were carved, with no little skill, the forms of the beasts of the forests they wandered in, and in which life must have been so hard and beset with so many dangers that we may well wonder that they had time or courage to think about art: so divine a thing is the spark of human intelligence.

What does all this mean? why did they do it and take all this trouble? Who taught them?

Indeed their teacher is not far to seek: whatever lived or grew about them: nay the mountains, the rocks themselves, the "bones of the earth" as the Northmen called them, had something about them which the must have dimly known for beauty; the things which were useful to them for food and fuel and clothes were ornamented: the day and the night, sunrise and sunset which showed to their dim minds as beings of passions like themselves; the serpent whose lurking malice and swift wrath they feared, and whom they worshipped lest he should slay them: all these had been fashioned fair and lovely by forces of which they knew nothing: and they, the latest-born and maybe the most terrible force of nature, how could they choose but take up the links of the chain and work as nature worked about them: many things she compelled them to, and this also.

This then was the birth of popular or ornamental art, the birth of man's intelligence.

Now the works of art I have just been alluding to belong to times of whose history they alone give us any glimpse, and we can have but a faint idea of anything that might have gone on between those days and the dawn of history, the dawn of civilization: of that dawn itself we know but little indeed, yet are to a certain extent helped out by the consideration of the various backward peoples of our time, some of whom at least one cannot help thinking might have had a chance of developing gradually into a condition somewhat like our past civilization if it had been their doom to be born into the world at a time when civilization has taken the form which it has now; the commercial form, under which all Society rests on a gigantic system of usury, pitiless and implacable, which is prepared to crush out of existence all peoples and communities that cannot speedily adapt themselves to its laws.

However that may be we can learn something from these survivals, if so they be, from the earlier condition of the world joined to the few historical hints we have left of that earlier condition, of the dawn of history: the lesson they teach us as to the growth of popular art seems to me to be something like this: the period is that of a state of things when Society has begun, when every man has had to give up some of his individuality for the sake of the advancement of the whole community: in that community division of labour has begun, though there is none of it—or scarcely any—in each occupation: a man has no longer to be his own provider in everything; the strong and young fare afield to hunt or fish, or herd the beasts of the community, or dig and sow and harvest in the strip of communal tillage, while the weak, the women, and the cripples stay at home to labour at the loom or the wheel, or the stithy.[1] So far at least has the division of labour gone. Now, rough as the hunter's life may be, he will have his joys however fierce and rude in his contention with wind and weather, his stealthy watching and final victory over the quarry: and the herdsman and tiller, although he has to take his share of rough torment from storm and frost and sun, yet has his eyes on beautiful things forever, and his ears often delighted by the multitudinous voice of nature as he goes to and fro through the changes of the year, nursing his hope of the harvest which is to be. With all such men, hunters, fishers, herdsmen, and husbandmen, it was well, and still may be, if they are not oppressed, but are allowed to have their due share of the goods which they have toiled to produce.

But how did it fare with their brethren, who sat within doors, paled by the lack of sun, down-hearted from want of air, with no excitement or promise of victory to stir their blood; surrounded by the blunders, the clumsiness, and the squalor of man instead of the order, deftness, and beauty of nature: hard indeed it seems it must be for them to forego all the brisk life and stir while they sit bowed over the loom

and every minute's work is like that of every other minute, no change or hope but in finishing the web that they may begin another; or to keep for ever moulding the pot of ugly grey or brown clay, no one of which is better or worse than another (unless it be quite spoiled): or to have no aim before them as they begrime themselves in the stithy but to make a knife that will cut like everybody else's knife: it is hard that they should be unwilling martyrs to the comfort of the commonwealth while others were leading a merry life, that they alone should miss the glory of the tales of perils and daring by flood and field, or the shouts [of] laughter that welcome the happy end of the vintage or the harvest. Their case surely must be that they are the slaves of slaves and as they sit at their dull tasks what can they hope for save the night and sleep in which to dream that they have grown strong and warlike, and the masters of such as they are in their waking hours?

Nay it was not so bad as that: whatever burdens folly and tyranny laid upon mankind in those rough times, this burden of dull and wasteful labour, unrelieved by any thought of what might be good in the work itself; unrelieved by any hope of praise for the special excellence of the work, was not laid on the craftsman for many ages, except in the quasi-penal labour which was laid on hostile conquered tribes under the ancient civilizations of Egypt and Mesopotamia; for the most part very different was the tale from the full one I have been telling of: labour found out a solace and a glory for the handicraftsman from the earliest times.

For note, that the goods which the hunter and the husbandman conquered from nature mostly perished in the using, unless they were of the kind that demanded more labour on them to make them useful to man: the hunter despoiled nature of the goods she had already produced; the husbandman helped her or compelled her to yield more than she was willing to yield unhelped or uncompelled; but neither of them created anything and their gettings were consumed in

---

[1] an anvil or forge.

the using, and the fame of them and joy in them died with them: but the craftsman by his labour fashioned something which without him would not have existed at all, and which was destined to last many years, nay for generations even: so that there needed to be no haste nor hurry in his work; he had time to think as he wrought at it, and to what should he entrust his thought for keeping and for communicating to other men rather than to the work which was growing beneath his hands, the thing he was making of whose life he was absolute master: where then was the dullness now? The flowers of the forest might glow in his web and its beast move over it: his imaginings of the tales of the priests and poets might be pictured on the dish or the pot he was fashioning; the sword hilt, the roof beam were no longer dead bronze and wood, but part of his soul made alive forever: and now no day was like another to him: hope was with him when he left his work in the evening that he might mend the day's failure or carry on its success the next day: hope wooed him to his work in the morning and helped him through the day's weariness.

And with all this he was grown to be no longer a slave of slaves, but a master; a man looked upon as better and more useful than the hunter or the tiller of the soil, deserving of plentiful thanks from the community.

And these thanks, the glory for his creations were indeed often his on strange terms, for the type of craftsman was sometimes exalted to the rank of a god swaying the terrible forces of nature forging the bolts of the world ruler, fashioning the furniture of the house of heaven; building the rampart which was to guard for ages the holy city of the younger Gods against the frost and fire giants of the North: but again and not without some countenance even from these older myths (note the lame and crafty Hephaes-

tus[1]) the type falls to the half-malignant and altogether guileful mountain spirit, conquering rather by cunning than force the huge giant and mighty warrior and still fully possessing the gift of miraculous power and creation.

Of course I do not mean to say that the primary intention was to make these craftsman-gods types of labour; Hephaestus, Thor, and Weland[2] had no doubt a wider and simpler origin than that but they received the special characteristics of the literary myths from ideas of handicraft and craftsmen that had been long in men's minds.

Such then it seems to me was the first origin of ornament on wares: not merely an attempt to escape from the wearisomeness of labour, but rather an expression of pleasure in the hope and sense of power and usefulness which men felt in the making of things in the childhood of the world.

Now it has been said, and surely with truth, that those men are the best and usefullest who never altogether throw off their childlike qualities even when they are grown old: and that same maxim I would apply to the race of man as well as to the individuals composing it; and if it were good that it should be so in other matters, and that the mirth and simplicity of earlier ages of the world should yet leave some reflection on our leisure, still more I think it is important that it should be preserved in our working time.

Nor indeed did that pleasure of labour fail man for many ages: I admit indeed that for a long time in the ancient world it was limited and indeed oppressed by the sternness of hieratic art; as notably for many centuries in Egypt, where the marvellous naturalism of its earlier days, in some branches at least, fell under the yoke a stiff though far from

---

[1] the Greek god of fire and patron of handicraftspeople, frequently alluded to in Homer's *Iliad*.

[2] Thor, the god of thunder, war, and strength in Norse mythology, and Weland the smith, a mythological character.

ignoble conventionalism: but even in that period we have enough left us outside the more pompous ornamentation of temples and tombs to show that on many sides art was still free, and labour abundantly illuminated by fancy and invention: much the same may be said of that art which was passed on through the whole of the valleys of Tigris and Euphrates and even extended to Cyprus and other of the islands by the people or peoples of Babylonia, and of which happy accident has preserved so many specimens in ruin mounds of Assyria: the pleasure of the artists who wrought the bas-reliefs for Assur-bani-pal at Koycinjik is too obvious [in] the shapes of animals at least [for] it to need many words from me here.[1]

The freer peoples who formed what was then the northern and western hem of civilization were as a matter of course less oppressed in their art by hieratic conventionalism, though they were not, nor indeed needed to be, wholly free from it: under the classical peoples of antiquity popular art had to run another danger of slavery, which in truth it did not wholly escape.

In popular art the expression of man's thoughts by his hand does for the most part fall far short of thoughts themselves; and this always the more as the race is nobler and the thought more exalted; in short all the more as the art, as popular art, is more worth having, as there is more hope of continued life and progress in it: I mean that between the rough, speedily-penciled work on a piece of archaic Greek pottery, or the shorthand for a field of flowers of the Persian weaver, or the rough stone-cutting, half-pathetic, half-humorous, of the mediaeval mason, between these things and the highly finished and, in its way, perfect ingenuity of a piece of Japanese drawing or lacquer, there is a whole world of difference, the real worth being on the side of the clumsier expression of the historic workman.

---

[1] a reference to the sculptured slabs depicting the lion hunting of King Assur-banipal, King of Assyria (c. 668–630 BC).

Now for a long while among the Greek and kindred peoples, art was wholly in the condition of its thought being far greater than its expression, deft and graceful (as amongst early art) that expression was: then came a period when the technical excellence (of the truest kind) advanced with wonderful speed; the standard of excellence in expression grew very high, and the feeling of a people cultivated very highly within narrow limits began to forbid any attempt at expression of thought which did not approach within the limits prescribed something like perfection: no man must attempt to do anything which he cannot do in such a way that it is almost impossible to pick a hole in its technical qualities: thus art was in the palmy days of the classic times divided strictly into a great expressive art practiced only by those who had mastered the means of expression, and a very limited ornamental art which was but an adjunct to the higher kind and in which there was nothing to express but complete submission to certain limited and well-known rules of proportion: such a state of things among a less gifted people would have gone far towards destroying art altogether; but among the Greeks this aristocracy of art was so numerous as to give us an impression at this distance of time of a great popular art existing among them; and doubtless the rules of art must have been unconsciously so well understood among the population, that what is called nowadays bad taste did not exist among them at all; a condition of art the easier to be brought about because of the great simplicity of the life they led in which what we now call luxury made no part.

Nevertheless you must understand that perfect as their art was it was barbarously and oppressively limited in scope, going step by step indeed with their social conditions the foundation of which was mere chattel slavery: when all is said what a mass of expression of human thought, what a world of beauty that exclusiveness shut out from the light of day. Absolute perfection in art is a vain hope; the day will never come when the hand of man can thoroughly express the best of the thoughts of man. Why then should we deprive ourselves therefore of all the fancy and imagination that lies in the aim of so many men of lesser capacity than that of great masters? Is it not better to say to all who have any genuine gifts however small, "courage! it is enough for a work of art if it show real skill of hand, genuine instinct for beauty, and some touch of originality; cooperation will show you how your smaller gifts may be used along with the greater ones."

Well the aristocratic exclusiveness of Greek art drew on it a heavy revenge enough: I have spoken of its first period during which the worth of its thought outwent its power of expression, and of its second, when the expression having reached a point approaching perfection, the exuberance of thought in it had to be repressed to satisfy the exclusive fastidiousness of the Greek mind: there remains yet a third period during which capacity of expression having reached its highest point could go no further, and when there was comparatively little to express by this perfected means, and the classical art was become academical and in fact all but dead.

By this time all domination had long passed away from the Greek name, and the Roman tax gatherer ruled the world of civilization; after a while more by the terror of the name of Rome than by any real power in the state: lower and lower fell the art which the Romans adopted from the Greeks, till at last it was redeemed from contempt only by the splendour, massiveness, and honest building of its great architectural and engineering works. In the meanwhile the great change drew near: the Roman landlords had turned all the people of civilization into their agricultural slaves, their hired servants and parasites, and the proletariat of the great cities who were fed on their bounty: before the operation was quite complete the state of things so brought about seemed likely to last for ever: for where was the foe to overturn it? But by the time it was complete the foe was at hand ready

for its destruction: for the Roman had reckoned without his host: he had subdued all civilization and made it his private slave; and now he found that whatever was respectable and desired the preservation of society would not fight; whereas whatever was against him and the stability of society, the starving slaves, the Christians, the barbarians of the East and the North were valiant and aggressive and were ready at every point to push forward what he considered anarchy and the disruption of the world, but which was at the worst the Medea's[1] caldron from which a new and vigorous Europe was to be born again: with that new birth of society, and faithfully following every stage of its fruitful death and change, a new art also was born: this art was at first clad in the body of the effete art which it took the place of; but yet was from the first startlingly different from it in soul and intention: as time went on it borrowed elements from the East and the North, and drew them together and moulded them into the Greco-Roman mass which was already revivified, and little by little the classical wrappings fell off from it, and left clear the strange and beautiful body of Byzantine art, the art of early Europe—of the time when feudality was shaping itself from the chaos of the ruins of old Rome.

From that city of New Rome it spread far and wide varying at first but little except as the materials in which it was wrought influenced it by their fineness or rudeness: in Sicily, Egypt, Spain, Persia it was modified by distinct eastern elements, all of them it seems referable to that art of the East which was carried wide about by the Arabs but was by no means Arab in origin but Persian rather: this influence abode with it and afterwards reacted strongly on the art of central and northern Europe which was born more directly of old or New Rome.

In the extreme North and Northwest of Europe it met with another modifying element in the shape of the Celtic or more probably pre-Celtic art, which

---

[1] a sorceress in Greek legend.

existed pure in Ireland, somewhat changed in England and Scandinavia by Teutonic translation: between this art, the representative of primitive ornamentation and the elaborate fretwork of Eastern art there is a certain sort of relationship; so that it might be doubted whether the complete ornament of the Middle-Ages does not owe some of its forms to this probably pre-Aryan art of Europe: but I think in fact that except in Scandinavia in the modified form above-mentioned its influence on Mediaeval art was not abiding, the equally elaborate but more logical and measured forms of the East taking its place.

However this may be it is certain that the great and in the main homogeneous art of the Middle Ages was both in form and in spirit a simple and direct development of the new-born art which sprang from the corrupt though still beautiful remains of Greco-Roman art; and it is to my mind certain also that it owed the form of that new birth to the incoming of Eastern or Persian ideas and handiwork which acted on it in a way not easy to trace I admit: that mingled art as I have said was still more permeated in some parts by the Eastern element, and in that condition in the 12th century especially was very powerful in fashioning Mediaeval art into what it presently became: nevertheless I cannot help recognizing a certain fitness about the name Gothic for indicating the work of the Middle Ages, though at first it may seem an absurd misnomer born of the hasty glance the antiquaries of our grandfather's time took of an art which they despised and were ignorant of. For besides that the Goths were as it were the iron of the spear that slew the Roman Empire, and from the most righteous slaying sprang Gothic Art; there is obvious in it, nay the very soul of it is that spirit of the North which makes us what we are at the best: the wild imagination, the love of nature, the scorn of pedantry, and stilted pompousness; the genuine, unashamed sentiment, and all this tempered by plenteous good humour and a love of homely and familiar things; a courage in short which is not

anxious to thrust anything which is human out of sight even in the most solemn times and places: these are the characteristics of Gothic art which pierce to the very heart of all those who are capable of feeling that manly love of man and his fair earthly home which is of all things that which most makes life worth living.

And now understand that that which makes Gothic art all this is its *freedom:* it was above all things the art of the people; the art of cooperation: no craftsman, who is a real one, is despised in it; there is room for every mind and every hand that belongs to a real man: something to express and some means of expressing it are all that is asked for: all the time this art lasts no handicraft lacks beauty for a moment, nor is anyone set to dull and slavish toil: things grow beautiful under the workman's hands without effort it would seem, and men do not know how to make an ugly thing: nowadays when we light on a piece of the household goods of this period we pay vast sums of money for it and treasure it up in a museum; for it teaches us—*us* who know everything else, this rough piece of handiwork done by an artisan who thought that the world was like a flat dish and that the sun went round the rim of it.

If this seems strange to you, let me remind you of one kind of work wrought by these craftsmen, which is both more accessible and more impressive than their moveable household goods: I mean the buildings which are [our] forefathers' and among some of which it is your rare good fortune to live: a good fortune which I hope will leave its impress in many an hour of sweet, indestructible pleasure on the future lives of every one of you.

Indeed they have had a hard time of it those ancient buildings of England raised once in such hope by the "Famous men and the fathers that begat us":[1] pious and religious people battered and half destroyed them; not understanding that the spirit

---

[1] Ecclesiastes 44:1.

which raised them was the essence of all religions: those who fought for our liberties blindly looked upon them as the strongholds of slavery and gave over their precious stones, the work of valiant souls and free hands, to the titled thieves who stole the public lands of England: The pedant of the 18th century, anti-poetical, ignorant of history, supposing that no art could exist outside the middle of the classical period, despised them, botched them, degraded them: the pedant of today, self-sufficient, the slave of money, ignorant he also of that real history which is no dead thing, but the living bond of the hopes of the past, the present, and the future, believes that from his study or his office he can re-create past times, and without a word of sympathy or a day of education can get from the machine-driven workman of today work like that of the free crafts-master of the Middle Ages: he while I speak is still busy in destroying the last remnants of our fathers' handicraft, and maybe he is the last as he is certainly the worst enemy they have had.

Yes even such a storm of folly and greed has swept continually over these glorious works into which was once builded the very soul of England: yet in spite of it all there they stand yet a token of the hope that was, and yet shall be the freedom and honour of labour. Bare as they have been stripped, wounded and patched up as they have been can we even think of them without being moved at the energy of co-operative art which reared them in a rude age by the hands of a scanty population?

For I say that glorious as they are in themselves they do betoken something more glorious still: for remember they do but represent the kind of building which was used throughout the country: when your chapel rose in its splendour there was not a cottage or a shed even on the way between Windsor and London which did not share in its beauty, humble as it might be. Now think what this means; we are so used to houses being generally ugly that it is difficult to imagine, every house for instance in London or the

suburbs more or less beautiful; not a chandler's shop at Hammersmith or Brixton but what was a work of art: there would be education for you: education which no books could give; amusement and happiness, to the builders as well as to the occupiers of such houses that no accumulation of wealth can now give to any richest man amongst us.

And I must tell you that if we have not this it is because we do not desire it: when we do desire it, and are ready to sacrifice greed and injustice for it we shall have this also as well as justice and goodwill between man and man.

Meanwhile you see I have taken you a long way from that first dawn of popular art: centuries we cannot count lie between the day when the cave-abider scratched his drawing of a mammoth on a mammoth's bone, and the day when the English masons and wood-carvers struck the last stroke before the Reformation at St. George's Chapel yonder. During all those ages whenever we catch a glimpse of the life of the people we find the popular arts progressive on the whole, and seldom failing in their first aim of lightening the toil of man by giving him pleasure in his daily work.

A long lapse of years indeed, while from the time when Sir Tho[ma]s More wrote his eloquent attack on commercialism and land-grabbing[1] till now, the days are few, the time short: but what has happened to popular art in that short while? What has happened to the popular arts I say in those three hundred years of struggle, mostly successful, for religious and political liberty; in those centuries of miraculous progress, during which England has grown from a semi-barbarous island kingdom into a mighty empire, the master of the minds of men as well as of their bodies?

I can tell you in three words what has happened to those arts: they have disappeared.

That is a strange story indeed and you may well

[1] The "attack" appears in Book I of *Utopia*.

doubt its truth, the change is so tremendous: but my whole opinion is this; to have popular art, or the art of the people, it must be made by and for the people, which means as I have said that man's handiwork is universally beautiful to the eye and elevating to the mind. But such art as pretends to be popular nowadays, do the hands and minds of the people fashion it? Do the people use it? Is the people rejoiced with the making and the using of it?

So far is this from being the case, that the people does not even know that such art exists or ever has existed; what pretence there is of Decorative Art is little touched by the people's hands, and not at all by their minds: they work at it not knowing what they do; like all other toilers nowadays their work is a grievous burden to them which they would cast off if they could. We cannot help knowing that not another hour's work would be done on the Decorative Arts today if it were not that the workers feared death by starvation if they left their work.

I hope you do not suppose that on these terms of labour you can have an art which has any life in it: if you do you are dreaming and will have rude awakening some day: meantime you well know what vast sums of money rich people will spend to isolate themselves from the tokens of increasing population, from the hovels in short which are being raised with such frightful speed all over civilized countries; and I do not wonder; if I were rich I should do the same myself; I should try to escape from the consequences of the system which had made me rich.

For when it comes to explaining why the labour on which depends the well-being of the arts or in other words the pleasure of life is in its present condition of slavishness I must tell you that since the 15th century a great change has taken place in the social condition of the people at large, which some people ignore, and which more still are contented with as a positive gain, and which they believe has brought the world of civilization into a social state which will endure as long as the world itself.

It would be impossible within the limits of such a lecture as this to show by what gradual means this change took place; to show how the chattel slavery of the classical times melted into the serfdom of the early Feudal period; how from those serfs were gradually developed the burgesses or corporations of the mediaeval towns, the yeomen and labourers of the fields, and the craftsmen of the guilds, which classes together with the feudal lords formed the society of the later Middle Ages: it will be enough for our present purpose to state that throughout the middle ages although there was a sharp distinction between the feudal lord and his inferior that distinction was rather arbitrary than real; that difficult, and except by means of ecclesiastical preferment almost impossible as it was to pass from one grade of society to another, there was no class which was by virtue of its position refined, and none which was mentally degraded by the same virtue: at the same time although in the later middle ages this hierarchical system had reached the inside of the craftguilds, and the craftsmen were divided into the privileged masters, with their privileged apprentices, and the journeymen who were unprivileged, there was no division of labour inside the guilds save that which arose from the learning of the craft: every full-instructed workman was master of his whole craft.

Neither outside the guilds was there any violent competition in buying and selling: the greater part of the goods made by the craftsmen were made for home consumption, and only the overplus of this came into the market: it was necessary therefore for the very existence of the craftsman that he should be skillful, intelligent, and thoughtful; nor was he driven by the exigencies of the competitive market which might demand cheapness from him at the cost of other qualities to forego the leisurely way of working which alone can produce a work of art: the universal spread of art made people good judges of wares and keen marketers moreover and cheap and nasty was in no demand.

Such I say was the condition of the artisan in the middle ages; it may be allowed that he was politically oppressed, superstitious, and ignorant—but he was an artist or free workman, using his brains for the pleasure and the solace of his working hours.

Passing over the gradual process which has changed him from what he was in the 15th century to what he is today let us look at the contrast of his position then and now, and glance at the state of Society which has produced it.

For in these days the system of hierarchical society has given place to a Society founded on what is called (miscalled I think) the system of free contract. Licence of competition almost complete has taken the place of the attempts to regulate life in accordance with a priori ideas of the duties men owe to one another. The distinctions between the classes [are] merged now into one distinction, that between rich and poor, or gentleman and non-gentleman: there is no insuperable bar to prevent a member of the poor or non-gentleman class rising into the rich or gentleman class: nay the thing is done every day, and in two generations the offspring of the person who has climbed up that ladder between rich and poor may become the equal of the greatest families of the Feudal aristocracy, most of whom, to say the truth have very slender pretentions to representing the families whose titles they bear: moreover there is felt to be no difference in cultivation and refinement between the titled gentry and the rich capitalists or their hangers-on of the professional classes: they are all gentlemen together, even when the latter are scarcely as well-to-do as some of the best-off of the lower classes.

On the other hand there is the great class of working men, among whom there is certainly great diversity as regards their wages, some of them as aforesaid earning as much as or more than *when they are at work* the poorer gentlemen; but whatever their grades may be as regards their money fortune they are all non-gentlemen, and do differ really and not conventionally from the class of gentlemen: their education, their leisure, their refinement, their religion is weighed in a different balance from [that] of the gentleman, nay they do not even speak the same dialect of the mother-tongue as he does: they are in all respects the lower classes, really and not conventionally I say, so that a working man is not fit company for a gentleman, or a gentleman for a working man.

Now this class division of the 19th century as opposed to that of the 14th was brought about by the gradual development of the system of commerce which is now complete or nearly so; the system as I said of unlimited licence of competition which supplanted the mediaeval system under which life was regulated by a conception of the duties men owed to each other and to the unseen powers.

I will not tonight give you any direct opinion as to the operation on the other sides of life of these two systems, but I am compelled by my subject to state to you that the effect of this change on popular or decorative art has been to destroy it.

This gulf between the rich and poor which is in fact a gulf between civilized and uncivilized people living in the same state and under laws nominally the same, this is the gulf which has swallowed up the popular arts; the art which raised our ancient buildings here and elsewhere, and under which every man's intelligence, were it great or small, was used and subordinated at once for the creation of a great work of art: whereas now it is accepted as a fact that whatever intelligence one of the non-gentleman class may possess is not and cannot be exercised during his working hours: in order to win that privilege he must raise himself out of his own class and become a gentleman.

Now the essence or soul of popular art is the due and worthy delight of each worker in his own handiwork, a delight which he feels he can communicate to other people, as it has been communicated to him by the thoughts of many generations of men under the name of Tradition.

If any of you care about art in any form I am sure you will allow that this reciprocal pleasure of communication is always present at the birth of a work of art: when you have been listening for instance to a beautiful piece of music could you possibly suppose that it was an irksome task to invent the sounds which were filling your whole soul with satisfaction or when you have been reading some beautiful passage of poetry, could you suppose that the strong and melodious words which were elevating your souls and opening new worlds to you, had been given forth from the writer's brain in a dull and pleasureless mood? Surely it is impossible that it should be so.

Yet remember, the artist's, the musician's, the poet's work is not easy, it is real labour enough unless he is a pretender: there are traps and pitfalls on the right hand and on the left into which his hope of creating a work of art may fall, and against which even the best man has to be laboriously on his guard: I say he is a workman or no artist: and on those grounds I claim some share of the divine pleasure of creation which accompanies it for all handicraftsmen, believing firmly that the making-good of this claim is a necessity for the world, if civilization is to be anything else than a name. For first, unless this claim is allowed and acted on, unless it is insisted upon as a necessary part of the organization of Society, it must be the *rule* that all things made by man for the use of his daily life will be ugly and base, will show wherever they are placed as mere blots on the beautiful face of the world.

And 2nd it will surely be but right and just that they should be ugly and base, for so done they will be but tokens of the enduring sorrow and slavery of the great mass of mankind: for all people not dishonest must work, and in one way or other their working hours must be the most important part of their lives: if therefore they have due hope, pleasure, and honour in their daily work their lives will on the whole be happy, if they lack that hope pleasure and honour their lives will be unhappy. It would therefore be unjust that art should come from the unhappy lives of the most of men: or in other words that the great mass of people should toil miserably for the pleasure of a few dishonest people.

Fortunately, you see, as far as the arts go that cannot be; it is a question of art and the happiness of the worker, or lack of art and his unhappiness.

In these days, then, in which man has obtained so much domination over the forces of nature, in which so much of what passes for wealth produced, in which Society taken as a whole either is or could be so rich: in these days what are the conditions of life for the working classes, that is to say for most men which would produce beauty and happiness for the world?

1st no honest or industrious man must be under Fear of poverty: the sordid troubles which this fear produces destroy imagination and intelligence, or turn them into other channels than the hope of giving *pleasure* to the world: every man therefore must be certain of earning a due livelihood, by which word I understand all things necessary for his mind as well as his body.

2nd all men must have due leisure: rest for body and mind; time for following according to their bent other occupations than the mere bread-winning one even if it be pleasant: and if their bread-winning work is of such a rough nature as of necessity to lack art or expression of pleasure in it, the daily hours of such labour must be *very* short.

3rd it follows from this last remark that all work in which art, or pleasure, is impossible should be done without as far as may be, that it should be looked on as a nuisance to be abated, a sickness of Society; as far as possible it should be done by machines: and machines should never be used for doing work in which men can take pleasure: whereas at present, as we all know too well, men do the work of machines, and machines of men—both disastrously.

4th those who are to produce beauty must live amidst beauty: their homes and surroundings must be clean, orderly, and in a word beautiful: this *should* be no hard matter to accomplish since the whole world is beautiful save where man has made it ugly.

5th all men should be educated, and have their due share in the stored-up knowledge of the world, so vastly greater now than in the days of art, but so much more unequally shared. All men I say should be educated not down to their "station in life" as people call it, that is according to the amount of money their parents may have, but according to their capacity.

6th when all these claims are allowed and acted on the last claim I make for labour will come of itself: that is, that there should be an end of class distinctions: that is to say that all crafts should be honourable and honoured, and that every man should be able to rise to eminence and fame by the exercise of his own craft, the work he understands best; whereas at present he can only rise to eminence by deserting his craft, by taking an undue share of the wealth of the world as wages for doing lighter work than his fellows; by becoming a capitalist as the phrase goes.

I will now sum up these conditions briefly: 1st extinction of poverty; 2nd leisure; 3rd avoidance of wasteful work; 4th care of the beauty of the earth; 5th education according to capacity, and 6th abolition of class distinctions, real, mind you, not formal.

To my mind these are the conditions of life for working men, or really for all men, under which we can have in these days once more popular art, or a happy life for most men. Is it worth while to strive to bring about this happy life? If it be, can we say that the price to be paid for it can be too high, whatever it may be?

You will have understood if you have followed my statement of the due conditions of labour that in my belief that price is the reconstruction of Society; for no mere palliatives of the evils of the present system will bring about those conditions. Furthermore I admit that such a great change would involve the sacrifice from many of us of things now much cherished: yet as I believe that those who uphold the present conditions of labour on the grounds of self-interest do so rather from stupidity than malice, so I think that their loss, or punishment, if you will, will be rather imaginary [than] real when the change comes: I think what we shall chiefly have to sacrifice will be the encumbrances, the troubles, the sorrows even which we now cherish as part of our wealth.

As to the means by which the Reconstruction is to be brought about, I must for more than one reason say nothing of them tonight; save this: that you yourselves in one way or other will as time goes on have offered to you opportunities of helping forward or of hindering that reconstruction; times when you will have to choose between the right hand and the left, and to range yourselves for or against the progress of the race of man: such chances are solemn times in the history of every man and it behooves us when we meet them to choose not influenced by our apparent self-interest but by our real sense of right and wrong: you may think that but a truism; yet I must tell you that in such matters it is the commonest thing to be said to anyone who thinks he ought to join some movement for the bettering of his fellows, "what will *you* do if this change happens": to my mind it is manhood and not rashness to answer such an objection by saying, what shall I do? Why have my fair share like my fellows.

I believe the time is at hand when each one of us of the well-to-do and rich classes will have to choose whether he will strive to have the great mass of men his equals and friends, or to keep them down as his slaves: when that time comes may we all remember this, that wretched and shameful as is the condition of a slave, there is one condition more wretched and shameful still—that of slave-holder.

—1969 (LECTURE 1886)

Oscar Wilde
1854 – 1900

Oscar Wilde was born in Ireland, attended Trinity College, Dublin, and graduated from Oxford in 1878. Wilde was an adherent of the "art for art's sake" movement (see Walter Pater), a position articulated in the essay, "The Critic as Artist" (1890). His major works include *The Picture of Dorian Gray* (1890), essays such as

"The Soul of Man Under Socialism" (1891), and a number of plays such as *Lady Windermere's Fan* (1892), *Salomé* (1894), and *The Importance of Being Earnest* (1895). Wilde's homosexuality led to a series of trials and in 1895 he was sentenced to two years in jail. He died in Paris.

❧❧❧

The Critic as Artist

With Some Remarks upon the
Importance of Doing Nothing

A DIALOGUE

PART I. PERSONS: *Gilbert and Ernest.*
SCENE: *the library of a house in Piccadilly, overlooking the Green Park.*

GILBERT: (*at the Piano*) My dear Ernest, what are you laughing at?

ERNEST: (*looking up*) At a capital story that I have just come across in this volume of Reminiscences that I have found on your table.

GILBERT: What is the book? Ah! I see. I have not read it yet. Is it good?

ERNEST: Well, while you have been playing, I have been turning over the pages with some amusement, though, as a rule, I dislike modern memoirs. They are generally written by people who have either entirely lost their memories, or have never done anything worth remembering; which, however, is, no doubt, the true explanation of their popularity, as the English public always feels perfectly at ease when a mediocrity is talking to it.

GILBERT: Yes: the public is wonderfully tolerant. It forgives everything except genius. But I must confess that I like all memoirs. I like them for their form, just

as much as for their matter. In literature mere egotism is delightful. It is what fascinates us in the letters of personalities so different as Cicero and Balzac, Flaubert and Berlioz, Byron and Madame de Sévigné.[1] Whenever we come across it, and, strangely enough, it is rather rare, we cannot but welcome it, and do not easily forget it. Humanity will always love Rousseau[2] for having confessed his sins, not to a priest, but to the world, and the couchant nymphs that Cellini[3] wrought in bronze for the castle of King Francis, the green and gold Perseus,[4] even, that in the open Loggia at Florence[5] shows the moon the dead terror that once turned life to stone, have not given it more pleasure than has that autobiography in

---

[1] Marcus Tullius Cicero (106–43 BC), the great Roman orator; Honoré de Balzac (1799–1850), celebrated French realist novelist; Gustave Flaubert (1821–80), French novelist; Hector Berlioz (1803–69), one of the central figures in French romantic music, who supplemented his earnings as a musician with his work as a critic and writer; Lord Byron (1788–1824), Romantic poet; Madame de Sévigné (1626–96), French writer and lady of fashion.

[2] Jean Jacques Rousseau (1712–78), the Swiss-French philosopher and political theorist who played a central role in the French Enlightenment, and helped shape nineteenth-century Romanticism by influencing such figures as Kant and Goethe.

[3] Benvenuto Cellini (1500–71), Florentine goldsmith and sculptor.

[4] Son of Zeus and Danae, he succeeded in beheading the Gorgon Medusa, and won Andromeda's hand in marriage when he destroyed the sea-monster threatening to devour her. Upon his death he was placed in the sky as a constellation by the goddess Athena.

[5] built between 1352–58 by Alberto Arnoldi, sculptor and architect. A "loggia" is an arcaded gallery.

which the supreme scoundrel of the Renaissance relates the story of his splendour and his shame. The opinions, the character, the achievements of the man, matter very little. He may be a sceptic like the gentle Sieur de Montaigne,[1] or a saint like the bitter son of Monica,[2] but when he tells us his own secrets he can always charm our ears to listening and our lips to silence. The mode of thought that Cardinal Newman[3] represented—if that can be called a mode of thought which seeks to solve intellectual problems by a denial of the supremacy of the intellect—may not, cannot, I think, survive. But the world will never weary of watching that troubled soul in its progress from darkness to darkness. The lonely church at Littlemore, where "the breath of the morning is damp, and worshippers are few," will always be dear to it, and whenever men see the yellow snapdragon blossoming on the wall of Trinity they will think of that gracious undergraduate who saw in the flower's sure recurrence a prophecy that he would abide for ever with the Benign Mother of his days—a prophecy that Faith, in her wisdom or her folly, suffered not to be fulfilled. Yes; autobiography is irresistible. Poor, silly, conceited Mr. Secretary Pepys[4] has chattered his way into the circle of the Immortals, and, conscious that indiscretion is the better part of valour, bustles about among them in that "shaggy purple gown with gold buttons and looped lace" which he is so fond of describing to us, perfectly at his ease, and prattling, to his own and our infinite pleasure, of the Indian blue petticoat that he bought for his wife, of the "good hog's harslet," and the "pleasant French fricassee of veal" that he loved to eat, of his game of bowls with Will Joyce, and his "gadding after beauties," and his reciting of *Hamlet* on a Sunday, and his playing of the viol on week days, and other wicked or trivial things. Even in actual life egotism is not without its attractions. When people talk to us about others they are usually dull. When they talk to us about themselves they are nearly always interesting, and if one could shut them up, when they become wearisome, as easily as one can shut up a book of which one has grown wearied, they would be perfect absolutely.

ERNEST: There is much virtue in that If, as Touchstone[5] would say. But do you seriously propose that every man should become his own Boswell?[6] What would become of our industrious compilers of Lives and Recollections in that case?

GILBERT: What has become of them? They are the pest of the age, nothing more and nothing less. Every great man nowadays has his disciples, and it is always Judas who writes the biography.

ERNEST: My dear fellow!

GILBERT: I am afraid it is true. Formerly we used to canonise our heroes. The modern method is to vulgarise them. Cheap editions of great books may be delightful, but cheap editions of great men are absolutely detestable.

ERNEST: May I ask, Gilbert, to whom you allude?

GILBERT: Oh! To all our second-rate *littérateurs*. We are overrun by a set of people who, when poet or painter passes away, arrive at the house along with the undertaker, and forget that their one duty is to behave as mutes. But we won't talk about them. They are the mere body-snatchers of literature. The dust is given to one, and the ashes to another, and the soul is out of their reach. And now, let me play Chopin[7]

---

[1] Michel Seigneur de Montaigne (1533–92), French essayist who was the initiator and most accomplished master of the essay as a modern literary form.

[2] St. Augustine (354–430): "The bitter son of Monica."

[3] English prelate and writer, John Henry Cardinal Newman (1801–90). The allusions to Newman's early years refer to and paraphrase his celebrated spiritual autobiography, *Apologia pro Vita Sua* (1864).

[4] Samuel Pepys (1633–1703), English public official and author of the renowned English *Diary*.

[5] the jocular clown in Shakespeare's *As You Like It*.

[6] James Boswell (1740–95), Scottish author of *The Life of Samuel Johnson* (1791).

[7] Frédéric François Chopin (1810–49), Franco-Polish composer.

to you, or Dvořák?[1] Shall I play you a fantasy by Dvořák? He writes passionate, curiously-coloured things.

ERNEST: No; I don't want music just at present. It is far too indefinite. Besides, I took the Baroness Bernstein down to dinner last night, and, though absolutely charming in every other respect, she insisted on discussing music as if it were actually written in the German language. Now, whatever music sounds like, I am glad to say that it does not sound in the smallest degree like German. There are forms of patriotism that are really quite degrading. No; Gilbert, don't play any more. Turn round and talk to me. Talk to me till the white-horned day comes into the room. There is something in your voice that is wonderful.

GILBERT (*rising from the piano*): I am not in a mood for talking to-night. I really am not. How horrid of you to smile! Where are the cigarettes? Thanks. How exquisite these single daffodils are! They seem to made of amber and cool ivory. They are like Greek things of the best period. What was the story in the confessions of the remorseful Academician[2] that made you laugh? Tell it to me. After playing Chopin, I feel as if I had been weeping over sins that I had never committed, and mourning over tragedies that were not my own. Music always seems to me to produce that effect. It creates for one a past of which one has been ignorant, and fills one with a sense of sorrows that have been hidden from one's tears. I can fancy a man who had led a perfectly commonplace life, hearing by chance some curious piece of music, and suddenly discovering that his soul, without his being conscious of it, had passed through terrible experiences, and known fearful joys, or wild romantic loves, or great renunciations. And so tell me this story, Ernest. I want to be amused.

ERNEST: Oh! I don't know that it is of any importance. But I thought it a really admirable illustration of the true value of ordinary art-criticism. It seems that a lady once gravely asked the remorseful Academician, as you call him, if his celebrated picture of "A Spring-day at Whiteley's," or "Waiting for the Last Omnibus," or some subject of that kind, was all painted by hand?

GILBERT: And was it?

ERNEST: You are quite incorrigible. But, seriously speaking, what is the use of art-criticism? Why cannot the artist be left alone, to create a new world if he wishes it, or, if not, to shadow forth the world which we already know, and of which, I fancy, we would each one of us be wearied if Art, with her fine spirit of choice and delicate instinct of selection, did not, as it were, purify it for us, and give to it a momentary perfection. It seems to me that the imagination spreads, or should spread, a solitude around it, and works best in silence and in isolation. Why should the artist be troubled by the shrill clamour of criticism? Why should those who cannot create take upon themselves to estimate the value of creative work? What can they know about it? If a man's work is easy to understand, an explanation is unnecessary....

GILBERT: And if his work is incomprehensible, an explanation is wicked.

ERNEST: I did not say that.

GILBERT: Ah! but you should have. Nowadays, we have so few mysteries left to us that we cannot afford to part with one of them. The members of the Browning Society, like the theologians of the Broad Church Party,[3] or the authors of Mr. Walter Scott's Great Writers Series, seem to me to spend their time in trying to explain their divinity away. Where one had hoped that Browning was a mystic they have sought to show that he was simply inarticulate. Where one had fancied that he had something to

---

[1]   Antonín Dvořák (1841–1904), Czech composer.

[2]   not identified; almost certainly a Wildean spoof.

[3]   a liberal Anglican party.

conceal, they have proved that he had but little to reveal. But I speak merely of his incoherent work. Taken as a whole the man was great. He did not belong to the Olympians, and had all the incompleteness of the Titan.[1] He did not survey, and it was but rarely that he could sing. His work is marred by struggle, violence and effort, and he passed not from emotion to form, but from thought to chaos. Still, he was great. He has been called a thinker, and was certainly a man who was always thinking, and always thinking aloud; but it was not thought that fascinated him, but rather the processes by which thought moves. It was the machine he loved, not what the machine makes. The method by which the fool arrives at his folly was as dear to him as the ultimate wisdom of the wise. So much, indeed, did the subtle mechanism of the mind fascinate him that he despised language, or looked upon it as an incomplete instrument of expression. Rhyme, that exquisite echo which in the Muse's hollow hill creates and answers its own voice; rhyme, which in the hands of the real artist becomes not merely a material element of metrical beauty, but a spiritual element of thought and passion also, waking a new mood, it may be, or stirring a fresh train of ideas, or opening by mere sweetness and suggestion of sound some golden door at which the Imagination itself had knocked in vain; rhyme, which can turn man's utterance to the speech of gods; rhyme, the one chord we have added to the Greek lyre, became in Robert Browning's hands a grotesque, misshapen thing, which at times made him masquerade in poetry as a low comedian, and ride Pegasus[2] too often with his tongue in his cheek. There are moments when he wounds us by monstrous music. Nay, if he can only get his music by

breaking the strings of his lute, he breaks them, and they snap in discord, and no Athenian tettix, making melody from tremulous wings, lights on the ivory horn to make the movement perfect, or the interval less harsh. Yet, he was great: and though he turned language into ignoble clay, he made from it men and women that live. He is the most Shakespearian creature since Shakespeare. If Shakespeare could sing with myriad lips, Browning could stammer through a thousand mouths. Even now, as I am speaking, and speaking not against him but for him, there glides through the room the pageant of his persons. There, creeps Fra Lippo Lippi with his cheeks still burning from some girl's hot kiss. There, stands dread Saul with the lordly male-sapphires gleaming in his turban. Mildred Tresham is there, and the Spanish monk, yellow with hatred, and Blougram, and Ben Ezra, and the Bishop of St. Praxed's. The spawn of Setebos gibbers in the corner, and Sebald, hearing Pippa pass by, looks on Ottima's haggard face, and loathes her and his own sin, and himself. Pale as the white satin of his doublet, the melancholy king watches with dreamy treacherous eyes too loyal Strafford pass forth to his doom, and Andrea[3] shudders as he hears the cousin's whistle in the garden, and bids his perfect wife go down. Yes, Browning was great. And as what will he be remembered? As a poet? Ah, not as a poet! He will be remembered as a writer of fiction, as the most supreme writer of fiction, it may be, that we have ever had. His sense of dramatic situation was unrivalled, and, if he could not answer his own problems, he could at least put problems forth, and what more should an artist do? Considered from the point of view of a creator of character he ranks next to him who made Hamlet. Had he been articulate, he might have sat beside him. The only man who can touch the hem of his garment is George Meredith. Meredith is a prose Browning, and

---

[1] a member of the race of gods that sprang from the union between Uranus and Gaia, Sky and Earth. Ruling, according to Greek mythology, the primeval world, their position of supremacy was usurped by a new race of divinities led by Zeus, the Olympians.

[2] the immortal winged horse that was born of the blood that fell from Medusa's neck when she was decapitated by Perseus.

[3] a litany of Browning's most memorable dramatic personae.

so is Browning. He used poetry as a medium for writing in prose.

ERNEST: There is something in what you say, but there is not everything in what you say. In many points you are unjust.

GILBERT: It is difficult not to be unjust to what one loves. But let us return to the particular point at issue. What was it that you said?

ERNEST: Simply this: that in the best days of art there were no art-critics.

GILBERT: I seem to have heard that observation before, Ernest. It has all the vitality of error and all the tediousness of an old friend.

ERNEST: It is true. Yes: there is no use your tossing your head in that petulant manner. It is quite true. In the best days of art there were no art-critics. The sculptor hewed from the marble block the great white-limbed Hermes[1] that slept within it. The waxers and gilders of images gave tone and texture to the statue, and the world, when it saw it, worshipped and was dumb. He poured the glowing bronze into the mould of sand, and the river of red metal cooled into noble curves and took the impress of the body of a god. With enamel or polished jewels he gave sight to the sightless eyes. The hyacinth-like curls grew crisp beneath his graver. And when, in some dim frescoed fane, or pillared sunlit portico, the child of Leto[2] stood upon his pedestal, those who passed by, διὰ λαμπροτάτου βαίνοντες ἁβρῶς αἰθέρος [treading delicately through the bright air], became conscious of a new influence that had come across their lives, and dreamily, or with a sense of strange and quickening joy, went to their homes or daily labour, or wandered, it may be, through the city gates to that nymph-haunted meadow where young Phaedrus bathed his feet, and, lying there on the soft grass, beneath the tall wind-whispering planes and flowering *agnus castus*,[3] began to think of the wonder of beauty, and grew silent with unaccustomed awe. In those days the artist was free. From the river valley he took the fine clay in his fingers, and with a little tool of wood or bone, fashioned it into forms so exquisite that the people gave them to the dead as their playthings, and we find them still in the dusty tombs on the yellow hillside by Tanagra, with the faint gold and the fading crimson still lingering about hair and lips and raiment. On a wall of fresh plaster, stained with bright sandyx or mixed with milk and saffron, he pictured one who trod with tired feet the purple white-starred fields of asphodel,[4] one "in whose eyelids lay the whole of the Trojan War," Polyxena, the daughter of Priam;[5] or figured Odysseus, the wise and cunning, bound by tight cords to the mast-step, that he might listen without hurt to the singing of the Sirens, or wandering by the clear river of Acheron, where the ghosts of fishes flitted over the pebbly bed; or showed the Persian in trews and mitre flying before the Greek at Marathon,[6] or the galleys clashing their beaks of brass in the little Salaminian bay. He drew with silver-point and charcoal upon parchment and prepared cedar. Upon ivory and rose-coloured terra-cotta he painted with wax, making the wax fluid with juice of olives, and with heated irons making it firm. Panel and marble and linen canvas became wonderful as his brush swept across them; and life seeing her own image, was still, and dared not speak. All life, indeed, was his, from the merchants seated in the market-place to the cloaked shepherd lying on the hill; from the

---

[1] The son of Zeus and Atlas's daughter Maia, Hermes was the messenger of Zeus, the guide of the souls of the dead to the underworld, the protector of travelers, the god of chance and profit, and the patron deity of thieves and merchants.

[2] Apollo.

[3] a shrub with finger-shaped leaves and slender violet flowers.

[4] a plant with large white flowers and a proliferation of long leaves. The ancient Greeks planted asphodels near tombs, regarding them as the form of food preferred by the dead.

[5] the king of Troy at the time of the Trojan War; father of Paris, who instigated the battle when he abducted Helen, the wife of Menelaus.

[6] the city founded by Marathon, the son of Epopcus, king of Sicyon.

nymph hidden in the laurels and the faun that pipes at noon, to the king whom, in long green-curtained litter, slaves bore upon oil-bright shoulders, and fanned with peacock fans. Men and women, with pleasure or sorrow in their faces, passed before him. He watched them, and their secret became his. Through form and colour he re-created a world.

All subtle arts belonged to him also. He held the gem against the revolving disk, and the amethyst became the purple couch for Adonis,[1] and across the veined sardonyx sped Artemis[2] with her hounds. He beat out the gold into roses, and strung them together for necklace or armlet. He beat out the gold into wreaths for the conqueror's helmet, or into palmates for the Tyrian[3] robe, or into masks for the royal dead. On the back of the silver mirror he graved Thetis[4] borne by her Nereids,[5] or love-sick Phaedra[6] with her nurse, or Persephone,[7] weary of memory, putting poppies in her hair. The potter sat in his shed, and, flower-like from the silent wheel, the vase rose up beneath his hands. He decorated the base and stem and ears with pattern of dainty olive-leaf, or foliated acanthus,[8] or curved and crested wave. Then in black or red he painted lads wrestling, or in the race: knights in full armour, with strange heraldic shields and curious visors, leaning from shell-shaped chariot over rearing steeds: the gods seated at the feast or working their miracles: the heroes in their victory or in their pain. Sometimes he would etch in thin vermilion lines upon a ground of white the languid bridegroom and his bride, with Eros[9] hovering round them—an Eros like one of Donatello's[10] angels, a little laughing thing with gilded or with azure wings. On the curved side he would write the name of his friend. ΚΑΛΟΣ ΑΛΚΙΒΙΑΔΗΣ [fair Alcibiades][11] or ΚΑΛΟΣ ΧΑΡΜΙΔΗΣ [fair Charmides] tells us the story of his days. Again, on the rim of the wide flat cup he would draw the stag browsing, or the lion at rest, as his fancy willed it. From the tiny perfume-bottle laughed Aphrodite at her toilet, and, with bare-limbed Maenads[12] in his train, Dionysus[13] danced round the wine-jar on naked must-stained feet, while, satyr-like, the old Silenus[14] sprawled upon the bloated skins, or shook that magic spear which was tipped with a fretted fir-cone, and wreathed with dark ivy. And no one came to trouble the artist at his work. No irresponsible chatter disturbed him. He

---

[1] Beloved by the quarreling goddesses Aphrodite and Persephone, Adonis was attacked and killed by a wild boar while in Aphrodite's possession. To commemorate his beauty and her sorrow, Aphrodite made the blood-red anemone spring from the blood that spilled at his death.

[2] Daughter of Zeus and Leto, twin sister of Apollo, Artemis was the virgin goddess of hunting and archery, and, ironically, the protector of all animals, children, and helpless creatures.

[3] from the city of Tyre, in southwest Lebanon, on the Mediterranean.

[4] A beautiful nereid, she became the mother of Achilles, whom it is said she dipped in the River Styx to render invulnerable. However, having forgotten to anoint the heel by which she held him, she ensured his death.

[5] sea nymphs; the fifty daughters of Nereus and his wife Doris.

[6] daughter of Minos and wife of Theseus. When Phaedra's stepson, Hippolytus, spurned her incestuous love, she secured his doom by accusing him of rape, and then hung herself. Her story has been dramatized by Euripides, Seneca, and Racine.

[7] The daughter of Zeus and Demeter in Greek mythology, Persephone became the queen of the Underworld when she was abducted by the god Hades. In order to placate the devastated mother and daughter, Zeus, who had sanctioned the kidnaping, decreed that Persephone would spend four months a year with Hades, and the remainder with her mother. Originally a fertility tale, the myth of Persephone came to symbolize the renewal of life after death.

[8] common name for the Acanthaceae, a family of perennial shrubs and herbs, most of which are tropical.

[9] the Greek god of carnal love.

[10] Italian sculptor and innovator in Renaissance art.

[11] Athenian statesman and general (c. 450–404 BC).

[12] female followers of Dionysus, who executed the Dionysian rites in an orgiastic frenzy of singing, dancing, and music.

[13] Greek god of wine.

[14] Possessing the tail, nose, and ears of a horse, Silenus was a companion of the Maenads and, as a result, a participant in the revels of Dionysus.

was not worried by opinions. By the Ilyssus, says Arnold somewhere, there was no Higginbotham. By the Ilyssus, my dear Gilbert, there were no silly art congresses bringing provincialism to the provinces and teaching the mediocrity how to mouth. By the Ilyssus there were no tedious magazines about art, in which the industrious prattle of what they do not understand. On the reed-grown banks of that little stream strutted no ridiculous journalism monopolising the seat of judgment when it should be apologising in the dock. The Greeks had no art-critics.

GILBERT: Ernest, you are quite delightful, but your views are terribly unsound. I am afraid that you have been listening to the conversation of some one older than yourself. That is always a dangerous thing to do, and if you will allow it to degenerate into a habit you will find it absolutely fatal to any intellectual development. As for modern journalism, it is not my business to defend it. It justifies its own existence by the great Darwinian principle of the survival of the vulgarest. I have merely to do with literature.

ERNEST: But what is the difference between literature and journalism?

GILBERT: Oh! journalism is unreadable, and literature is not read. That is all. But with regard to your statement that the Greeks had no art-critics, I assure you that is quite absurd. It would be more just to say that the Greeks were a nation of art-critics.

ERNEST: Really?

GILBERT: Yes, a nation of art-critics. But I don't wish to destroy the delightfully unreal picture that you have drawn of the relation of the Hellenic artist to the intellectual spirit of his age. To give an accurate description of what has never occurred is not merely the proper occupation of the historian, but the inalienable privilege of any man of parts and culture. Still less do I desire to talk learnedly. Learned conversation is either the affectation of the ignorant or the profession of the mentally unemployed. And, as for what is called improving conversation, that is merely the foolish method by which the still more foolish

philanthropist feebly tries to disarm the just rancour of the criminal classes. No: let me play to you some mad scarlet thing by Dvorák. The pallid figures on the tapestry are smiling at us, and the heavy eyelids of my bronze Narcissus[1] are folded in sleep. Don't let us discuss anything solemnly. I am but too conscious of the fact that we are born in an age when only the dull are treated seriously, and I live in terror of not being misunderstood. Don't degrade me into the position of giving you useful information. Education is an admirable thing, but it is well to remember from time to time that nothing that is worth knowing can be taught. Through the parted curtains of the window I see the moon like a clipped piece of silver. Like gilded bees the stars cluster round her. The sky is a hard hollow sapphire. Let us go out into the night. Thought is wonderful, but adventure is more wonderful still. Who knows but we may meet Prince Florizel of Bohemia, and hear the fair Cuban tell us that she is not what she seems?

ERNEST: You are horribly wilful. I insist on your discussing this matter with me. You have said that the Greeks were a nation of art-critics. What art-criticism have they left us?

GILBERT: My dear Ernest, even if not a single fragment of art-criticism has come down to us from Hellenic or Hellenistic days, it would be none the less true that the Greeks were a nation of art-critics, and that they invented the criticism of art just as they invented the criticism of everything else. For, after all, what is our primary debt to the Greeks? Simply the critical spirit. And, this spirit, which they exercised on questions of religion and science, of ethics and metaphysics, of politics and education, they exercised on questions of art also, and, indeed, of the two supreme and highest arts, they have left us the most flawless system of criticism that the world has ever seen.

---

[1] a variety of showy-blossomed plants indigenous to the Mediterranean and Asia.

ERNEST: But what are the two supreme and highest arts?

GILBERT: Life and Literature, life and the perfect expression of life. The principles of the former, as laid down by the Greeks, we may not realise in an age so married by false ideals as our own. The principles of the latter, as they laid them down, are, in many cases, so subtle that we can hardly understand them. Recognising that the most perfect art is that which most fully mirrors man in all his infinite variety, they elaborated the criticism of language, considered in the light of the mere material of that art, to a point to which we, with our accentual system of reasonable or emotional emphasis, can barely if at all attain; studying, for instance, the metrical movements of a prose as scientifically as a modern musician studies harmony and counterpoint, and, I need hardly say, with much keener aesthetic instinct. In this they were right, as they were right in all things. Since the introduction of printing, and the fatal development of the habit of reading amongst the middle and lower classes of this country, there has been a tendency in literature to appeal more and more to the eye, and less and less to the ear which is really the sense which, from the standpoint of pure art, it should seek to please, and by whose canons of pleasure it should abide always. Even the work of Mr. Pater,[1] who is, on the whole, the most perfect master of English prose now creating amongst us, is often more like a piece of mosaic than a passage in music, and seems, here and there, to lack the true rhythmical life of words and the fine freedom and richness of effect that such rhythmical life produces. We, in fact, have made writing a definite mode of composition, and have treated it as a form of elaborate design. The Greeks, upon the other hand, regarded writing simply as a method of chronicling. Their test was always the spoken word in its musical and metrical relations. The voice was the medium, and the ear the critic. I

have sometimes thought that the story of Homer's blindness might be really an artistic myth, created in critical days, and serving to remind us, not merely that the great poet is always a seer, seeing less with the eyes of the body than he does with the eyes of the soul, but that he is a true singer also, building his song out of music, repeating each line over and over again to himself till he has caught the secret of its melody, chaunting in darkness the words that are winged with light. Certainly, whether this be so or not, it was to his blindness, as an occasion, if not as a cause, that England's great poet owed much of the majestic movement and sonorous splendour of his later verse. When Milton could no longer write he began to sing. Who would match the measures of *Comus* with the measures of *Samson Agonistes*, or of *Paradise Lost* or *Regained*? When Milton became blind he composed, as every one should compose, with the voice purely, and so the pipe or reed of earlier days became that mighty many-stopped organ whose rich reverberant music has all the stateliness of Homeric verse, if it seeks not to have its swiftness, and is the one imperishable inheritance of English literature sweeping through all the ages, because above them, and abiding with us ever, being immortal in its form. Yes: writing has done much harm to writers. We must return to the voice. That must be our test, and perhaps then we shall be able to appreciate some of the subtleties of Greek art-criticism.

As it now is, we cannot do so. Sometimes, when I have written a piece of prose that I have been modest enough to consider absolutely free from fault, a dreadful thought comes over me that I may have been guilty of the immortal effeminacy of using trochaic and tribrachic movements, a crime for which a learned critic of the Augustan age censures with most just severity the brilliant if somewhat paradoxical Hegesias.[2] I grow cold when I think of it, and

---

[1] Walter Horatio Pater (1839–94), British essayist and critic.

[2] a Greek historian and orator whose pompous oratory was abhorred by ancient critics (c. 300 or 250 BC).

wonder to myself if the admirable ethical effect of the prose of that charming writer, who once in a spirit of reckless generosity towards the uncultivated portion of our community proclaimed the monstrous doctrine that conduct is three-fourths of life, will not some day be entirely annihilated by the discovery that the paeons have been wrongly placed.

ERNEST: Ah! now you are flippant.

GILBERT: Who would not be flippant when he is gravely told that the Greeks had no art-critics? I can understand it being said that the constructive genius of the Greeks lost itself in criticism, but not that the race to whom we owe the critical spirit did not criticise. You will not ask me to give you a survey of Greek art criticism from Plato to Plotinus.[1] The night is too lovely for that, and the moon, if she heard us, would put more ashes on her face than are there already. But think merely of one perfect little work of aesthetic criticism, Aristotle's *Treatise on Poetry*. It is not perfect in form, for it is badly written, consisting perhaps of notes dotted down for an art lecture, or of isolated fragments destined for some larger book, but in temper and treatment it is perfect, absolutely. The ethical effect of art, its importance to culture, and its place in the formation of character, had been done once for all by Plato; but here we have art treated, not from the moral, but from the purely aesthetic point of view. Plato had, of course, dealt with many definitely artistic subjects, such as the importance of unity in a work of art, the necessity for tone and harmony, the aesthetic value of appearances, the relation of the visible arts to the external world, and the relation of fiction to fact. He first perhaps stirred in the soul of man that desire that we have not yet satisfied, the desire to know the connection between Beauty and Truth, and the place of Beauty in the moral and intellectual order of the Kosmos. The problems of idealism and realism, as he sets them forth, may seem to many to be somewhat

barren of result in the metaphysical sphere of abstract being in which he places them, but transfer them to the sphere of art, and you will find that they are still vital and full of meaning. It may be that it is as a critic of Beauty that Plato is destined to live, and that by altering the name of the sphere of his speculation we shall find a new philosophy. But Aristotle, like Goethe,[2] deals with art primarily in its concrete manifestations, taking Tragedy, for instance, and investigating the material it uses, which is language, its subject-matter, which is life, the method by which it works, which is action, the conditions under which it reveals itself, which are those of theatric presentation, its logical structure, which is plot, and its final aesthetic appeal, which is to the sense of beauty realised through the passions of pity and awe. That purification and spiritualising of the nature which he calls κάθαρσις [catharsis] is, as Goethe saw, essentially aesthetic, and is not moral, as Lessing[3] fancied. Concerning himself primarily with the impression that the work of art produces, Aristotle sets himself to analyse that impression, to investigate its source, to see how it is engendered. As a physiologist and psychologist, he knows that the health of a function resides in energy. To have a capacity for a passion and not to realise it, is to make oneself incomplete and limited. The mimic spectacle of life that Tragedy affords cleanses the bosom of much "perilous stuff," and by presenting high and worthy objects for the exercise of the emotions purifies and spiritualises the man; nay, not merely does it spiritualise him, but it initiates him also into noble feelings of which he might else have known nothing, the word κάθαρσις having, it has sometimes seemed to me, a definite allusion to the rite of initiation, if indeed that be not, as I am occasionally tempted to fancy, its true and

1 Hellenistic philosopher and founder of Neoplatonism (205–70).

2 Johann Wolfgang von Goethe (1749–1832), German dramatist, poet, novelist, and scientist, best known for his dramatic poem *Faust*.

3 Gotthold Ephraim Lessing (1729–81), German philosopher and dramatist.

only meaning here. This is of course a mere outline of the book. But you see what a perfect piece of aesthetic criticism it is. Who indeed but a Greek could have analysed art so well? After reading it, one does not wonder any longer that Alexandria devoted itself so largely to art-criticism, and that we find the artistic temperaments of the day investigating every question of style and manner discussing the great Academic schools of painting, for instance, such as the school of Sicyon, that sought to preserve the dignified traditions of the antique mode, or the realistic and impressionist schools, that aimed at reproducing actual life, or the elements of ideality in portraiture, or the artistic value of the epic form in an age so modern as theirs, or the proper subject-matter for the artist. Indeed, I fear that the inartistic temperaments of the days busied themselves also in matters of literature and art, for the accusations of plagiarism were endless, and such accusations proceed either from the thin colourless lips of impotence, or from the grotesque mouths of those who, possessing nothing of their own, fancy that they can gain a reputation for wealth by crying out that they have been robbed. And I assure you, my dear Ernest, that the Greeks chattered about painters quite as much as people do nowadays, and had their private views, and shilling exhibitions, and Arts and Crafts guilds, and Pre-Raphaelite movements, and movements towards realism, and lectured about art, and wrote essays on art, and produced their art-historians, and their archaeologists, and all the rest of it. Why, even the theatrical managers of travelling companies brought their dramatic critics with them when they went on tour, and paid them very handsome salaries for writing laudatory notices. Whatever, in fact, is modern in our life we owe to the Greeks. Whatever is an anachronism is due to mediaevalism. It is the Greeks who have given us the whole system of art-criticism, and how fine their critical instinct was, may be seen from the fact that the material they criticised with most care was, as I have already said, language.

For the material that painter or sculptor uses is meagre in comparison with that of words. Words have not merely music as sweet as that of viol and lute, colour as rich and vivid as any that makes lovely for us the canvas of the Venetian or the Spaniard, and plastic form no less sure and certain than that which reveals itself in marble or in bronze but thought and passion and spirituality are theirs also, are theirs indeed alone. If the Greeks had criticised nothing but language, they would still have been the great art-critics of the world. To know the principles of the highest art is to know the principles of all the arts.

But I see that the moon is hiding behind a sulphur-coloured cloud. Out of a tawny mane of drift she gleams like a lion's eye. She is afraid that I will talk to you of Lucian[1] and Longinus,[2] of Quintilian[3] and Dionysus, of Pliny[4] and Fronto and Pausanias, of all those who in the antique world wrote or lectured upon art matters. She need not be afraid. I am tired of my expedition into the dim, dull abyss of facts. There is nothing left for me now but the divine μονόχρονος ἡδονή [undivided pleasure] of another cigarette. Cigarettes have at least the charm of leaving one unsatisfied.

ERNEST: Try one of mine. They are rather good. I get them direct from Cairo. The only use of our *attachés* is that they supply their friends with excellent tobacco. And as the moon has hidden herself, let us talk a little longer. I am quite ready to admit that I was wrong in what I said about the Greeks. They were, as you have pointed out, a nation of art-critics. I ac-

---

[1] Greek prose writer famous for his satiric dialogues (c. 125, d. after 180).

[2] Greek writer of *On the Sublime*, an important work of literary criticism defining the characteristics of what would now be referred to as loftiness of style.

[3] Marcus Fabius Quintilianus (c. 35–95), Roman teacher and theoretician.

[4] Pliny the Younger (62?–c. 113), Roman statesman and orator whose letters provide an intimate reflection of Roman life.

knowledge it, and I feel a little sorry for them. For the creative faculty is higher than the critical. There is really no comparison between them.

GILBERT: The antithesis between them is entirely arbitrary. Without the critical faculty, there is no artistic creation at all, worthy of the name. You spoke a little while ago of that fine spirit of choice and delicate instinct of selection by which the artist realises life for us, and gives to it a momentary perfection. Well, that spirit of choice, that subtle tact of omission, is really the critical faculty in one of its most characteristic moods, and no one who does not possess this critical faculty can create anything at all in art. Arnold's definition of literature as a criticism of life, was not very felicitous in form, but it showed how keenly he recognised the importance of the critical element in all creative work.

ERNEST: I should have said that great artists worked unconsciously, that they were "wiser then they knew," as, I think, Emerson[1] remarks somewhere.

GILBERT: It is really not so, Ernest. All fine imaginative work is self-conscious and deliberate. No poet sings because he must sing. At least, no great poet does. A great poet sings because he chooses to sing. It is so now, and it has always been so. We are sometimes apt to think that the voices that sounded at the dawn of poetry were simpler, fresher and more natural than ours, and that the world which the early poets looked at, and through which they walked, had a kind of poetical quality of its own, and almost without changing could pass into song. The snow lies thick now upon Olympus, and its steep scarped sides are bleak and barren, but once, we fancy, the white feet of the Muses brushed the dew from the anemo-nes[2] in the morning, and at evening came Apollo[3] to sing to the shepherds in the vale. But in this we are merely lending to other ages what we desire, or think we desire, for our own. Our historical sense is at fault. Every century that produces poetry is, so far, an artificial century, and the work that seems to us to be the most natural and simple product of its time is always the result of the most self-conscious effort. Believe me, Ernest, there is no fine art without self-consciousness, and self-consciousness and the critical spirit are one.

ERNEST: I see what you mean, and there is much in it. But surely you would admit that the great poems of the early world, the primitive, anonymous collective poems, were the result of the imagination of races, rather than of the imagination of individuals?

GILBERT: Not when they became poetry. Not when they received a beautiful form. For there is no art where there is no style, and no style where there is no unity, and unity is of the individual. No doubt Homer had old ballads and stories to deal with, as Shakespeare had chronicles and plays and novels from which to work, but they were merely his rough material. He took them, and shaped them into song. They became his, because he made them lovely. They were built out of music,

> And so not built after all,
> And therefore built for ever.

The longer one studies life and literature, the more strongly one feels that behind everything that is wonderful stands the individual, and that it is not the moment that makes the man, but the man who creates the age. Indeed, I am inclined to think that each myth and legend that seems to us to spring out of the wonder, or terror, or fancy of tribe and nation,

---

[1] Ralph Waldo Emerson (1803–82), one of America's most influential writers and thinkers.

[2] herbs containing a poisonous compound that was once used to treat bruises and fevers.

[3] Son of Zeus and Leto, and twin brother of Artemis, he was the principal god of prophecy, the arts (particularly music), and archery.

was in its origin the invention of one single mind. The curiously limited number of the myths seems to me to point to this conclusion. But we must not go off into questions of comparative mythology. We must keep to criticism. And what I want to point out is this. An age that has no criticism is either an age in which art is immobile, hieratic, and confined to the reproduction of formal types, or an age that possesses no art at all. There have been critical ages that have not been creative, in the ordinary sense of the word, ages in which the spirit of man has sought to set in order the treasures of his treasure-house, to separate the gold from the silver, and the silver from the lead, to count over the jewels, and to give names to the pearls. But there has never been a creative age that has not been critical also. For it is the critical faculty that invents fresh forms. The tendency of creation is to repeat itself. It is to the critical instinct that we owe each new school that springs up, each new mould that art finds ready to its hand. There is really not a single form that art now uses that does not come to us from the critical spirit of Alexandria, where these forms were either stereotyped or invented or made perfect. I say Alexandria, not merely because it was there that the Greek spirit became most self-conscious, and indeed ultimately expired in scepticism and theology, but because it was to that city, and not to Athens, that Rome turned for her models, and it was through the survival, such as it was, of the Latin language that culture lived at all. When, at the Renaissance, Greek literature dawned upon Europe, the soil had been in some measure prepared for it. But, to get rid of the details of history, which are always wearisome and usually inaccurate, let us say generally, that the forms of art have been due to the Greek critical spirit. To it we owe the epic, the lyric, the entire drama in every one of its developments, including burlesque, the idyll, the romantic novel, the novel of adventure, the essay, the dialogue, the oration, the lecture, for which perhaps we should not forgive them, and the epigram, in all the wide mean-

ing of that word. In fact, we owe it everything, except the sonnet, to which, however, some curious parallels of thought-movement may be traced in the Anthology, American journalism, to which no parallel can be found anywhere, and the ballad in sham Scotch dialect, which one of our most industrious writers has recently proposed should be made the basis for a final and unanimous effort on the part of our second-rate poets to make themselves really romantic. Each new school, as it appears, cries out against criticism, but it is to the critical faculty in man that it owes its origin. The mere creative instinct does not innovate, but reproduces.

ERNEST: You have been talking of criticism as an essential part of the creative spirit, and I now fully accept your theory. But what of criticism outside creation? I have a foolish habit of reading periodicals, and it seems to me that most modern criticism is perfectly valueless.

GILBERT: So is most modern creative work also. Mediocrity weighing mediocrity in the balance, and incompetence applauding its brother—that is the spectacle which the artistic activity of England affords us from time to time. And yet, I feel I am a little unfair in this matter. As a rule, the critics—I speak, of course, of the higher class, of those in fact who write for the sixpenny papers—are far more cultured than the people whose work they are called upon to review. This is, indeed, only what one would expect, for criticism demands infinitely more cultivation than creation does.

ERNEST: Really?

GILBERT: Certainly. Anybody can write a three-volumed novel. It merely requires a complete ignorance of both life and literature. The difficulty that I should fancy the reviewer feels is the difficulty of sustaining any standard. Where there is no style a standard must be impossible. The poor reviewers are apparently reduced to be the reporters of the police-court of literature, the chroniclers of the doings of the habitual criminals of art. It is sometimes said of them that they do not read all through the works they are called upon to criticise. They do not. Or at least they should not. If they did so, they would become confirmed misanthropes, or if I may borrow a phrase from one of the pretty Newnham graduates,[1] confirmed womanthropes for the rest of their lives. Nor is it necessary. To know the vintage and quality of a wine one need not drink the whole cask. It must be perfectly easy in half an hour to say whether a book is worth anything or worth nothing. Ten minutes are really sufficient, if one has the instinct for form. Who wants to wade through a dull volume? One tastes it, and that is quite enough—more than enough, I should imagine. I am aware that there are many honest workers in painting as well as in literature who object to criticism entirely. They are quite right. Their work stands in no intellectual relation to their age. It brings us no new element of pleasure. It suggests no fresh departure of thought, or passion, or beauty. It should not be spoken of. It should be left to the oblivion that it deserves.

ERNEST: But, my dear fellow—excuse me for interrupting you—you seem to me to be allowing your passion for criticism to lead you a great deal too far. For, after all, even you must admit that it is much more difficult to do a thing than to talk about it.

GILBERT: More difficult to do a thing than to talk about it? Not at all. That is a gross popular error. It is very much more difficult to talk about a thing than to do it. In the sphere of actual life that is of course obvious. Anybody can make history. Only a great man can write it. There is no mode of action, no form of emotion, that we do not share with the lower animals. It is only by language that we rise above them, or above each other—by language, which is the parent, and not the child, of thought. Action, indeed, is always easy, and when presented to us in its most aggravated, because most continuous form, which I

take to be that of real industry, becomes simply the refuge of people who have nothing whatsoever to do. No, Ernest, don't talk about action. It is a blind thing dependent on external influences, and moved by an impulse of whose nature it is unconscious. It is a thing incomplete in its essence, because limited by accident, and ignorant of its direction, being always at variance with its aim. Its basis is the lack of imagination. It is the last resource of those who know not how to dream.

ERNEST: Gilbert, you hold the world as if it were a crystal ball. You hold it in your hand, and reverse it to please a wilful fancy. You do nothing but re-write history.

GILBERT: The one duty we owe to history is to rewrite it. That is not the least of the tasks in store for the critical spirit. When we have fully discovered the scientific laws that govern life, we shall realise that the one person who has more illusions than the dreamer is the man of action. He, indeed, knows neither the origin of his deeds nor their results. From the field in which he thought that he had sown thorns, we have gathered our vintage, and the fig-tree that he planted for our pleasure is as barren as the thistle, and more bitter. It is because Humanity has never known where it was going that it has been able to find its way.

ERNEST: You think, then, that in the sphere of action a conscious aim is a delusion?

GILBERT: It is worse than a delusion. If we lived long enough to see the results of our actions it may be that those who call themselves good would be sickened with a dull remorse, and those whom the world calls evil stirred by a noble joy. Each little thing that we do passes into the great machine of life which may grind our virtues to powder and make them worthless, or transform our sins into elements of a new civilisation, more marvellous and more splendid than any that has gone before. But men are the slaves of words. They rage against Materialism, as they call it, forgetting that there has been no material improvement that has

---

[1] Newnham College, the first woman's college to be founded at Cambridge University.

not spiritualised the world, and that there have been few, if any, spiritual awakenings that have not wasted the world's faculties in barren hopes, and fruitless aspirations, and empty or trammelling creeds. What is termed Sin is an essential element of progress. Without it the world would stagnate, or grow old, or become colourless. By its curiosity Sin increases the experience of the race. Through its intensified assertion of individualism, it saves us from monotony of type. In its rejection of the current notions about morality, it is one with the higher ethics. And as for the virtues! What are the virtues? Nature, M. Renan[1] tells us, cares little about chastity, and it may be that it is to the shame of the Magdalen, and not to their own purity, that the Lucretias[2] of modern life owe their freedom from stain. Chastity, as even those of whose religion it makes a formal part have been compelled to acknowledge, creates a multitude of evils. The mere existence of conscience, that faculty of which people prate so much nowadays, and are so ignorantly proud, is a sign of our imperfect development. It must be merged in instinct before we become fine. Self-denial is simply a method by which man arrests his progress, and self-sacrifice a survival of the mutilation of the savage, part of that old worship of pain which is so terrible a factor in the history of the world, and which even now makes its victims day by day, and has its altars in the land. Virtues! Who knows what the virtues are? Not you. Not I. Not any one. It is well for our vanity that we slay the criminal, for if we suffered him to live he might show us what we had gained by his crime. It is well for his peace that the saint goes to his martyrdom. He is spared the sight of the horror of his harvest.

ERNEST: Gilbert, you sound too harsh a note. Let us go back to the more gracious fields of literature. What was it you said? That it was more difficult to talk about a thing than to do it?

GILBERT (*after a pause*): Yes: I believe I ventured upon that simple truth. Surely you see now that I am right? When man acts he is a puppet. When he describes he is a poet. The whole secret lies in that. It was easy enough on the sandy plains by windy Ilion[3] to send the notched arrow from the painted bow, or to hurl against the shield of hide and flamelike brass the long ash-handled spear. It was easy for the adulterous queen to spread the Tyrian carpets for her lord, and then, as he lay couched in the marble bath, to throw over his head the purple net, and call to her smooth-faced lover to stab through the meshes at the heart that should have broken at Aulis.[4] For Antigone[5] even, with Death waiting for her as her bridegroom, it was easy to pass through the tainted air at noon, and climb the hill, and strew with kindly earth the wretched naked corpse that had no tomb. But what of those who wrote about these things? What of those who gave them reality, and made them live for ever? Are they not greater than the men and women they sing of? "Hector that sweet knight is dead," and Lucian tells us how in the dim under-world Menippus saw the bleaching skull of Helen, and marvelled that it was for so grim a favour that all those horned ships were launched, those beautiful mailed men laid low, those towered cities brought to dust. Yet, every day the swanlike daughter of Leda[6] comes out on the battlements, and looks down at the tide of war. The greybeards wonder at her loveliness, and she stands by the side of the king. In his chamber

---

[1] Ernest Renan (1823–92), French historian and philologist, known for his *Life of Jesus.*

[2] refers to Lucretia Borgia (1480–1519), whose beauty and kindness won her great esteem in spite of the stories of her crimes that were circulated, but unfounded.

[3] the city of Troy.

[4] an allusion to the story of Clytemnestra and Agamemnon.

[5] daughter of Oedipus, king of Thebes, and his wife and mother Jocasta. The tragic story of her death sentence and suicide figures in Sophocles's plays *Oedipus at Colonus* and *Antigone.*

[6] Helen of Troy, who was said to have hatched from an egg because the god Zeus had made love to her mother in the form of a swan.

of stained ivory lies her leman. He is polishing his dainty armour, and combing the scarlet plume. With squire and page, her husband passes from tent to tent. She can see his bright hair, and hears, or fancies that she hears, that clear cold voice. In the courtyard below, the son of Priam[1] is buckling on his brazen cuirass. The white arms of Andromache[2] are around his neck. He sets his helmet on the ground, lest their babe should be frightened. Behind the embroidered curtains of his pavilion sits Achilles,[3] in perfumed raiment, while in harness of gilt and silver the friend of his soul arrays himself to go forth to the fight. From a curiously carven chest that his mother Thetis had brought to his ship-side, the Lord of the Myrmidons takes out that mystic chalice that the lip of man had never touched, and cleanses it with brimstone, and with fresh water cools it, and, having washed his hands, fills with black wine its burnished hollow, and spills the thick grape-blood upon the ground in honour of Him whom at Dodona barefooted prophets worshipped, and prays to Him, and knows not that he prays in vain, and that by the hands of two knights from Troy, Panthous'[4] son, Euphorbus, whose love-locks were looped with gold, and the Priamid, the lion-hearted, Patroklus, the comrade of comrades, must meet his doom. Phantoms, are they? Heroes of mist and mountain? Shadows in a song? No: they are real. Action! What is action? It dies at the moment of its energy. It is a base concession to fact. The world is made by the singer for the dreamer.

ERNEST: While you talk it seems to me to be so.

GILBERT: It is so in truth. On the mouldering citadel of Troy lies the lizard like a thing of green bronze.

The owl has built her nest in the palace of Priam. Over the empty plain wander shepherd and goatherd with their flocks, and where, on the surfaced, oily sea, οἶνοψ πόντος [wine-coloured sea], as Homer calls it, copper-prowed and streaked with vermilion, the great galleys of the Danaoi came in their gleaming crescent, the lonely tunny-fisher sits in his little boat and watches the bobbing corks of his net. Yet, every morning the doors of the city are thrown open, and on foot, or in horse-drawn chariot, the warriors go forth to battle, and mock their enemies from behind their iron masks. All day long the fight rages, and when night comes the torches gleam by the tents, and the cresset burns in the hall. Those who live in marble or on painted panel, know of life but a single exquisite instant, eternal indeed in its beauty, but limited to one note of passion or one mood of calm. Those whom the poet makes live have their myriad emotions of joy and terror, of courage and despair, of pleasure and of suffering. The seasons come and go in glad or saddening pageant, and with winged or leaden feet the years pass by before them. They have their youth and their manhood, they are children, and they grow old. It is always dawn for St. Helena,[5] as Veronese saw her at the window. Through the still morning air the angels bring her the symbol of God's pain. The cool breezes of the morning lift the gilt threads from her brow. On that little hill by the city of Florence, where the lovers of Giorgione[6] are lying, it is always the solstice of noon, of noon made so languorous by summer suns that hardly can the slim naked girl dip into the marble tank the round bubble of clear glass, and the long fingers of the lute-player rest idly upon the chords. It is twilight always for the dancing nymphs whom Corot[7] set free among the

---

[1] Hector, the eldest son.

[2] wife of Hector, her dramatic tale is depicted in Euripides's tragedy *Andromache*.

[3] central Greek hero in the *Iliad*.

[4] Trojan elder and priest of Apollo; his three sons, Polydamas, Euphorbus, and Hypereno, were Trojan warriors.

---

[5] Mother of Constantine I, she is said to have discovered the True Cross and the Holy Sepulchre in Jerusalem (c. 248–328?).

[6] Venetian painter (c. 1478–1510).

[7] Jean-Baptiste Camille Corot (1796–1875), French landscape painter who celebrated the countryside without romanticizing it.

silver poplars of France. In eternal twilight they move, those frail diaphanous figures, whose tremulous white feet seem not to touch the dew-drenched grass they tread on. But those who walk in epos, drama, or romance, see through the labouring months the young moons wax and wane, and watch the night from evening unto morning star, and from sunrise unto sunsetting, can note the shifting day with all its gold and shadow. For them, as for us, the flowers bloom and wither, and the Earth, that Green-tressed Goddess as Coleridge calls her, alters her raiment for their pleasure. The statue is concentrated to one moment of perfection. The image stained upon the canvas possesses no spiritual element of growth or change. If they know nothing of death, it is because they know little of life, for the secrets of life and death belong to those, and those only, whom the sequence of time affects, and who possess not merely the present but the future, and can rise or fall from a past of glory or of shame. Movement, that problem of the visible arts, can be truly realised by Literature alone. It is Literature that shows us the body in its swiftness and the soul in its unrest.

ERNEST: Yes; I see now what you mean. But, surely, the higher you place the creative artist, the lower must the critic rank.

GILBERT: Why so?

ERNEST: Because the best that he can give us will be but an echo of rich music, a dim shadow of clear-outlined form. It may, indeed, be that life is chaos, as you tell me that it is; that its martyrdoms are mean and its heroisms ignoble; and that it is the function of Literature to create, from the rough material of actual existence, a new world that will be more marvellous, more enduring, and more true than the world that common eyes look upon, and through which common natures seek to realise their perfection. But surely, if this new world has been made by the spirit and touch of a great artist, it will be a thing so complete and perfect that there will be nothing left for the critic to do. I quite understand now, and

indeed admit most readily, that it is far more difficult to talk about a thing than to do it. But it seems to me that this sound and sensible maxim, which is really extremely soothing to one's feelings, and should be adopted as its motto by every Academy of Literature all over the world, applies only to the relations that exist between Art and Life, and not to any relations that there may be between Art and Criticism.

GILBERT: But, surely, Criticism is itself an art. And just as artistic creation implies the working of the critical faculty, and, indeed, without it cannot be said to exist at all, so Criticism is really creative in the highest sense of the word. Criticism is, in fact, both creative and independent.

ERNEST: Independent?

GILBERT: Yes; independent. Criticism is no more to be judged by any low standard of imitation or resemblance than is the work of poet or sculptor. The critic occupies the same relation to the work of art that he criticises as the artist does to the visible world of form and colour, or the unseen world of passion and of thought. He does not even require for the perfection of his art the finest materials. Anything will serve his purpose. And just as out of the sordid and sentimental amours of the silly wife of a small country doctor in the squalid village of Yonville-l'Abbaye, near Rouen, Gustave Flaubert was able to create a classic,[1] and make a masterpiece of style, so, from subjects of little or no importance, such as the pictures in this year's Royal Academy, or in any year's Royal Academy for that matter, Mr. Lewis Morris's poems, M. Ohnet's novels, or the plays of Mr. Henry Arthur Jones,[2] the true critic can, if it be his pleasure so to

---

[1] *Madame Bovary*.

[2] Sir Lewis Morris (1833–1907), a lacklustre, but popular writer of mythological and religious poetry. Georges Ohnet (1848–1918), a fashionable French novelist of the late nineteenth century. Henry Arthur Jones (1851–1929), a celebrated English dramatist whose principal successes were the melodramatic *The Silver King* (1882), *The Case of Rebellious Susan* (1894), *Michael and His Lost Angel* (1896), and *The Liars* (1897).

direct or waste his faculty of contemplation, produce work that will be flawless in beauty and instinct with intellectual subtlety. Why not? Dullness is always an irresistible temptation for brilliancy, and stupidity is the permanent *Bestia Trionfans* that calls wisdom from its cave. To an artist so creative as the critic, what does subject-matter signify? No more and no less than it does to the novelist and the painter. Like them, he can find his motives everywhere. Treatment is the test. There is nothing that has not in it suggestion or challenge.

ERNEST: But is Criticism really a creative art?

GILBERT: Why should it not be? It works with materials, and puts them into a form that is at once new and delightful. What more can one say of poetry? Indeed, I would call criticism a creation within a creation. For just as the great artists, from Homer and Aeschylus,[1] down to Shakespeare and Keats, did not go directly to life for their subject-matter, but sought for it in myth, and legend, and ancient tale, so the critic deals with materials that others have, as it were, purified for him, and to which imaginative form and colour have been already added. Nay, more, I would say that the highest Criticism, being the purest form of personal impression, is in its way more creative than creation, as it has least reference to any standard external to itself, and is, in fact, its own reason for existing, and, as the Greeks would put it, in itself, and to itself, an end. Certainly, it is never trammelled by any shackles of verisimilitude. No ignoble considerations of probability, that cowardly concession to the tedious repetitions of domestic or public life, affect it ever. One may appeal from fiction unto fact. But from the soul there is no appeal.

ERNEST: From the soul?

GILBERT: Yes, from the soul. That is what the highest criticism really is, the record of one's own soul. It is more fascinating than history, as it is concerned simply with oneself. It is more delightful than philosophy, as its subject is concrete and not abstract, real and not vague. It is the only civilised form of autobiography, as it deals not with the events, but with the thoughts of one's life; not with life's physical accidents of deed or circumstance, but with the spiritual moods and imaginative passions of the mind. I am always amused by the silly vanity of those writers and artists of our day who seem to imagine that the primary function of the critic is to chatter about their second-rate work. The best that one can say of most modern creative art is that it is just a little less vulgar than reality, and so the critic, with his fine sense of distinction and sure instinct of delicate refinement, will prefer to look into the silver mirror or through the woven veil, and will turn his eyes away from the chaos and clamour of actual existence, though the mirror be tarnished and the veil be torn. His sole aim is to chronicle his own impressions. It is for him that pictures are painted, books written, and marble hewn into form.

ERNEST: I seem to have heard another theory of Criticism.

GILBERT: Yes: it has been said by one whose gracious memory we all revere, and the music of whose pipe once lured Proserpina from her Sicilian fields, and made those white feet stir, and not in vain, the Cumnor cowslips, that the proper aim of Criticism is to see the object as in itself it really is. But this is a very serious error, and takes no cognisance of Criticism's most perfect form, which is in its essence purely subjective, and seeks to reveal its own secret and not the secret of another. For the highest Criticism deals with art not as expressive but as impressive purely.

ERNEST: But is that really so?

GILBERT: Of course it is. Who cares whether Mr. Ruskin's views on Turner[2] are sound or not? What

---

1 Athenian tragic poet (525–456 BC).

2 Joseph Mallord William Turner (1775–1851), the foremost English romantic landscape painter.

does it matter? That mighty and majestic prose of his, so fervid and so fiery-coloured in its noble eloquence, so rich in its elaborate symphonic music, so sure and certain, at its best, in subtle choice of word and epithet, is at least as great a work of art as any of those wonderful sunsets that bleach or rot on their corrupted canvases in England's [Tate] Gallery; greater indeed, one is apt to think at times, not merely because its equal beauty is more enduring, but on account of the fuller variety of its appeal, soul speaking to soul in those long-cadenced lines, not through form and colour alone, though through these, indeed, completely and without loss, but with intellectual and emotional utterance, with lofty passion and with loftier thought, with imaginative insight, and with poetic aim; greater, I always think, even as Literature is the greater art. Who, again, cares whether Mr. Pater has put into the portrait of Monna Lisa something that Lionardo never dreamed of? The painter may have been merely the slave of an archaic smile, as some have fancied, but whenever I pass into the cool galleries of the Palace of the Louvre, and stand before that strange figure "set in its marble chair in that cirque of fantastic rocks, as in some faint light under sea," I murmur to myself, "She is older than the rocks among which she sits; like the vampire, she has been dead many times, and learned the secrets of the grave; and has been a diver in deep seas, and keeps their fallen day about her; and trafficked for strange webs with Eastern merchants; and, as Leda, was the mother of Helen of Troy, and as St. Anne, the mother of Mary; and all this has been to her but as the sound of lyres and flutes, and lives only in the delicacy with which it has moulded the changing lineaments, and tinged the eyelids and the hands." And I say to my friend, "The presence that thus so strangely rose beside the waters is expressive of what in the ways of a thousand years man had come to desire"; and he answers me, "Hers is the head upon which all 'the ends of the world are come,' and the eyelids are a little weary."

And so the picture becomes more wonderful to us than it really is, and reveals to us a secret of which, in truth, it knows nothing, and the music of the mystical prose is as sweet in our ears as was that flute-player's music that lent to the lips of La Gioconda those subtle and poisonous curves. Do you ask me what Lionardo would have said had any one told him of this picture that "all the thoughts and experience of the world had etched and moulded there in that which they had of power to refine and make expressive the outward form, the animalism of Greece, the lust of Rome, the reverie of the Middle Age with its spiritual ambition and imaginative loves, the return of the Pagan world, the sins of the Borgias?"[1] He would probably have answered that he had contemplated none of these things, but had concerned himself simply with certain arrangements of lines and masses, and with new and curious colour-harmonies of blue and green. And it is for this very reason that the criticism which I have quoted is criticism of the highest kind. It treats the work of art simply as a starting-point for a new creation. It does not confine itself—let us at least suppose so for the moment—to discovering the real intention of the artist and accepting that as final. And in this it is right, for the meaning of any beautiful created thing is, at least, as much in the soul of him who looks at it, as it was in his soul who wrought it. Nay, it is rather the beholder who lends to the beautiful thing its myriad meanings, and makes it marvellous for us, and sets it in some new relation to the age, so that it becomes a vital portion of our lives, and a symbol of what we pray for, or perhaps of what, having prayed for, we fear that we may receive. The longer I study, Ernest, the more clearly I see that the beauty of the visible arts is, as the beauty of music, impressive primarily, and that it may be marred, and indeed often is so, by any excess of intellectual intention on the part of the

---

[1] Spanish-Italian family whose members include Popes Calixtus III and Alexander VI, and the infamous Lucretia Borgia.

artist. For when the work is finished it has, as it were, an independent life of its own, and may deliver a message far other than that which was put into its lips to say. Sometimes, when I listen to the overture to *Tannhäuser*,[1] I seem indeed to see that comely knight treading delicately on the flower-strewn grass, and to hear the voice of Venus calling to him from the caverned hill. But at other times it speaks to me of a thousand different things, of myself, it may be, and my own life, or of the lives of others whom one has loved and grown weary of loving, or of the passions that man has known, or of the passions that man has not known, and so has sought for. To-night it may fill one with that ΕΡΩΣ ΤΩΝ ΑΔΥΝΑΤΩΝ, that *Amour de l'Impossible*, which falls like a madness on many who think they live securely and out of reach of harm, so that they sicken suddenly with the poison of unlimited desire, and, in the infinite pursuit of what they may not obtain, grow faint and swoon or stumble. Tomorrow, like the music of which Aristotle and Plato tell us, the noble Dorian music of the Greek, it may perform the office of a physician, and give us an anodyne against pain, and heal the spirit that is wounded, and "bring the soul into harmony with all right things." And what is true about music is true about all the arts. Beauty has as many meanings as man has moods. Beauty is the symbol of symbols. Beauty reveals everything, because it expresses nothing. When it shows us itself, it shows us the whole fiery-coloured world.

ERNEST: But is such work as you have talked about really criticism?

GILBERT: It is the highest Criticism, for it criticises not merely the individual work of art, but Beauty itself, and fills with wonder a form which the artist may have left void, or not understood, or understood incompletely.

ERNEST: The highest Criticism, then, is more creative than creation, and the primary aim of the critic is to

see the object as in itself it really is not; that is your theory, I believe?

GILBERT: Yes, that is my theory. To the critic the work of art is simply a suggestion for a new work of its own, that need not necessarily bear any obvious resemblance to the thing it criticises. The one characteristic of a beautiful form is that one can put into it whatever one wishes, and see in it whatever one chooses to see; and the Beauty, that gives to creation its universal and aesthetic element, makes the critic a creator in his turn, and whispers of a thousand different things which were not present in the mind of him who carved the statue or painted the panel or graved the gem.

It is sometimes said by those who understand neither the nature of the highest Criticism nor the charm of the highest Art, that the pictures that the critic loves most to write about are those that belong to the anecdotage of painting, and that deal with scenes taken out of literature or history. But this is not so. Indeed, pictures of this kind are far too intelligible. As a class, they rank with illustrations, and even considered from this point of view are failures, as they do not stir the imagination, but set definite bounds to it. For the domain of the painter is, as I suggested before, widely different from that of the poet. To the latter belongs life in its full and absolute entirety; not merely the beauty that men look at, but the beauty that men listen to also; not merely the momentary grace of form or the transient gladness of colour, but the whole sphere of feeling, the perfect cycle of thought. The painter is so far limited that it is only through the mask of the body that he can show us the mystery of the soul; only through conventional images that he can handle ideas; only through its physical equivalents that he can deal with psychology. And how inadequately does he do it then, asking us to accept the torn turban of the Moor for the noble rage of Othello, or a dotard in a storm for the wild madness of Lear! Yet it seems as if nothing could stop him. Most of our

---

[1] an opera written by the German composer Richard Wagner.

elderly English painters spend their wicked and wasted lives in poaching upon the domain of the poets, marring their motives by clumsy treatment, and striving to render, by visible form or colour, the marvel of what is invisible, the splendour of what is not seen. Their pictures are, as a natural consequence, insufferably tedious. They have degraded the invisible arts into the obvious arts, and the one thing not worth looking at is the obvious. I do not say that poet and painter may not treat of the same subject. They have always done so, and will always do so. But while the poet can be pictorial or not, as he chooses, the painter must be pictorial always. For a painter is limited, not to what he sees in nature, but to what upon canvas may be seen.

And so, my dear Ernest, pictures of this kind will not really fascinate the critic. He will turn from them to such works as make him brood and dream and fancy, to works that possess the subtle quality of suggestion, and seem to tell one that even from them there is an escape into a wider world. It is sometimes said that the tragedy of an artist's life is that he cannot realise his ideal. But the true tragedy that dogs the steps of most artists is that they realise their ideal too absolutely. For, when the ideal is realised, it is robbed of its wonder and its mystery, and becomes simply a new starting-point for an ideal that is other than itself. This is the reason why music is the perfect type of art. Music can never reveal its ultimate secret. This, also, is the explanation of the value of limitations in art. The sculptor gladly surrenders imitative colour, and the painter the actual dimensions of form, because by such renunciations they are able to avoid too definite a presentation of the Real, which would be mere imitation, and too definite a realisation of the Ideal, which would be too purely intellectual. It is through its very incompleteness that Art becomes complete in beauty, and so addresses itself, not to the faculty of recognition nor to the faculty of reason, but to the aesthetic sense alone, which, while accepting both reason and recognition as stages of

apprehension, subordinates them both to a pure synthetic impression of the work of art as a whole, and, taking whatever alien emotional elements the work may possess, uses their very complexity as a means by which a richer unity may be added to the ultimate impression itself. You see, then, how it is that the aesthetic critic rejects those obvious modes of art that have but one message to deliver, and having delivered it become dumb and sterile, and seeks rather for such modes as suggest reverie and mood, and by their imaginative beauty make all interpretations true, and no interpretation final. Some resemblance, no doubt, the creative work of the critic will have to the work that has stirred him to creation, but it will be such resemblance as exists, not between Nature and the mirror that the painter of landscape or figure may be supposed to hold up to her, but between Nature and the work of the decorative artist. Just as on the flowerless carpets of Persia, tulip and rose blossom indeed and are lovely to look on, though they are not reproduced in visible shape or line; just as the pearl and purple of the sea-shell is echoed in the church of St. Mark at Venice; just as the vaulted ceiling of the wondrous chapel at Ravenna[1] is made gorgeous by the gold and green and sapphire of the peacock's tail, though the birds of Juno[2] fly not across it; so the critic reproduces the work that he criticises in a mode that is never imitative, and part of whose charm may really consist in the rejection of resemblance, and shows us in this way not merely the meaning but also the mystery of Beauty, and, by transforming each art into literature, solves once for all the problem of Art's unity.

But I see it is time for supper. After we have discussed some Chambertin and a few ortolans, we

---

[1] a city in north-central Italy famous for its fifth- and sixth-century mosaics.

[2] Roman goddess of light and childbirth, the sister and wife of her male counterpart, Jupiter.

will pass on to the question of the critic considered in the light of the interpreter.

ERNEST: Ah! you admit, then, that the critic may occasionally be allowed to see the object as in itself it really is.

GILBERT: I am not quite sure. Perhaps I may admit it after supper. There is a subtle influence in supper.
—1890

Arthur Symons
1865 – 1945

Arthur Symons was a poet and critic associated with the variously named "Aesthetic" or "Decadent" or "Symbolist" movement. This involves, among other things, a love of beauty, the substitution of suggestion for statement, dim sadness, profound sensuality, and the reliance on symbols. His *Symbolist Movement In Literature* (1899), preceded by the earlier condensed version, "The Decadent Movement in Literature" (1893), was important in defining "Symbolist" theories and for introducing French writers and their literary ideas to England.

❧❧❧

The Decadent Movement in Literature [1]

The latest movement in European literature has been called by many names, none of them quite exact or comprehensive—Decadence, Symbolism, Impressionism, for instance. It is easy to dispute over words, and we shall find that Verlaine[2] objects to being called a Decadent, Maeterlinck[3] to being called a Symbolist, Huysmans[4] to being called an Impressionist. These terms, as it happens, have been adopted as the badge of little separate cliques, noisy, brainsick young people who haunt the brasseries of the Boulevard Saint-Michel, and exhaust their ingenuities in theorizing over the works they cannot write. But, taken frankly as epithets which express their own meaning, both Impressionism and Symbolism convey some notion of that new kind of literature which is perhaps more broadly characterized by the word Decadence. The most representative literature of the day—the writing which appeals to, which has done so much to form, the younger generation—is certainly not classic, nor has it any relation with that old antithesis of the Classic, the Romantic. After a fashion it is no doubt a decadence; it has all the qualities that mark the end of great periods, the qualities that we find in the Greek, the Latin, decadence: an intense self-consciousness, a restless curiosity in research, an over-subtilizing refinement upon refinement, a spiritual and moral perversity. If what we call the classic is indeed the supreme art—those qualities of perfect simplicity, perfect sanity, perfect proportion, the supreme qualities—then this representative literature of to-day, interesting, beautiful, novel as it is, is really a new and beautiful and interesting disease.

Healthy we cannot call it, and healthy it does not wish to be considered. The Goncourts,[5] in their prefaces, in their *Journal*, are always insisting on their own malady, *la névrose*.[6] It is in their work, too, that Huysmans notes with delight "*le style tacheté et faisandé*"—high-flavoured and spotted with corruption—which he himself possesses in the highest degree. "Having desire without light, curiosity without wisdom, seeking God by strange ways, by ways traced by the hands of men; offering rash incense upon the high places to an unknown God, who is the God of darkness"—that is how Ernest Hello,[7] in one of his apocalyptic moments, characterizes the nineteenth century. And this unreason of the soul—of which Hello himself is so curious a vic-

---

[1] (1893): a preliminary and condensed version of his later book, *The Symbolist Movement in Literature* (1899).

[2] Paul Verlaine (1844–96), French symbolist.

[3] Maurice Maeterlinck (1862–1949), Belgian poet and dramatist.

[4] Joris Karl Huysmans (1848–1907), French poet, an early Naturalist and later Decadent.

[5] brothers Edmond Louis Antonine Huot de Goncourt (1822–96) and Jules Alfred Huot de Goncourt (1830–70).

[6] "neurosis."

[7] (1828–85).

tim—this unstable, equilibrium, which has overbalanced so many brilliant intelligences into one form or another of spiritual confusion, is but another form of the *maladie fin de siècle*.[1] For its very disease of form, this literature is certainly typical of a civilization grown over-luxurious, over-inquiring, too languid for the relief of action, too uncertain for any emphasis in opinion or in conduct. It reflects all the moods, all the manners, of a sophisticated society; its very artificiality is a way of being true to nature; simplicity, sanity, proportion—the classic qualities—how much do we possess them in our life, our surroundings, that we should look to find them in our literature—so evidently the literature of a decadence?

Taking the word Decadence, then, as most precisely expressing the general sense of the newest movement in literature, we find that the terms Impressionism and Symbolism define correctly enough the two main branches of that movement. Now Impressionist and Symbolist have more in common than either supposes; both are really working on the same hypothesis, applied in different directions. What both seek is not general truth merely, but *la vérité vraie*, the very essence of truth—the truth of appearances to the senses, of the visible world to the eyes that see it; and the truth of spiritual things to the spiritual vision. The Impressionist, in literature as in painting, would flash upon you in a new, sudden way so exact an image of what you have just seen, just as you have seen it, that you may say, as a young American sculptor, a pupil of Rodin,[2] said to me on seeing for the first time a picture of Whistler's,[3] "Whistler seems to think his picture upon canvas—and there it is!" Or you may find, with Sainte-Beuve, writing of Goncourt, the "soul of the landscape"—the soul of whatever corner

of the visible world has to be realized. The Symbolist, in this new, sudden way, would flash upon you the "soul" of that which can be apprehended only by the soul—the finer sense of things unseen, the deeper meaning of things evident. And naturally, necessarily, this endeavour after a perfect truth to one's impression, to one's intuition—perhaps an impossible endeavour—has brought with it, in its revolt from ready-made impressions and conclusions, a revolt from the ready-made of language, from the bondage of traditional form, of a form become rigid. In France, where this movement began and has mainly flourished, it is Goncourt who was the first to invent a style in prose really new, impressionistic, a style which was itself almost sensation. It is Verlaine who has invented such another new style in verse.

The work of the brothers De Goncourt—twelve novels, eleven or twelve studies in the history of the eighteenth century, six or seven books about art, the art mainly of the eighteenth century and of Japan, two plays, some volumes of letters and of fragments, and a *Journal* in six volumes—is perhaps in its intention and its consequences the most revolutionary of the century. No one has ever tried so deliberately to do something new as the Goncourts; and the final word in the summing up which the survivor has placed at the head of the *Préfaces et Manifestes* is a word which speaks of *tentatives, enfin, où les deux frères ont cherchés à faire du neuf, ont fait leurs efforts pour doter les diverses branches de la littérature de quelque chose que n'avaient point songé à trouver leurs prédécesseurs*.[4] And in the preface to *Chérie*, in that pathetic passage which tells of the two brothers (one mortally stricken, and within a few months of death) taking their daily walk in the Bois de Boulogne, there is a definite demand on posterity. "The search after *reality* in literature, the resurrection of eighteenth-

---

[1] "the malady of the turn of the century."

[2] Auguste Rodin (1840–1917), French sculptor.

[3] James Abbott McNeill Whistler (1834–1903), American-born painter who worked mainly in England.

[4] "attempts, then, by which the two brothers have tried to make something new, have made efforts to bestow upon the various forms of literature something which their predecessors had never dreamed of finding."

century art, the triumph of *Japonisme*—are not these," said Jules, "the three great literary and artistic movements of the second half of the nineteenth century? And it is we who brought them about, these three movements. Well, when one has done that, it is difficult indeed not to be *somebody* in the future." Nor, even, is this all. What the Goncourts have done is to specialize vision, so to speak, and to subtilize language to the point of rendering every detail in just the form and colour of the actual impression. Edmond de Goncourt once said to me—varying, if I remember rightly, an expression he had put into the *Journal*—"My brother and I invented an opera-glass: the young people nowadays are taking it out of our hands."

An opera-glass—a special, unique way of seeing things—that is what the Goncourts have brought to bear upon the common things about us; and it is here that they have done the "something new," here more than anywhere. They have never sought "to see life steadily and see it whole": their vision has always been somewhat feverish, with the diseased sharpness of over-excited nerves. "We do not hide from ourselves that we have been passionate, nervous creatures, unhealthily impressionable," confesses the *Journal*. But it is this morbid intensity in seeing and seizing things that has helped to form that marvellous style—"a style perhaps too ambitious of impossibilities," as they admit—a style which inherits some of its colour from Gautier,[1] some of its fine outline from Flaubert,[2] but which has brought light and shadow into the colour, which has softened outline in the magic of atmosphere. With them words are not merely colour and sound, they live. That search after *l'image peinte, l'épithète rare*, is not (as with Flaubert) a search after harmony of phrase for its own sake; it is a desperate endeavour to give sensation, to flash the impression of the moment, to preserve the very heat

and motion of life. And so, in analysis as in description, they have found out a way of noting the fine shades; they have broken the outline of the conventional novel in chapters, with its continuous story, in order to indicate—sometimes in a chapter of half a page—this and that revealing moment, this or that significant attitude or accident or sensation. For the placid traditions of French prose they have had but little respect: their aim has been but one, that of giving (as M. Edmond de Goncourt tells us in the preface to *Chérie*) *"une langue rendant nos idées, d'une façon distincte de celui-ci ou de celui-là, une langue personelle, une langue portant notre signature."*[3]

What Goncourt has done in prose—inventing absolutely a new way of saying things, to correspond with that new way of seeing things, which he has found—Verlaine has done in verse. In a famous poem, *Art Poétique*,[4] he has himself defined his own ideal of the poetic art:

> Car nous voulons la Nuance encor.
> Pas la Couleur, rien que la Nuance!
> Oh! la Nuance seule fiancé
> Le rêve au rêve et la flûte au cor![5]

Music first of all and before all, he insists; and then, not colour, but *la nuance*, the last fine shade. Poetry is to be something vague, intangible, evanescent, a winged soul in flight "toward other skies and other loves." To express the inexpressible he speaks of beautiful eyes behind a veil, of the palpitating sunlight of noon, of the blue swarm of clear stars in a cool autumn sky: and the verse in which he makes

---

[1] Theophile Gautier (1811–72), French poet, novelist, and critic.

[2] Gustave Flaubert (1821–80), French novelist.

---

[3] "a language rendering our ideas in a manner distinct from this one or that, a personal language, a language bearing our signature."

[4] "Art Poétique" was published in *Jadis et naguère* (1855).

[5] "Never the color, always the shade,
Always the nuance is supreme!
Only by shade is the trothal made
Between the flute and horn, of dream with dream!"

(ll. 13–16)

this confession of faith has the exquisite troubled beauty—*"sans rien en lui qui pèse ou qui pose"*[1]—which he commends as the essential quality of verse. In a later poem of poetical counsel he tells us that art should, first of all, be absolutely clear, absolutely sincere: *L'art, mes enfants, c'est d'être absolument soi-même.*[2] The two poems, with their seven years' interval—an interval which means so much in the life of a man like Verlaine—give us all that there is of theory in the work of the least theoretical, the most really instinctive, of poetical innovators. Verlaine's poetry has varied with his life; always in excess—now furiously sensual, now feverishly devout—he has been constant only to himself, to his own self-contradictions. For, with all the violence, turmoil, and disorder of a life which is almost the life of a modern Villon,[3] Paul Verlaine has always retained that childlike simplicity, and, in his verse, which has been his confessional, that fine sincerity, of which Villon may be thought to have set the example in literature.

Beginning his career as a Parnassian[4] with the *Poèmes Saturniens*, Verlaine becomes himself, in his exquisite first manner, in the *Fêtes Galantes*, caprices after Watteau,[5] followed, a year later, by *La Bonne Chanson*, a happy record of too confident a lover's happiness. *Romances sans Paroles*, in which the poetry of Impressionism reaches its very highest point, is more *tourmenté*, goes deeper, becomes more poignantly personal. It is the poetry of sensation, of evocation: poetry which paints as well as sings, and which paints as Whistler paints, seeming to think the colour and outlines upon the canvas, to think them

only, and they are there. The mere magic of words—words which evoke pictures, which recall sensations—can go no further; and in his next book, *Sagesse*, published after seven years' wanderings and sufferings, there is a grayer manner of more deeply personal confession—that "sincerity, and the impression of the moment followed to the letter," which he has defined in a prose criticism on himself as his main preference in regard to style. "Sincerity and the impression of the moment followed to the letter," mark the rest of Verlaine's work, whether the sentiment be that of passionate friendship, as in *Amour*, of love, human and divine, as in *Bonheur*, of the mere lust of the flesh, as in *Parallèlement* and *Chansons pour Elle*.[6] In his very latest verse the quality of simplicity has become exaggerated, has become, at times, childish; the once exquisite depravity of style has lost some of its distinction; there is no longer the same delicately vivid "impression of the moment" to render. Yet the very closeness with which it follows a lamentable career gives a curious interest to even the worst of Verlaine's work. And how unique, how unsurpassable in its kind, is the best! *"Et tout le reste est littérature!"* was the cry, supreme and contemptuous, of that early *Art Poétique*; and compared with Verlaine at his best, all other contemporary work in verse seems not yet disenfranchised from mere "literature." To fix the last fine shade, the quintessence of things; to fix it fleetingly; to be a disembodied voice, and yet the voice of a human soul: that is the ideal of Decadence, and it is what Paul Verlaine has achieved.

And certainly, so far as achievement goes, no other poet of the actual group in France can be named beside him or near him. But in Stephane Mallarmé, with his supreme pose as the supreme poet, and his two or three pieces of exquisite verse and delicately artificial prose to show by way of

---

[1] "with nothing heavy and nothing at rest."

[2] "Art, my children, is to be absolutely one's self."

[3] François Villon (c. 1431–after 1463?), Medieval French poet.

[4] Parnassianism, a poetic movement of the Second Empire and early Third Empire, bridges Romanticism and Symbolism in French literature. Parnassians rejected Romantic lyricism in favour of a more impersonal, objective, and positivistic form of artistic expression.

[5] Antoine Watteau (1684–1721), French painter.

---

[6] Symons here cites works of Verlaine published between 1866 and 1891.

result, we have the prophet and pontiff of the movement, the mystical and theoretical leader of the great emancipation. No one has ever dreamed such beautiful, impossible dreams as Mallarmé: no one has ever so possessed his soul in the contemplation of masterpieces to come. All his life he has been haunted by the desire to create, not so much something new in literature, as a literature which should itself be a new art. He has dreamed of a work into which all the arts should enter, and achieve themselves by a mutual interdependence—a harmonizing of all the arts into one supreme art—and he has theorized with infinite subtlety over the possibilities of doing the impossible. Every Tuesday for the last twenty years he has talked more fascinatingly, more suggestively, than anyone else has ever done, in that little room in the Rue de Rome, to that little group of eager young poets. "A seeker after something in the world, that is there in no satisfying measure or not at all," he has carried his contempt for the usual, the conventional, beyond the point of literary expression, into the domain of practical affairs. Until the publication, quite recently, of a selection of *Vers et Prose*, it was only possible to get his poems in a limited and expensive edition, lithographed in facsimile of his own clear and elegant handwriting. An aristocrat of letters, Mallarmé has always looked with intense disdain on the indiscriminate accident of universal suffrage. He has wished neither to be read nor to be understood by the bourgeois intelligence, and it is with some deliberateness of intention that he has made both issues impossible. Catulle Mendès [1] defines him admirably as "a difficult author," and in his latest period he has succeeded in becoming absolutely unintelligible. His early poems, *L'Après-midi d'un Faune, Hérodiade,* for example, and some exquisite sonnets, and one or two fragments of perfectly polished verse, are written in a language which has nothing in common with every-day language—symbol within symbol, image within image; but symbol and image achieve themselves in expression without seeming to call for the necessity of a key. The latest poems (in which punctuation is sometimes entirely suppressed, for our further bewilderment) consist merely of a sequence of symbols, in which every word must be taken in a sense with which its ordinary significance has nothing to do. Mallarmé's contortion of the French language, so far as mere style is concerned, is curiously similar to the kind of depravation which was undergone by the Latin language in its decadence. It is, indeed, in part a reversion to Latin phraseology, to the Latin construction, and it has made, of the colour and flowing French language, something irregular, unquiet, expressive, with sudden surprising felicities, with nervous starts and lapses, with new capacities for the exact noting of sensation. Alike to the ordinary and to the scholarly reader it is painful, intolerable; a jargon, a massacre. Supremely self-confident, and backed, certainly, by an ardent following of the younger generation, Mallarmé goes on his way, experimenting more and more audaciously, having achieved by this time, at all events, a style wholly his own. Yet the *chef d'œuvre inconnu* [2] seems no nearer completion, the impossible seems no more likely to be done. The two or three beautiful fragments remain, and we will still hear the voice in the Rue de Rome.

Probably it is as a voice, an influence, that Mallarmé will be remembered. His personal magnetism has had a great deal to do with the making of the very newest French literature; few literary beginners in Paris have been able to escape the rewards and punishments of his contact, his suggestion. One of the young poets who form that delightful Tuesday evening coterie said to me, "We owe much to Mallarmé, but he has kept us all back three years." That is where the danger of so inspiring, so helping a person-

---

[1] Catulle Mendès (1841–1909), French poet, novelist, playwright, and critic.

[2] "the unknown masterpiece."

ality comes in. The work even of Henri de Regnier,[1] who is the best of the disciples, has not entirely got clear from the influence that has shown his fine talent the way to develop. Perhaps it is in the verse of men who are not exactly following in the counsel of the master—who might disown him, whom he might disown—that one sees most clearly the outcome of his theories, the actual consequences of his practice. In regard to the construction of verse, Mallarmé has always remained faithful to the traditional syllabic measurement; but the freak of the discovery of *le vers libre* is certainly the natural consequence of his experiments upon the elasticity of rhythm, upon the power of resistance of the caesura. *Le vers libre* in the hands of most of the experimenters becomes merely rhymeless, irregular prose. I never really understood the charm that may be found in this apparently structureless rhythm until I heard Dujardin[2] read aloud the as yet unpublished conclusion of a dramatic poem in several parts. It was rhymed, but rhymes with some irregularity, and the rhythm was purely and simply a vocal effect. The rhythm came and went as the spirit moved. You might deny that it was rhythm at all; and yet, read as I heard it read, in a sort of slow chant, it produced on me the effect of really beautiful verse. But *vers libres* in the hands of a sciolist are the most intolerably and easy and annoying of poetical exercises. Even in the case of *Le Pèlerin Passionné*[3] I cannot see the justification of what is merely regular syllabic verse lengthened or shortened arbitrarily, with the Alexandrine always evident in the background as the footrule of the new metre. In this hazardous experiment Jean Moréas,[4]

whose real talent lies in quite another direction, has brought nothing into literature but an example of deliberate singularity for singularity's sake. I seem to find the measure of the man in a remark I once heard him make in a café, where we were discussing the technique of metre: "You, Verlaine!" he cried, leaning across the table, "have only written lines of sixteen syllables; *I* have written lines of twenty syllables!" And turning to me, he asked anxiously if Swinburne had ever done that—had written a line of twenty syllables.

That is indeed the measure of the man, and it points a criticism upon not a few of the busy little *littérateurs* who are founding new *revues* every other week in Paris. These people have nothing to say, but they are resolved to say something, and to say it in the newest mode. They are Impressionists because it is the fashion, Symbolists because it is the vogue, Decadents because Decadence is in the very air of the cafés. And so, in their manner, they are mile-posts on the way of this new movement, telling how far it has gone. But to find a new personality, a new way of seeing things, among the young writers who are starting up on every hand, we must turn from Paris to Brussels—to the so-called Belgian Shakespeare, Maurice Maeterlinck. Maeterlinck was discovered to the general French public by Octave Mirbeau,[5] in an article in the *Figaro*,[6] August 24, 1890, on the publication of *La Princesse Maleine*. "*Maurice Maeterlinck nous a donné l'œuvre la plus géniale de ce temps, et la plus extraordinaire et la plus naïve aussi, comparable et—oserai-je le dire?—supérieure en beauté à ce qui il y a de plus beau dans Shakespeare. . . plus tragique que* Macbeth, *plus extraordinaire en pensée que* Hamlet."[7]

---

[1] Henri de Régnier (1864–1936), French poet of the Symbolist school.

[2] Édouard Dujardin (1861–1949), French symbolist poet, novelist, dramatist, and critic.

[3] not identified.

[4] Jean Moréas (1856–1910), (pseudonym of Iannis Papadiamantopoulous), Greek-born French symbolist who wrote the manifesto of the movement (*Le Figaro*, 18 September 1886).

[5] Octave Mirbeau (1848–1917), anarchistic French journalist, novelist, and art critic.

[6] *Le Figaro* is a Parisian daily newspaper.

[7] "Maurice Maeterlinck has given us the most ingenious masterpiece of the age as well as the most extraordinary, and also the most naive, comparable and, dare I say it?, superior in beauty to that which is most beautiful in Shakespeare...more tragic that *Macbeth*, more extraordinary

That is how the enthusiast announced his discovery. In truth, Maeterlinck is not a Shakespeare, and the Elizabethan violence of his first play is of the school of Webster and Tourneur rather than of Shakespeare. As a dramatist he has but one note, that of fear; he has but one method, that of repetition. In *La Princesse Maleine* there is a certain amount of action —action which is certainly meant to reinvest the terrors of *Macbeth* and of *Lear*. In *L'Intruse* and *Les Aveugles*[1] the scene is stationary, the action but reflected upon the stage, as if from another plane. In *Les Sept Princesses*[2] the action, such as it is, is "such stuff as dreams are made of," and is, literally, in great part seen through a window.

This window, looking out upon the unseen—an open door, as in *L'Intruse,* through which Death, the intruder, may come invisibly—how typical of the new kind of symbolic and impressionistic drama which Maeterlinck has invented! I say invented, a little rashly. The real discoverer of this new kind of drama was that strange, inspiring man of genius whom Maeterlinck, above all others, delights to honour, Villiers de l'Isle-Adam. Imagine a combination of Swift, of Poe, and of Coleridge, and you will have some idea of the extraordinary, impossible poet and cynic who, after a life of brilliant failure, has left a series of unfinished works in every kind of literature; among the finished achievements one volume of short stories, *Contes Cruels*, which is an absolute masterpiece. Yet, apart from this, it was the misfortune of Villiers never to attain the height of his imaginings, and even *Axel*, the work of a lifetime, is an achievement only half achieved. Only half achieved, or achieved only in the work of others; for, in its mystical intention, its remoteness from any kind of outward reality, *Axel* is undoubtedly the origin of the symbolistic drama. This drama, in

Villiers, is of pure symbol, of sheer poetry. It has an exalted eloquence which we find in none of his followers. As Maeterlinck has developed it, it is a drama which appeals directly to the sensations—sometimes crudely, sometimes subtly —playing its variations upon the very nerves themselves. The "vague spiritual fear" which it creates out of our nervous apprehension is unlike anything that has ever been done before, even by Hoffmann, even by Poe. It is an effect of atmosphere—an atmosphere in which outlines change and become mysterious, in which a word quietly uttered makes one start, in which all one's mental activity becomes concentrated on something, one knows not what, something slow creeping, terrifying, which comes nearer and nearer, an impending nightmare.

La Princesse Maleine, it is said, was written for a theatre of marionettes, and it is certainly with the effect of marionettes that these sudden exclamatory people come and go. Maleine, Hjalmar, Uglyane— these are no men and women, but a masque of shadows, a dance of silhouettes behind the white sheet of the "Chat Noir," and they have the fantastic charm of these enigmatical semblances, "luminous, gemlike, ghostlike," with, also, their somewhat mechanical eeriness. The personages of *L'Intruse*, of *Les Aveugles*—in which the spiritual terror and physical apprehension which are common to all Maeterlinck's work have become more interior—are mere abstractions, typifying age, infancy, disaster, but with scarcely a suggestion of individual character. And the style itself is a sort of abstraction, all the capacities of language being deliberately abandoned for a simplicity which, in its calculated repetition, is like the drip, drip, of a tiny stream of water. Maeterlinck is difficult to quote, but here, in English, is a passage from Act I. of *La Princesse Maleine*, which will indicate something of this monotonous style:—

"I cannot see you. Come hither, this is more light here; lean back your head a little towards the sky.

---

in thought than *Hamlet*."

[1] both published in 1890.

[2] 1891.

You too are strange to-night! It is as though my eyes were opened to-night! It is as though my heart were half opened to-night! But I think you are strangely beautiful! But you are strangely beautiful, Uglyane! It seems to me that I have never looked on you till now! But I think you are strangely beautiful! There is something about you. . . Let us go elsewhither—under the light—come!"

As an experiment in a new kind of drama, these curious plays do not seem to exactly achieve themselves on the stage; it is difficult to imagine how they could ever be made so impressive, when thus externalized, as they are when all is left to the imagination. *L'Intruse* for instance, seemed, as one saw it acted, too faint in outline, with too little carrying power for scenic effect. But Maeterlinck is by no means anxious to be considered merely or mainly as a dramatist. A brooding poet, a mystic, a contemplative spectator of the comedy of death—that is how he presents himself to us in his work; and the introduction which he has prefixed to his translation of *L'Ornement des Noces Spirituelles*, of Ruysbroeck *l'Admirable*, shows how deeply he has studied the mystical writers of all ages, and how much akin to theirs is his own temper. Plato and Plotinus,[1] St. Bernard[2] and Jacob Boehm,[3] Coleridge and Novalis[4]—he knows them all, and it is with a sort of reverence that he sets himself to the task of translating the astonishing Flemish mystic of the thirteenth century, known till now only by the fragments translated into French by Ernest Hello from a sixteenth-century Latin version. This translation and this introduction help to explain the real character of Maeterlinck's dramatic work, dramatic as to form, by a sort of accident, but essentially mystical.

Partly akin to Maeterlinck by race, more completely alien from him in temper than it is possible to express, Joris Karl Huysmans demands a prominent place in any record of the Decadent movement. His work, like that of the Goncourts, is largely determined by the *maladie fin de siècle*—the diseased nerves that, in his case, have given a curious personal quality of pessimism to his outlook on the world, his view of life. Part of his work—*Marthe, Les Sœurs Vatard, En Menage, A Vau-l'eau*[5]—is a minute and searching study of the minor discomforts, the commonplace miseries of life, as seen by a peevishly disordered vision, delighting, for its own self-torture, in the insistent contemplation of human stupidity, of the sordid in existence. Yet these books do but lead up to the unique masterpiece, the astonishing caprice of *A Rebours*, in which he has concentrated all that is delicately depraved, all that is beautifully, curiously poisonous, in modern art. *A Rebours* is the history of a typical Decadent—a study, indeed, after a real man, but a study which seizes the type rather than the personality. In the sensations and ideas of Des Esseintes[6] we see the sensations and ideas of the effeminate, overcivilized, deliberately abnormal creature who is the last product of our society: partly the father, partly the offspring, of the perverse art that he adores. Des Esseintes creates for his solace, in the wilderness of a barren and profoundly uncomfortable world, an artificial paradise. His Thebaide raffinée[7] is furnished elaborately for candle-light, equipped with the pictures, the books, that satisfy his sense of the exquisitely abnormal. He delights in the

---

[1] Plotinus (205–70), Neoplatonist philosopher.

[2] St. Bernard of Clairvaux (1090–1153), influential theologian of the soul's journey.

[3] Jacob Boehm, Jakob Boehme (1575–1624), German Lutheran and mystic.

[4] pseudonym of Friedrich Freiherr von Hardenberg (1772–1801), German philosopher and Romantic poet.

[5] works published between 1876 and 1882.

[6] the hero of *A Rebours*.

[7] a refined or sophisticated version of the Theban world represented by the Sophoclean trilogy—*Oedipus the King, Oedipus at Colonus*, and *Antigone*.

Latin of Apuleius[1] and Petronius,[2] in the French of Baudelaire, Goncourt, Verlaine, Mallarmé, Villiers; in the pictures of Gustave Moreau,[3] of Odilon Redon.[4] He delights in the beauty of strange, unnatural flowers, in the melodic combination of scents, in the imagined harmonies of the sense of taste. And at last, exhausted by these spiritual and sensory debauches in the delights of the artificial, he is left (as we close the book) with a brief, doubtful choice before him—madness or death, or else a return to nature, to the normal life.

Since *A Rebours*, Huysmans has written one other remarkable book, *La-Bas*, a study in the hysteria and mystical corruption of contemporary Black Magic. But it is on that one exceptional achievement, *A Rebours,* that his fame will rest; it is there he has expressed not merely himself, but an epoch. And he has done so in a style which carries the modern experiments upon language to their furthest development. Formed upon Goncourt and Flaubert, it has sought for novelty, *l'image peinte*, the exactitude of colour, the forcible precision of epithet, wherever words, images, or epithets are to be found. Barbaric in its profusion, violent in its emphasis, wearying in its splendour, it is—especially in regard to things seen—extraordinarily expressive, with all the shades of a painter's palette. Elaborately and deliberately perverse, it is in its very perversity that Huysmans' work—so fascinating, so repellent, so instinctively artificial—comes to represent, as the work of no other writer can be said to do, the main tendencies, the chief results, of the Decadent movement in literature.

—1893

The Symbolist Movement in Literature [5]

INTRODUCTION

"It is in and through Symbols that man, consciously or unconsciously, lives, works, and has his being: those ages, moreover, are accounted the noblest which can the best recognise symbolical worth, and prize it highest."　　CARLYLE.[6]

Without symbolism there can be no literature; indeed, not even language. What are words themselves but symbols, almost as arbitrary as the letters which compose them, mere sounds of the voice to which we have agreed to give certain significations, as we have agreed to translate these sounds by those combination of letters? Symbolism began with the first words uttered by the first man, as he named every living thing; or before them, in heaven, when God named the world into being. And we see, in these beginnings, precisely what Symbolism in literature really is: a form of expression, at the best but approximate, essentially but arbitrary, until it has obtained the force of a convention, for an unseen reality apprehended by the consciousness. It is sometimes permitted to us to hope our convention is indeed the reflection rather than merely the sign of that unseen reality. We have done much if we have found a recognisable sign.

"A symbol," says Comte Goblet d'Alviella,[7] in his book on *The Migration of Symbols,* "might be defined as a representation which does not aim at being a reproduction." Originally, as he points out, used by the Greeks to denote "the two halves of the tablet they divided between themselves as a pledge of

---

[1] Apuleius (flourished c. 155 AD), Roman writer.

[2] Petronius Arbiter (d. 65 AD), Roman politician and writer.

[3] Gustave Moreau (1826–98), French Symbolist painter.

[4] Odilon Redon (1840–1916), French Symbolist painter.

[5] originally published in 1899. Two selections follow: the "Introduction" and Chapter 1, "Stéphane Mallarmé."

[6] *Sartor Resartus*, "Symbols" 3.3, which initially appeared in serial form in *Fraser's Magazine* from November 1833 to August 1834.

[7] *The Migration of Symbols* (1894), by Comte Eugene Goblet d'Alviella (1846–1925).

hospitality," it came to be used of every sign, formula, or rite by which those initiated in any mystery made themselves secretly known to one another. Gradually the word extended its meaning, until it came to denote every conventional representation of idea by form, of the unseen by the visible. "In a Symbol," says Carlyle, "there is concealment and yet revelation: hence therefore, by Silence and by Speech acting together, comes a double significance." And, in that fine chapter of Sartor Resartus, he goes further, vindicating for the word its full value: "In the Symbol proper, what we can call a Symbol, there is ever, more or less distinctly and directly, some embodiment and revelation of the Infinite; the Infinite is made to blend itself with the Finite, to stand visible, and as it were, attainable there."

It is in such a sense as this that the word Symbolism has been used to describe a movement which, during the last generation, has profoundly influenced the course of French literature. All such words, used of anything so living, variable, and irresponsible as literature, are, as symbols themselves must so often be, mere compromises, mere indications. Symbolism, as seen in the writers of our day, would have no value if it were not seen also, under one disguise or another, in every great imaginative writer. What distinguishes the Symbolism of our day from the Symbolism of the past is that it has now become conscious of itself, in a sense in which it was unconscious even in Gérard de Nerval,[1] to whom I trace the particular origin of the literature which I call Symbolist. The forces which mould the thought of men change, or men's resistance to them slackens; with the change of men's thought comes a change of literature, alike in its inmost essence and in its outward form: after the world has starved its soul long enough in the contemplation and the re-arrangement of material things, comes the turn of the soul; and with it comes the literature of which I write in this volume, a literature in which the visible world is no longer a reality, and the unseen world is no longer a dream.

The great epoch in French literature which preceded this epoch was that of the offshoot of Romanticism which produced Baudelaire, Flaubert, the Goncourts, Taine, Zola, Leconte de Lisle.[2] Taine was the philosopher both of what had gone before him and of what came immediately after; so that he seems to explain at once Flaubert and Zola. It was the age of Science, the age of material things; and words, with that facile elasticity which there is in them, did miracles in the exact representation of everything that visibly existed, exactly as it existed. Even Baudelaire, in whom the spirit is always an uneasy guest at the orgy of life, had a certain theory of Realism which tortures many of his poems into strange, metallic shapes, and fills them with imitative odours, and disturbs them with a too deliberate rhetoric of the flesh. Flaubert, the one impeccable novelist who has ever lived, was resolute to be the novelist of a world in which art, formal art, was the only escape from the burden of reality, and in which the soul was of use mainly as the agent of fine literature. The Goncourts caught at Impressionism to render the fugitive aspects of a world which existed only as a thing of flat spaces, and angles, and coloured movement, in which sun and shadow were the artists; as moods, no less flitting, were the artists of the merely receptive consciousness of men and women. Zola has tried to build in brick and mortar inside the covers of a book; he is quite sure that the soul is a nervous fluid, which he is quite sure some man of science is about to catch for us, as a man of science has bottled the air, a

---

[1] Gérard de Nerval (1808–55), the pseudonym of Gérard Labrunie, French poet and writer of periodical literature.

[2] Charles Baudelaire (1821–67), Gustave Flaubert (1821–80), the brothers Edmond Louis Antonine Huot de Goncourt (1822–96) and Jules Alfred Huot de Goncourt (1830–70), French novelists and historians; Hippolyté Adolphe Taine (1828–93), French critic and historian; Émile Zola (1840–1902), French novelist, founder of Naturalism; Charles-Marie Leconte de Lisle (1818–94), French poet and leading figure in the Parnassian movement of French poetry.

pretty, blue liquid. Leconte de Lisle turned the world to stone, but saw, beyond the world, only a pause from misery in a Nirvana never subtilised to the Eastern ecstasy. And, with all these writers, form aimed above all things at being precise, at saying rather than suggesting, at saying what they had to say so completely that nothing remained over, which it might be the business of the reader to divine. And so they have expressed, finally, a certain aspect of the world; and some of them have carried style to a point beyond which the style that says, rather than suggests, cannot go. The whole of that movement comes to a splendid funeral in Heredia's[1] sonnets, in which the literature of form says its last word, and dies.

Meanwhile, something which is vaguely called Decadence had come into being. That name, rarely used with any precise meaning, was usually either hurled as a reproach or hurled back as a defiance. It pleased some young men in various countries to call themselves Decadents, with all the thrill of unsatisfied virtue masquerading as uncomprehended vice. As a matter of fact, the term is in its place only when applied to style; to that ingenious deformation of the language, in Mallarmé,[2] for instance, which can be compared with what we are accustomed to call the Greek and Latin of the Decadence. No doubt perversity of form and perversity of matter are often found together, and, among the lesser men especially, experiment was carried far, not only in the direction of style. But a movement which in this sense might be called Decadent could but have been a straying aside from the main road of literature. Nothing, not even conventional virtue, is so provincial as conventional vice; and the desire to "bewilder the middle classes" is itself middle-class. The interlude, half a mock-interlude, of Decadence, diverted the attention of the critics while something more serious was in preparation. That something more serious has crys-

tallised, for the time, under the form of Symbolism, in which art returns to the one pathway, leading through beautiful things to the eternal beauty.

In most of the writers whom I have dealt with as summing up in themselves all that is best in Symbolism, it will be noticed that the form is very carefully elaborated, and seems to count for at least as much as in those writers of whose over-possession by form I have complained. Here, however, all this elaboration comes from a very different motive, and leads to other ends. There is such a thing as perfecting form that form may be annihilated. All the art of Verlaine[3] is in bringing verse to a bird's song, the art of Mallarmé in bringing verse to the song of an orchestra. In Villiers de l'Isle-Adam drama becomes an embodiment of spiritual forces, in Maeterlinck[4] not even their embodiment, but the remote sound of their voices. It is all an attempt to spiritualise literature, to evade the old bondage of rhetoric, the old bondage of exteriority. Description is banished that beautiful things may be evoked, magically; the regular beat of verse is broken in order that words may fly, upon subtler wings. Mystery is no longer feared, as the great mystery in whose midst we are islanded was feared by those to whom that unknown sea was only a great void. We are coming closer to nature, as we seem to shrink from it with something of horror, disdaining to catalogue the trees of the forest. And as we brush aside the accidents of daily life, in which men and women imagine that they are alone touching reality, we come closer to humanity, to everything in humanity, to everything in humanity that may have begun before the world and may outlast it.

Here, then, in this revolt against exteriority, against rhetoric, against a materialistic tradition; in this endeavour to disengage the ultimate essence, the soul, of whatever exists and can be realised by the consciousness; in this dutiful waiting upon every

---

[1] José-Maria de Heredia (1842–1905), Cuban-born French poet.

[2] Stéphane Mallarmé (1842–98).

[3] Paul Verlaine (1844–96), French symbolist.

[4] Maurice Maeterlinck (1862–1949), Belgian poet and dramatist.

symbol by which the soul of things can be made visible; literature, bowed down by so many burdens, may at last attain liberty, and its authentic speech. In attaining this liberty, it accepts a heavier burden; for in speaking to us so intimately, so solemnly, as only religion had hitherto spoken to us, it becomes itself a kind of religion, with all the duties and responsibilities of the sacred ritual.

STÉPHANE MALLARMÉ

I

Stéphane Mallarmé was one of those who love literature too much to write it except by fragments; in whom the desire of perfection brings its own defeat. With either more or less ambition he would have done more to achieve himself; he was always divided between an absolute aim at the absolute, that is, the unattainable, and a too logical disdain for the compromise by which, after all, literature is literature. Carry the theories of Mallarmé to a practical conclusion, multiply his powers in a direct ratio, and you have Wagner.[1] It is his failure not to be Wagner. And, Wagner having existed, it was for him to be something more, to complete Wagner. Well, not being able to be that, it was a matter of sincere indifference to him whether he left one or two little, limited masterpieces of formal verse and prose, the more or the less. It was "the work" that he dreamed of, the new art, more than a new religion, whose precise form in the world he was never quite able to settle.

Un auteur difficile, in the phrase of M. Catulle Mendès,[2] it has always been to what he himself calls "a labyrinth illuminated by flowers" that Mallarmé has felt it due to their dignity to invite his readers. To their own dignity, and also to his. Mallarmé was obscure, not so much because he wrote differently, as

because he thought differently, from other people. His mind was elliptical, and, relying with undue confidence on the intelligence of his readers, he emphasised the effect of what was unlike other people in his mind by resolutely ignoring even the links of connection that existed between them. Never having aimed at popularity, he never needed, as most writers need, to make the first advances. He made neither intrusion upon nor concession to those who, after all, were not obliged to read him. And when he spoke, he considered it neither needful nor seemly to listen in order to hear whether he was heard. To the charge of obscurity he replied, with sufficient disdain, that there are many who do not know how to read—except the newspaper, he adds, in one of those disconcerting, oddly-printed parentheses, which makes his work, to those who rightly apprehend it, so full of wise limitations, so safe from hasty or seemingly final conclusions. No one in our time has more significantly vindicated the supreme right of the artist in the aristocracy of letters; wilfully, perhaps, not always wisely, but nobly, logically. Has not every artist shrunk from that making of himself "a motley to the view," that handing over of his naked soul to the laughter of the multitude? But who, in our time, has wrought so subtle a veil, shining on this side, where the few are, a thick cloud on the other, where are the many? The oracles have always had the wisdom to hide their secrets in the obscurity of many meanings, or of what has seemed meaningless; and might it not, after all, be the finest epitaph for a self-respecting man of letters to be able to say, even after the writing of many books: I have kept my secret, I have not betrayed myself to the multitude?

But to Mallarmé, certainly, there might be applied the significant warning of Rossetti:

> Yet woe to thee if once thou yield
> Unto the act of doing nought![3]

---

[1] Richard Wagner (1813–83), German composer.

[2] Catulle Mendès (1841–1909), French poet, novelist, dramatist, and critic.

---

[3] not identified.

After a life of persistent devotion to literature, he has left enough poems to make a single small volume (less, certainly, than a hundred poems in all), a single volume of prose, a few pamphlets, and a prose translation of the poems of Poe. It is because among these there are masterpieces, poems which are among the most beautiful poems written in our time, prose which has all the subtlest qualities of prose, that, quitting the abstract point of view, we are forced to regret the fatal enchantments, fatal for him, of theories which are so greatly needed by others, so valuable for our instruction, if we are only a little careful in putting them into practice.

In estimating the significance of Stéphane Mallarmé, it is necessary to take into account not only his verse and prose, but, almost more than these, the Tuesdays of the Rue de Rome, in which he gave himself freely to more than one generation. No one who has ever climbed those four flights of stairs will have forgotten the narrow, homely interior, elegant with a sort of scrupulous Dutch comfort; the heavy, carved furniture, the tall clock, the portraits, Manet's, Whistler's, on the walls; the table on which the china bowl, odorous with tobacco, was pushed from hand to hand; above all, the rocking-chair, Mallarmé's, from which he would rise quietly, to stand leaning his elbow on the mantelpiece, while one hand, the hand which did not hold the cigarette, would sketch out one of those familiar gestures: *un peu de prêtre, un peu de danseuse* (in M. Rodenbach's[1] admirable phrase)*, avec lesquels il avait l'air chaque fois d'*entrer *dans la conversation, comme on entre en scène.* One of the best talkers of our time, he was, unlike most other fine talkers, harmonious with his own theories in giving no monologues, in allowing every liberty to his guests, to the conversation; in his perfect readiness to follow the slightest indication, to embroider upon

[1] Georges Rodenbach (1855–98), Belgian Symbolist poet and novelist. "A bit of priest, a bit of dancer, with which he seemed each time to enter into the conversation, as one enters on stage."

any frame, with any material presented to him. There would have been something almost of the challenge of the improvisatore in this easily moved alertness of mental attitude, had it not been for the singular gentleness with which Mallarmé's intelligence moved, in these considerable feats, with the half-apologetic negligence of the perfect acrobat. He seemed to be no more than brushing the dust off your own ideas, settling, arranging them a little, before he gave them back to you, surprisingly luminous. It was only afterwards that you realised how small had been your own part in the matter, as well as what it meant to have enlightened without dazzling you. But there was always the feeling of comradeship, the comradeship of a master, whom, while you were there at least, you did not question; and that very feeling lifted you, in your own estimation, nearer to art.

Invaluable, it seems to me, those Tuesdays must have been to the young men of two generations who have been making French literature; they were unique, certainly, in the experience of the young Englishman who was always so cordially received there, with so flattering a cordiality. Here was a house in which art, literature, was the very atmosphere, a religious atmosphere; and the master of the house, in his just a little solemn simplicity, a priest. I never heard the price of a book mentioned, or the number of thousand francs which a popular author had been paid for his last volume; here, in this one literary house, literature was unknown as a trade. And, above all, the questions that were discussed were never, at least, in Mallarmé's treatment, in his guidance of them, other than essential questions, considerations of art in the abstract, of literature before it coagulates into a book, of life as its amusing and various web spins the stuff of art. When, indeed, the conversation, by some untimely hazard, drifted too near to one, became for a moment, perhaps inconveniently, practical, it was Mallarmé's solicitous politeness to wait, a little constrained, almost uneasy, rolling his cigarette in silence, until the disturbing moment had passed.

There were other disturbing moments, sometimes. I remember one night, rather late, the sudden irruption of M. de Heredia, coming on after a dinner-party, and seating himself, in his well-filled evening dress, precisely in Mallarmé's favourite chair. He was intensely amusing, voluble, floridly vehement; Mallarmé, I am sure, was delighted to see him; but the loud voice was a little trying to his nerves, and then he did not know what to do without his chair. He was like a cat that has been turned out of its favourite corner, as he roamed uneasily about the room, resting an unaccustomed elbow on the sideboard, visibly at a disadvantage.

For the attitude of those young men, some of them no longer exactly young, who frequented the Tuesdays, was certainly the attitude of the disciple. Mallarmé never exacted it, he seemed never to notice it; yet it meant to him, all the same, a good deal; as it meant, and in the best sense, a good deal to them. He loved art with a supreme disinterestedness, and it was for the sake of art that he wished to be really a master. For he knew that he had something to teach, that he had found out some secrets worth knowing, that he had discovered a point of view which he could to some degree perpetuate in those young men who listened to him. And to them this free kind of apprenticeship was, beyond all that it gave in direct counsels, in the pattern of work, a noble influence. Mallarmé's quiet, laborious life was for some of them the only counterpoise to the Bohemian example of the *d'Harcourt*[1] or the *Taverne*, where art is loved, but with something of haste, in a very changing devotion. It was impossible to come away from Mallarmé's without some tranquillising influence from that quiet place, some impersonal ambition towards excellence, the resolve, at least, to write a

sonnet, a page of prose, that should be in its own way as perfect as one could make it, worthy of Mallarmé.

II

"Poetry," said Mallarmé, "is the language of a state of crisis"; and all his poems are the evocation of a passing ecstasy, arrested in mid-flight. This ecstasy is never the mere instinctive cry of the heart, the simple human joy or sorrow, which, like the Parnassians, but for not quite the same reason, he did not admit in poetry. It is a mental transposition of emotion or sensation, veiled with atmosphere, and becoming, as it becomes a poem, pure beauty. Here, for instance, in a poem which I have translated line for line, and almost word for word, a delicate emotion, a figure vaguely divined, a landscape magically evoked, blend in a single effect.

SIGH

My soul, calm sister, towards thy brow, whereon
    scarce grieves
An autumn strewn already with its russet leaves,
And towards the wandering sky of thine angelic
    eyes,
Mounts, as in melancholy gardens may arise
Some faithful fountain sighing whitely towards the
    blue!
—Towards the blue pale and pure that sad
    October knew,
When, in those depths, it mirrored languors
    infinite,
And agonising leaves upon the waters white,
Windily drifting, traced a furrow cold and dun,
Where, in one long last ray, lingered the yellow
    sun.

Another poem comes a little closer to nature, but with what exquisite precautions, and with what surprising novelty in its unhesitating touch on actual things!

---

[1] Eugène d'Harcourt (1859–1918), French composer.

SEA-WIND

The flesh is sad, alas! and all the books are read.
Flight, only flight! I feel that birds are wild to
    tread
The floor of unknown foam, and to attain the
    skies!
Nought, neither ancient gardens mirrored in
    the eyes,
Shall hold this heart that bathes in waters its
    delight,
O nights! nor yet my waking lamp, whose lonely
    light
Shadows the vacant paper, whiteness profits
    best,
Nor the young wife who rocks her baby on her
    breast.
I will depart. O steamer, swaying rope and spar,
Lift anchor for exotic lands that lie afar!
A weariness, outworn by cruel hopes, still clings
To the last farewell handerchief's last beckonings!
And are not these, the masts inviting storms,
    not these
That an awakening wind bends over wrecking
    seas,
Lost, not a sail, a sail, a flowering isle, ere long?
But, O my heart, hear thou, hear thou the sailor's
    song!

These (need I say?) belong to the earlier period, in which Mallarmé had not yet withdrawn his light into the cloud; and to the same period belong the prose-poems, one of which, perhaps the most exquisite, I will translate here.

AUTUMN LAMENT

"Ever since Maria left me, for another star—which? Orion, Altair, or thou, green Venus?—I have always cherished solitude. How many long days have I passed, alone with my cat! By *alone*, I mean without a material being, and my cat is a mystical companion, a spirit. I may say, then, that I have passed long days alone with my cat, and alone, with one of the last writers of the Roman decadence; for since the white creature is no more, strangely and singularly, I have loved all that may be summed up in the word: fall. Thus, in the year, my favourite season is during those last languid summer days which come just before the autumn; and, in the day, the hour when I take my walk is the hour when the sun lingers before fading, with rays of copper-yellow on the grey walls, and of copper-red on the window-panes. And, just so, the literature from which my soul demands delight must be the poetry dying out of the last moments of Rome, provided, nevertheless, that it breathes nothing of the rejuvenating approach of the Barbarians, and does not stammer the infantile Latin of the first Christian prose.

"I read, then, one of those beloved poems (whose streaks of rouge have more charm for me than the fresh cheek of youth), and buried my hand in the fur of the pure animal, when a barrel-organ began to sing, languishingly and melancholy, under my window. It played in the long alley of poplars, whose leaves seem mournful to me even in spring, since Maria passed that way with the tapers, for the last time. Yes, sad people's instrument, truly: the piano glitters, the violin brings one's torn fibres to the light, but the barrel-organ, in the twilight of memory, has set me despairingly dreaming. While it murmured a gaily vulgar air, such as puts mirth into the heart of the suburbs, an old-fashioned, an empty air, how came it that its refrain went to my very soul, and made me weep like a romantic ballad? I drank it in, and I did not throw a penny out of the window, for fear of disturbing my own impression, and of perceiving that the instrument was not singing by itself."

Between these characteristic, clear, and beautiful poems, in verse and in prose, and the opaque darkness of the later writings, come one or two poems, perhaps the finest of all, in which already clearness is "a secondary grace," but in which a subtle rapture finds incomparable expression. *L'Après-midi d'un Faune* and *Hérodiade* have already been introduced, in different ways, to English readers: the former by Mr. Gosse,[1] in a detailed analysis; the latter by a translation into verse. And Debussy,[2] in his new music, has taken *L'Après-midi d'un Faune* almost for his new point of departure, interpreting it, at all events, faultlessly. In these two poems I find Mallarmé at the moment when his own desire achieves itself; when he attains Wagner's ideal, that "the most complete work of the poet should be that which, in its final achievement, becomes a perfect music": every word is a jewel, scattering and recapturing sudden fire, every image is a symbol, and the whole poem is visible music. After this point began that fatal "last period" which comes to most artists who have thought too curiously, or dreamed too remote dreams, or followed a too wandering beauty. Mallarmé had long been too conscious that all publication is "almost a speculation, on one's modesty, for one's silence": that "to unclench the fists, breaking one's sedentary dream, for a ruffling face to face with the idea," was after all unnecessary to his own conception of himself, a mere way of convincing the public that one exists; and having achieved, as he thought, "the right to abstain from doing anything exceptional," he devoted himself, doubly, to silence. Seldom condescending to write, he wrote now only for himself, and in a manner which certainly saved him from intrusion. Some of Meredith's[3] poems, and occasional passages of his prose, can alone give in English some faint idea of the later prose and verse of Mallarmé. The verse could not, I think, be translated; of the prose, in which an extreme lucidity of thought comes to us but glimmeringly through the entanglements of

a construction, part Latin, part English, I shall endeavour to translate some fragments, in speaking of the theoretic writings, contained in the two volumes of *Vers et Prose* and *Divagations*.

III

It is the distinction of Mallarmé to have aspired after an impossible liberation of the soul of literature from what is fretting and constraining in "the body of that death," which is the mere literature of words. Words, he has realised, are of value only as a notation of the free breath of the spirit; words, therefore, must be employed with an extreme care, in their choice and adjustment, in setting them to reflect and chime upon one another; yet least of all for their own sake, for what they can never, except by suggestion, express. "Every soul is a melody," he has said, "which needs to be readjusted; and for that are the flute or the viol of each." The word, treated indeed with a kind of "adoration," as he says, is so regarded in a magnificent sense, in which it is apprehended as a living thing, itself the vision rather than the reality; at least the philtre of the evocation. The word, chosen as he chooses it, is for him a liberating principle, by which the spirit is extracted from matter; takes form, perhaps assumes immortality. Thus an artificiality, even in the use of words, that seeming artificiality which comes from using words as if they had never been used before, that chimerical search after the virginity of language, is but the paradoxical outward sign of extreme discontent with even the best of their service. Writers who use words fluently, seeming to disregard their importance, do so from an unconscious confidence in their expressiveness, which the scrupulous thinker, the precise dreamer, can never place in the most carefully chosen among them. To evoke, by some elaborate, instantaneous magic of language, without the formality of an after all impossible description; to be, rather than to express: that is what Mallarmé has consistently, and from the first, sought in verse and prose. And he has sought this

---

[1] Sir Edward (William) Gosse (1849–1928), English critic, poet, and biographer.

[2] Claude Debussy (1862–1918), French composer.

[3] George Meredith (1828–1909), novelist and poet.

wandering, illusive, beckoning butterfly, the soul of dreams, over more and more entangled ground; and it has led him into the depths of many forests, far from the sunlight. To say that he has found what he sought is impossible; but (is it possible to avoid saying?) how heroic a search, and what marvellous discoveries by the way!

I think I understand, though I cannot claim his own authority for my supposition, the way in which Mallarmé wrote verse, and the reason why it became more and more abstruse, more and more unintelligible. Remember his principle: that to name is to destroy, to suggest is to create. Note, further, that he condemns the inclusion in verse of anything but, "for example, the horror of the forest, or the silent thunder afloat in the leaves; not the intrinsic, dense wood of the trees." He has received, then, a mental sensation: let it be the horror of the forest. This sensation begins to form in his brain, at first probably no more than a rhythm, absolutely without words. Gradually thought begins to concentrate itself (but with an extreme care, lest it should break the tension on which all depends) upon the sensation, already struggling to find its own consciousness. Delicately, stealthily, with infinitely timid precaution, words present themselves, at first in silence. Every word seems like a desecration, seems, the clearer it is, to throw back the original sensation farther and farther into the darkness. But, guided always by the rhythm, which is the executive soul (as, in Aristotle's definition, the soul is the form of the body), words come slowly, one by one, shaping the message. Imagine the poem already written down, at least composed. In its very imperfection, it is clear, it shows the links by which it has been riveted together; the whole process of its construction can be studied. Now most writers would be content; but with Mallarmé the work has only begun. In the final result there must be no sign of the making, there must be only the thing made. He works over it, word by word, changing a word here, for its colour, which is not precisely the colour

required, a word there, for the break it makes in the music. A new image occurs to him, rarer, subtler, than the one he has used; the image is transferred. By the time the poem has reached, as it seems to him, a flawless unity, the steps of the progress have been only too effectually effaced; and while the poet, who has seen the thing from the beginning, still sees the relation of point to point, the reader, who comes to it only in its final stage, finds himself in a not unnatural bewilderment. Pursue this manner of writing to its ultimate development; start with an enigma, and then withdraw the key of the enigma; and you arrive, easily, at the frozen impenetrability of those latest sonnets, in which the absence of all punctuation is scarcely a recognisable hindrance.

That, I fancy to myself, was his actual way of writing; here, in what I prefer to give as a corollary, is the theory. "Symbolist, Decadent, or Mystic, the schools thus called by themselves, or thus hastily labelled by our information-press, adopt, for meeting-place, the point of an Idealism which (similarly as in fugues, in sonatas) rejects the 'natural' materials, and, as brutal, a direct thought ordering them; to retain no more than suggestion. To be instituted, a relation between images, exact; and that therefrom should detach itself a third aspect, fusible and clear, offered to the divination. Abolished, the pretension, æsthetically an error, despite its dominion over almost all the masterpieces, to enclose within the subtle paper other than, for example, the horror of the forest, or the silent thunder afloat in the leaves; not the intrinsic, dense wood of the trees. Some few bursts of personal pride, veridically trumpeted, awaken the architecture of the palace, alone habitable; not of stone, on which the pages would close but ill." For example (it is his own): "I say: a flower! and out of the oblivion to which my voice consigns every contour, so far as anything save the known calyx, musically arises, idea, and exquisite, the one flower absent from all bouquets." "The pure work," then, "implies the elocutionary disappearance of the poet, who yields place to the words, immobilised by the shock of their inequality; they take light from mutual reflection, like an actual train of fire over precious stones, replacing the old lyric afflatus or the enthusiastic personal direction of the phrase." "The verse which out of many vocables remakes an entire word, new, unknown to the language, and as if magical, attains this isolation of speech." Whence, it being "music which rejoins verse, to form, since Wagner, Poetry," the final conclusion: "That we are now precisely at the moment of seeking, before that breaking up of the large rhythms of literature, and their scattering in articulate, almost instrumental, nervous waves, an art which shall complete the transposition, into the Book, of the symphony, or simply recapture our own: for, it is not in elementary sonorities of brass, strings, wood, unquestionably, but in the intellectual word at its utmost, that, fully and evidently, we should find, drawing to itself all the correspondences of the universe, the supreme Music."

Here, literally translated, in exactly the arrangement of the original, are some passages out of the theoretic writings, which I have brought together, to indicate what seem to me the main lines of Mallarmé's doctrine. It is the doctrine which, as I have already said, had been divined by Gérard de Nerval; but what, in Gérard, was pure vision, becomes in Mallarmé a logical sequence of meditation. Mallarmé was not a mystic, to whom anything came unconsciously; he was a thinker, in whom an extraordinary subtlety of mind was exercised on always explicit, though by no means the common, problems. "A seeker after something in the world, that is there in no satisfying measure, or not at all," he pursued his search with unwearying persistence, with a sharp mental division of dream and idea, certainly very lucid to himself, however he may have failed to render his expression clear to others. And I, for one,

cannot doubt that he was, for the most part, entirely right in his statement and analysis of the new conditions under which we are now privileged or condemned to write. His obscurity was partly his failure to carry out the spirit of his own directions; but, apart from obscurity, which we may all be fortunate enough to escape, is it possible for a writer, at the present day, to be quite simple, with the old, objective simplicity, in either thought or expression? To be *naïf*, to be archaic, is not to be either natural or simple; I affirm that it is not natural to be what is called "natural" any longer. We have no longer the mental attitude of those to whom a story was but a story, and all stories good; we have realised, since it was proved to us by Poe, not merely that the age of epics is past, but that no long poem was ever written; the finest long poem in the world being but a series of short poems linked together by prose. And, naturally, we can no longer write what we can no longer accept. Symbolism, implicit in all literature from the beginning, as it is implicit in the very words we use, comes to us now, at last quite conscious of itself, offering us the only escape from our many imprisonments. We find a new, an older, sense in the so worn out forms of things; the world, which we can no longer believe in as the satisfying material object it was to our grandparents, becomes transfigured with a new light; words, which long usage had darkened almost out of recognition, take fresh lustre. And it is on the lines of that spiritualising of the word, that perfecting of form in its capacity for allusion and suggestion, that confidence in the eternal correspondences between the visible and the invisible universe, which Mallarmé taught, and too intermittently practised, that literature must now move, if it is in any sense to move forward.

—1899

Alice Meynell
1847 – 1922

Alice Meynell was a poet, journalist, and political activist, particularly in support of the non-militant suffragists. Her first volume of poetry, *Preludes* (1875), was admired by Tennyson and Ruskin, and through her later work she became friends with fellow-poets Francis Thompson, Coventry Patmore, and George Meredith. Her best poems, reflecting the Victorian themes of the ambiguity of motherhood, the fallen woman, and the social and political ramifications of motherhood (she bore eight children), are personal and lyrical.

೮ꍏ೮

Tennyson [1]

Fifty years after Tennyson's birth he was saluted a great poet by that unanimous acclamation which includes mere clamour. Fifty further years, and his centenary was marked by a new detraction. It is sometimes difficult to distinguish the obscure but not unmajestic law of change from the sorry custom of reaction. Change hastes not and rests not, reaction beats to and fro, flickering about the moving mind of the world. Reaction—the paltry precipitancy of the multitude—rather than the novelty of change, has brought about a ferment and corruption of opinion on Tennyson's poetry. It may be said that opinion is the same now as it was in the middle of the nineteenth century—the same, but turned. All that was not worth having of admiration then has soured into detraction now. It is of no more significance, acrid, than it was, sweet. What the herding of opinion gave yesterday it is able to take away to-day, that and no more.

But besides the common favour-disfavour of the day, there is the tendency of educated opinion, once disposed to accept the whole of Tennyson's poetry as though he could not be "parted from himself," and now disposed to reject the whole, on the same plea. But if ever there was a poet who needed to be thus "parted"—the word is his own—it is he who wrote both narrowly for his time and liberally for all time, and who—this is the more important character of his poetry—had both a style and a manner: a masterly style, a magical style, a too dainty manner, nearly a trick; a noble landscape and in it figures something ready-made. He is a subject for our alternatives of feeling, nay, our conflicts, as is hardly another poet. We may deeply admire and wonder, and, in another line or hemistich, grow indifferent or slightly averse. He sheds the luminous suns of dreams upon men and women who would do well with footlights; waters their way with rushing streams of Paradise and cataracts from visionary hills; laps them in divine darkness; leads them into those touching landscapes, "the lovely that are not beloved," long grey fields, cool sombre summers, and meadows thronged with unnoticeable flowers; speeds his carpet knight—or is that hardly a just name for one whose sword "smites" so well?—upon a carpet of authentic wild flowers; pushes his rovers, in costume, from off blossoming shores, on the keels of old romance. The style and the manner, I have said, run side by side. If we may take one poet's too violent phrase, and consider poets to be "damned to poetry," why, then, Tennyson is condemned by a couple of sentences, "to run concurrently." We have the style and the manner locked together at times in a single stanza, locked and yet not mingled. There should be no danger for the more judicious reader lest impatience at the peculiar Tennyson trick should involve the great Tennyson style in a sweep of protest. Yet the danger has in fact

---

[1] first published in *Hearts of Controversy*, 1917.

proved real within the present and recent years, and seems about to threaten still more among the less judicious. But it will not long prevail. The vigorous little nation of lovers of poetry, alive one by one within the vague multitude of the nation of England, cannot remain finally insensible to what is at once majestic and magical in Tennyson. For those are not qualities they neglect in their other masters. How, valuing singleness of heart in the sixteenth century, splendour in the seventeenth, composure in the eighteenth; how, with a spiritual ear for the note—commonly called Celtic, albeit it is the most English thing in the world—the wild wood note of the remoter song; how, with the educated sense of style, the liberal sense of ease; how, in a word, fostering Letters and loving Nature, shall that choice nation within England long disregard these virtues in the nineteenth-century master? How disregard him, for more than the few years of reaction, for the insignificant reasons of his bygone taste, his insipid courtliness, his prettiness, or what not? It is no dishonour to Tennyson, for it is a dishonour to our education, to disparage a poet who wrote but the two—had he written no more of their kind—lines of "The Passing of Arthur," of which, before I quote them, I will permit myself the personal remembrance of a great contemporary author's opinion. Meredith, speaking to me of the high-water mark of English style in poetry and prose, cited those lines as topmost in poetry:

On one side lay the ocean, and on one
Lay a great water, and the moon was full.[1]

Here is no taint of manner, no pretty posture or habit, but the simplicity of poetry and the simplicity of Nature, something on the yonder side of imagery. It is to be noted that this noble passage is from Tennyson's generally weakest kind of work—blank verse; and should thus be a sign that the laxity of so

many parts of the "Idylls" and other blank verse poems was a kind of unnecessary fault. Lax this form of poetry undoubtedly is with Tennyson. His blank verse is often too easy; it cannot be said to fly, for the paradoxical reason that it has no weight; it slips by, without halting or tripping indeed, but also without the friction of the movement of vitality. This quality, which is so near to a fault, this quality of ease, has come to be disregarded in our day. That Horace Walpole overpraised this virtue is not good reason that we should hold it for a vice. Yet we do more than undervalue it; and several of our authors, in prose and poetry, seem to find much merit in the manifest difficulty; they will not have a key to turn, though closely and tightly, in oiled wards; let the reluctant iron catch and grind, or they would even prefer to pick you the lock.

But though we may think it time that the quality once overprized should be restored to a more proportionate honour, our great poet Tennyson shows us that of all merits ease is, unexpectedly enough, the most dangerous. It is not only, with him, that the wards are oiled, it is also that the key turns loosely. This is true of much of the beautiful "Idylls," but not of their best passages, nor of such magnificent blank verse as that of the close of "A Vision of Sin," or of "Lucretius." As to the question of ease, we cannot have a better maxim than Coventry Patmore's saying that poetry "should confess, but not suffer from, its difficulties."[2] Tennyson is always an artist, and the finish of his work is one of the principal notes of his versification. How this finish comports with the excessive ease of his prosody remains his own peculiar secret. Ease, in him, does not mean that he has any unhandsome slovenly ways. On the contrary, he resembles rather the warrior with the pouncet box.[3]

---

[1] *Idylls of the King*, "The Passing of Arthur," ll. 170–80.

[2] not identified.

[3] a small box with a perforated lid for perfumes. For "the warrior with the pouncet box" see 1 *Henry IV*. 1.3. 36–41.

Tennyson certainly *worked*, and the exceeding ease of his blank verse comes perhaps of this little paradox—that he makes somewhat too much show of the hiding of his art.

In the first place the poet with the great welcome style and the little unwelcome manner, Tennyson is, in the second place, the modern poet who withstood France. (That is, of course, modern France—France since the Renaissance. From medieval Provence there is not an English poet who does not own inheritance.) It was some time about the date of the Restoration that modern France began to be modish in England. A ruffle at the court of Charles, a couplet in the ear of Pope, a *tour de phrase* from Mme de Sévigné[1] much to the taste of Walpole, later the good example of French painting—rich interest paid for the loan of our Constable's initiative—later still a scattering of French taste, French critical business, over all the shallow places of our literature—these have all been phases of a national vanity of ours, an eager and anxious fluttering or jostling to be foremost and French. Matthew Arnold's essay on criticism fostered this anxiety, and yet I find in this work of his a lack of easy French knowledge, such as his misunderstanding of the word *brutalité*, which means no more, or little more, than roughness. Matthew Arnold, by the way, knew so little of the French character as to altogether ignorant of French provincialism, French practical sense, and French "convenience." "Convenience" is his dearest word of contempt, "practical sense" his next dearest, and he throws them a score of times in the teeth of the English. Strange is the irony of truth. For he bestows those withering words on the nation that has the fifty religions, and attributes "ideas"—as the antithesis of "convenience" and "practical sense"—to the nation that has the fifty sauces. And not for a moment does he suspect himself of this blunder, so manifest as to

be disconcerting to his reader. One seems to hear an incurably English accent in all this, which indeed is reported, by his acquaintance, of Matthew Arnold's actual speaking of French. It is certain that he has not the interest of familiarity with the language, but only the interest of strangeness. Now, while we meet the effect of the French coat in our seventeenth century, of the French light verse in our earlier eighteenth century, and of French philosophy in our later, of the French revolution in our Wordsworth, of the French painting in our nineteenth-century studios, of French fiction—and the dregs are still running—in our libraries, of French poetry in our Swinburne, of French criticism in our Arnold, Tennyson shows the effect of nothing French whatever. Not the Elizabethans, not Shakespeare, not Jeremy Taylor,[2] not Milton, not Shelley were (in their art, not in their matter) more insular in their time. France, by the way, has more than appreciated the homage of Tennyson's contemporaries; Victor Hugo avers, in *Les Misérables*, that our people imitate his people in all things, and in particular he rouses in us a delighted laughter of surprises by asserting that the London street-boy imitates the Parisian street-boy. There is, in fact, something of a street-boy in some of our late more literary mimicries.

We are apt to judge a poet too exclusively by his imagery. Tennyson is hardly a great master of imagery. He has more imagination than imagery. He sees the thing, with so luminous a mind's eye, that it is sufficient to him; he needs not to see it more beautifully by a similitude. "A clear-walled city" is enough; "meadows" are enough—indeed Tennyson reigns for ever over all meadows; "the happy birds that change their sky"; "Bright Phosphor, fresher for the night"; "Twilight and evening bell"; "the stillness of the central sea"; "that friend of mine who lives in God"; "the solitary morning"; "Four grey walls and four

---

[1] Marie de Rabutin-Chantel Sévigné (1626–96), French letter-writer and Salonist.

[2] Jeremy Taylor (1613–67), Anglican clergyman and religious writer.

grey towers"; "Watched by weeping queens"; these are enough, illustrious, and needing not illustration.

If we do not see Tennyson to be the lonely, the first, the *one* that he is, this is because of the throng of his following, though a number that are of that throng hardly know, or else would deny, their flocking. But he added to our literature not only in the way of cumulation, but by the advent of his single genius. He is one of the few fountain-head poets of the world. The new landscape which was his—the lovely unbeloved—is, it need hardly be said, the matter of his poetry and not its inspiration. It may have seemed to some readers that it is the novelty, in poetry, of this homely unscenic scenery—this Lincolnshire quality—that accounts for Tennyson's freshness of vision. But it is not so. Tennyson is fresh also in scenic scenery; he is fresh with the things that others have outworn; mountains, desert islands, castles, elves, what you will that is conventional. Where are there more divinely poetic lines than those, which will never be wearied with quotation, beginning, "A splendour falls"? What castle walls have stood in such a light of old romance, where in all poetry is there a sound wilder than that of those faint "horns of elfland"? Here is the remoteness, the beyond, the light delirium, not of disease but of more rapturous and delicate health, the closer secret of poetry. This most English of modern poets has been taunted with his mere gardens. He loved, indeed, the "lazy lilies,"[1] of the exquisite garden of "The Gardener's Daughter," but he betook his ecstatic English spirit also far afield and overseas; to the winter places of his familiar nightingale:

> When first the liquid note beloved of men
> Comes flying over many a windy wave;[2]

to the lotus-eaters' shore; to the outland landscapes of "The Palace of Art"—the "clear-walled city by the sea," the "pillared town," the "full-fed river";[3] to the "pencilled valleys" of Monte Rosa;[4] to the "vale in Ida,"[5] to that tremendous upland in the "Vision of Sin":

> At last I heard a voice upon the slope
> Cry to the summit, Is there any hope?
> To which an answer pealed from that high land,
> But in a tongue no man could understand.[6]

The Cleopatra of "The Dream of Fair Women" is but a ready-made Cleopatra, but when in the shades of her forest she remembers the sun of the world, she leaves the page of Tennyson's poorest manner and becomes one with Shakespeare's queen:

> We drank the Libyan sun to sleep.[7]

Nay, there is never a passage of manner but a great passage of style rebukes our dislike and recalls our heart again. The dramas, less than the lyrics, and even less than the "Idylls," are matter for the true Tennysonian. Their action is, at its liveliest, rather vivacious than vital, and the sentiment, whether in "Becket" or in "Harold," is not only modern, it is fixed within Tennyson's own peculiar score or so of years. But that he might have answered, in drama, to a stronger stimulus, a sharper spur, than his time administered, may be guessed from a few passages of "Queen Mary," and from the dramatic terror of the arrow in "Harold." The line has appeared in prophetic frag-

---

[1] l. 42.

[2] *Idylls of the King*, "The Marriage of Geraint," ll. 336–37.

---

[3] l. 97, l. 124, l. 73.

[4] "The Daisy," l. 67.

[5] "Œnone," l. 1.

[6] ll. 219–22.

[7] l. 145.

ments in earlier scenes, and at the moment of doom it is the outcry of unquestionable tragedy:

Sanguelac—Sanguelac—the arrow—
  the arrow!—Away![1]

Tennyson is also an eminently all-intelligible poet. Those whom he puzzles or confounds must be a flock with an incalculable liability to go wide of any road—"down all manner of streets," as the desperate drover cries in the anecdote. But what are streets, however various, to the ways of error that a great flock will take in open country—minutely, individually wrong, making mistakes upon hardly perceptible occasions, or none—"minute fortuitous variations in any possible direction," as used to be said in exposition of the Darwinian theory? A vast outlying public, like that of Tennyson, may make you as many blunders as it has heads; but the accurate clear poet proved his meaning to all accurate perceptions. Where he hesitates, his is the sincere pause of process and uncertainty. It has been said that Tennyson, midway between the student of material science and the mystic, wrote and thought according to an age that wavered, with him, between the two minds, and that men have now taken one way or the other. Is this indeed true, and are men so divided and so sure? Or have they not rather already turned, in numbers, back to the parting, or meeting, of eternal roads? The religious question that arises upon experience of death has never been asked with more sincerity and attention than by him. If "In Memoriam" represents the mind of yesterday it represents no less the mind of to-morrow. It is true that pessimism and insurrection in their ignobler forms—nay, in the ignoblest form of a fashion—have, or had but yesterday, the control of the popular pen. Trivial pessimism or trivial optimism, it matters little which prevails. For those who follow the one habit to-day would have

followed the other in a past generation. Fleeting as they are, it cannot be within their competence to neglect or reject the philosophy of "In Memoriam." To the dainty stanzas of that poem, it is true, no great struggle of reasoning was to be committed, nor would any such dispute be judiciously entrusted to the rhymes of a song of sorrow. Tennyson here proposes, rather than closes with, the ultimate question of our destiny. The conflict, for which he proves himself strong enough, is in that magnificent poem of a thinker, "Lucretius." But so far as "In Memoriam" attempts, weighs, falters, and confides, it is true to the experience of human anguish and intellect.

I say intellect advisedly. Not for him such blunders of thought as Coleridge's in "The Ancient Mariner" or Wordsworth's in "Hartleap Well." Coleridge names the sun, moon, and stars as when, in a dream, the sleeping imagination is threatened with some significant illness. We see them in his great poem as apparitions. Coleridge's senses are infinitely and transcendently spiritual. But a candid reader must be permitted to think the mere story silly. The wedding-guest might rise the morrow morn a sadder but he assuredly did not rise a wiser man.

As for Wordsworth, the most beautiful stanzas of "Hartleap Well" are fatally rebuked by the truths of Nature. He shows us the ruins of an aspen wood, a blighted hollow, a dreary place, forlorn because an innocent stag, hunted, had there broken his heart in a leap from the rocks above; grass would not grow there.

This beast not unobserved by Nature fell,
His death was mourned by sympathy divine.[2]

And the signs of that sympathy are cruelly asserted by the poet to be these woodland ruins—cruelly, because the daily sight of the world blossoming over the

---

[1] *Harold* 3.1.402.

[2] ll. 163–64.

agonies of beast and bird is made less tolerable to us by such a fiction.

> The Being that is in the clouds and air
>
> .   .   .   .   .
>
> Maintains a deep and reverential care
> For the unoffending creature whom He loves.[1]

The poet offers us as a proof of that "reverential care," the visible alteration of Nature at the scene of suffering—an alteration we have to dispense with every day we pass in the woods. We are tempted to ask whether Wordsworth himself believed in the sympathy he asks us—on such grounds!—to believe in? Did he think his faith to be worthy of no more than a fictitious sign and a false proof?

Nowhere in the whole of Tennyson's thought is there such an attack upon our reason and our heart. He is more serious than the solemn Wordsworth.

And this poem, with all else that Tennyson wrote, tutors, with here and there a subtle word, this nature-loving nation to perceive land, light, sky, and ocean, as he perceived. To this we return, upon this we dwell. He has been to us, firstly, the poet of two geniuses—a small and an immense; secondly, the modern poet who answered in the negative that most significant modern question, French or not French? But he was, before the outset of all our study of him, of all our love of him, the poet of landscape, and this he is more dearly than pen can describe him. This eternal character of his is keen in the verse that is winged to meet a homeward ship with her "dewy decks," and in the sudden island landscape,

> The clover sod,
> That takes the sunshine and the rains,
> Or where the kneeling hamlet drains
> The chalice of the grapes of God.

It is poignant in the garden-night:

> A breeze began to tremble o'er
> The large leaves of the sycamore,
>
> .   .   .   .   .
>
> And gathering freshlier overhead,
> Rocked the full-foliaged elm, and swung
> The heavy-folded rose, and flung
> The lilies to and fro, and said
>   "The dawn, the dawn," and died away.[2]

His are the exalted senses that sensual poets know nothing of. I think the sense of hearing as well as the sense of sight, has never been more greatly exalted than by Tennyson:

> As from beyond the limit of the world,
>   Like the last echo born of a great cry.[3]

As to this garden-character so much decried I confess that the "lawn" does not generally delight me, the word nor the thing. But in Tennyson's page the word is wonderful, as though it had never been dull: "The mountain lawn was dewy-dark."[4] It is not that he brings the mountains too near or ranks them in his own peculiar garden-plot, but that the word withdraws to summits, withdraws into dreams; the lawn is aloft, alone, and as wild as ancient snow. It is the same with many another word or phrase changed, by passing into his vocabulary, into something rich and strange. His own especially is the March month—his "roaring moon." His is the spirit of the dawning month of flowers and storms; the golden, soft names of daffodil and crocus are caught by the gale as you speak them in his verse, in a fine disproportion with the energy and gloom. His was a new apprehension of nature, an increase in the number, and not only in the sum, of our national apprehensions of poetry in nature. Unaware of a separate angel

---

[1] l. 165, ll. 167–68.

[2] *In Memoriam*, 1.10.12, ll. 13–16, ll. 54–61.

[3] *Idylls of the King*, "The Passing of Arthur," ll. 458–59.

[4] "Œnone," l. 48.

of modern poetry is he who is insensible to the Tennyson note—the new note that we reaffirm even with the notes of Vaughan, Traherne,[1] Wordsworth, Coleridge, Blake well in our ears—the Tennyson note of splendour, all-distinct. He showed the perpetually transfigured landscape in transfiguring words. He is the captain of our dreams. Others have lighted a candle in England, he lit a sun. Through him our daily suns, and also the backward and historic suns long since set, which he did not sing, are magnified; and he bestows upon us an exalted retrospection. Through him Napoleon's sun of Austerlitz rises, for us, with a more brilliant menace upon arms and the plain; through him Fielding's "most melancholy sun" lights the dying man to the setting-forth on that last voyage of his with such an immortal gleam, denying hope, as would not have lighted, for us, the memory of that seaward morning, had our poetry not undergone the illumination, the transcendent sunrise, of Tennyson's genius.

Emerson knew that the poet speaks adequately then only when he speaks "a little wildly, or with the flower of the mind." Tennyson, the clearest-headed of poets, is our wild poet; wild, notwithstanding that little foppery we know of in hi0m—that walking delicately, like Agag;[2] wild, notwithstanding the work, the ease, the neatness, the finish; notwithstanding the assertion of manliness which, in asserting, somewhat misses the mark; a wilder poet than the rough, than the sensual, than the defiant, than the accuser, than the denouncer. Wild flowers are his—great poet— wild winds, wild lights, wild heart, wild eyes!

—1917

---

[1] Henry Vaughan (1622–95), Welsh poet; Thomas Traherne (c.1638–74), poet and religious writer.

[2] King of the Amalekites, 1 Samuel 15:32.

Robert Browning [3]

It says much for the power of Browning that he was able to leaven the mass of cultivated people by means of a comparatively little knot of readers. That he should be popular in any literal sense of the word had always been an impossibility which Browning very frankly accepted. Too obscure to be understood without unusual power of thought and especially without unusual mobility of mind, on the part of his reader, his work is also seldom musical enough to haunt the memory; and these two defects, if defects they be, have become proverbial with regard to him, and inseparable from his name. Yet he has, now and then, written verse in which a difficult thought has been expressed pellucidly, and verse ringing with true significant music, and occasionally even with a too obvious and insistent tune; but these exceptions are very naturally lost sight of in his prevailing practice. Now, in our opinion no author should be blamed for obscurity, nor should any pains be grudged in the effort to understand him, provided that he has done his best to be intelligible. Difficult thoughts are quite distinct from difficult words. Difficulty of thought is the very heart of poetry. Those who complain of it would restrict poetry to literal narrative for its epics, to unanalysed—and therefore ultimately to unrealized and conventional—passion for its drama, and to songs for its lyrics. Doubtless narrative, dramas of primary passion, and singable songs are all excellent things; masterpieces have been done in these ways—but in the past—in a fresher, broader, and simpler time than ours. Those masterpieces bring their own age with them, as it were, into our hearts; we ourselves assume a singleness of mind as we read them; they are neither too obvious nor too unthoughtful to interest us; but it is far otherwise with modern work which is laid upon the same lines.

---

[3] first published in *The Pen*, 1880.

Our age is not simple—we inherit so much from other ages; and our language has lost the freshness of its early literature—reasons why the poetry of our time should be complex in thought and should depend upon something more mental than the charm of form sufficient in the lyrics of the Elizabethans. The English language was once so beautiful, so fresh and free, that any well-composed group of English words would make a poem. But some of the vitality has been written out of the language since then; it is richer now than ever, but it has lost that youthfulness of form; and though the poems of those other times cannot themselves cease to be fresh to us, nothing can now be written of exactly their character. Beauty of manner must therefore be secondary in modern poetry to importance of thought; and no true thinking is altogether easy. Granted that modern poetry must be thoughtful or nothing, and that thought is difficult, we shall here have a sufficient apology for more than half Browning's obscurity. The rest must, as usual, be ascribed to the mere construction of his phrases; he has his own way of dropping out articles and other little words, which leads to grammatical ambiguities never, perhaps, suspected by the author himself and greatly to be lamented; grammatical obscurity is, perhaps, the one obscurity of which a reader has a right to complain. The same habit of contraction adds greatly to the tenseness of the verse, and it is this tenseness which we might wish to see relaxed. Even when his thought is closest, the words might fit it a little less tightly, we think; but Browning's mannerisms are not, as mannerisms, displeasing, for they are full of himself—of one of the most original personalities of contemporary literature. He, like Tennyson, is essential, not accidental, in English poetry.

Browning is, as a poet, distinctively a man of the world; we use the term in the sense in which it is employed by men when they intend praise; he is keenly interested in things as they are; he is impartial and has a masculine tolerance and patience which belong essentially to the dramatic genius; he prefers to be shrewd rather than profound in the mental analysis which delights him; there are heights in the human soul that tempt this explorer less than level ways—provided these are intricate enough. Browning is distinctively human, but not in the sense which the word generally bears; he is not exactly gentle or sympathetic, or penetrated with the pathos of the human tragedy; he is curious in human things, interested, experimental, and he preserves a sane cheerfulness altogether characteristic of himself. This last, which supports him through pages upon pages of inquiries and experiments as to the mental processes of a spirit-rapping cheat also inspires him with poems on death, now heroically grotesque, now ecstatic.

> I would hate that death bandaged my eyes, and
> forebore,
>   And bade me creep past,
> No! Let me taste the whole of it, fare like my peers,
>   The heroes of old,
> Bear the brunt, in a minute pay glad life's arrears
>   Of pain, darkness, and cold.
>
>   .   .   .   .   .
>
> The fiend-voices that rave
>   Shall dwindle, shall blend,
> Shall change, shall become first a peace out of pain,
>   Then a light, then thy breast,
> O thou soul of my soul! I shall clasp thee again,
>   And with God be the rest![1]

In the following the "little minute's sleep" is past:

> "What! and is it you again?" quoth I.
> "I again; whom else did you expect?" quoth
>   she.

---

[1] "Prospice," ll. 15–28.

Then he tells her how much relieved he is to be rid of life and he sketches his own epitaph:

> "Afflictions sore long time be bore; do end," quoth I.
> I end with "Love is all and death is nought," quoth she.[1]

He carries this same temper of mind through his study of Bishop Blougram's sophistries, and through the resignation of *Any Wife to Any Husband*. And surely Browning's work loses something by this equanimity, this large tolerance of his. A mind less serene, whole, scientific, and independent might oftener be touched, or hurt, or discouraged into seeking a lofty and lovely ideal which is rare in his poetry. Not that Browning cannot conceive it, but that he is too closely and intently at work with things as they are to attend to it.

But no one who has not followed him through his labours of analysis, can understand the pleasure of the more studious reader at hearing Browning's cool, strong, argumentative voice break in the rare note of emotion, caused by his own sudden rise to a higher moral and mental beauty than lies in the path of a man of the world. When this happens, not the feeling only, but the verse softens and relaxes; for his style, like his thought, is knotted—is as knotty, indeed, as a fugue. But when that higher, fresher thought comes, it brings with it its own inevitable music. No poet has written fuller, more important, and more significant music than Browning at these rare moments. For instance, in that fine drama, *The Return of the Druses*, there is some difficulty in the character of Anael with her double love and her half-deliberate delusion, so that much of the verse allotted to her is intricate enough; but where strong single feeling rises in the heart of this exiled Druse girl, what exquisite music sweeps out indeliberately!—

> Dost thou snow-swathe thee kinglier, Lebanon,
> Than in my dreams?[2]

English poetry might in vain be searched for a nobler cadence. In *Pippa Passes* (to our mind the most beautiful, though not therefore necessarily the most intellectual, of all Browning's works) such music is too frequent to allow us to choose examples; it occurs in *Balaustion's Adventure*, now and then, and less frequently elsewhere. Far more strongly accented musical pieces occur now and then in his work; *Evelyn Hope* and *A Lover's Quarrel* are as melodious—except for an occasional jerk—as the warmest admirers of insistently rhythmic verse could possibly require; but these bear the same relation to the higher music of which we have just spoken, as is borne by a tune of Rossini's[3] to one of Schumann's[4] significant sentences of notes.

—1913

from *The Rhythm of Life*

If life is not always poetical, it is at least metrical. Periodicity rules over the mental experience of man, according to the path of the orbit of his thoughts. Distances are not gauged, ellipses not measured, velocities not ascertained, times not known. Nevertheless, the recurrence is sure. What the mind suffered last week, or last year, it does not suffer now; but it will suffer again next week or next year. Happiness is not a matter of events; it depends upon the tides of the mind. Disease is metrical,

---

[1] a series of somewhat misquoted lines from the "Epilogue" of *Fifine at the Fair* (ll. 7–8, 30–31).

[2] 2.179–80.

[3] Gioachino Antonio Rossini (1792–1868), Italian composer.

[4] Robert Schumann (1810–56), German composer, pianist, and conductor.

closing in at shorter and shorter periods towards death, sweeping abroad at longer and longer intervals towards recovery. Sorrow for one cause was intolerable yesterday, and will be intolerable to-morrow; to-day it is easy to bear, but the cause has not passed. Even the burden of a spiritual distress unsolved is bound to leave the heart to a temporary peace; and remorse itself does not remain—it returns. Gaiety takes us by a dear surprise. If we had made a course of notes of its visits, we might have been on the watch, and would have had an expectation instead of a discovery. No one makes such observations; in all the diaries of students of the interior world, there have never come to light the records of the Kepler[1] of such cycles. But Thomas à Kempis[2] knew of the recurrences, if he did not measure them. In his cell alone with the elements—"What wouldst thou more than these? for out of these were all things made"— he learnt the stay to be found in the depth of the hour of bitterness, and the remembrance that restrains the soul at the coming of the moment of delight, giving it a more conscious welcome, but presaging for it an inexorable flight. And "rarely, rarely comest thou,"[3] sighed Shelley, not to Delight merely, but to the Spirit of Delight. Delight can be compelled beforehand, called, and constrained to our service—Ariel can be bound to a daily task; but such artificial violence throws life out of metre, and it is not the spirit that is thus compelled. *That* flits upon an orbit elliptically or parabolically or hyperbolically curved, keeping no man knows what trysts with Time.

It seems fit that Shelley and the author of the "Imitation"[4] should both have been keen and simple enough to perceive these flights, and to guess at the order of this periodicity. Both souls were in close touch with the spirits of their several worlds, and no deliberate human rules, no infractions of the liberty and law of the universal movement, kept from them the knowledge of recurrences. *Eppur si muove*.[5] They knew that presence does not exist without absence; they knew that what is just upon its flight of farewell is already on its long path of return. They knew that what is approaching to the very touch is hastening towards departure. "O wind," cried Shelley, in autumn,

> O wind,
> If winter comes can spring be far behind?[6]

They knew that the flux is equal to the reflux; that to interrupt with unlawful recurrences, out of time, is to weaken the impulse of onset and retreat; the sweep and impetus of movement. To live in constant efforts after an equal life, whether the equality be sought in mental production, or in spiritual sweetness, or in the joy of the senses, is to live without either rest or full activity. The souls of certain of the saints, being singularly simple and single, have been in the most complete subjection to the law of periodicity. Ecstasy and desolation visited them by seasons. They endured, during spaces of vacant time, the interior loss of all for which they had sacrificed the world. They rejoiced in the uncovenanted beatitude of sweetness alighting in their hearts. Like them are the poets whom, three times or ten times in the course of a long life, the Muse has approached, touched, and forsaken. And yet hardly like them; not always so docile, nor so wholly prepared for the departure, the brevity, of the golden and irrevocable hour. Few poets have fully recognized the metrical absence of

---

[1] Johann Kepler (1571–1630), German mathematician who proposed early laws of planetary motion.

[2] Thomas à Kempis (c. 1380–1471), German mystic.

[3] "Song" 1.

[4] Thomas à Kempis's "Of the Imitation of Christ."

[5] a version of the words spoken (quietly?) by Galileo following his recantation of his theory of the earth's movement: "And yet, it moves."

[6] "Ode to the West Wind" (1820), ll. 69–70.

their Muse. For full recognition is expressed in one only way—silence.

It has been found that several tribes in Africa and in America worship the moon, and not the sun; a great number worship both; but no tribes are known to adore the sun, and not the moon. On her depend the tides; and she is Selene, mother of Herse, bringer of the dews that recurrently irrigate lands where rain is rare. More than any other companion of earth is she the Measurer. Early Indo-Germanic languages knew her by that name. Her metrical phases are the symbol of the order of recurrence. Constancy in approach and in departure is the reason of her inconstancies. Juliet[1] will not receive a vow spoken in invocation of the moon; but Juliet did not live to know that love itself has tidal times—lapses and ebbs which are due to the metrical rule of the interior heart, but which the lover vainly and unkindly attributes to some outward alteration in the beloved. For man—except those elect already named—is hardly aware of periodicity. The individual man either never learns it fully, or learns it late. And he learns it so late, because it is a matter of cumulative experience upon which cumulative evidence is long lacking. It is in the after-part of each life that the law is learnt so definitely as to do away with the hope or fear of continuance. That young sorrow comes so near to despair is a result of this young ignorance. So is the early hope of great achievement. Life seems so long, and its capacity so great, to one who knows nothing of all the intervals it needs must hold—intervals between aspirations, between actions, pauses as inevitable as the pauses of sleep. And life looks impossible to the young unfortunate, unaware of the inevitable and unfailing refreshment. It would be for their peace to learn that there is a tide in the affairs of men, in a sense more subtle—if it is not too audacious to add a meaning to Shakespeare—than the phrase was meant to contain. Their joy is flying away from them on its way home; their life will wax and wane; and if they would be wise, they must wake and rest in its phases, knowing that they are ruled by the law that commands all things—a sun's revolutions and the rhythmic pangs of maternity.

—1913

---

[1] *Romeo and Juliet* 2.2.109–11: "O! swear not by the moon, the inconstant moon, / That monthly changes in her circled orb, / Lest that thy love prove likewise variable."

Elizabeth Robins
1862 – 1952

The American-born Elizabeth Robins moved to England in 1889 and achieved fame as England's foremost Ibsen actress, having particular success as Hedda Gabler (1891). She was also Ibsen's first English producer.

As well, Robins was a prolific writer of feminist plays, novels, and essays. "Woman's Secret" is from her 1913 collection of essays, *Way Stations*.

❧❧❧

Woman's Secret

BY WAY OF PREFACE

With all the sense of partisanship that the Women's Movement in England may arouse in certain natures, there is one occasional feature of it (a feature far more infrequent than has been alleged) that some of us deprecate. It is the assumption that men have consciously and deliberately initiated all the injustices from which women suffer. This is at once to suppose men more powerful than they have ever been, and more wrong-headed.

So far as I know them, the great majority of the women leaders in reforms share a sense of painful wincing when they hear women talking as if all men were in a conscious conspiracy against the other sex.

Realising our own imperfections, a sense of something very like shame descends upon us on those occasions when we are asked to listen to pleas that would make out all women to be Angels of Light and all men Princes of Darkness.

Looking as far into the matter as we are able, we find the chief difference between ourselves and men to lie in the fact that men are expected to struggle against adverse circumstance, whereas they have made it our chief virtue not to struggle.

Nevertheless, when we begin to inquire into the origin of the order under which we live, we cannot believe in our hearts that men really ever got together and said: "Go to! we'll enslave the women!" On the contrary, we find a difficulty in doubting that we all merely followed our lines of least resistance, and that these lines brought women so constantly to the exercise of patience at the cradle and the hearth, and brought men so constantly to the exercise of physical force on the battlefield or in the chase, that the hands of each became subdued to that they worked in.

Women's hands, as civilisation advanced, grew softer and smaller; men's grew larger and more muscular as they exercised their power to grip or strike. The arrangement between the sexes seems to have come about without blame or credit on either side. It was the best working arrangement the uncivilised could devise. The trouble with it to-day is that it long ago served its purpose, and became outworn. We all, men and women alike, have arrived at a place where we must devise something better. But we shall not come by any fair understanding of the past, or by any helpful scheme of betterment for the future, till women realise and frankly admit that men, equally with themselves, are victims of circumstance.

The object of these pages is twofold. One is to put forward a plea which, if it were generally allowed, might serve better than anything else to do away with age-old misunderstanding. My second object is to set forth what seems to be the chief reason for the too long continuance of the situation in which we find ourselves, and to suggest that the cause of it is women's inarticulateness in the past.

To speak of her as inarticulate is not to forget that she has long been called the voluble sex. Her supposed inability to keep a secret is with many an unchallenged article of faith. Yet no secret has ever been better kept than the woman's, as those may dimly have divined who speak of the sex as enigmatic.

In every tongue, at various stages of the world's progress, we have had the man's views upon every subject within sight—including woman. What the woman thought of it all, no deepest delver in dusty archives, or among ruins of dead cities, has ever brought to light. The sagas, the histories, song, epitaph, and story—the world's garnered treasure of record, whether it be of the life of action or the life of the spirit—they are all but so many reflections of the mind of man.

From India to Egypt, from Greece to Yucatan, the learned are labouring to bring the Past to light. All over the civilised world are those who wait with eagerness to hear of the recovery of some lost masterpiece—thrilling when the cable tells of a Menander[1] speaking for himself at last, instead of through the mouths of others. All the learned world waits to hear what men of the Minoan civilisation felt and thought. But the living may wait till they, too, are dust; or, while their brief day lasts, they may read all the books in all the tongues of earth, con every record in clay or stone or papyrus, and still know only half the story. Schliemann[2] may uncover one Troy after another, six separate cities deep, and never come the nearer to what Helen thought. All that is not silence is the voice of man.

Some would wrest the significance of this into a reproach to woman, seeing in it the most sweeping of all the indictments against her belated claim to stand—in civilised communities—on an equal

footing with her brother man. But to read history so is to understand man's part in it as little as woman's.

If I were one of the dominant sex, I think I would not be so sure, as many good men seem to be, that they are competent to speak for women. If I were a man, and cared to know the world I live in, I almost think it would make me a shade uneasy—the weight of that long silence of one-half the world; even more uneasy if, being a man, I should come to realise the strange persistence of the woman in her immemorial rôle. When I should hear women chattering, I almost think I might not feel it so acute in me to note that with all their words they so seldom "say anything." What if they know better? What if it is by that means they have kept their secret? For let no one think the old rule of feminine dissimulation is even yet superseded.

Some measure we get of the profundity of that abyss of silence when we see, even in these emancipated times, how little of what woman really thinks and feels gets over the footlights of the world's big stage.

Let us remember it is only yesterday that women in any number began to write for the public prints. But in taking up the pen, what did this new recruit conceive to be her task? To proclaim her own or other women's actual thoughts and feelings? Far from it. Her task, as she naturally and even inevitably conceived it, was to imitate as nearly as possible the method, but above all the point of view, of man.

She wrote her stories as she fashioned her gowns and formed her manners, and for the same reason; in literature following meekly in the steps of the forgotten Master, the first tribal story-teller, inventor of that chimera, "the man's woman."

There was no insuperable difficulty in the way of her playing "the sedulous ape," as is amply demonstrated by the serried ranks of competent and popular woman-novelists.

---

[1] Menander (342–293 BC), Greek comic poet.

[2] Heinrich Schliemann (1822–90), German archaeologist, excavated the traditional site of Troy in 1871 and eventually discovered the remains of earlier cities at the same site.

She is still held to be in no way so highly flattered as by hearing that men can hardly credit her book to be the work of a woman.

The realisation that she had access to a rich and as yet unrifled storehouse may have crossed her mind, but there were cogent reasons for concealing her knowledge. With the wariness of ages, which has come to be instinct, she contented herself with echoing the old fables, presenting to a man-governed world puppets as nearly as possible like those that had from the beginning found such favour in men's sight.

Contrary to the popular impression, to say in print what she thinks is the last thing the woman-novelist or journalist is commonly so rash as to attempt. In print, even more than elsewhere (unless she is reckless), she must wear the aspect that shall have the best chance of pleasing her brothers. Her publishers are not women. Even the professional readers and advisers of publishers are men. The critics in the world outside, men. Money, reputation—these are vested in men. If a woman would win a little at their hands, she must walk warily, and not too much displease them. But I put it to my brothers: Is that the spirit of the faithful chronicler? Is it not far more the spirit of the notorious flatterers and liars who, in the times gone by, addressed those abject prefaces to powerful patrons—testimonials which make us laugh or blush according to our temper? Little as we can judge of those princes and nobles from the starving men of letters who licked their boots, hardly more can men discover to-day what women really think of them from the fairy-tales of feminine spinning, however much the spinster "makes faces," as Stevenson would say, and pretends, "Now I am being Realistic!"

What she is really doing is her level best to play the man's game, and seeing how nearly like him she can do it. So conscious is she it is *his* game she is trying her hand at, that she is prone to borrow his very name to set upon her title-page. She does so, not only that she may get courage from it to talk deep and go a-swashbuckling now and then, but for the purpose of reassuring the man. Here is something quite in your line, she implies; for lo! my name is "George."

Her instinct for the mask is abundantly justified.

No view is more widely accepted than that every woman's book is but a naïve attempt to extend her own little personality.

We do not commonly find the man-made hero confounded with the author. When a man takes some small section of the arc of a character or a dramatic situation, and (capable of intellectual honesty, and precisely of leaving himself out of the Saga) if he follows the curve so rigidly that he describes the complete circle, his faithful projection of the illusion of life is rewarded by his critics' saying: "What a power of imagination the fellow has!"

If a woman but attempts this honourable task—an affair of strong self-control and of almost mathematical accuracy—if she happens to bring it off, her critics pat her on the back with an absent-minded air, while they look about for "personal experience."

Or they do not even look about. They are content to say: "This is so like the real thing it must be a piece of verbatim reporting, done by a person whose merit is a retentive memory. These life-like scenes are autobiography. The heroine is naturally the writer's self, made to look as she think she looks, or as she wishes to heaven she might!"

The opinions, the aspirations of this character or that—they are the woman-novelist's own. The fact that, as the books multiply, her heroines are found to be widely different in outer aspect and in spirit—that is a trifle easily negligible. If there is no heroine, why, then the woman-writer must be the boy of the story. Otherwise it must be that she has imagination, which is plainly preposterous.

If a woman had written "Macbeth," it would have been obvious that she had murdered her husband; or, if he wasn't her husband, the more shame!

Until society is differently constituted let no one expect that women in general will adventure lightly upon truth-telling in their books.

The older generation may even have the excuse that the doom of the false witness has overtaken them. In the end they believe their own lies.

Even the young and clear-eyed may stand abashed before the great new task, and for another generation the woman may still write her book but to weave another veil, the while she makes her bread—or perhaps her cake.

If the faculty for telling the truth is in itself a kind of genius, as has been said, the use of our mere talent for reproducing the current ideals has certainly been the safer exercise. It cannot be too strongly emphasised that whatever special knowledge we had, whatever was new to the world of letters or disquieting to private life, women writers have kept to themselves as successfully as did the Egyptian women buried thirty centuries ago beneath those tons of granite whereon men graved their version of the ended story.

Of one form of testimonial man has been chary. Often touchingly ready to invest some woman with every gentle virtue, he has usually made an exception of humour. Some show of excuse he has had from two causes. Humour is of humble origin, ethically speaking, and seems to have been sired by cruelty—the pleasure in another's pain or loss of dignity that found diversion in the ruder kinds of horseplay. It seems likely enough that woman's natural sympathy and her sheltering compassion may have prevented her from sharing the bumpkin view of comedy which, in the spacious times behind us, found in Jew-baiting and insanity side-splitting entertainments. Woman may be pardoned for wondering if it may not have been in part her humaner instinct about some of the stock jokes of the race that earned her the reputation of a constitutional lack of humour.

In these slightly more enlightened days, when the less inarticulate—called by men "the exceptional woman"—has been allowed this quality of humour so long withheld, she has take her "exceptionalness" here, as elsewhere, on trust. For any wide knowledge of her own sex is, perhaps, the newest of all woman's acquisitions. Almost every woman has known certain men very well indeed. Other women have been, even for her, the enigma they remained to men.

Now we begin to see that this same sense of humour—being a "small-arm," light, and adapted to delicate handling—seems to be an even commoner blade in the feminine armoury than in that loftier hall where are ranged the heavy artillery—the crossbows and blunderbusses of the other sex.

But since woman's field of action has been the home, she found out millenniums ago that humour there makes for success only under the strictest rules.

She has learned to welcome it as a sign of unbending in her lord. She has even cultivated it (in him) by a process, pelican-like, of offering her own breast; or, to modify the figure, she made her contribution to the domestic cheer by submitting herself to be the target for his pleasantry.

She must have early seen how, when the bow is in the other hand, and her arrow finds *him* out, the point is so little appreciated that she has been fain to give up marksmanship.

If she needed consoling for the resultant rumour of her lack of skill, she has found it in the reflection that no man has ever been known to long for humour in his nearest relations, least of all in the wife of his bosom.

The notion that woman is without this faculty is merely one of the many ways in which men advertise her success in keeping her mental processes to herself. A slave's accomplishment, perhaps. Certainly women have learnt few lessons as well.

What wonder that the age we live in is significant and revolutionary beyond any other, since for the first time since the dawn of civilisation the world is beginning—barely beginning—to be told what the secretive half of the human race really thinks and feels.

That we are not monkeys disporting ourselves in trees is due, so say the wise, to the home-making proclivities of one branch of the anthropoid family. This home-making proclivity was nothing else than the female's instinct to provide the best possible environment for her young—an added tenderness for those weakest breeding in her an added inventiveness.

This was the frail-seeming but sure foundation on which arose the many mansions of human achievement.

A case might be made out by anyone so foolish as to wish to divide responsibility and to apportion merit—a case to prove that civilisation is peculiarly women's affair. Certainly it is difficult to see how the upbuilding of the race could have come about without its passing through two phases, which owed their initiation not to masculine but to feminine development. These two aspects of the same significant tendency were:—

1. The woman's giving up of brute competition (where she excelled, be it remembered);

2. Her specialising in the home (accepting the yoke of silence and of service).

Woman purchased civilisation at the price of her liberty.

When our immemorial forefathers and foremothers lived in cave and tree-crotch, the female asked no consideration and got no quarter, not even in the performance of her vital function. She had no need of either. She was (in spite of the drain on her physical resources) quite equal to the task of taking care of both herself and her progeny.

So well able was she to bear the double burden—this major share in the perpetuation of the species—that where it was a question of protecting her young, she was accounted a foe more terrible than any male of her kind.[1]

No nonsense in those days about her being the weaker sex.

No hint of her being a creature for whom special allowances must be made—till she, the first specialist, began to specialise. Not till she gave up gambolling in the airy leafage and took to making a home; to nursing not alone the young, but the sick and the old; making rude coverings as shelter from the cold, brooding long upon the dead, domesticating fire for her first handmaiden; not till then did she cease to compete on the lower plane of brute strength and cunning with the male.

If these first women, making their wholly instinctive choice, had not "chosen" the keeping of the hearthstone warm by staying at home to feed the fire; if women of the past had not sat by the sick and suffered with the dying, not only would there never have been a Woman Question, there would never have been a Civilisation.

Now, civilisation means control. It means a harnessing of forces in external nature and in the spirit of mankind. Woman, with the child to teach her, practised the first lessons in the New Learning on herself. She engraved the strange new maxims on her savage heart. Be patient; be patient; and again and always, and down to the dark, mysterious end, be patient. Above all, let the fierce grown-up child, man, suppose he is a hero and a king. He is above all things vain; and if he is to do his new work of bringing in the food and defending the house against the enemy—if he is to do these things in good heart—he must be allowed to think himself a monstrous fine fellow. No douche of cold criticism or shaft of wit must be turned upon him. That they sometimes were; that the early woman now and then forgot her part, and was promptly reminded of it by an exercise of brute force, is proved by those amenities of mediæval argument—the ducking-stool and the gossips' bridle.

---

[1] "This was published before Mr. Kipling's tribute to 'the sex.'" (Robins's note.)

Since her tongue was the one thing men feared most, no variety of female has had more scorn heaped on her than the woman who had a grievance and dared talk about it. The silent woman was the paragon. Oh, well for the man who praised her that he could not see her heart! The truth about himself and the mind of his mate, these were things to be hidden. For the rest, he was ruled by the two primal hungers, though clumsily and at cost. His greed in both paid him back in disease. If even to-day he explodes in rage at hearing fragments of the long-suppressed truth, who can blame the instinct of self-preservation that has held the woman silent hitherto upon inconvenient themes?

From those dim ages wherein the beginnings of speech took shape—the day when the first phrases were spoken instead of barked or brayed or chattered—from that day to this, amongst women, they have been few and far between who betrayed the conspiracy of silence about the things that matter. Innocent or crafty, she has filled the void with pretty twittering. In all recorded history only a single voice here and there to rouse in men a gaping wonder and a deep disquiet. Then all made smooth and soothed again by some form of that phrase, "An exceptional woman," with the prompt rider, "sexless." And so you others, beware!

Since it is by sex you live, take heed lest in some unwary hour you, too, become exceptional, and so, by a well-known philological necessity, decline through "singularity" to "egregiousness" and "insolence."

If I have admitted that hitherto men have had little opportunity of knowing that their point of view is not the only possible one, it seems necessary to add that they do not make the presentation of another an easy matter. There is no woman, I imagine, however old or isolated, who does not value the good opinion of men. Her mistake has been that she has valued it beyond a thing more valuable.

Many a mere looker-on at the game must have been stung by the reception accorded the little handful of women who have ventured into the public arena, not as artists, story-tellers, or mere commentators upon manners, but as earnest and practical contributors to the gravest problems of life.

If upon those who are erroneously held to represent the prevailing temper of the Forward Party among women—if, upon a few, a sense of the discouragement administered by men presses so hard that, here and there, it finds expression in bitterness—that result is surely natural enough.

My point is that it is not only "natural." Like most unreflective, instinctive revelations it has its special significance. This particular manifestation is perhaps more valuable than even the inquiring mind has realised.

If men find themselves publicly represented by women as being *en masse* not very noble or very effectual, they should see in the circumstance a proof merely that a woman here and there has followed the masculine example in taking certain instances for the type of creation's mould.

Yet here again we have a case where it has made a vast difference when the shoe was on the other foot.

When a man proclaims his poor opinion of women, lumping them all together in a general condemnation (after the fashion of certain so-called philosophers), saying the worst he can of all because he has had bad luck with one or two, he is not told that he is an hysterical or a narrow-minded creature.

Misogynist views have not been held to be so much a failure of intelligence or good temper in the man, as a failure, black and all-unpardonable, in women.

No one seems to have resented the ludicrous unfairness of the Kundry *motif* [1] in Art. Public

---

[1] Robins refers here to Richard Wagner's *Parsifal*, first produced in 1882. In the story of Parsifal and the Holy Grail, Kundry is a strange woman who entertains a conflicted moral allegiance to both the Christian brotherhood of knights who guard the Grail and to Klingsor,

opinion canonised the superficial Augustine,[1] who in his ignoble estimate of women hesitated to spare even his long-suffering and most excellent mother.

He, too, was called a saint who, with such generous urbanity, said of woman that she was: "A necessary evil, a natural temptation, a desirable calamity, a domestic peril, a deadly fascination, and a painted ill."[2]

If we do not blame the disappointed man for thinking meanly of women, neither should we in justice, or in logic, blame the woman who has found men falling too far below her ideal for her to accept stolidly her disillusionment. If man has not scrupled to show his seamy side to woman, why should woman scruple to admit the seamy side? Will the would ever arrive at a fair estimate of both sides till the day comes when woman presents her view without fear and without reproach?

In the occasional bitterness—so much less common among the Suffragists, for instance, than has been supposed—there may be for the wise man a degree of enlightenment that soft words could never bring. His enlightenment may be hoped quietly to rectify the current view of woman's contentment with her false position. In default of such peaceful readjustment, woman's reaction from the enforced attitude of subservience can hardly fail to result in making more general and more prolonged such temporary unfairness as may already exist in her judgment of men.

The swing of the pendulum to the opposite extreme from the old deification of the masculine principle, might even (contrary to our faith) seem to be the only way of arriving at that fairness of each to each, the equilibrium of the future.

Which consideration brings me to my plea: that men should for our common good embrace such opportunity as comes their way of taking a turn at trying to understand some of the points of view possible to the opposite sex. I would like to ask them to remember that if our parts had been reversed, if woman had been the dominant partner, men would have exercised precisely those arts of dissimulation and of long silence, alternated with brief outbursts of bitterness, that always characterise the unfree. When the few women who can bring themselves to speak out plain, do so in men's hearing, even those who wish well only to themselves—if there are such men—should listen with a little of the patience that, for centuries untold, women have bestowed upon masculine utterances.

The fairer-minded will remember, too, that exposition is an art difficult to the novice. As in the other arts, skill in this comes only by the practice we have been denied. Advocacy is a profession whose doors are still closed on women. Our brothers must therefore try to see though our imperfections of presentment something of that truth we have so long and so religiously withheld.

—1913

---

a knight who has been rejected by the brotherhood and who seeks revenge for this rejection. Because she seeks to seduce Parsifal in the interest of Klingsor, but ultimately dies repentant, Kundry participates in the traditional angel/whore dialectic of female representation.

[1] St. Augustine of Hippo (354–430), bishop and philosopher.

[2] "What else is a woman but a foe to friendship, a cosmic punishment, a necessary evil, a natural temptation, a desirable calamity, a domestic peril, a delectable detriment, a deadly fascination, a painted ill!" St. John Chrysostom (c. 347–407), Bishop and Doctor.

Thomas Hardy
1840 – 1928

Thomas Hardy was born and lived most of his life in rural Dorsetshire. Although now best known for his fiction (e.g. *The Return of the Native* [1878], *The Mayor of Casterbridge* [1886], *Tess of the d'Urbervilles* [1891], and

Jude the Obscure [1895]), Hardy began and ended his career as a poet. His early poetry and some new works were published in *Wessex Poems* (1898), followed over the years by seven volumes of lyrics and narratives.

⟋⟍⟋⟍

Apology [1]
Preface to *Late Lyrics and Earlier*

The launching of a volume of this kind in neo-Georgian days by one who began writing in mid-Victorian, and has published nothing to speak of for some years, may seem to call for a few words of excuse or explanation. Whether or no, readers may feel assured that a new book is submitted to them with great hesitation at so belated a date. Insistent practical reasons, however, among which were requests from some illustrious men of letters who are in sympathy with my productions, the accident that several of the poems have already seen the light, and that dozens of them have been lying about for years, compelled the course adopted, in spite of the natural disinclination of a writer whose works have been so frequently regarded askance by a pragmatic section here and there, to draw attention to them once more.

I do not know that it is necessary to say much on the contents of the book, even in deference to suggestions that will be mentioned presently. I believe that those readers who care for my poems at all—readers to whom no passport is required—will care for this new instalment of them, perhaps the last, as much as for any that have preceded them. Moreover, in the eyes of a less friendly class the pieces, though a very mixed collection indeed, contain, so far as I am able to see, little or nothing in technic or teaching that can be considered a Star-Chamber matter, or so

much as agitating to a ladies' school; even though, to use Wordsworth's observation in his Preface to *Lyrical Ballads*, such readers may suppose "that by the act of writing in verse an author makes a formal engagement that he will gratify certain known habits of association: that he not only thus apprises the reader that certain classes of ideas and expressions will be found in his book, but that others will be carefully excluded."

It is true, nevertheless, that some grave, positive, stark, delineations are interspersed among those of the passive, lighter, and traditional sort presumably nearer to stereotyped tastes. For—while I am quite aware that a thinker is not expected, and, indeed, is scarcely allowed, now more than heretofore, to state all that crosses his mind concerning existence in this universe, in his attempts to explain or excuse the presence of evil and the incongruity of penalizing the irresponsible—it must be obvious to open intelligences that, without denying the beauty and faithful service of certain venerable cults, such disallowance of "obstinate questionings" and "blank misgivings" tends to a paralysed intellectual stalemate. Heine observed nearly a hundred years ago that the soul has her eternal rights; that she will not be darkened by statutes, nor lullabied by the music of bells. And what is to-day, in allusions to the present author's pages, alleged to be "pessimism" is, in truth, only such "questionings" in the exploration of reality, and is the first step towards the soul's betterment, and the body's also.

---

[1] published in 1922 as a preface to Hardy's *Late Lyrics and Earlier*.

If I may be forgiven for quoting my own old words, let me repeat what I printed in this relation more than twenty years ago, and wrote much earlier, in a poem entitled "In Tenebris":[1]

If way to the Better there be, it exacts a full look at the Worst:

that is to say, by the exploration of reality, and its frank recognition stage by stage along the survey, with an eye to the best consummation possible: briefly, evolutionary meliorism. But it is called pessimism nevertheless; under which word, expressed with condemnatory emphasis, it is regarded by many as some pernicious new thing (though so old as to underlie the Gospel scheme, and even to permeate the Greek drama); and the subject is charitably left to decent silence, as if further comment were needless.

Happily there are some who feel such Levitical[2] passing-by to be, alas, by no means a permanent dismissal of the matter; that comment on where the world stands is very much the reverse of needless in these disordered years of our prematurely afflicted century: that amendment and not madness lies that way. And looking down the future these few hold fast to the same: that whether the human and kindred animal races survive till the exhaustion or destruction of the globe, or whether these races perish and are succeeded by others before that conclusion comes, pain to all upon it, tongued or dumb, shall be kept down to a minimum by loving-kindness, operating through scientific knowledge, and actuated by the modicum of free will conjecturally possessed by organic life when the mighty necessitating forces—unconscious or other—that have "the balancings of the clouds," happen to be in equilibrium, which may or may not be often.

To conclude this question I may add that the argument of the so-called optimists is neatly summarized in a stern pronouncement against me by my friend Mr. Frederic Harrison[3] in a late essay of his, in the words: "This view of life is not mine." The solemn declaration does not seem to me to be so annihilating to the said "view" (really a series of fugitive impressions which I have never tried to coordinate) as is complacently assumed. Surely it embodies a too human fallacy quite familiar in logic. Next, a knowing reviewer, apparently a Roman Catholic young man, speaks, with some rather gross instances of the *suggestio falsi* in his whole article, of "Mr. Hardy refusing consolation," the "dark gravity of his ideas," and so on. When a Positivist and a Romanist agree there must be something wonderful in it, which should make a poet sit up. But…O that 'twere possible!

I would not have alluded in this place or anywhere else to such casual personal criticisms—for casual and unreflecting they must be—but for the satisfaction of two or three friends in whose opinion a short answer was deemed desirable, on account of the continual repetition of these criticisms, or more precisely, quizzings. After all, the serious and truly literary inquiry in this connection is: Should a shaper of such stuff as dreams are made on disregard considerations of what is customary and expected, and apply himself to the real function of poetry, the application of ideas to life (in Matthew Arnold's familiar phrase)?[4] This bears more particularly on what has been called the "philosophy" of these poems—usually reproved as "queer." Whoever the author may be that undertakes such application of ideas in this "philosophic" direction—where it is specially required—glacial judgments must inevitably fall upon him amid opinion whose arbiters largely decry individuality, to whom *ideas* are oddities to

---

[1] published 1895–96.

[2] Luke 10:30–37: the parable of the Good Samaritan, in which a Levite looks on a wounded man and passes him by.

[3] Frederic Harrison (1831–1923), historian and popular philosopher.

[4] From *On Translating Homer*.

smile at, who are moved by a yearning the reverse of that of the Athenian inquirers on Mars Hill;[1] and stiffen their features not only at sound of a new thing, but at a restatement of old things in new terms. Hence should anything of this sort in the following adumbrations seem "queer"—should any of them seem to good Panglossians[2] to embody strange and disrespectful conceptions of this best of all possible worlds, I apologize; but cannot help it.

Such divergences, which, though piquant for the nonce, it would be affectation to say are not saddening and discouraging likewise, may, to be sure, arise sometimes from superficial aspect only, writer and reader seeing the same thing at different angles. But in palpable cases of divergence they arise, as already said, whenever a serious effort is made towards that which the authority I have cited—who would now be called old-fashioned, possibly even parochial —affirmed to be what no good critic could deny as the poet's province, the application of ideas to life. One might shrewdly guess, by the by, that in such recommendation the famous writer may have overlooked the cold-shouldering results upon an enthusiastic disciple that would be pretty certain to follow his putting the high aim in practice, and have forgotten the disconcerting experience of Gil Blas with the Archbishop.[3]

To add a few more words to what has already taken up too many, there is a contingency liable to miscellanies of verse that I have never seen mentioned, so far as I can remember; I mean the chance little shocks that may be caused over a book of various character like the present and its predecessors by the juxtaposition of unrelated, even discordant, effusions; poems perhaps years apart in the making, yet facing each other. An odd result of this has been that dramatic anecdotes of a satirical and humorous intention following verse in graver voice, have been read as misfires because they raise the smile that they were intended to raise, the journalist, deaf to the sudden change of key, being unconscious that he is laughing with the author and not at him. I admit that I did not foresee such contingencies as I ought to have done, and that people might not perceive when the tone altered. But the difficulties of arranging the themes in a graduated kinship of moods would have been so great that irrelation was almost unavoidable with efforts so diverse. I must trust for right note-catching to those finely-touched spirits who can divine without half a whisper, whose intuitiveness is proof against all the accidents of inconsequence. In respect of the less alert, however, should any one's train of thought be thrown out of gear by a consecutive piping of vocal reeds in jarring tonics, without a semiquaver's rest between, and be led thereby to miss the writer's aim and meaning in one out of two contiguous compositions, I shall deeply regret it.

Having at last, I think, finished with the personal points that I was recommended to notice, I will forsake the immediate object of this Preface; and, leaving *Late Lyrics* to whatever fate it deserves, digress for a few moments to more general considerations. The thoughts of any man of letters concerned to keep poetry alive cannot but run uncomfortably on the precarious prospects of English verse at the present day. Verily the hazards and casualties surrounding the birth and setting forth of almost every modern creation in numbers are ominously like those of one of Shelley's paper-boats on a windy lake. And a forward conjecture scarcely permits the hope of a better time, unless men's tendencies should change. So indeed of all art, literature, and "high thinking"

---

[1] the Areopagus, or Hill of Ares (Mars), in Athens, the site of the state tribunal.

[2] Pangloss, the optimistic philosopher of Voltaire's *Candide*, held that this was the best of all possible worlds.

[3] In LeSage's novel, *The Adventures of Gil Blas*, the Archbishop of Granada asks Gil Blas's view of his sermons, then strongly resents the opinions when given.

nowadays. Whether owing to the barbarizing of taste in the younger minds by the dark madness of the late war, the unabashed cultivation of selfishness in all classes, the plethoric growth of knowledge simultaneously with the stunting of wisdom, "a degrading thirst after outrageous stimulation" (to quote Wordsworth again), or from any other cause, we seem threatened with a new Dark Age.

I formerly thought, like other much exercised writers, that so far as literature was concerned a partial cause might be impotent or mischievous criticism; the satirizing of individuality, the lack of whole-seeing in contemporary estimates of poetry and kindred work, the knowingness affected by junior reviewers, the overgrowth of meticulousness in their peerings for an opinion, as if it were a cultivated habit in them to scrutinize the tool-marks and be blind to the building, to hearken for the key-creaks and be deaf to the diapason, to judge the landscape by a nocturnal exploration with a flash-lantern. In other words, to carry on the old game of sampling the poem or drama by quoting the worst line or worst passage only, in ignorance or not of Coleridge's proof that a versification of any length neither can be nor ought to be all poetry;[1] of reading meanings into a book that its author never dreamt of writing there. I might go on interminably.

But I do not now think any such temporary obstructions to be the cause of the hazard, for these negligences and ignorances, though they may have stifled a few true poets in the run of generations, disperse like stricken leaves before the wind of next week, and are no more heard of again in the region of letters than their writers themselves. No: we may be convinced that something of the deeper sort mentioned must be the cause.

In any event poetry, pure literature in general, religion—I include religion, in its essential and undogmatic sense, because poetry and religion touch each other; are, indeed, often but different names for the same thing—these, I say, the visible signs of mental and emotional life, must like all other things keep moving, becoming; even though at present, when belief in witches of Endor is displacing the Darwinian theory and "the truth that shall make you free," men's minds appear, as above noted, to be moving backwards rather than on. I speak somewhat sweepingly, and should except many thoughtful writers in verse and prose; also men in certain worthy but small bodies of various denominations, and perhaps in the homely quarter where advance might have been the very least expected a few years back— the English Church—if one reads it rightly as showing evidence of "removing those things that are shaken," in accordance with the wise Epistolary recommendation to the Hebrews.[2] For since the historic and once august hierarchy of Rome some generation ago lost its chance of being the religion of the future by doing otherwise, and throwing over the little band of New Catholics who were making a struggle for continuity by applying the principle of evolution to their own faith, joining hands with modern science, and outflanking the hesitating English instinct towards liturgical restatement (a flank march which I at the time quite expected to witness, with the gathering of many millions of waiting agnostics into its fold); since then, one may ask, what other purely English establishment than the Church, of sufficient dignity and footing, with such strength of old association, such scope for transmutability, such architectural spell, is left in this country to keep the shreds of morality together?[3]

---

[1] See *Biographia Literaria* 14: "a poem of any length neither can be, or ought to be, all poetry."

[2] See Hebrews 12:27.

[3] "However, one must not be too sanguine in reading signs, and since the above was written evidence that the Church will go far in the removal of 'things that are shaken' has not been encouraging." (Hardy's note.)

It may indeed be a forlorn hope, a mere dream, that of an alliance between religion, which must be retained unless the world is to perish, and complete rationality, which must come, unless also the world is to perish, by means of the interfusing effect of poetry—"the breath and finer spirit of all knowledge; the impassioned expression of science,"[1] as it was defined by an English poet who was quite orthodox in his ideas. But if it be true, as Comte[2] argued, that advance is never in a straight line, but in a looped orbit, we may, in the aforesaid ominous moving backward, be doing it *pour mieux sauter,* drawing back for a spring. I repeat that I forlornly hope so, notwithstanding the supercilious regard of hope by

Schopenhauer, von Hartmann, and other philosophers down to Einstein who have my respect. But one dares not prophesy. Physical, chronological, and other contingencies keep me in these days from critical studies and literary circles

> Where once we held debate, a band
> Of youthful friends, on mind and art [3]

(if one may quote Tennyson in this century). Hence I cannot know how things are going so well as I used to know them, and the aforesaid limitations must quite prevent my knowing henceforward.
—FEBRUARY, 1922

---

[1] slightly garbled quotation from Wordsworth's "Preface to the Second Edition of *Lyrical Ballads*." It should read: "the impassioned expression which is in the countenance of all science."

[2] Auguste Comte (1798–1857), best known for positivist philosophy.

[3] from Tennyson's description of his friends at Cambridge (*In Memoriam*, 87).

Index of First Lines

Index of Authors and Titles